ROUGH GUIDES **PHRASEBOOK**

SWEDISH

Contacting the Editors

Every effort has been made to provide accurate information in this publication, but changes are inevitable. The publisher cannot be responsible for any resulting loss, inconvenience or injury.
We would appreciate it if readers would call our attention to any errors or outdated information. We also welcome your suggestions; if you come across a relevant expression not in our phrase book, please contact us at:**hello@insightguides.com**

Cover & Interior Design: Slawomir Krajewski
Head of Production: Rebeka Davies
Production Manager: Rebecca Hancock
Picture Researcher: Slawomir Krajewski
Cover Photo: all shutterstock

Interior Photos: all shutterstock

CONTENTS

INTRODUCTION

PRACTICALITIES

ON THE WAY

LEISURE TIME

SAFE TRAVEL

FOOD

PEOPLE

DICTIONARY

PRONUNCIATION

This section is designed to familiarize you with the sounds of Swedish using our simplified phonetic transcription. You'll find the pronunciation of the Swedish letters and sounds explained below, together with their 'imitated' equivalents. To use this system, found throughout the phrase book, simply read the pronunciation as if it were English, noting any special rules below.

The Swedish alphabet has 29 letters, the last three of which are the vowels **å**, **ä** and **ö**. Unlike English, the letter **y** is a vowel, meaning that Swedish has nine vowels. Swedish vowels are pure vowel sounds, as opposed to being a combination of two sounds (diphthongs) as they often are in English. Diphthongs occur only in dialects such as **Gotländska** (spoken on the island of Gotland), **Skånska** (spoken in the southern province of Skåne) and **Dalmål** (spoken in Dalarna, a province roughly in the middle of the country).
Swedish has very consistent rules with respect to the sounding of individual letters, i.e. all the letters should be pronounced distinctly, even vowels and consonants at the ends of words. The Swedish language is often referred to as a 'musical' language due to the fact that the intonation and rhythm moves up and down, giving the language a musical quality. Despite this stress, pronunciation is quite consistent. Most words with two or more syllables have primary stress on the first syllable of the word, and this can be followed by a secondary stress on the second syllable. There are also a number of words with two or more syllables which do not have stress on the first syllable, but often on the last. Stress has been noted in the phonetic transcription with underlining.

CONSONANTS

Letter	Approximate Pronunciation	Symbol	Example	Pronunciation
c	like s in sit	s	**cykel**	*sew • kerl**
g	1. before o, å, a and u, like g in get	g	**gata**	*gah • ta*
	2. before i, e, ö and ä, like y in yet	y	**get**	*yet*
	3. after r and l, like y in yet	y	**borg**	*bohry*
j	1. soft, like y in yet	y	**jag**	*yahg*
	2. after r and l, like y in yet	y	**familj**	*fah • mihly*
k	1. before o, å, a and u, like k in keep	k	**katt**	*kat*
	2. before i, e, ö and ä, like ch in chew		**köpa**	*chur • pa*
q	like k in keep	k	**Blomquist**	*bloom • kvihst*
r	strong, almost trilled, r		**röd**	*rurd*
s	like s in see	s	**sitta**	*siht • a*
w	like v in very	v	**wennergren**	*vehn • eh • grehn*
z	like s in suit	s	**zebra**	*see • bra*

Letters b, d, f, h, m, n, p, t, v and x are pronounced as in English.
*Bold indicates a lengthening of the sound — emphasis on the vowel sound.

CONSONANT CLUSTERS

Letter	Approximate Pronunciation	Symbol	Example	Pronunciation
ch	like sh in ship	**sh**	**check**	*shehk*
ck	like ck in tick	**k**	**flicka**	*flih • ka*
dj, gj, hj, lj	like y in yet	**y**	**djur**	*yeur*
sj, skj, stj, sch, ch	like sh in shop	**sh**	**sjal**	*shahl*
sk	1. before o, å, a and u, like sk in skip	**sk**	**skala**	*skah • la*
	2. before i, e, ö and ä, like sh in ship	**sh**	**skära**	*shai • ra*
tj	like sh followed by ch	**shch**	**tjock**	*shchohk*

VOWELS

Letter	Approximate Pronunciation	Symbol	Example	Pronunciation
a	1. when long, like a in father	**ah**	**dag**	*dahg*
	2. when short, like a in cat	**a**	**katt**	*kat*
e	1. when long, like ee in beer	**ee**	**veta**	*vee • ta*
	2. when short, like e in fell	**eh**	**ett**	*eht*

Letter	Approximate Pronunciation	Symbol	Example	Pronunciation
i	1. when long, like ee in see	**ee**	**bil**	*beel*
	2. when short, like i in bit	**ih**	**mitt**	*miht*
o	1. when long, like oa in coat	**oa**	**sko**	*sk**oa***
	2. like the exclamation oh	**oh**	**font**	*fohnt*
u	1. when long, eu in feud	**eu**	**ruta**	*<u>reu</u>•ta*
	2. when short, like u in up	**uh**	**uppe**	*<u>uh</u>•per*
y	like ew in new	**ew**	**byta**	*<u>bew</u>•ta*
å	1. when long, like oa in oar	**oa**	**gå**	*g**oa***
	2. when short, like o in hot	**oh**	**åtta**	*<u>oh</u>•ta*
ä	1. when long, like ai in air	**ai**	**här**	*hair*
	2. when short, like e in set	**eh**	**säng**	*sehng*
ö	1. when long, like u in cure	**ur**	**smör**	*sm**ur***
	2. when short, like u in nut	**uh**	**rött**	*ruhrt*

Swedish vowels are divided into two groups: hard and soft. **A, o, u** and **å** are hard vowels; **e, i, y, ä** and **ö** are soft vowels. Vowels can also be pronounced either long or short. When a vowel is pronounced 'long' the sound is longer, but also more open and rounder. The 'short' vowel sounds are more closed, literally a 'shorter' sound than a long vowel. An easy rule to remember is that if the vowel is followed by a single consonant, as in **stad** (city), it is long. If the vowel is followed by a double consonant, as in **katt** (cat), the vowel is short. The exception to this rule is with the consonants **m** and **n**.

Swedish is spoken throughout Sweden as well as in the coastal regions of Finland and Estonia. While written Swedish has been standardized, there are characteristic spoken dialects in certain regions such as Gotland, Skåne and Dalarna. Other languages, in addition to Swedish, are also spoken in Sweden, such as Finnish, which is spoken in some communities in Northern Sweden, and the Sámi (Lappish) languages, which are spoken in Sámi communities throughout Northern Norway, Sweden, Finland and Russia. Swedish, Norwegian, Danish, Icelandic and Faroese (spoken on the Faroe Islands) are all derived from Old Norse, the language spoken prior to the Viking Age. Over time, the Scandinavian languages developed from this common language. Danish, Norwegian and Swedish are separate and distinct languages but remain close enough that they are mutually intelligible. The Finnish and Sámi languages belong to a different language family, to which Hungarian also belongs.

HOW TO USE THE APP

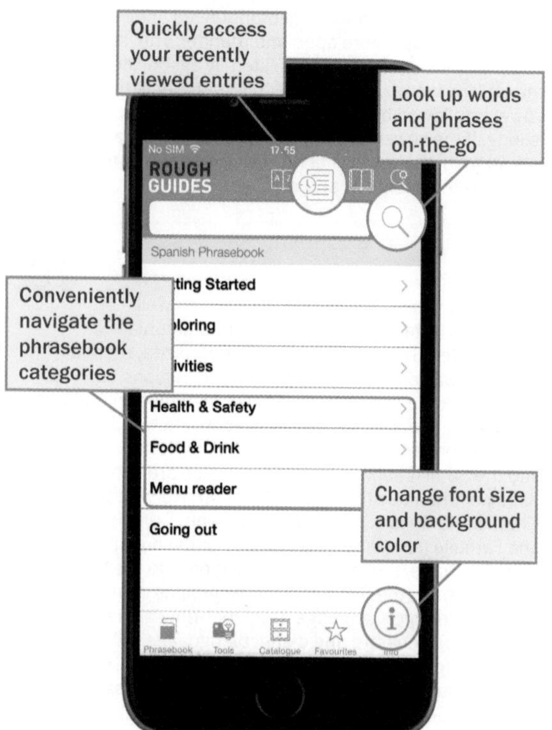
Quickly access your recently viewed entries
Look up words and phrases on-the-go
No SIM
17:55
ROUGH GUIDES
Spanish Phrasebook
Conveniently navigate the phrasebook categories
Health & Safety
Food & Drink
Menu reader
Going out
Change font size and background color
Phrasebook
Tools
Catalogue
Favourites

Save the most useful everyday words and phrases to your Favorites

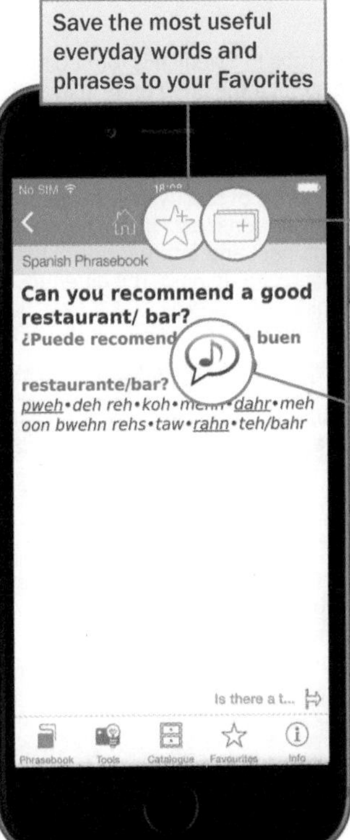

Use the Flash Cards Quiz to learn and memorize new words easily

Take all digital advantages of the app: listen to words and phrases pronounced by native speakers

To learn how to Activate the app, see the inside back cover of this phrasebook.

GRAMMAR

REGULAR VERBS

The present tense of regular verbs in Swedish is formed by adding either -**r** or -**er** to the stem. If the stem ends in **a**, add an -**r**, if it ends in a consonant add -**er**. The past tense is formed by adding either -**de** or -**te** to the basic form. If the basic form ends in a **p**, **t**, **k** or **s**, add -**te**, if not then add -**de**. The future is formed by adding the present tense of **ska** (will) + the verb in the infinitive. This applies to all persons (e.g., I, you, he, she, it, etc.). Following are the present, past and future forms of the verbs **att köpa** (to buy) and **att fråga** (to ask). The different conjugation endings are in bold.

	PRESENT	PAST	FUTURE
att köpa (to buy)	**köper**	**köpte**	*ska köpa*
att fråga (to ask)	**frågar**	**frågade**	*ska fråga*

PRONOUNS

I	**jag**	**it (common/neuter)**	**den/det**
you (sing., inf,)	**du**	**we**	**vi**
he	**han**	**you (pl.)**	**ni**
she	**hon**	**they**	**de**

In Swedish there are two terms for 'you': **du** (singular/informal) and **ni** (plural/informal). Both are used when talking to relatives, friends, colleagues, children, between young people and in work situations. The plural form, **ni**, is used in more formal situations to refer to one or more persons. Its use has however become less frequent, so nowadays you will hear most people address each other with **du**.

IRREGULAR VERBS

There are a number of irregular verbs in Swedish; these must be memorized. Like regular verbs, however, the irregular verb form remains the same, irrespective of person. The table below shows the present, past and future conjugations for a number of important, useful irregular verbs.

	PRESENT	PAST	FUTURE
att vara (to be)	**är**	**var**	*ska vara*
att ha (to have)	**har**	**hade**	*ska ha*
att komma (to come)	**kommer**	**kom**	*ska komma*
att göra (to do)	**gör**	**gjorde**	*ska göra*
att gå (to go/walk)	**går**	**gick**	*ska gå*

sing. = singular, inf. = informal, pl. = plural

WORD ORDER

Swedish is similar to English in terms of word order for simple sentences, i.e. it follows the subject-verb-object pattern.
Example:
Sara läser en bok. Sara is reading a book.
When the sentence doesn't begin with a subject, the word order changes; the verb and the subject are inverted.
Example:
Nu läser Sara en bok. Now Sara is reading a book.
However, **nu** could just as well be placed at the end of the sentence, e.g. **Sara läser en bok nu.**
Questions are formed by reversing the order of the subject and verb:
Du ser katten. You see the cat.
Ser du katten? Do you see the cat?

NEGATIONS

A statement can be negated by inserting the word **inte** after the verb:
Jag talar svenska. I speak Swedish.
Jag talar inte svenska. I do not speak Swedish.

NOUNS & ARTICLES

The indefinite article (a, an) is expressed with **en** for common nouns and with **ett** for neuter nouns. Generally, common nouns can be both feminine and masculine (e.g. people, animals, etc.); neuter nouns have no gender (e.g. house, roof, etc.). However, there are several exceptions to this rule.
In Swedish, there are five different endings used to form plural nouns; three correspond to common gender nouns and two to neuter gender nouns. The following rules apply to nouns in the indefinite singular.

1. **en** words that end in -**a** take an -**or** ending
2. **en** words that end in -**e** take an -**ar** ending
3. **en** words with stress on the last vowel take an -**er** ending
4. **ett** words that end in a vowel take an -**n** ending
5. **ett** words that end in a consonant take no additional ending

Common gender nouns that end in a consonant are not covered by the rules above. These words will take either an -**ar** ending or an -**er** ending. The nouns which fall into this category will simply need to be memorized.

SINGULAR INDEFINITE	PLURAL INDEFINITE
en flicka (a girl)	**flick*or***
en timme (an hour)	**timm*ar***
en telefon (a telephone)	**telefon*er***
ett konto (an account)	**konto*n***
ett hus (a house)	**hus**
en bil (a car)	**bil*ar***

Definite articles: where in English we say 'the car', the Swedes say the equivalent of 'car-the', i.e. they tag the definite article onto the end of the noun. In the singular, common nouns take an -**en** ending, neuter nouns an -**et** ending. In the plural, common nouns add an -**na** and neuter nouns take an -**en** ending, neuter nouns an -**et** ending. In the plural, common nouns add an -**na** and neuter nouns take an -**en**.

	SINGULAR	PLURAL
common gender	**katten** the cat	**katterna** the cats
neuter gender	**tåget** the train	**tågen** the trains

DEMONSTRATIVE ADJECTIVES

	SINGULAR	NEUTER	PLURAL
this/these	**min**	**mitt**	**mina**
these/those	**den**	**det**	**de**
	denna bil (this car)	**deta hus** (this house)	

POSSESSIVE ADJECTIVES

	COMMON	NEUTER	PLURAL
my	**min**	**mitt**	**mina**
your (sing.)	**din**	**ditt**	**dina**
our	**vår**	**vårt**	**våra**
his	**hans**	**ditt**	**dina**
hers		**hennes**	
its		**dess/dess**	
their		**deras**	
your (pl.)	**er**	**ert**	**era**

ADVERBS & ADVERBIAL EXPRESSIONS

Adverbs are generally formed by adding **-t** to the corresponding adjective.
Snabb quick
Hon går snabbt. She walks quickly.

PRACTICALITIES

THE BASICS

NUMBERS

NEED TO KNOW

0	**noll** *nohl*
1	**ett** *eht*
2	**två** *tv**oa***
3	**tre** *tree*
4	**fyra** *few • ra*
5	**fem** *fehm*
6	**sex** *sehx*
7	**sju** *sheu*
8	**åtta** *oh • ta*
9	**nio** *nee • oa*
10	**tio** *tee • oa*
11	**elva** *ehl • va*
12	**tolv** *tohlv*
13	**tretton** *treh • tohn*
14	**fjorton** *fyeur • tohn*
15	**femton** *fehm • tohn*

16	**sexton** *sehx • tohn*
17	**sjutton** *sheu • tohn*
18	**arton** *ar • tohn*
19	**nitton** *nih • tohn*
20	**tjugo** *shcheu • goa*
21	**tjugoett** *shcheu • goa • eht*
22	**tjugotvå** *shcheu • goa • tvoa*
30	**trettio** *treh • tee • oa*
31	**trettioett** *treh • tee • oa • eht*
40	**fyrtio** *fuhr • tee • oa*
50	**femtio** *fehm • tee • oa*
60	**sextio** *sehx • tee • oa*
70	**sjuttio** *sheu • tee • oa*
80	**åttio** *oh • tee • oa*
90	**nittio** *nih • tee • oa*
100	**hundra** *huhn • dra*
101	**hundraett** *huhn • dra • eht*
200	**två hundra** *tvoa huhn • dra*
500	**fem hundra** *fehm huhn • dra*
1,000	**ett tusen** *eht teu • sehn*
10,000	**tio tusen** *tee • oa teu • sehn*
1,000,000	**en miljon** *ehn mihl • yoan*

ORDINAL NUMBERS

first	**första** *furs • ta*
second	**andra** *an • dra*
third	**tredje** *tree • dyer*

fourth	**fjärde** *fyair • der*
fifth	**femte** *fehm • ter*
once	**en gång** *ehn goang*
twice	**två gånger** *tvoa goang • ehr*
three times	**tre gånger** *tree goang • ehr*

TIME

NEED TO KNOW

What time is it?	**Hur mycket är klockan?** *heur mew • ker air kloh • kan*
It's noon [midday].	**Klockan är tolv.** *kloh • kan air tolv*
Midnight.	**Midnatt.** *meed • nat*
From 9 o'clock to 5 o'clock.	**Från nio till sjutton.** *froan nee • oa tihl sheu • tohn*
It's twenty after [past] four.	**Den är tjugo över fyra.** *dehn air shcheu • goa ur • ver few • ra*
It's a quarter to nine.	**Den är kvart i nio.** *dehn air kvart ee nee • oa*
5:30 a.m.	**Halv sex på morgonen.** *halv sehx poa mor • oh • nehn*
5:30 p.m.	**Halv sex på kvällen.** *halv sehx poa kveh • lehn*

Sweden officially follows the 24-hour clock. Formal communication, such as public transporation schedules and TV programming, follows this system. However, in ordinary conversation, time is generally expressed as shown above, often with the addition of **på morgonen** (in the morning), **på förmiddagen** (mid-morning), **på eftermiddagen** (in the afternoon), **på kvällen** (in the evening) and **på natten** (at night).

DAYS

NEED TO KNOW

Monday **måndag**
moan • dahg

Tuesday **tisdag**
tees • dahg

Wednesday **onsdag**
oans • dahg

Thursday **torsdag**
toash • dahg

Friday **fredag**
free • dahg

Saturday **lördag**
lurr • dahg

Sunday **söndag**
surn • dahg

DATES

yesterday	**igår** *ee • goar*
today	**idag** *ee • dahg*
tomorrow	**imorgon** *ee • mo • ron*
day	**dag** *dahg*
week	**vecka** *veh • ka*
month	**månad** *moa • nad*
year	**år** *oar*

MONTHS

January	**januari** *ya • neu • ah • ree*
February	**februari** *fehb • reu • ah • ree*
March	**mars** *mash*
April	**april** *ap • rihl*
May	**maj** *maiy*
June	**juni** *yeu • nee*
July	**juli** *yeu • lee*

August	**augusti** *a • guhss • tee*
September	**september** *sehp • tehm • behr*
October	**oktober** *ohk • toa • behr*
November	**november** *noh • vehm • behr*
December	**december** *dee • sehm • behr*

Sweden follows a day-month-year format instead of the month-day-year format used in the U.S.
E.g.: July 25, 2008; **25/07/08** = 7/25/2008 in the U.S.

SEASONS

spring	**vår** *voar*
summer	**sommar** *soh • mar*
fall [autumn]	**höst** *huhst*
winter	**vinter** *vihn • tehr*

HOLIDAYS

January 1: **Nyårsdagen** New Year's Day
January 6: **Trettondagen** Epiphany
May 1: **Första maj** May Day
June 6: **Flaggans dag** Flag Day

December 25: **Juldagen** Christmas Day
December 26: **Annandag jul** Boxing Day
Moveable dates include:
Långfredagen Good Friday
Kristi himmelfärdsdag Ascension
Pingstdagen Whitsunday
Allhelgonadagen All Saints' Day
Midsommardagen Midsummer Day

The two most important holidays in Sweden are Midsummer and Christmas. **Midsommardagen** (Midsummer) is celebrated with midsummer poles (similar to the may pole) and traditional songs and dances. Traditional food includes **matjesill** (pickled herring), fresh fish and schnapps. For **Juldagen** (Christmas), special cakes and other delicious treats are prepared, such as **pepparkakor** (ginger cookies), **saffranbullar** (saffron buns) and **julbord** (Christmas **smörgåsbord,** a festive buffet). Though not an official holiday, **Luciadagen** (St. Lucia Day) on December 13 marks the beginning of the Chirstmas season. Swedes also celebrate the beginning of spring on April 30, which is known as **Valborgsmässoafton,** with huge bonfires, fireworks and singing. June 6 is **Flaggans dag** (Flag Day), the national day of Sweden. Streets are decorated with yellow and blue, the colors of the Swedish flag, patriotic speeches are made and traditional games and meals are enjoyed.

ARRIVAL & DEPARTURE

NEED TO KNOW

I'm here on vacation [holiday]/business. **Jag är här på semester/ affärsresa.**
Yahg air hair poa seh • mehs • ter/ a • fairs • ree • sa

I'm going to... **Jag ska resa till...**
yahg skah ree • sa tihl...

I'm staying at a hotel/youth hostel. **Jag bor på hotell/vandrarhem.**
yahg boar poa hoh • tehl/ vahnd • rar • hehm

BORDER CONTROL

I'm just passing through. **Jag är bara på genomresa.**
yahg air bah • ra poa ye • nohm • ree • sa

I would like to declare... **Jag skulle vilja förtulla...**
yahg skuh • ler vihl • ya furr • tuh • la...

I have nothing to declare. **Jag har inget att förtulla.**
yahg hahr ihng • eht at furr • tuh • la

YOU MAY HEAR...

Er biljett/Ert pass, tack. *eer bihl • yeht/ eert pas tak*	Your ticket/ passport, please.
Vad är syftet med ert besök? *vahd air sewf • tet meed ehrt beh • surk*	What's the purpose of your visit?
Var bor du? *vahr boar deu*	Where are you staying?
Hur länge ska du stanna? *heur lehng • er skah deu stan • a*	How long are you staying?
Vem är du här med? *vehm air deu hair meed*	Who are you here with?
Metta le iniziali/Firmi qui. *meht • tah leh ee • nee • tsyah • lee/ feer • mee kwee*	Initial/Sign here.

YOU MAY SEE...

TULL	customs
TAXFRIA VAROR	duty-free goods
VAROR ATT FÖRTULLA	goods to declare
INGET ATT FÖRTULLA	nothing to declare
PASSKONTROLL	passport control
POLIS	police

YOU MAY HEAR...

Har du något att förtulla? *hahr deu noa • goht at furr • tuh • la*	Anything to declare?
Du måste betala tull för det här. *deu mos • ter beh • tah • la tuhl furr dee hair*	You must pay duty on this.
Var snäll och öppna den här väskan. *vahr snehl ohk urp • na dehn hair vehs • kan*	Please open this bag.

MONEY

NEED TO KNOW

Where's...?	**Var ligger...?** *vahr lih • gehr...*
the ATM	**bankomaten** *bank • oa • mah • tehn*
the bank	**banken** *bank • ehn*
the currency exchange office	**växelkontoret** *vehx • ehl • kohn • toar • eht*
What time does the bank open/close?	**När öppnar/stänger banken?** *nair urp • nahr/stehng • ehr bank • ehn*
I'd like to change dollars/pounds into kronor.	**Jag skulle vilja växla dollar/pund till kronor.** *yahg skuh • ler vihl • ya vehx • la doh • lar/pund tihl kroa • nohr*
I want to cash some traveler's checks [cheques].	**Jag skulle vilja lösa in några resecheckar.** *yahg skuh • ler vihl • yalur • sa ihn noa • gra ree • seh • sheh • kar*

AT THE BANK

Can I exchange foreign currency here?	**Kan jag växla pengar här?** *kan yahg vehx • la pehng • ar hair*
What's the exchange rate?	**Vad är växelkursen?** *vahd air vehx • ehl • keur • shehn*
I think there's a mistake.	**Jag tror det är ett misstag.** *Yahg troar dee air eht mis • tagh*
How much is the fee?	**Hur mycket är expeditionsavgiften?** *Heur mew • ker air ehx • peh • dee • shoans • afv • yihf • tehn*
I've lost my traveler's checks.	**Jag har tappat mina resecheckar.** *Yahg hahr ta • pat mee • na ree • seh • sheh • kar*
I've lost my card.	**Jag har tappat mitt kort.** *yahg hahr ta • pat miht koart*
My credit cards have been stolen.	**Mina kreditkort är stulna.** *mee • na kreh • deet • koart air steul • na*
My card doesn't work.	**Mitt kort fungerar inte.** *miht koart fuhn • gee • rar ihn • ter*
The ATM ate my card.	**Uttagsautomaten tog mitt kort.** *eut • tahgs • ah • toa • mah • tehn toagh mith koart.*

For Numbers, see page 22.

YOU MAY SEE...

SÄTT IN KORTET	insert card
AVBESTÄLLA	cancel
RENSA	clear
ENTER	enter
PINKOD	PIN
TA UT	withdraw
FRÅN CHEKKONTO	from checking [current] account
FRÅN SPARKONTO	from savings account
KVITTOT	receipt

Cash can be obtained from a **Bankomat** (ATM) with MasterCard, Visa, Eurocard, American Express and other international credit cards or with a debit card. It is also possible to exchange traveler's checks in Sweden. In recent years, it has become quite common for the banks to refer customers with traveler's checks to the nearest **växelkontor** (currency exchange business) such as Forex or X-Change. These businesses are often located near or in points of departure/arrival such as airports or train stations, but can also be found in city centers. Remember to bring your passport with you for identification when you want to exchange money or cash traveler's checks. Most banks close at 3:00 p.m., though some are open later one day a week, often on Thursdays.

YOU MAY SEE...

Unlike the majority of other European Union countries, Sweden has not adopted the euro as its national currency. Sweden's monetary unit is the **krona** (singular) or **kronor** (plural) abbreviated to **SEK**.
The **krona** is divided into **öre**.
Coins: 50 **öre**,1 **krona**, 5 and 10 **kronor**
Banknotes: 20, 50,100, 500 and 1000 **kronor**

CONVERSATION

NEED TO KNOW

Hello!	**Hej!** *hay*
How are you?	**Hur står det till?** *heur stoar dee tihl*
Fine, thanks. And you?	**Bra, tack. Och du?** *brah tak ohk deu*
Excuse me!	**Ursäkta!** *eur • shehk • ta*
Do you speak English?	**Talar du engelska?** *tah • lar deu ehng • ehl • ska*
What's your name?	**Vad heter du?** *vahd hee • tehr deu*
My name is...	**Jag heter...** *yahg hee • tehr...*

Nice to meet you.	**Trevligt att träffas.** *treev • lihgt at trehf • as.*
Where are you from?	**Var kommer du ifrån?** *vahr ko • mehr deu ee • froan*
I'm from the U.S./U.K.	**Jag kommer från USA/ Storbritannien.** *yahg koh • mehr froan eu ehs ah/ stoap • bree • tan • yehn*
What do you do?	**Vad sysslar du med?** *vahd sews • lar deu meed*
I work for…	**Jag jobbar på.** *yahg yohb • ar poa…*
I'm a student.	**Jag är student.** *yahg air stuh • dent*
I'm retired.	**Jag är pensionär.** *yahg air pang • shoa • nair*
Do you like…?	**Tycker du om…?** *tew • kehr deu ohm…*
Goodbye.	**Hej då.** *hay • doa*
See you later.	**Vi ses.** *vee sees*

LANGUAGE DIFFICULTIES

Do you speak English?	**Talar du engelska?** *tah • lar deu ehng • ehl • ska*
Does anyone here speak English?	**Talar någon engelska här?** *tah • lar noa • gohn ehng • ehl • ska hair*
I don't speak Swedish.	**Jag talar inte svenska.** *yahg tah • lar ihn • ter svehn • ska*
Could you speak more slowly?	**Kan du tala lite långsammare?** *kan deu tah • la lee • ter loang • sam • a • rer*
Could you repeat that?	**Kan du upprepa det?** *kan deu uhp • ree • pah dee*
Excuse me?	**Ursäkta?** *eur • shehk • ta*
What was that?	**Vad var det?** *vahd vahr dee*
Can you spell it?	**Kan du stava det?** *kahn deu stah • va deht*
Write it down, please.	**Skriv ner det, tack.** *skreev neer dee tak*
Can you translate this for me?	**Kan du översätta det här?** *kan deu ur • ver • seh • ta deet hair*
What does this/that mean?	**Vad betyder det här/där?** *vad beh • tew • der dee hair/dair*
I understand.	**Jag förstår.** *yahg furr • stoar*
I don't understand.	**Jag förstår inte.** *yahg furr • stoar ihn • ter*
Do you understand?	**Förstår du?** *furr • stoar deu*

YOU MAY HEAR...

Jag talar bara lite engelska. *yahg tah • lar bah • ra lee • ter ehng • ehl • ska*	I speak only a little English.
Jag talar inte engelska. *yahg tah • lar in • ter ehng • ehl • ska*	I don't speak English.

MAKING FRIENDS

Swedes shake hands when greeting someone and when saying goodbye; this applies for meeting new people but is also often the case with colleagues or acquaintances. When you meet someone for the first time, shake hands and give your name. As in many countries, titles are more commonly used by the older generation, but you will sometimes hear **herr** (Mr.), **fru** (Mrs.) and **fröken** (Miss) used, as well as professional titles, e.g., **doktor** (doctor), **ingenjör** (engineer), etc.

Hello.	**Hej.** *hay*
Good morning.	**God morgon.** *goad mor • on*
Good afternoon.	**God middag.** *goad mi • dahg*
Good evening.	**God afton.** *goad af • tohn*
My name is...	**Jag heter...** *yahg hee • tehr...*
What's your name?	**Vad heter du?** *vahd hee • tehr deu*

I'd like to introduce you to...	**Får jag presentera...** *foar yahg preh • sehn • tee • ra...*
Pleased to meet you.	**Trevligt att träffas.** *treev • lihgt at treh • fas*
How are you?	**Hur står det till?** *heur stoar dee tihl*
Fine, thanks.	**Bra, tack.** *brah tak*
And you?	**Och du?** *ohk deu*

TRAVEL TALK

I'm here...	**Jag är här...** *yahg air hair...*
on business	**på affärsresa** *poa a • fairs • ree • sa*
on vacation [holiday]	**på semester** *poa seh • mehs • tehr*
studying	**för studier** *furr steu • de • ehr*
I'm staying for...	**Jag ska stanna i...** *yahg skah sta • na ee...*
I've been here..	**Jag har varit här i...** *yahg hahr vah • riht hair ee...*
a day	**en dag** *ehn dahg*
a week	**en vecka** *ehn veh • ka*
a month	**en månad** *ehn moa • nad*
Where are you from?	**Var kommer du ifrån?** *vahr koh • mehr deu ee • froan*
I'm from.	**Jag kommer från.** *yahg koh • mehr froan...*

For Numbers, see page 22.

PERSONAL

Who are you here with?	**Vem är du här med?** *vehm air deu hair meed*
I'm on my own.	**Jag är ensam.** *yahg air ehn • sam*
I'm with…	**Jag är här med…** *yahg air hair meed…*
my husband/wife	**min man/fru** *mihn man/freu*
my boyfriend	**min pojkvän** *mihn povk • vehn*
girlfriend	**flickvän** *flihk • vehn*
a friend/friends	**en vän/vänner** *ehn vehn/venhn • ehr*
a colleague	**en kollega** *ehn koh • lee • ga/*
colleagues	**kolleger** *koh • lee • goahr*
When's your birthday?	**När fyller du år?** *nair fewl • ehr deu* ***oa****r*
How old are you?	**Hur gammal är du?** *heur gah • mal air deu*
I'm…	**Jag är…** *yahg air…*
single	**ogift** *oa • yift*
in a relationship	**i ett förhållande** *ee eht furr • hoal • an • der*
engaged	**förlovad** *fuhr • loh • vad*

married	**gift** *yihft*
divorced	**skild** *shihld*
separated	**separerad** *seh • pa • ree • rad*
I'm a widow/ widower.	**Jag är änka/änkling.** *yahg air ehng • ka/ehnak • lihna*
Do you have children/ grandchildren?	**Har du barn/barnbarn?** *hahr deu bahrn/bahrn • bahrn*

For Numbers, see page 22.

WORK & SCHOOL

What do you do?	**Vad sysslar du med?** *vahd sews • lar deu meed*
What are you studying?	**Vad läser du?** *vahd lai • sehr deu*
I'm studying...	**Jag läser...** *yahg lai • sehr...*
I work full time/ part time.	**Jag arbetar heltid/deltid.** *yahg ahr • beh • tar hehl • teed/dehl • teed*
I work at home.	**Jag arbetar hemifrån.** *yahg ahr • beh • tar hehm • ih • froan*
I'm unemployed.	**Jag är arbetslös.** *yahg air ar • behts • lus*
Who do you work for?	**Vilken firma jobbar du på?** *vihl • kehn fihr • ma yohb • ar deu poa*
I work for...	**Jag jobbar på...** *yahg yohb • ar poa...*
Here's my business card.	**Här är mitt kort.** *hair air miht koahrt*

WEATHER

What's the weather forecast for tomorrow?	**Vad är väderleksrapporten för imorgon?** *vahd air vair • dehr • leeks • ra • pohr • tehn furr ee • mo • ron*
What beautiful/ terrible weather!	**Vilket vackert/förskräckligt väder!** *vihl • keht va • kert/furr • skrehk • ligt vair • dehr*
It's...	**Det är...** *dee air...*
hot/cold	**varmt/kallt** *varmt/kahlt*
cool/warm	**svalt/varmt** *svahlt/varmt*
rainy/sunny	**regnigt/soligt** *rehng • nihkt/soal • ikt*
snowy/icy	**snöigt/halt** *snur • ikt/hahlt*
Do I need a jacket/ an umbrella?	**Behöver jag en jacka/ett paraply?** *beh • hur • ver yahg ehn yah • ka/eht pa • ra • plew*

CLARION HOTEL

ON THE WAY

GETTING AROUND

NEED TO KNOW

How do I get to town?	**Hur kommer jag till staden?** *heur koh • mehr yahg tihl stahd • ehn*
Where is...?	**Var ligger...?** *vahr lih • gehr...*
the airport	**flygplatsen** *flewg • plats • ehn*
the train [railway] station	**järnvägsstationen** *yairn • vehgs • sta • shoa • nehn*
the bus station	**bussterminalen** *bus • tehr • mee • nah • lehn*
the subway [underground] station	**tunnelbanestationen** *teu • nehl • bah • neh • sta • shoan • ehn*
How far is it?	**Hur långt är det?** *heur loangt air dee*
Where can I buy tickets?	**Var kan jag köpa biljetter?** *vahr kan yahg chur • pa bil • yeht • tehr*

One-way [single]/ round-trip [return].	**Enkel/Retur.** *ehng • kehl/reh • teur*
How much does it cost?	**Hur mycket kostar det?** *heur mew • ker kos • tar d**ee***
Are there any discounts?	**Finns det några rabatter?** *fihns d**ee** n**oa** • gra ra • bat • ehr*
Which gate?	**Vid vilken gate?** *veed vihl • kehn gayt*
Which line?	**Vilken kö?** *vihl • kehn k**ur***
Which platform?	**Vilken plattform?** *vihl • kehn plat • fohrm*
Where can I get a taxi?	**Var kan jag få tag på en taxi?** *vahr kan yahg f**oa** tahg p**oa** ehn tax • ee*
Please take me to this address.	**Var snäll och kör mig till denna address.** *vahr snehl ohk ch**ur**r may tihl deh • na ad • rehs*
Where can I rent a car?	**Var kan jag hyra en bil?** *vahr kan yahg hew • ra ehn beel*
I'd like a map.	**Jag skulle vilja ha en karta.** *Yahg skuh • ler vihl • ya h**ah** ehn kahr • ta*

TICKETS

When is...to	**När går...till Uppsala?** *nair g**oa**r...tihl uhp • sah • la Uppsala?*
the (first) bus	**(första) bussen** *(f**ur**s • ta) buhs • ehn*

the (next) flight	**(nästa) flyg** *(nehs • ta) flewg*
the (last) train	**(sista) tåget** *(sihs • ta) toa • geht*
Where can I buy tickets?	**Var kan jag köpa biljetter?** *vahr kan yahg chur • pa bihl • yeht • er*
One ticket/Two tickets, please.	**En biljett/Två biljetter, tack.** *ehn bil • yet/tvoa bil • yeht • er tak*
For today/tomorrow.	**Till dagens/imorgon.** *tihl dah • gens/ee • mo • ron*
...ticket.	**...biljett.** *...bihl • yeht*
A one-way [single]	**En enkel** *ehn ehng • kehl*
A return-trip	**En retur** *ehn reh • teur*
A first class	**En första klass** *ehn furr • sta klas*
A business class	**En i affärsklass** *Ehn ee a • fairs • klas*
An economy class	**En turist klass** *ehn tuh • rihst klas*
How much does it cost?	**Hur mycket kostar det?** *heur mew • ker kos • tar dee*
Is there a discount for...?	**Blir det rabatt för...?** *bleer dee ra • bat furr...*
children	**barn** *bahrn*
students	**studerande** *steu • dee • ran • der*
senior citizens	**pensionärer** *pan • shoa • nair • ehr*
tourists	**turister** *tuh • rihst • ehr*

The express bus/ express train, please.	**Expressbussen/expresståget, tack.** *Ehx • prehs • buhs • ehn/ ehx • prehs • toa • geht, tak*
The local bus/train, please.	**Lokalbussen/tåget, tack.** *Loh • kahl • buhs • en/toa • geht, tak*
I have an e-ticket.	**Jag har en e-biljett.** *yahg hahr ehn ee • bihl • yet*
Can I buy a ticket on the bus/train?	**Kan jag köpa en biljett på bussen/ tåget?** *kan yahg chur • pa ehn bihl • yeht poa bus • ehn/toa • geht*
Do I have to stamp the ticket before boarding?	**Ska jag stämpla biljetten innan jag går ombord?** *Skah yahg stehm • pla bil • yet • ehn • ihn • ahn • yahg • goar • ohm • bohrd*
How long is this ticket valid?	**Hur länge gäller denna biljett?** *Heur lehng • er yeh • lehr deh • na bihl • yet*
Can I return on the same ticket?	**Kan jag åka tillbaka med samma biljett?** *Kahn yahg oak • ha tihl • bah • ka mehd sam • a bihl • yet*
I'd like to...my reservation.	**Jag skulle vilja...min bokning.** *Yahg skuh • ler vihl • ya...mihn boak • nihng*
cancel	**avbeställa** *afv • beh • steh • la*
change	**ändra** *ehn • dra*
confirm	**bekräfta** *beh • krehf • ta*

AIRPORT TRANSFER

How much is a taxi to the airport?	**Vad kostar en taxi till flygplatsen?** *Vahd kos • tar ehn tax • ee tihl flewg • plat • sehn*
To...Airport, please.	**Till...Flygplats, tack.** *tihl...flewg • plats tak*
My airline is...	**Mitt flygbolag är...** *miht flewg • boa • lahg air...*
My flight leaves at...	**Mitt flyg avgår klockan...** *miht flewg afv•goar kloh • kan...*
I'm in a rush.	**Jag har bråttom.** *yahg hahr broa • tohm*
Can you take an alternate route?	**Kan du köra någon annan väg?** *kan deu chur • ra noa • gohn an • nan vehg*
Can you drive faster/ slower?	**Kan du köra lite fortare/långsammare?** *kan deu chur • ra lee • ter foar • ta • rer/ loang • sam • a • rer*

YOU MAY HEAR...

Vilket flygbolag reser du med? *vihl • keht flewg • boa • lahg ree • sehr deu meed*	What airline are you flying?
Inrikes eller utrikes? *in • ree • kehs ehl • er eut • ree • kehs*	Domestic or International?
Vilken terminal? *vihl • kehn tehr • mee • nahl*	What terminal?

CHECKING IN

Where is check-in?	**Var är incheckningen?** *vahr air in • shehk • nihng • ehn*
My name is...	**Jag heter...** *yahg hee • ter...*
I'm going to...	**Jag ska resa till...** *yahg skah ree • sa tihl...*
I have...	**Jag har....** *Yahg hahr...*
one suitcase	**en resväska** *ehn rehs • vehs • ka*
two suitcases	**två resväskor** *tvoh rehs • vehs • kohr*
one piece of hand luggage	**ett handbagage** *eht hand • ba • gah • sh*
How much luggage is allowed?	**Hur mycket gratis bagage får man ha?** *heur mew • ker grah • tihs ba • goash foar man hah*
Is that pounds or kilos?	**Är det i pund eller kilo?** *Air deht ee pund ehl • er cheeh • loh*
Which terminal/ gate does flight... leave from?	**Vid vilken terminal/gate går flygnummer...?** *veed vihl • kehn tehr • mee • nahl/gayt goar flewg • nuhm • ehr...*
I'd like a window/ an aisle seat.	**Jag skulle vilja ha en fönsterplats/ plats i mittgången.** *yahg skuh • ler vihl • ya hah ehn furns • tehr • plats/plats ee miht • goang • ehn*
When do we leave/ arrive?	**När avgår vi/är vi framme?** *nair afv • goar vee/air vee fra • mer*

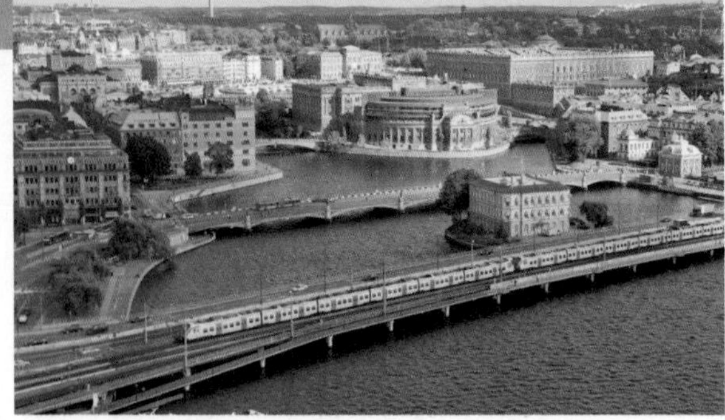

Is flight...delayed?	**Är det någon försening på flyg...?** *air d**ee** noa • gohn furr • seen • ihng p**oa** fl**ew**g...*
How late will it be?	**Hur försenat är det?** *heur furr • seen • at air d**ee***

YOU MAY SEE...

ANKOMST	arrivals
AVGÅNG	departures
BAGAGEUTLÄMNING	baggage claim
INRIKESFLYG	domestic flights
UTRIKESFLYG	international flights
CHECKA IN	check-in
CHECKA IN E-BILJETT	e-ticket check-in
AVGÅNGSGATER	departure gates

YOU MAY HEAR...

Nästa! *nehs • ta*	Next!
Er biljett/Ert pass, tack. *eer bihl • yet/ eert pas tak*	Your ticket/ passport, please.
Hur mycket bagage har du? *heur mew • ker ba • goash hahr deu*	How much luggage do you have?
Du har övervikt. *deu hahr **ur** • vehr • vikt*	You have excess luggage.
Det där är för tungt/för stort handbagage. *d**ee** dair air f**urr** teungt/f**urr** st**oa**rt hand • ba • goash*	That's too heavy/large for a carry-on [to carry on board].
Packade du väskorna själv? *pa • ka • der deu vehs • kohr • na shehlv*	Did you pack these bags yourself?
Har någon gett er något att ta med? *hahr n**oa** • gohn yeht eer n**oa** • goht at tah meed*	Did anyone give you anything to carry?
Töm era fickor, tack. *turm ee • ra fihk • ohr tak*	Empty your pockets, please.
Ta av er skorna, tack. *ta afv eer skoar • na tak*	Take off your shoes, please.
Nu är ni välkommna att borda flight nummer... *neu air nee vail • kohm • na at bohr • da flajt nuhm • ehr...*	Now boarding flight...

LUGGAGE

Where is/are...?	**Var finns...?** *vahr fihns...*
the luggage carts [trolleys]	**bagagekärrorna** *ba • goash • chair • ohr • na*
the luggage lockers	**förvaringsskåpen** *furr • vah • rihng • sk**oa**p • ehn*
the baggage claim	**bagageutlämningen** *ba • goash • eut • lehm • nihng • ehn*
I've lost my baggage.	**Jag har förlorat mitt bagage.** *yahg hahr furr • loa • rat miht ba • goash*
My baggage has been stolen.	**Mitt bagage har blivit stulet.** *miht ba • goash hahr blee • viht steu • leht*
My suitcase was damaged.	**Min resväska blev skadad.** *Mihn rees • vehs • ka bleev skah • dad*

FINDING YOUR WAY

Where is...?	**Var finns...?** *vahr fihns...*
the currency exchange office	**växelkontoret** *vehx • ehl • kohn • t**oa**r • eht*
the car hire	**biluthyrningen** *beel • **eu**t • h**ew**r • nihng • ehn*
the exit	**utgången** *eut • g**oa**ng • ehn*
the taxi	**taxin** *tax • een*
Is there...into town?	**Finns det...in till stan?** *fihns d**ee**...ihn tihl stahn*
a bus	**en buss** *ehn buhs*

a train	**ett tåg** *eht toag*
a subway	**tunnelbana** *tuh • nehl • bah • na*

For Asking Directions, see page 64.

YOU MAY SEE...

PLATTFORM	platform
SPÅR	tracks
INFORMATION	information
BILJETTKONTOR	ticket office
ANKOMST	arrival
AVGÅNG	departure

TRAIN

How do I get to the train station?	**Hur kommer jag till järnvägsstationen?** *heur koh • mehr yahg tihl yairn • vaigs • sta • shoa • nehn*
How far is it?	**Hur långt är det?** *heur loangt air dee*
Where is/are...?	**Var finns...?** *vahr fihns...*
the ticket office	**biljettkontoret** *bihl • yet • kohn • toar • eht*
the luggage lockers	**förvaringsskåpen** *furr • vah • rihng • skoap • ehn*
the platforms	**plattformarna** *plat • fohr • mar • na*
Could I have a schedule [timetable], please?	**Kan jag få en tidtabell, tack?** *kan yahg foa ehn teed • ta • behl tak*

How long is the trip?	**Hur lång tid tar resan?** *heur loang teed tahr ree • san*
Is it a direct train?	**Är det ett direkttåg?** *air deh • ta eht dihr • ekt • toag*
Do I have to change trains?	**Behöver jag byta tåg?** *beh • hur • vehr yahg bew • ta toag*
Is the train on time?	**Är tåget i tid?** *air toag • het ee tihd*

For Time, see page 24.

Statens järnvägar or **SJ** (the Swedish State Railway) operates an extensive network covering the entire country, while also offering international connections to Oslo, Copenhagen and Berlin. The X2000 train, which reaches speeds up to 200 km/h, serves many of Sweden's greater cities and towns. Long-distance trains have restaurant cars and/or buffets, and there are also sleepers and couchettes for both first and second class. The system is reliable and comfortable, and offers a wide range of travel options with respect to schedule and cost. Discount tickets are available for young children, families, students and senior citizens. Special travel cards and programs are also available. On some trains, marked **R** or **IC**, you must reserve a seat by purchasing a **sittplatsbiljett** in addition to your travel ticket. For extraordinary scenery, try the northern **Inlandsbanan** (Inland Railway) service, which runs from Mora in Dalarna to Gällivare beyond the Arctic circle. The **Vildmarksexpressen** (Wilderness Express) has old 1930s coaches and a gourmet restaurant, and runs on the same line between Östersund and Gällivare, with stops and excursions.

DEPARTURES

Which platform does the train to...leave from?	**Vilken plattform går tåget till...från?** *Vihl • kehn plat • fohrm goar tao • geht froan*
When is the train to...?	**När går tåget till...?** *nair goar toa • geht tihl...*
Is this the right platform for...?	**Är det här rätta plattformen till...?** *air dee hair reh • ta plat • fohr • mehn tihl...*
Where is platform...?	**Var är plattform...?** *vahr air plat • fohrm...*
Where do I change for...?	**Var måste jag byta till...?** *vahr mos • ter yahg bew • ta tihl...*

ON BOARD

Can I sit here/open the window?	**Kan jag sitta här/öppna fönstret?** *Kan yahg sihta hair/urp • na fuhns • streht*
Is this seat taken?	**Är den här platsen upptagen?** *air dehn hair plats • ehn uhp • tah • gehn*
That's my seat.	**Det där är min plats.** *dee dair air mihn plats*
Here's my reservation.	**Här är min bokning.** *Hair air meen boak • nihng*

BUS

Where's the bus station?	**Var är bussterminalen?** *vahr air bus • tehr • mih • nahl • ehn*
How far is it?	**Hur långt är det?** *heur loangt air dee*
How do I get to...?	**Hur kommer jag till...?** *heur koh • mehr yahg tihl...*

Does the bus stop at...?	**Stannar bussen vid...?** *stan • ar buhs • en veed...*
Could you tell me when to get off?	**Kan du tala om för mig när jag ska stiga av?** *kan deu tah • la ohm furr may nair yahg skah stee • ga afv*
Do I have to change buses?	**Behöver jag byta buss?** *beh • hur • vehr yahg bew • ta buhs*
Stop here, please.	**Stanna här, tack.** *sta • na hair tak*

For Tickets, see page 45.

YOU MAY HEAR...

Påstigning! *poa • steeg • nihng*	All aboard!
Biljetter, tack. *bihl • yet • er tak*	Tickets, please.
Du måste byta i... *deu moss • ter bew • ta ee...*	You have to change in...
Nästa hållplats... *nehs • ta hoal • plats...*	Next stop...

YOU MAY SEE...

BUSSHÅLLPLATS	bus stop
INGÅNG/UTGÅNG	enter/exit
STÄMPLA ER BILJETT	stamp your ticket

Public transportation in Sweden is an excellent and well-maintained system that includes **bussar** (buses), **tunnelbanan** (subways), **spårvagnar** (trams) and **tåg** (trains). All of these run frequently, usually between 5:00 a.m. and midnight on weekdays and a bit later on weekends. Most cities and towns have a bus system, though only a few have trams and subways. While it is possible to purchase single tickets for the different modes of public transportation, it is more cost efficient to purchase a card or set of tickets if you are going to be using a particular network frequently. Most major cities have websites that provide up to date information on routes, tickets and prices; many of the sites have English as a language option.

SUBWAY

Where's the nearest subway [underground] station?	**Var är närmaste tunnelbanestation?** *Vahr air nair • mas • ter tuh • nehl • bah • neh • sta • sh**oa**n*
Which direction?	**Åt vilket håll?** *Oat vihl • keht hohl*
Can I have a map of the subway [underground], please?	**Kan jag få en tunnelbanekarta, tack?** *Kan yahg f**oa** ehn tuh • nehl • bah • neh • kahr • ta tak*
Which line should I take for...?	**Vilken linje ska jag ta till...?** *vihl • kehn leen • yeh skah yahg tah tihl...*
Where do I change for...?	**Var måste jag byta till...?** *vahr mos • ter yahg b**ew** • ta tihl...*

Is this the train to…?	**Är det här tåget till…?** *air d**ee** hair <u>toa</u> • geht tihl…*
How many stops to…?	**Hur många hållplatser är det till...?** *Heur moh • ngah hohl • plat • sehr air deht tihl...*
Where are we?	**Var är vi?** *vahr air vee*

For Tickets, see page 45.

The subway in Stockholm is efficient and easy to use. It runs from 5:00 a.m. to midnight on weekdays. Tickets are valid for one hour from the time they are stamped and can be bought from ticket booths; discount cards can be purchased from **Pressbyrån** (a newsstand). Tickets can also be purchased at **SL Centers**, some tourist offices and certain grocery stores. The public transportation websites will have information on these retailers and businesses and what types of tickets they sell. Day and multi-day cards are also available. Subway and bus tickets in Stockholm are interchangeable.

YOU MAY SEE...

LIVBÅT	life boat
FLYTVÄST	life jacket
ACTIVERA HANDBROMSEN	use parking brake
LÄMNA INTE VÄRDESAKER I BILEN	do not leave valuables in your car

BOAT & FERRY

When is the car ferry to Gotland leaving?	**Hur dags går bilfärjan till Gotland?** *heur daks g**oa**r beel • fair • yan tihl goht • land*
Where are the life jackets?	**Var finns flytvästarna?** *vahr fihns flewt • vehs • tar • na*
Can I take my car?	**Kan jag ta med min bil?** *Kahn yahg tah mehd meen bihl*
Can I drive on to the ferry now?	**Får jag köra ombord nu?** *f**oa**r yahg ch**ur** • ra ohm bohrd neu*
What time is the next sailing?	**Hur dags går nästa?** *Heur daks goar nehs • ta*
Can I book a seat/ cabin?	**Kan jag boka en plats/hytt?** *Kahn yahg boa • ka plats/hewt*
How long is the trip?	**Hur lång är resan?** *heur l**oa**ng air ree • san*
Where should I park?	**Var ska jag parkera?** *vahr skah yahg par • **kee** • ra*

Regular boat and ferry services, carrying cars and passengers, link Sweden to neighboring countries such as Norway, Denmark and Germany as well as to the U.K. Ferry services from Stockholm to the vacation destinations of Åland and Gotland in the Baltic Sea are very popular, as are ferries to Finland, Estonia and Latvia. Not to be missed are the ferry and steamer trips from Stockholm to the many surrounding islands, known as **Skärgården** (the Archipelago).

TAXI

Where can I get a taxi?	**Var kan jag få tag på en taxi?** *vahr kan yahg foa tahg p**oa** ehn tax • ee*
I'd like a taxi now/for tomorrow at...	**Jag skulle vilja ha en taxi nu/imorgon klockan...** *yahg skuh • ler vihl • ya hah ehn tax • ee neu/ee • mo • ron kloh • kan...*
Can you send a taxi?	**Kan du skicka en taxi?** *Kahn deu shih • ka ehn tax • ee*
Do you have the number for a taxi?	**Har du numret till taxi?** *Hahr deu nuhm • reht tihl tax • ee*
Pick me up at... (place/time)	**Hämta mig vid/klockan...** *hehm • ta may veed/kloh • kan...*
I'm going to...	**Jag ska resa till...** *yahg skah ree • sa tihl...*
this address	**denna adress** *deh • na ad • rehs*
the airport	**flygplatsen** *fl**ewg** • plat • sehn*
the train station	**järnvägsstationen** *y**air**n • vaigs • sta • sh**oa** • nehn*
I'm late.	**Jag är sen.** *yahg air seen*
Can you drive faster/ slower?	**Kan du köra fortare/långsammare?** *Kan deu ch**ur** • ra fohrt • a • rer/ loang • sam • a • rer*
Stop/Wait here.	**Stanna/Vänta här.** *sta • na/vehn • ta hair*
How much?	**Hur mycket kostar det?** *heur mew • ker kos • tar dee*
You said it would cost...kronor.	**Du sa att det skulle kosta...kronor.** *deu sah at **dee** skuh • ler kos • ta... kr**oa** • nohr*

Keep the change. **Behåll växeln.**
be • hoal vehx • ehln

A receipt, please. **Kvittot, tack.**
kvih • tot tak

Taxis can be found at stands marked **Taxi.** You can also flag down a taxi in the street, especially near hotels and bus and train stations. Calling a taxi by phone is a third option; numbers are available from your concierge or a local phone book. The sign **Ledig** (free), when lit, indicates that the taxi is available.

YOU MAY HEAR...

Vart vill du åka? Where to?
vart vihl deu ***oa*** *• ka*

Vilken adress? What's the address?
vihl • kehn ad • rehs

BICYCLE & MOTORBIKE

I'd like to hire... **Jag skulle vilja hyra...**
*yahg skuh • ler vihl • ya h*_**ew**_ *• ra...*

a bicycle **en cykel**
ehn sew • kehl

a moped **en moped**
ehn moh • peed

a motorbike **en motorcykel**
*ehn m*_**oa**_ *• tohr • sew • kehl*

How much per day/ week?	**Hur mycket kostar det per dag/vecka?** *heur mew • ker kos • tar dee pair dahg/ veh • ka*
Can I have a helmet/ lock?	**Kan jag få en hjälm/ett cykelås?** *kan yahg foa ehn yehlm/eht sew • kehl • loas*

YOU MAY HEAR...

Har du ett internationellt körkort? *hahr deu eht in • tehr • na • shoa • nehlt churr • koart*	Do you have an international driver's license?
Kan jag få se ert pass, tack? *kan yahg foa see eert pas tak*	May I see your passport, please?
Vill du ha en försäkring? *vil deu hah ehn furr • sair • krihng*	Do you want insurance?
Det blir en handpenning på... *dee bleer ehn hand • peh • nihng poa...*	There is a deposit of...
Underteckna här, tack. *uhn • der • tehk • na hair tak*	Please sign here.

CAR HIRE

Where can I hire a car?	**Var kan jag hyra en bil?** *vahr kan yahg hew • ra ehn beel*
I'd like to hire...	**Jag skulle vilja hyra...** *yahg skuh • ler vihl • ya hew • ra...*
a cheap/small car	**en billig/liten bil** *en bihl • eeg/lee • tehn beel*
a 2-/4-door car	**en bil med två/fyra dörrar** *ehn beel meed tvoa/few • ra dur • rar*

an automatic/ manual car	**en bil med automatväxel/ manuell** *ehn beel meed ah • toa • maht • vehx • ehl/ mah • nuh • ehl*
a car with air-conditioning	**en bil med luftkonditionering** *ehn beel meed luhft • kohn • dee • shoa • neer • ihng*
a car seat	**en bilbarnstol** *ehn beel • barn • stoal*
How much does it cost...?	**Hur mycket kostar det...?** *heur mew • ker kos • tar dee...*
per day/week	**per dag/vecka** *pair dahg/veh • ka*
per kilometer	**per kilometer** *pair chee • loh • mee • ter*
How much does it cost...?	**Hur mycket kostar det...?** *heur mew • ker kos • tar dee...*
for unlimited mileage	**för obegränsade mil** *furr oa • beh • grehn • sa • deh • meel*
with insurance	**med försäkring** *meed furr • sair • krihng*
Are there any special weekend rates?	**Har ni särskilda helgrabatter?** *hahr nee sair • shihl • da hely • ra • bat • ehr*

FUEL STATION

Where's the next fuel station, please?	**Ursäkta, var är närmaste bensinstation?** *eur • shehk • ta vahr air nair • mas • the behn • seen • sta • shoan*
Fill it up, please.	**Fyll tanken, tack.** *feyl tan • kehn tak*
...liters, please.	**...liter, tack.** *...lee • tehr tak*

I'll pay in cash/by credit card.	**Jag betalar kontant/med kreditkort.** *Yahg beh • tah • lar kohn • tant/meed kreh • deet • koart*

YOU MAY SEE...

VANLIG	regular
PREMIUM	premium [super]
DIESEL	diesel

ASKING DIRECTIONS

Is this the road to...?	**Är det här vägen till...?** *air dee hair vair • gehn tihl...*
How far is it to...?	**Hur långt är det till...?** *heur loangt air d**ee** tihl...*
Where's...?	**Var ligger...?** *vahr lih • gehr...*
...Street	**...gata** *...gah • ta*
this address	**denna adress** *deh • na ad • rehs*
the highway [motorway]	**motorvägen** *m**oa** • tohr • vair • gehn*
Can you show me on the map?	**Kan du visa mig på kartan?** *kan deu vee • sa may p**oa** kahr • tan*
I'm lost.	**Jag har kommit vilse.** *yahg hahr koh • miht vihl • ser*

YOU MAY HEAR...

rakt fram *rahkt fram*	straight ahead
till vänster *tihl vehn • stehr*	on/to the left
till höger *tihl hur • gehr*	on/to the right
i/runt hörnan *ee/ruhnt hur • nan*	on/around the corner
mitt emot *miht ee • moat*	opposite
bakom *bah • kohm*	behind
bredvid *breh • veed*	next to
efter *ehf • tehr*	after
norr/söder *nohr/sur • dehr*	north/south
öster/väster *urs • tehr/vehs • tehr*	east/west
vid trafikljusen *veed tra • feek • yeus • ehn*	at the traffic light
vid avfarten *veed afv • far • tehn*	at the exit

YOU MAY SEE...

	STOPP	stop
	LÄMNA FÖRETRÄDE	give way
	PARKERING FÖRBJUDEN	no parking
	**FARLIG KURVA**	dangerous curve 
	**ENKELRIKTAT**	one way
	**INGEN INFART**	no entry
	**OMKÖRNING FÖRBJUDEN**	no passing
	U-SVÄNG FÖRBJUDEN	no U-turn
	**ÖVERGÅNGSSTÄLLE FÖR FOTGÄNGARE**	pedestrian crossing

PARKING

Can I park here? **Får jag parkera här?**
foar yahg par • kee • ra hair

Is there a parking lot [car park] nearby? **Finns det en parkeringsplats i närheten?**
fihns dee ehn par • kee • rihngs • plats ee nair • hee • tehn

Where's...?	**Var ligger...?** *Vahr lih • gehr...*
the parking garage	**parkeringshuset** *par-kee • rihngs • huhseht*
the parking meter	**parkeringsautomaten** *par • kee • rihngs ah • toa • mah • tehn*
How much does it cost...?	**Hur mycket koster det...?** *h**eu**r mew • ker kos • tar d**ee**...*
per hour	**per timme** *pair tihm • er*
per day	**per dag** *pair dahg*
overnight	**över natten** ***ur*** *• vehr na • tehn*

Street parking, parking lots and, in some cases, parking garages will be available in most of Sweden's cities and larger towns. Street parking is generally metered in city centers and downtown areas. A blue circular sign with a red slash tells you where parking is prohibited. There will be signs indicating whether or not parking is free. In places where parking is metered, a ticket allowing you to park for a specific period of time will need to be purchased. If this is the case, tickets can be purchased from a **biljettautomat** (ticket machine). You pay for the amount of time you want to park and then place the ticket on the driver's side of the car, on the dashboard, so that the ticket is in plain sight. In some cases, parking may be free, and there will be signs posted with time limits, usually two or three hours.

BREAKDOWN & REPAIR

My car broke down/ won't start.	**Min bil har gått sönder/startar inte.** *min beel hahr goat surn • dehr/star • tar in • ter*
Can you fix it today?	**Kan ni laga den idag?** *kan nee lah • ga dehn ee • dahg*
When will it be ready?	**När blir den färdig?** *nair bleer dehn fair • dihg*
How much?	**Hur mycket kostar det?** *heur mew • ker kos • tar dee*
I have a puncture/ flat tyre (tire).	**Jag har punktering.** *Yahg hahr puhng • teh • rihng*

ACCIDENTS

There's been an accident.	**Det har hänt en olycka.** *dee hahr hehnt ehn oa • lew • ka*
Call an ambulance/ the police.	**Ring efter en ambulans/polisen.** *rihng ehf • ter ehn am • beu • lans/ poa • lee • sehn*

PLACES TO STAY

NEED TO KNOW

Can you recommend a hotel in...?	**Kan du rekommendera ett hotel i...?** *kan deu reh • koh • mehn • dee • ra eht hoh • tehl ee...*
I have a reservation.	**Jag har bokat rum.** *yahg hahr boa • kat ruhm*
My name is...	**Jag heter...** *yahg hee • tehr...*
Do you have a room...?	**Har ni ett ledigt rum...?** *hahr nee eht lee • dihgt ruhm...*
for one/two	**för en person/två personer** *furr ehn pehr • shoan/tvoa pehr • shoan • ehr*
with a bathroom	**med badrum** *meed bahd • ruhm*
with air-conditioning	**med luftkonditionering** *meed luhft • kohn • dee • shoa • neer • ihng*
For tonight.	**För ikväll.** *furr ee • kvehl*
For two nights.	**För två nätter.** *furr tvoa neh • tehr*
For one week.	**För en vecka.** *furr ehn veh • ka*
How much?	**Hur mycket kostar det?** *heur mew • ker kos • tar dee*

Do you have anything cheaper?	**Har ni någonting billigare?** *hahr nee noa • gohn • tihng bihl • ee • ga • rer*
When's check-out?	**När måste vi checka ut?** *nair mos • ter vee sheh • ka eut*
Can I leave this in the safe?	**Kan jag lämna detta i kassaskåpet?** *Kan yahg lehm • na deh • ta ee ka • sah • skoa • peht*
Could we leave our baggage here until...?	**Kan vi lämna vårt bagage här till klockan...?** *kan vee lehm • na voart ba • goash hair tihl kloh • kan...*
Could I have the bill/ receipt, please?	**Kan jag få räkningen/kvittot, tack?** *Kan yahg foa rairk • nihng • en/kvih • toht tak*
I'll pay in cash/by credit card.	**Jag betalar kontant/med kreditkort.** *Yahg beh • tah • lar kohn • tant/meed kreh • deet • koart*

SOMEWHERE TO STAY

Can you recommend a hotel in…?	**Kan du rekommendera ett hotel i…?** *kan deu reh • koh • mehn • dee • ra eht hoh • tehl ee…*
a hostel	**ett vandrarhem** *eht vand • rar • hehm*
a campsite	**en kampingplats** *ehn kam • pihng • plats*
a bed and breakfast	**rum med frukost** *ruhm mehd fruh • kohst*
What is it near?	**Vad finns det i närheten?** *vahd fihns dee ee nair • hee • tehn*
How do I get there?	**Hur kommer jag dit?** *heur koh • mehr yahg deet*

AT THE HOTEL

I have a reservation.	**Jag har bokat rum.** *yahg hahr boh • kat ruhm*
My name is…	**Jag heter…** *yahg hee • tehr…*
Do you have a room…?	**Har ni ett rum…?** *hahr nee eht ruhm…*
with a bathroom/ shower	**med bad/dusch** *meed bahd/deush*
with air-conditioning	**med luftkonditionering** *meed luhft • kohn • dee • shoa • neer • ihng*
that's smoking/ non-smoking	**för rökare/icke-rökare** *furr rur • kah • rer/ ih • keh rur • ka • rer*
For tonight.	**För ikväll.** *furr ee • kvehl*

YOU MAY HEAR...

Ert pass/kreditkort, tack. *ehrt pas/ kreh • deet • koart tak*	Your passport/ credit card, please.
Kan du fylla i den här blanketten. *kan deu few • la ee dehn hair blan • keh • tehn*	Please fill out this form.
Skriv under här. *skreev uhn • der hair*	Sign here.

For two nights.	**För två nätter.** *furr tvoa neh • tehr*
For one week.	**För en vecka.** *furr ehn veh • ka*
Does the hotel have...?	**Finns det...på hotellet?** *fihns dee...poa hoh • tehl • eht*
a computer	**en dator** *ehn dah • tohr*
an elevator [lift]	**en hiss** *ehn hihs*
(wireless) internet service	**(trådlös) internet** *(troad • lurs) in • tehr • net*
room service	**rumservice** *ruhm • sehr • vihs*
a pool	**en simbassäng** *ehn sihm • ba • sehng*
a gym	**ett gym** *eht ym*
I need...	**Jag behöver...** *yahg beh • hur • vehr...*
an extra bed	**en extra säng** *ehn ehx • tra sehng*

a cot	**en tältsäng** *ehn tehlt • sehng*
a crib	**en barnsäng** *ehn bahrn • sehng*

For Numbers, see page 22.

PRICE

How much per night/week?	**Vad kostar det per natt/vecka?** *Vahd kos • tar dee pair nat/veh • ka*
Does the price include breakfast/ sales tax [VAT]?	**Ingår frukost/moms i priset?** *ihn • goar fruh • kohst/mohms ee pree • seht*
Are there any discounts?	**Ger ni rabatter?** *Yehr nee ra • bat·ehr*

PREFERENCES

Can I see the room?	**Kan jag se rummet?** *Kan yahg seh ruhm • eht*
I'd like a…room.	**Jag skulle vilja ha ett…rum.** *Yahg skuh • ler vihl • ya hah eht …ruhm*
better	**bättre** *beh • treh*
bigger	**större** *stuh • reh*
cheaper	**billigare** *bihl • ee • ga • rer*
quieter	**tystare** *tews • tah • rer*
I'll take it.	**Ja tar det.** *Yahg tahr deht*
No, I won't take it.	**Nej, jag tar inte det.** *Nay, yahg tahr deht in • ter*

There is a wide range of places to stay in Sweden, from luxury to budget. Budget options include **privatrum** (private rooms), much like bed and breakfasts, or **stugor** (cabins) and **lägenheter** (apartments). Cabins and apartments are usually rented out on a weekly basis, but one- or two-night stays may also be an option. Information can be found at the local tourist office; you may also see signs along the road indicating that there is a vacancy in a cabin nearby. Motorists can look for **motel** (motels); these are reasonably priced with restaurants and car-friendly facilities. When looking for somewhere to stay in university towns such as Stockholm, Göteborg or Lund, staying at a **sommarhotel** (summer hotel) can be a good choice. Student dormitories are open to tourists in the summer and are a good option if you are traveling in a group. Families can enjoy a **familjehotell** (a family hotel), which has special rates for groups sharing the same room (three to six beds). These only operate during the summer months. All-inclusive accommodation is also available in the form of a **turisthotell** (tourist hotel) or **pensionat** (boarding house). These are clean and comfortable hotels or guesthouses that are often found at summer resorts and winter sport areas. Sweden also offers first class and deluxe hotels, usually found in larger cities and towns. Prices and amenities vary but the standards are usually high. Breakfast is usually included. When booking somewhere to stay during the summer months and high tourist season it is important to book in advance.

QUESTIONS

Where's...?	**Var ligger...?** *vahr lih • gehr...*
the bar	**baren** *bah • rehn*
the bathroom [toilet]	**toaletten** *toa • ah • leh • tehn*
the elevator [lift]	**hissen** *his • ehn*
Can I have...?	**Kan jag få...?** *kan yahg foa...*
a blanket	**ett täcke** *eht teh • ker*
an iron	**ett strykjärn** *eht strewk • yairn*
the room key/ key card	**rumsnyckeln/nyckelkortet** *Ruhms • new • kehl/new • kehl • koart*
a pillow	**en kudde** *ehn keu • der*
soap	**tvål** *tvoal*
toilet paper	**toalettpapper** *toa • ah • leht • pa • pehr*
a towel	**en handduk** *ehn han • deuk*
Can I use this adapter here?	**Kan jag använda den här adaptern här?** *kan yahg an • vehn • da dehn hair a • dap • tern hair*
How do I turn on the lights?	**Hur tänder man lamporna?** *heur tehn • der man lam • pohr • na*
Could you wake me at...?	**Kan ni väcka mig klockan...?** *kan nee veh • ka may kloh • kan...*

Could I have my things from the safe?	**Kan jag få mina saker från kassaskåpet?** *kan yahg f**oa** mee • na sah • ker fr**oa**n ka • sa • sk**oa** • peht*
Is there any mail/a message for me?	**Finns det någon post/eht meddelande till mig?** *fihns d**ee** n**oa** • gohn pohst/eht meed • d**ee**l • an • der tihl may*
Do you have a laundry service?	**Har ni tvättservice?** *hahr nee tveht • sehr • vihs*

YOU MAY SEE...

TRYCK	push
DRAG	pull
WC	restroom [toilet]
DAMTOALETT	women's restroom
HERRTOALETT	men's restroom
DUSCH	shower
HISS	elevator [lift]
TRAPPOR	stairs
TVÄTT	laundry
VAR GOD STÖR EJ	do not disturb
BRANDUTGÅNG	fire door
NÖDUTGÅNG	emergency exit
TELEFONVÄCKNING	wake-up call

PROBLEMS

There's a problem.	**Jag har ett problem.** *yahg hahr eht proh • bleem*
I've lost my key/ key card.	**Jag har tappat bort min nyckel/mitt nyckelkort.** *yahg hahr ta • pat bort mihn new • kehl/ miht new • kehl • koart*
I've locked myself out of my room.	**Jag har låst ut mig ur rummet.** *yahg hahr loast eut may eur ruhm • eht*
There's no hot water/ toilet paper.	**Det finns inget varmvatten/ toalettpapper.** *dee fihns ihng • eht varmt • va • tehrn/ toa • ah • leht • pa • per*
The room is dirty.	**Rummet är smutsigt.** *ruhm • eht air smuht • siht*
There are bugs in our room.	**Det finns insekter på vårt rum.** *dee fihns ihn • sehk • tehr poa voart ruhm*
Can you fix...?	**Kan ni laga...?** *kan nee lah • ga...*
the air-conditioning	**luftkonditioneringen** *luhft • kohn • dee • shoa • neer • ihng • ehn*
the fan	**fläkten** *flehk • tehn*
the heating	**värmen** *vair • mehn*
the light	**lampan** *lahm • pan*
the TV	**teven** *teh • veen*
the toilet	**toaletten** *toa • ah • leh • tehn*

I'd like to move to another room. **Jag skulle vilja flytta till ett annat rum.**
yahg skuh • ler vihl • ya flew • ta tihl eht an • at ruhm

...is/are broken. **...är trasig.**
...air trah • sihg

Throughout Sweden the current is 230-volt, 50-cycle AC. If you bring your own electrical appliances, buy a continental adapter plug (round pins) before leaving home. You may also need a transformer appropriate to the wattage of the appliance.

CHECKING OUT

When do we need to check out? **När måste vi checka ut?**
nair mos • ter vee sheh • ka eut

Could we leave our baggage here until...? **Kan vi lämna vårt bagage här till klockan...?**
kan vee lehm • na voart ba • goash hair tihl kloh • kan...

Can I have an itemized bill/receipt? **Kan jag få en specificerad räkning/ett specificerad kvitto?**
kan yahg foa ehn speh • seh • fee • ee • rad rairk • ning/eht speh • seh • fee • ee • rad kvih • toh

I think there's a mistake in this bill. **Jag tror det måste vara fel på notan.**
*Yahg troar d**ee** mos • ter vah • ra feel p**oa** noa • tan.*

I'll pay in cash/by credit card. **Jag betalar kontant/med kreditkort.**
Yahg beh • tah • lar • kohn • tant/meed kreh • deet • koart

A service charge as well as **moms** (sales tax) is included in hotel and restaurant bills, but you are expected to round up a restaurant bill to the nearest **krona**. Tipping is generally not expected, but it's always appreciated if the service has been exceptionally good. It is customary to give a small tip to hairdressers, barbers, taxi drivers and porters.

RENTING

I've reserved an apartment/a room.	**Jag har bokat en lägenhet/ett rum.** *Yahg hahr boh • kat ehn lair • gehn • h**ee**t/ eht ruhm*
My name is...	**Jag heter...** *yahg hee • tehr...*
Can I have the key/ key card?	**Kan jag få nyckeln/nyckelkortet?** *kan yahg f**oa** new • kehln/ new • kehl • koar • teht*
Are there...?	**Finns det...?** *fihns d**ee**...*
dishes	**porslin** *poarsh • leen*
pillows	**kuddar** *keu • dar*
sheets	**lakan** *lah • kan*
towels	**handdukar** *han • **deu** • kar*
utensils	**bestick** *beh • stihk*

When do I put out the bins/recycling?	**När ska jag ställa ut soporna/ återvinning?** *nair skah yahg steh • la eut soa • pohr • na/ oat • ehr • vihn • ing*
...has broken down.	**...har gått sönder.** *...hahr goat surn • dehr*
How does...work?	**Hur fungerar...?** *heur fuhn • geh • rar...*
the air-conditioner	**luftkonditioneringen** *luhft • kohn • dee • shoa • neer • ihng • ehn*
the dishwasher	**diskmaskinen** *dihsk • ma • shee • nehn*
the freezer	**frysen** *frew • sen*
the heater	**värmeelementet** *vair • meh • ehl • eh • mehn • teht*
the microwave	**mikrovågsugnen** *mik • roh • voags • eung • nehn*
How does...work?	**Hur fungerar...?** *heur fuhn • geh • rar...*
the refrigerator	**kylskåpet** *kewl • skoa • peht*
the stove	**spisen** *spee • sehn*
the washing machine	**tvättmaskinen** *tveht • mah • shee • nehn*

DOMESTIC ITEMS

I'd like...	**Jag skulle vilja ha...** *yahg skuh • ler vihl • ya hah...*
an adapter	**en adapter** *ehn a • dap • tehr*
aluminum	**aluminiumfolie** *ah • leu • mee • nee • um • foh • lyer* foil

a bottle opener	**en flasköppnare** *ehn flask • urp • na • rer*
a broom	**en sopborste** *ehn sop • borsh • ter*
a can opener	**en konservöppnare** *ehn kohn • serv • urp • na • rer*
cleaning supplies	**städutrustning** *staird • eut • reust • nihng*
a corkscrew	**en korkskruv** *ehn kohrk • skreuv*
detergent	**tvättmedel** *tveht • mee • dehl*
dishwashing liquid	**diskmedel** *disk • mee • dehl*
bin bags	**soppåsar** *sop • poa • sar*
a light bulb	**en glödlampa** *ehn glurd • lam • pa*
matches	**tändstickor** *tehnd • stih • kohr*
a mop	**en skurmopp** *ehn skewr • mop*
napkins	**pappersservetter** *pa • pers • sahr • veh • ter*
plastic wrap [cling film]	**plastfolie** *plast • foh • lyer*
a plunger	**en vaskrensare** *ehn vask • rehn • sa • rer*
scissors	**en sax** *ehn sax*
a vacuum cleaner	**en dammsugare** *ehn damm • seu • ga • rer*

For In the Kitchen, see page 199.

If you are looking for something comfortable and reasonably priced, **Svenska Turistföreningen** or **STF** (the Swedish Tourist Club) is an excellent place to start. Here you can search for accommodations such as **vandrarhem** (youth hostels). If you are a member of **STF** or Hostelling International you get a member discount. Generally, room options include dormitory style rooms, split male and female, as well as smaller private rooms or family rooms. You are usually expected to bring your own towels and sheets as these usually are not provided, but can be rented. Shared kitchen facilities are often available, so that you can buy food at the local supermarket and prepare your own meals. Some hostels offer breakfast.

AT THE HOSTEL

Do you have any places left for tonight?	**Finns det några lediga platser ikväll?** *fihns dee noa • gra lee • dih • ga plats • ehr ee • kvehl*
Can I have...?	**Kan jag få...?** *kan yahg foa...*
a single/double room	**ett enkelrum/dubbelrum** *eht hng • kehl • ruhm/duh • behl • ruhm*
a blanket	**ett täcke** *eht tehk • er*
a pillow	**en kudde** *ehn keu • der*
sheets	**lakan** *lah • kan*
a towel	**en handduk** *ehn han • deuk*

What time are the doors locked?	**När stängs ytterdörrarna?** *nair stehngs ew • ter • dur • ar • na*
Do I need a membership card?	**Behöver jag medlemskort?** *beh • hur • vehr yahg mehd • lehms • koart*
Here's my international student card.	**Här är mitt internationella studentkort.** *hair air miht in • tehr • na • shoa • nehl • ah stuh • dehnt • koart*

GOING CAMPING

Can I camp here?	**Får man tälta här?** *foar man tehl • ta hair*
Is there a campsite near here?	**Finns det en campingplats i närheten?** *fihns dee ehn kam • pihng • plats ee nair • hee • tehn*
What is the charge per day/week?	**Vad kostar det per dag/vecka?** *vahd kos • tar dee pair dahg/veh • ka*
Are there...?	**Finns det...?** *fihns dee...*
cooking facilities	**kokmöjligheter** *koak • mury • lihg • hee • tehr*
electrical outlets	**nätuttag** *nairt • eut • tahg*
laundry facilities	**tvättmöjligheter** *tveht • mury • lig • hee • tehr*
showers	**dusch** *deush*
tents for hire	**tält för uthyrning** *tehlt furr eut • hewr • nihng*
Where can I empty the chemical toilet?	**Var kan jag tömma den kemiska toaletten?** *vahr kan yahg tur • ma dehn sheh • mihs • ka toa • ah • leh • tehn*

For Domestic Items, see page 80.

YOU MAY SEE...

DRICKSVATTEN	drinking water
INGEN CAMPING	no camping
INGEN GRILLNING	no barbeques
INGEN ÖPPEN ELD	no fires

COMMUNICATIONS

NEED TO KNOW

Where's an internet cafe?	**Var finns det ett internetkafé?** *vahr fihns d**ee** eht ihn • tehr • neht • ka • feh*
Can I access the internet/check e-mail here?	**Kan jag komma ut på internet/ kola e-post här?** *kan yahg koh • ma eut p**oa** ihn • tehr • neht/koa • la ee • pohst hair*
How much per hour/ half hour?	**Hur mycket kostar det per timme/ halvtimme?** *heur mew • ker kos • tar d**ee** pair tihm • er/halv • tihm • er*
How do I connect/ log on?	**Hur loggar jag in?** *heur loh • gar yag ihn*
Can I have a phone card?	**Kan jag få ett telefonkort?** *kan yahg foa eht teh • leh • foan • koart*

Can I have your phone number?	**Kan jag få ditt telefonnummer?** *kan yahg foa diht teh • leh • foan • nuhm • ehr*
Here's my number/ e-mail address.	**Här är mitt nummer/min e-postadress.** *hair air miht nuhm • ehr/mihn ee • pohst • ad • rehs*
Call me.	**Var snäll och ring mig.** *vahr snehl ohk ring may*
E-mail me.	**Skicka en e-post till mig.** *shih • ka ehn ee • pohst tihl may*
Hello. This is...	**Hej. Det här är...** *hay dee hair air...*
I'd like to speak to...	**Jag skulle vilja tala med...** *yahg skuh • ler vihl • ya tah • la meed...*
Repeat that, please.	**Kan du upprepa det, tack.** *kan deu uhp • ree • pa dee tak*
I'll be in touch.	**Jag hör av mig snart.** *yahg hur afv may snahrt*
Goodbye.	**Hej då.** *hay doa*
Where is the post office?	**Var ligger posten?** *vahr lih • gehr pohs • tehn*
I'd like to send this to...	**Jag skulle vilja skicka det här till...** *yahg skuh • ler vihl • ya shih • ka dee hair tihl...*

ONLINE

Where's an internet cafe?	**Var finns det ett internetcafe?** *vahr fihns deht eht ihn • tehr • neht • ka • feh*
Does it have wireless internet?	**Finns det trådlös internet där?** *fihns d**ee** troad • lurs ihn • tehr • neht dair*
What is the WiFi password?	**Vilket är WiFi-lösenordet?** *vihl • keht wai • fai-lur • sehn • oarde*
Is the WiFi free?	**Är WiFi gratis?** *air wai • fain grah • tihs*
Do you have bluetooth?	**Har ni blåtand?** *hahr nee bloa • tand*
How do I turn the computer on/off?	**Hur sätter jag på/stänger jag av datorn?** *heur seh • tehr yahg poa/stehng • her yahg afv dah • torn*
Can I print?	**Kan jag skriva ut?** *kan yahg skree • va **eu**t*
Can I...?	**Kan jag...?** *kahn yahg...*
access the internet	**gå ut på internet** *goa eut poa ihn • tehr • neth*

check my e-mail	**kolla min e-post** *kohla meen eh • pohst*
plug in/charge my laptop/iPhone/ iPad/BlackBerry?	**sätta i/ladda min laptop/iPhone/ iPad/BlackBerry** *sehta ih/ladha meen laptop/iPad/ BlackBerry*
access Skype?	**använda Skype** *an • vehn • a Skype*
How much per half hour/hour?	**Hur mycket kostar det per halvtimme/ timme?** *Heur mew • keh koh • star deht pehr halv • tihm • er/tih • mer*
How do I...?	**Hur gör man för att...?** *heur y**ur**r man f**ur**r at...*
connect/ disconnect	**koppla upp/koppla ner** *kohp • la uhp/kohp • la nehr*
log on/off	**logga in/ut** *loh • ga ihn/**eu**t*
type this symbol	**skriva in det här tecknet** *skree • va ihn d**ee** hair tehk • neht*
What's your e-mail?	**Vad har du för e-postadress?** *vahd hahr deu f**ur**r ee • pohst • ad • rehs*
My e-mail is...	**Min e-postadress är...** *mihn ee • pohst • ad • rehs air...*
Do you have a scanner?	**Har ni en skanner?** *Hahr nee ehn ska • nehr*

SOCIAL MEDIA

Are you on Facebook/Twitter?	**Finns du på Facebook/Twitter?** *Fihns deu poa Facebook/Twitter*
What's your user name?	**Vilket användarnamn har du?** *Vihl • keht an • vehn • dar • namn hahr deu*
I'll add you as a friend.	**Jag lägger till dig som vän.** *yahg lehg • ehr tihl day sohm vehn*

I'll follow you on Twitter.	**Jag följer dig på Twitter.** *Yahg fuhl • yehr day poa Twitter*
Are you following...?	**Följer du...?** *Fuhl • yehr deu...*
I'll put the pictures on Facebook/Twitter.	**Jag lägger ut bilderna på Facebook/ Twitter.** *yahg lehg • ehr eut bihl • dehr • na poa Facebook/Twitter*
I'll tag you in the pictures.	**Jag taggar bilderna.** *yahg ta • gar bihl • dehr • na*

YOU MAY SEE...

STÄNG	close
RADERA	delete
E-POST	e-mail
UTGÅNG	exit
HJÄLP	help
INSTANT MESSENGER	instant messenger
INTERNET	internet
LOGGA IN	login
NYTT MEDDELANDE	new message
AV/PÅ	on/off
ÖPPNA	open
SKRIV UT	print
SPARA	save
SKICKA	send
ANVÄNDARNAMN	username
LÖSENORD	password
TRÅDLÖS INTERNET	wireless internet

PHONE

A phone card/ prepaid phone please.	**Ett telefonkort, tack.** *eht teh • leh • foan • koart tak*
How much does it cost?	**Hur mycket kostar det?** *heur mew • ker kos • tar dee*
What's the area/ country code for...?	**Vad är riktnumret/landskoden till...?** *vahd air rikt • nuhm • reht/ lands • koa • dehn tihl...*
What's the number for Information?	**Vilket nummer är det till Nummerbyrån?** *vihl • keht nuhm • ehr air dee tihl nuhm • ehr • bew • roan*
I'd like the number for...	**Jag skulle vilja ha numret till...** *yahg skuh • ler vihl • ya hah nuhm • reht tihl...*
I'd like to call collect [reverse the charges].	**Jag vill ringa ett mottagaren-betalar-samtal.** *yahg vihl rihng • a eht moh • tah • ga • ren be • tah • lar-sam • tahl*
My phone doesn't work here.	**Min telefon fungerar inte här.** *mihn teh • leh • foan fuhn • geh • rar ihn • ter hair*
What network are you on?	**Vilket nätverk använder du?** *vihl • keht neht • vehrk an • vehn • der deu*
Is it 3G?	**Är det 3G?** *air deht treh • geh*
I have run out of credit/minutes.	**Jag har inte mer pengar/minuter på kortet.** *yahg hahr ihn • ther meer pehng • ar/ mih • nuh • tehr poa koart • eht*
Can I buy some credit?	**Kan jag fylla på kortet?** *kahn yahg fewlah poa koart • et*

Do you have a phone charger?	**Har du/ni en telefonladdare?** *Hahr deu/nee ehn teh • leh • foan • lad • ar • eh*
Can I have your number?	**Kan jag få ditt telefonnummer?** *kan yahg foa diht teh • leh • foan • nuhm • ehr*
Here's my number.	**Här är mitt nummer.** *hair air miht nuhm • ehr*
Please call me.	**Var snäll och ring mig.** *vahr snehl ohk rihng may*
Please text me.	**Var snäll och skicka ett sms till mig.** *Vahr snehl ohk shih • ka eht ehs • ehm • ehs tihl may*
I'll call you.	**Jag ringer dig.** *yahg rihng • ehr day*
I'll text you.	**Jag skickar ett sms till dig.** *yahg shih • kar eht ehs • ehm • ehs tihl day*

TELEPHONE ETIQUETTE

Hello. This is...	**Hej. Det här är...** *hay dee hair air...*
I'd like to speak to...	**Jag skulle vilja tala med...** *yahg skuh • ler vihl • ya tah • la meed...*
Extension...	**Anknytning...** *an • knewt • nihng...*
Speak louder/more slowly.	**Var snäll och tala högre/långsammare.** *vahr snehl ohk tah • la hur • greh/ loang • sam • a • rer*
Can you repeat that?	**Kan du upprepa det?** *kan deu uhp • ree • pa dee*
I'll call back later.	**Jag ringer senare.** *yahg rihng • ehr see • na • rer*
Goodbye.	**Hej då.** *hay doa*

YOU MAY HEAR...

Vem är det? *vehm air dee*	Who's calling?
Ett ögonblick. *eht ur•gohn•blihk*	One moment.
Tyvärr, är han/hon inte här. *tew•vair air hahn/hoan ihn•ter hair*	I'm afraid he/she is not in.
Han/Hon kan inte komma till telefonen. *hahn/hoan kan ihn•ter koh•ma tihl teh•leh•foan•ehn*	He/She can't come to the phone.
Vill du lämna ett meddelande? *vihl deu lehm•na eht mee•dee•lan•der*	Would you like to leave a message?
Ring tillbaka senare/om tio minuter. *rihng tihl•bah•ka see•na•rer/ ohm tee•oah mih•neu•tehr*	Call back later/ in 10 minutes.
Kan han/hon ringa upp dig? *kan hahn/ hoan rihng•a uhp day*	Can he/she call you back?
Vad är ditt telefonnummer? *vahd air dihtteh•leh•foan•nuhm•her*	What's your number?

FAX

Can I send/receive a fax here?	**Kan man skicka/ta emot fax här?** *kan man shih•ka/ta ee•moat fax hair*
What's the fax number?	**Vad är ditt faxnummer?** *vahd air diht fax•nuhm•ehr*
Please fax this to...	**Var snäll och faxa det här till...** *vahr snehl ohk fax•ah dee hair tihl...*

To call the U.S. or Canada from Sweden, dial 00 + 1 + area code + phone number. To call the U.K., dial 00 + 44 + area code (minus first 0) + phone number. Information on area codes for Sweden and international dialing codes can be found in the phone book and are usually available at hotels and youth hostels. The emergency number in Sweden is 112.

POST

Where's the post office/mailbox?
Var ligger posten/postlådan?
vahr lih • gehr pohs • tehn/pohst • loa • dan

A stamp for this postcard/letter, please.
Kan jag få ett frimärke till det här vykortet/brevet, tack.
*kan yahg f**oa** eht free • mair • ker tihl d**ee** hair vew • koar • teht/ bree • veht tak*

How much does it cost?
Hur mycket kostar det?
*heur mew • ker kos • tar d**ee***

I want to send this package by airmail/ express.
Jag vill skicka det här paketet med flygpost/express.
*yahg vihl shih • ka d**ee** hair pa • kee • teht meed fl**ew**g • pohst/ehx • prehs*

The receipt, please.
Kvittot, tack.
kvih • toht tak

YOU MAY HEAR...

Fyll i tulldeklarationen, tack. *fewl ee tuhl • deh • klar • a • shoa • nehn tak*	Please fill out the customs declaration form.
Vad är värdet? *vahd air vair • deht*	What's the value?
Vad finns inuti? *vahd fihns ihn • eu • tee*	What's inside?

Posten (the post office) is easy to find, just look for the blue **Post** sign with a yellow horn. Mailboxes are bright yellow. Business hours are 9:00 a.m. to 6:00 p.m. and on Saturdays, until 1:00 p.m. Like many other stores and business, you will need to take a number and wait for it to be called or displayed on a screen before you can be helped. Stamps can be purchased at **Pressbyrån** (newsstand chain) as well as some grocery stores.

SIGHTSEEING

NEED TO KNOW

Where's the tourist information office?	**Var ligger turistinformationen?** *vahr lih • gehr teu • rihst • ihn • fohr • ma • shoan • ehn*
What are the main points of interest?	**Vad finns det för sevärdheter?** *vahd fihns d**ee** f**ur**r see • vaird • hee • tehr*
Do you have tours in English?	**Finns det några turer på engelska?** *fihns d**ee** noa • gra teu • rehr p**oa** ehng • ehl • ska*
Can I have a map/ guide, please?	**Kan jag få en karta/guide, tack?** *kan yahg f**oa** ehn kahr • ta/gujd tak*

TOURIST INFORMATION

Do you have any information on...?	**Har ni information om...?** *hahr nee ihn • for • ma • sh**oa**n om...*
Can you recommend...?	**Kan ni rekommendera...?** *kan nee reh • koh • mehn d**ee** • ra...*

There are tourist information offices in all large cities and towns. These are usually marked by a green sign with an **I**. For general information, Sweden's official tourism website is a good place to start. Here you can find information on accommodation, attractions and activities as well as cultural and historical information. Most cities have their own tourist boards and websites, where you can request brochures, maps and more prior to your arrival. Also look for **Stockholmskortet** (the Stockholm Card) if you will be spending several days in the city. For one fee, you have access to musems, events and transportation throughout the city. You can choose whether you want the card for 24, 48 or 72 hours. The equivalent in Göteborg is **Göteborgs Passet.**

a boat trip	**en båttur** *ehn b**oa**t • teur*
an excursion	**en rundtur** *ehn ruhnd • teur*
a sightseeing tour	**en sightseeingtur** *ehn sight • see • ihng • teur*

ON TOUR

I'd like to go on the tour to…	**Jag vill följa med på turen till…** *yahg vihl furl • ja meed p**oa** teu • ren tihl…*
When's the next tour?	**När går nästa rundresa?** *nair goar nehsta ruhnd • rehsa*
Are there tours in English?	**Finns det någon tur på engelska?** *fihns d**ee** n**oa** • gohn teur p**oa** ehng • ehl • ska*

Is there an English-speaking guide/ audio guide?	**Finns det en engelsktalande guide/ ljudguide?** *fihns deht ehn ehng • ehlsk • tah • lan • de gahyd/ aw • dee • oh gahyd*
What time do we leave/return?	**När åker vi/kommer vi tillbaka?** *nair oak • er vee/koh • mehr vee tihl • bah • ka*
We'd like to have a look at...	**Vi skulle vilja se...** *vee skuh • ler vihl • ya see...*
Can we stop here...?	**Kan vi stanna här...?** *kan vee sta • na hair...*
to take photographs	**för att ta foton** *furr at tah foa • tohn*
to buy souvenirs	**för att köpa souvenirer** *furr at chur • pa seu • veh • nee • rehr*
to use the toilets	**för att gå på toaletten** *furr at goa poa toa • ah • leh • tehn*
Is there access for the disabled?	**Finns det tillgång för rörelsehindrade?** *fihns dee tihl • goang furr rurr • ehl • ser • hihn • dra • der*

For Tickets, see page 45.

SEEING THE SIGHTS

Where is...?	**Var ligger...?** *vahr lih • gehr...*
the battleground	**slagfältet** *slahg • fehl • teht*
the botanical garden	**botaniska trädgården** *boa • tan • ihs • ska traird • goar • dehn*
Where is...?	**Var ligger...?** *vahr lih • gehr...*
the castle	**slottet** *sloht • eht*

the downtown area	**centrum** *sehn • truhm*
the fountain	**fontänen** *fohn • tairn • ehn*
the library	**biblioteket** *bihb • lee • oa • teek • eht*
the market	**torget** *tohr • yeht*
the museum	**museet** *muh • see • eht*
the old town	**gamla stan** *gam • la stahn*
the opera house	**operan** *oap • eh • ran*
the palace	**slottet** *sloht • eht*
the park	**parken** *park • ehn*
the shopping area	**Et affärscentrumet** *eht a • ffairs • sehn • truhm • eht*
the town hall	**stadshuset** *stads • heus • eht*
Can you show me on the map?	**Kan du visa mig på kartan?** *kan deu vee • sa may poa kahr • tan*

It's...	**Det är...** *det air...*
amazing	**fantastiskt** *fan • ta • stihskt*
beautiful	**vackert** *va • kehrt*
boring	**trist** *trihst*
interesting	**intressant** *in • treh • sant*
magnificent	**storslaget** *stoar • slahg • eht*
romantic	**romantiskt** *roh • man • tihskt*
strange	**konstigt** *kohn • stihgt*
stunning	**förbluffande** *furr·bluh·fahnder*
terrible	**hemskt** *hehmskt*
ugly	**fult** *feult*
I (don't) like it.	**Jag tycker (inte) om den/det.** *yahg tew • kehr (in • ter) ohm dehn/dee*

For Asking Directions, see page 64.

RELIGIOUS SITES

Where is...?	**Var är...?** *vahr air...*
the cathedral	**domkyrkan** *dohm • chewr • kahn*
the church	**kyrkan** *chewr • kan*

the mosque	**moskén** *mos • kehn*
the shrine	**altaret** *alt • a • reht*
the synagogue	**synagogan** *sihn • a • gohg • an*
the temple	**templet** *tehmp • leht*
What time is mass/ the service?	**Hur dags är mässan/gudstjänsten?** *heur daks air mehs • an/ geuds • tjain • stehn*

LEISURE TIME

SHOPPING

NEED TO KNOW

Where is the market/ mall [shopping centre]?	**Var ligger orget/affärscentrumet?** *vahr lih • gehr tohr • yeht/ a • ffairs • sehn • truhm • eht*
I'm just looking.	**Jag tittar bara.** *yahg tih • tar bah • ra*
Can you help me?	**Kan du hjälpa mig?** *kan deu yehlp • a may*
I'm being helped.	**Jag får hjälp, tack.** *yahg foar yehlp tak*
How much does it cost?	**Hur mycket kostar det?** *heur mew • ker kos • tar det*
This/That one, thanks.	**Den här/där, tack.** *dehn hair/dair tak*
That's all, thanks.	**Det var allt, tack.** *dee vahr alt tak*
Where do I pay?	**Var kan jag betala?** *vahr kan yahg beh • tah • la*
I'll pay in cash/by credit card.	**Jag vill betala kontant/med kreditkort.** *yahg vihl beh • tah • la kohn • tant/meed kreh • deet • koart*
A receipt, please.	**Kvittot, tack.** *kvih • tot tak*

AT THE SHOPS

Where is...?	**Var finns...?** *vahr fihns...*

the antiques store	**antikaffären** *an • teek • a • ffair • ehn*
the bakery	**bageriet** *bahg • eh • ree • eht*
the bookstore	**bokhandeln** *boak • han • dehln*
the clothing store	**klädaffären** *klaird • a • ffair • ehn*
the delicatessen	**delikatessaffären** *dehl • eh • ka • tehs • a • fair • ehn*
the department store	**varuhuset** *vahr • eu • heus • eht*
the health food store	**hälsokostaffären** *hehl • soa • kost • a • fair • ehn*
the jeweler	**juveleraren** *yeu • veh • lee • rar • ehn*
the liquor store [off-licence]	**systembolaget** *sews • teem • boa • lahg • eht*
the market	**torget** *tohr • yeht*
the pastry shop	**konditoriet** *kohn • deh • toh • ree • eht*
the pharmacy [chemist]	**apoteket** *a • poa • tee • keht*
the produce [grocery] store	**livsmedelsaffären** *lihvs • mee • dehls • a • fair • ehn*
the shoe store	**skoaffären** *skoa • a • fair • ehn*
the shopping mall [shopping centre]	**affärscentrumet** *a • ffairs • sehn • truhm • eht*
the souvenir store	**souvenirbutiken** *seu • veh • neer • buh • tee • kehn*
the supermarket	**snabbköpet** *snab • chur • peht*

Although Sweden still has many small, specialty shops, **Köpcentrum** (malls) are becoming more and more common, especially in larger towns. Many chain and department stores, such as **Åhléns** and **Kappahl** and **Hennes & Mauritz**, have branches all over the country, all of which sell quality goods. In the well-established Stockholm department store **NK**, you can find almost anything, though it can be quite expensive. Designer goods can be found at **DesignTorget** in Stockholm. For traditional handicrafts look for signs with **hemslöjd** (handicraft); in Stockholm, these can be found at **Svensk Hemslöjd** and **Svenskt Hantverk** (traditional handicraft stores). Many towns have colorful markets, where you can buy anything from fresh fruit and vegetables to flowers and handicrafts. **Julmarknaden** (Christmas market) in Stockholm in the Old Town and **Skansen** (outdoor park and museum), are historic shopping areas.

Where is...?	**Var finns...?** *vahr fihns...*
the tobacconist	**tobaksaffären** *toa • baks • a • ffair • ehn*
the toy store	**leksaksaffären** *leek • sahks • a • fair • ehn*

ASK AN ASSISTANT

When do you open/ close?	**När öppnar/stänger ni?** *nair uhp • nar/stehng • er nee*
Where is...?	**Var finns...?** *vahr fihns...*

the cashier [cash desk]	**kassan** *kah • san*
the escalator	**rulltrappan** *ruhl • tra • pan*
the elevator [lift]	**hissen** *his • ehn*
the fitting room	**provrummet** *proav • ruhm • eht*
the store directory [guide]	**informationen** *in • for • ma • shoa • nehn*
Can you help me?	**Kan du hjälpa mig?** *kan deu yehl • pa may*
I'm just looking.	**Jag tittar bara.** *yahg tih • tar bah • ra*
I'm being helped.	**Tack, jag får hjälp.** *tak yahg foar yehlp*
Do you have any…?	**Har ni några…?** *hahr nee noa • gra…*
Could you show me…?	**Kan du visa mig några…?** *kan deu vee • sa may noa • gra…*
Can you ship/ wrap it?	**Kan du skicka/slå in det?** *kan deu shih • ka dee/sloa ihn dee*
How much does it cost?	**Hur mycket kostar det?** *heur mew • kerht kos • tar dee*
That's all, thanks.	**Det var allt, tack.** *dee vahr alt tak*

For Clothes & Accessories, see page 114.

PERSONAL PREFERENCES

I want something…	**Jag skulle vilja ha något…** *yahg skuh • ler vihl • ya hah noa • goht…*

YOU MAY HEAR...

Kan jag hjälpa er? *kan yahg yehl • pa her*	Can I help you?
Ett ögonblick, tack. *eht ur • gohn • blihk tak*	Just a moment, please.
Vad vill ni beställa? *vahd vihl nee beh • steh • la*	What would you like?
Något annat? *noa • goht an • nat*	Anything else?

cheap/expensive	**billigt/dyrt** *bihl • igt/dewyt*
larger/smaller	**större/mindre** *sturr • er/mihn • drer*
from this region	**från denna region** *frohn deh • na regheoan*
Is it real?	**Är den äkta?** *air dehn aik • ta*
Could you show me this/that?	**Kan du visa mig den här/där?** *kan deu vee • sa may dehn hair/dair*
That's not quite what I want.	**Det är inte riktigt vad jag vill ha.** *dee air ihn • ter rihk • tikt vahd yahg vihl hah*
I don't like it.	**Jag tycker inte om det.** *yahg tew • kehr ihn • ter ohm dee*
That's too expensive.	**Det är för dyrt.** *dee air furr dewrt*
I'd like to think about it.	**Jag behöver tänka på det.** *Yahg beh • hur • vehr tehng • ka poa dee*
I'll take it.	**Jag tar den.** *yahg tahr dehn*

YOU MAY SEE...

ÖPPET/STÄNGT	open/closed
STÄNGT FÖR LUNCH	closed for lunch
PROVRUM	fitting room
KASSÖR/KASSÖRSKA	cashier
ENDAST KONTANT	cash only
VI TAR KREDITKORT	credit cards accepted
AFFÄRSTID	business hours
UTGÅNG	exit

PAYING & BARGAINING

How much does it cost?	**Hur mycket kostar det?** *heur mew • ker kos • tar dee*
I'll pay...	**Jag betalar...** *yahg beh • tah • lar...*
in cash	**kontant** *kohn • tant*
by credit card	**med kreditkort** *meed kreh • deet • koart*
by traveler's check [cheque]	**med en resecheck** *meed ehn ree • seh • shehk*
The receipt, please.	**Kvittot, tack.** *kvih • toht tak*
That's too much.	**Det är för mycket.** *dee air furr mew • ker*
I'll give you...	**Jag kan ge er...** *yahg kan yee ehr...*

I only have...kronor.	**Jag har bara...kronor.** *yahg hahr bah • ra...kroa • nohr*
Is that your best price?	**Är det ditt bästa pris?** *air deht diht beh • sta prihs*
Can you give me a discount?	**Kan du ge mig rabatt?** *kan deu yee may ra • bat*

For Numbers, see page 22.

YOU MAY HEAR...

Hur vill ni betala? *heur vihl nee beh • tah • la*	How are you paying?
Ditt kreditkort har avvisats. *diht kreh • dith • koart hahr ahv • veesahts*	Your credit card has been declined.
ID, tack. *ee • deh, tak.*	ID, please.
Vi tar inte kreditkort. *Vee tahr ihnte kreh • diht • koart*	We don't accept credit cards.
Bara kontanter, tack. *bah • ra kohn • tan • tehr tak*	Cash only, please.
Har du mindre växel? *hahr deu mihn • drer vehx • ehl*	Do you have any smaller change?

MAKING A COMPLAINT

I'd like…	**Jag skulle vilja…** *yahg skuh • ler vihl • ya…*
to exchange this	**byta den här** *bew • ta dehn hair*
to return this	**återlämna den här** *oa • tehr • lehm • na dehn hair*
a refund	**ha pengarna tillbaka** *hah pehng • ar • na tihl • bah • ka*
to see the manager	**få träffa butikschefen** *foa treh • fa beu • teeks • sheef • ehn*

SERVICES

Can you recommend…?	**Kan du rekommendera…?** *kan deu reh • koh • mehn • dee • ra…*
a barber	**en herrfrisör** *ehn hair • fri • surr*
a dry cleaner	**en kemtvätt** *ehn shehm • tveht*
a hairdresser	**en damfrisör** *ehn dahm • free • surr*
a laundromat [launderette]	**en snabbtvätt** *ehn snab • tveht*
a nail salon	**en nagelvårdssalong** *ehn nah • gehl • voards • sa • loang*
a spa	**ett spa** *eht spah*
a travel agency	**en resebyrå** *ehn ree • seh • bew • roa*
Can you…this?	**Kan ni…den här?** *kan nee…dehn hair*

alter	**ändra på** *ehn • dra poa*
clean	**göra ren** *yur • ra reen*
mend	**laga** *lah • ga*
press	**stryka** *strew • ka*
When will it be ready?	**När blir det klart?** *nair bleer dee klahrt*

HAIR & BEAUTY

I'd like…	**Jag vill…** *yahg vihl…*
an appointment for today/ tomorrow	**boka en tid till idag/imorgon** *boa • ka ehn teed tihl ee • dahg/ ee • mo • ron*
some colour/ highlights	**färg/slingor** *fehry/slihng • ohr*
my hair styled/ blow-dried	**få en ny frisyr/föning** *foa ehn new free • sewr/funeeng*
a hair cut	**få en klippning** *foa ehn klihp • nihng*
an eyebrow/ a bikini wax	**en vaxning av ögonbrynen/bikinilinjen** *ehn vaks • nihng afv ur • gonn • brew • nehn/ beh • kee • nee • leen • yehn*
a facial	**en ansiktsbehandling** *ehn an • sihkts • beh • hand • lihng*
a manicure/ pedicure	**en manikyr/pedikyr** *ehn ma • nee • kewr/pehd • ee • kewr*
a (sports) massage	**(tränings) massage** *(trair • nihngs •) ma • sahsh*
a trim, please…	**en klippning, tack…** *ehn klihp • nihng, tak*

Don't cut it too short.	**Klipp det inte för kort.**
	klihp dee ihn • ter furr koart
Shorter here.	**Kortare här.**
	koar • ta • rer hair
Do you do...?	**Ger ni...?**
	yehr nee...
acupuncture	**akupunktur**
	a • keu • puhnk • teur
aromatherapy	**aroma-terapi**
	a • roa • ma • teh • ra • pee
oxygen treatment	**syrebehandling**
	sew • reh • beh • hand • lihng
Is there a sauna?	**Finns det bastu?**
	fihns dee bas • teu

Spas and wellness centers are becoming increasingly popular. There are many to choose from, both in urban and rural areas. It is possible to find spas that offer everything from traditional massage, such as the Swedish massage, which focuses on circulation and relaxation, to yoga, exercise and more. Some are even eco-friendly. Many spas and health centers also have gyms, pools and saunas.

ANTIQUES

How old is this?	**Hur gammalt är det här?**
	heur gam • alt air dee hair
Do you have anything from the ... era?	**Har ni något från ... perioden?**
	hahr nee noh • goht frohn ... per • eeoh • dehn
Will I have problems with customs?	**Får jag problem i tullen?**
	foar yahg proa • bleem ee tuh • lehn

Is there a certificate of authenticity?	**Finns det ett äkthetsbevis?** *fihns dee eht ehkt • heets • beh • vees*
Can you ship/wrap it?	**Kan ni skicka/packa in det?** *kahn nee shih • ka/paka ihn deht*

CLOTHING

I'd like…	**Jag skulle vilja ha…** *yahg skuh • ler vihl • ya hah…*
Can I try this on?	**Kan jag prova den här?** *kan yahg proa • va dehn hair*
It doesn't fit.	**Den passar inte.** *dehn pas • ar ihn • ter*
It's too…	**Den är för…** *dehn air furr…*
big	**stor** *stoar*
small	**liten** *lee • tehn*
short	**kort** *kort*
long	**lång** *loang*
tight	**liten** *leetehn*
loose	**stor** *stohr*
Do you have this in size…?	**Har ni den här i storlek…?** *hahr nee dehn hair ee stoar • leek…*
Do you have this in a bigger/smaller size?	**Har ni den här i en större/en mindre storlek?** *hahr nee dehn hair ee ehn stur • re/ehn mihn • drer stoar • leek*

For Numbers, see page 22.

YOU MAY SEE...

HERRKLÄDER	men's clothing
DAMKLÄDER	women's clothing
BARNKLÄDER	children's clothing

YOU MAY HEAR...

Du klär jättebra i den. *Deu klair jai • teh • brah i dehn*	That looks great on you.
Hur sitter den? *huhr sih • tehr dehn*	How does it fit?
Vi har inte din storlek. *Vee hahr ihnte deen stohr • lehk*	We don't have your size.

COLORS

I'm looking for something in...	**Jag söker något i...** *yahg **sur** • ker **noa** • goht ee...*
beige	**beige** *beesh*
black	**svart** *svart*
blue	**blått** *bloat*
brown	**brunt** *br**eu**nt*
gray	**grått** *groat*

green	**grönt** *grurnt*
orange	**orange** *oa • ransh*
pink	**rosa** *roa • sa*
purple	**lila** *lee • la*
red	**rött** *ruhrt*
white	**vitt** *vit*
yellow	**gult** *geult*
I'm looking for something in…	**Jag söker något i…** *yahg sur • ker noa • goht ee…*

CLOTHES & ACCESSORIES

a backpack	**ryggsäck** *rewg • sehk*
a belt	**skärp** *shairp*
a bikini	**bikini** *bih • kee • nee*
a blouse	**blus** *bleus*
a bra	**behå** *beh • hoa*
briefs [underpants]	**kalsonger [underbyxor]** *khal • sohn • gehr [uhn • dehr • bew • xohr]*
panties	**trosor** *troh·sohr*
a coat	**rock** *rohk*

a dress	**klänning** *klehn • ihng*
a hat	**hatt** *hat*
a jacket	**jacka** *ya • ka*
jeans	**jeans** *jeens*
pajamas	**pyjamas** *pew • ya • mas*
pants [trousers]	**byxor** *bewx • ohr*
panty hose [tights]	**strumpbyxor** *struhmp • bewx • ohr*
a purse [handbag]	**handväska** *hand • vehs • ka*
a raincoat	**regnkappa** *rehngn • kap • a*
a scarf	**halsduk** *hals • deuk*
a shirt	**skjorta** *shoar • ta*
shorts	**shorts** *shohrts*
a skirt	**kjol** *choal*
socks	**sockar** *soh • kar*
stockings	**strumpor** *stuhm • pohr*
a suit (jacket and pants)	**kostym** *kos • tewm*
a suit (jacket and skirt)	**dräkt** *drehkt*

sunglasses	**solglasögon** *soal • glahs • **ur** • gohn*
a sweater	**tröja** *trur • ya*
a sweatshirt	**sweatshirt** *sweat • shirt swimming*
swimming trunks	**badbyxor** *bahd • bewx • ohr*
a swimsuit	**baddräkt** *bahd • drehkt*
a T-shirt	**T-skjorta** *tee • shoarta*
a tie	**slips** *slihps*
underpants (men's/women's)	**kalsonger/trosor** *kal • soang • ehr/troa • sohr*
underwear	**underkläder** *uhn • dehr • klai • dehr*

FABRIC

I'd like…	**Jag skulle vilja ha…** *yahg skuh • ler vihl • ya hah…*
cotton	**bomull** *boam • uhl*
denim	**denim** *dehn • ihm*
lace	**spets** *spehts*
leather	**läder** *lair • der*
linen	**linne** *lih • ner*
silk	**siden** *see • dehn*

wool	**ull** *uhl*
Is it machine washable?	**Kan det tvättas i maskin?** *kan dee tveht • as ee ma • sheen*

SHOES

I'd like...	**Jag skulle vilja ha...** *yahg skuh • ler vihl • ya hah...*
high-heeled/ flat shoes	**högklackade/lågklackade skor** *hurg • klak • a • der/loag • klak • a • der skoar*
boots	**stövlar** *stuhv • lar*
I'd like...	**Jag skulle vilja ha...** *yahg skuh • ler vihl • ya hah...*
loafers	**loafers** *loa • fers*
sandals	**sandaler** *san • dahl • ehr*
shoes	**skor** *skoar*
slippers	**tofflor** *toff • lohr*
sneakers	**träningsskor** *trair • nihngs • skoar*
In size...	**I storlek...** *ee stoar • leek...*

For Numbers, see page 22.

SIZES

Small (S)	**liten** *leet • ehn*

Medium (M)	**medium** *mee • dee • uhm*
large (L)	**stor** *stoar*
extra large (XL)	**extra stor** *ehx • tra stoar*
petite	**petite** *peh • teet*
plus size	**plus-storlek** *pleus • stoar • leek*

NEWSAGENT & TOBACCONIST

Do you sell English language books/ newspapers?	**Säljer ni böcker/tidningar på engelska?** *sehl • yehr nee bur • kehr/teed • nihng • ar poa ehng • ehl • ska*
I'd like...	**Jag skulle vilja ha...** *yahg skuh • ler vihl • ya hah...*
candy [sweets]	**godis [sötsaker]** *goa • dihs [sut • sahk • ehr]*
some chewing gum	**tuggummi** *tuhg • guh • mee*
a chocolate bar	**en chokladkaka** *ehn shohk • lahd • kahka*
some cigars	**några cigarrer** *noa • gra see • gahr • er*
a pack/carton of cigarettes	**ett paket/en limpa cigaretter** *eht pak • eht/ehn lihm • pa sih • ga • reht • her*
a lighter	**en tändare** *ehn tehn • da • rehr*
a magazine	**en veckotidning** *ehn veh • koa • teed • nihng*
matches	**tändstickor** *tehnd • stik • ohr*

a newspaper	**en tidning** *ehn teed • nihng*
a pen	**en penna** *ehn peh • na*
a postcard	**ett vykort** *eht vew • koart*
a road/town map of...	**en vägkarta/stadskarta över...** *ehn vairg • kahr • ta/stats • kahr • ta ur • vehr...*
some stamps	**några frimärken** *noa • gra free • mair • kehn*

PHOTOGRAPHY

I'm looking for... camera.	**Jag skulle vilja köpa...kamera.** *yahg skuh • ler vihl • ya chur • pa... kah • meh • ra*
an automatic	**en automatisk** *ehn ah • toa • mah • tihsk*
a digital	**en digital** *ehn dih • gih • tahl*
a disposable	**en engångs** *ehn een • goangs*
I'd like...	**Jag skulle vilja ha...** *yahg skuh • ler vihl • ya hah...*
a battery	**ett batteri** *eht ba • teh • ree*
a digital print	**ett digitalt kort** *eht dih • gih • tahlt koart*
a memory card	**ett minneskort** *eht mihn • ehs • koart*
Can I print digital photos here?	**Kan jag skriva ut digitala foton här?** *kan yahg skree • va eut dih • gih • tah • la foh • toan hair*

SOUVENIRS

candlesticks	**ljusstakar** *yeus • stah • kar*
Christmas decorations	**juldekorationer** *yeul • dehk • oh • ra • shoan • ehr*
clogs	**träskor** *trair • skoar*
crystal (glass)	**kristallglas** *kree • stal • glahs*
a Dala horse (red wooden horse)	**en dalahäst** *ehn dah • la • hehst*
dolls	**dockor** *dok • oar*
glassware	**glasföremål** *glahs • furr • reh • moal*
handicrafts	**hemslöjd** *hehm • sluhyd*
horn work	**något i horn** *noa • goht ee hoarn*
jewelry	**smycken** *smew • kehn*
porcelain	**porslin** *pohrsh • leen*
pottery	**keramik** *cheh • ra • meek*
reindeer antlers	**renhorn** *reen • hoarn*
Sami handicrafts	**sameslöjd** *sah • meh • sluhyd*
smoked salmon	**rökt lax** *rurkt lax*
a tablecloth	**en duk** *ehn deuk*

textiles	**textil** *tehx • teel*
wood carvings	**träfigurer** *trair • fih • geu • rehr*
a wooden knife	**en träkniv** *ehn trair • kneev*
a wooden spoon	**en träsked** *ehn trair • sheed*
Can I see this/that?	**Får jag se på den här/där?** *foar yahg she poa dehn hair/dair*
The one in the window/display case.	**Den i fönstret/vitrinet.** *dehn ee furn • streht/vi • treen • eht*
I'd like…	**Jag skulle vilja ha…** *yahg skuh • ler vihl • ya hah…*
a battery	**ett batteri** *eht ba • teh • ree*
a bracelet	**ett armband** *eht arm • band*
a brooch	**en brosch** *ehn broash*
earrings	**örhängen** *ur • hehng • ehn*
a necklace	**ett halsband** *eht hals • band*
a ring	**en ring** *ehn rihng*
a watch	**en armbandsklocka** *ehn arm • bands • kloh • ka*
copper	**koppar** *kohpp • ar*
crystal (quartz)	**kristall** *krihs • tall*

When it comes to souvenirs, whether you are looking for something traditional or modern, you are sure to find just the thing in Sweden. **Träslöjd** (woodwork), **hemslöjd** (handicrafts), **keramik** (ceramics) and Swedish crystal are popular, traditional souvenirs. The **dalahäst** (Dala horse) is perhaps one of the most famous and ubiquitous souvenirs; traditionally, its color is a reddish-orange, but the horses can now be found in a wide range of colors and sizes. Sweden is known for its design, which is evident in its selection of **porslin** (fine china) and ceramics. Some well-known manufacturers include **Höganäs Keramik** and **Rörstrand**, the latter being the second oldest porcelain manufacturer in Europe, founded in 1746. Sweden is also famous for its glass and crystal, both with respect to design and to quality. **Glasriket** (the kingdom of glass) located in Småland, in southeastern Sweden, has around 15 glass factories, including some of the most famous glassworks in Sweden, such as **Kosta Boda**, **Orrefors** and **Nybro**. Factory tours are often available. In addition to the traditional Swedish handicrafts mentioned above, **sameslöjd** (**Sámi** handicraft) is something that should not be overlooked. The **Sámi** are known for their beautiful crafts, which include jewelry and knives carved from reindeer antlers, jewelry made from beaded pewter and reindeer leather as well as a wide range of clothing in reindeer leather and different types of fur.

diamond	**diamant** *dee • a • mant*
white/yellow gold	**vitt/rött guld** *viht/rurtt geuld*

pearl	**pärla** *pair • la*
I'd like...	**Jag skulle vilja ha...** *yahg skuh • ler vihl • ya hah...*
pewter	**tenn** *teen*
platinum	**platina** *plah • tee • na*
sterling silver	**äkta silver** *ehk • ta sihl • vehr*
Is this real?	**Är den här äkta?** *air dehn hair ehk • ta*
Can you engrave it?	**Kan ni gravera den?** *kan nee gra • vee • ra dehn*

SPORT & LEISURE

NEED TO KNOW

When's the game?	**När börjar matchen?** *nair bur • yar ma • shchehn*
Where's...?	**Var ligger...?** *vahr lih • gehr...*
the beach	**stranden** *stran • dehn*
Where's...?	**Var ligger...?** *vahr lih • gehr...*
the park	**parken** *park • ehn*
the pool	**simbassängen** *sihm • ba • sehng • ehn*

Is it safe to swim/ dive here?	**Kan man simma/dyka här utan risk?** *kan man sihmm • a/dew • ka hair eu • tan rihsk*
Can I rent [hire] golf clubs?	**Kan man hyra golfklubbor?** *kan man hew • ra gohlf • kluh • bohr*
How much per hour?	**Vad kostar det per timme?** *vahd kos • tar dee pair tihm • er*
How far is it to...?	**Hur långt är det till...?** *heur loangt air dee tihl...*
Can you show me on the map?	**Kan du visa mig på kartan?** *kan deu vee sa may poa kahr • tan*

WATCHING SPORT

When's...?	**När börjar...?** *nair bur • yar...*
the baseball game	**basebollmatchen** *base • bohl • mat • shehn*
the basketball game	**basketbollmatchen** *bahs • keht • bohl • ma • shchehn*

Sports and recreation are popular, and there are excellent sports facilities everywhere, ranging from **golf** (golf), **fiske** (fishing), **tennis** (tennis) and **fotboll** (soccer) to **skidåkning** (skiing) and **ishockey** (ice hockey). Tourist offices should have contact information for the various sports facilities in your area. Swedes also love the great outdoors, and the country has much to offer when it comes to **bergklättring** (mountain climbing), **vandring** (hiking), **ridsport** (horsebackriding), **cykelåkning** (cycling), **paddla kanot** (canoeing) and **segling** (boating). Whether you are looking for a day hike or planning a longer trip, some great choices include **Kebnekaise**, which is Sweden's highest mountain, **Kungsleden**, **Bohusleden** or **Padjelantleden**. There are a lot of options for cyclists, both amateurs and professionals, and popular cycle routes include **Kustlinjen** and **Sverigeleden**.

the boxing match	**boxningsmatchen** *boax • nihngs • matsh • ehn*
the cricket game	**cricketspelet** *cricket • matsh • ehn*
the cycling race	**cykeltävlingen** *sew • kehl • taiv • lihng • ehn*
the golf tournament	**golfspelet** *golf • spee • leht*
the soccer [football] game	**fotbollsmatchen** *foat • bohls • ma • shchehn*
the tennis match	**tennismatchen** *tehn • ihs • ma • shchehn*
the volleyball game	**volleybollspelet** *voh • lee • bohl • spee • leht*

Which teams are playing?	**Vilka lag spelar?** *vihl • ka lahg spee • lar*
Where's the stadium?	**Var ligger idrottsarenan?** *vahr lih • gehr ee • drohts • a • ree • nan*
Where's the horsetrack/ racetrack?	**Var finns hästkapplöpnings/ kapplöpningsbanan?** *Vahr fihns hehst • kap • luhp • nihngs/ kahp • luhp • nihgs • bahn • an*
Where can I place a bet?	**Var kan jag spela lotto?** *vahr kan yahg spee • la loh • toa*

PLAYING SPORT

Is there...nearby?	**Finns det...i närheten?** *fihns dee...ee nair • hee • ten*
a golf course	**en golfbana** *ehn gohlf • bah • na*
a gym	**ett gym** *eht yim*
a park	**en park** *ehn park*
a tennis court	**en tennisbana** *ehn tehn • ihs • bah • nohr*
How much per...?	**Hur mycket kostar det per...?** *heur mew • ker kos • tar dee pair...*
day	**dag** *dahg*
hour	**timme** *tihm • er*
game	**spel** *speel*
round	**runda** *ruhn • da*
Can I rent [hire]...?	**Kan man hyra...?** *kan man hew • ra...*

golf clubs	**klubbor** *kluhb • ohr*
equipment	**utrustning** *eut • ruhst • nihng*
a racket	**en racket** *ehn ra • keht*

AT THE BEACH/POOL

Where's the beach/ pool?	**Var är stranden/simbassängen?** *vahr air stran • dehn/ sihm • ba • sehng • ehn*
Is there a…here?	**Finns det…här?** *fihns dee…hair*
a kiddie [paddling] pool	**en barnbassäng** *ehn bahrn • bah • sehng*
an indoor/ outdoor pool	**en inomhuspool/utomhuspool** *ehn in • ohm • heus • poal/ eut • ohm • heus • poal*
a lifeguard	**en livräddare** *leev • rehd • a • rer*
Is it safe to swim/ dive?	**Kan man simma/dyka här utan risk?** *Kan man sihm • a/dew • ka hair eu • tan rihsk*
Is it safe for children?	**Är det barnsäkert?** *air dee bahrn • sair • kert*
I want to hire…	**Jag skulle vilja hyra…** *yahg skuh • ker vihl • ya hew • ra…*
a deck chair	**en solstol** *ehn soal • stoal*
diving equipment	**dykutrustning** *dewk • uht • ruhst • nihng*
a jet ski	**en jetski** *ehn jeht • skee*

a motorboat	**en motorbåt** *ehn moa • tor • boat*
a rowboat	**en roddbåt** *ehn rohd • boat*
snorkeling equipment	**snorklingsutrustning** *snoh • rklihngs • uht • ruhst • nihng*
a surfboard	**en surfbräda** *ehn suhrf • brair • da*
a towel	**en handduk** *ehn hand • deuk*
an umbrella	**en solparasol** *ehn soal • pa • ra • sohl*
water skis	**vattenskidor** *va • tehrn • shee • dohr*
a windsurfer	**en vindsurfare** *ehn vihnd • suhr • fa • reh*

For Traveling with Children, see page 134.

A significant portion of the Swedish coastline is rough, covered with granite rocks and cliffs and dotted with beaches. Most of the sandy beaches are found in the south and on the southwest coasts. Around Stockholm you can swim and dive from the small islands in the archipelago — and you can even swim in the water around Stockholm itself. Inland lakes, coastal areas and the popular archipelagos of Stockholm and the West Coast are perfect for boaters, canoeists and kayakers alike.

WINTER SPORTS

A lift pass for a day/ five days, please.	**Ett liftpass för en dag/för fem dagar, tack.** *eht lihft • pas furr ehn dahg/furr fehm dahg • ar tak*
Where's the ice rink?	**Var ligger isbanan?** *vahr lee • gehr ihs • bahn • an*
Are there lessons?	**Kan man få lektioner?** *kan man foa lehk • shoa • nehr*
How much?	**Hur mycket?** *huhr mew • keh*
I'm a beginner.	**Jag är nybörjare.** *yahg air new • bur • yah • reh*
I'm experienced.	**Jag har erfarenhet.** *yahg hahr air • fah • rehn • heet*

Swedes grow up with skiing: cross-country in the south and downhill in the north. There are many excellent ski resorts in the north, offering superb skiing and first-class facilities. Many hotels offer three- to seven-day package deals, including transportation and accommodation. In June, try **Riksgränsen** for a taste of skiing in the midnight sun.

Långfärdsbussar (long-distance buses) are efficient, relatively cheap and run daily to all major towns and resorts. Most of the major ski resorts also offer other winter sport activities like snowmobile safaris, snowshoeing and dog sledding tours. **Ishotellet** (Ice Hotel), though not a ski resort specifically, does offer several of these activities.

I'd like to hire...	**Jag skulle vilja hyra...** *yahg skuh • ler vihl • ya hew • ra...*
boots	**skidpjäxor** *sheed • pyeaix • ohr*
a helmet	**en hjälm** *ehn yehlm*
ice skates	**skridskor** *skrih • skohr*
poles	**stavar** *stah • var*
skis	**skidor** *shee • dohr*
a snowboard	**en snowboard** *ehn snow • board*
snowshoes	**pjäxor** *pyaix • ohr*
These are too big/ small.	**De här är för stora/små.** *dehm hair air furr stoa • ra/smoa*
A trail [piste] map, please.	**En karta över spåren, tack.** *ehn kahr • ta ur • vehr spoa • rehn tak*

YOU MAY SEE...

DRAGLIFT	drag lift
ÄGGLIFT	cable car
STOLLIFT	chair lift
NYBÖRJARE	novice
MELLANNIVÅ	intermediate
AVANCERAD	expert
SPÅRET STÄNGD	trail [piste] closed

OUT IN THE COUNTRY

I'd like a map of...	**Jag skulle vilja ha en karta över...** *yahg <u>skuh</u> • ler <u>vihl</u> • ya hah ehn <u>kahr</u> • ta <u>**ur**</u> • vehr...*
this region	**denna region** *<u>dehn</u> • a reh • <u>g**io**an</u>*
walking routes	**vandringsleder** *<u>van</u> • drihngs • <u>lee</u> • dehr*
cycle routes	**cykeleder** *<u>sew</u> • kehl • <u>lee</u> • dehr*
the trails	**spåren** *<u>sp**oa**</u> • rehn*
Is it easy/difficult?	**Är det lätt/svårt?** *air d**ee** leht/sv**oa**rt*
Is it far/steep?	**Är det långt/brant?** *air d**ee** loangt/brant*
How far is it to...?	**Hur långt är det till...?** *heur <u>loangt</u> air d**ee** tihl...*
Can you show me on the map?	**Kan du visa mig på kartan?** *kan deu <u>vee</u> • sa may p**oa** <u>kahr</u> • tan*
I'm lost.	**Jag har kommit vilse.** *yahg hahr <u>koh</u> • miht <u>vihl</u> • ser*

Where's...?	**Var ligger...?** *vahr lih • gehr...*
the bridge	**bron** *broan*
the cave	**grottan** *groht • an*
the cliff	**klippa** *klihp • an*
the farm	**bondgården** *boand • goard • ehn*
the field	**åkern** *oak • ern*
the footpath	**fotvandringsleden** *foat • vand • rihngs • lee • dehn*
the forest	**skogen** *skoag • ehn*
the hill	**berget** *behr • yeht*
the lake	**sjön** *shurn*
the mountain	**berget** *behr • yeht*
the mountain pass	**bergspasset** *berys • pas • eht*
the mountain range	**bergskedjan** *berys • chee • dyan*
the nature reserve	**naturreservatet** *na • teur • res • her • vah • teht*
the panorama	**panoraman** *pan • o • rah • man*
the park	**parken** *park • ehn*
the path	**stigen** *stee • gehn*

Where's...?	**Var ligger...?** *vahr lih • gehr...*
the peak	**toppen** *tohp • ehn*
the picnic area/ rest area	**picknickområdet/rastplatsen** *pihk • nihk • ohm • roa • det/rast • plats • ehn*
the pond	**dammen** *dah • mehn*
the river	**floden** *fload • ehn*
the sea	**havet** *hafv • eht*
the hot spring	**den varma källan** *dehn var • ma cheh • lan*
the valley	**dalen** *dahl • ehn*
the viewpoint	**utsiktspunkten** *eut • sihkts • peunk • tehn*
the village	**byn** *bewn*
the vineyard	**vinodlingen** *vihn • ohd • lihng • ehn*
the waterfall	**vattenfallet** *va • tehrn • fal*

TRAVELING WITH CHILDREN

NEED TO KNOW

Is there a discount for kids?	**Har ni barnrabatt?** *hahr nee bahrn • rah • bat*
Can you recommend a babysitter?	**Kan du rekommendera en barnvakt?** *kan deu reh • koh • mehn • dee • ra ehn bahrn • vakt*
Could I have a highchair?	**Kan jag få en barnstol, tack?** *kan yahg foa ehn bahrn • stoal tak*
Where can I change the baby?	**Var kan jag byta på babyn?** *vahr kan yahg bew • ta poa bai • been*
Where's...?	**Var ligger...?** *vahr lih • gehr...*
the amusement park	**nöjesfältet** *nury • ehs • fehl • teht*
the arcade	**arkadhallen** *ar • kahd • ha • lehn*
the kiddie [paddling] pool	**barnbassängen** *bahrn • ba • sehng • ehn*
the park	**parken** *park • kehn*
the playground	**lekplatsen** *leek • plats • ehn*
the zoo	**djurparken** *yeur • park • ehn*
Are kids allowed?	**Får man ta barnen med?** *foar man tah bahr • nehn meed*
Is it safe for kids?	**Är det barnsäkert?** *air det bahrn • sair • kert*

YOU MAY HEAR...

Vad gullig! *vahd geul • ig*	How cute!
Vad heter han/hon? *vahd hee • tehr han/hoan*	What's his/her name?
Hur gammal är han/hon? *heur gam • al air han/hoan*	How old is he/she?

OUT & ABOUT

Can you recommend something for kids?	**Kan du föreslå något för barn?** *kan deu furr • reh • sloa noa • goht furr bahrn*
Where's...?	**Var är...?** *Vahr air...*
the amusement park	**nöjesparken** *nuy • ehs • pahr • kehn*
the arcade	**gallerian** *gah • le • ree • an*
the kiddie [paddling] pool	**barnbassängen/plaskdammen** *bah • rn • ba • sehng • ehn/ plask • da • mehn*
the park	**parken** *par • kehn*
the playground	**lekplatsen** *lehk • plat • sehn*
the zoo	**djurparken** *yeur • par • kehn*
Are kids allowed?	**Tillåts barn?** *tihl • oats bahrn*
Is it safe for kids?	**Är det säkert för barn?** *air deht seh • kehrt furr bahrn*

Is it suitable for… year olds?	**Passar det för…-åringar?** *pas • ar dee furr…oa • rihng • ar*

For Numbers, see page 22.

BABY ESSENTIALS

Do you have…?	**Har ni…?** *hahr nee…*
a baby bottle	**en nappflaska** *ehn nap • flas • ka*
baby food	**babymat** *behy • bih • maht*
baby wipes	**våtservetter för barn** *voat • ser • veht • er furrbahrn*
a car seat	**en bilbarnstol** *ehn beel • bahrn • stoal*
a children's menu	**en barnmeny** *ehn bahrn • meh • new*
a children's portion	**en barnportion** *bahrn • pohrt • shoan*
a highchair	**en barnstol** *ehn bahrn • stoal*

a crib	**en barnsäng** *ehn bahrn • sehng*
diapers [nappies]	**blöjor** *blury • ohr*
formula	**välling** *vehl • ihng*
a pacifier [dummy]	**en napp** *ehn nap*
a playpen	**ett lekrum** *eht leek • ruhm*
a stroller [pushchair]	**en sittvagn** *ehn siht • vangn*
Can I breastfeed the baby here?	**Får jag amma barnet här?** *foar yahg ah • ma bahr • neht hair*
Where can I change the baby?	**Var kan jag byta på babyn?** *vahr kan yahg bew • ta poa bai • been*

For Dining with Children, see page 168.

BABYSITTING

Can you recommend a reliable babysitter?	**Kan du rekommendera en pålitlig barnvakt?** *kaun deu re • koh • mehn • dee • rahra ehn poa • leet • lihg bahrn • vakt*
What's the charge?	**Vad kostar det?** *vahd kos • tar dee*
We'll be back by...	**Vi kommer tillbaka** *Vee koh • mehr tihl • bah • ka*
I'll pick them up at...	**Jag hämtar dem...** *yahg hehm • tar dehm...*
I can be reached at...	**Du kan nå mig på...** *deu kan noa may poa...*

For Time, see page 24

SAFE TRAVEL

EMERGENCIES

NEED TO KNOW

Help!	**Hjälp!** *yelp*
Go away!	**Ge er iväg!** *yeh ehr ee • vairg*
Stop thief!	**Stoppa tjuven!** *stop • a shcheu • vehn*
Get a doctor!	**Hämta en läkare!** *hehm • ta ehn lair • ka • rer*
Fire!	**Det brinner!** *dee brihn • ehr*
I'm lost.	**Jag har gått vilse.** *yahg hahr goat vihl • ser*
Can you help me?	**Kan du hjälpa mig?** *kan deu yehl • pa may*

YOU MAY HEAR...

Fyll i blanketten, tack. *fewl ee blan • keht • ehn tak*	Please fill out this form.
Er legitimation, tack. *ehr lehg • ee • tih • ma • shoan tak*	Your identification, please.
När/Var hände det? *nair/vahr hehn • dehr dee*	When/Where did it happen?
Hur ser han/hon ut? *hewr seer han/hoan eut*	What does he/she look like?

POLICE

In an emergency, dial: **112.**
This number will connect you to the police, the fire brigade or an ambulance.

NEED TO KNOW

Call the police!	**Ring polisen!** *rihng poa • lee • sehn*
Where's the nearest police station?	**Var ligger närmaste polisstation?** *vahr lih • gehr nair • mas • ter poo • lees • sta • shoan*
There's been an accident.	**Det har hänt en olycka.** *det hahr hehnt ehn oa • lewk • a*
I've been attacked.	**Jag har blivit anfallen.** *jahg hahr blee • viht an • fa • lehn*
My child is missing.	**Mitt barn har kommit bort.** *miht bahrn hahr koh • miht bohrt*
I need...	**Jag behöver...** *yahg beh • hur • vehr...*
an interpreter	**en tolk** *ehn tohlk*
to contact my lawyer	**kontakta min advokat** *kohn • tak • ta mihn ad • voh • kaht*
to make a phone call	**ringa ett samtal** *rihng • a eht sam • tahl*
I'm innocent.	**Jag är oskyldig.** *yahg air oa • shewl • dihg*

CRIME & LOST PROPERTY

I want to report…	**Jag vill anmäla…** *yahg vihl an • mair • la…*
a mugging	**ett överfall** *eht **ur** • vehr • fal*
a rape	**en våldtäkt** *ehn vohld • tehkt*
a theft	**ett rån** *eht r**oa**n*
I've been robbed/ mugged.	**Jag har blivit rånad/överfallen.** *yahg hahr blee • viht r**oa** • nad/ **ur** • veh • fal • ehn*
I've lost…	**Jag har tappet…** *yahg hahr tah • pat…*
My…has been stolen.	**Någon har stulit…** *n**oa** • gohn hahr steu • liht…*
backpack	**min ryggsäck** *mihn rewg • sehk*
bicycle	**min cykel** *mihn sew • kehl*
camera	**min kamera** *mihn kah • meh • ra*

rental car	**min bil/hyrbil** *mihn beel/hewr • beel*
computer	**min dator** *mihn dah • tohr*
credit cards	**mina kreditkort** *mee • na kre • deet • koart*
jewelry	**mina smycken** *mee • na smew • ken*
money	**mina pengar** *mee • na pehng • ar*
passport	**mitt pass** *miht pas*
purse [handbag]	**min portmonnä** *mihn pohrt • mo • nai*
traveler's checks [cheques]	**mina resecheckar** *mee • na ree • seh • shehk • ar*
wallet	**min plånbok** *mihn ploan • boak*
I need a police report for my insurance.	**Jag behöver en polisanmälan till min försäkring.** *yahg beh • hu • vehr ehn poal • ees • an • mailan tihl meen furr • sehk·rihng*
Where is the British/ American/Irish embassy?	**Var ligger den brittiska/amerikanska ambassaden?** *var ligger den brittiska/amerikanska ambassaden?*

HEALTH

NEED TO KNOW

I'm sick [ill].	**Jag är sjuk.** *yahg air sheuk*
I need an English-speaking doctor.	**Jag behöver en engelsktalande läkare.** *yahg beh • hur • vehr ehn ehng • ehlsk • tahl • an • der lair • ka • rer*
It hurts here.	**Det gör ont här.** *dee yurr oant hair*
I have a stomachache.	**Jag har ont i magen.** *yahg hahr oant ee mah • gehn*

FINDING A DOCTOR

Can you recommend a doctor/dentist?	**Kan du rekommendera en läkare/tandläkare?** *kan deu reh • koh • mehn • dee • ra ehn lair • ka • rer/tand • lair • ka • rer*
Can the doctor come to see me here?	**Kan doktorn komma och undersöka mig här?** *kan dohk • torn koh • ma ohk eun • der • sur • ka may hair*
I need an English-speaking doctor.	**Jag behöver en engelsktalande läkare.** *yahg beh • uv • ehr en eeng • ehlsk • tah • lan • de leh • ka • re*
What are their office hours?	**Vilka är deras öppettider?** *vihl • ka air dee • ras ur • peh • tee • dehr*

Can I make an appointment for...?	**Kan jag boka en tid...?** *kan yahg boa • ka ehn teed...*
today	**idag** *ee • dahg*
tomorrow	**imorgon** *ee • mo • ron*
as soon as possible	**så snart som möjligt** *soa snahrt som mury • ligt*
It's urgent.	**Det är brådskande.** *dee air broas • kan • der*

SYMPTOMS

I'm...	**Jag...** *yahg...*
bleeding	**blöder** *blur • dehr*
constipated	**är förstoppad** *air furr • stop • ad*
dizzy	**har yrsel** *hahr ewr • sehl*
nauseous	**mår illa** *moar ihl • la*

vomiting	**kräks** *krairks*
It hurts here.	**Det gör ont här.** *dee yurr oant hair*
I have…	**Jag har…** *yahg hahr…*
an allergic reaction	**en allergisk reaktion** *ehn a • lehr • gihsk ree • ak • shoan*
chest pain	**ont i bröstet** *oant ee brurs • teht*
cramps	**kramper** *kram • pehr*
diarrhea	**diarré** *dee • ar • ee*
an earache	**ont i örat** *oant ee ur • rat*
a fever	**feber** *fee • behr*
pain	**ont** *oant*
a rash	**ett utslag** *eht eut • slahg*
a sprain	**en stukning** *ehn steuk • nihng*
some swelling	**en lätt svullnad** *ehn leht sveul • nad*
a stomachache	**ont i magen** *oant ee mah • gehn*
sunstroke	**solsting** *soal • stihng*
I've been sick [ill] for…days.	**Jag har varit sjuk i…dagar.** *yahg hahr vah • riht sheuk ee…dah • gar*

For Numbers, see page 22.

YOU MAY HEAR...

Vad är det för fel? *vahd air dee fur feel*	What's wrong?
Var gör det ont? *vahr yur dee oant*	Where does it hurt?
Gör det ont här? *yur deht ohnt hehr*	Does it hurt here?
Tar du någon annan medicin? *tahr deu noa • gohn an • an meh • dih • seen*	Are you taking any other medication?
Är du allergisk mot något? *air deu a • lehr • gihsk moat noa • goht*	Are you allergic to anything?
Öppna munnen. *urp • na muhn • ehn*	Open your mouth.
Andas djupt. *an • das yeupt*	Breathe deeply.
Hosta, tack. *hoas • ta, tak*	Cough, please.
Du behöver åka till sjukhuset. *deu beh • hur • vehr oa • ka tihl sjeuk • heu • seht*	You need to go to the hospital.

CONDITIONS

I'm anemic/diabetic.	**Jag är anemisk/diabetiker.** *yahg air a • nee • mihsk/ dee • a • beh • tih • ker*
I'm epileptic.	**Jag har epilepsi.** *yahg hahr eh • pih • leh • psi*

I'm allergic to antibiotics/ penicillin.	**Jag är allergisk mot antibiotika/ penicillin.** *yahg air a • lehr • gihsk moat an • tih • bee • oa • tee • ka/ pehn • eh • si • leen*
I have...	**Jag har...** *yahg hahr...*
arthritis	**artrit** *ar • treet*
asthma	**astma** *as • ma*
high/low blood pressure	**högt/låg blodtryck** *hurgt/loagt bload • trewk*
a heart condition	**hjärtproblem** *yairt • proa • bleem*
I'm taking... (medicine).	**Jag tar...(medicin).** *yahg tahr...(meh • dee • seen)*

TREATMENT

Can you prescribe a generic drug [unbranded medication]?	**Kan du skriva ut ett generiskt läkemedel [generika]?** *Kahn deu skrih • va eut eht gehn • eh • rih • skt lai • keh • meh • dehl [gehn • eh • rih • ka]*
Where can I get it?	**Var hittar jag det?** *vahr hih • tar yahg deht*
Do I need a prescription/ medicine?	**Behöver jag ett recept/medicin?** *beh • hur • vehr yahg eht reh • sehpt/ meh • dih • sihn*

For Pharmacy, see page 151.

HOSPITAL

Please notify my family.	**Var snäll och underrätta min familj.** *vahr snehl ohk eun • der • rehta mihn fa • mily*
I'm in pain.	**Jag har ont.** *yahg hahr oant*
I need a doctor/nurse.	**Jag behöver en läkare/sjuksköterska.** *yahg beh • hur • vehr ehn lair • ka • rer/ sheuk • shur • ter • ska*
When are visiting hours?	**När är det besökstid?** *nair air dee beh • surks • teed*
I'm visiting...	**Jag vill besöka...** *yahg vihl beh • sur • ka...*

DENTIST

I've broken a tooth/lost a filling.	**Jag har brutit av en tand/tappat en plomb.** *yahg hahr breu • tiht afv ehn tand/tap • at ehn plohmb*
This tooth hurts.	**Den här tanden gör ont.** *dehn hair tan • dehn yur oant*
Can you fix this denture?	**Kan du reparera den här tandprotesen?** *kan deu reh • pa • ree • ra dehn hair tand • proh • tees • ehn*

GYNECOLOGIST

I have menstrual cramps/a vaginal infection.	**Jag har mens värk/en vaginal infektion.** *yahg hahr mens vehrk/ehn va • gih • nahl ihn • fehk • shoan*
I missed my period.	**Min mens har inte kommit.** *mihn mehns hahr ihn • ter koh • miht*

I'm on the Pill.	**Jag tar p-piller.** *yahg tahr pee • pihl • ler*
I'm (...months) pregnant.	**Jag är (...månader) gravid.** *Yahg air (...moh • na • dehr) gra • veed*
I'm (not) pregnant.	**Jag är (inte) gravid.** *yahg air (ihn • ter) gra • veed*
I haven't had my period for...months.	**Jag har inte haft mens på... månader.** *yahg hahr ihn • ter haft mehns p**oa**... m**oa** • na • dehr*

For Numbers, see page 22.

OPTICIAN

I've lost...	**Jag har tappat...** *yahg hahr tap • at...*
a contact lens	**en kontaktlins** *ehn kohn • takt • lihns*
my glasses	**mina glasögon** *mee • na glahs • **ur** • gohn*
a lens	**en lins** *ehn lihns*

PAYMENT & INSURANCE

How much does it cost?	**Hur mycket kostar det?** *heur mew • ker kos • tar d**ee***
Can I pay by credit card?	**Kan jag betala med kreditkort?** *kan yahg beh • tah • la meed kreh • deet • koart*
I have insurance.	**Jag har försäkring.** *yahg hahr f**urr** • sair • krihng*

Can I have a receipt for my insurance?	**Kan jag få ett kvitto för mitt försäkringsbolag?** *kan yahg foa eht kvih • toh furr miht furr • sair • krihngs • boa • lahg*

PHARMACY

NEED TO KNOW

Where's the nearest pharmacy?	**Var är närmaste apotek?** *vahr air nair • mas • teh a • poa • teek*
What time does the pharmacy open/close?	**När öppnar/stänger apoteket?** *nair urp • nar/ stehng • ehr a • poa • tee • keht*
What would you recommend for...?	**Vad kan du rekommendera för...?** *vahd kan deu reh • koh • mehn • dee • ra furr...*
How much should I take?	**Hur mycket ska jag ta?** *heur mew • ker skah yahg tah*
Can you fill [make up] this prescription for me?	**Kan ni göra iordning det här receptet åt mig?** *kan nee yur • ra ee oard • nihng dee hair reh • sehp • teht oat may*
I'm allergic to...	**Jag är allergisk mot...** *yahg air a • lehr • gihsk moat...*

WHAT TO TAKE

How much should I take?	**Hur mycket ska jag ta?** *heur mew • ker skah yahg tah*

How many times a day should I take it?	**Hur många gånger om dagen ska jag ta det?** *heur moang • a goang • er ohm dah • gehn skah yahg tah dee*
Is it suitable for children?	**Är det lämpligt för barn?** *air dee lehmp • lihgt furr bahrn*
I'm taking... (medicine).	**Jag tar...(medicin).** *yahg tahr...(meh • dee • seen)*
Are there side effects?	**Ger det några biverkningar?** *yehr dee noa • gra bee • vehrk • nihng • ar*
I'd like some medicine for...	**Jag behöver medicin mot...** *yahg beh • hur • vehr meh • dih • seen moat...*
a cold	**en förkylning** *ehn furr • chewl • nihng*
a cough	**hosta** *hoas • ta*
diarrhea	**diarré** *dee • a • reh*
a headache	**huvudvärk** *huh • vuhd • vairk*
an insect bite	**ett insektbett** *eht in • sekt • beht*
motion sickness	**åksjuka** *oak • sheu • ka*
a sore throat	**halsont** *hals • oant*
a sunburn	**solbränna** *soal • brehn • a*
a toothache	**tandvärk** *tand • vairk*
an upset stomach	**ont i magen** *oant ee mah • gehn*

In addition to filling prescriptions, **apotek** (pharmacies) sell over-the-counter medication as well as their own brands of toiletries and cosmetics. Almost all pharmacies are open on weekdays, but not all are open late in the evening or on weekends. Business hours vary considerably depending on the pharmacy. Generally, business hours are between 9:00 a.m. and 5:00 p.m. on weekdays. Pharmacies that are open in the evening usually close around 9:00 p.m., and weekend hours are generally from 10:00 a.m. to 4:00 p.m.

YOU MAY SEE...

EN GÅNG/TRE GÅNGER PER DAG	once/three times a day
TABLETTER	tablets
DROPPAR TESKEDAR	drop teaspoons
FÖRE/EFTER/TILLSAMMANS MED MÅLTIDER	before/after/ with meals
PÅ FASTANDE MAGE	on an empty stomach
SVÄLJS HELA	swallow whole
KAN ORSAKA DÅSIGHET	may cause drowsniness
ENDAST FÖR UTVÄRTES BRUK	for external use only

BASIC SUPPLIES

I'd like...	**Jag skulle vilja ha...** *yahg skuh • ler vihl • ya hah...*
acetaminophen [paracetamol]	**acetominofen** *a • seht • a • mihn • oa • fehn*
antiseptic cream	**antiseptisk salva** *an • tih • sehp • tihsk sal • va*
aspirin	**huvudvärkstabletter** *heu • vuhd • vairks • ta • bleh • ter*
bandage [plasters]	**gasbinda** *gahs • bihn • da*
a comb	**kam** *kam*
condoms	**kondomer** *kohn • doa • mehr*
contact lens solution	**kontaktlinsvätska** *kohn • takt • lins • veht • ska*
deodorant	**deodorant** *dee • oa • deh • rant*
a hairbrush	**en hårborste** *ehn hoar • bohrsh • ter*
hair spray	**hårspray** *hoar • spray*
ibuprofen	**ibuprofen** *ee • beu • proa • fehn*
insect repellent	**myggolja** *mewg • ohl • ya*
a nail file	**en nagelfil** *ehn nah • gehl • feel*
a (disposable) razor	**en (engångs)-rakhyvel** *ehn (een • goangs) • rahk • hew • vehl*
razor blades	**rakblad** *rahk • blahd*

sanitary napkins [towels]	**bindor** *bin • dohr*
shampoo/	**schampo** *sham • poa*
conditioner	**hårbalsam** *hoar • bal • sam*
soap	**tvål** *tvoal*
sunscreen	**solskyddskräm** *soal • shewds • krairm*
tampons	**tamponger** *tam • poang • ehr*
tissue	**papper näsdukar** *pa • pehrs • nairs • deu • kar*
toilet paper	**toalettpapper** *toa • a • leht • pa • pehr*
a toothbrush	**tandborste** *tand • bohr • ster*
toothpaste	**tandkräm** *tand • krairm*

For Baby Essentials, see page 136.

CHILD HEALTH & EMERGENCY

Can you recommend a pediatrician?	**Kan du rekommendera en barnläkare?** *kan deu reh • koh • men • dee • ra ehn bahrn • lairk • a • rer*
My child is allergic to…	**Mitt barn är allergiskt mot…** *miht bahrn air a • lehr • gisk moat…*
My child is missing.	**Mitt barn har kommit bort.** *miht bahrn hahr koh • miht bohrt*
Have you seen a boy/girl?	**Har du sett en pojke/flicka?** *hahr deu seht ehn poy • ker/flih • ka*

DISABLED TRAVELERS

NEED TO KNOW

Is there...? **Finns det...?**
fihns det...

access for the disabled **ingång för rörelsehindrade**
in • goang furr rur • rehl • seh • hihn • dra • der

a wheelchair ramp **en rullstolsramp**
ehn reul • stoals • ramp

a disabled-accessible toilet **en handikappanpassad toalett**
ehn hand • ee • kap • an • pas • ad toa • ah • leht

I need... **Jag behöver...**
yahg beh • hur • ver...

assistance **hjälp**
yehlp

an elevator [lift] **en hiss**
ehn hihs

a ground floor room **ett rum på bottenvåningen**
eht ruhm poa boh • tehrn • voa • nihng • hen

ASKING FOR ASSISTANCE

I'm disabled. **Jag är handikappad.**
yahg air hand • ee • kap • ad

I'm deaf. **Jag är döv.**
yahg air durv

I'm visually/hearing impaired.	**Jag är synskadad/hörselskadad.** *yahg air sewn • skah • dad/ hur • sel • skah • dad*
I'm unable to walk far/use the stairs.	**Jag kan inte gå långt/gå i trappor.** *yahg kan ihn • ter goa loangt/goa ee trap • ohr*
Can I bring my wheelchair?	**Kan jag ta med min rullstol?** *kan yahg tah meed mihn ruhl • stoal*
Are guide dogs permitted?	**Är det tillåtet med ledarhund?** *air dee tihl • loa • teht meed leed • ar • huhnd*
Can you help me?	**Kan du hjälpa mig?** *kan deu yehl • pa may*
Could you open/hold the door?	**Kan du öppna/hålla upp dörren?** *kan deu urp • na/hoa • la uhp dur • rehn*

For Health, see page 144.

FOOD

EATING OUT

NEED TO KNOW

Can you recommend a good restaurant/bar?	**Kan du rekommendera en bra restaurang/pub?** *kan deu reh • koh • mehn • dee • ra ehn brah rehs • teu • rang/peub*
Is there a traditional Swedish/an inexpensive restaurant nearby?	**Finns det något värdshus/någon billigare restaurang i närheten?** *fihns dee noa • goht vairds • heus/ noa • gohn bihl • ih • ga • rer rehs • teu • rang ee nair • hee • tehn*
A table for..., please.	**Ett bord för..., tack.** *eht bohrd furr...tak*
Could we sit...?	**Får vi sitta...?** *foar vee siht • a...*
here/there	**här/där** *hair/dair*
outside	**ute** *eu • ter*

in a non-smoking area	**vid bord för icke-rökare** *veed bohrd furr ee • keh • rur • ka • rer*
I'm waiting for someone.	**Jag väntar på någon.** *yahg vairn • tar poa noa • gohn*
Where are the toilets?	**Var finns toaletten?** *vahr fihns toa • ah • leh • tehn*
A menu, please.	**En meny, tack.** *ehn meh • neu tak*
What do you recommend?	**Vad rekommenderar du?** *vahd reh • koh • mehn • dee • rar deu*
I'd like...	**Jag skulle vilja ha...** *yahg skuh • ler vihl • ya hah...*
Some more..., please.	**Lite mer..., tack.** *lee • ter meer...tak*
Enjoy your meal.	**Smaklig måltid.** *smahk • lihg moal • teed*
The check [bill], please.	**Kan jag få räkningen, tack.** *kan yahg foa rairk • nihng • ehn tak*
Is service included?	**Är serveringsavgiften inräknad?** *air ser • veeh • rihngs • afv • yihf • tehn ihn • rairk • nad*
Can I pay by credit card?	**Kan jag betala med kreditkort?** *kan yahg beh • tah • la meed kreh • deet • koart*
Can I have the receipt, please?	**Kan jag få kvittot, tack?** *kan yahg foa kvih • toht tak*
Thank you.	**Tack.** *tak*

WHERE TO EAT

Can you recommend...?	**Kan du rekommendera...?** *kan deu reh • koh • mehn • dee • ra...*
a restaurant	**en restaurang** *ehn rehs • teu • rang*
a bar	**en bar** *ehn bahr*
a cafe	**ett kafé** *eht ka • feh*
a fast-food place	**en grillbar** *ehn grihl • bahr*
a steakhouse	**ett stekhus** *eht steek • heus*
a cheap restaurant	**en billig restaurang** *en bihl • eeg reh • stah • eu • rahng*
an expensive restaurant	**en dyr restaurang** *ehn dewr reh • stah • eu • rahng*

When it comes to eating out, there are many options, ranging from fast-food stands to five-star restaurants. If you are looking for a quick bite to eat, then a **gatukök** (fast-food stand) is an easy choice. If you are looking for more traditional cuisine, this can be found at a **värdshus** (roadside restaurant), **kafé** (cafe) or **restaurang** (restaurant).

RESERVATIONS & PREFERENCES

I'd like to reserve a table...	**Jag skulle vilja boka ett bord...** *yahg skuh • ler vihl • ya boh • ka eht bohrd...*
for two	**för två** *furr tv**oa***
for this evening	**till ikväll** *tihl ee • kvehl*
for tomorrow at...	**imorgon klockan...** *ee • mo • ron kloh • kan...*
A table for two, please.	**Kan jag få ett bord för två tack.** *kan yahg f**oa** eht bohrd f**urr** tv**oa** tak*
We have a reservation.	**Vi har bokat ett bord.** *vee hahr boa • kat eht bohrd*
My name is...	**Jag heter...** *yahg hee • tehr...*
Could we sit...?	**Får vi sitta...?** *f**oa**r vee siht • a...*
here/there	**här/där** *hair/dair*
outside	**ute** *eu • ter*
in a non-smoking area	**vid bord för icke-rökare** *veed bohrd f**urr** ee • keh • rur • kah • rer*
by the window	**vid fönstret** *veed furns • treht*
in the shade	**i skuggan** *ee skuh • gan*
in the sun	**i solen** *ee sohl • ehn*
Where are the restrooms [toilets]?	**Var finns toaletten?** *vahr fihns toa • ah • leh • tehn*

YOU MAY HEAR...

Har ni bokat? *hahr nee boh • kat*	Do you have a reservation?
Hur många blir ni? *heur moang • a bleer nee*	How many?
Rökare eller icke-rökare? *rur • ka • rer ehl • ehr ee • keh • rur • ka • rer*	Smoking or non-smoking?
Vill ni beställa? *vihl nee beh • steh • la*	Are you ready to order?
Vad vill ni beställa? *vahd vihl nee beh • steh • la*	What would you like?
Jag kan rekommendera... *yahg kan reh • koh • mehn • dee • ra...*	I recommend...
Smaklig måltid. *smahk • lihg moal • teed*	Enjoy your meal.

HOW TO ORDER

Excuse me!	**Ursäkta!** *eur • shehk • ta*
We're ready to order.	**Vi vill gärna beställa.** *vee vihl yair • na beh • steh • la*
May I see the wine list?	**Kan jag få se vinlistan?** *kan yahg foa see veen • lihs • tan*
I'd like...	**Jag skulle vilja ha...** *yahg skuh • ler vihl • ya hah...*
a bottle of...	**en flaska...** *ehn flahs • ka...*
a glass of...	**ett glas...** *eht glahs...*

a carafe of...	**en karaff...** *ehn kah • raf...*
The menu, please.	**En meny, tack.** *ehn meh • neu tak*
Do you have...?	**Har ni...?** *hahr nee...*
a menu in English	**en meny på engelska** *ehn meh • neu poa ehng • ehl • ska*
a fixed price menu	**en meny med fast pris** *ehn meh • neu meed fast prees*
a children's menu	**en barnmeny** *ehn bahrn • meh • neu*
What do you recommend?	**Vad rekommenderar ni?** *vahd reh • koh • mehn • dee • rar nee*
What's this?	**Vad är det här?** *vahd air dee hair*
What's in it?	**Vad är det i den?** *vahd air dee ee dehn*
Is it spicy?	**Är den kryddstark?** *air dehn kreyd • stark*
I'd like...	**Jag skulle vilja ha...** *yahg skuh • ler vihl • ya hah...*
More..., please.	**Lite mer..., tack.** *lee • teh meer...tak*
With/Without...	**Med/Utan...** *meed/eu • tan...*
I can't have...	**Jag kan inte äta mat som innehåller...** *yahg kan ihn • ter air • ta maht som ih • neh • hoal • lehr...*
rare	**blodig** *bloa • dihg*
medium	**medium** *mee • dee • uhm*
well done	**genomstekt** *ye • nom • steekt*

It's to go [take away]. **Jag ska ta den med mig.**
yahg skah tah dehn meed may

For Drinks, see page 200.

YOU MAY SEE...

KUVERTAVGIFT	cover charge
FAST PRIS	fixed-price
MENY	menu
DAGENS MENY	menu of the day
DRICKS (INTE) INRÄKNAD	service (not) included
SPECIALITETER	specials

COOKING METHODS

baked **bakad**
bah • kad

boiled **kokt**
koakt

braised **bräserad**
braeh • seeh • rad

breaded **panerad**
pah • neeh • rad

creamed **rörd**
rurd

diced **i bitar**
ee bee • tar

filleted **filead**
fih • leeh • ad

fried **stekt**
steekt

grilled	**grillad** *grihl • ad*
poached	**pocherad** *poa • sheeh • rad*
roasted	**ugnstekt** *eungn • steekt*
sautéed	**stekt** *steekt*
smoked	**rökt** *rurkt*
steamed	**ångkokt** *oang • koakt*
stewed	**stuvad** *steu • vad*
stuffed	**fylld** *fewld*

DIETARY REQUIREMENTS

I am...	**Jag är...** *yahg air...*
diabetic	**diabetiker** *dee • a • beh • tih • ker*
lactose intolerant	**laktosintolerant** *lak • toas • in • toh • leh • rant*
vegetarian	**vegetarian** *veh • geh • ta • ree • ahn*
vegan	**vegan** *veh • gahn*
I'm allergic to...	**Jag är allergisk mot...** *yahg air a • lehr • gihsk moat...*
I can't eat food that contains...	**Jag kan inte äta mat som innehåller...** *yahg kan ihn • ter air • ta maht som ihn • neh • hoa • lehr...*

dairy	**mejeriprodukter** *may • eh • ree • proh • duhk • tehr*
gluten	**gluten** *glue • tehn*
nut	**nöt** *nurt*
pork	**fläskkött** *flehsk • churt*
shellfish	**skaldjur** *skahl • yeur*
spicy food	**kryddad mat** *krew • dad maht*
wheat	**vete** *veeh • te*
Is it halal/kosher?	**Är det halal/kosher?** *air deht ha • lal/kosh • ehr*
Do you have...?	**Har ni...?** *hahr nee*
skimmed milk	**lättmjölk** *leht • myulk*
whole milk	**standardmjölk** *stahn • dardh • myulk*
soya milk	**sojamjölk** *soh • ya • myulk*

DINING WITH CHILDREN

Do you have a children's menu?	**Har ni en barnmeny?** *hahr nee ehn bahrn • meh • neu*
Can you bring a high chair, please?	**Kan jag få en barnstol, tack?** *kan yahg foa ehn bahrn • stoal tak*
Where can I feed/ change the baby?	**Var kan jag mata/byta på babyn?** *vahr kan yahg mah • ta/bew • ta poa bai • been*

Can you warm this?	**Kan ni värma det här?** *kan nee vair • ma dee hair*

For Traveling with Children, see page 134.

HOW TO COMPLAIN

How much longer will our food be?	**Hur länge till behöver vi vänta?** *heur lehng • er tihl beh • hur • ver vee vehn • ta*
We can't wait any longer.	**Vi kan inte vänta längre.** *vee kan ihn • t'er vehn • ta lehng • rer*
We're leaving.	**Vi går nu.** *vee goar neu*
That's not what I ordered.	**Det här har jag inte beställt.** *dee hair hahr yahg ihn • ter beh • stehlt*
I asked for…	**Jag beställde…** *yahg beh • stehl • der…*
I can't eat this.	**Jag kan inte äta det här.** *yahg kan ihn • ter air • ta dee hair*
This is too…	**Det här är för…** *dee hair air furr…*
cold/hot	**kallt/varmt** *kalt/varmt*
salty/spicy	**salt/kryddat** *salt/krew • dat*
tough/bland	**segt/smaklöst** *sekt/smahk • lurst*
This isn't clean/ fresh.	**Det här är inte rent/färskt.** *dee hair air ihn • ter reent/fairskt*

PAYING

The check [bill], please.	**Kan jag få räkningen, tack.** *kan yahg foa rairk • nihng • ehn tak*

We'd like to pay separately.	**Vi vill betala var för sig.** *vee vihl beh • tah • la vahr f**urr** say*
It's all together.	**Allt tillsammans.** *alt tihl • saa • mans*
Is service included?	**Är serveringsavgiften inräknad?** *air sehr • veeh • rihngs • afv • yihf • ten ihn • rairk • nad*
What's this amount for?	**Vad står den här summan för?** *vahd st**oa**r dehn hair suhm • an f**urr***
I didn't have that. I had…	**Jag åt inte det. Jag åt...** *yahg **oa**t ihn • ter d**ee** yahg **oa**t…*
Can I pay by credit card?	**Kan jag betala med kreditkort?** *kan yahg beh • tah • la meed kreh • deet • koart*
Can I have an itemized bill/ a receipt?	**Kan jag få en specificerad räkning/ett kvitto?** *kan yahg f**oa** ehn speh • seh • fee • ee • rad rairk • nihng/eht kvih • toh*
That was a very good meal.	**Det var en mycket god måltid.** *d**ee** vahr ehn mew • ker goad m**oa**l • teed*
I've already paid.	**Jag har redan betalat.** *yahg hahr reh • dan beh • tah • lat*

MEALS & COOKING

BREAKFAST

apelsin *a • pehl • seen*	orange
bacon *bay • kohn*	bacon

bröd *brurd*	bread
filmjölk *feel • myurlk*	thick yogurt
frukostflingor *fruh • kohst • flihng • or*	(cold) cereal
fruktjuice *fruhkt • yoas*	fruit juice
grapefrukt *grape • fruhkt*	grapefruit
gröt *grurt*	(hot) cereal
havregryn *hafv • reh • greun*	oatmeal
honung *hoa • neung*	honey
kaffe... *ka • fer...*	coffee...
med mjölk *meed myurlk*	with milk
med socker *meed soh • ker*	with sugar
med sötningsmedel *meed surt • nihngs • mee • dehl*	with artificial sweetener
utan koffein *eu • tan koh • feen*	decaf
kallskuret *kal • skeu • reht*	cold cuts [charcuterie]
kokt ägg *koakt ehg*	boiled egg
korv *kohrv*	sausage
marmelad *mar • meh • lahd*	marmalade

mjölk *myurlk*	milk
muffin *muh • fihn*	muffin
müsli *mews • lee*	granola [muesli]
omelett *ohm • eh • leht*	omelet
ost *oast*	cheese
rostat bröd *roahs • tat brurd*	toast
småbröd *smoa • brurd*	roll
smör *smur*	butter
stekt ägg *steekt ehg*	fried egg

Frukost (breakfast) is usually served from 7:00 to 10:00 a.m. Hotels and guesthouses offer a large buffet selection of cheese, cold meat, bread, eggs, cereals and **filmjölk** (thick yogurt). **Lunch** (lunch) is served from as early as 11:00 a.m. Although many Swedes have a warm meal at lunchtime, some opt for a sandwich or a salad. This is the best time to try the **dagens rätt** (specialty of the day). **Middag** (dinner) is normally eaten early, around 6:00 or 7:00 p.m., though many restaurants continue serving until late, especially at the weekend. Many Swedes will also eat a meal later in the evening, referred to as **kvällsmål;** this evening meal usually includes sandwiches, yogurt or soup.

sylt *sewlt*	jam
thé *tee*	tea
vatten *va • tehrn*	water
yoghurt *yoh • geurt*	yogurt
ägg *ehg*	egg
äggröra *ehg • rur • ra*	scrambled eggs
äpple *ehp • leh*	apple

APPETIZERS

färska räkor *fair • ska rair • kohr*	unshelled shrimp [prawns], served with toast, butter and mayonnaise
förrätt *furr • reht*	appetizer [starter]
gravlax *grafv • lax*	marinated salmon
löjrom *lurj • rohm*	bleak roe, served with chopped, raw onions and sour cream and eaten on toast
rökt lax *rurkt lax*	smoked salmon
sill *sihl*	marinated herring

sillbricka *sihl • brih • ka*	variety of marinated herring
S.O.S. (smör, ost och sill) *ehs oa ehs (smur oast ohk sil)*	a small plate of marinated herring, bread, butter and cheese
toast skagen *toast skah • gehn*	toast with chopped shrimp [prawns] in mayonnaise, topped with bleak roe
viltpastej *vihlt • pa • stay*	game pâté

SOUP

buljong *beul • yong*	broth
fisksoppa *fihsk • sop • a*	fish soup
grönsakssoppa *grurn • sahks • sohp • a*	vegetable soup
kall soppa *kal sohp • a*	cold soup
kycklingsoppa *chewk • lihng • sohp • a*	chicken soup
kött och grönsakssoppa *churt • oa • grurn • sahk • sohp • a*	meat and vegetable soup
köttsoppa *churt • sohp • a*	a hearty soup of beef, vegetables and dumplings
löksoppa *lurk • sohp • a*	onion soup
nyponsoppa *new • pohn • sohp • a*	rose-hip soup

oxsvanssoppa — oxtail soup
oax • svans • sohp • a

potatissoppa — potato soup
poa • tah • tihs • sohp • a

rörd soppa — cream soup
rurrd sohp • a

sparrissoppa — asparagus soup
spa • rihs • sohp • a

spenatsoppa — a rich soup made from spinach, potatoes, milk and cream
speh • nat • sohp • a

tomatsoppa — tomato soup
toa • maht • soh • pa

ärtsoppa — green or yellow pea soup
airt • sohp • a

FISH & SEAFOOD

abborre — perch
ah • bohr • er

ansjovis — anchovy
an • shoa • vees

blåmussla — blue mussel
bloa • muhs • la

braxen — sea bream
brak • sehn

böckling — smoked Baltic herring
burk • lihng

fisk — fish
fihsk

forell — trout
foa • rehl

färska räkor — unshelled shrimp [prawns]
fairs • ka rair • kohr

gravlax *grafv • lax*	marinated salmon
gädda *yeh • da*	sea perch
halstrad fisk *hal • strahd fihsk*	grilled fish
halstrad forell med färskpotatis *hal • strad foa • rehl med fairsk • poa • tah • tihs*	grilled trout with new potatoes
havsabborre *hafs • a • boh • rer*	sea bass
hummer *huhm • ehr*	lobster
hälleflundra *heh • leh • fleun • dra*	halibut
inlagd sill *ihn • lagd sil*	marinated (pickled) herring
Janssons frestelse *yahn • sons frehs • tehl • ser*	casserole with potatoes and anchovies
kammussla *kam • muhs • la*	scallop
kolja *kohl • ya*	haddock
krabba *kra • ba*	crab
kräfta *krehf • ta*	crayfish
kummel *keu • mel*	hake
lax *lax*	salmon

löjrom *lury • rohm*	bleak roe with chopped, raw onions and sour cream; served on toast
makrill *mak • rihl*	mackerel
marulk *mahr • eulk*	monkfish
matjesill *ma • shcheh • sihl*	marinated herring
multe *muhl • ter*	mullet
mussla *muhs • la*	mussel
mört *murt*	roach (type of fish)
ostron *oas • tron*	oyster
piggvar *pihg • vahr*	turbot
rimmad lax med stuvad potatis *rihm • ahd lax meed steu • vad poa • tah • tihs*	lightly salted salmon with creamed potatoes and dill
rocka *roh • ka*	ray (type of fish)
räkor *rair • kohr*	shrimp [prawns]
röding *rur • dihng*	char
rödspätta *rurd • speh • ta*	plaice
rökt fisk *rurkt fisk*	smoked fish

rökt lax *rurkt lax*	smoked salmon
rökt ål *rurkt oal*	smoked eel
sardin *sar • deen*	sardine
sill *sihl*	herring
sillbricka *sihl • brih • ka*	variety of marinated herring
sillsallad *sihl • sal • ad*	beet and herring salad
sjötunga *sjur • tuhng • a*	sole
skaldjur *skahl • yeur*	shellfish
skaldjurssallad *skahl • yeurs • sal • ad*	shellfish salad
skarpsill *skarp • sihl*	herring
småsill *smoa • sihl*	herring
S.O.S. (smör, ost och sill) *ehs oa ehs (smur oast ohk sihl)*	small plate of marinated herring, bread, butter and cheese
stekt fisk *steekt fisk*	fried fish
strömming *struhrm • ihng*	sprats (small Baltic herring) filleted and sandwiched in pairs with dill and butter in the middle

strömmingsflundra *strurm • ihngs • fleun • dra*	Baltic herring, filleted and sandwiched in pairs, fried, with dill and butter filling
stuvad abborre *steu • vad a • boh • rer*	perch poached with onion, parsley and lemon
tonfisk *toan • fihsk*	tuna
torsk *tohrshk*	cod
ugnsbakad fisk *eungns • bah • kad fihsk*	oven-baked fish
vitling *veet • lihng*	whiting
västkustsallad *vehst • kuhst • sal • ad*	west coast salad, with shrimp [prawns] and mussels
ål *oal*	eel
ångkokt fisk *oang • koakt fisk*	steamed fish

MEAT & POULTRY

anka *ang • ka*	duck
bacon *bay • kon*	bacon
biffkött *bihf • churt*	beef
biffstek *bihf • steek*	steak

bog *boag*	shoulder (cut of meat)
broiler *broy • lehr*	spring chicken
entrecote *an • treh • koat*	sirloin steak
falukorv *fah • leu • kohrv*	lightly spiced sausage
fasan *fa • sahn*	pheasant
filé *fih • leh*	filet mignon
fläsk *flehsk*	pork
fläskben *flehsk • been*	ham bone
fläskfilé *flehsk • fih • leh*	fillet of pork
fläskkarré *flehsk • ka • reh*	pork loin
fläskkorv *flehsk • kohrv*	spicy, boiled pork sausage
fläsklägg *flehsk • lehg*	knuckle of pork
fågel *foa • gehl*	poultry
får *foar*	mutton
get *yeet*	kid (goat)
grillad kyckling *grihl • ahd chewk • lihng*	grilled chicken
gås *goas*	goose

hamburgare *ham • beur • ya • rer*	hamburger
hare *hah • rer*	rabbit
hjort *yohrt*	deer
isterband *ihs • tehr • band*	sausage of pork, barley and beef
kalkon *kal • koan*	turkey
kallskuret *kal • skeu • reht*	cold cuts [charcuterie]
kalops *ka • lohps*	beef stew
kalvkött *kalv • churt*	veal
kalvsylta *kalv • sewl • ta*	cold veal in jelly
karré *ka • reh*	tenderloin
kokt skinka *koakt shihng • ka*	boiled ham
korv *kohrv*	sausage
kotlett *koht • lehtt*	cutlet
kyckling *chewk • lihng*	chicken
kycklingbröst *chewk • lihng • brurst*	chicken breast
kycklinglever *chewk • lihng • lee • vehr*	chicken liver
kåldomar med gräddsås och lingon *koal • dohl • mar meed grehd • soas ohk*	chopped [minced] meat and rice

lihng • ohn	stuffed in cabbage leaves
kött *churt*	meat
köttbulle *churt • buh • ler*	meatball
köttfärs *churt • fairs*	chopped [minced] beef
lamm *lamm*	lamb
lammgryta *lamm • grew • ta*	lamb stew
lever *lee • vehr*	liver
leverpastej *lee • vehr pa • stay*	liver pâté
lägg *lehg*	shank (top of leg)
lövbiff *lurv • bihf*	fried, thinly sliced beef, with onions
medaljong *meh • dal • yong*	small fillet of cut meat
njure *nyeu • rer*	kidney
nötkött *nurt • churt*	red meat
oxkött *oax • churt*	ox
oxrullad *oax • reu • lahd*	braised roll of beef
oxsvans *oax • svans*	oxtail
pannbiff *pan • bihf*	beef patty

prinskorv *prihns • kohrv*	small pork sausage
pärlhöns *pairl • hurns*	guinea fowl
ragu *ra • guh*	beef stew
rapphöna *rap • hurna*	partridge
ren *reen*	reindeer
renstek med svampsås *reen • steek meed svamp • soas*	roast reindeer with mushroom sauce
revbensspjäll *reev • beens • spehl*	spareribs
rostbiff *rohst • bihf*	roast beef
rumpstek *ruhmp • steek*	rump steak
rådjur *roa • yeur*	venison
rådjursstek *roa • yeur • steek*	roast of venison
rökt renstek *rurkt reen • steek*	smoked reindeer
rökt skinka *rurkt shihng • ka*	smoked ham
sadel *sah • dehl*	saddle (cut of meat)
salamikorv *sa • lah • mee • kohrv*	salami
schnitzel *shniht • sehl*	escallope
sillsallad *sihl • sal • ad*	beet and herring salad

sjömansbiff *shur • mans • bihf*	casserole of fried beef, onions and potatoes, braised in beer
skinka *shihng • ka*	ham
spädgris *spaird • grees*	an unweaned piglet
stekt kyckling *steekt chewk • lihng*	fried chicken (not breaded)
T-benstek *tee • been • steek*	T-bone steak
tunga *tuhng • a*	tongue (cow)

If you've never heard of typical Swedish food, you may at least be familiar with the famous **smörgåsbord** — it is a buffet meal on a grand scale, presented on a large, beautifully decorated table. You start at one end of the table, usually the one with the cold seafood dishes, marinated herring, **Janssons frestelse** (literally, Jansson's temptation, a potato and anchovies casserole) and salad. Then you work your way through the cold meat, meatballs, sausage, omelets and vegetables. Finally, you end at the cheeseboard and desserts. You're welcome to start all over again; the price is set, and you can eat as much as you like. You will find that the Swedes tend to drink **akvavit** (aquavit) or beer with the feast, although an accompanying glass of wine is becoming more common for those who find **akvavit** too strong.

At Christmas time, the **smörgåsbord** becomes a **julbord** (Christmas buffet), popular in homes and restaurants alike.

ugnsstekt kyckling roast chicken
eungn • steekt chewk • lihng
vaktel quail
vak • tehl
varmkorv hot dog
varm • kohrv
wienerschnitzel breaded veal cutlet
vee • nehr • shniht • sehl
vildand wild duck
vihld • and
vilt game
vihlt
älg moose
ehly
älgfilé fillet of moose
ehly • fih • leh
älgstek moose roast
ehly • steek
älgstek med svampsås roast moose with mushroom sauce
ehly • steek meed svamp • soas

VEGETABLES & STAPLES

avokado avocado
a • voh • kah • doa
basilika basil
ba • sih • lee • ka
blandsallad mixed salad
bland • sal • ad
blomkål cauliflower
bloam • koal
bouquet garni mixed herbs
boh • keh gar • nee
böna... ...bean
bur • na...

bond *boand*	broad
bryt *brewt*	kidney
grön *grurn*	green
vax *vax*	butter
broccoli *broh • koh • lee*	broccoli
brysselkål *brew • sehl • koal*	Brussel sprout
bröd *brurd*	bread
bönskott *burn • skoht*	bean sprout
champinjon *sham • pihn • yoan*	mushroom
chilipeppar *shee • lih • peh • par*	chili pepper
dragon *dra • goan*	tarragon
endiv *an • deev*	endive
fullkornsmjöl *fuhl • kohrns • myurl*	whole wheat flour
fänkål *fehn • koal*	fennel
färskpotatis *fairsk • poa • tah • this*	new potato
gräslök *grairs • lurk*	chive
grön paprika *grurn pah • pree • ka*	green pepper

grönsak *grurn • sahk*	vegetable
grönsallad *grurn • sal • ad*	lettuce
gurka *geur • ka*	cucumber
haricots verts *ar • ee • koh • vair*	green bean
honung *hoa • neung*	honey
ingefära *ih • ng • eh • fai • ra*	ginger
kanel *ka • neel*	cinnamon
kantarell *kan • ta • rehl*	chanterelle mushroom
kapris *ka • prees*	caper
kikärta *cheek • air • ta*	chickpea
kokt potatis *koakt poa • tah • tihs*	boiled potato
kronärtskocka *kroan • airts • koh • ka*	artichoke
kryddpeppar *krewd • peh • par*	allspice
kummin *keu • meen*	caraway
kål *koal*	cabbage
kålrot *koal • roht*	turnip
källkrasse *chehl • kra • ser*	watercress

körvel *chur • vehl*	chervil
lagerblad *lah • gehr • blahd*	bay leaf
lins *lihns*	lentil
lök *l**ur**k*	onion
majs *mays*	sweet corn
mjöl *my**ur**l*	flour
morot *moa • roht*	carrot
muskot *muhs • koht*	nutmeg
mynta *mewn • ta*	mint (herb)
nejlika *nay • lih • ka*	clove
nudel *neu • dehl*	noodle
olja och vinäger *oal • ya ohk vee • **nai** • gehr*	oil and vinegar
palsternacka *pal • stehr • na • ka*	parsnip
paprika ***pah** • prih • ka*	pepper (fresh)
pasta *pas • ta*	pasta
persilja *pair • shihl • ya*	parsley
potatis *poa • tah • tihs*	potato

potatissallad *poa • tah • tihs • sal • ad*	potato salad
pumpa *puhm • pa*	pumpkin
purjolök *peur • yoh • lurk*	leek
ris *rees*	rice
rosmarin *roas • ma • reen*	rosemary
rova *roa • va*	turnip
rädisa *raid • dih • sa*	radish
röd paprika *rurd pah • pree • ka*	sweet red pepper
rödbeta *rurd • bee • ta*	beet
rödkål *rurd • koal*	red cabbage
salladshuvud *sal • ads • heu • vuhd*	head of lettuce
saltgurka *salt • geur • ka*	salted, pickled gherkin
salvia *sal • vee • a*	sage
schalottenlök *sha • loh • tehn • lurk*	shallot [spring onion]
selleri *seh • leh • ree*	celery
sirap *seh • rap*	syrup
skogssvamp *skoags • svamp*	field mushroom

smör — butter
smurr

sockerärta — sugar snap pea [mangetout]
soh • kehr • air • ta

sparris — asparagus
spar • ihs

spenat — spinach
speh • naht

squash — squash (vegetable)
skoawsh

svamp — mushroom
svamp

sötpotatis — sweet potato
surt • poa • tah • tihs

timjan — thyme
tihm • yan

tomat — tomato
toa • maht

tomater och lök — tomato and onion salad
toa • mah • ter ohk lurk

vanilj — vanilla
va • nihly

vattenkrasse — watercress
kra • ser

vetemjöl — wheat flour (regular)
vee • teh • mjurl

vild champinjon — wild mushroom
vihl • da sham • pihn • yoan

vitkål — white cabbage
veet • koal

vitlök — garlic
veet • lurk

vårlök — shallot [spring onion]
voar • lurk

zucchini — zucchini [courgette]
seu • kee • nee
äggplanta — eggplant [aubergine]
ehg • plan • ta
ärta — peas
air • ta
ättiksgurka — pickled gherkin
eh • tiks • geur • kah

FRUIT

ananas — pineapple
an • a • nas
apelsin — orange
a • pehl • seen
aprikos — apricot
a • prih • koas
banan — banana
ba • nahn
bigarrå — sweet morello cherry
bih • ga • roa
björnbär — blackberry
byurn • bair
blå vindruva — black grape
bloa veen • dreu • va
blåbär — blueberry
bloa • bair
citron — lemon
see • troan
dadel — date
dahd • ehl
enbär — juniper berry
een • bair
fikon — fig
fee • kohn

frukt *fruhkt*	fruit
grapefrukt *grape • fruhkt*	grapefruit
grön vindruva *grurn veen • dreu • va*	green grape
hallon *hal • ohn*	raspberry
hasselnöt *ha • sehl • nurt*	hazelnut
hjortron *yoahr • tron*	cloudberry
jordgubbe *yoard • guh • ber*	strawberry
jordnöt *yoard • nurt*	peanut
katrinplommon *ka • treen • ploa • mohn*	prune
kiwifrukt *kee • vee • fruhkt*	kiwi
kokosnöt *koa • kos • nurt*	coconut
krusbär *kreus • bair*	gooseberry
körsbär *churs • bair*	cherry
lingon *lihng • ohn*	lingonberry
mandarin *man • da • reen*	tangerine/ mandarin orange
mandel *man • dehl*	almond
(vatten)melon *(va • tehrn)meh • loan*	(water)melon

mullbär *muhl • bair*	mulberry
nektarin *nehk • ta • reen*	nectarine
oliv *o • leev*	olive
persika *pairsh • ih • ka*	peach
plommon *plohm • on*	plum
pomegranat äpple *pom • eh • gra • naht • ehp • leh*	pomegranate
päron *pai • rohn*	pear
rabarber *rah • bar • behr*	rhubarb
russin *ruh • sihn*	raisin
röd vinbär *rurd veen • bair*	red currant
smultron *smeul • trohn*	wild strawberry
sultana *suhl • tahn • a*	sultana raisin
svart vinbär *svart veen • bair*	black currant
valnöt *vahl • nurt*	walnut
vinbär *veen • bair*	currant
vindruva *veen • dreu • va*	grape
äpple *ehp • leh*	apple

CHEESE

fårost *foar • oast*	ewe's milk cheese
getost *yeet • oast*	goat cheese
grevé *greh • vee*	a semi-hard cheese similar to gouda and emmentaler
herrgårdsost *hehr • goards • oast*	a semi-hard cheese with large holes and a nutty flavor
kryddost *krewd • oast*	a sharp, strong cheese with caraway seeds
mesost *mees • oast*	a soft, sweet, yellowish whey cheese
mjukost *myeuk • oast*	soft cheese
ost *oast*	cheese
ostbricka *oast • brih • ka*	cheese plate
prästost *prehst • oast*	hard cheese with a strong, rich flavor
svecia *sveh • see • a*	semi-hard cheeses
västerbotten *vehs • tehr • boh • tehrn*	a sharp, tangy, hard and very strong cheese from the north of Sweden

ädelost *air • dehl • oast*	a blue cheese with a sharp taste, similar to Roquefort

DESSERT

efterrätt *ehf • tehr • reht*	dessert
friterad camembert med hjortronsylt *free • tee • rad cam • ehm • behrt meed yoh • tron • sewlt*	deep-fried camembert with cloudberry jam
fruktsallad *fruhkt • sal • ad*	fruit salad
glass *glas*	ice cream
jordgubbar med grädde *yoard • guhb • ar meed greh • deh*	strawberries and cream
kaka *kah • ka*	cake
mandeltårta *man • dehl • toar • ta*	almond tart
marängsviss *mah • rehng • svis*	meringue with whipped cream and chocolate sauce
mjuk pepparkaka *myeuk peh • par • kah • ka*	soft ginger cake
ostkaka *oast • kah • ka*	traditional southern Sweden curd cake
tårta *toarta*	sponge-based fruit or cream cake
våffla (med sylt och grädde) *vohf • la meed sewlt ohk greh • der*	waffle (with jam and whipped cream)
äppelpaj *eh • pehl • pay*	apple tart

äppelkaka *eh • pehl • kah • ka*	apple cake
äppelring *ehp • ehl • rihng*	apple fritter

SAUCES & CONDIMENTS

peppar *peh • par*	pepper
salt *salt*	salt
senap *see • nap*	mustard
socker *soh • kehr*	sugar
sötningsmedel *surt • nihngs • mee • dehl*	artificial sweetener
ketchup *keht • shuhp*	ketchup

AT THE MARKET

Where are the carts [trolleys]/baskets?	**Var finns shoppingvagnarna/ shoppingkorgarna?** *vahr fihns shoh • pihng • vagn • nar • na/ shoh • pihng • kohr • yar • na*
Where is/are...?	**Var finns...?** *vahr fihns...*
I'd like some of this/that.	**Jag skulle vilja ha lite av det här/ det där.** *yahg skuh • ler vihl • ya hah lee • teh afv dee hair/dee dair*
Can I taste it?	**Får jag smaka?** *foar yahg smah • ka*
I'd like...	**Jag skulle vilja ha...** *yahg skuh • ler vihl • ya hah...*

a kilo/half-kilo of…	**ett kilo/halvt kilo…** *eht chee • loh/halft chee • loh…*
a liter/half-liter of…	**en liter/halv liter…** *ehn lee • ter/halv lee • ter…*
a piece of…	**en bit av…** *ehn beet afv…*
a slice of…	**en skiva av…** *ehn shee • va afv…*
More/Less than that.	**Mer/Mindre än det där.** *meer/mihn • dreh ehn dee dair*
How much does it cost?	**Hur mycket kostar det?** *heur mew • ker kos • tar dee*
Where do I pay?	**Var kan jag betala?** *vahr kan yahg beh • tah • la*
Can I have a bag?	**Kan jag få en påse?** *kan yahg foa ehn poa • seh*
I'm being helped.	**Tack, jag har fått hjälp.** *tak yahg hahr foat yehlp*

YOU MAY HEAR…

Kan jag hjälpa er? *kan yahg yehl • pa eer*	Can I help you?
Vad vill ni beställa? *vahd vihl nee beh • steh • la*	What would you like?
Något annat? *noa • goht an • nat*	Anything else?
Det kostar…kronor. *dee kos • tar…kroa • nohr*	That's…kronor.

Measurements in Europe are metric — and that applies to the weight of food too. If you tend to think in pounds and ounces, it's worth brushing up on what the equivalent is before you go shopping for fruit and veg in markets and supermarkets. Five hundred grams, or half a kilo, is a common quantity to order, and that converts to just over a pound (17.65 ounces, to be precise).

Although Sweden still has many small, specialty shops, they are slowly giving way to **köpcentrum** (shopping centers), especially in larger towns. You can still find markets that sell fresh fruit and vegetables as well as flowers and some handicrafts. **Julmarknaden** (the traditional Christmas market) in Stockholm is reminiscent of times gone by. Supermarkets can be found in most large towns, cities and suburbs. **Närbutiker** (corner shops), as well as **Pressbyrån** (newsstand chain) sell a good range of food. In Stockholm, **Östermalmshallen** and **Hötorgshallen** (market halls) sell fresh meat — including reindeer and moose — fish and poultry. Swedes enjoy a variety of fish and seafood, and one will find a good selection in most restaurants and supermarkets. If you visit Sweden in August, you will no doubt enjoy a **kräftkalas** (crayfish party). There is not much meat on a crayfish, but when helped down with a few glasses of **akvavit** (aquavit) and some salad and cheese, it makes for an unforgettable evening.

IN THE KITCHEN

bottle opener	**flasköppnare** *flask • eup • na • rehr*
bowl	**djup tallrik** *yeup tal • rihk*
can opener	**konservöppnare** *kohn • sehrv • urp • nah • rer*
corkscrew	**korkskruv** *kohrk • skreuv*
cup	**kopp** *kohp*
fork	**gaffel** *gahf • ehl*
frying pan	**stekpanna** *steek • pan • na*
glass	**glas** *glahs*
knife	**kniv** *kneev*
measuring cup/ spoon	**mått/måttsked** *moat/moat • sheed*
napkin	**servett** *sehr • vehtt*
plate	**tallrik** *tal • rihk*
pot	**gryta** *grew • ta*
saucepan	**kastrull** *kas • truhl*
spatula	**steekspade** *steek • spah • der*
spoon	**sked** *sheed*

DRINKS

NEED TO KNOW

May I see the wine list/drink menu?	**Kan jag få se vinlistan/ drinklistan?** *kan yahg foa see veen • lihs • tan/ drihnk • lihs • tan*
What do you recommend?	**Vad rekommenderar ni?** *vahd reh • koh • mehn • dee • rar nee*
I'd like a bottle/glass of red/white wine.	**Jag skulle vilja ha en flaska/ett glas rött/ vitt vin.** *yahg skuh • ler vihl • ya hah ehn flas • ka/ eht glahs ruhrt/viht veen*
The house wine, please.	**Husets vin, tack.** *heu • sehts veen tak*
Another bottle/glass, please.	**En flaska/Ett glas till, tack.** *ehn flas • ka/eht glahs tihl tak*
I'd like a local beer.	**Jag skulle vilja ha en öl från trakten.** *yahg skuh • ler vihl • ya hah ehn url fron trak • tehn*
Let me buy you a drink.	**Får jag bjuda på en drink.** *foar yahg byeu • da poa ehn drihnk*
Cheers!	**Skål!** *skoal*
A coffee/tea, please.	**En kopp kaffe/te, tack.** *ehn kohp ka • fer/tee tak*
Black.	**Svart.** *Svart*
With…	**Med…** *meed…*

milk	**mjölk** *myuhlk*
sugar	**socker** *soh • kehr*
artificial sweetener	**sötningsmedel** *surt • nihngs • mee • dehl*
decaf	**utan koffein** *eu • tan koh • feen*
..., please.	**..., tack.** *...tak*
Juice	**Juice** *yoas*
Soda	**sodavatten** *soa • da • va • tehrn*
Sparkling water	**Vatten med kolsyra** *va • tehrn meed koal • sew • ra*
Still water	**Vatten utan kolsyra** *va • tehrn eu • tan koal • sew • ra*
Is the tap water safe to drink?	**Kan man dricka kranvattnet?** *kan man drih • ka krahn • vat • neht*

NON-ALCOHOLIC DRINKS

alkoholfri dryck — non-alcoholic drink
al • ko • hoal • free drewk

ananasjuice — pineapple juice
an • a • nas • yoas

apelsinjuice — orange juice
a • pehl • seen • yoas

cola — cola
koa • la

fruktjuice — fruit juice
fruhkt • yoas

juice *yoas*	juice
kaffe *ka • fer*	coffee
läsk *lehsk*	soft drink
milkshake *milk • shake*	milk shake
mineralvatten *mihn • eh • rahl • va • tehrn*	mineral water
mjölk *myurlk*	milk
saft *saft*	squash (fruit cordial)
sockerdricka *soh • kehr • drih • ka*	lemonade
sodavatten *soa • da • va • tehrn*	soda water

For afternoon tea (usually enjoyed with lemon) or coffee you can do no better than the typical Swedish **konditori** (patisserie or coffee shop). Help yourself to as many cups as you like while indulging in a slice of **prinsesstårta** (sponge cake with cream and custard, covered with green marzipan), **mazarin** (almond tart, topped with icing) or a **wienerbröd** (Danish pastry). Try **saffransbullar** (saffron buns) and **pepparkakor** (ginger cookies) at Christmas. Most **konditori** are self-service, but some of the more elegant ones and those in hotels provide full service. Coffee is definitely the national drink, and it is always freshly brewed. It is commonly drunk black, but ask for **mjölk** (milk) or **grädde** (cream) if you like it that way.

thé med mjölk/citron — tea with milk/lemon
tee meed myurlk/ see • troan

tomatjuice — tomato juice
toa • maht • yoas

tonic — tonic water
toh • nihk

varmchoklad — hot chocolate
varm shoa • klahd

vatten med/utan kolsyra — sparkling/still water
va • tehrn meed/ eu • tan koal • sew • ra

YOU MAY HEAR...

Får jag bjuda på en drink? — Can I buy you a drink?
foar yahg bjeu • da pao ehn drink

Med mjölk/socker? — With milk/sugar?
meed myurlk/soh • ker

Vatten med/utan kolsyra? — Sparkling/Still water?
va • tehrn meed/ eu • tan koal • sew • ra

APERITIFS, COCKTAILS & LIQUEURS

akvavit — aquavit, the famous Swedish grain- or potato-based spirit
a • kva • veet

cognac — brandy
kohn • yak

gin — gin
jihn

glögg *glurg*	mulled wine with port and spices, served hot
herrgårdsakvavit *hair • goards • a • kva • veet*	aquavit, flavored with caraway seeds and whisky
likör *lih • kurr*	liqueur
portvin *port • veen*	port
punsch *peunsh*	sweet liqueur
rom *rohm*	rum
sherry *sheh • ree*	sherry
skåne *skoa • ner*	aquavit, flavored with aniseed and caraway seeds
sprit *spreet*	spirits
vermouth *vehr • meutt*	vermouth
vodka… *vod • ka…*	vodka…
med is *meed ees*	on the rocks [with ice]
med tonic *meed toh • nihk*	with tonic water
med vatten *meed va • tehrn*	with water
whisky *vihs • kee*	whisky

BEER

burköl — canned beer
buhrk • url

fatöl — draft [draught]
faht • url

lättöl — light beer
leht • url

öl på flaska — bottled beer local/imported
url poa fla • ska

utan alkohol — non-alcoholic
uh • tan al • koh • hohl

Beer is probably the most popular alcoholic drink in Sweden, and there are many good Swedish breweries. Beer with an alcohol content above 3%, called **starköl**, can only be bought in **Systembolaget** (state liquor store); **lättöl** and **folköl**, which are below 3% alcohol content, can be bought in grocery stores and supermarkets. You will find many well known international beers, but the most common are Carlsberg, Heineken and Swedish brews such as Pripps and Falcon.

WINE

dessertvin — dessert wine
deh • sair • veen

husets vin — house wine
heu • sehts veen

mousserande — sparkling
moa • see • ran • der

rosé — blush [rosé]
roh • seh

rött — red
ruhrt

sött — sweet
suhrt

torrt — dry
tohrt

vitt — white
viht

champagne — champagne
shahm • pany

ON THE MENU

abborre — perch
ah • bohr • er

akvavit — aquavit, the famous Swedish grain- or potato-based spirit
a • kva • veet

alkoholfri dryck — non-alcoholic drink
al • ko • hoal • free drewk

ananas — pineapple
an • a • nas

ananasjuice — pineapple juice
an • a • nas • yoas

anka — duck
ang • ka

ansjovis — anchovy
an • shoa • vees

apelsin — orange
a • pehl • seen

apelsinjuice *a • pehl • <u>seen</u> • yoas*	orange juice
aprikos *a • prih • <u>koas</u>*	apricot
avokado *a • voh • <u>kah</u> • doa*	avocado
bacon *<u>bay</u> • kon*	bacon
bakelse *<u>bah</u> • kehl • sehr*	piece of cake
bakverk *<u>bahk</u> • verk*	pastry
banan *ba • <u>nahn</u>*	banana
basilika *ba • sih • <u>lee</u> • ka*	basil
biffkött *<u>bihf</u> • churt*	beef
biffstek *<u>bif</u> • steek*	steak
bigarrå *bih • ga • <u>roa</u>*	sweet morello cherry
bit *beet*	slice

björnbär *byurn • bair*	blackberry
blandade *blan • da • der*	assorted
blandade grönsaker *blan • da • der grurn • sah • kehr*	mixed vegetables
blandade kryddor *blan • da • der krew • dohr*	mixed herbs
blandade nötter *blan • da • der nur • tehr*	assorted nuts
blandsallad *bland • sal • ad*	mixed salad
blodig *bloa • dihg*	rare
blomkål *bloam • koal*	cauliflower
blå vindruva *bloa veen • dreu • va*	black grape
blåbär *bloa • bair*	blueberry
blåbärssylt *bloa • bairs • sewlt*	blueberry jam
blåmussla *bloa • muhs • la*	blue mussel
bog *boag*	shoulder (cut of meat)
bondböna *boand • bur • nohr*	broad bean
bordsvin *boards • veen*	table wine
bouquet garni *boh • keh gar • nee*	mixed herbs
braxen *brak • sehn*	sea bream

broccoli *broh • loh • lee*	broccoli
broiler *broy • lehr*	spring chicken
brylépudding *brew • lee • peu • dihng*	crème brulee
brysselkål *brew • sehl • koal*	brussel sprout
brytböna *brewt • bur • na*	kidney bean
brännvin *brehn • veen*	aquavit, grain or potato based spirit
bröd *brurd*	bread
brödsmulor *brurd • smeu • lohr*	bread crumbs
bröst *brurst*	breast
buljong *buhl • yong*	broth
bulle *buh • ler*	bun
burköl *buhrk • url*	canned beer
bål *boal*	punch
böckling *burk • lihng*	smoked herring
böna *bur • na*	bean [pulses]
bönskott *burn • skoht*	bean sprout
champinjon *sham • pihn • yoan*	mushroom

chilipeppar *shee • lih • peh • par*	chili pepper
chips *shihps*	potato chips [crisps]
choklad *shoa • klahd*	chocolate
citron *see • troan*	lemon
citronjuice *see • troan • yoas*	lemon juice
cognac *kohn • yak*	brandy
cola *koa • la*	cola
dadel *dahd • ehl*	date
dagens meny *dah • gehns meh • neu*	menu of the day
dagens rätt *dah • gehns rairtt*	speciality of the day
dessertvin *deh • sair • veen*	dessert wine
dillsås *dihl • soas*	dill sauce
dragon *dra • goan*	tarragon
dryck med alkohol *drewk meed al • ko • hoal*	alcoholic drink
efterrätt *ehf • tehr • rairt*	dessert
en halv flaska *ehn halv fla • ska*	half bottle
enbär *een • bair*	juniper berry

endiv — endive
an • deev

entrecote — sirloin steak
an • treh • koa

falukorv — lightly spiced sausage
fah • leu • kohrv

fasan — pheasant
fa • sahn

fatöl — draft [draught] beer
faht • url

fikon — fig
fee • kohn

filé — filet mignon
fih • leh

filmjölk — thick yogurt
feel • mjurlk

fisk — fish
fihsk

fisk och skaldjur — fish and seafood
fihsk • ohk • skahl • yeur

fisksoppa — fish soup
fihsk • sop • a

fläsk — pork
flehsk

fläskben — ham bone
flehsk • been

fläskfilé — fillet of pork
flehsk • fih • leh

fläskkarré — pork loin
flehsk • ka • reh

fläskkorv — spicy, boiled pork sausage
flehsk • kohrv

fläsklägg — knuckle of pork
flehsk • lehg

fläskpannkaka *flehsk • pan • kah • ka*	thick pancake filled with bacon
forell *foa • rehl*	trout
franskbröd *fransk • brurd*	French bread
friterad camembert med hjortronsylt *free • tee • rad cam • ehm • behrt meed yoh • tron • sewlt*	deep-fried Camembert with cloudberry jam
frukost *fruh • kohst*	breakfast
frukostflingor *fruhkost • flihng • ohr*	(cold) cereal
frukt *fruhkt*	fruit
fruktjuice *fruhkt • yoas*	fruit juice
fruktsallad *fruhkt • sal • ad*	fruit salad
fullkornsmjöl *fuhl • kohrns • myurl*	whole wheat flour
fylld (med) *fewld (meed)*	stuffed (with)
fylld oliv *fewld o • leev*	stuffed olive
fylligt *few • liht*	full-bodied (wine)
fågel *foa • gehl*	poultry
får *foar*	mutton
fårost *foar • oast*	ewe's milk cheese
fänkål *fehn • koal*	fennel

färsk (frukt) *fehrsk (fruhkt)*	fresh (fruit)
färsk fikon *fairsk fee • kohn*	fresh fig
färska räkor *fairs • ka rair • kohr*	unshelled shrimp [prawns]
färskpotatis *fairsk • poa • tah • tihs*	new potato
förlorat ägg *furr • loa • rat ehg*	poached egg
förrätt *furr • rairt*	appetizer [starter]
garnering *gar • nee • rihng*	garnish
gelé *sheh • leh*	jelly
get *yeet*	kid (goat)
getost *yeet • oast*	goat cheese
gin *jihn*	gin
glass *glas*	ice cream
glutenfritt *glue • tehn • friht*	gluten free
glögg *glurg*	mulled wine with port and spices, served hot
grapefrukt *grahp • fruhkt*	grapefruit
gratinerad *gra • tih • nee • rad*	au gratin
gratäng *gra • tehng*	casserole

gravlax *grafv • lax*	marinated salmon
grevé *greh • veh*	semi-hard cheese
grillad kyckling *grihl • ahd chewk • lihng*	grilled chicken
grillspett *grihl • speht*	skewer
gryta *grew • ta*	pot roast, stew or casserole
grädde *greh • der*	cream
gräddfil *grehd • feel*	sour cream
gräslök *grairs • lurk*	chive
grön böna *grur • na bur • na*	green bean
grön paprika *grurn pah • pree • ka*	green pepper
grön vindruva *grurn veen • dreu • va*	green grape
grönsak *grurn • sahk*	vegetable
grönsakssoppa *grurn • sahks • sohp • a*	vegetable soup
grönsallad *grurn • sal • ad*	green salad
gröt *grurt*	(hot) cereal
gurka *geur • ka*	cucumber
gås *goas*	goose

gädda *yeh • da*	sea perch
hallon *hal • ohn*	raspberry
halstrad fisk *hal • strahd fihsk*	grilled fish
halstrad forell med färskpotatis *hal • strad foa • rehl med fairsk • poa • tah • this*	grilled trout with new potatoes
hamburgare *ham • beur • ya • rer*	hamburger
hare *hah • rer*	rabbit
haricots verts *ar • ee • koh • vair*	string beans
hasselbackspotatis *ha • sehl • baks • poa • tah • tihs*	oven-baked potato, coated in bread crumbs
hasselnöt *ha • sehl • nurt*	hazelnut
havre *hafv • rer*	oats
havregryn *hafv • reh • greun*	oatmeal
havsabborre *hafs • a • boh • rer*	sea bass
hemlagad *hehm • lah • gad*	homemade
herrgårdsakvavit *hair • goards • a • kva • veet*	aquavit flavored with caraway seeds and whisky
herrgårdsost *hehr • goards • oast*	semi-hard cheese with a nutty flavor
hett *heht*	hot (temperature)

hjort *yohrt*	deer
hjortron *yoahr • tron*	cloudberry
hjortron sylt *yoar • trohn • sewlt*	cloudberry jam
honung *hoa • neung*	honey
hovmästarsås *hoav • mehs • tar • soas*	dill sauce
hummer *huhm • ehr*	lobster
husets specialitet *heu • sehts speh • sih • al • ee • teet*	specialty of the house
husets vin *heu • sehts veen*	house wine
huvudrätt *heu • vuhd • rait*	main course
hårdkokt ägg *hoard • kohkt ehg*	hard-boiled egg
hårt bröd *hoart brurd*	crispbread
hälleflundra *heh • leh • fleun • dra*	halibut
ingefära *ih • ng • eh • fai • ra*	ginger
inlagd i ättika (vinäger) *ihn • lahgd ee eh • tih • ka*	marinated in vinegar
inlagd sill *ihn • lahgd sil*	marinated (pickled) herring
is *ees*	ice
isterband *ihs • tehr • band*	sausage of pork, barley and beef

Janssons frestelse *yahn • sons frehs • tehl • ser*	casserole with potatoes and anchovies
jordgubbar med grädde *yoard • guhb • ar meed greh • deh*	strawberries and cream
jordgubbe *yoard • guh • ber*	strawberry
jordnöt *yoard • nurt*	peanut
juice *yoas*	juice
julbord *yeul • board*	buffet of hot and cold Swedish specialties served at Christmas time
kaffe *ka • fer*	coffee
kaka *kah • ka*	cake
kalkon *kal • koan*	turkey
kall soppa *kal sohp • a*	cold soup
kallskuret *kal • skeu • reht*	cold cuts
kalops *ka • lohps*	beef stew
kalvbräss *kalv • brehs*	sweetbread
kalvkött *kalv • churt*	veal
kalvsylta *kalv • sewl • ta*	cold veal in jelly
kammussla *kam • muhs • la*	scallop

kanderad frukt *kan • deeh • rahd fruhkt*	candied fruit
kanel *ka • neel*	cinnamon
kantarell *kan • ta • rehl*	chanterelle mushroom
kapris *ka • prees*	caper
karaff *ka • raff*	carafe
karameller *ka • ra • mehl • ehr*	candy [sweets]
karré *ka • reh*	tenderloin
katrinplommon *ka • treen • ploa • mohn*	prune
kex *kehx*	cookie [biscuit]
kikärta *cheek • air • ta*	chickpea
kiwifrukt *kee • vee • fruhkt*	kiwi
klimp *klihmp*	dumpling
kokosnöt *koa • kos • nurt*	coconut
kokt katrinplommon *koakt ka • treen • ploa • mohn*	stewed prune
kokt potatis *koakt poa • tah • tihs*	boiled potato
kokt skinka *koakt shihng • ka*	boiled ham
kokt ägg *koakt ehg*	boiled egg

kolja *kohl • ya*	haddock
kolsyrad *koal • **sew** • rad*	carbonated
kompott *kom • poht*	stewed fruit
konserverad frukt *kon • ser • vee • rad fruhkt*	canned fruit
korv *kohrv*	sausage
kotlett *koht • lehtt*	cutlet
krabba *kra • ba*	crab
kronärtskocka *kr**oa**n • airts • koh • ka*	artichoke
kroppkaka *kropp • kah • ka*	potato dumpling, filled with bacon and onions
krusbär *kreus • bair*	gooseberry
krydda *krew • da*	spice
kryddad *krew • dad*	spicy
kryddad pepparsås *krew • dahd peh • par • s**oa**s*	hot pepper sauce
kryddost *krewd • oast*	sharp, strong cheese with caraway seeds
kryddpeppar *krewd • peh • par*	allspice
kryddstarkt *krewd • starkt*	spicy

kräfta *krehf • ta*	crayfish
kummel *keu • mel*	hake
kummin *keu • meen*	caraway
kvark *kvark*	fresh curd cheese
kyckling *chewk • lihng*	chicken
kycklingbröst *chewk • lihng • brurst*	chicken breast
kycklinglever *chewk • lihng • lee • vehr*	chicken liver
kycklingsoppa *chewk • lihng • sohp • a*	chicken soup
kyld dryck *chewl drewk*	cold drink
kylt *chewlt*	chilled (wine, etc.)
kål *koal*	cabbage
kåldolmar *koal • dohl • mar*	cabbage leaves stuffed with chopped [minced] meat and rice
kålrot *koal • roht*	turnip
källkrasse *chehl • kra • se*	watercress
körsbär *churs • bair*	cherry
körvel *chur • vehl*	chervil

kött *churt*	meat
kött och grönsakssoppa *churt • oa • grurn • sahk • sohp • a*	meat and vegetable soup soup
köttbulle *churt • buh • ler*	meatball
köttfärs *churt • fairs*	chopped [minced] beef
köttsoppa *churt • sohp • a*	beef and vegetable soup with dumplings
köttsås *churt • soas*	meat sauce
lagerblad *lah • gehr • blahd*	bay leaf
lageröl *lah • ger • url*	lager
lamm *lamm*	lamb
lammgryta *lamm • grew • ta*	lamb stew
landgång *land • goang*	long open-faced sandwich
lax *lax*	salmon
lever *lee • vehr*	liver
leverpastej *lee • vehr pa • stay*	liver pâté
lingon *lihng • ohn*	lingonberry
lingonsylt *lihng • ohn • sewlt*	lingonberry jam

lins *lihns*	lentil
likör *lih • kurr*	liqueur
lägg *lehg*	shank (top of leg)
läsk *lehsk*	soft drink
lättöl *leht • ur*	light beer
löjrom *lury • rohm*	bleak roe with chopped, raw onions and sour cream; served on toast
lök *lurk*	onion
löksoppa *lurk • sohp • a*	onion soup
lövbiff *lurv • bihf*	fried, thinly sliced beef, with onions
majonnäs *may • oha • nairs*	mayonnaise
majs *mays*	sweet corn
makrill *mahk • rihl*	mackerel
mandarin *man • da • reen*	tangerine/ mandarin orange
mandel *man • dehl*	almond
mandeltårta *man • dehl • toar • ta*	almond tart
marmelad *mahr • meh • lahd*	marmalade

marsipan *mahr • sih • pahn*	marzipan
marulk *mahr • eulk*	monkfish
maräng *mah • rehng*	meringue
marängsviss *mah • rehng • svihs*	meringue served with cream and chocolate sauce
matjesill *ma • shcheh • sihl*	marinated herring
med citron *meed see • troan*	with lemon
med florsocker *meed floar • soh • ker*	with icing
med grädde *meed greh • der*	with cream
med is *meed ees*	with ice
med kolsyra *meed koal • sew • ra*	carbonated (drink)
med mjölk *meed myurlk*	with milk
med socker *meed soh • kehr*	with sugar
med tonic *meed toh • nihk*	with tonic water
med vatten *meed va • tehrn*	with water
med vitlök *meed veet • lurk*	with garlic
medaljong *meh • dal • yong*	small fillet of cut meat
medium *meh • dee • yuhm*	medium

mellanmål
meh • lan • moal — snack

(vatten)melon
(va • tehrn)meh • loan — (water)melon

meny
meh • neu — menu

mesost
mees • oast — soft, sweet whey cheese

middag
mih • dahg — dinner

milkshake
milk • shake — milk shake

mineralvatten
mih • neh • rahl • va • tehrn — mineral water

mjuk pepparkaka
myeuk peh • par • kah • ka — soft ginger cake

mjukost
myeuk • oast — soft cheese

mjöl
myurl — flour

mjölk
myurlk — milk

mogen
moa • gehn — ripe

morot
moa • roht — carrot

mousserande
moa • see • ran • der — sparkling (wine)

muffin
muh • fihn — muffin

mullbär
muhl • bair — mulberry

multe
muhl • ter — mullet

munk — donut
muhnk

muskot — nutmeg
muhs • koht

müsli — granola [muesli]
mews • lee

mussla — mussel
muhs • la

mustigt — full-bodied (wine)
muhs • tihkt

mycket kryddad — highly seasoned
mew • keht krew • dad

mycket torrt — very dry (wine, etc.)
mew • keht tohrt

mynta — mint (herb)
mewn • ta

mäktig — rich (sauce)
mehk • tihg

mördegstårta — tart (sweet or savory)
muhr • deegs • toar • ta

mört — roach (type of fish)
murtt

nejlika — clove
nay • lih • ka

nektarin — nectarine
nehk • ta • reen

njure — kidney
nyeu • rer

nudel — noodle
neu • dehl

nyponsoppa — rose-hip soup
new • pohn • sohp • a

nötkött — red meat
nurt • churt

odlade champinjon *oad • lah • der sham • peen • yoan*	cultivated mushroom
ojäst bröd *oa • yairst brurd*	unleavened bread
oliv *o • leev*	olive
olja och vinäger *oal • ya ohk vee • nai • gehr*	oil and vinegar
omelett *om • eh • leht*	omelet
ost *oast*	cheese
ostbricka *oast • brih • ka*	cheese plate
ostkaka *oast • kah • ka*	curd cake served with jam
ostkex *oast • kehx*	cheese cracker
ostron *oa • strohn*	oyster
oxkött *oax • churt*	ox
oxrullad *oax • reu • lahd*	braised roll of beef
oxsvans *oax • svans*	oxtail
oxsvanssoppa *oax • svans • sohp • a*	oxtail soup
paj *pay*	pie
palsternacka *pal • stehr • na • ka*	parsnip
pannbiff *pan • bihf*	beef patty

pannkaka *pan • kah • ka*	pancake
paprika *pah • prih • ka*	pepper (fresh)
pasta *pas • ta*	pasta
pastarätt *pas • ta • rairt*	pasta dish
pastej *pa • stay*	pâté
peppar *peh • par*	pepper (condiment)
pepparkaka *peh • par • kah • ka*	ginger cookie
pepparrotssås *peh • pa • roat • soas*	horseradish sauce
persika *pair • shih • ka*	peach
persilja *pair • shihl • ya*	parsley
piggvar *pihg • vahr*	turbot
pitabröd *pee • ta • brurd*	pita bread
plommon *ploa • mohn*	plum
plättar *pleh • tar*	small pancakes served with jam and whipped cream
pomegranat äpple *pom • eh • gra • naht • ehp • leh*	pomegranate
pommes frites *pohm • friht*	French fries
portion *pohrt • shoan*	portion

portvin *pohrt • veen*	port
potatis *poa • tah • tihs*	potato
potatismos *poa • tah • tihs • moas*	mashed potatoes
potatissoppa *poa • tah • tihs • sohp • a*	potato soup
prinsesstårta *prihn • sehs • toar • ta*	sponge cake with (vanilla) custard, whipped cream and jam, covered in light green marzipan
prinskorv *prihns • kohrv*	small pork sausage
prästost *prehst • oast*	hard cheese with a strong, rich flavor
pumpa *puhm • pa*	pumpkin
punsch *peunsh*	sweet liqueur
purjolök *peur • yoh • lurk*	leek
pytt i panna *pewt • ee • pa • na*	chunks of fried meat, onion and potatoes
på beställning *poa beh • stehl • nihng*	made on request
pärlande *pair • lan • der*	sparkling
pärlhöns *pairl • hurns*	guinea fowl
päron *pai • rohn*	pear

rabarber *rah • bar • behr*	rhubarb
ragu *ra • gue*	beef stew
rapphöna *rap • hurna*	partridge
ren *reen*	reindeer
renat *ree • nat*	flavorless, clear spirit (aquavit)
renstek *reen • steek*	roast reindeer
revbensspjäll *reev • beens • spehl*	spare ribs
riktigt blodig *rihk • tihgt bloa • dihg*	very rare
rimmad lax *rih • mad lax*	lightly salted salmon
ris *rees*	rice
rocka *roh • ka*	ray (type of fish)
rom *rohm*	rum
rosé *roh • seh*	blush (wine)
rosmarin *roas • ma • reen*	rosemary
rostat bröd *rohs • tat brurd*	toast
rostbiff *rohst • bihf*	roast beef
rova *roa • va*	turnip

rumpstek *ruhmp • steek*	rump steak
russin *ruh • sihn*	raisin
rå *roa*	raw
rådjur *roa • yeur*	venison
rådjursstek *roa • yeur • steek*	roast of venison
rågbröd *roag • brurd*	rye bread
rädisa *raid • dih • sa*	radish
räkor *rair • kohr*	shrimp [prawns]
rätt *reht*	dish
röd paprika *rurd pah • pree • ka*	sweet red pepper
röd vinbär *rurd veen • bair*	red currant
rödbeta *rurd • bee • ta*	beet
röding *rur • dihng*	char
rödkål *rurd • koal*	red cabbage
rödspätta *rurd • speh • ta*	plaice
rökt fisk *rurkt fisk*	smoked fish
rökt lax *rurkt lax*	smoked salmon

rökt renstek — smoked reindeer
rurkt reen • steek

rökt skinka — smoked ham
rurkt shihng • ka

rökt ål — smoked eel
rurkt oal

rörd soppa — cream soup
rurrd sohp • a

rött — red (wine)
rurt

sadel — saddle (cut of meat)
sah • dehl

saffransbullar — Christmas saffron buns
sa • frans • buh • lar

saft — squash (fruit cordial)
saft

salamikorv — salami
sa • lah • mee • kohrv

sallad — salad
sal • ad

salladshuvud — head of lettuce
sal • ads • heu • vuhd

salt — salt
salt

saltade jordnötter — salted peanuts
sal • ta • der yoard • nur • ter

saltgurka — salted, pickled gherkin
salt • geur • ka

salvia — sage
sal • vee • a

sardin — sardine
sar • deen

schalottenlök — shallot
sha • loh • tehn • lurk

schnitzel *shniht • sehl*	escallope
selleri *seh • leh • ree*	celery
senap *see • nap*	mustard
sherry *sheh • ree*	sherry
sill *sihl*	herring
sillbricka *sihl • brih • ka*	variety of marinated herring
sillsallad *sihl • sal • ad*	beet and herring salad
sirap *seh • rap*	syrup
sjömansbiff *shur • mans • bihf*	casserole of fried beef, onions and potatoes, braised in beer
sjötunga *sjur • teung • a*	sole
skaldjur *skahl • yeur*	shellfish
skaldjurssallad *skahl • yeurs • sal • ad*	shellfish salad
skarpsill *skarp • sihl*	herring
skinka *skihng • ka*	ham
skogssvamp *skoags • svamp*	field mushroom
sky *shewy*	gravy

skåne *skoa • ner*	type of aquavit flavored with aniseed and caraway
smultron *smeul • trohn*	wild strawberry
småbröd *smoa • brurd*	roll
småkaka *smoa • kah • ka*	cookie [biscuit]
smårätt *smoa • rairt*	snack
småsill *smoa • sihl*	herring
smör *smur*	butter
smördeg *smur • deeg*	pastry
smörgås *smur • goas*	Swedish open-faced sandwich
snigel *sneeg • ehl*	snail
socker *soh • kehr*	sugar
sockerdricka *soh • kehr • drih • ka*	lemonade
sockerkaka *soh • kehr • kah • ka*	sponge cake
sockerärta *soh • kehr • air • ta*	sugar snap pea [mangetout]
sodavatten *soa • da • va • tehrn*	soda water
soppa *sohp • a*	soup

S.O.S. (smör, ost och sill) *ehs oa ehs (smur oast ohk sihl)*	small plate of marinated herring, read, butter and cheese
sparris *spar • ihs*	asparagus
sparrissoppa *spa • rihs • sohp • a*	asparagus soup
specialitet för landsdelen *speh • sih • ahl • ih • teet furr lands • deel • ehn*	local specialty
spenat *speh • naht*	spinach
spenatsoppa *speh • naht • sohp • a*	spinach soup
sprit *spreet*	spirits
spädgris *spaird • grees*	unweaned piglet
squash *skoawsh*	squash (vegetable)
stark *stark*	strong (flavor)
starkt kryddad *starkt krew • dad*	hot (spicy)
stek *steek*	roast
stekt fisk *steekt fisk*	fried fish
stekt kyckling *steekt chewk • lihng*	fried chicken (not breaded)
stekt potatis *steekt poa • tah • tihs*	sautéed potato
stekt ägg *steekt ehg*	fried egg

strömming *strurm • ihng*	sprats (small Baltic herring)
strömmingsflundra *strurm • ihngs • fleun • dra*	Baltic herring, filleted and sandwiched in pairs, fried, with dill and butter filling
stuvad abborre *steu • vad a • bohr • er*	perch poached with onion, parsley and lemon
sufflé *suh • fleh*	soufflé
sultana *suhl • tahn • a*	sultana raisin
sur *seur*	sour
svamp *svamp*	mushroom
svart vinbär *svart veen • bair*	black currant
svecia *sveh • see • a*	semi-hard cheese
svensk punsch *sven • sk peunsh*	Swedish punch (sweet liqueur)
sylt *sewlt*	jam
sås *soas*	sauce
sötningsmedel *surt • nihngs • mee • dehl*	artificial sweetener
sötpotatis *surt • poa • tah • tihs*	sweet potato
sötsur sås *surt • seur soas*	sweet-and-sour sauce

sött *suht*	sweet
T-benstek *<u>tee</u> • been • steek*	T-bone steak
thé *tee*	tea
timjan *tihm • <u>yan</u>*	thyme
toast skagen *toast <u>skah</u> • gehn*	toast with chopped shrimp in mayonnaise, topped with bleak roe
tomat *toa • <u>maht</u>*	tomato
tomater och lök *toa • <u>mah</u> • ter ohk lurk*	tomato and onion salad
tomatjuice *toa • <u>maht</u> • yoas*	tomato juice
tomatsoppa *toa • <u>maht</u> • soh • pa*	tomato soup
tomatsås *toa • <u>maht</u> • soas*	tomato sauce
tonfisk *<u>toan</u> • fihsk*	tuna
tonic *<u>toh</u> • nihk*	tonic water
torkade dadel *<u>tohr</u> • ka • der <u>dah</u> • dehl*	dried date
torkade fikon *<u>tohr</u> • ka • der <u>fee</u> • kohn*	dried fig
torrt *tohrt*	dry
torsk *torshk*	cod

tunga *tuhng • a*	tongue (cow)
tunn sås *tuhnn soas*	light (sauce)
tunnbröd *tuhnn • brurd*	Swedish flat bread, can be soft or crispy
tårta *toarta*	sponge-based fruit or cream cake
ugnsbakad fisk *eungns • bah • kad fihsk*	oven-baked fish
ugnsstekt kyckling *eungn • steekt chewk • lihng*	roast chicken
ugnsstekt potatis *eungn • steekt poa • tah • tihs*	roast potato
utan koffein *eu • tan ko • feen*	decaffeinated
vaktel *vak • tehl*	quail
valfria tillbehör *vahl • free • a tihl • beh • hurr*	choice of side dishes
valnöt *vahl • nurt*	walnut
vanilj *va • nihly*	vanilla
vaniljsås *va • nihly • soas*	vanilla sauce, often like custard
varmchoklad *varm shoa • klahd*	hot chocolate
varmkorv *varm kohrv*	hot dog
varmrätt *varm • rairt*	warm meal, usually main course
varmt *varmt*	hot

vatten *va • tehrn*	water
vattenkrasse *va • tehrn • kra • ser*	watercress
vaxböna *vax • bur • na*	butter bean
vegetarisk meny *vehg • eh • tah • risk meh • neu*	vegetarian menu
vermouth *vehr • meutt*	vermouth
vetemjöl *vee • teh • mjurl*	wheat flour (regular)
whisky *vihs • kee*	whisky
wienerbröd *vee • nehr • brurd*	Danish pastry
wienerschnitzel *vee • nehr • shniht • sehl*	breaded veal cutlet
vild champinjon *vihl • da sham • pihn • yoan*	wild mushroom
vildand *vihld • and*	wild duck
vilt *vihlt*	game
viltpastej *vihlt • pa • stay*	game pâté
vin *veen*	wine
vinaigrettesås *vih • neh • greht • soas*	vinaigrette [French dressing]
vinbär *veen • bair*	currant
vindruva *veen • dreu • va*	grape

vinlista
veen • lihs • ta
wine list

vispgrädde
visp • greh • der
whipped cream

vit sås
veet soas
white sauce

vitkål
veet • koal
white cabbage

vitkålssallad
veet • koal • sal • ad
coleslaw

vitling
veet • lihng
whiting

vitlök
veet • lurk
garlic

vitlöksmajonnäs
veet • lurks • may • oa • nairs
garlic mayonnaise

vitlökssås
veet • lurk • soas
garlic sauce

vinbär
veen • bair
currant

vindruva
veen • dreu • va
grape

vinlista
veen • lihs • ta
wine list

vispgrädde
visp • greh • der
whipped cream

vitt
viht
white (wine)

vitt bröd
viht brurd
white bread

vodka
vod • ka
vodka

vol au vent
vohl • oa • vahnt
vol-au-vent (pastry filled with meat or fish)

våffla (med sylt och grädde) *vohf • la meed sewlt ohk greh • der* — waffle (with jam and whipped cream)

vårlök *voar lurk* — shallot [spring onion]

västerbotten *vehs • tehr • boh • tehn* — strong, tangy, hard cheese

västkustsallad *vehst • kuhst • sal • ad* — west coast salad, with shrimp [prawns] and mussels

yoghurt *yoa • geurt* — yogurt

zucchini *seu • kee • nee* — zucchini [courgette]

ål *oal* — eel

ångkokt fisk *oang • koakt fisk* — steamed fish

ädelost *air • dehl • oast* — blue cheese

ägg *ehg* — egg

äggplanta *ehg • plan • ta* — eggplant [aubergine]

äggula *ehg • geu • la* — egg yolk

äggröra *ehg • rur • ra* — scrambled egg

äggvita *ehg • vee • ta* — egg white

älg *ehly* — moose

älgfilé *ehly • fih • leh* — fillet of moose

älgstek *ehly • steek*	moose roast
älgstek med svampsås *ehly • steek meed svamp • soas*	roast moose with mushroom sauce
äppelkaka *eh • pehl • kah • ka*	apple cake
äppelpaj *ehp • ehl • pay*	apple tart
äppelring *ehp • ehl • rihng*	apple fritter
äpple *ehp • leh*	apple
ärta *air • ta*	pea
ärtsoppa *airt • sohp • a*	green or yellow pea soup
ättiksgurka *eh • tihks • geur • ka*	sweet, pickled gherkins
öl *url*	beer
öl på flaska *url poa fla • ska*	bottled beer

PEOPLE

GOING OUT

NEED TO KNOW

Do you have a program of events?	**Har ni ett evenemangsprogram?** *hahr nee eht eh • vehn • eh • mangs • proa • gram*
What's playing at the movies [cinema] tonight?	**Vad visas på bio ikväll?** *vahd vee • sas poa bee • oa ee • kvehl*
Where's...?	**Var ligger...?** *vahr lih • gehr...*
the downtown area	**centrum** *sehn • truhm*
the bar	**baren** *bah • rehn*
the dance club	**diskoteket** *dis • koh • tee • keht*

ENTERTAINMENT

Can you recommend...?	**Kan du rekommendera...?** *kan deu reh • koh • mehn • dee • ra...*
a concert	**en konsert** *ehn kohn • sair*
a movie	**en film** *ehn film*
an opera	**en opera** *ehn oa • peh • ra*
a play	**en teaterpjäs** *ehn tee • ah • tehr • pjais*

When does it start/end? **När börjar/slutar den?**
*nair **bur** • yar/sleu • tar dehn*

What's the dress code? **Vilken klädsel gäller?**
vihl • kehn klaid • sehl gehl • lehr

I like... **Jag tycker om...**
yahg tew • kehr ohm...

classical music **klassisk musik**
klas • isk meu • seek

folk music **folkmusik**
folk • meu • seek

jazz **jazz**
yas

pop music **popmusik**
pop • meu • seek

rap **rap**
rap

For Tickets, see page 45.

YOU MAY HEAR...

Stäng av mobiltelefonen, tack.
*stehng afv mo • beel • teh • leh • **foa** • nen tak*
Turn off your cell [mobile] phones, please.

NIGHTLIFE

What's there to do at night?	**Vad kan man göra på kvällarna?** *vahd kan man yur • ra poa kvehl • ar • na*
Can you recommend...?	**Kan du rekommendera...?** *kan deu reh • koh • mehn • dee • ra...*
a bar	**en bar** *ehn bahr*
a casino	**ett kasino** *eht ka • see • noh*
a dance club	**ett diskotek** *eht dis • koh • tehk*
a gay club	**en gayklubb** *ehn gay • kluhb*
a jazz club	**en jazzklubb** *ehn yas • kluhb*
a club with local music	**en klubb med lokal musik** *ehn kluhb meed lo • kahl meu • seek*
a nightclub	**en nattklubb** *ehn nat • kluhb*
Is there live music?	**Spelar man livemusik där?** *spee • lar man live • meu • seek dair*
How do I get there?	**Hur kan jag komma dit?** *heur kan yahg koh • ma deet*
Is there a cover charge?	**Är det kuvertavgift?** *air de keu • vair • afv • yihft*
Let's go dancing.	**Vi går ut och dansar.** *vee goar eut ohk dan • sar*
Is this area safe at night?	**Är detta område säkert på natten?** *ehr deh • ta ohm • roh • deh seh • kehrt poh na • tehn*

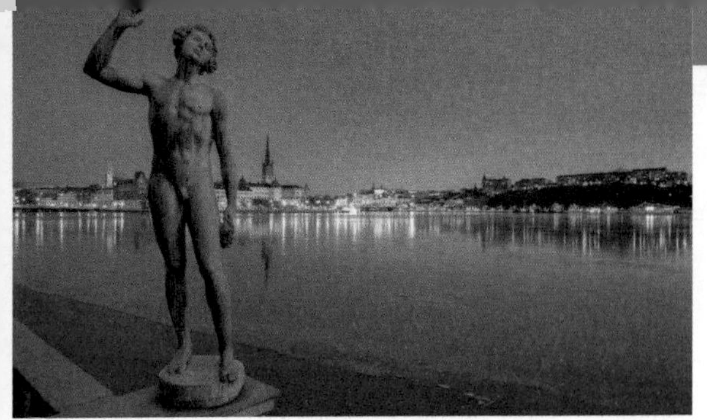

Sweden has produced several world famous pop and rock bands, and music is an important part of contemporary culture and entertainment. The government generously supports independent musicians, as well as smaller music groups, orchestras and symphonies. In larger cities and towns you'll easily find concerts and performances to attend, and information should be listed at the tourist office or its webpage regarding upcoming concerts and events. If you are traveling in Sweden during the summer, attending a music festival is an unforgettable experience. **The Peace & Love Festival** in Borlänge, just two hours from Stockholm, is popular among the younger crowd. Stockholm is home to **Ung08**, which is Europe's largest youth festival, geared toward 13-19 year olds. **The Hultsfred Festival**, in southern Sweden, is the oldest and largest festival. There are also a host of other music festivals covering everything from folk music, to pop and jazz.

ROMANCE

NEED TO KNOW

Would you like to go out for a drink/ dinner?	**Har du lust att ta en drink/gå ut och äta?** *hahr deu luhst at tah ehn drihnk/goa eut ohk air • ta*
What are your plans for tonight/ tomorrow?	**Vad har du för planer för ikväll/ imorgon?** *vahd hahr deu furr plah • nehr furr ee • kvehl/ee • mo • ron*
Can I have your number?	**Kan jag få ditt telefonnummer?** *kan yahg foa diht teh • leh • foan • nuhm • ehr*
May I join you?	**Får jag göra dig sällskap?** *foar yahg yurra dihg sehl • skahp*
Can I buy you a drink?	**Får jag bjuda på en drink?** *foar yahg byeu • da poa ehn drihnk*
I like you.	**Jag gillar dig.** *yahg yihi • ar day*
I love you.	**Jag älskar dig.** *yahg ehl • skar day*

THE DATING GAME

Would you like to...?	**Har du lust att...?** *hahr deu luhst at...*
go out for coffee	**gå ut och ta en kopp kaffe** *goa eut ohk tah ehn kohp ka • fer*

go for a drink **ta en drink**
tah ehn drihnk

go out for a meal **gå ut och äta**
*g**oa** eut ohk air • ta*

What are your plans for...? **Vad har du för planer för...?**
vahd hahr deu furr plah • nehr furr...

today **idag**
ee • dahg

tonight **ikväll**
ee • kvehl

tomorrow **imorgon**
ee • mo • ron

this weekend **den här helgen**
dehn hair hehl • yehn

Where would you like to go? **Vart vill du gå?**
*vart vihl deu g**oa***

I'd like to go to... **Jag skulle vilja gå till...**
*yahg skuh • ler vihl • ya g**oa** tihl...*

Do you like...? **Tycker du om...?**
tew • kehr deu ohm...

Can I have your number/e-mail? **Kan jag få ditt nummer/din e-post?**
*kan yahg f**oa** diht nuhm • ehr/dihn ee • pohst*

Are you on Facebook/ Twitter? **Finns du på Facebook/Twitter?**
fihns deu poa Facebook/Twitter

Can I join you? **Får jag följa med?**
*f**oa**r yahg furl • ya meed*

You're very attractive. **Du är väldigt snygg.**
deu air vehl • dihkt snewgg

You look great! **Vad du ser vacker ut!**
vahd deu seer va • kehr eut

Shall we go somewhere quieter? **Ska vi gå till ett lugnare ställe?**
*skah vee g**oa** tihl eht luhng • na • rer stehl • ler*

For Communications, see page 84.

ACCEPTING & REJECTING

Thank you. I'd love to.	**Tack, det vill jag gärna.** *tak d**ee** vihl yahg yair • na*
Where should we meet?	**Var ska vi träffas?** *vahr skah vee treh • fas*
I'll meet you at the bar/your hotel.	**Vi träffas i baren/på ditt hotell.** *vee treh • fas ee bahr • en/p**oa** diht hoh • tehl*
I'll come by at…	**Jag kommer…** *yahg koh • mehr…*
What's your address?	**Vilken address har du?** *Vihl • kehn ahd • rehs hahr deu*
Thank you, but I'm busy.	**Tack, men jag är upptagen.** *tak men yahg air uhp • tah • gehn*
I'm not interested.	**Jag är inte intresserad.** *yahg air in • ter in • treh • see • rad*
Leave me alone, please!	**Kan du lämna mig ifred, tack!** *kan deu lehm • na may ee • freed tak*
Stop bothering me!	**Sluta störa mig!** *sluh • ta stur • ra may*

GETTING INTIMATE

Can I hug/kiss you?	**Får jag krama/kysa dig?** *foar yahg krah • ma/chews • a day*
Yes.	**Ja.** *yah*
No.	**Nej.** *nay*
Stop!	**Stopp!** *stop*

SEXUAL PREFERENCES

Are you gay?	**Är du gay?** *air deu gay*
I'm…	**Jag är…** *yahg air…*
heterosexual	**heterosexuell** *heh • tehr • ro • sehk • shew • ehl*
homosexual	**homosexuell** *hoh • moa • sehk • shew • ehl*
bisexual	**bisexuell** *bee • sehk • shew • ehl*
Do you like men/ women?	**Gillar du män/kvinnor?** *yih • lahr deu mehn/kvih • nohr*

For Grammar, see page 14.

Öpp

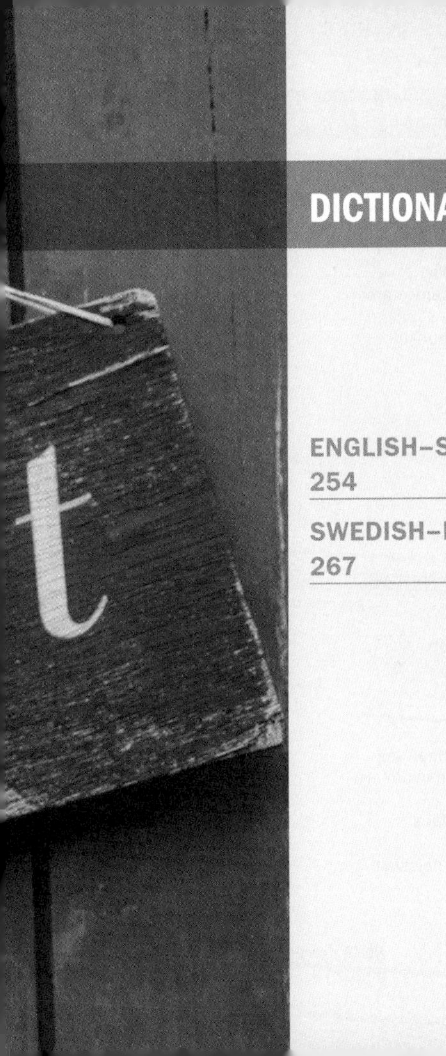

DICTIONARY

ENGLISH–SWEDISH

A

about (approximately) omkring
accept *v* acceptera
accident olycka
accommodation logi
acetaminophen paracetamol
across över
acupuncture akupunktur
adapter adapter
address *n* adress
adopt *v* adoptera
after efter
age ålder
air conditioning luftkonditionering
air mail flygpost
airline flygbolag
airport flygplats
aisle seat plats i mittgången
all alla
allergic allergisk
allergic reaction allergisk reaktion
allergy allergi
allow *v* tillåta
alter *v* ändra på
alternate route annan väg
aluminum foil aluminiumfolie
a.m. fm
ambulance ambulans
amount summa
amusement park nöjesfält
and och
anemic anemisk
animal djur
another annan
antiques store antikaffär
antiseptic cream antiseptisk salva
anyone någon
anything något
apartment lägenhet
apologize *v* be om ursäkt
appliance apparat
approve *v* godkänna
area code riktnummer
aromatherapy aroma-terapi
arrival ankomst
arrive *v* anlända
ask *v* fråga
aspirin huvudvärkstablett
asthma astma
at vid
ATM Bankomat
attack *n* anfall
audio guide audioguide
authentic äkta
automatic automatisk
available ledig
away iväg

B

baby baby
baby bottle nappflaska
baby formula välling
baby wipes våtservetter för barn

adj adjective
adv adverb
BE British English
n noun
v verb

babysitter barnvakt
backpack ryggsäck
bad dålig
bag (shopping) påse
baggage cart bagagekärra
baggage claim bagageutlämning
bakery bageri
band (music group) band
bandage (gauze) gasbinda
bank bank
bank charge bankavgift
banknote sedel
bar bar
barber herrfrisör
bath bad
bathroom badrum; **(toilet)** toalett
battery batteri
battlefield slagfält
be *v* vara
beach strand
beautiful vacker
become *v* bli
bed *n* säng
before före
begin *v* börja
behind bakom
belt skärp
between mellan
big stor
bicycle cykel
bicycle lock cykelås
bikini bikini
bill *n* **(restaurant bill)** nota; **(hotel, invoice)** räkning
birthday födelsedag
bite *n* bett; *v* **(bite)** bita; *v* **(chew)** tugga
black svart
blanket *n* täcke
bleed *v* blöda
blood blod
blood pressure blodtryck
blouse blus
board *v* **(flight)** borda
boarding house pensionat
boarding pass (airport) boardingkort
boat båt
boat tour båttur
book bok
bookstore bokhandel
boots stövlar
boring trist
botanical garden botanisk trädgård
bottle flaska
bottle opener flasköppnare
bowl djup tallrik
boy pojke
boyfriend pojkvän
bra behå
bracelet armband
break *v* gå sönder
breakdown *v* **(car)** gå sönder
breastfeed *v* amma
breathe andas
bridge bro
bring ta med
broken (broken) sönder; **(damaged)** trasig
brooch brosch
broom sopborste
brown brun
burn *v* brinna
bus buss
bus route busslinje
bus station bussterminal
bus stop busshållplats
business center businesscenter
business hours öppettider
business trip affärsresa
busy upptagen
but men
buy *v* köpa

C

cabin stuga
cafe kafé
calender kalender
call *v* **(phone)** ringa
calm lugn
camera kamera
camping bed tältsäng
can *n* burk; *v* **(be able to)** kan
can opener konservöppnare
cancel *v* avbeställa
car bil
car deck (ferry) bildäck
car ferry bilfärja
car park [BE] parkeringsplats
car rental biluthyrning
car seat bilbarnstol
carafe karaff
card *n* kort
carry on *n* **(luggage)** handbagage
cash kontant
cashier (male) kassör; **(female)** kassörska
casino kasino
castle slott
cathedral katedral
cave grotta
cell phone mobiltelefon
ceramics keramik
certificate of authenticity äkthetsbevis
chair lift stollift
change *n* **(money)** växel; *v* **(transportation; a baby)** byta; *v* **(reservation)** ändra;
cheap billig
check in *v* checka in
check in desk (airport) incheckning
check out *v* checka ut
checking account checkkonto
chemical toilet kemisk toalett
chemist [BE] apotek
chest bröstet
child barn
child's cot [BE] barnsäng
children's menu barnmeny
church kyrka
cigar cigarr
cinema [BE] bio
city (city) stad; **(downtown)** centrum
city map stadskarta
classical music klassiskmusik
clean *n* ren
cleaning supplies städutrustning
clear *v* **(computer)** rensa
cliff klippa
cling film [BE] plastfolie
clock klocka
close *v* stänga
closed stängt
clothing store klädaffär
coat rock
coffee shop konditori
coin mynt
cold (illness) förskylning; **(temperature)** kall
colleague kollega
color färg
comb kam
come *v* komma
company (business) firma; **(companionship)** sällskap
computer dator
concert konsert
conditioner hårbalsam
condom kondom
conference konferens
conference room konferensrum
confirm *v* **(reservation)** bekräfta
contact lens solution kontaktlinsvätska

contain *v* innehålla
contraceptive preventivmedel
convention hall kongresshall
cooking facilities kokmöjligheter
cool (temperature) sval
copy *n* kopia
copy machine kopieringsautomat
corkscrew korkskruv
correct rätt
cost *v* kosta
cotton bomull
cough *n* hosta; v hosta
country code landsnummer
cover charge kuvertavgift
credit card kreditkort
crib barnsäng
cross country skiing längdåkning
crystal (glass) kristallglas
cup kopp
culture kultur
currency valuta
currency exchange office växelkontor
customs tull
customs declaration form tulldeklaration
cute *adj* gullig
cycling cykelåkning

D

dala horse dalahäst
damage *v* **(damage)** skada; *n* **(harm)** skada
dance *v* dansa
dance club diskotek
day ticket dagsbiljett
day trip dagstur
deaf döv
debit card bankkort
declare *v* **(customs)** förtulla
deck chair solstol
deep djup
delay *n* försening
delete *v* **(computer)** radera
delicatessen delikatessaffär
denim denim
dentist tandläkare
denture tandprotes
deodorant deodorant
depart v **(train)** avgå
department store varuhus
departure (airport) avgång
departure gate avgångsgate
deposit handpenning
desire *adj* gärna; *n* lust
detour trafikomläggning
develop *v* **(photos)** framkalla
diabetic *n* diabetiker
dial *v* **(number)** slå
diamond diamant
diaper blöja
diarrhea diarré
diesel diesel
difficult svårt
digital digital
digital print digitalt kort
dirty smutsig
disabled rörelsehindrad
disabled accessible toilet [BE] handicappanpassad toalett
discount rabatt
discount card rabattkort
dish detergent diskmedel
dishwasher diskmaskin
display case vitrin
disposable camera engångskamera
disturb *v* störa
dive *v* dyka
divide *v* dela
diving equipment dykarutrustning
divorced skild
dizzy yr

do *v* **(do something)** göra; **(work with)** syssla med
do not disturb var god stör ej
doctor doktor
doll docka
dollar dollar
domestic (travel) inrikes
domestic flight inrikes flyg
domestic partner sambo
door dörr
dosage dosering
downtown centrum
dress klänning
dress code klädsel
drive v köra
driver's license körkort
drops (medication) droppar
dry cleaner kemtvätt
dubbed dubbad
duty free taxfri
duty free good taxfri vara

E

each varje
ear öra
earring örhänge
east öster
easy lätt
eat *v* äta
economy class turist klass
electrical outlet nätuttag
elevator hiss
e-mail e-post
e-mail address e-postadress
emergency nödsituation
emergency brake nödbroms
emergency exit nödutgång
English engelska
engrave *v* gravera
enter *n* **(entrance)** ingång; **(computer)** enter
entertainment underhållning
equipment utrustning
escalator rulltrappa
e-ticket e-biljett
European Union (EU) europeiska unionen
event händelse
examine *v* **(medical)** undersöka
excess baggage överviktsbagage
exchange rate växelkursen
excuse me (attention, pardon) ursäkta; **(to get past)** ursäkta mig
exit *n* **(way out)** utgång
expensive dyr
expert avancerad
express express
express mail expresspost
extension (phone) anknytning
eyeglasses glasögon

F

fabric tyg
family familj
fan (ventilation) fläkt
fantastic *adj* fantastisk
fare biljettpris
farm bondgård
fast fort
fax fax
fax machine fax machine
female kvinna
ferry färja
fever feber
field fält
fill *v* **(prescription)** göra i ordning
filling (dental) plomb
film [BE] film
fire exit brandutgång
first första
fishing fiske
fit *v* **(clothing)** passa
fitting room provrum

fix *v* laga
fixed price fast pris
flat [BE] lägenhet
flight flyg
flight number flygnummer
floor (level) våning
football [BE] fotboll
for (someone) för
foreign currency utländsk valuta
forest skog
forget *v* glömma
fork gaffel
form *n* blankett
fountain fontän
free (available) ledig
free of charge gratis
freezer frys
friend vän
from ifrån
frying pan stekpanna
fun rolig
function *v* **(work)** fungera
further (more) ytterliggare

G

game spel
garbage sopor
garbage bag soppåse
gasoline bensin
gas station bensinstation
gate (boarding) gate
genuine äkta
get off (train) stiga av
gift shop presentaffär
gift present
girlfriend flickvän
give *v* ge
glass (drinking) glas
gold guld
golf golf
golf club golfklubba
golf course golfbana
good *adj* bra
goodbye hej då
greengrocer [BE] livsmedelsaffär
grocery store livsmedelsaffär
group grupp
guest gäst
guide (brochure) guide; (person) guide
guide dog ledarhund
gym gym

H

hair cut klippning
hair dryer hårtork
hair style frisyr
hairbrush hårborste
hairdresser damfrisör
hairspray hårspray
half halv
handbag [BE] handväska
handicapped rörelsehindrade
handicapped accessible toilet handicappanpassad toalett
handicraft hantverk
handmade handgjord
hat hatt
have *v* ha
health food store hälsokostaffär
hearing impaired hörselskadad
heat värme
helmet hjälm
help *n* hjälp; *v* hjälpa
here här
hi hej
highchair barnstol
highway motorväg
hike *v* vandra
hiking vandring
hill kulle
hire *v* [BE] rent
holiday [BE] **(vacation)** semester
holiday (celebration) helgdag

horseback riding ridsport
hospital sjukhus
hot varm
hotel hotell
hour timme
husband man

I

ibuprofen ibuprofen
ice hockey ishockey
identification (idenitification) legitimation; **(ID card)** ID-kort
ill [BE] sjuk
in i
included (in the price) inkluderad
indoor pool inomhusbassäng
information desk information
innocent oskyldig
insect insekt
insect bite insektbett
insect repellent mygg olja
inside inuti
instant messenger instant messenger
instructor instruktör
insurance försäkring
interesting intressant
international (travel) utrikes
international driver's license internationellt körkort
internet internet
internet cafe internetkafé
interpreter tolk
iron *n* **(clothes)** strykjärn; *v* **(clothes)** stryka
itemized bill specificerad räkning

J

jacket jacka
jeans jeans
jet ski jetski
jeweler juvelerare
jewelry smycken
job jobb

K

keep *v* behålla
key nyckel
key card nyckelkort
kiddie pool barnbassäng
kiss *v* kyssa
kitchen kök
knife kniv
krona (Swedish currency) krona

L

lace spets
lactose intolerant laktosinterant
ladies' restroom damtoilett
ladieswear damkläder
lake sjö
last sista
late sen
launderette [BE] snabbtvätt
laundromat snabbtvätt
laundry tvätt
laundry detergent tvättmedel
laundry facilities tvättmöjligheter
lawyer advokat
leather läder
leave *v* lämna
left (direction) vänster
lesson lektion
letter brev
library bibliotek
life boat livbåt
life jacket flytväst
lifeguard livräddare
lift (ski) lift
lift [BE] *n* **(elevator)** hiss
lift pass liftkort
light (lamp) lampa
light bulb glödlampa
lighter tändare
like *v* gilla

line (bus) linje
linen linne
live *v* bo
loafers loafers
lock *v* låsa
log on logga in
log out logga ut
long *adj* lång; *adv* länge
lose *v* **(lost luggage)** förlora; *v* **(drop, lose)** tappa
lost *n* vilse
lost property office [BE] hittegodsexpedition
lost and found hittegodsexpedition
lottery lotto
love *v* älska
luggage locker förvaringsskåp

M

mail post
mailbox postlåda
manager chef
manicure manikyr
many många
map karta
market marknad
married gift
mass mässan
match (fire) tändsticka
meal måltid
mean *v* **(signify)** betyda
measuring spoon måttsked
medicine medicin
medium medium
meet *v* träffa
meeting sammanträde
memory card minneskort
men's restroom herrtoalett
menstrual cramps mensvärk
menstruation mens
menswear herrkläder
menu meny
message meddelande
microwave mikrovågsugn
minimum minimum
Miss fröken
mistake misstag
mobile phone [BE] mobiltelefon
moment ögonblick
mop *n* skurmop
moped moped
mosque moské
motel motell
motion sickness åksjuka
motorboat motorbåt
motorcycle motocykel
motorway [BE] motorväg
mountain berg
mouth mun
movie film
movies bio
Mr. herr
Mrs. fru
mugging överfall
multi-day card flerdagskort
museum museum
must måste

N

nail file nagelfil
nail salon nagelvårdssalong
name *n* namn
napkin servett
nappy [BE] blöja
nature reserve naturreservat
nearby nära
necklace halsband
need *v* behöva
new ny
newspaper tidning
newsstand tidningskiosk
next nästa
next to bredvid

nice *adj* snäll
no (not allowed) ej
nobody ingen
no smoking rökning förbjuden
north norr
not inte
not included (in the price) inte inkluderad
nothing inget
number nummer
nurse sjuksköterska

O

off av
old gammal
on (switch) på
one way (street) enkelriktad
one-way ticket enkel biljett
only bara
open *n* öppet; *v* öppna
opening hours [BE] öppettider
opera opera
opposite mitt emot
optician optiker
or eller
orchestra orkester
order *v* beställa
other andra
outdoor utomhus
outdoor pool utomhusbassäng
outside ute
overnight delivery (mail) expressutdelning
oxygen treatment syrebehandling

P

pacifier napp
package paket
paddling pool [BE] barnbassäng
pajamas pyjamas
panorama panorama
pants byxor
panty hose strumpbyxor
paper napkin papperservett
parcel [BE] paket
park *n* park; *v* parkera
parking parkering
parking lot parkeringsplats
passport pass
passport control passkontroll
password (computer) lösenord
pay phone telefonautomat
pay *v* betala
peak (mountain) top
pearl pärla
pedestrian crossing övergångsställe för fotgängare
pedestrian fotgängare
pedicure pedikyr
pen kulspetspenna
per per
per day per dag
per week per vecka
performance (music, theater) föreställning
person person
petite petit
petrol [BE] bensin
petrol station [BE] bensinstation
pewter tenn
pharmacy apotek
phone call samtal
phone card telefonkort
phone number telefonnummer
photo foto
pick up *v* **(person/thing)** hämta
picnic area picknickområde
piece bit
pill tablett
pillow kudde
PIN PIN kod
pink rosa
piste [BE] spår

place *n* ställe
plan *n* plan
plaster [BE] plåster
plastic wrap plastfolie
platform (train) plattform
platinum platina
plate tallrik
play *n* **(theater)** teaterpjäs;*v* spela
playground lekplats
playpen lekrum
pleasant trevlig
please (request) snälla; **(invitation)** varsågod
plunger vaskrensare
pocket *n* ficka
point of interest sevärdhet
police polis
police report polisrapport
police station polisstation
pond damm
post office postkontor
postage porto
postcard vykort
pot (cooking pot) gryta; (saucepan) kastrull
pound sterling engelsk pund
pregnant gravid
premium (gas) premium
prescription recept
price pris
print (computer) skriva ut
private privat
private room privatrum
problem problem
produce store matbutik
program (events) program
pub pub
public transportation allmänna kommunikationer
pull dra
purple lila
purpose syfte
purse (large) handväska, **(small)** portmonnä
push tryck
pushchair [BE] sittvagn

R

racket (tennis) racket
railroad järnväg
railway [BE] järnväg
rain regn
raincoat regnkappa
rap rap
rape *n* våldtäkt
rapids fors
rash *n* utslag
(disposable) razor (engångs) rakhyvel
reach *v* nå
read *v* läsa
ready färdig
receipt kvitto
receive *v* ta emot
receptionist receptionist
recommend *v* rekommendera
refrigderator kylskåp
region region
regular gas vanlig
relationship (romantic) förhållande
rent *n* hyra; *v* hyra
repair *v* reparera
repairs (car) reparationer
repeat *v* upprepa
report *v* **(crime)** anmäla
reservation bokning
reserved reserverad
rest area rastplats
restroom (sign) WC
restaurant restaurang
return *v* **(give back)** återlämna
return ticket [BE] retur **(biljett)**

reverse charge call [BE] ba-samtal
right (correct) rätt; **(direction)** höger
ring (jewelry) ring
river flod
road väg
road map vägkarta
romantic romantisk
room rum
room service rumservice
round *n* **(golf)** runda
round-trip ticket retur biljett
rubbish [BE] sopor

S

safe *n* kassaskåp
sailing segling
sandals sandaler
sanitary napkin binda
saucepan kastrull
sauna bastu
save *v* **(collect)** spara
scarf halsduk
schedule tidsschema
scissors sax
sea hav
seat (on train) plats
seat number platsnummer
seat reservation (train) sittplatsbiljett
seminar seminarium
send *v* skicka
separated (couple) separerad
service serveringsavgift
service charge (bank) expeditionsavgift
sex sex
shampoo shampoo
sheet lakan
shoe store skoaffär
shoes skor
shopping basket shoppingkorg
shopping cart shoppingvagn
shopping centre [BE] shoppingcenter
shopping mall shoppingcenter
shorts shorts
show *v* visa
shower dusch
sick sjuk
side effect biverkning
sightseeing tour sightseeingtur
sign *v* undertäckna
silk siden
SIM card (cell phone) SIM kort
single ticket [BE] enkel **(biljett)**
sit *v* sitta
size storlek
skiing skidåkning
skirt kjol
slice *n* skiva
slippers tofflor
slippery (icy) hal
slow *adj* långsam
small liten
sneakers träningsskor
snorkeling equipment snorkelutrustning
snow snö
snowboard snowboard
snowshoes pjäxor
soap tvål
soccer fotboll
sock socka
something något
soon snart
soother [BE] napp
sore throat halsont
sorry förlåt
south söder
souvenir souvenir
spa spa
spatula stekspade

speak *v* tala
spoon sked
sports massage träningsmassage
spouse (female) maka; **(male)** make
sprain stukning
square (town feature) torg
stadium stadion
stair trappa
stamp *n* frimärke
stamp your ticket stämpla er biljett
start *v* **(car)** starta
stay *n* stanna
steakhouse stekhus
steep brant
stolen stulen
stomach magen
stomachache ont i magen
stop *n* **(bus stop)** bushållplats; v stanna
store *n* butik; *v* förvara
strange konstig
stream å
street gata
stroller sittvagn
student studerande
study *v* läsa
stunning jättesnygg
subtitle text
suburb förort
subway tunnelbana
subway station tunnelbanestation
suitable lämplig
suitcase resväska
sunburn solbränna
sunglasses solglasögon
sunstroke solsting
super [BE] **(gas)** premium
supermarket snabbköp
surfboard surfbräda
sweater tröja
sweatshirt sweatshirt
Swedish *adj* svensk; **(language)** svenska
swelling svullnad
swim *v* simma
swimming pool simbassäng
swimming trunks badbyxor
swimsuit baddräkt
symbol (computer) tecken
symphony (orchestra) symfoni
synagogue synagoga

T

table bord
tablecloth duk
take *v* ta
take out *v* ta ut
taken (occupied) upptagen
tampon tampong
tax skatt
taxi taxi
teaspoon tesked
temperature temperatur
temple tempel
tennis tennis
tennis court tennisbana
terminal (airport) terminal
terrible förskräcklig
text message sms
textiles textil
thank you tack
theft rån
thief tjuv
think *v* tänka
ticket biljett
ticket machine biljettautomat
ticket office biljettkontor
tie *n* slips
tights [BE] strumpbyxor
timetable [BE] tidsschema

tip (service) dricks
tissue näsduk
to till
tobacconist tobaksaffär
toilet [BE] toalett; **(sign)** WC
toilet paper toalettpapper
tooth tand
toothbrush tandborste
toothpaste tandkräm
tour tur
tourist turist
tourist attraction turistattraktion
tourist information turistinformation
tourist office turistbyrå
town hall stadshus
toy store leksaksaffär
track (railroad) spår
trail spår
train *n* tåg
train station järnvägsstation
tram spårvagn
translate *v* översätta
travel *v* **(travel)** resa; **(drive)** åka
travel agency resebyrå
travel agent (female) resebyråkvinna; **(male)** resebyråman
travel sickness [BE] åksjuka
traveler's check resecheck
traveller's cheque [BE] resecheck
treat *v* **(to a meal)** bjuda
trim (hair) putsning
trip *n* resa
trolley [BE] bagagekärra
trouser [BE] byxor
try *v* prova
turn off *v* stänga av
turn on *v* sätta på

U

ugly ful
umbrella (standard) paraply; **(sun)** solparasol
underground [BE] tunnelbana
underground station [BE] tunnelbanestation
understand *v* förstå
underwear (general) underkläder
unfortunately tyvärr
United Kingdom Storbritanien
unlimited (mileage) obegränsad
until tills
urgent brådskande
United State Förenta Staterna
use *v* använda
username användarnamn
utensil bestick

V

vacancy ledigt rum
vacation semester
vacuum cleaner dammsugare
vaginal infection vaginal infektion
valley dal
valuable värdesak
value *n* värde
vegetarian vegetarian
viewpoint utsiktspunkt
village by
visit *n* besök; *v* besöka
visiting hours besökstid
visitor besökare
visitor besökare
visually impaired syn skadad
vomit *v* kräkas

W

wait vänta
wake up *v* vakna

wake-up call telefonväckning
walk *n* promenad; *v* gå
wallet plånbok
want *v* vilja
washing machine tvättmaskin
waterfall vattenfall
weather forecast väderleksrapport
weekend helg
welcome välkommen
west väster
wheelchair rullstol
wheelchair ramp rullstolsramp
when när
where var
which vilken
white vitt
who vem
widow änka
widower änkling
window fönster
window seat fönsterplats
windsurfing vindsurfa
wireless internet trådlös internet
with med
withdrawal (bank) uttag
wood trä
wool ull
work from home *v* arbeta hemifrån
wrap *v* **(present)** slå in
write *v* skriva
wrong fel

Y

yellow gul
yes ja
yield lämna företräde
youth hostel vandrarhem

Z

zoo djurpark

SWEDISH–ENGLISH

A

acceptera *v* accept
adapter adapter
adoptera *v* adopt
adress *n* address
advokat lawyer
affärscentrum shopping mall [centre BE]
affärsresa business trip
akupunktur acupuncture
alla all
allergi allergy
allergisk allergic
allergisk reaktion allergic reaction
allmänna kommunikationer public transportation
alternativ väg alternate route
aluminiumfolie aluminum foil
ambulans ambulance
amma *v* breastfeed
andas breathe
andra other
anemisk anemic
anfall *n* attack
anknytning extension (phone)
ankomst arrival
anlända *v* arrive
anmäla *v* report (crime)

annan another
antikaffär antiques store
antiseptisk salva antiseptic cream
använda *v* use
användarnamn username
apotek pharmacy [chemist BE]
apparat appliance
arbeta hemifrån *v* work from home
armband bracelet
aroma-terapi aromatherapy
astma asthma
audioguide audio guide
automatisk automatic
av off
avancerad expert
avbeställa *v* cancel
avgå *v* depart (plane)
avgång departure
avgångsgate departure gate

B

baby baby
bad bath
badbyxor swim trunks
baddräkt swim suit
badrum bathroom [toilet BE]
bagagekärra baggage cart [trolley BE]
bagageutlämning baggage claim
bageri bakery
bakom behind
band band (music group)
bank bank
bankavgift bank charge
bankkort debit card
Bankomat ATM
bar bar
bara only (just)
barn child
barnbassäng kiddie pool [paddling pool BE]
barnmeny children's menu
barnstol highchair
barnsäng crib [child's cot BE]
barnvakt babysitter
bastu sauna
batteri battery
be om ursäkt *v* apologize
behå bra
behålla *v* keep
behöva *v* need
bekräfta *v* confirm (reservation)
bensin gasoline [petrol BE]
bensinstation gas station [petrol station BE]
berg mountain
bergklättring rock climbing
bestick utensil
beställa *v* order
besök *n* visit
besöka *v* visit
besökare visitor
besökstid visiting hours
betala *v* pay
bett *n* bite
betyda mean (signify)
bibliotek library
bikini bikini
bil car
bilbarnstol car seat
bildäck car deck (ferry)
bilfärja car ferry
biljett ticket
biljettautomat ticket machine
biljettkontor ticket office
biljettpris fare
billig cheap
bilsäte car seat
biluthyrning car rental
binda sanitary napkin [towel BE]
bio movies [cinema BE]

bit piece
bita *v* bite
biverkning side effect
bjuda *v* treat (to a meal)
blankett *n* form
bli *v* become
blod blood
blodtryck blood pressure
blus blouse
blöda bleed
blöja diaper [nappy BE]
bo *v* live
boardingkort boarding pass
bok book
bokhandel bookstore
bokning reservation (travel, restaurant)
bomull cotton
bondgård farm
bord table
borda *v* board (flight)
botanisk trädgård botanical garden
bra *adj* good
brandutgång fire exit
brant steep
bredvid next to
brev letter
brinna *v* burn
bro bridge
brosch brooch
brun brown
brådskande urgent
bröstet chest
burk *n* can
businesscenter business center
buss bus
busshållplats bus stop [request stop BE]
busslinje bus route
bussterminal bus station
butik *n* store
by village
byta *v* change (baby, connection)
byxor pants [trouser BE]
båt boat
båttur boat tour
börja *v* begin

C

centrum downtown
checka in check in (airport)
checka ut check out (hotel)
chef manager
cigarr cigar
cykel bicycle
cykelåkning cycling
cykelås bicycle lock

D

dagsbiljett day ticket
dagstur day trip
dal valley
dalahäst dala horse
damfrisör hairdresser
damkläder ladieswear
damtoalett ladies' restroom
damm pond
dammsugare vacuum cleaner
dansa *v* dance
dator computer
dela divide
delikatessaffär delicatessen
denim denim
deodorant deodorant
diabetiker *n* diabetic
diamant diamond
diarré diarrhea
diesel diesel
digital digital
digitalt kort digital print
diskmedel dish detergent
diskmaskin dishwasher
djup deep

djup tallrik bowl
djur animal
djurpark zoo
docka doll
doktor doctor
dollar dollar
dosering dosage
dra pull
dricks tip (service)
droppar drops (medication)
dubbad dubbed
duk table cloth
dusch shower
dyka *v* dive
dykarutrustning diving equipment
dyr expensive
dålig bad
dörr door
döv deaf

E

e-biljett e-ticket
efter after
ej no (do not...)
eller or
endast only (nothing but)
engelska English
engelsk pund pound sterling
engångskamera disposable camera
enkel biljett one-way trip [single ticket BE]
enkelriktad one way (street)
enter enter (computer)
e-post e-mail
e-postadress e-mail address
europeiska unionen European Union (EU)
expeditionsavgift service charge (bank)
express express
expresspost express mail
expressutdelning overnight delivery (mail)

F

familj family
fantastisk *adj* fantastic
fast pris fixed price
fax fax
fax machine fax machine
feber fever
fel wrong
ficka *n* pocket
film movie [film BE]
fiske fishing
flaska bottle
flasköppnare bottle opener
flerdagskort multi-day card
flickvän girlfriend
flod river
flyg flight
flygbolag airline
flygnummer flightnumber
flygplats airport
flygpost airmail
fläkt fan
fm a.m.
fontän fountain
fors rapids
fort fast
fotboll soccer [football BE]
fotgängare pedestrian
foto photo
framkalla *v* develop (photos)
fri free
frimärken stamps
frisyr hair style
fru Mrs.
frys freezer
fråga ask
från from...
fröken Miss

ful ugly
fungera *v* function (work)
fylla *v* fill
fält field
färdig ready
färg color
färja ferry
födelsedag birthday
fönster window
fönsterplats window seat
för tung/stor too much, excess (baggage)
före before
Förenta Staterna United States
föreställning performance (music, theater)
förhållande relationship (romantic)
förlora *v* lose
förlåt sorry
försening *n* delay
förskräcklig terrible
förskylning cold (sick)
första first
förstå *v* understand
försäkring insurance
förtulla *v* declare (customs)
förvaringsskåp luggage locker
förort suburb

G

gaffel fork
gammal *adj* old, *n* age
gasbinda bandage (gauze)
gata street
gate gate (boarding)
ge *v* give
gift married
gilla *v* like
glas glass (drinking)
glasögon eyeglasses
glödlampa light bulb
glömma *v* forget
godkänna *v* approve
golf golf
golfbana golf course
golfklubb golf club
gratis free of charge
gravera *v* engrave
gravid pregnant
grotta cave
grupp group
gryta pot (cooking)
guide guide (brochure); guide (person)
gul yellow
guld gold
gullig *adj* cute
gym gym
gå *v* walk, leave
gå sönder break; breakdown (car)
gärna *adj* desire
göra *v* do

H

ha *v* have
hal slippery (icy)
halsband necklace
halsduk scarf
halsont sore throat
halv halv
handbagage carry on
handgjord handmade
handicappanpassad toalett handicapped accessible toilet [disabled BE]
handpenning deposit
handväska purse [hand bag BE]
hantverk handicraft
hatt hat
hav sea
hej hi
hej då goodbye
helg weekend

helgdag holiday (celebration)
hemifrån work from home
hemlagad homemade (food)
herr Mr.
herrfrisör barber
herrkläder menswear
herrtoalett men's restroom
iss elevator [lift BE]
hittegodsexpedition lost-and-found [lost property office BE]
hjälm helmet
hjälp *n* help
hjälpa *v* help
hosta *n* cough; *v* to cough
hotell hotel
huvudvärkstablett aspirin
hyra rent [hire BE]
hårbalsam conditioner
hårborste hairbrush
hårspray hairspray
hårtork hair dryer
hälsokostaffär health food store
hämta *v* pick up (thing/person)
händelse event
här here
höger right (direction)
hörselskadad hearing impaired

I

i in
ibuprofen ibuprofen
ID-kort identification
ifrån from
incheckning check in desk (airport)
information information desk
ingen nobody (sg)
inget nothing
ingång entrance
inkluderad included (in the price)
innehålla contain
inomhusbassäng indoor swimming pool
inrikes domestic (travel)
inrikes flyg domestic flight
insekt insect
insektbett insect bite
instant messenger instant messenger
instruktör instructor
inte not
inte inkluderad not included (in the price)
internationellt
körkort international driver's license
internet internet
internetkafé internet café
intressant interesting
inuti inside
ishockey ice hockey
iväg away

J

ja yes
jacka jacket
jeans jeans
jetski jet ski
jobb job
juvelerare jeweler
järnväg railroad [railway BE]
järnvägsstation train station
jättesnygg stunning

K

kafé café
kalender calendar
kall cold (temperature)
kam comb
kamera camera
kan *v* can (be able to)
karaff carafe
karta map

kasino casino
kassaskåp *n* safe
kassör cashier (male)
kassörska cashier (female)
kastrull saucepan (cooking)
katedral cathedral
kemisk toalett chemical toilet
kemtvätt dry cleaner
keramik ceramics
kjol skirt
klassiskmusik classical music
klippa cliff
klippning hair cut
klocka(n) clock
klädaffär clothing store
klädsel dress code
klänning dress
kniv knife
kokmöjligheter cooking facilities
kollega colleague
komma *v* come
konditori coffee shop
kondom condom
konferens conference
konferensrum conference room
kongresshall convention hall
konsert concert
konservöppnare can opener
konstig strange
kontaktlinsvätska contact lens solution
kontant *n* cash
kopia *n* copy
kopieringsautomat copy machine
kopp cup
korkskruv corkscrew
kort *n* card, *adj* short
kosta *v* cost
kostym suit (jacket/pants)
kreditkort credit card
kristallglas crystal (glass)
krona krona (Swedish currency)
kräkas *v* vomit
kudde pillow
kulle hill
kulspetspenna pen
kultur culture
kuvertavgift cover charge
kvinna female
kvitto receipt
kylskåp refridgerator
kyrka church
kyssa *v* kiss
kök kitchen
köpa *v* buy
köra drive
körkort driver's license

L

laga *v* fix
lakan sheet
laktosintolerant lactose intolerant
lampa light (lamp)
landsnummer country code
ledarhund guide dog
ledig available
ledigt rum vacancy
legitimation identification
lekplats playground
lekrum playpen
leksaksaffär toy store
lektion lesson
liftkort liftpass
lila purple
linje line
linne linen
liten small
livbåt life boat
livräddare lifeguard
livsmedelsaffär grocery store [greengrocer BE]
loafers loafers

logga in log on (connect to internet)
logga ut log out
logi accommodation
lotto lottery
luftkonditionering air conditioning
lugn calm
lust *n* desire
lyft lift (ski)
lång long
långsam slow
låsa *v* lock
läder leather
lägenhet apartment [flat BE]
lämna *v* leave
lämna före träde yield
lämplig suitable
längdåkning cross country skiing
länge long (time)
läsa *v* (book) read; (school) study
lätt easy
lösenord password

M

magen stomach
maka spouse (female)
make spouse (male)
man husband, man
manikyr manicure
marknad market
matbutik produce store (general store) [grocer BE]
med with
meddelande message
medicin medicine
medium medium
mellan between
men but
mens menstruation
mensvärk menstrual cramps
meny menu
mikrovågsugn microwave
minimum minimum (requirement)
minneskort memory card
misstag mistake
mitt emot opposite
mobiltelefon cell phone [mobile phone BE]
moms sales tax [VAT BE]
moped moped
moské mosque
motel motel
motorcykel motorcycle
motorbåt motorboat
motorväg highway [motorway BE]
mun mouth
museum museum
mygg olja insect repellent
mynt coin
måltid meal
många many
måste must
måttsked measuring spoon
mässan mass (catholic)

N

nagelfil nail file
nagelvårdssalong nail salon
namn *n* name
napp pacifer [soother BE]
nappflaska baby bottle
naturreservat nature reserve
norr north
nota bill (restaurant)
nummer number
ny new
nyckel key
nyckelkort key card
nå *v* reach
någon anyone
något anything, something
när when
nära nearby

näsduk tissue
nästa next
nätuttag electrical outlet
nödbroms emergency brake
nödsituation emergency
nödutgång emergency exit
nöjesfält amusement park

O

obegränsad unlimited (mileage)
och and
olycka accident
omkring about (approximately)
ont i magen stomachache
opera opera
optiker optician
orkester orchestra

P

paket package [parcel BE]
panorama panorama
pappersservett paper napkin
paracetamol acetaminophen
paraply umbrella
park park
parkering parking
parkering på gatan street parking
parkeringsplats (one or several) parking lot [car park BE]
pass passport
passa *v* fit
passkontroll passport control
pedikyr pedicure
pensionat boarding house
per per
per dag per day
per vecka per week
person person
petit petite
picknickområde picnic area
PIN kod PIN code
pjäxor snowshoes
plan *n* plan
plastfolie plastic wrap [cling film BE]
platina platinum
plats seat (on train)
plats i mittgången aisle seat
platsnummer seat number
plattform platform (train)
plomb filling
plånbok wallet
pojke boy
pojkvän boyfriend
polis police
polisrapport police report
polisstation police station
porto postage
post mail
postkontor post office
postlåda mail box
premium premium [super BE] (gas)
presentaffär gift shop
present gift
preventivmedel contraceptive
pris price
privat private
privatrum private room
problem problem
program progam (events)
prova *v* try
provrum fitting room
pub pub
putsning trim (hair)
pyjamas pajamas
på on (switch)
påse bag
pärla pearl

R

rabatt discount
rabattkort discount card

racket racket (tennis)
radera delete (computer)
(engångs)rakhyvel (disposable) razor
rap rap
rastplats rest area
recept prescription
receptionist receptionist
region region
regn rain
regnkappa raincoat
rekommendera *v* recommend
ren adj clean
rensa clear (computer, ATM), clean
reparationer repairs (car)
reparera *v* repair
resa *v* travel, *n* trip
resebyrå travel agency
resebyråkvinna travel agent (female)
resebyråman travel agent (male)
resecheck traveler's check [traveller's cheque BE]
reserverad reserved
restaurang restaurant
resväska suitcase
retur (biljett) round-trip ticket [return ticket BE]
ridsport horseback riding
riktnummer area code
ring ring (jewelry)
ringa *v* call (phone)
rock coat
rolig fun
romantisk romantic
rosa pink
rullstol wheelchair
rullstolsramp wheelchair ramp
rulltrappa escalator
rum room
rumservice room service
runda *v* round (golf)
ryggsäck backpack
rån theft
räkning bill (hotel, invoice)
rätt correct
rökning förbjuden no smoking
rörelsehindrad disabled

S

sambo domestic partner
sammanträde meeting
samtal phone call
sandaler sandals
sax scissors
sedel banknote
segling sailing
semester vacation
seminarium seminar
sen late
separerad separated (couple)
serveringsavgift service
servett napkin
sevärdhet point of interest
sex sex
shampoo shampoo
shoppingcenter shopping mall [shopping centre BE]
shoppingkorg shopping basket
shoppingvagn shopping cart
shorts shorts
siden silk
sightseeingtur sightseeing tour
simbassäng swimming pool
SIM kort SIM card (cell phone)
simma *v* swim
sista last
sitta *v* sit
sittplatsbiljett seat reservation (train)
sittvagn stroller [pushchair BE]
sjuk sick [ill BE]
sjukhus hospital

sjuksköterska nurse
sjö lake
skada *n* damage, *v* harm
skatt tax
sked spoon
skicka *v* send
skidåkning skiing
skild divorced
skiva *n* slice
skoaffär shoe store
skog forest
skor shoes
skriva write
skriva ut print
skurmop *n* mop
skyldig innocent
skärp belt
slagfält battlefield
slips tie
slott castle
slå *v* (phone number) dial
slå in *v* wrap (present)
sms text message
smutsig dirty
smycken jewelry
snabbköp supermarket
snabbtvätt Laundromat [launderette BE]
snart soon
snorkelutrustning snorkeling equipment
snowboard snowboard
snäll *adj* nice
snälla (request) please
snö snow
socka sock
solbränna sunburn
solglasögon sunglasses
solsting sunstroke
solstol deck chair
sopborste broom
sopor garbage (garbage disposal) [rubbish BE]
soppåse garbage bag
souvenir souvenir
spa spa
spara *v* save
specifierad räkning itemized bill
spel game
spela *v* play
spets lace
spår trail [piste BE]; track (railroad)
spårvagn tram
stad city
stadion stadium
stadshus town hall
stadskarta city map
stanna *n* stay; *v* stop
starta *v* start
stekhus steakhouse
stekpanna frying pan
stekspade spatula
stiga av get off (train)
stollift chair lift
stor big
Storbritannien United Kingdom
storlek size
strand beach
strumpbyxor panty hose [tights BE]
strykjärn iron (clothes)
studerande student
stuga cabin
stukning *n* sprain
stulen stolen
städutrustning cleaning supplies
ställe place
stämpla er biljett stamp your ticket
stäng av turn off
stänga *v* close
stängt closed
störa disturb

stövlar boots
summa amount
surfbräda surfboard
sval cool (temperature)
svart black
sweatshirt sweatshirt
svensk *adj* swedish
svenska *adj* swedish; (language) Swedish
svullnad swelling
svårt difficult
syfte purpose
symfoni symphony (orchestra)
syn skadad visually impaired
synagoga synagogue
syrebehandling oxygen treatment
syssla med *v* do (work with)
sällskap company (companionship)
säng bed
sätta på turn on
söder south
sönder broken

T

ta *v* take
ta emot *v* receive
ta med bring
ta ut take out
tablett pill (tablet)
tack thank you
tala *v* speak
tallrik plate
tampong tampon
tand tooth
tandborste toothbrush
tandkräm toothpaste
tandläkare dentist
tandprotes dentures
tappa *v* lose; drop
taxfri duty free
taxfri vara duty free good
taxi taxi
teaterpjäs play (theater)
tecken symbol (computer)
telefon katalog telephone catalog
telefonautomat pay phone
telefonkort phone card
telefonnummer phone number
telefonväckning wake up call
temperatur temperature
tempel temple
tenn pewter
tennis tennis
tennisbana tennis court
terminal terminal (airport)
tesked teaspoon
text subtitle
textil textiles
tidning newspaper
tidningskiosk newsstand
tidsschema schedule [timetable BE]
till to
tills until
tillåta *v* allow
timme hour
toalett bathroom [toilet BE]
toalettpapper toilet paper
tobaksaffär tobacconist
tofflor slippers
tolk interpreter
top peak (moutain)
torg square (town feature)
trappa stair
trasig broken (damaged)
trevlig pleasant
trist boring
tryck push
trådlös internet wireless internet
trä wood
träffa *v* meet
träfigur wood carvings

en knife
sage sports
sneakers
den spoon
en clogs
on customs
form
ubway [underground
tation subway
erground station BE]
conomy class
on tourist attraction
rist office
ation tourist
washing machine
aundry detergent
ter laundry facilities
nately
ket
ping bed
er
atch (fire)

entertainment
underwear (general)
examine (medical)
v sign

upprepa *v* repeat
upptagen busy
ursäkta *v* excuse me (to get attention, pardon me)
ursäkta mig excuse me (to get past)
ute outside
utgång exit way out
utländsk valuta foreign currency
utomhus outdoor
utomhusbassäng outdoor pool
utrikes international (travel)
utrustning equipment
utsiktspunkt view point
utslag *n* rash
uttag withdrawal (bank)

V

vacker beautiful
vaginal infektion vaginal infection
vakna *v* wake up
valuta currency
vandra *v* hike
vandrarhem youth hostel
vandring hiking
vanlig regular gas
var where
var god stör ej do not disturb
vara *v* be
varje each
varm hot
varsågod (invitation) please
varuhus department store
vaskrensare plunger
vattenfall waterfall
WC (sign) restroom [toilet BE]
veckotidning magazine
vegetarian vegetarian
vem who
vid at
vilja *v* want

vilken which
vilse lost
visa *v* show
vitrin display case
vitt white
vykort postcard
våldtäkt *n* rape
våning floor (level, etage in building)
våtservetter för barn baby wipes
väderleksrapport weather forecast
väg road
vägkarta road map
välkommen welcome
välling baby formula
vän friend
vänster left (direction)
vänta wait
värde *n* value
värdesak *n* valuable
värme heat
väska bag
väster west
växel *n* change (money)
växelkontor currency exchange office
växelkursen exchange rate
växla change money

Y

yr dizzy
ytterliggare further (more)

Å

å stream
åka *v* travel, drive (motor vehicle)
åksjuka motion sickness [travel sickness BE]
ålder age
återlämna *v* return (give back)
äkta authentic
äkthetsbevis certifica authenticity
älska *v* love
ändra *v* change (reser
ändra på *v* alter
änka widow
änkling widower
äta *v* eat

Ö

ögonblick (one) mom
öppet open
öppettider business h [opening hours BE]
öppna *v* open
öra ear
öre öre (Swedish curr
örhänge earring
öster east
över across (the road)
överfall mugging
övergångsställe för f pedestrian crossing
översätta *v* translate
överviktsbagage exc

GUIDED TOUR OF *LITERATURE & COMPOSITION*, SECOND EDITION

"Why read literature? To many of us, that question seems as strange as asking "Why breathe?" Literature has been part of our life, family, school, and community for as long as we can remember. Of course, there are those who argue that what today's students need is preparation for the "real world," but in the push for practical university and workplace preparedness we sometimes overlook the importance of cultivating students' critical thinking skills and imaginations. Literature offers a chance to investigate ourselves and others, to study human nature, and to encounter complex and compelling ideas. How better to reflect on the demands of contemporary life than to study William Wordsworth's "The World Is Too Much with Us" alongside Nathalie Handal's "Caribe in Nueva York"? And does not the proffered wisdom of William Shakespeare, Emily Dickinson, Richard Blanco, and Natasha Trethewey provide important preparation for surviving and thriving in this complex world?

Literary analysis is an intellectual discipline that hones students' thinking by requiring them to probe a text deeply and analyze the means that writers employ to achieve their effects. Along with preparing students for the rigors of an Advanced Placement® exam, learning how to analyze a text and articulate a perspective prepares students for life, both in academia and in the workplace. This preparation and exploration are what we hope students achieve when they use *Literature & Composition* because it specifically targets the development of the skills and habits of mind that are the keys to their success in an Advanced Placement® Literature course."

— Carol Jago, Renée H. Shea, Lawrence Scanlon, and Robin Dissin Aufses

Welcome to *Literature & Composition*, Second Edition, a textbook designed specifically for the AP® English Literature & Composition course. We offer this guided tour of the book to introduce you to its structure and features.

NEW TO THIS EDITION

NEW! Chapter 4 — Close Reading: Analyzing Poetry — takes students step-by-step through the process of reading and writing close analyses of poetry. The instruction emphasizes the connection between the elements of style and meaning, providing solid preparation for Free Response Question 1 on the AP® Literature exam.

NEW! Texts in Context sections are fascinating casebooks that open up engaging avenues of investigation into the meaning of each chapter's Classic Text and the complex ideas it grapples with.

- **Chapter 5:** *The Metamorphosis* and the Modernist Vision
- **Chapter 6:** *Heart of Darkness* and the Legacy of Colonialism
- **Chapter 7:** *The Importance of Being Earnest* and the Satiric Tradition
- **Chapter 8:** *Hamlet* and the Evolution of Character
- **Chapter 9:** *Frankenstein* and the Ethics of Creation
- **Chapter 10:** *Othello* through Critical Lenses

MORE! Paired Poems, offering a wider range of selections for you and more practice for your students. There are now two or three sets of paired poems in each thematic chapter.

NEW! A full-color design, featuring visuals in their original format alongside the texts they inform. An analytical question connects each image back to the text, bringing both works to life, fostering creative analysis, and serving as a springboard to textual analysis.

MORE! Full-length works appear in *Literature & Composition*, Second Edition. With the addition of *Frankenstein* and *Othello*, this edition offers nine full-length works to prepare students for the open question of the AP® Literature exam:

- Susan Glaspell, *Trifles*
- August Wilson, *Fences*
- Franz Kafka, *The Metamorphosis*
- Joseph Conrad, *Heart of Darkness*
- James Joyce, *The Dead*
- Oscar Wilde, *The Importance of Being Earnest*
- William Shakespeare, *Hamlet*
- **NEW!** Mary Shelley, *Frankenstein*
- **NEW!** William Shakespeare, *Othello*

STRUCTURE OF *LITERATURE & COMPOSITION*, SECOND EDITION

Skill-Building Opening Chapters

1 Literature as Conversation: The Active Reader
2 The Big Picture: Analyzing Fiction and Drama
3 Close Reading: Analyzing Passages of Fiction
4 Close Reading: Analyzing Poetry

These opening chapters scaffold key skills for AP® success: reading closely, thinking critically, and writing persuasive literary analyses. Each chapter uses brief and accessible texts to introduce key concepts, then provides multiple opportunities for students to practice those skills.

Thematic Readings Chapters

5 Home and Family
6 Identity and Culture
7 Love and Relationships
8 Conformity and Rebellion
9 Tradition and Progress
10 War and Peace

Using readings that range from approachable to highly challenging works of recognized literary merit, along with rigorous guided literary analysis tasks, these chapters allow students to hone and master the skills built in the opening chapters.

Helpful Reference Section

MLA Guidelines for a List of Works Cited
Glossary

These brief reference guides give students and teachers resources for reinforcing documentation habits and clarifying key terminology.

INSIDE THE OPENING CHAPTERS (CHS. 1–4)

The four opening chapters introduce strategies and scaffolding that guide students toward deep reading of difficult texts while fostering an understanding of key literary terms and analytical techniques. Many students today need more support than ever, and with that in mind, we designed these opening chapters to be highly practical, approachable, and activity oriented. Chapters 2, 3, and 4 are designed to introduce the skills needed on the three essay prompts on the AP® Literature exam. These approaches to reading and writing are revisited repeatedly in the subsequent thematic chapters through the discussion and close-reading questions that follow each piece of literature and deepened through the Texts in Context sections, Close Reading workshops, and Suggestions for Writing prompts at the end of each thematic chapter.

Chapter 1 — Literature as Conversation: The Active Reader

In this chapter, we explore the purpose of literary analysis, introducing close-reading tools like annotation, reading journals, and think-aloud dialogues. These approaches and habits of mind lead to both insightful analysis and thoughtful conversation between and among the reader, the work, and its author.

Chapter 2 — The Big Picture: Analyzing Fiction and Drama

This chapter teaches students to analyze the major elements of fiction and drama — focusing on important literary elements such as character, setting, and theme — and includes instruction for writing the type of thoughtful, interpretive, complex literary analysis required by the open question on the AP® Literature exam.

Chapter 3 — Close Reading: Analyzing Passages of Fiction

In this chapter, we include instruction on close analysis, revealing how the elements of style create meaning in fiction. Students are also introduced to the process of writing a close-analysis essay on a passage of prose, the type of essay required by Free Response Question 2 on the AP® Literature exam.

NEW! Chapter 4 — Close Reading: Analyzing Poetry

This brand-new chapter provides step-by-step support in the type of literary analysis that is often the hardest for students to master, introducing students to close-reading strategies that connect the elements of style to meaning in poetry and offering instruction on writing a close analysis of both a single poem and a comparison and contrast of two poems.

INSIDE THE THEMATIC READINGS CHAPTERS (CHS. 5–10)

So often on the AP® Literature exam, students score poorly because they discuss stylistic and literary elements without connecting their analysis to meaning or acknowledging the complexity of the work. This portion of *Literature & Composition* is organized thematically to signal that ideas are central and that meaning is ultimately what literature is about.

The themes in this book — home and family, identity and culture, love and relationships, conformity and rebellion, tradition and progress, and war and peace — are those our students have found engaging and that are explored in many longer works of literature, both classic and contemporary. They are designed to foster classroom conversation, encourage students to ponder enduring questions, and promote connections not only between and among the texts themselves but also with the vibrant cultural conversations going on in the world today.

The thematic arrangement of this book offers students the opportunity to consider big questions — social, political, economic, aesthetic, and literary — through the eyes of William Shakespeare and Naomi Shihab Nye, Walt Whitman and Amit Majmudar, Franz Kafka and Gwendolyn Brooks, whose literary texts offer compelling perspectives on complex human issues. As students grapple with these issues, they read the literature closely and even reread one text in light of another.

The selections in *Literature & Composition*, Second Edition, range from the approachable to the challenging, and everything in between, to give students of various skill levels points of entry and opportunities to join the conversation.

Thematic Chapter Overview

Each thematic chapter includes the following key elements:

5 HOME AND FAMILY 148

*A **universal theme** designed to focus students' interpretation of the literature in the chapter.*

*A **Central Text** — a major work by a world-renowned author — is a rich work of exceptional literary merit that opens and anchors the chapter.*

*A **Classic Text** — a full-length work written before 1915 that exposes students to the challenging diction and syntax of earlier literature, which often appears on the AP® Literature exam.*

***NEW!** A **Texts in Context** section that explores intriguing interpretations and insights into important works — such as* Frankenstein *and ethics or* Othello *and critical literary perspectives — and is designed to enrich students' understanding of the complex issues each work illuminates.*

*A diverse collection of **Poetry,** spanning the sixteenth century to the present day, all exploring different angles of the chapter's theme.*

*A collection of **Fiction** — three short stories per chapter, from literary classics like Herman Melville's "Bartleby, the Scrivener" to fresh new finds like Phil Klay's "Ten Kliks South."*

*Two or more sets of **Paired Poems** to compare and contrast — a key AP® Literature skill.*

*A **Close Reading** section with exercises that focus on building stylistic analysis skills.*

***Suggestions for Writing** — from simulated AP® Literature exam prompts to longer essay assignments, research projects, creative writing ideas, and more — these prompts give students all the practice they need to hone their reading and writing skills.*

Central and Classic Texts Spark Discussion and Foster Critical Thinking

A Central Text and a Classic Text of significant literary merit begin and anchor each thematic chapter. These works invite students to delve deeply into the theme, forming a foundation for interpreting the stories and poems in the rest of the chapter. The Classic Texts challenge students to read literature from an earlier time, written for a very different audience than today's, with syntax and vocabulary that may be unfamiliar. These Classic Texts, which include such works as *Heart of Darkness*, *Hamlet*, *Frankenstein*, and *The Importance of Being Earnest*, enlarge students' background knowledge by offering windows into other times and other worlds.

Central Texts range from selections written by late twentieth-century writers, such as August Wilson and Flannery O'Connor, to pieces written by celebrated contemporary authors, such as Edwidge Danticat and Jhumpa Lahiri.

Texts in Context — Support for Reading Classic Texts

Designed specifically to broaden student understanding of complex, classic works of literature, Texts in Context sections ask students to apply high-level thinking skills to a collection of fiction, poetry, nonfiction, and visual texts that provide new insights into the chapter's Classic Text. Exploring connections between, among, and beyond the Texts in Context encourages students to consider the Classic Text in a new light — and guides them to deeper, more nuanced interpretations of its meaning that take into account a variety of literary, artistic, cultural, political, and historical issues. Through a series of questions and writing prompts, students are invited to enter the literary conversation and express their viewpoints on the big ideas reflected in these readings.

Paired Poems — Key Practice in Comparison and Contrast

Two or more pairs of poems in each thematic chapter provide practice in comparison and contrast, an essential AP® Literature skill. These pairings encourage students to explore different types of connections, whether the poems have similar topics, rely on similar allusions, represent different perspectives on the same subject, or even express similar emotions through different styles. These pairs help students go beyond surface similarities in order to understand both poems in greater depth.

Fiction and Poetry — Fresh and Familiar Selections

The Central Texts and Classic Texts are followed by a collection of rich, rigorous short stories and poems that appeal to sixteen- to eighteen-year-olds. These texts span the ages, drawing from work both familiar and fresh, building on classics by writers such as Emily Dickinson and Nathaniel Hawthorne but also departing from the usual fare by offering literature by authors from around the world, such as Warsan Shire, Chimamanda Ngozi Adichie, and Zbigniew Herbert, as well as a wealth of new American voices — including Gregory Pardlo, Natalie Diaz, and Phil Klay. Bridging the old and the new emphasizes that many questions and issues — about the nature of war or the concept of identity, for example — have captivated and puzzled humanity through the ages and across cultures.

Contemporary writers, such as Robin Coste Lewis, Karen Russell, Sandra Cisneros, and Sherman Alexie, continue to explore these issues.

Probing Questions — Targeted Practice for Key AP® Literature Skills

Throughout the book there are guided questions designed to direct students' reading and scaffold their emerging interpretation of the works.

The Central Texts and Classic Texts are followed by these types of questions:

- **Questions for Discussion** invite students to investigate the text, probing the work for meaning, and direct their attention to important ideas in the story, poem, or play.
- **Questions on Style and Structure** focus students on the technical and artistic aspects of the work. Responding to these questions will help them begin to analyze the tools writers employ to achieve an effect and prepare them for the kinds of essay and multiple-choice questions they will face on exams.
- **Suggestions for Writing** offer students multiple opportunities to use writing to explore their developing understanding of a text. In every set of writing suggestions, students are offered one or more questions resembling those on the AP® exam, and in some cases, students are asked to try their hand at the techniques the author has used.

Texts in Context sections contain questions after each individual text, culminating in a set of **Literature in Conversation** questions that encourage students to draw connections between, among, and beyond the Classic Text and Texts in Context.

Other selections in the book are accompanied by **Exploring the Text** questions that call for close, careful reading and ask students to discuss and interpret the work. These questions allow students to practice what they have learned in the opening chapters and to broaden their experience of literature.

Close Reading Hones Literary Analysis Skills

The Close Reading section at the end of each thematic chapter breaks down the close-reading process to explore how a writer uses elements of style to create meaning. Focusing on particular aspects of writing — connotation, figurative language, irony, tone, syntax, and imagery — this section offers students explanations of these elements using examples taken from the readings in the chapter. For instance, by scrutinizing how Mary Shelley, Hanif Kureishi, and Gerard Manley Hopkins employ syntax to convey meaning, students deepen their understanding of how literary texts work. The exercises that follow give students firsthand experience with the concepts and practice in analyzing works for a specific element of style, before inviting them to try out the technique in their own writing.

- **Chapter 5:** Connotation
- **Chapter 6:** Figurative Language
- **Chapter 7:** Irony
- **Chapter 8:** Tone
- **Chapter 9:** Syntax
- **Chapter 10:** Imagery

Suggestions for Writing — AP®-style Literary Analysis and Beyond

The Suggestions for Writing at the end of each chapter are prompts for longer writing projects. Expanding on the skills introduced in the opening chapters, these prompts give students the opportunity to practice the kind of writing required on the AP® exam and beyond. Most of these projects require students to use multiple literary sources — an important skill for their work in college classes.

Visual Texts — Images with a Purpose

We believe that visual literacy is crucial to being able to understand and analyze our world and that images in a textbook should not be mere decoration or even illustration. We made it our goal in this edition of *Literature & Composition* for every visual text to have a clear, authentic pedagogical purpose. Images were carefully selected to inform the reading of a print text, suggest new ideas, provide additional context, extend an understanding to the real world, or encourage students to make interesting connections.

This 2016 production of Giuseppe Verdi's opera *Otello*, based on *Othello*, takes place in a refugee camp. **Why do you think the director chose this setting? What parallels might be drawn between the struggles of refugees and those of Othello?**

Lluis Gene/AFP/Getty Images

WORLD-CLASS SUPPORT FOR TEACHERS

Teacher's Edition

Written by teachers for teachers, the Teacher's Edition offers essential tools and tips from master teachers, including suggestions for building context, approaches for close reading, places to check for understanding, and teaching ideas designed to engage students and differentiate instruction. All of this support is placed in the margins of the book, so you always have it right where you need it.

Teacher's Resource Flash Drive

This handy flash drive contains additional teacher and student resources for *Literature & Composition*, Second Edition, including:

- Suggested responses to questions
- Classroom strategies and how-tos
- Vocabulary support
- Key passages for annotation
- AP®-style essay prompts

Test Bank for AP® English Literature and Composition

Covering every piece in the thematic chapters, and including more than 1,200 simulated AP® multiple-choice questions, this test bank is our biggest ever for AP® Literature. This test bank is integrated into the e-book or available in ExamView format.

The ExamView Test Generator lets you quickly create paper, Internet, and LAN-based tests. You can create and format a test in minutes in a fully customizable platform that lets you enter your own questions, edit existing questions, set time limits, incorporate multimedia, and scramble both answer choice and question order to prevent cheating. Detailed results feed directly into a gradebook.

YOUR E-BOOK SOLUTION

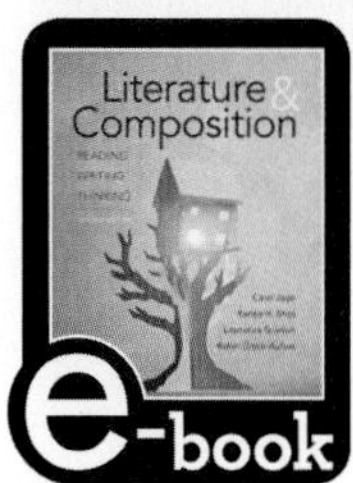

Literature & Composition, Second Edition, has an interactive e-book that offers the accessibility you want and the flexibility you need. The format features page fidelity that ensures the e-book matches the print text and allows each user to download and read the e-book on multiple devices. Use it on a PC or Mac, an iPad, or an Android tablet. All notes and assignments automatically sync to the device upon logging in. And our platform makes it supremely easy to communicate with your class, provide assignments, notes, and feedback, or give quizzes. Contact us for the latest digital options to support this text on your device of choice.

Teacher's Edition e-Book—The Ultimate Teacher's Resource

The Teacher's Edition of *Literature & Composition*, Second Edition, is also available in the e-book format, putting all of the teacher support materials right where you need them.

ACKNOWLEDGMENTS

We would like to thank the talented team at Bedford, Freeman, and Worth. We've relied on their expertise, enjoyed their enthusiasm, and appreciated their encouragement more than we can say. Their support started at the top with Publisher Ann Heath and Vice President of Sales Paul Altier. To say a simple thanks to Lisa Erdely, senior marketing manager, is to deal in understatement. Her unflagging determination, faith in the project, and creativity sustained us throughout this revision.

Since it does indeed take a village, we are grateful for the efforts of a supportive team. Our editorial assistant, Corrina Santos, is also a fine researcher and general problem solver. Our gifted and innovative media editor, Kim Morté, keeps us in the second decade of the twenty-first century. We are enormously thankful to Peter Jacoby, senior project editor, and Denise Quirk, copy editor, for their meticulous and tireless attention to details of language and design.

We have had the stunningly good luck to work with two remarkable Bedford editors. To Nathan Odell, who has been with us since the start of *Literature & Composition*, we send a thankful praise song for being a cheerleader, a taskmaster, a diplomat, at once an advocate and a chief skeptic, a perfectionist, and the best of friends — as well as our "dear reader." To Caitlin Kaufman, who led the team for this revision, we send continuous applause for her knowledge of contemporary writers, generous work ethic, commitment to ensuring that all students see themselves in the literature they study, and — most of all — her unfaltering vision for how to improve this book for students and teachers alike.

We are fortunate to have had the assistance of some amazing teachers at key times in this project, especially with the development of the Teacher's Edition and Teacher's Resource Flash Drive. Our thanks to Carlos Escobar, Charise Hallberg, Julie Horger, Maura Kelly, Steve Klinge, Mark Leidner, and Tom Tucker.

We are grateful to the reviewers who always kept us anchored in the world of the classroom reality and generously shared their amazing experience and expertise for both the first and second editions of *Literature & Composition*. Our thanks to Lance Balla, Barbara Bloy, Helen Boyd, Barbra A. Brooks-Barker, Brian Burnett, Chasidy Burton, Betsy Butler, Mary Calkin, Caryl Catzlaff, Jolinda Collins, Shirley Counsil, Cathy A. D'Agostino, Peter Drewniany, Jennifer Dooley, Carol Elsen, Michael Feuer, Andrew Foster, Elizabeth Gonsalves, Kelly E. Guilfoil, James Hausman III, David Herring, Jennifer Hiller, Allyson Howard, Erica Jacobs, Jan Kelly, Carol Krause, Tom Lippi, Joan Mangan, Kelsey Mapes, Marie Leone Meyer, Nancy Monroe, Tracy Mosca, Skip Nicholson, Jeffrey Nienaber, Sherlayne Nuckols, Frazier L. O'Leary Jr., Deborah Parker, Julia Parsons, Linda A. Pavich, Bill Pell, Catherine Pfaff, Sally P. Pfeifer, Amy Regis, Kyle Reynolds, Linda Rood, Jaclynn Rozansky, Heidi Rubin de la Borbolla, Edward Schmieder, Bobbi Scott, Conni Shelnut, Deborah Shepard, Pat Sherbert, William Smith, Larissa Snyder, Virginia Allen Speaks, Al Stout, Doranna Tindle, Karen Van Duyn, Addison Welp, Luke Wiseman, Carol Yoakley-Terrell, and David Youngblood. We are deeply grateful for spouses, children, friends, and family who have supported our efforts, given up their weekends and evenings to advise us, and kept the faith that this project was absolutely worthwhile and would eventually be finished!

Finally, we would like to thank our students over the years, including more than a few who have become admirable teachers themselves, for honoring the tradition of reading and writing that gives meaning to our lives.

This is the book we committed ourselves to developing for you and your students. We've brought to the task our many years of working with high school and college students as well as our deep love of literature, reading, and writing. We hope *Literature & Composition* helps you and your students and that you enjoy using it as much as we enjoyed writing it.

Best Wishes,

Carol Jago
Renée H. Shea
Lawrence Scanlon
Robin Dissin Aufses

CONTENTS

3 CLOSE READING: ANALYZING PASSAGES OF FICTION 78

4 CLOSE READING: ANALYZING POETRY 106

5 HOME AND FAMILY 148

Contents

CONTENTS BY GENRE

Fiction

Poetry

Drama

Nonfiction

Visual Texts

Book, Magazine, and Playbill Covers

Cartoons

Collage

Digital Art

Engravings, Murals, and Paintings

Maps

Photographs

Posters

Sculpture

Tapestry

Literature & Composition

READING

WRITING

THINKING

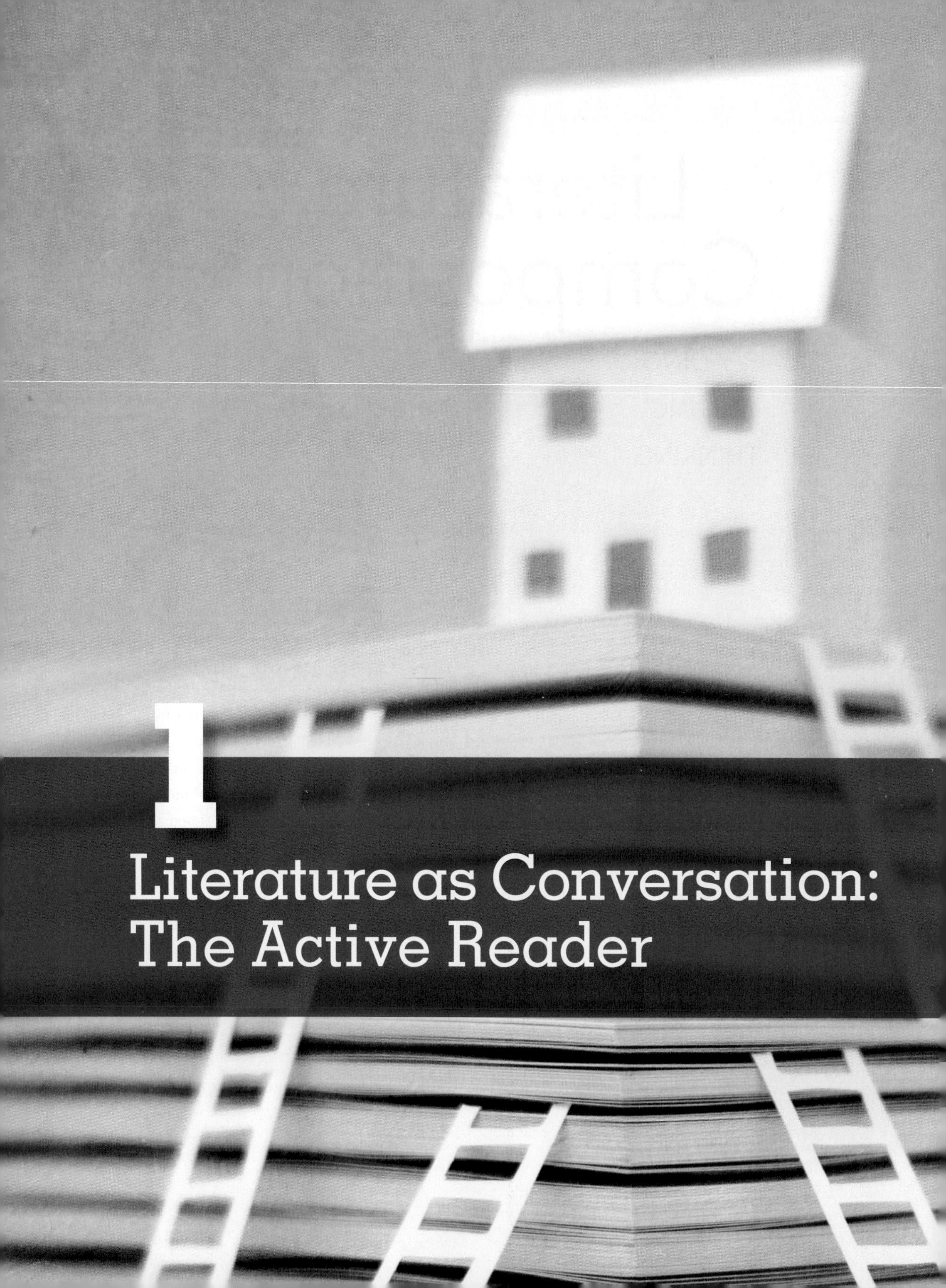

1 Literature as Conversation: The Active Reader

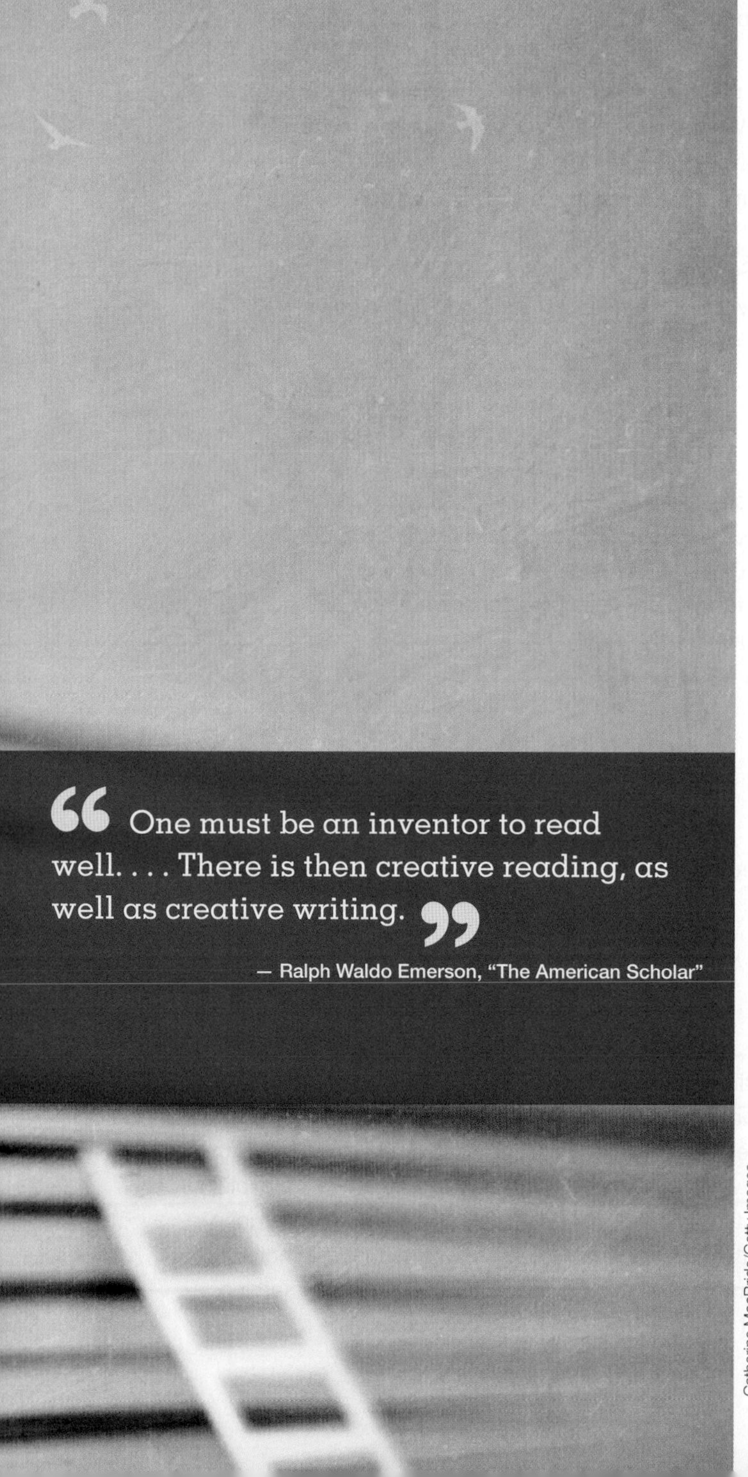

“One must be an inventor to read well. . . . There is then creative reading, as well as creative writing.”
— Ralph Waldo Emerson, “The American Scholar”

Catherine MacBride/Getty Images

We often think of reading as a solitary activity, a private moment. Reading poetry might even be a kind of meditation. Yet reading is also social, because even when we read sitting alone, we're in conversation — with both ourselves and the author. What we're reading might give voice to a feeling or an experience we've actually had, it might challenge our own beliefs, or it might invite us to enter an entirely unfamiliar world. And sometimes we extend that conversation by discussing what we read with friends or with classmates, whether online, in person, or in writing.

Generally, we do two types of reading. We read to gather information, and we read to discover ideas and appreciate the writer's craft. You might, for instance, read to figure out how to use all the features of a smart phone or determine what to do if your pet swallows a squeaky ball. You're looking for clear, accurate information. The second type of reading involves actively seeking a deeper understanding of the multiple layers in a text by exploring the language the author uses. It is a collaboration between the reader, the text, and the author to create meaning. Think of a piece of music.

The composer writes the score (the text), but it isn't until the musician plays it, or interprets it, that the music comes to life and takes on meaning. Bringing our own insight, expertise, and emotion into a work of literature is called being an active reader, and it is the type of reading we need to do with literature — whether poems, novels, stories, or plays. Active reading will be our focus throughout this book, and it is the foundation of discussing, analyzing, and writing about literature. It is the creative reading of creative writing.

Just because active reading is a creative process doesn't mean we skip the basic level of comprehending what's going on. Whether it's a poem or story, our first reading is usually pretty slow going, because we're trying to keep track of who's who, what the setting is, and what's happening. But at the same time, we're noticing connections between the words on the page and the big ideas and themes. We're looking at the details — we're starting to analyze. So, active readers interact with both the content and the craft — not only do they look at *what* a text means, they also examine *how* a text conveys that meaning.

Telling It Slant

One of the most famous mantras in creative writing is "show, don't tell." Creative, complex literature (the kind you're going to read in this book) doesn't tell readers what to think or feel — it *makes* them think; it *makes* them feel. Writers have to make their point through action, setting, language, and other tools to create impressions, emotions, and experiences. As the poet Emily Dickinson said:

> Tell all the truth but tell it slant —
> Success in Circuit lies
> Too bright for our infirm Delight
> The Truth's superb surprise
>
> As Lightning to the Children eased
> With explanation kind
> The Truth must dazzle gradually
> Or every man be blind —
>
> [c. 1868]

Dickinson suggests that indirection is the way toward "truth," more like a process of discovery than steps in an instruction manual. But why in a poem about "truth" do we find the word "lies"? Why must truth reveal itself — or be revealed "with explanation kind," the way we explain lightning to children while trying not to frighten them? the way we explain lightning to children while trying not to frighten them? In this short, somewhat enigmatic poem, Dickinson may be getting at the heart of what literature is: texts that ask more questions than they answer, that draw us in to explore them. In fact, reading something that disrupts our expectations might make us question a tradition, undermine a stereotype, broaden our sense of what is "right," or maybe make us see gray areas instead of black and white.

Such experiences can make us more empathetic, a crucial skill in navigating the complex social relationships in our personal and professional lives. Just as making sense of our lives and world requires going beyond a surface understanding, actively reading literary texts means being able to infer meanings that may only be suggested, to understand the significance of symbolic gestures, to comprehend not just what happens but what it means.

ACTIVITY

Discuss how "Spring in the Classroom" by Mary Oliver "tell[s] all the truth but tell[s] it slant."

Spring in the Classroom

MARY OLIVER

Elbows on dry books, we dreamed
Past Miss Willow Bangs, and lessons, and windows,
To catch all day glimpses and guesses of the greening woodlot,
Its secrets and increases,
Its hidden nests and kind.
And what warmed in us was no book-learning,
But the old mud blood murmuring,
Loosening like petals from bone sleep.
So spring surrounded the classroom, and we suffered to be kept indoors,
Droned through lessons, carved when we could with jackknives
Our pulsing initials into the desks, and grew
Angry to be held so, without pity and beyond reason,
By Miss Willow Bangs, her eyes two stones behind glass,
Her legs thick, her heart
In love with pencils and arithmetic.

So it went — one gorgeous day lost after another
While we sat like captives and breathed the chalky air
And the leaves thickened and birds called
From the edge of the world — till it grew easy to hate,
To plot mutiny, even murder. Oh, we had her in chains,
We had her hanged and cold, in our longing to be gone!
And then one day, Miss Willow Bangs, we saw you
As we ran wild in our three o'clock escape
Past the abandoned swings; you were leaning
All furry and blooming against the old brick wall
In the Art Teacher's arms.

[1972]

BECOMING AN ACTIVE READER

The more we read and reread, the more we "hear" the poem or passage in our head, and the more deeply we're likely to understand the language, the ideas, and how they connect. We certainly notice more details each time we return to the text. But how do you immerse yourself in the language and enjoy and explore the ideas at the same time? In this section, we'll discuss three strategies for active, engaged reading that you can apply to poetry, drama, and fiction. Each one involves a different way to connect with the text: annotating, journaling, and having a dialogue with a partner. You may find some of these more to your liking than others, and you might adapt or change them a bit to make them more useful to your own purposes. In any case, these strategies can help you process a piece of literature, and they will promote creative reading that leads to spirited discussions and lays the foundation for insightful writing.

Annotation

Annotation is the most important technique and habit of mind to develop as you become an active reader. Annotation is simply the process of noting, right on the text itself, words that strike you, phrases that confuse or thrill you, or places where you want to talk back to the speaker, a character, or even the author. Annotation is your running commentary as a reader. Ideally, you can write on the text itself, but if not, sticky notes will do. If you are reading on a screen, there will likely be various ways to annotate through color-coding and marginal notes and comments. Try to avoid just highlighting, because it doesn't require you to respond in words. Annotation is about writing down *your* observations, *your* questions. Highlighting alone can't do that — though it calls attention to details in a text, it doesn't require a reader's response.

Why bother to do this? In their best-selling book, *How to Read a Book*, scholars and avid readers Mortimer Adler and Charles van Doren sum it up:

> Why is marking a book indispensable to reading it? First, it keeps you awake — not merely conscious, but wide awake. Second, reading, if it is active, is thinking, and thinking tends to express itself in words, spoken or written. The person who says he knows what he thinks but cannot express it usually does not know what he thinks. Third, writing your reactions down helps you to remember the thoughts of the author.

What you as a reader get from annotation is a deeper understanding, and one that is more likely to stick in your memory. You can then use that knowledge to help inform your discussions with others, or improve your writing about the text.

Once you finish, your annotation might look like a jumble of ideas. Sometimes it is helpful to make annotation a two-step process: annotate directly onto the text first, then write a paragraph summing up your observations. This informal writing can help you explore your thoughts and bring together the observations you made during the annotation.

Let's try annotating Shakespeare's Sonnet 29:

Could mean money, could mean luck.

Probably not literal eyes

Powerful image

Shoeless? Look this up.

Lots of self pity.

Like "fortune" in line one, mixing the idea of money with other good things

Meaning handsome, I guess?

No idea what art and scope refer to here.

This "yet" seems to be a turning point.

Is that just a shortened "happily"?

Vivid image

Another reference to heaven. Last time it was "deaf," now there is singing.

Weird to bring "sullen" back in here when everything else is so uplifting.

Back to the money thing!

Ah, so that is why he was talking about money, to set up this last line. Now I'm seeing a double-meaning in the word "state," meaning both what a king rules over, and simply "situation."

When, in disgrace with fortune and men's eyes,
I all alone beweep my outcast state,
And trouble deaf heaven with my bootless cries,
And look upon myself, and curse my fate,
Wishing me like to one more rich in hope,
Featur'd like him, like him with friends possess'd,
Desiring this man's art and that man's scope,
With what I most enjoy contented least;
Yet in these thoughts myself almost despising,
Haply I think on thee, and then my state,
Like to the lark at break of day arising
From sullen earth, sings hymns at heaven's gate;
For thy sweet love remember'd such wealth brings
That then I scorn to change my state with kings.

[1609]

While the annotation definitely shows an active, engaged reader, there are so many insights and ideas and questions and observations — it's a bit of a noisy process. So, to begin sorting through and organizing, as well as figuring out what you need to do next to deepen your understanding, let's write a paragraph or two of exploratory writing. This will help you sift through your observations and order your thoughts.

As I reached the end of the poem, I noticed that he has been playing with this idea of money throughout to set up that line about being richer than a king at the end. So, looking back at the beginning we see "fortune" in line 1, "rich in hope" in line 5, "friends possess'd" in line 6, "man's scope" in line 7 (which I'm thinking means the scope of his wealth? still not entirely sure), and obviously "wealth" in the second-to-last line. These are all references to possessions and wealth that establish the speaker as poor in so many ways, but rich in love because he has this person—his love. The other interesting thing is how he treated heaven: first it's deaf, and then it's a place with a lark singing hymns at its gates. That was an interesting reversal. Also, apparently "bootless" means futile.

ACTIVITY

Following is another sonnet, "Golden Retrievals" by Mark Doty. Take the poem through the two-step annotation process we have just discussed. Look for things you find interesting, language you find powerful, and lines that are confusing or compelling.

Golden Retrievals

MARK DOTY

Fetch? Balls and sticks capture my attention
seconds at a time. Catch? I don't think so.
Bunny, tumbling leaf, a squirrel who's — oh
joy — actually scared. Sniff the wind, then

I'm off again: muck, pond, ditch, residue
of any thrillingly dead thing. And you?
Either you're sunk in the past, half our walk,
thinking of what you never can bring back,

or else you're off in some fog concerning
— tomorrow, is that what you call it? My work:
to unsnare time's warp (and woof!), retrieving,
my haze-headed friend, you. This shining bark,

a Zen master's bronzy gong, calls you here,
entirely, now: bow-wow, bow-wow, bow-wow.

[1998]

Reading Journal

A basic reading journal contains just two columns: on the left, you identify a phrase, line, or passage; on the right, you comment on it. If you're keeping a journal to keep you focused as you read an entire novel, you will probably write as you read. But if you're journaling as preparation for analyzing a shorter passage or a poem, you'll have a chance to read it first, then write in your journal as you reread. When it comes time to write, the reading journal is one way for you to keep a record of passages that will become your textual evidence in your essay. When you're writing under time constraints, you probably won't be able to do a formal journal, but the habit of mind that you develop by practicing journal writing should instill an analytical approach that leads to strong interpretive writing.

Remember that you're "commenting" as an active reader, so you might ask questions, record personal reactions, note a striking image or phrase, investigate patterns or shifts that puzzle you, explore multiple meanings, or reflect on something that bothers or unsettles you. Sometimes it can be helpful to paraphrase a complicated passage, but avoid just paraphrasing the entire piece — that's not going to help you understand the nuances of the text.

Let's look at an example based on a reading of the following passage, taken from the short story "Everyday Use" by Alice Walker. It takes place in the 1960s, and in this early section of the story, Mama, the narrator, is anticipating her precocious daughter Dee's visit home from college.

from **Everyday Use**

ALICE WALKER

You've no doubt seen those TV shows where the child who has "made it" is confronted, as a surprise, by her own mother and father, tottering in weakly from backstage. (A pleasant surprise, of course: What would they do if parent and child came on the show only to curse out and insult each other?) On TV mother and child embrace and smile into each other's faces. Sometimes the mother and father weep, the child wraps them in her arms and leans across the table to tell how she would not have made it without their help. I have seen these programs.

Sometimes I dream a dream in which Dee and I are suddenly brought together on a TV program of this sort. Out of a dark and soft-seated limousine I am ushered into a bright room filled with many people. There I meet a smiling, gray, sporty man like Johnny Carson who shakes my hand and tells me what a fine girl I have. Then we are on the stage and Dee is embracing me with tears in her eyes. She pins on my dress a large orchid, even though she has told me once that she thinks orchids are tacky flowers.

In real life I am a large, big-boned woman with rough, man-working hands. In the winter I wear flannel nightgowns to bed and overalls during the day. I can kill and clean a hog as mercilessly as a man. My fat keeps me hot in zero weather. I can work outside all day, breaking ice to get water for washing; I can eat pork liver cooked over the open fire minutes after it comes steaming from the hog. One winter I knocked a bull calf straight in the brain between the eyes with a sledge hammer and had the meat hung up to chill before nightfall. But of course all this does not show on television. I am the way my daughter would want me to be: a hundred pounds lighter, my skin like an uncooked barley pancake. My hair glistens in the hot bright lights. Johnny Carson has much to do to keep up with my quick and witty tongue.

But that is a mistake. I know even before I wake up. Who ever knew a Johnson with a quick tongue? Who can even imagine me looking a strange white man in the eye? It seems to me I have talked to them always with one foot raised in flight, with my head fumed in whichever way is farthest from them. Dee, though. She would always look anyone in the eye. Hesitation was no part of her nature.

[1973]

Text	Commentary
"those TV shows where the child who has 'made it' is confronted, as a surprise, by her own mother and father."	Sounds like a reality show, or more like the old Oprah shows — very emotional and dramatic.
"dream a dream"	Might have just said, "I dream" — but repetition emphasizes that Mama feels it's unlikely this will ever happen.
"Out of a dark and soft-seated limousine I am ushered into a bright room filled with many people."	The setting feels unreal, contrast of dark and light, comfort and discomfort.
"Johnny Carson has much to do to keep up with my quick and witty tongue."	Who is Johnny Carson? An important reference?
"In real life I am a large, big-boned woman . . . nightfall."	Mama describes herself as anything but fancy or sophisticated. She's a hard-working, physically powerful woman. She seems proud of it — no apology.
"I am the way my daughter would want me to be."	Contrast between reality and dream. Maybe a typical mother-daughter conflict?
"I am . . . a hundred pounds lighter, my skin like an uncooked barley pancake . . . my quick and witty tongue."	Mama believes her daughter wishes she fit in with mainstream culture, more sophisticated and urbane.
"Who can even imagine me looking a strange white man in the eye?"	More contrast between mother and daughter, between Dee's idea of what her mother should be and who she really is.
"Hesitation was no part of her nature."	Mama seems proud of Dee, even though she knows Dee is embarrassed by her.

If you go back over this journal, what patterns do you see? That contrast between mother and daughter is pretty obvious, but it's also a signal of something more complex. Mama recognizes how her daughter sees her and seems to appreciate Dee's more assertive personality, even dreams of pleasing her. Yet Dee — the talented college girl — fails to reciprocate with much appreciation of her mother.

Notice, too, that as you start to discern patterns or bigger ideas, you're doing so with textual evidence — the quotations on the left side — to back up an emerging interpretation.

"Everyday Use," a fairly contemporary story, is pretty accessible. The reference to the Johnny Carson show, one of the original late-night talk shows, might be unfamiliar, but most of the vocabulary is probably familiar to you, and the sentence structure is straightforward. When you read poetry, the reading journal can help you to understand literally what is going on and then begin to interpret.

ACTIVITY

Read "The Harlem Dancer," a poem by the Jamaican-born Harlem Renaissance poet Claude McKay. Engage with the text by commenting on language or ideas and posing questions about anything that you feel you don't understand or about interpretations that you begin to develop.

The Harlem Dancer

CLAUDE McKAY

Applauding youths laughed with young prostitutes
And watched her perfect, half-clothed body sway;
Her voice was like the sound of blended flutes
Blown by black players upon a picnic day.
She sang and danced on gracefully and calm,
The light gauze hanging loose about her form;
To me she seemed a proudly-swaying palm
Grown lovelier for passing through a storm.
Upon her swarthy neck black shiny curls
Luxuriant fell; and tossing coins in praise,
The wine-flushed, bold-eyed boys, and even the girls,
Devoured her shape with eager, passionate gaze;
But looking at her falsely-smiling face,
I knew her self was not in that strange place.

[1917]

Think-Aloud Dialogue

The techniques we've discussed so far are things you can do when you are reading alone. This strategy, in contrast, is collaborative (as the name *dialogue* suggests). The purpose of a think-aloud dialogue is to take the sort of commentary — ideas, questions, revelations — that you have been doing on paper as annotations or a reading journal, and turn them into an oral conversation with a partner — who can then agree, disagree, add to the idea, contribute an observation of his or her own, and move the conversation forward.

Step one of doing a think-aloud is to take turns reading with a partner. You might read a sentence, or a line of poetry, or just a few words. Just keep to small chunks that invite discussion. The person reading also initiates the commentary on what he or she has just read. The partner can then respond, both to the text and the reader's commentary. Keep this process going until you've finished the text.

As the reader and commentator, you can pose questions about anything that confuses you, whether it's a vocabulary word, a complex sentence, or an idea. You might note specific uses of language that strike you as especially powerful or vivid. You might even paraphrase a line that is perplexing or complicated. The key is to respond directly to each other, and build on your partner's comments — to have a conversation.

We opened this chapter with Ralph Waldo Emerson's assertion that there is "creative reading as well as creative writing." We explored that idea, discussing ways to become an active, engaged — and creative — reader. Whether you're reading a contemporary novel that immediately grabs your interest or an older poem that might take some time to appreciate, you've practiced a few approaches to active reading: annotation, a reading journal, and a think-aloud dialogue.

ACTIVITY

With a partner, try a think-aloud dialogue with the opening of *Swamplandia!*, a novel by Karen Russell about a family-owned alligator-wrestling theme park in the Florida Everglades.

from Swamplandia!

KAREN RUSSELL

Our mother performed in starlight. Whose innovation this was I never discovered. Probably it was Chief Bigtree's idea, and it was a good one — to blank the follow spot and let a sharp moon cut across the sky, unchaperoned; to kill the microphone; to leave the stage lights' tin eyelids scrolled and give the tourists in the stands a chance to enjoy the darkness of our island; to encourage the whole stadium to gulp air along with Swamplandia!'s star performer, the world-famous alligator wrestler Hilola Bigtree. Four times a week, our mother climbed the ladder above the Gator Pit in a green two-piece bathing suit and stood on the edge of the diving board, breathing. If it was windy, her long hair flew around her face, but the rest of her stayed motionless. Nights in the swamp were dark and star-lepered — our island was thirty-odd miles off the grid of mainland lights — and although your naked eye could easily find the ball of Venus and the sapphire hairs of the Pleiades, our mother's body was just lines, a smudge against the palm trees.

[2011]

ACTIVITY

Take a few moments to reflect on the reading strategies in this chapter.

- **Do you find one of these more comfortable or useful to you than another? Why?**
- **Does one strategy seem to apply more naturally to fiction than poetry?**
- **Is one more helpful in a limited time frame, another more likely to keep you focused when you have less structured time?**
- **Are there other strategies you've used on your own or in another class that you think are useful additions to your repertoire?**

Discuss these questions as you reflect upon the work you've done in this chapter. You might want to use a passage from a poem or novel you know as an example in support of your viewpoint.

2
The Big Picture: Analyzing Fiction and Drama

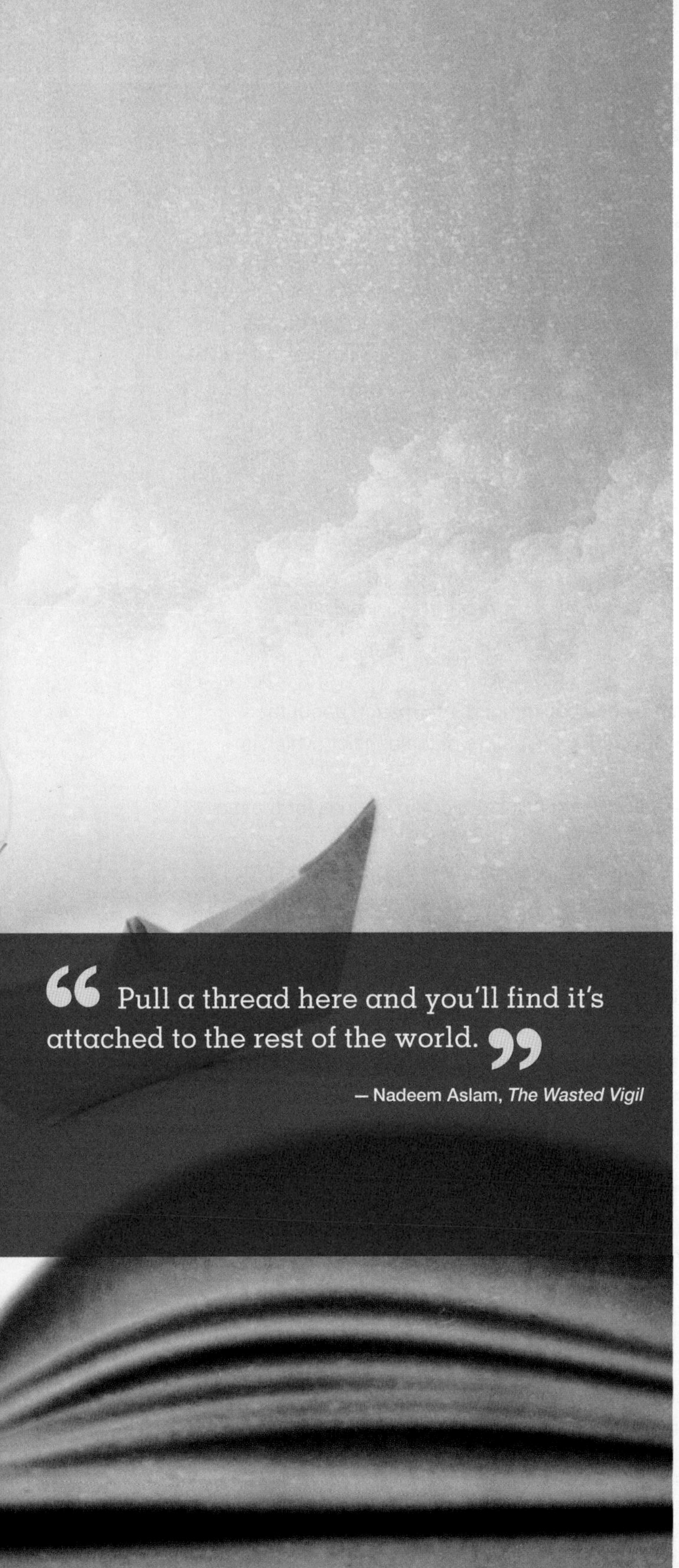

"Pull a thread here and you'll find it's attached to the rest of the world."
— Nadeem Aslam, *The Wasted Vigil*
Catherine MacBride/Getty Images

When someone asks us about a novel, play, or short story, we usually respond by describing what happened, retelling the plot in our own words. After all, who doesn't enjoy a good page-turner? But in literary fiction and drama, the way the story is told and the ideas the piece explores may be just as important as the events of the plot. In these pieces, plots may be built on conflicts within a character or between characters, which play out in a particular setting. The story is told to us from a certain point of view. Sometimes there are symbols that carry more than a literal meaning. An author uses these elements to deliver a message or theme. By studying how each of these literary elements works, both individually and together, we can begin to understand how they produce the meaning of the work as a whole.

ELEMENTS OF FICTION

Plot

Essentially, **plot** is what happens in a **narrative**. Yet plot is more than a series of events; authors must arrange **conflicts**, complications, and resolutions to create logical cause-and-effect relationships. Readers must understand not just *what* is happening but also *why* it's happening. A plot must be believable, though it doesn't have to be realistic.

A conventional narrative — whether in a short story, novel, or play — typically involves five main stages:

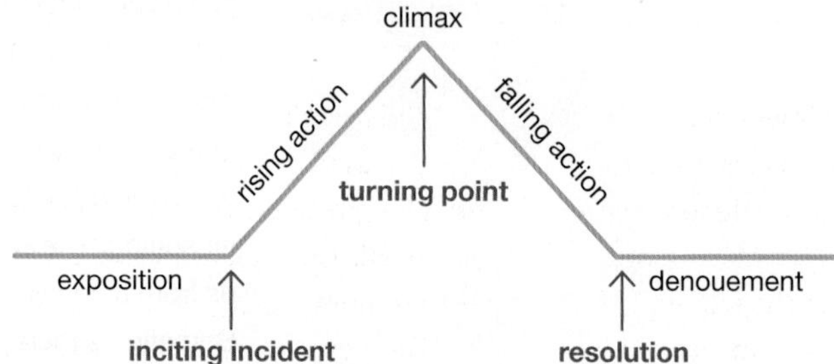

- **Exposition:** This opening section provides background information about the characters, setting, and situation, describing the nature of the conflict, which is generally an unstable situation.
- **Rising action**: After an inciting incident, the conflict and complications for the main character begin to build.
- **Climax**: The climax occurs when the emotional tension or **suspense** of the plot reaches its peak. The climax may include a turning point where the fortunes of the protagonist improve (in **comedy**) or worsen (in **tragedy**). Building to the climax usually occupies most of a story, and what follows is comparatively brief.
- **Falling action**: This section details the result (or fallout) of the climax or turning point. In this phase, the conflict gets resolved.
- **Denouement** (pronounced *day-noo-mah*): This French word means "untying the knot." In this often very brief phase, the conflict has been resolved, and balance is restored to the world of the story. In fairy tales, this phase is often represented by a single sentence: "And they lived happily ever after." The denouement was traditionally used to tell "the moral of the story," but writers in the twentieth and twenty-first centuries frequently close without this final **resolution**, leaving readers to ponder the possible meanings of what came before.

It bears repeating that this is a structure for traditional narratives and was originally used to describe ancient Greek and Shakespearean plays. Most modern stories do not follow this model exactly, and it can be interesting to investigate how and where they depart from it.

Plot may follow a chronological sequence, particularly in realistic fiction and drama, but sometimes writers deliberately present events in a manner that requires readers to assemble them into a cohesive pattern. A story may begin ***in medias res,*** a Latin term meaning "in the middle of the action" — that is, just as an important event is about to take place. Homer's *Iliad*, for example, opens not in the first year of the Trojan War but after nine years of fighting. Writers may also employ **flashback** to describe events that have taken place before the story begins, or **foreshadowing** to hint at things that might happen later in the story.

Let's look at a short story, "One of These Days" by Gabriel García Márquez, a Nobel Prize–winning author from Colombia.

One of These Days

GABRIEL GARCÍA MÁRQUEZ

Monday dawned warm and rainless. Aurelio Escovar, a dentist without a degree, and a very early riser, opened his office at six. He took some false teeth, still mounted in their plaster mold, out of the glass case and put on the table a fistful of instruments which he arranged in size order, as if they were on display. He wore a collarless striped shirt, closed at the neck with a golden stud, and pants held up by suspenders. He was erect and skinny, with a look that rarely corresponded to the situation, the way deaf people have of looking.

When he had things arranged on the table, he pulled the drill toward the dental chair and sat down to polish the false teeth. He seemed not to be thinking about what he was doing, but worked steadily, pumping the drill with his feet, even when he didn't need it.

After eight he stopped for a while to look at the sky through the window, and he saw two pensive buzzards who were drying themselves in the sun on the ridgepole of the house next door. He went on working with the idea that before lunch it would rain again. The shrill voice of his eleven-year-old son interrupted his concentration.

"Papa."

"What?" 5

"The Mayor wants to know if you'll pull his tooth."

"Tell him I'm not here."

He was polishing a gold tooth. He held it at arm's length, and examined it with his eyes half closed. His son shouted again from the little waiting room.

"He says you are, too, because he can hear you."

The dentist kept examining the tooth. Only 10
when he had put it on the table with the finished work did he say:

"So much the better."

He operated the drill again. He took several pieces of a bridge out of a cardboard box where he kept the things he still had to do and began to polish the gold.

"Papa."

"What?"

He still hadn't changed his expression. 15

"He says if you don't take out his tooth, he'll shoot you."

Without hurrying, with an extremely tranquil movement, he stopped pedaling the drill, pushed it away from the chair, and pulled the lower drawer of the table all the way out. There was a revolver. "OK," he said. "Tell him to come and shoot me."

He rolled the chair over opposite the door, his hand resting on the edge of the drawer. The Mayor appeared at the door. He had shaved the left side of his face, but the other side, swollen and in pain, had a five-day-old beard. The dentist saw many nights of desperation in his dull eyes. He closed the drawer with his fingertips and said softly:

"Sit down."

"Good morning," said the Mayor.

"Morning," said the dentist.

While the instruments were boiling, the Mayor leaned his skull on the headrest of the chair and felt better. His breath was icy. It was a poor office: an old wooden chair, the pedal drill, a glass case with ceramic bottles. Opposite the chair was a window with a shoulder-high cloth curtain. When he felt the dentist approach, the Mayor braced his heels and opened his mouth.

Aurelio Escovar turned his head toward the light. After inspecting the infected tooth, he closed the Mayor's jaw with a cautious pressure of his fingers.

"It has to be without anesthesia," he said.

"Why?"

"Because you have an abscess."

The Mayor looked him in the eye. "All right," he said, and tried to smile. The dentist did not return the smile. He brought the basin of sterilized instruments to the worktable and took them out of the water with a pair of cold tweezers, still without hurrying. Then he pushed the spittoon with the tip of his shoe, and went to wash his hands in the washbasin. He did all this without looking at the Mayor. But the Mayor didn't take his eyes off him.

It was a lower wisdom tooth. The dentist spread his feet and grasped the tooth with the hot forceps. The Mayor seized the arms of the chair, braced his feet with all his strength, and felt an icy void in his kidneys, but didn't make a sound. The dentist moved only his wrist. Without rancor, rather with a bitter tenderness, he said:

"Now you'll pay for our twenty dead men."

The Mayor felt the crunch of bones in his jaw, and his eyes filled with tears. But he didn't breathe until he felt the tooth come out. Then he saw it through his tears. It seemed so foreign to his pain that he failed to understand his torture of the five previous nights.

Bent over the spittoon, sweating, panting, he unbuttoned his tunic and reached for the handkerchief in his pants pocket. The dentist gave him a clean cloth.

"Dry your tears," he said.

The Mayor did. He was trembling. While the dentist washed his hands, he saw the crumbling ceiling and a dusty spider web with spider's eggs and dead insects. The dentist returned, drying his hands. "Go to bed," he said, "and gargle with salt water." The Mayor stood up, said goodbye with a casual military salute, and walked toward the door, stretching his legs, without buttoning up his tunic.

"Send the bill," he said.

"To you or the town?"

The Mayor didn't look at him. He closed the door and said through the screen:

"It's the same damn thing."

[1962]

This very short story takes place over a few hours, and the plot seems quite simple: a poor dentist pulls the wisdom tooth of the mayor. Yet even this brief story more or less follows the conventional narrative structure. Márquez opens with two paragraphs of exposition that introduce Aurelio Escovar and his dental office. When Escovar tells his son to lie to the mayor and say he is not in, we recognize conflict — something's amiss. The dentist goes about his work until his son tells him that the mayor has threatened to shoot him if he does not pull the tooth. The dentist makes his revolver available and agrees to attend to the mayor. Suspense is mounting by this point because of the potentially volatile situation.

In less than a page, a visit to the dentist has become a matter of life and death. The action rises as the dentist prepares for the extraction and denies the mayor anesthesia, and reaches a climax when the dentist tells the mayor that he will "pay for our twenty dead men" (para. 29) as he pulls the tooth. Experiencing such acute pain that he tears up, the mayor seems to have been defanged, literally and figuratively, and the dentist emerges victorious. However, the story does not end at this climactic moment. The falling action occurs when the dentist asks if the bill should go to the mayor or the town, and the mayor replies that they are the same thing. This plot unfolds and ends without a denouement; in fact, the ending suggests that the conflict is not entirely over. Nonetheless, in the world of this story, a shootout was averted, and order has been restored.

The following questions will help guide your analysis of plot:

- Is the plot arranged in chronological order, or does it begin *in medias res*?
- Does the plot involve a flashback? If so, what is its purpose?
- What is the nature of the conflict?
- What conditions at the outset make the situation unstable?
- Is the conflict external or internal?
- What is the high point, or climax?
- How is the conflict resolved? If there is no resolution, why not?
- Is there a denouement? If not, why is the story inconclusive?
- What patterns do you find in the plot's structure?

ACTIVITY

Choose a fairy tale, legend, or folktale and analyze its plot. Identify specific parts of the plot, such as exposition, rising action, climax, falling action, and denouement, and examine whether the plot employs flashbacks or begins in medias res.

Character

Character and plot go hand in hand because the conflict that structures a plot usually arises between two or more characters, as we saw in "One of These Days." In a plot with an external conflict, the story usually has a **protagonist**, or main character, who is in conflict with another person, called the **antagonist**. A conflict may also be internal, such as those in which a character struggles with temptation or tries to reconcile two incompatible traits. The main characters in a literary work grow or change over the course of the story or play; in fact, that change often structures the plot. The clearest example of character change structuring a plot is seen in a **coming-of-age story**, also called a **bildungsroman**, which chronicles how a young character grows from innocence to experience. For a character's growth to be believable, it must be clearly motivated by the circumstances of the story. Sometimes the change is gradual and sometimes it is sudden, as with an **epiphany**, a term Irish author James Joyce used to describe when a character suddenly realizes something significant about life.

Characters commonly fall into two categories: round (also called dynamic) or flat (also called static). The protagonist is typically a **round character**, one who exhibits a range of emotions and changes over the course of the story. Round characters have multiple personality traits and thus resemble real people. **Flat characters** embody only one or two traits and provide a background for the protagonist's actions. A common type of flat character is the **foil**, a contrasting character who allows the protagonist to stand out more distinctly. **Stock characters** may represent stereotypes, such as the absent-minded professor or the town drunk, occasionally providing comic relief.

Developing Character

Authors can reveal character either directly or indirectly. **Direct characterization** occurs when a narrator explicitly describes the background, motivation, temperament, or appearance of a character. In Jane Austen's *Pride and Prejudice*, for instance, we are told directly that Mrs. Bennet "was a woman of mean understanding, little information, and uncertain temper. When she was discontented, she fancied herself nervous. The business of her life was to get her daughters married." **Indirect characterization** occurs when an author shows rather than tells us what a character is like through what he or she says, does, or thinks, or what others say about the character.

Let's take a look at another excerpt from *Pride and Prejudice* by Jane Austen. Notice the way Austen directly and indirectly characterizes Mr. Darcy.

from Pride and Prejudice

JANE AUSTEN

Mr. Bingley was good looking and gentlemanlike; he had a pleasant countenance, and easy, unaffected manners. His sisters were fine women, with an air of decided fashion. His brother-in-law, Mr. Hurst, merely looked the gentleman; but his friend Mr. Darcy soon drew the attention of the room by his fine, tall person, handsome features, noble mien; and the report which was in general circulation within five minutes after his entrance, of his having ten thousand a year. The gentlemen pronounced him to be a fine figure of a man, the ladies declared he was much handsomer than Mr. Bingley, and he was looked at with great admiration for about half the evening, till his manners gave a disgust which turned the tide of his popularity; for he was discovered to be proud, to be above his company, and above being pleased; and not all his large estate in Derbyshire could then save him from having a most forbidding, disagreeable countenance, and being unworthy to be compared with his friend.

Mr. Bingley had soon made himself acquainted with all the principal people in the room; he was lively and unreserved, danced every dance, was angry that the ball closed so early, and talked of giving one himself at Netherfield. Such amiable qualities must speak for themselves. What a contrast between him and his friend! Mr. Darcy danced only once with Mrs. Hurst and once with Miss Bingley, declined being introduced to any other lady, and spent the rest of the evening in walking about the room, speaking occasionally to one of his own party. His character was decided. He was the proudest, most disagreeable man in the world, and every body hoped that he would never come there again. Amongst the most violent against him was Mrs. Bennet, whose dislike of his general behaviour was sharpened into particular resentment by his having slighted one of her daughters.

Elizabeth Bennet had been obliged, by the scarcity of gentlemen, to sit down for two dances; and during part of that time, Mr. Darcy had been standing near enough for her to overhear a conversation between him and Mr. Bingley, who came from the dance for a few minutes to press his friend to join it.

"Come, Darcy," said he, "I must have you dance. I hate to see you standing about by yourself in this stupid manner. You had much better dance."

5 "I certainly shall not. You know how I detest it, unless I am particularly acquainted with my partner. At such an assembly as this, it would be insupportable. Your sisters are engaged, and there is not another woman in the room whom it would not be a punishment to me to stand up with."

"I would not be so fastidious as you are," cried Bingley, "for a kingdom! Upon my honour, I never met with so many pleasant girls in my life, as I have this evening; and there are several of them, you see, uncommonly pretty."

"*You* are dancing with the only handsome girl in the room," said Mr. Darcy, looking at the eldest Miss Bennet.

"Oh! she is the most beautiful creature I ever beheld! But there is one of her sisters sitting down just behind you, who is very pretty, and I dare say, very agreeable. Do let me ask my partner to introduce you."

"Which do you mean?" and turning round, he looked for a moment at Elizabeth, till catching her eye, he withdrew his own and coldly said, "She is tolerable; but not handsome enough to tempt *me*; and I am in no humour at present to give consequence to young ladies who are slighted by other men. You had better return to your partner and enjoy her smiles, for you are wasting your time with me."

[1813]

Austen's narrator offers direct commentary on the physical appearance of Mr. Darcy, noting his "fine, tall person, handsome features, noble mien," and points out that he is quite wealthy. The narrator also explains that Darcy's "manners gave a disgust which turned the tide of his popularity" (para. 1). But much of the characterization is indirect: we see Darcy in action. Bingley acts as a foil, or contrasting character, with his warmth emphasizing Darcy's cool, aloof nature. The dialogue between Bingley and Darcy allows the latter to speak for himself, and what he says further characterizes him as arrogant. His meeting Elizabeth's eye, then turning away with a judgmental comment, suggests his inflated sense of self-importance.

The following questions will help guide your analysis of character:

- Who are the main characters in this story? Who is the protagonist? Who is the antagonist?
- What do we know about them? How does the author provide that information? Are the descriptions and characterizations direct or indirect?
- What is their relationship to each other?
- How do they change from beginning to end?
- What is the function of the minor characters?
- Do some characters see themselves differently from the way readers see them? If so, how?

ACTIVITY

***Fools Crow*, a bildungsroman by Great Plains Indian writer James Welch, begins by introducing the protagonist, White Man's Dog, who will later earn the name Fools Crow. Discuss the direct and indirect methods Welch uses to characterize him in the following passage.**

from Fools Crow

JAMES WELCH

Now that the weather had changed, the moon of the falling leaves turned white in the blackening sky and White Man's Dog was restless. He chewed the stick of dry meat and watched Cold Maker gather his forces. The black clouds moved in the north in circles, their dance a slow deliberate fury. It was almost night, and he looked back down into the flats along the Two Medicine River. The lodges of the Lone Eaters were illuminated by cooking fires within. It was that time of evening when even the dogs rest and the horses graze undisturbed along the grassy banks.

White Man's Dog raised his eyes to the west and followed the Backbone of the World from south to north until he could pick out Chief Mountain. It stood a little apart from the other mountains, not as tall as some but strong, its square granite face a landmark to all who passed. But it was more than a landmark to the Pikunis, Kainahs and Siksikas, the three tribes of the Blackfeet, for it was on top of Chief Mountain that the blackhorn skull pillows of the great warriors still lay. On those skulls Eagle Head and Iron Breast had dreamed their visions in the long-ago, and the animal helpers had made them strong in spirit and fortunate in war.

Not so lucky was White Man's Dog. He had little to show for his eighteen winters. His father, Rides-at-the-door, had many horses and three wives. He himself had three horses and no wives. His animals were puny, not a blackhorn runner among them. He owned a musket and no powder and his animal helper was weak.

[1986]

Setting

Setting indicates the time and place, the when and where, of a literary text. Author Eudora Welty described it as "the named, identified, concrete, exact and exacting, and therefore credible, gathering spot of all that has been felt, is about to be experienced." It includes such objective facts as the nation or town, date and time, weather and season in which the story occurs. If events occur on a dark and stormy night, we can reasonably expect a dark and stormy tale. If the action opens on a spring morning in a sunlit glade, it is likely that the author is preparing us for a lighter tale, establishing a contrast between different settings in the story, or being ironic. In order to understand how setting relates to the meaning of the work as a whole, you will have to consider the thematic significance of things that might at first seem merely physical and objective. The most important thing is that you pay attention to the details — the sights and sounds, textures and tones, colors and shapes.

In the following passage from Edgar Allan Poe's "The Masque of the Red Death," Poe describes the castle where Prince Prospero and his friends seclude themselves in an attempt to escape the plague that is threatening the community. Notice how the physical details of the description create a sinister and foreboding atmosphere.

from **The Masque of the Red Death**

EDGAR ALLAN POE

It was a voluptuous scene, that masquerade. But first let me tell of the rooms in which it was held. There were seven — an imperial suite. In many palaces, however, such suites form a long and straight vista, while the folding doors slide back nearly to the walls on either hand, so that the view of the whole extent is scarcely impeded. Here the case was very different; as might have been expected from the duke's love of the *bizarre*. The apartments were so irregularly disposed that the vision embraced but little more than one at a time. There was a sharp turn at every twenty or thirty yards, and at each turn a novel effect. To the right and left, in the middle of each wall, a tall and narrow Gothic window looked out upon a closed corridor which pursued the windings of the suite. These windows were of stained glass whose color varied in accordance with the prevailing hue of the decorations of the chamber into which it opened. That at the eastern extremity was hung, for example, in blue — and vividly blue were its windows. The second chamber was purple in its ornaments and tapestries, and here the panes were purple. The third was green throughout, and so were the casements. The fourth was furnished and lighted with orange — the fifth with white — the sixth with violet. The seventh apartment was closely shrouded in black velvet tapestries that hung all over the ceiling and down the walls, falling in heavy folds upon a carpet of the same material and hue. But in this chamber only, the color of the windows failed to correspond with the decorations. The panes here were scarlet — a deep blood color. Now in no one of the seven apartments was there any lamp or candelabrum, amid the profusion of golden ornaments that lay scattered to and fro or depended from the roof. There was no light of any kind emanating from lamp or candle within the suite of chambers. But in the corridors that followed the suite, there stood, opposite to each window, a heavy tripod, bearing a brazier of fire that projected its rays through the tinted glass and so glaringly illumined the room. And thus were produced a multitude of gaudy and fantastic appearances. But in the western or black chamber the effect of the fire-light that streamed upon the dark hangings through the blood-tinted panes was ghastly in the extreme, and produced so wild a look upon the countenances of those who entered, that there were few of the company bold enough to set foot within its precincts at all.

It was in this apartment, also, that there stood against the western wall, a gigantic clock of ebony. Its pendulum swung to and fro with a dull, heavy, monotonous clang; and when the minute-hand made the circuit of the face, and the hour was to be stricken, there came from the brazen lungs of the clock a sound which was clear and loud and deep and exceedingly musical, but of so peculiar a note and emphasis that, at each lapse of an hour, the musicians of the orchestra were constrained to pause, momentarily, in their performance, to hearken to the sound; and thus the waltzers perforce ceased their evolutions; and there was a brief disconcert of the whole gay company; and, while the chimes of the clock yet rang, it was observed that the giddiest grew pale, and the more aged and sedate passed their hands over their brows as if in confused revery or meditation. But when the echoes had fully ceased, a light laughter at once pervaded the assembly; the musicians looked at each other and smiled as if at their own nervousness and folly, and made whispering vows, each to the other, that the next chiming of the clock should produce in them no similar emotion; and then, after the lapse of sixty minutes (which embrace three thousand and six hundred seconds of the Time that flies), there came yet another chiming of the clock, and then were the same disconcert and tremulousness and meditation as before.

[1845]

The first paragraph takes us on a detailed tour of the suite, telling us what is on our right and left, how many yards of space are between various apartments, what is on the walls, where the windows are, what colors the curtains are, and the like. As we realize the difficulty of navigating from apartment to apartment and note the colors, culminating in "scarlet — a deep blood color," we recognize that the setting is opulent yet oppressive; it is filled with the trappings of wealth yet seems to entrap its residents. Poe deepens the atmosphere of foreboding by telling us what is *not* there — no gentle light "from lamp or candle"; instead, illumination is by fire, a hellish glow that is "ghastly in the extreme."

After he has given us a view of this odd suite, Poe zeroes in on one particular part of the furnishings: a large, black pendulum clock, whose sound rang with "so peculiar a note and emphasis" that it reminded the residents every hour of their own mortality. Poe's description of the setting is literal, but when we analyze those details, an atmosphere of menace, even doom, is revealed.

Historical Context

A novel, short story, or play may be set in a historical era — a time and place that has its own political, economic, or social upheavals. In many cases, historical context goes unstated; it is part of the knowledge that the author expects the reader to bring to the text. For instance, in John Steinbeck's novel *The Grapes of Wrath*, we follow the Joad family as they migrate from middle America to California, along the legendary Route 66, on a search for work, prosperity, and stability.

from **The Grapes of Wrath**

JOHN STEINBECK

Highway 66 is the main migrant road. 66 — the long concrete path across the country, waving gently up and down on the map, from Mississippi to Bakersfield — over the red lands and the gray lands, twisting up into the mountains, crossing the Divide and down into the bright and terrible desert, and across the desert to the mountains again, and into the rich California valleys.

66 is the path of a people in flight, refugees from dust and shrinking land, from the thunder of tractors and shrinking ownership, from the desert's slow northward invasion, from the twisting winds that howl up out of Texas, from the

floods that bring no richness to the land and steal what little richness is there. From all of these the people are in flight, and they come into 66 from the tributary side roads, from the wagon tracks and the rutted country roads. 66 is the mother road, the road of flight.

Clarksville and Ozark and Van Buren and Fort Smith on 64, and there's an end of Arkansas. And all the roads into Oklahoma City, 66 down from Tulsa, 270 up from McAlester. 81 from Wichita Falls south, from Enid north. Edmond, McLoud, Purcell. 66 out of Oklahoma City; El Reno and Clinton, going west on 66. Hydro, Elk City, and Texola; and there's an end to Oklahoma. 66 across the Panhandle of Texas. Shamrock and McLean, Conway and Amarillo, the yellow. Wildorado and Vega and Boise, and there's an end of Texas. Tucumcari and Santa Rosa and into the New Mexican mountains to Albuquerque, where the road comes down from Santa Fe. Then down the gorged Rio Grande to Los Lunas and west again on 66 to Gallup, and there's the border of New Mexico.

[1939]

In this description, we get a good sense of the physical setting. The first paragraph, one long sentence that rambles along like the road itself, describes Highway 66 — it goes from Mississippi to Bakersfield, California — and sets a mood with the sensory images of the "long concrete path." In the second paragraph, the narrator introduces the people who follow this road in the hope of finding something better than the desolation of the drought that has worsened their economic hardship. The word *flight* appears three times, so we get a clear sense of movement from one thing to another, though what that thing is, we're not sure. The third paragraph consists almost entirely of names of places along Highway 66. Even if we do not know these towns, we still get a clear sense of movement, of going from one stop to the next.

What is unstated is the reason for the migration, though it is implied when the narrator describes the migrating families as "refugees from dust and shrinking land" (para. 2). This passage refers to the great migration of families to California as a result of the Dust Bowl, a historic drought combined with severe storms that destroyed much of the farmland in middle America during the Great Depression of the 1930s. This historical setting, not just Route 66 but the context of the Dust Bowl and the Great Depression, makes the story of the Joad family emblematic of an entire era in American history.

Sometimes historical settings are not implicit but explicit — with dates and places clearly identified. In the following passage from *Call It Sleep* by Henry Roth, the setting is essential to the novel's exploration of the Jewish American experience in early twentieth-century America.

from **Call It Sleep**

HENRY ROTH

The small white steamer, *Peter Stuyvesant*, that delivered the immigrants from the stench and throb of the steerage to the stench and the throb of New York tenements, rolled slightly on the water beside the stone quay in the lee of the weathered barracks and new brick buildings of Ellis Island. Her skipper was waiting for the last of the officials, laborers and guards to embark upon her before he cast off and started for Manhattan. Since this was Saturday afternoon and this the last trip she would make for the week-end, those left behind might have to stay over till Monday. Her whistle bellowed its hoarse warning. A few figures in overalls sauntered from the high doors of the immigration quarters and down the grey pavement that led to the dock.

It was May of the year 1907, the year that was destined to bring the greatest number of immigrants to the shores of the United States. All that day, as on all the days since spring began, her decks had been thronged by hundreds upon hundreds of foreigners, natives from almost every land in the world. . . .

[1934]

From the first sentence, we are placed in New York City, arriving via a steamer filled with immigrants. The entrance to the United States through Ellis Island where the "immigration quarters" are is also our entrance into the novel. Roth opens the next paragraph with a specific date — 1907, which marked the high point of immigration during that era. As the paragraph continues, the narrator of this autobiographical novel describes the crowds of immigrants aboard the ship, then focuses on a woman and her child. Thus, the historical setting provides a particular context for the life that is beginning as these two characters step onto a new land.

Cultural Environment

Setting may also establish the cultural environment of a work — the manners, mores, customs, rituals, and codes of conduct. In some instances, this cultural environment is based on an actual period, culture, or community. In other instances, an author has to invent a new culture, as in the case of George Orwell's novel *1984*:

from **1984**

GEORGE ORWELL

It was a bright cold day in April, and the clocks were striking thirteen. Winston Smith, his chin nuzzled into his breast in an effort to escape the vile wind, slipped quickly through the glass doors of Victory Mansions, though not quickly enough to prevent a swirl of gritty dust from entering along with him.

The hallway smelt of boiled cabbage and old rag mats. At one end of it a colored poster, too large for indoor display, had been tacked to the wall. It depicted simply an enormous face, more than a meter wide: the face of a man of about forty-five, with a heavy black mustache and ruggedly handsome features. Winston made for the stairs. It was no use trying the lift. Even at the best of times it was seldom working, and at present the electric current was cut off during daylight hours. It was part of the economy drive in preparation for Hate Week. The flat was seven flights up, and Winston, who was thirty-nine, and had a varicose ulcer above his right ankle, went slowly, resting several times on the way. On each landing, opposite the lift shaft, the poster with the enormous face gazed from the wall. It was one of those pictures which are so contrived that the eyes follow you about when you move. BIG BROTHER IS WATCHING YOU, the caption beneath it ran.

Inside the flat a fruity voice was reading out a list of figures which had something to do with the production of pig iron. The voice came from an oblong metal plaque like a dulled mirror which formed part of the surface of the right-hand wall. Winston turned a switch and the voice sank somewhat, though the words were still distinguishable. The instrument (the telescreen, it was called) could be dimmed, but there was no way of shutting it off completely.

He moved over to the window: a smallish, frail figure, the meagerness of his body merely emphasized by the blue overalls which were the uniform of the Party. His hair was very fair, his face naturally sanguine, his skin roughened by coarse soap and blunt razor blades and the cold of the winter that had just ended.

Outside, even through the shut window pane, the world looked cold. Down in the street little eddies of wind were whirling dust and torn paper into spirals, and though the sun was shining and the sky a harsh blue, there seemed to be no color in anything except the posters that were plastered everywhere. The black-mustachio'd face gazed down from every commanding corner. There was one on the house front immediately opposite. BIG BROTHER IS WATCHING YOU, the caption said, while the dark eyes looked deep into Winston's own. Down at street level another poster, torn at one corner, flapped fitfully in the wind, alternately covering and uncovering the single word INGSOC. In the far distance a helicopter skimmed down between the roofs, hovered for an instant like a bluebottle, and darted away again with a curving flight. It was the Police Patrol, snooping into people's windows. The patrols did not matter, however. Only the Thought Police mattered.

[1949]

From the very beginning of this novel, when the clocks strike thirteen, we know we're in a different world. For *1984*, Orwell created a social environment in which the values we take for granted are dispensed with. In their place is a society built on surveillance and **propaganda**, with odd customs and institutions such as Hate Week and the Thought Police. It's an environment where the "telescreen" broadcasting Big Brother's voice can be "dimmed" but cannot be silenced; the omnipresent drone of the voice is part of the setting. Posters of Big Brother are everywhere, and the sound of a helicopter is a reminder of the constant surveillance. Of course, Orwell's point was to warn us of one possible future for our world, and the shocking comparisons between the society of his novel and our own society is one of the main reasons that *1984* continues to be so powerful and so disturbing.

The following questions will help guide your analysis of setting:

- What is the geographical setting? The time, place, weather, season? Why is it important?
- What historical context or social environment is being depicted, and what background information is required to understand the situation?
- What details of the setting does the author use to create atmosphere or mood?
- How does the setting seem to relate to the themes?

ACTIVITY

Authors often use setting as another means of developing a character. Discuss the interaction between setting and character in the following passage from *Tess of the D'Urbervilles* by Thomas Hardy. The context is that the unmarried Tess, who lives in a traditional nineteenth-century village in rural England, has recently had a child. Pay close attention to the way the narrator uses setting to comment on Tess's situation.

from Tess of the D'Urbervilles

THOMAS HARDY

The bedroom which she shared with some of the children formed her retreat more continually than ever. Here, under her few square yards of thatch, she watched winds, and snows, and rains, gorgeous sunsets, and successive moons at their full. So close kept she that at length almost everybody thought she had gone away.

The only exercise that Tess took at this time was after dark; and it was then, when out in the woods, that she seemed least solitary. She knew how to hit to a hair's-breadth that moment of evening when the light and the darkness are so evenly balanced that the constraint of day and the suspense of night neutralize each other, leaving absolute mental liberty. It is then that the plight of being alive becomes attenuated to its least possible dimensions. She had no fear of the shadows; her sole idea seemed to be to shun mankind — or rather that cold accretion called the world, which, so terrible in the mass, is so unformidable, even pitiable, in its units.

On these lonely hills and dales her quiescent glide was of a piece with the element she moved in. Her flexuous and stealthy figure became an integral part of the scene. At times her whimsical fancy would intensify natural processes around her till they seemed a part of her own story. Rather they became a part of it; for the world is only a psychological phenomenon, and what they seemed they were. The midnight airs and gusts, moaning amongst the tightly-wrapped buds and bark of the winter twigs, were formulae of bitter reproach. A wet day was the expression of irremediable grief at her weakness in the mind of some vague ethical being whom she could not class definitely as the God of her childhood, and could not comprehend as any other.

But this encompassment of her own characterization, based on shreds of convention, peopled by phantoms and voices antipathetic to her, was a sorry and mistaken creation of Tess's fancy — a cloud of moral hobgoblins by which she was terrified without reason. It was they that were out of harmony with the actual world, not she. Walking among the sleeping birds in the hedges, watching the skipping rabbits on a moonlit warren, or standing under a pheasant-laden bough, she looked upon herself as a figure of Guilt intruding into the haunts of Innocence. But all the while she was making a distinction where there was no difference. Feeling herself in antagonism she was quite in accord. She had been made to break an accepted social law, but no law known to the environment in which she fancied herself such an anomaly.

[1891]

Point of View

Point of view is the perspective through which a story is told. This perspective determines what the reader knows as well as the manner in which the story is told. Writers of fiction most commonly use first- and third-person narrators. Second-person narrators are rare but not unheard of, as in Jay McInerney's novel *Bright Lights, Big City*, which begins as follows:

> You are not the kind of guy who would be at a place like this at this time of the morning. But here you are, and you cannot say that the terrain is entirely unfamiliar, although the details are fuzzy.

Second-person point of view puts the reader right in the story, but it is rarely used (and is often viewed as a gimmick), perhaps because it makes the reading experience too literal — you are not just asked to imagine a character, you are told that you *are* the character.

First-Person Point of View

A first-person narrator tells a story using first-person pronouns such as *I* and *we*. From this point of view, we see the world from a single character's perspective (usually the main character's, though it can be a minor character's). The first-person narrator gives us a vivid on-the-spot view of what is happening. Just be careful not to confuse a first-person narrator with the author. In most cases, a first-person narrator is every bit as much a creation of the writer's imagination as any other character.

Let's examine a passage from *The Beautiful Things That Heaven Bears*, the first novel by Ethiopian-born Dinaw Mengestu, in which the main character is preparing to have dinner with his neighbor and her daughter.

from **The Beautiful Things That Heaven Bears**

DINAW MENGESTU

I went home early and changed into a neatly pressed button-down white shirt and a pair of slightly worn gray wool slacks Kenneth had handed down to me. The cuff links, a holdover from my father's days in the Ethiopian government, had the old Ethiopian flag with the Lion of Judah and his crooked crown on it. They were the only things of my father I had left. He used to keep them in a small gray jewelry box with the lid open on top of the dresser in his bedroom, although I can't remember ever having seen him wear them. What I can remember is him holding them out to me and saying with a slight, sarcastic lilt to his voice, "Someday all this will be yours." I don't think he ever actually intended for them to become heirlooms. They were just cheap cuff links from an old, decaying regime, but you hold on to what you can and hope the meaning comes later.

Before leaving the house I stood in front of my bathroom mirror and practiced my introduction. I brushed forward the edges of my thinning hair and patted down the sides of my small Afro. My reflection stared back disapprovingly. I had aged, but there was nothing distinguished about me. The laugh lines around my mouth had burrowed in, and there was more of my forehead than I cared to show. I smiled and tried to find a hint of a younger and better version of myself, but there was no doing. He was gone.

[2007]

Notice how the first-person viewpoint helps reveal the speaker's character. We see the world through his eyes. The first paragraph shows us how meticulous he is as he chooses what to wear; he is not wealthy, yet he takes care to choose clothes that are ironed and to wear cuff links that belonged to his father. The way he remembers his father adds to our understanding of this character, who is living a long way from Ethiopia, where he grew up. The second paragraph continues the studied concern with how he looks, though it adds more self-criticism. He stands before the mirror and assesses himself, as though he's looking at another person entirely. He worries about his aging and searches to find traces of his younger self. These details and his admission that he is practicing the way he will introduce himself betray his insecurity.

Imagine how different the story would be if it had been told in the third person with a narrator explaining how Sepha (the main character's name) is feeling. Let's just change the pronouns in one section:

> Sepha's reflection stared back disapprovingly. He had aged, but there was nothing distinguished about him. . . . He smiled and tried to find a hint of a younger and better version of himself, but there was no doing.

It's essentially the same information, yet note the difference in authority. The third-person narrator's observations are more convincing, because they seem like objective observations. With first-person narration, we don't know if the narrator's perceptions of his own looks are accurate or if they just reflect his lack of confidence, since his perceptions are obviously subjective. The first-person viewpoint in this passage makes the character seem more vulnerable — a guy going on a first date and worried about the impression he'll make.

One quirk of first-person narration (and occasionally third-person narration) is that the author might choose to tell the story from the perspective of someone who is naive, mentally ill, biased, corrupt, or downright immoral. A narrator of this sort is called an **unreliable narrator**. An author might use an unreliable narrator to distinguish the character's point of view from his or her own, or to make an ironic point. In *Adventures of Huckleberry Finn*, Huck tells the story from a perspective that is sometimes naive, sometimes mischievous, and certainly ironic, as demonstrated in the following passage.

from Adventures of Huckleberry Finn

MARK TWAIN

The Widow Douglas, she took me for her son, and allowed she would sivilize me; but it was rough living in the house all the time, considering how dismal regular and decent the widow was in all her ways; and so when I couldn't stand it no longer, I lit out. I got into my old rags, and my sugar-hogshead again, and was free and satisfied. But Tom Sawyer, he hunted me up and said he was going to start a band of robbers, and I might join if I would go back to the widow and be respectable. So I went back.

The widow she cried over me, and called me a poor lost lamb, and she called me a lot of other names, too, but she never meant no harm by it. She put me in them new clothes again, and I couldn't do nothing but sweat and sweat, and feel all cramped up. Well, then, the old thing commenced again. The widow rung a bell for supper, and you had to come to time. When you got to the table you couldn't go right to eating, but you had to wait for the widow to tuck down her head and grumble a little over the victuals, though there warn't really anything the matter with them. That is, nothing only everything was cooked by itself. In a barrel of odds and ends it is different; things get mixed up, and the juice kind of swaps around, and the things go better.

[1885]

In this passage, Huck tells us about his time with the Widow Douglas, particularly her efforts to "sivilize" him. Huck's point of view gives us a skewed version of what it means to be "respectable." He calls the widow "regular and decent" but thinks she is "dismal." Later in the passage, instead of telling us that the widow says grace over dinner, Huck tells us that the widow would "tuck down her head and grumble a little over the victuals, though there warn't really anything the matter with them." The reason Huck tolerates all of this civilizing is so he'll be respectable enough to join Tom Sawyer's band of robbers. What irony! Twain is using Huck's naive perspective to satirize the ways of "regular and decent" folk. Twain's point seems to be that the trappings of respectability are not what make you a good person; indeed, that's just about enough to qualify you for membership in a band of robbers. The thing to remember is that we are seeing this world through the eyes of the naive and mischievous Huckleberry Finn, who is a tool of the great satirist Mark Twain — which means that as readers we need to stay alert or will miss the ironic complexity of this story.

Third-Person Point of View

A third-person narrator tells the story using the third-person pronouns *he*, *she*, and *it*. This type of narrator views all events in a story from a distance and does not play a role in the actual plot. When the narrator is **omniscient**, readers have access to what all the characters are thinking and feeling. A **limited omniscient narrator** tells us what just one major or minor character is thinking and feeling. This perspective both conceals and reveals. While it restricts how much readers know, it can also give readers insight into who a character is and how that character sees the world. In "Miss Brill" by Katherine Mansfield, we see through the eyes of an aging woman sitting in a park in a vacation town in France, observing others around her. We experience all of the action and characters through her perspective.

from Miss Brill

KATHERINE MANSFIELD

Oh, how fascinating it was! How she enjoyed it! How she loved sitting here, watching it all! It was like a play. It was exactly like a play. Who could believe the sky at the back wasn't painted? But it wasn't till a little brown dog trotted on solemn and then slowly trotted off, like a little "theatre" dog, a little dog that had been drugged, that Miss Brill discovered what it was that made it so exciting. They were all on the stage. They weren't only the audience, not only looking on; they were acting. Even she had a part and came every Sunday. No doubt somebody would have noticed if she hadn't been there; she was part of the performance after all. How strange she'd never thought of it like that before! And yet it explained why she made such a point of starting from home at just the same time each week — so as not to be late for the performance — and it also explained why she had quite a queer, shy feeling at telling her English pupils how she spent her Sunday afternoons. No wonder! Miss Brill nearly laughed out loud. She was on the stage. She thought of the old invalid gentleman to whom she read the newspaper four afternoons a week while he slept in the garden. She had got quite used to the frail head on the cotton pillow, the hollowed eyes, the open mouth, and the high pinched nose. If he'd been dead she mightn't have noticed for weeks; she wouldn't have minded. But suddenly he knew he was having the paper read to him by an actress! "An actress!" The old head lifted; two points of light quivered in the old eyes. "An actress — are ye?" And Miss Brill smoothed the newspaper as though it were the manuscript of her part and said gently: "Yes, I have been an actress for a long time."

[1920]

In this passage, Miss Brill (whose first name is never revealed) feels like part of the world she is observing. Priding herself on her ability to notice the rich details all around her, she does not see herself as a solitary or pitiful figure. We get to know her as a vibrant, joyful, appreciative, perhaps even contemplative person. Soon after, however, she overhears a young couple laughing at her, a slight that causes her to question whether she really has a part in this world that belongs to the young. We never know the motivation or level of awareness of any other character because the limited omniscient third-person viewpoint is that of Miss Brill.

Another variation on the third-person perspective involves an **objective narrator** (also called a neutral narrator), who recounts only what characters say and do, offering no insight into their thinking or analysis of events; all interpretation is left to the reader. In the short story "The Lottery," author Shirley Jackson uses this perspective to stand back and suspend judgment on an incident that turns ugly and violent: individuals are participating in a lottery to determine which member of the community will be stoned to death. Notice that the objectivity emphasizes the community's willingness to go along with this "tradition."

from The Lottery

SHIRLEY JACKSON

The lottery was conducted — as were the square dances, the teen-age club, the Halloween program — by Mr. Summers, who had time and energy to devote to civic activities. He was a round-faced, jovial man and he ran the coal business, and people were sorry for him, because he had no children and his wife was a scold. When he arrived in the square, carrying the black wooden box, there was a murmur of conversation among the villagers, and he waved and called, "Little late today, folks." The postmaster, Mr. Graves, followed him, carrying a three-legged stool, and the stool was put in the center of the square and Mr. Summers set the black box down on it. The villagers kept their distance, leaving a space between themselves and the stool, and when Mr. Summers said, "Some of you fellows want to give me a hand?" there was a hesitation before two men, Mr. Martin and his oldest son, Baxter, came forward to hold the box steady on the stool while Mr. Summers stirred up the papers inside it.

[1948]

The characters' actions are described straightforwardly but without any commentary on why they do what they do or how they feel about it. There is no tone of approval or disapproval. Somehow, the detached reporting makes the horror of what is being reported even more striking because the failure to express an opinion suggests the narrator's acceptance.

Stream of Consciousness

Stream of consciousness is a narrative technique characteristic of such twentieth-century writers as William Faulkner, James Joyce, and Virginia Woolf, and such contemporary writers as Toni Morrison and Cormac McCarthy. It takes readers inside the mind of a narrator, recounting thoughts, impressions, and feelings, from either a first-person or a third-person limited omniscient perspective. The reader is privy to exactly what the character is thinking, without the filters of causality or logic. Such interior monologues are often characterized by fragments, swift (or entirely absent) transitions, and a free association of ideas. Stream of consciousness writing is almost never the only narrative technique at work in a novel. Typically, the writer takes readers in and out of the stream, shifting back and forth between interior monologue and other points of view. In the following passage from *Ulysses,* Joyce takes us into the mind of Leopold Bloom as he walks through the streets of Dublin, Ireland. Among the things already on his mind are his wife, Molly, her father, Old Tweedy, and a funeral that he will attend later in the day.

from **Ulysses**

JAMES JOYCE

He crossed to the bright side, avoiding the loose cellarflap of number seventy five. The sun was nearing the steeple of George's church. Be a warm day I fancy. Specially in these black clothes feel it more. Black conducts, reflects (refracts is it ?), the heat. But I couldn't go in that light suit. Make a picnic of it. His eyelids sank quietly often as he walked in happy warmth. Boland's breadvan delivering with trays our daily but she prefers yesterday's loaves turnovers crisp crowns hot. Makes you feel young. Somewhere in the east: early morning: set off at dawn, travel round in front of the sun steal a day's march on him. Keep it up for ever never grow a day older technically. Walk along a strand, strange land, come to a city gate, sentry there, old ranker too, old Tweedy's big moustaches leaning on a long kind of a spear. Wander through awned streets. Turbaned faces going by. Dark caves of carpet shops, big man, Turko the terrible, seated crosslegged smoking a coiled pipe. Cries of sellers in the streets. Drink water scented with fennel, sherbet. Wander along all day. Might meet a robber or two. Well, meet him. Getting on to sundown. The shadows of the mosques along the pillars: priest with a scroll rolled up. A shiver of the trees, signal, the evening wind. I pass on. Fading gold sky. A mother watches from her doorway. She calls her children home in their dark language. High wall: beyond strings twanged. Night sky moon, violet, colour of Molly's new garters. Strings. Listen. A girl playing one of those instruments what do you call them: dulcimers. I pass.

Probably not a bit like it really. Kind of stuff you read: in the track of the sun. Sunburst on the titlepage. He smiled, pleasing himself.

[1922]

While this narrative technique gives us access to an intimate perspective, it also requires us to pay close attention and participate in the reading to a greater degree than usual. Notice how we hear the narration directly from Bloom's thoughts, as he experiences them. We hear and see what he hears and sees. His senses prompt his imagination to create a daydream, and the reader is carried along with it, catching glimpses of "the dark caves of carpet shops," "the shadows of the mosques along the pillars," "a shiver of the trees," and the "fading gold sky" — until Bloom's rational mind brings him back: "Probably not a bit like it really." Yet that narration offers no overt causality or other stated connections among Bloom's perceptions and ideas. At first, stream of consciousness can be challenging to read, because making order out of what seems confusing is largely left to the reader. But, once you have fully entered the narrative, you may come to appreciate the heightened state of awareness it conveys.

ACTIVITY

Read "Seeing Eye," a short story by Brad Watson. What is the point of view from which the story is told? Discuss the effect this viewpoint has on the overall story.

Seeing Eye

BRAD WATSON

The dog came to the curb's edge and stopped. The man holding on to his halter stopped beside him. Across the street, the signal flashed the words "Don't Walk." The dog saw the signal but paid little notice. He was trained to see what mattered: the absence of moving traffic. The signal kept blinking. The cars kept driving through the intersection. He watched the cars, listened to the intensity of their engines, the arid whine of their tires. He listened for something he'd become accustomed to hearing, the buzz and tumbling of switches from the box on the pole next to them. The dog associated it with the imminent stopping of the cars. He looked back over his right shoulder at the man, who stood with his head cocked, listening to the traffic.

A woman behind them spoke up.

"Huh," she said. "The light's stuck."

The dog looked at her, then turned back to watch the traffic, which continued to rush through the intersection without pause.

"I'm going down a block," the woman said. She 5
spoke to the man. "Would you like me to show you a detour? No telling how long this light will be."

"No, thank you," the man said. "We'll just wait a little bit. Right, Buck?" The dog looked back over his shoulder at the man, then watched the woman walk away.

"Good luck," the woman said. The dog's ears stood up and he stiffened for just a second.

"She said 'luck,' not 'Buck,'" the man said, laughing easily and reaching down to scratch the dog's ears. He gripped the loose skin on Buck's neck with his right hand and gave it an affectionate shake. He continued to hold the halter guide loosely with his left.

The dog watched the traffic rush by.

"We'll just wait here, Buck," the man said. 10
"By the time we go a block out of our way, the light will've fixed itself." He cleared his throat and cocked his head, as if listening for something. The dog dipped his head and shifted his shoulders in the halter.

The man laughed softly.

"If we went down a block, I'll bet that light would get stuck, too. We'd be following some kind of traveling glitch across town. We could go for miles, and then end up in some field, and a voice saying, 'I suppose you're wondering why I've summoned you here.'"

It was the longest they'd ever stood waiting for traffic to stop. The dog saw people across the street wait momentarily, glance around, then leave. He watched the traffic. It began to have a hypnotic effect upon him: the traffic, the blinking crossing signal. His focus on the next move, the crossing, on the implied courses of the pedestrians around them and those still waiting at the opposite curb, on the potential obstructions ahead, dissolved into the rare luxury of wandering attention.

The sounds of the traffic grinding through the intersection were diminished to a small aural dot in the back of his mind, and he became aware of the regular bleat of a slow-turning box fan in an open window of the building behind them. Odd scents distinguished themselves in his nostrils and blended into a rich funk that swirled about the pedestrians who stopped next to them, a secret aromatic history that eddied about him even as the pedestrians muttered among themselves and moved on.

The hard clean smell of new shoe leather seeped from the air-conditioned stores, overlaying the drift of worn leather and grime that eased from tiny musty pores in the sidewalk. He snuffled at them and sneezed. In a trembling confusion he was aware of all that was carried in the breeze, the strong odor of tobacco and the sharp rake of its smoke, the gasoline and exhaust fumes and the stench of aging rubber, the fetid waves that rolled through it all from garbage bins in the alleys and on the backstreet curbs.

He lowered his head and shifted his shoulders in the harness like a boxer.

"Easy, Buck," the man said.

Sometimes in their room the man paced the floor and seemed to say his words in time with his steps until he became like a lulling clock to Buck as he lay resting beneath the dining table. He dozed to the man's mumbling and the sifting sound of his fingers as they grazed the pages of his book. At times in their dark room the man sat on the edge of his cot and scratched Buck's ears and spoke to him. "Panorama, Buck," he would say. "That's the most difficult to recall. I can see the details, with my hands, with my nose, my tongue. It brings them back. But the big picture. I feel like I must be replacing it with something phony, like a Disney movie or something." Buck looked up at the man's shadowed face in the dark room, at his small eyes in their sallow depressions.

On the farm where he'd been raised before his training at the school, Buck's name had been Pete. The children and the old man and the woman had tussled with him, thrown sticks, said, "Pete! Good old Pete." They called out to him, mumbled the name into his fur. But now the man always said "Buck" in the same tone of voice, soft and gentle. As if the man were speaking to himself. As if Buck were not really there.

"I miss colors, Buck," the man would say. "It's getting harder to remember them. The blue planet. I remember that. Pictures from space. From out in the blackness."

Looking up from the intersection, Buck saw birds dart through the sky between buildings as quickly as they slipped past the open window at dawn. He heard their high-pitched cries so clearly that he saw their beady eyes, their barbed tongues flicking between parted beaks. He salivated at the dusky taste of a dove once he'd held in his mouth. And in his most delicate bones he felt the murmur of some incessant activity, the low hum beyond the visible world. His hackles rose and his muscles tingled with electricity.

There was a metallic whirring, like a big fat June bug stuck on its back, followed by the dull clunk of the switch in the traffic control box. Cars stopped. The lane opened up before them, and for a moment no one moved, as if the empty-eyed vehicles were not to be trusted, restrained only by some fragile miracle of faith. He felt the man carefully regrip the leather harness. He felt the activity of the world spool down into the tight and rifled tunnel of their path.

"Forward, Buck," said the man.

He leaned into the harness and moved them into the world.

[1996]

Layered Points of View

Not every story has a straightforward first- or third-person point of view. Often a novel is told through multiple layered perspectives. In her novel *A Crime in the Neighborhood*, Suzanne Berne tells the story from the viewpoint of a woman, Marsha, who recalls a violent crime that occurred when she was an adolescent. In the following passage, Marsha is remembering an encounter between a suspicious neighbor and her mother, who is waiting for guests to arrive for a barbecue.

from **A Crime in the Neighborhood**

SUZANNE BERNE

"I think I would like a little more wine, thank you," [my mother] added after a moment, and held out her cup.

As he bent to refill her cup, their eyes met and she smiled up at him. "It's still early," she told him. "They might still come."

"Yes," he said.

Two stories above them, I propped my chin on the back of a hand, leaning on the windowsill. Had she remembered to turn off the burner from under the pan of hamburger meat? Had she noticed, on her way out, if the freezer door was ajar?

When I look back I don't have trouble understanding how my mother got herself into Mr. Green's yard that night. All the time she had been preparing dinner she must have been glancing out the kitchen window, watching him as he sat alone in his unsteady chair, stiff khaki shirt fading into the early evening. I suppose it was the cumulative effect of that vision that finally made her fumble toward the door as if the hamburger meat had already burned, as if the whole house were filled with smoke. Because as I recall it now there *was* something dire in the sight of Mr. Green that evening. Something powerful enough to send my mother rushing from the house, barefoot half-dressed. . . . What must have made my mother's eyes sting that summer evening, what must have made her almost run to the kitchen door, had to be the fury of mortal fear — the fear that comes from understanding all at once that you are by yourself in a vast world, and that one day something worse than anything that has ever happened before will happen.

[1998]

The narrator begins recounting the story through dialogue between her mother and Mr. Green, dialogue that the narrator reconstructs from memory but presents as though it were just occurring. Her narrative voice intrudes from "[t]wo stories above them," as she remembers herself as a young girl looking down from an upstairs window, where she watched the encounter and wondered if her mother "remembered to turn off the burner from under the pan of hamburger meat." In the next paragraph, the narrator reminds us that an older, more mature person is telling the story as a flashback: "When I look back. . . ." What follows is hardly the consciousness of the young girl at the windowsill but that of an adult who is remembering the story and reflecting on how it influenced her.

Another layered technique is to introduce a story using another story, called a **narrative frame** or frame story. A narrative frame establishes who is telling the main story and under what circumstances. Narrative frames usually create a shift in perspective. If the frame story is told in first-person present tense, perhaps the main story will be told as a flashback, or in third person as something that happened to someone else. When a frame is used to pass on a secondhand story, the reader is left to wonder if the narrator is getting everything right, or if he or she is misremembering or embellishing the tale. Emily Brontë uses a narrative frame for her novel *Wuthering Heights*. The book's primary narrator is a gentleman named Lockwood, who has come to live at Thrushcross Grange. His mysterious landlord, Heathcliff, lives at neighboring Wuthering Heights. In a journal, Lockwood records the story told to him by Mrs. Dean, a former servant of the Earnshaws, the family that originally owned Wuthering Heights. In the following excerpt, the novel moves from the frame to the story within it as Lockwood talks with Mrs. Dean. At the end of the passage, she begins to narrate the story within the story.

from **Wuthering Heights**

EMILY BRONTË

"Oh, I'll turn the talk on my landlord's family!" I thought to myself. "A good subject to start — and that pretty girl-widow, I should like to know her history; whether she be a native of the country, or, as is more probable, an exotic that the surly indigenae will not recognise for kin."

With this intention I asked Mrs. Dean why Heathcliff let Thrushcross Grange, and preferred living in a situation and residence so much inferior.

"Is he not rich enough to keep the estate in good order?" I enquired.

"Rich, sir!" she returned. "He has, nobody knows what money, and every year it increases. Yes, yes, he's rich enough to live in a finer house than this; but he's very near — close-handed; and, if he had meant to flit to Thrushcross

Grange, as soon as he heard of a good tenant, he could not have borne to miss the change of getting a few hundreds more. It is strange people should be so greedy, when they are alone in the world!"

"He had a son, it seems?"

"Yes, he had one — he is dead."

"And that young lady, Mrs. Heathcliff, is his widow?"

"Yes."

"Where did she come from originally?"

"Why, sir, she is my late master's daughter; Catherine Linton was her maiden name. I nursed her, poor thing! I did wish Mr. Heathcliff would remove here, and then we might have been together again."

"What, Catherine Linton!" I exclaimed, astonished. But a minute's reflection convinced me it was not my ghostly Catherine. "Then," I continued, "my predecessor's name was Linton?"

"It was."

"And who is that Earnshaw, Hareton Earnshaw, who lives with Mr. Heathcliff? are they relations?"

"No; he is the late Mr. Linton's nephew."

"The young lady's cousin, then?"

"Yes; her husband was her cousin also — one, on the mother's — the other, on the father's side — Heathcliff married Mr. Linton's sister."

"I see the house at Wuthering Heights has 'Earnshaw' carved over the front door. Are they an old family?"

"Very old, sir; and Hareton is the last of them, as our Miss Cathy is of us — I mean, of the Lintons. Have you been to Wuthering Heights? I beg pardon for asking; but I should like to hear how she is."

"Mrs. Heathcliff? she looked very well, and very handsome; yet, I think, not very happy."

"Oh dear, I don't wonder! And how did you like the master?"

"A rough fellow, rather, Mrs. Dean. Is not that his character?"

"Rough as a saw-edge, and hard as whinstone! The less you meddle with him the better."

"He must have had some ups and downs in life to make him such a churl. Do you know anything of his history?"

"It's a cuckoo's, sir — I know all about it; except where he was born, and who were his parents, and how he got his money, at first — And Hareton has been cast out like an unfledged dunnock — The unfortunate lad is the only one, in all this parish, that does not guess how he has been cheated!"

"Well, Mrs. Dean, it will be a charitable deed to tell me something of my neighbors — I feel I shall not rest, if I go to bed; so be good enough to sit and chat an hour."

"Oh, certainly, sir! I'll just fetch a little sewing, and then I'll sit as long as you please. But you've caught cold, I saw you shivering, and you must have some gruel to drive it out."

The worthy woman bustled off, and I crouched nearer the fire: my head felt hot, and the rest of me chill: moreover I was excited, almost to a pitch of foolishness through my nerves and brain. This caused me to feel, not uncomfortable, but rather fearful, as I am still, of serious effects from the incidents of to-day and yesterday.

She returned presently, bringing a smoking basin and a basket of work; and, having placed the former on the hob, drew in her seat, evidently pleased to find me so companionable.

Before I came to live here, she commenced, waiting no further invitation to her story; I was almost always at Wuthering Heights. . . .

[1847]

When a writer uses a narrative frame, there is often a thematic link between the frame and the main narrative. Both Lockwood and Mrs. Dean wish to understand how the past haunts as well as shapes the present, and to make sense of the present state of affairs at Wuthering Heights. With a frame of this sort, this story gets told in several different ways:

- Lockwood narrates his move to Thrushcross Grange and his first encounter with his landlord, Heathcliff, at neighboring Wuthering Heights.
- Lockwood asks Mrs. Dean about Heathcliff and Catherine and their histories. He records her story in a journal, quoting and paraphrasing her as she narrates up to the present.
- Within Mrs. Dean's story, other characters — including Catherine and Heathcliff — also narrate, telling stories within the story.
- Lockwood narrates the final section of the book, using the details of the story he has been told by Mrs. Dean to make sense of contemporary events.

This complex storytelling technique effectively draws a connection between Mrs. Dean and Lockwood as it moves between the frame and the main narrative. It also draws a connection between Lockwood and Heathcliff that goes well beyond that of landlord and tenant as Lockwood learns about Heathcliff's past — and perhaps most significantly, between Lockwood and the reader, who must try to make sense of strange and intriguing characters and events.

The following questions will help guide your analysis of point of view, and will become important when you come to the frame tales included in this book: *Heart of Darkness* (p. 327) and *Frankenstein* (p. 848).

- Is the point of view first person (*I*) or third person (*he*, *she*, *it*)?
- Is the narrator a participant or an observer in the story?
- If the point of view is first person, how reliable is the narrator?
- If the perspective is third person, is the narrator omniscient or limited omniscient?
- Does the point of view shift during the course of the story? If so, what is the impact?
- If the piece has a narrative frame, how does it relate thematically to the main narrative?

ACTIVITY

The following passage is from Colm Tóibín's novel *Brooklyn*, which takes place in the mid-twentieth century. Discuss how the setting, as told from the third-person limited omniscient point of view, characterizes the narrator, a young woman who has recently immigrated to Brooklyn from a small town in Ireland.

from Brooklyn

COLM TÓIBÍN

She liked the morning air and the quietness of these few leafy streets, streets that had shops only on the corners, streets where people lived, where there were three or four apartments in each house and where she passed women accompanying their children to school as she went to work. As she walked along, however, she knew she was getting close to the real world, which had wider streets and more traffic. Once she arrived at Atlantic Avenue, Brooklyn began to feel like a strange place to her, with so many gaps between buildings and so many derelict buildings. And then suddenly, when she arrived at Fulton Street, there would be so many people crowding to cross the street, and in such dense clusters, that on the first morning she thought a fight had broken out or someone was injured and they had gathered to get a good view.

[2009]

Symbol

Literary texts sometimes include objects, places, events, or even characters that carry meanings or associations beyond the literal. These **symbols** allow the author to draw connections to themes and ideas in the story, and often point the way to the meaning of the work as a whole. In literature and art, a symbol stands in for a meaning suggested more than specified, evoked more than defined or stated; it approaches a meaning signified but not explained. A symbol begins as something literal in the story, like the glass slipper in *Cinderella*. That literal thing then takes on metaphorical significance – it represents an idea (or ideas). What ideas does Cinderella's glass slipper represent? It's unique and beautiful, perhaps like Cinderella herself, amidst a sea of the usual ho-hum courtiers. It's fragile, like the brief spell that turned Cinderella into a princess. Or perhaps you read the story differently and find another meaning in the symbol of the glass slipper; symbols are frequently opportunities for interpretation.

You might have realized as you were reading the paragraph above that symbols are metaphorical. This is correct, but they are not the same as verbal metaphors. Verbal metaphors are isolated to the sentence or line where the metaphor is written. They are created by words and they are a matter of style. Symbols work on a larger scale. They are metaphors created from objects in the story, or literary elements like setting and character, and they tend to develop throughout a story, rather than existing in only one line.

Let's look at an example of symbolism that happens to include both a symbolic character and a symbolic setting, from Ernest Hemingway's short story, "The End of Something."

from The End of Something

ERNEST HEMINGWAY

In the old days Hortons Bay was a lumbering town. No one who lived in it was out of sound of the big saws in the mill by the lake. Then one year there were no more logs to make lumber. The lumber schooners came into the bay and were loaded with the cut of the mill that stood stacked in the yard. All the piles of lumber were carried away. The big mill building had all its machinery that was removable taken out and hoisted on board one of the schooners by the men who had worked in the mill. The schooner moved out of the bay toward the open lake carrying the two great saws, the travelling carriage that hurled the logs against the revolving, circular saws and all the rollers, wheels, belts and iron piled on a hull-deep load of lumber. Its open hold covered with canvas and lashed tight, the sails of the schooner filled and it moved out into the open lake, carrying with it everything that had made the mill a mill and Hortons Bay a town.

The one-story bunk houses, the eating-house, the company store, the mill offices, and the big mill itself stood deserted in the acres of sawdust that covered the swampy meadow by the shore of the bay.

Ten years later there was nothing of the mill left except the broken white limestone of its foundations showing through the swampy second growth as Nick and Marjorie rowed along the shore. They were trolling along the edge of the channel-bank where the bottom dropped off suddenly from sandy shallows to twelve feet of dark water. They were trolling on their way to the point to set night lines for rainbow trout.

"There's our old ruin, Nick," Marjorie said.

Nick, rowing, looked at the white stone in the green trees.

"There it is," he said.

"Can you remember when it was a mill?" Marjorie asked.

"I can just remember," Nick said.

"It seems more like a castle," Marjorie said.

[1924]

At this point in the story, Nick doesn't reply other than to say that the fish aren't biting. But already, the reader who notices the symbol of the lumber mill knows what the "something" in the title refers to. A perceptive reader will recognize how the town and the mill were once thriving, full of activity and energy, but are now hollow and empty. As symbols, the town and the mill and the activity all stand in for the deterioration of the relationship between Nick and Marjorie. When Marjorie proclaims, "There's our old ruin, Nick," she might as well be saying, "There's a symbol for our relationship." Marjorie's attempt to recall the life suggested by the opening symbolism is an effort to recapture the "castle" that once was — but the old symbol doesn't speak to Nick at all.

While recognizing symbols in literature is essential, it's equally important to avoid making your study of a short story, novel, or play just a hunt for common symbols. Symbols work by association and always fit into the context of the work as a whole, so be careful not to jump to conclusions. There is no secret code that says that water always symbolizes rebirth, for instance. Water might symbolize rebirth in one work but could suggest purity or infinite possibility in another. Some symbols are unique to specific texts, such as the green light at the end of the dock in *The Great Gatsby*.

ACTIVITY

Think of a movie that includes a symbol. Discuss what the symbol means and how it connects to the meaning of the work as a whole.

Symbol and Allegory

Sometimes you will read fiction in which nearly everything is symbolic, and the objects that work as symbols carry fixed meanings. Such symbols — ones that encompass an entire work — create allegories. An **allegory** is a literary work that portrays abstract ideas in concrete ways. Allegories often contain **archetypes**, cultural symbols that have become universally understood and recognized. Common examples include a garden, a dark forest, a desert, a mentor, a journey, or a quest. Allegorical characters are frequently personifications of abstract ideas, with names that often refer to those ideas. Unnamed allegorical characters are usually archetypes — for example, a particular father, mother, or child may represent the concepts of fatherhood, motherhood, or childhood.

Below is an example of a highly symbolic allegorical passage that relies on such archetypes, from Stephen King's book, *The Gunslinger*.

from The Gunslinger

STEPHEN KING

The man in black fled across the desert, and the gunslinger followed.

The desert was the apotheosis of all deserts, huge, standing to the sky for what looked like eternity in all directions. It was white and blinding and waterless and without feature save for the faint, cloudy haze of the mountains which sketched themselves on the horizon and the devil-grass which brought sweet dreams, nightmares, death. An occasional tombstone sign pointed the way, for once the drifted track that cut its way through the thick crust of alkali had been a highway. Coaches and buckas had followed it. The world had moved on since then. The world had emptied.

[1978]

To begin with, we have the archetype of a journey across a desert. We also have a "man in black" as a symbolic figure representing evil itself, while "the gunslinger" is a symbolic archetype of a hero, inspired by American westerns. The desert is a symbolic setting, and King is very direct about what it represents: "The world had emptied." This is not just a barren landscape, it is death itself. With this passage, King sets the stage. We know as readers that the story unfolding is about more than just two men following each other in the desert, it is a battle of good versus evil, an allegory of life versus death.

The following questions will help guide your analysis of symbols:

- What objects does the writer seem to emphasize, through description, repetition, or placement in the story?
- What might be symbolic about the setting? What characters or aspects of a character might be symbolic? What events might be symbolic?
- Is there a recurring pattern, or **motif**, of images or events?
- How does your symbolic interpretation fit with the context of the story?

ACTIVITY

Read the following short story by Naguib Mahfouz (1911–2006), an Egyptian writer and winner of the Nobel Prize. As you read, consider the title of the story as well as its symbolism. How might the story be considered an allegory? In what ways does it serve as a symbolic representation of the narrator's life?

Half a Day

NAGUIB MAHFOUZ

I proceeded alongside my father, clutching his right hand, running to keep up with the long strides he was taking. All my clothes were new: the black shoes, the green school uniform, and the red tarboosh. My delight in my new clothes, however, was not altogether unmarred, for this was no feast day but the day on which I was to be cast into school for the first time.

My mother stood at the window watching our progress, and I would turn toward her from time to time, as though appealing for help. We walked along a street lined with gardens; on both sides were extensive fields planted with crops, prickly pears, henna trees, and a few date palms.

"Why school?" I challenged my father openly. "I shall never do anything to annoy you."

"I'm not punishing you," he said, laughing. "School's not a punishment. It's the factory that makes useful men out of boys. Don't you want to be like your father and brothers?"

I was not convinced. I did not believe there 5
was really any good to be had in tearing me away from the intimacy of my home and throwing me into this building that stood at the end of the road like some huge, high-walled fortress, exceedingly stern and grim.

When we arrived at the gate we could see the courtyard, vast and crammed full of boys and girls. "Go in by yourself," said my father, "and join them. Put a smile on your face and be a good example to others."

I hesitated and clung to his hand, but he gently pushed me from him. "Be a man," he said. "Today you truly begin life. You will find me waiting for you when it's time to leave."

I took a few steps, then stopped and looked but saw nothing. Then the faces of boys and girls came into view. I did not know a single one of them, and none of them knew me. I felt I was a stranger who had lost his way. But glances of curiosity were directed toward me, and one boy approached and asked, "Who brought you?"

"My father," I whispered.

"My father's dead," he said quite simply. 10

I did not know what to say. The gate was closed, letting out a pitiable screech. Some of the children burst into tears. The bell rang. A lady came along, followed by a group of men. The men began sorting us into ranks. We were formed into an intricate pattern in the great courtyard surrounded on three sides by high buildings of several floors; from each floor we were overlooked by a long balcony roofed in wood.

"This is your new home," said the woman. "Here too there are mothers and fathers. Here there is everything that is enjoyable and beneficial to knowledge and religion. Dry your tears and face life joyfully."

We submitted to the facts, and this submission brought a sort of contentment. Living beings were drawn to other living beings, and from the first moments my heart made friends with such boys as were to be my friends and fell in love with such girls as I was to be in love with, so that it seemed my misgivings had had no basis. I had never imagined school would have this rich variety. We played all sorts of different games: swings, the vaulting horse, ball games. In the music room we chanted our first songs. We also had our first introduction to language. We saw a globe of the Earth, which revolved and showed the various continents and countries. We started learning the numbers. The story of the Creator of the universe was read to us, we were told of His present world and of His Hereafter, and we heard examples of what He said. We ate delicious food, took a little nap, and woke up to go on with friendship and love, play and learning.

As our path revealed itself to us, however, we did not find it as totally sweet and unclouded as we had presumed. Dust-laden winds and unexpected accidents came about suddenly, so we had to be watchful, at the ready, and very patient. It was not all a matter of playing and fooling around. Rivalries could bring about pain and hatred or give rise to fighting. And while the lady would sometimes smile, she would often scowl and scold. Even more frequently she would resort to physical punishment.

In addition, the time for changing one's mind was over and gone and there was no question of ever returning to the paradise of home. Nothing lay ahead of us but exertion, struggle, and perseverance. Those who were able took advantage of the opportunities for success and happiness that presented themselves amid the worries.

The bell rang announcing the passing of the day and the end of work. The throngs of children rushed toward the gate, which was opened again. I bade farewell to friends and sweethearts and passed through the gate. I peered around but found no trace of my father, who had promised to be there. I stepped aside to wait. When I had waited for a long time without avail, I decided to return home on my own. After I had taken a few steps, a middle-aged man passed by, and I realized at once that I knew him. He came toward me, smiling, and shook me by the hand, saying, "It's a long time since we last met—how are you?"

With a nod of my head, I agreed with him and in turn asked, "And you, how are you?"

"As you can see, not all that good, the Almighty be praised!"

Again he shook me by the hand and went off. I proceeded a few steps, then came to a startled halt. Good Lord! Where was the street lined with gardens? Where had it disappeared to? When did all these vehicles invade it? And when did all these hordes of humanity come to rest upon its surface? How did these hills of refuse come to cover its sides? And where were the fields that bordered it? High buildings had taken over, the street surged with children, and disturbing noises shook the air. At various points stood conjurers showing off their tricks and making snakes appear from baskets. Then there was a band announcing the opening of a circus, with clowns and weight lifters walking in front. A line of trucks carrying central security troops crawled majestically by. The siren of a fire engine shrieked, and it was not clear how the vehicle would cleave its way to reach the blazing fire. A battle raged between a taxi driver and his passenger, while the passenger's wife called out for help and no one answered. Good God! I was in a daze. My head spun. I almost went crazy. How could all this have happened in half a day, between early morning and sunset? I would find the answer at home with my father. But where was my home? I could see only tall buildings and hordes of people. I hastened on to the crossroads between the gardens and Abu Khoda. I had to cross Abu Khoda to reach my house, but the stream of cars would not let up. The fire engine's siren was shrieking at full pitch as it moved at a snail's pace, and I said to myself, "Let the fire take its pleasure in what it consumes." Extremely irritated, I wondered when I would be able to cross. I stood there a long time, until the young lad employed at the ironing shop on the corner came up to me. He stretched out his arm and said gallantly, "Grandpa, let me take you across."

[1989]

Theme

When we talk about the way a work of literature raises a question or explores an issue in addition to telling a story, we are talking about theme. The rich works you read in school usually have several themes, which are revealed through the piece's plot, character, setting, point of view, and symbols.

Identifying and articulating themes is not a simple process. Literary critic Northrop Frye used the term "the educated imagination" to describe the intersection of skills and knowledge with creativity. Think about the previous sections of this chapter as having educated your imagination so that now you're ready to uncover the themes of complex novels, plays, short stories, and even poems. As you come up with a theme for a piece of writing, you are inevitably interpreting it; thus, the theme you find may not be the same one others find. There can be many themes in a work — not just one "answer" waiting to be discovered.

Let's put some of these ideas to work by examining the themes of a short story by Pulitzer Prize–winning author Edward P. Jones.

The First Day

EDWARD P. JONES

On an otherwise unremarkable September morning, long before I learned to be ashamed of my mother, she takes my hand and we set off down New Jersey Avenue to begin my very first day of school. I am wearing a checkeredlike blue-and-green cotton dress, and scattered about these colors are bits of yellow and white and brown. My mother has uncharacteristically spent nearly an hour on my hair that morning, plaiting and replaiting so that now my scalp tingles. Whenever I turn my head quickly, my nose fills with the faint smell of Dixie Peach hair grease. The smell is somehow a soothing one now and I will reach for it time and time again before the morning ends. All the plaits, each with a blue barrette near the tip and each twisted into an uncommon sturdiness, will last until I go to bed that night, something that has never happened before. My stomach is full of milk and oatmeal sweetened with brown sugar. Like everything else I have on, my pale green slip and underwear are new, the underwear having come three to a plastic package with a little girl on the front who appears to be dancing. Behind my ears, my mother, to stop my whining, has dabbed the stingiest bit of her gardenia perfume, the last present my father gave her before he disappeared into memory. Because I cannot smell it, I have only her word that the perfume is there. I am also wearing yellow socks trimmed with thin lines of black and white around the tops. My shoes are my greatest joy, black patent-leather miracles, and when one is nicked at the toe later that morning in class, my heart will break.

I am carrying a pencil, a pencil sharpener, and a small ten-cent tablet with a black-and-white speckled cover. My mother does not believe that a girl in kindergarten needs such things, so I am taking them only because of my insistent whining and because they are presents from our neighbors, Mary Keith and Blondelle Harris. Miss Mary and Miss Blondelle are watching my two younger sisters until my mother returns. The women are as precious to me as my mother and sisters. Out playing one day, I have overheard an older child, speaking to another child, call Miss Mary and Miss Blondelle a word that is brand new to me. This is my mother: When I say the word in fun to one of my sisters, my mother slaps me across the mouth and the word is lost for years and years.

All the way down New Jersey Avenue, the sidewalks are teeming with children. In my neighborhood, I have many friends, but I see none of them as my mother and I walk. We cross New York Avenue, we cross Pierce Street, and we cross L and K, and still I see no one who knows my name. At I Street, between New Jersey Avenue and Third Street, we enter Seaton Elementary School, a timeworn, sad-faced building across the street from my mother's church, Mt. Carmel Baptist.

Just inside the front door, women out of the advertisements in *Ebony* are greeting other parents and children. The woman who greets us has pearls thick as jumbo marbles that come down almost to her navel, and she acts as if she had known me all my life, touching my shoulder, cupping her hand under my chin. She is enveloped in a perfume that I only know is not gardenia. When, in answer to her question, my mother tells her that we live at 1227 New Jersey Avenue, the woman first seems to be picturing in her head where we live. Then she shakes her head and says that we are at the wrong school, that we should be at Walker-Jones.

My mother shakes her head vigorously. "I want her to go here," my mother says. "If I'da wanted her someplace else, I'da took her there." The woman continues to act as if she has known me all my life, but she tells my mother that we live beyond the area that Seaton serves. My mother is not convinced and for several more minutes she questions the woman about why I cannot attend Seaton. For as many Sundays as I can remember, perhaps even Sundays when I was in her womb, my mother has pointed across I Street to Seaton as we come and go to Mt. Carmel. "You gonna go there and learn about the whole world." But one of the guardians of that place is saying no, and no again. I am learning this about my mother: The higher up on the scale of respectability a person is — and teachers are rather high up in her eyes — the less she is liable to let them push her around. But finally, I see in her eyes the closing gate, and she takes my hand and we leave the building. On the steps, she stops as people move past us on either side.

"Mama, I can't go to school?"

She says nothing at first, then takes my hand again and we are down the steps quickly and nearing New Jersey Avenue before I can blink. This is my mother: She says, "One monkey don't stop no show."

Walker-Jones is a larger, newer school and I immediately like it because of that. But it is not across the street from my mother's church, her rock, one of her connections to God, and I sense her doubts as she absently rubs her thumb over the back of her hand. We find our way to the crowded auditorium where gray metal chairs are set up in the middle of the room. Along the wall to the left are tables and other chairs. Every chair seems occupied by a child or adult. Somewhere in the room a child is crying, a cry that rises above the buzz-talk of so many people. Strewn about the floor are dozens and dozens of pieces of white paper, and people are walking over them without any thought of picking them up. And seeing this lack of concern, I am all of a sudden afraid.

"Is this where they register for school?" my mother asks a woman at one of the tables.

The woman looks up slowly as if she has heard this question once too often. She nods. She is tiny, almost as small as the girl standing beside her. The woman's hair is set in a mass of curlers and all of those curlers are made of paper money, here a dollar bill, there a five-dollar bill. The girl's hair is arrayed in curls, but some of them are beginning to droop and this makes me happy. On the table beside the woman's pocketbook is a large notebook, worthy of someone in high school, and looking at me looking at the notebook, the girl places her hand possessively on it. In her other hand she holds several pencils with thick crowns of additional erasers.

"These the forms you gotta use?" my mother asks the woman, picking up a few pieces of the paper from the table. "Is this what you have to fill out?"

The woman tells her yes, but that she need fill out only one.

"I see," my mother says, looking about the room. Then: "Would you help me with this form? That is, if you don't mind."

The woman asks my mother what she means.

"This form. Would you mind helpin me fill it out?"

The woman still seems not to understand.

"I can't read it. I don't know how to read or write, and I'm askin you to help me." My mother looks at me, then looks away. I know almost all of her looks, but this one is brand new to me. "Would you help me, then?"

The woman says Why sure, and suddenly she appears happier, so much more satisfied with everything. She finishes the form for her daughter and my mother and I step aside to wait for her. We find two chairs nearby and sit. My mother is now diseased, according to the girl's eyes, and until the moment her mother takes her and the form to the front of the auditorium, the girl never stops looking at my mother. I stare back at her. "Don't stare," my mother says to me. "You know better than that."

Another woman out of the *Ebony* ads takes the woman's child away. Now, the woman says upon returning, let's see what we can do for you two.

My mother answers the questions the woman reads off the form. They start with my last name, and then on to the first and middle names. This is school, I think. This is going to school. My mother slowly enunciates each word of my name. This is my mother: As the questions go on, she takes from her pocketbook document after document, as if they will support my right to attend school, as if she has been saving them up for just this moment. Indeed, she takes out more papers than I have ever seen her do in other places: my birth certificate, my baptismal record, a doctor's letter concerning my bout with chicken pox, rent receipts, records of immunization, a letter about our public assistance payments, even her marriage license — every single paper that has anything even remotely to do with my five-year-old life. Few of the papers are needed here, but it does not matter and my mother continues to pull out the documents with the purposefulness of a magician pulling out a long string of scarves. She has learned that money is the beginning and end of everything in this world, and when the woman finishes, my mother offers her fifty cents, and the woman accepts it without hesitation. My mother and I are just about the last parent and child in the room.

My mother presents the form to a woman sitting in front of the stage, and the woman looks at it and writes something on a white card, which she gives to my mother. Before long, the woman who has taken the girl with the drooping curls appears from behind us, speaks to the sitting woman, and introduces herself to my mother and me. She's to be my teacher, she tells my mother. My mother stares.

We go into the hall, where my mother kneels down to me. Her lips are quivering. "I'll be back to pick you up at twelve o'clock. I don't want you to go nowhere. You just wait right here. And listen to every word she say." I touch her lips and press them together. It is an old, old game between us. She puts my hand down at my side, which is not part of the game. She stands and looks a second at the teacher, then she turns and walks away. I see where she has darned one of her socks the night before. Her shoes make loud sounds in the hall. She passes through the doors and I can still hear the loud sounds of her shoes. And even when the teacher turns me toward the classrooms and I hear what must be the singing and talking of all the children in the world, I can still hear my mother's footsteps above it all.

[1992]

To uncover the themes of a story, you will have to rely on your observations, find portions of the work that seem significant or meaningful, and then explain why you think they are significant. Although literary elements often work together to create a theme, we're going to go element by element, in order to demonstrate a relatively systematic way of looking for themes.

Let's start with the plot of this story, which is pretty straightforward: an uneducated mother takes her daughter to the first day of kindergarten; they are refused admission to one school and have to go to another, where a kindly person assists the mother in filling out the necessary forms; the mother leaves the child at school, telling her to pay close attention to the teacher. That's pretty much it. Yet within that plot, we can see quite a few events that seem to have deeper significance and could point toward possible themes. For instance, why would a mother who cannot read do her utmost, overcoming obstacle after obstacle, to get her child into school? This seems a bit paradoxical, more than a little heartwarming, and definitely important. Is the author's message that perhaps the people who truly understand the importance of an education are the ones who haven't had the benefit of one?

Who are the characters in this story? The main characters are the mother and the daughter. The other characters are all female, mostly teachers. Where are the men in this story? That is definitely a question worth exploring, but let's stick to the mother and the daughter for now. How does the daughter change or develop because of the action of the plot? Think about the title: "The First Day." We can ask: the first day of what? Literally, it's the first day of school, but it is also the first day that the narrator is leaving her family and entering society as a whole. It's the first day that her education and her fate are being transferred from her mother to the female teachers, who are minor but important characters in this story. These observations suggest a number of themes, especially the importance of community in raising a child.

The story's setting is a poor neighborhood of Washington, D.C., and we're given details about the school the mother wants her daughter to attend — the school that is directly across from her church. Why is the proximity of the church important to the setting? How does it reveal a theme? The narrator tells us that the church is very important to her mother — it is her "rock" — so it's clear that the mother wants the daughter to go to the nearby school because it is familiar, safe, protected, and in a community she trusts. This aspect of the setting reinforces the theme we uncovered when looking at character: community is important in raising a child. But it also goes further, speaking to the mother's anxiety about letting her daughter go.

Point of view can often be a difficult platform for interpretation, but in this story, it is especially interesting. The narrator is the daughter, recalling the incident from the vantage point of adulthood. But the narrator is more specific about her point of view. She says that these events occurred "long before [she] learned to be ashamed of [her] mother" (para. 1). The word "learned" seems significant, given the context of this story about education. We think of education as being "book learning," but it's clear that some part of the narrator's education has involved "learning" to be ashamed of her mother. Yet as she's telling this story, she does not seem ashamed; she seems proud of her mother's heroic journey, proud that her mother overcame so many obstacles in order to make sure her daughter had a bright future. So one theme might involve the changing perspectives we have regarding our parents: When we are young, we think they are strong and infallible, but we grow to see their flaws as we become part of the world rather than just part of a family; it takes time to come back around to respect and appreciate all the things our parents have done on our behalf.

Not every story operates through symbols, and although this short piece may not have many, the narrator's shoes could certainly be symbolic. She says, "My shoes are my greatest joy, black patent-leather miracles, and when one is nicked at the toe later that morning in class, my heart will break" (para. 1). Perhaps the fate of these shoes mirrors her relationship with her mother. Before going out into the world, she is proud of her mother, yet in the process of going to school, meeting other people, and learning new things, just like the shiny shoes, her mother's image gets nicked. Perhaps that change is what really breaks her heart. So, one theme might be that on the first day of school, we are letting go of our parents just as much as they are letting go of us.

As you can see, as you consider themes, you often move beyond the text to draw conclusions about the real world. "The First Day," for example, suggests something about the role of education in our lives that goes beyond this particular five-year-old's first day in kindergarten. Isn't this story really about the role education can play in parent-child relationships, when the child's education outpaces that of the parent? Maybe Jones is asking us to think about what happened later, as the narrator aged, was successful at school, went on to college. Her mother may be one hundred percent supportive of her daughter's education. Yet, those very opportunities can divide and separate the two, as the daughter's experiences diverge from those of her mother. The narrator is looking back with obvious love and appreciation for her mother, yet Jones does not give us the story of what took place between "the first day" and the point from which the narrator remembers it.

There is no magic formula for finding a novel, play, or short story's themes other than observation and interpretation — and, of course, rereading. Nevertheless, here are a few suggestions to keep in mind as you try to articulate themes.

1. *Subject and theme are not the same*. The subject of Jones's story may be a little girl's first day of school, but the theme is what the work says about the subject. Thus, you should state a theme as a complete sentence (or two). For instance, "Once a child enters school, teachers, peers, and society as a whole take over some of the responsibility for raising that child. While this can expand a child's horizons and create opportunities for him or her, it can also test the bond between parent and child."

2. *Avoid clichés*. Even though "love conquers all" may indeed be a theme of Jones's story, try to state it in a more original and sophisticated way. Clichés are lazy statements that ignore the complexity of a literary text.
3. *Do not ignore contradictory details*. You don't want to claim, for instance, that the theme of Jones's story is about how a little girl came to be ashamed of her mother, since the mother is portrayed heroically in the story.
4. *A theme is not a moral*. It may sometimes be tempting to extract "the moral of the story" (which is likely to be a cliché). Resist! Writers of drama and fiction — and poetry — work indirectly. If a writer wanted to convey an idea directly, he or she would write an editorial for a newspaper. Those who choose to write a literary work do so to explore ideas indirectly through plots, characters, settings, points of view, symbols, and the like.
5. *A literary work almost always has more than one theme*. Notice how many themes we have already discussed for this very short story. It is likely that you will think of even more as you bring your own ideas and experiences to the piece.
6. *Themes can be questions.* Author Toni Morrison has said that she does not write to put forth answers but to explore questions. You'll read some works that present an intellectual or a moral dilemma, or pose a conundrum that you are not obligated to answer. Questions "The First Day" poses might be these: Why must parenting always involve loss? Do those who lack education value it more than those who take it for granted? When do children begin to understand and appreciate their parents?

ACTIVITY

Read the following short story by Antiguan-American writer Jamaica Kincaid and try to articulate at least three possible themes.

Girl

JAMAICA KINCAID

Wash the white clothes on Monday and put them on the stone heap; wash the color clothes on Tuesday and put them on the clothesline to dry; don't walk barehead in the hot sun; cook pumpkin fritters in very hot sweet oil; soak your little cloths right after you take them off; when buying cotton to make yourself a nice blouse, be sure that it doesn't have gum on it, because that way it won't hold up well after a wash; soak salt fish overnight before you cook it; is it true that you sing benna in Sunday school?; always eat your food in such a way that it won't turn someone else's stomach; on Sundays try to walk like a lady and not like the slut you are so bent on becoming; don't sing benna in Sunday school; you mustn't speak to wharf-rat boys, not even to give directions; don't eat fruits on the street — flies will follow you; *but I don't sing benna on Sundays at all and never in Sunday school*; this is how to sew on a button; this is how to make a buttonhole for the button you have just sewed on; this is how to hem a dress when you see the hem coming down and so to prevent yourself from looking like the slut I know you are so bent on becoming; this is how you iron your father's khaki shirt so that it doesn't have a crease; this is how you iron your father's khaki pants so that they don't have a crease; this is how you grow okra — far from the house, because okra tree harbors red ants; when you are growing dasheen, make sure it gets plenty of water or else it makes your throat itch when you are eating it; this is how you sweep a corner; this is how you sweep a whole house; this is how you sweep a yard; this is how you smile to someone you don't like too much; this is how you smile to someone you don't like at all; this is how you smile to someone you like completely; this is how you set a table for tea; this is how you set a table for dinner; this is how you set a table for dinner with an important guest; this is how you set a table for lunch; this is how you set a table for breakfast; this is how to behave in the presence of men who don't know you very well, and this way they won't recognize immediately the slut I have warned you against becoming; be sure to wash every day, even if it is with your own spit; don't squat down to play marbles — you are not a boy, you know; don't pick people's flowers — you might catch something; don't throw stones at blackbirds, because it might not be a blackbird at all; this is how to make a bread pudding; this is how to make doukona; this is how to make pepper pot; this is how to make a good medicine for a cold; this is how to make a good medicine to throw away a child before it even becomes a child; this is how to catch a fish; this is how to throw back a fish you don't like, and that way something bad won't fall on you; this is how to bully a man; this is how a man bullies you; this is how to love a man, and if this doesn't work there are other ways, and if they don't work don't feel too bad about giving up; this is how to spit up in the air if you feel like it, and this is how to move quick so that it doesn't fall on you; this is how to make ends meet; always squeeze bread to make sure it's fresh; *but what if the baker won't let me feel the bread?*; you mean to say that after all you are really going to be the kind of woman who the baker won't let near the bread?

[1978]

ANALYZING DRAMA

Analyzing drama is quite similar to analyzing fiction: both require consideration of plot, character, setting, symbol, and theme. However, there are some differences. The most important difference is that point of view is not a major concern in drama, because few plays have a narrator. If there is one, he or she is likely presented as a character who occasionally steps out to speak to the audience. Another major difference is that a play is a theatrical as well as a literary experience. When we read a play, we imagine the performance: the actors creating the characters and reading the lines, the director interpreting the atmosphere and physical setting on stage, and especially the interaction between the performers and the audience. When we see a play on stage, we are literally seeing how other people read, imagine, and interpret that play, and that inevitably adds to the meaning of the work. Let's look at some other ways that analyzing drama is different from analyzing fiction.

Plot

Plot works similarly in drama as in fiction. In fact, our traditional concept of how to structure a plot (p. 16) was developed by studying classic works from Greek drama and Shakespeare's plays. Drama, however, is often broken into **acts**, and acts are further divided into **scenes**. Acts and scenes structure a play, and it can be revealing to consider why the acts and scenes are divided as they are.

Character

Since a play does not have a narrator, **dialogue**, or the conversation between two or more characters, becomes an essential way to reveal character. Though playwrights attempt to represent normal speech patterns and usage, dramatic dialogue is usually different from normal human conversation. Every minute on stage must be used to the greatest advantage, so conversations must be pointed and charged with meaning. When reading drama, you should try to isolate three elements of dialogue: (1) the content of what is being said; (2) the way it is being said, including both the language and the stage directions for delivering the line; and (3) the reaction and response from other characters.

In *Pygmalion* by George Bernard Shaw, the two central characters, Eliza Doolittle and Henry Higgins, come from different worlds: she is a Cockney flower girl, Higgins is a professor of phonetics (pronunciation). Higgins bets that he can "make a duchess of this draggle-tailed guttersnipe" in six months, and he wins the bet. The following dialogue takes place as Eliza realizes that she's a fish out of water in both her new world and her old world. In this exchange, notice how the dialogue characterizes Eliza and Henry. You might want to read the lines aloud to get a better sense of the pacing and rhythm, noting that Shaw uses spacing to emphasize some words.

from **Pygmalion**

GEORGE BERNARD SHAW

ELIZA *tries to control herself and feel indifferent as she rises and walks across to the hearth to switch off the lights. By the time she gets there she is on the point of screaming. She sits down in Higgins's chair and holds on hard to the arms. Finally she gives way and flings herself furiously on the floor raging.*

HIGGINS *[in despairing wrath outside]*: What the devil have I done with my slippers? *[He appears at the door].*

LIZA *[snatching up the slippers, and hurling them at him one after the other with all her force]*: There are your slippers. And there. Take your slippers; and may you never have a day's luck with them!

HIGGINS *[astounded]*: What on earth—! *[He comes to her].* Whats the matter? Get up. *[He pulls her up].* Anything wrong?

LIZA *[breathless]*: Nothing wrong—with y o u. Ive won your bet for you, havnt I? Thats enough for you. *I* dont matter, I suppose.

HIGGINS Y o u won my bet! You! Presumptuous insect! *I* won it. What did you throw those slippers at me for?

LIZA Because I wanted to smash your face. Id like to kill you, you selfish brute. Why didnt you leave me where you picked me out of—in the gutter? You thank God its all over, and that now you can throw me back again there, do you? *[She crisps her fingers frantically].*

HIGGINS *[looking at her in cool wonder]*: The creature i s nervous, after all.

LIZA *[gives a suffocated scream of fury, and instinctively darts her nails at his face]*: !!

HIGGINS *[catching her wrists]*: Ah! would you? Claws in, you cat. How dare you shew your temper to me? Sit down and be quiet. *[He throws her roughly into the easy-chair].*

LIZA *[crushed by superior strength and weight]*: Whats to become of me? Whats to become of me?

HIGGINS How the devil do I know whats to become of you? What does it matter what becomes of you?

LIZA You dont care. I know you dont care. You wouldnt care if I was dead. I'm nothing to you — not so much as them slippers.

HIGGINS *[thundering]*: T h o s e slippers.

LIZA *[with bitter submission]*: Those slippers. I didnt think it made any difference now.

A pause. **ELIZA** *hopeless and crushed.* **HIGGINS** *a little uneasy.*

HIGGINS *[in his loftiest manner]*: Why have you begun going on like this? May I ask whether you complain of your treatment here?

LIZA No.

HIGGINS Has anybody behaved badly to you? Colonel Pickering? Mrs. Pearce? Any of the servants?

LIZA No.

HIGGINS I presume you dont pretend that I have treated you badly.

LIZA No.

HIGGINS I am glad to hear it. *[He moderates his tone].* Perhaps youre tired after the strain of the day. Will you have a glass of champagne? *[He moves towards the door].*

LIZA No. *[Recollecting her manners]* Thank you.

HIGGINS *[good-humored again]*: This has been coming on you for some days. I suppose it was natural for you to be anxious about the garden party. But thats all over now. *[He pats her kindly on the shoulder. She writhes].* Theres nothing more to worry about.

LIZA No. Nothing more for y o u to worry about. *[She suddenly rises and gets away from him by going to the piano bench, where she sits and hides her face].* Oh God! I wish I was dead.

HIGGINS *[staring after her in sincere surprise]*: Why? in heaven's name, why? *[Reasonably, going to her]* Listen to me, Eliza. All this irritation is purely subjective.

LIZA I dont understand. Im too ignorant.

HIGGINS Its only imagination. Low spirits and nothing else. Nobodys hurting you. Nothings wrong. You go to bed like a good girl and sleep it off. Have a little cry and say your prayers: that will make you comfortable.

LIZA I heard y o u r prayers. "Thank God its all over!"

HIGGINS *[impatiently]*: Well, dont you thank God its all over? Now you are free and can do what you like.

LIZA *[pulling herself together in desperation]*: What am I fit for? What have you left me fit for? Where am I to go? What am I to do? What's to become of me?

[1913]

Perhaps what is most striking in this dialogue is that Higgins never really hears Liza. She is despondent and trying to figure out how she's going to live the rest of her life, while he's trying to find his slippers. When she hurls the slippers at him along with the wish that they never bring him anything good, he responds with utter surprise, asking, "Anything wrong?" The understatement in this scene is humorous, yet as the dialogue continues, we realize that Higgins completely lacks empathy for the young woman, who is his student — and his subject. In the face of her anger, he responds indignantly that she has stepped out of her place: "Presumptuous insect," he calls her. She accuses him of not caring at all about her, and he responds by correcting her diction. He counters her emotion with sheer logic, asking her if she has been treated badly by anyone during her stay with him. Since she cannot point to any concrete act of mistreatment, he concludes that her problem is simply stress, which he dismisses as "purely subjective." Ultimately, he treats her as if she were a child, sending her off to bed to have a good cry and get some rest. The dialogue has not only shown us the quintessential failure to communicate but also characterized Higgins as cerebral and detached and Liza as a woman in the midst of an identity crisis.

Another important technique that playwrights use to reveal character is the **soliloquy** — a **monologue** in which a character, alone on the stage, reveals his or her thoughts or emotions, as if the character is thinking out loud. Through a soliloquy, a playwright can reveal to the audience a character's motivation, intent, or even doubt. For example, in William Shakespeare's *Richard III*, Richard — Duke of Gloucester, brother to King Edward IV, and later King Richard III of England — opens the play with the following soliloquy.

from Richard III

WILLIAM SHAKESPEARE

Enter **RICHARD DUKE OF GLOUCESTER,** *solus*

RICHARD Now is the winter of our discontent
Made glorious summer by this son of [1] York,
And all the clouds that loured[2] upon our house
In the deep bosom of the ocean buried.
Now are our brows bound with victorious wreaths,
Our bruisèd arms hung up for monuments,
Our stern alarums changed to merry meetings,
Our dreadful marches to delightful measures.[3]
Grim-visaged war[4] hath smoothed his wrinkled front,
And now, instead of mounting barbèd[5] steeds
To fright the souls of fearful adversaries,
He[6] capers[7] nimbly in a lady's chamber
To the lascivious[8] pleasing of a lute.
But I that am not shaped for sportive tricks
Nor made to court an amorous looking-glass,
I that am rudely stamped and want love's majesty
To strut before a wanton[9] ambling nymph,
I that am curtailed of this fair proportion,
Cheated of feature by dissembling[10] nature,
Deformed, unfinished, sent before my time

[1] **sun of York:** a pun on "son" and reference to the King. — Eds.
[2] **lour'd:** scowled. — Eds.
[3] **measures:** stately dances. — Eds.
[4] **Grim-visaged war:** Mars (Ares), the Greek god of war. — Eds.
[5] **barbed steeds:** armored horses. — Eds.
[6] **he:** Mars (Ares). — Eds.
[7] **capers:** frolics about. — Eds.
[8] **lascivious:** seductive. — Eds.
[9] **wanton:** lewd. — Eds.
[10] **dissembling:** lying, deceitful. — Eds.

Into this breathing world scarce half made up,
And that so lamely and unfashionable[11]
That dogs bark at me as I halt by them,
Why, I, in this weak piping[12] time of peace,
Have no delight to pass away the time,
Unless to see my shadow in the sun
And descant[13] on mine own deformity.
And therefore, since I cannot prove a lover
To entertain these fair well-spoken days,
I am determinèd to prove a villain
And hate the idle pleasures of these days.

[1593]

[11] **unfashionable:** misshapen, ugly. — Eds.
[12] **piping:** the pipe was associated with peace, the fife with war. — Eds.
[13] **descant:** to comment at length, to discourse, to riff on an idea or theme. — Eds.

This soliloquy reveals that Richard, the play's main character, has villainous intent. In his deformity, he feels out of place, at odds with his surroundings, and expresses jealousy and disdain for those not "curtailed of this fine proportion." Richard prefers "dreadful marches" to "delightful measures," expressing his scorn for "glorious summer" and for his brother the king. The duplicity that puts the plot in motion and creates the conflict of the play is clear to the audience but not to other characters, resulting in **dramatic irony**. The audience has become privy to Richard's inner thoughts. When he says, "I am determinèd to prove a villain," he lets the audience in on his plans. The audience knows the king is in danger. Without a narrator to give us access to the mind of a character, a soliloquy is the perfect way to expose his or her inner workings, struggles, reflections, and intentions.

Setting

Setting is different in a play because there is a physical set to consider. The playwright has to keep this in mind when writing and be realistic about what most theaters will be able to stage. In modern plays, we usually find fairly explicit information about the setting, which a director can use to create a set and which we, as readers, can use to build a mental image. In *A Doll's House* by Henrik Ibsen, for instance, the scenery for act I is described in considerable detail:

from **A Doll's House**

HENRIK IBSEN

A comfortable room, tastefully but not expensively furnished. A door to the right in the back wall leads to the entryway; another to the left leads to HELMER'S *study. Between these doors, a piano. Midway in the left-hand wall a door, and further back a window. Near the window a round table with an armchair and a small sofa. In the right-hand wall, toward the rear, a door, and nearer the foreground a porcelain stove with two armchairs and a rocking chair beside it. Between the stove and the side door, a small table. Engravings on the walls. An étagère with china figures and other small art objects; a small bookcase with richly bound books; the floor carpeted; a fire burning in the stove. It is a winter day.*

[A bell rings in the entryway; shortly after we hear the door being unlocked. NORA *comes into the room, humming happily to herself; she is wearing street clothes and carries an armload of packages, which she puts down on the table to the right. She has left the hall door open, and through it a Delivery Boy is seen holding a Christmas tree and a basket, which he gives to the Maid who let them in.]*

[1879]

Ibsen's instructions indicate where doors and windows are, the location of a piano, the placement of a rocker next to two armchairs. At the same time, some of the directions are subject to interpretation, such as this being a "comfortable room, tastefully but not expensively furnished." That part is left to the reader's — or set designer's — imagination.

ACTIVITY

Read the opening stage directions that Lorraine Hansberry wrote for her play *A Raisin in the Sun*. What is the connection between the setting and the characters? How does this opening section suggest ideas likely to be explored during the course of the play?

from A Raisin in the Sun

LORRAINE HANSBERRY

The Younger living room would be a comfortable and well-ordered room if it were not for a number of indestructible contradictions to this state of being. Its furnishings are typical and undistinguished and their primary feature now is that they have clearly had to accommodate the living of too many people for too many years — and they are tired. Still, we can see that at some time, a time probably no longer remembered by the family (except perhaps for Mama), the furnishings of this room were actually selected with care and love and even hope — and brought to this apartment and arranged with taste and pride.

That was a long time ago. Now the once loved pattern of the couch upholstery has to fight to show itself from under acres of crocheted doilies and couch covers which have themselves finally come to be more important than the upholstery. And here a table or a chair has been moved to disguise the worn places in the carpet; but the carpet has fought back by showing its weariness, with depressing uniformity, elsewhere on its surface.

Weariness has, in fact, won in this room. Everything has been polished, washed, sat on, used, scrubbed too often. All pretenses but living itself have long since vanished from the very atmosphere of this room.

Moreover, a section of this room, for it is not really a room unto itself, though the landlord's lease would make it seem so, slopes backward to provide a small kitchen area, where the family prepares the meals that are eaten in the living room proper, which must also serve as dining room. The single window that has been provided for these "two" rooms is located in this kitchen area. The sole natural light the family may enjoy in the course of a day is only that which fights its way through this little window.

At left, a door leads to a bedroom which is shared by Mama and her daughter, Beneatha. At right, opposite, is a second room (which in the beginning of the life of this apartment was probably a breakfast room) which serves as a bedroom for Walter and his wife, Ruth.

TIME *Sometime between World War II and the present.*

PLACE *Chicago's Southside.*

AT RISE *It is morning dark in the living room. Travis is asleep on the make-down bed at center. An alarm clock sounds from within the bedroom at right, and presently Ruth enters from that room and closes the door behind her. She crosses sleepily toward the window. As she passes her sleeping son she reaches down and shakes him a little. At the window she raises the shade and a dusky Southside morning light comes in feebly. She fills a pot with water and puts it on to boil. She calls to the boy, between yawns, in a slightly muffled voice.*

Ruth is about thirty. We can see that she was a pretty girl, even exceptionally so, but now it is apparent that life has been little that she expected, and disappointment has already begun to hang in her face. In a few years, before thirty-five even, she will be known among her people as a "settled woman."

She crosses to her son and gives him a good, final, rousing shake.

[1959]

Symbol

In drama, symbols are intended to be visually represented on stage, making them even more clear and powerful than symbols in fiction. These symbols may be part of the setting, character, or even the plot. Let's return to the stage directions for *A Doll's House*. Ibsen opens act II by shifting the setting just slightly:

> *Same room. Beside the piano the Christmas tree now stands stripped of ornament, burned-down candle stubs on its ragged branches.* NORA'S *street clothes lie on the sofa.* NORA, *alone in the room, moves restlessly about; at last she stops at the sofa and picks up her coat.*

Notice the change in the Christmas tree from act I to act II. The Christmas tree and its degradation become a symbol of the intensifying conflict going on in the household.

In drama, any item used by an actor or as part of scenery is called a **prop** — short for "theatrical property," because props are items owned not by the actors but by the theater or troupe. Props may simply add to a character's appearance (a pipe held by a detective) or to the atmosphere created by the setting (an old rocking chair), but they frequently function as symbols. In August Wilson's 1987 play *The Piano Lesson*, the piano is a central symbol of the play. Wilson emphasizes its importance in his opening directions to the play:

> *Dominating the parlor is an old upright piano. On the legs of the piano, carved in the manner of African sculpture, are mask-like figures resembling totems. The carvings are rendered with a grace and power of invention that lifts them out of the realm of craftsmanship and into the realm of art.*

Wilson reveals the symbolic meaning of the piano through the course of the play. Purchased through an exchange for slaves, the piano symbolizes the treatment of slaves not as human beings but as property. The piano becomes the site of conflict when a family member wants to sell it to purchase land. How the characters view the piano tells us something about them and their values. Wilson scholar Sandra Shannon describes its importance: "a 135-year-old piano that is simultaneously the Charles family heirloom and a unifying device for the play . . . [it is] the center of the play's conflict as well as its symbolic core."

When considering the relationship between setting and symbol, it is good to keep in mind the principle that has come to be called "Chekhov's gun." Playwright Anton Chekhov said, "If in the first act you have hung a pistol on the wall, then in the following one it should be fired. Otherwise don't put it there." Chekhov is suggesting that symbols should be intentional, not misleading.

Elements of the plot itself can work as symbols, especially in performance. In *The Gin Game*, which won the 1978 Pulitzer Prize for Drama, playwright D. L. Coburn depicts two characters, Weller and Fonsia, in a home for the elderly. As they become acquainted, their conversation becomes increasingly adversarial, a battle of sorts. Here is one exchange close to the end of the play:

---

from **The Gin Game**

D. L. COBURN

WELLER *[Sitting down]*: Well, come on, I'll play you a hand of gin.

FONSIA You know, Weller, you can be such an . . . an enjoyable person to be with — you've got a wonderful sense of humor . . . If it wasn't for that damn gin game.

WELLER My goodness, Fonsia. Such language.

FONSIA Weller, I've played all the cards I'm going to play.

WELLER Now, Fonsie, I'm not going to argue with you. We're playing gin! *[**FONSIA** gets to her feet.]*

FONSIA That's it, Weller! You're not going to drop this gin game business . . . and I'm not going to play. So there's no reason for us to sit here and fight over it. I'll just go on in.

WELLER You stay right where you are.

FONSIA It's the only thing I know to do.

WELLER What do you mean, it's the only thing you know to do?? You came out here, didn't you? *[**WELLER** is now on his feet.]*

FONSIA Yes, I did. But certainly not to play gin. All I wanted . . .

WELLER All you wanted to do was manipulate me! We've been playing your game . . . NOW WE'RE GONNA PLAY MINE.

[1976]

In the course of the play — seventeen hands of gin rummy — these characters drop their pleasant façades and reveal their controlling and bitter natures. The recreational activity of playing cards transforms into something larger than a mere game. As the audience reads or watches the play, the card game that moves the plot forward comes to symbolize the battle with life and aging that the characters are waging. Weller thinks he has gotten a bad hand, and he tries to change his luck, if only symbolically, by winning at gin rummy. The play asks: Do you play your cards by being honest? by bluffing and lying? Can you strategize and control the game, or is it all a matter of luck? No wonder the author described the card game as "the engine that drives the play."

ACTIVITY

Theme functions similarly in drama as it does in fiction. Choose a play you have read or a movie you have recently seen and articulate at least two of its themes, paying careful attention to character, dialogue, setting, and symbol.

FROM ANALYSIS TO ESSAY: WRITING AN INTERPRETIVE ESSAY

Let's take a look at a short play. As you read it, consider the literary elements we have discussed: plot, character, setting, and symbol. Try to formulate at least two or three thematic statements that could become the thesis for an interpretive essay.

Trifles

SUSAN GLASPELL

Characters

GEORGE HENDERSON *county attorney*
HENRY PETERS *sheriff*
LEWIS HALE *a neighboring farmer*
MRS. PETERS
MRS. HALE

SCENE *The kitchen in the now abandoned farmhouse of John Wright, a gloomy kitchen, and left without having been put in order — unwashed pans under the sink, a loaf of bread outside the breadbox, a dish towel on the table — other signs of incompleted work. At the rear the outer door opens and the* SHERIFF *comes in followed by the* COUNTY ATTORNEY *and* HALE. *The* SHERIFF *and* HALE *are men in middle life, the* COUNTY ATTORNEY *is a young man; all are much bundled up and go at once to the stove. They are followed by the two women — the* SHERIFF*'s wife first; she is a slight wiry woman, a thin nervous face.* MRS. HALE *is larger and would ordinarily be called more comfortable looking, but she is disturbed now and looks fearfully about as she enters. The women have come in slowly, and stand close together near the door.*

COUNTY ATTORNEY *[rubbing his hands]*: This feels good. Come up to the fire, ladies.

MRS. PETERS *[after taking a step forward]*: I'm not — cold.

SHERIFF *[unbuttoning his overcoat and stepping away from the stove as if to mark the beginning of official business]*: Now, Mr. Hale, before we move things about, you explain to Mr. Henderson just what you saw when you came here yesterday morning.

COUNTY ATTORNEY By the way, has anything been moved? Are things just as you left them yesterday?

SHERIFF *[looking about]*: It's just about the same. When it dropped below zero last night I thought I'd better send Frank out this morning to make a fire for us — no use getting pneumonia with a big case on, but I told him not to touch anything except the stove — and you know Frank.

COUNTY ATTORNEY Somebody should have been left here yesterday.

SHERIFF Oh — yesterday. When I had to send Frank to Morris Center for that man who went crazy — I want you to know I had my hands full yesterday. I knew you could get back from Omaha by today and as long as I went over everything here myself —

COUNTY ATTORNEY Well, Mr. Hale, tell just what happened when you came here yesterday morning.

HALE Harry and I had started to town with a load of potatoes. We came along the road from my place and as I got here I said, "I'm going to see if I can't get John Wright to go in with me on a party telephone." I spoke to Wright about it once before and he put me off, saying folks talked too much anyway, and all he asked was peace and quiet — I guess you know about how much he talked himself; but I thought maybe if I went to the house and talked about it before his wife, though I said to Harry that I didn't know as what his wife wanted made much difference to John —

COUNTY ATTORNEY Let's talk about that later, Mr. Hale. I do want to talk about that, but tell now just what happened when you got to the house.

HALE I didn't hear or see anything; I knocked at the door, and still it was all quiet inside. I knew they must be up, it was past eight o'clock. So I knocked again, and I thought I heard somebody say, "Come in." I wasn't sure, I'm not sure yet, but I opened the door — this door *[indicating the door by which the two women are still standing]* and there in that rocker — *[pointing to it]* sat Mrs. Wright. *[They all look at the rocker.]*

COUNTY ATTORNEY What — was she doing?

HALE She was rockin' back and forth. She had her apron in her hand and was kind of — pleating it.

COUNTY ATTORNEY And how did she — look?

HALE Well, she looked queer.

COUNTY ATTORNEY How do you mean — queer?

HALE Well, as if she didn't know what she was going to do next. And kind of done up.

COUNTY ATTORNEY How did she seem to feel about your coming?

HALE Why, I don't think she minded — one way or other. She didn't pay much attention. I said, "How do, Mrs. Wright, it's cold, ain't it?" And she said, "Is it?" — and went on kind of pleating at her apron. Well, I was surprised; she didn't ask me to come up to the stove, or to set down, but just sat there, not even looking at me, so I said, "I want to see John." And then she — laughed. I guess you would call it a laugh. I thought of Harry and the team outside, so I said a little sharp: "Can't I see John?" "No," she says, kind o' dull like. "Ain't he home?" says I. "Yes," says she, "he's home." "Then why can't I see him?" I asked her, out of patience. "'Cause he's dead," says she. "*Dead?*" says I. She just nodded her head, not getting a bit excited, but rockin' back and forth. "Why — where is he?" says I, not knowing what to say. She just pointed upstairs — like that *[himself pointing to the room above]*. I started for the stairs, with the idea of going up there. I walked from there to here — then I says, "Why, what did he die of?" "He died of a rope round his neck," says she, and just went on pleatin' at her apron. Well, I went out and called Harry. I thought I might — need help. We went upstairs and there he was lyin' —

COUNTY ATTORNEY I think I'd rather have you go into that upstairs, where you can point it all out. Just go on now with the rest of the story.

HALE Well, my first thought was to get that rope off. It looked . . . *[stops; his face twitches]* . . . but Harry, he went up to him, and he said, "No, he's dead all right, and we'd better not touch anything." So we went back downstairs. She was still sitting that same way. "Has anybody been notified?" I asked. "No," says she, unconcerned. "Who did this, Mrs. Wright?" said Harry. He said it businesslike — and she stopped pleatin' of her apron. "I don't know," she says. "You don't *know*?" says Harry. "No," says she. "Weren't you sleepin' in the bed with him?" says Harry. "Yes," says she, "but I was on the inside." "Somebody slipped a rope round his neck and strangled him and you didn't wake up?" says Harry. "I didn't wake up," she said after him. We must 'a' looked as if we didn't see how that could be, for after a minute she said, "I sleep sound." Harry was going to ask her more questions but I said maybe we ought to let her tell her story first to the coroner, or the sheriff, so Harry went fast as he could to Rivers' place, where there's a telephone.

COUNTY ATTORNEY And what did Mrs. Wright do when she knew that you had gone for the coroner?

HALE She moved from the rocker to that chair over there *[pointing to a small chair in the corner]* and just sat there with her hands held together and looking down. I got a feeling that I ought to make some conversation, so I said I had come in to see if John wanted to put in a telephone, and at that she started to laugh, and then she stopped and looked at me — scared. *[The* **COUNTY ATTORNEY**, *who has had his notebook out, makes a note.]* I dunno, maybe it wasn't scared. I wouldn't like to say it was. Soon Harry got back, and then Dr. Lloyd came and you, Mr. Peters, and so I guess that's all I know that you don't.

COUNTY ATTORNEY *[looking around]*: I guess we'll go upstairs first — and then out to the barn and around there. *[To the* **SHERIFF**.*]* You're convinced that there was nothing important here — nothing that would point to any motive?

SHERIFF Nothing here but kitchen things. *[The* **COUNTY ATTORNEY**, *after again looking around the kitchen, opens the door of a cupboard closet. He gets up on a chair and looks on a shelf. Pulls his hand away, sticky.]*

COUNTY ATTORNEY Here's a nice mess. *[The women draw nearer.]*

MRS. PETERS *[to the other woman]*: Oh, her fruit; it did freeze. *[To the Lawyer.]* She worried about that when it turned so cold. She said the fire'd go out and her jars would break.

SHERIFF *[rises]*: Well, can you beat the woman! Held for murder and worryin' about her preserves.

COUNTY ATTORNEY I guess before we're through she may have something more serious than preserves to worry about.

HALE Well, women are used to worrying over trifles. *[The two women move a little closer together.]*

COUNTY ATTORNEY *[with the gallantry of a young politician]*: And yet, for all their worries, what would we do without the ladies? *[The women do not unbend. He goes to the sink, takes a dipperful of water from the pail, and pouring it into a basin, washes his hands. Starts to wipe them on the roller towel, turns it for a cleaner place.]* Dirty towels! *[Kicks his foot against the pans under the sink.]* Not much of a housekeeper, would you say, ladies?

MRS. HALE *[stiffly]*: There's a great deal of work to be done on a farm.

COUNTY ATTORNEY To be sure. And yet *[with a little bow to her]* I know there are some Dickson county farmhouses which do not have such roller towels. *[He gives it a pull to expose its full length again.]*

MRS. HALE Those towels get dirty awful quick. Men's hands aren't always as clean as they might be.

COUNTY ATTORNEY Ah, loyal to your sex, I see. But you and Mrs. Wright were neighbors. I suppose you were friends, too.

MRS. HALE *[shaking her head]*: I've not seen much of her of late years. I've not been in this house — it's more than a year.

COUNTY ATTORNEY And why was that? You didn't like her?

MRS. HALE I liked her all well enough. Farmers' wives have their hands full, Mr. Henderson. And then —

COUNTY ATTORNEY Yes — ?

MRS. HALE *[looking about]*: It never seemed a very cheerful place.

COUNTY ATTORNEY No — it's not cheerful. I shouldn't say she had the homemaking instinct.

MRS. HALE Well, I don't know as Wright had, either.

COUNTY ATTORNEY You mean that they didn't get on very well?

MRS. HALE No, I don't mean anything. But I don't think a place'd be any cheerfuller for John Wright's being in it.

COUNTY ATTORNEY I'd like to talk more of that a little later. I want to get the lay of things upstairs now. *[He goes to the left where three steps lead to a stair door.]*

SHERIFF I suppose anything Mrs. Peters does'll be all right. She was to take in some clothes for her, you know, and a few little things. We left in such a hurry yesterday.

COUNTY ATTORNEY Yes, but I would like to see what you take, Mrs. Peters, and keep an eye out for anything that might be of use to us.

MRS. PETERS Yes, Mr. Henderson. *[The women listen to the men's steps on the stairs, then look about the kitchen.]*

MRS. HALE I'd hate to have men coming into my kitchen, snooping around and criticizing. *[She arranges the pans under sink which the Lawyer had shoved out of place.]*

MRS. PETERS Of course it's no more than their duty.

MRS. HALE Duty's all right, but I guess that deputy sheriff that came out to make the fire might have got a little of this on. *[Gives the roller towel a pull.]* Wish I'd thought of that sooner. Seems mean to talk about her for not having things slicked up when she had to come away in such a hurry.

MRS. PETERS *[who has gone to a small table in the left rear corner of the room, and lifted one end of a towel that covers a pan]*: She had bread set. *[Stands still.]*

MRS. HALE *[eyes fixed on a loaf of bread beside the breadbox, which is on a low shelf at the other side of the room. Moves slowly toward it.]*: She was going to put this in there. *[Picks up loaf, then abruptly drops it. In a manner of returning to familiar things.]* It's a shame about her fruit. I wonder if it's all gone. *[Gets up on the chair and looks.]* I think there's some here that's all right, Mrs. Peters. Yes — here; *[holding it toward the window]* this is cherries, too. *[Looking again.]* I declare I believe that's the only one. *[Gets down, bottle in her hand. Goes to the sink and wipes it off on the outside.]* She'll feel awful bad after all her hard work in the hot weather. I remember the afternoon I put up my cherries last summer. *[She puts the bottle on the big kitchen table, center of the room. With a sigh, is about to sit down in the rocking-chair. Before she is seated realizes what chair it is; with a slow look at it, steps back. The chair which she has touched rocks back and forth.]*

MRS. PETERS Well, I must get those things from the front room closet. *[She goes to the door at the right, but after looking into the other room, steps back.]* You coming with me, Mrs. Hale? You could help me carry them. *[They go in the other room; reappear,* **MRS. PETERS** *carrying a dress and skirt,* **MRS. HALE** *following with a pair of shoes.]* My, it's cold in there. *[She puts the clothes on the big table, and hurries to the stove.]*

MRS. HALE *[examining the skirt]*: Wright was close. I think maybe that's why she kept so much to herself. She didn't even belong to the Ladies' Aid. I suppose she felt she couldn't do her part, and then you don't enjoy things when you feel shabby. I heard she used to wear pretty clothes and be lively, when she was Minnie Foster, one of the town girls singing in the choir. But that — oh, that was thirty years ago. This all you want to take in?

MRS. PETERS She said she wanted an apron. Funny thing to want, for there isn't much to get you dirty in jail, goodness knows. But I suppose just to make her feel more natural. She said they was in the top drawer in this cupboard. Yes, here. And then her little shawl that always hung behind the door. *[Opens stair door and looks.]* Yes, here it is. *[Quickly shuts door leading upstairs.]*

MRS. HALE *[abruptly moving toward her]*: Mrs. Peters?

MRS. PETERS Yes, Mrs. Hale?

MRS. HALE Do you think she did it?

MRS. PETERS *[in a frightened voice]*: Oh, I don't know.

MRS. HALE Well, I don't think she did. Asking for an apron and her little shawl. Worrying about her fruit.

MRS. PETERS *[starts to speak, glances up, where footsteps are heard in the room above. In a low voice]*: Mr. Peters says it looks bad for her. Mr. Henderson is awful sarcastic in a speech and he'll make fun of her sayin' she didn't wake up.

MRS. HALE: Well, I guess John Wright didn't wake when they was slipping that rope under his neck.

MRS. PETERS No, it's strange. It must have been done awful crafty and still. They say it was such a — funny way to kill a man, rigging it all up like that.

MRS. HALE That's just what Mr. Hale said. There was a gun in the house. He says that's what he can't understand.

MRS. PETERS Mr. Henderson said coming out that what was needed for the case was a motive; something to show anger, or — sudden feeling.

MRS. HALE *[who is standing by the table]*: Well, I don't see any signs of anger around here. *[She puts her hand on the dish towel which lies on the table, stands looking down at table, one-half of which is clean, the other half messy.]* It's wiped to here. *[Makes a move as if to finish work, then turns and looks at loaf of bread outside the breadbox. Drops towel. In that voice of coming back to familiar things.]* Wonder how they are finding things upstairs. I hope she had it a little more red-up up there. You know, it seems kind of *sneaking*. Locking her up in town and then coming out here and trying to get her own house to turn against her!

MRS. PETERS But, Mrs. Hale, the law is the law.

MRS. HALE I s'pose 'tis. *[Unbuttoning her coat.]* Better loosen up your things, Mrs. Peters. You won't feel them when you go out. *[**MRS. PETERS** takes off her fur tippet, goes to hang it on hook at back of room, stands looking at the under part of the small corner table.]*

MRS. PETERS She was piecing a quilt. *[She brings the large sewing basket and they look at the bright pieces.]*

MRS. HALE It's a log cabin pattern. Pretty, isn't it? I wonder if she was goin' to quilt it or just knot it? *[Footsteps have been heard coming down the stairs. The **SHERIFF** enters followed by **HALE** and the **COUNTY ATTORNEY**.]*

SHERIFF They wonder if she was going to quilt it or just knot it! *[The men laugh, the women look abashed.]*

COUNTY ATTORNEY *[rubbing his hands over the stove]*: Frank's fire didn't do much up there, did it? Well, let's go out to the barn and get that cleared up. *[The men go outside.]*

MRS. HALE *[resentfully]*: I don't know as there's anything so strange, our takin' up our time with little things while we're waiting for them to get the evidence. *[She sits down at the big table smoothing out a block with* *decision.]* I don't see as it's anything to laugh about.

MRS. PETERS *[apologetically]*: Of course they've got awful important things on their minds. *[Pulls up a chair and joins Mrs. Hale at the table.]*

MRS. HALE *[examining another block]*: Mrs. Peters, look at this one. Here, this is the one she was working on, and look at the sewing! All the rest of it has been so nice and even. And look at this! It's all over the place! Why, it looks as if she didn't know what she was about! *[After she has said this they look at each other, then start to glance back at the door. After an instant* **MRS. HALE** *has pulled at a knot and ripped the sewing.]*

MRS. PETERS Oh, what are you doing, Mrs. Hale?

MRS. HALE *[mildly]*: Just pulling out a stitch or two that's not sewed very good. *[Threading a needle.]* Bad sewing always made me fidgety.

MRS. PETERS *[nervously]*: I don't think we ought to touch things.

MRS. HALE I'll just finish up this end. *[Suddenly stopping and leaning forward.]* Mrs. Peters?

MRS. PETERS Yes, Mrs. Hale?

MRS. HALE What do you suppose she was so nervous about?

MRS. PETERS Oh — I don't know. I don't know as she was nervous. I sometimes sew awful queer when I'm just tired. *[***MRS. HALE** *starts to say something, looks at* **MRS. PETERS**, *then goes on sewing.]* Well, I must get these things wrapped up. They may be through sooner than we think. *[Putting apron and other things together.]* I wonder where I can find a piece of paper, and string. *[Rises.]*

MRS. HALE In that cupboard, maybe.

MRS. PETERS *[looking in cupboard]*: Why, here's a bird-cage. *[Holds it up.]* Did she have a bird, Mrs. Hale?

MRS. HALE Why, I don't know whether she did or not — I've not been here for so long. There was a man around last year selling canaries cheap, but I don't know as she took one; maybe she did. She used to sing real pretty herself.

MRS. PETERS *[glancing around]*: Seems funny to think of a bird here. But she must have had one, or why would she have a cage? I wonder what happened to it?

MRS. HALE I s'pose maybe the cat got it.

MRS. PETERS No, she didn't have a cat. She's got that feeling some people have about cats — being afraid of them. My cat got in her room and she was real upset and asked me to take it out.

MRS. HALE My sister Bessie was like that. Queer, ain't it?

MRS. PETERS *[examining the cage]*: Why, look at this door. It's broke. One hinge is pulled apart.

MRS. HALE *[looking too]*: Looks as if someone must have been rough with it.

MRS. PETERS Why, yes. *[She brings the cage forward and puts it on the table.]*

MRS. HALE I wish if they're going to find any evidence they'd be about it. I don't like this place.

MRS. PETERS But I'm awful glad you came with me, Mrs. Hale. It would be lonesome for me sitting here alone.

MRS. HALE It would, wouldn't it? *[Dropping her sewing.]* But I tell you what I do wish, Mrs. Peters. I wish I had come over sometimes when she was here. I — *[looking around the room]* — wish I had.

MRS. PETERS But of course you were awful busy, Mrs. Hale — your house and your children.

MRS. HALE I could've come. I stayed away because it weren't cheerful — and that's why I ought to have come. I — I've never liked this place. Maybe because it's down in a hollow and you don't see the road. I dunno what it is, but it's a lonesome place and always was. I wish I had come over to see Minnie Foster sometimes. I can see now — *[Shakes her head.]*

MRS. PETERS Well, you mustn't reproach yourself, MRS. HALE. Somehow we just don't see how it is with other folks until — something turns up.

MRS. HALE Not having children makes less work — but it makes a quiet house, and Wright out to work all day, and no company when he did come in. Did you know John Wright, Mrs. Peters?

MRS. PETERS Not to know him; I've seen him in town. They say he was a good man.

MRS. HALE Yes — good; he didn't drink, and kept his word as well as most, I guess, and paid his debts. But he was a hard man, Mrs. Peters. Just to pass the time of day with him — *[Shivers.]* Like a raw wind that gets to the bone. *[Pauses, her eye falling on the cage.]* I should think she would 'a' wanted a bird. But what do you suppose went with it?

MRS. PETERS I don't know, unless it got sick and died. *[She reaches over and swings the broken door, swings it again, both women watch it.]*

MRS. HALE You weren't raised round here, were you? *[**MRS. PETERS** shakes her head.]* You didn't know — her?

MRS. PETERS Not till they brought her yesterday.

MRS. HALE She — come to think of it, she was kind of like a bird herself — real sweet and pretty, but kind of timid and — fluttery. How — she — did — change. *[Silence: then as if struck by a happy thought and relieved to get back to everyday things.]* Tell you what, Mrs. Peters, why don't you take the quilt in with you? It might take up her mind.

MRS. PETERS Why, I think that's a real nice idea, Mrs. Hale. There couldn't possibly be any objection to it, could there? Now, just what would I take? I wonder if her patches are in here — and her things. *[They look in the sewing basket.]*

MRS. HALE Here's some red. I expect this has got sewing things in it. *[Brings out a fancy box.]* What a pretty box. Looks like something somebody would give you. Maybe her scissors are in here. *[Opens box. Suddenly puts her hand to her nose.]* Why — *[**MRS. PETERS** bends nearer, then turns her face away.]* There's something wrapped up in this piece of silk.

MRS. PETERS Why, this isn't her scissors.

MRS. HALE *[lifting the silk]*: Oh, Mrs. Peters — it's — *[**MRS. PETERS** bends closer.]*

MRS. PETERS It's the bird.

MRS. HALE *[jumping up]*: But, Mrs. Peters — look at it! Its neck! Look at its neck! It's all — other side *to*.

MRS. PETERS Somebody — wrung — its — neck. *[Their eyes meet. A look of growing comprehension, of horror. Steps are heard outside. **MRS. HALE** slips box under quilt pieces, and sinks into her chair. Enter **SHERIFF** and **COUNTY ATTORNEY**. **MRS. PETERS** rises.]*

COUNTY ATTORNEY *[as one turning from serious things to little pleasantries]*: Well, ladies, have you decided whether she was going to quilt it or knot it?

MRS. PETERS We think she was going to — knot it.

COUNTY ATTORNEY Well, that's interesting, I'm sure. *[Seeing the bird-cage.]* Has the bird flown?

MRS. HALE *[putting more quilt pieces over the box]*: We think the — cat got it.

COUNTY ATTORNEY *[preoccupied]*: Is there a cat? *[**MRS. HALE** glances in a quick covert way at **MRS. PETERS**.]*

MRS. PETERS Well, not now. They're superstitious, you know. They leave.

COUNTY ATTORNEY *[to **SHERIFF PETERS**, continuing an interrupted conversation]*: No sign at all of anyone having come from the outside. Their own rope. Now let's go up again and go over it piece by piece. *[They start upstairs.]* It would have to have been someone who knew just the — *[**MRS. PETERS**

sits down. The two women sit there not looking at one another, but as if peering into something and at the same time holding back. When they talk now it is in the manner of feeling their way over strange ground, as if afraid of what they are saying, but as if they cannot help saying it.]

MRS. HALE She liked the bird. She was going to bury it in that pretty box.

MRS. PETERS *[in a whisper]*: When I was a girl — my kitten — there was a boy took a hatchet, and before my eyes — and before I could get there — *[Covers her face an instant.]* If they hadn't held me back I would have — *[catches herself, looks upstairs where steps are heard, falters weakly]* — hurt him.

MRS. HALE *[with a slow look around her]*: I wonder how it would seem never to have had any children around. *[Pause.]* No, Wright wouldn't like the bird — a thing that sang. She used to sing. He killed that, too.

MRS. PETERS *[moving uneasily]*: We don't know who killed the bird.

MRS. HALE I knew John Wright.

MRS. PETERS It was an awful thing was done in this house that night, Mrs. Hale. Killing a man while he slept, slipping a rope around his neck that choked the life out of him.

MRS. HALE His neck. Choked the life out of him. *[Her hand goes out and rests on the bird-cage.]*

MRS. PETERS *[with rising voice]*: We don't know who killed him. We don't *know*.

MRS. HALE *[her own feeling not interrupted]*: If there'd been years and years of nothing, then a bird to sing to you, it would be awful — still, after the bird was still.

MRS. PETERS *[something within her speaking]*: I know what stillness is. When we homesteaded in Dakota, and my first baby died — after he was two years old, and me with no other then —

MRS. HALE *[moving]*: How soon do you suppose they'll be through looking for the evidence?

MRS. PETERS I know what stillness is. *[Pulling herself back.]* The law has got to punish crime, Mrs. Hale.

MRS. HALE *[not as if answering that]*: I wish you'd seen Minnie Foster when she wore a white dress with blue ribbons and stood up there in the choir and sang. *[A look around the room.]* Oh, I *wish* I'd come over here once in a while! That was a crime! That was a crime! Who's going to punish that?

MRS. PETERS *[looking upstairs]*: We mustn't — take on.

MRS. HALE I might have known she needed help! I know how things can be — for women. I tell you, it's queer, Mrs. Peters. We live close together and we live far apart. We all go through the same things — it's all just a different kind of the same thing. *[Brushes her eyes, noticing the bottle of fruit, reaches out for it.]* If I was you I wouldn't tell her her fruit was gone. Tell her it *ain't*. Tell her it's all right. Take this in to prove it to her. She — she may never know whether it was broke or not.

MRS. PETERS *[takes the bottle, looks about for something to wrap it in; takes petticoat from the clothes brought from the other room, very nervously begins winding this around the bottle. In a false voice]*: My, it's a good thing the men couldn't hear us. Wouldn't they just laugh! Getting all stirred up over a little thing like a — dead canary. As if that could have anything to do with — with — wouldn't they *laugh*! *[The men are heard coming down stairs.]*

MRS. HALE *[under her breath]*: Maybe they would — maybe they wouldn't.

COUNTY ATTORNEY No, Peters, it's all perfectly clear except a reason for doing it. But you know juries when it comes to women. If there was some definite thing. Something to show — something to make a story about — a thing that would connect up with this strange way of doing it — *[The women's eyes meet for an instant. Enter* Hale *from outer door.]*

HALE Well, I've got the team around. Pretty cold out there.

COUNTY ATTORNEY I'm going to stay here a while by myself. *[To the Sheriff.]* You can send Frank out for me, can't you? I want to go over everything. I'm not satisfied that we can't do better.

SHERIFF Do you want to see what Mrs. Peters is going to take in? *[The Lawyer goes to the table, picks up the apron, laughs.]*

COUNTY ATTORNEY Oh, I guess they're not very dangerous things the ladies have picked out. *[Moves a few things about, disturbing the quilt pieces which cover the box. Steps back.]* No, Mrs. Peters doesn't need supervising. For that matter a sheriff's wife is married to the law. Ever think of it that way, Mrs. Peters?

MRS. PETERS Not — just that way.

SHERIFF *[chuckling]*: Married to the law. *[Moves toward the other room.]* I just want you to come in here a minute, George. We ought to take a look at these windows.

COUNTY ATTORNEY *[scoffingly]*: Oh, windows!

SHERIFF We'll be right out, Mr. Hale. *[**HALE** goes outside. The **SHERIFF** follows the **COUNTY ATTORNEY** into the other room. Then **MRS. HALE** rises, hands tight together, looking intensely at **MRS. PETERS**, whose eyes make a slow turn, finally meeting **MRS. HALE**'s. A moment **MRS. HALE** holds her, then her own eyes point the way to where the box is concealed. Suddenly **MRS. PETERS** throws back quilt pieces and tries to put the box in the bag she is wearing. It is too big. She opens box, starts to take bird out, cannot touch it, goes to pieces, stands there helpless. Sound of a knob turning in the other room. **MRS. HALE** snatches the box and puts it in the pocket of her big coat. Enter **COUNTY ATTORNEY** and **SHERIFF**.]*

COUNTY ATTORNEY *[facetiously]:* Well, Henry, at least we found out that she was not going to quilt it. She was going to — what is it you call it, ladies?

MRS. HALE *[her hand against her pocket]*: We call it — knot it, Mr. Henderson.

Curtain

[1916]

Analyzing Literary Elements

In *Trifles*, two plots run parallel: the men have an off-stage story as they hunt for clues to the murder of Mr. Wright; the women have an on-stage story as they unravel the life of Mrs. Wright. The tension in the story's plot has to do with the rate at which Mrs. Hale and Mrs. Peters come to understand what has happened. Suspense builds as the two women, and the audience, figure out who killed Mr. Wright and why. The suspense is heightened by the moral dilemma of whether the women should conceal incriminating evidence — and whether they'll get caught doing it. Of course, one reason the men in the story don't figure out what happened is that they dismiss the things the women say as mere trifles.

Trifles has two female characters — Mrs. Hale and Mrs. Peters — and three male characters — Mr. Hale, the sheriff, and the county attorney. Mr. and Mrs. Wright, though not on stage, have a presence as well. Over the course of the play, Mrs. Hale and Mrs. Peters change, feeling less certain about their own beliefs, disappointed in themselves for not being better friends to Mrs. Wright, and empathetic to her desperate loneliness. The men don't change. We learn about all of the characters through their conversation, especially in the way the conversation changes when the men are involved.

The setting of *Trifles* helps us understand character and also moves the plot along. The play takes place in an empty farmhouse, but the setting is more complicated than that. The men go to the bedroom where the murder occurred, while the women focus on the kitchen. Both the men and the women note the disheveled condition in which Mrs. Wright left it, yet the women are protective of her as well, understanding that she probably wouldn't have left such a mess if she hadn't been unexpectedly taken from her home. They also come to understand that the mess (which is a part of the setting) may be a sign of the "sudden feeling" the sheriff and attorney are looking for. We learn that the community is close and that Mrs. Peters is a newcomer. Mrs. Hale has known the woman under suspicion for many years, and it is through that familiarity that she understands what has happened and makes the decision she does.

Certain symbols are repeated in *Trifles.* The cold is brutal and unrelenting. The characters move toward the stove whenever possible, and the cold is a repeated subject of conversation. Mr. Wright is depicted as being cold and unloving, making the cold a clear symbol of a life without affection or even company. Other symbols might be Mrs. Wright's quilt pieces, the choice between quilting and knotting, the dead bird and the broken birdcage, the preserves (or trifles), and even the half-done chores. Each of these things is more fraught with meaning than it at first seems.

So, although the subject of *Trifles* is the unraveling of a mystery and the decision to protect the murderer, some of its themes might be:

- Sexism can make people blind to the truth.
- People may take desperate measures when they feel trapped in a loveless marriage, in a cold, isolated house, or in a society that doesn't value them.
- Someone who is a criminal by one set of social standards might be a victim according to another set of social standards. Or, in other words, justice is not always the same as the rule of law.

ACTIVITY

Working in groups, choose a passage from *Trifles* that you think is pivotal to one of the themes, then act it out or read the lines in a way that dramatizes that theme.

Developing a Thesis Statement

Now that we have analyzed how the literary elements of the play work together to express its themes, it's time to turn those themes into a thesis statement. First and foremost, remember that you are analyzing the elements of the work in order to arrive at an interpretation; you should not be summarizing the work. Simply retelling what happened or making an observation does not amount to an interpretation. Stating that Mrs. Peters seems to change her mind over the course of the play is not enough. You would be better off claiming that she changes her mind as the result of seeing justice in a different way. If you start right off with a thesis statement that argues for an interpretation of the play's meaning, you will guard against summary. Let's examine a few examples of thesis statements that would result in summary, and consider how they could be turned into interpretive thesis statements.

SUMMARY: In *Trifles*, the women notice evidence that the men do not.

INTERPRETATION: In *Trifles*, the differences in the evidence the men and women notice suggest different worldviews and value systems.

The summary statement simply tells what happened during the course of the play, but the interpretive statement takes that same point and explains *why* it happened. It answers the question: Why do the women notice evidence that the men do not? Here's another one:

SUMMARY: Mrs. Hale and Mrs. Peters discover a birdcage and dead canary, which provide clues to what actually happened to Mr. Wright.

INTERPRETATION: When Mrs. Hale and Mrs. Peters discover a birdcage and a dead canary wrapped in silk, they associate the silenced songbird with the joyless and repressed life that might have motivated Mrs. Wright to murder her husband.

The summary statement is accurate, but it is not an interpretation. You might ask yourself the following questions: Can I write a whole essay on this idea? Would anyone else see this point differently? If the answer to both questions is yes, then you're probably writing an interpretation. If the answer is no, you're probably in the realm of fact, or comprehension, rather than interpretation. Anyone who reads the play can tell you that these women discover a birdcage and a dead canary and see both as clues to understanding the murder. What else is there to say? If you ask yourself further questions, you'll get beyond summary and move toward interpretation. Why were the birdcage and the dead canary clues? What is the connection between the canary, the birdcage, and Mrs. Wright? An interpretation will reveal these connections, while a summary will not.

Remember when formulating your thesis that you are writing about how literary elements such as plot, character, setting, and symbol illuminate the meaning of the work as a whole. Thus, you are always balancing the two: literary elements and interpretation.

Let's develop a thesis in response to the following prompt.

In a conventional murder mystery, the point of the story is to figure out who the culprit is. The mystery in Susan Glaspell's play *Trifles* is unconventional, as the culprit is apprehended before the play even begins. However, as Mrs. Hale and Mrs. Peters unravel the mystery of why the murder took place, the play's themes are

> revealed. Discuss how Susan Glaspell uses the mystery in *Trifles* to reveal a theme of her play.

A good starting point is to figure out exactly what is being asked — that is, to deconstruct the prompt. In this case, you're being asked to consider the murder-mystery plot not as an end in itself but as a means of developing a theme. A murder mystery is all about the law, because somebody has to be held accountable for the crime. Yet in *Trifles*, Mrs. Hale and Mrs. Peters begin to question the law. As they unravel the mystery, they aren't so sure that "the law is the law." So maybe Glaspell is asking us to reflect on the relationship between law and justice or to link justice and punishment. Did Mrs. Wright do wrong in being her husband's judge, jury, and executioner? Was living with him punishment enough for her wrongdoing? Did she choose a punishment that fit his "crime"? These are complex questions — questions not definitively answered in the play but ones that it raises.

When you're trying to fit ideas and insights such as these into a single sentence, it's likely to be pretty awkward at first, and that's fine. We call this first attempt a working thesis. For example, you might come up with this:

> The murder mystery in *Trifles* is solved, but it is not so easy to answer the questions that the mystery raises about law, justice, and punishment, and whether hard-and-fast rules that govern human relations are always appropriate or fair.

This is a start, but it's a long, rambling sentence that could use some focus. At this point, you probably need to decide whether you're going to argue that Glaspell takes a definite stand on these issues. The play ends inconclusively — Mrs. Wright is neither convicted nor exonerated — which makes it difficult to say that the play (or its author) takes a stand on these issues. A better route, then, is to argue that Glaspell asks her audience/readers to explore these issues:

> In *Trifles*, the murder mystery is the means Glaspell uses to explore whether the rule of law is always the same as justice.

ACTIVITY

Discuss whether each of the following thesis statements is interpretation or summary. Then discuss whether the interpretive statements clearly focus on how literary elements contribute to the meaning of the work as a whole. Suggest improvements to those thesis statements that you find faulty or weak.

1. *Trifles* is a play about isolation and loneliness.
2. The broken birdcage in *Trifles* functions both as a clue to the circumstances of the murder and as a symbol that illuminates the role of Mrs. Wright in her marriage.
3. The character of Mrs. Peters, the wife of the sheriff, undergoes a significant change during the course of *Trifles*, a play set during a time when women were defined primarily through their husbands.

4. The frigid setting of Susan Glaspell's *Trifles* contributes to the characterization of all three women: it highlights the cold and isolated existence of the absent Mrs. Wright, while evoking the sympathetic responses of Mrs. Hale and Mrs. Peters.
5. Even though we never actually meet her, Mrs. Wright exerts a powerful presence in *Trifles.*
6. In the opening scene of *Trifles*, the men dominate the room as they stand near the stove, while the women remain near the door and quietly tolerate the cold.
7. The absent Mrs. Wright, suspected of murder in Susan Glaspell's *Trifles*, embodies the idea that loneliness, abuse, and isolation can lead a person to despair and even violence.
8. In *Trifles*, the male authority figures, including the sheriff himself, dismiss the female characters' investigation into the murder of Mr. Wright.
9. The kitchen, the dead bird, and the knots in the quilt have symbolic significance for the overall meaning of *Trifles*.
10. In *Trifles*, the discovery of the dead bird is a pivotal complication, especially for Mrs. Peters, that changes how the women view the role of the law.

Planning an Interpretive Essay

Regardless of whether you are given a specific prompt to respond to or are assigned a more general topic on a literary work, your main points will grow out of your thesis statement. Expressing these points as topic sentences moves the essay along and makes it more cohesive. Let's return to our thesis on justice:

> In *Trifles*, the murder mystery is the means Glaspell uses to explore whether the rule of law is always the same as justice.

This thesis indicates that you will first discuss the murder mystery as a plot device, and then explain how it contributes to the theme. If you were jotting down notes to structure your essay, they might look something like this:

- Solving the murder is not really the point of the story. Suspect is detained, and case is pretty much closed right from the beginning.
- Seem to be different ways of investigating for men and women. Men doing police work. Women looking at "trifles."
- Women suppress evidence. Defy men's justice. Empathize with Mrs. Wright.
- Birdcage and dead bird symbolize Mrs. Wright (former singer) and her desolate life with Mr. Wright.

These blocks of notes may not neatly transform into clear topic sentences, but they do suggest a logical progression. If we turn them into complete sentences — in some cases, separating ideas; in others, combining them — we end up with an outline:

TOPIC SENTENCE 1

Although Mr. Hale retells the circumstances of finding the body, questions arise concerning Mrs. Wright's indifferent behavior and the way her husband died.

TOPIC SENTENCE 2

During the investigation, the men follow rules to gather evidence, supporting one another's assumptions about what is significant, while the women quietly observe the surroundings, noticing important clues that the men dismiss as "trifles."

TOPIC SENTENCE 3

Identifying with Mrs. Wright, the women withhold judgment and instead try to understand what might have motivated her.

TOPIC SENTENCE 4

The birdcage and the dead canary, clues to the mystery, also symbolize the quiet oppression of Mrs. Wright.

TOPIC SENTENCE 5

The play's conclusion serves as closure to the mystery, but it is the investigative process that proves to be more illuminating.

Of course, this is bare bones, not yet a fully developed essay, but these five topic sentences show a progression of thought. Going well beyond summary, they examine plot, setting, and character. Each resulting analytic paragraph will contribute to the overall interpretation.

ACTIVITY

Sometimes you will be asked to consider how a quotation applies to a piece of literature. Choosing one of the following quotations, develop a thesis statement and four points explaining how it applies to *Trifles*.

- "The writers, I do believe, who get the best and most lasting response from their readers are the writers who offer a happy ending through moral development. By a happy ending, I do not mean mere fortunate events — a marriage or a last minute rescue from death — but some kind of spiritual reassessment or moral reconciliation, even with the self, even at death." — Fay Weldon
- "In a dark time, the eye begins to see." — Theodore Roethke
- "All literature is protest." — Richard Wright
- "Literature is the question minus the answer." — Roland Barthes

Supporting Your Interpretation

Whether you are writing with the text in hand or from memory, the same principle should guide your writing: be specific. If you refer to a character as "what's-his-name" or refer to a setting in general terms, you're not likely to be convincing. We've said it before, but it bears repeating: active reading and rereading are essential. Citing examples and explicitly explaining how they illustrate and support your interpretation are key to a successful essay that analyzes a literary work. The more you explain *how* rather than state *that*, the stronger your essay will be.

At this point, you know that you should avoid summary in your essay, but how much information should you give your readers about the work's plot or characters? One helpful guideline is to assume that your reader has read the text but has not necessarily thought too much about it. By doing so, you won't have to recount the plot or describe the characters. Thomas Foster, the author of *How to Read Literature Like a Professor*, suggests writing for the person who sits in front of you in class.

Let's start with a sample paragraph developed from the third topic sentence in the outline in the previous section:

> Identifying with Mrs. Wright, the women withhold judgment and instead try to understand what might have motivated her. Mrs. Hale and Mrs. Peters look around the house, especially the kitchen, and notice the fruit Mrs. Wright has canned and the quilt she is stitching. They talk about the fact that the couple had no children and that Mr. Wright was not a communicative husband. They also discuss incidents from their own past when they felt strong emotions that might have made them do something uncharacteristic or rash.

The paragraph holds a clear focus, and the information is drawn from the play. However, it is very general; thus, much of it seems like summary. Yes, it is true that the women look around the house; the details of their noticing the canned fruit and quilt are promising, but *so what*? What can you infer from their actions? How do these events reveal some of the themes that anchor the play? Similarly, the women do talk about the loneliness of a couple with no children living in such isolation; again, though, *so what*? How do these remembrances help them to understand Mrs. Wright's motivation, which is the focus established in the topic sentence? Answering these questions will help you move from the *what* to the *so what*.

The most important part of supporting your argument involves explaining your examples and discussing the ways the details you recount or quote connect to your thesis statement and topic sentences. You do this by including sentences of explanation, sometimes called commentary or analysis, for each of your examples — and making those examples as concrete as possible. Consider this revision of the previous developmental paragraph:

> Identifying with Mrs. Wright, the women withhold judgment and instead try to understand what might have motivated her. They discuss how hard life must have been for Minnie in a house with no children and with John, who was cold and distant. The Wright house is located in a hollow, and the road cannot even be seen, so Mrs. Hale and

Mrs. Peters begin to understand how the isolation and sense of entrapment could have led Mrs. Wright to snap. They can see how the only means of escape might have been to kill her captor, Mr. Wright. Mrs. Peters furthers the link between them and Mrs. Wright by sharing a time when Mrs. Peters herself felt the desire to hurt a boy who butchered her kitten with a hatchet. The women realize that they too might have been driven to violence under Mrs. Wright's circumstances.

Notice how specific this paragraph is, with its inclusion of examples drawn from the play. Even without direct quotations, this paragraph provides support for the interpretive point made in the topic sentence.

ACTIVITY

Revise the paragraph below using quotations from *Trifles*. Explain whether you think the direct quotations make the paragraph more convincing.

The dramatic tension in *Trifles* is created by the difference between how the men see the situation at the Wrights' house and how the women see it. The men—Hale, the county attorney, and the sheriff—dismiss the messiness of the farmhouse as chronic bad housekeeping. They do not see that it may offer a clue to what happened. Their attitude toward Mrs. Wright's quilting is similarly dismissive. The women, on the other hand, read into and beyond the mess. They see the half-wiped table, the bread outside the breadbox, and the one patch that is badly sewn as signs that Mrs. Wright was unhappy and under stress. The men dwell on what they see as a trifling dilemma (to quilt or knot), while the women look into Mrs. Wright's sewing box and find the dead bird. The men's consideration of all domestic matters as trivial prevents them from seeing that there was a story, even a possible motive that could prove Mrs. Wright guilty. The suspense in the play arises from the possibility that either one of the men will become more perceptive or that one of the women will break under the pressure of what they have discovered.

A Sample Interpretive Essay

The student essay on pages 75–76 was written in class in response to the following prompt.

In a conventional murder mystery, the point of the story is to figure out who the culprit is. The mystery in Susan Glaspell's play *Trifles* is unconventional, as the culprit is apprehended before the play even begins. However, as Mrs. Hale and Mrs. Peters unravel the mystery of why the murder took place, the play's themes are revealed. Discuss how Susan Glaspell uses the mystery in *Trifles* to reveal a theme of her play.

Examine the essay carefully before responding to the revision questions that follow it.

Student Essay on *Trifles*

Aneyn M. O'Grady

Trifles is a play by Susan Glaspell written in 1916. John Wright, a farm owner, has recently been murdered at night in his bed, strangled by a rope. His wife, Minnie Wright, the only person confirmed present at the time of death, is accused of the homicide. The characters go to the Wright home the day after the murder. While at the house, there are two separate but parallel narratives. One involves the men (the sheriff, the county attorney, and Mr. Hale) who focus on the investigation, searching for a motive. The other involves the women (Mrs. Peters, the sheriff's wife, and Mrs. Hale) who are there to collect things Mrs. Wright requested. They, unlike the men, treat the house like a home, instead of a crime scene. Focusing their attention on seemingly insignificant details, Mrs. Peters and Mrs. Hale ironically discover the truth behind the murder. This one-scene play thus centers on a mystery as well as the relations between men and women at the time. The symbolism in the play helps to solve the murder but also gives the author an opportunity to discuss the roles and duties of a husband and wife, and to question how they should interact.

Although Mr. Hale retells the circumstances of finding the body, questions arise concerning Mrs. Wright's indifferent behavior and the way her husband died. Despite the presence of a gun, a rope was used to kill him. This alternative method is more passionate and emotionally involved. It allows the killer to have complete control and power over the victim. The play is set in the kitchen: a housewife's main domain and responsibility. Traditionally it is her duty to keep it clean, but Mrs. Wright's kitchen is completely unkempt, an act of defiance against her role as a wife, imposed by society. The half-cleaned table shows the conflict that exists in Mrs. Wright's character. The clean part is proof of an accepting housewife whereas the messy part represents her rebellious side. Mrs. Wright, by killing her husband, frees herself from the one person who held her to her "housewife" persona. She still asks for her apron, symbol of a housewife, proving that she cannot forget this "good wife" image even in jail.

During the investigation, the men follow rules to gather evidence, supporting one another's assumptions about what is significant, while the women quietly observe the surroundings, noticing important clues that the men dismiss as "trifles." The men are at the Wright house out of an obligation with a professional goal. With their minds set on what they consider more important things, they pay little attention to what preoccupies the women. First the women notice the fruit preserves and how this will upset Mrs. Wright. They then comment on the uncleanness of the kitchen. These worries appear to be unnecessary until they find the quilt. The alteration in sewing presents the transformation in Mrs. Wright's character. At first the stitches are perfect and clean, normal. They then become erratic, hinting at nervousness. This alludes to Minnie's crisis and emotional instability, which could have led her to killing her husband. Mrs. Hale and Mrs. Peters wonder whether or not Mrs. Wright planned to quilt or knot the patches together. The sheriff scoffs at this inquiry, yet it alludes to Mrs. Wright's decision to knot the rope around Mr. Wright's neck. The women exchange information necessary to solving the murder, yet their conversations are seen as foolish female chatter by their husbands and the county attorney.

Identifying with Mrs. Wright, the women withhold judgment and instead try to understand what might have motivated her. They discuss how hard life must have been for Minnie in a house with no children and with John, who was cold and distant. The Wright house is located in a hollow, and the road cannot even be seen, so Mrs. Hale and Mrs. Peters begin to understand how the isolation and sense of entrapment could have led Mrs. Wright to snap. They can see how the only means of escape might have been to kill her captor, Mr. Wright. Mrs. Peters furthers the link between them and Mrs. Wright by sharing a time when Mrs. Peters herself felt the desire to hurt a boy who butchered her kitten with a hatchet. The women realize that they too might have been driven to violence under Mrs. Wright's circumstances.

The birdcage and the dead canary are key symbols and discoveries to the plot. Mrs. Hale and Mrs. Peters automatically associate the canary with Mrs. Wright. The bird reminds them of Minnie's old life as a young girl in the choir who loved to sing, full of life. This addresses a contrasting portrait with the person she has become after becoming a married woman. John Wright is accused of having killed the canary, since he disliked anything that made music or sang. This is linked to the way he metaphorically killed Minnie Foster, the joyful carefree spirit of Mrs. Wright. The canary represents the only hope and joy left in her life, yet her husband took that away from her too. Mrs. Wright intended to bury the canary, an act also symbolizing the burial of a part of her. By strangling Mr. Wright, Mrs. Wright forces their roles to be reversed. John Wright becomes the submissive, helpless creature, just like the canary. Mrs. Wright then becomes like a cat, an animal that she disliked.

The play's conclusion serves as closure to the mystery, but it is the investigation process that proves to be more illuminating. The men are responsible for carrying out business in society, leaving the women to content themselves with their household, children, and other activities deemed frivolous. The characters of both sexes have different reasons for entering the Wright house. The men have legal interests, whereas the women are only there to collect personal effects for Mrs. Wright. Left no other option by their husbands looking for evidence, the women focus their energy on trifles, such as the sewing in a quilt or the presence of an empty birdcage. As they make attempts to tidy up — their natural instinct — Mrs. Hale and Mrs. Peters think of their own situations as wives. They are in the house of a woman who refused to take orders from her husband any longer, to be unhappy, and think of trivial things men do not care about. The irony in the end is that these very things that the men do not notice, that they do not think of, hold the answer to solving the murder.

QUESTIONS

1. This essay does not have a distinctive title. What might be a title that captures the main point of the essay?
2. Identify a paragraph that is especially effective. What particular qualities of that paragraph make it effective?
3. Identify a weak paragraph. How might you revise it to improve it?
4. Is there a logical progression to the paragraphs? How might you change the order to improve the essay?
5. The conclusion is a relatively long paragraph with substantive analysis. In what ways does it function as a developmental paragraph? Should the student have written another paragraph as a conclusion? Discuss this point by considering the purpose of a concluding paragraph.

ACTIVITY

Choose one of the following prompts and write an interpretive essay using "One of These Days" (pp. 17–18), "Seeing Eye" (pp. 34–36), "The First Day" (pp. 45–48), "Half a Day" (pp. 43–44), "Girl" (pp. 50–51), or *Trifles* (pp. 59–67).

- Explain how the opening scene or first few paragraphs of the play or short story introduce a central idea or theme.
- Analyze how the author uses literary techniques in his or her work to challenge the status quo in a society or community.
- Discuss how the author's use of time in constructing a story's plot — especially in medias res and flashbacks — contributes to the meaning of the work as a whole.

3
Close Reading: Analyzing Passages of Fiction

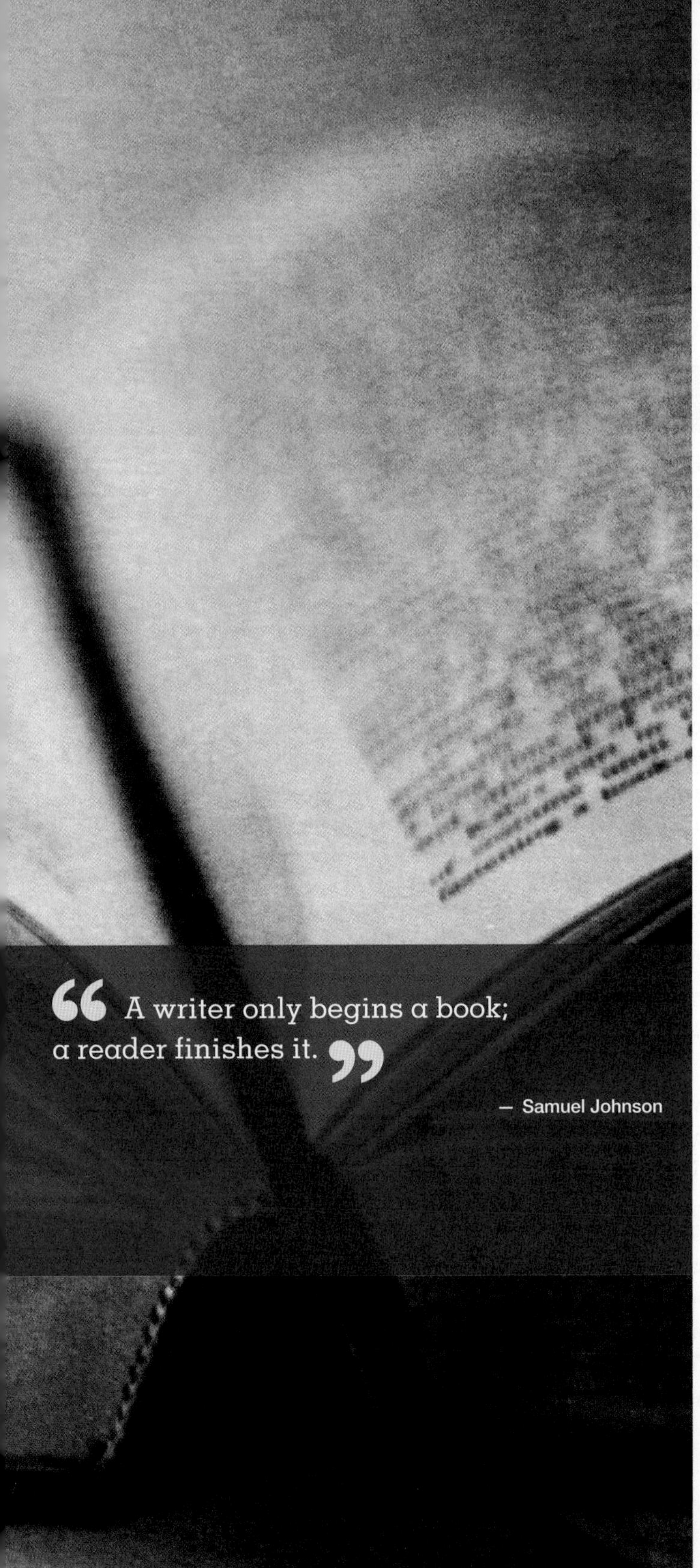

“A writer only begins a book; a reader finishes it.”
— Samuel Johnson

Catherine MacBride/Getty Images

In Chapter 2, we explored the “big picture” of fiction and drama: that is, how character, plot, setting, point of view, and theme all contribute to the meaning of an entire work. In this chapter, we'll show you *how* a writer expresses these narrative elements in prose, analyzing the stylistic resources of language that work together to create meaning. By looking at the various parts of a short passage of fiction, we begin to appreciate a writer's artistry and understand how he or she uses various literary techniques to make a statement, suggest an emotion, or convey an idea. In short, we are moving from a panoramic view to a close-up.

Close reading, sometimes called explication of text, means developing an understanding of a work that is based on its small details and the larger ideas those details evoke, add up to, or suggest. Essential to close reading is observation — taking note of what catches your attention as you read and then asking questions about why a phrase or scene strikes you. The texts you are asked to read closely are often not that long, which means you can read them several times. Each time you read a passage, you will notice more and more. Building on the strategies to promote active reading we discussed in Chapter 1, this chapter will offer ways to deepen your awareness of the specific literary elements authors use to express their ideas. We'll move from identifying these elements to analyzing their effect on us as readers, then show you how to approach writing a close analysis essay that shares your insights. Let's start with what you notice when you first read a passage from a short story or a novel.

FROM FIRST IMPRESSIONS TO QUESTIONS

Take a close look at this excerpt from *The Great Gatsby* by F. Scott Fitzgerald, a novel you might already know. The book takes place on and around Long Island, New York, in the 1920s and is narrated by Nick Carraway, a young man of relatively modest means whose wealthy friends and family treat him as a confidant. This passage appears near the beginning of the book — in it, Nick goes to visit Tom Buchanan, his cousin's husband and a former classmate from their years together at Yale University. As you read, pay careful attention to the specific language Fitzgerald uses to set the scene and jot down your first impressions. You should also note any unfamiliar vocabulary, and, if possible, look it up. If you are able to work only with the passage itself, do your best to use the surrounding context to figure out the words, phrases, or usages that confuse you. Finally, try and tune in to the way the language of the passage affects you as you read; for instance, do specific words or phrases carry an emotional meaning? Do they create a certain feeling or atmosphere?

from The Great Gatsby

F. SCOTT FITZGERALD

And so it happened that on a warm windy evening I drove over to East Egg to see two old friends whom I scarcely knew at all. Their house was even more elaborate than I expected, a cheerful red-and-white Georgian Colonial mansion, overlooking the bay. The lawn started at the beach and ran toward the front door for a quarter of a mile, jumping over sun-dials and brick walks and burning gardens — finally when it reached the house drifting up the side in bright vines as though from the momentum of its run. The front was broken by a line of French windows, glowing now with reflected gold and wide open to the warm windy afternoon, and Tom Buchanan in riding clothes was standing with his legs apart on the front porch.

He had changed since his New Haven years. Now he was a sturdy straw-haired man of thirty with a rather hard mouth and a supercilious manner. Two shining arrogant eyes had established dominance over his face and gave him the appearance of always leaning aggressively forward. Not even the effeminate swank of his riding clothes could hide the enormous power of that body — he seemed to fill those glistening boots until he strained the top lacing, and you could see a great pack of muscle shifting when his shoulder moved under his thin coat. It was a body capable of enormous leverage — a cruel body.

His speaking voice, a gruff husky tenor, added to the impression of fractiousness he conveyed. There was a touch of paternal contempt in it, even toward people he liked — and there were men at New Haven who had hated his guts.

"Now, don't think my opinion on these matters is final," he seemed to say, "just because I'm stronger and more of a man than you are." We were in the same senior society, and while we were never intimate I always had the impression that he approved of me and wanted me to like him with some harsh, defiant wistfulness of his own.

We talked for a few minutes on the sunny porch.

"I've got a nice place here," he said, his eyes flashing about restlessly.

Turning me around by one arm, he moved a broad flat hand along the front vista, including in its sweep a sunken Italian garden, a half acre of deep, pungent roses, and a snub-nosed motor-boat that bumped the tide offshore.

"It belonged to Demaine, the oil man." He turned me around again, politely and abruptly. "We'll go inside."

We walked through a high hallway into a bright rosy-colored space, fragilely bound into the house by French windows at either end. The windows were ajar and gleaming white against the fresh grass outside that seemed to grow a little way into the house. A breeze blew through the room, blew curtains in at one end and out the other like pale flags, twisting them up toward the frosted wedding-cake of the ceiling, and then rippled over the wine-colored rug, making a shadow on it as wind does on the sea.

The only completely stationary object in the room was an enormous couch on which two young women were buoyed up as though upon an anchored balloon. They were both in white, and their dresses were rippling and fluttering as if they had just been blown back in after a short flight around the house. I must have stood for a few moments listening to the whip and snap of the curtains and the groan of a picture on the wall. Then there was a boom as Tom Buchanan shut the rear windows and the caught wind died out about the room, and the curtains and the rugs and the two young women ballooned slowly to the floor.

[1925]

You probably notice, first of all, that the narrative is told from one person's viewpoint, a first person account. As we discussed in Chapter 2, narrative perspective is a key element of fiction because it is our first point of entry into any fictional world — and it's essential to close reading. In this case, the narrator, Nick Carraway, is paying a visit to "two old friends," whom, strangely, he "scarcely knew at all." Is this contrast a source of tension? We don't know at this point, but it's worth noting so that we're on the lookout as we read on for any other potential contradictions or conflicts.

Fitzgerald, through his narrator, gives us a detailed description of the "Georgian Colonial mansion" that overlooks the bay. The lawn is given human-like characteristics through a series of verbs: "ran," "jumping," "reached," and "drifting." The French windows, "glowing now with reflected gold," are as open as the spacious lawn to the wind. Is this a peaceful scene? An idyllic one? One where the house is in harmony with nature or at odds with it? These are good questions to explore, even if you can't answer them yet.

Then, into the scene strides Tom Buchanan, who is center stage for the next two paragraphs. What words stand out? Is there a pattern to them? Words and phrases that Nick uses to describe Tom and his behavior include: "sturdy," "supercilious," "aggressively," "swank," "enormous power," "cruel," and "contempt." Most of these suggest something negative, possibly menacing.

In the next few paragraphs, Fitzgerald moves from straight description to dialogue, both imagined ("he seemed to say") and actual. You may wonder why Tom doesn't ask the narrator — whom he has not seen for some time — any personal questions. Instead, Tom focuses on himself: he gestures toward his property, which he points out (without being asked) belonged to an "oil man." Does this boast point to a contrast between the idea that rich men must be inherently confident and Tom's apparently insecure need to call attention to his wealth? Could Tom's physically intimidating appearance and behavior mask a desire to be liked and admired?

In the following two paragraphs, Fitzgerald returns to description as Nick and Tom walk inside the mansion. What words stand out here? You might note the odd use of "fragile" in the description of the "rosy-colored space, fragilely bound into the house by French windows." That sense of something tenuous or insubstantial intensifies as Nick notices the windows left "ajar" and the breeze blowing through the room that twists the curtains up "toward the frosted wedding-cake of the ceiling." What does that image suggest? Portraying a building's structural support as icing does not exactly imply that it's sturdy. Why does the breeze, which we might expect to create a sense of openness, even freedom, "rippl[e]" over the rug like "a shadow"? Maybe that shadow suggests menace in the midst of such opulence.

In the final paragraph of this excerpt, we meet two women sitting on the couch, which we're told is the "only completely stationary object in the room." They are "buoyed up as though upon an anchored balloon," an image that is reinforced by their dresses "rippling and fluttering as if they had just been blown back in after a short flight around the house." Something seems off balance here; nothing holds still or stays in focus. Everything is flimsy or in flux, despite the fact that the mansion itself is stationary, and its furnishings are the best money can buy. Why does the setting seem so dream-like? Is Fitzgerald asking us to consider what money can (and cannot) achieve?

By paying attention to striking language choices and asking questions, we have gathered textual evidence to begin interpreting the passage. In this case, we see this scene as the narrator does. The way Fitzgerald uses language shows us an expensive house dominated by a powerful man who alternates between insecurity and "paternal contempt" for others. Open and spacious, the house seems to be a place where its privileged occupants live in luxury but without purpose.

TALKING WITH THE TEXT

By exploring what catches your attention, you're already starting to develop a kind of interior conversation with the text that explores what the writer is doing and why. To become a more careful reader, the most helpful thing you can do is read, read, and reread, but we can also practice strategies to help you fully engage with a text every time you turn to it. One important point to keep in mind is that your goal is not simply to identify and list **literary elements** — although you may spot some — but to analyze their effect. In other words, how do the writer's choices help craft the work's meaning?

As we mentioned at the beginning of this chapter, the first step to close reading is observing carefully and asking questions. These can be simple ones (such as the meaning of unfamiliar words) or more complex ones (such as the meaning suggested by figurative language). Below are some questions you may find helpful to keep in mind as you read any text for the first time:

- From whose viewpoint is the story being told? What beliefs or biases might the narrator have?
- Who are the characters, and how are they described? Can you sense any conflicts or contradictions within or between individuals?
- Where and when does the story take place? What is striking about the language the author uses to present the time and setting?

Asking yourself these questions will jump start your close reading, but you should also come up with your own questions and independent observations as you read and reread a work. When you talk back to the text in this way, you begin to engage with it on new levels, opening avenues of inquiry that will lead you to analysis. If you're having trouble delving into a text, consider trying the following approaches:

- Pose questions about things that confuse you. Are there aspects of the setting that do not seem to fit with the rest of the narrative? Are characters behaving in ways that appear unusual, particularly in light of what else the author has revealed about them?
- Make connections within the passage. Note any repetitions, patterns, contrasts, or points of tension, especially between and among characters.
- Note striking, unusual, or distinctive word choices. Keep an eye out for language that signals a change of some sort in the narrative.

Once you've gone through the text carefully by reading, questioning, and examining how the language contributes to meaning, you have a strong foundation for either contributing to a discussion in a larger group or preparing to write about the piece.

ACTIVITY

Read the following passage from the novel *Their Eyes Were Watching God* by Zora Neale Hurston. In this scene, the central character, Janie, has just come from the funeral of her husband, a prominent figure in a Florida town where he owned a store and served as mayor.

As you read, write down your observations about Hurston's language choices and develop questions about the passage. What kind of setting does Hurston establish in this passage? Based on this passage, what words would you use to describe Janie?

from Their Eyes Were Watching God

ZORA NEALE HURSTON

Janie starched and ironed her face and came set in the funeral behind her veil. It was like a wall of stone and steel. . . . All things concerning death and burial were said and done. Finish. End. Never-more. Darkness. Deep hole. Dissolution. Eternity. Weeping and wailing outside. Inside the expensive black folds were resurrection and life. She did not reach outside for anything, nor did the things of death reach inside to disturb her calm. She sent her face to Joe's funeral, and herself went rollicking with the springtime across the world. . . .

Most of the day she was at the store, but at night she was there in the big house and sometimes it creaked and cried all night under the weight of lonesomeness. Then she'd lie awake in bed asking lonesomeness some questions. . . . She had been getting ready for her great journey to the horizons in search of *people*; it was important to all the world that she should find them and they find her. But she had been whipped like a cur dog. . . . [Her grandmother] had taken the biggest thing God ever made, the horizon — for no matter how far a person can go the horizon is still way beyond you — and pinched it in to such a little bit of a thing that she could tie it about her granddaughter's neck tight enough to choke her. She hated the old woman who had twisted her so in the name of love. Most humans didn't love one another nohow, and this mislove was so strong that even common blood couldn't overcome it all the time. She had found a jewel down inside herself and she had wanted to walk where people could see her and gleam it around. But she had been set in the marketplace to sell.

[1937]

LITERARY ELEMENTS

The point of close reading is to go beyond merely summarizing what happens or simply identifying the literary techniques the writer employs in a piece of prose. To perform close analysis, we must understand how a writer's stylistic choices convey a work's message or meaning. Once you begin to analyze literature closely, you will see how all of the parts of a piece of literature work together, from overall characterization and tone to individual word choices.

Let's look closely at this excerpt from *My Ántonia* by Willa Cather, a novel about early settlers in the American West, narrated by a young boy who moves from Virginia to Nebraska to be brought up by his grandparents.

from **My Ántonia**

WILLA CATHER

I sat down in the middle of the garden, where snakes could scarcely approach unseen, and leaned my back against a warm yellow pumpkin. There were some ground-cherry bushes growing along the furrows, full of fruit. I turned back the papery triangular sheaths that protected the berries and ate a few. All about me giant grasshoppers, twice as big as any I had ever seen, were doing acrobatic feats among the dried vines. The gophers scurried up and down the ploughed ground. There in the sheltered draw-bottom the wind did not blow very hard, but I could hear it singing its humming tune up on the level, and I could see the tall grasses wave. The earth was warm under me, and warm as I crumbled it through my fingers. Queer little red bugs came out and moved in slow squadrons around me. Their backs were polished vermilion, with black spots. I kept as still as I could. Nothing happened. I did not expect anything to happen. I was something that lay under the sun and felt it, like the pumpkins, and I did not want to be anything more. I was entirely happy. Perhaps we feel like that when we die and become a part of something entire, whether it is sun and air, or goodness and knowledge. At any rate, that is happiness; to be dissolved into something complete and great. When it comes to one, it comes as naturally as sleep.

[1918]

After even an initial reading of such a descriptive passage, you probably have a sense of how comfortable the narrator feels in this natural environment. But how does Cather convey that feeling? To answer that question, we need to get more specific about exactly what literary and stylistic elements are at work. Understanding these concepts will give you things to be on the lookout for as you close-read, as well as the vocabulary to help you describe what you see. Most important, these elements provide essential evidence for close literary analysis and help you support your interpretation of the meaning of a work. It's likely you know some of these terms, but others may be new to you. Examples for all of these concepts, and more, are available in the glossary at the back of this book.

Diction

Authors choose their words carefully to convey precise meanings. We call these word choices the author's **diction**. A word can have more than one dictionary definition, or **denotation**, so when you analyze diction, you must consider all of a word's possible meanings. If some words have associations, or **connotations**, beyond the dictionary definitions, you should ask how those relate to the meaning of the piece. Sometimes a word's connotations will reveal another layer of meaning; sometimes they will affect the tone, as in the case of either **formal** or **informal diction**, which is sometimes called **slang**, or **colloquial**, language. Diction can also be **abstract** or **concrete**. While the passage from *My Ántonia* is entirely narrative, it's important to note the function diction serves as part of dialogue in prose. The characters' spoken words are also the author's language choices, and you should think critically about their effect on the reader.

Let's look at some of the diction choices Cather makes. The passage begins in a garden where it would be hard for a snake to "approach unseen." The narrator is outdoors on a sheltered part of a prairie farm, so the garden and the snake are examples of concrete details. But snakes and gardens also carry other meanings. It is hard not to think of the Garden of Eden and of sheltered, childlike innocence. Perhaps the most striking detail is the narrator leaning back "against a warm yellow pumpkin" and slowly eating berries after "turn[ing] back the papery triangular sheaths that protected them." The language itself conveys a sense of ease and trust.

Below, we've included some questions that will help you fully explore the effect of diction in a piece of prose:

- Which of the important words (verbs, nouns, adjectives, and adverbs) in the passage are general and abstract, and which are specific and concrete?
- Are important words and phrases formal, informal, colloquial, or slang?
- Are there words with strong connotations, words we might refer to as "loaded"? What are those connotations?

Figurative Language

Language that is not literal is called figurative, as in a figure of speech. Sometimes this kind of language is called *metaphorical* because it explains or expands on an idea by comparing it to something else. **Similes** make such comparisons by using the words *like*, *as*, or *than* (e.g., *love is like a rose; love is lighter than air*), while **metaphors** directly state that one thing is another (e.g., *love is a battlefield*). **Personification** is a figure of speech in which a concept, an object, or an animal is given human characteristics (e.g., *love is blind*). When a metaphor is extended over several lines in a work, it's called an **extended metaphor** or a conceit.

Other forms of figurative language include **overstatement** (or **hyperbole**), **understatement, paradox** (a statement that seems contradictory but actually reveals a surprising truth), and **irony**. There are a few different types of **irony**, but **verbal irony** is the most common. It occurs when a speaker says one thing but really means something else, or when there is a noticeable incongruity between what is expected and what is said.

Personification prevails in the passage from *My Ántonia*. The narrator describes the grasshoppers "doing acrobatic feats" as though they are people, and hears the wind "singing its humming tune" as the tall grasses "wave." Taken together, all these examples from the natural world seem to the narrator like friendly companions, suggesting his comfort and perhaps even that he believes he is a part of their world. In the next sentence, when he "crumble[s]" the earth between his fingers, the line between human and natural worlds blurs.

The following questions will help you take a closer look at the figurative language in a short story or passage of prose:

- Which words and/or phrases are used literally, and which are used figuratively?
- Does the figurative language evoke a specific feeling or mood? Is it consistent throughout the passage?

Imagery

Imagery creates a vivid mental picture or a physical sensation by appealing to one or more of the five senses: that is, how something looks, feels, sounds, smells, or tastes. In considering imagery, look carefully at how the sense impressions are created. Also pay attention to patterns of images that are repeated throughout a work. Often writers use figurative language to make their descriptions even more vivid. In the Cather passage, the narrator hears the wind and feels the warmth of the earth, but the keenest images are visual: he sees the grasshoppers jumping and the tall grasses waving. Let's take a closer look at this description in particular:

> Queer little red bugs came out and moved in slow squadrons around me. Their backs were polished vermilion, with black spots.

The imagery tells us that these are little red bugs with black spots, but consider what is added with the words "squadrons" and "polished vermilion," both figurative descriptions. Our imagination is piqued by the self-sufficiency of an army of bugs, painted bright red, going about their business, oblivious to the human presence of the narrator. With such striking images, the narrator suggests a heightened sensory awareness of his experience.

ACTIVITY

In this passage from the nineteenth-century novel *Middlemarch* by George Eliot (pen name of Mary Ann Evans), Will Ladislaw – a charming and talented young man who has neither property nor a profession – meets Dorothea Brooke Casaubon, the lovely wife of an older and self-absorbed scholar. Discuss how the diction and figurative language in this paragraph raise the emotional temperature of Will's meeting with Dorothea.

---

from Middlemarch

GEORGE ELIOT

Will, the moment before, had been low in the depths of boredom, and, obliged to help Mr. Brooke in arranging "documents" about hanging sheep-stealers, was exemplifying the power our minds have of riding several horses at once by inwardly arranging measures towards getting a lodging for himself in Middlemarch and cutting short his constant residence at the Grange; while there flitted through all these steadier images a tickling vision of a sheep-stealing epic written with Homeric particularity. When Mrs. Casaubon was announced he started up as from an electric shock, and felt a tingling at his finger-ends. Any one observing him would have seen a change in his complexion, in the adjustment of his facial muscles, in the vividness of his glance, which might have made them imagine that every molecule in his body had passed the message of a magic touch. And so it had. For effective magic is transcendent nature; and who shall measure the subtlety of those touches which convey the quality of soul as well as body, and make a man's passion for one woman differ from his passion for another as joy in the morning light over valley and river and white mountain-top differs from joy among Chinese lanterns and glass pannels? Will, too, was made of very impressible stuff. The bow of a violin drawn near him cleverly, would at one stroke change the aspect of the world for him, and his point of view shifted as easily as his mood. Dorothea's entrance was the freshness of morning.

[1874]

Syntax

Syntax is the arrangement of words into phrases, clauses, and sentences. When we read closely, we consider whether the sentences in a work are long or short, **simple** or **complex**. The sentence might also be **cumulative**, beginning with an independent clause and followed by subordinate clauses or phrases that add detail; or **periodic**, beginning with subordinate clauses or phrases that build toward the main clause. The word order can be the traditional subject-verb-object order or **inverted** (e.g., verb-subject-object or object-subject-verb). You might also look at syntactic patterns, such as several long sentences followed by a short sentence.

The Cather passage is almost entirely composed of straightforward, declarative sentences that follow a subject-verb-object pattern. Only in the last three sentences, when Cather departs from the concrete natural world, does she deviate from this structure. Note the immediate contrast between short, perhaps even abrupt sentences — for instance, "Nothing happened," and "I was entirely happy" — and the longer ones that follow: "Perhaps we feel like that when we die and become a part of something entire, whether it is sun and air, or goodness and knowledge. At any rate, that is happiness: to be dissolved into something complete and great." Those two sentences, which seem to accumulate details as part of the speaker's natural thought processes, almost seem like an incantation. The syntax itself reinforces the narrator's progress from observation to reflection or even meditation. By the end of the passage, we have a sense of the narrator's ease as he seems to float from idea to idea. Note, too, that the shifts in syntax parallel shifts in diction. In the shorter, more straightforward sentences, the narrator is a keen observer of details in the natural world; as he moves into longer, more reflective thoughts, his language becomes more abstract. He has moved from the external physical world to the interior realm of thought.

When you begin to look at the syntax in a work of prose, you may find the following questions helpful:

- What is the order of the words in the sentences? Are they in the usual subject-verb-object order, or are they inverted?
- Are nouns or verbs more prevalent in the passage?

- What are the sentences like? Do their meanings build periodically or cumulatively?
- How do the sentences connect their words, phrases, and clauses?
- How is the passage organized? Is it chronological? Does it move from concrete to abstract language or vice versa? Or does it follow some other pattern?

Tone and Mood

Tone reflects the author's attitude toward the subject of the work. **Mood** is the feeling the reader experiences as a result of the tone. Closely related, tone and mood evoke emotions and are created by the writer's style choices. Both must be inferred by taking into account the effect of various literary elements, including setting, details, diction, figurative language, and syntax. When you describe the tone and mood of a work, try to use at least two precise words, rather than words that are vague and general, such as *happy*, *sad*, or *different*. Though there are many possibilities, a pair of adjectives with similar connotations (e.g., *detached and bitter*), a pair of contrasting adjectives (e.g., *detached but optimistic*), and an adverb-adjective combination (e.g., *bitterly detached*) are all effective and versatile. When analyzing the Cather passage, for instance, you might say that the joyful and contented tone creates a reflective, peaceful mood.

Although there are nearly infinite ways to describe the tone of a work, some common words used to express tone include: *mysterious*, *contemptuous*, *optimistic*, *pessimistic*, *detached*, *nostalgic*, *bitter*, *arrogant*, *playful*, *impassioned*, *restrained*, *somber*, and *indignant*.

ACTIVITY

Read the following brief passage from the short story "A White Heron" by Sarah Orne Jewett. Choose three of the literary elements we've just discussed and analyze how Jewett uses them to dramatize the young Sylvia's adventure.

from A White Heron

SARAH ORNE JEWETT

Half a mile from home, at the farther edge of the woods, where the land was highest, a great pine-tree stood, the last of its generation. Whether it was left for a boundary mark, or for what reason, no one could say; the woodchoppers who had felled its mates were dead and gone long ago, and a whole forest of sturdy trees, pines and oaks and maples, had grown again. But the stately head of this old pine towered above them all and made a landmark for sea and shore miles and miles away. Sylvia knew it well. She had always believed that whoever climbed to the top of it could see the ocean; and the little girl had often laid her hand on the great rough trunk and looked up wistfully at those dark boughs that the wind always stirred, no matter how hot and still the air might be below. Now she thought of the tree with a new excitement, for why, if one climbed it at break of day, could not one see all the world, and easily discover from whence the white heron flew, and mark the place, and find the hidden nest?

What a spirit of adventure, what wild ambition! What fancied triumph and delight and glory for the later morning when she could make known the secret! It was almost too real and too great for the childish heart to bear. . . .

There was the huge tree asleep yet in the paling moonlight, and small and silly Sylvia began with utmost bravery to mount to the top of it, with tingling, eager blood coursing the channels of her whole frame, with her bare feet and fingers, that pinched and held like bird's claws to the monstrous ladder reaching up, up, almost to the sky itself. First she must mount the white oak tree that grew alongside, where she was almost lost among the dark branches and the green leaves heavy and wet with dew; a bird fluttered off its nest, and a red squirrel ran to and fro and scolded pettishly at the harmless house-breaker. Sylvia felt her way easily. She had often climbed there, and knew that higher still one of the oak's upper branches chafed against the pine trunk, just where its lower boughs were set close together. There, when she made the dangerous pass from one tree to the other, the great enterprise would really begin.

She crept out along the swaying oak limb at last, and took the daring step across into the old pine-tree. The way was harder than she thought; she must reach far and hold fast, the sharp dry twigs caught and held her and scratched her like angry talons, the pitch made her thin little fingers clumsy and stiff as she went round and round the tree's great stem, higher and higher upward. The sparrows and robins in the woods below were beginning to wake and twitter to the dawn, yet it seemed much lighter there aloft in the pine-tree, and the child knew she must hurry if her project were to be of any use.

The tree seemed to lengthen itself out as she 5
went up, and to reach farther and farther upward. It was like a great main-mast to the voyaging earth; it must truly have been amazed that morning through all its ponderous frame as it felt this determined spark of human spirit wending its way from higher branch to branch. Who knows how steadily the least twigs held themselves to advantage this light, weak creature on her way! The old pine must have loved his new dependent. More than all the hawks, and bats, and moths, and even the sweet voiced thrushes, was the brave, beating heart of the solitary gray-eyed child. And the tree stood still and frowned away the winds that June morning while the dawn grew bright in the east.

Sylvia's face was like a pale star, if one had seen it from the ground, when the last thorny bough was past, and she stood trembling and tired but wholly triumphant, high in the tree-top. Yes, there was the sea with the dawning sun making a golden dazzle over it, and toward that glorious east flew two hawks with slow-moving pinions. How low they looked in the air from that height when one had only seen them before far up, and dark against the blue sky. Their gray feathers were as soft as moths; they seemed only a little way from the tree, and Sylvia felt as if she too could go flying away among the clouds. Westward, the woodlands and farms reached miles and miles into the distance; here and there were church steeples, and white villages, truly it was a vast and awesome world.

[1886]

CONNECTING LITERARY ELEMENTS OF STYLE

Following is an excerpt from *Far from the Madding Crowd* by the British writer Thomas Hardy. In this passage, the farmer Gabriel Oak observes Bathsheba Everdene, a young woman on her way to a neighboring farm, when she is left alone in the wagon carrying her household belongings. The "wagoner," or driver, has gone back to retrieve a missing part of the horse-drawn wagon. As you read through this passage, think about how the literary techniques and style elements we've just discussed reveal Bathsheba's character.

from **Far from the Madding Crowd**

THOMAS HARDY

The girl on the summit of the load sat motionless, surrounded by tables and chairs with their legs upwards, backed by an oak settle, and ornamented in front by pots of geraniums, myrtles, and cactuses, together with a caged canary — all probably from the windows of the house just vacated. There was also a cat in a willow basket, from the partly-opened lid of which she gazed with half-closed eyes, and affectionately surveyed the small birds around.

The handsome girl waited for some time idly in her place, and the only sound heard in the stillness was the hopping of the canary up and down the perches of its prison. Then she looked attentively downwards. It was not at the bird, nor at the cat; it was at an oblong package tied in paper, and lying between them. She turned her head to learn if the wagoner were coming. He was not yet in sight; and then her eyes crept back to the package, her thoughts seeming to run upon what was inside it. At length she drew the article into her lap, and untied the paper covering; a small swing looking-glass was disclosed, in which she proceeded to survey herself attentively. Then she parted her lips and smiled.

It was a fine morning, and the sun lighted up to a scarlet glow the crimson jacket she wore, and painted a soft lustre upon her bright face and black hair. The myrtles, geraniums, and cactuses packed around her were fresh and green, and at such a leafless season they invested the whole concern of horses, wagon, furniture, and girl, with a peculiar charm of rarity. What possessed her to indulge in such a performance in the sight of the sparrows, blackbirds, and unperceived farmer, who were alone its spectators — whether the smile began as a factitious one, to test her capacity in that art, nobody knows; it ended certainly in a real smile. She blushed at herself, and seeing her reflection blush, blushed the more.

The change from the customary spot and necessary occasion of such an act — from the dressing hour in a bedroom to a time of travelling out-of-doors — lent to the idle deed a novelty it certainly did not intrinsically possess. The picture was a delicate one. Woman's prescriptive infirmity had stalked into the sunlight, which had invested it with the freshness of an originality. A cynical inference was irresistible by Gabriel Oak as he regarded the scene, generous though he fain would have been. There was no necessity whatever for her looking in the glass. She did not adjust her hat, or pat her hair, or press a dimple into shape, or do one thing to signify that any such intention had been her motive in taking up the glass. She simply observed herself as a fair product of nature in a feminine direction, her expressions seeming to glide into far-off though likely dramas in which men would play a part — vistas of probable triumphs — the smiles being of a phase suggesting that hearts were imagined as lost and won. Still, this was but conjecture, and the whole series of actions were so idly put forth as to make it rash to assert that intention had any part in them at all.

The wagoner's steps were heard returning. 5
She put the glass in the paper, and the whole again into its place.

[1864]

What strikes you immediately? Bathsheba's vanity? The rural scene? A sense of mystery? Our initial questions and impressions lead us to consider the writer's craft — the *how* of Bathsheba's characterization. Notice that the narration is third person — Bathsheba is described as "the girl" — so we're not witnessing this scene from her perspective. While the reader isn't in Gabriel's mind, there is a sense of seeing Bathsheba from his perspective, as she is unaware of his gaze. She is outside, atop a horse-drawn wagon, on her way from one place to another, and in transition.

Let's look at how you might annotate the passage as you read.

The girl on the summit of the load sat motionless, surrounded by tables and chairs with their legs upwards, backed by an oak settle, and ornamented in front by pots of geraniums, myrtles, and cactuses, together with a caged canary — all probably from the windows of the house just vacated. There was also a cat in a willow basket, from the partly-opened lid of which she gazed with half-closed eyes, and affectionately surveyed the small birds around.

Concrete detail.

The cat's partially concealed and watching birds. Prey and predator!

The handsome girl waited for some time idly in her place, and the only sound heard in the stillness was the hopping of the canary up and down the perches of its prison. Then she looked attentively downwards. It was not at the bird, nor at the cat; it was at an oblong package tied in paper, and lying between them. She turned her head to learn if the wagoner were coming. He was not yet in sight; and her eyes crept back to the package, her thoughts seeming to run upon what was inside it. At length she drew the article into her lap, and untied the paper covering; a small swing looking-glass was disclosed, in which she proceeded to survey herself attentively. She parted her lips and smiled.

It's quiet — almost like we, as readers, are spying on her.

Interesting word choice. Is she lazy? Complacent?

Why is the birdcage compared to prison here?

These words and phrases all connote secrecy.

Suggests a secret revealed.

It was a fine morning, and the sun lighted up to a scarlet glow the crimson jacket she wore, and painted a soft lustre upon her bright face and black hair. The myrtles, geraniums, and cactuses packed around her were fresh and green, and at such a

Natural world in full bloom — sensual imagery of color and sound.

These words and phrases all suggest vitality, vividness. Sun seems complicit in emphasizing her beauty.

leafless season they invested the whole concern of horses, wagon, furniture, and girl, with a peculiar charm of rarity. What possessed her to indulge in such a performance in the sight of the sparrows, blackbirds, and unperceived farmer, who were alone its spectators, — whether the smile began as a factitious one, to test her capacity in that art, nobody knows; it ended certainly in a real smile. She blushed at herself, and seeing her reflection blush, blushed the more.

The change from the customary spot and necessary occasion of such an act — from the dressing hour in a bedroom to a time of travelling out of doors — lent to the idle deed a novelty it certainly did not intrinsically possess. The picture was a delicate one. Woman's prescriptive infirmity had stalked into the sunlight, which had invested it with the freshness of an originality. A cynical inference was irresistible by Gabriel Oak as he regarded the scene, generous though he fain would have been. There was no necessity whatever for her looking in the glass. She did not adjust her hat, or pat her hair, or press a dimple into shape, or do one thing to signify that any such intention had been her motive in taking up the glass. She simply observed herself as a fair product of nature in a feminine direction, her expressions seeming to glide into far-off though likely dramas in which men would play a part — vistas of probable triumphs — the smiles being of a phase suggesting that hearts were imagined as lost and won. Still, this was but conjecture, and the whole series of actions were so idly put forth as to make it rash to assert that intention had any part in them at all.

The wagoner's steps were heard returning. She put the glass in the paper, and the whole again into its place.

Odd word. Is she acting?

Maybe her audience?

Meaning artificial?

More suggestion of performance and artifice — is she aware she's being watched?

Repetition. Blushing suggests bloom, spring-like, maybe even sexuality.

So she's behaving inappropriately because she's outside?

Second time "idle" has been used to describe Bathsheba and/or her actions!

Meaning? Infirmity = weakness or frailty? Prescriptive = accepted?

Why is the scene "delicate"? Is Bathsheba fragile? Sensitive? Does she need someone to take care of her?

Pure vanity: no purpose except to admire herself.

Another reference to performance and acting.

She's the star of her own show!

So everything I just read was pure speculation?

There's that word again! This is the third time it appears.

More secrecy.

From the first paragraph, we note the detailed description of the setting, particularly Bathsheba's belongings in the wagon: from furniture and plants to her cat and canary. The concrete details used to describe the "caged canary" (whose cage is later termed a "prison") and the cat "with half-closed eyes" who "affectionately surveyed the small birds around" are unsettling at best, perhaps even foreboding. Prey and predator are present in this seemingly ordinary scene.

In the next paragraph, Hardy uses language that connotes secrecy. He reminds us that only the sound of the canary hopping in its cage breaks the silence of the landscape. Bathsheba's eyes "crept" to the "package" that we learn is a mirror. She didn't simply reach down and unwrap it; instead, she "drew the article into her lap," as though hoping to escape notice. When the glass is finally in plain view, it is "disclosed," suggesting a secret revealed.

In the third paragraph, Hardy calls attention to Bathsheba's blushing, a characteristic we typically associate (certainly in Victorian times, when the novel was written) with feminine behavior. Hardy repeats the word three times — "She blushed at herself and seeing her reflection blush, blushed the more" — as Bathsheba smiles openly at her reflection. She may be blushing at her own beauty or at her own vanity, but in either case, Hardy's repetition calls our attention to the fact that she's interacting with her own image.

Blushing also connotes the bloom of youth, which Hardy picks up in the sensual images of a spring morning: the sun on her jacket "lighted up to a scarlet glow" and "painted a soft lustre" on her skin and hair. Hardy's sentences are long and flowing accumulations of sights and sounds — "myrtles, geraniums, and cactuses," closely followed by the "horses, wagon, furniture, and girl" — that lend a breathless quality to the scene. In fact, Bathsheba herself seems to reflect her environment. Her youth intensifies this mood of expectation and new beginnings — and possibly signals an awakening.

Subtle reminders in paragraphs three and four indicate there may be a distance between what we see and what is actually true, adding complexity to the passage. Hardy uses the word "performance" to describe Bathsheba's behavior, suggesting inauthenticity; similarly, in the fourth paragraph he uses the phrase "such an act." Hardy even says her smile might have begun "as a factitious one" — that is, contrived or artificial.

Then, amid all of this description, Hardy presents readers with an assertion: "Woman's prescriptive infirmity had stalked into the sunlight, which had invested it with the freshness of an originality." That "prescriptive infirmity" is likely vanity. Bathsheba, we're told, is not looking into the mirror for any practical reason, such as fixing her hair, but rather simply to observe herself "as a fair product of nature in a feminine direction." Her thoughts aren't described as introspective but instead "[seem] to glide" into "dramas in which men would play a part." These "dramas" link back to the "performance" mentioned in paragraph three. But the next sentence makes this judgment of her character seem less objective; Hardy specifies that this portrayal of her inner thoughts is "just conjecture" on Gabriel's part. By the end of the passage, Gabriel acknowledges that this young woman's "intention" is not clear, though we've seen enough to imagine that she might be quite shrewd and, at the very least, understands the power of her attractiveness. Even though variations of the word *idle* appear three times in the passage, her behavior seems calculated and practiced rather than nonchalant.

When we put all of these elements of style together — the concrete details, the lush descriptions of a spring morning, and images of performance and artifice — we get a picture of a young woman who is shrewd yet vulnerable. Hardy characterizes Bathsheba as someone who seems to recognize her own youthful beauty and the potential power it confers, yet we feel some unease about what will happen to her next.

ACTIVITY

Consider this opening section from *A House for Mr. Biswas* by V. S. Naipaul, who won the Nobel Prize for literature in 2001. This novel traces the life of Mohan Biswas during a time of colonial rule in Trinidad. How does Naipaul employ literary elements to develop the character of Mr. Biswas and convey the significance that owning a home has for him?

from A House for Mr. Biswas

V. S. NAIPAUL

Mr. Biswas was forty-six, and had four children. He had no money. His wife Shama had no money. On the house in Sikkim Street Mr. Biswas owed, and had been owing for four years, three thousand dollars. . . .

Since they had moved to the house Shama had learned a new loyalty, to him and to their children; away from her mother and sisters, she was able to express this without shame, and to Mr. Biswas this was a triumph almost as big as the acquiring of his own house.

He thought of the house as his own, though for years it had been irretrievably mortgaged. And during these months of illness and despair he was struck again and again by the wonder of being in his own house, the audacity of it: to walk in through his own front gate, to bar entry to whoever he wished, to close his doors and windows every night, to hear no noises except those of his family, to wander freely from room to room and about his yard, instead of being condemned, as before, to retire the moment he got home to the crowded room in one or the other of Mrs. Tulsi's houses, crowded with Shama's sisters, their husbands, their children. As a boy he had moved from one house of strangers to another; and since his marriage he felt he had lived nowhere but in the houses of the Tulsis, at Hanuman House in Arwacas, in the decaying wooden house at Shorthills, in the clumsy concrete house in Port of Spain. And now at the end he found himself in his own house, on his own half-lot of land, his own portion of the earth. That he should have been responsible for this seemed to him, in these last months, stupendous.

[1961]

FROM ANALYSIS TO ESSAY: WRITING A CLOSE ANALYSIS ESSAY

Most of the time, you will write a literary analysis essay in response to an assignment that provides both a fiction passage and a prompt. These analyses usually revolve around characterization, though they take a number of forms. Most often, you will be asked to analyze how a writer uses literary elements to reveal a person's character. Some essay prompts will ask you to focus on the effect that a setting (like the landscape or the cultural environment) or a specific event (such as another character's death or a dramatic revelation) has on a character. You might also be asked about connections between or among characters, often in terms of how a central character is developed through interactions with minor characters or how a complex relationship (such as that of a husband and wife or parent and child) is portrayed.

For this section, we're going to focus on "Reunion," a short story written in 1962 by John Cheever. It centers on a meeting between the narrator, Charlie, and his father, whom he has not seen for three years. Start out by perusing the entire story just to get an initial sense of what's going on. As we discussed earlier, a few general questions are relevant to focus your reading on any fictional text, including this one:

- From whose viewpoint is the story being told? What beliefs or biases might the narrator have?
- Who are the characters, and how are they described? Can you sense any conflicts or contradictions within or between individuals?
- Where and when does the story take place? What is striking about the language the author uses to present the time and setting?

Reunion

JOHN CHEEVER

The last time I saw my father was in Grand Central Station. I was going from my grandmother's in the Adirondacks to a cottage on the Cape that my mother had rented, and I wrote my father that I would be in New York between trains for an hour and a half, and asked if we could have lunch together. His secretary wrote to say that he would meet me at the information booth at noon, and at twelve o'clock sharp I saw him coming through the crowd. He was a stranger to me — my mother divorced him three years ago and I hadn't been with him since — but as soon as I saw him I felt that he was my father, my flesh and blood, my future and my doom. I knew that when I was grown I would be something like him; I would have to plan my campaigns within his limitations. He was a big, good-looking man, and I was terribly happy to see him again. He struck me on the back and shook my hand. "Hi, Charlie," he said. "Hi, boy. I'd like to take you up to my club, but it's in the Sixties, and if you have to catch an early train I guess we'd better get something to eat around here." He put his arm around me, and I smelled my father the way my mother sniffs a rose. It was a rich compound of whiskey, after-shave lotion, shoe polish, woolens, and the rankness of a mature male. I hoped that someone would see us together. I wished that we could be photographed. I wanted some record of our having been together.

We went out of the station and up a side street to a restaurant. It was still early, and the place was empty. The bartender was quarreling with a delivery boy, and there was one very old waiter in a red coat down by the kitchen door. We sat down, and my father hailed the waiter in a loud voice. "*Kellner!*"[1] he shouted. *"Garçon!*[2] *Cameriere!*[3] *You!"* His boisterousness in the empty restaurant seemed out of place. "Could we have a little service here!" he shouted. "Chop-chop." Then he clapped his hands. This caught the waiter's attention, and he shuffled over to our table.

"Were you clapping your hands at me?" he asked.

"Calm down, calm down, *sommelier*,"[4] my father said. "If it isn't too much to ask of you — if it wouldn't be too much above and beyond the call of duty, we would like a couple of Beefeater Gibsons."

"I don't like to be clapped at," the waiter said.

"I should have brought my whistle," my father said. "I have a whistle that is audible only to the ears of old waiters. Now, take out your little pad and your little pencil and see if you can get this straight: two Beefeater Gibsons. Repeat after me: two Beefeater Gibsons."

"I think you'd better go somewhere else," the waiter said quietly.

"That," said my father, "is one of the most brilliant suggestions I have ever heard. Come on, Charlie, let's get the hell out of here."

I followed my father out of that restaurant into another. He was not so boisterous this time. Our drinks came, and he cross-questioned me about the baseball season. He then struck the edge of his empty glass with his knife and began shouting again. *"Garçon! Kellner! Cameriere! You!* Could we trouble you to bring us two more of the same."

"How old is the boy?" the waiter asked.

"That," my father said, "is none of your God-damned business."

"I'm sorry, sir," the waiter said, "but I won't serve the boy another drink."

"Well, I have some news for you," my father said. "I have some very interesting news for you. This doesn't happen to be the only restaurant in New York. They've opened another on the corner. Come on, Charlie."

He paid the bill, and I followed him out of that restaurant into another. Here the waiters wore pink jackets like hunting coats, and there was a lot of horse tack on the walls. We sat down, and my father began to shout again. "Master of the hounds! Tallyhoo and all that sort of thing. We'd like a little something in the way of a stirrup cup. Namely, two Bibson Geefeaters."

"Two Bibson Geefeaters?" the waiter asked, smiling.

"You know damned well what I want," my father said angrily. "I want two Beefeater Gibsons, and make it snappy. Things have changed in jolly old England. So my friend the duke tells me. Let's see what England can produce in the way of a cocktail."

"This isn't England," the waiter said.

"Don't argue with me," my father said. "Just do as you're told."

"If there is one thing I cannot tolerate," my father said, "it is an impudent domestic. Come on, Charlie."

The fourth place we went to was Italian. "*Buon giorno,*"[5] my father said. "*Per favore, possiamo avere due cocktail americani, forti, forti. Molto gin, poco vermut.*"[6]

[1] ***Kellner:*** "Waiter" in German. — Eds.

[2] ***Garçon:*** "Waiter" in French. — Eds.

[3] ***Cameriere:*** "Waiter" in Italian. — Eds.

[4] ***Sommelier:*** The waiter or waitress who serves wine at a restaurant. — Eds.

[5] ***Buon giorno:*** "Good day" in Italian — Eds.

[6] ***Per favore, possiamo avere due cocktail americani, forti, forti. Molto gin, poco vermut:*** Italian for "Please, can we have two American cocktails, very strong. Lots of gin, just a little vermouth." — Eds.

"I don't understand Italian," the waiter said.

"Oh, come off it," my father said. "You understand Italian, and you know damned well you do. *Vogliamo due cocktail americani. Subito.*"[7]

The waiter left us and spoke with the captain, who came over to our table and said, "I'm sorry, sir, but this table is reserved."

"All right," my father said. "Get us another table."

"All the tables are reserved," the captain said.

"I get it," my father said. "You don't desire our patronage. Is that it? Well, the hell with you. *Vada all'inferno.*[8] Let's go, Charlie."

"I have to get my train," I said.

"I'm sorry, sonny," my father said. "I'm terribly sorry." He put his arm around me and pressed me against him. "I'll walk you back to the station. If there had only been time to go up to my club."

"That's all right, Daddy," I said.

"I'll get you a paper," he said. "I'll get you a paper to read on the train."

Then he went up to a newsstand and said, "Kind sir, will you be good enough to favor me with one of your God-damned, no-good, ten-cent afternoon papers?" The clerk turned away from him and stared at a magazine cover. "Is it asking too much, kind sir," my father said, "is it asking too much for you to sell me one of your disgusting specimens of yellow journalism?"

"I have to go, Daddy," I said. "It's late."

"Now, just wait a second, sonny," he said. "Just wait a second. I want to get a rise out of this chap."

"Goodbye, Daddy," I said, and I went down the stairs and got my train, and that was the last time I saw my father.

[1962]

[7] ***Vogliamo due cocktail americani. Subito:*** Italian for "We want two American cocktails. Immediately." — Eds.

[8] ***Vada all'inferno:*** Italian for "Go to hell." — Eds.

Preparing to Write

Most of the time, you'll be given a prompt or a writing assignment that will focus your analysis. For instance, in this case, your teacher may assign the following prompt:

> In a well-written essay, analyze the literary elements that John Cheever uses to characterize the complex relationship between father and son in "Reunion."

Before starting to analyze at a deeper level and beginning your written response, it's helpful to put into a sentence or two just what is going on in this story. We might sum up "Reunion" as follows:

> In "Reunion," the narrator, who seems to have been a teenager at the time, remembers his final meeting with his father, whom he hadn't seen in three years. His father drank too much, behaved badly, and disappointed his son.

That's actually it — the outline of what happens in the story. But the emotional wallop, the part that makes us feel the experience and think about it, comes from the style and structure that Cheever uses to tell this brief tale. To get to the deeper layer required by such an assignment, you might reread the story carefully before consolidating your observations and insights into a graphic organizer.

A graphic organizer helps break a work into more manageable sections for close reading. Since you'll probably have more observations than you can discuss in a single, relatively brief essay, you can focus by returning to the prompt. What are you asked to do?

In this case, you must discuss the relationship between the two central characters, Charlie and his father. With this in mind, you can use a graphic organizer to begin exploring how Cheever portrays them. Structuring your close reading in this way helps you move beyond simply describing the author's language choices to analysis that connects style with its effect and meaning. Your teacher may divide the text for you, or you may discover natural divisions as you begin your analysis. In this case, the story divides fairly naturally between narrative sections and sections composed entirely of dialogue.

Lines	**Element of Style**	**Effect or Function**
"The last time I saw my father was in Grand Central Station."	Straightforward, factual, nonjudgmental sentence. Same phrase appears at beginning and end: it frames the story.	The narrator starts out with factual-sounding reporting and does not directly criticize his father's behavior. The framing unifies the story and contributes to a sad, reflective tone.
". . . he was my father, my flesh and blood, my future and my doom. . . . I would have to plan my campaigns within his limitations."	Strong, emotional language. Metaphor of war suggested by "my campaigns."	The narrative expresses conflicting emotions: he feels the blood bond with his father, yet this is his "doom," which suggests he's terrified of that bond. He longs for a good relationship yet seems to feel at war with his father.
"He was a big, good-looking, man. . . ." "I smelled my father the way my mother sniffs a rose. . . ." "I wished that we could be photographed."	Description of the father, including a simile, includes both physical detail and figurative language.	Charlie admires his father and is hopeful that this meeting will be a positive turning point in their relationship.
"a loud voice," "boisterousness" "shouted," "clapped his hands"	Vivid language to describe the father's behavior.	The father is portrayed as a rude, arrogant, sarcastic man. The narrator recognizes the inappropriate and obnoxious behavior yet never speaks up to criticize his father.
"*Kellner . . . Garçon! Cameriere!*" "*sommelier*" "*Per favore, possiamo . . .*" "*Vogliamo due cocktail . . .*" "*Vada all'inferno.*"	Dialogue shows the father using various languages in the restaurant.	When the father uses these phrases to belittle wait staff, his pompous behavior shows him to be both boorish and insecure. He's a show-off.

(*continued*)

Lines	Element of Style	Effect or Function
"I should have brought my whistle . . . that is audible only to the ears of old waiters." "You know damned well what I want . . . two Beefeater Gibsons, and make it snappy."	Dialogue shows Charlie's father addressing wait staff sarcastically and condescendingly.	Charlie is embarrassed by his father's boorish and increasingly drunken behavior, yet he says nothing to his father about it.
"I'd like to take you up to my club, but it's in the Sixties, and if you have to catch an early train . . ." " . . . he cross-questioned me about the baseball season." "I'm sorry, sonny. . . . I'm terribly sorry."	Dialogue between father and son is actually mostly monologue. Father makes excuses, fails to connect on an emotional level, and apologizes.	This dialogue shows the father's ineffectuality as a parent. But it also shows him to be insecure and pitiful.

A graphic organizer helps you prepare to write, but you won't be able to use every idea there in a focused, coherent close analysis essay — especially if you face time or length constraints. This graphic organizer, for instance, suggests more than one approach to analyzing the relationship between father and son. It illustrates the conflicting emotions the narrator expresses toward his relationship with his father — his hopeful anticipation of their meeting contrasts with his fear of the bond between them; the narrator's admiration is tempered by his dread of becoming like his father. It also shows how an essay might focus on the father's character, offering a perspective of him as both obnoxious and pitiful — not entirely a villain, though certainly a disappointing parent. As you move forward, you must decide what direction you want your essay to take.

Developing a Thesis Statement

Now that we've organized our observations in writing, let's return to the prompt:

> In a well-written essay, analyze the literary elements that John Cheever uses to characterize the complex relationship between father and son in "Reunion".

Even with an assignment as specific as this one, there's no "right answer," and certainly more than one way to write an effective response. But, as the prompt states, your essay must link your interpretation of the father-son relationship to literary elements of style. In effect, you are building a kind of literary argument with references from the text that show how the language and structure of this story develop and reinforce the complexity of the relationship between Charlie and his father. This means that a **thesis statement** that merely restates the prompt will not be effective:

> In "Reunion," John Cheever uses several literary devices to characterize the complex relationship between Charlie and his father.

A strong thesis also goes beyond a summary of the story:

> In "Reunion," an adult narrator looks back on his last meeting with his father.

The thesis above fails to identify any literary elements that Cheever employs, but more important, pure plot description does not leave room for you to develop an analysis.

A successful thesis will focus on specific characteristics of the story's language and structure, so that in the body of the essay you can analyze how they help convey your interpretation of the father-son relationship at the center of the story. However, you must be careful not to make your thesis so narrow that you'll run out of things to say about it as you write your essay:

> In "Reunion," Cheever uses dialogue to characterize the last meeting between a teenage boy and his father.

Although this thesis identifies a literary element — dialogue — it's short on analysis. It does not go far enough because there's no interpretation of the meaning of the complex relationship at the heart of the story. Dialogue is certainly one of the literary techniques you could examine in your analysis of that relationship, but it's not enough to anchor an entire essay.

Before you determine what literary or style elements you'll discuss, you need to decide on an interpretation of the kind of relationship Cheever depicts in "Reunion." Otherwise, your essay will likely boil down to a list of literary elements that don't relate to each other or convey a larger insight into the story. In this case, let's consider the idea of "doom." Charlie's memory of his last meeting with his father haunts him, as does the idea of his father, whom Charlie calls his "doom." Cheever depicts the boy's growing disappointment as he sees the effect of his father's increasingly rude and obnoxious behavior — yet we don't see the man as simply a villain but rather as a boastful, insecure man who does not know how to be a father. He may be a sad case, but he's Charlie's "flesh and blood" and will inevitably influence who the boy becomes. Here's the start of a thesis that captures that idea:

> In "Reunion," John Cheever depicts a son who is haunted by both his father's failures and his own fear of repeating them.

How does Cheever convey this idea? We can point to the reflective, wistful tone of a narrator looking back on a remembered experience, the lively dialogue that re-creates the embarrassing and disappointing experience during this last meeting, a setting that suggests a point of transition, and diction that hints at the narrator's ambivalence toward his father. Listing all of these would make a pretty long and potentially confusing thesis, but if you blend some of the literary elements together, you can craft one that fully responds to the prompt:

> Through the narrator's emotional descriptions, colorful dialogue, and wistful tone, Cheever depicts a son who is haunted by both his father's failures and his fear of repeating them himself.

Organizing a Close Analysis Essay

Keep in mind that your initial thesis — what we call a "working thesis" — isn't set in stone and may change as you draft your essay. But a clear working thesis can guide you and serve as a solid essay outline. Your essay can be organized around literary elements, with one paragraph on emotional language, one on dialogue, and one on tone. In each paragraph, make sure you discuss both the element and its effect; do not simply define and illustrate the literary or style element but explain how it conveys meaning.

Integrating Quotations

Literary analysis, as you know, requires textual references, either via direct quotations or paraphrased references to the story. When you're writing an analysis or interpretation of a work, the text is your evidence. Quotations that are carefully chosen and incorporated into your own writing provide persuasive support for your thesis. Take care to avoid quoting big chunks of text, because your voice (not the author's) should prevail in a close analysis essay — that is, you must offer thoughtful commentary on what you quote. One way you might check to make sure that you're analyzing a work is to highlight all your quotations from the text. The paragraph below quotes from "Reunion":

> Cheever's narrator describes his father in striking language. His father was "a big, good-looking man," who "was a rich compound of whiskey, after-shave lotion, shoe polish, woolens, and the rankness of a mature male." Charlie uses strong verbs to capture his father's "boisterousness": he "hailed the waiter in a loud voice," he "cross-questioned me," and "struck the edge of his empty glass with his knife and began shouting."

Except for the topic sentence, this paragraph is almost entirely made up of quotations from "Reunion." In fact, it probably feels as though you're rereading Cheever's story. There is no commentary, which leaves the reader without a clear understanding of the essay writer's interpretation. At best, the paragraph reads like a list that catalogs examples of striking language throughout the story.

Compare that paragraph to the one that follows. While both share a similar structure and even use the same quotations, the essay writer's original commentary is what moves the following paragraph toward analysis. Notice how the writer interprets the effect Cheever's language choices have on the story.

> Cheever's narrator describes his father in striking language. Charlie begins by describing his father as "a big, good-looking man." In many ways a general description, this is the way the teenager sees him in terms of size and overall appearance. But the narrator brings in a more mature perspective in his memory of a man who "was a rich compound of whiskey, after-shave lotion, shoe polish, woolens, and the rankness of a mature male." The "mature male" description is clearly not something the narrator would have understood when he was younger, but it is the way he now remembers his father. As their reunion continues, Charlie uses strong verbs to capture his father's "boisterousness": he "hailed the waiter in a loud voice," he "cross-questioned me," and "struck the edge of his empty glass with his knife and began shouting." There's no sugar-coating the father's behavior as the narrator describes his father in the precise terms of recollection that remains, years later, both dramatic and painful.

A Sample Close Analysis Essay

Read the sample essay here, and respond to the questions at the end.

A "Reunion" Gone Wrong

"Reunion," a short story written by John Cheever in 1962, begins and ends in Grand Central Station in New York City, a place of transition and movement, a place people pass through on their way to various other destinations. For Charlie, the narrator who recalls his younger self, this "reunion" is more than just a meeting: it's his last hope of salvaging a strained relationship with his father. Through the narrator's emotional descriptions, colorful dialogue, and wistful tone, Cheever depicts a son who is haunted by both his father's failures and his fear of repeating them himself.

At the outset, the language Charlie uses to remember this experience is heavy with emotion that shows his hopeful anticipation mixed with dread. After explaining that he initiated the meeting, he calls his father a "stranger," yet he then describes the moment he sees him in the train station as one of profound recognition. Charlie "felt he was my father, my flesh and blood." This realization is, however, both a reassurance and a warning. On the one hand, the narrator has arranged this "reunion" because he is optimistic about establishing a relationship with his estranged father despite the divorce and the absence of three years. On the other hand, however, he fears that his father is his "future" and "doom." Believing he is unable to avoid becoming "something like" his father, he seems to feel trapped. He even uses the language of battle in his description of his reaction to his father's behavior during their last meeting: "I would have to plan my campaigns," he thinks, "within his limitations." The diction he uses to describe his father also points to this ambivalence. Charlie is "terribly happy," an odd combination of words; he says he smells his father "the way my mother sniffs a rose," but includes the scent of "the rankness of a mature male" among his recollections. The verbs that capture his anticipation—"hoped," "wished," and "wanted"—all suggest yearning, though not realization.

Cheever characterizes the father with lively dialogue that shows him to be belligerent and rude, though also pitifully insecure. The father bullies waiters in one restaurant after another, showing off by spouting basic phrases of foreign languages, whether French, Italian, or German. He tries to mock the waiters with sarcastic comments that often devolve into curse words and spark contentious encounters. When waiters at each location try to avoid conflict by either deflecting his accusations or courteously asking him to leave, Charlie's father deliberately tries to create confrontations. In an oddly similar fashion, he cannot have a conversation with his son. Only once does he ask Charlie a question, and it's not personal: it's about baseball. While he offers to buy his son a newspaper, he is so obnoxious toward the newsstand attendant that the son simply tries to get away, saying that he has to get his train.

By the end of the story, Cheever's melancholy tone suggests a role reversal between Charlie and his father. At the outset, Charlie is the boy, looking forward to seeing his father, who has arranged the meeting through his secretary rather than directly communicating with his son. Charlie accepts what is given him. Recognizing that his father is a "stranger," Charlie still wishes for a photograph of the two of them, wanting "some record of our having been together." In his heart, Charlie knows this meeting is not the start of anything lasting. Yet, throughout his father's blustering, bullying, and obnoxious behavior fueled by drinking, Charlie speaks not a word of criticism to his father and lets the man's words and actions speak for themselves. As Charlie's father becomes increasingly pathetic, he becomes the child, desperately seeking approval. Charlie becomes the adult when he insists that he has a train to catch and tells his father, "It's late." Without recriminations or a childish outburst of anger, Charlie turns and goes in a new direction — alone.

In slightly more than a thousand words of sparse language, painful dialogue, and a circular narrative arc, Cheever leaves his readers wondering if Charlie will echo his father's behavior. At the end of the story, the narrator recounts the moment when he refuses to stay with his father any longer: "'I have to go, Daddy,' I said. 'It's late.'" He calls him "Daddy," the way a young child usually refers to his father, but as readers, we hear the longing in that choice. And we know that it is too "late" to save this meeting. Even at the end, which loops back to the beginning — "that was the last time I saw my father" — it's not clear whether Charlie will be able to escape the legacy his father represents, but, as narrator of this story, he has shown himself to be a resolute young man and a reflective older one.

QUESTIONS

1. Examine the relationship between the thesis and the topic sentences. Do you think the basic structure of the essay is effective or ineffective? Why?
2. How does the essay support its argument with evidence from the text? Cite a paragraph that you find especially persuasive and explain why.
3. The essay writer argues that Cheever uses dialogue to characterize the father in the third paragraph of this essay. To what extent do you think that the textual evidence, which is entirely paraphrased without any direct quotations, supports this interpretation?
4. In the second-to-last paragraph, the writer discusses the role reversal of Charlie and his father. Does the thesis prepare us as readers for this paragraph? If you think it's a valid point, should it have been incorporated into the thesis or presented as the conclusion to the essay?
5. What is another argument you might make based on a close reading of "Reunion"? It does not have to contradict this writer's interpretation entirely but rather offer another way to read the story or a different conclusion from the one drawn in this sample essay.

ACTIVITY

The following passage is from the opening chapter of *Song of Solomon* by Toni Morrison. Macon Dead is standing outside and watching his estranged sister Pilate, along with her daughter and granddaughter, through a window. Write an essay analyzing how Morrison conveys the conflicted relationship between the observer and the observed in this scene.

from Song of Solomon

TONI MORRISON

He turned back and walked slowly toward Pilate's house. They were singing some melody that Pilate was leading. A phrase that the other two were taking up and building on. Her powerful contralto, Reba's piercing soprano in counterpoint, and the soft voice of the girl, Hagar, who must be about ten or eleven now, pulled him like a carpet tack under the influence of a magnet.

Surrendering to the sound, Macon moved closer. He wanted no conversation, no witness, only to listen and perhaps to see the three of them, the source of that music that made him think of fields and wild turkey and calico. Treading as lightly as he could, he crept up to the side window where the candlelight flickered lowest, and peeped in. Reba was cutting her toenails with a kitchen knife or a switchblade, her long neck bent almost to her knees. The girl, Hagar, was braiding her hair, while Pilate, whose face he could not see because her back was to the window, was stirring something in a pot. Wine pulp, perhaps. Macon knew it was not food she was stirring, for she and her daughters ate like children. Whatever they had a taste for. No meal was ever planned or balanced or served. Nor was there any gathering at the table. Pilate might bake hot bread and each one of them would eat it with butter whenever she felt like it. Or there might be grapes, left over from the winemaking, or peaches for days on end. If one of them bought a gallon of milk they drank it until it was gone. If another got a half bushel of tomatoes or a dozen ears of corn, they ate them until they were gone too. They ate what they had or came across or had a craving for. Profits from their wine-selling evaporated like sea water in a hot wind — going for junk jewelry for Hagar, Reba's gifts to men, and he didn't know what all.

Near the window, hidden by the dark, he felt the irritability of the day drain from him and relished the effortless beauty of the women singing in the candlelight. Reba's soft profile, Hagar's hands moving, moving in her heavy hair, and Pilate. He knew her face better than he knew his own. Singing now, her face would be a mask; all emotion and passion would have left her features and entered her voice. But he knew that when she was neither singing nor talking, her face was animated by her constantly moving lips. She chewed things. As a baby, as a very young girl, she kept things in her mouth — straw from brooms, gristle, buttons, seeds, leaves, string, and her favorite, when he could find some for her, rubber bands and India rubber erasers. Her lips were alive with small movements. If you were close to her, you wondered if she was about to smile or was she merely shifting a straw from the baseline of her gums to her tongue. Perhaps she was dislodging a curl of rubber band from inside her cheek, or was she really smiling? From a distance she appeared to be whispering to herself, when she was only nibbling or splitting tiny seeds with her front teeth. Her lips were darker than her skin, wine-stained, blueberry-dyed, so her face had a cosmetic look — as though she had applied a very dark lipstick neatly and blotted away its shine on a scrap of newspaper.

As Macon felt himself softening under the weight of memory and music, the song died down. The air was quiet and yet Macon Dead could not leave. He liked looking at them freely this way. They didn't move. They simply stopped singing and Reba went on paring her toenails, Hagar threaded and un-threaded her hair, and Pilate swayed like a willow over her stirring.

[1977]

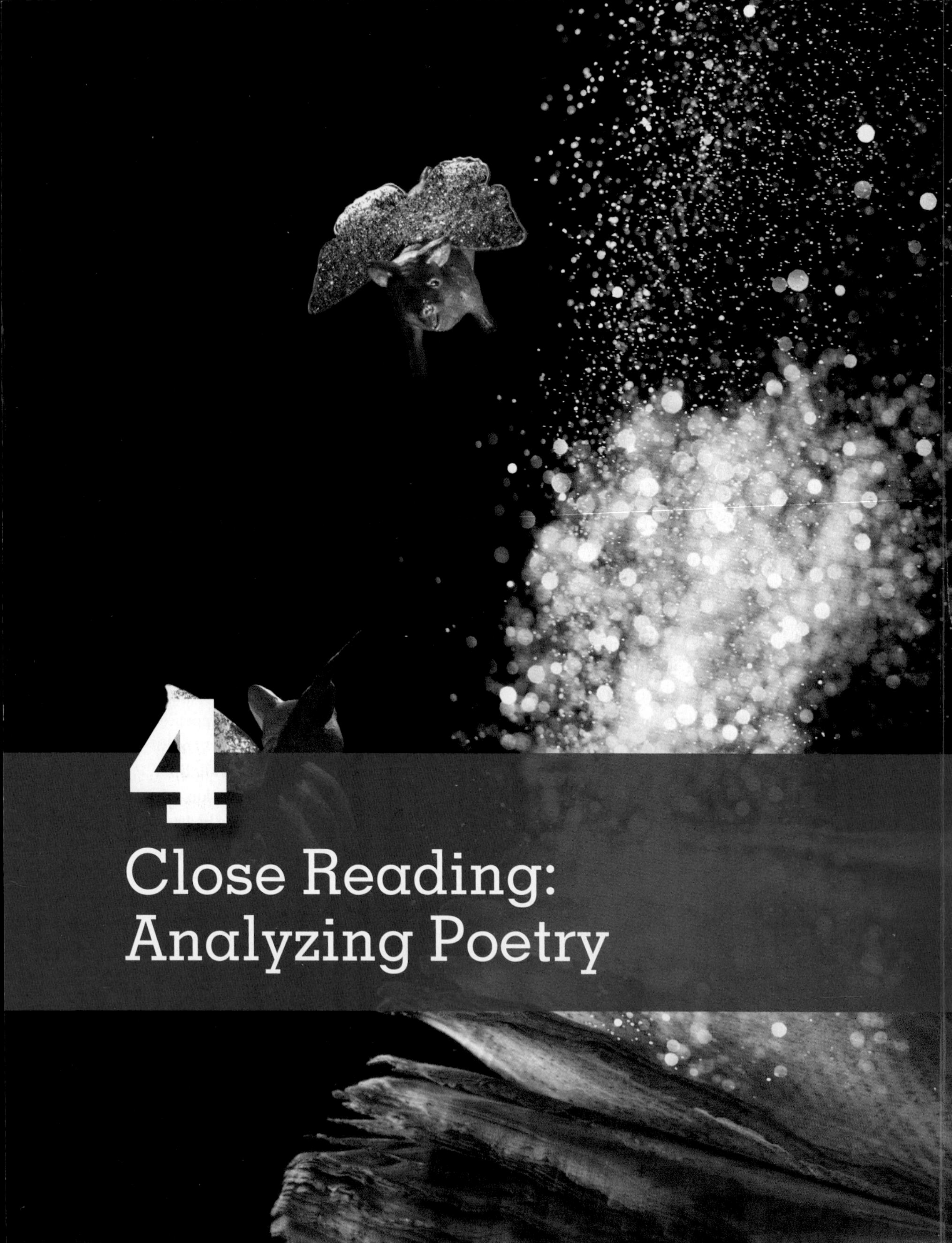

4
Close Reading: Analyzing Poetry

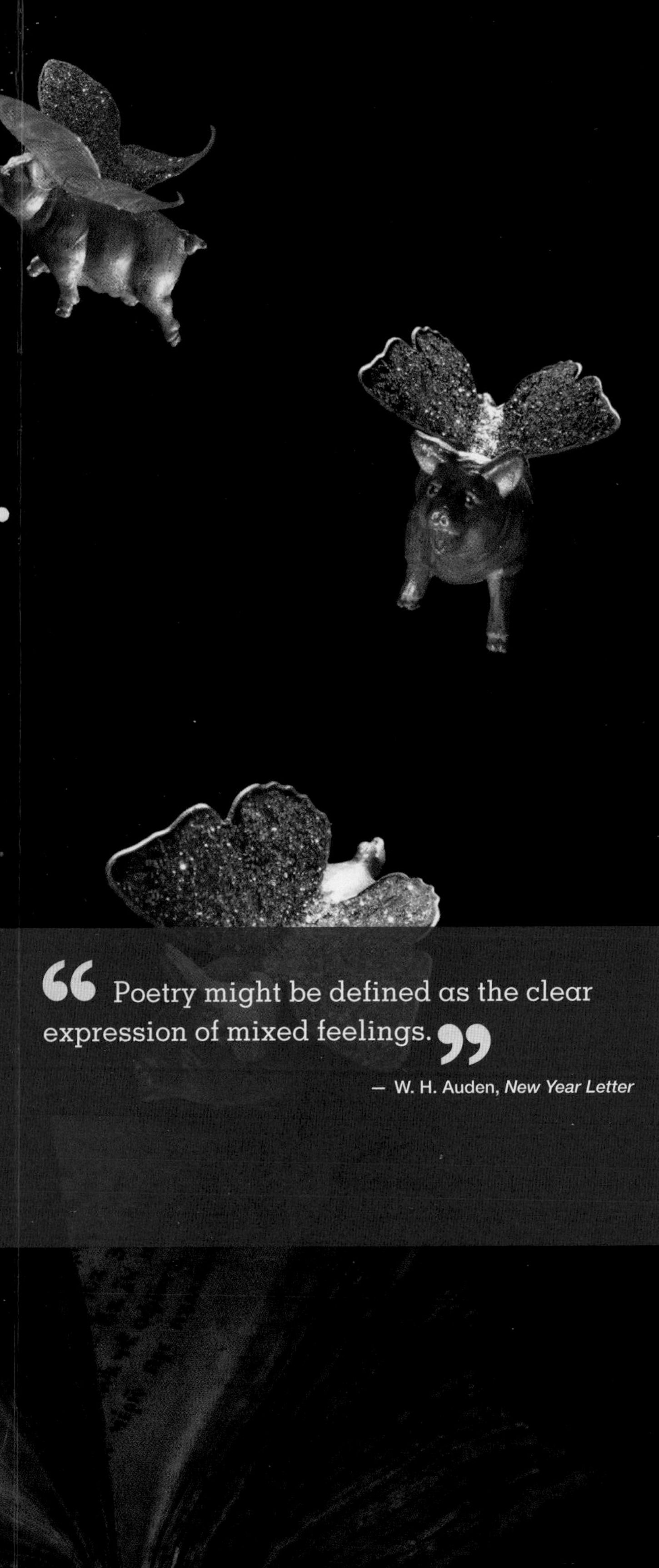

Poetry might be defined as the clear expression of mixed feelings.
— W. H. Auden, New Year Letter
Floriana/Getty Images

The language and structure of poetry are often more compressed than prose; most poems say a lot in a small amount of space. While both forms of writing convey meaning that runs deeper than the literal, the stories, emotions, and ideas that poetry expresses often seem much less straightforward. However, many poems do contain familiar narrative arcs, and all poetry uses language that is rich and will reward an active reader. Every word matters, which is why it's a good idea to read a poem more than once in a sitting. Of course, the most important step — even before the ones we offer in this chapter — is to open your heart and mind to the emotional effects of the work, which will be both satisfying and helpful in getting you started.

As you read poetry, keep in mind some of the ways you will be asked to respond to it. Nearly always, you will be asked to closely analyze a poem — in other words, you must interpret not just *what* a poem means, but *how* that meaning is created. Often, this will involve analyzing the speaker's attitude toward an idea expressed in the poem. You may also be asked to examine how elements of the poem connect to a larger meaning or to analyze the relationship between two ideas in a single poem. Another common objective of close analysis is to study more than one poem at a time, typically through comparison and contrast of the ways each work treats a common theme or idea. Above all, the key to close analysis is making connections between style and meaning.

In this chapter, we suggest three steps you can use to help you begin the study of a new poem:

1. First, we recommend reading a poem at its most literal level to form a basic understanding of it — this will help you discover the poem's main subject and provide the foundation for your analysis.
2. Second, we will show you how to locate the speaker of a poem, along with his or her attitude toward its subject. This will help form the basis of your interpretation of the poem's meaning.
3. Third, we will walk you through how to read a poem for its stylistic details, demonstrating how each of the major poetic elements of style contributes to a poem's meaning. This last step is crucial: it connects style to meaning by providing evidence for your interpretation of the poem — no close analysis is complete without it.

Usually, you will be asked to put your analysis in writing, and this process directly connects to how we approach reading poetry in this chapter. When you write a close analysis essay, you start with the larger ideas you've discovered and use the small details — the words themselves and how they're arranged — to support your interpretation of the meaning of the piece. Later in the chapter, we illustrate how to craft a thesis statement and write an effective close analysis essay, including strategies for organizing the essay and guidance on how to integrate quotations seamlessly into your writing. Let's start with some strategies for approaching a poem on your first read-through.

STEP 1: READING FOR LITERAL MEANING

Before you can begin to analyze a poem, you must identify its subject. In other words, what is the poem about? Your answer should distill the poem's main idea or ideas into a sentence, phrase, or even just a word — this short summary will provide the foundation for your interpretation of its meaning.

One of the most effective ways to determine a poem's subject is to read it with an eye toward the literal meaning of the words on the page. Some questions to help you do this on your first read include:

- What is happening in the poem?
- What do you visualize as you read?
- What does it make you think about?
- Do you have an emotional reaction to it?

With those questions in mind, let's take a look at "Digging," by Nobel laureate Seamus Heaney.

Digging

SEAMUS HEANEY

Between my finger and my thumb
The squat pen rests; snug as a gun.

Under my window, a clean rasping sound
When the spade sinks into gravelly ground:
My father, digging. I look down

Till his straining rump among the flowerbeds
Bends low, comes up twenty years away
Stooping in rhythm through potato drills
Where he was digging.

The coarse boot nestled on the lug, the shaft
Against the inside knee was levered firmly.
He rooted out tall tops, buried the bright edge deep
To scatter new potatoes that we picked
Loving their cool hardness in our hands.

By God, the old man could handle a spade.
Just like his old man.

My grandfather cut more turf in a day
Than any other man on Toner's bog.
Once I carried him milk in a bottle
Corked sloppily with paper. He straightened up
To drink it, then fell to right away
Nicking and slicing neatly, heaving sods
Over his shoulder, going down and down
For the good turf. Digging.

The cold smell of potato mould, the squelch and slap
Of soggy peat, the curt cuts of an edge
Through living roots awaken in my head.
But I've no spade to follow men like them.

Between my finger and my thumb
The squat pen rests.
I'll dig with it.

[1966]

Before you begin rereading "Digging," consider the title; it may provide a useful clue about the poem's subject. A poem's title can also serve as its first line (though this is not the case with "Digging"). Keep in mind, however, that titles can be misleading, ironic, or indirect. Taking note of the title is just one of many approaches to understanding a poem, and it should happen alongside the other reading strategies we include here. In "Digging," the title is only part of the story — we know by the second line that the poem's speaker is holding a pen, not a shovel — but it gives us a way into the poem by raising questions for the reader to explore: who's digging, and why?

If you find that the poem is confusing or difficult to follow, it may be helpful to look for full sentences that extend past the line and stanza breaks — those sentences may reveal a story. Notice that, in "Digging," the poem's first stanza can be read as one sentence:

> "Between my finger and my thumb the squat pen rests; snug as a gun."

The poem's second sentence ends in the middle of line 5:

> "Under my window, a clean rasping sound when the spade sinks into gravelly ground: my father, digging."

The next sentence goes on until line 9:

> "I look down till his straining rump among the flowerbeds bends low, comes up twenty years away stooping in rhythm through potato drills where he was digging."

Follow the pattern yourself on your next read-through. After one or two readings, you've probably noticed that "Digging" is about more than just digging. In fact, there's a story here — one that spans generations but is compressed into just fifteen sentences:

> "Between my finger and my thumb the squat pen rests; snug as a gun. Under my window, a clean rasping sound when the spade sinks into gravelly ground: my father, digging. I look down till his straining rump among the flowerbeds bends low, comes up twenty years away stooping in rhythm through potato drills where he was digging. The coarse boot nestled on the lug, the shaft against the inside knee was levered firmly. He rooted out tall tops, buried the bright edge deep to scatter new potatoes that we picked, loving their cool hardness in our hands. By God, the old man could handle a spade. Just like his old man. My grandfather cut more turf in a day than any other man on Toner's bog. Once I carried him milk in a bottle corked sloppily with paper. He straightened up to drink it, then fell to right away nicking and slicing neatly, heaving sods over his shoulder, going down and down for the good turf. Digging. The cold smell of potato mould, the squelch and slap of soggy peat, the curt cuts of an edge through living roots awaken in my head. But I've no spade to follow men like them. Between my finger and my thumb the squat pen rests. I'll dig with it."

You may discover, after breaking a poem down into sentences, that you can immediately identify its subject. However, if this is not the case, another useful exercise to try — particularly when a poem's narrative does not appear to be linear, or when it does not appear to follow any narrative pattern whatsoever — is paraphrasing. By putting the poem in your own words, it may be easier to spot whether it has a narrative arc, and if so, identify its most important aspects. This will help clarify the poem's subject. A paraphrase of "Digging," for example, may look something like this:

> The speaker is holding a pen and looks out his window, maybe taking a break from writing, where he sees his father in the garden. The speaker then remembers his father digging potatoes twenty years earlier. His father was very good at digging potatoes. This observation brings to mind his grandfather cutting turf and a time that the speaker brought him some milk. The speaker remembers the smells he associates with digging potatoes and turf. The speaker doesn't dig turf or potatoes. He is a writer and uses a pen to dig.

Once you've paraphrased a poem, you can take a step back and look at the bigger picture. What stands out most in this paraphrase? In this case, we can see that the poem's subject is more complex than the simple act of digging. The speaker's connection to his family, and his family's connection to the land, is clear: the bulk of the paragraph is about his observation of his father and grandfather physically digging into the earth in a few different outdoor settings. The contrast between what the speaker is doing and what he is observing is stark — in this paraphrase his present-day actions only come into focus in the first sentence and again in the final two. In both places, the speaker is clearly not performing manual labor; instead, he carries a pen. When he uses his pen to dig, he does not mean in the literal sense. Based on this information, here's one way you might phrase the subject of the poem:

> In "Digging," the speaker's thoughts about his father and grandfather lead him to contemplate different ways of digging.

ACTIVITY

Read Christina Rossetti's "Promises like Pie Crust," keeping in mind that the title reflects an old English proverb: "Promises are like pie-crust, made to be broken." Paraphrase the poem and identify its subject.

Promises like Pie-Crust

CHRISTINA GEORGINA ROSSETTI

Promise me no promises,
So will I not promise you;
Keep we both our liberties,
Never false and never true:
Let us hold the die uncast,
Free to come as free to go;
For I cannot know your past,
And of mine what can you know?

You, so warm, may once have been
Warmer towards another one;
I, so cold, may once have seen
Sunlight, once have felt the sun:
Who shall show us if it was
Thus indeed in time of old?
Fades the image from the glass
And the fortune is not told.

If you promised, you might grieve
For lost liberty again;
If I promised, I believe
I should fret to break the chain:
Let us be the friends we were,
Nothing more but nothing less;
Many thrive on frugal fare
Who would perish of excess.

[1861]

STEP 2: CONSIDERING THE SPEAKER

Once you have identified the subject of a poem, the next step is to think about who the speaker is. A poem's speaker provides its "voice"; when we read a poem, we are viewing the world from the speaker's perspective. It may be tempting to jump to the conclusion that the speaker and poet are the same, but most often the speaker is a persona, or character, created by the poet. And even when the speaker is the poet, it's often the poet in a particular mood, with a particular purpose or attitude, telling a particular story at a particular time. In "Digging," we can guess that the speaker is probably the poet, largely because he seems to be a writer — he's got a pen in his hand. The poem begins with him at his desk looking out the window. By the end of the poem we know the speaker wants to communicate something more than that he is taking a break from writing; interestingly, the focus comes back to the pen he uses to do his work.

Developing a clear idea of who the speaker is helps clarify his or her attitude toward the poem's subject. The connection you make between speaker and subject forms the basis for your interpretation of the poem's meaning — before you begin to explore *how* a writer creates meaning, you must first develop your own idea of what that meaning is.

Let's look at "Digging" again. How does the subject of the poem — family and different ways of digging — connect with the speaker's writerly persona? Below, we discuss some elements that are key to understanding the speaker's attitude.

Diction

Writers of poetry make conscious word choices, depending often on the connotations and denotations of the words they choose. **Denotation** refers to a word's explicit meaning, while **connotation** refers to the associations a word carries. Together, these word choices work in concert to create **diction**. Literary language is richer than everyday language, so reading poetry requires bringing those associations to the surface, while at the same time remaining alert to the concrete meanings of the words in the poem.

A poem's diction provides a direct link to the speaker's attitude, and, in turn, some of the poem's bigger ideas. As you consider diction, try to locate the words with strong connotations and think about how these added layers affect the poem's meaning.

If you're not sure how to find the diction that gives a poem its depth and power, look for word choices that appeal to one or more of your five senses. In "Digging," for instance, Heaney uses words that create rich, immediate visual images for the reader: the "squat pen" (l. 2), the "gravelly ground" (l. 4), his father's "straining rump" (l. 6), the "bright edge" of the shovel (l. 12), and the recurrence of the "squat pen" at the end of the poem (l. 30). Consider how those words develop the character of the speaker and affect how we see his father and grandfather. They are typically associated with hard, sharp, and solid surfaces; they not only point to the difficulty of manual labor, but also highlight the physical strength of the speaker's father and grandfather.

Many of Heaney's other word choices relate to sound: the "clean rasping sound" (l. 3) of the speaker's father digging in the garden mirrors the "nicking and slicing" (l. 22) of his grandfather's shovel as it cuts through turf. The "squelch and slap" (l. 25) made by the soggy peat when his grandfather heaved it over his shoulder is less mechanical, but no less vivid — all of these sounds remind the reader that the digging the speaker's family has traditionally done is physically demanding.

Throughout the poem, Heaney's diction emphasizes the speaker's connections to rural Irish life and conveys what are, for him, the familiar sounds of home. His language choices portray the speaker as a man who admires his father and grandfather and has deep respect for the grueling work they have done. The title, "Digging," a word used several times in the poem, has connotations as well — such as depth or discovery — and invites us to consider how a poet could dig.

Shifts

When we think about the speaker's attitude toward the subject of a poem, it can also be helpful to look at the **shifts**, which indicate some kind of change, often in the speaker's perspective. You might see a shift in verb tense, a shift from past to present, a shift in tone — from exuberant to melancholy, maybe — or even a change in speaker or point of view. Spotting these shifts can help focus your analysis.

You'll notice that "Digging" starts in the present tense, with the speaker looking out the window and seeing his father digging in the flowerbeds. But when his father "comes up twenty years away," the tense changes to the past and stays there for the next three stanzas. The second-to-last stanza of the poem moves back to the present, and the final line is in the future tense. The speaker has, perhaps, used these memories to consider his own vocation and its connection to the work done by his father and grandfather.

You might also have seen another series of shifts, from reality (the speaker looking out his window) to memory (those cool hard potatoes) and imagination (from the flowerbeds to the potato drills) and even to legend ("My grandfather cut more turf in a day / Than any other man on Toner's bog"). The speaker sifts through these memories and myths to see where he fits. This shift might suggest that despite the passing of time and the flexibility of memory, the speaker feels close to his father and grandfather, and can conjure their presence when he needs to.

You may detect yet another shift in the tone of the second-to-last stanza, a sort of unpleasant quality to the grandfather's digging: "the squelch and slap / of soggy peat, the curt cuts of an edge." When the speaker says he has "no spade to follow men like him" could there be a bit of relief? He, unlike the other men in his family, will work indoors, at a desk, looking out a window.

Tone and Mood

The speaker's attitude toward the subject of a poem is expressed by the poem's tone and mood. **Tone** provides the emotional coloring of a work and is a direct reflection of the speaker's attitude; diction is often the primary contributor to a poem's tone, but all of the writer's style choices affect it. **Mood** is the feeling the reader experiences as a result of the tone. If you are unsure of how to read a poem's tone, its mood — the way you feel about it — will help point you in the right direction. For instance, the speaker's description of his memories in "Digging" might call to mind your own childhood or family history, and the nostalgia typically associated with times past. The fact that both you and the speaker are sitting comfortably (you are reading; the speaker is writing) while his family labors outside may sharpen your view of the contrast between the speaker's occupation and that of his forebears.

There are many other ways to identify the tone of a work, and if you have a solid understanding of the poem's subject and the identity of its speaker, it may be clear to you before you begin to look closely at the poet's language choices. But, as we mentioned earlier, examining a poem's diction is an excellent place to start, and "Digging" is no exception. Throughout the poem, the speaker uses words that connote strength and ruggedness to describe his father and grandfather — these choices suggest he admires them, and his admiration implies he may be nostalgic for an earlier time. This same language also communicates the difficulty of the work, and the phrases that appeal to the reader's sense of sound bring home the fact that the men in the speaker's family have traditionally made their living from arduous physical labor. Despite the fact that the speaker describes his pen as a blunt, "squat" instrument — not unlike a shovel — the contrast between the digging his father and grandfather have done and the digging the speaker plans to do with his pen is striking. We can feel the speaker's nostalgia as he thinks wistfully about his father and grandfather. But we also sense some ambivalence: the speaker's deep respect for the tradition of manual labor in his family seems a bit at odds with the idea that writing is a worthwhile pursuit.

As you can see, a poem can be interpreted in several ways — there is no single "right" way to approach deciphering the speaker's attitude toward the subject. Your job is to defend your interpretation of a poem's meaning with evidence from the work itself.

ACTIVITY

Read "My Heart and I" by Elizabeth Barrett Browning. What is the speaker's situation in this poem? How does her repeated reference to "my heart and I," as though her heart were separate from her, reveal her attitude toward her experiences? Consider how the poem's tone and/or shifts contribute to the speaker's perspective.

My Heart and I

ELIZABETH BARRETT BROWNING

Enough! we're tired, my heart and I;
We sit beside the headstone thus,
And wish the name were carved for us;
The moss reprints more tenderly
The hard types of the mason's knife,
As Heaven's sweet life renews earth's life,
With which we're tired, my heart and I.

You see we're tired, my heart and I;
We dealt with books, we trusted men,
And in our own blood drenched the pen,
As if such colors could not fly.
We walked too straight for fortune's end,
We loved too true to keep a friend;
At last we're tired, my heart and I.

How tired we feel, my heart and I;
We seem of no use in the world;
Our fancies hang gray and uncurled
About men's eyes indifferently;
Our voice, which thrilled you so, will let
You sleep; our tears are only wet;
What do we here, my heart and I?

So tired, so tired, my heart and I;
It was not thus in that old time
When Ralph sat with me 'neath the lime
To watch the sun set from the sky:
"Dear Love, you're looking tired," he said;
I, smiling at him, shook my head;
'Tis now we're tired, my heart and I.

So tired, so tired, my heart and I!
Though now none takes me on his arm
To fold me close and kiss me warm,
Till each quick breath ends in a sigh
Of happy languor. Now, alone
We lean upon his graveyard stone,
Uncheered, unkissed, my heart and I.

Tired out we are, my heart and I.
Suppose the world brought diadems
To tempt us, crusted with loose gems
Of powers and pleasures? Let it try.
We scarcely care to look at even
A pretty child, o' God's blue heaven,
We feel so tired, my heart and I.

Yet, who complains? My heart and I?
In this abundant earth no doubt
Is little room for things worn out;
Disdain them, break them, throw them by;
And if before the days grew rough,
We once were loved, then — well enough
I think we've fared, my heart and I.

[1862]

STEP 3: READING FOR DETAIL

Determining the subject of a poem and the speaker's attitude toward it will help you form an original opinion about the meaning of the work. However, a truly effective close analysis incorporates support from the text itself — that is, you must show *how* the poem's meaning is created, using the poet's language, style, and structure choices as evidence.

You may be familiar with many of the terms used to analyze poetry, sometimes called the elements of style. As you strengthen your familiarity with them, keep in mind that close analysis is more than just a treasure hunt for where examples of these elements occur. Remember, all style elements help convey the speaker's attitude, and successful close analysis considers the effect that each style element has on the tone and meaning of the poem. Below, we work with "To an Athlete Dying Young," by A. E. Housman, to examine how several of its style elements help create and reinforce meaning. Examples for all of these concepts, and more, are available in the glossary at the back of the book.

To an Athlete Dying Young

A. E. HOUSMAN

The time you won your town the race
We chaired you through the market-place;
Man and boy stood cheering by,
And home we brought you shoulder-high.

To-day, the road all runners come,
Shoulder-high we bring you home,
And set you at your threshold down,
Townsman of a stiller town.

Smart lad, to slip betimes away
From fields where glory does not stay
And early though the laurel grows
It withers quicker than the rose.

Eyes the shady night has shut
Cannot see the record cut,
And silence sounds no worse than cheers
After earth has stopped the ears:

Now you will not swell the rout
Of lads that wore their honours out,
Runners whom renown outran
And the name died before the man.

So set, before its echoes fade,
The fleet foot on the sill of shade,
And hold to the low lintel up
The still-defended challenge-cup.

And round that early-laurelled head
Will flock to gaze the strengthless dead,
And find unwithered on its curls
The garland briefer than a girl's.

[1896]

Figurative Language

As we discussed in Chapter 3, language that is not literal is called figurative. Often such language is called *metaphorical* because it explains or expands on an idea by making a direct comparison between unlike things. **Similes** make such comparisons by using the words *like*, *as*, or *than* (e.g., *cold as ice*), while **metaphors** directly state that one thing is another (e.g., *an icy glare*). An **extended metaphor**, or conceit, is one that spans several lines of a work. Let's look back at the poem's last two stanzas:

> So set, before its echoes fade,
> The fleet foot on the sill of shade,
> And hold to the low lintel up
> The still-defended challenge cup.
>
> And round that early-laurelled head
> Will flock to gaze the strengthless dead,
> And find unwithered on its curls
> The garland briefer than a girl's.

Here, Housman develops a metaphor in which the speaker compares the burial of the young athlete to walking through a door — the "sill of shade." His trophy will be displayed at the "low lintel" (the beam across the top of a door), a metaphor for the edge of his coffin. In the next stanza his "garland briefer than a girl's" will be admired by the "strengthless dead," the crowd he will meet in the afterlife. This metaphor implies that dying young is a blessing because it keeps youthful achievements alive — the athlete will never know when the cheering stops or that his records have been broken.

Sometimes a poet will **personify** an object or idea, giving it human qualities. A good example of this can be found in the fourth stanza of Housman's poem:

> Eyes the shady night has shut
> Cannot see the record cut,
> And silence sounds no worse than cheers
> After earth has stopped the ears:

Here, "the shady night" — death — "has shut" the eyes of the young athlete. Personifying death in this way gives it a gentler quality, in keeping with the idea of death as a blessing.

Imagery

As we discussed in Chapter 3, **imagery** is language that appeals to any of the five senses. When you read poetry, it's important to think about how impressions of sensory experiences are created. Often, patterns of images are repeated throughout a poem. As you consider poetic imagery, it may be helpful to begin by asking yourself whether the images are concrete, or whether they depend on figurative language to come alive. Two of the strongest images in "To an Athlete Dying Young" are of the young athlete on two different days. In the first stanza he is held shoulder high in a chair and marched before the cheering crowd, having just won a race:

> The time you won your town the race
> We chaired you through the market-place;
> Man and boy stood cheering by,
> And home we brought you shoulder-high.

In the second stanza he is also held shoulder high, but this time in his coffin by pallbearers:

> To-day, the road all runners come,
> Shoulder-high we bring you home,
> And set you at your threshold down,
> Townsman of a stiller town.

Let's think about what the mirroring of these two images suggests. The first image is quite concrete — the speaker remembers the cheers when the young athlete was carried home "shoulder-high" after his success in the race. The second image, of the athlete in a coffin held "shoulder high," is more abstract. He is lowered into a much "stiller town": a grave. That he is carried shoulder-high in both a victory parade and his funeral march suggests that an early death has preserved his glory; he will always be remembered as a young athlete in his prime.

ACTIVITY

Read "XIV" by Nobel laureate Derek Walcott and identify the ways the poem's figurative language and imagery convey the importance of the event the speaker describes.

XIV

DEREK WALCOTT

With the frenzy of an old snake shedding its skin,
the speckled road, scored with ruts, smelling of mold,
twisted on itself and reentered the forest
where the dasheen leaves thicken and folk stories begin.
Sunset would threaten us as we climbed closer
to her house up the asphalt hill road, whose yam vines
wrangled over gutters with the dark reek of moss,
the shutters closing like the eyelids of that mimosa
called Ti-Marie; then — lucent as paper lanterns,
lamplight glowed through the ribs, house after house —
there was her own lamp at the black twist of the path.
There's childhood, and there's childhood's aftermath.
She began to remember at the minute of the fireflies,
to the sound of pipe water banging in kerosene tins,
stories she told to my brother and myself.
Her leaves were the libraries of the Caribbean.
The luck that was ours, those fragrant origins!
Her head was magnificent, Sidone. In the gully of her voice
shadows stood up and walked, her voice travels my shelves.
She was the lamplight in the stare of two mesmerized boys
still joined in one shadow, indivisible twins.

[1984]

Structure

Poetic Syntax

Syntax — the arrangement of words into phrases, clauses, and sentences — is another style element that applies to both prose and poetry. For example, Housman uses **inversion** in several places, perhaps to maintain the rhyme scheme but also to emphasize a point. When he writes, "And home we brought you shoulder-high" (l. 4), the shift in expected word order ("We brought you home") emphasizes "home," which is further reinforced through repetition two lines later: "Shoulder-high we bring you home." The first home is the triumphant return of the living athlete; the second is the home he will inhabit in the cemetery.

When you analyze poetry, you will want to be on the lookout for **enjambment** (also called a run-on line, when one line ends without a pause and must continue into the next line to complete its meaning) and **caesura** (a pause within a line of poetry, sometimes punctuated, sometimes not). You can see an example of enjambment in lines 17–18 of "To an Athlete Dying Young":

> Now you will not swell the route
> Of lads that wore their honours out,

There is also an instance of caesura in line 9:

> Smart lad, to slip betimes away

You can see how the continuation of the sentence in the first example echoes the procession winding through the town. The caesura in the second example reflects the unexpected death of the athlete.

You will also want to pay attention to syntactic patterns such as line length: are the poem's lines long, short, or a combination of the two? The lines in Housman's poem are generally short, which could be seen as a comment on the short life of the athlete.

Meter

The lines in structured poems often follow a regular pattern of **rhythm** called a **meter**. Literally, meter counts the measure of a line, referring to the pattern of stressed or unstressed syllables, combinations of which we call **feet**. **Iambic** meter is by far the most common in English. An iamb is a poetic foot of two syllables with the stress, or accent, on the second, as in the word "again," or the phrase "by far." The two most common metric patterns are **iambic pentameter**, in which a line consists of five iambic feet, and **iambic tetrameter**, which measures four iambic feet. "To an Athlete Dying Young," is in iambic tetrameter. Each of its lines follows a rhythm of four beats, each one an iambic foot with the emphasis on the second syllable:

> Thĕ tíme | yŏu wón | yŏur tówn | thĕ ráce
> Wĕ cháired | yŏu thróugh | thĕ már | kĕt-pláce.

You can probably see and even feel how the meter, with its steadily flowing pace, mimics a procession or march. It would sound odd and halting if you were to emphasize the first syllable instead:

> Thé tĭme | yóu wŏn | yóur tŏwn | thé rănce

Form

Poetry is sometimes written in conventional forms that can give you hints about how the structure relates to the meaning of the poem. When you recognize a traditional form, consider whether it maintains the conventions or defies them. One way to approach this is to ask yourself whether the poem's content strikes you as traditional or unusual. Looking at the connection between form and content through this lens will help inform your analysis.

When you look at the structure of a poem that is not in a traditional form, try to figure out how it is organized. Is it a narrative, in which the action dictates the structure? Are the stanzas chronological, cause and effect, or question and answer? What is the relationship between them? Look for word or sentence patterns or patterns of imagery that might reveal the relationships among the stanzas. Ultimately, what you should be on the lookout for is how the structure reinforces the meaning of the poem. "To An Athlete Dying Young," for instance, is quite traditional: it has four-line stanzas that rhyme; its narrative is chronological; and it develops a particular idea metaphorically. The poem addresses the age-old question of how to make meaning from the death of a young person, and this traditional form suits Housman's purpose.

Although poems have many specialized forms, the most common is the **sonnet**. Traditionally written as love poems, the sonnet form has been used for a wide variety of purposes, including war poems, protest poems, and parodies. Sonnets generally consist of fourteen lines, usually in iambic pentameter, as you may observe in the opening lines of Shakespeare's Sonnet 29 in Chapter 1 (p. 7):

> Whĕn, iń | dĭs- graće | wĭth fόr- | tŭne anď | mĕn's eýes
> Ĭ all | ă- lońe | bĕ - weép | mў out- | căst staťe.

There are two classic types of sonnet. The **Italian**, or **Petrarchan**, **sonnet** is divided into an octave (eight lines) rhyming *abba, abba* and a sestet (six lines) with a variety of different rhyme schemes: *cdcdcd*, *cdecde*, or *cddcdd*. Traditionally, the octave raises an issue or expresses a doubt, and the sestet resolves the issue or doubt. The shift from the first to the second section is called the "turn." The **English**, or **Shakespearean**, **sonnet** consists of three four-line stanzas and a couplet at the end. This type of sonnet rhymes *abab*, *cdcd*, *efef*, *gg*. The third stanza usually provides the turn, and the last two lines often close the sonnet with a witty remark.

Other common traditional forms include:

- **Elegy.** A contemplative poem, usually for someone who has died.
- **Lyric.** A short poem expressing the personal thoughts or feelings of a first-person speaker.
- **Ode.** A form of poetry used to meditate on or address a single object or condition. It originally followed strict rules of rhythm and rhyme, but by the Romantic period it was more flexible.
- **Villanelle.** A form of poetry in which five **tercets**, or three-line stanzas (rhyme scheme *aba*), are followed by a quatrain (rhyme scheme *abaa*). At the end of tercets two and four, the first line of tercet one is repeated. At the end of tercets three and five, the last line of tercet one is repeated. These two repeated lines, called *refrain lines*, are repeated again to conclude the quatrain. Much of the power of this form lies in its repeated lines and their subtly shifting sense or meaning over the course of the poem.

ACTIVITY

Read the poem "Sonnet" by Alice Moore Dunbar-Nelson and consider the relationship between form and meaning. Describe the ways the poem's content does and does not conform to the traditions of the sonnet form. Next, explain how the poem's form reflects the speaker's attitude toward springtime.

Sonnet

ALICE MOORE DUNBAR-NELSON

I had no thought of violets of late,
The wild, shy kind that spring beneath your feet
In wistful April days, when lovers mate

And wander through the fields in raptures sweet.
The thought of violets meant florists' shops,
And bows and pins, and perfumed papers fine;
And garish lights, and mincing little fops
And cabarets and songs, and deadening wine.
So far from sweet real things my thoughts had strayed,
I had forgot wide fields, and clear brown streams;
The perfect loveliness that God has made,—
Wild violets shy and Heaven-mounting dreams.
And now—unwittingly, you've made me dream
Of violets, and my soul's forgotten gleam.

[1922]

Sound

Sound is the musical quality of poetry. It can be created through some of the other techniques we discuss, such as rhyme, enjambment, and caesura. It can also be created by word choice, especially through **alliteration** (the repetition of initial consonant sounds in a sequence of words or syllables), **assonance** (the repetition of vowel sounds in a sequence of words or syllables), **consonance** (identical consonant sounds in nearby words that follow different vowel sounds), and **onomatopoeia** (use of a word that refers to a sound and whose pronunciation mimics that sound). Sound can also be created by rhythm and **cadence** (similar to rhythm, but related to the rise and fall of the voice). Like all of the elements of style, the key to analysis is to connect the sound of the poem to its meaning. Take a look at the alliteration in stanzas 4 and 5 of "To an Athlete Dying Young":

> Eyes the shady night has shut
> Cannot see the record cut,
> And silence sounds no worse than cheers
> After earth has stopped the ears:
>
> Now you will not swell the rout
> Of lads that wore their honours out,
> Runners whom renown outran
> And the name died before the man.

Within these stanzas, consider these two lines in particular: "And silence sounds no worse than cheers" (l. 15) and "Runners whom renown outran" (l. 19). The repetition of the *s* and *r* sounds quiet the poem, evoking the sound of somber, lowered voices at a funeral. You'll also see how the rhythm, created by the poem's meter, marches the poem forward, much like a funeral procession.

Rhyme

As you know, some poems **rhyme** and some — those written in **free verse** — do not. Rhyme at the end of a line is called **end rhyme**, while rhyme within a line of poetry is called **internal rhyme**. There is an example of both in the first two lines of "To an Athlete Dying Young":

> The time you won your town the race
> We chaired you through the market-place;

The last two words of each line, "race" and "market-place," are end rhymes, while "you" and "through" in the second line is an instance of internal rhyme.

Sometimes a rhyme is visual; you can see it though the sounds of the two words don't rhyme. When an author uses poetic license to rhyme words that do not sound quite the same, it is called **near rhyme**, also known as **slant rhyme**. Lines 5 and 6 of Housman's poem contains a good example:

> To-day, the road all runners come,
> Shoulder-high we bring you home,

Rhyme is usually notated using letters of the alphabet; you use one letter for each sound that rhymes. For instance, a simple **quatrain** or four-line stanza might rhyme *abab*, meaning that every other line rhymes. Or it might be arranged as **couplets** that rhyme *aabb*; the first two lines rhyme with each other and the second two lines rhyme with each other. The pattern of rhyme for an entire poem is called its rhyme scheme. It can be useful to consider the effects of rhyme in a poem by charting its rhyme scheme; reading a rhyming poem out loud is also helpful. Notice how the consistent *aabb* rhyme scheme in "To an Athlete Dying Young" contributes to the rhythm of the procession — the young athlete's funeral march.

ACTIVITY

Read "The Century Quilt" by Marilyn Nelson. Describe how the poem's sound and musicality help convey the importance of the quilt to the speaker.

The Century Quilt

MARILYN NELSON

My sister and I were in love
with Meema's Indian blanket.
We fell asleep under army green
issued to Daddy by Supply.
When Meema came to live with us
she brought her medicines, her cane,
and the blanket I found on my sister's bed
the last time I visited her.
I remembered how I'd planned to inherit
that blanket, how we used to wrap ourselves
at play in its folds and be chieftains
and princesses.

Now I've found a quilt
I'd like to die under;
Six Van Dyke brown squares,
two white ones, and one square
the yellowbrown of Mama's cheeks.
Each square holds a sweet gum leaf

whose fingers I imagine
would caress me into the silence.

I think I'd have good dreams
for a hundred years under this quilt,
as Meema must have, under her blanket,
dreamed she was a girl again in Kentucky
among her yellow sisters,
their grandfather's white family
nodding at them when they met.
When their father came home from his store
they cranked up the pianola
and all of the beautiful sisters
giggled and danced.
She must have dreamed about Mama
when the dancing was over:
a lanky girl trailing after her father
through his Oklahoma field.

Perhaps under this quilt
I'd dream of myself,
of my childhood of miracles,
of my father's burnt umber pride,
my mother's ochre gentleness.
Within the dream of myself
perhaps I'd meet my son
or my other child, as yet unconceived.
I'd call it The Century Quilt,
after its pattern of leaves.

[1985]

CONNECTING POETIC ELEMENTS OF STYLE

Now that we've considered some of the specific techniques poets use to convey meaning, let's look at a poem by Robert Herrick, "Delight in Disorder," in which he describes the appeal of dressing in a way that is careless — or seemingly so.

Delight in Disorder

ROBERT HERRICK

A sweet disorder in the dress
Kindles in clothes a wantonness.
A lawn[1] about the shoulders thrown
Into a fine distraction;
An erring lace, which here and there
Enthralls the crimson stomacher,[2]
A cuff neglectful, and thereby
Ribbons to flow confusedly;
A winning wave, deserving note,
In the tempestuous petticoat;

[1]Linen scarf. — EDS.
[2]A piece of stiff, embroidered cloth worn over the stomach. — EDS.

A careless shoestring, in whose tie
I see a wild civility;
Do more bewitch me than when art
Is too precise in every part.

[1648]

This is a great poem for practicing close reading. Written over 350 years ago, it may seem difficult at first. Some of the vocabulary, such as *lawn* and *stomacher*, is unfamiliar to readers today. Other words, such as *petticoat*, may be **archaic**, but you have probably come across them before. As always, if you don't know what something means, you should look it up. Let's look at how you might briefly annotate the poem as you read:

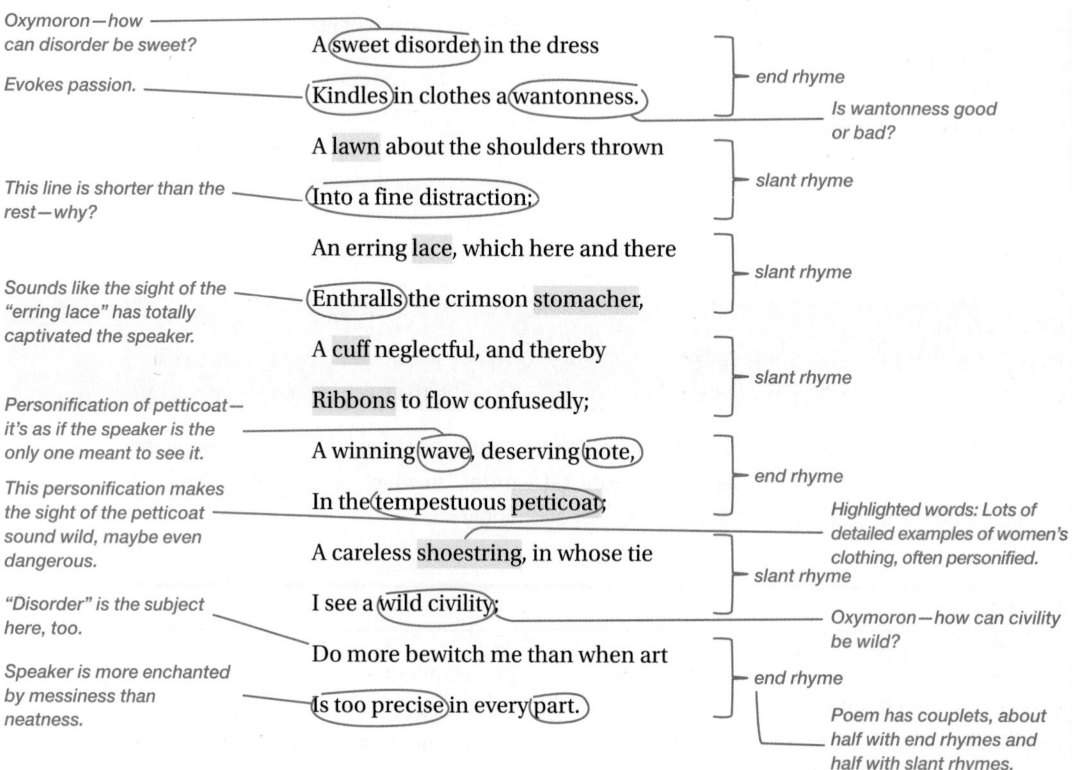

Oxymoron—how can disorder be sweet?
A sweet disorder in the dress
Evokes passion.
Kindles in clothes a wantonness.
end rhyme
Is wantonness good or bad?
A lawn about the shoulders thrown
This line is shorter than the rest—why?
Into a fine distraction;
slant rhyme
An erring lace, which here and there
slant rhyme
Sounds like the sight of the "erring lace" has totally captivated the speaker.
Enthralls the crimson stomacher,
A cuff neglectful, and thereby
slant rhyme
Ribbons to flow confusedly;
Personification of petticoat—it's as if the speaker is the only one meant to see it.
A winning wave, deserving note,
end rhyme
This personification makes the sight of the petticoat sound wild, maybe even dangerous.
In the tempestuous petticoat;
Highlighted words: Lots of detailed examples of women's clothing, often personified.
A careless shoestring, in whose tie
slant rhyme
"Disorder" is the subject here, too.
I see a wild civility;
Oxymoron—how can civility be wild?
Do more bewitch me than when art
end rhyme
Speaker is more enchanted by messiness than neatness.
Is too precise in every part.
Poem has couplets, about half with end rhymes and half with slant rhymes.

If we take this poem a line at a time, we see that the speaker uses the first two lines (which form a full sentence) to make a kind of argument. He says that "sweet disorder" in the way someone dresses "kindles . . . a wantonness." The verb "kindles" means to light up, awaken, or arouse, and "wantonness" can mean flirting or even lewdness. By the next line, it's clear that the speaker is talking about women's clothing in particular: "A lawn about the shoulders thrown." He continues to describe in detail a woman's clothing — style, color, and fabric. Every example he gives is different: lawn, lace, crimson stomacher, cuff, ribbons, petticoat, and shoestring. Together, they could almost form an outfit — the only thing missing is the actual dress. The last two lines break from description, however, as the speaker notes the effect such clothing has on him.

It may take a couple of readings to realize that the speaker is giving his views on messiness in women's clothing and that he finds it attractive. He seems at first a bit ambivalent — is the "wantonness" good or bad? Wanton dress calls to mind wanton behavior, which has mostly negative connotations, but the speaker is obviously inspired by it. He waits until very close to the end of the poem to give his final verdict: dress that appears careless is bewitching. When you take a closer look at the work, you will see how this attitude is created and reinforced by Herrick's style choices.

On your second or third reading, you might have noticed the personification. The speaker notes the "fine distraction" of the scarf thrown over the woman's shoulders, a "cuff" that is "neglectful," ribbons that "flow confusedly," and a "tempestuous petticoat." Similarly, the "erring lace," a mere decoration, takes surprisingly deliberate action when it "[e]nthralls the crimson stomacher." This personification suggests that the clothes reflect qualities of the person wearing them.

Two **oxymorons** (paradoxes made up of two seemingly contradictory words) support the possibility that something is going on other than just a literal description of clothing. The opening line refers to a "sweet disorder," but most would consider disorder unsettling, hardly "sweet"; later, the speaker sees a "wild civility," another seeming contradiction, because how can "civility" — or courteous behavior — be "wild"? The clothing he describes hints at finery; the woman wearing it is most likely wealthy and dresses with a certain amount of decorum. However, the way she wears her clothing is wild: the lawn is "thrown" over her shoulders, and the lace on her stomacher is "erring" — it "enthralls," or holds, the stomacher only "here and there," implying it is not securely fastened to the dress. The petticoat is another typical detail of women's clothing at the time — the bigger the skirt, the better the woman's social standing. However, petticoats are worn beneath a dress and not meant to be seen in public. Using them to give the speaker a "wave" he finds "winning," or charming, is definitely a flirtatious gesture.

Note the words suggesting passion: *kindles, wantonness, crimson, tempestuous,* and *bewitch*. Is this poem actually about seduction? If so, its indirect manner is not overtly sexual or vulgar but flirtatious, sly, even mischievous. Alliteration adds a teasing singsong quality: "Delight . . . Disorder," "winning wave," and "precise . . . part." Further, the symmetry of the alliteration brings a bit of order into the description of disorder — but only a bit.

We might look to the structure of the poem for further evidence of the playful tone. The structure seems regular and predictable. The fourteen lines are presented in seven rhymed pairs, or couplets, most having eight syllables. The opening and closing couplets have exactly rhyming final syllables ("dress" / "wantonness" and "art" / "part"). Notice the neatly repeating **parallel structure** of lines 3, 5, 7, 9, and 11. However, there are inconsistencies within the poem. Some of the rhymes are only near rhymes (e.g., lines 11 and 12: "tie" does not rhyme with "civility"). The poem's lines are in iambic tetrameter, but the rhythm is not always even. The evenness of the opening line, for instance ("A sweet disorder in the dress") is violated by line 10 ("In the tempestuous petticoat"). It seems Herrick's contention that "disorder" can be "sweet" is reflected in the structure of the poem.

Or, put in more thematic terms, Herrick might be reminding us that appearances can be deceiving, that perfection may not be as appealing as charming imperfections. Or, since the cultural values of his time dictated strict outward propriety, he might be telling his readers that passion lurks just beneath the veneer of polite society.

ACTIVITY

Read and annotate "Bright Star" by John Keats. Then identify the subject of the poem, establish the speaker's attitude toward the subject, and analyze how the poem's style elements convey that attitude. Be sure to support your analysis with examples from the poem.

Bright Star, would I were stedfast as thou art—

JOHN KEATS

Bright Star, would I were stedfast as thou art—
Not in lone splendor hung aloft the night,
And watching, with eternal lids apart,
Like nature's patient, sleepless Eremite,[1]
The moving waters at their priestlike task
Of pure ablution round earth's human shores,
Or gazing on the new soft-fallen masque
Of snow upon the mountains and the moors—
No—yet still stedfast, still unchangeable
Pillow'd upon my fair love's ripening breast,
To feel for ever its soft swell and fall,
Awake for ever in a sweet unrest,
Still, still to hear her tender-taken breath,
And so live ever—or else swoon to death—

[1820]

[1]Hermit, particularly one under a religious vow.—Eds.

FROM ANALYSIS TO ESSAY: WRITING A CLOSE ANALYSIS ESSAY

Earlier in this chapter, we outlined steps to help you read a poem. We suggested identifying its subject, determining the speaker's attitude toward that subject, and then looking at how the language of the poem conveys that attitude to create meaning. This kind of close reading is good preparation for writing about poetry. In this part of the chapter, we will show you how to use the observations you've made in your close reading to put together a clear, effective analysis essay.

The purpose of a close analysis essay is to examine how a poem's style helps convey its meaning. Often, the key to achieving this lies in analyzing the speaker's attitude toward an idea or theme expressed by the poem—typically, the poem's subject—or examining the relationship between two ideas within a poem. Regardless of the specific task you are asked to perform, a successful close analysis essay always connects a poem's style elements to its meaning.

Let's take a look at "Woodchucks" by Maxine Kumin. Begin by following the steps we outlined earlier in the chapter: read the poem literally to identify the subject, establish the speaker's attitude toward that subject, and read it again to consider how the style elements convey the speaker's attitude.

Woodchucks

MAXINE KUMIN

Gassing the woodchucks didn't turn out right.
The knockout bomb from the Feed and Grain Exchange
was featured as merciful, quick at the bone
and the case we had against them was airtight,
both exits shoehorned shut with puddingstone,
but they had a sub-sub-basement out of range.

Next morning they turned up again, no worse
for the cyanide than we for our cigarettes
and state-store Scotch, all of us up to scratch.
They brought down the marigolds as a matter of course
and then took over the vegetable patch
nipping the broccoli shoots, beheading the carrots.

The food from our mouths, I said, righteously thrilling
to the feel of the .22, the bullets' neat noses.
I, a lapsed pacifist fallen from grace
puffed with Darwinian pieties for killing,
now drew a bead on the littlest woodchuck's face.
He died down in the everbearing roses.

Ten minutes later I dropped the mother. She
flipflopped in the air and fell, her needle teeth
still hooked in a leaf of early Swiss chard.
Another baby next. O one-two-three
the murderer inside me rose up hard,
the hawkeye killer came on stage forthwith.

There's one chuck left. Old wily fellow, he keeps
me cocked and ready day after day after day.
All night I hunt his humped-up form. I dream
I sight along the barrel in my sleep.
If only they'd all consented to die unseen
gassed underground the quiet Nazi way.

[1972]

Preparing to Write

Let's start by summarizing the work in one sentence, just to be sure you know what's going on.

> In "Woodchucks" the speaker is stymied and disturbed by the difficulty of exterminating the woodchucks that are taking over her garden.

Even this quick paraphrase engages in a certain level of interpretation — not only does it state that the poem is about killing woodchucks, but it also draws the inference that the speaker has some ambivalence about her situation.

Now that we've clarified the subject of the poem, our next consideration should be deepening our understanding of the speaker. Who is she, and what is her attitude toward killing the woodchucks in her garden? She has already tried one method of getting rid of the woodchucks, and now she's making the case for escalating her efforts. You'll probably notice a sense of us against them as she justifies her actions. The speaker describes the crimes committed by the woodchucks, how they "took over the vegetable patch / nipping the broccoli shoots, beheading the carrots." She describes herself as "righteously thrilling" when she picks up her gun; you may find her quite self-righteous. It's clear that her attitude toward the woodchucks is anger and frustration, but you might also get a sense of mixed feelings about her actions against them.

You have probably noticed some things about the poem as a whole, such as its short lines, strong verbs, and vivid images. Keep those things in mind as you take a look at the following graphic organizer, where we examine the way specific elements of style and structure add layers of meaning to Kumin's poem and support one interpretation of the work.

Creating a graphic organizer is one way to approach deciding which style elements to focus on in your analysis. This pre-writing strategy will help you break the poem down into specific areas for commentary — line or stanza divisions provide natural breaking points. The graphic organizer on pages 129–32 first paraphrases what the poem is saying, then identifies a style element by name or description, and finally considers its effect: how does it help establish the speaker's attitude? How does it help convey meaning? Setting up your close reading in such a structured way guides you through an analysis that does not stop with simple restatement or even identification of elements of style but links them to effect and meaning.

There is no denying that completing a detailed graphic organizer like this one takes time. But understanding a text with layers of meaning requires time and attention to detail, especially if you are preparing to write about it. Plus, once you have examined the work so closely, you'll have already found ideas and evidence to use in your essay.

Lines	Paraphrase	Element of Style	Effect or Function
"Gassing the woodchucks didn't turn out right."	Killing the woodchucks didn't work.	Informal, conversational diction—concrete and straightforward.	Introduces the poem's subject, draws the reader into the speaker's world immediately.
"The knockout bomb from the Feed and Grain Exchange / was featured as merciful, quick at the bone / and the case against them was airtight, / both exits shoehorned shut with puddingstone, / but they had a sub-sub-basement out of range."	The gas was supposed to give the woodchucks a quick and painless death, but never reached them.	Play on words: the "case" against the woodchucks is "airtight," much as the woodchucks' underground home is made airtight to poison them.	Dark humor downplays the fact that the speaker is killing living creatures.
		"The "case" and the "sub-sub-basement" ascribe human behavior to the woodchucks.	Humanizing the woodchucks could hint at ambivalence, or it could suggest that the speaker believes it's fair to wage war against them because they aren't simply defenseless animals.
"Next morning they turned up again, no worse / for the cyanide than we for our cigarettes / and state-store Scotch, all of us up to scratch."	The next morning, the woodchucks were in the garden again.	More informal diction—also clarifies point of view: "we," rather than just first-person "I."	Use of "we" makes reader complicit in everything the speaker does.
		Comparison: "cyanide" to "state-store Scotch"—neither has an apparent effect on woodchucks or speaker.	Comparison of poison to alcohol again downplays the fact that the speaker was trying to kill the woodchucks.
		The only instance in which "us" describes both humans and woodchucks.	Grouping the woodchucks and humans together suggests that woodchucks are as hardy as humans.

(continued)

Lines	Paraphrase	Element of Style	Effect or Function
"They brought down the marigolds as a matter of course / and then took over the vegetable patch / nipping the broccoli shoots, beheading the carrots."	The woodchucks destroyed the flowers and the vegetable patch.	Use of "they" and repeated dependent clauses with strong and/or violent verbs: "brought down," "took over," "nipping," and "beheading."	Portrays woodchucks as an enemy army, evoking speaker's feelings of anger and indignation.
"The food from our mouths, I said, righteously thrilling / to the feel of the .22, the bullets' neat noses."	The speaker picked up a gun to shoot the woodchucks.	Concrete imagery: "the .22" and "the bullets' neat noses." The speaker is "thrilling."	Heightens visceral thrill of contemplating violent action.
		Sentence fragment: "The food from our mouths."	The speaker justifies killing by suggesting the woodchucks are taking the food from the mouths of her own family.
"I, a lapsed pacifist fallen from grace / puffed with Darwinian pieties for killing, / now drew a bead on the littlest woodchuck's face."	The speaker used to be a pacifist. But she had reasons for killing the woodchucks. She aimed at the smallest woodchuck.	The speaker uses abstract diction to describe herself as a "lapsed pacifist fallen from grace" whose new "Darwinian pieties" compel her to pick up a gun.	Abstractions could mean the speaker is viewing her actions from a critical distance and is self-aware—or they could simply cloak the speaker's delight in violence with rhetoric that justifies killing the woodchucks.
		Diction: "puffed"	The verb "puffed" hints at speaker's sense of self-righteousness.
		Violent imagery: the speaker "drew a bead," aiming her gun at a woodchuck.	The speaker is not sugarcoating her actions; the woodchucks are the enemy, and she is at war with them.

Lines	Paraphrase	Element of Style	Effect or Function
"He died down in the everbearing roses."	The smallest woodchuck died.	Short, declarative sentence. Diction: "everbearing"	The brevity of the sentence echoes the finality of death; perhaps the speaker enjoys the irony, as everbearing roses bloom all season long.
"Ten minutes later I dropped the mother. She / flipflopped in the air and fell, her needle teeth / still hooked in a leaf of early Swiss chard."	The speaker shot an adult woodchuck next. The bullet knocked the woodchuck off the ground. The woodchuck still had food in its teeth.	Concrete, brutal imagery used to describe woodchuck: "flipflopped," "needle teeth," "hooked." Informal diction: "dropped"	The woodchucks are portrayed as increasingly aggressive and tenacious opponents. This informal word choice implies that the killing is casual and comes easily to the speaker. It also draws the reader into the scene.
"Another baby next. O one-two-three / the murderer inside me rose up hard, / the hawkeye killer came on stage forthwith."	The speaker shot another small woodchuck next. The speaker began to feel like a murderer.	Theatrical diction describes the speaker's actions: "murderer in me" and "hawkeye killer" who "came on stage."	Speaker distances herself from the killings. It wasn't her essential self; it was something "in her," performing the deed "on stage." This suggests her ambivalence about her behavior.
"There's one chuck left. Old wily fellow, he keeps / me cocked and ready day after day after day."	Only one old woodchuck is still alive. The speaker looks for it every day.	Repetition of "day"; the speaker is "cocked and ready."	There is a sense of the need for eternal vigilance, on guard for the enemy.

(*continued*)

Lines	Paraphrase	Element of Style	Effect or Function
"All night I hunt his humped-up form. I dream / I sight along the barrel in my sleep."	The speaker dreams of shooting the oldest woodchuck.	Violent diction used to describe the speaker's dreams about the last woodchuck standing: "hunt" and "sight along the barrel."	The "dream" could point to the speaker's obsession with killing the woodchucks, or it could indicate her actions have begun to haunt her.
"If only they'd all consented to die unseen / gassed underground the quiet Nazi way."	The speaker wishes the gas had worked, and that the woodchucks had died somewhere out of sight.	Draws a parallel between killing rodents and Nazi war crimes of gassing people.	Emphasizes speaker's uneasiness with having to kill the woodchucks in an active fashion, leaving her obsessed with doing it and feeling repulsed by her actions.

Creating a graphic organizer is good preparation for writing, but it's important to remember that you won't be able to use every single idea in a clear and cohesive close analysis essay. The graphic organizer above identifies more style elements than you could likely use in a single essay — particularly if there are limits on time and length. As you begin to plan your essay, you must decide which style elements best support your thesis.

Developing a Thesis Statement

When it comes time to write a close analysis essay, the first thing to do is formulate a **thesis statement**. Your thesis statement will reflect your interpretation of the meaning of the work and should incorporate the style elements you plan to use to support it. You may end up changing your thesis statement as you go, but having an idea of your argument will help you stay focused. Your teacher will likely have provided you with a prompt or an assignment, and if you've done a thorough job of reading and taking notes in the form of annotation or a graphic organizer, you will probably have more ideas than you can actually use in the essay. For example, your reading may have revealed the vivid imagery and sense of irony in the poem. You may have also noticed allusions to history, and underlying themes — like guilt and violence — that highlight the speaker's ambivalence and self-doubt. Another prominent feature of the poem is its syntax: the long conversational sentences interspersed with short simple ones. Does this pattern suggest self-justification? There are several ways to approach this poem and many possible interpretations.

Let's say your teacher has assigned you the following prompt:

> Write an essay in which you analyze how the style and structure of Maxine Kumin's "Woodchucks" convey the speaker's attitude toward killing the woodchucks in her garden.

Remember, your thesis must be an interpretation of the meaning of the poem that you will support with evidence from the text. You should avoid creating a thesis statement that is so broad that it just restates the prompt:

> Maxine Kumin uses style and structure to convey the speaker's attitude toward killing the woodchucks in her poem "Woodchucks."

Not only does this thesis fail to mention the specific elements the writer plans to discuss, it also fails to interpret the speaker's attitude toward killing the woodchucks. The thesis needs to focus on specific characteristics of the poem's style and structure, so that in the body of the essay you can analyze how they help convey your interpretation of the speaker's attitude.

On the other hand, it is important not to narrow your thesis so much that there is nothing to say about it:

> In "Woodchucks" the speaker's diction is violent and defensive.

Although this thesis isolates a style element — diction — it does not interpret the speaker's attitude toward killing the woodchucks, nor does it recognize the complexity of the poem. You could not discuss a thesis like this for long before running out of things to say. A good thesis should be expressed clearly and should inform the reader of the essay's purpose. It is the backbone of your essay, and everything will connect to it.

Working with the prompt above, let's consider how Kumin develops the speaker's persona and how that voice conveys the speaker's attitude toward killing the woodchucks in her garden. Looking back at what we've noted about "Woodchucks" in the graphic organizer, we get a sense of mounting aggression as the speaker demonizes the woodchucks. But first she expresses her disappointment that the "knockout bomb from the Feed and Grain Exchange" was ineffective. You'll have noted that the end of the poem comes back to the gas, with the speaker lamenting that the woodchucks didn't "die unseen / gassed underground the quiet Nazi way." That may make us rethink what we first saw as a progression in the speaker's aggression. What does this regret suggest about the speaker's feelings toward her own actions? Is killing with gas really any different from killing with a gun?

We might also look at Kumin's diction choices. Her word choices are conversational; we get the sense that the speaker is a weekend gardener, annoyed that the woodchucks are getting in the way of her hobby. After all, she and her friends are smokers and drinkers, not subsistence farmers. The language of killing is hard and unambiguous: she "dropped" and "drew a bead" on each woodchuck with the rifle; her "murderer inside . . . rose up hard." But she also considers the woodchucks fair game: they are taking the "food from our mouths," "nipping the broccoli," and "beheading the carrots." These language choices suggest that aggression is close to the surface and can rise quickly when people feel their interests are threatened.

The rhyme scheme is interesting too: *abc*, *acb*, which sounds like just enough of a sing-song to soothe a troubled soul. There's a funny sort of delay in the second set of three lines when the *b* rhyme becomes the *c* rhyme. That hesitation may reflect the speaker's self-doubt:

Gassing the woodchucks didn't turn out right. *a*
The knockout bomb from the Feed and Grain Exchange *b*
was featured as merciful, quick at the bone *c*
and the case we had against them was airtight, *a*
both exits shoehorned shut with puddingstone, *c*
but they had a sub-sub-basement out of range. *b*

Remembering that it is always important to address a work's complexity, we might develop the following thesis statement in response to the original prompt:

> Write an essay in which you analyze how the style and structure of Maxine Kumin's "Woodchucks" convey the speaker's attitude toward killing the woodchucks in her garden.

> In "Woodchucks" the diction, imagery, and rhyme scheme help convey the speaker's ambivalent attitude toward her own violent behavior, showing that killing sight unseen is not, perhaps, so different from picking up a gun and pulling the trigger.

Organizing a Close Analysis Essay

Once you have an idea for a thesis statement — and, remember, this "working thesis" can change at any time — look back at the text and your notes, keeping in mind the ideas that inspired your thesis as you prepare to support it. Your essay might be organized around the style elements, with a paragraph each on diction, imagery, and rhyme scheme, for example. Or you could approach it a different way: you might group your ideas according to the ways Kumin shows the changes in the speaker's attitude toward her actions, with one paragraph on her justifications, one on her ambivalence and self-doubt, and another on what's implied by her actions.

You've probably noticed that the thesis statement we've suggested is likely to lead to a five-paragraph essay. Perhaps you've been warned to stay away from this organization because it is formulaic or prescriptive. We agree: stay away from the formulaic or prescriptive. However, the five-paragraph essay may or may not fall into that category. There's no rule that says that every question or topic will fit neatly into an introduction, three body (or developmental) paragraphs, and a conclusion. Yet if you happen to have three points to make, you'll end up with five paragraphs that could form a cogent and insightful essay.

Integrating Quotations

Close analysis, as you know, requires references to the text, and you should think of the language of a poem as evidence to support your thesis. When you quote directly from a poem in your analysis, use a forward slash mark to indicate a line break. The key is to choose quotations carefully and integrate them as seamlessly as possible into your own writing, avoiding big chunks of text. Just remember that your voice should prevail in a close analysis essay — that is, you must offer thoughtful commentary on what you quote. One way you might check to make sure that you're providing sufficient analysis of a work is to highlight all your quotations from the text. Here's an example of a paragraph that quotes from "Woodchucks."

> The violent word choices in "Woodchucks" help create a battle scene in the poem, illustrating the change the speaker undergoes as the war between human and nature escalates. The woodchucks are "no worse for the cyanide," still "nipping the broccoli shoots, beheading the carrots." The speaker references World War II, including "the quiet Nazi way" and "gassing." She also takes up arms, "thrilling / to the feel of the .22," "[draws] a bead" on a baby woodchuck, then triumphs again as she "drop[s] the mother," whose body "flipflop[s] in the air." She feels the "murderer inside" and like a "hawkeye killer." She stays "cocked and ready day after day after day" as she "hunts [the old woodchuck's] humped up form."

Apart from the topic sentence, the paragraph consists primarily of a string of quotations. There is no commentary on the text, and as a result very little to guide the reader to an understanding of the essay writer's interpretation. Instead, this paragraph reads more like a list that catalogs instances of violent language throughout the poem.

Compare that paragraph to the one below. While the structure and some of the quotations remain essentially the same, original commentary moves the paragraph beyond a string of quotes to a discussion of the effect of Kumin's language choices.

> The violent word choices in "Woodchucks" help create a battle scene in the poem, illustrating the change the speaker undergoes as the war between human and nature escalates. The woodchucks, on a rampage, are "nipping the broccoli shoots" and "beheading the carrots." Their actions against the speaker's garden, as well as the speaker's response, are acts of war, and casualties follow. The speaker's references to World War II bring the battle to a new level, as words like "gassing" and "Nazi" remind us that

wartime atrocities take place both seen and unseen. The speaker sees herself as a soldier who must accomplish her mission, though she is aware that her actions are over the top. There is, however, no denying a certain sense of glee as the speaker prepares to fight. She finds the .22 "thrilling" and is proud of being able to "[draw] a bead" as she "dropped the mother." She believes she is an even match for the woodchucks and assumes that the playing field is level because they attacked her first. While she is honest enough with herself to see that there is a "murderer inside her," she's not quite self-aware enough to know that the war against the old woodchuck, which keeps her "cocked and ready day after day after day," has dehumanized her. Both through her actions and the language used to describe them, the speaker's uneasy relationship with nature is made clear.

Documenting Sources

In a close analysis essay, you are likely only writing about one text, so you won't need a formal Works Cited page. Your teacher may ask you to use line numbers to identify where your quotations can be found, but with a short poem or passage of fiction it may be unnecessary. If you do add line numbers, they should go in parentheses after the quotation mark and before your punctuation, like this:

The youngest woodchuck dies in the "everbearing roses" (l. 18).

The speaker seems to feel no remorse as she sees "the littlest woodchuck's face. / He died down in the everbearing roses" (ll.19-20).

A Sample Close Analysis Essay

Read the sample essay here, and respond to the questions at the end.

The Art of War in "Woodchucks"

Antoine Assaf

What can prompt a man to become cruel? In "Woodchucks," the poet Maxine Kumin describes the speaker's lust to kill the woodchucks in her garden. Her desire and the method she uses grow from a simple, merciful execution to a bloody massacre. The poem's diction, imagery, and rhyme scheme all help convey the speaker's ambivalent attitude toward her own violent behavior, showing that killing sight unseen is not, perhaps, so different from picking up a gun and pulling the trigger.

The violent word choices in "Woodchucks" help create a battle scene in the poem, illustrating the change the speaker undergoes as the war between human and nature escalates. The woodchucks, on a rampage, are "nipping the broccoli shoots" and “beheading the carrots” (l. 12). Their actions against the speaker’s garden, as well as the speaker’s response, are acts of war, and casualties follow. The speaker’s references to World War II bring the battle to a new level, as words like “gassing” (l. 1) and “Nazi” (l. 30) remind us that wartime atrocities take place both seen and unseen. The speaker sees herself as a soldier who must accomplish her mission, though she is not without the awareness that her actions are over the top. There is, however, no denying a certain sense of glee as the speaker prepares to fight. She finds taking up the .22 “thrilling” (l. 13) and is proud of being able to “[draw] a bead” (l. 17) and “[drop] the mother” (l. 19). She believes she is an even match for the woodchucks and assumes that the playing field is level because they attacked her first. While she is honest enough with herself to see that there is a “murderer inside [her]” (l. 23), she’s not quite self-aware enough to know that the war against the old woodchuck, which keeps her “cocked and ready day after day after day” (l. 26), has dehumanized her. Both through her actions and the language used to describe them, the speaker’s uneasy relationship with nature is made clear.

The poem’s imagery suggests that even though the poem presents a sort of victory of human over nature, the speaker does not seem proud of what she has done. The baby dying in the “everbearing roses” (l. 18) smacks of infanticide, a cruelty beyond war. The speaker presents herself as indulging in bad habits such as “cigarettes / and state-store Scotch” (ll. 8-9) as a way of justifying her use of “cyanide” (l. 8). She sees herself as a “hawkeye killer” (l. 24), an image that evokes a predator stalking its prey and suggests a natural power that she didn’t know she had. She wishes, finally, that the woodchucks had “consented to die unseen / gassed underground the quiet Nazi way” (ll. 29-30). This image circles back to the first line of the poem: “Gassing the woodchucks didn’t turn out right,” highlighting the speaker’s regret and discomfort at the battle she seems forced to fight. She is, in fact, haunted by the surviving woodchuck’s “humped up form” (l. 27).

“Woodchucks” has a somewhat unusual rhyme scheme, which echoes the speaker’s mixed feelings about what she’s doing. The first three lines are *abc* and the second are *acb*, so the second line rhymes with the sixth line and the third line rhymes with the fifth. This pattern continues through the whole poem. So the poem is both balanced and unbalanced — a bit like the situation of the speaker. Part of her believes that her war against the woodchucks is fair; another part of her is not so sure.

One of the aims of “Woodchucks” seems to be to describe the speaker’s loss of innocence. She is faced with having to protect what she believes is her territory, but she is forced to acknowledge that the woodchucks won’t give it up so easily. She is ambivalent about her part in the war against the woodchucks, though the poem’s language leaves no doubt that war it is.

QUESTIONS

1. Examine the relationship between the thesis and the topic sentences. Do you think the basic structure of the essay is effective or ineffective? Why?
2. How does the essay support its argument with evidence from the text? Cite evidence that you find especially effective and explain why.
3. The writer argues that the poem's language, imagery, and rhyme scheme illustrate the speaker's ambivalence. To what extent do you think that the textual evidence supports this interpretation?
4. What is another argument you might make based on a close reading of "Woodchucks"? It does not have to contradict this writer's interpretation entirely but rather offer another way to read the poem or a different conclusion from the one drawn in this sample essay.

ACTIVITY

Read the following poem by William Stafford. Then use the close reading techniques you've learned to generate ideas for a thesis statement and several topic sentences for a close analysis essay that examines the speaker's attitude toward humanity's role in the natural world.

Traveling through the Dark

WILLIAM STAFFORD

Traveling through the dark I found a deer
dead on the edge of the Wilson River road.
It is usually best to roll them into the canyon:
that road is narrow; to swerve might make more dead.

By glow of the tail-light I stumbled back of the car
and stood by the heap, a doe, a recent killing;
she had stiffened already, almost cold.
I dragged her off; she was large in the belly.

My fingers touching her side brought me the reason —
her side was warm; her fawn lay there waiting,
alive, still, never to be born.
Beside that mountain road I hesitated.

The car aimed ahead its lowered parking lights;
under the hood purred the steady engine.
I stood in the glare of the warm exhaust turning red;
around our group I could hear the wilderness listen.

I thought hard for us all — my only swerving —,
then pushed her over the edge into the river.

[1962]

WORKING WITH TWO TEXTS: THE COMPARISON AND CONTRAST ESSAY

You have probably written comparison and contrast essays in English or other classes. Essay questions that ask you to compare and contrast two poems or prose passages are common in the classroom as well as on standardized tests. They require close reading, of course, but as you read you will also be looking for elements that the two works have in common — or that set them apart. The prompt will frequently give you an idea of what connects the two texts on the surface — often the subjects are the same — but your task is to develop an argument that goes beyond those surface similarities or differences.

Since you have already worked with two poems that are about animals, let's consider what else "Woodchucks" and "Traveling through the Dark" have in common, as well as what makes them different. As you plan a comparison and contrast essay, you might want to make a graphic organizer, such as the one below, that will help you generate ideas about the similarities and differences in situation, speaker, imagery, or tone, to name a few.

Title	"Woodchucks"	"Traveling through the Dark"
Situation	Killing woodchucks who are pests in the garden	Disposing of a dead deer on the side of the road
Speaker (Point of View)	First person. The speaker describes her escalating war against the woodchucks eating her vegetables.	Also first person. The speaker finds the dead deer and decides what to do with its body.
Imagery	Violent: "nipping the broccoli shoots, beheading the carrots" (l. 12); "She / flipflopped in the air and fell, her needle teeth / still hooked in a leaf of early Swiss chard" (ll. 19-21).	Contemplative, a bit detached: "She had stiffened already, almost cold" (l. 7); "My fingers touching her side brought me the reason / her side was warm . . . " (ll. 9-10); "The car aimed ahead its lowered parking lights; / under the hood purred the steady engine" (ll. 13-14).
Tone	Aggressive, but also conspiratorial and defensive: "and the case we had against them was airtight" (l. 4); "all of us up to scratch" (l. 9); "I dropped the mother" (l. 19); "the murderer inside me" (l. 23).	Gentle and resigned: "I thought hard for us all" (l. 17); "her fawn lay there waiting, / alive, still, never to be born" (ll. 10-11).

Syntax	Combination of short and long sentences with the enjambment of complete sentences throughout ("They brought down the marigolds as a matter of course / and then took over the vegetable patch / nipping the broccoli shoots, beheading the carrots"). Mirrors the natural flow of a conversation.	Two- and three-line sentences, some of which are compound sentences, connected with colons or semicolons. Suggests the attempt to respond reasonably to sadness and possible danger.

ACTIVITY

After rereading "Woodchucks" and "Traveling through the Dark," continue to fill in the chart with your own observations about some of the poems' other similarities and differences. You might add rows for theme, rhythm, allusion, figurative language, or other characteristics that you find significant.

Developing a Thesis Statement

Developing your thesis depends in large measure on the question you're asked. If your assignment is simply to compare and contrast these two poems, it's up to you to determine if you want to focus primarily on differences or similarities and then decide which areas or literary elements you will analyze. Keep in mind that the purpose of putting two works (or ideas) next to each other is usually to emphasize something that is not immediately obvious. For instance, the fact that both of these poems are about nature is pretty obvious; there's probably not much point in contrasting a woodchuck and a deer. However, if you examine how the speaker sees each animal, you'll discover more interesting issues, such as how one poem is largely in the moment and contemplates violence while the other seems to recall a past that still reverberates. One poem rages and rationalizes; the other presents memories and reflections. One is aggressive in tone, while the other is more contemplative.

If you are given a prompt, you'll have clearer direction, but it is still up to you to determine the specifics of your analysis. Suppose you are given the following essay assignment:

> The effects of humans on the natural world figure prominently in both Maxine Kumin's "Woodchucks" and William Stafford's "Traveling through the Dark." In an essay, compare and contrast the two poems, analyzing the literary devices each writer uses to explore the speaker's attitude toward the natural world.

Even though this prompt is quite specific, it leaves many questions and decisions up to you. First, it directs you to analyze the literary devices, but it does not indicate which ones. Whether the prompt asks for “literary devices,” “style devices,” “literary techniques,” “resources of language,” “literary elements,” “poetic elements,” or “formal elements,” you’re being asked to consider the writer’s language. Second, it asks that you “explore the speaker’s attitude toward the natural world,” but it doesn’t indicate what that attitude is. So before you can craft a thesis, you need to analyze the poems carefully and think about the themes. How is the relationship between the animals and the humans in each poem similar or different? Usually you want to begin by finding the common ground, and then noting the differences. For instance, you could claim that in both of these poems the speaker attempts to communicate the complexity of humans’ relationship to the natural world. The ways each poem represents that complexity are, however, quite different. For instance, in Kumin’s poem, the speaker is aggressive, defensively justifying her actions, while the speaker in Stafford’s poem observes, reports, and regrets.

Remember that your thesis should not be too broad:

> Animals are central to both poems, but the poets present them in different ways.

Your thesis should not focus too narrowly on the meaning of the poems without specifying which resources of language you intend to discuss:

> In both poems, animals help dramatize the relationship humans have with nature; however, each speaker’s relationship is different.

Nor should your thesis focus too narrowly on the resources of language and ignore the speakers’ attitudes:

> In these two poems, the point of view, images, and rhythmic structure are different.

If we balance the two components — attention to the resources of language and attention to meaning — we’ll come up with a working thesis:

> In both poems, the speakers’ relationships to animals are the means the poets use to dramatize our relationship to nature; however, the diction, the imagery, and the rhythm of the two poems convey very different experiences.

This is only a working thesis, a draft to be used as a starting point — you can tell by the awkward language and repetition. It identifies the specific resources of language the writer will discuss and begins to develop an interpretation of how the poets are using those resources. The following revised thesis statement attempts, in a succinct fashion, to narrow our scope of interpretation while maintaining focus on the resources of language that the poems share:

> In these two poems, the diction, imagery, and rhythm reveal the complicated relationships between humans and nature, but a world of difference separates each speaker’s experience.

Organizing a Comparison and Contrast Essay

After you have created a thesis statement for your comparison and contrast essay, you need to consider how to organize your essay. In general, you have two alternatives: text-by-text, or element-by-element.

Text-by-Text Organization

One way to organize a comparison and contrast essay about two literary works is to divide it into a discussion of the works one by one. In the first developmental, or body, paragraphs, you could, for instance, discuss literary elements in "Woodchucks," and then in the next paragraphs, discuss how those same elements are used similarly or differently in "Traveling through the Dark." If you are under time constraints, you might write only one paragraph for each poem, but be careful that you don't try to include too much in a single paragraph. Instead, be sure that your paragraphs are clearly focused and supported and that you draw connections between the two texts.

Let's consider an outline for an essay responding to the prompt about "Woodchucks" and "Traveling through the Dark."

THESIS

Although both Kumin and Stafford depict humanity's relationship to nature as troubled, the diction, imagery, and rhythm in both poems show each speaker's vastly different perspective on that relationship.

TOPIC SENTENCE 1

In "Woodchucks," the speaker's angry and aggressive tone suggests that the relationship between humans and animals is inherently hostile.

TOPIC SENTENCE 2

In "Traveling through the Dark," the gentle and elegiac tone suggests the sadness of the unbridgeable gap between humans and nature.

If you are faced with time constraints or a restricted length, you might find this text-by-text approach especially useful. An essay developed from this outline, for instance, addresses the prompt and, with the inclusion of strong textual support, could result in an insightful reading of the two poems. Its structure is essentially two sections — one poem, then the next. This logical pattern can be effective as long as the introduction and conclusion emphasize the connections between the two poems that are analyzed in the body paragraphs.

Element-by-Element Organization

The alternative is to organize the paragraphs around the literary elements you want to discuss. In the case of the thesis we're working with here, you could analyze the diction in both poems, then the imagery in both poems, then the rhythmic structure in both poems.

Should each paragraph refer to both works? In most instances, yes, but there are no hard and fast rules. If you have a lot to say about one of the literary elements you're analyzing, then break the discussion into two paragraphs, one on each poem. As always, form follows function when you are organizing an essay. Rather than a template, your own ideas and the material should guide your decisions about the best way to present an analysis.

The chief advantage of this element-by-element organization is that you are comparing and contrasting as you go, rather than waiting until the end. After a topic sentence that focuses on the point you want to make, you would offer evidence from both poems, reminding the reader of the impact of the difference or similarity.

Consider this outline for an essay organized according to literary elements:

THESIS

Although both Kumin and Stafford depict humanity's relationship to nature as troubled, the diction, imagery, and rhythm in both poems show each speaker's vastly different perspective on that relationship.

TOPIC SENTENCE 1

Though both poems are told from a first-person point of view, the diction in each poem conveys the vast difference in the type of connection each speaker has to nature.

TOPIC SENTENCE 2

While the two poets create vivid images of the natural world, the difference in the images reflects the speakers' divergent views of the relationship between humans and nature.

TOPIC SENTENCE 3

The rhythm and syntax of each poem reflect each speaker's unique take on humanity's uneasy relationship to nature.

Transitions

Because you must juggle two works in a comparison and contrast essay, it is especially important that your transitions are effective. Here are some words and phrases you might use to help keep your work and its intentions clear:

COMPARISON TRANSITIONS	CONTRAST TRANSITIONS
in comparison	in contrast
compared to	on the one hand . . . on the other hand
like	conversely
similar to	on the contrary
likewise	unlike
also	however
similarly	although

COMPARISON TRANSITIONS	CONTRAST TRANSITIONS
in the same way	yet
as in . . . , so in the other	still
moreover	but
	even though
	nevertheless
	regardless
	despite
	while

Documenting Sources

In a comparison and contrast essay, you will have two sources, so while you probably won't need a formal Works Cited page, you might be asked to use parenthetical citations in which you identify the work by the writer's name and the line number:

> Described as "stiffened already, almost cold" (Stafford l. 7), the deer . . .
>
> Described as "humped up" (Kumin l. 27), the old woodchuck haunts . . .

If the author of the work is introduced in the sentence, just use the line number:

> Kumin describes the surviving woodchuck as an "Old wily fellow" (l. 25).

A Sample Comparison and Contrast Essay

Following is a sample essay that follows the element-by-element form of comparison. Read it, and then discuss the questions that follow.

Human Nature: Two Perspectives

Javier Echevarria

The relationship between humans and nature can be very complex, and it often varies from individual to individual. These feelings can range from awe and admiration in the face of nature's immensity and power for some people to peacefulness and reflection in others. In "Woodchucks" by Maxine Kumin, the speaker is confronted by a plague of woodchucks, and the poem explores the events that take place in the garden. In William Stafford's poem "Traveling through the Dark," the speaker is confronted by a dead deer as he drives on a lonely road. While both Kumin and Stafford's poems portray scenes of death, the imagery used to describe these deaths sheds light on the starkly different relationships that the two speakers have with nature.

In "Woodchucks," the imagery used is mainly that of a battlefield, suggesting that the relationship between humans and nature is one of war and destruction. The opening word, "gassing" (l. 1), takes the reader into a world of suffering and aggressiveness. Like soldiers, who are prisoners of their trenches, the woodchucks have no escape because "both exits" are "shoehorned shut with puddingstone" (l. 5). The poem's imagery then continues to be structured around the mutual retaliations between woodchucks and speaker. Indeed, nature — in the form of the woodchucks — is quick to answer to the attacks. Like a rising army, the woodchucks counterattack by "nipping the broccoli shoots, beheading the carrots" (l. 12). Besides the clear images of two confronting, warring factions, the sense of being in the middle of a battlefield is reinforced through military expressions such as "out of range" (l. 6), "took over" (l. 11), "beheading" (l. 12), and "hawkeye killer" (l. 24). The reader is also exposed to the perverse satisfaction that the speaker gets out of the mass killing: "the murderer inside me rose up hard" (l. 23) and "righteously thrilling to the feel of the .22" (l. 14). The speaker is aware of the excitement that emanates from her cruelty, but she doesn't embrace it without remorse. Whereas at first she mocks her old self for being too gentle on the woodchucks and drums up "pieties for killing" (l. 16), she soon regrets her actions and wishes "they'd all consented to die unseen / gassed underground the quiet Nazi way" (ll. 29-30). The reader is thus offered the image of a soldier who walks into battle confident and serene, but comes out of it troubled by the bloodthirsty excitement she experienced. Since her desire to kill seems to come from within, the conflict between nature and humans is depicted as inevitable.

In "Traveling through the Dark," imagery illustrates an unexpected funeral over which the speaker presides. Right from the beginning, the speaker is aware of the right thing to do: "It is usually best to roll them into the canyon" (l. 3). Combining his first reaction with the fact that he "stood by the heap" (l. 6) which had "stiffened already, almost cold" (l.7), the scene parallels a funeral. Indeed, the doe is "a recent killing" (l. 6), and the speaker feels the need to send her back to nature. His respectful tone, conveyed by his actions, adds to the funeral-like atmosphere. In this scenery of death, however, the speaker finds a spark of life: "her fawn lay there waiting, / alive" (ll. 10-11). The speaker's hesitation to do what he knows is "usually best" shows he is saddened by the events. He could try to help the fawn even though it is likely to be a lost cause. The personification of nature shows both his respect for it as well as his sense of intimidation, suggesting he possibly believes the natural world is judging him: "I could hear the wilderness listen" (l. 16). Although he doesn't directly address the dilemma regarding the fawn's life, several hints show that he is perfectly aware of the situation and the responsibilities that emanate from it: "around our group" (l. 16) and "I thought hard for us all" (l. 17). The line between life and death, mirrored by the belly of the doe, becomes blurry for the speaker. The diction, reflecting silence and death, contributes to the sense that the scene is a spiritual burial of the doe, and greatly contrasts with the living creature inside her: "alive, still" (l. 11). Although the speaker seems to be respectful of nature, his ultimate decision to sacrifice the fawn along with its mother ends the poem on a melancholy note, which conveys the message that humans and nature are not meant to interact.

The image of war created by "Woodchucks" and the funeral ceremony that seems to take place in "Traveling through the Dark" offer a window into two completely different attitudes toward the natural world. On one side, the speaker of "Woodchucks" takes a sadistic pleasure in exterminating the animals one by one. Nature is thus presented as inherently hostile to humans, and vice-versa, it is suggested that humans have an innate desire for cruelty. This sharply contrasts with the respectful attitude of the speaker in "Traveling through the Dark." Although both speakers discuss similar events, namely the death of animals, putting the poems side by side and contrasting their differences enable the reader to appreciate the spectrum of emotions that can be felt toward nature.

QUESTIONS

1. Is the introduction effective? What about the thesis statement? Explain why or why not. If you believe it is not effective, how could it be improved?
2. In what ways are transitions used within this essay to emphasize the similarities and differences between the poems?
3. Paragraphs 2 and 3 discuss diction as well as vivid imagery. Should diction have been specified in the thesis? Explain.
4. Do you agree with the essay's argument? Explain why or why not. Which parts of the interpretation do you find most persuasive? Questionable?
5. What other literary elements might you have used to make a similar argument?
6. What suggestions can you offer for polishing the essay?

ACTIVITY

Read "in the inner city" by Lucille Clifton and "The City's Love" by Claude McKay, two poems in which a speaker characterizes urban life. Plan and write a comparison and contrast essay in which you analyze the style elements that reveal the relationship between the speaker and the city in each poem.

in the inner city

LUCILLE CLIFTON

in the inner city
or
like we call it
home
we think a lot about uptown

and the silent nights
and the houses straight as
dead men
and the pastel lights
and we hang on to our no place
happy to be alive
and in the inner city
or
like we call it
home

[1969]

The City's Love

CLAUDE McKAY

For one brief golden moment rare like wine,
The gracious city swept across the line;
Oblivious of the color of my skin,
Forgetting that I was an alien guest,
She bent to me, my hostile heart to win,
Caught me in passion to her pillowy breast;
The great, proud city, seized with a strange love,
Bowed down for one flame hour my pride to prove.

[1922]

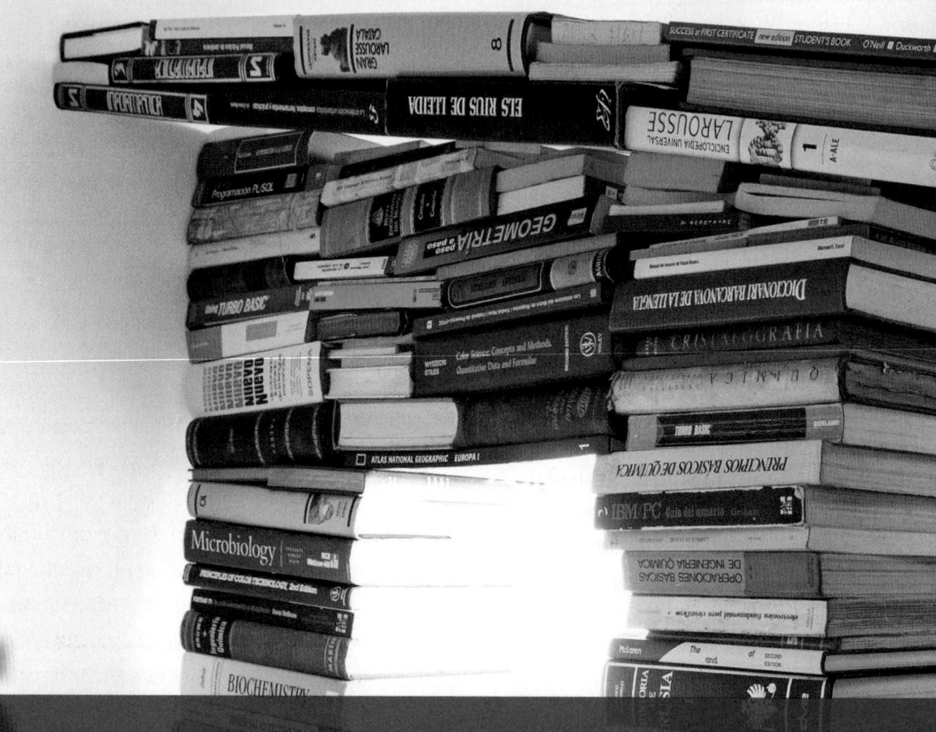

5
Home and Family

> “Happy families are all alike; every unhappy family is unhappy in its own way.”
>
> — Leo Tolstoy, *Anna Karenina*

Artur Debat/Getty Images

What makes a house a home? “Home” suggests sanctuary, loved ones, nourishment — a place where everybody knows your name. The term is woven deep into our language as well as our consciousness. Consider the connotations of *homemade* and *homespun*. Home can offer refuge from the hostile world, or it can be a prison. People living together inevitably — sometimes intentionally — rub one another the wrong way. This chafing provides writers with rich material for art. (Remember, without conflict there is no story.) Are these writers working through their own failed relationships with mothers, fathers, and siblings? Sometimes. Are they exploring their conflicted feelings toward a home they left behind? Maybe. Are they holding up a mirror that allows us to see our own homes and families in a new light? Most certainly.

Though the trappings of home and family differ across cultures, human families have much in common. Legend has it that a man from Czechoslovakia, after watching a production of August Wilson’s *Fences* (set in Pittsburgh in the 1950s), approached the playwright and asked him, “How did you know about my family?” Wilson may not have known that particular man’s family, but he knew about families and how the sins of the father play out in the lives of sons.

The readings in this chapter explore the theme of home and family within a broad range of contexts. Franz Kafka's modernist masterpiece, *The Metamorphosis*, is told from the point of view of a son whose transformation into a large bug renders him unable to support his middle-class family in the rapidly changing cityscape they call home. You'll also find several selections of modernist fiction, poetry, and art that reflect early twentieth–century perceptions of human experience, particularly in urban centers — these works will help you explore the place *The Metamorphosis* occupies within modernist tradition. In Langston Hughes's poem "Mother to Son," the speaker uses her own suffering as an example to chide her son, "So boy, don't you turn back. / Don't you set down on the steps / 'Cause you finds it's kinder hard." Alice Munro's "The Progress of Love" looks at family through the stories characters tell, retell, and revise about their shared memories. Let the literature on the following pages take you into other homes and families so that you can return to your own with new eyes.

Fences

AUGUST WILSON

AP Photo/Ted S. Warren

August Wilson (1945–2005) was born in Pittsburgh to a white father and an African American mother. When his father died in 1965, he changed his legal name (Frederick August Kittel) to August Wilson, assuming his mother's maiden name. Brought up by his mother, he spent his early years in the Hill — a poor, multiracial district of Pittsburgh, the setting for his later work. His formal education ended when he dropped out of high school at the age of fifteen. He was largely self-educated, becoming acquainted with the works of leading African American writers through the Carnegie Library. He cofounded the Black Horizon Theater in the Hill District in 1968, and vowed to become a writer. This ambition was realized during the 1980s, when Wilson began writing *The Pittsburgh Cycle* — a remarkable collection of partially interconnected plays. Collectively, the plays portray the twentieth century from an African American perspective. The cycle garnered many awards, including two Pulitzer Prizes (for *Fences* in 1985 and *The Piano Lesson* in 1989); the tenth and final play, *Radio Golf*, was performed a few months before his death. Wilson's influence lies in his ability, through larger-than-life characters and intense, perceptive characterization, to create a universal dimension in which issues of race and family in America are examined. In *Fences*, Troy Maxson embodies one of those larger-than-life characters.

For Lloyd Richards, who adds to whatever he touches

When the sins of our fathers visit us
We do not have to play host.
We can banish them with forgiveness
As God, in His Largeness and Laws.

— August Wilson

Characters

TROY MAXSON

JIM BONO, *Troy's friend*

ROSE, *Troy's wife*

LYONS, *Troy's oldest son by previous marriage*

GABRIEL, *Troy's brother*

CORY, *Troy and Rose's son*

RAYNELL, *Troy's daughter*

SETTING The setting is the yard which fronts the only entrance to the Maxson household, an ancient two-story brick house set back off a small alley in a big-city neighborhood. The entrance to the house is gained by two or three steps leading to a wooden porch badly in need of paint.

A relatively recent addition to the house and running its full width, the porch lacks congruence. It is a sturdy porch with a flat roof. One or two chairs of dubious value sit at one end where the kitchen window opens onto the porch. An old-fashioned icebox stands silent guard at the opposite end.

The yard is a small dirt yard, partially fenced, except for the last scene, with a wooden sawhorse, a pile of lumber, and other fence-building

equipment set off to the side. Opposite is a tree from which hangs a ball made of rags.
A baseball bat leans against the tree. Two oil drums serve as garbage receptacles and sit near the house at right to complete the setting.

THE PLAY Near the turn of the century, the destitute of Europe sprang on the city with tenacious claws and an honest and solid dream. The city devoured them. They swelled its belly until it burst into a thousand furnaces and sewing machines, a thousand butcher shops and bakers' ovens, a thousand churches and hospitals and funeral parlors and money-lenders. The city grew. It nourished itself and offered each man a partnership limited only by his talent, his guile, and his willingness and capacity for hard work. For the immigrants of Europe, a dream dared and won true.

The descendants of African slaves were offered no such welcome or participation. They came from places called the Carolinas and the Virginias, Georgia, Alabama, Mississippi, and Tennessee. They came strong, eager, searching. The city rejected them and they fled and settled along the riverbanks and under bridges in shallow, ramshackle houses made of sticks and tarpaper. They collected rags and wood. They sold the use of their muscles and their bodies. They cleaned houses and washed clothes, they shined shoes, and in quiet desperation and vengeful pride, they stole, and lived in pursuit of their own dream. That they could breathe free, finally, and stand to meet life with the force of dignity and whatever eloquence the heart could call upon.

By 1957, the hard-won victories of the European immigrants had solidified the industrial might of America. War had been confronted and won with new energies that used loyalty and patriotism as its fuel. Life was rich, full, and flourishing. The Milwaukee Braves won the World Series, and the hot winds of change that would make the sixties a turbulent, racing, dangerous, and provocative decade had not yet begun to blow full.

ACT I

Scene 1

It is 1957. **TROY** *and* **BONO** *enter the yard, engaged in conversation.* **TROY** *is fifty-three years old, a large man with thick, heavy hands; it is this largeness that he strives to fill out and make an accommodation with. Together with his blackness, his largeness informs his sensibilities and the choices he has made in his life.*

Of the two men, **BONO** *is obviously the follower. His commitment to their friendship of thirty-odd years is rooted in his admiration of* **TROY***'s honesty, capacity for hard work, and his strength, which* **BONO** *seeks to emulate.*

It is Friday night, payday, and the one night of the week the two men engage in a ritual of talk and drink. **TROY** *is usually the most talkative and at times he can be crude and almost vulgar, though he is capable of rising to profound heights of expression. The men carry lunch buckets and wear or carry burlap aprons and are dressed in clothes suitable to their jobs as garbage collectors.*

BONO Troy, you ought to stop that lying!

TROY I ain't lying! The nigger had a watermelon this big. (*He indicates with his hands.*) Talking about . . . "What watermelon, Mr. Rand?" I liked to fell out! "What watermelon, Mr. Rand?" . . . And it sitting there big as life.

BONO What did Mr. Rand say?

TROY Ain't said nothing. Figure if the nigger too dumb to know he carrying a watermelon, he wasn't gonna get much sense out of him. Trying to hide that great big old watermelon under his coat. Afraid to let the white man see him carry it home.

BONO I'm like you . . . I ain't got no time for them kind of people.

TROY Now what he look like getting mad cause he see the man from the union talking to Mr. Rand?

BONO He come to me talking about . . . "Maxson gonna get us fired." I told him to get away from me with that. He walked away from me calling you a troublemaker. What Mr. Rand say?

TROY Ain't said nothing. He told me to go down the Commissioner's office next Friday. They called me down there to see them.

BONO Well, as long as you got your complaint filed, they can't fire you. That's what one of them white fellows tell me.

TROY I ain't worried about them firing me. They gonna fire me cause I asked a question? That's all I did. I went to Mr. Rand and asked him, "Why? Why you got the white mens driving and the colored lifting?" Told him, "What's the matter, don't I count? You think only white fellows got sense enough to drive a truck. That ain't no paper job! Hell, anybody can drive a truck. How come you got all whites driving and the colored lifting?" He told me "take it to the union." Well, hell, that's what I done! Now they wanna come up with this pack of lies.

BONO I told Brownie if the man come and ask him any questions . . . just tell the truth! It ain't nothing but something they done trumped up on you cause you filed a complaint on them.

TROY Brownie don't understand nothing. All I want them to do is change the job description. Give everybody a chance to drive the truck. Brownie can't see that. He ain't got that much sense.

BONO How you figure he be making out with that gal be up at Taylors' all the time . . . that Alberta gal?

TROY Same as you and me. Getting just as much as we is. Which is to say nothing.

BONO It is, huh? I figure you doing a little better than me . . . and I ain't saying what I'm doing.

TROY Aw, nigger, look here . . . I know you. If you had got anywhere near that gal, twenty minutes later you be looking to tell somebody. And the first one you gonna tell . . . that you gonna want to brag to . . . is me.

BONO I ain't saying that. I see where you be eyeing her.

TROY I eye all the women. I don't miss nothing. Don't never let nobody tell you Troy Maxson don't eye the women.

BONO You been doing more than eyeing her. You done bought her a drink or two.

TROY Hell yeah, I bought her a drink! What that mean? I bought you one, too. What that mean cause I buy her a drink? I'm just being polite.

BONO It's all right to buy her one drink. That's what you call being polite. But when you wanna be buying two or three . . . that's what you call eyeing her.

TROY Look here, as long as you known me . . . you ever known me to chase after women?

BONO Hell yeah! Long as I done known you. You forgetting I knew you when.

TROY Naw, I'm talking about since I been married to Rose?

BONO Oh, not since you been married to Rose. Now, that's the truth, there. I can say that.

TROY All right then! Case closed.

BONO I see you be walking up around Alberta's house. You supposed to be at Taylors' and you be walking up around there.

TROY What you watching where I'm walking for? I ain't watching after you.

BONO I seen you walking around there more than once.

TROY Hell, you liable to see me walking anywhere! That don't mean nothing cause you see me walking around there.

BONO Where she come from anyway? She just kinda showed up one day.

TROY Tallahassee. You can look at her and tell she one of them Florida gals. They got some big healthy women down there. Grow them right up out the ground. Got a little bit of Indian in her. Most of them niggers down in Florida got some Indian in them.

BONO I don't know about that Indian part. But she damn sure big and healthy. Woman wear some big stockings. Got them great big old legs and hips as wide as the Mississippi River.

TROY Legs don't mean nothing. You don't do nothing but push them out of the way. But them hips cushion the ride!

BONO Troy, you ain't got no sense.

TROY It's the truth! Like you riding on Goodyears!

ROSE *enters from the house. She is ten years younger than* **TROY**, *her devotion to him stems from her recognition of the possibilities of her life without him: a succession of abusive men and their babies, a life of partying and running the streets, the Church, or aloneness with its attendant pain and frustration. She recognizes* **TROY**'*s spirit as a fine and illuminating one and she either ignores or forgives his faults, only some of which she recognizes. Though she doesn't drink, her presence is an integral part of the Friday night rituals. She alternates between the porch and the kitchen, where supper preparations are under way.*

ROSE What you all out here getting into?

TROY What you worried about what we getting into for? This is men talk, woman.

ROSE What I care what you all talking about? Bono, you gonna stay for supper?

BONO No, I thank you, Rose. But Lucille say she cooking up a pot of pigfeet.

TROY Pigfeet! Hell, I'm going home with you! Might even stay the night if you got some pigfeet. You got something in there to top them pigfeet, Rose?

ROSE I'm cooking up some chicken. I got some chicken and collard greens.

TROY Well, go on back in the house and let me and Bono finish what we was talking about. This is men talk. I got some talk for you later. You know what kind of talk I mean. You go on and powder it up.

ROSE Troy Maxson, don't you start that now!

TROY (*puts his arm around her*): Aw, woman . . . come here. Look here, Bono . . . when I met this woman . . . I got out that place, say, "Hitch up my pony, saddle up my mare . . . there's a woman out there for me somewhere. I looked here. Looked there. Saw Rose and latched on to her." I latched on to her and told her — I'm gonna tell you the truth — I told her, "Baby, I don't wanna marry, I just wanna be your man." Rose told me . . . tell him what you told me, Rose.

ROSE I told him if he wasn't the marrying kind, then move out the way so the marrying kind could find me.

TROY That's what she told me. "Nigger, you in my way. You blocking the view! Move out the way so I can find me a husband." I thought it over two or three days. Come back —

ROSE Ain't no two or three days nothing. You was back the same night.

TROY Come back, told her . . . "Okay, baby . . . but I'm gonna buy me a banty rooster and put him out there in the backyard . . . and when he see a stranger come, he'll flap his wings and crow . . ." Look here, Bono, I could watch the front door by myself . . . it was that back door I was worried about.

ROSE Troy, you ought not talk like that. Troy ain't doing nothing but telling a lie.

TROY Only thing is . . . when we first got married . . . forget the rooster . . . we ain't had no yard!

BONO I hear you tell it. Me and Lucille was staying down there on Logan Street. Had two rooms with the outhouse in the back. I ain't mind the outhouse none. But when that goddamn wind blow through there in the winter . . . that's what I'm talking about! To this day I wonder why in the hell I ever stayed down there for six long years. But see, I didn't know I could do no better. I thought only white folks had inside toilets and things.

ROSE There's a lot of people don't know they can do no better than they doing now. That's just something you got to learn. A lot of folks still shop at Bella's.

TROY Ain't nothing wrong with shopping at Bella's. She got fresh food.

ROSE I ain't said nothing about if she got fresh food. I'm talking about what she charge. She charge ten cents more than the A&P.

TROY The A&P ain't never done nothing for me. I spends my money where I'm treated right. I go down to Bella, say, "I need a loaf of bread, I'll pay you Friday." She give it to me. What sense that make when I got money to go and spend it somewhere else and ignore the person who done right by me? That ain't in the Bible.

ROSE We ain't talking about what's in the Bible. What sense it make to shop there when she overcharge?

TROY You shop where you want to. I'll do my shopping where the people been good to me.

ROSE Well, I don't think it's right for her to overcharge. That's all I was saying.

BONO Look here . . . I got to get on. Lucille going be raising all kind of hell.

TROY Where you going, nigger? We ain't finished this pint. Come here, finish this pint.

BONO Well, hell, I am . . . if you ever turn the bottle loose.

TROY (*hands him the bottle*): The only thing I say about the A&P is I'm glad Cory got that job down there. Help him take care of his school clothes and things. Gabe done moved out and things getting tight around here. He got that job. . . . He can start to look out for himself.

ROSE Cory done went and got recruited by a college football team.

TROY I told that boy about that football stuff. The white man ain't gonna let him get nowhere with that football. I told him when he first come to me with it. Now you come telling me he done went and got more tied up in it. He ought to go and get recruited in how to fix cars or something where he can make a living.

ROSE He ain't talking about making no living playing football. It's just something the boys in school do. They gonna send a recruiter by to talk to you. He'll tell you he ain't talking about making no living playing football. It's a honor to be recruited.

TROY It ain't gonna get him nowhere. Bono'll tell you that.

BONO If he be like you in the sports . . . he's gonna be all right. Ain't but two men ever played baseball as good as you. That's Babe Ruth and Josh Gibson.[1] Them's the only two men ever hit more home runs than you.

TROY What it ever get me? Ain't got a pot to piss in or a window to throw it out of.

ROSE Times have changed since you was playing baseball, Troy. That was before the war. Times have changed a lot since then.

TROY How in hell they done changed?

ROSE They got lots of colored boys playing ball now. Baseball and football.

BONO You right about that, Rose. Times have changed, Troy. You just come along too early.

TROY There ought not never have been no time called too early! Now you take that fellow . . . what's that fellow they had playing right field for the Yankees back then? You know who I'm talking about, Bono. Used to play right field for the Yankees.

ROSE Selkirk?

TROY Selkirk! That's it! Man batting .269, understand? .269. What kind of sense that make? I was hitting .432 with thirty-seven home runs! Man batting .269 and playing right field for the Yankees! I saw Josh Gibson's daughter yesterday. She walking around with raggedy shoes on her feet. Now I bet you Selkirk's daughter ain't walking around with raggedy shoes on her feet! I bet you that!

---

[1] Josh Gibson (1911–1947) was a baseball player in the Negro leagues. — EDS.

ROSE They got a lot of colored baseball players now. Jackie Robinson was the first. Folks had to wait for Jackie Robinson.

TROY I done seen a hundred niggers play baseball better than Jackie Robinson. Hell, I know some teams Jackie Robinson couldn't even make! What you talking about Jackie Robinson. Jackie Robinson wasn't nobody. I'm talking about if you could play ball then they ought to have let you play. Don't care what color you were. Come telling me I come along too early. If you could play . . . then they ought to have let you play.

TROY *takes a long drink from the bottle.*

ROSE You gonna drink yourself to death. You don't need to be drinking like that.

TROY Death ain't nothing. I done seen him. Done wrassled with him. You can't tell me nothing about death. Death ain't nothing but a fastball on the outside corner. And you know what I'll do to that! Lookee here, Bono . . . am I lying? You get one of them fastballs, about waist high, over the outside corner of the plate where you can get the meat of the bat on it . . . and good god! You can kiss it goodbye. Now, am I lying?

BONO Naw, you telling the truth there. I seen you do it.

TROY If I'm lying . . . that 450 feet worth of lying! (*Pause.*) That's all death is to me. A fastball on the outside corner.

ROSE I don't know why you want to get on talking about death.

TROY Ain't nothing wrong with talking about death. That's part of life. Everybody gonna die. You gonna die, I'm gonna die. Bono's gonna die. Hell, we all gonna die.

ROSE But you ain't got to talk about it. I don't like to talk about it.

TROY You the one brought it up. Me and Bono was talking about baseball . . . you tell me I'm gonna drink myself to death. Ain't that right, Bono? You know I don't drink this but one night out of the week. That's Friday night. I'm gonna drink just enough to where I can handle it. Then I cuts it loose. I leave it alone. So don't you worry about me drinking myself to death. 'Cause I ain't worried about Death. I done seen him. I done wrestled with him.

Look here, Bono . . . I looked up one day and Death was marching straight at me. Like Soldiers on Parade! The Army of Death was marching straight at me. The middle of July, 1941. It got real cold just like it be winter. It seem like Death himself reached out and touched me on the shoulder. He touch me just like I touch you. I got cold as ice and Death standing there grinning at me.

ROSE Troy, why don't you hush that talk.

TROY I say . . . what you want, Mr. Death? You be wanting me? You done brought your army to be getting me? I looked him dead in the eye. I wasn't fearing nothing. I was ready to tangle. Just like I'm ready to tangle now. The Bible say be ever vigilant. That's why I don't get but so drunk. I got to keep watch.

ROSE Troy was right down there in Mercy Hospital. You remember he had pneumonia? Laying there with a fever talking plumb out of his head.

TROY Death standing there staring at me . . . carrying that sickle in his hand. Finally he say, "You want bound over for another year?" See, just like that . . . "You want bound over for another year?" I told him, "Bound over hell! Let's settle this now!"

It seem like he kinda fell back when I said that, and all the cold went out of me. I reached down and grabbed that sickle and threw it just as far as I could throw it . . . and me and him commenced to wrestling.

We wrestled for three days and three nights. I can't say where I found the strength from. Every time it seemed like he was gonna get the best of me, I'd reach way down deep inside myself and find the strength to do him one better.

In this painting entitled *Amerika (Baseball)*, how does artist R. B. Kitaj introduce elements of threat and menace? How does his depiction of baseball reflect or challenge Troy Maxson's relationship with the sport?

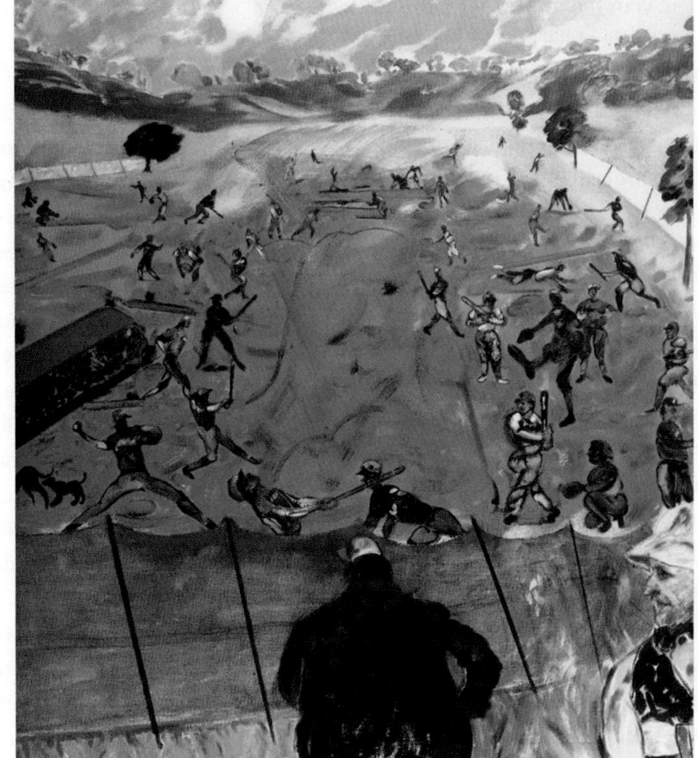

R. B. Kitaj, Amerika (Baseball), 1983–1984. Oil on canvas. 58 × 58 inches. Collection Yale University Art Gallery. © the Estate of R. B. Kitaj, Courtesy Marlborough Gallery, New York.

ROSE Every time Troy tell that story he find different ways to tell it. Different things to make up about it.

TROY I ain't making up nothing. I'm telling you the facts of what happened. I wrestled with Death for three days and three nights and I'm standing here to tell you about it. (*Pause.*) All right. At the end of the third night we done weakened each other to where we can't hardly move. Death stood up, throwed on his robe . . . had him a white robe with a hood on it. He throwed on that robe and went off to look for his sickle. Say, "I'll be back." Just like that. "I'll be back." I told him, say, "Yeah, but . . . you gonna have to find me!" I wasn't no fool. I wan't going looking for him. Death ain't nothing to play with. And I know he's gonna get me. I know I got to join his army . . . his camp followers. But as long as I keep my strength and see him coming . . . as long as I keep up my vigilance . . . he's gonna have to fight to get me. I ain't going easy.

BONO Well, look here, since you got to keep up your vigilance . . . let me have the bottle.

TROY Aw hell, I shouldn't have told you that part. I should have left out that part.

ROSE Troy be talking that stuff and half the time don't even know what he be talking about.

TROY Bono know me better than that.

BONO That's right. I know you. I know you got some Uncle Remus[2]

[2] Fictional narrator in books by Joel Chandler Harris that retell traditional black folktales featuring Brer Rabbit. — EDS.

in your blood. You got more stories than the devil got sinners.

TROY Aw hell, I done seen him too! Done talked with the devil.

ROSE Troy, don't nobody wanna be hearing all that stuff.

LYONS *enters the yard from the street. Thirty-four years old,* **TROY**'*s son by a previous marriage, he sports a neatly trimmed goatee, sport coat, white shirt, tieless and buttoned at the collar. Though he fancies himself a musician, he is more caught up in the rituals and "idea" of being a musician than in the actual practice of the music. He has come to borrow money from* **TROY**, *and while he knows he will be successful, he is uncertain as to what extent his lifestyle will be held up to scrutiny and ridicule.*

LYONS Hey, Pop.

TROY What you come "Hey, Popping" me for?

LYONS How you doing, Rose? (*He kisses her.*) Mr. Bono. How you doing?

BONO Hey, Lyons . . . how you been?

TROY He must have been doing all right. I ain't seen him around here last week.

ROSE Troy, leave your boy alone. He come by to see you and you wanna start all that nonsense.

TROY I ain't bothering Lyons. (*Offers him the bottle.*) Here . . . get you a drink. We got an understanding. I know why he come by to see me and he know I know.

LYONS Come on, Pop . . . I just stopped by to say hi . . . see how you was doing.

TROY You ain't stopped by yesterday.

ROSE You gonna stay for supper, Lyons? I got some chicken cooking in the oven.

LYONS No, Rose . . . thanks. I was just in the neighborhood and thought I'd stop by for a minute.

TROY You was in the neighborhood all right, nigger. You telling the truth there. You was in the neighborhood cause it's my payday.

LYONS Well, hell, since you mentioned it . . . let me have ten dollars.

TROY I'll be damned! I'll die and go to hell and play blackjack with the devil before I give you ten dollars.

BONO That's what I wanna know about . . . that devil you done seen.

LYONS What . . . Pop done seen the devil? You too much, Pops.

TROY Yeah, I done seen him. Talked to him too!

ROSE You ain't seen no devil. I done told you that man ain't had nothing to do with the devil. Anything you can't understand, you want to call it the devil.

TROY Look here, Bono . . . I went down to see Hertzberger about some furniture. Got three rooms for two-ninety-eight. That what it say on the radio. "Three rooms . . . two-ninety-eight." Even made up a little song about it. Go down there . . . man tell me I can't get no credit. I'm working every day and can't get no credit. What to do? I got an empty house with some raggedy furniture in it. Cory ain't got no bed. He's sleeping on a pile of rags on the floor. Working every day and can't get no credit. Come back here — Rose'll tell you — madder than hell. Sit down . . . try to figure what I'm gonna do. Come a knock on the door. Ain't been living here but three days. Who know I'm here? Open the door . . . devil standing there bigger than life. White fellow . . . white fellow . . . got on good clothes and everything. Standing there with a clipboard in his hand. I ain't had to say nothing. First words come out of his mouth was . . . "I understand you need some furniture and can't get no credit." I liked to fell over. He say, "I'll give you all the credit you want, but you got to pay the interest on it." I told him, "Give me three rooms worth and charge whatever you want." Next day a truck pulled up here and two men unloaded them three rooms. Man what drove the truck give me a book. Say send ten dollars, first of every month to the address in the book and everything will be all right. Say if I miss a payment the devil was coming back and it'll be hell to pay. That was fifteen years ago. To this day . . . the first of the month I send my ten dollars, Rose'll tell you.

ROSE Troy lying.

TROY I ain't never seen that man since. Now you tell me who else that could have been but the devil? I ain't sold my soul or nothing like that, you understand. Naw, I wouldn't have truck with the devil about nothing like that. I got my furniture and pays my ten dollars the first of the month just like clockwork.

BONO How long you say you been paying this ten dollars a month?

TROY Fifteen years!

BONO Hell, ain't you finished paying for it yet? How much the man done charged you?

TROY Ah hell, I done paid for it. I done paid for it ten times over! The fact is I'm scared to stop paying it.

ROSE Troy lying. We got that furniture from Mr. Glickman. He ain't paying no ten dollars a month to nobody.

TROY Aw hell, woman. Bono know I ain't that big a fool.

LYONS I was just getting ready to say . . . I know where there's a bridge for sale.

TROY Look here, I'll tell you this . . . it don't matter to me if he was the devil. It don't matter if the devil give credit. Somebody has got to give it.

ROSE It ought to matter. You going around talking about having truck with the devil . . . God's the one you gonna have to answer to. He's the one gonna be at the Judgment.

LYONS Yeah, well, look here, Pop . . . let me have that ten dollars. I'll give it back to you. Bonnie got a job working at the hospital.

TROY What I tell you, Bono? The only time I see this nigger is when he wants something. That's the only time I see him.

LYONS Come on, Pop, Mr. Bono don't want to hear all that. Let me have the ten dollars. I told you Bonnie working.

TROY What that mean to me? "Bonnie working." I don't care if she working. Go ask her for the ten dollars if she working. Talking about "Bonnie working." Why ain't you working?

LYONS Aw, Pop, you know I can't find no decent job. Where am I gonna get a job at? You know I can't get no job.

TROY I told you I know some people down there. I can get you on the rubbish if you want to work. I told you that the last time you came by here asking me for something.

LYONS Naw, Pop . . . thanks. That ain't for me. I don't wanna be carrying nobody's rubbish. I don't wanna be punching nobody's time clock.

TROY What's the matter, you too good to carry people's rubbish? Where you think that ten dollars you talking about come from? I'm just supposed to haul people's rubbish and give my money to you cause you too lazy to work. You too lazy to work and wanna know why you ain't got what I got.

ROSE What hospital Bonnie working at? Mercy?

LYONS She's down at Passavant working in the laundry.

TROY I ain't got nothing as it is. I give you that ten dollars and I got to eat beans the rest of the week. Naw . . . you ain't getting no ten dollars here.

LYONS You ain't got to be eating no beans. I don't know why you wanna say that.

TROY I ain't got no extra money. Gabe done moved over to Miss Pearl's paying her the rent and things done got tight around here. I can't afford to be giving you every payday.

LYONS I ain't asked you to give me nothing. I asked you to loan me ten dollars. I know you got ten dollars.

TROY Yeah, I got it. You know why I got it? Cause I don't throw my money away out there in the streets. You living the fast life . . . wanna be a musician . . . running around in them clubs and things . . . then, you learn to take care of yourself. You ain't gonna find me

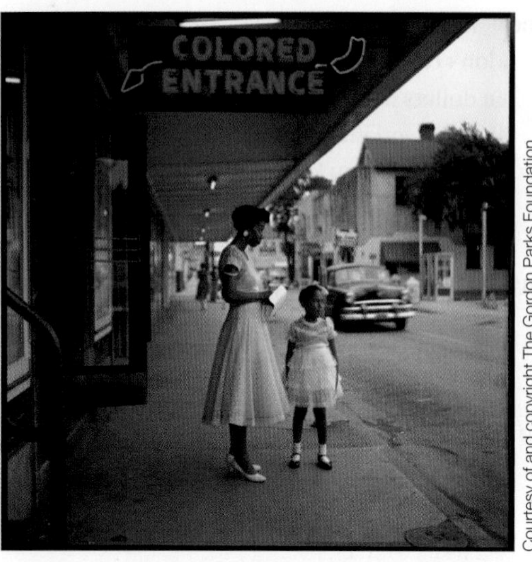

Gordon Parks took this photograph in 1956 as part of his Segregation Series, which was published in *Life* magazine. The series focused on an African American family living in Mobile, Alabama, documenting everyday life in the Jim Crow–era south. **How does this photograph illustrate some of the challenges and tensions Troy, Rose, and their family face? How does it contribute to your understanding of Troy's character in particular?**

going and asking nobody for nothing. I done spent too many years without.

LYONS You and me is two different people, Pop.

TROY I done learned my mistake and learned to do what's right by it. You still trying to get something for nothing. Life don't owe you nothing. You owe it to yourself. Ask Bono. He'll tell you I'm right.

LYONS You got your way of dealing with the world . . . I got mine. The only thing that matters to me is the music.

TROY Yeah, I can see that! It don't matter how you gonna eat . . . where your next dollar is coming from. You telling the truth there.

LYONS I know I got to eat. But I got to live too. I need something that gonna help me to get out of the bed in the morning. Make me feel like I belong in the world. I don't bother nobody. I just stay with the music cause that's the only way I can find to live in the world. Otherwise there ain't no telling what I might do. Now I don't come criticizing you and how you live. I just come by to ask you for ten dollars. I don't wanna hear all that about how I live.

TROY Boy, your mamma did a hell of a job raising you.

LYONS You can't change me, Pop. I'm thirty-four years old. If you wanted to change me, you should have been there when I was growing up. I come by to see you . . . ask for ten dollars and you want to talk about how I was raised. You don't know nothing about how I was raised.

ROSE Let the boy have ten dollars, Troy.

TROY (*to* **LYONS**): What the hell you looking at me for? I ain't got no ten dollars. You know what I do with my money. (*To* **ROSE**.) Give him ten dollars if you want him to have it.

ROSE I will. Just as soon as you turn it loose.

TROY (*handing* **ROSE** *the money*): There it is. Seventy-six dollars and forty-two cents. You see this, Bono? Now, I ain't gonna get but six of that back.

ROSE You ought to stop telling that lie. Here, Lyons. (*She hands him the money.*)

LYONS Thanks, Rose. Look . . . I got to run . . . I'll see you later.

TROY Wait a minute. You gonna say, "thanks, Rose" and ain't gonna look to see where she got that ten dollars from? See how they do me, Bono?

LYONS I know she got it from you, Pop. Thanks. I'll give it back to you.

TROY There he go telling another lie. Time I see that ten dollars . . . he'll be owing me thirty more.

LYONS See you, Mr. Bono.

BONO Take care, Lyons!

LYONS Thanks, Pop. I'll see you again.

LYONS *exits the yard.*

TROY I don't know why he don't go and get him a decent job and take care of that woman he got.

BONO He'll be all right, Troy. The boy is still young.

TROY The *boy* is thirty-four years old.

ROSE Let's not get off into all that.

BONO Look here . . . I got to be going. I got to be getting on. Lucille gonna be waiting.

TROY (*puts his arm around* **ROSE**): See this woman, Bono? I love this woman. I love this woman so much it hurts. I love her so much . . . I done run out of ways of loving her. So I got to go back to basics. Don't you come by my house Monday morning talking about time to go to work . . . 'cause I'm still gonna be stroking!

ROSE Troy! Stop it now!

BONO I ain't paying him no mind, Rose. That ain't nothing but gin-talk. Go on, Troy. I'll see you Monday.

TROY Don't you come by my house, nigger! I done told you what I'm gonna be doing.

The lights go down to black.

Scene 2

The lights come up on **ROSE** *hanging up clothes. She hums and sings softly to herself. It is the following morning.*

ROSE (*sings*): Jesus, be a fence all around me every day
Jesus, I want you to protect me as I travel on my way.
Jesus, be a fence all around me every day.

TROY *enters from the house.*

Jesus, I want you to protect me
As I travel on my way.
(*To* **TROY**.) 'Morning. You ready for breakfast? I can fix it soon as I finish hanging up these clothes?

TROY I got the coffee on. That'll be all right. I'll just drink some of that this morning.

ROSE That 651 hit yesterday. That's the second time this month. Miss Pearl hit for a dollar . . . seem like those that need the least always get lucky. Poor folks can't get nothing.

TROY Them numbers don't know nobody. I don't know why you fool with them. You and Lyons both.

ROSE It's something to do.

TROY You ain't doing nothing but throwing your money away.

ROSE Troy, you know I don't play foolishly. I just play a nickel here and a nickel there.

TROY That's two nickels you done thrown away.

ROSE Now I hit sometimes . . . that makes up for it. It always comes in handy when I do hit. I don't hear you complaining then.

TROY I ain't complaining now. I just say it's foolish. Trying to guess out of six hundred ways which way the number gonna come. If I had all the money niggers, these Negroes, throw away on numbers for one week — just one week — I'd be a rich man.

ROSE Well, you wishing and calling it foolish ain't gonna stop folks from playing numbers. That's one thing for sure. Besides . . . some good things come from playing numbers. Look where Pope done bought him that restaurant off of numbers.

TROY I can't stand niggers like that. Man ain't had two dimes to rub together. He walking around with his shoes all run over bumming money for cigarettes. All right. Got lucky there and hit the numbers . . .

ROSE Troy, I know all about it.

TROY Had good sense, I'll say that for him. He ain't throwed his money away. I seen niggers hit the numbers and go through two thousand dollars in four days. Man bought him that restaurant down there . . . fixed it up real nice . . . and then didn't want nobody to come in it! A Negro go in there and can't get no kind of service. I seen a white fellow come in there and order a bowl of stew. Pope picked all the meat out the pot for him. Man ain't had nothing but a bowl of meat! Negro come behind him and ain't got nothing but the potatoes and carrots. Talking about what numbers do for people, you picked a wrong example. Ain't done nothing but make a worser fool out of him than he was before.

ROSE Troy, you ought to stop worrying about what happened at work yesterday.

TROY I ain't worried. Just told me to be down there at the Commissioner's office on Friday. Everybody think they gonna fire me. I ain't worried about them firing me. You ain't got to worry about that. (*Pause.*) Where's Cory? Cory in the house? (*Calls.*) Cory?

ROSE He gone out.

TROY Out, huh? He gone out 'cause he know I want him to help me with this fence. I know how he is. That boy scared of work.

GABRIEL *enters. He comes halfway down the alley and, hearing* **TROY**'*s voice, stops.*

TROY (*continues*): He ain't done a lick of work in his life.

ROSE He had to go to football practice. Coach wanted them to get in a little extra practice before the season start.

TROY I got his practice . . . running out of here before he get his chores done.

ROSE Troy, what is wrong with you this morning? Don't nothing set right with you. Go on back in there and go to bed . . . get up on the other side.

TROY Why something got to be wrong with me? I ain't said nothing wrong with me.

ROSE You got something to say about everything. First it's the numbers . . . then it's the way the man runs his restaurant . . . then you done got on Cory. What's it gonna be next? Take a look up there and see if the weather suits you . . . or is it gonna be how you gonna put up the fence with the clothes hanging in the yard.

TROY You hit the nail on the head then.

ROSE I know you like I know the back of my hand. Go on in there and get you some coffee . . . see if that straighten you up. 'Cause you ain't right this morning.

TROY *starts into the house and sees* **GABRIEL**. **GABRIEL** *starts singing.* **TROY**'*s brother, he is seven years younger than* **TROY**. *Injured in World War II, he has a metal plate in his head. He carries an old trumpet tied around his waist and believes with every fiber of his being that he is the Archangel Gabriel. He carries a chipped basket with an assortment of discarded fruits and vegetables he has picked up in the strip district and which he attempts to sell.*

GABRIEL (*singing*): Yes, ma am, I got plums
You ask me how I sell them
Oh ten cents apiece
Three for a quarter
Come and buy now
'Cause I'm here today
And tomorrow I'll be gone

GABRIEL *enters.*

Hey, Rose!

ROSE How you doing, Gabe?

GABRIEL There's Troy . . . Hey, Troy!

TROY Hey, Gabe.

Exit into kitchen.

ROSE (*to* **GABRIEL**): What you got there?

GABRIEL You know what I got, Rose. I got fruits and vegetables.

ROSE (*looking in basket*): Where's all these plums you talking about?

GABRIEL I ain't got no plums today, Rose. I was just singing that. Have some tomorrow. Put me in a big order for plums. Have enough plums tomorrow for St. Peter and everybody.

TROY *reenters from kitchen, crosses to steps.*

(*to* **ROSE**.) Troy's mad at me.

TROY I ain't mad at you. What I got to be mad at you about? You ain't done nothing to me.

GABRIEL I just moved over to Miss Pearl's to keep out from in your way. I ain't mean no harm by it.

TROY Who said anything about that? I ain't said anything about that.

GABRIEL You ain't mad at me, is you?

TROY Naw . . . I ain't mad at you, Gabe. If I was mad at you I'd tell you about it.

GABRIEL Got me two rooms. In the basement. Got my own door too. Wanna see my key? (*He holds up a key.*) That's my own key! Ain't nobody else got a key like that. That's my key! My two rooms!

TROY Well, that's good, Gabe. You got your own key . . . that's good.

ROSE You hungry, Gabe? I was just fixing to cook Troy his breakfast.

GABRIEL I'll take some biscuits. You got some biscuits? Did you know when I was in heaven . . . every morning me and St. Peter would sit down by the gate and eat some big fat biscuits? Oh, yeah! We had us a good time. We'd sit there and eat us them biscuits and then St. Peter would go off to sleep and tell me to wake him up when it's time to open the gates for the judgment.

ROSE Well, come on . . . I'll make up a batch of biscuits.

ROSE *exits into the house.*

GABRIEL Troy . . . St. Peter got your name in the book. I seen it. It say . . . Troy Maxson. I say . . . I know him! He got the same name like what I got. That's my brother!

TROY How many times you gonna tell me that, Gabe?

GABRIEL Ain't got my name in the book. Don't have to have my name. I done died and went to heaven. He got your name though. One morning St. Peter was looking at his book . . . marking it up for the judgment . . . and he let me see your name. Got it in there under M. Got Rose's name . . . I ain't seen it like I seen yours . . . but I know it's in there. He got a great big book. Got everybody's name what was ever been born. That's what he told me. But I seen your name. Seen it with my own eyes.

TROY Go on in the house there. Rose going to fix you something to eat.

GABRIEL Oh, I ain't hungry. I done had breakfast with Aunt Jemimah. She come by and cooked me up a whole mess of flapjacks. Remember how we used to eat them flapjacks?

TROY Go on in the house and get you something to eat now.

GABRIEL I got to sell my plums. I done sold some tomatoes. Got me two quarters. Wanna see? (*He shows* **TROY** *his quarters.*) I'm gonna save them and buy me a new horn so St. Peter can hear me when it's time to open the gates. (**GABRIEL** *stops suddenly. Listens.*) Hear that? That's the hellhounds. I got to chase them out of here. Go on get out of here! Get out!

GABRIEL *exits singing.*

Better get ready for the judgment
Better get ready for the judgment
My Lord is coming down

ROSE *enters from the house.*

TROY He's gone off somewhere.

GABRIEL (*offstage*): Better get ready for the
judgment
Better get ready for the judgment morning
Better get ready for the judgment
My God is coming down

ROSE He ain't eating right. Miss Pearl say she can't get him to eat nothing.

TROY What you want me to do about it, Rose? I done did everything I can for the man. I can't make him get well. Man got half his head blown away . . . what you expect?

ROSE Seem like something ought to be done to help him.

TROY Man don't bother nobody. He just mixed up from that metal plate he got in his head. Ain't no sense for him to go back into the hospital.

ROSE Least he be eating right. They can help him take care of himself.

TROY Don't nobody wanna be locked up, Rose. What you wanna lock him up for? Man go over there and fight the war . . . messin' around with them Japs, get half his head blown off . . . and they give him a lousy three thousand dollars. And I had to swoop down on that.

ROSE Is you fixing to go into that again?

TROY That's the only way I got a roof over my head . . . cause of that metal plate.

ROSE Ain't no sense you blaming yourself for nothing. Gabe wasn't in no condition to manage that money. You done what was right by him. Can't nobody say you ain't done what was right by him. Look how long you took care of him . . . till he wanted to have his own place and moved over there with Miss Pearl.

TROY That ain't what I'm saying, woman! I'm just stating the facts. If my brother didn't have that metal plate in his head . . . I wouldn't have a pot to piss in or a window to throw it out of. And I'm fifty-three years old. Now see if you can understand that!

TROY *gets up from the porch and starts to exit the yard.*

ROSE Where you going off to? You been running out of here every Saturday for weeks. I thought you was gonna work on this fence?

TROY I'm gonna walk down to Taylors'. Listen to the ball game. I'll be back in a bit. I'll work on it when I get back.

He exits the yard. The lights go to black.

Scene 3

The lights come up on the yard. It is four hours later. **ROSE** *is taking down the clothes from the line.* **CORY** *enters carrying his football equipment.*

ROSE Your daddy like to had a fit with you running out of here this morning without doing your chores.

CORY I told you I had to go to practice.

ROSE He say you were supposed to help him with this fence.

CORY He been saying that the last four or five Saturdays, and then he don't never do nothing, but go down to Taylors. Did you tell him about the recruiter?

ROSE Yeah, I told him.

CORY What he say?

ROSE He ain't said nothing too much. You get in there and get started on your chores before he gets back. Go on and scrub down them steps before he gets back here hollering and carrying on.

CORY I'm hungry. What you got to eat, Mama?

ROSE Go on and get started on your chores. I got some meat loaf in there. Go on and make you a sandwich . . . and don't leave no mess in there.

CORY *exits into the house.* **ROSE** *continues to take down the clothes.* **TROY** *enters the yard and sneaks up and grabs her from behind.*

Troy! Go on, now. You liked to scared me to death. What was the score of the game? Lucille had me on the phone and I couldn't keep up with it.

TROY What I care about the game? Come here, woman. (*He tries to kiss her.*)

ROSE I thought you went down Taylors' to listen to the game. Go on, Troy! You supposed to be putting up this fence.

TROY (*attempting to kiss her again*): I'll put it up when I finish with what is at hand.

ROSE Go on, Troy. I ain't studying you.

TROY (*chasing after her*): I'm studying you . . . fixing to do my homework!

ROSE Troy, you better leave me alone.

TROY Where's Cory? That boy brought his butt home yet?

ROSE He's in the house doing his chores.

TROY (*calling*): Cory! Get your butt out here, boy!

ROSE *exits into the house with the laundry.* **TROY** *goes over to the pile of wood, picks up a board, and starts sawing.* **CORY** *enters from the house.*

TROY You just now coming in here from leaving this morning?

CORY Yeah, I had to go to football practice.

TROY Yeah, what?

CORY Yessir.

TROY I ain't but two seconds off you noway. The garbage sitting in there overflowing . . . you ain't done none of your chores . . . and you come in here talking about "Yeah."

CORY I was just getting ready to do my chores now, Pop . . .

TROY Your first chore is to help me with this fence on Saturday. Everything else come after that. Now get that saw and cut them boards.

CORY *takes the saw and begins cutting the boards.* **TROY** *continues working. There is a long pause.*

CORY Hey, Pop . . . why don't you buy a TV?

TROY What I want with a TV? What I want one of them for?

CORY Everybody got one. Earl, Ba Bra . . . Jesse!

TROY I ain't asked you who had one. I say what I want with one?

CORY So you can watch it. They got lots of things on TV. Baseball games and everything. We could watch the World Series.

TROY Yeah . . . and how much this TV cost?

CORY I don't know. They got them on sale for around two hundred dollars.

TROY Two hundred dollars, huh?

CORY That ain't that much, Pop.

TROY Naw, it's just two hundred dollars. See that roof you got over your head at night? Let me tell you something about that roof. It's been over ten years since that roof was last tarred. See now . . . the snow come this winter and sit up there on that roof like it is . . . and it's gonna seep inside. It's just gonna be a little bit . . . ain't gonna hardly notice it. Then the next thing you know, it's gonna be leaking all over the house. Then the wood rot from all that water and you gonna need a whole new roof. Now, how much you think it cost to get that roof tarred?

CORY I don't know.

TROY Two hundred and sixty-four dollars . . . cash money. While you thinking about a TV, I got to be thinking about the roof . . . and whatever else go wrong here. Now if you had two hundred dollars, what would you do . . . fix the roof or buy a TV?

CORY I'd buy a TV. Then when the roof started to leak . . . when it needed fixing . . . I'd fix it.

TROY Where you gonna get the money from? You done spent it for a TV. You gonna sit up and watch the water run all over your brand new TV.

CORY Aw, Pop. You got money. I know you do.

TROY Where I got it at, huh?

CORY You got it in the bank.

TROY You wanna see my bankbook? You wanna see that seventy-three dollars and twenty-two cents I got sitting up in there.

CORY You ain't got to pay for it all at one time. You can put a down payment on it and carry it on home with you.

TROY Not me. I ain't gonna owe nobody nothing if I can help it. Miss a payment and they come and snatch it right out your house. Then what you got? Now, soon as I get two hundred dollars clear, then I'll buy a TV. Right now, as soon as I get two hundred and sixty-four dollars, I'm gonna have this roof tarred.

CORY Aw . . . Pop!

TROY You go on and get you two hundred dollars and buy one if ya want it. I got better things to do with my money.

CORY I can't get no two hundred dollars. I ain't never seen two hundred dollars.

TROY I'll tell you what . . . you get you a hundred dollars and I'll put the other hundred with it.

CORY All right, I'm gonna show you.

TROY You gonna show me how you can cut them boards right now.

CORY *begins to cut the boards. There is a long pause.*

CORY The Pirates won today. That makes five in a row.

TROY I ain't thinking about the Pirates. Got an all-white team. Got that boy . . . that Puerto Rican boy . . . Clemente. Don't even half-play him. That boy could be something if they give him a chance. Play him one day and sit him on the bench the next.

CORY He gets a lot of chances to play.

TROY I'm talking about playing regular. Playing every day so you can get your timing. That's what I'm talking about.

CORY They got some white guys on the team that don't play every day. You can't play everybody at the same time.

TROY If they got a white fellow sitting on the bench . . . you can bet your last dollar he can't play! The colored guy got to be twice as good before he get on the team. That's why I don't want you to get all tied up in them sports. Man on the team and what it get him? They got colored on the team and don't use them. Same as not having them. All them teams the same.

CORY The Braves got Hank Aaron and Wes Covington. Hank Aaron hit two home runs today. That makes forty-three.

TROY Hank Aaron ain't nobody. That what you supposed to do. That's how you supposed to play the game. Ain't nothing to it. It's just a matter of timing . . . getting the right follow-through. Hell, I can hit forty-three home runs right now!

CORY Not off no major-league pitching, you couldn't.

TROY We had better pitching in the Negro leagues. I hit seven home runs off of Satchel Paige. You can't get no better than that!

CORY Sandy Koufax. He's leading the league in strikeouts.

TROY I ain't thinking of no Sandy Koufax.

CORY You got Warren Spahn and Lew Burdette. I bet you couldn't hit no home runs off of Warren Spahn.

TROY I'm through with it now. You go on and cut them boards. (*Pause.*) Your mama tell me you done got recruited by a college football team? Is that right?

CORY Yeah. Coach Zellman say the recruiter gonna be coming by to talk to you. Get you to sign the permission papers.

TROY I thought you supposed to be working down there at the A&P. Ain't you suppose to be working down there after school?

CORY Mr. Stawicki say he gonna hold my job for me until after the football season. Say starting next week I can work weekends.

TROY I thought we had an understanding about this football stuff? You suppose to keep up with your chores and hold that job down at the A&P. Ain't been around here all day on a Saturday. Ain't none of your chores done . . . and now you telling me you done quit your job.

CORY I'm going to be working weekends.

TROY You damn right you are! And ain't no need for nobody coming around here to talk to me about signing nothing.

CORY Hey, Pop . . . you can't do that. He's coming all the way from North Carolina.

TROY I don't care where he coming from. The white man ain't gonna let you get nowhere with that football noway. You go on and get your book-learning so you can work yourself up in that A&P or learn how to fix cars or build houses or something, get you a trade. That way you have something can't nobody take away from you. You go on and learn how to put your hands to some good use. Besides hauling people's garbage.

CORY I get good grades, Pop. That's why the recruiter wants to talk with you. You got to keep up your grades to get recruited. This way I'll be going to college. I'll get a chance . . .

TROY First you gonna get your butt down there to the A&P and get your job back.

CORY Mr. Stawicki done already hired somebody else 'cause I told him I was playing football.

TROY You a bigger fool than I thought . . . to let somebody take away your job so you can play some football. Where you gonna get your money to take out your girlfriend and what-not? What kind of foolishness is that to let somebody take away your job?

CORY I'm still gonna be working weekends.

TROY Naw . . . naw. You getting your butt out of here and finding you another job.

CORY Come on, Pop! I got to practice. I can't work after school and play football too. The team needs me. That's what Coach Zellman say . . .

TROY I don't care what nobody else say. I'm the boss . . . you understand? I'm the boss around here. I do the only saying what counts.

CORY Come on, Pop!

TROY I asked you . . . did you understand?

CORY Yeah . . .

TROY What?!

CORY Yessir.

TROY You go on down there to that A&P and see if you can get your job back. If you can't do both . . . then you quit the football team. You've got to take the crookeds with the straights.

CORY Yessir. (*Pause.*) Can I ask you a question?

TROY What the hell you wanna ask me? Mr. Stawicki the one you got the questions for.

CORY How come you ain't never liked me?

TROY Liked you? Who the hell say I got to like you? What law is there say I got to like you? Wanna stand up in my face and ask a damn fool-ass question like that. Talking about liking somebody. Come here, boy, when I talk to you.

CORY *comes over to where* **TROY** *is working. He stands slouched over and* **TROY** *shoves him on his shoulder.*

Straighten up, goddammit! I asked you a question . . . what law is there say I got to like you?

CORY None.

TROY Well, all right then! Don't you eat every day? (*Pause.*) Answer me when I talk to you! Don't you eat every day?

CORY Yeah.

TROY Nigger, as long as you in my house, you put that sir on the end of it when you talk to me!

CORY Yes . . . sir.

TROY You eat every day.

CORY Yessir!

TROY Got a roof over your head.

CORY Yessir!

TROY Got clothes on your back.

CORY Yessir.

TROY Why you think that is?

CORY Cause of you.

TROY Ah, hell I know it's cause of me . . . but why do you think that is?

CORY (*hesitant*): Cause you like me.

TROY Like you? I go out of here every morning . . . bust my butt . . . putting up with them crackers every day . . . cause I like you? You are the biggest fool I ever saw. (*Pause.*) It's my job. It's my responsibility! You understand that? A man got to take care of his family. You live in my house . . . sleep you behind on my bedclothes . . . fill you belly up with my food . . . cause you my son. You my flesh and blood. Not cause I like you! Cause it's my duty to take care of you. I owe a responsibility to you! Let's get this straight right here . . . before it go along any further . . . I ain't got to like you. Mr. Rand don't give me my money come payday cause he likes me. He give me cause he owe me. I done give you everything I had to give you. I gave you your life! Me and your mama worked that out between us. And liking your black ass wasn't part of the bargain. Don't you try and go through life worrying about if somebody like you or not. You best be making sure they doing right by you. You understand what I'm saying, boy?

CORY Yessir.

TROY Then get the hell out of my face, and get on down to that A&P.

ROSE *has been standing behind the screen door for much of the scene. She enters as* **CORY** *exits.*

ROSE Why don't you let the boy go ahead and play football, Troy? Ain't no harm in that. He's just trying to be like you with the sports.

TROY I don't want him to be like me! I want him to move as far away from my life as he can get. You the only decent thing that ever happened to me. I wish him that. But I don't wish him a thing else from my life. I decided seventeen years ago that boy wasn't getting involved in no sports. Not after what they did to me in the sports.

ROSE Troy, why don't you admit you was too old to play in the major leagues? For once . . . why don't you admit that?

TROY What do you mean too old? Don't come telling me I was too old. I just wasn't the right color. Hell, I'm fifty-three years old and can do better than Selkirk's .269 right now!

ROSE How's was you gonna play ball when you were over forty? Sometimes I can't get no sense out of you.

TROY I got good sense, woman. I got sense enough not to let my boy get hurt over playing no sports. You been mothering that boy too much. Worried about if people like him.

ROSE Everything that boy do . . . he do for you. He wants you to say "Good job, son." That's all.

TROY Rose, I ain't got time for that. He's alive. He's healthy. He's got to make his own way. I made mine. Ain't nobody gonna hold his hand when he get out there in that world.

ROSE Times have changed from when you was young, Troy. People change. The world's changing around you and you can't even see it.

TROY (*slow, methodical*): Woman . . . I do the best I can do. I come in here every Friday. I carry a sack of potatoes and a bucket of lard. You all line up at the door with your hands out. I give you the lint from my pockets. I give you my sweat and my blood. I ain't got no tears. I done spent them. We go upstairs in that room at night . . . and I fall down on you and try to blast a hole into forever. I get up Monday morning . . . find my lunch on the table. I go out. Make my way. Find my strength to carry me through to the next Friday. (*Pause.*) That's all I got, Rose. That's all I got to give. I can't give nothing else.

TROY *exits into the house. The lights go down to black.*

Scene 4

It is Friday. Two weeks later. **CORY** *starts out of the house with his football equipment. The phone rings.*

CORY (*calling*): I got it! (*He answers the phone and stands in the screen door talking.*) Hello? Hey, Jesse. Naw . . . I was just getting ready to leave now.

ROSE (*calling*): Cory!

CORY I told you, man, them spikes is all tore up. You can use them if you want, but they ain't no good. Earl got some spikes.

ROSE (*calling*): Cory!

CORY (*calling to* **ROSE**): Mam? I'm talking to Jesse. (*Into phone.*) When she say that? (*Pause.*) Aw, you lying, man. I'm gonna tell her you said that.

ROSE (*calling*): Cory, don't you go nowhere!

CORY I got to go to the game, Ma! (*Into the phone.*) Yeah, hey, look, I'll talk to you later. Yeah, I'll meet you over Earl's house. Later. Bye, Ma.

CORY *exits the house and starts out the yard.*

ROSE Cory, where you going off to? You got that stuff all pulled out and thrown all over your room.

CORY (*in the yard*): I was looking for my spikes. Jesse wanted to borrow my spikes.

ROSE Get up there and get that cleaned up before your daddy get back in here.

CORY I got to go to the game! I'll clean it up *when I get back.*

CORY *exits.*

ROSE That's all he need to do is see that room all messed up.

ROSE *exits into the house.* **TROY** *and* **BONO** *enter the yard.* **TROY** *is dressed in clothes other than his work clothes.*

BONO He told him the same thing he told you. Take it to the union.

TROY Brownie ain't got that much sense. Man wasn't thinking about nothing. He wait until I confront them on it . . . then he wanna come crying seniority. (*Calls.*) Hey, Rose!

BONO I wish I could have seen Mr. Rand's face when he told you.

TROY He couldn't get it out of his mouth! Liked to bit his tongue! When they called me down there to the Commissioner's office . . . he thought they was gonna fire me. Like everybody else.

BONO I didn't think they was gonna fire you. I thought they was gonna put you on the warning paper.

TROY Hey, Rose! (*To* **BONO**.) Yeah, Mr. Rand like to bit his tongue.

TROY *breaks the seal on the bottle, takes a drink, and hands it to* **BONO**.

BONO I see you run right down to Taylors' and told that Alberta gal.

TROY (*calling*): Hey Rose! (*To* **BONO**.) I told everybody. Hey, Rose! I went down there to cash my check.

ROSE (*entering from the house*): Hush all that hollering, man! I know you out here. What they say down there at the Commissioner's office?

TROY You supposed to come when I call you, woman. Bono'll tell you that. (*To* **BONO**.) Don't Lucille come when you call her?

ROSE Man, hush your mouth. I ain't no dog . . . talk about "come when you call me."

TROY (*puts his arm around* **ROSE**): You hear this, Bono? I had me an old dog used to get uppity like that. You say, "C'mere, Blue!" . . . and he just lay there and look at you. End up getting a stick and chasing him away trying to make him come.

ROSE I ain't studying you and your dog. I remember you used to sing that old song.

TROY (*he sings*): Hear it ring! Hear it ring! I had a dog his name was Blue.

ROSE Don't nobody wanna hear you sing that old song.

TROY (*sings*): You know Blue was mighty true.

ROSE Used to have Cory running around here singing that song.

BONO Hell, I remember that song myself.

TROY (*sings*): You know Blue was a good old dog.
Blue treed a possum in a hollow log.
That was my daddy's song. My daddy made up that song.

ROSE I don't care who made it up. Don't nobody wanna hear you sing it.

TROY (*makes a song like calling a dog*): Come here, woman.

ROSE You come in here carrying on, I reckon they ain't fired you. What they say down there at the Commissioner's office?

TROY Look here, Rose . . . Mr. Rand called me into his office today when I got back from talking to them people down there . . . it come from up top . . . he called me in and told me they was making me a driver.

ROSE Troy, you kidding!

TROY No I ain't. Ask Bono.

ROSE Well, that's great, Troy. Now you don't have to hassle them people no more.

LYONS *enters from the street.*

TROY Aw hell, I wasn't looking to see you today. I thought you was in jail. Got it all over the front page of the *Courier* about them raiding Sefus's place . . . where you be hanging out with all them thugs.

LYONS Hey, Pop . . . that ain't got nothing to do with me. I don't go down there gambling. I go down there to sit in with the band. I ain't got nothing to do with the gambling part. They got some good music down there.

TROY They got some rogues . . . is what they got.

LYONS How you been, Mr. Bono? Hi, Rose.

BONO I see where you playing down at the Crawford Grill tonight.

ROSE How come you ain't brought Bonnie like I told you? You should have brought Bonnie with you, she ain't been over in a month of Sundays.

LYONS I was just in the neighborhood . . . thought I'd stop by.

TROY Here he come . . .

BONO Your daddy got a promotion on the rubbish. He's gonna be the first colored driver. Ain't got to do nothing but sit up there and read the paper like them white fellows.

LYONS Hey, Pop . . . if you knew how to read you'd be all right.

BONO Naw . . . naw . . . you mean if the nigger knew how to *drive* he'd be all right. Been fighting with them people about driving and ain't even got a license. Mr. Rand know you ain't got no driver's license?

TROY Driving ain't nothing. All you do is point the truck where you want it to go. Driving ain't nothing.

BONO Do Mr. Rand know you ain't got no driver's license? That's what I'm talking about. I ain't asked if driving was easy. I asked if Mr. Rand know you ain't got no driver's license.

TROY He ain't got to know. The man ain't got to know my business. Time he find out, I have two or three driver's licenses.

LYONS (*going into his pocket*): Say, look here, Pop . . .

TROY I knew it was coming. Didn't I tell you, Bono? I know what kind of "Look here, Pop" that was. The nigger fixing to ask me for some money. It's Friday night. It's my payday. All them rogues down there on the avenue . . . the ones that ain't in jail . . . and Lyons is hopping in his shoes to get down there with them.

LYONS See, Pop . . . if you give somebody else a chance to talk sometimes, you'd see that I was fixing to pay you back your ten dollars like I told you. Here . . . I told you I'd pay you when Bonnie got paid.

TROY Naw . . . you go ahead and keep that ten dollars. Put it in the bank. The next time you feel like you wanna come by here and ask me for something . . . you go on down there and get that.

LYONS Here's your ten dollars, Pop. I told you I don't want you to give me nothing. I just wanted to borrow ten dollars.

TROY Naw . . . you go on and keep that for the next time you want to ask me.

LYONS Come on, Pop . . . here go your ten dollars.

ROSE Why don't you go on and let the boy pay you back, Troy?

LYONS Here you go, Rose. If you don't take it I'm gonna have to hear about it for the next six months. (*He hands her the money.*)

ROSE You can hand yours over here too, Troy.

TROY You see this, Bono. You see how they do me.

BONO Yeah, Lucille do me the same way.

GABRIEL *is heard singing offstage. He enters.*

GABRIEL Better get ready for the Judgment! Better get ready for . . . Hey! . . . Hey! . . . There's Troy's boy!

LYONS How are you doing, Uncle Gabe?

GABRIEL Lyons . . . The King of the Jungle! Rose . . . hey, Rose. Got a flower for you. (*He takes a rose from his pocket.*) Picked it myself. That's the same rose like you is!

ROSE That's right nice of you, Gabe.

LYONS What you been doing, Uncle Gabe?

GABRIEL Oh, I been chasing hellhounds and waiting on the time to tell St. Peter to open the gates.

LYONS You been chasing hellhounds, huh? Well . . . you doing the right thing, Uncle Gabe. Somebody got to chase them.

GABRIEL Oh, yeah . . . I know it. The devil's strong. The devil ain't no pushover. Hellhounds snipping at everybody's heels. But I got my trumpet waiting on the Judgment time.

LYONS Waiting on the Battle of Armageddon, huh?

GABRIEL Ain't gonna be too much of a battle when God get to waving that Judgment sword. But the people's gonna have a hell of a time trying to get into heaven if them gates ain't open.

LYONS (*putting his arm around* **GABRIEL**): You hear this, Pop. Uncle Gabe, you all right!

GABRIEL (*laughing with* **LYONS**): Lyons! King of the Jungle.

ROSE You gonna stay for supper, Gabe? Want me to fix you a plate?

GABRIEL I'll take a sandwich, Rose. Don't want no plate. Just wanna eat with my hands. I'll take a sandwich.

ROSE How about you, Lyons? You staying? Got some short ribs cooking.

LYONS Naw, I won't eat nothing till after we finished playing. (*Pause.*) You ought to come down and listen to me play Pop.

TROY I don't like that Chinese music. All that noise.

ROSE Go on in the house and wash up, Gabe . . . I'll fix you a sandwich.

GABRIEL (*to* **LYONS**, *as he exits*): Troy's mad at me.

LYONS What you mad at Uncle Gabe for, Pop?

ROSE He thinks Troy's mad at him cause he moved over to Miss Pearl's.

TROY I ain't mad at the man. He can live where he want to live at.

LYONS What he move over there for? Miss Pearl don't like nobody.

ROSE She don't mind him none. She treats him real nice. She just don't allow all that singing.

TROY She don't mind that rent he be paying . . . that's what she don't mind.

ROSE Troy, I ain't going through that with you no more. He's over there cause he want to have his own place. He can come and go as he please.

TROY Hell, he could come and go as he please here. I wasn't stopping him. I ain't put no rules on him.

ROSE It ain't the same thing, Troy. And you know it.

GABRIEL *comes to the door.*

Now, that's the last I wanna hear about that. I don't wanna hear nothing else about Gabe and Miss Pearl. And next week . . .

GABRIEL I'm ready for my sandwich, Rose.

ROSE And next week . . . when that recruiter come from that school . . . I want you to sign that paper and go on and let Cory play football. Then that'll be the last I have to hear about that.

TROY (*to* **ROSE** *as she exits into the house*): I ain't thinking about Cory nothing.

LYONS What . . . Cory got recruited? What school he going to?

TROY That boy walking around here smelling his piss . . . thinking he's grown. Thinking he's gonna do what he want, irrespective of what I say. Look here, Bono . . . I left the Commissioner's office and went down to the A&P . . . that boy ain't working down there. He lying to me. Telling me he got his job back . . . telling me he working weekends . . . telling me he working after school . . . Mr. Stawicki tell me he ain't working down there at all!

LYONS Cory just growing up. He's just busting at the seams trying to fill out your shoes.

TROY I don't care what he's doing. When he get to the point where he wanna disobey me . . . then it's time for him to move on. Bono'll tell you that. I bet he ain't never disobeyed his daddy without paying the consequences.

BONO I ain't never had a chance. My daddy came on through . . . but I ain't never knew him to see him . . . or what he had on his mind or where he went. Just moving on through. Searching out the New Land. That's what the old folks used to call it. See a fellow moving around from place to place . . . woman to woman . . . called it searching out the New Land. I can't say if he ever found it. I come along, didn't want no kids. Didn't know if I was gonna be in one place long enough to fix on them right as their daddy. I figured I was going searching too. As it turned out I been hooked up with Lucille near about as long as your daddy been with Rose. Going on sixteen years.

TROY Sometimes I wish I hadn't known my daddy. He ain't cared nothing about no kids. A kid to him wasn't nothing. All he wanted was for you to learn how to walk so he could start you to working. When it come time for eating . . . he ate first. If there was anything left over, that's what you got. Man would sit down and eat two chickens and give you the wing.

LYONS You ought to stop that, Pop. Everybody feed their kids. No matter how hard times is . . . everybody care about their kids. Make sure they have something to eat.

TROY The only thing my daddy cared about was getting them bales of cotton in to Mr. Lubin. That's the only thing that mattered to him. Sometimes I used to wonder why he was living. Wonder why the devil hadn't come and got him. "Get them bales of cotton in to Mr. Lubin" and find out he owe him money . . .

LYONS He should have just went on and left when he saw he couldn't get nowhere. That's what I would have done.

TROY How he gonna leave with eleven kids? And where he gonna go? He ain't knew how to do nothing but farm. No, he was trapped and I think he knew it. But I'll say this for him . . . he felt a responsibility toward us. Maybe he ain't treated us the way I felt he should have . . . but without that responsibility he could have walked off and left us . . . made his own way.

BONO A lot of them did. Back in those days what you talking about . . . they walk out their front door and just take on down one road or another and keep on walking.

LYONS There you go! That's what I'm talking about.

BONO Just keep on walking till you come to something else. Ain't you never heard of nobody having the walking blues? Well, that's what you call it when you just take off like that.

TROY My daddy ain't had them walking blues! What you talking about? He stayed right there with his family. But he was just as evil as he could be. My mama couldn't stand him. Couldn't stand that evilness. She run off when I was about eight. She sneaked off one night after he had gone to sleep. Told me she was coming back for me. I ain't never seen her no more. All his women run off and left him. He wasn't good for nobody.

When my turn come to head out, I was fourteen and got to sniffing around Joe Canewell's daughter. Had us an old mule we called Greyboy. My daddy sent me out to do some plowing and I tied up Greyboy and went to fooling around with Joe Canewell's daughter. We done found us a nice little spot, got real cozy with each other. She about thirteen and we done figured we was grown anyway . . . so we down there enjoying ourselves . . . ain't thinking about nothing. We didn't know Greyboy had got loose and wandered back to the house and my daddy was looking for me. We down there by the creek enjoying ourselves when my daddy come up on us. Surprised us. He had them leather straps off the mule and commenced to whupping me like there was no tomorrow. I jumped up, mad and embarrassed. I was scared of my daddy. When he commenced to whupping on me . . . quite naturally I run to get out of the way. (*Pause.*) Now I thought he was mad cause I ain't done my work. But I see where he was chasing me off so he could have the gal for himself. When I see what the matter of it was, I lost all fear of my daddy. Right there is where I become a man . . . at fourteen years of age. (*Pause.*) Now it was my turn to run him off. I picked up them same reins that he had used on me. I picked up them reins and commenced to whupping on him. The gal jumped up and run off . . . and when my daddy turned to face me, I could see why the devil had never come to get him . . . cause he was the devil himself. I don't know what happened. When I woke up, I was laying right there by the creek, and Blue . . . this old dog we had . . . was licking my face. I thought I was blind. I couldn't see nothing. Both my eyes were swollen shut. I laid there and cried. I didn't know what I was gonna do. The only thing I knew was the time had come for me to leave my daddy's house. And right there the world suddenly got big. And it was a long time before I could cut it down to where I could handle it.

Part of that cutting down was when I got to the place where I could feel him kicking in

This painting by Jacob Lawrence is from his Migration Series, which depicts the migration of African Americans from the rural south to northern urban centers over the course of several decades, beginning around 1915. **How might this work offer insight into the experience that shaped Troy's father?**

my blood and knew that the only thing that separated us was the matter of a few years.

GABRIEL *enters from the house with a sandwich.*

LYONS What you got there, Uncle Gabe?

GABRIEL Got me a ham sandwich. Rose gave me a ham sandwich.

TROY I don't know what happened to him. I done lost touch with everybody except Gabriel. But I hope he's dead. I hope he found some peace.

LYONS That's a heavy story, Pop. I didn't know you left home when you was fourteen.

TROY And didn't know nothing. The only part of the world I knew was the forty-two acres of Mr. Lubin's land. That's all I knew about life.

LYONS Fourteen's kinda young to be out on your own. (*Phone rings.*) I don't even think I was ready to be out on my own at fourteen. I don't know what I would have done.

TROY I got up from the creek and walked on down to Mobile. I was through with farming. Figured I could do better in the city. So I walked the two hundred miles to Mobile.

LYONS Wait a minute . . . you ain't walked no two hundred miles, Pop. Ain't nobody gonna walk no two hundred miles. You talking about some walking there.

BONO That's the only way you got anywhere back in them days.

LYONS Shhh. Damn if I wouldn't have hitched a ride with somebody!

TROY Who you gonna hitch it with? They ain't had no cars and things like they got now. We talking about 1918.

ROSE (*entering*): What you all out here getting into?

TROY (*to* **ROSE**): I'm telling Lyons how good he got it. He don't know nothing about this I'm talking.

ROSE Lyons, that was Bonnie on the phone. She say you supposed to pick her up.

LYONS Yeah, okay, Rose.

TROY I walked on down to Mobile and hitched up with some of them fellows that was heading this way. Got up here and found out . . . not only couldn't you get a job . . . you couldn't find no place to live. I thought I was in freedom. Shhh. Colored folks living down there on the riverbanks in whatever kind of shelter they could find for themselves. Right down there under the Brady Street Bridge. Living in shacks made of sticks and tarpaper. Messed around there and went from bad to worse. Started stealing. First it was food. Then I figured, hell, if I steal money I can buy me some food. Buy me some shoes too! One thing led to another. Met your mama. I was young and anxious to be a man. Met your mama and had you. What I do that for? Now I got to worry about feeding you and her. Got to steal three times as much. Went out one day looking for somebody to rob . . . that's what I was, a robber. I'll tell you the truth. I'm ashamed of it today. But it's the truth. Went to rob this fellow . . . pulled out my knife . . . and he pulled out a gun. Shot me in the chest. I felt just like somebody had taken a hot branding iron and laid it on me. When he shot me I jumped at him with my knife. They told me I killed him and they put me in the penitentiary and locked me up for fifteen years. That's where I met Bono. That's where I learned how to play baseball. Got out that place and your mama had taken you and went on to make life without me. Fifteen years was a long time for her to wait. But that fifteen years cured me of that robbing stuff. Rose'll tell you. She asked me when I met her if I had gotten all that foolishness out of my system. And I told her, "Baby, it's you and baseball all what count with me." You hear me, Bono? I meant it too. She say, "Which one comes first?" I told her, "Baby, ain't no doubt it's baseball . . . but you stick and get old with me and we'll both outlive this baseball." Am I right, Rose? And it's true.

ROSE Man, hush your mouth. You ain't said no such thing. Talking about, "Baby, you know you'll always be number one with me." That's what you was talking.

TROY You hear that, Bono. That's why I love her.

BONO Rose'll keep you straight. You get off the track, she'll straighten you up.

ROSE Lyons, you better get on up and get Bonnie. She waiting on you.

LYONS (*gets up to go*): Hey, Pop, why don't you come on down to the Grill and hear me play?

TROY I ain't going down there. I'm too old to be sitting around in them clubs.

BONO You got to be good to play down at the Grill.

LYONS Come on, Pop . . .

TROY I got to get up in the morning.

LYONS You ain't got to stay long.

TROY Naw, I'm gonna get my supper and go on to bed.

LYONS Well, I got to go. I'll see you again.

TROY Don't you come around my house on my payday.

ROSE Pick up the phone and let somebody know you coming. And bring Bonnie with you. You know I'm always glad to see her.

LYONS Yeah, I'll do that, Rose. You take care now. See you, Pop. See you, Mr. Bono. See you, Uncle Gabe.

GABRIEL Lyons! King of the Jungle!

LYONS *exits.*

TROY Is supper ready, woman? Me and you got some business to take care of. I'm gonna tear it up too.

ROSE Troy, I done told you now!

TROY (*puts his arm around* **BONO**): Aw hell, woman . . . this is Bono. Bono like family. I done known this nigger since . . . how long I done know you?

BONO It's been a long time.

TROY I done know this nigger since Skippy was a pup. Me and him done been through some times.

BONO You sure right about that.

TROY Hell, I done know him longer than I known you. And we still standing shoulder to shoulder. Hey, look here, Bono . . . a man can't ask for no more than that. (*Drinks to him.*) I love you, nigger.

BONO Hell, I love you too . . . I got to get home see my woman. You got yours in hand. I got to go get mine.

BONO *starts to exit as* **CORY** *enters the yard, dressed in his football uniform. He gives* **TROY** *a hard, uncompromising look.*

CORY What you do that for, Pop?

He throws his helmet down in the direction of **TROY**.

ROSE What's the matter? Cory . . . what's the matter?

CORY Papa done went up to the school and told Coach Zellman I can't play football no more. Wouldn't even let me play the game. Told him to tell the recruiter not to come.

ROSE Troy . . .

TROY What you Troying me for. Yeah, I did it. And the boy know why I did it.

CORY Why you wanna do that to me? That was the one chance I had.

ROSE Ain't nothing wrong with Cory playing football, Troy.

TROY The boy lied to me. I told the nigger if he wanna play football . . . to keep up his chores and hold down that job at the A&P. That was the conditions. Stopped down there to see Mr. Stawicki . . .

CORY I can't work after school during the football season, Pop! I tried to tell you that Mr. Stawicki's holding my job for me. You don't never want to listen to nobody. And then you wanna go and do this to me!

TROY I ain't done nothing to you. You done it to yourself.

CORY Just cause you didn't have a chance! You just scared I'm gonna be better than you, that's all.

TROY Come here.

ROSE Troy . . .

CORY *reluctantly crosses over to* **TROY**.

TROY All right! See. You done made a mistake.

CORY I didn't even do nothing!

TROY I'm gonna tell you what your mistake was. See . . . you swung at the ball and didn't hit it. That's strike one. See, you in the batter's box now. You swung and you missed. That's strike one. Don't you strike out!

Lights fade to black.

ACT II

Scene 1

The following morning. **CORY** *is at the tree hitting the ball with the bat. He tries to mimic* **TROY**, *but his swing is awkward, less sure.* **ROSE** *enters from the house.*

ROSE Cory, I want you to help me with this cupboard.

CORY I ain't quitting the team. I don't care what Poppa say.

ROSE I'll talk to him when he gets back. He had to go see about your Uncle Gabe. The police done arrested him. Say he was disturbing the peace. He'll be back directly. Come on in here and help me clean out the top of this cupboard.

CORY *exits into the house.* **ROSE** *sees* **TROY** *and* **BONO** *coming down the alley.*

Troy . . . what they say down there?

TROY Ain't said nothing. I give them fifty dollars and they let him go. I'll talk to you about it. Where's Cory?

ROSE He's in there helping me clean out these cupboards.

TROY Tell him to get his butt out here.

TROY *and* **BONO** *go over to the pile of wood.* **BONO** *picks up the saw and begins sawing.*

TROY (*to* **BONO**): All they want is the money. That makes six or seven times I done went down there and got him. See me coming they stick out their hands.

BONO Yeah. I know what you mean. That's all they care about . . . that money. They don't care about what's right. (*Pause.*) Nigger, why you got to go and get some hard wood? You ain't doing nothing but building a little old fence. Get you some soft pine wood. That's all you need.

TROY I know what I'm doing. This is outside wood. You put pine wood inside the house. Pine wood is inside wood. This here is outside wood. Now you tell me where the fence is gonna be?

BONO You don't need this wood. You can put it up with pine wood and it'll stand as long as you gonna be here looking at it.

TROY How you know how long I'm gonna be here, nigger? Hell, I might just live forever. Live longer than old man Horsely.

BONO That's what Magee used to say.

TROY Magee's a damn fool. Now you tell me who you ever heard of gonna pull their own teeth with a pair of rusty pliers.

BONO The old folks . . . my granddaddy used to pull his teeth with pliers. They ain't had no dentists for the colored folks back then.

TROY Get clean pliers! You understand? Clean pliers! Sterilize them! Besides we ain't living back then. All Magee had to do was walk over to Doc Goldblum's.

BONO I see where you and that Tallahassee gal . . . that Alberta . . . I see where you all done got tight.

TROY What you mean "got tight"?

BONO I see where you be laughing and joking with her all the time.

TROY I laughs and jokes with all of them, Bono. You know me.

BONO That ain't the kind of laughing and joking I'm talking about.

CORY *enters from the house.*

CORY How you doing, Mr. Bono?

TROY Cory? Get that saw from Bono and cut some wood. He talking about the wood's too hard to cut. Stand back there, Jim, and let that young boy show you how it's done.

BONO He's sure welcome to it.

CORY *takes the saw and begins to cut the wood.*

Whew-e-e! Look at that. Big old strong boy. Look like Joe Louis. Hell, must be getting old the way I'm watching that boy whip through that wood.

CORY I don't see why Mama want a fence around the yard noways.

TROY Damn if I know either. What the hell she keeping out with it? She ain't got nothing nobody want.

BONO Some people build fences to keep people out . . . and other people build fences to keep people in. Rose wants to hold on to you all. She loves you.

TROY Hell, nigger, I don't need nobody to tell me my wife loves me. Cory . . . go on in the house and see if you can find that other saw.

CORY Where's it at?

TROY I said find it! Look for it till you find it!

CORY *exits into the house.*

What's that supposed to mean? Wanna keep us in?

BONO Troy . . . I done known you seem like damn near my whole life. You and Rose both. I done know both of you all for a long time. I remember when you met Rose. When you was hitting them baseball out the park. A lot of them old gals was after you then. You had the pick of the litter. When you picked Rose, I was happy for you. That was the first time I knew you had any sense. I said . . . My man Troy knows what he's doing . . . I'm gonna follow this nigger . . . he might take me somewhere. I been following you too. I done learned a whole heap of things about life watching you. I done learned how to tell where the shit lies. How to tell it from the alfalfa. You done learned me a lot of things. You showed me how to not make the same mistakes . . . to take life as it comes along and keep putting one foot in front of the other. (*Pause.*) Rose a good woman, Troy.

TROY Hell, nigger, I know she a good woman. I been married to her for eighteen years. What you got on your mind, Bono?

BONO I just say she a good woman. Just like I say anything. I ain't got to have nothing on my mind.

TROY You just gonna say she a good woman and leave it hanging out there like that? Why you telling me she a good woman?

BONO She loves you, Troy. Rose loves you.

TROY You saying I don't measure up. That's what you trying to say. I don't measure up cause I'm seeing this other gal. I know what you trying to say.

BONO I know what Rose means to you, Troy.

I'm just trying to say I don't want to see you mess up.

TROY Yeah, I appreciate that, Bono. If you was messing around on Lucille I'd be telling you the same thing.

BONO Well, that's all I got to say. I just say that because I love you both.

TROY Hell, you know me . . . I wasn't out there looking for nothing. You can't find a better woman than Rose. I know that. But seems like this woman just stuck onto me where I can't shake her loose. I done wrestled with it, tried to throw her off me . . . but she just stuck on tighter. Now she's stuck on for good.

BONO You's in control . . . that's what you tell me all the time. You responsible for what you do.

TROY I ain't ducking the responsibility of it. As long as it sets right in my heart . . . then I'm okay. Cause that's all I listen to. It'll tell me right from wrong every time. And I ain't talking about doing Rose no bad turn. I love Rose. She done carried me a long ways and I love and respect her for that.

BONO I know you do. That's why I don't want to see you hurt her. But what you gonna do when she find out? What you got then? If you try and juggle both of them . . . sooner or later you gonna drop one of them. That's common sense.

TROY Yeah, I hear what you saying, Bono. I been trying to figure a way to work it out.

BONO Work it out right, Troy. I don't want to be getting all up between you and Rose's business . . . but work it so it come out right.

TROY Ah hell, I get all up between you and Lucille's business. When you gonna get that woman that refrigerator she been wanting? Don't tell me you ain't got no money now. I know who your banker is. Mellon don't need that money bad as Lucille want that refrigerator. I'll tell you that.

BONO Tell you what I'll do . . . when you finish building this fence for Rose . . . I'll buy Lucille that refrigerator.

TROY You done stuck your foot in your mouth now!

TROY *grabs up a board and begins to saw.* **BONO** *starts to walk out the yard.*

Hey, nigger . . . where you going?

BONO I'm going home. I know you don't expect me to help you now. I'm protecting my money. I wanna see you put that fence up by yourself. That's what I want to see. You'll be here another six months without me.

TROY Nigger, you ain't right.

BONO When it comes to my money . . . I'm right as fireworks on the Fourth of July.

TROY All right, we gonna see now. You better get out your bankbook.

BONO *exits, and* **TROY** *continues to work.* **ROSE** *enters from the house.*

ROSE What they say down there? What's happening with Gabe?

TROY I went down there and got him out. Cost me fifty dollars. Say he was disturbing the peace. Judge set up a hearing for him in three weeks. Say to show cause why he shouldn't be recommitted.

ROSE What was he doing that cause them to arrest him?

TROY Some kids was teasing him and he run them off home. Say he was howling and carrying on. Some folks seen him and called the police. That's all it was.

ROSE Well, what's you say? What'd you tell the judge?

TROY Told him I'd look after him. It didn't make no sense to recommit the man. He stuck out his big greasy palm and told me to give him fifty dollars and take him on home.

ROSE Where's he at now? Where'd he go off to?

TROY He's gone about his business. He don't need nobody to hold his hand.

ROSE Well, I don't know. Seem like that would be the best place for him if they did put him into the hospital. I know what you're gonna say. But that's what I think would be best.

TROY The man done had his life ruined

fighting for what? And they wanna take and lock him up. Let him be free. He don't bother nobody.

ROSE Well, everybody got their own way of looking at it I guess. Come on and get your lunch. I got a bowl of lima beans and some cornbread in the oven. Come and get something to eat. Ain't no sense you fretting over Gabe.

ROSE *turns to go into the house.*

TROY Rose . . . got something to tell you.

ROSE Well, come on . . . wait till I get this food on the table.

TROY Rose!

She stops and turns around.

I don't know how to say this. (*Pause.*) I can't explain it none. It just sort of grows on you till it gets out of hand. It starts out like a little bush . . . and the next thing you know it's a whole forest.

ROSE Troy . . . what is you talking about?

TROY I'm talking, woman, let me talk. I'm trying to find a way to tell you . . . I'm gonna be a daddy. I'm gonna be somebody's daddy.

ROSE Troy . . . you're not telling me this? You're gonna be . . . what?

TROY Rose . . . now . . . see . . .

ROSE You telling me you gonna be somebody's daddy? You telling your *wife* this?

GABRIEL *enters from the street. He carries a rose in his hand.*

GABRIEL Hey, Troy! Hey, Rose!

ROSE I have to wait eighteen years to hear something like this.

GABRIEL Hey, Rose . . . I got a flower for you. (*He hands it to her.*) That's a rose. Same rose like you is.

ROSE Thanks, Gabe.

GABRIEL Troy, you ain't mad at me is you? Them bad mens come and put me away. You ain't mad at me is you?

TROY Naw, Gabe, I ain't mad at you.

ROSE Eighteen years and you wanna come with this.

GABRIEL (*takes a quarter out of his pocket*): See what I got? Got a brand new quarter.

TROY Rose . . . it's just . . .

ROSE Ain't nothing you can say, Troy. Ain't no way of explaining that.

GABRIEL Fellow that give me this quarter had a whole mess of them. I'm gonna keep this quarter till it stop shining.

ROSE Gabe, go on in the house there. I got some watermelon in the Frigidaire. Go on and get you a piece.

GABRIEL Say, Rose . . . you know I was chasing hellhounds and them bad mens come and get me and take me away. Troy helped me. He come down there and told them they better let me go before he beat them up. Yeah, he did!

ROSE You go on and get you a piece of watermelon, Gabe. Them bad mens is gone now.

GABRIEL Okay, Rose . . . gonna get me some watermelon. The kind with the stripes on it.

GABRIEL *exits into the house.*

ROSE Why, Troy? Why? After all these years to come dragging this in to me now. It don't make no sense at your age. I could have expected this ten or fifteen years ago, but not now.

TROY Age ain't got nothing to do with it, Rose.

ROSE I done tried to be everything a wife should be. Everything a wife could be. Been married eighteen years and I got to live to see the day you tell me you been seeing another woman and done fathered a child by her. And you know I ain't never wanted no half nothing in my family. My whole family is half. Everybody got different fathers and mothers . . . my two sisters and my brother. Can't hardly tell who's who. Can't never sit down and talk about Papa and Mama. It's your papa and your mama and my papa and my mama . . .

TROY Rose . . . stop it now.

ROSE I ain't never wanted that for none of my children. And now you wanna drag your behind in here and tell me something like this.

TROY You ought to know. It's time for you to know.

ROSE Well, I don't want to know, goddamn it!

TROY I can't just make it go away. It's done now. I can't wish the circumstance of the thing away.

ROSE And you don't want to either. Maybe you want to wish me and my boy away. Maybe that's what you want? Well, you can't wish us away. I've got eighteen years of my life invested in you. You ought to have stayed upstairs in my bed where you belong.

TROY Rose . . . now listen to me . . . we can get a handle on this thing. We can talk this out . . . come to an understanding.

ROSE All of a sudden it's "we." Where was "we" at when you was down there rolling around with some godforsaken woman? "We" should have come to an understanding before you started making a damn fool of yourself. You're a day late and a dollar short when it comes to an understanding with me.

TROY It's just . . . She gives me a different idea . . . a different understanding about myself. I can step out of this house and get away from the pressures and problems . . . be a different man. I ain't got to wonder how I'm gonna pay the bills or get the roof fixed. I can just be a part of myself that I ain't never been.

ROSE What I want to know . . . is do you plan to continue seeing her. That's all you can say to me.

TROY I can sit up in her house and laugh. Do you understand what I'm saying. I can laugh out loud . . . and it feels good. It reaches all the way down to the bottom of my shoes. (*Pause.*) Rose, I can't give that up.

ROSE Maybe you ought to go on and stay down there with her . . . if she's a better woman than me.

TROY It ain't about nobody being a better woman or nothing. Rose, you ain't the blame. A man couldn't ask for no woman to be a better wife than you've been. I'm responsible for it. I done locked myself into a pattern trying to take care of you all that I forgot about myself.

ROSE What the hell was I there for? That was my job, not somebody else's.

TROY Rose, I done tried all my life to live decent . . . to live a clean . . . hard . . . useful life. I tried to be a good husband to you. In every way I knew how. Maybe I come into the world backwards, I don't know. But . . . you born with two strikes on you before you come to the plate. You got to guard it closely . . . always looking for the curve ball on the inside corner. You can't afford to let none get past you. You can't afford a call strike. If you going down . . . you going down swinging. Everything lined up against you. What you gonna do. I fooled them, Rose. I bunted. When I found you and Cory and a halfway decent job . . . I was safe. Couldn't nothing touch me. I wasn't gonna strike out no more. I wasn't going back to the penitentiary. I wasn't gonna lay in the streets with a bottle of wine. I was safe. I had me a family. A job. I wasn't gonna get that last strike. I was on first looking for one of them boys to knock me in. To get me home.

ROSE You should have stayed in my bed, Troy.

TROY Then when I saw that gal . . . she firmed up my backbone. And I got to thinking that if I tried . . . I just might be able to steal second. Do you understand after eighteen years I wanted to steal second.

ROSE You should have held me tight. You should have grabbed me and held on.

TROY I stood on first base for eighteen years and I thought . . . well, goddamn it . . . go on for it!

ROSE We're not talking about baseball! We're talking about you going off to lay in bed with another woman . . . and then bring it home to me. That's what we're talking about. We ain't talking about no baseball.

TROY Rose, you're not listening to me. I'm trying the best I can to explain it to you. It's not easy for me to admit that I been standing in the same place for eighteen years.

ROSE I been standing with you! I been right here with you, Troy. I got a life too. I gave eighteen years of my life to stand in the same spot with you. Don't you think I ever wanted other things? Don't you think I had dreams and hopes? What about my life? What about me. Don't you think it ever crossed my mind to want to know other men? That I wanted to lay up somewhere and forget about my responsibilities? That I wanted someone to make me laugh so I could feel good? You not the only one who's got wants and needs. But I held on to you, Troy. I took all my feelings, my wants and needs, my dreams . . . and I buried them inside you. I planted a seed and watched and prayed over it. I planted myself inside you and waited to bloom. And it didn't take me no eighteen years to find out the soil was hard and rocky and it wasn't never gonna bloom.

But I held on to you, Troy. I held you tighter. You was my husband. I owed you everything I had. Every part of me I could find to give you. And upstairs in that room . . . with the darkness falling in on me . . . I gave everything I had to try and erase the doubt that you wasn't the finest man in the world. And wherever you was going . . . I wanted to be there with you. Cause you was my husband. Cause that's the only way I was gonna survive as your wife. You always talking about what you give . . . and what you don't have to give. But you take too. You take . . . and don't even know nobody's giving!

ROSE *turns to exit into the house;* **TROY** *grabs her arm.*

TROY You say I take and don't give!

ROSE Troy! You're hurting me!

TROY You say I take and don't give!

ROSE Troy . . . you're hurting my arm! Let go!

TROY I done give you everything I got. Don't you tell that lie on me.

ROSE Troy!

TROY Don't you tell that lie on me!

CORY *enters from the house.*

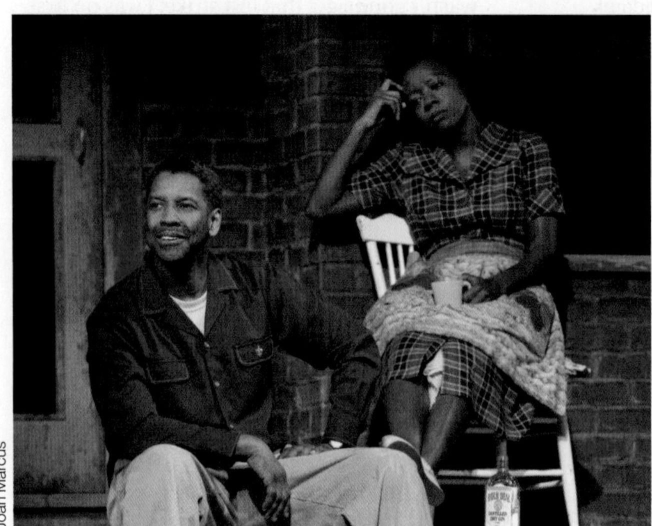

Joan Marcus

This photograph is from a 2010 stage production of *Fences* starring Denzel Washington as Troy and Viola Davis as Rose. **In what ways does this photograph from a stage production of *Fences* capture the relationship between Troy and Rose?**

CORY Mama!

ROSE Troy. You're hurting me.

TROY Don't you tell me about no taking and giving.

CORY *comes up behind* **TROY** *and grabs him.* **TROY**, *surprised, is thrown off balance just as* **CORY** *throws a glancing blow that catches him on the chest and knocks him down.* **TROY** *is stunned, as is* **CORY**.

ROSE Troy. Troy. No!

TROY *gets to his feet and starts at* **CORY**.

Troy . . . no. Please! Troy!

ROSE *pulls on* **TROY** *to hold him back.* **TROY** *stops himself.*

TROY (*to* **CORY**): All right. That's strike two. You stay away from around me, boy. Don't you strike out. You living with a full count. Don't you strike out.

TROY *exits out the yard as the lights go down.*

Scene 2

It is six months later, early afternoon. **TROY** *enters from the house and starts to exit the yard.* **ROSE** *enters from the house.*

ROSE Troy, I want to talk to you.

TROY All of a sudden, after all this time, you want to talk to me, huh? You ain't wanted to talk to me for months. You ain't wanted to talk to me last night. You ain't wanted no part of me then. What you wanna talk to me about now?

ROSE Tomorrow's Friday.

TROY I know what day tomorrow is. You think I don't know tomorrow's Friday? My whole life I ain't done nothing but look to see Friday coming and you got to tell me it's Friday.

ROSE I want to know if you're coming home.

TROY I always come home, Rose. You know that. There ain't never been a night I ain't come home.

ROSE That ain't what I mean . . . and you know it. I want to know if you're coming straight home after work.

TROY I figure I'd cash my check . . . hang out at Taylors' with the boys . . . maybe play a game of checkers . . .

ROSE Troy, I can't live like this. I won't live like this. You livin' on borrowed time with me. It's been going on six months now you ain't been coming home.

TROY I be here every night. Every night of the year. That's 365 days.

ROSE I want you to come home tomorrow after work.

TROY Rose . . . I don't mess up my pay. You know that now. I take my pay and I give it to you. I don't have no money but what you give me back. I just want to have a little time to myself . . . a little time to enjoy life.

ROSE What about me? When's my time to enjoy life?

TROY I don't know what to tell you, Rose. I'm doing the best I can.

ROSE You ain't been home from work but time enough to change your clothes and run out . . . and you wanna call that the best you can do?

TROY I'm going over to the hospital to see Alberta. She went into the hospital this afternoon. Look like she might have the baby early. I won't be gone long.

ROSE Well, you ought to know. They went over to Miss Pearl's and got Gabe today. She said you told them to go ahead and lock him up.

TROY I ain't said no such thing. Whoever told you that is telling a lie. Pearl ain't doing nothing but telling a big fat lie.

ROSE She ain't had to tell me. I read it on the papers.

TROY I ain't told them nothing of the kind.

ROSE I saw it right there on the papers.

TROY What it say, huh?

ROSE It said you told them to take him.

TROY Then they screwed that up, just the way they screw up everything. I ain't worried about what they got on the paper.

ROSE Say the government send part of his check to the hospital and the other part to you.

TROY I ain't got nothing to do with that if that's the way it works. I ain't made up the rules about how it work.

ROSE You did Gabe just like you did Cory. You wouldn't sign the paper for Cory . . . but you signed for Gabe. You signed that paper.

The telephone is heard ringing inside the house.

TROY I told you I ain't signed nothing, woman! The only thing I signed was the release form. Hell, I can't read, I don't know what they had on that paper! I ain't signed nothing about sending Gabe away.

ROSE I said send him to the hospital . . . you said let him be free . . . now you done went down there and signed him to the hospital for half his money. You went back on yourself, Troy. You gonna have to answer for that.

TROY See now . . . you been over there talking to Miss Pearl. She done got mad cause she ain't getting Gabe's rent money. That's all it is. She's liable to say anything.

ROSE Troy, I seen where you signed the paper.

TROY You ain't seen nothing I signed. What she doing got papers on my brother anyway? Miss Pearl telling a big fat lie. And I'm gonna tell her about it too! You ain't seen nothing I signed. Say . . . you ain't seen nothing I signed.

ROSE *exits into the house to answer the telephone. Presently she returns.*

ROSE Troy . . . that was the hospital. Alberta had the baby.

TROY What she have? What is it?

ROSE It's a girl.

TROY I better get on down to the hospital to see her.

ROSE Troy . . .

TROY Rose . . . I got to go see her now. That's only right . . . what's the matter . . . the baby's all right, ain't it?

ROSE Alberta died having the baby.

TROY Died . . . you say she's dead? Alberta's dead?

ROSE They said they done all they could. They couldn't do nothing for her.

TROY The baby? How's the baby?

ROSE They say it's healthy. I wonder who's gonna bury her.

TROY She had family, Rose. She wasn't living in the world by herself.

ROSE I know she wasn't living in the world by herself.

TROY Next thing you gonna want to know if she had any insurance.

ROSE Troy, you ain't got to talk like that.

TROY That's the first thing that jumped out your mouth. "Who's gonna bury her?" Like I'm fixing to take on that task for myself.

ROSE I am your wife. Don't push me away.

TROY I ain't pushing nobody away. Just give me some space. That's all. Just give me some room to breathe.

ROSE *exits into the house.* **TROY** *walks about the yard.*

TROY (*with a quiet rage that threatens to consume him*): All right . . . Mr. Death. See now . . . I'm gonna tell you what I'm gonna do. I'm gonna take and build me a fence around this yard. See? I'm gonna build me a fence around what belongs to me. And then I want you to stay on the other side. See? You stay over there until you're ready for me. Then you come on. Bring your army. Bring your sickle. Bring your wrestling clothes. I ain't gonna fall down on my vigilance this time. You ain't gonna sneak up on me no more. When you ready for me . . . when the top of your list say Troy Maxson . . . that's when you come around here. You come up and knock on the front door. Ain't nobody else got nothing to do with this. This is between you and me. Man to man. You stay on the other side of that fence until you ready for me. Then you come up and knock on the front door. Anytime you want. I'll be ready for you.

The lights go down to black.

Scene 3

The lights come up on the porch. It is late evening three days later. **ROSE** *sits listening to the ball game waiting for* **TROY**. *The final out of the game is made and* **ROSE** *switches off the radio.* **TROY** *enters the yard carrying an infant wrapped in blankets. He stands back from the house and calls.*

ROSE *enters and stands on the porch. There is a long, awkward silence, the weight of which grows heavier with each passing second.*

TROY Rose . . . I'm standing here with my daughter in my arms. She ain't but a wee bittie little old thing. She don't know nothing about grownups' business. She innocent . . . and she ain't got no mama.

ROSE What you telling me for, Troy?

She turns and exits into the house.

TROY Well . . . I guess we'll just sit out here on the porch.

He sits down on the porch. There is an awkward indelicateness about the way he handles the baby. His largeness engulfs and seems to swallow it. He speaks loud enough for **ROSE** *to hear.*

A man's got to do what's right for him. I ain't sorry for nothing I done. It felt right in my heart. (*To the baby.*) What you smiling at? Your daddy's a big man. Got these great big old hands. But sometimes he's scared. And right now your daddy's scared cause we sitting out here and ain't got no home. Oh, I been homeless before. I ain't had no little baby with me. But I been homeless. You just be out on the road by your lonesome and you see one of them trains coming and you just kinda go like this . . .

He sings as a lullaby.

Please, Mr. Engineer let a man ride the line
Please, Mr. Engineer let a man ride the line
I ain't got no ticket please let me ride the blinds

ROSE *enters from the house.* **TROY**, *hearing her steps behind him, stands and faces her.*

She's my daughter, Rose. My own flesh and blood. I can't deny her no more than I can deny them boys. (*Pause.*) You and them boys is my family. You and them and this child is all I got in the world. So I guess what I'm saying is . . . I'd appreciate it if you'd help me take care of her.

ROSE Okay, Troy . . . you're right. I'll take care of your baby for you . . . cause . . . like you say . . . she's innocent . . . and you can't visit the sins of the father upon the child. A motherless child has got a hard time. (*She takes the baby from him.*) From right now . . . this child got a mother. But you a womanless man.

ROSE *turns and exits into the house with the baby. Lights go down to black.*

Scene 4

It is two months later. **LYONS** *enters from the street. He knocks on the door and calls.*

LYONS Hey, Rose! (*Pause.*): Rose!

ROSE (*from inside the house*): Stop that yelling. You gonna wake up Raynell. I just got her to sleep.

LYONS I just stopped by to pay Papa this twenty dollars I owe him. Where's Papa at?

ROSE He should be here in a minute. I'm getting ready to go down to the church. Sit down and wait on him.

LYONS I got to go pick up Bonnie over her mother's house.

ROSE Well, sit it down there on the table. He'll get it.

LYONS (*enters the house and sets the money on the table*): Tell Papa I said thanks. I'll see you again.

ROSE All right, Lyons. We'll see you.

LYONS *starts to exit as* **CORY** *enters.*

CORY Hey, Lyons.

LYONS What's happening, Cory? Say man, I'm sorry I missed your graduation. You know

I had a gig and couldn't get away. Otherwise, I would have been there, man. So what you doing?

CORY I'm trying to find a job.

LYONS Yeah I know how that go, man. It's rough out here. Jobs are scarce.

CORY Yeah, I know.

LYONS Look here, I got to run. Talk to Papa . . . he know some people. He'll be able to help get you a job. Talk to him . . . see what he say.

CORY Yeah . . . all right, Lyons.

LYONS: You take care. I'll talk to you soon. We'll find some time to talk.

LYONS exits the yard. CORY wanders over to the tree, picks up the bat, and assumes a batting stance. He studies an imaginary pitcher and swings. Dissatisfied with the result, he tries again. TROY enters. They eye each other for a beat. CORY puts the bat down and exits the yard. TROY starts into the house as ROSE exits with RAYNELL. She is carrying a cake.

TROY I'm coming in and everybody's going out.

ROSE I'm taking this cake down to the church for the bake sale. Lyons was by to see you. He stopped by to pay you your twenty dollars. It's laying in there on the table.

TROY (*going into his pocket*): Well . . . here go this money.

ROSE Put it in there on the table, Troy. I'll get it.

TROY What time you coming back?

ROSE Ain't no use in you studying me. It don't matter what time I come back.

TROY I just asked you a question, woman. What's the matter . . . can't I ask you a question?

ROSE Troy, I don't want to go into it. Your dinner's in there on the stove. All you got to do is heat it up. And don't you be eating the rest of them cakes in there. I'm coming back for them. We having a bake sale at the church tomorrow.

ROSE exits the yard. TROY sits down on the steps, takes a pint bottle from his pocket, opens it, and drinks. He begins to sing

TROY Hear it ring! Hear it ring!
Had an old dog his name was Blue
You know Blue was mighty true
You know Blue was a good old dog
Blue trees a possum in a hollow log
You know from that he was a good old dog

BONO enters the yard.

BONO Hey, Troy.

TROY Hey, what's happening, Bono?

BONO I just thought I'd stop by to see you.

TROY What you stop by and see me for? You ain't stopped by in a month of Sundays. Hell, I must owe you money or something.

BONO Since you got your promotion I can't keep up with you. Used to see you every day. Now I don't even know what route you working.

TROY They keep switching me around. Got me out in Greentree now . . . hauling white folks' garbage.

BONO Greentree, huh? You lucky, at least you ain't got to be lifting them barrels. Damn if they ain't getting heavier. I'm gonna put in my two years and call it quits.

TROY I'm thinking about retiring myself.

BONO You got it easy. You can *drive* for another five years.

TROY It ain't the same, Bono. It ain't like working the back of the truck. Ain't got nobody to talk to . . . feel like you working by yourself. Naw, I'm thinking about retiring. How's Lucille?

BONO She all right. Her arthritis get to acting up on her sometime. Saw Rose on my way in. She going down to the church, huh?

TROY Yeah, she took up going down there. All them preachers looking for somebody to fatten their pockets. (*Pause.*) Got some gin here.

BONO Naw, thanks. I just stopped by to say hello.

TROY Hell, nigger . . . you can take a drink. I ain't never known you to say no to a drink. You ain't got to work tomorrow.

BONO I just stopped by. I'm fixing to go over to

Skinner's. We got us a domino game going over his house every Friday.

TROY Nigger, you can't play no dominoes. I used to whup you four games out of five.

BONO Well, that learned me. I'm getting better.

TROY Yeah? Well, that's all right.

BONO Look here . . . I got to be getting on. Stop by sometime, huh?

TROY Yeah, I'll do that, Bono. Lucille told Rose you bought her a new refrigerator.

BONO Yeah, Rose told Lucille you had finally built your fence . . . so I figured we'd call it even.

TROY I knew you would.

BONO Yeah . . . okay. I'll be talking to you.

TROY Yeah, take care, Bono. Good to see you. I'm gonna stop over.

BONO Yeah. Okay, Troy.

BONO *exits.* **TROY** *drinks from the bottle.*

TROY Old Blue died and I dig his grave
Let him down with a golden chain
Every night when I hear old Blue bark
I know Blue treed a possum in Noah's Ark.
Hear it ring! Hear it ring!

CORY *enters the yard. They eye each other for a beat.* **TROY** *is sitting in the middle of the steps.* **CORY** *walks over.*

CORY I got to get by.

TROY Say what? What's you say?

CORY You in my way. I got to get by.

TROY You got to get by where? This is my house. Bought and paid for. In full. Took me fifteen years. And if you wanna go in my house and I'm sitting on the steps . . . you say excuse me. Like your mama taught you.

CORY Come on, Pop . . . I got to get by.

CORY *starts to maneuver his way past* **TROY**. **TROY** *grabs his leg and shoves him back.*

TROY You just gonna walk over top of me?

CORY I live here too!

TROY (*advancing toward him*): You just gonna walk over top of me in my own house?

CORY I ain't scared of you.

TROY I ain't asked if you was scared of me. I asked you if you was fixing to walk over top of me in my own house? That's the question. You ain't gonna say excuse me? You just gonna walk over top of me?

CORY If you wanna put it like that.

TROY How else am I gonna put it?

CORY I was walking by you to go into the house cause you sitting on the steps drunk, singing to yourself. You can put it like that.

TROY Without saying excuse me???

CORY *doesn't respond.*

I asked you a question. Without saying excuse me???

CORY I ain't got to say excuse me to you. You don't count around here no more.

TROY Oh, I see . . . I don't count around here no more. You ain't got to say excuse me to your daddy. All of a sudden you done got so grown that your daddy don't count around here no more . . . Around here in his own house and yard that he done paid for with the sweat of his brow. You done got so grown to where you gonna take over. You gonna take over my house. Is that right? You gonna wear my pants. You gonna go in there and stretch out on my bed. You ain't got to say excuse me cause I don't count around here no more. Is that right?

CORY That's right. You always talking this dumb stuff. Now, why don't you just get out my way?

TROY I guess you got someplace to sleep and something to put in your belly. You got that, huh? You got that? That's what you need. You got that, huh?

CORY You don't know what I got. You ain't got to worry about what I got.

TROY You right! You one hundred percent right! I done spent the last seventeen years worrying about what you got. Now it's your turn, see? I'll tell you what to do. You grown . . . we done established that. You a man. Now, let's see you act like one. Turn your behind around and walk out this yard. And when you get out there in the alley . . . you can forget about this house. See? Cause this is my house. You go on and be a man and get your own house. You can forget about this. Cause this is mine. You go on and get yours cause I'm through with doing for you.

CORY You talking about what you did for me . . . what'd you ever give me?

TROY Them feet and bones! That pumping heart, nigger! I give you more than anybody else is ever gonna give you.

CORY You ain't never gave me nothing! You ain't never done nothing but hold me back. Afraid I was gonna be better than you. All you ever did was try and make me scared of you. I used to tremble every time you called my name. Every time I heard your footsteps in the house. Wondering all the time . . . what's Papa gonna say if I do this? . . . What's he gonna say if I do that? . . . What's Papa gonna say if I turn on the radio? And Mama, too . . . she tries . . . but she's scared of you.

TROY You leave your mama out of this. She ain't got nothing to do with this.

CORY I don't know how she stand you . . . after what you did to her.

TROY I told you to leave your mama out of this!

He advances toward **CORY**.

CORY What you gonna do . . . give me a whupping? You can't whup me no more. You're too old. You just an old man.

TROY (*shoves him on his shoulder*): Nigger! That's what you are. You just another nigger on the street to me!

CORY You crazy! You know that?

TROY Go on now! You got the devil in you. Get on away from me!

CORY You just a crazy old man . . . talking about I got the devil in me.

TROY Yeah, I'm crazy! If you don't get on the other side of that yard . . . I'm gonna show you how crazy I am! Go on . . . get the hell out of my yard.

CORY It ain't your yard. You took Uncle Gabe's money he got from the army to buy this house and then you put him out.

This photograph of James Earl Jones as Troy Maxson in the 1987 Broadway production of *Fences* is entitled, "Troy Maxson takes a swing at death." **How does this image capture the ambiguity of a central metaphor in the play?**

TROY (*advances on* **CORY**): Get your black ass out of my yard!

TROY'*s advance backs* **CORY** *up against the tree.* **CORY** *grabs up the bat.*

CORY I ain't going nowhere! Come on . . . put me out! I ain't scared of you.

TROY That's my bat!

CORY Come on!

TROY Put my bat down!

CORY Come on, put me out.

CORY *swings at* **TROY**, *who backs across the yard.*

What's the matter? You so bad . . . put me out!

TROY *advances toward* **CORY**.

CORY (*backing up*): Come on! Come on!

TROY You're gonna have to use it! You wanna draw that bat back on me . . . you're gonna have to use it.

CORY Come on! . . . Come on!

CORY *swings the bat at* **TROY** *a second time. He misses.* **TROY** *continues to advance toward him.*

TROY You're gonna have to kill me! You wanna draw that bat back on me. You're gonna have to kill me.

CORY, *backed up against the tree, can go no farther.* **TROY** *taunts him. He sticks out his head and offers him a target.*

Come on! Come on!

CORY *is unable to swing the bat.* **TROY** *grabs it.*

TROY Then I'll show you.

CORY *and* **TROY** *struggle over the bat. The struggle is fierce and fully engaged.* **TROY** *ultimately is the stronger and takes the bat from* **CORY** *and stands over him ready to swing. He stops himself.*

Go on and get away from around my house.

CORY, *stung by his defeat, picks himself up, walks slowly out of the yard and up the alley.*

CORY Tell Mama I'll be back for my things.

TROY They'll be on the other side of that fence.

CORY *exits.*

TROY I can't taste nothing. Helluljah! I can't taste nothing no more. (**TROY** *assumes a batting posture and begins to taunt Death, the fastball on the outside corner.*) Come on! It's between you and me now! Come on! Anytime you want! Come on! I be ready for you . . . but I ain't gonna be easy.

The lights go down on the scene.

Scene 5

The time is 1965. The lights come up in the yard. It is the morning of **TROY**'*s funeral. A funeral plaque with a light hangs beside the door. There is a small garden plot off to the side. There is noise and activity in the house as* **ROSE**, **LYONS**, *and* **BONO** *have gathered. The door opens and* **RAYNELL**, *seven years old, enters dressed in a flannel nightgown. She crosses to the garden and pokes around with a stick.* **ROSE** *calls from the house.*

ROSE Raynell!

RAYNELL Mam?

ROSE What you doing out there?

RAYNELL Nothing.

ROSE *comes to the door.*

ROSE Girl, get in here and get dressed. What you doing?

RAYNELL Seeing if my garden growed.

ROSE I told you it ain't gonna grow overnight. You got to wait.

RAYNELL It don't look like it never gonna grow. Dag!

ROSE I told you a watched pot never boils. Get in here and get dressed.

RAYNELL This ain't even no pot, Mama.

ROSE You just have to give it a chance. It'll grow. Now you come on and do what I told you. We got to be getting ready. This ain't no morning to be playing around. You hear me?

RAYNELL Yes, Mam.

ROSE *exits into the house.* **RAYNELL** *continues to poke at her garden with a stick.* **CORY** *enters. He is dressed in a Marine corporal's uniform, and carries a duffel bag. His posture is that of a military man, and his speech has a clipped sternness.*

CORY (*to* **RAYNELL**): Hi. (*Pause.*) I bet your name is Raynell.

RAYNELL Uh huh.

CORY Is your mama home?

RAYNELL *runs up on the porch and calls through the screen door.*

RAYNELL Mama . . . there's some man out here. Mama?

ROSE *comes to the door.*

ROSE Cory? Lord have mercy! Look here, you all!

ROSE *and* **CORY** *embrace in a tearful reunion as* **BONO** *and* **LYONS** *enter from the house dressed in funeral clothes.*

BONO Aw, looka here . . .

ROSE Done got all grown up!

CORY Don't cry, Mama. What you crying about?

ROSE I'm just so glad you made it.

CORY Hey Lyons. How you doing, Mr. Bono.

LYONS *goes to embrace* **CORY**.

LYONS Look at you, man. Look at you. Don't he look good, Rose. Got them Corporal stripes.

ROSE What took you so long?

CORY You know how the Marines are, Mama. They got to get all their paperwork straight before they let you do anything.

ROSE Well, I'm sure glad you made it. They let Lyons come. Your Uncle Gabe's still in the hospital. They don't know if they gonna let him out or not. I just talked to them a little while ago.

LYONS A Corporal in the United States Marines.

BONO Your daddy knew you had it in you. He used to tell me all the time.

LYONS Don't he look good, Mr. Bono?

BONO Yeah, he remind me of Troy when I first met him. (*Pause.*) Say, Rose, Lucille's down at the church with the choir. I'm gonna go down and get the pallbearers lined up. I'll be back to get you all.

ROSE Thanks, Jim.

CORY See you, Mr. Bono.

LYONS (*with his arm around* **RAYNELL**): Cory . . . look at Raynell. Ain't she precious? She gonna break a whole lot of hearts.

ROSE Raynell, come and say hello to your brother. This is your brother, Cory. You remember Cory.

RAYNELL No, Mam.

CORY She don't remember me, Mama.

ROSE Well, we talk about you. She heard us talk about you. (*To* **RAYNELL**.) This is your brother, Cory. Come on and say hello.

RAYNELL Hi.

CORY Hi. So you're Raynell. Mama told me a lot about you.

ROSE You all come on into the house and let me fix you some breakfast. Keep up your strength.

CORY I ain't hungry, Mama.

LYONS You can fix me something, Rose. I'll be in there in a minute.

ROSE Cory, you sure you don't want nothing? I know they ain't feeding you right.

CORY No, Mama . . . thanks. I don't feel like eating. I'll get something later.

ROSE Raynell . . . get on upstairs and get that dress on like I told you.

ROSE *and* **RAYNELL** *exit into the house.*

LYONS So . . . I hear you thinking about getting married.

CORY Yeah, I done found the right one, Lyons. It's about time.

LYONS Me and Bonnie been split up about four years now. About the time Papa retired. I guess she just got tired of all them changes I was putting her through. (*Pause.*) I always knew you was gonna make something out yourself. Your head was always in the right direction. So . . . you gonna stay in . . . make it a career . . . put in your twenty years?

CORY I don't know. I got six already, I think that's enough.

LYONS Stick with Uncle Sam and retire early. Ain't nothing out here. I guess Rose told you what happened with me. They got me down the workhouse. I thought I was being slick cashing other people's checks.

CORY How much time you doing?

LYONS They give me three years. I got that beat now. I ain't got but nine more months. It ain't so bad. You learn to deal with it like anything else. You got to take the crookeds with the straights. That's what Papa used to say. He used to say that when he struck out. I seen him strike out three times in a row . . . and the next time up he hit the ball over the grandstand. Right out there in Homestead Field. He wasn't satisfied hitting in the seats . . . he want to hit it over everything! After the game he had two hundred people standing around waiting to shake his hand.

You got to take the crookeds with the straights. Yeah, Papa was something else.

CORY You still playing?

LYONS Cory . . . you know I'm gonna do that. There's some fellows down there we got us a band . . . we gonna try and stay together when we get out . . . but yeah, I'm still playing. It still helps me to get out of bed in the morning. As long as it do that I'm gonna be right there playing and trying to make some sense out of it.

ROSE (*calling*): Lyons, I got these eggs in the pan.

LYONS Let me go on and get these eggs, man. Get ready to go bury Papa. (*Pause.*) How you doing? You doing all right?

CORY nods. LYONS touches him on the shoulder and they share a moment of silent grief. LYONS exits into the house. CORY wanders about the yard. RAYNELL enters.

RAYNELL Hi.

CORY Hi.

RAYNELL Did you used to sleep in my room?

CORY Yeah . . . that used to be my room.

RAYNELL That's what Papa call it. "Cory's room." It got your football in the closet.

ROSE comes to the door.

ROSE Raynell, get in there and get them good shoes on.

RAYNELL Mama, can't I wear these? Them other one hurt my feet.

ROSE Well, they just gonna have to hurt your feet for a while. You ain't said they hurt your feet when you went down to the store and got them.

RAYNELL They didn't hurt then. My feet done got bigger.

ROSE Don't you give me no backtalk now. You get in there and get them shoes on.

RAYNELL exits into the house.

Ain't too much changed. He still got that piece of rag tied to that tree. He was out here swinging that bat. I was just ready to go back in the house. He swung that bat and then he just fell over. Seem like he swung it and stood there with this grin on his face . . . and then he just fell over. They carried him on down to the hospital, but I knew there wasn't no need . . . why don't you come on in the house?

CORY Mama . . . I got something to tell you. I don't know how to tell you this . . . but I've got to tell you . . . I'm not going to Papa's funeral.

ROSE Boy, hush your mouth. That's your daddy you talking about. I don't want hear that kind of talk this morning. I done raised you to come to this? You standing there all healthy and grown talking about you ain't going to your daddy's funeral?

CORY Mama . . . listen . . .

ROSE I don't want to hear it, Cory. You just get that thought out of your head.

CORY I can't drag Papa with me everywhere I go. I've got to say no to him. One time in my life I've got to say no.

ROSE Don't nobody have to listen to nothing like that. I know you and your daddy ain't seen eye to eye, but I ain't got to listen to that kind of talk this morning. Whatever was between you and your daddy . . . the time has come to put it aside. Just take it and set it over there on the shelf and forget about it. Disrespecting your daddy ain't gonna make you a man, Cory. You got to find a way to come to that on your own. Not going to your daddy's funeral ain't gonna make you a man.

CORY The whole time I was growing up . . . living in his house . . . Papa was like a shadow that followed you everywhere. It weighed on you and sunk into your flesh. It would wrap around you and lay there until you couldn't tell which one was you anymore. That shadow digging in your flesh. Trying to crawl in. Trying to live through you. Everywhere I looked, Troy Maxson was staring back at me . . . hiding under the bed . . . in the closet. I'm just saying I've got to find a way to get rid of that shadow, Mama.

ROSE You just like him. You got him in you good.

CORY Don't tell me that, Mama.

ROSE You Troy Maxson all over again.

CORY I don't want to be Troy Maxson. I want to be me.

ROSE You can't be nobody but who you are, Cory. That shadow wasn't nothing but you growing into yourself. You either got to grow into it or cut it down to fit you. But that's all you got to make life with. That's all you got to measure yourself against that world out there. Your daddy wanted you to be everything he wasn't . . . and at the same time he tried to make you into everything he was. I don't know if he was right or wrong . . . but I do know he meant to do more good than he meant to do harm. He wasn't always right. Sometimes when he touched he bruised. And sometimes when he took me in his arms he cut.

When I first met your daddy I thought . . . Here is a man I can lay down with and make a baby. That's the first thing I thought when I seen him. I was thirty years old and had done seen my share of men. But when he walked up to me and said, "I can dance a waltz that'll make you dizzy," I thought, Rose Lee, here is a man that you can open yourself up to and be filled to bursting. Here is a man that can fill all them empty spaces you been tipping around the edges of. One of them empty spaces was being somebody's mother.

I married your daddy and settled down to cooking his supper and keeping clean sheets on the bed. When your daddy walked through the house he was so big he filled it up. That was my first mistake. Not to make him leave some room for me. For my part in the matter. But at that time I wanted that. I wanted a house that I could sing in. And that's what your daddy gave me. I didn't know to keep up his strength I had to give up little pieces of mine. I did that. I took on his life as mine and mixed up the pieces so that you couldn't hardly tell which was which anymore. It was my choice. It was my life and I didn't have to live it like that. But that's what life offered me in the way of being a woman and I took it. I grabbed hold of it with both hands.

August Wilson has said that this collage by African American artist Romare Bearden inspired *Fences*. **What elements in this work do you see reflected in the play? What characteristics do the two share?**

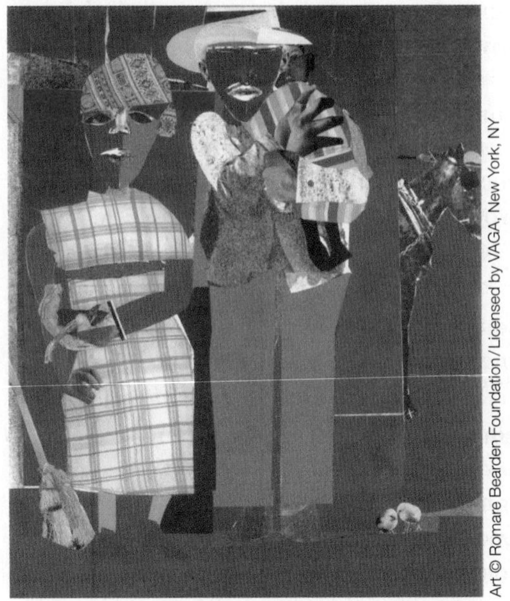

By the time Raynell came into the house, me and your daddy had done lost touch with one another. I didn't want to make my blessing off of nobody's misfortune . . . but I took on to Raynell like she was all them babies I had wanted and never had.

The phone rings.

Like I'd been blessed to relive a part of my life. And if the Lord see fit to keep up my strength . . . I'm gonna do her just like your daddy did you . . . I'm gonna give her the best of what's in me.

RAYNELL (*entering, still with her old shoes*): Mama . . . Reverend Tollivier on the phone.

ROSE *exits into the house.*

RAYNELL Hi.

CORY Hi.

RAYNELL You in the Army or the Marines?

CORY Marines.

RAYNELL Papa said it was the Army. Did you know Blue?

CORY Blue? Who's Blue?

RAYNELL Papa's dog what he sing about all the time.

CORY (*singing*): Hear it ring! Hear it ring!
I had a dog his name was Blue
You know Blue was mighty true
You know Blue was a good old dog
Blue treed a possum in a hollow log
You know from that he was a good old dog.
Hear it ring! Hear it ring!

RAYNELL *joins in singing.*

CORY AND RAYNELL Blue treed a possum out on a limb
Blue looked at me and I looked at him
Grabbed that possum and put him in a sack
Blue stayed there till I came back
Old Blue's feets was big and round
Never allowed a possum to touch the ground.
Old Blue died and I dug his grave
I dug his grave with a silver spade
Let him down with a golden chain
And every night I call his name
Go on Blue, you good dog you
Go on Blue, you good dog you

RAYNELL Blue laid down and died like a man
Blue laid down and died . . .

BOTH Blue laid down and died like a man
Now he's treeing possums in the Promised Land
I'm gonna tell you this to let you know
Blue's gone where the good dogs go
When I hear old Blue bark
When I hear old Blue bark
Blue treed a possum in Noah's Ark
Blue treed a possum in Noah's Ark.

ROSE *comes to the screen door.*

ROSE Cory, we gonna be ready to go in a minute.

CORY (*to* **RAYNELL**): You go on in the house and change them shoes like Mama told you so we can go to Papa's funeral.

RAYNELL Okay, I'll be back.

RAYNELL *exits into the house.* **CORY** *gets up and crosses over to the tree.* **ROSE** *stands in the screen door watching him.* **GABRIEL** *enters from the alley.*

GABRIEL (*calling*): Hey, Rose!

ROSE Gabe?

GABRIEL I'm here, Rose. Hey Rose, I'm here!

ROSE *enters from the house.*

ROSE Lord . . . Look here, Lyons!

LYONS See, I told you, Rose . . . I told you they'd let him come.

CORY How you doing, Uncle Gabe?

LYONS How you doing, Uncle Gabe?

GABRIEL Hey, Rose. It's time. It's time to tell St. Peter to open the gates. Troy, you ready? You ready, Troy. I'm gonna tell St. Peter to open the gates. You get ready now.

GABRIEL, *with great fanfare, braces himself to blow. The trumpet is without a mouthpiece. He puts the end of it into his mouth and blows with great force, like a man who has been waiting some twenty-odd years for this single moment. No sound comes out of the trumpet. He braces himself and blows again with the same result. A third time he blows. There is a weight of impossible description that falls away and leaves him bare and exposed to a frightful realization. It is a trauma that a sane and normal mind would be unable to withstand. He begins to dance. A slow, strange dance, eerie and life-giving. A dance of atavistic signature and ritual.* **LYONS** *attempts to embrace him.* **GABRIEL** *pushes* **LYONS** *away. He begins to howl in what is an attempt at song, or perhaps a song turning back into itself in an attempt at speech. He finishes his dance and the gates of heaven stand open as wide as God's closet.*

That's the way that go!

[1985]

QUESTIONS FOR DISCUSSION

1. Troy Maxson's last name makes subtle reference to the Mason-Dixon Line – the imaginary line that in the 1820s divided slave states from free states. How does this allusion to history help prepare you for the play's themes? What are the connotations of other characters' names – for example, *Rose* and *Gabriel*?
2. What is the significance of the biblical and supernatural allusions that appear throughout the play? Consider the story of Troy getting furniture from the devil, and the behavior and history of Gabriel.
3. In the stage directions for act I, scene 1, August Wilson describes Troy as "a large man with thick, heavy hands; it is this largeness that he strives to fill out and make an accommodation with." How does this description establish the character of Troy? Consider also Troy's encounters with Death – the way he taunts Death to come and get him, asserting that he will go down swinging. What might Wilson be saying about Troy's character with these descriptions?
4. How does Rose's assertion in act I, scene 1, that "Times have changed" (l. 240) set the mood for the action that follows? How does it anticipate the themes Wilson will explore more specifically through his characters and the action of the play?
5. How do you interpret Lyons's response to his father's criticism of his lifestyle: "I know I got to eat. But I got to live too. I need something that gonna help me to get out of the bed in the morning. Make me feel like I belong in the world" (I.1.560–63)? Discuss what it is that makes each of the central characters feel some sense of belonging in the world: Troy, Rose, Lyons, and Cory.
6. What role does Bono play in the development of Troy's character? Pick a scene that you think shows Bono's role most clearly, and then explain.
7. At the opening of act I, scene 2, Rose is hanging up clothes in the early morning, humming and singing to herself. Her song imploring Jesus to "be a fence all around me every day" reflects one of the play's important themes. How do different characters relate to and define fences? Whom do fences keep out, and whom do they enclose? Consider also how fences relate to baseball. Explain why this is an appropriate title for the play.
8. In act I, scene 3, Troy explains why he refuses to sign Cory's recruitment papers: "The white man ain't gonna let you get nowhere with that football noway. You go on and get your book-learning so you can work yourself up in that A&P or learn how to fix cars or build houses or something, get you a trade. That way you have something can't nobody take away from you. You go on and learn how to put your hands to some good use. Besides hauling people's garbage" (ll. 194–203). Could there be more to his refusal than the explanation he offers? Explain.
9. What is the significance of Troy's triumph at work, earning the right to drive the garbage truck (act I, scene 4)? What is ironic about this victory? How and why does his promotion affect his relationship with Bono?
10. Why do you think the playwright chose not to have Alberta make an appearance on stage? How does she appear in your imagination? How would you describe her?
11. Is Troy a hypocrite? Do his relationships with Alberta and Cory make his assertions regarding family responsibilities and duty ring false?
12. When Cory returns after Troy's death, he tells Rose, "I can't drag Papa with me everywhere I go. I've got to say no to him" (II.5.166–67). What finally convinces Cory to attend Troy's funeral? What does his attending the funeral suggest about what Cory's future might hold and what kind of home and family he will have? Has he said "no" to his father?

QUESTIONS ON STYLE AND STRUCTURE

1. Three texts, all written by Wilson, precede the actual opening of the play: a four-line poem, a description of the setting, and a more discursive piece entitled "The Play." Although these texts provide specific information, they also raise larger issues. What are some of these? Pay particular attention to the language Wilson uses ("in His Largeness and Laws," "the porch lacks congruence," "The city devoured them," "new energies that used loyalty and patriotism as its fuel").
2. In act I, scene 1, Troy's friend Bono chides him about "that Alberta gal" (ll. 54–55). What is significant about

the introduction of this complicating element before we meet Troy's wife? What might this foreshadow in the play? How does this teasing introduce a complication within the play's exposition?

3. Early in the play (act I, scene 1), Wilson's stage direction for Rose indicates that she "alternates between the porch and the kitchen." Throughout the play, she is associated with food and preparation. Examine specific passages and examples, and discuss how Wilson uses this association to develop the character of Rose.
4. Why do you think Wilson holds off until the end of act I to have Troy reveal his past and his own confrontation with his father at age fourteen? Why does Wilson have Troy tell the story as a flashback to Lyons and Bono rather than to Cory? Pay special attention to Troy's tone; how does this section contribute to your understanding of his character?
5. Much of the play is concerned with money: earning it, owing it, paying for things. Yet Wilson alerts us to a metaphorical level when Troy insists, "Life don't owe you nothing. You owe it to yourself" (I.1.552–53). Discuss how the language of commerce — debt, payment, purchase, cheating — develops important themes in the play.
6. What do you think is the climax of *Fences*? Explain your reasoning.
7. Much of *Fences* is written in dialect, depicting the natural speech patterns of the characters in the play. In one example, Troy teases Rose with: "I'm studying you . . . fixing to do my homework!" (I.3.35–36). In other instances, Wilson brings in dialect through songs the characters recall or sing. How does the dialect affect your understanding of the play? Do you find that the style of the characters' language, which reflects the period when the action occurs, dates the play for contemporary viewers?
8. In act II, scene 1, Troy uses baseball metaphors ("steal second," "stood on first base for eighteen years") to explain his affair with Alberta to Rose. How is this use of language consistent with Troy's character? On what basis does Rose reject the comparison? Consider the metaphor she chooses as she counters with an explanation of how she has tried to live her life.
9. Wilson has described *Fences* as having a "blues aesthetic." Songs, and particularly the blues, play an important role in Wilson's plays. Where do you see the influence of the blues on *Fences*? Is it in the diction? the syntax? the themes? the structure? Or does it show itself in some other way?
10. The character of Gabriel has puzzled readers, audiences, and even directors; one even suggested that he be dropped from the script to keep from confusing audiences. Some see him as a spiritual presence with a visible link to the African past. What elements of plot and character depend on him? Explain how you do or do not see Gabriel as essential to *Fences*. Include the final scene in your interpretation.

SUGGESTIONS FOR WRITING

1. Rose is a character who has provoked a great deal of controversy: some see her as a strong matriarch who holds her family together, while others argue that she enables Troy's worst behaviors. Write an essay explaining your view of Rose. Consider both her assertion that she "ain't never wanted no half nothing in [her] family" (II.1.275–76) and her decision to bring Raynell into the Maxson family.
2. In the description of Troy Maxson that precedes the play, Wilson writes, "at times he can be crude and almost vulgar, though he is capable of rising to profound heights of expression." Write an essay analyzing the character of Troy as embodying this tension. Discuss which inclination you believe ultimately prevails.
3. Tragic heroes possess a character flaw or commit an error of judgment that leads to their downfall and a reversal of fortune. Write an essay explaining why you believe that Troy is a tragic hero, paying careful attention to ways in which this play diverges from the classical model.
4. *Fences* is most often interpreted as a "generational play." In fact, August Wilson scholar Sandra Shannon describes a 1997 production in Beijing with an all-Chinese cast in which both audience members and actors found that "their connections to *Fences* seemed to have had more to do with the shifting of a powerful nation's economic and generational center from one determined by tradition to one responding to the trappings of

modernization." Discuss the generational conflicts in this play, and consider how they are reflective of more universal experiences than ones specific to the African American experience.

5. Write a eulogy to be read at Troy Maxson's funeral. Include details from his life that would help mourners see that "he meant to do more good than he meant to do harm" (II.5.207–9). Choose the speaker of your eulogy carefully. It could be any of the characters in the play, or someone else entirely.
6. Imagine that ten years have elapsed since Troy's death, and Cory and Lyons return home to celebrate Rose's birthday. Write a dialogue between the half brothers in which they reminisce about their father.
7. Troy Maxson took part in the Great Migration of rural blacks from the South to urban centers in the North. The artist Jacob Lawrence has chronicled this journey in his Migration Series. The series is housed in the Museum of Modern Art in New York, but the images are available online at www.phillipscollection.org/migration_series. Choose one painting that particularly appeals to you, and write about how it helps you visualize the historical movement.
8. Throughout the play, Troy uses baseball metaphors to explain how he thinks and feels. Try omitting the metaphor and rewriting Troy's speech to Rose in act II, scene 1, more literally (beginning with "But . . . you born with two strikes on you before you come to the plate" on lines 341–42). How does the loss of the baseball metaphor affect the power of the speech?
9. The time frame of *Fences* spans several major historical moments for African Americans in the nineteenth and twentieth centuries: Reconstruction, the Great Migration, the Great Depression, and the civil rights movement. Write an essay explaining how the historical and social forces of these eras are reflected either in the play as a whole or in the character of Troy Maxson.

The Metamorphosis

FRANZ KAFKA

Translated by Alexis Walker

Photo by ullstein bild/ullstein bild via Getty Images

Born in Prague, Czechoslovakia, to middle-class Jewish parents, Franz Kafka (1883–1924) spoke Czech in his childhood but studied in German-speaking schools. He graduated from the Charles-Ferdinand University in Prague with a law degree. Kafka was employed for many years at the Workers' Accident Insurance Institute, and he wrote after his working hours. He published *The Metamorphosis* (1915) and *The Penal Colony* (1919) during his lifetime. After his death from tuberculosis, three other novels were published, despite his request that the manuscripts be destroyed: *The Trial* (1925), *The Castle* (1926), and *Amerika* (1927). Over the course of his life, Kafka wrote hundreds of letters to family and close friends, including his father, with whom he had a strained and formal relationship. Michiko Kakutani, Pulitzer Prize–winning critic for the *New York Times*, has said that Kafka's letters and works of fiction share "the same nervous attention to minute particulars; the same paranoid awareness of shifting balances of power; the same atmosphere of emotional suffocation — combined, surprisingly enough, with moments of boyish ardor and delight."

I

When Gregor Samsa awoke in his bed one morning from unquiet dreams, he found himself transformed into an enormous insect.* He lay on a back as hard as armor and saw, when he raised his head slightly, a jutting brown underbelly divided into arching segments. The bedcovers could barely cover it; they threatened to slide off altogether. His many legs, pitifully thin in comparison with the rest of his bulk, fluttered helplessly before his eyes.

"What has happened to me?" he thought. It wasn't a dream. His room — a decent enough room for a person, if slightly too small — lay quietly between the four familiar walls. Over the table on which was spread his unpacked collections of fabric samples — Samsa was a traveling salesman — hung the picture that he had recently cut out of an illustrated magazine and fit into an attractive gilt frame. The picture was of a woman clad in a fur hat and a fur stole; she sat upright and held out to the viewer a thick fur muff into which her entire forearm disappeared.

Gregor's gaze then directed itself to the window. The dreary weather — one could hear raindrops hit the metal awning over the window — made him quite melancholy. "What if I slept a bit longer and forgot all this foolishness," he thought. But that was altogether

* Translator's note: The closest English equivalents to the German word Kafka uses here (*Ungeziefer*) are "vermin" and "pest"—the German word denotes parasitic and otherwise objectionable creatures (including fleas, lice, rats, mice, etc.) and connotes uncleanness. "Insect" is a compromise: though at once more specific and less evocative than the original, it sidesteps problems of agreement ("vermin" being almost always plural in English) and of tone ("pest" being more colloquial than the German *Ungeziefer*).

impossible, because he was used to sleeping on his right side, and his current condition made working himself into this position impossible. No matter how vigorously he swung himself over to the right, he immediately rolled again onto his back. He tried what seemed hundreds of times, closing his eyes in order to avoid having to see his wriggling legs. He finally gave up only when he began to feel in his side a small dull ache that he had never felt before.

"Oh, God," he thought, "what a strenuous profession I've chosen — traveling day in, day out! The demands of business are far greater on the road than they are at the home office, and I'm burdened with the annoyances of travel besides: the worry about train connections; the irregular, bad meals; a social life limited to passing acquaintances who never become real friends. To hell with it!" He felt an itch on his belly, and he shoved himself back against the bedpost so he could lift his head more easily. He found the spot that itched: it was covered with small white dots that he couldn't identify. He went to touch the spot with one of his legs but drew it back immediately, because the touch made him shudder.

He slid back into his former position. "This early rising," he thought, "can make you into a complete idiot. A man needs his sleep. Other travelers live like women in a harem. When, for example, I go back to my hotel during the course of the morning to write up orders, these gentlemen are just sitting down to breakfast. I should try that with the Director: I'd be fired on the spot. Who knows, though — that might be good for me. If it weren't for my parents, I would have given notice long ago: I would have confronted the Director and given him a piece of my mind. He would have fallen off his chair! It's incredible the way he has of sitting perched at his reading desk and speaking from on high to employees who, on top of everything, have to draw very near owing to his slight deafness. Oh well, I shouldn't give up hope altogether: once I have the money to pay off my parents' debt — it should only be another five or six years — I'll definitely do it. Then I'll make my big break. In the meantime, I have to get up — my train leaves at five."

And he looked over at the alarm clock that ticked on the bureau. "God in heaven!" he thought. It was six-thirty, and the hands of the clock went quietly on; it was even later than six-thirty — it was closer to six-forty-five. Shouldn't the alarm have gone off? He could see from the bed that it was correctly set for four o'clock; it must have gone off. But was it possible to sleep peacefully through that furniture-rattling noise? Of course, he hadn't actually slept peacefully, but he had no doubt for that reason slept more deeply. But what should he do now? The next train left at seven o'clock. In order to catch that one, he'd have to rush like a madman, and his samples weren't packed up yet. He hardly felt alert or energetic enough. And even if he caught the train, he wouldn't avoid the Director's wrath, because the office porter had been waiting at the five-o'clock train and would long since have reported his failure to appear. The porter was completely under the Director's thumb — he had neither a backbone nor brains. What if Gregor were to report himself sick? But that would be highly awkward and suspicious, because he had not been sick once in five years of service. The Director would certainly come with the insurance doctor. He would reproach his parents for their lazy son and dismiss all rejoinders by referring them to the doctor, who considered all people completely healthy, but work-averse. And would he be so wrong in this case? Gregor actually felt completely fine, despite a fatigue completely unwarranted after such a long sleep. He even had a powerful appetite.

As he thought all this over hurriedly, without being able to decide whether to leave his bed — the clock had just struck six-forty-five — there was a knock on the door near the head of his bed. "Gregor," he heard — it was his mother — "it's a quarter to seven. Weren't you going on a trip?" What a gentle voice! Gregor was terrified when he heard his answer. It was unmistakably in his old voice, but had mixed in, as if from down deep, an irrepressible, painful, squeaking noise, which allowed words to be heard clearly when first uttered, but as they resonated, distorted them to such an extent that they were difficult to understand. Gregor had wanted to answer in detail and explain everything, but in light of the circumstances he limited himself to saying: "Yes, yes, thanks, Mother, I'm getting up." The wooden door seemed to make the change in Gregor's voice imperceptible outside the room, because his mother was satisfied with his explanation and shuffled away. But through this brief exchange the other family members had become aware that Gregor was unexpectedly still at home, and his father was already knocking on one side door — lightly, but with his fist. "Gregor, Gregor," he called, "What's going on?" And after a short pause he urged again, with a deeper voice: Gregor! Gregor!" At the other side door, his sister fretted softly: "Gregor? Are you ill? Do you need something?" To both sides, Gregor answered, "I'm just about ready to go," and he made an effort to ban anything conspicuous from his voice by the most painstaking enunciation and by inserting long pauses between individual words. His father returned to his breakfast, but his sister whispered: "Gregor, open up, I beg you." Gregor had no intention of opening the door, however — instead he gave thanks for his habitual precaution, born of much travel, of locking all doors during the night, even at home.

First he wanted to get up, quietly and undisturbed, get dressed, and above all eat breakfast — only then did he want to think over what came next, because he could see that he would come to no reasonable conclusions as long as he lay in bed. In the past he had often felt one mild pain or another while lying in bed, possibly from lying in an awkward position, that proved to be sheer imagination once he got up. He was eager to see how today's fantasies would gradually resolve themselves. He didn't doubt in the least that the change in his voice was nothing more than the harbinger of a hearty cold, one of the occupational hazards of traveling salesmen.

Throwing off the covers was perfectly simple: he only needed to puff himself up a bit and they fell off on their own. But doing more than that was difficult, especially because he was so strangely broad. He would normally have used his arms and hands to get up; now, he had only the many little legs which were continuously moving in every direction and which he could not seem to control. If he meant to bend one, it would be the first one to stretch itself out, if he finally succeeded in enforcing his will with one leg, all the rest of them worked furiously, as if liberated, in extreme, painful agitation. "You can't just lie here in bed doing nothing," Gregor said to himself.

10 At first he intended to get out of the bed with the lower part of his body foremost, but this lower part, which he had moreover not yet seen and of which he could not form a proper mental image, proved too difficult to move. It went extremely slowly. When, nearly frantic, he finally gathered his strength and recklessly shoved himself forward, he misjudged the direction and violently struck the lower bed post. The burning pain he felt convinced him that the lower part of his body was at least at the moment the most sensitive part.

He afterwards attempted to get his upper body out of bed and carefully turned his head towards the edge of the bed. This he could do easily, and in spite of its bulk and weight, the mass of his body finally slowly followed the direction of his head. But when he held his head at last free of the bed, he became afraid to shift further in this direction, because if he ultimately let himself fall like that, it would be a miracle if his head were not injured. And now, of all times, he could not afford to lose consciousness; he would rather remain in bed.

After continued effort, however, he found himself lying exactly as before, and heaved a sigh. He saw his little legs struggling against one another even more furiously, if that were possible, and he saw no way of introducing calm and order to this anarchy. At this point he repeated to himself that he could not possibly lie in bed any longer and that it would be most sensible to risk everything, even if there were only the smallest hope of thereby freeing himself from bed. At the same time, however, he kept reminding himself that calm deliberation was always better than rash decision-making. All the while he tried hard to focus on the view from the window, but unfortunately there was little encouragement or cheer to gain from the sight of the morning fog, which shrouded even the opposite side of the narrow street. "Already seven o'clock," he said to himself with the latest striking of the alarm clock, "already seven o'clock and still such fog." And he lay quiet a short while, breathing shallowly, as if he thought complete stillness might restore things to their true and natural state.

After a bit, however, he said to himself, "Before it strikes seven-fifteen, I must without fail be completely out of bed. For one thing, someone from the company will have come by then to inquire after me, because the office opens before seven." And he concentrated his efforts toward swinging his entire body out of the bed all at the same time. If he let himself fall out of bed in this manner, his head, which he would raise sharply during the fall, would presumably remain uninjured. His back seemed to be hard; nothing would happen to it in the fall onto the carpet. His greatest source of misgiving was anticipation of the loud crash that would follow, which would probably arouse anxiety, if not terror, beyond the doors. That would have to be risked, however.

When, by rocking back and forth, Gregor moved halfway off of the bed — the new method was more a game than an exertion — it occurred to him how simple everything would be if someone would come help him. Two strong people — he thought of his father and the servant girl — would be more than adequate. They would only have to shove their arms under his domed back, pry him up out of bed, prop up his bulk by crouching low, and then help him complete the turn over onto the floor, where hopefully his little legs would gain some sense of purpose. Quite apart from the fact that the doors were locked, though, should he really call for help? In spite of his predicament he couldn't suppress a smile at the thought.

He was already so far along that he could hardly maintain his balance when he rocked forcefully. Very soon he would have to make a final decision, because in five minutes it would be seven-fifteen. Just then the front doorbell rang. "That's someone from the company," he said to himself and virtually froze, though his little legs only danced more hurriedly. Everything remained quiet for a moment. "They're not opening the door," Gregor said to himself, momentarily carried away by some absurd hope. But then, naturally, as always, the servant girl directed her firm step to the door and opened it. Gregor needed to hear only the first word of greeting from the visitor and he already knew who it was — the Deputy Director himself. Why was Gregor condemned to work at a company where the least infraction immediately attracted the greatest suspicion? Were all employees then without exception scoundrels; were there among them no loyal, devoted individuals who, when they had merely missed a few morning hours of service, would become so tormented by pangs of conscience that they would be frankly unable to leave their beds? Wouldn't it really have been enough to send an apprentice to inquire — if indeed this inquiry were necessary at all? Did the Deputy Director himself have to come, thereby showing the entire innocent family that the investigation of this suspicious situation could only be entrusted to the Deputy Director himself? And more as a result of the agitation into which this line of thought transported Gregor, than as a result of a proper decision, he swung himself with all his might out of the bed. There was a loud thump, but no actual crash. The fall was muffled a bit by the carpet, and his back was more elastic than Gregor had thought — these things accounted for the fairly inconspicuous dull thump. He had failed only to raise his head carefully enough and had struck it. He twisted it back and forth and rubbed it into the carpet out of anger and pain.

"Something happened inside there," said the Deputy Director in the room to the left. Gregor tried to imagine something similar to what had happened to him today happening to the Deputy Director; it really was possible, after all. But as if in cruel response to this question the Deputy Director took a few decisive steps in the next room, making his patent leather boots creak. From the room to the right Gregor's sister whispered to inform him: "Gregor, the Deputy Director is here." "I know," said Gregor to himself; but he did not dare to raise his voice loud enough for his sister to hear.

"Gregor," his father now said from the room to the left, "the Deputy Director has come and inquires as to why you did not leave with the early morning train. We don't know what we should say to him. Furthermore, he wants to speak to you directly. So please open the door. He will surely have the goodness to excuse the disorder of your room." "Good morning, Mr. Samsa," the Deputy Director called out at the same time in a friendly manner. "He is not well," his mother said to the Deputy Director, while his father still spoke at the door, "he is not well, believe me, sir. Why would Gregor otherwise miss a train? The boy has nothing in his head but the company. I almost worry that he never goes out at night; he has been in the city eight days now, but he was at home every night. He sits with us at the table and quietly reads the newspaper or studies train schedules. Busying himself with woodworking is as far as he goes in the way of amusement. In the course of two, three evenings, for example, he cut himself a small frame; you would be astounded at how pretty it is. It's hanging in his room; you will see it right away, when Gregor opens up. I am happy, in any case, that you're here, Deputy Director. We could not have persuaded Gregor to open the door alone; he is so stubborn; and there's certainly something wrong with him, although he denied it this morning." "I'm coming right away," said Gregor slowly and carefully, while not moving at all, in order not to miss a word of the conversation. "Otherwise, dear woman, I can't explain it myself, either," said the Deputy Director. "Hopefully it's nothing serious. Though I must say, that we businessmen — either fortunately or unfortunately, as you will — must often ignore a trivial indisposition in the interest of business." "So can the Deputy Director come in to see you?" asked his impatient father, knocking again at the door. "No," said Gregor. In the room to the left there arose an awkward silence; in the room to the right, his sister began sobbing.

Why didn't his sister join the others? She had most likely just now arisen from bed and had not yet begun to get dressed. And why was she crying? Because he did not stand up and let the Deputy Director in; because he was in danger of losing his position and because the Director would then persecute his parents with the old demands? Those were unnecessary worries, for the time being. Gregor was still here and did not in the least contemplate leaving his family. At the moment he was lying on the carpet, and no one who was aware of his condition would seriously request that he let the

Deputy Director in. Gregor could not possibly be dismissed just for this minor breach of politeness; he could easily find a suitable excuse later. And it seemed to Gregor far more reasonable to leave him in peace now, instead of disturbing him with tears and entreaties. But it was the uncertainty of it all that distressed the others and so excused their behavior.

"Mr. Samsa," the Deputy Director now called in a raised voice, "what's the matter? You barricade yourself there in your room, answer merely with yes and no, burden your parents with profound, unnecessary worries and — this only mentioned incidentally — neglect your business responsibilities in an unheard-of way. I speak here in the name of your parents and your Director and earnestly request of you an immediate, clear explanation. I am amazed; I am amazed. I thought I knew you as a quiet, reasonable person, and now you suddenly begin to exhibit extraordinary capriciousness. The Director told me early this morning of a possible explanation for your dereliction — it related to the cash account recently entrusted to you — but I actually almost gave him my word of honor that this explanation could not be accurate. Now, however, I see your incomprehensible stubbornness here, and I lose any desire to vouch for you in the least. And your position is not the most secure. I originally had the intention of saying all of this just between the two of us, but since you force me to waste my time here needlessly, I don't know why your parents should not also hear it. Your performance recently has been very unsatisfying. It is not the time of the year, of course, to do extraordinary business, we recognize that; but there is no time of year in which to do *no* business, Mr. Samsa — there cannot be."

"But, sir," called out Gregor, beside himself, forgetting everything else in his agitation, "I'll open up immediately, this instant. A mild indisposition — an attack of dizziness — has kept me from getting up. I'm still lying in bed. I'm completely recovered now, though. I'm climbing out of bed right now. Just one moment of patience! I thought things were not quite back to normal yet. But I'm already well again. How it can suddenly come over a person! I was fine yesterday evening, my parents know that, or perhaps I should say that yesterday evening I had a slight premonition of it. It must have been easy to see in me. Why didn't I report it to the office yesterday! But one always thinks that one can ride out illness without having to stay home. Sir! Spare my parents! There is no basis for all the reproaches you've made against me; no one said anything about them to me before now. Perhaps you haven't seen the latest orders that I sent in. In any case, I will be starting my trip on the eight o'clock train. These few hours of rest have strengthened me. Don't let me hold you up, though, sir; I'll soon be in the office myself, and please have the goodness to say so, and to send my greetings to the Director."

And while Gregor hurriedly blurted all this out, hardly knowing what he said, he moved effortlessly closer to the chest, thanks to the practice he had had in bed, and attempted to raise himself against it to an upright position. He actually wanted to open the door, actually wanted to let them see him and to speak with the Deputy Director. He was eager to know what they all would say to him when they finally saw him, after so much urging. Would they be afraid? If so, Gregor would be absolved of responsibility and could relax. If they took it all in stride, however, then, too, he would have no cause for worry, and he really could be at the train station at eight, if he hurried. At first he simply slid a few times down the side of the slippery chest; finally, however, he gave himself one last swing and stood upright. He ignored the pain in his lower body, despite the fact that it burned. Now he let himself fall against the back of a nearby chair and held tight to its sides with his legs. This helped him regain his self-control, and he stayed quiet, so that he could hear the Deputy Director speak.

GREG WOOD / AFP / Getty Images

The Metamorphosis has been adapted many times, as both play and opera. In this photograph from a stage production, the characters, including Gregor, are all dressed in everyday clothing. **Why do you think this production does not represent Gregor's physical transformation? How do you think the viewer's experience of Gregor's transformation is affected by the fact that the actor who plays him is still clearly human?**

"Did you understand one word?" the Deputy Director asked his parents. "Surely he's making fun of us?" "For God's sake," cried his mother in the midst of tears, "he might be seriously ill, and we're all plaguing him. Grete! Grete!" she then screamed. "Mother?" called his sister from the other side. They were communicating through Gregor's room. "You must go fetch the doctor this minute. Gregor is ill. Quickly, to the doctor. Did you hear Gregor speak just now?" "That was the voice of an animal," said the Deputy Director, noticeably quiet, by contrast with the screaming of his mother. "Anna! Anna!" called his father towards the kitchen, clapping his hands, "Get a locksmith immediately!" And the two girls ran, their skirts rustling, through the foyer — how had his sister gotten dressed so quickly? — and flung the apartment door open. There was no noise of the door slamming; they had probably left it open, as was usual in apartments where some great misfortune had occurred.

Gregor had become much calmer, however. It was true that they didn't understand his speech, but it sounded clear enough to him, clearer than previously, perhaps because his ear had adjusted to it. But they did still believe that something was wrong with him, and they were prepared to help him. He was pleased by the confidence and certainty with which the first arrangements had been made. He felt drawn once again into the circle of humanity and expected great things from both the doctor and the locksmith, without really making a distinction between them. In order to develop the clearest possible voice for the decisive discussions to come, he coughed a bit, although he tried to do this in a muted fashion, because this, too, might sound very different from a human cough — he no longer trusted himself to judge. It had now fallen completely silent in the next room. His parents might have been sitting at the table, whispering with the Deputy Director, or perhaps they were all pressed against the door, listening.

Using the chair, Gregor slowly shoved himself forward, and then let go, throwing himself against the door, and holding himself upright against it. The balls of his feet had some sticky substance on them. He took a moment to recover from the exertion. Then he applied himself to turning the key in the lock. Unfortunately, it seemed as if he had no real teeth — what then could he grip the key with? — but his jaws, on the other hand, were powerful. With their help he started to turn the key. He paid no attention to the fact that he obviously did some harm to himself in the process — a brown discharge came out from his mouth, flowing over the key and dripping on the floor. "Listen now," said the Deputy Director in the next room, "he's turning the key." That encouraged Gregor greatly, but all of them should have cheered him on, his father and mother, too: "Come on, Gregor," they should have called, "keep at it, keep working the lock!" And imagining that all his efforts were being watched with rapt attention, he recklessly bit down on the key with all his might. He danced around the lock, following the key as it turned; holding himself upright entirely with his mouth, he either pulled up on the key or forced it down with the full weight of his body, as necessary. The crisp click of the lock finally snapping back elated him. Breathing a sigh of relief he said to himself, "I didn't even need the locksmith," and he laid his head on the door handle, in order to open the door.

Because he had to open the door in this way, he was not yet visible even when it was opened wide. If he didn't want to fall flat on his back just before his entrance into the next room, he would first have to slowly make his way around the open panel of the double door. He was still busy with this difficult maneuver and had not yet had a moment to think of the others, when he heard the Deputy Director force out a loud "Oh!" It sounded like a gust of wind. Now he could also see the Deputy, who was nearest the door — he pressed his hand to his open mouth and slowly shrank back, as if an invisible, irresistible force drove him. His mother — who stood, despite the presence of the Deputy Director, with her hair still loose, and sticking up in parts from her night's sleep — first looked at his father with her hands clasped; then she walked two steps towards Gregor and sank to the ground in the midst of her billowing skirts, her face completely hidden, sunk upon her breast. His father balled his fist with a fierce expression, as if he wanted to knock Gregor back into his room; then he looked uncertainly around the living room, covered his eyes with his hands, and sobbed so that his powerful chest shook.

Gregor had not yet entered the outer room; instead, he leaned from within against the door panel that was still fastened, so that only half of his body and his head, craned to one side in order to see them, were visible. It had become much brighter outside in the meantime: one could clearly see a section of the endless, gray-black building — it was a hospital — that stood across the street, its severe, uniform windows breaking up its facade. The rain still fell, but only in large, singly visible and singly plummeting drops. The table teemed with breakfast dishes; his father considered breakfast the most important meal of the day, and he protracted it for hours reading various periodicals. On the wall just opposite hung a photograph of Gregor from his military days, which showed him dressed as a lieutenant, with a carefree smile, his hand on his dagger, his bearing and his uniform commanding respect. The door to the foyer was open, and because the door to the apartment was open as well, one could see the outer hall and the top of the staircase leading downwards.

"Now," said Gregor — and he was well aware that he was the only one remaining calm — "I will just get dressed, pack my samples up, and be off. Will you all allow me to go? Deputy

Director, you see that I'm not obstinate and that I want to work. Traveling is demanding, but I couldn't live without it. Where do you intend to go now, Deputy Director? To the office? Yes? Will you report everything accurately? A person might be unable to work for a time, but it is precisely then that one must consider his past accomplishments and keep in mind that once the hindrance is past, he will certainly work even harder and more efficiently. I owe a great deal to the Director — you know that only too well. On the other hand, I have the care of my parents and sister. I'm in a fix, but I'll work my way out again. But please don't make it more difficult for me than it already is. Take my part in the office! I know the traveling salesmen aren't popular. People think we earn a huge amount of money and lead grand lives. People just don't have any particular reason to think this prejudice through carefully. You, however, Deputy Director, you have a better perspective on how things work than most of the staff — I might say, confidentially, a better perspective than even the Director himself, who, in his capacity as owner, can easily be misled in his judgment about an employee. You know very well that the traveling salesman, because he is away from the office the better part of the year, easily falls victim to gossip, to chance misfortune, and groundless complaints. It's impossible for him to defend himself against these complaints, as he ordinarily learns nothing of them; it's only when he comes home at the end of a trip completely exhausted that he feels the terrible consequences, whose origins he can't divine, in his very body. Deputy Director, don't leave without saying one word that shows me that you agree with me at least in part!"

But the Deputy Director had turned away at Gregor's first words, and was staring back at Gregor over one twitching shoulder, his mouth agape. During Gregor's speech he had not stood still for a moment, but, never taking his eyes off of Gregor, moved steadily but surreptitiously towards the door, as if there were some secret prohibition against leaving the room. He had already reached the foyer, and judging by the sudden movement with which he pulled his foot out of the room at his last step, one would have thought his sole was on fire. Once in the foyer, he stretched his hand out towards the staircase as if divine deliverance awaited him there.

Gregor realized that the Deputy Director could under no circumstances be allowed to leave this way, if his position at the company were not to be endangered. His parents didn't understand this as well as he did. They had over the years persuaded themselves that he was guaranteed permanent employment in the company, and besides, they had so much to do in dealing with their own distress at the moment, that their foresight had vanished. But Gregor had this foresight. The Deputy Director must be detained, calmed, persuaded, and finally won over — the future of Gregor and his family depended on it. If only his sister were here! She was clever: she was already crying when Gregor was still calmly lying on his back. And the Deputy Director, that ladies' man, would surely have let her sway him: she would have closed the apartment door and talked him out of his fear in the foyer. But his sister was not there, so Gregor would have to handle it himself. And without thinking about the fact that he had no idea yet how well he could move, without thinking that his speech was possibly — well, very probably — incomprehensible, he let go of the door panel, forcing himself through the opening, and headed for the Deputy Director, who was already at the landing in the hall and hugging himself in a comical manner. With a small cry, scrambling in vain for something to hold on to, Gregor immediately fell down onto his many little legs. This had hardly happened, when for the first time that morning he felt a sense of physical well-being. His little legs had solid ground beneath them; they obeyed him completely, as he noted to his delight. They even strove to carry him where he wanted to go.

Suddenly, he believed that the ultimate relief of all his suffering was at hand. But at that moment, as he lay on the floor trembling with suppressed energy, close to his mother and directly opposite her, she sprang up — she who had seemed so lost in thought — with her arms outstretched, her fingers splayed, and cried out: "Help, for God's sake, help!" She kept her head turned towards him, as if she wanted to be able to see him better, but, following a contradictory impulse, she ran heedlessly backwards, forgetting that the table full of dishes lay behind her. She quickly sat down when she reached it, as if absent-mindedly, seeming not to notice that next to her the coffeepot had been knocked over and coffee was streaming freely out onto the carpet.

"Mother, Mother," Gregor said softly, and looked up at her. The Deputy Director vanished from his mind momentarily, and he couldn't stop himself from snapping his jaws at the empty air several times at the sight of the flowing coffee. His mother began screaming again over this, fled from the table, and fell into the arms of his father, who was hurrying towards her. But Gregor had no time then for his parents. The Deputy Director was already on the stairs. His chin on the railing, he looked back one last time. Gregor took a running start, in order to have the best chance of catching up to him. The Deputy Director must have sensed something, as he sprang down several steps and then disappeared. "Ahh!" he screamed; it echoed throughout the entire stairwell.

Unfortunately, the flight of the Deputy Director seemed to have completely unhinged his father, who up until then had been relatively self-controlled. Instead of running after the Deputy Director or at least not restraining Gregor from pursuing him, with his right hand he grabbed the walking stick that the Deputy Director had left behind on an armchair together with his hat and coat; with his left hand he picked up a large newspaper from the table; then, stamping his feet, he began to drive Gregor back into his room by swatting at him with the stick and the newspaper. None of Gregor's pleas helped — none of his pleas were understood. The more submissively he bowed his head, the more vigorously his father stamped his feet. Across the room, despite the cool weather, his mother had thrown open a window and, leaning far out of the window, pressed her face into her hands. Between the street and the stairwell there arose a strong cross-draft: the window curtains flew up; the newspapers on the table rustled, and a few pages fluttered to the floor. His father drove him back mercilessly, spitting out hissing noises like a wild beast. Gregor, however, still was unpracticed in moving backwards, so he went very slowly. If he had only been allowed time to turn around, he would have gone immediately back into his room, but he was afraid of making his father impatient. At every moment the stick in his father's hand threatened to deal him a fatal blow to his back or head. Finally, however, Gregor found he had no choice, as he noted with terror that he seemed unable to keep going in the right direction when he moved backwards. He therefore began, with frequent side-glances at his father, to turn around as quickly as he could, which was actually very slowly. His father might have understood his good intentions, because he did not disturb him while he was doing this; in fact, he actually directed him here and there from a distance with the point of his stick. If only there weren't this unbearable hissing from his father! It unnerved Gregor completely. He was already almost completely turned around when, listening to his hissing, he made a mistake and turned a bit in the wrong direction. When he was finally, fortunately, headfirst at the opening of the door, it appeared that his body was too wide to go through without further ado. In his present state of mind it was naturally far from occurring to his father to open the other door panel in order to make a wide enough passageway for Gregor. He was obsessed merely with getting

Gregor into his room as quickly as possible. He would never have allowed the preparations necessary for Gregor to raise himself up and possibly go through the door that way. Instead, making a great deal of noise, he drove Gregor forward as if there were no obstacle before him. The noise coming from behind Gregor didn't sound any longer like the voice of his father. It was clearly no laughing matter, so Gregor forced himself — happen what would — through the door. One side of his body was hoisted upwards. He lay crookedly in the doorway. One of his flanks was rubbed raw, and on the white door ugly smears remained behind. He was soon stuck fast, and couldn't move at all anymore. His little legs hung twitching on one side, and those on the other side were pressed painfully against the floor. Then his father liberated him with a powerful shove from behind, and he flew, bleeding heavily, a long way into his room. The door was slammed shut with the stick, and then it was finally quiet.

II

It was already twilight when Gregor awoke from a deep, dreamless sleep. He would not have arisen much later even without having been disturbed, for he felt well rested and no longer sleepy, but it seemed to him that he had been awakened by the sounds of a fleeting footstep and of the door to the foyer carefully being shut. The glare from the electric street lamp outside lay palely here and there on the ceiling of his room and on the upper surfaces of the furniture, but down by Gregor it was dark. He shoved himself slowly towards the door, awkwardly groping with the feelers he had just then come to appreciate, in order to see what had happened there. His left side seemed to be a single, long, unpleasantly taut scar, and he had to positively limp on his row of legs. One leg had been seriously injured during the events of the morning: it dragged limply behind him.

It was only when he was at the door that he realized what had actually lured him there: it was the smell of something edible. Standing there was a basin filled with fresh milk, swimming with small pieces of white bread. He could almost have laughed for joy, for he was even hungrier than he had been that morning. He immediately dunked his head in the milk nearly up to his eyes. But he soon pulled back, disappointed. It wasn't only that his tender left side made it hard for him to eat — for it seemed he was able to eat only if his entire panting body cooperated — it was rather that the milk, which had always been his favorite drink, and which his sister certainly placed here for that reason, didn't taste good to him at all. He turned away from the basin with something like revulsion and crept back into the middle of the room.

The gas lamps had been turned on in the living room, as Gregor saw through the crack in the door. Whereas ordinarily at this hour his father would read the afternoon paper out loud to his mother and sometimes to his sister, now there wasn't a sound. Perhaps the reading, which his sister had frequently told him and wrote him about, had lately dropped out of their routine. It was completely quiet, though the apartment was certainly not empty. "What a quiet life the family leads," Gregor said to himself and felt great pride, as he stared into the darkness before him, that he had been able to provide his parents and his sister with such a life, in such a nice apartment. But what if terror now drove away all quiet, all prosperity, all contentment? Rather than surrender to such thoughts, Gregor preferred to move about, so he crawled back and forth in the room.

Once during the long evening one of the side doors and later the other was opened a crack and then hastily shut again. Someone had probably needed to come in, but had then thought better of it. Gregor now stopped directly in front of the door to the living room, determined somehow to get the hesitant visitor to come in, or at least to find out who it was, but the doors were not opened again and Gregor waited in vain. Early on, when the doors were locked, everyone had wanted to come in; now, when he had unlocked one door and the others had clearly been unlocked during the day, no one came, and the keys had been moved to the outside.

It was late at night before the light in the living room was turned out, and it was now clear that his parents and sister had been awake until then, for all three could clearly be heard departing on tiptoes. Now surely no one would come to see Gregor until morning; he therefore had quite a while in which to consider undisturbed how he should newly arrange his life. But he was uneasy lying flat on the ground in the high-ceilinged open room. He did not know why this should be, for he had lived in the room for five years already. Half unconsciously, and not without some shame, he scurried under the sofa where, despite the fact that his back was a bit crushed and he could no longer lift his head, he immediately felt more comfortable, regretting only that his body was too broad to fit completely underneath.

He remained there the entire night. He spent part of it in a light sleep, out of which hunger kept jolting him awake, and part of it awake, consumed by worries and by vague hopes that all led to the same conclusion: that for the time being he should keep calm and, by exercising patience and the greatest consideration for his family, try to make bearable the unpleasantness that he would in his present condition inevitably cause them.

Early the next morning — it was nearly still night — Gregor had a chance to test the firmness of his resolve, for his sister, already half-dressed, opened the door leading from the foyer and looked tensely inside. She couldn't find him right away, but when she noticed him under the sofa — God, he had to be someplace, he couldn't have just flown away — she was so shocked that without being able to stop herself, she slammed the door shut again. But as if she regretted her behavior, she opened the door again immediately, and came inside on tiptoe, as if she were in the presence of someone severely ill, or even a complete stranger. Gregor shoved his head forward just to the edge of the sofa and watched her. He wondered whether she would notice that he had left the milk standing, though not from lack of hunger, and whether she would bring him some other food that suited him better. If she didn't do it on her own, he would rather starve than make her aware of it, although he felt a strong urge to shoot out from beneath the sofa, throw himself at her feet, and beg her for something good to eat. But his sister, with some amazement, right away noticed the still full basin: only a bit of milk had been spilled around its edges. She picked it up immediately, though with a rag, not with her bare hands, and took it away. Gregor was extremely curious to see what she would bring as a replacement and thought a great deal about it. He could never have guessed, however, what his sister in her goodness actually did. In order to test his preferences, she brought him an entire assortment of foods spread out on an old newspaper. There were old, half-rotten vegetables; bones from last night's meal, covered with congealed white sauce; a few raisins and almonds; a cheese that Gregor had declared inedible two days before; a piece of dry bread, a piece of bread smeared with butter, and a piece with butter and salt. Beside this she placed the basin that seemed now to be designated permanently for Gregor, which she had filled with water. And out of tact, because she knew Gregor would not eat in front of her, she departed hastily, even going so far as to turn the key in the lock, just so that Gregor would know that he could make himself as comfortable as he wanted. Gregor's legs quivered, now that the meal lay waiting. His wounds must moreover have completely healed. He felt no impairment now, and was astonished at this, thinking of how he had cut himself very slightly with a knife more than a month ago, and how the wound

Alison Czinkota

How does this work, by artist Alison Czinkota, characterize Gregor's sister Grete as she offers him food?

had still hurt him considerably the day before yesterday. "Am I less sensitive than before?" he wondered, and sucked greedily at the cheese, to which he had found himself urgently drawn, before everything else. In rapid succession, amidst tears of joy, he devoured the cheese, the vegetables, and the sauce. He didn't like the taste of the fresh foods, however — he couldn't even bear their smell, and dragged the foods that he wanted to eat a bit farther away. He had long since finished everything and lay lazily in the same spot when his sister slowly turned the key in the lock, as a sign that he should withdraw. That jolted him awake immediately, though he was almost dozing, and he hurried back under the sofa. But it took great self-control for him to remain under the sofa even for the brief time that his sister was in the room, for his body had swelled a bit with the ample meal, and he could hardly breathe in the narrow space. Half-suffocating, he looked out with slightly bulging eyes as his sister, who noticed nothing, swept up with a broom not just the remainder of the food Gregor had eaten, but also the food that he had not even touched, as if this were no longer useable. She put it all in a container that she closed with a wooden lid, and then carried everything out. She had hardly turned around when Gregor pulled himself out from under the sofa and exhaled.

In this way Gregor now received his daily meals: the first in the morning, while his parents and the servant girl still slept, and the second after the common midday meal, for his parents slept a bit afterwards, and his sister sent the serving girl away on one errand or another. It was not that the others wanted him to starve, but experiencing his meals at secondhand might have been all they could bear; or perhaps his sister simply wanted to spare them even this minor source of sorrow, since they were already suffering enough.

With what kinds of excuses they had managed to get the doctor and the locksmith out of the apartment the first morning, Gregor didn't manage to find out. Because no one could understand him, it didn't occur to anyone — not even to his sister — that he could understand them, so he had to content himself, when his sister was in his room, with listening to her occasional sighs and appeals to the saints. It was only later, when she had gotten used to things a bit — getting used to them completely was out of the question, of course — that Gregor sometimes seized on a remark that was meant in a friendly way or that could be taken that way. "Today he liked it," she said, if he had made a real dent in the meal, while in the contrary case, which occurred ever more frequently of late, she used to say almost sadly: "Everything untouched again."

Though Gregor could not learn any news directly, he overheard some from the rooms next door. The moment he heard voices, he immediately ran to the door and pressed his entire body up against it. Especially in the early days, there was no conversation that did not somehow, if only indirectly, relate to him. For two days there were consultations at every meal about what they should do; between meals, too, they discussed the same thing. There were always at least two family members at home, because no one wanted to remain home alone, and they couldn't under any circumstances all leave the apartment at the same time. On the very first day the girl who cooked for them had begged his mother on bended knee — it wasn't exactly clear what and how much she knew of what had happened — to dismiss her. As she departed fifteen minutes later, she tearfully thanked them for her dismissal, as if for the greatest favor that had ever been done her, and swore a terrible oath, without anyone having asked her to do so, not to betray the least of what she knew to anyone.

Now his sister had to do the cooking, together with his mother. This didn't take much effort, however, because they ate practically nothing. Gregor heard them again and again urge each other to eat and receive no other answer than "Thanks, I've had enough," or something similar. It seemed they didn't drink anything, either. His sister often asked his father if he would like a beer, cheerfully offering to get it herself. When his father said nothing, she offered to send the porter for it, in case he didn't want to trouble her. When his father finally uttered a firm "No," the subject was dropped.

In the course of the first few days his father explained their entire financial situation and their prospects to his mother and to his sister. Now and then he stood up from the table and took various documents and notebooks out of the small safe that he had rescued from the bankruptcy of his business five years before. He could be heard opening the complicated lock and closing it again after removing what he sought. His father's explanations contained the first heartening news that Gregor had heard since his imprisonment. He had been under the impression that his father had absolutely nothing left over from his business. As least, he had said nothing to the contrary, and Gregor had certainly never asked him about it. Gregor's concern at the time of the bankruptcy had been to arrange everything so that the family could forget as soon as possible the financial misfortune that had brought them to a state of complete despair. And so he had begun to work with pronounced fervor. Practically overnight he was elevated from a minor clerk into a traveling salesman, which naturally gave him completely different financial prospects. His successes at work translated directly into cash that he could lay on the table at home before his astonished and pleased family. Those had been fine times, but they had never recurred, at least not with the same warm feelings, although Gregor later earned so much money that he was in a position to support the entire family, and he did so. They simply got used to it — the family, as well as Gregor. They gratefully accepted his money, and he gladly offered it, but that special warmth did not reappear. Only his sister remained close to Gregor. Because she loved music very much, unlike Gregor, and could play the violin movingly, he secretly planned to send her to the conservatory next year, despite the great cost, which would have to be made up somehow. The conservatory came up often in conversations with his sister during Gregor's brief stays in the city, but only as a beautiful dream whose realization was unthinkable. His parents didn't even like to hear them utter those innocent musings. But Gregor had given it a good deal of thought and intended to announce his decision with due ceremony on Christmas Eve.

These thoughts, completely futile in his present situation, went through his head while he clung to the door and listened. Sometimes, from sheer exhaustion, he could listen no more and would let his head fall against the door, but then immediately catch himself, for even the faint noise that he made in doing so was heard next door and caused them all to fall silent. "What's he doing now?" said his father after a pause, obviously turned towards the door. Only then was the interrupted conversation gradually taken up again.

Gregor now learned — for his father tended to repeat himself often in his explanations, partly because he had not concerned himself with these matters for a long while, and partly, too, because his mother didn't immediately understand everything the first time — that despite all their misfortunes, a certain sum, though a very small one, was left over from the old days. The untouched interest on the sum had moreover in the meantime allowed it to grow a bit. Besides this, the money that Gregor had brought home every month — he had only kept a few florins for himself — had not been completely exhausted and had accumulated into a small amount of capital. Gregor, behind the door, nodded eagerly, overjoyed at this unexpected foresight and thriftiness. It occurred to him that he might have used that extra money to further pay down the debt his father owed the Director, bringing closer the day that he could quit his job, but the way his father had arranged things was no doubt better.

The sum that had been saved was not, however, large enough to allow his family to live off of the interest. It would have been enough to support them for a year, or at most two years, but no longer. The sum really shouldn't be touched: it should be set aside for emergencies. To live, money would have to be earned. His father was a healthy but old man, who had not worked now for five years and couldn't in any case take on too much. During these five years, which had been the first free time of his hardworking but unsuccessful life, he had put on a great deal of weight and had become downright sluggish. But was his elderly mother supposed to earn money now — his mother, who suffered from asthma, for whom even a stroll through the apartment was considerable exertion, and who spent every other day on the sofa by the open window, gasping for breath? Or his sister, who at seventeen was still a child, and whose lifestyle up to that point had consisted of dressing herself neatly, sleeping late, helping out in the household, taking part in a few modest pleasures, and above all playing the violin? Whenever the conversation turned towards the necessity of earning money, Gregor left the door and threw himself on the leather sofa that stood nearby, for he burned with shame and sorrow.

Often he lay there the long night through, though he was unable to sleep for a moment and just scratched for hours at the leather. Or he would go to great pains to shove an armchair to the window, then crawl up to the windowsill and, bolstered by the armchair, lean against the window. He did so only in some kind of nostalgia for the feeling of freedom he had previously found in looking out the window, for the fact was that every day he saw things that were even a short distance away less and less clearly. He could no longer see the hospital that lay across the way, whose all too massive prospect he had earlier cursed. If he had not known very well that he lived in the quiet, but distinctly urban Charlotte Street, he could have believed that he looked out of his window into a desert in which the gray sky and the gray earth merged indistinguishably. His alert sister only had to see the armchair standing by the window twice before she began to shove the chair precisely back to the spot by the window after she straightened up the room. She even left the inner casement open from then on.

If Gregor had been able to speak to his sister and thank her for everything she had to do for him, he would have been able to bear her assistance more easily; as it was, however, it caused him some pain. His sister tried to hide the awkwardness of the whole thing as much as possible, and the longer it went on, the better she succeeded, but Gregor felt everything more acutely as time went on. Even her entrance was terrible for him. She had hardly entered, when, without even taking the time to shut the doors, though she otherwise took such pains to spare everyone the sight of Gregor's room, she ran to the window and hastily flung it open, as if she were suffocating. Then she remained for a time by the window, cold as it still was, and breathed deeply. With this running and commotion she alarmed Gregor twice daily. He trembled under the sofa the entire time and yet he knew very well that she would gladly have spared him, if only it had been possible to stay in a room where Gregor was with the windows closed.

Once — one month had already passed since Gregor's transformation, and there was no longer any reason for his sister to be astonished by his appearance — she came a bit earlier than usual and encountered Gregor as he was staring out the window, motionless and perfectly positioned to frighten someone. Gregor would not have been surprised if she had not come in, since his position hindered her from immediately opening the window, but she not only refrained from coming in, she actually turned around and locked the door. A stranger would have thought that Gregor had lain in wait for her and tried to bite her. Gregor naturally hid himself immediately under the sofa, but he had to wait until midday for her return, and she seemed then more agitated than usual. He realized from this that his appearance was still unbearable to her and that it would remain so — that she had to steel herself to keep from running at the sight of even the small portion of his body that jutted out from beneath the sofa. In order to spare her the sight, one day he dragged a sheet onto the sofa — it took him four hours to do so — and arranged it in such a way that he was completely covered. His sister could not have seen him even if she bent down. If the sheet had not been necessary, in her opinion, she could have removed it, for it obviously couldn't be pleasant for Gregor to block himself off so completely. But she left the sheet where it was, and Gregor thought he even noticed a grateful glance when he once carefully lifted the sheet with his head in order to see how his sister liked the new arrangement.

In the first two weeks his parents could not bring themselves to come in to see him, and he often heard them praise his sister's current industry, whereas they had previously complained a great deal about her, as she had then seemed to them a rather idle girl. In those early days, both his father and his mother often waited in front of Gregor's room while his sister straightened up, and as soon as she came out, she had to tell them precisely what it looked like in the room, what Gregor had eaten, how he had behaved, and whether there were perhaps any slight improvement in his condition. His mother also wanted to visit Gregor early on, but his father and sister dissuaded her with sound reasons to which Gregor listened very attentively, and which he completely supported. Later, however, she had to be restrained with force. When she cried out, "Let me in to see Gregor; he's my poor son! Don't you understand that I must go to him?" Gregor thought that it might be good if his mother did come in — not every day, of course, but perhaps once a week. After all, she knew how to do things much better than his sister, who, despite her courage, was still only a child, and who likely took on such a heavy burden only out of childish thoughtlessness.

Gregor's wish to see his mother was soon fulfilled. During the day, for his parents' sake, Gregor did not want to show himself at the window, but he did not have much room to crawl in the few square meters of floor space. It was hard enough for him to bear lying quietly during the night, and eating soon gave him not the least bit of pleasure, so in order to distract himself, he had adopted the habit of crawling across the walls and ceiling. He especially liked hanging upside down from the ceiling. It was completely different from lying on the floor: he could breathe more freely; his entire body swayed gently; and in the nearly happy distraction in which he found himself above, it sometimes happened that he unexpectedly let himself fall and crashed to the ground. But these days he had better control of his body, so he did not hurt himself even in a great fall. His sister immediately noticed the new amusement that Gregor had found for himself — he left a trace of stickiness behind him here and there while crawling — and so she got it in her head to allow him to crawl to his utmost by removing the furniture that hindered it, especially the chest of drawers and desk. She was not capable of doing this herself, however. She didn't dare ask her father for help. The servant girl would certainly not help her: this roughly sixteen-year-old girl had stuck it out quite bravely since the dismissal of the former cook, but she had asked for the privilege of keeping the kitchen door always locked and only having to open it when specifically asked. So his sister had no choice but to enlist her mother one time when her father was absent. With cries of great joy his mother approached, but fell silent at the door of Gregor's room. His sister checked first, of course, to see that the room was in order; only then did she let her mother enter. In great haste, Gregor pulled the sheet lower and gathered more material around him. It looked like a sheet had merely been carelessly thrown over the sofa. Gregor also refrained from spying out from under the sheet. He deprived himself of the sight of his mother and took his pleasure entirely from the fact that she had come. "Come on, you can't see him," said his sister, and she apparently led her mother in by the hand. Gregor then heard the two frail women shove the heavy old chest of drawers from its place. His sister reserved the greatest part of the labor for herself, ignoring the warnings of her mother, who feared that she would overexert herself. It took a very long time. After fifteen minutes of work, his mother said that they should just leave the chest where it was, first, because it was too heavy — they wouldn't be finished before his father returned, and so would end up leaving the chest in the middle of the room, where it would block Gregor at every turn — and second, because it was not at all certain that they were doing Gregor a favor by removing the furniture. It seemed to her rather the opposite: the sight of the empty wall oppressed her heart. Why should Gregor not feel the same way? He had been used to the room's furniture for so long, that he would surely feel lost in an empty room. "And isn't it so," concluded his mother very softly — almost whispering, as if she wanted to keep Gregor, of whose precise whereabouts she wasn't certain, from hearing even the sound of her voice, for she was convinced that he could not understand the words — "isn't it so, that by removing the furniture we seem to be saying that we give up all hope of his recovery, and abandon him absolutely? I think it would be best if we left the room in exactly the same condition it was in before, so that when Gregor returns to us, he'll find

And me without
a Twitter account.
klossner

John Klossner The New Yorker Collection/ The Cartoon Bank

How does the cartoonist suggest that *The Metamorphosis* has become part of our popular culture — perhaps even for those who haven't read the novella?

everything unchanged, and so more easily forget what's happened in the meantime."

In listening to his mother's words, Gregor realized that the lack of any direct human communication over the course of the past two months, together with the monotonous life he led in the midst of the family, must have deranged his mind; otherwise he couldn't explain why he had earnestly desired that his room be emptied. Did he really want to let them transform the warm room, comfortably outfitted with inherited furnishings, into a cave? Granted, he would be able to crawl undisturbed in all directions, but he would at the same time forget, quickly and completely, his human past. He was already close to forgetting it, but his mother's voice, so long unheard, had roused him. Nothing should be removed; everything had to stay. He could not afford to lose the good influence the furniture had on his condition. If the furniture hindered him from carrying on his mindless crawling about, that was no drawback, it was rather a great advantage.

But his sister was unfortunately of a different opinion. She had become accustomed, not completely without justification, to playing the expert when it came to discussing anything that concerned Gregor with her parents. And so her mother's advice now led her to insist on the removal not only of the chest and the desk, which was all she had first intended, but of all of the furniture, with the exception of the indispensable sofa. Of course, it was not just childish stubbornness and the hard-won self-confidence she had recently and unexpectedly acquired that determined her on this course: she had actually observed that Gregor needed a great deal of room to crawl around in, and that he did not use the furniture at all, as far as she could see. It might also have been the romantic nature of girls of her age, which sought some outlet at every opportunity, and made her want Gregor's situation to be even more terrifying, so that she could do even more than before to help him. For in a space in which Gregor, completely alone, ruled the empty walls, no person but Grete would dare to enter.

And so she did not allow herself to be swayed by her mother, who faltered from sheer uneasiness at being in the room, soon fell silent, and finally helped his sister as much as she was able in shoving the chest out of the room. Gregor could spare the chest if he must, but the desk had to stay. The women had hardly left the room with the chest, pushing at it and gasping for air, when Gregor stuck his head out from under the sofa, in order to see where he could intervene, as carefully and as considerately as possible. But unfortunately it was his mother who returned first, while Grete in the next room gripped the chest and rocked it back and forth alone, without, naturally, being able to move it from its spot. His mother was not, however, used to the sight of Gregor — he might have made her sick — so Gregor, alarmed, rushed back to the opposite end of the sofa. He could not, however, prevent the sheet from moving a bit at the front. That was enough to put his mother on the alert. She froze, stood still a moment, and then returned to Grete.

Though Gregor kept telling himself that nothing extraordinary was happening — a few pieces of furniture were merely being moved around — he soon realized that this continual back and forth on the part of the women, their soft calls to one another, and the scraping of the furniture on the floor affected him like the greatest of commotions closing in on him from all sides. However closely he drew in his head and legs and however firmly he pressed his body to the floor, he realized he couldn't stand it much longer. They were emptying out his room; they were taking from him everything that he held dear. They had carried out the chest which held his fret saw and other tools; they were already working free the desk from the grooves it had worn into the floor — the desk at which he had written his exercises as a student at trade school, at secondary school, and even at primary school. At this point he did not have the patience to contemplate the women's good intentions, the existence of which he had at any rate almost forgotten. Exhausted, they worked now in complete silence, and only the heavy tread of their feet could be heard.

And so he burst forth from under the sofa — the women were just leaning against the desk in the next room, in order to catch their breath — though he changed the direction of his charge four times, for he really did not know what to save first. On one otherwise empty wall he distinctly saw the picture of the woman dressed entirely in furs. He crept hurriedly up to it and pressed himself against the glass, which held him fast and soothed his hot belly. At least no one could take away this picture, which Gregor now completely covered with his body. He turned his head towards the door of the living room in order to observe the women on their return.

They weren't allowing themselves much rest and so came back directly. Grete had put her arm around her mother and seemed practically to carry her. "Well, what should we take now?" said Grete and looked around. Then her glance met Gregor's as he clung to the wall. She maintained her composure — surely only due to her mother's presence — bent her face to her mother, in order to keep her from looking around, and said hastily, a tremor in her voice, "Come, let's go back in the living room for a moment." Grete's intention was clear to Gregor: she wanted to bring her mother to safety and then chase him down off of the wall. Well, she could try! He would sit on the picture and not give it up. He would rather spring in Grete's face.

But Grete's words had for the first time really unsettled his mother. She moved to the side, spotted the giant brown fleck on the flowered wallpaper, and cried out in a screeching, raw voice, before she was really fully conscious that it was Gregor that she saw, "Oh my God; oh my God!" She then fell onto the sofa with widespread arms, as if she were altogether giving up, and didn't move. "Gregor, you — !" cried his sister with a raised fist and piercing gaze. They were the first words she had directly addressed to Gregor since his transformation. She ran into the next room in order to get some scent with which she could wake her mother out of her faint. Gregor wanted to help, too — there was still time to save the picture — but he was stuck to the glass and had to tear himself free. He, too, ran into the next room, as if he could give his sister some advice, as in earlier days, but then he had to stand helplessly behind her while she rummaged through various bottles. She was startled when she turned around; a bottle fell to the floor and broke. A sliver of glass cut Gregor's face, and some burning medicine spilled over him. Grete took as many bottles as she could carry and ran with them in to her mother. She then slammed the door shut with her foot. Gregor was now shut off from his mother, who was through his fault possibly near death. He couldn't open the door, if he did not want to chase away his sister, who had to remain with his mother. He had nothing left to do but wait. Oppressed by self-reproaches and worry, he began to crawl. He crawled over everything — walls, furniture, and ceiling — and finally, in his despair, he fell, the entire room spinning around him, onto the center of the large table.

A short time passed, and Gregor lay limply there. All around was quiet. Perhaps that was a good sign. Then the bell rang. The servant girl was naturally locked into her kitchen, and so Grete had to go open the door. His father had returned. "What happened?" were his first words. The look on Grete's face betrayed everything to him. Grete answered with a muffled voice — she was obviously pressing her face against her father's chest. "Mother fainted, but she's already better. Gregor broke out." "I was waiting for this," said his father, "I always said it would happen, but you women didn't want to hear it." It was clear to Gregor that his father had interpreted Grete's all-too-brief announcement in the worst possible way, and assumed that Gregor had been guilty of some act of violence. Therefore Gregor had to try to mollify his father, for he had neither the time nor the ability to enlighten him. And so he fled to the door of his room and pressed against it, so that his father could see immediately on leaving the hallway that Gregor had every intention of returning right away to his room. It would not be necessary to drive him back, just to open the door, and he would disappear instantly.

But his father was not in the mood to notice such subtleties: "Ah!" he cried out on entering, in a tone that made him seem at once furious and glad. Gregor drew his head back from the door and turned it toward his father. His father's appearance was different from the way he remembered it. Lately, due to his new habit of crawling about, Gregor had concerned himself less with the goings-on in the rest of the apartment; he should therefore really have been prepared to encounter new developments. But still, still, was this really his father? The same man who lay, tired out, buried deep in his bed, when Gregor was all set to go on a business trip? The man who, dressed in a nightshirt, had greeted him when he returned in the evenings from an easy chair, and, unable to stand up, only raised his arms to show his joy at his return? The man who, on the rare walks he took together with Gregor and his mother on a few Sundays and the most important holidays of the year, walked packed into his old coat even more slowly than they did, though they walked slowly enough, laboring forward with a deliberately placed cane, and who nearly always stopped when he wanted to say something, gathering his companions around him? Now, he was quite well put together. He was dressed in the kind of close-fitting blue uniform with gold buttons that doormen at the banking houses wore; over the high stiff collar of the coat his pronounced double chin protruded; under his bushy eyebrows the glance of his dark eyes sprang forth fresh and alert; the formerly disheveled white hair was combed flat into a painfully exact, shining part. He threw his hat, which bore a gold monogram — probably that of a bank — in an arc across the room and onto the sofa. He moved towards Gregor, the ends of his long coat pushed back, his hands in his pants pockets, his face grim. He probably did not know himself what he planned to do. In any case he lifted his feet unusually high, and Gregor was astonished at the gigantic size of the soles of his boots. But he didn't let his astonishment distract him. He had known from the first day of his new life that his father considered the greatest severity appropriate in dealing with him. And so he ran away from his father. He froze when his father stood still and hurried forward again when his father moved a muscle. In this way they circled the room several times, without anything decisive happening; the whole thing moved at such a slow tempo that it didn't even look like a pursuit. For the time being, Gregor stayed on the floor. He was afraid that his father might consider flight toward the walls or the ceiling as particular wickedness. But Gregor realized that he couldn't keep up even this pace for long, for when his father took a single step, he had to carry out myriad movements. He soon felt short of breath; his lungs had not been reliable even in the old days. As he staggered forward, he could barely keep his eyes open, so hard did he try to concentrate his energy for running. In his dullness he was simply unable to think of any other means of deliverance. He had almost forgotten already that the walls were open to him, though they were obstructed here by painstakingly carved furniture full of points and sharp edges. Suddenly something lightly thrown flew just past him and rolled ahead. It was an apple. Another immediately followed. Gregor froze in fear. Running further was pointless, for his father had decided to bombard him. He had filled his

How might this painting by Francis Bacon, a twentieth-century artist, be interpreted as "Kafkaesque"? Note construction, line, and color as well as the central image.

Francis Bacon *Head VI,* 1949/Arts Council Collection, Southbank Centre, London, UK/Bridgeman Images. Artwork: © The Estate of Francis Bacon. All rights reserved./DACS, London/ARS, NY 2016. Image: Bridgeman Images.

pockets from the fruit bowl on the credenza and now threw apple after apple, without for the time being aiming very carefully. These small red apples rolled around on the ground, knocking into each other as if charged with electricity. A weakly thrown apple strafed Gregor's back, but glanced off without doing any harm. One that flew immediately in its wake actually embedded itself in his back, however. Gregor tried to drag himself forward, as if he could outrun the unbelievable pain by changing position, but he felt as if he were nailed to the spot and lay sprawled upon the ground, in complete distraction of all of his senses. With his last conscious glance he watched as the door to his room was ripped open and, ahead of his screaming sister, his mother ran out of the room in her slip — for his sister had undressed her to let her breathe freely while in her faint — and raced towards his father, her untied skirts slipping down to the floor one after another; he watched as, stumbling on the skirts, she embraced his father, fully at one with him — but Gregor's vision now failed him utterly — and, with her hands clasped around the back of his head, begged him to spare Gregor's life.

III

The deep injury from which Gregor had suffered for over a month — the apple remained embedded in his flesh as a visible memento, as no one dared to remove it — seemed to have reminded even his father that despite his present sad and repulsive state, Gregor was a member of the family who should not be treated as an enemy. The law of familial obligation dictated, rather, that one had to swallow one's revulsion and be tolerant, simply be tolerant.

And though Gregor had probably permanently lost some mobility through his injury, and now, like an invalid, took many, many minutes to cross his room — crawling on high was out of the question — this degeneration in his condition brought with it a compensation that was to his mind completely satisfactory. Toward evening they now opened the living room door so that, lying in the darkness of his room and invisible from the living room, he could watch the entire family at the lighted table and listen to their conversation by general consent, as it were — a complete change from the early days when he used to watch the door like a hawk an hour or two before they gathered.

Of course, the conversations were not as lively as in earlier days. Gregor used to recall them longingly in the small hotel rooms where he had had to throw himself, exhausted, into the damp bedclothes. These days everything was mostly very quiet. His father fell asleep in his armchair soon after the evening meal; his mother and sister urged one another to silence. His mother now sewed fine lingerie for a boutique, bending close to her work under the light. His sister, who had taken a job as a salesclerk, studied stenography and French at night, in order to find a better position one day. Sometimes his father awoke and, as if he didn't realize that he had been sleeping, would say to his mother: "How long you're sewing again today!" Then he would fall asleep again immediately, while his mother and sister exchanged tired smiles.

With a kind of stubbornness his father refused to take off his work uniform when he returned home, and while his nightshirt hung, useless, on a clothes hook, he dozed at his place fully clothed, as if he were always on duty and awaited the call of his superiors. As a result, the uniform, which hadn't been new in the first place, became less than pristine, despite the care his mother and sister took with it. Gregor often spent whole evenings looking at the badly stained coat, its oft-polished gold buttons shining, in which the old man slept highly uncomfortably, but quietly.

As soon as the clock struck ten, his mother tried to wake his father by speaking softly to him, and tried to persuade him to go to bed, for he couldn't sleep well there, and a good sleep was absolutely essential, since he had to be at work by six. But in the stubbornness that had come over him since he became a bank employee, he always insisted on remaining longer where he was, although he regularly fell asleep again, and required much effort to persuade in exchanging the armchair for his bed. His mother and sister could press him with gentle remonstrances as much as they liked — for a quarter of an hour at a time he slowly shook his head, his eyes closed, and refused to stand up. His mother plucked at his sleeve, and whispered endearments in his ear; his sister left her work in order to help her mother, but got nowhere with him. He only sank deeper into his armchair. Only when the women grasped him under the arms would he open his eyes, look in turn at Gregor's mother and sister, and say, "What a life. This is the peace and quiet of my old age." And bracing himself against the women, he hoisted himself up laboriously, as if he were his own greatest burden, and allowed himself to be led to the door. He waved them off then and went on under his own power, but Gregor's mother would hastily throw down her sewing and his sister her quill in order to run after him and be of further help to him.

Who in this overworked and overtired family had time to worry about Gregor more than was absolutely necessary? The household was ever more reduced in circumstances. The servant girl had been dismissed, and a gigantic, bony servant with white hair that fluttered about her head came in the mornings and the evenings to do the hardest labor. Everything else his mother took care of, in addition to her abundant sewing work. It even came to pass that various pieces of family jewelry, which his mother and sister had previously worn with pleasure at parties and celebrations, were sold, as Gregor learned one evening from a general conversation about the prices obtained. Their greatest source of complaint, however, was that the apartment, far too large for them under the circumstances, could not be left, because it was unthinkable that Gregor be relocated. But Gregor realized that it was not consideration for him that hindered a relocation, for they could have transported him easily in a suitable carton with a few air holes. What really kept the family from changing apartments was despair, and the thought that they had been afflicted by misfortune such as had struck no one in their circle of relatives and acquaintances. They did everything that the world demanded of poor people — his father fetched breakfast for the junior bank clerks; his mother dedicated herself to making underwear for strangers; his sister ran back and forth behind the counter at the beck and call of customers — but they could do no more than that. And the wound in his back began to hurt Gregor anew when his mother and sister would return from putting his father to bed, let their work lie, and huddle close together, cheek to cheek. His mother, gesturing towards Gregor's room, said, "Close the door, Grete," and Gregor was in the dark again, while next door the women mingled tears or stared, dry-eyed and numb, down at the table.

Gregor passed the days and nights nearly without sleep. Sometimes he considered taking the affairs of the family in hand again, the next time the door was opened. After some time, he thought again about the Director and the Deputy Director, the clerks and the apprentices, the slow-witted porter, two or three friends from other companies, a chambermaid from a hotel in the provinces — a dear, fleeting memory — and a cashier from a hat store whom he had courted seriously, though too slowly. They reappeared in his thoughts together with strangers or people he had already forgotten, but instead of helping him and his family, they all remained detached, and he was glad when they disappeared. At other times, however, he was not in the mood to worry about his family. He was filled with rage at the poor care they took of him, and though he could think of nothing for which he had an appetite, he made plans to reach the pantry and take what was due him, even if he were not hungry. Without considering any longer what might especially please Gregor, mornings and afternoons before returning to the store his sister hurriedly shoved any old kind of food into his room with her foot, only in order to sweep it out with a whisk of the broom in the evenings, indifferent as to whether it might have been merely tasted or — as was usually the case — it remained completely untouched. Her cleaning of the room, which she now always did in the evening, could not have been done any more hastily. Smears of dirt ran along the walls, and here and there lay balls of dust and filth. In the early days Gregor used to position himself upon the arrival of his sister in a particularly grubby corner, in order to reproach her. But he could have remained there for weeks, and his sister would still not have changed her ways. She saw the dirt as well as he did, but she had simply decided to leave it there. At the same time, with a touchiness entirely new to her that had now possessed the entire family, she was vigilant in making sure that the straightening of Gregor's room was left to her. His mother once undertook a thorough cleaning of Gregor's room, which had required several buckets of water — the moisture bothered Gregor, and he lay broad, embittered, and unmoving on top of the sofa — but his mother did not go unpunished. That evening his sister had hardly registered the change in Gregor's room when, highly insulted, she ran into the living room, and despite her mother's beseechingly raised hands, broke into a spasm of tears that his parents — his father had naturally been frightened out of his seat — at first simply watched, helpless with astonishment. Then they, too, were affected: on one side, his father reproached his mother for not leaving the cleaning of Gregor's room to his sister; on the other side, he shouted at his sister that she would never be allowed to clean Gregor's room again. In the meantime, his mother tried to drag his father, who was beside himself with agitation, into the bedroom; his sister, racked by sobs, hammered the table with her small fists; and Gregor hissed loudly with fury that no one thought to close the door and so spare him the scene and the noise.

But even if his sister, exhausted from her work, could no longer manage to care for Gregor as she had earlier, his mother would still not have had to intervene in order to keep Gregor from being neglected. For there was still the servant. This old widow, who had weathered the worst in her long life with the help of a powerful frame, felt no especial revulsion towards Gregor. Without exactly being curious, she had once by chance opened the door to Gregor's room and stood staring at the sight of him, her hands folded across her chest. Gregor was completely taken by surprise, and despite the fact that no one was chasing him, he began to run back and forth. Since that time, she hadn't missed a chance to open the door quickly in the morning and the evening to look in at Gregor. At first she called him over to her with words that she probably considered friendly, like "Come on over here, you old dung beetle!" or "Look at the old dung beetle!" Gregor did not respond to such overtures, but remained motionless in his place, as if the door had not even been opened. If only they would order this servant to clean his room daily, instead of letting her needlessly disturb him at will! Once in the early morning — a hard rain, perhaps already a sign of the coming spring, beat on the windowpanes — Gregor became so embittered when the servant began to speak that he turned towards her, as if to attack, though slowly and feebly. Instead of being afraid, however, the servant simply lifted high into the air a chair that stood in reach of the door. As she stood there with her mouth opened wide, it was clear that she intended to shut her mouth only after the chair in her hands had come down on Gregor's back. "That's it, then?" she asked, as Gregor turned around again, and she put the chair quietly back in its corner.

Gregor now ate almost nothing. When he happened to pass by the food prepared for him, he sometimes idly took a bite and held it in his mouth for an hour or so, only to spit most of it out again. At first he thought that his sorrow over the state of his room kept him from eating, but he had actually reconciled himself very soon to the changes. The family had gotten into the habit of putting into his room things that wouldn't fit anywhere else: there were now many such things, as they had rented one room in the apartment out to three lodgers. These three serious gentlemen — all three had full beards, as Gregor discovered once by looking through the crack in the door — were painfully focused on order, not only in their room, but, simply because they had taken lodgings there, in the entire household, especially in the kitchen. They would not put up with useless or dirty things. And in any case, they had brought with them most of their own furnishings. For this reason, many things that were not saleable, but that the family did not want to throw away, had become superfluous. All of this made its way into Gregor's room — even, eventually, the ash bin and the rubbish bin from the kitchen. The servant, who was always in a rush, simply slung anything that was at the moment unuseable into Gregor's room. Fortunately Gregor usually saw only the relevant object and the hand that held it. The servant might once have intended to take the things out again when time and opportunity permitted, or perhaps to throw them all out together once and for all, but in practice they lay wherever they were tossed, unless Gregor wound his way through the clutter and stirred it up — first because he had no other place to crawl, and later with growing pleasure, although after such forays, tired to death and full of sorrow, he could not stir for hours.

Because the lodgers sometimes took their evening meal in the common living room, the living room door remained closed on some evenings. Gregor managed without it very well. On some evenings when it was open he did not even take advantage of it, but without the family's knowing it, lay in the darkest corner of his room. Once, however, the servant left the door to his room open a bit, and it remained open, even as the lodgers came in that evening and the light was turned on. They sat at the head of the table, where in former days his father, mother, and Gregor had eaten, unfolded their napkins, and took their knives and forks in hand. His mother immediately appeared in the doorway with a dish of meat and his sister directly behind her with a dish piled high with potatoes. The steaming food gave off a rich smell. The lodgers bent over the dishes placed before them as if they wanted to check them before eating, and the one in the middle, whom the other two appeared to consider an authority, actually cut off a piece of meat still in the serving dish, obviously to test whether it were tender enough, or whether it might perhaps need to be sent back to the kitchen. He was satisfied, and mother and sister, who had watched the proceedings tensely, breathed again and smiled.

The family themselves ate in the kitchen. Nevertheless, his father, before he went into the kitchen, came into the room and made a single long bow while circling the table, cap in hand. The lodgers all rose together and murmured something into their beards. When they were alone again, they ate in near total silence. It seemed strange to Gregor that, among all the various sounds of eating, he could pick out the sound of their chewing teeth—it was as if Gregor were thereby reminded that one needed teeth in order to eat, and that one could do nothing with even the most beautiful toothless jaws. "I do have an appetite," said Gregor sorrowfully to himself, "but not for these things. How these lodgers feed themselves, while I'm dying of hunger!"

On this very evening, though Gregor did not remember having heard it once before during that whole time, the violin sounded from the kitchen. The lodgers had already finished their meal. The middle one had pulled out a newspaper and given each of the others one page. They now read, leaning back, and smoked. As the violin began to play, they became alert, arose and went on tiptoes to the hall door, where they stood pressed up against one another. They must have heard them in the kitchen, for his father called out: "Do you gentlemen perhaps dislike the playing? It can be stopped immediately." "On the contrary," said the lodger in the middle, "wouldn't the young lady like to come out and play here in this room, where it's much more comfortable and convenient?" "Oh, please!" called his father, as if he were the violin player. The lodgers moved back into the room and waited. His father soon came in with the music stand, his mother with the music, and his sister with the violin. His sister quietly prepared to play. His parents, who had never rented a room out before and so exaggerated the courtesy due the lodgers, did not dare to sit on their own chairs. His father leaned against the door, his right hand stuck between two buttons of his fastened livery coat. His mother, however, accepted a chair offered by one of the lodgers, and sat off in the corner where he had happened to place the chair.

His sister began to play. His father and mother, on either side of her, followed every note, attentive to the movements of her hands. Gregor, drawn by the music, had ventured a bit further forward. His head was already in the living room. He hardly wondered at himself for being so inconsiderate towards the others of late; earlier, this consideration had been a great source of pride. And just now he had more reason than before to hide himself. Because of the dust everywhere in his room that flew up at the least movement, he was himself covered in dust. Threads, hairs, and bits of leftover food stuck to his back and sides. His general apathy was much too great for him now to lie on his back and scrub himself on the carpet, as he used to do several times a day. Despite his condition, however, he had no qualms about advancing a bit onto the immaculate living room floor.

But no one paid any attention to him. His family was entirely absorbed in the playing of the violin. The lodgers, on the other hand, who had at first, their hands in their pants pockets, taken up positions inconveniently close to his sister's music stand, in order to see all the notes, soon withdrew to the window, their heads bowed amidst whispered conversation, and remained there with Gregor's father worriedly observing them. It was now painfully obvious that they were disappointed in what they had

This painting, by Yosl Bergner, depicts Gregor's reaction to Grete's violin: "The music gripped him — was he then an animal?" **How does Bergner's work address this question?**

assumed would be a beautiful or entertaining performance, and that they were sick of the entire production and now allowed their quiet to be disturbed only out of politeness. The way they all blew their cigar smoke out of their mouths and noses indicated great irritation. But his sister played so beautifully! Her face was turned to the side; her gaze followed the lines of notes, searching and sorrowful. Gregor crept further forward and held his head close to the floor, in order to meet her gaze if possible. The music gripped him — was he then an animal? He felt as if he were being guided to the sustenance he had unknowingly desired. He was determined to press on all the way to his sister, to pull on her skirt and let her know that she could come into his room with her violin. No one here knew how to appreciate her playing the way he did. He wanted never to let her out of his room again, at least not as long as he lived. His terrifying shape would finally be of some use to him: he would be at all doors of his room at once, hissing at all intruders. His sister, though, would not be forced, but would rather stay with him willingly. She would sit next to him on the sofa, her ear inclined towards him, and he would confide in her that he had intended to send her to the conservatory, and that, were it not for the misfortune that had occurred, he had intended to announce it to everyone last Christmas — Christmas had surely passed already? — ignoring any possible objections. After this declaration, his sister would surely burst into tears of emotion, and Gregor would lift himself up to her shoulder and kiss her neck, which she now left uncovered, without ribbon or collar, since she had begun working at the store.

"Mr. Samsa!" called the middle lodger and without wasting another word, pointed at Gregor, who was slowly inching his way forward. The violin fell silent. The middle lodger smiled at first, shaking his head at his friends, and then looked down again at Gregor. His father seemed to consider it more urgent to reassure the lodgers than to drive Gregor back, despite the fact that they seemed calm and more entertained by Gregor than by the violin. He hurried over to them and tried with outspread arms to urge them into their room; at the same time, he wanted to block their view of Gregor with his body. They actually became a bit angry now, though it was unclear whether this was over his father's behavior or over the dawning recognition that, unbeknownst to them, they had all the while had a neighbor like Gregor. They asked his father for an explanation, raised their arms, pulled agitatedly at their beards and only reluctantly retreated into their room. In the meantime his sister had come out of the trance into which she had fallen after her playing had been so suddenly broken off. For a time she had held her violin and bow in her limply hanging hands and continued to stare at the music, as if she were still playing. Now, all at once, she pulled herself together, laid the instrument in the lap of her mother, who, short of breath and gasping for air, was still seated, and ran into the next room, which the lodgers were now approaching more quickly at the urging of her father. Under her practiced hands, the covers and pillows flew high in the air and arranged themselves. Before the lodgers had reached the room, she was finished readying the beds and had slipped out. His father's stubbornness seemed to have returned to the extent that he forgot all respect that he owed his lodgers. He kept urging them and urging them, until finally at the threshold the gentleman in the middle resoundingly stamped his foot and so brought his father to a standstill. "I hereby declare," he said, and, raising his hand, sought the gaze of Gregor's mother and sister, as well, "that, in consideration of the revolting conditions existing in this apartment and this family" — and here, without a moment's hesitation, he spat on the ground — "I give notice this instant. I will naturally pay absolutely nothing for the days I have lived here; on the contrary, I will consider bringing charges against you, which will — believe me — be very easy to prove." He fell silent and stared straight ahead, as if he were waiting for something. His two friends then obliged him by chiming in with the words: "We, too, give notice this instant." At that, he seized the door handle and shut the door with a crash.

His father staggered to his chair, his hands stretched out before him, and fell into it. It looked as if he were stretching himself out for his usual evening nap, but his head, sharply, ceaselessly nodding, showed that he was not sleeping at all. Gregor had lain all this time in the same spot where the lodgers had discovered him. His disappointment at the failure of his plans — perhaps, though, too, the weakness caused by his long hunger — made it impossible for him to move. He was distinctly afraid that in the next moment everything was going to come crashing down on top of him. He waited. Not even the violin roused him, which slipped from his mother's trembling fingers and fell from her lap, emitting a ringing tone.

"My dear parents," said his sister and struck her hand on the table by way of preamble, "we can't go on like this. If you can't see it, I can. I don't want to use the name of my brother in front of this monster, so let me just say this: we have to try to get rid of it. We have tried as much as humanly possible to care for it and to put up with it. I don't think it could reproach us in the least."

"She is absolutely right," said his father under his breath. His mother, who seemed not to have caught her breath yet, began to emit a muffled cough into the hand she held before her, a crazed expression in her eyes.

His sister hurried to his mother and put her hand to her forehead. His sister's words seemed to have put his father's thoughts in a surer course. He sat up straight, fiddling with his uniform cap amongst the plates that still sat on the table from the lodgers' evening meal, and looked for a time down at the quiet Gregor.

"We must try to get rid of it," his sister finally said to his father, for his mother heard nothing in the midst of her coughing. "It's going to kill you both; I can see it coming. When people have to work as hard as we do, they can't bear this kind of constant torture at home. I can't bear it any more." And she began crying so hard that her tears flowed down her mother's face, where she began mechanically wiping them away with her hand.

"But my child," said his father, sympathetically and with striking compassion, "what should we do?"

His sister only shrugged her shoulders as a sign of the helplessness that had during her crying spell taken the place of her former certainty. "But if he understood us — " his father said, half questioningly. His sister, in the midst of her tears, waved her hand violently as a sign that that was out of the question.

"If he understood us," his father repeated, and by closing his eyes, tried to absorb her certainty that it was impossible, "then we might be able to arrive at some arrangement with him. But as things stand — "

"It has to go," cried his sister. "That is the only way, father. You must simply try to rid yourself of the thought that it's Gregor. Our real misfortune is that we believed it for so long. But how can it be Gregor? If it were Gregor, he would have seen long ago that such an animal cannot live with people and he would have left voluntarily. We would then have had no brother, but we could have lived on and honored his memory. But this beast persecutes us, drives off the lodgers, and obviously wants to take over the apartment and force us to sleep out in the alley. Just look, Father," she suddenly screamed, "he's starting again!" And in a state of terror totally incomprehensible to Gregor, his sister abandoned his mother and practically vaulted off her chair, as if she would rather sacrifice her than remain in Gregor's vicinity. She hurried behind her father who, agitated entirely through her behavior, stood up as well and half raised his arms as if to protect her.

But it wasn't at all Gregor's intent to upset anyone, especially not his sister. He had just begun to turn himself around in order to make his way back into his room. Of course, that procedure looked peculiar enough, because his ailing condition meant that in order to turn even with difficulty he had to help with his head, which he lifted repeatedly and braced against the ground. He paused and looked around. His good intentions seemed to be recognized: it had only been a momentary fright. They all looked at him, silent and sorrowful. His mother lay in her chair, her legs stretched before her and pressed together; her eyes were nearly falling shut from exhaustion. His father and sister sat next to one another, his sister with her hand laid around her father's neck.

"Maybe they'll allow me to turn around now," thought Gregor, and started to work on it again. He could not suppress the wheezing caused by his exertion, and he had to stop and rest now and then. No one rushed him: he was left to his own devices. When he had completed the turn, he immediately headed straight back. He was astonished by the vast distance that divided him from his room, and he could not grasp how in his weakened condition he had put the entire distance behind him, almost without noticing it. Focused solely on crawling as quickly as possible, he hardly noticed that no word and

Photo © PVDE / Bridgeman Images

Kafka insisted that the cover of *The Metamorphosis* not include a visual representation of Gregor in his transformed state. **In what ways do you think that this first-edition cover captures the spirit and ideas of the novella?**

no outcry from his family disturbed him. He turned his head only when he was already at the door — not all the way, for he felt his neck getting stiff, but enough to see that nothing had changed behind him, except for the fact that his sister had stood up. His last glance fell on his mother, who was now fast asleep.

He was hardly in his room when the door was hastily pushed to, bolted fast and locked. The sudden noise behind him frightened Gregor so much that his legs buckled beneath him. It was his sister who had rushed to do it. She had stood, waiting, and had suddenly sprung forward, light-footed — Gregor had not even heard her coming — crying out to her parents "Finally!" as she turned the key in the lock.

"And now?" Gregor asked himself, and looked around in the dark. He soon discovered that he could no longer move at all. He didn't wonder at this; on the contrary, it had seemed unnatural to him that he had actually been able to move before on such thin legs. Besides that, however, he felt relatively comfortable. He did have pains all over his body, but it seemed to him that they were becoming weaker and weaker and would finally die away altogether. He could hardly feel the rotten apple in his back or the inflamed surrounding area, which was now completely covered in moist dust. He thought of his family with compassion and love. His conviction that he had to disappear was even more definite than his sister's. He remained in this state of empty and peaceful contemplation until the clock tower struck three. He experienced once more the approach of daylight outside the window. Then, unwilled, his head sank fully down, and from his nostrils his last breath weakly streamed forth.

When the servant came in the early morning — though she had often been asked to refrain from doing so, she slammed all the doors out of sheer vigor and haste, to such an extent that it was not possible to sleep quietly anywhere in the apartment once she had arrived — she noticed nothing unusual at first in her morning visit to Gregor. She thought that he intentionally lay there motionless because he found her behavior insulting; she credited him with all manner of intelligence. As she happened to be holding her long broom in her hand, she tried to tickle Gregor with it from the door. When she met with no response, she became irritated and poked him a bit. Only when she had shoved him from his spot without meeting any resistance did she become alert. She soon understood the situation. Her eyes widened, and she whistled out loud. It wasn't long before she had flung the door of the master bedroom open and called loudly into the darkness: "Look, everyone, it's kicked the bucket; it's lying there, dead as a doornail!"

The Samsas sat bolt upright in bed and had first to overcome their alarm at the servant's behavior before they could understand her report. Then, however, they climbed hurriedly out of bed, one on each side. Mr. Samsa threw the blanket over his shoulders; Mrs. Samsa emerged in her nightgown. In this manner they entered Gregor's room. In the meantime Grete had opened the door to the living room, where she had been sleeping since the arrival of the lodgers. She was completely dressed, as if she had not slept; her pale face confirmed the impression. "Dead?" said Mrs. Samsa, and looked questioningly up at the servant, although she could have made her own investigation or even have recognized the fact without making any investigation. "I'd say so," said the servant, and as proof, she pushed Gregor's corpse further to one side with the broom. Mrs. Samsa moved as if she wanted to hold her back, but she didn't. "Well," said Mr. Samsa, "now we can thank God." He crossed himself, and the three women followed his example. Grete, who did not take her eyes from the corpse, said: "Just look at how thin he was. He hadn't eaten anything for so long. The food came out just the way it went in." Gregor's body was indeed completely flat and dry; it was really only possible to see it now that he was off his legs and nothing else distracted the eye.

"Come, Grete, come sit with us for a bit," said Mrs. Samsa with a wistful smile, and Grete followed her parents into their bedroom, though not without looking back at the corpse. The servant shut the door and opened the window wide. Despite the early morning the fresh air already had something mild mixed in it. It was, after all, already the end of March.

The three lodgers emerged from their room and looked in amazement for their breakfast. It had been forgotten. "Where is breakfast?" the middlemost of the men asked the servant sullenly. She laid a finger to her lips and then silently and hastily signaled to the men that they might come into Gregor's room. They came and stood around Gregor's corpse in the now completely bright room, their hands in the pockets of their somewhat shabby coats.

The door to the bedroom opened then, and Mr. Samsa appeared in his livery with his wife on one arm and his daughter on the other. They had all been crying; Grete pressed her face from time to time to her father's arm.

"Leave my apartment immediately!" said Mr. Samsa and pointed to the door, without letting the women leave his side. "What do you mean?" said the middle lodger, somewhat dismayed, and smiled mawkishly. The two others held their hands behind their backs and rubbed them together continuously, as if in joyful expectation of a great fight, which would, they were sure, end favorably for them. "I mean exactly what I say," answered Mr. Samsa, and advanced in a line with his companions toward the lodger. He stood quietly, at first, and looked at the ground, as if the things in his head were arranging themselves in a new order. "Then we'll go," he said and looked up at Mr. Samsa, as if a sudden access of humility required him to seek renewed approval even for this decision. Mr. Samsa merely nodded shortly several times, his eyes wide and staring. At this, the man immediately walked with long strides into the foyer. His two friends had listened at first, their hands completely still, and they now skipped after him directly, as if in fear that Mr. Samsa could step in front of them in the foyer and disrupt their connection to their leader. In the hall all three of them took their hats from the rack, drew their walking sticks from the stand, bowed mutely, and left the apartment. In what proved to be a completely unnecessary precaution, Mr. Samsa walked out with the two women onto the landing. Leaning on the railing, they watched as the three men slowly but steadily descended the stairs, disappearing on every floor at the turning of the stairwell, and emerging again after a few moments. The lower they went, the more the Samsa family lost interest in them, and as a butcher's boy carrying his burden on his head with dignity passed them and then climbed high above them, Mr. Samsa left the landing with the women and they all returned, as if freed from a burden, to their apartment.

They decided to spend the day resting and taking a stroll. They had not only earned this rest from work, they absolutely needed it. And so they sat at the table and wrote three letters of excuse, Mr. Samsa to the bank directors, Mrs. Samsa to her employer, and Grete to her supervisor. While they were writing the servant entered in order to say that she was leaving, as her morning work was finished. Writing, the three of them merely nodded at first, without looking up; only when the servant failed to depart did they look up angrily. "Well?" asked Mr. Samsa. The servant stood in the door, smiling, as if she had some great piece of good news to report to the family, but would only do so if she were thoroughly interrogated. The nearly upright little ostrich feather on her hat, which had annoyed Mr. Samsa the entire time she had been employed there, waved freely in all directions. "Well, what do you want?" asked Mrs. Samsa, for whom the servant had the most respect. "Well," the servant answered, and could not say more right away, fairly bursting with friendly laughter, "well, you needn't worry about getting rid of that thing next door. It's all been taken care of." Mrs. Samsa and Grete bent to their letters again, as if they wanted to continue writing. Mr. Samsa, who saw that the servant was about to begin describing everything in great detail, decisively headed this off with an outstretched hand. Since she was not going to be allowed to tell her story, she suddenly remembered her great haste, and, obviously deeply insulted, called out, "'Bye, everyone," then spun around wildly and left the apartment amidst a terrific slamming of doors.

"Tonight we're firing her," said Mr. Samsa, but received no answer either from his wife or from his daughter, for the servant seemed to have disturbed their but newly restored calm. They rose, went to the window, and remained there, their arms around each other. Mr. Samsa turned in his chair as they went and quietly observed them for a while. Then he called out, "Well, come over here. Let what's past be past. And take some care of me, for once." The women obeyed immediately, hurrying over to him and caressing him, and then quickly finished their letters.

Then all three of them left the apartment together, which they had not done for months, and took a trolley to the open air beyond the city. The car they sat in was drenched with warm sunlight. Leaning back comfortably in their seats, they discussed their future prospects, and it emerged that these were not at all bad on closer inspection, for all three of their positions were altogether favorable at present and, most importantly, had great potential for the future. The greatest improvement of their present situation would have to come, naturally, from a change of apartments. They would want a smaller and cheaper apartment, but one that was better located and generally more convenient than their current apartment, which Gregor had originally found for them. While they conversed in this way, it occurred to both Mr. and Mrs. Samsa in the same moment in looking at their ever more lively daughter that despite the recent ordeals that had made her cheeks so pale, she had blossomed into a pretty and well-developed young woman. Becoming quieter and almost unconsciously communicating through glances, they realized that it would soon be time to look for a good husband for her. And it seemed to them a confirmation of their new dreams and good intentions, when, at the end of their journey, their daughter rose first and stretched her young body.

[1915]

QUESTIONS FOR DISCUSSION

1. The story opens, "When Gregor Samsa awoke in his bed one morning from unquiet dreams, he found himself transformed into an enormous insect." When you first read those lines, did you find them humorous? When did you begin to understand the serious intent, or did the fantastic or surreal situation make it difficult for you to take the story seriously? Could this "metamorphosis" be a dream?
2. Among Gregor's responses to his transformation, we see anxiety, frustration, and surprise, but not shock. In fact, we're told that Gregor "was eager to see how today's fantasies would gradually resolve themselves" (para. 8). What do you think Franz Kafka's purpose might be in not presenting Gregor as horrified by the discovery that he has transformed into an insect?
3. What does Kafka's choice to make Gregor a traveling salesman suggest? What details of Gregor's professional life do we learn, and how might his profession connect to his turning into a bug? Consider Kafka's description of Gregor as "condemned to work at a company where the least infraction immediately attracted the greatest suspicion" (para. 15).
4. What information does Gregor learn about the family's "entire financial situation and their prospects" (para. 43)? How would you characterize

Gregor's reaction to this revelation? Why do you think he does not react with more anger or resentment?

5. How does each family member initially react to Gregor's transformation? What do their responses say about each of them? How do those reactions change or intensify over the course of the novella?

6. Who do you believe holds the most power in this story of the Samsa family, and why? Does the balance of power shift over time? In what ways could Gregor's transformation be seen as a way to obtain power?

7. In the opening paragraph of Part III, Gregor is described as "a member of the family who should not be treated as an enemy. The laws of familial obligation dictated, rather, that one had to swallow one's revulsion and be tolerant, simply be tolerant." From whose perspective is this statement written? How do you interpret that "familial obligation"? Do you think it is meant to be an indictment of his family? Why or why not?

8. Kafka refers to the new jobs that Gregor's parents and sister take on as "everything that the world demanded of poor people" (para. 66). In what light does Kafka portray them here? Is he suggesting they are admirable for taking care of themselves? Is he taking a sarcastic tone about the fact that they have to work? Explain, using details from the text to support your answer.

9. When Grete plays her violin, Gregor is "drawn by the music" (para. 73) and enters the living room. We witness this scene from his perspective: "The music gripped him — was he then an animal?" (para. 74). How do you answer that question? How do you think Kafka answers it?

10. What qualities from before his metamorphosis does Gregor retain, particularly in his death scene (paras. 84–88)? Does Kafka present this final act in such a way that we could interpret it as a suicide or murder? Or does Gregor just fade away?

11. How do the minor characters contribute to the themes — such as the dissolution of the family or dehumanization of the urban work force — in *The Metamorphosis*? Consider the Deputy Director, the Samsa family's servants, and the boarders.

12. In what ways does Grete's transformation parallel Gregor's? In what ways does it differ? Would her "metamorphosis" have been possible had Gregor remained the dutiful salesman going to work each day? Why or why not?

13. How do you interpret the final paragraph of *The Metamorphosis*? Do you think that Kafka wanted his readers to see the ending as a positive new beginning, a resigned statement that life goes on, or an indictment of our failure to accept difference? Or is it something else? Cite specific passages to support your response.

14. While *The Metamorphosis* has many traditional narrative elements — a logical plot, a coherent sense of time and place, characters developed over the course of the work — Kafka departs from tradition in the way he combines vastly different elements of the grotesque with the everyday, presenting the beautiful alongside the disgusting. Find two examples of such juxtapositions and discuss how they contribute to one of Kafka's central themes.

QUESTIONS ON STYLE AND STRUCTURE

1. By the end of Part I, has Kafka made us root for Gregor? What literary techniques does Kafka employ to build sympathy for him? Cite specific passages to explain how Kafka elicits your response.

2. *The Metamorphosis* contains many references to sleep and dreams. The first sentence of the novella begins with the phrase, "When Gregor Samsa awoke in his bed one morning from unquiet dreams. . . ." Might Kafka be suggesting that Gregor's metamorphosis is entirely a dream? Identify at least four passages and explain how they support or challenge this interpretation.

3. *The Metamorphosis* is told in the third person, but we are privy to what Gregor is thinking and feeling. How does this point of view affect the reader's understanding of his situation? Cite specific passages to support your response.

4. What elements of irony do you find in paragraph 6? Pay special attention to the people who govern Gregor's life — that is, those who make rules and those who affect his sense of self-worth. What other examples of irony do you find in the story? Analyze the effect of at least two.

5. The concept of time is central to the novella's opening. What references to time — clocks, deadlines,

numbers that control Gregor's day, schedules — do you find in Part I? What assertion might Kafka be making with this language and these images?

6. Beginning in paragraph 9, Kafka describes, in great detail, Gregor's difficulties with moving and manipulating his new, unfamiliar body as he tries to get out of bed. What do you believe is Kafka's purpose in providing such a vivid description of his physical movements, and what is the effect? Is the humor intentional, or are these descriptions meant to evoke pity? Explain.

7. The events in the novella take place almost entirely within the Samsa apartment, though we see the hospital from the window. What is the significance of this setting? What does Kafka achieve by limiting it in this way? Why do you think Kafka describes in such rich detail the surroundings that are "home" to the Samsa family?

8. How does Kafka use images of freedom and entrapment to develop his theme(s) in *The Metamorphosis*? Identify several specific examples and analyze their effect.

9. Speech — language — is central to the story of *The Metamorphosis*. When Gregor first tries to speak, he is "terrified" because his "old voice" is mixed with "an irrepressible, painful, squeaking noise" (para. 7). How does Kafka develop this relationship between voice and power (or the lack of both)?

10. How does Kafka employ humor in *The Metamorphosis*? Is the tone outright sarcastic, or is it more subtle? Would you characterize it as hilarious comedy? as dark humor? Discuss at least two examples of Kafka's skillful use of different types of humor in the novella and the purpose they serve.

11. The final paragraph of Part I is filled with physical and psychological violence. To what extent has Kafka prepared readers for this violence? How does the language describing Gregor and his father's confrontation serve Kafka's purpose? How does the scene that ends Part II — in which Gregor's father pummels him with apples — both parallel and depart from the last paragraph of Part I?

12. Where is the tipping point in the plot — a shift, an event, or revelation that signals a significant change? Consider how the three "sections" structure the novella. If you had to point to a paragraph or two as the climax of the novella, which would you choose, and why?

SUGGESTIONS FOR WRITING

1. Why does Gregor feel "drawn once again into the circle of humanity" (para. 23)? What does this transitory hope suggest about Gregor? In what ways does Kafka signal the gradual diminution of his humanity? What elements of humanity, if any, does Gregor retain until the very end? Be sure to analyze the text of the novella and avoid plot summary.

2. How does the motif of money shape the relationships between and among the members of the Samsa family? In your response, explain whether you believe Kafka suggests that the dissolution of the family is the result or cause of a culture dominated by materialism.

3. One critic made this point about Kafka's work: "As political estrangement becomes more and more the norm of Western society, and as capitalism, as Kafka said, becomes 'the condition of the world and the soul,' Kafka's fears will more and more provide the frame in which we read his work." Write an essay analyzing how this commentary affects your interpretation of *The Metamorphosis*.

4. In a lecture delivered to new college students at the outset of their first semester, Professor Warren Breckman discussed *The Metamorphosis*, which all incoming students were required to read over the summer:

> Kafka's *The Metamorphosis* strikes me as a particularly well-chosen novel . . . and I say this not only because the adult life into which you are entering will inevitably have its Kafkaesque moments. Rather, with its exploration of identity, of belonging and exclusion, of tolerance and intolerance, *The Metamorphosis* raises many questions for people like you, students who are facing a time of transition and transformation. Of course, my hope is that your education . . . will not transform you into beetles, but into less earth-bound creatures. Nonetheless, the tale of the unfortunate Gregor Samsa can make us think more deeply about our own identity, about the fluidity of what we take to be stable and fixed, and about the perils and miracles of our own metamorphoses.

What is his central point? Explain why you agree or disagree with him that *The Metamorphosis* would be an appropriate — and compelling — text for new college students to read and discuss with their peers and professors.

5. When he was thirty-six, Kafka wrote a "Letter to his Father" ("Brief an den Vater"), a long document in which he took stock of their troubled relationship. He never sent the letter and it remained unpublished until recently. At one point, he recalls an incident that took place when he was six years old. He had kept his parents awake by repeatedly asking for water, and in response his exasperated father left him on the balcony of their apartment for a while, dressed only in his pajamas. Kafka admits that his father rarely applied physical punishment, yet the threat of violence, particularly psychological, was all around. He wrote, "For years to come, I suffered agonies when I imagined how this giant man, my father, the ultimate authority, could come, for practically no reason, and carry me from my bed to the *Pawlatsche* [balcony] at night, and that I was such a nothing to him." Research the relationship between Kafka and his father further, then write an essay that examines how it influenced and may even be reflected in *The Metamorphosis*.

6. In his essay "The Beetle and the Fly," filmmaker David Cronenberg compares the plight of Gregor with that of the protagonist in his movie *The Fly*:

> In the movie I co-wrote and directed of George Langelaan's short story *The Fly*, I have our hero Seth Brundle, played by Jeff Goldblum, say, while deep in the throes of his transformation into a hideous fly/human hybrid, "I'm an insect who dreamt he was a man and loved it. But now the dream is over, and the insect is awake." He is warning his former lover that he is now a danger to her, a creature with no compassion and no empathy. He has shed his humanity like the shell of a cicada nymph, and what has emerged is no longer human. He is also suggesting that to be a human, a self-aware consciousness, is a dream that cannot last, an illusion. Gregor too has trouble clinging to what is left of his humanity, and as his family begins to feel that this thing in Gregor's room is no longer Gregor, he begins to feel the same way.

After watching the film, consider this quotation as you compare and contrast the concept of "metamorphosis" in both works. What social commentary does each work provide? In what ways does *The Fly* depart from *The Metamorphosis*? Consider such elements as theme, narrative structure, and characterization.

7. Develop your own interpretation of *The Metamorphosis* using multimedia tools — audio, visual, or both. Explain why you made the choices you did.

8. Both *The Metamorphosis* by Franz Kafka and "The Yellow Wallpaper" (1892) by Charlotte Perkins Gilman explore themes of confinement and alienation. After reading "The Yellow Wallpaper," compare and contrast each work's treatment of the outsider. Pay particular attention to what forces frustrate the protagonists, how the transformation of each is a response to those forces, and whether you interpret each narrative's ending as bleak or more optimistic.

9. A reader sent the following letter to Franz Kafka in 1917:

> Dear Sir:
>
> You have made me unhappy.
>
> I bought your "Metamorphosis" as a gift for my cousin. But she is incapable of understanding the story. My cousin gave it to her mother who doesn't understand it either. Her mother gave the book to my other cousin, who also didn't find an explanation. Now they have written to me. They expect me to explain the story to them since I am the Ph.D. in the family. But I am at a loss to explain it.
>
> Sir! I have spent months in the trenches exchanging blows with the Russians without batting an eyelash. But I could not stand losing my good name with my cousins. Only you can help me. You must do it since you are the one who landed me in this mess. So please tell me what my cousin should think about Metamorphosis.
>
> Most respectfully yours,
>
> Dr. Siegfried Wolff

Many would agree with Dr. Wolff's cousin that *The Metamorphosis* resists interpretation, or at least a single or literal reading. How would you explain the "story" of the novella to someone else? How might Kafka? Write a letter to Dr. Wolff in Kafka's voice, advising him what to tell his cousin.

TEXTS IN CONTEXT

The Metamorphosis and the Modernist Vision

"Make it new!" — an exhortation poet Ezra Pound made in 1928 — has since become the battle cry of what we now refer to as the modernist movement. Although it is difficult to point to an actual date when the period began, the turn of the twentieth century saw a dramatic series of culture shocks that brought about changes in every sphere. Industrialization that shifted demographics from the country to the city, rapid social and political change, and advances in science and technology had exerted a profound influence by the early 1900s.

Usually dated by the reign of Britain's Queen Victoria (1837–1901), the Victorian age saw many advances in medical, scientific, and technological knowledge as well as rapid industrialization and a boom in urban populations. The late Victorian era in particular was characterized by European imperial expansion, mainly into Africa and Asia, spurred by nationalistic pride. This struggle for power among European nations colonizing other continents placed an increasing strain on diplomatic relations, creating tension that would eventually lead to open conflict.

Victoria's reign also saw the rise of socialism, liberalism, and organized feminism — all challenges to long-established western European social, economic, and political systems. While other European countries, including France and Italy, experienced a series of political revolutions in the mid-nineteenth century, Britain's political landscape shifted toward popular democracy as voting rights expanded incrementally; by 1884, men had attained near-universal suffrage. At the turn of the century, much of the western world was wrestling with groundbreaking ideas of the late 1800s: Sigmund Freud's notion of the unconscious mind (the id), Karl Marx's socialism, Charles Darwin's theory of natural selection, and Friedrich Nietzsche's nihilist mantra — "God is

Underwood Archives/UIG/Bridgeman Images

Industrialization during the nineteenth century spurred rapid urban expansion. Its effects are evident in the above photograph, taken in 1900, which shows laundry hung out to dry in a Manhattan tenement. **What does the physical landscape of the city, as seen here, suggest about the psychological environment for urban residents?**

dead" — that reflected a growing secularization in society.

Perhaps the most destabilizing influence during the early twentieth century was World War I. One of the bloodiest wars in recorded history, and the first to play out on a global scale, it introduced a deadly combination of primitive trench-warfare tactics and modern weaponry — by its finish, nearly 9 million people had died. It was also one of the most politically bewildering conflicts the world had ever seen. Though it began as a struggle between the Austro-Hungarian Empire and Serbia, a tangled web of alliances quickly dragged Russia, Great Britain, France, Germany, Italy, the Ottoman Empire, Japan, Bulgaria, and ultimately the United States into the fray. For many, the death and destruction of the Great War that ravaged Europe from 1914 to 1918 raised doubts about widely accepted beliefs in science, politics, and religion. The technological advances made possible by industrialization had produced deadly weapons that caused destruction on a previously unimaginable scale; imperialist policies and nationalistic fervor had led to irreparable global conflict. Faith in the established political and social order of the Victorian era dwindled.

Private Collection/Archives Charmet/Bridgeman Images

This image shows the ruins of the French city of Verdun after eight months of bombardment from the German and French armies. The Battle of Verdun was one of World War I's longest and bloodiest battles, lasting from February 21 to December 18, 1916. **How might this devastation have prompted a desire not simply to rebuild what was destroyed but to rethink a way of life or values?**

This general uncertainty about the nature of reality contributed to a growing sense of alienation and fragmentation in the wake of World War I. Artists, musicians, and writers made a radical break with the past and sought new ways to interpret the now-unfamiliar world they confronted. Many rejected the so-called "realistic" depiction of human experience in both the written and visual arts of the nineteenth century. Traditional art forms suddenly seemed incapable of representing the mystery, complexity, and uncertainty of modern life.

Many cite the 1913 Armory Show, the first large exhibition of modern art in America, as the start of the modernist movement. The three-city exhibition started in New York City's 69th Regiment Armory, then went on to Chicago and Boston. It featured the works of European modern artists — including Henri Matisse, Marcel Duchamp, and Pablo Picasso — and the show shocked many Americans who, accustomed to realistic art, were perplexed by experimental and abstract expression.

Modernism is now known for its abstract art, symbolic poetry, and stream-of-consciousness prose — all meant to represent the subjective experience of modern life rather than the objective reality of it. These efforts were driven by innovation in form and content. Although both writers and visual artists experimented in many different forms, the modernists' vision shares certain characteristics:

- a belief that traditional religious and social institutions such as the family had broken down;
- a view of urban society as fostering a mechanistic, materialistic culture;
- a sense of anonymity and alienation brought on, in part, by the banality of bourgeois life; and
- a conviction that there is no such thing as absolute truth, only relative and subjective perceptions.

While these ideas may seem to add up to a fairly bleak view, modernists believed that their willingness to innovate, to "make it new," and to experiment with forms more attuned to the social and political realities of the era could be a transformative, even healing experience. Writers, for instance, emphasized and validated the individual's perception of reality, often exploring characters' rich inner lives through the stream-of-consciousness narrative technique. This method of narration describes in words the flow of thoughts in the minds of the characters. Writers such as James Joyce, Virginia Woolf, Jean Toomer, and William Faulkner used stream of consciousness to paint characters' perceptions and observations as elements that propel the narrative forward through association rather than causality.

Modernist writers and artists often found the collage a mode of expression suited to their philosophical beliefs. In visual art, a collage is a work created by materials and objects glued to a flat surface. In poetry, this technique is called fragmentation, where diverse pieces or images come together — or don't — in a way that mirrors the disjointed, chaotic modern world. In both cases, the collage abandons the logical relationships that typically order a work of art — such as cause-and-effect, chronology, and subordination — to express a less coherent view of reality, one that highlights subjective individual experience. The poet Ezra Pound coined the term "imagism" to characterize an early twentieth century style of poetry that sought to replace the abstract, often decorative language of the nineteenth century with clear, concise, concrete images. Pound's famous two-line poem, "In a Station of the Metro," epitomized the tenets of this movement:

> The apparition   of these faces   in the crowd :
> Petals   on a wet, black   bough .

Pound observes a scene in the subway, then recasts — and elevates — it as a powerful image. Such overall economy of language, apt metaphors, and precisely observed detail were what imagist poets like Ezra Pound, H. D., Richard Aldington, William Carlos Williams, and Amy Lowell strove to create.

Franz Kafka's *The Metamorphosis*, written in 1912 and published in 1915, is a work forever poised on the cusp of modernism. In this section, you will consider the novella in the context of other literature and art from approximately the same period. You'll have an opportunity to see how others interpret the dictum to "make it new" as well as how each writer and artist builds on the traditions and conventions of the past. We begin with an excerpt from a famous essay called "Tradition and the Individual Talent" by T. S. Eliot. In it, he argues against rejecting the past but instead urges his audience to redefine the relationship between past and present.

TEXTS IN CONTEXT

T. S. Eliot / from *Tradition and the Individual Talent* (nonfiction)
Otto Dix / *Der Krieg* ("The War") (painting)
Robert Burns / *A Red, Red Rose* and **H. D.** / *Sea Rose* (poetry)
Amy Lowell / *A London Thoroughfare. 2 A.M.* and *The Emperor's Garden* (poetry)
Fernand Léger / *La Ville* ("The City") (painting)
T. S. Eliot / *The Love Song of J. Alfred Prufrock* (poetry)
Virginia Woolf / from *Mrs. Dalloway* (fiction)

from Tradition and the Individual Talent

T. S. ELIOT

Poet, dramatist, and critic Thomas Stearns Eliot (1888–1965) was born and raised in St. Louis, Missouri. He moved to England when he was twenty-five to attend Oxford University after studying at Harvard University and eventually became a British subject. His most famous works include "The Love Song of J. Alfred Prufrock" (1915), "The Wasteland" (1922), "Ash Wednesday" (1930), "Burnt Norton" (1941), "Little Gidding" (1942), "Four Quartets" (1943), and the play *Murder in the Cathedral* (1935). He was awarded the Nobel Prize for Literature in 1948. Eliot is considered one of the great poetic innovators of the twentieth century and is closely associated with the modernist movement — especially in his stream-of-consciousness style steeped in literary allusions and mythological references. Eliot believed that such complex poetry was necessary in order to reflect the complexities of modern civilization, but he also considered tradition to be an ongoing process that united the past with the present. His essay "Tradition and the Individual Talent" explores the complex relationship between a poet's historical context and the value of that poet's unique voice.

In English writing we seldom speak of tradition, though we occasionally apply its name in deploring its absence. We cannot refer to "the tradition" or to "a tradition"; at most, we employ the adjective in saying that the poetry of So-and-so is "traditional" or even "too traditional." Seldom, perhaps, does the word appear except in a phrase of censure. . . .

[W]hen we praise a poet, upon those aspects of his work in which he least resembles anyone else. In these aspects or parts of his work we pretend to find what is individual, what is the peculiar essence of the man. We dwell with satisfaction upon the poet's difference from his predecessors, especially his immediate predecessors; we endeavour to find something that can be isolated in order to be enjoyed. Whereas if we approach a poet without this prejudice we shall often find that not only the best, but the most individual parts of his work may be those in which the dead poets, his ancestors, assert their immortality most vigorously. And I do not mean the impressionable period of adolescence, but the period of full maturity.

Yet if the only form of tradition, of handing down, consisted in following the ways of the immediate generation before us in a blind or timid adherence to its successes, "tradition" should positively be discouraged. We have seen many such simple currents soon lost in the sand; and novelty is better than repetition. Tradition is a matter of much wider significance. It cannot be inherited, and if you want it you must obtain it by great labour. It involves, in the first place, the historical sense, which we may call nearly indispensable to anyone who would continue to be a poet beyond his twenty-fifth year; and the historical sense involves a perception, not only of the pastness of the past, but of its presence; the historical sense compels a man to write not merely with his own generation in his bones, but with a feeling that the whole of the literature of Europe from Homer and within it the whole of the literature of his own country has a simultaneous existence and composes a simultaneous order. This historical sense, which is a sense of the timeless as well as of the temporal together, is what makes a writer traditional. And it is at the same time what makes a writer most acutely conscious of his place in time, of his contemporaneity.

No poet, no artist of any art, has his complete meaning alone. His significance, his appreciation is the appreciation of his relation to the dead poets and artists. You cannot value him alone; you must set him, for contrast and comparison, among the dead.

[1920]

QUESTIONS

1. How does T. S. Eliot's concept of "tradition" fuse past and present?
2. How does he challenge the view that the value of a work of art should be measured by its departure from its predecessors?
3. To what extent does the final paragraph of this excerpt argue that an artist must pay tribute — either by reflecting or refuting — the ideas of his or her predecessors?
4. How does Eliot's concept of the presence of the past apply to musical artists? Choose a musician or band, contemporary or past, with whom you are familiar, and discuss.

Der Krieg ("The War")

OTTO DIX

Otto Dix (1891–1969) was a German artist known for his vivid depictions of the brutality of war. Dix volunteered as a machine-gunner during World War I and was sent to the Western Front in the autumn of 1915. He was at the Battle of the Somme in France, one of the bloodiest in military history. After the war, Dix taught at Dresden Academy. His paintings, done in the modernist style called German expressionism, reflected the horror of his war experiences. When the Nazis came to power in the early 1930s, they viewed his work as detrimental to the rise of militarism; thus, he was dismissed from his teaching position and denigrated in the German press. Some of his paintings were destroyed; other works, hidden away, have only recently been rediscovered. After being conscripted into the German national militia near the end of World War II, Dix was captured by French troops and held until February of 1946. He later returned to Germany, where his reputation as an artist was restored, and continued to create antiwar paintings until his death in 1969. The following triptych of paintings, titled *Der Krieg* ("The War"), is the culmination of a portfolio of antiwar paintings and drawings completed between 1924 and 1932.

[1932]

QUESTIONS

1. Although the paintings are not entirely representational, there are several recognizable elements. What are they? Be very specific in identifying the images — both figures and the setting — that make up this triptych.
2. What elements of deliberate distortion do you see in the paintings? How effective is this technique in comparison to more realistic depictions of wartime scenes?
3. How do the color and composition of the paintings contribute to their hallucinatory, nightmarish quality?
4. What details of these paintings support the argument that Otto Dix depicts the depravity and barbarity of war in the early twentieth century?
5. What narrative do these panels seem to tell? Do these images add up to a coherent, linear storyline? Consider the way Dix handles time: do these panels follow a chronology or conflate different times?
6. Although Dix's *Der Krieg* specifically depicts the trench warfare of World War I, it has been seen as one of the most powerful indictments of war in general. To what extent is it still relevant to contemporary conflicts? Explain, using details from the triptych.

A Red, Red Rose

ROBERT BURNS

Robert Burns (1759–1796) was a poet and lyricist who remains a folk hero in his native Scotland to this day. Burns often wrote in the Scottish dialect, and his song "Auld Lang Syne" still commemorates the end of the calendar year in many places throughout the world. His most famous poem, "A Red, Red Rose," also became a popular ballad. In it, Burns describes a rose as a symbol of romantic love and beauty, a traditional treatment of the flower. For centuries before and since, a rose tended either to represent a speaker's beloved and his passion for her, or recalled the Virgin Mary's purity in Christian theology. "A Red, Red Rose" typifies the kind of conventional interpretation of symbol that modernist poets would later question and subvert.

O my luve's like a red, red rose
    That's newly sprung in June;
O my luve's like the melodie
    That's sweetly play'd in tune.

As fair art thou, my bonie lass,
    So deep in luve am I;
And I will luve thee still, my dear,
    Till a' the seas gang dry.

Till a' the seas gang dry, my dear.
    And the rocks melt wi' the sun:
O I will love thee still, my dear,
    While the sands o' life shall run.

And fare-thee-weel, my only luve:
    And fare-thee-weel awhile!
And I will come again, my luve,
    Tho' 'twere ten thousand mile!

O my luve's like a red, red rose
    That's newly sprung in June;
O my luve's like the melodie
    That's sweetly play'd in tune.

[1794]

QUESTIONS

1. What tone does the opening simile establish?
2. What other similes accumulate during the poem to support and enhance the opening one?
3. As a twenty-first–century reader, which of these similes do you find the most original and moving? Why?
4. Do you believe that relying upon the rose's traditional associations increases or decreases its symbolic value? Explain.

Sea Rose

H. D.

H. D. (1886–1961), pen name of Hilda Doolittle, was an influential American poet and novelist known for her association with imagism, a modernist literary movement that came to prominence in the early twentieth century. Imagists rejected overly sentimental, decorative language in favor of direct and succinct expression. Such poets often focused an entire poem on a single image, as H.D. does in the following poem, "Sea Rose." This poem undermines the stereotype of roses as symbols of beauty, romance, and purity by framing the image in concrete, unsentimental terms that renew its power.

Rose, harsh rose,
marred and with stint of petals,
meagre flower, thin,
sparse of leaf,

more precious
than a wet rose
single on a stem —
you are caught in the drift.

Stunted, with small leaf,
you are flung on the sand,
you are lifted
in the crisp sand
that drives in the wind.

Can the spice-rose
drip such acrid fragrance
hardened in a leaf?

[1916]

QUESTIONS

1. In what ways does the opening stanza (ll. 1–4) defy our expectations based on the traditional way of seeing and writing about a rose? Cite specific language choices.
2. Who is the speaker in this poem? Who (or what) is being addressed?
3. How do you interpret the line, "you are caught in the drift" (l. 8)?
4. What is the impact of comparing the sea rose to two other roses? How does the sea rose compare?
5. What do you think the speaker anticipates as the response to the poem's final rhetorical question (ll. 14–16)?
6. What is the effect of the sparse, perhaps even stark, language of the poem? What is the difference, for instance, between "flung on the sand" and "flung harshly on the cold sand"?
7. Do you think the sea rose, as depicted in this poem, is beautiful? Why or why not?
8. What does the sea rose symbolize in this poem? In what ways does it both evoke and subvert traditional associations with the rose?

A London Thoroughfare. 2 A.M. and The Emperor's Garden

AMY LOWELL

Amy Lowell (1874–1925) was an American poet from Brookline, Massachusetts. She was born into a prominent family, sister to the astronomer Percival Lowell and Harvard president Abbott Lawrence Lowell. As a poet, Lowell was an early advocate for free verse and eventually embraced the imagist movement, which favored direct expression over decorative language. Lowell published eight collections of poetry in her lifetime, and three more were published after her death at age fifty-one, including *What's O'Clock*, for which she was posthumously awarded the Pulitzer Prize in 1926. In both "A London Thoroughfare. 2 A.M." and "The Emperor's Garden," Lowell blends unsentimental and blunt language with vivid imagery to evoke the alienating forces of modernity.

A London Thoroughfare. 2 A.M.

They have watered the street,
It shines in the glare of lamps,
Cold, white lamps,
And lies
Like a slow-moving river,
Barred with silver and black.
Cabs go down it,
One,
And then another.
Between them I hear the shuffling of feet.
Tramps doze on the window-ledges,
Night-walkers pass along the sidewalks.
The city is squalid and sinister,
With the silver-barred street in the midst,
Slow-moving,
A river leading nowhere.

Opposite my window,
The moon cuts,
Clear and round,
Through the plum-coloured night.
She cannot light the city;
It is too bright.
It has white lamps,
And glitters coldly.

I stand in the window and watch the moon.
She is thin and lustreless,
But I love her.
I know the moon,
And this is an alien city.

[1914]

The Emperor's Garden

Once, in the sultry heats of midsummer,
An emperor caused the miniature mountains in his garden
To be covered with white silk,
That so crowned
They might cool his eyes
With the sparkle of snow.

[1917]

QUESTIONS

1. How would you characterize the speaker of "A London Thoroughfare. 2 A.M."? How does she depict the city? Does she use primarily literal or figurative language? Cite examples to support your response.
2. Where does a shift occur in "A London Thoroughfare. 2 A.M."? What is the relationship between what happens before and after that shift?
3. Summarize the poem "The Emperor's Garden." To what extent do you think your summary captures Amy Lowell's purpose or ideas?
4. How does Lowell appeal to the senses in "The Emperor's Garden"? Cite specific words and images.
5. Add at least five of the following modifiers to "The Emperor's Garden": *sweltering, falling, gentle, sparkling, deep blue, bright, wise, sensuous.* How do these additional descriptions change the effect the poem has on you?
6. Lowell believed that "concentration is of the very essence of poetry" and strove to "produce poetry that is hard and clear, never blurred nor indefinite." Based on these two poems, explain why you believe she did or did not imbue her own work with these qualities.
7. Judging from these examples, is it more important to feel or to understand imagist poetry — or is that a false dichotomy? Can one response to art exist without the other? Explain.

La Ville ("The City")

FERNAND LÉGER

Fernand Léger (1881–1955) was a French painter and sculptor. He was born in Normandy to farmers and served on the front lines for the French army during World War I. Like many artists associated with the modernist movement, Léger's work blended abstract and recognizable figures to evoke the great changes wrought by urbanization, the first World War, and the increasing speed and apparent chaos of modern life. While Léger embraced recognizable subject matter later in his career, he also experimented with bold primary colors and geometric shapes to render it unfamiliar. In his famous painting, *La Ville* ("The City"), Léger reflects the vivid but disorienting and claustrophobic feeling of urban spaces in the early twentieth century.

The Philadelphia Museum of Art / Art Resource, NY

[1919]

QUESTIONS

1. What elements of urban life can you discern in this painting?
2. How do the colors and geometric patterns in this painting capture the artist's sense of movement in the city?
3. What do the broken texts and images suggest about the artist's perception of urban spaces?
4. One critic described this painting as a "utopian billboard for machine-age urban life." What elements of the work might support such an interpretation?
5. On the next page is a cityscape painted in 1877 by Gustave Caillebotte entitled *Paris Street; Rainy Day*. It exemplifies the type of realistic work that Fernand Léger believed no longer accurately portrayed urban life. How does it contrast with the cityscape of *La Ville*? Consider the geometry that structures the paintings, the figures, and the viewer's perspective in both works.

Gustave Caillebotte, French, 1848–1894, Paris Street; Rainy Day, 1877, Oil on canvas, 212.2 × 276.2 cm (83 1/2 × 108 3/4 in.), Charles H. and Mary F. S. Worcester Collection, 1964.336, The Art Institute of Chicago

The Love Song of J. Alfred Prufrock

T. S. ELIOT

Poet, dramatist, and critic Thomas Stearns Eliot (1888–1965) was born and raised in St. Louis, Missouri. He moved to England when he was twenty-five to attend Oxford University after studying at Harvard University and eventually became a British subject. His most famous works include "The Love Song of J. Alfred Prufrock" (1915), "The Wasteland" (1922), "Ash Wednesday" (1930), "Burnt Norton" (1941), "Little Gidding" (1942), "Four Quartets" (1943), and the play *Murder in the Cathedral* (1935). He was awarded the Nobel Prize for Literature in 1948. Eliot is considered one of the great poetic innovators of the twentieth century and is closely associated with the modernist movement — especially in his use of stream of consciousness, a technique he employs in "The Love Song of J. Alfred Prufrock" to depict a speaker wandering through the streets of a city on a foggy night. Eliot did not compromise when it came to the language of poetry, believing that it should represent the complexities of modern civilization. "The Love Song of J. Alfred Prufrock," a poem begun when Eliot was a college student and published when he was twenty-eight, is considered one of those works that epitomize the cultural significance of poetry.

S'io credesse che mia risposta fosse
A persona che mai tornasse al mondo,
Questa fiamma staria senza più scosse.
Ma perciocchè giammai di questo fondo

Non tornò vivo alcun, s'i'odo il vero,
Senza tema d'infamia ti rispondo.[1]

Let us go then, you and I,
When the evening is spread out against the sky
Like a patient etherized upon a table;
Let us go, through certain half-deserted streets,
The muttering retreats
Of restless nights in one-night cheap hotels
And sawdust restaurants with oyster-shells:
Streets that follow like a tedious argument
Of insidious intent
To lead you to an overwhelming question . . .
Oh, do not ask, "What is it?"
Let us go and make our visit.

In the room the women come and go
Talking of Michelangelo.

The yellow fog that rubs its back upon the window-panes,
The yellow smoke that rubs its muzzle on the window-panes
Licked its tongue into the corners of the evening,
Lingered upon the pools that stand in drains,
Let fall upon its back the soot that falls from chimneys,
Slipped by the terrace, made a sudden leap,
And seeing that it was a soft October night,
Curled once about the house, and fell asleep.

And indeed there will be time
For the yellow smoke that slides along the street,
Rubbing its back upon the window-panes;
There will be time, there will be time
To prepare a face to meet the faces that you meet;
There will be time to murder and create,
And time for all the works and days of hands[2]
That lift and drop a question on your plate:
Time for you and time for me,
And time yet for a hundred indecisions,
And for a hundred visions and revisions,
Before the taking of a toast and tea.

---

[1] From Dante's *Inferno*, canto XXVII, 61–66. The words are spoken by Guido da Montefeltro, who was condemned to hell for providing false counsel to Pope Boniface VII. When asked to identify himself, Guido responded, "If I thought my answers were given to anyone who could ever return to the world, this flame would shake no more; but since none ever did return above from this depth, if what I hear is true, without fear of infamy I answer thee." He does not know that Dante will return to earth to report on what he has seen and heard. — EDS.

[2] Reference to the title of a poem about agricultural life by the early Greek poet Hesiod. — EDS.

In the room the women come and go
Talking of Michelangelo.

And indeed there will be time
To wonder, "Do I dare?" and, "Do I dare?"
Time to turn back and descend the stair,
With a bald spot in the middle of my hair —

[They will say: "How his hair is growing thin!"]
My morning coat, my collar mounting firmly to the chin,
My necktie rich and modest, but asserted by a simple pin —
[They will say: "But how his arms and legs are thin!"]
Do I dare
Disturb the universe?
In a minute there is time
For decisions and revisions which a minute will reverse.

For I have known them all already, known them all:
Have known the evenings, mornings, afternoons,
I have measured out my life with coffee spoons;
I know the voices dying with a dying fall
Beneath the music from a farther room.
 So how should I presume?

And I have known the eyes already, known them all —
The eyes that fix you in a formulated phrase.
And when I am formulated, sprawling on a pin,
When I am pinned and wriggling on the wall,
Then how should I begin
To spit out all the butt-ends of my days and ways?
 And how should I presume?

And I have known the arms already, known them all —
Arms that are braceleted and white and bare
[But in the lamplight, downed with light brown hair!]
Is it perfume from a dress
That makes me so digress?
Arms that lie along a table, or wrap about a shawl.
 And should I then presume?
 And how should I begin?

Shall I say, I have gone at dusk through narrow streets,
And watched the smoke that rises from the pipes
Of lonely men in shirt-sleeves, leaning out of windows? . . .

. . . . .

I should have been a pair of ragged claws
Scuttling across the floors of silent seas.

And the afternoon, the evening, sleeps so peacefully!
Smoothed by long fingers,
Asleep . . . tired . . . or it malingers,
Stretched on the floor, here beside you and me.
Should I, after tea and cakes and ices,
Have the strength to force the moment to its crisis?
But though I have wept and fasted, wept and prayed,
Though I have seen my head (grown slightly bald) brought in upon a platter,[3]
I am no prophet — and here's no great matter;
I have seen the moment of my greatness flicker,
And I have seen the eternal Footman hold my coat, and snicker,
And in short, I was afraid.

And would it have been worth it, after all,
After the cups, the marmalade, the tea,
Among the porcelain, among some talk of you and me,
Would it have been worth while
To have bitten off the matter with a smile,
To have squeezed the universe into a ball
To roll it toward some overwhelming question,
To say: "I am Lazarus,[4] come from the dead,
Come back to tell you all, I shall tell you all" —
If one, settling a pillow by her head,
    Should say: "That is not what I meant at all.
    That is not it, at all."

And would it have been worth it, after all,
Would it have been worth while,
After the sunsets and the dooryards and the sprinkled streets,
After the novels, after the teacups, after the skirts that trail along the floor —
And this, and so much more? —
It is impossible to say just what I mean!
But as if a magic lantern threw the nerves in patterns on a screen:
Would it have been worth while
If one, settling a pillow or throwing off a shawl,
And turning toward the window, should say:
    "That is not it at all,
    That is not what I meant, at all."

. . . . .

[3] From Matthew 14:1–11. King Herod ordered the beheading of John the Baptist at the request of Herod's wife and daughter. — EDS.

[4] From John 11:1–44. Lazarus was raised from the dead by Jesus. — EDS.

No! I am not Prince Hamlet, nor was meant to be;
Am an attendant lord, one that will do
To swell a progress, start a scene or two,
Advise the prince: no doubt, an easy tool,
Deferential, glad to be of use,
Politic, cautious, and meticulous;
Full of high sentence, but a bit obtuse;
At times, indeed, almost ridiculous —
Almost, at times, the Fool.
I grow old . . . I grow old . . .
I shall wear the bottoms of my trousers rolled.

Shall I part my hair behind? Do I dare to eat a peach?

I shall wear white flannel trousers, and walk upon the beach.
I have heard the mermaids singing, each to each.

I do not think that they will sing to me.

I have seen them riding seaward on the waves
Combing the white hair of the waves blown back
When the wind blows the water white and black.
We have lingered in the chambers of the sea
By sea-girls wreathed with seaweed red and brown
Till human voices wake us, and we drown.

[1917]

QUESTIONS

1. We can assume that the speaker of the poem is Prufrock. What kind of person is he? Try to describe him in three or four words. What qualities of his character do you think he unknowingly reveals through his perceptions and observations?
2. How does T. S. Eliot set the tone in the poem's first stanza? Look carefully at both the figurative language and concrete details.
3. The "yellow fog" that is the subject of the poem's third stanza has the qualities of a cat. Is this association threatening, comforting, or both? How does your interpretation of the fog affect your reading of the poem as a whole?
4. You may notice that the images are arranged from top to bottom — the description goes from the sky to the streets in the opening stanza and progresses from the windowpanes to the drains in the third. What is the effect of the way Eliot's speaker, Prufrock, guides the reader's eye and imagination?
5. The middle section of the poem (ll. 37–86) moves from the chaotic city setting into the fragmented, anxiety-ridden mind of the speaker. How is Prufrock's physical description developed in lines 37–44? How do his physical characteristics connect to his emotional state?
6. In what ways is "The Love Song of J. Alfred Prufrock" a poem about time? Read through the text and look for references to time — particularly aging, the meaning of time, and the word *time* itself. What might Eliot be asserting or questioning about the meaning of time?
7. How does this poem reflect modernist concerns about the loss of emotional connections and alienation? To what extent does Eliot explore the reasons why such estrangement occurs? To what extent does he offer a solution?

from **Mrs. Dalloway**

VIRGINIA WOOLF

Virginia Woolf (1882–1941) was a renowned novelist, critic, and essayist closely associated with the modernist movement. Her most famous works are the novels *Mrs. Dalloway* (1925) and *To the Lighthouse* (1927), and also many nonfiction essays, including *A Room of One's Own* (1929). In *Mrs. Dalloway*, Woolf experiments with stream of consciousness, the quintessential modernist narrative mode also used by T. S. Eliot, James Joyce, Henry James, and others. In the following excerpt from the opening of *Mrs. Dalloway*, Woolf takes the reader into the mind of Clarissa Dalloway, an upper-class British woman planning a dinner party against the backdrop of the profound losses England suffered in World War I.

Mrs. Dalloway said she would buy the flowers herself.

For Lucy had her work cut out for her. The doors would be taken off their hinges; Rumpelmayer's men were coming. And then, thought Clarissa Dalloway, what a morning — fresh as if issued to children on a beach.

What a lark! What a plunge! For so it had always seemed to her, when, with a little squeak of the hinges, which she could hear now, she had burst open the French windows and plunged at Bourton into the open air. How fresh, how calm, stiller than this of course, the air was in the early morning; like the flap of a wave; the kiss of a wave; chill and sharp and yet (for a girl of eighteen as she then was) solemn, feeling as she did, standing there at the open window, that something awful was about to happen; looking at the flowers, at the trees with the smoke winding off them and the rooks rising, falling; standing and looking until Peter Walsh said, "Musing among the vegetables?" — was that it? — "I prefer men to cauliflowers" — was that it? He must have said it at breakfast one morning when she had gone out on to the terrace — Peter Walsh. He would be back from India one of these days, June or July, she forgot which, for his letters were awfully dull; it was his sayings one remembered; his eyes, his pocket-knife, his smile, his grumpiness and, when millions of things had utterly vanished — how strange it was! — a few sayings like this about cabbages.

She stiffened a little on the kerb, waiting for Durtnall's van to pass. A charming woman, Scrope Purvis thought her (knowing her as one does know people who live next door to one in Westminster); a touch of the bird about her, of the jay, blue-green, light, vivacious, though she was over fifty, and grown very white since her illness. There she perched, never seeing him, waiting to cross, very upright.

For having lived in Westminster — how many 5
years now? over twenty, — one feels even in the midst of the traffic, or waking at night, Clarissa was positive, a particular hush, or solemnity; an indescribable pause; a suspense (but that might be her heart, affected, they said, by influenza) before Big Ben strikes. There! Out it boomed. First a warning, musical; then the hour, irrevocable. The leaden circles dissolved in the air. Such fools we are, she thought, crossing Victoria Street. For Heaven only knows why one loves it so, how one sees it so, making it up, building it round one, tumbling it, creating it every moment afresh; but the veriest frumps, the most dejected of miseries sitting on doorsteps (drink their downfall) do the same; can't be dealt with, she felt positive, by Acts of Parliament for that very reason: they love life. In people's eyes, in the swing, tramp, and trudge; in the bellow and the uproar; the carriages, motor cars, omnibuses,

vans, sandwich men shuffling and swinging; brass bands; barrel organs; in the triumph and the jingle and the strange high singing of some aeroplane overhead was what she loved; life; London; this moment of June.

For it was the middle of June. The War was over, except for some one like Mrs. Foxcroft at the Embassy last night eating her heart out because that nice boy was killed and now the old Manor House must go to a cousin; or Lady Bexborough who opened a bazaar, they said, with the telegram in her hand, John, her favourite, killed; but it was over; thank Heaven — over. It was June. The King and Queen were at the Palace. And everywhere, though it was still so early, there was a beating, a stirring of galloping ponies, tapping of cricket bats; Lords, Ascot, Ranelagh and all the rest of it; wrapped in the soft mesh of the grey-blue morning air, which, as the day wore on, would unwind them, and set down on their lawns and pitches the bouncing ponies, whose forefeet just struck the ground and up they sprung, the whirling young men, and laughing girls in their transparent muslins who, even now, after dancing all night, were taking their absurd woolly dogs for a run; and even now, at this hour, discreet old dowagers were shooting out in their motor cars on errands of mystery; and the shopkeepers were fidgeting in their windows with their paste and diamonds, their lovely old sea-green brooches in eighteenth-century settings to tempt Americans (but one must economise, not buy things rashly for Elizabeth), and she, too, loving it as she did with an absurd and faithful passion, being part of it, since her people were courtiers once in the time of the Georges, she, too, was going that very night to kindle and illuminate; to give her party. But how strange, on entering the Park, the silence; the mist; the hum; the slow-swimming happy ducks; the pouched birds waddling; and who should be coming along with his back against the Government buildings, most appropriately, carrying a despatch box stamped with the Royal Arms, who but Hugh Whitbread; her old friend Hugh — the admirable Hugh!

"Good-morning to you, Clarissa!" said Hugh, rather extravagantly, for they had known each other as children. "Where are you off to?"

"I love walking in London," said Mrs. Dalloway. "Really it's better than walking in the country."

[1925]

QUESTIONS

1. *Mrs. Dalloway* is set in London, which is the focus of this opening section. How does Clarissa feel about the city? Cite specific words and passages to support your response.
2. Where does Virginia Woolf conflate or shift between the past and the present in this passage? What is the effect of these conflations and shifts?
3. What is the purpose of the conflicting emotions and contradictory actions in this passage? Identify two and discuss their effect.
4. Woolf intended to write a novel that underscored the profound change in life after World War I. How does the style of this passage make the reader experience the dislocation and disruption that the author believed characterized post–World War I London?

LITERATURE IN CONVERSATION
The Metamorphosis and the Modernist Vision

1. In what ways is *The Metamorphosis* by Franz Kafka a modernist work? Consider how it embodies some of the characteristics of this movement as well as ways in which its style and structure might prefigure later works like *Mrs. Dalloway*.
2. Modernism is, in many ways, a reaction to and preoccupation with the impact urbanization had on traditional beliefs and human relationships. Discuss how urban life is depicted in both *The Metamorphosis* and at least one other work from these Texts in Context.
3. In the introduction to this section, we discussed the collage as a form modernists used to capture the fragmentation of life in the early twentieth century. Discuss how at least two of these works might be seen as "collages," either visual or written.
4. In their effort to "make it new" and reveal the fissures of life in the early twentieth century, do the artists you've explored — including Kafka — present a bleak view of life in an age of rapid change, a hopeful perspective that results from facing change and trauma, or a little of both? In short, is modernism primarily optimistic or pessimistic? Consider at least two texts in your response.
5. Research another element of or influence on the modernist movement, such as cubism, Sigmund Freud's work on the impact of the unconscious, Albert Einstein's theory of relativity, composer Igor Stravinsky's *The Rite of Spring*, or playwright Bertolt Brecht's *The Threepenny Opera*. What characteristics of modernism do they express?
6. *The Metamorphosis* and the texts in this section primarily represent European and American perspectives on early twentieth-century life, but the effects of modernism were global. Research one of the following writers and artists and discuss the form modernism takes in his or her work: Mexican poet Octavio Paz (1914–1998), Indian painters Amrita Sher-Gil (1913–1941) and Jamini Roy (1887–1972), Russian poet Anna Akhmatova (1889–1966), Martinique poet Aimé Césaire (1913–2008), Japanese novelist Jun'ichirō Tanizaki (1886–1965), and Japanese poet Chika Sagawa (1911–1936).

FICTION

I Stand Here Ironing

TILLIE OLSEN

Tillie Olsen (1913–2007) was born in Nebraska, the daughter of Russian Jewish immigrants. Her parents were active socialists who fled Russia after the attempted revolution of 1905. She recalled, "It was a rich childhood from the standpoint of ideas." She attended high school but abandoned formal education after the eleventh grade. Later in life, as an influential writer, she received nine honorary degrees from colleges and universities. Political activism and responsibilities as a wife and mother made Olsen's writing sporadic. She published *Tell Me a Riddle* (1961), a series of four interconnected stories (the first of which is "I Stand Here Ironing"), *Yonnondio: From the Thirties* (1974), and *Silences* (1978), a nonfiction work about her life and the obstacles to writing that caused her own silences. Olsen was influential in the founding of the Feminist Press in 1970. Later work included *Mother to Daughter, Daughter to Mother, Mothers on Mothering: A Daybook and Reader* (1984), and *Mothers and Daughters: That Special Quality: An Exploration in Photographs* (1987). Perhaps her most famous story, "I Stand Here Ironing" focuses on the struggle of a working-class mother.

I stand here ironing, and what you asked me moves tormented back and forth with the iron.

"I wish you would manage the time to come in and talk with me about your daughter. I'm sure you can help me understand her. She's a youngster who needs help and whom I'm deeply interested in helping."

"Who needs help." . . . Even if I came, what good would it do? You think because I am her mother I have a key, or that in some way you could use me as a key? She has lived for nineteen years. There is all that life that has happened outside of me, beyond me.

And when is there time to remember, to sift, to weigh, to estimate, to total? I will start and there will be an interruption and I will have to gather it all together again. Or I will become engulfed with all I did or did not do, with what should have been and what cannot be helped.

She was a beautiful baby. The first and only 5
one of our five that was beautiful at birth. You do not guess how new and uneasy her tenancy in her now-loveliness. You did not know her all those years she was thought homely, or see her poring over her baby pictures, making me tell her over and over how beautiful she had been — and would be, I would tell her — and was now, to the seeing eye. But the seeing eyes were few or nonexistent. Including mine.

I nursed her. They feel that's important nowadays, I nursed all the children, but with her, with all the fierce rigidity of first motherhood, I did like the books then said. Though her cries battered me to trembling and my breasts ached with swollenness, I waited till the clock decreed.

Why do I put that first? I do not even know if it matters, or if it explains anything.

She was a beautiful baby. She blew shining bubbles of sound. She loved motion, loved light, loved color and music and textures. She would lie on the floor in her blue overalls patting the surface so hard in ecstasy her hands and feet would blur. She was a miracle to me, but when she was eight months old I had to leave her daytimes with the woman downstairs to whom she was no miracle at all, for I worked or looked for work and for Emily's father, who "could no longer endure" (he wrote in his good-bye note) "sharing want with us."

I was nineteen. It was the pre-relief, pre-WPA world of the depression. I would start running as soon as I got off the streetcar, running up the stairs, the place smelling sour, and awake or asleep to startle awake, when she saw me she would break into a clogged weeping that could not be comforted, a weeping I can hear yet.

After a while I found a job hashing at night so I could be with her days, and it was better. But it came to where I had to bring her to his family and leave her.

It took a long time to raise the money for her fare back. Then she got chicken pox and I had to wait longer. When she finally came, I hardly knew her, walking quick and nervous like her father, looking like her father, thin, and dressed in a shoddy red that yellowed her skin and glared at the pockmarks. All the baby loveliness gone.

She was two. Old enough for nursery school they said, and I did not know then what I know now — the fatigue of the long day, and the lacerations of group life in the kinds of nurseries that are only parking places for children.

Except that it would have made no difference if I had known. It was the only place there was. It was the only way we could be together, the only way I could hold a job.

And even without knowing, I knew. I knew the teacher that was evil because all these years it has curdled into my memory, the little boy hunched in the corner, her rasp, "why aren't you outside, because Alvin hits you? that's no reason, go out, scaredy." I knew Emily hated it even if she did not clutch and implore "don't go Mommy" like the other children, mornings.

She always had a reason why we should stay home. Momma, you look sick. Momma, I feel sick. Momma, the teachers aren't there today, they're sick. Momma, we can't go, there was a fire there last night. Momma, it's a holiday today, no school, they told me. But never a direct protest, never rebellion.

I think of our others in their three-, four-year-oldness — the explosions, the tempers, the denunciations, the demands — and I feel suddenly ill. I put the iron down. What in me demanded that goodness in her? And what was the cost, the cost to her of such goodness?

The old man living in the back once said in his gentle way: "You should smile at Emily more when you look at her." What *was* in my face when I looked at her? I loved her. There were all the acts of love.

It was only with the others I remembered what he said, and it was the face of joy, and not of care or tightness or worry I turned to them — too late for Emily. She does not smile easily, let alone almost always as her brothers and sisters do. Her face is closed and sombre, but when she wants, how fluid. You must have seen it in her pantomimes, you spoke of her rare gift for comedy on the stage that rouses laughter out of the audience so dear they applaud and applaud and do not want to let her go.

Where does it come from, that comedy? There was none of it in her when she came back to me that second time, after I had to send her away again. She had a new daddy now to learn to love, and I think perhaps it was a better time.

Except when we left her alone nights, telling ourselves she was old enough.

"Can't you go some other time, Mommy, like tomorrow?" she would ask. "Will it be just a little while you'll be gone? Do you promise?"

The time we came back, the front door open, the clock on the floor in the hall. She rigid awake. "It wasn't just a little while. I didn't cry. Three times I called you, just three times, and then I ran downstairs to open the door so you could come faster. The clock talked loud. I threw it away, it scared me what it talked."

She said the clock talked loud again that night I went to the hospital to have Susan. She was delirious with the fever that comes before red measles, but she was fully conscious all the week I was gone and the week after we were home when she could not come near the new baby or me.

She did not get well. She stayed skeleton thin, not wanting to eat, and night after night she had nightmares. She would call for me, and I would rouse from exhaustion to sleepily call back: "You're all right, darling, go to sleep, it's just a dream," and if she still called, in a sterner voice, "now go to sleep, Emily, there's nothing to hurt you." Twice, only twice, when I had to get up for Susan anyhow, I went in to sit with her.

Now when it is too late (as if she would let me hold her and comfort her like I do the others) I get up and go to her at once at her moan or restless stirring. "Are you awake, Emily? Can I get you something?" And the answer is always the same: "No, I'm all right, go back to sleep, Mother."

They persuaded me at the clinic to send her away to a convalescent home in the country where "she can have the kind of food and care you can't manage for her, and you'll be free to concentrate on the new baby." They still send children to that place. I see pictures on the society page of sleek young women planning affairs to raise money for it, or dancing at the affairs, or decorating Easter eggs or filling Christmas stockings for the children.

They never have a picture of the children so I do not know if the girls still wear those gigantic red bows and the ravaged looks on the every other Sunday when parents can come to visit "unless otherwise notified" — as we were notified the first six weeks.

Oh it is a handsome place, green lawns and tall trees and fluted flower beds. High up on the balconies of each cottage the children stand, the girls in their red bows and white dresses, the boys in white suits and giant red ties. The parents stand below shrieking up to be heard and the children shriek down to be heard, and between them the invisible wall "Not To Be Contaminated by Parental Germs or Physical Affection."

There was a tiny girl who always stood hand in hand with Emily. Her parents never came. One visit she was gone. "They moved her to Rose Cottage," Emily shouted in explanation. "They don't like you to love anybody here."

She wrote once a week, the labored writing of a seven-year-old. "I am fine. How is the baby. If I write my leter nicly I will have a star. Love." There never was a star. We wrote every other day, letters she could never hold or keep but only hear read — once. "We simply do not have room for children to keep any personal possessions," they patiently explained when we pieced one Sunday's shrieking together to plead how much it would mean to Emily, who loved so to keep things, to be allowed to keep her letters and cards.

Each visit she looked frailer. "She isn't eating," they told us.

(They had runny eggs for breakfast or mush with lumps, Emily said later, I'd hold it in my mouth and not swallow. Nothing ever tasted good, just when they had chicken.)

It took us eight months to get her released home, and only the fact that she gained back so little of her seven lost pounds convinced the social worker.

I used to try to hold and love her after she came back, but her body would stay stiff, and after a while she'd push away. She ate little. Food sickened her, and I think much of life too. Oh she had physical lightness and brightness, twinkling by on skates, bouncing like a ball up and down up and down over the jump rope, skimming over the hill; but these were momentary.

She fretted about her appearance, thin and dark and foreign-looking at a time when every little girl was supposed to look or thought she should look a chubby blonde replica of Shirley Temple. The doorbell sometimes rang for her, but no one seemed to come and play in the house or to be a best friend. Maybe because we moved so much.

There was a boy she loved painfully through two school semesters. Months later she told me how she had taken pennies from my purse to buy him candy. "Licorice was his favorite and I brought him some every day, but he still liked Jennifer better'n me. Why, Mommy?" The kind of question for which there is no answer.

School was a worry for her. She was not glib or quick in a world where glibness and quickness were easily confused with ability to learn. To her overworked and exasperated teachers she was an overconscientious "slow learner" who kept trying to catch up and was absent entirely too often.

I let her be absent, though sometimes the illness was imaginary. How different from my now-strictness about attendance with the others. I wasn't working. We had a new baby. I was home anyhow. Sometimes, after Susan grew old enough, I would keep her home from school, too, to have them all together.

Mostly Emily had asthma, and her breathing, harsh and labored, would fill the house with a curiously tranquil sound. I would bring the two old dresser mirrors and her boxes of collections to her bed. She would select beads and single earrings, bottle tops and shells, dried flowers and pebbles, old postcards and scraps, all sorts of oddments; then she and Susan would play Kingdom, setting up landscapes and furniture, peopling them with action.

Those were the only times of peaceful companionship between her and Susan. I have edged away from it, that poisonous feeling between them, that terrible balancing of hurts and needs I had to do between the two, and did so badly, those earlier years.

Oh there were conflicts between the others too, each one human, needing, demanding, hurting, taking — but only between Emily and Susan, no, Emily toward Susan that corroding resentment. It seems so obvious on the surface, yet it is not obvious; Susan, the second child, Susan, golden- and curly-haired and chubby, quick and articulate and assured, everything in appearance and manner Emily was not; Susan, not able to resist Emily's precious things, losing or sometimes clumsily breaking them; Susan telling jokes and riddles to company for applause while Emily sat silent (to say to me later: that was *my* riddle, Mother, I told it to Susan); Susan, who for all the five years' difference in age was just a year behind Emily in developing physically.

I am glad for that slow physical development that widened the difference between her and her contemporaries, though she suffered over it. She was too vulnerable for that terrible world of youthful competition, of preening and parading, of constant measuring of yourself against every other, of envy, "If I had that copper hair," "If I had that skin. . . ." She tormented herself enough about not looking like the others, there was enough of unsureness, the having to be conscious of words before you speak, the constant caring — what are they thinking of me? without having it all magnified by the merciless physical drives.

Ronnie is calling. He is wet and I change him. It is rare there is such a cry now. That time of motherhood is almost behind me when the ear is not one's own but must always be racked and listening for the child cry, the child call. We sit for a while and I hold him, looking out over the city spread in charcoal with its soft aisles of light. "*Shoogily,*" he breathes and curls closer. I carry him back to bed, asleep. *Shoogily*. A funny word, a family word, inherited from Emily, invented by her to say: *comfort*.

In this and other ways she leaves her seal, I say aloud. And startle at my saying it. What do I mean? What did I start to gather together, to try and make coherent? I was at the terrible, growing years. War years. I do not remember them well. I was working, there were four smaller ones now, there was not time for her. She had to help be a mother, and housekeeper, and shopper. She had to get her seal. Mornings of crisis and near hysteria trying to get lunches packed, hair combed, coats and shoes found, everyone to school or Child Care on time, the baby ready for transportation. And always the paper scribbled on by a smaller one, the book looked at by Susan then mislaid, the homework not done. Running out to that huge school where she was one, she was lost, she was a drop; suffering over the unpreparedness, stammering and unsure in her classes.

There was so little time left at night after the kids were bedded down. She would struggle over books, always eating (it was in those years she developed her enormous appetite that is legendary in our family) and I would be ironing, or preparing food for the next day, or writing V-mail to Bill, or tending the baby. Sometimes, to make me laugh, or out of her despair, she would imitate happenings or types at school.

I think I said once: "Why don't you do something like this in the school amateur show?" One morning she phoned me at work, hardly understandable through the weeping: "Mother, I did it. I won, I won; they gave me first prize; they clapped and clapped and wouldn't let me go."

Now suddenly she was Somebody, and as imprisoned in her difference as she had been in anonymity.

She began to be asked to perform at other high schools, even in colleges, then at city and statewide affairs. The first one we went to, I only recognized her that first moment when thin, shy, she almost drowned herself into the curtains. Then: Was this Emily? The control, the command, the convulsing and deadly clowning, the spell, then the roaring, stamping audience, unwilling to let this rare and precious laughter out of their lives.

Afterwards: You ought to do something about her with a gift like that — but without money or knowing how, what does one do? We have left it all to her, and the gift has so often eddied inside, clogged and clotted, as been used and growing.

She is coming. She runs up the stairs two at a time with her light graceful step, and I know she is happy tonight. Whatever it was that occasioned your call did not happen today.

"Aren't you ever going to finish the ironing, Mother? Whistler painted his mother in a rocker. I'd have to paint mine standing over an ironing board." This is one of her communicative nights and she tells me everything and nothing as she fixes herself a plate of food out of the icebox.

She is so lovely. Why did you want me to come in at all? Why were you concerned? She will find her way.

She starts up the stairs to bed. "Don't get me up with the rest in the morning." "But I thought you were having midterms." "Oh, those," she comes back in, kisses me, and says quite lightly, "in a couple of years when we'll all be atom-dead they won't matter a bit."

She has said it before. She *believes* it. But because I have been dredging the past, and all that compounds a human being is so heavy and meaningful in me, I cannot endure it tonight.

I will never total it all. I will never come in to say: She was a child seldom smiled at. Her father left me before she was a year old. I had to work her first six years when there was work, or I sent her home and to his relatives. There were years she had care she hated. She was dark and thin and foreign-looking in a world where the prestige went to blondeness and curly hair and dimples, she was slow where glibness was prized. She was a child of anxious, not proud, love. We were poor and could not afford for her the soil of easy growth. I was a young mother,

I was a distracted mother. There were other children pushing up, demanding. Her younger sister seemed all that she was not. There were years she did not want me to touch her. She kept too much in herself, her life was such she had to keep too much in herself. My wisdom came too late. She has much to her and probably little will come of it. She is a child of her age, of depression, of war, of fear.

Let her be. So all that is in her will not bloom — but in how many does it? There is still enough left to live by. Only help her to know — help make it so there is cause for her to know — that she is more than this dress on the ironing board, helpless before the iron.

[1961]

EXPLORING THE TEXT

1. How is the setting of the story's frame, a woman standing at an ironing board, critical to the story's themes?
2. What structural purpose do the interruptions in the narrator's interior monologue serve in the story? For instance, "Ronnie is calling. He is wet and I change him" in paragraph 43. Notice, too, how the speaker's use of run-on sentences and made-up words — such as "four-year-oldness" (para. 16) — contrasts with short declarative sentences such as "She was a beautiful baby" (paras. 5 and 8), "I was nineteen" (para. 9), and "She was two" (para. 12). What is the effect of this juxtaposition?
3. The "you" the narrator addresses at the beginning of the story refers to a teacher concerned about Emily's welfare. At first the narrator seems somewhat defensive (as in the third paragraph, when she sarcastically responds to the teacher's request). How does the relationship between the narrator and the teacher evolve over the course of the story, so that by the end the narrator beseeches, "Only help her to know — help make it so there is cause for her to know" (para. 56)? To what extent might the narrator be addressing the reader as well as the teacher?
4. What do you make of the repeated references to quantitative matters in this story — for instance, "to sift, to weigh, to estimate, to total" in paragraph 4? Find other examples of this motif in the story, and explain its significance.
5. In the final lines of the story, the narrator calls her daughter "a child of her age, of depression, of war, of fear" (para. 55). How have historical events affected Emily's development? How have they imposed limitations on her? How have they made her strong?
6. Why does Tillie Olsen give us so much specific detail about Emily's appearance? How do these descriptions contribute to her characterization? How is her appearance related to the choices she makes to distinguish herself, to stand out? What does the narrator mean when she says of Emily, "Now suddenly she was Somebody, and as imprisoned in her difference as she had been in anonymity" (para. 47)?
7. What, finally, is the narrator's assessment of her own performance as a mother? Do you think she believes she has been a good mother to her children? Overall, is the story hopeful or hopeless?
8. Rarely do we hear Emily speak in this story. Instead, we hear others' comments about and reactions to her, including her mother's. How do you think Emily would characterize her relationship with her mother? Do you think she would blame her mother or circumstances beyond their control for the difficulties she has experienced?

The Moths

HELENA MARÍA VIRAMONTES

Helena María Viramontes (b. 1949) grew up as one of nine children in East Los Angeles. She has a BA from Immaculate Heart College, an MFA from the University of California, Irvine, and is currently a professor of English at Cornell University. Her mother's plight — raising nine children with a husband who "showed all that is bad in being male" — moved Helena to write of Chicana women's struggles. While writing for several underground literary publications, Viramontes published her first collection of short stories, *The Moths and Other Stories*, in 1985. In 1995, her first novel, *Under the Feet of Jesus*, was published, followed by *Their Dogs Came with Them* in 2007. The latter is her most ambitious work, drawing on her teenage years, the explosive decade of the 1960s, and the lives of young women coming of age at the height of *El Movimiento*, the fight for Latino civil rights in America. The story included here is the title piece from her 1985 collection about the relationship between a young woman and her *abuelita*, or grandmother.

I was fourteen years old when Abuelita requested my help. And it seemed only fair. Abuelita had pulled me through the rages of scarlet fever by placing, removing and replacing potato slices on the temples of my forehead; she had seen me through several whippings, an arm broken by a dare jump off Tío Enrique's tool-shed, puberty, and my first lie. Really, I told Amá, it was only fair.

Not that I was her favorite granddaughter or anything special. I wasn't even pretty or nice like my older sisters and I just couldn't do the girl things they could do. My hands were too big to handle the fineries of crocheting or embroidery and I always pricked my fingers or knotted my colored threads time and time again while my sisters laughed and called me bull hands with their cute waterlike voices. So I began keeping a piece of jagged brick in my sock to bash my sisters or anyone who called me bull hands. Once, while we all sat in the bedroom, I hit Teresa on the forehead, right above her eyebrow and she ran to Amá with her mouth open, her hand over her eye while blood seeped between her fingers. I was used to the whippings by then.

I wasn't respectful either. I even went so far as to doubt the power of Abuelita's slices, the slices she said absorbed my fever. "You're still alive, aren't you?" Abuelita snapped back, her pasty gray eye beaming at me and burning holes in my suspicions. Regretful that I had let secret questions drop out of my mouth, I couldn't look into her eyes. My hands began to fan out, grow like a liar's nose until they hung by my side like low weights. Abuelita made a balm out of dried moth wings and Vicks and rubbed my hands, shaped them back to size and it was the strangest feeling. Like bones melting. Like sun shining through the darkness of your eyelids. I didn't mind helping Abuelita after that, so Amá would always send me over to her.

In the early afternoon Amá would push her hair back, hand me my sweater and shoes, and tell me to go to Mama Luna's. This was to avoid another fight and another whipping, I knew. I would deliver one last direct shot on Marisela's arm and jump out of our house, the slam of the screen door burying her cries of anger, and I'd gladly go help Abuelita plant her wild lilies or jasmine or heliotrope or cilantro or hierbabuena[1] in red Hills Brothers coffee cans.

[1] Also yerba buena, or "good herb," a plant in the mint family that is steeped to make a tea-like beverage. — EDS.

Abuelita would wait for me at the top step of her porch holding a hammer and nail and empty coffee cans. And although we hardly spoke, hardly looked at each other as we worked over root transplants, I always felt her gray eye on me. It made me feel, in a strange sort of way, safe and guarded and not alone. Like God was supposed to make you feel.

5 On Abuelita's porch, I would puncture holes in the bottom of the coffee cans with a nail and a precise hit of a hammer. This completed, my job was to fill them with red clay mud from beneath her rose bushes, packing it softly, then making a perfect hole, four fingers round, to nest a sprouting avocado pit, or the spidery sweet potatoes that Abuelita rooted in mayonnaise jars with toothpicks and daily water, or prickly chayotes[2] that produced vines that twisted and wound all over her porch pillars, crawling to the roof, up and over the roof, and down the other side, making her small brick house look like it was cradled within the vines that grew pear-shaped squashes ready for the pick, ready to be steamed with onions and cheese and butter. The roots would burst out of the rusted coffee cans and search for a place to connect. I would then feed the seedlings with water.

But this was a different kind of help, Amá said, because Abuelita was dying. Looking into her gray eye, then into her brown one, the doctor said it was just a matter of days. And so it seemed only fair that these hands she had melted and formed found use in rubbing her caving body with alcohol and marihuana, rubbing her arms and legs, turning her face to the window so that she could watch the Bird of Paradise blooming or smell the scent of clove in the air. I toweled her face frequently and held her hand for hours. Her gray wiry hair hung over the mattress. Since I could remember, she'd kept her long hair in braids. Her mouth was vacant and when she slept, her eyelids never closed all the way. Up close, you could see her gray eye beaming out the window, staring hard as if to remember everything. I never kissed her. I left the window open when I went to the market.

Across the street from Jay's Market there was a chapel. I never knew its denomination, but I went in just the same to search for candles. I sat down on one of the pews because there were none. After I cleaned my fingernails, I looked up at the high ceiling. I had forgotten the vastness of these places, the coolness of the marble pillars and the frozen statues with blank eyes. I was alone. I knew why I had never returned.

That was one of Apá's biggest complaints. He would pound his hands on the table, rocking the sugar dish or spilling a cup of coffee and scream that if I didn't go to mass every Sunday to save my goddamn sinning soul, then I had no reason to go out of the house, period. Punto final.[3] He would grab my arm and dig his nails into me to make sure I understood the importance of catechism. Did he make himself clear? Then he strategically directed his anger at Amá for her lousy ways of bringing up daughters, being disrespectful and unbelieving, and my older sisters would pull me aside and tell me if I didn't get to mass right this minute, they were all going to kick the holy shit out of me. Why am I so selfish? Can't you see what it's doing to Amá, you idiot? So I would wash my feet and stuff them in my black Easter shoes that shone with Vaseline, grab a missal and veil, and wave good-bye to Amá.

I would walk slowly down Lorena to First to Evergreen, counting the cracks on the cement. On Evergreen I would turn left and walk to Abuelita's. I liked her porch because it was shielded by the vines of the chayotes and I could get a good look at the people and car traffic on

[2] Pear-shaped vegetable similar to a cucumber. — EDS.

[3] Final point, period. — EDS.

Evergreen without them knowing. I would jump up the porch steps, knock on the screen door as I wiped my feet and call Abuelita? mi Abuelita? As I opened the door and stuck my head in, I would catch the gagging scent of toasting chile on the placa.[4] When I entered the sala,[5] she would greet me from the kitchen, wringing her hands in her apron. I'd sit at the corner of the table to keep from being in her way. The chiles made my eyes water. Am I crying? No, Mama Luna, I'm sure not crying. I don't like going to mass, but my eyes watered anyway, the tears dropping on the tablecloth like candle wax. Abuelita lifted the burnt chiles from the fire and sprinkled water on them until the skins began to separate. Placing them in front of me, she turned to check the menudo.[6] I peeled the skins off and put the flimsy, limp looking green and yellow chiles in the molcajete[7] and began to crush and crush and twist and crush the heart out of the tomato, the clove of garlic, the stupid chiles that made me cry, crushed them until they turned into liquid under my bull hand. With a wooden spoon, I scraped hard to destroy the guilt, and my tears were gone. I put the bowl of chile next to a vase filled with freshly cut roses. Abuelita touched my hand and pointed to the bowl of menudo that steamed in front of me. I spooned some chile into the menudo and rolled a corn tortilla thin with the palms of my hands. As I ate, a fine Sunday breeze entered the kitchen and a rose petal calmly feathered down to the table.

10 I left the chapel without blessing myself and walked to Jay's. Most of the time Jay didn't have much of anything. The tomatoes were always soft and the cans of Campbell soups had rusted spots on them. There was dust on the tops of cereal boxes. I picked up what I needed: rubbing alcohol, five cans of chicken broth, a big bottle of Pine Sol. At first Jay got mad because I thought I had forgotten the money. But it was there all the time, in my back pocket.

When I returned from the market, I heard Amá crying in Abuelita's kitchen. She looked up at me with puffy eyes. I placed the bags of groceries on the table and began putting the cans of soup away. Amá sobbed quietly. I never kissed her. After a while, I patted her on the back for comfort. Finally: "¿Y mi Amá?"[8] she asked in a whisper, then choked again and cried into her apron.

Abuelita fell off the bed twice yesterday, I said, knowing that I shouldn't have said it and wondering why I wanted to say it because it only made Amá cry harder. I guess I became angry and just so tired of the quarrels and beatings and unanswered prayers and my hands just there hanging helplessly by my side. Amá looked at me again, confused, angry, and her eyes were filled with sorrow. I went outside and sat on the porch swing and watched the people pass. I sat there until she left. I dozed off repeating the words to myself like rosary prayers: when do you stop giving when do you start giving when do you . . . and when my hands fell from my lap, I awoke to catch them. The sun was setting, an orange glow, and I knew Abuelita was hungry.

There comes a time when the sun is defiant. Just about the time when moods change, inevitable seasons of a day, transitions from one color to another, that hour or minute or second when the sun is finally defeated, finally sinks into the realization that it cannot with all its power to heal or burn, exist forever, there comes an illumination where the sun and earth meet, a final burst of burning red orange fury reminding us that although endings are inevitable, they are necessary for rebirths, and when that time came,

[4] Plate. — EDS.

[5] Living room. — EDS.

[6] Traditional Mexican soup made with tripe. — EDS.

[7] Stone bowl used for grinding foods or spices, similar to a mortar and pestle. — EDS.

[8] "And my Mama?" — EDS.

just when I switched on the light in the kitchen to open Abuelita's can of soup, it was probably then that she died.

The room smelled of Pine Sol and vomit and Abuelita had defecated the remains of her cancerous stomach. She had turned to the window and tried to speak, but her mouth remained open and speechless. I heard you, Abuelita, I said, stroking her cheek, I heard you. I opened the windows of the house and let the soup simmer and overboil on the stove. I turned the stove off and poured the soup down the sink. From the cabinet I got a tin basin, filled it with lukewarm water and carried it carefully to the room. I went to the linen closet and took out some modest bleached white towels. With the sacredness of a priest preparing his vestments, I unfolded the towels one by one on my shoulders. I removed the sheets and blankets from her bed and peeled off her thick flannel nightgown. I toweled her puzzled face, stretching out the wrinkles, removing the coils of her neck, toweled her shoulders and breasts. Then I changed the water. I returned to towel the creases of her stretch-marked stomach, her sporadic vaginal hairs, and her sagging thighs. I removed the lint from between her toes and noticed a mapped birthmark on the fold of her buttock. The scars on her back which were as thin as the life lines on the palms of her hands made me realize how little I really knew of Abuelita. I covered her with a thin blanket and went into the bathroom. I washed my hands, and turned on the tub faucets and watched the water pour into the tub with vitality and steam. When it was full, I turned off the water and undressed. Then, I went to get Abuelita.

15 She was not as heavy as I thought and when I carried her in my arms, her body fell into a V, and yet my legs were tired, shaky, and I felt as if the distance between the bedroom and bathroom was miles and years away. Amá, where are you?

I stepped into the bathtub one leg first, then the other. I bent my knees slowly to descend into the water slowly so I wouldn't scald her skin. There, there, Abuelita, I said, cradling her, smoothing her as we descended, I heard you. Her hair fell back and spread across the water like eagle's wings. The water in the tub overflowed and poured onto the tile of the floor. Then the moths came. Small, gray ones that came from her soul and out through her mouth fluttering to light, circling the single dull light bulb of the bathroom. Dying is lonely and I wanted to go to where the moths were, stay with her and plant chayotes whose vines would crawl up her fingers and into the clouds; I wanted to rest my head on her chest with her stroking my hair, telling me about the moths that lay within the soul and slowly eat the spirit up; I wanted to return to the waters of the womb with her so that we would never be alone again. I wanted. I wanted my Amá. I removed a few strands of hair from Abuelita's face and held her small light head within the hollow of my neck. The bathroom was filled with moths, and for the first time in a long time I cried, rocking us, crying for her, for me, for Amá, the sobs emerging from the depths of anguish, the misery of feeling half born, sobbing until finally the sobs rippled into circles and circles of sadness and relief. There, there, I said to Abuelita, rocking us gently, there, there.

[1985]

EXPLORING THE TEXT

1. The story opens with the narrator's grandmother applying potato slices to the narrator's fevered brow. Compare this opening with the conclusion of the story. What is the significance of the contrast between the gentleness at the beginning and end of the story, and the rough treatment the narrator typically gives to family members ("I hit Teresa on the forehead," para. 2) and receives from them ("He would grab my arm and dig his nails into me," para. 8)?
2. How does the work Abuelita asks the narrator to do — planting, cooking — help the teenager deal with her pent-up anger?
3. As the narrator cares for her dying grandmother, she begins to ask herself, "when do you stop giving when do you start giving" (para. 12), continuing the repetition of the word "when" throughout the following paragraph. What is the significance of this repetition for the fourteen-year-old narrator? What might she be questioning in her own life?
4. Trace the references to hands in this story. How do you interpret the poultice balm of moth wings that Abuelita uses to shape the narrator's hands back into shape? What is the significance of this act?
5. What is the role of religion and spirituality in this story? Why does the narrator think to herself when she is in the chapel, "I was alone. I knew why I had never returned" (para. 7)? What conflicts does religion cause in her family?
6. Note the references throughout to Amá, the narrator's mother. When Amá is crying in Abuelita's kitchen, why does the narrator choose not to kiss her? Why at the end does the narrator say, "I wanted. I wanted my Amá" (para. 16)? What is the nature of the relationship among these three generations of women? What does the narrator want it to be?
7. What do the moths represent in the story?
8. Describe the ways in which the narrator is an outcast in her own family. What does her grandmother seem to understand that the girl's immediate family members do not?
9. Does the narrator's fearlessness about death strike you as unusual? Why do you think she is comfortable enough to bathe her dead Abuelita? Consider the sensuous descriptions throughout the story.

The Progress of Love

ALICE MUNRO

Alice Munro (b. 1931) is a Nobel Prize–winning Canadian writer, known primarily for her short stories. Munro was born in Ontario and began writing as a teenager, publishing her first story in 1950 while studying English and journalism at the University of Western Ontario. Munro's first story collection, *Dance of the Happy Shades* (1968), won the Governor General's Award, then Canada's highest literary prize. Her publications include fourteen original short story collections, a novel, and numerous major awards. Munro won the 1998 National Book Critics Circle Award for her story collection *The Love of a Good Woman*. For her contributions to the short story genre and to literature as a whole, Munro won the 2009 Man Booker International Prize and the 2013 Nobel Prize in Literature. Munro's stories are often set in Ontario, feature a strong regional focus, and present characters against a backdrop of deeply rooted customs and traditions. They also often employ a nonchronological structure reflecting the psychological complexity of memory and experience. In "The Progress of Love," Munro follows a narrator's nonlinear memories and reflections to examine a lifetime of changing family dynamics.

I got a call at work, and it was my father. This was not long after I was divorced and started in the real-estate office. Both of my boys were in school. It was a hot enough day in September.

My father was so polite, even in the family. He took time to ask me how I was. Country manners. Even if somebody phones up to tell you your house is burning down, they ask first how you are.

"I'm fine," I said. "How are you?"

"Not so good, I guess," said my father, in his old way — apologetic but self-respecting. "I think your mother's gone."

I knew that "gone" meant "dead." I knew that. But for a second or so I saw my mother in her black straw hat setting off down the lane. The word "gone" seemed full of nothing but a deep relief and even an excitement — the excitement you feel when a door closes and your house sinks back to normal and you let yourself loose into all the free space around you. That was in my father's voice, too — behind the apology, a queer sound like a gulped breath. But my mother hadn't been a burden — she hadn't been sick a day — and far from feeling relieved at her death, my father took it hard. He never got used to living alone, he said. He went into the Netterfield County Home quite willingly.

He told me how he found my mother on the couch in the kitchen when he came in at noon. She had picked a few tomatoes, and was setting them on the windowsill to ripen; then she must have felt weak, and lain down. Now, telling this, his voice went wobbly — meandering, as you would expect — in his amazement. I saw in my mind the couch, the old quilt that protected it, right under the phone.

"So I thought I better call you," my father said, and he waited for me to say what he should do now.

My mother prayed on her knees at midday, at night, and first thing in the morning. Every day opened up to her to have God's will done in it. Every night she totted up what she'd done and said and thought, to see how it squared with Him. That kind of life is dreary, people think, but they're missing the point. For one thing, such a life can never be boring. And nothing can happen to you that you can't make use of. Even if you're racked by troubles, and sick and poor and ugly, you've got your soul to carry through life like a treasure on a platter. Going upstairs to pray after the noon meal, my mother would be full of energy and expectation, seriously smiling.

She was saved at a camp meeting when she was fourteen. That was the same summer that her own mother — my grandmother — died. For a few years, my mother went to meetings with a lot of other people who'd been saved, some who'd been saved over and over again, enthusiastic old sinners. She could tell stories about what went on at those meetings, the singing and hollering and wildness. She told about one old man getting up and shouting, "Come down, O Lord, come down among us now! Come down through the roof and I'll pay for the shingles!"

She was back to being just an Anglican, a serious one, by the time she got married. She was twenty-five then, and my father was thirty-eight. A tall good-looking couple, good dancers, good card-players, sociable. But serious people — that's how I would try to describe them. Serious the way hardly anybody is anymore. My father was not religious in the way my mother was. He was an Anglican, an Orangeman, a Conservative, because that's what he had been brought up to be. He was the son who got left on the farm with his parents and took care of them till they died. He met my mother, he waited for her, they married; he thought himself lucky then to have a family to work for. (I have two brothers, and I had a baby sister who died.) I have a feeling that my father never slept with any woman before my mother, and never with her until he married her. And he had to wait, because my mother wouldn't get married until she had paid back to her own father every cent he had spent on her since her mother died. She had kept track of everything — board, books, clothes — so that she could pay it back. When she married, she had no nest egg, as teachers usually did, no hope chest, sheets, or dishes. My father used to say, with a somber, joking face, that he had hoped to get a woman with money in the bank. "But you take the money in the bank, you have to take the face that goes with it," he said, "and sometimes that's no bargain."

The house we lived in had big, high rooms, with dark-green blinds on the windows. When the blinds were pulled down against the sun, I used to like to move my head and catch the light flashing through the holes and cracks. Another thing I liked looking at was chimney stains, old or fresh, which I could turn into animals, people's faces, even distant cities. I told my own two boys about that, and their father, Dan Casey, said, "See, your mom's folks were so poor, they couldn't afford TV, so they got these stains on the ceiling — your mom had to watch the stains on the ceiling!" He always liked to kid me about thinking poor was anything great.

When my father was very old, I figured out that he didn't mind people doing new sorts of things — for instance, my getting divorced — as much as he minded them having new sorts of reasons for doing them.

Thank God he never had to know about the commune.

"The Lord never intended," he used to say. Sitting around with the other old men in the Home, in the long, dim porch behind the spirea bushes, he talked about how the Lord never intended for people to tear around the country on motorbikes and snowmobiles. And how the Lord never intended for nurses' uniforms to be pants. The nurses didn't mind at all. They called him "Handsome," and told me he was a real old sweetheart, a real old religious gentleman. They marvelled at his thick black hair, which he kept until he died. They washed and combed it beautifully, wet-waved it with their fingers.

Sometimes, with all their care, he was a little unhappy. He wanted to go home. He worried about the cows, the fences, about who was getting up to light the fire. A few flashes of meanness — very few. Once, he gave me a sneaky, unfriendly look when I went in; he said, "I'm surprised you haven't worn all the skin off your knees by now."

I laughed. I said, "What doing? Scrubbing floors?"

"Praying!" he said, in a voice like spitting.

He didn't know who he was talking to.

I don't remember my mother's hair being anything but white. My mother went white in her twenties, and never saved any of her young hair, which had been brown. I used to try to get her to tell what color brown.

"Dark."

"Like Brent, or like Dolly?" Those were two workhorses we had, a team.

"I don't know. It wasn't horsehair."

"Was it like chocolate?"

"Something like."

"Weren't you sad when it went white?"

"No. I was glad."

"Why?"

"I was glad that I wouldn't have hair anymore that was the same color as my father's."

Hatred is always a sin, my mother told me. Remember that. One drop of hatred in your soul will spread and discolor everything like a drop of black ink in white milk. I was struck by that and meant to try it, but knew I shouldn't waste the milk.

* * *

All these things I remember. All the things I know, or have been told, about people I never even saw. I was named Euphemia, after my mother's mother. A terrible name, such as nobody has nowadays. At home they called me

Phemie, but when I started to work, I called myself Fame. My husband, Dan Casey, called me Fame. Then in the bar of the Shamrock Hotel, years later, after my divorce, when I was going out, a man said to me, "Fame, I've been meaning to ask you, just what is it you are famous for?"

"I don't know," I told him. "I don't know, unless it's for wasting my time talking to jerks like you."

After that I thought of changing it altogether, to something like Joan, but unless I moved away from here, how could I do that?

In the summer of 1947, when I was twelve, I helped my mother paper the downstairs bedroom, the spare room. My mother's sister, Beryl, was coming to visit us. These two sisters hadn't seen each other for years. Very soon after their mother died, their father married again. He went to live in Minneapolis, then in Seattle, with his new wife and his younger daughter, Beryl. My mother wouldn't go with them. She stayed on in the town of Ramsay, where they had been living. She was boarded with a childless couple who had been neighbors. She and Beryl had met only once or twice since they were grown up. Beryl lived in California.

The paper had a design of cornflowers on a white ground. My mother had got it at a reduced price, because it was the end of a lot. This meant we had trouble matching the pattern, and behind the door we had to do some tricky fitting with scraps and strips. This was before the days of pre-pasted wallpaper. We had a trestle table set up in the front room, and we mixed the paste and swept it onto the back of the paper with wide brushes, watching for lumps. We worked with the windows up, screens fitted under them, the front door open, the screens door closed. The country we could see through the mesh of screens and the wavery old window glass was all hot and flowering — milkweed and wild carrot in the pastures, mustard rampaging in the clover, some fields creamy with the buckwheat people grew then. My mother sang. She sang a song she said her own mother used to sing when she and Beryl were little girls.

"I once had a sweetheart, but now I have none.
He's gone and he's left me to weep and to moan.
He's gone and he's left me, but contented I'll be,
For I'll get another one, better than he!"

I was excited because Beryl was coming, a visitor, all the way from California. Also, because I had gone to town in late June to write the Entrance Examinations, and was hoping to hear soon that I had passed with honors. Everybody who had finished Grade 8 in the country schools had to go into town to write those examinations. I loved that — the rustling sheets of foolscap, the important silence, the big stone high-school building, all the old initials carved in the desks, darkened with varnish. The first burst of summer outside, the green and yellow light, the townlike chestnut trees, and honeysuckle. And all it was was this same town, where I have lived now more than half my life. I wondered at it. And at myself, drawing maps with ease and solving problems, knowing quantities of answers. I thought I was so clever. But I wasn't clever enough to understand the simplest thing. I didn't even understand that examinations made no difference in my case. I wouldn't be going to high school. How could I? That was before there were school buses; you had to board in town. My parents didn't have the money. They operated on very little cash, as many farmers did then. The payments from the cheese factory were about all that came in regularly. And they didn't think of my life going in that direction, the high-school direction. They thought that I would stay at home and help my mother, maybe hire out to help women in the neighborhood who were sick or having a baby. Until such time as I got married. That was what they were waiting to tell me when I got the results of the examinations.

You would think my mother might have a different idea, since she had been a schoolteacher herself. But she said God didn't care. God isn't interested in what kind of job or what kind of education anybody has, she told me. He doesn't care two hoots about that, and it's what He cares about that matters.

This was the first time I understood how God could become a real opponent, not just some kind of nuisance or large decoration.

My mother's name as a child was Marietta. That continued to be her name, of course, but until Beryl came I never heard her called by it. My father always said Mother. I had a childish notion — I knew it was childish — that Mother suited my mother better than it did other mothers. Mother, not Mama. When I was away from her, I could not think what my mother's face was like, and this frightened me. Sitting in school, just over a hill from home, I would try to picture my mother's face. Sometimes I thought that if I couldn't do it, that might mean my mother was dead. But I had a sense of her all the time, and would be reminded of her by the most unlikely things — an upright piano, or a tall white loaf of bread. That's ridiculous, but true.

Marietta, in my mind, was separate, not swallowed up in my mother's grownup body. Marietta was still running around loose up in her town of Ramsay, on the Ottawa River. In that town, the streets were full of horses and puddles, and darkened by men who came in from the bush on weekends. Loggers. There were eleven hotels on the main street, where the loggers stayed, and drank.

The house Marietta lived in was halfway up a steep street climbing from the river. It was a double house, with two bay windows in front, and a wooden trellis that separated the two front porches. In the other half of the house lived the Sutcliffes, the people Marietta was to board with after her mother died and her father left town. Mr. Sutcliffe was an Englishman, a telegraph operator. His wife was German. She always made coffee instead of tea. She made strudel. The dough for the strudel hung down over the edges of the table like a fine cloth. It sometimes looked to Marietta like a skin.

Mrs. Sutcliffe was the one who talked Marietta's mother out of hanging herself.

Marietta was home from school that day, because it was Saturday. She woke up late and heard the silence in the house. She was always scared of that — a silent house — and as soon as she opened the door after school she would call, "Mama! Mama!" Often her mother wouldn't answer. But she would be there. Marietta would hear with relief the rattle of the stove grate or the steady slap of the iron.

That morning, she didn't hear anything. She came downstairs, and got herself a slice of bread and butter and molasses, folded over. She opened the cellar door and called. She went into the front room and peered out the window, through the bridal fern. She saw her little sister, Beryl, and some other neighborhood children rolling down the bit of grassy terrace to the sidewalk, picking themselves up and scrambling to the top and rolling down again.

"Mama?" called Marietta. She walked through the house to the back yard. It was late spring, the day was cloudy and mild. In the sprouting vegetable gardens, the earth was damp, and the leaves on the trees seemed suddenly full-sized, letting down drops of water left over from the rain of the night before.

"Mama?" calls Marietta under the trees, under the clothesline.

At the end of the yard is a small barn, where they keep firewood, and some tools and old furniture. A chair, a straight-backed wooden chair, can be seen through the open doorway. On the chair, Marietta sees her mother's feet, her mother's black laced shoes. Then the long, printed cotton summer work dress, the apron, the rolled-up sleeves. Her mother's shiny-looking white arms, and neck, and face.

Her mother stood on the chair and didn't answer. She didn't look at Marietta, but smiled and tapped her foot, as if to say, "Here I am, then. What are you going to do about it?" Something looked wrong about her, beyond the fact that she was standing on a chair and smiling in this queer, tight way. Standing on an old chair with back rungs missing, which she had pulled out to the middle of the barn floor, where it teetered on the bumpy earth. There was a shadow on her neck.

The shadow was a rope, a noose on the end of a rope that hung down from a beam overhead.

"Mama?" says Marietta, in a fainter voice "Mama. Come down, please." Her voice is faint because she fears that any yell or cry might jolt her mother into movement, cause her to step off the chair and throw her weight on the rope. But even if Marietta wanted to yell she couldn't. Nothing but this pitiful thread of a voice is left to her — just as in a dream when a beast or a machine is bearing down on you.

"Go and get your father."

That was what her mother told her to do, and Marietta obeyed. With terror in her legs, she ran. In her nightgown, in the middle of a Saturday morning, she ran. She ran past Beryl and the other children, still tumbling down the slope. She ran along the sidewalk, which was at that time a boardwalk, then on the unpaved street, full of last night's puddles. The street crossed the railway tracks. At the foot of the hill, it intersected the main street of the town. Between the main street and the river were some warehouses and the buildings of small manufacturers. That was where Marietta's father had his carriage works. Wagons, buggies, sleds were made there. In fact, Marietta's father had invented a new sort of sled to carry logs in the bush. It had been patented. He was just getting started in Ramsay. (Later on, in the States, he made money. A man fond of hotel bars, barbershops, harness races, women, but not afraid of work — give him credit.)

Marietta did not find him at work that day. The office was empty. She ran out into the yard where the men were working. She stumbled in the fresh sawdust. The men laughed and shook their heads at her. No. Not here. Not a-here right now. No. Why don't you try upstreet? Wait. Wait a minute. Hadn't you better get some clothes on first?

They didn't mean any harm. They didn't have the sense to see that something must be wrong. But Marietta never could stand men laughing. There were always places she hated to go past, let alone into, and that was the reason. Men laughing. Because of that, she hated barbershops, hated their smell. (When she started going to dances later on with my father, she asked him not to put any dressing on his hair, because the smell reminded her.) A bunch of men standing out on the street, outside a hotel, seemed to Marietta like a clot of poison. You tried not to hear what they were saying, but you could be sure it was vile. If they didn't say anything, they laughed and vileness spread out from them — poison — just the same. It was only after Marietta was saved that she could walk right past them. Armed by God, she walked through their midst and nothing stuck to her, nothing scorched her; she was safe as Daniel.

Now she turned and ran, straight back the way she had come. Up the hill, running to get home. She thought she had made a mistake leaving her mother. Why did her mother tell her to go? Why did she want her father? Quite possibly so that she could greet him with the sight of her own warm body swinging on the end of a rope. Marietta should have stayed — she should have stayed and talked her mother out of it. She should have run to Mrs. Sutcliffe, or any neighbor, not wasted time this way. She hadn't thought who could help, who could even believe what she was talking about. She had the idea that all families except her own lived in peace, that threats and miseries didn't exist in other people's houses, and couldn't be explained there.

A train was coming into town. Marietta had to wait. Passengers looked out at her from its windows. She broke out wailing in the faces of those strangers. When the train passed, she continued up the hill — a spectacle, with her hair uncombed, her feet bare and muddy, in her nightgown, with a wild, wet face. By the time she ran into her own yard, in sight of the barn, she was howling. "Mama!" she was howling. "Mama!"

Nobody was there. The chair was standing just where it had been before. The rope was dangling over the back of it. Marietta was sure that her mother had gone ahead and done it. Her mother was already dead — she had been cut down and taken away.

But warm, fat hands settled down on her shoulders, and Mrs. Sutcliffe said, "Marietta. Stop the noise. Marietta. Child. Stop the crying. Come inside. She is well, Marietta. Come inside and you will see."

Mrs. Sutcliffe's foreign voice said, "Mari-et-cha," giving the name a rich, important sound. She was as kind as could be. When Marietta lived with the Sutcliffes later, she was treated as the daughter of the household, and it was a household just as peaceful and comfortable as she had imagined other households to be. But she never felt like a daughter there.

In Mrs. Sutcliffe's kitchen, Beryl sat on the floor eating a raisin cookie and playing with the black-and-white cat, whose name was Dickie. Marietta's mother sat at the table, with a cup of coffee in front of her.

"She was silly," Mrs. Sutcliffe said. Did she mean Marietta's mother or Marietta herself? She didn't have many English words to describe things.

Marietta's mother laughed, and Marietta blacked out. She fainted, after running all that way uphill, howling, in the warm, damp morning. Next thing she knew, she was taking black, sweet coffee from a spoon held by Mrs. Sutcliffe. Beryl picked Dickie up by the front legs and offered him as a cheering present. Marietta's mother was still sitting at the table.

Her heart was broken. That was what I always heard my mother say. That was the end of it. Those words lifted up the story and sealed it shut. I never asked, Who broke it? I never asked, What was the men's poison talk? What was the meaning of the word "vile"?

Marietta's mother laughed after not hanging herself. She sat at Mrs. Sutcliffe's kitchen table long ago and laughed. Her heart was broken.

I always had a feeling, with my mother's talk and stories, of something swelling out behind. Like a cloud you couldn't see through, or get to the end of. There was a cloud, a poison, that had touched my mother's life. And when I grieved my mother, I became part of it. Then I would beat my head against my mother's stomach and breasts, against her tall, firm front, demanding to be forgiven. My mother would tell me to ask God. But it wasn't God, it was my mother I had to get straight with. It seemed as if she knew something about me that was worse, far worse, than ordinary lies and tricks and meanness; it was a really sickening shame. I beat against my mother's front to make her forget that.

My brothers weren't bothered by any of this. I don't think so. They seemed to me like cheerful savages, running around free, not having to learn much. And when I just had the two boys myself, no daughters, I felt as if something could stop now — the stories, and griefs, the old puzzles you can't resist or solve.

Aunt Beryl said not to call her Aunt. "I'm not used to being anybody's aunt, honey. I'm not even anybody's momma. I'm just me. Call me Beryl."

Beryl had started out as a stenographer, and now she had her own typing and bookkeeping business, which employed many girls. She had arrived with a man friend, whose name was Mr. Florence. Her letter had said that she would be getting a ride with a friend, but she hadn't said whether the friend would be staying or going on. She hadn't even said if it was a man or a woman.

Mr. Florence was staying. He was a tall, thin man with a long, tanned face, very light-colored eyes, and a way of twitching the corner of his mouth that might have been a smile.

He was the one who got to sleep in the room that my mother and I had papered, because he was the stranger, and a man. Beryl had to sleep with me. At first we thought that Mr. Florence was quite rude, because he wasn't used to our way of talking and we weren't used to his. The first morning, my father said to Mr. Florence, "Well, I hope you got some kind of a sleep on that old bed in there?" (The spare-room bed was heavenly, with a feather tick.) This was Mr. Florence's cue to say that he had never slept better.

Mr. Florence twitched. He said, "I slept on worse."

His favorite place to be was in his car. His car was a royal-blue Chrysler, from the first batch turned out after the war. Inside it, the upholstery and floor covering and roof and door padding were all pearl gray. Mr. Florence kept the names of those colors in mind and corrected you if you said just "blue" or "gray."

"Mouse skin is what it looks like to me," said Beryl rambunctiously. "I tell him it's just mouse skin!"

The car was parked at the side of the house, under the locust trees. Mr. Florence sat inside with the windows rolled up, smoking, in the rich new-car smell.

"I'm afraid we're not doing much to entertain your friend," my mother said.

"I wouldn't worry about him," said Beryl. She always spoke about Mr. Florence as if there was a joke about him that only she appreciated. I wondered long afterward if he had a bottle in the glove compartment and took a nip from time to time to keep his spirits up. He kept his hat on.

Beryl herself was being entertained enough for two. Instead of staying in the house and talking to my mother, as a lady visitor usually did, she demanded to be shown everything there was to see on a farm. She said that I was to take her around and explain things, and see that she didn't fall into any manure piles.

I didn't know what to show. I took Beryl to the icehouse, where chunks of ice the size of dresser drawers, or bigger, lay buried in sawdust. Every few days, my father would chop off a piece of ice and carry it to the kitchen, where it melted in a tin-lined box and cooled the milk and butter.

Beryl said she had never had any idea ice came in pieces that big. She seemed intent on finding things strange, or horrible, or funny.

"Where in the world do you get ice that big?"

I couldn't tell if that was a joke.

"Off of the lake," I said.

"Off of the lake! Do you have lakes up here that have ice on them all summer?"

I told her how my father cut the ice on the lake every winter and hauled it home, and buried it in sawdust, and that kept it from melting.

Beryl said, "That's amazing!"

"Well, it melts a little," I said. I was deeply disappointed in Beryl.

"That's really amazing."

Beryl went along when I went to get the cows. A scarecrow in white slacks (this was what my father called her afterward), with a white sun hat tied under her chin by a flaunting red ribbon. Her fingernails and toenails — she wore sandals — were painted to match the ribbon. She wore the small, dark sunglasses people wore at that time. (Not the people I knew — they didn't own sunglasses.) She had a big red mouth, a loud laugh, hair of an unnatural color and a high gloss, like cherry wood. She was so noisy and shiny, so glamorously got up, that it was hard to tell whether she was good-looking, or happy, or anything.

We didn't have any conversation along the cowpath, because Beryl kept her distance from the cows and was busy watching where she stepped. Once I had them all tied in their stalls, she came closer. She lit a cigarette. Nobody smoked in the barn. My father and other farmers chewed tobacco there instead. I didn't see how I could ask Beryl to chew tobacco.

"Can you get the milk out of them or does your father have to?" Beryl said. "Is it hard to do?"

I pulled some milk down through the cow's teat. One of the barn cats came over and waited. I shot a thin stream into its mouth. The cat and I were both showing off.

"Doesn't that hurt?" said Beryl. "Think if it was you."

I had never thought of a cow's teat as corresponding to any part of myself, and was shaken by this indecency. In fact, I could never grasp a warm, warty teat in such a firm and casual way again.

Beryl slept in a peach-colored rayon nightgown trimmed with écru lace. She had a robe to match. She was just as careful about the word "écru" as Mr. Florence was about his royal blue and pearl gray.

I managed to get undressed and put on my nightgown without any part of me being exposed at any time. An awkward business. I left my underpants on, and hoped that Beryl had done the same. The idea of sharing my bed with a grownup was a torment to me. But I did get to see the contents of what Beryl called her beauty kit. Hand-painted glass jars contained puffs of cotton wool, talcum powder, milky lotion, ice-blue astringent. Little pots of red and mauve rouge — rather greasy-looking. Blue and black pencils. Emery boards, a pumice stone, nail polish with an overpowering smell of bananas, face powder in a celluloid box shaped like a shell, with the name of a dessert — Apricot Delight.

I had heated some water on the coal-oil stove we used in summertime. Beryl scrubbed her face clean, and there was such a change that I almost expected to see makeup lying in strips in the washbowl, like the old wallpaper we had soaked and peeled. Beryl's skin was pale now, covered with fine cracks, rather like the shiny mud at the bottom of puddles drying up in early summer.

"Look what happened to my skin," she said. "Dieting. I weighed a hundred and sixty-nine pounds once, and I took it off too fast and my face fell in on me. Now I've got this cream, though. It's made from a secret formula and you can't even buy it commercially. Smell it. See, it doesn't smell all perfumy. It smells serious."

She was patting the cream on her face with puffs of cotton wool, patting away until there was nothing to be seen on the surface.

"It smells like lard," I said.

"Christ Almighty, I hope I haven't been paying that kind of money to rub lard on my face. Don't tell your mother I swear."

She poured clean water into the drinking glass and wet her comb, then combed her hair wet and twisted each strand round her finger, clamping the twisted strand to her head with two crossed pins. I would be doing the same myself, a couple of years later.

"Always do your hair wet, else it's no good doing it up at all," Beryl said. "And always roll it under even if you want it to flip up. See?"

When I was doing my hair up — as I did for years — I sometimes thought of this, and thought that of all the pieces of advice people had given me, this was the one I had followed most carefully.

We put the lamp out and got into bed, and Beryl said, "I never knew it could get so dark. I've never known a dark that was as dark as this." She was whispering. I was slow to understand that she was comparing country nights to city nights, and I wondered if the darkness in Netterfield County could really be greater than that in California.

"Honey?" whispered Beryl. "Are there any animals outside?"

"Cows," I said.

"Yes, but wild animals? Are there bears?"

"Yes," I said. My father had once found bear tracks and droppings in the bush, and the apples had all been torn off a wild apple tree. That was years ago, when he was a young man.

Beryl moaned and giggled. "Think if Mr. Florence had to go out in the night and he ran into a bear!"

Next day was Sunday. Beryl and Mr. Florence drove my brothers and me to Sunday school in the Chrysler. That was at ten o'clock in the morning. They came back at eleven to bring my parents to church.

"Hop in," Beryl said to me. "You, too," she said to the boys. "We're going for a drive."

Beryl was dressed up in a satiny ivory dress with red dots, and a red-lined frill over the hips, and red high-heeled shoes. Mr. Florence wore a pale-blue summer suit.

"Aren't you going to church?" I said. That was what people dressed up for, in my experience.

Beryl laughed. "Honey, this isn't Mr. Florence's kind of religion."

I was used to going straight from Sunday school into church, and sitting for another hour and a half. In summer, the open windows let in the cedary smell of the graveyard and the occasional, almost sacrilegious sound of a car swooshing by on the road. Today we spent this time driving through country I had never seen before. I had never seen it, though it was less than twenty miles from home. Our truck went to the cheese factory, to church, and to town on Saturday nights. The nearest thing to a drive was when it went to the dump. I had seen the near end of Bell's Lake, because that was where my father cut the ice in winter. You couldn't get close to it in summer; the shoreline was all choked up with bulrushes. I had thought that the other end of the lake would look pretty much the same, but when we drove there today, I saw cottages, docks and boats, dark water reflecting the trees. All this and I hadn't known about it. This, too, was Bell's Lake. I was glad to have seen it at last, but in some way not altogether glad of the surprise.

Finally, a white frame building appeared, with verandas and potted flowers, and some twinkling poplar trees in front. The Wildwood Inn. Today the same building is covered with stucco and done up with Tudor beams and called the Hideaway. The poplar trees have been cut down for a parking lot.

On the way back to the church to pick up my parents, Mr. Florence turned in to the farm next to ours, which belonged to the McAllisters. The McAllisters were Catholics. Our two families were neighborly but not close.

"Come on, boys, out you get," said Beryl to my brothers. "Not you," she said to me. "You stay put." She herded the little boys up to the porch, where some McAllisters were watching. They were in their raggedy home clothes, because their church, or Mass, or whatever it was, got out early. Mrs. McAllister came out and stood listening, rather dumbfounded, to Beryl's laughing talk.

Beryl came back to the car by herself. "There," she said. "They're going to play with the neighbor children."

Play with McAllisters? Besides being Catholics, all but the baby were girls.

"They've still got their good clothes on," I said.

"So what? Can't they have a good time with their good clothes on? I do!"

My parents were taken by surprise as well. Beryl got out and told my father he was to ride in the front seat, for the legroom. She got into the back, with my mother and me. Mr. Florence turned again onto the Bell's Lake road, and Beryl announced that we were all going to the Wildwood Inn for dinner.

"You're all dressed up, why not take advantage?" she said. "We dropped the boys off with your neighbors. I thought they might be too young to appreciate it. The neighbors were happy to have them." She said with a further emphasis that it was to be their treat. Hers and Mr. Florence's.

"Well, now," said my father. He probably didn't have five dollars in his pocket. "Well, now. I wonder do they let the farmers in?"

He made various jokes along this line. In the hotel dining room, which was all in white — white tablecloths, white painted chairs — with sweating glass water pitchers and high, whirring fans, he picked up a table napkin the size of a diaper and spoke to me in a loud whisper, "Can you tell me what to do with this thing? Can I put it on my head to keep the draft off?"

Of course he had eaten in hotel dining rooms before. He knew about table napkins and pie forks. And my mother knew — she wasn't even a country woman, to begin with. Nevertheless this was a huge event. Not exactly a pleasure — as Beryl must have meant it to be — but a huge, unsettling event. Eating a meal in public, only a few miles from home, eating in a big room full of people you didn't know, the food served by a stranger, a snippy-looking girl who was probably a college student working at a summer job.

"I'd like the rooster," my father said. "How long has he been in the pot?" It was only good manners, as he knew it, to joke with people who waited on him.

"Beg your pardon?" the girl said.

"Roast chicken," said Beryl. "Is that okay for everybody?"

Mr. Florence was looking gloomy. Perhaps he didn't care for jokes when it was his money that was being spent. Perhaps he had counted on something better than ice water to fill up the glasses.

The waitress put down a dish of celery and olives, and my mother said, "Just a minute while I give thanks." She bowed her head and said quietly but audibly, "Lord, bless this food to our use, and us to Thy service, for Christ's sake. Amen." Refreshed, she sat up straight and passed the dish to me, saying, "Mind the olives. There's stones in them."

Beryl was smiling around at the room.

The waitress came back with a basket of rolls.

"Parker House!" Beryl leaned over and breathed in their smell. "Eat them while they're hot enough to melt the butter!"

Mr. Florence twitched, and peered into the butter dish. "Is that what this is — butter? I thought it was Shirley Temple's curls."

His face was hardly less gloomy than before, but it was a joke, and his making it seemed to convey to us something of the very thing that had just been publicly asked for — a blessing.

"When he says something funny," said Beryl — who often referred to Mr. Florence as "he" even when he was right there — "you notice how he always keeps a straight face? That reminds me of Mama. I mean of our mama, Marietta's and mine. Daddy, when he made a joke you could see it coming a mile away — he couldn't keep it off his face — but Mama was another story. She could look so sour. But she could joke on her deathbed. In fact, she did that very thing. Marietta, remember when she was in bed in the front room the spring before she died?"

"I remember she was in bed in that room," my mother said. "Yes."

"Well, Daddy came in and she was lying there in her clean nightgown, with the covers off, because the German lady from next door had just been helping her take a wash, and she was still there tidying up the bed. So Daddy wanted to be cheerful, and he said, 'Spring must be coming. I saw a crow today.' This must have been in March. And Mama said quick as a shot, 'Well, you better cover me up then, before it looks in that window and gets any ideas!' The German lady — Daddy said she just about dropped the basin. Because it was true, Mama was skin and bones; she was dying. But she could joke."

Mr. Florence said, "Might as well when there's no use to cry."

"But she could carry a joke too far, Mama could. One time, one time, she wanted to give Daddy a scare. He was supposed to be interested in some girl that kept coming around to the works. Well, he was a big good-looking man. So Mama said, 'Well, I'll just do away with myself, and you can get on with her and see how you like it when I come back and haunt you.' He told her not to be so stupid, and he went off downtown. And Mama went out to the barn and climbed on a chair and put a rope around her neck. Didn't she, Marietta? Marietta went looking for her and she found her like that!"

My mother bent her head and put her hands in her lap, almost as if she was getting ready to say another grace.

"Daddy told me all about it, but I can remember anyway. I remember Marietta tearing off down the hill in her nightie, and I guess the German lady saw her go, and she came out and was looking for Mama, and somehow we all ended up in the barn — me, too, and some kids I was playing with — and there was Mama up on a chair preparing to give Daddy the fright of his life. She'd sent Marietta after him. And the German lady starts wailing, 'Oh, Missus, come down Missus, think of your little *kindren*' — '*kindren*' is the German for 'children' — 'think of your *kindren*,' and so on. Until it was me standing there — I was just a little squirt, but I was the one noticed that rope. My eyes followed that rope up and up and I saw it was just hanging over the beam, just flung there — it wasn't tied at all! Marietta hadn't noticed that, the German lady hadn't noticed it. But I just spoke up and said, 'Mama, how are you going to manage to hang yourself without that rope tied around the beam?' "

Mr. Florence said, "That'd be a tough one."

"I spoiled her game. The German lady made coffee and we went over there and had a few treats, and, Marietta, you couldn't find Daddy after all, could you? You could hear Marietta howling, coming up the hill, a block away."

"Natural for her to be upset," my father said.

"Sure it was. Mama went too far."

"She meant it," my mother said. "She meant it more than you give her credit for."

"She meant to get a rise out of Daddy. That was their whole life together. He always said she was a hard woman to live with, but she had a lot of character. I believe he missed that, with Gladys."

"I wouldn't know," my mother said, in that particularly steady voice with which she always spoke of her father. "What he did say or didn't say."

"People are dead now," said my father. "It isn't up to us to judge."

"I know," said Beryl. "I know Marietta's always had a different view."

My mother looked at Mr. Florence and smiled quite easily and radiantly. "I'm sure you don't know what to make of all these family matters."

The one time that I visited Beryl, when Beryl was an old woman, all knobby and twisted up with arthritis, Beryl said, "Marietta got all Daddy's looks. And she never did a thing with herself. Remember her wearing that old navy-blue crêpe dress when we went to the hotel that time? Of course, I know it was probably all she had, but did it have to be all she had? You know, I was scared of her somehow. I couldn't stay in a room alone with her. But she had outstanding looks." Trying to remember an occasion when I had noticed my mother's looks, I thought of the time in the hotel, my mother's pale-olive skin against the heavy white, coiled hair, her open, handsome face smiling at Mr. Florence — as if he was the one to be forgiven.

I didn't have a problem right away with Beryl's story. For one thing, I was hungry and greedy, and a lot of my attention went to the roast chicken and gravy and mashed potatoes laid on the plate with an ice-cream scoop and the bright diced vegetables out of a can, which I thought much superior to those fresh from the garden. For dessert, I had a butterscotch sundae, an agonizing choice over chocolate. The others had plain vanilla ice cream.

Why shouldn't Beryl's version of the same event be different from my mother's? Beryl was strange in every way — everything about her was slanted, seen from a new angle. It was my mother's version that held, for a time. It absorbed Beryl's story, closed over it. But Beryl's story didn't vanish; it stayed sealed off for years, but it wasn't gone. It was like the knowledge of that hotel and dining room. I knew about it now, though I didn't think of it as a place to go back to. And indeed, without Beryl's or Mr. Florence's money, I couldn't. But I knew it was there.

The next time I was in the Wildwood Inn, in fact, was after I was married. The Lions Club had a banquet and dance there. The man I had married, Dan Casey, was a Lion. You could get a drink there by that time. Dan Casey wouldn't have gone anywhere you couldn't. Then the place was remodelled into the Hideaway, and now they have strippers every night but Sunday. On Thursday nights, they have a male stripper. I go there with people from the real-estate office to celebrate birthdays or other big events.

The farm was sold for five thousand dollars in 1965. A man from Toronto bought it, for a hobby farm or just an investment. After a couple of years, he rented it to a commune. They stayed there, different people drifting on and off, for a dozen years or so. They raised goats and sold the milk to the health-food store that had opened up in town. They painted a rainbow across the side of the barn that faced the road. They hung tie-dyed sheets over the windows, and let the long grass and flowering weeds reclaim the yard. My parents had finally got electricity in, but these people didn't use it. They preferred oil lamps and the wood stove, and taking their dirty clothes to town. People said they wouldn't know how to handle lamps or wood fires, and they would burn the place down. But they didn't. In fact, they didn't manage badly. They kept the house and barn in some sort of repair and they worked a big garden. They even dusted their potatoes against blight — though I heard that there was some sort of row about this and some of the stricter members left. The place actually looked a lot better than many of the farms round about that were still in the hands of the original families. The McAllister son had started a wrecking business on their place. My own brothers were long gone.

I knew I was not being reasonable, but I had the feeling that I'd rather see the farm suffer outright neglect — I'd sooner see it in the hands of hoodlums and scroungers — than see that rainbow on the barn, and some letters that looked Egyptian painted on the wall of the house. That seemed a mockery. I even disliked the sight of those people when they came to town — the men with their hair in ponytails, and with holes in their overalls that I believed were cut on purpose, and the women with long hair and no makeup and their meek, superior expressions. What do you know about life, I felt like asking them. What makes you think you can come here and mock my father and mother and their life and their poverty? But when I thought of the rainbow and those letters, I knew they weren't trying to mock or imitate my parents' life. They had displaced that life, hardly knowing it existed. They had set up in its place these beliefs and customs of their own, which I hoped would fail them.

That happened, more or less. The commune disintegrated. The goats disappeared. Some of the women moved to town, cut their hair, put on makeup, and got jobs as waitresses or cashiers to support their children. The Toronto man put the place up for sale, and after about a year it was sold for more than ten times what he had paid for it. A young couple from Ottawa bought it. They have painted the outside a pale gray with oyster trim, and have put in skylights and a handsome front door with carriage lamps on either side. Inside, they've changed it around so much that I've been told I'd never recognize it.

I did get in once, before this happened, during the year that the house was empty and for sale. The company I work for was handling it, and I had a key, though the house was being shown by another agent. I let myself in on a Sunday afternoon. I had a man with me, not a client but a friend — Bob Marks, whom I was seeing a lot at the time.

"This is that hippie place," Bob Marks said when I stopped the car. "I've been by here before."

He was a lawyer, a Catholic, separated from his wife. He thought he wanted to settle down and start up a practice here in town. But there already was one Catholic lawyer. Business was slow. A couple of times a week, Bob Marks would be fairly drunk before supper.

"It's more than that," I said. "It's where I was born. Where I grew up." We walked through the weeds, and I unlocked the door.

He said that he had thought, from the way I talked, that it would be farther out.

"It seemed farther then."

All the rooms were bare, and the floors swept clean. The woodwork was freshly painted — I was surprised to see no smudges on the glass. Some new panes, some old wavy ones. Some of the walls had been stripped of their paper and painted. A wall in the kitchen was painted a deep blue, with an enormous dove on it. On a wall in the front room, giant sunflowers appeared, and a butterfly of almost the same size.

Bob Marks whistled. "Somebody was an artist."

"If that's what you want to call it," I said, and turned back to the kitchen. The same wood stove was there. "My mother once burned up three thousand dollars," I said. "She burned three thousand dollars in that stove."

He whistled again, differently. "What do you mean? She threw in a check?"

"No, no. It was in bills. She did it deliberately. She went into town to the bank and she had them give it all to her, in a shoebox. She brought it home and put it in the stove. She put it in just a few bills at a time, so it wouldn't make too big a blaze. My father stood and watched her."

"What are you talking about?" said Bob Marks. "I thought you were so poor."

"We were. We were very poor."

"So how come she had three thousand dollars? That would be like thirty thousand today. Easily. More than thirty thousand today."

"It was her legacy," I said. "It was what she got from her father. Her father died in Seattle and left her three thousand dollars, and she burned it up because she hated him. She didn't want his money. She hated him."

"That's a lot of hate," Bob Marks said.

"That isn't the point. Her hating him, or whether he was bad enough for her to have a right to hate him. Not likely he was. That isn't the point."

"Money," he said. "Money's always the point."

"No. My father letting her do it is the point. To me it is. My father stood and watched and he never protested. If anybody had tried to stop her, he would have protected her. I consider that love."

"Some people would consider it lunacy."

I remember that that had been Beryl's opinion, exactly.

I went into the front room and stared at the butterfly, with its pink-and-orange wings. Then I went into the front bedroom and found two human figures painted on the wall. A man and a woman holding hands and facing straight ahead. They were naked, and larger than life size.

"It reminds me of that John Lennon and Yoko Ono picture," I said to Bob Marks, who had come in behind me. "That record cover, wasn't it?" I didn't want him to think that anything he had said in the kitchen had upset me.

Bob Marks said, "Different color hair."

That was true. Both figures had yellow hair painted in a solid mass, the way they do it in the comic strips. Horsetails of yellow hair curling over their shoulders and little pigs' tails of yellow hair decorating their not so private parts. Their skin was a flat beige pink and their eyes a staring blue, the same blue that was on the kitchen wall.

I noticed that they hadn't quite finished peeling the wallpaper away before making this painting. In the corner, there was some paper left that matched the paper on the other walls—a modernistic design of intersecting pink and gray and mauve bubbles. The man from Toronto must have put that on. The paper underneath hadn't been stripped off when this new paper went on. I could see an edge of it, the cornflowers on a white ground.

"I guess this was where they carried on their sexual shenanigans," Bob Marks said, in a tone familiar to me. That thickened, sad, uneasy, but determined tone. The not particularly friendly lust of middle-aged respectable men.

I didn't say anything. I worked away some of the bubble paper to see more of the cornflowers. Suddenly I hit a loose spot, and ripped away a big swatch of it. But the cornflower paper came, too, and a little shower of dried plaster.

"Why is it?" I said. "Just tell me, why is it that no man can mention a place like this without getting around to the subject of sex in about two seconds flat? Just say the words 'hippie' or 'commune' and all you guys can think about is screwing! As if there wasn't anything at all behind it but orgies and fancy combinations and non-stop screwing! I get so sick of that—it's all so stupid it just makes me sick!"

In the car, on the way home from the hotel, we sat as before—the men in the front seat, the women in the back. I was in the middle, Beryl and my mother on either side of me. Their heated bodies pressed against me, through cloth; their smells crowded out the smells of the cedar bush we passed through, and the pockets of bog, where Beryl exclaimed at the water lilies. Beryl smelled of all those things in pots and bottles. My mother smelled of flour and hard soap and the warm crêpe of her good dress and the kerosene she had used to take the spots off.

"A lovely meal," my mother said. "Thank you, Beryl. Thank you, Mr. Florence."

"I don't know who is going to be fit to do the milking," my father said. "Now that we've all ate in such style."

"Speaking of money," said Beryl—though nobody actually had been—"do you mind my asking what you did with yours? I put mine in real estate. Real estate in California—you can't lose. I was thinking you could get an electric stove, so you wouldn't have to bother with a fire in summer or fool with that coal-oil thing, either one."

All the other people in the car laughed, even Mr. Florence.

"That's a good idea, Beryl," said my father. "We could use it to set things on till we get the electricity."

"Oh, Lord," said Beryl. "How stupid can I get?"

"And we don't actually have the money, either," my mother said cheerfully, as if she was continuing the joke.

But Beryl spoke sharply. "You wrote me you got it. You got the same as me."

My father half turned in his seat. "What money are you talking about?" he said. "What's this money?"

"From Daddy's will," Beryl said. "That you got last year. Look, maybe I shouldn't have asked. If you had to pay something off, that's still a good use, isn't it? It doesn't matter. We're all family here. Practically."

"We didn't have to use it to pay anything off," my mother said. "I burned it."

Then she told how she went into town in the truck, one day almost a year ago, and got them to give her the money in a box she had brought along for the purpose. She took it home, and put it in the stove and burned it.

My father turned around and faced the road ahead.

I could feel Beryl twisting beside me while my mother talked. She was twisting, and moaning a little, as if she had a pain she couldn't suppress. At the end of the story, she let out a sound of astonishment and suffering, an angry groan.

"So you burned up money!" she said. "You burned up money in the stove."

My mother was still cheerful. "You sound as if I'd burned up one of my children."

"You burned their chances. You burned up everything the money could have got for them."

"The last thing my children need is money. None of us need his money."

"That's criminal," Beryl said harshly. She pitched her voice into the front seat: "Why did you let her?"

"He wasn't there," my mother said. "Nobody was there."

My father said, "It was her money, Beryl."

"Never mind," Beryl said. "That's criminal."

"Criminal is for when you call in the police," Mr. Florence said. Like other things he had said that day, this created a little island of surprise and a peculiar gratitude.

Gratitude not felt by all.

"Don't you pretend this isn't the craziest thing you ever heard of," Beryl shouted into the front seat. "Don't you pretend you don't think so! Because it is, and you do. You think just the same as me!"

My father did not stand in the kitchen watching my mother feed the money into the flames. It wouldn't appear so. He did not know about it—it seems fairly clear, if I remember everything, that he did not know about it until that Sunday afternoon in Mr. Florence's Chrysler, when my mother told them all together. Why, then, can I see the scene so clearly, just as I described it to Bob Marks (and to others—he was not the first)? I see my father standing by the table in the middle of the room—the table with the drawer in it for knives and forks, and the scrubbed oilcloth on top—and there is the box of money on the table. My mother is carefully dropping the bills into the fire. She holds the stove lid by the blackened lifter in one hand. And my father, standing by, seems not just to be permitting her to do this but to be protecting her. A solemn scene, but not crazy. People doing something that seems to them natural and necessary. At least, one of them is doing what seems natural and necessary, and the other believes that the important thing is for that person to be free, to go ahead. They understand that other people might not think so. They do not care.

How hard it is for me to believe that I made that up. It seems so much the truth it is the truth; it's what I believe about them. I haven't stopped believing it. But I have stopped telling that story. I never told it to anyone again after telling it to Bob Marks. I don't think so. I didn't stop just because it wasn't, strictly speaking, true. I stopped because I saw that I had to give up expecting people to see it the way I did. I had to give up expecting them to approve of any part of what was done. How could I even say that I approved of it myself? If I had been the sort of person who approved of that, who could do it, I wouldn't have done all I have done—run away from home to work in a restaurant in town when I was fifteen, gone to night school to learn typing and bookkeeping, got into the real-estate office, and finally become a licensed agent. I wouldn't be divorced. My father wouldn't have died in the county home. My hair would be white, as it has been naturally for years, instead of a color called Copper Sunrise. And not one of these things would I change, not really, if I could.

Bob Marks was a decent man — good-hearted, sometimes with imagination. After I had lashed out at him like that, he said, "You don't need to be so tough on us." In a moment, he said, "Was this your room when you were a little girl?" He thought that was why the mention of the sexual shenanigans had upset me.

And I thought it would be just as well to let him think that. I said yes, yes, it was my room when I was a little girl. It was just as well to make up right away. Moments of kindness and reconciliation are worth having, even if the parting has to come sooner or later. I wonder if those moments aren't more valued, and deliberately gone after, in the setups some people like myself have now, than they were in those old marriages, where love and grudges could be growing underground, so confused and stubborn, it must have seemed they had forever.

[1986]

EXPLORING THE TEXT

1. Why do you think the story is called "The Progress of Love"? What kind of progress does Euphemia make (or not make)?
2. "The Progress of Love" spans three distinct time periods. Considering both the changes in the setting and the character of the narrator, Euphemia, identify each period. How does Alice Munro characterize each one? How do her language choices signal each transition through time?
3. Novelist and short story writer Lorrie Moore has said, "If short stories are about life and novels are about the world, one can see Munro's capacious stories as being a little about both: fate and time and love are the things she is most interested in, as well as their unexpected outcomes." In what ways is "The Progress of Love" about life? In what ways is it about fate?
4. Take a careful look at paragraph 158. How do Munro's diction and syntax choices help her achieve her purpose here? How do they create the tone and mood? What does the passage add to the story?
5. When she relays the story of how Marietta's mother almost hanged herself (paras. 40–61), Euphemia presents the event as Marietta's version of what happened. How does Euphemia use that story to characterize her mother's family life and the relationship between her mother's parents? How might it be connected to Marietta's deep religious faith? Compare Euphemia's telling to Beryl's version of the same event (paras. 141–53). How do the two differ? What remains the same in both versions of the story?
6. Among the themes examined in "The Progress of Love" are self-delusion, personal identity, religious faith, family obligations, marriage, gender, and family. Choose one or two of these themes — or one that's not mentioned here — and discuss how Munro addresses and develops it. You might consider the ways she uses characterization, setting, dialogue, or point of view to build the theme or themes you have chosen.
7. This story contains several misunderstandings, or at least miscommunications. Trace one or two of them. What point do you think they make about the "progress of love"?
8. The narrator, who has already had three different names — Euphemia, Phemie, and Fame — says she would like to change her name to something simple like Joan but then asks herself, "unless I moved away from here, how could I do that?" (para. 32). What does this hesitation suggest about her character? How does it relate to some of the story's themes?
9. Compare Euphemia's twelve-year-old self to her present-day self. What characteristics remain the same? How do we know what happens — and doesn't happen — to her? What is the effect of having certain events (like her family's decision not to send Euphemia to school) happen offstage? Why do you think Fame (as she is known in adulthood) continues to tell some stories as truth even though she knows they are not, in fact, true?

POETRY

On My First Son

BEN JONSON

Ben Jonson (1572–1637) was a dominant force in English theater for much of his adult life and was widely regarded as the equal of Shakespeare. Born in London to an indigent widowed mother, he was encouraged to attend college. However, financial considerations compelled him to become a bricklayer, a trade Jonson "could not endure." He ultimately joined the army and fought for the Protestant cause in Holland. Returning to England in 1592, he took the London theater by storm. He tried his hand at both acting and directing, but it was in writing that he excelled. His early tragedies have not survived the ages, but his later comedies have, including *Every Man in His Humour* (1598), which was performed by a cast that included William Shakespeare, as well as *Volpone* (1606), *The Alchemist* (1610), and *Bartholomew Fair* (1614). He also wrote many masques (a genre now extinct) for the court of King James I and Queen Anne. "On My First Son" is an epitaph written after the death of Jonson's first son, Benjamin, at the age of seven.

Farewell, thou child of my right hand,[1] and joy;
My sin was too much hope of thee, loved boy:
Seven years thou wert lent to me, and I thee pay,
Exacted by thy fate, on the just day.
O could I lose all father now! For why
Will man lament the state he should envy,
To have so soon 'scaped world's and flesh's rage,
And, if no other misery, yet age?
Rest in soft peace, and asked, say, "Here doth lie
Ben Jonson his best piece of poetry."
For whose sake henceforth all his vows be such
As what he loves may never like too much.

[1616]

[1]Benjamin means "son of my right hand" in Hebrew. — EDS.

EXPLORING THE TEXT

1. In line 2 the speaker calls hope a "sin." How can this be?
2. How do you interpret the metaphor in lines 3–4, in which Ben Jonson compares his son's life to a loan? What does this comparison suggest about the speaker's faith and his resulting views on life?
3. How does the speaker attempt to console himself over the loss of his son? Identify language in the poem that demonstrates your point.
4. What does the speaker mean when he asks, "O could I lose all father now!" (l. 5)?
5. Why do you think the speaker calls his son "his best piece of poetry" (l. 10)? What does this suggest about the value he places on his poetry?
6. What do you make of the final lines of the epitaph? To whom does the "his" in line 11 refer to? What is the difference between the words "love" and "like" in the last line? What does the speaker vow in that line?

Before the Birth of One of Her Children

ANNE BRADSTREET

In 1630, Anne Bradstreet (1612/13–1678) and her husband, Simon, the son of a nonconformist minister, sailed to Massachusetts with Anne's parents. With *The Tenth Muse Lately Sprung Up in America* (1650) — possibly published in England without her knowledge — she became the first female poet in America. Because the Puritan community disdained female intellectual ambition, it was thought advisable to append the words "By a Gentle Woman in Those Parts," to reassure readers that Bradstreet was a diligent Puritan mother. Bradstreet's most remarkable poetry consists of thirty-five short reflective poems, explicit in their description of familial and marital love. Some of these appeared in the 1678 edition of *The Tenth Muse*; others remained hidden in her notebook until they were published in 1867. The twentieth century saw renewed interest in America's first female poet with John Berryman's poem "Homage to Mistress Bradstreet" (1956) and new editions of her work in 1967 and 1981. The mother of eight children, she writes of impending childbirth with apprehension and acceptance of the will of God in "Before the Birth of One of Her Children."

All things within this fading world hath end,
Adversity doth still our joys attend;
No ties so strong, no friends so dear and sweet,
But with death's parting blow is sure to meet.
The sentence past is most irrevocable,
A common thing, yet oh, inevitable.
How soon, my Dear, death may my steps attend,
How soon't may be thy lot to lose thy friend,
We both are ignorant, yet love bids me
These farewell lines to recommend to thee,
That when that knot's untied that made us one,
I may seem thine, who in effect am none.
And if I see not half my days that's due,
What nature would, God grant to yours and you;
The many faults that well you know I have
Let be interred in my oblivious grave;
If any worth or virtue were in me,
Let that live freshly in thy memory
And when thou feel'st no grief, as I no harms,
Yet love thy dead, who long lay in thine arms,
And when thy loss shall be repaid with gains
Look to my little babes, my dear remains.
And if thou love thyself, or loved'st me,
These O protect from stepdame's injury.
And if chance to thine eyes shall bring this verse,
With some sad sighs honor my absent hearse;
And kiss this paper for thy love's dear sake,
Who with salt tears this last farewell did take.

[1678]

EXPLORING THE TEXT

1. Anne Bradstreet had borne eight children, had lost two, and was battling tuberculosis when she wrote this poem. How are those circumstances reflected in the sentiments expressed in the poem? How is the poem itself not only last wishes but also a legacy to her children?
2. Restate the following line into simple language: "Adversity doth still our joys attend" (l. 2). What might the speaker mean by that statement in general, and how might it apply to her situation in particular?
3. How do you interpret the paradox in line 21? Explain the double meaning of "remains" in line 22.
4. Why do you think Bradstreet adds "if thou love thyself" to her qualification "or loved'st me" (l. 23)? What additional power does the "or" invoke?
5. Although the poem is presented without stanza breaks, it falls into sections. What are they? How do they form a sort of argument that the speaker is making?
6. How would you describe the tone of this poem? Try using a pair of words, such as "cautiously optimistic" or "fearful yet hopeful."

Sonnet: On Receiving a Letter Informing Me of the Birth of a Son

SAMUEL TAYLOR COLERIDGE

Samuel Taylor Coleridge (1772–1834) was an influential English poet and literary critic best known for his poems *The Rime of the Ancient Mariner* and *Kubla Khan*. Coleridge studied at Cambridge University but never received a degree. Throughout his life, Coleridge battled anxiety and depression and suffered from neuralgic and rheumatic pains. He was treated for these conditions with laudanum, which fostered an opium addiction. In 1795, Coleridge met poet William Wordsworth and in 1798, Coleridge and Wordsworth published a joint volume of poetry, *Lyrical Ballads*, signaling the beginning of the English romantic age. Although he was primarily known as a poet, most of Coleridge's poetry was not published until after his death, and he likely considered himself a philosopher and critic first. Coleridge's travels throughout Europe brought him into contact with transcendentalism, the critical philosophy of Immanuel Kant, and the German classical poet Friedrich Schiller, whose dramatic trilogy *Wallenstein* Coleridge translated into English. Coleridge was also an influential Shakespearean, delivering a series of lectures in 1810–1811. Before his seminal lecture on *Hamlet* in January 1812, critical consensus had been that *Hamlet* was one of Shakespeare's inferior works. In 1816, Coleridge finished *Biographia Literaria*, a volume blending autobiography, dissertations, and criticism. Coleridge died in 1834, leaving behind his unpublished *Opus Maximum*, a post-Kantian philosophical treatise. In "Sonnet: On Receiving a Letter Informing Me of the Birth of a Son," Coleridge reflects with his trademark mix of rapture and melancholy on the premature birth of his son Hartley.

When they did greet me father, sudden awe
Weigh'd down my spirit: I retired and knelt
Seeking the throne of grace, but inly felt
No heavenly visitation upwards draw
My feeble mind, nor cheering ray impart.
Ah me! before the Eternal Sire I brought
Th' unquiet silence of confused thought
And hopeless feelings: my o'erwhelmed heart
Trembled, and vacant tears stream'd down my face.
And now once more, O Lord! to thee I bend,
Lover of souls! and groan for future grace,
That ere my babe youth's perilous maze have trod,
Thy overshadowing Spirit may descend,
And he be born again, a child of God!

[1796]

EXPLORING THE TEXT

1. Trace the speaker's emotional state throughout the poem. What is his predominant emotion? How is that emotion communicated? Consider in particular the oxymoron ("unquiet silence") in line 7 or the strange turn of speech ("vacant tears") in line 9.
2. How would you characterize the speaker's attitude toward the news of his son's birth? What words or phrases are most revealing about his attitude?
3. What does the speaker wish for his son? Why do you think that wish seems so urgent for the speaker?
4. Look carefully at the punctuation in the first line. How would the meaning of the line change if there were a comma after "me"? How does that slight ambiguity connect with the rest of the poem?
5. How does the sonnet form suit the subject matter? Be sure to consider the rhyme scheme (abba, cddc, efe, gfg).
6. Where does the poem deviate from the expected ten-syllable lines? What do you think these digressions from the sonnet form signal about the speaker's emotional state? How do they help convey the speaker's attitude?
7. In 1802, Samuel Taylor Coleridge wrote the "Letter to Sara Hutchinson," which was later published in part as "Dejection: An Ode." The unpublished part included the following lines:

   Those little Angel Children (woe is me!)
   There have been hours, when feeling how they bind
   And pluck out the Wing-feathers of my Mind . . .
   I have half-wish'd they never had been born!

   Compare these lines to the poem above. What seeds of Coleridge's ambivalence do you see in the sonnet?

We Are Seven

WILLIAM WORDSWORTH

William Wordsworth (1770–1850) is one of the most famous and influential poets of the Western world and one of the premier Romantics. Widely known for his reverence of nature and the power of his lyrical verse, he lived in the Lake District of northern England, where he was inspired by the natural beauty of the landscape. With Samuel Taylor Coleridge, he published *Lyrical Ballads* in 1798; the collection, which changed the direction of English poetry, begins with Coleridge's "Rime of the Ancient Mariner" and includes Wordsworth's "Lines Composed a Few Miles above Tintern Abbey." Among Wordsworth's other most famous works are "The World Is Too Much with Us" (p. 447), a sonnet; "Ode: Intimations of Immortality"; and "The Prelude, or Growth of a Poet's Mind," an autobiographical poem. "We Are Seven" first appeared in *Lyrical Ballads*.

—A simple Child,
That lightly draws its breath,
And feels its life in every limb,
What should it know of death?

I met a little cottage Girl:
She was eight years old, she said;
Her hair was thick with many a curl
That clustered round her head.

She had a rustic, woodland air,
And she was wildly clad:
Her eyes were fair, and very fair;
—Her beauty made me glad.

"Sisters and brothers, little Maid,
How many may you be?"
"How many? Seven in all," she said,
And wondering looked at me.

"And where are they? I pray you tell."
She answered, "Seven are we;
And two of us at Conway dwell,
And two are gone to sea.

"Two of us in the church-yard lie,
My sister and my brother;
And, in the church-yard cottage, I
Dwell near them with my mother."

"You say that two at Conway dwell,
And two are gone to sea,
Yet ye are seven! — I pray you tell,
Sweet Maid, how this may be."

Then did the little Maid reply,
"Seven boys and girls are we;
Two of us in the church-yard lie,
Beneath the church-yard tree."

"You run about, my little Maid,
Your limbs they are alive;
If two are in the church-yard laid,
Then ye are only five."

"Their graves are green, they may be seen,"
The little Maid replied,
"Twelve steps or more from my mother's door,
And they are side by side.

"My stockings there I often knit,
My kerchief there I hem;
And there upon the ground I sit,
And sing a song to them.

"And often after sunset, Sir,
When it is light and fair,
I take my little porringer,
And eat my supper there.

"The first that died was sister Jane;
In bed she moaning lay,
Till God released her of her pain;
And then she went away.

"So in the church-yard she was laid;
And, when the grass was dry,
Together round her grave we played,
My brother John and I.

"And when the ground was white with snow,
And I could run and slide,
My brother John was forced to go,
And he lies by her side."

"How many are you, then," said I,
"If they two are in heaven?"
Quick was the little Maid's reply,
"O Master! we are seven."

"But they are dead; those two are dead!
Their spirits are in heaven!"
'T was throwing words away; for still
The little Maid would have her will,
And said, "Nay, we are seven!"

[1798]

EXPLORING THE TEXT

1. What concrete details help the reader picture the "little cottage Girl"? For instance, what does the speaker mean in line 11 when he says, "Her eyes were fair, and very fair"? Why is the setting important to the tale being told?
2. In the first stanza, the speaker raises a question that is explored in subsequent stanzas through a dialogue between him and the little girl. Note how the speaker asks again and again how many children are in the little girl's family and how her answer never wavers. What effect does this repetition have on your understanding of the poem?
3. How would you characterize the little girl's attitude toward her dead sister and brother? What is the logic leading to her conclusion that "we are seven"? Does William Wordsworth present the girl sympathetically or critically?
4. What does the girl understand about the nature of family and the death of family members that the

ostensibly more experienced speaker has yet to learn? By the end, has she altered the speaker's view?

5. In his preface to *Lyrical Ballads* (1802), Wordsworth states that he wants his poetry to be written in "the real language of men," not the more elaborate language associated with elevated literary efforts. How well does "We Are Seven" achieve this goal? Is the regular rhyme and rhythm scheme in keeping with this goal? What about the repetition? What examples of figurative language do you find?

A Prayer for My Daughter

WILLIAM BUTLER YEATS

William Butler Yeats (1865–1939) was born in Dublin to a middle-class Protestant family with strong connections to England. The young Yeats spent his childhood in the west of Ireland, a region that remained a profound influence on his work. Yeats began as a playwright, founding the Irish Literary Theatre in 1899, and wrote several plays celebrating Irish cultural tradition. The most important of these are *Cathleen ni Houlihan* (1902), *The King's Threshold* (1904), and *Deirdre* (1907). His early plays earned him the Nobel Prize for Literature in 1923. By 1912, he had turned to writing poetry. Profoundly influenced by the poetry of William Blake, Yeats's work reflects Ireland's rich mythology and a fascination with the occult. His collections include *The Wild Swans at Coole* (1919), *Michael Robartes and the Dancer* (1921), *The Tower* (1928), and *The Winding Stair* (1933). Written at the age of fifty-four, "A Prayer for My Daughter" (1919) reflects the uncertainties of an aging father raising a daughter in a tumultuous world.

Once more the storm is howling, and half hid
Under this cradle-hood and coverlid
My child sleeps on. There is no obstacle
But Gregory's wood and one bare hill
Whereby the haystack- and roof-levelling wind,
Bred on the Atlantic, can be stayed;
And for an hour I have walked and prayed
Because of the great gloom that is in my mind.

I have walked and prayed for this young child an hour
And heard the sea-wind scream upon the tower,
And under the arches of the bridge, and scream
In the elms above the flooded stream;
Imagining in excited reverie
That the future years had come,
Dancing to a frenzied drum,
Out of the murderous innocence of the sea.

May she be granted beauty and yet not
Beauty to make a stranger's eye distraught,
Or hers before a looking-glass, for such,
Being made beautiful overmuch,
Consider beauty a sufficient end,
Lose natural kindness and maybe
The heart-revealing intimacy
That chooses right, and never find a friend.

Helen being chosen found life flat and dull
And later had much trouble from a fool,
While that great Queen, that rose out of the spray,
Being fatherless could have her way
Yet chose a bandy-leggèd smith for man.
It's certain that fine women eat
A crazy salad with their meat
Whereby the Horn of Plenty is undone.

In courtesy I'd have her chiefly learned;
Hearts are not had as a gift but hearts are earned
By those that are not entirely beautiful;
Yet many, that have played the fool
For beauty's very self, has charm made wise.
And many a poor man that has roved,
Loved and thought himself beloved,
From a glad kindness cannot take his eyes.

May she become a flourishing hidden tree
That all her thoughts may like the linnet be,
And have no business but dispensing round
Their magnanimities of sound,
Nor but in merriment begin a chase,
Nor but in merriment a quarrel.
O may she live like some green laurel
Rooted in one dear perpetual place.

My mind, because the minds that I have loved,
The sort of beauty that I have approved,
Prosper but little, has dried up of late,
Yet knows that to be choked with hate
May well be of all evil chances chief.
If there's no hatred in a mind
Assault and battery of the wind
Can never tear the linnet from the leaf.

An intellectual hatred is the worst,
So let her think opinions are accursed.
Have I not seen the loveliest woman born
Out of the mouth of Plenty's horn,
Because of her opinionated mind
Barter that horn and every good
By quiet natures understood
For an old bellows full of angry wind?

Considering that, all hatred driven hence,
The soul recovers radical innocence
And learns at last that it is self-delighting,
Self-appeasing, self-affrighting,
And that its own sweet will is Heaven's will;
She can, though every face should scowl
And every windy quarter howl
Or every bellows burst, be happy still.

And may her bridegroom bring her to a house
Where all's accustomed, ceremonious;
For arrogance and hatred are the wares
Peddled in the thoroughfares.
How but in custom and in ceremony
Are innocence and beauty born?
Ceremony's a name for the rich horn,
And custom for the spreading laurel tree.

[1919]

EXPLORING THE TEXT

1. What contrasts does the opening stanza establish? Consider the settings inside and outside, as well as the speaker's frame of mind.
2. Why is the speaker skeptical of "Being made beautiful overmuch" (l. 20)? What does he see as the dangers of extraordinary beauty? How do the allusions to Helen of Troy and Aphrodite ("that great Queen, that rose out of the spray," l. 27) support the speaker's views on beauty?
3. What does the speaker mean when he wishes for his daughter to "become a flourishing hidden tree" with thoughts "like the linnet be" (ll. 41–42)? What does this wish suggest about the future he envisions for his child? How do you interpret his desire that she be "Rooted in one dear perpetual place" (l. 48)? What are the alternatives to being a hidden tree with thoughts like a linnet?
4. What is the effect of the repeated construction "May she" (ll. 17, 41, 47)? What difference would it have made if William Butler Yeats had written "I hope she"?
5. In stanza 5, the speaker says, "In courtesy I'd have her chiefly learned" (l. 33). What is the meaning he attaches to the term "courtesy"? How might his concept of courtesy sum up the qualities he believes lead to a satisfying life?
6. Examine Yeats's use of figurative language. How do you interpret the image of the "Horn of Plenty" (l. 32), for instance, or "like some green laurel / Rooted in one dear perpetual place" (ll. 47–48)?

What does the oxymoron "murderous innocence" (l. 16) mean? What effect does the personification of nature have?

7. What are the values the speaker wants his daughter to embrace? Which ones does he want her to avoid?
8. Based on the poem's final two stanzas, how would you describe the father's vision of an ideal woman? Pay careful attention to his use of the word "innocence" in these stanzas.
9. What might the setting of this poem represent? How does this setting affect the tone of this poem?
10. Why is this poem entitled "A Prayer for My Daughter"? What elements of prayer are embodied here?
11. Is the vision that Yeats favors for his daughter one that reflects stereotypical views of women? What elements of the poem might lend themselves to such an interpretation? What is your interpretation?

Mother to Son

LANGSTON HUGHES

Langston Hughes (1902–1967) grew up in the African American community of Joplin, Missouri. He spent a year at Columbia University and became involved with the Harlem movement, but was shocked by the endemic racial prejudice at the university and subsequently left. Hughes traveled for several years, spending some time in Paris before returning to the United States. He completed his BA at Pennsylvania's Lincoln University in 1929, after which he returned to Harlem for the remainder of his life. Hughes's output was prolific in verse, prose, and drama. His first volume of poetry, *The Weary Blues*, was published in 1926. This collection contained "The Negro Speaks of Rivers," perhaps his most famous poem. His first novel, *Not Without Laughter* (1930), won the Harmon Gold Medal for literature. He is remembered for his celebration of the uniqueness of African American culture, which found expression in "The Negro Artist and the Racial Mountain" (1926), published in the *Nation*, and in the poem "My People." He also wrote children's poetry, musicals, and opera. This poem, "Mother to Son," expresses a mother's advice to her son with its famous refrain, "Life for me ain't been no crystal stair."

Well, son, I'll tell you:
Life for me ain't been no crystal stair.
It's had tacks in it,
And splinters,
And boards torn up,
And places with no carpet on the floor—
Bare.
But all the time
I'se been a-climbin' on,
And reachin' landin's,
And turnin' corners,
And sometimes goin' in the dark
Where there ain't been no light.

So boy, don't you turn back.
Don't you set down on the steps
'Cause you finds it's kinder hard.
Don't you fall now—
For I'se still goin', honey,
I'se still climbin',
And life for me ain't been no crystal stair.

[1922]

EXPLORING THE TEXT

1. What is the overall message the mother is trying to convey to her son?
2. Based on details in the poem, how would you characterize the mother?
3. The poem's speaker employs an extended metaphor to explain her life to her son. What do you think the "crystal stair" symbolizes (l. 2)? Why do you think the poet has chosen to repeat this image in the final line? What might the details of tacks, splinters, landings, and corners represent? What does the inclusion of these images suggest about the mother's relationship with her son?
4. What effect do colloquial expressions and dialect have on your understanding of the speaker? What effect do they have on the meaning of the poem?
5. How old is the son being addressed? Does he seem to be at some sort of crossroads? Cite specific textual evidence to support your viewpoint.
6. Is the mother in this poem lecturing, apologizing, advising, pleading, showing affection, criticizing? How would you characterize the tone of the poem?
7. Even though the poem is presented without stanza breaks, there are "turns," or shifts. What are they? Try reciting or performing the poem; where would you emphasize the pauses? How do these breaks influence or emphasize meaning?

The Writer

RICHARD WILBUR

Richard Wilbur (b. 1921) is an American poet and translator. He grew up in New York City and graduated from Amherst College in 1942. After serving in the army during World War II, Wilbur attended graduate school at Harvard University and went on to teach at Wellesley College, Wesleyan University, and Smith College. Wilbur has published thirteen poetry collections. *Things of This World* (1957) won a Pulitzer Prize and a National Book Award. Wilbur won a second Pulitzer Prize for his *New and Collected Poems* (1989). He has also written two books of prose and translated numerous plays by the French dramatists Molière, Jean Racine, and Pierre Corneille. Wilbur's poetry often illuminates epiphany in everyday experiences, a quality on full display in "The Writer."

In her room at the prow of the house
Where light breaks, and the windows are tossed with linden,
My daughter is writing a story.

I pause in the stairwell, hearing
From her shut door a commotion of typewriter-keys
Like a chain hauled over a gunwale.

Young as she is, the stuff
Of her life is a great cargo, and some of it heavy:
I wish her a lucky passage.

But now it is she who pauses,
As if to reject my thought and its easy figure.
A stillness greatens, in which

The whole house seems to be thinking,
And then she is at it again with a bunched clamor
Of strokes, and again is silent.

I remember the dazed starling
Which was trapped in that very room, two years ago;
How we stole in, lifted a sash

And retreated, not to affright it;
And how for a helpless hour, through the crack of the door,
We watched the sleek, wild, dark

And iridescent creature
Batter against the brilliance, drop like a glove
To the hard floor, or the desk-top.

And wait then, humped and bloody.
For the wits to try it again; and how our spirits
Rose when, suddenly sure,

It lifted off from a chair-back,
Beating a smooth course for the right window
And clearing the sill of the world.

It is always a matter, my darling,
Of life or death, as I had forgotten. I wish
What I wished you before, but harder.

[1969]

EXPLORING THE TEXT

1. You probably noticed that the central image of the first three stanzas of "The Writer" is the house depicted as a ship at sea. What mood does the image set? What diction choices develop that image, and how might they be connected to the poem's subject? What does the image tell you about the speaker's family life? about the life of a writer?
2. What do you make of the word "passage" in line 9? What are some of its possible meanings? How do the word's multiple meanings help the speaker comment on the act of writing?
3. The story of the starling in the room is at once literal and metaphoric. What do you think it represents? Explain your answer.
4. What do you think the speaker means by "easy figure" (l.11)? Consider several possible meanings.
5. At the end of the poem, the speaker says, "I wish / What I wished you before, but harder." What do you think that wish was? What do you think the speaker means by "but harder"?
6. What is the connection between the speaker's attitude toward writing and his attitude toward his daughter? How do Richard Wilbur's language choices help develop this connection?
7. In an interview with the *Paris Review*, Wilbur said that "there has to be a sudden, confident sense that there is an exploitable and interesting relationship between something perceived out there and something in the way of incipient meaning within you. . . . Noting a likeness or resemblance between two things in nature can provide this freshness, but I think there must be more." In what ways does "The Writer" take the relationship between "something out there" and something within the speaker to a level beyond just resemblance?

My Father's Song

SIMON J. ORTIZ

Simon J. Ortiz (b. 1941) is the author of more than twenty-five books of poetry, short fiction, and nonfiction. A member of the Acoma Pueblo tribe, Ortiz grew up near Albuquerque, New Mexico. He attended Fort Lewis College, served three years in the military, and then attended the University of New Mexico before earning an MFA in writing from the University of Iowa in 1969. Since 1968, Ortiz has taught creative writing and Native American literature at many institutions, and he currently teaches at Arizona State University, where he is the founder and coordinator of the Indigenous Speakers Series. His most well-known works are the poetry collection *From Sand Creek* (1981), which won a Pushcart Prize, and *Woven Stone* (1992), a work that combines poetry and prose from three of his previous books. In "My Father's Song," Ortiz evokes both the power of familial memory and a tender reverence for nature.

Wanting to say things,
I miss my father tonight.
His voice, the slight catch,
the depth from his thin chest,
the tremble of emotion

in something he has just said
to his son, his song:

We planted corn one Spring at Acu —
we planted several times
but this one particular time
I remember the soft damp sand
in my hand.

My father had stopped at one point
to show me an overturned furrow;
the plowshare had unearthed
the burrow nest of a mouse
in the soft moist sand.

Very gently, he scooped tiny pink animals
into the palm of his hand
and told me to touch them.
We took them to the edge
of the field and put them in the shade
of a sand moist clod.

I remember the very softness
of cool and warm sand and tiny alive mice
and my father saying things.

[1977]

EXPLORING THE TEXT

1. "My Father's Song" has two different speakers. How can you tell which is which? How are the speakers different? How are they the same? Is there a point where the two meld together?
2. Why do you think the speaker calls his memory of his father a song?
3. Why do you think the poem opens with "Wanting to say things, / I miss my father tonight"? What do you think has made this particular night so important? What are some of the specific things the speaker misses about his father?
4. Simon J. Ortiz is considered a master of tactile imagery. Find examples of it in "My Father's Song." How are those images created and reinforced?
5. How does the structure of "My Father's Song" help convey what the speaker misses about his father?
6. Ortiz is a member of the Acoma Pueblo tribe. "Acu" (l. 8) is another word for Acoma. What aspects of this poem seem particularly tied to Native American culture and traditions? What aspects of it are universal?

My Father and the Figtree

NAOMI SHIHAB NYE

Naomi Shihab Nye (b. 1952) is a Palestinian American poet, novelist, editor, and political activist. Her works for children include the picture book *Sitti's Secret* (1994) and the novel *Habibi* (1997). Her poetry collections include *Different Ways to Pray* (1980), *Fuel* (1998), *19 Varieties of Gazelle: Poems of the Middle East* (2002), *You and Yours* (2005), *Honeybee* (2008), and *Tender Spot: Selected Poems* (2009). Nye describes herself as "a wandering poet" and has been a visiting writer all over the world. Her many awards include four Pushcart Prizes, the Jane Addams Children's Book award, and the Paterson Poetry Prize. Nye was elected a Chancellor of the Academy of American Poets in 2009, and in 2013 she was awarded both the Robert Creeley Award and the NSK Neustadt Prize for Children's Literature. In "My Father and the Figtree," a poem from her collection *Different Ways to Pray*, the speaker chronicles changes in her father's life through his cultural associations with a fig tree.

For other fruits my father was indifferent.
He'd point at the cherry trees and say,
"See those? I wish they were figs."
In the evening he sat by our beds
weaving folktales like vivid little scarves.
They always involved a figtree.
Even when it didn't fit, he'd stick it in.
Once Joha[1] was walking down the road
and he saw a figtree.
Or, he tied his camel to a figtree and went to sleep.
Or, later when they caught and arrested him,
his pockets were full of figs.

At age six I ate a dried fig and shrugged.
"That's not what I'm talking about!" he said,
"I'm talking about a fig straight from the earth
gift of Allah! — on a branch so heavy
it touches the ground.
I'm talking about picking the largest, fattest, sweetest fig
in the world and putting it in my mouth."
(Here he'd stop and close his eyes.)

Years passed, we lived in many houses,
none had figtrees.
We had lima beans, zucchini, parsley, beets.
"Plant one!" my mother said,
but my father never did.

---

[1] A trickster character in Middle East folktales. — EDS.

He tended garden half-heartedly, forgot to water,
let the okra get too big.
"What a dreamer he is. Look how many
things he starts and doesn't finish."

The last time he moved, I had a phone call,
My father, in Arabic, chanting a song
I'd never heard. "What's that?"
He took me out back to the new yard.
There, in the middle of Dallas, Texas,
a tree with the largest, fattest,
sweetest figs in the world.
"It's a figtree song!" he said,
plucking his fruits like ripe tokens,
emblems, assurance
of a world that was always his own.

[1980]

EXPLORING THE TEXT

1. What does the fig tree mean to the speaker's father? Why is the speaker's father "indifferent" (l. 1) to other fruits? What does the fig tree mean to the speaker? How do you know?
2. Describe how the poem shifts after the speaker says, "Years passed, we lived in many houses / none had figtrees" (ll. 20–21). What has changed in the speaker's attitude toward her father?
3. Why does the father refuse to plant a fig tree and instead "He tended garden halfheartedly, forgot to water, / let the okra get too big" (ll. 26–27)?
4. How do you interpret the final two lines? Why are figs "emblems, assurance / of a world that was always his own"? Do you have tokens or emblems of your background that make your world your own? Describe them.
5. What qualities of traditional storytelling do you see in "My Father and the Figtree"? What does Naomi Shihab Nye's use of what is traditionally a prose form tell us about the speaker's father? About the speaker?
6. In what ways does "My Father and the Figtree" connect the natural world to the immigrant experience? How does that connection help ease the difficulty of displacement for the speaker and her father?
7. Apart from two similes, Nye uses very little figurative language in this poem. Why do you think she decided to limit the poem in this way? What other resources of language does Nye use to give the poem its power?

Wild Geese

MARY OLIVER

Mary Oliver (b. 1935) was born in Maple Heights, Ohio, an affluent suburb of Cleveland. She attended Ohio State University and Vassar College, but did not complete her degree. Nonetheless, she has held several teaching positions at colleges, including Bennington College. Oliver published her first volume, *No Voyage, and Other Poems*, in 1963 at the age of twenty-eight, and in 1984 won the Pulitzer Prize with *American Primitive* (1983). Following a period of silence, she published a considerable body of prose and verse between 1990 and 2006, winning the Christopher Award and the L. L. Winship/PEN New England Award for *House of Light* (1990), and the National Book Award for *New and Selected Poems* (1992). These were followed by *White Pine* (1994), *West Wind* (1997), *Winter Hours: Prose, Prose Poems, and Poems* (1999), *Owls and Other Fantasies: Poems and Essays* (2003), *Why I Wake Early* (2004), and *Thirst* (2006), *Red Bird* (2008), and, most recently, *Felicity* (2015). The sense of community with nature is ever-present in her work, as in "Wild Geese," a poem exploring the place of humankind in "the family of things."

You do not have to be good.
You do not have to walk on your knees
for a hundred miles through the desert, repenting.
You only have to let the soft animal of your body love what it loves.
Tell me about despair, yours, and I will tell you mine.
Meanwhile the world goes on.
Meanwhile the sun and the clear pebbles of the rain
are moving across the landscapes,
over the prairies and the deep trees,
the mountains and the rivers.
Meanwhile the wild geese, high in the clean blue air,
are heading home again.
Whoever you are, no matter how lonely,
the world offers itself to your imagination,
calls to you like the wild geese, harsh and exciting—
over and over announcing your place
in the family of things.

[1986]

EXPLORING THE TEXT

1. Why do you think Mary Oliver chose to address readers directly as "You" in the opening lines of her poem? What effect does this have on your reading of the poem?

2. Even in the absence of a regular rhyme scheme or rhythm, the language of this poem seems to have an incantatory or hypnotic quality. How does Oliver achieve this effect?

3. Why does Oliver compare the way the world calls to us with the call of wild geese? What do wild geese represent in this poem? Why is it important that they "are heading home again" (l. 12)? Are the geese metaphorical? What might Oliver be suggesting about homing instincts in both birds and humans?

4. What does the phrase "no matter how lonely" (l. 13) suggest about the speaker's assumptions regarding her audience? What does the phrase suggest about the poem's purpose? How does that description link to the opening sentence?

5. How do you interpret the line "the world offers itself to your imagination" (l. 14)?

6. How does the nature imagery throughout this poem help us understand what Oliver means by "the family of things" (l. 17)? Overall, do you find this poem sad or hopeful?

My Father's Geography

AFAA MICHAEL WEAVER

Afaa Michael Weaver (b. 1951) is a poet, short story writer, and editor from Baltimore, Maryland. He earned a BA in literature from Excelsior College and an MA in playwriting and theater at Brown University. Weaver has published fourteen full-length poetry collections and has been awarded a Pew Fellowship in the Arts (1998), a Fulbright Scholarship to study in Taiwan (2002), the Kingsley Tufts Poetry Award (2014), and several Pushcart Prizes (2008, 2013, 2014). Weaver was also the first poet named an elder of the Cave Canem Foundation, an organization active in promoting African American poets. Weaver is currently an Alumnae Professor of English at Simmons College. In "My Father's Geography" Weaver explores his own connection to and separation from Africa while abroad in Europe.

I was parading the Côte d'Azur,
hopping the short trains from Nice to Cannes,
following the maze of streets in Monte Carlo
to the hill that overlooks the ville.[1]

A woman fed me paté in the afternoon,
calling from her stall to offer me more.
At breakfast I talked in French with an old man
about what he loved about America — the Kennedys.

On the beaches I walked and watched
topless women sunbathe and swim,
loving both home and being so far from it.

At a phone looking to Africa over the Mediterranean,
I called my father, and, missing me, he said,
"You almost home boy. Go on cross that sea!"

[1992]

[1] City. — EDS.

EXPLORING THE TEXT

1. Why do you think the poem is titled "My Father's Geography"?
2. How would you characterize the speaker? What kind of person is he? How is he defined by his travels? by his relationship with his father?
3. What does the speaker mean when he says he loves "both home and being so far from it" (l. 12)?
4. What are some possible meanings for the phrase "missing me" (l. 13)? What effect do those different meanings have on your understanding of the father's exhortation in the last line?
5. You may have noticed that "My Father's Geography" has fourteen lines. What other aspects of the poem might qualify it as a sonnet? How does that form contribute to the meaning of the poem? In what ways does the poem defy the formal conventions of a sonnet? How does this deviation from form affect the poem?

The Hammock

LI-YOUNG LEE

Li-Young Lee (b. 1957) was born to an elite Chinese family. His great-grandfather had been China's first republican president (1912–1916), and his father had been a personal physician to Mao Zedong. Despite the latter association, his family fled from China when the People's Republic was established in 1948, settling in Jakarta, where Lee was born. An increasing anti-Chinese movement in Indonesia drove the family from the country, and after a futile search for a permanent home in turbulent Asia, they settled in the United States in 1964. Lee was educated at the University of Pittsburgh, where he began to write. He later attended the University of Arizona and the State University of New York at Brockport. Lee's first collection of poetry was *Rose* (1986), which won the Delmore Schwartz Memorial Award from New York University. This was followed by *The City in Which I Love You* (1990), which won the Lamont Poetry Prize; *Book of My Nights* (2001); and his most recent publication, *Behind My Eyes* (2008). He has also published a personal memoir, *The Wingéd Seed: A Remembrance* (1995). Like much of Lee's poetry, "The Hammock," first published in the *Kenyon Review*, explores the interplay of the eternal and the everyday.

When I lay my head in my mother's lap
I think how day hides the stars,
the way I lay hidden once, waiting
inside my mother's singing to herself. And I remember
how she carried me on her back
between home and the kindergarten,
once each morning and once each afternoon.

I don't know what my mother's thinking.

When my son lays his head in my lap, I wonder:
Do his father's kisses keep his father's worries
from becoming his? I think, *Dear God,* and remember
there are stars we haven't heard from yet:
They have so far to arrive. *Amen,*
I think, and I feel almost comforted.

I've no idea what my child is thinking.

Between two unknowns, I live my life.
Between my mother's hopes, older than I am
by coming before me, and my child's wishes, older than I am
by outliving me. And what's it like?
Is it a door, and good-bye on either side?
A window, and eternity on either side?
Yes, and a little singing between two great rests.

[2000]

EXPLORING THE TEXT

1. What are the connotations of the word *hammock*? How do these connotations contribute to your understanding of the poem?
2. Find the visual and tactile images in the poem. What do these images suggest about the relationships described? Pay careful attention to the descriptions of physical positions.
3. Why do you think the poet chose to italicize the words "*Dear God*" (l. 11) and "*Amen*" (l. 13)? What does this tell you about the speaker's attitude toward his subject? How does this point the way to the poem's tone?
4. Why do the stars "have so far to arrive" (l. 13)? Those stars are in the same stanza as the father's "kisses" (l. 10) and "worries" (l. 10). How might the three be related?
5. What evidence is there in the poem — both words and images — of the speaker's tentativeness? For example, he feels "almost comforted" in line 14. He asks two questions at the very end and replies, "Yes" (l. 22) — but to which question is he responding? What is the source of this uncertainty? Does the speaker ultimately get beyond it, embrace it, or resign himself to it?
6. How did you interpret the poem's final stanza? What are the "two unknowns" (l. 16)? What are the "two great rests" (l. 22)? What do these images suggest about how the speaker lives his life?
7. Examine the structure of this poem by comparing stanzas one and three to stanzas two and four. How does the shape of the poem reflect its title and theme?

Whose Mouth Do I Speak With

SUZANNE RANCOURT

Suzanne Rancourt (b. 1959) is a Native American poet, educator, and elder of the Abenaki Bear Clan. She grew up in west central Maine and has served in the U.S. Marine Corps and U.S. Army. Rancourt earned an MFA in poetry from Vermont College and an MA in Educational Psychology from the University at Albany, SUNY. Her first book of poems, *Billboard in the Clouds* (2001), won the Native Writers' Circle of the Americas First Book Award. Her work has also been featured in several anthologies, including *The Journal of Military Experience, Vol. 2* (2012) and *In the Trenches: The Psychological Impact of War* (2015). Rancourt is also the managing editor for *Blue Streak: A Journal of Military Poetry*. In "Whose Mouth Do I Speak With," Rancourt's speaker reflects on her Native American heritage, bringing to life a childhood memory of her father.

I can remember my father bringing home spruce gum.
He worked in the woods and filled his pockets
with golden chunks of pitch.
For his children
he provided this special sacrament
and we'd gather at his feet, around his legs,
bumping his lunchbox, and his empty thermos rattled inside.
Our skin would stick to Daddy's gluey clothing
and we'd smell like Mumma's Pine Sol.
We had no money for store bought gum
but that's all right.
The spruce gum
was so close to chewing amber
as though in our mouths we held the eyes of Coyote
and how many other children had fathers
that placed on their innocent, anxious tongues
the blood of trees?

[2004]

EXPLORING THE TEXT

1. Spruce gum is the sap of the spruce tree that has hardened into resin; it is sometimes chewed like gum. When it hardens further, it becomes amber. According to one blogger from Maine, "You can't forget how the gum first crumbles, releasing a powerful taste of the spruce forest, then comes back together and settles down (after you spit out the impurities) into a nice, long lasting, lavender colored chew." How does this description of spruce gum inform your reading of the poem? What do you think spruce gum represents for the speaker?
2. Why does the speaker refer to her father bringing home spruce gum as a "sacrament" (l. 5)? How is the idea of a sacrament developed throughout the poem?
3. Consider the poem's imagery. What senses do the images appeal to? How does the imagery convey the speaker's attitude toward her father? her

childhood? What does the imagery imply about the larger meanings these memories have for her as an adult?

4. In Native American tradition, Coyote (l. 14) is often a trickster, usually imagined and portrayed with yellow — or amber — eyes. How does Coyote connect some of the images in "Whose Mouth Do I Speak With"?

5. How does the poem answer the question of the poem's title? In what ways is the answer left open to interpretation? Whose mouth does the speaker speak with?

My Husband

REBECCA HAZELTON

Rebecca Hazelton (b. 1978) is an award-winning poet, editor, and critic. After attending Davidson College, Hazelton went on to earn an MFA from the University of Notre Dame and a PhD from Florida State University. Hazelton was a 2010–2011 Jay C. and Ruth Hall Poetry Fellow at the University of Wisconsin–Madison Creative Writing Institute, and her third full-length book of poetry, *Vow* (2012), won the Cleveland State Poetry Center Open Competition Prize. She is the author of two other full-length books of poetry, *Fair Copy* (2012) and *Bad Star* (2013). She has taught at Beloit College and Oklahoma State University. In "My Husband," Hazelton's speaker paints a vivid, idealized portrait of her husband.

My husband in the house.
          My husband on the lawn,
pushing the mower, 4th of July, the way
          my husband's sweat wends like Crown Royale
to the waistband
of his shorts,
          the slow motion shake of the head the water
running down his chest,
          all of this lit like a Poison[1] video:
Cherry Pie[2] his cutoffs his blond hair his air guitar crescendo.
My husband
at the PTA meeting.
          My husband warming milk
          at 3 a.m. while I sleep.
My husband washing the white Corvette the bare chest and the soap,
          the objectification of my husband
by the pram pushers
and mailman.
          My husband at Home Depot asking

[1] An American rock band that was particularly popular from the mid-1980s to the mid-1990s. — EDS.

[2] A popular song by the rock band Warrant, recorded in 1990. The music video includes a blonde woman in cutoffs playing the air guitar. It was banned from a Canadian TV network for being "offensively sexist." — EDS.

where the bolts are,
the nuts, the screws,
my god, it's filthy
my husband reading from the news,
my husband cooking French toast, Belgian waffles,
my husband for all
nationalities.
My husband with a scotch, my husband
with his shoes off,
his slippers on, my husband's golden
leg hairs in the glow of a reading lamp.
My husband bearded, my husband shaved, the way my husband
taps out the razor, the small hairs
in the sink,
my husband with tweezers
to my foot,
to the splinter I carried
for years,
my husband chiding me
for waiting
to remove what pained me,
my husband brandishing aloft
the sliver to the light, and laughing.

[2015]

EXPLORING THE TEXT

1. The poem opens with a long, detailed description of the speaker's husband mowing the lawn, "all of this lit like a Poison video" (l. 9). What aspects of "My Husband" are like a music video? Consider film techniques such as framing, close-ups, and lighting. How do those details help Rebecca Hazelton paint a picture of her feelings about her husband?
2. What might the "sliver" in the poem's last line represent? Why do you think the husband is laughing?
3. Look carefully at the structure of "My Husband." What do you notice about the position of the lines and the lengths of the lines? What effect do those choices have on the poem's mood?
4. How would you describe the tone of "My Husband"? Consider Hazelton's use of repetition, varying line lengths, imagery, and hyperbole.
5. Discuss whether you think "My Husband" objectifies the speaker's husband, supporting your position with evidence from the poem itself.

PAIRED POEMS

My Papa's Waltz

THEODORE ROETHKE

Theodore Roethke (1908–1963) was born in Saginaw, Michigan. His early years spent in the family greenhouse business brought him close to nature and to his father, who died suddenly when Roethke was fifteen, a loss that looms large in the poem "My Papa's Waltz." After graduating from the University of Michigan, he did brief stints at law school and at Harvard University before the Great Depression compelled him to find work teaching at Lafayette College. He continued to teach throughout his life. Roethke first became popular after favorable reviews for *Open House* in 1941. He then won numerous prizes for his work throughout the 1950s and 1960s, including National Book Awards for both *Words for the Wind* (1957) and *The Far Field* (1964). The meeting of the mystical and the natural is at the center of his work — a meeting that fascinated such earlier poets as William Blake and William Wordsworth, both of whom were strong influences on Roethke's poetry. "My Papa's Waltz" is his most famous, and oft-interpreted, poem.

The whiskey on your breath
Could make a small boy dizzy;
But I hung on like death:
Such waltzing was not easy.

We romped until the pans
Slid from the kitchen shelf;
My mother's countenance
Could not unfrown itself.

The hand that held my wrist
Was battered on one knuckle;
At every step you missed
My right ear scraped a buckle.

You beat time on my head
With a palm caked hard by dirt,
Then waltzed me off to bed
Still clinging to your shirt.

[1948]

EXPLORING THE TEXT

1. How would you characterize the relationship between the father and the son in this poem?
2. Consider the two figures of speech in the poem: the simile of "hung on like death" (l. 3) and the metaphor of "waltzing" throughout the poem. What do they add to the story line of the poem? Imagine, for instance, if the title were changed to "My Papa" or "Dancing with My Father."
3. How do you interpret the lines "My mother's countenance / Could not unfrown itself" (ll. 7–8)? Is she angry? jealous? worried? frightened? disapproving? Why doesn't she take action or step in?
4. Manuscripts show that Theodore Roethke started writing this poem as a portrait of a daughter and her father. Explain why you think having a girl at the center of this poem would or would not affect your response to it.
5. What is the effect of the regular rhyme and rhythm scheme of the poem? In what ways does it mimic a waltz?
6. Some interpret this poem to be about an abusive father-son relationship, while others read it quite differently. How do you interpret it? Use textual evidence from the poem to explain your reading.

Those Winter Sundays

ROBERT HAYDEN

Born Asa Bundy Sheffey in Detroit, Michigan, Robert Hayden (1913–1980) was raised both in a dysfunctional family and in an equally dysfunctional foster home just next door. The turmoil of his childhood was complicated by his extreme nearsightedness, which excluded him from most activities other than reading. Hayden attended Detroit City College (now Wayne State University) before studying under W. H. Auden in the graduate English program at the University of Michigan. In 1976, he was appointed consultant in poetry to the Library of Congress, a post that was the forerunner to that of U.S. poet laureate. His first volume, *Heart-Shape in the Dust* (1940), took its voice from the Harlem Renaissance and impressed W. H. Auden with its originality. Later work continued to garner critical praise, including his epic poem on the *Amistad* mutiny, "Middle Passage," and *A Ballad of Remembrance* (1962), which includes his most famous poem, "Those Winter Sundays."

Sundays too my father got up early
and put his clothes on in the blueblack cold,
then with cracked hands that ached
from labor in the weekday weather made
banked fires blaze. No one ever thanked him.

I'd wake and hear the cold splintering, breaking.
When the rooms were warm, he'd call,
and slowly I would rise and dress,
fearing the chronic angers of that house,

Speaking indifferently to him,
who had driven out the cold
and polished my good shoes as well.
What did I know, what did I know
of love's austere and lonely offices?

[1962]

EXPLORING THE TEXT

1. What are the different time frames of this poem, and when does the poem shift from flashback to present day? How does Robert Hayden keep this shift from seeming abrupt?
2. What does the line "fearing the chronic angers of that house" (l. 9) suggest about the son's relationship with his father and the kind of home he grew up in?
3. What is the meaning of "love's austere and lonely offices" (l. 14)? What effect does Hayden achieve by choosing such an uncommon, somewhat archaic term as "offices"?
4. What is the tone of this poem? How do the specific details of the setting the speaker describes contribute to that tone? Consider also how the literal descriptions act as metaphors. What, for instance, is "blueblack cold" (l. 2)?
5. Notice the poem's shift between father and son, from "him" to "I." How does this alternation contribute to your understanding of the poem?
6. What contrasts do you see in the poem? Identify at least three, and discuss how they work individually and collectively.
7. What is the son's feeling about his father? Could this poem be read as a son's belated thank you? Explain your answer. What does the adult speaker in the poem understand about his father that he did not as a child? What is the effect of the repetition in the last two lines?
8. In poetry, the lyric is usually a short poem expressing personal feelings and may take the form of a song set to music. What music would you choose to convey the tone and themes of "Those Winter Sundays"?

FOCUS ON COMPARISON AND CONTRAST

1. "My Papa's Waltz" and "Those Winter Sundays" are both poems in which the speakers remember their fathers. What are the similarities in their descriptions of their fathers? What are the differences?
2. One poem rhymes; the other doesn't. How does the choice to rhyme or not affect the meaning of each poem? How does that decision affect the character of the speaker?
3. How would you characterize the mood in each of these poems? How do they differ from each other? What are the similarities?

WRITING ASSIGNMENT

In "My Papa's Waltz" and "Those Winter Sundays," each speaker contemplates his fraught relationship with his father, sharing memories of their interactions. Read both poems carefully. Then write an essay in which you compare and contrast the poems, analyzing the techniques each poet uses to depict the speaker's attitude toward his father.

Turtle Soup

MARILYN CHIN

Marilyn Chin (b. 1955) is a prominent Chinese American poet, writer, and translator who grew up in Portland, Oregon, after her family emigrated from Hong Kong. She earned a BA from the University of Massachusetts and an MFA from the University of Iowa. Chin has won numerous awards for her poetry, including the Radcliffe Institute Fellowship at Harvard, two National Endowment for the Arts grants, the Stegner Fellowship, five Pushcart Prizes, and a Fulbright Fellowship to study in Taiwan. Chin is the author of four books of poetry: *Dwarf Bamboo* (1987), *The Phoenix Gone, the Terrace Empty* (1994), *Rhapsody in Plain Yellow* (2002), and *Hard Love Province* (2014). She has also published one book of interlinked stories, *Revenge of the Mooncake Vixen* (2009), and has translated works by early modern Chinese poet Ai Qing and the early modern Japanese poet Gōzō Yoshimasu. Chin's own work explores Asian American feminism and bicultural identity. In "Turtle Soup," Chin presents a dinner scene that captures a moment of conflict between two cultures and two generations.

You go home one evening tired from work,
and your mother boils you turtle soup.
Twelve hours hunched over the hearth
(who knows what else is in that cauldron).

You say, "Ma, you've poached the symbol of long life;
that turtle lived four thousand years, swam
the Wei, up the Yellow, over the Yangtze.[1]
Witnessed the Bronze Age,[2] the High Tang[3]
grazed on splendid sericulture."[4]
(So, she boils the life out of him.)

"All our ancestors have been fools.
Remember Uncle Wu who rode ten thousand miles
to kill a famous Manchu[5] and ended up
with his head on a pole? Eat, child,
its liver will make you strong."

"Sometimes you're the life, sometimes the sacrifice."
Her sobbing is inconsolable.
So, you spread that gentle napkin
over your lap in decorous Pasadena.

---

[1] Rivers that are a part of the Grand Canal in China. — EDS.

[2] 3000 BC - 1000 BC. — EDS.

[3] Period of time during the Tang Dynasty when Chinese poetry flourished. — EDS.

[4] Raising silkworms in order to produce silk. — EDS.

[5] A Chinese ethnic minority. — EDS.

Baby, some high priestess has got it wrong.
The golden decal on the green underbelly
says "Made in Hong Kong."

Is there nothing left but the shell
and humanity's strange inscriptions,
the songs, the rites, the oracles?

for Ben Huang

[1993]

EXPLORING THE TEXT

1. Who is the speaker of "Turtle Soup"? Who is the audience — the "you" the poem addresses? How does Marilyn Chin's use of the pronoun "you" complicate the character of the speaker?
2. Consider Chin's diction choices. What effect do words and phrases such as "cauldron," "symbol," "sacrifice," "high priestess," "inscriptions," "rites," and "oracles" have on the mood of the poem?
3. What do the references to Chinese history, art, culture, and geography in the second stanza tell us about the speaker? What does her mother's response — "All our ancestors have been fools" — suggest about the relationship between the speaker and her mother? about the mother's attitude toward the history and traditions the speaker cites?
4. What is the effect of the parentheses in the last lines of the first and second stanzas? Why do you think the poet chose to use them?
5. What do you make of the "Made in Hong Kong" decal in line 22? What does it suggest about the speaker's opinion of authenticity? What might her mother think of it?
6. What do you think "'Sometimes you're the life, sometimes the sacrifice'" (l. 16) means? Why does that statement cause the speaker to "spread that gentle napkin / over [her] lap in decorous Pasadena" (ll. 18–19)?
7. What role does food — the turtle soup — and the idea of nourishment play in the poem? How does the poet move from the scene of her mother cooking a meal to commenting on "humanity's strange inscriptions / the songs, the rites, the oracles?" (ll. 24–25)?

Peaches

ADRIENNE SU

Adrienne Su (b. 1967) is an American poet from Atlanta, Georgia. She earned a BA from Harvard University and an MFA from the University of Virginia. Su's first book, *Middle Kingdom* (1997), was translated into Chinese and published in China in 2006. She is the author of two other poetry collections: *Sanctuary* (2006) and *Having None of It* (2009). Su's writing has earned many awards, including a National Endowment for the Arts Fellowship and residences at the Fine Arts Works Center and The Frost Place. Her poems have been anthologized in *The New American Poets* (2000), *The Pushcart Prize XXIV* (2000), and *Asian-American Poetry: The Next Generation* (2004). She currently teaches at Dickinson College. In "Peaches," Su reflects on her heritage as a child of Chinese immigrants growing up in the American South.

A crate of peaches straight from the farm
has to be maintained, or eaten in days.
Obvious, but in my family, they went so fast,
I never saw the mess that punishes delay.

I thought everyone bought fruit by the crate,
stored it in the coolest part of the house,
then devoured it before any could rot.
I'm from the Peach State, and to those

who ask *But where are you from originally*,
I'd like to reply *The homeland of the peach*,
but I'm too nice, and they might not look it up.
In truth, the reason we bought so much

did have to do with being Chinese — at least
Chinese in that part of America, both strangers
and natives on a lonely, beautiful street
where food came in stackable containers

and fussy bags, unless you bothered to drive
to the source, where the same money landed
a bushel of fruit, a twenty-pound sack of rice.
You had to drive anyway, each house surrounded

by land enough to grow your own, if lawns
hadn't been required. At home I loved to stare
into the extra freezer, reviewing mountains
of foil-wrapped meats, cakes, juice concentrate,

mysterious packets brought by house guests
from New York Chinatown, to be transformed
by heat, force, and my mother's patient effort,
enough to keep us fed through flood or storm,

provided the power stayed on, or fire and ice
could be procured, which would be labor-intensive,
but so was everything else my parents did.
Their lives were labor, they kept this from the kids,

who grew up to confuse work with pleasure,
to become typical immigrants' children,
taller than their parents and unaware of hunger
except when asked the odd, perplexing question.

[2015]

EXPLORING THE TEXT

1. What do you think the speaker means when she says that the peaches "went so fast / I never saw the mess that punishes delay" (ll. 3–4)? How does that line comment on more than just a crate of peaches?
2. The speaker says she comes from the Peach State, which is Georgia. Why is she asked where she originally comes from? How does the family's way of buying peaches by the crate complicate her answer to that question?
3. Consider the poem's syntax. What effect does Adrienne Su's use of enjambment have on the poem's tone? Why might she have placed stanza breaks mid-sentence?
4. What do you think the "odd, perplexing question" in the poem's last line is?
5. How does this poem comment on contemporary American life? What contrasts does the speaker make with the life of her parents as immigrants from China?
6. In an essay about food in poetry, Su writes:

   > Food has been a topic of poetry for many centuries and in many cultures; the notion that food writing and poetry writing are totally separate ventures is a recent development. Much of our knowledge of eating habits, culinary practices, and food taboos throughout history and around the world comes from poetry. Food in poetry also functions as a powerful symbol of spiritual and moral states. . . .

   How does the food in "Peaches" provide information about eating habits, culinary practices, and food taboos? Does it function as a "symbol of spiritual or moral states"? Explain your answer.

FOCUS ON COMPARISON AND CONTRAST

1. Compare the tone of "Turtle Soup" to that of "Peaches." Are there any similarities?
2. Both poems address themes of family, cultural tradition, and Chinese American experience through food. What are the similarities in how the poets choose to address those themes? What are the differences?
3. While the narrative of "Turtle Soup" centers on a mother-daughter relationship, "Peaches" focuses primarily on the speaker's memories of growing up in Georgia. However, both poems illuminate a gap between the speaker's generation and that of her parents. Compare and contrast the speaker in each poem. How are their attitudes toward their parents' generation similar? How are they different?

WRITING ASSIGNMENT

"Turtle Soup" and "Peaches" both examine intergenerational family relationships through the lens of food. Compare and contrast the two poems, analyzing the techniques each poet uses to convey the nature of the speaker's relationship with her family.

CONNOTATION

"Diversity Blooms in Outer Suburbs." This headline from the *Washington Post* captures the power of connotation. The article uses the words "grows" and "increases" throughout, yet "Blooms" in the headline connotes more than growth: it's positive growth, a flowering. Just as journalists use the power of connotative meaning to draw in readers, writers of literary texts — poems, plays, stories, and novels — make language choices that influence their readers' responses. What is the difference, for instance, between *labor* and *work*? between *lady* and *woman*? between *pail* and *bucket*? You can be sure that writers think about these differences and make deliberate choices.

Paying attention to connotation often leads to an interpretation, or a better understanding of the mood of a piece — especially when it comes to verb choices. Consider the following sentences from the "Play" opening of *Fences* (p. 152):

> **THE PLAY** Near the turn of the century, the destitute of Europe *sprang* on the city with tenacious claws and an honest and solid dream. The city *devoured* them.

If Wilson had used words that were less evocative, the sentence would be far less vivid. For instance:

> Near the turn of the century, the destitute of Europe *arrived* in the city with *ambition* and an honest and solid dream. The city *absorbed* them.

"Sprang" suggests a feeling that "arrived" does not; "tenacious claws" carries a visual image that the less expressive "ambition" does not; and certainly "devoured" evokes an exciting and almost aggressive quality that the more neutral "absorbed" does not.

Connotation may work individually or cumulatively. Notice in the following paragraph from the "Play" section of the opening of *Fences* how the connotations of several words together suggest upheaval and progress:

> By 1957, the hard-won victories of the European immigrants had solidified the industrial might of America. War had been confronted and won with new energies that used loyalty and patriotism as its fuel. Life was rich, full, and flourishing. The Milwaukee Braves won the World Series, and the hot winds of change that would make the sixties a turbulent, racing, dangerous, and provocative decade had not yet begun to blow full.

Notice how a few word substitutions can change the mood of the paragraph:

> By 1957, the hard-won victories of the European immigrants had *built up* the industrial *strength* of America. War had been *fought* and won with new energies that used loyalty and patriotism as its fuel. Life was rich, full, and *improving*. The Milwaukee Braves won the World Series, and the *growing* change that would make the sixties an *unstable*, *exciting*, dangerous, and *controversial* decade had not yet begun to *happen*.

The following exercises will help you examine how precisely chosen words can convey meaning.

EXERCISE 1

Discuss the differences in connotations in the following groups of words:

a. skinny, slender, svelte, gaunt, slim, lithe

b. dog, pooch, canine, pup

c. run, bolt, race, sprint, dash

d. alleged, reported, maintained, contended, claimed

e. rich, affluent, prosperous, wealthy

f. kids, descendants, children, progeny, offspring

EXERCISE 2

A. What do the connotations of the underlined words and phrases suggest about the home life that the speaker describes in Robert Hayden's "Those Winter Sundays"?

> Sundays too my father got up early
> and put his clothes on in the blueblack cold,
> then with cracked hands that ached
> from labor in the weekday weather made
> banked fires blaze. No one ever thanked him.
>
> I'd wake and hear the cold splintering, breaking.
> When the rooms were warm, he'd call,
> and slowly I would rise and dress,
> fearing the chronic angers of that house,
>
> Speaking indifferently to him,
> who had driven out the cold
> and polished my good shoes as well.
> What did I know, what did I know
> of love's austere and lonely offices?

B. What connotations contribute to the ambivalence the narrator of Alice Munro's "The Progress of Love" feels about her Aunt Beryl?

> A scarecrow in white slacks (this is what my father called her afterward), with a white sun hat tied under her chin by a flaunting red ribbon. Her fingernails and toenails — she wore sandals — were painted to match the ribbon. She wore the small, dark sunglasses people wore at that time. (Not the people I knew — they didn't own sunglasses.) She had a big red mouth, a loud laugh, hair of an unnatural color and a high gloss, like cherry wood. She was so noisy and shiny, so glamorously got up, that it was hard to tell whether she was good looking, or happy, or anything.

EXERCISE 3

Examine the following words from Marilyn Chin's poem "Turtle Soup." What connotations do these words suggest to you? Write each word on a piece of paper and cluster any associations that come to you, using the model cluster below as a template.

- boiled
- poached
- cauldron
- underbelly
- rites

MODEL CLUSTER

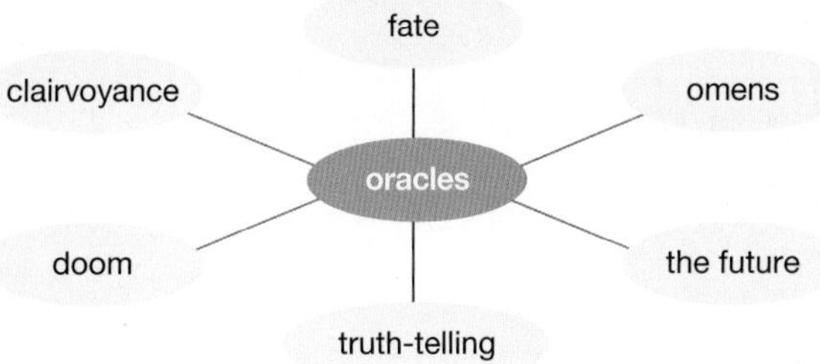

How do the connotations of these words contribute to the poem's tone? What inferences can you draw regarding the meaning of the poem based on Chin's choice of words? Turn to a partner and share your findings.

EXERCISE 4

Reread Mary Oliver's poem "Wild Geese." How do the connotations of words in that poem contribute to its meaning? For instance, the word *animal* can often have negative connotations, but how is it used in line 4? Find other words with denotations and connotations that are important to the meaning of "Wild Geese."

EXERCISE 5

Write two short paragraphs. In the first, describe something about your family or home that you like or appreciate. In the second, describe something about your family or home that you find annoying. In both paragraphs, choose words with connotations that convey your attitude toward your subjects.

HOME AND FAMILY

1. Select three texts from this chapter that you found particularly memorable, and in a well-organized essay, analyze how the writers have explored the theme of home and family.
2. Compare and contrast how two of the poets in this chapter have used resources of language such as diction, syntax, and imagery to express their ideas regarding the theme of home and family.
3. Several of the works in this chapter (including *Fences*, "The Moths," "The Progress of Love," "The Hammock," and "Peaches") explore multigenerational family units. Using two or three different selections, discuss the ties that keep families together as well as those that challenge the connections among multiple generations.
4. Select a text from the chapter that depicts a conflict between a parent and a child. Craft an essay in which you analyze the source of the conflict, and explore how this tension contributes to the meaning of the work as a whole.
5. Selecting three or four texts from the chapter, write an essay arguing whether families are more alike or different regardless of specific culture, ethnic background, or time period.
6. Choose one of the following quotations, and explain why it fits your beliefs about family in general or your family in particular.
   a. "Nobody has ever before asked the nuclear family to live all by itself in a box the way we do. With no relatives, no support, we've put it in an impossible situation."

      — Margaret Mead

   b. "If the family were a fruit, it would be an orange, a circle of sections, held together but separable — each segment distinct."

      — Letty Cottin Pogrebin

   c. "Important families are like potatoes. The best parts are underground."

      — Francis Bacon
7. Choose one of the poems addressed (directly or indirectly) to an absent party (for instance, the poems by Anne Bradstreet, William Butler Yeats, Langston Hughes, or Robert Hayden), and respond by writing a poem in the absent person's voice.
8. Search a museum website for images of home and family. Find a painting or photograph that conveys an image of family in marked contrast to that depicted by any text in this chapter. Explain the two perspectives of family.
9. Select a character from one of the texts in this chapter and a problem or difficulty from another text. In the voice of the character you've chosen, offer advice on how to solve or address the problem.
10. Write an essay in which you compare and contrast the dinner scene in "The Progress of Love" with a dinner scene in another work, such as F. Scott Fitzgerald's *The Great Gatsby*, Jane Austen's *Pride and Prejudice*, Toni Morrison's *Song of Solomon*, or Charles Dickens's *Great Expectations*.

6
Identity and Culture

> “No man, for any considerable period, can wear one face to himself, and another to the multitude, without finally getting bewildered as to which may be the true.”
>
> —Nathaniel Hawthorne, *The Scarlet Letter*

Chris Carlson/Getty Images

What makes us who we are? While our identity is shaped by our interests, personality, and talents, much of how we define ourselves is dependent on the culture that surrounds us. Gender, race, age, religion, national allegiance, geography, language, class, and ethnicity all play a role. In this chapter, the readings explore the many different ways that culture influences who we are.

In previous generations, immigrants tried to assimilate to their new country as quickly as possible, but newer generations are holding on to the traditions and identities of their homeland. Is defining identity based on difference a divisive or a constructive force in society? Some argue for cosmopolitanism — for people to be citizens of the world — in order to foster a greater sense of shared identity. Would that discourage cultural discrimination and bias, or would it erode local community values and ties? In contemporary literature, cross-cultural writers such as Jhumpa Lahiri — associated with both Indian and American culture — are part of the canon of the twenty-first century. Her characters and their level of comfort in more than one culture reflect the benefits and difficulties of living in a global community. Lahiri's "Interpreter of Maladies," as well as other stories in this chapter, asks: do we create an identity — or inherit one?

Many of the readings in this chapter explore identities that are not shaped by culture but are in conflict with it, from Ralph Waldo Emerson's "The Apology," to Kamau Brathwaite's "Ogun," to Mahmoud Darwish's "Identity Card." Some, such as Natalie Diaz's "The Facts of Art" and Gregory Pardlo's "Written by Himself," confront one-dimensional narratives; others, such as Nathalie Handal's "Caribe in Nueva York," celebrate the polyglot world of a big city where multiple cultures coexist — sometimes without conflict, sometimes with. The selections in the Texts in Context section in this chapter, as well as Joseph Conrad's *Heart of Darkness* itself, explore the assumptions and motivations of European colonial powers in Africa and the short- and longer-term consequences for both the colonized and the colonizer.

Whether we come to these texts from a single cultural tradition or read them through a multicultural lens, close, careful reading of these works reminds us that literature gives us glimpses into the conflicts and struggles that are an integral part of forming our identities.

Interpreter of Maladies

JHUMPA LAHIRI

Venturelli / GC Images / Getty Images

Born in London in 1967, Jhumpa Lahiri immigrated with her Bengali parents to Boston and then Kingston, Rhode Island. She received a BA in English literature from Barnard College and graduated from Boston University with master's degrees in English, creative writing, and comparative literature and a PhD in Renaissance studies. Lahiri has garnered critical acclaim and commercial success with two short-story collections — *Interpreter of Maladies* (1999) and *Unaccustomed Earth* (2008) — and two novels, *The Namesake* (2003) and *The Lowland* (2013). Her debut story collection, *Interpreter of Maladies*, won the PEN/Hemingway Award and the 2000 Pulitzer Prize for Fiction, making Lahiri the youngest person ever to win that prestigious award. *New York Times* critic Michiko Kakutani called Lahiri "a writer of uncommon elegance and poise," who made "a precocious debut" with this short story collection. Lahiri feels strong ties to England, India, and the United States, yet says, "No country is my motherland. I always find myself in exile in whichever country I travel to. . . ." She explores this theme in much of her fiction, including this title story from *Interpreter of Maladies*.

At the tea stall Mr. and Mrs. Das bickered about who should take Tina to the toilet. Eventually Mrs. Das relented when Mr. Das pointed out that he had given the girl her bath the night before. In the rearview mirror Mr. Kapasi watched as Mrs. Das emerged slowly from his bulky white Ambassador, dragging her shaved, largely bare legs across the back seat. She did not hold the little girl's hand as they walked to the rest room.

They were on their way to see the Sun Temple at Konarak. It was a dry, bright Saturday, the mid-July heat tempered by a steady ocean breeze, ideal weather for sightseeing. Ordinarily Mr. Kapasi would not have stopped so soon along the way, but less than five minutes after he'd picked up the family that morning in front of Hotel Sandy Villa, the little girl had complained. The first thing Mr. Kapasi had noticed when he saw Mr. and Mrs. Das, standing with their children under the portico of the hotel, was that they were very young, perhaps not even thirty. In addition to Tina they had two boys, Ronny and Bobby, who appeared very close in age and had teeth covered in a network of flashing silver wires. The family looked Indian but dressed as foreigners did, the children in stiff, brightly colored clothing and caps with translucent visors. Mr. Kapasi was accustomed to foreign tourists; he was assigned to them regularly because he could speak English. Yesterday he had driven an elderly couple from Scotland, both with spotted faces and fluffy white hair so thin it exposed their sunburnt scalps. In comparison, the tanned, youthful faces of Mr. and Mrs. Das were all the more striking. When he'd introduced himself, Mr. Kapasi had pressed his palms together in greeting, but Mr. Das squeezed hands like an American so that Mr. Kapasi felt it in his elbow. Mrs. Das, for her part, had flexed one side of her mouth, smiling dutifully at Mr. Kapasi, without displaying any interest in him.

As they waited at the tea stall, Ronny, who looked like the older of the two boys, clambered suddenly out of the back seat, intrigued by a goat tied to a stake in the ground.

"Don't touch it," Mr. Das said. He glanced up from his paperback tour book, which said "INDIA" in yellow letters and looked as if it had been published abroad. His voice, somehow tentative and a little shrill, sounded as though it had not yet settled into maturity.

"I want to give it a piece of gum," the boy called back as he trotted ahead.

Mr. Das stepped out of the car and stretched his legs by squatting briefly to the ground. A clean-shaven man, he looked exactly like a magnified version of Ronny. He had a sapphire blue visor, and was dressed in shorts, sneakers, and a T-shirt. The camera slung around his neck, with an impressive telephoto lens and numerous buttons and markings, was the only complicated thing he wore. He frowned, watching as Ronny rushed toward the goat, but appeared to have no intention of intervening. "Bobby, make sure that your brother doesn't do anything stupid."

"I don't feel like it," Bobby said, not moving. He was sitting in the front seat beside Mr. Kapasi, studying a picture of the elephant god taped to the glove compartment.

"No need to worry," Mr. Kapasi said. "They are quite tame." Mr. Kapasi was forty-six years old, with receding hair that had gone completely silver, but his butterscotch complexion and his unlined brow, which he treated in spare moments to dabs of lotus-oil balm, made it easy to imagine what he must have looked like at an earlier age. He wore gray trousers and a matching jacket-style shirt, tapered at the waist, with short sleeves and a large pointed collar, made of a thin but durable synthetic material. He had specified both the cut and the fabric to his tailor — it was his preferred uniform for giving tours because it did not get crushed during his long hours behind the wheel. Through the windshield he watched as Ronny circled around the goat, touched it quickly on its side, then trotted back to the car.

"You left India as a child?" Mr. Kapasi asked when Mr. Das had settled once again into the passenger seat.

"Oh, Mina and I were both born in America," Mr. Das announced with an air of sudden confidence. "Born and raised. Our parents live here now, in Assansol. They retired. We visit them every couple years." He turned to watch as the little girl ran toward the car, the wide purple bows of her sundress flopping on her narrow brown shoulders. She was holding to her chest a doll with yellow hair that looked as if it had been chopped, as a punitive measure, with a pair of dull scissors. "This is Tina's first trip to India, isn't it, Tina?"

"I don't have to go to the bathroom anymore," Tina announced.

"Where's Mina?" Mr. Das asked.

Mr. Kapasi found it strange that Mr. Das should refer to his wife by her first name when speaking to the little girl. Tina pointed to where Mrs. Das was purchasing something from one of the shirtless men who worked at the tea stall. Mr. Kapasi heard one of the shirtless men sing a phrase from a popular Hindi love song as Mrs. Das walked back to the car, but she did not appear to understand the words of the song, for she did not express irritation, or embarrassment, or react in any other way to the man's declarations.

He observed her. She wore a red-and-white-checkered skirt that stopped above her knees, slip-on shoes with a square wooden heel, and a close-fitting blouse styled like a man's undershirt. The blouse was decorated at chest-level with a calico appliqué in the shape of a strawberry. She was a short woman, with small hands like paws, her frosty pink fingernails painted to match her lips, and was slightly plump in her figure. Her hair, shorn only a little longer than her husband's, was parted far to one side. She was wearing large dark brown sunglasses with a pinkish tint to them, and carried a big straw bag,

Consider the description of Mrs. Das in paragraph 14. **In what ways does this painting reflect how she is viewed by other characters in the story?**

Art © Wayne Thiebaud/Licensed by VAGA, New York, NY Private Collection/Bridgeman Images

almost as big as her torso, shaped like a bowl, with a water bottle poking out of it. She walked slowly, carrying some puffed rice tossed with peanuts and chili peppers in a large packet made from newspapers. Mr. Kapasi turned to Mr. Das.

"Where in America do you live?"

"New Brunswick, New Jersey."

"Next to New York."

"Exactly. I teach middle school there."

"What subject?"

"Science. In fact, every year I take my students on a trip to the Museum of Natural History in New York City. In a way we have a lot in common, you could say, you and I. How long have you been a tour guide, Mr. Kapasi?"

"Five years."

Mrs. Das reached the car. "How long's the trip?" she asked, shutting the door.

"About two and a half hours," Mr. Kapasi replied.

At this Mrs. Das gave an impatient sigh, as if she had been traveling her whole life without pause. She fanned herself with a folded Bombay film magazine written in English.

"I thought that the Sun Temple is only eighteen miles north of Puri," Mr. Das said, tapping on the tour book.

"The roads to Konarak are poor. Actually it is a distance of fifty-two miles," Mr. Kapasi explained.

Mr. Das nodded, readjusting the camera strap where it had begun to chafe the back of his neck.

Before starting the ignition, Mr. Kapasi reached back to make sure the cranklike locks on the inside of each of the back doors were secured. As soon as the car began to move the little girl began to play with the lock on her side, clicking it with some effort forward and backward, but Mrs. Das said nothing to stop her. She sat a bit slouched at one end of the back seat, not offering her puffed rice to anyone. Ronny and Tina sat on either side of her, both snapping bright green gum.

"Look," Bobby said as the car began to gather speed. He pointed with his finger to the tall trees that lined the road. "Look."

"Monkeys!" Ronny shrieked. "Wow!"

They were seated in groups along the branches, with shining black faces, silver bodies, horizontal eyebrows, and crested heads. Their long gray tails dangled like a series of ropes among the leaves. A few scratched themselves with black leathery hands, or swung their feet, staring as the car passed.

"We call them the hanuman," Mr. Kapasi said. "They are quite common in the area."

As soon as he spoke, one of the monkeys leaped into the middle of the road, causing Mr. Kapasi to brake suddenly. Another bounced onto the hood of the car, then sprang away. Mr. Kapasi beeped his horn. The children began to get excited, sucking in their breath and covering their faces partly with their hands. They had never seen monkeys outside of a zoo, Mr. Das explained. He asked Mr. Kapasi to stop the car so that he could take a picture.

While Mr. Das adjusted his telephoto lens, Mrs. Das reached into her straw bag and pulled out a bottle of colorless nail polish, which she proceeded to stroke on the tip of her index finger.

The little girl stuck out a hand. "Mine too. Mommy, do mine too."

"Leave me alone," Mrs. Das said, blowing on her nail and turning her body slightly. "You're making me mess up."

The little girl occupied herself by buttoning and unbuttoning a pinafore on the doll's plastic body.

"All set," Mr. Das said, replacing the lens cap.

The car rattled considerably as it raced along the dusty road, causing them all to pop up from their seats every now and then, but Mrs. Das continued to polish her nails. Mr. Kapasi eased up on the accelerator, hoping to produce a smoother ride. When he reached for the gear-shift the boy in front accommodated him by swinging his hairless knees out of the way. Mr. Kapasi noted that this boy was slightly paler than the other children. "Daddy, why is the driver sitting on the wrong side in this car, too?" the boy asked.

"They all do that here, dummy," Ronny said.

"Don't call your brother a dummy," Mr. Das said. He turned to Mr. Kapasi. "In America, you know . . . it confuses them."

"Oh yes, I am well aware," Mr. Kapasi said. As delicately as he could, he shifted gears again, accelerating as they approached a hill in the road. "I see it on *Dallas*, the steering wheels are on the left-hand side."

"What's *Dallas*?" Tina asked, banging her now naked doll on the seat behind Mr. Kapasi.

"It went off the air," Mr. Das explained. "It's a television show."

They were all like siblings, Mr. Kapasi thought as they passed a row of date trees. Mr. and Mrs. Das behaved like an older brother and sister, not parents. It seemed that they were in charge of the children only for the day; it was hard to believe they were regularly responsible for anything other than themselves. Mr. Das tapped on his lens cap, and his tour book, dragging his thumbnail occasionally across the pages so that they made a scraping sound. Mrs. Das continued to polish her nails. She had still not removed her sunglasses. Every now and then Tina renewed her plea that she wanted her nails done, too, and so at one point Mrs. Das flicked a drop of polish on the little girl's finger before depositing the bottle back inside her straw bag.

"Isn't this an air-conditioned car?" she asked, still blowing on her hand. The window on Tina's side was broken and could not be rolled down.

"Quit complaining," Mr. Das said. "It isn't so hot."

"I told you to get a car with air-conditioning," Mrs. Das continued. "Why do you do this, Raj, just to save a few stupid rupees. What are you saving us, fifty cents?"

Their accents sounded just like the ones Mr. Kapasi heard on American television programs, though not like the ones on *Dallas*.

"Doesn't it get tiresome, Mr. Kapasi, showing people the same thing every day?" Mr. Das asked, rolling down his own window all the way. "Hey, do you mind stopping the car. I just want to get a shot of this guy."

Mr. Kapasi pulled over to the side of the road as Mr. Das took a picture of a barefoot man, his head wrapped in a dirty turban, seated on top of a cart of grain sacks pulled by a pair of bullocks. Both the man and the bullocks were emaciated. In the back seat Mrs. Das gazed out another window, at the sky, where nearly transparent clouds passed quickly in front of one another.

"I look forward to it, actually," Mr. Kapasi said as they continued on their way. "The Sun Temple is one of my favorite places. In that way it is a reward for me. I give tours on Fridays and Saturdays only. I have another job during the week."

"Oh? Where?" Mr. Das asked.

"I work in a doctor's office."

"You're a doctor?"

"I am not a doctor. I work with one. As an interpreter."

"What does a doctor need an interpreter for?"

"He has a number of Gujarati patients. My father was Gujarati, but many people do not speak Gujarati in this area, including the doctor.

And so the doctor asked me to work in his office, interpreting what the patients say."

"Interesting. I've never heard of anything like that." Mr. Das said.

Mr. Kapasi shrugged. "It is a job like any other."

"But so romantic," Mrs. Das said dreamily, breaking her extended silence. She lifted her pinkish brown sunglasses and arranged them on top of her head like a tiara. For the first time, her eyes met Mr. Kapasi's in the rearview mirror: pale, a bit small, their gaze fixed but drowsy.

Mr. Das craned to look at her. "What's so romantic about it?"

"I don't know. Something." She shrugged, knitting her brows together for an instant. "Would you like a piece of gum, Mr. Kapasi?" she asked brightly. She reached into her straw bag and handed him a small square wrapped in green-and-white-striped paper. As soon as Mr. Kapasi put the gum in his mouth a thick sweet liquid burst onto his tongue.

"Tell us more about your job, Mr. Kapasi," Mrs. Das said.

"What would you like to know, madame?"

"I don't know," she shrugged, munching on some puffed rice and licking the mustard oil from the corners of her mouth. "Tell us a typical situation." She settled back in her seat, her head tilted in a patch of sun, and closed her eyes. "I want to picture what happens."

"Very well. The other day a man came in with a pain in his throat."

"Did he smoke cigarettes?"

"No. It was very curious. He complained that he felt as if there were long pieces of straw stuck in his throat. When I told the doctor he was able to prescribe the proper medication."

"That's so neat."

"Yes," Mr. Kapasi agreed after some hesitation.

"So these patients are totally dependent on you," Mrs. Das said. She spoke slowly, as if she were thinking aloud. "In a way, more dependent on you than the doctor."

"How do you mean? How could it be?"

"Well, for example, you could tell the doctor that the pain felt like a burning, not straw. The patient would never know what you had told the doctor, and the doctor wouldn't know that you had told the wrong thing. It's a big responsibility."

"Yes, a big responsibility you have there, Mr. Kapasi," Mr. Das agreed.

Mr. Kapasi had never thought of his job in such complimentary terms. To him it was a thankless occupation. He found nothing noble in interpreting people's maladies, assiduously translating the symptoms of so many swollen bones, countless cramps of bellies and bowels, spots on people's palms that changed color, shape, or size. The doctor, nearly half his age, had an affinity for bell-bottom trousers and made humorless jokes about the Congress party. Together they worked in a stale little infirmary where Mr. Kapasi's smartly tailored clothes clung to him in the heat, in spite of the blackened blades of a ceiling fan churning over their heads.

The job was a sign of his failings. In his youth he'd been a devoted scholar of foreign languages, the owner of an impressive collection of dictionaries. He had dreamed of being an interpreter for diplomats and dignitaries, resolving conflicts between people and nations, settling disputes of which he alone could understand both sides. He was a self-educated man. In a series of notebooks, in the evenings before his parents settled his marriage, he had listed the common etymologies of words, and at one point in his life he was confident that he could converse, if given the opportunity, in English, French, Russian, Portuguese, and Italian, not to mention Hindi, Bengali, Orissi, and Gujarati. Now only a handful of European phrases remained in his memory, scattered words for things like saucers and chairs. English was the only non-Indian language he spoke fluently anymore. Mr. Kapasi knew it was not a remarkable talent. Sometimes he feared that his children knew better English than he did, just from watching television. Still, it came in handy for the tours.

He had taken the job as an interpreter after his first son, at the age of seven, contracted typhoid — that was how he had first made the acquaintance of the doctor. At the time Mr. Kapasi had been teaching English in a grammar school, and he bartered his skills as an interpreter to pay the increasingly exorbitant medical bills. In the end the boy had died one evening in his mother's arms, his limbs burning with fever, but then there was the funeral to pay for, and the other children who were born soon enough, and the newer, bigger house, and the good schools and tutors, and the fine shoes and the television, and the countless other ways he tried to console his wife and to keep her from crying in her sleep, and so when the doctor offered to pay him twice as much as he earned at the grammar school, he accepted. Mr. Kapasi knew that his wife had little regard for his career as an interpreter. He knew it reminded her of the son she'd lost, and that she resented the other lives he helped, in his own small way, to save. If ever she referred to his position, she used the phrase "doctor's assistant," as if the process of interpretation were equal to taking someone's temperature, or changing a bedpan. She never asked him about the patients who came to the doctor's office, or said that his job was a big responsibility.

For this reason it flattered Mr. Kapasi that Mrs. Das was so intrigued by his job. Unlike his wife, she had reminded him of its intellectual challenges. She had also used the word "romantic." She did not behave in a romantic way toward her husband, and yet she had used the word to describe him. He wondered if Mr. and Mrs. Das were a bad match, just as he and his wife were. Perhaps they, too, had little in common apart from three children and a decade of their lives. The signs he recognized from his own marriage were there — the bickering, the indifference, the protracted silences. Her sudden interest in him, an interest she did not express in either her husband or her children, was mildly intoxicating. When Mr. Kapasi thought once again about how she had said "romantic," the feeling of intoxication grew.

He began to check his reflection in the rearview mirror as he drove, feeling grateful that he had chosen the gray suit that morning and not the brown one, which tended to sag a little in the knees. From time to time he glanced through the mirror at Mrs. Das. In addition to glancing at her face he glanced at the strawberry between her breasts, and the golden brown hollow in her throat. He decided to tell Mrs. Das about another patient, and another: the young woman who had complained of a sensation of raindrops in her spine, the gentleman whose birthmark had begun to sprout hairs. Mrs. Das listened attentively, stroking her hair with a small plastic brush that resembled an oval bed of nails, asking more questions, for yet another example. The children were quiet, intent on spotting more monkeys in the trees, and Mr. Das was absorbed by his tour book, so it seemed like a private conversation between Mr. Kapasi and Mrs. Das. In this manner the next half hour passed, and when they stopped for lunch at a roadside restaurant that sold fritters and omelette sandwiches, usually something Mr. Kapasi looked forward to on his tours so that he could sit in peace and enjoy some hot tea, he was disappointed. As the Das family settled together under a magenta umbrella fringed with white and orange tassels, and placed their orders with one of the waiters who marched about in tricornered caps, Mr. Kapasi reluctantly headed toward a neighboring table.

"Mr. Kapasi, wait. There's room here," Mrs. Das called out. She gathered Tina onto her lap, insisting that he accompany them. And so, together, they had bottled mango juice and sandwiches and plates of onions and potatoes deep-fried in graham-flour batter. After finishing two omelette sandwiches Mr. Das took more pictures of the group as they ate.

"How much longer?" he asked Mr. Kapasi as he paused to load a new roll of film in the camera.

"About half an hour more."

By now the children had gotten up from the table to look at more monkeys perched in a nearby tree, so there was a considerable space between Mrs. Das and Mr. Kapasi. Mr. Das placed the camera to his face and squeezed one eye shut, his tongue exposed at one corner of his mouth. "This looks funny, Mina, you need to lean in closer to Mr. Kapasi."

She did. He could smell a scent on her skin, like a mixture of whiskey and rosewater. He worried suddenly that she could smell his perspiration, which he knew had collected beneath the synthetic material of his shirt. He polished off his mango juice in one gulp and smoothed his silver hair with his hands. A bit of the juice dripped onto his chin. He wondered if Mrs. Das had noticed.

She had not. "What's your address, Mr. Kapasi?" she inquired, fishing for something inside her straw bag.

"You would like my address?"

"So we can send you copies," she said. "Of the pictures." She handed him a scrap of paper which she had hastily ripped from a page of her film magazine. The blank portion was limited, for the narrow strip was crowded by lines of text and a tiny picture of a hero and heroine embracing under a eucalyptus tree.

The paper curled as Mr. Kapasi wrote his address in clear, careful letters. She would write to him, asking about his days interpreting at the doctor's office, and he would respond eloquently, choosing only the most entertaining anecdotes, ones that would make her laugh out loud as she read them in her house in New Jersey. In time she would reveal the disappointment of her marriage, and he his. In this way their friendship would grow, and flourish. He would possess a picture of the two of them, eating fried onions under a magenta umbrella, which he would keep, he decided, safely tucked between the pages of his Russian grammar. As his mind raced, Mr. Kapasi experienced a mild and pleasant shock. It was similar to a feeling he used to experience long ago when, after months of translating with the aid of a dictionary, he would finally read a passage from a French novel, or an Italian sonnet, and understand the words, one after another, unencumbered by his own efforts. In those moments Mr. Kapasi used to believe that all was right with the world, that all struggles were rewarded, that all of life's mistakes made sense in the end. The promise that he would hear from Mrs. Das now filled him with the same belief.

When he finished writing his address Mr. Kapasi handed her the paper, but as soon as he did so he worried that he had either misspelled his name, or accidentally reversed the numbers of his postal code. He dreaded the possibility of a lost letter, the photograph never reaching him, hovering somewhere in Orissa, close but ultimately unattainable. He thought of asking for the slip of paper again, just to make sure he had written his address accurately, but Mrs. Das had already dropped it into the jumble of her bag.

They reached Konarak at two-thirty. The temple, made of sandstone, was a massive pyramid-like structure in the shape of a chariot. It was dedicated to the great master of life, the sun, which struck three sides of the edifice as it made its journey each day across the sky. Twenty-four giant wheels were carved on the north and south sides of the plinth. The whole thing was drawn by a team of seven horses, speeding as if through the heavens. As they approached, Mr. Kapasi explained that the temple had been built between A.D. 1243 and 1255, with the efforts of twelve hundred artisans, by the great ruler of the Ganga dynasty, King Narasimhadeva the First, to commemorate his victory against the Muslim army.

"It says the temple occupies about a hundred and seventy acres of land," Mr. Das said, reading from his book.

"It's like a desert," Ronny said, his eyes wandering across the sand that stretched on all sides beyond the temple.

"The Chandrabhaga River once flowed one mile north of here. It is dry now," Mr. Kapasi said, turning off the engine.

95 They got out and walked toward the temple, posing first for pictures by the pair of lions that flanked the steps. Mr. Kapasi led them next to one of the wheels of the chariot, higher than any human being, nine feet in diameter.

" 'The wheels are supposed to symbolize the wheel of life,' " Mr. Das read. " 'They depict the cycle of creation, preservation, and achievement of realization.' Cool." He turned the page of his book. " 'Each wheel is divided into eight thick and thin spokes, dividing the day into eight equal parts. The rims are carved with designs of birds and animals, whereas the medallions in the spokes are carved with women in luxurious poses, largely erotic in nature.' "

What he referred to were the countless friezes of entwined naked bodies, making love in various positions, women clinging to the necks of men, their knees wrapped eternally around their lovers' thighs. In addition to these were assorted scenes from daily life, of hunting and trading, of deer being killed with bows and arrows and marching warriors holding swords in their hands.

It was no longer possible to enter the temple, for it had filled with rubble years ago, but they admired the exterior, as did all the tourists Mr. Kapasi brought there, slowly strolling along each of its sides. Mr. Das trailed behind, taking pictures. The children ran ahead, pointing to figures of naked people, intrigued in particular by the Nagamithunas, the half-human, half-serpentine couples who were said, Mr. Kapasi told them, to live in the deepest waters of the sea. Mr. Kapasi was pleased that they liked the temple, pleased especially that it appealed to Mrs. Das. She stopped every three or four paces, staring silently at the carved lovers, and the processions of elephants, and the topless female musicians beating on two-sided drums.

Though Mr. Kapasi had been to the temple countless times, it occurred to him, as he, too, gazed at the topless women, that he had never seen his own wife fully naked. Even when they had made love she kept the panels of her blouse hooked together, the string of her petticoat knotted around her waist. He had never admired the backs of his wife's legs the way he now admired those of Mrs. Das, walking as if for his benefit alone. He had, of course, seen plenty of bare limbs before, belonging to the American and European ladies who took his tours. But Mrs. Das was different. Unlike the other women, who had an interest only in the temple, and kept their noses buried in a guide-book, or their eyes behind the lens of a camera, Mrs. Das had taken an interest in him.

100 Mr. Kapasi was anxious to be alone with her, to continue their private conversation, yet he felt nervous to walk at her side. She was lost behind her sunglasses, ignoring her husband's requests that she pose for another picture, walking past her children as if they were strangers. Worried that he might disturb her, Mr. Kapasi walked ahead, to admire, as he always did, the three life-sized bronze avatars of Surya, the sun god, each emerging from its own niche on the temple facade to greet the sun at dawn, noon, and evening. They wore elaborate headdresses, their languid, elongated eyes closed, their bare chests draped with carved chains and amulets. Hibiscus petals, offerings from previous visitors, were strewn at their gray-green feet. The last statue, on the northern wall of the temple, was Mr. Kapasi's favorite. This Surya had a tired expression, weary after a hard day of work, sitting astride a horse with folded legs. Even his horse's eyes were drowsy. Around his body were smaller sculptures of women in pairs, their hips thrust to one side.

"Who's that?" Mrs. Das asked. He was startled to see that she was standing beside him.

"He is the Astachala-Surya," Mr. Kapasi said. "The setting sun."

"So in a couple of hours the sun will set right here?" She slipped a foot out of one of her square-heeled shoes, rubbed her toes on the back of her other leg.

"That is correct."

105 She raised her sunglasses for a moment, then put them back on again. "Neat."

Mr. Kapasi was not certain exactly what the word suggested, but he had a feeling it was a favorable response. He hoped that Mrs. Das had understood Surya's beauty, his power. Perhaps they would discuss it further in their letters. He would explain things to her, things about India, and she would explain things to him about America. In its own way this correspondence would fulfill his dream, of serving as an interpreter between nations. He looked at her straw bag, delighted that his address lay nestled among its contents. When he pictured her so many thousands of miles away he plummeted, so much so that he had an overwhelming urge to wrap his arms around her, to freeze with her, even for an instant, in an embrace witnessed by his favorite Surya. But Mrs. Das had already started walking.

"When do you return to America?" he asked, trying to sound placid.

"In ten days."

He calculated: A week to settle in, a week to develop the pictures, a few days to compose her letter, two weeks to get to India by air. According to his schedule, allowing room for delays, he would hear from Mrs. Das in approximately six weeks' time.

The family was silent as Mr. Kapasi drove them back, a little past four-thirty, to Hotel Sandy Villa. The children had bought miniature granite versions of the chariot's wheels at a souvenir stand, and they turned them round in their hands. Mr. Das continued to read his book. Mrs. Das untangled Tina's hair with her brush and divided it into two little ponytails.

Mr. Kapasi was beginning to dread the thought of dropping them off. He was not prepared to begin his six-week wait to hear from Mrs. Das. As he stole glances at her in the rear-view mirror, wrapping elastic bands around Tina's hair, he wondered how he might make the tour last a little longer. Ordinarily he sped back to Puri using a shortcut, eager to return home, scrub his feet and hands with sandalwood soap, and enjoy the evening newspaper and a cup of tea that his wife would serve him in silence. The thought of that silence, something to which he'd long been resigned, now oppressed him. It was then that he suggested visiting the hills at Udayagiri and Khandagiri, where a number of monastic dwellings were hewn out of the ground, facing one another across a defile. It was some miles away, but well worth seeing, Mr. Kapasi told them.

"Oh yeah, there's something mentioned about it in this book," Mr. Das said. "Built by a Jain king or something."

"Shall we go then?" Mr. Kapasi asked. He paused at a turn in the road. "It's to the left."

How might this Mandala of the sun god Surya, Mr. Kapasi's favorite figure, represent the sensuality and longing that he has for a life outside the boundaries of his job and family?

bpk, Berlin / Museum fuer Asiatische Kunst, Staatliche Museen, Berlin, Germany / Art Resource, NY

Mr. Das turned to look at Mrs. Das. Both of them shrugged.

"Left, left," the children chanted.

Mr. Kapasi turned the wheel, almost delirious with relief. He did not know what he would do or say to Mrs. Das once they arrived at the hills. Perhaps he would tell her what a pleasing smile she had. Perhaps he would compliment her strawberry shirt, which he found irresistibly becoming. Perhaps, when Mr. Das was busy taking a picture, he would take her hand.

He did not have to worry. When they got to the hills, divided by a steep path thick with trees, Mrs. Das refused to get out of the car. All along the path, dozens of monkeys were seated on stones, as well as on the branches of the trees. Their hind legs were stretched out in front and raised to shoulder level, their arms resting on their knees.

"My legs are tired," she said, sinking low in her seat. "I'll stay here."

"Why did you have to wear those stupid shoes?" Mr. Das said. "You won't be in the pictures."

"Pretend I'm there."

"But we could use one of these pictures for our Christmas card this year. We didn't get one of all five of us at the Sun Temple. Mr. Kapasi could take it."

"I'm not coming. Anyway, those monkeys give me the creeps."

"But they're harmless," Mr. Das said. He turned to Mr. Kapasi. "Aren't they?"

"They are more hungry than dangerous," Mr. Kapasi said. "Do not provoke them with food, and they will not bother you."

Mr. Das headed up the defile with the children, the boys at his side, the little girl on his shoulders. Mr. Kapasi watched as they crossed paths with a Japanese man and woman, the only other tourists there, who paused for a final photograph, then stepped into a nearby car and drove away. As the car disappeared out of view some of the monkeys called out, emitting soft whooping sounds, and then walked on their flat black hands and feet up the path. At one point a group of them formed a little ring around Mr. Das and the children. Tina screamed in delight. Ronny ran in circles around his father. Bobby bent down and picked up a fat stick on the ground. When he extended it, one of the monkeys approached him and snatched it, then briefly beat the ground.

"I'll join them," Mr. Kapasi said, unlocking the door on his side. "There is much to explain about the caves."

"No. Stay a minute," Mrs. Das said. She got out of the back seat and slipped in beside Mr. Kapasi. "Raj has his dumb book anyway." Together, through the windshield, Mrs. Das and Mr. Kapasi watched as Bobby and the monkey passed the stick back and forth between them.

"A brave little boy," Mr. Kapasi commented.

"It's not so surprising," Mrs. Das said.

"No?"

"He's not his."

"I beg your pardon?"

"Raj's. He's not Raj's son."

Mr. Kapasi felt a prickle on his skin. He reached into his shirt pocket for the small tin of lotus-oil balm he carried with him at all times, and applied it to three spots on his forehead. He knew that Mrs. Das was watching him, but he did not turn to face her. Instead he watched as the figures of Mr. Das and the children grew smaller, climbing up the steep path, pausing every now and then for a picture, surrounded by a growing number of monkeys.

"Are you surprised?" The way she put it made him choose his words with care.

"It's not the type of thing one assumes," Mr. Kapasi replied slowly. He put the tin of lotus-oil balm back in his pocket.

"No, of course not. And no one knows, of course. No one at all. I've kept it a secret for eight whole years." She looked at Mr. Kapasi, tilting her chin as if to gain a fresh perspective. "But now I've told you."

Mr. Kapasi nodded. He felt suddenly parched, and his forehead was warm and slightly numb from the balm. He considered asking Mrs. Das for a sip of water, then decided against it.

“We met when we were very young,” she said. She reached into her straw bag in search of something, then pulled out a packet of puffed rice. “Want some?”

140 “No, thank you.”

She put a fistful in her mouth, sank into the seat a little, and looked away from Mr. Kapasi, out the window on her side of the car. “We married when we were still in college. We were in high school when he proposed. We went to the same college, of course. Back then we couldn’t stand the thought of being separated, not for a day, not for a minute. Our parents were best friends who lived in the same town. My entire life I saw him every weekend, either at our house or theirs. We were sent upstairs to play together while our parents joked about our marriage. Imagine! They never caught us at anything, though in a way I think it was all more or less a setup. The things we did those Friday and Saturday nights, while our parents sat downstairs drinking tea . . . I could tell you stories, Mr. Kapasi.”

As a result of spending all her time in college with Raj, she continued, she did not make many close friends. There was no one to confide in about him at the end of a difficult day, or to share a passing thought or a worry. Her parents now lived on the other side of the world, but she had never been very close to them, anyway. After marrying so young she was overwhelmed by it all, having a child so quickly, and nursing, and warming up bottles of milk and testing their temperature against her wrist while Raj was at work, dressed in sweaters and corduroy pants, teaching his students about rocks and dinosaurs. Raj never looked cross or harried, or plump as she had become after the first baby.

Always tired, she declined invitations from her one or two college girlfriends, to have lunch or shop in Manhattan. Eventually the friends stopped calling her, so that she was left at home all day with the baby, surrounded by toys that made her trip when she walked or wince when she sat, always cross and tired. Only occasionally did they go out after Ronny was born, and even more rarely did they entertain. Raj didn’t mind; he looked forward to coming home from teaching and watching television and bouncing Ronny on his knee. She had been outraged when Raj told her that a Punjabi friend, someone whom she had once met but did not remember, would be staying with them for a week for some job interviews in the New Brunswick area.

Bobby was conceived in the afternoon, on a sofa littered with rubber teething toys, after the friend learned that a London pharmaceutical company had hired him, while Ronny cried to be freed from his playpen. She made no protest when the friend touched the small of her back as she was about to make a pot of coffee, then pulled her against his crisp navy suit. He made love to her swiftly, in silence, with an expertise she had never known, without the meaningful expressions and smiles Raj always insisted on afterward. The next day Raj drove the friend to JFK. He was married now, to a Punjabi girl, and they lived in London still, and every year they exchanged Christmas cards with Raj and Mina, each couple tucking photos of their families into the envelopes. He did not know that he was Bobby’s father. He never would.

145 “I beg your pardon, Mrs. Das, but why have you told me this information?” Mr. Kapasi asked when she had finally finished speaking, and had turned to face him once again.

“For God’s sake, stop calling me Mrs. Das. I’m twenty-eight. You probably have children my age.”

“Not quite.” It disturbed Mr. Kapasi to learn that she thought of him as a parent. The feeling he had had toward her, that had made him check his reflection in the rearview mirror as they drove, evaporated a little.

“I told you because of your talents.” She put the packet of puffed rice back into her bag without folding over the top.

“I don’t understand,” Mr. Kapasi said.

"Don't you see? For eight years I haven't been able to express this to anybody, not to friends, certainly not to Raj. He doesn't even suspect it. He thinks I'm still in love with him. Well, don't you have anything to say?"

"About what?"

"About what I've just told you. About my secret, and about how terrible it makes me feel. I feel terrible looking at my children, and at Raj, always terrible. I have terrible urges, Mr. Kapasi, to throw things away. One day I had the urge to throw everything I own out the window, the television, the children, everything. Don't you think it's unhealthy?"

He was silent.

"Mr. Kapasi, don't you have anything to say? I thought that was your job."

"My job is to give tours, Mrs. Das."

"Not that. Your other job. As an interpreter."

"But we do not face a language barrier. What need is there for an interpreter?"

"That's not what I mean. I would never have told you otherwise. Don't you realize what it means for me to tell you?"

"What does it mean?"

"It means that I'm tired of feeling so terrible all the time. Eight years, Mr. Kapasi, I've been in pain eight years. I was hoping you could help me feel better, say the right thing. Suggest some kind of remedy."

He looked at her, in her red plaid skirt and strawberry T-shirt, a woman not yet thirty, who loved neither her husband nor her children, who had already fallen out of love with life. Her confession depressed him, depressed him all the more when he thought of Mr. Das at the top of the path, Tina clinging to his shoulders, taking pictures of ancient monastic cells cut into the hills to show his students in America, unsuspecting and unaware that one of his sons was not his own. Mr. Kapasi felt insulted that Mrs. Das should ask him to interpret her common, trivial little secret. She did not resemble the patients in the doctor's office, those who came glassy-eyed and desperate, unable to sleep or breathe or urinate with ease, unable, above all, to give words to their pains. Still, Mr. Kapasi believed it was his duty to assist Mrs. Das. Perhaps he ought to tell her to confess the truth to Mr. Das. He would explain that honesty was the best policy. Honesty, surely, would help her feel better, as she'd put it. Perhaps he would offer to preside over the discussion, as a mediator. He decided to begin with the most obvious question, to get to the heart of the matter, and so he asked, "Is it really pain you feel, Mrs. Das, or is it guilt?"

She turned to him and glared, mustard oil thick on her frosty pink lips. She opened her mouth to say something, but as she glared at Mr. Kapasi some certain knowledge seemed to pass before her eyes, and she stopped. It crushed him; he knew at that moment that he was not even important enough to be properly insulted. She opened the car door and began walking up the path, wobbling a little on her square wooden heels, reaching into her straw bag to eat handfuls of puffed rice. It fell through her fingers, leaving a zigzagging trail, causing a monkey to leap down from a tree and devour the little white grains. In search of more, the monkey began to follow Mrs. Das. Others joined him, so that she was soon being followed by about half a dozen of them, their velvety tails dragging behind.

Mr. Kapasi stepped out of the car. He wanted to holler, to alert her in some way, but he worried that if she knew they were behind her, she would grow nervous. Perhaps she would lose her balance. Perhaps they would pull at her bag or her hair. He began to jog up the path, taking a fallen branch in his hand to scare away the monkeys. Mrs. Das continued walking, oblivious, trailing grains of puffed rice. Near the top of the incline, before a group of cells fronted by a row of squat stone pillars, Mr. Das was kneeling on the ground, focusing the lens of his camera. The children stood under the arcade, now hiding, now emerging from view.

"Wait for me," Mrs. Das called out. "I'm coming."

Tina jumped up and down. "Here comes Mommy!"

"Great," Mr. Das said without looking up. "Just in time. We'll get Mr. Kapasi to take a picture of the five of us."

Mr. Kapasi quickened his pace, waving his branch so that the monkeys scampered away, distracted, in another direction.

"Where's Bobby?" Mrs. Das asked when she stopped.

Mr. Das looked up from the camera. "I don't know, Ronny, where's Bobby?"

Ronny shrugged. "I thought he was right here."

"Where is he?" Mrs. Das repeated sharply. "What's wrong with all of you?"

They began calling his name, wandering up and down the path a bit. Because they were calling, they did not initially hear the boy's screams. When they found him, a little farther down the path under a tree, he was surrounded by a group of monkeys, over a dozen of them, pulling at his T-shirt with their long black fingers. The puffed rice Mrs. Das had spilled was scattered at his feet, raked over by the monkeys' hands. The boy was silent, his body frozen, swift tears running down his startled face. His bare legs were dusty and red with welts from where one of the monkeys struck him repeatedly with the stick he had given to it earlier.

"Daddy, the monkey's hurting Bobby," Tina said.

Mr. Das wiped his palms on the front of his shorts. In his nervousness he accidentally pressed the shutter on his camera; the whirring noise of the advancing film excited the monkeys, and the one with the stick began to beat Bobby

bpk, Berlin/Bayerische Staatsgemaeldesammlungen, Munich, Germany/Art Resource, NY

Gabriel Cornelius von Max titled this painting *Monkeys as Judges of Art*, but in "Interpreter of Maladies," the monkeys are judges of a different sort. **How might this crowded pack of creatures reflect the way Lahiri uses the monkeys in her story? Are they foolish, menacing, absurd, all of these combined, or something else entirely?**

DeAgostini/Getty Images

How does this photograph of the Konark Sun Temple enhance your understanding of the excursion that is the center of "Interpreter of Maladies"? Consider the ways this site might be a means to explore the collision of religious tradition and tourism or the clash between insider and outsider.

more intently. "What are we supposed to do? What if they start attacking?"

"Mr. Kapasi," Mrs. Das shrieked, noticing him standing to one side. "Do something, for God's sake, do something!"

Mr. Kapasi took his branch and shooed them away, hissing at the ones that remained, stomping his feet to scare them. The animals retreated slowly, with a measured gait, obedient but unintimidated. Mr. Kapasi gathered Bobby in his arms and brought him back to where his parents and siblings were standing. As he carried him he was tempted to whisper a secret into the boy's ear. But Bobby was stunned, and shivering with fright, his legs bleeding slightly where the stick had broken the skin. When Mr. Kapasi delivered him to his parents, Mr. Das brushed some dirt off the boy's T-shirt and put the visor on him the right way. Mrs. Das reached into her straw bag to find a bandage which she taped over the cut on his knee. Ronny offered his brother a fresh piece of gum. "He's fine. Just a little scared, right, Bobby?" Mr. Das said, patting the top of his head.

"God, let's get out of here," Mrs. Das said. She folded her arms across the strawberry on her chest. "This place gives me the creeps."

"Yeah. Back to the hotel, definitely," Mr. Das agreed.

"Poor Bobby," Mrs. Das said. "Come here a second. Let Mommy fix your hair." Again she reached into her straw bag, this time for her hairbrush, and began to run it around the edges of the translucent visor. When she whipped out the hairbrush, the slip of paper with Mr. Kapasi's address on it fluttered away in the wind. No one but Mr. Kapasi noticed. He watched as it rose, carried higher and higher by the breeze, into the trees where the monkeys now sat, solemnly observing the scene below. Mr. Kapasi observed it too, knowing that this was the picture of the Das family he would preserve forever in his mind.

[1999]

QUESTIONS FOR DISCUSSION

1. The dictionary defines *malady* as "an unwholesome or desperate condition." What are the various "maladies" in this story, and how are they represented? Pay particular attention to the contrast between the literal and figurative notions of sickness and how what constitutes a "malady" changes as the story develops.
2. What issues does Lahiri raise through her portrayal of children and the relationships between parents and children in this story? How has the death of

Mr. Kapasi's eldest son affected his relationship with his wife? At one point, Mr. Kapasi thinks that Mr. and Mrs. Das act more as "siblings" (para. 45) than parents to their children. Why does he draw that conclusion? What does that conclusion suggest about the Das family?

3. "Interpreter of Maladies" explores the impact of immigration, including the result of an imagined rather than an experienced homeland. How does the Das family imagine India? Why does Lahiri emphasize the taking of photographs during the family's vacation?

4. What do we normally think of when considering the job of an "interpreter"? How does Mr. Kapasi's job at the infirmary expand this definition? Why does he view that job as "a thankless occupation," "a sign of his failings" (paras. 76–77)?

5. After Mr. Kapasi asks Mrs. Das if she is feeling pain or guilt, Lahiri writes, "She turned to him and glared, mustard oil thick on her frosty pink lips. She opened her mouth to say something, but as she glared at Mr. Kapasi some certain knowledge seemed to pass before her eyes, and she stopped" (para. 162). What is Lahiri's attitude toward Mrs. Das at this juncture? What is the "certain knowledge" she realizes?

6. Trace the changes in Mr. Kapasi and Mrs. Das's relationship. How do her responses to her own family mirror shifts in her relationship to Mr. Kapasi? How do you interpret the ending of the story? Were you expecting it? What does the final sentence mean: "Mr. Kapasi observed it too, knowing that this was the picture of the Das family he would preserve forever in his mind" (para. 179)?

7. What is the moral responsibility of Mrs. Das? Should she tell her husband that Bobby is not his biological child? Should she tell the biological father? Should she tell Bobby? Do you sympathize with Mrs. Das when she tells Mr. Kapasi that she has "been in pain eight years" (para. 160)? In what ways has her silence been a kind of punishment for her?

8. Why does Lahiri choose the Sun Temple at Konarak as the central setting for her story? Research this sacred monument to learn more about it, including the sun god Surya. How does the information you learn add to your understanding of Lahiri's choice? Why do you think she chose this temple rather than a more famous one (to westerners, at least), such as the Taj Mahal?

QUESTIONS ON STYLE AND STRUCTURE

1. In the opening paragraph, Lahiri takes the reader right into the action and introduces all three major characters. What impression do the details she chooses give?

2. Lahiri provides physical descriptions of characters, particularly their clothing, in elaborate detail. What do these descriptions say about each of them? Pay particular attention to the carefully tailored suit Mr. Kapasi wears and to Mrs. Das's outfit. (Why, for instance, does Lahiri describe her wearing her sunglasses "on top of her head like a tiara" [para. 61] and having "small hands like paws" [para. 14]?)

3. Why does Lahiri begin accumulating details about language from the very beginning? We learn that Mr. Kapasi speaks English, he helps the doctor with patients who speak Gujarati, he finds it "strange" (para. 13) that Mr. Das refers to his wife by her first name to his children. Identify other examples throughout the story. What point is Lahiri making with these details?

4. How does Lahiri's description of the Sun Temple function in the story (para. 91)? Note that she begins by providing background information, shows her characters interacting, and describes the temple as being "filled with rubble years ago" (para. 98).

5. How does Lahiri use Mr. Kapasi's dreams and imaginings to develop his character? Why does his dream "of being an interpreter for diplomats and dignitaries, resolving conflicts between people and nations" (para. 77) seem sad — or does it? Pay special attention to his fantasies about Mrs. Das, such as the paragraph beginning, "The paper curled as Mr. Kapasi wrote his address in clear, careful letters. She would write to him . . ." (para. 89), and his calculations about how long it would be before he received her first letter (para. 109).

6. Dramatic irony is created when a reader knows something that the characters in the story do not; thus, some of the words and actions in a story would have a different meaning for the reader than they do for the characters. For example, once we learn of Mr. Kapasi's hope for a relationship with Mrs. Das (para. 89), his actions take on a different meaning for us than for her. Identify several other

examples of dramatic irony in the story, and discuss their effect on Lahiri's tone.

7. Photographs capture a moment in time and preserve it for record and reflection; we usually think of personal and family photos as positive. How does Lahiri's use of photographs contribute to the development of her theme(s)?

8. The final dramatic scene with the monkeys is a complex one, involving interaction among all the characters. What role does each character play through both words and action? As a reader, did you ever feel that something dreadful was about to happen? What is Lahiri's purpose in presenting the scene as she does?

9. The story is divided into three sections. If you think of each section as a chapter, how would you describe these divisions? What is Lahiri's purpose in making these divisions rather than telling the story as one continuous narrative?

10. The story touches on the past, present, and future (especially in the fantasy life of Mr. Kapasi) of all three central characters. Instead of presenting these as sequential narratives, however, Lahiri interweaves them. What is the effect of this technique?

SUGGESTIONS FOR WRITING

1. Discuss the difficulty of meaningful communication as a theme of "Interpreter of Maladies," specifically the interpretations and misinterpretations that occur during the course of the story. Consider the role that cultural differences, immigration and assimilation, and the dynamics of relationships play in hindering communication.

2. Even at middle age, Mr. Kapasi does not have a clear identity. Discuss the conflicts within his life, both internal and external, that contribute to his shifting and uncertain sense of who he is and where he belongs.

3. Write an essay characterizing the tone of this story. Pay particular attention to how Lahiri uses descriptive detail, dialogue, and visual images to develop tone.

4. In paragraphs 76–80, Lahiri describes Mr. Kapasi's musings after Mrs. Das tells him that she finds his job as an interpreter between a physician and his patients "romantic" and "a big responsibility." Write an essay analyzing the literary techniques Lahiri uses in these paragraphs to characterize Mr. Kapasi.

5. Lahiri has described the short story as "a middle ground between poetry and the novel" because it has "purity and intensity," "a ruthless distilled quality," "a compression and concentration that is akin to poetry." Discuss how these characteristics apply to "Interpreter of Maladies," specifically how the language of this short story is similar to what we associate with poetry.

6. *Diaspora* is a term that originally referred to the scattered Jewish community after the Babylonian exile (587 B.C.E.) and later to the Christians dispersed across the Greco-Roman world in the first century C.E. Today we use it more generally to refer to the movement, migration, or scattering of people from their original homelands. Discuss "Interpreter of Maladies" as a story about the struggle of being part of a diaspora in the late twentieth century.

7. During the story, we learn details about Mrs. Kapasi from her husband's perspective. According to Mr. Kapasi, theirs was "a bad match" (para. 79). His wife never asks him about his patients or says that his job is "a big responsibility" (para. 78). She serves him his evening cup of tea "in silence" (para. 111). We are given these bits of information, but we never get to see things from her point of view. Let her speak! Write a description of Mr. Kapasi in the voice of his wife.

8. Watch *The Namesake* (PG-13), and discuss the similar concerns found in that film and "Interpreter of Maladies." Pay particular attention to the clash of traditional culture and contemporary values, the responsibility of one generation to preserve and communicate its traditional culture to another, the role of women, and the relationship between parents and children.

Heart of Darkness

JOSEPH CONRAD

Corbis

Born Józef Teodor Konrad Walecz Korzeniowski to Polish parents living in the Russian-occupied Ukraine, Joseph Conrad (1857–1924) is considered one of the finest British writers. In addition to the novella *Heart of Darkness,* his most famous works include the novels *Lord Jim* (1900), *Nostromo* (1904), and *The Secret Agent* (1907). Remarkably, Conrad only became fluent in English in his twenties. After the death of his parents when he was nine, Conrad was raised and supported by a maternal uncle in Krakow. At seventeen — to avoid conscription into the Russian army — he joined the French merchant marines and began a fifteen-year career as a seaman. His travels and experiences with the French and later British Merchant Navy provided material for many stories and novels. In 1889, Conrad served as captain for a steamboat traveling up the Congo River, fulfilling his childhood wish to visit Africa. Much of what Conrad witnessed on this journey is reflected in *Heart of Darkness*, and like Marlow, he contracted an illness in Africa that affected him for the remainder of his life. *Heart of Darkness* was written in 1899 and first appeared in serial form. In 1902, the entire work was published in *Youth: A Narrative with Two Other Stories.*

1

The *Nellie*, a cruising yawl, swung to her anchor without a flutter of the sails, and was at rest. The flood had made, the wind was nearly calm, and being bound down the river, the only thing for it was to come to and wait for the turn of the tide.

The sea-reach of the Thames stretched before us like the beginning of an interminable waterway. In the offing[1] the sea and the sky were welded together without a joint, and in the luminous space the tanned sails of the barges drifting up with the tide seemed to stand still in red clusters of canvas sharply peaked, with gleams of varnished sprits.[2] A haze rested on the low shores that ran out to sea in vanishing flatness. The air was dark above Gravesend, and farther back still seemed condensed into a mournful gloom, brooding motionless over the biggest, and the greatest, town on earth.

The Director of Companies was our captain and our host. We four affectionately watched his back as he stood in the bows looking to seaward. On the whole river there was nothing that looked half so nautical. He resembled a pilot, which to a seaman is trustworthiness personified. It was difficult to realize his work was not out there in the luminous estuary, but behind him, within the brooding gloom.

Between us there was, as I have already said somewhere, the bond of the sea. Besides holding our hearts together through long periods of separation, it had the effect of making us tolerant of each other's yarns — and even convictions. The Lawyer — the best of old fellows — had, because of his many years and many virtues, the only cushion on deck, and was lying on the

[1] At a distance, but within sight. — EDS.

[2] Poles that are part of the mast assembly. — EDS.

only rug. The Accountant had brought out already a box of dominoes, and was toying architecturally with the bones. Marlow sat cross-legged right aft, leaning against the mizzen-mast. He had sunken cheeks, a yellow complexion, a straight back, an ascetic aspect, and, with his arms dropped, the palms of hands outwards, resembled an idol. The director, satisfied the anchor had good hold, made his way aft and sat down amongst us. We exchanged a few words lazily. Afterwards there was silence on board the yacht. For some reason or other we did not begin that game of dominoes. We felt meditative, and fit for nothing but placid staring. The day was ending in a serenity of still and exquisite brilliance. The water shone pacifically; the sky, without a speck, was a benign immensity of unstained light; the very mist on the Essex marshes was like a gauzy and radiant fabric, hung from the wooded rises inland, and draping the low shores in diaphanous folds. Only the gloom to the west, brooding over the upper reaches, became more sombre every minute, as if angered by the approach of the sun.

5 And at last, in its curved and imperceptible fall, the sun sank low, and from glowing white changed to a dull red without rays and without heat, as if about to go out suddenly, stricken to death by the touch of that gloom brooding over a crowd of men.

Forthwith a change came over the waters, and the serenity became less brilliant but more profound. The old river in its broad reach rested unruffled at the decline of day, after ages of good service done to the race that peopled its banks, spread out in the tranquil dignity of a waterway leading to the uttermost ends of the earth. We looked at the venerable stream not in the vivid flush of a short day that comes and departs for ever, but in the august light of abiding memories. And indeed nothing is easier for a man who has, as the phrase goes, "followed the sea" with reverence and affection, than to evoke the great spirit of the past upon the lower reaches of the Thames. The tidal current runs to and fro in its unceasing service, crowded with memories of men and ships it had borne to the rest of home or to the battles of the sea. It had known and served all the men of whom the nation is proud, from Sir Francis Drake[3] to Sir John Franklin,[4] knights all, titled and untitled — the great knights-errant of the sea. It had borne all the ships whose names are like jewels flashing in the night of time, from the *Golden Hind*[5] returning with her round flanks full of treasure, to be visited by the Queen's Highness and thus pass out of the gigantic tale, to the *Erebus* and *Terror*,[6] bound on other conquests — and that never returned. It had known the ships and the men. They had sailed from Deptford, from Greenwich, from Erith — the adventurers and the settlers; kings' ships and the ships of men on 'Change; captains, admirals, the dark "interlopers" of the Eastern trade, and the commissioned "generals" of East India fleets. Hunters for gold or pursuers of fame, they all had gone out on that stream, bearing the sword, and often the torch, messengers of the might within the land, bearers of a spark from the sacred fire. What greatness had not floated on the ebb of that river into the mystery of an unknown earth! . . . The dreams of men, the seed of commonwealths, the germs of empires.

The sun set; the dusk fell on the stream, and lights began to appear along the shore. The Chapman lighthouse, a three-legged thing erect on a mud-flat, shone strongly. Lights of ships moved in the fairway — a great stir of lights going up and going down. And farther west on the upper reaches the place of the monstrous town was still marked ominously on the sky, a

[3] Sir Francis Drake (1540–1596), English captain famous for defeating the Spanish Armada and sailing around the world. — EDS.

[4] Sir John Franklin (1786–1847), English naval officer who charted portions of the Arctic and died searching for the Northwest Passage. — EDS.

[5] Sir Francis Drake's ship. — EDS.

[6] Sir John Franklin's ships, lost in the Arctic. — EDS.

brooding gloom in sunshine, a lurid glare under the stars.

"And this also," said Marlow suddenly, "has been one of the dark places of the earth."

He was the only man of us who still "followed the sea." The worst that could be said of him was that he did not represent his class. He was a seaman, but he was a wanderer, too, while most seamen lead, if one may so express it, a sedentary life. Their minds are of the stay-at-home order, and their home is always with them — the ship; and so is their country — the sea. One ship is very much like another, and the sea is always the same. In the immutability of their surroundings the foreign shores, the foreign faces, the changing immensity of life, glide past, veiled not by a sense of mystery but by a slightly disdainful ignorance; for there is nothing mysterious to a seaman unless it be the sea itself, which is the mistress of his existence and as inscrutable as Destiny. For the rest, after his hours of work, a casual stroll or a casual spree on shore suffices to unfold for him the secret of a whole continent, and generally he finds the secret not worth knowing. The yarns of seamen have a direct simplicity, the whole meaning of which lies within the shell of a cracked nut. But Marlow was not typical (if his propensity to spin yarns be excepted), and to him the meaning of an episode was not inside like a kernel but outside, enveloping the tale which brought it out only as a glow brings out a haze, in the likeness of one of these misty halos that sometimes are made visible by the spectral illumination of moonshine.

10 His remark did not seem at all surprising. It was just like Marlow. It was accepted in silence. No one took the trouble to grunt even; and presently he said, very slow —

"I was thinking of very old times, when the Romans first came here, nineteen hundred years ago — the other day. . . . Light came out of this river since — you say Knights? Yes; but it is like a running blaze on a plain, like a flash of lightning in the clouds. We live in the flicker — may it last as long as the old earth keeps rolling! But darkness was here yesterday. Imagine the feelings of a commander of a fine — what d'ye call 'em? — trireme in the Mediterranean, ordered suddenly to the north; run overland across the Gauls in a hurry; put in charge of one of these craft the legionaries — a wonderful lot of handy men they must have been, too — used to build, apparently by the hundred, in a month or two, if we may believe what we read. Imagine him here — the very end of the world, a sea the colour of lead, a sky the colour of smoke, a kind of ship about as rigid as a concertina[7] — and going up this river with stores, or orders, or what you like. Sand-banks, marshes, forests, savages, — precious little to eat fit for a civilized man, nothing but Thames water to drink. No Falernian wine here, no going ashore. Here and there a military camp lost in a wilderness, like a needle in a bundle of hay — cold, fog, tempests, disease, exile, and death, — death skulking in the air, in the water, in the bush. They must have been dying like flies here. Oh, yes — he did it. Did it very well, too, no doubt, and without thinking much about it either, except afterwards to brag of what he had gone through in his time, perhaps. They were men enough to face the darkness. And perhaps he was cheered by keeping his eye on a chance of promotion to the fleet at Ravenna by and by, if he had good friends in Rome and survived the awful climate. Or think of a decent young citizen in a toga — perhaps too much dice, you know — coming out here in the train of some prefect, or tax-gatherer, or trader even, to mend his fortunes. Land in a swamp, march through the woods, and in some inland post feel the savagery, the utter savagery, had closed round him, — all that mysterious life of the wilderness that stirs in the forest, in the jungles, in the hearts of wild men. There's no initiation either into such mysteries. He has to

[7] Small accordion. — EDS.

live in the midst of the incomprehensible, which is also detestable. And it has a fascination, too, that goes to work upon him. The fascination of the abomination — you know, imagine the growing regrets, the longing to escape, the powerless disgust, the surrender, the hate."

He paused.

"Mind," he began again, lifting one arm from the elbow, the palm of the hand outwards, so that, with his legs folded before him, he had the pose of a Buddha preaching in European clothes and without a lotus-flower — "Mind, none of us would feel exactly like this. What saves us is efficiency — the devotion to efficiency. But these chaps were not much account, really. They were no colonists; their administration was merely a squeeze, and nothing more, I suspect. They were conquerors, and for that you want only brute force — nothing to boast of, when you have it, since your strength is just an accident arising from the weakness of others. They grabbed what they could get for the sake of what was to be got. It was just robbery with violence, aggravated murder on a great scale, and men going at it blind — as is very proper for those who tackle a darkness. The conquest of the earth, which mostly means the taking it away from those who have a different complexion or slightly flatter noses than ourselves, is not a pretty thing when you look into it too much. What redeems it is the idea only. An idea at the back of it; not a sentimental pretence but an idea; and an unselfish belief in the idea — something you can set up, and bow down before, and offer a sacrifice to. . . ."

He broke off. Flames glided in the river, small green flames, red flames, white flames, pursuing, overtaking, joining, crossing each other — then separating slowly or hastily. The traffic of the great city went on in the deepening night upon the sleepless river. We looked on, waiting patiently — there was nothing else to do till the end of the flood; but it was only after a long silence, when he said, in a hesitating voice, "I suppose you fellows remember I did once turn fresh-water sailor for a bit," that we knew we were fated, before the ebb began to run, to hear about one of Marlow's inconclusive experiences.

"I don't want to bother you much with what happened to me personally," he began, showing in this remark the weakness of many tellers of tales who seem so often unaware of what their audience would best like to hear; "yet to understand the effect of it on me you ought to know how I got out there, what I saw, how I went up that river to the place where I first met the poor chap. It was the farthest point of navigation and the culminating point of my experience. It seemed somehow to throw a kind of light on everything about me — and into my thoughts. It was sombre enough, too — and pitiful — not extraordinary in any way — not very clear either. No, not very clear. And yet it seemed to throw a kind of light.

"I had then, as you remember, just returned to London after a lot of Indian Ocean, Pacific, China Seas — a regular dose of the East — six years or so, and I was loafing about, hindering you fellows in your work and invading your homes, just as though I had got a heavenly mission to civilize you. It was very fine for a time, but after a bit I did get tired of resting. Then I began to look for a ship — I should think the hardest work on earth. But the ships wouldn't even look at me. And I got tired of that game, too.

"Now when I was a little chap I had a passion for maps. I would look for hours at South America, or Africa, or Australia, and lose myself in all the glories of exploration. At that time there were many blank spaces on the earth, and when I saw one that looked particularly inviting on a map (but they all look that) I would put my finger on it and say, When I grow up I will go there. The North Pole was one of these places, I remember. Well, I haven't been there yet, and shall not try now. The glamour's off.

Other places were scattered about the Equator, and in every sort of latitude all over the two hemispheres. I have been in some of them, and . . . well, we won't talk about that. But there was one yet — the biggest, the most blank, so to speak — that I had a hankering after.

"True, by this time it was not a blank space any more. It had got filled since my boyhood with rivers and lakes and names. It had ceased to be a blank space of delightful mystery — a white patch for a boy to dream gloriously over. It had become a place of darkness. But there was in it one river especially, a mighty big river, that you could see on the map, resembling an immense snake uncoiled, with its head in the sea, its body at rest curving afar over a vast country, and its tail lost in the depths of the land. And as I looked at the map of it in a shop-window, it fascinated me as a snake would a bird — a silly little bird. Then I remembered there was a big concern, a Company for trade on that river. Dash it all! I thought to myself, they can't trade without using some kind of craft on that lot of fresh water — steamboats! Why shouldn't I try to get charge of one? I went on along Fleet Street, but could not shake off the idea. The snake had charmed me.

"You understand it was a Continental concern, that Trading society; but I have a lot of relations living on the Continent, because it's cheap and not so nasty as it looks, they say.

"I am sorry to own I began to worry them. This was already a fresh departure for me. I was not used to get things that way, you know. I always went my own road and on my own legs where I had a mind to go. I wouldn't have believed it of myself; but, then — you see — I felt somehow I must get there by hook or by crook. So I worried them. The men said 'My dear fellow,' and did nothing. Then — would you believe it? — I tried the women. I, Charlie Marlow, set the women to work — to get a job. Heavens! Well, you see, the notion drove me. I had an aunt, a dear enthusiastic soul. She wrote: 'It will be delightful. I am ready to do anything, anything for you. It is a glorious idea. I know the wife of a very high personage in the Administration, and also a man who has lots of influence with,' etc., etc. She was determined to make no end of fuss to get me appointed skipper of a river steamboat, if such was my fancy.

"I got my appointment — of course; and I got it very quick. It appears the Company had received news that one of their captains had been killed in a scuffle with the natives. This was my chance, and it made me the more anxious to go. It was only months and months afterwards, when I made the attempt to recover what was left of the body, that I heard the original quarrel arose from a misunderstanding about some hens. Yes, two black hens. Fresleven — that was the fellow's name, a Dane — thought himself wronged somehow in the bargain, so he went ashore and started to hammer the chief of the village with a stick. Oh, it didn't surprise me in the least to hear this, and at the same time to be told that Fresleven was the gentlest, quietest creature that ever walked on two legs. No doubt he was; but he had been a couple of years already out there engaged in the noble cause, you know, and he probably felt the need at last of asserting his self-respect in some way. Therefore he whacked the old nigger mercilessly, while a big crowd of his people watched him, thunderstruck, till some man — I was told the chief's son — in desperation at hearing the old chap yell, made a tentative jab with a spear at the white man — and of course it went quite easy between the shoulder-blades. Then the whole population cleared into the forest, expecting all kinds of calamities to happen, while, on the other hand, the steamer Fresleven commanded left also in a bad panic, in charge of the engineer, I believe. Afterwards nobody seemed to trouble much about Fresleven's remains, till I got out and stepped into his shoes. I couldn't let it rest, though; but when an opportunity offered at last to meet my predecessor, the grass growing through his ribs was tall enough to hide his bones. They were all there. The supernatural being had not been touched after he fell. And the village was deserted, the huts gaped black, rotting, all askew within the fallen enclosures. A calamity had come to it, sure enough. The people had vanished. Mad terror had scattered them, men, women, and children, through the bush, and they had never returned. What became of the hens I don't know either. I should think the cause of progress got them, anyhow. However, through this glorious affair I got my appointment, before I had fairly begun to hope for it.

"I flew around like mad to get ready, and before forty-eight hours I was crossing the Channel to show myself to my employers, and sign the contract. In a very few hours I arrived in a city that always makes me think of a whited sepulchre.[8] Prejudice no doubt. I had no difficulty in finding the Company's offices. It was the biggest thing in the town, and everybody I met was full of it. They were going to run an over-sea empire, and make no end of coin by trade.

"A narrow and deserted street in deep shadow, high houses, innumerable windows with venetian blinds, a dead silence, grass sprouting between the stones, imposing carriage archways right and left, immense double doors standing ponderously ajar. I slipped through one of these cracks, went up a swept and ungarnished staircase, as arid as a desert, and opened the first door I came to. Two women, one fat and the other slim, sat on straw-bottomed chairs, knitting black wool. The slim one got up and walked straight at me — still knitting with downcast eyes — and only just as I began to think of getting out of her way, as you would for a somnambulist,[9] stood still, and looked up. Her dress was as plain as an umbrella-cover, and she turned round without a word and preceded me into a waiting-room. I gave my name, and looked about. Deal table in the middle, plain chairs all round the walls, on one end a large shining map, marked with all the colours of a rainbow. There was a vast amount of red — good to see at any time, because one knows that some real work is done in there, a deuce[10] of a lot of blue, a little green, smears of orange, and, on the East Coast, a purple patch, to show where the jolly pioneers of progress drink the jolly lager-beer. However, I wasn't going into any of these. I was going into the yellow. Dead in the centre. And the river was there — fascinating — deadly — like a snake. Ough! A door opened, a white-haired secretarial head, but wearing a compassionate expression, appeared, and a skinny forefinger beckoned me into the sanctuary. Its light was dim, and a heavy writing-desk squatted in the middle. From behind that structure came out an impression of pale plumpness in a frock-coat. The great man himself. He was five feet six, I should judge, and had his grip on the handle-end of ever so many millions. He shook hands, I fancy, murmured vaguely, was satisfied with my French. *Bon voyage.*

"In about forty-five seconds I found myself again in the waiting-room with the compassionate secretary, who, full of desolation and sympathy, made me sign some document. I believe I undertook amongst other things not to disclose any trade secrets. Well, I am not going to.

"I began to feel slightly uneasy. You know I am not used to such ceremonies, and there was something ominous in the atmosphere. It was just as though I had been let into some conspiracy — I don't know — something not quite right; and I was glad to get out. In the outer room the two women knitted black wool feverishly. People were arriving, and the younger one was walking back and forth introducing them. The old one sat on her chair. Her flat cloth slippers were propped up on a foot-warmer, and a

[8] Crypt, tomb, mausoleum. — EDS.

[9] Sleepwalker. — EDS.

[10] Mild word for devil. — EDS.

cat reposed on her lap. She wore a starched white affair on her head, had a wart on one cheek, and silver-rimmed spectacles hung on the tip of her nose. She glanced at me above the glasses. The swift and indifferent placidity of that look troubled me. Two youths with foolish and cheery countenances were being piloted over, and she threw at them the same quick glance of unconcerned wisdom. She seemed to know all about them and about me, too. An eerie feeling came over me. She seemed uncanny and fateful. Often far away there I thought of these two, guarding the door of Darkness, knitting black wool as for a warm pall, one introducing, introducing continuously to the unknown, the other scrutinizing the cheery and foolish faces with unconcerned old eyes. *Ave*![11] Old knitter of black wool. *Morituri te salutant*.[12] Not many of those she looked at ever saw her again — not half, by a long way.

"There was yet a visit to the doctor. 'A simple formality,' assured me the secretary, with an air of taking an immense part in all my sorrows. Accordingly a young chap wearing his hat over the left eyebrow, some clerk I suppose, — there must have been clerks in the business, though the house was as still as a house in a city of the dead — came from somewhere upstairs, and led me forth. He was shabby and careless, with ink-stains on the sleeves of his jacket, and his cravat was large and billowy, under a chin shaped like the toe of an old boot. It was a little too early for the doctor, so I proposed a drink, and thereupon he developed a vein of joviality. As we sat over our vermouths he glorified the Company's business, and by and by I expressed casually my surprise at him not going out there. He became very cool and collected all at once. 'I am not such a fool as I look, quoth Plato to his disciples,' he said sententiously, emptied his glass with great resolution, and we rose.

"The old doctor felt my pulse, evidently thinking of something else the while. 'Good, good for there,' he mumbled, and then with a certain eagerness asked me whether I would let him measure my head. Rather surprised, I said Yes, when he produced a thing like calipers and got the dimensions back and front and every way, taking notes carefully. He was an unshaven little man in a threadbare coat like a gaberdine, with his feet in slippers, and I thought him a harmless fool. 'I always ask leave, in the interests of science, to measure the crania of those going out there,' he said. 'And when they come back, too?' I asked. 'Oh, I never see them,' he remarked; 'and, moreover, the changes take place inside, you know.' He smiled, as if at some quiet joke. 'So you are going out there. Famous. Interesting, too.' He gave me a searching glance, and made another note. 'Ever any madness in your family?' he asked, in a matter-of-fact tone. I felt very annoyed. 'Is that question in the interests of science, too?' 'It would be,' he said, without taking notice of my irritation, 'interesting for science to watch the mental changes of individuals, on the spot, but . . .' 'Are you an alienist?' I interrupted. 'Every doctor should be — a little,' answered that original, imperturbably. 'I have a little theory which you Messieurs who go out there must help me to prove. This is my share in the advantages my country shall reap from the possession of such a magnificent dependency. The mere wealth I leave to others. Pardon my questions, but you are the first Englishman coming under my observation . . .' I hastened to assure him I was not in the least typical. 'If I were,' said I, 'I wouldn't be talking like this with you.' 'What you say is rather profound, and probably erroneous,' he said, with a laugh. 'Avoid irritation more than exposure to the sun. Adieu. How do you English say, eh? Good-bye. Ah! Good-bye. Adieu. In the tropics one must before everything keep calm.' . . . He lifted a warning forefinger. . . . '*Du calme, du calme. Adieu.*'

[11] Latin: "Hail!" — EDS.

[12] Latin: "We who are about to die salute you." — EDS.

"One thing more remained to do — say goodbye to my excellent aunt. I found her triumphant. I had a cup of tea — the last decent cup of tea for many days — and in a room that most soothingly looked just as you would expect a lady's drawing-room to look, we had a long quiet chat by the fireside. In the course of these confidences it became quite plain to me I had been represented to the wife of the high dignitary, and goodness knows to how many more people besides, as an exceptional and gifted creature — a piece of good fortune for the Company — a man you don't get hold of every day. Good heavens! and I was going to take charge of a two-penny-half-penny river-steamboat with a penny whistle attached! It appeared, however, I was also one of the Workers, with a capital — you know. Something like an emissary of light, something like a lower sort of apostle. There had been a lot of such rot let loose in print and talk just about that time, and the excellent woman, living right in the rush of all that humbug, got carried off her feet. She talked about 'weaning those ignorant millions from their horrid ways,' till, upon my word, she made me quite uncomfortable. I ventured to hint that the Company was run for profit.

"'You forget, dear Charlie, that the labourer is worthy of his hire,' she said, brightly. It's queer how out of touch with truth women are. They live in a world of their own, and there has never been anything like it, and never can be. It is too beautiful altogether, and if they were to set it up it would go to pieces before the first sunset. Some confounded fact we men have been living contentedly with ever since the day of creation would start up and knock the whole thing over.

"After this I got embraced, told to wear flannel, be sure to write often, and so on — and I left. In the street — I don't know why — a queer feeling came to me that I was an impostor. Odd thing that I, who used to clear out for any part of the world at twenty-four hours' notice, with less thought than most men give to the crossing of a street, had a moment — I won't say of hesitation, but of startled pause, before this commonplace affair. The best way I can explain it to you is by saying that, for a second or two, I felt as though, instead of going to the centre of a continent, I were about to set off for the centre of the earth.

"I left in a French steamer, and she called in every blamed port they have out there, for, as far as I could see, the sole purpose of landing soldiers and custom-house officers. I watched the coast. Watching a coast as it slips by the ship is like thinking about an enigma. There it is before you — smiling, frowning, inviting, grand, mean, insipid, or savage, and always mute with an air of whispering, Come and find out. This one was almost featureless, as if still in the making, with an aspect of monotonous grimness. The edge of a colossal jungle, so dark-green as to be almost black, fringed with white surf, ran straight, like a ruled line, far, far away along a blue sea whose glitter was blurred by a creeping mist. The sun was fierce, the land seemed to glisten and drip with steam. Here and there grayish-whitish specks showed up clustered inside the white surf, with a flag flying above them perhaps. Settlements some centuries old, and still no bigger than pinheads on the untouched expanse of their background. We pounded along, stopped, landed soldiers; went on, landed custom-house clerks to levy toll in what looked like a God-forsaken wilderness, with a tin shed and a flag-pole lost in it; landed more soldiers — to take care of the custom-house clerks, presumably. Some, I heard, got drowned in the surf; but whether they did or not, nobody seemed particularly to care. They were just flung out there, and on we went. Every day the coast looked the same, as though we had not moved; but we passed various places — trading places — with names like Gran' Bassam, Little Popo; names that seemed to belong to some sordid farce acted in front of a sinister back-cloth. The idleness of a passenger, my isolation amongst all these men with whom I had no point of contact, the oily and languid sea,

What is most striking to you about this 1907 photograph of soldiers in the Belgian Congo? In what ways does it reflect the relationship between European and African societies as depicted in *Heart of Darkness*?

the uniform sombreness of the coast, seemed to keep me away from the truth of things, within the toil of a mournful and senseless delusion. The voice of the surf heard now and then was a positive pleasure, like the speech of a brother. It was something natural, that had its reason, that had a meaning. Now and then a boat from the shore gave one a momentary contact with reality. It was paddled by black fellows. You could see from afar the white of their eyeballs glistening. They shouted, sang; their bodies streamed with perspiration; they had faces like grotesque masks — these chaps; but they had bone, muscle, a wild vitality, an intense energy of movement, that was as natural and true as the surf along their coast. They wanted no excuse for being there. They were a great comfort to look at. For a time I would feel I belonged still to a world of straightforward facts; but the feeling would not last long. Something would turn up to scare it away. Once, I remember, we came upon a man-of-war anchored off the coast. There wasn't even a shed there, and she was shelling the bush. It appears the French had one of their wars going on thereabouts. Her ensign dropped limp like a rag; the muzzles of the long six-inch guns stuck out all over the low hull; the greasy, slimy swell swung her up lazily and let her down, swaying her thin masts. In the empty immensity of earth, sky, and water, there she was, incomprehensible, firing into a continent. Pop, would go one of the six-inch guns; a small flame would dart and vanish, a little white smoke would disappear, a tiny projectile would give a feeble screech — and nothing happened. Nothing could happen. There was a touch of insanity in the proceeding, a sense of lugubrious drollery in the sight; and it was not dissipated by somebody on board assuring me earnestly there was a camp of natives — he called them enemies! — hidden out of sight somewhere.

"We gave her her letters (I heard the men in that lonely ship were dying of fever at the rate of three a day) and went on. We called at some more places with farcical names, where the merry dance of death and trade goes on in a still and earthy atmosphere as of an overheated catacomb; all along the formless coast bordered by dangerous surf, as if Nature herself had tried to ward off intruders; in and out of rivers, streams of death in life, whose banks were rotting into mud, whose waters, thickened into slime, invaded the contorted mangroves, that seemed to writhe at us in the extremity of an impotent despair. Nowhere did we stop long enough to get a particularized impression, but the general sense of vague and oppressive wonder grew upon me. It was like a weary pilgrimage amongst hints for nightmares.

"It was upward of thirty days before I saw the mouth of the big river. We anchored off the seat of the government. But my work would not begin till some two hundred miles farther on. So as soon as I could I made a start for a place thirty miles higher up.

"I had my passage on a little sea-going steamer. Her captain was a Swede, and knowing me for a seaman, invited me on the bridge. He was a young man, lean, fair, and morose, with lanky hair and a shuffling gait. As we left the miserable little wharf, he tossed his head contemptuously at the shore. 'Been living there?' he asked. I said, 'Yes.' 'Fine lot these government chaps — are they not?' he went on, speaking English with great precision and considerable bitterness. 'It is funny what some people will do for a few francs a month. I wonder what becomes of that kind when it goes up country?' I said to him I expected to see that soon. 'So-o-o!' he exclaimed. He shuffled athwart, keeping one eye ahead vigilantly. 'Don't be too sure,' he continued. 'The other day I took up a man who hanged himself on the road. He was a Swede, too.' 'Hanged himself! Why, in God's name?' I cried. He kept on looking out watchfully. 'Who knows? The sun too much for him, or the country perhaps.'

"At last we opened a reach. A rocky cliff appeared, mounds of turned-up earth by the shore, houses on a hill, others with iron roofs, amongst a waste of excavations, or hanging to the declivity. A continuous noise of the rapids above hovered over this scene of inhabited devastation. A lot of people, mostly black and naked, moved about like ants. A jetty projected into the river. A blinding sunlight drowned all this at times in a sudden recrudescence of glare. 'There's your Company's station,' said the Swede, pointing to three wooden barrack-like structures on the rocky slope. 'I will send your things up. Four boxes did you say? So. Farewell.'

"I came upon a boiler wallowing in the grass, then found a path leading up the hill. It turned aside for the boulders, and also for an under-sized railway-truck lying there on its back with its wheels in the air. One was off. The thing looked as dead as the carcass of some animal. I came upon more pieces of decaying machinery, a stack of rusty rails. To the left a clump of trees made a shady spot, where dark things seemed to stir feebly. I blinked, the path was steep. A horn tooted to the right, and I saw the black people run. A heavy and dull detonation shook the ground, a puff of smoke came out of the cliff, and that was all. No change appeared on the face of the rock. They were building a railway. The cliff was not in the way or anything; but this objectless blasting was all the work going on.

"A slight clinking behind me made me turn my head. Six black men advanced in a file, toiling up the path. They walked erect and slow, balancing small baskets full of earth on their heads, and the clink kept time with their footsteps. Black rags were wound round their loins, and the short ends behind waggled to and fro like tails. I could see every rib, the joints of their limbs were like knots in a rope; each had an iron collar on his neck, and all were connected together with a chain whose bights[13] swung between them, rhythmically clinking. Another report from the cliff made me think suddenly of that ship of war I had seen firing into a continent. It was the same kind of ominous voice; but these men could by no stretch of imagination be called enemies. They were called criminals, and the outraged law, like the bursting shells, had come to them, an insoluble mystery from the sea. All their meagre breasts panted together, the violently dilated nostrils quivered, the eyes stared stonily uphill. They passed me within six

[13] The middle part of a chain. — EDS.

inches, without a glance, with that complete, deathlike indifference of unhappy savages. Behind this raw matter one of the reclaimed, the product of the new forces at work, strolled despondently, carrying a rifle by its middle. He had a uniform jacket with one button off, and seeing a white man on the path, hoisted his weapon to his shoulder with alacrity. This was simple prudence, white men being so much alike at a distance that he could not tell who I might be. He was speedily reassured, and with a large, white, rascally grin, and a glance at his charge, seemed to take me into partnership in his exalted trust. After all, I also was a part of the great cause of these high and just proceedings.

"Instead of going up, I turned and descended to the left. My idea was to let that chain-gang get out of sight before I climbed the hill. You know I am not particularly tender; I've had to strike and to fend off. I've had to resist and to attack sometimes — that's only one way of resisting — without counting the exact cost, according to the demands of such sort of life as I had blundered into. I've seen the devil of violence, and the devil of greed, and the devil of hot desire; but, by all the stars! these were strong, lusty, red-eyed devils, that swayed and drove men — men, I tell you. But as I stood on this hillside, I foresaw that in the blinding sunshine of that land I would become acquainted with a flabby, pretending, weak-eyed devil of a rapacious and pitiless folly. How insidious he could be, too, I was only to find out several months later and a thousand miles farther. For a moment I stood appalled, as though by a warning. Finally I descended the hill, obliquely, towards the trees I had seen.

"I avoided a vast artificial hole somebody had been digging on the slope, the purpose of which I found it impossible to divine. It wasn't a quarry or a sandpit, anyhow. It was just a hole. It might have been connected with the philanthropic desire of giving the criminals something to do. I don't know. Then I nearly fell into a very narrow ravine, almost no more than a scar in the hillside. I discovered that a lot of imported drainage-pipes for the settlement had been tumbled in there. There wasn't one that was not broken. It was a wanton smash-up. At last I got under the trees. My purpose was to stroll into the shade for a moment; but no sooner within than it seemed to me I had stepped into the gloomy circle of some Inferno. The rapids were near, and an uninterrupted, uniform, headlong, rushing noise filled the mournful stillness of the grove, where not a breath stirred, not a leaf moved, with a mysterious sound — as though the tearing pace of the launched earth had suddenly become audible.

"Black shapes crouched, lay, sat between the trees leaning against the trunks, clinging to the earth, half coming out, half effaced within the dim light, in all the attitudes of pain, abandonment, and despair. Another mine on the cliff went off, followed by a slight shudder of the soil under my feet. The work was going on. The work! And this was the place where some of the helpers had withdrawn to die.

"They were dying slowly — it was very clear. They were not enemies, they were not criminals, they were nothing earthly now, — nothing but black shadows of disease and starvation, lying confusedly in the greenish gloom. Brought from all the recesses of the coast in all the legality of time contracts, lost in uncongenial surroundings, fed on unfamiliar food, they sickened, became inefficient, and were then allowed to crawl away and rest. These moribund shapes were free as air — and nearly as thin. I began to distinguish the gleam of the eyes under the trees. Then, glancing down, I saw a face near my hand. The black bones reclined at full length with one shoulder against the tree, and slowly the eyelids rose and the sunken eyes looked up at me, enormous and vacant, a kind of blind, white flicker in the depths of the orbs, which died out slowly. The man seemed young — almost a boy — but you know with them it's hard to tell. I found nothing else to do but to offer him

In 2013, artist Matt Kish illustrated several scenes from *Heart of Darkness*. **Discuss how the image below illustrates the following quotation from paragraph 41: "They were dying slowly — it was very clear. They were not enemies, they were not criminals, they were nothing earthly now, — nothing but black shadows of disease and starvation, lying confusedly in the greenish gloom."**

Matt Kish

one of my good Swede's ship's biscuits I had in my pocket. The fingers closed slowly on it and held — there was no other movement and no other glance. He had tied a bit of white worsted round his neck — Why? Where did he get it? Was it a badge — an ornament — a charm — a propitiatory act? Was there any idea at all connected with it? It looked startling round his black neck, this bit of white thread from beyond the seas.

"Near the same tree two more bundles of acute angles sat with their legs drawn up. One, with his chin propped on his knees, stared at nothing, in an intolerable and appalling manner: his brother phantom rested its forehead, as if overcome with a great weariness; and all about others were scattered in every pose of contorted collapse, as in some picture of a massacre or a pestilence. While I stood horror-struck, one of these creatures rose to his hands and knees, and went off on all-fours towards the river to drink. He lapped out of his hand, then sat up in the sunlight, crossing his shins in front of him, and after a time let his woolly head fall on his breastbone.

"I didn't want any more loitering in the shade, and I made haste towards the station. When near the buildings I met a white man, in such an unexpected elegance of get-up that in the first moment I took him for a sort of vision. I saw a high starched collar, white cuffs, a light alpaca jacket, snowy trousers, a clean necktie, and varnished boots. No hat. Hair parted, brushed, oiled, under a green-lined parasol held in a big white hand. He was amazing, and had a penholder behind his ear.

"I shook hands with this miracle, and I learned he was the Company's chief accountant, and that all the book-keeping was done at this station. He had come out for a moment, he said, 'to get a breath of fresh air.' The expression sounded wonderfully odd, with its suggestion of sedentary desk-life. I wouldn't have mentioned the fellow to you at all, only it was from his lips that I first heard the name of the man who is so indissolubly connected with the memories of that time. Moreover, I respected the fellow. Yes; I respected his collars, his vast cuffs, his brushed hair. His appearance was certainly that of a hair-dresser's dummy; but in the great demoralization of the land he kept up his appearance. That's backbone. His starched collars and got-up shirt-fronts were achievements of character. He had been out nearly three years; and, later, I could not help asking him how he managed to sport such linen. He had just the faintest blush, and said modestly, 'I've been teaching one of the native women about the station. It was difficult. She had a distaste for the work.' Thus this man had verily accomplished something. And he was devoted to his books, which were in apple-pie order.

"Everything else in the station was in a muddle, — heads, things, buildings. Strings of dusty niggers with splay feet arrived and departed; a stream of manufactured goods, rubbishy cottons, beads, and brass-wire set into the depths of darkness, and in return came a precious trickle of ivory.

"I had to wait in the station for ten days — an eternity. I lived in a hut in the yard, but to be out of the chaos I would sometimes get into the accountant's office. It was built of horizontal planks, and so badly put together that, as he bent over his high desk, he was barred from neck to heels with narrow strips of sunlight. There was no need to open the big shutter to see. It was hot there, too; big flies buzzed fiendishly, and did not sting, but stabbed. I sat generally on the floor, while, of faultless appearance (and even slightly scented), perching on a high stool, he wrote, he wrote. Sometimes he stood up for exercise. When a truckle-bed with a sick man (some invalid agent from up-country) was put in there, he exhibited a gentle annoyance. 'The groans of this sick person,' he said, 'distract my attention. And without that it is extremely difficult to guard against clerical errors in this climate.'

"One day he remarked, without lifting his head, 'In the interior you will no doubt meet Mr. Kurtz.' On my asking who Mr. Kurtz was, he said he was a first-class agent; and seeing my disappointment at this information, he added slowly, laying down his pen, 'He is a very remarkable person.' Further questions elicited from him that Mr. Kurtz was at present in charge of a trading post, a very important one, in the true ivory-country, at 'the very bottom of there. Sends in as much ivory as all the others put together . . .' He began to write again. The sick man was too ill to groan. The flies buzzed in a great peace.

"Suddenly there was a growing murmur of voices and a great tramping of feet. A caravan had come in. A violent babble of uncouth sounds burst out on the other side of the planks. All the carriers were speaking together, and in the midst of the uproar the lamentable voice of the chief agent was heard 'giving it up' tearfully for the twentieth time that day. . . . He rose slowly. 'What a frightful row,'[14] he said. He crossed the room gently to look at the sick man, and returning, said to me, 'He does not hear.' 'What! Dead?' I asked, startled. 'No, not yet,' he answered, with great composure. Then, alluding with a toss of the head to the tumult in the station-yard, 'When one has got to make correct entries, one comes to hate those savages — hate them to the death.' He remained thoughtful for a moment. 'When you see Mr. Kurtz,' he went on, 'tell him from me that everything here' — he glanced at the desk — 'is very satisfactory. I don't like to write to him — with those messengers of ours you never know who may get hold of your letter — at that Central Station.' He stared at me for a moment with his mild, bulging eyes. 'Oh, he will go far, very far,' he began again. 'He will be somebody in the Administration before long. They, above — the Council in Europe, you know — mean him to be.'

"He turned to his work. The noise outside had ceased, and presently in going out I stopped at the door. In the steady buzz of flies the homeward-bound agent was lying flushed and insensible; the other, bent over his books, was making correct entries of perfectly correct transactions; and fifty feet below the doorstep I could see the still tree-tops of the grove of death.

"Next day I left that station at last, with a caravan of sixty men, for a two-hundred-mile tramp.

[14] Racket. — EDS.

"No use telling you much about that. Paths, paths, everywhere; a stamped-in network of paths spreading over the empty land, through long grass, through burnt grass, through thickets, down and up chilly ravines, up and down stony hills ablaze with heat; and a solitude, a solitude, nobody, not a hut. The population had cleared out a long time ago. Well, if a lot of mysterious niggers armed with all kinds of fearful weapons suddenly took to travelling on the road between Deal and Gravesend, catching the yokels right and left to carry heavy loads for them, I fancy every farm and cottage thereabouts would get empty very soon. Only here the dwellings were gone, too. Still I passed through several abandoned villages. There's something pathetically childish in the ruins of grass walls. Day after day, with the stamp and shuffle of sixty pair of bare feet behind me, each pair under a 60-lb. load. Camp, cook, sleep, strike camp, march. Now and then a carrier dead in harness, at rest in the long grass near the path, with an empty water-gourd and his long staff lying by his side. A great silence around and above. Perhaps on some quiet night the tremor of far-off drums, sinking, swelling, a tremor vast, faint; a sound weird, appealing, suggestive, and wild — and perhaps with as profound a meaning as the sound of bells in a Christian country. Once a white man in an unbuttoned uniform, camping on the path with an armed escort of lank Zanzibaris, very hospitable and festive — not to say drunk. Was looking after the upkeep of the road he declared. Can't say I saw any road or any upkeep, unless the body of a middle-aged negro, with a bullet-hole in the forehead, upon which I absolutely stumbled three miles farther on, may be considered as a permanent improvement. I had a white companion, too, not a bad chap, but rather too fleshy and with the exasperating habit of fainting on the hot hillsides, miles away from the least bit of shade and water. Annoying, you know, to hold your own coat like a parasol over a man's head while he is coming-to. I couldn't help asking him once what he meant by coming there at all. 'To make money, of course. What do you think?' he said, scornfully. Then he got fever, and had to be carried in a hammock slung under a pole. As he weighed sixteen stone I had no end of rows with the carriers. They jibbed, ran away, sneaked off with their loads in the night — quite a mutiny. So, one evening, I made a speech in English with gestures, not one of which was lost to the sixty pairs of eyes before me, and the next morning I started the hammock off in front all right. An hour afterwards I came upon the whole concern wrecked in a bush — man, hammock, groans, blankets, horrors. The heavy pole had skinned his poor nose. He was very anxious for me to kill somebody, but there wasn't the shadow of a carrier near. I remembered the old doctor — 'It would be interesting for science to watch the mental changes of individuals, on the spot.' I felt I was becoming scientifically interesting. However, all that is to no purpose. On the fifteenth day I came in sight of the big river again, and hobbled into the Central Station. It was on a back water surrounded by scrub and forest, with a pretty border of smelly mud on one side, and on the three others enclosed by a crazy fence of rushes. A neglected gap was all the gate it had, and the first glance at the place was enough to let you see the flabby devil was running that show. White men with long staves in their hands appeared languidly from amongst the buildings, strolling up to take a look at me, and then retired out of sight somewhere. One of them, a stout, excitable chap with black moustaches, informed me with great volubility and many digressions, as soon as I told him who I was, that my steamer was at the bottom of the river. I was thunderstruck. What, how, why? Oh, it was 'all right.' The 'manager himself' was there. All quite correct. 'Everybody had behaved splendidly! splendidly!' — 'you must,' he said in agitation, 'go and see the general manager at once. He is waiting!'

"I did not see the real significance of that wreck at once. I fancy I see it now, but I am not sure — not at all. Certainly the affair was too stupid — when I think of it — to be altogether natural. Still . . . But at the moment it presented itself simply as a confounded nuisance. The steamer was sunk. They had started two days before in a sudden hurry up the river with the manager on board, in charge of some volunteer skipper, and before they had been out three hours they tore the bottom out of her on stones, and she sank near the south bank. I asked myself what I was to do there, now my boat was lost. As a matter of fact, I had plenty to do in fishing my command out of the river. I had to set about it the very next day. That, and the repairs when I brought the pieces to the station, took some months.

"My first interview with the manager was curious. He did not ask me to sit down after my twenty-mile walk that morning. He was commonplace in complexion, in feature, in manners, and in voice. He was of middle size and of ordinary build. His eyes, of the usual blue, were perhaps remarkably cold, and he certainly could make his glance fall on one as trenchant and heavy as an axe. But even at these times the rest of his person seemed to disclaim the intention. Otherwise there was only an indefinable, faint expression of his lips, something stealthy — a smile — not a smile — I remember it, but I can't explain. It was unconscious, this smile was, though just after he had said something it got intensified for an instant. It came at the end of his speeches like a seal applied on the words to make the meaning of the commonest phrase appear absolutely inscrutable. He was a common trader, from his youth up employed in these parts — nothing more. He was obeyed, yet he inspired neither love nor fear, nor even respect. He inspired uneasiness. That was it! Uneasiness. Not a definite mistrust — just — uneasiness — nothing more. You have no idea how effective such a . . . a . . . faculty can be. He had no genius for organizing, for initiative, or for order even. That was evident in such things as the deplorable state of the station. He had no learning, and no intelligence. His position had come to him — why? Perhaps because he was never ill . . . He had served three terms of three years out there . . . Because triumphant health in the general rout of constitutions is a kind of power in itself. When he went home on leave he rioted on a large scale — pompously. Jack ashore[15] — with a difference — in externals only. This one could gather from his casual talk. He originated nothing, he could keep the routine going — that's all. But he was great. He was great by this little thing that it was impossible to tell what could control such a man. He never gave that secret away. Perhaps there was nothing within him. Such a suspicion made one pause — for out there there were no external checks. Once when various tropical diseases had laid low almost every 'agent' in the station, he was heard to say, 'Men who come out here should have no entrails.' He sealed the utterance with that smile of his, as though it had been a door opening into a darkness he had in his keeping. You fancied you had seen things — but the seal was on. When annoyed at meal-times by the constant quarrels of the white men about precedence, he ordered an immense round table to be made, for which a special house had to be built. This was the station's mess-room. Where he sat was the first place — the rest were nowhere. One felt this to be his unalterable conviction. He was neither civil nor uncivil. He was quiet. He allowed his 'boy' — an overfed young negro from the coast — to treat the white men, under his very eyes, with provoking insolence.

"He began to speak as soon as he saw me. I had been very long on the road. He could not wait. Had to start without me. The up-river stations had to be relieved. There had been so many delays already that he did not know who was dead and who was alive, and how they got on — and so on, and so on. He paid no attention

[15] Shorthand for a sailor (Jack) on shore leave. From the traditional sea chantey about a drunken sailor, "Get Up Jack! John, Sit Down!" — EDS.

to my explanations, and, playing with a stick of sealing-wax, repeated several times that the situation was 'very grave, very grave.' There were rumours that a very important station was in jeopardy, and its chief, Mr. Kurtz, was ill. Hoped it was not true. Mr. Kurtz was . . . I felt weary and irritable. Hang Kurtz, I thought. I interrupted him by saying I had heard of Mr. Kurtz on the coast. 'Ah! So they talk of him down there,' he murmured to himself. Then he began again, assuring me Mr. Kurtz was the best agent he had, an exceptional man, of the greatest importance to the Company; therefore I could understand his anxiety. He was, he said, 'very, very uneasy.' Certainly he fidgeted on his chair a good deal, exclaimed, 'Ah, Mr. Kurtz!' broke the stick of sealing-wax and seemed dumfounded by the accident. Next thing he wanted to know 'how long it would take to' . . . I interrupted him again. Being hungry, you know, and kept on my feet too, I was getting savage. 'How can I tell?' I said. 'I haven't even seen the wreck yet — some months, no doubt.' All this talk seemed to me so futile. 'Some months,' he said. 'Well, let us say three months before we can make a start. Yes. That ought to do the affair.' I flung out of his hut (he lived all alone in a clay hut with a sort of verandah) muttering to myself my opinion of him. He was a chattering idiot. Afterwards I took it back when it was borne in upon me startlingly with what extreme nicety he had estimated the time requisite for the 'affair.'

"I went to work the next day, turning, so to speak, my back on that station. In that way only it seemed to me I could keep my hold on the redeeming facts of life. Still, one must look about sometimes; and then I saw this station, these men strolling aimlessly about in the sunshine of the yard. I asked myself sometimes what it all meant. They wandered here and there with their absurd long staves in their hands, like a lot of faithless pilgrims bewitched inside a rotten fence. The word 'ivory' rang in the air, was whispered, was sighed. You would think they were praying to it. A taint of imbecile rapacity blew through it all, like a whiff from some corpse. By Jove! I've never seen anything so unreal in my life. And outside, the silent wilderness surrounding this cleared speck on the earth struck me as something great and invincible, like evil or truth, waiting patiently for the passing away of this fantastic invasion.

"Oh, these months! Well, never mind. Various things happened. One evening a grass shed full of calico, cotton prints, beads, and I don't know what else, burst into a blaze so suddenly that you would have thought the earth had opened to let an avenging fire consume all that trash. I was smoking my pipe quietly by my dismantled steamer, and saw them all cutting capers in the light, with their arms lifted high, when the stout man with moustaches came tearing down to the river, a tin pail in his hand, assured me that everybody was 'behaving splendidly, splendidly,' dipped about a quart of water and tore back again. I noticed there was a hole in the bottom of his pail.

"I strolled up. There was no hurry. You see the thing had gone off like a box of matches. It had been hopeless from the very first. The flame had leaped high, driven everybody back, lighted up everything — and collapsed. The shed was already a heap of embers glowing fiercely. A nigger was being beaten near by. They said he had caused the fire in some way; be that as it may, he was screeching most horribly. I saw him, later, for several days, sitting in a bit of shade looking very sick and trying to recover himself: afterwards he arose and went out — and the wilderness without a sound took him into its bosom again. As I approached the glow from the dark I found myself at the back of two men, talking. I heard the name of Kurtz pronounced, then the words, 'take advantage of this unfortunate accident.' One of the men was the manager. I wished him a good evening. 'Did you ever see anything like it — eh? it is incredible,' he said, and walked off. The other man remained. He was a first-class agent, young, gentlemanly, a bit reserved, with a forked little beard and a hooked nose. He was stand-offish with the other agents, and they on their side said he was the manager's spy upon them. As to me, I had hardly ever spoken to him before. We got into talk, and by and by we strolled away from the hissing ruins. Then he asked me to his room, which was in the main building of the station. He struck a match, and I perceived that this young aristocrat had not only a silver-mounted dressing-case but also a whole candle all to himself. Just at that time the manager was the only man supposed to have any right to candles. Native mats covered the clay walls; a collection of spears, assegais,[16] shields, knives was hung up in trophies. The business entrusted to this fellow was the making of bricks — so I had been informed; but there wasn't a fragment of a brick anywhere in the station, and he had been there more than a year — waiting. It seems he could not make bricks without something, I don't know what — straw maybe. Anyways, it could not be found there, and as it was not likely to be sent from Europe, it did not appear clear to me what he was waiting for. An act of special creation perhaps. However, they were all waiting — all the sixteen or twenty pilgrims of them — for something; and upon my word it did not seem an uncongenial occupation, from the way they took it, though the only thing that ever came to them was disease — as far as I could see. They beguiled the time by backbiting and intriguing against each other in a foolish kind of way. There was an air of plotting about that station, but nothing came of it, of course. It was as unreal as everything else — as the philanthropic pretence of the whole concern, as their talk, as their government, as their show of work. The only real feeling was a desire to get appointed to a trading-post where ivory was to be had, so that they could earn percentages. They intrigued and slandered and hated each other only on that account, — but as to effectually lifting a little finger — oh, no. By heavens! there is something after all in the world allowing one man to steal a horse while another must not look at a halter. Steal a horse straight out. Very well. He has done it. Perhaps he can ride. But there is a way of looking at a halter that would provoke the most charitable of saints into a kick.

"I had no idea why he wanted to be sociable, but as we chatted in there it suddenly occurred to me the fellow was trying to get at something — in fact, pumping me. He alluded constantly to Europe, to the people I was supposed to know there — putting leading questions as to my acquaintances in the sepulchral city, and so on. His little eyes glittered like mica discs — with curiosity — though he tried to keep up a bit of superciliousness. At first I was astonished, but very soon I became awfully curious to see what he would find out from me. I couldn't possibly imagine what I had in me to make it worth his while. It was very pretty to see how he baffled himself, for in truth my body was full only of chills, and my head had nothing in it but that wretched steamboat business. It was evident he took me for a perfectly shameless prevaricator. At last he got angry, and, to conceal a movement of furious annoyance, he yawned. I rose. Then I noticed a small sketch in oils, on a panel, representing a woman, draped and blindfolded, carrying a lighted torch. The background was sombre — almost black. The movement of the woman was stately, and the effect of the torch-light on the face was sinister.

"It arrested me, and he stood by civilly, holding an empty half-pint champagne bottle (medical comforts) with the candle stuck in it. To my question he said Mr. Kurtz had painted this — in this very station more than a year ago — while waiting for means to go to his trading-post. 'Tell me, pray,' said I, 'who is this Mr. Kurtz?'

" 'The chief of the Inner Station,' he answered in a short tone, looking away. 'Much obliged,' I said, laughing. 'And you are the

[16] African spears with short shafts and long blades. — EDS.

brickmaker of the Central Station. Everyone knows that.' He was silent for a while. 'He is a prodigy,' he said at last. 'He is an emissary of pity, and science, and progress, and devil knows what else. We want,' he began to declaim suddenly, 'for the guidance of the cause intrusted to us by Europe, so to speak, higher intelligence, wide sympathies, a singleness of purpose.' 'Who says that?' I asked. 'Lots of them,' he replied. 'Some even write that; and so *he* comes here, a special being, as you ought to know.' 'Why ought I to know?' I interrupted, really surprised. He paid no attention. 'Yes. To-day he is chief of the best station, next year he will be assistant-manager, two years more and . . . but I daresay you know what he will be in two years' time. You are of the new gang — the gang of virtue. The same people who sent him specially also recommended you. Oh, don't say no. I've my own eyes to trust.' Light dawned upon me. My dear aunt's influential acquaintances were producing an unexpected effect upon that young man. I nearly burst into a laugh. 'Do you read the Company's confidential correspondence?' I asked. He hadn't a word to say. It was great fun. 'When Mr. Kurtz,' I continued, severely, 'is General Manager, you won't have the opportunity.'

"He blew the candle out suddenly, and we went outside. The moon had risen. Black figures strolled about listlessly, pouring water on the glow, whence proceeded a sound of hissing; steam ascended in the moonlight, the beaten nigger groaned somewhere. 'What a row the brute makes!' said the indefatigable man with the moustaches, appearing near us. 'Serve him right. Transgression — punishment — bang! Pitiless, pitiless. That's the only way. This will prevent all conflagrations for the future. I was just telling the manager . . .' He noticed my companion, and became crestfallen all at once. 'Not in bed yet,' he said, with a kind of servile heartiness; 'it's so natural. Ha! Danger — agitation.' He vanished. I went on to the river-side, and the other followed me. I heard a scathing murmur at my ear, 'Heap of muffs — go to.' The pilgrims could be seen in knots gesticulating, discussing. Several had still their staves in their hands. I verily believe they took these sticks to bed with them. Beyond the fence the forest stood up spectrally in the moonlight, and through the dim stir, through the faint sounds of that lamentable courtyard, the silence of the land went home to one's very heart — its mystery, its greatness, the amazing reality of its concealed life. The hurt nigger moaned feebly somewhere near by, and then fetched a deep sigh that made me mend my pace away from there. I felt a hand introducing itself under my arm. 'My dear sir,' said the fellow, 'I don't want to be misunderstood, and especially by you, who will see Mr. Kurtz long before I can have that pleasure. I wouldn't like him to get a false idea of my disposition. . . .'

"I let him run on, this papier-mâché Mephistopheles, and it seemed to me that if I tried I could poke my forefinger through him, and would find nothing inside but a little loose dirt, maybe. He, don't you see, had been planning to be assistant-manager by and by under the present man, and I could see that the coming of that Kurtz had upset them both not a little. He talked precipitately, and I did not try to stop him. I had my shoulders against the wreck of my steamer, hauled up on the slope like a carcass of some big river animal. The smell of mud, of primeval mud, by Jove! was in my nostrils, the high stillness of primeval forest was before my eyes; there were shiny patches on the black creek. The moon had spread over everything a thin layer of silver — over the rank grass, over the mud, upon the wall of matted vegetation standing higher than the wall of a temple, over the great river I could see through a sombre gap glittering, glittering, as it flowed broadly by without a murmur. All this was great, expectant, mute, while the man jabbered about himself. I wondered whether the stillness on the face of the immensity looking at us two were meant as an appeal or as a menace. What were we who had strayed in here? Could we handle that dumb thing, or would it handle us? I felt how big, how confoundedly big, was that thing that couldn't talk, and perhaps was deaf as well. What was in there? I could see a little ivory coming out from there, and I had heard Mr. Kurtz was in there. I had heard enough about it, too — God knows! Yet somehow it didn't bring any image with it — no more than if I had been told an angel or a fiend was in there. I believed it in the same way one of you might believe there are inhabitants in the planet Mars. I knew once a Scotch sailmaker who was certain, dead sure, there were people in Mars. If you asked him for some idea how they looked and behaved, he would get shy and mutter something about 'walking on all-fours.' If you as much as smiled, he would — though a man of sixty — offer to fight you. I would not have gone so far as to fight for Kurtz, but I went for him near enough to a lie. You know I hate, detest, and can't bear a lie, not because I am straighter than the rest of us, but simply because it appalls me. There is a taint of death, a flavour of mortality in lies — which is exactly what I hate and detest in the world — what I want to forget. It makes me miserable and sick, like biting something rotten would do. Temperament, I suppose. Well, I went near enough to it by letting the young fool there believe anything he liked to imagine as to my influence in Europe. I became in an instant as much of a pretence as the rest of the bewitched pilgrims. This simply because I had a notion it somehow would be of help to that Kurtz whom at the time I did not see — you understand. He was just a word for me. I did not see the man in the name any more than you do. Do you see him? Do you see the story? Do you see anything? It seems to me I am trying to tell you a dream — making a vain attempt, because no relation of a dream can convey the dream-sensation, that commingling of absurdity, surprise, and bewilderment in a tremor of struggling revolt, that notion of being captured by the incredible which is of the very essence of dreams. . . ."

He was silent for a while.

". . . No, it is impossible; it is impossible to convey the life-sensation of any given epoch of one's existence — that which makes its truth, its meaning — its subtle and penetrating essence. It is impossible. We live as we dream — alone. . . ."

He paused again as if reflecting, then added —

"Of course in this you fellows see more than I could then. You see me, whom you know. . . ."

It had become so pitch dark that we listeners could hardly see one another. For a long time already he, sitting apart, had been no more to us than a voice. There was not a word from anybody. The others might have been asleep, but I was awake. I listened, I listened on the watch for the sentence, for the word, that would give me the clue to the faint uneasiness inspired by this narrative that seemed to shape itself without human lips in the heavy night-air of the river.

". . . Yes — I let him run on," Marlow began again, "and think what he pleased about the powers that were behind me. I did! And there was nothing behind me! There was nothing but that wretched, old, mangled steamboat I was leaning against, while he talked fluently about 'the necessity for every man to get on.' 'And when one comes out here, you conceive, it is not to gaze at the moon.' Mr. Kurtz was a 'universal genius,' but even a genius would find it easier to work with 'adequate tools — intelligent men.' He did not make bricks — why, there was a physical impossibility in the way — as I was well aware; and if he did secretarial work for the manager, it was because 'no sensible man rejects wantonly the confidence of his superiors.' Did I see it? I saw it. What more did I want? What I really wanted was rivets, by heaven! Rivets. To get on with the work — to stop the hole. Rivets I wanted. There were cases of them down at the coast — cases — piled up — burst — split! You kicked a loose rivet at every second step in that station yard on the hillside. Rivets had rolled into the grove of death. You could fill your pockets with rivets for the trouble of stooping down — and there wasn't one rivet to be found where it was wanted. We had plates that would do, but nothing to fasten them with. And every week the messenger, a lone negro, letter-bag on shoulder and staff in hand, left our station for the coast. And several times a week a coast caravan came in with trade goods — ghastly glazed calico that made you shudder only to look at it, glass beads value about a penny a quart, confounded spotted cotton handkerchiefs. And no rivets. Three carriers could have brought all that was wanted to set that steamboat afloat.

"He was becoming confidential now, but I fancy my unresponsive attitude must have exasperated him at last, for he judged it necessary to inform me he feared neither God nor devil, let alone any mere man. I said I could see that very well, but what I wanted was a certain quantity of rivets — and rivets were what really Mr. Kurtz wanted, if he had only known it. Now letters went to the coast every week. . . . 'My dear sir,' he cried, 'I write from dictation.' I demanded rivets. There was a way — for an intelligent man. He changed his manner; became very cold, and suddenly began to talk about a hippopotamus; wondered whether sleeping on board the steamer (I stuck to my salvage night and day) I wasn't disturbed. There was an old hippo that had the bad habit of getting out on the bank and roaming at night over the station grounds. The pilgrims used to turn out in a body and empty every rifle they could lay hands on at him. Some even had sat up o' nights for him. All this energy was wasted, though. 'That animal has a charmed life,' he said; 'but you can say this only of brutes in this country. No man — you apprehend me? — no man here bears a charmed life.' He stood there for a moment in the moonlight with his delicate hooked nose set a little askew, and his mica eyes glittering without a wink, then, with a curt Good-night, he strode off. I could see he was disturbed and considerably puzzled, which made me feel more hopeful than I had been for days. It was a great comfort to turn from that chap to my influential friend, the battered, twisted, ruined, tin-pot steamboat. I clambered on board. She rang under my feet like an empty Huntley & Palmer biscuit-tin kicked along a gutter; she was nothing so solid in make, and rather less pretty in shape, but I had expended enough hard work on her to make me love her. No influential friend would have served me better. She had given me a chance to come out a bit — to find out what I could do. No, I don't like work. I had rather laze about and think of all the fine things that can be done. I don't like work — no man does — but I like what is in the work — the chance to find yourself. Your own reality — for yourself, not for others — what no other man can ever know. They can only see the mere show, and never can tell what it really means.

"I was not surprised to see somebody sitting aft, on the deck, with his legs dangling over the mud. You see I rather chummed with the few mechanics there were in that station, whom the other pilgrims naturally despised — on account of their imperfect manners, I suppose. This was the foreman — a boiler-maker by trade — a good worker. He was a lank, bony, yellow-faced man, with big intense eyes. His aspect was worried, and his head was as bald as the palm of my hand; but his hair in falling seemed to have stuck to his chin, and had prospered in the new locality, for his beard hung down to his waist. He was a widower with six young children (he had left them in charge of a sister of his to come out there), and the passion of his life was pigeon-flying. He was an enthusiast and a connoisseur. He would rave about pigeons. After work hours he used sometimes to come over from his hut for a talk about his children and his pigeons; at work, when he had to crawl in the mud under the bottom of the steamboat, he would tie up that beard of his in a kind of white serviette[17] he brought for the purpose. It had loops to go over his ears. In the

[17] Table napkin. — EDS.

evening he could be seen squatted on the bank rinsing that wrapper in the creek with great care, then spreading it solemnly on a bush to dry.

"I slapped him on the back and shouted, 'We shall have rivets!' He scrambled to his feet exclaiming, 'No! Rivets!' as though he couldn't believe his ears. Then in a low voice, 'You . . . eh?' I don't know why we behaved like lunatics. I put my finger to the side of my nose and nodded mysteriously. 'Good for you!' he cried, snapped his fingers above his head, lifting one foot. I tried a jig. We capered on the iron deck. A frightful clatter came out of that hulk, and the virgin forest on the other bank of the creek sent it back in a thundering roll upon the sleeping station. It must have made some of the pilgrims sit up in their hovels. A dark figure obscured the lighted doorway of the manager's hut, vanished, then, a second or so after, the doorway itself vanished, too. We stopped, and the silence driven away by the stamping of our feet flowed back again from the recesses of the land. The great wall of vegetation, an exuberant and entangled mass of trunks, branches, leaves, boughs, festoons, motionless in the moonlight, was like a rioting invasion of soundless life, a rolling wave of plants, piled up, crested, ready to topple over the creek, to sweep every little man of us out of his little existence. And it moved not. A deadened burst of mighty splashes and snorts reached us from afar, as though an ichthyosaurus had been taking a bath of glitter in the great river. 'After all,' said the boiler-maker in a reasonable tone, 'why shouldn't we get the rivets?' Why not, indeed! I did not know of any reason why we shouldn't. 'They'll come in three weeks,' I said, confidently.

"But they didn't. Instead of rivets there came an invasion, an infliction, a visitation. It came in sections during the next three weeks, each section headed by a donkey carrying a white man in new clothes and tan shoes, bowing from that elevation right and left to the impressed pilgrims. A quarrelsome band of footsore sulky niggers trod on the heels of the donkey; a lot of tents, camp-stools, tin boxes, white cases, brown bales would be shot down in the courtyard, and the air of mystery would deepen a little over the muddle of the station. Five such instalments came, with their absurd air of disorderly flight with the loot of innumerable outfit shops and provision stores, that, one would think, they were lugging, after a raid, into the wilderness for equitable division. It was an inextricable mess of things decent in themselves but that human folly made look like the spoils of thieving.

"This devoted band called itself the Eldorado Exploring Expedition, and I believe they were sworn to secrecy. Their talk, however, was the talk of sordid buccaneers: it was reckless without hardihood, greedy without audacity, and cruel without courage; there was not an atom of foresight or of serious intention in the whole batch of them, and they did not seem aware these things are wanted for the work of the world. To tear treasure out of the bowels of the land was their desire, with no more moral purpose at the back of it than there is in burglars breaking into a safe. Who paid the expenses of the noble enterprise I don't know; but the uncle of our manager was leader of that lot.

"In exterior he resembled a butcher in a poor neighbourhood, and his eyes had a look of sleepy cunning. He carried his fat paunch with ostentation on his short legs, and during the time his gang infested the station spoke to no one but his nephew. You could see these two roaming about all day long with their heads close together in an everlasting confab.

"I had given up worrying myself about the rivets. One's capacity for that kind of folly is more limited than you would suppose. I said Hang!—and let things slide. I had plenty of time for meditation, and now and then I would give some thought to Kurtz. I wasn't very interested in him. No. Still, I was curious to see whether this man, who had come out equipped with moral ideas of some sort, would climb to the top after all and how he would set about his work when there."

2

"One evening as I was lying flat on the deck of my steamboat, I heard voices approaching—and there were the nephew and the uncle strolling along the bank. I laid my head on my arm again, and had nearly lost myself in a doze, when somebody said in my ear, as it were: 'I am as harmless as a little child, but I don't like to be dictated to. Am I the manager—or am I not? I was ordered to send him there. It's incredible.' . . . I became aware that the two were standing on the shore alongside the forepart of the steamboat, just below my head. I did not move; it did not occur to me to move: I was sleepy. 'It *is* unpleasant,' grunted the uncle. 'He has asked the Administration to be sent there,' said the other, 'with the idea of showing what he could do; and I was instructed accordingly. Look at the influence that man must have. Is it not frightful?' They both agreed it was frightful, then made several bizarre remarks: 'Make rain and fine weather—one man—the Council—by the nose'—bits of absurd sentences that got the better of my drowsiness, so that I had pretty near the whole of my wits about me when the uncle said, 'The climate may do away with this difficulty for you. Is he alone there?' 'Yes,' answered the manager; 'he sent his assistant down the river with a note to me in these terms: "Clear this poor devil out of the country, and don't bother sending more of that sort. I had rather be alone than have the kind of men you can dispose of with me." It was more than a year ago. Can you imagine such impudence!' 'Anything since then?' asked the other, hoarsely. 'Ivory,' jerked the nephew; 'lots of it—prime sort—lots—most annoying, from him.' 'And with that?' questioned the heavy rumble. 'Invoice,' was the reply fired out, so to speak. Then silence. They had been talking about Kurtz.

"I was broad awake by this time, but, lying perfectly at ease, remained still, having no inducement to change my position. 'How did that ivory come all this way?' growled the elder man, who seemed very vexed. The other explained that it had come with a fleet of canoes in charge of an English half-caste clerk Kurtz had with him; that Kurtz had apparently intended to return himself, the station being by that time bare of goods and stores, but after coming three hundred miles, had suddenly decided to go back, which he started to do alone in a small dugout with four paddlers, leaving the half-caste to continue down the river with the ivory. The two fellows there seemed astounded at anybody attempting such a thing. They were at a loss for an adequate motive. As to me, I seemed to see Kurtz for the first time. It was a distinct glimpse: the dugout, four paddling savages, and the lone white man turning his back suddenly on the headquarters, on relief, on thoughts of home—perhaps; setting his face towards the depths of the wilderness, towards his empty and desolate station. I did not know the motive. Perhaps he was just simply a fine fellow who stuck to his work for its own sake. His name, you understand, had not been pronounced once. He was 'that man.' The half-caste, who, as far as I could see, had conducted a difficult trip with great prudence and pluck, was invariably alluded to as 'that scoundrel.' The 'scoundrel' had reported that the 'man' had been very ill—had recovered imperfectly. . . . The two below me moved away then a few paces, and strolled back and forth at some little distance. I heard: 'Military post—doctor—two hundred miles—quite alone now—unavoidable delays—nine months—no news—strange rumours.' They approached again, just as the manager was saying, 'No one, as far as I know, unless a species of wandering trader—a pestilential fellow, snapping ivory from the natives.' Who was it they were talking about now? I gathered in snatches that this was some man supposed to be in Kurtz's district, and of whom the manager did not approve. 'We will not be free from unfair competition till one of these fellows is hanged for an example,' he said. 'Certainly,' grunted the other; 'get him hanged! Why not? Anything — anything can be done in this country. That's what I say; nobody here, you understand, *here*, can endanger your position. And why? You stand the climate — you outlast them all. The danger is in Europe; but there before I left I took care to ——' They moved off and whispered, then their voices rose again. 'The extraordinary series of delays is not my fault. I did my best.' The fat man sighed. 'Very sad.' 'And the pestiferous absurdity of his talk,' continued the other; 'he bothered me enough when he was here. "Each station should be like a beacon on the road towards better things, a centre for trade of course, but also for humanizing, improving, instructing." Conceive you — that ass! And he wants to be manager! No, it's — ' Here he got choked by excessive indignation, and I lifted my head the least bit. I was surprised to see how near they were — right under me. I could have spat upon their hats. They were looking on the ground, absorbed in thought. The manager was switching his leg with a slender twig: his sagacious relative lifted his head. 'You have been well since you came out this time?' he asked. The other gave a start. 'Who? I? Oh! Like a charm — like a charm. But the rest — oh, my goodness! All sick. They die so quick, too, that I haven't the time to send them out of the country — it's incredible!' 'H'm. Just so,' grunted the uncle. 'Ah! my boy, trust to this — I say, trust to this.' I saw him extend his short flipper of an arm for a gesture that took in the forest, the creek, the mud, the river, — seemed to beckon with a dishonouring flourish before the sunlit face of the land a treacherous appeal to the lurking death, to the hidden evil, to the profound darkness of its heart. It was so startling that I leaped to my feet and looked back at the edge of the forest, as though I had expected an answer of some sort to that black display of confidence. You know the foolish notions that come to one sometimes. The high stillness confronted these two figures with its ominous patience, waiting for the passing away of a fantastic invasion.

"They swore aloud together — out of sheer fright, I believe — then pretending not to know anything of my existence, turned back to the station. The sun was low; and leaning forward side by side, they seemed to be tugging painfully uphill their two ridiculous shadows of unequal length, that trailed behind them slowly over the tall grass without bending a single blade.

"In a few days the Eldorado Expedition went into the patient wilderness, that closed upon it as the sea closes over a diver. Long afterwards the news came that all the donkeys were dead. I know nothing as to the fate of the less valuable animals. They, no doubt, like the rest of us, found what they deserved. I did not inquire. I was then rather excited at the prospect of meeting Kurtz very soon. When I say very soon I mean it comparatively. It was just two months from the day we left the creek when we came to the bank below Kurtz's station.

"Going up that river was like travelling back to the earliest beginnings of the world, when vegetation rioted on the earth and the big trees were kings. An empty stream, a great silence, an impenetrable forest. The air was warm, thick, heavy, sluggish. There was no joy in the brilliance of sunshine. The long stretches of the waterway ran on, deserted, into the gloom of overshadowed distances. On silvery sandbanks hippos and alligators sunned themselves side by side. The broadening waters flowed through a mob of wooded islands; you lost your way on that river as you would in a desert, and butted all day long against shoals, trying to find the channel, till you thought yourself bewitched and cut off for ever from everything you had known once — somewhere — far away — in another existence perhaps. There were moments when one's past came back to one, as it will sometimes when you have not a moment to spare to yourself; but it came in the shape of an unrestful and noisy dream, remembered with wonder amongst the overwhelming realities of this strange world of plants, and water, and silence. And this stillness of life did not in the least resemble a peace. It was the stillness of an implacable force brooding over an inscrutable intention. It looked at you with a vengeful aspect. I got used to it afterwards; I did not see it any more; I had no time. I had to keep guessing at the channel; I had to discern, mostly by inspiration, the signs of hidden banks; I watched for sunken stones; I was learning to clap my teeth smartly before my heart flew out, when I shaved by a fluke some infernal sly old snag that would have ripped the life out of the tin-pot steamboat and drowned all the pilgrims; I had to keep a look-out for the signs of dead wood we could cut up in the night for next day's steaming. When you have to attend to things of that sort, to the mere incidents of the surface, the reality — the reality, I tell you — fades. The inner truth is hidden — luckily, luckily. But I felt it all the same; I felt often its mysterious stillness watching me at my monkey tricks, just as it watches you fellows performing on your respective tight-ropes for — what is it? half-a-crown a tumble——"

"Try to be civil, Marlow," growled a voice, and I knew there was at least one listener awake besides myself.

"I beg your pardon. I forgot the heartache which makes up the rest of the price. And indeed what does the price matter, if the trick be well done? You do your tricks very well. And I didn't do badly either, since I managed not to sink that steamboat on my first trip. It's a wonder to me yet. Imagine a blindfolded man set to drive a van over a bad road. I sweated and shivered over that business considerably, I can tell you. After all, for a seaman, to scrape the bottom of the thing that's supposed to float all the time under his care is the unpardonable sin. No one may know of it, but you never forget the thump — eh? A blow on the very heart. You remember it, you dream of it, you wake up at night and think of it — years after — and go hot and cold all over. I don't pretend to say that steamboat floated all the time. More than once she had to wade for a bit, with twenty cannibals splashing around and pushing. We had enlisted some of these chaps on the way for a crew. Fine fellows — cannibals — in their place. They were men one could work with, and I am grateful to them. And, after all, they did not eat each other before my face: they had brought along a provision of hippo-meat which went rotten, and made the mystery of the wilderness stink in my nostrils. Phoo! I can sniff it now. I had the manager on board and three or four pilgrims with their staves — all complete. Sometimes we came upon a station close by the bank, clinging to the skirts of the unknown, and the white men rushing out of a tumble-down hovel, with great gestures of joy and surprise and welcome, seemed very strange — had the appearance of being held there captive by a spell. The word ivory would ring in the air for a while — and on we went again into the silence, along empty reaches, round the still bends, between the high walls of our winding way, reverberating in hollow claps the ponderous beat of the stern-wheel. Trees, trees, millions of trees, massive, immense, running up high; and at their foot, hugging the bank against the stream, crept the little begrimed steamboat, like a sluggish beetle crawling on the floor of a lofty portico. It made you feel very small, very lost, and yet it was not altogether depressing, that feeling. After all, if you were small, the grimy beetle crawled on — which was just what you wanted it to do. Where the pilgrims imagined it crawled to I don't know. To some place where they expected to get something, I bet! For me it crawled towards Kurtz — exclusively; but when the steam-pipes started leaking we crawled very slow. The reaches opened before us and closed behind, as if the forest had stepped leisurely across the water to bar the way for our return. We penetrated deeper and deeper into the heart of darkness. It was very quiet there. At night sometimes the roll of drums behind the curtain of trees would run up the river and remain sustained faintly, as if hovering in the air high over our heads, till the first break of day. Whether it meant war, peace, or prayer we could not tell. The dawns were heralded by the descent of a chill stillness; the wood-cutters slept, their fires burned low; the snapping of a twig would make you start. We were wanderers on a prehistoric earth, on an earth that wore the aspect of an unknown planet. We could have fancied ourselves the first of men taking possession of an accursed inheritance, to be subdued at the cost of profound anguish and of excessive toil. But suddenly, as we struggled round a bend, there would be a glimpse of rush walls, of peaked grass-roofs, a burst of yells, a whirl of black limbs, a mass of hands clapping, of feet stamping, of bodies swaying, of eyes rolling, under the droop of heavy and motionless foliage. The steamer toiled along slowly on the edge of a black and incomprehensible frenzy. The prehistoric man was cursing us, praying to us, welcoming us — who could tell? We were cut off from the comprehension of our surroundings; we glided past like phantoms, wondering and secretly appalled, as sane men would be before an enthusiastic outbreak in a madhouse. We could not understand because we were too far and could not remember, because we were travelling in the night of first ages, of those ages that are gone, leaving hardly a sign — and no memories.

"The earth seemed unearthly. We are accustomed to look upon the shackled form of a conquered monster, but there — there you could look at a thing monstrous and free. It was unearthly, and the men were ——No, they were not inhuman. Well, you know, that was the worst of it — this suspicion of their not being inhuman. It would come slowly to one. They howled and leaped, and spun, and made horrid faces; but what thrilled you was just the thought of their humanity — like yours — the thought of your

What interpretation of *Heart of Darkness* does this cover illustration by Mike Mignola suggest?

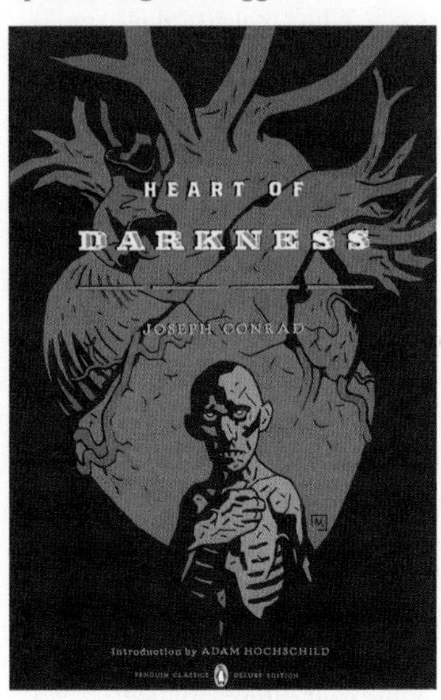

remote kinship with this wild and passionate uproar. Ugly. Yes, it was ugly enough; but if you were man enough you would admit to yourself that there was in you just the faintest trace of a response to the terrible frankness of that noise, a dim suspicion of there being a meaning in it which you — you so remote from the night of first ages — could comprehend. And why not? The mind of man is capable of anything—because everything is in it, all the past as well as all the future. What was there after all? Joy, fear, sorrow, devotion, valour, rage — who can tell? — but truth — truth stripped of its cloak of time. Let the fool gape and shudder — the man knows, and can look on without a wink. But he must at least be as much of a man as these on the shore. He must meet that truth with his own true stuff — with his own inborn strength. Principles won't do. Acquisitions, clothes, pretty rags — rags that would fly off at the first good shake. No; you want a deliberate belief. An appeal to me in this fiendish row — is there? Very well; I hear; I admit, but I have a voice, too, and for good or evil mine is the speech that cannot be silenced. Of course, a fool, what with sheer fright and fine sentiments, is always safe. Who's that grunting? You wonder I didn't go ashore for a howl and a dance? Well, no — I didn't. Fine sentiments, you say? Fine sentiments, be hanged! I had no time. I had to mess about with white-lead and strips of woollen blanket helping to put bandages on those leaky steam-pipes — I tell you. I had to watch the steering, and circumvent those snags, and get the tin-pot along by hook or by crook. There was surface-truth enough in these things to save a wiser man. And between whiles I had to look after the savage who was fireman. He was an improved specimen; he could fire up a vertical boiler. He was there below me, and, upon my word, to look at him was as edifying as seeing a dog in a parody of breeches and a feather hat, walking on his hind-legs. A few months of training had done for that really fine chap. He squinted at the steam-gauge and at the water-gauge with an evident effort of intrepidity — and he had filed teeth, too, the poor devil, and the wool of his pate shaved into queer patterns, and three ornamental scars on each of his cheeks. He ought to have been clapping his hands and stamping his feet on the bank, instead of which he was hard at work, a thrall to strange witchcraft, full of improving knowledge. He was useful because he had been instructed; and what he knew was this — that should the water in that transparent thing disappear, the evil spirit inside the boiler would get angry through the greatness of his thirst, and take a terrible vengeance. So he sweated and fired up and watched the glass fearfully (with an impromptu charm, made of rags, tied to his arm, and a piece of polished bone, as big as a watch, stuck flat-ways through his lower lip), while the wooded banks slipped past us slowly, the short noise was left behind, the interminable miles of silence — and we crept on, towards Kurtz. But the snags were thick, the water was treacherous and shallow, the boiler seemed indeed to have a sulky devil in it, and thus neither that fireman nor I had any time to peer into our creepy thoughts.

"Some fifty miles below the Inner Station we came upon a hut of reeds, an inclined and melancholy pole, with the unrecognizable tatters of what had been a flag of some sort flying from it, and a neatly stacked wood-pile. This was unexpected. We came to the bank, and on the stack of firewood found a flat piece of board with some faded pencil-writing on it. When deciphered it said: 'Wood for you. Hurry up. Approach cautiously.' There was a signature, but it was illegible — not Kurtz — a much longer word. 'Hurry up.' Where? Up the river? 'Approach cautiously.' We had not done so. But the warning could not have been meant for the place where it could be only found after approach. Something was wrong above. But what — and how much? That was the question. We commented adversely upon the imbecility of that telegraphic style. The bush around said nothing, and would not let us look very far, either. A torn curtain of red twill hung in the doorway of the hut, and flapped sadly in our faces. The dwelling was dismantled; but we could see a white man had lived there not very long ago. There remained a rude table — a plank on two posts; a heap of rubbish reposed in a dark corner, and by the door I picked up a book. It had lost its covers, and the pages had been thumbed into a state of extremely dirty softness; but the back had been lovingly stitched afresh with white cotton thread, which looked clean yet. It was an extraordinary find. Its title was, *An Inquiry into some Points of Seamanship*, by a man Towser, Towson — some such name — Master in his Majesty's Navy. The matter looked dreary reading enough, with illustrative diagrams and repulsive tables of figures, and the copy was sixty years old. I handled this amazing antiquity with the greatest possible tenderness, lest it should dissolve in my hands. Within,

Towson or Towser was inquiring earnestly into the breaking strain of ships' chains and tackle, and other such matters. Not a very enthralling book; but at the first glance you could see there a singleness of intention, an honest concern for the right way of going to work, which made these humble pages, thought out so many years ago, luminous with another than a professional light. The simple old sailor, with his talk of chains and purchases, made me forget the jungle and the pilgrims in a delicious sensation of having come upon something unmistakably real. Such a book being there was wonderful enough; but still more astounding were the notes pencilled in the margin, and plainly referring to the text. I couldn't believe my eyes! They were in cipher! Yes, it looked like cipher. Fancy a man lugging with him a book of that description into this nowhere and studying it — and making notes — in cipher at that! It was an extravagant mystery.

"I had been dimly aware for some time of a worrying noise, and when I lifted my eyes I saw the wood-pile was gone, and the manager, aided by all the pilgrims, was shouting at me from the river-side. I slipped the book into my pocket. I assure you to leave off reading was like tearing myself away from the shelter of an old and solid friendship.

"I started the lame engine ahead. 'It must be this miserable trader — this intruder,' exclaimed the manager, looking back malevolently at the place we had left. 'He must be English,' I said. 'It will not save him from getting into trouble if he is not careful,' muttered the manager darkly. I observed with assumed innocence that no man was safe from trouble in this world.

"The current was more rapid now, the steamer seemed at her last gasp, the stern-wheel flopped languidly, and I caught myself listening on tiptoe for the next beat of the boat, for in sober truth I expected the wretched thing to give up every moment. It was like watching the last flickers of a life. But still we crawled. Sometimes I would pick out a tree a little way ahead to measure our progress towards Kurtz by, but I lost it invariably before we got abreast. To keep the eyes so long on one thing was too much for human patience. The manager displayed a beautiful resignation. I fretted and fumed and took to arguing with myself whether or no I would talk openly with Kurtz; but before I could come to any conclusion it occurred to me that my speech or my silence, indeed any action of mine, would be a mere futility. What did it matter what any one knew or ignored? What did it matter who was manager? One gets sometimes such a flash of insight. The essentials of this affair lay deep under the surface, beyond my reach, and beyond my power of meddling.

"Towards the evening of the second day we judged ourselves about eight miles from Kurtz's station. I wanted to push on; but the manager looked grave, and told me the navigation up there was so dangerous that it would be advisable, the sun being very low already, to wait where we were till next morning. Moreover, he pointed out that if the warning to approach cautiously were to be followed, we must approach in daylight — not at dusk, or in the dark. This was sensible enough. Eight miles meant nearly three hours' steaming for us, and I could also see suspicious ripples at the upper end of the reach. Nevertheless, I was annoyed beyond expression at the delay, and most unreasonably, too, since one night more could not matter much after so many months. As we had plenty of wood, and caution was the word, I brought up in the middle of the stream. The reach was narrow, straight, with high sides like a railway cutting. The dusk came gliding into it long before the sun had set. The current ran smooth and swift, but a dumb immobility sat on the banks. The living trees, lashed together by the creepers and every living bush of the undergrowth, might have been changed into stone, even to the slenderest twig, to the lightest leaf. It was not sleep — it seemed unnatural, like a state of trance. Not the faintest sound of any kind could be heard. You looked on amazed, and began to suspect yourself of being deaf — then the night came suddenly, and struck you blind as well. About three in the morning some large fish leaped, and the loud splash made me jump as though a gun had been fired. When the sun rose there was a white fog, very warm and clammy, and more blinding than the night. It did not shift or drive; it was just there, standing all round you like something solid. At eight or nine, perhaps, it lifted as a shutter lifts. We had a glimpse of the towering multitude of trees, of the immense matted jungle, with the blazing little ball of the sun hanging over it — all perfectly still — and then the white shutter came down again, smoothly, as if sliding in greased grooves. I ordered the chain, which we had begun to heave in, to be paid out again. Before it stopped running with a muffled rattle, a cry, a very loud cry, as of infinite desolation, soared slowly in the opaque air. It ceased. A complaining clamour, modulated in savage discords, filled our ears. The sheer unexpectedness of it made my hair stir under my cap. I don't know how it struck the others: to me it seemed as though the mist itself had screamed, so suddenly, and apparently from all sides at once, did this tumultuous and mournful uproar arise. It culminated in a hurried outbreak of almost intolerably excessive shrieking, which stopped short, leaving us stiffened in a variety of silly attitudes, and obstinately listening to the nearly as appalling and excessive silence. 'Good God! What is the meaning——' stammered at my elbow one of the pilgrims, — a little fat man, with sandy hair and red whiskers, who wore side-spring boots, and pink pyjamas tucked into his socks. Two others remained open-mouthed a whole minute, then dashed into the little cabin, to rush out incontinently and stand darting scared glances, with Winchesters at 'ready' in their hands. What we could see was just the steamer we were on, her outlines blurred as though she had been on the point of dissolving, and a misty strip of water, perhaps two feet broad, around her — and that was all. The rest of the world was nowhere, as far as our eyes and ears were concerned. Just nowhere. Gone, disappeared; swept off without leaving a whisper or a shadow behind.

"I went forward, and ordered the chain to be hauled in short, so as to be ready to trip the anchor and move the steamboat at once if necessary. 'Will they attack?' whispered an awed voice. 'We will be all butchered in this fog,' murmured another. The faces twitched with the strain, the hands trembled slightly, the eyes forgot to wink. It was very curious to see the contrast of expressions of the white men and of the black fellows of our crew, who were as much strangers to that part of the river as we, though their homes were only eight hundred miles away. The whites, of course greatly discomposed, had besides a curious look of being painfully shocked by such an outrageous row. The others had an alert, naturally interested expression; but their faces were essentially quiet, even those of the one or two who grinned as they hauled at the chain. Several exchanged short, grunting phrases, which seemed to settle the matter to their satisfaction. Their headman, a young, broad-chested black, severely draped in dark-blue fringed cloths, with fierce nostrils and his hair all done up artfully in oily ringlets, stood near me. 'Aha!' I said, just for good fellowship's sake. 'Catch 'im,' he snapped, with a bloodshot widening of his eyes and a flash of sharp teeth — 'catch 'im. Give 'im to us.' 'To you, eh?' I asked; 'what would you do with them?' 'Eat 'im!' he said, curtly, and, leaning his elbow on the rail, looked out into the fog in a dignified and profoundly pensive attitude. I would no doubt have been properly horrified, had it not occurred to me that he and his chaps must be very hungry: that they must have been growing increasingly hungry for at least this month past. They had been engaged for six months (I don't think a single one of them had any clear idea of time, as we at the end of countless ages have. They still belonged to the beginnings of time — had no inherited experience to teach them as it were), and of course, as long as there was a piece of paper written over in accordance with some farcical law or other made down the river, it didn't enter anybody's head to trouble how they would live. Certainly they had brought with them some rotten hippo-meat, which couldn't have lasted very long, anyway, even if the pilgrims hadn't, in the midst of a shocking hullabaloo, thrown a considerable quantity of it overboard. It looked like a high-handed proceeding; but it was really a case of legitimate self-defence. You can't breathe dead hippo waking, sleeping, and eating, and at the same time keep your precarious grip on existence. Besides that, they had given them every week three pieces of brass wire, each about nine inches long; and the theory was they were to buy their provisions with that currency in river-side villages. You can see how *that* worked. There were either no villages, or the people were hostile, or the director, who like the rest of us fed out of tins, with an occasional old he-goat thrown in, didn't want to stop the steamer for some more or less recondite reason. So, unless they swallowed the wire itself, or made loops of it to snare the fishes with, I don't see what good their extravagant salary could be to them. I must say it was paid with a regularity worthy of a large and honourable trading company. For the rest, the only thing to eat — though it didn't look eatable in the least — I saw in their possession was a few lumps of some stuff like half-cooked dough, of a dirty lavender colour, they kept wrapped in leaves, and now and then swallowed a piece of, but so small that it seemed done more for the looks of the thing than for any serious purpose of sustenance. Why in the name of all the gnawing devils of hunger they didn't go for us — they were thirty to five — and have a good tuck-in for once, amazes me now when I think of it. They were big powerful men, with not much capacity to weigh the consequences, with courage, with strength, even yet, though their skins were no longer glossy and their muscles no longer hard. And I saw that something restraining, one of those human secrets that baffle probability, had come into play there. I looked at them with a swift quickening of interest — not because it occurred to me I might be eaten by them before very long, though I own to you that just then I perceived — in a new light, as it were — how unwholesome the pilgrims looked, and I hoped, yes I positively hoped, that my aspect was not so — what shall I say? — so — unappetizing: a touch of fantastic vanity which fitted well with the dream-sensation that pervaded all my days at that time. Perhaps I had a little fever, too. One can't live with one's finger everlastingly on one's pulse. I had often 'a little fever,' or a little touch of other things — the playful paw-strokes of the wilderness, the preliminary trifling before the more serious onslaught which came in due course. Yes; I looked at them as you would on any human being, with a curiosity of their impulses, motives, capacities, weaknesses, when brought to the test of an inexorable physical necessity. Restraint! What possible restraint? Was it superstition, disgust, patience, fear — or some kind of primitive honour? No fear can stand up to hunger, no patience can wear it out, disgust simply does not exist where hunger is; and as to superstition, beliefs, and what you may call principles, they are less than chaff in a breeze. Don't you know the devilry of lingering starvation, its exasperating torment, its black thoughts, its sombre and brooding ferocity? Well, I do. It takes a man all his inborn strength to fight hunger properly. It's really easier to face bereavement, dishonour, and the perdition of one's soul — than this kind of prolonged hunger. Sad, but true. And these chaps, too, had no earthly reason for any kind of scruple. Restraint! I would just as soon have expected restraint from a hyena prowling amongst the corpses of a battlefield. But there was the fact facing me — the fact dazzling, to be seen, like the foam on the depths of the sea, like a ripple on an unfathomable enigma, a mystery greater — when I thought of it — than the curious, inexplicable note of desperate grief in this savage clamour that had swept by us on the river-bank, behind the blind whiteness of the fog.

"Two pilgrims were quarrelling in hurried whispers as to which bank. 'Left.' 'No, no; how can you? Right, right, of course.' 'It is very serious,' said the manager's voice behind me; 'I would be desolated if anything should happen to Mr. Kurtz before we came up.' I looked at him, and had not the slightest doubt he was sincere. He was just the kind of man who would wish to preserve appearances. That was his restraint. But when he muttered something about going on at once, I did not even take the trouble to answer him. I knew, and he knew, that it was impossible. Were we to let go our hold of the bottom, we would be absolutely in the air — in space. We wouldn't be able to tell where we were going to — whether up or down stream, or across — till we fetched against one bank or the other, — and then we wouldn't know at first which it was. Of course I made no move. I had no mind for a smash-up. You couldn't imagine a more deadly place for a shipwreck. Whether drowned at once or not, we were sure to perish speedily in one way or another. 'I authorize you to take all the risks,' he said, after a short silence. 'I refuse to take any,' I said, shortly; which was just the answer he expected, though its tone might have surprised him. 'Well, I must defer to your judgment. You are captain,' he said, with marked civility. I turned my shoulder to him in sign of my appreciation, and looked into the fog. How long would it last? It was the most hopeless look-out. The approach to this Kurtz grubbing for ivory in the wretched bush was beset by as many dangers as though he had been an enchanted princess sleeping in a fabulous castle. 'Will they attack, do you think?' asked the manager, in a confidential tone.

"I did not think they would attack, for several obvious reasons. The thick fog was one. If they left the bank in their canoes they would get lost in it, as we would be if we attempted to move. Still, I had also judged the jungle of both banks quite impenetrable — and yet eyes were in it, eyes that had seen us. The river-side bushes were certainly very thick; but the undergrowth behind was evidently penetrable. However, during the short lift I had seen no canoes anywhere in the reach — certainly not abreast of the steamer. But what made the idea of attack inconceivable to me was the nature of the noise — of the cries we had heard. They had not the fierce character boding immediate hostile intention. Unexpected, wild, and violent as they had been, they had given me an irresistible impression of sorrow. The glimpse of the steamboat had for some reason filled those savages with unrestrained grief. The danger, if any, I expounded, was from our proximity to a great human passion let loose. Even extreme grief may ultimately vent itself in violence — but more generally takes the form of apathy. . . .

"You should have seen the pilgrims stare! They had no heart to grin, or even to revile me: but I believe they thought me gone mad — with fright, maybe. I delivered a regular lecture. My dear boys, it was no good bothering. Keep a look-out? Well, you may guess I watched the fog for the signs of lifting as a cat watches a mouse; but for anything else our eyes were of no more use to us than if we had been buried miles deep in a heap of cotton-wool. It felt like it, too — choking, warm, stifling. Besides, all I said, though it sounded extravagant, was absolutely true to fact. What we afterwards alluded to as an attack was really an attempt at repulse. The action was very far from being aggressive — it was not even defensive, in the usual sense: it was undertaken under the stress of desperation, and in its essence was purely protective.

"It developed itself, I should say, two hours after the fog lifted, and its commencement was at a spot, roughly speaking, about a mile and a half below Kurtz's station. We had just floundered and flopped round a bend, when I saw an islet, a mere grassy hummock of bright green, in the middle of the stream. It was the only thing of the kind; but as we opened the reach more, I perceived it was the head of a long sandbank, or rather of a chain of shallow patches stretching down the middle of the river. They were discoloured, just awash, and the whole lot was seen just under the water, exactly as a man's backbone is seen running down the middle of his back under the skin. Now, as far as I did see, I could go to the right or to the left of this. I didn't know either channel, of course. The banks looked pretty well alike, the depth appeared the same; but as I had been informed the station was on the west side, I naturally headed for the western passage.

"No sooner had we fairly entered it than I became aware it was much narrower than I had supposed. To the left of us there was the long uninterrupted shoal, and to the right a high, steep bank heavily overgrown with bushes. Above the bush the trees stood in serried ranks. The twigs overhung the current thickly, and from distance to distance a large limb of some tree projected rigidly over the stream. It was then well on in the afternoon, the face of the forest was gloomy, and a broad strip of shadow had already fallen on the water. In this shadow we steamed up — very slowly, as you may imagine. I sheered her well inshore — the water being deepest near the bank, as the sounding-pole informed me.

"One of my hungry and forbearing friends was sounding in the bows just below me. This steamboat was exactly like a decked scow. On the deck, there were two little teak-wood houses, with doors and windows. The boiler was in the fore-end, and the machinery right astern. Over the whole there was a light roof, supported on stanchions. The funnel projected through that roof, and in front of the funnel a small cabin built of light planks served for a pilot-house. It contained a couch, two camp-stools, a loaded Martini-Henry leaning in one corner, a tiny table, and the steering-wheel. It had a wide door in front and a broad shutter at each side. All these were always thrown open, of course. I spent my days perched up there on the extreme fore-end of that roof, before the door. At night I slept, or tried to, on the couch. An athletic black belonging to some coast tribe, and educated by my poor predecessor, was the helmsman. He sported a pair of brass earrings, wore a blue cloth wrapper from the waist to the ankles, and thought all the world of himself. He was the most unstable kind of fool I had ever seen. He steered with no end of a swagger while you were by; but if he lost sight of you, he became instantly the prey of an abject funk, and would let that cripple of a steamboat get the upper hand of him in a minute.

"I was looking down at the sounding-pole, and feeling much annoyed to see at each try a little more of it stick out of that river, when I saw my poleman give up the business suddenly, and stretch himself flat on the deck, without even taking the trouble to haul his pole in. He kept hold on it though, and it trailed in the water. At the same time the fireman, whom I could also see below me, sat down abruptly before his furnace and ducked his head. I was amazed. Then I had to look at the river mighty quick, because there was a snag in the fairway. Sticks, little sticks, were flying about — thick: they were whizzing before my nose, dropping below me, striking behind me against my pilot-house. All this time the river, the shore, the woods, were very quiet — perfectly quiet. I could only hear the heavy splashing thump of the stern-wheel and the patter of these things. We cleared the snag clumsily. Arrows, by Jove! We were being shot at! I stepped in quickly to close the shutter on the land-side. That fool-helmsman, his hands on the spokes, was lifting his knees high, stamping his feet, champing his mouth, like a reined-in horse. Confound him! And we were staggering within ten feet of the bank. I had to lean right out to swing the heavy shutter, and I saw a face amongst the leaves on the level with my own, looking at me very fierce and steady; and then suddenly, as though a veil had been removed from my eyes, I made out, deep in the tangled gloom, naked breasts, arms, legs, glaring eyes, — the bush was swarming with human limbs in movement, glistening, of bronze colour. The twigs shook, swayed, and rustled, the arrows flew out of them, and then the shutter came to. 'Steer her straight,' I said to the helmsman. He held his head rigid, face forward; but his eyes rolled, he kept on lifting and setting down his feet gently, his mouth foamed a little. 'Keep quiet!' I said in a fury. I might just as well have ordered a tree not to sway in the wind. I darted out. Below me there was a great scuffle of feet on the iron deck; confused exclamations; a voice screamed, 'Can you turn back?' I caught sight of a V-shaped ripple on the water ahead. What? Another snag! A fusillade burst out under my feet. The pilgrims had opened with their Winchesters, and were simply squirting lead into that bush. A deuce of a lot of smoke came up and drove slowly forward. I swore at it. Now I couldn't see the ripple or the snag either. I stood in the doorway, peering, and the arrows came in swarms. They might have been poisoned, but they looked as though they wouldn't kill a cat. The bush began to howl. Our wood-cutters raised a warlike whoop; the report of a rifle just at my back deafened me. I glanced over my shoulder, and the pilot-house was yet full of noise and smoke when I made a dash at the wheel. The fool-nigger had dropped everything, to throw the shutter open and let off that Martini-Henry. He stood before the wide opening, glaring, and I yelled at him to come back, while I straightened the sudden twist out of that steamboat. There was no room to turn even if I had wanted to, the snag was somewhere very near ahead in that confounded smoke, there was no time to lose, so I just crowded her into the bank — right into the bank, where I knew the water was deep.

"We tore slowly along the overhanging bushes in a whirl of broken twigs and flying leaves. The fusillade below stopped short, as I had foreseen it would when the squirts got empty. I threw my head back to a glinting whizz that traversed the pilot-house, in at one shutter-hole and out at the other. Looking past that mad helmsman, who was shaking the empty rifle and yelling at the shore, I saw vague forms of men running bent double, leaping, gliding, distinct, incomplete, evanescent. Something big appeared in the air before the shutter, the rifle went overboard, and the man stepped back swiftly, looked at me over his shoulder in an extraordinary, profound, familiar manner, and fell upon my feet. The side of his head hit the wheel twice, and the end of what appeared a long cane clattered round and knocked over a little camp-stool. It looked as though after wrenching that thing from somebody ashore he had lost his balance in the effort. The thin smoke had blown away, we were clear of the snag, and looking ahead I could see that in another hundred yards or so I would be free to sheer off, away from the bank; but my feet felt so very warm and wet that I had to look down. The man had rolled on his back and stared straight up at me; both his hands clutched that cane. It was the shaft of a spear that, either thrown or lunged through the opening, had caught him in the side just below the ribs; the blade had gone in out of sight, after making a frightful gash; my shoes were full; a pool of blood lay very still, gleaming dark-red under the wheel; his eyes shone with an amazing lustre. The fusillade burst out again. He looked at me anxiously, gripping the spear like something precious, with an air of being afraid I would try to take it away from him. I had to make an effort to free my eyes from his gaze and attend to the steering. With one hand I felt above my head for the line of the steam whistle, and jerked out screech after screech hurriedly. The tumult of angry and warlike yells was checked instantly, and then from the depths of the woods went out such a tremulous and prolonged wail of mournful fear and utter despair as may be imagined to follow the flight of the last hope from the earth. There was a great commotion in the bush; the shower of arrows stopped, a few dropping shots rang out sharply — then silence, in which the languid beat of the stern-wheel came plainly to my ears. I put the helm hard a-starboard at the moment when the pilgrim in pink pyjamas, very hot and agitated, appeared in the doorway. 'The manager sends me ——' he began in an official tone, and stopped short. 'Good God!' he said, glaring at the wounded man.

"We two whites stood over him, and his lustrous and inquiring glance enveloped us both. I declare it looked as though he would presently put to us some question in an understandable language; but he died without uttering a sound, without moving a limb, without twitching a muscle. Only in the very last moment, as though in response to some sign we could not see, to some whisper we could not hear, he frowned heavily, and that frown gave to his black death-mask an inconceivably sombre, brooding, and menacing expression. The lustre of inquiring glance faded swiftly into vacant glassiness. 'Can you steer?' I asked the agent eagerly. He looked very dubious; but I made a grab at his arm, and he understood at once I meant him to steer whether or no. To tell you the truth, I was morbidly anxious to change my shoes and socks. 'He is dead,' murmured the fellow, immensely impressed. 'No doubt about it,' said I, tugging like mad at the shoe-laces. 'And by the way, I suppose Mr. Kurtz is dead as well by this time.'

"For the moment that was the dominant thought. There was a sense of extreme disappointment, as though I had found out I had been striving after something altogether without a substance. I couldn't have been more disgusted if I had travelled all this way for the sole purpose of talking with Mr. Kurtz. Talking with . . . I flung one shoe overboard, and became aware that that was exactly what I had been looking forward to — a talk with Kurtz. I made the strange discovery that I had never imagined him as doing, you know, but as discoursing. I didn't say to myself, 'Now I will never see him,' or 'Now I will never shake him by the hand,' but, 'now I will never hear him.' The man presented himself as a voice. Not of course that I did not connect him with some sort of action. Hadn't I been told in all the tones of jealousy and admiration that he had collected, bartered, swindled, or stolen more ivory than all the other agents together? That was not the point. The point was in his being a gifted creature, and that of all his gifts the one that stood out preeminently, that carried with it a sense of real presence, was his ability to talk, his words — the gift of expression, the bewildering, the illuminating, the most exalted and the most contemptible, the pulsating stream of light, or the deceitful flow from the heart of an impenetrable darkness.

"The other shoe went flying unto the devil-god of that river. I thought, By Jove! it's all over. We are too late; he has vanished — the gift has vanished, by means of some spear, arrow, or club. I will never hear that chap speak after all, — and my sorrow had a startling extravagance of emotion, even such as I had noticed in the howling sorrow of these savages in the bush. I couldn't have felt more of lonely desolation somehow, had I been robbed of a belief or had missed my destiny in life. . . . Why do you sigh in this beastly way, somebody? Absurd? Well, absurd. Good Lord! mustn't a man ever ——Here, give me some tobacco." . . .

There was a pause of profound stillness, then a match flared, and Marlow's lean face appeared, worn, hollow, with downward folds and dropped eyelids, with an aspect of concentrated attention; and as he took vigorous draws at his pipe, it seemed to retreat and advance out of the night in the regular flicker of the tiny flame. The match went out.

"Absurd!" he cried. "This is the worst of trying to tell. . . . Here you all are, each moored with two good addresses, like a hulk with two anchors, a butcher round one corner, a policeman round another, excellent appetites, and temperature normal — you hear — normal from year's end to year's end. And you say, Absurd! Absurd be — exploded! Absurd! My dear boys, what can you expect from a man who out of sheer nervousness had just flung overboard a pair of new shoes! Now I think of it, it is amazing I did not shed tears. I am, upon the whole, proud of my fortitude. I was cut to the quick at the idea of having lost the inestimable privilege of listening to the gifted Kurtz. Of course I was wrong. The privilege was waiting for me. Oh, yes, I heard more than enough. And I was right, too. A voice. He was very little more than a voice. And I heard — him — it — this voice — other voices — all of them were so little more than voices — and the memory of that time itself lingers around me, impalpable, like a dying vibration of one immense jabber, silly, atrocious, sordid, savage, or simply mean, without any kind of sense. Voices, voices — even the girl herself — now ——"

He was silent for a long time.

"I laid the ghost of his gifts at last with a lie," he began, suddenly. "Girl! What? Did I mention a girl? Oh, she is out of it — completely. They — the women I mean—are out of it—should be out of it. We must help them to stay in that beautiful world of their own, lest ours gets worse. Oh, she had to be out of it. You should have heard the disinterred body of Mr. Kurtz saying, 'My Intended.' You would have perceived directly then how completely she was out of it. And the lofty frontal bone of Mr. Kurtz! They say the hair goes on growing sometimes, but this — ah — specimen, was impressively bald. The wilderness had patted him on the head, and, behold, it was like a ball — an ivory ball; it had caressed him, and — lo! — he had withered; it had taken him, loved him, embraced him, got into his veins, consumed his flesh, and sealed his soul to its own by the inconceivable ceremonies of some devilish initiation. He was its spoiled and pampered favourite. Ivory? I should think so. Heaps of it, stacks of it. The old mud shanty was bursting with it. You would think there was not a single tusk left either above or below the ground in the whole country. 'Mostly fossil,' the manager had remarked, disparagingly. It was no more fossil than I am; but they call it fossil when it is dug up. It appears these niggers do bury the tusks sometimes — but evidently they couldn't bury this parcel deep enough to save the gifted Mr. Kurtz from his fate. We filled the steamboat with it, and had to pile a lot on the deck. Thus he could see and enjoy as long as he could see, because the appreciation of this favour had remained with him to the last. You should have heard him say, 'My ivory.' Oh, yes, I heard him. 'My Intended, my ivory, my station, my river, my ——' everything belonged to him. It made me hold my breath in expectation of hearing the wilderness burst into a prodigious peal of laughter that would shake the fixed stars in their places. Everything belonged to him — but that was a trifle. The thing was to know what he belonged to, how many powers of darkness claimed him for their own. That was the reflection that made you creepy all over. It was impossible — it was not good for one either — trying to imagine. He had taken a high seat amongst the devils of the land — I mean literally. You can't understand. How could you? — with solid pavement under your feet, surrounded by kind neighbours ready to cheer you or to fall on you, stepping delicately between the butcher and the policeman, in the holy terror of scandal and gallows and lunatic asylums — how can you imagine what particular region of the first ages a man's untrammelled feet may take him into by the way of solitude — utter solitude without a policeman — by the way of silence — utter silence, where no warning voice of a kind neighbour can be heard whispering of public opinion? These little things make all the great difference. When they are gone you must fall back upon your own innate strength, upon your own capacity for faithfulness.

Of course you may be too much of a fool to go wrong — too dull even to know you are being assaulted by the powers of darkness. I take it, no fool ever made a bargain for his soul with the devil: the fool is too much of a fool, or the devil too much of a devil — I don't know which. Or you may be such a thunderingly exalted creature as to be altogether deaf and blind to anything but heavenly sights and sounds. Then the earth for you is only a standing place — and whether to be like this is your loss or your gain I won't pretend to say. But most of us are neither one nor the other. The earth for us is a place to live in, where we must put up with sights, with sounds, with smells, too, by Jove! — breathe dead hippo, so to speak, and not be contaminated. And there, don't you see? your strength comes in, the faith in your ability for the digging of unostentatious holes to bury the stuff in — your power of devotion, not to yourself, but to an obscure, back-breaking business. And that's difficult enough. Mind, I am not trying to excuse or even explain — I am trying to account to myself for — for — Mr. Kurtz — for the shade of Mr. Kurtz. This initiated wraith from the back of Nowhere honoured me with its amazing confidence before it vanished altogether. This was because it could speak English to me. The original Kurtz had been educated partly in England, and — as he was good enough to say himself — his sympathies were in the right place. His mother was half-English, his father was half-French. All Europe contributed to the making of Kurtz; and by and by I learned that, most appropriately, the International Society for the Suppression of Savage Customs had intrusted him with the making of a report, for its future guidance. And he had written it, too. I've seen it. I've read it. It was eloquent, vibrating with eloquence, but too high-strung, I think. Seventeen pages of close writing he had found time for! But this must have been before his — let us say — nerves, went wrong, and caused him to preside at certain midnight dances ending with unspeakable rites, which — as far as I reluctantly gathered from what I heard at various times — were offered up to him — do you understand? — to Mr. Kurtz himself. But it was a beautiful piece of writing. The opening paragraph, however, in the light of later information, strikes me now as ominous. He began with the argument that we whites, from the point of development we had arrived at, 'must necessarily appear to them [savages] in the nature of supernatural beings — we approach them with the might as of a deity,' and so on, and so on. 'By the simple exercise of our will we can exert a power for good practically unbounded,' etc., etc. From that point he soared and took me with him. The peroration was magnificent, though difficult to remember, you know. It gave me the notion of an exotic Immensity ruled by an august Benevolence. It made me tingle with enthusiasm. This was the unbounded power of eloquence — of words — of burning noble words. There were no practical hints to interrupt the magic current of phrases, unless a kind of note at the foot of the last page, scrawled evidently much later, in an unsteady hand, may be regarded as the exposition of a method. It was very simple, and at the end of that moving appeal to every altruistic sentiment it blazed at you, luminous and terrifying, like a flash of lightning in a serene sky: 'Exterminate all the brutes!' The curious part was that he had apparently forgotten all about that valuable postscriptum, because, later on, when he in a sense came to himself, he repeatedly entreated me to take good care of 'my pamphlet' (he called it), as it was sure to have in the future a good influence upon his career. I had full information about all these things, and, besides, as it turned out, I was to have the care of his memory. I've done enough for it to give me the indisputable right to lay it, if I choose, for an everlasting rest in the dust-bin of progress, amongst all the sweepings and, figuratively speaking, all the dead cats of civilization. But then, you see, I can't choose. He won't be forgotten. Whatever he was, he was not common. He had the power to charm or frighten rudimentary souls into an aggravated witch-dance in his honour; he could also fill the small souls of the pilgrims with bitter misgivings: he had one devoted friend at least, and he had conquered one soul in the world that was neither rudimentary nor tainted with self-seeking. No; I can't forget him, though I am not prepared to affirm the fellow was exactly worth the life we lost in getting to him. I missed my late helmsman awfully, — I missed him even while his body was still lying in the pilot-house. Perhaps you will think it passing strange this regret for a savage who was no more account than a grain of sand in a black Sahara. Well, don't you see, he had done something, he had steered; for months I had him at my back — a help — an instrument. It was a kind of partnership. He steered for me — I had to look after him, I worried about his deficiencies, and thus a subtle bond had been created, of which I only became aware when it was suddenly broken. And the intimate profundity of that look he gave me when he received his hurt remains to this day in my memory — like a claim of distant kinship affirmed in a supreme moment.

"Poor fool! If he had only left that shutter alone. He had no restraint, no restraint — just like Kurtz — a tree swayed by the wind. As soon as I had put on a dry pair of slippers, I dragged him out, after first jerking the spear out of his side, which operation I confess I performed with my eyes shut tight. His heels leaped together over the little door-step; his shoulders were pressed to my breast; I hugged him from behind desperately. Oh! he was heavy, heavy; heavier than any man on earth, I should imagine. Then without more ado I tipped him overboard. The current snatched him as though he had been a wisp of grass, and I saw the body roll over twice before I lost sight of it for ever. All the pilgrims and the manager were then congregated on the awning-deck about the pilot-house, chattering at each other like a flock of excited magpies, and there was a scandalized murmur at my heartless promptitude. What they wanted to keep that body hanging about for I can't guess. Embalm it, maybe. But I had also heard another, and a very ominous, murmur on the deck below. My friends the wood-cutters were likewise scandalized, and with a better show of reason — though I admit that the reason itself was quite inadmissible. Oh, quite! I had made up my mind that if my late helmsman was to be eaten, the fishes alone should have him. He had been a very second-rate helmsman while alive, but now he was dead he might have become a first-class temptation, and possibly cause some startling trouble. Besides, I was anxious to take the wheel, the man in pink pyjamas showing himself a hopeless duffer at the business.

"This I did directly the simple funeral was over. We were going half-speed, keeping right in the middle of the stream, and I listened to the talk about me. They had given up Kurtz, they had given up the station; Kurtz was dead, and the station had been burnt — and so on — and so on. The red-haired pilgrim was beside himself with the thought that at least this poor Kurtz had been properly avenged. 'Say! We must have made a glorious slaughter of them in the bush. Eh? What do you think? Say?' He positively danced, the bloodthirsty little gingery beggar. And he had nearly fainted when he saw the wounded man! I could not help saying, 'You made a glorious lot of smoke, anyhow.' I had seen, from the way the tops of the bushes rustled and flew, that almost all the shots had gone too high. You can't hit anything unless you take aim and fire from the shoulder; but these chaps fired from the hip with their eyes shut. The retreat, I maintained — and I was right — was caused by the screeching of the steam-whistle. Upon this they forgot Kurtz, and began to howl at me with indignant protests.

"The manager stood by the wheel murmuring confidentially about the necessity of getting well away down the river before dark at all events, when I saw in the distance a clearing on the river-side and the outlines of some sort of building. 'What's this?' I asked. He clapped his hands in wonder. 'The station!' he cried. I edged in at once, still going half-speed.

"Through my glasses I saw the slope of a hill interspersed with rare trees and perfectly free from undergrowth. A long decaying building on the summit was half buried in the high grass; the large holes in the peaked roof gaped black from afar; the jungle and the woods made a background. There was no enclosure or fence of any kind; but there had been one apparently, for near the house half-a-dozen slim posts remained in a row, roughly trimmed, and with their upper ends ornamented with round carved balls. The rails, or whatever there had been between, had disappeared. Of course the forest surrounded all that. The river-bank was clear, and on the water-side I saw a white man under a hat like a cart-wheel beckoning persistently with his whole arm. Examining the edge of the forest above and below, I was almost certain I could see movements—human forms gliding here and there. I steamed past prudently, then stopped the engines and let her drift down. The man on the shore began to shout, urging us to land. 'We have been attacked,' screamed the manager. 'I know—I know. It's all right,' yelled back the other, as cheerful as you please. 'Come along. It's all right. I am glad.'

"His aspect reminded me of something I had seen—something funny I had seen somewhere. As I manœuvred to get alongside, I was asking myself, 'What does this fellow look like?' Suddenly I got it. He looked like a harlequin. His clothes had been made of some stuff that was brown holland[18] probably, but it was covered with patches all over, with bright patches, blue, red, and yellow—patches on the back, patches on the front, patches on elbows, on knees; coloured binding around his jacket, scarlet edging at the bottom of his trousers; and the sunshine made him look extremely gay and wonderfully neat withal, because you could see how beautifully all this patching had been done. A beardless, boyish face, very fair, no features to speak of, nose peeling, little blue eyes, smiles and frowns chasing each other over that open countenance like sunshine and shadow on a wind-swept plain. 'Look out, captain!' he cried; 'there's a snag lodged in here last night.' What! Another snag? I confess I swore shamefully. I had nearly holed my cripple, to finish off that charming trip. The harlequin on the bank turned his little pug-nose up to me. 'You English?' he asked, all smiles. 'Are you?' I shouted from the wheel. The smiles vanished, and he shook his head as if sorry for my disappointment. Then he brightened up. 'Never mind!' he cried, encouragingly. 'Are we in time?' I asked. 'He is up there,' he replied, with a toss of the head up the hill, and becoming gloomy all of a sudden. His face was like the autumn sky, overcast one moment and bright the next.

110 "When the manager, escorted by the pilgrims, all of them armed to the teeth, had gone to the house this chap came on board. 'I say, I don't like this. These natives are in the bush,' I said. He assured me earnestly it was all right. 'They are simple people,' he added; 'well, I am glad you came. It took me all my time to keep them off.' 'But you said it was all right,' I cried. 'Oh, they meant no harm,' he said; and as I stared he corrected himself, 'Not exactly.' Then vivaciously, 'My faith, your pilot-house wants a clean-up!' In the next breath he advised me to keep enough steam on the boiler to blow the whistle in case of any trouble. 'One good screech will do more for you than all your rifles. They are simple people,' he repeated. He rattled away at such a rate he quite overwhelmed me. He seemed to be trying to make up for lots of silence, and actually hinted, laughing, that such was the case. 'Don't you talk with Mr. Kurtz?' I said. 'You don't talk with that man—you listen to him,' he exclaimed with severe exaltation. 'But now——' He waved his arm, and in the twinkling of an eye was in the uttermost depths of

[18] Unbleached linen. — EDS.

"The Rhodes Colossus," a cartoon published in the British magazine *Punch* in 1892, depicts Cecil Rhodes—a British financier, statesman, and empire builder—straddling everything on the continent between Cape Town, South Africa and Cairo, Egypt. **In what ways do the cartoon's visual elements and its message relate to Marlow's experiences? What themes do the two texts share?**

THE RHODES COLOSSUS

STRIDING FROM CAPE TOWN TO CAIRO.

*** Mr. Rhodes had announced his intention to continue the telegraph northwards across the Zambesi to Uganda, then, crossing the Soudan, to complete the overland telegraph line from Cape Town to Cairo.

Private Collection / Bridgeman Images

despondency. In a moment he came up again with a jump, possessed himself of both my hands, shook them continuously, while he gabbled: 'Brother sailor . . . honour . . . pleasure . . . delight . . . introduce myself . . . Russian . . . son of an arch-priest . . . Government of Tambov . . . What? Tobacco! English tobacco; the excellent English tobacco! Now, that's brotherly. Smoke? Where's a sailor that does not smoke?'

"The pipe soothed him, and gradually I made out he had run away from school, had gone to sea in a Russian ship; ran away again; served some time in English ships; was now reconciled with the arch-priest. He made a point of that. 'But when one is young one must see things, gather experience, ideas; enlarge the mind.' 'Here!' I interrupted. 'You can never tell! Here I met Mr. Kurtz,' he said, youthfully solemn and reproachful. I held my tongue after that. It appears he had persuaded a Dutch trading-house on the coast to fit him out with stores and goods, and had started for the interior with a light heart, and no more idea of what would happen to him than a baby. He had been wandering about that river for nearly two years alone, cut off from everybody and everything. 'I am not so young as I look. I am twenty-five,' he said. 'At first old Van Shuyten would tell me to go to the devil,' he narrated with keen enjoyment; 'but I stuck to him, and talked and talked, till at last he got afraid I would talk the hind-leg off his favourite dog, so he gave me some cheap things and a few guns, and told me he hoped he would never see my face again. Good old Dutchman, Van Shuyten. I've sent him one small lot of ivory a year ago, so that he can't call me a little thief when I get back. I hope he got it. And for the rest I don't care. I had some wood stacked for you. That was my old house. Did you see?'

"I gave him Towson's book. He made as though he would kiss me, but restrained himself. 'The only book I had left, and I thought I had lost it,' he said, looking at it ecstatically. 'So many accidents happen to a man going about alone, you know. Canoes get upset sometimes — and sometimes you've got to clear out so quick when the people get angry.' He thumbed the pages. 'You made notes in Russian?' I asked. He nodded. 'I thought they were written in cipher,' I said. He laughed, then became serious. 'I had lots of trouble to keep these people off,' he said. 'Did they want to kill you?' I asked. 'Oh, no!' he cried, and checked himself. 'Why did they attack us?' I pursued. He hesitated, then said shame-facedly, 'They don't want him to go.' 'Don't they?' I said, curiously. He nodded a nod full of mystery and wisdom. 'I tell you,' he cried, 'this man has enlarged my mind.' He opened his arms wide, staring at me with his little blue eyes that were perfectly round."

3

"I looked at him, lost in astonishment. There he was before me, in motley, as though he had absconded from a troupe of mimes, enthusiastic, fabulous. His very existence was improbable, inexplicable, and altogether bewildering. He was an insoluble problem. It was inconceivable how he had existed, how he had succeeded in getting so far, how he had managed to remain — why he did not instantly disappear. 'I went a little farther,' he said, 'then still a little farther — till I had gone so far that I don't know how I'll ever get back. Never mind. Plenty time. I can manage. You take Kurtz away quick — quick — I tell you.' The glamour of youth enveloped his particoloured rags, his destitution, his loneliness, the essential desolation of his futile wanderings. For months — for years — his life hadn't been worth a day's purchase; and there he was gallantly, thoughtlessly alive, to all appearance indestructible solely by the virtue of his few years and of his unreflecting audacity. I was seduced into something like admiration — like envy. Glamour urged him on, glamour kept him unscathed. He surely wanted nothing from the wilderness but space to breathe in and to push on through. His need was to exist, and to move onwards at the greatest possible risk, and with a maximum of privation. If the absolutely pure, uncalculating, unpractical spirit of adventure had ever ruled a human being, it ruled this be-patched youth. I almost envied him the possession of this modest and clear flame. It seemed to have consumed all thought of self so completely, that even while he was talking to you, you forgot that it was he — the man before your eyes — who had gone through these things. I did not envy him his devotion to Kurtz, though. He had not meditated over it. It came to him, and he accepted it with a sort of eager fatalism. I must say that to me it appeared about the most dangerous thing in every way he had come upon so far.

"They had come together unavoidably, like two ships becalmed near each other, and lay rubbing sides at last. I suppose Kurtz wanted an audience, because on a certain occasion, when encamped in the forest, they had talked all night, or more probably Kurtz had talked. 'We talked of everything,' he said, quite transported at the recollection. 'I forgot there was such a thing as sleep. The night did not seem to last an hour. Everything! Everything! . . . Of love too.' 'Ah, he talked to you of love!' I said, much amused. 'It isn't what you think,' he cried, almost passionately. 'It was in general. He made me see things — things.'

"He threw his arms up. We were on deck at the time, and the headman of my wood-cutters, lounging near by, turned upon him his heavy and glittering eyes. I looked around, and I don't know why, but I assure you that never, never before, did this land, this river, this jungle, the very arch of this blazing sky, appear to me so hopeless and so dark, so impenetrable to human thought, so pitiless to human weakness. 'And, ever since, you have been with him, of course?' I said.

"On the contrary. It appears their intercourse had been very much broken by various causes. He had, as he informed me proudly, managed to nurse Kurtz through two illnesses (he alluded to it as you would to some risky feat), but as a rule Kurtz wandered alone, far in the depths of the forest. 'Very often coming to this station, I had to wait days and days before he would turn up,' he said. 'Ah, it was worth waiting for! — sometimes.' 'What was he doing? exploring or what?' I asked. 'Oh, yes, of course'; he had discovered lots of villages, a lake, too — he did not know exactly in what direction; it was dangerous to inquire too much — but mostly his expeditions had been for ivory. 'But he had no goods to trade with by that time,' I objected. 'There's a good lot of cartridges left even yet,' he answered, looking away. 'To speak plainly, he raided the country,' I said. He nodded. 'Not alone, surely!' He muttered something about the villages round that lake. 'Kurtz got the tribe to follow him, did he?' I suggested. He fidgeted a little. 'They adored him,' he said. The tone of these words was so extraordinary that I looked at him searchingly. It was curious to see his mingled eagerness and reluctance to speak of Kurtz. The man filled his life, occupied his thoughts, swayed his emotions. 'What can you expect?' he burst out; 'he came to them with thunder and lightning, you know — and they had never seen anything like it — and very terrible. He could be very terrible. You can't judge Mr. Kurtz as you would an ordinary man. No, no, no! Now — just to give you an idea — I don't mind telling you, he wanted to shoot me, too, one day — but I don't judge him.' 'Shoot you!' I cried. 'What for?' 'Well, I had a small lot of ivory the chief of that village near my house gave me. You see I used to shoot game for them. Well, he wanted it, and wouldn't hear reason. He declared he would shoot me unless I gave him the ivory and then cleared out of the country, because he could do so, and had a fancy for it, and there was nothing on earth to prevent him killing whom he jolly well pleased. And it was true, too. I gave him the ivory. What did I care! But I didn't clear out. No, no. I couldn't leave him. I had to be careful, of course, till we got friendly again for a time. He had his second illness then. Afterwards I had to keep out of the way; but I didn't mind. He was living for the most part in those villages on the lake. When he came down to the river, sometimes he would take to me, and sometimes it was better for me to be careful. This man suffered too much. He hated all this, and somehow he couldn't get away. When I had a chance I begged him to try and leave while there was time; I offered to go back with him. And he would say yes, and then he would remain; go off on another ivory hunt; disappear for weeks; forget himself amongst these people — forget himself — you know.' 'Why! he's mad,' I said. He protested indignantly. Mr. Kurtz couldn't be mad. If I had heard him talk, only two days ago, I wouldn't dare hint at such a thing. . . . I had taken up my binoculars while we talked, and was looking at the shore, sweeping the limit of the forest at each side and at the back of the house. The consciousness of there being people in that bush, so silent, so quiet — as silent and quiet as the ruined house on the hill — made me uneasy. There was no sign on the face of nature of this amazing tale that was not so much told as suggested to me in desolate exclamations, completed by shrugs, in interrupted phrases, in hints ending in deep sighs. The woods were unmoved, like a mask — heavy, like the closed door of a prison — they looked with their air of hidden knowledge, of patient expectation, of unapproachable silence. The Russian was explaining to me that it was only lately that Mr. Kurtz had come down to the river, bringing along with him all the fighting men of that lake tribe. He had been absent for several months — getting himself adored, I suppose — and had come down unexpectedly, with the intention to all appearance of making a raid either across the river or down stream. Evidently the appetite for more ivory had got the better of the — what shall I say? — less material aspirations. However he had got much worse suddenly. 'I heard he was lying helpless, and so I came up — took my chance,' said the Russian. 'Oh, he is bad, very bad.' I directed my glass to the house. There were no signs of life, but there was the ruined roof, the long mud wall peeping above the grass, with three little square window-holes, no two of the same size; all this brought within reach of my hand, as it were. And then I made a brusque movement, and one of the remaining posts of that vanished fence leaped up in the field of my glass. You remember I told you I had been struck at the distance by certain attempts at ornamentation, rather remarkable in the ruinous aspect

In paragraph 116, the manager tells Marlow, "Well, he wanted it, and wouldn't hear reason. He declared he would shoot me unless I gave him the ivory and then cleared out of the country, because he could do so, and had a fancy for it, and there was nothing on earth to prevent him killing whom he jolly well pleased. And it was true, too. I gave him the ivory. What did I care!" **How does this photograph of the early twentieth-century ivory trade in the Belgian Congo reflect and/or challenge the details of the manager's story?**

of the place. Now I had suddenly a nearer view, and its first result was to make me throw my head back as if before a blow. Then I went carefully from post to post with my glass, and I saw my mistake. These round knobs were not ornamental but symbolic; they were expressive and puzzling, striking and disturbing — food for thought and also for vultures if there had been any looking down from the sky; but at all events for such ants as were industrious enough to ascend the pole. They would have been even more impressive, those heads on the stakes, if their faces had not been turned to the house. Only one, the first I had made out, was facing my way. I was not so shocked as you may think. The start back I had given was really nothing but a movement of surprise. I had expected to see a knob of wood there, you know. I returned deliberately to the first I had seen — and there it was, black, dried, sunken, with closed eyelids, — a head that seemed to sleep at the top of that pole, and with the shrunken dry lips showing a narrow white line of the teeth, was smiling, too, smiling continuously at some endless and jocose dream of that eternal slumber.

"I am not disclosing any trade secrets. In fact, the manager said afterwards that Mr. Kurtz's methods had ruined the district. I have no opinion on that point, but I want you clearly to understand that there was nothing exactly profitable in these heads being there. They only showed that Mr. Kurtz lacked restraint in the gratification of his various lusts, that there was something wanting in him — some small matter which, when the pressing need arose, could not be found under his magnificent eloquence. Whether he knew of this deficiency himself I can't say. I think the knowledge came to him at last — only at the very last. But the wilderness had found him out early, and had taken on him a terrible vengeance for the fantastic invasion. I think it had whispered to him things about himself which he did not know, things of which he had no conception till he took counsel with this great solitude — and the whisper had proved irresistibly fascinating. It echoed loudly within him because he was hollow at the core. . . . I put down the glass, and the head that had appeared near enough to be spoken to seemed at once to have leaped away from me into inaccessible distance.

"The admirer of Mr. Kurtz was a bit crestfallen. In a hurried, indistinct voice he began to assure me he had not dared to take these — say, symbols — down. He was not afraid of the natives; they would not stir till Mr. Kurtz gave the word. His ascendancy was extraordinary. The camps of these people surrounded the place, and the chiefs came every day to see him. They would crawl. . . . 'I don't want to know anything of the ceremonies used when approaching Mr. Kurtz,' I shouted. Curious, this feeling that came over me that such details would be more intolerable than those heads drying on the stakes under Mr. Kurtz's windows. After all, that was only a savage sight, while I seemed at one bound to have been transported into some lightless region of subtle horrors, where pure, uncomplicated savagery was a positive relief, being something that had a right to exist — obviously — in the sunshine. The young man looked at me with surprise. I suppose it did not occur to him that Mr. Kurtz was no idol of mine. He forgot I hadn't heard any of these splendid monologues on, what was it? on love, justice, conduct of life — or what not. If it had come to crawling before Mr. Kurtz, he crawled as much as the veriest savage of them all. I had no idea of the conditions, he said: these heads were the heads of rebels. I shocked him excessively by laughing. Rebels! What would be the next definition I was to hear? There had been enemies, criminals, workers — and these were rebels. Those rebellious heads looked very subdued to me on their sticks. 'You don't know how such a life tries a man like Kurtz,' cried Kurtz's last disciple. 'Well, and you?' I said. 'I! I! I am a simple man. I have no great thoughts. I want nothing from anybody. How can you compare me to . . . ?' His feelings were too much for speech, and suddenly he broke down. 'I don't understand,' he groaned. 'I've been doing my best to keep him alive, and that's enough. I had no hand in all this. I have no abilities. There hasn't been a drop of medicine or a mouthful of invalid food for months here. He was shamefully abandoned. A man like this, with such ideas. Shamefully! Shamefully! I — I — haven't slept for the last ten nights . . .'

"His voice lost itself in the calm of the evening. The long shadows of the forest had slipped downhill while we talked, had gone far beyond the ruined hovel, beyond the symbolic row of stakes. All this was in the gloom, while we down there were yet in the sunshine, and the stretch of the river abreast of the clearing glittered in a still and dazzling splendour, with a murky and overshadowed bend above and below. Not a living soul was seen on the shore. The bushes did not rustle.

"Suddenly round the corner of the house a group of men appeared, as though they had come up from the ground. They waded waist-deep in the grass, in a compact body, bearing an improvised stretcher in their midst. Instantly, in the emptiness of the landscape, a cry arose whose shrillness pierced the still air like a sharp arrow flying straight to the very heart of the land; and, as if by enchantment, streams of human beings — of naked human beings — with spears in their hands, with bows, with shields, with wild glances and savage movements, were poured into the clearing by the dark-faced and pensive forest. The bushes shook, the grass swayed for a time, and then everything stood still in attentive immobility.

" 'Now, if he does not say the right thing to them we are all done for,' said the Russian at my elbow. The knot of men with the stretcher had stopped, too, halfway to the steamer, as if petrified. I saw the man on the stretcher sit up, lank and with an uplifted arm, above the shoulders of the bearers. 'Let us hope that the man who can talk so well of love in general will find some particular reason to spare us this time,' I said. I resented bitterly the absurd danger of our situation, as if to be at the mercy of that atrocious phantom had been a dishonouring necessity. I could not hear a sound, but through my glasses I saw the thin arm extended commandingly, the lower jaw moving, the eyes of that apparition shining darkly far in its bony head that nodded with grotesque jerks. Kurtz — Kurtz — that means short in German — don't it? Well, the name was as true as everything else in his life — and death. He looked at least seven feet long. His covering had fallen off, and his body emerged from it pitiful and appalling as from a winding-sheet. I could see the cage of his ribs all astir, the bones of his arm waving. It was as though an animated image of death carved out of old ivory had been shaking its hand with menaces at a motionless crowd of men made of dark and glittering bronze. I saw him open his mouth wide — it gave him a weirdly voracious aspect, as though he had wanted to swallow all the air, all the earth, all the men before him. A deep voice reached me faintly. He must have been shouting. He fell back suddenly. The stretcher shook as the bearers staggered forward again, and almost at the same time I noticed that the crowd of savages was vanishing without any perceptible movement of retreat, as if the forest that had ejected these beings so suddenly had drawn them in again as the breath is drawn in a long aspiration.

"Some of the pilgrims behind the stretcher carried his arms — two shot-guns, a heavy rifle, and a light revolver-carbine — the thunderbolts of that pitiful Jupiter. The manager bent over him murmuring as he walked beside his head. They laid him down in one of the little cabins — just a room for a bedplace and a camp-stool or two, you know. We had brought his belated correspondence, and a lot of torn envelopes and open letters littered his bed. His hand roamed feebly amongst these papers. I was struck by the fire of his eyes and the composed languor of his expression. It was not so much the exhaustion of disease. He did not seem in pain. This shadow looked satiated and calm, as though for the moment it had had its fill of all the emotions.

"He rustled one of the letters, and looking straight in my face said, 'I am glad.' Somebody had been writing to him about me. These special recommendations were turning up again. The volume of tone he emitted without effort, almost without the trouble of moving his lips, amazed me. A voice! a voice! It was grave, profound, vibrating, while the man did not seem capable of a whisper. However, he had enough strength in him — factitious no doubt — to very nearly make an end of us, as you shall hear directly.

"The manager appeared silently in the doorway; I stepped out at once and he drew the curtain after me. The Russian, eyed curiously by the pilgrims, was staring at the shore. I followed the direction of his glance.

"Dark human shapes could be made out in the distance, flitting indistinctly against the gloomy border of the forest, and near the river two bronze figures, leaning on tall spears, stood in the sunlight under fantastic head-dresses of spotted skins, warlike and still in statuesque repose. And from right to left along the lighted shore moved a wild and gorgeous apparition of a woman.

"She walked with measured steps, draped in striped and fringed cloths, treading the earth proudly, with a slight jingle and flash of barbarous ornaments. She carried her head high; her hair was done in the shape of a helmet; she had brass leggings to the knee, brass wire gauntlets to the elbow, a crimson spot on her tawny cheek, innumerable necklaces of glass beads on her neck; bizarre things, charms, gifts of witch-men, that hung about her, glittered and trembled at every step. She must have had the value of several elephant tusks upon her. She was savage and superb, wild-eyed and magnificent; there was something ominous and stately in her deliberate progress. And in the hush that had fallen suddenly upon the whole sorrowful land, the immense wilderness, the colossal body of the fecund and mysterious life seemed to look at her, pensive, as though it had been looking at the image of its own tenebrous and passionate soul.

"She came abreast of the steamer, stood still, and faced us. Her long shadow fell to the water's edge. Her face had a tragic and fierce aspect of wild sorrow and of dumb pain mingled with the fear of some struggling, half-shaped resolve. She stood looking at us without a stir, and like the wilderness itself, with an air of brooding over an inscrutable purpose. A whole minute passed, and then she made a step forward. There was a low jingle, a glint of yellow metal, a sway of fringed draperies, and she stopped as if her heart had failed her. The young fellow by my side growled. The pilgrims murmured at my back. She looked at us all as if her life had depended upon the unswerving steadiness of her glance. Suddenly she opened her bared arms and threw them up rigid above her head, as though in an uncontrollable desire to touch the sky, and at the same time the swift shadows darted out on the earth, swept around on the river, gathering the steamer into a shadowy embrace. A formidable silence hung over the scene.

"She turned away slowly, walked on, following the bank, and passed into the bushes to the left. Once only her eyes gleamed back at us in the dusk of the thickets before she disappeared.

"'If she had offered to come aboard I really think I would have tried to shoot her,' said the man of patches, nervously. 'I have been risking my life every day for the last fortnight to keep her out of the house. She got in one day and kicked up a row about those miserable rags I picked up in the storeroom to mend my clothes with. I wasn't decent. At least it must have been that, for she talked like a fury to Kurtz for an hour, pointing at me now and then. I don't understand the dialect of this tribe. Luckily for me, I fancy Kurtz felt too ill that day to care, or there would have been mischief. I don't understand. . . . No — it's too much for me. Ah, well, it's all over now.'

"At this moment I heard Kurtz's deep voice behind the curtain: 'Save me! — save the ivory, you mean. Don't tell me. Save *me*! Why, I've had to save you. You are interrupting my plans now. Sick! Sick! Not so sick as you would like to believe. Never mind. I'll carry my ideas out yet — I will return. I'll show you what can be done. You with your little peddling notions — you are interfering with me. I will return. I. . . .'

"The manager came out. He did me the honour to take me under the arm and lead me aside. 'He is very low, very low,' he said. He considered it necessary to sigh, but neglected to be consistently sorrowful. 'We have done all we could for him — haven't we? But there is no disguising the fact, Mr. Kurtz has done more harm than good to the Company. He did not see the time was not ripe for vigorous action. Cautiously, cautiously — that's my principle. We must be cautious yet. The district is closed to us for a time. Deplorable! Upon the whole, the trade will suffer. I don't deny there is a remarkable quantity of ivory — mostly fossil. We must save it, at all events — but look how precarious the position is — and why? Because the method is unsound.' 'Do you,' said I, looking at the shore, 'call it "unsound method"?' 'Without doubt,' he exclaimed, hotly. 'Don't you?' . . . 'No method at all,' I murmured after a while. 'Exactly,' he exulted. 'I anticipated this. Shows a complete want of judgment. It is my duty to point it out in the proper quarter.' 'Oh,' said I, 'that fellow — what's his name? — the brickmaker, will make a readable report for you.' He appeared confounded for a moment. It seemed to me I had never breathed an atmosphere so vile, and I turned mentally to Kurtz for relief — positively for relief. 'Nevertheless I think Mr. Kurtz is a remarkable man,' I said with emphasis. He started, dropped on me a cold heavy glance, said very quietly, 'He *was*,' and turned his back on me. My hour of favour was over; I found myself lumped along with Kurtz as a partisan of methods for which the time was not ripe: I was unsound! Ah! but it was something to have at least a choice of nightmares.

"I had turned to the wilderness really, not to Mr. Kurtz, who, I was ready to admit, was as good as buried. And for a moment it seemed to me as if I also were buried in a vast grave full of unspeakable secrets. I felt an intolerable weight oppressing my breast, the smell of the damp earth, the unseen presence of victorious corruption, the darkness of an impenetrable night. . . . The Russian tapped me on the shoulder. I heard him mumbling and stammering something about 'brother seaman — couldn't conceal — knowledge of matters that would affect Mr. Kurtz's reputation.' I waited. For him evidently Mr. Kurtz was not in his grave; I suspect that for him Mr. Kurtz was one of the immortals. 'Well!' said I at last, 'speak out. As it happens, I am Mr. Kurtz's friend — in a way.'

"He stated with a good deal of formality that had we not been 'of the same profession,' he would have kept the matter to himself without regard to consequences. 'He suspected there was an active ill will towards him on the part of these white men that ——' 'You are right,' I said, remembering a certain conversation I had overheard. 'The manager thinks you ought to be hanged.' He showed a concern at this intelligence which amused me at first. 'I had better get out of the way quietly,' he said, earnestly. 'I can do no more for Kurtz now, and they would soon find some excuse. What's to stop them? There's a military post three hundred miles from here.' 'Well, upon my word,' said I, 'perhaps you had better go if you have any friends amongst the savages near by.' 'Plenty,' he said. 'They are simple people — and I want nothing, you know.' He stood biting his lip, then: 'I don't want any harm to happen to these whites here, but of course I was thinking of Mr. Kurtz's reputation — but you are a brother seaman and ——' 'All right,' said I, after a time. 'Mr. Kurtz's reputation is safe with me.' I did not know how truly I spoke.

"He informed me, lowering his voice, that it was Kurtz who had ordered the attack to be made on the steamer. 'He hated sometimes the idea of being taken away — and then again. . . . But I don't understand these matters. I am a simple man. He thought it would scare you away — that you would give it up, thinking him dead. I could not stop him. Oh, I had an awful time of it this last month.' 'Very well,' I said. 'He is all right now.' 'Ye-e-es,' he muttered, not very convinced apparently. 'Thanks,' said I; 'I shall keep my eyes open.' 'But quiet — eh?' he urged, anxiously. 'It would be awful for his reputation if anybody here ——' I promised a complete discretion with great gravity. 'I have a canoe and three black fellows waiting not very far. I am off. Could you give me a few Martini-Henry cartridges?' I could, and did, with proper secrecy. He helped himself, with a wink at me, to a handful of my tobacco. 'Between sailors — you know — good English tobacco.' At the door of the pilot-house he turned round — 'I say, haven't you a pair of shoes you could spare?' He raised one leg. 'Look.' The soles were tied with knotted strings sandal-wise under his bare feet. I rooted out an old pair, at which he looked with admiration before tucking it under his left arm. One of his pockets (bright red) was bulging with cartridges, from the other (dark blue) peeped 'Towson's Inquiry,' etc., etc. He seemed to think himself excellently well equipped for a renewed encounter with the wilderness. 'Ah! I'll never, never meet such a man again. You ought to have heard him recite poetry — his own, too, it was, he told me. Poetry!' He rolled his eyes at the recollection of these delights. 'Oh, he enlarged my mind!' 'Good-bye,' said I. He shook hands and vanished in the night. Sometimes I ask myself whether I had ever really seen him — whether it was possible to meet such a phenomenon! . . .

"When I woke up shortly after midnight his warning came to my mind with its hint of danger that seemed, in the starred darkness, real enough to make me get up for the purpose of having a look round. On the hill a big fire burned, illuminating fitfully a crooked corner of the station-house. One of the agents with a picket[19] of a few of our blacks, armed for the purpose, was keeping guard over the ivory; but deep within the forest, red gleams that wavered, that seemed to sink and rise from the ground amongst confused columnar shapes of intense blackness, showed the exact position of the camp where Mr. Kurtz's adorers were keeping their uneasy vigil. The monotonous beating of a big drum filled the air with muffled shocks and a lingering vibration. A steady droning sound of many men chanting each to himself some weird incantation came out from the black, flat wall of the woods as the humming of bees comes out of a hive, and had a strange narcotic effect upon my half-awake senses. I believe I dozed off leaning over the rail, till an abrupt burst of yells, an overwhelming outbreak of a pent-up and mysterious frenzy, woke me up in a bewildered wonder. It was cut short all at once, and the low droning went on with an effect of audible and soothing silence. I glanced casually into the little cabin. A light was burning within, but Mr. Kurtz was not there.

"I think I would have raised an outcry if I had believed my eyes. But I didn't believe them at first — the thing seemed so impossible. The fact is I was completely unnerved by a sheer blank fright, pure abstract terror, unconnected with any distinct shape of physical danger. What made this emotion so overpowering was — how shall I define it? — the moral shock I received, as if something altogether monstrous, intolerable to thought and odious to the soul, had been thrust upon me unexpectedly. This lasted of course the merest fraction of a second, and then the usual sense of commonplace, deadly danger, the possibility of a sudden onslaught and massacre, or something of the kind, which I saw impending, was positively welcome and composing. It pacified me, in fact, so much, that I did not raise an alarm.

"There was an agent buttoned up inside an ulster and sleeping on a chair on deck within three feet of me. The yells had not awakened him; he snored very slightly; I left him to his slumbers and leaped ashore. I did not betray Mr. Kurtz — it was ordered I should never betray him — it was written I should be loyal to the nightmare of my choice. I was anxious to deal with this shadow by myself alone, — and to this day I don't know why I was so jealous of sharing with any one the peculiar blackness of that experience.

"As soon as I got on the bank I saw a trail — a broad trail through the grass. I remember the exultation with which I said to myself, 'He can't walk — he is crawling on all-fours — I've got him.' The grass was wet with dew. I strode rapidly with clenched fists. I fancy I had some vague notion of falling upon him and giving him a drubbing. I don't know. I had some imbecile thoughts. The knitting old woman with the cat obtruded herself upon my memory as a most improper person to be sitting at the other end of such an affair. I saw a row of pilgrims squirting lead in the air out of Winchesters held to the hip. I thought I would never get back to the steamer, and imagined myself living alone and unarmed in the woods to an advanced age. Such silly things — you know. And I remember I confounded the beat of the drum with the beating of my heart, and was pleased at its calm regularity.

"I kept to the track though — then stopped to listen. The night was very clear; a dark blue space, sparkling with dew and starlight, in which black things stood very still. I thought I could see a kind of motion ahead of me. I was strangely cocksure of everything that night. I actually left the track and ran in a wide semicircle (I verily believe chuckling to myself) so as to get in front of that stir, of that motion I had seen — if indeed I had seen anything. I was circumventing Kurtz as though it had been a boyish game.

[19] Small group of soldiers. — EDS.

In 2013, artist Matt Kish illustrated several scenes from *Heart of Darkness*. **Discuss how the image below interprets the following quotation from paragraph 138: "As soon as I got on the bank I saw a trail—a broad trail through the grass. I remember the exultation with which I said to myself, 'He can't walk—he is crawling on all-fours—I've got him.'"**

Matt Kish

140 "I came upon him, and, if he had not heard me coming, I would have fallen over him, too, but he got up in time. He rose, unsteady, long, pale, indistinct, like a vapour exhaled by the earth, and swayed slightly, misty and silent before me; while at my back the fires loomed between the trees, and the murmur of many voices issued from the forest. I had cut him off cleverly; but when actually confronting him I seemed to come to my senses, I saw the danger in its right proportion. It was by no means over yet. Suppose he began to shout? Though he could hardly stand, there was still plenty of vigour in his voice. 'Go away — hide yourself,' he said, in that profound tone. It was very awful. I glanced back. We were within thirty yards from the nearest fire. A black figure stood up, strode on long black legs, waving long black arms, across the glow. It had horns — antelope horns, I think — on its head. Some sorcerer, some witch-man, no doubt: it looked fiend-like enough. 'Do you know what you are doing?' I whispered. 'Perfectly,' he answered, raising his voice for that single word: it sounded to me far off and yet loud, like a hail through a speaking-trumpet. If he makes a row we are lost, I thought to myself. This clearly was not a case for fisticuffs, even apart from the very natural aversion I had to beat that Shadow — this wandering and tormented thing. 'You will be lost,' I said — 'utterly lost.' One gets sometimes such a flash of inspiration, you know. I did say the right thing, though indeed he could not have been more irretrievably lost than he was at this very moment, when the foundations of our intimacy were being laid — to endure — to endure — even to the end — even beyond.

"'I had immense plans,' he muttered irresolutely. 'Yes,' said I; 'but if you try to shout I'll smash your head with ——' There was not a stick or stone near. 'I will throttle you for good,' I corrected myself. 'I was on the threshold of great things,' he pleaded, in a voice of longing, with a wistfulness of tone that made my blood run cold. 'And now for this stupid scoundrel ——' 'Your success in Europe is assured in any case,' I affirmed, steadily. I did not want to have the throttling of him, you understand — and indeed it would have been very little use for any practical purpose. I tried to break the spell — the heavy, mute spell of the wilderness — that seemed to draw him to its pitiless breast by the awakening of forgotten and brutal instincts, by the memory of gratified and monstrous passions. This alone, I was convinced, had driven him out to the edge of the forest, to the bush, towards the gleam of fires, the throb of drums, the drone of weird incantations; this alone had beguiled his unlawful soul beyond the bounds of permitted aspirations. And, don't you see, the terror of the position was not in being knocked on the head — though I had a very lively sense of that danger, too — but in this, that I had to deal with a being to whom I could not appeal in the name of anything high or low. I had, even like the niggers, to invoke him — himself — his own exalted and incredible degradation. There was nothing either above or below him, and I knew it. He had kicked himself loose of the earth. Confound the man! he had kicked the very earth to pieces. He was alone, and I before him did not know whether I stood on the ground or floated in the air. I've been telling you what we said — repeating the phrases we pronounced — but what's the good? They were common everyday words — the familiar, vague sounds exchanged on every waking day of life. But what of that? They had behind them, to my mind, the terrific suggestiveness of words heard in dreams, of phrases spoken in nightmares. Soul! If anybody had ever struggled with a soul, I am the man. And I wasn't arguing with a lunatic either. Believe me or not, his intelligence was perfectly clear — concentrated, it is true, upon himself with horrible intensity, yet clear; and therein was my only chance — barring, of course, the killing him there and then, which wasn't so good, on account of unavoidable noise. But his soul was mad. Being alone in the wilderness, it had looked within itself, and, by heavens! I tell you, it had gone mad. I had — for my sins, I suppose — to go through the ordeal of looking into it myself. No eloquence could have been so withering to one's belief in mankind as his final burst of sincerity. He struggled with himself, too. I saw it — I heard it. I saw the inconceivable mystery of a soul that knew no restraint, no faith, and no fear, yet struggling blindly with itself. I kept my head pretty well; but when I had him at last stretched on the couch, I wiped my forehead, while my legs shook under me as though I had carried half a ton on my back down that hill. And yet I had only supported him, his bony arm clasped round my neck — and he was not much heavier than a child.

"When next day we left at noon, the crowd, of whose presence behind the curtain of trees I had been acutely conscious all the time, flowed out of the woods again, filled the clearing, covered the slope with a mass of naked, breathing, quivering, bronze bodies. I steamed up a bit, then swung downstream, and two thousand eyes followed the evolutions of the splashing, thumping, fierce river-demon beating the water with its terrible tail and breathing black smoke into the air. In front of the first rank, along the river, three men, plastered with bright red earth from head to foot, strutted to and fro restlessly. When we came abreast again, they faced the river, stamped their feet, nodded their horned heads, swayed their scarlet bodies; they shook towards the fierce river-demon a bunch of black feathers, a mangy skin with a pendent tail — something that looked like a dried gourd; they shouted periodically together strings of amazing words that resembled no sounds of human language; and the deep murmurs of the crowd, interrupted suddenly, were like the responses of some satanic litany.

"We had carried Kurtz into the pilot-house: there was more air there. Lying on the couch, he stared through the open shutter. There was an eddy in the mass of human bodies, and the woman with helmeted head and tawny cheeks rushed out to the very brink of the stream. She put out her hands, shouted something, and all that wild mob took up the shout in a roaring chorus of articulated, rapid, breathless utterance.

"'Do you understand this?' I asked.

"He kept on looking out past me with fiery, longing eyes, with a mingled expression of wistfulness and hate. He made no answer, but I saw a smile, a smile of indefinable meaning, appear on his colourless lips that a moment after twitched convulsively. 'Do I not?' he said slowly, gasping, as if the words had been torn out of him by a supernatural power.

"I pulled the string of the whistle, and I did this because I saw the pilgrims on deck getting out their rifles with an air of anticipating a jolly lark. At the sudden screech there was a movement of abject terror through that wedged mass of bodies. 'Don't! don't you frighten them away,' cried someone on deck disconsolately. I pulled the string time after time. They broke and ran, they leaped, they crouched, they swerved, they dodged the flying terror of the sound. The three red chaps had fallen flat, face down on the shore, as though they had been shot dead. Only the barbarous and superb woman did not so much as flinch, and stretched tragically her bare arms after us over the sombre and glittering river.

"And then that imbecile crowd down on the deck started their little fun, and I could see nothing more for smoke.

"The brown current ran swiftly out of the heart of darkness, bearing us down towards the sea with twice the speed of our upward progress; and Kurtz's life was running swiftly, too, ebbing, ebbing out of his heart into the sea of inexorable time. The manager was very placid, he had no vital anxieties now, he took us both in with a comprehensive and satisfied glance: the 'affair' had come off as well as could be wished. I saw the time approaching when I would be left alone of the party of 'unsound method.' The pilgrims looked upon me with disfavour. I was, so to speak, numbered with the dead. It is strange how I accepted this unforeseen partnership, this choice of nightmares forced upon me in the tenebrous land invaded by these mean and greedy phantoms.

"Kurtz discoursed. A voice! a voice! It rang deep to the very last. It survived his strength to hide in the magnificent folds of eloquence the barren darkness of his heart. Oh, he struggled! he struggled! The wastes of his weary brain were haunted by shadowy images now — images of wealth and fame revolving obsequiously round his unextinguishable gift of noble and lofty expression. My Intended, my station, my career, my ideas — these were the subjects for the occasional utterances of elevated sentiments. The shade of the original Kurtz frequented the bedside of the hollow sham, whose fate it was to be buried presently in the mould of primeval earth. But both the diabolic love and the unearthly hate of the mysteries it had penetrated fought for the possession of that soul satiated with primitive emotions, avid of lying fame, of sham distinction, of all the appearances of success and power.

"Sometimes he was contemptibly childish. He desired to have kings meet him at railway-stations on his return from some ghastly Nowhere, where he intended to accomplish great things. 'You show them you have in you something that is really profitable, and then there will be no limits to the recognition of your ability,' he would say. 'Of course you must take care of the motives — right motives — always.' The long reaches that were like one and the same reach, monotonous bends that were exactly alike, slipped past the steamer with their multitude of secular trees looking patiently after this grimy fragment of another world, the forerunner of change, of conquest, of trade, of massacres, of blessings. I looked ahead — piloting. 'Close the shutter,' said Kurtz suddenly one day; 'I can't bear to look at this.' I did so. There was a silence. 'Oh, but I will wring your heart yet!' he cried at the invisible wilderness.

"We broke down — as I had expected — and had to lie up for repairs at the head of an island. This delay was the first thing that shook Kurtz's confidence. One morning he gave me a packet of papers and a photograph — the lot tied together with a shoe-string. 'Keep this for me,' he said. 'This noxious fool' (meaning the manager) 'is capable of prying into my boxes when I am not looking.' In the afternoon I saw him. He was lying on his back with closed eyes, and I withdrew quietly, but I heard him mutter, 'Live rightly, die, die . . .' I listened. There was nothing more. Was he rehearsing some speech in his sleep, or was it a fragment of a phrase from some newspaper article? He had been writing for the papers and meant to do so again, 'for the furthering of my ideas. It's a duty.'

"His was an impenetrable darkness. I looked at him as you peer down at a man who is lying at the bottom of a precipice where the sun never shines. But I had not much time to give him, because I was helping the engine-driver to take to pieces the leaky cylinders, to straighten a bent connecting-rod, and in other such matters. I lived in an infernal mess of rust, filings, nuts, bolts, spanners, hammers, ratchet-drills — things I abominate, because I don't get on with them. I tended the little forge we fortunately had aboard; I toiled wearily in a wretched scrap-heap—unless I had the shakes too bad to stand.

"One evening coming in with a candle I was startled to hear him say a little tremulously, 'I am lying here in the dark waiting for death.' The light was within a foot of his eyes. I forced myself to murmur, 'Oh, nonsense!' and stood over him as if transfixed.

"Anything approaching the change that came over his features I have never seen before, and hope never to see again. Oh, I wasn't touched. I was fascinated. It was as though a veil had been rent. I saw on that ivory face the expression of sombre pride, of ruthless power, of craven terror — of an intense and hopeless despair. Did he live his life again in every detail of desire, temptation, and surrender during that supreme moment of complete knowledge? He cried in a whisper at some image, at some vision — he cried out twice, a cry that was no more than a breath —

" 'The horror! The horror!'

"I blew the candle out and left the cabin. The pilgrims were dining in the mess-room, and I took my place opposite the manager, who lifted his eyes to give me a questioning glance, which I successfully ignored. He leaned back, serene, with that peculiar smile of his sealing the unexpressed depths of his meanness. A continuous shower of small flies streamed upon the lamp, upon the cloth, upon our hands and faces. Suddenly the manager's boy put his insolent black head in the doorway, and said in a tone of scathing contempt —

" 'Mistah Kurtz — he dead.'

"All the pilgrims rushed out to see. I remained, and went on with my dinner. I believe I was considered brutally callous. However, I did not eat much. There was a lamp in there — light, don't you know — and outside it was so beastly, beastly dark. I went no more near the remarkable man who had pronounced a judgment upon the adventures of his soul on this earth. The voice was gone. What else had been there? But I am of course aware that next day the pilgrims buried something in a muddy hole.

"And then they very nearly buried me.

"However, as you see, I did not go to join Kurtz there and then. I did not. I remained to

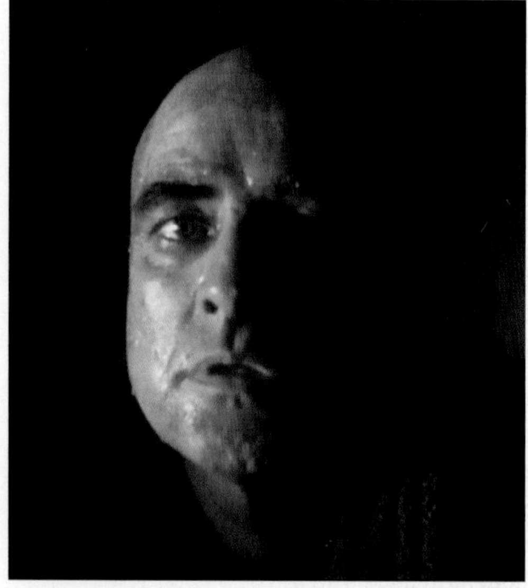

This movie still shows Marlon Brando as Colonel Kurtz in *Apocalypse Now*, a film based on *Heart of Darkness* that takes place during the Vietnam War. **How do the composition, pose, and colors in this image evoke the character of Kurtz as Conrad describes him?**

dream the nightmare out to the end, and to show my loyalty to Kurtz once more. Destiny. My destiny! Droll thing life is — that mysterious arrangement of merciless logic for a futile purpose. The most you can hope from it is some knowledge of yourself — that comes too late — a crop of unextinguishable regrets. I have wrestled with death. It is the most unexciting contest you can imagine. It takes place in an impalpable grayness, with nothing underfoot, with nothing around, without spectators, without clamour, without glory, without the great desire of victory, without the great fear of defeat, in a sickly atmosphere of tepid scepticism, without much belief in your own right, and still less in that of your adversary. If such is the form of ultimate wisdom, then life is a greater riddle than some of us think it to be. I was within a hair's breadth of the last opportunity for pronouncement, and I found with humiliation that probably I would have nothing to say. This is the reason why I affirm that Kurtz was a remarkable man. He had something to say. He said it. Since I had peeped over the edge myself, I understand better the meaning of his stare, that could not see the flame of the candle, but was wide enough to embrace the whole universe, piercing enough to penetrate all the hearts that beat in the darkness. He had summed up — he had judged. 'The horror!' He was a remarkable man. After all, this was the expression of some sort of belief; it had candour, it had conviction, it had a vibrating note of revolt in its whisper, it had the appalling face of a glimpsed truth — the strange commingling of desire and hate. And it is not my own extremity I remember best — a vision of grayness without form filled with physical pain, and a careless contempt for the evanescence of all things — even of this pain itself. No! It is his extremity that I seem to have lived through. True, he had made that last stride, he had stepped over the edge, while I had been permitted to draw back my hesitating foot. And perhaps in this is the whole difference; perhaps all the wisdom, and all truth, and all sincerity, are just compressed into that inappreciable moment of time in which we step over the threshold of the invisible. Perhaps! I like to think my summing-up would not have been a word of careless contempt. Better his cry — much better. It was an affirmation, a moral victory paid for by innumerable defeats, by abominable terrors, by abominable satisfactions. But it was a victory! That is why I have remained loyal to Kurtz to the last, and even beyond, when a long time after I heard once more, not his own voice, but the echo of his magnificent eloquence thrown to me from a soul as translucently pure as a cliff of crystal.

"No, they did not bury me, though there is a period of time which I remember mistily, with a shuddering wonder, like a passage through some inconceivable world that had no hope in it and no desire. I found myself back in the sepulchral city resenting the sight of people hurrying through the streets to filch a little money from each other, to devour their infamous cookery, to gulp their unwholesome beer, to dream their insignificant and silly dreams. They trespassed upon my thoughts. They were intruders whose knowledge of life was to me an irritating pretence, because I felt so sure they could not possibly know the things I knew. Their bearing, which was simply the bearing of commonplace individuals going about their business in the assurance of perfect safety, was offensive to me like the outrageous flauntings of folly in the face of a danger it is unable to comprehend. I had no particular desire to enlighten them, but I had some difficulty in restraining myself from laughing in their faces, so full of stupid importance. I daresay I was not very well at that time. I tottered about the streets — there were various affairs to settle — grinning bitterly at perfectly respectable persons. I admit my behaviour was inexcusable, but then my temperature was seldom normal in these days. My dear aunt's endeavours to 'nurse up my strength' seemed altogether beside the mark. It was not my strength that wanted nursing, it was my imagination that wanted soothing. I kept the bundle of papers given me by Kurtz, not knowing exactly what to do with it. His mother had died lately, watched over, as I was told, by his Intended. A clean-shaved man, with an official manner and wearing gold-rimmed spectacles, called on me one day and made inquiries, at first circuitous, afterwards suavely pressing, about what he was pleased to denominate certain 'documents.' I was not surprised, because I had had two rows with the manager on the subject out there. I had refused to give up the smallest scrap out of that package, and I took the same attitude with the spectacled man. He became darkly menacing at last, and with much heat argued that the Company had the right to every bit of information about its 'territories.' And said he, 'Mr. Kurtz's knowledge of unexplored regions must have been necessarily extensive and peculiar — owing to his great abilities and to the deplorable circumstances in which he had been placed: therefore ——' I assured him Mr. Kurtz's knowledge, however extensive, did not bear upon the problems of commerce or administration. He invoked then the name of science. 'It would be an incalculable loss if,' etc., etc. I offered him the report on the 'Suppression of Savage Customs,' with the postscriptum torn off. He took it up eagerly, but ended by sniffing at it with an air of contempt. 'This is not what we had a right to expect,' he remarked. 'Expect nothing else,' I said. 'There are only private letters.' He withdrew upon some threat of legal proceedings, and I saw him no more; but another fellow, calling himself Kurtz's cousin, appeared two days later, and was anxious to hear all the details about his dear relative's last moments. Incidentally he gave me to understand that Kurtz had been essentially a great musician. 'There was the making of an immense success,' said the man, who was an organist, I believe, with lank gray hair flowing over a greasy coat-collar. I had no reason to doubt his statement; and to this day I am unable to say what was Kurtz's profession, whether he ever had any — which was the greatest of his talents. I had taken him for a painter who wrote for the papers, or else for a journalist who could paint — but even the cousin (who took snuff during the interview) could not tell me what he had been — exactly. He was a universal genius — on that point I agreed with the old chap, who thereupon blew his nose noisily into a large cotton handkerchief and withdrew in senile agitation, bearing off some family letters and memoranda without importance. Ultimately a journalist anxious to know something of the fate of his 'dear colleague' turned up. This visitor informed me Kurtz's proper sphere ought to have been politics 'on the popular side.' He had furry straight eyebrows, bristly hair cropped short, an eye-glass on a broad ribbon, and, becoming expansive, confessed his opinion that Kurtz really couldn't write a bit — 'but heavens! how that man could talk. He electrified large meetings. He had faith — don't you see? — he had the faith. He could get himself to believe anything — anything. He would have been a splendid leader of an extreme party.' 'What party?' I asked. 'Any party,' answered the other. 'He was an — an — extremist.' Did I not think so? I assented. Did I know, he asked, with a sudden flash of curiosity, 'what it was that had induced him to go out there?' 'Yes,' said I, and forthwith handed him the famous Report for publication, if he thought fit. He glanced through it hurriedly, mumbling all the time, judged 'it would do,' and took himself off with this plunder.

"Thus I was left at last with a slim packet of letters and the girl's portrait. She struck me as beautiful — I mean she had a beautiful expression. I know that the sunlight can be made to lie, too, yet one felt that no manipulation of light and pose could have conveyed the delicate shade of truthfulness upon those features. She seemed ready to listen without mental reservation, without suspicion, without a thought for herself. I concluded I would go and give her back her portrait and those letters myself. Curiosity? Yes; and also some other feeling perhaps. All that had been Kurtz's had passed out of my hands: his soul, his body, his station, his plans, his ivory, his career. There remained only his memory and his Intended — and I wanted to give that up, too, to the past, in a way — to surrender personally all that remained of him with me to that oblivion which is the last word of our common fate. I don't defend myself. I had no clear perception of what it was I really wanted. Perhaps it was an impulse of unconscious loyalty, or the fulfilment of one of those ironic necessities that lurk in the facts of human existence. I don't know. I can't tell. But I went.

"I thought his memory was like the other memories of the dead that accumulate in every man's life — a vague impress on the brain of shadows that had fallen on it in their swift and final passage; but before the high and ponderous door, between the tall houses of a street as still and decorous as a well-kept alley in a cemetery, I had a vision of him on the stretcher, opening his mouth voraciously, as if to devour all the earth with all its mankind. He lived then before me; he lived as much as he had ever lived — a shadow insatiable of splendid appearances, of frightful realities; a shadow darker than the shadow of the night, and draped nobly in the folds of a gorgeous eloquence. The vision seemed to enter the house with me — the stretcher, the phantom-bearers, the wild crowd of obedient worshippers, the gloom of the forests, the glitter of the reach between the murky bends, the beat of the drum, regular and muffled like the beating of a heart — the heart of a conquering darkness. It was a moment of triumph for the wilderness, an invading and vengeful rush which, it seemed to me, I would have to keep back alone for the salvation of another soul. And the memory of what I had heard him say afar there, with the horned shapes stirring at my back, in the glow of fires, within the patient woods, those broken phrases came back to me, were heard again in their ominous and terrifying simplicity. I remembered his abject pleading, his abject threats, the colossal scale of his vile desires, the meanness, the torment, the tempestuous anguish of his soul. And later on I seemed to see his collected languid manner, when he said one day, 'This lot of ivory now is really mine. The Company did not pay for it. I collected it myself at a very great personal risk. I am afraid they will try to claim it as theirs though. H'm. It is a difficult case. What do you think I ought to do — resist? Eh? I want

How does this image from a German stage adaptation of *Heart of Darkness* depict the central conflict of Conrad's novella? Consider the stage design, the placement of the two men, and the colors of both the costumes and the set in your response.

Photo by Lieberenz / ullstein bild via Getty Images

no more than justice.' . . . He wanted no more than justice — no more than justice. I rang the bell before a mahogany door on the first floor, and while I waited he seemed to stare at me out of the glassy panel — stare with that wide and immense stare embracing, condemning, loathing all the universe. I seemed to hear the whispered cry, 'The horror! The horror!'

"The dusk was falling. I had to wait in a lofty drawing-room with three long windows from floor to ceiling that were like three luminous and bedraped columns. The bent gilt legs and backs of the furniture shone in indistinct curves. The tall marble fireplace had a cold and monumental whiteness. A grand piano stood massively in a corner; with dark gleams on the flat surfaces like a sombre and polished sarcophagus. A high door opened — closed. I rose.

"She came forward, all in black, with a pale head, floating towards me in the dusk. She was in mourning. It was more than a year since his death, more than a year since the news came; she seemed as though she would remember and mourn for ever. She took both my hands in hers and murmured, 'I had heard you were coming.' I noticed she was not very young — I mean not girlish. She had a mature capacity for fidelity, for belief, for suffering. The room seemed to have grown darker, as if all the sad light of the cloudy evening had taken refuge on her forehead. This fair hair, this pale visage, this pure brow, seemed surrounded by an ashy halo from which the dark eyes looked out at me. Their glance was guileless, profound, confident, and trustful. She carried her sorrowful head as though she were proud of that sorrow, as though she would say, I — I alone know how to mourn for him as he deserves. But while we were still shaking hands, such a look of awful desolation came upon her face that I perceived she was one of those creatures that are not the playthings of Time. For her he had died only yesterday. And, by Jove! the impression was so powerful that for me, too, he seemed to have died only yesterday — nay, this very minute. I saw her and him in the same instant of time — his death and her sorrow — I saw her sorrow in the very moment of his death. Do you understand? I saw them together — I heard them together. She had said, with a deep catch of the breath, 'I have survived' while my strained ears seemed to hear distinctly, mingled with her tone of despairing regret, the summing up whisper of his eternal condemnation. I asked myself what I was doing there, with a sensation of panic in my heart as though I had blundered into a place of cruel and absurd mysteries not fit for a human being to behold. She motioned me to a chair. We sat down. I laid the packet gently on the little table, and she put her hand over it. . . . 'You knew him well,' she murmured, after a moment of mourning silence.

" 'Intimacy grows quickly out there,' I said. 'I knew him as well as it is possible for one man to know another.'

" 'And you admired him,' she said. 'It was impossible to know him and not to admire him. Was it?'

" 'He was a remarkable man,' I said, unsteadily. Then before the appealing fixity of her gaze, that seemed to watch for more words on my lips, I went on, 'It was impossible not to ——'

" 'Love him,' she finished eagerly, silencing me into an appalled dumbness. 'How true! how true! But when you think that no one knew him so well as I! I had all his noble confidence. I knew him best.'

" 'You knew him best,' I repeated. And perhaps she did. But with every word spoken the room was growing darker, and only her forehead, smooth and white, remained illumined by the unextinguishable light of belief and love.

" 'You were his friend,' she went on. 'His friend,' she repeated, a little louder. 'You must have been, if he had given you this, and sent you to me. I feel I can speak to you — and oh! I must speak. I want you — you who have heard his last words — to know I have been worthy of him. . . . It is not pride. . . . Yes! I am proud to know I understood him better than any one on earth — he told me so himself. And since his mother died I have had no one — no one — to — to ——'

"I listened. The darkness deepened. I was not even sure whether he had given me the right bundle. I rather suspect he wanted me to take care of another batch of his papers which, after his death, I saw the manager examining under the lamp. And the girl talked, easing her pain in the certitude of my sympathy; she talked as thirsty men drink. I had heard that her engagement with Kurtz had been disapproved by her people. He wasn't rich enough or something. And indeed I don't know whether he had not been a pauper all his life. He had given me some reason to infer that it was his impatience of comparative poverty that drove him out there.

"'. . . Who was not his friend who had heard him speak once?' she was saying. 'He drew men towards him by what was best in them.' She looked at me with intensity. 'It is the gift of the great,' she went on, and the sound of her low voice seemed to have the accompaniment of all the other sounds, full of mystery, desolation, and sorrow, I had ever heard — the ripple of the river, the soughing of the trees swayed by the wind, the murmurs of the crowds, the faint ring of incomprehensible words cried from afar, the whisper of a voice speaking from beyond the threshold of an eternal darkness. 'But you have heard him! You know!' she cried.

"'Yes, I know,' I said with something like despair in my heart, but bowing my head before the faith that was in her, before that great and saving illusion that shone with an unearthly glow in the darkness, in the triumphant darkness from which I could not have defended her — from which I could not even defend myself.

"'What a loss to me — to us!' — she corrected herself with beautiful generosity; then added in a murmur, 'To the world.' By the last gleams of twilight I could see the glitter of her eyes, full of tears — of tears that would not fall.

"'I have been very happy — very fortunate — very proud,' she went on. 'Too fortunate. Too happy for a little while. And now I am unhappy for — for life.'

"She stood up; her fair hair seemed to catch all the remaining light in a glimmer of gold. I rose, too.

"'And of all this,' she went on, mournfully, 'of all his promise, and of all his greatness, of his generous mind, of his noble heart, nothing remains — nothing but a memory. You and I——'

"'We shall always remember him,' I said, hastily.

"'No!' she cried. 'It is impossible that all this should be lost — that such a life should be sacrificed to leave nothing — but sorrow. You know what vast plans he had. I knew of them, too — I could not perhaps understand — but others knew of them. Something must remain. His words, at least, have not died.'

"'His words will remain,' I said.

"'And his example,' she whispered to herself. 'Men looked up to him — his goodness shone in every act. His example ——'

"'True,' I said; 'his example, too. Yes, his example. I forgot that.'

"'But I do not. I cannot — I cannot believe — not yet. I cannot believe that I shall never see him again, that nobody will see him again, never, never, never.'

"She put out her arms as if after a retreating figure, stretching them back and with clasped pale hands across the fading and narrow sheen of the window. Never see him! I saw him clearly enough then. I shall see this eloquent phantom as long as I live, and I shall see her, too, a tragic and familiar Shade, resembling in this gesture another one, tragic also, and bedecked with powerless charms, stretching bare brown arms over the glitter of the infernal stream, the stream of darkness. She said suddenly very low, 'He died as he lived.'

"'His end,' said I, with dull anger stirring in me, 'was in every way worthy of his life.'

"'And I was not with him,' she murmured. My anger subsided before a feeling of infinite pity.

"'Everything that could be done ——' I mumbled.

"'Ah, but I believed in him more than any one on earth — more than his own mother, more than — himself. He needed me! Me! I would have treasured every sigh, every word, every sign, every glance.'

190 "I felt like a chill grip on my chest. 'Don't,' I said, in a muffled voice.

"'Forgive me. I — I — have mourned so long in silence — in silence. . . . You were with him — to the last? I think of his loneliness. Nobody near to understand him as I would have understood. Perhaps no one to hear. . . .'

"'To the very end,' I said, shakily. 'I heard his very last words. . . .' I stopped in a fright.

"'Repeat them,' she murmured in a heart-broken tone. 'I want — I want — something — something — to — to live with.'

"I was on the point of crying at her, 'Don't you hear them?' The dusk was repeating them in a persistent whisper all around us, in a whisper that seemed to swell menacingly like the first whisper of a rising wind. 'The horror! the horror!'

195 "'His last word — to live with,' she insisted. 'Don't you understand I loved him — I loved him — I loved him!'

"I pulled myself together and spoke slowly.

"'The last word he pronounced was — your name.'

"I heard a light sigh and then my heart stood still, stopped dead short by an exulting and terrible cry, by the cry of inconceivable triumph and of unspeakable pain. 'I knew it — I was sure!' . . . She knew. She was sure. I heard her weeping; she had hidden her face in her hands. It seemed to me that the house would collapse before I could escape, that the heavens would fall upon my head. But nothing happened. The heavens do not fall for such a trifle. Would they have fallen, I wonder, if I had rendered Kurtz that justice which was his due? Hadn't he said he wanted only justice? But I couldn't. I could not tell her. It would have been too dark — too dark altogether. . . ."

Marlow ceased, and sat apart, indistinct and silent, in the pose of a meditating Buddha. Nobody moved for a time. "We have lost the first of the ebb," said the Director, suddenly. I raised my head. The offing was barred by a black bank of clouds, and the tranquil waterway leading to the uttermost ends of the earth flowed sombre under an overcast sky — seemed to lead into the heart of an immense darkness.

[1902]

QUESTIONS FOR DISCUSSION

1. Apart from Marlow, Kurtz, and Fresleven the Dane, all of the characters in *Heart of Darkness* are nameless, and most are referred to by their occupations: *Accountant*, *Lawyer*, *Brickmaker*, *Manager*, *Fireman*, even the *Intended*. Why might Joseph Conrad have done this? What might this choice suggest about Conrad's attitude toward work and identity? What do the named characters have in common? What was Conrad's purpose in naming them?
2. Why do you think Marlow begins his tale of a journey to the heart of darkness with an account of London in "very old times, when the Romans first came here" (para. 11)? What is the connection between London in Roman times and the English colonization of Africa?
3. Why do the two women who guard the doors of the Company's office (para. 25) remind Marlow of the greeting gladiators offered to the Roman emperor, "*Ave! Morituri te salutant*" ("Hail! We who are about to die salute you")? What does the recollection suggest about Marlow's attitude toward his new job and his life in general?
4. Marlow's aunt believes he is going to Africa as "an emissary of light" (para. 28). Does Marlow agree with her description? Does he change his attitude? Where is the irony in his aunt's comment?

5. When Marlow arrives at Central Station after a two-hundred-mile trek, he meets the manager and finds that the man "inspired uneasiness" (para. 53). Why does Marlow respond this way? What does Marlow make of the fact that the manager was "never ill"? What do you think Conrad is saying about the manager by making him resistant to tropical disease?

6. In paragraph 58, Marlow describes a painting Kurtz made of "a woman, draped and blindfolded, carrying a lighted torch." What message was Kurtz sending with this painting? At this point in the story, do you think Marlow would agree or disagree with this message? Why?

7. What does the Eldorado Exploring Expedition (paras. 72–73) represent to Marlow?

8. In paragraph 80, Marlow begins his journey on the steamboat to Kurtz. Why does he find the practical work of navigation steadying? Why does he remember so many concrete details of this work?

9. How does Marlow respond to the cannibals under his control (paras. 82–83)? Consider also the cannibals' resistance to hunger, as Marlow describes it in paragraph 89. What does he mean by the "remote kinship" he feels? How is Marlow's response both typical and atypical of other Europeans in the story?

10. What is the significance of Marlow's comparison of Kurtz to "an enchanted princess sleeping in a fabulous castle" (para. 90)?

11. Discuss the ways in which Marlow is both attracted to and repulsed by the idea of Kurtz.

12. What is the significance of Marlow's leaving his steamboat to follow Kurtz to the bonfire in the forest?

13. How have Kurtz's methods become "unsound" (para. 131)? What evidence do you find to support the manager's assessment?

14. What significance do you attach to the illness that overtakes Marlow following Kurtz's death? Remember that the manager was able to survive in Africa without succumbing to illness. What does this contrast suggest about the metaphorical role that illness plays in the story? What does this contrast say about the characters of these two men?

15. How do you interpret Kurtz's dying words, "The horror! The horror!" (para. 155) ? How do you think Marlow interprets them?

16. How does Marlow's visit with Kurtz's Intended complete his journey?

17. What qualities does Marlow possess that allow him to go to the heart of darkness and return, whereas Kurtz could neither survive nor return?

18. Marlow insists in paragraph 62 that he hates lies, yet at the end of his tale he lies to Kurtz's Intended, telling her that the last words on Kurtz's lips were not "The horror!" but her name. Why? How does Marlow justify this lie to himself?

QUESTIONS ON STYLE AND STRUCTURE

1. Marlow's tale of his journey into the heart of darkness is set within the "frame" of four travelers on the *Nellie* waiting for the tide to turn so they can head out to sea. How does this narrative frame affect your interpretation of Marlow's storytelling?

2. Conrad introduces the reader to Marlow with a short description in paragraph 4: "Marlow sat cross-legged right aft, leaning against the mizzen-mast. He had sunken cheeks, a yellow complexion, a straight back, an ascetic aspect, and, with his arms dropped, the palms of hands outwards, resembled an idol." What does this description suggest to you about Marlow's character?

3. Marlow's fascination with Africa began with a white patch on maps he pored over as a boy (para. 18). In this description, he uses several figures of speech: "It had ceased to be a blank space of delightful mystery"; "a mighty big river, that you could see on the map, resembling an immense snake"; "it fascinated me as a snake would a bird." What does Marlow's language suggest about how he sees the African continent — particularly the river and the role it would play in his life?

4. In paragraph 21, Marlow recalls Fresleven, the steamboat captain whose place Marlow has taken, and describes the events surrounding the man's death as a "glorious affair." How do the details in Marlow's account suggest the opposite — that what occurred was anything but glorious?

5. Marlow calls the offices of his employer a "whited sepulchre" (para. 22). What do you infer from this image? What might it symbolize? How does the

description of the street leading to the offices and the offices themselves develop or dispute this metaphor?

6. Why do you think Conrad juxtaposes a description of dying natives (paras. 40–42) with a description of the meticulously attired chief accountant (para. 43)? How does the proximity of these two descriptions help you visualize the Company's station?

7. What does the double negative in the sentence "It was unearthly, and the men were——No, they were not inhuman" (para. 83) suggest about Marlow's response to the Africans he encounters? What does it suggest about Marlow's state of mind at this point in his journey?

8. As the steamboat approaches Inner Station (para. 88), a white fog surrounds Marlow's company, "very warm and clammy, and more blinding than the night. . . . The rest of the world was nowhere, as far as our eyes and ears were concerned. Just nowhere. Gone, disappeared; swept off without leaving a whisper or a shadow behind." What might this white fog symbolize?

9. What does Kurtz's repetition of "my" in "My Intended, my ivory, my station, my river" (para. 104) and "My Intended, my station, my career, my ideas" (para. 149) reveal about him? What do you think Conrad is suggesting about men like Kurtz?

10. Marlow says of the harlequin-like character who greets him at Inner Station, "His face was like the autumn sky, overcast one moment and bright the next" (para. 109). What does the simile help you understand about the young man's character?

11. Explain what Marlow means when he says, "Kurtz discoursed. A voice! a voice! It rang deep to the very last. It survived his strength to hide in the magnificent folds of eloquence the barren darkness of his heart" (para. 149).

12. In paragraphs 100–103, Conrad returns readers to the deck of the *Nellie*, reminding them of the frame for Marlow's story. Why do you think the author chose to do so at this point in the tale?

13. In paragraph 108, Marlow at first mistakes shrunken human heads for ivory ornaments. What is the significance of the heads themselves as well as Marlow's misperception? Is the description of the heads (para. 116) poetic? Grisly? Refer to specific choices in diction and syntax that support your interpretation.

14. Why does Conrad set the face-to-face encounter between Kurtz and Marlow in a forest with the two of them alone? Marlow says, "the foundations of our intimacy were being laid — to endure — to endure — even to the end — even beyond" (para. 140). How does Conrad's use of repetition and dashes contribute to your understanding of Marlow's comment?

15. In paragraphs 140–141, Marlow describes his initial interaction with Kurtz. The description is filled with contrasts in Marlow's responses to and impressions of Kurtz, such as his "exalted and incredible degradation." Identify other oxymorons, and discuss whether you interpret the oxymorons as true conflicts or paradoxes — that is, only seemingly contradictory.

16. Marlow asserts that Kurtz "is a remarkable man" (para. 131). He calls Kurtz's dying words "an affirmation, a moral victory paid for by innumerable defeats, by abominable terrors, by abominable satisfactions. But it was a victory! That is why I have remained loyal to Kurtz" (para. 160). How do you interpret Marlow's use of the word "victory" in this passage? What does he mean by "loyalty" specifically in this passage but also elsewhere in the text?

17. Compare the descriptions of the two women in Kurtz's life — the one in Africa and his Intended in England. Pay special attention to how the women respond to Kurtz's departure and their expressions of grief. Do you find either of these descriptions to be stereotypes of women? Cite specific passages to support your response.

18. How do you interpret the final paragraph of the novel? Why does Conrad give the last spoken word to the Director?

19. In paragraphs 11–13, Conrad foreshadows what Marlow experiences on his own journey into the heart of darkness. What did you make of this passage when you first read it? How do you interpret it now upon rereading and in light of the whole tale?

20. Marlow first refers to Kurtz as "the poor chap" (para. 15). In retrospect, do you think this is an accurate description, an understatement, an ironic comment, or a combination of all three?

SUGGESTIONS FOR WRITING

1. Choose one of the following tensions in *Heart of Darkness* and write an essay that traces its evolution throughout the novel: appearance vs. reality, primitivism vs. civilization, light vs. dark, or innocence vs. experience.
2. This novella is both an actual journey and a psychological one. Write an essay discussing Marlow's psychological journey. What changes does he experience? Pay particular attention to the values he claims to have yet violates or abandons. In what ways does he learn to accept ambiguities?
3. Marlow's initial encounter with Africans occurs as he travels along the coast of the continent. Write an essay explaining how the language Conrad employs to describe the natives and the colonials conveys Marlow's emerging attitudes toward these two groups. For example, what is the significance of using the word "Pop" to describe the sound of six-inch guns firing into the continent (para. 31)? How is this first encounter with Africans reflective of what can occur when cultures collide?
4. Analyze Marlow's obsession with Kurtz. Why does he pursue Kurtz? Why does he defend and attempt to save him? Why does he choose Kurtz over the other colonials? What do Kurtz and Marlow have in common?
5. In paragraph 104, we hear Marlow's analysis of Kurtz. Write an essay analyzing the literary devices Conrad uses to achieve his purpose in this passage.
6. Many nineteenth- and twentieth-century writers (e.g., Friedrich Nietzsche, Mark Twain, Honoré de Balzac, Henrik Ibsen, Thomas Hardy, and Stephen Crane) express a tragic conception of human life — that its purpose is impenetrable, its joys and sorrows meaningless. Write an essay exploring your interpretation of Conrad's conception of human life.
7. Conrad has been taken to task by some feminist readers and critics who claim that the few women he does depict are passive and stereotyped. Write a dramatic monologue in the voice of Marlow's aunt, Kurtz's mistress in Africa, or his Intended to explain what Conrad left out — or failed to understand — about that character.
8. Imagine that Marlow kept a blog as he made his journey up the river to Kurtz. Write five to eight posts in the voice of Marlow, or create a real blog with Marlow as its author.
9. The complex narration is a distinctive quality of *Heart of Darkness.* Write an essay explaining how this narrative strategy reflects the theme(s) in the novel.

TEXTS IN CONTEXT

Heart of Darkness and the Legacy of Colonialism

In the early 1800s, European countries controlled 35 percent of the world, but by 1914, that number had risen to nearly 85 percent and included parts of Africa, Asia, Latin America, and the Caribbean. During the late nineteenth and early twentieth centuries, European nations — locked in economic and political competition with each other, each struggling for dominance — renewed their efforts to expand into other parts of the world, especially in Africa and Asia. This imperialist drive to colonize foreign lands was bolstered by popular belief in pseudoscientific theories, such as social Darwinism, which cast Western Europeans as part of a dominant white race and justified the conquest of other peoples. Though not without its critics, the prevailing view of the era held that the quest for empire was not only the result of inevitable natural law but also a "civilizing mission" to bring Western government, technology, and social values to new colonies. This attitude is reflected in much of the writing and art of the late 1800s and early 1900s, which often portrayed non-European peoples as backward and primitive. Take, for instance, Rudyard Kipling's poem "The White Man's Burden," in which he refers to nonwhite peoples across the globe, collectively, as "half devil and half child." There was little room in the Western European mindset for the acceptance or even appreciation of the customs, beliefs, and lifestyles of people on other continents as being equal to their European counterparts.

This 1907 photograph, entitled "Mrs. Davis in a Borrowed 'Hammock,' the Local Means of Transportation on the West Coast," was most likely taken by the American writer and journalist Richard Harding Davis for his book, *The Congo and Coasts of Africa*, which documented Belgian atrocities of the era. **To what extent does this photograph undermine the premise of Richard Harding Davis's book? What aspects of *Heart of Darkness* undermine its commentary on colonialism?**

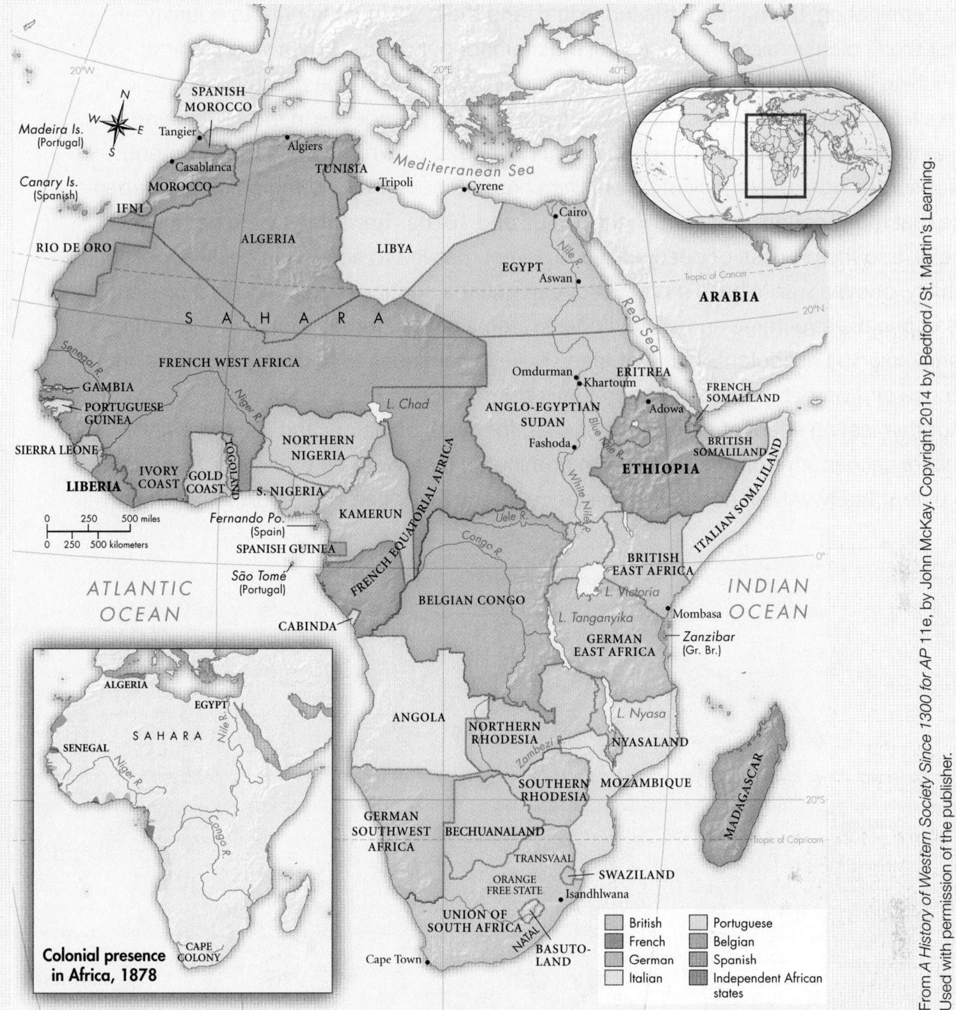

This map shows the partition of Africa by European colonial powers between 1880 and 1914. **Judging from this map, which European countries stood to gain the most power from expanding their empires by colonizing Africa? Consider strategic location and natural resources in particular.**

The consequences of this mindset for colonized peoples were dire. The result, in Africa, was the wholesale parceling of lands and the subjugation of its peoples at the hands of Western European nations — particularly Great Britain, France, Belgium, Germany, and Italy. The concept of bringing Western government and technology to other parts of the globe was merely a justification that disguised the political and economic maneuvering for resources, living space, and wealth. By the year 1900, only two African countries remained independent of colonial rule: Ethiopia, which successfully defended itself from the Italians, and Liberia, a nation created in 1821 by freed American slaves.

Though brutal, Europe's near-total possession of African lands was relatively short lived. Africans were able to turn liberal European political philosophies — such as self-determination, the rights of the individual, and the basic human right to equality — against their colonial rulers in successful bids for independence. Egypt was the first, establishing its own government in 1922, and after World War II the process of decolonization swiftly accelerated. Most African nations won independence in the 1960s, and by 1975 almost every single country on the continent had its own sovereign government.

Not surprisingly, the legacy of colonialism has extended beyond the political independence that many countries gained in the 1960s and 1970s. Transitions were not always peaceful, and the process of decolonization sometimes led to economic decline, political instability, or even war. What's more, European nations continued to maintain a presence in the economic structures and educational systems of their former colonies — creating a system known as neocolonialism that many believe continues to undermine political independence and perpetuate Western economic domination to the present day.

Another lasting effect of colonialism is that, for much of history, the literary, artistic, and historical narrative of Africa has been dominated by a Western paradigm. During the early part of the twentieth century, for instance, many European artists turned to African

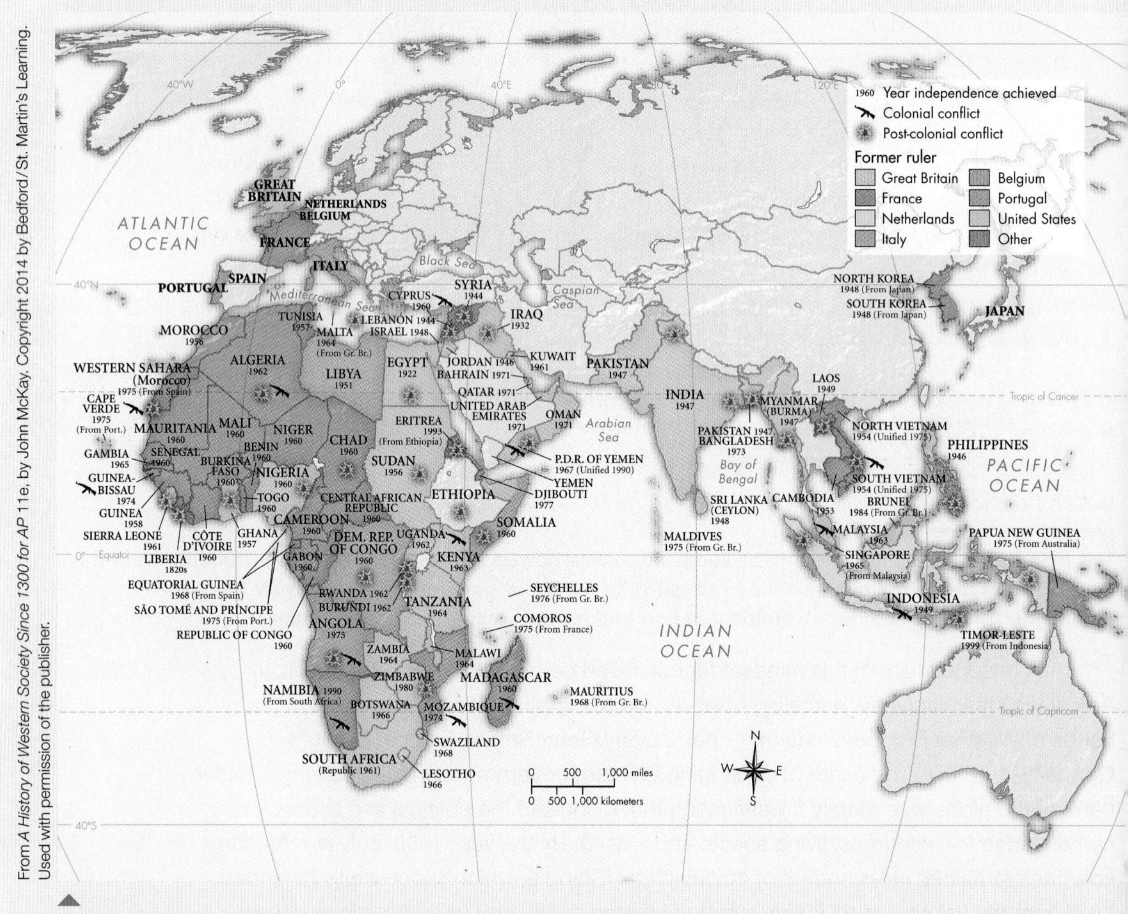

This map shows the decolonization of Africa and Asia from 1947 to the present day. **How does this map illustrate the consequences of colonization that *Heart of Darkness* anticipated? Consider conflicts both during and after colonial rule along with the dates of independence depicted here.**

art for inspiration. Believing that Western culture lacked vitality and originality, many of these artists took African masks and sculptures that were shown in Europe as a result of colonial conquest and exploratory expeditions as inspiration for their own art. At the time, however, these objects were treated as artifacts rather than as original artworks from vibrant cultures with rich traditions. On its website, the Metropolitan Museum of Art explains this phenomenon: “While these artists knew nothing of the original meaning and function of the West and Central African sculptures they encountered, they . . . adapted these qualities to their own efforts to move beyond the naturalism that had defined Western art since the Renaissance.” Thus the work these Western artists produced as a result was well received as *art*, whereas the original African works were portrayed as mere relics of primitive cultures.

It’s also all too easy to encounter only the Western narrative in literature — one that, for all the beautiful work it has produced, is not only incomplete but has often failed to recognize that colonized cultures have equally rich histories, art, myths, legends, and literature. In a TEDTalk titled “The Danger of a Single Story,” contemporary Nigerian author Chimimanda Ngozi Adichie warns against relying on just one perspective:

> It is impossible to talk about the single story without talking about power. There is a word, an Igbo word, that I think about whenever I think about the power structures of the world, and it is “nkali.” It’s a noun that loosely translates to “to be greater than another.” Like our economic and political worlds, stories too are defined by the principle of nkali: How they are told, who tells them, when they’re told, how many stories are told, are really dependent on power. . . . Stories matter. Many stories matter. Stories have been used to dispossess and to malign, but stories can also be used to empower and to humanize. Stories can break the dignity of a people, but stories can also repair that broken dignity. . . . [W]hen we reject the single story, when we realize that there is never a single story about any place, we regain a kind of paradise.

When we read, it is important to consider the perspective of the narrative. Though many interpret *Heart of Darkness* as critical of imperialism, it is also a product of its time, a piece that helped build the very tradition of the “single story” Adichie cautions against. Drawn from Conrad’s own era all the way to the present, the following texts not only provide context for a deeper understanding of *Heart of Darkness* but also comment in various ways on the assumptions and motivations of European colonial powers in Africa and the short- and longer-term consequences for both the colonized and the colonizer.

TEXTS IN CONTEXT

Chinua Achebe / *An Image of Africa* (nonfiction)
Rudyard Kipling / *The White Man’s Burden* (poetry)
H. T. Johnson / *The Black Man’s Burden* (poetry)
Fang Ngil Mask, Gabon and **Amadeo Modigliani** / *Tête* (“Head”) (sculpture)
and *Portrait of Jeanne Hébuterne* (painting)
Doris Lessing / *The Old Chief Mshlanga* (fiction)
Felix Mnthali / *The Stranglehold of English Lit* (poetry)
Léopold Senghor / *In Memoriam* (poetry)
Binyavanga Wainaina / *How to Write about Africa* (nonfiction)

An Image of Africa

CHINUA ACHEBE

Chinua Achebe (1930–2013) is the most widely read African writer of his generation, primarily for his debut novel, *Things Fall Apart* (1958). His novels, poetry, and criticism examine the clash of cultures during the colonial era, especially the conflict between traditional tribal values and Christianity. He also addressed the politics and alienation of the postcolonial period in Nigeria in his later works, such as *No Longer at Ease* (1960) and *A Man of the People* (1966). Achebe taught at Bard College in New York from 1990 to 2008, and served as a professor of Africana Studies at Brown University from 2009 until his death in 2013. In "An Image of Africa," originally delivered as a lecture at the University of Massachusetts in 1975, Achebe criticized Joseph Conrad for being "a bloody racist" in his portrayal of Africa and Africans in *Heart of Darkness*.

It was a fine autumn morning at the beginning of this academic year such as encouraged friendliness to passing strangers. Brisk youngsters were hurrying in all directions, many of them obviously freshmen in their first flush of enthusiasm. An older man, going the same way as I, turned and remarked to me how very young they came these days. I agreed. Then he asked me if I was a student too. I said no, I was a teacher. What did I teach? African literature. Now that was funny, he said, because he never had thought of Africa as having that kind of stuff, you know. By this time I was walking much faster. "Oh well," I heard him say finally, behind me, "I guess I have to take your course to find out."

A few weeks later I received two very touching letters from high school children in Yonkers, New York, who — bless their teacher — had just read *Things Fall Apart*. One of them was particularly happy to learn about the customs and superstitions of an African tribe.

I propose to draw from these rather trivial encounters rather heavy conclusions which at first sight might seem somewhat out of proportion to them: But only at first sight.

The young fellow from Yonkers, perhaps partly on account of his age but I believe also for much deeper and more serious reasons, is obviously unaware that the life of his own tribesmen in Yonkers, New York, is full of odd customs and superstitions and, like everybody else in his culture, imagines that he needs a trip to Africa to encounter those things.

5 The other person being fully my own age could not be excused on the grounds of his years. Ignorance might be a more likely reason; but here again I believe that something more willful than a mere lack of information was at work. For did not that erudite British historian and Regius Professor at Oxford, Hugh Trevor-Roper, pronounce a few years ago that African history did not exist?

If there is something in these utterances more than youthful experience, more than a lack of factual knowledge, what is it? Quite simply it is the desire — one might indeed say the need — in Western psychology to set Africa up as a foil in Europe, a place of negations at once remote and vaguely familiar in comparison with which Europe's own state of spiritual grace will be manifest.

This need is not new: which should relieve us of considerable responsibility and perhaps make us even willing to look at this phenomenon dispassionately. I have neither the desire nor, indeed, the competence to do so with the tools of the social and biological sciences.

But, I can respond, as a novelist, to one famous book of European fiction, Joseph Conrad's *Heart of Darkness*, which better than any other work I know displays that Western desire and need which I have just spoken about. Of course, there are whole libraries of books devoted to the same purpose, but most of them are so obvious and so crude that few people worry about them today. Conrad, on the other hand, is undoubtedly one of the great stylists of modern fiction and a good storyteller into the bargain. His contribution therefore falls automatically into a different class — permanent literature — read and taught and constantly evaluated by serious academics. *Heart of Darkness* is indeed so secure today that a leading Conrad scholar has numbered it "among the half-dozen greatest short novels in the English language." I will return to this critical opinion in due course because it may seriously modify my earlier suppositions about who may or may not be guilty in the things of which I will now speak.

Heart of Darkness projects the image of Africa as "the other world," the antithesis of Europe and therefore of civilization, a place where a man's vaunted intelligence and refinement are finally mocked by triumphant bestiality. The book opens on the River Thames, tranquil, resting peacefully "at the decline of day after ages of good service done to the race that peopled its banks." But the actual story takes place on the River Congo, the very antithesis of the Thames. The River Congo is quite decidedly not a River Emeritus. It has rendered no service and enjoys no old-age pension. We are told that "going up that river was like travelling back to the earliest beginning of the world."

Is Conrad saying then that these two rivers are very different, one good, the other bad? Yes, but that is not the real point. What actually worries Conrad is the lurking hint of kinship, of common ancestry. For the Thames, too, "has been one of the dark places of the earth." It conquered its darkness, of course, and is now at peace. But if it were to visit its primordial relative, the Congo, it would run the terrible risk of hearing grotesque, suggestive echoes of its own forgotten darkness, and of falling victim to an avenging recrudescence of the mindless frenzy of the first beginnings.

10 I am not going to waste your time with examples of Conrad's famed evocation of the African atmosphere. In the final consideration it amounts to no more than a steady, ponderous, fake-ritualistic repetition of two sentences, one about silence and the other about frenzy. An example of the former is "It was the stillness of an implacable force brooding over an inscrutable intention" and of the latter, "The steamer toiled along slowly on the edge of a black and incomprehensible frenzy." Of course, there is a judicious change of adjective from time to time so that instead of "inscrutable," for example, you might have "unspeakable," etc., etc.

The eagle-eyed English critic, F. R. Leavis, drew attention nearly thirty years ago to Conrad's "adjectival insistence upon inexpressible and incomprehensible mystery." That insistence must not be dismissed lightly, as many Conrad critics have tended to do, as a mere stylistic flaw. For it raises serious questions of artistic good faith. When a writer, while pretending to record scenes, incidents and their impact, is in reality engaged in inducing hypnotic stupor in his readers through a bombardment of emotive words and other forms of trickery, much more has to be at stake than stylistic felicity. Generally, normal readers are well armed to detect and resist such underhand activity. But Conrad chose his subject well — one which was guaranteed not to put him in conflict with the psychological predisposition of his readers or raise the need for him to contend with their resistance. He chose the role of purveyor of comforting myths.

The most interesting and revealing passages in *Heart of Darkness* are, however, about people.

I must quote a long passage from the middle of the story in which representatives of Europe in a steamer going down the Congo encounter the denizens of Africa:

> We were wanderers on a prehistoric earth, on an earth that wore the aspect of an unknown planet. We could have fancied ourselves the first of men taking possession of an accursed inheritance, to be subdued at the cost of profound anguish and of excessive toil. But suddenly, as we struggled round a bend, there would be a glimpse of rush walls, of peaked grass-roofs, a burst of yells, a whirl of black limbs, a mass of hands clapping, of feet stamping, of bodies swaying, of eyes rolling, under the droop of heavy and motionless foliage. The steamer toiled along slowly on the edge of a black and incomprehensible frenzy. The prehistoric man was cursing us, praying to us, welcoming us — who could tell? We were cut off from the comprehension of our surroundings; we glided past like phantoms, wondering and secretly appalled, as sane men would be before an enthusiastic outbreak in a madhouse. We could not understand because we were too far and could not remember because we were travelling in the night of first ages, of those ages that are gone, leaving hardly a sign — and no memories.
>
> The earth seemed unearthly. We are accustomed to look upon the shackled form of a conquered monster, but there — there you could look at a thing monstrous and free. It was unearthly, and the men were —— No, they were not inhuman. Well, you know, that was the worst of it — this suspicion of their not being inhuman. It would come slowly to one. They howled and leaped, and spun, and made horrid faces; but what thrilled you was just the thought of their humanity — like yours — the thought of your remote kinship with this wild and passionate uproar. Ugly. Yes, it was ugly enough; but if you were man enough you would admit to yourself that there was in you just the faintest trace of a response to the terrible frankness of that noise, a dim suspicion of there being a meaning in it which you — you so remote from the night of first ages — could comprehend.

Herein lies the meaning of *Heart of Darkness* and the fascination it holds over the Western mind: "What thrilled you was just the thought of their humanity — like yours . . . Ugly."

Having shown us Africa in the mass, Conrad then zeros in on a specific example, giving us one of his rare descriptions of an African who is not just limbs or rolling eyes:

> And between whiles I had to look after the savage who was fireman. He was an improved specimen; he could fire up a vertical boiler. He was there below me, and, upon my word, to look at him was as edifying as seeing a dog in a parody of breeches and a feather hat, walking on his hind-legs. A few months of training had done for that really fine chap. He squinted at the steam-gauge and at the water-gauge with an evident effort of intrepidity — and he had filed his teeth, too, the poor devil, and the wool of his pate shaved into queer patterns, and three ornamental scars on each of his cheeks. He ought to have been clapping his hands and stamping his feet on the bank, instead of which he was hard at work, a thrall to strange witchcraft, full of improving knowledge.

As everybody knows, Conrad is a romantic on the side. He might not exactly admire savages clapping their hands and stamping their feet but they have at least the merit of being in their place, unlike this dog in a parody of breeches. For Conrad, things (and persons) being in their place is of the utmost importance.

Towards the end of the story, Conrad lavishes great attention quite unexpectedly on an African woman who has obviously been some kind of mistress to Mr. Kurtz and now presides (if I may be permitted a little imitation of Conrad) like a formidable mystery over the inexorable imminence of his departure:

> She was savage and superb, wild-eyed and magnificent. . . . She stood looking at us without a stir, and like the wilderness itself, with an air of brooding over an inscrutable purpose.

This Amazon is drawn in considerable detail, albeit of a predictable nature, for two reasons. First, she is in her place and so can win Conrad's special brand of approval; and second, she fulfills a structural requirement of the story; she is a savage counterpart to the refined, European woman with whom the story will end:

> She came forward, all in black, with a pale head, floating towards me in the dusk. She was in mourning. . . . She took both my hands in hers and murmured, "I had heard you were coming." . . . She had a mature capacity for fidelity, for belief, for suffering.

15 The difference in the attitude of the novelist to these two women is conveyed in too many direct and subtle ways to need elaboration. But perhaps the most significant difference is the one implied in the author's bestowal of human expression to the one and the withholding of it from the other. It is clearly not part of Conrad's purpose to confer language on the "rudimentary souls" of Africa. They only "exchanged short grunting phrases" even among themselves but mostly they were too busy with their frenzy. There are two occasions in the book, however, when Conrad departs somewhat from his practice and confers speech, even English speech, on the savages. The first occurs when cannibalism gets the better of them:

> "Catch 'im," he snapped, with a bloodshot widening of his eyes and a flash of sharp teeth—"catch 'im. Give 'im to us." "To you, eh?" I asked; "what would you do with them?" "Eat 'im!" he said, curtly. . . .

The other occasion is the famous announcement:

> "Mistah Kurtz—he dead."

At first sight, these instances might be mistaken for unexpected acts of generosity from Conrad. In reality, they constitute some of his best assaults. In the case of the cannibals, the incomprehensible grunts that had thus far served them for speech suddenly proved inadequate for Conrad's purpose of letting the European glimpse the unspeakable craving in their hearts. Weighing the necessity for consistency in the portrayal of the dumb brutes against the sensational advantages of securing their conviction by clear, unambiguous evidence issuing out of their own mouth, Conrad chose the latter. As for the announcement of Mr. Kurtz's death by the "insolent black head in the doorway," what better or more appropriate *finis* could be written to the horror story of that wayward child of civilization who willfully had given his soul to the powers of darkness and "taken a high seat amongst the devils of the land" than the proclamation of his physical death by the forces he had joined?

It might be contended, of course, that the attitude to the African in *Heart of Darkness* is not Conrad's but that of his fictional narrator, Marlow, and that far from endorsing it Conrad might indeed be holding it up to irony and criticism. Certainly, Conrad appears to go to considerable pains to set up layers of insulation between himself and the moral universe of his story. He has, for example, a narrator behind a narrator. The primary narrator is Marlow but his account is given to us through the filter of a second, shadowy person. But if Conrad's intention is to draw a *cordon sanitaire*[1] between himself and the moral and psychological malaise of his narrator, his care seems to me totally wasted because he neglects

[1] Quarantine line.—EDS.

to hint however subtly or tentatively at an alternative frame of reference by which we may judge the actions and opinions of his characters. It would not have been beyond Conrad's power to make that provision if he had thought it necessary. Marlow seems to me to enjoy Conrad's complete confidence — a feeling reinforced by the close similarities between their careers.

Marlow comes through to us not only as a witness of truth, but one holding those advanced and humane views appropriate to the English liberal tradition which required all Englishmen of decency to be deeply shocked by atrocities in Bulgaria or the Congo of King Leopold of the Belgians or wherever. Thus Marlow is able to toss out such bleeding-heart sentiments as these:

> They were dying slowly — it was very clear. They were not enemies, they were not criminals, they were nothing earthly now, — nothing but black shadows of disease and starvation, lying confusedly in the greenish gloom. Brought from all the recesses of the coast in all the legality of time contracts, lost in uncongenial surroundings, fed on unfamiliar food, they sickened, became inefficient, and were then allowed to crawl away and rest.

The kind of liberalism espoused here by Marlow/Conrad touched all the best minds of the age in England, Europe, and America. It took different forms in the minds of different people but almost always managed to sidestep the ultimate question of equality between white people and black people. That extraordinary missionary, Albert Schweitzer[2], who sacrificed brilliant careers in music and theology in Europe for a life of service to Africans in much the same area as Conrad writes about, epitomizes the ambivalence. In a comment which I have often quoted but must quote one last time, Schweitzer says: "The African is indeed my brother but my junior brother." And so he proceeded to build a hospital appropriate to the needs of junior brothers with standards of hygiene reminiscent of medical practice in the days before the germ theory of disease came into being. Naturally, he became a sensation in Europe and America. Pilgrims flocked, and I believe still flock even after he has passed on, to witness the prodigious miracle in Lamberene, on the edge of the primeval forest.

Conrad's liberalism would not take him quite as far as Schweitzer's, though. He would not use the word "brother" however qualified; the farthest he would go was "kinship." When Marlow's African helmsman falls down with a spear in his heart he gives his white master one final disquieting look.

> And the intimate profundity of that look he gave me when he received his hurt remains to this day in my memory — like a claim of distant kinship affirmed in a supreme moment.

It is important to note that Conrad, careful as ever with his words, is not talking so much about *distant kinship* as about someone *laying a claim* on it. The black man lays a claim on the white man which is well-nigh intolerable. It is the laying of this claim which frightens and at the same time fascinates Conrad, ". . . the thought of their humanity — like yours . . . Ugly."

The point of my observations should be quite clear by now, namely, that Conrad was a bloody racist. That this simple truth is glossed over in criticism of his work is due to the fact that white racism against Africa is such a normal way of thinking that its manifestations go completely undetected. Students of *Heart of Darkness* will often tell you that Conrad is concerned not so much with Africa as with the deterioration of one European mind caused by solitude and sickness. They will point out to you that Conrad is, if anything, less charitable to the

[2] Albert Schweitzer (1875–1965) was a French-German humanitarian, theologian, organist, missionary, and medical doctor who was awarded the Nobel Peace Prize in 1952. — EDS.

Europeans in the story than he is to the natives. A Conrad student told me in Scotland last year that Africa is merely a setting for the disintegration of the mind of Mr. Kurtz.

20 Which is partly the point: Africa as setting and backdrop which eliminates the African as human factor. Africa as a metaphysical battlefield devoid of all recognizable humanity, into which the wandering European enters at his peril. Of course, there is a preposterous and perverse kind of arrogance in thus reducing Africa to the role of props for the breakup of one petty European mind. But that is not even the point. The real question is the dehumanization of Africa and Africans which this age-long attitude has fostered and continues to foster in the world. And the question is whether a novel which celebrates this dehumanization, which depersonalizes a portion of the human race, can be called a great work of art. My answer is: No, it cannot. I would not call that man an artist, for example, who composes an eloquent instigation to one people to fall upon another and destroy them. No matter how striking his imagery or how beautiful his cadences fall, such a man is no more a great artist than another may be called a priest who reads the mass backwards or a physician who poisons his patients. All those men in Nazi Germany who lent their talent to the service of virulent racism whether in science, philosophy, or the arts have generally and rightly been condemned for their perversions. The time is long overdue for taking a hard look at the work of creative artists who apply their talents, alas often considerable as in the case of Conrad, to set people against people. This, I take it, is what Yevtushenko[3] is after when he tells us that a poet cannot be a slave trader at the same time, and gives the striking example of Arthur Rimbaud[4], who was fortunately honest enough to give up any pretenses to poetry when he opted for slave trading. For poetry surely can only be on the side of man's deliverance and not his enslavement; for the brotherhood and unity of all mankind and against the doctrines of Hitler's master races or Conrad's "rudimentary souls."

Last year was the fiftieth anniversary of Conrad's death. He was born in 1857, the very year in which the first Anglican missionaries were arriving among my own people in Nigeria. It was certainly not his fault that he lived his life at a time when the reputation of the black man was at a particularly low level. But even after due allowances have been made for all the influences of contemporary prejudice on his sensibility, there remains still in Conrad's attitude a residue of antipathy to black people which his peculiar psychology alone can explain. His own account of his first encounter with a black man is very revealing:

> A certain enormous buck nigger encountered in Haiti fixed my conception of blind, furious, unreasoning rage, as manifested in the human animal to the end of my days. Of the nigger I used to dream for years afterwards.

Certainly, Conrad had a problem with niggers. His inordinate love of that word itself should be of interest to psychoanalysts. Sometimes his fixation on blackness is equally interesting, as when he gives us this brief description:

> A black figure stood up, strode on long black legs, waving long black arms.

As though we might expect a black figure striding along on black legs to have *white* arms! But so unrelenting is Conrad's obsession.

---

[3] Yevgeny Yevtushenko (b. 1933) is a Russian poet most famous for the poem "Babi Yar," which criticized the Soviet regime's refusal to acknowledge atrocities committed during World War II. The poem's title refers to a ravine in Kiev, Ukraine, where 100,000–150,000 people were massacred during the war. It is perhaps best known as the site of the 1941 Nazi massacre of nearly 34,000 Jews during a two-day span. — EDS.

[4] Arthur Rimbaud (1854–1891) was a French poet known for his experimental writing. He began writing poetry at age seventeen; he abandoned the pursuit entirely at age twenty-one. — EDS.

As a matter of interest, Conrad gives us in *A Personal Record* what amounts to a companion piece to the buck nigger of Haiti. At the age of sixteen Conrad encountered his first Englishman in Europe. He calls him "my unforgettable Englishman" and describes him in the following manner:

> [his] calves exposed to the public gaze . . . dazzled the beholder by the splendor of their marble-like condition and their rich tone of young ivory. . . . The light of a headlong, exalted satisfaction with the world of men . . . illumined his face . . . and triumphant eyes. In passing he cast a glance of kindly curiosity and a friendly gleam of big, sound, shiny teeth . . . his white calves twinkled sturdily.

Irrational love and irrational hate jostling together in the heart of that tormented man. But whereas irrational love may at worst engender foolish acts of indiscretion, irrational hate can endanger the life of the community. Naturally, Conrad is a dream for psychoanalytic critics. Perhaps the most detailed study of him in this direction is by Bernard C. Meyer, MD. In this lengthy book, Dr. Meyer follows every conceivable lead (and sometimes inconceivable ones) to explain Conrad. As an example, he gives us long disquisitions on the significance of hair and haircutting in Conrad. And yet not even one word is spared for his attitude to black people. Not even the discussion of Conrad's anti-Semitism was enough to spark off in Dr. Meyer's mind those other dark and explosive thoughts. Which only leads one to surmise that Western psychoanalysts must regard the kind of racism displayed by Conrad as absolutely normal despite the profoundly important work done by Frantz Fanon in the psychiatric hospitals of French Algeria.

Whatever Conrad's problems were, you might say he is now safely dead. Quite true. Unfortunately, his heart of darkness plagues us still. Which is why an offensive and totally deplorable book can be described by a serious scholar as "among the half-dozen greatest short novels in the English language," and why it is today perhaps the most commonly prescribed novel in the twentieth-century literature courses in our own English Department here. Indeed the time is long overdue for a hard look at things.

There are two probable grounds on which what I have said so far may be contested. The first is that it is no concern of fiction to please people about whom it is written. I will go along with that. But I am not talking about pleasing people. I am talking about a book which parades in the most vulgar fashion prejudices and insults from which a section of mankind has suffered untold agonies and atrocities in the past and continues to do so in many ways and many places today. I am talking about a story in which the very humanity of black people is called in question. It seems to me totally inconceivable that great art or even good art could possibly reside in such unwholesome surroundings.

Secondly, I may be challenged on the grounds of actuality. Conrad, after all, sailed down the Congo in 1890, when my own father was still a babe in arms, and recorded what he saw. How could I stand up in 1975, fifty years after his death, and purport to contradict him? My answer is that as a sensible man I will not accept just any traveller's tales solely on the grounds that I have not made the journey myself. I will not trust the evidence even of a man's very eyes when I suspect them to be as jaundiced as Conrad's. And we also happen to know that Conrad was, in the words of his biographer, Bernard C. Meyer, "notoriously inaccurate in the rendering of his own history."

But more important by far is the abundant testimony about Conrad's savages which we could gather if we were so inclined from other sources and which might lead us to think that these people must have had other occupations besides merging into the evil forest or materializing out of it simply to plague Marlow and his dispirited band. For as it happened, soon after

Conrad had written his book an event of far greater consequence was taking place in the art world of Europe. This is how Frank Willett, a British art historian, describes it:

> Gauguin[5] had gone to Tahiti, the most extravagant individual act of turning to a non-European culture in the decades immediately before and after 1900, when European artists were avid for new artistic experiences, but it was only about 1904–5 that African art began to make its distinctive impact. One piece is still identifiable; it is a mask that had been given to Maurice Vlaminck in 1905. He records that Derain was "speechless" and "stunned" when he saw it, bought it from Vlaminck and in turn showed it to Picasso and Matisse, who were also greatly affected by it. Ambroise Vollard then borrowed it and had it cast in bronze. . . . The revolution of twentieth century art was under way!

The mask in question was made by other savages living just north of Conrad's River Congo. They have a name, the Fang people, and are without a doubt among the world's greatest masters of the sculptured form. As you might have guessed, the event to which Frank Willett refers marked the beginning of cubism and the infusion of new life into European art that had run completely out of strength.

The point of all this is to suggest that Conrad's picture of the people of the Congo seems grossly inadequate even at the height of their subjection to the ravages of King Leopold's International Association for the Civilization of Central Africa. Travellers with closed minds can tell us little except about themselves. But even those not blinkered, like Conrad, with xenophobia can be astonishingly blind.

Let me digress a little here. One of the greatest and most intrepid travellers of all time, Marco Polo, journeyed to the Far East from the Mediterranean in the thirteenth century and spent twenty years in the court of Kublai Khan in China. On his return to Venice he set down in his book entitled *Description of the World* his impressions of the peoples and places and customs he had seen. There are at least two extraordinary omissions in his account. He says nothing about the art of printing unknown as yet in Europe but in full flower in China. He either did not notice it at all or if he did, failed to see what use Europe could possibly have for it. Whatever reason, Europe had to wait another hundred years for Gutenberg. But even more spectacular was Marco Polo's omission of any reference to the Great Wall of China nearly four thousand miles long and already more than one thousand years old at the time of his visit. Again, he may not have seen it; but the Great Wall of China is the only structure built by man which is visible from the moon! Indeed, travellers can be blind.

As I said earlier, Conrad did not originate the image of Africa which we find in his book. It was and is the dominant image of Africa in the Western imagination and Conrad merely brought the peculiar gifts of his own mind to bear on it. For reasons which can certainly use close psychological inquiry, the West seems to suffer deep anxieties about the precariousness of its civilization and to have a need for constant reassurance by comparing it with Africa. If Europe, advancing in civilization, could cast a backward glance periodically at Africa trapped in primordial barbarity, it could say with faith and feeling: There go I but for the grace of God. Africa is to Europe as the picture is to Dorian Gray[6] — a carrier onto whom the master unloads his physical and moral deformities so that he may go forward, erect and immaculate. Consequently, Africa is something to be avoided just as the picture has to be hidden away to

[5] Eugène Henri Paul Gauguin (1848–1903), French Post-Impressionist painter, moved to Tahiti toward the end of his life. — EDS.

[6] A reference to the Oscar Wilde novel *The Picture of Dorian Gray* (1890). The titular character, Dorian Gray, sells his soul to remain forever young and beautiful while a full-length portrait of him ages instead. — EDS.

safeguard the man's jeopardous integrity. Keep away from Africa, or else! Mr. Kurtz of *Heart of Darkness* should have heeded that warning and the prowling horror in his heart would have kept its place, chained to its lair. But he foolishly exposed himself to the wild irresistible allure of the jungle and lo! the darkness found him out.

In my original conception of this talk I had thought to conclude it nicely on an appropriately positive note in which I would suggest from my privileged position in African and Western culture some advantages the West might derive from Africa once it rid its mind of old prejudices and began to look at Africa not through a haze of distortions and cheap mystification but quite simply as a continent of people — not angels, but not rudimentary souls either — just people, often highly gifted people and often strikingly successful in their enterprise with life and society. But as I thought more about the stereotype image, about its grip and pervasiveness, about the willful tenacity with which the West holds it to its heart; when I thought of your television and the cinema and newspapers, about books read in schools and out of school, of churches preaching to empty pews about the need to send help to the heathen in Africa, I realized that no easy optimism was possible. And there is something totally wrong in offering bribes to the West in return for its good opinion of Africa. Ultimately, the abandonment of unwholesome thoughts must be its own and only reward. Although I have used the word *willful* a few times in this talk to characterize the West's view of Africa, it may well be that what is happening at this stage is more akin to reflex action than calculated malice. Which does not make the situation more, but less, hopeful. Let me give you one last and really minor example of what I mean.

Last November the *Christian Science Monitor* carried an interesting article written by its Education Editor on the serious psychological and learning problems faced by little children who speak one language at home and then go to school where something else is spoken. It was a wide-ranging article taking in Spanish-speaking children in this country, the children of migrant Italian workers in Germany, the quadrilingual phenomenon in Malaysia, and so on. And all this while the article speaks unequivocally about *language*. But then out of the blue sky comes this:

> In London there is an enormous immigration of children who speak Indian or Nigerian dialects, or some other native language.

I believe that the introduction of *dialects*, which is technically erroneous in the context, is almost a reflex action caused by an instinctive desire of the writer to downgrade the discussion to the level of Africa and India. And this is quite comparable to Conrad's withholding of language from his rudimentary souls. Language is too grand for these chaps; let's give them dialects. In all this business a lot of violence is inevitably done to words and their meaning. Look at the phrase "native language" in the above excerpt. Surely the only native language possible in London is Cockney English. But our writer obviously means something else — something Indians and Africans speak.

Perhaps a change will come. Perhaps this is the time when it can begin, when the high optimism engendered by the breathtaking achievements of Western science and industry is giving way to doubt and even confusion. There is just the possibility that Western man may begin to look seriously at the achievements of other people. I read in the papers the other day a suggestion that what America needs at this time is somehow to bring back the extended family. And I saw in my mind's eye future African Peace Corps Volunteers coming to help you set up the system.

Seriously, although the work which needs to be done may appear too daunting, I believe that it is not one day too soon to begin. And where better than at a university?

[1975]

QUESTIONS

1. What is the purpose of the anecdotes that open this essay?
2. Chinua Achebe acknowledges that Joseph Conrad's literary talents and *Heart of Darkness* have some merit. What are the positive qualities he concedes?
3. What is Achebe's basic interpretation of *Heart of Darkness*? What are his objections to traditional interpretations?
4. What does Achebe mean when he asserts that although Conrad is dead, "his heart of darkness plagues us still" (para. 23)?
5. What is the purpose of Achebe bringing Albert Schweitzer and Marco Polo into this analysis?
6. What textual evidence, including tone, can you cite to illustrate that Achebe felt that his university audience would not be entirely hostile or even unreceptive to his argument? What does Achebe mean when he refers to his "privileged position in African and Western culture" (para. 30)?
7. Find points in Achebe's argument that you agree with as well as those with which you disagree. Pay particular attention to whether Achebe believes that Conrad's condemnation of the colonizers is as clear as his devaluation of the natives.

The White Man's Burden

RUDYARD KIPLING

Winner of the Nobel Prize for Literature in 1907, Rudyard Kipling (1865–1936) is best known for the children's classic *The Jungle Book* (1894). Kipling was born in Bombay, educated in England, and lived for many years in India as a reporter for Anglo-Indian newspapers. Although Kipling demonstrates both understanding and appreciation of Indian culture in many of his works, "The White Man's Burden" famously summarizes the Eurocentric expansionist ideology of the time. Kipling originally wrote the poem for Queen Victoria's Diamond Jubilee in 1897, ultimately publishing it two years later in the popular magazine *McClure's*.

Take up the White Man's burden —
Send forth the best ye breed —
Go, bind your sons to exile
To serve your captives' need;
To wait, in heavy harness,
On fluttered folk and wild —
Your new-caught sullen peoples,
Half devil and half child.

Take up the White Man's burden —
In patience to abide,
To veil the threat of terror
And check the show of pride;
By open speech and simple,
An hundred times made plain,
To seek another's profit
And work another's gain.

Take up the White Man's burden —
The savage wars of peace —
Fill full the mouth of Famine,
And bid the sickness cease;
And when your goal is nearest
(The end for others sought)
Watch sloth and heathen folly
Bring all your hope to nought.

Take up the White Man's burden —
No iron rule of kings,
But toil of serf and sweeper —
The tale of common things.
The ports ye shall not enter,
The roads ye shall not tread,
Go, make them with your living
And mark them with your dead.

Take up the White Man's burden,
And reap his old reward —
The blame of those ye better
The hate of those ye guard —
The cry of hosts ye humour
(Ah, slowly?) toward the light: —
"Why brought ye us from bondage,
Our loved Egyptian night?"

Take up the White Man's burden —
Ye dare not stoop to less —
Nor call too loud on Freedom
To cloak your weariness.
By all ye will or whisper,
By all ye leave or do,
The silent sullen peoples
Shall weigh your God and you.

Take up the White Man's burden!
Have done with childish days —
The lightly-proffered laurel,
The easy ungrudged praise:
Comes now, to search your manhood
Through all the thankless years,
Cold, edged with dear-bought wisdom,
The judgment of your peers.

[1899]

QUESTIONS

1. The poem is written as a series of imperatives addressed to "you"; to whom is the speaker addressing these exhortations?
2. How are "others" — nonwhites — depicted in this poem? Cite specific descriptions and images.
3. What exactly is the "burden" alluded to in the title?

The Black Man's Burden

H. T. JOHNSON

Among the many replies to Kipling's poem was "The Black Man's Burden," a poem written by African American clergyman and editor H. T. Johnson. The poem was published in the *Christian Recorder* in 1899.

Pile on the Black Man's burden,
'Tis nearest at your door;
Why heed long-bleeding Cuba
Or dark Hawaii's shore?
Halt ye your fearless armies
Which menace feeble folks,
Who fight with clubs and arrows
And brook your rifle's smokes.

Pile on the Black Man's burden,
His wail with laughter drown,
You've sealed the Red Man's problem
And now take up the Brown.
In vain ye seek to end it
With bullets, blood or death —
Better by far defend it
With honor's holy breath.

Pile on the Black Man's burden,
His back is broad though sore;
What though the weight oppress him,
He's borne the like before.
Your Jim-Crow laws and customs,
And fiendish midnight deed,
Though winked at by the nation,
Will some day trouble breed.

Pile on the Black Man's burden,
At length 'twill Heaven pierce;
Then on you or your children
Will reign God's judgments fierce.
Your battleships and armies
May weaker ones appall,
But God Almighty's justice
They'll not disturb at all.

[1899]

QUESTIONS

1. What direct links, apart from the titles, with Rudyard Kipling's poem do you see? Some have read H. T. Johnson's poem as a parody of Kipling's. Explain why you would agree or disagree with this assessment.
2. Both poems use second person ("you" and "your"), but who is the "you" in Kipling's poem and who is the "you" in Johnson's?
3. What is the "it" referred to in lines 13 and 15 of this poem? Why does Johnson call for "defend[ing] it / With honor's holy breath" (ll. 15–16)?

Fang Ngil Mask, Gabon

Ngil masks were worn by the members of the Fang tribe in Gabon. The Ngil was a secret religious society that acted in a judiciary and a police capacity — they discovered and punished sorcerers, but they also brokered peace between rival clans and villages. After a period of violence and unrest, the French banned these masks in 1910.

The Israel Museum, Jerusalem, Israel, The Arthur and Madeleine Chalette Lejwa Collection / Bridgeman Images

[c. 1900]

Tête and Portrait of Jeanne Hébuterne

AMEDEO MODIGLIANI

Amedeo Modigliani (1884–1920), an Italian painter and sculptor who worked mainly in France, was one of the early twentieth-century European artists who integrated African art's bold lines and open designs into his own work. Believed to have encountered African masks at archaeological exhibits in Paris, Modigliani found in the aesthetics of that art a purity of form that inspired his own work. Below are Modigliani's sculpture entitled *Tête* (1912) and a later painting, *Portrait of Jeanne Hébuterne* (1918).

Tête ("Head")

MIGUEL MEDINA/AFP/Getty Images

[1912]

Portrait of Jeanne Hébuterne

PrivateCollection/Bridgeman Images

[1918]

QUESTIONS

1. How would you describe the characteristics of the Fang Ngil mask, and what effects do they have on the viewer? Do you consider it beautiful? Explain in terms of the criteria that define beauty for you.
2. In what ways would you consider "Tête" a tribute, a copy, an inspiration, an appreciation, an idealization, an appropriation, or a remix of the Fang Ngil mask? Or is it something else? What about the portrait Amedeo Modigliani painted? Would you apply the same term to describe its relationship to the mask? Why or why not?

3. The term "primitivism" has been used to describe African art displayed in Europe during this period, a term now considered problematic. Intended to contrast the "natural" with the "civilized," Primitivism refers to the belief that Western European society had been corrupted by industrialization and urbanization, and that cultures perceived as undeveloped held more value. To what extent do you find this term inaccurate or even offensive? Why? Use the Fang Ngil mask and Modigliani's work to explain your viewpoint.
4. It is not an exaggeration to say that African art such as the Fang Ngil mask reached a European audience largely because of nineteenth-century colonialism. European governments considered it within their authority to bring back African works, usually without permission or payment. Many were displayed initially as artifacts in archaeological museums, though eventually they made their way into art museums and were recognized as genuine works of art. In this context, how do you view the artistic legacy of colonialism? Is it largely positive or essentially negative? Does the respect and appreciation we now have not only for pre–twentieth-century African art itself, but for its influence on Western artists, mitigate in any way the initial Western attitude toward the work and the means by which it was acquired? Explain.

The Old Chief Mshlanga

DORIS LESSING

Winner of the 2007 Nobel Prize in Literature, Doris Lessing (1919–2013) was born in Persia (now Iran) to British parents. In 1925, the family moved to Rhodesia (now Zimbabwe), from which many of the stories in her prolific career emerge. Lessing moved to London in 1949 and began publishing her work, including *The Grass Is Singing* (1949) and her breakout work *A Golden Notebook* (1962), which became a feminist manifesto. Lessing continued to write fiction, autobiography, drama (including an opera), and graphic novels; her latest work was the novel *Alfred and Emily*, published in 2008. "The Old Chief Mshlanga" was originally published in 1951 in Lessing's second book, *This Was the Old Chief's Country*, a collection of short stories set in Zimbabwe.

They were good, the years of ranging the bush over her father's farm which, like every white farm, was largely unused, broken only occasionally by small patches of cultivation. In between, nothing but trees, the long sparse grass, thorn and cactus and gully, grass and outcrop and thorn. And a jutting piece of rock which had been thrust up from the warm soil of Africa unimaginable eras of time ago, washed into hollows and whorls by sun and wind that had traveled so many thousands of miles of space and bush, would hold the weight of a small girl whose eyes were sightless for anything but a pale willowed river, a pale gleaming castle — a small girl singing: "Out flew the web and floated wide, the mirror cracked from side to side . . ."

Pushing her way through the green aisles of the mealie stalks,[1] the leaves arching like cathedrals veined with sunlight far overhead, with the packed red earth underfoot, a fine lace of red starred witchweed would summon up a black bent figure croaking premonitions: the Northern witch, bred of cold Northern forests, would stand before her among the mealie fields, and it was the mealie fields that faded and fled, leaving her among the gnarled roots of an oak, snow falling thick and soft and white, the woodcutter's

[1] Corn. — EDS.

fire glowing red welcome through crowding tree trunks.

A white child, opening its eyes curiously on a sun-suffused landscape, a gaunt and violent landscape, might be supposed to accept it as her own, to take the msasa trees and the thorn trees as familiars, to feel her blood running free and responsive to the swing of the seasons.

This child could not see a msasa tree, or the thorn, for what they were. Her books held tales of alien fairies, her rivers ran slow and peaceful, and she knew the shape of the leaves of an ash or an oak, the names of the little creatures that lived in English streams, when the words "the veld" meant strangeness, though she could remember nothing else.

5 Because of this, for many years, it was the veld that seemed unreal; the sun was a foreign sun, and the wind spoke a strange language.

The black people on the farm were as remote as the trees and the rocks. They were an amorphous black mass, mingling and thinning and massing like tadpoles, faceless, who existed merely to serve, to say "Yes, Baas," take their money, and go. They changed season by season, moving from one farm to the next, according to their outlandish needs, which one did not have to understand, coming from perhaps hundreds of miles north or east, passing on after a few months — where? Perhaps even as far away as the fabled gold mines of Johannesburg, where the pay was so much better than the few shillings a month and the double handful of mealie meal twice a day which they earned in that part of Africa.

The child was taught to take them for granted: the servants in the house would come running a hundred yards to pick up a book if she dropped it. She was called "Nkosikaas" — Chieftainess, even by the black children her own age.

Later, when the farm grew too small to hold her curiosity, she carried a gun in the crook of her arm and wandered miles a day, from vlei to vlei,[2] from kopje to kopje,[3] accompanied by two dogs: the dogs and the gun were an armor against fear. Because of them she never felt fear.

If a native came into sight along the kaffir[4] paths half a mile away, the dogs would flush him up a tree as if he were a bird. If he expostulated (in his uncouth language which was by itself ridiculous) that was cheek. If one was in a good mood, it could be a matter for laughter. Otherwise one passed on, hardly glancing at the angry man in the tree.

10 On the rare occasions when white children met together they could amuse themselves by hailing a passing native in order to make a buffoon of him; they could set the dogs on him and watch him run; they could tease a small black child as if he were a puppy — save that they would not throw stones and sticks at a dog without a sense of guilt.

Later still, certain questions presented themselves in the child's mind; and because the answers were not easy to accept, they were silenced by an even greater arrogance of manner.

It was even impossible to think of the black people who worked about the house as friends, for if she talked to one of them, her mother would come running anxiously: "Come away; you mustn't talk to natives."

It was this instilled consciousness of danger, of something unpleasant, that made it easy to laugh out loud, crudely, if a servant made a mistake in his English or if he failed to understand an order — there is a certain kind of laughter that is fear, afraid of itself.

One evening, when I was about fourteen, I was walking down the side of a mealie field that had been newly plowed, so that the great red clods showed fresh and tumbling to the vlei beyond, like a choppy red sea; it was that

---

[2] Marsh or lake. — EDS.

[3] Rocky mounds exposed by erosion. — EDS.

[4] Former generic term for South African blacks, now derogatory. — EDS.

hushed and listening hour, when the birds send long sad calls from tree to tree, and all the colors of earth and sky and leaf are deep and golden. I had my rifle in the curve of my arm, and the dogs were at my heels.

In front of me, perhaps a couple of hundred yards away, a group of three Africans came into sight around the side of a big ant-heap. I whistled the dogs close in to my skirts and let the gun swing in my hand, and advanced, waiting for them to move aside, off the path, in respect for my passing. But they came on steadily, and the dogs looked up at me for the command to chase. I was angry. It was "cheek" for a native not to stand off a path, the moment he caught sight of you.

In front walked an old man, stooping his weight on to a stick, his hair grizzled white, a dark red blanket slung over his shoulders like a cloak. Behind him came two young men, carrying bundles of pots, assegais,[5] hatchets.

The group was not a usual one. They were not natives seeking work. These had an air of dignity, of quietly following their own purpose. It was the dignity that checked my tongue. I walked quietly on, talking softly to the growling dogs, till I was ten paces away. Then the old man stopped, drawing his blanket close.

"Morning, Nkosikaas," he said, using the customary greeting for any time of the day.

"Good morning," I said. "Where are you going?" My voice was a little truculent.

The old man spoke in his own language, then one of the young men stepped forward politely and said in careful English: "My Chief travels to see his brothers beyond the river."

A Chief! I thought, understanding the pride that made the old man stand before me like an equal — more than an equal, for he showed courtesy, and I showed none.

The old man spoke again, wearing dignity like an inherited garment, still standing ten paces off, flanked by his entourage, not looking at me (that would have been rude) but directing his eyes somewhere over my head at the trees.

"You are the little Nkosikaas from the farm of Baas Jordan?"

"That's right," I said.

"Perhaps your father does not remember," said the interpreter for the old man, "but there was an affair with some goats. I remember seeing you when you were . . ." The young man held his hand at knee level and smiled.

We all smiled.

"What is your name?" I asked.

"This is Chief Mshlanga," said the young man.

"I will tell my father that I met you," I said.

The old man said: "My greetings to your father, little Nkosikaas."

"Good morning," I said politely, finding the politeness difficult, from lack of use.

"Morning, little Nkosikaas," said the old man, and stood aside to let me pass.

I went by, my gun hanging awkwardly, the dogs sniffing and growling, cheated of their favorite game of chasing natives like animals.

Not long afterwards I read in an old explorer's book the phrase: "Chief Mshlanga's country." It went like this: "Our destination was Chief Mshlanga's country, to the north of the river; and it was our desire to ask his permission to prospect for gold in his territory."

The phrase "ask his permission" was so extraordinary to a white child, brought up to consider all natives as things to use, that it revived those questions, which could not be suppressed: they fermented slowly in my mind.

On another occasion one of those old prospectors who still move over Africa looking for neglected reefs, with their hammers and tents, and pans for sifting gold from crushed rock, came to the farm and, in talking of the old days, used that phrase again: "This was the Old Chief's country," he said. "It stretched from those mountains over there way back to the river, hundreds of miles of country." That was his

[5] A pole used as a weapon like a javelin or a spear. — EDS.

name for our district: "The Old Chief's Country"; he did not use our name for it—a new phrase which held no implication of usurped ownership.

As I read more books about the time when this part of Africa was opened up, not much more than fifty years before, I found Old Chief Mshlanga had been a famous man, known to all the explorers and prospectors. But then he had been young; or maybe it was his father or uncle they spoke of—I never found out.

During that year I met him several times in the part of the farm that was traversed by natives moving over the country. I learned that the path up the side of the big red field where the birds sang was the recognized highway for migrants. Perhaps I even haunted it in the hope of meeting him: being greeted by him, the exchange of courtesies, seemed to answer the questions that troubled me.

Soon I carried a gun in a different spirit; I used it for shooting food and not to give me confidence. And now the dogs learned better manners. When I saw a native approaching, we offered and took greetings; and slowly that other landscape in my mind faded, and my feet struck directly on the African soil, and I saw the shapes of tree and hill clearly, and the black people moved back, as it were, out of my life: it was as if I stood aside to watch a slow intimate dance of landscape and men, a very old dance, whose steps I could not learn.

But I thought: this is my heritage, too; I was bred here; it is my country as well as the black man's country; and there is plenty of room for all of us, without elbowing each other off the pavements and roads.

It seemed it was only necessary to let free that respect I felt when I was talking with Old Chief Mshlanga, to let both black and white people meet gently, with tolerance for each other's differences: it seemed quite easy.

Then, one day, something new happened. Working in our house as servants were always three natives: cook, houseboy, garden boy. They used to change as the farm natives changed: staying for a few months, then moving on to a new job, or back home to their kraals.[6] They were thought of as "good" or "bad" natives; which meant: how did they behave as servants? Were they lazy, efficient, obedient, or disrespectful? If the family felt good-humored, the phrase was: "What can you expect from raw black savages?" If we were angry, we said: "These damned niggers, we would be much better off without them."

One day, a white policeman was on his rounds of the district, and he said laughingly: "Did you know you have an important man in your kitchen?"

"What!" exclaimed my mother sharply. "What do you mean?"

"A Chief's son." The policeman seemed amused. "He'll boss the tribe when the old man dies."

"He'd better not put on a Chief's son act with me," said my mother.

When the policeman left, we looked with different eyes at our cook: he was a good worker, but he drank too much at weekends—that was how we knew him.

He was a tall youth, with very black skin, like black polished metal, his tightly growing black hair parted white man's fashion at one side, with a metal comb from the store stuck into it; very polite, very distant, very quick to obey an order. Now that it had been pointed out, we said: "Of course, you can see. Blood always tells."

My mother became strict with him now she knew about his birth and prospects. Sometimes, when she lost her temper, she would say: "You aren't the Chief yet, you know." And he would answer her very quietly, his eyes on the ground: "Yes, Nkosikaas."

[6] Literally, corrals for animals; often used in colonial southern Africa to refer to tribal homesteads in which huts were built in a circle. — EDS.

One afternoon, he asked for a whole day off, instead of the customary half-day, to go home next Sunday.

"How can you go home in one day?"

"It will take me half an hour on my bicycle," he explained.

I watched the direction he took; and the next day I went off to look for this kraal; I understood he must be Chief Mshlanga's successor: there was no other kraal near enough our farm.

Beyond our boundaries on that side the country was new to me. I followed unfamiliar paths past kopjes that till now had been part of the jagged horizon, hazed with distance. This was Government land, which had never been cultivated by white men; at first I could not understand why it was that it appeared, in merely crossing the boundary, I had entered a completely fresh type of landscape. It was a wide green valley, where a small river sparkled, and vivid water-birds darted over the rushes. The grass was thick and soft to my calves, the trees stood tall and shapely.

I was used to our farm, whose hundred of acres of harsh eroded soil bore trees that had been cut for the mine furnaces and had grown thin and twisted, where the cattle had dragged the grass flat, leaving innumerable crisscrossing trails that deepened each season into gullies, under the force of the rains.

This country had been left untouched, save for prospectors whose picks had struck a few sparks from the surface of the rocks as they wandered by; and for migrant natives whose passing had left, perhaps, a charred patch on the trunk of a tree where their evening fire had nestled.

It was very silent: a hot morning with pigeons cooing throatily, the midday shadows lying dense and thick with clear yellow spaces of sunlight between and in all that wide green parklike valley, not a human soul but myself.

I was listening to the quick regular tapping of a woodpecker when slowly a chill feeling seemed to grow up from the small of my back to my shoulders, in a constricting spasm like a shudder, and at the roots of my hair a tingling sensation began and ran down over the surface of my flesh, leaving me goosefleshed and cold, though I was damp with sweat. Fever? I thought; then uneasily, turned to look over my shoulder; and realized suddenly that this was fear. It was extraordinary, even humiliating. It was a new fear. For all the years I had walked by myself over this country I had never known a moment's uneasiness; in the beginning because I had been supported by a gun and the dogs, then because I had learned an easy friendliness for the Africans I might encounter.

I had read of this feeling, how the bigness and silence of Africa, under the ancient sun, grows dense and takes shape in the mind, till even the birds seem to call menacingly, and a deadly spirit comes out of the trees and the rocks. You move warily, as if your very passing disturbs something old and evil, something dark and big and angry that might suddenly rear and strike from behind. You look at groves of entwined trees; and picture the animals that might be lurking there; you look at the river running slowly, dropping from level to level through the vlei, spreading into pools where at night the buck come to drink, and the crocodiles rise and drag them by their soft noses into underwater caves. Fear possessed me. I found I was turning round and round, because of that shapeless menace behind me that might reach out and take me; I kept glancing at the files of kopjes which, seen from a different angle, seemed to change with every step so that even known landmarks, like a big mountain that had sentineled my world since I first became conscious of it, showed an unfamiliar sunlit valley among its foothills. I did not know where I was. I was lost. Panic seized me. I found I was spinning round and round, staring anxiously at this tree and that, peering up at the sun which appeared to have moved into an eastern slant, shedding the sad yellow light of sunset. Hours must have passed! I looked at my watch and found that this state of meaningless terror had lasted perhaps ten minutes.

The point was that it was meaningless. I was not ten miles from home: I had only to take my way back along the valley to find myself at the fence; away among the foothills of the kopjes gleamed the roof of a neighbor's house, and a couple of hours' walking would reach it. This was the sort of fear that contracts the flesh of a dog at night and sets him howling at the full moon. It had nothing to do with what I thought or felt; and I was more disturbed by the fact that I could become its victim than of the physical sensation itself: I walked steadily on, quieted, in a divided mind, watching my own pricking nerves and apprehensive glances from side to side with a disgusted amusement. Deliberately I set myself to think of this village I was seeking, and what I should do when I entered it — if I could find it, which was doubtful, since I was walking aimlessly and it might be anywhere in the hundreds of thousands of acres of bush that stretched about me. With my mind on that village, I realized that a new sensation was added to the fear: loneliness. Now such a terror of isolation invaded me that I could hardly walk; and if it were not that I came over the crest of a small rise and saw a village below me, I should have turned and gone home. It was a cluster of thatched huts in a clearing among trees. There were neat patches of mealies and pumpkins and millet, and cattle grazed under some trees at a distance. Fowls scratched among the huts, dogs lay sleeping on the grass, and goats friezed a kopje that jutted up beyond a tributary of the river lying like an enclosing arm round the village.

As I came close I saw the huts were lovingly decorated with patterns of yellow and red and ochre mud on the walls; and the thatch was tied in place with plaits of straw.

This was not at all like our farm compound, a dirty and neglected place, a temporary home for migrants who had no roots in it.

And now I did not know what to do next. I called a small black boy, who was sitting on a log playing a stringed gourd, quite naked except for the strings of blue beads round his neck, and said: "Tell the Chief I am here." The child stuck his thumb in his mouth and stared shyly back at me.

For minutes I shifted my feet on the edge of what seemed a deserted village, till at last the child scuttled off, and then some women came. They were draped in bright cloths, with brass glinting in their ears and on their arms. They also stared, silently; then turned to chatter among themselves.

I said again: "Can I see Chief Mshlanga?" I saw they caught the name; they did not understand what I wanted. I did not understand myself.

At last I walked through them and came past the huts and saw a clearing under a big shady tree, where a dozen old men sat cross-legged on the ground, talking. Chief Mshlanga was leaning back against the tree, holding a gourd in his hand, from which he had been drinking. When he saw me, not a muscle of his face moved, and I could see he was not pleased: perhaps he was afflicted with my own shyness, due to being unable to find the right forms of courtesy for the occasion. To meet me, on our own farm, was one thing; but I should not have come here. What had I expected? I could not join them socially: the thing was unheard of. Bad enough that I, a white girl, should be walking the veld alone as a white man might: and in this part of the bush where only Government officials had the right to move.

Again I stood, smiling foolishly, while behind me stood the groups of brightly clad, chattering women, their faces alert with curiosity and interest, and in front of me sat the old men, with old lined faces, their eyes guarded, aloof. It was a village of ancients and children and women. Even the two young men who kneeled beside the Chief were not those I had seen with him previously: the young men were all away working on the white men's farms and mines, and the Chief must depend on relatives who were temporarily on holiday for his attendants.

"The small white Nkosikaas is far from home," remarked the old man at last.

"Yes," I agreed, "it is far." I wanted to say: "I have come to pay you a friendly visit, Chief Mshlanga." I could not say it. I might now be feeling an urgent helpless desire to get to know these men and women as people, to be accepted by them as a friend, but the truth was I had set out in a spirit of curiosity: I had wanted to see the village that one day our cook, the reserved and obedient young man who got drunk on Sundays, would one day rule over.

"The child of Nkosi Jordan is welcome," said Chief Mshlanga.

"Thank you," I said, and could think of nothing more to say. There was a silence, while the flies rose and began to buzz around my head; and the wind shook a little in the thick green tree that spread its branches over the old men.

"Good morning," I said at last. "I have to return now to my home."

"Morning, little Nkosikaas," said Chief Mshlanga.

I walked away from the indifferent village, over the rise past the staring amber-eyed goats, down through the tall stately trees into the great rich green valley where the river meandered and the pigeons cooed tales of plenty and the woodpecker tapped softly.

The fear had gone; the loneliness had set into stiff-necked stoicism; there was now a queer hostility in the landscape, a cold, hard, sullen indomitability that walked with me, as strong as a wall, as intangible as smoke; it seemed to say to me: you walk here as a destroyer. I went slowly homewards, with an empty heart: I had learned that if one cannot call a country to heel like a dog, neither can one dismiss the past with a smile in an easy gush of feeling, saying: I could not help it, I am also a victim.

I only saw Chief Mshlanga once again.

One night my father's big red land was trampled down by small sharp hooves, and it was discovered that the culprits were goats from Chief Mshlanga's kraal. This had happened once before, years ago.

My father confiscated all the goats. Then he sent a message to the old Chief that if he wanted them he would have to pay for the damage.

He arrived at our house at the time of sunset one evening, looking very old and bent now, walking stiffly under his regally draped blanket, leaning on a big stick. My father sat himself down in his big chair below the steps of the house; the old man squatted carefully on the ground before him, flanked by his two young men.

The palaver was long and painful, because of the bad English of the young man who interpreted, and because my father could not speak dialect, but only kitchen kaffir.

From my father's point of view, at least two hundred pounds' worth of damage had been done to the crop. He knew he could not get the money from the old man. He felt he was entitled to keep the goats. As for the old Chief, he kept repeating angrily: "Twenty goats! My people cannot lose twenty goats! We are not rich, like the Nkosi Jordan, to lose twenty goats at once."

My father did not think of himself as rich, but rather as very poor. He spoke quickly and angrily in return, saying that the damage done meant a great deal to him, and that he was entitled to the goats.

At last it grew so heated that the cook, the Chief's son, was called from the kitchen to be interpreter, and now my father spoke fluently in English, and our cook translated rapidly so that the old man could understand how very angry my father was. The young man spoke without emotion, in a mechanical way, his eyes lowered, but showing how he felt his position by a hostile uncomfortable set of the shoulders.

It was now in the late sunset, the sky a welter of colors, the birds singing their last songs, and the cattle, lowing peacefully, moving past us towards their sheds for the night. It was the hour when Africa is most beautiful; and here was this pathetic, ugly scene, doing no one any good.

At last my father stated finally: "I'm not going to argue about it. I am keeping the goats."

The old Chief flashed back in his own language: "That means that my people will go hungry when the dry season comes."

"Go to the police, then," said my father, and looked triumphant.

There was, of course, no more to be said.

The old man sat silent, his head bent, his hands dangling helplessly over his withered knees. Then he rose, the young men helping him, and he stood facing my father. He spoke once again, very stiffly; and turned away and went home to his village.

"What did he say?" asked my father of the young man, who laughed uncomfortably and would not meet his eyes.

"What did he say?" insisted my father.

Our cook stood straight and silent, his brows knotted together. Then he spoke. "My father says: All this land, this land you call yours, is his land; and belongs to our people."

Having made this statement, he walked off into the bush after his father, and we did not see him again.

Our next cook was a migrant from Nyasaland, with no expectations of greatness.

Next time the policeman came on his rounds he was told this story. He remarked: "That kraal has no right to be there; it should have been moved long ago. I don't know why no one has done anything about it. I'll have a chat with the Native Commissioner next week. I'm going over for tennis on Sunday, anyway."

Sometime later we heard that Chief Mshlanga and his people had been moved two hundred miles east, to a proper Native Reserve; the Government land was going to be opened up for white settlement soon.

I went to see the village again, about a year afterwards. There was nothing there. Mounds of red mud, where the huts had been, had long swathes of rotting thatch over them, veined with the red galleries of the white ants. The pumpkin vines rioted everywhere, over the bushes, up the lower branches of trees so that the great golden balls rolled underfoot and dangled overhead: it was a festival of pumpkins. The bushes were crowding up, the new grass sprang vivid green.

The settler lucky enough to be allotted the lush warm valley (if he chose to cultivate this particular section) would find, suddenly, in the middle of a mealie field, the plants were growing fifteen feet tall, the weight of the cobs dragging at the stalks, and wonder what unsuspected vein of richness he had struck.

[1951]

QUESTIONS

1. We see this story through the eyes of a young white girl. To what extent does she represent the whites' view of Africa?
2. Why does Doris Lessing emphasize the role of language in this story? For instance, the ease the narrator felt in laughing out loud "if a servant made a mistake in his English" (para. 13); her father's inability to "speak dialect" except for "kitchen kaffir" (para. 80); and the angry retort that the "old Chief flashed back in his own language" to her father near the end (para. 86).
3. What passages can you find that indicate the young narrator's recognition of the complexity of her position? Why, for example, does she describe Chief Mshlanga as "wearing dignity like an inherited garment" (para. 22)?

4. What evidence is there of the narrator's appreciation for the physical beauty of the African landscape? What does Lessing suggest when the narrator characterizes the landscape with a mixture of images of Africa and Europe, such as "green aisles of the mealie stalks, the leaves arching like cathedrals" (para. 2)?
5. How do you respond to the narrator's thoughts: "this is my heritage, too; I was bred here; it is my country as well as the black man's country; and there is plenty of room for all of us" (para. 40)? Do you think Lessing agrees with her?
6. What does the ending of this story suggest about the likely future of the colonists?

The Stranglehold of English Lit

FELIX MNTHALI

A Malawian poet, novelist, and playwright, Felix Mnthali (b. 1933) was educated in Lesotho and Canada, and has taught at the University of Ibadan, Malawi University, and the University of Botswana. Among his best-known works are *When Sunset Comes to Saptiwa* (1980) — a collection of poems — and the novels *My Dear Anniversary* (1992) and *Yoranivyoto* (1998). The following poem is from *Echoes from Obadan* (privately printed in 1961).

(For Molara Ogundipe-Leslie)

Those questions, sister,
those questions
stand
stab
jab
and gore
too close to the centre!

For if we had asked
why Jane Austen's people
carouse all day
and do no work

would Europe in Africa
have stood
the test of time?
and would she still maul
the flower of our youth
in the south?
Would she?

Your elegance of deceit,
Jane Austen,
lulled the sons and daughters
of the dispossessed
into a calf-love
with irony and satire
around imaginary people.

While history went on mocking
the victims of branding irons
and sugar-plantations
that made Jane Austen's people
wealthy beyond compare!

Eng. Lit., my sister,
was more than a cruel joke —
it was the heart
of alien conquest.

How could questions be asked
at Makerere and Ibadan,
Dakar and Ford Hare —
with Jane Austen
at the centre?
How could they be answered?

[1961]

QUESTIONS

1. Why do you think Felix Mnthali chose Jane Austen as the author cited in this poem?
2. Who is the "sister" (l. 1) the speaker addresses?
3. Why does the speaker assert that "Eng. Lit." (l. 31) "was the heart / of alien conquest" (ll. 33–34)?
4. What is the nature of the power that Mnthali believes literature holds?

In Memoriam

LÉOPOLD SENGHOR

Translated by Melvin Dixon

A prolific poet and influential statesman, Léopold Sedar Senghor (1906–2001) was born in Dakar, Senegal, and educated in France. He served in the French army during World War II, was captured, and spent two years in Nazi concentration camps. After the war, Senghor served several terms as the Senegalese representative to the French National Assembly when Senegal was under French rule before returning to his native land as a leader of the independence movement. In 1960, he became the first democratically elected president of Senegal, a post he held for nearly twenty years. With fellow poets and intellectuals Aimé Cesaire and Léon Damas, Senghor founded the movement known as Négritude, a reaction against colonial domination and a celebration of African culture and aesthetics. "In Memoriam," first published in 1945 and then published in translation as part of his *Collected Poems* (1998), explores the conflict Senghor felt between his Catholic faith and his Senegalese heritage.

Today is Sunday.
I fear the crowd of my fellows with such faces of stone.
From my glass tower filled with headaches and impatient Ancestors,
I contemplate the roofs and hilltops in the mist.
In the stillness — somber, naked chimneys.
Below them my dead are asleep and my dreams turn to ashes.
All my dreams, blood running freely down the streets
And mixing with blood from the butcher shops.
From this observatory like the outskirts of town
I contemplate my dreams lost along the streets,
Crouched at the foot of the hills like the guides of my race
On the rivers of the Gambia[1] and the Saloum[2]
And now on the Seine[3] at the foot of these hills.
Let me remember my dead!

[1] A river in West Africa that runs through Guinea, Senegal, and Gambia. — EDS.
[2] A river in Senegal that flows into the Atlantic Ocean. — EDS.
[3] A river in France that runs through Paris to the English Channel. — EDS.

Yesterday was All Saints' Day, the solemn anniversary of the Sun,
And I had no dead to honor in any cemetery.
O Forefathers! You who have always refused to die,
Who knew how to resist Death from the Sine[4] to the Seine,
And now in the fragile veins of my indomitable blood,
Guard my dreams as you did your thin-legged migrant sons!
O Ancestors! Defend the roofs of Paris in this dominical fog,
The roofs that protect my dead.
Let me leave this tower so dangerously secure
And descend to the streets, joining my brothers
Who have blue eyes and hard hands.

[1945/1998]

[4] A river in Senegal. — EDS.

QUESTIONS

1. What feeling does the simple opening statement — "Today is Sunday" — establish? What is the added significance that the previous day was All Saints' Day?
2. What words and images does Senghor's speaker use to describe the city and people of Paris? What ambivalence does the speaker seem to have toward both?
3. How does the speaker characterize his dreams? Are they "ashes" (l. 6) and "lost" (l. 10), or do they remain alive in his "indomitable blood" (l. 19)? Or somewhere in between the two? Consider the connotative language, metaphor, and personification as you prepare your response.
4. The speaker pleads, "Let me remember my dead!" (l. 14). How do you interpret this line? Is it a rhetorical question, a criticism of himself, a plea to his "fellow" Parisians? Something else?
5. What shift in both form and tone does line 17 – "O Forefathers!" – signal?
6. How would you describe the relationship the speaker has with his ancestors? What does he mean when he states that they "always refused to die" (l. 17)?
7. At the end of the poem, the speaker asks to leave "this tower so dangerously secure" to join his blue-eyed "brothers" who have "hard hands," an expression that, in Senegal, is a metaphor for hate and meanness. Given these final lines, has the speaker resolved the tension between the alienation he feels in Paris with the soothing assurance of the ancestors? Explain.
8. Some have interpreted this poem as a prayer. Explain with specific textual references why you agree or disagree.

How to Write about Africa

BINYAVANGA WAINAINA

Binyavanga Wainaina (b. 1971) lives in Nairobi, Kenya. He is the founding editor of the literary and political magazine *Kwani?* and won the Caine Prize for African Writing in 2002 for his short story "Discovering Home." In 2008, the *Atlanta Journal-Constitution* named him a person worth watching in politics, entertainment, and the arts. A sought-after speaker, he was

writer-in-residence at Union College in Schenectady, New York, for the years 2005–2008, and at Williams College in Williamstown, Massachusetts, in fall 2008. This article appeared in a 2005 issue of *Granta* magazine, before spreading rapidly over the Internet and through e-mail.

Always use the word 'Africa' or 'Darkness' or 'Safari' in your title. Subtitles may include the words 'Zanzibar', 'Masai', 'Zulu', 'Zambezi', 'Congo', 'Nile', 'Big', 'Sky', 'Shadow', 'Drum', 'Sun' or 'Bygone'. Also useful are words such as 'Guerrillas', 'Timeless', 'Primordial' and 'Tribal'. Note that 'People' means Africans who are not black, while 'The People' means black Africans.

Never have a picture of a well-adjusted African on the cover of your book, or in it, unless that African has won the Nobel Prize. An AK-47, prominent ribs, naked breasts: use these. If you must include an African, make sure you get one in Masai or Zulu or Dogon dress.

In your text, treat Africa as if it were one country. It is hot and dusty with rolling grasslands and huge herds of animals and tall, thin people who are starving. Or it is hot and steamy with very short people who eat primates. Don't get bogged down with precise descriptions. Africa is big: fifty-four countries, nine hundred million people who are too busy starving and dying and warring and emigrating to read your book. The continent is full of deserts, jungles, highlands, savannahs and many other things, but your reader doesn't care about all that, so keep your descriptions romantic and evocative and unparticular.

Make sure you show how Africans have music and rhythm deep in their souls, and eat things no other humans eat. Do not mention rice and beef and wheat; monkey-brain is an African's cuisine of choice, along with goat, snake, worms and grubs and all manner of game meat. Make sure you show that you are able to eat such food without flinching, and describe how you learn to enjoy it — because you care.

5 Taboo subjects: ordinary domestic scenes, love between Africans (unless a death is involved), references to African writers or intellectuals, mention of school-going children who are not suffering from yaws or Ebola fever or female genital mutilation.

Throughout the book, adopt a *sotto* voice, in conspiracy with the reader, and a sad *I-expected-so-much* tone. Establish early on that your liberalism is impeccable, and mention near the beginning how much you love Africa, how you fell in love with the place and can't live without her. Africa is the only continent you can love — take advantage of this. If you are a man, thrust yourself into her warm virgin forests. If you are a woman, treat Africa as a man who wears a bush jacket and disappears off into the sunset. Africa is to be pitied, worshipped or dominated. Whichever angle you take, be sure to leave the strong impression that without your intervention and your important book, Africa is doomed.

Your African characters may include naked warriors, loyal servants, diviners and seers, ancient wise men living in hermitic splendour. Or corrupt politicians, inept polygamous travel-guides, and prostitutes you have slept with. The Loyal Servant always behaves like a seven-year-old and needs a firm hand; he is scared of snakes, good with children, and always involving you in his complex domestic dramas. The Ancient Wise Man always comes from a noble tribe (not the money-grubbing tribes like the Gikuyu, the Igbo or the Shona). He has rheumy eyes and is close to the Earth. The Modern African is a fat man who steals and works in the visa office, refusing to give work permits to qualified Westerners who really care about Africa. He is an enemy of development, always using his government job to make it difficult for pragmatic and good-hearted expats to set up NGOs or Legal Conservation Areas. Or he is an Oxford-educated intellectual turned serial-killing politician in a Savile Row suit. He is a cannibal who likes Cristal champagne, and his mother is a rich witch-doctor who really runs the country.

Among your characters you must always include The Starving African, who wanders the refugee camp nearly naked, and waits for the benevolence of the West. Her children have flies on their eyelids and pot bellies, and her breasts are flat and empty. She must look utterly helpless. She can have no past, no history; such diversions ruin the dramatic moment. Moans are good. She must never say anything about herself in the dialogue except to speak of her (unspeakable) suffering. Also be sure to include a warm and motherly woman who has a rolling laugh and who is concerned for your well-being. Just call her Mama. Her children are all delinquent. These characters should buzz around your main hero, making him look good. Your hero can teach them, bathe them, feed them; he carries lots of babies and has seen Death. Your hero is you (if reportage), or a beautiful, tragic international celebrity/aristocrat who now cares for animals (if fiction).

Bad Western characters may include children of Tory cabinet ministers, Afrikaners, employees of the World Bank. When talking about exploitation by foreigners, mention the Chinese and Indian traders. Blame the West for Africa's situation. But do not be too specific.

10 Broad brushstrokes throughout are good. Avoid having the African characters laugh, or struggle to educate their kids, or just make do in mundane circumstances. Have them illuminate something about Europe or America in Africa. African characters should be colourful, exotic, larger than life — but empty inside, with no dialogue, no conflicts or resolutions in their stories, no depth or quirks to confuse the cause.

Describe, in detail, naked breasts (young, old, conservative, recently raped, big, small) or mutilated genitals, or enhanced genitals. Or any kind of genitals. And dead bodies. Or, better, naked dead bodies. And especially rotting naked dead bodies. Remember, any work you submit in which people look filthy and miserable will be referred to as the "real Africa," and you want that on your dust jacket. Do not feel queasy about this: you are trying to help them to get aid from the West. The biggest taboo in writing about Africa is to describe or show dead or suffering white people.

Animals, on the other hand, must be treated as well rounded, complex characters. They speak (or grunt while tossing their manes proudly) and have names, ambitions and desires. They also have family values: *see how lions teach their children?* Elephants are caring, and are good feminists or dignified patriarchs. So are gorillas. Never, ever say anything negative about an elephant or a gorilla. Elephants may attack people's property, destroy their crops, and even kill them. Always take the side of the elephant. Big cats have public-school accents. Hyenas are fair game and have vaguely Middle Eastern accents. Any short Africans who live in the jungle or desert may be portrayed with good humour (unless they are in conflict with an elephant or chimpanzee or gorilla, in which case they are pure evil).

After celebrity activists and aid workers, conservationists are Africa's most important people. Do not offend them. You need them to invite you to their thirty thousand-acre game ranch or "conservation area," and this is the only way you will get to interview the celebrity activist. Often a book cover with a heroic-looking conservationist on it works magic for sales. Anybody white, tanned and wearing khaki who once had a pet antelope or a farm is a conservationist, one who is preserving Africa's rich heritage. When interviewing him or her, do not ask how much funding they have; do not ask how much money they make off their game. Never ask how much they pay their employees.

Readers will be put off if you don't mention the light in Africa. And sunsets, the African sunset is a must. It is always big and red. There is always a big sky. Wide empty spaces and game are critical—Africa is the Land of Wide Empty Spaces. When writing about the plight of flora and fauna, make sure you mention that Africa is overpopulated. When your main character is in a desert or jungle living with indigenous peoples (anybody short), it is okay to mention that Africa has been severely depopulated by Aids and War (use caps).

You'll also need a nightclub called Tropicana, where mercenaries, evil nouveau riche Africans and prostitutes and guerrillas and expats hang out. 15

Always end your book with Nelson Mandela saying something about rainbows or renaissances. Because you care.

[2005]

QUESTIONS

1. Binyavanga Wainaina writes in imperative sentences, giving what seem to be commands or issuing edicts. To whom is he speaking?
2. Identify and discuss several of the stereotypes that Wainaina describes. Are you familiar with any of these from movies you've seen? television shows? *Heart of Darkness*? "The Old Chief Mshlanga"? children's films or plays?
3. At what point did you realize Wainaina's ironic tone — from the very outset? Find examples of hyperbole and understatement. What other techniques does he use to develop his satire? Consider the imperative sentence form, sentence fragments, choice of details, and visual images.
4. Explain whether you think Wainaina would have been more successful in making his point if he had written without satire — that is, more like Chinua Achebe in "An Image of Africa."
5. Discuss whether you think Wainaina goes too far. How do you interpret the ending comment about Nelson Mandela? As you answer that question, ask yourself if the audience Wainaina addresses as "you" is actually his audience.

LITERATURE IN CONVERSATION
Heart of Darkness and the Legacy of Colonialism

1. How do you think Joseph Conrad would respond to Felix Mnthali's poem "The Stranglehold of English Lit"? Would he agree wholeheartedly, disagree entirely, claim that great literature is universal, or perhaps see his novel as the exception that could promote useful dialogue? Write a response in Conrad's voice.
2. There is much debate as to whether *Heart of Darkness* is a racist book that has no place in the high school or college classroom, or an important window onto the Eurocentric tradition and its own heart of darkness. Drawing from Chinua Achebe's essay and at least one other piece you have read — whether in this chapter or elsewhere — write an essay taking a position in that debate.
3. Write an essay analyzing at least three different types of cultural clashes or conflicts that result from colonialism and its legacy. Refer to at least three texts from this book in your response.
4. So much of the literature and commentary about colonialism centers around its impact on large populations. Some of the texts in this chapter, however, explore its consequences for individuals. Write an essay discussing the way at least two of these texts provide insight into the influence of colonialism on the individual.
5. Albert Memmi examines at length the destructive nature of colonialism for the colonizer in his book, *The Colonizer and the Colonized*. Using at least two texts chosen from this conversation or *Heart*

of Darkness, discuss why you agree or disagree with the analysis he presents here:

> It is impossible for him [the colonizer] not to be aware of the constant illegitimacy of his status. It is, moreover, in a way a double illegitimacy. A foreigner, having come to land by the accidents of history, he has succeeded not merely in creating a place for himself but also in taking away that of the inhabitant, granting himself astounding privileges to the detriment of those rightfully entitled to them. And this is not by virtue of local laws, which in a certain way legitimize this inequality by tradition, but by upsetting the established rules and substituting his own. He thus appears doubly unjust. He is a privileged being and an illegitimately privileged one; that is, a usurper. Furthermore, this is so, not only in the eyes of the colonized, but in his own as well.

6. Write an essay examining how three of the stereotypes identified in Binyavanga Wainaina's "How to Write about Africa" are either illustrated or challenged by at least two other texts in this conversation.

7. Select a contemporary film set in Africa. As you watch it, consider whether — and to what extent — the film stereotypes African peoples and cultures or, conversely, provides a valid and meaningful representation. Then, write a script that imagines a dialogue between three or four of the authors from this conversation. In it, they have also just watched the film, and they discuss the nature and effect of its portrayal of African peoples and cultures.

FICTION

Young Goodman Brown

NATHANIEL HAWTHORNE

One of America's major voices of the nineteenth century, Nathaniel Hawthorne (1804–1864) was born in Salem, Massachusetts, into a family whose ancestors had participated in the Salem witch trials of the seventeenth century. He graduated from Bowdoin College in Maine, where he was a classmate of the poet Henry Wadsworth Longfellow and future president of the United States Franklin Pierce, who remained Hawthorne's lifelong friend. For several years after college, Hawthorne wrote sketches and stories and worked as a surveyor in the Customs House in Boston. In 1837, he published a volume of stories, *Twice-Told Tales*, followed by *Mosses from an Old Manse* (1846) — named for his house, which had belonged to Ralph Waldo Emerson. The years 1850 and 1851 saw the publication of Hawthorne's major works, *The Scarlet Letter* and *The House of the Seven Gables*. Hawthorne's writing is often allegorical and contains many of the elements of the supernatural; in fact, he referred to his books as "romances" rather than novels. Among his most famous stories are "My Kinsman, Major Molineux," "Rappaccini's Daughter," and "Young Goodman Brown," included here.

Young Goodman Brown came forth at sunset into the street of Salem village; but put his head back, after crossing the threshold, to exchange a parting kiss with his young wife. And Faith, as the wife was aptly named, thrust her own pretty head into the street, letting the wind play with the pink ribbons of her cap while she called to Goodman Brown.

"Dearest heart," whispered she, softly and rather sadly, when her lips were close to his ear, "prithee put off your journey until sunrise and sleep in your own bed to-night. A lone woman is troubled with such dreams and such thoughts that she's afeard of herself sometimes. Pray tarry with me this night, dear husband, of all nights in the year."

"My love and my Faith," replied young Goodman Brown, "of all nights in the year, this one night must I tarry away from thee. My journey, as thou callest it, forth and back again, must needs be done 'twixt now and sunrise. What, my sweet, pretty wife, dost thou doubt me already, and we but three months married?"

"Then God bless you!" said Faith, with the pink ribbons; "and may you find all well when you come back."

5 "Amen!" cried Goodman Brown. "Say thy prayers, dear Faith, and go to bed at dusk, and no harm will come to thee."

So they parted; and the young man pursued his way until, being about to turn the corner by the meeting-house, he looked back and saw the head of Faith still peeping after him with a melancholy air, in spite of her pink ribbons.

"Poor little Faith!" thought he, for his heart smote him. "What a wretch am I to leave her on such an errand! She talks of dreams, too. Methought as she spoke there was trouble in her face, as if a dream had warned her what work is to be done to-night. But no, no; 't would kill her to think it. Well, she's a blessed angel on earth; and after this one night I'll cling to her skirts and follow her to heaven."

With this excellent resolve for the future, Goodman Brown felt himself justified in making more haste on his present evil purpose. He had taken a dreary road, darkened by all the gloomiest trees of the forest, which barely stood aside to let the narrow path creep through, and closed immediately behind. It was all as lonely as could be; and there is this peculiarity in such a solitude, that the traveler knows not who may be concealed by the innumerable trunks and the thick boughs overhead; so that with lonely footsteps he may yet be passing through an unseen multitude.

"There may be a devilish Indian behind every tree," said Goodman Brown to himself; and he glanced fearfully behind him as he added, "What if the devil himself should be at my very elbow!"

His head being turned back, he passed a crook of the road, and, looking forward again, beheld the figure of a man, in grave and decent attire, seated at the foot of an old tree. He arose at Goodman Brown's approach and walked onward side by side with him.

"You are late, Goodman Brown," said he. "The clock of the Old South was striking as I came through Boston, and that is full fifteen minutes agone."

"Faith kept me back a while," replied the young man, with a tremor in his voice, caused by the sudden appearance of his companion, though not wholly unexpected.

It was now deep dusk in the forest, and deepest in that part of it where these two were journeying. As nearly as could be discerned, the second traveller was about fifty years old, apparently in the same rank of life as Goodman Brown, and bearing a considerable resemblance to him, though perhaps more in expression than features. Still they might have been taken for father and son. And yet, though the elder person was as simply clad as the younger, and as simple in manner too, he had an indescribable air of one who knew the world, and who would not have felt abashed at the governor's dinner table or in King William's court, were it possible that his affairs should call him thither. But the only thing about him that could be fixed upon as remarkable was his staff, which bore the likeness of a great black snake, so curiously wrought that it might almost be seen to twist and wriggle itself like a living serpent. This, of course, must have been an ocular deception, assisted by the uncertain light.

"Come, Goodman Brown!" cried his fellow-traveller, "this is a dull pace for the beginning of a journey. Take my staff, if you are so soon weary."

"Friend," said the other, exchanging his slow pace for a full stop, "having kept covenant by meeting thee here, it is my purpose now to return whence I came. I have scruples touching the matter thou wot'st[1] of."

"Sayest thou so?" replied he of the serpent, smiling apart. "Let us walk on, nevertheless, reasoning as we go; and if I convince thee not thou shalt turn back. We are but a little way in the forest yet."

"Too far! too far!" exclaimed the goodman, unconsciously resuming his walk. "My father never went into the woods on such an errand, nor his father before him. We have been a race of honest men and good Christians since the days of the martyrs; and shall I be the first of the name of Brown that ever took this path and kept — "

"Such company, thou wouldst say," observed the elder person, interpreting his pause. "Well said, Goodman Brown! I have been as well acquainted with your family as with ever a one among the Puritans; and that's no trifle to say. I helped your grandfather, the constable, when he lashed the Quaker woman so smartly through the streets of Salem; and it was I that brought your father a pitch-pine knot, kindled at my own hearth, to set fire to an Indian village, in

[1]Know. — EDS.

King Philip's war.[2] They were my good friends, both; and many a pleasant walk have we had along this path, and returned merrily after midnight. I would fain be friends with you for their sake."

"If it be as thou sayest," replied Goodman Brown, "I marvel they never spoke of these matters; or, verily, I marvel not, seeing that the least rumor of the sort would have driven them from New England. We are a people of prayer, and good works to boot, and abide no such wickedness."

"Wickedness or not," said the traveller with the twisted staff, "I have a very general acquaintance here in New England. The deacons of many a church have drunk the communion wine with me; the selectmen of divers towns make me their chairman; and a majority of the Great and General Court are firm supporters of my interest. The governor and I, too — But these are state secrets."

"Can this be so?" cried Goodman Brown, with a stare of amazement at his undisturbed companion. "Howbeit, I have nothing to do with the governor and council; they have their own ways, and are no rule for a simple husbandman like me. But, were I to go on with thee, how should I meet the eye of that good old man, our minister, at Salem village? Oh, his voice would make me tremble both Sabbath day and lecture day."

Thus far the elder traveller had listened with due gravity; but now burst into a fit of irrepressible mirth, shaking himself so violently that his snake-like staff actually seemed to wriggle in sympathy.

"Ha! ha! ha!" shouted he again and again; then composing himself, "Well, go on, Goodman Brown, go on; but, prithee, don't kill me with laughing."

"Well, then, to end the matter at once," said Goodman Brown, considerably nettled, "there is my wife, Faith. It would break her dear little heart; and I'd rather break my own."

"Nay, if that be the case," answered the other, "e'en go thy ways, Goodman Brown. I would not for twenty old women like the one hobbling before us that Faith should come to any harm."

As he spoke he pointed his staff at a female figure on the path, in whom Goodman Brown recognized a very pious and exemplary dame, who had taught him his catechism in youth, and was still his moral and spiritual adviser, jointly with the minister and Deacon Gookin.

"A marvel, truly, that Goody[3] Cloyse should be so far in the wilderness at nightfall," said he. "But with your leave, friend, I shall take a cut through the woods until we have left this Christian woman behind. Being a stranger to you, she might ask whom I was consorting with and whither I was going."

"Be it so," said his fellow-traveller. "Betake you to the woods, and let me keep the path."

Accordingly the young man turned aside, but took care to watch his companion, who advanced softly along the road until he had come within a staff's length of the old dame. She, meanwhile, was making the best of her way, with singular speed for so aged a woman, and mumbling some indistinct words — a prayer, doubtless — as she went. The traveller put forth his staff and touched her withered neck with what seemed the serpent's tail.

"The devil!" screamed the pious old lady.

"Then Goody Cloyse knows her old friend?" observed the traveller, confronting her and leaning on his writhing stick.

"Ah, forsooth, and is it your worship indeed?" cried the good dame. "Yea, truly is it, and in the very image of my old gossip, Goodman Brown, the grandfather of the silly fellow that now is. But — would your worship believe it? — my broomstick hath strangely disappeared, stolen, as I suspect, by that unhanged witch, Goody Cory, and that, too,

[2] War between Native Americans and New England colonists. The Native American leader was known as King Philip. — EDS.

[3] Short for "goodwife," archaic form of *missus*. — EDS.

when I was all anointed with the juice of smallage, and cinquefoil, and wolf's-bane—"

"Mingled with fine wheat and the fat of a new-born babe," said the shape of old Goodman Brown.

"Ah, your worship knows the recipe," cried the old lady, cackling aloud. "So, as I was saying, being all ready for the meeting, and no horse to ride on, I made up my mind to foot it; for they tell me there is a nice young man to be taken into communion to-night. But now your good worship will lend me your arm, and we shall be there in a twinkling."

"That can hardly be," answered her friend. "I may not spare you my arm, Goody Cloyse; but here is my staff, if you will."

So saying, he threw it down at her feet, where, perhaps, it assumed life, being one of the rods which its owner had formerly lent to the Egyptian magi. Of this fact, however, Goodman Brown could not take cognizance. He had cast up his eyes in astonishment, and, looking down again, beheld neither Goody Cloyse nor the serpentine staff, but his fellow-traveller alone, who waited for him as calmly as if nothing had happened.

"That old woman taught me my catechism," said the young man; and there was a world of meaning in this simple comment.

They continued to walk onward, while the elder traveller exhorted his companion to make good speed and persevere in the path, discoursing so aptly that his arguments seemed rather to spring up in the bosom of his auditor than to be suggested by himself. As they went, he plucked a branch of maple to serve for a walking stick, and began to strip it of the twigs and little boughs, which were wet with evening dew. The moment his fingers touched them they became strangely withered and dried up as with a week's sunshine. Thus the pair proceeded, at a good free pace, until suddenly, in a gloomy hollow of the road, Goodman Brown sat himself down on the stump of a tree and refused to go any farther.

"Friend," he said, stubbornly, "my mind is made up. Not another step will I budge on this errand. What if a wretched old woman do choose to go to the devil when I thought she was going to heaven: is that any reason why I should quit my dear Faith and go after her?"

"You will think better of this by and by," said his acquaintance, composedly. "Sit here and rest yourself a while; and when you feel like moving again, there is my staff to help you along."

Without more words, he threw his companion the maple stick, and was as speedily out of sight as if he had vanished into the deepening gloom. The young man sat a few moments by the roadside, applauding himself greatly, and thinking with how clear a conscience he should meet the minister in his morning walk, nor shrink from the eye of good old Deacon Gookin. And what calm sleep would be his that very night, which was to have been spent so wickedly, but so purely and sweetly now, in the arms of Faith! Amidst these pleasant and praiseworthy meditations, Goodman Brown heard the tramp of horses along the road, and deemed it advisable to conceal himself within the verge of the forest, conscious of the guilty purpose that had brought him thither, though now so happily turned from it.

On came the hoof tramps and the voices of the riders, two grave old voices, conversing soberly as they drew near. These mingled sounds appeared to pass along the road, within a few yards of the young man's hiding-place; but, owing doubtless to the depth of the gloom at that particular spot, neither the travellers nor their steeds were visible. Though their figures brushed the small boughs by the wayside, it could not be seen that they intercepted, even for a moment, the faint gleam from the strip of bright sky athwart which they must have passed. Goodman Brown alternately crouched and stood on tiptoe, pulling aside the branches and thrusting forth his head as far as he durst without discerning so much as a shadow. It vexed him the more, because he could have sworn, were such a thing possible, that he recognized the voices of the minister and Deacon Gookin, jogging along quietly, as they were wont to do, when bound to some ordination or ecclesiastical council. While yet within hearing, one of the riders stopped to pluck a switch.

"Of the two, reverend sir," said the voice like the deacon's, "I had rather miss an ordination dinner than to-night's meeting. They tell me that some of our community are to be here from Falmouth and beyond, and others from Connecticut and Rhode Island, besides several of the Indian powwows, who, after their fashion, know almost as much deviltry as the best of us. Moreover, there is a goodly young woman to be taken into communion."

"Mighty well, Deacon Gookin!" replied the solemn old tones of the minister. "Spur up, or we shall be late. Nothing can be done, you know, until I get on the ground."

The hoofs clattered again; and the voices, talking so strangely in the empty air, passed on through the forest, where no church had ever been gathered or solitary Christian prayed. Whither, then, could these holy men be journeying so deep into the heathen wilderness? Young Goodman Brown caught hold of a tree for support, being ready to sink down on the ground, faint and overburdened with the heavy sickness of his heart. He looked up to the sky, doubting whether there really was a heaven above him. Yet there was the blue arch, and the stars brightening in it.

"With heaven above and Faith below, I will yet stand firm against the devil!" cried Goodman Brown.

While he still gazed upward into the deep arch of the firmament and had lifted his hands to pray, a cloud, though no wind was stirring, hurried across the zenith and hid the brightening stars. The blue sky was still visible, except directly overhead, where this black mass of cloud was sweeping swiftly northward. Aloft in the air, as if from the depths of the cloud, came a confused and doubtful sound of voices. Once the listener fancied that he could distinguish the accents of towns-people of his own, men and women, both pious and ungodly, many of whom he had met at the communion table, and had seen others rioting at the tavern. The next moment, so indistinct were the sounds, he doubted whether he had heard aught but the murmur of the old forest, whispering without a wind. Then came a stronger swell of those familiar tones, heard daily in the sunshine at Salem village, but never until now from a cloud of night. There was one voice, of a young woman, uttering lamentations, yet with an uncertain sorrow, and entreating for some favor, which, perhaps, it would grieve her to obtain; and all the unseen multitude, both saints and sinners, seemed to encourage her onward.

"Faith!" shouted Goodman Brown, in a voice of agony and desperation; and the echoes of the forest mocked him, crying, "Faith! Faith!" as if bewildered wretches were seeking her all through the wilderness.

The cry of grief, rage, and terror was yet piercing the night, when the unhappy husband held his breath for a response. There was a scream, drowned immediately in a louder murmur of voices, fading into far-off laughter, as the dark cloud swept away, leaving the clear and silent sky above Goodman Brown. But something fluttered lightly down through the air and caught on the branch of a tree. The young man seized it, and beheld a pink ribbon.

"My Faith is gone!" cried he after one stupefied moment. "There is no good on earth; and sin is but a name. Come, devil; for to thee is this world given."

And, maddened with despair, so that he laughed loud and long, did Goodman Brown grasp his staff and set forth again, at such a rate that he seemed to fly along the forest path rather than to walk or run. The road grew wilder and drearier and more faintly traced, and vanished at length, leaving him in the heart of the dark wilderness, still rushing onward with the instinct that guides mortal man to evil. The whole forest was peopled with frightful sounds — the creaking of the trees, the howling of wild beasts, and the yell of Indians; while sometimes the wind tolled like a distant church bell, and sometimes gave a broad roar around the traveller, as if all Nature were laughing him to scorn. But he was himself the chief horror of the scene, and shrank not from its other horrors.

"Ha! ha! ha!" roared Goodman Brown when the wind laughed at him. "Let us hear which will laugh loudest. Think not to frighten me with your deviltry. Come witch, come wizard, come Indian powwow, come devil himself, and here comes Goodman Brown. You may as well fear him as he fear you."

In truth, all through the haunted forest, there could be nothing more frightful than the figure of Goodman Brown. On he flew among the black pines, brandishing his staff with frenzied gestures, now giving vent to an inspiration of horrid blasphemy, and now shouting forth such laughter as set all the echoes of the forest laughing like demons around him. The fiend in his own shape is less hideous than when he rages in the breast of man. Thus sped the demoniac on his course, until, quivering among the trees, he saw a red light before him, as when the felled trunks and branches of a clearing have been set on fire, and throw up their lurid blaze against the sky, at the hour of midnight. He paused, in a lull of the tempest that had driven him onward, and heard the swell of what seemed a hymn, rolling solemnly from a distance with the weight of many voices. He knew the tune; it was a familiar one in the choir of the village meeting-house. The verse died heavily away, and was lengthened by a chorus, not of human voices, but of all the sounds of the benighted wilderness pealing in awful harmony together. Goodman Brown cried out, and his cry was lost to his own ear, by its unison with the cry of the desert.

In the interval of silence he stole forward until the light glared full upon his eyes. At one extremity of an open space, hemmed in by the dark wall of the forest, arose a rock, bearing some rude, natural resemblance either to an altar or a pulpit, and surrounded by four blazing pines, their tops aflame, their stems untouched, like candles at an evening meeting. The mass of foliage that had overgrown the summit of the rock was all on fire, blazing high into the night and fitfully illuminating the whole field. Each pendent twig and leafy festoon was in a blaze. As the red light arose and fell, a numerous congregation alternately shone forth, then disappeared in shadow, and again grew, as it were, out of the darkness, peopling the heart of the solitary woods at once.

"A grave and dark-clad company," quoth 55
Goodman Brown.

In truth they were such. Among them, quivering to and fro between gloom and splendor, appeared faces that would be seen next day at the council board of the province, and others which, Sabbath after Sabbath, looked devoutly heavenward, and benignantly over the crowded pews, from the holiest pulpits in the land. Some affirm that the lady of the governor was there. At least there were high dames well known to her, and wives of honored husbands, and widows, a great multitude, and ancient maidens, all of excellent repute, and fair young girls, who trembled lest their mothers should espy them. Either the sudden gleams of light flashing over the obscure field bedazzled Goodman Brown, or he recognized a score of the church members of Salem village famous for their especial sanctity. Good old Deacon Gookin had arrived, and waited at the skirts of that venerable saint, his revered pastor. But, irreverently consorting with these grave, reputable, and pious people, these elders of the church, these chaste dames and dewy virgins, there were men of dissolute lives and women of spotted fame, wretches given over to all mean and filthy vice, and suspected even of horrid crimes. It was strange to see that the good shrank not from the wicked, nor were the sinners abashed by the saints. Scattered also among their pale-faced enemies were the Indian priests, or powwows, who had often scared their native forest with more hideous incantations than any known to English witchcraft.

"But where is Faith?" thought Goodman Brown; and, as hope came into his heart, he trembled.

Another verse of the hymn arose, a slow and mournful strain, such as the pious love, but joined to words which expressed all that our nature can conceive of sin, and darkly hinted at far more. Unfathomable to mere mortals is the lore of fiends. Verse after verse was sung; and still the chorus of the desert swelled between like the deepest tone of a mighty organ; and with the final peal of that dreadful anthem there came a sound, as if the roaring wind, the rushing streams, the howling beasts, and every other voice of the unconcerted wilderness were mingling and according with the voice of guilty man in homage to the prince of all. The four blazing pines threw up a loftier flame, and obscurely discovered shapes and visages of horror on the smoke wreaths above the impious assembly. At the same moment the fire on the rock shot redly forth and formed a glowing arch above its base, where now appeared a figure. With reverence be it spoken, the figure bore no slight similitude, both in garb and manner, to some grave divine[4] of the New England churches.

"Bring forth the converts!" cried a voice that echoed through the field and rolled into the forest.

At the word, Goodman Brown stepped forth from the shadow of the trees and approached the congregation, with whom he felt a loathful brotherhood by the sympathy of all that was wicked in his heart. He could have well-nigh sworn that the shape of his own dead father beckoned him to advance, looking downward from a smoke wreath, while a woman, with dim features of despair, threw out her hand to warn him back. Was it his mother? But he had no power to retreat one step, nor to resist, even in thought, when the minister and good old Deacon Gookin seized his arms and led him to the blazing rock. Thither came also the slender form of a veiled female, led between Goody Cloyse, that pious teacher of the catechism, and Martha Carrier, who had received the devil's promise to be queen of hell. A rampant hag was she. And there stood the proselytes beneath the canopy of fire.

"Welcome, my children," said the dark figure, "to the communion of your race. Ye have found thus young your nature and your destiny. My children, look behind you!"

They turned; and flashing forth, as it were, in a sheet of flame, the fiend worshippers were seen; the smile of welcome gleamed darkly on every visage.

"There," resumed the sable form, "are all whom ye have reverenced from youth. Ye deemed them holier than yourselves and shrank from your own sin, contrasting it with their lives of righteousness and prayerful aspirations heavenward. Yet here are they all in my worshipping assembly. This night it shall be granted you to know their secret deeds: how hoary-bearded elders of the church have whispered wanton words to the young maids of their households; how many a woman, eager for widows' weeds, has given her husband a drink at bedtime and let him sleep his last sleep in her bosom; how beardless youths have made haste to inherit their fathers' wealth; and how fair damsels — blush not, sweet ones — have dug little graves in the garden, and bidden me, the sole guest, to an infant's funeral. By the sympathy of your human hearts for sin ye shall scent out all the places — whether in church, bedchamber, street, field, or forest — where crime

[4] Theologian, or member of the clergy. — EDS.

has been committed, and shall exult to behold the whole earth one stain of guilt, one mighty blood spot. Far more than this. It shall be yours to penetrate, in every bosom, the deep mystery of sin, the fountain of all wicked arts, and which inexhaustibly supplies more evil impulses than human power — than my power at its utmost — can make manifest in deeds. And now, my children, look upon each other."

They did so; and, by the blaze of the hell-kindled torches, the wretched man beheld his Faith, and the wife her husband, trembling before that unhallowed altar.

"Lo, there ye stand, my children," said the figure, in a deep and solemn tone, almost sad with its despairing awfulness, as if his once angelic nature could yet mourn for our miserable race. "Depending upon one another's hearts, ye had still hoped that virtue were not all a dream. Now are ye undeceived. Evil is the nature of mankind. Evil must be your only happiness. Welcome again, my children, to the communion of your race."

"Welcome," repeated the fiend worshippers, in one cry of despair and triumph.

And there they stood, the only pair, as it seemed, who were yet hesitating on the verge of wickedness in this dark world. A basin was hollowed, naturally, in the rock. Did it contain water, reddened by the lurid light? or was it blood? or, perchance, a liquid flame? Herein did the shape of evil dip his hand and prepare to lay the mark of baptism upon their foreheads, that they might be partakers of the mystery of sin, more conscious of the secret guilt of others, both in deed and thought, than they could now be of their own. The husband cast one look at his pale wife, and Faith at him. What polluted wretches would the next glance show them to each other, shuddering alike at what they disclosed and what they saw!

"Faith! Faith!" cried the husband, "look up to heaven, and resist the wicked one."

Whether Faith obeyed he knew not. Hardly had he spoken when he found himself amid calm night and solitude, listening to a roar of the wind which died heavily away through the forest. He staggered against the rock, and felt it chill and damp; while a hanging twig, that had been all on fire, besprinkled his cheek with the coldest dew.

The next morning young Goodman Brown came slowly into the street of Salem village, staring around him like a bewildered man. The good old minister was taking a walk along the graveyard to get an appetite for breakfast and meditate his sermon, and bestowed a blessing, as he passed, on Goodman Brown. He shrank from the venerable saint as if to avoid an anathema. Old Deacon Gookin was at domestic worship, and the holy words of his prayer were heard through the open window. "What God doth the wizard pray to?" quoth Goodman Brown. Goody Cloyse, that excellent old Christian, stood in the early sunshine at her own lattice, catechizing a little girl who had brought her a pint of morning's milk. Goodman Brown snatched away the child as from the grasp of the fiend himself. Turning the corner by the meeting-house, he spied the head of Faith, with the pink ribbons, gazing anxiously forth, and bursting into such joy at sight of him that she skipped along the street and almost kissed her husband before the whole village. But Goodman Brown looked sternly and sadly into her face, and passed on without a greeting.

Had Goodman Brown fallen asleep in the forest, and only dreamed a wild dream of a witch-meeting?

Be it so if you will; but, alas! it was a dream of evil omen for young Goodman Brown. A stern, a sad, a darkly meditative, a distrustful, if not a desperate man did he become from the night of that fearful dream. On the Sabbath day, when the congregation were singing a holy psalm, he could not listen because an anthem of sin rushed loudly upon his ear and drowned all the blessed strain. When the minister spoke from the pulpit with power and fervid eloquence, and, with his hand on the open Bible, of the sacred truths of our religion, and of saint-like lives and triumphant deaths, and of future bliss or misery unutterable, then did Goodman Brown turn pale, dreading lest the roof should thunder down upon the gray blasphemer and his hearers. Often, awaking suddenly at midnight, he shrank from the bosom of Faith; and at morning or eventide, when the family knelt down at prayer, he scowled and muttered to himself, and gazed sternly at his wife, and turned away. And when he had lived long, and was borne to his grave a hoary corpse, followed by Faith, an aged woman, and children and grandchildren, a goodly procession, besides neighbors not a few, they carved no hopeful verse upon his tombstone, for his dying hour was gloom.

[1835]

EXPLORING THE TEXT

1. What is the significance of the names Goodman Brown and Faith, especially in such statements as "Faith kept me back a while" in paragraph 12 and "My Faith is gone!" in paragraph 50?
2. Nathaniel Hawthorne presents contrasting imagery in the story. What, for example, is the effect of juxtaposing "melancholy air" with "pink ribbons" (para. 6)? How do the various contrasts develop a theme?
3. Discuss the imagery developed in paragraph 8. What effect does it create?
4. In paragraph 37, the narrator remarks, "there was a world of meaning in this simple comment." What is the "world of meaning" he is referring to?
5. What is the nature of Goodman Brown's quest? Where is he going? Why? In paragraph 41, the reader learns that Goodman Brown was "conscious of the guilty purpose that had brought him thither, though now so happily turned from it." How conscious is he? Does he happily turn from it?
6. Paragraph 53 begins: "In truth, all through the haunted forest, there could be nothing more frightful than the figure of Goodman Brown." Does that description refer more to how others might see him or to how he sees himself? What does Hawthorne mean when he points out that the "fiend in his own shape is less hideous than when he rages in the breast of man"? Why at the end of the paragraph is his cry "lost to his own ear, by its unison with the cry of the desert"?
7. Paragraph 71 reads, in its entirety: "Had Goodman Brown fallen asleep in the forest, and only dreamed a wild dream of a witch-meeting?" Do you believe it was a dream, or did Goodman Brown actually live his experience? Explain. What is the effect of Goodman Brown's experience, whether it was a dream or not?
8. Considering the symbolism, discuss the story as an allegory. How might Goodman Brown's quest serve as a symbolic representation of the development of his identity?
9. Herman Melville, author of *Moby-Dick*, admired Hawthorne's work immensely, and stated that Hawthorne says "NO! in Thunder." How does "Young Goodman Brown" fit Melville's characterization?

Where Are You Going, Where Have You Been?

JOYCE CAROL OATES

Joyce Carol Oates (b. 1938) received a typewriter at age fourteen and wrote "novel after novel" in high school and college. She was the youngest author ever to receive the National Book Award — for her novel *Them* (1969). Currently a professor of creative writing at Princeton University, Oates is highly prolific, having published more than thirty novels, including *Black Water* (1992), *We Were the Mulvaneys* (1996), *The Falls* (2004), and *Little Bird*

of Heaven (2009). She has written several mystery novels under the pseudonyms Rosamond Smith and Lauren Kelly. Her most recent short story collection, *Lovely, Dark, Deep* (2014), was a finalist for the Pulitzer Prize. Oates is also a literary and social critic who has written on such wide-ranging subjects as the poetry of Emily Dickinson, the fiction of James Joyce, and the life of boxer Mike Tyson. "Where Are You Going, Where Have You Been?" is typical of her work, which often explores the violence and suspense lurking beneath ordinary family life. This story is based on the factual case of a psychopath known as the Pied Piper of Tucson. In an interview with the *New York Times*, Oates described him:

> The Pied Piper mimicked teenagers in their talk, dress, and behavior, but he was not a teenager — he was a man in his early thirties. Rather short, he stuffed rags in his leather boots to give himself height. (And sometimes walked unsteadily as a consequence: did none among his admiring constituency notice?) He charmed his victims as charismatic psychopaths have always charmed their victims, to the bewilderment of others who fancy themselves free of all lunatic attractions. The Pied Piper of Tucson: a trashy dream, a tabloid archetype, sheer artifice, comedy, cartoon — surrounded, however improbably, and finally tragically, by real people. You think that, if you look twice, he won't be there. But there he is.

For Bob Dylan

Her name was Connie. She was fifteen and she had a quick nervous giggling habit of craning her neck to glance into mirrors, or checking other people's faces to make sure her own was all right. Her mother, who noticed everything and knew everything and who hadn't much reason any longer to look at her own face, always scolded Connie about it. "Stop gawking at yourself, who are you? You think you're so pretty?" she would say. Connie would raise her eyebrows at these familiar complaints and look right through her mother, into a shadowy vision of herself as she was right at that moment: she knew she was pretty and that was everything. Her mother had been pretty once too, if you could believe those old snapshots in the album, but now her looks were gone and that was why she was always after Connie.

"Why don't you keep your room clean like your sister? How've you got your hair fixed — what the hell stinks? Hair spray? You don't see your sister using that junk."

Her sister June was twenty-four and still lived at home. She was a secretary in the high school Connie attended, and if that wasn't bad enough — with her in the same building — she was so plain and chunky and steady that Connie had to hear her praised all the time by her mother and her mother's sisters. June did this, June did that, she saved money and helped clean the house and cooked and Connie couldn't do a thing, her mind was all filled with trashy daydreams. Their father was away at work most of the time and when he came home he wanted supper and he read the newspaper at supper and after supper he went to bed. He didn't bother talking much to them, but around his bent head Connie's mother kept picking at her until Connie wished her mother was dead and she herself was dead and it was all over. "She makes me want to throw up sometimes," she complained to her friends. She had a high, breathless, amused voice which made everything she said a little forced, whether it was sincere or not.

There was one good thing: June went places with girl friends of hers, girls who were just as plain and steady as she, and so when Connie wanted to do that her mother had no objections. The father of Connie's best girl friend drove the girls the three miles to town and left them off at a shopping plaza, so that they could walk through the stores or go to a movie, and when he came to pick them up again at eleven he never bothered to ask what they had done.

5 They must have been familiar sights, walking around that shopping plaza in their shorts and flat ballerina slippers that always scuffed the sidewalk, with charm bracelets jingling on their thin wrists; they would lean together to whisper and laugh secretly if someone passed by who amused or interested them. Connie had long dark blond hair that drew anyone's eye to it, and she wore part of it pulled up on her head and puffed out and the rest of it she let fall down her back. She wore a pullover jersey blouse that looked one way when she was at home and another way when she was away from home. Everything about her had two sides to it, one for home and one for anywhere that was not home: her walk that could be childlike and bobbing, or languid enough to make anyone think she was hearing music in her head, her mouth which was pale and smirking most of the time, but bright and pink on these evenings out, her laugh which was cynical and drawling at home — "Ha, ha, very funny" — but high-pitched and nervous anywhere else, like the jingling of the charms on her bracelet.

Sometimes they did go shopping or to a movie, but sometimes they went across the highway, ducking fast across the busy road, to a drive-in restaurant where older kids hung out. The restaurant was shaped like a big bottle, though squatter than a real bottle, and on its cap was a revolving figure of a grinning boy who held a hamburger aloft. One night in midsummer they ran across, breathless with daring, and right away someone leaned out a car window and invited them over, but it was just a boy from high school they didn't like. It made them feel good to be able to ignore him. They went up through the maze of parked and cruising cars to the bright-lit, fly-infested restaurant, their faces pleased and expectant as if they were entering a sacred building that loomed out of the night to give them what haven and what blessing they yearned for. They sat at the counter and crossed their legs at the ankles, their thin shoulders rigid with excitement, and listened to the music that made everything so good: the music was always in the background like music at a church service, it was something to depend upon.

A boy named Eddie came in to talk with them. He sat backwards on his stool, turning himself jerkily around in semi-circles and then stopping and turning again, and after a while he asked Connie if she would like something to eat. She said she did and so she tapped her friend's arm on her way out — her friend pulled her face up into a brave droll look — and Connie said she would meet her at eleven, across the way. "I just hate to leave her like that," Connie said earnestly, but the boy said that she wouldn't be alone for long. So they went out to his car and on the way Connie couldn't help but let her eyes wander over the windshields and faces all around her, her face gleaming with the joy that had nothing to do with Eddie or even this place; it might have been the music. She drew her shoulders up and sucked in her breath with the pure pleasure of being alive, and just at that moment she happened to glance at a face just a few feet from hers. It was a boy with shaggy black hair, in a convertible jalopy painted gold. He stared at her and then his lips widened into a grin. Connie slit her eyes at him and turned away, but she couldn't help glancing back and there he was still watching her. He wagged a finger and laughed and said, "Gonna get you, baby," and Connie turned away again without Eddie noticing anything.

She spent three hours with him, at the restaurant where they ate hamburgers and drank Cokes in wax cups that were always sweating, and then down an alley a mile or so away, and when he left her off at five to eleven only the movie house was still open at the plaza. Her girl friend was there, talking with a boy. When Connie came up the two girls smiled at each other and Connie said, "How was the movie?" and the girl said, "*You* should know." They rode off with the girl's father, sleepy and pleased, and Connie couldn't help but look at the darkened shopping plaza with its big empty parking lot and its signs that were faded and ghostly now, and over at the drive-in restaurant where cars were still circling tirelessly. She couldn't hear the music at this distance.

Next morning June asked her how the movie was and Connie said, "So-so."

10 She and that girl and occasionally another girl went out several times a week that way, and the rest of the time Connie spent around the house — it was summer vacation — getting in her mother's way and thinking, dreaming, about the boys she met. But all the boys fell back and dissolved into a single face that was not even a face, but an idea, a feeling, mixed up with the urgent insistent pounding of the music and the humid night air of July. Connie's mother kept dragging her back to the daylight by finding things for her to do or saying suddenly, "What's this about the Pettinger girl?"

And Connie would say nervously, "Oh, her. That dope." She always drew thick clear lines between herself and such girls, and her mother was simple and kindly enough to believe her. Her mother was so simple, Connie thought, that it was maybe cruel to fool her so much. Her mother went scuffling around the house in old bedroom slippers and complained over the telephone to one sister about the other, then the other called up and the two of them complained about the third one. If June's name was mentioned her mother's tone was approving, and if Connie's name was mentioned it was disapproving. This did not really mean she disliked Connie and actually Connie thought that her mother preferred her to June because she was prettier, but the two of them kept up a pretense of exasperation, a sense that they were tugging and struggling over something of little value to either of them. Sometimes, over coffee, they were almost friends, but something would come up — some vexation that was like a fly buzzing suddenly around their heads — and their faces went hard with contempt.

One Sunday Connie got up at eleven — none of them bothered with church — and washed her hair so that it could dry all day long, in the sun. Her parents and sister were going to a barbecue at an aunt's house and Connie said no, she wasn't interested, rolling her eyes, to let mother know just what she thought of it. "Stay home alone then," her mother said sharply. Connie sat out back in a lawn chair and watched them drive away, her father quiet and bald, hunched around so that he could back the car out, her mother with a look that was still angry and not at all softened through the windshield, and in the back seat poor old June all dressed up as if she didn't know what a barbecue was, with all the running yelling kids and the flies. Connie sat with her eyes closed in the sun, dreaming and dazed with the warmth about her as if this were a kind of love, the caresses of love, and her mind slipped over onto thoughts of the boy she had been with the night before and how nice he had been, how sweet it always was, not the way someone like June would suppose but sweet, gentle, the way it was in movies and promised in songs; and when she opened her eyes she hardly knew where she was, the back yard ran off into weeds and a fenceline of trees and behind it the sky was perfectly blue and still. The asbestos "ranch house" that was now three years old startled her — it looked small. She shook her head as if to get awake.

It was too hot. She went inside the house and turned on the radio to drown out the quiet. She sat on the edge of her bed, barefoot, and listened for an hour and a half to a program called XYZ Sunday Jamboree, record after record of hard, fast, shrieking songs she sang along with, interspersed by exclamations from "Bobby King": "An' look here you girls at Napoleon's — Son and Charley want you to pay real close attention to this song coming up!"

And Connie paid close attention herself, bathed in a glow of slow-pulsed joy that seemed to rise mysteriously out of the music itself and lay languidly about the airless little room, breathed in and breathed out with each gentle rise and fall of her chest.

15 After a while she heard a car coming up the drive. She sat up at once, startled, because it couldn't be her father so soon. The gravel kept crunching all the way in from the road — the driveway was long — and Connie ran to the window. It was a car she didn't know. It was an open jalopy, painted a bright gold that caught the sun opaquely. Her heart began to pound and her fingers snatched at her hair, checking it, and she whispered "Christ. Christ," wondering how bad she looked. The car came to a stop at the side door and the horn sounded four short taps as if this were a signal Connie knew.

She went into the kitchen and approached the door slowly, then hung out the screen door, her bare toes curling down off the step. There were two boys in the car and now she recognized the driver: he had shaggy, shabby black hair that looked crazy as a wig and he was grinning at her.

"I ain't late, am I?" he said.

"Who the hell do you think you are?" Connie said.

"Toldja I'd be out, didn't I?"

20 "I don't even know who you are."

She spoke sullenly, careful to show no interest or pleasure, and he spoke in a fast bright monotone. Connie looked past him to the other boy, taking her time. He had fair brown hair, with a lock that fell onto his forehead. His sideburns gave him a fierce, embarrassed look, but so far he hadn't even bothered to glance at her. Both boys wore sunglasses. The driver's glasses were metallic and mirrored everything in miniature.

"You wanta come for a ride?" he said.

Connie smirked and let her hair fall loose over one shoulder.

"Don'tcha like my car? New paint job," he said. "Hey."

25 "What?"

"You're cute."

She pretended to fidget, chasing flies away from the door.

"Don'tcha believe me, or what?" he said.

"Look, I don't even know who you are," Connie said in disgust.

30 "Hey, Ellie's got a radio, see. Mine's broke down." He lifted his friend's arm and showed her the little transistor the boy was holding, and now Connie began to hear the music. It was the same program that was playing inside the house.

"Bobby King?" she said.

"I listen to him all the time. I think he's great."

"He's kind of great," Connie said reluctantly.

"Listen, that guy's *great*. He knows where the action is."

35 Connie blushed a little, because the glasses made it impossible for her to see just what this boy was looking at. She couldn't decide if she liked him or if he was just a jerk, and so she dawdled in the doorway and wouldn't come down or go back inside. She said, "What's all that stuff painted on your car?"

"Can'tcha read it?" He opened the door very carefully, as if he was afraid it might fall off. He slid out just as carefully, planting his feet firmly on the ground, the tiny metallic world in his glasses slowing down like gelatine hardening and in the midst of it Connie's bright green blouse. "This here is my name, to begin with," he said. ARNOLD FRIEND was written in tar-like black letters on the side, with a drawing of a round grinning face that reminded Connie of a pumpkin, except it wore sunglasses. "I wanta introduce myself, I'm Arnold Friend and that's my real name and I'm gonna be your friend, honey, and inside the car's Ellie Oscar, he's kinda shy." Ellie brought his transistor up to his shoulder and balanced it there. "Now these numbers are a secret code, honey," Arnold Friend explained. He read off the numbers 33, 19, 17 and raised his eyebrows at her to see what she thought of that, but she didn't think much of it. The left rear fender had been smashed and around it was written, on the gleaming gold background: DONE BY CRAZY WOMAN DRIVER. Connie had to laugh at that. Arnold Friend was pleased at her laughter and looked up at her. "Around the other side's a lot more — you wanta come and see them?"

"No."

"Why not?"

"Why should I?"

"Don'tcha wanta see what's on the car? 40
Don'tcha wanta go for a ride?"

"I don't know."

"Why not?"

"I got things to do."

"Like what?"

"Things." 45

He laughed as if she had said something funny. He slapped his thighs. He was standing in a strange way, leaning back against the car as if he were balancing himself. He wasn't tall, only an inch or so taller than she would be if she came down to him. Connie liked the way he was dressed, which was the way all of them dressed: tight faded jeans stuffed into black, scuffed boots, a belt that pulled his waist in and showed how lean he was, and a white pull-over shirt that was a little soiled and showed the hard small muscles of his arms and shoulders. He looked as if he probably did hard work, lifting and carrying things. Even his neck looked muscular. And his face was a familiar face, somehow: the jaw and chin and cheeks slightly darkened, because he hadn't shaved for a day or two, and the nose long and hawk-like, sniffing as if she were a treat he was going to gobble up and it was all a joke.

"Connie, you ain't telling the truth. This is your day set aside for a ride with me and you know it," he said, still laughing. The way he straightened and recovered from his fit of laughing showed that it had been all fake.

"How do you know what my name is?" she said suspiciously.

"It's Connie."

"Maybe and maybe not." 50

"I know my Connie," he said, wagging his finger. Now she remembered him even better, back at the restaurant, and her cheeks warmed at the thought of how she sucked in her breath just at the moment she passed him — how she must have looked to him. And he had remembered her. "Ellie and I come out here especially for you," he said. "Ellie can sit in back. How about it?"

"Where?"

"Where what?"

"Where're we going?"

He looked at her. He took off the sunglasses 55
and she saw how pale the skin around his eyes was, like holes that were not in shadow but instead in light. His eyes were like chips of broken glass that catch the light in an amiable way. He smiled. It was as if the idea of going for a ride somewhere, to some place, was a new idea to him.

"Just for a ride, Connie sweetheart."

"I never said my name was Connie," she said.

"But I know what it is. I know your name and all about you, lots of things," Arnold Friend said. He had not moved yet but stood still leaning back against the side of his jalopy. "I took a special interest in you, such a pretty girl, and found out all about you like I know your parents and sister are gone somewheres and I know where and how long they're going to be gone, and I know who you were with last night, and your best friend's name is Betty. Right?"

He spoke in a simple lilting voice, exactly as if he were reciting the words to a song. His smile assured her that everything was fine. In the car Ellie turned up the volume on his radio and did not bother to look around at them.

"Ellie can sit in the back seat," Arnold Friend said. He indicated his friend with a casual jerk of his chin, as if Ellie did not count and she could not bother with him.

"How'd you find out all that stuff ?" Connie said.

"Listen: Betty Schultz and Tony Fitch and Jimmy Pettinger and Nancy Pettinger," he said, in a chant. "Raymond Stanley and Bob Hutter — "

"Do you know all those kids?"

"I know everybody."

"Look, you're kidding. You're not from around here."

"Sure."

"But — how come we never saw you before?"

"Sure you saw me before," he said. He looked down at his boots, as if he were a little offended. "You just don't remember."

"I guess I'd remember you," Connie said.

"Yeah?" He looked up at this, beaming. He was pleased. He began to mark time with the music from Ellie's radio, tapping his fists lightly together. Connie looked away from his smile to the car, which was painted so bright it almost hurt her eyes to look at it. She looked at that name, ARNOLD FRIEND. And up at the front fender was an expression that was familiar — MAN THE FLYING SAUCERS. It was an expression kids had used the year before, but didn't use this year. She looked at it for a while as if the words meant something to her that she did not yet know.

"What're you thinking about? Huh?" Arnold Friend demanded. "Not worried about your hair blowing around in the car, are you?"

"No."

"Think I maybe can't drive good?"

"How do I know?"

"You're a hard girl to handle. How come?" he said. "Don't you know I'm your friend? Didn't you see me put my sign in the air when you walked by?"

"What sign?"

"My sign." And he drew an X in the air, leaning out toward her. They were maybe ten feet apart. After his hand fell back to his side the X was still in the air, almost visible. Connie let the screen door close and stood perfectly still inside it, listening to the music from her radio and the boy's blend together. She stared at Arnold Friend. He stood there so stiffly relaxed, pretending to be relaxed, with one hand idly on the door handle as if he were keeping himself up that way and had no intention of ever moving again. She recognized most things about him, the tight jeans that showed his thighs and buttocks and the greasy leather boots and the tight shirt, and even that slippery friendly smile of his, that sleepy dreamy smile that all the boys used to get across ideas they didn't want to put into words. She recognized all this and also the singsong way he talked, slightly mocking, kidding, but serious and a little melancholy, and she recognized the way he tapped one fist against the other in homage to the perpetual music behind him. But all these things did not come together.

She said suddenly, "Hey, how old are you?"

His smile faded. She could see then that he wasn't a kid, he was much older — thirty, maybe more. At this knowledge her heart began to pound faster.

"That's a crazy thing to ask. Can'tcha see I'm your own age?"

"Like hell you are."

"Or maybe a coupla years older, I'm eighteen."

"Eighteen?" she said doubtfully.

He grinned to reassure her and lines appeared at the corners of his mouth. His teeth were big and white. He grinned so broadly his eyes became slits and she saw how thick the lashes were, thick and black as if painted with a black tar-like material. Then he seemed to become embarrassed, abruptly, and looked over his shoulder at Ellie. "*Him*, he's crazy," he said. "Ain't he a riot, he's a nut, a real character." Ellie was still listening to the music. His sunglasses told nothing about what he was thinking. He wore a bright orange shirt unbuttoned halfway to show his chest, which was a pale, bluish chest and not muscular like Arnold Friend's. His shirt collar was turned up all around and the very tips of the collar pointed out past his chin as if they were protecting him. He was pressing the transistor radio up against his ear and sat there in a kind of daze, right in the sun.

“He's kinda strange,” Connie said. 85

“Hey, she says you're kinda strange! Kinda strange!” Arnold Friend cried. He pounded on the car to get Ellie's attention. Ellie turned for the first time and Connie saw with shock that he wasn't a kid either — he had a fair, hairless face, cheeks reddened slightly as if the veins grew too close to the surface of his skin, the face of a forty-year-old baby. Connie felt a wave of dizziness rise in her at this sight and she stared at him as if waiting for something to change the shock of the moment, make it all right again. Ellie's lips kept shaping words, mumbling along with the words blasting his ear.

“Maybe you two better go away,” Connie said faintly.

“What? How come?” Arnold Friend cried. “We come out here to take you for a ride. It's Sunday.” He had the voice of the man on the radio now. It was the same voice, Connie thought. “Don'tcha know it's Sunday all day and honey, no matter who you were with last night today you're with Arnold Friend and don't you forget it! — Maybe you better step out here,” he said, and this last was in a different voice. It was a little flatter, as if the heat was finally getting to him.

“No. I got things to do.”

“Hey.” 90

“You two better leave.”

“We ain't leaving until you come with us.”

“Like hell I am — ”

“Connie, don't fool around with me. I mean — I mean, don't fool *around*,” he said, shaking his head. He laughed incredulously. He placed his sunglasses on top of his head, carefully, as if he were indeed wearing a wig, and brought the stems down behind his ears. Connie stared at him, another wave of dizziness and fear rising in her so that for a moment he wasn't even in focus but was just a blur, standing there against his gold car, and she had the idea that he had driven up the driveway all right but had come from nowhere before that and belonged nowhere and that everything about him and even the music that was so familiar to her was only half real.

“If my father comes and sees you — ” 95

“He ain't coming. He's at a barbecue.”

“How do you know that?”

“Aunt Tillie's. Right now they're — uh — they're drinking. Sitting around,” he said vaguely, squinting as if he were staring all the way to town and over to Aunt Tillie's back yard. Then the vision seemed to clear and he nodded energetically. “Yeah. Sitting around. There's your sister in a blue dress, huh? And high heels, the poor sad bitch — nothing like you, sweetheart! And your mother's helping some fat woman with the corn, they're cleaning the corn — husking the corn — ”

“What fat woman?” Connie cried.

“How do I know what fat woman. I don't 100
know every goddamn fat woman in the world!” Arnold Friend laughed.

“Oh, that's Mrs. Hornby. . . . Who invited her?” Connie said. She felt a little light-headed. Her breath was coming quickly.

“She's too fat. I don't like them fat. I like them the way you are, honey,” he said, smiling sleepily at her. They stared at each other for a while, through the screen door. He said softly, “Now what you're going to do is this: you're going to come out that door. You're going to sit up front with me and Ellie's going to sit in the back, the hell with Ellie, right? This isn't Ellie's date. You're my date. I'm your lover, honey.”

"What? You're crazy—"

"Yes, I'm your lover. You don't know what that is but you will," he said. "I know that too. I know all about you. But look: it's real nice and you couldn't ask for nobody better than me, or more polite. I always keep my word. I'll tell you how it is, I'm always nice at first, the first time. I'll hold you so tight you won't think you have to try to get away or pretend anything because you'll know you can't. And I'll come inside you where it's all secret and you'll give in to me and you'll love me—"

105 "Shut up! You're crazy!" Connie said. She backed away from the door. She put her hands against her ears as if she'd heard something terrible, something not meant for her. "People don't talk like that, you're crazy," she muttered. Her heart was almost too big now for her chest and its pumping made sweat break out all over her. She looked out to see Arnold Friend pause and then take a step toward the porch lurching. He almost fell. But, like a clever drunken man, he managed to catch his balance. He wobbled in his high boots and grabbed hold of one of the porch posts.

"Honey?" he said. "You still listening?"

"Get the hell out of here!"

"Be nice, honey. Listen."

"I'm going to call the police—"

110 He wobbled again and out of the side of his mouth came a fast spat curse, an aside not meant for her to hear. But even this "Christ!" sounded forced. Then he began to smile again. She watched this smile come, awkward as if he were smiling from inside a mask. His whole face was a mask, she thought wildly, tanned down onto his throat but then running out as if he had plastered make-up on his face but had forgotten about his throat.

"Honey—? Listen, here's how it is. I always tell the truth and I promise you this: I ain't coming in that house after you."

"You better not! I'm going to call the police if you—if you don't—"

"Honey," he said, talking right through her voice, "honey, I'm not coming in there but you are coming out here. You know why?"

She was panting. The kitchen looked like a place she had never seen before, some room she had run inside but which wasn't good enough, wasn't going to help her. The kitchen window had never had a curtain, after three years, and there were dishes in the sink for her to do—probably—and if you ran your hand across the table you'd probably feel something sticky there.

115 "You listening, honey? Hey?"

"—going to call the police—"

"Soon as you touch the phone I don't need to keep my promise and can come inside. You won't want that."

She rushed forward and tried to lock the door. Her fingers were shaking. "But why lock it," Arnold Friend said gently, talking right into her face. "It's just a screen door. It's just nothing." One of his boots was at a strange angle, as if his foot wasn't in it. It pointed out to the left, bent at the ankle. "I mean, anybody can break through a screen door and glass and wood and iron or anything else if he needs to, anybody at all and specially Arnold Friend. If the place got lit up with a fire, honey, you'd come runnin' out into my arms, right into my arms an' safe at home—like you knew I was your lover and'd stopped fooling around, I don't mind a nice shy girl but I don't like no fooling around." Part of those words were spoken with a slight rhythmic lilt, and Connie somehow recognized them—the echo of a song from last year, about a girl rushing into her boy friend's arms and coming home again—

Connie stood barefoot on the linoleum floor, staring at him. "What do you want?" she whispered.

120 "I want you," he said.

"What?"

"Seen you that night and thought, that's the one, yes sir. I never needed to look any more."

"But my father's coming back. He's coming to get me. I had to wash my hair first—" She spoke in a dry, rapid voice, hardly raising it for him to hear.

"No, your daddy is not coming and yes, you had to wash your hair and you washed it for me. It's nice and shining and all for me. I thank you, sweetheart," he said, with a mock bow, but again he almost lost his balance. He had to bend and adjust his boots. Evidently his feet did not go all the way down; the boots must have been stuffed with something so that he would seem taller. Connie stared out at him and behind him at Ellie in the car, who seemed to be looking off toward Connie's right, into nothing. Then Ellie said, pulling the words out of the air one after another as if he were just discovering them, "You want me to pull out the phone?"

"Shut your mouth and keep it shut," Arnold Friend said, his face red from bending over or maybe from embarrassment because Connie had seen his boots. "This ain't none of your business."

"What — what are you doing? What do you want?" Connie said. "If I call the police they'll get you, they'll arrest you — "

"Promise was not to come in unless you touch that phone, and I'll keep that promise," he said. He resumed his erect position and tried to force his shoulders back. He sounded like a hero in a movie, declaring something important. He spoke too loudly and it was as if he were speaking to someone behind Connie. "I ain't made plans for coming in that house where I don't belong but just for you to come out to me, the way you should. Don't you know who I am?"

"You're crazy," she whispered. She backed away from the door but did not want to go into another part of the house, as if this would give him permission to come through the door. "What do you . . . You're crazy, you . . ."

"Huh? What're you saying, honey?"

Her eyes darted everywhere in the kitchen. She could not remember what it was, this room.

"This is how it is, honey: you come out and we'll drive away, have a nice ride. But if you don't come out we're gonna wait till your people come home and then they're all going to get it."

"You want that telephone pulled out?" Ellie said. He held the radio away from his ear and grimaced, as if without the radio the air was too much for him.

"I toldja shut up, Ellie," Arnold Friend said, "you're deaf, get a hearing aid, right? Fix yourself up. This little girl's no trouble and's gonna be nice to me, so Ellie keep to yourself, this ain't your date — right? Don't hem in on me, don't hog, don't crush, don't bird dog, don't trail me," he said in a rapid, meaningless voice, as if he were running through all the expressions he'd learned but was no longer sure which one of them was in style, then rushing on to new ones, making them up with his eyes closed. "Don't crawl under my fence, don't squeeze in my chipmunk hole, don't sniff my glue, suck my popsicle, keep your own greasy fingers on yourself!" He shaded his eyes and peered in at Connie, who was backed against the kitchen table. "Don't mind him, honey, he's just a creep. He's a dope. Right? I'm the boy for you and like I said, you come out here nice like a lady and give me your hand, and nobody else gets hurt, I mean, your nice old bald-headed daddy and your mummy and your sister in her high heels. Because listen: why bring them in this?"

"Leave me alone," Connie whispered.

"Hey, you know that old woman down the road, the one with the chickens and stuff — you know her?"

"She's dead!"

"Dead? What? You know her?" Arnold Friend said.

"She's dead — "

"Don't you like her?"

"She's dead — she's — she isn't here any more — "

"But don't you like her, I mean, you got something against her? Some grudge or something?" Then his voice dipped as if he were conscious of rudeness. He touched the sunglasses on top of his head as if to make sure they were still there. "Now you be a good girl."

"What are you going to do?"

"Just two things, or maybe three," Arnold Friend said. "But I promise it won't last long and you'll like me that way you get to like people you're close to. You will. It's all over for you here, so come on out. You don't want your people in any trouble, do you?"

She turned and bumped against a chair or something, hurting her leg, but she ran into the back room and picked up the telephone. Something roared in her ear, a tiny roaring, and she was so sick with fear that she could do nothing but listen to it — the telephone was clammy and very heavy and her fingers groped down to the dial but were too weak to touch it. She began to scream into the phone, into the roaring. She cried out, she cried for her mother, she felt her breath start jerking back and forth in her lungs as if it were something Arnold Friend was stabbing her with again and again with no tenderness. A noisy sorrowful wailing rose all about her and she was locked inside it the way she was locked inside this house.

After a while she could hear again. She was sitting on the floor, with her wet back against the wall.

Arnold Friend was saying from the door, "That's a good girl. Put the phone back."

She kicked the phone away from her.

"No, honey. Pick it up. Put it back right."

She picked it up and put it back. The dial tone stopped.

"That's a good girl. Now you come outside."

She was hollow with what had been fear but what was now just an emptiness. All that screaming had blasted it out of her. She sat, one leg cramped under her, and deep inside her brain was something like a pinpoint of light that kept going and would not let her relax. She thought, I'm not going to see my mother again. She thought, I'm not going to sleep in my bed again. Her bright green blouse was all wet.

Arnold Friend said, in a gentle-loud voice that was like a stage voice, "The place where you came from ain't there any more, and where you had in mind to go is cancelled out. This place you are now — inside your daddy's house — is nothing but a cardboard box I can knock down any time. You know that and always did know it. You hear me?"

She thought, I have got to think. I have got to know what to do.

"We'll go out to a nice field, out in the country here where it smells so nice and it's sunny," Arnold Friend said. "I'll have my arms tight around you so you won't need to try to get away and I'll show you what love is like, what it does. The hell with this house! It looks solid all right," he said. He ran a fingernail down the screen and the noise did not make Connie shiver, as it would have the day before. "Now put your hand on your heart, honey. Feel that? That feels solid too but we know better. Be nice to me, be sweet like you can because what else is there for a girl like you but to be sweet and pretty and give in? — and get away before her people get back?"

She felt her pounding heart. Her hand seemed to enclose it. She thought for the first time in her life that it was nothing that was hers, that belonged to her, but just a pounding, living thing inside this body that wasn't really hers either.

"You don't want them to get hurt," Arnold Friend went on. "Now get up, honey. Get up all by yourself."

She stood.

"Now turn this way. That's right. Come over to me — Ellie, put that away, didn't I tell you? You dope. You miserable creepy dope," Arnold Friend said. His words were not angry but only part of an incantation. The incantation was kindly. "Now come out through the kitchen to me honey and let's see a smile, try it, you're a brave sweet little girl and now they're eating corn and hotdogs cooked to bursting over an outdoor fire, and they don't know one thing about you and never did and honey you're better than them because not a one of them would have done this for you."

Connie felt the linoleum under her feet; it was cool. She brushed her hair back out of her eyes. Arnold Friend let go of the post tentatively and opened his arms for her, his elbows pointing in toward each other and his wrists limp, to show that this was an embarrassed embrace and a little mocking, he didn't want to make her self-conscious.

160 She put out her hand against the screen. She watched herself push the door slowly open as if she were back safe somewhere in the other doorway, watching this body and this head of long hair moving out into the sunlight where Arnold Friend waited.

"My sweet little blue-eyed girl," he said in a half-sung sigh that had nothing to do with her brown eyes but was taken up just the same by the vast sunlit reaches of the land behind him and on all sides of him — so much land that Connie had never seen before and did not recognize except to know that she was going to it.

[1966]

EXPLORING THE TEXT

1. Explain why you think Connie is or is not a typical teenage girl, as Oates depicts her early in the story. Which of her qualities strike you as specific to an earlier time period, and which seem more characteristic of teenagers in general? How is Connie distancing herself from her family and her perception of their values? Pay particular attention to the contrasts Oates draws in paragraph 5.
2. What part does June play in Connie's characterization? What elements of Connie's character and struggle to construct an identity independent of her family does June's presence emphasize?
3. How is Arnold Friend characterized by the external descriptions Oates provides of his physical features and his clothes? What does his dialogue add? Is he a three-dimensional character or a stereotypical one? Examine the passage where Connie first sees him (para. 7). Why is she drawn to Arnold Friend?
4. How is music used throughout the story, especially to develop character and setting? Why is music so important to Connie? What does Oates mean when she writes in paragraph 94 that "even the music that was so familiar to her [Connie] was only half real"? Why does Oates describe Arnold as having "the voice of the man on the radio now" (para. 88)? What is the significance of Connie's later recognition that Arnold spoke "with a slight rhythmic lilt, . . . [his words] the echo of a song from last year" (para. 118)?
5. What does Arnold Friend mean when he tells Connie, "The place where you came from ain't there any more, and where you had in mind to go is cancelled out" (para. 152)? What does *place* mean in this context, and how is Connie's identity destined by it?
6. Suspense builds throughout this story. How does Oates generate and control that suspense? At which points does the suspense increase with particular intensity?
7. How does Oates convey the mounting fear Connie feels in the last pages of the story? Note the ways in which she shifts from Connie being the agent of her own actions to Connie being just an observer, such as, "She watched herself push the door slowly open" (para. 160). By the end, is Connie acting out of concern for her family or blind fear? What or who is controlling her actions?
8. Oates does not provide closure in this story. Why? Does the indeterminate ending add to or diminish the story's power?
9. Oates has called this story "a realistic allegory." What does that description mean? What allegorical elements do you see in the story?
10. Oates says she based her story on three Tucson, Arizona, murders committed by Charles Schmid, "the Pied Piper of Tucson," in the 1960s. Research this incident and explore how the facts match the fiction. How does this link to an actual incident influence your reading of the story?
11. Oates dedicates the story to Bob Dylan and says she was inspired by his song "It's All Over Now, Baby Blue." Listen to the song, paying special attention to the lyrics. Why do you think Oates found this song compelling?

Apollo

CHIMAMANDA NGOZI ADICHIE

Chimamanda Ngozi Adichie (b. 1977) is one of her generation's most promising African writers. Adichie's first novel, *Purple Hibiscus* (2003), was awarded the Commonwealth Writers' Prize for Best First Book. Her second novel, *Half of a Yellow Sun* (2006), which is set during the Biafran civil war in Nigeria (1967–1970), won the Orange Prize for Fiction in 2007; the novel is dedicated to her two grandfathers, who died in the war. Adichie was awarded a MacArthur Foundation Fellowship in 2008, and *The Thing Around Your Neck*, her first collection of short stories, was published to acclaim in 2009. Her third novel, *Americanah*, was selected as one of the ten best books of 2013 by the *New York Times Book Review* and won a National Book Critics Circle Award. Adichie reached new audiences when a portion of her 2013 TEDx talk entitled "We Should All Be Feminists" was heavily sampled in the Beyoncé song "***Flawless" later that year. Adichie currently divides her time between the United States and Nigeria, where she grew up and attended medical school at the University of Nigeria for two years before coming to America. She has also earned an MFA in creative writing from Johns Hopkins University and an MA in African studies from Yale University. Adichie describes fellow Nigerian writer Chinua Achebe as her hero, and many consider her his literary heir. "Apollo" is set in Nigeria and examines issues of social class and self-discovery as the narrator recalls a formative childhood experience.

Twice a month, like a dutiful son, I visited my parents in Enugu, in their small overfurnished flat that grew dark in the afternoon. Retirement had changed them, shrunk them. They were in their late eighties, both small and mahogany-skinned, with a tendency to stoop. They seemed to look more and more alike, as though all the years together had made their features blend and bleed into one another. They even smelled alike — a menthol scent, from the green vial of Vicks VapoRub they passed to each other, carefully rubbing a little in their nostrils and on aching joints. When I arrived, I would find them either sitting out on the veranda overlooking the road or sunk into the living-room sofa, watching Animal Planet. They had a new, simple sense of wonder. They marvelled at the wiliness of wolves, laughed at the cleverness of apes, and asked each other, "Ifukwa?[1] Did you see that?"

They had, too, a new, baffling patience for incredible stories. Once, my mother told me that a sick neighbor in Abba, our ancestral home town, had vomited a grasshopper — a living, writhing insect, which, she said, was proof that wicked relatives had poisoned him. "Somebody texted us a picture of the grasshopper," my father said. They always supported each other's stories. When my father told me that Chief Okeke's young house help had mysteriously died, and the story around town was that the chief had killed the teen-ager and used her liver for moneymaking rituals, my mother added, "They say he used the heart, too."

Fifteen years earlier, my parents would have scoffed at these stories. My mother, a professor of political science, would have said "Nonsense" in her crisp manner, and my father, a professor of education, would merely have snorted, the stories not worth the effort of speech. It puzzled me that they had shed those old selves, and

[1] Igbo for "Did you see that?" — EDS.

become the kind of Nigerians who told anecdotes about diabetes cured by drinking holy water.

Still, I humored them and half listened to their stories. It was a kind of innocence, this new childhood of old age. They had grown slower with the passing years, and their faces lit up at the sight of me and even their prying questions — "When will you give us a grandchild? When will you bring a girl to introduce to us?" — no longer made me as tense as before. Each time I drove away, on Sunday afternoons after a big lunch of rice and stew, I wondered if it would be the last time I would see them both alive, if before my next visit I would receive a phone call from one of them telling me to come right away. The thought filled me with a nostalgic sadness that stayed with me until I got back to Port Harcourt. And yet I knew that if I had a family, if I could complain about rising school fees as the children of their friends did, then I would not visit them so regularly. I would have nothing for which to make amends.

5 During a visit in November, my parents talked about the increase in armed robberies all over the east. Thieves, too, had to prepare for Christmas. My mother told me how a vigilante mob in Onitsha had caught some thieves, beaten them, and torn off their clothes — how old tires had been thrown over their heads like necklaces, amid shouts for petrol and matches, before the police arrived, fired shots in the air to disperse the crowd, and took the robbers away. My mother paused, and I waited for a supernatural detail that would embellish the story. Perhaps, just as they arrived at the police station, the thieves had turned into vultures and flown away.

"Do you know," she continued, "one of the armed robbers, in fact the ring leader, was Raphael? He was our houseboy years ago. I don't think you'll remember him."

I stared at my mother. "Raphael?"

"It's not surprising he ended like this," my father said. "He didn't start well."

My mind had been submerged in the foggy lull of my parents' storytelling, and I struggled now with the sharp awakening of memory.

10 My mother said again, "You probably won't remember him. There were so many of those houseboys. You were young."

But I remembered. Of course I remembered Raphael.

Nothing changed when Raphael came to live with us, not at first. He seemed like all the others, an ordinary-looking teen from a nearby village. The houseboy before him, Hyginus, had been sent home for insulting my mother. Before Hyginus was John, whom I remembered because he had not been sent away; he had broken a plate while washing it and, fearing my mother's anger, had packed his things and fled before she came home from work. All the houseboys treated me with the contemptuous care of people who disliked my mother. Please come and eat your food, they would say — I don't want trouble from Madam. My mother regularly shouted at them, for being slow, stupid, hard of hearing; even her bell-ringing, her thumb resting on the red knob, the shrillness searing through the house, sounded like shouting. How difficult could it be to remember to fry the eggs differently, my father's plain and hers with onions, or to put the Russian dolls back on the same shelf after dusting, or to iron my school uniform properly?

I was my parents' only child, born late in their lives. "When I got pregnant, I thought it was menopause," my mother told me once. I must have been around eight years old, and did not know what "menopause" meant. She had a brusque manner, as did my father; they had about them the air of people who were quick to dismiss others. They had met at the University of Ibadan, married against their families' wishes — his thought her too educated, while hers preferred a wealthier suitor — and spent their lives in an intense and intimate competition over who published more, who won at badminton, who had the last word in an argument. They often read aloud to each other in the evening, from journals or newspapers, standing rather than sitting in the parlor, sometimes pacing, as though about to spring at a new idea. They drank Mateus rosé — that dark, shapely bottle always seemed to be resting on a table near them — and left behind glasses faint with reddish dregs. Throughout my childhood, I worried about not being quick enough to respond when they spoke to me.

I worried, too, that I did not care for books. Reading did not do to me what it did to my parents, agitating them or turning them into vague beings lost to time, who did not quite notice when I came and went. I read books only enough to satisfy them, and to answer the kinds of unexpected questions that might come in the middle of a meal — What did I think of Pip?[2] Had Ezeulu[3] done the right thing? I sometimes felt like an interloper in our house. My bedroom had bookshelves, stacked with the overflow books that did not fit in the study and the corridor, and they made my stay feel transient, as though I were not quite where I was supposed to be. I sensed my parents' disappointment in the way they glanced at each other when I spoke about a book, and I knew that what I had said was not incorrect but merely ordinary, uncharged with their brand of originality. Going to the staff club with them was an ordeal: I found badminton boring, the shuttlecock seemed to me an unfinished thing, as though whoever had invented the game had stopped halfway.

15 What I loved was kung fu. I watched "Enter the Dragon" so often that I knew all the lines, and I longed to wake up and be Bruce Lee. I would kick and strike at the air, at imaginary enemies who had killed my imaginary family. I would pull my mattress onto the floor, stand on two thick books — usually hardcover copies of "Black Beauty" and "The Water-Babies" — and leap onto the mattress, screaming "Haaa!" like Bruce Lee. One day, in the middle of my practice, I looked up to see Raphael standing in the doorway, watching me. I expected a mild reprimand. He had made my bed that morning, and now the room was in disarray. Instead, he smiled, touched his chest, and brought his finger to his tongue, as though tasting his own blood. My favorite scene. I stared at Raphael with the pure thrill of unexpected pleasure. "I watched the film in the other house where I worked," he said. "Look at this."

He pivoted slightly, leaped up, and kicked, his leg straight and high, his body all taut grace. I was twelve years old and had, until then, never felt that I recognized myself in another person.

Raphael and I practiced in the back yard, leaping from the raised concrete soakaway[4] and landing on the grass. Raphael told me to suck in my belly, to keep my legs straight and my fingers precise. He taught me to breathe. My previous attempts, in the enclosure of my room, had felt stillborn. Now, outside with Raphael, slicing the air with my arms, I could feel my practice become real, with soft grass below and high sky above, and the endless space mine to conquer. This was truly happening. I could become a black belt one day. Outside the kitchen door was a high open veranda, and I wanted to jump off its flight of six steps and try a flying kick. "No," Raphael said. "That veranda is too high."

On weekends, if my parents went to the staff club without me, Raphael and I watched Bruce Lee videotapes, Raphael saying, "Watch it! Watch it!" Through his eyes, I saw the films anew; some moves that I had thought merely competent became luminous when he said, "Watch it!" Raphael knew what really mattered; his wisdom lay easy on his skin. He rewound the

[2] The protagonist of the novel *Great Expectations* by Charles Dickens. — EDS.

[3] The protagonist of the novel *Arrow of God* by Chinua Achebe. — EDS.

[4] A covered chamber with porous walls that drains excess water by allowing it to soak into the ground slowly. — EDS.

sections in which Bruce Lee used a nunchaku, and watched unblinking, gasping at the clean aggression of the metal-and-wood weapon.

"I wish I had a nunchaku[5]," I said.

"It is very difficult to use," Raphael said firmly, and I felt almost sorry to have wanted one.

Not long afterward, I came back from school one day and Raphael said, "See." From the cupboard he took out a nunchaku — two pieces of wood, cut from an old cleaning mop and sanded down, held together by a spiral of metal springs. He must have been making it for at least a week, in his free time after his housework. He showed me how to use it. His moves seemed clumsy, nothing like Bruce Lee's. I took the nunchaku and tried to swing it, but only ended up with a thump on my chest. Raphael laughed. "You think you can just start like that?" he said. "You have to practice for a long time."

At school, I sat through classes thinking of the wood's smoothness in the palm of my hand. It was after school, with Raphael, that my real life began. My parents did not notice how close Raphael and I had become. All they saw was that I now happened to play outside, and Raphael was, of course, part of the landscape of outside: weeding the garden, washing pots at the water tank. One afternoon, Raphael finished plucking a chicken and interrupted my solo practice on the lawn. "Fight!" he said. A duel began, his hands bare, mine swinging my new weapon. He pushed me hard. One end hit him on the arm, and he looked surprised and then impressed, as if he had not thought me capable. I swung again and again. He feinted and dodged and kicked. Time collapsed. In the end, we were both panting and laughing. I remember, even now, very clearly, the smallness of his shorts that afternoon, and how the muscles ran wiry like ropes down his legs.

On weekends, I ate lunch with my parents. I always ate quickly, dreaming of escape and hoping that they would not turn to me with one of their test questions. At one lunch, Raphael served white disks of boiled yam on a bed of greens, and then cubed pawpaw[6] and pineapple.

"The vegetable was too tough," my mother said. "Are we grass-eating goats?" She glanced at him. "What is wrong with your eyes?"

It took me a moment to realize that this was not her usual figurative lambasting — "What is that big object blocking your nose?" she would ask, if she noticed a smell in the kitchen that he had not. The whites of Raphael's eyes were red. A painful, unnatural red. He mumbled that an insect had flown into them.

"It looks like Apollo[7]," my father said.

My mother pushed back her chair and examined Raphael's face. "Ah-ah! Yes, it is. Go to your room and stay there."

Raphael hesitated, as though wanting to finish clearing the plates.

"Go!" my father said. "Before you infect us all with this thing."

Raphael, looking confused, edged away from the table. My mother called him back. "Have you had this before?"

"No, Madam."

"It's an infection of your conjunctiva, the thing that covers your eyes," she said. In the midst of her Igbo words, "conjunctiva" sounded sharp and dangerous. "We're going to buy medicine for you. Use it three times a day and stay in your room. Don't cook until it clears." Turning to me, she said, "Okenwa, make sure you don't go near him. Apollo is very infectious." From her perfunctory tone, it was clear that she did not imagine I would have any reason to go near Raphael.

Later, my parents drove to the pharmacy in town and came back with a bottle of eye drops,

[5] Often known as "nunchucks," a Japanese weapon used in martial arts. — EDS.

[6] Another word for papaya fruit. — EDS.

[7] The popular name for seasonal conjunctivitis, a contagious infection of the eyes. — EDS.

which my father took to Raphael's room in the boys' quarters, at the back of the house, with the air of someone going reluctantly into battle. That evening, I went with my parents to Obollo Road to buy akara[8] for dinner; when we returned, it felt strange not to have Raphael open the front door, not to find him closing the living-room curtains and turning on the lights. In the quiet kitchen, our house seemed emptied of life. As soon as my parents were immersed in themselves, I went out to the boys' quarters and knocked on Raphael's door. It was ajar. He was lying on his back, his narrow bed pushed against the wall, and turned when I came in, surprised, making as if to get up. I had never been in his room before. The exposed light bulb dangling from the ceiling cast sombre shadows.

"What is it?" he asked.

"Nothing. I came to see how you are."

He shrugged and settled back down on the bed. "I don't know how I got this. Don't come close."

But I went close.

"I had Apollo in Primary 3," I said. "It will go quickly, don't worry. Have you used the eye drops this evening?"

He shrugged and said nothing. The bottle of eye drops sat unopened on the table.

"You haven't used them at all?" I asked.

"No."

"Why?"

He avoided looking at me. "I cannot do it."

Raphael, who could disembowel a turkey and lift a full bag of rice, could not drip liquid medicine into his eyes. At first, I was astonished, then amused, and then moved. I looked around his room and was struck by how bare it was — the bed pushed against the wall, a spindly table, a gray metal box in the corner, which I assumed contained all that he owned.

"I will put the drops in for you," I said. I took the bottle and twisted off the cap.

"Don't come close," he said again.

I was already close. I bent over him. He began a frantic blinking.

"Breathe like in kung fu," I said.

I touched his face, gently pulled down his lower left eyelid, and dropped the liquid into his eye. The other lid I pulled more firmly, because he had shut his eyes tight.

"Ndo,[9]" I said. "Sorry."

He opened his eyes and looked at me, and on his face shone something wondrous. I had never felt myself the subject of admiration. It made me think of science class, of a new maize shoot growing greenly toward light. He touched my arm. I turned to go.

"I'll come before I go to school," I said.

In the morning, I slipped into his room, put in his eye drops, and slipped out and into my father's car, to be dropped off at school.

By the third day, Raphael's room felt familiar to me, welcoming, uncluttered by objects. As I put in the drops, I discovered things about him that I guarded closely: the early darkening of hair above his upper lip, the ringworm patch in the hollow between his jaw and his neck. I sat on the edge of his bed and we talked about "Snake in the Monkey's Shadow." We had discussed the film many times, and we said things that we had said before, but in the quiet of his room they felt like secrets. Our voices were low, almost hushed. His body's warmth cast warmth over me.

He got up to demonstrate the snake style, and afterward, both of us laughing, he grasped my hand in his. Then he let go and moved slightly away from me.

"This Apollo has gone," he said.

His eyes were clear. I wished he had not healed so quickly.

I dreamed of being with Raphael and Bruce Lee in an open field, practicing for a fight. When

[8] Fried bean cakes, a popular Nigerian breakfast food and snack. — EDS.

[9] Igbo for "sorry." — EDS.

I woke up, my eyes refused to open. I pried my lids apart. My eyes burned and itched. Each time I blinked, they seemed to produce more pale ugly fluid that coated my lashes. It felt as if heated grains of sand were under my eyelids. I feared that something inside me was thawing that was not supposed to thaw.

My mother shouted at Raphael, "Why did you bring this thing to my house? Why?" It was as though by catching Apollo he had conspired to infect her son. Raphael did not respond. He never did when she shouted at him. She was standing at the top of the stairs, and Raphael was below her.

"How did he manage to give you Apollo from his room?" my father asked me.

"It wasn't Raphael. I think I got it from somebody in my class," I told my parents.

"Who?" I should have known my mother would ask. At that moment, my mind erased all my classmates' names.

"Who?" she asked again.

"Chidi Obi," I said finally, the first name that came to me. He sat in front of me and smelled like old clothes.

"Do you have a headache?" my mother asked.

"Yes."

My father brought me Panadol. My mother telephoned Dr. Igbokwe. My parents were brisk. They stood by my door, watching me drink a cup of Milo that my father had made. I drank quickly. I hoped that they would not drag an armchair into my room, as they did every time I was sick with malaria, when I would wake up with a bitter tongue to find one parent inches from me, silently reading a book, and I would will myself to get well quickly, to free them.

Dr. Igbokwe arrived and shined a torch in my eyes. His cologne was strong; I could smell it long after he'd gone, a heady scent close to alcohol that I imagined would worsen nausea. After he left, my parents created a patient's altar by my bed — on a table covered with cloth, they put a bottle of orange Lucozade, a blue tin of glucose, and freshly peeled oranges on a plastic tray.

They did not bring the armchair, but one of them was home throughout the week that I had Apollo. They took turns putting in my eye drops, my father more clumsily than my mother, leaving sticky liquid running down my face. They did not know how well I could put in the drops myself. Each time they raised the bottle above my face, I remembered the look in Raphael's eyes that first evening in his room, and I felt haunted by happiness.

My parents closed the curtains and kept my room dark. I was sick of lying down. I wanted to see Raphael, but my mother had banned him from my room, as though he could somehow make my condition worse. I wished that he would come and see me. Surely he could pretend to be putting away a bedsheet, or bringing a bucket to the bathroom. Why didn't he come? He had not even said sorry to me. I strained to hear his voice, but the kitchen was too far away and his voice, when he spoke to my mother, was too low.

Once, after going to the toilet, I tried to sneak downstairs to the kitchen, but my father loomed at the bottom of the stairs.

"Kedu?[10]" He asked. "Are you all right?"

"I want water," I said.

"I'll bring it. Go and lie down."

Finally, my parents went out together. I had been sleeping, and woke up to sense the emptiness of the house. I hurried downstairs and to the kitchen. It, too, was empty. I wondered if Raphael was in the boys' quarters; he was not supposed to go to his room during the day, but maybe he had, now that my parents were away. I went out to the open veranda. I heard Raphael's voice before I saw him, standing near the tank, digging his foot into the sand, talking to Josephine, Professor Nwosu's house help. Professor Nwosu sometimes sent eggs from his

[10] Igbo for "How are you?" — EDS.

poultry, and never let my parents pay for them. Had Josephine brought eggs? She was tall and plump; now she had the air of someone who had already said goodbye but was lingering. With her, Raphael was different — the slouch in his back, the agitated foot. He was shy. She was talking to him with a kind of playful power, as though she could see through him to things that amused her. My reason blurred.

"Raphael!" I called out.

He turned. "Oh. Okenwa. Are you allowed to come downstairs?"

He spoke as though I were a child, as though we had not sat together in his dim room.

"I'm hungry! Where is my food?" It was the first thing that came to me, but in trying to be imperious I sounded shrill.

Josephine's face puckered, as though she were about to break into slow, long laughter. Raphael said something that I could not hear, but it had the sound of betrayal. My parents drove up just then, and suddenly Josephine and Raphael were roused. Josephine hurried out of the compound, and Raphael came toward me. His shirt was stained in the front, orangish, like palm oil from soup. Had my parents not come back, he would have stayed there mumbling by the tank; my presence had changed nothing.

"What do you want to eat?" he asked.

"You didn't come to see me."

"You know Madam said I should not go near you."

Why was he making it all so common and ordinary? I, too, had been asked not to go to his room, and yet I had gone, I had put in his eye drops every day.

"After all, you gave me the Apollo," I said.

"Sorry." He said it dully, his mind elsewhere.

I could hear my mother's voice. I was angry that they were back. My time with Raphael was shortened, and I felt the sensation of a widening crack.

"Do you want plantain or yam?" Raphael asked, not to placate me but as if nothing serious had happened. My eyes were burning again. He came up the steps. I moved away from him, too quickly, to the edge of the veranda, and my rubber slippers shifted under me. Unbalanced, I fell. I landed on my hands and knees, startled by the force of my own weight, and I felt the tears coming before I could stop them. Stiff with humiliation, I did not move.

My parents appeared.

"Okenwa!" my father shouted.

I stayed on the ground, a stone sunk in my knee. "Raphael pushed me."

"What?" My parents said it at the same time, in English. "What?"

There was time. Before my father turned to Raphael, and before my mother lunged at him as if to slap him, and before she told him to go pack his things and leave immediately, there was time. I could have spoken. I could have cut into that silence. I could have said that it was an accident. I could have taken back my lie and left my parents merely to wonder.

[2015]

EXPLORING THE TEXT

1. Okenwa, the narrator, explains that he visits his parents "twice a month, like a dutiful son" (para. 1) and that if he had fulfilled their wish for him to marry and have a family, he wouldn't visit as often, because he "would have nothing for which to make amends" (para. 4). What do these details suggest about Okenwa? What motivates him? What other details in the story's opening characterize him?
2. Okenwa describes how his parents have changed, noting that they seem shrunken, with a "tendency to stoop" (para. 1), and they now have a "baffling patience for incredible stories" (para. 2). Reread

the story's opening (paras. 1–11) and look for other specific descriptions of how they have changed, as well as how Okenwa regards them. What do these details suggest about how Okenwa views his parents?

3. At the end of the first section, when Okenwa's mother suggests he probably doesn't remember Raphael, Okenwa thinks, "But I remembered. Of course I remembered Raphael" (para. 11). What is the effect of this repetition, especially right before the flashback begins? Considering what we learn about Okenwa and his parents in the first section, why do you think Adichie presents the story of Okenwa and Raphael as a flashback?

4. Of his childhood, Okenwa says, "I was twelve years old and had, until then, never felt that I recognized myself in another person" (para. 16), and "I had never felt myself the subject of admiration" (para. 51). What do those remarks suggest about the relationship between him and his parents? How would you describe that relationship? Discuss details that support your view.

5. Clearly Okenwa looks up to Raphael. Consider his attitude: would you call it a fascination? A "crush"? Idolatry? An infatuation? Admiration? Something else? Explain, using details from the text to support your perspective.

6. Raphael is an archangel with healing powers who appears in the religious texts of several faiths, including Christianity, Judaism, and Islam. Why do you think Adichie chose to give the houseboy such a name? How does this choice contribute to your understanding of his character?

7. In paragraph 80, Okenwa describes the moment when he feels betrayed by Raphael. Read this paragraph closely, noticing the descriptions of Josephine's face, Raphael's shirt, and of both characters' movements. Why do you think this moment is described so vividly? How do the details emphasize Okenwa's disappointing experience of betrayal?

8. In the final section of the story, Okenwa wonders why Raphael "was . . . making it all so common and ordinary" (para. 84). How does that thought reflect the story's theme(s)?

9. Compare and contrast the interactions between Okenwa and Raphael in two key scenes: when Okenwa visits an ailing Raphael (paras. 35–52) and when Okenwa approaches Raphael outside in the final section of the story (paras. 76–88). How would you characterize their interaction in each of these two scenes? How do the dialogue and detail in each section create two very different impressions of their relationship?

10. Why do you believe Okenwa tells his parents that Raphael pushed him? What do the diction and syntax in the last paragraph convey about Okenwa's decision to lie?

11. What is Adichie's attitude toward Okenwa and his family? Consider in particular the description of Okenwa's adolescent view of his parents in paragraphs 13 and 14. What attitude might the author be expressing about the characters when she has Okenwa explain that his parents "had about them the air of people who were quick to dismiss others" (para. 13) and that he "sometimes felt like an interloper in our house" (para. 14)? What other details in these paragraphs suggest the author's attitude?

12. When Raphael comes down with Apollo, the whites of his eyes are described as "a painful, unnatural red" (para. 26), and Okenwa's mother warns him that the disease is "very infectious" (para. 33). Later, when Raphael has recovered from the infection, he cuts short Okenwa's visit to his room by simply stating, "This Apollo has gone" (para. 57). What possible meaning(s) does Apollo bring to the story? Why do you think the story is named after this infection?

13. References to the famous martial artist Bruce Lee play a central role in this story. As a child, Okenwa "longed to wake up and be Bruce Lee" (para. 15), and Okenwa and Raphael bond over their admiration for him. What is the significance of the many allusions to Bruce Lee throughout the story? What does it say about both Okenwa and Raphael that they are drawn to this powerful figure and mimic his kung fu moves?

POETRY

The Quiet Life

ALEXANDER POPE

Alexander Pope (1688–1744) is generally considered the eighteenth century's greatest English poet. Known for satirical verse, Pope was the first writer to be able to live off the proceeds of his work — namely, his very popular translation of Homer's *Iliad*. Pope was a Roman Catholic, and the anti-Catholic sentiment and laws of his time dictated — and limited — his formal education. He read widely on his own, learning French, Italian, Latin, and Greek. Critics attacked Pope's version of Shakespeare's works, and he responded with *The Dunciad* — a scathing satire of the literary establishment that brought him enemies and even threats of physical violence. Pope's work goes in and out of fashion, but some of his words are so ingrained in the English language that they are considered proverbs by those unfamiliar with his work. "A little learning is a dangerous thing," "To err is human, to forgive, divine," and "For fools rush in where angels fear to tread" are from *Essay on Criticism*; "Hope springs eternal in the human breast" and "The proper study of mankind is man" are both found in *Essay on Man*. In the following poem, the young Pope considers the virtues of defining oneself within a small and bounded environment.

Happy the man whose wish and care
A few paternal acres bound,
Content to breathe his native air
In his own ground.

Whose herds with milk, whose fields with bread,
Whose flocks supply him with attire;
Whose trees in summer yield him shade,
In winter, fire.

Blest, who can unconcern'dly find
Hours, days, and years, slide soft away
In health of body; peace of mind;
Quiet by day;

Sound sleep by night; study and ease
Together mix'd; sweet recreation,
And innocence, which most does please
With meditation.

Thus let me live, unseen, unknown;
Thus unlamented let me die;
Steal from the world, and not a stone
Tell where I lie.

[1709]

EXPLORING THE TEXT

1. What are the values that the speaker espouses? What is the implicit contrast in values raised in the last stanza?
2. How does the speaker of this poem construct his identity? What resources does he draw on to determine who he is?
3. How does the form of the poem reinforce the theme of balance?
4. This poem is notable for its use of inversions, or anastrophe. How does this syntax impact the mood of the poem? How does it contribute to the overall meaning of the poem? Explain.
5. Today's Green movement may not have the same pastoral ideals as those found in this poem, yet there are some similarities. What are they? Do you think Alexander Pope would approve of or even embrace this movement?

The World Is Too Much with Us

WILLIAM WORDSWORTH

William Wordsworth (1770–1850) is one of the most famous and influential poets of the Western world and one of the premier Romantics. Widely known for his reverence of nature and the power of his lyrical verse, he lived in the Lake District of northern England, where he was inspired by the natural beauty of the landscape. With Samuel Taylor Coleridge, he published *Lyrical Ballads* in 1798; the collection, which changed the direction of English poetry, begins with Coleridge's "Rime of the Ancient Mariner" and includes Wordsworth's "Lines Composed a Few Miles above Tintern Abbey." Among Wordsworth's other famous works are "The World Is Too Much with Us," a sonnet; "Ode: Intimations of Immortality"; and "The Prelude or Growth of a Poet's Mind," an autobiographical poem. "The World Is Too Much with Us," written around 1802 and published in 1807, criticizes society for being materialistic and estranged from nature.

The world is too much with us; late and soon,
Getting and spending, we lay waste our powers:
Little we see in Nature that is ours;
We have given our hearts away, a sordid boon!
This Sea that bares her bosom to the moon;
The winds that will be howling at all hours,
And are up-gathered now like sleeping flowers;
For this, for everything, we are out of tune;
It moves us not. — Great God! I'd rather be
A Pagan suckled in a creed outworn;
So might I, standing on this pleasant lea,
Have glimpses that would make me less forlorn;
Have sight of Proteus rising from the sea;
Or hear old Triton[1] blow his wreathèd horn.

[1807]

---

[1] In Greek mythology, both Proteus and Triton were gods of the sea and sons of Poseidon. — EDS.

EXPLORING THE TEXT

1. "The World Is Too Much with Us" is a traditional Petrarchan sonnet. In what ways does the rigid form enhance William Wordsworth's passionate message? Is his passion at all repressed by the sonnet form? How does the sestet answer the octave? What other shifts or transitions do you notice in the poem?
2. Why does the speaker feel that his sense of self is compromised? Why does he claim that "we lay waste our powers" (l. 2)? What could "we" do to reclaim our identity?
3. What effect does the speaker achieve by personifying the wind and the sea?
4. Discuss the impact that any of the following word replacements might have on the poem: "selling and buying" for "getting and spending" (l. 2); "screeching" for "howling" (l. 6); "napping flowers" for "sleeping flowers" (l. 7); "fed" for "suckled" (l. 10); and "sad" for "forlorn" (l. 12). Consider connotation as you discuss the changes in effect.
5. What effect do the references to mythology have? How are they connected to Wordsworth's conviction that materialism causes an estrangement from nature that may have dire results?
6. According to critic Camille Paglia, line 8's "we are out of tune" contains a "buried image": the body as Aeolian or wind harp, played upon and vibrated by nature. How does that image — and its related metaphor — add to Wordsworth's argument about the loss of self that results from "late and soon, / Getting and spending" (ll. 1–2)?

The Apology

RALPH WALDO EMERSON

Ralph Waldo Emerson (1803–1882), perhaps best known for his essay "Self-Reliance," was one of America's most influential thinkers and writers. After graduating from Harvard Divinity School, he followed nine generations of his family into the ministry but practiced for only a few years. Known as a great orator, Emerson made his living as a popular lecturer on a wide range of topics, from politics to religion to art. From 1821 to 1826, he taught in city and country schools, and later served on a number of school boards, including the Concord School Committee and the Board of Overseers of Harvard College. Central to Emerson's thought is recognizing the spiritual relationship between humans and the natural world. In 1836, he and other like-minded intellectuals such as Henry David Thoreau founded the Transcendental Club, and that same year Emerson published his influential essay "Nature," which expresses the central philosophy of what came to be known as Transcendentalism. In his 1837 speech entitled "The American Scholar," which Oliver Wendell Holmes Sr. called America's "intellectual Declaration of Independence," Emerson urged American writers to develop their own style rather than emulating the European masters. With the tumult of the Industrial Revolution as a backdrop, Emerson poses an alternative way of being in the world in his poem "The Apology."

Think me not unkind and rude
    That I walk alone in grove and glen;
I go to the god of the wood
    To fetch his word to men.

Tax not my sloth that I
    Fold my arms beside the brook;

Each cloud that floated in the sky
  Writes a letter in my book.

Chide me not, laborious band,
  For the idle flowers I brought;
Every aster in my hand
  Goes home loaded with a thought.

There was never mystery
  But 'tis figured in the flowers;
Was never secret history
  But birds tell it in the bowers.

One harvest from thy field
  Homeward brought the oxen strong;
A second crop thine acres yield,
  Which I gather in a song.

[1847]

EXPLORING THE TEXT

1. Ralph Waldo Emerson's sentence structure (imperatives) and his references to "thy" and "thine" in the last stanza suggest that the speaker is addressing someone. Who is the person or group he is addressing?
2. The poem is structured as a contrast between two roles or two identities that define a member of a community. What are the central contrasts?
3. How does the regularity of the form, particularly the rhyme scheme, reinforce the point Emerson is making?
4. What is meant by "god of the wood / To fetch his word to men" (ll. 3–4)? Why does Emerson not capitalize "god"? If his audience is a conventionally religious one, more likely to expect the familiar phrase "the Word of God," what are the implications of his making such a change?
5. What are the central images of this poem, and why are they fitting given the time period in which it was written?
6. How would you describe the tone of the poem? Is it playful? Defensive? Sentimental? You might capture it better in a phrase (an adjective-noun combination) than in a single word. Refer to specific language in the poem that supports your choice.
7. The word *apology* has a number of nuances in its meaning. We think of it most commonly as an admission of error accompanied by an expression of regret. Closely related is *apologia*, which does not suggest guilt or error but is instead a desire to make clear the grounds for a belief or position. How might each of these apply to this poem? Which do you think Emerson most likely intended?

I'm Nobody! Who are you?

EMILY DICKINSON

Born into a prominent family in Amherst, Massachusetts, Emily Dickinson (1830–1886) received some formal education at Amherst Academy and Mount Holyoke Female Seminary (which became Mount Holyoke College). Throughout her lifetime, Dickinson was a shy and reclusive person, who preferred to remain within her close family circle. In 1862, she enclosed four poems in a letter to literary critic and abolitionist Thomas Wentworth Higginson, who had written a piece in the *Atlantic Monthly* that included practical advice for young writers. Her letter began, "Mr. Higginson, – Are you too deeply occupied to say if my verse is alive? The mind is so near itself it cannot see distinctly, and I have none to ask. Should you think it breathed, and had you the leisure to tell me, I should feel quick gratitude." Dickinson didn't sign the letter, but instead enclosed her name on a card inside a smaller envelope. Dickinson wrote over seventeen hundred poems, but only ten were published in her lifetime.

I'm Nobody! Who are you?
Are you — Nobody — too?
Then there's a pair of us!
Don't tell! they'd advertise — you know!

How dreary — to be — Somebody!
How public — like a Frog —
To tell one's name — the livelong June —
To an admiring Bog!

[c. 1861]

EXPLORING THE TEXT

1. What characteristics do you typically associate with people who identify themselves as "Nobodies"? By addressing the reader directly ("Who are you?"), how does the poem invite the reader to reexamine what it means to be "a nobody"?
2. How does society commonly treat its "Nobodies"? Why do you think the speaker is worried that "they'd advertise" (l. 4)?
3. Where do you find evidence of irony in the poem?
4. In the second stanza, the speaker uses a simile to express her contempt for a certain type of behavior. What is that behavior, and how does the simile reinforce her point?
5. How does what we know about Emily Dickinson's shyness invite an autobiographical reading of this poem?
6. Compare and contrast this poem with "The Quiet Life" by Alexander Pope (p. 446). What resources of language do the two poets employ to express the kind of life that each believes is most valuable?

Heritage

COUNTEE CULLEN

An important figure during the Harlem Renaissance, Countee Cullen (1903–1946) grew up in New York City. At fifteen, he was adopted by Reverend Frederick A. Cullen, pastor of Harlem's largest congregation. Cullen graduated Phi Beta Kappa from New York University in 1923 and received an MA from Harvard University in 1926; he traveled to France as a Guggenheim Fellow after graduation. His published collections include *Color* (1925), *Copper Sun* (1927), *The Ballad of the Brown Girl* (1928), *The Black Christ and Other Poems* (1929), and *The Medea and Some Other Poems* (1935). He also wrote fiction, including the novel *One Way to Heaven* (1931) and the play *St. Louis Woman* (1946). Cullen differed from many other poets of this period because he wrote in the lyric tradition of John Keats, his favorite poet. Race was, however, a central concern of his work. He ends "Yet Do I Marvel," one of his most famous poems, with the lines: "Yet do I marvel at this curious thing: / To make a poet black, and bid him sing!" In "Heritage," he explores his African heritage and how he understands and balances that legacy with the Judeo-Christian tradition of his religion and education.

(For Harold Jackman)

What is Africa to me:
Copper sun or scarlet sea,
Jungle star or jungle track,
Strong bronzed men, or regal black
Women from whose loins I sprang
When the birds of Eden sang?
One three centuries removed
From the scenes his fathers loved,
Spicy grove, cinnamon tree,
What is Africa to me?

So I lie, who all day long
Want no sound except the song
Sung by wild barbaric birds
Goading massive jungle herds,
Juggernauts of flesh that pass
Trampling tall defiant grass
Where young forest lovers lie,
Plighting troth beneath the sky.
So I lie, who always hear,
Though I cram against my ear
Both my thumbs, and keep them there,
Great drums throbbing through the air.
So I lie, whose fount of pride,
Dear distress, and joy allied,
Is my somber flesh and skin,
With the dark blood dammed within
Like great pulsing tides of wine
That, I fear, must burst the fine
Channels of the chafing net
Where they surge and foam and fret.

Africa? A book one thumbs
Listlessly, till slumber comes.
Unremembered are her bats
Circling through the night, her cats
Crouching in the river reeds,
Stalking gentle flesh that feeds
By the river brink; no more
Does the bugle-throated roar
Cry that monarch claws have leapt
From the scabbards where they slept.
Silver snakes that once a year
Doff the lovely coats you wear,
Seek no covert in your fear
Lest a mortal eye should see;
What's your nakedness to me?
Here no leprous flowers rear
Fierce corollas in the air;
Here no bodies sleek and wet,
Dripping mingled rain and sweat,
Tread the savage measures of
Jungle boys and girls in love.
What is last year's snow to me,
Last year's anything? The tree
Budding yearly must forget
How its past arose or set—
Bough and blossom, flower, fruit,
Even what shy bird with mute
Wonder at her travail there,
Meekly labored in its hair.
One three centuries removed
From the scenes his fathers loved,
Spice grove, cinnamon tree,
What is Africa to me?

So I lie, who find no peace
Night or day, no slight release
From the unremittant beat
Made by cruel padded feet

Walking through my body's street.
Up and down they go, and back,
Treading out a jungle track.
So I lie, who never quite
Safely sleep from rain at night—
I can never rest at all
When the rain begins to fall;
Like a soul gone mad with pain
I must match its weird refrain;
Ever must I twist and squirm,
Writhing like a baited worm,
While its primal measures drip
Through my body, crying, "Strip!
Doff this new exuberance.
Come and dance the Lover's Dance!"
In an old remembered way
Rain works on me night and day.

Quaint, outlandish heathen gods
Black men fashion out of rods,
Clay, and brittle bits of stone,
In a likeness like their own,
My conversion came high-priced;
I belong to Jesus Christ,
Preacher of humility;
Heathen gods are naught to me.

Father, Son, and Holy Ghost,
So I make an idle boast;
Jesus of the twice-turned cheek,
Lamb of God, although I speak
With my mouth thus, in my heart
Do I play a double part.
Ever at Thy glowing altar
Must my heart grow sick and falter,
Wishing He I served were black,
Thinking then it would not lack
Precedent of pain to guide it,
Let who would or might deride it;
Surely then this flesh would know
Yours had borne a kindred woe.
Lord, I fashion dark gods, too,
Daring even to give You
Dark despairing features where,
Crowned with dark rebellious hair,
Patience wavers just so much as
Mortal grief compels, while touches
Quick and hot, of anger, rise
To smitten cheek and weary eyes.
Lord, forgive me if my need
Sometimes shapes a human creed.

All day long and all night through,
One thing only must I do:
Quench my pride and cool my blood,
Lest I perish in the flood.
Lest a hidden ember set
Timber that I thought was wet
Burning like the dryest flax,
Melting like the merest wax,
Lest the grave restore its dead.
Not yet has my heart or head
In the least way realized
They and I are civilized.

[1925]

EXPLORING THE TEXT

1. Read a part of the poem aloud and listen to the beat and the sound. Countee Cullen uses the traditional form of rhyming couplets (*aabbccddee* . . .); is this regular beat calming or unsettling? What is the effect of sustaining the rhyming couplets and the rhythm throughout the poem?
2. What is the impact of the repetition used in the poem? Note the repeated question "What is Africa to me?" Other examples of repetition include the repeated phrase "So I lie" and the italicized quatrains. How does the repetition work in conjunction with the rhyming couplets and rhythm?
3. What specific details describe Africa? Start with the opening descriptions that Cullen presents as contrasts. As the poem progresses, what visual picture emerges? Is it noteworthy that some details

are inaccurate, such as the fact that the cinnamon tree referred to in the refrain is not, in fact, native to Africa? Is the depiction stereotypical? Consider how a person would learn about Africa in the early 1920s.

4. What does the speaker mean by his description of Africa as "A book one thumbs / Listlessly, till slumber comes" (ll. 31–32)?
5. Starting with line 85, the speaker struggles to reconcile his Christian beliefs with "heathen gods." What is the nature of his struggle? Why do you think he raises the issue of religion in the very last part of the poem?
6. In addition to differing religious beliefs, what other dualities in cultural values do you find in the poem? If you interpret the poem as the inner struggle of the speaker trying to construct his identity, what are the conflicts the speaker experiences?
7. How do you interpret the italicized ending of the poem? Pay special attention to the word "civilized" (l. 128). Why might Cullen have chosen to end his poem with this word? Ultimately, what is Africa to the speaker?
8. How would you describe the tone of the poem? Try using two or three words to make your description more precise, such as *sad yet hopeful*, or *admiringly critical*. Cite specific passages to support your response.

The Most of It

ROBERT FROST

Though Robert Frost (1874–1963) is considered the quintessential New England poet, he was born in San Francisco. After the death of his father when Frost was eleven years old, the family moved to Massachusetts. Frost attended Dartmouth College and Harvard University, but in both cases left early to support his family. He delivered newspapers, farmed, did factory work, and taught high school and college, but he considered poetry to be his true calling. Frost won four Pulitzer Prizes for his collections *New Hampshire: A Poem with Notes and Grace Notes* (1924), *Collected Poems* (1931), *A Further Range* (1937), and *A Witness Tree* (1943), and in 1961 he spoke at the inauguration of President John F. Kennedy. Frost's poetry often examines social and philosophical commentary through its realistic evocation of rural life. Frost's work is also known for its command of American colloquial speech. Both of these qualities are on full display in "The Most of It."

He thought he kept the universe alone;
For all the voice in answer he could wake
Was but the mocking echo of his own
From some tree-hidden cliff across the lake.
Some morning from the boulder-broken beach
He would cry out on life, that what it wants
Is not its own love back in copy speech,
But counter-love, original response.
And nothing ever came of what he cried
Unless it was the embodiment that crashed
In the cliff's talus[1] on the other side,

[1] Sloping debris. — EDS.

And then in the far distant water splashed,
But after a time allowed for it to swim,
Instead of proving human when it neared
And someone else additional to him,
As a great buck[2] it powerfully appeared,
Pushing the crumpled water up ahead,
And landed pouring like a waterfall,
And stumbled through the rocks with horny tread,
And forced the underbrush—and that was all.

[1942]

[2] An adult male deer, moose, or elk. — EDS.

EXPLORING THE TEXT

1. Who is the "he" introduced at the beginning? How would you describe the dramatic situation? Why did he think that "he kept the universe alone"? What is he doing? What does he wish for?
2. Why do you believe the echo in line 3 is "mocking"?
3. Imagine that the poem ended with line 9: "And nothing ever came of what he cried." How would this ending change your understanding of the poem?
4. What is the "embodiment" indicated in line 10? Explain.
5. This poem consists of just three sentences. What happens in the last sentence (ll. 10-20)? Paraphrase the events.
6. Is there a physical "buck" (l. 16) in the poem, or does the buck represent something else? What about the "waterfall" in line 18? How do you interpret these lines? What effect do they have on the poem's meaning?
7. After reading the poem in its entirety, carefully consider the concluding phrase: "and that was all." How do you interpret this phrase? How does it relate to the title of the poem?
8. How would you describe the setting of this poem? What resources of language does Robert Frost use to set the scene where the events depicted take place?
9. How would you describe the speaker's tone? What is his attitude toward the man in the poem? Toward nature? Explain.

Fern Hill

DYLAN THOMAS

Dylan Thomas (1914–1953) was born in Wales, spent much of his life in London, and gained a following in the United States, where he often lectured and gave readings. He wrote his first volume of poetry when he was only twenty and published steadily throughout his lifetime. His works include *The Map of Love* (1939); *Portrait of the Artist as a Young Dog* (1940); *Deaths and Entrances* (1946); *In Country Sleep* (1952); and the posthumous *Under Milk Wood: A Play for Voices* (1954), which features characters from the fictional Welsh fishing village of Llareggub. During World War II, Thomas wrote scripts for documentary films, and after the war he was a literary commentator for BBC radio. He died in New York

City at the age of thirty-nine of complications from alcoholism. Thomas was a popular and flamboyant figure, known for his spirited readings — especially his famous reading of "Do not go gentle into that good night," one of his most beloved poems. His other works include *A Child's Christmas in Wales*, published posthumously in 1955, and "Fern Hill."

Now as I was young and easy under the apple boughs
About the lilting house and happy as the grass was green,
    The night above the dingle starry,
        Time let me hail and climb
    Golden in the heydays of his eyes,
And honored among wagons I was prince of the apple towns
And once below a time I lordly had the trees and leaves
        Trail with daisies and barley
    Down the rivers of the windfall light.

And as I was green and carefree, famous among the barns
About the happy yard and singing as the farm was home,
    In the sun that is young once only,
        Time let me play and be
    Golden in the mercy of his means,
And green and golden I was huntsman and herdsman, the calves
Sang to my horn, the foxes on the hills barked clear and cold,
        And the sabbath rang slowly
    In the pebbles of the holy streams.

All the sun long it was running, it was lovely, the hay
Fields high as the house, the tunes from the chimneys, it was air
    And playing, lovely and watery
        And fire green as grass.
    And nightly under the simple stars
As I rode to sleep the owls were bearing the farm away,
All the moon long I heard, blessed among stables, the nightjars
    Flying with the ricks, and the horses
        Flashing into the dark.

And then to awake, and the farm, like a wanderer white
With the dew, come back, the cock on his shoulder; it was all
    Shining, it was Adam and maiden,
        The sky gathered again
    And the sun grew round that very day.
So it must have been after the birth of the simple light
In the first, spinning place, the spellbound horses walking warm
    Out of the whinnying green stable
        On to the fields of praise.

And honored among foxes and pheasants by the gay house
Under the new made clouds and happy as the heart was long,
In the sun born over and over,
I ran my heedless ways,
My wishes raced through the house-high hay
And nothing I cared, at my sky-blue trades, that time allows
In all his tuneful turning so few and such morning songs
Before the children green and golden
Follow him out of grace,

Nothing I cared, in the lamb white days, that time would take me
Up to the swallow-thronged loft by the shadow of my hand,
In the moon that is always rising,
Nor that riding to sleep
I should hear him fly with the high fields
And wake to the farm forever fled from the childless land.
Oh as I was young and easy in the mercy of his means,
Time held me green and dying
Though I sang in my chains like the sea.

[1946]

EXPLORING THE TEXT

1. A narrative about youth and age, this poem opens with "Now as I was young and easy" and ends with the speaker looking back on the time that he "was young and easy" (l. 52). What are the major divisions or events in the process of growing older that he recounts? You might consider the structure of the poem as six verse paragraphs.
2. Color plays a key role in this poem, especially green. List the images of green that Dylan Thomas uses. What patterns do you see? What do you make of seeming contradictions such as "fire green as grass" (l. 22) or "green and dying" (l. 53)? How does Thomas develop his ideas through the use of this color?
3. How does Thomas use imagery of light to mark the speaker's changing perception? Consider specific references to "light" (ll. 9 and 33) and related references, such as "golden" (ll. 5, 14, 15, and 44) and "Shining" (l. 30). What contrasts does he draw with these?
4. What is the effect of Thomas's personification of time? How does he characterize it?
5. The poem opens with a simple country scene "under the apple boughs," yet there are allusions to royalty. What is Thomas's purpose in creating this juxtaposition?
6. How does the biblical allusion to "Adam and maiden" (l. 30) contribute to the development of the poem?
7. Thomas creates striking images with unusual phrasing and combinations. How do you interpret "the rivers of the windfall light" (l. 9), "All the sun long" (l. 19), "a wanderer white / With the dew" (ll. 28–29), and "my sky-blue trades" (l. 42)? Can you find other phrases that are similarly vibrant?
8. How would you characterize the tone of the final three lines — depressing? resigned? nostalgic? defiant? Is the overall tone of the poem positive or negative?
9. Do you think Thomas is using this poem to pay tribute to the natural world and all it can teach us, or is he using the idyllic country setting as a symbol for a more abstract concept? Cite specific passages and language to support your response.
10. Are "Fern Hill" and "The Quiet Life" by Alexander Pope (p. 446) more similar or different in their themes?

We Real Cool

GWENDOLYN BROOKS

Born in Topeka, Kansas, and raised in Chicago, Gwendolyn Brooks (1917–2000) was author of more than twenty books of poetry, including her breakout work, *A Street in Bronzeville* (1945), and *Annie Allen* (1949), for which she became the first African American author to receive the Pulitzer Prize. In 1968, she was named poet laureate of the state of Illinois, and from 1985 to 1986 she served as consultant in poetry to the Library of Congress — the first African American woman to hold this position. Much of Brooks's work focuses on Chicago's urban landscape and culture, reflecting the speech patterns and expressions of the African American neighborhoods of Chicago's South Side, where she lived. While depicting the gritty reality of urban poverty, her poems express an affirmation of life. A frequent visitor and reader in public schools throughout her career, Brooks strove to help inner-city children find the poetry in their lives. Her awareness of the cultural forces that defined their experience — particularly the lives of young men — is clear in "We Real Cool," a poem that remains relevant over half a century after Brooks wrote it.

The Pool Players.
Seven at the Golden Shovel.

We real cool. We
Left school. We

Lurk late. We
Strike straight. We

Sing sin. We
Thin gin. We

Jazz June. We
Die soon.

[1960]

EXPLORING THE TEXT

1. Why do you think Gwendolyn Brooks chose to attach the epigraph "The Pool Players. Seven at the Golden Shovel" to her poem? How did this information — coming where it does at the beginning of the text — influence your reading of the poem?
2. How many times is the pronoun "We" repeated in the poem? What does the placement of the pronoun suggest about the poet's attitude toward the young men? What does the repetition and placement of "We" suggest about the pool players' sense of themselves — their identity?
3. How does Brooks's use of monosyllabic words, alliteration, and internal rhyme contribute to your understanding of these "cool" young men?
4. In an interview in *Contemporary Literature* 11:1 (Winter 1970), Brooks offers stage directions for how "We Real Cool" should be read aloud:

   > First of all, let me tell you how that's supposed to be said, because there's a reason why I set it out as I did. These are people who are essentially saying "Kilroy is here. We are." But they're a little uncertain of the strength of their identity. The "We" — you're supposed to stop

after the "We" and think about their validity, and of course there's no way for you to tell whether it should be said softly or not, I suppose, but I say it rather softly because I want to represent their basic uncertainty, which they don't bother to question every day, of course.

How do the poet's instructions contribute to your experience of the poem?

5. What does this poem's abrupt and rapid-fire rhythm suggest about these young men's lives?
6. In his 1942 painting entitled *Pool Parlor*, artist Jacob Lawrence depicts a group of young men playing the game. In what ways is his depiction similar to and different from that of Brooks's characterization? Pay special attention to the sense of risk that Brooks expresses; to what extent does Lawrence suggest a similar menace — or does he?

Identity Card

MAHMOUD DARWISH

Translated from Arabic by Denys Johnson-Davies

One of the most prominent poets of the Arab world, Mahmoud Darwish (1941–2008) was born in what was then the British Mandate of Palestine. When Egypt, Iraq, Jordan, Lebanon, and Syria declared war on the newly established State of Israel, following the 1948 termination of the British Mandate, Darwish's family fled to Lebanon. When they returned two years later, their village had been destroyed, they had missed a census, and they had lost their citizenship. Darwish's political activities, in addition to his lack of citizenship, resulted in several arrests, and eventually exile. He later served on the executive committee of the controversial Palestinian Liberation Organization (PLO). His first book of poetry, *Asafir bila ajnihah* (*Sparrows without Wings*), was published when he was nineteen. He wrote in Arabic but spoke French, English, and Hebrew. In an interview in 2000, Darwish described how he viewed the intersection of poetry and politics: "I don't think there is any role for poetry [in a Palestinian state]. Poems can't establish a state. But they can establish a metaphorical homeland in the minds of the people. I think my poems have built some houses in this landscape." In 2008, he was given the equivalent of a state funeral by the Palestine Authority and was buried in Ramallah. Written in 1964, "Identity Card" was inspired by an incident in which an Israeli soldier asked Darwish for his papers.

Put it on record.
    I am an Arab
And the number of my card is fifty thousand
I have eight children
And the ninth is due after summer.
What's there to be angry about?

Put it on record.
    I am an Arab
Working with comrades of toil in a quarry.
I have eight children
For them I wrest the loaf of bread,
The clothes and exercise books
From the rocks
And beg for no alms at your door,
    Lower not myself at your doorstep.
    What's there to be angry about?

Put it on record.
    I am an Arab.
I am a name without a title,
Patient in a country where everything
Lives in a whirlpool of anger.
    My roots
    Took hold before the birth of time
    Before the burgeoning of the ages,
    Before cypress and olive trees,
    Before the proliferation of weeds.

My father is from the family of the plough
    Not from highborn nobles.
And my grandfather was a peasant
    Without line or genealogy.
My house is a watchman's hut
    Made of sticks and reeds.
Does my status satisfy you?
    I am a name without a surname.

Put it on record.
    I am an Arab.
Colour of hair: jet black.
Colour of eyes: brown.
My distinguishing features:
    On my head the *'iqal* cords over a *keffiyeh*[1]
    Scratching him who touches it.
My address:
    I'm from a village, remote, forgotten,
    Its streets without name
    And all its men in the fields and quarry.
    What's there to be angry about?

Put it on record.
    I am an Arab.
You stole my forefathers' vineyards
    And land I used to till,
    I and all my children,
    And you left us and all my grandchildren
    Nothing but these rocks.
    Will your government be taking them too
    As is being said?

So!
    Put it on record at the top of page one:
    I don't hate people,
    I trespass on no one's property.

And yet, if I were to become hungry
    I shall eat the flesh of my usurper.
    Beware, beware of my hunger
    And of my anger!

[1964/1980]

[1] A *keffiyeh* is a traditional Arab headdress. It is held in place by a cord called an *'iqal*. — EDS.

EXPLORING THE TEXT

1. Think about the identity cards you carry (driver's license, school ID). Why do you carry these cards? What do they reveal about your identity? What information does and does not appear there? Given only the information listed on your identity cards, what might a stranger assume about your identity?
2. To whom does the poem seem to be addressed? Support your view with specific evidence from the poem.
3. What effect does the repetition of the lines "Put it on record. / I am an Arab" have on you as a reader? How does the repetition contribute to the poem's meaning?
4. The meaning of the line "What's there to be angry about?" (ll. 6, 16, and 46) becomes increasingly ironic as the poem progresses. Discuss how these six words shift in meaning depending on their placement within the poem.
5. Explain how "And yet" in line 60 marks a turning point in the poem and a warning from the speaker to his audience.
6. Do some research on the history of Arab-Israeli relations. How does your research change your reading of this poem?

Ogun

KAMAU BRATHWAITE

Edward Kamau (E. K.) Brathwaite (b. 1930) is a poet, playwright, critic, and historian whose work explores the links between his West Indian and African heritages. Born and raised on the Caribbean island of Barbados, he was educated at Pembroke College, Cambridge, and received his PhD from the University of Sussex. Recipient of both Guggenheim and Fulbright fellowships and winner of numerous awards, Brathwaite worked in the Ministry of Education in Ghana and has taught at the University of the West Indies, the University of Nairobi, Boston University, and Yale University. He is currently a professor emeritus of comparative literature at New York University. Brathwaite's publications include *The Arrivants: A New World Trilogy* (1973), *Black + Blues* (1976), *Mother Poem* (1977), *Sun Poem* (1982), *X/Self* (1987), and *The Zea Mexican Diary* (1993). His 2006 collection of poetry, *Born to Slow Horses*, won the International Griffin Poetry Prize. Part of the judges' citation read: "Here political realities turn into musical complexities, voices overlap, history becomes mythology, spirits appear in photographs." Much of his poetry celebrates the oral tradition and shows the influence of jazz, particularly the works of Charlie Parker and John Coltrane. In the following poem, Brathwaite meditates on the preference for the new over the traditional — represented here by Ogun, the Yoruba and Afro-Caribbean creator-god.

My uncle made chairs, tables, balanced doors on, dug out
coffins, smoothing the white wood out

with plane and quick sandpaper until
it shone like his short-sighted glasses.

The knuckles of his hands were silvered knobs of nails hit, hurt and flat-

tened out with blast of heavy hammer. He was knock-knee'd, flat-
footed and his clip clop sandals slapped across the concrete

flooring of his little shop where canefield mulemen and a fleet
of Bedford lorry drivers dropped in to scratch themselves and talk.

There was no shock of wood, no beam
of light mahogany his saw teeth couldn't handle.

When shaping squares for locks, a key hole
care tapped rat tat tat upon the handle

of his humpbacked chisel. Cold
world of wood caught fire as he whittled: rectangle

window frames, the intersecting x of folding chairs, triangle

trellises, the donkey
box-cart in its squeaking square.

But he was poor and most days he was hungry.
Imported cabinets with mirrors, formica table

tops, spine-curving chairs made up of tubes, with hollow
steel-like bird bones that sat on rubber ploughs,

thin beds, stretched not on boards, but blue high-tensioned cables,
were what the world preferred.

And yet he had a block of wood that would have baffled them.
With knife and gimlet care he worked away at this on Sundays,

explored its knotted hurts, cutting his way
along its yellow whorls until his hands could feel

how it had swelled and shivered, breathing air,
its weathered green burning rings of time,

its contoured grain still tuned to roots and water.
And as he cut, he heard the creak of forests:

green lizard faces gulped, grey memories with moth
eyes watched him from their shadows, soft

liquid tendrils leaked among the flowers
and a black rigid thunder he had never heard within his hammer

came stomping up the trunks. And as he worked within his shattered
Sunday shop, the wood took shape: dry shuttered

eyes, slack anciently everted lips, flat
ruined face, eaten by pox, ravaged by rat

and woodworm, dry cistern mouth, cracked
gullet crying for the desert, the heavy black

enduring jaw; lost pain, lost iron;
emerging woodwork image of his anger.

[1969]

EXPLORING THE TEXT

1. What is the literal situation being described in this poem? Who is the subject, and what is he doing?
2. Read the poem aloud and just try to listen. How does the sound affect your understanding? Identify and discuss the effects of alliteration, onomatopoeia, and line breaks.
3. The poem contains references to the tools of both the carpenter's and the sculptor's craft. Does this specialized language enhance your response to the poem, or is it a distraction? Consider terms such as "plane" (l. 3) and "gimlet" (l. 28).
4. Identify the figurative language in the poem. There is a great deal of concrete descriptive detail but few actual figures of speech. Why do you think the poet chose to use so few metaphors and similes?
5. The poem has a three-part structure: the opening, a transition, and a final section. Where are these divisions? How does this structure reinforce the ideas or themes of the poem?
6. The poem is narrated by an outside observer, a family member describing the subject. What is the relationship between the speaker, the title, and the subject? How would the overall impact of the poem change if the subject himself were the speaker?
7. How do you interpret the ending of the poem, beginning with line 39: "And as he worked . . ."? Try crafting a sentence that could serve as the thesis for an interpretive essay on "Ogun."

Caribe in Nueva York

NATHALIE HANDAL

Nathalie Handal (b. 1969) — a Palestinian American poet, playwright, editor, and critic — has lived in Europe, the United States, the Caribbean, Latin America, and the Middle East, and is fluent in several languages. After earning a BA in international relations and communications at Simmons College in Boston and an MFA at Bennington College in Vermont, she did postgraduate work at the University of London in English and drama. Based in New York City and Paris, she is currently a professor at Columbia University and part of the Low-Residency MFA Faculty at Sierra Nevada College. Handal has published several poetry collections and is the editor of *The Poetry of Arab Women: A Contemporary Anthology* (2000), which won the PEN Oakland/Josephine Miles Award. Handal coedited with Tina Chang and Ravi Shankar *Language for a New Century: Contemporary Poetry from the Middle East, Asia, and Beyond* (2008). An active theater director and producer, Handal has been a playwright-in-residence for the New York Theatre Workshop and Vassar College. Her most recent works have been produced at the John F. Kennedy Center for the Performing Arts, the Bush Theatre, and Westminster Abbey in London. Her debut collection, *The Lives of Rain* (2005), includes a series of poems on the consequences of displacement in Palestine itself as well as others on the Palestinian diaspora. In the following poem from that collection, she explores the experience of multiple identities, a theme that runs throughout her work.

Un Caribeño tells me:
we are spoiled here
we eat burgers, fries
arroz y habichuelas negras, plátanos[1]
for two dollars and ninety-nine cents
others starve, looking for a few bits —
We forget hunger . . .
I love America
but I dream of mangoes
Café Santo Domingo, merengue,
salsa, bachata, son[2]
I can't forget the sun on my back
in my eyes
but this is Nueva York in winter
and I can't see the beautiful brown legs
of *las mulatas* [3]
can't see their curves as they move
in the streets of Brooklyn, Bronx,
in the Upper West
Washington Heights . . .
Now I eat at Lenny's Bagels and Gray's Papaya
I look at the Hudson
instead of the Caribbean waters, *los malecones.*[4]
Proud of Gloria, Shakira, Mark, JLo
Juan Luís Guerra, Celia Cruz [5] . . .
I dream of *la tierra* [6]
where we were born,
I walk Central Park
with our islands in my pockets
and my gloves on.

[2005]

[1] *arroz,* rice; *habichuelas negras,* black beans; *plátanos,* plantains.
[2] *son,* typical music from Cuba.
[3] women of multiracial heritage. — EDS.
[4] *los malecones,* waterfront boulevards.
[5] Gloria, Shakira, Mark, JLo, Juan Luís Guerra, Celia Cruz are all Latino performers/musicians.
[6] *tierra,* land.

EXPLORING THE TEXT

1. Who are the two speakers in the poem?
2. Identify at least three different cultures or ethnicities referred to directly or indirectly through allusion. How does Nathalie Handal refer to them (e.g., language, food, place)? How do these contribute to the point Handal is making?
3. The speaker alternates between first-person singular and plural. Who are "we" or "our" meant to include?
4. How do you interpret the juxtaposition of the following lines: "We forget hunger . . . / I love America" (ll. 7–8)? Is Handal's speaker callous? resigned? arrogant? ambivalent?
5. What is Handal's purpose in using Spanish in this poem? In the notes, she explains some of the language and allusions but not everything. Why? Depending on whether or not you knew the meaning of "Un Caribeño" (a male from the Caribbean), how would your understanding or experience of the poem change?
6. What is the meaning of the final image — "our islands in my pockets / and my gloves on" (ll. 29–30)? Is this a sad or a hopeful image? Explain whether you find it a fitting way to close the poem.

The Facts of Art

NATALIE DIAZ

Natalie Diaz (b. 1978) is an American poet and language activist. She is Mojave and an enrolled member of the Gila River Indian community. After attending Old Dominion University in Norfolk, Virginia, on an athletic scholarship, Diaz went on to play professional basketball in Austria, Portugal, Spain, Sweden, and Turkey. She returned to Old Dominion

University and earned an MFA in writing. Her debut book of poetry, *When My Brother Was an Aztec* (2012), powerfully evokes the Native American experience by blending of personal and mythical imagery. Diaz's work has been featured in *Best New Poets*, and she received the Nimrod/Hardman Pablo Neruda Prize for Poetry and the Tobias Wolff Award for Fiction. She is part of the Institute of American Indian Arts low-residency MFA faculty in Santa Fe, New Mexico, and currently splits her time between Princeton, New Jersey, and Mohave Valley, Arizona, where she works with the last speakers of the Mojave language to teach and revitalize the Mojave language. "The Facts of Art," from her debut collection of poetry, uses vivid imagery to reveal the brutal history that is often hidden by western conceptions of art.

woven plaque basket with sunflower design, Hopi,
Arizona, before 1935

from an American Indian basketry exhibit in
Portsmouth, Virginia

The Arizona highway sailed across the desert —
a gray battleship drawing a black wake,
halting at the foot of the orange mesa,
unwilling to go around.

Hopi men and women — brown, and small, and claylike
— peered down from their tabletops at yellow tractors, water trucks,
and white men blistered with sun — red as fire ants — towing
sunscreen-slathered wives in glinting Airstream trailers
in caravans behind them.

Elders knew these BIA[1] roads were bad medicine — knew too
that young men listen less and less, and these young Hopi men
needed work, hence set aside their tools, blocks of cottonwood root
and half-finished Koshari the clown katsinas,[2] then
signed on with the Department of Transportation,

were hired to stab drills deep into the earth's thick red flesh
on First Mesa[3], drive giant sparking blades across the mesas' faces,
run the drill bits so deep they smoked, bearding all the Hopi men
in white — *Bad spirits,* said the Elders —

The blades caught fire, burned out — *Ma'saw[4] is angry,* the Elders said.
New blades were flown in by helicopter. While Elders dreamed
their arms and legs had been cleaved off and their torsos were flung
over the edge of a dinner table, the young Hopi men went
back to work cutting the land into large chunks of rust.

[1] Bureau of Indian Affairs. — EDS.
[2] Katsinas, in Hopi religious tradition, are dolls carved out of cottonwood root into depictions of the Katsinam, or Hopi spirit messengers. Koshari is a trickster katsina. — EDS.
[3] One of three mesas that unite the system of villages on the Arizona Hopi Reservation. — EDS.
[4] A Hopi deity who serves as guardian of the earth. — EDS.

Nobody noticed at first — not the white workers,
not the Indian workers — but in the mounds of dismantled mesa,
among the clods and piles of sand,
lay the small gray bowls of babies' skulls.

Not until they climbed to the bottom did they see
the silvered bones glinting from the freshly sliced dirt-and-rock wall —
a mausoleum mosaic, a sick tapestry: the tiny remains
roused from death's dusty cradle, cut in half, cracked,
wrapped in time-tattered scraps of blankets.

Let's call it a day, the white foreman said.
That night, all the Indian workers got sad-drunk — got sick
— while Elders sank to their kivas[5] in prayer. Next morning,
as dawn festered on the horizon, state workers scaled the mesas,
knocked at the doors of pueblos that had them, hollered
into those without them,

demanding the Hopi men come back to work — then begging them —
then buying them whiskey — begging again — finally sending their white
wives up the dangerous trail etched into the steep sides
to buy baskets from Hopi wives and grandmothers
as a sign of treaty.

When that didn't work, the state workers called the Indians lazy,
sent their sunhat-wearing wives back up to buy more baskets —
katsinas too — then called the Hopis *good-for-nothings,*
before begging them back once more.

We'll try again in the morning, the foreman said.
But the Indian workers never returned —
The BIA's and DOT's[6] calls to work went unanswered,
as the fevered Hopis stayed huddled inside.

The small bones half-buried in the crevices of mesa —
in the once-holy darkness of silent earth and always-night —
smiled or sighed beneath the moonlight, while white women
in Airstream trailers wrote letters home

praising their husbands' patience, describing the lazy savages:
such squalor in their stone and plaster homes — cobs of corn stacked
floor to ceiling against crumbling walls — their devilish ceremonies
and the barbaric way they buried their babies,
oh, and those beautiful, beautiful baskets.

[2012]

---

[5]Large rooms, either partially or wholly underground, used for Hopi religious ceremonies. — EDS.

[6]Department of Transportation. — EDS.

EXPLORING THE TEXT

1. Note that the Hopi men *and* women are presented together in line 5; not so the Elders and the young men, and not so the white men and their wives. How does the poet characterize each of these groups? Why might she have chosen to establish these contrasts early in the poem?
2. How does the figurative language set the scene and contribute to the tone and mood in the first two stanzas?
3. At first the state workers try what might be considered bribery to convince the Hopis to return to work. When that fails, they resort to derision. What might Natalie Diaz be suggesting by this swift change in their perspective?
4. Pay close attention to the syntax and structure of the poem. Why do you think Diaz chose to write such complex sentences, breaking them across both lines and stanzas? What mood does this help create? What does it suggest about the poet's attitude toward the events the poem describes?
5. The image of white women in Airstream trailers appears both near the beginning and end of the poem: first, as the white men are arriving, "towing /sunscreen-slathered wives in glinting Airstream trailers" (ll. 7-8); then, after the Hopis refused to return to work, "white women/in Airstream trailers wrote letters home" (ll. 54–55). Compare and contrast the context in which each of these images appear. Why do you think Diaz chose to repeat this image in particular? What effect does each image, taken on its own, have on the poem? What effect do the images have when taken together?
6. The final two stanzas are expressed in a single cumulative sentence that includes a lengthy adverbial clause beginning in line 54. What is the effect of the poet's decision to conclude the poem with an account of the white women's letters home rather than the "small bones" (l.52)? Explain.
7. Now that you've read the poem, what do you make of the title? What, in the context of this poem, are the "facts" of art? How does the title express or relate to the themes the poem explores?
8. What do the Hopi baskets represent? What elements of style does Diaz use to convey that meaning to readers?

Dolorosa

MOLLY ROSE QUINN

Molly Rose Quinn (b. 1988) is an American poet who was raised in Memphis, Tennessee. She earned an MFA in poetry from Sarah Lawrence College, and her poems have appeared in *Black Warrior Review*, *The Offing*, *PEN Poetry Series*, and elsewhere. Quinn has taught writing at the Sackett Street Writers' Workshop and co-organizes the Moby-Dick Marathon NYC, an annual marathon reading of Melville's classic novel. She is currently the director of public programming at Housing Works Bookstore Café, a volunteer-run nonprofit bookstore in Manhattan dedicated to fighting AIDS and homelessness. In "Dolorosa," Quinn evokes the wildness of adolescence in the context of a rigid religious tradition.

(The Chapel at St. Mary's School for Girls)

where the pillar falls at the edge of morning the teachers
beg us to tug down our skirts they offer their palms
for our gumballs and your god is here to say that beauty
is easy like cutting teeth and your legs and your legs
and yours and I in the pew wish to scrape down
to nothing cuff myself kneel better and what could be

worthier hair voice and loudly I beg for ascendancy
dear classmates your legs in neat rows pray as you do
with fists up and the sun in here bare pray for safety
the teen saint she is the girl to win it all for I beg my
mariology[1] as she sets the way that girl she never once
begged for sparing she begged for death like wine
she begged the best she supplicated she died this dying
begs for me I give it such pleasure and legs and the pew
and the alb[2] and the bread and all other objects beg to be
candles when you are a candle you can beg to be lit
each of you in the pew you beg to be lit I'll never shine
bigger as we know teenagers beg to be begged and we do
you girls you begged me to hold you begged me to take
what I took you beg bigger and better and for that
you'll be queens the chimes chime and bells bell
and dear god I know I can be the greatest girl ever
by anointing all alone and being loved the very best
and she says what is so good about anger god killed
my son for himself I suppose and this halo it's nothing
I asked for and of course she'll be lying and your legs
and your legs and yours tanned and the best thing all year.

[2013]

---

[1] The study of the Virgin Mary. — EDS.

[2] A white garment worn by leaders in the Catholic church. — EDS.

EXPLORING THE TEXT

1. This poem is notable for its odd juxtapositions and jumbles of objects and images. For example, consider the "legs and the pew / and the alb and the bread" (ll. 14-15). What is the intent and effect of this technique? Explain, using at least two examples from the poem.
2. What effect does the poem's run-on, stream-of-consciousness style have on your interpretation of its meaning? How does it help shape the mood of the poem?
3. How does the tone shift after the speaker says, "dear classmates your legs in neat rows pray as you do / with fists up and the sun in here bare pray for safety" (ll. 8-9)? Explain.
4. Who is "she" in line 24? What is significant about the statement the speaker attributes to her?
5. In an interview for web-based Brooklyn Poets, Molly Rose Quinn said, "More than church this is a poem of womanhood. The legs and hair." What do you think Quinn means by that? How do the language and structure of the poem reflect your understanding of this statement?
6. The word "begs" (or forms of it) appears more than a dozen times in this poem. Similarly, "legs" appears several times as well. What is the effect of such repetition and rhyme? How does it contribute to your understanding of the poem?
7. How would you characterize the speaker of the poem? What is the speaker's attitude toward the church? womanhood? her teachers? her classmates?
8. According to the author, the title of the poem "refers to *STABAT MATER DOLOROSA*, a thirteenth-century hymn, a meditation on the suffering of Mary during the crucifixion of Christ." Why might Quinn have decided to name the poem after that song, which translates as "the mother stood weeping"? In what ways does the poem explore themes of suffering and faith?

Written by Himself

GREGORY PARDLO

Gregory Pardlo (b. 1968) is an American poet whose second volume of poetry, *Digest,* won the 2015 Pulitzer Prize for Poetry. *Digest* was also shortlisted for the 2015 NAACP Image Award and was a finalist for the Hurston-Wright Legacy Award. His first book of poems, *Totem*, won the *American Poetry Review*/Honickman Prize in 2007, and he also translated *Pencil of Rays and Spiked Mace* (2004) by the Danish poet Niels Lyngsø. Pardlo grew up in Willingboro, New Jersey, and received a BA in English from Rutgers University–Camden and an MFA from New York University. In 2016, Pardlo moved from his teaching post at Columbia University to Rutgers University-Camden. "Written by Himself," selected for *The Best American Poetry* (2010), blends myth and modernity to evoke the act of self-creation.

I was born in minutes in a roadside kitchen a skillet
whispering my name. I was born to rainwater and lye;
I was born across the river where I
was borrowed with clothespins, a harrow tooth,[1]
broadsides[2] sewn in my shoes. I returned, though
it please you, through no fault of my own,
pockets filled with coffee grounds and eggshells.
I was born still and superstitious; I bore an unexpected burden.
I gave birth, I gave blessing, I gave rise to suspicion.
I was born abandoned outdoors in the heat-shaped air,
air drifting like spirits and old windows.
I was born a fraction and a cipher and a ledger entry;
I was an index of first lines when I was born.
I was born waist-deep stubborn in the water crying
                    ain't I a woman and a brother I was born
to this hall of mirrors, this horror story I was
born with a prologue of references, pursued
by mosquitoes and thieves, I was born passing
off the problem of the twentieth century: I was born.
I read minds before I could read fishes and loaves;[3]
I walked a piece of the way alone before I was born.

[2014]

---

[1] A piece of farm equipment used to make plowed land level. — EDS.

[2] A large sheet of paper with a public announcement printed on one side. — EDS.

[3] A reference to the biblical story in which Jesus feeds five thousand people with only two fish and five loaves of bread. — EDS.

EXPLORING THE TEXT

1. *The Narrative of the Life of Frederick Douglass,* an 1845 autobiography by the former slave who became a leader in the abolition movement, often appears with the subtitle *Written by Himself*. Why do you think Gregory Pardlo took that phrase as the title for his poem? How does knowing that influence your understanding and appreciation of the poem?
2. What might Pardlo mean by "I was born"? What is the effect of the anaphora, or repetition, of that phrase? Why do you think the poet chose to use that phrase to both open and conclude the poem?
3. The poem presents a collage of both related and seemingly unrelated images. Which ones might refer to literal experiences? Which ones are most mysterious? Explain.
4. Carefully note Pardlo's inconsistent use of punctuation. What do you make of the enjambment in lines 5 to 6 and again in lines 18 to 19? How does this technique help reinforce the poem's meaning?
5. Pardlo has said, "I accept that my identity is a digest of discourses and that my engagement with the world is mediated through these discourses." How does the poem, and especially the voice of its speaker, reflect that statement? What discourses are present in the poem, and how do they mediate the poet's communication with the reader?

Half-Mexican

JUAN FELIPE HERRERA

Juan Felipe Herrera (b. 1948) is a poet, performer, writer, cartoonist, teacher, and activist. He has been the United States poet laureate since 2015. The son of farm workers, Herrera grew up in California's San Joaquín and Salinas Valleys. He earned a BA in social anthropology from the University of California, Los Angeles, and an MFA from the Iowa Writers' Workshop. Herrera's publications include fourteen collections of poetry and eleven other books of prose, short stories, young adult novels, and picture books for children. His 2007 book *187 Reasons Mexicanos Can't Cross the Border: Undocuments 1971–2007* blends both Spanish and English text to examine cultural hybridity along the U.S.–Mexico border. His numerous awards include a Guggenheim Fellowship, two National Endowment for the Arts Fellowships, and the 2008 National Book Critics Circle Award in poetry for *Half the World in Light*. In 2012, Herrera was appointed California poet laureate by Governor Jerry Brown. He currently holds the Tomás Rivera Endowed Chair in the Creative Writing Department at the University of California, Riverside, and directs the Art and Barbara Culver Center for the Arts in Riverside. "Half-Mexican," from his most recent collection of poetry, *Notes on the Assemblage* (2015), explores the dual consciousness of Mexican American identity.

Odd to be a half-Mexican, let me put it this way
I am Mexican + Mexican, then there's the question of the half
To say Mexican without the half, well it means another thing
One could say *only Mexican*

Then think of pyramids — obsidian flaw, flame etchings, goddesses with
Flayed visages claw feet & skulls as belts — these are not Mexican
They are existences, that is to say
Slavery, sinew, hearts shredded sacrifices for the continuum
Quarks[1] & galaxies, the cosmic milk that flows into trees
Then darkness

What is the other — yes
It is Mexican too, yet it is formless, it is speckled with particles
European pieces? To say colony or power is incorrect
Better to think of Kant[2] in his tiny room
Shuffling in his black socks seeking out the notion of time
Or Einstein re-working the erroneous equation[3]
Concerning the way light bends — all this has to do with
The half, the half-thing when you are a half-being

Time
Light

How they stalk you & how you beseech them
All this becomes your lifelong project, that is
You are Mexican. One half Mexican the other half
Mexican, then the half against itself.

[2015]

[1] Subatomic particles that combine to form protons and neutrons. — EDS.
[2] Immanuel Kant (1724–1804) was a German philosopher, often considered the central figure of modern philosophy. — EDS.
[3] Albert Einstein's well-known Theory of Relativity, summarized by the equation $E = mc^2$, has since been proven incorrect. — EDS.

EXPLORING THE TEXT

1. Juan Felipe Herrera writes "One could say *only Mexican* / Then think of pyramids — obsidian flaw, flame etchings, goddesses with / Flayed visages claw feet & skulls as belts — these are not Mexican / They are existences . . ." (ll. 4-7). What point do you think Herrera makes in those lines? To what extent does the poem contradict itself in later lines? How does it explore and clarify the meaning of "Mexican"?
2. Discussing his early reading of poetry in an interview with the *New York Times*, Herrera has said, "Any poem that said, 'Hello, I'm here, how are you?' was one I didn't even want to read. I wanted to fly with symbols and metaphors and see trees in the shape of flying saucers." How does "Half-Mexican" live up to the poet's requirements for poetry? Explain.
3. Select what you consider to be the most striking image in the poem. How does it contribute to the overall effect that the poem has on you?
4. If you were to divide this poem into two distinct poems, where would you do so, and what title would you give to each? How is the speaker's persona affected by this division? Explain.
5. What do the references to Kant and Einstein suggest about how the speaker sees himself? About his relationship to the world around him?

6. This poem may at first strike the reader as confusing — perhaps intentionally so. In a *New York Times* review of Herrera's poems, Harvard professor Stephen Burt writes, "Trying to break down old borders and orders, Herrera risks making his poetry, simply, a mess. . . . Herrera's best work seems not formless but endlessly fertile, open-ended, full of beginnings. . . ." Is this poem "a mess"? Or is it "fertile" but not "formless"? Explain, using the text of the poem to support your response.

PAIRED POEMS

When I consider how my light is spent

JOHN MILTON

Often grouped with William Shakespeare and Geoffrey Chaucer as one of the giants of English literature, John Milton (1608–1674) is best known for his epic poem *Paradise Lost*. He studied independently for five years after receiving his MA from Cambridge University, then traveled through Europe. When he returned to England, the country was in a state of flux. Milton supported the Puritans and Oliver Cromwell and wrote pamphlets on many political issues, such as free speech and censorship. Milton's eyesight began to deteriorate, however, and by 1652 he was blind. In 1657, the poet Andrew Marvell — most famous for "To His Coy Mistress" — became his assistant. After the Restoration in 1660, when Charles II resumed the throne, Milton was arrested for his Puritan activities but escaped imprisonment and execution. He devoted the remainder of his life to writing, publishing his masterpiece, *Paradise Lost*, in 1667 and its sequel, *Paradise Regained*, in 1671. "When I consider how my light is spent," written the year Milton lost his sight, is a meditation on that loss.

When I consider how my light is spent,
  Ere half my days, in this dark world and wide,
  And that one talent which is death to hide
  Lodged with me useless, though my soul more bent
To serve therewith my Maker, and present
  My true account, lest he returning chide;
  "Doth God exact day-labor, light denied?"
  I fondly ask; but Patience to prevent
That murmur, soon replies, "God doth not need
  Either man's work or his own gifts; who best
  Bear his mild yoke, they serve him best. His state
Is kingly. Thousands at his bidding speed
  And post o'er land and ocean without rest:
  They also serve who only stand and wait."

[c. 1655]

EXPLORING THE TEXT

1. This poem is structured through several voices. Who is the speaker in lines 1–6? in line 7? in lines 9–14?
2. Milton uses familiar words in ways that are unfamiliar to twenty-first-century readers. What do "bent" (l. 4) and "exact" (l. 7) mean, for instance? What other examples can you find? Define them.
3. What does the speaker mean by the "mild yoke" (l. 11)?
4. How would you describe the movement or change in the speaker's attitude toward his blindness from the beginning to the end of the poem?
5. The last line of the poem is frequently quoted as a kind of motto for those who are not in the midst of action but are nevertheless involved, whether the situation is war or a more personal plight. Explain why you think Milton would find this use of the line true to his poem.

A Blind Man

JORGE LUIS BORGES

Translated by Alastair Reid

Jorge Luis Borges (1899–1986) was an extremely influential Argentine short-story writer, essayist, poet, translator, and figure in Spanish-language literature. When Borges was fifteen, his family left Argentina for Switzerland, where Borges was educated at the Collège de Genève. He returned to Argentina in 1921 and began publishing poems and stories. Borges's best-known books, *Ficciones* (1944) and *El Aleph* (1949), are compilations of short stories interconnected by common themes, including dreams, labyrinths, mirrors, philosophy, and religion. He is considered one of the first writers to embrace magical realism — a genre in which realistic narrative seamlessly blends with elements of fantasy. In 1955, he was appointed director for the National Public Library and professor of English literature at the University of Buenos Aires. In 1961, he gained international reknown by winning the Formentor group's first *Prix International* prize, which he shared with playwright Samuel Beckett. In 1971, Borges won the Jerusalem Prize for the Freedom of the Individual in Society. Borges went completely blind when he was fifty-five, an event the speaker of "A Blind Man" contemplates as he considers the impact of perception on identity.

I do not know what face is looking back
whenever I look at the face in the mirror;
I do not know what old face seeks its image
in silent and already weary anger.
Slow in my blindness, with my hand I feel
the contours of my face. A flash of light
gets through to me. I have made out your hair,

color of ash and at the same time, gold.
I say again that I have lost no more
than the inconsequential skin of things.
These wise words come from Milton, and are noble,
but then I think of letters and of roses.
I think, too, that if I could see my features,
I would know who I am, this precious afternoon.

[1975/1999]

EXPLORING THE TEXT

1. How would you describe the speaker in the poem? What is he doing, and why?
2. What is the effect of the oxymoron in line 4?
3. The speaker states, "I have lost no more/than the inconsequential skin of things" (ll. 8–9). Is the idea presented in those lines contradicted by that presented in the concluding couplet? Explain.
4. How would you describe the tone of this poem? How would you explain the mood?

FOCUS ON COMPARISON AND CONTRAST

1. In "A Blind Man," Jorge Luis Borges refers to "wise words . . . from Milton" that "are noble" (l. 11). Based on your reading of "When I consider how my light is spent," what are the noble and wise words to which Borges refers?
2. How effective would "When I consider how my light is spent" be as a title for Borges's poem? How effective would "A Blind Man" be as the title of Milton's? How do these two titles underscore the differences in each speaker's attitude toward his blindness?
3. These poems share both a similar form and similar subject. How else are they alike? How do they differ in their approach? How would you describe the tone and mood of each?

WRITING ASSIGNMENT

In each of these poems, the speaker explores his identity after losing his sight. Write an essay that compares and contrasts the two poems. Considering the fact that Borges refers to Milton's poem, discuss the attitudes each speaker expresses toward his blindness, analyzing the style elements each writer uses to present that attitude.

History Lesson and Southern History

NATASHA TRETHEWEY

Natasha Trethewey (b. 1966) is a Pulitzer Prize–winning American poet. She grew up in Mississippi and went on to study at the University of Georgia, Hollins University, and the University of Massachusetts, Amherst. Trethewey's first book, *Domestic Work* (2000), won the First Annual Cave Canem Foundation Poetry Prize. Trethewey is the author of four other books of poetry, including *Native Guard* (2006), for which she won the 2007 Pulitzer Prize for Poetry. In 2012 Trethewey was named both the United States poet laureate and the poet laureate of Mississippi. Trethewey has also earned fellowships from the National Endowment for the Arts, the John Simon Guggenheim Memorial Foundation, and the Rockefeller Foundation. Her poetry is known for its blending of free verse with traditional forms like the sonnet and villanelle. In both "Southern History" and "History Lesson," Trethewey uses concise, evocative imagery and lyricism to paint two memories that explore the legacy of race in America.

History Lesson

I am four in this photograph, standing
on a wide strip of Mississippi beach,
my hands on the flowered hips

of a bright bikini. My toes dig in,
curl around wet sand. The sun cuts
the rippling Gulf in flashes with each

tidal rush. Minnows dart at my feet
glinting like switchblades. I am alone
except for my grandmother, other side

of the camera, telling me how to pose.
It is 1970, two years after they opened
the rest of this beach to us,

forty years since the photograph
where she stood on a narrow plot
of sand marked *colored,* smiling,

her hands on the flowered hips
of a cotton meal-sack dress.

[2000]

EXPLORING THE TEXT

1. What is the dramatic situation presented in the poem? What is the speaker doing as she speaks the lines to the reader?
2. How much of what the speaker says is from observation and how much is from memory? Explain, using language from the poem.
3. What is the effect of the contrasting images of the "wide strip," (l. 2) and the "narrow plot" (l. 14)?
4. Why does the poet repeat "flowered hips" in lines 3 and 16? How does the repetition of the image help convey the speaker's attitude toward each of the two photographs described?
5. Why do you think the poem is titled "History Lesson"? What lesson does the poem teach?

Southern History

Before the war, they were happy, he said,
quoting our textbook. (This was senior-year

history class.) *The slaves were clothed, fed,*
and better off under a master's care.

I watched the words blur on the page. No one
raised a hand, disagreed. Not even me.

It was late; we still had Reconstruction
to cover before the test, and — luckily —

three hours of watching *Gone with the Wind.*
History, the teacher said, *of the old South —*

a true account of how things were back then.
On screen a slave stood big as life: big mouth,

bucked eyes, our textbook's grinning proof — a lie
my teacher guarded. Silent, so did I.

[2006]

EXPLORING THE TEXT

1. Why do you believe the poet says that the words from the textbook "blur on the page" (l. 5)? Is it because the lesson is dull or boring, as the anticipation that "luckily" there was to be a "three hour" movie might suggest, or is there another reason (ll. 8–9)? Explain.
2. What is the implication of the statement, "we still had Reconstruction / to cover before the test" (ll. 7–8)?
3. What is the "lie" in line 13? Explain.
4. The speaker uses the phrases "Not even me" (l. 6) and "so did I" (l. 14) to describe her inaction. How do you think the speaker feels about her silence? Why do you think she confesses it? Explain.
5. This poem maintains many features of the sonnet form, but the line breaks do not conform to tradition. Why might the poet deliberately use line breaks to disguise this poem as something other than a sonnet? What does this choice suggest about the speaker's attitude toward the experience the poem describes? Explain.
6. Why do you think the poet makes use of italics in some lines and not in others? What effect does this device have on the tone and mood of the poem?
7. The question of accuracy and bias in history textbooks has recently become a much-debated national issue in the United States. How does Natasha Trethewey's poem, "Southern History," contribute to the discussion of how history is perceived and taught in American classrooms?

FOCUS ON COMPARISON AND CONTRAST

1. While both poems are written in the first person, the speakers have very different voices. How would you compare and contrast the two speakers? Do they share a common concern? Explain.
2. Although the titles differ, both poems are concerned with the idea of "history." It could be said that both poems present a "history lesson." Could "Southern History" as accurately be titled

"History Lesson"? Explain, using details from both poems.

3. The speaker in "Southern History" speaks in the past tense, while "History Lesson" is told in the present tense. How do the different tenses affect the overall tone and meaning of each poem?

WRITING ASSIGNMENT

In each of these poems, Natasha Tretheway reflects on history and its meaning. Write an essay in which you compare and contrast the two works, analyzing how the poet uses resources of language to question just what "history" means.

Where You Fell

JENNIFER FUMIKO CAHILL

Jennifer Fumiko Cahill (b. 1972) is an American writer and a native of New York State. She earned a BA at the University of California, Santa Barbara, and an MFA in writing from Columbia University. Cahill lived in Tokyo for more than a decade, where she taught writing at Temple University's Japan Campus. Her poems have appeared in such journals as *Boulevard*, *Arts and Letters*, *The Southern Review*, *Gulf Coast*, and *Prairie Schooner*, and her fiction has been anthologized in *Tomo: Friendship Through Fiction — An Anthology of Japan Teen Stories*. In "Where You Fell," which won the 2007 Robert Watson Literary Prize for poetry, Cahill evokes a ritual of grief.

The snow held your shape like bedding,
the shadow of your hand over your head ruined
by the feet of the men who found and carried you.

I stayed in your house for a day, following your habits,
coatless to the shed and back. I finished the wood
you'd begun to split, feeling the heft of the axe

as you felt it. We are always becoming what
we lose. They will say they saw a fox whisper
into your ear. They will never come back.

I pawed the snow to form your hand again,
your sleeping profile. Then I pressed my face
to the mold of your cheek and I became you.

[2007]

EXPLORING THE TEXT

1. Who is the "you" of the title? What has evidently happened to him or her? What might be the speaker's relationship with him or her? How do you know?
2. What might the speaker mean by, "We are always becoming what / we lose" (ll. 7-8)? How does this statement reflect the poem's meaning?
3. What do lines 8-9 — "They will say they saw a fox whisper / into your ear. They will never come back" — suggest about how the speaker views the experience of loss?
4. How would you describe the tone of the poem? Explain, using language from the poem as evidence.

Imprint

DARA BARNAT

Dara Barnat (b. 1979) is an American-Israeli poet and translator who divides her time between New York and Tel Aviv. She earned a PhD from Tel Aviv University, where she teaches poetry and creative writing. Her poems have appeared in *diode*, *Poet Lore*, *Crab Orchard Review*, *Flyway*, and the *Collagist*, and her translations from Hebrew appear or are forthcoming in *Lilith*, *Bridges: A Jewish Feminist Journal*, *International Poetry Review*, *Women in Judaism*, and *Ezra*. Barnat's chapbook, *Headwind Migration*, was released by Pudding House Publications in 2009.

I hear you're gone and I fall with you —

in that place part of me stays,

like a hand in clay,

even as I make rice for dinner, boil water,

measure the grains,

pour wine, set out flowers with all their petals.

The imprint holds the loss of everything.

It holds what we thought was joy.

[2015]

EXPLORING THE TEXT

1. What do you take the first line of the poem to mean?
2. What is the effect of the speaker's description of small mundane rituals in lines 4-6?
3. What kind of paradox does the speaker illustrate in line 7? What is its effect? How does it reflect the poem's meaning?
4. How would you describe the tone of the final line of the poem? How does that final thought affect the poem's meaning? What does it suggest about the speaker?

FOCUS ON COMPARISON AND CONTRAST

1. Compare and contrast the way the speaker of each poem seeks to make a connection with another person. How are the speakers alike? In what ways do they differ?
2. These poems share a common image: that of an imprint that remains visible after the person who made it has left the spot. Discuss the way that each poet uses the image as a central focus, and analyze how that image contributes to the overall effect of each poem.

WRITING ASSIGNMENT

Write an essay in which you compare and contrast "Where You Fell" and "Imprint," analyzing how each poet uses a central image to explore themes of identity and loss.

FIGURATIVE LANGUAGE

As you learned in Chapters 3 and 4, figurative language refers to any language that goes beyond the literal. Such literary devices, or *tropes*, as metaphor, simile, and personification, "turn" meaning of words from the literal to the figurative. These techniques don't exist for the sake of a treasure hunt; they exist because they help writers say what they want to say in a way that is vivid and forceful. They provide meaning beyond the denotation of the words, they elicit emotional responses, they add another level of meaning or nuance, and they bring descriptions to life. Figurative language should not simply be added as decoration or ornamentation to create a more elaborate style. In the best writing, figurative language works subtly to express an idea while opening the work up to interpretation.

Many writers and critics use the term *metaphor* to refer to figurative language in general, as Robert Frost does in his essay "Education by Poetry." He says, "unless you are at home in the metaphor . . . you are not safe anywhere. Because you are not at ease with figurative values: you don't know the metaphor in its strength and its weakness." Frost is pointing out that figurative language deeply influences the way we think and view the world by highlighting relationships among different objects, actions, and ideas.

Sometimes we use figurative language in everyday speech or in our own persuasive writing to appeal to a shared understanding between audience and author. For instance, sports metaphors call on common values; therefore, most of us know what someone means when proclaiming, "We're in a marathon, not a sprint." A writer signals that he believes his life is more than half over when he entitles his memoir *The Fifth Inning*, as did poet E. Ethelbert Miller; and we all know that things are going well when someone declares, "We've got them on the ropes!" These metaphors make sense to us even if we don't know very much about track, baseball, or boxing.

Figurative language is playful, but like a good joke, it takes finesse, and in the hands of a careless writer, it can be pretty dreadful. Websites abound with metaphors that have gone awry. One site featuring bad lines from mystery novels includes, "Her parting words lingered heavily inside me like last night's Taco Bell" and "The killer was a misplaced comma in the jaunty, happy sentence that made up the party crowd." Another site devoted to metaphors from romance novels offers us, "Claire felt swept away by this dark stranger, a helpless dust bunny in the roaring cacophony of his gas-powered leaf blower." Sometimes people just get carried away and mix their metaphors, as did one media figure, who declared, "I knew enough to realize that the alligators were in the swamp and that it was time to circle the wagons."

But who's to say that these are "bad" or "ineffective," while others are original, elegant, and insightful? Sometime it is a matter of taste, time period, or occasion. The more you read and analyze literature, the more astute you will become about what works and what does not, though different interpretations are one of the pleasures of literature. In her book *Illness as Metaphor*, Susan Sontag points out the military metaphors we use to describe cancer: cancer cells are "invasive," and the body's "defenses" must be summoned to "defeat" the "enemy." While she argues that such language "contributes to the excommunicating and stigmatizing of the ill," others might find the metaphors effective because they suggest a battle leading toward victory — and health.

Remember that identifying and naming examples of figurative language are only a small part of analysis; it is their effect on meaning that is important.

In "Where Are You Going, Where Have You Been?" by Joyce Carol Oates, the similes add layers of complexity to the character of Arnold Friend.

> He looked at her. He took off the sunglasses and she saw how pale the skin around his eyes was, like holes that were not in shadow but instead in light. His eyes were like chips of broken glass that catch the light in an amiable way. He smiled.

That his skin looks "like holes" and his eyes look "like chips of broken glass" evokes a sense of unease, hinting at Friend's malevolence. However, the similes also provide images that explain Connie's fascination with Friend: his skin is "not in shadow but instead in light," and the broken glass of his eyes "catch[es] the light in an amiable way."

In "The Facts of Art," Natalie Diaz begins with a metaphor that suggests swift and powerful forward movement:

> The Arizona highway sailed across the desert —
> a gray battleship drawing a black wake,
> halting at the foot of the orange mesa,
> unwilling to go around.

The personification that follows the metaphor imbues that sense of movement with its own will, both expressing a feeling of inevitability and hinting at a looming conflict.

The following exercises will help you begin to analyze figurative language and understand its effects on meaning and clarity. Remember, it is not enough to simply recognize a technique; the effective close reader should understand how that technique creates layers of meaning and provokes an emotional reaction.

EXERCISE 1

In each of the following sentences or excerpts, choose the simile or metaphor that you think is the most meaningful and explain why. Then explain why you think the author used the simile or metaphor he or she did.

1. My mind had been submerged in the foggy lull of my parents' storytelling, and I struggled now with the sharp awakening of memory. ("Apollo")
2. I am a name without a title,
   Patient in a country where everything
   Lives in a whirlpool of anger.
   ("Identity Card")
3. Arnold Friend said, in a gentle-loud voice that was like a stage voice, "The place where you came from ain't there any more, and where you had in mind to go is cancelled out. This place you are now — inside your daddy's house — is nothing but a cardboard box I can knock down any time. You know that and always did know it. You hear me?" ("Where Are You Going, Where Have You Been?")
4. I dream of *la tierra*
   where we were born,
   I walk Central Park
   with our islands in my pockets
   and my gloves on.
   ("Caribe in Nueva York")
5. I came upon him, and, if he had not heard me coming, I would have fallen over him, too, but he got up in time. He rose, unsteady, long, pale, indistinct, like a vapour exhaled by the earth, and

swayed slightly, misty and silent before me; while at my back the fires loomed between the trees, and the murmur of many voices issued from the forest. (*Heart of Darkness*)

6. "Look," Bobby said as the car began to gather speed. He pointed with his finger to the tall trees that lined the road. "Look."

   "Monkeys!" Ronny shrieked. "Wow!"

   They were seated in groups along the branches, with shining black faces, silver bodies, horizontal eyebrows, and crested heads. Their long gray tails dangled like a series of ropes among the leaves. A few scratched themselves with black leathery hands, or swung their feet, staring as the car passed. ("Interpreter of Maladies")

7. But after a time allowed for it to swim,
   Instead of proving human when it neared
   And someone else additional to him
   As a great buck it powerfully appeared,
   Pushing the crumpled water up ahead,
   And landed pouring like a waterfall,
   And stumbled through the rocks with horny tread,
   And forced the underbrush — and that was all.
   ("The Most of It")

EXERCISE 2

Identify the figurative language in the following selections, and then label each as metaphor, simile, personification, apostrophe, metonymy, and so on. Discuss their effects on the meaning of the passage and the ways in which they evoke a response from the reader.

1. Twice a month, like a dutiful son, I visited my parents in Enugu, in their small overfurnished flat that grew dark in the afternoon. Retirement had changed them, shrunk them. They were in their late eighties, both small and mahogany-skinned, with a tendency to stoop. ("Apollo")

2. This Sea that bares her bosom to the moon;
   The winds that will be howling at all hours,
   And are up-gathered now like sleeping flowers;
   For this, for everything, we are out of tune;
   It moves us not.
   ("The World Is Too Much with Us")

3. I was born abandoned outdoors in the heat-shaped air,
   air drifting like spirits and old windows.
   I was born a fraction and a cipher and a ledger entry;
   I was an index of first lines when I was born.
   ("Written by Himself")

4. The whole forest was peopled with frightful sounds — the creaking of the trees, the howling of wild beasts, and the yell of Indians; while sometimes the wind tolled like a distant church bell, and sometimes gave a broad roar around the traveller, as if all Nature were laughing him to scorn. ("Young Goodman Brown")

5. she begged the best she supplicated she died this dying
   begs for me I give it such pleasure and legs and the pew
   and the alb and the bread and all other objects beg to be

candles when you are a candle you can beg to be lit
each of you in the pew you beg to be lit I'll never shine
bigger as we know teenagers beg to be begged
("Dolorosa")

6. Not until they climbed to the bottom did they see
the silvered bones glinting from the freshly sliced dirt-and-rock wall —
a mausoleum mosaic, a sick tapestry: the tiny remains
roused from death's dusty cradle, cut in half, cracked,
wrapped in time-tattered scraps of blankets.
("The Facts of Art")

7. I do not know what face is looking back
whenever I look at the face in the mirror;
I do not know what old face seeks its image
in silent and already weary anger.
("A Blind Man")

8. The yarns of seamen have a direct simplicity, the whole meaning of which lies within the shell of a cracked nut. But Marlow was not typical (if his propensity to spin yarns be excepted), and to him the meaning of an episode was not inside like a kernel but outside, enveloping the tale which brought it out only as a glow brings out a haze, in the likeness of one of these misty halos that sometimes are made visible by the spectral illumination of moonshine. (*Heart of Darkness*)

9. It was a great comfort to turn from that chap to my influential friend, the battered, twisted, ruined, tin-pot steamboat. I clambered on board. She rang under my feet like an empty Huntley & Palmer biscuit-tin kicked along a gutter; she was nothing so solid in make, and rather less pretty in shape, but I had expended enough hard work on her to make me love her. No influential friend would have served me better. She had given me a chance to come out a bit — to find out what I could do. (*Heart of Darkness*)

EXERCISE 3

Following is a passage from *Heart of Darkness* (p. 328). Identify the figurative language and discuss its effect. Focus on why it adds nuance and complexity to the passage rather than simply ornamentation.

> Forthwith a change came over the waters, and the serenity became less brilliant but more profound. The old river in its broad reach rested unruffled at the decline of day, after ages of good service done to the race that peopled its banks, spread out in the tranquil dignity of a waterway leading to the uttermost ends of the earth. We looked at the venerable stream not in the vivid flush of a short day that comes and departs for ever, but in the august light of abiding memories. And indeed nothing is easier for a man who has, as the phrase goes, "followed the sea" with reverence and affection, than to evoke the great spirit of the past upon the lower reaches of the Thames. The tidal current runs to and fro in its unceasing service, crowded with memories of men and ships it had borne to the rest of home or to the battles of the sea. It had known and served all the men of whom the nation is proud, from Sir Francis Drake to Sir John Franklin, knights all, titled

and untitled — the great knights-errant of the sea. It had borne all the ships whose names are like jewels flashing in the night of time, from the *Golden Hind* returning with her round flanks full of treasure, to be visited by the Queen's Highness and thus pass out of the gigantic tale, to the *Erebus* and *Terror*, bound on other conquests — and that never returned. It had known the ships and the men. They had sailed from Deptford, from Greenwich, from Erith — the adventurers and the settlers; kings' ships and the ships of men on 'Change; captains, admirals, the dark "interlopers" of the Eastern trade, and the commissioned "generals" of East India fleets. Hunters for gold or pursuers of fame, they all had gone out on that stream, bearing the sword, and often the torch, messengers of the might within the land, bearers of a spark from the sacred fire. What greatness had not floated on the ebb of that river into the mystery of an unknown earth! . . . The dreams of men, the seed of commonwealths, the germs of empires.

EXERCISE 4

Rewrite the following passage from *Heart of Darkness* (p. 347) by eliminating the figurative language and making the description as literal as you can. Discuss the effect of your revision.

We stopped, and the silence driven away by the stamping of our feet flowed back again from the recesses of the land. The great wall of vegetation, an exuberant and entangled mass of trunks, branches, leaves, boughs, festoons, motionless in the moonlight, was like a rioting invasion of soundless life, a rolling wave of plants, piled up, crested, ready to topple over the creek, to sweep every little man of us out of his little existence.

EXERCISE 5

Jumpa Lahiri's "Interpreter of Maladies" (p. 311) introduces its main characters in prose that is notably descriptive, though there is little figurative language. Rewrite the following passage by adding carefully selected figurative language, and explain the choices you have made. How do your additions change the meaning of the passage? The story? Why do you think Lahiri chose to avoid figurative language?

At the tea stall Mr. and Mrs. Das bickered about who should take Tina to the toilet. Eventually Mrs. Das relented when Mr. Das pointed out that he had given the girl her bath the night before. In the rearview mirror Mr. Kapasi watched as Mrs. Das emerged slowly from his bulky white Ambassador, dragging her shaved, largely bare legs across the back seat. She did not hold the little girl's hand as they walked to the rest room.

They were on their way to see the Sun Temple at Konarak. It was a dry, bright Saturday, the mid-July heat tempered by a steady ocean breeze, ideal weather for sight-seeing. Ordinarily Mr. Kapasi would not have stopped so soon along the way, but less than five minutes after he'd picked up the family that morning in front of Hotel Sandy Villa, the little girl had complained. The first thing Mr. Kapasi had noticed when he saw Mr. and Mrs. Das, standing with their children under the portico of the hotel, was that they were very young, perhaps not even thirty. In addition to Tina they had two boys,

Ronny and Bobby, who appeared very close in age and had teeth covered in a network of flashing silver wires. The family looked Indian but dressed as foreigners did, the children in stiff, brightly colored clothing and caps with translucent visors. Mr. Kapasi was accustomed to foreign tourists; he was assigned to them regularly because he could speak English. Yesterday he had driven an elderly couple from Scotland, both with spotted faces and fluffy white hair so thin it exposed their sunburnt scalps. In comparison, the tanned, youthful faces of Mr. and Mrs. Das were all the more striking. When he'd introduced himself, Mr. Kapasi had pressed his palms together in greeting, but Mr. Das squeezed hands like an American so that Mr. Kapasi felt it in his elbow. Mrs. Das, for her part, had flexed one side of her mouth, smiling dutifully at Mr. Kapasi, without displaying any interest in him.

EXERCISE 6

Both Dylan Thomas's "Fern Hill" (p. 454) and Molly Rose Quinn's "Dolorosa" (p. 466) present characters reflecting back on youthful experience. Reread the poems and discuss how each uses figurative language to describe adolescent experience and explore its impact on each speaker's identity.

EXERCISE 7

Gregory Pardlo's "Written by Himself" (p. 468) uses a series of metaphors that reflect the personal identity of the speaker. Create a series of metaphors that express important, perhaps contradictory aspects of your identity.

IDENTITY AND CULTURE

1. Look again at the quotation by Nathaniel Hawthorne that begins this chapter. Using two of the texts you have studied in this chapter, discuss the conflict that results from trying to assume an identity based on the expectations of others rather than being true to oneself.
2. Many of the texts you've read in this chapter explore the dissonance that results from cultural clashes, particularly the conflicts experienced by those who are moving — by choice or by coercion—from one culture to another. Discuss the nature of that clash by focusing on three different texts.
3. Philosopher Theodor Adorno wrote that for those in exile, their writing becomes a kind of home: "In his text, the writer sets up house. . . . For [the person] who no longer has a homeland, writing becomes a place to live." Discuss what you think Adorno means, referring to at least two of the texts in this chapter as part of your interpretation.
4. Author James Baldwin wrote: "An identity would seem to be arrived at by the way in which the person faces and uses his experience." Discuss this quotation by referring to at least one of the texts you've read in this chapter and your own experience.
5. Most Americans believe that they are the master of their own destiny and that anyone can create and re-create him- or herself. To what extent do you believe that identity is the result of free choice rather than something determined by factors out of our control, such as race, gender, and ethnicity? Include references to at least three of the texts studied in this chapter in your response.
6. Emily Dickinson begins her poem: "I'm Nobody! Who are you? / Are you — Nobody — too?" Write a response that answers her question from the point of view of a protagonist from one of the stories in this chapter. Include references to the text of the story to support your response.
7. Identity theft is the fastest-growing type of fraud in the United States today. The term is most commonly used to refer to the crime of someone pretending to be you in order to buy goods and services in your name, or to access your bank or credit card accounts. What does this definition say about us? Is our "identity" determined by the objective data of our income, the goods and services we purchase, and the bank accounts and credit cards that give us access to those? Is it possible to "steal" someone's identity? Write an essay explaining your opinion. Refer to two or more texts from this chapter in your response.
8. Go to the National Portrait Gallery website (npg .si.edu), and select a portrait that either appeals to you or puzzles you. Write about what you see in the portrait and what the visual details suggest to you about the person's identity and culture.
9. Is a person's perceived identity a result of his or her "history"? How much is what we regard as "history" responsible for how others perceive us and for how we perceive ourselves?

7
Love and Relationships

Ay me! for aught that I could ever read,
Could ever hear by tale or history,
The course of true love never did run smooth.
— William Shakespeare, *A Midsummer Night's Dream*

Chris Dale/Getty Images

What is it about love and relationships that has captured the imaginations of poets and writers throughout the ages? Why are we drawn to love stories, even when they so often end in tears? The literature in this chapter explores the many ways people find love, keep love, or keep it from falling apart. As Elizabeth Bishop explains, sometimes love "may look like (*Write* it!) like disaster."

Love and relationships, particularly romantic relationships, are frequently the subject of humorous and satirical literature. Why might this be the case? Is it the subject of love itself that is held up for satire, or the conventions imposed on romantic and other types of relationships, which remind us of the complexity of human nature, that lend themselves to satire? In *The Importance of Being Earnest*, Oscar Wilde pokes fun at the trappings of Victorian courtship and marital rules of engagement. As you chuckle over a young lady's determination to marry a man named Ernest, you may find yourself reflecting on the cultural mores that circumscribe contemporary courtship. The Texts in Context in this chapter invite you to consider the ways in which satire shines a light on human folly and encourages change for the better.

A common variation on the theme of love and relationships is shattered dreams. In James Joyce's "The Dead," Gretta Conroy recalls the sudden death of her first love at seventeen. In "Woman Hollering Creek," Sandra Cisneros portrays a relationship that began with a young girl's dreams of true love but ended in abuse. In "Bliss," Katherine Mansfield invites us to watch Bertha Young's dreams of her perfect life shatter in an evening. In his inimitably laconic manner, the poet Billy Collins uses the analogy of "weighing the dog" to describe his feelings of loss after a love affair goes wrong.

If there is a constant among the many variations on the theme of love and relationships, it can be found in the words of William Shakespeare, "The course of true love never did run smooth." Even the reassurances of John Donne's "A Valediction: Forbidding Mourning" have been reinterpreted by Adrienne Rich in a poem with the same title. How do we recognize true love? Can you ever be sure? We hope that reading this literature will help you navigate your relationships. Don't be surprised if in the process you shed a few tears.

The Dead

JAMES JOYCE

Berenice Abbott / Getty Images

James Augustine Aloysius Joyce (1882–1941) was born near Dublin, Ireland. Although Joyce's work is inextricably connected to Ireland, and nearly all of it takes place in Dublin, he lived in Italy and France for most of his adult life. His short stories and novels reflect his inner turmoil about both his native country and the Roman Catholic Church in which he was raised. Joyce used stream of consciousness, an onslaught of tiny details, and both accessible and obscure allusions to literature, history, and politics to create the recognizable world of his fiction, but as he told a friend, "the ideas are always simple." His most famous works — *Dubliners* (1914), *Portrait of the Artist as a Young Man* (1916), *Ulysses* (1922), and even *Finnegans Wake* (1939) — tell us what it means to be a father, a son, a husband, a writer. "The Dead" is the last story in *Dubliners*, a collection about life in Dublin that captures both the city's romance and its monotony. Joyce once said, "When you remember that Dublin has been a capital for thousands of years, that it is the 'second' city of the British Empire, that it is nearly three times as big as Venice, it seems strange that no artist has given it to the world." "The Dead" is set at a dinner party for the Feast of the Epiphany, thrown annually by two aging sisters and the grown niece they raised; it follows their nephew, Gabriel Conroy, and his wife, Gretta, throughout the evening. A brilliant stylist and observer of human nature, Joyce captures the bittersweet and transient nature of several different kinds of love in "The Dead."

Lily, the caretaker's daughter, was literally run off her feet. Hardly had she brought one gentleman into the little pantry behind the office on the ground floor and helped him off with his overcoat than the wheezy hall-door bell clanged again and she had to scamper along the bare hallway to let in another guest. It was well for her she had not to attend to the ladies also. But Miss Kate and Miss Julia had thought of that and had converted the bathroom upstairs into a ladies' dressing-room. Miss Kate and Miss Julia were there, gossiping and laughing and fussing, walking after each other to the head of the stairs, peering down over the banisters and calling down to Lily to ask her who had come.

It was always a great affair, the Misses Morkan's annual dance. Everybody who knew them came to it, members of the family, old friends of the family, the members of Julia's choir, any of Kate's pupils that were grown up enough and even some of Mary Jane's pupils too. Never once had it fallen flat. For years and years it had gone off in splendid style as long as anyone could remember; ever since Kate and Julia, after the death of their brother Pat, had left the house in Stoney Batter and taken Mary Jane, their only niece, to live with them in the dark gaunt house on Usher's Island, the upper part of which they had rented from Mr Fulham, the cornfactor on the ground floor. That was a good thirty years ago if it was a day. Mary Jane, who was then a little girl in short clothes, was now the main prop of the household, for she had the organ in Haddington Road. She had been through the Academy and gave a pupils' concert every year in the upper room of the Ancient Concert Rooms. Many of her pupils belonged to the better-class families on the Kingstown and Dalkey line. Old as they were, her aunts also did their share. Julia, though she was quite grey, was still the leading soprano in Adam and Eve's,[1] and Kate, being too feeble to go about much, gave music lessons to beginners on the old square piano in the back room. Lily, the caretaker's daughter, did housemaid's work for them. Though their life was modest they believed in eating well; the best of everything: diamond-bone sirloins, three-shilling tea and the best bottled stout. But Lily seldom made a mistake in the orders so that she got on well with her three mistresses. They were fussy, that was all. But the only thing they would not stand was back answers.

Of course they had good reason to be fussy on such a night. And then it was long after ten o'clock and yet there was no sign of Gabriel and his wife. Besides they were dreadfully afraid that Freddy Malins might turn up screwed. They would not wish for worlds that any of Mary Jane's pupils should see him under the influence; and when he was like that it was sometimes very hard to manage him. Freddy Malins always came late but they wondered what could be keeping Gabriel: and that was what brought them every two minutes to the banisters to ask Lily had Gabriel or Freddy come.

— O, Mr Conroy, said Lily to Gabriel when she opened the door for him, Miss Kate and Miss Julia thought you were never coming. Goodnight, Mrs Conroy.

— I'll engage they did, said Gabriel, but they forget that my wife here takes three mortal hours to dress herself.

He stood on the mat, scraping the snow from his goloshes, while Lily led his wife to the foot of the stairs and called out:

— Miss Kate, here's Mrs Conroy.

Kate and Julia came toddling down the dark stairs at once. Both of them kissed Gabriel's wife, said she must be perished alive and asked was Gabriel with her.

— Here I am as right as the mail, Aunt Kate! Go on up. I'll follow, called out Gabriel from the dark.

He continued scraping his feet vigorously while the three women went upstairs, laughing, to the ladies' dressing-room. A light fringe of snow lay like a cape on the shoulders of his overcoat and like toecaps on the toes of his goloshes; and, as the buttons of his overcoat slipped with a squeaking noise through the snow-stiffened frieze, a cold fragrant air from out-of-doors escaped from crevices and folds.

— Is it snowing again, Mr Conroy? asked Lily.

She had preceded him into the pantry to help him off with his overcoat. Gabriel smiled at the three syllables she had given his surname and glanced at her. She was a slim, growing girl, pale in complexion and with hay-coloured hair. The gas in the pantry made her look still paler. Gabriel had known her when she was a child and used to sit on the lowest step nursing a rag doll.

— Yes, Lily, he answered, and I think we're in for a night of it.

He looked up at the pantry ceiling, which was shaking with the stamping and shuffling of feet on the floor above, listened for a moment to the piano and then glanced at the girl, who was folding his overcoat carefully at the end of a shelf.

— Tell me, Lily, he said in a friendly tone, do you still go to school?

---

[1] Commonly used name for the Church of the Immaculate Conception in Merchant's Quay, Dublin, a Roman Catholic church that is run by the Franciscans. — EDS.

—O no, sir, she answered. I'm done schooling this year and more.

—O, then, said Gabriel gaily, I suppose we'll be going to your wedding one of these fine days with your young man, eh?

The girl glanced back at him over her shoulder and said with great bitterness:

—The men that is now is only all palaver and what they can get out of you.

20 Gabriel coloured as if he felt he had made a mistake and, without looking at her, kicked off his goloshes and flicked actively with his muffler at his patent-leather shoes.

He was a stout tallish young man. The high colour of his cheeks pushed upwards even to his forehead where it scattered itself in a few formless patches of pale red; and on his hairless face there scintillated restlessly the polished lenses and the bright gilt rims of the glasses which screened his delicate and restless eyes. His glossy black hair was parted in the middle and brushed in a long curve behind his ears where it curled slightly beneath the groove left by his hat.

When he had flicked lustre into his shoes he stood up and pulled his waistcoat down more tightly on his plump body. Then he took a coin rapidly from his pocket.

—O Lily, he said, thrusting it into her hands, it's Christmas-time, isn't it? Just . . . here's a little . . . .

He walked rapidly towards the door.

25 —O no, sir! cried the girl, following him. Really, sir, I wouldn't take it.

—Christmas-time! Christmas-time! said Gabriel, almost trotting to the stairs and waving his hand to her in deprecation.

The girl, seeing that he had gained the stairs, called out after him:

—Well, thank you, sir.

He waited outside the drawing-room door until the waltz should finish, listening to the skirts that swept against it and to the shuffling of feet. He was still discomposed by the girl's bitter and sudden retort. It had cast a gloom over him which he tried to dispel by arranging his cuffs and the bows of his tie. Then he took from his waistcoat pocket a little paper and glanced at the headings he had made for his speech. He was undecided about the lines from Robert Browning for he feared they would be above the heads of his hearers. Some quotation that they could recognise from Shakespeare or from the Melodies would be better. The indelicate clacking of the men's heels and the shuffling of their soles reminded him that their grade of culture differed from his. He would only make himself ridiculous by quoting poetry to them which they could not understand. They would think that he was airing his superior education. He would fail with them just as he had failed with the girl in the pantry. He had taken up a wrong tone. His whole speech was a mistake from first to last, an utter failure.

30 Just then his aunts and his wife came out of the ladies' dressing-room. His aunts were two small plainly dressed old women. Aunt Julia was an inch or so the taller. Her hair, drawn low over the tops of her ears, was grey; and grey also, with darker shadows, was her large flaccid face. Though she was stout in build and stood erect her slow eyes and parted lips gave her the appearance of a woman who did not know where she was or where she was going. Aunt Kate was more vivacious. Her face, healthier than her sister's, was all puckers and creases, like a shrivelled red apple, and her hair, braided in the same old-fashioned way, had not lost its ripe nut colour.

They both kissed Gabriel frankly. He was their favourite nephew, the son of their dead elder sister, Ellen, who had married T. J. Conroy of the Port and Docks.

—Gretta tells me you're not going to take a cab back to Monkstown to-night, Gabriel, said Aunt Kate.

—No, said Gabriel, turning to his wife, we had quite enough of that last year, hadn't we? Don't you remember, Aunt Kate, what a cold Gretta got out of it? Cab windows rattling all the way, and the east wind blowing in after we passed Merrion. Very jolly it was. Gretta caught a dreadful cold.

Aunt Kate frowned severely and nodded her head at every word.

— Quite right, Gabriel, quite right, she said. You can't be too careful.

— But as for Gretta there, said Gabriel, she'd walk home in the snow if she were let.

Mrs Conroy laughed.

— Don't mind him, Aunt Kate, she said. He's really an awful bother, what with green shades for Tom's eyes at night and making him do the dumb-bells, and forcing Eva to eat the stirabout.[2] The poor child! And she simply hates the sight of it! . . . O, but you'll never guess what he makes me wear now!

She broke out into a peal of laughter and glanced at her husband, whose admiring and happy eyes had been wandering from her dress to her face and hair. The two aunts laughed heartily too, for Gabriel's solicitude was a standing joke with them.

— Goloshes! said Mrs Conroy. That's the latest. Whenever it's wet underfoot I must put on my goloshes. To-night even he wanted me to put them on, but I wouldn't. The next thing he'll buy me will be a diving suit.

Gabriel laughed nervously and patted his tie reassuringly while Aunt Kate nearly doubled herself, so heartily did she enjoy the joke. The smile soon faded from Aunt Julia's face and her mirthless eyes were directed towards her nephew's face. After a pause she asked:

— And what are goloshes, Gabriel?

— Goloshes, Julia! exclaimed her sister. Goodness me, don't you know what goloshes are? You wear them over your . . . over your boots, Gretta, isn't it?

— Yes, said Mrs Conroy. Guttapercha things. We both have a pair now. Gabriel says everyone wears them on the continent.

[2] Porridge. — EDS.

— O, on the continent, murmured Aunt Julia, nodding her head slowly.

Gabriel knitted his brows and said, as if he were slightly angered:

— It's nothing very wonderful but Gretta thinks it very funny because she says the word reminds her of Christy Minstrels.

— But tell me, Gabriel, said Aunt Kate, with brisk tact. Of course, you've seen about the room. Gretta was saying . . .

— O, the room is all right, replied Gabriel. I've taken one in the Gresham.

— To be sure, said Aunt Kate, by far the best thing to do. And the children, Gretta, you're not anxious about them?

— O, for one night, said Mrs Conroy. Besides, Bessie will look after them.

— To be sure, said Aunt Kate again. What a comfort it is to have a girl like that, one you can depend on! There's that Lily, I'm sure I don't know what has come over her lately. She's not the girl she was at all.

Gabriel was about to ask his aunt some questions on this point but she broke off suddenly to gaze after her sister who had wandered down the stairs and was craning her neck over the banisters.

— Now, I ask you, she said, almost testily, where is Julia going? Julia! Julia! Where are you going?

Julia, who had gone halfway down one flight, came back and announced blandly:

— Here's Freddy.

At the same moment a clapping of hands and a final flourish of the pianist told that the waltz had ended. The drawing-room door was opened from within and some couples came out. Aunt Kate drew Gabriel aside hurriedly and whispered into his ear:

— Slip down, Gabriel, like a good fellow and see if he's all right, and don't let him up if he's screwed. I'm sure he's screwed. I'm sure he is.

Gabriel went to the stairs and listened over the banisters. He could hear two persons talking in the pantry. Then he recognized Freddy Malins' laugh. He went down the stairs noisily.

60 —It's such a relief, said Aunt Kate to Mrs Conroy, that Gabriel is here. I always feel easier in my mind when he's here. . . . Julia, there's Miss Daly and Miss Power will take some refreshment. Thanks for your beautiful waltz, Miss Daly. It made lovely time.

A tall wizen-faced man, with a stiff grizzled moustache and swarthy skin, who was passing out with his partner said:

—And may we have some refreshment, too, Miss Morkan?

—Julia, said Aunt Kate summarily, and here's Mr Browne and Miss Furlong. Take them in, Julia, with Miss Daly and Miss Power.

—I'm the man for the ladies, said Mr Browne, pursing his lips until his moustache bristled and smiling in all his wrinkles. You know, Miss Morkan, the reason they are so fond of me is—

65 He did not finish his sentence, but, seeing that Aunt Kate was out of earshot, at once led the three young ladies into the back room. The middle of the room was occupied by two square tables placed end to end, and on these Aunt Julia and the caretaker were straightening and smoothing a large cloth. On the sideboard were arrayed dishes and plates, and glasses and bundles of knives and forks and spoons. The top of the closed square piano served also as a side-board for viands and sweets. At a smaller side-board in one corner two young men were standing, drinking hop-bitters.

Mr Browne led his charges thither and invited them all, in jest, to some ladies' punch, hot, strong and sweet. As they said they never took anything strong he opened three bottles of lemonade for them. Then he asked one of the young men to move aside, and, taking hold of the decanter, filled out for himself a goodly measure of whisky. The young men eyed him respectfully while he took a trial sip.

—God help me, he said, smiling, it's the doctor's orders.

His wizened face broke into a broader smile, and the three young ladies laughed in musical echo to his pleasantry, swaying their bodies to and fro, with nervous jerks of their shoulders. The boldest said:

—O, now, Mr Browne, I'm sure the doctor never ordered anything of the kind.

70 Mr Browne took another sip of his whisky and said, with sidling mimicry:

—Well, you see, I'm like the famous Mrs Cassidy, who is reported to have said: *Now, Mary Grimes, if I don't take it, make me take it, for I feel I want it.*

His hot face had leaned forward a little too confidentially and he had assumed a very low Dublin accent so that the young ladies, with one instinct, received his speech in silence. Miss Furlong, who was one of Mary Jane's pupils, asked Miss Daly what was the name of the pretty waltz she had played; and Mr Browne, seeing that he was ignored, turned promptly to the two young men who were more appreciative.

A red-faced young woman, dressed in pansy, came into the room, excitedly clapping her hands and crying:

—Quadrilles! Quadrilles!

75 Close on her heels came Aunt Kate, crying:

—Two gentlemen and three ladies, Mary Jane!

—O, here's Mr Bergin and Mr Kerrigan, said Mary Jane. Mr Kerrigan, will you take Miss Power? Miss Furlong, may I get you a partner, Mr Bergin. O, that'll just do now.

—Three ladies, Mary Jane, said Aunt Kate.

The two young gentlemen asked the ladies if they might have the pleasure, and Mary Jane turned to Miss Daly.

80 —O, Miss Daly, you're really awfully good, after playing for the last two dances, but really we're so short of ladies to-night.

—I don't mind in the least, Miss Morkan.

—But I've a nice partner for you, Mr Bartell D'Arcy, the tenor. I'll get him to sing later on. All Dublin is raving about him.

—Lovely voice, lovely voice! said Aunt Kate.

As the piano had twice begun the prelude to the first figure Mary Jane led her recruits quickly from the room. They had hardly gone when Aunt Julia wandered slowly into the room, looking behind her at something.

85 —What is the matter, Julia? asked Aunt Kate anxiously. Who is it?

Julia, who was carrying in a column of table-napkins, turned to her sister and said, simply, as if the question had surprised her:

—It's only Freddy, Kate, and Gabriel with him.

In fact right behind her Gabriel could be seen piloting Freddy Malins across the landing. The latter, a young man of about forty, was of Gabriel's size and build, with very round shoulders. His face was fleshy and pallid, touched with colour only at the thick hanging lobes of his ears and at the wide wings of his nose. He had coarse features, a blunt nose, a convex and receding brow, tumid and protruded lips. His heavy-lidded eyes and the disorder of his scanty hair made him look sleepy. He was laughing heartily in a high key at a story which he had been telling Gabriel on the stairs and at the same time rubbing the knuckles of his left fist backwards and forwards into his left eye.

—Good-evening, Freddy, said Aunt Julia.

90 Freddy Malins bade the Misses Morkan good-evening in what seemed an offhand fashion by reason of the habitual catch in his voice and then, seeing that Mr Browne was grinning at him from the sideboard, crossed the room on rather shaky legs and began to repeat in an undertone the story he had just told to Gabriel.

—He's not so bad, is he? said Aunt Kate to Gabriel.

Gabriel's brows were dark, but he raised them quickly and answered:

—O no, hardly noticeable.

DEA / G. DAGLI ORTI / Getty Images

A lively dance imported from France, the quadrille includes four couples dancing in square sets. Immensely popular throughout the nineteenth century and into the early twentieth, it often adapted music from stage plays and was thought to be quite flirtatious. **What does the quadrille dancing in *The Dead* (paras. 74–84) reveal about the social customs in Dublin society at the time? In what ways does this illustration reflect those customs?**

—Now, isn't he a terrible fellow! she said. And his poor mother made him take the pledge on New Year's Eve. But come on, Gabriel, into the drawing-room.

95 Before leaving the room with Gabriel she signalled to Mr Browne by frowning and shaking her forefinger in warning to and fro. Mr Browne nodded in answer and, when she had gone, said to Freddy Malins:

—Now, then, Teddy, I'm going to fill you out a good glass of lemonade just to buck you up.

Freddy Malins, who was nearing the climax of his story, waved the offer aside impatiently but Mr Browne, having first called Freddy Malins' attention to a disarray in his dress, filled out and handed him a full glass of lemonade. Freddy Malins' left hand accepted the glass mechanically, his right hand being engaged in the mechanical readjustment of his dress. Mr Browne, whose face was once more wrinkling with mirth, poured out for himself a glass of whisky while Freddy Malins exploded, before he had well reached the climax of his story, in a kink of high-pitched bronchitic laughter and, setting down his untasted and overflowing glass, began to rub the knuckles of his left fist backwards and forwards into his left eye, repeating words of his last phrase as well as his fit of laughter would allow him.

. . . .

Gabriel could not listen while Mary Jane was playing her Academy piece, full of runs and difficult passages, to the hushed drawing-room. He liked music but the piece she was playing had no melody for him and he doubted whether it had any melody for the other listeners, though they had begged Mary Jane to play something. Four young men, who had come from the refreshment-room to stand in the doorway at the sound of the piano, had gone away quietly in couples after a few minutes. The only persons who seemed to follow the music were Mary Jane herself, her hands racing along the key-board or lifted from it at the pauses like those of a priestess in momentary imprecation, and Aunt Kate standing at her elbow to turn the page.

Gabriel's eyes, irritated by the floor, which glittered with beeswax under the heavy chandelier, wandered to the wall above the piano. A picture of the balcony scene in *Romeo and Juliet* hung there and beside it was a picture of the two murdered princes in the Tower which Aunt Julia had worked in red, blue and brown wools when she was a girl. Probably in the school they had gone to as girls that kind of work had been taught, for one year his mother had worked for him as a birthday present a waistcoat of purple tabinet, with little foxes' heads upon it, lined with brown satin and having round mulberry buttons. It was strange that his mother had had no musical talent though Aunt Kate used to call her the brains carrier of the Morkan family. Both she and Julia had always seemed a little proud of their serious and matronly sister. Her photograph stood before the pierglass. She had an open book on her knees and was pointing out something in it to Constantine who, dressed in a man-o'-war suit, lay at her feet. It was she who had chosen the names of her sons for she was very sensible of the dignity of family life. Thanks to her, Constantine was now senior curate in Balbriggan and, thanks to her, Gabriel himself had taken his degree in the Royal University. A shadow passed over his face as he remembered her sullen opposition to his marriage. Some slighting phrases she had used still rankled in his memory; she had once spoken of Gretta as being country cute and that was not true of Gretta at all. It was Gretta who had nursed her during all her last long illness in their house at Monkstown.

He knew that Mary Jane must be near the 100
end of her piece, for she was playing again the opening melody with runs of scales after every bar and while he waited for the end the resentment died down in his heart. The piece ended with a trill of octaves in the treble and a final deep octave in the bass. Great applause greeted

Mary Jane as, blushing and rolling up her music nervously, she escaped from the room. The most vigorous clapping came from the four young men in the doorway who had gone away to the refreshment-room at the beginning of the piece but had come back when the piano had stopped.

Lancers were arranged. Gabriel found himself partnered with Miss Ivors. She was a frank-mannered, talkative young lady, with a freckled face and prominent brown eyes. She did not wear a low-cut bodice and the large brooch which was fixed in the front of her collar bore on it an Irish device.

When they had taken their places she said abruptly:

— I have a crow to pluck with you.

— With me? said Gabriel.

She nodded her head gravely.

— What is it? asked Gabriel, smiling at her solemn manner.

— Who is G. C.? answered Miss Ivors, — turning her eyes upon him.

Gabriel coloured and was about to knit his brows, as if he did not understand, when she said bluntly:

— O, innocent Amy! I have found out that you write for *The Daily Express*. Now, aren't you ashamed of yourself?

— Why should I be ashamed of myself? asked Gabriel, blinking his eyes and trying to smile.

— Well, I'm ashamed of you, said Miss Ivors frankly. To say you'd write for a rag like that. I didn't think you were a West Briton.[3]

A look of perplexity appeared on Gabriel's face. It was true that he wrote a literary column every Wednesday in *The Daily Express*, for which he was paid fifteen shillings. But that did not make him a West Briton surely. The books he received for review were almost more welcome than the paltry cheque. He loved to feel the covers and turn over the pages of newly printed books. Nearly every day when his teaching in the college was ended he used to wander down the quays to the second-hand booksellers, to Hickey's on Bachelor's Walk, to Webb's or Massey's on Aston's Quay, or to O'Clohissey's in the by-street. He did not know how to meet her charge. He wanted to say that literature was above politics. But they were friends of many years' standing and their careers had been parallel, first at the University and then as teachers: he could not risk a grandiose phrase with her. He continued blinking his eyes and trying to smile and murmured lamely that he saw nothing political in writing reviews of books.

When their turn to cross had come he was still perplexed and inattentive. Miss Ivors promptly took his hand in a warm grasp and said in a soft friendly tone:

— Of course, I was only joking. Come, we cross now.

When they were together again she spoke of the University question[4] and Gabriel felt more at ease. A friend of hers had shown her his review of Browning's poems. That was how she had found out the secret: but she liked the review immensely. Then she said suddenly:

— O, Mr Conroy, will you come for an excursion to the Aran Isles this summer? We're going to stay there a whole month. It will be splendid out in the Atlantic. You ought to come. Mr Clancy is coming, and Mr Kilkelly and Kathleen Kearney. It would be splendid for Gretta too if she'd come. She's from Connacht, isn't she?

— Her people are, said Gabriel shortly.

— But you will come, won't you? said Miss Ivors, laying her warm hand eagerly on his arm.

[3] A native of Ireland, but sympathetic to England. — EDS.

[4] The question of providing an adequate higher education to Catholics in Ireland, given that Trinity College required Protestant exams to be passed. — EDS.

—The fact is, said Gabriel, I have just arranged to go—

—Go where? asked Miss Ivors.

—Well, you know, every year I go for a cycling tour with some fellows and so—

—But where? asked Miss Ivors.

—Well, we usually go to France or Belgium or perhaps Germany, said Gabriel awkwardly.

—And why do you go to France and Belgium, said Miss Ivors, instead of visiting your own land?

—Well, said Gabriel, it's partly to keep in touch with the languages and partly for a change.

—And haven't you your own language to keep in touch with—Irish? asked Miss Ivors.

—Well, said Gabriel, if it comes to that, you know, Irish is not my language.

Their neighbours had turned to listen to the cross-examination. Gabriel glanced right and left nervously and tried to keep his good humour under the ordeal which was making a blush invade his forehead.

—And haven't you your own land to visit, continued Miss Ivors, that you know nothing of, your own people, and your own country?

—O, to tell you the truth, retorted Gabriel suddenly, I'm sick of my own country, sick of it!

—Why? asked Miss Ivors.

Gabriel did not answer, for his retort had heated him.

—Why? repeated Miss Ivors.

They had to go visiting together and, as he had not answered her, Miss Ivors said warmly:

—Of course, you've no answer.

Gabriel tried to cover his agitation by taking part in the dance with great energy. He avoided her eyes, for he had seen a sour expression on her face. But when they met in the long chain he was surprised to feel his hand firmly pressed. She looked at him from under her brows for a moment quizzically until he smiled. Then, just as the chain was about to start again, she stood on tiptoe and whispered into his ear:

—West Briton!

When the lancers were over Gabriel went away to a remote corner of the room where Freddy Malins' mother was sitting. She was a stout, feeble old woman with white hair. Her voice had a catch in it like her son's and she stuttered slightly. She had been told that Freddy had come and that he was nearly all right. Gabriel asked her whether she had had a good crossing. She lived with her married daughter in Glasgow and came to Dublin on a visit once a year. She answered placidly that she had had a beautiful crossing and that the captain had been most attentive to her. She spoke also of the beautiful house her daughter kept in Glasgow, and of all the friends they had there. While her tongue rambled on Gabriel tried to banish from his mind all memory of the unpleasant incident with Miss Ivors. Of course the girl or woman, or whatever she was, was an enthusiast, but there was a time for all things. Perhaps he ought not to have answered her like that. But she had no right to call him a West Briton before people, even in joke. She had tried to make him ridiculous before people, heckling him and staring at him with her rabbit's eyes.

He saw his wife making her way towards him through the waltzing couples. When she reached him she said into his ear:

—Gabriel, Aunt Kate wants to know won't you carve the goose as usual. Miss Daly will carve the ham and I'll do the pudding.

—All right, said Gabriel.

—She's sending in the younger ones first as soon as this waltz is over so that we'll have the table to ourselves.

—Were you dancing? asked Gabriel.

—Of course I was. Didn't you see me? What words had you with Molly Ivors?

—No words. Why? Did she say so?

—Something like that. I'm trying to get that Mr D'Arcy to sing. He's full of conceit, I think.

—There were no words, said Gabriel moodily, only she wanted me to go for a trip to the west of Ireland and I said I wouldn't.

His wife clasped her hands excitedly and gave a little jump.

—O, do go, Gabriel, she cried. I'd love to see Galway again.

—You can go if you like, said Gabriel coldly.

She looked at him for a moment, then turned to Mrs Malins and said:

—There's a nice husband for you, Mrs Malins.

While she was threading her way back across the room Mrs Malins, without adverting to the interruption, went on to tell Gabriel what beautiful places there were in Scotland and beautiful scenery. Her son-in-law brought them every year to the lakes and they used to go fishing. Her son-in-law was a splendid fisher. One day he caught a fish, a beautiful big big fish, and the man in the hotel boiled it for their dinner.

Gabriel hardly heard what she said. Now that supper was coming near he began to think again about his speech and about the quotation. When he saw Freddy Malins coming across the room to visit his mother Gabriel left the chair free for him and retired into the embrasure of the window. The room had already cleared and from the back room came the clatter of plates and knives. Those who still remained in the drawing-room seemed tired of dancing and were conversing quietly in little groups. Gabriel's warm, trembling fingers tapped the cold pane of the window. How cool it must be outside! How pleasant it would be to walk out alone, first along by the river and then through the park! The snow would be lying on the branches of the trees and forming a bright cap on the top of the Wellington Monument. How much more pleasant it would be there than at the supper-table!

He ran over the headings of his speech: Irish hospitality, sad memories, the Three Graces, Paris, the quotation from Browning. He repeated to himself a phrase he had written in his review: *One feels that one is listening to a thought-tormented music.* Miss Ivors had praised the review. Was she sincere? Had she really any life of her own behind all her propagandism? There had never been any ill-feeling between them until that night. It unnerved him to think that she would be at the supper-table, looking up at him while he spoke with her critical quizzing eyes. Perhaps she would not be sorry to see him fail in his speech. An idea came into his mind and gave him courage. He would say, alluding to Aunt Kate and Aunt Julia: *Ladies and Gentlemen, the generation which is now on the wane among us may have had its faults but for my part I think it had certain qualities of hospitality, of humour, of humanity, which the new and very serious and hypereducated generation that is growing up around us seems to me to lack.* Very good: that was one for Miss Ivors. What did he care that his aunts were only two ignorant old women?

A murmur in the room attracted his attention. Mr Browne was advancing from the door, gallantly escorting Aunt Julia, who leaned upon his arm, smiling and hanging her head. An irregular musketry of applause escorted her also as far as the piano and then, as Mary Jane seated herself on the stool, and Aunt Julia, no longer smiling, half turned so as to pitch her voice fairly into the room, gradually ceased. Gabriel recognized the prelude. It was that of an old song of Aunt Julia's—*Arrayed for the Bridal.* Her voice, strong and clear in tone, attacked with great spirit the runs which embellish the air and though she sang very rapidly she did not miss even the smallest of the grace notes. To follow the voice, without looking at the singer's face, was to feel and share the excitement of swift and secure flight. Gabriel applauded loudly with all the others at the close of the song and loud applause was borne in from the invisible supper-table. It sounded so genuine that a little colour struggled into Aunt Julia's face as she bent to replace in the music-stand the old leather-bound song-book that had her initials on the cover.

Freddy Malins, who had listened with his head perched sideways to hear her better, was still applauding when everyone else had ceased and talking animatedly to his mother who nodded her head gravely and slowly in acquiescence. At last, when he could clap no more, he stood up suddenly and hurried across the room to Aunt Julia whose hand he seized and held in both his hands, shaking it when words failed him or the catch in his voice proved too much for him.

—I was just telling my mother, he said, I never heard you sing so well, never. No, I never heard your voice so good as it is tonight. Now! Would you believe that now? That's the truth. Upon my word and honour that's the truth. I never heard your voice sound so fresh and so . . . so clear and fresh, never.

Aunt Julia smiled broadly and murmured something about compliments as she released her hand from his grasp. Mr Browne extended his open hand towards her and said to those who were near him in the manner of a showman introducing a prodigy to an audience:

—Miss Julia Morkan, my latest discovery!

He was laughing very heartily at this himself when Freddy Malins turned to him and said:

—Well, Browne, if you're serious you might make a worse discovery. All I can say is I never heard her sing half so well as long as I am coming here. And that's the honest truth.

—Neither did I, said Mr Browne. I think her voice has greatly improved.

Aunt Julia shrugged her shoulders and said with meek pride:

—Thirty years ago I hadn't a bad voice as voices go.

—I often told Julia, said Aunt Kate emphatically, that she was simply thrown away in that choir. But she never would be said by me.

She turned as if to appeal to the good sense of the others against a refractory child while Aunt Julia gazed in front of her, a vague smile of reminiscence playing on her face.

—No, continued Aunt Kate, she wouldn't be said or led by anyone, slaving there in that choir night and day, night and day. Six o'clock on Christmas morning! And all for what?

—Well, isn't it for the honour of God, Aunt Kate? asked Mary Jane, twisting round on the piano-stool and smiling.

Aunt Kate turned fiercely on her niece and said:

—I know all about the honour of God, Mary Jane, but I think it's not at all honourable for the pope to turn out the women out of the choirs that have slaved there all their lives and put little whippersnappers of boys over their heads. I suppose it is for the good of the Church if the pope does it. But it's not just, Mary Jane, and it's not right.

She had worked herself into a passion and would have continued in defence of her sister for it was a sore subject with her but Mary Jane, seeing that all the dancers had come back, intervened pacifically:

—Now, Aunt Kate, you're giving scandal to Mr Browne who is of the other persuasion.

Aunt Kate turned to Mr Browne, who was grinning at this allusion to his religion, and said hastily:

—O, I don't question the pope's being right. I'm only a stupid old woman and I wouldn't presume to do such a thing. But there's such a thing as common everyday politeness and gratitude. And if I were in Julia's place I'd tell that Father Healy straight up to his face . . .

—And besides, Aunt Kate, said Mary Jane, we really are all hungry and when we are hungry we are all very quarrelsome.

—And when we are thirsty we are also quarrelsome, added Mr Browne.

—So that we had better go to supper, said Mary Jane, and finish the discussion afterwards.

On the landing outside the drawing-room Gabriel found his wife and Mary Jane trying to persuade Miss Ivors to stay for supper. But Miss Ivors, who had put on her hat and was buttoning

"Arrayed for the Bridal" is a song by George Linley based on Vincenzo Bellini's Italian opera *I Puritani* (*The Puritans*). It is an epithalamium, a song or poem in praise of the bride and bridegroom that prays for their prosperity. In "The Dead," Aunt Julia Morkan sings this song beautifully in spite of Gabriel's concern that she is well past her prime, both physically and intellectually. **In what ways could this illustration on the sheet music reflect James Joyce's characterization of Aunt Julia? Joyce's characterization of Dublin society?**

Sheridan Libraries / Levy / Gado / Getty Images

her cloak, would not stay. She did not feel in the least hungry and she had already overstayed her time.

— But only for ten minutes, Molly, said Mrs Conroy. That won't delay you.

— To take a pick itself, said Mary Jane, after all your dancing.

— I really couldn't, said Miss Ivors.

— I am afraid you didn't enjoy yourself at all, said Mary Jane hopelessly.

— Ever so much, I assure you, said Miss Ivors, but you really must let me run off now.

— But how can you get home? asked Mrs Conroy.

— O, it's only two steps up the quay.

Gabriel hesitated a moment and said:

— If you will allow me, Miss Ivors, I'll see you home if you really are obliged to go.

But Miss Ivors broke away from them.

— I won't hear of it, she cried. For goodness sake go in to your suppers and don't mind me. I'm quite well able to take care of myself.

— Well, you're the comical girl, Molly, said Mrs Conroy frankly.

— *Beannacht libh,*[5] cried Miss Ivors, with a laugh, as she ran down the staircase.

Mary Jane gazed after her, a moody puzzled expression on her face, while Mrs Conroy leaned over the banisters to listen for the hall-door. Gabriel asked himself was he the cause of her abrupt departure. But she did not seem to be in ill humour: she had gone away laughing. He stared blankly down the staircase.

At that moment Aunt Kate came toddling out of the supper-room, almost wringing her hands in despair.

— Where is Gabriel? she cried. Where on earth is Gabriel? There's everyone waiting in there, stage to let, and nobody to carve the goose!

— Here I am, Aunt Kate! cried Gabriel, with sudden animation, ready to carve a flock of geese, if necessary.

A fat brown goose lay at one end of the table and at the other end, on a bed of creased paper strewn with sprigs of parsley, lay a great ham, stripped of its outer skin and peppered over with crust crumbs, a neat paper frill round its shin and beside this was a round of spiced beef. Between these rival ends ran parallel lines of side-dishes: two little minsters of jelly, red and yellow; a

[5] An Irish blessing used to say goodbye. — EDS.

shallow dish full of blocks of blancmange and red jam, a large green leaf-shaped dish with a stalk-shaped handle, on which lay bunches of purple raisins and peeled almonds, a companion dish on which lay a solid rectangle of Smyrna figs, a dish of custard topped with grated nutmeg, a small bowl full of chocolates and sweets wrapped in gold and silver papers and a glass vase in which stood some tall celery stalks. In the centre of the table there stood, as sentries to a fruit-stand which upheld a pyramid of oranges and American apples, two squat old-fashioned decanters of cut glass, one containing port and the other dark sherry. On the closed square piano a pudding in a huge yellow dish lay in waiting, and behind it were three squads of bottles of stout and ale and minerals drawn up according to the colours of their uniforms, the first two black, with brown and red labels, the third and smallest squad white, with transverse green sashes.

Gabriel took his seat boldly at the head of the table and, having looked to the edge of the carver, plunged his fork firmly into the goose. He felt quite at ease now for he was an expert carver and liked nothing better than to find himself at the head of a well-laden table.

— Miss Furlong, what shall I send you? he asked. A wing or a slice of the breast?

— Just a small slice of the breast.

— Miss Higgins, what for you?

— O, anything at all, Mr Conroy.

While Gabriel and Miss Daly exchanged plates of goose and plates of ham and spiced beef Lily went from guest to guest with a dish of hot floury potatoes wrapped in a white napkin. This was Mary Jane's idea and she had also suggested apple sauce for the goose but Aunt Kate had said that plain roast goose without apple sauce had always been good enough for her and she hoped she might never eat worse. Mary Jane waited on her pupils and saw that they got the best slices and Aunt Kate and Aunt Julia opened and carried across from the piano bottles of stout and ale for the gentlemen and bottles of minerals for the ladies. There was a great deal of confusion and laughter and noise, the noise of orders and counter-orders, of knives and forks, of corks and glass-stoppers. Gabriel began to carve second helpings as soon as he had finished the first round without serving himself. Everyone protested loudly, so that he compromised by taking a long draught of stout for he had found the carving hot work. Mary Jane settled down quietly to her supper but Aunt Kate and Aunt Julia were still toddling round the table, walking on each other's heels, getting in each other's way and giving each other unheeded orders. Mr Browne begged of them to sit down and eat their suppers and so did Gabriel but they said there was time enough so that, at last, Freddy Malins stood up and, capturing Aunt Kate, plumped her down on her chair amid general laughter.

When everyone had been well served Gabriel said, smiling:

— Now, if anyone wants a little more of what vulgar people call stuffing let him or her speak.

A chorus of voices invited him to begin his own supper and Lily came forward with three potatoes which she had reserved for him.

— Very well, said Gabriel amiably, as he took another preparatory draught, kindly forget my existence, ladies and gentlemen, for a few minutes.

He set to his supper and took no part in the conversation with which the table covered Lily's removal of the plates. The subject of talk was the opera company which was then at the Theatre Royal. Mr Bartell D'Arcy, the tenor, a dark-complexioned young man with a smart moustache, praised very highly the leading contralto of the company but Miss Furlong thought she had a rather vulgar style of production. Freddy Malins said there was a negro chieftain singing in the second part of the Gaiety pantomime who had one of the finest tenor voices he had ever heard.

— Have you heard him? he asked Mr Bartell D'Arcy across the table.

— No, answered Mr Bartell D'Arcy carelessly.

— Because, Freddy Malins explained, now I'd be curious to hear your opinion of him. I think he has a grand voice.

— It takes Teddy to find out the really good things, said Mr Browne familiarly to the table.

— And why couldn't he have a voice too? asked Freddy Malins sharply. Is it because he's only a black?

Nobody answered this question and Mary Jane led the table back to the legitimate opera. One of her pupils had given her a pass for *Mignon*. Of course it was very fine, she said, but it made her think of poor Georgina Burns. Mr Browne could go back farther still, to the old Italian companies that used to come to Dublin — Tietjens, Ilma de Murzka, Campanini, the great Trebelli, Giuglini, Ravelli, Aramburo. Those were the days, he said, when there was something like singing to be heard in Dublin. He told too of how the top gallery of the old Royal used to be packed night after night, of how one night an Italian tenor had sung five encores to *Let Me Like a Soldier Fall*, introducing a high C every time, and of how the gallery boys would sometimes in their enthusiasm unyoke the horses from the carriage of some great *prima donna* and pull her themselves through the streets to her hotel. Why did they never play the grand old operas now, he asked, *Dinorah, Lucrezia Borgia*? Because they could not get the voices to sing them: that was why.

— O, well, said Mr Bartell D'Arcy, I presume there are as good singers to-day as there were then.

— Where are they? asked Mr Browne defiantly.

— In London, Paris, Milan, said Mr Bartell D'Arcy warmly. I suppose Caruso, for example, is quite as good, if not better than any of the men you have mentioned.

— Maybe so, said Mr Browne. But I may tell you I doubt it strongly.

— O, I'd give anything to hear Caruso sing, said Mary Jane.

— For me, said Aunt Kate, who had been picking a bone, there was only one tenor. To please me, I mean. But I suppose none of you ever heard of him.

— Who was he, Miss Morkan? asked Mr Bartell D'Arcy politely.

— His name, said Aunt Kate, was Parkinson. I heard him when he was in his prime and I think he had then the purest tenor voice that was ever put into a man's throat.

— Strange, said Mr Bartell D'Arcy. I never even heard of him.

— Yes, yes, Miss Morkan is right, said Mr Browne. I remember hearing of old Parkinson, but he's too far back for me.

— A beautiful pure sweet mellow English tenor, said Aunt Kate with enthusiasm.

Gabriel having finished, the huge pudding was transferred to the table. The clatter of forks and spoons began again. Gabriel's wife served out spoonfuls of the pudding and passed the plates down the table. Midway down they were held up by Mary Jane, who replenished them with raspberry or orange jelly or with blancmange and jam. The pudding was of Aunt Julia's making and she received praises for it from all quarters. She herself said that it was not quite brown enough.

— Well, I hope, Miss Morkan, said Mr Browne, that I'm brown enough for you because, you know, I'm all brown.

All the gentlemen, except Gabriel, ate some of the pudding out of compliment to Aunt Julia. As Gabriel never ate sweets the celery had been left for him. Freddy Malins also took a stalk of celery and ate it with his pudding. He had been told that celery was a capital thing for the blood and he was just then under doctor's care. Mrs Malins, who had been silent all through the supper, said that her son was going down to Mount Melleray in a week or so. The table then spoke of Mount Melleray, how bracing the air was down there, how hospitable the monks were and how they never asked for a penny-piece from their guests.

—And do you mean to say, asked Mr Browne incredulously, that a chap can go down there and put up there as if it were a hotel and live on the fat of the land and then come away without paying a farthing?

—O, most people give some donation to the monastery when they leave, said Mary Jane.

—I wish we had an institution like that in our Church, said Mr Browne candidly.

He was astonished to hear that the monks never spoke, got up at two in the morning and slept in their coffins. He asked what they did it for.

—That's the rule of the order, said Aunt Kate firmly.

—Yes, but why? asked Mr Browne.

Aunt Kate repeated that it was the rule, that was all. Mr Browne still seemed not to understand. Freddy Malins explained to him, as best he could, that the monks were trying to make up for the sins committed by all the sinners in the outside world. The explanation was not very clear for Mr Browne grinned and said:

—I like that idea very much but wouldn't a comfortable spring bed do them as well as a coffin?

—The coffin, said Mary Jane, is to remind them of their last end.

As the subject had grown lugubrious it was buried in a silence of the table during which Mrs Malins could be heard saying to her neighbour in an indistinct undertone:

—They are very good men, the monks, very pious men.

The raisins and almonds and figs and apples and oranges and chocolates and sweets were now passed about the table and Aunt Julia invited all the guests to have either port or sherry. At first Mr Bartell D'Arcy refused to take either but one of his neighbours nudged him and whispered something to him upon which he allowed his glass to be filled. Gradually as the last glasses were being filled the conversation ceased. A pause followed, broken only by the noise of the wine and by unsettlings of chairs. The Misses Morkan, all three, looked down at the tablecloth. Someone coughed once or twice and then a few gentlemen patted the table gently as a signal for silence. The silence came and Gabriel pushed back his chair and stood up.

The patting at once grew louder in encouragement and then ceased altogether. Gabriel leaned his ten trembling fingers on the tablecloth and smiled nervously at the company. Meeting a row of upturned faces he raised his eyes to the chandelier. The piano was playing a waltz tune and he could hear the skirts sweeping against the drawing-room door. People, perhaps, were standing in the snow on the quay outside, gazing up at the lighted windows and listening to the waltz music. The air was pure there. In the distance lay the park where the trees were weighted with snow. The Wellington Monument wore a gleaming cap of snow that flashed westward over the white field of Fifteen Acres.

He began:

—Ladies and Gentlemen.

—It has fallen to my lot this evening, as in years past, to perform a very pleasing task but a task for which I am afraid my poor powers as a speaker are all too inadequate.

—No, no! said Mr Browne.

—But, however that may be, I can only ask you to-night to take the will for the deed and to lend me your attention for a few moments while I endeavour to express to you in words what my feelings are on this occasion.

—Ladies and Gentlemen. It is not the first time that we have gathered together under this hospitable roof, around this hospitable board. It is not the first time that we have been the recipients—or perhaps, I had better say, the victims—of the hospitality of certain good ladies.

Number 15 Ushers Island, the home of Joyce's real-life grand-aunts who were the models for the Morkan Sisters, is now owned by Brendan Kilty (far left) who opens it for celebrations of Joyce and his work. In this picture, the feast from "The Dead" was recreated as part of the centennial celebrations of *Dubliners* in 2014. **How does the sumptuousness of the food and drink presented connect to the theme of hospitality in "The Dead"? Why do you think this aspect of the story continues to resonate with readers over a century later?**

He made a circle in the air with his arm and paused. Everyone laughed or smiled at Aunt Kate and Aunt Julia and Mary Jane who all turned crimson with pleasure. Gabriel went on more boldly:

— I feel more strongly with every recurring year that our country has no tradition which does it so much honour and which it should guard so jealously as that of its hospitality. It is a tradition that is unique as far as my experience goes (and I have visited not a few places abroad) among the modern nations. Some would say, perhaps, that with us it is rather a failing than anything to be boasted of. But granted even that, it is, to my mind, a princely failing, and one that I trust will long be cultivated among us. Of one thing, at least, I am sure. As long as this one roof shelters the good ladies aforesaid — and I wish from my heart it may do so for many and many a long year to come — the tradition of genuine warm-hearted courteous Irish hospitality, which our forefathers have handed down to us and which we must hand down to our descendants, is still alive among us.

A hearty murmur of assent ran round the table. It shot through Gabriel's mind that Miss Ivors was not there and that she had gone away discourteously: and he said with confidence in himself:

— Ladies and Gentlemen.

— A new generation is growing up in our midst, a generation actuated by new ideas and new principles. It is serious and enthusiastic for these new ideas and its enthusiasm, even when it is misdirected, is, I believe, in the main sincere. But we are living in a sceptical and, if I may use the phrase, a thought-tormented age: and sometimes I fear that this new generation, educated or hypereducated as it is, will lack those qualities of humanity, of hospitality, of kindly humour which belonged to an older day. Listening to-night to the names of all those great singers of the past it seemed to me, I must confess, that we were living in a less spacious age. Those days might, without exaggeration, be called spacious days: and if they are gone beyond recall let us hope, at least, that in gatherings such as this we shall still speak of them with pride and affection, still cherish in our hearts the memory of those dead and gone great ones whose fame the world will not willingly let die.

—Hear, hear! said Mr Browne loudly.

—But yet, continued Gabriel, his voice falling into a softer inflection, there are always in gatherings such as this sadder thoughts that will recur to our minds: thoughts of the past, of youth, of changes, of absent faces that we miss here to-night. Our path through life is strewn with many such sad memories: and were we to brood upon them always we could not find the heart to go on bravely with our work among the living. We have all of us living duties and living affections which claim, and rightly claim, our strenuous endeavours.

—Therefore, I will not linger on the past. I will not let any gloomy moralising intrude upon us here to-night. Here we are gathered together for a brief moment from the bustle and rush of our everyday routine. We are met here as friends, in the spirit of good-fellowship, as colleagues, also, to a certain extent, in the true spirit of *camaraderie*, and as the guests of—what shall I call them?—the Three Graces of the Dublin musical world.

The table burst into applause and laughter at this sally. Aunt Julia vainly asked each of her neighbours in turn to tell her what Gabriel had said.

—He says we are the Three Graces, Aunt Julia, said Mary Jane.

Aunt Julia did not understand but she looked up, smiling, at Gabriel, who continued in the same vein:

—Ladies and Gentlemen.

—I will not attempt to play to-night the part that Paris played on another occasion. I will not attempt to choose between them. The task would be an invidious one and one beyond my poor powers. For when I view them in turn, whether it be our chief hostess herself, whose good heart, whose too good heart, has become a byword with all who know her, or her sister, who seems to be gifted with perennial youth and whose singing must have been a surprise and a revelation to us all to-night, or, last but not least, when I consider our youngest hostess, talented, cheerful, hard-working and the best of nieces, I confess, Ladies and Gentlemen, that I do not know to which of them I should award the prize.

Gabriel glanced down at his aunts and, seeing the large smile on Aunt Julia's face and the tears which had risen to Aunt Kate's eyes, hastened to his close. He raised his glass of port gallantly, while every member of the company fingered a glass expectantly, and said loudly:

—Let us toast them all three together. Let us drink to their health, wealth, long life, happiness and prosperity and may they long continue to hold the proud and self-won position which they hold in their profession and the position of honour and affection which they hold in our hearts.

All the guests stood up, glass in hand, and turning towards the three seated ladies, sang in unison, with Mr Browne as leader:

For they are jolly gay fellows,
For they are jolly gay fellows,
For they are jolly gay fellows,
Which nobody can deny.

Aunt Kate was making frank use of her handkerchief and even Aunt Julia seemed moved. Freddy Malins beat time with his pudding-fork and the singers turned towards one another, as if in melodious conference, while they sang with emphasis:

Unless he tells a lie,
Unless he tells a lie.

Then, turning once more towards their hostesses, they sang:

For they are jolly gay fellows,
For they are jolly gay fellows,

For they are jolly gay fellows,
Which nobody can deny.

The acclamation which followed was taken up beyond the door of the supper-room by many of the other guests and renewed time after time, Freddy Malins acting as officer with his fork on high.

The piercing morning air came into the hall where they were standing so that Aunt Kate said:

— Close the door, somebody. Mrs Malins will get her death of cold.

— Browne is out there, Aunt Kate, said Mary Jane.

— Browne is everywhere, said Aunt Kate, lowering her voice.

Mary Jane laughed at her tone.

— Really, she said archly, he is very attentive.

— He has been laid on here like the gas, said Aunt Kate in the same tone, all during the Christmas.

She laughed herself this time good-humouredly and then added quickly:

— But tell him to come in, Mary Jane, and close the door. I hope to goodness he didn't hear me.

At that moment the hall-door was opened and Mr Browne came in from the doorstep, laughing as if his heart would break. He was dressed in a long green overcoat with mock astrakhan cuffs and collar and wore on his head an oval fur cap. He pointed down the snow-covered quay from where the sound of shrill prolonged whistling was borne in.

— Teddy will have all the cabs in Dublin out, he said.

Gabriel advanced from the little pantry behind the office, struggling into his overcoat and, looking round the hall, said:

— Gretta not down yet?

— She's getting on her things, Gabriel, said Aunt Kate.

— Who's playing up there? asked Gabriel.

— Nobody. They're all gone.

— O no, Aunt Kate, said Mary Jane. Bartell D'Arcy and Miss O'Callaghan aren't gone yet.

— Someone is strumming at the piano, anyhow, said Gabriel.

Mary Jane glanced at Gabriel and Mr Browne and said with a shiver:

— It makes me feel cold to look at you two gentlemen muffled up like that. I wouldn't like to face your journey home at this hour.

— I'd like nothing better this minute, said Mr Browne stoutly, than a rattling fine walk in the country or a fast drive with a good spanking goer between the shafts.

— We used to have a very good horse and trap at home, said Aunt Julia sadly.

— The never-to-be-forgotten Johnny, said Mary Jane, laughing.

Aunt Kate and Gabriel laughed too.

— Why, what was wonderful about Johnny? asked Mr Browne.

— The late lamented Patrick Morkan, our grandfather, that is, explained Gabriel, commonly known in his later years as the old gentleman, was a glue-boiler.

— O, now, Gabriel, said Aunt Kate, laughing, he had a starch mill.

— Well, glue or starch, said Gabriel, the old gentleman had a horse by the name of Johnny. And Johnny used to work in the old gentleman's mill, walking round and round in order to drive the mill. That was all very well; but now comes the tragic part about Johnny. One fine day the old gentleman thought he'd like to drive out with the quality to a military review in the park.

— The Lord have mercy on his soul, said Aunt Kate compassionately.

— Amen, said Gabriel. So the old gentleman, as I said, harnessed Johnny and put on his very best tall hat and his very best stock collar and drove out in grand style from his ancestral mansion somewhere near Back Lane, I think.

Everyone laughed, even Mrs Malins, at Gabriel's manner and Aunt Kate said:

— O, now, Gabriel, he didn't live in Back Lane, really. Only the mill was there.

— Out from the mansion of his forefathers, continued Gabriel, he drove with Johnny. And everything went on beautifully until Johnny came in sight of King Billy's statue: and whether he fell in love with the horse King Billy sits on or whether he thought he was back again in the mill, anyhow he began to walk round the statue.

Gabriel paced in a circle round the hall in his goloshes amid the laughter of the others.

— Round and round he went, said Gabriel, and the old gentleman, who was a very pompous old gentleman, was highly indignant. *Go on, sir! What do you mean, sir? Johnny! Johnny! Most extraordinary conduct! Can't understand the horse!*

The peals of laughter which followed Gabriel's imitation of the incident were interrupted by a resounding knock at the hall-door. Mary Jane ran to open it and let in Freddy Malins. Freddy Malins, with his hat well back on his head and his shoulders humped with cold, was puffing and steaming after his exertions.

— I could only get one cab, he said.

— O, we'll find another along the quay, said Gabriel.

— Yes, said Aunt Kate. Better not keep Mrs Malins standing in the draught.

Mrs Malins was helped down the front steps by her son and Mr Browne and, after many manoeuvres, hoisted into the cab. Freddy Malins clambered in after her and spent a long time settling her on the seat, Mr Browne helping him with advice. At last she was settled comfortably and Freddy Malins invited Mr Browne into the cab. There was a good deal of confused talk, and then Mr Browne got into the cab. The cabman settled his rug over his knees, and bent down for the address. The confusion grew greater and the cabman was directed differently by Freddy Malins and Mr Browne, each of whom had his head out through a window of the cab. The difficulty was to know where to drop Mr Browne along the route and Aunt Kate, Aunt Julia and Mary Jane helped the discussion from the doorstep with cross-directions and contradictions and abundance of laughter. As for Freddy Malins he was speechless with laughter. He popped his head in and out of the window every moment, to the great danger of his hat, and told his mother how the discussion was progressing till at last Mr Browne shouted to the bewildered cabman above the din of everybody's laughter:

— Do you know Trinity College?

— Yes, sir, said the cabman.

— Well, drive bang up against Trinity College gates, said Mr Browne, and then we'll tell you where to go. You understand now?

— Yes, sir, said the cabman.

— Make like a bird for Trinity College.

— Right, sir, cried the cabman.

The horse was whipped up and the cab rattled off along the quay amid a chorus of laughter and adieus.

Gabriel had not gone to the door with the others. He was in a dark part of the hall gazing up the staircase. A woman was standing near the top of the first flight, in the shadow also. He could not see her face but he could see the terracotta and salmonpink panels of her skirt which the shadow made appear black and white. It was his wife. She was leaning on the banisters, listening to something. Gabriel was surprised at her stillness and strained his ear to listen also. But he could hear little save the noise of laughter and dispute on the front steps, a few chords struck on the piano and a few notes of a man's voice singing.

He stood still in the gloom of the hall, trying to catch the air that the voice was singing and gazing up at his wife. There was grace and mystery in her attitude as if she were a symbol of something. He asked himself what is a woman standing on the stairs in the shadow, listening to distant music, a symbol of. If he were a painter he would paint her in that attitude. Her blue felt hat would show off the bronze of her hair against the darkness and the dark panels of her skirt would show off the light ones. *Distant Music* he would call the picture if he were a painter.

The hall-door was closed; and Aunt Kate, Aunt Julia and Mary Jane came down the hall, still laughing.

— Well, isn't Freddy terrible? said Mary Jane. He's really terrible.

Gabriel said nothing but pointed up the stairs towards where his wife was standing. Now that the hall-door was closed the voice and the piano could be heard more clearly. Gabriel held up his hand for them to be silent. The song seemed to be in the old Irish tonality and the singer seemed uncertain both of his words and of his voice. The voice, made plaintive by distance and by the singer's hoarseness, faintly illuminated the cadence of the air with words expressing grief:

> O, the rain falls on my heavy locks
> And the dew wets my skin,
> My babe lies cold . . .

— O, exclaimed Mary Jane. It's Bartell D'Arcy singing, and he wouldn't sing all the night. O, I'll get him to sing a song before he goes.

— O do, Mary Jane, said Aunt Kate.

Mary Jane brushed past the others and ran to the staircase but before she reached it the singing stopped and the piano was closed abruptly.

— O, what a pity! she cried. Is he coming down, Gretta?

Gabriel heard his wife answer yes and saw her come down towards them. A few steps behind her were Mr Bartell D'Arcy and Miss O'Callaghan.

— O, Mr D'Arcy, cried Mary Jane, it's downright mean of you to break off like that when we were all in raptures listening to you.

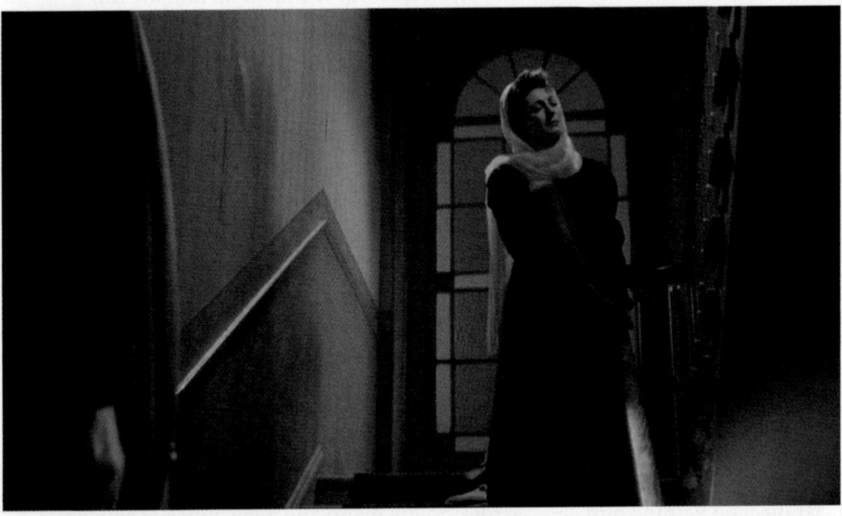

Anjelica Huston, daughter of director John Huston, played Gretta Conroy in the 1987 film version of "The Dead." **How does this image capture Gretta's response to the music and the memories it evokes for her?**

—I have been at him all the evening, said Miss O'Callaghan, and Mrs Conroy too and he told us he had a dreadful cold and couldn't sing.

—O, Mr D'Arcy, said Aunt Kate, now that was a great fib to tell.

—Can't you see that I'm as hoarse as a crow? said Mr D'Arcy roughly.

He went into the pantry hastily and put on his overcoat. The others, taken aback by his rude speech, could find nothing to say. Aunt Kate wrinkled her brows and made signs to the others to drop the subject. Mr D'Arcy stood swathing his neck carefully and frowning.

—It's the weather, said Aunt Julia, after a pause.

—Yes, everybody has colds, said Aunt Kate readily, everybody.

—They say, said Mary Jane, we haven't had snow like it for thirty years; and I read this morning in the newspapers that the snow is general all over Ireland.

—I love the look of snow, said Aunt Julia sadly.

—So do I, said Miss O'Callaghan. I think Christmas is never really Christmas unless we have the snow on the ground.

—But poor Mr D'Arcy doesn't like the snow, said Aunt Kate, smiling.

Mr D'Arcy came from the pantry, fully swathed and buttoned, and in a repentant tone told them the history of his cold. Everyone gave him advice and said it was a great pity and urged him to be very careful of his throat in the night air. Gabriel watched his wife, who did not join in the conversation. She was standing right under the dusty fanlight and the flame of the gas lit up the rich bronze of her hair which he had seen her drying at the fire a few days before. She was in the same attitude and seemed unaware of the talk about her. At last she turned towards them and Gabriel saw that there was colour on her cheeks and that her eyes were shining. A sudden tide of joy went leaping out of his heart.

—Mr D'Arcy, she said, what is the name of that song you were singing?

—It's called *The Lass of Aughrim*, said Mr D'Arcy, but I couldn't remember it properly. Why? Do you know it?

—*The Lass of Aughrim*, she repeated. I couldn't think of the name.

—It's a very nice air, said Mary Jane. I'm sorry you were not in voice to-night.

—Now, Mary Jane, said Aunt Kate, don't annoy Mr D'Arcy. I won't have him annoyed.

Seeing that all were ready to start she shepherded them to the door where good-night was said:

—Well, good-night, Aunt Kate, and thanks for the pleasant evening.

—Good-night, Gabriel. Good-night, Gretta!

—Good-night, Aunt Kate, and thanks ever so much. Good-night, Aunt Julia.

—O, good-night, Gretta, I didn't see you.

—Good-night, Mr D'Arcy. Good-night, Miss O'Callaghan.

—Good-night, Miss Morkan.

—Good-night, again.

—Good-night, all. Safe home.

—Good-night. Good-night.

The morning was still dark. A dull yellow light brooded over the houses and the river; and the sky seemed to be descending. It was slushy underfoot; and only streaks and patches of snow lay on the roofs, on the parapets of the quay and on the area railings. The lamps were still burning redly in the murky air and, across the river, the palace of the Four Courts stood out menacingly against the heavy sky.

She was walking on before him with Mr Bartell D'Arcy, her shoes in a brown parcel tucked under one arm and her hands holding her skirt up from the slush. She had no longer any grace of attitude but Gabriel's eyes were still bright with happiness. The blood went bounding along his veins; and the thoughts went rioting through his brain, proud, joyful, tender, valorous.

She was walking on before him so lightly and so erect that he longed to run after her noiselessly, catch her by the shoulders and say something foolish and affectionate into her ear. She seemed to him so frail that he longed to defend her against something and then to be alone with her. Moments of their secret life together burst like stars upon his memory. A heliotrope envelope was lying beside his breakfast-cup and he was caressing it with his hand. Birds were twittering in the ivy and the sunny web of the curtain was shimmering along the floor: he could not eat for happiness. They were standing on the crowded platform and he was placing a ticket inside the warm palm of her glove. He was standing with her in the cold, looking in through a grated window at a man making bottles in a roaring furnace. It was very cold. Her face, fragrant in the cold air, was quite close to his; and suddenly she called out to the man at the furnace:

— Is the fire hot, sir?

But the man could not hear with the noise of the furnace. It was just as well. He might have answered rudely.

A wave of yet more tender joy escaped from his heart and went coursing in warm flood along his arteries. Like the tender fires of stars moments of their life together, that no one knew of or would ever know of, broke upon and illumined his memory. He longed to recall to her those moments, to make her forget the years of their dull existence together and remember only their moments of ecstasy. For the years, he felt, had not quenched his soul or hers. Their children, his writing, her household cares had not quenched all their souls' tender fire. In one letter that he had written to her then he had said: *Why is it that words like these seem to me so dull and cold? Is it because there is no word tender enough to be your name?*

Like distant music these words that he had written years before were borne towards him from the past. He longed to be alone with her. When the others had gone away, when he and she were in the room in their hotel, then they would be alone together. He would call her softly:

— Gretta!

Perhaps she would not hear at once: she would be undressing. Then something in his voice would strike her. She would turn and look at him. . . .

At the corner of Winetavern Street they met a cab. He was glad of its rattling noise as it saved him from conversation. She was looking out of the window and seemed tired. The others spoke only a few words, pointing out some building or street. The horse galloped along wearily under the murky morning sky, dragging his old rattling box after his heels, and Gabriel was again in a cab with her, galloping to catch the boat, galloping to their honeymoon.

As the cab drove across O'Connell Bridge Miss O'Callaghan said:

— They say you never cross O'Connell Bridge without seeing a white horse.

— I see a white man this time, said Gabriel.

— Where? asked Mr Bartell D'Arcy.

Gabriel pointed to the statue,[6] on which lay patches of snow. Then he nodded familiarly to it and waved his hand.

— Good-night, Dan, he said gaily.

When the cab drew up before the hotel Gabriel jumped out and, in spite of Mr Bartell D'Arcy's protest, paid the driver. He gave the man a shilling over his fare. The man saluted and said:

— A prosperous New Year to you, sir.

— The same to you, said Gabriel cordially.

She leaned for a moment on his arm in getting out of the cab and while standing at the curbstone, bidding the others good-night. She leaned lightly on his arm, as lightly as when she had danced with him a few hours before. He had felt proud and happy then, happy that she was his, proud of her grace and wifely carriage. But now, after the kindling again of so many memories, the first touch of her body, musical and strange and perfumed, sent through him a keen

[6] Statue of Daniel O'Connell (1775–1847), an Irish lawyer who fought for Catholic rights. — EDS.

pang of lust. Under cover of her silence he pressed her arm closely to his side; and, as they stood at the hotel door, he felt that they had escaped from their lives and duties, escaped from home and friends and run away together with wild and radiant hearts to a new adventure.

An old man was dozing in a great hooded chair in the hall. He lit a candle in the office and went before them to the stairs. They followed him in silence, their feet falling in soft thuds on the thickly carpeted stairs. She mounted the stairs behind the porter, her head bowed in the ascent, her frail shoulders curved as with a burden, her skirt girt tightly about her. He could have flung his arms about her hips and held her still for his arms were trembling with desire to seize her and only the stress of his nails against the palms of his hands held the wild impulse of his body in check. The porter halted on the stairs to settle his guttering candle. They halted too on the steps below him. In the silence Gabriel could hear the falling of molten wax into the tray and the thumping of his own heart against his ribs.

The porter led them along a corridor and opened a door. Then he set his un-stable candle down on a toilet-table and asked at what hour they were to be called in the morning.

— Eight, said Gabriel.

The porter pointed to the tap of the electric-light and began a muttered apology, but Gabriel cut him short.

— We don't want any light. We have light enough from the street. And I say, he added, pointing to the candle, you might remove that handsome article, like a good man.

The porter took up his candle again, but slowly for he was surprised by such a novel idea. Then he mumbled good-night and went out. Gabriel shot the lock to.

A ghostly light from the street lamp lay in a long shaft from one window to the door. Gabriel threw his overcoat and hat on a couch and crossed the room towards the window. He looked down into the street in order that his emotion might calm a little. Then he turned and leaned against a chest of drawers with his back to the light. She had taken off her hat and cloak and was standing before a large swinging mirror, unhooking her waist. Gabriel paused for a few moments, watching her, and then said:

— Gretta!

She turned away from the mirror slowly and walked along the shaft of light towards him. Her face looked so serious and weary that the words would not pass Gabriel's lips. No, it was not the moment yet.

— You looked tired, he said.

— I am a little, she answered.

— You don't feel ill or weak?

— No, tired: that's all.

She went on to the window and stood there, looking out. Gabriel waited again and then, fearing that diffidence was about to conquer him, he said abruptly:

— By the way, Gretta!

— What is it?

— You know that poor fellow Malins? he said quickly.

— Yes. What about him?

— Well, poor fellow, he's a decent sort of chap after all, continued Gabriel in a false voice. He gave me back that sovereign I lent him and I didn't expect it really. It's a pity he wouldn't keep away from that Browne, because he's not a bad fellow at heart.

He was trembling now with annoyance. Why did she seem so abstracted? He did not know how he could begin. Was she annoyed, too, about something? If she would only turn to him or come to him of her own accord! To take her as she was would be brutal. No, he must see some ardour in her eyes first. He longed to be master of her strange mood.

— When did you lend him the pound? she asked, after a pause.

Gabriel strove to restrain himself from breaking out into brutal language about the sottish Malins and his pound. He longed to cry to her from his soul, to crush her body against his, to overmaster her. But he said:

— O, at Christmas, when he opened that little Christmas-card shop in Henry Street.

He was in such a fever of rage and desire that he did not hear her come from the window. She stood before him for an instant, looking at him strangely. Then, suddenly raising herself on tiptoe and resting her hands lightly on his shoulders, she kissed him.

— You are a very generous person, Gabriel, she said.

Gabriel, trembling with delight at her sudden kiss and at the quaintness of her phrase, put his hands on her hair and began smoothing it back, scarcely touching it with his fingers. The washing had made it fine and brilliant. His heart was brimming over with happiness. Just when he was wishing for it she had come to him of her own accord. Perhaps her thoughts had been running with his. Perhaps she had felt the impetuous desire that was in him and then the yielding mood had come upon her. Now that she had fallen to him so easily he wondered why he had been so diffident.

He stood, holding her head between his hands. Then, slipping one arm swiftly about her body and drawing her towards him, he said softly:

— Gretta, dear, what are you thinking about?

She did not answer nor yield wholly to his arm. He said again, softly:

— Tell me what it is, Gretta. I think I know what is the matter. Do I know?

She did not answer at once. Then she said in an outburst of tears:

— O, I am thinking about that song, *The Lass of Aughrim.*

She broke loose from him and ran to the bed and, throwing her arms across the bed-rail, hid her face. Gabriel stood stock-still for a moment in astonishment and then followed her. As he passed in the way of the cheval-glass he caught sight of himself in full length, his broad, well-filled shirt-front, the face whose expression always puzzled him when he saw it in a mirror and his glimmering gilt-rimmed eyeglasses. He halted a few paces from her and said:

— What about the song? Why does that make you cry?

She raised her head from her arms and dried her eyes with the back of her hand like a child. A kinder note than he had intended went into his voice.

— Why, Gretta? he asked.

— I am thinking about a person long ago who used to sing that song.

— And who was the person long ago? asked Gabriel, smiling.

— It was a person I used to know in Galway when I was living with my grandmother, she said.

The smile passed away from Gabriel's face. A dull anger began to gather again at the back of his mind and the dull fires of his lust began to glow angrily in his veins.

— Someone you were in love with? he asked ironically.

— It was a young boy I used to know, she answered, named Michael Furey. He used to sing that song, *The Lass of Aughrim.* He was very delicate.

Gabriel was silent. He did not wish her to think that he was interested in this delicate boy.

— I can see him so plainly, she said after a moment. Such eyes as he had: big dark eyes! And such an expression in them — an expression!

— O then, you were in love with him? said Gabriel.

— I used to go out walking with him, she said, when I was in Galway.

A thought flew across Gabriel's mind.

— Perhaps that was why you wanted to go to Galway with that Ivors girl? he said coldly.

She looked at him and asked in surprise:

— What for?

Her eyes made Gabriel feel awkward. He shrugged his shoulders and said:

— How do I know? To see him perhaps.

She looked away from him along the shaft of light towards the window in silence.

—He is dead, she said at length. He died when he was only seventeen. Isn't it a terrible thing to die so young as that?

—What was he? asked Gabriel, still ironically.

—He was in the gasworks, she said.

Gabriel felt humiliated by the failure of his irony and by the evocation of this figure from the dead, a boy in the gasworks. While he had been full of memories of their secret life together, full of tenderness and joy and desire, she had been comparing him in her mind with another. A shameful consciousness of his own person assailed him. He saw himself as a ludicrous figure, acting as a pennyboy for his aunts, a nervous well-meaning sentimentalist, orating to vulgarians and idealising his own clownish lusts, the pitiable fatuous fellow he had caught a glimpse of in the mirror. Instinctively he turned his back more to the light lest she might see the shame that burned upon his forehead.

He tried to keep up his tone of cold interrogation but his voice when he spoke was humble and indifferent.

—I suppose you were in love with this Michael Furey, Gretta, he said.

—I was great with him at that time, she said.

Her voice was veiled and sad. Gabriel, feeling now how vain it would be to try to lead her whither he had purposed, caressed one of her hands and said, also sadly:

—And what did he die of so young, Gretta? Consumption, was it?

—I think he died for me, she answered.

A vague terror seized Gabriel at this answer as if, at that hour when he had hoped to triumph, some impalpable and vindictive being was coming against him, gathering forces against him in its vague world. But he shook himself free of it with an effort of reason and continued to caress her hand. He did not question her again for he felt that she would tell him of herself. Her hand was warm and moist: it did not respond to his touch but he continued to caress it just as he had caressed her first letter to him that spring morning.

—It was in the winter, she said, about the beginning of the winter when I was going to leave my grandmother's and come up here to the convent. And he was ill at the time in his lodgings in Galway and wouldn't be let out and his people in Oughterard were written to. He was in decline, they said, or something like that. I never knew rightly.

She paused for a moment and sighed.

—Poor fellow, she said. He was very fond of me and he was such a gentle boy. We used to go out together, walking, you know, Gabriel, like the way they do in the country. He was going to study singing only for his health. He had a very good voice, poor Michael Furey.

—Well; and then? asked Gabriel.

—And then when it came to the time for me to leave Galway and come up to the convent he was much worse and I wouldn't be let see him so I wrote a letter saying I was going up to Dublin and would be back in the summer and hoping he would be better then.

She paused for a moment to get her voice under control and then went on:

—Then the night before I left I was in my grandmother's house in Nuns' Island, packing up, and I heard gravel thrown up against the window. The window was so wet I couldn't see so I ran downstairs as I was and slipped out the back into the garden and there was the poor fellow at the end of the garden, shivering.

—And did you not tell him to go back? asked Gabriel.

—I implored of him to go home at once and told him he would get his death in the rain. But he said he did not want to live. I can see his eyes as well as well! He was standing at the end of the wall where there was a tree.

—And did he go home? asked Gabriel.

—Yes, he went home. And when I was only a week in the convent he died and he was buried in Oughterard where his people came from. O, the day I heard that, that he was dead!

She stopped, choking with sobs, and, overcome by emotion, flung herself face downward on the bed, sobbing in the quilt. Gabriel held her hand for a moment longer, irresolutely, and then, shy of intruding on her grief, let it fall gently and walked quietly to the window.

She was fast asleep.

Gabriel, leaning on his elbow, looked for a few moments unresentfully on her tangled hair and half-open mouth, listening to her deep-drawn breath. So she had had that romance in her life: a man had died for her sake. It hardly pained him now to think how poor a part he, her husband, had played in her life. He watched her while she slept as though he and she had never lived together as man and wife. His curious eyes rested long upon her face and on her hair: and, as he thought of what she must have been then, in that time of her first girlish beauty, a strange friendly pity for her entered his soul. He did not like to say even to himself that her face was no longer beautiful but he knew that it was no longer the face for which Michael Furey had braved death.

Perhaps she had not told him all the story. His eyes moved to the chair over which she had thrown some of her clothes. A petticoat string dangled to the floor. One boot stood upright, its limp upper fallen down: the fellow of it lay upon its side. He wondered at his riot of emotions of an hour before. From what had it proceeded? From his aunt's supper, from his own foolish speech, from the wine and dancing, the merry-making when saying good-night in the hall, the pleasure of the walk along the river in the snow. Poor Aunt Julia! She, too, would soon be a shade with the shade of Patrick Morkan and his horse. He had caught that haggard look upon her face for a moment when she was singing Arrayed for the Bridal. Soon, perhaps, he would be sitting in that same drawing-room, dressed in black, his silk hat on his knees. The blinds would be drawn down and Aunt Kate would be sitting beside him, crying and blowing her nose and telling him how Julia had died. He would cast about in his mind for some words that might console her, and would find only lame and useless ones. Yes, yes: that would happen very soon.

The air of the room chilled his shoulders. He stretched himself cautiously along under the sheets and lay down beside his wife. One by one they were all becoming shades. Better pass boldly into that other world, in the full glory of some passion, than fade and wither dismally with age. He thought of how she who lay beside him had locked in her heart for so many years that image of her lover's eyes when he had told her that he did not wish to live.

Generous tears filled Gabriel's eyes. He had never felt like that himself towards any woman but he knew that such a feeling must be love. The tears gathered more thickly in his eyes and in the partial darkness he imagined he saw the form of a young man standing under a dripping tree. Other forms were near. His soul had approached that region where dwell the vast hosts of the dead. He was conscious of, but could not apprehend, their wayward and flickering existence. His own identity was fading out into a grey impalpable world: the solid world itself which these dead had one time reared and lived in was dissolving and dwindling.

A few light taps upon the pane made him turn to the window. It had begun to snow again. He watched sleepily the flakes, silver and dark, falling obliquely against the lamplight. The time had come for him to set out on his journey westward. Yes, the newspapers were right: snow was general all over Ireland. It was falling on every part of the dark central plain, on the treeless hills, falling softly upon the Bog of Allen and, farther westward, softly falling into the dark mutinous Shannon waves. It was falling, too, upon every part of the lonely churchyard on the hill where Michael Furey lay buried. It lay thickly drifted on the crooked crosses and headstones, on the spears of the little gate, on the barren thorns. His soul swooned slowly as he heard the snow falling faintly through the universe and faintly falling, like the descent of their last end, upon all the living and the dead.

[1914]

QUESTIONS FOR DISCUSSION

1. "The Dead" opens with "Lily, the caretaker's daughter," taking the guests' coats. She is the first character with whom Gabriel interacts, and Gabriel is rattled by their conversation. Reread the story's first few pages, looking carefully at the way James Joyce describes Lily's role in the Morkan household. Why do you think she answers Gabriel so sharply? Why do you think Gabriel gives her money? Why is Gabriel "discomposed by the girl's bitter and sudden retort" (para. 29)?
2. The Morkan sisters' party takes place on the Feast of the Epiphany, celebrated on January 6 and commemorating the visit of the Magi, or Three Kings, to the baby Jesus. Although the feast day has different interpretations and is celebrated in different ways, all churches agree that it commemorates the manifestation of Christ to the world. Why might Joyce have chosen this particular feast day on which to set "The Dead"?
3. Who do you think the dead are in "The Dead"?
4. What are some of the significant moments in the story when Gabriel feels he is different from others? When does he seek to isolate himself from interaction, and how are those moments described? Why is he hesitant to quote Robert Browning in his speech (para. 29)?
5. In paragraphs 37–45, Gabriel, Gretta, Aunt Kate, and Aunt Julia discuss Gabriel's excessive caution, including his insistence that his wife wear "goloshes." Reread this section and pay particular attention to the aunts' responses. Are they playfully mocking or critical of their "favorite nephew"? How does Gabriel respond? What does this interaction suggest about their relationship?
6. In paragraphs 207–24, the party guests discuss the local music scene, past and present. In a way, it is a discussion of high culture versus popular culture. What do the guests' opinions on music reveal about them? What might Joyce have thought about the conflict between high and popular culture?
7. Gabriel watches his wife at the top of the stairs: "There was grace and mystery in her attitude as if she were a symbol of something. He asked himself what is a woman standing on the stairs in the shadow, listening to distant music, a symbol of" (para. 314). Try to answer Gabriel's question.
8. Do Gabriel and Gretta seem mismatched? Consider how she interacts with his family, whether he is defensive about her background, and how he responds to finding out that she has a history that she had not previously shared with him. Do you think she should have told him? Will Gretta's revelation change her and Gabriel's relationship?
9. As the tenor Mr. Bartell D'Arcy is leaving the party, he speaks rudely to his hosts (paras. 323–24). Look closely at how everyone responds to his behavior. Why do they make excuses for him? Are they merely being polite, or do their responses suggest their awareness of his social status? Do their responses indicate something else entirely, and if so, what?
10. Joyce said that he added "The Dead" to *Dubliners* to provide uplift to a collection that many found dreary. Yet its title hardly suggests uplift. What was your emotional response to "The Dead"? In what ways might it be uplifting?
11. Joyce said that one of the purposes of "The Dead" was to reproduce Dublin's "ingenuous

insularity and its hospitality." Discuss what he might have meant by "ingenuous insularity" and whether you think the phrase is positive or negative. Reread Gabriel's comments on this topic (para. 248) and find examples of the guests' interactions that illustrate Dublin's insularity and hospitality.

12. Identify key moments in the story when music and dance are involved. What part do music and dance play in the way the characters relate to one another in this story?

13. To what extent do you think Joyce judges the characters in "The Dead"? Explain, referring to specific passages to support your response.

14. As with much of Joyce's work, "The Dead" has many autobiographical elements. Like Gretta, Joyce's wife, Nora, was from Galway, in western Ireland. She had two loves before Joyce, both of whom, like Michael Furey, died young. How does this knowledge impact your view of the story?

QUESTIONS ON STYLE AND STRUCTURE

1. Joyce wrote one play, *My Brilliant Career,* which he sent to William Archer, Norwegian playwright Henrik Ibsen's English translator, for criticism. The play is lost, but in a letter that survived, Archer stated that he was concerned that Joyce began with a large canvas but in the end focused on only a few people. This criticism became a virtue in Joyce's later works. What is the connection between the large canvas of the party — and Dublin — and the focus on Gabriel at the story's end? What possible layers of meaning does this approach add to the story?

2. How does Joyce create the atmosphere of the party? Look carefully at the detailed descriptions of the hostesses, guests, servants, house, music, and food. What tone does he create through his descriptions? Identify moments when Joyce might be expressing a particular attitude toward the party and its participants.

3. How does Joyce use subtle details to create his characters? Find examples in which a gesture, a color, or an item of clothing helps explain a character.

4. Amid the swirl of the Morkan sisters' party, several guests come into focus. What roles do characters such as Freddy Malins, his mother, Miss Ivors, Mr. Browne, and the tenor Mr. D'Arcy play in the story?

5. In paragraph 10, Joyce evokes all five senses. Look for other paragraphs or sentences with this kind of vivid imagery. In addition to making the story come to life, what is the effect of these passages? How do the images come together to help Joyce make a bigger statement about Dublin? about the Irish?

6. Once Gabriel arrives at the party, he reports on much of the action, as well as his reaction to certain events. How does Joyce balance Gabriel's self-criticism with his open-mindedness about his aunts' party and the other guests?

7. Joyce injects politics into "The Dead" in the scene in which Gabriel dances with Miss Ivors, an Irish nationalist (paras. 101–37). Trace the way Miss Ivors exposes Gabriel as the anonymous book reviewer G.C. for the *Daily Express*, and the way Gabriel defends himself. Gabriel notes that "they were friends of many years' standing and their careers had been parallel, first at the University and then as teachers: he could not risk a grandiose phrase with her" (para. 112). How do these details from the narrator shape how we interpret Gabriel's response? What do these details suggest about how the perception of the power balance in a relationship can impact interactions?

8. For a story called "The Dead," there is quite a bit of humor. How does Gabriel's willingness, for example, to "carve a flock of geese, if necessary" (para. 195) help develop his character and also the character of Dublin society? Find other examples of Joyce's sly sense of humor.

9. The dinner, which is the centerpiece of "The Dead" (paras. 196–239), is filled with sensuous details. How does Joyce pace the description so that the reader is caught up not only in the food but in the swirl of conversation and conviviality?

10. Analyze Gabriel's speech (paras. 242–61). Do you think it is overly sentimental? How do you think Gabriel feels about his audience? In what ways does he pitch the speech to them? What assumptions about the audience drive the speech?

11. How does the tone of the story shift at the end of the party? Examine the way Joyce makes the transition from the party to Gabriel's very private contemplation of Gretta.

12. What do the details of Gabriel's imaginary painting of Gretta reveal about his feelings for his wife (para. 314)?

13. Identify examples of images of snow and fire in "The Dead," and discuss their effect. How do these image patterns further the development of the themes in the story?

14. Joyce is famous for having invented *epiphany* as a literary term. He defined it as the "sudden revelation of the whatness of a thing," the moment in which "the soul of the commonest object . . . seems to us radiant . . . a sudden spiritual manifestation [either] in the vulgarity of speech or of a gesture or in a memorable phrase of the mind itself." What is Gabriel's epiphany? What causes it?

SUGGESTIONS FOR WRITING

1. Write an essay in which you discuss how the party that is the setting for "The Dead" reveals the values of the characters and the society in which they live.

2. Develop an argument that asserts one of the story's possible points about romantic love or marriage. Write an essay that analyzes how the literary elements in the story — characterization, point of view, figurative language, and so on — reinforce this idea.

3. Choose two or more minor characters in the story and analyze the significance of how they relate or fail to relate to one another.

4. In *Transitions: Narratives in Modern Irish Culture*, Irish scholar Richard Kearney argues that the crisis of twentieth-century Irish culture is defined by a clash between "revivalism and modernism," between those who "seek to revive the past" and those who turn to a cosmopolitan or international perspective and thereby "seek to rewrite or repudiate it altogether." Using "The Dead," support, challenge, or qualify Kearney's claim.

5. Identify significant descriptions of the setting throughout the story and write an essay analyzing how these details impact the tone and meaning of the work.

6. Choose a passage in the story that on a first reading may have seemed insignificant or even mundane, but on additional readings takes on significant meaning. Write an essay that closely analyzes the details of the passage, arguing for the passage's significance to the work as a whole.

7. View John Huston's film version of "The Dead," which stars his daughter Anjelica Huston as Gretta Conroy. Write a review in which you evaluate Mr. Huston's interpretation of Joyce's story.

8. Make a mix CD of the music mentioned in "The Dead," including any modern versions of the songs. Then write the liner notes.

The Importance of Being Earnest: A Trivial Comedy for Serious People

OSCAR WILDE

Time Life Pictures / Getty Images

Oscar Fingal O'Flahertie Wills Wilde was born in Dublin in 1854. At the age of sixteen, Wilde won the Royal School Scholarship to Trinity College Dublin, where he won several awards as a scholar of ancient Greek before receiving a scholarship to Magdalen College, Oxford. Here he became engaged with the aesthetic, or decadence, movement, whose commitment to beauty and art for art's sake conflicted with the strict morality and restraint of the Victorian era. After graduating, Wilde moved to London, where he married Constance Lloyd and had two sons. Wilde established himself as a writer, publishing two children's books and, in 1890, his only novel, *The Picture of Dorian Gray*. The explicit characterization of evil and the underlying homoerotic subculture it depicted were condemned by Victorian English society. Wilde, amused by the reaction of his critics, turned more decisively to social and political satire, and in 1891–1892 he wrote his first play, *Lady Windermere's Fan*. Its immediate success established his direction as a playwright, and in the following three years he wrote *A Woman of No Importance* (1893), *An Ideal Husband* (1895), and *The Importance of Being Earnest* (1895). Wilde's later years were less happy. In 1895, he was caught in a homosexual relationship (at the time a criminal offense), which eventually led to a two-year sentence in Reading jail. After his release, he published "The Ballad of Reading Gaol" (1898), a profound reflection on the nature of sin and the need for charity. Effectively an outcast from Britain, Wilde lived in Paris under an assumed name until his death from meningitis in November 1900. *The Importance of Being Earnest* is considered one of the finest satirical plays written in the English language.

The Persons of the Play

JOHN WORTHING, J.P. *of the Manor House, Woolton, Hertfordshire*
ALGERNON MONCRIEFF *his friend*
REV. CANON CHASUBLE, D.D. *rector of Woolton*
MERRIMAN *butler to Mr. Worthing*
LANE *Mr. Moncrieff's manservant*
LADY BRACKNELL
HON. GWENDOLEN FAIRFAX *her daughter*
CECILY CARDEW *John Worthing's ward*
MISS PRISM *her governess*

The Scenes of the Play

ACT I *Algernon Moncrieff's Flat in Half-Moon Street, W.*
ACT II *The Garden at the Manor House, Woolton*
ACT III *Morning Room at the Manor House, Woolton*

ACT I

(*Scene: Morning room in Algernon's flat in Half Moon Street. The room is luxuriously and artistically furnished. The sound of a piano is heard in the adjoining room.* **LANE** *is arranging afternoon tea on the table, and after the music has ceased,* **ALGERNON** *enters.*)

ALGERNON Did you hear what I was playing, Lane?

LANE I didn't think it polite to listen, sir.

ALGERNON I'm sorry for that, for your sake. I don't play accurately — anyone can play accurately — but I play with wonderful expression. As far as the piano is concerned, sentiment is my forte. I keep science for Life.

LANE Yes, sir.

ALGERNON And, speaking of the science of Life, have you got the cucumber sandwiches cut for Lady Bracknell?

LANE Yes, sir. (*Hands them on a salver.*)

ALGERNON (*inspects them, takes two, and sits down on the sofa*): Oh! — by the way, Lane, I see from your book that on Thursday night, when Lord Shoreham and Mr. Worthing were dining with me, eight bottles of champagne are entered as having been consumed.

LANE Yes, sir; eight bottles and a pint.

ALGERNON Why is it that at a bachelor's establishment the servants invariably drink the champagne? I ask merely for information.

LANE I attribute it to the superior quality of the wine, sir. I have often observed that in married households the champagne is rarely of a first-rate brand.

ALGERNON Good heavens! Is marriage so demoralizing as that?

LANE I believe it *is* a very pleasant state, sir. I have had very little experience of it myself up to the present. I have only been married once. That was in consequence of a misunderstanding between myself and a young person.

ALGERNON (*languidly*): I don't know that I am much interested in your family life, Lane.

LANE No, sir; it is not a very interesting subject. I never think of it myself.

ALGERNON Very natural, I am sure. That will do, Lane, thank you.

LANE Thank you, sir. (**LANE** *goes out.*)

ALGERNON Lane's views on marriage seem somewhat lax. Really, if the lower orders don't set us a good example, what on earth is the use of them? They seem, as a class, to have absolutely no sense of moral responsibility.

(*Enter* **LANE**.)

LANE Mr. Ernest Worthing.

(*Enter* **JACK**. **LANE** *goes out.*)

ALGERNON How are you, my dear Ernest? What brings you up to town?

JACK Oh, pleasure, pleasure! What else should bring one anywhere? Eating as usual, I see, Algy!

ALGERNON (*stiffly*): I believe it is customary in good society to take some slight refreshment at five o'clock. Where have you been since last Thursday?

JACK (*sitting down on the sofa*): In the country.

ALGERNON What on earth do you do there?

JACK (*pulling off his gloves*): When one is in town one amuses oneself. When one is in the country one amuses other people. It is excessively boring.

ALGERNON And who are the people you amuse?

JACK (*airily*): Oh, neighbors, neighbors.

ALGERNON Got nice neighbors in your part of Shropshire?

JACK Perfectly horrid! Never speak to one of them.

ALGERNON How immensely you must amuse them! (*Goes over and takes sandwich.*) By the way, Shropshire is your county, is it not?

JACK Eh? Shropshire? Yes, of course. Hallo! Why all these cups? Why cucumber sandwiches? Why such reckless extravagance in one so young? Who is coming to tea?

ALGERNON Oh! merely Aunt Augusta and Gwendolen.

JACK How perfectly delightful!

ALGERNON Yes, that is all very well; but I am afraid Aunt Augusta won't quite approve of your being here.

JACK May I ask why?

ALGERNON My dear fellow, the way you flirt with Gwendolen is perfectly disgraceful. It is almost as bad as the way Gwendolen flirts with you.

JACK I am in love with Gwendolen. I have come up to town expressly to propose to her.

ALGERNON I thought you had come up for pleasure? — I call that business.

JACK How utterly unromantic you are!

ALGERNON I really don't see anything romantic in proposing. It is very romantic to be in love. But there is nothing romantic about a definite proposal. Why, one may be accepted. One usually is, I believe. Then the excitement is all over. The very essence of romance is uncertainty. If ever I get married, I'll certainly try to forget the fact.

JACK I have no doubt about that, dear Algy. The Divorce Court was specially invented for people whose memories are so curiously constituted.

ALGERNON Oh! there is no use speculating on that subject. Divorces are made in heaven — (**JACK** *puts out his hand to take a sandwich.* **ALGERNON** *at once interferes.*) Please don't touch the cucumber sandwiches. They are ordered specially for Aunt Augusta. (*Takes one and eats it.*)

JACK Well, you have been eating them all the time.

ALGERNON That is quite a different matter. She is my aunt. (*Takes plate from below.*) Have some bread and butter. The bread and butter is for Gwendolen. Gwendolen is devoted to bread and butter.

JACK (*advancing to table and helping himself*): And very good bread and butter it is too.

ALGERNON Well, my dear fellow, you need not eat as if you were going to eat it all. You behave as if you were married to her already. You are not married to her already, and I don't think you ever will be.

JACK Why on earth do you say that?

ALGERNON Well, in the first place, girls never marry the men they flirt with. Girls don't think it right.

JACK Oh, that is nonsense!

ALGERNON It isn't. It is a great truth. It accounts for the extraordinary number of bachelors that one sees all over the place. In the second place, I don't give my consent.

JACK Your consent!

ALGERNON My dear fellow, Gwendolen is my first cousin. And before I allow you to marry her, you will have to clear up the whole question of Cecily. (*Rings bell.*)

© MBI/Alamy Stock Photo

In a guide to making the perfect cucumber sandwich published in the English newspaper the *Guardian*, reporter Felicity Cloake asserts, "They glory in their own delicacy: rumour suggests the nutritional redundancy of a thin, white bread sandwich filled with a fruit that's 96% water was intended to celebrate the sedentary lifestyles of the Victorian upper crust." **How might the cucumber sandwich pictured here and described in *The Importance of Being Earnest* be interpreted as a comment on the preoccupations of the characters in the play?**

JACK Cecily! What on earth do you mean? What do you mean, Algy, by Cecily! I don't know anyone of the name of Cecily.

(*Enter* **LANE**.)

ALGERNON Bring me that cigarette case Mr. Worthing left in the smoking room the last time he dined here.

LANE Yes, sir. (**LANE** *goes out.*)

JACK Do you mean to say you have had my cigarette case all this time? I wish to goodness you had let me know. I have been writing frantic letters to Scotland Yard about it. I was very nearly offering a large reward.

ALGERNON Well, I wish you would offer one. I happen to be more than usually hard up.

JACK There is no good offering a large reward now that the thing is found.

(*Enter* **LANE** *with the cigarette case on a salver.* **ALGERNON** *takes it at once.* **LANE** *goes out.*)

ALGERNON I think that is rather mean of you, Ernest, I must say. (*Opens case and examines it.*) However, it makes no matter, for, now that I look at the inscription inside, I find that the thing isn't yours after all.

JACK Of course it's mine. (*Moving to him.*) You have seen me with it a hundred times, and you have no right whatsoever to read what is written inside. It is a very ungentlemanly thing to read a private cigarette case.

ALGERNON Oh! it is absurd to have a hard-and-fast rule about what one should read and what one shouldn't. More than half of modern culture depends on what one shouldn't read.

JACK I am quite aware of the fact, and I don't propose to discuss modern culture. It isn't the sort of thing one should talk of in private. I simply want my cigarette case back.

ALGERNON Yes; but this isn't your cigarette case. This cigarette case is a present from someone of the name of Cecily, and you said you didn't know anyone of that name.

JACK Well, if you want to know, Cecily happens to be my aunt.

ALGERNON Your aunt!

JACK Yes. Charming old lady she is, too. Lives at Tunbridge Wells. Just give it back to me, Algy.

ALGERNON (*retreating to back of sofa*): But why does she call herself little Cecily if she is your aunt and lives at Tunbridge Wells? (*Reading.*) "From little Cecily with her fondest love."

JACK (*moving to sofa and kneeling upon it*): My dear fellow, what on earth is there in that? Some aunts are tall, some aunts are not tall. That is a matter that surely an aunt may be allowed to decide for herself. You seem to think that every aunt should be exactly like your aunt! That is absurd! For heaven's sake give me back my cigarette case. (*Follows* **ALGERNON** *round the room.*)

ALGERNON Yes. But why does your aunt call you her uncle? "From little Cecily, with her fondest love to her dear Uncle Jack." There is no objection, I admit, to an aunt being a small aunt, but why an aunt, no matter what her size may be, should call her own nephew her uncle, I can't quite make out. Besides, your name isn't Jack at all; it is Ernest.

JACK It isn't Ernest; it's Jack.

ALGERNON You have always told me it was Ernest. I have introduced you to everyone as Ernest. You answer to the name of Ernest. You look as if your name was Ernest. You are the most earnest looking person I ever saw in my life. It is perfectly absurd your saying that your name isn't Ernest. It's on your cards. Here is one of them (*taking it from case*) "Mr. Ernest Worthing, B.4, The Albany." I'll keep this as a proof that your name is Ernest if ever you attempt to deny it to me, or to Gwendolen, or to anyone else. (*Puts the card in his pocket.*)

JACK Well, my name is Ernest in town and Jack in the country, and the cigarette case was given to me in the country.

ALGERNON Yes, but that does not account for the fact that your small Aunt Cecily, who lives at Tunbridge Wells, calls you her dear uncle. Come, old boy, you had much better have the thing out at once.

JACK My dear Algy, you talk exactly as if you were a dentist. It is very vulgar to talk like a dentist when one isn't a dentist. It produces a false impression.

ALGERNON Well, that is exactly what dentists always do. Now, go on! Tell me the whole thing. I may mention that I have always suspected you of being a confirmed and secret Bunburyist; and I am quite sure of it now.

JACK Bunburyist? What on earth do you mean by a Bunburyist?

ALGERNON I'll reveal to you the meaning of that incomparable expression as soon as you are kind enough to inform me why you are Ernest in town and Jack in the country.

JACK Well, produce my cigarette case first.

ALGERNON Here it is. (*Hands cigarette case.*) Now produce your explanation, and pray make it improbable. (*Sits on sofa.*)

JACK My dear fellow, there is nothing improbable about my explanation at all. In fact it's perfectly ordinary. Old Mr. Thomas Cardew, who adopted me when I was a little boy, made me in his will guardian to his granddaughter, Miss Cecily Cardew. Cecily, who addresses me as her uncle from motives of respect that you could not possibly appreciate, lives at my place in the country under the charge of her admirable governess, Miss Prism.

ALGERNON Where is that place in the country, by the way?

JACK That is nothing to you, dear boy. You are not going to be invited — I may tell you candidly that the place is not in Shropshire.

ALGERNON I suspected that, my dear fellow! I have Bunburyed all over Shropshire on two separate occasions. Now, go on. Why are you Ernest in town and Jack in the country?

JACK My dear Algy, I don't know whether you will be able to understand my real motives. You are hardly serious enough. When one is placed in the position of guardian, one has to adopt a very high moral tone on all subjects. It's one's duty to do so. And as a high moral tone can hardly be said to conduce very much to either one's health or one's happiness, in order to get up to town I have always pretended to have a younger brother of the name of Ernest, who lives in the Albany, and gets into the most dreadful scrapes. That, my dear Algy, is the whole truth pure and simple.

ALGERNON The truth is rarely pure and never simple. Modern life would be very tedious if it were either, and modern literature a complete impossibility!

JACK That wouldn't be at all a bad thing.

ALGERNON Literary criticism is not your forte, my dear fellow. Don't try it. You should leave that to people who haven't been at a university. They do it so well in the daily papers. What you really are is a Bunburyist. I was quite right in saying you were a Bunburyist. You are one of the most advanced Bunburyists I know.

JACK What on earth do you mean?

ALGERNON You have invented a very useful younger brother called Ernest, in order that you may be able to come up to town as often as you like. I have invented an invaluable permanent invalid called Bunbury, in order that I may be able to go down into the country whenever I choose. Bunbury is perfectly invaluable. If it wasn't for Bunbury's extraordinary bad health, for instance, I wouldn't be able to dine with you at Willis's tonight, for I have been really engaged to Aunt Augusta for more than a week.

JACK I haven't asked you to dine with me anywhere tonight.

ALGERNON I know. You are absurdly careless about sending out invitations. It is very foolish of you. Nothing annoys people so much as not receiving invitations.

JACK You had much better dine with your Aunt Augusta.

ALGERNON I haven't the smallest intention of doing anything of the kind. To begin with, I dined there on Monday, and once a week is quite enough to dine with one's own relations. In the second place, whenever I do dine there I am always treated as a member of the family, and sent down with[1] either no woman at all, or two. In the third place, I know perfectly well whom she will place me next to, tonight. She will place me next Mary Farquhar, who always flirts with her own husband across the dinner table. That is not very pleasant. Indeed, it is not even decent — and that sort of thing is enormously on the increase. The amount of women in London who flirt with their own husbands is perfectly scandalous. It looks so bad. It is simply washing one's clean linen in public. Besides, now that I know you to be a confirmed Bunburyist I naturally want to talk to you about Bunburying. I want to tell you the rules.

JACK I'm not a Bunburyist at all. If Gwendolen accepts me, I am going to kill my brother, indeed I think I'll kill him in any case. Cecily is a little too much interested in him. It is rather a bore. So I am going to get rid of Ernest. And I strongly advise you to do the same with Mr. — with your invalid friend who has the absurd name.

ALGERNON Nothing will induce me to part with Bunbury, and if you ever get married, which seems to me extremely problematic, you will be very glad to know Bunbury. A man who marries without knowing Bunbury has a very tedious time of it.

JACK That is nonsense. If I marry a charming girl like Gwendolen, and she is the only girl I ever saw in my life that I would marry, I certainly won't want to know Bunbury.

ALGERNON Then your wife will. You don't seem to realize, that in married life three is company and two is none.

JACK (*sententiously*): That, my dear young friend, is the theory that the corrupt French drama has been propounding for the last fifty years.

ALGERNON Yes; and that the happy English home has proved in half the time.

JACK For heaven's sake, don't try to be cynical. It's perfectly easy to be cynical.

ALGERNON My dear fellow, it isn't easy to be anything nowadays. There's such a lot of beastly competition about. (*The sound of an electric bell is heard.*) Ah! that must be Aunt Augusta. Only relatives, or creditors, ever ring in that Wagnerian[2] manner. Now, if I get her out of the way for ten minutes, so that you can have an opportunity for proposing to Gwendolen, may I dine with you tonight at Willis's?

JACK I suppose so, if you want to.

ALGERNON Yes, but you must be serious about it. I hate people who are not serious about meals. It is so shallow of them.

(*Enter* **LANE**.)

LANE Lady Bracknell and Miss Fairfax.

(**ALGERNON** *goes forward to meet them. Enter* **LADY BRACKNELL** *and* **GWENDOLEN**.)

LADY BRACKNELL Good afternoon, dear Algernon, I hope you are behaving very well.

ALGERNON I'm feeling very well, Aunt Augusta.

LADY BRACKNELL That's not quite the same thing. In fact the two things rarely go together.

(*Sees* **JACK** *and bows to him with icy coldness.*)

ALGERNON (*to* **GWENDOLEN**): Dear me, you are smart!

[1] Assigned a woman to accompany into the dining room. — EDS.

[2] German composer Richard Wagner's most famous operatic work is the *Ring* Cycle, from which we get the stereotypical operatic image of a bellowing soprano wearing a Viking helmet. — EDS.

GWENDOLEN I am always smart! Aren't I, Mr. Worthing?

JACK You're quite perfect, Miss Fairfax.

GWENDOLEN Oh! I hope I am not that. It would leave no room for developments, and I intend to develop in many directions.

*(***GWENDOLEN** *and* **JACK** *sit down together in the corner.)*

LADY BRACKNELL I'm sorry if we are a little late, Algernon, but I was obliged to call on dear Lady Harbury. I hadn't been there since her poor husband's death. I never saw a woman so altered; she looks quite twenty years younger. And now I'll have a cup of tea, and one of those nice cucumber sandwiches you promised me.

ALGERNON Certainly, Aunt Augusta. (*Goes over to tea table.*)

LADY BRACKNELL Won't you come and sit here, Gwendolen?

GWENDOLEN Thanks, Mama, I'm quite comfortable where I am.

ALGERNON (*picking up empty plate in horror*): Good heavens! Lane! Why are there no cucumber sandwiches? I ordered them specially.

LANE (*gravely*): There were no cucumbers in the market this morning, sir. I went down twice.

ALGERNON No cucumbers!

AANE No, sir. Not even for ready money.

ALGERNON That will do, Lane, thank you.

LANE Thank you, sir. (*Goes out.*)

ALGERNON I am greatly distressed, Aunt Augusta, about there being no cucumbers, not even for ready money.

LADY BRACKNELL It really makes no matter, Algernon. I had some crumpets with Lady Harbury, who seems to me to be living entirely for pleasure now.

ALGERNON I hear her hair has turned quite gold from grief.

LADY BRACKNELL It certainly has changed its color. From what cause I, of course, cannot say. (**ALGERNON** *crosses and hands tea.*) Thank you. I've quite a treat for you tonight, Algernon. I am going to send you down with Mary Farquhar. She is such a nice woman, and so attentive to her husband. It's delightful to watch them.

ALGERNON I am afraid, Aunt Augusta, I shall have to give up the pleasure of dining with you tonight after all.

LADY BRACKNELL (*frowning*): I hope not, Algernon. It would put my table completely out. Your uncle would have to dine upstairs. Fortunately he is accustomed to that.

ALGERNON It is a great bore, and, I need hardly say, a terrible disappointment to me, but the fact is I have just had a telegram to say that my poor friend Bunbury is very ill again. (*Exchanges glances with* **JACK.**) They seem to think I should be with him.

LADY BRACKNELL It is very strange. This Mr. Bunbury seems to suffer from curiously bad health.

ALGERNON Yes; poor Bunbury is a dreadful invalid.

LADY BRACKNELL Well, I must say, Algernon, that I think it is high time that Mr. Bunbury made up his mind whether he was going to live or to die. This shilly-shallying with the question is absurd. Nor do I in any way approve of the modern sympathy with invalids. I consider it morbid. Illness of any kind is hardly a thing to be encouraged in others. Health is the primary duty of life. I am always telling that to your poor uncle, but he never seems to take much notice — as far as any improvement in his ailments goes. I should be much obliged if you would ask Mr. Bunbury, from me, to be kind enough not to have a relapse on Saturday, for I rely on you to arrange my music for me. It is my last reception, and one wants something that will encourage conversation, particularly at the end of the season when everyone has practically said whatever they had to say, which, in most cases, was probably not much.

ALGERNON I'll speak to Bunbury, Aunt Augusta, if he is still conscious, and I think I can promise you he'll be all right by Saturday. Of course the music is a great difficulty. You see, if one plays good music, people don't listen, and if one plays bad music people don't talk. But I'll run over the program I've drawn out, if you will kindly come into the next room for a moment.

LADY BRACKNELL Thank you, Algernon. It is very thoughtful of you. (*Rising, and following* **ALGERNON**.) I'm sure the program will be delightful, after a few expurgations. French songs I cannot possibly allow. People always seem to think that they are improper, and either look shocked, which is vulgar, or laugh, which is worse. But German sounds a thoroughly respectable language, and indeed, I believe is so. Gwendolen, you will accompany me.

GWENDOLEN Certainly, Mama.

(**LADY BRACKNELL** *and* **ALGERNON** *go into the music room.* **GWENDOLEN** *remains behind.*)

JACK Charming day it has been, Miss Fairfax.

GWENDOLEN Pray don't talk to me about the weather, Mr. Worthing. Whenever people talk to me about the weather, I always feel quite certain that they mean something else. And that makes me so nervous.

JACK I do mean something else.

GWENDOLEN I thought so. In fact, I am never wrong.

JACK And I would like to be allowed to take advantage of Lady Bracknell's temporary absence—

GWENDOLEN I would certainly advise you to do so. Mama has a way of coming back suddenly into a room that I have often had to speak to her about.

JACK (*nervously*): Miss Fairfax, ever since I met you I have admired you more than any girl—I have ever met since—I met you.

GWENDOLEN Yes, I am quite aware of the fact. And I often wish that in public, at any rate, you had been more demonstrative. For me you have always had an irresistible fascination. Even before I met you I was far from indifferent to you. (**JACK** *looks at her in amazement.*) We live, as I hope you know, Mr. Worthing, in an age of ideals. The fact is constantly mentioned in the more expensive monthly magazines, and has reached the provincial pulpits I am told: And my ideal has always been to love someone of the name of Ernest. There is something in that name that inspires absolute confidence. The moment Algernon first mentioned to me that he had a friend called Ernest, I knew I was destined to love you.

JACK You really love me, Gwendolen?

GWENDOLEN Passionately!

JACK Darling! You don't know how happy you've made me.

GWENDOLEN My own Ernest!

JACK But you don't mean to say that you couldn't love me if my name wasn't Ernest?

GWENDOLEN But your name is Ernest.

JACK Yes, I know it is. But supposing it was something else? Do you mean to say you couldn't love me then?

GWENDOLEN (*glibly*): Ah! that is clearly a metaphysical speculation, and like most metaphysical speculations has very little reference at all to the actual facts of real life, as we know them.

JACK Personally, darling, to speak quite candidly, I don't much care about the name of Ernest—I don't think the name suits me at all.

GWENDOLEN It suits you perfectly. It is a divine name. It has a music of its own. It produces vibrations.

JACK Well, really, Gwendolen, I must say that I think there are lots of other much nicer names. I think Jack, for instance, a charming name.

GWENDOLEN Jack? — No, there is very little music in the name Jack, if any at all, indeed. It does not thrill. It produces absolutely no vibrations — I have known several Jacks, and they all, without exception, were more than usually plain. Besides, Jack is a notorious domesticity for John! And I pity any woman who is married to a man called John. She would probably never be allowed to know the entrancing pleasure of a single moment's solitude. The only really safe name is Ernest.

JACK Gwendolen, I must get christened at once — I mean we must get married at once. There is no time to be lost.

GWENDOLEN Married, Mr. Worthing?

JACK (*astounded*): Well — surely. You know that I love you, and you led me to believe, Miss Fairfax, that you were not absolutely indifferent to me.

GWENDOLEN I adore you. But you haven't proposed to me yet. Nothing has been said at all about marriage. The subject has not even been touched on.

JACK Well — may I propose to you now?

GWENDOLEN I think it would be an admirable opportunity. And to spare you any possible disappointment, Mr. Worthing, I think it only fair to tell you quite frankly beforehand that I am fully determined to accept you.

JACK Gwendolen!

GWENDOLEN Yes, Mr. Worthing, what have you got to say to me?

JACK You know what I have got to say to you.

GWENDOLEN Yes, but you don't say it.

JACK Gwendolen, will you marry me? (*Goes on his knees.*)

GWENDOLEN Of course I will, darling. How long you have been about it! I am afraid you have had very little experience in how to propose.

JACK My own one, I have never loved anyone in the world but you.

GWENDOLEN Yes, but men often propose for practice. I know my brother Gerald does. All my girlfriends tell me so. What wonderfully blue eyes you have, Ernest! They are quite, quite blue. I hope you will always look at me just like that, especially when there are other people present.

(*Enter* **LADY BRACKNELL**.)

LADY BRACKNELL Mr. Worthing! Rise, sir, from this semirecumbent posture. It is most indecorous.

GWENDOLEN Mama! (*He tries to rise; she restrains him.*) I must beg you to retire. This is no place for you. Besides, Mr. Worthing has not quite finished yet.

LADY BRACKNELL Finished what, may I ask?

GWENDOLEN I am engaged to Mr. Worthing, Mama. (*They rise together.*)

LADY BRACKNELL Pardon me, you are not engaged to anyone. When you do become engaged to someone, I, or your father, should his health permit him, will inform you of the fact. An engagement should come on a young girl as a surprise, pleasant or unpleasant, as the case may be. It is hardly a matter that she could be allowed to arrange for herself — And now I have a few questions to put to you, Mr. Worthing. While I am making these inquiries, you, Gwendolen, will wait for me below in the carriage.

GWENDOLEN (*reproachfully*): Mama!

LADY BRACKNELL In the carriage, Gwendolen! (**GWENDOLEN** *goes to the door. She and* **JACK** *blow kisses to each other behind* **LADY BRACKNELL**'*s back.* **LADY BRACKNELL** *looks vaguely about as if she could not understand what the noise was. Finally turns round.*) Gwendolen, the carriage!

GWENDOLEN Yes, Mama.

(*Goes out, looking back at* **JACK**.)

LADY BRACKNELL (*sitting down*): You can take a seat, Mr. Worthing. (*Looks in her pocket for notebook and pencil.*)

JACK Thank you, Lady Bracknell, I prefer standing.

LADY BRACKNELL (*pencil and notebook in hand*): I feel bound to tell you that you are not down on my list of eligible young men, although I have the same list as the dear Duchess of Bolton has. We work together, in fact. However, I am quite ready to enter your name, should your answers be what a really affectionate mother requires. Do you smoke?

JACK Well, yes, I must admit I smoke.

LADY BRACKNELL I am glad to hear it. A man should always have an occupation of some kind. There are far too many idle men in London as it is. How old are you?

JACK Twenty-nine.

LADY BRACKNELL A very good age to be married at. I have always been of opinion that a man who desires to get married should know either everything or nothing. Which do you know?

JACK (*after some hesitation*): I know nothing, Lady Bracknell.

LADY BRACKNELL I am pleased to hear it. I do not approve of anything that tampers with natural ignorance. Ignorance is like a delicate exotic fruit; touch it and the bloom is gone. The whole theory of modern education is radically unsound. Fortunately in England, at any rate, education produces no effect whatsoever. If it did, it would prove a serious danger to the upper classes, and probably lead to acts of violence in Grosvenor Square. What is your income?

JACK Between seven and eight thousand a year.

LADY BRACKNELL (*makes a note in her book*): In land, or in investments?

JACK In investments, chiefly.

LADY BRACKNELL That is satisfactory. What between the duties expected of one during one's lifetime, and the duties exacted from one after one's death, land has ceased to be either a profit or a pleasure. It gives one position, and prevents one from keeping it up. That's all that can be said about land.

JACK I have a country house with some land, of course, attached to it, about fifteen hundred acres, I believe; but I don't depend on that for my real income. In fact, as far as I can make out, the poachers are the only people who make anything out of it.

LADY BRACKNELL A country house! How many bedrooms? Well, that point can be cleared up afterwards. You have a town house, I hope? A girl with a simple, unspoiled nature, like Gwendolen, could hardly be expected to reside in the country.

JACK Well, I own a house in Belgrave Square, but it is let by the year to Lady Bloxham. Of course, I can get it back whenever I like, at six months' notice.

LADY BRACKNELL Lady Bloxham? I don't know her.

JACK Oh, she goes about very little. She is a lady considerably advanced in years.

LADY BRACKNELL Ah, nowadays that is no guarantee of respectability of character. What number in Belgrave Square?

JACK 149.

LADY BRACKNELL (*shaking her head*): The unfashionable side. I thought there was something. However, that could easily be altered.

JACK Do you mean the fashion, or the side?

LADY BRACKNELL (*sternly*): Both, if necessary, I presume. What are your politics?

JACK Well, I am afraid I really have none. I am a Liberal Unionist.

LADY BRACKNELL Oh, they count as Tories. They dine with us. Or come in the evening, at any rate. Now to minor matters. Are your parents living?

JACK I have lost both my parents.

LADY BRACKNELL Both? To lose one parent may be regarded as a misfortune — to lose *both* seems like carelessness. Who was your father? He was evidently a man of some wealth. Was he born in what the Radical papers call the purple of commerce, or did he rise from the ranks of the aristocracy?

JACK I am afraid I really don't know. The fact is, Lady Bracknell, I said I had lost my parents. It would be nearer the truth to say that my parents seem to have lost me — I don't actually know who I am by birth. I was — well, I was found.

LADY BRACKNELL Found!

JACK The late Mr. Thomas Cardew, an old gentleman of a very charitable and kindly disposition, found me, and gave me the name of Worthing, because he happened to have a first-class ticket for Worthing in his pocket at the time. Worthing is a place in Sussex. It is a seaside resort.

LADY BRACKNELL Where did the charitable gentleman who had a first-class ticket for this seaside resort find you?

JACK (*gravely*): In a handbag.

LADY BRACKNELL A handbag?

JACK (*very seriously*): Yes, Lady Bracknell. I was in a handbag — a somewhat large, black leather handbag, with handles to it — an ordinary handbag in fact.

LADY BRACKNELL In what locality did this Mr. James, or Thomas, Cardew come across this ordinary handbag?

JACK In the cloakroom at Victoria Station. It was given to him in mistake for his own.

LADY BRACKNELL The cloakroom at Victoria Station?

JACK Yes. The Brighton line.

LADY BRACKNELL The line is immaterial. Mr. Worthing, I confess I feel somewhat bewildered by what you have just told me. To be born, or at any rate bred, in a handbag, whether it had handles or not, seems to me to display a contempt for the ordinary decencies of family life that reminds one of the worst excesses of the French Revolution. And I presume you know what that unfortunate movement led to? As for the particular locality in which the handbag was found, a cloakroom at a railway station might serve to conceal a social indiscretion — has probably, indeed, been used for that purpose before now — but it could hardly be regarded as an assured basis for a recognized position in good society.

JACK May I ask you then what you would advise me to do? I need hardly say I would do anything in the world to ensure Gwendolen's happiness.

LADY BRACKNELL I would strongly advise you, Mr. Worthing, to try and acquire some relations as soon as possible, and to make a definite effort to produce at any rate one parent, of either sex, before the season is quite over.

JACK Well, I don't see how I could possibly manage to do that. I can produce the handbag at any moment. It is in my dressing room at home. I really think that should satisfy you, Lady Bracknell.

LADY BRACKNELL Me, sir! What has it to do with me? You can hardly imagine that I and Lord Bracknell would dream of allowing our only daughter — a girl brought up with the utmost care — to marry into a cloakroom, and form an alliance with a parcel? Good morning, Mr. Worthing!

(**LADY BRACKNELL** *sweeps out in majestic indignation.*)

JACK Good morning! (**ALGERNON**, *from the other room, strikes up the Wedding March.* **JACK** *looks perfectly furious, and goes to the door.*) For goodness' sake don't play that ghastly tune, Algy. How idiotic you are!

(*The music stops, and* **ALGERNON** *enters cheerily.*)

ALGERNON Didn't it go off all right, old boy? You don't mean to say Gwendolen refused you? I know it is a way she has. She is always refusing people. I think it is most ill-natured of her.

JACK Oh, Gwendolen is as right as a trivet. As far as she is concerned, we are engaged. Her mother is perfectly unbearable. Never met such a Gorgon[3] — I don't really know what a Gorgon is like, but I am quite sure that Lady Bracknell is one. In any case, she is a monster, without being a myth, which is rather unfair. I beg your pardon, Algy, I suppose I shouldn't talk about your own aunt in that way before you.

ALGERNON My dear boy, I love hearing my relations abused. It is the only thing that makes me put up with them at all. Relations are simply a tedious pack of people, who haven't got the remotest knowledge of how to live, nor the smallest instinct about when to die.

JACK Oh, that is nonsense!

ALGERNON It isn't!

JACK Well, I won't argue about the matter. You always want to argue about things.

ALGERNON That is exactly what things were originally made for.

JACK Upon my word, if I thought that, I'd shoot myself — (*A pause.*) You don't think there is any chance of Gwendolen becoming like her mother in about a hundred and fifty years, do you, Algy?

ALGERNON All women become like their mothers. That is their tragedy. No man does. That's his.

JACK Is that clever?

ALGERNON It is perfectly phrased! and quite as true as any observation in civilized life should be.

JACK I am sick to death of cleverness. Everybody is clever nowadays. You can't go anywhere without meeting clever people. The thing has become an absolute public nuisance. I wish to goodness we had a few fools left.

ALGERNON We have.

JACK I should extremely like to meet them. What do they talk about?

ALGERNON The fools? Oh! about the clever people, of course.

JACK What fools!

ALGERNON By the way, did you tell Gwendolen the truth about your being Ernest in town, and Jack in the country?

JACK (*in a very patronizing manner*): My dear fellow, the truth isn't quite the sort of thing one tells to a nice sweet refined girl. What extraordinary ideas you have about the way to behave to a woman!

ALGERNON The only way to behave to a woman is to make love to her if she is pretty, and to someone else if she is plain.

JACK Oh, that is nonsense.

ALGERNON What about your brother? What about the profligate Ernest?

JACK Oh, before the end of the week I shall have got rid of him. I'll say he died in Paris of apoplexy. Lots of people die of apoplexy, quite suddenly, don't they?

ALGERNON Yes, but it's hereditary, my dear fellow. It's a sort of thing that runs in families. You had much better say a severe chill.

JACK You are sure a severe chill isn't hereditary, or anything of that kind?

ALGERNON Of course it isn't!

JACK Very well, then. My poor brother Ernest is carried off suddenly in Paris, by a severe chill. That gets rid of him.

ALGERNON But I thought you said that — Miss Cardew was a little too much interested in your poor brother Ernest? Won't she feel his loss a good deal?

JACK Oh, that is all right. Cecily is not a silly romantic girl, I am glad to say. She has got a capital appetite, goes on long walks, and pays no attention at all to her lessons.

ALGERNON I would rather like to see Cecily.

JACK I will take very good care you never do. She is excessively pretty, and she is only just eighteen.

---

[3] Protective deities in Greek mythology, gorgons (like Medusa) often had serpents for hair and could turn people to stone with a look. — EDS.

ALGERNON Have you told Gwendolen yet that you have an excessively pretty ward who is only just eighteen?

JACK Oh! one doesn't blurt these things out to people. Cecily and Gwendolen are perfectly certain to be extremely great friends. I'll bet you anything you like that half an hour after they have met, they will be calling each other sister.

ALGERNON Women only do that when they have called each other a lot of other things first. Now, my dear boy, if we want to get a good table at Willis's, we really must go and dress. Do you know it is nearly seven?

JACK (*irritably*): Oh! it always is nearly seven.

ALGERNON Well, I'm hungry.

JACK I never knew you when you weren't—

ALGERNON What shall we do after dinner? Go to a theater?

JACK Oh, no! I loathe listening.

ALGERNON Well, let us go to the Club?

JACK Oh, no! I hate talking.

ALGERNON Well, we might trot round to the Empire[4] at ten?

JACK Oh, no! I can't bear looking at things. It is so silly.

ALGERNON Well, what shall we do?

JACK Nothing!

ALGERNON It is awfully hard work doing nothing. However, I don't mind hard work where there is no definite object of any kind.

(*Enter* **LANE.**)

LANE Miss Fairfax.

(*Enter* **GWENDOLEN. LANE** *goes out.*)

ALGERNON Gwendolen, upon my word!

GWENDOLEN Algy, kindly turn your back. I have something very particular to say to Mr. Worthing.

ALGERNON Really, Gwendolen, I don't think I can allow this at all.

[4]Empire Theatre. — EDS.

GWENDOLEN Algy, you always adopt a strictly immoral attitude towards life. You are not quite old enough to do that. (**ALGERNON** *retires to the fireplace.*)

JACK My own darling!

GWENDOLEN Ernest, we may never be married. From the expression on Mama's face I fear we never shall. Few parents nowadays pay any regard to what their children say to them. The old-fashioned respect for the young is fast dying out. Whatever influence I ever had over Mama, I lost at the age of three. But although she may prevent us from becoming man and wife, and I may marry someone else, and marry often, nothing that she can possibly do can alter my eternal devotion to you.

JACK Dear Gwendolen!

GWENDOLEN The story of your romantic origin, as related to me by Mama, with unpleasing comments, has naturally stirred the deeper fibers of my nature. Your Christian name has an irresistible fascination. The simplicity of your character makes you exquisitely incomprehensible to me. Your town address at the Albany I have. What is your address in the country?

JACK The Manor House, Woolton, Hertfordshire.

(**ALGERNON**, *who has been carefully listening, smiles to himself, and writes the address on his shirt cuff. Then picks up the Railway Guide.*)

GWENDOLEN There is a good postal service, I suppose? It may be necessary to do something desperate. That of course will require serious consideration. I will communicate with you daily.

JACK My own one!

GWENDOLEN How long do you remain in town?

JACK Till Monday.

GWENDOLEN Good! Algy, you may turn round now.

ALGERNON Thanks, I've turned round already.

GWENDOLEN You may also ring the bell.

JACK You will let me see you to your carriage, my own darling?

GWENDOLEN Certainly.

JACK (*To* **LANE**, *who now enters*): I will see Miss Fairfax out.

LANE Yes, sir. (**JACK** *and* **GWENDOLEN** *go off.*)

(**LANE** *presents several letters on a salver to* **ALGERNON**. *It is to be surmised that they are bills, as* **ALGERNON**, *after looking at the envelopes, tears them up.*)

ALGERNON A glass of sherry, Lane.

LANE Yes, sir.

ALGERNON Tomorrow, Lane, I'm going Bunburying.

LANE Yes, sir.

ALGERNON I shall probably not be back till Monday. You can put up my dress clothes, my smoking jacket, and all the Bunbury suits —

LANE Yes, sir. (*Handing sherry.*)

ALGERNON I hope tomorrow will be a fine day, Lane.

LANE It never is, sir.

ALGERNON Lane, you're a perfect pessimist.

LANE I do my best to give satisfaction, sir.

(*Enter* **JACK**. **LANE** *goes off.*)

JACK There's a sensible, intellectual girl! the only girl I ever cared for in my life. (**ALGERNON** *is laughing immoderately.*) What on earth are you so amused at?

ALGERNON Oh, I'm a little anxious about poor Bunbury, that is all.

JACK If you don't take care, your friend Bunbury will get you into a serious scrape some day.

ALGERNON I love scrapes. They are the only things that are never serious.

JACK Oh, that's nonsense, Algy. You never talk anything but nonsense.

ALGERNON Nobody ever does.

(**JACK** *looks indignantly at him, and leaves the room.* **ALGERNON** *lights a cigarette, reads his shirt cuff, and smiles.*)

Aubrey Beardsley (1872–1898) was an English illustrator whose drawings often emphasized the grotesque, the decadent, and the erotic. In response to Wilde's boast that he never had to look anything up, Beardsley drew *Oscar Wilde at Work*, which shows the playwright at his desk surrounded by reference works. **How does Beardsley poke fun at some of the same ideas that Wilde satirizes in *The Importance of Being Earnest*?**

Lordprice Collection / Alamy

ACT II

(*Scene: Garden at the Manor House. A flight of gray stone steps leads up to the house. The garden, an old-fashioned one, full of roses. Time of year, July. Basket chairs, and a table covered with books, are set under a large yew tree.* **MISS PRISM** *discovered seated at the table.* **CECILY** *is at the back watering flowers.*

MISS PRISM (*calling*): Cecily, Cecily! Surely such a utilitarian occupation as the watering of flowers is rather Moulton's duty than yours? Especially at a moment when intellectual pleasures await you. Your German grammar is on the table. Pray open it at page fifteen. We will repeat yesterday's lesson.

CECILY (*coming over very slowly*): But I don't like German. It isn't at all a becoming language. I know perfectly well that I look quite plain after my German lesson.

MISS PRISM Child, you know how anxious your guardian is that you should improve yourself in every way. He laid particular stress on your German, as he was leaving for town yesterday. Indeed, he always lays stress on your German when he is leaving for town.

CECILY Dear Uncle Jack is so very serious! Sometimes he is so serious that I think he cannot be quite well.

MISS PRISM (*drawing herself up*): Your guardian enjoys the best of health, and his gravity of demeanor is especially to be commended in one so comparatively young as he is. I know no one who has a higher sense of duty and responsibility.

CECILY I suppose that is why he often looks a little bored when we three are together.

MISS PRISM Cecily! I am surprised at you. Mr. Worthing has many troubles in his life. Idle merriment and triviality would be out of place in his conversation. You must remember his constant anxiety about that unfortunate young man his brother.

CECILY I wish Uncle Jack would allow that unfortunate young man, his brother, to come down here sometimes. We might have a good influence over him, Miss Prism. I am sure you certainly would. You know German, and geology, and things of that kind influence a man very much.

(**CECILY** *begins to write in her diary.*)

MISS PRISM (*shaking her head*): I do not think that even I could produce any effect on a character that according to his own brother's admission is irretrievably weak and vacillating. Indeed I am not sure that I would desire to reclaim him. I am not in favor of this modern mania for turning bad people into good people at a moment's notice. As a man sows so let him reap. You must put away your diary, Cecily. I really don't see why you should keep a diary at all.

CECILY I keep a diary in order to enter the wonderful secrets of my life. If I didn't write them down, I should probably forget all about them.

MISS PRISM Memory, my dear Cecily, is the diary that we all carry about with us.

CECILY Yes, but it usually chronicles the things that have never happened, and couldn't possibly have happened. I believe that Memory is responsible for nearly all the three-volume novels that Mudie sends us.

MISS PRISM Do not speak slightingly of the three-volume novel, Cecily. I wrote one myself in earlier days.

CECILY Did you really, Miss Prism? How wonderfully clever you are! I hope it did not end happily? I don't like novels that end happily. They depress me so much.

MISS PRISM The good ended happily, and the bad unhappily. That is what Fiction means.

CECILY I suppose so. But it seems very unfair. And was your novel ever published?

MISS PRISM Alas! no. The manuscript unfortunately was abandoned. I use the word in the sense of lost or mislaid. To your work, child, these speculations are profitless.

CECILY (*smiling*): But I see dear Dr. Chasuble coming up through the garden.

MISS PRISM (*rising and advancing*): Dr. Chasuble! This is indeed a pleasure.

(*Enter* **CANON CHASUBLE.**)

CHASUBLE And how are we this morning? Miss Prism, you are, I trust, well?

CECILY Miss Prism has just been complaining of a slight headache. I think it would do her so much good to have a short stroll with you in the park, Dr. Chasuble.

MISS PRISM Cecily, I have not mentioned anything about a headache.

CECILY No, dear Miss Prism, I know that, but I felt instinctively that you had a headache. Indeed I was thinking about that, and not about my German lesson, when the Rector came in.

CHASUBLE I hope, Cecily, you are not inattentive.

CECILY Oh, I am afraid I am.

CHASUBLE That is strange. Were I fortunate enough to be Miss Prism's pupil, I would hang upon her lips. (**MISS PRISM** *glares.*) I spoke metaphorically. — My metaphor was drawn from bees. Ahem! Mr. Worthing, I suppose, has not returned from town yet?

MISS PRISM We do not expect him till Monday afternoon.

CHASUBLE Ah yes, he usually likes to spend his Sunday in London. He is not one of those whose sole aim is enjoyment, as, by all accounts, that unfortunate young man his brother seems to be. But I must not disturb Egeria[5] and her pupil any longer.

MISS PRISM Egeria? My name is Laetitia, Doctor.

CHASUBLE (*bowing*): A classical allusion merely, drawn from the Pagan authors. I shall see you both no doubt at Evensong?

MISS PRISM I think, dear Doctor, I will have a stroll with you. I find I have a headache after all, and a walk might do it good.

CHASUBLE With pleasure, Miss Prism, with pleasure. We might go as far as the schools and back.

MISS PRISM That would be delightful. Cecily, you will read your Political Economy in my absence. The chapter on the Fall of the Rupee you may omit. It is somewhat too sensational. Even these metallic problems have their melodramatic side.

(*Goes down the garden with* **DR. CHASUBLE.**)

[5] Roman goddess of water. — EDS.

CECILY (*picks up books and throws them back on table*): Horrid Political Economy! Horrid Geography! Horrid, horrid German!

(*Enter* **MERRIMAN** *with a card on a salver.*)

MERRIMAN Mr. Ernest Worthing has just driven over from the station. He has brought his luggage with him.

CECILY (*takes the card and reads it*): "Mr. Ernest Worthing, B.4, The Albany, W." Uncle Jack's brother! Did you tell him Mr. Worthing was in town?

MERRIMAN Yes, Miss. He seemed very much disappointed. I mentioned that you and Miss Prism were in the garden. He said he was anxious to speak to you privately for a moment.

CECILY Ask Mr. Ernest Worthing to come here. I suppose you had better talk to the housekeeper about a room for him.

MERRIMAN Yes, Miss. (**MERRIMAN** *goes off.*)

CECILY I have never met any really wicked person before. I feel rather frightened. I am so afraid he will look just like everyone else.

(*Enter* **ALGERNON**, *very gay and debonair.*)

He does!

ALGERNON (*raising his hat*): You are my little cousin Cecily, I'm sure.

CECILY You are under some strange mistake. I am not little. In fact, I believe I am more than usually tall for my age. (**ALGERNON** *is rather taken aback.*) But I am your cousin Cecily. You, I see from your card, are Uncle Jack's brother, my cousin Ernest, my wicked cousin Ernest.

ALGERNON Oh! I am not really wicked at all, cousin Cecily. You mustn't think that I am wicked.

CECILY If you are not, then you have certainly been deceiving us all in a very inexcusable manner. I hope you have not been leading a double life, pretending to be wicked and being really good all the time. That would be hypocrisy.

ALGERNON (*looks at her in amazement*): Oh! Of course I have been rather reckless.

CECILY I am glad to hear it.

ALGERNON In fact, now you mention the subject, I have been very bad in my own small way.

CECILY I don't think you should be so proud of that, though I am sure it must have been very pleasant.

ALGERNON It is much pleasanter being here with you.

CECILY I can't understand how you are here at all. Uncle Jack won't be back till Monday afternoon.

ALGERNON That is a great disappointment. I am obliged to go up by the first train on Monday morning. I have a business appointment that I am anxious— to miss.

CECILY Couldn't you miss it anywhere but in London?

ALGERNON No: the appointment is in London.

CECILY Well, I know, of course, how important it is not to keep a business engagement, if one wants to retain any sense of the beauty of life, but still I think you had better wait till Uncle Jack arrives. I know he wants to speak to you about your emigrating.

ALGERNON About my what?

CECILY Your emigrating. He has gone up to buy your outfit.

ALGERNON I certainly wouldn't let Jack buy my outfit. He has no taste in neckties at all.

CECILY I don't think you will require neckties. Uncle Jack is sending you to Australia.

ALGERNON Australia! I'd sooner die.

CECILY Well, he said at dinner on Wednesday night, that you would have to choose between this world, the next world, and Australia.

ALGERNON Oh, well! The accounts I have received of Australia and the next world are not particularly encouraging. This world is good enough for me, Cousin Cecily.

CECILY Yes, but are you good enough for it?

ALGERNON I'm afraid I'm not that. That is why I want you to reform me. You might make that your mission, if you don't mind, Cousin Cecily.

CECILY I'm afraid I've no time, this afternoon.

ALGERNON Well, would you mind my reforming myself this afternoon?

CECILY It is rather quixotic of you. But I think you should try.

ALGERNON I will. I feel better already.

CECILY You are looking a little worse.

ALGERNON That is because I am hungry.

CECILY How thoughtless of me. I should have remembered that when one is going to lead an entirely new life, one requires regular and wholesome meals. Won't you come in?

ALGERNON Thank you. Might I have a buttonhole[6] first? I never have any appetite unless I have a buttonhole first.

CECILY A Maréchal Niel?[7]

ALGERNON No, I'd sooner have a pink rose.

CECILY Why? (*Cuts a flower.*)

ALGERNON Because you are like a pink rose, Cousin Cecily.

CECILY I don't think it can be right for you to talk to me like that. Miss Prism never says such things to me.

ALGERNON Then Miss Prism is a shortsighted old lady. (**CECILY** *puts the rose in his buttonhole.*) You are the prettiest girl I ever saw.

CECILY Miss Prism says that all good looks are a snare.

ALGERNON They are a snare that every sensible man would like to be caught in.

CECILY Oh! I don't think I would care to catch a sensible man. I shouldn't know what to talk to him about.

(*They pass into the house.* **MISS PRISM** *and* **DR. CHASUBLE** *return.*)

MISS PRISM You are too much alone, dear Dr. Chasuble. You should get married.

---

[6] Boutonniere. — EDS.

[7] A yellow rose. — EDS.

A misanthrope I can understand — a womanthrope, never!

CHASUBLE (*with a scholar's shudder*): Believe me, I do not deserve so neologistic a phrase. The precept as well as the practice of the Primitive Church was distinctly against matrimony.

MISS PRISM (*sententiously*): That is obviously the reason why the Primitive Church has not lasted up to the present day. And you do not seem to realize, dear Doctor, that by persistently remaining single, a man converts himself into a permanent public temptation. Men should be more careful; this very celibacy leads weaker vessels astray.

CHASUBLE But is a man not equally attractive when married?

MISS PRISM No married man is ever attractive except to his wife.

CHASUBLE And often, I've been told, not even to her.

MISS PRISM That depends on the intellectual sympathies of the woman. Maturity can always be depended on. Ripeness can be trusted. Young women are green. (**DR. CHASUBLE** *starts.*) I spoke horticulturally. My metaphor was drawn from fruits. But where is Cecily?

CHASUBLE Perhaps she followed us to the schools.

(*Enter* **JACK** *slowly from the back of the garden. He is dressed in the deepest mourning, with crepe hatband and black gloves.*)

MISS PRISM Mr. Worthing!

CHASUBLE Mr. Worthing?

MISS PRISM This is indeed a surprise. We did not look for you till Monday afternoon.

JACK (*shakes* **MISS PRISM'S** *hand in a tragic manner*): I have returned sooner than I expected. Dr. Chasuble, I hope you are well?

CHASUBLE Dear Mr. Worthing, I trust this garb of woe does not betoken some terrible calamity?

JACK My brother.

MISS PRISM More shameful debts and extravagance?

CHASUBLE Still leading his life of pleasure?

JACK (*shaking his head*): Dead!

CHASUBLE Your brother Ernest dead?

JACK Quite dead.

MISS PRISM What a lesson for him! I trust he will profit by it.

CHASUBLE Mr. Worthing, I offer you my sincere condolence. You have at least the consolation of knowing that you were always the most generous and forgiving of brothers.

JACK Poor Ernest! He had many faults, but it is a sad, sad blow.

CHASUBLE Very sad indeed. Were you with him at the end?

JACK No. He died abroad; in Paris, in fact. I had a telegram last night from the manager of the Grand Hotel.

CHASUBLE Was the cause of death mentioned?

JACK A severe chill, it seems.

MISS PRISM As a man sows, so shall he reap.

CHASUBLE (*raising his hand*): Charity, dear Miss Prism, charity! None of us are perfect. I myself am peculiarly susceptible to drafts. Will the interment take place here?

JACK No. He seems to have expressed a desire to be buried in Paris.

CHASUBLE In Paris! (*Shakes his head.*) I fear that hardly points to any very serious state of mind at the last. You would no doubt wish me to make some slight allusion to this tragic domestic affliction next Sunday. (*Jack presses his hand convulsively.*) My sermon on the meaning of the manna in the wilderness can be adapted to almost any occasion, joyful, or, as in the present case, distressing. (*All sigh.*) I have preached it at harvest celebrations, christenings, confirmations, on days of humiliation and festal days. The last time I delivered it was in the Cathedral, as a charity sermon on behalf of the Society for the Prevention of Discontent among the

Upper Orders. The Bishop, who was present, was much struck by some of the analogies I drew.

JACK Ah! that reminds me, you mentioned christenings I think, Dr. Chasuble? I suppose you know how to christen all right? (**DR. CHASUBLE** *looks astounded.*) I mean, of course, you are continually christening, aren't you?

MISS PRISM It is, I regret to say, one of the Rector's most constant duties in this parish. I have often spoken to the poorer classes on the subject. But they don't seem to know what thrift is.

CHASUBLE But is there any particular infant in whom you are interested, Mr. Worthing? Your brother was, I believe, unmarried, was he not?

JACK Oh yes.

MISS PRISM (*bitterly*): People who live entirely for pleasure usually are.

JACK But it is not for any child, dear Doctor. I am very fond of children. No! the fact is, I would like to be christened myself, this afternoon, if you have nothing better to do.

CHASUBLE But surely, Mr. Worthing, you have been christened already?

JACK I don't remember anything about it.

CHASUBLE But have you any grave doubts on the subject?

JACK I certainly intend to have. Of course I don't know if the thing would bother you in any way, or if you think I am a little too old now.

CHASUBLE Not at all. The sprinkling, and, indeed, the immersion of adults is a perfectly canonical practice.

JACK Immersion!

CHASUBLE You need have no apprehensions. Sprinkling is all that is necessary, or indeed I think advisable. Our weather is so changeable. At what hour would you wish the ceremony performed?

JACK Oh, I might trot round about five if that would suit you.

CHASUBLE Perfectly, perfectly! In fact I have two similar ceremonies to perform at that time. A case of twins that occurred recently in one of the outlying cottages on your own estate. Poor Jenkins the carter, a most hard-working man.

JACK Oh! I don't see much fun in being christened along with other babies. It would be childish. Would half-past five do?

CHASUBLE Admirably! Admirably! (*Takes out watch.*) And now, dear Mr. Worthing, I will not intrude any longer into a house of sorrow. I would merely beg you not to be too much bowed down by grief. What seem to us bitter trials are often blessings in disguise.

MISS PRISM This seems to me a blessing of an extremely obvious kind.

(*Enter* **CECILY** *from the house.*)

CECILY Uncle Jack! Oh, I am pleased to see you back. But what horrid clothes you have got on! Do go and change them.

MISS PRISM Cecily!

CHASUBLE My child! my child!

(**CECILY** *goes towards* **JACK**; *he kisses her brow in a melancholy manner.*)

CECILY What is the matter, Uncle Jack? Do look happy! You look as if you had toothache, and I have got such a surprise for you. Who do you think is in the dining room? Your brother!

JACK Who?

CECILY Your brother Ernest. He arrived about half an hour ago.

JACK What nonsense! I haven't got a brother.

CECILY Oh, don't say that. However badly he may have behaved to you in the past he is still your brother. You couldn't be so heartless as to disown him. I'll tell him to come out. And you will shake hands with him, won't you, Uncle Jack? (*Runs back into the house.*)

CHASUBLE These are very joyful tidings.

MISS PRISM After we had all been resigned to his loss, his sudden return seems to me peculiarly distressing.

JACK My brother is in the dining room? I don't know what it all means. I think it is perfectly absurd.

(*Enter* **ALGERNON** *and* **CECILY** *hand in hand. They come slowly up to* **JACK**.)

JACK Good heavens! (*Motions* **ALGERNON** *away*.)

ALGERNON Brother John, I have come down from town to tell you that I am very sorry for all the trouble I have given you, and that I intend to lead a better life in the future.

(**JACK** *glares at him and does not take his hand*.)

CECILY Uncle Jack, you are not going to refuse your own brother's hand?

JACK Nothing will induce me to take his hand. I think his coming down here disgraceful. He knows perfectly well why.

CECILY Uncle Jack, do be nice. There is some good in everyone. Ernest has just been telling me about his poor invalid friend Mr. Bunbury whom he goes to visit so often. And surely there must be much good in one who is kind to an invalid, and leaves the pleasures of London to sit by a bed of pain.

JACK Oh! he has been talking about Bunbury, has he?

CECILY Yes, he has told me all about poor Mr. Bunbury, and his terrible state of health.

JACK Bunbury! Well, I won't have him talk to you about Bunbury or about anything else. It is enough to drive one perfectly frantic.

ALGERNON Of course I admit that the faults were all on my side. But I must say that I think that Brother John's coldness to me is peculiarly painful. I expected a more enthusiastic welcome, especially considering it is the first time I have come here.

CECILY Uncle Jack, if you don't shake hands with Ernest I will never forgive you.

JACK Never forgive me?

CECILY Never, never, never!

JACK Well, this is the last time I shall ever do it.

(*Shakes with* **ALGERNON** *and glares*.)

CHASUBLE It's pleasant, is it not, to see so perfect a reconciliation? I think we might leave the two brothers together.

MISS PRISM Cecily, you will come with us.

CECILY Certainly, Miss Prism. My little task of reconciliation is over.

CHASUBLE You have done a beautiful action today, dear child.

MISS PRISM We must not be premature in our judgments.

CECILY I feel very happy. (*They all go off*.)

JACK You young scoundrel, Algy, you must get out of this place as soon as possible. I don't allow any Bunburying here.

(*Enter* **MERRIMAN**.)

MERRIMAN I have put Mr. Ernest's things in the room next to yours, sir. I suppose that is all right?

JACK What?

MERRIMAN Mr. Ernest's luggage, sir. I have unpacked it and put it in the room next to your own.

JACK His luggage?

MERRIMAN Yes, sir. Three portmanteaus, a dressing case, two hatboxes, and a large luncheon basket.

ALGERNON I am afraid I can't stay more than a week this time.

JACK Merriman, order the dog cart at once. Mr. Ernest has been suddenly called back to town.

MERRIMAN Yes, sir. (*Goes back into the house*.)

ALGERNON What a fearful liar you are, Jack. I have not been called back to town at all.

JACK Yes, you have.

ALGERNON I haven't heard anyone call me.

JACK Your duty as a gentleman calls you back.

ALGERNON My duty as a gentleman has never interfered with my pleasures in the smallest degree.

JACK I can quite understand that.

ALGERNON Well, Cecily is a darling.

JACK You are not to talk of Miss Cardew like that. I don't like it.

ALGERNON Well, I don't like your clothes. You look perfectly ridiculous in them. Why on earth don't you go up and change? It is perfectly childish to be in deep mourning for a man who is actually staying for a whole week in your house as a guest. I call it grotesque.

JACK You are certainly not staying with me for a whole week as a guest or anything else. You have got to leave — by the four-five train.

ALGERNON I certainly won't leave you so long as you are in mourning. It would be most unfriendly. If I were in mourning you would stay with me, I suppose. I should think it very unkind if you didn't.

JACK Well, will you go if I change my clothes?

ALGERNON Yes, if you are not too long. I never saw anybody take so long to dress, and with such little result.

JACK Well, at any rate, that is better than being always overdressed as you are.

ALGERNON If I am occasionally a little overdressed, I make up for it by being always immensely overeducated.

JACK Your vanity is ridiculous, your conduct an outrage, and your presence in my garden utterly absurd. However, you have got to catch the four-five, and I hope you will have a pleasant journey back to town. This Bunburying, as you call it, has not been a great success for you. (*Goes into the house.*)

ALGERNON I think it has been a great success. I'm in love with Cecily, and that is everything.

(*Enter* **CECILY** *at the back of the garden. She picks up the can and begins to water the flowers.*)

But I must see her before I go, and make arrangements for another Bunbury. Ah, there she is.

CECILY Oh, I merely came back to water the roses. I thought you were with Uncle Jack.

ALGERNON He's gone to order the dog cart for me.

CECILY Oh, is he going to take you for a nice drive?

ALGERNON He's going to send me away.

CECILY Then have we got to part?

ALGERNON I am afraid so. It's a very painful parting.

CECILY It is always painful to part from people whom one has known for a very brief space of time. The absence of old friends one can endure with equanimity. But even a momentary separation from anyone to whom one has just been introduced is almost unbearable.

ALGERNON Thank you.

(*Enter* **MERRIMAN.**)

MERRIMAN The dog cart is at the door, sir.

(**ALGERNON** *looks appealingly at* **CECILY.**)

CECILY It can wait, Merriman — for — five minutes.

MERRIMAN Yes, Miss. (*Exit* **MERRIMAN.**)

ALGERNON I hope, Cecily, I shall not offend you if I state quite frankly and openly that you seem to me to be in every way the visible personification of absolute perfection.

CECILY I think your frankness does you great credit, Ernest. If you will allow me, I will copy your remarks into my diary. (*Goes over to table and begins writing in diary.*)

ALGERNON Do you really keep a diary? I'd give anything to look at it. May I?

CECILY Oh no. (*Puts her hand over it.*) You see, it is simply a very young girl's record of her own thoughts and impressions, and consequently meant for publication. When it appears in volume form I hope you will order a copy. But pray, Ernest, don't stop. I delight in taking down from dictation. I have reached "absolute perfection." You can go on. I am quite ready for more.

ALGERNON (*somewhat taken aback*): Ahem! Ahem!

CECILY Oh, don't cough, Ernest. When one is dictating one should speak fluently and not cough. Besides, I don't know how to spell a cough.

(*Writes as* **ALGERNON** *speaks.*)

ALGERNON (*speaking very rapidly*): Cecily, ever since I first looked upon your wonderful and incomparable beauty, I have dared to love you wildly, passionately, devotedly, hopelessly.

CECILY I don't think that you should tell me that you love me wildly, passionately, devotedly, hopelessly. Hopelessly doesn't seem to make much sense, does it?

ALGERNON Cecily!

(*Enter* **MERRIMAN**.)

MERRIMAN The dog cart is waiting, sir.

ALGERNON Tell it to come round next week, at the same hour.

MERRIMAN (*looks at* **CECILY**, *who makes no sign*): Yes, sir. (**MERRIMAN** *retires.*)

CECILY Uncle Jack would be very much annoyed if he knew you were staying on till next week, at the same hour.

ALGERNON Oh, I don't care about Jack. I don't care for anybody in the whole world but you. I love you, Cecily. You will marry me, won't you?

CECILY You silly boy! Of course. Why, we have been engaged for the last three months.

ALGERNON For the last three months?

CECILY Yes, it will be exactly three months on Thursday.

ALGERNON But how did we become engaged?

CECILY Well, ever since dear Uncle Jack first confessed to us that he had a younger brother who was very wicked and bad, you of course have formed the chief topic of conversation between myself and Miss Prism. And of course a man who is much talked about is always very attractive. One feels there must be something in him after all. I daresay it was foolish of me, but I fell in love with you, Ernest.

ALGERNON Darling! And when was the engagement actually settled?

CECILY On the 14th of February last. Worn out by your entire ignorance of my existence, I determined to end the matter one way or the other, and after a long struggle with myself I accepted you under this dear old tree here. The next day I bought this little ring in your name, and this is the little bangle with the true lovers' knot I promised you always to wear.

ALGERNON Did I give you this? It's very pretty, isn't it?

CECILY Yes, you've wonderfully good taste, Ernest. It's the excuse I've always given for your leading such a bad life. And this is the box in which I keep all your dear letters.

(*Kneels at table, opens box, and produces letters tied up with blue ribbon.*)

ALGERNON My letters! But, my own sweet Cecily, I have never written you any letters.

CECILY You need hardly remind me of that, Ernest. I remember only too well that I was forced to write your letters for you. I wrote always three times a week, and sometimes oftener.

ALGERNON Oh, do let me read them, Cecily!

CECILY Oh, I couldn't possibly. They would make you far too conceited. (*Replaces box.*) The three you wrote me after I had broken off the engagement are so beautiful, and so badly spelled, that even now I can hardly read them without crying a little.

ALGERNON But was our engagement ever broken off?

CECILY Of course it was. On the 22nd of last March. You can see the entry if you like. (*Shows diary.*) "Today I broke off my engagement with Ernest. I feel it is better to do so. The weather still continues charming."

ALGERNON But why on earth did you break it off? What had I done? I had done nothing at all. Cecily, I am very much hurt indeed to hear you broke it off. Particularly when the weather was so charming.

CECILY It would hardly have been a really serious engagement if it hadn't been broken off at least once. But I forgave you before the week was out.

ALGERNON (*crossing to her, and kneeling*): What a perfect angel you are, Cecily.

CECILY You dear romantic boy. (*He kisses her; she puts her fingers through his hair.*) I hope your hair curls naturally, does it?

ALGERNON Yes, darling, with a little help from others.

CECILY I am so glad.

ALGERNON You'll never break off our engagement again, Cecily?

CECILY I don't think I could break it off now that I have actually met you. Besides, of course, there is the question of your name.

ALGERNON (*nervously*): Yes, of course.

CECILY You must not laugh at me, darling, but it had always been a girlish dream of mine to love someone whose name was Ernest. (**ALGERNON** *rises,* **CECILY** *also.*) There is something in that name that seems to inspire absolute confidence. I pity any poor married woman whose husband is not called Ernest.

ALGERNON But, my dear child, do you mean to say you could not love me if I had some other name?

CECILY But what name?

ALGERNON Oh, any name you like — Algernon — for instance —

CECILY But I don't like the name of Algernon.

ALGERNON Well, my own dear, sweet, loving little darling, I really can't see why you should object to the name of Algernon. It is not at all a bad name. In fact, it is rather an aristocratic name. Half of the chaps who get into the Bankruptcy Court are called Algernon. But seriously, Cecily — (*moving to her*) — if my name was Algy, couldn't you love me?

CECILY (*rising*): I might respect you, Ernest, I might admire your character, but I fear that I should not be able to give you my undivided attention.

ALGERNON Ahem! Cecily! (*Picking up hat.*) Your Rector here is, I suppose, thoroughly experienced in the practice of all the rites and ceremonials of the Church?

CECILY Oh yes. Dr. Chasuble is a most learned man. He has never written a single book, so you can imagine how much he knows.

ALGERNON I must see him at once on a most important christening — I mean on most important business.

CECILY Oh!

ALGERNON I shan't be away more than half an hour.

CECILY Considering that we have been engaged since February the 14th, and that I only met you today for the first time, I think it is rather hard that you should leave me for so long a period as half an hour. Couldn't you make it twenty minutes?

ALGERNON I'll be back in no time.

(*Kisses her and rushes down the garden.*)

CECILY What an impetuous boy he is! I like his hair so much. I must enter his proposal in my diary.

(*Enter* **MERRIMAN.**)

MERRIMAN A Miss Fairfax has just called to see Mr. Worthing. On very important business, Miss Fairfax states.

CECILY Isn't Mr. Worthing in his library?

MERRIMAN Mr. Worthing went over in the direction of the Rectory some time ago.

CECILY Pray ask the lady to come out here; Mr. Worthing is sure to be back soon. And you can bring tea.

MERRIMAN Yes, miss. (*Goes out.*)

CECILY Miss Fairfax! I suppose one of the many good elderly women who are associated with Uncle Jack in some of his philanthropic work in London. I don't quite like women who are interested in philanthropic work. I think it is so forward of them.

(*Enter* **MERRIMAN**.)

MERRIMAN Miss Fairfax.

(*Enter* **GWENDOLEN**. *Exit* **MERRIMAN**.)

CECILY (*advancing to meet her*): Pray let me introduce myself to you. My name is Cecily Cardew.

GWENDOLEN Cecily Cardew? (*Moving to her and shaking hands.*) What a very sweet name! Something tells me that we are going to be great friends. I like you already more than I can say. My first impressions of people are never wrong.

CECILY How nice of you to like me so much after we have known each other such a comparatively short time. Pray sit down.

GWENDOLEN (*still standing up*): I may call you Cecily, may I not?

CECILY With pleasure!

GWENDOLEN And you will always call me Gwendolen, won't you?

CECILY If you wish.

GWENDOLEN Then that is all quite settled, is it not?

CECILY I hope so.

(*A pause. They both sit down together.*)

GWENDOLEN Perhaps this might be a favorable opportunity for my mentioning who I am. My father is Lord Bracknell. You have never heard of Papa, I suppose?

CECILY I don't think so.

GWENDOLEN Outside the family circle, Papa, I am glad to say, is entirely unknown. I think that is quite as it should be. The home seems to me to be the proper sphere for the man. And certainly once a man begins to neglect his domestic duties he becomes painfully effeminate, does he not? And I don't like that. It makes men so very attractive. Cecily, Mama, whose views on education are remarkably strict, has brought me up to be extremely shortsighted; it is part of her system, so do you mind my looking at you through my glasses?

CECILY Oh! not at all, Gwendolen. I am very fond of being looked at.

GWENDOLEN (*after examining* **CECILY** *carefully through a lorgnette*): You are here on a short visit I suppose?

CECILY Oh no! I live here.

GWENDOLEN (*severely*): Really? Your mother, no doubt, or some female relative of advanced years, resides here also?

CECILY Oh no! I have no mother, nor, in fact, any relations.

GWENDOLEN Indeed?

CECILY My dear guardian, with the assistance of Miss Prism, has the arduous task of looking after me.

GWENDOLEN Your guardian?

CECILY Yes, I am Mr. Worthing's ward.

GWENDOLEN Oh! It is strange he never mentioned to me that he had a ward. How secretive of him! He grows more interesting hourly. I am not sure, however, that the news inspires me with feelings of unmixed delight. (*Rising and going to her.*) I am very fond of you, Cecily; I have liked you ever since I met you! But I am bound to state that now that I know that you are Mr. Worthing's ward, I cannot help expressing a wish you were — well, just a little older than you seem to be — and not quite so very alluring in appearance. In fact, if I may speak candidly —

CECILY Pray do! I think that whenever one has anything unpleasant to say, one should always be quite candid.

GWENDOLEN Well, to speak with perfect candor, Cecily, I wish that you were fully forty-two, and more than usually plain for your age. Ernest has a strong upright nature.

He is the very soul of truth and honor. Disloyalty would be as impossible to him as deception. But even men of the noblest possible moral character are extremely susceptible to the influence of the physical charms of others. Modern, no less than Ancient History, supplies us with many most painful examples of what I refer to. If it were not so, indeed, History would be quite unreadable.

CECILY I beg your pardon, Gwendolen, did you say Ernest?

GWENDOLEN Yes.

CECILY Oh, but it is not Mr. Ernest Worthing who is my guardian. It is his brother — his elder brother.

GWENDOLEN (*sitting down again*): Ernest never mentioned to me that he had a brother.

CECILY I am sorry to say they have not been on good terms for a long time.

GWENDOLEN Ah! that accounts for it. And now that I think of it I have never heard any man mention his brother. The subject seems distasteful to most men. Cecily, you have lifted a load from my mind. I was growing almost anxious. It would have been terrible if any cloud had come across a friendship like ours, would it not? Of course you are quite, quite sure that it is not Mr. Ernest Worthing who is your guardian?

CECILY Quite sure. (*A pause.*) In fact, I am going to be his.

GWENDOLEN (*inquiringly*): I beg your pardon?

CECILY (*rather shy and confidingly*): Dearest Gwendolen, there is no reason why I should make a secret of it to you. Our little county newspaper is sure to chronicle the fact next week. Mr. Ernest Worthing and I are engaged to be married.

GWENDOLEN (*quite politely, rising*): My darling Cecily, I think there must be some slight error. Mr. Ernest Worthing is engaged to me. The announcement will appear in the *Morning Post* on Saturday at the latest.

CECILY (*very politely, rising*): I am afraid you must be under some misconception. Ernest proposed to me exactly ten minutes ago. (*Shows diary.*)

GWENDOLEN (*examines diary through her lorgnette carefully*): It is certainly very curious, for he asked me to be his wife yesterday afternoon at 5:30. If you would care to verify the incident, pray do so. (*Produces diary of her own.*) I never travel without my diary. One should always have something sensational to read in the train. I am so sorry, dear Cecily, if it is any disappointment to you, but I am afraid *I* have the prior claim.

CECILY It would distress me more than I can tell you, dear Gwendolen, if it caused you any mental or physical anguish, but I feel bound to point out that since Ernest proposed to you he clearly has changed his mind.

GWENDOLEN (*meditatively*): If the poor fellow has been entrapped into any foolish promise I shall consider it my duty to rescue him at once, and with a firm hand.

CECILY (*thoughtfully and sadly*): Whatever unfortunate entanglement my dear boy may have got into, I will never reproach him with it after we are married.

GWENDOLEN Do you allude to me, Miss Cardew, as an entanglement? You are presumptuous. On an occasion of this kind it becomes more than a moral duty to speak one's mind. It becomes a pleasure.

CECILY Do you suggest, Miss Fairfax, that I entrapped Ernest into an engagement? How dare you? This is no time for wearing the shallow mask of manners. When I see a spade I call it a spade.

GWENDOLEN (*satirically*): I am glad to say that I have never seen a spade. It is obvious that our social spheres have been widely different.

(*Enter* **MERRIMAN**, *followed by the Footman. He carries a salver, tablecloth, and plate stand.* **CECILY** *is about to retort. The presence of the* *servants exercises a restraining influence, under which both girls chafe.*)

MERRIMAN Shall I lay tea here as usual, miss?

CECILY (*sternly, in a calm voice*): Yes, as usual.

(**MERRIMAN** *begins to clear table and lay cloth. A long pause.* **CECILY** *and* **GWENDOLEN** *glare at each other.*)

GWENDOLEN Are there many interesting walks in the vicinity, Miss Cardew?

CECILY Oh! Yes! a great many. From the top of one of the hills quite close one can see five counties.

GWENDOLEN Five counties! I don't think I should like that. I hate crowds.

CECILY (*sweetly*): I suppose that is why you live in town?

(**GWENDOLEN** *bites her lip, and beats her foot nervously with her parasol.*)

GWENDOLEN (*looking round*): Quite a well-kept garden this is, Miss Cardew.

CECILY So glad you like it, Miss Fairfax.

GWENDOLEN I had no idea there were any flowers in the country.

CECILY Oh, flowers are as common here, Miss Fairfax, as people are in London.

GWENDOLEN Personally I cannot understand how anybody manages to exist in the country, if anybody who is anybody does. The country always bores me to death.

CECILY Ah! This is what the newspapers call agricultural depression, is it not? I believe the aristocracy are suffering very much from it just at present. It is almost an epidemic amongst them, I have been told. May I offer you some tea, Miss Fairfax?

GWENDOLEN (*with elaborate politeness*): Thank you. (*Aside.*) Detestable girl! But I require tea!

CECILY (*sweetly*): Sugar?

GWENDOLEN (*superciliously*): No, thank you. Sugar is not fashionable anymore.

(**CECILY** *looks angrily at her, takes up the tongs, and puts four lumps of sugar into the cup.*)

CECILY (*severely*): Cake or bread and butter?

GWENDOLEN (*in a bored manner*): Bread and butter, please. Cake is rarely seen at the best houses nowadays.

CECILY (*cuts a very large slice of cake, and puts it on the tray*): Hand that to Miss Fairfax.

(**MERRIMAN** *does so, and goes out with Footman.* **GWENDOLEN** *drinks the tea and makes a grimace. Puts down cup at once, reaches out her hand to the bread and butter, looks at it, and finds it is cake. Rises in indignation.*)

GWENDOLEN You have filled my tea with lumps of sugar, and though I asked most distinctly for bread and butter, you have given me cake. I am known for the gentleness of my disposition, and the extraordinary sweetness of my nature, but I warn you, Miss Cardew, you may go too far.

CECILY (*rising*): To save my poor, innocent, trusting boy from the machinations of any other girl there are no lengths to which I would not go.

GWENDOLEN From the moment I saw you I distrusted you. I felt that you were false and deceitful. I am never deceived in such matters. My first impressions of people are invariably right.

CECILY It seems to me, Miss Fairfax, that I am trespassing on your valuable time. No doubt you have many other calls of a similar character to make in the neighborhood.

(*Enter* **JACK**.)

GWENDOLEN (*catching sight of him*): Ernest! My own Ernest!

JACK Gwendolen! Darling! (*Offers to kiss her.*)

GWENDOLEN (*draws back*): A moment! May I ask if you are engaged to be married to this young lady? (*Points to* **CECILY**.)

JACK (*laughing*): To dear little Cecily! Of course not! What could have put such an idea into your pretty little head?

GWENDOLEN Thank you. You may! (*Offers her cheek.*)

CECILY (*very sweetly*): I knew there must be some misunderstanding, Miss Fairfax. The gentleman whose arm is at present round your waist is my dear guardian, Mr. John Worthing.

GWENDOLEN I beg your pardon?

CECILY This is Uncle Jack.

GWENDOLEN (*receding*): Jack! Oh!

(*Enter* **ALGERNON**.)

CECILY Here is Ernest.

ALGERNON (*goes straight over to Cecily without noticing anyone else*): My own love! (*Offers to kiss her.*)

CECILY (*drawing back*): A moment, Ernest! May I ask you — are you engaged to be married to this young lady?

ALGERNON (*looking round*): To what young lady? Good heavens! Gwendolen!

CECILY Yes! to good heavens, Gwendolen, I mean to Gwendolen.

ALGERNON (*laughing*): Of course not! What could have put such an idea into your pretty little head?

CECILY Thank you. (*Presenting her cheek to be kissed.*) You may. (**ALGERNON** *kisses her.*)

GWENDOLEN I felt there was some slight error, Miss Cardew. The gentleman who is now embracing you is my cousin, Mr. Algernon Moncrieff.

CECILY (*breaking away from* **ALGERNON**): Algernon Moncrieff! Oh!

(*The two girls move towards each other and put their arms round each other's waists as if for protection.*)

CECILY Are you called Algernon?

ALGERNON I cannot deny it.

CECILY Oh!

GWENDOLEN Is your name really John?

JACK (*standing rather proudly*): I could deny it if I liked. I could deny anything if I liked. But my name certainly is John. It has been John for years.

CECILY (*to* **GWENDOLEN**): A gross deception has been practiced on both of us.

GWENDOLEN My poor wounded Cecily!

CECILY My sweet wronged Gwendolen!

GWENDOLEN (*slowly and seriously*): You will call me sister, will you not?

(*They embrace.* **JACK** *and* **ALGERNON** *groan and walk up and down.*)

CECILY (*rather brightly*): There is just one question I would like to be allowed to ask my guardian.

GWENDOLEN An admirable idea! Mr. Worthing, there is just one question I would like to be permitted to put to you. Where is your brother Ernest? We are both engaged to be married to your brother Ernest, so it is a matter of some importance to us to know where your brother Ernest is at present.

JACK (*slowly and hesitatingly*): Gwendolen — Cecily — it is very painful for me to be forced to speak the truth. It is the first time in my life that I have ever been reduced to such a painful position, and I am really quite inexperienced in doing anything of the kind. However, I will tell you quite frankly that I have no brother Ernest. I have no brother at all. I never had a brother in my life, and I certainly have not the smallest intention of ever having one in the future.

CECILY (*surprised*): No brother at all?

JACK (*cheerily*): None!

GWENDOLEN (*severely*): Had you never a brother of any kind?

JACK (*pleasantly*): Never. Not even of any kind.

GWENDOLEN I am afraid it is quite clear, Cecily, that neither of us is engaged to be married to anyone.

CECILY It is not a very pleasant position for a young girl suddenly to find herself in. Is it?

GWENDOLEN Let us go into the house. They will hardly venture to come after us there.

CECILY No, men are so cowardly, aren't they?

(*They retire into the house with scornful looks.*)

JACK This ghastly state of things is what you call Bunburying, I suppose?

ALGERNON Yes, and a perfectly wonderful Bunbury it is. The most wonderful Bunbury I have ever had in my life.

JACK Well, you've no right whatsoever to Bunbury here.

ALGERNON That is absurd. One has a right to Bunbury anywhere one chooses. Every serious Bunburyist knows that.

JACK Serious Bunburyist! Good heavens!

ALGERNON Well, one must be serious about something, if one wants to have any amusement in life. I happen to be serious about Bunburying. What on earth you are serious about I haven't got the remotest idea. About everything, I should fancy. You have such an absolutely trivial nature.

JACK Well, the only small satisfaction I have in the whole of this wretched business is that your friend Bunbury is quite exploded. You won't be able to run down to the country quite so often as you used to do, dear Algy. And a very good thing too.

ALGERNON Your brother is a little off color, isn't he, dear Jack? You won't be able to disappear to London quite so frequently as your wicked custom was. And not a bad thing either.

JACK As for your conduct towards Miss Cardew, I must say that your taking in a sweet, simple, innocent girl like that is quite inexcusable. To say nothing of the fact that she is my ward.

ALGERNON I can see no possible defense at all for your deceiving a brilliant, clever, thoroughly experienced young lady like Miss Fairfax. To say nothing of the fact that she is my cousin.

JACK I wanted to be engaged to Gwendolen, that is all. I love her.

ALGERNON Well, I simply wanted to be engaged to Cecily. I adore her.

JACK There is certainly no chance of your marrying Miss Cardew.

ALGERNON I don't think there is much likelihood, Jack, of you and Miss Fairfax being united.

JACK Well, that is no business of yours.

ALGERNON If it was my business, I wouldn't talk about it. (*Begins to eat muffins.*) It is very vulgar to talk about one's business. Only people like stockbrokers do that, and then merely at dinner parties.

JACK How you can sit there, calmly eating muffins when we are in this horrible trouble, I can't make out. You seem to me to be perfectly heartless.

ALGERNON Well, I can't eat muffins in an agitated manner. The butter would probably get on my cuffs. One should always eat muffins quite calmly. It is the only way to eat them.

JACK I say it's perfectly heartless your eating muffins at all, under the circumstances.

ALGERNON When I am in trouble, eating is the only thing that consoles me. Indeed, when I am in really great trouble, as anyone who knows me intimately will tell you, I refuse everything except food and drink. At the present moment I am eating muffins because I am unhappy. Besides, I am particularly fond of muffins. (*Rising.*)

JACK (*rising*): Well, that is no reason why you should eat them all in that greedy way.

(*Takes muffins from* **ALGERNON.**)

ALGERNON (*offering tea cake*): I wish you would have tea cake instead. I don't like tea cake.

JACK Good heavens! I suppose a man may eat his own muffins in his own garden.

ALGERNON But you have just said it was perfectly heartless to eat muffins.

JACK I said it was perfectly heartless of you, under the circumstances. That is a very different thing.

ALGERNON That may be, but the muffins are the same. (*He seizes the muffin dish from* **JACK**.)

JACK Algy, I wish to goodness you would go.

ALGERNON You can't possibly ask me to go without having some dinner. It's absurd. I never go without my dinner. No one ever does, except vegetarians and people like that. Besides I have just made arrangements with Dr. Chasuble to be christened at a quarter to six under the name of Ernest.

JACK My dear fellow, the sooner you give up that nonsense the better. I made arrange ments this morning with Dr. Chasuble to be christened myself at 5.30, and I naturally will take the name of Ernest. Gwendolen would wish it. We can't both be christened Ernest. It's absurd. Besides, I have a perfect right to be christened if I like. There is no evidence at all that I have ever been christened by anybody. I should think it extremely probable I never was, and so does Dr. Chasuble. It is entirely different in your case. You have been christened already.

ALGERNON Yes, but I have not been christened for years.

JACK Yes, but you have been christened. That is the important thing.

ALGERNON Quite so. So I know my constitution can stand it. If you are not quite sure about your ever having been christened, I must say I think it rather dangerous your venturing on it now. It might make you very unwell. You can hardly have forgotten that someone very closely connected with you was very nearly carried off this week in Paris by a severe chill.

JACK Yes, but you said yourself that a severe chill was not hereditary.

ALGERNON It usen't to be, I know — but I dare-say it is now. Science is always making wonderful improvements in things.

JACK (*picking up the muffin dish*): Oh, that is nonsense; you are always talking nonsense.

ALGERNON Jack, you are at the muffins again! I wish you wouldn't. There are only two left. (*Takes them.*) I told you I was particularly fond of muffins.

JACK But I hate tea cake.

ALGERNON Why on earth then do you allow tea cake to be served up for your guests? What ideas you have of hospitality!

JACK Algernon! I have already told you to go. I don't want you here. Why don't you go!

ALGERNON I haven't quite finished my tea yet! and there is still one muffin left.

(**JACK** *groans, and sinks into a chair.* **ALGERNON** *still continues eating.*)

ACT III

(*Scene: Morning room at the Manor House.* **GWENDOLEN** *and* **CECILY** *are at the window, looking out into the garden.*)

GWENDOLEN The fact that they did not follow us at once into the house, as anyone else would have done, seems to me to show that they have some sense of shame left.

CECILY They have been eating muffins. That looks like repentance.

GWENDOLEN (*after a pause*): They don't seem to notice us at all. Couldn't you cough?

CECILY But I haven't got a cough.

GWENDOLEN They're looking at us. What effrontery!

CECILY They're approaching. That's very forward of them.

GWENDOLEN Let us preserve a dignified silence.

CECILY Certainly. It's the only thing to do now.

(*Enter* **JACK** *followed by* **ALGERNON**. *They whistle some dreadful popular air from a British opera.*)

GWENDOLEN This dignified silence seems to produce an unpleasant effect.

CECILY A most distasteful one.

GWENDOLEN But we will not be the first to speak.

CECILY Certainly not.

GWENDOLEN Mr. Worthing, I have something very particular to ask you. Much depends on your reply.

CECILY Gwendolen, your common sense is invaluable. Mr. Moncrieff, kindly answer me the following question. Why did you pretend to be my guardian's brother?

ALGERNON In order that I might have an opportunity of meeting you.

CECILY (*to* **GWENDOLEN**): That certainly seems a satisfactory explanation, does it not?

GWENDOLEN Yes, dear, if you can believe him.

CECILY I don't. But that does not affect the wonderful beauty of his answer.

GWENDOLEN True. In matters of grave importance, style, not sincerity, is the vital thing. Mr. Worthing, what explanation can you offer to me for pretending to have a brother? Was it in order that you might have an opportunity of coming up to town to see me as often as possible?

JACK Can you doubt it, Miss Fairfax?

GWENDOLEN I have the gravest doubts upon the subject. But I intend to crush them. This is not the moment for German skepticism. (*Moving to* **CECILY**.) Their explanations appear to be quite satisfactory, especially Mr. Worthing's. That seems to me to have the stamp of truth upon it.

CECILY I am more than content with what Mr. Moncrieff said. His voice alone inspires one with absolute credulity.

GWENDOLEN Then you think we should forgive them?

CECILY Yes. I mean no.

GWENDOLEN True! I had forgotten. There are principles at stake that one cannot surrender. Which of us should tell them? The task is not a pleasant one.

CECILY Could we not both speak at the same time?

GWENDOLEN An excellent idea! I nearly always speak at the same time as other people. Will you take the time from me?

CECILY Certainly.

(**GWENDOLEN** *beats time with uplifted finger.*)

GWENDOLEN AND CECILY (*speaking together*): Your Christian names are still an insuperable barrier. That is all!

JACK AND ALGERNON (*speaking together*): Our Christian names! Is that all? But we are going to be christened this afternoon.

GWENDOLEN (*to* **JACK**): For my sake you are prepared to do this terrible thing?

JACK I am!

CECILY (*to* **ALGERNON**): To please me you are ready to face this fearful ordeal?

ALGERNON I am!

GWENDOLEN How absurd to talk of the equality of the sexes! Where questions of self-sacrifice are concerned, men are infinitely beyond us.

JACK We are! (*Clasps hands with* **ALGERNON**.)

CECILY They have moments of physical courage of which we women know absolutely nothing.

GWENDOLEN (*to* **JACK**): Darling!

ALGERNON (*to* **CECILY**): Darling!

(*They fall into each other's arms.*)

(*Enter* **MERRIMAN**. *When he enters he coughs loudly, seeing the situation.*)

MERRIMAN Ahem! Ahem! Lady Bracknell!

JACK Good heavens!

(*Enter* **LADY BRACKNELL**. *The couples separate in alarm. Exit* **MERRIMAN**.)

LADY BRACKNELL Gwendolen! What does this mean?

GWENDOLEN Merely that I am engaged to be married to Mr. Worthing, Mama.

LADY BRACKNELL Come here. Sit down. Sit down immediately. Hesitation of any kind is a sign of mental decay in the young, of physical weakness in the old. (*Turns to* **JACK**.) Apprised, sir, of my daughter's sudden flight by her trusty maid, whose confidence I purchased by means of a small coin, I followed her at once by a luggage train. Her unhappy father is, I am glad to say, under the impression that she is attending a more than usually lengthy lecture by the University

Extension Scheme on the influence of a permanent income on thought. I do not propose to undeceive him. Indeed I have never undeceived him on any question. I would consider it wrong. But of course, you will clearly understand that all communication between yourself and my daughter must cease immediately from this moment. On this point, as indeed on all points, I am firm.

JACK I am engaged to be married to Gwendolen, Lady Bracknell!

LADY BRACKNELL You are nothing of the kind, sir. And now, as regards Algernon! — Algernon!

ALGERNON Yes, Aunt Augusta.

LADY BRACKNELL May I ask if it is in this house that your invalid friend Mr. Bunbury resides?

ALGERNON (*stammering*): Oh! No! Bunbury doesn't live here. Bunbury is somewhere else at present. In fact, Bunbury is dead.

LADY BRACKNELL Dead! When did Mr. Bunbury die? His death must have been extremely sudden.

ALGERNON (*airily*): Oh! I killed Bunbury this afternoon. I mean poor Bunbury died this afternoon.

LADY BRACKNELL What did he die of?

ALGERNON Bunbury? Oh, he was quite exploded.

LADY BRACKNELL Exploded! Was he the victim of a revolutionary outrage? I was not aware that Mr. Bunbury was interested in social legislation. If so, he is well punished for his morbidity.

ALGERNON My dear Aunt Augusta, I mean he was found out! The doctors found out that Bunbury could not live, that is what I mean — so Bunbury died.

LADY BRACKNELL He seems to have had great confidence in the opinion of his physicians. I am glad, however, that he made up his mind at the last to some definite course of action, and acted under proper medical advice. And now that we have finally got rid of this Mr. Bunbury, may I ask, Mr. Worthing, who is that young person whose hand my nephew Algernon is now holding in what seems to me a peculiarly unnecessary manner?

JACK That lady is Miss Cecily Cardew, my ward.

(**LADY BRACKNELL** *bows coldly to* **CECILY.**)

ALGERNON I am engaged to be married to Cecily, Aunt Augusta.

LADY BRACKNELL I beg your pardon?

CECILY Mr. Moncrieff and I are engaged to be married, Lady Bracknell.

LADY BRACKNELL (*with a shiver, crossing to the sofa and sitting down*): I do not know whether there is anything peculiarly exciting in the air of this particular part of Hertfordshire, but the number of engagements that go on seems to me considerably above the proper average that statistics have laid down for our guidance. I think some preliminary inquiry on my part would not be out of place. Mr. Worthing, is Miss Cardew at all connected with any of the larger railway stations in London? I merely desire information. Until yesterday I had no idea that there were any families or persons whose origin was a Terminus. (**JACK** *looks perfectly furious, but restrains himself.*)

JACK (*in a clear, cold voice*): Miss Cardew is the grand-daughter of the late Mr. Thomas Cardew of 149, Belgrave Square, S.W.; Gervase Park, Dorking, Surrey; and the Sporran, Fifeshire, N.B.

LADY BRACKNELL That sounds not unsatisfactory. Three addresses always inspire confidence, even in tradesmen. But what proof have I of their authenticity?

JACK I have carefully preserved the Court Guides of the period. They are open to your inspection, Lady Bracknell.

LADY BRACKNELL (*grimly*): I have known strange errors in that publication.

JACK Miss Cardew's family solicitors are Messrs. Markby, Markby, and Markby.

LADY BRACKNELL Markby, Markby, and Markby? A firm of the very highest position in their profession. Indeed I am told that one of the Mr. Markbys is occasionally to be seen at dinner parties. So far I am satisfied.

JACK (*very irritably*): How extremely kind of you, Lady Bracknell! I have also in my possession, you will be pleased to hear, certificates of Miss Cardew's birth, baptism, whooping cough, registration, vaccination, confirmation, and the measles; both the German and the English variety.

LADY BRACKNELL Ah! A life crowded with incident I see; though perhaps somewhat too exciting for a young girl. I am not myself in favor of premature experiences. (*Rises, looks at her watch.*) Gwendolen! the time approaches for our departure. We have not a moment to lose. As a matter of form, Mr. Worthing, I had better ask you if Miss Cardew has any little fortune?

JACK Oh! about a hundred and thirty thousand pounds in the Funds. That is all. Good-bye, Lady Bracknell. So pleased to have seen you.

LADY BRACKNELL (*sitting down again*): A moment, Mr. Worthing. A hundred and thirty thousand pounds! And in the Funds! Miss Cardew seems to me a most attractive young lady, now that I look at her. Few girls of the present day have any really solid qualities, any of the qualities that last, and improve with time. We live, I regret to say, in an age of surfaces. (*To* **CECILY**.) Come over here, dear. (**CECILY** *goes across.*) Pretty child! your dress is sadly simple, and your hair seems almost as Nature might have left it. But we can soon alter all that. A thoroughly experienced French maid produces a really marvelous result in a very brief space of time. I remember recommending one to young Lady Lancing, and after three months her own husband did not know her.

JACK (*aside*): And after six months nobody knew her.

LADY BRACKNELL (*glares at* **JACK** *for a few moments. Then bends, with a practiced smile, to* **CECILY**): Kindly turn round, sweet child. (**CECILY** *turns completely round.*) No, the side view is what I want. (**CECILY** *presents her profile.*) Yes, quite as I expected. There are distinct social possibilities in your profile. The two weak points in our age are its want of principle and its want of profile. The chin a little higher, dear. Style largely depends on the way the chin is worn. They are worn very high, just at present. Algernon!

ALGERNON Yes, Aunt Augusta!

LADY BRACKNELL There are distinct social possibilities in Miss Cardew's profile.

ALGERNON Cecily is the sweetest, dearest, prettiest girl in the whole world. And I don't care twopence about social possibilities.

LADY BRACKNELL Never speak disrespectfully of Society, Algernon. Only people who can't get into it do that. (*To* **CECILY**.) Dear child, of course you know that Algernon has nothing but his debts to depend upon. But I do not approve of mercenary marriages. When I married Lord Bracknell I had no fortune of any kind. But I never dreamed for a moment of allowing that to stand in my way. Well, I suppose I must give my consent.

ALGERNON Thank you, Aunt Augusta.

LADY BRACKNELL Cecily, you may kiss me!

CECILY (*kisses her*): Thank you, Lady Bracknell.

LADY BRACKNELL You may also address me as Aunt Augusta for the future.

CECILY Thank you, Aunt Augusta.

LADY BRACKNELL The marriage, I think, had better take place quite soon.

ALGERNON Thank you, Aunt Augusta.

CECILY Thank you, Aunt Augusta.

LADY BRACKNELL To speak frankly, I am not in favor of long engagements. They give people the opportunity of finding out each other's character before marriage, which I think is never advisable.

JACK I beg your pardon for interrupting you, Lady Bracknell, but this engagement is quite out of the question. I am Miss Cardew's guardian, and she cannot marry without my

Sara Krulwich / The New York Times / Redux Pictures

Charles Isherwood's *New York Times* review of the 2011 production of *The Importance of Being Earnest* begins, "Within the seconds of sweeping onstage, and with a wordless gesture as funny as it is subtle, the great actor Brian Bedford proves beyond question that gender is of no importance whatsoever in portraying the imposing Lady Bracknell. . . ." **What is your first reaction to this photo from the play? How does this casting choice reflect Wilde's characterization of Lady Bracknell? In what ways might it connect to the themes of the play?**

consent until she comes of age. That consent I absolutely decline to give.

LADY BRACKNELL Upon what grounds may I ask? Algernon is an extremely, I may almost say an ostentatiously, eligible young man. He has nothing, but he looks everything. What more can one desire?

JACK It pains me very much to have to speak frankly to you, Lady Bracknell, about your nephew, but the fact is that I do not approve at all of his moral character. I suspect him of being untruthful.

(**ALGERNON** *and* **CECILY** *look at him in indignant amazement.*)

LADY BRACKNELL Untruthful! My nephew Algernon? Impossible! He is an Oxonian.[8]

JACK I fear there can be no possible doubt about the matter. This afternoon, during my temporary absence in London on an important question of romance, he obtained admission to my house by means of the false pretense of being my brother. Under an assumed name he drank, I've just been informed by my butler, an entire pint bottle of my Perrier-Jouêt, Brut, '89; a wine I was specially reserving for myself. Continuing his disgraceful deception, he succeeded in the course of the afternoon in alienating the affections of my only ward. He subsequently stayed to tea, and devoured every single muffin. And what makes his conduct all the more heartless is, that he was perfectly well aware from the first that I have no brother, that I never had a brother, and that I don't intend to have a brother, not even of any kind. I distinctly told him so myself yesterday afternoon.

LADY BRACKNELL Ahem! Mr. Worthing, after careful consideration I have decided entirely to overlook my nephew's conduct to you.

JACK That is very generous of you, Lady Bracknell. My own decision, however, is unalterable. I decline to give my consent.

LADY BRACKNELL (*to* **CECILY**): Come here, sweet child. (**CECILY** *goes over.*) How old are you, dear?

CECILY Well, I am really only eighteen, but I always admit to twenty when I go to evening parties.

LADY BRACKNELL You are perfectly right in making some slight alteration. Indeed, no woman should ever be quite accurate about her age. It

[8] Educated at Oxford University. — EDS.

looks so calculating — (*In a meditative manner.*) Eighteen but admitting to twenty at evening parties. Well, it will not be very long before you are of age and free from the restraints of tutelage. So I don't think your guardian's consent is, after all, a matter of any importance.

JACK Pray excuse me, Lady Bracknell, for interrupting you again, but it is only fair to tell you that according to the terms of her grandfather's will Miss Cardew does not come legally of age till she is thirty-five.

LADY BRACKNELL That does not seem to me to be a grave objection. Thirty-five is a very attractive age. London society is full of women of the very highest birth who have, of their own free choice, remained thirty-five for years. Lady Dumbleton is an instance in point. To my own knowledge she has been thirty-five ever since she arrived at the age of forty, which was many years ago now. I see no reason why our dear Cecily should not be even still more attractive at the age you mention than she is at present. There will be a large accumulation of property.

CECILY Algy, could you wait for me till I was thirty-five?

ALGERNON Of course I could, Cecily. You know I could.

CECILY Yes, I felt it instinctively, but I couldn't wait all that time. I hate waiting even five minutes for anybody. It always makes me rather cross. I am not punctual myself, I know, but I do like punctuality in others, and waiting, even to be married, is quite out of the question.

ALGERNON Then what is to be done, Cecily?

CECILY I don't know, Mr. Moncrieff.

LADY BRACKNELL My dear Mr. Worthing, as Miss Cardew states positively that she cannot wait till she is thirty-five — a remark which I am bound to say seems to me to show a somewhat impatient nature — I would beg of you to reconsider your decision.

JACK But my dear Lady Bracknell, the matter is entirely in your own hands. The moment you consent to my marriage with Gwendolen, I will most gladly allow your nephew to form an alliance with my ward.

LADY BRACKNELL (*rising and drawing herself up*): You must be quite aware that what you propose is out of the question.

JACK Then a passionate celibacy is all that any of us can look forward to.

LADY BRACKNELL That is not the destiny I propose for Gwendolen. Algernon, of course, can choose for himself. (*Pulls out her watch.*) Come, dear; (**GWENDOLEN** *rises*) we have already missed five, if not six, trains. To miss any more might expose us to comment on the platform.

(*Enter* **DR. CHASUBLE.**)

CHASUBLE Everything is quite ready for the christenings.

LADY BRACKNELL The christenings, sir! Is not that somewhat premature?

CHASUBLE (*looking rather puzzled, and pointing to* **JACK** *and* **ALGERNON**): Both these gentlemen have expressed a desire for immediate baptism.

LADY BRACKNELL At their age? The idea is grotesque and irreligious! Algernon, I forbid you to be baptized. I will not hear of such excesses. Lord Bracknell would be highly displeased if he learned that that was the way in which you wasted your time and money.

CHASUBLE Am I to understand then that there are to be no christenings at all this afternoon?

JACK I don't think that, as things are now, it would be of much practical value to either of us, Dr. Chasuble.

CHASUBLE I am grieved to hear such sentiments from you, Mr. Worthing. They savor of the heretical views of the Anabaptists,[9] views that I have completely refuted in four of my

[9] Protestant Christian sect that baptized adult believers only, not infants. — EDS.

This image, taken from director Oliver Parker's 2002 film adaptation of *The Importance of Being Earnest*, shows Rupert Everett as Algernon, Dame Judi Dench as Lady Bracknell, and Reese Witherspoon as Cecily. **How do these actors' facial expressions reflect the characters they play?**

unpublished sermons. However, as your present mood seems to be one peculiarly secular, I will return to the church at once. Indeed, I have just been informed by the pew opener that for the last hour and a half Miss Prism has been waiting for me in the vestry.

LADY BRACKNELL (*starting*): Miss Prism! Did I hear you mention a Miss Prism?

CHASUBLE Yes, Lady Bracknell. I am on my way to join her.

LADY BRACKNELL Pray allow me to detain you for a moment. This matter may prove to be one of vital importance to Lord Bracknell and myself. Is this Miss Prism a female of repellent aspect, remotely connected with education?

CHASUBLE (*somewhat indignantly*): She is the most cultivated of ladies, and the very picture of respectability.

LADY BRACKNELL It is obviously the same person. May I ask what position she holds in your household?

CHASUBLE (*severely*): I am a celibate, madam.

JACK (*interposing*): Miss Prism, Lady Bracknell, has been for the last three years Miss Cardew's esteemed governess and valued companion.

LADY BRACKNELL In spite of what I hear of her, I must see her at once. Let her be sent for.

CHASUBLE (*looking off*): She approaches; she is nigh.

(*Enter* **MISS PRISM** *hurriedly.*)

MISS PRISM I was told you expected me in the vestry, dear Canon. I have been waiting for you there for an hour and three-quarters.

(*Catches sight of* **LADY BRACKNELL**, *who has fixed her with a stony glare.* **MISS PRISM** *grows pale and quails. She looks anxiously round as if desirous to escape.*)

LADY BRACKNELL (*in a severe, judicial voice*): Prism! (**MISS PRISM** *bows her head in shame.*) Come here, Prism! (**MISS PRISM** *approaches in a humble manner.*) Prism! Where is that baby? (*General consternation. The Canon starts back in horror.* **ALGERNON** *and* **JACK** *pretend to be anxious to shield* **CECILY** *and* **GWENDOLEN** *from hearing the details of a terrible public scandal.*) Twenty-eight years ago, Prism, you left Lord Bracknell's house, Number 104, Upper Grosvenor Street, in charge of a perambulator that contained a baby, of the male sex. You never returned. A few weeks later, through the elaborate investigations of the Metropolitan police, the perambulator was discovered at midnight, standing by itself in a remote corner of Bayswater. It contained the manuscript of a three-volume novel of more than usually revolting sentimentality. (**MISS PRISM** *starts in involuntary indignation.*) But the baby was not there! (*Everyone looks at* **MISS PRISM.**) Prism! Where is that baby? (*A pause.*)

MISS PRISM Lady Bracknell, I admit with shame that I do not know. I only wish I did. The plain facts of the case are these. On the morning of the day you mention, a day that is forever branded on my memory, I prepared as usual to take the baby out in its perambulator. I had also with me a somewhat old, but capacious handbag in which I had intended to place the manuscript of a work of fiction that I had written during my few unoccupied hours. In a moment of mental abstraction, for which I never can forgive myself, I deposited the manuscript in the bassinette, and placed the baby in the handbag.

JACK (*who has been listening attentively*): But where did you deposit the handbag?

MISS PRISM Do not ask me, Mr. Worthing.

JACK Miss Prism, this is a matter of no small importance to me. I insist on knowing where you deposited the handbag that contained that infant.

MISS PRISM I left it in the cloakroom of one of the larger railway stations in London.

JACK What railway station?

MISS PRISM (*quite crushed*): Victoria. The Brighton line. (*Sinks into a chair.*)

JACK I must retire to my room for a moment. Gwendolen, wait here for me.

GWENDOLEN If you are not too long, I will wait here for you all my life. (*Exit* **JACK** *in great excitement.*)

CHASUBLE What do you think this means, Lady Bracknell?

LADY BRACKNELL I dare not even suspect, Dr. Chasuble. I need hardly tell you that in families of high position strange coincidences are not supposed to occur. They are hardly considered the thing.

(*Noises heard overhead as if someone was throwing trunks about. Everyone looks up.*)

CECILY Uncle Jack seems strangely agitated.

CHASUBLE Your guardian has a very emotional nature.

LADY BRACKNELL This noise is extremely unpleasant. It sounds as if he was having an argument. I dislike arguments of any kind. They are always vulgar, and often convincing.

CHASUBLE (*looking up*): It has stopped now. (*The noise is redoubled.*)

LADY BRACKNELL I wish he would arrive at some conclusion.

GWENDOLEN This suspense is terrible. I hope it will last.

(*Enter* **JACK** *with a handbag of black leather in his hand.*)

JACK (*rushing over to* **MISS PRISM**): Is this the handbag, Miss Prism? Examine it carefully before you speak. The happiness of more than one life depends on your answer.

MISS PRISM (*calmly*): It seems to be mine. Yes, here is the injury it received through the upsetting of a Gower Street omnibus in younger and happier days. Here is the stain on the lining caused by the explosion of a temperance beverage, an incident that occurred at Leamington. And here, on the lock, are my initials. I had forgotten that in an extravagant mood I had had them placed there. The bag is undoubtedly mine. I am delighted to have it so unexpectedly restored to me. It has been a great inconvenience being without it all these years.

JACK (*in a pathetic voice*): Miss Prism, more is restored to you than this handbag. I was the baby you placed in it.

MISS PRISM (*amazed*): You?

JACK (*embracing her*): Yes — mother!

This gouache painting of the climactic revelation of the handbag is by English illustrator Frank Marsden Lea (1900–1967). **How does Lea capture the mood of the scene? Consider color, line, and composition.**

LOOK AND LEARN (A & B IMAGES) / Private Collection / Bridgeman Images

MISS PRISM (*recoiling in indignant astonishment*): Mr. Worthing! I am unmarried!

JACK Unmarried! I do not deny that is a serious blow. But after all, who has the right to cast a stone against one who has suffered? Cannot repentance wipe out an act of folly? Why should there be one law for men, and another for women? Mother, I forgive you. (*Tries to embrace her again.*)

MISS PRISM (*still more indignant*): Mr. Worthing, there is some error. (*Pointing to* **LADY BRACKNELL.**) There is the lady who can tell you who you really are.

JACK (*after a pause*): Lady Bracknell, I hate to seem inquisitive, but would you kindly inform me who I am?

LADY BRACKNELL I am afraid that the news I have to give you will not altogether please you. You are the son of my poor sister, Mrs. Moncrieff, and consequently Algernon's elder brother.

JACK Algy's elder brother! Then I have a brother after all. I knew I had a brother! I always said I had a brother! Cecily, — how could you have ever doubted that I had a brother? (*Seizes hold of* **ALGERNON.**) Dr. Chasuble, my unfortunate brother. Miss Prism, my unfortunate brother. Gwendolen, my unfortunate brother. Algy, you young scoundrel, you will have to treat me with more respect in the future. You have never behaved to me like a brother in all your life.

ALGERNON Well, not till today, old boy, I admit. I did my best, however, though I was out of practice. (*Shakes hands.*)

GWENDOLEN (*to* **JACK**): My own! But what own are you? What is your Christian name, now that you have become someone else?

JACK Good heavens! — I had quite forgotten that point. Your decision on the subject of my name is irrevocable, I suppose?

GWENDOLEN I never change, except in my affections.

CECILY What a noble nature you have, Gwendolen!

JACK Then the question had better be cleared up at once. Aunt Augusta, a moment. At the time when Miss Prism left me in the handbag, had I been christened already?

LADY BRACKNELL Every luxury that money could buy, including christening, had been lavished on you by your fond and doting parents.

JACK Then I was christened! That is settled. Now, what name was I given? Let me know the worst.

LADY BRACKNELL Being the eldest son you were naturally christened after your father.

JACK (*irritably*): Yes, but what was my father's Christian name?

LADY BRACKNELL (*meditatively*): I cannot at the present moment recall what the General's Christian name was. But I have no doubt he had one. He was eccentric, I admit. But only in later years. And that was the result of the Indian climate, and marriage, and indigestion, and other things of that kind.

JACK Algy! Can't you recollect what our father's Christian name was?

ALGERNON My dear boy, we were never even on speaking terms. He died before I was a year old.

JACK His name would appear in the Army Lists of the period, I suppose, Aunt Augusta?

LADY BRACKNELL The General was essentially a man of peace, except in his domestic life. But I have no doubt his name would appear in any military directory.

JACK The Army Lists of the last forty years are here. These delightful records should have been my constant study. (*Rushes to bookcase and tears the books out.*) M. Generals — Mallam, Maxbohm, Magley, what ghastly names they have — Markby, Migsby, Mobbs, Moncrieff! Lieutenant 1840, Captain, Lieutenant-Colonel, Colonel, General 1869, Christian names, Ernest John. (*Puts book very quietly down and speaks quite calmly.*) I always told you, Gwendolen, my name was Ernest, didn't I? Well, it is Ernest after all. I mean it naturally is Ernest.

LADY BRACKNELL Yes, I remember now that the General was called Ernest. I knew I had some particular reason for disliking the name.

GWENDOLEN Ernest! My own Ernest! I felt from the first that you could have no other name!

JACK Gwendolen, it is a terrible thing for a man to find out suddenly that all his life he has been speaking nothing but the truth. Can you forgive me?

GWENDOLEN I can. For I feel that you are sure to change.

JACK My own one!

CHASUBLE (*to* **MISS PRISM**): Laetitia! (*Embraces her.*)

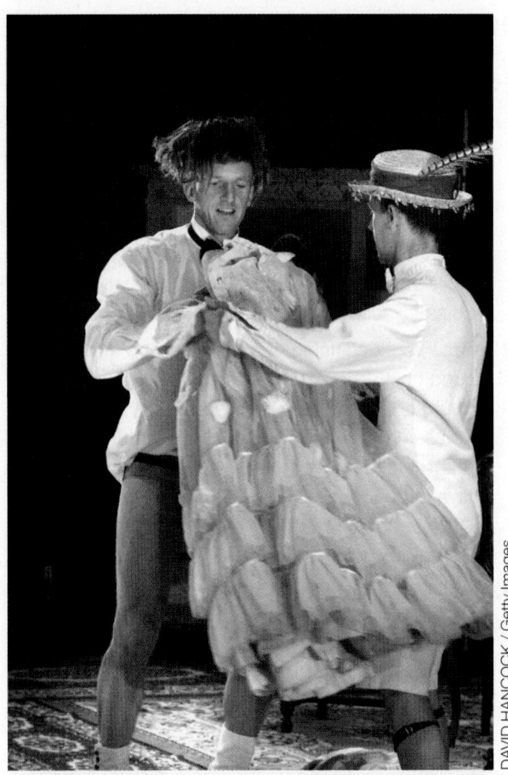

DAVID HANCOCK / Getty Images

This photo shows British actors David Woods (left) and Jon Haynes (right) in an unconventional version of the closing scene of *The Importance of Being Earnest*. In this 2006 adaptation of the play, performed in Sydney, Australia, the actors made nine costume changes, and this avant-garde version included a mixture of musical genres, cross-dressing, and, of course, Oscar Wilde's biting wit. **What aspects of the play lend themselves to revision and updating? Which do you think should be staged conventionally?**

MISS PRISM (*enthusiastically*): Frederick! At last!

ALGERNON Cecily! (*Embraces her.*) At last!

JACK Gwendolen! (*Embraces her.*) At last!

LADY BRACKNELL My nephew, you seem to be displaying signs of triviality.

JACK On the contrary, Aunt Augusta, I've now realized for the first time in my life the vital Importance of Being Earnest.

[1895]

QUESTIONS FOR DISCUSSION

1. In Oscar Wilde's time, "earnestness" — sober behavior, a serious turn of mind — was valued as an important character trait. How does Wilde undermine this value? Consider when the characters are earnest and when they are not. How does the pun on *earnest* and *Ernest* seen throughout the play, as well as Gwendolen's and Cecily's fascination with the name Ernest, further this satirization?
2. At the very beginning of act I, Algernon states, "I don't play accurately — anyone can play accurately — but I play with wonderful expression" (ll. 4–7). How does this comment establish a theme for the play? In what other ways throughout the play is Algernon not accurate but expressive? Are other characters also not accurate but expressive?
3. How does Wilde portray the relationship between Algernon and his servant Lane in act I? What do their conversations suggest about class differences and the society in which the play is set? Is there some irony in their interactions?
4. What is the significance of Jack's leading a double life, with one persona for the city and another for the country? How is this similar to what Algernon has created with his invalid friend Bunbury? How is it different? What is ironic about Algernon later impersonating Jack's alter ego, Ernest?
5. What do the scenes of Algernon and Jack jostling over cucumber sandwiches (act I) and muffins (act II) suggest about their characters and their priorities? Explain how Wilde uses these props to produce a comic effect.
6. Look closely at the exchange in act II between Cecily and Gwendolen in which they both believe they are engaged to the same man (ll. 858–71). What self-contradicting values do their cutting remarks about city life and country life reveal?
7. As suggested in the subtitle, Wilde treats trivial things with gravity and grave things trivially. At what point does earnestness border on ridiculousness? Find examples to support your opinion.
8. Compare and contrast the female characters in the play — Cecily and Gwendolen with Lady Bracknell and Miss Prism. What is Wilde's attitude toward women in this play? Compare and contrast that attitude with his attitude toward Algernon and Jack. Does Wilde seem to have more sympathy for the women or for the men? Is one gender portrayed as more foolish, more clever, more self-aware, more naive? When devising your answer, consider the different schemes with which male and female characters deceive others and themselves throughout the play.
9. In satire, human folly is held up to ridicule. Though humorous, a satire's purpose is to critique — often seriously — that which it mocks. How does Lady Bracknell's interview of Jack as a prospective suitor in act I satirize "modern education"? Where else in the play does Wilde satirize education?
10. How does Wilde make *The Importance of Being Earnest* funny? Identify what you consider to be the most humorous part of the play, and explain your choice. Now, think about the purpose of the humor in this play. Find instances where Wilde uses humor to satirize some of the more ridiculous aspects of society.
11. What do you think was Wilde's purpose for writing this play? Consider that he may have had more than a single purpose in mind. Who might have been his intended audience?
12. What does this play have to tell us about our own society? Is the play still relevant? Explain.

QUESTIONS ON STYLE AND STRUCTURE

1. How does the scene description for act I prepare the reader for Wilde's satire of Victorian society? Throughout the first act, how do specific stage directions contribute to the play's tone?
2. Consider the invented word *Bunburyist*. Why is the term used so many times in quick succession in act I (ll. 230–38; 288–91) and with such relish? How many variations (different parts of speech, different definitions) does the word undergo? Why does a made-up term play such an important role in this play?
3. Compare and contrast the alternating dialogues between Miss Prism and Chasuble and between Algernon and Cecily in the beginning of act II. How do these exchanges advance the plot? How do they reveal some of the play's themes?

4. Generally, this play sticks to the conventions of the comedy of manners — a satiric form of drama that lampoons social conventions. However, it occasionally becomes a farce, marked by wholly absurd situations, slapstick, raucous wordplay, and innuendo. Identify a shift to farce in the play. How does it contribute to the plot? What is its effect on the tone of the play?
5. Though he is mentioned several times, Lord Bracknell never appears in the play. How do other characters' descriptions of him allow us to construct an image of the man? What does this stylistic choice accomplish in terms of theme, characterization, and plot advancement? Consider how these elements would change if he actually appeared on the stage.
6. What effect does the shift in setting from the city to the country in act II have on the plot's development? How does this structure develop the play's themes?
7. What purpose do the minor characters of Miss Prism and Canon Chasuble serve in the play? How are their names a clue to their respective roles? During their stroll in act II, how does their diction differ from that of the main characters? What does their dialogue tell you about their relationship, their values, and the larger institutions they represent?
8. Explain the role of the black handbag in the play. What other objects serve as important props, and how do they advance the plot?
9. A hallmark of Wilde's style is his use of the epigram — a short, witty, often paradoxical statement designed to surprise the audience. *The Importance of Being Earnest* is full of such lines, such as the following line from act I: "To lose one parent may be regarded as a misfortune — to lose *both* seems like carelessness" (ll. 719–21). Identify three examples of epigrams in the play, and consider the purpose of each statement. What role do epigrams serve collectively, and how do they affect the tone of the play?
10. How do the final moments of the play conform to the "happily every after" conventions of romantic comedy? How do they deviate from (or comment on) such conventions?

SUGGESTIONS FOR WRITING

1. Write an essay in which you explore how Oscar Wilde employs irony to satirize the social conventions of his time. Offer examples from the play to illustrate your point. In your response, consider what purpose a satire like *The Importance of Being Earnest* serves. To what extent is satire a valuable objective in art? Is satire the means or the end in *The Importance of Being Earnest* — or both? Explain.
2. Reread the final act of *The Importance of Being Earnest.* Then, focusing particularly on the play's conclusion, write an essay in which you explain how Wilde uses three literary devices — overstatement (hyperbole), understatement, and irony, for example — to critique the values of Victorian society.
3. As a comedy of manners, *The Importance of Being Earnest* pokes fun at the behavior and affectations of a social class obsessed with appearances and, of course, earnestness. But can Wilde's play also be read as a satire of a satire? Write an essay in which you analyze various ways in which *The Importance of Being Earnest* transcends the comedy of manners genre.
4. What does *The Importance of Being Earnest* suggest about love and marriage in the world it depicts? Consider the characters' relationships and their wide range of assertions about marriage and courtship.
5. Some critics have argued that Wilde's play, while written in the late 1800s, depicts a cultural transition to the twentieth century. How might this work be read as a segue between the nineteenth and twentieth centuries in terms of the nineteenth-century cultural values it satirizes and the twentieth-century values *The Importance of Being Earnest* depicts or predicts? Some outside research may be required.
6. Write a contemporary version of act II's scene between Cecily and Gwendolen in which they first meet (ll. 747–967). Consider your setting for this meeting. Carefully rename the characters. What might they chat about? Pay particular attention to your characters' speech patterns. What do these suggest about your characters' beliefs and values, as well as those of the society they represent?

TEXTS IN CONTEXT

The Importance of Being Earnest and the Satiric Tradition

In one of the most famous essays of all time, Jonathan Swift (1667–1745) suggested that the answer to poverty and starvation in Ireland, then under British rule, was to eat the children. He pointed out the advantages of such a plan, often in graphic detail — for instance: "A child will make two dishes at an entertainment for friends; and when the family dines alone, the fore or hind quarter will make a reasonable Dish; and seasoned with a little Pepper and Salt, will be very good Boiled on the fourth day. . . ."

Today, the idea is so outrageous that we can immediately recognize that Swift's suggestion is not a serious one. But at the time, many, including the queen of England, failed to recognize that he was satirizing the inhumane attitudes and policies of the British government toward its non-British subjects. His essay was, in fact, a perfect example of **satire:** writing or art that employs irony, wit, and usually humor to expose societal shortcomings, human folly, or injustice. In an article for the *New York Review of Books*, Tim Parks frames the purpose of satire as work that attempts "to bring about change through ridicule; or if change is too grand an aspiration, we might say that it seeks to give us a fresh perspective on the absurdities and evils we live among, such that we are eager for change." At its best, satire is a social corrective. Even in the early 1700s, though, Swift was far from the first satirist. Satire is as old as language itself, a time-honored artistic tradition, and yet it is always relevant. In the fourth century B.C., the Greek playwright Aristophanes wrote the antiwar play *Lysistrata*, in which soldiers' wives refuse to have sex with them until they quit fighting the Peloponnesian War. Modern productions of the play have protested the United States' involvement in Iraq, and contemporary director Spike Lee adapted *Lysistrata* for his 2015 film *Chi-Raq*, in which women use a similar strategy to stop gang violence in Chicago. Swift, Aristophanes, and Lee make us laugh, but the works of all three speak to serious issues and strive to bring about change. Some would argue that satire prevails in today's pop culture. Whether it's social commentary in animated form in *The Simpsons*, the wordplay of rap and hip-hop music, or the biting wit of the online faux-news source known as the *Onion*, satire pricks the public conscience by reminding us of our own ridiculous or unfair behavior.

We usually characterize satire as one of two types. The more gentle, witty, playful — or **Horatian** — satire seeks to criticize with what we might call sympathetic laughter. Named for the Roman poet Horace, such satire often points out vanity, foolish behavior, superficiality, or self-absorption. The second type of satire, named for the Roman poet Juvenal, is angry, usually sarcastic in tone, often bitter. While Horatian satire is tolerant in its recognition of human foibles, **Juvenalian** satire can be harsh, even contemptuous, in its disgust with a specific behavior, policy, or practice. Below, we take a closer look at some important elements that help create satiric art and writing of both types.

Funny Times

What assumption does this cartoonist make about his audience?

Elements of Satire

Humor

Humor comes in all shapes and sizes, from the physical comedy of slapstick to subtle wit. By presenting criticism humorously, a writer can avoid moralizing or preaching. In fact, skillful humor can make us recognize a failing in ourselves or our own social or political traditions that we might not have seen (or seen as a problem).

Irony

Irony — an incongruity between expectation and reality, or what is said and what is truly meant — is another key component of satire, and we discuss it in-depth in the Close Reading section at the end of this chapter (p. 626). Writers often use techniques such as **hyperbole**, **caricature**, and **understatement** (pp. 626–27) to achieve this irony. One short example of light-hearted irony is Emily Dickinson's nineteenth-century poem "Fame is a bee":

> Fame is a bee,
>   It has a song —
> It has a sting —
>   Ah, too, it has a wing.

The poem is almost a wink, a quick, lively song that makes us smile. It demonstrates **reversal**, a technique of irony where expectations are upended for effect, in this case fame stinging (negative), but then taking flight (positive). But is this poem actually satire? It lacks the scale of the social critique mounted by Swift or Aristophanes, yet it does poke fun at the notion of fame — which is not always good! Indeed, we might think of Dickinson's poem as a clear-eyed look predicting today's celebrity worship.

Parody

Parody, another element of satire, is an imitation or a mockery to achieve a comic effect. Sometimes peoples' behavior is parodied; other times, works of literature, art, or events are mocked. The popular *Lord of the Rings* trilogy by J.R.R. Tolkien, for instance, was parodied by Henry Beard and Douglas C. Kenney in their novel *Bored of the Rings*. While parody falls flat if you are unfamiliar with the work being parodied, in this case, all the context a reader needs is in both titles.

Crossing the Line

Where is the line between a gentle corrective, a passionate criticism, and an offensive attack? Frequently, it's a matter of the relationship between speaker or author and audience. What's funny to a young person may offend a member of an older generation. A political satire may be entirely legitimate in terms of the issue being criticized, yet an audience who feels the means of the satire has gone too far may render it ineffective. For instance, a lampoon, a sharp, often virulent satire directed against an individual or a society as a whole, may come off as gratuitous, unjust, or malicious. Think about **farce** — a comic dramatic work using buffoonery and horseplay and typically including crude characterization and ludicrously improbable situations. At its best, a farce may appear not only funny but also contain deeper implications by satirizing weaknesses of humans and human society. At its worst, a farce devolves into improbable coincidences, vulgar humor, and pointless chaos.

And much depends upon the time period and cultural milieu. Published in 1884, *The Adventures of Huckleberry Finn* by Mark Twain, now considered an American classic by most, was banned by the Concord Public Library, which declared it "trash suitable only for the slums." Bret Easton Ellis's 1991 novel *American Psycho*, a scathing (and horrific) indictment of capitalism and consumer culture, features a murderous Wall Street banker who treats everything — humans, animals, and objects alike — as a commodity. When the book was first published, Ellis received hate mail and death threats. Even today, you must be over age eighteen to purchase the book in some countries.

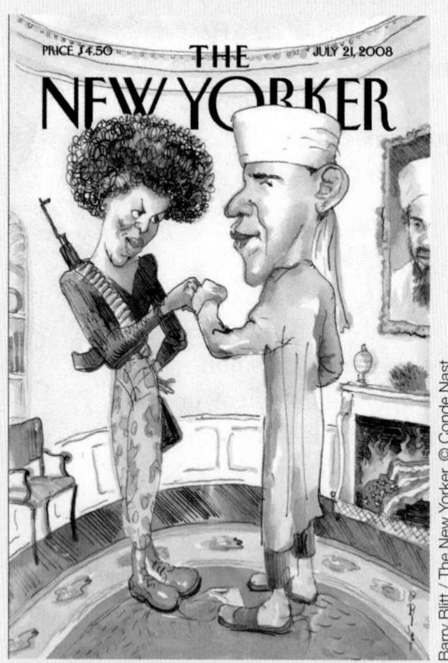

Barry Blitt / The New Yorker, © Conde Nast

Which two elements of this cover do you think would have been most likely to cause misunderstanding of the artist's intent?

Determining how far satire should go — and what methods are most effective — can have consequences more far-reaching than a literary exercise or a bad theatre review. The French satirical weekly magazine *Charlie Hebdo* considered no government, cultural, religious, or social issue off limits — regardless of left or right political preferences. As a result of its publication of controversial cartoons of Muhammad, the magazine's headquarters were the target of terrorist attacks that in 2015 resulted in the deaths of twelve people.

Although not tragic in its outcome, the *New Yorker* magazine published a cover entitled "The Politics of Fear" that depicted then presidential candidate Barack Obama and his wife Michelle fist-bumping. She was sporting a huge Afro, strapped with ammunition, and carrying an assault rifle; he was in Muslim dress, wearing a caftan and taqiyah. They're shown in the Oval Office with a portrait of Osama Bin Laden above the fireplace, where the American flag is burning. According to Bill Blitt, who drew the cover, it "satirizes the use of scare tactics and misinformation in the Presidential election to derail Barack Obama's campaign." Negative responses from both sides of the political aisle called it tasteless and insulting. Was it effective? It certainly got people talking, but the talk was less about how ridiculous Obama-related fear mongering was (as the artist says was his intent) and more about its offensiveness.

As you analyze satire, and maybe even write your own, keep in mind that effective satire is not destructive, but constructive. Let's return to the master satirist Jonathan Swift for the last word. In his poem entitled "Verses on the Death of Dr. Swift," he imagines how he would like to be remembered, denying any malicious intent in his works and claiming his purpose was always correction.

As with a moral view design'd
To cure the vices of mankind,
His vein, ironically grave,
Exposed the fool, and lash'd the knave. . . .

Yet malice never was his aim;
He lash'd the vice, but spared the name;
No individual could resent,
Where thousands equally were meant;
His satire points at no defect,
But what all mortals may correct. . . .

TEXTS IN CONTEXT

George Bernard Shaw / from *An Old New Play and a New Old One* (nonfiction)
The *Onion* / *School "Fine," U.S. Teens Report* (fiction)
Jane Austen / from *Pride and Prejudice* (fiction)
Jonathan Swift / *A Satirical Elegy on the Death of a Late Famous General* (poetry)
"I Want You" World War I Poster and "I Want Out" Anti–Vietnam War Poster (posters)
Sherman Alexie / *How to Write the Great American Indian Novel* (poetry)
Ishmael Reed / *Points of View* (poetry)
Matthea Harvey / *PROM KING AND QUEEN SEEK U.N. RECOGNITION OF THEIR OWN COUNTRY . . . PROMVANIA!* (poetry)

from An Old New Play and a New Old One

GEORGE BERNARD SHAW

Born in Ireland, George Bernard Shaw (1856–1950) was a prolific playwright, music and drama critic, and political commentator. He was the author of more than sixty plays, including *Man and Superman* (1902) and *Pygmalion* (1912). The latter was made into two films, and the screenplay Shaw wrote for the first film won an Academy Award. He was awarded the Nobel Prize for Literature in 1925. The following review of Oscar Wilde's *The Importance of Being Earnest* appeared in the *Saturday Review* in 1895.

I do not suppose it to be Mr. Wilde's first play: he is too susceptible to fine art to have begun otherwise than with a strenuous imitation of a great dramatic poem, Greek or Shakespearian; but it was perhaps the first which he designed for practical commercial use at the West End theatres. The evidence of this is abundant. The play has a plot — a gross anachronism; there is a scene between the two girls in the second act quite in the literary style of Mr. Gilbert, and almost inhuman enough to have been conceived by him; the humour is adulterated by stock mechanical fun to an extent that absolutely scandalizes one in a play with such an author's name to it; and the punning title and several of the more farcical passages recall the epoch of the late H. J. Byron. The whole has been varnished, and here and there veneered, by the author of "A Woman of no Importance"; but the general effect is that of a farcical comedy dating from the seventies, unplayed during that period because it was too clever and too decent, and brought up to date as far as possible by Mr. Wilde in his now completely formed style. Such is the impression left by the play on me. But I find other critics, equally entitled to respect, declaring that "The Importance of Being Earnest" is a strained effort of Mr. Wilde's at ultra-modernity, and that it could never have been written but for the opening up of entirely new paths in drama last year by "Arms and the Man." At which I confess to a chuckle.

I cannot say that I greatly cared for "The Importance of Being Earnest." It amused me, of course; but unless comedy touches me as well as amuses me, it leaves me with a sense of having wasted my evening. I go to the theatre to be moved to laughter, not to be tickled or bustled into it; and that is why, though I laugh as much as anybody at a farcical comedy, I am out of spirits before the end of the second act, and out of temper before the end of the third, my miserable mechanical laughter intensifying these symptoms at every outburst. If the public ever becomes intelligent enough to know when it is really enjoying itself and when it is not, there will be an end of farcical comedy. Now in "The Importance of Being Earnest" there is a good deal of this rib-tickling: for instance, the lies, the deceptions, the cross purposes, the sham mourning, the christening of the two grown-up men, the muffin eating, and so forth. These could only have been raised from the farcical plane by making them occur to characters who had, like Don Quixote, convinced us of their reality and obtained some hold on our sympathy. But that unfortunate moment of Gilbertism breaks our belief in the humanity of the play. Thus we are thrown back on the force and daintiness of its wit, brought home by an exquisitely grave, natural, and unconscious execution on the part of the actors. Alas! the latter is not forthcoming. Mr. Kinsey Peile as a man-servant, and Miss Irene Vanbrugh as

Gwendolen Fairfax, alone escaped from a devastating consciousness of Mr. Wilde's reputation, which more or less preoccupied all the rest, except perhaps Miss Millard, with whom all comedy is a preoccupation, since she is essentially a sentimental actress. In such passages as the Gilbertian quarrel with Gwendolen, her charm rebuked the scene instead of enhancing it. The older ladies were, if they will excuse my saying so, quite maddening. The violence of their affectation, the insufferable low comedy soars and swoops of the voice, the rigid shivers of elbow, shoulder, and neck, which are supposed on the stage to characterize the behaviour of ladies after the age of forty, played havoc with the piece. In Miss Rose Leclerq a good deal of this sort of thing is only the mannerism of a genuine if somewhat impossible style; but Miss Leclerq was absent through indisposition on the night of my visit; so that I had not her style to console me.

Mr. Aynesworth's easy-going "Our Boys" style of play suited his part rather happily; and Mr. Alexander's graver and more refined manner made the right contrast with it. But Mr. Alexander, after playing with very nearly if not quite perfect conviction in the first two acts, suddenly lost confidence in the third, and began to spur up for a rattling finish. From the moment that began, the play was done with. The speech in which Worthing forgives his supposed mother, and the business of searching the army lists, which should have been conducted with subdued earnestness, was bustled through to the destruction of all verisimilitude and consequently all interest. That is the worst of having anyone who is not an inveterate and hardened comedian in a leading comedy part. His faith, patience, and relish begin to give out after a time; and he finally commits the unpardonable sin against the author of giving the signal that the play is over ten minutes before the fall of the curtain, instead of speaking the last line as if the whole evening were still before the audience.

Mr. Alexander does not throw himself genuinely into comedy: he condescends to amuse himself with it; and in the end he finds that he cannot condescend enough. On the whole I must decline to accept "The Importance of Being Earnest" as a day less than ten years old; and I am altogether unable to perceive any uncommon excellence in its presentation.

[1895]

QUESTIONS

1. Overall, what is George Bernard Shaw's primary criticism of the play? Why does he conclude that it lacks any "uncommon excellence"?
2. What do you think he means by this description: "The play has a plot — a gross anachronism"?
3. Shaw admits to being "amused" by the play, but why does he believe that satirical work that elicits no more than such a response is inadequate? Based on this review, what does Shaw expect of satire?
4. In a letter to a biographer of Oscar Wilde in 1916, Shaw characterized *The Importance of Being Earnest* as "extremely funny" but "essentially hateful," and called it a "heartless play." Given the standards for satirical drama that Shaw asserts in this review, what do you think he meant by these negative descriptions?

School "Fine," U.S. Teens Report

THE ONION

The *Onion* is a digital media company that publishes fake articles on a range of local, national, and international current events, both real and fictional. It is structured in the same way as many real newspapers, with traditional news reports, op-ed pieces, interviews, and editorials. The following article, published on October 25, 2000, appeared after actual research reported that U.S. students ranked far below their international counterparts in achievement tests, yet still expressed confidence in their skills and abilities.

WASHINGTON, DC — According to results of a survey released Monday by the Department Of Education, most U.S. teenagers characterize their education as "fine."

The survey, conducted by the Office of Educational Research and Improvement (OERI), polled more than 2,000 public-school attendees between the ages of 14 and 18. The students were asked a wide variety of questions about their educational experience, ranging from the subjects they were studying to their feelings about homework, to what they had for lunch that day.

To the question, "How was school today?" 68 percent of participants responded "fine," while 18 percent answered "good" and 10 percent "okay." The remaining 4 percent replied with a shrug.

"This is the highest 'fine' response we've ever gotten since these surveys were first conducted in the 1960s," said Jeanette Franks, an OERI researcher who supervised the survey. "By comparison, in last year's survey, just 44 percent said school was 'fine' today, while 41 percent said, 'ehh,' and 15 percent said, 'I 'unno.' This year, the 'I 'unnos' didn't even rank."

5 "The findings of this survey should be heartening to parents and educators nationwide," Education Secretary Richard Riley said. "Children are our greatest natural resource, and for a majority of them to feel that they are receiving a fine education is wonderful news."

U.S. students also expressed optimism about their ability to succeed in school. Asked if they expect to do well on upcoming algebra tests, 87 percent said, "Sure." Asked if they were prepared for English exams, 51 percent responded "Yeah" and 40 percent "I guess."

Students were even more enthusiastic about America's hard-working educators, with 71 percent characterizing their social-studies teachers as "incredibly fascinating" and earth-science teachers as "not at all boring." A full 82 percent said that their civics class is "so important, I don't want to miss a second of it."

According to Franks, America's teens have an unusually strong sense of the importance of their education and the vital role it plays in becoming productive members of society.

"We asked our survey participants if what they were learning in school was helping them become better people and giving them a sense of values and concern for the community," Franks said. "A whopping 89 percent answered, 'Sure,' with the remaining 11 percent split among 'Yeah, sure,' 'Sure, I guess,' and, 'Sure. Whatever.' "

10 Despite the welcome results, the Department Of Education is refusing to rest on its laurels.

"Yes, my department is extremely pleased by the poll's results, but we still have a long way to go," Riley said. "I, for one, will not rest until every child in America feels that school is 'fine.' In this, the richest and most powerful nation on the planet, no child should receive an education that is merely 'ehh.' Our kids deserve better."

[2000]

QUESTIONS

1. What elements of traditional news reporting are included in this article? Which names are those of real people and which are fictional? Does it matter? Why or why not?
2. When do you think a reader who did not know this article was from the *Onion* would first realize that it is satirical and not serious? What tips the reader off? Would you characterize the reporter's voice as serious? What elements of satire prevail in this piece?
3. What exactly is the issue being satirized? What is the corrective action, if any, that the article asserts or suggests?
4. As a student in a U.S. high school, do you find this piece funny? offensive? silly? In other words, how effective do you think it is as a work of satire? Explain.
5. Scott Dikkers, the *Onion*'s co-founder and former editor-in-chief, responded to a question about the distinction between satirical and offensive humor by characterizing it as "ambiguous." "Humor," he said, "comes when you hone in on the truth, especially when people are trying to avoid that truth." He cited the example of a headline that ran shortly after the tragic shootings at Columbine High School: "Columbine jocks safely resume bullying." To what extent do you agree that the line between effective and offensive satire is "ambiguous," and to what extent do you think that the example he used supports his position?

from **Pride and Prejudice**

JANE AUSTEN

Jane Austen (1775–1817), a writer renowned for her witty social satires, published *Pride and Prejudice* in 1813. More than two hundred years later, it remains one of the most popular novels in the English language — there have been several film adaptations and a number of retellings published, including *Pride and Prejudice with Zombies*, a 2009 novel made into a film in 2016, and *Eligible* (2016), a novel by Curtis Sittenfeld that reimagines the setting as a reality show. In the following scene, Mr. Collins, a clergyman, proposes marriage to his cousin Elizabeth Bennet. Since laws of the day prohibited women from inheriting property, the Bennet estate could only be passed down to the closest male relative — in this case, Mr. Collins. Elizabeth, despite her family's precarious financial position, has vowed she will marry for love only.

"Believe me, my dear Miss Elizabeth, that your modesty, so far from doing you any disservice, rather adds to your other perfections. You would have been less amiable in my eyes had there *not* been this little unwillingness; but allow me to assure you, that I have your respected mother's permission for this address. You can hardly doubt the purport of my discourse, however your natural delicacy may lead you to dissemble; my attentions have been too marked to be mistaken. Almost as soon as I entered the house, I singled you out as the companion of my future life. But before I am run away with by my feelings on this subject, perhaps it would be advisable for me to state my reasons for marrying — and, moreover, for coming into Hertfordshire with the design of selecting a wife, as I certainly did."

The idea of Mr. Collins, with all his solemn composure, being run away with by his feelings, made Elizabeth so near laughing, that she could not use the short pause he allowed in any attempt to stop him farther, and he continued : —

"My reasons for marrying are, first, that I think it a right thing for every clergyman in easy circumstances (like myself) to set the example of matrimony in his parish; secondly, that I am convinced it will add very greatly to my happiness; and thirdly — which perhaps I ought to have mentioned earlier, that it is the particular advice and recommendation of the very noble lady whom I have the honor of calling patroness. Twice has she condescended to give me her opinion (unasked too!) on this subject; and it was but the very Saturday night before I left Hunsford — between our pools at quadrille, while Mrs. Jenkinson was arranging Miss de Bourgh's footstool, that she said, 'Mr. Collins, you must marry. A clergyman like you must marry. — Choose properly, choose a gentlewoman for *my* sake; and for your *own*, let her be an active, useful sort of person, not brought up high, but able to make a small income go a good way. This is my advice. Find such a woman as soon as you can, bring her to Hunsford, and I will visit her.' Allow me, by the way, to observe, my fair cousin, that I do not reckon the notice and kindness of Lady Catherine de Bourgh as among the least of the advantages in my power to offer. You will find her manners beyond anything I can describe; and your wit and vivacity, I think, must be acceptable to her, especially when tempered with the silence and respect which her rank will inevitably excite. Thus much for my general intention in favor of matrimony; it remains to be told why my views were directed to Longbourn instead of my own neighborhood, where I assure you there are many amiable young women. But the fact is, that being, as I am, to inherit this estate after the death of your honored father (who, however, may live many years longer), I could not satisfy myself without resolving to choose a wife from among his daughters, that the loss to them might be as little as possible, when the melancholy event takes place — which, however, as I have already said, may not be for several years. This has been my motive, my fair cousin, and I flatter myself it will not sink me in your esteem. And now nothing remains for me but to assure you in the most animated language of the violence of my affection. To fortune I am perfectly indifferent, and shall make no demand of that nature on your father, since I am well aware that it could not be complied with; and that one thousand pounds in the 4 per cents., which will not be yours till after your mother's decease, is all that you may ever be entitled to. On that head, therefore, I shall be uniformly silent; and you may assure yourself that no ungenerous reproach shall ever pass my lips when we are married."

It was absolutely necessary to interrupt him now.

5 "You are too hasty, sir," she cried. "You forget that I have made no answer. Let me do it without further loss of time. Accept my thanks for the compliment you are paying me. I am very sensible of the honor of your proposals, but it is impossible for me to do otherwise than decline them."

"I am not now to learn," replied Mr. Collins, with a formal wave of the hand, "that it is usual with young ladies to reject the addresses of the man whom they secretly mean to accept, when he first applies for their favor; and that sometimes the refusal is repeated a second or even a third time. I am therefore by no means discouraged by what you have just said, and shall hope to lead you to the altar ere long."

"Upon my word, sir," cried Elizabeth, "your hope is rather an extraordinary one after my declaration. I do assure you that I am not one of those young ladies (if such young ladies there are) who are so daring as to risk their happiness on the chance of being asked a second time. I am perfectly serious in my refusal. You could not make *me* happy, and I am convinced that I am the last woman in the world who would make *you* so. Nay, were your friend Lady Catherine to know me, I am persuaded she would find me in every respect ill qualified for the situation."

"Were it certain that Lady Catherine would think so," said Mr. Collins very gravely — "but I cannot imagine that her ladyship would at all disapprove of you. And you may be certain that when I have the honor of seeing her again, I shall speak in the highest terms of your modesty, economy, and other amiable qualifications."

"Indeed, Mr. Collins, all praise of me will be unnecessary. You must give me leave to judge for myself, and pay me the compliment of believing what I say. I wish you very happy and very rich, and by refusing your hand, do all in my power to prevent your being otherwise. In making me the offer, you must have satisfied the delicacy of your feelings with regard to my family, and may take possession of Longbourn estate whenever it falls, without any self-reproach. This matter may be considered, therefore, as finally settled." And rising as she thus spoke, she would have quitted the room, had not Mr. Collins thus addressed her:

"When I do myself the honor of speaking to you next on the subject, I shall hope to receive a more favorable answer than you have now given me; though I am far from accusing you of cruelty at present, because I know it to be the established custom of your sex to reject a man on the first application, and perhaps you have even now said as much to encourage my suit as would be consistent with the true delicacy of the female character."

"Really, Mr. Collins," cried Elizabeth with some warmth, "you puzzle me exceedingly. If what I have hitherto said can appear to you in the form of encouragement, I know not how to express my refusal in such a way as may convince you of its being one."

"You must give me leave to flatter myself, my dear cousin, that your refusal of my addresses is merely words of course. My reasons for believing it are briefly these: — It does not appear to me that my hand is unworthy your acceptance, or that the establishment I can offer would be any other than highly desirable. My situation in life, my connections with the family of De Bourgh, and my relationship to your own, are circumstances highly in my favor; and you should take it into further consideration, that in spite of your manifold attractions, it is by no means certain that another offer of marriage may ever be made you. Your portion is unhappily so small, that it will in all likelihood undo the effects of your loveliness and amiable qualifications. As I must therefore conclude that you are not serious in your rejection of me, I shall choose to attribute it to your wish of increasing my love by suspense, according to the usual practice of elegant females."

"I do assure you, sir, that I have no pretensions whatever to that kind of elegance which consists in tormenting a respectable man. I would rather be paid the compliment of being believed sincere. I thank you again and again for the honor you have done me in your proposals, but to accept them is absolutely impossible. My feelings in every respect forbid it. Can I speak plainer? Do not consider me now as an elegant female, intending to plague you, but as a rational creature, speaking the truth from her heart."

"You are uniformly charming!" cried he, with an air of awkward gallantry; "and I am persuaded that when sanctioned by the express authority of both your excellent parents, my proposals will not fail of being acceptable."

To such perseverance in wilful self-deception Elizabeth would make no reply, and immediately and in silence withdrew; determined, that if he persisted in considering her repeated refusals as flattering encouragement, to apply to her father, whose negative might be uttered in such a manner as must be decisive, and whose behavior at least could not be mistaken for the affectation and coquetry of an elegant female.

[1813]

QUESTIONS

1. In what ways does Mr. Collins present his proposal as a business transaction? To what extent do you think the proposal is purely a parody of an earnest marriage proposal?
2. What examples of humor do you find in this proposal? Identify examples of both hyperbole and understatement and explain their effect.
3. Jane Austen's sharp wit is at work through irony, both verbal and dramatic, in this scene. Identify some examples of these and discuss how they contribute to the characterization of Mr. Collins. Consider, especially, the narrative point of view in the passage.
4. How would you characterize Mr. Collins's diction? Does it help portray him as a caricature? If so, what is he a caricature of? Clergymen? Men of a certain class? Men in general? Cite specific evidence from the text to support your response.
5. While this passage is comic in many ways, the humor reminds us of serious social and economic realities of the time. Where exactly does Austen remind us that there is more at work here than the desire to make her audience laugh?

A Satirical Elegy on the Death of a Late Famous General

JONATHAN SWIFT

Perhaps best known for *Gulliver's Travels* (1726), which has mistakenly come to be thought of as a children's novel, Jonathan Swift (1667–1745) was born in Ireland to English parents. He was educated at Trinity College, Dublin, was ordained a minister, and was appointed dean of Saint Patrick's cathedral in Dublin in 1713. For years he addressed the political problems of his day by publishing pamphlets on contemporary social issues, some of them anonymously. Among these pamphlets is the well-known essay "A Modest Proposal for Preventing the Children of Poor People in Ireland from Being a Burden to Their Parents or Country, and for Making Them Beneficial to the Publick," widely known as "A Modest Proposal." As a model of elegant prose and cogent argument, it has gained deserved fame. The subject of "A Satirical Elegy on the Death of a Late Famous General" is John Churchill, the first Duke of Marlborough, whom Swift believed had prolonged the War of the Spanish Succession (1701–1714) for his own profit and glory.

His Grace! impossible! what, dead!
Of old age too, and in his bed!
And could that mighty warrior fall,
And so inglorious, after all?
Well, since he's gone, no matter how,
The last loud trump must wake him now;
And, trust me, as the noise grows stronger,
He'd wish to sleep a little longer.
And could he be indeed so old
As by the newspapers we're told?
Threescore,[1] I think, is pretty high;
'Twas time in conscience he should die!
This world he cumber'd long enough;
He burnt his candle to the snuff;
And that's the reason, some folks think,
He left behind so great a stink.
Behold his funeral appears,
Nor widow's sighs, nor orphan's tears,
Wont[2] at such times each heart to pierce,
Attend the progress of his hearse.
But what of that? his friends may say
He had those honours in his day.

[1] Sixty years. — EDS.

[2] Accustomed. — EDS.

True to his profit[3] and his pride,
He made them weep before he died.
Come hither, all ye empty things!
Ye bubbles raised by breath of kings!
Who float upon the tide of state;
Come hither, and behold your fate!
Let Pride be taught by this rebuke,
How very mean[4] a thing's a duke;
From all his ill-got honours flung,
Turn'd to that dirt from whence he sprung.

[1722]

[3] Profession. — EDS.

[4] Contemptible. — EDS.

QUESTIONS

1. Who is the speaker — the "I" — of the poem? How would you describe his attitude toward the general expressed in the first few lines?
2. What comment does the speaker make about the general's age? Why is it "time in conscience he should die" (l. 12)?
3. Why are there no widows or orphans following the funeral procession? What, then, are the "honours" that the general had "in his day" (l. 22)?
4. How does the poem shift at line 25? Who are the "bubbles raised by breath of kings" (l. 26)?
5. What strategies of satire does Jonathan Swift use most extensively in this poem? Identify and discuss the effect of at least two.
6. Was Swift satirizing one individual exclusively, or was he targeting a larger issue? How would you describe the object of his satire? Consider lines 25–32 in your response.
7. An elegy is a lament for the dead, usually a reflection on the life of the departed that portrays him or her in a positive light. How does this poem upend the expected content of an elegy?
8. One critic described Swift's elegy as "a poem so angry it sometimes forgets to be satirical." What do you think that statement means? Do you think the poem is successful as a work of satire? Explain, with specific reference to the text.

"I Want You" World War I Poster and "I Want Out" Anti–Vietnam War Poster

The original Uncle Sam "I Want You" poster, created by artist and illustrator James Montgomery Flagg, first graced the cover of a 1916 issue of *Leslie's Weekly*, a popular newsmagazine of the day. Over four million copies of the poster were printed between 1917 and 1918 as the United States entered World War I. In this iconic image, Uncle Sam commands, "I want YOU" with a pointed finger and stern face to summon recruits. It became a symbol of the patriotic duty to serve and defend America, intended to rally young men around the cause. The re-imagined poster — published anonymously in 1971 by the Committee to Unsell the War, a campaign that protested military involvement in Vietnam — proclaims, "I want OUT."

SWIM INK 2 LLC / Private Collection / Bridgeman Images

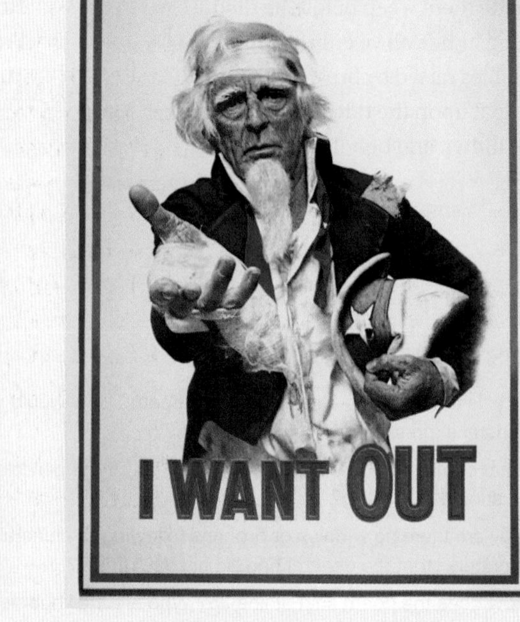

Private Collection / Peter Newark American Pictures / Bridgeman Images

[1916/1971]

QUESTIONS

1. Fifty-five years after the original poster appeared, the newer American icon looks bandaged and battered. What details in this version support the proclamation, "I want out!"?
2. How does the 1971 reinterpretation reverse and invert the gestures of the original poster? Would you characterize it as a parody of the original? Explain.
3. Kat Kinsman, a writer, blogger, and political humorist, says that humor such as we see in the 1971 poster is essential to making people reconsider their views. "These images are hyperbolic," she admits. "But I tend to think that if you can get people laughing, you can get them thinking." To what extent do you agree or disagree with her view? Use details from the 1971 poster to support your response.

How to Write the Great American Indian Novel

SHERMAN ALEXIE

A Spokane/Coeur d'Alene Indian, Sherman Alexie (b. 1966) grew up on the Spokane Indian reservation in Wellpinit, Washington. He graduated from Washington State University with a BA in American Studies. Alexie has published fourteen books of poetry and short stories about life on the reservation and the relationship between the Indian and mainstream communities, including his first collection of short stories, *The Lone Ranger and Tonto Fistfight in Heaven* (1993), which received a PEN/Hemingway Award for Best First Book of Fiction. In 1997, Alexie wrote the screenplay for what became the award-winning film *Smoke Signals* (1998), based on his short story "This Is What It Means to Say Phoenix,

Arizona." *The Absolutely True Diary of a Part-Time Indian* (2007) was awarded the National Book Award for young people's literature in 2007. *War Dances*, his 2009 book of short stories and poems, won the PEN/Faulkner Award for Fiction, and in 2015 he and David Lehman edited *The Best American Poetry*, an annually published anthology. He is well known for his sense of humor and performance ability, winning the World Heavyweight Poetry Bout competition four years in a row. In this poem, originally published in the *New Yorker*, Alexie addresses the question of how to represent Native Americans in some imagined "great American Indian novel."

All of the Indians must have tragic features: tragic noses, eyes, and arms.
Their hands and fingers must be tragic when they reach for tragic food.

The hero must be a half-breed, half white and half Indian, preferably
from a horse culture. He should often weep alone. That is mandatory.

If the hero is an Indian woman, she is beautiful. She must be slender
and in love with a white man. But if she loves an Indian man

then he must be a half-breed, preferably from a horse culture.
If the Indian woman loves a white man, then he has to be so white

that we can see the blue veins running through his skin like rivers.
When the Indian woman steps out of her dress, the white man gasps

at the endless beauty of her brown skin. She should be compared to nature:
brown hills, mountains, fertile valleys, dewy grass, wind, and clear water.

If she is compared to murky water, however, then she must have a secret.
Indians always have secrets, which are carefully and slowly revealed.

Yet Indian secrets can be disclosed suddenly, like a storm.
Indian men, of course, are storms. They should destroy the lives

of any white women who choose to love them. All white women love
Indian men. That is always the case. White women feign disgust

at the savage in blue jeans and T-shirt, but secretly lust after him.
White women dream about half-breed Indian men from horse cultures.

Indian men are horses, smelling wild and gamey. When the Indian man
unbuttons his pants, the white woman should think of topsoil.

There must be one murder, one suicide, one attempted rape.
Alcohol should be consumed. Cars must be driven at high speeds.

Indians must see visions. White people can have the same visions
if they are in love with Indians. If a white person loves an Indian

then the white person is Indian by proximity. White people must carry
an Indian deep inside themselves. Those interior Indians are half-breed

and obviously from horse cultures. If the interior Indian is male
then he must be a warrior, especially if he is inside a white man.

If the interior Indian is female, then she must be a healer, especially if she is inside
a white woman. Sometimes there are complications.

An Indian man can be hidden inside a white woman. An Indian woman
can be hidden inside a white man. In these rare instances,

everybody is a half-breed struggling to learn more about his or her horse culture.
There must be redemption, of course, and sins must be forgiven.

For this, we need children. A white child and an Indian child, gender
not important, should express deep affection in a childlike way.

In the Great American Indian novel, when it is finally written,
all of the white people will be Indians and all of the Indians will be ghosts.

[1996]

QUESTIONS

1. Whom do you think Sherman Alexie intends as the audience for this poem? Is the speaker addressing people who write about Native Americans or people who are themselves Native Americans? What aspects of the poem support your viewpoint?
2. Structurally, the poem is a series of injunctions about what "must" be done, and what is "mandatory," when writing about Native Americans. How does Alexie juxtapose romantic as well as violent imagery, and to what effect?
3. Where in popular culture do you see the stereotypes that Alexie calls up in his poem? Choose two stereotypes and provide examples of each at work in a movie, television show, or advertisement from the present or past. How does Alexie's humor use Native American stereotypes to expose issues that plague Native American culture and expose biases in society at large?
4. How would you describe the overall tone of the poem? Does Alexie maintain this same tone throughout, or does it shift? If so, where and how?
5. This poem was referred to by one critic as "a devastating contemporary satire." What exactly is Alexie satirizing? Pay particular attention to the notions of "complications," "redemption," and "ghosts" that he raises.

Points of View

ISHMAEL REED

Born in Chattanooga, Tennessee, in 1938, Ishmael Reed is known for using humor to expose human absurdities, particularly racial bias. He's published more than twenty books of poetry, essays, novels, and plays, and is the recipient of numerous awards, including a "genius grant" from the MacArthur Foundation and the Lifetime Achievement Award from the National Poetry Association. Professor Emeritus at the University of California, Berkeley, and a community activist, Reed currently blogs for the *San Francisco Chronicle*.

The pioneers and the indians
disagree about a lot of things
for example, the pioneer says that
when you meet a bear in the woods
you should yell at him and if that
doesn't work, you should fell him
The indians say that you should
whisper to him softly and call him by
loving nicknames
No one's bothered to ask the bear
what he thinks

[2007]

QUESTIONS

1. To what extent do you think "Points of View" is a poem about race? Taking your response into account as support, what exactly is Ishmael Reed satirizing in this poem?
2. How does Reed use reversal to maintain a humorous tone? Does this tone undercut or enhance the point he is making? Explain.
3. One critic described Reed's poems as "'edutainments' — forms of surprise, revelation, and frequent hilarity." In what ways do you see this poem as a synergy of education and entertainment?

PROM KING AND QUEEN SEEK U.N. RECOGNITION OF THEIR OWN COUNTRY . . . PROMVANIA!

MATTHEA HARVEY

Matthea Harvey (b. 1973) was born in Germany and moved to the United States from England when she was eight. She received a BA from Harvard University and an MFA from the Iowa Writers' Workshop. She has published five books of poetry and currently teaches at Sarah Lawrence University. "PROM KING AND QUEEN SEEK U.N. RECOGNITION OF THEIR OWN COUNTRY . . . PROMVANIA!" takes its title from an article in a satiric newspaper.

Most August Council of Member Nations,
please accept this petition and attendant corsages —
roses for the ladies' wrists, magnetized magnolias
for the men's lapels. The dewdrops are glue and won't
drip. Lauren, my queen, your tiara's dents are sadly
spotlit under these fluorescents, (Sarah should
never have said that about your glorious ass), but aside
from the usual border disputes with Homecoming and
Sadie Hawkins, we're committed to peace. Pinky-swear.
Yes, of course you have questions. We know how to

spike punch to perfection and if a large percentage
of our national debt stems from the nightly balloon-falls
we require, there is much to admire in our high school
treasurer's thrift — she orders streamers in bulk and
the prom court runners-up (we'd never call them losers)
collect faux-fetti from the hole punches in the English wing.
The right to have a perfect prom is inalienable, right?
One of these nights, it's going to happen — there'll be no ex
dancing by, starry-eyed, with her strapless inching toward
topless (expect sanctions, Santana!), no need to photoshop
added sparkle onto our CVS scepters. Press your hand to your
cheek but pretend it's someone else's hand. Vote yes.

[2014]

QUESTIONS

1. Who is the speaker of the poem? How effective is that speaker? Explain.
2. In this poem, trivial subjects, characters, and events are treated ceremoniously, with the elevated language and elaborate devices characteristic of classic heroic literature. What examples of this style does Matthea Harvey poke fun at in this poem? Identify and discuss the effect of at least two examples. Consider such strategies as wordplay, hyperbole, and juxtaposition.
3. Who do you believe is the intended audience for this poem? Explain.
4. How might this poem qualify as an example of effective Horatian satire?

LITERATURE IN CONVERSATION
The Importance of Being Earnest and the Satiric Tradition

1. George Bernard Shaw criticized *The Importance of Being Earnest* because he felt it lacked the serious social criticism that would qualify it as a satire. What do you think? Explain your position on the effectiveness of the play as a satire.
2. Analyze the methods that Oscar Wilde employs to satirize courtship and marriage in *The Importance of Being Earnest*. Consider at least three and discuss why each is appropriate to the subject.
3. In what ways are the excerpt from Jane Austen's *Pride and Prejudice* and the article from the *Onion* more alike than different, despite the fact that they were written nearly two hundred years apart? Consider the elements of satire evident in each.
4. Compare and contrast the satiric methods in two of the poems you've read in this section.
5. The poems by Sherman Alexie and Ishmael Reed both present minority views within a majority culture. Compare and contrast their purposes and methods. Which do you think delivers the more powerful message, and why?
6. Both Jonathan's Swift's "Elegy" and the 1971 Uncle Sam poster convey an antiwar message, though they take different approaches. Discuss why and how each is appropriate and effective for its own time period, culture, and audience.
7. Both Matthea Harvey's "PROMVANIA" poem and the *Onion* article satirize the typical American high school experience. Which text do you find more appealing — and more likely to cause students such as you to become critically aware of their behavior and/or attitudes? Explain with specific textual references.

8. Write your own work of satire on an issue in your local community or the larger community that you believe is in need of reform. You might choose an individual who is running for office or is in a leadership position, or you can focus on a practice or policy that you believe is unfair or inappropriate. Address a specific audience by indicating the occasion or place where you would present the satire (e.g., a speech to a specific group, a blog post on a particular site, an article in a local newspaper or magazine).

9. Analyze the strategies and effectiveness of a popular comedian of your choosing. Consider the audience to whom he or she appeals, the targets of the satire, and the strategies used to express it. Pay close attention to the historical and cultural context and its effect on what is considered "acceptable." How does or did the comedian ever stir up controversy by crossing the line of good taste or acceptable topics? Feel free to choose your own, but suggestions include Aziz Ansari, Lenny Bruce, Hannibal Buress, George Carlin, Margaret Cho, Louis C.K., Stephen Colbert, Lena Dunham, Cameron Esposito, Tina Fey, Zach Galifianakis, Dick Gregory, Whoopi Goldberg, Kevin Hart, Jen Kirkman, Eddie Murphy, Tig Notaro, John Oliver, Amy Poehler, Brian Regan, Chris Rock, Sarah Silverman, Amy Schumer, Jon Stewart, Jessica Williams, or Steven Wright.

10. Write an evaluation of a satiric news source. Consider whether the source presents itself as credible journalism or clearly a spoof. Discuss who or what you believe are the main targets of the satire, and who the audience is. Which methods of satire (e.g., caricature, lampoon, wordplay) are most prevalent, and to what effect?

11. Write an essay supporting or challenging one of the following quotations about satire. Choose at least two of the works you've analyzed in this section, in addition to *The Importance of Being Earnest*, as part of your discussion.

    a. "Satire is traditionally the weapon of the powerless against the powerful." — Molly Ivins

    b. "Praise undeserved, is satire in disguise." — Alexander Pope

    c. "You can't make up anything anymore. The world itself is a satire. All you're doing is recording it." — Art Buchwald

    d. "Satire should, like a polished razor keen, / Wound with a touch that's scarcely felt or seen." — Lady Mary Wortley Montague

    e. "Good satire comes from anger. It comes from a sense of injustice, that there are wrongs in the world that need to be fixed." — Carl Hiaasen

    f. "For something to be funny, the audience has to be in a position to sense the truth of it. It has to be primed. Satire can crystallize what's already in the air, but it can't really put it there." — Garry Trudeau

FICTION

Bliss

KATHERINE MANSFIELD

Katherine Mansfield (1888–1923) was born in New Zealand. Never the favorite child of her parents, she considered herself "an ugly duckling" and saw her family as being "for trade," while she was "for art." She was educated in Wellington at the exclusive Miss Swainson's school, and in London, where she attended Queen's College. Mansfield's early stories began to appear in the magazine *New Age* in 1910 and were published in the collection *In a German Pension* (1911). She collaborated in editing two literary magazines: *Rhythm* (with John Murry) and *Signature* (with D. H. Lawrence). After a period of traveling in Europe and sporadic writing, Mansfield published *Bliss and Other Stories* (1920) and *The Garden Party* (1922). In 1918, she married John Murry and, through him, became part of the Garsington set — the English literary group that included Lady Ottoline Morrell, D. H. Lawrence, Aldous Huxley, and Leonard and Virginia Woolf. Her celebrity was short lived. She was diagnosed with tuberculosis in 1919, and her final years were spent in search of specialist medical help and a climate that would ameliorate her condition. Her ability to paint a scene with economy and a deft touch, combined with a perceptive eye for tension beneath a calm surface, is revealed in "Bliss."

Although Bertha Young was thirty she still had moments like this when she wanted to run instead of walk, to take dancing steps on and off the pavement, to bowl a hoop, to throw something up in the air and catch it again, or to stand still and laugh at — nothing — at nothing, simply.

What can you do if you are thirty and, turning the corner of your own street, you are overcome, suddenly, by a feeling of bliss — absolute bliss! — as though you'd suddenly swallowed a bright piece of that late afternoon sun and it burned in your bosom, sending out a little shower of sparks into every particle, into every finger and toe? . . .

Oh, is there no way you can express it without being "drunk and disorderly"? How idiotic civilization is! Why be given a body if you have to keep it shut up in a case like a rare, rare fiddle?

"No, that about the fiddle is not quite what I mean," she thought, running up the steps and feeling in her bag for the key — she's forgotten it, as usual — and rattling the letter-box. "It's not what I mean, because — Thank you, Mary" — she went into the hall. "Is nurse back?"

"Yes, M'm." 5

"And has the fruit come?"

"Yes, M'm. Everything's come."

"Bring the fruit up to the dining-room, will you? I'll arrange it before I go upstairs."

It was dusky in the dining-room and quite chilly. But all the same Bertha threw off her coat; she could not bear the tight clasp of it another moment, and the cold air fell on her arms.

But in her bosom there was still that bright 10
glowing place — that shower of little sparks coming from it. It was almost unbearable. She hardly dared to breathe for fear of fanning it higher, and yet she breathed deeply, deeply. She hardly dared to look into the cold mirror — but she did look, and it gave her back a woman, radiant, with smiling, trembling lips, with big,

dark eyes and an air of listening, waiting for something . . . divine to happen . . . that she knew must happen . . . infallibly.

Mary brought in the fruit on a tray and with it a glass bowl, and a blue dish, very lovely, with a strange sheen on it as though it had been dipped in milk.

"Shall I turn on the light, M'm?"

"No, thank you. I can see quite well."

There were tangerines and apples stained with strawberry pink. Some yellow pears, smooth as silk, some white grapes covered with a silver bloom and a big cluster of purple ones. These last she had bought to tone in with the new dining-room carpet. Yes, that did sound rather far-fetched and absurd, but it was really why she had bought them. She had thought in the shop: "I must have some purple ones to bring the carpet up to the table." And it had seemed quite sense at the time.

When she had finished with them and had made two pyramids of these bright round shapes, she stood away from the table to get the effect — and it really was most curious. For the dark table seemed to melt into the dusky light and the glass dish and the blue bowl to float in the air. This, of course in her present mood, was so incredibly beautiful. . . . She began to laugh.

"No, no. I'm getting hysterical." And she seized her bag and coat and ran upstairs to the nursery.

Nurse sat at a low table giving Little B her supper after her bath. The baby had on a white flannel gown and a blue woollen jacket, and her dark, fine hair was brushed up into a funny little peak. She looked up when she saw her mother and began to jump.

"Now, my lovey, eat it up like a good girl," said Nurse, setting her lips in a way that Bertha knew, and that meant she had come into the nursery at another wrong moment.

"Has she been good, Nanny?"

"She's been a little sweet all the afternoon," whispered Nanny. "We went to the park and I sat down on a chair and took her out of the pram and a big dog came along and put his head on my knee and she clutched its ear, tugged it. Oh, you should have seen her."

Bertha wanted to ask if it wasn't rather dangerous to let her clutch at a strange dog's ear. But she did not dare to. She stood watching them, her hands by her side, like the poor little girl in front of the rich little girl with the doll.

The baby looked up at her again, stared, and then smiled so charmingly that Bertha couldn't help crying:

"Oh, Nanny, do let me finish giving her her supper while you put the bath things away."

"Well, M'm, she oughtn't to be changed hands while she's eating," said Nanny, still whispering. "It unsettles her; it's very likely to upset her."

How absurd it was. Why have a baby if it has to be kept — not in a case like a rare, rare fiddle — but in another woman's arms?

"Oh, I must!" said she.

Very offended, Nanny handed her over.

"Now, don't excite her after her supper. You know you do, M'm. And I have such a time with her after!"

Thank heaven! Nanny went out of the room with the bath towels.

"Now I've got you to myself, my little precious," said Bertha, as the baby leaned against her.

She ate delightfully, holding up her lips for the spoon and then waving her hands. Sometimes she wouldn't let the spoon go; and sometimes, just as Bertha had filled it, she waved it away to the four winds.

When the soup was finished Bertha turned round to the fire.

"You're nice — you're very nice!" said she, kissing her warm baby. "I'm fond of you. I like you."

And, indeed, she loved Little B so much — her neck as she bent forward, her exquisite toes as they shone transparent in the firelight — that all her feeling of bliss came back again, and again she didn't know how to express it — what to do with it.

"You're wanted on the telephone," said Nanny, coming back in triumph and seizing *her* Little B.

Down she flew. It was Harry.

"Oh, is that you, Ber? Look here. I'll be late. I'll take a taxi and come along as quickly as I can, but get dinner put back ten minutes — will you? All right?"

"Yes, perfectly. Oh, Harry!"

"Yes?"

What had she to say? She'd nothing to say. She only wanted to get in touch with him for a moment. She couldn't absurdly cry: "Hasn't it been a divine day!"

"What is it?" rapped out the little voice.

"Nothing. *Entendu*," said Bertha, and hung up the receiver, thinking how more than idiotic civilization was.

They had people coming to dinner. The Norman Knights — a very sound couple — he was about to start a theater, and she was awfully keen on interior decoration, a young man, Eddie Warren, who had just published a little book of poems and whom everybody was asking to dine, and a "find" of Bertha's called Pearl Fulton. What Miss Fulton did, Bertha didn't know. They had met at the club and Bertha had fallen in love with her, as she always did fall in love with beautiful women who had something strange about them.

The provoking thing was that, though they had been about together and met a number of times and really talked, Bertha couldn't yet make her out. Up to a certain point Miss Fulton was rarely, wonderfully frank, but the certain point was there, and beyond that she would not go.

Was there anything beyond it? Harry said "No." Voted her dullish, and "cold like all blond women, with a touch, perhaps, of anæmia of the brain." But Bertha wouldn't agree with him; not yet, at any rate.

"No, the way she has of sitting with her head a little on one side, and smiling, has something behind it, Harry, and I must find out what that something is."

"Most likely it's a good stomach," answered Harry.

He made a point of catching Bertha's heels with replies of that kind . . . "liver frozen, my dear girl," or "pure flatulence," or "kidney disease," . . . and so on. For some strange reason Bertha liked this, and almost admired it in him very much.

She went into the drawing-room and lighted the fire; then, picking up the cushions, one by one, that Mary had disposed so carefully, she threw them back on to the chairs and the couches. That made all the difference; the room came alive at once. As she was about to throw the last one she surprised herself by suddenly hugging it to her, passionately, passionately. But it did not put out the fire in her bosom. Oh, on the contrary!

The windows of the drawing-room opened on to a balcony overlooking the garden. At the far end, against the wall, there was a tall, slender pear tree in fullest, richest bloom; it stood perfect, as though becalmed against the jade-green sky. Bertha couldn't help feeling, even from this distance, that it had not a single bud or a faded petal. Down below, in the garden beds, the red and yellow tulips, heavy with flowers, seemed to lean upon the dusk. A grey cat, dragging its belly, crept across the lawn, and a black one, its shadow, trailed after. The sight of them, so intent and so quick, gave Bertha a curious shiver.

"What creepy things cats are!" she stammered, and she turned away from the window and began walking up and down. . . .

How strong the jonquils smelled in the warm room. Too strong? Oh, no. And yet, as though overcome, she flung down on a couch and pressed her hands to her eyes.

"I'm too happy—too happy!" she murmured.

And she seemed to see on her eyelids the lovely pear tree with its wide open blossoms as a symbol of her own life.

Really—really—she had everything. She was young. Harry and she were as much in love as ever, and they got on together splendidly and were really good pals. She had an adorable baby. They didn't have to worry about money. They had this absolutely satisfactory house and garden. And friends—modern, thrilling friends, writers and painters and poets or people keen on social questions—just the kind of friends they wanted. And then there were books, and there was music, and she had found a wonderful little dressmaker, and they were going abroad in the summer, and their new cook made the most superb omelettes. . . .

"I'm absurd! Absurd!" She sat up; but she felt quite dizzy, quite drunk. It must have been the spring.

Yes, it was the spring. Now she was so tired she could not drag herself upstairs to dress.

A white dress, a string of jade beads, green shoes and stockings. It wasn't intentional. She had thought of this scheme hours before she stood at the drawing-room window.

Her petals rushed softly into the hall, and she kissed Mrs. Norman Knight, who was taking off the most amusing orange coat with a procession of black monkeys round the hem and up the fronts.

". . . Why! Why! Why is the middle-class so stodgy—so utterly without a sense of humor! My dear, it's only a fluke that I am here at all—Norman being the protective fluke. For my darling monkeys so upset the train that it rose to a man and simply ate me with its eyes. Didn't laugh—wasn't amused—that I should have loved. No, just stared—and bored me through and through."

"But the cream of it was," said Norman, pressing a large tortoiseshell-rimmed monocle into his eye, "you don't mind me telling this, Face, do you?" (In their home and among their friends they called each other Face and Mug.) "The cream of it was when she, being full fed, turned to the woman beside her and said: 'Haven't you ever seen a monkey before?'"

"Oh, yes!" Mrs. Norman Knight joined in the laughter. "Wasn't that too absolutely creamy?"

And a funnier thing still was that now her coat was off she did look like a very intelligent monkey—who had even made that yellow silk dress out of scraped banana skins. And her amber earrings; they were like little dangling nuts.

"This is a sad, sad fall!" said Mug, pausing in front of Little B's perambulator. "When the perambulator comes into the hall——" and he waved the rest of the quotation away.

The bell rang. It was lean, pale Eddie Warren (as usual) in a state of acute distress.

"It *is* the right house, *isn't* it?" he pleaded.

"Oh, I think so—I hope so," said Bertha brightly.

"I have had such a *dreadful* experience with a taxi-man; he was *most* sinister. I couldn't get him to *stop*. The *more* I knocked and called the *faster* he went. And *in* the moonlight this *bizarre* figure with the *flattened* head *crouching* over the *lit-tle* wheel. . . ."

He shuddered, taking off an immense white silk scarf. Bertha noticed that his socks were white, too—most charming.

"But how dreadful!" she cried.

"Yes, it really was," said Eddie, following her into the drawing-room. "I saw myself *driving* through Eternity in a *timeless* taxi."

He knew the Norman Knights. In fact, he was going to write a play for N. K. when the theater scheme came off.

"Well, Warren, how's the play?" said Norman Knight, dropping his monocle and giving his eye a moment in which to rise to the surface before it was screwed down again.

And Mrs. Norman Knight: "Oh, Mr. Warren, what happy socks!"

"I *am* so glad you like them," said he, staring at his feet. "They seem to have got so *much* whiter since the moon rose." And he turned his lean sorrowful young face to Bertha. "There *is* a moon, you know."

She wanted to cry: "I am sure there is—often—often!"

He really was a most attractive person. But so was Face, crouched before the fire in her banana skins, and so was Mug, smoking a cigarette and saying as he flicked the ash: "Why doth the bridegroom tarry?"

"There he is, now."

Bang went the front door open and shut. Harry shouted: "Hullo, you people. Down in five minutes." And they heard him swarm up the stairs. Bertha couldn't help smiling; she knew how he loved doing things at high pressure. What, after all, did an extra five minutes matter? But he would pretend to himself that they mattered beyond measure. And then he would make a great point of coming into the drawing-room, extravagantly cool and collected.

Harry had such a zest for life. Oh, how she appreciated it in him. And his passion for fighting—for seeking in everything that came up against him another test of his power and of his courage—that, too, she understood. Even when it made him just occasionally, to other people, who didn't know him well, a little ridiculous perhaps. . . . For there were moments when he rushed into battle where no battle was. . . . She talked and laughed and positively forgot until he had come in (just as she had imagined) that Pearl Fulton had not turned up.

"I wonder if Miss Fulton has forgotten?"

"I expect so," said Harry. "Is she on the 'phone?"

"Ah! There's a taxi, now." And Bertha smiled with that little air of proprietorship that she always assumed while her women finds were new and mysterious. "She lives in taxis."

"She'll run to fat if she does," said Harry coolly, ringing the bell for dinner. "Frightful danger for blond women."

"Harry—don't," warned Bertha, laughing up at him.

Came another tiny moment, while they waited, laughing and talking, just a trifle too much at their ease, a trifle too unaware. And then Miss Fulton, all in silver, with a silver fillet binding her pale blond hair, came in smiling, her head a little on one side.

"Am I late?"

"No, not at all," said Bertha. "Come along." And she took her arm and they moved into the dining-room.

What was there in the touch of that cool arm that could fan—fan—start blazing—blazing—the fire of bliss that Bertha did not know what to do with?

Miss Fulton did not look at her; but then she seldom did look at people directly. Her heavy eyelids lay upon her eyes and the strange half smile came and went upon her lips as though she lived by listening rather than seeing. But Bertha knew, suddenly, as if the longest, most intimate look had passed between them—as if they had said to each other: "You, too?"—that Pearl Fulton, stirring the beautiful red soup in the grey plate, was feeling just what she was feeling.

And the others? Face and Mug, Eddie and Harry, their spoons rising and falling—dabbing their lips with their napkins, crumbling bread, fiddling with the forks and glasses and talking.

"I met her at the Alpha shore—the weirdest little person. She'd not only cut off her hair, but she seemed to have taken a dreadfully good snip off her legs and arms and her neck and her poor little nose as well."

"Isn't she very *liée* with Michael Oat?"

"The man who wrote *Love in False Teeth*?"

"He wants to write a play for me. One act. One man. Decides to commit suicide. Gives all the reasons why he should and why he shouldn't. And just as he has made up his mind either to do it or not to do it — curtain. Not half a bad idea."

"What's he going to call it — 'Stomach Trouble'?"

"I *think* I've come across the *same* idea in a lit-tle French review, *quite* unknown in England."

No, they didn't share it. They were dears — dears — and she loved having them there, at her table, and giving them delicious food and wine. In fact, she longed to tell them how delightful they were, and what a decorative group they made, how they seemed to set one another off and how they reminded her of a play by Chekhov!

Harry was enjoying his dinner. It was part of his — well, not his nature, exactly, and certainly not his pose — his — something or other — to talk about food and to glory in his "shameless passion for the white flesh of the lobster" and "the green of pistachio ices — green and cold like the eyelids of Egyptian dancers."

When he looked up at her and said: "Bertha, this is a very admirable *soufflée*!" she almost could have wept with child-like pleasure.

Oh, why did she feel so tender toward the whole world tonight? Everything was good — was right. All that happened seemed to fill again her brimming cup of bliss.

And still, in the back of her mind, there was the pear tree. It would be silver now, in the light of poor dear Eddie's moon, silver as Miss Fulton, who sat there turning a tangerine in her slender fingers that were so pale a light seemed to come from them.

What she simply couldn't make out — what was miraculous — was how she should have guessed Miss Fulton's mood so exactly and so instantly. For she never doubted for a moment that she was right, and yet what had she to go on? Less than nothing.

"I believe this does happen very, very rarely between women. Never between men," thought Bertha. "But while I am making coffee in the drawing-room perhaps she will 'give a sign.'"

What she meant by that she did not know, and what would happen after that she could not imagine.

While she thought like this she saw herself talking and laughing. She had to talk because of her desire to laugh.

"I must laugh or die."

But when she noticed Face's funny little habit of tucking something down the front of her bodice — as if she kept a tiny, secret hoard of nuts there, too — Bertha *had to dig her nails* into her hands — so as not to laugh too much.

It was over at last. And: "Come and see my new coffee machine," said Bertha.

"We only have a new coffee machine once a fortnight," said Harry. Face took her arm this time; Miss Fulton bent her head and followed after.

The fire had died down in the drawing-room to a red, flickering "nest of baby phoenixes," said Face.

"Don't turn up the light for a moment. It is so lovely." And down she crouched by the fire again. She was always cold . . . "without her little red flannel jacket, of course," thought Bertha.

At that moment Miss Fulton "gave the sign."

"Have you a garden?" said the cool, sleepy voice.

This was so exquisite on her part that all Bertha could do was to obey. She crossed the room, pulled the curtains apart, and opened those long windows.

"There!" she breathed.

And the two women stood side by side looking at the slender, flowering tree. Although it was so still it seemed, like the flame of a candle, to stretch up, to point, to quiver in the bright air, to grow taller and taller as they gazed — almost to touch the rim of the round, silver moon.

How long did they stand there? Both, as it were, caught in that circle of unearthly light, understanding each other perfectly, creatures of another world, and wondering what they were to do in this one with all this blissful treasure that burned in their bosoms and dropped, in silver flowers, from their hair and hands?

Forever — for a moment? And did Miss Fulton murmur: "Yes. Just *that*." Or did Bertha dream it?

Then the light was snapped on and Face made the coffee and Harry said: "My dear Mrs. Knight, don't ask me about my baby. I never see her. I shan't feel the slightest interest in her until she has a lover," and Mug took his eye out of the conservatory for a moment and then put it under glass again and Eddie Warren drank his coffee and set down the cup with a face of anguish as though he had drunk and seen the spider.

"What I want to do is to give the young men a show. I believe London is simply teeming with first-chop, unwritten plays. What I want to say to 'em is: 'Here's the theater. Fire ahead.'"

"You know, my dear, I am going to decorate a room for the Jacob Nathans. Oh, I am so tempted to do a fried-fish scheme, with the backs of the chairs shaped like frying pans and lovely chip potatoes embroidered all over the curtains."

"The trouble with our young writing men is that they are still too romantic. You can't put out to sea without being seasick and wanting a basin. Well, why won't they have the courage of those basins?"

"A *dreadful* poem about a *girl* who was *violated* by a beggar *without* a nose in a lit-tle wood. . . ."

Miss Fulton sank into the lowest, deepest chair and Harry handed round the cigarettes.

From the way he stood in front of her shaking the silver box and saying abruptly: "Egyptian? Turkish? Virginian? They're all mixed up," Bertha realized that she not only bored him; he really disliked her. And she decided from the way Miss Fulton said: "No, thank you, I won't smoke," that she felt it, too, and was hurt.

"Oh, Harry, don't dislike her. You are quite wrong about her. She's wonderful, wonderful. And, besides, how can you feel so differently about someone who means so much to me? I shall try to tell you when we are in bed tonight what has been happening. What she and I have shared."

At those last words something strange and almost terrifying darted into Bertha's mind. And this something blind and smiling whispered to her: "Soon these people will go. The house will be quiet — quiet. The lights will be out. And you and he will be alone together in the dark room — the warm bed. . . ."

She jumped up from her chair and ran over to the piano.

"What a pity someone does not play!" she cried. "What a pity somebody does not play."

For the first time in her life Bertha Young desired her husband.

Oh, she loved him — she'd been in love with him, of course, in every other way, but just not in that way. And, equally, of course, she'd understood that he was different. They'd discussed it so often. It had worried her dreadfully at first to find that she was so cold, but after a time it had not seemed to matter. They were so frank with each other — such good pals. That was the best of being modern.

But now — ardently! ardently! The word ached in her ardent body! Was this what that feeling of bliss had been leading up to? But then — then —

"My dear," said Mrs. Norman Knight, "you know our shame. We are the victims of time and train. We live in Hampstead. It's been so nice."

"I'll come with you into the hall," said Bertha. "I love having you. But you must not miss the last train. That's so awful, isn't it?"

"Have a whisky, Knight, before you go?" called Harry.

"No, thanks, old chap."

Bertha squeezed his hand for that as she shook it.

"Good night, good-bye," she cried from the top step, feeling that this self of hers was taking leave of them forever.

When she got back into the drawing-room the others were on the move.

". . . Then you can come part of the way in my taxi."

"I shall be *so* thankful *not* to have to face *another* drive *alone* after my *dreadful* experience."

"You can get a taxi at the rank just at the end of the street. You won't have to walk more than a few yards."

"That's comfort. I'll go and put on my coat."

Miss Fulton moved toward the hall and Bertha was following when Harry almost pushed past.

"Let me help you."

Bertha knew that he was repenting his rudeness — she let him go. What a boy he was in some ways — so impulsive — so simple.

And Eddie and she were left by the fire.

"I *wonder* if you have seen Bilks' *new* poem called *Table d'Hôte,*" said Eddie softly. "It's *so* wonderful. In the last Anthology. Have you got a copy? I'd *so* like to *show* it to you. It begins with an *incredibly* beautiful line: 'Why Must it Always be Tomato Soup?'"

"Yes," said Bertha. And she moved noiselessly to a table opposite the drawing-room door and Eddie glided noiselessly after her. She picked up the little book and gave it to him; they had not made a sound.

While he looked it up she turned her head toward the hall. And she saw . . . Harry with Miss Fulton's coat in his arms and Miss Fulton with her back turned to him and her head bent. He tossed the coat away, put his hands on her shoulders, and turned her violently to him. His lips said: "I adore you," and Miss Fulton laid her moonbeam fingers on his cheeks and smiled her sleepy smile. Harry's nostrils quivered; his lips curled back in a hideous grin while he whispered: "Tomorrow," and with her eyelids Miss Fulton said: "Yes."

"Here it is," said Eddie. "'Why Must it Always be Tomato Soup?' It's so *deeply* true, don't you feel? Tomato soup is so *dreadfully* eternal."

"If you prefer," said Harry's voice, very loud, from the hall, "I can 'phone you a cab to come to the door."

"Oh, no. It's not necessary," said Miss Fulton, and she came up to Bertha and gave her the slender fingers to hold.

"Good-bye. Thank you so much."

"Good-bye," said Bertha.

Miss Fulton held her hand a moment longer.

"Your lovely pear tree!" she murmured.

And then she was gone, with Eddie following, like the black cat following the grey cat.

"I'll shut up shop," said Harry, extravagantly cool and collected.

"Your lovely pear tree — pear tree — pear tree!"

Bertha simply ran over to the long windows.

"Oh, what is going to happen now?" she cried.

But the pear tree was as lovely as ever and as full of flower and as still.

[1920]

EXPLORING THE TEXT

1. What are the denotations and connotations of the word *bliss*? Why does Bertha admonish herself for "getting hysterical" (para. 16)? Is her bliss the same as the "zest for life" (para. 80) she ascribes to her husband?
2. What is your impression of Bertha from the opening section of the story? What holds her attention? Be on the lookout for conflicts and contradictions. What does she mean when she says, "Why be given a body if you have to keep it shut up in a case like a rare, rare fiddle" (para. 3)? Does that question undermine her professions of bliss?
3. How would you describe Bertha's relationship with her baby? her husband? her baby's nurse? What do these relationships reveal about Bertha's role within her family circle?
4. Reread the account of the dinner party. Look for details that offer insight into the relationships among these characters. What conclusions can you draw about these people and the society they represent?
5. How does the character of Pearl Fulton evolve? Does Katherine Mansfield depict her negatively? What qualities does Bertha note initially? When did you begin to suspect that Pearl and Harry were having an affair? Does Mansfield give us clues?
6. Trace the pear tree throughout the story. It is introduced in a simple description but eventually becomes important as a symbol; what does it symbolize? Also trace how the tree works as a structural marker in the story.
7. Do Bertha and Harry love each other? Consider the nature of their relationship, particularly her realization that she wants more intimacy (paras. 128–33). Use examples from the story to defend your response.
8. At the end of the story, Bertha cries, "Oh, what is going to happen now?" (para. 163). What do you think is going to happen? How does the final sentence – "But the pear tree was as lovely as ever and as full of flower and as still" – point the way to an answer to what happens next? What effect does this kind of ending have on you as a reader?
9. One critic analyzes the theme of "Bliss" as follows: "While 'on the surface' the story outlines the happiness of this dainty, middle-class housewife, the author is surreptitiously interrogating the rigid nature of accepted male and female roles." What do you think she means? Explain why you agree or disagree with this interpretation.

A Rose for Emily

WILLIAM FAULKNER

William Faulkner (1897–1962) is considered one of the finest American writers of the twentieth century. Born in New Albany, Mississippi, Faulkner grew bored with education in his early teens, joining first the Canadian and then the British Royal Air Force during the First World War – though he never saw action. Faulkner's writing is distinctly southern and often set in Jefferson, Mississippi. While living in New Orleans, Faulkner wrote his first novel, *Soldier's Pay* (1926). Over the next three years, he published *Mosquitoes* (1927) and *The Sound and the Fury* (1929), which established his reputation. The following decade saw Faulkner at his most prolific. *As I Lay Dying* (1930), *Sanctuary* (1931), and *Light in August* (1932), together with collections of poems and short stories, preceded publication of *Absalom, Absalom!* in 1936. During spells in Hollywood, he also established himself as a masterly screenwriter. In 1949, he was awarded the Nobel Prize for Literature. The story "A Rose for Emily" demonstrates Faulkner's uniquely subtle style and his ability to mingle truth with fiction.

I

When Miss Emily Grierson died, our whole town went to her funeral: the men through a sort of respectful affection for a fallen monument, the women mostly out of curiosity to see the inside of her house, which no one save an old manservant — a combined gardener and cook — had seen in at least ten years.

It was a big, squarish frame house that had once been white, decorated with cupolas and spires and scrolled balconies in the heavily lightsome style of the seventies, set on what had once been our most select street. But garages and cotton gins had encroached and obliterated even the august names of that neighborhood; only Miss Emily's house was left, lifting its stubborn and coquettish decay above the cotton wagons and the gasoline pumps — an eyesore among eyesores. And now Miss Emily had gone to join the representatives of those august names where they lay in the cedar-bemused cemetery among the ranked and anonymous graves of Union and Confederate soldiers who fell at the battle of Jefferson.

Alive, Miss Emily had been a tradition, a duty, and a care; a sort of hereditary obligation upon the town, dating from that day in 1894 when Colonel Sartoris, the mayor — he who fathered the edict that no Negro woman should appear on the streets without an apron — remitted her taxes, the dispensation dating from the death of her father on into perpetuity. Not that Miss Emily would have accepted charity. Colonel Sartoris invented an involved tale to the effect that Miss Emily's father had loaned money to the town, which the town, as a matter of business, preferred this way of repaying. Only a man of Colonel Sartoris' generation and thought could have invented it, and only a woman could have believed it.

When the next generation, with its more modern ideas, became mayors and aldermen, this arrangement created some little dissatisfaction. On the first of the year they mailed her a tax notice. February came, and there was no reply. They wrote her a formal letter, asking her to call at the sheriff's office at her convenience. A week later the mayor wrote her himself, offering to call or to send his car for her, and received in reply a note on paper of an archaic shape, in a thin, flowing calligraphy in faded ink, to the effect that she no longer went out at all. The tax notice was also enclosed, without comment.

5 They called a special meeting of the Board of Aldermen. A deputation waited upon her, knocked at the door through which no visitor had passed since she ceased giving china-painting lessons eight or ten years earlier. They were admitted by the old Negro into a dim hall from which a stairway mounted into still more shadow. It smelled of dust and disuse — a close, dank smell. The Negro led them into the parlor. It was furnished in heavy, leather-covered furniture. When the Negro opened the blinds of one window, they could see that the leather was cracked; and when they sat down, a faint dust rose sluggishly about their thighs, spinning with slow motes in the single sun-ray. On a tarnished gilt easel before the fireplace stood a crayon portrait of Miss Emily's father.

They rose when she entered — a small, fat woman in black, with a thin gold chain descending to her waist and vanishing into her belt, leaning on an ebony cane with a tarnished gold head. Her skeleton was small and spare; perhaps that was why what would have been merely plumpness in another was obesity in her. She looked bloated, like a body long submerged in motionless water, and of that pallid hue. Her eyes, lost in the fatty ridges of her face, looked like two small pieces of coal pressed into a lump of dough as they moved from one face to another while the visitors stated their errand.

She did not ask them to sit. She just stood in the door and listened quietly until the spokesman came to a stumbling halt. Then they could hear the invisible watch ticking at the end of the gold chain.

Her voice was dry and cold. "I have no taxes in Jefferson. Colonel Sartoris explained it to me. Perhaps one of you can gain access to the city records and satisfy yourselves."

"But we have. We are the city authorities, Miss Emily. Didn't you get a notice from the sheriff, signed by him?"

"I received a paper, yes," Miss Emily said. "Perhaps he considers himself the sheriff. . . . I have no taxes in Jefferson."

"But there is nothing on the books to show that, you see. We must go by the — "

"See Colonel Sartoris. I have no taxes in Jefferson."

"But, Miss Emily — "

"See Colonel Sartoris." (Colonel Sartoris had been dead almost ten years.) "I have no taxes in Jefferson. Tobe!" The Negro appeared. "Show these gentlemen out."

II

So she vanquished them, horse and foot, just as she had vanquished their fathers thirty years before about the smell. That was two years after her father's death and a short time after her sweetheart — the one we believed would marry her — had deserted her. After her father's death she went out very little; after her sweetheart went away, people hardly saw her at all. A few of the ladies had the temerity to call, but were not received, and the only sign of life about the place was the Negro man — a young man then — going in and out with a market basket.

"Just as if a man — any man — could keep a kitchen properly," the ladies said; so they were not surprised when the smell developed. It was another link between the gross, teeming world and the high and mighty Griersons.

A neighbor, a woman, complained to the mayor, Judge Stevens, eighty years old.

"But what will you have me do about it, madam?" he said.

"Why, send her word to stop it," the woman said. "Isn't there a law?"

"I'm sure that won't be necessary," Judge Stevens said. "It's probably just a snake or a rat that nigger of hers killed in the yard. I'll speak to him about it."

The next day he received two more complaints, one from a man who came in diffident deprecation. "We really must do something about it, Judge. I'd be the last one in the world to bother Miss Emily, but we've got to do something." That night the Board of Aldermen met — three graybeards and one younger man, a member of the rising generation.

"It's simple enough," he said. "Send her word to have her place cleaned up. Give her a certain time to do it in, and if she don't . . ."

"Dammit, sir," Judge Stevens said, "will you accuse a lady to her face of smelling bad?"

So the next night, after midnight, four men crossed Miss Emily's lawn and slunk about the house like burglars, sniffing along the base of the brickwork and at the cellar openings while one of them performed a regular sowing motion with his hand out of a sack slung from his shoulder. They broke open the cellar door and sprinkled lime there, and in all the outbuildings. As they recrossed the lawn, a window that had been dark was lighted and Miss Emily sat in it, the light behind her, and her upright torso motionless as that of an idol. They crept quietly across the lawn and into the shadow of the locusts that lined the street. After a week or two the smell went away.

That was when people had begun to feel really sorry for her. People in our town, remembering how old lady Wyatt, her great-aunt, had gone completely crazy at last, believed that the Griersons held themselves a little too high for what they really were. None of the young men were quite good enough for Miss Emily and such. We had long thought of them as a tableau,

Miss Emily a slender figure in white in the background, her father a spraddled silhouette in the foreground, his back to her and clutching a horsewhip, the two of them framed by the back-flung front door. So when she got to be thirty and was still single, we were not pleased exactly, but vindicated; even with insanity in the family she wouldn't have turned down all of her chances if they had really materialized.

When her father died, it got about that the house was all that was left to her; and in a way, people were glad. At last they could pity Miss Emily. Being left alone, and a pauper, she had become humanized. Now she too would know the old thrill and the old despair of a penny more or less.

The day after his death all the ladies prepared to call at the house and offer condolence and aid, as is our custom. Miss Emily met them at the door, dressed as usual and with no trace of grief on her face. She told them that her father was not dead. She did that for three days, with the ministers calling on her, and the doctors, trying to persuade her to let them dispose of the body. Just as they were about to resort to law and force, she broke down, and they buried her father quickly.

We did not say she was crazy then. We believed she had to do that. We remembered all the young men her father had driven away, and we knew that with nothing left, she would have to cling to that which had robbed her, as people will.

III

She was sick for a long time. When we saw her again, her hair was cut short, making her look like a girl, with a vague resemblance to those angels in colored church windows — sort of tragic and serene.

30 The town had just let the contracts for paving the sidewalks, and in the summer after her father's death they began the work. The construction company came with niggers and mules and machinery, and a foreman named Homer Barron, a Yankee — a big, dark, ready man, with a big voice and eyes lighter than his face. The little boys would follow in groups to hear him cuss the niggers, and the niggers singing in time to the rise and fall of picks. Pretty soon he knew everybody in town. Whenever you heard a lot of laughing anywhere about the square, Homer Barron would be in the center of the group. Presently, we began to see him and Miss Emily on Sunday afternoons driving in the yellow-wheeled buggy and the matched team of bays from the livery stable.

At first we were glad that Miss Emily would have an interest, because the ladies all said, "Of course a Grierson would not think seriously of a Northerner, a day laborer." But there were still others, older people, who said that even grief could not cause a real lady to forget *noblesse oblige* — without calling it *noblesse oblige*. They just said, "Poor Emily. Her kinsfolk should come to her." She had some kin in Alabama; but years ago her father had fallen out with them over the estate of old lady Wyatt, the crazy woman, and there was no communication between the two families. They had not even been represented at the funeral.

And as soon as the old people said, "Poor Emily," the whispering began. "Do you suppose it's really so?" they said to one another. "Of course it is. What else could . . ." This behind their hands; rustling of craned silk and satin behind jalousies closed upon the sun of Sunday afternoon as the thin, swift clop-clop-clop of the matched team passed: "Poor Emily."

She carried her head high enough — even when we believed that she was fallen. It was as if she demanded more than ever the recognition of her dignity as the last Grierson; as if it had wanted that touch of earthiness to reaffirm her imperviousness. Like when she bought the rat poison, the arsenic. That was over a year after they had begun to say "Poor Emily," and while the two female cousins were visiting her.

"I want some poison," she said to the druggist. She was over thirty then, still a slight woman, though thinner than usual, with cold, haughty black eyes in a face the flesh of which was strained across the temples and about the eye-sockets as you imagine a lighthouse-keeper's face ought to look. "I want some poison," she said.

"Yes, Miss Emily. What kind? For rats and such? I'd recom——"

"I want the best you have. I don't care what kind."

The druggist named several. "They'll kill anything up to an elephant. But what you want is——"

"Arsenic," Miss Emily said. "Is that a good one?"

"Is . . . arsenic? Yes, ma'am. But what you want——"

"I want arsenic."

The druggist looked down at her. She looked back at him, erect, her face like a strained flag. "Why, of course," the druggist said. "If that's what you want. But the law requires you to tell what you are going to use it for."

Miss Emily just stared at him, her head tilted back in order to look him eye for eye, until he looked away and went and got the arsenic and wrapped it up. The Negro delivery boy brought her the package; the druggist didn't come back. When she opened the package at home there was written on the box, under the skull and bones: "For rats."

IV

So the next day we all said, "She will kill herself"; and we said it would be the best thing. When she had first begun to be seen with Homer Barron, we had said, "She will marry him." Then we said, "She will persuade him yet," because Homer himself had remarked — he liked men, and it was known that he drank with the younger men in the Elks' Club — that he was not a marrying man. Later we said, "Poor Emily" behind the jalousies as they passed on Sunday afternoon in the glittering buggy, Miss Emily with her head high and Homer Barron with his hat cocked and a cigar in his teeth, reins and whip in a yellow glove.

Then some of the ladies began to say that it was a disgrace to the town and a bad example to the young people. The men did not want to interfere, but at last the ladies forced the Baptist minister — Miss Emily's people were Episcopal — to call upon her. He would never divulge what happened during that interview, but he refused to go back again. The next Sunday they again drove about the streets, and the following day the minister's wife wrote to Miss Emily's relations in Alabama.

So she had blood-kin under her roof again and we sat back to watch developments. At first nothing happened. Then we were sure that they were to be married. We learned that Miss Emily had been to the jeweler's and ordered a man's toilet set in silver, with the letters H. B. on each piece. Two days later we learned that she had bought a complete outfit of men's clothing, including a nightshirt, and we said, "They are married." We were really glad. We were glad because the two female cousins were even more Grierson than Miss Emily had ever been.

So we were not surprised when Homer Barron — the streets had been finished some time since — was gone. We were a little disappointed that there was not a public blowing-off, but we believed that he had gone on to prepare for Miss Emily's coming, or to give her a chance to get rid of the cousins. (By that time it was a cabal, and we were all Miss Emily's allies to help circumvent the cousins.) Sure enough, after another week they departed. And, as we had expected all along, within three days Homer Barron was back in town. A neighbor saw the Negro man admit him at the kitchen door at dusk one evening.

And that was the last we saw of Homer Barron. And of Miss Emily for some time. The Negro man went in and out with the market basket, but the front door remained closed. Now and then we would see her at a window for a moment, as the men did that night when they sprinkled the lime, but for almost six months she did not appear on the streets. Then we knew that this was to be expected too; as if that quality of her father which had thwarted her woman's life so many times had been too virulent and too furious to die.

When we next saw Miss Emily, she had grown fat and her hair was turning gray. During the next few years it grew grayer and grayer until it attained an even pepper-and-salt iron-gray, when it ceased turning. Up to the day of her death at seventy-four it was still that vigorous iron-gray, like the hair of an active man.

From that time on her front door remained closed, save for a period of six or seven years, when she was about forty, during which she gave lessons in china-painting. She fitted up a studio in one of the downstairs rooms, where the daughters and granddaughters of Colonel Sartoris' contemporaries were sent to her with the same regularity and in the same spirit that they were sent to church on Sundays with a twenty-five-cent piece for the collection plate. Meanwhile her taxes had been remitted.

Then the newer generation became the backbone and the spirit of the town, and the painting pupils grew up and fell away and did not send their children to her with boxes of color and tedious brushes and pictures cut from the ladies' magazines. The front door closed upon the last one and remained closed for good. When the town got free postal delivery, Miss Emily alone refused to let them fasten the metal numbers above her door and attach a mailbox to it. She would not listen to them.

Daily, monthly, yearly we watched the Negro grow grayer and more stooped, going in and out with the market basket. Each December we sent her a tax notice, which would be returned by the post office a week later, unclaimed. Now and then we would see her in one of the downstairs windows — she had evidently shut up the top floor of the house — like the carven torso of an idol in a niche, looking or not looking at us, we could never tell which. Thus she passed from generation to generation — dear, inescapable, impervious, tranquil, and perverse.

And so she died. Fell ill in the house filled with dust and shadows, with only a doddering Negro man to wait on her. We did not even know she was sick; we had long since given up trying to get information from the Negro. He talked to no one, probably not even to her, for his voice had grown harsh and rusty, as if from disuse.

She died in one of the downstairs rooms, in a heavy walnut bed with a curtain, her gray head propped on a pillow yellow and moldy with age and lack of sunlight.

V

The Negro met the first of the ladies at the front door and let them in, with their hushed, sibilant voices and their quick, curious glances, and then he disappeared. He walked right through the house and out the back and was not seen again.

The two female cousins came at once. They held the funeral on the second day, with the town coming to look at Miss Emily beneath a mass of bought flowers, with the crayon face of her father musing profoundly above the bier and the ladies sibilant and macabre; and the very old men — some in their brushed Confederate uniforms — on the porch and the lawn, talking of Miss Emily as if she had been a contemporary of theirs, believing that they had danced with her and courted her perhaps, confusing time with its mathematical progression, as the old do, to whom all the past is not a diminishing road but, instead, a huge meadow which no winter ever quite touches, divided from them now by the narrow bottleneck of the most recent decade of years.

Already we knew that there was one room in that region above stairs which no one had seen in forty years, and which would have to be forced. They waited until Miss Emily was decently in the ground before they opened it.

The violence of breaking down the door seemed to fill this room with pervading dust. A thin, acrid pall as of the tomb seemed to lie everywhere upon this room decked and furnished as for a bridal: upon the valance curtains of faded rose color, upon the rose-shaded lights, upon the dressing table, upon the delicate array of crystal and the man's toilet things backed with tarnished silver, silver so tarnished that the monogram was obscured. Among them lay a collar and tie, as if they had just been removed, which, lifted, left upon the surface a pale crescent in the dust. Upon a chair hung the suit, carefully folded; beneath it the two mute shoes and the discarded socks.

The man himself lay in the bed.

For a long while we just stood there, looking down at the profound and fleshless grin. The body had apparently once lain in the attitude of an embrace, but now the long sleep that outlasts love, that conquers even the grimace of love, had cuckolded him. What was left of him, rotted beneath what was left of the nightshirt, had become inextricable from the bed in which he lay; and upon him and upon the pillow beside him lay that even coating of the patient and biding dust.

Then we noticed that in the second pillow 60
was the indentation of a head. One of us lifted something from it, and leaning forward, that faint and invisible dust dry and acrid in the nostrils, we saw a long strand of iron-gray hair.

[1931]

EXPLORING THE TEXT

1. "A Rose for Emily" is narrated in first-person plural. Why do you think William Faulkner chose "we" rather than "I" as the voice for the story? How might this narrative strategy be related to the description of Emily as "a tradition, a duty, and a care; a sort of hereditary obligation upon the town" (para. 3)?
2. Trace the timeline of this story, and then analyze why the author decided to recount the tale in this manner. How does the order of the telling help shape the story's meaning? What details foreshadow the story's conclusion? What governs the five-part division of the story?
3. Discuss how this story might be viewed as a conflict between North and South. Keep in mind that Homer Barron is a construction foreman and a northerner, while Emily Grierson comes from a genteel southern family. How might the physical descriptions of Miss Emily relate to this theme?
4. Look at paragraph 55. How do the diction, syntax, and imagery in this paragraph reinforce one of the story's themes?
5. How is Miss Emily "a fallen monument" (para. 1)? To what is she a monument? Why is she repeatedly called an "idol"? What connection can you draw between these images and one of the story's themes?
6. Describe Emily's relationship with her father. What details in the story support your view? How does this relationship influence the development of events in the story?
7. Did the story's ending surprise you? Explain why Miss Emily did what she did.
8. In an interview, Faulkner described the conflict of Miss Emily: she "had broken all the laws of her tradition, her background, and she had finally broken the law of God too. . . . And she knew she was doing wrong, and that's why her own life was wrecked. Instead of murdering one lover, and then to go on and take another and when she used him up to murder him, she was expiating her crime." How might this story be seen as expiation?

Woman Hollering Creek

SANDRA CISNEROS

Born in Chicago, the only girl among seven children, Sandra Cisneros (b. 1954) spent her early life in both Chicago and Mexico before her family eventually settled in Humboldt Park, a Puerto Rican neighborhood of Chicago. Cisneros earned a bachelor's degree from Loyola University and an MFA from the University of Iowa. Set in Humboldt Park, her most famous work is *The House on Mango Street* (1984), which won the American Book Award and established her reputation. Her other works include *My Wicked, Wicked Ways* (1987), *Woman Hollering Creek and Other Stories* (1991), *Hairs / Pelitos* (1994), *Loose Woman: Poems* (1994), *Caramelo* (2002), *Vintage Cisneros* (2004), the children's book *Bravo Bruno* (2011), *Have You Seen Marie?* (2012), and *A House of My Own* (2015). Cisneros received fellowships from the National Endowment for the Arts in 1981 and 1988, and won a MacArthur Fellowship in 1995. Since 2007, the Alfredo Cisneros Del Moral Foundation, whose name commemorates Ms. Cisneros's father, has awarded over $75,000 to writers born or living in Texas. This work prompted Cisneros to recall, "In my own experience, grants not only allowed me time to write but, more importantly, confirmed I was indeed a writer at precarious moments when my own faith in my art wobbled." Cisneros has taught at the high school level in Chicago, was a writer-in-residence at Our Lady of the Lake University in San Antonio, and currently lives in central Mexico. In the title story from her collection, *Woman Hollering Creek*, Cisneros re-creates the lives of women living on both sides of the U.S.-Mexico border through a series of sketches set around San Antonio.

The day Don Serafín gave Juan Pedro Martínez Sánchez permission to take Cleófilas Engriqueta DeLeón Hernández as his bride, across her father's threshold, over several miles of dirt road and several miles of paved, over one border and beyond to a town *en el otro lado* — on the other side — already did he divine the morning his daughter would raise her hand over her eyes, look south, and dream of returning to the chores that never ended, six good-for-nothing brothers, and one old man's complaints.

He had said, after all, in the hubbub of parting: I am your father, I will never abandon you. He had said that, hadn't he, when he hugged and then let her go. But at the moment Cleófilas was busy looking for Chela, her maid of honor, to fulfill her bouquet conspiracy. She would not remember her father's parting words until later. *I am your father, I will never abandon you.*

Only now as a mother did she remember. Now, when she and Juan Pedrito sat by the creek's edge. How when a man and a woman love each other, sometimes that love sours. But a parent's love for a child, a child's for its parents, is another thing entirely.

This is what Cleófilas thought evenings when Juan Pedro did not come home, and she lay on her side of the bed listening to the hollow roar of the interstate, a distant dog barking, the pecan trees rustling like ladies in stiff petticoats — *shh-shh-shh, shh-shh-shh* — soothing her to sleep.

5 In the town where she grew up, there isn't very much to do except accompany the aunts and godmothers to the house of one or the other to play cards. Or walk to the cinema to see this week's film again, speckled and with one hair quivering annoyingly on the screen. Or to the center of town to order a milk shake that will

appear in a day and a half as a pimple on her backside. Or to the girlfriend's house to watch the latest *telenovela* episode and try to copy the way the women comb their hair, wear their makeup.

But what Cleófilas has been waiting for, has been whispering and sighing and giggling for, has been anticipating since she was old enough to lean against the window displays of gauze and butterflies and lace, is passion. Not the kind on the cover of the *¡Alarma!* magazines, mind you, where the lover is photographed with the bloody fork she used to salvage her good name. But passion in its purest crystalline essence. The kind the books and songs and *telenovelas* describe when one finds, finally, the great love of one's life, and does whatever one can, must do, at whatever the cost.

Tú o Nadie. "You or No One." The title of the current favorite *telenovela.* The beautiful Lucía Méndez having to put up with all kinds of hardships of the heart, separation and betrayal, and loving, always loving no matter what, because *that* is the most important thing, and did you see Lucía Méndez on the Bayer aspirin commercials — wasn't she lovely? Does she dye her hair do you think? Cleófilas is going to go to the *farmacía* and buy a hair rinse; her girlfriend Chela will apply it — it's not that difficult at all.

Because you didn't watch last night's episode when Lucía confessed she loved him more than anyone in her life. In her life! And she sings the song "You or No One" in the beginning and end of the show. *Tú o Nadie.* Somehow one ought to live one's life like that, don't you think? You or no one. Because to suffer for love is good. The pain all sweet somehow. In the end.

Seguín. She had liked the sound of it. Far away and lovely. Not like *Monclova. Coahuila.* Ugly.

10 *Seguín, Tejas.* A nice sterling ring to it. The tinkle of money. She would get to wear outfits like the woman on the *tele,* like Lucía Méndez. And have a lovely house, and wouldn't Chela be jealous.

And yes, they will drive all the way to Laredo to get her wedding dress. That's what they say. Because Juan Pedro wants to get married right away, without a long engagement since he can't take off too much time from work. He has a very important position in Seguin with, with . . . a beer company, I think. Or was it tires? Yes, he has to be back. So they will get married in the spring when he can take off work, and then they will drive off in his new pickup — did you see it? — to their new home in Seguin. Well, not exactly new, but they're going to repaint the house. You know newlyweds. New paint and new furniture. Why not? He can afford it. And later on add maybe a room or two for the children. May they be blessed with many.

Well, you'll see. Cleófilas has always been so good with her sewing machine. A little *rrrr, rrrr, rrrr* of the machine and *¡zas!* Miracles. She's always been so clever, that girl. Poor thing. And without even a mama to advise her on things like her wedding night. Well, may God help her. What with a father with a head like a burro, and those six clumsy brothers. Well, what do you think! Yes, I'm going to the wedding. Of course! The dress I want to wear just needs to be altered a teensy bit to bring it up to date. See, I saw a new style last night that I thought would suit me. Did you watch last night's episode of *The Rich Also Cry*? Well, did you notice the dress the mother was wearing?

La Gritona. Such a funny name for such a lovely *arroyo.* But that's what they called the creek that ran behind the house. Though no one could say whether the woman had hollered from anger or pain. The natives only knew the *arroyo* one crossed on the way to San Antonio, and then once again on the way back, was called Woman Hollering, a name no one from these parts questions, little less understood. *Pues, allá de los indios, quién sabe*[1] — who knows, the townspeople shrugged, because it was of no concern to their lives how this trickle of water received its curious name.

---

[1] Well, that's from the Indians, who knows? — EDS.

"What do you want to know for?" Trini the laundromat attendant asked in the same gruff Spanish she always used whenever she gave Cleófilas change or yelled at her for something. First for putting too much soap in the machines. Later, for sitting on a washer. And still later, after Juan Pedrito was born, for not understanding that in this country you cannot let your baby walk around with no diaper and his pee-pee hanging out, it wasn't nice, *¿entiendes? Pues.*[2]

15 How could Cleófilas explain to a woman like this why the name Woman Hollering fascinated her. Well, there was no sense talking to Trini.

On the other hand there were the neighbor ladies, one on either side of the house they rented near the *arroyo.* The woman Soledad on the left, the woman Dolores on the right.

The neighbor lady Soledad liked to call herself a widow, though how she came to be one was a mystery. Her husband had either died, or run away with an ice-house floozie, or simply gone out for cigarettes one afternoon and never came back. It was hard to say which since Soledad, as a rule, didn't mention him.

In the other house lived *la señora* Dolores, kind and very sweet, but her house smelled too much of incense and candles from the altars that burned continuously in memory of two sons who had died in the last war and one husband who had died shortly after from grief. The neighbor lady Dolores divided her time between the memory of these men and her garden, famous for its sunflowers — so tall they had to be supported with broom handles and old boards; red red cockscombs, fringed and bleeding a thick menstrual color; and, especially, roses whose sad scent reminded Cleófilas of the dead. Each Sunday *la señora* Dolores clipped the most beautiful of these flowers and arranged them on three modest headstones at the Seguin cemetery.

The neighbor ladies, Soledad, Dolores, they might've known once the name of the *arroyo* before it turned English but they did not know now. They were too busy remembering the men who had left through either choice or circumstance and would never come back.

20 Pain or rage, Cleófilas wondered when she drove over the bridge the first time as a newlywed and Juan Pedro had pointed it out. *La Gritona,* he had said, and she had laughed. Such a funny name for a creek so pretty and full of happily ever after.

The first time she had been so surprised she didn't cry out or try to defend herself. She had always said she would strike back if a man, any man, were to strike her.

But when the moment came, and he slapped her once, and then again, and again; until the lip split and bled an orchid of blood, she didn't fight back, she didn't break into tears, she didn't run away as she imagined she might when she saw such things in the *telenovelas.*

In her own home her parents had never raised a hand to each other or to their children. Although she admitted she may have been brought up a little leniently as an only daughter — *la consentida,* the princess — there were some things she would never tolerate. Ever.

Instead, when it happened the first time, when they were barely man and wife, she had been so stunned, it left her speechless, motionless, numb. She had done nothing but reach up to the heat of her mouth and stare at the blood on her hand as if even then she didn't understand.

25 She could think of nothing to say, said nothing. Just stroked the dark curls of the man who wept and would weep like a child, his tears of repentance and shame, this time and each.

The men at the ice house. From what she can tell, from the times during her first year when still a newlywed she is invited and accompanies her husband, sits mute beside their conversation, waits and sips a beer until it grows warm, twists a paper napkin into a knot, then another into a fan, one into a rose, nods her head, smiles,

[2] Understand? Good. — EDS.

yawns, politely grins, laughs at the appropriate moments, leans against her husband's sleeve, tugs at his elbow, and finally becomes good at predicting where the talk will lead, from this Cleófilas concludes each is nightly trying to find the truth lying at the bottom of the bottle like a gold doubloon on the sea floor.

They want to tell each other what they want to tell themselves. But what is bumping like a helium balloon at the ceiling of the brain never finds its way out. It bubbles and rises, it gurgles in the throat, it rolls across the surface of the tongue, and erupts from the lips — a belch.

If they are lucky, there are tears at the end of the long night. At any given moment, the fists try to speak. They are dogs chasing their own tails before lying down to sleep, trying to find a way, a route, an out, and — finally — get some peace.

In the morning sometimes before he opens his eyes. Or after they have finished loving. Or at times when he is simply across from her at the table putting pieces of food into his mouth and chewing. Cleófilas thinks, this is the man I have waited my whole life for.

Not that he isn't a good man. She has to remind herself why she loves him when she changes the baby's Pampers, or when she mops the bathroom floor, or tries to make the curtains for the doorways without doors, or whiten the linen. Or wonder a little when he kicks the refrigerator and says he hates this shitty house and is going out where he won't be bothered with the baby's howling and her suspicious questions, and her requests to fix this and this and this because if she had any brains in her head she'd realize he's been up before the rooster earning his living to pay for the food in her belly and the roof over her head and would have to wake up again early the next day so why can't you just leave me in peace, woman.

He is not very tall, no, and he doesn't look like the men on the *telenovelas.* His face still scarred from acne. And he has a bit of a belly from all the beer he drinks. Well, he's always been husky.

This man who farts and belches and snores as well as laughs and kisses and holds her. Somehow this husband whose whiskers she finds each morning on the sink, whose shoes she must air each evening on the porch, this husband who cuts his fingernails in public, laughs loudly, curses like a man, and demands each course of dinner be served on a separate plate like at his mother's, as soon as he gets home, on time or late, and who doesn't care at all for music or *telenovelas* or romance or roses or the moon floating pearly over the *arroyo*, or through the bedroom window for that matter, shut the blinds and go back to sleep, this man, this father, this rival, this keeper, this lord, this master, this husband till kingdom come.

A doubt. Slender as a hair. A washed cup set back on the shelf wrong-side-up. Her lipstick, and body talc, and hairbrush all arranged in the bathroom a different way.

No. Her imagination. The house the same as always. Nothing.

Coming home from the hospital with her new son, her husband. Something comforting in discovering her house slippers beneath the bed, the faded housecoat where she left it on the bathroom hook. Her pillow. Their bed.

Sweet sweet homecoming. Sweet as the scent of face powder in the air, jasmine, sticky liquor.

Smudged fingerprint on the door. Crushed cigarette in a glass. Wrinkle in the brain crumpling to a crease.

Sometimes she thinks of her father's house. But how could she go back there? What a disgrace. What would the neighbors say? Coming home like that with one baby on her hip and one in the oven. Where's your husband?

The town of gossips. The town of dust and despair. Which she has traded for this town of gossips. This town of dust, despair. Houses farther apart perhaps, though no more privacy because of it. No leafy *zócalo*[3] in the center of the town, though the murmur of talk is clear enough all the same. No huddled whispering on the church steps each Sunday. Because here the whispering begins at sunset at the ice house instead.

This town with its silly pride for a bronze pecan the size of a baby carriage in front of the city hall. TV repair shop, drugstore, hardware, dry cleaner's, chiropractor's, liquor store, bail bonds, empty storefront, and nothing, nothing, nothing of interest. Nothing one could walk to, at any rate. Because the towns here are built so that you have to depend on husbands. Or you stay home. Or you drive. If you're rich enough to own, allowed to drive, your own car.

There is no place to go. Unless one counts the neighbor ladies. Soledad on one side, Dolores on the other. Or the creek.

Don't go out there after dark, *mi'jita*. Stay near the house. *No es bueno para la salud.*[4] *Mala suerte*. Bad luck. *Mal aire.* You'll get sick and the baby too. You'll catch a fright wandering about in the dark, and then you'll see how right we were.

The stream sometimes only a muddy puddle in the summer, though now in the springtime, because of the rains, a good-size alive thing, a thing with a voice all its own, all day and all night calling in its high, silver voice. Is it La Llorona, the weeping woman? La Llorona, who drowned her own children. Perhaps La Llorona is the one they named the creek after, she thinks, remembering all the stories she learned as a child.

La Llorona calling to her. She is sure of it. Cleófilas sets the baby's Donald Duck blanket on the grass. Listens. The day sky turning to night. The baby pulling up fist-fuls of grass and laughing. La Llorona. Wonders if something as quiet as this drives a woman to the darkness under the trees.

What she needs is . . . and made a gesture as if to yank a woman's buttocks to his groin.

Maximiliano, the foul-smelling fool from across the road, said this and set the men laughing, but Cleófilas just muttered, *Grosero,* and went on washing dishes.

She knew he said it not because it was true, but more because it was he who needed to sleep with a woman, instead of drinking each night at the ice house and stumbling home alone.

Maximiliano who was said to have killed his wife in an ice-house brawl when she came at him with a mop. I had to shoot, he said — she was armed.

Their laughter outside the kitchen window. Her husband's, his friends'. Manolo, Beto, Efraín, el Perico. Maximiliano.

Was Cleófilas just exaggerating as her husband always said? It seemed the newspapers were full of such stories. This woman found on the side of the interstate. This one pushed from a moving car. This one's cadaver, this one unconscious, this one beaten blue. Her ex-husband, her husband, her lover, her father, her brother, her uncle, her friend, her co-worker. Always. The same grisly news in the pages of the dailies. She dunked a glass under the soapy water for a moment — shivered.

He had thrown a book. Hers. From across the room. A hot welt across the cheek. She could forgive that. But what stung more was the fact it was *her* book, a love story by Corín Tellado, what she loved most now that she lived in the U.S., without a television set, without the *telenovelas.*

Except now and again when her husband was away and she could manage it, the few episodes glimpsed at the neighbor lady Soledad's house because Dolores didn't care for that sort of thing, though Soledad was often kind enough to retell what had happened on what episode of *María de Nadie,* the poor Argentine country girl who had the ill fortune of falling in love with the beautiful son of the Arrocha family, the very family she worked for, whose roof she slept under and whose floors she vacuumed, while in that same house, with the dust brooms

---

[3] Town square. — EDS.

[4] It's not good for your health. — EDS.

and floor cleaners as witnesses, the square-jawed Juan Carlos Arrocha had uttered words of love, I love you, María, listen to me, *mi querida*,[5] but it was she who had to say No, no, we are not of the same class, and remind him it was not his place nor hers to fall in love, while all the while her heart was breaking, can you imagine.

Cleófilas thought her life would have to be like that, like a *telenovela*, only now the episodes got sadder and sadder. And there were no commercials in between for comic relief. And no happy ending in sight. She thought this when she sat with the baby out by the creek behind the house. Cleófilas de . . . ? But somehow she would have to change her name to Topazio, or Yesenia, Cristal, Adriana, Stefania, Andrea, something more poetic than Cleófilas. Everything happened to women with names like jewels. But what happened to a Cleófilas? Nothing. But a crack in the face.

Because the doctor has said so. She has to go. To make sure the new baby is all right, so there won't be any problems when he's born, and the appointment card says next Tuesday. Could he please take her. And that's all.

No, she won't mention it. She promises. If the doctor asks she can say she fell down the front steps or slipped when she was out in the backyard, slipped out back, she could tell him that. She has to go back next Tuesday, Juan Pedro, please, for the new baby. For their child.

She could write to her father and ask maybe for money, just a loan, for the new baby's medical expenses. Well then if he'd rather she didn't. All right, she won't. Please don't anymore. Please don't. She knows it's difficult saving money with all the bills they have, but how else are they going to get out of debt with the truck payments? And after the rent and the food and the electricity and the gas and the water and the who-knows-what, well, there's hardly anything left. But please, at least for the doctor visit. She won't ask for anything else. She has to. Why is she so anxious? Because.

Because she is going to make sure the baby is not turned around backward this time to split her down the center. Yes. Next Tuesday at five-thirty. I'll have Juan Pedrito dressed and ready. But those are the only shoes he has. I'll polish them, and we'll be ready. As soon as you come from work. We won't make you ashamed.

Felice? It's me, Graciela.

No, I can't talk louder. I'm at work.

Look, I need kind of a favor. There's a patient, a lady here who's got a problem.

Well, wait a minute. Are you listening to me or what?

I can't talk real loud 'cause her husband's in the next room.

Well, would you just listen?

I was going to do this sonogram on her — she's pregnant, right? — and she just starts crying on me. *Híjole*,[6] Felice! This poor lady's got black-and-blue marks all over. I'm not kidding.

From her husband. Who else? Another one of those brides from across the border. And her family's all in Mexico.

Shit. You think they're going to help her? Give me a break. This lady doesn't even speak English. She hasn't been allowed to call home or write or nothing. That's why I'm calling you.

She needs a ride.

Not to Mexico, you goof. Just to the Greyhound. In San Anto.

No, just a ride. She's got her own money. All you'd have to do is drop her off in San Antonio on your way home. Come on, Felice. Please? If we don't help her, who will? I'd drive her myself, but she needs to be on that bus before her husband gets home from work. What do you say?

I don't know. Wait.

Right away, tomorrow even.

Well, if tomorrow's no good for you . . .

[5]My beloved. — EDS.

[6] Interjection: gosh or jeez. — EDS.

It's a date, Felice. Thursday. At the Cash N Carry off I-10. Noon. She'll be ready.

Oh, and her name's Cleófilas.

I don't know. One of those Mexican saints, I guess. A martyr or something.

75 Cleófilas. C-L-E-O-F-I-L-A-S. Cle. O. Fi. Las. Write it down.

Thanks, Felice. When her kid's born she'll have to name her after us, right?

Yeah, you got it. A regular soap opera sometimes. *Qué vida, comadre. Bueno bye.*

All morning that flutter of half-fear, half-doubt. At any moment Juan Pedro might appear in the doorway. On the street. At the Cash N Carry. Like in the dreams she dreamed.

There was that to think about, yes, until the woman in the pickup drove up. Then there wasn't time to think about anything but the pickup pointed toward San Antonio. Put your bags in the back and get in.

80 But when they drove across the *arroyo*, the driver opened her mouth and let out a yell as loud as any mariachi. Which startled not only Cleófilas, but Juan Pedrito as well.

Pues, look how cute. I scared you two, right? Sorry. Should've warned you. Every time I cross that bridge I do that. Because of the name, you know. Woman Hollering. *Pues*, I holler. She said this in a Spanish pocked with English and laughed. Did you ever notice, Felice continued, how nothing around here is named after a woman? Really. Unless she's the Virgin. I guess you're only famous if you're a virgin. She was laughing again.

That's why I like the name of that *arroyo*. Makes you want to holler like Tarzan, right?

Everything about this woman, this Felice, amazed Cleófilas. The fact that she drove a pickup. A pickup, mind you, but when Cleófilas asked if it was her husband's, she said she didn't have a husband. The pickup was hers. She herself had chosen it. She herself was paying for it.

I used to have a Pontiac Sunbird. But those cars are for *viejas*.[7] Pussy cars. Now this here is a real car.

85 What kind of talk was that coming from a woman? Cleófilas thought. But then again, Felice was like no woman she'd ever met. Can you imagine, when we crossed the *arroyo* she just started yelling like crazy, she would say later to her father and brothers. Just like that. Who would've thought?

Who would've? Pain or rage, perhaps, but not a hoot like the one Felice had just let go. Makes you want to holler like Tarzan, Felice had said.

Then Felice began laughing again, but it wasn't Felice laughing. It was gurgling out of her own throat, a long ribbon of laughter, like water.

[1991]

[7]Old ladies. — EDS.

EXPLORING THE TEXT

1. What do you learn about Cleófilas in the very first section of the story, which is told as a flashback? What are the contrasts between "then" and "now" that Sandra Cisneros establishes in this section? What is the tone of the story's opening, and how does Cisneros use sentence structure and language to convey this?
2. Paragraph 21 begins with "The first time she had been so surprised she didn't cry out or try to defend herself." Why might Cisneros choose not to identify what the specific action was? Why didn't Cleófilas behave as she thought she would and was instead "speechless, motionless, numb" (para. 24)?
3. In her new home in Texas, Cleófilas lives between Dolores and Soledad. In Spanish, *dolores* means "sorrow" and *soledad* means "solitude." What does the author's choice of these names for neighbors suggest about Cleófilas's life in this Texas town? What other evidence can you find to support this interpretation of Cleófilas's life in Seguin?

4. Why are *telenovelas* important in this story? What role do they play in women's lives? How do they affect Cleófilas's views about love and relationships?
5. How does Cisneros's language reveal her attitude toward the men in the story? Does she condemn them? Pay particular attention to the section describing "The men at the ice house" (paras. 26–28). For instance, what does the metaphor "the fists try to speak" (para. 28) suggest about the men in this story and the lives they lead?
6. What can you infer about the characters of Felice and Graciela based on their phone conversation? What is significant about Cleófilas's experience in the truck with Felice at the story's end? How do the two women serve as foils to Cleófilas?
7. Analyze the role La Gritona (Woman Hollering Creek) plays in the story. What does it symbolize? How does the meaning of the symbol change over the course of the story?
8. In this story, Cisneros often makes use of compelling sentence fragments. Find a passage in which fragments play a significant role and explain their impact on the meaning of the passage.
9. What references do you find to speaking up, staying silent, being heard or not heard, whispering, yelling, speaking in different languages, and telling stories? How do these descriptions work together to develop the theme of finding voice?

POETRY

They flee from me

SIR THOMAS WYATT

Sir Thomas Wyatt (1503–1542) was born at Allington Castle in Kent, one of three children of Sir Henry Wyatt, a courtier during the reigns of Henry VII and Henry VIII. Sir Thomas Wyatt was educated privately before attending St. John's College, Cambridge, where he excelled in Greek and Latin verse but did not earn a degree. Like his father, he served as a courtier to King Henry VIII, eventually being named an ambassador. His poetry is largely imitative of Roman models but represented a novel form in English literature. In particular, Wyatt invented the English sonnet, later imitated by William Shakespeare and countless other poets. Published posthumously, *Songes and Sonnettes* (1557) greatly influenced sixteenth- and seventeenth-century writers. "They flee from me" is a subtle, cynical examination of how relationships between lovers change; it has been interpreted by some scholars as an allegory for political shifts of power as well.

They flee from me, that sometime did me seek,
With naked foot stalking in my chamber.
I have seen them, gentle, tame, and meek,
That now are wild, and do not remember
That sometime they put themselves in danger
To take bread at my hand; and now they range,
Busily seeking with a continual change.

Thankèd be fortune it hath been otherwise,
Twenty times better; but once in special,
In thin array, after a pleasant guise,
When her loose gown from her shoulders did fall,
And she me caught in her arms long and small,
Therewithall[1] sweetly did me kiss
And softly said, "Dear heart, how like you this?"

It was no dream, I lay broad waking.
But all is turned, thorough[2] my gentleness,
Into a strange fashion of forsaking;
And I have leave to go, of[3] her goodness,
And she also to use newfangleness.[4]
But since that I so kindly[5] am served,
I fain[6] would know what she hath deserved.

[1557]

[1] With all that. — EDS.
[2] Through. — EDS.
[3] Out of (thanks to). — EDS.
[4] Fondness for new things, fickleness. — EDS.
[5] Graciously (ironic), also naturally or fittingly. — EDS.
[6] Gladly. — EDS.

EXPLORING THE TEXT

1. In the first stanza, the speaker in the poem talks of women taking "bread at my hand" (l. 6). What does this image suggest about his attitude toward women? What does it suggest about women's attitudes toward him?
2. What seems to have changed in the balance of power between man and woman in the second stanza? How does the speaker feel about this change?
3. In line 14, a woman addresses the speaker as "dear heart." Keeping in mind that a hart is a male red deer often hunted in Sir Thomas Wyatt's time, how could this line be interpreted as more than a simple endearment? Have the roles of hunter and hunted been reversed?
4. Each stanza in the poem ends with a rhymed couplet. Explain how each couplet encapsulates the previous lines in the stanza.
5. At the time Wyatt wrote this poem, women lacked most of the legal and social rights that we now practically take for granted. How does Wyatt use figurative language and imagery to portray the imbalance of power between men and women in intimate relationships?

Leave me, O Love, which reachest but to dust

SIR PHILIP SIDNEY

"The poet-soldier" and "worthiest knight that lived," Sir Philip Sidney (1554–1586) was born in Kent, England, to an influential English family. Educated at Christ Church College, Oxford, he had by the age of twenty-one traveled extensively in Europe and developed acquaintanceships with influential courtiers in many European capitals, eventually serving

as a diplomat for Queen Elizabeth I. He withdrew from the royal court in 1580 and wrote *Astrophel and Stella* (c. 1590), a cycle of 108 sonnets and 11 songs; *The Countess of Pembroke's Arcadia* (c. 1593), which was unfinished at his death; and *The Defence of Poesie* (c. 1595), which argued that poetry represented truth more honestly than did history or science: "Now for the poet, he nothing affirmeth, and therefore never lieth." "Leave me, O Love, which reachest but to dust" is from *Certain Sonnets* (c. 1598).

Leave me, O Love which reachest but to dust;
And thou, my mind, aspire to higher things;
Grow rich in that which never taketh rust,
Whatever fades but fading pleasure brings.
Draw in thy beams, and humble all thy might
To that sweet yoke where lasting freedoms be;
Which breaks the clouds and opens forth the light,
That doth both shine and give us sight to see.
O take fast hold; let that light be thy guide
In this small course which birth draws out to death,
And think how evil becometh him to slide,
Who seeketh heav'n, and comes of heav'nly breath.
 Then farewell, world; thy uttermost I see;
 Eternal Love, maintain thy life in me.

[c.1598]

EXPLORING THE TEXT

1. In his sonnet, Sir Philip Sidney uses apostrophe, addressing "Love" directly in the first line, "thou, my mind" in the second line, and "Eternal Love" in the last line. What effect do these direct addresses have on your understanding of the poem?
2. Explain the admonition, "And thou, my mind, aspire to higher things" (l. 2). What does Sidney mean by "higher things"?
3. How do you interpret the paradox, or apparent contradiction, of "Draw in thy beams, and humble all thy might / To that sweet yoke where lasting freedoms be" (ll. 5–6)? How is it possible to be free while wearing a yoke?
4. What kind of love does the speaker in the poem wish to leave behind? Why?
5. Based on your reading of the sonnet, what relationship do you think the speaker in the poem values most?

The Flea

JOHN DONNE

John Donne (1572–1631) was born in London to a prosperous family. He was educated by Jesuits and attended both Oxford and Cambridge, where he studied law. His satires (written 1593–1595) and the poems later collected as *Songs and Sonnets* reflect life among the barristers. Donne was ordained in the Church of England in 1615 and became a renowned preacher. His sermons were published in three volumes — *LXXX Sermons* (1640), *Fifty Sermons* (1649), and *XXVI Sermons* (1661) — though today only his poetry is widely read. Donne's poems were not collected in his lifetime; indeed, only when he was short of funds in 1613–1614 did he attempt to gather them together, writing to friends that "I am made a Rhapsoder of mine own rags, and that cost me more diligence, to seek them, than it did to make them." Eventually published as *Poems* in 1633, they met with immediate acclaim. Donne has since been regarded as the most important of the metaphysical poets — a loose confederation of artists who relied on wit and incongruous, often startling imagery (metaphysical conceits), as you will see in "The Flea."

Mark[1] but this flea, and mark in this
How little that which thou deny'st me is;
It sucked me first, and now sucks thee,
And in this flea our two bloods mingled be;
Thou know'st that this cannot be said
A sin, nor shame, nor loss of maidenhead,
    Yet this enjoys before it woo,
    And pampered swells with one blood made of two,
    And this, alas, is more than we would do.

Oh stay,[2] three lives in one flea spare,
Where we almost, yea more than, married are.
This flea is you and I, and this
Our marriage bed, and marriage temple is;
Though parents grudge, and you, we're met
And cloistered in these living walls of jet.
    Though use[3] make you apt to kill me,
    Let not to that, self-murder added be,
    And sacrilege, three sins in killing three.

Cruel and sudden, hast thou since
Purpled thy nail in blood of innocence?
Wherein could this flea guilty be,
Except in that drop which it sucked from thee?
Yet thou triumph'st, and say'st that thou
Find'st not thyself, nor me, the weaker now;
    'Tis true; then learn how false, fears be;
    Just so much honor, when thou yield'st to me,
    Will waste, as this flea's death took life from thee.

[1633]

[1] Notice. — EDS.
[2] Stop. — EDS.
[3] Habit. — EDS.

EXPLORING THE TEXT

1. In order to make sense of "The Flea," you will need to read not only between the lines but also before the poem begins. What has occurred before the first stanza?
2. "The Flea" employs an extended metaphor as the center of its argument in this seduction poem. What is the metaphor? How does John Donne develop it? How does it make his argument more convincing?
3. What do the lines "Thou know'st that this cannot be said / A sin, nor shame, nor loss of maidenhead" (ll. 5–6) tell you about the woman in the poem and how she is responding to the speaker's wooing of her?
4. What does the speaker mean when he says "three lives in one flea" (l. 10)?
5. Consider the three sets of indented lines. Taken together, what argument do they make? How does each set differ from the preceding lines in the stanza?
6. Paraphrase the final five lines of the poem. What is the speaker's argument?
7. What is beguiling about the use of a flea to plead one's case as a lover?
8. How would you describe the overall tone of this poem?

To the Virgins, to Make Much of Time

ROBERT HERRICK

Robert Herrick (1591–1674) was one of six children born to a prosperous family in London. After his father's presumed suicide in 1592, he was separated from his mother and brought up in the Presbyterian household of his uncle. After serving six years of a ten-year apprenticeship with his uncle, a goldsmith, Herrick entered St. John's College, Cambridge, when he was twenty-two and transferred to Trinity Hall three years later, receiving his BA in 1617 and an MA in 1620. In 1623, he was ordained; and in 1640, *The severall Poems written by Master Robert Herrick* appeared. The bulk of his work was published in *His Noble Numbers* (1647) and *Hesperides; or, The Works Both Human and Divine of Robert Herrick, Esq.* (1648). The range of subject is broad; over twelve hundred short poems in many forms — derived from Roman and Greek poetry — give remarkable insight into Herrick's joyful interpretation of God's gifts. Like his contemporary Andrew Marvell, Herrick was influenced by classical models. Unlike Marvell and the metaphysical poets, however, he adopted a simple, pastoral style. Central to this poem and to much of his work are his religious faith and a celebration of the divine, though brief, gift of life.

Gather ye rose-buds while ye may,
    Old Time is still a-flying;
And this same flower that smiles today,
    Tomorrow will be dying.

The glorious lamp of heaven, the sun,
    The higher he's a-getting,
The sooner will his race be run,
    And nearer he's to setting.

That age is best which is the first,
    When youth and blood are warmer;
But being spent, the worse, and worst
    Times still succeed the former.

Then be not coy, but use your time,
    And while ye may, go marry;
For having lost but once your prime,
    You may for ever tarry.

[1648]

EXPLORING THE TEXT

1. The poem opens with the speaker urging virgins to "Gather ye rose-buds" (l. 1). What do the rosebuds symbolize? What is the urgency?
2. Describe the rhyming pattern and rhythm of Robert Herrick's poem. What effect do they produce, and how does that contribute to the poem's meaning?
3. In the second stanza, the speaker compares the course of a day to a race. How does this comparison add evidence to the point being made in the first stanza?
4. What can you infer about the speaker's attitude toward aging from the following lines: "That age is best which is the first" (l. 9) and "and worst / Times still succeed the former" (ll. 11–12)?
5. In the final stanza, the speaker offers instructions and a warning. Is his advice still relevant? How might you update or reply to his admonitions?

She Walks in Beauty

LORD BYRON

In a short life, George Gordon Byron (1788–1824) staked his claim as one of the greatest romantic poets in the English language, became an exile from his own country and a national hero in Greece (where a suburb of Athens is named after him), and gave his name to the adjective *Byronic*, which refers to his mercurial, romantic, and tragic character. Born in London, he inherited the barony of Byron at the age of ten, becoming Lord Byron. As a child, he displayed an idleness and mischievous temperament that continued at Trinity College, Cambridge, where he kept a bear in protest of college regulations forbidding undergraduates to keep dogs. The first commercial edition of his work was *Hours of Idleness* (1807), which met with savage reviews, prompting his satirical response, *English Bards and Scotch Reviewers* (1809). His reputation grew with the publication of *The Corsair* (1814), which sold ten thousand copies on the day of its release. In 1816, Byron left England for Italy, where he spent time with Percy Bysshe Shelley and Mary Shelley. In 1821, he published *The Prophecy of Dante*, three cantos of *Don Juan*, *Marino Faliero*, *Sardanapalus*, *The Two Foscari*, and *Cain*. Originally written as a song lyric, "She Walks in Beauty" clearly expresses Byron's love of beauty.

I

She walks in Beauty, like the night
 Of cloudless climes[1] and starry skies;
And all that's best of dark and bright
 Meet in her aspect and her eyes:
Thus mellowed to that tender light
 Which Heaven to gaudy day denies.

II

One shade the more, one ray the less,
Had half impaired the nameless grace
Which waves in every raven tress,
 Or softly lightens o'er her face;
Where thoughts serenely sweet express,
How pure, how dear their dwelling-place.

III

And on that cheek, and o'er that brow,
 So soft, so calm, yet eloquent,
The smiles that win, the tints that glow,
 But tell of days in goodness spent,
A mind at peace with all below,
 A heart whose love is innocent!

[1814]

[1] Climates. — EDS.

EXPLORING THE TEXT

1. What is it about the phrase "like the night" (l. 1) that immediately draws readers into the poem?
2. What does the alliteration of "cloudless climes" and "starry skies" (l. 2) contribute to the poem's effect?
3. How does the poem invite us to view the night in a new light? What lines in the poem support your interpretation? For instance, what is the denotation and connotation of the adjective "gaudy" (l. 6)? How does Lord Byron's use of this descriptor for day help us understand what he is trying to say about night? How does it help you see the woman the speaker describes?
4. What do you know about this unnamed woman who "walks in Beauty" (l. 1)? What can you infer from the line "So soft, so calm, yet eloquent" (l. 14)?
5. Paraphrase the last stanza of the poem. How do you interpret Byron's final exclamation mark?
6. What do you imagine is the speaker's relationship to the woman he describes?

Love is not all

EDNA ST. VINCENT MILLAY

Edna St. Vincent Millay (1892–1950) was born in Maine. In 1912, she entered her poem "Renascence" in a competition, winning fourth place and inclusion in *The Lyric Year*, which earned her acclaim and a scholarship to Vassar College. The poem would be included in her first collection, *Renascence and Other Poems*, published in 1917. After graduating, Vincent (as she insisted on being called) moved to Greenwich Village — then New York's bohemian district. To this period belong her short-story collection (written as Nancy Boyd), *A Few Figs from Thistles* (1920); her first verse play, *The Lamp and the Bell* (1921); and a play in one act, *Aria da Capo* (1920). After an extended trip to Europe, she returned to New York and published *The Harp Weaver and Other Poems* (1923). That year she won the Pulitzer Prize for Poetry, one of the first women to be so honored. She also wrote the libretto of one of the few American grand operas, *The King's Henchman* (1927). Sympathetic to Marxism-Leninism, she was active in protests against the execution of Sacco and Vanzetti, addressing the issue in *The Buck in the Snow* (1928). "Love is not all," written in 1931, is a beautifully objective assessment of a traditional subject of poetry in which she leads the reader gently but inexorably to her own position.

Love is not all: it is not meat nor drink
Nor slumber nor a roof against the rain;
Nor yet a floating spar to men that sink
And rise and sink and rise and sink again;
Love can not fill the thickened lung with breath,
Nor clean the blood, nor set the fractured bone;
Yet many a man is making friends with death
Even as I speak, for lack of love alone.
It well may be that in a difficult hour,
Pinned down by pain and moaning for release,

Or nagged by want past resolution's power,
I might be driven to sell your love for peace,
Or trade the memory of this night for food.
It well may be. I do not think I would.

[1931]

EXPLORING THE TEXT

1. Explain the argument expressed in the first six lines of this sonnet. Why do you think Edna St. Vincent Millay begins her love poem by defining what love is not? Why do you think Millay chose to write this poem as a sonnet?
2. What is the poem's situation — that is, where is the speaker in relation to the person she is addressing? Characterize the relationship of the two based on the information the poem provides.
3. "Love is not all" depends on an extended metaphor. What is it? How does Millay make it seem possible?
4. In lines 9–14 of the sonnet, Millay imagines a series of hypothetical situations. Describe how the speaker's tone shifts in these final lines.
5. What do you make of the tentativeness of the final line, "It well may be. I do not think I would"? Why are these words more intriguing than a declaration of "Never!" would be?
6. How does the tone of the poem reflect Millay's attitude toward love? How would you describe this tone?

Siren Song

MARGARET ATWOOD

Margaret Atwood (b. 1939) was born in Ottawa and spent much of her childhood in northern Quebec. She earned her undergraduate degree at Victoria College (now University) of the University of Toronto and an MA at Radcliffe College (Harvard University). Atwood is a prolific writer in many forms, including poetry, literary criticism, and fiction. She is the author of more than fifteen collections of poetry including early works like *Double Persephone* (1961), *The Circle Game* (1964), *Expeditions* (1965), *Speeches for Doctor Frankenstein* (1966), and *The Animals in That Country* (1968), and later works like *Interlunar* (1984), *Morning in the Burned House* (1995), *Eating Fire: Selected Poems 1965–1995* (1998), and *The Door* (2007). Atwood's first novel, *The Edible Woman* (1969), is at once frightening and comic. Eight more novels followed — *Surfacing* (1972), *Lady Oracle* (1976), *Life Before Man* (1979), *Bodily Harm* (1981), *The Handmaid's Tale* (1985), *Cat's Eye* (1988), *The Robber Bride* (1993), and *Alias Grace* (1996) — many of them winning awards and recognition, including being named finalists for the Booker Prize, before *The Blind Assassin* (2000) won the Booker Prize. Recent novels include *The Year of the Flood* (2009), *MaddAddam* (2013), *Scribbler Moon* (2014), *The Heart Goes Last* (2015), and *Hag-Seed* (2016). With her wry, satirical, and mischievous sense of humor, Atwood has the ability to blend the prosaic with pure fantasy. Much of Atwood's poetry draws from myth and legend. In "Siren Song" Atwood adopts the voice of a siren, one of three birdlike women from Greek mythology whose irresistible songs would lure passing sailors toward a rocky coast where they would be shipwrecked.

This is the one song everyone
would like to learn: the song
that is irresistible:

the song that forces men
to leap overboard in squadrons
even though they see beached skulls

the song nobody knows
because anyone who had heard it
is dead, and the others can't remember.

Shall I tell you the secret
and if I do, will you get me
out of this bird suit?

I don't enjoy it here
squatting on this island
looking picturesque and mythical

with these two feathery maniacs,
I don't enjoy singing
this trio, fatal and valuable.

I will tell the secret to you,
to you, only to you.
Come closer. This song

is a cry for help: Help me!
Only you, only you can,
you are unique

at last. Alas
it is a boring song
but it works every time.

[1974]

EXPLORING THE TEXT

1. What is the appeal of the siren song? Why is it that it "works every time" (l. 27)? What is the appeal of the siren's age-old tactic for a modern audience?
2. Based on the way the siren addresses the reader, what can you infer about her audience?
3. The mythical sirens were creatures of mystery. How does Atwood's diction demystify them? Cite specific examples from the text.
4. Describe the tone of the poem. Look carefully at Atwood's use of hyperbole and understatement.
5. What stereotypes of women does Atwood draw upon in this poem?
6. Discuss how Atwood's poem can be read as a response to Homer. How might it be a protest against his depiction of the sirens?

One Art

ELIZABETH BISHOP

Elizabeth Bishop (1911–1979) was born in Worcester, Massachusetts, before finally settling in Boston. She attended Vassar College, where she earned a BA and met poet Marianne Moore, who dissuaded her from medical school in favor of life as a poet. Bishop published her first collection of poetry, *North and South* (1946), after traveling in Europe and North Africa. During an extended trip to Brazil, she published her second collection, *A Cold Spring* (1955), with the poems of *North and South* in a single volume. This won her the Pulitzer Prize in 1956. Bishop lived in Brazil for fifteen years; translated the Brazilian work *Minha vida de menina* as *The Diary of Helena Morely* (1957); and described her life in Brazil in her third collection of poetry, *Questions of Travel* (1965). Her last collection, *Geography III*, was published in 1976. Elizabeth Bishop's work amounts to little more than one hundred carefully crafted poems. She was recognized by her peers as a poet of exceptional talent but did not

achieve popular recognition until after her death, with the publication of *The Complete Poems, 1927–1979* (1983). The modified villanelle "One Art" (from *Geography III*) reflects on the experience of losing.

The art of losing isn't hard to master;
so many things seem filled with the intent
to be lost that their loss is no disaster.

Lose something every day. Accept the fluster
of lost door keys, the hour badly spent.
The art of losing isn't hard to master.

Then practice losing farther, losing faster:
places, and names, and where it was you meant
to travel. None of these will bring disaster.

I lost my mother's watch. And look! my last, or
next-to-last, of three loved houses went.
The art of losing isn't hard to master.

I lost two cities, lovely ones. And, vaster,
some realms I owned, two rivers, a continent.
I miss them, but it wasn't a disaster.

—Even losing you (the joking voice, a gesture
I love) I shan't have lied. It's evident
the art of losing's not too hard to master
though it may look like (*Write* it!) like disaster.

[1976]

EXPLORING THE TEXT

1. What are the denotations of the word *lose*? What are its connotations? Consider various forms of the word. What are the different ways Elizabeth Bishop uses it in "One Art"?
2. Bishop's "One Art" is a modified villanelle. How has she modified it? Why might she have modified it? How does this form contribute to the poem's meaning?
3. Find examples of hyperbole in this poem. How does the use of hyperbole communicate the author's attitude toward her subject?
4. To whom is the parenthetical "(*Write* it!)" (l. 19) addressed? What is the effect of the repetition of "like" in this final line?
5. According to Bishop, why is losing an art, and why is it important to master? Are you convinced by her argument? How can you apply it to your own life?

Movement Song

AUDRE LORDE

Audre Lorde (1934–1992) was an influential American writer, radical feminist, and civil rights activist. Lorde grew up in New York City, the daughter of Caribbean immigrants from Barbados and Carriacou. She attended the National University of Mexico, Hunter College, and Columbia University, where she earned a master's degree in library science in 1961. She wrote more than fifteen books, including the poetry collections *The First Cities* (1968), *Cables to Rage* (1970), and *Our Dead Behind Us* (1986), and the essay collections *The Cancer Journals* (1980), *Sister Outsider: Essays and Speeches* (1984), and *A Burst of Light* (1988). In "Movement Song" Lorde mixes fantastical imagery with characteristic forthrightness to bid a mournful goodbye to a lover.

I have studied the tight curls on the back of your neck
moving away from me
beyond anger or failure
your face in the evening schools of longing
through mornings of wish and ripen
we were always saying goodbye
in the blood in the bone over coffee
before dashing for elevators going
in opposite directions
without goodbyes.

Do not remember me as a bridge nor a roof
as the maker of legends
nor as a trap
door to that world
where black and white clericals
hang on the edge of beauty in five oclock elevators
twitching their shoulders to avoid other flesh
and now
there is someone to speak for them
moving away from me into tomorrows
morning of wish and ripen
your goodbye is promise of lightning
in the last angels hand
unwelcome and warning
the sands have run out against us
we were rewarded by journeys
away from each other
into desire
into mornings alone
where excuse and endurance mingle
conceiving decision.
Do not remember me
as disaster
nor as the keeper of secrets
I am a fellow rider in the cattle cars
watching
you move slowly out of my bed
saying we cannot waste time
only ourselves.

[1982]

EXPLORING THE TEXT

1. The poem opens with the imagery of the speaker studying "the tight curls on the back of your neck/moving away from me" (ll. 1–2). What does this specific imagery convey about how the speaker feels?
2. The speaker refers to "dashing for elevators" (l. 8) in the first stanza and "five oclock elevators" (l. 16) in the second stanza. What do these references suggest about why they are always saying goodbye? What does the poet convey by referring to the elevators as "cattle cars" (l.35) at the end of the poem?
3. The speaker mentions several ways in which she does not want to be remembered. Identify these and consider what they suggest as a whole. What do these examples communicate about how she *does* want to be remembered?
4. Make note of the role time plays in the poem, including references to morning and evening. What attitude does the poem express about time and how we experience our days?
5. What is suggested by the metaphor "your goodbye is a promise of lightning / in the last angels hand" (ll. 23–24)? How does it contribute to the tone of the last stanza?
6. Note the short, choppy lines throughout the poem, as well as the poet's choice to omit punctuation where it might normally be included. How do these form choices help shape the tone?
7. The poem is titled "Movement Song." What sort of movement is represented in the poem? What does this movement suggest about the speaker's relationship to her former lover?
8. What does this poem convey about the challenge of maintaining relationships while fulfilling the demands of daily life?

Weighing the Dog

BILLY COLLINS

Billy Collins (b. 1941) served as poet laureate of the United States from 2001 through 2003 and as New York state poet from 2004 through 2006. He has published fourteen collections of poetry, including *The Art of Drowning* (1995), *Picnic, Lightning* (1998), *Nine Horses* (2002), and most recently *Voyage* (2014). Collins has received fellowships from the National Endowment for the Arts and the Guggenheim Foundation, and was chosen in 1992 as a "Literary Lion" of the New York Public Library. Collins, who actively promotes poetry in the schools, edited *Poetry 180: A Turning Back to Poetry* (2003) — an anthology of contemporary poems available online that aims to increase high school students' appreciation and enjoyment of poetry. Collins currently teaches in the MFA program at Stony Brook Southampton. Poet Stephen Dunn has said of Collins, "We seem to always know where we are in a Billy Collins poem, but not necessarily where he is going." Such is the case with "Weighing the Dog."

It is awkward for me and bewildering for him
as I hold him in my arms in the small bathroom,
balancing our weight on the shaky blue scale,

but this is the way to weigh a dog and easier
than training him to sit obediently on one spot
with his tongue out, waiting for the cookie.

With pencil and paper I subtract my weight
from our total to find out the remainder that is his,
and I start to wonder if there is an analogy here.

It could not have to do with my leaving you
though I never figured out what you amounted to
until I subtracted myself from our combination.
You held me in your arms more than I held you
through all those awkward and bewildering months
and now we are both lost in strange and distant neighborhoods.

[1991]

EXPLORING THE TEXT

1. Where does this poem shift from being a poem about a man and his dog to being a poem about something else, something more? What is this something else?
2. The speaker suggests that weighing the dog is an analogy in line 9 and then denies it in line 10. How does that denial actually extend the analogy?
3. How does the structure of the poem's first six lines mirror its subject? Look especially at the way Billy Collins creates balance in each line.
4. Whom does the speaker blame for the failure of his relationship? What evidence in the poem can you find to support your view?
5. Collins is considered a poet who makes poetry seem easy. Explain whether you think "Weighing the Dog" is an "easy" poem.

I'm a Fool to Love You

CORNELIUS EADY

Cornelius Eady (b. 1954) is an award-winning American poet from Rochester, New York. He is the author of seven full-length poetry collections, including *Kartunes* (1980), *The Gathering of My Name* (1991), which was nominated for a Pulitzer Prize; *The Autobiography of a Jukebox: Poems* (1997); and most recently, *Hardheaded Weather: New and Selected Poems* (2008). Eady's work is known for its exploration of race and class as well as its engagement with the blues and jazz musical traditions, and he has received grants from the National Endowment for the Arts, the Guggenheim Foundation, the Rockefeller Foundation, and the Lila Wallace–Reader's Digest Fund. Eady also co-founded Cave Canem Foundation in 1996, a nonprofit organization dedicated to the promotion of African American poets. He has taught at Sarah Lawrence College, New York University, William and Mary, Notre Dame, and Sweet Briar College, and he currently holds the Miller Family Endowed Chair in Literature and Writing at the University of Missouri-Columbia. In "I'm a Fool to Love You," Eady evokes the blues to examine the difficult romantic choices the speaker's mother was forced to make.

Some folks will tell you the blues is a woman,
Some type of supernatural creature.
My mother would tell you, if she could,
About her life with my father,
A strange and sometimes cruel gentleman.
She would tell you about the choices
A young black woman faces.
Is falling in with some man
A deal with the devil
In blue terms, the tongue we use
When we don't want nuance
To get in the way,
When we need to talk straight?
My mother chooses my father
After choosing a man
Who was, as we sing it,
Of no account.
This man made my father look good,
That's how bad it was.
He made my father seem like an island
In the middle of a stormy sea,
He made my father look like a rock.
And is the blues the moment you realize
You exist in a stacked deck,
You look in a mirror at your young face,
The face my sister carries,
And you know it's the only leverage
You've got?
Does this create a hurt that whispers
How you going to do?
Is the blues the moment
You shrug your shoulders
And agree, a girl without money
Is nothing, dust
To be pushed around by any old breeze?
Compared to this,
My father seems, briefly,
To be a fire escape.
This is the way the blues works
Its sorry wonders,
Makes trouble look like
A feather bed,
Makes the wrong man's kisses
A healing.

[1997]

EXPLORING THE TEXT

1. The speaker describes his father as a "strange and sometimes cruel gentleman" (l. 5) who, to his mother, appeared to be "an island/in the middle of a stormy sea" (ll. 20–21) and "a fire escape" (l. 38). What do these descriptions, especially the two metaphors, convey about his mother's life and the options she had?
2. In line 9, the speaker characterizes falling in love with a man as a "deal with a devil." How does the depiction of his mother's experience reinforce this idea?
3. How do you interpret the "blue terms" in line 10? Why is it "the tongue we use / When we don't want nuance / To get in the way, / When we need to talk straight" (ll. 10–13)?
4. In line 24, the speaker shifts from describing his mother in third person to second person, or "you." How does this shift contribute to the emotional impact of the poem?
5. Throughout the poem, the speaker poses questions, though without the punctuation of question marks. What effect does this syntactical choice have on the poem? To what extent does the speaker answer those questions — or are they entirely rhetorical?
6. What ironic language does the poet use in lines 39–44 to end the poem? How do these ironic statements reinforce the speaker's attitude toward relationships?
7. The speaker refers to "the blues," or a deep sadness, throughout the poem. However, this is also an allusion to blues music, which has had a significant influence on Cornelius Eady's poetry. Research the characteristics of the blues genre and identify the ways in which this poem reflects that musical tradition. Consider diction, theme, and the poem's title.

This was once a love poem

JANE HIRSHFIELD

Jane Hirshfield (b. 1953) was born in New York City. She earned her BA at Princeton University, where she was introduced to classical-era Japanese and Chinese literature. Hirshfield then spent eight years in full-time practice of Zen during her twenties. Her first published collection of poems was *Alaya* (1982). Since then, she has published nine other volumes of poetry, including *Given Sugar, Given Salt* (2001), a finalist for the National Book Critics Circle Award, *After* (2006), *Come, Thief: Poems* (2013), and *The Beauty: Poems* (2015). Hirshfield has also written a collection of essays on poetic craft, *Nine Gates: Entering the Mind of Poetry* (1997). She lives in the San Francisco Bay Area and has taught in the Bennington MFA Writing Seminars, at the University of California, Berkeley, and at the University of San Francisco. "This was once a love poem" speaks to the impermanence of life, a prominent theme in Hirshfield's work.

This was once a love poem,
before its haunches thickened, its breath grew short,
before it found itself sitting,
perplexed and a little embarrassed,
on the fender of a parked car,
while many people passed by without turning their heads.

It remembers itself dressing as if for a great engagement.
It remembers choosing these shoes,
this scarf or tie.

Once, it drank beer for breakfast,
drifted its feet
in a river side by side with the feet of another.

Once it pretended shyness, then grew truly shy,
dropping its head so the hair would fall forward,
so the eyes would not be seen.

It spoke with passion of history, of art.
It was lovely then, this poem.
Under its chin, no fold of skin softened.
Behind the knees, no pad of yellow fat.
What it knew in the morning it still believed at nightfall.
An unconjured confidence lifted its eyebrows, its cheeks.

The longing has not diminished.
Still it understands. It is time to consider a cat,
the cultivation of African violets or flowering cactus.

Yes, it decides:
Many miniature cacti, in blue and red painted pots.
When it finds itself disquieted
by the pure and unfamiliar silence of its new life,
it will touch them — one, then another —
with a single finger outstretched like a tiny flame.

[2001]

EXPLORING THE TEXT

1. How does Jane Hirshfield's use of a prose form reinforce the poem's meaning? Look closely at the first line.
2. How did the personification in the poem help you to grasp what had happened in the relationship?
3. Trace the changes the speaker describes in the character and behavior of the poem over the course of the love affair. What do the changes represent for the speaker?
4. Describe how the poem shifts with the following lines: "An unconjured confidence lifted its eyebrows, its cheeks. / The longing has not diminished. / Still it understands" (ll. 21–23). What has changed in the speaker's attitude?
5. Why is it "time to consider a cat" (l. 23)? What does buying a cat represent to the speaker in the poem? Why do you think the speaker decides in favor of cactus plants over African violets or a cat?

Lisa

DAVID HERNANDEZ

David Hernandez (b. 1971) is an American poet and novelist from Burbank, California. He earned a BA at California State University, Long Beach, and has taught at the University of California, Irvine, Antioch University, and California State University, Long Beach. He is the author of three books of poetry, *A House Waiting for Music* (2003), *Always Danger* (2006), and *Hoodwinked* (2011), and two young adult novels, *Suckerpunch* (2008) and *No More Us for You* (2009). In 2011, Hernandez was awarded a National Endowment for the Arts Fellowship for Poetry. He currently teaches at California State University, Fullerton. Hernandez's work is known for finding the beautiful in the ordinary with humor and lyrical precision.

Last night I traced with my finger
the long scar on my love's stomach
as if I was following a road on a map.
I heard the scream of tires, saw the flash

of chrome, her six-year-old body
a rag doll bleeding at the seams.
It is foolish of me to wish
I was there before it happened, to reach

back thirty years, clasp her small hand
and pull her away from that speeding car
that turned her organs into bruised fruit.
How easily she could have missed

her seventh birthday, the lit candles waiting
for her to blow out their tiny flames.
How easily I could've spent last night
in a crowded bar instead,

my shoulders brushing against strangers,
a man on the jukebox
singing his heart out to a woman
with the prettiest eyes he's ever seen.

[2003]

EXPLORING THE TEXT

1. As the speaker imagines his love's childhood accident, he compares her to "a rag doll bleeding at the seams" (l. 6) and later compares her organs to "bruised fruit" (l. 11). How do these vivid metaphors convey the speaker's emotions about her traumatic experience?
2. What is the effect of the repetition of "How easily" in lines 12 and 15? How does that repetition contribute to the tone of the poem?
3. The poet inserts stanza breaks in the middle of sentences, breaking up words that should be read together. Examine each of the stanza breaks. Why do you think the poet included them at those particular points? How do they affect your understanding of the poem?
4. Most of the poem employs vivid and specific imagery, but the description of the bar in the last stanza is vague by comparison. Why do you think the poet uses such a generic and almost clichéd description to end the poem?
5. What attitude does the poem express about the role of fate in romantic relationships? Explain how the author uses poetic devices to convey that attitude.

Urban Renewal XVIII

MAJOR JACKSON

Major Jackson (b. 1968) is an American poet and professor from Philadelphia, Pennsylvania. He earned degrees from Temple University and the University of Oregon. His first book, *Leaving Saturn* (2002), won the 2001 Cave Canem Poetry Prize and was a finalist for a National Books Critics Circle Award. His second and third books, *Hoops* (2006) and *Holding Company* (2010), were both finalists for an NAACP Image Award for Outstanding Literary Work – Poetry. His most recent book is *Roll Deep* (2015). Jackson's other awards include a 1995 Pew Fellowship in the Arts, a 2003 Whiting Writers' Award, and a 2013 Guggenheim

Fellowship. Jackson is currently Richard Dennis Green and Gold Professor of English at the University of Vermont, teaches at the Bennington Writing Seminars, and serves as the poetry editor of the *Harvard Review*. In "Urban Renewal XVIII," the speaker remembers the overwhelming mixture of longing and insecurity that characterize adolescent desire.

How untouchable the girls arm-locked strutting
up the main hall of Central High unopposed
for decades looked. I flattened myself against
the wall, unnerved by their cloudsea of élan,[1]
which pounced upon any timid girl regrettably
in their way, their high-wattage lifting slow motion
like curls of light strands of honey. The swagger
behind their blue-tinted sunglasses and low-rider
jeans hurt boys like me, so vast the worlds
between us, even the slightest whiff of recognition,
an accidental side glance, an unintended tongue-piercing
display of Juicy Fruit chew, was intoxicating
and could wildly cast a chess-playing geek into
a week-long surmise of inner doubts, likelihoods,
and depressions. You might say my whole life led
to celebrating youth and how it snubs and rebuffs.
Back then I learned to avoid what I feared
and to place my third-string hopes on a game-winning
basketball shot, sure it would slow them to a stop,
pan their lip-glossed smiles, blessing me with their cool.

[2006]

[1] Stylish flair. — EDS.

EXPLORING THE TEXT

1. The first sentence of the poem (ll. 1–3) is structured in an unusual, almost unnatural way. Why do you think the poet chose this word order? What does the syntax of the sentence emphasize?
2. Though the speaker presents the events of the poem as his own experience, he situates it in the "main hall of Central High" (l. 2) and suggests the girls were "unopposed / for decades" (ll. 2–3). What does this general setting and time period suggest about the girls the speaker describes?
3. The speaker describes the girls' "swagger" (l. 7) as "intoxicating" (l. 12). What details and images throughout the poem reinforce this description?
4. The poem shifts in line 15 from relating the speaker's experience in adolescence to reflecting on how it has influenced him. Within the context of his experience, how do you interpret lines 15–16: "You might say my whole life led / to celebrating youth and how it snubs and rebuffs"?
5. What does this poem communicate about the dynamics between boys and girls during adolescence? What resources of language does the poet use to make his point(s)?

For Women Who Are Difficult to Love

WARSAN SHIRE

Poet Warsan Shire (b. 1988) won the Brunel University African Poetry Prize in 2013 and went on to be named the first Young Poet Laureate for London in 2014, and Poet in Residence for Queensland, Australia. She is the author of several poetry pamphlets, including *Teaching My Mother How to Give Birth* (2011), and *Her Blue Body* (2015, Limited Edition), as well as an audio book of poems, *the seven stages of being lonely* (2012). Her work appears in both mainstream and independent publications and covers a broad range of subjects. In an interview, the self-described "artistic activist" has said she writes "character-driven poetry" in order to "tell the stories of those people, especially refugees and immigrants, that otherwise wouldn't be told." Already a bestselling poet, Shire gained additional international attention when her poetry was used to adapt and narrate Beyoncé's 2016 visual album, *Lemonade*.

you are a horse running alone
and he tries to tame you
compares you to an impossible highway
to a burning house
says you are blinding him
that he could never leave you
forget you
want anything but you
you dizzy him, you are unbearable
every woman before or after you
is doused in your name
you fill his mouth
his teeth ache with memory of taste
his body just a long shadow seeking yours
but you are always too intense
frightening in the way you want him
unashamed and sacrificial
he tells you that no man can live up to the one who
lives in your head
and you tried to change didn't you?
closed your mouth more
tried to be softer
prettier
less volatile, less awake
but even when sleeping you could feel
him travelling away from you in his dreams
so what did you want to do love
split his head open?

you can't make homes out of human beings
someone should have already told you that
and if he wants to leave
then let him leave
you are terrifying
and strange and beautiful
something not everyone knows how to love.

[2012]

EXPLORING THE TEXT

1. The poem opens with direct address to "you" and goes on to offer a combination of observation, accusation, and advice. Who do you imagine the speaker is? Is the "you" she addresses singular, collective, or both? What specific elements of text support your responses?
2. Within the first 14 lines, how is the relationship between the man and woman characterized? What contradictions do you notice? How do you interpret the metaphor "his body just a long shadow seeking yours" (l. 14)?
3. What shift in idea, attitude, or tone does the "but" (l. 15) signal?
4. In lines 27–28, the speaker asks a question: "so what did you want to do love / split his head open?" Is "love" an affectionate reference to the "you" here, or might the speaker be personifying love? Since the speaker never directly answers this question, how does it function in the poem?
5. Tensions exist throughout the poem — such as the friction between what exists and what is imagined. What other tensions do you see? Pay close attention to the language choices Shire makes to express contradictions, paradoxes, and conflicts. What is the overall impact of these? Are they resolved by the poem's end?
6. How do you interpret the line "you don't make homes out of human beings" in the context of this poem?
7. After reading and analyzing the poem, how do you interpret its title? Is it a dare, an insult, a sardonic joke, a straightforward description, or something else entirely?
8. One reviewer characterized Shire as "an emotional cartographer." To what extent does this description apply to "For Women Who Are Difficult to Love"?
9. One critic speculated that Shire's work is so popular because what she has to say crosses lines of gender, race, and nationality. In what ways does this poem transcend such socially prescribed boundaries?
10. What would "you" have to say? Or "him"? Write your own poem in the voice of the one(s) spoken to or spoken about responding to the speaker in this poem.

Chess

AIMEE NEZHUKUMATATHIL

Aimee Nezhukumatathil [Nez-ZOO-koo-mah-tah-TILL] (b. 1974) is an Asian American poet known for her accessible style and lush descriptions. Born in Chicago, Nezhukumatathil earned a BA and MFA from Ohio State University. *Miracle Fruit* (2003), her first full-length poetry collection, won the Tupelo Press Prize, *ForeWord* magazine's Book of the Year Award in poetry, and the Global Filipino Award. Her other books of poetry include *At the Drive-In*

Volcano (2007) and *Lucky Fish* (2011). Nezhukumatathil's poetry draws on her Filipina and South Indian background and often concerns love, loss, and landscape. Nezhukumatathil is currently an associate professor at the State University of New York–Fredonia, where she teaches creative writing and environmental literature. In "Chess," Nezhukumatathil makes imaginative leaps to compare the highly ordered and austere game of chess to the messier, more personal exchanges of a romantic relationship.

Exactly four different men have tried
to teach me how to play. I could never
tell the difference between a rook
or bishop, but I knew the horse meant

knight. And that made sense to me,
because a horse *is* night: soot-hoof
and nostril, dark as a sabled evening
with no stars, bats, or moon blooms.

It's a night in Ohio where a man sleeps
alone one week and the next, the woman
he will eventually marry leans her body
into his for the first time, leans a kind

of faith, too — filled with white crickets
and bouquets of wild carrot. And
the months and the honeyed years
after that will make all the light

and dark squares feel like tiles
for a kitchen they can one day build
together. Every turn, every sacrificial
move — all the decoys, the castling,

the deflections — these will be both
riotous and unruly, the exact opposite
of what she thought she ever wanted
in the endgame of her days.

[2015]

EXPLORING THE TEXT

1. In the first two lines, the speaker asserts, "Exactly four different men have tried / to teach me how to play." Why do you think she is so precise about the exact number? What do you think the speaker is suggesting by pointing out that all of these men have tried to teach her to play chess and failed?
2. Aside from the reference to the setting of Ohio in line 9, the description of the relationship between the man and the woman in the poem is left deliberately vague. What is the effect of this lack of detail in the poet's description of the couple?
3. The faith that the woman has in the man early in the relationship is "filled with white crickets / and bouquets of wild carrot" (ll. 13–14). What does this imagery convey about her initial attitude toward the relationship? How does this imagery contrast with that used to describe the game of chess in lines 6–8?
4. The first two stanzas of the poem are a first-person discussion of chess, while the rest of the poem is a third-person description of a relationship. How are these two parts related? How does the game of chess function as a metaphor for what the couple's relationship becomes?
5. How does the poem shift starting in line 19? Consider shifts in sound, rhythm, and tone. What attitude does the end of the poem express about relationships, and how do these literary devices reinforce that attitude?

PAIRED POEMS

My mistress' eyes are nothing like the sun

WILLIAM SHAKESPEARE

William Shakespeare (1564–1616) was born in Stratford-upon-Avon, England. Little is known of his life aside from the fact that he married Anne Hathaway when he was eighteen, worked as an actor-playwright in London, and retired in 1613. His plays fall into four principal categories: early comedies (1585–1594), more sophisticated comedies and histories (1595–1599), the great tragedies (1599–1607), and the final phase (1608–1613). His most accomplished works — including *Hamlet* (1601), *Othello* (1604), *King Lear* (1605), and *Macbeth* (1606) — belong to the third period. In his time, his contemporaries, and likely Shakespeare himself, looked to his sonnets and other poems as the more important works. The 154 sonnets were written at various stages in Shakespeare's life, but when and to whom they were written remain unclear. William Wordsworth believed that only through the sonnets could one understand Shakespeare. The following selection is Sonnet 130.

My mistress' eyes are nothing like the sun;
Coral is far more red than her lips' red;
If snow be white, why then her breasts are dun;
If hairs be wires, black wires grow on her head.
I have seen roses damasked red and white,
But no such roses see I in her cheeks;
And in some perfumes is there more delight
Than in the breath that from my mistress reeks.
I love to hear her speak, yet well I know
That music hath a far more pleasing sound;
I grant I never saw a goddess go:
My mistress, when she walks, treads on the ground.
    And yet, by heaven, I think my love as rare
    As any she belied with false compare.

[1609]

EXPLORING THE TEXT

1. Why do you think the speaker chooses to catalog his mistress's shortcomings?
2. Explain the turn the sonnet takes in the final couplet. How do these lines invite readers to reassess the first twelve lines?
3. How would you describe the tone in the first twelve lines? How does the tone shift in the final couplet? What resources of language does the author use to create this contrast in tone?

My ugly love
Sonnet XX

PABLO NERUDA

Translated by Stephen Tapscott

Pablo Neruda (1904–1973) — "the greatest poet of the 20th century in any language," according to Colombian writer Gabriel García Márquez — was born Neftalí Ricardo Reyes y Basoalto in Parral, Chile. He studied French and trained to be a teacher at the University of Chile in Santiago, but instead adopted the name Pablo Neruda and devoted himself to writing. His first published collection, *Crepusculario* (1923), was followed by *Veinte poemas de amor y una cancion desesperada* (1924), his most translated work. *Residencia en la tierra* (1933) established his reputation, and his experience of fascism in Spain inspired *España en el corazón* (1937). His ambitious *Canto general* — 250 poems combined into an epic about South America — was published in Mexico City in 1950. The collection includes "Alturas de Macchu Picchu" (1944), a monumental poem celebrating South America's cultures but condemning its social systems. He was elected to the Chilean Senate in 1945 but was forced to go into hiding in 1948 for anti-government statements; after more than a year, he was finally able to flee the country. He describes the period of exile that followed in *Las uvas y el viento* (1954); and later, in *Extravagario* (1958), he reexamines his loyalty to the Communist Party. Neruda was awarded the Nobel Prize for Literature in 1971. The poem "My ugly love" — included in *Cien sonetos de amor* (1959) — was dedicated to his wife Matilde Urrutia and is a tender, passionate hymn addressing the reality of love after the beauty of youth has flown.

My ugly love, you're a messy chestnut.
My beauty, you are pretty as the wind.
Ugly: your mouth is big enough for two mouths.
Beauty: your kisses are fresh as new melons.

Ugly: where *did* you hide your breasts?
They're meager, two little scoops of wheat.
I'd much rather see two moons across your chest,
two huge proud towers.

Ugly: not even the sea contains things like your toenails.
Beauty: flower by flower, star by star, wave by wave,
Love, I've made an inventory of your body:

My ugly one, I love you for your waist of gold;
my beauty, for the wrinkle on your forehead.
My Love: I love you for your clarity, your dark.

[1959/1986]

EXPLORING THE TEXT

1. How does the juxtaposition of the woman's beauty and ugliness affect your understanding of the speaker's love?
2. Why do you think Pablo Neruda put the line "Love, I've made an inventory of your body" (l. 11) where he did? Why not at the beginning?
3. Why do you think the speaker departs from describing physical qualities in the final line? How did you interpret this line?

FOCUS ON COMPARISON AND CONTRAST

1. What do these poems have in common in terms of their descriptions of the beloved? What is similar about the two poets' use of imagery?
2. How does the structure of Pablo Neruda's sonnet differ from the structure of William Shakespeare's sonnet? What effect do these differences have on your reading of the poems?
3. Compare the use of alternating positive and negative imagery in the two sonnets. What is different about the way this technique is used in "My ugly love" as compared to how it's used in "My mistress' eyes are nothing like the sun"?
4. Compare the tone employed by the speaker in the Neruda sonnet as he addresses his beloved with the tone employed by the speaker in the Shakespearean sonnet as he addresses a third party. Given your findings, what purpose, other than pitching woo, might these two poems serve?

WRITING ASSIGNMENT

"My mistress' eyes are nothing like the sun" and "My ugly love" are both concerned with beauty and love. In a well-written essay, compare and contrast the poems, analyzing the relationship of beauty in each. In your essay, consider elements such as imagery, structure, and tone.

A Valediction: Forbidding Mourning

JOHN DONNE

John Donne (1572–1631) was born in London to a prosperous family. He was educated by Jesuits and attended both Oxford and Cambridge, where he studied law. His satires (written 1593–1595) and the poems later collected as *Songs and Sonnets* reflect life among the barristers. Donne was ordained in the Church of England in 1615 and became a renowned preacher. His sermons were published in three volumes — *LXXX Sermons* (1640), *Fifty Sermons* (1649), and *XXVI Sermons* (1661) — though today only his poetry is widely read. Donne's poems were not collected in his lifetime; indeed, only when he was short of funds in 1613–1614 did he attempt to gather them together, writing to friends that "I am made a Rhapsoder of mine own rags, and that cost me more diligence, to seek them, than it did to make them." Eventually published as *Poems* in 1633, they met with immediate acclaim. Donne has since been regarded as the most important of the metaphysical poets — a loose confederation of artists who relied on wit and incongruous, often startling imagery (known as metaphysical conceits). Donne's poetry was often of a personal nature, focusing in particular on love in his earlier works. He wrote "A Valediction: Forbidding Mourning" to his pregnant wife, Anne, before leaving England on a trip to Europe in 1611 or 1612.

As virtuous men pass mildly 'away,
And whisper to their souls to go,
Whilst some of their sad friends do say,
The breath goes now, and some say, no:

So let us melt, and make no noise,
No tear-floods, nor sigh-tempests move.
'Twere profanation of our joys
To tell the laity[1] our love.

Moving of th' earth brings harms and fears,
Men reckon what it did and meant,
But trepidation of the spheres,
Though greater far, is innocent.

Dull sublunary[2] lovers' love
(Whose soul is sense) cannot admit
Absence, because it doth remove
Those things which elemented it.

But we by a love, so much refined,
That ourselves know not what it is,
Inter-assured of the mind,
Care less, eyes, lips, and hands to miss.

Our two souls therefore, which are one,
Though I must go, endure not yet
A breach, but an expansion,
Like gold to aery thinness beat.

If they be two, they are two so
As stiff twin compasses are two,
Thy soul the fixed foot, makes no show
To move, but doth, if the other do.

And though it in the centre sit,
Yet when the other far doth roam,
It leans, and hearkens after it,
And grows erect, as that comes home.

Such wilt thou be to me, who must
Like th' other foot, obliquely run.
Thy firmness makes my circle just,
And makes me end, where I begun.

[c. 1611]

[1] Ordinary people. — EDS.

[2] Relating to earthly concerns (as opposed to higher-minded, spiritual ones). — EDS.

EXPLORING THE TEXT

1. The poem opens with a description of how "virtuous men" die (ll. 1–4). What does this stanza suggest about how these men part from their lives? How does that description set the tone for a poem about how the speaker believes he and his beloved should face parting from each other?
2. In line 6, the speaker suggests to his beloved that they not resort to "tear-floods" or "sigh-tempests" as they part. What is the effect of the references to storms in this context?
3. In lines 13–20, the speaker suggests their love is more "refined" than those of "dull sublunary lovers." Why does he suggest these "dull" lovers are unable to bear being apart? How would you describe his attitude in these two stanzas?

4. John Donne uses a simile in line 24 to explain that in their parting, their connected souls will be "like gold to aery thinness beat." What is expressed about their parting in this comparison? How does the simile reinforce the argument he is making?
5. The poem ends with the sort of "conceit" metaphysical poets are known for, an extended simile that compares the speaker and his beloved to the two legs of a compass used to draw circles. What significant words are used to describe the compass and its actions? What does this comparison as a whole suggest about the speaker's relationship to the woman he is addressing?
6. How does Donne use the structure of his poem to build his argument? Consider the consistent form of the stanzas, as well as the conjunctions at the beginning of some stanzas, such as "So" (l. 5), "But" (l. 17), and "And" (l. 29). Furthermore, consider how he organizes the major comparisons throughout the poem. How do they build on each other in a logical order?

A Valediction Forbidding Mourning

ADRIENNE RICH

Adrienne Rich (1929–2012) was born in Baltimore, Maryland, and grew up in a household in which she was encouraged to read and write poetry. She received a BA in English from Radcliffe College (Harvard University). During her senior year at Radcliffe, poet W. H. Auden selected her first collection of poems, *A Change of World* (1951), for the Yale Series of Younger Poets Award. She published many collections of poetry and essays during her career, including the 1963 volume *Snapshots of a Daughter-in-Law: Poems 1954–1962*, which established her as a poet concerned with feminism, politics, and social justice. She won the National Book Award in 1974 for *Diving into the Wreck: Poems 1971–1972.* Rather than accepting the award by herself, she was accompanied by the other nominated feminist poets, Audre Lorde and Alice Walker, and the three accepted the award on behalf of all women. When the National Endowment for the Arts granted her the National Medal of Arts in 1997, Rich turned down the award as a protest against social injustice. The *New York Times* has called Rich "a poet of towering reputation and towering rage" and deemed her "among the most influential writers of the feminist movement."

My swirling wants. Your frozen lips.
The grammar turned and attacked me.
Themes, written under duress.
Emptiness of the notations.

They gave me a drug that slowed the healing of wounds.

I want you to see this before I leave:
the experience of repetition as death
the failure of criticism to locate the pain

the poster in the bus that said:
my bleeding is under control.

A red plant in a cemetery of plastic wreaths.

A last attempt: the language is a dialect called metaphor.
These images go unglossed: hair, glacier, flashlight.
When I think of a landscape I am thinking of a time.
When I talk of taking a trip I mean forever.
I could say: those mountains have a meaning
but further than that I could not say.

To do something very common, in my own way.

[1970]

EXPLORING THE TEXT

1. What does the first stanza suggest about the speaker's experience with writing? Make note of Adrienne Rich's diction and the actions that are described. How would you characterize the tone of these lines?
2. What is ironic about line 5, which states, "They gave me a drug that slowed the healing of wounds"? Who do you think "they" refers to? What does this line suggest about the speaker's experience?
3. In the third stanza, the speaker continues to describe her experience as a writer, using words such as "death" (l. 7), "pain" (l. 8), and "bleeding" (l. 10). What is the effect of using words that evoke physical experience to describe an intellectual pursuit? How might this reinforce the attitude she is expressing about her experience as a writer?
4. In line 11, Rich offers the image of "A red plant in a cemetery of plastic wreaths." How is the "red plant" a significant contrast to the "cemetery of plastic wreaths"? Within the context of the poem, what might each image represent?
5. What is the speaker suggesting when she says, "When I think of a landscape I am thinking of a time. / When I talk of taking a trip I mean forever" (lines 14–15)? How is the tone of this stanza different from the tone of the first stanza?
6. What does the speaker seem to be declaring about her future in the last line of the poem? What is ironic about the speaker's use of the phrase "very common" to describe what she intends to do? If this is a poem about bidding farewell, what do you believe she is saying goodbye to?
7. Why do you believe Rich uses John Donne's title for her poem? How does this allusion to his poem impact your experience with and understanding of Rich's poem?

FOCUS ON COMPARISON AND CONTRAST

1. Compare and contrast the emotional state of the speakers in these two poems. How do John Donne and Adrienne Rich use diction and detail to characterize how their speakers feel? Aside from gender, how else are the speakers of these two poems different? What do they have in common?
2. Consider the differences in the form that each poem takes. Donne uses quatrains with regular meter and rhyme, while Rich dispenses with formal pattern and rhyme, even setting single lines off as their own stanzas. How do these different formal choices impact your interpretation of these poems?
3. Compare and contrast the tone of each poem, considering how the imagery as a whole contributes to each.

WRITING ASSIGNMENT

"A Valediction: Forbidding Mourning" by John Donne and "A Valediction Forbidding Mourning" by Adrienne Rich both deal with bidding farewell to someone or something. Read each poem carefully. Then, write an essay comparing and contrasting the two poems, analyzing how each poet uses style elements to convey the attitudes each speaker expresses toward the idea of parting and separation.

IRONY

Irony is an incongruity between expectation and reality. It can be tricky to spot. It helps to know that there are several kinds: *verbal irony*, in which there is an incongruity between what the speaker says and what he or she means; *situational irony*, in which there is a discrepancy between what seems fitting and what actually happens (the examples in Alanis Morissette's 1995 song "Ironic" are failed attempts at situational irony); and *dramatic irony*, in which the contrast is between what a character says or thinks and what the audience (or readers) know to be true. In all of these cases, the reader or observer plays a key role. Irony only occurs if the audience perceives the discrepancy. If you make an ironic comment and your audience takes it at face value, the attempt at irony has failed. In this section, we'll focus on verbal irony — acknowledging that it can often be difficult to identify, particularly when reading a work from an earlier time period or a society that is not entirely familiar to us.

Playful, Satiric, and Sarcastic Irony

Irony is a tool that can be used for many purposes. We might think about these as a continuum, depending on how good natured (or mean spirited) the irony is, ranging from playful humor that reminds us of our shared human frailties, to **satire** that exposes a social issue, to bitter **sarcasm** that ridicules and demeans its target. Take these three headlines from the satiric newspaper the *Onion*, for example:

Playful

> "Simple Task of Going to Post Office Feels Like Weight of 10,000 Boulders"

Satiric

> "KFC No Longer Permitted to Use Word 'Eat' in Advertisements"

Sarcastic

> "Teenage Rebels Seize Control of Food Court's Corner Table"

Of course, irony often achieves more than one of these purposes, which is what makes it such a powerful verbal weapon.

Irony works by creating some kind of humor — whether it results in a smile, a belly laugh, or a wince — but it's important to recognize that irony usually serves a serious function, as Oscar Wilde reminds us in his subtitle to *The Importance of Being Earnest: A Trivial Comedy for Serious People*. By bringing together contrasting ideas, an author can use irony to reveal hypocrisy or injustice, and sometimes even lobby for social change, however subtly.

Ways to Create an Ironic Tone

Examining specific techniques writers use to create irony is a helpful step toward understanding both what irony is and how an author develops an ironic tone. There are an unlimited number of ways to create irony, but the following are some common techniques.

Hyperbole, or overstatement, is more than simple exaggeration or a lie: it is exaggeration in the service of truth. Like a well-crafted metaphor, it should suggest a deeper meaning. Hyperbole is ironic because there is an incongruity between what is literally said and what is actually meant. **Caricature** is a specific type of hyperbole: a representation in which the subject's distinctive features are deliberately exaggerated to yield a comic or even grotesque effect. In literature, caricatures may result in characters who are deliberately one-dimensional, even stereotypes; yet if done skillfully, a caricature calls attention to a character's faults or foibles.

The opposite of hyperbole — **understatement** — has a similar effect. Both of these are at work in the following exchange in act II of *The Importance of Being Earnest*:

> **GWENDOLEN:** Cecily Cardew? (*Moving to her and shaking hands.*) What a very sweet name! Something tells me that we are going to be great friends. I like you already more than I can say. My first impressions of people are never wrong.
>
> **CECILY:** How nice of you to like me so much after we have known each other such a comparatively short time. Pray sit down.
>
> GWENDOLEN (*still standing up*): I may call you Cecily, may I not?

Cecily uses understatement in this exchange to respond to Gwendolen's hyperbolic greeting. It's not that they've known each other "such a comparatively short time"; they've known each other for mere seconds. Cecily is subtly pointing out Gwendolen's insincerity and frivolousness, without being rude. Understatement is often used to cloak a wry jab in politeness. Note that in this case, as in most, understatement tends to be more subtle than hyperbole.

Juxtaposition — placing two ideas or words side by side to emphasize their incongruity — is another of the ironist's strategies. In the opening dialogue between Lane and Algernon, Wilde juxtaposes a seemingly philosophical subject — the "science of Life" — with the trivial concern of food to be served for tea. Algernon asks Lane, "And, speaking of the science of Life, have you got the cucumber sandwiches cut for Lady Bracknell?" Juxtaposing something so serious with something so trivial alerts us to Algernon's lack of priorities. This lays the foundation for Wilde's criticism of the hypocrisy of Victorian morality.

Wordplay can be an important way to create the humor that is essential to much of irony. **Puns** (deliberately misusing words that sound alike) or double entendres (expressions with two meanings) are common. Here's an example from act I:

> **JACK:** My dear Algy, you talk exactly as if you were a dentist. It is very vulgar to talk like a dentist when one isn't a dentist. It produces a false impression.
>
> **ALGERNON:** Well, that is exactly what dentists always do.

The expression "false impression" is a double entendre — a dentist uses plaster to take a "negative" impression of a patient's teeth. Algernon uses the double entendre playfully here to verbally spar with Jack and show off his cleverness. We see, too, that Wilde is using this playful wittiness to characterize Algernon as a bit frivolous and more than a little fond of himself.

Another way to create irony is through strained or false logic, most often through a **non sequitur**, which is technically defined as a conclusion that does not follow logically from the premises; it is a logical fallacy. In literature, a non sequitur is a reply or remark that does not have any relevance to what preceded it. In *The Importance of Being Earnest*, Wilde characterizes Cecily as being a less than thoughtful person in remarks such as the following: "Oh yes. Dr. Chasuble is a most learned man. He has never written a single book, so you can imagine how much he knows." Her three points (Dr. Chasuble is "most learned," he has never written a book, thus we "can imagine how much he knows") are so logically unrelated as to be humorous. The irony stems from the incongruity between the statement that Dr. Chasuble is "most learned" and what is really meant: he has never written a book, so whether he is smart or not is up to our imagination.

Though irony comes in many forms, they all have one thing in common — a significant distance between what is said and what is true.

The irony occurs when the reader notices that gap. Irony pervades *The Importance of Being Earnest*, as Wilde accumulates and deepens his satire of Victorian society — particularly marriage. In many of the other texts you have read, irony is perceptible in specific lines or passages and, in some cases, results in an overall ironic tone. The following exercises will help you practice recognizing irony and the ways it is created.

EXERCISE 1

We speak ironically every day, saying the opposite of what we actually mean in a tone of voice that reveals our true meaning. Turn to a partner and practice saying the following lines ironically. Consider how tone of voice, gestures, and facial expression convey irony.

- "Yeah, right."
- "I can't wait."
- "That's a great idea."
- "He's a shy one."
- "You saved the day."
- "That's very interesting."

EXERCISE 2

Identify the ironic techniques of hyperbole, understatement, juxtaposition, wordplay, and non sequitur in the following excerpts from readings in this chapter.

1. ALGERNON: Why is it that at a bachelor's establishment the servants invariably drink the champagne? I ask merely for information.

   LANE: I attribute it to the superior quality of the wine, sir. I have often observed that in married households the champagne is rarely of a first-rate brand. (*The Importance of Being Earnest*, I. ll. 15–18)

2. LADY BRACKNELL: . . . Do you smoke?

   JACK: well, yes, I must admit I smoke.

   LADY BRACKNELL: I am glad to hear it. A man should always have an occupation of some kind. There are far too many idle men in London as it is. (*The Importance of Being Earnest*, I. ll. 395–98)

3. Colonel Sartoris invented an involved tale to the effect that Miss Emily's father had loaned money to the town, which the town, as a matter of business, preferred this way of repaying. Only a man of Colonel Sartoris' generation and thought could have invented it, and only a woman could have believed it.

   When the next generation, with its more modern ideas, became mayors and aldermen, this arrangement created some little dissatisfaction. ("A Rose for Emily," paras. 3–4)

4. It's a date, Felice. Thursday. At the Cash N Carry off I-10. Noon. She'll be ready.

   Oh, and her name's Cleófilas.

   I don't know. One of those Mexican saints, I guess. A martyr or something.

   Cleófilas. C-L-E-O-F-I-L-A-S. Cle. O. Fi. Las. Write it down.

   Thanks, Felice. When her kid's born she'll have to name her after us, right?

   Yeah, you got it. A regular soap opera sometimes. *Qué vida, comadre. Bueno bye.*

   ("Woman Hollering Creek," paras. 72–77)

5. Oh stay, three lives in one flea spare,
Where we almost, yea more than, married are.
This flea is you and I, and this
Our marriage bed, and marriage temple is. ("The Flea," ll. 10–14)

6. I lost two cities, lovely ones. And, vaster,
some realms I owned, two rivers, a continent.
I miss them, but it wasn't a disaster.
("One Art," ll. 13–15)

EXERCISE 3

Explain how the author uses irony to make a serious comment in each of the following excerpts from readings in this chapter.

1. **ALGERNON:** She will place me next Mary Farquhar, who always flirts with her own husband across the dinner table. That is not very pleasant. Indeed, it is not even decent — and that sort of thing is enormously on the increase. The amount of women in London who flirt with their own husbands is perfectly scandalous. It looks so bad. It is simply washing one's clean linen in public.
(*The Importance of Being Earnest*, I. ll. 197–201)

2. **LADY BRACKNELL:** London society is full of women of the very highest birth who have, of their own free choice, remained thirty-five for years. Lady Dumbleton is an instance in point. To my own knowledge she has been thirty-five ever since she arrived at the age of forty, which was many years ago now.
(*The Importance of Being Earnest*, III. ll. 210–13)

3. **JACK:** I am sick to death of cleverness. Everybody is clever nowadays. You can't go anywhere without meeting clever people. The thing has become an absolutely public nuisance. I wish to goodness we had a few fools left.
ALGERNON: We have.
JACK: I should extremely like to meet them. What do they talk about?
ALGERNON: The fools? Oh! about the clever people, of course.
JACK: What fools!
(*The Importance of Being Earnest*, I. ll. 513–19)

4. When the soup was finished Bertha turned round to the fire.
"You're nice — you're very nice!" said she, kissing her warm baby. "I'm fond of you. I like you."
And, indeed she loved Little B so much — her neck as she bent forward, her exquisite toes as they shone transparent in the firelight — that all her feelings of bliss came back again, and again she didn't know how to express it — what to do with it.
"You're wanted on the telephone," said Nanny, coming back in triumph and seizing *her* Little B. ("Bliss," paras. 32–35)

5. "I have had such a *dreadful* experience with a taxi-man; he was *most* sinister. I couldn't get him to *stop*. The *more* I knocked and called the *faster* he went. . . ."
"But how dreadful!" she cried.
"Yes, it really was," said Eddie, following her into the drawing-room. "I saw myself *driving* through Eternity in a *timeless* taxi." ("Bliss," paras. 68–71)

6. But please, at least for the doctor visit. She won't ask for anything else. She has to. Why is she so anxious? Because.

   Because she is going to make sure the baby is not turned around backward this time to split her down the middle. Yes. Next Tuesday at five-thirty. I'll have Juan Pedrito dressed and ready. But those are the only shoes he has. I'll polish them, and we'll be ready. As soon as you come from work. We won't make you ashamed. ("Woman Hollering Creek," paras. 55–56)

7. It is awkward for me and bewildering for him
   as I hold him in my arms in the small bathroom,
   balancing our weight on the shaky blue scale,

   but this is the way to weigh a dog and easier
   than training him to sit obediently on one spot
   with his tongue out, waiting for the cookie.

   ("Weighing the Dog," ll. 1–6)

EXERCISE 4

In her poem "Siren Song," Margaret Atwood uses a number of strategies to develop an ironic tone, starting with the irony of the situation itself. Explain how the ironic tone, including some humor, conveys a serious message. Consider how Atwood prepares her reader for the final punch line.

EXERCISE 5

Write a poem praising a person, a place, or an event in an ironic tone, showing that your true intent is to poke fun at or criticize your subject. Try to use some of the strategies discussed in this section.

LOVE AND RELATIONSHIPS

1. Setting can play an important role in the development or deterioration of relationships as depicted in literature. Write an essay in which you explore the impact of setting on at least three of the works in this chapter. Analyze how the setting contributes to the meaning of the work as a whole.
2. Choose two poems from this chapter that posit contrasting views on romantic love. Write an essay in which you analyze the contrasting attitudes toward the subject. Consider how poetic devices in each piece help to convey the speaker's particular viewpoint.
3. Many of the texts in this chapter comment on inequities in the power of men and women in romance and marriage. Concentrating on three texts, write an essay analyzing the consequences of such inequities. Consider similarities as well as differences.
4. An often-quoted piece of dialogue from the Oscar Wilde play *A Woman of No Importance* offers a cynical view of marriage: "One should always be in love. That is the reason one should never marry." Choose one short story in this chapter and analyze whether the story supports or refutes the cynical view of marriage expressed in this quotation. Include specific references to the text to support your analysis.
5. Many of the authors in this chapter explore the disconnect between physical attraction and true love. Using the literature in this chapter as evidence, write an essay arguing for or against the importance of physical attractiveness in a romantic relationship.
6. Song lyrics often use love and relationships as a theme. Choose a song from a recording artist whose work you enjoy, and analyze the lyrics in the same way you would a piece of literature. Discuss how the songwriter uses imagery, diction, syntax, allusion, and figurative language, and explain their effect on the song.
7. Using one of the poems in this chapter as a model, write a poem on the theme of love and relationships. You might write a poem that offers a twist on a mythological story of seduction or love, as Margaret Atwood does in "Siren Song," or write a poem based on an analogy, as Billy Collins does in "Weighing the Dog."
8. Watch a film that is considered a romantic comedy; then discuss some of the techniques the filmmaker uses to explore the theme of love and relationships. Compare and contrast those techniques with the ones encountered in this chapter, such as irony, farce, romantic imagery, stock characters, and predictable plot structures.
9. Choose one of the following quotations about love and relationships and write an essay analyzing the extent that it applies to at least two of the texts in this chapter.
   a. The beginning of love is to let those we love be perfectly themselves, and not to twist them to fit our own image. Otherwise we love only the reflection of ourselves we find in them.
      — Thomas Merton
   b. There is always some madness in love. But there is also always some reason in madness.
      — Friedrich Nietzsche
   c. Being deeply loved by someone gives you strength, while loving someone deeply gives you courage.
      — Lao Tzu
   d. A journey is like marriage. The certain way to be wrong is to think you control it.
      — John Steinbeck
   e. Marriage is a wonderful institution, but who wants to live in an institution?
      — Groucho Marx
   f. We are never so defenseless against suffering as when we love.
      — Sigmund Freud
   g. We love because it's the only true adventure.
      — Nikki Giovanni

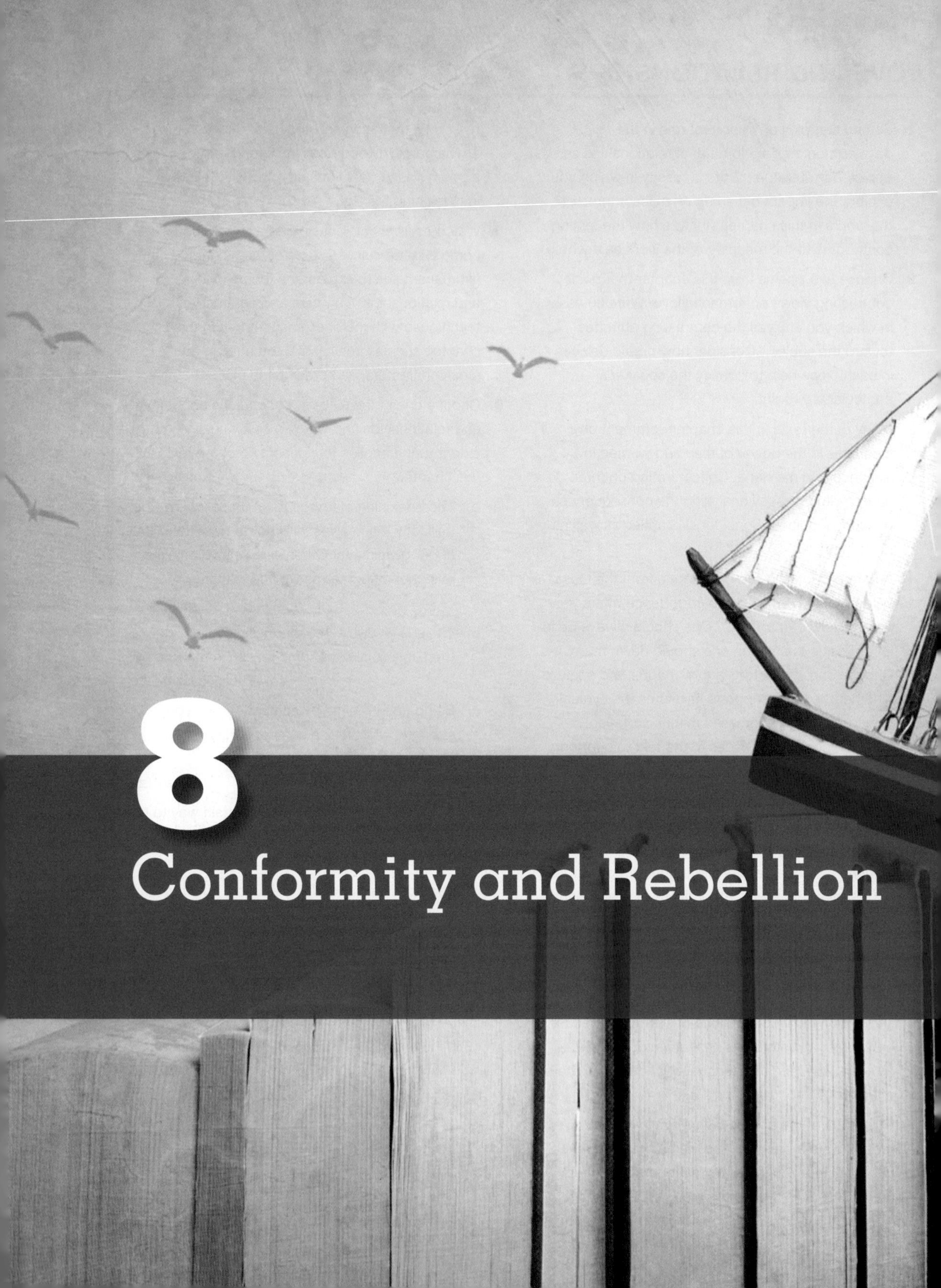

8
Conformity and Rebellion

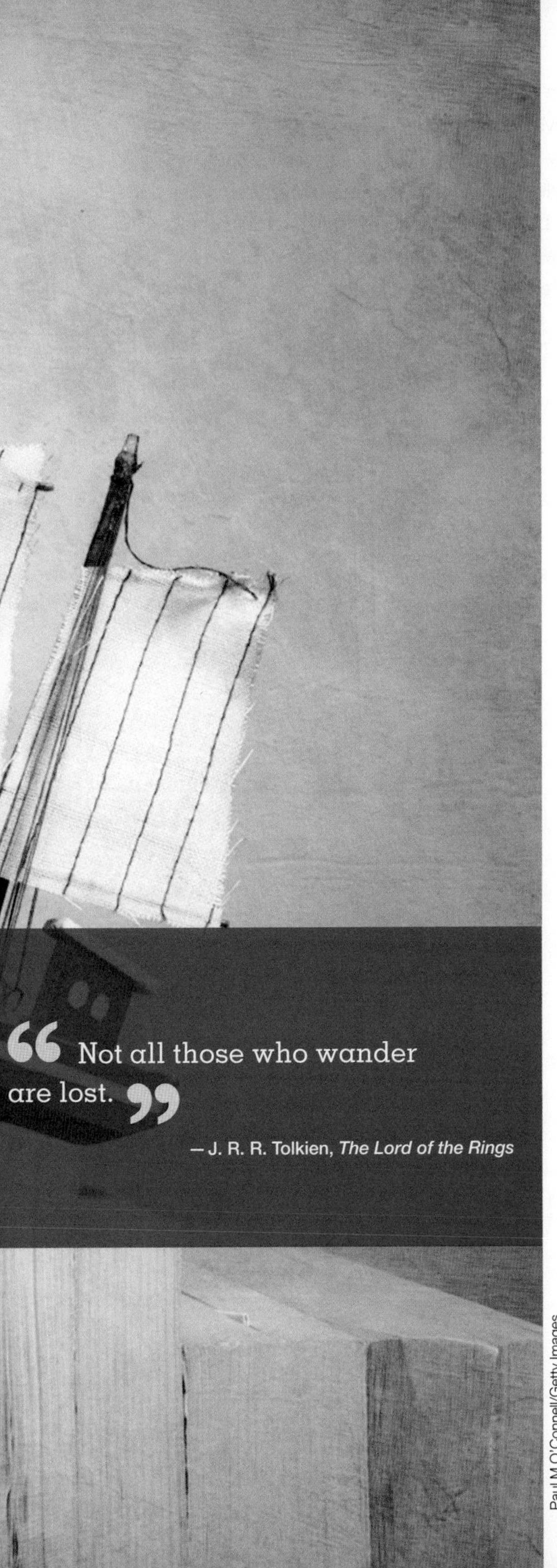

"Not all those who wander are lost."

— J. R. R. Tolkien, *The Lord of the Rings*

Paul M O'Connell/Getty Images

Much of the literature of the Western world might be said to express the struggle between conformity and rebellion. We find this theme in our earliest recorded texts. Genesis tells the story of Eve and Adam's refusal to conform — an act picked up centuries later in the opening lines of John Milton's epic poem, *Paradise Lost*: "Of man's first disobedience, and the fruit / Of that forbidden tree whose mortal taste / Brought death into the world, and all our woe." At the same time, however, we see obedience as a virtue. Without duty and order, without cooperation and teamwork, where would we be? We admire and respect those heroes who hold things together — figures such as Abraham Lincoln and Franklin Delano Roosevelt — as well as those who serve and protect us: police officers, firefighters, and soldiers. But we also look to heroes who rebel: Socrates, Nicolaus Copernicus, Galileo Galilei, Charles Darwin, Thomas Jefferson, Henry David Thoreau, Elizabeth Cady Stanton, Mahatma Gandhi, and Martin Luther King Jr. Our heroes are often those who, as Senator Robert F. Kennedy said, "dream of things that never were and ask, why not?" Sometimes the noblest rebellion is in conformity with a higher law.

The texts in this chapter present the ongoing struggle between the inertia of conformity and the challenges and promises of rebellion. The question of rebellion is explored in William Shakespeare's classic play *Hamlet*, and our Texts in Context consider Hamlet, his motivations, and the forces aligned against him from multiple angles.

The cost of conformity is revealed in Edwidge Danticat's modern story "The Book of the Dead." In "Bartleby, the Scrivener," Herman Melville demonstrates one man's rebellion against the expectations of others. Poems by Percy Bysshe Shelley and Gwendolyn Brooks address political conformity and rebellion, while a short story by Karen Russell and poems by Barbara Jane Reyes, Robin Coste Lewis, and Jamila Woods examine conformity to and rebellion against constraints of gender and race. In each of their poems, Wallace Stevens and E. E. Cummings consider the power that imagination has to transform the drabness of the mundane.

The Book of the Dead

EDWIDGE DANTICAT

Ernesto Ruscio / Getty Images

Born in Haiti in 1969, Edwidge Danticat immigrated to the United States when she was twelve and currently lives in Miami. She received her BA from Barnard College and her MFA from Brown University, where her thesis project became her first novel, *Breath, Eyes, Memory* (1994), which was an Oprah Winfrey Book Club selection in 1998. She has since written ten other books across a variety of genres, including collections of short stories, young adult novels, and nonfiction. Some of her most well-known works include the story collection *Krik? Krak!* (1995), which was nominated for the National Book Award; the novel *The Farming of Bones* (1998), which won an American Book Award; the novel-in-stories *The Dew Breaker* (2004); and her autobiography *Brother, I'm Dying* (2007), which won a National Book Critics Circle Award. In 2009, Danticat was awarded the prestigious MacArthur Fellowship. Danticat's works also include three young adult novels: *Behind the Mountains* (2002), *Anacaona, Golden Flower, Haiti, 1490* (2005), and *Untwine* (2015). She also edited *The Butterfly's Way: Voices from the Haitian Diaspora in the United States* (2001) and *Best American Essays* (2011). Themes of national identity, mother-daughter relationships, and diasporic politics are prominent in Danticat's work. "The Book of the Dead" is the first in a series of seven interrelated stories in *The Dew Breaker*. Dew breakers were Haitian militiamen, or Tonton Macoutes, who carried out the tyrannical policies of dictator François Duvalier in Haiti during the 1960s. They were called dew breakers because they usually struck at dawn.

My father is gone. I'm slouched in a cast-aluminum chair across from two men, one the manager of the hotel where we're staying and the other a policeman. They're both waiting for me to explain what's become of him, my father.

The hotel manager — MR. FLAVIO SALINAS, the plaque on his office door reads — has the most striking pair of chartreuse eyes I've ever seen on a man with an island Spanish lilt to his voice.

The police officer, Officer Bo, is a baby-faced, short, white Floridian with a potbelly.

"Where are you and your daddy from, Ms. Bienaimé?" Officer Bo asks, doing the best he can with my last name. He does such a lousy job that, even though he and I and Salinas are the only people in Salinas' office, at first I think he's talking to someone else.

I was born and raised in East Flatbush, 5
Brooklyn, and have never even been to my parents' birthplace. Still, I answer "Haiti" because it is one more thing I've always longed to have in common with my parents.

Officer Bo plows forward with, "You all the way down here in Lakeland from Haiti?"

"We live in New York," I say. "We were on our way to Tampa."

"To do what?" Officer Bo continues. "Visit?"

"To deliver a sculpture." I say. "I'm an artist, a sculptor."

I'm really not an artist, not in the way I'd like to be. I'm more of an obsessive wood-carver with a single subject thus far — my father.

My creative eye finds Manager Salinas' office gaudy. The walls are covered with orange-and-green wallpaper, briefly interrupted by a giant gold-leaf–bordered print of a Victorian cottage that resembles the building we're in.

Patting his light green tie, which brings out even more the hallucinatory shade of his eyes, Manager Salinas reassuringly tells me, "Officer Bo and I will do our best."

We start out with a brief description of my father: "Sixty-five, five feet eight inches, one hundred and eighty pounds, with a widow's peak, thinning salt-and-pepper hair, and velvet-brown eyes — "

"Velvet?" Officer Bo interrupts.

"Deep brown, same color as his complexion," I explain.

My father has had partial frontal dentures since he fell off his and my mother's bed and landed on his face ten years ago when he was having one of his prison nightmares. I mention that too. Just the dentures, not the nightmares. I also bring up the blunt, ropelike scar that runs from my father's right cheek down to the corner of his mouth, the only visible reminder of the year he spent in prison in Haiti.

"Please don't be offended by what I'm about to ask," Officer Bo says. "I deal with an older population here, and this is something that comes up a lot when they go missing. Does your daddy have any kind of mental illness, senility?"

I reply, "No, he's not senile."

"You have any pictures of your daddy?" Officer Bo asks.

My father has never liked having his picture taken. We have only a few of him at home, some awkward shots at my different school graduations, with him standing between my mother and me, his hand covering his scar. I had hoped to take some pictures of him on this trip, but he hadn't let me. At one of the rest stops I bought a disposable camera and pointed it at him anyway. As usual, he protested, covering his face with both hands like a little boy protecting his cheeks from a slap. He didn't want any more pictures taken of him for the rest of his life, he said, he was feeling too ugly.

"That's too bad," Officer Bo offers at the end of my too lengthy explanation. "He speaks English, your daddy? Can he ask for directions, et cetera?"

"Yes," I say.

"Is there anything that might make your father run away from you, particularly here in Lakeland?" Manager Salinas asks. "Did you two have a fight?"

I had never tried to tell my father's story in words before now, but my first completed sculpture of him was the reason for our trip: a three-foot mahogany figure of my father naked, kneeling on a half-foot-square base, his back arched like the curve of a crescent moon, his downcast eyes fixed on his very long fingers and the large palms of his hands. It was hardly revolutionary, rough and not too detailed, minimalist at best, but it was my favorite of all my attempted representations of my father. It was the way I had imagined him in prison.

The last time I had seen my father? The previous night, before falling asleep. When we pulled our rental car into the hotel's hedge-bordered parking lot, it was almost midnight. All the restaurants in the area were closed. There was nothing to do but shower and go to bed.

"It's like paradise here," my father had said when he'd seen our tiny room. It had the same orange-and-green wallpaper as Salinas' office, and the plush emerald carpet matched the walls. "Look, Ka," he said, his deep, raspy voice muted with exhaustion, "the carpet is like grass under our feet."

He'd picked the bed closest to the bathroom, removed the top of his gray jogging suit, and unpacked his toiletries. Soon after, I heard him humming loudly, as he always did, in the shower.

I checked on the sculpture, just felt it a little bit through the bubble padding and carton wrapping to make sure it was still whole. I'd used a piece of mahogany that was naturally flawed, with a few superficial cracks along what was now the back. I'd thought these cracks beautiful and had made no effort to sand or polish them away, as they seemed like the wood's own scars, like the one my father had on his face. But I was also a little worried about the cracks. Would they seem amateurish and unintentional, like a mistake? Could the wood come apart with simple movements or with age? Would the client be satisfied?

I closed my eyes and tried to picture the client to whom I was delivering the sculpture: Gabrielle Fonteneau, a Haitian American woman about my age, the star of a popular television series and an avid art collector. My friend Céline Benoit, a former colleague at the junior high school where I'm a substitute art teacher, had grown up with Gabrielle Fonteneau in Tampa and, at my request, on a holiday visit home had shown Gabrielle Fonteneau a snapshot of my *Father* piece and had persuaded her to buy it.

Gabrielle Fonteneau was spending the week away from Hollywood at her parents' house in Tampa. I took some time off, and both my mother and I figured that my father, who watched a lot of television, both at home and at his Nostrand Avenue barbershop, would enjoy meeting Gabrielle Fonteneau too. But when I woke up, my father was gone and so was the sculpture.

I stepped out of the room and onto the balcony overlooking the parking lot. It was a hot and muggy morning, the humid air laden with the smell of the freshly mowed tropical grass and sprinkler-showered hibiscus bordering the parking lot. My rental car too was gone. I hoped my father was driving around trying to find us some breakfast and would explain when he got back why he'd taken the sculpture with him, so I got dressed and waited. I watched a half hour of local morning news, smoked five mentholated cigarettes even though we were in a nonsmoking room, and waited some more.

All that waiting took two hours, and I felt guilty for having held back so long before going to the front desk to ask, "Have you seen my father?"

I feel Officer Bo's fingers gently stroking my wrist, perhaps to tell me to stop talking. Up close Officer Bo smells like fried eggs and gasoline, like breakfast at the Amoco.

"I'll put the word out with the other boys," he says. "Salinas here will be in his office. Why don't you go on back to your hotel room in case your daddy shows up there?"

Back in the room, I lie in my father's unmade bed. The sheets smell like his cologne, an odd mix of lavender and lime that I've always thought too pungent, but that he likes nonetheless.

I jump up when I hear the click from the electronic key in the door. It's the maid. She's a young Cuban woman who is overly polite, making up for her lack of English with deferential gestures: a great big smile, a nod, even a bow as she backs out of the room. She reminds me of my mother when she has to work on non-Haitian clients at her beauty shop, how she pays much more attention to those clients, forcing herself to laugh at jokes she barely understands and smiling at insults she doesn't quite grasp, all to avoid being forced into a conversation, knowing she couldn't hold up her end very well.

It's almost noon when I pick up the phone and call my mother at the salon. One of her employees tells me that she's not yet returned from the Mass she attends every day. After the Mass, if she has clients waiting, she'll walk the twenty blocks from the church to the salon. If she has no appointments, then she'll let her workers handle the walk-ins and go home for lunch. This was as close to retirement as my mother would ever come. This routine was her dream when she first started the shop. She had always wanted a life with room for daily Mass and long walks and the option of sometimes not going to work.

I call my parents' house. My mother isn't there either, so I leave the hotel number on the machine.

"Please call as soon as you can, Manman," I say. "It's about Papa."

It's early afternoon when my mother calls back, her voice cracking with worry. I had been sitting in that tiny hotel room, eating chips and candy bars from the vending machines, chain-smoking and waiting for something to happen, either for my father, Officer Bo, or Manager Salinas to walk into the room with some terrible news or for my mother or Gabrielle Fonteneau to call. I took turns imagining my mother screaming hysterically, berating both herself and me for thinking this trip with my father a good idea, then envisioning Gabrielle Fonteneau calling to say that we shouldn't have come on the trip. It had all been a joke. She wasn't going to buy a sculpture from me after all, especially one I didn't have.

"Where Papa?" Just as I expected, my mother sounds as though she's gasping for breath. I tell her to calm down, that nothing bad has happened. Papa's okay. I've just lost sight of him for a little while.

"How you lost him?" she asks.

"He got up before I did and disappeared," I say.

"How long he been gone?"

I can tell she's pacing back and forth in the kitchen, her slippers flapping against the Mexican tiles. I can hear the faucet when she turns it on, imagine her pushing a glass underneath it and filling it up. I hear her sipping the water as I say, "He's been gone for hours now. I don't even believe it myself."

"You call police?"

Now she's probably sitting at the kitchen table, her eyes closed, her fingers sliding back and forth across her forehead. She clicks her tongue and starts humming one of those mournful songs from the Mass, songs that my father, who attends church only at Christmas, picks up from her and also hums to himself in the shower.

My mother stops humming just long enough to ask, "What the police say?"

"To wait, that he'll come back."

There's a loud tapping on the line, my mother thumping her fingers against the phone's mouthpiece; it gives me a slight ache in my ear.

"He come back," she says with more certainty than either Officer Bo or Manager Salinas. "He not leave you like that."

I promise to call my mother hourly with an update, but I know she'll call me sooner than that, so I dial Gabrielle Fonteneau's cell phone. Gabrielle Fonteneau's voice sounds just as it does on television, but more silken, nuanced, and seductive without the sitcom laugh track.

"To think," my father once said while watching her show, in which she plays a smart-mouthed nurse in an inner-city hospital's maternity ward. "A Haitian-born actress with her own American television show. We have really come far."

"So nice of you to come all this way to personally deliver the sculpture," Gabrielle Fonteneau says. She sounds like she's in a place with cicadas, waterfalls, palm trees, and citronella candles to keep the mosquitoes away.

I realize that I too am in such a place, but I'm not able to enjoy it.

"Were you told why I like this sculpture so much?" Gabrielle Fonteneau asks. "It's regal and humble at the same time. It reminds me of my own father."

I hadn't been trying to delve into the universal world of fathers, but I'm glad my sculpture reminds Gabrielle Fonteneau of her father, for I'm not beyond the spontaneous fanaticism inspired by famous people, whose breezy declarations seem to carry so much more weight than those of ordinary mortals. I still had trouble believing I had Gabrielle Fonteneau's cell number, which Céline Benoit had made me promise not to share with anyone else, not even my father.

My thoughts are drifting from Gabrielle Fonteneau's father to mine when I hear her say, "So when will you get here? You have the directions, right? Maybe you can join us for lunch tomorrow, at around twelve."

"We'll be there," I say.

But I'm no longer so certain.

My father loves museums. When he's not working at his barbershop, he's often at the Brooklyn Museum. The Ancient Egyptian rooms are his favorites.

"The Egyptians, they was like us," he likes to say. The Egyptians worshiped their gods in many forms, fought among themselves, and were often ruled by foreigners. The pharaohs were like the dictators he had fled, and their queens were as beautiful as Gabrielle Fonteneau. But what he admires most about the Ancient Egyptians is the way they mourn their dead.

"They know how to grieve," he'd say, marveling at the mummification process that went on for weeks but resulted in corpses that survived thousands of years.

My whole adult life, I have struggled to find the proper manner of sculpting my father, a quiet and distant man who only came alive while standing with me most of the Saturday mornings of my childhood, mesmerized by the golden masks, the shawabtis, and the schist tablets, Isis, Nefertiti, and Osiris, the jackal-headed ruler of the underworld.

In ancient Egypt, a mummy mask with an idealized face would be placed over the head of a body to symbolize resurrection and passage to the afterlife. It was believed to provide protection from evil spirits on the journey to the afterworld ruled by Osiris. **What does Ka's father's obsession with ancient Egyptian culture say about his beliefs and hopes? To what extent do you think a mummy mask is emblematic of his character?**

ALESSANDRO VANNINI/Corbis via Getty Images

The sun is setting and my mother has called more than a dozen times when my father finally appears in the hotel room doorway. He looks like a much younger man and appears calm and rested, as if bronzed after a long day at the beach.

"Too smoky in here," he says.

I point to my makeshift ashtray, a Dixie cup filled with tobacco-dyed water and cigarette butts.

"Ka, let your father talk to you." He fans the smoky air with his hands, walks over to the bed, and bends down to unlace his sneakers. "Yon ti koze, a little chat."

"Where were you?" I feel my eyelids twitching, a nervous reaction I inherited from my epileptic mother. "Why didn't you leave a note? And Papa, where is the sculpture?"

"That is why we must chat," he says, pulling off his sand-filled sneakers and rubbing the soles of his large, calloused feet each in turn. "I have objections."

He's silent for a long time, concentrating on his foot massage, as though he'd been looking forward to it all day.

"I'd prefer you not sell that statue," he says at last. Then he turns away, picks up the phone, and calls my mother.

"I know she called you," he says to her in Creole. "She panicked. I was just walking, thinking."

I hear my mother loudly scolding him, telling him not to leave me again. When he hangs up, he grabs his sneakers and puts them back on.

"Where's the sculpture?" My eyes are twitching so badly now I can barely see.

"We go," he says. "I take you to it."

We walk out to the parking lot, where the hotel sprinkler is once more at work, spouting water onto the grass and hedges like centrifugal rain. The streetlights are on now, looking brighter and brighter as the dusk deepens around them. New hotel guests are arriving. Others are leaving for dinner, talking loudly as they walk to their cars.

As my father maneuvers our car out of the parking lot, I tell myself that he might be ill, mentally ill, even though I'd never detected any signs of it before, beyond his prison nightmares.

When I was eight years old and my father had the measles for the first time in his life, I overheard him say to a customer on the phone, "Maybe serious. Doctor tell me, at my age, measles can kill."

This was the first time I realized that my father could die. I looked up the word "kill" in every dictionary and encyclopedia at school, trying to understand what it really meant, that my father could be eradicated from my life.

My father stops the car on the side of the highway near a man-made lake, one of those marvels of the modern tropical city, with curved stone benches surrounding a stagnant body of water. There's scant light to see by except a half-moon. Stomping the well-manicured grass, my father heads toward one of the benches. I sit down next to him, letting my hands dangle between my legs.

Here I am a little girl again, on some outing with my father, like his trips to the botanic garden or the zoo or the Egyptian statues at the museum. Again, I'm there simply because he wants me to be. I knew I was supposed to learn something from these childhood outings, but it took me years to realize that ultimately my father was doing his best to be like other fathers, to share as much of himself with me as he could.

I glance over at the lake. It's muddy and dark, and there are some very large pink fishes bobbing back and forth near the surface, looking as though they want to leap out and trade places with us.

"Is this where the sculpture is?" I ask.

"In the water," he says.

"Okay," I say calmly. But I know I'm already defeated. I know the piece is already lost. The cracks have probably taken in so much water that the wood has split into several chunks and plunged to the bottom. All I can think of saying is something glib, something I'm not even sure my father will understand.

"Please know this about yourself," I say. "You're a very harsh critic."

My father attempts to smother a smile. He scratches his chin and the scar on the side of his face, but says nothing. In this light the usually chiseled and embossed-looking scar appears deeper than usual, yet somehow less threatening, like a dimple that's spread out too far.

Anger is a wasted emotion, I've always thought. My parents would complain to each other about unjust politics in New York, but they never got angry at my grades, at all the Cs I got in everything but art classes, at my not eating my vegetables or occasionally vomiting my daily spoonful of cod-liver oil. Ordinary anger, I've always thought, is useless. But now I'm deeply angry. I want to hit my father, beat the craziness out of his head.

"Ka," he says, "I tell you why I named you Ka."

Yes, he'd told me, many, many times before. Now does not seem like a good time to remind me, but maybe he's hoping it will calm me, keep me from hating him for the rest of my life.

"Your mother not like the name at all," he says. "She say everybody tease you, people take pleasure repeating your name, calling you Kaka, Kaka, Kaka."

This too I had heard before.

"Okay," I interrupt him with a quick wave of my hands. "I've got it."

"I call you Ka," he says, "because in Egyptian world — "

A ka is a double of the body, I want to complete the sentence for him — the body's companion through life and after life. It guides the body through the kingdom of the dead. That's what I tell my students when I overhear them referring to me as Teacher Kaka.

"You see, ka is like soul," my father now says. "In Haiti is what we call good angel, ti bon anj. When you born, I look at your face, I think, here is my ka, my good angel."

I'm softening a bit. Hearing my father call me his good angel is the point at which I often stop being apathetic.

"I say rest in Creole," he prefaces, "because my tongue too heavy in English to say things like this, especially older things."

"Fine," I reply defiantly in English.

"Ka," he continues in Creole, "when I first saw your statue, I wanted to be buried with it, to take it with me into the other world."

"Like the Ancient Egyptians," I continue in English.

He smiles, grateful, I think, that in spite of everything, I can still appreciate his passions.

"Ka," he says, "when I read to you, with my very bad accent, from *The Book of the Dead*, do you remember how I made you read some chapters to me too?"

But this recollection is harder for me to embrace. I had been terribly bored by *The Book of the Dead*. The images of dead hearts being placed on scales and souls traveling aimlessly down fiery underground rivers had given me my own nightmares. It had seemed selfish of him not to ask me what I wanted to listen to before going to bed, what I wanted to read and have read to me. But since he'd recovered from the measles and hadn't died as we'd both feared, I'd vowed to myself to always tolerate, even indulge him, letting him take me places I didn't enjoy and read me things I cared nothing about, simply to witness the joy they gave him, the kind of bliss that might keep a dying person alive. But maybe he wasn't going to be alive for long. Maybe this is what *this* outing is about. Perhaps my "statue," as he called it, is a sacrificial offering, the final one that he and I would make together before he was gone.

"Are you dying?" I ask my father. It's the one explanation that would make what he's done seem insignificant or even logical. "Are you ill? Are you going to die?"

What would I do now, if this were true? I'd find him the best doctor, move back home with him and my mother. I'd get a serious job, find a boyfriend, and get married, and I'd never complain again about his having dumped my sculpture in the lake.

Like me, my father tends to be silent a moment too long during an important conversation and then say too much when less should be said. I listen to the wailing of crickets and cicadas, though I can't tell where they're coming from. There's the highway, and the cars racing by, the half-moon, the lake dug up from the depths of the ground — with my sculpture now at the bottom of it, the allée of royal palms whose shadows intermingle with the giant fishes on the surface of that lake, and there is me and my father.

"Do you recall the judgment of the dead," my father speaks up at last, "when the heart of a person is put on a scale? If it's heavy, the heart, then this person cannot enter the other world."

It is a testament to my upbringing, and perhaps the Kaka and good angel story has something to do with this as well, that I remain silent now, at this particular time.

"I don't deserve a statue," my father says. But at this very instant he does look like one, like the Madonna of humility, contemplating her losses in the dust, or an Ancient Egyptian funerary priest, kneeling with his hands prayerfully folded on his lap.

"Ka," he says, "when I took you to the Brooklyn Museum, I would stand there for hours admiring them. But all you noticed was how there were pieces missing from them, eyes, noses, legs, sometimes even heads. You always noticed more what was not there than what was."

Of course, this way of looking at things was why I ultimately began sculpting in the first place, to make statues that would amaze my father even more than these ancient relics.

"Ka, I am like one of those statues," he says.

"An Ancient Egyptian?" I hear echoes of my loud, derisive laugh only after I've been laughing for a while. It's the only weapon I have now, the only way I know to take my revenge on my father.

"Don't do that," he says, frowning, irritated, almost shouting over my laughter. "Why do that? If you are mad, let yourself be mad. Why do you always laugh like a clown when you are angry?"

I tend to wave my hands about wildly when I laugh, but I don't notice I'm doing that now until he reaches over to grab them. I quickly move them away, but he ends up catching my right wrist, the same wrist Officer Bo had stroked earlier to make me shut up. My father holds on to it so tightly now that I feel his fingers crushing the bone, almost splitting it apart, and I can't laugh anymore.

"Let go," I say, and he releases my wrist quickly. He looks down at his own fingers, then lowers his hand to his lap.

My wrist is still throbbing. I keep stroking it to relieve some of the pain. It's the ache there that makes me want to cry more than anything, not so much this sudden, uncharacteristic flash of anger from my father.

"I'm sorry," he says. "I did not want to hurt you. I did not want to hurt anyone."

I keep rubbing my wrist, hoping he'll feel even sorrier, even guiltier for grabbing me so hard, but even more for throwing away my work.

"Ka, I don't deserve a statue," he says again, this time much more slowly, "not a whole one, at least. You see, Ka, your father was the hunter, he was not the prey."

I stop stroking my wrist, sensing something coming that might hurt much more. He's silent again. I don't want to prod him, feed him any cues, urge him to speak, but finally I get tired of the silence and feel I have no choice but to ask, "What are you talking about?"

I immediately regret the question. Is he going to explain why he and my mother have no close friends, why they've never had anyone over to the house, why they never speak of any relatives in Haiti or anywhere else, or have never returned there or, even after I learned Creole from them, have never taught me anything else about the country beyond what I could find out on my own, on the television, in newspapers, in books? Is he about to tell me why Manman is so pious? Why she goes to daily Mass? I am not sure I want to know anything more than the little they've chosen to share with me all these years, but it is clear to me that he needs to tell me, has been trying to for a long time.

"We have a proverb," he continues. "One day for the hunter, one day for the prey. Ka, your father was the hunter, he was not the prey."

Each word is now hard-won as it leaves my father's mouth, balanced like those hearts on the Ancient Egyptian scales.

"Ka, I was never in prison," he says.

"Okay," I say, sounding like I am fourteen again, chanting from what my mother used to call the meaningless adolescent chorus, just to sound like everyone else my age.

"I was working in the prison," my father says. And I decide not to interrupt him again until he's done.

Stranded in the middle of this speech now, he has to go on. "It was one of the prisoners inside the prison who cut my face in this way," he says.

My father now points to the long, pitted scar on his right cheek. I am so used to his hands covering it up that this new purposeful motion toward it seems dramatic and extreme, almost like raising a veil.

"This man who cut my face," he continues, "I shot and killed him, like I killed many people."

I'm amazed that he managed to say all of this in one breath, like a monologue. I wish I too had had some rehearsal time, a chance to have learned what to say in response.

There is no time yet, no space in my brain to allow for whatever my mother might have to confess. Was she huntress or prey? A thirty-year-plus disciple of my father's coercive persuasion? She'd kept to herself even more than he had, like someone who was nurturing a great pain that

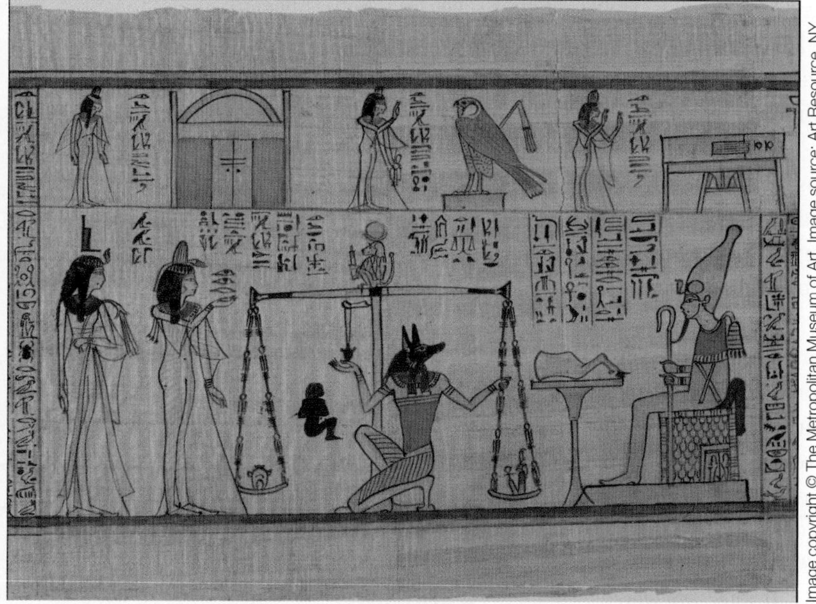

This funerary papyrus depicts the "weighing of hearts" practice in the Egyptian *Book of the Dead:* Osiris, god of the afterlife, would measure the weight of the heart of the deceased against that of a feather. If the heart weighed more, it would be judged heavy with wrongdoing and eaten by Ammat, the demon god under the scales, thus barring the deceased from the afterlife. **Why would such a practice appeal to Ka's father? What does his fascination with it suggest about the way he thinks of his past?**

she could never speak about. Yet she had done her best to be a good mother to me, taking charge of feeding and clothing me and making sure my hair was always combed, leaving only what she must have considered my intellectual development to my father.

When I was younger, she'd taken me to Mass with her on Sundays. Was I supposed to have been praying for my father all that time, the father who was the hunter and not the prey?

I think back to "The Negative Confession" ritual from *The Book of the Dead*, a ceremony that was supposed to take place before the weighing of hearts, giving the dead a chance to affirm that they'd done only good things in their lifetime. It was one of the chapters my father read to me most often. Now he was telling me I should have heard something beyond what he was reading. I should have removed the negatives.

"I am not a violent man," he had read. "I have made no one weep. I have never been angry without cause. I have never uttered any lies. I have never slain any men or women. I have done no evil."

And just so I will be absolutely certain of what I'd heard, I ask my father, "And those nightmares you were always having, what were they?"

"Of what I," he says, "your father, did to others."

Another image of my mother now fills my head, of her as a young woman, a woman my age, taking my father in her arms. At what point did she decide that she loved him? When did she know that she was supposed to have despised him?

"Does Manman know?" I ask.

"Yes," he says. "I explained, after you were born."

I am the one who drives the short distance back to the hotel. The ride seems drawn out, the cars in front of us appear to be dawdling. I honk impatiently, even when everyone except me is driving at a normal speed. My father is silent, not even telling me, as he has always done whenever he's been my passenger, to calm down, to be careful, to take my time.

As we are pulling into the hotel parking lot, I realize that I haven't notified Officer Bo and Manager Salinas that my father has been found. I decide that I will call them from my room. Then, before we leave the car, my father says, "Ka, no matter what, I'm still your father, still your mother's husband. I would never do these things now."

And this to me is as meaningful a declaration as his other confession. It was my first inkling that maybe my father was wrong in his own representation of his former life, that maybe his past offered more choices than being either hunter or prey.

When we get back to the hotel room, I find messages from both Officer Bo and Manager Salinas. Their shifts are over, but I leave word informing them that my father has returned.

While I'm on the phone, my father slips into the bathroom and runs the shower at full force. He is not humming.

When it seems he's never coming out, I call my mother at home in Brooklyn.

"Manman, how do you love him?" I whisper into the phone.

My mother is clicking her tongue and tapping her fingers against the mouthpiece again. Her soft tone makes me think I have awakened her from her sleep.

"He tell you?" she asks.

"Yes," I say.

"Everything?"

"Is there more?"

"What he told you he want to tell you for long time," she says, "you, his good angel."

It has always amazed me how much my mother and father echo each other, in their speech, their actions, even in their businesses. I wonder how much more alike they could possibly be. But why shouldn't they be alike? Like all parents, they were a society of two, sharing a series of private codes and associations, a past that even if I'd been born in the country of their birth, I still wouldn't have known, couldn't have known, thoroughly. I was a part of them. Some might say I belonged to them. But I wasn't them.

"I don't know, Ka." My mother is whispering now, as though there's a chance she might also be overheard by my father. "You and me, we save him. When I meet him, it made him stop hurt the people. This how I see it. He a seed thrown in rock. You, me, we make him take root."

As my mother is speaking, this feeling comes over me that I sometimes have when I'm carving, this sensation that my hands don't belong to me at all, that something else besides my brain and muscles is moving my fingers, something bigger and stronger than myself, an invisible puppetmaster over whom I have no control. I feel as though it's this same puppetmaster that now forces me to lower the phone and hang up, in midconversation, on my mother.

As soon as I put the phone down, I tell myself that I could continue this particular conversation at will, in a few minutes, a few hours, a few days, even a few years. Whenever I'm ready.

My father walks back into the room, his thinning hair wet, his pajamas on. My mother does not call me back. Somehow she must know that she has betrayed me by not sharing my confusion and, on some level, my feeling that my life could have gone on fine without my knowing these types of things about my father.

When I get up the next morning, my father's already dressed. He's sitting on the edge of the bed, his head bowed, his face buried in his palms, his forehead shadowed by his fingers. If I were sculpting him at this moment, I would carve a praying mantis, crouching motionless, seeming to pray, while actually waiting to strike.

With his back to me now, my father says, "Will you call that actress and tell her we have it no more, the statue?"

"We were invited to lunch there," I say. "I believe we should go and tell her in person."

He raises his shoulders and shrugs.

"Up to you," he says.

We start out for Gabrielle Fonteneau's house after breakfast. It's not quite as hot as the previous morning, but it's getting there. I crank up the AC at full blast, making it almost impossible for us to have a conversation, even if we wanted to.

The drive seems longer than the twenty-four hours it took to get to Lakeland from New York. I quickly grow tired of the fake lakes, the fenced-in canals, the citrus groves, the fan-shaped travelers' palms, the highway so imposingly neat. My father turns his face away from me and takes in the tropical landscape, as though he will never see it again. I know he's enjoying the live oaks with Spanish moss and bromeliads growing in their shade, the yellow trumpet flowers and flame vines, the tamarinds and jacaranda trees we speed by, because he expressed his admiration for them before, on the first half of our journey.

As we approach Gabrielle Fonteneau's house, my father breaks the silence in the car by saying, "Now you see, Ka, why your mother and me, we have never returned home."

The Fonteneaus' house is made of bricks and white coral, on a cul-de-sac with a row of banyans separating the two sides of the street.

My father and I get out of the car and follow a concrete path to the front door. Before we can knock, an older woman appears in the doorway. It's Gabrielle Fonteneau's mother. She resembles Gabrielle Fonteneau, or the way Gabrielle looks on television, with stunning almond eyes, skin the color of sorrel and spiraling curls brushing the sides of her face.

"We've been looking out for you," she says with a broad smile.

When Gabrielle's father joins her in the doorway, I realize where Gabrielle Fonteneau gets her height. He's more than six feet tall.

Mr. Fonteneau extends his hands, first to my father and then to me. They're relatively small, half the size of my father's.

We move slowly through the living room, which has a cathedral ceiling and walls covered with Haitian paintings with subjects ranging from market scenes and first communions to weddings and wakes. Most remarkable is a life-size portrait of Gabrielle Fonteneau sitting on a canopy-covered bench in what seems like her parents' garden.

Out on the back terrace, which towers over a nursery of azaleas, hibiscus, dracaenas, and lemongrass, a table is set for lunch.

Mr. Fonteneau asks my father where he is from in Haiti, and my father lies. In the past, I thought he always said he was from a different province each time because he'd really lived in all of those places, but I realize now that he says this to reduce the possibility of anyone identifying him, even though thirty-seven years and a thinning head of widow-peaked salt-and-pepper hair shield him from the threat of immediate recognition.

When Gabrielle Fonteneau makes her entrance, in an off-the-shoulder ruby dress, my father and I both rise from our seats.

"Gabrielle," she coos, extending her hand to my father, who leans forward and kisses it before spontaneously blurting out, "My dear, you are one of the most splendid flowers of Haiti."

Gabrielle Fonteneau looks a bit flustered. She tilts her head coyly and turns toward me.

"Welcome," she says.

During the meal of conch, fried plantains, and mushroom rice, Mr. Fonteneau tries to draw my father into conversation by asking him, in Creole, when he was last in Haiti.

"Thirty-seven years," my father answers with a mouthful of food.

"No going back for you?" asks Mrs. Fonteneau.

"I have not yet had the opportunity," my father replies.

"We go back every year," says Mrs. Fonteneau, "to a beautiful place overlooking the ocean, in the mountains of Jacmel."

"Have you ever been to Jacmel?" Gabrielle Fonteneau asks me.

I shake my head no.

"We're fortunate," Mrs. Fonteneau says, "that we have a place to go where we can say the rain is sweeter, the dust is lighter, our beaches prettier."

"So now we are tasting rain and weighing dust?" Mr. Fonteneau says and laughs.

"There's nothing like drinking the sweet juice from a coconut fetched from your own tree." Mrs. Fonteneau's eyes are lit up now as she puts her fork down to better paint the picture for us. She's giddy, her voice grows louder and higher, and even her daughter is absorbed, smiling and recollecting with her mother.

"There's nothing like sinking your hand in sand from the beach in your own country," Mrs. Fonteneau is saying. "It's a wonderful feeling, wonderful."

I imagine my father's nightmares. Maybe he dreams of dipping his hands in the sand on a beach in his own country and finding that what he comes up with is a fistful of blood.

After lunch, my father asks if he can have a closer look at the Fonteneaus' garden. While he's taking the tour, I make my confession about the sculpture to Gabrielle Fonteneau.

She frowns as she listens, fidgeting, shifting her weight from one foot to the other, as though she's greatly annoyed that so much of her valuable time had been so carelessly squandered on me. Perhaps she's wondering if this was just an elaborate scheme to meet her, perhaps she wants us out of her house as quickly as possible.

"I don't usually have people come into my house like this," she says, "I promise you."

"I appreciate it," I say. "I'm grateful for your trust and I didn't mean to violate it."

"I guess if you don't have it, then you don't have it," she says. "But I'm very disappointed. I really wanted to give that piece to my father."

"I'm sorry," I say.

"I should have known something was off," she says, looking around the room, as if for something more interesting to concentrate on. "Usually when people come here to sell us art, first of all they're always carrying it with them and they always show it to us right away. But since you know Céline I overlooked that."

"There was a sculpture," I say, aware of how stupid my excuse was going to sound. "My father didn't like it, and he threw it away."

She raises her perfectly arched eyebrows, as if out of concern for my father's sanity, or for my own. Or maybe it's another indirect signal that she now wants us out of her sight.

"We're done, then," she says, looking directly at my face. "I have to make a call. Enjoy the rest of your day."

Gabrielle Fonteneau excuses herself, disappearing behind a closed door. Through the terrace overlooking the garden, I see her parents guiding my father along rows of lemongrass. I want to call Gabrielle Fonteneau back and promise her that I will make her another sculpture, but I can't. I don't know that I will be able to work on anything for some time. I have lost my subject, the prisoner father I loved as well as pitied.

In the garden Mr. Fonteneau snaps a few sprigs of lemongrass from one of the plants, puts them in a plastic bag that Mrs. Fonteneau is holding. Mrs. Fonteneau hands the bag of lemongrass to my father.

Watching my father accept with a nod of thanks, I remember the chapter "Driving Back Slaughters" from *The Book of the Dead*, which my father sometimes read to me to drive away my fear of imagined monsters. It was a chapter full of terrible lines like "My mouth is the keeper of both speech and silence. I am the child who travels the roads of yesterday, the one who has been wrought from his eye."

I wave to my father in the garden to signal that we should leave now, and he slowly comes toward me, the Fonteneaus trailing behind him.

With each step forward, he rubs the scar on the side of his face, and out of a strange reflex I scratch my face in the same spot.

Maybe the last person my father harmed had dreamed moments like this into my father's future, strangers seeing that scar furrowed into his face and taking turns staring at it and avoiding it, forcing him to conceal it with his hands, pretend it's not there, or make up some lie about it, to explain.

Out on the sidewalk in front of the Fonteneaus' house, before we both take our places in the car, my father and I wave good-bye to Gabrielle Fonteneau's parents, who are standing in their doorway. Even though I'm not sure they understood the purpose of our visit, they were more than kind, treating us as though we were old friends of their daughter's, which maybe they had mistaken us for.

As the Fonteneaus turn their backs to us and close their front door, I look over at my father, who's still smiling and waving. When he smiles the scar shrinks and nearly disappears into the folds of his cheek, which used to make me wish he would never stop smiling.

Once the Fonteneaus are out of sight, my father reaches down on his lap and strokes the plastic bag with the lemongrass the Fonteneaus had given him. The car is already beginning to smell too much like lemongrass, like air freshener overkill.

"What will you use that for?" I ask.

"To make tea," he says, "for Manman and me."

I pull the car away from the Fonteneaus' curb, dreading the rest stops, the gas station, the midway hotels ahead for us. I wish my mother were here now, talking to us about some miracle she'd just heard about in a sermon at the Mass. I wish my sculpture were still in the trunk. I wish I hadn't met Gabrielle Fonteneau, that I still had that to look forward to somewhere else, sometime in the future. I wish I could give my father whatever he'd been seeking in telling me his secret. But my father, if anyone could, must have already understood that confessions do not lighten living hearts.

I had always thought that my father's only ordeal was that he'd left his country and moved to a place where everything from the climate to the language was so unlike his own, a place where he never quite seemed to fit in, never appeared to belong. The only thing I can grasp now, as I drive way beyond the speed limit down yet another highway, is why the unfamiliar might have been so comforting, rather than distressing, to my father. And why he has never wanted the person he was, is, permanently documented in any way. He taught himself to appreciate the enormous weight of permanent markers by learning about the Ancient Egyptians. He had gotten to know them, through their crypts and monuments, in a way that he wanted no one to know him, no one except my mother and me, we, who are now his kas, his good angels, his masks against his own face.

[2004]

QUESTIONS FOR DISCUSSION

1. Edwidge Danticat does not name the Tonton Macoutes or refer to François Duvalier in her story, yet this background is essential to the dew breaker's life in Haiti as well as in the United States. Why isn't Danticat more explicit about the historical context?
2. How do you interpret the title of the story? How does it both refer to the ancient Egyptian *Book of the Dead* and go beyond that reference? Why is Ka's father drawn to this culture?
3. Ka's father offers one explanation for why he destroyed her sculpture. Do you believe him? What are other possible explanations for his action?
4. Ka has a somewhat different relationship with her mother than she has with her father. How would you characterize each of these relationships? Do you think it would have mattered to Ka if her mother rather than her father had revealed to her his past as "hunter" rather than "prey"? Explain your answer.
5. How much does Ka's mother know about her husband? Is it significant that he told her about his past after they were married and had their daughter?
6. Once her father has revealed his secret identity to her, Ka immediately turns to thoughts of her mother: "There is no time yet, no space in my brain to allow for whatever my mother might have to confess. Was she huntress or prey?" (para. 133). Why does Ka shift to her mother before responding to her father in either words or thoughts?
7. How has Ka's relationship with her father changed by the end of the story? Explain whether you believe she will forgive him. Even if she does, do you think it will impact their relationship? Do you think she would rather not have known about his past?
8. Will Ka do another sculpture of her father in the future? If you think not, explain your reasoning. If you think so, explain what you think the sculpture might look like.
9. Ka says that her father, "if anyone could, must have already understood that confessions do not lighten living hearts" (para. 213). Why does she think he would understand this? And if he does understand this, why does he reveal his past to her?
10. Who are the victimizers and who are the victims in this story? Is such a classification appropriate or even possible under these circumstances?
11. Danticat poses powerful questions about blame, guilt, forgiveness, healing, and redemption in "The Book of the Dead." Is she arguing that Ka should forgive her father? Has he forgiven himself? Does forgiveness — by his daughter or his wife or even himself — mean that he is not morally culpable for his actions as a young man?

QUESTIONS ON STYLE AND STRUCTURE

1. "The Book of the Dead" opens with the simple sentence, "My father is gone." How is this sentence explained, echoed, and explored throughout the story?
2. Why do you think Danticat chose to tell this story through Ka rather than through her father or an omniscient narrator who might have revealed the feelings of Ka, her mother, and her father?
3. What elements of mystery are present in the story? As the story begins, Ka is trying to locate her father, who has gone missing. When do you realize that he has not been hurt, taken ill, or become the victim of a violent crime but that he has left on his own? Is this an effective way to begin the story, or do you think it is misleading? What are some of the clues Ka has about her father's identity? What information about her parents and the way the family lives in New York changes meaning when Ka learns about her father's past in Haiti?
4. When her father reveals his past, he begins by referring to himself in the first person ("I don't deserve a statue"), then shifts to the third person ("your father was the hunter, he was not the prey") (para. 121). Why? What does that change in perspective suggest?
5. Ka describes the material she chose for her sculpture: "a piece of mahogany that was naturally flawed, with a few superficial cracks along what was now the back. I'd thought these cracks beautiful and had made no effort to sand or polish them away, as they seemed like the wood's own scars, like the one my father had on his face" (para. 28). What does this passage suggest about Ka's intuition about her father? What does it suggest about her ability to accept imperfection? Has her father tried to "polish away" his own scars up until this point?
6. What is the function of the minor characters of Gabrielle Fonteneau and her parents? How does Danticat weave them into the structure of the story, and how do they contribute to the development of the story's themes? As you explore their role, ask yourself why Danticat did not simply structure the story so that Ka and her father chose not to visit the Fonteneaus after the sculpture was destroyed.
7. In an interview in *The Caribbean Writer*, Danticat talks about silence:

   > Silence is at the core of a story like this, just as it is during the dictatorship. There's so much you're not allowed to say. The Duvaliers silenced — by killing a whole generation and stunning many of the survivors into silence. . . . Migration also silences you. You're in a country where you don't speak the language, don't know the names of things, so there is a silencing there as well . . . [yet] that these characters tell their stories in different ways, to the reader, to other people, breaks that silence.

   Discuss the role of silence and voice in "The Book of the Dead," paying special attention to who chooses to speak and when, and the use of Haitian Creole in exchanges between Ka and her parents.
8. What does Ka mean when she thinks back to "The Negative Confession" ritual from *The Book of the Dead*: "Now he was telling me I should have heard something beyond what he was reading. I should have removed the negatives" (para. 135)?
9. After his confession, her father assures Ka that "no matter what, I'm still your father, still your mother's husband. I would never do these things now" (para. 143). Why does she think that this statement "is as meaningful a declaration as his other confession" (para. 144)? What does she mean when she thinks, "It was my first inkling that maybe my father was wrong in his own representation of his former life, that maybe his past offered more choices than being either hunter or prey" (para. 144)?
10. Who or what is the "puppetmaster" in paragraph 157, in which Ka describes how she feels when talking to her mother about her father's past:

    > As my mother is speaking, this feeling comes over me that I sometimes have when I'm carving, this sensation that my hands don't belong to me at all, that something else besides my brain and muscles is moving my fingers, something bigger and stronger than myself, an invisible puppetmaster over whom I have no control. I feel as though it's this same puppetmaster that now forces me to lower the phone and hang up, in midconversation, on my mother.
11. How do you interpret the final paragraph of the story? Does it end on a hopeful note? What does Danticat mean by "the enormous weight of permanent markers"? How are the dew breaker's "good angels" "his masks against his own face"?

SUGGESTIONS FOR WRITING

1. Write an essay discussing the ways in which this new information about her father shakes Ka's own identity. Consider her various responses from feeling that her "life could have gone on fine without . . . knowing these types of things about [her] father" (para. 159), to imagining that she feels a scar in the same place on her face as her father's.
2. Do a close reading of the passage in which Ka's father reveals that he was "the hunter . . . not the prey" (paras. 110–41). Discuss how Danticat conveys the confusion Ka is feeling as her father makes this revelation to her.
3. Write an essay comparing and contrasting "The Book of the Dead" with another work in which a character's relationship to events in the past contributes to the meaning of the work. Consider how these events positively or negatively affect the present actions, attitudes, or values of Ka or her father and a character from another work.
4. Discuss "The Book of the Dead" in terms of how Michiko Kakutani, a book reviewer for the *New York Times*, has characterized the story: "A tale that simultaneously unfolds to become a philosophical meditation on the possibility of redemption and the longing of victims and victimizers alike to believe in the promise of new beginnings held forth by the American Dream."
5. Write an essay explaining whether you think that Ka should forgive her father. Center your discussion on "The Book of the Dead," but explore the concept of forgiveness, healing, and redemption through research into other areas, such as the documentary "As We Forgive" — about reconciliation efforts in Rwanda — and the Amy Biehl Foundation in South Africa.
6. Draw, paint, sculpt, or digitally create your interpretation of Ka's sculpture of her father. Explain what information in Danticat's story led you to your design and how you might have changed her original sculpture to fit your interpretation of the story.
7. Watch Jonathan Demme's documentary *The Agronomist*, the true story of Jean Dominique, a Haitian radio journalist and human rights activist. Write an essay discussing how this film expands your understanding of "The Book of the Dead."

Hamlet, Prince of Denmark

WILLIAM SHAKESPEARE

National Portrait Gallery, London, UK/Bridgeman Images

William Shakespeare (1564–1616) was born in Stratford-upon-Avon, England. Little is known of his life aside from the fact that he married Anne Hathaway when he was eighteen, worked as an actor-playwright in London, and retired in 1613. His plays fall into four principal categories: early comedies (1585–1594), more sophisticated comedies and histories (1595–1599), the great tragedies (1599–1607), and the final phase (1608–1613). His most accomplished works — including *Hamlet* (1601), *Othello* (1604), *King Lear* (1605), and *Macbeth* (1606) — belong to the third period. Yet in his time, his contemporaries — and likely Shakespeare himself — looked to his sonnets and other poems as the more important works. The 154 sonnets were written at various stages in Shakespeare's life, but when and to whom they were written remain unclear. While William Wordsworth believed that only through the sonnets could one understand Shakespeare, *Hamlet* is Shakespeare's most famous work, and is regarded by many to be his finest. It has been performed, adapted, and studied more than any other play in the English language.

[*Dramatis Personae*

CLAUDIUS *King of Denmark*
HAMLET *son to the late and nephew to the present king*
POLONIUS *lord chamberlain*
HORATIO *friend to Hamlet*
LAERTES *son to Polonius*
VOLTIMAND, **CORNELIUS**, **ROSENCRANTZ**, **GUILDENSTERN**, **OSRIC** } *courtiers*
A GENTLEMAN
A PRIEST
MARCELLUS, **BERNARDO** } *officers*
FRANCISCO *a soldier*
REYNALDO *servant to Polonius*
PLAYERS
TWO CLOWNS *grave-diggers*
FORTINBRAS *Prince of Norway*
A CAPTAIN
ENGLISH AMBASSADORS
GERTRUDE *Queen of Denmark, and mother to Hamlet*
OPHELIA, *daughter to Polonius*
LORDS, LADIES, OFFICERS, SOLDIERS, SAILORS, MESSENGERS, *and other* **ATTENDANTS**
GHOST *of Hamlet's father*

SCENE: *Denmark.*]

ACT I

[Scene i: *Elsinore. A platform° before the castle.*]

Enter **BERNARDO** *and* **FRANCISCO**, *two sentinels.*

BERNARDO Who's there?
FRANCISCO Nay, answer me:° stand, and unfold yourself.
BERNARDO Long live the king!°
FRANCISCO Bernardo?
BERNARDO He.
FRANCISCO You come most carefully upon your hour.
BERNARDO 'Tis now struck twelve; get thee to bed, Francisco.
FRANCISCO For this relief much thanks: 'tis bitter cold,
And I am sick at heart.
BERNARDO Have you had quiet guard?
FRANCISCO Not a mouse stirring.
BERNARDO Well, good night.
If you do meet Horatio and Marcellus,
The rivals° of my watch, bid them make haste.

Enter **HORATIO** *and* **MARCELLUS**.

FRANCISCO I think I hear them. Stand, ho! Who is there?
HORATIO Friends to this ground.
MARCELLUS And liegemen to the Dane.
FRANCISCO Give you° good night.
MARCELLUS O, farewell, honest soldier:
Who hath reliev'd you?
FRANCISCO Bernardo hath my place.
Give you good night. *Exit* **FRANCISCO**.
MARCELLUS Holla! Bernardo!
BERNARDO Say,
What, is Horatio there?
HORATIO A piece of him.
BERNARDO Welcome, Horatio: welcome, good Marcellus.
MARCELLUS What, has this thing appear'd again to-night?
BERNARDO I have seen nothing.
MARCELLUS Horatio says 'tis but our fantasy,
And will not let belief take hold of him
Touching this dreaded sight, twice seen of us:
Therefore I have entreated him along
With us to watch the minutes of this night;
That if again this apparition come,
He may approve° our eyes and speak to it.
HORATIO Tush, tush, 'twill not appear.
BERNARDO Sit down awhile;
And let us once again assail your ears,
That are so fortified against our story
What we have two nights seen.
HORATIO Well, sit we down,
And let us hear Bernardo speak of this.
BERNARDO Last night of all,
When yond same star that's westward from the pole°
Had made his course t' illume that part of heaven
Where now it burns, Marcellus and myself,
The bell then beating one, —

Enter **GHOST**.

MARCELLUS Peace, break thee off; look, where it comes again!
BERNARDO In the same figure, like the king that's dead.
MARCELLUS Thou art a scholar;° speak to it, Horatio.
BERNARDO Looks 'a not like the king? mark it, Horatio.

Act I, Scene i. **platform:** A level space on the battlements of the royal castle at Elsinore, a Danish seaport; now Helsingör. **2 me:** This is emphatic, since Francisco is the sentry. **3 Long live the king:** Either a password or greeting; Horatio and Marcellus use a different one in line 15. **13 rivals:** Partners. **16 Give you:** God give you.

29 approve: Corroborate. **36 pole:** Polestar. **42 scholar:** Exorcisms were performed in Latin, which Horatio as an educated man would be able to speak.

HORATIO Most like: it harrows° me with fear and wonder.
BERNARDO It would be spoke to.°
MARCELLUS Speak to it, Horatio.
HORATIO What art thou that usurp'st this time of night,
Together with that fair and warlike form
In which the majesty of buried Denmark°
Did sometimes march? by heaven I charge thee, speak!
MARCELLUS It is offended.
BERNARDO See it stalks away!
HORATIO Stay! speak, speak! I charge thee, speak! *Exit* **GHOST.**
MARCELLUS 'Tis gone, and will not answer.
BERNARDO How now, Horatio! you tremble and look pale:
Is not this something more than fantasy?
What think you on 't?
HORATIO Before my God, I might not this believe
Without the sensible and true avouch
Of mine own eyes.
MARCELLUS Is it not like the king?
HORATIO As thou art to thyself:
Such was the very armour he had on
When he the ambitious Norway combated;
So frown'd he once, when, in an angry parle,
He smote° the sledded Polacks° on the ice.
'Tis strange.
MARCELLUS Thus twice before, and jump° at this dead hour,
With martial stalk hath he gone by our watch.
HORATIO In what particular thought to work I know not;
But in the gross and scope° of my opinion,
This bodes some strange eruption to our state.

44 harrows: Lacerates the feelings. **45 It . . . to:** A ghost could not speak until spoken to. **48 buried Denmark:** The buried king of Denmark. **63 smote:** Defeated. **sledded Polacks:** Polanders using sledges. **65 jump:** Exactly. **68 gross and scope:** General drift.

MARCELLUS Good now,° sit down, and tell me, he that knows,
Why this same strict and most observant watch
So nightly toils° the subject° of the land,
And why such daily cast° of brazen cannon,
And foreign mart° for implements of war;
Why such impress° of shipwrights, whose sore task
Does not divide the Sunday from the week;
What might be toward, that this sweaty haste
Doth make the night joint-labourer with the day:
Who is't that can inform me?
HORATIO That can I;
At least, the whisper goes so. Our last king,
Whose image even but now appear'd to us,
Was, as you know, by Fortinbras of Norway,
Thereto prick'd on° by a most emulate° pride,
Dar'd to the combat; in which our valiant Hamlet—
For so this side of our known world esteem'd him—
Did slay this Fortinbras; who, by a seal'd compact,
Well ratified by law and heraldry,°
Did forfeit, with his life, all those his lands
Which he stood seiz'd° of, to the conqueror:
Against the which, a moiety competent°
Was gaged by our king; which had return'd
To the inheritance of Fortinbras,
Had he been vanquisher; as, by the same comart,°
And carriage° of the article design'd,
His fell to Hamlet. Now, sir, young Fortinbras,
Of unimproved° mettle hot and full,°

70 Good now: An expression denoting entreaty or expostulation. **72 toils:** Causes or makes to toil. **subject:** People, subjects. **73 cast:** Casting, founding. **74 mart:** Buying and selling, traffic. **75 impress:** Impressment. **83 prick'd on:** Incited. **emulate:** Rivaling. **87 law and heraldry:** Heraldic law, governing combat. **89 seiz'd:** Possessed. **90 moiety competent:** Adequate or sufficient portion. **93 comart:** Joint bargain. **94 carriage:** Import, bearing. **96 unimproved:** Not turned to account. **hot and full:** Full of fight.

Hath in the skirts of Norway here and there
Shark'd up° a list of lawless resolutes,°
For food and diet,° to some enterprise
That hath a stomach in't; which is no other —
As it doth well appear unto our state —
But to recover of us, by strong hand
And terms compulsatory, those foresaid lands
So by his father lost: and this, I take it,
Is the main motive of our preparations,
The source of this our watch and the chief head
Of this post-haste and romage° in the land.

BERNARDO I think it be no other but e'en so:
Well may it sort° that this portentous figure
Comes armed through our watch; so like the king
That was and is the question of these wars.

HORATIO A mote° it is to trouble the mind's eye.
In the most high and palmy state° of Rome,
A little ere the mightiest Julius fell,
The graves stood tenantless and the sheeted dead
Did squeak and gibber in the Roman streets:
As stars with trains of fire° and dews of blood,
Disasters° in the sun; and the moist star°
Upon whose influence Neptune's empire° stands
Was sick almost to doomsday with eclipse:
And even the like precurse° of fear'd events,
As harbingers preceding still the fates
And prologue to the omen coming on,
Have heaven and earth together demonstrated
Unto our climatures and countrymen. —

Enter **GHOST.**

But soft, behold! lo, where it comes again!
I'll cross° it, though it blast me. Stay, illusion!
If thou hast any sound, or use of voice,
Speak to me! *It° spreads his arms.*
If there be any good thing to be done,
That may to thee do ease and grace to me,
Speak to me!
If thou art privy to thy country's fate,
Which, happily, foreknowing may avoid,
O, speak!
Or if thou hast uphoarded in thy life
Extorted treasure in the womb of earth,
For which, they say, you spirits oft walk in death, *The cock crows.*
Speak of it:° stay, and speak! Stop it, Marcellus.

MARCELLUS Shall I strike at it with my partisan?°

HORATIO Do, if it will not stand.

BERNARDO 'Tis here!

HORATIO 'Tis here!

MARCELLUS 'Tis gone! [*Exit* **GHOST.**]
We do it wrong, being so majestical,
To offer it the show of violence;
For it is, as the air, invulnerable,
And our vain blows malicious mockery.

BERNARDO It was about to speak, when the cock crew.°

HORATIO And then it started like a guilty thing
Upon a fearful summons. I have heard,
The cock, that is the trumpet to the morn,
Doth with his lofty and shrill-sounding throat
Awake the god of day; and, at his warning,
Whether in sea or fire, in earth or air,
Th' extravagant and erring° spirit hies
To his confine:° and of the truth herein

---

98 Shark'd up: Got together in haphazard fashion. **resolutes:** Desperadoes. **99 food and diet:** No pay but their keep. **107 romage:** Bustle, commotion. **109 sort:** Suit. **112 mote:** Speck of dust. **113 palmy state:** Triumphant sovereignty. **117 stars . . . fire:** I.e., comets. **118 Disasters:** Unfavorable aspects. **moist star:** The moon, governing tides. **119 Neptune's empire:** The sea. **121 precurse:** Heralding.

127 cross: Meet, face, thus bringing down the evil influence on the person who crosses it. **129 It:** The Ghost, or perhaps Horatio. **133–139 If . . . it:** Horatio recites the traditional reasons why ghosts might walk. **140 partisan:** Long-handled spear with a blade having lateral projections. **147 cock crew:** According to traditional ghost lore, spirits returned to their confines at cockcrow. **154 extravagant and erring:** Wandering. Both words mean the same thing. **155 confine:** Place of confinement.

This present object made probation.°

MARCELLUS It faded on the crowing of the cock.
Some say that ever 'gainst° that season comes
Wherein our Saviour's birth is celebrated,
The bird of dawning singeth all night long:
And then, they say, no spirit dare stir abroad;
The nights are wholesome; then no planets strike,°
No fairy takes,° nor witch hath power to charm,
So hallow'd and so gracious° is that time.

HORATIO So have I heard and do in part believe it.
But, look, the morn, in russet mantle clad,
Walks o'er the dew of yon high eastward hill:
Break we our watch up; and by my advice,
Let us impart what we have seen to-night
Unto young Hamlet; for, upon my life,
This spirit, dumb to us, will speak to him.
Do you consent we shall acquaint him with it,
As needful in our loves, fitting our duty?

MARCELLUS Let's do 't, I pray; and I this morning know
Where we shall find him most conveniently. *Exeunt.*

[Scene ii: *A room of state in the castle.*]

Flourish. Enter **CLAUDIUS**, *King of Denmark,* **GERTRUDE** *the Queen,* **COUNCILORS, POLONIUS** *and his son* **LAERTES, HAMLET**, *cum aliis*° [*including* **VOLTIMAND** *and* **CORNELIUS**].

KING Though yet of Hamlet our dear brother's death
The memory be green, and that it us befitted
To bear our hearts in grief and our whole kingdom
To be contracted in one brow of woe,
Yet so far hath discretion fought with nature
That we with wisest sorrow think on him,
Together with remembrance of ourselves.
Therefore our sometime sister, now our queen,
Th' imperial jointress° to this warlike state,
Have we, as 'twere with a defeated joy, —
With an auspicious and a dropping eye,
With mirth in funeral and with dirge in marriage,
In equal scale weighing delight and dole, —
Taken to wife: nor have we herein barr'd
Your better wisdoms, which have freely gone
With this affair along. For all, our thanks.
Now follows, that° you know, young Fortinbras,
Holding a weak supposal° of our worth,
Or thinking by our late dear brother's death
Our state to be disjoint° and out of frame,°
Colleagued° with this dream of his advantage,°
He hath not fail'd to pester us with message,
Importing° the surrender of those lands
Lost by his father, with all bands of law,
To our most valiant brother. So much for him.
Now for ourself and for this time of meeting:
Thus much the business is: we have here writ
To Norway, uncle of young Fortinbras, —
Who, impotent and bed-rid, scarcely hears
Of this his nephew's purpose, — to suppress
His further gait° herein; in that the levies,
The lists and full proportions, are all made
Out of his subject:° and we here dispatch
You, good Cornelius, and you, Voltimand,
For bearers of this greeting to old Norway;
Giving to you no further personal power
To business with the king, more than the scope

---

156 probation: Proof, trial. **158 'gainst:** Just before. **162 planets strike:** It was thought that planets were malignant and might strike travelers by night. **163 No fairy takes:** It was thought that fairies would steal babies. **164 gracious:** Full of goodness.
Scene ii. cum aliis: With others.

9 jointress: Woman possessed of a jointure, or joint tenancy of an estate. **17 that:** That which. **18 weak supposal:** Low estimate. **20 disjoint:** Distracted, out of joint. **frame:** Order. **21 Colleagued:** added to. **dream . . . advantage:** Visionary hope of success. **23 Importing:** Purporting, pertaining to. **31 gait:** Proceeding. **33 Out of his subject:** At the expense of Norway's subjects (collectively).

Of these delated° articles allow.
Farewell, and let your haste commend your duty.

CORNELIUS } **VOLTIMAND** } In that and all things will we show our duty.

KING We doubt it nothing: heartily farewell.
[*Exeunt* **VOLTIMAND** *and* **CORNELIUS.**]
And now, Laertes, what's the news with you?
You told us of some suit; what is't, Laertes?
You cannot speak of reason to the Dane,°
And lose your voice:° what wouldst thou beg, Laertes,
That shall not be my offer, not thy asking?
The head is not more native° to the heart,
The hand more instrumental° to the mouth,
Than is the throne of Denmark to thy father.
What wouldst thou have, Laertes?

LAERTES My dread lord,
Your leave and favour to return to France;
From whence though willingly I came to Denmark,
To show my duty in your coronation,
Yet now, I must confess, that duty done,
My thoughts and wishes bend again toward France
And bow them to your gracious leave and pardon.°

KING Have you your father's leave? What says Polonius?

POLONIUS He hath, my lord, wrung from me my slow leave
By laboursome petition, and at last
Upon his will I seal'd my hard consent:
I do beseech you, give him leave to go.

KING Take thy fair hour, Laertes; time be thine,
And thy best graces spend it at thy will!
But now, my cousin° Hamlet, and my son,—

HAMLET [*aside*]: A little more than kin, and less than kind!°

KING How is it that the clouds still hang on you?

HAMLET Not so, my lord; I am too much in the sun.°

QUEEN Good Hamlet, cast thy nighted colour off,
And let thine eye look like a friend on Denmark.
Do not for ever with thy vailed lids
Seek for thy noble father in the dust:
Thou know'st 'tis common; all that lives must die,
Passing through nature to eternity.

HAMLET Ay, madam, it is common.°

QUEEN If it be,
Why seems it so particular with thee?

HAMLET Seems, madam! nay, it is; I know not "seems."
'Tis not alone my inky cloak, good mother,
Nor customary suits° of solemn black,
Nor windy suspiration° of forc'd breath,
No, nor the fruitful river in the eye,
Nor the dejected 'haviour of the visage,
Together with all forms, moods, shapes of grief,
That can denote me truly: these indeed seem,
For they are actions that a man might play:
But I have that within which passeth show;
These but the trappings and the suits of woe.

KING 'Tis sweet and commendable in your nature, Hamlet,
To give these mourning duties to your father:
But, you must know, your father lost a father;
That father lost, lost his, and the survivor bound

---

38 delated: Expressly stated. **44 the Dane:** Danish king. **45 lose your voice:** Speak in vain. **47 native:** Closely connected, related. **48 instrumental:** Serviceable. **56 leave and pardon:** Permission to depart. **64 cousin:** Any kin not of the immediate family.

65 A little . . . kind: My relation to you has become more than kinship warrants; it has also become unnatural. **67 I am . . . sun:** (1) I am too much out of doors, (2) I am too much in the sun of your grace (ironical), (3) I am too much of a son to you. Possibly an allusion to the proverb "Out of heaven's blessing into the warm sun"; i.e., Hamlet is out of house and home in being deprived of the kingship. **74 Ay . . . common:** It is common, but it hurts nevertheless; possibly a reference to the commonplace quality of the queen's remark. **78 customary suits:** Suits prescribed by custom for mourning. **79 windy suspiration:** Heavy sighing.

In filial obligation for some term
To do obsequious° sorrow: but to persever
In obstinate condolement° is a course
Of impious stubbornness; 'tis unmanly grief;
It shows a will most incorrect° to heaven,
A heart unfortified, a mind impatient,
An understanding simple and unschool'd:
For what we know must be and is as common
As any the most vulgar thing° to sense,
Why should we in our peevish opposition
Take it to heart? Fie! 'tis a fault to heaven,
A fault against the dead, a fault to nature,
To reason most absurd; whose common theme
Is death of fathers, and who still hath cried,
From the first corse° till he that died to-day,
"This must be so." We pray you, throw to earth
This unprevailing° woe, and think of us
As of a father: for let the world take note,
You are the most immediate° to our throne;
And with no less nobility° of love
Than that which dearest father bears his son,
Do I impart° toward you. For your intent
In going back to school in Wittenberg,°
It is most retrograde° to our desire:
And we beseech you, bend you° to remain
Here, in the cheer and comfort of our eye,
Our chiefest courtier, cousin, and our son.

QUEEN Let not thy mother lose her prayers, Hamlet:
I pray thee, stay with us; go not to Wittenberg.

HAMLET I shall in all my best obey you, madam.

KING Why, 'tis a loving and a fair reply:
Be as ourself in Denmark. Madam, come;
This gentle and unforc'd accord of Hamlet
Sits smiling to my heart: in grace whereof,
No jocund health that Denmark drinks to-day,
But the great cannon to the clouds shall tell,
And the king's rouse° the heaven shall bruit again,°
Re-speaking earthly thunder. Come away.

Flourish. Exeunt all but **HAMLET**.

HAMLET O, that this too too solid flesh would melt,
Thaw and resolve itself into a dew!
Or that the Everlasting had not fix'd
His canon 'gainst self-slaughter! O God! God!
How weary, stale, flat and unprofitable,
Seem to me all the uses of this world!
Fie on't! ah fie! 'tis an unweeded garden,
That grows to seed; things rank and gross in nature
Possess it merely.° That it should come to this!
But two months dead: nay, not so much, not two:
So excellent a king; that was, to this,
Hyperion° to a satyr; so loving to my mother
That he might not beteem° the winds of heaven
Visit her face too roughly. Heaven and earth!
Must I remember? why, she would hang on him,
As if increase of appetite had grown
By what it fed on: and yet, within a month —
Let me not think on't — Frailty, thy name is woman! —
A little month, or ere those shoes were old
With which she followed my poor father's body,
Like Niobe,° all tears: — why she, even she —
O God! a beast, that wants discourse of reason,°
Would have mourn'd longer — married with my uncle,

---

92 obsequious: Dutiful. **93 condolement:** Sorrowing. **95 incorrect:** Untrained, uncorrected. **99 vulgar thing:** Common experience. **105 corse:** Corpse. **107 unprevailing:** Unavailing. **109 most immediate:** Next in succession. **110 nobility:** High degree. **112 impart:** The object is apparently love (l. 110). **113 Wittenberg:** Famous German university founded in 1502. **114 retrograde:** Contrary. **115 bend you:** Incline yourself (imperative).

127 rouse: Draft of liquor. **bruit again:** Echo. **137 merely:** Completely, entirely. **140 Hyperion:** God of the sun in the older regime of ancient gods. **141 beteem:** Allow. **149 Niobe:** Tantalus's daughter, who boasted that she had more sons and daughters than Leto; for this, Apollo and Artemis slew her children. She was turned into stone by Zeus on Mount Sipylus. **150 discourse of reason:** Process or faculty of reason.

My father's brother, but no more like my
father
Than I to Hercules: within a month:
Ere yet the salt of most unrighteous tears
Had left the flushing in her galled° eyes,
She married. O, most wicked speed, to post
With such dexterity° to incestuous sheets!
It is not nor it cannot come to good:
But break, my heart; for I must hold my tongue.

Enter **HORATIO**, **MARCELLUS**, *and* **BERNARDO**.

HORATIO Hail to your lordship!

HAMLET
YE DANE.
A GHOST STORY.
PRICE 3/-
LONDON

Private Collection / © Look and Learn / Peter Jackson Collection / Bridgeman Images

This illustration graces the cover of a nineteenth-century English production program booklet for *Hamlet ye Dane: A Ghost Story*. **What is the relationship between the image and the title on this booklet cover? How is Hamlet portrayed here, and what might an audience expect upon seeing such a program?**

155 galled: Irritated. **157 dexterity:** Facility.

HAMLET I am glad to see
you well:
Horatio! — or I do forget myself.
HORATIO The same, my lord, and your poor
servant ever.
HAMLET Sir, my good friend; I'll change that
name with you:°
And what make you from Wittenberg, Horatio?
Marcellus?
MARCELLUS My good lord —
HAMLET I am very glad to see you. Good even, sir.
But what, in faith, make you from Wittenberg?
HORATIO A truant disposition, good my lord.
HAMLET I would not hear your enemy say so,
Nor shall you do my ear that violence,
To make it truster of your own report
Against yourself: I know you are no truant.
But what is your affair in Elsinore?
We'll teach you to drink deep ere you depart.
HORATIO My lord, I came to see your father's
funeral.
HAMLET I prithee, do not mock me,
fellow-student;
I think it was to see my mother's wedding.
HORATIO Indeed, my lord, it follow'd hard°
upon.
HAMLET Thrift, thrift, Horatio! the funeral bak'd
meats°
Did coldly furnish forth the marriage tables.
Would I had met my dearest° foe in heaven
Or ever I had seen that day, Horatio!
My father! — methinks I see my father.
HORATIO Where, my lord?
HAMLET In my mind's eye,
Horatio.
HORATIO I saw him once; 'a° was a goodly king.
HAMLET 'A was a man, take him for all in all,
I shall not look upon his like again.

163 I'll . . . you: I'll be your servant, you shall be my friend; also explained as "I'll exchange the name of friend with you." **179 hard:** Close. **180 bak'd meats:** Meat pies. **182 dearest:** Direst. The adjective *dear* in Shakespeare has two different origins: O.E. *deore*, "beloved," and O.E. *deor*, "fierce." *Dearest* is the superlative of the second. **186 'a:** He.

HORATIO My lord, I think I saw him yesternight.
HAMLET Saw? who?
HORATIO My lord, the king your father.
HAMLET The king my father!
HORATIO Season your admiration° for a while
With an attent ear, till I may deliver,
Upon the witness of these gentlemen,
This marvel to you.
HAMLET For God's love, let me hear.
HORATIO Two nights together had these gentlemen,
Marcellus and Bernardo, on their watch,
In the dead waste and middle of the night,
Been thus encount'red. A figure like your father,
Armed at point exactly, cap-a-pe,°
Appears before them, and with solemn march
Goes slow and stately by them: thrice he walk'd
By their oppress'd° and fear-surprised eyes,
Within his truncheon's° length; whilst they, distill'd°
Almost to jelly with the act° of fear,
Stand dumb and speak not to him. This to me
In dreadful secrecy impart they did;
And I with them the third night kept the watch:
Where, as they had deliver'd, both in time,
Form of the thing, each word made true and good,
The apparition comes: I knew your father;
These hands are not more like.
HAMLET But where was this?
MARCELLUS My lord, upon the platform where we watch'd.
HAMLET Did you not speak to it?
HORATIO My lord, I did;
But answer made it none: yet once methought
It lifted up it° head and did address
Itself to motion, like as it would speak;
But even then the morning cock crew loud,
And at the sound it shrunk in haste away,
And vanish'd from our sight.
HAMLET 'Tis very strange.
HORATIO As I do live, my honour'd lord, 'tis true;
And we did think it writ down in our duty
To let you know of it.
HAMLET Indeed, indeed, sirs, but this troubles me.
Hold you the watch to-night?
MARCELLUS / **BERNARDO** We do, my lord.
HAMLET Arm'd, say you?
MARCELLUS / **BERNARDO** Arm'd, my lord.
HAMLET From top to toe?
MARCELLUS / **BERNARDO** My lord, from head to foot.
HAMLET Then saw you not his face?
HORATIO O, yes, my lord; he wore his beaver° up.
HAMLET What, look'd he frowningly?
HORATIO A countenance more
In sorrow than in anger.
HAMLET Pale or red?
HORATIO Nay, very pale.
HAMLET And fix'd his eyes upon you?
HORATIO Most constantly.
HAMLET I would I had been there.
HORATIO It would have much amaz'd you.
HAMLET Very like, very like. Stay'd it long?
HORATIO While one with moderate haste might tell a hundred.
MARCELLUS / **BERNARDO** Longer, longer.
HORATIO Not when I saw't.

---

192 Season your admiration: Restrain your astonishment.
200 cap-a-pe: From head to foot. **203 oppress'd:** Distressed.
204 truncheon: Officer's staff. **distill'd:** Softened, weakened.
205 act: Action.

216 it: Its. **229 beaver:** Visor on the helmet.

HAMLET His beard was grizzled, — no?
HORATIO It was, as I have seen it in his life,
A sable° silver'd.
HAMLET I will watch to-night;
Perchance 'twill walk again.
HORATIO I warr'nt it will.
HAMLET If it assume my noble father's person,
I'll speak to it, though hell itself should gape
And bid me hold my peace. I pray you all,
If you have hitherto conceal'd this sight,
Let it be tenable in your silence still;
And whatsoever else shall hap to-night,
Give it an understanding, but no tongue:
I will requite your loves. So, fare you well:
Upon the platform, 'twixt eleven and twelve,
I'll visit you.
ALL Our duty to your honour.
HAMLET Your loves, as mine to you: farewell.
Exeunt [all but **HAMLET**].
My father's spirit in arms! all is not well;
I doubt° some foul play: would the night were come!
Till then sit still, my soul: foul deeds will rise,
Though all the earth o'erwhelm them, to men's eyes. *Exit.*

[Scene iii: *A room in* **POLONIUS***'s house.*]

Enter **LAERTES** *and* **OPHELIA**, *his sister.*

LAERTES My necessaries are embark'd: farewell:
And, sister, as the winds give benefit
And convoy is assistant,° do not sleep,
But let me hear from you.
OPHELIA Do you doubt that?
LAERTES For Hamlet and the trifling of his favour,
Hold it a fashion° and a toy in blood,°
A violet in the youth of primy° nature,
Forward,° not permanent, sweet, not lasting,
The perfume and suppliance of a minute;°
No more.
OPHELIA No more but so?
LAERTES Think it no more:
For nature, crescent,° does not grow alone
In thews° and bulk, but, as this temple° waxes,
The inward service of the mind and soul
Grows wide withal. Perhaps he loves you now,
And now no soil° nor cautel° doth besmirch
The virtue of his will: but you must fear,
His greatness weigh'd,° his will is not his own;
For he himself is subject to his birth:
He may not, as unvalued persons do,
Carve for himself; for on his choice depends
The safety and health of this whole state;
And therefore must his choice be circumscrib'd
Unto the voice and yielding° of that body
Whereof he is the head. Then if he says he loves you,
It fits your wisdom so far to believe it
As he in his particular act and place
May give his saying deed;° which is no further
Than the main voice of Denmark goes withal.
Then weigh what loss your honour may sustain,
If with too credent° ear you list his songs,
Or lose your heart, or your chaste treasure open
To his unmast'red° importunity.
Fear it, Ophelia, fear it, my dear sister,
And keep you in the rear of your affection,
Out of the shot and danger of desire.
The chariest° maid is prodigal enough,
If she unmask her beauty to the moon:
Virtue itself 'scapes not calumnious strokes:
The canker galls the infants of the spring,°

---

239 sable: Black color. **254 doubt:** Fear. **Scene iii. 3 convoy is assistant:** Means of conveyance are available. **6 fashion:** Custom, prevailing usage. **toy in blood:** Passing amorous fancy. **7 primy:** In its prime. **8 Forward:** Precocious.

9 suppliance of a minute: Diversion to fill up a minute. **11 crescent:** Growing, waxing. **12 thews:** Bodily strength; **temple:** Body. **15 soil:** Blemish. **cautel:** Crafty device. **17 greatness weigh'd:** High position considered. **23 voice and yielding:** Assent, approval. **27 deed:** Effect. **30 credent:** Credulous. **32 unmast'red:** Unrestrained. **36 chariest:** Most scrupulously modest. **39 The canker . . . spring:** The cankerworm destroys the young plants of spring.

Too oft before their buttons° be disclos'd,°
And in the morn and liquid dew° of youth
Contagious blastments° are most imminent.
Be wary then; best safety lies in fear:
Youth to itself rebels, though none else near.

OPHELIA I shall the effect of this good lesson keep,
As watchman to my heart. But, good my brother,
Do not, as some ungracious° pastors do,
Show me the steep and thorny way to heaven;
Whiles, like a puff'd° and reckless libertine,
Himself the primrose path of dalliance treads,
And recks° not his own rede.°

Enter **POLONIUS.**

LAERTES O, fear me not.
I stay too long: but here my father comes.
A double° blessing is a double grace;
Occasion° smiles upon a second leave.

POLONIUS Yet here, Laertes? aboard, aboard, for shame!
The wind sits in the shoulder of your sail,
And you are stay'd for. There; my blessing with thee!
And these few precepts° in thy memory
Look thou character.° Give thy thoughts no tongue,
Nor any unproportion'd° thought his act.
Be thou familiar, but by no means vulgar.°
Those friends thou hast, and their adoption tried,
Grapple them to thy soul with hoops of steel;
But do not dull thy palm with entertainment
Of each new-hatch'd, unfledg'd° comrade. Beware
Of entrance to a quarrel, but being in,
Bear't that th' opposed may beware of thee.
Give every man thy ear, but few thy voice;
Take each man's censure, but reserve thy judgement.
Costly thy habit as thy purse can buy,
But not express'd in fancy;° rich, not gaudy;
For the apparel oft proclaims the man,
And they in France of the best rank and station
Are of a most select and generous chief in that.°
Neither a borrower nor a lender be;
For loan oft loses both itself and friend,
And borrowing dulleth edge of husbandry.°
This above all: to thine own self be true,
And it must follow, as the night the day,
Thou canst not then be false to any man.
Farewell: my blessing season° this in thee!

LAERTES Most humbly do I take my leave, my lord.

POLONIUS The time invites you; go; your servants tend.

LAERTES Farewell, Ophelia; and remember well
What I have said to you.

OPHELIA 'Tis in my memory lock'd,
And you yourself shall keep the key of it.

LAERTES Farewell. *Exit* **LAERTES.**

POLONIUS What is 't, Ophelia, he hath said to you?

OPHELIA So please you, something touching the Lord Hamlet.

POLONIUS Marry, well bethought:
'Tis told me, he hath very oft of late
Given private time to you; and you yourself
Have of your audience been most free and bounteous:
If it be so, as so't is put on° me,
And that in way of caution, I must tell you,

---

40 buttons: Buds. **disclos'd:** Opened. **41 liquid dew:** I.e., time when dew is fresh. **42 blastments:** Blights. **47 ungracious:** Graceless. **49 puff'd:** Bloated. **51 recks:** Heeds. **rede:** Counsel. **53 double:** I.e., Laertes has already bade his father good-bye. **54 Occasion:** Opportunity. **58 precepts:** Many parallels have been found to the series of maxims that follow, one of the closer being that in Lyly's *Euphues*. **59 character:** Inscribe. **60 unproportion'd:** Inordinate. **61 vulgar:** Common. **65 unfledg'd:** Immature.

71 express'd in fancy: Fantastical in design. **74 Are . . . that:** *Chief* is usually taken as a substantive meaning "head," "eminence." **77 husbandry:** Thrift. **81 season:** Mature. **94 put on:** Impressed on.

You do not understand yourself so clearly
As it behooves my daughter and your honour.
What is between you? give me up the truth.

OPHELIA He hath, my lord, of late made many tenders°
Of his affection to me.

POLONIUS Affection! pooh! you speak like a green girl,
Unsifted° in such perilous circumstance.
Do you believe his tenders,° as you call them?

OPHELIA I do not know, my lord, what I should think.

POLONIUS Marry, I will teach you: think yourself a baby;
That you have ta'en these tenders° for true pay,
Which are not sterling.° Tender° yourself more dearly;
Or — not to crack the wind° of the poor phrase,
Running it thus — you'll tender me a fool.°

OPHELIA My lord, he hath importun'd me with love
In honourable fashion.

POLONIUS Ay, fashion° you may call it; go to, go to.

OPHELIA And hath given countenance° to his speech, my lord,
With almost all the holy vows of heaven.

POLONIUS Ay, springes° to catch woodcocks.° I do know,
When the blood burns, how prodigal the soul
Lends the tongue vows: these blazes, daughter,
Giving more light than heat, extinct in both,
Even in their promise, as it is a-making,
You must not take for fire. From this time
Be somewhat scanter of your maiden presence;
Set your entreatments° at a higher rate
Than a command to parley.° For Lord Hamlet,
Believe so much in him,° that he is young,
And with a larger tether may he walk
Than may be given you: in few,° Ophelia,
Do not believe his vows; for they are brokers,°
Not of that dye° which their investments° show,
But mere implorators of° unholy suits,
Breathing° like sanctified and pious bawds,
The better to beguile. This is for all:
I would not, in plain terms, from this time forth,
Have you so slander° any moment leisure,
As to give words or talk with the Lord Hamlet.
Look to 't, I charge you: come your ways.

OPHELIA I shall obey, my lord. *Exeunt.*

[Scene iv: *The platform.*]

Enter **HAMLET**, **HORATIO**, *and* **MARCELLUS**.

HAMLET The air bites shrewdly; it is very cold.

HORATIO It is a nipping and an eager air.

HAMLET What hour now?

HORATIO I think it lacks of twelve.

MARCELLUS No, it is struck.

HORATIO Indeed? I heard it not: then it draws near the season
Wherein the spirit held his wont to walk.

A flourish of trumpets, and two pieces go off.

What does this mean, my lord?

HAMLET The king doth wake° to-night and takes his rouse,°
Keeps wassail,° and the swagg'ring up-spring° reels;°

---

99 tenders: Offers. **102 Unsifted:** Untried. **103 tenders:** Offers. **106 tenders:** Promises to pay. **107 sterling:** Legal currency. **Tender:** Hold. **108 crack the wind:** I.e., run it until it is broken-winded. **109 tender . . . fool:** Show me a fool (for a daughter). **112 fashion:** Mere form, pretense. **113 countenance:** Credit, support. **115 springes:** Snares. **woodcocks:** Birds easily caught, type of stupidity.

122 entreatments: Conversations, interviews. **123 command to parley:** Mere invitation to talk. **124 so . . . him:** This much concerning him. **126 in few:** Briefly. **127 brokers:** Go-betweens, procurers. **128 dye:** Color or sort. **investments:** Clothes. **129 implorators of:** Solicitors of. **130 Breathing:** Speaking. **133 slander:** Bring disgrace or reproach upon. **Scene iv. 8 wake:** Stay awake, hold revel. **rouse:** Carouse, drinking bout. **9 wassail:** Carousal. **up-spring:** Last and wildest dance at German merry-makings. **reels:** Reels through.

And, as he drains his draughts of Rhenish°
down,
The kettle-drum and trumpet thus bray out
The triumph of his pledge.°

HORATIO Is it a custom?

HAMLET Ay, marry, is 't:
But to my mind, though I am native here
And to the manner born,° it is a custom
More honour'd in the breach than the
observance.
This heavy-headed revel east and west
Makes us traduc'd and tax'd of other nations:
They clepe° us drunkards, and with swinish
phrase°
Soil our addition;° and indeed it takes
From our achievements, though perform'd at
height,
The pith and marrow of our attribute.°
So, oft it chances in particular men,
That for some vicious mole of nature° in
them,
As, in their birth — wherein they are not
guilty,
Since nature cannot choose his origin —
By the o'ergrowth of some complexion,
Oft breaking down the pales° and forts of
reason,
Or by some habit that too much o'er-leavens°
The form of plausive° manners, that these
men,
Carrying, I say, the stamp of one defect,
Being nature's livery,° or fortune's star,° —
Their virtues else — be they as pure as grace,
As infinite as man may undergo —
Shall in the general censure take corruption
From that particular fault: the dram of eale°
Doth all the noble substance of a doubt
To his own scandal.°

Enter **GHOST**.

HORATIO Look, my lord, it comes!

HAMLET Angels and ministers of grace° defend
us!
Be thou a spirit of health or goblin damn'd,
Bring with thee airs from heaven or blasts
from hell,
Be thy intents wicked or charitable,
Thou com'st in such a questionable° shape
That I will speak to thee: I'll call thee Hamlet,
King, father, royal Dane: O, answer me!
Let me not burst in ignorance; but tell
Why thy canoniz'd° bones, hearsed° in death,
Have burst their cerements;° why the
sepulchre,
Wherein we saw thee quietly interr'd,
Hath op'd his ponderous and marble jaws,
To cast thee up again. What may this mean,
That thou, dead corse, again in complete
steel
Revisits thus the glimpses of the moon,°
Making night hideous; and we fools of
nature°
So horridly to shake our disposition
With thoughts beyond the reaches of our
souls?
Say, why is this? wherefore? what should we
do?

[**GHOST**] *beckons* [**HAMLET**].

HORATIO It beckons you to go away with it,
As if it some impartment° did desire
To you alone.

---

10 Rhenish: Rhine wine. **12 triumph . . . pledge:** His glorious achievement as a drinker. **15 to . . . born:** Destined by birth to be subject to the custom in question. **19 clepe:** Call. **with swinish phrase:** By calling us swine. **20 addition:** Reputation. **22 attribute:** Reputation. **24 mole of nature:** Natural blemish in one's constitution. **28 pales:** Palings (as of a fortification). **29 o'er-leavens:** Induces a change throughout (as yeast works in bread). **30 plausive:** Pleasing. **32 nature's livery:** Endowment from nature. **fortune's star:** The position in which one is placed by fortune, a reference to astrology. The two phrases are aspects of the same thing.

36–38 the dram . . . scandal: A famous crux: *dram of eale* has had various interpretations, the preferred one being probably "a dram of evil." **39 ministers of grace:** Messengers of God. **43 questionable:** Inviting question or conversation. **47 canoniz'd:** Buried according to the canons of the church. **hearsed:** Coffined. **48 cerements:** Grave-clothes. **53 glimpses of the moon:** The earth by night. **54 fools of nature:** Mere men, limited to natural knowledge. **59 impartment:** Communication.

MARCELLUS Look, with what courteous action
It waves you to a more removed° ground:
But do not go with it.
HORATIO No, by no means.
HAMLET It will not speak; then I will follow it.
HORATIO Do not, my lord!
HAMLET Why, what should be the fear?
I do not set my life at a pin's fee;
And for my soul, what can it do to that,
Being a thing immortal as itself?
It waves me forth again: I'll follow it.
HORATIO What if it tempt you toward the flood, my lord,
Or to the dreadful summit of the cliff
That beetles o'er° his base into the sea,
And there assume some other horrible form,
Which might deprive your sovereignty of reason°
And draw you into madness? think of it:
The very place puts toys of desperation,°
Without more motive, into every brain
That looks so many fathoms to the sea
And hears it roar beneath.
HAMLET It waves me still.
Go on; I'll follow thee.
MARCELLUS You shall not go, my lord.
HAMLET Hold off your hands!
HORATIO Be rul'd; you shall not go.
HAMLET My fate cries out,
And makes each petty artere° in this body
As hardy as the Nemean lion's° nerve.°
Still am I call'd. Unhand me, gentlemen.

61 removed: Remote. **71 beetles o'er:** Overhangs threateningly. **73 deprive . . . reason:** Take away the sovereignty of your reason. It was thought that evil spirits would sometimes assume the form of departed spirits in order to work madness in a human creature. **75 toys of desperation:** Freakish notions of suicide. **82 artere:** Artery. **83 Nemean lion's:** The Nemean lion was one of the monsters slain by Hercules. **nerve:** Sinew, tendon. The point is that the arteries which were carrying the spirits out into the body were functioning and were as stiff and hard as the sinews of the lion.

By heaven, I'll make a ghost of him that lets° me!
I say, away! Go on; I'll follow thee.
Exeunt **GHOST** *and* **HAMLET**.
HORATIO He waxes desperate with imagination.
MARCELLUS Let's follow; 'tis not fit thus to obey him.
HORATIO Have after. To what issue° will this come?
MARCELLUS Something is rotten in the state of Denmark.
HORATIO Heaven will direct it.°
MARCELLUS Nay, let's follow him. *Exeunt.*

[Scene v: *Another part of the platform.*]

Enter **GHOST** *and* **HAMLET**.

HAMLET Whither wilt thou lead me? speak; I'll go no further.
GHOST Mark me.
HAMLET I will.
GHOST My hour is almost come,
When I to sulphurous and tormenting flames
Must render up myself.
HAMLET Alas, poor ghost!
GHOST Pity me not, but lend thy serious hearing
To what I shall unfold.
HAMLET Speak; I am bound to hear.
GHOST So art thou to revenge, when thou shalt hear.
HAMLET What?
GHOST I am thy father's spirit,
Doom'd for a certain term to walk the night,
And for the day confin'd to fast° in fires,
Till the foul crimes done in my days of nature
Are burnt and purg'd away. But that I am forbid
To tell the secrets of my prison-house,

85 lets: Hinders. **89 issue:** Outcome. **91 it:** I.e., the outcome. **Scene v. 11 fast:** Probably, do without food. It has been sometimes taken in the sense of doing general penance.

I could a tale unfold whose lightest word
Would harrow up thy soul, freeze thy young blood,
Make thy two eyes, like stars, start from their spheres,°
Thy knotted° and combined° locks to part
And each particular hair to stand an end,
Like quills upon the fretful porpentine:°
But this eternal blazon° must not be
To ears of flesh and blood. List, list, O, list!
If thou didst ever thy dear father love —

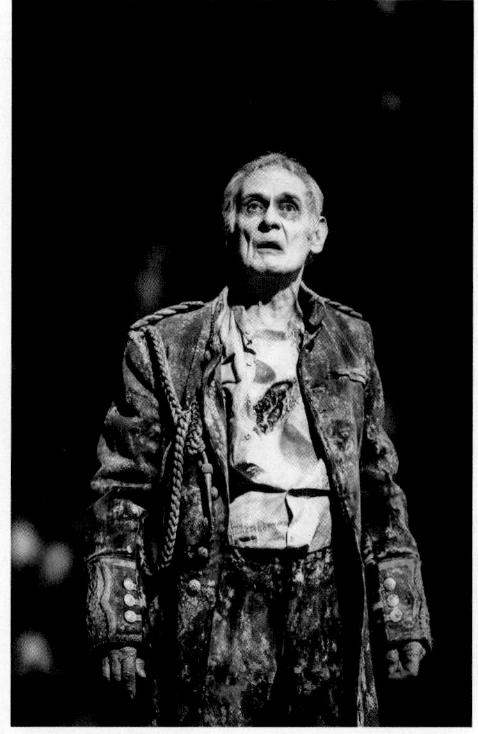

In this image, from a 2015 stage production of Hamlet, actor Karl Johnson plays the ghost of King Hamlet. **How do the wardrobe and makeup choices presented here characterize the ghost? Why do you think he is portrayed in this way?**

17 spheres: Orbits. **18 knotted:** Perhaps intricately arranged. **combined:** Tied, bound. **20 porpentine:** Porcupine. **21 eternal blazon:** Promulgation or proclamation of eternity, revelation of the hereafter.

HAMLET O God!
GHOST Revenge his foul and most unnatural° murder.
HAMLET Murder!
GHOST Murder most foul, as in the best it is;
But this most foul, strange and unnatural.
HAMLET Haste me to know't, that I, with wings as swift
As meditation or the thoughts of love,
May sweep to my revenge.
GHOST I find thee apt;
And duller shouldst thou be than the fat weed°
That roots itself in ease on Lethe wharf,°
Wouldst thou not stir in this. Now, Hamlet, hear:
'Tis given out that, sleeping in my orchard,
A serpent stung me; so the whole ear of Denmark
Is by a forged process of my death
Rankly abus'd: but know, thou noble youth,
The serpent that did sting thy father's life
Now wears his crown.
HAMLET O my prophetic soul!
My uncle!
GHOST Ay, that incestuous, that adulterate° beast,
With witchcraft of his wit, with traitorous gifts, —
O wicked wit and gifts, that have the power
So to seduce! — won to his shameful lust
The will of my most seeming-virtuous queen:
O Hamlet, what a falling-off was there!
From me, whose love was of that dignity
That it went hand in hand even with the vow
I made to her in marriage, and to decline
Upon a wretch whose natural gifts were poor
To those of mine!
But virtue, as it never will be moved,
Though lewdness court it in a shape of heaven,

25 unnatural: I.e., pertaining to fratricide. **32 fat weed:** Many suggestions have been offered as to the particular plant intended, including asphodel; probably a general figure for plants growing along rotting wharves and piles. **33 Lethe wharf:** Bank of the river of forgetfulness in Hades. **42 adulterate:** Adulterous.

So lust, though to a radiant angel link'd,
Will sate itself in a celestial bed,
And prey on garbage.
But, soft! methinks I scent the morning air;
Brief let me be. Sleeping within my orchard,
My custom always of the afternoon,
Upon my secure° hour thy uncle stole,
With juice of cursed hebona° in a vial,
And in the porches of my ears did pour
The leperous° distilment; whose effect
Holds such an enmity with blood of man
That swift as quicksilver it courses through
The natural gates and alleys of the body,
And with a sudden vigour it doth posset°
And curd, like eager° droppings into milk,
The thin and wholesome blood: so did it mine;
And a most instant tetter bark'd about,
Most lazar-like,° with vile and loathsome crust,
All my smooth body.
Thus was I, sleeping, by a brother's hand
Of life, of crown, of queen, at once dispatch'd:°
Cut off even in the blossoms of my sin,
Unhous'led,° disappointed,° unanel'd,°
No reck'ning made, but sent to my account
With all my imperfections on my head:
O, horrible! O, horrible! most horrible!°
If thou hast nature in thee, bear it not;
Let not the royal bed of Denmark be
A couch for luxury° and damned incest.
But, howsomever thou pursues this act,
Taint not thy mind,° nor let thy soul contrive
Against thy mother aught: leave her to heaven
And to those thorns that in her bosom lodge,
To prick and sting her. Fare thee well at once!
The glow-worm shows the matin° to be near,
And 'gins to pale his uneffectual fire:°
Adieu, adieu, adieu! remember me. [*Exit.*]

HAMLET O all you host of heaven! O earth! what else?
And shall I couple° hell? O, fie! Hold, hold, my heart;
And you, my sinews, grow not instant old,
But bear me stiffly up. Remember thee!
Ay, thou poor ghost, whiles memory holds a seat
In this distracted globe.° Remember thee!
Yea, from the table of my memory
I'll wipe away all trivial fond records,
All saws° of books, all forms, all pressures° past,
That youth and observation copied there;
And thy commandment all alone shall live
Within the book and volume of my brain,
Unmix'd with baser matter: yes, by heaven!
O most pernicious woman!
O villain, villain, smiling, damned villain!
My tables,°—meet it is I set it down,
That one may smile, and smile, and be a villain;
At least I am sure it may be so in Denmark:
[*Writing.*]
So, uncle, there you are. Now to my word;°
It is "Adieu, adieu! remember me,"
I have sworn't.

Enter **HORATIO** *and* **MARCELLUS.**

HORATIO My lord, my lord—

MARCELLUS Lord Hamlet,—

HORATIO Heavens secure him!

HAMLET So be it!

MARCELLUS Hillo, ho, ho,° my lord!

HAMLET Hillo, ho, ho, boy! come, bird, come.

MARCELLUS How is't, my noble lord?

61 secure: Confident, unsuspicious. **62 hebona:** Generally supposed to mean "henbane," conjectured *hemlock; ebenus,* meaning "yew." **64 leperous:** Causing leprosy. **68 posset:** Coagulate, curdle. **69 eager:** Sour, acid. **72 lazar-like:** Leperlike. **75 dispatch'd:** Suddenly bereft. **77 Unhous'led:** Without having received the sacrament. **disappointed:** Unready, without equipment for the last journey. **unanel'd:** Without having received extreme unction. **80 O . . . horrible:** Many editors give this line to Hamlet; Garrick and Sir Henry Irving spoke it in that part. **83 luxury:** Lechery. **85 Taint . . . mind:** Probably, deprave not thy character, do nothing except in the pursuit of a natural revenge.

89 matin: Morning. **90 uneffectual fire:** Cold light. **93 couple:** Add. **97 distracted globe:** Confused head. **100 saws:** Wise sayings. **pressures:** Impressions stamped. **107 tables:** Probably a small portable writing-tablet carried at the belt. **110 word:** Watchword. **115 Hillo, ho, ho:** A falconer's call to a hawk in air.

HORATIO What news, my lord?
HAMLET O, wonderful!
HORATIO Good my lord, tell it.
HAMLET No; you will reveal it.
HORATIO Not I, my lord, by heaven.
MARCELLUS Nor I, my lord.
HAMLET How say you, then; would heart of man once think it?
But you'll be secret?
HORATIO } **MARCELLUS** } Ay, by heaven, my lord.
HAMLET There's ne'er a villain dwelling in all Denmark
But he's an arrant° knave.
HORATIO There needs no ghost, my lord, come from the grave
To tell us this.
HAMLET Why, right; you are in the right;
And so, without more circumstance at all,
I hold it fit that we shake hands and part:
You, as your business and desire shall point you;
For every man has business and desire,
Such as it is; and for my own poor part,
Look you, I'll go pray.
HORATIO These are but wild and whirling words, my lord.
HAMLET I am sorry they offend you, heartily;
Yes, 'faith, heartily.
HORATIO There's no offence, my lord.
HAMLET Yes, by Saint Patrick,° but there is, Horatio,
And much offence too. Touching this vision here,
It is an honest° ghost, that let me tell you:
For your desire to know what is between us,
O'ermaster 't as you may. And now, good friends,
As you are friends, scholars and soldiers,
Give me one poor request.
HORATIO What is 't, my lord? we will.
HAMLET Never make known what you have seen to-night.
HORATIO } **MARCELLUS** } My lord, we will not.
HAMLET Nay, but swear 't.
HORATIO In faith,
My lord, not I.
MARCELLUS Nor I, my lord, in faith.
HAMLET Upon my sword.°
MARCELLUS We have sworn, my lord, already.
HAMLET Indeed, upon my sword, indeed.

GHOST *cries under the stage.*

GHOST Swear.
HAMLET Ah, ha, boy! say'st thou so? art thou there, truepenny?°
Come on — you hear this fellow in the cellarage —
Consent to swear.
HORATIO Propose the oath, my lord.
HAMLET Never to speak of this that you have seen,
Swear by my sword.
GHOST [*beneath*]: Swear.
HAMLET Hic et ubique?° then we'll shift our ground.
Come hither, gentlemen,
And lay your hands again upon my sword:
Swear by my sword,
Never to speak of this that you have heard.
GHOST [*beneath*]: Swear by his sword.
HAMLET Well said, old mole! canst work i' th' earth so fast?
A worthy pioner!° Once more remove, good friends.
HORATIO O day and night, but this is wondrous strange!

---

124 arrant: Thoroughgoing. **136 Saint Patrick:** St. Patrick was keeper of Purgatory and patron saint of all blunders and confusion. **138 honest:** I.e., a real ghost and not an evil spirit.

147 sword: I.e., the hilt in the form of a cross. **150 truepenny:** Good old boy, or the like. **156 Hic et ubique?:** Here and everywhere? **163 pioner:** Digger, miner.

HAMLET And therefore as a stranger give it
welcome.
There are more things in heaven and earth,
Horatio,
Than are dreamt of in your philosophy.
But come;
Here, as before, never, so help you mercy,
How strange or odd soe'er I bear myself,
As I perchance hereafter shall think meet
To put an antic° disposition on,
That you, at such times seeing me, never shall,
With arms encumb'red° thus, or this
head-shake,
Or by pronouncing of some doubtful
phrase,
As "Well, well, we know," or "We could, an if
we would,"
Or "If we list to speak," or "There be, an if they
might,"
Or such ambiguous giving out,° to note°
That you know aught of me: this not to do,
So grace and mercy at your most need help
you,
Swear.

GHOST [*beneath*]: Swear.

HAMLET Rest, rest, perturbed spirit! [*They
swear.*] So, gentlemen,
With all my love I do commend me to you:
And what so poor a man as Hamlet is
May do, t' express his love and friending° to
you,
God willing, shall not lack. Let us go in
together;
And still your fingers on your lips, I pray.
The time is out of joint: O cursed spite,
That ever I was born to set it right!
Nay, come, let's go together. *Exeunt.*

ACT II

[Scene i: *A room in* POLONIUS*'s house.*]

Enter old **POLONIUS** *with his man* [**REYNALDO**].

POLONIUS Give him this money and these
notes, Reynaldo.

REYNALDO I will, my lord.

POLONIUS You shall do marvellous wisely, good
Reynaldo,

INDIVISION CHARMET/Private Collection/Bridgeman Images

This 1884 watercolor was made for the set design of act I in a French production of Hamlet. **How is the setting portrayed here? How do the set designer's choices reflect the meaning of the events that have taken place thus far?**

172 antic: Fantastic. **174 encumb'red:** Folded or entwined.
178 giving out: Profession of knowledge. **to note:** To give a sign.

186 friending: Friendliness.

Before you visit him, to make inquire
Of his behaviour.

REYNALDO My lord, I did intend it.

POLONIUS Marry, well said; very well said. Look you, sir,
Inquire me first what Danskers° are in Paris;
And how, and who, what means, and where they keep,°
What company, at what expense; and finding
By this encompassment° and drift° of question
That they do know my son, come you more nearer
Than your particular demands will touch it:°
Take° you as 'twere, some distant knowledge of him;
As thus, "I know his father and his friends,
And in part him": do you mark this, Reynaldo?

REYNALDO Ay, very well, my lord.

POLONIUS "And in part him; but" you may say "not well:
But, if 't be he I mean, he's very wild;
Addicted so and so": and there put on° him
What forgeries° you please; marry, none so rank
As may dishonour him; take heed of that;
But, sir, such wanton,° wild and usual slips
As are companions noted and most known
To youth and liberty.

REYNALDO As gaming, my lord.

POLONIUS Ay, or drinking, fencing,° swearing, quarrelling,
Drabbing;° you may go so far.

REYNALDO My lord, that would dishonour him.

POLONIUS 'Faith, no; as you may season it in the charge.
You must not put another scandal on him,
That he is open to incontinency;°
That's not my meaning: but breathe his faults so quaintly°
That they may seem the taints of liberty,°
The flash and outbreak of a fiery mind,
A savageness in unreclaimed° blood,
Of general assault.°

REYNALDO But, my good lord,—

POLONIUS Wherefore should you do this?

REYNALDO Ay, my lord,
I would know that.

POLONIUS Marry, sir, here's my drift;
And, I believe, it is a fetch of wit:°
You laying these slight sullies on my son,
As 'twere a thing a little soil'd i' th' working,
Mark you,
Your party in converse, him you would sound,
Having ever° seen in the prenominate° crimes
The youth you breathe of guilty, be assur'd
He closes with you in this consequence;°
"Good sir," or so, or "friend," or "gentleman,"
According to the phrase or the addition
Of man and country.

REYNALDO Very good, my lord.

POLONIUS And then, sir, does 'a this—'a does—what was I about to say? By the mass, I was about to say something: where did I leave?

REYNALDO At "closes in the consequence," at "friend or so," and "gentleman."

POLONIUS At "closes in the consequence," ay, marry;
He closes thus: "I know the gentleman;
I saw him yesterday, or t' other day,

Act II, Scene i. **7 Danskers:** Danske was a common variant for "Denmark"; hence "Dane." **8 keep:** Dwell. **10 encompassment:** Roundabout talking. **drift:** Gradual approach or course. **11–12 come . . . it:** I.e., you will find out more this way than by asking pointed questions. **13 Take:** Assume, pretend. **19 put on:** Impute to. **20 forgeries:** Invented tales. **22 wanton:** Sportive, unrestrained. **25 fencing:** Indicative of the ill repute of professional fencers and fencing schools in Elizabethan times. **26 Drabbing:** Associating with immoral women.

30 incontinency: Habitual loose behavior. **31 quaintly:** Delicately, ingeniously. **32 taints of liberty:** Blemishes due to freedom. **34 unreclaimed:** Untamed. **35 general assault:** Tendency that assails all untrained youth. **38 fetch of wit:** Clever trick. **43 ever:** At any time. **prenominate:** Before-mentioned. **45 closes . . . consequence:** Agrees with you in this conclusion.

Or then, or then; with such, or such; and, as you say,
There was 'a gaming; there o'ertook in 's rouse;°
There falling out at tennis": or perchance,
"I saw him enter such a house of sale,"
Videlicet,° a brothel, or so forth.
See you now;
Your bait of falsehood takes this carp of truth:
And thus do we of wisdom and of reach,°
With windlasses° and with assays of bias,°
By indirections° find directions° out:
So by my former lecture° and advice,
Shall you my son. You have me, have you not?

REYNALDO My lord, I have.

POLONIUS God bye ye;° fare ye well.

REYNALDO Good my lord!

POLONIUS Observe his inclination in yourself.°

REYNALDO I shall, my lord.

POLONIUS And let him ply his music.°

REYNALDO Well, my lord.

POLONIUS Farewell! *Exit* **REYNALDO.**

Enter **OPHELIA.**

How now, Ophelia! what's the matter?

OPHELIA O, my lord, my lord, I have been so affrighted!

POLONIUS With what, i' th' name of God?

OPHELIA My lord, as I was sewing in my closet,°
Lord Hamlet, with his doublet° all unbrac'd;°
No hat upon his head; his stockings foul'd,
Ungart'red, and down-gyved° to his ankle;
Pale as his shirt; his knees knocking each other;
And with a look so piteous in purport
As if he had been loosed out of hell
To speak of horrors, — he comes before me.

POLONIUS Mad for thy love?

OPHELIA My lord, I do not know;
But truly, I do fear it.

POLONIUS What said he?

OPHELIA He took me by the wrist and held me hard;
Then goes he to the length of all his arm;
And, with his other hand thus o'er his brow,
He falls to such perusal of my face
As 'a would draw it. Long stay'd he so;
At last, a little shaking of mine arm
And thrice his head thus waving up and down,
He rais'd a sigh so piteous and profound
As it did seem to shatter all his bulk°
And end his being: that done, he lets me go:
And, with his head over his shoulder turn'd,
He seem'd to find his way without his eyes;
For out o' doors he went without their helps,
And, to the last, bended their light on me.

POLONIUS Come, go with me: I will go seek the king.
This is the very ecstasy of love,
Whose violent property° fordoes° itself
And leads the will to desperate undertakings
As oft as any passion under heaven
That does afflict our natures. I am sorry.
What, have you given him any hard words of late?

OPHELIA No, my good lord, but, as you did command,
I did repel his letters and denied
His access to me.

POLONIUS That hath made him mad.
I am sorry that with better heed and judgement

---

59 o'ertook in 's rouse: Overcome by drink. **62 Videlicet:** Namely. **65 reach:** Capacity, ability. **66 windlasses:** I.e., circuitous paths. **assays of bias:** Attempts that resemble the course of the bowl, which, being weighted on one side, has a curving motion. **67 indirections:** Devious courses. **directions:** Straight courses, i.e., the truth. **68 lecture:** Admonition. **70 bye ye:** Be with you. **72 Observe . . . yourself:** In your own person, not by spies; or conform your own conduct to his inclination; or test him by studying yourself. **74 ply his music:** Probably to be taken literally. **78 closet:** Private chamber. **79 doublet:** Close-fitting coat. **unbrac'd:** Unfastened.

81 down-gyved: Fallen to the ankles (like gyves or fetters). **96 bulk:** Body. **104 property:** Nature. **fordoes:** Destroys.

I had not quoted° him: I fear'd he did but trifle,
And meant to wrack thee; but, beshrew my jealousy!°
By heaven, it is as proper to our age
To cast beyond° ourselves in our opinions
As it is common for the younger sort
To lack discretion. Come, go we to the king:
This must be known; which, being kept close, might move
More grief to hide than hate to utter love.°
Come. *Exeunt.*

[Scene ii: *A room in the castle.*]

Flourish. Enter **KING** *and* **QUEEN, ROSENCRANTZ,** *and* **GUILDENSTERN** [*with others*].

KING Welcome, dear Rosencrantz and Guildenstern!
Moreover that° we much did long to see you,
The need we have to use you did provoke
Our hasty sending. Something have you heard
Of Hamlet's transformation; so call it,
Sith° nor th' exterior nor the inward man
Resembles that it was. What it should be,
More than his father's death, that thus hath put him
So much from th' understanding of himself,
I cannot dream of: I entreat you both,
That, being of so young days° brought up with him,
And sith so neighbour'd to his youth and haviour,
That you vouchsafe your rest° here in our court
Some little time: so by your companies
To draw him on to pleasures, and to gather,
So much as from occasion you may glean,
Whether aught, to us unknown, afflicts him thus,
That, open'd, lies within our remedy.

QUEEN Good gentlemen, he hath much talk'd of you;
And sure I am two men there are not living
To whom he more adheres. If it will please you
To show us so much gentry° and good will
As to expend your time with us awhile,
For the supply and profit° of our hope,
Your visitation shall receive such thanks
As fits a king's remembrance.

ROSENCRANTZ Both your majesties
Might, by the sovereign power you have of us,
Put your dread pleasures more into command
Than to entreaty.

GUILDENSTERN But we both obey,
And here give up ourselves, in the full bent°
To lay our service freely at your feet,
To be commanded.

KING Thanks, Rosencrantz and gentle Guildenstern.

QUEEN Thanks, Guildenstern and gentle Rosencrantz:
And I beseech you instantly to visit
My too much changed son. Go, some of you,
And bring these gentlemen where Hamlet is.

GUILDENSTERN Heavens make our presence and our practices
Pleasant and helpful to him!

QUEEN Ay, amen!

Exeunt **ROSENCRANTZ** *and* **GUILDENSTERN** [*with some* **ATTENDANTS**].

Enter **POLONIUS.**

---

113 quoted: Observed. **111 beshrew my jealousy:** Curse my suspicions. **116 cast beyond:** Overshoot, miscalculate. **119–120 might . . . love:** I.e., I might cause more grief to others by hiding the knowledge of Hamlet's love to Ophelia than hatred to me and mine by telling of it. **Scene ii. 2 Moreover that:** Besides the fact that. **6 Sith:** Since. **11 of . . . days:** From such early youth. **13 vouchsafe your rest:** Please to stay.

22 gentry: Courtesy. **24 supply and profit:** Aid and successful outcome. **30 in . . . bent:** To the utmost degree of our mental capacity.

POLONIUS Th' ambassadors from Norway, my good lord,
Are joyfully return'd.
KING Thou still hast been the father of good news.
POLONIUS Have I, my lord? I assure my good liege,
I hold my duty, as I hold my soul,
Both to my God and to my gracious king:
And I do think, or else this brain of mine
Hunts not the trail of policy so sure
As it hath us'd to do, that I have found
The very cause of Hamlet's lunacy.
KING O, speak of that; that do I long to hear.
POLONIUS Give first admittance to th' ambassadors;
My news shall be the fruit to that great feast.
KING Thyself do grace to them, and bring them in. [*Exit* **POLONIUS**.]
He tells me, my dear Gertrude, he hath found
The head and source of all your son's distemper.
QUEEN I doubt° it is no other but the main;°
His father's death, and our o'erhasty marriage.
KING Well, we shall sift him.

Enter **AMBASSADORS** [**VOLTIMAND** *and* **CORNELIUS**, *with* **POLONIUS**].

Welcome, my good friends!
Say, Voltimand, what from our brother Norway?
VOLTIMAND Most fair return of greetings and desires.
Upon our first, he sent out to suppress
His nephew's levies; which to him appear'd
To be a preparation 'gainst the Polack;
But, better look'd into, he truly found
It was against your highness: whereat griev'd,
That so his sickness, age and impotence
Was falsely borne in hand,° sends out arrests
On Fortinbras; which he, in brief, obeys;
Receives rebuke from Norway, and in fine°
Makes vow before his uncle never more
To give th' assay° of arms against your majesty.
Whereon old Norway, overcome with joy,
Gives him three score thousand crowns in annual fee,
And his commission to employ those soldiers,
So levied as before, against the Polack:
With an entreaty, herein further shown, [*Giving a paper.*]
That it might please you to give quiet pass
Through your dominions for this enterprise,
On such regards of safety and allowance°
As therein are set down.
KING It likes° us well;
And at our more consider'd° time we'll read,
Answer, and think upon this business.
Meantime we thank you for your well-took labour:
Go to your rest; at night we'll feast together:
Most welcome home!

Exeunt **AMBASSADORS**.

POLONIUS This business is well ended.
My liege, and madam, to expostulate
What majesty should be, what duty is,
Why day is day, night night, and time is time,
Were nothing but to waste night, day and time.
Therefore, since brevity is the soul of wit,°
And tediousness the limbs and outward flourishes,°
I will be brief: your noble son is mad:
Mad call I it; for, to define true madness,
What is 't but to be nothing else but mad?
But let that go.

---

56 doubt: Fear. **main:** Chief point, principal concern.

67 borne in hand: Deluded. **69 in fine:** In the end. **71 assay:** Assault, trial (of arms). **79 safety and allowance:** Pledges of safety to the country and terms of permission for the troops to pass. **80 likes:** Pleases. **81 consider'd:** Suitable for deliberation. **90 wit:** Sound sense or judgment. **91 flourishes:** Ostentation, embellishments.

QUEEN More matter, with less art.
POLONIUS Madam, I swear I use no art at all.
That he is mad, 'tis true: 'tis true 'tis pity;
And pity 'tis 'tis true: a foolish figure;°
But farewell it, for I will use no art.
Mad let us grant him, then: and now remains
That we find out the cause of this effect,
Or rather say, the cause of this defect,
For this effect defective comes by cause:
Thus it remains, and the remainder thus.
Perpend.°
I have a daughter — have while she is mine —
Who, in her duty and obedience, mark,
Hath given me this: now gather, and surmise.
[*Reads the letter.*] "To the celestial and my soul's idol, the most beautified Ophelia," —
That's an ill phrase, a vile phrase; "beautified" is a vile phrase: but you shall hear.
Thus: [*Reads.*]
"In her excellent white bosom, these, & c."
QUEEN Came this from Hamlet to her?
POLONIUS Good madam, stay awhile; I will be faithful. [*Reads.*]
"Doubt thou the stars are fire;
Doubt that the sun doth move;
Doubt truth to be a liar;
But never doubt I love.
"O dear Ophelia, I am ill at these numbers;° I have not art to reckon° my groans: but that I love thee best, O most best, believe it. Adieu.
"Thine evermore, most dear lady, whilst this machine° is to him,
HAMLET."
This, in obedience, hath my daughter shown me,
And more above,° hath his solicitings,
As they fell out° by time, by means° and place,
All given to mine ear.
KING But how hath she
Receiv'd his love?
POLONIUS What do you think of me?
KING As of a man faithful and honourable.
POLONIUS I would fain prove so. But what might you think,
When I had seen this hot love on the wing —
As I perceiv'd it, I must tell you that,
Before my daughter told me — what might you,
Or my dear majesty your queen here, think,
If I had play'd the desk or table-book,°
Or given my heart a winking,° mute and dumb,
Or look'd upon this love with idle sight;
What might you think? No, I went round to work,
And my young mistress thus I did bespeak:°
"Lord Hamlet is a prince, out of thy star;°
This must not be": and then I prescripts gave her,
That she should lock herself from his resort,
Admit no messengers, receive no tokens.
Which done, she took the fruits of my advice;
And he, repelled — a short tale to make —
Fell into a sadness, then into a fast,
Thence to a watch,° thence into a weakness,
Thence to a lightness,° and, by this declension,°
Into the madness wherein now he raves,
And all we mourn for.
KING Do you think 'tis this?
QUEEN It may be, very like.
POLONIUS Hath there been such a time — I would fain know that —
That I have positively said "'Tis so,"
When it prov'd otherwise?
KING Not that I know.

---

98 figure: Figure of speech. **105 Perpend:** Consider. **121 ill . . . numbers:** Unskilled at writing verses. **122 reckon:** Number metrically, scan. **125 machine:** Bodily frame. **127 more above:** Moreover. **128 fell out:** Occurred. **means:** Opportunities (of access).

138 play'd . . . table-book: I.e., remained shut up, concealed this information. **139 given . . . winking:** Given my heart a signal to keep silent. **142 bespeak:** Address. **143 out . . . star:** Above thee in position. **150 watch:** State of sleeplessness. **151 lightness:** Lightheadedness. **declension:** Decline, deterioration.

POLONIUS [*pointing to his head and shoulder*]: Take this from this, if this be otherwise:
If circumstances lead me, I will find
Where truth is hid, though it were hid indeed
Within the centre.°

KING How may we try it further?

POLONIUS You know, sometimes he walks four hours together
Here in the lobby.

QUEEN So he does indeed.

POLONIUS At such a time I'll loose my daughter to him:
Be you and I behind an arras° then;
Mark the encounter: if he love her not
And be not from his reason fall'n thereon,°
Let me be no assistant for a state,
But keep a farm and carters.

KING We will try it.

Enter **HAMLET** [*reading on a book*].

QUEEN But, look, where sadly the poor wretch comes reading.

POLONIUS Away, I do beseech you both, away:

Exeunt **KING** *and* **QUEEN** [*with* **ATTENDANTS**].

I'll board° him presently. O, give me leave.
How does my good Lord Hamlet?

HAMLET Well, God-a-mercy.

POLONIUS Do you know me, my lord?

HAMLET Excellent well; you are a fishmonger.°

POLONIUS Not I, my lord.

HAMLET Then I would you were so honest a man.

POLONIUS Honest, my lord!

HAMLET Ay, sir; to be honest, as this world goes, is to be one man picked out of ten thousand.

POLONIUS That's very true, my lord.

HAMLET For if the sun breed maggots in a dead dog, being a good kissing carrion,°—Have you a daughter?

POLONIUS I have, my lord.

HAMLET Let her not walk i' the sun:° conception° is a blessing: but as your daughter may conceive—Friend, look to 't.

POLONIUS [*aside*]: How say you by° that? Still harping on my daughter: yet he knew me not at first; 'a said I was a fishmonger: 'a is far gone, far gone: and truly in my youth I suffered much extremity for love; very near this. I'll speak to him again. What do you read, my lord?

HAMLET Words, words, words.

POLONIUS What is the matter,° my lord?

HAMLET Between who?°

POLONIUS I mean, the matter that you read, my lord.

HAMLET Slanders, sir: for the satirical rogue says here that old men have grey beards, that their faces are wrinkled, their eyes purging° thick amber and plum-tree gum and that they have a plentiful lack of wit, together with most weak hams: all which, sir, though I most powerfully and potently believe, yet I hold it not honesty° to have it thus set down, for yourself, sir, should be old as I am, if like a crab you could go backward.

POLONIUS [*aside*]: Though this be madness, yet there is method in 't.—Will you walk out of the air, my lord?

HAMLET Into my grave.

POLONIUS Indeed, that's out of the air. [*Aside.*]
How pregnant sometimes his replies

---

163 centre: Middle point of the earth. **167 arras:** Hanging, tapestry. **169 thereon:** On that account. **174 board:** Accost. **178 fishmonger:** An opprobrious expression meaning "bawd," "procurer."

187 good kissing carrion: I.e., a good piece of flesh for kissing (?). **190 i' the sun:** In the sunshine of princely favors. **191 conception:** Quibble on "understanding" and "pregnancy." **193 by:** Concerning. **201 matter:** Substance. **202 Between who:** Hamlet deliberately takes *matter* as meaning "basis of dispute." **207 purging:** discharging. **211 honesty:** Decency.

are! a happiness° that often madness hits on, which reason and sanity could not so prosperously° be delivered of. I will leave him, and suddenly contrive the means of meeting between him and my daughter. — My honourable lord, I will most humbly take my leave of you.

HAMLET You cannot, sir, take from me any thing that I will more willingly part withal: except my life, except my life, except my life.

Enter **GUILDENSTERN** *and* **ROSENCRANTZ**.

POLONIUS Fare you well, my lord.

HAMLET These tedious old fools!

POLONIUS You go to seek the Lord Hamlet; there he is.

ROSENCRANTZ [*to* **POLONIUS**]: God save you, sir! [*Exit* **POLONIUS.**]

GUILDENSTERN My honoured lord!

ROSENCRANTZ My most dear lord!

HAMLET My excellent good friends! How dost thou, Guildenstern? Ah, Rosencrantz! Good lads, how do ye both?

ROSENCRANTZ As the indifferent° children of the earth.

GUILDENSTERN Happy, in that we are not over-happy;
On Fortune's cap we are not the very button.

HAMLET Nor the soles of her shoe?

ROSENCRANTZ Neither, my lord.

HAMLET Then you live about her waist, or in the middle of her favours?

GUILDENSTERN 'Faith, her privates° we.

HAMLET In the secret parts of Fortune? O, most true; she is a strumpet. What's the news?

ROSENCRANTZ None, my lord, but that the world's grown honest.

HAMLET Then is doomsday near: but your news is not true. Let me question more in

This photograph is a still from the 1921 silent movie based on *Hamlet* with Danish actress Asta Nielsen in the title role. In this version, Prince Hamlet is actually a princess, and Polonius and Queen Gertrude — fearing the king's death has left no successor to the throne — hatch a political plot to disguise the princess as a man. To complicate matters, Hamlet falls in love with Horatio, and because Horatio is interested in Ophelia, Hamlet envies her. **What aspects of Hamlet's character does Nielsen evoke here? Why do you think the film's creators chose to alter the plot of the play the way they did?**

---

221 happiness: Felicity of expression. **223 prosperously:** Successfully.

240 indifferent: Ordinary. **247 privates:** I.e., ordinary men (sexual pun on *private parts*).

particular: what have you, my good friends, deserved at the hands of Fortune, that she sends you to prison hither?

GUILDENSTERN Prison, my lord!

HAMLET Denmark's a prison.

ROSENCRANTZ Then is the world one.

HAMLET A goodly one; in which there are many confines,° wards and dungeons, Denmark being one o' the worst.

ROSENCRANTZ We think not so, my lord.

HAMLET Why, then, 'tis none to you; for there is nothing either good or bad, but thinking makes it so: to me it is a prison.

ROSENCRANTZ Why then, your ambition makes it one; 'tis too narrow for your mind.

HAMLET O God, I could be bounded in a nutshell and count myself a king of infinite space, were it not that I have bad dreams.

GUILDENSTERN Which dreams indeed are ambition, for the very substance of the ambitious° is merely the shadow of a dream.

HAMLET A dream itself is but a shadow.

ROSENCRANTZ Truly, and I hold ambition of so airy and light a quality that it is but a shadow's shadow.

HAMLET Then are our beggars bodies, and our monarchs and outstretched heroes the beggars' shadows. Shall we to the court? for, by my fay,° I cannot reason.°

ROSENCRANTZ, **GUILDENSTERn** We'll wait upon° you.

HAMLET No such matter: I will not sort° you with the rest of my servants, for, to speak to you like an honest man, I am most dreadfully attended.° But, in the beaten way of friendship,° what make you at Elsinore?

ROSENCRANTZ To visit you, my lord: no other occasion.

HAMLET Beggar that I am, I am ever poor in thanks; but I thank you: and sure, dear friends, my thanks are too dear a° half-penny. Were you not sent for? Is it your own inclining? Is it a free visitation? Come, come, deal justly with me: come, come; nay, speak.

GUILDENSTERN What should we say, my lord?

HAMLET Why, any thing, but to the purpose. You were sent for; and there is a kind of confession in your looks which your modesties have not craft enough to colour: I know the good king and queen have sent for you.

ROSENCRANTZ To what end, my lord?

HAMLET That you must teach me. But let me conjure° you, by the rights of our fellowship, by the consonancy of our youth,° by the obligation of our ever-preserved love, and by what more dear a better proposer° could charge you withal, be even and direct with me, whether you were sent for, or no?

ROSENCRANTZ [*aside to* **GUILDENSTERN**]: What say you?

HAMLET [*aside*]: Nay, then, I have an eye of you. — If you love me, hold not off.

GUILDENSTERN My lord, we were sent for.

HAMLET I will tell you why; so shall my anticipation prevent your discovery,° and your secrecy to the king and queen moult no feather. I have of late — but wherefore I know not — lost all my mirth, forgone all custom of exercises; and indeed it goes so heavily with my disposition that this goodly frame, the earth, seems to me a sterile promontory, this most excellent

---

262 confines: Places of confinement. **275–276 very . . . ambitious:** That seemingly most substantial thing which the ambitious pursue. **285 fay:** Faith. **reason:** Argue. **286 wait upon:** Accompany. **287 sort:** Class. **290 dreadfully attended:** Poorly provided with servants. **290–291 in the . . . friendship:** As a matter of course among friends.

296 a: I.e., at a. **310 conjure:** Adjure, entreat. **311 consonancy of our youth:** The fact that we are of the same age. **313 better proposer:** One more skillful in finding proposals. **322 prevent your discovery:** Forestall your disclosure.

canopy, the air, look you, this brave o'erhanging firmament, this majestical roof fretted° with golden fire, why, it appeareth nothing to me but a foul and pestilent congregation of vapours. What a piece of work is a man! how noble in reason! how infinite in faculties!° in form and moving how express° and admirable! in action how like an angel! in apprehension° how like a god! the beauty of the world! the paragon of animals! And yet, to me, what is this quintessence° of dust? man delights not me: no, nor woman neither, though by your smiling you seem to say so.

ROSENCRANTZ My lord, there was no such stuff in my thoughts.

HAMLET Why did you laugh then, when I said "man delights not me"?

ROSENCRANTZ To think, my lord, if you delight not in man, what lenten° entertainment the players shall receive from you: we coted° them on the way; and hither are they coming, to offer you service.

HAMLET He that plays the king shall be welcome; his majesty shall have tribute of me; the adventurous knight shall use his foil and target;° the lover shall not sigh gratis; the humorous man° shall end his part in peace; the clown shall make those laugh whose lungs are tickle o' the sere;° and the lady shall say her mind freely, or the blank verse shall halt for 't.° What players are they?

ROSENCRANTZ Even those you were wont to take delight in, the tragedians of the city.

HAMLET How chances it they travel? their residence,° both in reputation and profit, was better both ways.

ROSENCRANTZ I think their inhibition° comes by the means of the late innovation.°

HAMLET Do they hold the same estimation they did when I was in the city? are they so followed?

ROSENCRANTZ No, indeed, are they not.

HAMLET How° comes it? do they grow rusty?

ROSENCRANTZ Nay, their endeavour keeps in the wonted pace: but there is, sir, an aery° of children, little eyases,° that cry out on the top of question,° and are most tyrannically° clapped for 't: these are now the fashion, and so berattle° the common stages° — so they call them — that many wearing rapiers° are afraid of goose-quills° and dare scarce come thither.

HAMLET What, are they children? who maintains 'em? how are they escoted?° Will they pursue the quality° no longer than they can sing?° will they not say afterwards, if they should grow themselves to common° players — as it is most like, if their means are no better — their writers do them wrong, to make them exclaim against their own succession?°

ROSENCRANTZ 'Faith, there has been much to do on both sides; and the nation holds it

---

332 fretted: Adorned. **336 faculties:** Capacity. **337 express:** Well-framed (?), exact (?). **339 apprehension:** Understanding. **342 quintessence:** The fifth essence of ancient philosophy, supposed to be the substance of the heavenly bodies and to be latent in all things. **350 lenten:** Meager. **352 coted:** Overtook and passed beyond. **357 foil and target:** Sword and shield. **358 humorous man:** Actor who takes the part of the humor characters. **360 tickle o' the sere:** Easy on the trigger. **361–362 the lady . . . for 't:** The lady (fond of talking) shall have opportunity to talk, blank verse or no blank verse.

367 residence: Remaining in one place. **369 inhibition:** Formal prohibition (from acting plays in the city or, possibly, at court). **370 innovation:** The new fashion in satirical plays performed by boy actors in the "private" theaters. **375–405 How . . . load:** The passage is the famous one dealing with the War of the Theatres (1599–1602); namely, the rivalry between the children's companies and the adult actors. **377 aery.** Nest. **378 eyases:** Young hawks. **378–379 cry . . . question:** Speak in a high key dominating conversation; clamor forth the height of controversy; probably "excel"; perhaps intended to decry leaders of the dramatic profession. **379–380 tyrannically:** Outrageously. **381 berattle:** Berate. **381–382 common stages:** Public theaters. **382–383 many wearing rapiers:** Many men of fashion, who were afraid to patronize the common players for fear of being satirized by the poets who wrote for the children. **383 goose-quills:** I.e., pens of satirists. **386 escoted:** Maintained. **387 quality:** Acting profession. **387–388 no longer . . . sing:** I.e., until their voices change. **389 common:** Regular, adult. **393 succession:** Future careers.

no sin to tarre° them to controversy: there was, for a while, no money bid for argument,° unless the poet and the player went to cuffs° in the question.°

HAMLET Is't possible?

GUILDENSTERN O, there has been much throwing about of brains.

HAMLET Do the boys carry it away?°

ROSENCRANTZ Ay, that they do, my lord; Hercules and his load° too.

HAMLET It is not very strange; for my uncle is king of Denmark, and those that would make mows° at him while my father lived, give twenty, forty, fifty, a hundred ducats° a-piece for his picture in little.° 'Sblood, there is something in this more than natural, if philosophy could find it out.

A flourish [of trumpets within].

GUILDENSTERN There are the players.

HAMLET Gentlemen, you are welcome to Elsinore. Your hands, come then: the appurtenance of welcome is fashion and ceremony: let me comply° with you in this garb,° lest my extent° to the players, which, I tell you, must show fairly outwards, should more appear like entertainment than yours. You are welcome: but my uncle-father and aunt-mother are deceived.

GUILDENSTERN In what, my dear lord?

HAMLET I am but mad north-north-west:° when the wind is southerly I know a hawk from a handsaw.°

Enter **POLONIUS.**

POLONIUS Well be with you, gentlemen!

HAMLET Hark you, Guildenstern; and you too: at each ear a hearer: that great baby you see there is not yet out of his swaddling-clouts.°

ROSENCRANTZ Happily he is the second time come to them; for they say an old man is twice a child.

HAMLET I will prophesy he comes to tell me of the players; mark it. — You say right, sir: o' Monday morning;° 'twas then indeed.

POLONIUS My lord, I have news to tell you.

HAMLET My lord, I have news to tell you. When Roscius° was an actor in Rome, —

POLONIUS The actors are come hither, my lord.

HAMLET Buz, buz!°

POLONIUS Upon my honour, —

HAMLET Then came each actor on his ass, —

POLONIUS The best actors in the world, either for tragedy, comedy, history, pastoral, pastoral-comical, historical-pastoral, tragical-historical, tragical-comical-historical-pastoral, scene individable,° or poem unlimited:° Seneca° cannot be too heavy, nor Plautus° too light. For the law of writ and the liberty,° these are the only men.

HAMLET O Jephthah, judge of Israel,° what a treasure hadst thou!

POLONIUS What a treasure had he, my lord?

HAMLET Why,

"One fair daughter, and no more,
The which he loved passing well."

---

396 tarre: Set on (as dogs). **398 argument:** Probably, plot for a play. **399 went to cuffs:** Came to blows. **question:** Controversy. **403 carry it away:** Win the day. **405 Hercules . . . load:** Regarded as an allusion to the sign of the Globe Theatre, which was Hercules bearing the world on his shoulder. **408 mows:** Grimaces. **409 ducats:** Gold coins worth 9 shillings and 4 pence. **410 in little:** In miniature. **417 comply:** Observe the formalities of courtesy. **418 garb:** Manner. **extent:** Showing of kindness. **424 I am . . . north-north-west:** I am only partly mad, i.e., in only one point of the compass. **426 handsaw:** A proposed reading of *hernshaw* would mean "heron"; *handsaw* may be an early corruption of *hernshaw*. Another view regards *hawk* as the variant of *hack*, a tool of the pickax type, and *handsaw* as a saw operated by hand.

431 swaddling-clouts: Cloths in which to wrap a newborn baby. **437 o' Monday morning:** Said to mislead Polonius. **440 Roscius:** A famous Roman actor. **442 Buz, buz:** An interjection used at Oxford to denote stale news. **449 scene individable:** A play observing the unity of place. **450 poem unlimited:** A play disregarding the unities of time and place. **Seneca:** Writer of Latin tragedies, model of early Elizabethan writers of tragedy. **451 Plautus:** Writer of Latin comedy. **451–452 law . . . liberty:** Pieces written according to rules and without rules, i.e., "classical" and "romantic" dramas. **454 Jephthah . . . Israel:** Jephthah had to sacrifice his daughter; see Judges II.

POLONIUS [*aside*]: Still on my daughter.

HAMLET Am I not i' the right, old Jephthah?

POLONIUS If you call me Jephthah, my lord, I have a daughter that I love passing° well.

HAMLET Nay, that follows not.

POLONIUS What follows, then, my lord?

HAMLET Why,
"As by lot, God wot,"
and then, you know,
"It came to pass, as most like° it was," — the first row° of the pious chanson° will show you more; for look, where my abridgement comes.°

Enter the **PLAYERS.**

You are welcome, masters; welcome, all. I am glad to see thee well. Welcome, good friends. O, old friend! why, thy face is valanced° since I saw thee last: comest thou to beard me in Denmark? What, my young lady and mistress! By'r lady, your ladyship is nearer to heaven than when I saw you last, by the altitude of a chopine.° Pray God, your voice, like a piece of uncurrent° gold, be not cracked within the ring.° Masters, you are all welcome. We'll e'en to 't like French falconers, fly at any thing we see: we'll have a speech straight: come, give us a taste of your quality; come, a passionate speech.

FIRST PLAYER What speech, my good lord?

HAMLET I heard thee speak me a speech once, but it was never acted; or, if it was, not above once; for the play, I remember, pleased not the million; 'twas caviary to the general:° but it was — as I received it, and others, whose judgements in such matters cried in the top of° mine — an excellent play, well digested in the scenes, set down with as much modesty as cunning.° I remember, one said there were no sallets° in the lines to make the matter savoury, nor no matter in the phrase that might indict° the author of affectation; but called it an honest method, as wholesome as sweet, and by very much more handsome than fine.° One speech in 't I chiefly loved: 'twas Æneas' tale to Dido;° and thereabout of it especially, where he speaks of Priam's slaughter: if it live in your memory, begin at this line: let me see, let me see —
"The rugged Pyrrhus,° like th' Hyrcanian beast,"° —
'tis not so: — it begins with Pyrrhus: —
"The rugged Pyrrhus, he whose sable arms,
Black as his purpose, did the night resemble
When he lay couched in the ominous horse,°
Hath now this dread and black complexion smear'd
With heraldry more dismal; head to foot
Now is he total gules;° horridly trick'd°
With blood of fathers, mothers, daughters, sons,
Bak'd and impasted° with the parching streets,
That lend a tyrannous and a damned light
To their lord's murder: roasted in wrath and fire,

---

463 passing: Surpassingly. **469 like:** Probable. **470 row:** Stanza. **chanson:** Ballad. **472 abridgement comes:** Opportunity comes for cutting short the conversation. **476 valanced:** Fringed (with a beard). **480 chopine:** Kind of shoe raised by the thickness of the heel; worn in Italy, particularly at Venice. **482 uncurrent:** Not passable as lawful coinage. **482–483 cracked within the ring:** In the center of coins were rings enclosing the sovereign's head; if the coin was cracked within this ring, it was unfit for currency. **492–493 caviary to the general:** Not relished by the multitude.

495 cried in the top of: Spoke with greater authority than. **498 cunning:** Skill. **499 sallets:** Salads: here, spicy improprieties. **501 indict:** Convict. **502–504 as wholesome . . . fine:** Its beauty was not that of elaborate ornament, but that of order and proportion. **505 Æneas' tale to Dido:** The lines recited by the player are imitated from Marlowe and Nashe's *Dido Queen of Carthage* (II.i.214 ff.). They are written in such a way that the conventionality of the play within a play is raised above that of ordinary drama. **510 Pyrrhus.** A Greek hero in the Trojan War. **Hyrcanian beast:** The tiger; see Virgil, *Aeneid*, IV.266. **514 ominous horse:** Trojan horse. **517 gules:** Red, a heraldic term. **trick'd:** Spotted, smeared. **519 impasted:** Made into a paste.

And thus o'er-sized° with coagulate gore,
With eyes like carbuncles, the hellish Pyrrhus
Old grandsire Priam seeks."
So, proceed you.

POLONIUS 'Fore God, my lord, well spoken, with good accent and good discretion.

FIRST PLAYER "Anon he finds him
Striking too short at Greeks; his antique sword,
Rebellious to his arm, lies where it falls,
Repugnant° to command: unequal match'd,
Pyrrhus at Priam drives; in rage strikes wide;
But with the whiff and wind of his fell sword
Th' unnerved father falls. Then senseless Ilium,°
Seeming to feel this blow, with flaming top
Stoops to his base, and with a hideous crash
Takes prisoner Pyrrhus' ear: for, lo! his sword
Which was declining on the milky head
Of reverend Priam, seem'd i' th' air to stick:
So, as a painted tyrant,° Pyrrhus stood,
And like a neutral to his will and matter,°
Did nothing.
But, as we often see, against° some storm,
A silence in the heavens, the rack° stand still,
The bold winds speechless and the orb below
As hush as death, anon the dreadful thunder
Doth rend the region,° so, after Pyrrhus' pause,
Aroused vengeance sets him new a-work;
And never did the Cyclops' hammers fall
On Mars's armour forg'd for proof eterne°
With less remorse than Pyrrhus' bleeding sword
Now falls on Priam.
Out, out, thou strumpet, Fortune! All you gods,
In general synod,° take away her power;
Break all the spokes and fellies° from her wheel,
And bowl the round nave° down the hill of heaven,
As low as to the fiends!"

POLONIUS This is too long.

HAMLET It shall to the barber's, with your beard. Prithee, say on: he's for a jig° or a tale of bawdry,° or he sleeps: say on: come to Hecuba.°

FIRST PLAYER "But who, ah woe! had seen the mobled° queen — "

HAMLET "The mobled queen?"

POLONIUS That's good; "mobled queen" is good.

FIRST PLAYER "Run barefoot up and down, threat'ning the flames
With bisson rheum;° a clout° upon that head
Where late the diadem stood, and for a robe,
About her lank and all o'er-teemed° loins,
A blanket, in the alarm of fear caught up;
Who this had seen, with tongue in venom steep'd,
'Gainst Fortune's state would treason have pronounc'd:°
But if the gods themselves did see her then
When she saw Pyrrhus make malicious sport
In mincing with his sword her husband's limbs,
The instant burst of clamour that she made,
Unless things mortal move them not at all,
Would have made milch° the burning eyes of heaven,
And passion in the gods."

POLONIUS Look, whe'r he has not turned° his colour and has tears in 's eyes. Prithee, no more.

---

522 o'er-sized: Covered as with size or glue. **531 Repugnant:** Disobedient. **534 Then senseless Ilium:** Insensate Troy. **540 painted tyrant:** Tyrant in a picture. **541 matter:** Task. **543 against:** Before. **544 rack:** Mass of clouds. **547 region:** Assembly. **550 proof eterne:** External resistance to assault. **554 synod:** Assembly.

555 fellies: Pieces of wood forming the rim of a wheel. **556 nave:** Hub. **560 jig:** Comic performance given at the end or in an interval of a play. **561 bawdry:** Indecency. **562 Hecuba:** Wife of Priam, king of Troy. **563 mobled:** Muffled. **567 bisson rheum:** Blinding tears. **clout:** Piece of cloth. **569 o'er-teemed:** Worn out with bearing children. **572 pronounc'd:** Proclaimed. **578 milch:** Moist with tears. **580 turned:** Changed.

HAMLET 'Tis well; I'll have thee speak out the rest soon. Good my lord, will you see the players well bestowed? Do you hear, let them be well used; for they are the abstract° and brief chronicles of the time: after your death you were better have a bad epitaph than their ill report while you live.

POLONIUS My lord, I will use them according to their desert.

HAMLET God's bodykins,° man, much better: use every man after his desert, and who shall 'scape whipping? Use them after your own honour and dignity: the less they deserve, the more merit is in your bounty. Take them in.

POLONIUS Come, sirs.

HAMLET Follow him, friends: we'll hear a play tomorrow. [*Aside to First Player.*] Dost thou hear me, old friend; can you play the Murder of Gonzago?

FIRST PLAYER Ay, my lord.

HAMLET We'll ha 't to-morrow night. You could, for a need, study a speech of some dozen or sixteen lines,° which I would set down and insert in 't, could you not?

FIRST PLAYER Ay, my lord.

HAMLET Very well. Follow that lord; and look you mock him not. — My good friends, I'll leave you till night: you are welcome to Elsinore.

Exeunt **POLONIUS** *and* **PLAYERS.**

ROSENCRANTZ Good my lord!

Exeunt [**ROSENCRANTZ** *and* **GUILDENSTERN**].

HAMLET Ay, so, God bye to you. — Now I am alone.
O, what a rogue and peasant° slave am I!
Is it not monstrous that this player here,
But in a fiction, in a dream of passion,
Could force his soul so to his own conceit
That from her working all his visage wann'd,°
Tears in his eyes, distraction in 's aspect,
A broken voice, and his whole function suiting
With forms to his conceit?° and all for nothing!
For Hecuba!
What's Hecuba to him, or he to Hecuba,
That he should weep for her? What would he do,
Had he the motive and the cue for passion
That I have? He would drown the stage with tears
And cleave the general ear with horrid speech,
Make mad the guilty and appall the free,
Confound the ignorant, and amaze indeed
The very faculties of eyes and ears.
Yet I,
A dull and muddy-mettled° rascal, peak,°
Like John-a-dreams,° unpregnant of° my cause,
And can say nothing; no, not for a king.
Upon whose property° and most dear life
A damn'd defeat was made. Am I a coward?
Who calls me villain? breaks my pate across?
Plucks off my beard, and blows it in my face?
Tweaks me by the nose? gives me the lie i' th' throat,
As deep as to the lungs? who does me this?
Ha!
'Swounds, I should take it: for it cannot be
But I am pigeon-liver'd° and lack gall
To make oppression bitter, or ere this

---

587 abstract: Summary account. **591 bodykins:** Diminutive form of the oath "by God's body." **604–605 dozen or sixteen lines:** Critics have amused themselves by trying to locate Hamlet's lines. Lucianus's speech III.ii.283–285 is the best guess. **614 peasant:** Base.

618 wann'd: Grew pale. **621 his whole . . . conceit:** His whole being responded with forms to suit his thought. **632 muddy-mettled:** Dull-spirited. **peak:** Mope, pine. **633 John-a-dreams:** An expression occurring elsewhere in Elizabethan literature to indicate a dreamer. **unpregnant of:** Not quickened by. **635 property:** Proprietorship (of crown and life). **643 pigeon-liver'd:** The pigeon was supposed to secrete no gall; if Hamlet, so he says, had had gall, he would have felt the bitterness of oppression, and avenged it.

I should have fatted all the region kites°
With this slave's offal: bloody, bawdy villain!
Remorseless, treacherous, lecherous, kindless° villain!
O, vengeance!
Why, what an ass am I! This is most brave,
That I, the son of a dear father murder'd,
Prompted to my revenge by heaven and hell,
Must, like a whore, unpack my heart with words,
And fall a-cursing, like a very drab,°
A stallion!°
Fie upon 't! foh! About,° my brains! Hum, I have heard
That guilty creatures sitting at a play
Have by the very cunning of the scene
Been struck so to the soul that presently
They have proclaim'd their malefactions;
For murder, though it have no tongue, will speak
With most miraculous organ. I'll have these players
Play something like the murder of my father
Before mine uncle: I'll observe his looks:
I'll tent° him to the quick: if 'a do blench,°
I know my course. The spirit that I have seen
May be the devil:° and the devil hath power
T' assume a pleasing shape; yea, and perhaps
Out of my weakness and my melancholy,
As he is very potent with such spirits,°
Abuses me to damn me: I'll have grounds
More relative° than this:° the play's the thing
Wherein I'll catch the conscience of the king.

Exit.

---

645 region kites: Kites of the air. **647 kindless:** Unnatural. **653 drab:** Prostitute. **654 stallion:** Prostitute (male or female). **655 About:** About it, or turn thou right about. **664 tent:** Probe. **blench:** Quail, flinch. **666 May be the devil:** Hamlet's suspicion is properly grounded in the belief of the time. **669 spirits:** Humors. **671 relative:** Closely related, definite. **this:** I.e., the ghost's story.

ACT III

[Scene i: *A room in the castle.*]

Enter **KING, QUEEN, POLONIUS, OPHELIA, ROSENCRANTZ, GUILDENSTERN, LORDS.**

KING And can you, by no drift of conference,°
Get from him why he puts on this confusion,
Grating so harshly all his days of quiet
With turbulent and dangerous lunacy?

ROSENCRANTZ He does confess he feels himself distracted;
But from what cause 'a will by no means speak.

GUILDENSTERN Nor do we find him forward° to be sounded,
But, with a crafty madness, keeps aloof,
When we would bring him on to some confession
Of his true state.

QUEEN Did he receive you well?

ROSENCRANTZ Most like a gentleman.

GUILDENSTERN But with much forcing of his disposition.°

ROSENCRANTZ Niggard of question;° but, of our demands,
Most free in his reply.

QUEEN Did you assay° him
To any pastime?

ROSENCRANTZ Madam, it so fell out, that certain players
We o'er-raught° on the way: of these we told him;
And there did seem in him a kind of joy
To hear of it: they are here about the court,
And, as I think, they have already order
This night to play before him.

POLONIUS 'Tis most true:
And he beseech'd me to entreat your majesties
To hear and see the matter.

Act III, Scene i. 1 drift of conference: Device of conversation. **7 forward:** Willing. **11–12 forcing of his disposition:** I.e., against his will. **13 Niggard of question:** Sparing of conversation. **15 assay:** Try to win. **17 o'er-raught:** Overtook.

KING With all my heart; and it doth much content me
To hear him so inclin'd.
Good gentlemen, give him a further edge,°
And drive his purpose into these delights.

ROSENCRANTZ We shall, my lord.

Exeunt **ROSENCRANTZ** *and* **GUILDENSTERN.**

KING Sweet Gertrude, leave us too;
For we have closely° sent for Hamlet hither,
That he, as 'twere by accident, may here
Affront° Ophelia:
Her father and myself, lawful espials,°
Will so bestow ourselves that, seeing, unseen,
We may of their encounter frankly judge,
And gather by him, as he is behav'd,
If 't be th' affliction of his love or no
That thus he suffers for.

QUEEN I shall obey you.
And for your part, Ophelia, I do wish
That your good beauties be the happy cause
Of Hamlet's wildness:° so shall I hope your virtues
Will bring him to his wonted way again,
To both your honours.

OPHELIA Madam, I wish it may.

[*Exit* **QUEEN.**]

POLONIUS Ophelia, walk you here. Gracious,° so please you,
We will bestow ourselves. [*To* **OPHELIA.**] Read on this book;
That show of such an exercise° may colour°
Your loneliness. We are oft to blame in this, —
'Tis too much prov'd — that with devotion's visage
And pious action we do sugar o'er
The devil himself.

KING [*aside*] O, 'tis too true!
How smart a lash that speech doth give my conscience!
The harlot's cheek, beautied with plast'ring art,
Is not more ugly to° the thing° that helps it
Than is my deed to my most painted word:
O heavy burthen!

POLONIUS I hear him coming: let's withdraw, my lord.

[*Exeunt* **KING** *and* **POLONIUS.**]

Enter **HAMLET.**

HAMLET To be, or not to be: that is the question:
Whether 'tis nobler in the mind to suffer
The slings and arrows of outrageous fortune,
Or to take arms against a sea° of troubles,
And by opposing end them? To die: to sleep;
No more; and by a sleep to say we end
The heart-ache and the thousand natural shocks
That flesh is heir to, 'tis a consummation
Devoutly to be wish'd. To die, to sleep;
To sleep: perchance to dream: ay, there's the rub;
For in that sleep of death what dreams may come
When we have shuffled° off this mortal coil,°
Must give us pause: there's the respect°
That makes calamity of so long life;°
For who would bear the whips and scorns of time,°
Th' oppressor's wrong, the proud man's contumely,°
The pangs of despis'd° love, the law's delay,
The insolence of office° and the spurns°
That patient merit of th' unworthy takes,

---

26 edge: Incitement. **29 closely:** Secretly. **31 Affront:** Confront. **32 lawful espials:** Legitimate spies. **40 wildness:** Madness. **43 Gracious:** Your grace (addressed to the king). **45 exercise:** Act of devotion (the book she reads is one of devotion). **colour:** Give a plausible appearance to.

52 to: Compared to. **thing:** I.e., the cosmetic. **59 sea:** The mixed metaphor of this speech has often been commented on; a later emendation *siege* has sometimes been spoken on the stage. **67 shuffled:** Sloughed, cast. **coil:** Usually means "turmoil"; here, possibly "body" (conceived of as wound about the soul like rope); *clay, soil, veil,* have been suggested as emendations. **68 respect:** Consideration. **69 of . . . life:** So long-lived. **70 time:** The world. **71 contumely:** rudeness arising from arrogance or insolence; contemptuous treatment. **72 despis'd:** Rejected. **73 office:** Office-holders. **spurns:** Insults.

Robert Mankoff/The New Yorker Collection/The Cartoon Bank

This cartoon, which originally appeared in the *New Yorker*, reflects on Hamlet's most famous soliloquy. **Do you find it funny? What kind of audience does it suggest the cartoonist believes is familiar with Hamlet?**

When he himself might his quietus° make
With a bare bodkin?° who would fardels° bear,
To grunt and sweat under a weary life,
But that the dread of something after death,
The undiscover'd° country from whose bourn°
No traveller returns, puzzles the will
And makes us rather bear those ills we have
Than fly to others that we know not of?
Thus conscience° does make cowards of us all;
And thus the native hue° of resolution
Is sicklied o'er° with the pale cast° of thought,
And enterprises of great pitch° and moment°
With this regard° their currents° turn awry,
And lose the name of action — Soft you now!
The fair Ophelia! Nymph, in thy orisons°
Be all my sins rememb'red.

OPHELIA Good my lord,
How does your honour for this many a day?

HAMLET I humbly thank you; well, well, well.

OPHELIA My lord, I have remembrances of yours,
That I have longed long to re-deliver;
I pray you, now receive them.

HAMLET No, not I;
I never gave you aught.

OPHELIA My honour'd lord, you know right well you did;
And, with them, words of so sweet breath compos'd
As made the things more rich: their perfume lost,
Take these again; for to the noble mind
Rich gifts wax poor when givers prove unkind.
There, my lord.

HAMLET Ha, ha! are you honest?°

OPHELIA My lord?

HAMLET Are you fair?

OPHELIA What means your lordship?

HAMLET That if you be honest and fair, your honesty° should admit no discourse to° your beauty.

---

75 quietus: Acquittance; here, death. **76 bare bodkin:** Mere dagger; *bare* is sometimes understood as "unsheathed." **fardels:** Burdens. **79 undiscover'd:** undisclosed, unrevealed. **bourn:** Boundary. **83 conscience:** Probably, inhibition by the faculty of reason restraining the will from doing wrong. **84 native hue:** Natural color; metaphor derived from the color of the face. **85 sicklied o'er:** Given a sickly tinge. **cast:** Shade of color. **86 pitch:** Height (as of a falcon's flight). **moment:** Importance. **87 regard:** Respect, consideration. **currents:** Courses. **89 orisons:** Prayers.

103–109 are you honest . . . beauty: *Honest* meaning "truthful" and "chaste" and *fair* meaning "just, honorable" (l. 105) and "beauty" (l. 108) are not mere quibbles; the speech has the irony of a *double entendre*. **108 your honesty:** Your chastity. **discourse to:** Familiar intercourse with.

OPHELIA Could beauty, my lord, have better commerce° than with honesty?

HAMLET Ay, truly; for the power of beauty will sooner transform honesty from what it is to a bawd than the force of honesty can translate beauty into his likeness: this was sometime a paradox, but now the time° gives it proof. I did love you once.

OPHELIA Indeed, my lord, you made me believe so.

HAMLET You should not have believed me; for virtue cannot so inoculate° our old stock but we shall relish of it:° I loved you not.

OPHELIA I was the more deceived.

HAMLET Get thee to a nunnery: why wouldst thou be a breeder of sinners? I am myself indifferent honest;° but yet I could accuse me of such things that it were better my mother had not borne me: I am very proud, revengeful, ambitious, with more offences at my beck° than I have thoughts to put them in, imagination to give them shape, or time to act them in. What should such fellows as I do crawling between earth and heaven? We are arrant knaves, all; believe none of us. Go thy ways to a nunnery. Where's your father?

OPHELIA At home, my lord.

HAMLET Let the doors be shut upon him, that he may play the fool no where but in 's own house. Farewell.

OPHELIA O, help him, you sweet heavens!

HAMLET If thou dost marry, I'll give thee this plague for thy dowry: be thou as chaste as ice, as pure as snow, thou shalt not escape calumny. Get thee to a nunnery, go: farewell. Or, if thou wilt needs marry, marry a fool; for wise men know well enough what monsters° you make of them. To a nunnery, go, and quickly too. Farewell.

OPHELIA O heavenly powers, restore him!

HAMLET I have heard of your° paintings too, well enough; God hath given you one face, and you make yourselves another: you jig,° you amble, and you lisp; you nick-name God's creatures, and make your wantonness your ignorance.° Go to, I'll no more on 't; it hath made me mad. I say, we will have no more marriage: those that are married already, all but one,° shall live; the rest shall keep as they are. To a nunnery, go. *Exit.*

OPHELIA O, what a noble mind is here o'er-thrown!
The courtier's, soldier's, scholar's, eye, tongue, sword;
Th' expectancy and rose° of the fair state,
The glass of fashion and the mould of form,°
Th' observ'd of all observers,° quite, quite down!
And I, of ladies most deject and wretched,
That suck'd the honey of his music vows,
Now see that noble and most sovereign reason,
Like sweet bells jangled, out of time and harsh;
That unmatch'd form and feature of blown° youth
Blasted with ecstasy:° O, woe is me,
T' have seen what I have seen, see what I see!

Enter **KING** *and* **POLONIUS.**

---

111 commerce: Intercourse. **116 the time:** The present age. **121 inoculate:** Graft (metaphorical). **122 but . . . it:** I.e., that we do not still have about us a taste of the old stock; i.e., retain our sinfulness. **126 indifferent honest:** Moderately virtuous. **130 beck:** Command.

148 monsters: An allusion to the horns of a cuckold. **151 your:** Indefinite use. **154 jig:** Move with jerky motion; probably allusion to the *jig*, or song and dance, of the current stage. **155–156 make . . . ignorance:** I.e., excuse your wantonness on the ground of your ignorance. **159 one:** I.e., the king. **164 expectancy and rose:** Source of hope. **165 The glass . . . form:** The mirror of fashion and the pattern of courtly behavior. **166 observ'd . . . observers:** I.e., the center of attention in the court. **171 blown:** Blooming. **172 ecstasy:** Madness.

KING Love! his affections do not that way tend;
Nor what he spake, though it lack'd form a little,
Was not like madness. There's something in his soul,
O'er which his melancholy sits on brood;
And I do doubt° the hatch and the disclose°
Will be some danger: which for to prevent,
I have in quick determination
Thus set it down: he shall with speed to England,
For the demand of our neglected tribute:
Haply the seas and countries different
With variable° objects shall expel
This something-settled° matter in his heart,
Whereon his brains still beating puts him thus
From fashion of himself.° What think you on 't?

POLONIUS It shall do well: but yet do I believe
The origin and commencement of his grief
Sprung from neglected love. How now, Ophelia!
You need not tell us what Lord Hamlet said;
We heard it all. My lord, do as you please;
But, if you hold it fit, after the play
Let his queen mother all alone entreat him
To show his grief: let her be round° with him;
And I'll be plac'd, so please you, in the ear
Of all their conference. If she find him not,
To England send him, or confine him where
Your wisdom best shall think.

KING It shall be so:
Madness in great ones must not unwatch'd go. *Exeunt.*

[**Scene ii:** *A hall in the castle.*]

Enter **HAMLET** *and three of the* **PLAYERS.**

HAMLET Speak the speech, I pray you, as I pronounced it to you, trippingly on the tongue: but if you mouth it, as many of your° players do, I had as lief the town-crier spoke my lines. Nor do not saw the air too much with your hand, thus, but use all gently; for in the very torrent, tempest, and, as I may say, whirlwind of your passion, you must acquire and beget a temperance that may give it smoothness. O, it offends me to the soul to hear a robustious° periwig-pated° fellow tear a passion to tatters, to very rags, to split the ears of the groundlings,° who for the most part are capable of° nothing but inexplicable° dumb-shows and noise: I would have such a fellow whipped for o'er-doing Termagant;° it out-herods Herod:° pray you, avoid it.

FIRST PLAYER I warrant your honour.

HAMLET Be not too tame neither, but let your own discretion be your tutor: suit the action to the word, the word to the action; with this special observance, that you o'er-step not the modesty of nature: for any thing so overdone is from the purpose of playing, whose end, both at the first and now, was and is, to hold, as 't were, the mirror up to nature; to show virtue her own feature, scorn her own image, and the very age and body of the time his form and pressure.° Now this overdone, or come tardy off,° though it make the unskil-ful laugh, cannot but make the judicious grieve; the censure of the which one° must in your allowance o'erweigh a whole

---

178 doubt: Fear. **disclose:** Disclosure or revelation (by chipping of the shell). **184 variable:** Various. **185 something-settled:** Somewhat settled. **187 From . . . himself:** Out of his natural manner. **195 round:** Blunt.

Scene ii. 4 your: Indefinite use. **12 robustious:** Violent, boisterous. **periwig-pated:** Wearing a wig. **14 groundlings:** Those who stood in the yard of the theater. **15 capable of:** Susceptible of being influenced by. **16. inexplicable:** Of no significance worth explaining. **18 Termagant:** A god of the Saracens; a character in the St. Nicholas play, where one of his worshipers, leaving him in charge of goods, returns to find them stolen; whereupon he beats the god (or idol), which howls vociferously. **19 Herod:** Herod of Jewry; a character in *The Slaughter of the Innocents* and other cycle plays. The part was played with great noise and fury. **32 pressure:** Stamp, impressed character. **33 come tardy off:** Inadequately done. **35 the censure . . . one:** The judgment of even one of whom.

theatre of others. O, there be players that I have seen play, and heard others praise, and that highly, not to speak it profanely, that, neither having the accent of Christians nor the gait of Christian, pagan, nor man, have so strutted and bellowed that I have thought some of nature's journeymen° had made men and not made them well, they imitated humanity so abominably.

FIRST PLAYER I hope we have reformed that indifferently° with us, sir.

HAMLET O, reform it altogether. And let those that play your clowns speak no more than is set down for them; for there be of° them that will themselves laugh, to set on some quantity of barren° spectators to laugh too; though, in the mean time, some necessary question of the play be then to be considered: that's villanous, and shows a most pitiful ambition in the fool that uses it. Go, make you ready.

[*Exeunt* **PLAYERS.**]

Enter **POLONIUS, GUILDENSTERN,** *and* **ROSENCRANTZ.**

How now, my lord! will the king hear this piece of work?

POLONIUS And the queen too, and that presently.

HAMLET Bid the players make haste.

[*Exit* **POLONIUS.**]

Will you two help to hasten them?

ROSENCRANTZ
GUILDENSTERN } We will, my lord.

Exeunt they two.

HAMLET What ho! Horatio!

Enter **HORATIO.**

HORATIO Here, sweet lord, at your service.

HAMLET Horatio, thou art e'en as just° a man
As e'er my conversation cop'd withal.

HORATIO O, my dear lord, —

HAMLET Nay, do not think I flatter;
For what advancement may I hope from thee
That no revenue hast but thy good spirits,
To feed and clothe thee? Why should the poor be flatter'd?
No, let the candied tongue lick absurd pomp,
And crook the pregnant° hinges of the knee
Where thrift° may follow fawning. Dost thou hear?
Since my dear soul was mistress of her choice
And could of men distinguish her election,
S' hath seal'd thee for herself; for thou hast been
As one, in suff'ring all, that suffers nothing,
A man that fortune's buffets and rewards
Hast ta'en with equal thanks: and blest are those
Whose blood and judgement are so well commeddled,
That they are not a pipe for fortune's finger
To sound what stop° she please. Give me that man
That is not passion's slave, and I will wear him
In my heart's core, ay, in my heart of heart,
As I do thee. — Something too much of this. —
There is a play to-night before the king;
One scene of it comes near the circumstance
Which I have told thee of my father's death:
I prithee, when thou seest that act afoot,
Even with the very comment of thy soul°
Observe my uncle: if his occulted° guilt
Do not itself unkennel in one speech,
It is a damned° ghost that we have seen,
And my imaginations are as foul

---

44 journeymen: Laborers not yet masters in their trade.
48 indifferently: Fairly, tolerably. **51 of:** I.e., some among them.
53 barren: I.e., of wit.

67 just: Honest, honorable. **74 pregnant:** Pliant. **75 thrift:** Profit. **84 stop:** Hole in a wind instrument for controlling the sound. **92 very . . . soul:** Inward and sagacious criticism. **93 occulted:** Hidden. **95 damned:** In league with Satan.

As Vulcan's stithy.° Give him heedful note;
For I mine eyes will rivet to his face,
And after we will both our judgements join
In censure of his seeming.°

HORATIO Well, my lord:
If 'a steal aught the whilst this play is playing,
And 'scape detecting, I will pay the theft.

Enter trumpets and kettledrums, **KING, QUEEN, POLONIUS, OPHELIA,** [**ROSENCRANTZ, GUILDENSTERN,** *and others*].

HAMLET They are coming to the play; I must be idle:° Get you a place.

KING How fares our cousin Hamlet?

HAMLET Excellent, i' faith; of the chameleon's dish:° I eat the air, promise-crammed: you cannot feed capons so.

KING I have nothing with° this answer, Hamlet; these words are not mine.°

HAMLET No, nor mine now. [*To* **POLONIUS**.] My lord, you played once i' the university, you say?

POLONIUS That did I, my lord; and was accounted a good actor.

HAMLET What did you enact?

POLONIUS I did enact Julius Cæsar: I was killed i' the Capitol; Brutus killed me.

HAMLET It was a brute part of him to kill so capital a calf there. Be the players ready?

ROSENCRANTZ Ay, my lord; they stay upon your patience.

QUEEN Come hither, my dear Hamlet, sit by me.

HAMLET No, good mother, here's metal more attractive.

POLONIUS [*to the King*]: O, ho! do you mark that?

HAMLET Lady, shall I lie in your lap?
[*Lying down at* **OPHELIA**'*s feet.*]

OPHELIA No, my lord.

HAMLET I mean, my head upon your lap?

OPHELIA Ay, my lord.

HAMLET Do you think I meant country° matters?

OPHELIA I think nothing, my lord.

HAMLET That's a fair thought to lie between maids' legs.

OPHELIA What is, my lord?

HAMLET Nothing.

OPHELIA You are merry, my lord.

HAMLET Who, I?

OPHELIA Ay, my lord.

HAMLET O God, your only° jig-maker.° What should a man do but be merry? for, look you, how cheerfully my mother looks, and my father died within's two hours.

OPHELIA Nay, 'tis twice two months, my lord.

HAMLET So long? Nay then, let the devil wear black, for I'll have a suit of sables.° O heavens! die two months ago, and not forgotten yet? Then there's hope a great man's memory may outlive his life half a year: but, by 'r lady, 'a must build churches, then; or else shall 'a suffer not thinking on,° with the hobbyhorse, whose epitaph is "For, O, for, O, the hobbyhorse is forgot."°

The trumpets sound. Dumb show follows.

Enter a King and a Queen [very lovingly]; the Queen embracing him, and he her. [She kneels, and makes show of protestation unto him.] He takes her up, and declines his head upon her neck: he lies him down upon a bank of flowers: she, seeing him asleep, leaves him. Anon comes in another man, takes off his crown, kisses it, pours poison in the sleeper's ears, and leaves him. The

---

97 stithy: Smithy, place of *stiths* (anvils). **99 censure . . . seeming:** Judgment of his appearance or behavior. **104 idle:** Crazy, or not attending to anything serious. **106–107 chameleon's dish:** Chameleons were supposed to feed on air. (Hamlet deliberately misinterprets the king's "fares" as "feeds.") **109 have . . . with:** Make nothing of. **110 are not mine:** Do not respond to what I ask.

132 country: With a bawdy pun. **142 your only:** Only your. **jig-maker:** Composer of jigs (song and dance). **148 suit of sables:** Garments trimmed with the fur of the sable, with a quibble on *sable* meaning "black." **153–154 suffer . . . on:** Undergo oblivion. **155–156 "For . . . forgot":** Verse of a song occurring also in *Love's Labour's Lost*, III.i.30. The hobbyhorse was a character in the Morris Dance.

Queen returns; finds the King dead, makes passionate action. The Poisoner, with some three or four come in again, seems to condole with her. The dead body is carried away. The Poisoner woos the Queen with gifts: she seems harsh awhile, but in the end accepts love. [*Exeunt.*]

OPHELIA What means this, my lord?

HAMLET Marry, this is miching mallecho;° it means mischief.

OPHELIA Belike this show imports the argument of the play.

Enter **PROLOGUE.**

HAMLET We shall know by this fellow: the players cannot keep counsel; they'll tell all.

OPHELIA Will 'a tell us what this show meant?

HAMLET Ay, or any show that you'll show him: be not you ashamed to show, he'll not shame to tell you what it means.

OPHELIA You are naught, you are naught:° I'll mark the play.

PROLOGUE For us, and for our tragedy,
Here stooping° to your clemency,
We beg your hearing patiently. [*Exit.*]

HAMLET Is this a prologue, or the posy° of a ring?

OPHELIA 'Tis brief, my lord.

HAMLET As woman's love.

Enter [*two* **PLAYERS** *as*] *King and Queen.*

PLAYER KING Full thirty times hath Phoebus' cart gone round
Neptune's salt wash° and Tellus'° orbed ground,
And thirty dozen moons with borrowed° sheen
About the world have times twelve thirties been,
Since love our hearts and Hymen° did our hands
Unite commutual° in most sacred bands.

PLAYER QUEEN So many journeys may the sun and moon
Make us again count o'er ere love be done!
But, woe is me, you are so sick of late,
So far from cheer and from your former state,
That I distrust° you. Yet, though I distrust,
Discomfort you, my lord, it nothing must:
For women's fear and love holds quantity;°
In neither aught, or in extremity.
Now, what my love is, proof hath made you know;
And as my love is siz'd, my fear is so:
Where love is great, the littlest doubts are fear;
Where little fears grow great, great love grows there.

PLAYER KING 'Faith, I must leave thee, love, and shortly too;
My operant° powers their functions leave° to do:
And thou shalt live in this fair world behind,
Honour'd, belov'd; and haply one as kind
For husband shalt thou —

PLAYER QUEEN O, confound the rest!
Such love must needs be treason in my breast:
In second husband let me be accurst!
None wed the second but who kill'd the first.

HAMLET [*aside*]: Wormwood, wormwood.

PLAYER QUEEN The instances that second marriage move
Are base respects of thrift, but none of love:
A second time I kill my husband dead,
When second husband kisses me in bed.

PLAYER KING I do believe you think what now you speak;
But what we do determine oft we break.

---

158 miching mallecho: Sneaking mischief. **169 naught:** Indecent. **172 stooping:** Bowing. **174 posy:** Motto. **179 salt wash:** The sea. **Tellus:** Goddess of the earth (*orbed ground*). **180 borrowed:** I.e., reflected.

182 Hymen: God of matrimony. **183 commutual:** Mutually. **188 distrust:** Am anxious about. **190 holds quantity:** Keeps proportion between. **197 operant:** Active. **leave:** Cease.

Purpose is but the slave to memory,
Of violent birth, but poor validity:
Which now, like fruit unripe, sticks on the tree;
But fall, unshaken, when they mellow be.
Most necessary 'tis that we forget
To pay ourselves what to ourselves is debt:
What to ourselves in passion we propose,
The passion ending, doth the purpose lose.
The violence of either grief or joy
Their own enactures° with themselves destroy:
Where joy most revels, grief doth most lament;
Grief joys, joy grieves, on slender accident.
This world is not for aye,° nor 'tis not strange
That even our loves should with our fortunes change;
For 'tis a question left us yet to prove,
Whether love lead fortune, or else fortune love.
The great man down, you mark his favourite flies;
The poor advanc'd makes friends of enemies.
And hitherto doth love on fortune tend;
For who° not needs shall never lack a friend,
And who in want a hollow friend doth try,
Directly seasons° him his enemy.
But, orderly to end where I begun,
Our wills and fates do so contrary run
That our devices still are overthrown;
Our thoughts are ours, their ends° none of our own:
So think thou wilt no second husband wed;
But die thy thoughts when thy first lord is dead.

PLAYER QUEEN Nor earth to me give food, nor heaven light!
Sport and repose lock from me day and night!
To desperation turn my trust and hope!
An anchor's° cheer° in prison be my scope!
Each opposite° that blanks° the face of joy
Meet what I would have well and it destroy!
Both here and hence pursue me lasting strife,
If, once a widow, ever I be wife!

HAMLET If she should break it now!

PLAYER KING 'Tis deeply sworn. Sweet, leave me here awhile;
My spirits grow dull, and fain I would beguile
The tedious day with sleep.

[*Sleeps.*]

PLAYER QUEEN Sleep rock thy brain;
And never come mischance between us twain!

Exit.

HAMLET Madam, how like you this play?

QUEEN The lady doth protest too much, methinks.

HAMLET O, but she'll keep her word.

KING Have you heard the argument? Is there no offence in 't?

HAMLET No, no, they do but jest, poison in jest; no offence i' the world.

KING What do you call the play?

HAMLET The Mouse-trap. Marry, how? Tropically.° This play is the image of a murder done in Vienna: Gonzago° is the duke's name; his wife, Baptista: you shall see anon; 't is a knavish piece of work: but what o' that? your majesty and we that have free souls, it touches us not: let the galled jade° winch,° our withers° are unwrung.°

---

220 enactures: Fulfillments. **223 aye:** Ever. **230 who:** Whoever. **232 seasons:** Matures, ripens. **236 ends:** Results.

242 An anchor's: An anchorite's. **cheer:** Fare; sometimes printed as *chair*. **243 opposite:** Adverse thing. **blanks:** Causes to *blanch* or grow pale. **262 Tropically:** Figuratively, *trapically* suggests a pun on *trap* in *Mouse-trap* (l. 261). **263 Gonzago:** In 1538, Luigi Gonzago murdered the Duke of Urbano by pouring poisoned lotion in his ears. **268 galled jade:** Horse whose hide is rubbed by saddle or harness. **winch:** Wince. **withers:** The part between the horse's shoulder blades. **269 unwrung:** Not wrung or twisted.

Roy Miles Fine Paintings/Bridgeman Images

This nineteenth-century painting by Daniel Maclise portrays his vision of the play-within-the-play scene. **How do the details in this image illustrate the text of that scene? Particularly, what do the depictions of King Claudius, Hamlet, and Ophelia suggest about their characters?**

Enter **LUCIANUS.**

This is one Lucianus, nephew to the king.

OPHELIA You are as good as a chorus,° my lord.

HAMLET I could interpret between you and your love, if I could see the puppets dallying.°

OPHELIA You are keen, my lord, you are keen.

HAMLET It would cost you a groaning to take off my edge.

OPHELIA Still better, and worse.°

HAMLET So you mistake° your husbands. Begin, murderer; pox,° leave thy damnable faces, and begin. Come: the croaking raven doth bellow for revenge.

LUCIANUS Thoughts black, hands apt, drugs fit, and time agreeing;
Confederate° season, else no creature seeing;
Thou mixture rank, of midnight weeds collected,
With Hecate's° ban° thrice blasted, thrice infected,
Thy natural magic and dire property,
On wholesome life usurp immediately.

[*Pours the poison into the sleeper's ears.*]

HAMLET 'A poisons him i' the garden for his estate. His name's Gonzago: the story is extant, and written in very choice Italian: you shall see anon how the murderer gets the love of Gonzago's wife.

OPHELIA The king rises.

HAMLET What, frighted with false fire!°

QUEEN How fares my lord?

POLONIUS Give o'er the play.

KING Give me some light: away!

POLONIUS Lights, lights, lights!

Exeunt all but **HAMLET** *and* **HORATIO.**

HAMLET Why, let the strucken deer go weep,
The hart ungalled play;
For some must watch, while some must sleep:
Thus runs the world away.°
Would not this,° sir, and a forest of feathers°—if the rest of my fortunes turn Turk with° me—with two Provincial roses° on my razed° shoes,

271 chorus: In many Elizabethan plays, the action was explained by an actor known as the "chorus"; at a puppet show the actor who explained the action was known as an "interpreter," as indicated by the lines following. **274 dallying:** With sexual suggestion, continued in *keen* (sexually aroused), *groaning* (i.e., in pregnancy), and *edge* (i.e., sexual desire or impetuosity). **278 Still . . . worse:** More keen, less decorous. **279 mistake:** Err in taking. **280 pox:** An imprecation. **284 Confederate:** Conspiring (to assist the murderer). **286 Hecate:** The goddess of witchcraft. **ban:** Curse.

295 false fire: Fireworks, or a blank discharge. **300–303 Why . . . away:** Probably from an old ballad, with allusion to the popular belief that a wounded deer retires to weep and die. Cf. *As You Like It*, II.i.66. **304 this:** I.e., the play. **305 feathers:** Allusion to the plumes which Elizabethan actors were fond of wearing. **305–306 turn Turk with:** Go back on. **306–307 two Provincial roses:** Rosettes of ribbon like the roses of Provins near Paris, or else the roses of Provence. **307 razed:** Cut, slashed (by way of ornament).

get me a fellowship in a cry° of players,° sir?

HORATIO Half a share.°

HAMLET A whole one, I.

For thou dost know, O Damon° dear,
This realm dismantled° was
Of Jove himself; and now reigns here
A very, very° — pajock.°

HORATIO You might have rhymed.

HAMLET O good Horatio, I'll take the ghost's word for a thousand pound. Didst perceive?

HORATIO Very well, my lord.

HAMLET Upon the talk of the poisoning?

HORATIO I did very well note him.

HAMLET Ah, ha! Come, some music! come, the recorders!°

For if the king like not the comedy,
Why then, belike, he likes it not, perdy.°
Come, some music!

Enter **ROSENCRANTZ** *and* **GUILDENSTERN.**

GUILDENSTERN Good my lord, vouchsafe me a word with you.

HAMLET Sir, a whole history.

GUILDENSTERN The king, sir, —

HAMLET Ay, sir, what of him?

GUILDENSTERN Is in his retirement marvellous distempered.

HAMLET With drink, sir?

GUILDENSTERN No, my lord, rather with choler.°

HAMLET Your wisdom should show itself more richer to signify this to his doctor; for, for me to put him to his purgation would perhaps plunge him into far more choler.

308–309 fellowship . . . players: Partnership in a theatrical company. **308 cry:** Pack (as of hounds). **310 Half a share:** Allusion to the custom in dramatic companies of dividing the ownership into a number of shares among the householders. **312 Damon:** Symbol of loyalty and friendship in Greek myth. **313 dismantled:** Stripped, divested. **312–315 For . . . very:** Probably from an old ballad having to do with Damon and Pythias. **315 pajock:** Peacock (a bird with a bad reputation). Possibly the word was *patchock*, diminutive of *patch*, clown. **323 recorders:** Wind instruments of the flute kind. **325 perdy:** Corruption of *par dieu*. **335 choler:** Bilious disorder, with quibble on the sense "anger."

GUILDENSTERN Good my lord, put your discourse into some frame° and start not so wildly from my affair.

HAMLET I am tame, sir: pronounce.

GUILDENSTERN The queen, your mother, in most great affliction of spirit, hath sent me to you.

HAMLET You are welcome.

GUILDENSTERN Nay, good my lord, this courtesy is not of the right breed. If it shall please you to make me a wholesome° answer, I will do your mother's commandment; if not, your pardon and my return shall be the end of my business.

HAMLET Sir, I cannot.

GUILDENSTERN What, my lord?

HAMLET Make you a wholesome answer; my wit's diseased: but, sir, such answer as I can make, you shall command; or, rather, as you say, my mother: therefore no more, but to the matter:° my mother, you say, —

ROSENCRANTZ Then thus she says; your behaviour hath struck her into amazement and admiration.

HAMLET O wonderful son, that can so 'stonish a mother! But is there no sequel at the heels of this mother's admiration? Impart.

ROSENCRANTZ She desires to speak with you in her closet, ere you go to bed.

HAMLET We shall obey, were she ten times our mother. Have you any further trade with us?

ROSENCRANTZ My lord, you once did love me.

HAMLET And do still, by these pickers and stealers.°

ROSENCRANTZ Good my lord, what is your cause of distemper? you do, surely, bar the door upon your own liberty, if you deny your griefs to your friend.

HAMLET Sir, I lack advancement.

341 frame: Order. **350 wholesome:** Sensible. **360 matter:** Matter in hand. **373–374 pickers and stealers:** Hands, so called from the catechism "to keep my hands from picking and stealing."

ROSENCRANTZ How can that be, when you have the voice° of the king himself for your succession in Denmark?

HAMLET Ay, sir, but "While the grass grows,"° — the proverb is something musty.

Enter the Players with recorders.

O, the recorders! let me see one. To withdraw° with you: — why do you go about to recover the wind° of me, as if you would drive me into a toil?°

GUILDENSTERN O, my lord, if my duty be too bold, my love is too unmannerly.°

HAMLET I do not well understand that. Will you play upon this pipe?

GUILDENSTERN My lord, I cannot.

HAMLET I pray you.

GUILDENSTERN Believe me, I cannot.

HAMLET I beseech you.

GUILDENSTERN I know no touch of it, my lord.

HAMLET 'Tis as easy as lying: govern these ventages° with your fingers and thumb, give it breath with your mouth, and it will discourse most eloquent music. Look you, these are the stops.

GUILDENSTERN But these cannot I command to any utterance of harmony; I have not the skill.

HAMLET Why, look you now, how unworthy a thing you make of me! You would play upon me; you would seem to know my stops; you would pluck out the heart of my mystery; you would sound me from my lowest note to the top of my compass:° and there is much music, excellent voice, in this little organ;° yet cannot you make it speak. 'Sblood, do you think I am easier to be played on than a pipe? Call me what instrument you will, though you can fret° me, you cannot play upon me.

Enter **POLONIUS**.

God bless you, sir!

POLONIUS My lord, the queen would speak with you, and presently.

HAMLET Do you see yonder cloud that 's almost in shape of a camel?

POLONIUS By the mass, and 'tis like a camel, indeed.

HAMLET Methinks it is like a weasel.

POLONIUS It is backed like a weasel.

HAMLET Or like a whale?

POLONIUS Very like a whale.

HAMLET Then I will come to my mother by and by. [*Aside.*] They fool me to the top of my bent.° — I will come by and by.°

POLONIUS I will say so.

[*Exit.*]

HAMLET By and by is easily said.
Leave me, friends.

[*Exeunt all but* **HAMLET**.]

'Tis now the very witching time° of night,
When churchyards yawn and hell itself breathes out
Contagion to this world: now could I drink hot blood,
And do such bitter business as the day
Would quake to look on. Soft! now to my mother.
O heart, lose not thy nature; let not ever
The soul of Nero° enter this firm bosom:
Let me be cruel, not unnatural:
I will speak daggers to her, but use none;
My tongue and soul in this be hypocrites;
How in my words somever she be shent,°
To give them seals° never, my soul, consent!

Exit.

381 voice: Support. **383–384 "While . . . grows":** The rest of the proverb is "the silly horse starves." Hamlet may be destroyed while he is waiting for the succession to the kingdom. **385 withdraw:** Speak in private. **387 recover the wind:** Get to the windward side. **388 toil:** Snare. **389–390 if . . . unmannerly:** If I am using an unmannerly boldness, it is my love which occasions it. **399 ventages:** Stops of the recorders. **411 compass:** Range of voice. **413 organ:** Musical instrument, i.e., the pipe.

416 fret: Quibble on meaning "irritate" and the piece of wood, gut, or metal which regulates the fingering. **430–431 top of my bent:** Limit of endurance, i.e., extent to which a bow may be bent. **431 by and by:** Immediately. **435 witching time:** I.e., time when spells are cast. **441 Nero:** Murderer of his mother, Agrippina. **445 shent:** Rebuked. **446 give them seals:** Confirm with deeds.

[**Scene iii:** *A room in the castle.*]

Enter **KING, ROSENCRANTZ,** *and* **GUILDENSTERN.**

KING I like him not, nor stands it safe with us
To let his madness range. Therefore prepare you;
I your commission will forthwith dispatch,°
And he to England shall along with you:
The terms° of our estate° may not endure
Hazard so near us as doth hourly grow
Out of his brows.°

GUILDENSTERN We will ourselves provide:
Most holy and religious fear it is

Private Collection/Bridgeman Images

This 1915 lithograph from an illustrated edition of *Hamlet* shows King Claudius talking of having the prince killed. **What does this depiction suggest about how the artist viewed King Claudius? To what extent does the text of the play support this interpretation?**

To keep those many many bodies safe
That live and feed upon your majesty.

ROSENCRANTZ The single and peculiar° life is bound,
With all the strength and armour of the mind,
To keep itself from noyance;° but much more
That spirit upon whose weal depend and rest
The lives of many. The cess° of majesty
Dies not alone; but, like a gulf,° doth draw
What's near it with it: it is a massy wheel,
Fix'd on the summit of the highest mount,
To whose huge spokes ten thousand lesser things
Are mortis'd and adjoin'd; which, when it falls,
Each small annexment, petty consequence,
Attends° the boist'rous ruin. Never alone
Did the king sigh, but with a general groan.

KING Arm° you, I pray you, to this speedy voyage;
For we will fetters put about this fear,
Which now goes too free-footed.

ROSENCRANTZ We will haste us.

Exeunt **GENTLEMEN** [**ROSENCRANTZ** *and* **GUILDENSTERN**].

Enter **POLONIUS.**

POLONIUS My lord, he's going to his mother's closet:
Behind the arras° I'll convey° myself,
To hear the process;° I'll warrant she'll tax him home:°
And, as you said, and wisely was it said,
'Tis meet that some more audience than a mother,
Since nature makes them partial, should o'erhear

Scene iii. 3 dispatch: Prepare. **5 terms:** Condition, circumstances. **estate:** State. **7 brows:** Effronteries.

11 single and peculiar: Individual and private. **13 noyance:** Harm. **15 cess:** Decease. **16 gulf:** Whirlpool. **22 Attends:** Participates in. **24 Arm:** Prepare. **28 arras:** Screen of tapestry placed around the walls of household apartments. **convey:** Implication of secrecy, *convey* was often used to mean "steal." **29 process:** Proceedings. **tax him home:** Reprove him severely.

The speech, of vantage.° Fare you well, my
liege:
I'll call upon you ere you go to bed,
And tell you what I know.

KING Thanks, dear my lord.

Exit [**POLONIUS**].

O, my offence is rank, it smells to heaven;
It hath the primal eldest curse° upon't,
A brother's murder. Pray can I not,
Though inclination be as sharp as will:°
My stronger guilt defeats my strong intent;
And, like a man to double business bound,
I stand in pause where I shall first begin,
And both neglect. What if this cursed hand
Were thicker than itself with brother's blood,
Is there not rain enough in the sweet
heavens
To wash it white as snow? Whereto serves
mercy
But to confront° the visage of offence?
And what's in prayer but this two-fold force,
To be forestalled° ere we come to fall,
Or pardon'd being down? Then I'll look up;
My fault is past. But, O, what form of prayer
Can serve my turn? "Forgive me my foul
murder"?
That cannot be: since I am still possess'd
Of those effects for which I did the murder,
My crown, mine own ambition° and my
queen.
May one be pardon'd and retain th' offence?°
In the corrupted currents° of this world
Offence's gilded hand° may shove by justice,
And oft 'tis seen the wicked prize° itself
Buys out the law: but 'tis not so above;
There is no shuffling,° there the action lies°
In his true nature; and we ourselves
compell'd,
Even to the teeth and forehead° of our faults,
To give in evidence. What then? what rests?°
Try what repentance can: what can it not?
Yet what can it when one can not repent?
O wretched state! O bosom black as death!
O limed° soul, that, struggling to be free,
Art more engag'd!° Help, angels! Make assay!°
Bow, stubborn knees; and, heart with strings
of steel,
Be soft as sinews of the new-born babe!
All may be well.

[*He kneels.*]

Enter **HAMLET**.

HAMLET Now might I do it pat,° now he is
praying;
And now I'll do't. And so 'a goes to heaven;
And so am I reveng'd. That would be
scann'd:°
A villain kills my father; and for that,
I, his sole son, do this same villain send
To heaven.
Why, this is hire and salary, not revenge.
'A took my father grossly, full of bread;°
With all his crimes broad blown,° as flush° as
May;
And how his audit stands who knows save
heaven?
But in our circumstance and course° of
thought,
'Tis heavy with him: and am I then reveng'd,
To take him in the purging of his soul,
When he is fit and season'd for his passage?°
No!
Up, sword; and know thou a more horrid hent:°

---

33 of vantage: From an advantageous place. **37 primal eldest curse:** The curse of Cain, the first to kill his brother. **39 sharp as will:** I.e., his desire is as strong as his determination. **47 confront:** Oppose directly. **49 forestalled:** Prevented. **55 ambition:** I.e., realization of ambition. **56 offence:** Benefit accruing from offense. **57 currents:** Courses. **58 gilded hand:** Hand offering gold as a bribe. **59 wicked prize:** Prize won by wickedness. **61 shuffling:** Escape by trickery. **lies:** Is sustainable.

63 teeth and forehead: Very face. **64 rests:** Remains. **68 limed:** Caught as with birdlime. **69 engag'd:** Embedded. **assay:** Trial. **73 pat:** Opportunely. **74–75 would be scann'd:** Needs to be looked into. **80 full of bread:** Enjoying his worldly pleasures (see Ezekiel 16:49). **81 broad blown:** In full bloom. **flush:** Lusty. **83 in . . . course:** As we see it in our mortal situation. **86 fit . . . passage:** I.e., reconciled to heaven by forgiveness of his sins. **88 hent:** Seizing; or more probably, occasion of seizure.

Johan Persson/ArenaPal

This photograph, taken from a 2015 production of *Hamlet* starring Benedict Cumberbatch as the title character, depicts the moment Hamlet decides not to kill King Claudius while he is at prayer. **What does Cumberbatch's expression suggest about Hamlet's motive for walking away from the opportunity to avenge his father? What effect does the positioning of the painting of King Hamlet directly behind Cumberbatch achieve?**

When he is drunk asleep,° or in his rage,
Or in th' incestuous pleasure of his bed;
At game, a-swearing, or about some act
That has no relish of salvation in't;
Then trip him, that his heels may kick at heaven,
And that his soul may be as damn'd and black
As hell, whereto it goes. My mother stays:
This physic° but prolongs thy sickly days.
Exit.

KING [*Rising*]: My words fly up, my thoughts remain below:
Words without thoughts never to heaven go.
Exit.

89 **drunk asleep:** In a drunken sleep. 96 **physic:** Purging (by prayer).

[Scene iv: *The Queen's closet.*]

Enter [**QUEEN**] **GERTRUDE** *and* **POLONIUS.**

POLONIUS 'A will come straight. Look you lay° home to him:
Tell him his pranks have been too broad° to bear with,
And that your grace hath screen'd and stood between
Much heat° and him. I'll sconce° me even here.
Pray you, be round° with him.

HAMLET [*within*]: Mother, mother, mother!

QUEEN I'll warrant you,
Fear me not: withdraw, I hear him coming.
[**POLONIUS** *hides behind the arras.*]

Enter **HAMLET.**

Scene iv. 1 **lay:** Thrust. 2 **broad:** Unrestrained. 4 **Much heat:** I.e., the king's anger. **sconce:** Hide. 5 **round:** Blunt.

HAMLET Now, mother, what's the matter?
QUEEN Hamlet, thou hast thy father much offended.
HAMLET Mother, you have my father° much offended.
QUEEN Come, come, you answer with an idle tongue.
HAMLET Go, go, you question with a wicked tongue.
QUEEN Why, how now, Hamlet!
HAMLET What's the matter now?
QUEEN Have you forgot me?
HAMLET No, by the rood,° not so:
You are the queen, your husband's brother's wife;
And — would it were not so! — you are my mother.
QUEEN Nay, then, I'll set those to you that can speak.
HAMLET Come, come, and sit you down; you shall not budge;
You go not till I set you up a glass
Where you may see the inmost part of you.
QUEEN What wilt thou do? thou wilt not murder me?
Help, help, ho!
POLONIUS [*behind*]: What, ho! help, help; help!
HAMLET [*drawing*]: How now! a rat? Dead, for a ducat, dead!
[*Makes a pass through the arras.*]
POLONIUS [*behind*]: O, I am slain!
[*Falls and dies.*]
QUEEN O me, what hast thou done?
HAMLET Nay, I know not:
Is it the king?
QUEEN O, what a rash and bloody deed is this!
HAMLET A bloody deed! almost as bad, good mother,
As kill a king, and marry with his brother.
QUEEN As kill a king!
HAMLET Ay, lady, it was my word.
[*Lifts up the arras and discovers* **POLONIUS**.]
Thou wretched, rash, intruding fool, farewell!
I took thee for thy better: take thy fortune;
Thou find'st to be too busy is some danger.
Leave wringing of your hands: peace! sit you down,
And let me wring your heart; for so I shall,
If it be made of penetrable stuff,
If damned custom have not braz'd° it so
That it be proof and bulwark against sense.
QUEEN What have I done, that thou dar'st wag thy tongue
In noise so rude against me?
HAMLET Such an act
That blurs the grace and blush of modesty,
Calls virtue hypocrite, takes off the rose
From the fair forehead of an innocent love
And sets a blister° there, makes marriage-vows
As false as dicers' oaths: O, such a deed
As from the body of contraction° plucks
The very soul, and sweet religion° makes
A rhapsody° of words: heaven's face does glow
O'er this solidity and compound mass
With heated visage, as against the doom
Is thought-sick at the act.°
QUEEN Ay me, what act,
That roars so loud, and thunders in the index?°
HAMLET Look here, upon this picture, and on this.

9–10 thy father, my father: I.e., Claudius, the elder Hamlet. **14 rood:** Cross.

38 braz'd: Brazened, hardened. **45 sets a blister:** Brands as a harlot. **47 contraction:** The marriage contract. **48 religion:** Religious vows. **49 rhapsody:** Senseless string. **49–52 heaven's . . . act:** Heaven's face blushes to look down on this world, and Gertrude's marriage makes heaven feel as sick as though the day of doom were near. **53 index:** Prelude or preface.

The counterfeit presentment° of two
brothers.
See, what a grace was seated on this brow;
Hyperion's° curls; the front° of Jove himself;
An eye like Mars, to threaten and command;
A station° like the herald Mercury
New-lighted on a heaven-kissing hill;
A combination and a form indeed,
Where every god did seem to set his seal,
To give the world assurance° of a man:
This was your husband. Look you now, what
follows:
Here is your husband; like a mildew'd ear,°
Blasting his wholesome brother. Have you
eyes?
Could you on this fair mountain leave to feed,
And batten° on this moor?° Ha! have you eyes?
You cannot call it love; for at your age
The hey-day° in the blood is tame, it's
humble,

Musee des Beaux-Arts, Reims, France/Bridgeman Images

This 1855 painting by Eugène Delacroix portrays Hamlet's discovery that he has stabbed Polonius through the curtain. **How does Delacroix depict Hamlet's reaction here? What about that of Gertrude in the background? To what extent are those reactions represented in the text of the play itself?**

55 counterfeit presentment: Portrayed representation.
57 Hyperion's: The sun god's. **front:** Brow. **59 station:** Manner of standing. **63 assurance:** Pledge, guarantee.

65 mildew'd ear: See Genesis 41:5–7. **68 batten:** Grow fat. **moor:** Barren upland. **70 hey-day:** State of excitement.

And waits upon the judgement: and what judgement
Would step from this to this? Sense, sure, you have,
Else could you not have motion;° but sure, that sense
Is apoplex'd;° for madness would not err,
Nor sense to ecstasy was ne'er so thrall'd°
But it reserv'd some quantity of choice,°
To serve in such a difference. What devil was't
That thus hath cozen'd° you at hoodman-blind?°
Eyes without feeling, feeling without sight,
Ears without hands or eyes, smelling sans° all,
Or but a sickly part of one true sense
Could not so mope.°
O shame! where is thy blush? Rebellious hell,
If thou canst mutine° in a matron's bones,
To flaming youth let virtue be as wax,
And melt in her own fire: proclaim no shame
When the compulsive ardour gives the charge,°
Since frost itself as actively doth burn
And reason panders will.°

QUEEN O Hamlet, speak no more:
Thou turn'st mine eyes into my very soul;
And there I see such black and grained° spots
As will not leave their tinct.

HAMLET Nay, but to live
In the rank sweat of an enseamed° bed,
Stew'd in corruption, honeying and making love
Over the nasty sty, —

QUEEN O, speak to me no more;
These words, like daggers, enter in mine ears;
No more, sweet Hamlet!

HAMLET A murderer and a villain;
A slave that is not twentieth part the tithe
Of your precedent lord;° a vice of kings;°
A cutpurse of the empire and the rule,
That from a shelf the precious diadem stole,
And put it in his pocket!

QUEEN No more!

Enter **GHOST.**

HAMLET A king of shreds and patches,° —
Save me, and hover o'er me with your wings,
You heavenly guards! What would your gracious figure?

QUEEN Alas, he's mad!

HAMLET Do you not come your tardy son to chide,
That, laps'd in time and passion,° lets go by
Th' important° acting of your dread command?
O, say!

GHOST Do not forget: this visitation
Is but to whet thy almost blunted purpose.
But, look, amazement° on thy mother sits:
O, step between her and her fighting soul:
Conceit in weakest bodies strongest works:
Speak to her, Hamlet.

HAMLET How is it with you, lady?

QUEEN Alas, how is 't with you,
That you do bend your eye on vacancy
And with th' incorporal° air do hold discourse?
Forth at your eyes your spirits wildly peep;
And, as the sleeping soldiers in th' alarm,

72–73 Sense . . . motion: Sense and motion are functions of the middle or sensible soul, the possession of sense being the basis of motion. **74 apoplex'd:** Paralyzed. Mental derangement was thus of three sorts: apoplexy, ecstasy, and diabolic possession. **75 thrall'd:** Enslaved. **76 quantity of choice:** Fragment of the power to choose. **78 cozen'd:** Tricked, cheated. **hoodman-blind:** Blindman's buff. **80 sans:** Without. **82 mope:** Be in a depressed, spiritless state; act aimlessly. **84 mutine:** Mutiny, rebel. **87 gives the charge:** Delivers the attack. **89 reason panders will:** The normal and proper situation was one in which reason guided the will in the direction of good; here, reason is perverted and leads in the direction of evil. **91 grained:** Dyed in grain. **93 enseamed:** Loaded with grease, greased.

99 precedent lord: I.e., the elder Hamlet. **vice of kings:** Buffoon of kings; a reference to the vice, or clown, of the morality plays and interludes. **103 shreds and patches:** I.e., motley, the traditional costume of the vice. **108 laps'd . . . passion:** Having suffered time to slip and passion to cool; also explained as "engrossed in casual events and lapsed into mere fruitless passion, so that he no longer entertains a rational purpose." **109 important:** Urgent. **113 amazement:** Frenzy, distraction. **119 incorporal:** Immaterial.

Your bedded° hair, like life in excrements,°
Start up, and stand an° end. O gentle son,
Upon the heat and flame of thy distemper
Sprinkle cool patience. Whereon do you look?

HAMLET On him, on him! Look you, how pale he glares!
His form and cause conjoin'd,° preaching to stones,
Would make them capable. — Do not look upon me;
Lest with this piteous action you convert
My stern effects:° then what I have to do
Will want true colour;° tears perchance for blood.

QUEEN To whom do you speak this?

HAMLET Do you see nothing there?

QUEEN Nothing at all; yet all that is I see.

HAMLET Nor did you nothing hear?

QUEEN No, nothing but ourselves.

HAMLET Why, look you there! look, how it steals away!
My father, in his habit as he liv'd!
Look, where he goes, even now, out at the portal!

Exit **GHOST.**

QUEEN This is the very coinage of your brain:
This bodiless creation ecstasy
Is very cunning in.

HAMLET Ecstasy!
My pulse, as yours, doth temperately keep time,
And makes as healthful music: it is not madness
That I have utt'red: bring me to the test,
And I the matter will re-word,° which madness
Would gambol° from. Mother, for love of grace,
Lay not that flattering unction° to your soul,
That not your trespass, but my madness speaks:
It will but skin and film the ulcerous place,
Whiles rank corruption, mining° all within,
Infects unseen. Confess yourself to heaven;
Repent what's past; avoid what is to come;°
And do not spread the compost° on the weeds,
To make them ranker. Forgive me this my virtue;°
For in the fatness° of these pursy° times
Virtue itself of vice must pardon beg,
Yea, curb° and woo for leave to do him good.

QUEEN O Hamlet, thou hast cleft my heart in twain.

HAMLET O, throw away the worser part of it,
And live the purer with the other half.
Good night: but go not to my uncle's bed;
Assume a virtue, if you have it not.
That monster, custom, who all sense doth eat,
Of habits devil, is angel yet in this,
That to the use of actions fair and good
He likewise gives a frock or livery,
That aptly is put on. Refrain to-night,
And that shall lend a kind of easiness
To the next abstinence: the next more easy;
For use almost can change the stamp of nature,
And either . . . the devil, or throw him out°

---

122 bedded: Laid in smooth layers. **excrements:** The hair was considered an excrement or voided part of the body. **123 an:** On. **127 conjoin'd:** United. **129–130 convert . . . effects:** Divert me from my stern duty. For *effects*, possibly *affects* (affections of the mind). **131 want true colour:** Lack good reason so that (with a play on the normal sense of *colour*) I shall shed tears instead of blood.

144 re-word: Repeat in words. **145 gambol:** Skip away. **146 unction:** Ointment used medicinally or as a rite; suggestion that forgiveness for sin may not be so easily achieved. **149 mining:** Working under the surface. **151 what is to come:** I.e., the sins of the future. **152 compost:** Manure. **153 this my virtue:** My virtuous talk in reproving you. **154 fatness:** Grossness. **pursy:** Short-winded, corpulent. **156 curb:** Bow, bend the knee. **170** Defective line usually emended by inserting *master* after *either*.

With wondrous potency. Once more, good
night:
And when you are desirous to be bless'd,°
I'll blessing beg of you. For this same lord,
[*Pointing to* POLONIUS.]
I do repent: but heaven hath pleas'd it so,
To punish me with this and this with me,
That I must be their scourge and minister.
I will bestow him, and will answer well
The death I gave him. So, again, good night.
I must be cruel, only to be kind:
Thus bad begins and worse remains
behind.
One word more, good lady.

QUEEN What shall I do?

HAMLET Not this, by no means, that I bid you
do:
Let the bloat° king tempt you again to bed;
Pinch wanton on your cheek; call you his
mouse;
And let him, for a pair of reechy° kisses,
Or paddling in your neck with his damn'd
fingers,
Make you to ravel all this matter out,
That I essentially° am not in madness,
But mad in craft. 'Twere good you let him
know;
For who, that's but a queen, fair, sober,
wise,
Would from a paddock,° from a bat, a gib,°
Such dear concernings° hide? who would do
so?
No, in despite of sense and secrecy,
Unpeg the basket on the house's top,
Let the birds fly, and, like the famous ape,°
To try conclusions,° in the basket
creep,
And break your own neck down.

QUEEN Be thou assur'd, if words be made of
breath,
And breath of life, I have no life to breathe
What thou hast said to me.

HAMLET I must to England; you know that?

QUEEN Alack,
I had forgot: 'tis so concluded on.

HAMLET There's letters seal'd: and my two
schoolfellows,
Whom I will trust as I will adders fang'd,
They bear the mandate; they must sweep my
way,°
And marshal me to knavery. Let it work;
For 'tis the sport to have the enginer°
Hoist° with his own petar:° and 't shall go
hard
But I will delve one yard below their
mines,
And blow them at the moon: O, 'tis most
sweet,
When in one line two crafts° directly meet.
This man shall set me packing:°
I'll lug the guts into the neighbour room.
Mother, good night. Indeed this counsellor
Is now most still, most secret and most
grave,
Who was in life a foolish prating knave.
Come, sir, to draw° toward an end with
you.
Good night, mother.
Exeunt [*severally;* HAMLET *dragging
in* POLONIUS].

---

172 be bless'd: Become blessed, i.e., repentant. **183 bloat:** Bloated. **185 reechy:** Dirty, filthy. **188 essentially:** In my essential nature. **191 paddock:** Toad. **gib:** Tomcat. **192 dear concernings:** Important affairs. **195 the famous ape:** A letter from Sir John Suckling seems to supply other details of the story, otherwise not identified: "It is the story of the jackanapes and the partridges; thou starest after a beauty till it be lost to thee, then let'st out another, and starest after that till it is gone too."

196 conclusions: Experiments. **205 sweep my way:** Clear my path. **207 enginer:** Constructor of military works, or possibly artilleryman. **208 Hoist:** Blown up. **petar:** Defined as a small engine of war used to blow in a door or make a breach, and as a case filled with explosive materials. **211 two crafts:** Two acts of guile, with quibble on the sense of "two ships." **212 set me packing:** Set me to making schemes, set me to lugging (him), and, also, send me off in a hurry. **217 draw:** Come, with quibble on literal sense.

The photograph on the left was made to promote the 1990 Franco Zeffirelli film *Hamlet*, starring Glenn Close as Gertrude. The painting on the right is Leonardo da Vinci's iconic *Mona Lisa*, painted about a century before *Hamlet* was first performed. **What characteristics do these images share? How do they differ? Why do you think Close was photographed in a way that so vividly evokes da Vinci's famous work? What can you infer about Close's portrayal of Gertrude based on this choice?**

ACT IV

[Scene i: *A room in the castle.*]

Enter KING *and* QUEEN, *with* ROSENCRANTZ *and* GUILDENSTERN.

KING There's matter in these sighs, these profound heaves:
You must translate: 'tis fit we understand them.
Where is your son?

QUEEN Bestow this place on us a little while.

[*Exeunt* ROSENCRANTZ *and* GUILDENSTERN.]

Ah, mine own lord, what have I seen to-night!

KING What, Gertrude? How does Hamlet?

QUEEN Mad as the sea and wind, when both contend
Which is the mightier: in his lawless fit,
Behind the arras hearing something stir,
Whips out his rapier, cries, "A rat, a rat!"
And, in this brainish° apprehension,° kills
The unseen good old man.

KING O heavy deed!
It had been so with us, had we been there:
His liberty is full of threats to all;
To you yourself, to us, to every one.
Alas, how shall this bloody deed be answer'd?
It will be laid to us, whose providence°
Should have kept short,° restrain'd and out of haunt,°
This mad young man: but so much was our love,

Act IV, Scene i. 11 brainish: Headstrong, passionate. **apprehension:** Conception, imagination. **17 providence:** Foresight. **18 short:** I.e., on a short tether. **out of haunt:** Secluded.

We would not understand what was most fit;
But, like the owner of a foul disease,
To keep it from divulging,° let it feed
Even on the pith of life. Where is he gone?

QUEEN To draw apart the body he hath kill'd:
O'er whom his very madness, like some ore
Among a mineral° of metals base,
Shows itself pure; 'a weeps for what is done.

KING O Gertrude, come away!
The sun no sooner shall the mountains touch,
But we will ship him hence: and this vile deed
We must, with all our majesty and skill,
Both countenance and excuse. Ho, Guildenstern!

Enter **ROSENCRANTZ** *and* **GUILDENSTERN.**

Friends both, go join you with some further aid:
Hamlet in madness hath Polonius slain,
And from his mother's closet hath he dragg'd him:
Go seek him out; speak fair, and bring the body
Into the chapel. I pray you, haste in this.

[*Exeunt* **ROSENCRANTZ** *and* **GUILDENSTERN.**]

Come, Gertrude, we'll call up our wisest friends;
And let them know, both what we mean to do,
And what's untimely done . . .°
Whose whisper o'er the world's diameter,°
As level° as the cannon to his blank,°
Transports his pois'ned shot, may miss our name,
And hit the woundless° air. O, come away!
My soul is full of discord and dismay.

Exeunt.

22 divulging: Becoming evident. **26 mineral:** Mine. **40** Defective line; some editors add: *so, haply, slander*; others add: *for, haply, slander*; other conjectures. **41 diameter:** Extent from side to side. **42 level:** Straight. **blank:** White spot in the center of a target. **44 woundless:** Invulnerable.

[Scene ii: *Another room in the castle.*]

Enter **HAMLET.**

HAMLET Safely stowed.

ROSENCRANTZ, GUILDENSTERN [*within*]: Hamlet! Lord Hamlet!

HAMLET But soft, what noise? who calls on Hamlet? O, here they come.

Enter **ROSENCRANTZ** *and* **GUILDENSTERN.**

ROSENCRANTZ What have you done, my lord, with the dead body?

HAMLET Compounded it with dust, whereto 'tis kin.

ROSENCRANTZ Tell us where 'tis, that we may take it thence
And bear it to the chapel.

HAMLET Do not believe it.

ROSENCRANTZ Believe what?

HAMLET That I can keep your counsel° and not mine own. Besides, to be demanded of a sponge! what replication° should be made by the son of a king?

ROSENCRANTZ Take you me for a sponge, my lord?

HAMLET Ay, sir, that soaks up the king's countenance, his rewards, his authorities.° But such officers do the king best service in the end: he keeps them, like an ape an apple, in the corner of his jaw; first mouthed, to be last swallowed: when he needs what you have gleaned, it is but squeezing you, and, sponge, you shall be dry again.

ROSENCRANTZ I understand you not, my lord.

HAMLET I am glad of it: a knavish speech sleeps in a foolish ear.

ROSENCRANTZ My lord, you must tell us where the body is, and go with us to the king.

Scene ii. 13 keep your counsel: Hamlet is aware of their treachery but says nothing about it. **15 replication:** Reply. **20 authorities:** Authoritative backing.

HAMLET The body is with the king, but the king is not with the body.° The king is a thing —

GUILDENSTERN A thing, my lord!

HAMLET Of nothing: bring me to him. Hide fox, and all after.°

Exeunt.

[Scene iii: *Another room in the castle.*]

Enter **KING**, *and two or three.*

KING I have sent to seek him, and to find the body.
How dangerous is it that this man goes loose!
Yet must not we put the strong law on him:
He's lov'd of the distracted° multitude,
Who like not in their judgement, but their eyes;
And where 'tis so, th' offender's scourge° is weigh'd,°
But never the offence. To bear all smooth and even,
This sudden sending him away must seem
Deliberate pause:° diseases desperate grown
By desperate appliance are reliev'd,
Or not at all.

Enter **ROSENCRANTZ**, [**GUILDENSTERN**,] *and all the rest.*

How now! what hath befall'n?

ROSENCRANTZ Where the dead body is bestow'd, my lord,
We cannot get from him.

KING But where is he?

ROSENCRANTZ Without, my lord; guarded, to know your pleasure.

KING Bring him before us.

ROSENCRANTZ Ho! bring in the lord.

They enter [with **HAMLET**].

KING Now, Hamlet, where's Polonius?

HAMLET At supper.

KING At supper! where?

HAMLET Not where he eats, but where 'a is eaten: a certain convocation of politic° worms° are e'en at him. Your worm is your only emperor for diet: we fat all creatures else to fat us, and we fat ourselves for maggots: your fat king and your lean beggar is but variable service,° two dishes, but to one table: that's the end.

KING Alas, alas!

HAMLET A man may fish with the worm that hath eat of a king, and eat of the fish that hath fed of that worm.

KING What dost thou mean by this?

HAMLET Nothing but to show you how a king may go a progress° through the guts of a beggar.

KING Where is Polonius?

HAMLET In heaven; send thither to see: if your messenger find him not there, seek him i' the other place yourself. But if indeed you find him not within this month, you shall nose him as you go up the stairs into the lobby.

KING [*to some* **ATTENDANTS**]: Go seek him there.

HAMLET 'A will stay till you come.

[*Exeunt* **ATTENDANTS**.]

KING Hamlet, this deed, for thine especial safety, —
Which we do tender,° as we dearly grieve
For that which thou hast done, — must send thee hence
With fiery quickness: therefore prepare thyself;
The bark is ready, and the wind at help,
Th' associates tend, and everything is bent
For England.

---

34 The body . . . body: There are many interpretations; possibly, "The body lies in death with the king, my father; but my father walks disembodied"; or "Claudius has the bodily possession of kingship, but kingliness, or justice of inheritance, is not with him." **36 Hide . . . after:** An old signal cry in the game of hide-and-seek.
Scene iii. 4 distracted: I.e., without power of forming logical judgments. **6 scourge:** Punishment. **weigh'd:** Taken into consideration. **9 Deliberate pause:** Considered action.

21–22 convocation . . . worms: Allusion to the Diet of Worms (1521). **politic:** Crafty. **26 variable service:** A variety of dishes. **34 progress:** Royal journey of state. **46 tender:** Regard, hold dear.

HAMLET For England!
KING Ay, Hamlet.
HAMLET Good.
KING So is it, if thou knew'st our purposes.
HAMLET I see a cherub° that sees them. But, come; for England! Farewell, dear mother.
KING Thy loving father, Hamlet.
HAMLET My mother: father and mother is man and wife; man and wife is one flesh; and so, my mother. Come, for England!

Exit.

KING Follow him at foot;° tempt him with speed aboard;
Delay it not; I'll have him hence to-night:
Away! for every thing is seal'd and done
That else leans on th' affair: pray you, make haste. [*Exeunt all but the* KING.]
And, England, if my love thou hold'st at aught —
As my great power thereof may give thee sense,
Since yet thy cicatrice° looks raw and red
After the Danish sword, and thy free awe°
Pays homage to us — thou mayst not coldly set
Our sovereign process; which imports at full,
By letters congruing to that effect,
The present death of Hamlet. Do it, England;
For like the hectic° in my blood he rages,
And thou must cure me: till I know 'tis done,
Howe'er my haps,° my joys were ne'er begun.

Exit.

NATIONAL GEOGRAPHIC SOCIETY/Bridgeman Images

This photograph shows Kronborg Castle in Denmark, which was first built as a medieval fortress in the 1420s. Shortly before Shakespeare wrote *Hamlet*, King Frederick II had the structure rebuilt into a castle, and it became was the model for Elsinore in the play. **Why do you think Shakespeare might have chosen this location for the setting of this play? How does this image reflect its mood and themes?**

55 cherub: Cherubim are angels of knowledge. **60 at foot:** Close behind, at heel.

66 cicatrice: Scar. **67 free awe:** Voluntary show of respect. **72 hectic:** Fever. **74 haps:** Fortunes.

[Scene iv: *A plain in Denmark.*]

Enter **FORTINBRAS** *with his* **ARMY** *over the stage.*

FORTINBRAS Go, captain, from me greet the Danish king;
Tell him that, by his license,° Fortinbras
Craves the conveyance° of a promis'd march
Over his kingdom. You know the rendezvous.
If that his majesty would aught with us,
We shall express our duty in his eye;°
And let him know so.

CAPTAIN I will do't, my lord.

FORTINBRAS Go softly° on.

[*Exeunt all but* **CAPTAIN**.]

Enter **HAMLET**, **ROSENCRANTZ**, [**GUILDENSTERN**,] *&c.*

HAMLET Good sir, whose powers are these?

CAPTAIN They are of Norway, sir.

HAMLET How purpos'd, sir, I pray you?

CAPTAIN Against some part of Poland.

HAMLET Who commands them, sir?

CAPTAIN The nephew to old Norway, Fortinbras.

HAMLET Goes it against the main° of Poland, sir,
Or for some frontier?

CAPTAIN Truly to speak, and with no addition,
We go to gain a little patch of ground
That hath in it no profit but the name.
To pay five ducats, five, I would not farm it;°
Nor will it yield to Norway or the Pole
A ranker rate, should it be sold in fee.°

HAMLET Why, then the Polack never will defend it.

CAPTAIN Yes, it is already garrison'd.

HAMLET Two thousand souls and twenty thousand ducats
Will not debate the question of this straw:°
This is th' imposthume° of much wealth and peace,
That inward breaks, and shows no cause without
Why the man dies. I humbly thank you, sir.

CAPTAIN God be wi' you, sir.

[*Exit.*]

ROSENCRANTZ Will 't please you go, my lord?

HAMLET I'll be with you straight. Go a little before.

[*Exeunt all except* **HAMLET**.]

How all occasions° do inform against° me,
And spur my dull revenge! What is a man,
If his chief good and market of his time°
Be but to sleep and feed? a beast, no more.
Sure, he that made us with such large discourse,
Looking before and after, gave us not
That capability and god-like reason
To fust° in us unus'd. Now, whether it be
Bestial oblivion, or some craven scruple
Of thinking too precisely on th' event,
A thought which, quarter'd, hath but one part wisdom
And ever three parts coward, I do not know
Why yet I live to say "This thing 's to do";
Sith I have cause and will and strength and means
To do 't. Examples gross as earth exhort me:
Witness this army of such mass and charge
Led by a delicate and tender prince,
Whose spirit with divine ambition puff'd
Makes mouths at the invisible event,
Exposing what is mortal and unsure
To all that fortune, death and danger dare,
Even for an egg-shell. Rightly to be great
Is not to stir without great argument,

Scene iv. **2 license:** Leave. **3 conveyance:** Escort, convoy. **6 in his eye:** In his presence. **8 softly:** Slowly. **15 main:** Country itself. **20 farm it:** Take a lease of it. **22 fee:** Fee simple. **26 debate . . . straw:** Settle this trifling matter.

27 imposthume: Purulent abscess or swelling. **32 occasions:** Incidents, events. **inform against:** Generally defined as "show," "betray" (i.e., his tardiness); more probably *inform* means "take shape," as in *Macbeth*, II.i.48. **34 market of his time:** The best use he makes of his time, or that for which he sells his time. **39 fust:** Grow moldy.

But greatly to find quarrel in a straw
When honour's at the stake. How stand I then,
That have a father kill'd, a mother stain'd,
Excitements of° my reason and my blood,
And let all sleep? while, to my shame, I see
The imminent death of twenty thousand men,
That, for a fantasy and trick° of fame,
Go to their graves like beds, fight for a plot°
Whereon the numbers cannot try the cause,
Which is not tomb enough and continent
To hide the slain? O, from this time forth,
My thoughts be bloody, or be nothing worth!
Exit.

[Scene v: *Elsinore. A room in the castle.*]

Enter **HORATIO,** [**QUEEN**] **GERTRUDE,** *and a* **GENTLEMAN.**

QUEEN I will not speak with her.
GENTLEMAN She is importunate, indeed distract:
Her mood will needs be pitied.
QUEEN What would she have?
GENTLEMAN She speaks much of her father; says she hears
There's tricks° i' th' world; and hems, and beats her heart;°
Spurns enviously at straws;° speaks things in doubt,
That carry but half sense: her speech is nothing,
Yet the unshaped° use of it doth move
The hearers to collection;° they yawn° at it,
And botch° the words up fit to their own thoughts;
Which, as her winks, and nods, and gestures yield° them,
Indeed would make one think there might be thought,
Though nothing sure, yet much unhappily.°
HORATIO 'Twere good she were spoken with: for she may strew
Dangerous conjectures in ill-breeding minds.°
QUEEN Let her come in.
[*Exit* **GENTLEMAN.**]
[*Aside.*] To my sick soul, as sin's true nature is,
Each toy seems prologue to some great amiss:°
So full of artless jealousy is guilt,
It spills itself in fearing to be spilt.°

Enter **OPHELIA** [*distracted*].

OPHELIA Where is the beauteous majesty of Denmark?
QUEEN How now, Ophelia!
OPHELIA [*she sings*]: "How should I your true love know
From another one?
By his cockle hat° and staff,
And his sandal shoon."°
QUEEN Alas, sweet lady, what imports this song?
OPHELIA Say you? nay, pray you mark.
[*Song*] "He is dead and gone, lady,
He is dead and gone;
At his head a grass-green turf,
At his heels a stone."
O, ho!
QUEEN Nay, but, Ophelia —
OPHELIA Pray you, mark.
[*Sings.*] "White his shroud as the mountain snow" —

Enter **KING.**

58 Excitements of: Incentives to. **61 trick:** Toy, trifle. **62 plot:** Piece of ground. **Scene v. 5 tricks:** Deceptions. **heart:** I.e., breast. **6 Spurns . . . straws:** Kicks spitefully at small objects in her path. **8 unshaped:** Unformed, artless. **9 collection:** Inference, a guess at some sort of meaning. **yawn:** Wonder. **10 botch:** Patch. **11 yield:** Deliver, bring forth (her words).

13 much unhappily: Expressive of much unhappiness. **15 ill-breeding minds:** Minds bent on mischief. **18 great amiss:** Calamity, disaster. **19–20 So . . . spilt:** Guilt is so full of suspicion that it unskillfully betrays itself in fearing to be betrayed. **25 cockle hat:** Hat with cockleshell stuck in it as a sign that the wearer has been a pilgrim to the shrine of St. James of Compostella. The pilgrim's garb was a conventional disguise for lovers. **26 shoon:** Shoes.

QUEEN Alas, look here, my lord.

OPHELIA [*Song*]: "Larded° all with flowers;
Which bewept to the grave did not go
With true-love showers."

KING How do you, pretty lady?

OPHELIA Well, God 'ild° you! They say the owl° was a baker's daughter. Lord, we know what we are, but know not what we may be. God be at your table!

KING Conceit upon her father.

OPHELIA Pray let's have no words of this; but when they ask you what it means, say you this:
[*Song*] "To-morrow is Saint Valentine's day,
All in the morning betime,
And I a maid at your window,
To be your Valentine.°
Then up he rose, and donn'd his clothes,
And dupp'd° the chamber-door;
Let in the maid, that out a maid
Never departed more."

KING Pretty Ophelia!

OPHELIA Indeed, la, without an oath, I'll make an end on 't:
[*Sings.*] "By Gis° and by Saint Charity,
Alack, and fie for shame!
Young men will do 't, if they come to 't;
By cock,° they are to blame.
Quoth she, 'before you tumbled me,
You promis'd me to wed.'
'So would I ha' done, by yonder sun,
An thou hadst not come to my bed.' "

KING How long hath she been thus?

OPHELIA I hope all will be well. We must be patient: but I cannot choose but weep, to think they would lay him i' the cold ground. My brother shall know of it: and so I thank you for your good counsel. Come, my coach! Good night, ladies; good night, sweet ladies; good night, good night.
[*Exit.*]

KING Follow her close; give her good watch, I pray you.
[*Exit* **HORATIO.**]
O, this is the poison of deep grief; it springs
All from her father's death. O Gertrude, Gertrude,
When sorrows come, they come not single spies,
But in battalions. First, her father slain:
Next your son gone; and he most violent author
Of his own just remove: the people muddied,
Thick and unwholesome in their thoughts and whispers,
For good Polonius' death; and we have done but greenly,°
In hugger-mugger° to inter him: poor Ophelia
Divided from herself and her fair judgement,
Without the which we are pictures, or mere beasts:
Last, and as much containing as all these,
Her brother is in secret come from France;
Feeds on his wonder, keeps himself in clouds,°
And wants not buzzers° to infect his ear
With pestilent speeches of his father's death;
Wherein necessity, of matter beggar'd,°
Will nothing stick° our person to arraign
In ear and ear.° O my dear Gertrude, this,
Like to a murd'ring-piece,° in many places
Gives me superfluous death.
A noise within.

QUEEN Alack, what noise is this?

KING Where are my Switzers?° Let them guard the door.

Enter a **MESSENGER.**

---

38 Larded: Decorated. **42 God 'ild:** God yield or reward. **owl:** Reference to a monkish legend that a baker's daughter was turned into an owl for refusing bread to the Savior. **53 Valentine:** This song alludes to the belief that the first girl seen by a man on the morning of this day was his valentine or true love. **55 dupp'd:** Opened. **60 Gis:** Jesus. **63 cock:** Perversion of "God" in oaths.

84 greenly: Foolishly. **85 hugger-mugger:** Secret haste. **90 in clouds:** Invisible. **91 buzzers:** Gossipers. **93 of matter beggar'd:** Unprovided with facts. **94 nothing stick:** Not hesitate. **95 In ear and ear:** In everybody's ears. **96 murd'ring-piece:** Small cannon or mortar; suggestion of numerous missiles fired. **98 Switzers:** Swiss guards, mercenaries.

What is the matter?

MESSENGER Save yourself, my lord:
The ocean, overpeering° of his list,°
Eats not the flats with more impiteous haste
Than young Laertes, in a riotous head,
O'erbears your officers. The rabble call him lord;
And, as the world were now but to begin,
Antiquity forgot, custom not known,
The ratifiers and props of every word,°
They cry "Choose we: Laertes shall be king":
Caps, hands, and tongues, applaud it to the clouds:
"Laertes shall be king, Laertes king!"

A noise within.

QUEEN How cheerfully on the false trail they cry!
O, this is counter,° you false Danish dogs!

KING The doors are broke.

Enter **LAERTES** *with others.*

LAERTES Where is this king? Sirs, stand you all without.

DANES No, let's come in.

LAERTES I pray you, give me leave.

DANES We will, we will.

[*They retire without the door.*]

LAERTES I thank you: keep the door. O thou vile king,
Give me my father!

QUEEN Calmly, good Laertes.

LAERTES That drop of blood that's calm proclaims me bastard,
Cries cuckold to my father, brands the harlot
Even here, between the chaste unsmirched brow
Of my true mother.

KING What is the cause, Laertes,
That thy rebellion looks so giant-like?
Let him go, Gertrude; do not fear our person:
There's such divinity doth hedge a king,
That treason can but peep to° what it would,°
Acts little of his will. Tell me, Laertes,
Why thou art thus incens'd. Let him go, Gertrude.
Speak, man.

LAERTES Where is my father?

KING Dead.

QUEEN But not by him.

KING Let him demand his fill.

LAERTES How came he dead? I'll not be juggled with:
To hell, allegiance! vows, to the blackest devil!
Conscience and grace, to the profoundest pit!
I dare damnation. To this point I stand,
That both the worlds I give to negligence,°
Let come what comes; only I'll be reveng'd
Most throughly° for my father.

KING Who shall stay you?

LAERTES My will,° not all the world's:
And for my means, I'll husband them so well,
They shall go far with little.

KING Good Laertes,
If you desire to know the certainty
Of your dear father, is 't writ in your revenge,
That, swoopstake,° you will draw both friend and foe,
Winner and loser?

LAERTES None but his enemies.

KING Will you know them then?

LAERTES To his good friends thus wide I'll ope my arms;
And like the kind life-rend'ring pelican,°
Repast° them with my blood.

---

100 overpeering: Overflowing. **list:** Shore. **106 word:** Promise. **111 counter:** A hunting term meaning to follow the trail in a direction opposite to that which the game has taken.

125 peep to: I.e., look at from afar off. **would:** Wishes to do. **135 give to negligence:** He despises both the here and the hereafter. **137 throughly:** thoroughly. **138 My will:** He will not be stopped except by his own will. **143 swoopstake:** Literally, drawing the whole stake at once, i.e., indiscriminately. **147 pelican:** Reference to the belief that the pelican feeds its young with its own blood. **148 Repast:** Feed.

KING Why, now you speak
Like a good child and a true gentleman.
That I am guiltless of your father's death,
And am most sensibly in grief for it,
It shall as level to your judgement 'pear
As day does to your eye.

A noise within: "Let her come in."

LAERTES How now! what noise is that?

Enter **OPHELIA.**

O heat,° dry up my brains! tears seven times salt,
Burn out the sense and virtue of mine eye!
By heaven, thy madness shall be paid with weight,
Till our scale turn the beam. O rose of May!
Dear maid, kind sister, sweet Ophelia!
O heavens! is 't possible, a young maid's wits
Should be as mortal as an old man's life?
Nature is fine in love, and where 'tis fine,
It sends some precious instance of itself
After the thing it loves.

OPHELIA [*Song*]: "They bore him barefac'd on the bier;
Hey non nonny, nonny, hey nonny;
And in his grave rain'd many a tear:" —
Fare you well, my dove!

LAERTES Hadst thou thy wits, and didst persuade revenge,
It could not move thus.

OPHELIA [*sings*]: "You must sing a-down a-down,
An you call him a-down-a."
O, how the wheel° becomes it! It is the false steward,° that stole his master's daughter.

LAERTES This nothing's more than matter.

OPHELIA There's rosemary,° that's for remembrance; pray you, love, remember: and there is pansies,° that's for thoughts.

This painting of Ophelia, completed in 1910, is one of several by pre-Raphaelite artist John William Waterhouse. **What aspects of Ophelia's character does this painting evoke? What nuances of character do you believe are either ignored or exaggerated?**

LAERTES A document° in madness, thoughts and remembrance fitted.

OPHELIA There's fennel° for you, and columbines:° there's rue° for you; and here's some for me: we may call it herb of grace° o' Sundays: O, you must wear your rue with a difference. There's a daisy:° I would give you some violets,° but they

---

155 heat: Probably the heat generated by the passion of grief. **173 wheel:** Spinning wheel as accompaniment to the song refrain. **173–174 false steward:** The story is unknown. **176 rosemary:** Used as a symbol of remembrance both at weddings and at funerals. **178 pansies:** Emblems of love and courtship (from the French *pensée*).

179 document: Piece of instruction or lesson. **181 fennel:** Emblem of flattery. **182 columbines:** Emblem of unchastity (?) or ingratitude (?). **rue:** Emblem of repentance. It was usually mingled with holy water and then known as *herb of grace.* Ophelia is probably playing on the two meanings of *rue,* "repentant" and "even for ruth (pity)"; the former signification is for the queen, the latter for herself. **185 daisy:** Emblem of dissembling, faithlessness. **186 violets:** Emblems of faithfulness.

withered all when my father died: they say
'a made a good end, —
[*Sings.*] "For bonny sweet Robin is all my
joy."°

LAERTES Thought° and affliction, passion, hell
itself,
She turns to favour and to prettiness.

OPHELIA [*Song*]: "And will 'a not come again?°
And will 'a not come again?
No, no, he is dead:
Go to thy death-bed:
He never will come again.

"His beard was as white as snow,
All flaxen was his poll:°
He is gone, he is gone,
And we cast away° moan:
God ha' mercy on his soul!"

And of all Christian souls, I pray God. God be
wi' you. [*Exit.*]

LAERTES Do you see this, O God?

KING Laertes, I must commune with your grief,
Or you deny me right.° Go but apart,
Make choice of whom your wisest friends you
will,
And they shall hear and judge 'twixt you and
me:
If by direct or by collateral° hand
They find us touch'd,° we will our kingdom give,
Our crown, our life, and all that we call ours,
To you in satisfaction; but if not,
Be you content to lend your patience to us,
And we shall jointly labour with your soul
To give it due content.

LAERTES Let this be so;

This photo still is from the 1990 Franco Zeffirelli film *Hamlet* shows Helena Bonham Carter as Ophelia. Look carefully at her appearance, especially her hair and eyes. **How effectively does Carter capture Ophelia's madness here? How does her interpretation of Ophelia compare with that of Waterhouse (p. 710)?**

189 For . . . joy: Probably a line from a Robin Hood ballad.
190 Thought: Melancholy thought. **192 And . . . again:** This song appeared in the songbooks as "The Merry Milkmaids' Dumps."
198 poll: Head. **200 cast away:** Shipwrecked.

205 right: My rights. **208 collateral:** Indirect. **209 touch'd:** Implicated.

His means of death, his obscure funeral —
No trophy, sword, nor hatchment° o'er his bones,
No noble rite nor formal ostentation —
Cry to be heard, as 'twere from heaven to earth,
That I must call 't in question.

KING So you shall;
And where th' offence is let the great axe fall.
I pray you, go with me. *Exeunt.*

[Scene vi: *Another room in the castle.*]

Enter **HORATIO** *and others.*

HORATIO What are they that would speak with me?

GENTLEMAN Sea-faring men, sir: they say they have letters for you.

HORATIO Let them come in.

[*Exit* **GENTLEMAN.**]

I do not know from what part of the world
I should be greeted, if not from Lord Hamlet.

Enter **SAILORS.**

FIRST SAILOR God bless you, sir.

HORATIO Let him bless thee too.

FIRST SAILOR 'A shall sir, an 't please him. There's a letter for you, sir; it comes from the ambassador that was bound for England; if your name be Horatio, as I am let to know it is.

HORATIO [*reads*]: "Horatio, when thou shalt have overlooked this, give these fellows some means° to the king: they have letters for him. Ere we were two days old at sea, a pirate of very warlike appointment gave us chase. Finding ourselves too slow of sail, we put on a compelled valour, and in the grapple I boarded them: on the instant they got clear of our ship; so I alone became their prisoner. They have dealt with me like thieves of mercy:° but they knew what they did; I am to do a good turn for them. Let the king have the letters I have sent; and repair thou to me with as much speed as thou wouldest fly death. I have words to speak in thine ear will make thee dumb; yet are they much too light for the bore° of the matter. These good fellows will bring thee where I am. Rosencrantz and Guildenstern hold their course for England: of them I have much to tell thee. Farewell. He that thou knowest thine,

HAMLET."

Come, I will give you way for these your letters;
And do 't the speedier, that you may direct me
To him from whom you brought them.

Exeunt.

[Scene vii: *Another room in the castle.*]

Enter **KING** *and* **LAERTES.**

KING Now must your conscience° my acquittance seal,
And you must put me in your heart for friend,
Sith you have heard, and with a knowing ear,
That he which hath your noble father slain
Pursued my life.

LAERTES It well appears: but tell me
Why you proceeded not against these feats,
So criminal and so capital° in nature,
As by your safety, wisdom, all things else,
You mainly° were stirr'd up.

KING O, for two special reasons;
Which may to you, perhaps, seem much unsinew'd,°
But yet to me th' are strong. The queen his mother
Lives almost by his looks; and for myself —
My virtue or my plague, be it either which —

---

216 hatchment: Tablet displaying the armorial bearings of a deceased person. **Scene vi. 15 means:** Means of access. **23 thieves of mercy:** Merciful thieves.

30 bore: Caliber, importance. **Scene vii. 1 conscience:** Knowledge that this is true. **7 capital:** Punishable by death. **9 mainly:** Greatly. **10 unsinew'd:** Weak.

She's so conjunctive° to my life and soul,
That, as the star moves not but in his sphere,°
I could not but by her. The other motive,
Why to a public count° I might not go,
Is the great love the general gender° bear him;
Who, dipping all his faults in their affection,
Would, like the spring° that turneth wood to stone,
Convert his gyves° to graces; so that my arrows,
Too slightly timber'd° for so loud° a wind,
Would have reverted to my bow again,
And not where I had aim'd them.

LAERTES And so have I a noble father lost;
A sister driven into desp'rate terms,°
Whose worth, if praises may go back° again,
Stood challenger on mount° of all the age°
For her perfections: but my revenge will come.

KING Break not your sleeps for that: you must not think
That we are made of stuff so flat and dull
That we can let our beard be shook with danger
And think it pastime. You shortly shall hear more:
I lov'd your father, and we love ourself;
And that, I hope, will teach you to imagine —

Enter a MESSENGER *with letters.*

How now! what news?

MESSENGER Letters, my lord, from Hamlet:
These to your majesty; this to the queen.°

KING From Hamlet! who brought them?

MESSENGER Sailors, my lord, they say; I saw them not:
They were given me by Claudio;° he receiv'd them
Of him that brought them.

KING Laertes, you shall hear them.
Leave us. [*Exit* MESSENGER.]
[*Reads.*] "High and mighty, You shall know I am set naked° on your kingdom. To-morrow shall I beg leave to see your kingly eyes: when I shall, first asking your pardon thereunto, recount the occasion of my sudden and more strange return.

HAMLET."

What should this mean? Are all the rest come back?
Or is it some abuse, and no such thing?

LAERTES Know you the hand?

KING 'Tis Hamlet's character. "Naked!"
And in a postscript here, he says "alone."
Can you devise° me?

LAERTES I'm lost in it, my lord. But let him come;
It warms the very sickness in my heart,
That I shall live and tell him to his teeth,
"Thus didst thou."

KING If it be so, Laertes —
As how should it be so? how otherwise?° —
Will you be rul'd by me?

LAERTES Ay, my lord;
So you will not o'errule me to a peace.

KING To thine own peace. If he be now return'd,
As checking at° his voyage, and that he means
No more to undertake it, I will work him
To an exploit, now ripe in my device,
Under the which he shall not choose but fall:
And for his death no wind of blame shall breathe,

---

14 conjunctive: Conformable (the next line suggesting planetary conjunction). **15 sphere:** The hollow sphere in which, according to Ptolemaic astronomy, the planets were supposed to move. **17 count:** Account, reckoning. **18 general gender:** Common people. **20 spring:** I.e., one heavily charged with lime. **21 gyves:** Fetters; here, faults, or possibly, punishments inflicted (on him). **22 slightly timber'd:** Light. **loud:** Strong. **26 terms:** State, condition. **27 go back:** Return to Ophelia's former virtues. **28 on mount:** Set up on high, *mounted* (on horseback). **of all the age:** Qualifies *challenger* and not *mount.* **37 to the queen:** One hears no more of the letter to the queen.

40 Claudio: This character does not appear in the play. **44 naked:** Unprovided (with retinue). **55 devise:** Explain to. **60 As . . . otherwise?** How can this (Hamlet's return) be true? (yet) how otherwise than true (since we have the evidence of his letter)? Some editors read *How should it not be so*, etc., making the words refer to Laertes's desire to meet with Hamlet. **64 checking at:** Used in falconry of a hawk's leaving the quarry to fly at a chance bird; turn aside.

But even his mother shall uncharge the practice°
And call it accident.
LAERTES My lord, I will be rul'd;
The rather, if you could devise it so
That I might be the organ.°
KING It falls right.
You have been talk'd of since your travel much,
And that in Hamlet's hearing, for a quality
Wherein, they say, you shine: your sum of parts
Did not together pluck such envy from him
As did that one, and that, in my regard,
Of the unworthiest siege.°
LAERTES What part is that, my lord?
KING A very riband in the cap of youth,
Yet needful too; for youth no less becomes
The light and careless livery that it wears
Than settled age his sables° and his weeds,
Importing health and graveness. Two months since,
Here was a gentleman of Normandy: —
I have seen myself, and serv'd against, the French,
And they can well° on horseback: but this gallant
Had witchcraft in 't; he grew unto his seat;
And to such wondrous doing brought his horse,
As had he been incorps'd and demi-natur'd°
With the brave beast: so far he topp'd° my thought,
That I, in forgery° of shapes and tricks,
Come short of what he did.
LAERTES A Norman was 't?
KING A Norman.
LAERTES Upon my life, Lamord.°
KING The very same.
LAERTES I know him well: he is the brooch indeed
And gem of all the nation.
KING He made confession° of you,
And gave you such a masterly report
For art and exercise° in your defence°
And for your rapier most especial,
That he cried out, 'twould be a sight indeed,
If one could match you: the scrimers° of their nation,
He swore, had neither motion, guard, nor eye,
If you oppos'd them. Sir, this report of his
Did Hamlet so envenom with his envy
That he could nothing do but wish and beg
Your sudden coming o'er, to play° with you.
Now, out of this, —
LAERTES What out of this, my lord?
KING Laertes, was your father dear to you?
Or are you like the painting of a sorrow,
A face without a heart?
LAERTES Why ask you this?
KING Not that I think you did not love your father;
But that I know love is begun by time;
And that I see, in passages of proof,°
Time qualifies the spark and fire of it.
There lives within the very flame of love
A kind of wick or snuff that will abate it;
And nothing is at a like goodness still;
For goodness, growing to a plurisy,°
Dies in his own too much:° that we would do,
We should do when we would; for this "would" changes
And hath abatements° and delays as many
As there are tongues, are hands, are accidents;°

---

69 uncharge the practice: Acquit the stratagem of being a plot. **72 organ:** Agent, instrument. **78 siege:** Rank. **82 sables:** Rich garments. **86 can well:** Are skilled. **89 incorps'd and demi-natur'd:** Of one body and nearly of one nature (like the centaur). **90 topp'd:** Surpassed. **91 forgery:** Invention.

94 Lamord: This refers possibly to Pietro Monte, instructor to Louis XII's master of the horse. **97 confession:** Grudging admission of superiority. **99 art and exercise:** Skillful exercise. **defence:** Science of defense in sword practice. **102 scrimers:** Fencers. **107 play:** Fence. **114 passages of proof:** Proved instances. **119 plurisy:** Excess, plethora. **120 in his own too much:** Of its own excess. **122 abatements:** Diminutions. **123 accidents:** Occurrences, incidents.

And then this "should" is like a spendthrift° sigh,
That hurts by easing. But, to the quick o' th' ulcer:° —
Hamlet comes back: what would you undertake,
To show yourself your father's son in deed
More than in words?

LAERTES To cut his throat i' th' church.

KING No place, indeed, should murder sanctuarize;°
Revenge should have no bounds. But, good Laertes,
Will you do this, keep close within your chamber.
Hamlet return'd shall know you are come home:
We'll put on those shall praise your excellence
And set a double varnish on the fame
The Frenchman gave you, bring you in fine together
And wager on your heads: he, being remiss,
Most generous and free from all contriving,
Will not peruse the foils; so that, with ease,
Or with a little shuffling, you may choose
A sword unbated,° and in a pass of practice°
Requite him for your father.

LAERTES I will do 't:
And, for that purpose, I'll anoint my sword.
I bought an unction of a mountebank,°
So mortal that, but dip a knife in it,
Where it draws blood no cataplasm° so rare,
Collected from all simples° that have virtue
Under the moon,° can save the thing from death
That is but scratch'd withal: I'll touch my point
With this contagion, that, if I gall° him slightly,
It may be death.

KING Let's further think of this;
Weigh what convenience both of time and means
May fit us to our shape:° if this should fail,
And that our drift look through our bad performance,°
'Twere better not assay'd: therefore this project
Should have a back or second, that might hold,
If this should blast in proof.° Soft! let me see:
We'll make a solemn wager on your cunnings:°
I ha 't:
When in your motion you are hot and dry —
As make your bouts more violent to that end —
And that he calls for drink, I'll have prepar'd him
A chalice° for the nonce, whereon but sipping,
If he by chance escape your venom'd stuck,°
Our purpose may hold there. But stay, what noise?

Enter **QUEEN.**

QUEEN One woe doth tread upon another's heel,
So fast they follow: your sister's drown'd, Laertes.

LAERTES Drown'd! O, where?

QUEEN There is a willow° grows askant° the brook,
That shows his hoar° leaves in the glassy stream;
There with fantastic garlands did she make

---

124 spendthrift: An allusion to the belief that each sigh cost the heart a drop of blood. **125 quick o' th' ulcer:** Heart of the difficulty. **129 sanctuarize:** Protect from punishment; allusion to the right of sanctuary with which certain religious places were invested. **140 unbated:** Not blunted, having no button. **pass of practice:** Treacherous thrust. **143 mountebank:** Quack doctor. **145 cataplasm:** Plaster or poultice. **146 simples:** Herbs. **147 Under the moon:** I.e., when collected by moonlight to add to their medicinal value.

149 gall: Graze, wound. **152 shape:** Part we propose to act. **153 drift . . . performance:** Intention be disclosed by our bungling. **156 blast in proof:** Burst in the test (like a cannon). **157 cunnings:** Skills. **162 chalice:** Cup. **163 stuck:** Thrust (from *stoccado*) **168 willow:** For its significance of forsaken love. **askant:** Aslant. **169 hoar:** White (i.e., on the underside).

Of crow-flowers,° nettles, daisies, and long purples°
That liberal° shepherds give a grosser name,
But our cold maids do dead men's fingers call them:
There, on the pendent boughs her crownet° weeds
Clamb'ring to hang, an envious sliver° broke;
When down her weedy° trophies and herself
Fell in the weeping brook. Her clothes spread wide;
And, mermaid-like, awhile they bore her up:
Which time she chanted snatches of old lauds;°
As one incapable° of her own distress,
Or like a creature native and indued°
Upon that element: but long it could not be
Till that her garments, heavy with their drink,
Pull'd the poor wretch from her melodious lay
To muddy death.

LAERTES Alas, then, she is drown'd?

QUEEN Drown'd, drown'd.

LAERTES Too much of water hast thou, poor Ophelia,
And therefore I forbid my tears: but yet
It is our trick;° nature her custom holds,
Let shame say what it will: when these are gone,
The woman will be out.° Adieu, my lord:
I have a speech of fire, that fain would blaze,
But that this folly drowns it. *Exit.*

KING Let's follow, Gertrude:
How much I had to do to calm his rage!
Now fear I this will give it start again;
Therefore let 's follow. *Exeunt.*

Print Collector/Getty Images

Perhaps the most well-known painting of Ophelia is John Everett Millais's 1852 painting of her final moments. **How does Millais portray Ophelia in this work? Pay close attention to the expression on her face, her position in the water, and the way Millais used light and shadow.**

---

171 crow-flowers: Buttercups. **long purples:** Early purple orchids. **172 liberal:** Probably, free-spoken. **174 crownet:** Coronet; made into a chaplet. **175 sliver:** Branch. **176 weedy:** I.e., of plants. **179 lauds:** Hymns. **180 incapable:** Lacking capacity to apprehend. **181 indued:** Endowed with qualities fitting her for living in water.

189 trick: Way. **190–191 when . . . out:** When my tears are all shed, the woman in me will be satisfied.

ACT V

[Scene i: *A churchyard.*]

Enter two CLOWNS° [*with spades, &c.*].

FIRST CLOWN Is she to be buried in Christian burial when she wilfully seeks her own salvation?

SECOND CLOWN I tell thee she is; therefore make her grave straight:° the crowner° hath sat on her, and finds it Christian burial.

FIRST CLOWN How can that be, unless she drowned herself in her own defence?

SECOND CLOWN Why, 'tis found so.

FIRST CLOWN It must be "se offendendo";° it cannot be else. For here lies the point: if I drown myself wittingly,° it argues an act: and an act hath three branches;° it is, to act, to do, and to perform: argal,° she drowned herself wittingly.

SECOND CLOWN Nay, but hear you, goodman delver,°—

FIRST CLOWN Give me leave. Here lies the water; good: here stands the man; good: if the man go to this water, and drown himself, it is, will he, nill he, he goes,—mark you that; but if the water come to him and drown him, he drowns not himself: argal, he that is not guilty of his own death shortens not his own life.

SECOND CLOWN But is this law?

FIRST CLOWN Ay, marry, is 't; crowner's quest° law.

SECOND CLOWN Will you ha' the truth on 't? If this had not been a gentlewoman, she should have been buried out o' Christian burial.

FIRST CLOWN Why, there thou say'st:° and the more pity that great folk should have countenance° in this world to drown or hang themselves, more than their even° Christian. Come, my spade. There is no ancient gentlemen but gardeners, ditchers, and grave-makers: they hold up° Adam's profession.

SECOND CLOWN Was he a gentleman?

FIRST CLOWN 'A was the first that ever bore arms.

SECOND CLOWN Why, he had none.

FIRST CLOWN What, art a heathen? How dost thou understand the Scripture? The Scripture says "Adam digged": could he dig without arms? I'll put another question to thee: if thou answerest me not to the purpose, confess thyself°—

SECOND CLOWN Go to.°

FIRST CLOWN What is he that builds stronger than either the mason, the shipwright, or the carpenter?

SECOND CLOWN The gallows-maker; for that frame outlives a thousand tenants.

FIRST CLOWN I like thy wit well, in good faith: the gallows does well; but how does it well? it does well to those that do ill: now thou dost ill to say the gallows is built stronger than the church: argal, the gallows may do well to thee. To 't again, come.

SECOND CLOWN "Who builds stronger than a mason, a shipwright, or a carpenter?"

FIRST CLOWN Ay, tell me that, and unyoke.°

SECOND CLOWN Marry, now I can tell.

FIRST CLOWN To 't.

SECOND CLOWN Mass,° I cannot tell.

Act V, Scene i. Clowns: The word *clown* was used to denote peasants as well as humorous characters; here applied to the rustic type of clown. **5 straight:** Straightway, immediately; some interpret "from east to west in a direct line, parallel with the church." **crowner:** Coroner. **11 "se offendendo":** For *se defendendo*, term used in verdicts of justifiable homicide. **13 wittingly:** Intentionally. **14 three branches:** Parody of legal phraseology. **15 argal:** Corruption of *ergo*, therefore. **17 delver:** Digger. **27 quest:** Inquest.

32 there thou say'st: That's right. **34 countenance:** Privilege. **35 even:** Fellow. **38 hold up:** Maintain, continue. **48 confess thyself:** "And be hanged" completes the proverb. **49 Go to:** Perhaps, "begin," or some other form of concession. **63 unyoke:** After this great effort you may unharness the team of your wits. **66 Mass:** By the Mass.

Enter **HAMLET** *and* **HORATIO** [*at a distance*].

FIRST CLOWN Cudgel thy brains no more about it, for your dull ass will not mend his pace with beating; and, when you are asked this question next, say "a grave-maker": the houses he makes last till doomsday. Go, get thee in, and fetch me a stoup° of liquor.

[*Exit* **SECOND CLOWN**.] *Song.* [*He digs.*]

"In youth, when I did love, did love,
Methought it was very sweet,
To contract — O — the time, for — a — my behove,°
O, methought, there — a — was nothing — a — meet."

HAMLET Has this fellow no feeling of his business, that 'a sings at grave-making?

HORATIO Custom hath made it in him a property of easiness.°

HAMLET 'Tis e'en so: the hand of little employment hath the daintier sense.

FIRST CLOWN [*Song*]: "But age, with his stealing steps,
Hath claw'd me in his clutch,
And hath shipped me into the land
As if I had never been such."

[*Throws up a skull.*]

HAMLET That skull had a tongue in it, and could sing once: how the knave jowls° it to the ground, as if 'twere Cain's jaw-bone,° that did the first murder! This might be the pate of a politician,° which this ass now o'er-reaches;° one that would circumvent God, might it not?

HORATIO It might, my lord.

HAMLET Or of a courtier; which could say "Good morrow, sweet lord! How dost thou, sweet lord?" This might be my lord such-a-one, that praised my lord such-a-one's horse, when he meant to beg it; might it not?

HORATIO Ay, my lord.

HAMLET Why, e'en so: and now my Lady Worm's; chapless,° and knocked about the mazzard° with a sexton's spade: here's fine revolution, an we had the trick to see 't. Did these bones cost no more the breeding, but to play at loggats° with 'em? mine ache to think on 't.

FIRST CLOWN [*Song*]: "A pick-axe, and a spade, a spade,
For and° a shrouding sheet:
O, a pit of clay for to be made
For such a guest is meet."

[*Throws up another skull.*]

HAMLET There's another: why may not that be the skull of a lawyer? Where be his quiddities° now, his quillities,° his cases, his tenures,° and his tricks? why does he suffer this mad knave now to knock him about the sconce° with a dirty shovel, and will not tell him of his action of battery? Hum! This fellow might be in 's time a great buyer of land, with his statutes, his recognizances,° his fines, his double vouchers,° his recoveries:° is this the fine° of his fines, and the recovery of his recoveries, to have his fine pate full of fine dirt? will his vouchers vouch him no more of his purchases, and double ones too, than the length and breadth of a pair of indentures?° The very conveyances of his lands

---

72 stoup: Two-quart measure. **76 behove:** Benefit. **81 property of easiness:** A peculiarity that now is easy. **89 jowls:** Dashes. **90 Cain's jaw-bone:** Allusion to the old tradition that Cain slew Abel with the jawbone of an ass. **92 politician:** Schemer, plotter. **o'er-reaches:** Quibble on the literal sense and the sense "circumvent."

104 chapless: Having no lower jaw. **105 mazzard:** Head. **108 loggats:** A game in which six sticks are thrown to lie as near as possible to a stake fixed in the ground or block of wood on a floor. **111 For and:** And moreover. **116 quiddities:** Subtleties, quibbles. **quillities:** Verbal niceties, subtle distinctions. **117 tenures:** The holding of a piece of property or office, or the conditions or period of such holding. **119 sconce:** Head. **122–123 statutes, recognizances:** Legal terms connected with the transfer of land. **124 vouchers:** Persons called on to warrant a tenant's title. **recoveries:** Process for transfer of entailed estate. **fine:** The four uses of this word are as follows: (1) end, (2) legal process, (3) elegant, (4) small. **129–130 indentures:** Conveyances or contracts.

will scarcely lie in this box; and must the inheritor° himself have no more, ha?

HORATIO Not a jot more, my lord.

HAMLET Is not parchment made of sheep-skins?

HORATIO Ay, my lord, and of calf-skins° too.

HAMLET They are sheep and calves which seek out assurance in that.° I will speak to this fellow. Whose grave's this, sirrah?

FIRST CLOWN Mine, sir.
[*Sings.*] "O, a pit of clay for to be made
For such a guest is meet."

HAMLET I think it be thine, indeed; for thou liest in 't.

FIRST CLOWN You lie out on 't, sir, and therefore 't is not yours: for my part, I do not lie in 't, yet it is mine.

HAMLET Thou dost lie in 't, to be in 't and say it is thine: 'tis for the dead, not for the quick; therefore thou liest.

FIRST CLOWN 'Tis a quick lie, sir; 'twill away again, from me to you.

HAMLET What man dost thou dig it for?

FIRST CLOWN For no man, sir.

HAMLET What woman, then?

FIRST CLOWN For none, neither.

HAMLET Who is to be buried in 't?

FIRST CLOWN One that was a woman, sir; but, rest her soul, she's dead.

HAMLET How absolute° the knave is! we must speak by the card,° or equivocation° will undo us. By the Lord, Horatio, these three years I have taken note of it; the age is grown so picked° that the toe of the peasant comes so near the heel of the courtier, he galls° his kibe.° How long hast thou been a grave-maker?

132 inheritor: Possessor, owner. **135 calf-skins:** Parchments. **136 assurance in that:** Safety in legal parchments. **157 absolute:** Positive, decided. **158 by the card:** With precision, i.e., by the mariner's card on which the points of the compass were marked. **equivocation:** Ambiguity in the use of terms. **161 picked:** Refined, fastidious. **163 galls:** Chafes. **kibe:** Chilblain.

FIRST CLOWN Of all the day i' the year, I came to 't that day that our last king Hamlet overcame Fortinbras.

HAMLET How long is that since?

FIRST CLOWN Cannot you tell that? every fool can tell that: it was the very day that young Hamlet was born; he that is mad, and sent into England.

HAMLET Ay, marry, why was he sent into England?

FIRST CLOWN Why, because 'a was mad: 'a shall recover his wits there; or, if 'a do not, 'tis no great matter there.

HAMLET Why?

FIRST CLOWN 'Twill not be seen in him there; there the men are as mad as he.

HAMLET How came he mad?

FIRST CLOWN Very strangely, they say.

HAMLET How strangely?

FIRST CLOWN Faith, e'en with losing his wits.

HAMLET Upon what ground?

FIRST CLOWN Why, here in Denmark: I have been sexton here, man and boy, thirty years.°

HAMLET How long will a man lie i' the earth ere he rot?

FIRST CLOWN Faith, if 'a be not rotten before 'a die — as we have many pocky° corses now-a-days, that will scarce hold the laying in — 'a will last you some eight year or nine year: a tanner will last you nine year.

HAMLET Why he more than another?

FIRST CLOWN Why, sir, his hide is so tanned with his trade, that 'a will keep out water a great while; and your water is a sore decayer of your whoreson dead body. Here's a skull now hath lain you i' th' earth three and twenty years.

HAMLET Whose was it?

186 thirty years: This statement with that in lines 170–171 shows Hamlet's age to be thirty years. **191 pocky:** Rotten, diseased.

In this film still, taken from the 1948 movie *Hamlet*, Hamlet (played by Laurence Olivier) kneels to speak to the skull of Yorick. **Why do you think the director chose to film this scene as a close-up? What does the background suggest about how the film-makers wished their audience to view the setting?**

FIRST CLOWN A whoreson mad fellow's it was: whose do you think it was?

HAMLET Nay, I know not.

FIRST CLOWN A pestilence on him for a mad rogue! 'a poured a flagon of Rhenish on my head once. This same skull, sir, was Yorick's skull, the king's jester.

HAMLET This?

FIRST CLOWN E'en that.

HAMLET Let me see. [*Takes the skull.*] Alas, poor Yorick! I knew him, Horatio: a fellow of infinite jest, of most excellent fancy: he hath borne me on his back a thousand times; and now, how abhorred in my imagination it is! my gorge rises at it. Here hung those lips that I have kissed I know not how oft. Where be your gibes now? your gambols? your songs? your flashes of merriment, that were wont to set the table on a roar? Not one now, to mock your own grinning? quite chap-fallen? Now get you to my lady's chamber, and tell her, let her paint an inch thick, to this favour she must come; make her laugh at that. Prithee, Horatio, tell me one thing.

HORATIO What's that, my lord?

HAMLET Dost thou think Alexander looked o' this fashion i' the earth?

HORATIO E'en so.

HAMLET And smelt so? pah!

[*Puts down the skull.*]

HORATIO E'en so, my lord.

HAMLET To what base uses we may return, Horatio! Why may not imagination trace the noble dust of Alexander, till 'a find it stopping a bung-hole?

HORATIO 'Twere to consider too curiously,° to consider so.

HAMLET No, faith, not a jot; but to follow him thither with modesty enough, and likelihood to lead it: as thus: Alexander died,

---

240 curiously: Minutely.

Alexander was buried, Alexander returneth into dust; the dust is earth; of earth we make loam;° and why of that loam, whereto he was converted, might they not stop a beer-barrel?

Imperious° Cæsar, dead and turn'd to clay,
Might stop a hole to keep the wind away:
O, that that earth, which kept the world in awe,
Should patch a wall t'expel the winter's flaw!°
But soft! but soft awhile! here comes the king,

Enter **KING, QUEEN, LAERTES,** *and the Corse* [*of* **OPHELIA**, *in procession, with Priest, Lords, etc.*].

The queen, the courtiers: who is this they follow?
And with such maimed rites? This doth betoken
The corse they follow did with desp'rate hand
Fordo° it° own life: 'twas of some estate.
Couch° we awhile, and mark.
[*Retiring with* **HORATIO**.]

LAERTES What ceremony else?

HAMLET That is Laertes,
A very noble youth: mark.

LAERTES What ceremony else?

FIRST PRIEST Her obsequies have been as far enlarg'd°
As we have warranty: her death was doubtful;
And, but that great command o'ersways the order,
She should in ground unsanctified have lodg'd
Till the last trumpet; for charitable prayers,
Shards,° flints and pebbles should be thrown on her:
Yet here she is allow'd her virgin crants,°
Her maiden strewments° and the bringing home
Of bell and burial.°

LAERTES Must there no more be done?

FIRST PRIEST No more be done:
We should profane the service of the dead
To sing a requiem and such rest to her
As to peace-parted° souls.

LAERTES Lay her i' th' earth:
And from her fair and unpolluted flesh
May violets spring! I tell thee, churlish priest,
A minist'ring angel shall my sister be,
When thou liest howling.°

HAMLET What, the fair Ophelia!

QUEEN Sweets to the sweet: farewell!
[*Scattering flowers.*]
I hop'd thou shouldst have been my Hamlet's wife;
I thought thy bride-bed to have deck'd, sweet maid,
And not have strew'd thy grave.

LAERTES O, treble woe
Fall ten times treble on that cursed head,
Whose wicked deed thy most ingenious sense°
Depriv'd thee of! Hold off the earth awhile,
Till I have caught her once more in mine arms: [*Leaps into the grave.*]
Now pile your dust upon the quick and dead,
Till of this flat a mountain you have made,
T' o'ertop old Pelion,° or the skyish head
Of blue Olympus.

HAMLET [*Advancing*] What is he whose grief

---

246 loam: Clay paste for brickmaking. **249 Imperious:** Imperial. **252 flaw:** Gust of wind. **257 Fordo:** Destroy. **it:** Its. **258 Couch:** Hide, lurk. **262 enlarg'd:** Extended, referring to the fact that suicides are not given full burial rites. **267 Shards:** Broken bits of pottery. **268 crants:** Garlands customarily hung upon the biers of unmarried women.

269 strewments: Traditional strewing of flowers. **269–270 bringing . . . burial:** The laying to rest of the body, to the sound of the bell. **274 peace-parted:** Allusion to the text "Lord, now lettest thou thy servant depart in peace." **278 howling:** I.e., in hell. **284 ingenious sense:** Mind endowed with finest qualities. **289 Pelion:** Olympus, Pelion, and Ossa are mountains in the north of Thessaly.

Bears such an emphasis? whose phrase of sorrow
Conjures the wand'ring stars,° and makes them stand
Like wonder-wounded hearers? This is I,
Hamlet the Dane.

[*Leaps into the grave.*]

LAERTES The devil take thy soul!

[*Grappling with him.*]

HAMLET Thou pray'st not well.
I prithee, take thy fingers from my throat;
For, though I am not splenitive° and rash,
Yet have I in me something dangerous,
Which let thy wisdom fear: hold off thy hand.

KING Pluck them asunder.

QUEEN Hamlet, Hamlet!

ALL Gentlemen, —

HORATIO Good my lord, be quiet.

[*The* **ATTENDANTS** *part them, and they come out of the grave.*]

HAMLET Why, I will fight with him upon this theme
Until my eyelids will no longer wag.°

QUEEN O my son, what theme?

HAMLET I lov'd Ophelia: forty thousand brothers
Could not, with all their quantity° of love,
Make up my sum. What wilt thou do for her?

KING O, he is mad, Laertes.

QUEEN For love of God, forbear° him.

HAMLET 'Swounds,° show me what thou 'lt do:
Woo 't° weep? woo 't fight? woo 't fast? woo 't tear thyself?
Woo 't drink up eisel?° eat a crocodile?
I'll do 't. Dost thou come here to whine?
To outface me with leaping in her grave?
Be buried quick with her, and so will I:
And, if thou prate of mountains, let them throw
Millions of acres on us, till our ground,
Singeing his pate against the burning zone,°
Make Ossa like a wart! Nay, an thou 'lt mouth,
I'll rant as well as thou.

QUEEN This is mere madness:
And thus awhile the fit will work on him;
Anon, as patient as the female dove.
When that her golden couplets° are disclos'd,
His silence will sit drooping.

HAMLET Hear you, sir;
What is the reason that you use me thus?
I lov'd you ever: but it is no matter;
Let Hercules himself do what he may,
The cat will mew and dog will have his day.

KING I pray thee, good Horatio, wait upon him.

Exit **HAMLET** *and* **HORATIO**.

[*To* **LAERTES**.] Strengthen your patience in° our last night's speech;
We'll put the matter to the present push.°
Good Gertrude, set some watch over your son.
This grave shall have a living° monument:
An hour of quiet shortly shall we see;
Till then, in patience our proceeding be.

Exeunt.

[Scene ii: *A hall in the castle.*]

Enter **HAMLET** *and* **HORATIO**.

HAMLET So much for this, sir: now shall you see the other;
You do remember all the circumstance?

HORATIO Remember it, my lord!

HAMLET Sir, in my heart there was a kind of fighting,
That would not let me sleep: methought I lay

---

292 wand'ring stars: Planets. **297 splenitive:** Quick-tempered. **303 wag:** Move (not used ludicrously). **306 quantity:** Some suggest that the word is used in a deprecatory sense (little bits, fragments). **309 forbear:** Leave alone. **310 'Swounds:** Oath, "God's wounds." **311 Woo 't:** Wilt thou. **312 eisel:** Vinegar. Some editors have taken this to be the name of a river, such as the Yssel, the Weissel, or the Nile.

318 burning zone: Sun's orbit. **323 golden couplets:** The pigeon lays two eggs; the young when hatched are covered with golden down. **330 in:** By recalling. **331 present push:** Immediate test. **333 living:** Lasting; also refers (for Laertes's benefit) to the plot against Hamlet.

Worse than the mutines in the bilboes.°
Rashly,°
And prais'd be rashness for it, let us know,
Our indiscretion sometime serves us well,
When our deep plots do pall:° and that should learn us
There's a divinity that shapes our ends,
Rough-hew° them how we will, —

HORATIO That is most certain.

HAMLET Up from my cabin,
My sea-gown° scarf'd about me, in the dark
Grop'd I to find out them; had my desire,
Finger'd° their packet, and in fine° withdrew
To mine own room again; making so bold,
My fears forgetting manners, to unseal
Their grand commission; where I found, Horatio, —
O royal knavery! — an exact command,
Larded° with many several sorts of reasons
Importing Denmark's health and England's too,
With, ho! such bugs° and goblins in my life,°
That, on the supervise,° no leisure bated,°
No, not to stay the grinding of the axe,
My head should be struck off.

HORATIO Is 't possible?

HAMLET Here's the commission: read it at more leisure.
But wilt thou hear me how I did proceed?

HORATIO I beseech you.

HAMLET Being thus be-netted round with villanies, —
Ere I could make a prologue to my brains,
They had begun the play° — I sat me down,
Devis'd a new commission, wrote it fair:
I once did hold it, as our statists° do,
A baseness to write fair° and labour'd much
How to forget that learning, but, sir, now
It did me yeoman's° service: wilt thou know
Th' effect of what I wrote?

HORATIO Ay, good my lord.

HAMLET An earnest conjuration from the king,
As England was his faithful tributary,
As love between them like the palm might flourish,
As peace should still her wheaten garland° wear
And stand a comma° 'tween their amities,
And many such-like 'As'es° of great charge,°
That, on the view and knowing of these contents,
Without debatement further, more or less,
He should the bearers put to sudden death,
Not shriving-time° allow'd.

HORATIO How was this seal'd?

HAMLET Why, even in that was heaven ordinant.°
I had my father's signet in my purse,
Which was the model of that Danish seal;
Folded the writ up in the form of th' other,
Subscrib'd it, gave 't th' impression, plac'd it safely,
The changeling never known. Now, the next day
Was our sea-fight; and what to this was sequent°
Thou know'st already.

HORATIO So Guildenstern and Rosencrantz go to 't.

Scene ii. 6 mutines in the bilboes: Mutineers in shackles. **Rashly:** Goes with line 12. **9 pall:** Fail. **11 Rough-hew:** Shape roughly; it may mean "bungle." **13 sea-gown:** "A sea-gown, or a coarse, high-collered, and short-sleeved gowne, reaching down to the mid-leg, and used most by seamen and saylors" (Cotgrave, quoted by Singer). **15 Finger'd:** Pilfered, filched. **in fine:** Finally. **20 Larded:** Enriched. **22 bugs:** Bugbears. **such . . . life:** Such imaginary dangers if I were allowed to live. **23 supervise:** Perusal. **leisure bated:** Delay allowed. **30–31 prologue . . . play:** I.e., before I could begin to think, my mind had made its decision.

33 statists: Statesmen. **34 fair:** In a clear hand. **36 yeoman's:** I.e., faithful. **41 wheaten garland:** Symbol of peace. **42 comma:** Smallest break or separation. Here, *amity* begins and *amity* ends the period, and *peace* stands between like a dependent clause. The comma indicates continuity, link. **43 'As'es:** The "whereases" of a formal document, with play on the word *ass.* **charge:** Import, and burden. **47 shriving-time:** Time for absolution. **48 ordinant:** Directing. **54 sequent:** Subsequent.

HAMLET Why, man, they did make love to this employment;
They are not near my conscience; their defeat
Does by their own insinuation° grow:
'Tis dangerous when the baser nature comes
Between the pass° and fell incensed° points
Of mighty opposites.

HORATIO Why, what a king is this!

HAMLET Does it not, think thee, stand° me now upon—
He that hath kill'd my king and whor'd my mother,
Popp'd in between th' election° and my hopes,
Thrown out his angle° for my proper life,
And with such coz'nage°—is 't not perfect conscience,
To quit° him with this arm? and is 't not to be damn'd,
To let this canker° of our nature come
In further evil?

HORATIO It must be shortly known to him from England
What is the issue of the business there.

HAMLET It will be short: the interim is mine;
And a man's life's no more than to say "One."
But I am very sorry, good Horatio,
That to Laertes I forgot myself;
For, by the image of my cause, I see
The portraiture of his: I'll court his favours:
But, sure, the bravery° of his grief did put me
Into a tow'ring passion.

HORATIO Peace! who comes here?

Enter a **COURTIER** [**OSRIC**].

OSRIC Your lordship is right welcome back to Denmark.

59 **insinuation:** Interference. 61 **pass:** Thrust. **fell incensed:** Fiercely angered. 63 **stand:** Become incumbent. 65 **election:** The Danish throne was filled by election. 66 **angle:** Fishing line. 67 **coz'nage:** Trickery. 68 **quit:** Repay. 69 **canker:** Ulcer, or possibly the worm which destroys buds and leaves. 79 **bravery:** Bravado.

HAMLET I humbly thank you, sir. [*To* **HORATIO**.] Dost know this water-fly?°

HORATIO No, my good lord.

HAMLET Thy state is the more gracious; for 'tis a vice to know him. He hath much land, and fertile: let a beast be lord of beasts,° and his crib shall stand at the king's mess:° 'tis a chough;° but, as I say, spacious in the possession of dirt.

OSRIC Sweet lord, if your lordship were at leisure, I should impart a thing to you from his majesty.

HAMLET I will receive it, sir, with all diligence of spirit. Put your bonnet to his right use; 'tis for the head.

OSRIC I thank your lordship, it is very hot.

HAMLET No, believe me, 'tis very cold; the wind is northerly.

OSRIC It is indifferent° cold, my lord, indeed.

HAMLET But yet methinks it is very sultry and hot for my complexion.

OSRIC Exceedingly, my lord; it is very sultry,—as 'twere,—I cannot tell how. But, my lord, his majesty bade me signify to you that 'a has laid a great wager on your head: sir, this is the matter,—

HAMLET I beseech you, remember°—

[**HAMLET** *moves him to put on his hat.*]

OSRIC Nay, good my lord; for mine ease,° in good faith. Sir, here is newly come to court Laertes; believe me, an absolute gentleman, full of most excellent differences, of very soft° society and great showing:° indeed, to speak feelingly° of him, he is

82 **water-fly:** Vain or busily idle person. 87 **lord of beasts:** See Genesis 1:26, 28. 88 **his crib . . . mess:** He shall eat at the king's table and be one of the group of persons (usually four) constituting a *mess* at a banquet. 89 **chough:** Probably, chattering jackdaw; also explained as *chuff,* provincial boor or churl. 100 **indifferent:** Somewhat. 108 **remember:** I.e., remember thy courtesy; conventional phrase for "Be covered." 109 **mine ease:** Conventional reply declining the invitation of "Remember thy courtesy." 113 **soft:** Gentle. **showing:** Distinguished appearance. 114 **feelingly:** With just perception.

the card° or calendar of gentry,° for you shall find in him the continent of what part a gentleman would see.

HAMLET Sir, his definement° suffers no perdition° in you; though, I know, to divide him inventorially° would dozy° the arithmetic of memory, and yet but yaw° neither, in respect of his quick sail. But, in the verity of extolment, I take him to be a soul of great article;° and his infusion° of such dearth and rareness,° as, to make true diction of him, his semblable° is his mirror; and who else would trace° him, his umbrage,° nothing more.

OSRIC Your lordship speaks most infallibly of him.

HAMLET The concernancy,° sir? why do we wrap the gentleman in our more rawer breath?°

OSRIC Sir?

HORATIO [*aside to* **HAMLET**]: Is 't not possible to understand in another tongue?° You will do 't, sir, really.

HAMLET What imports the nomination° of this gentleman?

OSRIC Of Laertes?

HORATIO [*aside to* **HAMLET**]: His purse is empty already; all 's golden words are spent.

HAMLET Of him, sir.

OSRIC I know you are not ignorant—

HAMLET I would you did, sir; yet, in faith, if you did, it would not much approve° me. Well, sir?

OSRIC You are not ignorant of what excellence Laertes is—

HAMLET I dare not confess that, lest I should compare with him in excellence; but, to know a man well, were to know himself.°

OSRIC I mean, sir, for his weapon; but in the imputation° laid on him by them, in his meed° he's unfellowed.

HAMLET What's his weapon?

OSRIC Rapier and dagger.

HAMLET That's two of his weapons: but, well.

OSRIC The king, sir, hath wagered with him six Barbary horses: against the which he has impawned,° as I take it, six French rapiers and poniards, with their assigns, as girdle, hangers,° and so: three of the carriages, in faith, are very dear to fancy,° very responsive° to the hilts, most delicate° carriages, and of very liberal conceit.°

HAMLET What call you the carriages?

HORATIO [*aside to* **HAMLET**]: I knew you must be edified by the margent° ere you had done.

OSRIC The carriages, sir, are the hangers.

HAMLET The phrase would be more german° to the matter, if we could carry cannon by our sides: I would it might be hangers till then. But, on: six Barbary horses against six French swords, their assigns, and three liberal-conceited carriages; that's the French bet against the Danish. Why is this "impawned," as you call it?

OSRIC The king, sir, hath laid, that in a dozen passes between yourself and him, he shall not exceed you three hits: he hath laid on twelve for nine; and it would come to immediate trial, if your lordship would vouchsafe the answer.

---

115 card: Chart, map. **gentry:** Good breeding. **118 definement:** Definition. **119 perdition:** Loss, diminution. **120 divide him inventorially:** I.e., enumerate his graces. **dozy:** Dizzy. **121 yaw:** To move unsteadily (of a ship). **124 article:** Moment or importance. **infusion:** Infused temperament, character imparted by nature. **125 dearth and rareness:** Rarity. **126 semblable:** True likeness. **127 trace:** Follow. **128 umbrage:** Shadow. **130 concernancy:** Import. **131 breath:** Speech. **134–135 Is 't . . . tongue?:** I.e., can one converse with Osric only in this outlandish jargon? **137 nomination:** Naming. **145 approve:** Command.

150–152 but . . . himself: But to know a man as excellent were to know Laertes. **153 imputation:** Reputation. **154 meed:** Merit. **159–160 he has impawned:** He has wagered. **162 hangers:** Straps on the sword belt from which the sword hung. **163 dear to fancy:** Fancifully made. **164 responsive:** Probably, well balanced, corresponding closely. **165 delicate:** Fine in workmanship. **165–166 liberal conceit:** Elaborate design. **169 margent:** margin of a book, place for explanatory notes. **171 german:** Germane, appropriate.

HAMLET How if I answer "no"?

OSRIC I mean, my lord, the opposition of your person in trial.

HAMLET Sir, I will walk here in the hall: if it please his majesty, it is the breathing time° of day with me; let the foils be brought, the gentleman willing, and the king hold his purpose, I will win for him as I can; if not, I will gain nothing but my shame and the odd hits.

OSRIC Shall I re-deliver you e'en so?

HAMLET To this effect, sir; after what flourish your nature will.

OSRIC I commend my duty to your lordship.

HAMLET Yours, yours. [*Exit* **OSRIC**.] He does well to commend it himself; there are no tongues else for 's turn.

HORATIO This lapwing° runs away with the shell on his head.

HAMLET 'A did comply, sir, with his dug,° before 'a sucked it. Thus has he — and many more of the same breed that I know the drossy° age dotes on — only got the tune° of the time and out of an habit of encounter;° a kind of yesty° collection, which carries them through and through the most fann'd and winnowed° opinions; and do but blow them to their trial, the bubbles are out.°

Enter a **LORD**.

LORD My lord, his majesty commended him to you by young Osric, who brings back to him, that you attend him in the hall: he sends to know if your pleasure hold to play with Laertes, or that you will take longer time.

189 breathing time: Exercise period. **201 lapwing:** Peewit; noted for its wiliness in drawing a visitor away from its nest and its supposed habit of running about when newly hatched with its head in the shell; possibly an allusion to Osric's hat. **203 did comply . . . dug:** Paid compliments to his mother's breast. **206 drossy:** Frivolous. **tune:** Temper, mood. **207–208 habit of encounter:** Demeanor of social intercourse. **208 yesty:** Frothy. **210 fann'd and winnowed:** Select and refined. **211–212 blow . . . out:** I.e., put them to the test, and their ignorance is exposed.

HAMLET I am constant to my purposes; they follow the king's pleasure: if his fitness speaks, mine is ready; now or whensoever, provided I be so able as now.

LORD The king and queen and all are coming down.

HAMLET In happy time.°

LORD The queen desires you to use some gentle entertainment to Laertes before you fall to play.

HAMLET She well instructs me.

[*Exit* **LORD**.]

HORATIO You will lose this wager, my lord.

HAMLET I do not think so; since he went into France, I have been in continual practice; I shall win at the odds. But thou wouldst not think how ill all 's here about my heart: but it is no matter.

HORATIO Nay, good my lord, —

HAMLET It is but foolery; but it is such a kind of gain-giving,° as would perhaps trouble a woman.

HORATIO If your mind dislike any thing, obey it: I will forestall their repair hither, and say you are not fit.

HAMLET Not a whit, we defy augury: there's a special providence in the fall of a sparrow. If it be now, 'tis not to come; if it be not to come, it will be now; if it be not now, yet it will come: the readiness is all:° since no man of aught he leaves knows, what is 't to leave betimes? Let be.

A table prepared. [*Enter*] **TRUMPETS, DRUMS,** *and* **OFFICERS** *with cushions;* **KING, QUEEN,** [**OSRIC,**] *and all the* **STATE**; *foils, daggers,* [*and wine borne in;*] *and* **LAERTES**.

KING Come, Hamlet, come, and take this hand from me.

[*The* **KING** *puts* **LAERTES**'*s hand into* **HAMLET**'*s.*]

225 In happy time: A phrase of courtesy. **238 gain-giving:** Misgiving. **247 all:** All that matters.

HAMLET Give me your pardon, sir: I have done you wrong;
But pardon 't as you are a gentleman.
This presence° knows,
And you must needs have heard, how I am punish'd
With a sore distraction. What I have done,
That might your nature, honour and exception°
Roughly awake, I here proclaim was madness.
Was 't Hamlet wrong'd Laertes? Never Hamlet:
If Hamlet from himself be ta'en away,
And when he's not himself does wrong Laertes,
Then Hamlet does it not, Hamlet denies it.
Who does it, then? His madness: if 't be so,
Hamlet is of the faction that is wrong'd;
His madness is poor Hamlet's enemy.
Sir, in this audience,
Let my disclaiming from a purpos'd evil

In 1821, artist Eugène Delacroix painted a "self-portrait" — as Hamlet. **What does this imply about the fame and appeal of Shakespeare's play and its protagonist? What aspects of Hamlet's character do you believe Delacroix sought to represent in his self-portrait?**

FLAMMARION/Musee Eugene Delacroix, Paris, France/Bridgeman Images

253 presence: Royal assembly. **256 exception:** Disapproval.

Free me so far in your most generous thoughts,
That I have shot mine arrow o'er the house,
And hurt my brother.

LAERTES I am satisfied in nature,°
Whose motive, in this case, should stir me most
To my revenge: but in my terms of honour
I stand aloof; and will no reconcilement,
Till by some elder masters, of known honour,
I have a voice° and precedent of peace,
To keep my name ungor'd. But till that time,
I do receive your offer'd love like love,
And will not wrong it.

HAMLET I embrace it freely;
And will this brother's wager frankly play.
Give us the foils. Come on.

LAERTES Come, one for me.

HAMLET I'll be your foil,° Laertes: in mine ignorance
Your skill shall, like a star i' th' darkest night,
Stick fiery off° indeed.

LAERTES You mock me, sir.

HAMLET No, by this hand.

KING Give them the foils, young Osric. Cousin Hamlet,
You know the wager?

HAMLET Very well, my lord;
Your grace has laid the odds o' th' weaker side.

KING I do not fear it; I have seen you both:
But since he is better'd, we have therefore odds.

LAERTES This is too heavy, let me see another.

HAMLET This likes me well. These foils have all a length?

[*They prepare to play.*]

OSRIC Ay, my good lord.

KING Set me the stoups of wine upon that table.
If Hamlet give the first or second hit,
Or quit in answer of the third exchange,
Let all the battlements their ordnance fire;
The king shall drink to Hamlet's better breath;
And in the cup an union° shall he throw,
Richer than that which four successive kings
In Denmark's crown have worn. Give me the cups;
And let the kettle° to the trumpet speak,
The trumpet to the cannoneer without,
The cannons to the heavens, the heavens to earth,
"Now the king drinks to Hamlet." Come begin: *Trumpets the while.*
And you, the judges, bear a wary eye.

HAMLET Come on, sir.

LAERTES Come, my lord.

[*They play.*]

HAMLET One.

LAERTES No.

HAMLET
Judgement.

OSRIC A hit, a very palpable hit.

Drum, trumpets, and shot. Flourish. A piece goes off.

LAERTES Well; again.

KING Stay; give me drink. Hamlet, this pearl° is thine;
Here's to thy health. Give him the cup.

HAMLET I'll play this bout first; set it by awhile.
Come. [*They play.*] Another hit; what say you?

LAERTES A touch, a touch, I do confess 't.

KING Our son shall win.

QUEEN He's fat,° and scant of breath.
Here, Hamlet, take my napkin, rub thy brows:
The queen carouses° to thy fortune, Hamlet.

HAMLET Good madam!

---

269 nature: I.e., he is personally satisfied, but his honor must be satisfied by the rules of the code of honor. **274 voice:** Authoritative pronouncement. **280 foil:** Quibble on the two senses: "background which sets something off" and "blunted rapier for fencing." **282 Stick fiery off:** Stand out brilliantly.

297 union: Pearl. **300 kettle:** Kettledrum. **307 pearl:** I.e., the poison. **312 fat:** Not physically fit, out of training. Some earlier editors speculated that the term applied to the corpulence of Richard Burbage, who originally played the part, but the allusion now appears unlikely. Fat may also suggest "sweaty." **314 carouses:** Drinks a toast.

KING Gertrude, do not drink.

QUEEN I will, my lord; I pray you, pardon me.

[*Drinks.*]

KING [*aside*]: It is the poison'd cup: it is too late.

HAMLET I dare not drink yet, madam; by and by.

QUEEN Come, let me wipe thy face.

LAERTES My lord, I'll hit him now.

KING I do not think 't.

LAERTES [*aside*]: And yet 'tis almost 'gainst my conscience.

HAMLET Come, for the third, Laertes: you but dally;
I pray you, pass with your best violence;
I am afeard you make a wanton° of me.

LAERTES Say you so? come on.

[*They play.*]

OSRIC Nothing, neither way.

LAERTES Have at you now!

[**LAERTES** *wounds* **HAMLET**; *then, in scuffling, they change rapiers,° and* **HAMLET** *wounds* **LAERTES**.]

KING Part them; they are incens'd.

HAMLET Nay, come again.

[*The* **QUEEN** *falls.*]

OSRIC Look to the queen there, ho!

HORATIO They bleed on both sides. How is it, my lord?

OSRIC How is 't, Laertes?

LAERTES Why, as a woodcock° to mine own springe,° Osric;
I am justly kill'd with mine own treachery.

HAMLET How does the queen?

KING She swounds° to see them bleed.

QUEEN No, no, the drink, the drink, — O my dear Hamlet, —
The drink, the drink! I am poison'd.

[*Dies.*]

HAMLET O villany! Ho! let the door be lock'd:
Treachery! Seek it out.

[**LAERTES** *falls.*]

LAERTES It is here, Hamlet: Hamlet, thou art slain;
No med'cine in the world can do thee good;
In thee there is not half an hour of life;
The treacherous instrument is in thy hand,
Unbated° and envenom'd: the foul practice
Hath turn'd itself on me; lo, here I lie,
Never to rise again: thy mother's poison'd:
I can no more: the king, the king's to blame.

HAMLET The point envenom'd too!
Then, venom, to thy work.

[*Stabs the* **KING**.]

ALL Treason! treason!

KING O, yet defend me, friends; I am but hurt.

HAMLET Here, thou incestuous, murd'rous, damned Dane,
Drink off this potion. Is thy union here?
Follow my mother.

[**KING** *dies.*]

LAERTES He is justly serv'd;
It is a poison temper'd° by himself.
Exchange forgiveness with me, noble Hamlet:
Mine and my father's death come not upon thee,
Nor thine on me!

[*Dies.*]

HAMLET Heaven make thee free of it! I follow thee.
I am dead, Horatio. Wretched queen, adieu!
You that look pale and tremble at this chance,
That are but mutes° or audience to this act,
Had I but time — as this fell sergeant,° Death,
Is strict in his arrest — O, I could tell you —
But let it be. Horatio, I am dead;
Thou livest; report me and my cause aright
To the unsatisfied.

---

324 wanton: Spoiled child. **327 [S. D.] in scuffling, they change rapiers:** According to a widespread stage tradition, Hamlet receives a scratch, realizes that Laertes's sword is unbated, and accordingly forces an exchange. **332 woodcock:** As type of stupidity or as decoy. **springe:** Trap, snare. **334 swounds:** Swoons.

343 Unbated: Not blunted with a button. **354 temper'd:** Mixed. **361 mutes:** Performers in a play who speak no words. **362 sergeant:** Sheriff's officer.

HORATIO Never believe it:
I am more an antique Roman° than a Dane:
Here's yet some liquor left.

HAMLET As th' art a man,
Give me the cup: let go, by heaven, I'll ha 't.
O God! Horatio, what a wounded name,
Things standing thus unknown, shall live behind me!
If thou didst ever hold me in thy heart,
Absent thee from felicity awhile,
And in this harsh world draw thy breath in pain,
To tell my story.

A march afar off.

What warlike noise is this?

OSRIC Young Fortinbras, with conquest come from Poland,
To the ambassadors of England gives
This warlike volley.

HAMLET O, I die, Horatio;
The potent poison quite o'er-crows° my spirit:
I cannot live to hear the news from England;
But I do prophesy th' election lights
On Fortinbras: he has my dying voice;
So tell him, with th' occurrents,° more and less,
Which have solicited.° The rest is silence.

[*Dies.*]

HORATIO Now cracks a noble heart. Good night, sweet prince;
And flights of angels sing thee to thy rest!
Why does the drum come hither?

[*March within.*]

Enter **FORTINBRAS**, *with the* [*English*] **AMBASSADORS** [*and others*].

FORTINBRAS Where is this sight?

HORATIO What is it you would see?
If aught of woe or wonder, cease your search.

FORTINBRAS This quarry° cries on havoc.° O proud Death,
What feast is toward in thine eternal cell,
That thou so many princes at a shot
So bloodily hast struck?

FIRST AMBASSADOR The sight is dismal;
And our affairs from England come too late:
The ears are senseless that should give us hearing,
To tell him his commandment is fulfill'd,
That Rosencrantz and Guildenstern are dead:
Where should we have our thanks?

HORATIO Not from his mouth,°
Had it th' ability of life to thank you:
He never gave commandment for their death.
But since, so jump° upon this bloody question,°
You from the Polack wars, and you from England,
Are here arriv'd, give order that these bodies
High on a stage° be placed to the view;
And let me speak to th' yet unknowing world
How these things came about: so shall you hear
Of carnal, bloody, and unnatural acts,
Of accidental judgements, casual slaughters,
Of deaths put on by cunning and forc'd cause,
And, in this upshot, purposes mistook
Fall'n on th' inventors' heads: all this can I
Truly deliver.

FORTINBRAS Let us haste to hear it,
And call the noblest to the audience.
For me, with sorrow I embrace my fortune:
I have some rights of memory° in this kingdom,
Which now to claim my vantage doth invite me.

HORATIO Of that I shall have also cause to speak,

---

367 Roman: It was the Roman custom to follow masters in death. **379 o'er-crows:** Triumphs over. **383 occurrents:** Events, incidents. **384 solicited:** Moved, urged. **390 quarry:** Heap of dead. **cries on havoc:** Proclaims a general slaughter.

398 his mouth: I.e., the king's. **401 jump:** Precisely. **question:** Dispute. **404 stage:** Platform. **415 of memory:** Traditional, remembered.

And from his mouth whose voice will draw on more:°
But let this same be presently perform'd,
Even while men's minds are wild; lest more mischance,
On° plots and errors, happen.

FORTINBRAS Let four captains
Bear Hamlet, like a soldier, to the stage;
For he was likely, had he been put on,
To have prov'd most royal: and, for his passage,°
The soldiers' music and the rites of war
Speak loudly for him.
Take up the bodies: such a sight as this
Becomes the field,° but here shows much amiss.
Go, bid the soldiers shoot.

Exeunt [*marching, bearing off the dead bodies; after which a peal of ordnance is shot off*].

[c. 1600]

This modern watercolor by artist Jonathan Wolstenholme wittily depicts a "Shakespearean Scholar." **What do the details in the painting — the skull, the pen, the book's broken, "unhinged" spine — suggest about the play? Its central character? Those who study it?**

Private Collection/Bridgeman Images

418 voice . . . more: Vote will influence still others. **421 On:** On account of, or possibly, on top of, in addition to.

424 passage: Death. **428 field:** I.e., of battle.

QUESTIONS FOR DISCUSSION

1. What is the political situation in Denmark as the play begins? What information does Horatio provide beginning in line 79 of the opening scene? What further information do we learn from Claudius's speech that begins scene ii? (Note that throughout the play, King Claudius's speaking lines are indicated by only the title "King.")
2. How does Shakespeare characterize Horatio in the opening scenes? What are some of his chief qualities? How does Hamlet characterize Claudius? How does Hamlet compare Horatio and Claudius?
3. What does Hamlet's first soliloquy (I.ii.129–59) reveal about his state of mind? What is the source of his discontent?
4. What is the basis for both Laertes's and Polonius's objections to Ophelia's relationship with Hamlet? Which of their arguments seem most (and least) persuasive or fair? What does their treatment of Ophelia in act I, scene iii, reveal about their motivations? What does it suggest about their attitude toward Ophelia and toward women in general? How does class or station function in their arguments?
5. What do we learn from the Ghost in act I, scene v? If what he says is true, how does that reinforce what we have learned about the political situation in Denmark? How does Hamlet respond to the Ghost's instructions? What does he mean by saying, "O my prophetic soul!" (I.v.40)?
6. After listening to the Ghost speak, Hamlet wants to write about it, as indicated in act I, scene v, lines 107 and 108. How does this contrast with his remarks earlier in this speech? What does it suggest about his state of mind?
7. Why do you think Hamlet tells his companions he is likely to put on an "antic disposition" (I.v.172)? Is his behavior a deliberate strategy or a natural reaction to his anger and grief? Explain.
8. Compare the way Hamlet responds to Polonius in act II, scene ii, lines 176–233, with how he responds to his friends Rosencrantz and Guildenstern in lines 237–363. What do you learn about Hamlet from these responses?
9. In act III, scene i, lines 56–90, Hamlet delivers his famous "To be, or not to be" speech, arguably the most recognized passage in English literature. What is he contemplating? What inner conflict is he pondering? What conclusions does he reach?
10. Following his "To be, or not to be" soliloquy (III.i.56–89), why does Hamlet treat Ophelia so harshly? How does Ophelia describe Hamlet in lines 162–73? What does this description suggest about Hamlet before the time of the play? What does it suggest about the relationship between Hamlet and Ophelia?
11. What does the scene with the players (II.ii.473–611) reveal about Hamlet? How does the First Player's speech (II.ii.528–57) parallel Hamlet's situation?
12. Hamlet's speech to the players at the beginning of act III, scene ii, has often been interpreted as a sort of aside from Shakespeare containing his philosophy of acting. How else can it be interpreted? How do Hamlet's instructions tie in to some of the themes of the play?
13. In act III, scene iii, lines 73–96, Hamlet has a perfect opportunity to kill his uncle and avenge his murdered father. Instead, he makes a speech. Why does he hesitate in killing Claudius? Do you think we are meant to respect his piety or despise his cowardice? If you combine this incident with Hamlet's soliloquy at the end of act II, does it reveal something about Hamlet? about a theme of the play?
14. In act II, scene ii, lines 265–67, Hamlet says, "Why, then, 'tis none to you; for there is nothing either good or bad, but thinking makes it so." What assumptions underlie Hamlet's response? What does he mean? Do you agree with what he says? He then says to his old friends, "I am but mad north-north-west: when the wind is southerly I know a hawk from a handsaw" (II.ii.424–26). What does this remark suggest about Hamlet's madness, about his "antic disposition" (I.v.172)? Is he mad? Is he acting? Explain.
15. Why do you think the Ghost is visible to Horatio and the guards in act I, scenes i and iv, but not to Gertrude in act III, scene iv? Does the murder of Polonius in this scene make you reassess whether the Ghost is in fact a demon, and not the ghost of Hamlet's father?
16. What has driven Ophelia mad in act IV, scene v? What does her behavior suggest about the relationship between her and Hamlet? Cite specific lines to support your answer.

17. How does Laertes respond to his father's death? to Ophelia's? How do his responses compare to Hamlet's reaction to the death of *his* father?

18. Hamlet seems preoccupied with death for much of the play; what new insight does the graveyard scene (V.i.) reveal regarding his attitude toward mortality? toward life, fame, and accomplishment? How does this attitude connect to his central conflict in the play?

19. Why does Hamlet give his dying support to Fortinbras (V.ii.378–84)?

QUESTIONS ON STYLE AND STRUCTURE

1. The opening scene presents a great number of questions. How do these contribute to the mood of the scene and, ultimately, of the play itself?

2. Hamlet's first three lines (I.ii.65, 67, 74) are evasive answers using puns or other wordplay. What does this behavior reveal about his character and his state of mind?

3. How would you describe Claudius's opening speech (I.ii.1–39) and his reply to Hamlet (I. ii.87–117)? What does his use of imagery and juxtaposition in the first speech reveal about his purpose? What is the nature of his argument in the second?

4. How do the diction and imagery in the Ghost's speech to Hamlet (I.v.42–91) create a comparison between the two "gardens" before and after the entrance of the "serpents"?

5. In lines 321–44 of act II, scene ii, Hamlet delivers a lengthy explanation to Rosencrantz and Guildenstern, ending with a rhetorical question. What is the substance of this speech? How does the imagery that Hamlet uses transition his speech from an assessment of himself to that of mankind as a whole?

6. Claudius's aside in act III, scene i, lines 49–54, is the first definitive evidence of his guilt. Structurally, why do you think this revelation takes place halfway through the play as opposed to earlier (or later)?

7. Notice Hamlet's behavior toward Ophelia in act III, scene i. Why do you think – in dramatic, structural, and thematic terms – we have not observed a scene between Hamlet and Ophelia until this point?

8. In act II, scene i, Polonius says, "By indirections find directions out" (l. 64). What does he mean by that? How does such a comment reveal his character? Find another such witty or clever remark by another character, and explain how it reveals the character of its speaker.

9. Hamlet's four soliloquies (I.ii.129–59; II. ii.614–72; III.i.56–90; IV.iv.32–66) are remarkable for their style as well as their substance. Choose one of these monologues and discuss how its diction, figurative language, and imagery contribute to Hamlet's meaning and purpose.

10. Shakespeare occasionally gives two characters very similar lines or phrasings, the second instance reminding the reader or viewer of the first. In act IV, scene iv, for example, Hamlet wonders if he might be "thinking too precisely on th' event" (l. 41). In act V, scene i, Horatio says to Hamlet, "'Twere to consider too curiously, to consider so" (l. 240). What is the effect of these types of echoes throughout the play?

11. Do a close reading of one of Ophelia's songs in act IV, scene v, exploring how its form and content relate and respond to the action of the play (both actual and implied) and to Ophelia's state of mind. In your response, consider what has occurred offstage, as well as the possible or implied events to which she alludes. Why is she given song, as opposed to speech, in this instance?

SUGGESTIONS FOR WRITING

1. In *Hamlet*, as vengeance is applied, order is restored — or is it? Write an essay that discusses the symmetry at the end of the play, explaining how the plot of *Hamlet* makes an argument for or against revenge. Support your thesis with specific textual evidence.
2. While there are only two major female characters in *Hamlet* — Gertrude and Ophelia — they both play crucial roles. Write an essay in which you explain the importance of each of these women to the play, especially in terms of her relationship to Hamlet.
3. Recognize the immense importance of diction in *Hamlet* by making note of each instance of certain kinds of words. First, note words having to do with *appearances*, such as *play*, *act*, *seem*, *assume*, *show*, *reveal*, *appear*, *form*, *shape*, and *like* (for comparison), as well as references to *pictures*, *images*, *mirrors*, *faces*, and the like; then note references to clothing and fashion, such as *investments*, *trappings*, *suits*, and *fashion*, as well as references to *watching* and *spying* throughout the play. Through diction and the imagery it creates, trace the contrast between appearance and reality throughout the play, and write an essay explaining how that motif contributes to the meaning of the play as a whole.
4. Critic Northrop Frye said that *Hamlet* is Shakespeare's longest play because everyone in it (with the exceptions of Gertrude and Ophelia) "talks too much." Despite the calls to be brief from both the Ghost and Polonius, the characters do go on at length, and Hamlet certainly has a lot to say. Write an essay in which you explore why this play, for much of its length, focuses more on conversation and reflection than on action — and why this, in your opinion, contributes to a theme of the play. Support your position with textual evidence.
5. In *The Prince*, a Renaissance text from 1532, Niccolò Machiavelli writes:

    > A prince ought to be a fox in recognizing snares and a lion in driving off wolves. Those who assume the bearing of a lion alone lack understanding. It follows, then, that a wise prince cannot and should not keep his pledge when it is against his interest to do so and when his reasons for making the pledge are no longer operative. . . . But one must know how to mask this [fox-like] nature skillfully and be a great dissembler.

    In an essay, explore how both Hamlet and Claudius act in accordance with this advice. How do their tactics differ?
6. References to the macrocosm and the microcosm suggest that the same forces are at work within as without. In the play, a person is seen as a little world at the center of the world at large, where veins are rivers, and Hamlet speaks of his "distracted globe" (I.v.97). Find other references that reflect the presence of the macrocosm and the microcosm, and discuss their effect on the meaning of the play as a whole.
7. Consider the many conflicts in the play — for example, those between reason and passion, order and chaos, concealing and revealing, and honesty and deception. Choose one, and write an essay explaining how that conflict reveals a dominant theme of the play.
8. Hamlet's conversation with Rosencrantz and Guildenstern in act II, scene ii, contains a misunderstanding or disagreement surrounding the word *dream*; when Hamlet tells them he has had "bad dreams," Guildenstern equivocates *dream* with *ambition* (ll. 274–76). Write an essay in which you explore how this or other disagreements over meaning exacerbate the central conflicts of the play.
9. One interpretation of Hamlet's indecision involves the influence of multiple distracting events or motivations, which either directly delay him or confuse him to the point that he forgets his purpose. In an essay, explore how other characters in the play fall victim to distraction. Refer to specific incidents in the play, quoting from the text to support your essay.
10. The "To be, or not to be" soliloquy in act III, scene i (ll. 56–90) is perhaps the most famous monologue in the English language, yet its meaning is much debated. Write a close-analysis essay in which you interpret the speech. Consider Hamlet's prior soliloquy at the end of act II, scene ii; is this monologue a continuation of that scene, or a separate line of thought? Is Hamlet aware of his audience (Claudius and Polonius, hidden behind a

tapestry), or is he speaking to himself on the assumption that he is alone?

11. Read carefully "The Emperor of Ice-Cream," a 1922 poem by American poet Wallace Stevens, in which he includes words and phrases that appear in *Hamlet*. Write an essay that considers Stevens's poem as a meditation on mortality and also as a response to *Hamlet*. Make specific references to both texts in your essay.

> Call the roller of big cigars,
> The muscular one, and bid him whip
> In kitchen cups concupiscent curds.
> Let the wenches dawdle in such dress
> As they are used to wear, and let the boys
> Bring flowers in last month's newspapers.
> Let be be finale of seem.
> The only emperor is the emperor of ice-cream.
>
> Take from the dresser of deal,
> Lacking the three glass knobs, that sheet
> On which she embroidered fantails once
> And spread it so as to cover her face.
> If her horny feet protrude, they come
> To show how cold she is, and dumb.
> Let the lamp affix its beam.
> The only emperor is the emperor of ice-cream.

TEXTS IN CONTEXT

Hamlet and the Evolution of Character

Why do we read literature? There are many reasons, of course. We read for entertainment. We read for plot, for the *story*. We enjoy a gripping tale as the building suspense keeps us turning pages. We also read for information, for historical context, for instruction, and for edification. We also read to be challenged by provocative ideas, or to learn about a particular time period or an exotic place. Sometimes we read because we enjoy the style of a particular writer. But *character* is often the most appealing reason of them all. We remember the stories, the plots, the settings, the ideas, maybe even the style, of our favorite books and plays, but it is the characters that stay with us and continue to live inside our imaginations. We admire the heroes, we fear the villains; we follow the adventurers, the rebels, the provocative thinkers; we identify with and aspire to be like our favorites, and we care about them as we do about living people. We often see ourselves in the characters we encounter, confronting our own thoughts and beliefs as we read of theirs.

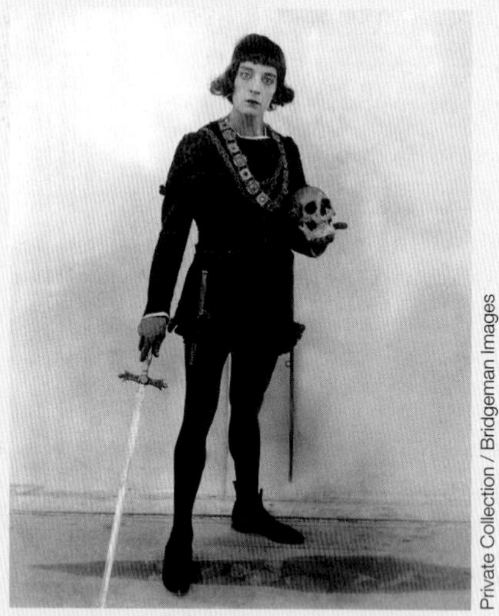

Private Collection / Bridgeman Images

Buster Keaton, a silent film star known for his physical comedy and deadpan expression, poses as Hamlet in a still for the 1922 film *Day Dreams*. **What characteristics of Hamlet do you see in this portrayal? How does Keaton convey them?**

Some literary characters tell their own stories — for instance, Lemuel Gulliver, David Copperfield, Jane Eyre, Huck Finn, and Janie Crawford. Others, such as Elizabeth Bennett, Raskolnikov, Hester Prynne, Bigger Thomas, and Harry Potter reach us via the perspective of an author as third-person narrator. Still others — Captain Ahab, Jay Gatsby, Atticus Finch — come to us from the perspective of other characters who narrate their own stories in the first-person. However we come to know literary characters, we recognize that *character* is one of the features of literature that makes us want to read, and likely the feature that we remember most. And perhaps no character in all of world literature has been studied as closely and extensively as Shakespeare's Hamlet.

But why is Hamlet widely regarded as the most compelling character in the history of literature? Is he heroic? Is he villainous? Is he rebellious? Is he indecisive? Do his thoughts and ideas provoke and challenge us? Do we identify with his situation and plight? Does he engage our sympathies? Do we care about him? For most readers, the answer to all of these questions is likely *yes*. Hamlet thinks and feels deeply, and his audience witnesses the profundity of his intellect and passion in his words. We perceive his humanity in his remarks about his youth with Yorick as well as in his bond with Horatio, and we feel his grief at the loss of his beloved father. His plans to avenge his father's ghost show how loyal and brave he intends to be; yet we also see how cruelly he treats Ophelia and his mother. His acerbic remarks about his uncle and his response to Polonius's death reveal his wit, which we enjoy even as we might find it disquieting. We sympathize with his revulsion toward the King — it puts his profound disgust with the world in perspective. And we understand the difficulty of the circumstances he faces; we know his disappointment and feel it with him. We see and feel all of this most pointedly in his soliloquies, those passages where we enter his mind and witness him alone with his tangled thoughts.

This portrait by F. Drummond Niblett, completed around 1910, depicts English actor Henry Irving in the role of Hamlet. **Why do you believe the artist chose to distort Irving's physical features in such a way? What do you make of Irving's pose and the expression on his face?**

Hamlet is clearly an intellectual. Upon seeing his father's ghost, his first thought is to write about it. His pleasures — and his profound pains — are those of the mind. Does this mean he thinks and talks too much, as many readers say? Is Horatio's remark, "'Twere to consider too curiously, to consider so" (V.i.240), an apt one? Is Hamlet's tendency to overthink, his "pale cast of thought" (III.i.85), what makes him "lose the name of action" (III.i.88)? Or is it fate, with its snares of coincidence and circumstance, that traps him, brands him as one of the "fools of nature" (I.iv.54)?

Many readers note Hamlet's self-centeredness and question whether he has actually lost his mind. Perhaps he is merely feigning madness as a stratagem. Regardless of whether Hamlet is sane, no reader can deny how wildly inconsistent he is in his behavior. Consider his statements of resolve beside his lack of action, his treatment of his old friends Rosencrantz and Guildenstern, and especially his interactions with

Ophelia. But should we be surprised to see such changes, such transformations of character? Is human nature — is *character* — consistent, or is it inconstant and inconsistent? In "On the Inconstancy of Our Actions," a sixteenth-century essay Shakespeare likely read, Michel de Montaigne wrestles with this very question:

> Sometimes I give my soul one visage, and sometimes another, according unto the posture or side I lay her in. If I speak diversely of myself, it is because I look diversely upon myself. All contrarieties are found in her, according to some turn or removing, and in some fashion or other. Shamefaced, bashful, insolent, chaste, luxurious, peevish, prattling, silent, fond, doting, labourious, nice, delicate, ingenious, slow, dull, froward,[1] humorous, debonair, wise, ignorant, false in words, true-speaking, both liberal, covetous, and prodigal. All these I perceive in some measure or other to be in mine, according as I stir or turn myself. And whosoever shall heedfully survey and consider himself shall find this volubility and discordance to be in himself, yea, and in his very judgement. I have nothing to say entirely, simply, and with solidity of myself, without confusion, disorder, blending, mingling; and in one word, *Distinguo*[2] is the most universal part of my logic. . . .
>
> We are all framed of flaps and patches, and of so shapeless and diverse a contexture, that every piece and every moment playeth his part. And there is as much difference found between us and ourselves as there is between ourselves and others.

Interpretations of *Hamlet* the play, and of Hamlet the character, are as diverse in kind as they are infinite in number. Hamlet may be a touchstone, a figure through which we view ourselves and others. He may be an impenetrable mystery. But while he is, after all, merely a vocabulary, a fictional creation, a figment of the imagination evoked by words printed in a book, he is also very real — he comes to life each time an actor takes his role on a stage or a reader turns a page. Each of the texts that follow addresses Hamlet as a character in literature, and in life. Read them carefully as you consider your own interpretation of the play, and of the person at its center.

TEXTS IN CONTEXT

Marjorie Garber / from *Hamlet: The Matter of Character* (nonfiction)
Sir Thomas Lawrence / *John Philip Kemble as Hamlet* (painting)
William Hazlitt / from *Characters of Shakespeare's Plays* (nonfiction)
English School / *Hamlet and the Ghost of His Father* (painting)
C. S. Lewis / from *Hamlet: The Prince or the Poem?* (nonfiction)
Zbigniew Herbert / *Elegy of Fortinbras* (poem)
Margaret Atwood / *Gertrude Talks Back* (fiction)
Meghan O'Rourke / from *Hamlet's Not Depressed, He's Grieving* (nonfiction)

[1] Moving or facing away from someone or something. — EDS.
[2] "I make a distinction." — EDS.

from Hamlet: The Matter of Character

MARJORIE GARBER

Marjorie Garber (b. 1944) is an American literary critic best known for her contributions to Shakespearean scholarship. Garber earned a BA at Swarthmore in 1966 and a PhD at Yale in 1969. Her first book, *Vested Interests: Cross-Dressing and Cultural Anxiety* (1991) was a groundbreaking theoretical work investigating the cultural rituals of and fascination with transvestitism. Since then Garber has written thirteen more books on a variety of topics related to sexuality, Shakespeare, and literature, including *Sex and Real Estate: Why We Love Houses* (2000), *Shakespeare After All* (2004), which was chosen by *Newsweek* as one of the ten best nonfiction books of 2004, and, most recently, *The Use and Abuse of Literature* (2011). Garber teaches at Harvard University. In the following excerpt, Garber examines Hamlet through several lenses, exploring how complex the notion of "character" really is.

One of the most contestatory problems for literary study in the past century has been the question of character, which can be divided into at least two equally troublesome parts: Can a literary character be considered and analyzed as if he or she were a "real" person, with motivations and a history, "mimetic" (that is, imitative) of "reality"? What dramatic effects and cues are given in the text that produce this illusion of roundedness or interiority? Or, from the opposite end of the spectrum, is a character — especially a dramatic character, a character in a play — nothing more, or less, than a piece of writing, identical to his or her lines in the play, and having no existence (psychic, gestural, conceptual, historical) beyond the lines he or she speaks?[1]

That the word "character" originally meant writing, or handwriting, and did so in Shakespeare's time, further complicates the issue — and certain theatrical and dramatic effects, like, for example, the soliloquy, obviously give the *illusion* of interiority, inwardness, personal history, and feelings, even though those effects, too, are purely fictional and gestural.

Literary characters have, over time, in a variety of kinds of works and kinds of readings, been regarded as *rounded, flat, symbolic, allegorical, realistic, representative, historical,* etc. Consider, just for example, the fact that in *Hamlet* the character of Claudius is never named but always given the speech prefix "King." Does that make him more symbolic, one-dimensional, allegorical? And what kind of a character is a Ghost?

In a phenomenon we might call "the Hamlet effect," much criticism of the play holds the mirror up to nature and finds the critic reflected there. Readers, scholars, and actors have over the years consistently identified with the character of Hamlet, finding in his gifts and his foibles an image of themselves. The English Romantic critic Samuel Taylor Coleridge famously observed, "I have a smack of Hamlet myself, if I may say so."[2] Goethe wrote of Hamlet in 1756:

> A lovely, pure, noble, and most moral nature, without the strength of nerve which forms a hero, sinks beneath a burden which it cannot

[1] There is an excellent essay on this question by the critic Alan Sinfield, called "When Is a Character Not a Character? Desdemona, Olivia, Lady Macbeth, and Subjectivity," in *Faultlines: Cultural Materialism and the Politics of Dissident Reading* (Berkeley: University of California Press, 1992), 52–79.

[2] Samuel Taylor Coleridge and Henry Nelson Coleridge, *Specimens of the Table Talk of Samuel Taylor Coleridge* (London: John Murray, 1836), 37.

> bear, and must not cast away. All duties are holy for him; the present is too hard. Impossibilities have been required of him; not in themselves impossibilities, but such for him. He winds, and turns, and torments himself; he advances and recoils; is ever put in mind, ever puts himself in mind; at last does all but lose his purpose from his thoughts; yet still without recovering his peace of mind.[3]

Some twenty years later, Coleridge drew a direct connection between the idea of Shakespearean character and the inner life of Hamlet:

> [O]ne of Shakespeare's modes of creating characters is, to conceive any intellectual or moral faculty in morbid excess, and then to place himself, Shakespeare, thus mutilated or diseased, under given circumstances. In Hamlet he seems to have wished to exemplify the moral necessity of a due balance between our attention to the objects of our senses, and our meditation on the workings of our minds, — an *equilibrium* between the real and the imaginary worlds. In Hamlet this balance is disturbed: . . . we see a great, an almost enormous, intellectual activity, and a proportionate aversion to real action . . . he vacillates from sensibility, and procrastinates from thought, and loses the power of action in the energy of resolve.[4]

Each critic describes a Hamlet who corresponds to something in himself. Goethe's Hamlet lacks "the strength of nerve which forms a hero," while Coleridge's Hamlet "procrastinates from thought, and loses the power of action in the energy of resolve." The time-honored question of Hamlet's delay is here linked to the question of character, in concepts like moral nature, weakness and greatness, an excess of sensibility, or a time "out of joint" for action. . . .

Freud's famous theory of the Oedipus 5
complex was founded not so much on Sophocles' play *Oedipus the King* as on Shakespeare's *Hamlet.*

Freud developed this theory initially in a correspondence with his friend and fellow doctor Wilhelm Fliess, dated October 15, 1897 (the same time as Ellis and shortly after Vining). In this letter, Freud wrote:

> I have found, in my own case, too, [the phenomenon of] being in love with my mother and jealous of my father, and I now consider it a universal event in early childhood. . . . If this is so, we can understand the gripping power of *Oedipus Rex*. . . . Everyone in the audience was once a budding Oedipus in fantasy and each recoils in horror from the dream fulfillment here transplanted into reality. . . .
>
> Fleetingly, the thought passed through my head that the same thing might be at the bottom of *Hamlet* as well. I am not thinking of Shakespeare's conscious intention, but believe, rather, that a real event stimulated the poet in his representation, in that his unconscious understood the unconscious of his hero. How does Hamlet the hysteric justify his words, "Thus conscience does make cowards of us all"? How does he explain his irresolution in avenging his father by the murder of his uncle — the same man who sends his courtiers [i.e., Rosencrantz and Guildenstern] to their death without a scruple and who is positively precipitate in murdering Laertes? How better than through the torment he suffers from the obscure memory that he himself had contemplated the same deed against his father out of passion for his mother?[5] . . .

[3] Johann Wolfgang von Goethe, *Wilhelm Meister's Apprenticeship*, trans. Thomas Carlyle (London: Olver & Boyd, 1824), 2: 75.

[4] Samuel Taylor Coleridge, *Notes and Lectures upon Shakespeare and the Old Dramatists* (New York, 1868), 4: 144.

[5] Sigmund Freud, *The Complete Letters of Sigmund Freud to Wilhelm Fliess*, ed. J. M. Masson (Cambridge: Harvard University Press, 1985), 272.

It was not until 1910 that Freud himself began to refer to this as the "Oedipus complex."[6] Suppose that he had termed it the "Hamlet complex" instead — how might views of the play and its character have altered? That year, 1910, was the same that Virginia Woolf would proclaim the beginning of a new modern era — tying the notion of modernity to *character.* "On or about December, 1910," wrote Woolf, "human character changed."[7] In that same year Freud's disciple and friend, the Welsh psychoanalyst Ernest Jones, had begun expanding the Oedipus theory into what would become an entire small book called *Hamlet and Oedipus.*[8]

The Freud-Jones theory of Hamlet and the Oedipus complex was to have enormous effects upon productions as well as readings and interpretations of the play. Laurence Olivier's classic treatment, made into a film in 1948, cut the roles of Fortinbras and Rosencrantz and Guildenstern completely, and reduced the script by about half. The political plot thus disappeared, replaced by an emphasis on character formed by family circumstances. The production was framed between the opening voice-over murmur, "[T]his is the tragedy of a man who could not make up his mind," and the final, or almost final, shot of the marital bed. . . .

In the course of the twentieth and twenty-first centuries, there have been at least three kinds of psychoanalytic readings associated with literature: a psychoanalysis of the author (Shakespeare's symptoms), a psychoanalysis of the character (Hamlet's symptoms), and a psychoanalysis of the text (the symptoms exhibited by *Hamlet* the *play*, like the splitting of characters into good father and bad father, or the linguistic symptoms like repetition, metaphor, or other figures of speech). In this last kind of reading the play is like a dream, an imaginative work made of signs and symbols, available for interpretation. It is really only this last kind of work that escapes from "character criticism" in the old speculative style, and moves toward an understanding of the text's multiplicities, the way it can be read and performed at different times in different ways, each persuasive. The business of the literary critic is not diagnosis but interpretation.

[2009]

---

[6] Sigmund Freud, "A Special Type of Object-Choice Made by Men" [1910], *The Standard Edition of the Complete Psychological Works of Sigmund Freud*, 24 vols., ed. and trans. James Strachey (London: Hogarth Press, 1953–74), 11: 171.

[7] Virginia Woolf, "Character in Fiction" (1924), *The Essays of Virginia Woolf, Vol. 3, 1919–1924*, ed. Andrew McNeillie (London: Hogarth Press, 1988), 421. *The Complete Works of Freud* would later be published by Virginia and Leonard Woolf's Hogarth Press and translated by Lytton Strachey's brother James. In 1924 the Hogarth Press took over the publication of the papers of the International Psycho-Analytical Institute, for which Jones was the general editor. We are talking here about a founding moment of modernity, in which the literary (and economic) interests of Bloomsbury crossed over into psychoanalysis, and made it available for the first time in English.

[8] Ernest Jones, *Hamlet and Oedipus* (New York: Norton, 1976).

QUESTIONS

1. Which of the two "equally troublesome parts" (para. 1) that Marjorie Garber explores most closely reflects your view of the question of literary *character*? Explain, using reference to literature that you have read.
2. What is "the Hamlet effect" (para. 4)? How does it relate to your reading of the play? Explain.
3. How does Johann Wolfgang von Goethe characterize Hamlet? How does Samuel Taylor Coleridge? Which of the two characterizations do you believe comes closest to the truth? Explain.
4. Of the three kinds of psychoanalytic readings that Garber discusses in the final paragraph — author, character, and text — which one interests you most? Which one is most helpful in illuminating Hamlet's character? Explain, using references to the text.

5. In the final paragraph, Garber writes: "The business of the literary critic is not diagnosis but interpretation." What does she mean? Replace "literary critic" with "student reader." Do you agree with the amended statement? Why or why not?
6. Garber includes a letter in which the founder of psychoanalysis, Sigmund Freud, reflects on both *Oedipus the King* and *Hamlet*. What does Freud suggest might be behind Hamlet's inaction regarding his father, King Hamlet? Does Freud's interpretation shed light on your understanding of Hamlet? Explain.
7. Hamlet certainly has reason to be disturbed. How likely do you think it is that part of his confusion stems from what we have come to call the Oedipus complex? To what extent might Freud's ideas be supported by what happens when Hamlet confronts Gertrude in act III, scene iv?
8. Garber writes, "It was not until 1910 that Freud himself began to refer to this as the 'Oedipus complex.' Suppose that he had termed it the 'Hamlet complex' instead — how might views of the play and its character have altered?" (para. 8). How would you answer Garber's question?

John Philip Kemble as Hamlet

SIR THOMAS LAWRENCE

Sir Thomas Lawrence (1769–1830) was a renowned English portrait painter and the fourth president of the Royal Academy of Arts. A child prodigy born in Bristol, by ten years old Lawrence was supporting his family with pastel portraits. At eighteen, he moved to London and began painting portraits in oils, receiving his first royal commission for a portrait of Queen Charlotte in 1790. He was named painter-in-ordinary to George III in 1792. Lawrence became an associate of the Royal Academy of Arts in 1791, and he became president in 1820. In 1814 he acquired the patronage of the Prince Regent (later King George IV) and was knighted in 1815. Throughout his life, Lawrence was known for his ability to capture the likeness of his subjects with romantic flair. In the portrait of John Philip Kemble as Hamlet, Lawrence uses high contrast between background and foreground to portray the Shakespearean character as well as the performer.

QUESTIONS

1. What do you see in this portrait? What details does the artist use to characterize this particular actor's portrayal of Hamlet? Which act, scene, and particular lines does the illustration depict?
2. How would you describe the expression on Kemble's face in this painting? What does the actor's gaze suggest about his interpretation of Hamlet?
3. Why do you think Sir Thomas Lawrence might have chosen to depict Hamlet as a lone figure? What does this choice suggest about Lawrence's attitude toward the actor and toward Hamlet? Explain.
4. Which features of Hamlet's character do you see displayed here? How does Kemble evidently see Hamlet? What about Lawrence?

Tate, London / Art Resource, NY

[1801]

from Characters of Shakespeare's Plays

WILLIAM HAZLITT

William Hazlitt (1778–1830) was an English writer widely acknowledged as the greatest literary and social critic of his age. The son of a Unitarian minister, Hazlitt went to Paris to pursue painting, but gradually convinced himself that he could not excel in his art. Encouraged by friends such as William Wordsworth, Samuel Taylor Coleridge, and Charles and Mary Lamb, Hazlitt turned to journalism and literature. Of all Hazlitt's voluminous writings, those which endure are his literary criticism and his essays on general topics. His most famous works are *Characters of Shakespeare's Plays* (1817), the first work of literary criticism to cover all of Shakespeare's plays; *Table-Talk* (1821), a book of general essays on topics ranging from art to philosophy; and *The Spirit of the Age: Or, Contemporary Portraits* (1825), a collection of character sketches portraying the leading intellectual, literary, and political figures of Hazlitt's time. In the following excerpt from *Characters of Shakespeare's Plays*, Hazlitt employs his characteristically clear yet poetic prose to paint the character of Hamlet as a marvel of emotional and verbal complexity.

Hamlet is a name: his speeches and sayings but the idle coinage of the poet's brain. What then, are they not real? They are as real as our own thoughts. Their reality is in the reader's mind. It is *we* who are Hamlet. This play has a prophetick truth, which is above that of history. Whoever has become thoughtful and melancholy, through his own mishaps or those of others; whoever has borne about with him the clouded brow of reflection, and thought himself "too much i' th' sun;" whoever has seen the golden lamp of day dimmed by envious mists rising in his own breast, and could find in the world before him only a dull blank with nothing left remarkable in it; whoever has known "the pangs of despised love, the insolence of office, or the spurns which patient merit of the unworthy takes;" he who has felt his mind sink within him, and sadness cling to his heart like a malady, who has had his hopes blighted and his youth staggered by the apparitions of strange things; who cannot be well at ease, while he sees evil hovering near him like a spectre; whose powers of action have been eaten up by thought, he to whom the universe seems infinite, and himself nothing; whose bitterness of soul makes him careless of consequences, and who goes to a play as his best resource to shove off, to a second remove, the evils of life by a mock representation of them — this is the true Hamlet. . . .

The character of Hamlet is itself a pure effusion of genius. It is not a character marked by strength of will or even of passion, but by refinement of thought and sentiment. Hamlet is as little of the hero as a man can well be: but he is a young and princely novice, full of high enthusiasm and quick sensibility — the sport of circumstances, questioning with fortune and refining on his own feelings, and forced from the natural bias of his disposition by the strangeness of his situation. He seems incapable of deliberate action, and is only hurried into extremities on the spur of the occasion, when he has no time to reflect, as in the scene where he kills Polonius, and again, where he alters the letters which Rosencraus and Guildenstern are taking with them to England, purporting his death. At other times, when he is most bound to act, he remains puzzled, undecided, and skeptical, dallies with his purposes, till the occasion is lost, and always finds some pretence to relapse into indolence and thoughtfulness again. For this reason he refuses to kill the King when he is at his prayers, and by a refinement in malice, which is in truth only an excuse for his own want of resolution, defers his revenge to some more fatal opportunity, when he shall be engaged in some act "that has no relish of salvation in it."

> "He kneels and prays,
> And now I'll do't, and so he goes to heaven,
> And so am I reveng'd: *that would be scann'd.*
> He kill'd my father, and for that,
> I, his sole son, send him to heaven.
> Why, this is reward, not revenge.
> Up sword and know thou a more horrid time,
> When he is drunk, asleep, or in a rage."

He is the prince of philosophical speculators, and because he cannot have his revenge perfect, according to the most refined idea his wish can form, he misses it altogether. So he scruples to trust the suggestions of the Ghost, contrives the scene of the play to have surer proof of his uncle's guilt, and then rests satisfied with this confirmation of his suspicions, and the success of his experiment, instead of acting upon it. Yet he is sensible of his own weakness, taxes himself with it, and tries to reason himself out of it.

> "How all occasions do inform against me,
> And spur my dull revenge! What is a man,
> If his chief good and market of his time
> Be but to sleep and feed? A beast; no more.
> Sure he that made us with such large discourse,
> Looking before and after, gave us not
> That capability and godlike reason
> To rust in us unus'd: now whether it be
> Bestial oblivion, or some craven scruple
> Of thinking too precisely on th' event, —
> A thought which quarter'd, hath but one part wisdom,
> And ever three parts coward; — I do not know
> Why yet I live to say, this thing's to do;
> Sith I have cause, and will, and strength, and means
> To do it. Examples gross as earth excite me:
> Witness this army of such mass and charge,
> Led by a delicate and tender prince,
> Whose spirit with divine ambition puff'd,
> Makes mouths at the invisible event,
> Exposing what is mortal and unsure
> To all that fortune, death, and danger dare,
> Even from an eggshell. 'Tis not to be great,
> Never to stir without great argument;
> But greatly to find quarrel in a straw,
> When honour's at the stake. How stand I then,
> That have a father kill'd, a mother stain'd,
> Excitements of my reason and my blood,
> And let all sleep, while to my shame I see
> The imminent death of twenty thousand men,
> That for a fantasy and trick of fame,
> Go to their graves like beds, fight for a plot
> Whereon the numbers cannot try the cause,
> Which is not tomb enough and continent
> To hide the slain? — O, from this time forth,
> My thoughts be bloody, or be nothing worth."

Still he does nothing; and this very speculation on his own infirmity only affords him another occasion for indulging it. It is not for any want of attachment to his father or abhorrence of his murder that Hamlet is thus dilatory, but it is more to his taste to indulge his imagination in reflecting upon the enormity of the crime and refining on his schemes of vengeance, than to put them into immediate practice. His ruling passion is to think, not to act: and any vague pretence that flatters this propensity instantly diverts him from his previous purposes. . . .

Shakspeare was thoroughly a master of the mixed motives of human character, and he here shews us the Queen, who was so criminal in some respects, not without sensibility and affection in other relations of life. — Ophelia is a character almost too exquisitely touching to be dwelt upon. Oh rose of May, oh flower too soon faded! Her love, her madness, her death, are described with the truest touches of tenderness and pathos. It is a character which nobody but Shakspeare could have drawn in the way that he has done, and to the conception of which there is not even the smallest approach, except in some of the old romantick ballads. Her brother, Laertes, is a character we do not like so well: he is too hot and cholerick, and somewhat rodomontade. Polonius is a perfect character in its kind; nor is there any foundation for the objections which have been made to the consistency of this part. It is said that he acts very foolishly and talks very sensibly. There is no inconsistency in that. Again, that he talks wisely at one time and foolishly at another; that his advice to Laertes is very sensible, and his advice to the King and Queen on the subject of Hamlet's madness very ridiculous. But he gives the one as a father, and is sincere in it; he gives the other as a mere courtier, a busybody, and is accordingly officious, garrulous, and impertinent. In short, Shakspeare has been accused of inconsistency in this and other characters, only because he has kept up the distinction which there is in nature, between the understandings and the moral habits of men, between the absurdity in their ideas and the absurdity of their motives. Polonius is not a fool, but he makes himself so. His folly, whether in his actions or speeches, comes under the head of impropriety of intention.

5 We do not like to see our author's plays acted, and least of all, HAMLET. There is no play that suffers so much in being transferred to the stage. Hamlet himself seems hardly capable of being acted. Mr. Kemble unavoidably fails in this character from want of ease and variety. The character of Hamlet is made up of undulating lines; it has the yielding flexibility of a "a wave o' th' sea." Mr. Kemble plays it like a man in armour, with a determined inveteracy of purpose, in one undeviating straight line, which is as remote from the natural grace and refined susceptibility of the character, as the sharp angles and abrupt starts which Mr. Kean introduces into the part. Mr. Kean's Hamlet is as much to splenetick and rash as Mr. Kemble's is too deliberate and formal. His manner is too strong and pointed. He throws a severity, approaching to virulence, into the common observations and answers. There is nothing of this in Hamlet. He is, as it were, wrapped up in his reflections, and only *thinks aloud*. There should therefore be no attempt to impress what he says upon others by a studied exaggeration of emphasis or manner; no *talking at* his hearers. There should be as much of the gentleman and scholar as possible infused into the part, and as little of the actor. A pensive air of sadness should sit reluctantly upon his brow, but no appearance of fixed and sullen gloom. He is full of weakness and melancholy, but there is no harshness in his nature. He is the most amiable of misanthropes.

[1818]

QUESTIONS

1. William Hazlitt opens with, "Hamlet is a name; his speeches and sayings but the idle coinage of the poet's brain. What, then, are they not real? They are as real as our own thoughts. Their reality is in the reader's mind. It is *we* who are Hamlet." Hazlitt then supports his assertion with the lengthy periodic sentence that begins with the phrase "Whoever has become thoughtful and melancholy, through his own mishaps or those of others . . ." and concludes with "this is the true Hamlet." Read that sentence carefully. Which of the situations that Hazlitt presents can you identify with? Choose two, and explain how your experience helps you understand Hamlet.
2. In paragraph 2 Hazlitt writes, "Hamlet is as little of the hero as a man can well be." How does Hazlitt support this claim? Do you agree with his assessment? Why do you believe Hamlet has had such an enormous impact on the reading world when his behavior is so un-heroic?
3. In paragraphs 2 through 4, Hazlitt analyzes Hamlet's inaction and comes to the conclusion that "his ruling passion is to think, not to act." What reasons does Hazlitt provide in his explanation? How is Hazlitt's explanation supported by examples from the play?
4. How does Hazlitt characterize Gertrude, Ophelia, Laertes, and Polonius? How do these characterizations figure into Hazlitt's analysis of Hamlet? Is that how you see these characters as well? Explain.
5. Why doesn't Hazlitt like to see Shakespeare's plays acted — especially *Hamlet*? Similarly, American novelist William Faulkner said that he preferred to read Shakespeare rather than see the plays acted. Do you prefer to read Shakespeare or to see a production? Explain.
6. Hamlet is "the most amiable of misanthropes," Hazlitt concludes. What does he mean by that? How accurately does that phrase describe Hamlet's character as you see it?

Hamlet and the Ghost of His Father

ENGLISH SCHOOL

Over the centuries since *Hamlet* was written, artistic renditions of its title character have been common throughout the western world. In this painting, an oil on canvas by an anonymous painter of the English school, the artist portrays Hamlet's father rising from flames to confront his son. The painting hangs in the Pushkin Museum in Moscow, Russia.

Pushkin Museum, Moscow, Russia/Bridgeman Images

[c. 19th century]

QUESTIONS

1. Who are the figures depicted in the painting? Describe each.
2. Identify the act, scene, and particular lines in *Hamlet* that the painting depicts. How accurately does the artist dramatize that scene? Does it depict the scene as you see it? Does the painting help you to understand the action taking place? Explain.
3. How does this painting represent Hamlet? Which of Hamlet's characteristics and qualities does the artist depict? How do you believe the artist wishes the reader to view him? Is that how you see Hamlet? Explain.

from Hamlet: The Prince or the Poem?

C. S. LEWIS

C. S. Lewis (1898 – 1963) was a British novelist, academic, critic, and Christian apologist. Born in Belfast, Ireland, Lewis served in the British army during World War I. After the war he graduated from Oxford University and was awarded a teaching position there. Lewis's early works include satires such as *The Screwtape Letters* (1942) and science fiction novels such as his successful Space Trilogy: *Out of the Silent Planet* (1938), *Perelandra* (1943), and *That Hideous Strength* (1945). Lewis was also a close friend of J.R.R. Tolkien. During World War II, Lewis gave popular radio broadcasts on his faith, which were later collected in *Mere Christianity* (1952). In the 1950s, Lewis began publishing the seven books that would comprise *The Chronicles of Narnia* children's series, beginning with *The Lion, The Witch and the Wardrobe* (1950). In "Hamlet: The Prince or the Poem?," a lecture delivered in 1942, Lewis argues that Hamlet's poetic manner of expression is the true marvel at the center of the play, and not necessarily the character of Hamlet himself.

For what, after all, is happening to us when we read any of Hamlet"s great speeches? We see visions of the flesh dissolving into a dew, of the world like an unweeded garden. We think of memory reeling in its "distracted globe." (I.v.97) We watch him scampering hither and thither like a maniac to avoid the voices wherewith he is haunted. Someone says "walk out of the air", (II.ii.216-217) and we hear the words "Into my grave" (II.ii.218) spontaneously respond to it. We think of being bounded in a nut-shell and king of infinite space: but for bad dreams. There's the trouble, for "I am most dreadfully attended". (II.ii.289-290) We see the picture of a dull and muddy-mettled rascal, a John-a-dreams,[1] somehow unable to move while ultimate dishonour is done him. We listen to his fear lest the whole thing may be an illusion due to melancholy. We get the sense of sweet relief at the words "shuffled off this mortal coil" (III.i.67) but mixed with the bottomless doubt about what may follow then. We think of bones and skulls, of women breeding sinners, and of how some, to whom all this experience is a sealed book, can yet dare death and danger "for an egg-shell." (IV.iv.53) But do we really enjoy these things, do we go back to them, because they show us Hamlet's character? Are they, from *that* point of view, so very interesting? Does the mere fact that a young man, literally haunted, dispossessed, and lacking friends, should feel thus, tell us anything remarkable? Let me put my question in another way. If instead of the speeches he actually utters about the firmament and man in his scene with Rosencrantz and Guildenstern Hamlet had merely said, "I don't seem to enjoy things the way I used to," and talked in that fashion throughout, should we find him interesting? I think the answer is "Not very." It may be replied that if he talked commonplace prose he would reveal his character less vividly. I am not so sure. He would certainly have revealed *something* less vividly; but would that something be himself? It seems to me that "this majestical roof" (II.ii.331-332) and "What a piece of work is a man!" (II.ii.334-335) give me primarily an impression not of the sort of person he must be to lose the estimation of things but of the things themselves and their great value; and that I should be able to discern, though with very faint interest, the same condition of loss in a personage who was quite unable so to put before me

[1] A dreamer who's out of touch with reality. — EDS.

what he was losing. And I do not think it true to reply that he would be a different character if he spoke less poetically. This point is often misunderstood. We sometimes speak as if the characters in whose mouths Shakespeare puts great poetry were poets: in the sense that Shakespeare was depicting men of poetical genius. But surely this is like thinking that Wagner's Wotan[2] is the dramatic portrait of a baritone? In opera song is the medium by which the representation is made and not part of the thing represented. The actors sing; the dramatic personages are feigned to be speaking. The only character who sings dramatically in *Figaro* is Cherubino.[3] Similarly in poetical drama poetry is the medium, not part of the delineated characters. While the actors speak poetry written for them by the poet, the dramatic personages are supposed to be merely talking. If ever there is occasion to *represent* poetry (as in the play scene from *Hamlet*), it is put into a different metre and strongly stylised so as to prevent confusion.

I trust that my conception is now becoming clear. I believe that we read Hamlet's speeches with interest chiefly because they describe so well a certain spiritual region through which most of us have passed and anyone in his circumstances might be expected to pass, rather than because of our concern to understand how and why this particular man entered it.

[1942]

[2] Richard Wagner (1813–1883) was a German composer most famous for "The Valkyrie," the second opera in the four-part *Ring of the Nibelung* cycle, which was based on Norse mythology. Wotan is the king of the gods in this story. — EDS.

[3] A lovestruck teenage page at court in *The Marriage of Figaro*, a four-act comic opera first composed in 1786 by Wolfgang Amadeus Mozart. Cherubino is often portrayed by a female singer.

QUESTIONS

1. How does C. S. Lewis characterize what we *see* when we read Hamlet? How does that view affect your interpretation of the play?
2. Lewis asks: "But do we really enjoy these things, do we go back to them, because they show us Hamlet's character?" (para. 1). How would you answer Lewis's question? Explain.
3. Do you agree with Lewis's assertion that if Hamlet were more plainspoken, readers wouldn't find him interesting? Why or why not?
4. Lewis says, "It seems to me that 'this majestical roof' (II.ii.331-332) and 'What a piece of work is a man' (II.ii.334-335) give me primarily an impression not of the sort of person he must be to lose the estimation of things but of the things themselves and their great value" (para. 1). What impression do you get from those phrases? How would you compare your response to Lewis's?
5. What point does Lewis make regarding the poetry Shakespearean characters speak? How does that point inform Lewis's discussion of Hamlet's character?
6. Are we, as Lewis suggests in paragraph 2, more interested in reading *Hamlet* to learn about ourselves than we are to learn about the particular character, Hamlet? Explain.

Elegy of Fortinbras

ZBIGNIEW HERBERT

Translated by Czeslaw Milosz

Zbigniew Herbert (1924 –1998) was a Polish poet, essayist, and dramatist known for his membership in the Polish resistance against both the Nazis during World War II and the Soviets in post-war Poland. Herbert earned a master's degree in economics at the University of Kraków and then a law degree at the Nicolaus Copernicus University in Torún. During the 1950s, Herbert worked many low-paying jobs because he refused to write within the framework of official Communist guidelines. In 1956, when widespread riots against the Soviet government brought about a political "thaw" in Poland, Herbert began publishing his work. His first collection of poetry was *The Chord of Light* (1956), which he followed with nine more books of poetry published in his lifetime and one published posthumously. Herbert also authored several books of essays and stories and four plays. In "Elegy of Fortinbras," the conquering prince of Norway addresses a recently deceased Hamlet.

To C.M.[1]

Now that we're alone we can talk prince man to man
though you lie on the stairs and see no more than a dead ant
nothing but black sun with broken rays
I could never think of your hands without smiling
and now that they lie on the stone like fallen nests
they are as defenseless as before The end is exactly this
The hands lie apart The sword lies apart The head apart
and the knight's feet in soft slippers

You will have a soldier's funeral without having been a soldier
the only ritual I am acquainted with a little
There will be no candles no singing only cannon-fuses and bursts
crepe dragged on the pavement helmets boots artillery horses drums drums I know
  nothing exquisite
those will be my manoeuvres before I start to rule
one has to take the city by the neck and shake it a bit

Anyhow you had to perish Hamlet you were not for life
you believed in crystal notions not in human clay
always twitching as if asleep you hunted chimeras
wolfishly you crunched the air only to vomit
you knew no human thing you did not know even how to breathe

---

[1] Herbert's friend, Czeslaw Milosz, also a dissident Polish poet. He translated much of Herbert's poetry, including "Elegy of Fortinbras," into English. — EDS.

Now you have peace Hamlet you accomplished what you had to
and you have peace The rest is not silence but belongs to me
you chose the easier part an elegant thrust
but what is heroic death compared with eternal watching
with a cold apple in one's hand on a narrow chair
with a view of the ant-hill and the clock's dial

Adieu prince I have tasks a sewer project
and a decree on prostitutes and beggars
I must also elaborate a better system of prisons
since as you justly said Denmark is a prison
I go to my affairs This night is born
a star named Hamlet We shall never meet
what I shall leave will not be worth a tragedy

It is not for us to greet each other or bid farewell we live on archipelagos
and that water these words what can they do what can they do prince

[1957]

QUESTIONS

1. How would you describe Fortinbras's stance in the poem? What is his attitude toward Hamlet? Which of the images in the first stanza best depict his tone? Explain.
2. What does Fortinbras mean when he says, "I know nothing exquisite" (l. 12)?
3. Fortinbras addresses Hamlet directly, saying "Anyhow you had to perish Hamlet you were not for life / you believed in crystal notions not in human clay" (ll. 15–16). What evidence in the text of *Hamlet* would support that statement? Explain.
4. Later in the poem, Fortinbras contradicts Hamlet: "The rest is not silence but belongs to me" (l. 21). Why does he say that? What does Fortinbras plan to do with "the rest"? Refer to stanzas 4 and 5 for details to support your answer.
5. How does the speaker contrast himself with Hamlet throughout the elegy? What does this contrast suggest about how Fortinbras views the role of a ruler? Explain, providing details from the text to support your answer.
6. In the final couplet of the poem, Fortinbras speaks of "archipelagos" (l. 33) and of "words" (l. 34). What is the significance of each of these words? Explain. What do these two lines suggest about how Fortinbras regards Hamlet? about how Zbigniew Herbert regards both Fortinbras and Hamlet? Explain.
7. Why do you think Herbert called this poem an elegy rather than a eulogy? What does this choice suggest about the perspective the poem takes on Hamlet and the significance of his life? What might this choice suggest about the poet's view of the role "crystal notions" (l. 16) play in human affairs?

Gertrude Talks Back

MARGARET ATWOOD

Margaret Atwood (b. 1939) was born in Ottawa and spent much of her childhood in northern Quebec. She earned her undergraduate degree at Victoria College (now University) of the University of Toronto and an MA at Radcliffe College (Harvard University). Atwood is a prolific writer in many forms, including poetry, literary criticism, and fiction. She is the author of more than fifteen collections of poetry including early works such as *Double Persephone* (1961), *The Circle Game* (1964), *Expeditions* (1965), *Speeches for Doctor Frankenstein* (1966), and *The Animals in That Country* (1968), and later works like *Interlunar* (1984), *Morning in the Burned House* (1995), *Eating Fire: Selected Poems 1965–1995* (1998), and *The Door* (2007). Atwood's first novel, *The Edible Woman* (1969), is at once frightening and comic. Eight more novels followed — *Surfacing* (1972), *Lady Oracle* (1976), *Life Before Man* (1979), *Bodily Harm* (1981), *The Handmaid's Tale* (1985), *Cat's Eye* (1988), *The Robber Bride* (1993), and *Alias Grace* (1996). Many of these were nominated for the Booker Prize before *The Blind Assassin* won it in 2000. Recent novels include *The Year of the Flood* (2009), *MaddAddam* (2013), *Scribbler Moon* (2014), *The Heart Goes Last* (2015), and *Hag-Seed* (2016). With her wry, satirical, and mischievous sense of humor, Atwood has the ability to blend the prosaic with pure fantasy. In "Gertrude Talks Back" Atwood imagines Hamlet from his mother's point of view.

I always thought it was a mistake, calling you Hamlet. I mean, what kind of a name is that for a young boy? It was your father's idea. Nothing would do but that you had to be called after him. Selfish. The other kids at school used to tease the life out of you. The nicknames! And those terrible jokes about pork.

I wanted to call you George.

I am *not* wringing my hands. I'm drying my nails.

Darling, please stop fidgeting with my mirror. That'll be the third one you've broken.

5 Yes, I've seen those pictures, thank you very much.

I *know* your father was handsomer than Claudius. High brow, aquiline nose and so on, looked great in uniform. But handsome isn't everything, especially in a man, and far be it from me to speak ill of the dead, but I think it's about time I pointed out to you that your dad just wasn't a whole lot of fun. Noble, sure, I grant you. But Claudius, well, he likes a drink now and then. He appreciates a decent meal. He enjoys a laugh, know what I mean? You don't always have to be tiptoeing around because of some holier-than-thou principle or something.

By the way, darling, I wish you wouldn't call your stepdad *the bloat king*. He does have a slight weight problem, and it hurts his feelings.

The rank sweat of a *what?* My bed is certainly not *enseamed,* whatever that might be! A nasty sty, indeed! Not that it's any of your business, but I change those sheets twice a week, which is more than you do, judging from that student slum pigpen in Wittenberg. I'll certainly never visit you *there* again without prior warning! I see that laundry of yours when you bring it home, and not often enough either, by a long shot! Only when you run out of black socks.

And let me tell you, everyone sweats at a time like that, as you'd find out very soon if you ever gave it a try. A real girlfriend would do you a heap of good. Not like that pasty-faced what's-her-name, all trussed up like a prize turkey in those touch-me-not corsets of hers. If you ask me, there's something off about that girl. Borderline. Any little shock could push her right over the edge.

10 Go get yourself someone more down-to-earth. Have a nice roll in the hay. Then you can talk to me about nasty sties.

No, darling, I am not *mad* at you. But I must say you're an awful prig sometimes. Just like your Dad. *The Flesh,* he'd say. You'd think it was dog dirt. You can excuse that in a young person, they are always so intolerant, but in someone his age it was getting, well, very hard to live with, and that's the understatement of the year.

Some days I think it would have been better for both of us if you hadn't been an only child. But you realize who you have to thank for *that.* You have no idea what I used to put up with. And every time I felt like a little, you know, just to warm up my aging bones, it was like I'd suggested murder.

Oh! You think *what?* You think Claudius murdered your Dad? Well, no wonder you've been so rude to him at the dinner table!

If I'd known *that,* I could have put you straight in no time flat.

15 It wasn't Claudius, darling.

It was me.

[1994]

QUESTIONS

1. How would you describe Gertrude's tone and stance in "Gertrude Talks Back"? How do you think Hamlet would respond?
2. How closely does Gertrude's characterization of Hamlet square with yours? Explain.
3. In paragraph 9 Gertrude talks about Ophelia. How would you compare what she says here with what she says in lines 330–34 of act V, scene i of *Hamlet*?
4. How does Gertrude characterize Hamlet's father? How plausible do you think her assessment is?
5. Were you surprised by the conclusion of the piece? Explain. To what extent is Atwood's interpretation plausible? How does it affect your view of Hamlet, and of *Hamlet*?

from **Hamlet's Not Depressed, He's Grieving**

MEGHAN O'ROURKE

Meghan O'Rourke (b. 1976) is an American nonfiction writer, poet, and critic from Brooklyn, New York. She is a graduate of Yale University, and earned an MFA in Creative Writing from Warren Wilson College. O'Rourke has worked as an editor for the *New Yorker* and the *Paris Review*, and is an occasional contributor to the *New York Times*. She is the author of two books of poetry — *Halflife* (2007) and *Once* (2011) — and a memoir about her mother's death, *The Long Goodbye* (2011). O'Rourke's numerous awards include the Lannan Literary Award (2007) and the Guggenheim Award for General Nonfiction (2014). Her writing has been praised for its nuanced examination of a broad range of topics, from gender bias in the

literary world, to the politics of marriage and divorce, to the place of grief and mourning in society. In "Hamlet's Not Depressed, He's Grieving," published in *Slate* in 2009, O'Rourke recalls the clarity and realism she found in *Hamlet* in the wake of the loss of her own parent.

I had a hard time sleeping right after my mother died. The nights were long and had their share of what C.S. Lewis, in his memoir *A Grief Observed*, calls "mad, midnight . . . entreaties spoken into the empty air." One of the things I did was read. I read lots of books about death and loss. But one said more to me about grieving than any other: *Hamlet.* I'm not alone in this. A colleague recently told me that after his mother died he listened over and over to a tape recording he'd made of the Kenneth Branagh film version.

I had always thought of Hamlet's melancholy as existential. I saw his sense that "the world is out of joint" as vague and philosophical. He's a depressive, self-obsessed young man who can't stop chewing at big metaphysical questions. But reading the play after my mother's death, I felt differently. Hamlet's moodiness and irascibility suddenly seemed deeply connected to the fact that his father has just died, and he doesn't know how to handle it. He is radically dislocated, stumbling through the world, trying to figure out where the walls are while the rest of the world acts as if nothing important has changed. I can relate. When Hamlet comes onstage he is greeted by his uncle with the worst question you can ask a grieving person: "How is it that the clouds still hang on you?" It reminded me of the friend who said, 14 days after my mother died, "Hope you're doing well." No wonder Hamlet is angry and cagey.

Hamlet is the best description of grief I've read because it dramatizes grief rather than merely describing it. Grief, Shakespeare understands, is a social experience. It's not just that Hamlet is sad; it's that everyone around him is unnerved by his grief. And Shakespeare doesn't flinch from that truth. He captures the way that people act as if sadness is bizarre when it is all too explainable. Hamlet's mother, Gertrude, tries to get him to see that his loss is "common." His uncle Claudius chides him to put aside his "unmanly grief." It's not just guilty people who act this way. Some are eager to get past the obvious rawness in your eyes or voice; why should they step into the flat shadows of your "sterile promontory"? Even if they wanted to, how could they? And this tension between your private sadness and the busy old world is a huge part of what I feel as I grieve — and felt most intensely in the first weeks of loss. Even if, as a friend helpfully pointed out, my mother wasn't murdered.

I am also moved by how much in *Hamlet* is about slippage — the difference between being and seeming, the uncertainty about how the inner translates into the outer. To mourn is to wonder at the strangeness that grief is not written all over your face in bruised hieroglyphics. And it's also to feel, quite powerfully, that you're not allowed to descend into the deepest fathom of your grief — that to do so would be taboo somehow. *Hamlet* is a play about a man whose grief is deemed unseemly.

5 Strangely, *Hamlet* somehow made me feel it was OK that I, too, had "lost all my mirth." My colleague put it better: "*Hamlet* is the grief-slacker's Bible, a knowing book that understands what you're going through and doesn't ask for much in return," he wrote to me. Maybe that's because the entire play is as drenched in grief as it is in blood. There is Ophelia's grief at Hamlet's angry withdrawal from her. There is Laertes'

grief that Polonius and Ophelia die. There is Gertrude and Claudius' grief, which is as fake as the flowers in a funeral home. Everyone is sad and messed up. *If only the court had just let Hamlet feel bad about his dad,* you start to feel, *things in Denmark might not have disintegrated so quickly!*

Hamlet also captures one of the aspects of grief I find it most difficult to speak about — the profound sense of ennui,[1] the moments of angrily feeling it is not worth continuing to live. After my mother died, I felt that abruptly, amid the chaos that is daily life, I had arrived at a terrible, insistent truth about the impermanence of the everyday. Everything seemed exhausting. Nothing seemed important. C.S. Lewis has a great passage about the laziness of grief, how it made him not want to shave or answer letters. At one point during that first month, I did not wash my hair for 10 days. Hamlet's soliloquy captures that numb exhaustion, and now I read it as a true expression of grief:

> O that this too too sullied flesh would melt,
> Thaw and resolve itself into a dew,
> Or that the Everlasting had not fix'd
> His canon 'gainst self-slaughter. O God! God!
> How weary, stale, flat, and unprofitable
> Seem to me all the uses of this world!

Those adjectives felt apt. And so, even, does the pained wish — in my case, thankfully fleeting — that one might melt away. Researchers have found that the bereaved are at a higher risk for suicideality (or suicidal thinking and behaviors) than the depressed. For many, that risk is quite acute. For others of us, this passage captures how passive a form those thoughts can take. Hamlet is less searching for death actively than he is wishing powerfully for the pain just to go away. And it is, to be honest, strangely comforting to see my own worst thoughts mirrored back at me — perhaps because I do not feel likely to go as far into them as Hamlet does. (So far, I have not accidentally killed anyone with a dagger, for example.)

The way Hamlet speaks conveys his grief as much as what he says. He talks in run-on sentences to Ophelia. He slips between like things without distinguishing fully between them — "to die, to sleep" and "to sleep, perchance to dream." He resorts to puns because puns free him from the terrible logic of normalcy, which has nothing to do with grief and cannot fully admit its darkness.

And Hamlet's madness, too, makes new sense. He goes mad because madness is the only method that makes sense in a world tyrannized by false logic. If no one can tell whether he is mad, it is because he cannot tell either. Grief is a bad moon, a sleeper wave. It's like having an inner combatant, a saboteur who, at the slightest change in the sunlight, or at the first notes of a jingle for a dog food commercial, will flick the memory switch, bringing tears to your eyes. No wonder Hamlet said, ". . . for there is nothing either good or bad, but thinking makes it so." Grief can also make you feel, like Hamlet, strangely flat. Nor is it ennobling, as *Hamlet* drives home. It makes you at once vulnerable and self-absorbed, needy and standoffish, knotted up inside, even punitive.

Like Hamlet, I, too, find it difficult to remember that my own "change in disposition" is connected to a distinct event. Most of the time, I just feel that I see the world more accurately than I used to. ("There are more things in heaven and earth, Horatio, / Than are dreamt of in your philosophy.") Pessimists, after all, are said to have a more realistic view of themselves in the world than optimists.

[2009]

[1]Listless boredom. — EDS.

QUESTIONS

1. Meghan O'Rourke says that as Hamlet mourns his beloved father's death, he feels as if "the rest of the world acts as if nothing important has changed" (para. 2). Cite the act, scene, and lines in the play that support O'Rourke's observation. Might this situation be responsible for Hamlet's seeming madness? In colloquial language, might the responses of everyone else, and especially Gertrude, be "driving him *crazy*"?
2. The 1948 film of *Hamlet* opens with a voice-over that says "This is the tragedy of a man who could not make up his mind." O'Rourke states: "Hamlet is a play about a man whose grief is deemed unseemly" (para. 4). While both of these statements capture neither the complexity of the play nor its protagonist, which assessment of Hamlet's character makes more sense to you? Explain.
3. In paragraph 5, O'Rourke writes, "*If only the court had just let Hamlet feel bad about his dad*, you start to feel, *things in Denmark might not have disintegrated so quickly!*" Do you agree with O'Rourke's assertion? Explain, using the text of the play to support your response.
4. According to O'Rourke, what accounts for Hamlet's "madness"(para. 8)? Do you agree with her that it "makes new sense"? Explain.
5. In the final paragraph, O'Rourke quotes Hamlet: "There are more things in heaven and earth, Horatio, / Than are dreamt of in your philosophy" (I.v.166). What does she imply here? Explain.

LITERATURE IN CONVERSATION
Hamlet and the Evolution of Character

1. Imagine that you have in your hands two copies of *Hamlet*, one with *Hamlet and the Ghost of His Father* as the cover art, the other with *John Philip Kemble as Hamlet*. What expectations would each induce in the reader? Which one more accurately depicts Hamlet's character as you see it? Explain.
2. In her essay on *Hamlet*, Marjorie Garber refers to the well-known 1948 film rendition of the play with distinctly Freudian overtones, and reminds us of the now infamous oversimplification of the "opening voice-over murmur, '[T]his is the tragedy of a man who could not make up his mind.'" The 1990 film adaptation – directed by Franco Zeffirelli and starring Mel Gibson as Hamlet, Glenn Close as Gertrude, and Helena Bonham Carter as Ophelia – also takes a similar tack. Why do you think that Freud has had such a powerful influence on interpretations of *Hamlet*?
3. In *The Prince,* a sixteenth-century text on how best to govern, author Niccolò Machiavelli asserts: "All men will see what you seem to be; only a few will know what you are." One question readers have pondered for centuries is whether Hamlet is, in fact, insane. At times he certainly seems to be, and acts accordingly. He says "my wit's diseased" (III.ii.355–356), but then he did say earlier that he would put "an antic disposition on" (I.v.172). To his mother, he says "I essentially am not in madness, / But mad in craft" (III.iv.188–89). To Rosencrantz and Guildenstern he says "I am but mad north-north-west. When the / wind is southerly I know a hawk from a handsaw" (II.ii.424–26). Using as evidence the text of *Hamlet* and two of the Texts in Context, answer the question: Is Hamlet mad?
4. Presented with a problem, Hamlet says "the time is out of joint" (I.iv.189), as if he is at the center of the world. About to die, he says, "the rest is silence" (V.ii.384), as if his death erases the world. These lines seem to suggest that Hamlet regards others as minor characters in the drama of his life. To what degree is Hamlet driven by self-centeredness and solipsism? Use both *Hamlet* and at least two other Texts in Context to support your argument.
5. In act III, scene I of the play, Ophelia describes Hamlet thusly:

   O, what a noble mind is here o'er-thrown!
   The courtier's, soldier's, scholar's eye, tongue,
   sword;
   Th' expectancy and rose of the fair state,

The glass of fashion and the mould of form,
Th' observed of all observers, quite, quite down!
And I, of ladies most deject and wretched,
That sucked the honey of his music vows,
Now see that noble and most sovereign reason
Like sweet bells jangled, out of tune and harsh;
That unmatched form and feature of blown youth
Blasted with ecstasy: O woe is me,
T' have seen what I have seen, see what I see!

Do you, as a reader, see what Ophelia has seen? Or do we as readers see only what she sees? Considering the perspectives the Texts in Context offer, how would you explain the vast difference between the Hamlet that Ophelia describes and the Hamlet that is?

6. C. S. Lewis contends that "we read Hamlet's speeches with interest chiefly because they describe so well a certain spiritual region through which most of us have passed and anyone in his circumstances might be expected to pass, rather than because of our concern to understand how and why this particular man entered it." Do you agree? What about the other writers in the Texts in Context, particularly William Hazlitt and Meghan O'Rourke? Explain.
7. One might separate the Texts in Context into two groups. In one, Garber, Hazlitt, Lewis, and O'Rourke provide a discussion and analysis of Hamlet's character; in the other group, the paintings and the pieces by Zbigniew Herbert and Margaret Atwood provide imaginative and artistic responses. Which of the two groups provides more insight into Hamlet's character? Explain.
8. Which of the Texts in Context has helped you the most to deepen your understanding of Hamlet, the character, and of *Hamlet*, the play? Explain.

FICTION

Bartleby, the Scrivener: A Story of Wall Street

HERMAN MELVILLE

Herman Melville (1819–1891), best known for his novel *Moby-Dick* (1851), was born in New York City. By the time he was in his early twenties, he went off to sea, sailing first to Liverpool, England, then to the Marquesas Islands and areas in the South Seas on a whaling ship. Based on his experiences, he wrote the novels *Typee* (1846) and *Omoo* (1847); *Redburn*, an autobiographical novel based on his first voyage, appeared in 1849. Largely self-educated, Melville read widely, especially William Shakespeare and Ralph Waldo Emerson, both of whom influenced *Moby-Dick*. In the book, Melville's narrator, Ishmael, tells of the epic quest of Captain Ahab after the white whale. Now widely regarded as one of the greatest novels of American literature for its gripping epic adventure and its profound metaphysical journey, it was not well received in its time, nor were the later novels *Pierre; or, The Ambiguities* (1852), *The Confidence Man* (1857), or *Billy Budd* (published posthumously in 1924). Although Melville is most known for his novels, later in his life he also wrote poems and many fine stories, including "Bartleby, the Scrivener," which reflects his experience of working on Wall Street.

I am a rather elderly man. The nature of my avocations, for the last thirty years, has brought me into more than ordinary contact with what would seem an interesting and somewhat singular set of men, of whom, as yet, nothing, that I know of, has ever been written — I mean, the law-copyists, or scriveners. I have known very many of them, professionally and privately, and, if I pleased, could relate diverse histories, at which good-natured gentlemen might smile, and sentimental souls might weep. But I waive the biographies of all other scriveners, for a few passages in the life of Bartleby, who was a scrivener, the strangest I ever saw, or heard of. While, of other law-copyists, I might write the complete life, of Bartleby nothing of that sort can be done. I believe that no materials exist, for a full and satisfactory biography of this man. It is an irreparable loss to literature. Bartleby was one of those beings of whom nothing is ascertainable, except from the original sources, and, in his case, those are very small. What my own astonished eyes saw of Bartleby, *that* is all I know of him, except, indeed, one vague report, which will appear in the sequel.

Ere introducing the scrivener, as he first appeared to me, it is fit I make some mention of myself, my *employés*, my business, my chambers, and general surroundings, because some such description is indispensable to an adequate understanding of the chief character about to be presented. Imprimis:[1] I am a man who, from his youth upwards, has been filled with a profound conviction that the easiest way of life is the best. Hence, though I belong to a profession proverbially energetic and nervous, even to turbulence, at times, yet nothing of that sort have I ever suffered to invade my peace. I am one of those unambitious lawyers who

[1]In the first place. — EDS.

never address a jury, or in any way draw down public applause; but, in the cool tranquillity of a snug retreat, do a snug business among rich men's bonds, and mortgages, and title-deeds. All who know me, consider me an eminently *safe* man. The late John Jacob Astor,[2] a personage little given to poetic enthusiasm, had no hesitation in pronouncing my first grand point to be prudence; my next, method. I do not speak it in vanity, but simply record the fact, that I was not unemployed in my profession by the late John Jacob Astor; a name which, I admit, I love to repeat; for it hath a rounded and orbicular sound to it, and rings like unto bullion. I will freely add, that I was not insensible to the late John Jacob Astor's good opinion.

Some time prior to the period at which this little history begins, my avocations had been largely increased. The good old office, now extinct in the State of New York, of a Master in Chancery, had been conferred upon me. It was not a very arduous office, but very pleasantly remunerative. I seldom lose my temper; much more seldom indulge in dangerous indignation at wrongs and outrages; but I must be permitted to be rash here and declare, that I consider the sudden and violent abrogation of the office of Master in Chancery, by the new Constitution, as a —— premature act; inasmuch as I had counted upon a life-lease of the profits, whereas I only received those of a few short years. But this is by the way.

My chambers were up stairs, at No. —— Wall Street. At one end, they looked upon the white wall of the interior of a spacious skylight shaft, penetrating the building from top to bottom.

5 This view might have been considered rather tame than otherwise, deficient in what landscape painters call "life." But, if so, the view from the other end of my chambers offered, at least, a contrast, if nothing more. In that direction, my windows commanded an unobstructed view of a lofty brick wall, black by age and everlasting shade; which wall required no spyglass to bring out its lurking beauties, but, for the benefit of all near-sighted spectators, was pushed up to within ten feet of my window-panes. Owing to the great height of the surrounding buildings, and my chambers being on the second floor, the interval between this wall and mine not a little resembled a huge square cistern.

At the period just preceding the advent of Bartleby, I had two persons as copyists in my employment, and a promising lad as an office-boy. First, Turkey; second, Nippers; third, Ginger Nut. These may seem names, the like of which are not usually found in the Directory. In truth, they were nicknames, mutually conferred upon each other by my three clerks, and were deemed expressive of their respective persons or characters. Turkey was a short, pursy Englishman, of about my own age — that is, somewhere not far from sixty. In the morning, one might say, his face was of a fine florid hue, but after twelve o'clock, meridian — his dinner hour — it blazed like a grate full of Christmas coals; and continued blazing — but, as it were, with a gradual wane — till six o'clock, P.M., or thereabouts; after which, I saw no more of the proprietor of the face, which, gaining its meridian with the sun, seemed to set with it, to rise, culminate, and decline the following day, with the like regularity and undiminished glory. There are many singular coincidences I have known in the course of my life, not the least among which was the fact, that, exactly when Turkey displayed his fullest beams from his red and radiant countenance, just then, too, at that critical moment, began the daily period when I considered his business capacities as seriously disturbed for the remainder of the twenty-four hours. Not that he was absolutely idle, or averse to business then; far from it. The difficulty was, he was apt to be

[2]Astor (1763–1848) was a fur trader and the richest American of his time. — EDS.

altogether too energetic. There was a strange, inflamed, flurried, flighty recklessness of activity about him. He would be incautious in dipping his pen into his inkstand. All his blots upon my documents were dropped there after twelve o'clock, meridian. Indeed, not only would he be reckless, and sadly given to making blots in the afternoon, but, some days, he went further, and was rather noisy. At such times, too, his face flamed with augmented blazonry, as if cannel coal had been heaped on anthracite. He made an unpleasant racket with his chair; spilled his sand-box; in mending his pens, impatiently split them all to pieces, and threw them on the floor in a sudden passion; stood up, and leaned over his table, boxing his papers about in a most indecorous manner, very sad to behold in an elderly man like him. Nevertheless, as he was in many ways a most valuable person to me, and all the time before twelve o'clock, meridian, was the quickest, steadiest creature, too, accomplishing a great deal of work in a style not easily to be matched — for these reasons, I was willing to overlook his eccentricities, though, indeed, occasionally, I remonstrated with him. I did this very gently, however, because, though the civilest, nay, the blandest and most reverential of men in the morning, yet, in the afternoon, he was disposed, upon provocation, to be slightly rash with his tongue — in fact, insolent. Now, valuing his morning services as I did, and resolved not to lose them — yet, at the same time, made uncomfortable by his inflamed ways after twelve o'clock — and being a man of peace, unwilling by my admonitions to call forth unseemly retorts from him, I took upon me, one Saturday noon (he was always worse on Saturdays) to hint to him, very kindly, that, perhaps, now that he was growing old, it might be well to abridge his labors; in short, he need not come to my chambers after twelve o'clock, but, dinner over, had best go home to his lodgings, and rest himself till tea-time. But no; he insisted upon his afternoon devotions. His countenance became intolerably fervid, as he oratorically assured me — gesticulating with a long ruler at the other end of the room — that if his services in the morning were useful, how indispensable, then, in the afternoon?

"With submission, sir," said Turkey, on this occasion, "I consider myself your right-hand man. In the morning I but marshal and deploy my columns; but in the afternoon I put myself at their head, and gallantly charge the foe, thus" — and he made a violent thrust with the ruler.

"But the blots, Turkey," intimated I.

"True; but, with submission, sir, behold these hairs! I am getting old. Surely, sir, a blot or two of a warm afternoon is not to be severely urged against gray hairs. Old age — even if it blot the page — is honorable. With submission, sir, we *both* are getting old."

This appeal to my fellow-feeling was hardly 10
to be resisted. At all events, I saw that go he would not. So, I made up my mind to let him stay, resolving, nevertheless, to see to it that, during the afternoon, he had to do with my less important papers.

Nippers, the second on my list, was a whiskered, sallow, and, upon the whole, rather piratical-looking young man, of about five-and-twenty. I always deemed him the victim of two evil powers — ambition and indigestion. The ambition was evinced by a certain impatience of the duties of a mere copyist, an unwarrantable usurpation of strictly professional affairs such as the original drawing up of legal documents. The indigestion seemed betokened in an occasional nervous testiness and grinning irritability, causing the teeth to audibly grind together over mistakes committed in copying; unnecessary maledictions, hissed, rather than spoken, in the heat of business; and especially by a continual discontent with the height of the table where he worked. Though of a very ingenious mechanical turn, Nippers could never get this table to suit him. He put chips under it, blocks of various sorts, bits of pasteboard, and at last went so far as to attempt an exquisite adjustment, by final pieces of folded blotting-paper. But no invention would answer. If, for the sake of easing his back, he brought the table-lid at a sharp angle well up towards his chin, and wrote there like a man using the steep roof of a Dutch house for his desk, then he declared that it stopped the circulation in his arms. If now he lowered the table to his waistbands, and stooped over it in writing, then there was a sore aching in his back. In short, the truth of the matter was, Nippers knew not what he wanted. Or, if he wanted anything, it was to be rid of a scrivener's table altogether. Among the manifestations of his diseased ambition was a fondness he had for receiving visits from certain ambiguous-looking fellows in seedy coats, whom he called his clients. Indeed, I was aware that not only was he, at times, considerable of a ward-politician, but he occasionally did a little business at the justices' courts, and was not unknown on the steps of the Tombs.[3] I have good reason to believe, however, that one individual who called upon him at my chambers, and who, with a grand air, he insisted was his client, was no other than a dun, and the alleged title-deed, a bill. But, with all his failings, and the annoyances he caused me, Nippers, like his compatriot Turkey, was a very useful man to me; wrote a neat, swift hand; and, when he chose, was not deficient in a gentlemanly sort of deportment. Added to this, he always dressed in a gentlemanly sort of way; and so, incidentally, reflected credit upon my chambers. Whereas, with respect to Turkey, I had much ado to keep him from being a reproach to me. His clothes were apt to look oily, and smell of eating-houses. He wore his pantaloons very loose and baggy in summer. His coats were execrable, his hat not to be handled. But while the hat was a thing of indifference to me, inasmuch as his natural civility and deference, as a dependent Englishman, always led him to doff it the moment he entered the room, yet his coat was another matter. Concerning his coats, I reasoned with him; but with no effect. The truth was, I suppose, that a man with so small an income could not afford to sport such a lustrous face and a lustrous coat at one and the same time. As Nippers once observed, Turkey's money went chiefly for red ink. One winter day, I presented Turkey with a highly respectable-looking coat of my own — a padded gray coat, of a most comfortable warmth, and which buttoned straight up from the knee to the neck. I thought Turkey would appreciate the favor, and abate his rashness and obstreperousness of afternoons. But no; I verily believe that buttoning himself up in so downy and blanket-like a coat had a pernicious effect upon him — upon the same principle that too much oats are bad for horses. In fact, precisely as a rash, restive horse is said to feel his oats, so Turkey felt his coat. It made him insolent. He was a man whom prosperity harmed.

Though, concerning the self-indulgent habits of Turkey, I had my own private surmises, yet, touching Nippers, I was well persuaded that, whatever might be his faults in other respects, he was, at least, a temperate young man. But indeed, nature herself seemed to have been his vintner, and, at his birth, charged him so thoroughly with an irritable, brandy-like disposition, that all subsequent potations were needless. When I consider how, amid the stillness of my chambers, Nippers would sometimes impatiently rise from his seat, and stooping over his table, spread his arms wide apart, seize the whole desk, and move it, and jerk it, with a grim, grinding motion on the floor, as if the table were a perverse voluntary agent, intent on thwarting and vexing him, I plainly perceive that, for Nippers, brandy-and-water were altogether superfluous.

It was fortunate for me that, owing to its peculiar cause — indigestion — the irritability

[3]A jail in New York City. — EDS.

and consequent nervousness of Nippers were mainly observable in the morning, while in the afternoon he was comparatively mild. So that, Turkey's paroxysms only coming on about twelve o'clock, I never had to do with their eccentricities at one time. Their fits relieved each other, like guards. When Nippers' was on, Turkey's was off; and vice versa. This was a good natural arrangement, under the circumstances.

Ginger Nut, the third on my list, was a lad, some twelve years old. His father was a carman, ambitious of seeing his son on the bench instead of a cart, before he died. So he sent him to my office, as student at law, errand-boy, cleaner, and sweeper, at the rate of one dollar a week. He had a little desk to himself, but he did not use it much. Upon inspection, the drawer exhibited a great array of the shells of various sorts of nuts. Indeed, to this quick-witted youth, the whole noble science of the law was contained in a nutshell. Not the least among the employments of Ginger Nut, as well as one which he discharged with the most alacrity, was his duty as cake and apple purveyor for Turkey and Nippers. Copying lawpapers being proverbially a dry, husky sort of business, my two scriveners were fain to moisten their mouths very often with Spitzenbergs, to be had at the numerous stalls nigh the Custom House and Post Office. Also, they sent Ginger Nut very frequently for that peculiar cake — small, flat, round, and very spicy — after which he had been named by them. Of a cold morning, when business was but dull, Turkey would gobble up scores of these cakes, as if they were mere wafers — indeed, they sell them at the rate of six or eight for a penny — the scrape of his pen blending with the crunching of the crisp particles in his mouth. Of all the fiery afternoon blunders and flurried rashness of Turkey, was his once moistening a ginger-cake between his lips, and clapping it on to a mortgage, for a seal. I came within an ace of dismissing him then. But he mollified me by making an oriental bow, and saying —

“With submission, sir, it was generous of me 15
to find you in stationery on my own account.”

Now my original business — that of a conveyancer and title hunter, and drawer-up of recondite documents of all sorts — was considerably increased by receiving the Master's office. There was now great work for scriveners. Not only must I push the clerks already with me, but I must have additional help.

In answer to my advertisement, a motionless young man one morning stood upon my office threshold, the door being open, for it was summer. I can see that figure now — pallidly neat, pitiably respectable, incurably forlorn! It was Bartleby.

After a few words touching his qualifications, I engaged him, glad to have among my corps of copyists a man of so singularly sedate an aspect, which I thought might operate beneficially upon the flighty temper of Turkey, and the fiery one of Nippers.

I should have stated before that ground-glass folding-doors divided my premises into two parts, one of which was occupied by my scriveners, the other by myself. According to my humor, I threw open these doors, or closed them. I resolved to assign Bartleby a corner by the folding-doors, but on my side of them, so as to have this quiet man within easy call, in case any trifling thing was to be done. I placed his desk close up to a small side-window in that part of the room, a window which originally had afforded a lateral view of certain grimy brick-yards and bricks, but which, owing to subsequent erections, commanded at present no view at all, though it gave some light. Within three feet of the panes was a wall, and the light came down from far above, between two lofty buildings, as from a very small opening in a dome. Still further to a satisfactory arrangement, I procured a high green folding screen, which might entirely isolate Bartleby from my sight, though not remove him from my voice. And thus, in a manner, privacy and society were conjoined.

At first, Bartleby did an extraordinary quantity of writing. As if long famishing for something to copy, he seemed to gorge himself on my documents. There was no pause for digestion. He ran a day and night line, copying by sunlight and by candle-light. I should have been quite delighted with his application, had he been cheerfully industrious. But he wrote on silently, palely, mechanically.

It is, of course, an indispensable part of a scrivener's business to verify the accuracy of his copy, word by word. Where there are two or more scriveners in an office, they assist each other in this examination, one reading from the copy, the other holding the original. It is a very dull, wearisome, and lethargic affair. I can readily imagine that, to some sanguine temperaments, it would be altogether intolerable. For example, I cannot credit that the mettlesome poet, Byron, would have contentedly sat down with Bartleby to examine a law document of, say five hundred pages, closely written in a crimpy hand.

Now and then, in the haste of business, it had been my habit to assist in comparing some brief document myself, calling Turkey or Nippers for this purpose. One object I had, in placing Bartleby so handy to me behind the screen, was, to avail myself of his services on such trivial occasions. It was on the third day, I think, of his being with me, and before any necessity had arisen for having his own writing examined, that, being much hurried to complete a small affair I had in hand, I abruptly called to Bartleby. In my haste and natural expectancy of instant compliance, I sat with my head bent over the original on my desk, and my right hand sideways, and somewhat nervously extended with the copy, so that, immediately upon emerging from his retreat, Bartleby might snatch it and proceed to business without the least delay.

In this very attitude did I sit when I called to him, rapidly stating what it was I wanted him to do — namely, to examine a small paper with me. Imagine my surprise, nay, my consternation, when, without moving from his privacy, Bartleby, in a singularly mild, firm voice, replied, "I would prefer not to."

I sat awhile in perfect silence, rallying my stunned faculties. Immediately it occurred to me that my ears had deceived me, or Bartleby had entirely misunderstood my meaning. I repeated my request in the clearest tone I could assume; but in quite as clear a one came the previous reply, "I would prefer not to."

"Prefer not to," echoed I, rising in high excitement, and crossing the room with a stride. "What do you mean? Are you moonstruck? I want you to help me compare this sheet here — take it," and I thrust it towards him.

"I would prefer not to," said he.

I looked at him steadfastly. His face was leanly composed; his gray eye dimly calm. Not a wrinkle of agitation rippled him. Had there been the least uneasiness, anger, impatience, or impertinence in his manner; in other words, had there been anything ordinarily human about him, doubtless I should have violently dismissed him from the premises. But as it was, I should have as soon thought of turning my pale plaster-of-paris bust of Cicero out of doors. I stood gazing at him awhile, as he went on with his own writing, and then reseated myself at my desk. This is very strange, thought I. What had one best do? But my business hurried me. I concluded to forget the matter for the present, reserving it for my future leisure. So, calling Nippers from the other room, the paper was speedily examined.

A few days after this, Bartleby concluded four lengthy documents, being quadruplicates of a week's testimony taken before me in my High Court of Chancery. It became necessary to examine them. It was an important suit, and great accuracy was imperative. Having all things arranged, I called Turkey, Nippers, and Ginger Nut, from the next room, meaning to place the four copies in the hands of my four clerks, while I should read from the original. Accordingly,

Turkey, Nippers, and Ginger Nut had taken their seats in a row, each with his document in his hand, when I called to Bartleby to join this interesting group.

"Bartleby! quick, I am waiting."

I heard a slow scrape of his chair legs on the uncarpeted floor, and soon he appeared standing at the entrance of his hermitage.

"What is wanted?" said he, mildly.

"The copies, the copies," said I, hurriedly. "We are going to examine them. There" — and I held towards him the fourth quadruplicate.

"I would prefer not to," he said, and gently disappeared behind the screen.

For a few moments I was turned into a pillar of salt, standing at the head of my seated column of clerks. Recovering myself, I advanced towards the screen, and demanded the reason for such extraordinary conduct.

"*Why* do you refuse?"

"I would prefer not to."

With any other man I should have flown outright into a dreadful passion, scorned all further words, and thrust him ignominiously from my presence. But there was something about Bartleby that not only strangely disarmed me, but, in a wonderful manner, touched and disconcerted me. I began to reason with him.

"These are your own copies we are about to examine. It is labor saving to you, because one examination will answer for your four papers. It is common usage. Every copyist is bound to help examine his copy. Is it not so? Will you not speak? Answer!"

"I prefer not to," he replied in a flute-like tone. It seemed to me that, while I had been addressing him, he carefully revolved every statement that I made; fully comprehended the meaning; could not gainsay the irresistible conclusion; but, at the same time, some paramount consideration prevailed with him to reply as he did.

"You are decided, then, not to comply with my request — a request made according to common usage and common sense?"

He briefly gave me to understand, that on that point my judgment was sound. Yes: his decision was irreversible.

It is not seldom the case that, when a man is browbeaten in some unprecedented and violently unreasonable way, he begins to stagger in his own plainest faith. He begins, as it were, vaguely to surmise that, wonderful as it may be, all the justice and all the reason is on the other side. Accordingly, if any disinterested persons are present, he turns to them for some reinforcement for his own faltering mind.

"Turkey," said I, "what do you think of this? Am I not right?"

"With submission, sir," said Turkey, in his blandest tone, "I think that you are."

"Nippers," said I, "what do *you* think of it?"

"I think I should kick him out of the office."

(The reader of nice perceptions will have perceived that, it being morning, Turkey's answer is couched in polite and tranquil terms, but Nippers replies in ill-tempered ones. Or, to repeat a previous sentence, Nippers' ugly mood was on duty, and Turkey's off.)

"Ginger Nut," said I, willing to enlist the smallest suffrage in my behalf, "what do *you* think of it?"

"I think, sir, he's a little *luny*," replied Ginger Nut, with a grin.

"You hear what they say," said I, turning towards the screen, "come forth and do your duty."

But he vouchsafed no reply. I pondered a moment in sore perplexity. But once more business hurried me. I determined again to postpone the consideration of this dilemma to my future leisure. With a little trouble we made out to examine the papers without Bartleby, though at every page or two Turkey deferentially dropped his opinion, that this proceeding was quite out of the common; while Nippers, twitching in his chair with a dyspeptic nervousness, ground out, between his set teeth, occasional hissing maledictions against the stubborn oaf behind the screen. And for his (Nippers') part, this was the first and the last time he would do another man's business without pay.

Meanwhile Bartleby sat in his hermitage, oblivious to everything but his own peculiar business there.

Some days passed, the scrivener being employed upon another lengthy work. His late remarkable conduct led me to regard his ways narrowly. I observed that he never went to dinner; indeed, that he never went anywhere. As yet I had never, of my personal knowledge, known him to be outside of my office. He was a perpetual sentry in the corner. At about eleven o'clock though, in the morning, I noticed that Ginger Nut would advance toward the opening in Bartleby's screen, as if silently beckoned thither by a gesture invisible to me where I sat. The boy would then leave the office, jingling a few pence, and reappear with a handful of ginger-nuts, which he delivered in the hermitage, receiving two of the cakes for his trouble.

He lives, then, on ginger-nuts, thought I; never eats a dinner, properly speaking; he must be a vegetarian, then, but no; he never eats even vegetables, he eats nothing but ginger-nuts. My mind then ran on in reveries concerning the probable effects upon the human constitution of living entirely on ginger-nuts. Ginger-nuts are so called, because they contain ginger as one of their peculiar constituents, and the final flavoring one. Now, what was ginger? A hot, spicy thing. Was Bartleby hot and spicy? Not at all. Ginger, then, had no effect upon Bartleby. Probably he preferred it should have none.

Nothing so aggravates an earnest person as a passive resistance. If the individual so resisted be of a not inhumane temper, and the resisting one perfectly harmless in his passivity, then, in the better moods of the former, he will endeavor charitably to construe to his imagination what proves impossible to be solved by his judgment. Even so, for the most part, I regarded Bartleby and his ways. Poor fellow! thought I, he means no mischief; it is plain he intends no insolence; his aspect sufficiently evinces that his eccentricities are involuntary. He is useful to me. I can get along with him. If I turn him away, the chances are he will fall in with some less indulgent employer, and then he will be rudely treated, and perhaps driven forth miserably to starve. Yes. Here I can cheaply purchase a delicious self-approval. To befriend Bartleby; to humor him in his strange wilfulness, will cost me little or nothing, while I lay up in my soul what will eventually prove a sweet morsel for my conscience. But this mood was not invariable with me. The passiveness of Bartleby sometimes irritated me. I felt strangely goaded on to encounter him in new opposition — to elicit some angry spark from him answerable to my own. But, indeed, I might as well have essayed to strike fire with my knuckles against a bit of Windsor soap. But one afternoon the evil impulse in me mastered me, and the following little scene ensued:

"Bartleby," said I, "when those papers are all copied, I will compare them with you."

"I would prefer not to."

"How? Surely you do not mean to persist in that mulish vagary?"

No answer.

I threw open the folding-doors nearby, and turning upon Turkey and Nippers, exclaimed:

"Bartleby a second time says, he won't examine his papers. What do you think of it, Turkey?"

It was afternoon, be it remembered. Turkey sat glowing like a brass boiler; his bald head steaming; his hands reeling among his blotted papers.

"Think of it?" roared Turkey. "I think I'll just step behind his screen, and black his eyes for him!"

So saying, Turkey rose to his feet and threw his arms into a pugilistic position. He was hurrying away to make good his promise, when I detained him, alarmed at the effect of incautiously rousing Turkey's combativeness after dinner.

"Sit down, Turkey," said I, "and hear what Nippers has to say. What do you think of it, Nippers? Would I not be justified in immediately dismissing Bartleby?"

"Excuse me, that is for you to decide, sir. I think his conduct quite unusual, and, indeed, unjust, as regards Turkey and myself. But it may only be a passing whim."

"Ah," exclaimed I, "you have strangely changed your mind, then — you speak very gently of him now."

"All beer," cried Turkey; "gentleness is effects of beer — Nippers and I dined together to-day. You see how gentle *I* am, sir. Shall I go and black his eyes?"

"You refer to Bartleby, I suppose. No, not to-day, Turkey," I replied; "pray, put up your fists."

I closed the doors, and again advanced towards Bartleby. I felt additional incentives tempting me to my fate. I burned to be rebelled against again. I remembered that Bartleby never left the office.

"Bartleby," said I, "Ginger Nut is away; just step around to the Post Office, won't you?" (it was but a three minutes' walk) "and see if there is anything for me."

"I would prefer not to."

"You *will* not?"

"I *prefer* not."

I staggered to my desk, and sat there in a deep study. My blind inveteracy returned. Was there any other thing in which I could procure myself to be ignominiously repulsed by this lean, penniless wight? — my hired clerk? What added thing is there, perfectly reasonable, that he will be sure to refuse to do?

"Bartleby!"

No answer.

"Bartleby," in a louder tone.

No answer.

"Bartleby," I roared.

Like a very ghost, agreeably to the laws of magical invocation, at the third summons, he appeared at the entrance of his hermitage.

"Go to the next room, and tell Nippers to come to me."

"I prefer not to," he respectfully and slowly said, and mildly disappeared.

"Very good, Bartleby," said I, in a quiet sort of serenely-severe self-possessed tone, intimating the unalterable purpose of some terrible retribution very close at hand. At the moment I half intended something of the kind. But upon the whole, as it was drawing towards my dinner-hour, I thought it best to put on my hat and walk home for the day, suffering much from perplexity and distress of mind.

Shall I acknowledge it? The conclusion of this whole business was, that it soon became a fixed fact of my chambers, that a pale young scrivener, by the name of Bartleby, had a desk there; that he copied for me at the usual rate of four cents a folio (one hundred words); but he was permanently exempt from examining the work done by him, that duty being transferred to Turkey and Nippers, out of compliment, doubtless, to their superior acuteness; moreover, said Bartleby was never, on any account, to be dispatched on the most trivial errand of any sort; and that even if entreated to take upon him such a matter, it was generally understood that he would "prefer not to" — in other words, that he would refuse point-blank.

As days passed on, I became considerably reconciled to Bartleby. His steadiness, his freedom from all dissipation, his incessant industry (except when he chose to throw himself into a standing revery behind his screen), his great stillness, his unalterableness of demeanor under all circumstances, made him a valuable acquisition. One prime thing was this — *he was always there* — first in the morning, continually through the day, and the last at night. I had a singular confidence in his honesty. I felt my most precious papers perfectly safe in his hands. Sometimes, to be sure, I could not, for the very soul of me, avoid falling into sudden spasmodic passions with him. For it was exceeding difficult to bear in mind all the time those strange peculiarities, privileges, and unheard-of exemptions, forming the tacit stipulations on Bartleby's part under which he remained in my office. Now and then, in the eagerness of dispatching pressing business, I would inadvertently summon Bartleby, in a short, rapid tone, to put his finger, say, on the incipient tie of a bit of red tape with which I was about compressing some papers. Of course, from behind the screen the usual answer, "I prefer not to," was sure to come; and then, how could a human creature, with the common infirmities of our nature, refrain from bitterly exclaiming upon such perverseness — such unreasonableness? However, every added repulse of this sort which I received only tended to lessen the probability of my repeating the inadvertence.

Here it must be said, that, according to the custom of most legal gentlemen occupying chambers in densely populated law buildings, there were several keys to my door. One was kept by a woman residing in the attic, which person weekly scrubbed and daily swept and dusted my apartments. Another was kept by Turkey for convenience sake. The third I sometimes carried in my own pocket. The fourth I knew not who had.

Now, one Sunday morning I happened to go to Trinity Church, to hear a celebrated preacher, and finding myself rather early on the ground I thought I would walk round to my chambers for a while. Luckily I had my key with me; but upon applying it to the lock, I found it resisted by something inserted from the inside. Quite surprised, I called out; when to my consternation a key was turned from within; and thrusting his lean visage at me, and holding the door ajar, the apparition of Bartleby appeared, in his shirt-sleeves, and otherwise in a strangely tattered *deshabille*, saying quietly that he was sorry, but he was deeply engaged just then, and — preferred not admitting me at present. In a brief word or two, he moreover added, that perhaps I had better walk round the block two or three times, and by that time he would probably have concluded his affairs.

Now, the utterly unsurmised appearance of Bartleby, tenanting my law-chambers of a Sunday morning, with his cadaverously gentlemanly nonchalance, yet withal firm and self-possessed, had such a strange effect upon me, that incontinently I slunk away from my own door, and did as desired. But not without sundry twinges of impotent rebellion against the mild effrontery of this unaccountable scrivener. Indeed, it was his wonderful mildness chiefly, which not only disarmed me, but unmanned me, as it were. For I consider that one, for the time, is sort of unmanned when he tranquilly permits his hired clerk to dictate to him, and order him away from his own premises. Furthermore, I was full of uneasiness as to what Bartleby could possibly be doing in my office in his shirt-sleeves, and in an otherwise dismantled condition of a Sunday morning. Was anything amiss going on? Nay, that was out of the question. It was not to be thought of for a moment that Bartleby was an immoral person. But what could he be doing there? — copying? Nay again, whatever might be his eccentricities, Bartleby was an eminently decorous person. He would be the last man to sit down to his desk in any state approaching to nudity. Besides, it was Sunday; and there was something about Bartleby that forbade the supposition that he would by any secular occupation violate the proprieties of the day.

Nevertheless, my mind was not pacified; and 90
full of a restless curiosity, at last I returned to the door. Without hindrance I inserted my key, opened it, and entered. Bartleby was not to be seen. I looked round anxiously, peeped behind his screen; but it was very plain that he was gone. Upon more closely examining the place, I surmised that for an indefinite period Bartleby

must have ate, dressed, and slept in my office, and that too without plate, mirror, or bed. The cushioned seat of a rickety old sofa in one corner bore the faint impress of a lean, reclining form. Rolled away under his desk, I found a blanket; under the empty grate, a blacking box and brush; on a chair, a tin basin, with soap and a ragged towel; in a newspaper a few crumbs of ginger-nuts and a morsel of cheese. Yes, thought I, it is evident enough that Bartleby has been making his home here, keeping bachelor's hall all by himself. Immediately then the thought came sweeping across me, what miserable friendlessness and loneliness are here revealed! His poverty is great; but his solitude, how horrible! Think of it. Of a Sunday, Wall Street is deserted as Petra;[4] and every night of every day it is an emptiness. This building, too, which of week-days hums with industry and life, at nightfall echoes with sheer vacancy, and all through Sunday is forlorn. And here Bartleby makes his home; sole spectator of a solitude which he has seen all populous — a sort of innocent and transformed Marius brooding among the ruins of Carthage?[5]

For the first time in my life a feeling of overpowering stinging melancholy seized me. Before, I had never experienced aught but a not unpleasing sadness. The bond of a common humanity now drew me irresistibly to gloom. A fraternal melancholy! For both I and Bartleby were sons of Adam. I remembered the bright silks and sparkling faces I had seen that day, in gala trim, swan-like sailing down the Mississippi of Broadway; and I contrasted them with the pallid copyist, and thought to myself, Ah, happiness courts the light, so we deem the world is gay; but misery hides aloof, so we deem that misery there is none. These sad fancyings — chimeras, doubtless, of a sick and silly brain — led on to other and more special thoughts, concerning the eccentricities of Bartleby. Presentiments of strange discoveries hovered round me. The scrivener's pale form appeared to me laid out, among uncaring strangers, in its shivering winding-sheet.

Suddenly I was attracted by Bartleby's closed desk, the key in open sight left in the lock.

I mean no mischief, seek the gratification of no heartless curiosity, thought I; besides, the desk is mine, and its contents, too, so I will make bold to look within. Everything was methodically arranged, the papers smoothly placed. The pigeon-holes were deep, and removing the files of documents, I groped into their recesses. Presently I felt something there, and dragged it out. It was an old bandanna hand-kerchief, heavy and knotted. I opened it, and saw it was a savings' bank.

I now recalled all the quiet mysteries which I had noted in the man. I remembered that he never spoke but to answer; that, though at intervals he had considerable time to himself, yet I had never seen him reading — no, not even a newspaper; that for long periods he would stand looking out, at his pale window behind the screen, upon the dead brick wall; I was quite sure he never visited any refectory or eating-house; while his pale face clearly indicated that he never drank beer like Turkey; or tea and coffee even, like other men; that he never went anywhere in particular that I could learn; never went out for a walk, unless, indeed, that was the case at present; that he had declined telling who he was, or whence he came, or whether he had any relatives in the world; that though so thin and pale, he never complained of ill-health. And more than all, I remembered a certain unconscious air of pallid — how shall I call it? — of pallid haughtiness, say, or rather an austere reserve about him, which had positively awed me into my tame compliance with his eccentricities, when I had

[4] Ancient Arabian city whose ruins were discovered in 1812. — EDS.

[5] Exiled Roman general Gaius Marius (157–86 B.C.E.) fled to the North African city-state of Carthage after a failed attempt to stop a civil war in Rome. Carthage had been destroyed by the Romans in the Third Punic War (149–146 B.C.E.). — EDS.

feared to ask him to do the slightest incidental thing for me, even though I might know, from his long-continued motionlessness, that behind his screen he must be standing in one of those dead-wall reveries of his.

Revolving all these things, and coupling them with the recently discovered fact, that he made my office his constant abiding place and home, and not forgetful of his morbid moodiness; revolving all these things, a prudential feeling began to steal over me. My first emotions had been those of pure melancholy and sincerest pity; but just in proportion as the forlornness of Bartleby grew and grew to my imagination, did that same melancholy merge into fear, that pity into repulsion. So true it is, and so terrible, too, that up to a certain point the thought or sight of misery enlists our best affections; but, in certain special cases, beyond that point it does not. They err who would assert that invariably this is owing to the inherent selfishness of the human heart. It rather proceeds from a certain hopelessness of remedying excessive and organic ill. To a sensitive being, pity is not seldom pain. And when at last it is perceived that such pity cannot lead to effectual succor, common sense bids the soul be rid of it. What I saw that morning persuaded me that the scrivener was the victim of innate and incurable disorder. I might give alms to his body; but his body did not pain him; it was his soul that suffered, and his soul I could not reach.

I did not accomplish the purpose of going to Trinity Church that morning. Somehow, the things I had seen disqualified me for the time from church-going. I walked homeward, thinking what I would do with Bartleby. Finally, I resolved upon this — I would put certain calm questions to him the next morning, touching his history, etc., and if he declined to answer them openly and unreservedly (and I supposed he would prefer not), then to give him a twenty dollar bill over and above whatever I might owe him, and tell him his services were no longer required; but that if in any other way I could assist him, I would be happy to do so, especially if he desired to return to his native place, wherever that might be, I would willingly help to defray the expenses. Moreover, if, after reaching home, he found himself at any time in want of aid, a letter from him would be sure of a reply.

The next morning came.

"Bartleby," said I, gently calling to him behind his screen.

No reply.

"Bartleby," said I, in a still gentler tone, "come here; I am not going to ask you to do anything you would prefer not to do — I simply wish to speak to you."

Upon this he noiselessly slid into view.

"Will you tell me, Bartleby, where you were born?"

"I would prefer not to."

"Will you tell me *anything* about yourself?"

"I would prefer not to."

"But what reasonable objection can you have to speak to me? I feel friendly towards you."

He did not look at me while I spoke, but kept his glance fixed upon my bust of Cicero, which, as I then sat, was directly behind me, some six inches above my head.

"What is your answer, Bartleby?" said I, after waiting a considerable time for a reply, during which his countenance remained immovable, only there was the faintest conceivable tremor of the white attenuated mouth.

"At present I prefer to give no answer," he said, and retired into his hermitage.

It was rather weak in me I confess, but his manner, on this occasion, nettled me. Not only did there seem to lurk in it a certain calm disdain, but his perverseness seemed ungrateful, considering the undeniable good usage and indulgence he had received from me.

Again I sat ruminating what I should do. Mortified as I was at his behavior, and resolved as I had been to dismiss him when I entered my office, nevertheless I strangely felt something superstitious knocking at my heart, and forbidding me to carry out my purpose, and denouncing me for a villain if I dared to breathe one bitter word against this forlornest of mankind. At last, familiarly drawing my chair behind his screen, I sat down and said: "Bartleby, never mind, then, about revealing your history; but let me entreat you, as a friend, to comply as far as may be with the usages of this office. Say now, you will help to examine papers tomorrow or next day: in short, say now, that in a day or two you will begin to be a little reasonable: — say so, Bartleby."

"At present I would prefer not to be a little reasonable," was his mildly cadaverous reply.

Just then the folding-doors opened, and Nippers approached. He seemed suffering from an unusually bad night's rest, induced by severer indigestion than common. He overheard those final words of Bartleby.

"*Prefer not*, eh?" gritted Nippers — "I'd *prefer* him, if I were you, sir," addressing me — "I'd *prefer* him; I'd give him preferences, the stubborn mule! What is it, sir, pray, that he *prefers* not to do now?"

Bartleby moved not a limb.

"Mr. Nippers," said I, "I'd prefer that you would withdraw for the present."

Somehow, of late, I had got into the way of involuntarily using this word "prefer" upon all sorts of not exactly suitable occasions. And I trembled to think that my contact with the scrivener had already and seriously affected me in a mental way. And what further and deeper aberration might it not yet produce? This apprehension had not been without efficacy in determining me to summary measures.

As Nippers, looking very sour and sulky, was departing, Turkey blandly and deferentially approached.

"With submission, sir," said he, "yesterday I was thinking about Bartleby here, and I think that if he would but prefer to take a quart of good ale every day, it would do much towards mending him, and enabling him to assist in examining his papers."

"So you have got the word, too," said I, slightly excited.

"With submission, what word, sir?" asked Turkey, respectfully crowding himself into the contracted space behind the screen, and by so doing, making me jostle the scrivener. "What word, sir?"

"I would prefer to be left alone here," said Bartleby, as if offended at being mobbed in his privacy.

"*That*'s the word, Turkey," said I — "*that's* it."

"Oh, *prefer*? oh yes — queer word. I never use it myself. But, sir, as I was saying, if he would but prefer — "

"Turkey," interrupted I, "you will please withdraw."

"Oh certainly, sir, if you prefer that I should."

As he opened the folding-door to retire, Nippers at his desk caught a glimpse of me, and asked whether I would prefer to have a certain paper copied on blue paper or white. He did not in the least roguishly accent the word "prefer." It was plain that it involuntarily rolled from his tongue. I thought to myself, surely I must get rid of a demented man, who already has in some degree turned the tongues, if not the heads of myself and clerks. But I thought it prudent not to break the dismission at once.

The next day I noticed that Bartleby did nothing but stand at his window in his dead-wall revery. Upon asking him why he did not write, he said that he had decided upon doing no more writing.

"Why, how now? what next?" exclaimed I, "do no more writing?"

"No more."

"And what is the reason?"

"Do you not see the reason for yourself ?" he indifferently replied.

I looked steadfastly at him, and perceived that his eyes looked dull and glazed. Instantly it occurred to me, that his unexampled diligence in copying by his dim window for the first few weeks of his stay with me might have temporarily impaired his vision.

I was touched. I said something in condolence with him. I hinted that of course he did wisely in abstaining from writing for a while; and urged him to embrace that opportunity of taking wholesome exercise in the open air. This, however, he did not do. A few days after this, my other clerks being absent, and being in a great hurry to dispatch certain letters by the mail, I thought that, having nothing else earthly to do, Bartleby would surely be less inflexible than usual, and carry these letters to the Post Office. But he blankly declined. So, much to my inconvenience, I went myself.

Still added days went by. Whether Bartleby's eyes improved or not, I could not say. To all appearance, I thought they did. But when I asked him if they did, he vouchsafed no answer. At all events, he would do no copying. At last, in replying to my urgings, he informed me that he had permanently given up copying.

"What!" exclaimed I; "suppose your eyes should get entirely well — better than ever before — would you not copy then?"

"I have given up copying," he answered, and slid aside.

He remained as ever, a fixture in my chamber. Nay — if that were possible — he became still more of a fixture than before. What was to be done? He would do nothing in the office; why should he stay there? In plain fact, he had now become a millstone to me, not only useless as a necklace, but afflictive to bear. Yet I was sorry for him. I speak less than truth when I say that, on his own account, he occasioned me uneasiness. If he would but have named a single relative or friend, I would instantly have written, and urged their taking the poor fellow away to some convenient retreat. But he seemed alone, absolutely alone in the universe. A bit of wreck in the mid-Atlantic. At length, necessities connected with my business tyrannized over all other considerations. Decently as I could, I told Bartleby that in six days' time he must unconditionally leave the office. I warned him to take measures, in the interval, for procuring some other abode. I offered to assist him in this endeavor, if he himself would but take the first step towards a removal. "And when you finally quit me, Bartleby," added I, "I shall see that you go not away entirely unprovided. Six days from this hour, remember."

At the expiration of that period, I peeped behind the screen, and lo! Bartleby was there.

I buttoned up my coat, balanced myself; advanced slowly towards him, touched his shoulder, and said, "The time has come; you must quit this place; I am sorry for you; here is money; but you must go."

"I would prefer not," he replied, with his back still towards me.

"You *must*."

He remained silent.

Now I had an unbounded confidence in this man's common honesty. He had frequently restored to me sixpences and shillings carelessly dropped upon the floor, for I am apt to be very reckless in such shirt-button affairs. The proceeding, then, which followed will not be deemed extraordinary.

"Bartleby," said I, "I owe you twelve dollars on account; here are thirty-two, the odd twenty are yours — Will you take it?" and I handed the bills towards him.

But he made no motion.

"I will leave them here, then," putting them under a weight on the table. Then taking my hat and cane and going to the door, I tranquilly turned and added — "After you have removed your things from these offices, Bartleby, you will of course lock the door — since every one is now gone for the day but you — and if you please, slip your key underneath the mat, so that I may have it in the morning. I shall not see you again; so good-bye to you. If, hereafter, in your new place of abode, I can be of any service to you, do not fail to advise me by letter. Good-bye, Bartleby, and fare you well."

But he answered not a word; like the last column of some ruined temple, he remained standing mute and solitary in the middle of the otherwise deserted room.

As I walked home in a pensive mood, my vanity got the better of my pity. I could not but highly plume myself on my masterly management in getting rid of Bartleby. Masterly I call it, and such it must appear to any dispassionate thinker. The beauty of my procedure seemed to consist in its perfect quietness. There was no vulgar bullying, no bravado of any sort, no choleric hectoring, and striding to and fro across the apartment, jerking out vehement commands for Bartleby to bundle himself off with his beggarly traps. Nothing of the kind. Without loudly bidding Bartleby depart — as an inferior genius might have done — I *assumed* the ground that depart he must; and upon that assumption built all I had to say. The more I thought over my procedure, the more I was charmed with it. Nevertheless, next morning, upon awakening, I had my doubts — I had somehow slept off the fumes of vanity. One of the coolest and wisest hours a man has, is just after he awakes in the morning. My procedure seemed as sagacious as ever — but only in theory. How it would prove in practice — there was the rub. It was truly a beautiful thought to have assumed Bartleby's departure; but, after all, that assumption was simply my own, and none of Bartleby's. The great point was, not whether I had assumed that he would quit me, but whether he would prefer to do so. He was more a man of preferences than assumptions.

After breakfast, I walked down town, arguing the probabilities pro and con. One moment I thought it would prove a miserable failure, and Bartleby would be found all alive at my office as usual; the next moment it seemed certain that I should find his chair empty. And so I kept veering about. At the corner of Broadway and Canal Street, I saw quite an excited group of people standing in earnest conversation.

"I'll take odds he doesn't," said a voice as I passed.

"Doesn't go? — done!" said I, "put up your money."

I was instinctively putting my hand in my pocket to produce my own, when I remembered that this was an election day. The words I had overheard bore no reference to Bartleby, but to the success or non-success of some candidate for the mayoralty. In my intent frame of mind, I had, as it were, imagined that all Broadway shared in my excitement, and were debating the same question with me. I passed on, very thankful that the uproar of the street screened my momentary absent-mindedness.

As I had intended, I was earlier than usual at my office door. I stood listening for a moment. All was still. He must be gone. I tried the knob. The door was locked. Yes, my procedure had worked to a charm; he indeed must be vanished. Yet a certain melancholy mixed with this: I was almost sorry for my brilliant success. I was fumbling under the door mat for the key, which Bartleby was to have left there for me, when accidentally my knee knocked against a panel, producing a summoning sound, and in response a voice came to me from within — "Not yet; I am occupied."

It was Bartleby.

I was thunderstruck. For an instant I stood like the man who, pipe in mouth, was killed one cloudless afternoon long ago in Virginia, by summer lightning; at his own warm open window he was killed, and remained leaning out there upon the dreamy afternoon, till some one touched him, when he fell.

"Not gone!" I murmured at last. But again obeying that wondrous ascendancy which the inscrutable scrivener had over me, and from which ascendancy, for all my chafing, I could not completely escape, I slowly went down stairs and out into the street, and while walking round the block, considered what I should next do in this unheard-of perplexity. Turn the man out by an actual thrusting I could not; to drive him away by calling him hard names would not do; calling in the police was an unpleasant idea; and yet, permit him to enjoy his cadaverous triumph over me — this, too, I could not think of. What was to be done? or, if nothing could be done, was there anything further that I could *assume* in the matter? Yes, as before I had prospectively assumed that Bartleby would depart, so now I might retrospectively assume that departed he was. In the legitimate carrying out of this assumption, I might enter my office in a great hurry, and pretending not to see Bartleby at all, walk straight against him as if he were air. Such a proceeding would in a singular degree have the appearance of a home-thrust. It was hardly possible that Bartleby could withstand such an application of the doctrine of assumption. But upon second thoughts the success of the plan seemed rather dubious. I resolved to argue the matter over with him again.

"Bartleby," said I, entering the office, with a quietly severe expression, "I am seriously displeased. I am pained, Bartleby. I had thought better of you. I had imagined you of such a gentlemanly organization, that in any delicate dilemma a slight hint would suffice — in short, an assumption. But it appears I am deceived. Why," I added, unaffectedly starting, "you have not even touched that money yet," pointing to it, just where I had left it the evening previous.

He answered nothing.

"Will you, or will you not, quit me?" I now demanded in a sudden passion, advancing close to him.

"I would prefer *not* to quit you," he replied, gently emphasizing the *not*.

"What earthly right have you to stay here? Do you pay any rent? Do you pay my taxes? Or is this property yours?"

He answered nothing.

"Are you ready to go on and write now? Are your eyes recovered? Could you copy a small paper for me this morning? or help examine a few lines? or step round to the Post Office? In a word, will you do anything at all, to give a coloring to your refusal to depart the premises?"

He silently retired into his hermitage.

I was now in such a state of nervous resentment that I thought it but prudent to check myself at present from further demonstrations. Bartleby and I were alone. I remembered the tragedy of the unfortunate Adams and the still more unfortunate Colt[6] in the solitary office of the latter; and how poor Colt, being dreadfully incensed by Adams, and imprudently permitting himself to get wildly excited, was at unawares hurried into his fatal act — an act which certainly no man could possibly deplore more than the actor himself. Often it had occurred to me in my ponderings upon the subject that had that altercation taken place in the public street, or at a private residence, it would not have terminated as it did. It was the circumstance of being alone in a solitary office, up stairs, of a building entirely unhallowed by humanizing domestic associations — an uncarpeted office, doubtless, of a dusty, haggard sort of appearance — this it must have been, which greatly helped to enhance the irritable desperation of the hapless Colt.

But when this old Adam of resentment rose in me and tempted me concerning Bartleby, I grappled him and threw him. How? Why, simply by recalling the divine injunction: "A new commandment give I unto you, that ye love one another." Yes, this it was that saved me. Aside from higher considerations, charity often operates as a vastly wise and prudent principle — a great safeguard to its possessor. Men have committed murder for jealousy's sake, and

---

[6] In a sensational case from 1841, John C. Colt (brother of Samuel Colt, inventor of the revolver) murdered a printer named Samuel Adams. Before his hanging, Colt committed suicide in the Tombs. — EDS.

anger's sake, and hatred's sake, and selfishness' sake, and spiritual pride's sake; but no man, that ever I heard of, ever committed a diabolical murder for sweet charity's sake. Mere self-interest, then, if no better motive can be enlisted, should, especially with high-tempered men, prompt all beings to charity and philanthropy. At any rate, upon the occasion in question, I strove to drown my exasperated feelings towards the scrivener by benevolently construing his conduct. Poor fellow, poor fellow! thought I, he don't mean anything; and besides, he has seen hard times, and ought to be indulged.

I endeavored, also, immediately to occupy myself, and at the same time to comfort my despondency. I tried to fancy, that in the course of the morning, at such time as might prove agreeable to him, Bartleby, of his own free accord, would emerge from his hermitage and take up some decided line of march in the direction of the door. But no. Half-past twelve o'clock came; Turkey began to glow in the face, overturn his inkstand, and become generally obstreperous; Nippers abated down into quietude and courtesy; Ginger Nut munched his noon apple; and Bartleby remained standing at his window in one of his profoundest dead-wall reveries. Will it be credited? Ought I to acknowledge it? That afternoon I left the office without saying one further word to him.

Some days now passed, during which, at leisure intervals I looked a little into "Edwards on the Will," and "Priestley on Necessity."[7] Under the circumstances, those books induced a salutary feeling. Gradually I slid into the persuasion that these troubles of mine, touching the scrivener, had been all predestined from eternity, and Bartleby was billeted upon me for some mysterious purpose of an all-wise Providence, which it was not for a mere mortal like me to fathom. Yes, Bartleby, stay there behind your screen, thought I; I shall persecute you no more; you are harmless and noiseless as any of these old chairs; in short, I never feel so private as when I know you are here. At last I see it, I feel it; I penetrate to the predestined purpose of my life. I am content. Others may have loftier parts to enact; but my mission in this world, Bartleby, is to furnish you with office-room for such period as you may see fit to remain.

170 I believe that this wise and blessed frame of mind would have continued with me, had it not been for the unsolicited and uncharitable remarks obtruded upon me by my professional friends who visited the rooms. But thus it often is, that the constant friction of illiberal minds wears out at last the best resolves of the more generous. Though to be sure, when I reflected upon it, it was not strange that people entering my office should be struck by the peculiar aspect of the unaccountable Bartleby, and so be tempted to throw out some sinister observations concerning him. Sometimes an attorney, having business with me, and calling at my office, and finding no one but the scrivener there, would undertake to obtain some sort of precise information from him touching my whereabouts; but without heeding his idle talk, Bartleby would remain standing immovable in the middle of the room. So after contemplating him in that position for a time, the attorney would depart, no wiser than he came.

Also, when a reference was going on, and the room full of lawyers and witnesses, and business driving fast, some deeply-occupied legal gentleman present, seeing Bartleby wholly unemployed, would request him to run round to his (the legal gentleman's) office and fetch some papers for him. Thereupon, Bartleby would tranquilly decline, and yet remain idle as before. Then the lawyer would give a great stare, and turn to me. And what could I say? At last I was made aware that all through the circle of my

[7] Jonathan Edwards, in *Freedom of the Will* (1754), and Joseph Priestley, in *Doctrine of Philosophical Necessity* (1777), argued that human beings lack free will. — EDS.

professional acquaintance, a whisper of wonder was running round, having reference to the strange creature I kept at my office. This worried me very much. And as the idea came upon me of his possibly turning out a long-lived man, and keeping occupying my chambers, and denying my authority; and perplexing my visitors; and scandalizing my professional reputation; and casting a general gloom over the premises; keeping soul and body together to the last upon his savings (for doubtless he spent but half a dime a day), and in the end perhaps outlive me, and claim possession of my office by right of his perpetual occupancy: as all these dark anticipations crowded upon me more and more, and my friends continually intruded their relentless remarks upon the apparition in my room; a great change was wrought in me. I resolved to gather all my faculties together, and forever rid me of this intolerable incubus.

Ere revolving any complicated project, however, adapted to this end, I first simply suggested to Bartleby the propriety of his permanent departure. In a calm and serious tone, I commended the idea to his careful and mature consideration. But, having taken three days to meditate upon it, he apprised me, that his original determination remained the same; in short, that he still preferred to abide with me.

What shall I do? I now said to myself, buttoning up my coat to the last button. What shall I do? what ought I to do? what does conscience say I *should* do with this man, or, rather, ghost. Rid myself of him, I must; go, he shall. But how? You will not thrust him, the poor, pale, passive mortal—you will not thrust such a helpless creature out of your door? you will not dishonor yourself by such cruelty? No, I will not, I cannot do that. Rather would I let him live and die here, and then mason up his remains in the wall. What, then, will you do? For all your coaxing, he will not budge. Bribes he leaves under your own paper-weight on your table; in short, it is quite plain that he prefers to cling to you.

Then something severe, something unusual must be done. What! surely you will not have him collared by a constable, and commit his innocent pallor to the common jail? And upon what ground could you procure such a thing to be done?—a vagrant, is he? What! he a vagrant, a wanderer, who refuses to budge? It is because he will *not* be a vagrant, then, that you seek to count him *as* a vagrant. That is too absurd. No visible means of support: there I have him. Wrong again: for indubitably he *does* support himself, and that is the only unanswerable proof that any man can show of his possessing the means so to do. No more, then. Since he will not quit me, I must quit him. I will change my offices; I will move elsewhere, and give him fair notice, that if I find him on my new premises I will then proceed against him as a common trespasser.

Acting accordingly, next day I thus addressed him: "I find these chambers too far from the City Hall; the air is unwholesome. In a word, I propose to remove my offices next week, and shall no longer require your services. I tell you this now, in order that you may seek another place."

He made no reply, and nothing more was said.

On the appointed day I engaged carts and men, proceeded to my chambers, and having but little furniture, everything was removed in a few hours. Throughout, the scrivener remained standing behind the screen, which I directed to be removed the last thing. It was withdrawn; and, being folded up like a huge folio, left him the motionless occupant of a naked room. I stood in the entry watching him a moment, while something from within me upbraided me.

I re-entered, with my hand in my pocket—and—and my heart in my mouth.

"Good-bye, Bartleby; I am going—good-bye, and God some way bless you; and take that," slipping something in his hand. But it dropped upon the floor, and then—strange to say — I tore myself from him whom I had so longed to be rid of.

Established in my new quarters, for a day or two I kept the door locked, and started at every footfall in the passages. When I returned to my rooms, after any little absence, I would pause at the threshold for an instant, and attentively listen, ere applying my key. But these fears were needless. Bartleby never came nigh me.

I thought all was going well, when a perturbed-looking stranger visited me, inquiring whether I was the person who had recently occupied rooms at No. —— Wall Street.

Full of forebodings, I replied that I was.

"Then, sir," said the stranger, who proved a lawyer, "you are responsible for the man you left there. He refuses to do any copying; he refuses to do anything; he says he prefers not to; and he refuses to quit the premises."

"I am very sorry, sir," said I, with assumed tranquillity, but an inward tremor, "but, really, the man you allude to is nothing to me — he is no relation or apprentice of mine, that you should hold me responsible for him."

"In mercy's name, who is he?"

"I certainly cannot inform you. I know nothing about him. Formerly I employed him as a copyist; but he has done nothing for me now for some time past."

"I shall settle him, then — good morning, sir."

Several days passed, and I heard nothing more; and, though I often felt a charitable prompting to call at the place and see poor Bartleby, yet a certain squeamishness, of I know not what, withheld me.

All is over with him, by this time, thought I, at last, when, through another week, no further intelligence reached me. But, coming to my room the day after, I found several persons waiting at my door in a high state of nervous excitement.

"That's the man — here he comes," cried the foremost one, whom I recognized as the lawyer who had previously called upon me alone.

"You must take him away, sir, at once," cried a portly person among them, advancing upon me, and whom I knew to be the landlord of No. —— Wall Street. "These gentlemen, my tenants, cannot stand it any longer; Mr. B ——," pointing to the lawyer, "has turned him out of his room, and he now persists in haunting the building generally, sitting upon the banisters of the stairs by day, and sleeping in the entry by night. Everybody is concerned; clients are leaving the offices; some fears are entertained of a mob; something you must do, and that without delay."

Aghast at this torrent, I fell back before it, and would fain have locked myself in my new quarters. In vain I persisted that Bartleby was nothing to me — no more than to any one else. In vain — I was the last person known to have anything to do with him, and they held me to the terrible account. Fearful, then, of being exposed in the papers (as one person present obscurely threatened), I considered the matter, and, at length, said, that if the lawyer would give me a confidential interview with the scrivener, in his (the lawyer's) own room, I would, that afternoon, strive my best to rid them of the nuisance they complained of.

Going up stairs to my old haunt, there was Bartleby silently sitting upon the banister at the landing.

"What are you doing here, Bartleby?" said I.

"Sitting upon the banister," he mildly replied.

I motioned him into the lawyer's room, who then left us.

"Bartleby," said I, "are you aware that you are the cause of great tribulation to me, by persisting in occupying the entry after being dismissed from the office?"

No answer.

"Now one of two things must take place. Either you must do something, or something must be done to you. Now what sort of business would you like to engage in? Would you like to re-engage in copying for some one?"

"No; I would prefer not to make any change."

"Would you like a clerkship in a dry-goods store?"

"There is too much confinement about that. No, I would not like a clerkship; but I am not particular."

"Too much confinement," I cried, "why, you keep yourself confined all the time!"

"I would prefer not to take a clerkship," he rejoined, as if to settle that little item at once.

"How would a bar-tender's business suit you? There is no trying of the eye-sight in that."

"I would not like it at all; though, as I said before, I am not particular."

His unwonted wordiness inspirited me. I returned to the charge.

"Well, then, would you like to travel through the country collecting bills for the merchants? That would improve your health."

"No, I would prefer to be doing something else."

"How, then, would going as a companion to Europe, to entertain some young gentleman with your conversation — how would that suit you?"

"Not at all. It does not strike me that there is anything definite about that. I like to be stationary. But I am not particular."

"Stationary you shall be, then," I cried, now losing all patience, and, for the first time in all my exasperating connection with him, fairly flying into a passion. "If you do not go away from these premises before night, I shall feel bound — indeed, I *am* bound — to — to quit the premises myself!" I rather absurdly concluded, knowing not with what possible threat to try to frighten his immobility into compliance. Despairing of all further efforts, I was precipitately leaving him, when a final thought occurred to me — one which had not been wholly unindulged before.

"Bartleby," said I, in the kindest tone I could assume under such exciting circumstances, "will you go home with me now — not to my office, but my dwelling — and remain there till we can conclude upon some convenient arrangement for you at our leisure? Come, let us start now, right away."

"No: at present I would prefer not to make any change at all."

I answered nothing; but, effectually dodging every one by the suddenness and rapidity of my flight, rushed from the building, ran up Wall Street towards Broadway, and, jumping into the first omnibus, was soon removed from pursuit. As soon as tranquillity returned, I distinctly perceived that I had now done all that I possibly could, both in respect to the demands of the landlord and his tenants, and with regard to my own desire and sense of duty, to benefit Bartleby, and shield him from rude persecution. I now strove to be entirely care-free and quiescent; and my conscience justified me in the attempt; though, indeed, it was not so successful as I could have wished. So fearful was I of being again hunted out by the incensed landlord and his exasperated tenants, that, surrendering my business to Nippers, for a few days, I drove about the upper part of the town and through the suburbs, in my rockaway; crossed over to Jersey City and Hoboken, and paid fugitive visits to Manhattanville and Astoria. In fact, I almost lived in my rockaway for the time.

When again I entered my office, lo, a note from the landlord lay upon the desk. I opened it with trembling hands. It informed me that the writer had sent to the police, and had Bartleby removed to the Tombs as a vagrant. Moreover, since I knew more about him than any one else, he wished me to appear at that place, and make a suitable statement of the facts. These tidings had a conflicting effect upon me. At first I was indignant; but, at last, almost approved. The landlord's energetic, summary disposition, had led him to adopt a procedure which I do not think I would have decided upon myself; and yet, as a last resort, under such peculiar circumstances, it seemed the only plan.

As I afterwards learned, the poor scrivener, when told that he must be conducted to the Tombs, offered not the slightest obstacle, but, in his pale, unmoving way, silently acquiesced.

Some of the compassionate and curious bystanders joined the party; and headed by one of the constables arm-in-arm with Bartleby, the silent procession filed its way through all the noise, and heat, and joy of the roaring thoroughfares at noon.

The same day I received the note, I went to the Tombs, or, to speak more properly, the Halls of Justice. Seeking the right officer, I stated the purpose of my call, and was informed that the individual I described was, indeed, within. I then assured the functionary that Bartleby was a perfectly honest man, and greatly to be compassionated, however unaccountably eccentric. I narrated all I knew, and closed by suggesting the idea of letting him remain in as indulgent confinement as possible, till something less harsh might be done — though, indeed, I hardly knew what. At all events, if nothing else could be decided upon, the almshouse must receive him. I then begged to have an interview.

Being under no disgraceful charge, and quite serene and harmless in all his ways, they had permitted him freely to wander about the prison, and, especially, in the inclosed grass-platted yards thereof. And so I found him there, standing all alone in the quietest of the yards, his face towards a high wall, while all around, from the narrow slits of the jail windows, I thought I saw peering out upon him the eyes of murderers and thieves.

"Bartleby!"

"I know you," he said, without looking round — "and I want nothing to say to you."

"It was not I that brought you here, Bartleby," said I, keenly pained at his implied suspicion. "And to you, this should not be so vile a place. Nothing reproachful attaches to you by being here. And see, it is not so sad a place as one might think. Look, there is the sky, and here is the grass."

"I know where I am," he replied, but would say nothing more, and so I left him.

As I entered the corridor again, a broad meat-like man, in an apron, accosted me, and, jerking his thumb over his shoulder, said — "Is that your friend?"

"Yes."

"Does he want to starve? If he does, let him live on the prison fare, that's all."

"Who are you?" asked I, not knowing what to make of such an unofficially speaking person in such a place.

"I am the grub-man. Such gentlemen as have friends here, hire me to provide them with something good to eat."

"Is this so?" said I, turning the turnkey.

He said it was.

"Well, then," said I, slipping some silver into the grub-man's hands (for so they called him), "I want you to give particular attention to my friend there; let him have the best dinner you can get. And you must be as polite to him as possible."

"Introduce me, will you?" said the grub-man, looking at me with an expression which seemed to say he was all impatience for an opportunity to give a specimen of his breeding.

Thinking it would prove of benefit to the scrivener, I acquiesced; and, asking the grub-man his name, went up with him to Bartleby.

"Bartleby, this is a friend; you will find him very useful to you."

"Your servant, sir, your servant," said the grub-man, making a low salutation behind his apron. "Hope you find it pleasant here, sir; nice grounds — cool apartments — hope you'll stay with us some time — try to make it agreeable. What will you have for dinner to-day?"

"I prefer not to dine to-day," said Bartleby, turning away. "It would disagree with me; I am unused to dinners." So saying, he slowly moved to the other side of the inclosure, and took up a position fronting the deadwall.

“How’s this?” said the grub-man, addressing me with a stare of astonishment. “He’s odd, ain’t he?”

“I think he is a little deranged,” said I, sadly.

“Deranged? deranged is it? Well, now, upon my word, I thought that friend of yourn was a gentleman forger; they are always pale and genteel-like, them forgers. I can’t help pity ’em — can’t help it, sir. Did you know Monroe Edwards?” he added, touchingly, and paused. Then, laying his hand piteously on my shoulder, sighed, “he died of consumption at Sing-Sing. So you weren’t acquainted with Monroe?”

“No, I was never socially acquainted with any forgers. But I cannot stop longer. Look to my friend yonder. You will not lose by it. I will see you again.”

Some few days after this, I again obtained admission to the Tombs, and went through the corridors in quest of Bartleby; but without finding him.

“I saw him coming from his cell not long ago,” said a turnkey, “may be he’s gone to loiter in the yards.”

So I went in that direction.

“Are you looking for the silent man?” said another turnkey, passing me. “Yonder he lies — sleeping in the yard there. ’Tis not twenty minutes since I saw him lie down.”

The yard was entirely quiet. It was not accessible to the common prisoners. The surrounding walls, of amazing thickness, kept off all sounds behind them. The Egyptian character of the masonry weighed upon me with its gloom. But a soft imprisoned turf grew under foot. The heart of the eternal pyramids, it seemed, wherein, by some strange magic, through the clefts, grass-seed, dropped by birds, had sprung.

Strangely huddled at the base of the wall, his knees drawn up, and lying on his side, his head touching the cold stones, I saw the wasted Bartleby. But nothing stirred. I paused; then went close up to him; stooped over, and saw that his dim eyes were open; otherwise he seemed profoundly sleeping. Something prompted me to touch him. I felt his hand, when a tingling shiver ran up my arm and down my spine to my feet.

The round face of the grub-man peered upon me now. “His dinner is ready. Won’t he dine to-day, either? Or does he live without dining?”

“Lives without dining,” said I, and closed the eyes.

“Eh! — He’s asleep, ain’t he?”

“With kings and counselors,”[8] murmured I.

There would seem little need for proceeding further in this history. Imagination will readily supply the meagre recital of poor Bartleby’s interment. But, ere parting with the reader, let me say, that if this little narrative has sufficiently interested him, to awaken curiosity as to who Bartleby was, and what manner of life he led prior to the present narrator’s making his acquaintance, I can only reply, that in such curiosity I fully share, but am wholly unable to gratify it. Yet here I hardly know whether I should divulge one little item of rumor, which came to my ear a few months after the scrivener’s decease. Upon what basis it rested, I could never ascertain; and hence, how true it is I cannot now tell. But, inasmuch as this vague report has not been without a certain suggestive interest to me, however sad, it may prove the same with some others; and so I will briefly mention it. The report was this: that Bartleby had been a subordinate clerk in the Dead Letter Office at Washington, from which he had been suddenly removed by a change in the administration. When I think over this rumor, hardly can I express the emotions which seize me. Dead letters! does it not sound like dead men? Conceive a man by nature and misfortune prone to a pallid hopelessness, can any business seem

[8] From Job 3:13–14: “then had I been at rest, / With kings and counselors of the earth, / which built desolate places for themselves.” — EDS.

more fitted to heighten it than that of continually handling these dead letters, and assorting them for the flames? For by the cart-load they are annually burned. Sometimes from out the folded paper the pale clerk takes a ring — the finger it was meant for, perhaps, moulders in the grave; a bank-note sent in swiftest charity — he whom it would relieve, nor eats nor hungers any more; pardon for those who died despairing; hope for those who died unhoping; good tidings for those who died stifled by unrelieved calamities. On errands of life, these letters speed to death.

Ah, Bartleby! Ah, humanity!

[1853]

EXPLORING THE TEXT

1. What effect does the opening paragraph have on you as a reader? What information do you learn? How does this paragraph embody "lawyerly language" — that is, language filled with qualifications and disclaimers?
2. The narrator's description of his three clerks — Turkey, Nippers, and Ginger Nut — might be summarized as a list of assets and liabilities, or credits and debits. What are the pluses and minuses of these characters, as Herman Melville presents them? What comparisons does he draw between and among the three workers? How do they set the stage for the introduction of Bartleby?
3. The narrator introduces Bartleby as "a motionless young man . . . pallidly neat, pitiably respectable, incurably forlorn!" (para. 17). How does he expand this description as the story develops? How does this initial characterization foreshadow Bartleby's end?
4. How and why does Bartleby's "passive resistance" (para. 55) stymie the lawyer-narrator? How do Bartleby's "preferences" make their way into the culture of the narrator's law office?
5. The narrator tells us that Bartleby "was more a man of preferences than assumptions" (para. 149). How does this worldview differ from the legal profession's belief in precedents and assumptions?
6. What significance does the subtitle, "A Story of Wall Street," have? Consider the literal walls in the office and in the Tombs that Melville describes.
7. The narrator characterizes himself as living the philosophy that "the easiest way of life is the best" (para. 2). Chart his changing responses to Bartleby throughout the story. Then consider the ways in which he validates or changes his initial philosophy. Does the narrator grow in self-awareness or deteriorate into self-delusion? How do you interpret his statement, "In vain I persisted that Bartleby was nothing to me — no more than to any one else" (para. 192)?
8. Humor, though often subtle and ironic, runs throughout the story. What examples of humor can you identify, and how do they work as commentary or characterization?
9. At the end of the story, the narrator offers the possibility that Bartleby's rejection of life has been brought on by his working in the Dead Letter Office, a place where mail with inscrutable or partial addresses is ultimately destroyed. Is this a plausible explanation? How does it fit thematically in the story, or case, that Melville has built?
10. How does this "Story of Wall Street" fit with the way we view Wall Street today? How do attitudes toward money and materialism inform this story? Does the characterization of the environment of Wall Street as mechanical and dehumanizing ring true in the twenty-first century?

Spunk

ZORA NEALE HURSTON

Zora Neale Hurston (1891–1960) came to prominence in the 1920s during the Harlem Renaissance. A novelist, folklorist, and anthropologist, she first gained attention with her short stories, including "Sweat" and "Spunk." She is best known for her novel *Their Eyes Were Watching God* (1937), set in Eatonville, Florida, where Hurston grew up; the town was the first incorporated African American community in the United States. She attended Howard University and won a scholarship to Barnard College in New York, living in Harlem throughout the 1920s; in 1936 she received a Guggenheim Fellowship. Her writing is known for its celebration of African American folk culture, as well as its use of authentic vernacular speech. Hurston, who died in poverty, was all but forgotten until Alice Walker took an interest in her. Walker's 1975 essay "Looking for Zora," published in *Ms.* magazine, described her personal journey to find Hurston's unmarked grave. The publication of this essay prompted a resurgence of interest in Hurston, including republication of many of her books. The following short story, Hurston's third, was published in Alain Locke's *The New Negro* (1925) — a collection of essays, poetry, fiction, drama, and visual texts, considered to be the manifesto of the Harlem Renaissance.

I

A giant of a brown-skinned man sauntered up the one street of the village and out into the palmetto thickets with a small pretty woman clinging lovingly to his arm.

"Looka theah, folkses!" cried Elijah Mosley, slapping his leg gleefully. "Theah they go, big as life an' brassy as tacks."

All the loungers in the store tried to walk to the door with an air of nonchalance but with small success.

"Now pee-eople!" Walter Thomas gasped. "Will you look at 'em!"

5 "But that's one thing Ah likes about Spunk Banks — he ain't skeered of nothin' on God's green footstool — *nothin'*! He rides that log down at saw-mill jus' like he struts 'round wid another man's wife — jus' don't give a kitty. When Tes' Miller got cut to giblets on that circle-saw, Spunk steps right up and starts ridin'. The rest of us was skeered to go near it."

A round-shouldered figure in overalls much too large came nervously in the door and the talking ceased. The men looked at each other and winked.

"Gimme some soda-water. Sass'prilla Ah reckon," the newcomer ordered, and stood far down the counter near the open pickled pig-feet tub to drink it.

Elijah nudged Walter and turned with mock gravity to the new-comer.

"Say, Joe, how's everything up yo' way? How's yo' wife?"

10 Joe started and all but dropped the bottle he was holding. He swallowed several times painfully and his lips trembled.

"Aw 'Lige, you oughtn't to do nothin' like that," Walter grumbled. Elijah ignored him.

"She jus' passed heah a few minutes ago goin' thata way," with a wave of his hand in the direction of the woods.

Now Joe knew his wife had passed that way. He knew that the men lounging in the general store had seen her, moreover, he knew that the men knew *he* knew. He stood there silent for a long moment staring blankly, with his Adam's apple twitching nervously up and down his throat. One could actually *see* the pain he was suffering, his eyes, his face, his hands, and even the dejected slump of his shoulders. He set the bottle down upon the counter. He didn't bang it, just eased it out of his hand silently and fiddled with his suspender buckle.

"Well, Ah'm goin' after her to-day. Ah'm goin' an' fetch her back. Spunk's done gone too fur."

15 He reached deep down into his trouser pocket and drew out a hollow ground razor, large and shiny, and passed his moistened thumb back and forth over the edge.

"Talkin' like a man, Joe. 'Course that's *yo'* fambly affairs, but Ah like to see grit in anybody."

Joe Kanty laid down a nickel and stumbled out into the street.

Dusk crept in from the woods. Ike Clarke lit the swinging oil lamp that was almost immediately surrounded by candle-flies. The men laughed boisterously behind Joe's back as they watched him shamble woodward.

"You oughtn't to said whut you said to him, 'Lige—look how it worked him up," Walter chided.

20 "And Ah hope it did work him up. Tain't even decent for a man to take and take like he do."

"Spunk will sho' kill him."

"Aw, Ah doan know. You never kin tell. He might turn him up an' spank him fur gettin' in the way, but Spunk wouldn't shoot no unarmed man. Dat razor he carried outa heah ain't gonna run Spunk down an' cut him, an' Joe ain't got the nerve to go to Spunk with it knowing he totes that Army .45. He makes that break outa heah to bluff us. He's gonna hide that razor behind the first palmetto root an' sneak back home to bed. Don't tell me nothin' 'bout that rabbit-foot colored man. Didn't he meet Spunk an' Lena face to face one day las week an' mumble sumthin' to Spunk 'bout lettin' his wife alone?"

"What did Spunk say?" Walter broke in. "Ah like him fine but tain't right the way he carries on wid Lena Kanty, jus' 'cause Joe's timid 'bout fightin'."

"You wrong theah, Walter. Tain't 'cause Joe's timid at all, it's 'cause Spunk wants Lena. If Joe was a passle of wile cats Spunk would tackle the job just the same. He'd go after *anything* he wanted the same way. As Ah wuz sayin' a minute ago, he tole Joe right to his face that Lena was his. 'Call her and see if she'll come. A woman knows her boss an' she answers when he calls.' 'Lena, ain't I yo' husband?' Joe sorter whines out. Lena looked at him real disgusted but she don't answer and she don't move outa her tracks. Then Spunk reaches out an' takes hold of her arm an' says: 'Lena, youse mine. From now on Ah works for you an' fights for you an' Ah never wants you to look to nobody for a crumb of bread, a stitch of close or a shingle to go over yo' head, but *me* long as Ah live. Ah'll git the lumber foh owah house to-morrow. Go home an git yo' things together!"

25 " 'Thass mah house,' Lena speaks up. 'Papa gimme that.'

" 'Well,' says Spunk, 'doan give up whut's yours, but when youse inside doan forgit youse mine, an' let no other man git outa his place wid you!'

"Lena looked up at him with her eyes so full of love that they wuz runnin' over, an' Spunk seen it an' Joe seen it too, and his lip started to tremblin' and his Adam's apple was galloping up and down his neck like a race horse. Ah bet he's wore out half a dozen Adam's apples since Spunk's been on the job with Lena. That's all he'll do. He'll be back heah after while swallowin' an' workin' his lips like he wants to say somethin' an' can't."

"But didn't he do *nothin'* to stop 'em?"

"Nope, not a frazzlin' thing—jus' stood there. Spunk took Lena's arm and walked off jus' like nothin' ain't happened and he stood there gazin' after them till they was outa sight. Now you know a woman don't want no man like that. I'm jus' waitin' to see whut he's goin' to say when he gits back."

II

But Joe Kanty never came back, never. The men in the store heard the sharp report of a pistol somewhere distant in the palmetto thicket and soon Spunk came walking leisurely, with his big black Stetson set at the same rakish angle and Lena clinging to his arm, came walking right into the general store. Lena wept in a frightened manner.

"Well," Spunk announced calmly, "Joe came out there wid a meat axe an' made me kill him."

He sent Lena home and led the men back to Joe — crumpled and limp with his right hand still clutching his razor.

"See mah back? Mah close cut clear through. He sneaked up an' tried to kill me from the back, but Ah got him, an' got him good, first shot," Spunk said.

The men glared at Elijah, accusingly.

"Take him up an' plant him in Stony Lonesome," Spunk said in a careless voice. "Ah didn't wanna shoot him but he made me do it. He's a dirty coward, jumpin' on a man from behind."

Spunk turned on his heel and sauntered away to where he knew his love wept in fear for him and no man stopped him. At the general store later on, they all talked of locking him up until the sheriff should come from Orlando, but no one did anything but talk.

A clear case of self-defense, the trial was a short one, and Spunk walked out of the court house to freedom again. He could work again, ride the dangerous log-carriage that fed the singing, snarling, biting circle-saw; he could stroll the soft dark lanes with his guitar. He was free to roam the woods again; he was free to return to Lena. He did all of these things.

III

"Whut you reckon, Walt?" Elijah asked one night later. "Spunk's gittin' ready to marry Lena!"

"Naw! Why, Joe ain't had time to git cold yit. Nohow Ah didn't figger Spunk was the marryin' kind."

"Well, he is," rejoined Elijah. "He done moved most of Lena's things — and her along wid 'em — over to the Bradley house. He's buying it. Jus' like Ah told yo' all right in heah the night Joe was kilt. Spunk's crazy 'bout Lena. He don't want folks to keep on talkin' 'bout her — thass reason he's rushin' so. Funny thing 'bout that bob-cat, wan't it?"

"What bob-cat, 'Lige? Ah ain't heered 'bout none."

"Ain't cher? Well, night befo' las' as they was goin' to bed, a big black bob-cat, black all over, you hear me, *black*, walked round and round that house and howled like forty, an' when Spunk got his gun an' went to the winder to shoot it, he says it stood right still an' looked him in the eye, an' howled right at him. The thing got Spunk so nervoused up he couldn't shoot. But Spunk says twan't no bob-cat nohow. He says it was Joe done sneaked back from Hell!"

"Humph!" sniffed Walter, "he oughter be nervous after what he done. Ah reckon Joe come back to dare him to marry Lena, or to come out an' fight. Ah bet he'll be back time and again, too. Know what Ah think? Joe wuz a braver man than Spunk."

There was a general shout of derision from the group.

"Thass a fact," went on Walter. "Lookit whut he done; took a razor an' went out to fight a man he knowed toted a gun an' wuz a crack shot, too; 'nother thing Joe wuz skeered of Spunk, skeered plumb stiff! But he went jes' the same. It took him a long time to get his nerve up. Tain't nothin' for Spunk to fight when he ain't skeered of nothin'. Now, Joe's done come back to have it out wid the man that's got all he ever had. Y'all know Joe ain't never had nothin' nor wanted nothin' besides Lena. It musta been a h'ant cause ain't nobody never seen no black bob-cat."

“ ’Nother thing,” cut in one of the men, “Spunk was cussin’ a blue streak to-day ’cause he ’lowed dat saw wuz wobblin’ — almos’ got ’im once. The machinist come, looked it over an said it wuz alright. Spunk musta been leanin t’wards it some. Den he claimed somebody pushed ’im but twan’t nobody close to ’im. Ah wuz glad when knockin’ off time came. I’m skeered of dat man when he gits hot. He’d beat you full of button holes as quick as he’s look atcher.”

IV

The men gathered the next evening in a different mood, no laughter. No badinage this time.

“Look, ’Lige, you goin’ to set up wid Spunk?”

“Naw, Ah reckon not, Walter. Tell yuh the truth, Ah’m a li’l bit skittish. Spunk died too wicket — died cussin’ he did. You know he thought he was done outa life.”

“Good Lawd, who’d he think done it?”

“Joe.”

“Joe Kanty? How come?”

“Walter, Ah b’leeve Ah will walk up thata way an’ set. Lena would like it Ah reckon.”

“But whut did he say, ’Lige?”

Elijah did not answer until they had left the lighted store and were strolling down the dark street.

“Ah wuz loadin’ a wagon wid scantlin’ right near the saw when Spunk fell on the carriage but ’fore Ah could git to him the saw got him in the body — awful sight. Me an’ Skint Miller got him off but it was too late. Anybody could see that. The fust thing he said wuz: ‘He pushed me, ’Lige — the dirty hound pushed me in the back!’ — he was spittin’ blood at ev’ry breath. We laid him on the sawdust pile with his face to the East so’s he could die easy. He helt mah han’ till the last, Walter, and said: ‘It was Joe, ’Lige . . . the dirty sneak shoved me . . . he didn’t dare come to mah face . . . but Ah’ll git the son-of-a-wood louse soon’s Ah get there an’ make hell too hot for him . . . Ah felt him shove me . . . !’ Thass how he died.”

“If spirits kin fight, there’s a powerful tussle goin’ on somewhere ovah Jordan ’cause Ah b’leeve Joe’s ready for Spunk an’ ain’t skeered any more — yas, Ah b’leeve Joe pushed ’im mahself.”

They had arrived at the house. Lena’s lamentations were deep and loud. She had filled the room with magnolia blossoms that gave off a heavy sweet odor. The keepers of the wake tipped about whispering in frightened tones. Everyone in the village was there, even old Jeff Kanty, Joe’s father, who a few hours before would have been afraid to come within ten feet of him, stood leering triumphantly down upon the fallen giant as if his fingers had been the teeth of steel that laid him low.

The cooling board consisted of three sixteen-inch boards on saw horses, a dingy sheet was his shroud.

The women ate heartily of the funeral baked meats and wondered who would be Lena’s next. The men whispered coarse conjectures between guzzles of whiskey.

[1925]

QUESTIONS

1. The story takes its title from the character Spunk Banks, but *spunk* also means gumption, or courage. Is this an appropriate title? Explain.
2. How does the dialect affect your reading and understanding of the story? Would Zora Neale Hurston have made her characters more credible — in 1925 — and broadened her audience if she had had them speak in so-called Standard English?
3. This intricate story is actually a series of stories or narrations. Identify the individual story lines, and explain how they are interrelated.

4. Examine the way Hurston allows the story to unfold through the conversations among the secondary characters. What information do they provide? What do they withhold?
5. Is there a character in the story that you consider fully formed, or round? What function do the flat or stereotyped characters play?
6. How does the story manifest Hurston's long-standing interest in folklore?
7. How is the African American community characterized in the story? Is Hurston celebrating and praising or criticizing and mocking the men and women she depicts?

The Prospectors

KAREN RUSSELL

Karen Russell (b. 1981) is a MacArthur Fellowship-winning American novelist and short story writer from Miami, Florida. She earned a BA in Spanish from Northwestern University in 2003 and an MFA from Columbia University in 2006. She is the author of two collections of short stories: *St. Lucy's Home for Girls Raised by Wolves* (2006) and *Vampires in the Lemon Grove* (2013). Her first novel, *Swamplandia!* (2011), was a finalist for the 2012 Pulitzer Prize, and she has also written a novella, *Sleep Donation* (2014). She has taught writing and literature at Columbia University, Williams College, Bard College, Bryn Mawr College, and Rutgers University-Camden. Russell's work is known for its surrealism and unconventional takes on common tropes found in ghost stories, fables, and fairy tales — evident in "The Prospectors," a short story that vividly evokes the intense bond of friendship between two young women.

The entire ride would take eleven minutes. That was what the boy had promised us, the boy who never showed.

To be honest, I hadn't expected to find the chairlift. Not through the maze of old-growth firs and not in the dwindling light. Not without our escort. A minute earlier, I'd been on the brink of suggesting that we give up and hike back to the logging road. But at the peak of our despondency we saw it: the lift, rising like a mirage out of the timber woods, its four dark cables striping the red sunset. Chairs were floating up the mountainside, forty feet above our heads. Empty chairs, upholstered in ice, swaying lightly in the wind. Sailing beside them, just as swiftly and serenely, a hundred chairs came down the mountain. As if a mirror were malfunctioning, each chair separating from a buckle-bright double. Nobody was manning the loading station; if we wanted to take the lift we'd have to do it alone. I squeezed Clara's hand.

A party awaited us at the peak. Or so we'd been told by Mr. No-Show, Mr. Nowhere, a French boy named Eugene de La Rochefoucauld.

"I bet his real name is Burt," Clara said angrily. We had never been stood up before. "I bet he's actually from Tennessee."

5 Well, he had certainly seemed European, when we met him coming down the mountain road on horseback, one week ago this night. He'd had that hat! Such a convincingly stupid goatee! He'd pronounced his name as if he were coughing up a jewel. Eugene de La

Rochefoucauld had proffered a nasally invitation: would we be his guests next Saturday night, at the gala opening of the Evergreen Lodge? We'd ride the new chairlift with him to the top of the mountain, and be among the first visitors to the marvellous new ski resort. The President himself might be in attendance.

Clara, unintimidated, had flirted back. "Two dates — is that not being a little greedy, Eugene?"

"No less would be acceptable," he'd said, smiling, "for a man of my stature." (Eugene was five feet four; we'd assumed he meant education, wealth.) The party was to be held seven thousand feet above Lucerne, Oregon, the mountain town where we had marooned ourselves, at nineteen and twenty-two; still pretty (Clara was beautiful), still young enough to attract notice, but penniless, living week to week in a "historic" boarding house. "Historic" had turned out to be the landlady's synonym for "haunted." "Turn-of-the-century sash windows," we'd discovered, meant "pneumonia holes."

We'd waited for Eugene for close to an hour, while Time went slinking around the forest, slyly rearranging its shadows; now a red glow clung to the huge branches of the Douglas firs. When I finally spoke, the bony snap in my voice startled us both.

"We don't need him, Clara."

"We don't?"

"No. We can get there on our own."

Clara turned to me with blue lips and flakes daggering her lashes. I felt a pang: I could see both that she was afraid of my proposal and that she could be persuaded. This is a terrible knowledge to possess about a friend. Nervously, I counted my silver and gold bracelets, meting out reasons for making the journey. If we did not make the trip, I would have to pawn them. I argued that it was riskier *not* to take this risk. (For me, at least; Clara had her wealthy parents waiting back in Florida. As much as we dared together, we never risked our friendship by bringing up that gulf.) I touched the fake red flower pinned to my black bun. What had we gone to all this effort for? We owed our landlady twelve dollars for January's rent. Did Clara prefer to wait in the drifts for our prince, that fake frog, Eugene, to arrive?

For months, all anybody in Lucerne had been able to talk about was this lodge, the centerpiece of a new ski resort on Mt. Joy. Another New Deal miracle. In his Fireside Chats, Roosevelt had promised us that these construction projects would lift us out of the Depression. Sometimes I caught myself squinting hungrily at the peak, as if the government money might be visible, falling from the actual clouds. Out-of-work artisans had flocked to northern Oregon: carpenters, masons, weavers, engineers. The Evergreen Lodge, we'd heard, had original stonework, carved from five thousand pounds of native granite. Its doors were cathedral huge, made of hand-cut ponderosa pine. Murals had been commissioned from local artists: scenes of mountain wildflowers, rearing bears. Quilts covered the beds, hand-crocheted by the New Deal men. I loved to picture their callused black thumbs on the bridally white muslin. Architecturally, what was said to stun every visitor was the main hall: a huge hexagonal chamber, with a band platform and "acres for dancing, at the top of the world!"

W.P.A.[1] workers cut trails into the side of Mt. Joy, assisted by the Civilian Conservation Corps boys from Camp Thistle and Camp Bountiful. I'd seen these young men around town, on leave from the woods, in their mud-caked boots and khaki shirts with the government logo. Their greasy faces clumped together like olives in a jar. They were the young mechanics who had wrenched the lift out of a snowy void and into skeletal, functioning existence. To raise bodies from the base of the mountain to the summit in

[1] The Works Progress Administration, formed in 1935 in order to help those financially affected by the Great Depression. — EDS.

eleven minutes! It sounded like one of Jules Verne's[2] visions.

"See that platform?" I said to Clara. "Stand there, and fall back into the next chair. I'll be right behind you."

At first, the climb was beautiful. An evergreen army held its position in the whipping winds. Soon, the woods were replaced by fields of white. Icy outcroppings rose like fangs out of a pink-rimmed sky. We rose, too, our voices swallowed by the cables' groaning. Clara was singing something that I strained to hear, and failed to comprehend.

Clara and I called ourselves the Prospectors. Our fathers, two very different kinds of gambler, had been obsessed with the Gold Rush, and we grew up hearing stories about Yukon fever and the Klondike stampeders. We knew the legend of the farmer who had panned out a hundred and thirty thousand dollars, the clerk who dug up eighty-five thousand, the blacksmith who discovered a haul of the magic metal on Rabbit Creek and made himself a hundred grand richer in a single hour. This period of American history held a special appeal for Clara's father, Mr. Finisterre, a bony-faced Portuguese immigrant to southwestern Florida who had wrung his modest fortune out of the sea-damp wallets of tourists. My own father had killed himself outside the dog track in the spring of 1931, and I'd been fortunate to find a job as a maid at the Hotel Finisterre.

Clara Finisterre was the only other maid on staff — a summer job. Her parents were strict and oblivious people. Their thousand rules went unenforced. They were very busy with their guests. A sea serpent, it was rumored, haunted the coastline beside the hotel, and ninety per cent of our tourism was serpent-driven. Amateur teratologists in Panama hats read the newspaper on the veranda, drinking orange juice and idly scanning the horizon for fins.

"Thank you," Mr. Finisterre whispered to me once, too sozzled to remember my name, "for keeping the secret that there is no secret." The black Atlantic rippled emptily in his eyeglasses.

Every night, Mrs. Finisterre hosted a cocktail hour: cubing green and orange melon, cranking songs out of the ivory gramophone, pouring bright malice into the fruit punch in the form of a mentally deranging Portuguese rum. She'd apprenticed her three beautiful daughters in the Light Arts, the Party Arts. Clara was her eldest. Together, the Finisterre women smoothed arguments and linens. They concocted banter, gab, palaver, patter — every sugary variety of small talk that dissolves into the night. I hated the cocktail hour, and, whenever I could, I escaped to beat rugs and sweep leaves on the hotel roof. One Monday, however, I heard footsteps ringing on the ladder. It was Clara. She saw me and froze.

Bruises were thickening all over her arms. They were that brilliant pansy-blue, the beautiful color that belies its origins. Automatically, I crossed the roof to her. We clacked skeletons; to call it an "embrace" would misrepresent the violence of our first collision. To soothe her, I heard myself making stupid jokes, babbling inanities about the weather, asking in my vague and meandering way what could be done to help her; I could not bring myself to say, plainly, *Who did this to you*? Choking on my only real question, I offered her my cardigan — the way you'd hand a sick person a tissue. She put it on. She buttoned all the buttons. You couldn't tell that anything was wrong now. This amazed me, that a covering so thin could erase her bruises. I'd half-expected them to bore holes through the wool.

"Don't worry, O.K.?" she said. "I promise, it's nothing."

"I won't tell," I blurted out — although of course I had nothing to tell beyond what I'd glimpsed. Night fell, and I was shivering now, so Clara held me. Something subtle and real shifted

---

[2] Jules Verne (1828–1905) was a French writer who greatly influenced the science fiction genre. — EDS.

inside our embrace — nothing detectable to an observer, but a change I registered in my bones. For the duration of our friendship, we'd trade off roles like this: anchor and boat, beholder and beheld. We must have looked like some Janus-faced statue, our chins pointing east and west. An unembarrassed silence seemed to be on loan to us from the distant future, where we were already friends. Then I heard her say, staring over my shoulder at the darkening sea: "What would you be, Aubby, if you lived somewhere else?"

"I'd be a prospector," I told her, without batting an eye. "I'd be a prospector of the prospectors. I'd wait for luck to strike them, and then I'd take their gold."

Clara laughed and I joined in, amazed — until this moment, I hadn't considered that my days at the hotel might be eclipsing other sorts of lives. Clara Finisterre was someone whom I thought of as having a fate to escape, but I wouldn't have dignified my own prospects that way, by calling them "a fate."

A week later, Clara took me to a débutante ball at a tacky mansion that looked rabid to me, frothy with white marble balconies. She introduced me as "my best friend, Aubergine." Thus began our secret life. We sifted through the closets and the jewelry boxes of our hosts. Clara tutored me in the social graces, and I taught Clara what to take, and how to get away with it.

One night, Clara came to find me on the roof. She was blinking muddily out of two black eyes. Who was doing this — Mr. Finisterre? Someone from the hotel? She refused to say. I made a deal with Clara: she never had to tell me who, but we had to leave Florida.

The next day, we found ourselves at the train station, with all our clothes and savings.

Those first weeks alone were an education. The West was very poor at that moment, owing to the Depression. But it was still home to many aspiring and expiring millionaires, and we made it our job to make their acquaintance. One aging oil speculator paid for our meals and our transit and required only that we absorb his memories; Clara nicknamed him the "allegedly legendary wit." He had three genres of tale: business victories; sporting adventures that ended in the death of mammals; and eulogies for his former virility.

We met mining captains and fishing captains, whose whiskers quivered like those of orphaned seals. The freckled heirs to timber fortunes. Glazy baronial types, with portentous and misguided names: Romulus and Creon, who were pleased to invite us to gala dinners, and to use us as their gloating mirrors. In exchange for this service, Clara and I helped ourselves to many fine items from their houses. Clara had a magic satchel that seemed to expand with our greed, and we stole everything it could swallow. Dessert spoons, candlesticks, a poodle's jewelled collar. We strode out of parties wearing our hostess's two-toned heels, woozy with adrenaline. Crutched along by Clara's sturdy charm, I was swung through doors that led to marmoreal courtyards and curtained salons and, in many cases, master bedrooms, where my skin glowed under the warm reefs of artificial lighting.

But winter hit, and our mining prospects dimmed considerably. The Oregon coastline was laced with ghost towns; two paper mills had closed, and whole counties had gone bankrupt. Men were flocking inland to the mountains, where the rumor was that the W.P.A. had work for construction teams. I told Clara that we needed to follow them. So we thumbed a ride with a group of work-starved Astoria teen-agers who had heard about the Evergreen Lodge. Gold dust had drawn the first prospectors to these mountains; those boys were after the weekly three-dollar salary. But if government money was snowing onto Mt. Joy, it had yet to reach the town below. I'd made a bad miscalculation, suggesting Lucerne. Our first night in town, Clara and I stared at our faces superimposed over the dark storefront windows. In the boarding house, we lay awake in the dark, pretending to believe in each other's theatrical sleep; only our bellies were honest, growling at each other. *Why did you bring us here*? Clara never dreamed of asking me. With her generous amnesia, she seemed already to have forgotten that leaving home had been my idea.

Day after day, I told Clara not to worry: "We just need one good night." We kept lying to each other, pretending that our hunger was part of the game. Social graces get you meagre results in a shuttered town. We started haunting the bars around the C.C.C.[3] camps. The gaunt men there had next to nothing, and I felt a pang lifting anything from them. Back in the boarding house, our fingers spidering through wallets, we barely spoke to each other. Clara and I began to disappear into adjacent rooms with strangers. *She was better off before*, my mind whispered. For the first time since we'd left Florida, it occurred to me that our expedition might fail.

The chairlift ascended seven thousand two hundred and fifty feet — I remembered this figure from the newspapers. It had meant very little to me in the abstract. But now I felt our height in the soles of my feet. For whole minutes, we lost sight of the mountain in an onrush of mist. Finally, hands were waiting to catch us. They shot out of the darkness, gripping me under the arms, swinging me free of the lift. Our empty chairs were whipped around by the huge bull wheel before starting the long flight downhill. Hands, wonderfully warm hands, were supporting my back.

"Eugene?" I called, my lips numb.

"Who's *You-Jean*?" a strange voice chuckled.

The man who was not Eugene turned out to be an ursine mountaineer. With his lantern held high, he peered into our faces. I recognized the drab green C.C.C. uniform. He looked about our age to me, although his face kept blurring in the snow. The lantern, battery powered, turned us all jaundiced shades of gold. He had no clue, he said, about any *Eugene*. But he'd been stationed here to escort guests to the lodge.

Out of the corner of my eye, I saw tears freezing onto Clara's cheeks. Already she was fluffing her hair, asking this government employee how he'd gotten the enviable job of escorting beautiful women across the snows. How quickly she was able to snap back into character! I could barely move my frozen tongue, and I trudged along behind them.

"How old are you girls?" the C.C.C. man asked, and "Where are you from?," and every lie that we told him made me feel safer in his company.

The lodge was a true palace. Its shadow alone seemed to cover fifty acres of snow. Electricity raised a yellowish aura around it, so that the resort loomed like a bubble pitched against the mountain sky. Its A-frame reared out of the woods with the insensate authority of any redwood tree. Lights blazed in every window. As we drew closer, we saw faces peering down at us from several of these.

The terror was still with us. The speed of the ascent. My blood felt carbonated. Six feet ahead of us, Not-Eugene, whose name we'd failed to catch, swung the battery-powered lamp above his head and guided us through a whale-gray tunnel made of ice. "Quite the runway to a party, eh?"

Two enormous polished doors blew inward, and we found ourselves in a rustic ballroom, with fireplaces in each corner shooting heat at us. Amethyst chandeliers sent lakes of light rippling across the dance floor; the stone chimneys looked like indoor caves. Over the bar, a mounted boar grinned tuskily down at us. Men mobbed us, handing us fizzing drinks, taking our coats. Deluged by introductions, we started giggling, handing our hands around: "Nilson, Pauley, Villanueva, Obadiah, Acker . . ." Proudly, each identified himself to us as one of the C.C.C.

[3] The Civilian Conservation Corps, formed in 1933 as a New Deal program that promoted environmental conservation. — EDS.

"tree soldiers" who had built this fantasy resort: masons and blacksmiths and painters and foresters. They were boys, I couldn't help but think, boys our age. More faces rose out of the shadows, beaming hard. I guessed that, like us, they'd been waiting for this night to come for some time. Someone lit two cigarettes, passed them our way.

I shivered now with expectation. Clara threaded her hand through mine and squeezed down hard — time to dive into the sea. We'd plunged into stranger waters, socially. How many nights had we spent together, listening to tourists speak in tongues, relieved of their senses by Mrs. Finisterre's rum punch? Most of the boys were already drunk — I could smell that. Some rocked on their heels, desperate to start dancing.

They led us toward the bar. Feeling came flooding back into my skin, and I kept laughing at everything these young men were saying, elated to be indoors with them. Clara had to pinch me through the puffed sleeve of my dress:

"Aubby? Are we the only girls here?"

Clara was right: where were the socialites we'd expected to see? The Oregon state forester, with his sullen red-lipped wife? The governor, the bank presidents? The ski experts from the Swiss Alps? Fifty-two paying guests, selected by lottery, had rooms waiting for them — we'd seen the list of names in Sunday's Oregon *Gazette*.

I turned to a man with wise amber eyes. He had unlined skin and a wispy blond mustache, but he smiled at us with the mellow despair of an old goat.

"Excuse me, sir. When does the celebration start?"

Clara flanked him on the left, smiling just as politely.

"Are we the first guests to arrive?"

But now the goat's eyes flamed: "Whadda you talkin' about? This party is *under way*, lady. You got twenty-six dancing partners to choose from out there — that ain't enough?"

The strength of his fury surprised us; backing up, I bumped my hip against a bannister. My hand closed on what turned out to be a tiny beaver, a carved ornament. Each cedar newel post had one.

"The woodwork is beautiful."

He grinned, soothed by the compliment.

"My supervisor is none other than O. B. Dawson."

"And your name?"

The thought appeared unbidden: *Later, you'll want to know what to scream.*

"Mickey Loatch. Got a wife, girls, I'm chagrined to say. Got three kids already, back in Osprey. I'm here so they can eat." Casually, he explained to us the intensity of his loneliness, the loneliness of the entire corps. They'd been driven by truck, eight miles each day, from Camp Thistle to the deep woods. For months at a time, they lived away from their families. Drinking water came from Lister bags; the latrines were saddle trenches. Everyone was glad, glad, glad, he said, to have the work. "There wasn't anything for us, until the Emerald Lodge project came along."

Mr. Loatch, I'd been noticing, had the strangest eyes I'd ever seen. They were a brilliant dark yellow, the color of that magic metal, gold.

Swallowing, I asked the man, "Excuse me, but I'm a bit confused. Isn't this the *Evergreen* Lodge?"

"The Evergreen Lodge?" the man said, exposing a mouthful of chewed pink sausage. "Where's dat, gurrls?" He laughed at his own cartoony voice.

A suspicion was coming into focus, a dreadful theory; I tried to talk it away, but the harder I looked, the keener it became. A quick scan of the room confirmed what I must have registered and ignored when I first walked through those doors. Were all of the boys' eyes this same hue? Trying to stay calm, I gripped Clara's hand and spun her around like a weathervane: gold, gold, gold, gold.

"Oh my God, Clara."

"Aubby? What's wrong with you?"

"Clara," I murmured, "I think we may have taken the wrong lift."

Two lodges existed on Mt. Joy. There was the Evergreen Lodge, which would be unveiled tonight, in a ceremony of extraordinary opulence, attended by the state forester and the President. Where Eugene was likely standing, on the balcony level, raising a flute for the champagne toast. There had once been, however, on the southeastern side of this same mountain, a second structure. This place lived on in local memory as demolished hope, as unconsummated blueprint. It was the failed original, crushed by an avalanche two years earlier, the graveyard of twenty-six workers from Company 609 of the Oregon Civilian Conservation Corps.

"Unwittingly," our landlady, who loved a bloody and unjust story, had told us over a pancake breakfast, "those workers were building their own casket." With tobogganing runs and a movie theatre, and more windows than Versailles, it was to have been even more impressive than the Evergreen Lodge. But the unfinished lodge had been completely covered in the collapse.

Mickey Loatch was still steering us around, showing off the stonework.

"Have you gals been to the Cloud Cap Inn? That's hitched to the mountain with wire cables. See, what we done is — "

"Mr. Loatch?" Swilling a drink, I steadied my voice. "How late does the chairlift run?"

"Oh dear." He pursed his lips. "You girls gotta be somewhere? I'm afraid you're stuck with us, at least until morning. You're the last we let up. They shut that lift down until dawn."

Next to me, I heard Clara in my ear: "Are you crazy? We just got here, and you're talking about leaving? Do you know how rude you sound?"

"They're dead."

"What are you talking about? Who's dead?"

"Everyone. Everyone but us."

Clara turned from me, her jaw tensing. At a nearby table, five green-clad boys were watching our conversation play out with detached interest, as if it were a sport they rarely followed. Clara wet her lips and smiled down at them, drumming her red nails on their table's glossy surface.

"This is so beautiful!" she cooed.

All five of the dead boys blushed.

"Excuse us," she fluttered. "Is there a powder room? My friend here is just a mess!"

"The Ladies Room" read a bronzed sign posted on an otherwise undistinguished door. At other parties, this room had always been our sanctuary. Once the door was shut, we stared at each other in the mirror, transferring knowledge across the glass. Her eyes were still brown, I noted with relief, and mine were blue. I worried that I might start screaming, but I bit back my panic, and I watched Clara do the same for me. "Your nose," I finally murmured. Blood poured in bright bars down her upper lip.

"I guess we must be really high up," she said, and started to cry.

"Shh, shh, shh . . ."

I wiped at the blood with a tissue.

"See?" I showed it to her. "At least we *are*, ah, at least we can still . . ."

Clara sneezed violently, and we stared at the reddish globules on the glass, which stood out with terrifying lucidity against the flat, unreal world of the mirror.

"What are we going to do, Aubby?"

I shook my head; a horror flooded through me until I could barely breathe.

Ordinarily, I would have handled the logistics of our escape — picked locks, counterfeited tickets. Clara would have corrected my lipstick and my posture, encouraging me to look more like a willowy seductress and less like a baseball umpire. But tonight it was Clara who formulated the plan. We had to tiptoe around the Emerald Lodge. We had to dim our own lights. And, most critical to our survival here, according to Clara: We had to persuade our dead hosts that we believed they were alive.

At first, I objected; I thought these workers deserved to know the truth about themselves.

"Oh?" Clara said. "How principled of you."

And what did I think was going to happen, she asked, if we told the men what we knew?

"I don't know. They'll let us go?"

Clara shook her head.

"Think about it, Aubby — what's keeping this place together?"

We had to be very cautious, very *amenable,* she argued. We couldn't challenge our hosts on any of their convictions. The Emerald Lodge was a real place, and they were breathing safely inside it. We had to admire their handiwork, she said. Continue to exclaim over the lintel arches and the wrought-iron grates, the beams and posts. As if they were real, as if they were solid. Clara begged me to do this. Who knew what might happen if we roused them from their dreaming? The C.C.C. workers' ghosts had built this place, Clara said; we were at their mercy. If the men discovered they were dead, we'd die with them. We needed to believe in their rooms until dawn — just long enough to escape them.

"Same plan as ever," Clara said. "How many hundreds of nights have we staked a claim at a party like this?"

Zero, I told her. On no occasion had we been the only living people.

"We'll charm them. We'll drink a little, dance a little. And then, come dawn, we'll escape down the mountain."

Somebody started pounding on the door: "Hey! What's the holdup, huh? Somebody fall in? You girls wanna dance or what?"

"Almost ready!" Clara shouted brightly.

On the dance floor, the amber-eyed ghosts were as awkward and as touching, as unconvincingly brash as any boys in history on the threshold of a party. Innocent hopefuls with their hats pressed to their chests.

"I feel sorry for them, Clara! They have no idea."

"Yes. It's terribly sad."

Her face hardened into a stony expression I'd seen on her only a handful of times in our career as prospectors.

"When we get back down the mountain, we can feel sad," she said. "Right now, we are going to laugh at all their jokes. We are going to celebrate this stupendous American landmark, the Emerald Lodge."

Clara's mother owned an etiquette book for women, the first chapter of which advises, *Make Your Date Feel Like He Is the Life of the Party!* People often mistake laughing girls for foolish creatures. They mistake our merriment for nerves or weakness, or the hysterical looning of desire. Sometimes, it is that. But not tonight. We could hold our wardens hostage, too, in this careful way. Everybody needs an audience.

At other parties, our hosts had always been very willing to believe us when we feigned interest in their endless rehearsals of the past. They used our black pupils to polish up their antique triumphs. Even an ogreish salmon-boat captain, a bachelor again at eighty-seven, was convinced that we were both in love with him. Nobody ever invited Clara and me to a gala to hear our honest opinions.

At the bar, a calliope of tiny glasses was waiting for me: honey and cherry and lemon. Flavored liquors, imported from Italy, the bartender smiled shyly. "Delicious!" I exclaimed, touching each to my lips. Clara, meanwhile, had been swept onto the dance floor. With her mauve lipstick in place and her glossy hair smoothed, she was shooting colors all around the room. Could you scare a dead boy with the vibrancy of your life? "Be careful," I mouthed, motioning her into the shadows. Boys in green beanies kept sidling up to her, vying for her attention. It hurt my heart to see them trying. Of course, news of their own death had not reached them — how could that news get up the mountain, to where the workers were buried under snow?

Perched on the barstool, I plaited my hair. I tried to think up some good jokes.

"Hullo. Care if I join you?"

This dead boy introduced himself as Lee Covey. Black bangs flopped onto his brow. He had the small, recessed, comically despondent face of a pug dog. I liked him immediately. And he was so funny that I did not have to theatricalize my laughter. Lee's voluble eyes made conversation feel almost unnecessary; his conviction that he was alive was contagious.

"I'm not much of a dancer," Lee apologized abruptly. As if to prove his point, he sent a glass crashing off the bar.

"Oh, that's O.K. I'm not, either. See my friend out there?" I asked. "In the green dress? She's the graceful one."

But Lee kept his golden eyes fixed on me, and soon it became difficult to say who was the mesmerist and who was succumbing to hypnosis. His Camp Thistle stories made me laugh so hard that I worried about falling off the barstool. Lee had a rippling laugh, like summer thunder; by this point I was very drunk. Lee started in on his family's sorry history: "Daddy the Dwindler, he spent it all, he lost everything we had, he turned me out of the house. It fell to me to support the family . . ."

I nodded, recognizing his story's contours. How had the other workers washed up here? I wondered. Did they remember their childhoods, their lives before the avalanche? Or had those memories been buried inside them?

It was the loneliest feeling, to watch the group of dead boys dancing. Coupled off, they held on to each other's shoulders. "For practice," Lee explained. They steered each other uncertainly around the hexagonal floor, swaying on currents of song.

"Say, how about it?" Lee said suddenly. "Let's give it a whirl — you only live once."

Seconds later, we were on the floor, jitterbugging in the center of the hall.

"Oh, oh, oh," he crooned.

When Lee and I kissed, it felt no different from kissing a living mouth. We sank into the rhythms of horns and strings and harmonicas, performed by a live band of five dead mountain brothers. With the naïve joy of all these ghosts, they tootled their glittery instruments at us.

A hand grabbed my shoulder.

"May I cut in?"

Clara dragged me off the floor.

Back in the powder room, Clara's eyes looked shiny, raccoon-beady. She was exhausted, I realized. Some grins are only reflexes, but others are courageous acts — Clara's was the latter. The clock had just chimed ten-thirty. The party showed no signs of slowing. At least the clock is moving, I pointed out. We tried to conjure a picture of the risen sun, piercing the thousand windows of the Emerald Lodge.

"You doing O.K.?"

"I have certainly been better."

"We're going to make it down the mountain."

"Of course we are."

Near the western staircase, Lee waited with a drink in hand. Shadows pooled unnaturally around his feet; they reminded me of peeling paint. If you stared too long, they seemed to curl slightly up from the floorboards.

"Jean! There you are!"

At the sound of my real name, I felt electrified — hadn't I introduced myself by a pseudonym? Clara and I had a telephone book of false names. It was how we dressed for parties. We chose alter egos for each other, like jewelry.

"It's Candy, actually." I smiled politely. "Short for Candace."

"Whatever you say, *Jean*," Lee said, playing lightly with my bracelet.

"Who told you that? Did my friend tell you that?"

"You did."

I blinked slowly at Lee, watching his grinning face come in and out of focus.

I'd had plenty more to drink, and I realized that I didn't remember half the things we'd talked about. What else, I wondered, had I let slip?

"How did you get that name, huh? It's a really pretty name, Jeannie."

I was unused to being asked personal questions. Lee put his arms around me, and then, unbelievably, I heard my voice in the darkness, telling the ghost a true story.

Jean, I told him, is what I prefer to go by. In Florida, most everybody called me Aubby.

My parents named me Aubergine. They wanted me to have a glamorous name. It was a luxury they could afford to give me, a spell of protection. "Aubergine" was a word that my father had learned during his wartime service, the French word for "dawn," he said. A name like that, they felt, would envelop me in an aura of mystery, from swaddling to shroud. One night, on a rare trip to a restaurant, we learned the truth from a fellow-diner, a bald, genteel eavesdropper.

"Aubergine," he said thoughtfully. "What an *interesting* name."

We beamed at him eagerly, my whole family.

"It is, of course, the French word for 'eggplant.' "

"Oh, darn!" my mother said, unable to contain her sorrow.

"Of course!" roared old dad.

But we were a family long accustomed to reversals of fortune; in fact, my father had gone bankrupt misapprehending various facts about the dog track and his own competencies.

"It suits you," the bald diner said, smiling and turning the pages of his newspaper. "You are a little fat, yes? Like an eggplant!"

"We call her Jean for short," my mother had smoothly replied.

Clara was always teasing me. "Don't fall in love with anybody," she'd say, and then we'd laugh for longer than the joke really warranted, because this scenario struck us both as so unlikely. But as I leaned against this ghost I felt my life falling into place. It was the spotlight of his eyes, those radiant beams, that gently drew motes from the past out of me — and I loved this. He had got me talking, and now I didn't want to shut up. His eyes grew wider and wider, golden nets woven with golden fibers. I told him about my father's suicide, my mother's death. At the last second, I bit my tongue, but I'd been on the verge of telling him about Clara's bruises, those mute blue coördinates. Not to solicit Lee's help — what could this phantom do? No, merely to keep him looking at me.

Hush, Aubby, I heard in Clara's tiny, moth-fluttery voice, which was immediately incinerated by the hot pleasure of Lee's gaze.

We kissed a second time. I felt our teeth click together; two warm hands cupped my cheeks. But when he lifted his face, his anguish leapt out at me. His wild eyes were like bees trapped on the wrong side of a window, bouncing along the glass. "You . . ." he began. He stroked at my cheek. "You feel . . ." Very delicately, he tried kissing me again. "You taste . . ." Some bewildered comment trailed off into silence. One hand smoothed over my dress, while the other rose to claw at his pale throat.

"How's that?" he whispered hoarsely in my ear. "Does that feel all right?"

Lee was so much in the dark. I had no idea how to help him. I wondered how honest I would have wanted Lee to be with me, if he were in my shoes. *Put him out of his misery*, country people say of sick dogs. But Lee looked very happy. Excited, even, about the future.

"Should we go upstairs, Jean?"

"But where did Clara go?" I kept murmuring. It took great effort to remember her name.

"Did she disappear on you?" Lee said, and winked. "Do you think she's found her way upstairs, too?"

Crossing the room, we spotted her. Her hands were clasped around the hog stubble of a large boy's neck, and they were swaying in the center of the hexagon. I waved at her, trying to get her attention, and she stared right through me. A smile played on her face, while the chandeliers plucked up the red in her hair, strumming even the subtlest colors out of her.

Grinning, Lee lifted a hand to his black eyebrow in a mock salute. His bloodless hand looked thin as paper. I had a sharp memory of standing at a bay window, in Florida, and feeling the night sky change direction on me — no longer lapping at the horizon but rolling inland. Something was pouring toward me now, a nothingness exhaled through the floury membrane of the boy. If Lee could see the difference in the transparency of our splayed hands, he wasn't letting on.

Now Clara was kissing her boy's plush lips. Her fingers were still knitted around his tawny neck. *Clara, Clara, we have abandoned our posts.* We shouldn't have kissed them; we shouldn't have taken that black water onboard. Lee may not have known that he was dead, but my body did; it seemed to be having some kind of stupefied reaction to the kiss. I felt myself sinking fast, sinking far below thought. The two boys swept us toward the stairs with a courtly synchronicity, their uniformed bodies tugging us into the shadows, where our hair and our skin and our purple and emerald party dresses turned suddenly blue, like two candles blown out.

And now I watched as Clara flowed up the stairs after her stocky dancing partner, laughing with genuine abandon, her neck flung back and her throat exposed. I followed right behind her, but I could not close the gap. I watched her ascent, just as I had on the lift. Groggily, I saw them moving down a posy-wallpapered corridor. Even squinting, I could not make out the watery digits on the doors. All these doors were, of course, identical. One swung open, then shut, swallowing Clara. I doubted we would find each other again. By now, however, I felt very calm. I let Lee lead me by the wrist, like a child, only my bracelets shaking.

Room 409 had natural wood walls, glowing with a piney shine in the low light. Lee sat down on a chair and tugged off his work boots, flushed with the yellow avarice of 4 A.M. Darkness flooded steadily out of him, and I absorbed it. "Jean," he kept saying, a word that sounded so familiar, although its meaning now escaped me. I covered his mouth with my mouth. I sat on the ghost boy's lap, kissing his neck, pretending to feel a pulse. Eventually, grumbling an apology, Lee stood and disappeared into the bathroom. I heard a faucet turn on; Lord knows what came pouring out of it. The room had a queen bed, and I pulled back a corner of the soft cotton quilt. It was so beautiful, edelweiss white. I slid in with my dress still pinned to me. I could not stop yawning; seconds from now, I'd drop off. I never wanted to go back out there, I decided. Why lie about this? There was no longer any chairlift waiting to carry us home, was there? No mountain, no fool's-gold moon. The Earth we'd left felt like a photograph. And was it such a terrible thing, to live at the lodge?

Something was descending slowly, like a heavy theatre curtain, inside my body; I felt my will to know the truth ebbing into a happy, warm insanity. We could all be dead — why not? We could be in love, me and a dead boy. We could be sisters here, Clara and I, equally poor and equally beautiful.

Lee had come back and was stroking my hair onto the pillow. "Want to take a little nap?" he asked.

I had never wanted anything more. But then I looked down at my red fingernails and noticed a tiny chip in the polish, exposing the translucent blue enamel. Clara had painted them for me yesterday morning, before the party — eons ago. *Clara,* I remembered. *What was happening to Clara*? I dug out of the heavy coverlet, struggling up. At precisely that moment, the door began to rattle in its frame; outside, a man was calling for Lee.

"He's here! He's here! He's here!" a baritone voice growled happily. "Goddammit, Lee, button up and get downstairs!"

Lee rubbed his golden eyes and palmed his curls. I stared at him uncomprehendingly.

"I regret the interruption, my dear. But this we cannot miss." He grinned at me, exposing a mouthful of holes. "You wanna have your picture taken, don'tcha?"

Clara and I found each other on the staircase. What had happened to her, in her room? That's a lock I can't pick. Even on ordinary nights, we often split up, and afterward we never discussed those unreal intervals in the boarding house. On our prospecting expeditions, whatever doors we closed stayed shut. Clara had her arm around her date, who looked doughier than I recalled, his round face almost featureless, his eyebrows vanished; even the point of his green toothpick seemed blurred. Lee ran up to greet him, and we hung back while the two men continued downstairs, racing each other to reach the photographer. This time we did not try to disguise our relief.

"I was falling asleep!" Clara said. "And I wanted to sleep so badly, Aubby, but then I remembered you were here somewhere, too."

"I was falling asleep," I said, "but then I remembered your face."

Clara redid my bun, and I straightened her hem. We were fine, we promised each other.

"I didn't get anything," Clara said. "But I'm not leaving empty-handed."

I gaped at her. Was she still talking about prospecting?

"You can't steal from this place."

Clara had turned to inspect a sculpted flower blooming from an iron railing; she tugged at it experimentally, as if she thought she might free it from the bannister.

"Clara, wake up. That's not — "

"No? That's not why you brought me here?"

She flicked her eyes up at me, her gaze limpid and accusatory. And I felt I'd become fluent in the language of eyes; now I saw what she'd known all along. What she'd been swallowing back on our prospecting trips, what she'd never once screamed at me, in the freezing boarding house: *You use me. Every party, you bait the hook, and I dangle. I let them, I am eaten, and what do I get? Some scrap metal?*

"I'm sorry, Clara . . ."

My apology opened outward, a blossoming horror. I'd used her bruises to justify leaving Florida. I'd used her face to open doors. Greed had convinced me I could take care of her up here, and then I'd disappeared on her. How long had Clara known what I was doing? I'd barely known myself.

But Clara, still holding my hand, pointed at the clock. It was 5 A.M.

"Dawn is coming." She gave me a wide, genuine smile. "We are going to get home."

Downstairs, the C.C.C. boys were shuffling around the dance floor, positioning themselves in a triangular arrangement. The tallest men knelt down, and the shorter men filed behind them. When they saw us watching from the staircase, they waved.

"Where you girls been? The photographer is *here.*"

The fires were still burning, the huge logs unconsumed. Even the walls, it seemed, were trembling in anticipation. This place wanted to go on shining in our living eyes, was that it? The dead boys feasted on our attention, but so did the entire structure.

Several of the dead boys grabbed us and hustled us toward the posed and grinning rows of uniformed workers. We spotted a tripod in the corner of the lodge, a man doubled over, his head swallowed by the black cover. He was wearing a flamboyant costume: a ragged black cape, made from the same smocky material as the camera cover, and bright-red satin trousers.

"Picture time!" his voice boomed.

Now the true light of the Emerald Lodge began to erupt in rhythmic bursts. We winced at the metallic flash, the sun above his neck. The workers stiffened, their lean faces plumped by grins. It was an inversion of the standard firing squad: two dozen men hunched before the photographer and his mounted cannon.

"*Cheese!*" the C.C.C. boys cried.

We squinted against the radiant detonations. These blasts were much brighter and louder than any shutter click on Earth.

With each flash, the men grew more definite: their chins sharpening, cheeks ripening around their smiles. Dim brows darkened to black arcs; the gold of their eyes deepened, as if each face were receiving a generous pour of whiskey. Was it life that these ghosts were drawing from the camera's light? No, these flashes — they imbued the ghosts with something else.

"Do not let him shoot you," I hissed, grabbing Clara by the elbow. We ran for cover. Every time the flashbulb illuminated the room, I flinched. "Did he get you? Did he get me?"

With an animal instinct, we knew to avoid that light. We could not let the photographer fix us in the frame, we could not let him capture us on whatever film still held them here, dancing jerkily on the hexagonal floor. *If that happens, we are done for*, I thought. *We are here forever.*

With his unlidded eye, the photographer spotted us where we had crouched behind the piano. Bent at the waist, his head cloaked by the wrinkling purple-black cover, he rotated the camera. Then he waggled his fingers at us, motioning us into the frame.

"Smile, ladies," Mickey Loatch ordered, as we darted around the cedar tables.

We never saw his face, but he was hunting us. This devil — excuse me, let us continue to call him "the party photographer," as I do not want to frighten anyone unduly — spun the tripod on its rolling wheels, his hairy hands gripping its sides, the cover flapping onto his shoulders like a strange pleated wig. His single blue lens kept fixing on our bodies. Clara dove low behind the wicker chairs and pulled me after her.

The C.C.C. boys who were assembled on the dance floor, meanwhile, stayed glacially frozen. Smiles floated muzzily around their faces. A droning rose from the room, a sound like dragonflies in summer, and I realized that we were hearing the men's groaning effort to stay in focus: to flood their faces with ersatz blood, to hold still, hold still, and smile.

Then the chair tipped; one of our pursuers had lifted Clara up, kicking and screaming, and began to carry her back to the dance floor, where men were shifting to make a place for her.

"Front and center, ladies," the company Captain called urgently. "Fix your dress, dear. The straps have gotten all twisted."

I had a terrible vision of Clara caught inside the shot with them, her eyes turning from brown to umber to the deathlessly sparkling gold.

"Stop!" I yelled. "Let her go! She — "

She's alive, I did not risk telling them.

"She does not photograph well!"

With aqueous indifference, the camera lifted its eye.

"Listen, forgive us, but we cannot be in your photograph!"

"Let *go!*" Clara said, cinched inside an octopus of restraining arms, every one of them pretending that this was still a game.

We used to pledge, with great passion, always to defend each other. We meant it, too. These were easy promises to make, when we were safely at the boarding house; but on this mountain even breathing felt dangerous.

But Clara pushed back. Clara saved us.

She directed her voice at every object in the lodge, screaming at the very rafters. Gloriously, her speech gurgling with saliva and blood and everything wet, everything living, she began to howl at them, the dead ones. She foamed red, my best friend, forming the words we had been stifling all night, the spell-bursting ones:

"It's done, gentlemen. It's over. Your song ended. You are news font; you are characters. I could read you each your own obituary. None of this — "

"Shut her up," a man growled.

"Shut up, shut up!" several others screamed.

She was chanting, one hand at her throbbing temple: "None of this, none of this, none of this *is!*"

Some men were thumbing their ears shut. Some had braced themselves in the doorframes, as they teach the children of the West to do during earthquakes. I resisted the urge to cover my own ears as she bansheed back at the shocked ghosts:

"Two years ago, there was an avalanche at your construction site. It was terrible, a tragedy. We were all so sorry . . ."

She took a breath.

"You are dead."

Her voice grew gentle, almost maternal — it was like watching the wind drop out of the world, flattening a full sail. Her shoulders fell, her palms turned out.

"You were all buried with this lodge."

Their eyes turned to us, incredulous. Hard and yellow, dozens of spiny armadillos. After a second, the C.C.C. company burst out laughing. Some men cried tears, they were howling so hard at Clara. Lee was among them, and he looked much changed, his face as smooth and flexibly white as an eel's belly.

These men — they didn't believe her!

And why should we ever have expected them to believe us, two female nobodies, two intruders? For these were the master carpenters, the master stonemasons and weavers, the master self-deceivers, the ghosts.

"Dead," one sad man said, as if testing the word out.

"Dead. Dead. Dead," his friends repeated, quizzically.

But the sound was a shallow production, as if each man were scratching at topsoil with the point of a shovel. Aware, perhaps, that if he dug with a little more dedication he would find his body lying breathless under this world's surface.

"Dead." "Dead."

"Dead."

"Dead."

"Dead."

"Dead."

They croaked like pond frogs, all across the ballroom. "Dead" was a foreign word which the boys could pronounce perfectly, soberly and matter-of-factly, without comprehending its meaning.

One or two of them, however, exchanged a glance; I saw a burly blacksmith cut eyes at the ruby-cheeked trumpet player. It was a guileful look, a what-can-be-done look.

So they knew; or they almost knew; or they'd buried the knowledge of their deaths, and we had exhumed it. Who can say what the dead do or do not know? Perhaps the knowledge of one's death, ceaselessly swallowed, is the very food you need to become a ghost. They burned that knowledge up like whale fat, and continued to shine on.

But then a quaking began to ripple across the ballroom floor. A chandelier, in its handsome zigzag frame, burst into a spray of glass above us. One of the pillars, three feet wide, cracked in two. Outside, from all corners, we heard a rumbling, as if the world were gathering its breath.

"Oh, God," I heard one of them groan. "It's happening again."

My eyes met Clara's, as they always do at parties. She did not have to tell me: *Run.*

On our race through the lodge, in all that chaos and din, Clara somehow heard another sound. A bright chirping. A sound like gold coins being tossed up, caught, and fisted. It stopped her cold. The entire building was shaking on its foundations, but through the tremors she spotted a domed cage, hanging in the foyer. On a tiny stirrup, a yellow bird was swinging. The cage was a wrought-iron skeleton, the handiwork of phantoms, but the bird, we both knew instantly, was real. It was agitating its wings in the polar air, as alive as we were. Its shadow was denser than anything in that ice palace. Its song split our eardrums. Its feathers burned into our retinas, rich with solar color, and its small body was stuffed with life.

At the Evergreen Lodge, on the opposite side of the mountain, two twelve-foot doors, designed and built by the C.C.C., stand sentry against the outside air — seven hundred pounds of hand-cut ponderosa pine, from Oregon's primeval woods. Inside the Emerald Lodge, we found their phantom twins, the dream originals. Those doors still worked, thank God. We pushed them open. Bright light, real daylight, shot onto our faces.

The sun was rising. The chairlift, visible across a pillowcase of fresh snow, was running.

We sprinted for it. Golden sunlight painted the steel cables. We raced across the platform, jumping for the chairs, and I will never know how fast or how far we flew to get back to Earth. In all our years of prospecting in the West, this was our greatest heist. Clara opened her satchel and lifted the yellow bird onto her lap, and I heard it shrieking the whole way down the mountain.

[2015]

EXPLORING THE TEXT

1. What are some of the possible meanings of "prospector" in the context of this story? Why do you believe Karen Russell used it as the title? In what ways are the various meanings illustrated in the story?
2. Trace the motif of "gold" in "The Prospectors." How is it used? What does it suggest about the characters of Aubby and Clara? about the wild west of the story's setting and the reasons the girls might have come to Oregon from Florida?
3. In paragraph 23 of the story, Aubby describes her friendship with Clara: "For the duration of our friendship, we'd trade off roles like this: anchor and boat, beholder and beheld. We must have looked like some Janus-faced statue, our chins pointing east and west." In what ways does the story's plot illustrate this assertion? How else does Russell reveal and develop the friendship between Aubby and Clara?
4. Consider the story's balance between reality and fantasy — for instance, the CCC did, in fact, build a lodge much like the one described in "The Prospectors" during the Great Depression. What do you think Russell meant to convey through the combination of the two? Do you think the story's end — with the girls flying down the mountain on a ski lift, carrying a yellow bird in its cage — falls into the category of reality or fantasy? Explain your answer.
5. We might expect Aubby and Clara to be more threatened by the situation at the Emerald Lodge than they seem to be, as they are outnumbered by dead men twenty to two. How would you describe their reaction? Why do you think Russell chose to portray their response in this way?
6. What connotations do the names of the characters in "The Prospectors" carry? Look up the meanings of or allusions made by the names Finisterre, La Rochefoucauld, Romulus, and Creon. Why do you think Russell chose those names for those characters? What do these names tell us about the characters themselves? For instance, what does it tell us about Aubby that her parents were fooled for so long about the meaning of the word "aubergine"?
7. How does Russell use the story's setting to explore themes of life and death, friendship, and humanity's relationship to nature?
8. In an interview in the *New Yorker*, where this story first appeared, Russell quoted philosopher Friedrich Nietzsche to explain the "dynamic that evolves between Aubby and Clara and their hosts: 'Let us beware of saying that death is the opposite of life. The living being is only a species of the dead, and a very rare species.'" In what ways does the story develop that theory? Did it seem convincing to you? Explain your answer.

POETRY

Sound and Sense

ALEXANDER POPE

Alexander Pope (1688–1744) is generally considered the eighteenth century's greatest English poet. Known for satirical verse, Pope was the first writer to be able to live off the proceeds of his work — namely, his very popular translation of Homer's *Iliad*. Pope was a Roman Catholic, and the anti-Catholic sentiment and laws of his time dictated — and limited — his formal education. He read widely on his own, learning French, Italian, Latin, and Greek. Critics attacked Pope's version of Shakespeare's works, and he responded with *The Dunciad* — a scathing satire of the literary establishment that brought him enemies and even threats of physical violence. Pope's work goes in and out of fashion, but some of his words are so ingrained in the English language that they are considered proverbs by those unfamiliar with his work. "Hope springs eternal in the human breast" and "The proper study of mankind is man" are both found in *An Essay on Man.* "A little learning is a dangerous thing," "To err is human, to forgive, divine," and "For fools rush in where angels fear to tread" are from *An Essay on Criticism,* as is the selection that follows. *An Essay on Criticism* is Pope's poem on the art of poetry, whose purpose was not so much to provide lessons for writers but to offer advice to critics.

True ease in writing comes from art, not chance,
As those move easiest who have learned to dance.
'Tis not enough no harshness gives offense,
The sound must seem an echo to the sense:
Soft is the strain when Zephyr[1] gently blows,
And the smooth stream in smoother numbers flows;
But when loud surges lash the sounding shore,
The hoarse, rough verse should like the torrent roar.
When Ajax[2] strives, some rock's vast weight to throw,
The line too labors, and the words move slow;
Not so, when swift Camilla[3] scours the plain,
Flies o'er th' unbending corn, and skims along the main.
Hear how Timotheus'[4] varied lays surprise,
And bid alternate passions fall and rise!
While, at each change, the son of Libyan Jove,[5]

[1] The west wind, after Zephyrus, the Greek god of the west wind. — EDS.
[2] Hero in the Trojan War and Homer's *Iliad.* — EDS.
[3] Warrior in Virgil's *Aeneid.* — EDS.
[4] Ancient Greek poet and musician, and character in John Dryden's poem "Alexander's Feast." — EDS.
[5] Alexander the Great, here a character in "Alexander's Feast." — EDS.

Now burns with glory, and then melts with love;
Now his fierce eyes with sparkling fury glow,
Now sighs steal out, and tears begin to flow;
Persians and Greeks like turns of nature found,
And the world's victor stood subdued by sound!
The pow'r of music all our hearts allow,
And what Timotheus was, is DRYDEN now.

[1711]

EXPLORING THE TEXT

1. Using allusions to classical mythology that he would have expected his readers to know, Alexander Pope makes his point in "Sound and Sense" by exemplifying the effects or defects he wants to direct attention to in bad or good poetry. For example, he uses alliteration — the gentle sound of *s* — when he describes Zephyr, the gentle west wind. Find other examples in the excerpt of alliteration and onomatopoeia. How do the sounds of the words illustrate the examples and provide lessons on "true ease in writing"?
2. Examine the rhyme scheme. Pope was famous for writing couplets (two rhyming lines). How do the series of couplets in this poem help Pope convey his message about the relationship between sound and sense?
3. Pope manipulates the sound of this poem by controlling the poem's rhythm. Find examples of the way he varies stress (or accent), mixes mono- and polysyllabic words, ends words in consonants that do not easily blend, or slows a line down with commas. Be sure to read the poem aloud to hear the effects of the poem's "sound."
4. "Sound and Sense" is a didactic poem, meaning it was written for the purpose of instructing its readers. However, it does contain lyrical language that expresses emotion. How does Pope use that lyrical language to achieve his didactic purpose in this poem?
5. What conclusions can you draw about Pope's view of the poet's obligations? What expectations do you think he had about the artist's place in society?

Song: To the Men of England

PERCY BYSSHE SHELLEY

The son of an English landowner and member of Parliament, Percy Bysshe Shelley (1792–1822) is considered one of the greatest lyric poets in English literature. Shelley fared poorly at Oxford, where he was said to have attended only a single lecture. Instead, he pursued his own interests, reading up to sixteen hours a day and writing pamphlets, gothic novels, and poetry. His controversial views, expounded in such pamphlets as *The Necessity of Atheism*, led to his expulsion from Oxford in 1811. After the suicide of his first wife in 1816, Shelley married Mary Wollstonecraft Godwin, who would later write *Frankenstein* (1818). In 1818, the couple moved to Italy, where Shelley maintained a tempestuous friendship with Lord Byron — a relationship that encouraged Shelley to vigorously pursue his writing. While in Italy, Shelley completed the verse drama *Prometheus Unbound* (1820), based on the lost

play by Aeschylus; *Adonais* (1821), a pastoral elegy for poet John Keats; the essay *The Philosophical View of Reform* (not published until 1920); and many poems, both lyrical and political. This poem, "Song: To the Men of England," contains many of the political sentiments that made Shelley such a controversial figure during his lifetime.

Men of England, wherefore plough
For the lords who lay ye low?
Wherefore weave with toil and care
The rich robes your tyrants wear?

Wherefore feed and clothe and save
From the cradle to the grave
Those ungrateful drones who would
Drain your sweat — nay, drink your blood?

Wherefore, Bees of England, forge
Many a weapon, chain, and scourge,
That these stingless drones may spoil
The forced produce of your toil?

Have ye leisure, comfort, calm,
Shelter, food, love's gentle balm?
Or what is it ye buy so dear
With your pain and with your fear?

The seed ye sow, another reaps;
The wealth ye find, another keeps;
The robes ye weave, another wears;
The arms ye forge, another bears.

Sow seed — but let no tyrant reap;
Find wealth — let no impostor heap;
Weave robes — let not the idle wear;
Forge arms — in your defence to bear.

Shrink to your cellars, holes, and cells —
In halls ye deck another dwells.
Why shake the chains ye wrought? Ye see
The steel ye tempered glance on ye.

With plough and spade and hoe and loom
Trace your grave and build your tomb
And weave your winding-sheet — till fair
England be your Sepulchre.

[1819]

EXPLORING THE TEXT

1. Who are the "Men of England" Percy Bysshe Shelley is speaking to, and what is his purpose in addressing them? How does Shelley characterize the "Men of England"?
2. The first half of this poem consists of four questions. Do you think they are rhetorical? Explain.
3. Drones, or male honeybees, do not collect nectar or pollen, but only mate with queens and perform secondary functions within the hive. Who do you think the "drones" in the poem represent? What other connotations of the word *drone* do you think apply?
4. Consider the series of objects that the speaker says are forged by the "Bees of England": "weapon, chain, and scourge" (l. 10). What do these items have in common? How do they differ?
5. Some of Shelley's language in the poem — "wherefore" and "ye," for example — was already archaic by the year of its composition. What effect do you think these word choices have on the tone and rhetorical impact of the poem?
6. Stanza 6 reverses the parallels of the declarative statements in the fifth stanza, making them imperative. How would you describe the speaker's tone in these stanzas?
7. How would you describe the poem's overall tone? How does the tone shift in the closing four stanzas?
8. "Song: To the Men of England" has been set to music and adopted as an anthem of the English labor movement. What elements of the poem make it especially suitable as a hymn or rallying cry? Do you think Shelley is advocating an armed rebellion or a more ambiguous refusal of the status quo?

Much Madness is divinest Sense—

EMILY DICKINSON

Born into a prominent family in Amherst, Massachusetts, Emily Dickinson (1830–1886) received some formal education at Amherst Academy and Mount Holyoke Female Seminary (which became Mount Holyoke College). Throughout her lifetime, Dickinson was a shy and reclusive person, who preferred to remain within her close family circle. In 1862, she enclosed four poems in a letter to literary critic and abolitionist Thomas Wentworth Higginson, who had written a piece in the *Atlantic Monthly* that included practical advice for young writers. Her letter began, "Mr. Higginson, — Are you too deeply occupied to say if my verse is alive? The mind is so near itself it cannot see distinctly, and I have none to ask. Should you think it breathed, and had you the leisure to tell me, I should feel quick gratitude." Dickinson didn't sign the letter, but instead enclosed her name on a card inside a smaller envelope. Dickinson wrote over seventeen hundred poems, but only ten were published in her lifetime. She defied traditional rules of poetry, never breaking rules out of mere carelessness. She was a master of whimsy, especially when dealing with serious topics, as in the following poem, "Much Madness is divinest Sense."

Much Madness is divinest Sense —
To a discerning Eye —
Much Sense — the starkest Madness —
'Tis the Majority
In this, as All, prevail —
Assent — and you are sane —
Demur — you're straightway dangerous —
And handled with a Chain —

[c. 1862]

EXPLORING THE TEXT

1. This poem relies on an inversion of the expected meanings of "sense" and "madness." Though the speaker does not explicitly tie the terms to any specific behavior or beliefs, can you find evidence indicating how the poem defines "madness"?
2. Do you think the poem presents an unresolvable paradox regarding "sense" and "madness"? How would you characterize the "discerning Eye" mentioned in line 2? Contrast this with the method of discernment practiced by the "Majority" in the poem.
3. Consider Emily Dickinson's choice of the word "demur" in line 7. How does choosing such a gentle term affect the meaning of the line? What do you make of the contrast between that word and the rest of the line?
4. To what extent does this poem speak to contemporary times? Are those who assent, or conform, regarded as sane; and those who rebel, or dissent, seen as dangerous? Use examples from current events to support your answer.
5. This poem could serve as an epigraph to one of the stories you have read in this chapter. Choose which story would be most appropriate, and explain why.

Disillusionment of Ten O'Clock

WALLACE STEVENS

Wallace Stevens (1879–1955) is considered one of the most important American modernist poets. Born in Reading, Pennsylvania, Stevens studied at Harvard University and graduated from New York Law School. He worked as a lawyer in New York and became vice president of one of the largest insurance businesses in Hartford, Connecticut. In addition to being a successful businessman, Stevens is regarded as one of the great poets of the twentieth century. His poetry collections include *Harmonium* (1923), *The Man with the Blue Guitar and Other Poems* (1937), *Transport to Summer* (1947), and *A Primitive Like an Orb* (1948). *Collected Poems* (1954) brought Stevens both a Pulitzer Prize and the National Book Award. Stevens's work is often described as meditative and philosophical. He was a poet of ideas, with a strong belief in the poet as someone with heightened powers. Stevens favored precision of imagery and clear, sharp language, rejecting the sentiment favored by the Romantic and Victorian poets.

The houses are haunted
By white night-gowns.
None are green,
Or purple with green rings,
Or green with yellow rings,
Or yellow with blue rings.
None of them are strange,
With socks of lace
And beaded ceintures.[1]
People are not going
To dream of baboons and periwinkles.
Only, here and there, an old sailor,
Drunk and asleep in his boots,
Catches tigers
In red weather.

[1923]

[1]Belts or sashes. — EDS.

EXPLORING THE TEXT

1. How do you interpret the poem's title? Consider Wallace Stevens's choice of words; why "ten o'clock" specifically? What are the connotations of "disillusionment," particularly with regard to Stevens's belief in the power and importance of imagination?
2. How would you characterize the speaker of the poem? What is his purpose, and to whom might he be speaking? Use textual evidence to support your analysis.
3. What do you think is the poem's unstated setting? What evidence in the text leads you to your conclusion?
4. Why don't the people in the poem dream? Why are they disillusioned? What are their lives like?

5. The speaker discusses various colors that the nightgowns are *not*; in fact, lines 3–11 are primarily about what is not found in these houses. What does this approach achieve in terms of the poem's mood and theme? How does it connect to the idea of "haunting" introduced in the opening line?
6. What do you think the poet is suggesting with the sudden leap from fairly mundane images of nightgowns to the absence of dreams of "baboons and periwinkles" (l. 11)?
7. In his poem "Someone Puts a Pineapple Together," Stevens proclaims, "Divest reality / Of its propriety." What does this statement mean? How does it apply to "Disillusionment of Ten O'Clock"?

anyone lived in a pretty how town

E. E. CUMMINGS

Edward Estlin (E. E.) Cummings (1894–1962) was an enormously prolific experimental poet. Born and raised in an affluent family in Cambridge, Massachusetts, he graduated from Cambridge Latin High School and received both a BA and an MA in English and classical studies from Harvard University. Before the United States entered World War I, Cummings, an avowed pacifist, volunteered as an ambulance driver in France, where he was held for a time in a detention camp — an experience that deepened his distrust of authority. *The Enormous Room* (1922), his first published work, is a fictional account of his imprisonment, followed in 1923 by his first collection of poems, *Tulips and Chimneys.* Cummings defied traditional rules of typography and punctuation in the pursuit of poetry that was both critical and whimsical. An immensely popular poet, he produced an extensive body of work including more than nine hundred poems. Critic Jenny Penberthy describes Cummings as "an unabashed lyricist, a modern cavalier love poet. But alongside his lyrical celebrations of nature, love, and the imagination are his satirical denouncements of tawdry, defiling, flat-footed, urban and political life — open terrain for invective and verbal inventiveness." Each of these verbal rebellions is on display in "anyone lived in a pretty how town," one of his most enduring poems, which blends wordplay, whimsy, and romance with sly criticism of the status quo.

anyone lived in a pretty how town
(with up so floating many bells down)
spring summer autumn winter
he sang his didn't he danced his did.

Women and men(both little and small)
cared for anyone not at all
they sowed their isn't they reaped their same
sun moon stars rain

children guessed(but only a few
and down they forgot as up they grew
autumn winter spring summer)
that noone loved him more by more

when by now and tree by leaf
she laughed his joy she cried his grief
bird by snow and stir by still
anyone's any was all to her

someones married their everyones
laughed their cryings and did their dance
(sleep wake hope and then)they
said their nevers they slept their dream

stars rain sun moon
(and only the snow can begin to explain
how children are apt to forget to remember
with up so floating many bells down)

one day anyone died i guess
(and noone stooped to kiss his face)
busy folk buried them side by side
little by little and was by was

all by all and deep by deep
and more by more they dream their sleep
noone and anyone earth by april
with by spirit and if by yes.

Women and men(both dong and ding)
summer autumn winter spring
reaped their sowing and went their came
sun moon stars rain

[1940]

EXPLORING THE TEXT

1. Who are the main characters in this poem? What are their names, and what is their relationship? Who is the "he" referred to in line 4 and the "him" in line 12? Who is the "she" referred to in line 14 and the "her" in line 16? Identify a passage in which the ambiguity of their identities results in multiple meanings. How does such ambiguity reinforce the poem's central themes?
2. Who are the other characters in the poem? Who are the conformists, and who are the nonconformists? What seems to be the difference in how they lived their lives? Use specific lines as evidence.
3. The poem exemplifies E. E. Cummings's experiments with syntax from its title onward. On first reading, a line such as "he sang his didn't he danced his did" (l. 4) can seem daunting, even unintelligible. How would additional punctuation or emphasis (e.g., "He sang his *didn't*; he danced his *did*") alter your reading of the line? Select another dense or challenging passage from the poem and try standardizing the punctuation or syntax, explaining your sense of the passage's meaning.
4. In the third stanza, which refers to the children growing up, the progression of the seasons begins with autumn. Why? Is the order of the seasons important in the first and last stanzas as well? Explain your response.
5. Discuss how the repeated phrase "with up so floating many bells down" mimics, through its unconventional syntax and word order, the image that it describes. Along with the repetition of the changing seasons, the poem contains many other images suggesting the passage of time. Which images most powerfully suggest change, aging, or other forms of transience? Which passages imply stasis?

Do not go gentle into that good night

DYLAN THOMAS

Dylan Thomas (1914–1953) was born in Wales, spent much of his life in London, and gained a following in the United States, where he often lectured and gave readings. He wrote his first volume of poetry when he was only twenty and published steadily throughout his lifetime. His works include *The Map of Love* (1939); *Portrait of the Artist as a Young Dog* (1940); *Deaths and Entrances* (1946); *In Country Sleep* (1952); and the posthumous *Under Milk Wood: A Play for Voices* (1954), which features characters from the fictional Welsh fishing village of Llareggub. During World War II, Thomas wrote scripts for documentary films, and after the war he was a literary commentator for BBC radio. He died in New York City at the age of thirty-nine of complications from alcoholism. Thomas was a popular and flamboyant figure, known for his spirited readings — especially his famous reading of "Do not go gentle into that good night," a poem addressed to his dying father.

Do not go gentle into that good night,
Old age should burn and rave at close of day;
Rage, rage against the dying of the light.

Though wise men at their end know dark is right,
Because their words had forked no lightning they
Do not go gentle into that good night.

Good men, the last wave by, crying how bright
Their frail deeds might have danced in a green bay,
Rage, rage against the dying of the light.

Wild men who caught and sang the sun in flight,
And learn, too late, they grieved it on its way,
Do not go gentle into that good night.

Grave men, near death, who see with blinding sight
Blind eyes could blaze like meteors and be gay,
Rage, rage against the dying of the light.

And you, my father, there on the sad height,
Curse, bless, me now with your fierce tears, I pray.
Do not go gentle into that good night.
Rage, rage against the dying of the light.

[1952]

EXPLORING THE TEXT

1. Much of the power of a villanelle, the form in which this poem is composed, resides in its repeated lines and their subtly shifting meaning over the course of the piece. How do Thomas's repeated lines change from stanza to stanza? You may consider theme, mood, imagery, and even grammatical structure to support your answer.
2. How do you interpret the images of natural forces that Dylan Thomas connects to the men described in the middle stanzas? Choose a stanza and explain how the particular metaphor develops the poem's themes.
3. Discuss the recurring images of light and darkness in the poem. What multiple meanings might these motifs convey? Explain, focusing on a specific passage or set of images.
4. Do you think the speaker's urgings are more for his father's benefit or for his own? How do you think the argument aids or harms them in dealing with the father's impending mortality?
5. Stanzas 2 through 5 are about "wise men," "good men," "wild men," and "grave men." How do they differ from one another in their response to death?
6. Thomas withholds the identity of the poem's subject until the final stanza. Why?
7. The rebellion embodied in the poem is not directed against any human authority or tradition but against death itself. Are there aspects of life that the speaker rejects as well in making his argument? Support your answer using specific passages from the text.

The Chicago *Defender* Sends a Man to Little Rock

GWENDOLYN BROOKS

Born in Topeka, Kansas, and raised in Chicago, Gwendolyn Brooks (1917–2000) was author of more than twenty books of poetry, including her breakout work, *A Street in Bronzeville* (1945), and *Annie Allen* (1949), for which she became the first African American author to receive the Pulitzer Prize. In 1968, she was named poet laureate of the state of Illinois, and from 1985 to 1986 she served as consultant in poetry to the Library of Congress — the first African American woman to hold this position. Much of Brooks's work focuses on Chicago's urban landscape and culture, reflecting the speech patterns and expressions of the African American neighborhoods of Chicago's South Side, where she lived. While depicting the gritty reality of urban poverty, her poems express an affirmation of life. In "The *Chicago Defender* Sends a Reporter to Little Rock, Fall 1957," Brooks contrasts the quaint lifestyle of a medium-sized city with its violent and frightening atmosphere of racial oppression, evoking the moral price of conformity in an unjust society.

Fall, 1957

In Little Rock the people bear
Babes, and comb and part their hair
And watch the want ads, put repair
To roof and latch. While wheat toast burns
A woman waters multiferns.

Time upholds or overturns
The many, tight, and small concerns.

In Little Rock the people sing
Sunday hymns like anything,
Through Sunday pomp and polishing.

And after testament and tunes,
Some soften Sunday afternoons
With lemon tea and Lorna Doones.[1]

I forecast
And I believe
Come Christmas Little Rock will cleave
To Christmas tree and trifle, weave,
From laugh and tinsel, texture fast.

In Little Rock is baseball; Barcarolle.[2]
That hotness in July . . . the uniformed figures raw and implacable
And not intellectual,

[1]A brand of shortbread cookies. — EDS.
[2]A type of folk music composed in the style of Venetian gondoliers. — EDS.

Batting the hotness or clawing the suffering dust.
The Open Air Concert, on the special twilight green . . .
When Beethoven is brutal or whispers to lady-like air.
Blanket-sitters are solemn, as Johann troubles to lean
To tell them what to mean. . . .

There is love, too, in Little Rock. Soft women softly
Opening themselves in kindness,
Or, pitying one's blindness,
Awaiting one's pleasure
In azure
Glory with anguished rose at the root. . . .
To wash away old semi-discomfitures.
They re-teach purple and unsullen blue.
The wispy soils go. And uncertain
Half-havings have they clarified to sures.

In Little Rock they know
Not answering the telephone is a way of rejecting life,
That it is our business to be bothered, is our business
To cherish bores or boredom, be polite
To lies and love and many-faceted fuzziness.

I scratch my head, massage the hate-I-had.
I blink across my prim and pencilled pad.
The saga I was sent for is not down.
Because there is a puzzle in this town.
The biggest News I do not dare
Telegraph to the Editor's chair:
"They are like people everywhere."

The angry Editor would reply
In hundred harryings of Why.

And true, they are hurling spittle, rock,
Garbage and fruit in Little Rock.
And I saw coiling storm a-writhe
On bright madonnas. And a scythe
Of men harassing brownish girls.
(The bows and barrettes in the curls
And braids declined away from joy.)

I saw a bleeding brownish boy. . . .

The lariat lynch-wish I deplored.

The loveliest lynchee was our Lord.

[1960]

EXPLORING THE TEXT

1. The poem's speaker is the reporter from the Chicago *Defender* (at that time the nation's largest African American newspaper) who has traveled to Little Rock, Arkansas, to cover the city's efforts to stop desegregation. What does the reporter's editor expect the story to be? What does the reporter find? What, finally, will the reporter's story be?
2. How would you characterize the diction in this poem? Consider the effect of the proper names, such as Lorna Doones, Barcarolle, Open Air Concert, and Beethoven. Why do you think Gwendolyn Brooks made the language choices she made? Why do you think she capitalized "Editor"?
3. Many of the speaker's observations relay details of everyday life. Do you think the speaker is observing the everyday life of Little Rock's white inhabitants, black inhabitants, or a combination of both? Explain how you know.
4. "The Chicago *Defender* Sends a Man to Little Rock" is written in ten-syllable (tetrameter) rhyming couplets. How does this traditional and accessible structure and rhyme scheme underscore the scene the poet sets? What point does Brooks make by structuring the poem in this way?
5. What changes in the poem at line 51? How does Brooks lead the reader up to that shift? Do you think the reporter has just seen more or is he trying to send his editor the story he thinks the editor wants? Explain your answer.
6. The last line of the poem — "The loveliest lynchee was our Lord" — made the poem famous and is often used in sermons. What do you make of this line? What effect does it have on the reader? How would the absence of that line change the poem's tone and meaning?
7. What does the poem aim to persuade the reader of? Do you think it succeeds? What argumentative strategies does it use?
8. In his 2011 book *Beautiful & Pointless: A Guide to Modern Poetry*, critic David Orr wrote that "Brooks herself would later become more skeptical of the conciliatory stance adopted" in "The Chicago *Defender* Sends a Man to Little Rock." Do you consider the poem's stance conciliatory? Why or why not?

Her Kind

ANNE SEXTON

Anne Sexton (1928–1974) was one of the most celebrated confessional poets to emerge in America during the 1960s and 1970s. Born in Newton, Massachusetts, she struggled through a childhood marked by family discord and, by some accounts, periodic abuse. Sexton grappled with depression and suicidal urges for much of her adult life. In 1957, at the suggestion of her therapist, she began attending meetings of poetry groups in Boston, where she met such poets as Robert Lowell, Maxine Kumin, and Sylvia Plath. Her work progressed very rapidly, and her first volume of poetry, *To Bedlam and Part Way Back* (1960), was published only a few years afterward. Her subsequent work gained considerable acclaim and a number of awards, culminating in the Pulitzer Prize for *Live or Die* (1967). Though much criticism of Sexton's poetry revolves around her mental illness and eventual suicide, the body of her work comprises a much broader range, including *Transformations* (1971), a collection of prose poems reimagining the Grimm brothers' fairy tales. "Her Kind," from *To Bedlam and Part Way Back*, is a daring experiment in point of view, exploring images of women as outcasts.

I have gone out, a possessed witch,
haunting the black air, braver at night;
dreaming evil, I have done my hitch
over the plain houses, light by light:
lonely thing, twelve-fingered, out of mind.
A woman like that is not a woman, quite.
I have been her kind.

I have found the warm caves in the woods,
filled them with skillets, carvings, shelves,
closets, silks, innumerable goods;
fixed the suppers for the worms and the elves:
whining, rearranging the disaligned.
A woman like that is misunderstood.
I have been her kind.

I have ridden in your cart, driver,
waved my nude arms at villages going by,
learning the last bright routes, survivor
where your flames still bite my thigh
and my ribs crack where your wheels wind.
A woman like that is not ashamed to die.
I have been her kind.

[1960]

EXPLORING THE TEXT

1. How would you characterize the speaker? Is the "I" referred to the same throughout the poem? Explain.
2. What is the speaker's attitude toward the "witch" in the opening lines? What particular descriptions seem the most sympathetic or unsympathetic?
3. Trace the point of view throughout this poem. Where does it shift? What perspectives are we offered?
4. Reading the poem in the context of this chapter's theme, what is the speaker — as well as the "kinds" of women with whom she identifies — rebelling against? What or whom do you think the speaker would identify with the notion of conformity?
5. This poem is rich in imagery. Analyze how the patterns of imagery in the first stanza relate to the meaning. How and why does the imagery shift in the third stanza?

The Day Lady Died

FRANK O'HARA

Frank O'Hara (1926–1966) grew up in Grafton, Massachusetts. After high school, he enlisted in the navy and served on a destroyer for most of World War II. While he was attending Harvard University on the GI Bill, his teacher, poet John Ciardi, recommended him for a graduate fellowship in comparative literature at the University of Michigan. After he received his master's degree, O'Hara moved to New York City, where he was at the center of New York's art and poetry worlds, writing for *Artnews* magazine and working both at the front desk and as an assistant curator at the Museum of Modern Art. O'Hara was inspired by city life as other poets have been inspired by nature. He once wrote, "I can't even enjoy a blade of grass unless I know there's a subway handy, or a record store or some other sign that people do not totally regret life." O'Hara's poetry collections include *City Winter and Other Poems* (1952); *Meditations in an Emergency* (1957); *Second Avenue* (1960); *Odes* (1960); and *Lunch Poems* (1964), from which the following poem about the death of jazz singer Billie Holiday is taken.

It is 12:20 in New York a Friday
three days after Bastille day, yes
it is 1959 and I go get a shoeshine
because I will get off the 4:19 in Easthampton
at 7:15 and then go straight to dinner
and I don't know the people who will feed me

I walk up the muggy street beginning to sun
and have a hamburger and a malted and buy
an ugly NEW WORLD WRITING to see what the poets
in Ghana are doing these days
                                        I go on to the bank
and Miss Stillwagon (first name Linda I once heard)
doesn't even look up my balance for once in her life
and in the GOLDEN GRIFFIN I get a little Verlaine
for Patsy with drawings by Bonnard although I do
think of Hesiod, trans. Richmond Lattimore or
Brendan Behan's new play or *Le Balcon* or *Les Nègres*
of Genet, but I don't, I stick with Verlaine
after practically going to sleep with quandariness

and for Mike I just stroll into the PARK LANE
Liquor Store and ask for a bottle of Strega and
then I go back where I came from to 6th Avenue
and the tobacconist in the Ziegfeld Theatre and
casually ask for a carton of Gauloises and a carton
of Picayunes, and a NEW YORK POST with her face on it

and I am sweating a lot by now and thinking of
leaning on the john door in the 5 SPOT
while she whispered a song along the keyboard
to Mal Waldron and everyone and I stopped breathing

[1964]

EXPLORING THE TEXT

1. It's probably safe to say that Frank O'Hara is the poem's speaker. Characterize him. From what you have read, how would you describe the rest of his day? the rest of his life?
2. The poem takes place on a summer day in New York City and provides plenty of details about the time and place. How does the vivid setting help create the poem's tone?
3. Except for the last two lines, the poem is in the present tense. How does the abrupt switch add another level of meaning to the poem?
4. O'Hara once described his work as "I do this I do that" poetry because his poems sometimes sound like diary entries. "The Day Lady Died" is from a collection called *Lunch Poems*. How is it more than a report of what someone did on his lunch hour?
5. "Lady" refers to jazz singer Billie Holiday, who died as a result of heroin addiction. O'Hara heard her sing at a club called Five Spot where she broke the law by singing a song with piano player Mal Waldron. Holiday had lost her cabaret license and wasn't supposed to sing where alcohol was served; she really did whisper her song. Does this information change the meaning of the poem? Explain.

Is About

ALLEN GINSBERG

Allen Ginsberg (1926–1997) was born in Newark, New Jersey. As a teenager, he began to read Walt Whitman, who, along with William Carlos Williams and William Blake, exerted an enormous influence on Ginsberg's writing. Ginsberg went to Columbia University on a scholarship to study law but changed his major to English. He became a major voice in the Beat movement, which included poets Gregory Corso and Lawrence Ferlinghetti, and novelists William S. Burroughs and Jack Kerouac, author of *On the Road* (1957). Ginsberg led a varied, unconventional life: he worked as a dishwasher, welder, and university professor; he was arrested several times for political protests; he spent time in a psychiatric institution; and he toured with Bob Dylan's band. Ginsberg's work is notable for its free expression and rejection of conformity and materialism. *Howl* (1955) created intense interest and controversy for both its style and its content. In 1957, the poem's publisher was charged with obscenity; however, the case was thrown out when the presiding judge ruled that *Howl* was of "redeeming social consequence." Ginsberg's other works include *Kaddish and Other Poems* (1961), which many regard as his finest, and the mixed-genre collection *The Fall of America*, which won a National Book Award in 1973. *Collected Poems 1947–1980* was published in 1984. "Is About," a poem that explains it all in quintessential Beat style, was first published in the *New Yorker*.

Dylan is about the Individual against the whole of creation
Beethoven is about one man's fist in the lightning clouds
The Pope is about abortion & the spirits of the dead . . .
Television is about people sitting in their living room looking at their things
America is about being a big Country full of Cowboys Indians Jews Negroes
 & Americans
Orientals Chicanos Factories skyscrapers Niagara Falls Steel Mills radios
 homeless Conservatives, don't forget
Russia is about Czars Stalin Poetry Secret Police Communism barefoot in
 the snow
But that's not really Russia it's a concept
A concept is about how to look at the earth from the moon
without ever getting there. The moon is about love & Werewolves, also Poe.
Poe is about looking at the moon from the sun
or else the graveyard
Everything is about something if you're a thin movie producer chain-
 smoking muggles
The world is about overpopulation, Imperial invasions, Biocide, Genocide,
 Fratricidal Wars, Starvation, Holocaust, mass injury & murder, high technology
Super science, atom Nuclear Neutron Hydrogen detritus, Radiation
 Compassion Buddha, Alchemy
Communication is about monopoly television radio movie newspaper
 spin on Earth, i.e. planetary censorship.

Universe is about Universe.
Allen Ginsberg is about confused mind writing down newspaper
headlines from Mars—
The audience is about salvation, the listeners are about sex, Spiritual
gymnastics, nostalgia for the Steam Engine & Pony Express
Hitler Stalin Roosevelt & Churchill are about arithmetic &
Quadrilateral equations, above all chemistry physics & chaos theory—
Who cares what it's all about?
I do! Edgar Allan Poe cares! Shelley cares! Beethoven & Dylan care.
Do you care? What are you about
or are you a human being with 10 fingers & two eyes?

[1996]

EXPLORING THE TEXT

1. "Is About" is, in a sense, a definition poem. Which definition seems most persuasive to you? How do you think the poem defines the title itself?
2. From among the characters who populate the poem (Dylan, Beethoven, the Pope, Poe, Buddha, Hitler, Stalin, Roosevelt, Churchill, and Shelley), select one you know well. Is the reference accurate, as you see it? How does it contribute to the meaning or effect of the poem?
3. What techniques does Allen Ginsberg employ to affect the tempo of each line? Consider line length, punctuation, and the sound of the words. How does the resulting pace inform your understanding of the poet's intentions or mood? Identify a list or a series of images or concepts in the poem that you find particularly striking. How does the juxtaposition of items in this list or series develop tension or resonance within the poem?
4. How does the element of surprise function in the poem? Identify an unexpected association or definition that particularly affected your reading or understanding of the speaker's intentions or ideas.
5. How would you describe the tone of the poem? How does Ginsberg create that tone?
6. How would you answer the last two questions of the poem (ll. 23–24)?
7. If asked, what would you say "Is About" is about?

Talk

TERRANCE HAYES

Terrance Hayes (b. 1971) is an American poet and educator. Born in Columbia, South Carolina, he earned a BA from Coker College and an MFA at the University of Pittsburgh. Hayes is the author of five books of poetry: *Muscular Music* (1999), which won both a Whiting Award and the Kate Tufts Discovery Award; *Hip Logic* (2002), which won the National Poetry Series; *Wind in a Box* (2006); *Lighthead* (2010), which won a National Book Award; and *How to Be Drawn* (2015). In 2009, Hayes won a Guggenheim Fellowship, and in 2014, he was named a MacArthur Foundation Fellow. Hayes's poetry is noted for its engagement with race in America, its nimble lyricism, its disarming humor, and its trenchant social observations. In "Talk," Hayes blends piercing honesty with imagery-laden narrative to recount and reconsider a moment of racial tension between the African American speaker and his white friend.

like a nigger now, my white friend, M, said
after my M.L.K. and Ronald Reagan impersonations,
the two of us alone and shirtless in the locker room,

and if you're thinking my knuckles knocked
a few times against his jaw or my fingers knotted
at his throat, you're wrong because I pretended

I didn't hear him, and when he didn't ask it again,
we slipped into our middle school uniforms
since it was November, the beginning

of basketball season, and jogged out
onto the court to play together
in that vision all Americans wish for

their children, and the point is we slipped
into our uniform harmony, and spit out *Go Team!*,
our hands stacked on and beneath the hands

of our teammates and that was as close
as I have come to passing for one
of the members of The Dream, my white friend

thinking I was so far from that word
that he could say it to me, which I guess
he could since I didn't let him taste the salt

and iron in the blood, I didn't teach him
what it's like to squint through a black eye,
and if I had I wonder if he would have grown

up to be the kind of white man who believes
all blacks are thugs or if he would have learned
to bite his tongue or let his belly be filled

by shame, but more importantly, would I be
the kind of black man who believes silence
is worth more than talk or that it can be

a kind of grace, though I'm not sure
that's the kind of black man I've become,
and in any case, M, wherever you are,

I'd just like to say I heard it, but let it go
because I was afraid to lose our friendship
or afraid we'd lose the game — which we did anyway.

[2006]

EXPLORING THE TEXT

1. What is the effect of having the title of the poem also function as its first word? Why do you think Terrance Hayes made this choice?
2. Characterize the speaker of "Talk." Explain how the poet develops his persona, considering both what is said in the poem and what is left unsaid.
3. What is the "vision Americans wish for / their children" (ll. 12–13)?
4. What does Hayes mean by "The Dream" (l. 18)? How does the context of the poem explain it?
5. Why do you think Hayes chose to extend sentences across both line and stanza breaks? How does this choice affect the way you read the poem? How does it help characterize the speaker?
6. What role does the sport of basketball occupy in the poem? How might the last two lines be a comment on larger issues?
7. A *New York Times* magazine profile of Hayes quotes him as addressing a group of high school students about poetry: "A poem is never about one thing. You want it to be as complicated as your feelings." What are some of the things "Talk" is about? In what ways does it reflect the speaker's complicated feelings?

To Be Walang Hiya

BARBARA JANE REYES

Barbara Jane Reyes (b. 1971) is an American poet born in Manila, Philippines, and raised in the San Francisco Bay area. She earned a BA in Ethnic Studies at UC Berkeley and an MFA at San Francisco State University. Reyes is the author of three books of poetry: *Gravities of Center* (2003), *Poeta en San Francisco* (2005), and *Diwata* (2010). Her work has been anthologized in many collections, including *Pinoy Poetics* (2004), *Asian Americans in the San Francisco Bay Area* (2004), and *100 Love Poems: Philippine Love Poetry Since 1905* (2004). Reyes lives in Oakland and has taught creative writing at Mills College and Philippine studies at the University of San Francisco. Her work is known for its exploration of the intersection of identity and culture. In "To Be Walang Hiya," the speaker reflects on the conflict between youthful expectation and the reality she must confront. "Walang hiya" is a phrase that carries several meanings in Tagalog, the language of the Philippines. It can be an adjective, meaning "to be without shame"; an interjection, meaning "shameless"; or a noun, meaning "an inconsiderate, rude, or selfish person."

Bubblegum lip gloss kissed,	Our lifelines, our mirrors,
I was never a singkil[1] *princess*	*These are Luminous Mysteries*[2] —
Knuckle cracking, polished toes,	Our notebooks, our language,
I was never a Santacruzan queen[3]	*To witness, to make way,*
Black eyeliner, push up bra	Our thirst and our wedding bands —
I was never a curtsying debutante	*To fill stone jars with water, to wed,*
Loud, gum-smacking babygirl	Our glamour and our armor.
I was never a tiaraed Miss Fil Am[4]	*To transfigure, dazzling as the sun.*

[2014]

[1] A complicated Philippine folk dance, traditionally performed only by women, and in earlier days only by royalty. It was considered a way to interest suitors. — EDS.

[2] Five prayers in the Catholic religion that reflect on important aspects of Christ's mission. — EDS.

[3] The Santa Cruzan is a beauty pageant held in many parts of the Philippines during the month of May. The queens in the pageants represent various Biblical queens, such as Esther and the Queen of Sheba, who performed heroic acts for their people. — EDS.

[4] A beauty pageant held in many cities in the United States whose winners are crowned Miss Filipino America. — EDS.

EXPLORING THE TEXT

1. How do you think the speaker of "To Be Walang Hiya" feels about the phrase and how its various meanings might apply to her? What does this title imply about social expectations for Filipino women?
2. How do the poem's images create a picture of the speaker? How do her various denials help shape her persona?
3. What do you think the speaker's attitude toward the "Santacruzan queen" (l. 4) is? How do you know? Why might the speaker have said she was "never a singkil princess" (l. 2)? What is the cumulative effect of the references to queens, princesses, and pageants?
4. The italicized lines all begin with "I was never." What qualities do the non-italicized lines have in common? How is their tone different from the rest of the poem? What language choices create that difference?
5. It is possible to read the poem two different ways — you can either read the lines in sequential order or read the left column before the right. How does the meaning change when the poem is read each way? What is the effect of the way the lines are broken up?

Art & Craft

ROBIN COSTE LEWIS

Robin Coste Lewis is an American poet born in Compton, California, with familial roots in New Orleans. She earned an MFA from New York University and a master's degree in Sanskrit and comparative religious literature from Harvard Divinity School. Her first book of poetry, *Voyage of the Sable Venus* (2015), which won the National Book Award, focuses on the history of race and Western art. Lewis has taught at Wheaton College, Hunter College, Hampshire College, and the New York University Low-Residency MFA in Paris. In her sonnet "Art & Craft," Lewis deftly portrays the compromises the speaker had to make as an adolescent in order to blend in at school.

I would figure out all the right answers
first, then gently mark a few of them wrong.
If a quiz had ten problems, I'd cancel
out one. When it had twenty, I'd bite my tongue

then leave at least two questions blank: __________ __________
A *B* was good, but an *A* was too good.
They'd kick your ass, call your big sister
slow, then stare over your desk, as if you'd

snaked out of a different hole. Knowing
taught me — quickly — to spell *community*
more honestly: *l-o-n-e-l-y*.
During Arts and Crafts, when Miss Larson allowed

the scissors out, I'd sneak a pair, then cut
my hair to stop me from growing too long.

[2015]

EXPLORING THE TEXT

1. Why do you think the poem is called "Art & Craft"? How is the title different from (or the same as) the Arts and Crafts session the speaker describes in line 12?
2. What is the effect of the two blanks that appear at the end of line 5? What words do these blanks evoke?
3. How would you characterize the speaker of "Art & Craft"? How does the poem reveal both her interior and exterior qualities?
4. This poem has 14 lines and could be considered a sonnet. What other qualities of the sonnet do you detect here? Consider the ways the poem plays with rhyme scheme, as well as the turn the last two lines take.
5. What do you think the speaker means when she says she would "cut / my hair to stop me from growing too long" (ll. 13–14)? How does that statement relate to the argument the poem makes?
6. "Art & Craft" is a poem from Robin Coste Lewis's National Book Award-winning collection, *Voyage of the Sable Venus*. The collection begins and ends with several lyric, often biographical, poems such as "Art & Craft" that, according to the National Book Foundation's website, consider "the roles desire and race play in the construction of self." How does this poem make those connections? The center of the book is a narrative made of the titles of artworks that are in some way connected to the black female figure in Western art. How might "Art & Craft," one of the lyric poems outside of the book's center, comment on the connection between art and self?

Ghazal for White Hen Pantry

JAMILA WOODS

Jamila Woods is an American poet, vocalist, and songwriter based in Chicago. She has a BA in Africana studies and theatre and performance studies from Brown University. As a musician, Woods is known for bringing choral layering to the hip-hip traditions of sampling and allusions. Her work with her band M&O has been featured by *OkayPlayer*, *SPIN*, *JET*, and *Ebony*. Woods is the author of a chapbook, *The Truth about Dolls* (2012), and her poetry has been featured in the anthologies *The Uncommon Core: Contemporary Poems for Learning & Living* (2013), *Courage: Daring Poems for Gutsy Girls* (2014), and *The Breakbeat Poets: New American Poetry in the Age of Hip-Hop* (2015). Woods currently works as the associate artistic director of Young Chicago Authors, a nonprofit organization behind the Louder Than a Bomb youth poetry slam festival. In "Ghazal for White Hen Pantry," Woods explores the struggle of an African American teenager trying to assert herself in a world still marred by racism. The ghazal, a form that originated in Arabic poetry, consists of rhyming couplets and a refrain. The second line of each couplet typically ends with the same word, and the penultimate words in the second line of each couplet also rhyme with each other.

beverly be the only south side you don't fit in
everybody in your neighborhood color of white hen

brown bag tupperware lunch don't fill you
after school cross the street, count quarters with white friends

you love 25¢ zebra cakes mom would never let you eat
you learn to white lie through white teeth at white hen

oreos in your palm, perm in your hair
everyone's irish in beverly, you just missin' the white skin

pray they don't notice your burnt toast, unwondered bread
you be the brownest egg ever born from the white hen

pantry in your chest where you stuff all the Black in
distract from the syllables in your name with a white grin

keep your consonants crisp, coffee milked, hands visible
never touch the holiday-painted windows of white hen

you made that mistake, scratched your initials in the paint
an unmarked crown victoria pulled up, full of white men

they grabbed your wrist & wouldn't show you a badge
the manager clucked behind the counter, thick as a white hen

they told your friends to run home, but called the principal on you
& you learned Black sins cost much more than white ones

[2015]

EXPLORING THE TEXT

1. Consider the word "you," which is repeated several times throughout the poem. Who do you think the "you" is? Explain your answer. Characterize the "you." What do we know about her?
2. What do you think the speaker means by "keep your consonants crisp, coffee milked, hands visible" (l. 13)? What do those actions represent or evoke?
3. White Hen Pantry is a now-defunct chain of convenience stores located throughout the Midwest and New England. How does Woods play with the image of the white hen? Look at the literal meaning — where she talks about it as a convenience store — and also look at white hen as an image, such as in lines 2, 10, and 18. How does she connect the two meanings?
4. Why do you think the word "Black" is capitalized in the last line of the poem?
5. A ghazal is an ancient Persian form of the lyric poem that has a fixed number of verses and a repeated rhyme. It is typically on the theme of love and, originally, was often set to music. The rules of the form are quite strict: the second line of every other couplet ends with the same word, and the word before *that* word has to rhyme with the others. In this poem, *hen* — or a rhyme with *hen* — is the last word of every couplet and rather than a rhyme, the word *white* is repeated. Find other ways that Jamila Woods has played with the traditional structure of a ghazal. What effect does this kind of remixing have on your understanding of the poem? Why do you think Woods broke some of the rules of the form? Do you think it's important to know these rules to understand the poem's meaning? Explain.
6. How does this poem comment on conformity and rebellion? What do the speaker's small acts of rebellion suggest about her attitude toward the expectations of others? How does the poet use language to express that attitude?

PAIRED POEMS

An Epitaph

MATTHEW PRIOR

English poet and diplomat Matthew Prior (1664–1721) was born in Wimborne Minster, East Dorset. He earned his BA at St. John's College, Cambridge, in 1686. He served England as under-secretary of state and as commissioner of trade, and became a member of Parliament in 1701. In 1713, he helped negotiate the Treaty of Utrecht, which became known as "Matt's Peace." He also served as ambassador in Paris. After the death of Queen Anne, he returned to England, where he was impeached by the Whigs and imprisoned for two years. He continued to write in confinement, composing his most famous work, *Alma; or, The Progress of the Mind* (1718). He is buried in Poets' Corner in Westminster Abbey. Today, Prior is remembered chiefly for his satires, of which "An Epitaph" is a prime example.

Interred beneath this marble stone
Lie sauntering Jack and idle Joan.
While rolling threescore years and one
Did round this globe their courses run;
If human things went ill or well;
If changing empires rose or fell;
The morning passed, the evening came,
And found this couple still the same.
They walked and ate, good folks: what then?
Why then they walked and ate again.
They soundly slept the night away;
They did just nothing all the day;
And having buried children four,
Would not take pains to try for more.
Nor sister either had, nor brother:
They seemed just tallied for each other.
    Their moral and economy
Most perfectly they made agree:
Each virtue kept its proper bound,
Nor trespassed on the other's ground.
Nor fame, nor censure they regarded:
They neither punished, nor rewarded.
He cared not what the footmen did;
Her maids she neither praised, nor chid:
So every servant took his course;
And bad at first, they all grew worse.
Slothful disorder filled his stable,
And sluttish plenty decked her table.
Their beer was strong; their wine was port;
Their meal was large; their grace was short.
They gave the poor the remnant-meat
Just when it grew not fit to eat.
    They paid the church and parish rate,[1]
And took, but read not the receipt;
For which they claimed their Sunday's due
Of slumbering in an upper pew.
    No man's defects sought they to know,
So never made themselves a foe.
No man's good deeds did they commend,
So never raised themselves a friend.
Nor cherished they relations poor:
That might decrease their present store;
Nor barn nor house did they repair:
That might oblige their future heir.
    They neither added, nor confounded;
They neither wanted, nor abounded.
Each Christmas they accompts did clear;
And wound their bottom[2] round the year.

[1] Church rate refers to tithing; parish rate, to taxes. — EDS.

[2] A ball of thread or yarn is sometimes called a *bottom*, here meaning they wrapped their affairs up tidily. — EDS.

Nor tear nor smile did they employ
At news of public grief or joy.
When bells were rung and bonfires made,
If asked, they ne'er denied their aid;
Their jug was to the ringers carried,
Whoever either died, or married.
Their billet[3] at the fire was found,
Whoever was deposed, or crowned.
Nor good, nor bad, nor fools, nor wise;
They would not learn, nor could advise;
Without love, hatred, joy, or fear,
They led — a kind of — as it were;
Nor wished, nor cared, nor laughed, nor cried;
And so they lived; and so they died.

[1718]

[3] Firewood. — Eds.

EXPLORING THE TEXT

1. How are Jack and Joan characterized in the poem? What is meant by the couplet, "Their moral and economy / Most perfectly they made agree" (ll. 17–18)? What are the effects of their mildness toward others and their conformity as expressed in lines 19–32?
2. Consider the different meanings of the word "grace" in line 30. Where else in the poem are wealth or plenty placed at odds with spirituality?
3. Line 60 says, "They led — a kind of — as it were." How might this line serve as a fitting summary of the poem? Explain.
4. What might have improved the lives of Jack and Joan?
5. "An Epitaph" is composed entirely of rhyming couplets with a steady rhythm. How does this form reinforce the themes of the poem?
6. This poem was written in part to satirize the landed gentry in early eighteenth-century England, as well as the conservative elected officials who supported them. How do you think the poem relates to the present day? If you were to imagine a contemporary Jack and Joan, how would you describe them?

The Unknown Citizen

W. H. AUDEN

Born in northern England to a doctor and a nurse, Wystan Hugh Auden (1907–1973) earned a scholarship to Oxford to study engineering. While there, he became interested in poetry — especially the modernist poetry of T. S. Eliot — and studied English instead. He was part of a group of poets known as the Oxford Group (and later, the Auden Generation), which included Stephen Spender and Louis MacNeice. During the 1930s, Auden traveled to Spain and China; became involved in political causes; and wrote prose, poetry, and plays. In 1939, Auden left England and became a United States citizen. *Another Time* (1940), the first book he wrote in America, contains some of his most famous poems, including "Musée des Beaux Arts" and "The Unknown Citizen." He won a Pulitzer Prize for *The Age of Anxiety* (1947) and a National Book Award for *The Shield of Achilles* (1955).

(To JS/07 M 378
This Marble Monument
Is Erected by the State)

He was found by the Bureau of Statistics to be
One against whom there was no official complaint,

And all the reports on his conduct agree
That, in the modern sense of an old-fashioned word, he was a saint,
For in everything he did he served the Greater Community.
Except for the War till the day he retired,
He worked in a factory and never got fired,
But satisfied his employers, Fudge Motors Inc.
Yet he wasn't a scab or odd in his views.
For his Union reports that he paid his dues,
(Our report on his Union shows it was sound)
And our Social Psychology workers found
That he was popular with his mates and liked a drink.
The Press are convinced that he bought a paper every day
And that his reactions to advertisements were normal in every way.
Policies taken out in his name prove that he was fully insured,
And his Health-card shows he was once in a hospital but left it cured.
Both Producers Research and High-Grade Living declare
He was fully sensible to the advantages of the Instalment Plan
And had everything necessary to the Modern Man,
A phonograph, a radio, a car and a frigidaire.
Our researchers into Public Opinion are content
That he held the proper opinions for the time of year;
When there was peace, he was for peace: when there was war, he went.
He was married and added five children to the population,
Which our Eugenist says was the right number for a parent of his generation.
And our teachers report that he never interfered with their education.
Was he free? Was he happy? The question is absurd:
Had anything been wrong, we should certainly have heard.

[1940]

EXPLORING THE TEXT

1. How do you interpret the modern definition of "sainthood" offered in line 4? How does the modern sense differ from the old-fashioned one?
2. Reread the poem, looking specifically for adjectives related to value judgments (i.e., good/bad, beautiful/ugly). How would you characterize the values Auden describes? What is missing from them?
3. What is suggested by the words "our" in lines 11, 12, 22, 26, and 27, and "we" in the final line of the poem?
4. Note the list of possessions given in line 21: "A phonograph, a radio, a car and a frigidaire." What would that list consist of if the poem were written today?
5. Note that some of the lines of the poem run on as if they're out of control; they seem too long. Why might the poet have chosen to write this way?
6. Do you find the poem humorous? Which is the most comical line? Which is the most ironic? Why?
7. What is Auden satirizing in this poem?

FOCUS ON COMPARISON AND CONTRAST

1. Compare and contrast the characters of Jack and Joan with the unknown citizen. What qualities do they share? What makes them different?
2. What is Matthew Prior's attitude toward conformity and rebellion? What is W. H. Auden's? Which attitude more nearly resembles your own? Support your position with textual evidence.
3. Prior's poem was written about three hundred years ago; Auden's, about seventy-five. While each speaks to its own time, they both seem highly relevant today. Which one feels more contemporary in style? Which one feels more current in content? Explain.

WRITING ASSIGNMENT

Write an essay that compares how Prior and Auden create mock elegies and epitaphs to satirize their subjects. As you write your essay, consider how each writer uses elements of style to achieve his purpose.

Penelope

CAROL ANN DUFFY

The first woman to be named Britain's poet laureate, Carol Ann Duffy was born to Irish Catholic parents in Glasgow, Scotland, in 1955. She grew up in England, earning a degree in philosophy in 1977, and published her first collection of poetry in 1985. *Mean Time* won the Whitbread Poetry Award in 1993, and *Rapture* won the T. S. Eliot Prize in 2005. Duffy has also edited many anthologies and written books for children, including *The Oldest Girl in the World* (2000), *The Hat* (2007), and *The Christmas Truce* (2011). Her work continues to be very popular; in fact, in 2005 the *Guardian* called her "the most popular living poet in Britain." She is currently the creative director of the Writing School at Manchester Metropolitan University. "Penelope" is from *The World's Wife*, Duffy's 1999 collection based on stories from history and mythology but written in the voice of women whose roles have been historically overshadowed by men. Penelope is Odysseus's wife in Homer's *Odyssey*. Penelope, who waited for twenty years for Odysseus to return from the Trojan War, famously kept her suitors at bay by promising to marry one when she had finished weaving a tapestry for her stepfather — but each night she unwove her work so that she never appeared to make progress.

At first, I looked along the road
hoping to see him saunter home
among the olive trees,
a whistle for the dog
who mourned him with his warm head on my knees.
Six months of this
and then I noticed that whole days had passed
without my noticing.
I sorted cloth and scissors, needle, thread,

thinking to amuse myself,
but found a lifetime's industry instead.
I sewed a girl
under a single star — cross-stitch, silver silk —
running after childhood's bouncing ball.
I chose between three greens for the grass;
a smoky pink, a shadow's grey
to show a snapdragon gargling a bee.
I threaded walnut brown for a tree,

my thimble like an acorn
pushing up through umber soil.
Beneath the shade
I wrapped a maiden in a deep embrace
with heroism's boy
and lost myself completely
in a wild embroidery of love, lust, loss, lessons learnt;
then watched him sail away
into the loose gold stitching of the sun.

And when the others came to take his place,
disturb my peace,
I played for time.
I wore a widow's face, kept my head down,
did my work by day, at night unpicked it.
I knew which hour of the dark the moon
would start to fray,
I stitched it.
Grey threads and brown

pursued my needle's leaping fish
to form a river that would never reach the sea.
I tricked it. I was picking out
the smile of a woman at the centre
of this world, self-contained, absorbed, content,
most certainly not waiting,
when I heard a far-too-late familiar tread outside the door.
I licked my scarlet thread
and aimed it surely at the middle of the needle's eye once more.

[1999]

EXPLORING THE TEXT

1. How does the speaker of the poem characterize herself in the first stanza? How is her missing husband, Odysseus, characterized?
2. What changes in the speaker's attitude in the second stanza?
3. How does figurative language contribute to the poem's meaning? Consider the effects of the simile that begins on line 19 and the metaphor developed in lines 21–27. How literal or figurative is her "embroidery"? Is she depicting the world she's living in? Is she creating a fictional world in which to live? Is she affecting the world itself? Explain with specific reference to the text.
4. Stanza 4 presents the suitors and Penelope's trick. How dependent on a reading of Homer's *Odyssey* is your understanding of this part of the poem? How dependent is the poem as a whole on that knowledge? If you are familiar with *The Odyssey*, how does this poem comment on and inform your reading of it?
5. Why is the "familiar tread" "far-too-late" (l. 43)?

The Wife of the Man of Many Wiles

A. E. STALLINGS

Born and raised in Decatur, Georgia, A. E. Stallings (b. 1968) is a MacArthur Fellowship-winning American poet and translator. Stallings is the author of three books of poetry, *Archaic Smile* (1999), *Hapax* (2006), and *Olives* (2012). She has also published *The Nature of Things* (2007), a verse translation of a work by the Roman poet and philosopher Lucretius. In 2011, she won a Guggenheim Fellowship and a MacArthur Foundation Fellowship. She currently lives and teaches in Athens, Greece, and she is a frequent contributor of both poetry and criticism to *Poetry* magazine. Stallings's poetry is known for its use of traditional meter and rhyme, and figures and ideas from classical mythology often figure prominently in her writing. In "The Wife of the Man of Many Wiles," Stallings brings to life the voice of Penelope, wife of the famously clever Odysseus, often identified in Homer's *Iliad* and *Odyssey* as "the man of many wiles."

Believe what you want to. Believe that I wove,
If you wish, twenty years, and waited, while you
Were knee-deep in blood, hip-deep in goddesses.

I've not much to show for twenty years' weaving —
I have but one half-finished cloth at the loom.
Perhaps it's the lengthy, meticulous grieving.

Explain how you want to. Believe I unravelled
At night what I stitched in the slow siesta,
How I kept them all waiting for me to finish,

The suitors, you call them. Believe what you want to.
Believe that they waited for me to finish,
Believe I beguiled them with nightly un-doings.

Believe what you want to. That they never touched me.
Believe your own stories, as you would have me do,
How you only survived by the wise infidelities.

Believe that each day you wrote me a letter
That never arrived. Kill all the damn suitors
If you think it will make you feel better.

[1999]

EXPLORING THE TEXT

1. How does the speaker characterize herself? How does that characterization differ from the way Penelope is typically described?
2. What is the effect of the repetition of the word "Believe"? Why do you think A. E. Stallings chose to begin five lines of the poem with it? How does it help develop the character of the speaker?
3. What liberties has Stallings taken to make the speaker — Penelope — sound like a contemporary woman? How does that help the poem make an argument?
4. Why do you think the title of the poem is "The Wife of the Man of Many Wiles"? Why do you think Stallings chose not to call it "Penelope," or even to mention the names Penelope or Odysseus anywhere in the poem?

FOCUS ON COMPARISON AND CONTRAST

1. Compare the tone of "Penelope" to that of "The Wife of the Man of Many Wiles." What are the similarities? What are the differences?
2. Both poems are told from the point of view of Penelope, the long-waiting wife of Odysseus. In what ways are the points of view the same? In what ways are they different?
3. Both poems also provide a glimpse of Odysseus. What do we learn about him in each poem? What do the two characterizations have in common?

WRITING ASSIGNMENT

Write an essay that compares and contrasts the ways that Carol Ann Duffy and A. E. Stallings use the ancient story of Penelope from *The Odyssey* to comment on relationships between husbands and wives.

TONE

When we read sophisticated, challenging literature, perhaps the most elusive feature of the work is tone — defined as the attitude of the speaker toward his or her subject. In conversation, we communicate tone by varying our inflections, raising or lowering our volume and pitch, emphasizing certain words and phrases, and using gestures and facial expressions. Think of a phrase as simple as "Well, thanks," and imagine how the tone could vary from enthusiastic to sincere to surprised to sarcastic. Or consider this response to a marriage proposal: "You're asking me to marry you?" The speaker might be replying in a tone of outraged disbelief or one of unalloyed joy. The tone in these examples would be made clear by the sound of the person's voice and his or her physical cues. Writers, however, must create and convey tone solely through words appearing on a printed page — or a computer screen — where readers need to "hear" the speaker's voice. When we read to ourselves, we need to internalize the sound of the text, listening with our "inner ear," as it were. We may ask, is the voice serious, ironic, facetious, or somber? Does it encourage, complain, admonish, or exhort? When we hear the text correctly — that is, when we pick up on the implied attitude — we are recognizing the tone.

Tone, then, is produced by details and descriptions; diction, especially the connotations of the words chosen; the arrangement of the words, including syntax or sounds resulting through juxtaposition or meter; imagery and figurative language; overall structure, whether in sentences or stanzas; and especially context. In other words, to determine the tone of a poem or prose passage, readers have to pay attention to all the choices a writer makes.

Author versus Speaker

When thinking about tone, it's important to remember that in literature, the speaker, whether a narrator or specific character, is not necessarily the author. Often an author will speak through a **persona**, or "mask," which is the voice and viewpoint an author adopts to deliver a story or poem. In other instances, the author might speak through a character. If you have read Jonathan Swift's essay "A Modest Proposal," for example, or watched clips from *The Colbert Report*, you know that there is a difference between author and speaker, person and persona.

In drama, where there is little or no third-person narration and exposition, it is through tone that an author gives us insight into the characters' thoughts and feelings. Listen to Hamlet as he reflects on the quickness with which his mother remarried after his father's death:

> O, most wicked speed, to post / With such dexterity to incestuous sheets! (I.ii.156–57)

Listen closely to the *sound* of the language Shakespeare wrote for his character, Hamlet. The *s* sounds spit the venomous words out. The reader knows right away the poison and bitterness with which Hamlet, not Shakespeare, is filled; thus has Shakespeare prepared the reader for Hamlet's future language and behavior.

Style and Tone

Whether you are reading poetry or prose, the small choices in diction, imagery, figurative language, and syntax are the most important guides to understanding the work's tone and, ultimately, to interpreting the work's meaning. Let's look at an excerpt from "Her Kind" by Anne Sexton. The poem begins:

> I have gone out, a possessed witch,
> haunting the black air, braver at night;
> dreaming evil, I have done my hitch
> over the plain houses, light by light:
> lonely thing, twelve-fingered, out of mind.
> A woman like that is not a woman, quite.
> I have been her kind.

The first thing that we might determine when thinking about tone is whether it is positive or negative; from there, we can fine-tune our reading. For instance, if we read through this poem quickly, we might think that the tone is positive: the speaker is reveling in being a witch. After all, what would make a witch happier than flying high above the plain (boring) houses on her broom at night, feeling brave, and "dreaming evil"? We could say that the tone is not only positive but also exultant and empowered. But why, then, is she called a "lonely thing" in line 5? This line simply doesn't fit with a positive interpretation. Like a good juror, a good reader does not ignore evidence. Let's look more carefully to arrive at a fuller understanding of the tone of this poem.

Do other choices in the poem reinforce the idea that it carries a lonesome tone? What do these choices add to it? In line 2, the witch admits that she's "braver at night." The use of the comparative "braver" makes us wonder why she isn't as brave during the day, when the world is awake and people are out and about. Perhaps it's because she is "twelve-fingered"? Whether we take this description literally or figuratively, it tells us that this witch is not a rebel but an outcast. Now the "plain houses" that she passes over become symbols of a normal life that is denied her. The tone has become not just one of loneliness but one of bitter longing for what's below: the life of a woman, not that of a witch. As you can see, an investigation into the tone of a poem can very quickly lead to an interpretation of the entire piece.

Shifts in Tone

Tone is rarely consistent throughout a work of literature. Authors may use shifts in tone to add another layer of meaning to a literary text. In Chapters 3 and 4, we discussed "turns," or places in a poem or passage that shift or change. These pivot points are frequently the heart of the interpretive matter, and very often what is shifting is the tone. Let's look at an example from "Song: To the Men of England" by Percy Bysshe Shelley. The poem begins:

> Men of England, wherefore plough
> For the lords who lay ye low?
> Wherefore weave with toil and care
> The rich robes your tyrants wear?

In these lines, the pleading, urging tone of the speaker's rhetorical questions is designed to enjoin his readers to action. The first six quatrains of the poem continue to speak in the encouraging, hortatory tone established in the first stanza, as the speaker pleads with his readers to change their lives; then the tone shifts for the final two stanzas, becoming admonitory and ironic, as if scolding any reader who is resigned, frustrated, and dismissive of his call to action. Note the shift from stanza 6 to stanzas 7 and 8:

> Sow seed — but let no tyrant reap;
> Find wealth — let no impostor heap;
> Weave robes — let not the idle wear;
> Forge arms — in your defence to bear.
>
> Shrink to your cellars, holes, and cells —
> In halls ye deck another dwells.
> Why shake the chains ye wrought? Ye see
> The steel ye tempered glance on ye.
>
> With plough and spade and hoe and loom
> Trace your grave and build your tomb
> And weave your winding-sheet — till fair
> England be your Sepulchre.

Tone in Fiction

In addition to using tone to convey their meaning, authors of fiction and other narratives use tone to subtly develop settings, characters, and even themes. Let's take a look at a passage from Karen Russell's contemporary short story "The Prospectors":

> Every night Mrs. Finisterre hosted a cocktail
> hour: cubing green and orange melon,

> cranking songs out of the ivory gramophone, pouring bright malice into the fruit punch in the form of a mentally deranging Portuguese rum. She's apprenticed her three beautiful daughters in the Light Arts, the Party Arts. Clara was her eldest. Together, the Finisterre women soothed arguments and linens. They concocted banter, gab, palaver, patter — every sugary variety of small talk that dissolves into the night. I hated the cocktail hour, and whenever I could, I escaped to beat rugs and sweep leaves on the hotel roof. One Monday, however, I heard footsteps ringing on the ladder. It was Clara. She saw me and froze. (para. 20)

Both the imagery and the diction are the keys to understanding the tone of the passage. The passage begins by setting the scene of a lively cocktail hour with music and bright-colored snacks. But don't miss the way Mrs. Finisterre pours "malice" rather than rum into the punch, or its "mentally deranging" effect. Mrs. Finisterre has "apprenticed" her daughters, whose work it is to keep the party going with "banter, gab, palaver, patter — every sugary variety of small talk." These words for conversation underscore the superficiality, even con game, aspect of the party. When Aubby, the narrator, says she hated the cocktail hour, and will in the next few paragraphs discover that Clara has been badly beaten, we are not surprised. We've felt the sinister undertone in the passage. It is the cocktail hour and the suggestion of enslavement, evil, and falseness, that help make Clara and Aubby's flight to the far west believable.

Words That Describe Tone

There are nearly endless ways to describe tone. You'll often need more than one word — perhaps an adverb and adjective combination (*bitterly angry, humorously proud*) or a contrasting pair (*admiring yet envious, distant but loving*). Following is a list of words that provides a good place to start. Each of these adjectives is useful for describing tones that you will encounter in literature. After looking up any that you don't know, separate them into two categories, one positive and one negative. Choose one of the stories from this chapter, and apply two of the words from the list to each of the main characters and three of the words to the narrator. Add to this list as you continue to read literature and respond to tone.

solemn	sad	generous	somber	grave
didactic	audacious	mocking	dispassionate	resigned
acidulous	bitter	dreamy	pedantic	reflective
earnest	caustic	pitiful	elevated	lofty
candid	nostalgic	wistful	questioning	colloquial
detached	sentimental	apologetic	objective	lugubrious
restrained	enthusiastic	urbane	facetious	ambivalent
melancholy	sarcastic	playful	apprehensive	elegiac
acerbic	bitter	aloof	irreverent	sardonic
indignant	argumentative	scornful	pensive	incredulous
insistent	self-deprecating	familiar	maudlin	diffident
disinterested	condescending	sanguine	bemused	ecstatic
speculative	laudatory	strident	grim	mournful
contentious	cynical	self-assured	forthright	admonitory
contemptuous	urgent	poignant	zealous	giddy
querulous	polemical	insipid	stolid	callow

The following exercises will help you discern tone and understand how it contributes to meaning.

EXERCISE 1

The tone of "The Day Lady Died" by Frank O'Hara can be characterized as casual and confiding. We might even say that it overshares — at least until the last stanza. The speaker has seen in the newspaper that Billie Holiday — the "Lady" of the title — has died. The tone changes drastically when the speaker remembers seeing Holiday perform. Perform the poem in a way that conveys your interpretation of its tone, being sure to change your tone as the tone of the poem changes.

EXERCISE 2

For each of the following passages identify the tone or tones, explain how the text delivers the tone(s), and explain how tone contributes to meaning.

1. KING: 'Tis sweet and commendable in your nature, Hamlet,
To give these mourning duties to your father:
But, you must know, your father lost a father;
That father lost, lost his, and the survivor bound
In filial obligation for some term
To do obsequious sorrow: but to persever
In obstinate condolement is a course
Of impious stubbornness; 'tis unmanly grief;
It shows a will most incorrect to heaven,
A heart unfortified, a mind impatient,
An understanding simple and unschool'd:
For what we know must be and is as common
As any the most vulgar thing to sense,
Why should we in our peevish opposition
Take it to heart? Fie! 'tis a fault to heaven,
A fault against the dead, a fault to nature,
To reason most absurd; whose common theme
Is death of fathers, and who still hath cried,
From the first corse till he that died to-day,
"This must be so." We pray you, throw to earth
This unprevailing woe, and think of us
As of a father. (William Shakespeare, *Hamlet*, I.ii.87–108)

2. OPHELIA: O, what a noble mind is here o'er-thrown!
The courtier's, soldier's, scholar's, eye, tongue, sword;
Th' expectancy and rose of the fair state,
The glass of fashion and the mould of form,
Th' observ'd of all observers, quite, quite, down!
And I, of ladies most deject and wretched,
That suck'd the honey of his music vows,
Now see that noble and most sovereign reason

Like sweet bells jangled, out of time and harsh;
That unmatch'd form and feature of blown youth
Blasted with ecstasy: O, woe is me,
T' have seen what I have seen, see what I see! (William Shakespeare, *Hamlet,* III.i. 162–73)

3. I had always thought that my father's only ordeal was that he'd left his country and moved to a place where everything from the climate to the language was so unlike his own, a place where he never quite seemed to fit in, never appeared to belong. The only thing I can grasp now, as I drive way beyond the speed limit down yet another highway, is why the unfamiliar might have been so comforting, rather than distressing, to my father. And why he has never wanted the person he was, is, permanently documented in any way. He taught himself to appreciate the enormous weight of permanent markers by learning about the Ancient Egyptians. He had gotten to know them, through their crypts and monuments, in a way that he wanted no one to know him, no one except my mother and me, we, who are now his kas, his good angels, his masks against his own face. (Edwidge Danticat, "The Book of the Dead," para. 214)

4. Somehow, of late, I had got into the way of involuntarily using this word "prefer" upon all sorts of not exactly suitable occasions. And I trembled to think that my contact with the scrivener had already and seriously affected me in a mental way. And what further and deeper aberration might it not yet produce? This apprehension had not been without efficacy in determining me to summary measures. (Herman Melville, "Bartleby the Scrivener," para.117)

5. Something was descending slowly, like a heavy theatre curtain, inside my body; I felt my will to know the truth ebbing into a happy, warm insanity. We could all be dead — why not? We could be in love, me and a dead boy. We could be sisters here, Clara and I, equally poor and equally beautiful. (Karen Russell, "The Prospectors," para. 164)

6. Now Joe knew his wife had passed that way. He knew that the men lounging in the general store had seen her, moreover, he knew that the men knew *he* knew. He stood there silent for a long moment staring blankly, with his Adam's apple twitching nervously up and down his throat. One could actually *see* the pain he was suffering, his eyes, his face, his hands, and even the dejected slump of his shoulders. He set the bottle down upon the counter. He didn't bang it, jus teased it out of his hand silently and fiddled with his suspender buckle. (Zora Neale Hurston, "Spunk" para. 13)

7. Believe what you want to. That they never touched me.
Believe your own stories, as you would have me do,
How you only survived by the wise infidelities.

Believe that each day you wrote me a letter
That never arrived. Kill all the damn suitors
If you think it will make you feel better. (A. E. Stallings, "The Wife of the Man of Many Wiles," ll. 16–21)

8. Who cares what it's all about?
I do! Edgar Allan Poe cares! Shelley cares! Beethoven & Dylan care.
Do you care? What are you about
or are you a human being with 10 fingers and two eyes? (Allen Ginsberg, "Is About," ll. 21–24)

EXERCISE 3

In the following soliloquy (I.v.98–108), Hamlet's tone shifts dramatically, whether because he is mad or feigning madness. Identify the tone, where it shifts, and how the shift in tone affects the meaning of the soliloquy.

> Yea, from the table of my memory
> I'll wipe away all trivial fond records,
> All saws of books, all forms, all pressures past,
> That youth and observation copied there;
> And thy commandment all alone shall live
> Within the book and volume of my brain,
> Unmix'd with baser matter; yes, by heaven!
> O most pernicious woman!
> O villain, villain, smiling, damned villain!
> My tables, — meet it is I set it down,
> That one may smile, and smile, and be a villain.

EXERCISE 4

Having read Edwidge Danticat's "Book of the Dead," look back at the first 24 paragraphs. Describe the tone of the passage and explain how Danticat creates that tone. Consider the way the tone provides information that will be important to the rest of the story. Where does it create mystery? Where does it offer clues?

EXERCISE 5

Write a poem or passage expressing your viewpoint on conformity and rebellion that either expresses a specific tone or shifts between or among tones. Discuss the resources of language you used to develop that tone or tonal shifts.

EXERCISE 6

Choose a poem or a passage from a story in this chapter and through the use of diction, syntax, and other features of writing that we have discussed, change the tone of the poem or passage you select, rewriting it as a parody of the original. You might take a serious poem or passage and make it facetious, change an ironic one so that its attitude is earnest, make a critical piece laudatory or an impassioned one objective — whichever is appropriate for your text.

CONFORMITY AND REBELLION

1. Thinking about the overall theme of this chapter, we may ask: Why do we conform? Certainly, we sometimes conform because of timidity, reluctance, ambition, or simply ease; but then there are times when we conform out of a sense of duty or responsibility, in the spirit of cooperation, or with a sense of sacrifice. Consider these ideas as they run through the selections in the chapter, and develop a thesis regarding the nature of conformity. Refer specifically to the texts of several of the chapter's selections to support your essay.
2. "What is a rebel? According to Albert Camus, it's "A man who says 'no.'" Among those who say "no" in this chapter are Melville's Bartleby; Hurston's Joe Kanty; the speakers in the poems by Percy Bysshe Shelley, Dylan Thomas, Barbara Jane Reyes, and Robin Coste Lewis; and, of course, Hamlet. What is the significance of Camus's question and answer? Consider how at least two of the characters or speakers in the chapter say "no," and write an essay in which you compare and contrast their rebellious actions or words, and draw conclusions about the consequences of their rebellion.
3. African American poet James Branch Cabell has said that "Poetry is man's rebellion against what he is." Consider what Cabell's statement means and how it illustrates a theme that runs through the poetry selections in this chapter. Then write an essay that compares and contrasts the ways the speakers in two poems in this chapter illustrate Cabell's meaning.
4. Identify three selections in the chapter that express a similar theme in terms of conformity and rebellion, or three selections that offer different perspectives. Write an essay that explains how each of the three writers uses different means to express the themes or perspectives that you identify. Consider such features as structure, diction, imagery, figurative language, and tone. Refer to specific passages in each text to support your essay.
5. When confronted with a great challenge, the easier path to take is often the one that conformity proffers. Hamlet expresses the difficulty of accepting such a challenge. At the end of act I, he says, "The time is out of joint: O cursed spite, / That ever I was born to set it right!" (I.v.189–90). Write an essay that compares and contrasts the way three characters in the chapter confront the challenge of "setting things right." Use specific examples from the texts to support your essay.
6. Enjoining his listeners, singer Bob Marley proclaims, "Emancipate yourself from mental slavery / None but ourselves can free our minds." Similarly, the speakers of the poems by Percy Bysshe Shelley, Emily Dickinson, Dylan Thomas, Allen Ginsberg, and A. E. Stallings address the reader directly, stating an imperative. Compare the ways that two of these poems enjoin the reader to action. Refer to the texts of the poems to support your answer. Consider both style and content as you write your essay.
7. In imitation of Carol Duffy or A. E. Stallings, write a poem from the point of view of a secondary character in an epic poem, a novel, or a play. Use that character's point of view to show how he or she might see the main character or the events of the narrative in a different light.
8. Which of the short stories in this chapter did you enjoy most? Read two more stories or a novel by Danticat, Melville, Hurston, or Russell. Then write an essay that discusses the nature of conformity as addressed in the works of your selected author.
9. Write a poem in imitation of Ginsberg's "Is About," using a similar structure but changing each of the names and places that begin the lines. Then answer the question, What is your poem about?

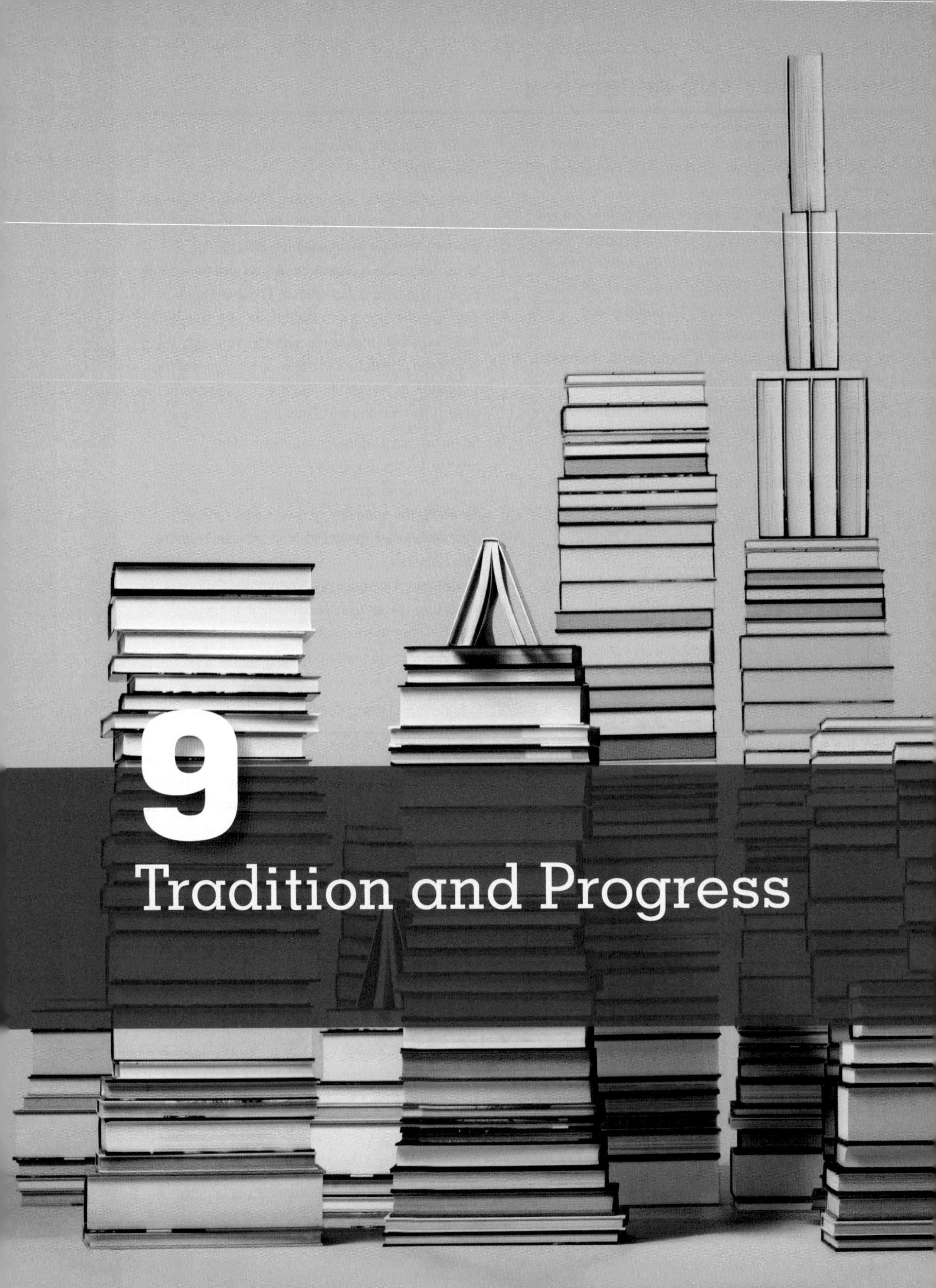

9 Tradition and Progress

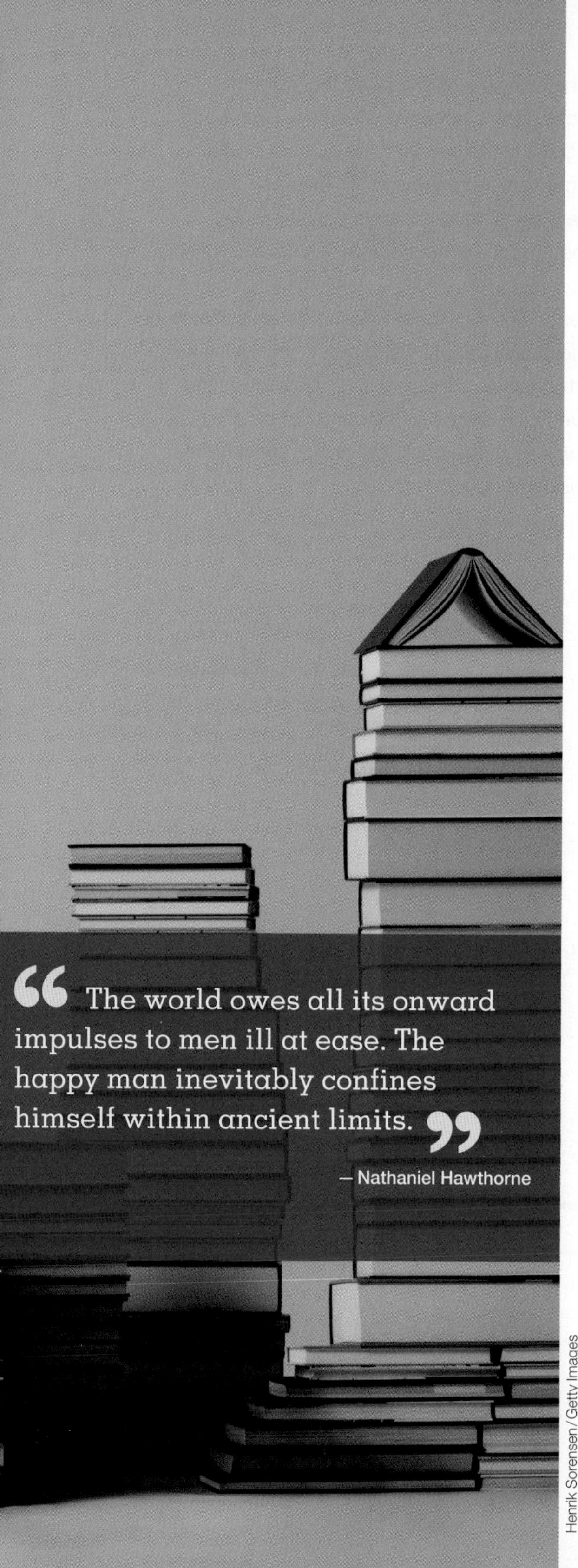

“The world owes all its onward impulses to men ill at ease. The happy man inevitably confines himself within ancient limits.”
— Nathaniel Hawthorne

Henrik Sorensen/Getty Images

There are few arenas in which the war between tradition and progress is as clearly fought as literature, where both the message and the medium — subject and style — take sides. The conflict between respect for traditional values and the human impulse to grow and change has been the subject of fiction and poetry for centuries. Even at first glance, a student of literature can tell the difference between a novel written in the nineteenth century and one written in the twentieth or twenty-first century; between a Shakespearean sonnet and a free-verse poem. In his essay “Tradition and the Individual Talent,” poet T. S. Eliot says, “If the only form of tradition, of handing down, consisted in following the ways of the immediate generation before us in a blind or timid adherence to its successes, ‘tradition’ should positively be discouraged.” The works in this chapter ask how we determine which traditions are worth keeping and which must be jettisoned for the sake of progress, and how the old and the new overlap in the meantime.

The works in this chapter honor both the new and the old. Mary Shelley’s *Frankenstein* could be considered the opening salvo in the contemporary discussion of the effects of modern science and technology, and the Texts in Context in this chapter explore the ethical issues technological process raises in Shelley’s work and beyond. Flannery O’Connor’s portrayal of the grandmother in “A Good Man Is Hard to Find” leaves us wondering if traditional values would have helped against the force of evil embodied in the character called The Misfit. Poems such as

Matthew Arnold's "Dover Beach" remind us that changes wrought by the Industrial Revolution had human costs and consequences, in the same way that May Swenson's "Goodbye, Goldeneye" points a finger at progress in the twentieth century. In "Indian Movie, New Jersey," Chitra Banerjee Divakaruni considers the conflict between the traditions of the country of one's birth and the ways of modern American life, while Richard Blanco's "Mother Country" celebrates America's multifaceted and ever-evolving cultural narrative.

In his 1985 essay "Where Is Our Dover Beach?" critic Roger Rosenblatt asks, "Who in Dover today would describe the world as various and beautiful and new? Yet how is the world less so than it was 134 years ago or a thousand, or the way it will be a thousand years hence, since its variety, beauty and novelty are always in the hands of people? . . . Everything," he says, "depends on how one wishes to live one's life, which still requires . . . constancy . . . and a good deal of courage besides."

A Good Man Is Hard to Find

FLANNERY O'CONNOR

Bridgeman Images

Flannery O'Connor (1925–1964) was born in Savannah, Georgia, and grew up on a farm in Milledgeville, Georgia. At the age of fifteen she lost her father to lupus, the same disease that would ultimately take her life at thirty-nine. In her short life, she would become one of the most acclaimed and widely read fiction writers of the twentieth century. After graduating from the Georgia State College for Women (now Georgia College & State University), she attended the Iowa Writers' Workshop. At twenty-six, after being diagnosed with a terminal form of lupus, O'Connor returned to the Georgia farm where she grew up. Despite her illness, she published three books — the story collection *A Good Man Is Hard to Find* (1955) and the novels *Wise Blood* (1952) and *The Violent Bear It Away* (1960) — before her death in 1964. Her later short stories were published posthumously as *Everything That Rises Must Converge* (1965). Most of O'Connor's stories are set in the American South, and critics often describe her writing as Southern gothic, a genre that adapts the traditional characters of the Deep South to life after the Civil War, with results often described as "grotesque." O'Connor famously questioned why this particular term was used to describe Southern stereotypes, arguing instead for the term "realistic." Her short stories examine the deep racial and religious divisions that exist among cultures generally lumped together as "Southern." The title story from *A Good Man Is Hard to Find* portrays a modern family on holiday and their encounter with The Misfit.

The dragon is by the side of the road, watching those who pass. Beware lest he devour you. We go to the Father of Souls, but it is necessary to pass by the dragon.

— St. Cyril of Jerusalem

The grandmother didn't want to go to Florida. She wanted to visit some of her connections in east Tennessee and she was seizing at every chance to change Bailey's mind. Bailey was the son she lived with, her only boy. He was sitting on the edge of his chair at the table, bent over the orange sports section of the *Journal*. "Now look here, Bailey," she said, "see here, read this," and she stood with one hand on her thin hip and the other rattling the newspaper at his bald head. "Here this fellow that calls himself The Misfit is aloose from the Federal Pen and headed toward Florida and you read here what it says he did to these people. Just you read it. I wouldn't take my children in any direction with a criminal like that aloose in it. I couldn't answer to my conscience if I did."

Bailey didn't look up from his reading so she wheeled around then and faced the children's mother, a young woman in slacks, whose face was as broad and innocent as a cabbage and was tied around with a green head-kerchief that had two points on the top like rabbit's ears. She was sitting on the sofa, feeding the baby his apricots out of a jar. "The children have been to Florida before," the old lady said. "You all ought to take them somewhere else for a change so they would see different parts of the world and be broad. They never have been to east Tennessee."

The children's mother didn't seem to hear her but the eight-year-old boy, John Wesley, a stocky child with glasses, said, "If you don't want to go to Florida, why dontcha stay at home?" He and the little girl, June Star, were reading the funny papers on the floor.

"She wouldn't stay at home to be queen for a day," June Star said without raising her yellow head.

"Yes and what would you do if this fellow, The Misfit, caught you?" the grandmother asked.

"I'd smack his face," John Wesley said.

"She wouldn't stay at home for a million bucks," June Star said. "Afraid she'd miss something. She has to go everywhere we go."

"All right, Miss," the grandmother said. "Just remember that the next time you want me to curl your hair."

June Star said her hair was naturally curly.

The next morning the grandmother was the first one in the car, ready to go. She had her big black valise that looked like the head of a hippopotamus in one corner, and underneath it she was hiding a basket with Pitty Sing, the cat, in it. She didn't intend for the cat to be left alone in the house for three days because he would miss her too much and she was afraid he might brush against one of the gas burners and accidentally asphyxiate himself. Her son, Bailey, didn't like to arrive at a motel with a cat.

She sat in the middle of the back seat with John Wesley and June Star on either side of her. Bailey and the children's mother and the baby sat in front and they left Atlanta at eight forty-five with the mileage on the car at 55890. The grandmother wrote this down because she thought it would be interesting to say how many miles they had been when they got back. It took them twenty minutes to reach the outskirts of the city.

The old lady settled herself comfortably, removing her white cotton gloves and putting them up with her purse on the shelf in front of the back window. The children's mother still had on slacks and still had her head tied up in a green kerchief, but the grandmother had on a navy blue straw sailor hat with a bunch of white violets on the brim and a navy blue dress with a small white dot in the print. Her collars and cuffs were white organdy trimmed with lace and at her neckline she had pinned a purple spray of cloth violets containing a sachet. In case of an accident, anyone seeing her dead on the highway would know at once that she was a lady.

She said she thought it was going to be a good day for driving, neither too hot nor too cold, and she cautioned Bailey that the speed limit was fifty-five miles an hour and that the patrolmen hid themselves behind billboards and small clumps of trees and sped out after you before you had a chance to slow down. She pointed out interesting details of the scenery: Stone Mountain; the blue granite that in some places came up to both sides of the highway; the brilliant red clay banks slightly streaked with purple; and the various crops that made rows of green lace-work on the ground. The trees were full of silver-white sunlight and the meanest of them sparkled. The children were reading comic magazines and their mother had gone back to sleep.

"Let's go through Georgia fast so we won't have to look at it much," John Wesley said.

"If I were a little boy," said the grandmother, "I wouldn't talk about my native state that way. Tennessee has the mountains and Georgia has the hills."

"Tennessee is just a hillbilly dumping ground," John Wesley said, "and Georgia is a lousy state too."

"You said it," June Star said.

"In my time," said the grandmother, folding her thin veined fingers, "children were more respectful of their native states and their parents

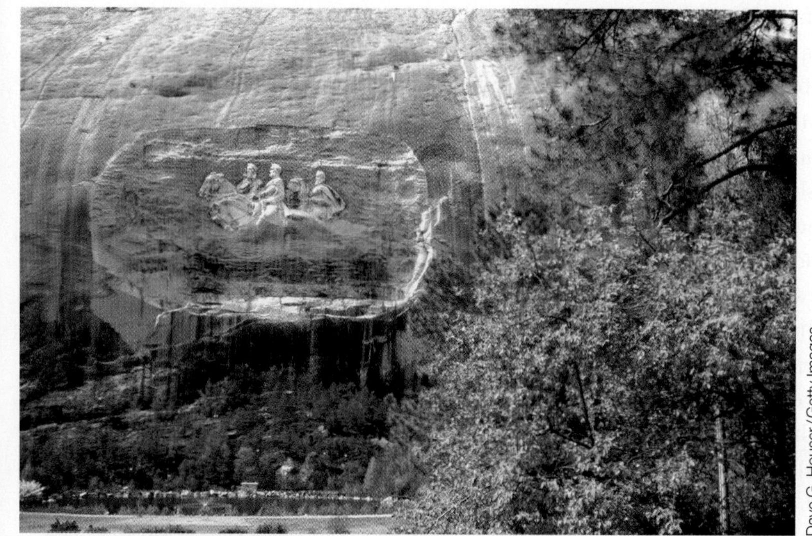

Dave G. Houser / Getty Images

This Confederate memorial rock relief depicting Robert E. Lee, Stonewall Jackson, and Jefferson Davis is carved into Stone Mountain in Atlanta, Georgia. It has long been the site of controversy — the Ku Klux Klan was revived there in 1915. Today, some view it as a celebration of Southern heritage, while others believe it is a reminder of slavery. In the story, the grandmother points out Stone Mountain as an interesting detail of scenery. **What does it suggest about the other characters, and the era in which they live, that no one else comments on it?**

and everything else. People did right then. Oh look at the cute little pickaninny!" she said and pointed to a Negro child standing in the door of a shack. "Wouldn't that make a picture, now?" she asked and they all turned and looked at the little Negro out of the back window. He waved.

"He didn't have any britches on," June Star said.

"He probably didn't have any," the grandmother explained. "Little niggers in the country don't have things like we do. If I could paint, I'd paint that picture," she said.

The children exchanged comic books.

The grandmother offered to hold the baby and the children's mother passed him over the front seat to her. She set him on her knee and bounced him and told him about the things they were passing. She rolled her eyes and screwed up her mouth and stuck her leathery thin face into his smooth bland one. Occasionally he gave her a far-away smile. They passed a large cotton field with five or six graves fenced in the middle of it, like a small island. "Look at the graveyard!" the grandmother said, pointing it out. "That was the old family burying ground. That belonged to the plantation."

"Where's the plantation?" John Wesley asked.

"Gone With the Wind," said the grandmother. "Ha. Ha."

When the children finished all the comic books they had brought, they opened the lunch and ate it. The grandmother ate a peanut butter sandwich and an olive and would not let the children throw the box and the paper napkins out the window. When there was nothing else to do they played a game by choosing a cloud and making the other two guess what shape it suggested. John Wesley took one the shape of a cow and June Star guessed a cow and John Wesley said, no, an automobile, and June Star said he didn't play fair, and they began to slap each other over the grandmother.

The grandmother said she would tell them a story if they would keep quiet. When she told a story, she rolled her eyes and waved her head and was very dramatic. She said once when she was a maiden lady she had been courted by a Mr. Edgar Atkins Teagarden from Jasper, Georgia. She said he was a very good-looking man and a gentleman and that he brought her a watermelon every Saturday afternoon with his initials cut in it, E. A. T. Well, one Saturday, she said, Mr. Teagarden brought the watermelon and there was nobody at home and he left it on the front porch and returned in his buggy to Jasper, but she never got the watermelon, she said, because a nigger boy ate it when he saw the initials, E. A. T.! This story tickled John Wesley's funny bone and he giggled and giggled but June Star didn't think it was any good. She said she wouldn't marry a man that just brought her a watermelon on Saturday. The grandmother said she would have done well to marry Mr. Teagarden because he was a gentleman and had bought Coca-Cola stock when it first came out and that he had died only a few years ago, a very wealthy man.

They stopped at The Tower for barbecued sandwiches. The Tower was a part stucco and part wood filling station and dance hall set in a clearing outside of Timothy. A fat man named Red Sammy Butts ran it and there were signs stuck here and there on the building and for miles up and down the highway saying, TRY RED SAMMY'S FAMOUS BARBECUE. NONE LIKE FAMOUS RED SAMMY'S! RED SAM! THE FAT BOY WITH THE HAPPY LAUGH. A VETERAN! RED SAMMY'S YOUR MAN!

Red Sammy was lying on the bare ground outside The Tower with his head under a truck while a gray monkey about a foot high, chained to a small chinaberry tree, chattered nearby. The monkey sprang back into the tree and got on the

Gone: An Historical Romance of a Civil War as It Occurred b'tween the Dusky Thighs of One Young Negress and Her Heart (1994) is a large-scale paper cutout of a scene depicting several aspects of Southern history by African American artist Kara Walker. **How does her "romantic" view of this history differ from the way the grandmother romanticizes the past in the American South? What aspects of this cutout reflect the South as O'Connor portrays it?**

highest limb as soon as he saw the children jump out of the car and run toward him.

Inside, The Tower was a long dark room with a counter at one end and tables at the other and dancing space in the middle. They all sat down at a board table next to the nickelodeon and Red Sam's wife, a tall burnt-brown woman with hair and eyes lighter than her skin, came and took their order. The children's mother put a dime in the machine and played "The Tennessee Waltz," and the grandmother said that tune always made her want to dance. She asked Bailey if he would like to dance but he only glared at her. He didn't have a naturally sunny disposition like she did and trips made him nervous. The grandmother's brown eyes were very bright. She swayed her head from side to side and pretended she was dancing in her chair. June Star said play something she could tap to so the children's mother put in another dime and played a fast number and June Star stepped out onto the dance floor and did her tap routine.

30 "Ain't she cute?" Red Sam's wife said, leaning over the counter. "Would you like to come be my little girl?"

"No I certainly wouldn't," June Star said. "I wouldn't live in a broken-down place like this for a million bucks!" and she ran back to the table.

"Ain't she cute?" the woman repeated, stretching her mouth politely.

"Aren't you ashamed?" hissed the grandmother.

Red Sam came in and told his wife to quit lounging on the counter and hurry up with these people's order. His khaki trousers reached just to his hip bones and his stomach hung over them like a sack of meal swaying under his shirt. He came over and sat down at a table nearby and let out a combination sigh and yodel. "You can't win," he said. "You can't win," and he wiped his sweating red face off with a gray handkerchief. "These days you don't know who to trust," he said. "Ain't that the truth?"

35 "People are certainly not nice like they used to be," said the grandmother.

"Two fellers come in here last week," Red Sammy said, "driving a Chrysler. It was a old beat-up car but it was a good one and these boys looked all right to me. Said they worked at the mill and you know I let them fellers charge the gas they bought? Now why did I do that?"

"Because you're a good man!" the grandmother said at once.

"Yes'm, I suppose so," Red Sam said as if he were struck with this answer.

His wife brought the orders, carrying the five plates all at once without a tray, two in each hand and one balanced on her arm. "It isn't a soul in this green world of God's that you can trust," she said. "And I don't count nobody out of that, not nobody," she repeated, looking at Red Sammy.

40 "Did you read about that criminal, The Misfit, that's escaped?" asked the grandmother.

"I wouldn't be a bit surprised if he didn't attact this place right here," said the woman. "If he hears about it being here, I wouldn't be none surprised to see him. If he hears it's two cent in the cash register, I wouldn't be a tall surprised if he . . ."

"That'll do," Red Sam said. "Go bring these people their Co'-Colas," and the woman went off to get the rest of the order.

"A good man is hard to find," Red Sammy said. "Everything is getting terrible. I remember the day you could go off and leave your screen door unlatched. Not no more."

He and the grandmother discussed better times. The old lady said that in her opinion Europe was entirely to blame for the way things were now. She said the way Europe acted you would think we were made of money and Red Sam said it was no use talking about it, she was exactly right. The children ran outside into the white sunlight and looked at the monkey in the lacy chinaberry tree. He was busy catching fleas on himself and biting each one carefully between his teeth as if it were a delicacy.

They drove off again into the hot afternoon. The grandmother took cat naps and woke up every few minutes with her own snoring. Outside of Toombsboro she woke up and recalled an old plantation that she had visited in this neighborhood once when she was a young lady. She said the house had six white columns across the front and that there was an avenue of oaks leading up to it and two little wooden trellis arbors on either side in front where you sat down with your suitor after a stroll in the garden. She recalled exactly which road to turn off to get to it. She knew that Bailey would not be willing to lose any time looking at an old house, but the more she talked about it, the more she wanted to see it once again and find out if the little twin arbors were still standing. "There was a secret panel in this house," she said craftily, not telling the truth but wishing that she were, "and the story went that all the family silver was hidden in it when Sherman[1] came through but it was never found . . ."

"Hey!" John Wesley said. "Let's go see it! We'll find it! We'll poke all the woodwork and find it! Who lives there? Where do you turn off at? Hey Pop, can't we turn off there?"

"We never have seen a house with a secret panel!" June Star shrieked. "Let's go to the house with the secret panel! Hey Pop, can't we go see the house with the secret panel!"

"It's not far from here, I know," the grandmother said. "It wouldn't take over twenty minutes."

Bailey was looking straight ahead. His jaw was as rigid as a horseshoe. "No," he said.

The children began to yell and scream that they wanted to see the house with the secret panel. John Wesley kicked the back of the front seat and June Star hung over her mother's shoulder and whined desperately into her ear that they never had any fun even on their vacation, that they could never do what THEY wanted to do. The baby began to scream and John Wesley kicked the back of the seat so hard that his father could feel the blows in his kidney.

"All right!" he shouted and drew the car to a stop at the side of the road. "Will you all shut up? Will you all just shut up for one second? If you don't shut up, we won't go anywhere."

"It would be very educational for them," the grandmother murmured.

"All right," Bailey said, "but get this: this is the only time we're going to stop for anything like this. This is the one and only time."

"The dirt road that you have to turn down is about a mile back," the grandmother directed. "I marked it when we passed."

"A dirt road," Bailey groaned.

After they had turned around and were headed toward the dirt road, the grandmother recalled other points about the house, the beautiful glass over the front doorway and the candle-lamp in the hall. John Wesley said that the secret panel was probably in the fireplace.

"You can't go inside this house," Bailey said. "You don't know who lives there."

"While you all talk to the people in front, I'll run around behind and get in a window," John Wesley suggested.

"We'll all stay in the car," his mother said.

They turned onto the dirt road and the car raced roughly along in a swirl of pink dust. The grandmother recalled the times when there were no paved roads and thirty miles was a day's journey. The dirt road was hilly and there were sudden washes in it and sharp curves on dangerous embankments. All at once they would be on a hill, looking down over the blue tops of trees for miles around, then the next minute, they would be in a red depression with the dust-coated trees looking down on them.

[1] Union general William Tecumseh Sherman (1820–1891) led a destructive campaign through Tennessee, Georgia, and the Carolinas during the Civil War. — EDS.

David G. Houser/Getty Images

The plantation house shown here, known as the Houmas, was built in the late eighteenth century. **What aspects of the Houmas, as shown in this photograph, reflect the grandmother's view of what Southern culture should be? What aspects reflect Southern culture as O'Connor depicts it in the story?**

"This place had better turn up in a minute," Bailey said, "or I'm going to turn around."

The road looked as if no one had traveled on it in months.

"It's not much farther," the grandmother said and just as she said it, a horrible thought came to her. The thought was so embarrassing that she turned red in the face and her eyes dilated and her feet jumped up, upsetting her valise in the corner. The instant the valise moved, the newspaper top she had over the basket under it rose with a snarl and Pitty Sing, the cat, sprang onto Bailey's shoulder.

The children were thrown to the floor and their mother, clutching the baby, was thrown out the door onto the ground; the old lady was thrown into the front seat. The car turned over once and landed right-side-up in a gulch off the side of the road. Bailey remained in the driver's seat with the cat — gray-striped with a broad white face and an orange nose — clinging to his neck like a caterpillar.

As soon as the children saw they could move their arms and legs, they scrambled out of the car, shouting, "We've had an ACCIDENT!" The grandmother was curled up under the dashboard, hoping she was injured so that Bailey's wrath would not come down on her all at once. The horrible thought she had had before the accident was that the house she had remembered so vividly was not in Georgia but in Tennessee.

Bailey removed the cat from his neck with both hands and flung it out the window against the side of a pine tree. Then he got out of the car and started looking for the children's mother. She was sitting against the side of the red gutted ditch, holding the screaming baby, but she only had a cut down her face and a broken shoulder. "We've had an ACCIDENT!" the children screamed in a frenzy of delight.

"But nobody's killed," June Star said with disappointment as the grandmother limped out of the car, her hat still pinned to her head but the broken front brim standing up at a jaunty angle and the violet spray hanging off the side. They all sat down in the ditch, except the children, to recover from the shock. They were all shaking.

"Maybe a car will come along," said the children's mother hoarsely.

"I believe I have injured an organ," said the grandmother, pressing her side, but no one answered her. Bailey's teeth were clattering. He had on a yellow sport shirt with bright blue parrots designed in it and his face was as yellow as the shirt. The grandmother decided that she would not mention that the house was in Tennessee.

The road was about ten feet above and they could see only the tops of the trees on the other side of it. Behind the ditch they were sitting in there were more woods, tall and dark and deep. In a few minutes they saw a car some distance away on top of a hill, coming slowly as if the occupants were watching them. The grandmother stood up and waved both arms dramatically to attract their attention. The car continued to come on slowly, disappeared around a bend and appeared again, moving even slower, on top of the hill they had gone over. It was a big black battered hearse-like automobile. There were three men in it.

It came to a stop just over them and for some minutes, the driver looked down with a steady expressionless gaze to where they were sitting, and didn't speak. Then he turned his head and muttered something to the other two and they got out. One was a fat boy in black trousers and a red sweat shirt with a silver stallion embossed on the front of it. He moved around on the right side of them and stood staring, his mouth partly open in a kind of loose grin. The other had on khaki pants and a blue striped coat and a gray hat pulled down very low, hiding most of his face. He came around slowly on the left side. Neither spoke.

The driver got out of the car and stood by the side of it, looking down at them. He was an older man than the other two. His hair was just beginning to gray and he wore silver-rimmed spectacles that gave him a scholarly look. He had a long creased face and didn't have on any shirt or undershirt. He had on blue jeans that were too tight for him and was holding a black hat and a gun. The two boys also had guns.

"We've had an ACCIDENT!" the children screamed.

The grandmother had the peculiar feeling that the bespectacled man was someone she knew. His face was as familiar to her as if she had known him all her life but she could not recall who he was. He moved away from the car and began to come down the embankment, placing his feet carefully so that he wouldn't slip. He had on tan and white shoes and no socks, and his ankles were red and thin. "Good afternoon," he said. "I see you all had you a little spill."

"We turned over twice!" said the grandmother.

"Oncet," he corrected. "We seen it happen. Try their car and see will it run, Hiram," he said quietly to the boy with the gray hat.

"What you got that gun for?" John Wesley asked. "Whatcha gonna do with that gun?"

"Lady," the man said to the children's mother, "would you mind calling them children to sit down by you? Children make me nervous. I want all you all to sit down right together there where you're at."

"What are you telling US what to do for?" June Star asked.

Behind them the line of woods gaped like a dark open mouth. "Come here," said their mother.

"Look here now," Bailey began suddenly, "we're in a predicament! We're in . . ."

The grandmother shrieked. She scrambled to her feet and stood staring. "You're The Misfit!" she said. "I recognized you at once!"

"Yes'm," the man said, smiling slightly as if he were pleased in spite of himself to be known, "but it would have been better for all of you, lady, if you hadn't of reckernized me."

Bailey turned his head sharply and said something to his mother that shocked even the children. The old lady began to cry and The Misfit reddened.

"Lady," he said, "don't you get upset. Sometimes a man says things he don't mean. I don't reckon he meant to talk to you thataway."

"You wouldn't shoot a lady, would you?" the grandmother said and removed a clean handkerchief from her cuff and began to slap at her eyes with it.

The Misfit pointed the toe of his shoe into the ground and made a little hole and then covered it up again. "I would hate to have to," he said.

"Listen," the grandmother almost screamed, "I know you're a good man. You don't look a bit like you have common blood. I know you must come from nice people!"

"Yes mam," he said, "finest people in the world." When he smiled he showed a row of strong white teeth. "God never made a finer woman than my mother and my daddy's heart was pure gold," he said. The boy with the red sweat shirt had come around behind them and was standing with his gun at his hip. The Misfit squatted down on the ground. "Watch them children, Bobby Lee," he said. "You know they make me nervous." He looked at the six of them huddled together in front of him and he seemed to be embarrassed as if he couldn't think of anything to say. "Ain't a cloud in the sky," he remarked, looking up at it. "Don't see no sun but don't see no cloud neither."

"Yes, it's a beautiful day," said the grandmother. "Listen," she said, "you shouldn't call yourself The Misfit because I know you're a good man at heart. I can just look at you and tell."

"Hush!" Bailey yelled. "Hush! Everybody shut up and let me handle this!" He was squatting in the position of a runner about to sprint forward but he didn't move.

"I pre-chate that, lady," The Misfit said and drew a little circle in the ground with the butt of his gun.

"It'll take a half a hour to fix this here car," Hiram called, looking over the raised hood of it.

"Well, first you and Bobby Lee get him and that little boy to step over yonder with you," The Misfit said, pointing to Bailey and John Wesley. "The boys want to ast you something," he said to Bailey. "Would you mind stepping back in them woods there with them?"

"Listen," Bailey began, "we're in a terrible predicament! Nobody realizes what this is," and his voice cracked. His eyes were as blue and intense as the parrots in his shirt and he remained perfectly still.

The grandmother reached up to adjust her hat brim as if she were going to the woods with him but it came off in her hand. She stood staring at it and after a second she let it fall on the ground. Hiram pulled Bailey up by the arm as if he were assisting an old man. John Wesley caught hold of his father's hand and Bobby Lee followed. They went off toward the woods and just as they reached the dark edge, Bailey turned and supporting himself against a gray naked pine trunk, he shouted, "I'll be back in a minute, Mamma, wait on me!"

"Come back this instant!" his mother shrilled but they all disappeared into the woods.

"Bailey Boy!" the grandmother called in a tragic voice but she found she was looking at The Misfit squatting on the ground in front of her. "I just know you're a good man," she said desperately. "You're not a bit common!"

"Nome, I ain't a good man," The Misfit said after a second as if he had considered her statement carefully, "but I ain't the worst in the world neither. My daddy said I was a different breed of dog from my brothers and sisters. 'You know,' Daddy said, 'it's some that can live their whole life out without asking about it and it's others has to know why it is, and this boy is one of the latters. He's going to be into everything!'" He put on his black hat and looked up suddenly and then away deep into the woods as if he were embarrassed again. "I'm sorry I don't have on a shirt before you ladies," he said, hunching his shoulders slightly. "We buried our clothes that we had on when we escaped and we're just making do until we can get better. We borrowed these from some folks we met," he explained.

"That's perfectly all right," the grandmother said. "Maybe Bailey has an extra shirt in his suitcase."

"I'll look and see terrectly," The Misfit said.

"Where are they taking him?" the children's mother screamed.

"Daddy was a card himself," The Misfit said. "You couldn't put anything over on him. He never got in trouble with the Authorities though. Just had the knack of handling them."

"You could be honest too if you'd only try," said the grandmother. "Think how wonderful it would be to settle down and live a comfortable life and not have to think about somebody chasing you all the time."

105 The Misfit kept scratching in the ground with the butt of his gun as if he were thinking about it. "Yes'm, somebody is always after you," he murmured.

The grandmother noticed how thin his shoulder blades were just behind his hat because she was standing up looking down on him. "Do you ever pray?" she asked.

He shook his head. All she saw was the black hat wiggle between his shoulder blades. "Nome," he said.

There was a pistol shot from the woods, followed closely by another. Then silence. The old lady's head jerked around. She could hear the wind move through the tree tops like a long satisfied insuck of breath. "Bailey Boy!" she called.

"I was a gospel singer for a while," The Misfit said. "I been most everything. Been in the arm service, both land and sea, at home and abroad, been twict married, been an undertaker, been with the railroads, plowed Mother Earth, been in a tornado, seen a man burnt alive oncet," and he looked up at the children's mother and the little girl who were sitting close together, their faces white and their eyes glassy; "I even seen a woman flogged," he said.

110 "Pray, pray," the grandmother began, "pray, pray . . ."

"I never was a bad boy that I remember of," The Misfit said in an almost dreamy voice, "but somewheres along the line I done something wrong and got sent to the penitentiary. I was buried alive," and he looked up and held her attention to him by a steady stare.

"That's when you should have started to pray," she said. "What did you do to get sent to the penitentiary that first time?"

"Turn to the right, it was a wall," The Misfit said, looking up again at the cloudless sky. "Turn to the left, it was a wall. Look up it was a ceiling, look down it was a floor. I forget what I done, lady. I set there and set there, trying to remember what it was I done and I ain't recalled it to this day. Oncet in a while, I would think it was coming to me, but it never come."

"Maybe they put you in by mistake," the old lady said vaguely.

115 "Nome," he said. "It wasn't no mistake. They had the papers on me."

"You must have stolen something," she said.

The Misfit sneered slightly. "Nobody had nothing I wanted," he said. "It was a head-doctor at the penitentiary said what I had done was kill my daddy but I known that for a lie. My daddy died in nineteen ought nineteen of the epidemic flu[2] and I never had a thing to do with it. He was buried in the Mount Hopewell Baptist churchyard and you can go there and see for yourself."

"If you would pray," the old lady said, "Jesus would help you."

"That's right," The Misfit said.

120 "Well then, why don't you pray?" she asked trembling with delight suddenly.

"I don't want no hep," he said. "I'm doing all right by myself."

Bobby Lee and Hiram came ambling back from the woods. Bobby Lee was dragging a yellow shirt with bright blue parrots in it.

"Thow me that shirt, Bobby Lee," The Misfit said. The shirt came flying at him and landed on his shoulder and he put it on. The grandmother couldn't name what the shirt reminded her of. "No, lady," The Misfit said while he was

[2] The influenza pandemic of 1918–19, the largest epidemic in history, killed between twenty and forty million people worldwide. — EDS.

buttoning it up, "I found out the crime don't matter. You can do one thing or you can do another, kill a man or take a tire off his car, because sooner or later you're going to forget what it was you done and just be punished for it."

The children's mother had begun to make heaving noises as if she couldn't get her breath. "Lady," he asked, "would you and that little girl like to step off yonder with Bobby Lee and Hiram and join your husband?"

"Yes, thank you," the mother said faintly. Her left arm dangled helplessly and she was holding the baby, who had gone to sleep, in the other. "Hep that lady up, Hiram," The Misfit said as she struggled to climb out of the ditch, "and Bobby Lee, you hold onto that little girl's hand."

"I don't want to hold hands with him," June Star said. "He reminds me of a pig."

The fat boy blushed and laughed and caught her by the arm and pulled her off into the woods after Hiram and her mother.

Alone with The Misfit, the grandmother found that she had lost her voice. There was not a cloud in the sky nor any sun. There was nothing around her but woods. She wanted to tell him that he must pray. She opened and closed her mouth several times before anything came out. Finally she found herself saying, "Jesus. Jesus," meaning, Jesus will help you, but the way she was saying it, it sounded as if she might be cursing.

"Yes'm," The Misfit said as if he agreed. "Jesus thown everything off balance. It was the same case with Him as with me except He hadn't committed any crime and they could prove I had committed one because they had the papers on me. Of course," he said, "they never shown me my papers. That's why I sign myself now. I said long ago, you get you a signature and sign everything you do and keep a copy of it. Then you'll know what you done and you can hold up the crime to the punishment and see do they match and in the end you'll have something to prove you ain't been treated right. I call myself The Misfit," he said, "because I can't make what all I done wrong fit what all I gone through in punishment."

There was a piercing scream from the woods, followed closely by a pistol report. "Does it seem right to you, lady, that one is punished a heap and another ain't punished at all?"

"Jesus!" the old lady cried. "You've got good blood! I know you wouldn't shoot a lady! I know

This religious sign was placed in front of a house on a highway between Columbus and Augusta, Georgia. Similar religious signs were placed along this highway at intervals of at least a mile and often much closer together — such signs were especially common during the Depression. **How does the grandmother use the language of signs like this to convince The Misfit to spare her?**

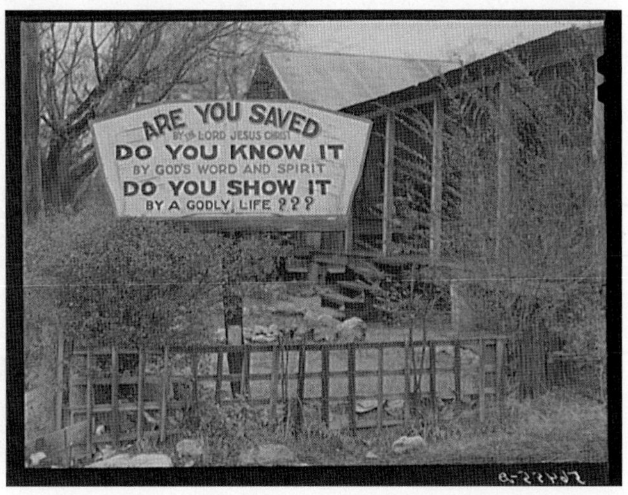

Library of Congress

you come from nice people! Pray! Jesus, you ought not to shoot a lady. I'll give you all the money I've got!"

"Lady," The Misfit said, looking beyond her far into the woods, "there never was a body that give the undertaker a tip."

There were two more pistol reports and the grandmother raised her head like a parched old turkey hen crying for water and called, "Bailey Boy, Bailey Boy!" as if her heart would break.

"Jesus was the only One that ever raised the dead," The Misfit continued, "and He shouldn't have done it. He thown everything off balance. If He did what He said, then it's nothing for you to do but thow away everything and follow Him, and if He didn't, then it's nothing for you to do but enjoy the few minutes you got left the best way you can — by killing somebody or burning down his house or doing some other meanness to him. No pleasure but meanness," he said and his voice had become almost a snarl.

"Maybe He didn't raise the dead," the old lady mumbled, not knowing what she was saying and feeling so dizzy that she sank down in the ditch with her legs twisted under her.

"I wasn't there so I can't say He didn't," The Misfit said. "I wisht I had of been there," he said, hitting the ground with his fist. "It ain't right I wasn't there because if I had of been there I would of known. Listen lady," he said in a high voice, "if I had of been there I would of known and I wouldn't be like I am now." His voice seemed about to crack and the grandmother's head cleared for an instant. She saw the man's face twisted close to her own as if he were going to cry and she murmured, "Why you're one of my babies. You're one of my own children!" She reached out and touched him on the shoulder. The Misfit sprang back as if a snake had bitten him and shot her three times through the chest. Then he put his gun down on the ground and took off his glasses and began to clean them.

Hiram and Bobby Lee returned from the woods and stood over the ditch, looking down at the grandmother who half sat and half lay in a puddle of blood with her legs crossed under her like a child's and her face smiling up at the cloudless sky.

Without his glasses, The Misfit's eyes were red-rimmed and pale and defenseless-looking.

Howard Schectman

This painting by artist Howard Schechtman illustrates the final scene in "A Good Man Is Hard to Find." **How closely does it match your own image of the story's last scene? What did the artist capture? What's missing?**

"Take her off and thow her where you thown the others," he said, picking up the cat that was rubbing itself against his leg.

"She was a talker, wasn't she?" Bobby Lee said, sliding down the ditch with a yodel.

140 "She would of been a good woman," The Misfit said, "if it had been somebody there to shoot her every minute of her life."

"Some fun!" Bobby Lee said.

"Shut up, Bobby Lee," The Misfit said. "It's no real pleasure in life."

[1955]

QUESTIONS FOR DISCUSSION

1. What tone does the epigraph set for the story? Reconsider it after you've read the story. How does your interpretation change?
2. What can you infer about the grandmother by reading the opening paragraph? What does she represent in the story? Consider the role she plays in her family as well as how she might embody a different era in the culture of the South. What does the grandmother mean when she tells The Misfit, "Why you're one of my babies. You're one of my own children" (para. 136)?
3. The main characters in a story usually have names. In this story, however, several main characters — The Misfit, the grandmother, and the children's mother — are unnamed. What is the purpose of not giving these characters names, referring to them only by their roles? How might leaving these characters unnamed connect to a theme of the story?
4. In what ways is the family in this story fairly typical in terms of the tensions and conflicts most families experience? How does Flannery O'Connor introduce comedy by depicting the differences between and among generations and relationships?
5. When Red Sammy says to the grandmother, "A good man is hard to find" (para. 43), what does he mean? Why did O'Connor choose this particular line for the story's title? Also consider why, in the final scene, the grandmother repeatedly tells The Misfit that she knows he is a "good man."
6. Discuss instances in which the grandmother's nostalgia for the past seems warranted and others in which it becomes limiting, even threatening. You might begin by considering some of the following: her desire to paint a picture of the "pickaninny" in the doorway, her story about Mr. Teagarden, her story of the house with the secret panel.
7. O'Connor has said that the short-story collection that included this story is about "original sin." What role does religion, specifically Christianity, play in this story? How do the grandmother's traditional views on salvation and prayer differ from The Misfit's? What does The Misfit mean when he asserts that "Jesus thown everything off balance" (paras. 129, 134)?
8. Were you surprised by the violence in the story? Why do you think O'Connor chose to leave the murders of everyone but the grandmother "off stage" rather than describing them directly? What is the impact of providing details about the shooting of the grandmother and describing her lifeless body?
9. How does The Misfit explain his behavior to the grandmother? Why does he shoot her precisely when he does? How do you interpret his assertion that "she would of been a good woman . . . if it had been somebody there to shoot her every minute of her life" (para. 140)? What does The Misfit understand about the grandmother's character?

QUESTIONS ON STYLE AND STRUCTURE

1. How does O'Connor use foreshadowing in "A Good Man Is Hard to Find"? What effect did the foreshadowing have on your first reading of the story? When you read about The Misfit in the first paragraph, did you think that you would meet him?
2. Contrast the description of the grandmother's outfit with the rest of the family's traveling attire (paras. 12, 69). What do the characters' clothes tell us about them? What is significant about The Misfit's appropriation of Bailey's parrot shirt (paras. 122–23)?
3. "'In my time,' said the grandmother, folding her thin veined fingers, 'children were more respectful of their native states and their parents and everything else. People did right then. Oh look at the cute little pickaninny!' she said and pointed to a Negro child standing in the door of a shack" (para. 18). What is ironic about this passage? How does the grandmother define "did right"? What evidence suggests a contrast between the character's and the author's perspectives of what it means to "do right"?
4. What is the purpose of the scene at Red Sammy's barbecue place? Consider the conversation between the grandmother and Red Sammy about the difficulty of finding a "good man." How does this scene develop the story's themes as well as plot?
5. Take another look at the allusion the grandmother makes to *Gone With the Wind* in paragraph 24. What deeper meaning can you find in her joke about the plantation? How does this joke affect your reading of the story?
6. Explain how the setting shifts once the family takes a detour off the main road. Why is this shift important to the story's plot? How does the shift in setting contribute to the shift in the story's tone?
7. Why do you think O'Connor chose to capitalize "ACCIDENT!" in the children's dialogue? After the accident, a slow-moving car appears on the horizon, "a big black battered hearse-like automobile" (para. 70). Why might the author have chosen not to use commas between these adjectives? How do the punctuation and alliteration contribute to the effect of this description?
8. The Misfit's words are often given a phonetic rendering:
   - "I pre-chate that, lady." (para. 92)
   - "The boys want to ast you something." (para. 94)
   - "I'll look and see terrectly." (para. 101)
   - "Nome." (para. 107)
   - "I . . . seen a man burnt alive oncet." (para. 109)
   - "I don't want no hep." (para. 121)

   What effect does this use of dialect have on your understanding of The Misfit's character? What other characters in the story speak in dialect, and what does it say about them?
9. Examine the following similes used in "A Good Man Is Hard to Find":
   - "whose face was as broad and innocent as a cabbage" (para. 2)
   - "her big black valise that looked like the head of a hippopotamus" (para. 10)
   - "His jaw was as rigid as a horseshoe." (para. 49)
   - "She could hear the wind move through the tree tops like a long satisfied insuck of breath." (para. 108)
   - "the grandmother raised her head like a parched old turkey hen crying for water" (para. 133)

   Choose three of these similes and explain how each comparison contributes to your ability to visualize the scene or character.
10. We stay close to the grandmother's point of view throughout most of the story. When does O'Connor move away from this perspective, and what effect does this have?

SUGGESTIONS FOR WRITING

1. Write an essay in which you analyze three literary devices or techniques O'Connor uses to characterize both the grandmother and her attitudes toward other characters in the story. Be sure to include specific evidence from the story to support your analysis.
2. Discuss how O'Connor plays out her theme of the struggle between good and evil in the characters of the grandmother and The Misfit. Explore the ways that each of these characters embodies elements of both good and evil.
3. Although this story has some universal themes, it is very much a story about the South — its values, traditions, and culture. Write an essay explaining how this is a Southern story.
4. Writing about violence in fiction, O'Connor claimed, "In my own stories I have found that violence is strangely capable of returning my characters to reality and preparing them to accept their moment of grace." Write an essay explaining whether you do or do not agree with this description as it applies to the grandmother, The Misfit, or both.
5. Write an essay offering two different interpretations of the ending of the story. Is it uplifting? cynical? bleak? hopeful? Have any of the characters been transformed? Then explain which of the interpretations you prefer. Include your understanding of The Misfit's final comment: "It's no real pleasure in life."
6. Write an essay that compares and contrasts the narrator in "A Good Man Is Hard to Find" with the narrator of another work of fiction in this chapter. In your response, consider some or all of the following: how each narrator feels about the characters he or she is describing; which character(s) he or she is most sympathetic toward; how close (or distant) the narrator is from the action; how the storyteller hopes you, the reader, will respond; and why this particular voice has been chosen.
7. You are an up-and-coming screenwriter who wants to adapt "A Good Man Is Hard to Find" for the big screen. Write a one-page proposal persuading a producer that this movie's story and themes will appeal to a wide audience and be timely in the twenty-first century. Include suggestions for a director, a few members of the cast, and a filming location.
8. Imagine that you are June Star or John Wesley, telling a school friend about your grandmother. Write a one-page soliloquy in which you characterize (through ranting about, imitating, or telling a story about) the old woman. Look closely at the children's speech patterns, and try to use both the syntax and the language that either child would.

Frankenstein

MARY SHELLEY

National Portrait Gallery, London, UK/Photo © Tarker/Bridgeman Images

Mary Shelley (1796–1851) was an English novelist, short story writer, dramatist, essayist, biographer, and travel writer. The daughter of political philosopher William Godwin and feminist philosopher Mary Wollstonecraft, Shelley grew up in London. Although best known for her Gothic novel *Frankenstein: or, The Modern Prometheus* (1818), she wrote many other works, including the historical novels *Valperga* (1823) and *Perkin Warbeck* (1830), the apocalyptic novel *The Last Man* (1826), the travel book *Rambles in Germany and Italy* (1844), and biographical articles for the widely circulated *Cabinet Cyclopædia* (1829–1846). In 1814, she began an affair with Percy Bysshe Shelley, who was married at the time; after his first wife's suicide in late 1816, the couple married. Mary and Percy Bysshe Shelley spent the summer of 1816 with Lord Byron and other friends in Geneva, Switzerland; because the weather was so often inclement, they were forced to stay inside and told ghost stories to entertain themselves. *Frankenstein* began as a ghost story, and Shelley finished the novel about a year later when she was nineteen. The tragedy of Victor Frankenstein, the ambitious scientist who creates life only to be horrified by his creation was, in many ways, the first of its kind. Many scholars consider it the earliest example of science fiction in English, and Shelley is often credited with inventing the genre.

Did I request thee, Maker, from my clay
To mould Me man? Did I solicit thee
From darkness to promote me?—

—*Paradise Lost* [X. 743–5]

LETTER I

To Mrs. Saville, England

St. Petersburgh, Dec. 11th, 17—.

You will rejoice to hear that no disaster has accompanied the commencement of an enterprise which you have regarded with such evil forebodings. I arrived here yesterday; and my first task is to assure my dear sister of my welfare, and increasing confidence in the success of my undertaking.

I am already far north of London; and as I walk in the streets of Petersburgh, I feel a cold northern breeze play upon my cheeks, which braces my nerves, and fills me with delight. Do you understand this feeling? This breeze, which has travelled from the regions towards which I am advancing, gives me a foretaste of those icy climes. Inspirited by this wind of promise, my day dreams become more fervent and vivid. I try in vain to be persuaded that the pole is the seat of frost and desolation; it ever presents itself to my imagination as the region of beauty and delight. There, Margaret, the sun is for ever visible; its broad disk just skirting the horizon, and diffusing a perpetual splendour. There—for with your leave, my sister, I will put some trust in preceding navigators—there snow and frost are banished; and, sailing over a calm sea, we may be wafted to a land surpassing in wonders and in beauty every region hitherto discovered on the habitable globe. Its productions and features may be without example, as the phenomena of the heavenly bodies undoubtedly are in those undiscovered solitudes. What may not be expected in a country of eternal light? I may there discover the wondrous power which attracts the needle; and may regulate a thousand celestial observations, that require only this voyage to render their seeming eccentricities consistent for ever. I shall satiate my ardent curiosity with the sight of a part of the world never before visited, and may tread a land never before imprinted by the foot of man. These are my enticements, and they are sufficient to conquer all fear of danger or death, and to induce me to commence this laborious voyage with the joy a child feels when he embarks in a little boat, with his holiday mates, on an expedition of discovery up his native river. But, supposing all these conjectures to be false, you cannot contest the inestimable benefit which I shall confer on all mankind to the last generation, by discovering a passage near the pole to those countries, to reach which at present so many months are requisite; or by ascertaining the secret of the magnet, which, if at all possible, can only be effected by an undertaking such as mine.

These reflections have dispelled the agitation with which I began my letter, and I feel my heart glow with an enthusiasm which elevates me to heaven; for nothing contributes so much to tranquillise the mind as a steady purpose, — a point on which the soul may fix its intellectual eye. This expedition has been the favourite dream of my early years. I have read with ardour the accounts of the various voyages which have been made in the prospect of arriving at the North Pacific Ocean through the seas which surround the pole. You may remember, that a history of all the voyages made for purposes of discovery composed the whole of our good uncle Thomas's library. My education was neglected, yet I was passionately fond of reading. These volumes were my study day and night, and my familiarity with them increased that regret which I had felt, as a child, on learning that my father's dying injunction had forbidden my uncle to allow me to embark in a seafaring life.

These visions faded when I perused, for the first time, those poets whose effusions entranced my soul, and lifted it to heaven. I also became a poet, and for one year lived in a Paradise of my own creation; I imagined that I also might obtain a niche in the temple where the names of Homer and Shakespeare are consecrated. You are well acquainted with my failure, and how heavily I bore the disappointment. But just at that time I inherited the fortune of my cousin, and my thoughts were turned into the channel of their earlier bent.

Six years have passed since I resolved on my 5
present undertaking. I can, even now, remember the hour from which I dedicated myself to this great enterprise. I commenced by inuring my body to hardship. I accompanied the whale-fishers on several expeditions to the North Sea; I voluntarily endured cold, famine, thirst, and want of sleep; I often worked harder than the common sailors during the day, and devoted my nights to the study of mathematics, the theory of medicine, and those branches of physical science from which a naval adventurer might derive the greatest practical advantage. Twice I actually hired myself as an under-mate in a Greenland whaler, and acquitted myself to admiration. I must own I felt a little proud, when my captain offered me the second dignity in the vessel, and entreated me to remain with the greatest earnestness; so valuable did he consider my services.

And now, dear Margaret, do I not deserve to accomplish some great purpose? My life might have been passed in ease and luxury; but I preferred glory to every enticement that wealth placed in my path. Oh, that some encouraging voice would answer in the affirmative! My courage and my resolution is firm; but my hopes fluctuate, and my spirits are often depressed. I am about to proceed on a long and difficult voyage, the emergencies of which will demand all my fortitude: I am required not only to raise the spirits of others, but sometimes to sustain my own, when theirs are failing.

This is the most favourable period for travelling in Russia. They fly quickly over the snow in their sledges; the motion is pleasant, and, in my opinion, far more agreeable than that of an English stage-coach. The cold is not excessive, if you are wrapped in furs, — a dress which I have already adopted; for there is a great difference between walking the deck and remaining seated motionless for hours, when no exercise prevents the blood from actually freezing in your veins. I have no ambition to lose my life on the post-road between St. Petersburgh and Archangel.[1]

I shall depart for the latter town in a fortnight or three weeks; and my intention is to hire a ship there, which can easily be done by paying the insurance for the owner, and to engage as many sailors as I think necessary among those who are accustomed to the whale-fishing. I do not intend to sail until the month of June; and when shall I return? Ah, dear sister, how can I answer this question? If I succeed, many, many months, perhaps years, will pass before you and I may meet. If I fail, you will see me again soon, or never.

Farewell, my dear, excellent Margaret. Heaven shower down blessings on you, and save me, that I may again and again testify my gratitude for all your love and kindness.

Your affectionate brother,
R. Walton.

LETTER II

To Mrs. Saville, England

Archangel, 28th March, 17 — .

How slowly the time passes here, encompassed as I am by frost and snow! yet a second step is taken towards my enterprise. I have hired a vessel, and am occupied in collecting my sailors; those whom I have already engaged appear to be men on whom I can depend, and are certainly possessed of dauntless courage.

But I have one want which I have never yet been able to satisfy; and the absence of the object of which I now feel as a most severe evil. I have no friend, Margaret: when I am glowing with the enthusiasm of success, there will be none to participate my joy; if I am assailed by disappointment, no one will endeavour to sustain me in dejection. I shall commit my thoughts to paper, it is true; but that is a poor medium for the communication of feeling. I desire the company of a man who could sympathise with me; whose eyes would reply to mine. You may deem me romantic, my dear sister, but I bitterly feel the want of a friend. I have no one near me, gentle yet courageous, possessed of a cultivated as well as of a capacious mind, whose tastes are like my own, to approve or amend my plans. How would such a friend repair the faults of your poor brother! I am too ardent in execution, and too impatient of difficulties. But it is a still greater evil to me that I am self-educated: for the first fourteen years of my life I ran wild on a common, and read nothing but our uncle Thomas's books of voyages. At that age I became acquainted with the celebrated poets of our own country; but it was only when it had ceased to be in my power to derive its most important benefits from such a conviction, that I perceived the necessity of becoming acquainted with more languages than that of my native country. Now I am twenty-eight, and am in reality more illiterate than many schoolboys of fifteen. It is true that I have thought more, and that my day dreams are more extended and magnificent; but they want (as the painters call it) *keeping*; and I greatly need a friend who would have sense enough not to despise me as romantic, and affection enough for me to endeavour to regulate my mind.

[1] A northern city in European Russia. — EDS.

Well, these are useless complaints; I shall certainly find no friend on the wide ocean, nor even here in Archangel, among merchants and seamen. Yet some feelings, unallied to the dross of human nature, beat even in these rugged bosoms. My lieutenant, for instance, is a man of wonderful courage and enterprise; he is madly desirous of glory: or rather, to word my phrase more characteristically, of advancement in his profession. He is an Englishman, and in the midst of national and professional prejudices, unsoftened by cultivation, retains some of the noblest endowments of humanity. I first became acquainted with him on board a whale vessel: finding that he was unemployed in this city, I easily engaged him to assist in my enterprise.

The master is a person of an excellent disposition, and is remarkable in the ship for his gentleness and the mildness of his discipline. This circumstance, added to his well known integrity and dauntless courage, made me very desirous to engage him. A youth passed in solitude, my best years spent under your gentle and feminine fosterage, has so refined the groundwork of my character, that I cannot overcome an intense distaste to the usual brutality exercised on board ship: I have never believed it to be necessary; and when I heard of a mariner equally noted for his kindliness of heart, and the respect and obedience paid to him by his crew, I felt myself peculiarly fortunate in being able to secure his services. I heard of him first in rather a romantic manner, from a lady who owes to him the happiness of her life. This, briefly, is his story. Some years ago, he loved a young Russian lady, of moderate fortune; and having amassed a considerable sum in prize-money, the father of the girl consented to the match. He saw his mistress once before the destined ceremony; but she was bathed in tears, and, throwing herself at his feet, entreated him to spare her, confessing at the same time that she loved another, but that he was poor, and that her father would never consent to the union. My generous friend reassured the suppliant, and on being informed of the name of her lover, instantly abandoned his pursuit. He had already bought a farm with his money, on which he had designed to pass the remainder of his life; but he bestowed the whole on his rival, together with the remains of his prize-money to purchase stock, and then himself solicited the young woman's father to consent to her marriage with her lover. But the old man decidedly refused, thinking himself bound in honour to my friend; who, when he found the father inexorable, quitted his country, nor returned until he heard that his former mistress was married according to her inclinations. "What a noble fellow!" you will exclaim. He is so; but then he is wholly uneducated: he is as silent as a Turk, and a kind of ignorant carelessness attends him, which, while it renders his conduct the more astonishing, detracts from the interest and sympathy which otherwise he would command.

Yet do not suppose, because I complain a little, or because I can conceive a consolation for my toils which I may never know, that I am wavering in my resolutions. Those are as fixed as fate; and my voyage is only now delayed until the weather shall permit my embarkation. The winter has been dreadfully severe; but the spring promises well, and it is considered as a remarkably early season; so that perhaps I may sail sooner than I expected. I shall do nothing rashly: you know me sufficiently to confide in my prudence and considerateness, whenever the safety of others is committed to my care.

15 I cannot describe to you my sensations on the near prospect of my undertaking. It is impossible to communicate to you a conception of the trembling sensation, half pleasurable and half fearful, with which I am preparing to depart. I am going to unexplored regions, to "the land of mist and snow;" but I shall kill no albatross, therefore do not be alarmed for my safety, or if I should come back to you as worn and woeful as the "Ancient

Mariner."[2] You will smile at my allusion; but I will disclose a secret. I have often attributed my attachment to, my passionate enthusiasm for, the dangerous mysteries of ocean, to that production of the most imaginative of modern poets. There is something at work in my soul, which I do not understand. I am practically industrious—painstaking;—a workman to execute with perseverance and labour:—but besides this, there is a love for the marvellous, a belief in the marvellous, intertwined in all my projects, which hurries me out of the common pathways of men, even to the wild sea and unvisited regions I am about to explore.

But to return to dearer considerations. Shall I meet you again, after having traversed immense seas, and returned by the most southern cape of Africa or America? I dare not expect such success, yet I cannot bear to look on the reverse of the picture. Continue for the present to write to me by every opportunity: I may receive your letters on some occasions when I need them most to support my spirits. I love you very tenderly. Remember me with affection, should you never hear from me again.

Your affectionate brother,
Robert Walton.

LETTER III

To Mrs. Saville, England

July 7th, 17—.

My dear Sister,
I write a few lines in haste, to say that I am safe, and well advanced on my voyage. This letter will reach England by a merchantman now on its homeward voyage from Archangel; more fortunate than I, who may not see my native land, perhaps, for many years. I am, however, in good spirits; my men are bold, and apparently firm of purpose; nor do the floating sheets of ice that continually pass us, indicating the dangers of the region towards which we are advancing, appear to dismay them. We have already reached a very high latitude; but it is the height of summer, and although not so warm as in England, the southern gales, which blow us speedily towards those shores which I so ardently desire to attain, breathe a degree of renovating warmth which I had not expected.

No incidents have hitherto befallen us that would make a figure in a letter. One or two stiff gales, and the springing of a leak, are accidents which experienced navigators scarcely remember to record; and I shall be well content if nothing worse happen to us during our voyage.

Adieu, my dear Margaret. Be assured, that for my own sake, as well as yours, I will not rashly encounter danger. I will be cool, persevering, and prudent.

But success *shall* crown my endeavours. Wherefore not? Thus far I have gone, tracing a secure way over the pathless seas: the very stars themselves being witnesses and testimonies of my triumph. Why not still proceed over the untamed yet obedient element? What can stop the determined heart and resolved will of man?

My swelling heart involuntarily pours itself out thus. But I must finish. Heaven bless my beloved sister!

R. W.

LETTER IV

To Mrs. Saville, England

August 5th, 17—.

So strange an accident has happened to us, that I cannot forbear recording it, although it is very probable that you will see me before these papers can come into your possession.

Last Monday (July 31st), we were nearly surrounded by ice, which closed in the ship on all

[2] A reference to Samuel Taylor Coleridge's epic poem, *The Rime of the Ancient Mariner*, first published in 1798. In it, an old sailor recounts a disastrous sea voyage; as his tale progresses, it becomes clear that the mariner is both the cause of the crew's misfortune and its only survivor.—EDS.

sides, scarcely leaving her the sea-room in which she floated. Our situation was somewhat dangerous, especially as we were compassed round by a very thick fog. We accordingly lay to, hoping that some change would take place in the atmosphere and weather.

About two o'clock the mist cleared away, and we beheld, stretched out in every direction, vast and irregular plains of ice, which seemed to have no end. Some of my comrades groaned, and my own mind began to grow watchful with anxious thoughts, when a strange sight suddenly attracted our attention, and diverted our solicitude from our own situation. We perceived a low carriage, fixed on a sledge and drawn by dogs, pass on towards the north, at the distance of half a mile: a being which had the shape of a man, but apparently of gigantic stature, sat in the sledge, and guided the dogs. We watched the rapid progress of the traveller with our telescopes, until he was lost among the distant inequalities of the ice.

This appearance excited our unqualified wonder. We were, as we believed, many hundred miles from any land; but this apparition seemed to denote that it was not, in reality, so distant as we had supposed. Shut in, however, by ice, it was impossible to follow his track, which we had observed with the greatest attention.

About two hours after this occurrence, we heard the ground sea; and before night the ice broke, and freed our ship. We, however, lay to until the morning, fearing to encounter in the dark those large loose masses which float about after the breaking up of the ice. I profited of this time to rest for a few hours.

In the morning, however, as soon as it was light, I went upon deck, and found all the sailors busy on one side of the vessel, apparently talking to some one in the sea. It was, in fact, a sledge, like that we had seen before, which had drifted towards us in the night, on a large fragment of ice. Only one dog remained alive; but there was a human being within it, whom the sailors were persuading to enter the vessel. He was not, as the other traveller seemed to be, a savage inhabitant of some undiscovered island, but an European. When I appeared on deck, the master said, "Here is our captain, and he will not allow you to perish on the open sea."

On perceiving me, the stranger addressed me in English, although with a foreign accent. "Before I come on board your vessel," said he, "will you have the kindness to inform me whither you are bound?"

You may conceive my astonishment on hearing such a question addressed to me from a man on the brink of destruction, and to whom I should have supposed that my vessel would have been a resource which he would not have exchanged for the most precious wealth the earth can afford. I replied, however, that we were on a voyage of discovery towards the northern pole.

Upon hearing this he appeared satisfied, and consented to come on board. Good God! Margaret, if you had seen the man who thus capitulated for his safety, your surprise would have been boundless. His limbs were nearly frozen, and his body dreadfully emaciated by fatigue and suffering. I never saw a man in so wretched a condition. We attempted to carry him into the cabin; but as soon as he had quitted the fresh air, he fainted. We accordingly brought him back to the deck, and restored him to animation by rubbing him with brandy, and forcing him to swallow a small quantity. As soon as he showed signs of life we wrapped him up in blankets, and placed him near the chimney of the kitchen stove. By slow degrees he recovered, and ate a little soup, which restored him wonderfully.

Two days passed in this manner before he was able to speak; and I often feared that his suffering had deprived him of understanding. When he had in some measure recovered, I removed him to my own cabin, and attended on him as much as my duty would permit. I never saw a more interesting creature: his eyes have generally an expression of wildness, and even madness; but there are moments when, if any one performs an act of kindness towards him, or does him any the most trifling service, his whole countenance is lighted up, as it were, with a beam of benevolence and sweetness that I never saw equalled. But he is generally melancholy and despairing; and sometimes he gnashes his teeth, as if impatient of the weight of woes that oppresses him.

When my guest was a little recovered, I had great trouble to keep off the men, who wished to ask him a thousand questions; but I would not allow him to be tormented by their idle curiosity, in a state of body and mind whose restoration evidently depended upon entire repose. Once, however, the lieutenant asked, Why he had come so far upon the ice in so strange a vehicle?

His countenance instantly assumed an aspect of the deepest gloom; and he replied, "To seek one who fled from me."

"And did the man whom you pursued travel in the same fashion?"

"Yes."

"Then I fancy we have seen him; for the day before we picked you up, we saw some dogs drawing a sledge, with a man in it, across the ice."

This aroused the stranger's attention; and he asked a multitude of questions concerning the route which the daemon, as he called him, had pursued. Soon after, when he was alone with me, he said, — "I have, doubtless, excited your curiosity, as well as that of these good people; but you are too considerate to make enquiries."

"Certainly; it would indeed be very impertinent and inhuman in me to trouble you with any inquisitiveness of mine."

"And yet you rescued me from a strange and perilous situation; you have benevolently restored me to life."

Soon after this he enquired if I thought that the breaking up of the ice had destroyed the other sledge? I replied, that I could not answer with any degree of certainty; for the ice had not broken until near midnight, and the traveller might have arrived at a place of safety before that time; but of this I could not judge.

From this time a new spirit of life animated the decaying frame of the stranger. He manifested the greatest eagerness to be upon deck, to watch for the sledge which had before appeared; but I have persuaded him to remain in the cabin, for he is far too weak to sustain the rawness of the atmosphere. I have promised that some one should watch for him, and give him instant notice if any new object should appear in sight.

Such is my journal of what relates to this strange occurrence up to the present day. The stranger has gradually improved in health, but is very silent, and appears uneasy when any one enters his cabin. Yet his manners are so conciliating and gentle, that the sailors are all interested in him, although they have had very little communication with him. For my own part, I begin to love him as a brother; and his constant and deep grief fills me with sympathy and compassion. He must have been a noble creature in his better days, being even now in wreck so attractive and amiable.

I said in one of my letters, my dear Margaret, that I should find no friend on the wide ocean; yet I have found a man who, before his spirit had been broken by misery, I should have been happy to have possessed as the brother of my heart.

I shall continue my journal concerning the stranger at intervals, should I have any fresh incidents to record.

August 13th, 17—.

My affection for my guest increases every day. He excites at once my admiration and my pity to an astonishing degree. How can I see so noble a creature destroyed by misery, without feeling the most poignant grief? He is so gentle, yet so wise; his mind is so cultivated; and when he speaks, although his words are culled with the choicest art, yet they flow with rapidity and unparalleled eloquence.

He is now much recovered from his illness, and is continually on the deck, apparently watching for the sledge that preceded his own. Yet, although unhappy, he is not so utterly occupied by his own misery, but that he interests himself deeply in the projects of others. He has frequently conversed with me on mine, which I have communicated to him without disguise. He entered attentively into all my arguments in favour of my eventual success, and into every minute detail of the measures I had taken to secure it. I was easily led by the sympathy which he evinced, to use the language of my heart; to give utterance to the burning ardour of my soul; and to say, with all the fervour that warmed me, how gladly I would sacrifice my fortune, my existence, my every hope, to the furtherance of my enterprise. One man's life or death were but a small price to pay for the acquirement of the knowledge which I sought; for the dominion I should acquire and transmit over the elemental foes of our race. As I spoke, a dark gloom spread over my listener's countenance. At first I perceived that he tried to suppress his emotion; he placed his hands before his eyes; and my voice quivered and failed me, as I beheld tears trickle fast from between his fingers, — a groan burst from his heaving breast. I paused; — at length he spoke, in broken accents: — "Unhappy man! Do you share my madness? Have you drank also of the intoxicating draught? Hear me, — let me reveal my tale, and you will dash the cup from your lips!"

Such words, you may imagine, strongly excited my curiosity; but the paroxysm of grief that had seized the stranger overcame his weakened powers, and many hours of repose and tranquil conversation were necessary to restore his composure.

Having conquered the violence of his feelings, he appeared to despise himself for being the slave of passion; and quelling the dark tyranny of despair, he led me again to converse concerning myself personally. He asked me the history of my earlier years. The tale was quickly told: but it awakened various trains of reflection. I spoke of my desire of finding a friend — of my thirst for a more intimate sympathy with a fellow mind than had ever fallen to my lot; and expressed my conviction that a man could boast of little happiness, who did not enjoy this blessing.

"I agree with you," replied the stranger; "we are unfashioned creatures, but half made up, if one wiser, better, dearer than ourselves — such a friend ought to be — do not lend his aid to perfectionate our weak and faulty natures. I once had a friend, the most noble of human creatures, and am entitled, therefore, to judge respecting friendship. You have hope, and the world before you, and have no cause for despair. But I — I have lost every thing, and cannot begin life anew."

As he said this, his countenance became expressive of a calm settled grief, that touched me to the heart. But he was silent, and presently retired to his cabin.

Even broken in spirit as he is, no one can feel more deeply than he does the beauties of nature. The starry sky, the sea, and every sight afforded by these wonderful regions, seems still to have the power of elevating his soul from earth. Such a man has a double existence: he may suffer misery, and be overwhelmed by disappointments; yet, when he has retired into himself, he will be like a celestial spirit, that has a halo around him, within whose circle no grief or folly ventures.

Will you smile at the enthusiasm I express concerning this divine wanderer? You would not, if you saw him. You have been tutored and refined by books and retirement from the world, and you are, therefore, somewhat fastidious; but this only renders you the more fit to appreciate the extraordinary merits of this wonderful man.

Sometimes I have endeavoured to discover what quality it is which he possesses, that elevates him so immeasurably above any other person I ever knew. I believe it to be an intuitive discernment; a quick but never-failing power of judgment; a penetration into the causes of things, unequalled for clearness and precision; add to this a facility of expression, and a voice whose varied intonations are soul-subduing music.

August 19, 17—.

Yesterday the stranger said to me, "You may easily perceive, Captain Walton, that I have suffered great and unparalleled misfortunes. I had determined, at one time, that the memory of these evils should die with me; but you have won me to alter my determination. You seek for knowledge and wisdom, as I once did; and I ardently hope that the gratification of your wishes may not be a serpent to sting you, as mine has been. I do not know that the relation of my disasters will be useful to you; yet, when I reflect that you are pursuing the same course, exposing yourself to the same dangers which have rendered me what I am, I imagine that you may deduce an apt moral from my tale; one that may direct you if you succeed in your undertaking, and console you in case of failure. Prepare to hear of occurrences which are usually deemed marvellous. Were we among the tamer scenes of nature, I might fear to encounter your unbelief, perhaps your ridicule; but many things will appear possible in these wild and mysterious regions, which would provoke the laughter of those unacquainted with the ever-varied powers of nature: — nor can I doubt but that my tale conveys in its series internal evidence of the truth of the events of which it is composed."

You may easily imagine that I was much gratified by the offered communication; yet I could not endure that he should renew his grief by a recital of his misfortunes. I felt the greatest eagerness to hear the promised narrative, partly from curiosity, and partly from a strong desire to ameliorate his fate, if it were in my power. I expressed these feelings in my answer.

"I thank you," he replied, "for your sympathy, but it is useless; my fate is nearly fulfilled. I wait but for one event, and then I shall repose in peace. I understand your feeling," continued he, perceiving that I wished to interrupt him; "but you are mistaken, my friend, if thus you will allow me to name you; nothing can alter my destiny: listen to my history, and you will perceive how irrevocably it is determined."

He then told me, that he would commence his narrative the next day when I should be at leisure. This promise drew from me the warmest thanks. I have resolved every night, when I am not imperatively occupied by my duties, to record, as nearly as possible in his own words, what he has related during the day. If I should be engaged, I will at least make notes. This manuscript will doubtless afford you the greatest pleasure: but to me, who know him, and who hear it from his own lips, with what interest and sympathy shall I read it in some future day! Even now, as I commence my task, his full-toned voice swells in my ears; his lustrous eyes dwell on me with all their melancholy sweetness; I see his thin hand raised in animation, while the lineaments of his face are irradiated by the soul within. Strange and harrowing must be his story; frightful the storm which embraced the gallant vessel on its course, and wrecked it — thus!

CHAPTER I

I am by birth a Genevese; and my family is one of the most distinguished of that republic. My ancestors had been for many years counsellors and syndics;[3] and my father had filled several public situations with honour and reputation. He was respected by all who knew him, for his integrity and indefatigable attention to public

[3] Government officials. — EDS.

business. He passed his younger days perpetually occupied by the affairs of his country; a variety of circumstances had prevented his marrying early, nor was it until the decline of life that he became a husband and the father of a family.

As the circumstances of his marriage illustrate his character, I cannot refrain from relating them. One of his most intimate friends was a merchant, who, from a flourishing state, fell, through numerous mischances, into poverty. This man, whose name was Beaufort, was of a proud and unbending disposition, and could not bear to live in poverty and oblivion in the same country where he had formerly been distinguished for his rank and magnificence. Having paid his debts, therefore, in the most honourable manner, he retreated with his daughter to the town of Lucerne, where he lived unknown and in wretchedness. My father loved Beaufort with the truest friendship, and was deeply grieved by his retreat in these unfortunate circumstances. He bitterly deplored the false pride which led his friend to a conduct so little worthy of the affection that united them. He lost no time in endeavouring to seek him out, with the hope of persuading him to begin the world again through his credit and assistance.

Beaufort had taken effectual measures to conceal himself; and it was ten months before my father discovered his abode. Overjoyed at this discovery, he hastened to the house, which was situated in a mean street, near the Reuss. But when he entered, misery and despair alone welcomed him. Beaufort had saved but a very small sum of money from the wreck of his fortunes; but it was sufficient to provide him with sustenance for some months, and in the mean time he hoped to procure some respectable employment in a merchant's house. The interval was, consequently, spent in inaction; his grief only became more deep and rankling, when he had leisure for reflection; and at length it took so fast hold of his mind, that at the end of three months he lay on a bed of sickness, incapable of any exertion.

His daughter attended him with the greatest tenderness; but she saw with despair that their little fund was rapidly decreasing, and that there was no other prospect of support. But Caroline Beaufort possessed a mind of an uncommon mould; and her courage rose to support her in her adversity. She procured plain work; she plaited straw; and by various means contrived to earn a pittance scarcely sufficient to support life.

Several months passed in this manner. Her father grew worse; her time was more entirely occupied in attending him; her means of subsistence decreased; and in the tenth month her father died in her arms, leaving her an orphan and a beggar. This last blow overcame her; and she knelt by Beaufort's coffin, weeping bitterly, when my father entered the chamber. He came like a protecting spirit to the poor girl, who committed herself to his care; and after the interment of his friend, he conducted her to Geneva, and placed her under the protection of a relation. Two years after this event Caroline became his wife.

There was a considerable difference between the ages of my parents, but this circumstance seemed to unite them only closer in bonds of devoted affection. There was a sense of justice in my father's upright mind, which rendered it necessary that he should approve highly to love strongly. Perhaps during former years he had suffered from the late-discovered unworthiness of one beloved, and so was disposed to set a greater value on tried worth. There was a show of gratitude and worship in his attachment to my mother, differing wholly from the doting fondness of age, for it was inspired by reverence for her virtues, and a desire to be the means of, in some degree, recompensing her for the sorrows she had endured, but which gave inexpressible grace to his behaviour to her. Every thing was made to yield to her wishes and her convenience. He strove to shelter her, as a fair exotic is sheltered by the gardener, from every rougher wind, and to surround her with all that could tend to excite pleasurable emotion in her soft and benevolent mind. Her health, and even the tranquillity of her hitherto constant spirit, had been shaken by what she had gone through. During the two years that had elapsed previous to their marriage my father had gradually relinquished all his public functions; and immediately after their union they sought the pleasant climate of Italy, and the change of scene and interest attendant on a tour through that land of wonders, as a restorative for her weakened frame.

From Italy they visited Germany and France. I, their eldest child, was born at Naples, and as an infant accompanied them in their rambles. I remained for several years their only child. Much as they were attached to each other, they seemed to draw inexhaustible stores of affection from a very mine of love to bestow them upon me. My mother's tender caresses, and my father's smile of benevolent pleasure while regarding me, are my first recollections. I was their plaything and their idol, and something better — their child, the innocent and helpless creature bestowed on them by Heaven, whom to bring up to good, and whose future lot it was in their hands to direct to happiness or misery, according as they fulfilled their duties towards me. With this deep consciousness of what they owed towards the being to which they had given life, added to the active spirit of tenderness that animated both, it may be imagined that while during every hour of my infant life I received a lesson of patience, of charity, and of self-control, I was so guided by a silken cord, that all seemed but one train of enjoyment to me.

For a long time I was their only care. My mother had much desired to have a daughter, but I continued their single offspring. When I was about five years old, while making an excursion beyond the frontiers of Italy, they passed a week on the shores of the Lake of Como. Their benevolent disposition often made them enter the cottages of the poor. This, to my mother, was more than a duty; it was a necessity, a passion, — remembering what she had suffered, and how she had been relieved, — for her to act in her turn the guardian angel to the afflicted. During one of their walks a poor cot in the foldings of a vale attracted their notice, as being singularly disconsolate, while the number of half-clothed children gathered about it, spoke of penury in its worst shape. One day, when my father had gone by himself to Milan, my mother, accompanied by me, visited this abode. She found a peasant and his wife, hard working, bent down by care and labour, distributing a scanty meal to five hungry babes. Among these there was one which attracted my mother far above all the rest. She appeared of a different stock. The four others were dark-eyed, hardy little vagrants; this child was thin, and very fair. Her hair was the brightest living gold, and, despite the poverty of her clothing, seemed to set a crown of distinction on her head. Her brow was clear and ample, her blue eyes cloudless, and her lips and the moulding of her face so expressive of sensibility and sweetness, that none could behold her without looking on her as of a distinct species, a being heaven-sent, and bearing a celestial stamp in all her features.

The peasant woman, perceiving that my mother fixed eyes of wonder and admiration on this lovely girl, eagerly communicated her history. She was not her child, but the daughter of a Milanese nobleman. Her mother was a German, and had died on giving her birth. The infant had been placed with these good people to nurse: they were better off then. They had not been long married, and their eldest child was but just born. The father of their charge was one of those Italians nursed in the memory of the antique glory of Italy, — one among the *schiavi ognor frementi,*[4] who exerted himself to obtain the liberty of his country. He became the victim

[4] Italian for "slaves ever trembling"; a reference to Austrian subjugation of Italians during the eighteenth and nineteenth centuries. — EDS.

of its weakness. Whether he had died, or still lingered in the dungeons of Austria, was not known. His property was confiscated, his child became an orphan and a beggar. She continued with her foster parents, and bloomed in their rude abode, fairer than a garden rose among dark-leaved brambles.

When my father returned from Milan, he found playing with me in the hall of our villa, a child fairer than pictured cherub — a creature who seemed to shed radiance from her looks, and whose form and motions were lighter than the chamois of the hills. The apparition was soon explained. With his permission my mother prevailed on her rustic guardians to yield their charge to her. They were fond of the sweet orphan. Her presence had seemed a blessing to them; but it would be unfair to her to keep her in poverty and want, when Providence afforded her such powerful protection. They consulted their village priest, and the result was, that Elizabeth Lavenza became the inmate of my parents' house — my more than sister — the beautiful and adored companion of all my occupations and my pleasures.

Every one loved Elizabeth. The passionate and almost reverential attachment with which all regarded her became, while I shared it, my pride and my delight. On the evening previous to her being brought to my home, my mother had said playfully, — "I have a pretty present for my Victor — to-morrow he shall have it." And when, on the morrow, she presented Elizabeth to me as her promised gift, I, with childish seriousness, interpreted her words literally, and looked upon Elizabeth as mine — mine to protect, love, and cherish. All praises bestowed on her, I received as made to a possession of my own. We called each other familiarly by the name of cousin. No word, no expression could body forth the kind of relation in which she stood to me — my more than sister, since till death she was to be mine only.

CHAPTER II

We were brought up together; there was not quite a year difference in our ages. I need not say that we were strangers to any species of disunion or dispute. Harmony was the soul of our companionship, and the diversity and contrast that subsisted in our characters drew us nearer together. Elizabeth was of a calmer and more concentrated disposition; but, with all my ardour, I was capable of a more intense application, and was more deeply smitten with the thirst for knowledge. She busied herself with following the aerial creations of the poets; and in the majestic and wondrous scenes which surrounded our Swiss home — the sublime shapes of the mountains; the changes of the seasons; tempest and calm; the silence of winter, and the life and turbulence of our Alpine summers, — she found ample scope for admiration and delight. While my companion contemplated with a serious and satisfied spirit the magnificent appearances of things, I delighted in investigating their causes. The world was to me a secret which I desired to divine. Curiosity, earnest research to learn the hidden laws of nature, gladness akin to rapture, as they were unfolded to me, are among the earliest sensations I can remember.

On the birth of a second son, my junior by seven years, my parents gave up entirely their wandering life, and fixed themselves in their native country. We possessed a house in Geneva, and a *campagne*[5] on Belrive, the eastern shore of the lake, at the distance of rather more than a league from the city. We resided principally in the latter, and the lives of my parents were passed in considerable seclusion. It was my temper to avoid a crowd, and to attach myself fervently to a few. I was indifferent, therefore, to my schoolfellows in general; but I united

[5] French for "countryside." — EDS.

myself in the bonds of the closest friendship to one among them. Henry Clerval was the son of a merchant of Geneva. He was a boy of singular talent and fancy. He loved enterprise, hardship, and even danger, for its own sake. He was deeply read in books of chivalry and romance. He composed heroic songs, and began to write many a tale of enchantment and knightly adventure. He tried to make us act plays, and to enter into masquerades, in which the characters were drawn from the heroes of Roncesvalles,[6] of the Round Table of King Arthur, and the chivalrous train who shed their blood to redeem the holy sepulchre from the hands of the infidels.

No human being could have passed a happier childhood than myself. My parents were possessed by the very spirit of kindness and indulgence. We felt that they were not the tyrants to rule our lot according to their caprice, but the agents and creators of all the many delights which we enjoyed. When I mingled with other families, I distinctly discerned how peculiarly fortunate my lot was, and gratitude assisted the development of filial love.

My temper was sometimes violent, and my passions vehement; but by some law in my temperature they were turned, not towards childish pursuits, but to an eager desire to learn, and not to learn all things indiscriminately. I confess that neither the structure of languages, nor the code of governments, nor the politics of various states, possessed attractions for me. It was the secrets of heaven and earth that I desired to learn; and whether it was the outward substance of things, or the inner spirit of nature and the mysterious soul of man that occupied me, still my enquiries were directed to the metaphysical, or, in its highest sense, the physical secrets of the world.

Meanwhile Clerval occupied himself, so to speak, with the moral relations of things. The busy stage of life, the virtues of heroes, and the actions of men, were his theme; and his hope and his dream was to become one among those whose names are recorded in story, as the gallant and adventurous benefactors of our species. The saintly soul of Elizabeth shone like a shrine-dedicated lamp in our peaceful home. Her sympathy was ours; her smile, her soft voice, the sweet glance of her celestial eyes, were ever there to bless and animate us. She was the living spirit of love to soften and attract: I might have become sullen in my study, rough through the ardour of my nature, but that she was there to subdue me to a semblance of her own gentleness. And Clerval — could aught ill entrench on the noble spirit of Clerval? — yet he might not have been so perfectly humane, so thoughtful in his generosity — so full of kindness and tenderness amidst his passion for adventurous exploit, had she not unfolded to him the real loveliness of beneficence, and made the doing good the end and aim of his soaring ambition.

I feel exquisite pleasure in dwelling on the recollections of childhood, before misfortune had tainted my mind, and changed its bright visions of extensive usefulness into gloomy and narrow reflections upon self. Besides, in drawing the picture of my early days, I also record those events which led, by insensible steps, to my after tale of misery: for when I would account to myself for the birth of that passion, which afterwards ruled my destiny, I find it arise, like a mountain river, from ignoble and almost forgotten sources; but, swelling as it proceeded, it became the torrent which, in its course, has swept away all my hopes and joys.

Natural philosophy is the genius that has regulated my fate; I desire, therefore, in this narration, to state those facts which led to my predilection for that science. When I was thirteen years of age, we all went on a party of pleasure to the baths near Thonon; the inclemency of the weather obliged us to remain a day confined to the inn. In this house I chanced to find a

[6] The site of a battle in the eleventh-century epic French poem, *The Song of Roland.* — EDS.

volume of the works of Cornelius Agrippa.[7] I opened it with apathy; the theory which he attempts to demonstrate, and the wonderful facts which he relates, soon changed this feeling into enthusiasm. A new light seemed to dawn upon my mind; and, bounding with joy, I communicated my discovery to my father. My father looked carelessly at the titlepage of my book, and said, "Ah! Cornelius Agrippa! My dear Victor, do not waste your time upon this; it is sad trash."

If, instead of this remark, my father had taken the pains to explain to me, that the principles of Agrippa had been entirely exploded, and that a modern system of science had been introduced, which possessed much greater powers than the ancient, because the powers of the latter were chimerical, while those of the former were real and practical; under such circumstances, I should certainly have thrown Agrippa aside, and have contented my imagination, warmed as it was, by returning with greater ardour to my former studies. It is even possible, that the train of my ideas would never have received the fatal impulse that led to my ruin. But the cursory glance my father had taken of my volume by no means assured me that he was acquainted with its contents; and I continued to read with the greatest avidity.

When I returned home, my first care was to procure the whole works of this author, and afterwards of Paracelsus[8] and Albertus Magnus.[9] I read and studied the wild fancies of these writers with delight; they appeared to me treasures known to few beside myself. I have described myself as always having been embued with a fervent longing to penetrate the secrets of nature. In spite of the intense labour and wonderful discoveries of modern philosophers, I always came from my studies discontented and unsatisfied. Sir Isaac Newton is said to have avowed that he felt like a child picking up shells beside the great and unexplored ocean of truth.

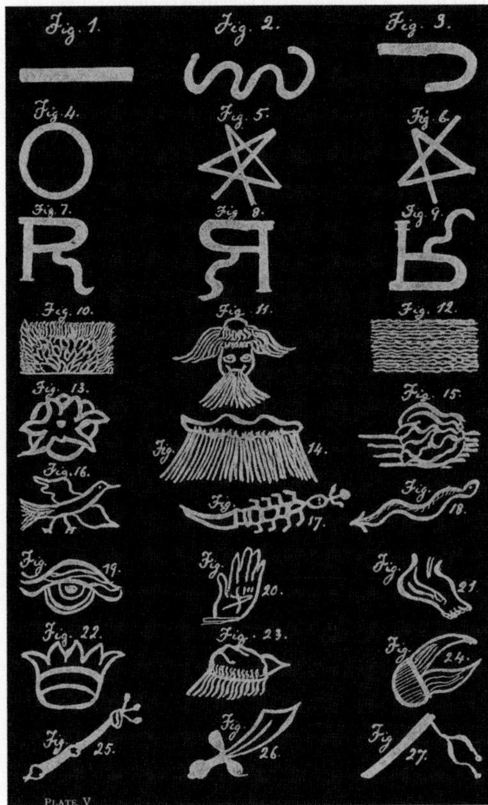

Culture Club / Getty Images

This artwork, titled *Character of Evil Spirits*, was inspired by Cornelius Agrippa's *The Fourth Book of Occult Philosophy* (1655). **In what ways might this interpretation of the content of the book, which Victor finds highly interesting, help shed light on his character?**

[7] Heinrich Cornelius Agrippa (1486–1535) was a German physician and occultist. — EDS.

[8] Theophrastus Bombastus von Hohenheim (1493–1541), also known as Paracelsus, was a Swiss physician who believed human beings could be produced through alchemy, a science dating to the medieval era that focused on turning common metals into gold, producing a universal healing elixir, and achieving immortality. — EDS.

[9] Albertus Magnus (1193–1280) was a German philosopher and theologian noted for his knowledge of Aristotle and the physical sciences, to whom many works on alchemy were (perhaps mistakenly) attributed. He later instructed Thomas Aquinas (1225–1274), a theologian who attempted to fuse tenets of Aristotelian philosophy with Roman Catholic principles. — EDS.

Those of his successors in each branch of natural philosophy with whom I was acquainted, appeared even to my boy's apprehensions, as tyros[10] engaged in the same pursuit.

The untaught peasant beheld the elements around him, and was acquainted with their practical uses. The most learned philosopher knew little more. He had partially unveiled the face of Nature, but her immortal lineaments were still a wonder and a mystery. He might dissect, anatomise, and give names; but, not to speak of a final cause, causes in their secondary and tertiary grades were utterly unknown to him. I had gazed upon the fortifications and impediments that seemed to keep human beings from entering the citadel of nature, and rashly and ignorantly I had repined.

But here were books, and here were men who had penetrated deeper and knew more. I took their word for all that they averred, and I became their disciple. It may appear strange that such should arise in the eighteenth century; but while I followed the routine of education in the schools of Geneva, I was, to a great degree, self taught with regard to my favourite studies. My father was not scientific, and I was left to struggle with a child's blindness, added to a student's thirst for knowledge. Under the guidance of my new preceptors, I entered with the greatest diligence into the search of the philosopher's stone and the elixir of life; but the latter soon obtained my undivided attention. Wealth was an inferior object; but what glory would attend the discovery, if I could banish disease from the human frame, and render man invulnerable to any but a violent death!

Nor were these my only visions. The raising of ghosts or devils was a promise liberally accorded by my favourite authors, the fulfilment of which I most eagerly sought; and if my incantations were always unsuccessful, I attributed the failure rather to my own inexperience and mistake, than to a want of skill or fidelity in my instructors. And thus for a time I was occupied by exploded systems, mingling, like an unadept, a thousand contradictory theories, and floundering desperately in a very slough of multifarious knowledge, guided by an ardent imagination and childish reasoning, till an accident again changed the current of my ideas.

When I was about fifteen years old we had retired to our house near Belrive, when we witnessed a most violent and terrible thunderstorm. It advanced from behind the mountains of Jura; and the thunder burst at once with frightful loudness from various quarters of the heavens. I remained, while the storm lasted, watching its progress with curiosity and delight. As I stood at the door, on a sudden I beheld a stream of fire issue from an old and beautiful oak, which stood about twenty yards from our house; and so soon as the dazzling light vanished, the oak had disappeared, and nothing remained but a blasted stump. When we visited it the next morning, we found the tree shattered in a singular manner. It was not splintered by the shock, but entirely reduced to thin ribands of wood. I never beheld any thing so utterly destroyed.

Before this I was not unacquainted with the more obvious laws of electricity. On this occasion a man of great research in natural philosophy was with us, and, excited by this catastrophe, he entered on the explanation of a theory which he had formed on the subject of electricity and galvanism, which was at once new and astonishing to me. All that he said threw greatly into the shade Cornelius Agrippa, Albertus Magnus, and Paracelsus, the lords of my imagination; but by some fatality the overthrow of these men disinclined me to pursue my accustomed studies. It seemed to me as if nothing would or could ever be known. All that had so long engaged my attention suddenly grew despicable. By one of those caprices of the mind, which we are perhaps most subject to in early

[10] Novices.—EDS.

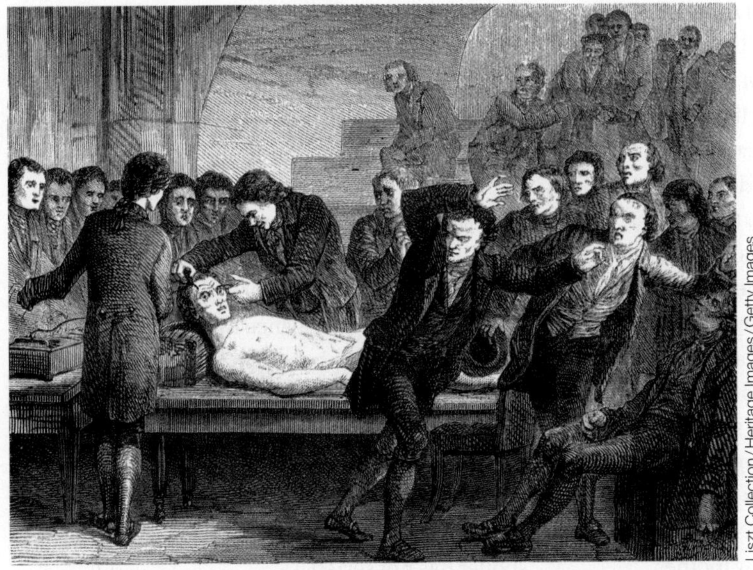

This engraving depicts Scottish doctor Andrew Ure performing one of several galvanic experiments on the corpse of Matthew Clydesdale, a recently executed murderer, in 1818. The electric current from Ure's galvanic battery stimulated Clydesdale's muscles, causing his limbs, chest, and face to move. As a result, some members of the audience fled, believing the dead man had been resurrected. **What do the events depicted in this engraving suggest about Frankenstein's new interest? What do they suggest about the direction the story is headed?**

youth, I at once gave up my former occupations; set down natural history and all its progeny as a deformed and abortive creation; and entertained the greatest disdain for a would-be science, which could never even step within the threshold of real knowledge. In this mood of mind I betook myself to the mathematics, and the branches of study appertaining to that science, as being built upon secure foundations, and so worthy of my consideration.

Thus strangely are our souls constructed, and by such slight ligaments are we bound to prosperity or ruin. When I look back, it seems to me as if this almost miraculous change of inclination and will was the immediate suggestion of the guardian angel of my life — the last effort made by the spirit of preservation to avert the storm that was even then hanging in the stars, and ready to envelop me. Her victory was announced by an unusual tranquillity and gladness of soul, which followed the relinquishing of my ancient and latterly tormenting studies. It was thus that I was to be taught to associate evil with their prosecution, happiness with their disregard.

It was a strong effort of the spirit of good; but it was ineffectual. Destiny was too potent, and her immutable laws had decreed my utter and terrible destruction.

CHAPTER III

When I had attained the age of seventeen, my parents resolved that I should become a student at the university of Ingolstadt.[11] I had hitherto attended the schools of Geneva; but my father thought it necessary, for the completion of my education, that I should be made acquainted

[11] A German city. — EDS.

with other customs than those of my native country. My departure was therefore fixed at an early date; but, before the day resolved upon could arrive, the first misfortune of my life occurred— an omen, as it were, of my future misery.

Elizabeth had caught the scarlet fever; her illness was severe, and she was in the greatest danger. During her illness, many arguments had been urged to persuade my mother to refrain from attending upon her. She had, at first, yielded to our entreaties; but when she heard that the life of her favourite was menaced, she could no longer control her anxiety. She attended her sick bed,—her watchful attentions triumphed over the malignity of the distemper,—Elizabeth was saved, but the consequences of this imprudence were fatal to her preserver. On the third day my mother sickened; her fever was accompanied by the most alarming symptoms, and the looks of her medical attendants prognosticated the worst event. On her death-bed the fortitude and benignity of this best of women did not desert her. She joined the hands of Elizabeth and myself:—"My children," she said, "my firmest hopes of future happiness were placed on the prospect of your union. This expectation will now be the consolation of your father. Elizabeth, my love, you must supply my place to my younger children. Alas! I regret that I am taken from you; and, happy and beloved as I have been, is it not hard to quit you all? But these are not thoughts befitting me; I will endeavour to resign myself cheerfully to death, and will indulge a hope of meeting you in another world."

She died calmly; and her countenance expressed affection even in death. I need not describe the feelings of those whose dearest ties are rent by that most irreparable evil; the void that presents itself to the soul; and the despair that is exhibited on the countenance. It is so long before the mind can persuade itself that she, whom we saw every day, and whose very existence appeared a part of our own, can have departed for ever—that the brightness of a beloved eye can have been extinguished, and the sound of a voice so familiar, and dear to the ear, can be hushed, never more to be heard. These are the reflections of the first days; but when the lapse of time proves the reality of the evil, then the actual bitterness of grief commences. Yet from whom has not that rude hand rent away some dear connection? and why should I describe a sorrow which all have felt, and must feel? The time at length arrives, when grief is rather an indulgence than a necessity; and the smile that plays upon the lips, although it may be deemed a sacrilege, is not banished. My mother was dead, but we had still duties which we ought to perform; we must continue our course with the rest, and learn to think ourselves fortunate, whilst one remains whom the spoiler has not seized.

My departure for Ingolstadt, which had been deferred by these events, was now again determined upon. I obtained from my father a respite of some weeks. It appeared to me sacrilege so soon to leave the repose, akin to death, of the house of mourning, and to rush into the thick of life. I was new to sorrow, but it did not the less alarm me. I was unwilling to quit the sight of those that remained to me; and, above all, I desired to see my sweet Elizabeth in some degree consoled.

She indeed veiled her grief, and strove to act the comforter to us all. She looked steadily on life, and assumed its duties with courage and zeal. She devoted herself to those whom she had been taught to call her uncle and cousins. Never was she so enchanting as at this time, when she recalled the sunshine of her smiles and spent them upon us. She forgot even her own regret in her endeavours to make us forget.

The day of my departure at length arrived. Clerval spent the last evening with us. He had endeavoured to persuade his father to permit him to accompany me, and to become my fellow student; but in vain. His father was a narrow-minded trader, and saw idleness and ruin in the aspirations and ambition of his son. Henry deeply felt the misfortune of being debarred from a liberal education. He said little; but when he spoke, I read in his kindling eye and in his animated glance a restrained but firm resolve, not to be chained to the miserable details of commerce.

We sat late. We could not tear ourselves away from each other, nor persuade ourselves to say the word "Farewell!" It was said; and we retired under the pretence of seeking repose, each fancying that the other was deceived: but when at morning's dawn I descended to the carriage which was to convey me away, they were all there — my father again to bless me, Clerval to press my hand once more, my Elizabeth to renew her entreaties that I would write often, and to bestow the last feminine attentions on her playmate and friend.

I threw myself into the chaise that was to convey me away, and indulged in the most melancholy reflections. I, who had ever been surrounded by amiable companions, continually engaged in endeavouring to bestow mutual pleasure — I was now alone. In the university, whither I was going, I must form my own friends, and be my own protector. My life had hitherto been remarkably secluded and domestic; and this had given me invincible repugnance to new countenances. I loved my brothers, Elizabeth, and Clerval; these were "old familiar faces;" but I believed myself totally unfitted for the company of strangers. Such were my reflections as I commenced my journey; but as I proceeded, my spirits and hopes rose. I ardently desired the acquisition of knowledge. I had often, when at home, thought it hard to remain during my youth cooped up in one place, and had longed to enter the world, and take my station among other human beings. Now my desires were complied with, and it would, indeed, have been folly to repent.

I had sufficient leisure for these and many other reflections during my journey to Ingolstadt, which was long and fatiguing. At length the high white steeple of the town met my eyes. I alighted, and was conducted to my solitary apartment, to spend the evening as I pleased.

The next morning I delivered my letters of introduction, and paid a visit to some of the principal professors. Chance — or rather the evil influence, the Angel of Destruction, which asserted omnipotent sway over me from the moment I turned my reluctant steps from my father's door — led me first to M. Krempe, professor of natural philosophy. He was an uncouth man, but deeply embued in the secrets of his science. He asked me several questions concerning my progress in the different branches of science appertaining to natural philosophy. I replied carelessly; and, partly in contempt, mentioned the names of my alchymists as the principal authors I had studied. The professor stared: "Have you," he said, "really spent your time in studying such nonsense?"

I replied in the affirmative. "Every minute," continued M. Krempe with warmth, "every instant that you have wasted on those books is utterly and entirely lost. You have burdened your memory with exploded systems and useless names. Good God! in what desert land have you lived, where no one was kind enough to inform you that these fancies, which you have so greedily imbibed, are a thousand years old, and as musty as they are ancient? I little expected, in this enlightened and scientific age, to find a disciple of Albertus Magnus and Paracelsus. My dear sir, you must begin your studies entirely anew."

So saying, he stept aside, and wrote down a list of several books treating of natural philosophy, which he desired me to procure; and dismissed me, after mentioning that in the beginning of the following week he intended to commence a course of lectures upon natural philosophy in its general relations, and that M. Waldman, a fellow-professor, would lecture upon chemistry the alternate days that he omitted.

I returned home, not disappointed, for I have said that I had long considered those authors useless whom the professor reprobated; but I returned, not at all the more inclined to recur to these studies in any shape. M. Krempe was a little, squat man, with a gruff voice and a repulsive countenance; the teacher, therefore, did not prepossess me in favour of his pursuits. In rather too philosophical and connected a strain, perhaps, I have given an account of the conclusions I had come to concerning them in my early years. As a child, I had not been content with the results promised by the modern professors of natural science. With a confusion of ideas only to be accounted for by my extreme youth, and my want of a guide on such matters, I had retrod the steps of knowledge along the paths of time, and exchanged the discoveries of recent enquirers for the dreams of forgotten alchymists. Besides, I had a contempt for the uses of modern natural philosophy. It was very different, when the masters of the science sought immortality and power; such views, although futile, were grand: but now the scene was changed. The ambition of the enquirer seemed to limit itself to the annihilation of those visions on which my interest in science was chiefly founded. I was required to exchange chimeras of boundless grandeur for realities of little worth.

Such were my reflections during the first two or three days of my residence at Ingolstadt, which were chiefly spent in becoming acquainted with the localities, and the principal residents in my new abode. But as the ensuing week commenced, I thought of the information which M. Krempe had given me concerning the lectures. And although I could not consent to go and hear that little conceited fellow deliver sentences out of a pulpit, I recollected what he had said of M. Waldman, whom I had never seen, as he had hitherto been out of town.

Partly from curiosity, and partly from idleness, I went into the lecturing room, which M. Waldman entered shortly after. This professor was very unlike his colleague. He appeared about fifty years of age, but with an aspect expressive of the greatest benevolence; a few grey hairs covered his temples, but those at the back of his head were nearly black. His person was short, but remarkably erect; and his voice the sweetest I had ever heard. He began his lecture by a recapitulation of the history of chemistry, and the various improvements made by different men of learning, pronouncing with fervour the names of the most distinguished discoverers. He then took a cursory view of the present state of the science, and explained many of its elementary terms. After having made a few preparatory experiments, he concluded with a panegyric upon modern chemistry, the terms of which I shall never forget:—

"The ancient teachers of this science," said he, "promised impossibilities, and performed nothing. The modern masters promise very little; they know that metals cannot be transmuted, and that the elixir of life is a chimera. But these philosophers, whose hands seem only made to dabble in dirt, and their eyes to pore over the microscope or crucible, have indeed performed miracles. They penetrate into the recesses of nature, and show how she works in her hiding places. They ascend into the heavens: they have discovered how the blood circulates, and the nature of the air we breathe. They have acquired new and almost unlimited powers; they can command the thunders of heaven, mimic the earthquake, and even mock the invisible world with its own shadows."

Such were the professor's words—rather let me say such the words of fate, enounced to destroy me. As he went on, I felt as if my soul were grappling with a palpable enemy; one by one the various keys were touched which formed the mechanism of my being: chord after chord was sounded, and soon my mind was filled with one thought, one conception, one purpose. So much has been done, exclaimed the soul of Frankenstein,—more, far more, will I achieve: treading in the steps already marked, I will pioneer a new way, explore unknown powers, and unfold to the world the deepest mysteries of creation.

I closed not my eyes that night. My internal being was in a state of insurrection and turmoil; I felt that order would thence arise, but I had no power to produce it. By degrees, after the morning's dawn, sleep came. I awoke, and my yesternight's thoughts were as a dream. There only remained a resolution to return to my ancient studies, and to devote myself to a science for which I believed myself to possess a natural talent. On the same day, I paid M. Waldman a visit. His manners in private were even more mild and attractive than in public; for there was a certain dignity in his mien during his lecture, which in his own house was replaced by the greatest affability and kindness. I gave him pretty nearly the same account of my former pursuits as I had given to his fellow-professor. He heard with attention the little narration concerning my studies, and smiled at the names of Cornelius Agrippa and Paracelsus, but without the contempt that M. Krempe had exhibited. He said, that "these were men to whose indefatigable zeal modern philosophers were indebted for most of the foundations of their knowledge. They had left to us, as an easier task, to give new names, and arrange in connected classifications, the facts which they in a great degree had been the instruments of bringing to light. The labours of men of genius, however erroneously directed, scarcely ever fail in ultimately turning to the solid advantage of mankind." I listened to his statement, which was delivered without any presumption or affectation; and then added, that his lecture had removed my prejudices against modern chemists; I expressed myself in measured terms, with the modesty and deference due from a youth to his instructor, without letting escape (inexperience in life would have made me ashamed) any of the enthusiasm which stimulated my intended labours. I requested his advice concerning the books I ought to procure.

"I am happy," said M. Waldman, "to have gained a disciple; and if your application equals your ability, I have no doubt of your success. Chemistry is that branch of natural philosophy in which the greatest improvements have been and may be made: it is on that account that I have made it my peculiar study; but at the same time I have not neglected the other branches of science. A man would make but a very sorry chemist if he attended to that department of human knowledge alone. If your wish is to become really a man of science, and not merely a petty experimentalist, I should advise you to apply to every branch of natural philosophy, including mathematics."

He then took me into his laboratory, and explained to me the uses of his various machines; instructing me as to what I ought to procure, and promising me the use of his own when I should have advanced far enough in the science not to derange their mechanism. He also gave me the list of books which I had requested; and I took my leave.

Thus ended a day memorable to me: it decided my future destiny.

CHAPTER IV

From this day natural philosophy, and particularly chemistry, in the most comprehensive sense of the term, became nearly my sole occupation. I read with ardour those works, so full of genius and discrimination, which modern enquirers have written on these subjects. I attended the lectures, and cultivated the acquaintance, of the men of science of the university; and I found even in M. Krempe a great deal of sound sense and real information, combined, it is true, with a repulsive physiognomy and manners, but not on that account the less valuable. In M. Waldman I found a true friend. His gentleness was never tinged by dogmatism; and his instructions were given with an air of frankness and good nature, that banished every idea of pedantry. In a thousand ways he smoothed for me the path of knowledge, and made the most abstruse enquiries clear and facile to my apprehension. My application was at first fluctuating and uncertain; it gained strength as I proceeded, and soon became so ardent and eager, that the stars often disappeared in the light of morning whilst I was yet engaged in my laboratory.

As I applied so closely, it may be easily conceived that my progress was rapid. My ardour was indeed the astonishment of the students, and my proficiency that of the masters. Professor Krempe often asked me, with a sly smile, how Cornelius Agrippa went on? whilst M. Waldman expressed the most heartfelt exultation in my progress. Two years passed in this manner, during which I paid no visit to Geneva, but was engaged, heart and soul, in the pursuit of some discoveries, which I hoped to make. None but those who have experienced them can conceive of the enticements of science. In other studies you go as far as others have gone before you, and there is nothing more to know; but in a scientific pursuit there is continual food for discovery and wonder. A mind of moderate capacity, which closely pursues one study, must infallibly arrive at great proficiency in that study; and I, who continually sought the attainment of one object of pursuit, and was solely wrapt up in this, improved so rapidly, that, at the end of two years, I made some discoveries in the improvement of some chemical instruments, which procured me great esteem and admiration at the university. When I had arrived at this point, and had become as well acquainted with the theory and practice of natural philosophy as depended on the lessons of any of the professors at Ingolstadt, my residence there being no longer conducive to my improvements, I thought of returning to my friends and my native town, when an incident happened that protracted my stay.

One of the phenomena which had peculiarly attracted my attention was the structure of the human frame, and, indeed, any animal endued with life. Whence, I often asked myself, did the principle of life proceed? It was a bold question, and one which has ever been considered as a mystery; yet with how many things are we upon the brink of becoming acquainted, if cowardice or carelessness did not restrain our enquiries. I revolved these circumstances in my mind, and determined thenceforth to apply myself more particularly to those branches of natural philosophy which relate to physiology. Unless I had been animated by an almost supernatural enthusiasm, my application to this study would have been irksome, and almost intolerable. To examine the causes of life, we must first have recourse to death. I became acquainted with the science of anatomy: but this was not sufficient; I must also observe the natural decay and corruption of the human body. In my education my father had taken the greatest precautions that my mind should be impressed with no supernatural horrors. I do not ever remember to have trembled at a tale of superstition, or to have feared the apparition of a spirit. Darkness had no effect upon my fancy; and a churchyard was to me merely the receptacle of bodies deprived of life, which, from being the seat of beauty and strength, had become food for the worm. Now I was led to examine the cause and progress of this decay, and forced to spend days and nights in vaults and charnel-houses.[12] My attention was fixed upon every object the most insupportable to the delicacy of the human feelings. I saw how the fine form of man was degraded and wasted; I beheld the corruption of death succeed to the blooming cheek of life; I saw how the worm inherited the wonders of the eye and brain. I paused, examining and analysing all the minutiae of causation, as exemplified in the change from life to death, and death to life, until from the midst of this darkness a sudden light broke in upon me — a light so brilliant and wondrous, yet so simple, that while I became dizzy with the immensity of the prospect which it illustrated, I was surprised, that among so many men of genius who had directed their enquiries towards

[12] Repositories for corpses and bones. — EDS.

the same science, that I alone should be reserved to discover so astonishing a secret.

Remember, I am not recording the vision of a madman. The sun does not more certainly shine in the heavens, than that which I now affirm is true. Some miracle might have produced it, yet the stages of the discovery were distinct and probable. After days and nights of incredible labour and fatigue, I succeeded in discovering the cause of generation and life; nay, more, I became myself capable of bestowing animation upon lifeless matter.

The astonishment which I had at first experienced on this discovery soon gave place to delight and rapture. After so much time spent in painful labour, to arrive at once at the summit of my desires, was the most gratifying consummation of my toils. But this discovery was so great and overwhelming, that all the steps by which I had been progressively led to it were obliterated, and I beheld only the result. What had been the study and desire of the wisest men since the creation of the world was now within my grasp. Not that, like a magic scene, it all opened upon me at once: the information I had obtained was of a nature rather to direct my endeavours so soon as I should point them towards the object of my search, than to exhibit that object already accomplished. I was like the Arabian[13] who had been buried with the dead, and found a passage to life, aided only by one glimmering, and seemingly ineffectual, light.

I see by your eagerness, and the wonder and hope which your eyes express, my friend, that you expect to be informed of the secret with which I am acquainted; that cannot be: listen patiently until the end of my story, and you will easily perceive why I am reserved upon that subject. I will not lead you on, unguarded and ardent as I then was, to your destruction and infallible misery. Learn from me, if not by my precepts, at least by my example, how dangerous is the acquirement of knowledge, and how much happier that man is who believes his native town to be the world, than he who aspires to become greater than his nature will allow.

When I found so astonishing a power placed within my hands, I hesitated a long time concerning the manner in which I should employ it. Although I possessed the capacity of bestowing animation, yet to prepare a frame for the reception of it, with all its intricacies of fibres, muscles, and veins, still remained a work of inconceivable difficulty and labour. I doubted at first whether I should attempt the creation of a being like myself, or one of simpler organization; but my imagination was too much exalted by my first success to permit me to doubt of my ability to give life to an animal as complex and wonderful as man. The materials at present within my command hardly appeared adequate to so arduous an undertaking; but I doubted not that I should ultimately succeed. I prepared myself for a multitude of reverses; my operations might be incessantly baffled, and at last my work be imperfect: yet, when I considered the improvement which every day takes place in science and mechanics, I was encouraged to hope my present attempts would at least lay the foundations of future success. Nor could I consider the magnitude and complexity of my plan as any argument of its impracticability. It was with these feelings that I began the creation of a human being. As the minuteness of the parts formed a great hindrance to my speed, I resolved, contrary to my first intention, to make the being of a gigantic stature; that is to say, about eight feet in height, and proportionably large. After having formed this determination, and having spent some months in successfully collecting and arranging my materials, I began.

No one can conceive the variety of feelings which bore me onwards, like a hurricane, in the

[13] A reference to the fourth of seven voyages of Sinbad in a seventeenth-century addition to a collection of Middle Eastern and South Asian stories, *One Thousand and One Nights*, whose earliest iterations date to the early eighth century. On his fourth voyage, Sinbad settles on an island where the custom when one spouse dies is to bury both together in a communal tomb. When Sinbad's young and beautiful wife dies, he is trapped underground with her body until an animal shows him an escape route. — EDS.

first enthusiasm of success. Life and death appeared to me ideal bounds, which I should first break through, and pour a torrent of light into our dark world. A new species would bless me as its creator and source; many happy and excellent natures would owe their being to me. No father could claim the gratitude of his child so completely as I should deserve theirs. Pursuing these reflections, I thought, that if I could bestow animation upon lifeless matter, I might in process of time (although I now found it impossible) renew life where death had apparently devoted the body to corruption.

These thoughts supported my spirits, while I pursued my undertaking with unremitting ardour. My cheek had grown pale with study, and my person had become emaciated with confinement. Sometimes, on the very brink of certainty, I failed; yet still I clung to the hope which the next day or the next hour might realise. One secret which I alone possessed was the hope to which I had dedicated myself; and the moon gazed on my midnight labours, while, with unrelaxed and breathless eagerness, I pursued nature to her hiding-places. Who shall conceive the horrors of my secret toil, as I dabbled among the unhallowed damps of the grave, or tortured the living animal to animate the lifeless clay? My limbs now tremble, and my eyes swim with the remembrance; but then a resistless, and almost frantic, impulse, urged me forward; I seemed to have lost all soul or sensation but for this one pursuit. It was indeed but a passing trance, that only made me feel with renewed acuteness so soon as, the unnatural stimulus ceasing to operate, I had returned to my old habits. I collected bones from charnel-houses; and disturbed, with profane fingers, the tremendous secrets of the human frame. In a solitary chamber, or rather cell, at the top of the house, and separated from all the other apartments by a gallery and staircase, I kept my workshop of filthy creation: my eye-balls were starting from their sockets in attending to the details of my employment. The dissecting room and the slaughter-house furnished many of my materials; and often did my human nature turn with loathing from my occupation, whilst, still urged on by an eagerness which perpetually increased, I brought my work near to a conclusion.

The summer months passed while I was thus engaged, heart and soul, in one pursuit. It was a most beautiful season; never did the fields bestow a more plentiful harvest, or the vines yield a more luxuriant vintage: but my eyes were insensible to the charms of nature. And the same feelings which made me neglect the scenes around me caused me also to forget those friends who were so many miles absent, and whom I had not seen for so long a time. I knew my silence disquieted them; and I well remembered the words of my father: "I know that while you are pleased with yourself, you will think of us with affection, and we shall hear regularly from you. You must pardon me if I regard any interruption in your correspondence as a proof that your other duties are equally neglected."

I knew well therefore what would be my father's feelings; but I could not tear my thoughts from my employment, loathsome in itself, but which had taken an irresistible hold of my imagination. I wished, as it were, to procrastinate all that related to my feelings of affection until the great object, which swallowed up every habit of my nature, should be completed.

I then thought that my father would be unjust if he ascribed my neglect to vice, or faultiness on my part; but I am now convinced that he was justified in conceiving that I should not be altogether free from blame. A human being in perfection ought always to preserve a calm and peaceful mind, and never to allow passion or a transitory desire to disturb his tranquillity. I do not think that the pursuit of knowledge is an exception to this rule. If the study to which you apply yourself has a tendency to weaken your affections, and to destroy your taste for those simple pleasures in which no alloy can possibly

Human dissection was prohibited in Britain before the sixteenth century and remained extremely restricted until the mid-eighteenth century, when a law was passed allowing physicians to dissect the bodies of executed murderers. This engraving by William Hogarth depicts such a dissection. However, legitimate access to cadavers remained extremely limited, and as a result, a black market developed and flourished until the Anatomy Act of 1832 dramatically increased the legal supply. **What does this engraving seem to suggest about the people performing the dissection? Given the crime and stigma surrounding dissection in Britain at the time *Frankenstein* was written, what might Shelley be suggesting about Victor by describing his forays into charnel houses to illegally obtain bodies?**

Musee d'Histoire de la Medecine, Paris, France / Archives Charmet / Bridgeman Images

mix, then that study is certainly unlawful, that is to say, not befitting the human mind. If this rule were always observed; if no man allowed any pursuit whatsoever to interfere with the tranquillity of his domestic affections, Greece had not been enslaved; Caesar would have spared his country; America would have been discovered more gradually; and the empires of Mexico and Peru had not been destroyed.

But I forget that I am moralising in the most interesting part of my tale; and your looks remind me to proceed.

My father made no reproach in his letters, and only took notice of my silence by enquiring into my occupations more particularly than before. Winter, spring, and summer passed away during my labours; but I did not watch the blossom or the expanding leaves — sights which before always yielded me supreme delight — so deeply was I engrossed in my occupation. The leaves of that year had withered before my work drew near to a close; and now every day showed me more plainly how well I had succeeded. But my enthusiasm was checked by my anxiety, and I appeared rather like one doomed by slavery to toil in the mines, or any other unwholesome trade, than an artist occupied by his favourite employment. Every night I was oppressed by a slow fever, and I became nervous to a most painful degree; the fall of a leaf startled me, and I shunned my fellow-creatures as if I had been guilty of a crime. Sometimes I grew alarmed at the wreck I perceived that I had become; the energy of my purpose alone sustained me: my labours would soon end, and I believed that exercise and amusement would then drive away incipient disease; and I promised myself both of these when my creation should be complete.

CHAPTER V

It was on a dreary night of November, that I beheld the accomplishment of my toils. With an anxiety that almost amounted to agony, I collected the instruments of life around me, that I might infuse a spark of being into the lifeless thing that lay at my feet. It was already one in the morning; the rain pattered dismally against the panes, and my candle was nearly burnt out, when, by the glimmer of the half-extinguished light, I saw the dull yellow eye of the creature open; it breathed hard, and a convulsive motion agitated its limbs.

How can I describe my emotions at this catastrophe, or how delineate the wretch whom with such infinite pains and care I had endeavoured to form? His limbs were in proportion, and I had selected his features as beautiful. Beautiful! — Great God! His yellow skin scarcely covered the work of muscles and arteries beneath; his hair was of a lustrous black, and flowing; his teeth of a pearly whiteness; but these luxuriances only formed a more horrid contrast with his watery eyes, that seemed almost of the same colour as the dun white sockets in which they were set, his shriveled complexion and straight black lips.

The different accidents of life are not so changeable as the feelings of human nature. I had worked hard for nearly two years, for the sole purpose of infusing life into an inanimate body. For this I had deprived myself of rest and health. I had desired it with an ardour that far exceeded moderation; but now that I had finished, the beauty of the dream vanished, and breathless horror and disgust filled my heart. Unable to endure the aspect of the being I had created, I rushed out of the room, and continued a long time traversing my bedchamber, unable to compose my mind to sleep. At length lassitude succeeded to the tumult I had before endured; and I threw myself on the bed in my clothes, endeavouring to seek a few moments of forgetfulness. But it was in vain; I slept, indeed, but I was disturbed by the wildest dreams. I thought I saw Elizabeth, in the bloom of health, walking in the streets of Ingolstadt. Delighted and surprised, I embraced her; but as I imprinted the first kiss on her lips, they became livid with the hue of death; her features appeared to change, and I thought that I held the corpse of my dead mother in my arms; a shroud enveloped her form, and I saw the graveworms crawling in the folds of the flannel. I started from my sleep with horror; a cold dew covered my forehead, my teeth chattered, and every limb became convulsed; when, by the dim and yellow light of the moon, as it forced its way through the window shutters, I beheld the wretch — the miserable monster whom I had created. He held up the curtain of the bed; and his eyes, if eyes they may be called, were fixed on me. His jaws opened, and he muttered some inarticulate sounds, while a grin wrinkled his cheeks. He might have spoken, but I did not hear; one hand was stretched out, seemingly to detain me, but I escaped, and rushed down stairs. I took refuge in the courtyard belonging to the house which I inhabited; where I remained during the rest of the night, walking up and down in the greatest agitation, listening attentively, catching and fearing each sound as if it were to announce the approach of the demoniacal corpse to which I had so miserably given life.

Oh! no mortal could support the horror of that countenance. A mummy again endued with animation could not be so hideous as that wretch. I had gazed on him while unfinished; he was ugly then; but when those muscles and joints were rendered capable of motion, it became a thing such as even Dante[14] could not have conceived.

[14] A reference to *The Inferno*, the first part of the three-part fourteenth-century poem *The Divine Comedy* by Dante Alighieri (1265–1321). In it, Dante tells of fantastical punishments and their effects on the people he meets as he is guided through hell by the Roman poet Virgil. — EDS.

I passed the night wretchedly. Sometimes my pulse beat so quickly and hardly, that I felt the palpitation of every artery; at others, I nearly sank to the ground through languor and extreme weakness. Mingled with this horror, I felt the bitterness of disappointment; dreams that had been my food and pleasant rest for so long a space were now become a hell to me; and the change was so rapid, the overthrow so complete!

Morning, dismal and wet, at length dawned, and discovered to my sleepless and aching eyes the church of Ingolstadt, its white steeple and clock, which indicated the sixth hour. The porter opened the gates of the court, which had that night been my asylum, and I issued into the streets, pacing them with quick steps, as if I sought to avoid the wretch whom I feared every turning of the street would present to my view. I did not dare return to the apartment which I inhabited, but felt impelled to hurry on, although drenched by the rain which poured from a black and comfortless sky.

I continued walking in this manner for some time, endeavouring, by bodily exercise, to ease the load that weighed upon my mind. I traversed the streets, without any clear conception of where I was, or what I was doing. My heart palpitated in the sickness of fear; and I hurried on with irregular steps, not daring to look about me: —

Like one who, on a lonely road,
    Doth walk in fear and dread,
And, having once turned round, walks on,
    And turns no more his head;
Because he knows a frightful fiend
    Doth close behind him tread.[15]

Continuing thus, I came at length opposite to the inn at which the various diligences and carriages usually stopped. Here I paused, I knew not why; but I remained some minutes with my eyes fixed on a coach that was coming towards me from the other end of the street. As it drew nearer, I observed that it was the Swiss diligence: it stopped just where I was standing; and, on the door being opened, I perceived Henry Clerval, who, on seeing me, instantly sprung out. "My dear Frankenstein," exclaimed he, "how glad I am to see you! how fortunate that you should be here at the very moment of my alighting!"

Nothing could equal my delight on seeing Clerval; his presence brought back to my thoughts my father, Elizabeth, and all those scenes of home so dear to my recollection. I grasped his hand, and in a moment forgot my horror and misfortune; I felt suddenly, and for the first time during many months, calm and serene joy. I welcomed my friend, therefore, in the most cordial manner, and we walked towards my college. Clerval continued talking for some time about our mutual friends, and his own good fortune in being permitted to come to Ingolstadt. "You may easily believe," said he, "how great was the difficulty to persuade my father that all necessary knowledge was not comprised in the noble art of book-keeping; and, indeed, I believe I left him incredulous to the last, for his constant answer to my unwearied entreaties was the same as that of the Dutch schoolmaster[16] in the Vicar of Wakefield: — 'I have ten thousand florins a year without Greek, I eat heartily without Greek.' But his affection for me at length overcame his dislike of learning, and he has permitted me to undertake a voyage of discovery to the land of knowledge."

"It gives me the greatest delight to see you; but tell me how you left my father, brothers, and Elizabeth."

"Very well, and very happy, only a little uneasy that they hear from you so seldom. By

[15] Coleridge's "Ancient Mariner" [Mary Shelley's note.]

[16] A reference to Chapter 20 of the 1766 novel *The Vicar of Wakefield* by Oliver Goldsmith (1730–1774). The book's plot is set in motion when the vicar has a sudden reversal in fortune and finds himself penniless. In Chapter 20, the vicar's son approaches the head professor of a university in Louvain, France, and offers his services as a master of the Greek language, only to find that the professor does not know and has no use for it. — EDS.

the by, I mean to lecture you a little upon their account myself. — But, my dear Frankenstein," continued he, stopping short, and gazing full in my face, "I did not before remark how very ill you appear; so thin and pale; you look as if you had been watching for several nights."

"You have guessed right; I have lately been so deeply engaged in one occupation, that I have not allowed myself sufficient rest, as you see; but I hope, I sincerely hope, that all these employments are now at an end, and that I am at length free."

I trembled excessively; I could not endure to think of, and far less to allude to, the occurrences of the preceding night. I walked with a quick pace, and we soon arrived at my college. I then reflected, and the thought made me shiver, that the creature whom I had left in my apartment might still be there, alive, and walking about. I dreaded to behold this monster; but I feared still more that Henry should see him. Entreating him, therefore, to remain a few minutes at the bottom of the stairs, I darted up towards my own room. My hand was already on the lock of the door before I recollected myself. I then paused; and a cold shivering came over me. I threw the door forcibly open, as children are accustomed to do when they expect a spectre to stand in waiting for them on the other side; but nothing appeared. I stepped fearfully in: the apartment was empty; and my bedroom was also freed from its hideous guest. I could hardly believe that so great a good fortune could have befallen me; but when I became assured that my enemy had indeed fled, I clapped my hands for joy, and ran down to Clerval.

We ascended into my room, and the servant presently brought breakfast; but I was unable to contain myself. It was not joy only that possessed me; I felt my flesh tingle with excess of sensitiveness, and my pulse beat rapidly. I was unable to remain for a single instant in the same place; I jumped over the chairs, clapped my hands, and laughed aloud. Clerval at first attributed my unusual spirits to joy on his arrival; but when he observed me more attentively, he saw a wildness in my eyes for which he could not account; and my loud, unrestrained, heartless laughter, frightened and astonished him.

"My dear Victor," cried he, "what, for God's sake, is the matter? Do not laugh in that manner. How ill you are! What is the cause of all this?"

"Do not ask me," cried I, putting my hands before my eyes, for I thought I saw the dreaded spectre glide into the room; "*he* can tell. — Oh, save me! save me!" I imagined that the monster seized me; I struggled furiously, and fell down in a fit.

Poor Clerval! what must have been his feelings? A meeting, which he anticipated with such joy, so strangely turned to bitterness. But I was not the witness of his grief; for I was lifeless, and did not recover my senses for a long, long time.

This was the commencement of a nervous fever, which confined me for several months. During all that time Henry was my only nurse. I afterwards learned that, knowing my father's advanced age, and unfitness for so long a journey, and how wretched my sickness would make Elizabeth, he spared them this grief by concealing the extent of my disorder. He knew that I could not have a more kind and attentive nurse than himself; and, firm in the hope he felt of my recovery, he did not doubt that, instead of doing harm, he performed the kindest action that he could towards them.

But I was in reality very ill; and surely nothing but the unbounded and unremitting attentions of my friend could have restored me to life. The form of the monster on whom I had bestowed existence was for ever before my eyes, and I raved incessantly concerning him. Doubtless my words surprised Henry: he at first believed them to be the wanderings of my disturbed imagination; but the pertinacity with which I continually recurred to the same subject persuaded him that my disorder indeed owed its origin to some uncommon and terrible event.

By very slow degrees, and with frequent relapses, that alarmed and grieved my friend, I recovered. I remember the first time I became capable of observing outward objects with any kind of pleasure, I perceived that the fallen leaves had disappeared, and that the young buds were shooting forth from the trees that shaded my window. It was a divine spring; and the season contributed greatly to my convalescence. I felt also sentiments of joy and affection revive in my bosom; my gloom disappeared, and in a short time I became as cheerful as before I was attacked by the fatal passion.

"Dearest Clerval," exclaimed I, "how kind, how very good you are to me. This whole winter, instead of being spent in study, as you promised yourself, has been consumed in my sick room. How shall I ever repay you? I feel the greatest remorse for the disappointment of which I have been the occasion; but you will forgive me."

"You will repay me entirely, if you do not discompose yourself, but get well as fast as you can; and since you appear in such good spirits, I may speak to you on one subject, may I not?"

I trembled. One subject! what could it be? Could he allude to an object on whom I dared not even think?

"Compose yourself," said Clerval, who observed my change of colour, "I will not mention it, if it agitates you; but your father and cousin would be very happy if they received a letter from you in your own hand-writing. They hardly know how ill you have been, and are uneasy at your long silence."

"Is that all, my dear Henry? How could you suppose that my first thought would not fly towards those dear, dear friends whom I love, and who are so deserving of my love."

"If this is your present temper, my friend, you will perhaps be glad to see a letter that has been lying here some days for you: it is from your cousin, I believe."

CHAPTER VI

Clerval then put the following letter into my hands. It was from my own Elizabeth: —

"My dearest Cousin,

"You have been ill, very ill, and even the constant letters of dear kind Henry are not sufficient to reassure me on your account. You are forbidden to write — to hold a pen; yet one word from you, dear Victor, is necessary to calm our apprehensions. For a long time I have thought that each post would bring this line, and my persuasions have restrained my uncle from undertaking a journey to Ingolstadt. I have prevented his encountering the inconveniences and perhaps dangers of so long a journey; yet how often have I regretted not being able to perform it myself! I figure to myself that the task of attending on your sick bed has devolved on some mercenary old nurse, who could never guess your wishes, nor minister to them with the care and affection of your poor cousin. Yet that is over now: Clerval writes that indeed you are getting better. I eagerly hope that you will confirm this intelligence soon in your own handwriting.

"Get well — and return to us. You will find a happy, cheerful home, and friends who love you dearly. Your father's health is vigorous, and he asks but to see you, — but to be assured that you are well; and not a care will ever cloud his benevolent countenance. How pleased you would be to remark the improvement of our Ernest! He is now sixteen, and full of activity and spirit. He is desirous to be a true Swiss, and to enter into foreign service; but we cannot part with him, at least until his elder brother returns to us. My uncle is not pleased with the idea of a military career in a distant country; but Ernest never had your powers of application. He looks upon study as an odious fetter; — his time is spent in the open air, climbing the hills or rowing on the lake. I fear that he will become an idler, unless we yield the point, and permit him to enter on the profession which he has selected.

"Little alteration, except the growth of our dear children, has taken place since you left us. The blue lake, and snow-clad mountains, they never change; — and I think our placid home, and our contented hearts are regulated by the same immutable laws. My trifling occupations take up my time and amuse me, and I am rewarded for any exertions by seeing none but happy, kind faces around me. Since you left us, but one change has taken place in our little household. Do you remember on what occasion Justine Moritz entered our family? Probably you do not; I will relate her history, therefore, in a few words. Madame Moritz, her mother, was a widow with four children, of whom Justine was the third. This girl had always been the favourite of her father; but, through a strange perversity, her mother could not endure her, and, after the death of M. Moritz, treated her very ill. My aunt observed this; and, when Justine was twelve years of age, prevailed on her mother to allow her to live at our house. The republican institutions of our country have produced simpler and happier manners than those which prevail in the great monarchies that surround it. Hence there is less distinction between the several classes of its inhabitants; and the lower orders, being neither so poor nor so despised, their manners are more refined and moral. A servant in Geneva does not mean the same thing as a servant in France and England. Justine, thus received in our family, learned the duties of a servant; a condition which, in our fortunate country, does not include the idea of ignorance, and a sacrifice of the dignity of a human being.

"Justine, you may remember, was a great favourite of yours; and I recollect you once remarked, that if you were in an ill-humour, one glance from Justine could dissipate it, for the same reason that Ariosto gives concerning the beauty of Angelica[17] — she looked so frank-hearted and happy. My aunt conceived a great attachment for her, by which she was induced to give her an education superior to that which she had at first intended. This benefit was fully repaid; Justine was the most grateful little creature in the world; I do not mean that she made any professions; I never heard one pass her lips; but you could see by her eyes that she almost adored her protectress. Although her disposition was gay, and in many respects inconsiderate, yet she paid the greatest attention to every gesture of my aunt. She thought her the model of all excellence, and endeavoured to imitate her phraseology and manners, so that even now she often reminds me of her.

"When my dearest aunt died, every one was too much occupied in their own grief to notice poor Justine, who had attended her during her illness with the most anxious affection. Poor Justine was very ill; but other trials were reserved for her.

"One by one, her brothers and sister died; and her mother, with the exception of her neglected daughter, was left childless. The conscience of the woman was troubled; she began to think that the deaths of her favourites was a judgment from heaven to chastise her partiality. She was a Roman Catholic; and I believe her confessor confirmed the idea which she had conceived. Accordingly, a few months after your departure for Ingolstadt, Justine was called home by her repentant mother. Poor girl! she wept when she quitted our house; she was much altered since the death of my aunt; grief had given softness and a winning mildness to her manners, which had before been remarkable for vivacity. Nor was her residence at her mother's house of a nature to restore her gaiety. The poor woman was very vacillating in her repentance. She sometimes begged Justine to forgive her unkindness, but much oftener accused her of having caused the deaths of her brothers and sister. Perpetual fretting at length threw Madame Moritz into a decline, which at first increased her

---

[17] The pagan heroine of the epic Italian romance *Orlando Furioso* (1532) by Lodovico Ariosto (1474–1535). Angelica's inability to reciprocate Orlando's love drives him mad. — EDS.

irritability, but she is now at peace for ever. She died on the first approach of cold weather, at the beginning of this last winter. Justine has returned to us; and I assure you I love her tenderly. She is very clever and gentle, and extremely pretty; as I mentioned before, her mien and her expressions continually remind me of my dear aunt.

"I must say also a few words to you, my dear cousin, of little darling William. I wish you could see him; he is very tall of his age, with sweet laughing blue eyes, dark eyelashes, and curling hair. When he smiles, two little dimples appear on each cheek, which are rosy with health. He has already had one or two little *wives*, but Louisa Biron is his favourite, a pretty little girl of five years of age.

"Now, dear Victor, I dare say you wish to be indulged in a little gossip concerning the good people of Geneva. The pretty Miss Mansfield has already received the congratulatory visits on her approaching marriage with a young Englishman, John Melbourne, Esq. Her ugly sister, Manon, married M. Duvillard, the rich banker, last autumn. Your favourite schoolfellow, Louis Manoir, has suffered several misfortunes since the departure of Clerval from Geneva. But he has already recovered his spirits, and is reported to be on the point of marrying a very lively pretty Frenchwoman, Madame Tavernier. She is a widow, and much older than Manoir; but she is very much admired, and a favourite with everybody.

"I have written myself into better spirits, dear cousin; but my anxiety returns upon me as I conclude. Write, dearest Victor, — one line — one word will be a blessing to us. Ten thousand thanks to Henry for his kindness, his affection, and his many letters: we are sincerely grateful. Adieu! my cousin; take care of your self; and, I entreat you, write!

"Elizabeth Lavenza.

"Geneva, March 18th, 17 — ."

"Dear, dear Elizabeth!" I exclaimed, when I had read her letter: "I will write instantly, and relieve them from the anxiety they must feel." I wrote, and this exertion greatly fatigued me; but my convalescence had commenced, and proceeded regularly. In another fortnight I was able to leave my chamber.

One of my first duties on my recovery was to introduce Clerval to the several professors of the university. In doing this, I underwent a kind of rough usage, ill befitting the wounds that my mind had sustained. Ever since the fatal night, the end of my labours, and the beginning of my misfortunes, I had conceived a violent antipathy even to the name of natural philosophy. When I was otherwise quite restored to health, the sight of a chemical instrument would renew all the agony of my nervous symptoms. Henry saw this, and had removed all my apparatus from my view. He had also changed my apartment; for he perceived that I had acquired a dislike for the room which had previously been my laboratory. But these cares of Clerval were made of no avail when I visited the professors. M. Waldman inflicted torture when he praised, with kindness and warmth, the astonishing progress I had made in the sciences. He soon perceived that I disliked the subject; but not guessing the real cause, he attributed my feelings to modesty, and changed the subject from my improvement, to the science itself, with a desire, as I evidently saw, of drawing me out. What could I do? He meant to please, and he tormented me. I felt as if he had placed carefully, one by one, in my view those instruments which were to be afterwards used in putting me to a slow and cruel death. I writhed under his words, yet dared not exhibit the pain I felt. Clerval, whose eyes and feelings were always quick in discerning the sensations of others, declined the subject, alleging, in excuse, his total ignorance; and the conversation took a more general turn. I thanked my friend from my heart, but I did not speak. I saw plainly that he was surprised, but he never attempted to draw my secret from me; and although I loved him with a mixture of affection and reverence that knew no bounds, yet I could never persuade myself to confide to him that event which was so often present to my recollection, but which I feared to detail to another would only impress more deeply.

M. Krempe was not equally docile; and in my condition at that time, of almost insupportable sensitiveness, his harsh blunt encomiums gave me even more pain than the benevolent approbation of M. Waldman. "D—n the fellow!" cried he; "why, M. Clerval, I assure you he has outstript us all. Ay, stare if you please; but it is nevertheless true. A youngster who, but a few years ago, believed in Cornelius Agrippa as firmly as in the gospel, has now set himself at the head of the university; and if he is not soon pulled down, we shall all be out of countenance.—Ay, ay," continued he, observing my face expressive of suffering, "M. Frankenstein is modest; an excellent quality in a young man. Young men should be diffident of themselves, you know, M. Clerval: I was myself when young; but that wears out in a very short time."

M. Krempe had now commenced an eulogy on himself, which happily turned the conversation from a subject that was so annoying to me.

Clerval had never sympathized in my tastes for natural science; and his literary pursuits differed wholly from those which had occupied me. He came to the university with the design of making himself complete master of the oriental languages, as thus he should open a field for the plan of life he had marked out for himself. Resolved to pursue no inglorious career, he turned his eyes toward the East, as affording scope for his spirit of enterprise. The Persian, Arabic, and Sanscrit languages engaged his attention, and I was easily induced to enter on the same studies. Idleness had ever been irksome to me, and now that I wished to fly from reflection, and hated my former studies, I felt great relief in being the fellow-pupil with my friend, and found not only instruction but consolation in the works of the orientalists. I did not, like him, attempt a critical knowledge of their dialects, for I did not contemplate making any other use of them than temporary amusement. I read merely to understand their meaning, and they well repaid my labours. Their melancholy is soothing, and their joy elevating, to a degree I never experienced in studying the authors of any other country. When you read their writings, life appears to consist in a warm sun and a garden of roses,—in the smiles and frowns of a fair enemy, and the fire that consumes your own heart. How different from the manly and heroical poetry of Greece and Rome!

Summer passed away in these occupations, 160
and my return to Geneva was fixed for the latter end of autumn; but being delayed by several accidents, winter and snow arrived, the roads were deemed impassable, and my journey was retarded until the ensuing spring. I felt this delay very bitterly; for I longed to see my native town and my beloved friends. My return had only been delayed so long, from an unwillingness to leave Clerval in a strange place, before he had become acquainted with any of its inhabitants. The winter, however, was spent cheerfully; and although the spring was uncommonly late, when it came its beauty compensated for its dilatoriness.

The month of May had already commenced, and I expected the letter daily which was to fix the date of my departure, when Henry proposed a pedestrian tour in the environs of Ingolstadt, that I might bid a personal farewell to the country I had so long inhabited. I acceded with pleasure to this proposition: I was fond of exercise, and Clerval had always been my favourite companion in the rambles of this nature that I had taken among the scenes of my native country.

We passed a fortnight in these perambulations: my health and spirits had long been restored, and they gained additional strength from the salubrious air I breathed, the natural incidents of our progress, and the conversation of my friend. Study had before secluded me from the intercourse of my fellow-creatures, and rendered me unsocial; but Clerval called forth the better feelings of my heart; he again taught me to love the aspect of nature, and the cheerful faces of children. Excellent friend! how sincerely did you love me, and endeavour to elevate my mind until it was on a level with your own! A selfish pursuit had cramped and narrowed me, until your gentleness and affection warmed and opened my senses; I became the same happy creature who, a few years ago, loved and beloved by all, had no sorrow or care. When happy, inanimate nature had the power of bestowing on me the most delightful sensations. A serene sky and verdant fields filled me with ecstasy. The present season was indeed divine; the flowers of spring bloomed in the hedges, while those of summer were already in bud. I was undisturbed by thoughts which during the preceding year had pressed upon me, notwithstanding my endeavours to throw them off, with an invincible burden.

Henry rejoiced in my gaiety, and sincerely sympathised in my feelings: he exerted himself to amuse me, while he expressed the sensations that filled his soul. The resources of his mind on this occasion were truly astonishing: his conversation was full of imagination; and very often, in imitation of the Persian and Arabic writers, he invented tales of wonderful fancy and passion. At other times he repeated my favourite poems, or drew me out into arguments, which he supported with great ingenuity.

We returned to our college on a Sunday afternoon: the peasants were dancing, and every one we met appeared gay and happy. My own spirits were high, and I bounded along with feelings of unbridled joy and hilarity.

CHAPTER VII

On my return, I found the following letter from my father:—

"My dear Victor,

"You have probably waited impatiently for a letter to fix the date of your return to us; and I was at first tempted to write only a few lines, merely mentioning the day on which I should expect you. But that would be a cruel kindness, and I dare not do it. What would be your surprise, my son, when you expected a happy and glad welcome, to behold, on the contrary, tears and wretchedness? And how, Victor, can I relate our misfortune? Absence cannot have rendered you callous to our joys and griefs; and how shall I inflict pain on my long absent son? I wish to prepare you for the woful news, but I know it is impossible; even now your eye skims over the page, to seek the words which are to convey to you the horrible tidings.

"William is dead!—that sweet child, whose smiles delighted and warmed my heart, who was so gentle, yet so gay! Victor, he is murdered!

"I will not attempt to console you; but will simply relate the circumstances of the transaction.

"Last Thursday (May 7th), I, my niece, and your two brothers, went to walk in Plainpalais. The evening was warm and serene, and we prolonged our walk farther than usual. It was already dusk before we thought of returning; and then we discovered that William and Ernest, who had gone on before, were not to be found. We accordingly rested on a seat until they should return. Presently Ernest came, and enquired if we had seen his brother: he said, that he had been playing with him, that William had run away to hide himself, and that he vainly sought for him, and afterwards waited for him a long time, but that he did not return.

"This account rather alarmed us, and we continued to search for him until night fell, when Elizabeth conjectured that he might have returned to the house. He was not there. We returned again, with torches; for I could not rest, when I thought that my sweet boy had lost himself, and was exposed to all the damps and dews of night; Elizabeth also suffered extreme anguish. About five in the morning I discovered my lovely boy, whom the night before I had seen blooming and active in health, stretched on the grass livid and motionless: the print of the murderer's finger was on his neck.

"He was conveyed home, and the anguish that was visible in my countenance betrayed the secret to Elizabeth. She was very earnest to see the corpse. At first I attempted to prevent her; but she persisted, and entering the room where it lay, hastily examined the neck of the victim, and clasping her hands exclaimed, 'O God! I have murdered my darling child!'

"She fainted, and was restored with extreme difficulty. When she again lived, it was only to weep and sigh. She told me, that that same evening William had teased her to let him wear a very valuable miniature that she possessed of your mother. This picture is gone, and was doubtless the temptation which urged the murderer to the deed. We have no trace of him at present, although our exertions to discover him are unremitted; but they will not restore my beloved William!

"Come, dearest Victor; you alone can console Elizabeth. She weeps continually, and accuses herself unjustly as the cause of his death; her words pierce my heart. We are all unhappy; but will not that be an additional motive for you, my son, to return and be our comforter? Your dear mother! Alas, Victor! I now say, Thank God she did not live to witness the cruel, miserable death of her youngest darling!

"Come, Victor; not brooding thoughts of vengeance against the assassin, but with feelings of peace and gentleness, that will heal, instead of festering, the wounds of our minds. Enter the house of mourning, my friend, but with kindness and affection for those who love you, and not with hatred for your enemies.

"Your affectionate and afflicted father,
"ALPHONSE FRANKENSTEIN.

"Geneva, May 12th, 17—."

Clerval, who had watched my countenance as I read this letter, was surprised to observe the despair that succeeded to the joy I at first expressed on receiving news from my friends. I threw the letter on the table, and covered my face with my hands.

"My dear Frankenstein," exclaimed Henry, when he perceived me weep with bitterness, "are you always to be unhappy? My dear friend, what has happened?"

I motioned to him to take up the letter, while I walked up and down the room in the extremest agitation. Tears also gushed from the eyes of Clerval, as he read the account of my misfortune.

"I can offer you no consolation, my friend," said he; "your disaster is irreparable. What do you intend to do?"

"To go instantly to Geneva: come with me, Henry, to order the horses."

During our walk, Clerval endeavoured to say a few words of consolation; he could only express his heartfelt sympathy. "Poor William!" said he, "dear lovely child, he now sleeps with his angel mother! Who that had seen him bright and joyous in his young beauty, but must weep over his untimely loss! To die so miserably; to feel the murderer's grasp! How much more a murderer, that could destroy such radiant innocence! Poor little fellow! one only consolation have we; his friends mourn and weep, but he is at rest. The pang is over, his sufferings are at an end for ever. A sod covers his gentle form, and he knows no pain. He can no longer be a subject for pity; we must reserve that for his miserable survivors."

Clerval spoke thus as we hurried through the streets; the words impressed themselves on my mind, and I remembered them afterwards in solitude. But now, as soon as the horses arrived, I hurried into a cabriolet, and bade farewell to my friend.

My journey was very melancholy. At first I wished to hurry on, for I longed to console and sympathise with my loved and sorrowing friends; but when I drew near my native town, I slackened my progress. I could hardly sustain the multitude of feelings that crowded into my mind. I passed through scenes familiar to my youth, but which I had not seen for nearly six years. How altered every thing might be during that time! One sudden and desolating change had taken place; but a thousand little circumstances might have by degrees worked other alterations, which, although they were done more tranquilly, might not be the less decisive. Fear overcame me; I dared not advance, dreading a thousand nameless evils that made me tremble, although I was unable to define them.

I remained two days at Lausanne, in this painful state of mind. I contemplated the lake: the waters were placid; all around was calm; and the snowy mountains, "the palaces of nature," were not changed. By degrees the calm and heavenly scene restored me, and I continued my journey towards Geneva.

The road ran by the side of the lake, which became narrower as I approached my native town. I discovered more distinctly the black sides of Jura, and the bright summit of Mont Blanc. I wept like a child. "Dear mountains! my own beautiful lake! how do you welcome your wanderer? Your summits are clear; the sky and lake are blue and placid. Is this to prognosticate peace, or to mock at my unhappiness?"

I fear, my friend, that I shall render myself tedious by dwelling on these preliminary circumstances; but they were days of comparative happiness, and I think of them with pleasure. My country, my beloved country! who but a native can tell the delight I took in again beholding thy streams, thy mountains, and, more than all, thy lovely lake!

Yet, as I drew nearer home, grief and fear again overcame me. Night also closed around; and when I could hardly see the dark mountains, I felt still more gloomily. The picture appeared a vast and dim scene of evil, and I foresaw obscurely that I was destined to become the most wretched of human beings. Alas! I prophesied truly, and failed only in one single circumstance, that in all the misery I imagined and dreaded, I did not conceive the hundredth part of the anguish I was destined to endure.

It was completely dark when I arrived in the environs of Geneva; the gates of the town were already shut; and I was obliged to pass the night at Secheron, a village at the distance of half a league from the city. The sky was serene; and, as I was unable to rest, I resolved to visit the spot where my poor William had been murdered. As I could not pass through the town, I was obliged to cross the lake in a boat to arrive at Plainpalais. During this short voyage I saw the lightnings playing on the summit of Mont Blanc in the most beautiful figures. The storm appeared to approach rapidly; and, on landing, I ascended a low hill, that I might observe its progress. It advanced; the heavens were clouded, and I soon felt the rain coming slowly in large drops, but its violence quickly increased.

I quitted my seat, and walked on, although the darkness and storm increased every minute, and the thunder burst with a terrific crash over my head. It was echoed from Salêve, the Juras, and the Alps of Savoy; vivid flashes of lightning dazzled my eyes, illuminating the lake, making it appear like a vast sheet of fire; then for an instant every thing seemed of a pitchy darkness, until the eye recovered itself from the preceding flash. The storm, as is often the case in Switzerland, appeared at once in various parts of the heavens. The most violent storm hung exactly north of the town, over that part of the lake which lies between the promontory of Belrive and the village of Copêt. Another storm enlightened Jura with faint flashes; and another darkened and sometimes disclosed the Môle, a peaked mountain to the east of the lake.

While I watched the tempest, so beautiful yet terrific, I wandered on with a hasty step. This noble war in the sky elevated my spirits; I clasped my hands, and exclaimed aloud, "William, dear angel! this is thy funeral, this thy dirge!" As I said these words, I perceived in the gloom a figure which stole from behind a clump of trees near me; I stood fixed, gazing intently; I could not be mistaken. A flash of lightning illuminated the object, and discovered its shape plainly to me: its gigantic stature, and the deformity of its aspect, more hideous than belongs to humanity, instantly informed me that it was the wretch, the filthy daemon, to whom I had given life. What did he there? Could he be (I shuddered at the conception) the murderer of my brother? No sooner did that idea cross my imagination, than I became convinced of its truth; my teeth chattered, and I was forced to lean against a tree for support. The figure passed me quickly, and I lost it in the gloom. Nothing in human shape could have destroyed that fair child. *He* was the murderer! I could not doubt it. The mere presence of the idea was an irresistible proof of the fact. I thought of pursuing the devil; but it would have been in vain, for another flash discovered him to me hanging among the rocks of the nearly perpendicular ascent of Mont Salêve, a hill that bounds Plainpalais on the south. He soon reached the summit, and disappeared.

I remained motionless. The thunder ceased; but the rain still continued, and the scene was enveloped in an impenetrable darkness. I revolved in my mind the events which I had until now sought to forget: the whole train of my progress towards the creation; the appearance of the work of my own hands alive at my bedside; its departure. Two years had now nearly elapsed since the night on which he first received life; and was this his first crime? Alas! I had turned loose into the world a depraved wretch, whose delight was in carnage and misery; had he not murdered my brother?

No one can conceive the anguish I suffered during the remainder of the night, which I spent, cold and wet, in the open air. But I did not feel the inconvenience of the weather; my imagination was busy in scenes of evil and despair. I considered the being whom I had cast among mankind, and endowed with the will and power to effect purposes of horror, such as the deed which he had now done, nearly in the light of my own vampire, my own spirit let loose from the grave, and forced to destroy all that was dear to me.

Day dawned; and I directed my steps towards the town. The gates were open, and I hastened to my father's house. My first thought was to discover what I knew of the murderer, and cause instant pursuit to be made. But I paused when I reflected on the story that I had to tell. A being whom I myself had formed, and endued with life, had met me at midnight among the precipices of an inaccessible mountain. I remembered also the nervous fever with which I had been seized just at the time that I dated my creation, and which would give an air of delirium to a tale otherwise so utterly improbable. I well knew that if any other had communicated such a relation to me, I should have looked upon it as the ravings of insanity. Besides, the strange nature of the animal would elude all pursuit, even if I were so far credited as to persuade my relatives to commence it. And then of what use would be pursuit? Who could arrest a creature capable of scaling the overhanging sides of Mont Salêve? These reflections determined me, and I resolved to remain silent.

It was about five in the morning when I entered my father's house. I told the servants not to disturb the family, and went into the library to attend their usual hour of rising.

Six years had elapsed, passed as a dream but for one indelible trace, and I stood in the same place where I had last embraced my father before my departure for Ingolstadt. Beloved and venerable parent! He still remained to me. I gazed on the picture of my mother, which stood over the mantel-piece. It was an historical subject, painted at my father's desire, and represented Caroline Beaufort in an agony of despair, kneeling by the coffin of her dead father. Her garb was rustic, and her cheek pale; but there was an air of dignity and beauty, that hardly permitted the sentiment of pity. Below this picture was a miniature of William; and my tears flowed when I looked upon it. While I was thus engaged, Ernest entered; he had heard me arrive, and hastened to welcome me. He expressed a sorrowful delight to see me: "Welcome, my dearest Victor," said he. "Ah! I wish you had come three months ago, and then you would have found us all joyous and delighted. You come to us now to share a misery which nothing can alleviate; yet your presence will, I hope, revive our father, who seems sinking under his misfortune; and your persuasions will induce poor Elizabeth to cease her vain and tormenting self-accusations. — Poor William! he was our darling and our pride!"

Tears, unrestrained, fell from my brother's eyes; a sense of mortal agony crept over my frame. Before, I had only imagined the wretchedness of my desolated home; the reality came on me as a new, and a not less terrible, disaster. I tried to calm Ernest; I enquired more minutely concerning my father, and her I named my cousin.

"She most of all," said Ernest, "requires consolation; she accused herself of having caused the death of my brother, and that made her very wretched. But since the murderer has been discovered — "

"The murderer discovered! Good God! how can that be? who could attempt to pursue him? It is impossible; one might as well try to overtake the winds, or confine a mountain-stream with a straw. I saw him too; he was free last night!"

"I do not know what you mean," replied my brother, in accents of wonder, "but to us the discovery we have made completes our misery. No one would believe it at first; and even now Elizabeth will not be convinced, notwithstanding all the evidence. Indeed, who would credit that Justine Moritz, who was so amiable, and fond of all the family, could suddenly become capable of so frightful, so appalling a crime?"

"Justine Moritz! Poor, poor girl, is she the accused? But it is wrongfully; every one knows that; no one believes it, surely, Ernest?"

"No one did at first; but several circumstances came out, that have almost forced conviction upon us; and her own behaviour has been so confused, as to add to the evidence of facts a weight that, I fear, leaves no hope for doubt. But she will be tried to-day, and you will then hear all."

He related that, the morning on which the murder of poor William had been discovered, Justine had been taken ill, and confined to her bed for several days. During this interval, one of the servants, happening to examine the apparel she had worn on the night of the murder, had discovered in her pocket the picture of my mother, which had been judged to be the temptation of the murderer. The servant instantly showed it to one of the others, who, without saying a word to any of the family, went to a magistrate; and, upon their deposition, Justine was apprehended. On being charged with the fact, the poor girl confirmed the suspicion in a great measure by her extreme confusion of manner.

This was a strange tale, but it did not shake my faith; and I replied earnestly, "You are all mistaken; I know the murderer. Justine, poor, good Justine, is innocent."

At that instant my father entered. I saw unhappiness deeply impressed on his countenance, but he endeavoured to welcome me cheerfully; and, after we had exchanged our mournful greeting, would have introduced some other topic than that of our disaster, had not Ernest exclaimed, "Good God, papa! Victor says that he knows who was the murderer of poor William."

"We do also, unfortunately," replied my father; "for indeed I had rather have been for ever ignorant than have discovered so much depravity and ingratitude in one I valued so highly."

"My dear father, you are mistaken; Justine is innocent."

"If she is, God forbid that she should suffer as guilty. She is to be tried to-day, and I hope, I sincerely hope, that she will be acquitted."

This speech calmed me. I was firmly convinced in my own mind that Justine, and indeed every human being, was guiltless of this murder. I had no fear, therefore, that any circumstantial evidence could be brought forward strong enough to convict her. My tale was not one to announce publicly; its astounding horror would be looked upon as madness by the vulgar. Did any one indeed exist, except I, the creator, who would believe, unless his senses convinced him, in the existence of the living monument of presumption and rash ignorance which I had let loose upon the world?

We were soon joined by Elizabeth. Time had altered her since I last beheld her; it had endowed her with loveliness surpassing the beauty of her childish years. There was the same candour, the same vivacity, but it was allied to an expression more full of sensibility and intellect. She welcomed me with the greatest affection. "Your arrival, my dear cousin," said she, "fills me with hope. You perhaps will find some means to justify my poor guiltless Justine. Alas! who is safe, if she be convicted of crime? I rely on her innocence as certainly as I do upon my own. Our misfortune is doubly hard to us; we have not only lost that lovely darling boy, but this poor girl, whom I sincerely love, is to be torn away by even a worse fate. If she is condemned, I never shall know joy more. But she will not, I am sure she will not; and then I shall be happy again, even after the sad death of my little William."

"She is innocent, my Elizabeth," said I, "and that shall be proved; fear nothing, but let your spirits be cheered by the assurance of her acquittal."

"How kind and generous you are! every one else believes in her guilt, and that made me wretched, for I knew that it was impossible: and to see every one else prejudiced in so deadly a manner rendered me hopeless and despairing." She wept.

"Dearest niece," said my father, "dry your tears. If she is, as you believe, innocent, rely on the justice of our laws, and the activity with which I shall prevent the slightest shadow of partiality."

CHAPTER VIII

We passed a few sad hours, until eleven o'clock, when the trial was to commence. My father and the rest of the family being obliged to attend as witnesses, I accompanied them to the court. During the whole of this wretched mockery of justice I suffered living torture. It was to be decided, whether the result of my curiosity and lawless devices would cause the death of two of my fellow-beings: one a smiling babe, full of innocence and joy; the other far more dreadfully murdered, with every aggravation of infamy that could make the murder memorable in horror. Justine also was a girl of merit, and possessed qualities which promised to render her life happy: now all was to be obliterated in an ignominous grave; and I the cause! A thousand times rather would I have confessed myself guilty of the crime ascribed to Justine; but I was absent when it was committed, and such a declaration would have been considered as the ravings of a madman, and would not have exculpated her who suffered through me.

The appearance of Justine was calm. She was dressed in mourning; and her countenance, always engaging, was rendered, by the solemnity of her feelings, exquisitely beautiful. Yet she appeared confident in innocence, and did not tremble, although gazed on and execrated by thousands; for all the kindness which her beauty might otherwise have excited, was obliterated in the minds of the spectators by the imagination of the enormity she was supposed to have committed. She was tranquil, yet her tranquillity was evidently constrained; and as her confusion had before been adduced as a proof of her guilt, she worked up her mind to an appearance of courage. When she entered the court, she threw her eyes round it, and quickly discovered where we were seated. A tear seemed to dim her eye when she saw us; but she quickly recovered herself, and a look of sorrowful affection seemed to attest her utter guiltlessness.

The trial began; and, after the advocate against her had stated the charge, several witnesses were called. Several strange facts combined against her, which might have staggered any one who had not such proof of her innocence as I had. She had been out the whole of the night on which the murder had been committed, and towards morning had been perceived by a market-woman not far from the spot where the body of the murdered child had been afterwards found. The woman asked her what she did there; but she looked very strangely, and only returned a confused and unintelligible answer. She returned to the house about eight o'clock; and, when one enquired where she had passed the night, she replied that she had been looking for the child, and demanded earnestly if any thing had been heard concerning him. When shown the body, she fell into violent hysterics, and kept her bed for several days. The picture was then produced, which the servant had found in her pocket; and when Elizabeth, in a faltering voice, proved that it was the same which, an hour before the child had been missed, she had placed round his neck, a murmur of horror and indignation filled the court.

Justine was called on for her defence. As the trial had proceeded, her countenance had altered. Surprise, horror, and misery were strongly expressed. Sometimes she struggled with her tears; but, when she was desired to plead, she collected her powers, and spoke, in an audible although variable voice.

"God knows," she said, "how entirely I am innocent. But I do not pretend that my protestations should acquit me: I rest my innocence on a plain and simple explanation of the facts which have been adduced against me; and I hope the character I have always borne will incline my judges to a favourable interpretation, where any circumstance appears doubtful or suspicious."

She then related that, by the permission of Elizabeth, she had passed the evening of the night on which the murder had been committed at the house of an aunt at Chêne, a village situated at about a league from Geneva. On her return, at about nine o'clock, she met a man, who asked her if she had seen any thing of the child who was lost. She was alarmed by this account, and passed several hours in looking for him, when the gates of Geneva were shut, and she was forced to remain several hours of the night in a barn belonging to a cottage, being unwilling to call up the inhabitants, to whom she was well known. Most of the night she spent here watching; towards morning she believed that she slept for a few minutes; some steps disturbed her, and she awoke. It was dawn, and she quitted her asylum, that she might again endeavour to find my brother. If she had gone near the spot where his body lay, it was without her knowledge. That she had been bewildered when questioned by the market-woman was not surprising, since she had passed a sleepless night, and the fate of poor William was yet uncertain. Concerning the picture she could give no account.

"I know," continued the unhappy victim, "how heavily and fatally this one circumstance weighs against me, but I have no power of explaining it; and when I have expressed my utter ignorance, I am only left to conjecture concerning the probabilities by which it might have been placed in my pocket. But here also I am checked. I believe that I have no enemy on earth, and none surely would have been so wicked as to destroy me wantonly. Did the murderer place it there? I know of no opportunity afforded him for so doing; or, if I had, why should he have stolen the jewel, to part with it again so soon?

"I commit my cause to the justice of my judges, yet I see no room for hope. I beg permission to have a few witnesses examined concerning my character; and if their testimony shall not overweigh my supposed guilt, I must be condemned, although I would pledge my salvation on my innocence."

Several witnesses were called, who had known her for many years, and they spoke well of her; but fear, and hatred of the crime of which they supposed her guilty, rendered them timorous, and unwilling to come forward. Elizabeth saw even this last resource, her excellent dispositions and irreproachable conduct, about to fail the accused, when, although violently agitated, she desired permission to address the court.

"I am," said she, "the cousin of the unhappy child who was murdered, or rather his sister, for I was educated by and have lived with his parents ever since and even long before his birth. It may therefore be judged indecent in me to come forward on this occasion; but when I see a fellow-creature about to perish through the cowardice of her pretended friends, I wish to be allowed to speak, that I may say what I know of her character. I am well acquainted with the accused. I have lived in the same house with her, at one time for five, and at another for nearly two years. During all that period she appeared to me the most amiable and benevolent of human creatures. She nursed Madame Frankenstein, my aunt, in her last illness, with the greatest affection and care; and afterwards attended her own mother during a tedious illness, in a manner that excited the admiration of all who knew her; after which she again lived in my uncle's house, where she was beloved by all the family. She was warmly attached to the child who is now dead, and acted towards him like a most affectionate mother. For my own part, I do not hesitate to say, that, notwithstanding all the evidence produced against her, I believe and rely on her perfect innocence. She had no temptation for such an action: as to the bauble on which the chief proof rests, if she had earnestly desired it, I should have willingly given it to her; so much do I esteem and value her."

A murmur of approbation followed Elizabeth's simple and powerful appeal; but it was excited by her generous interference, and not in favour of poor Justine, on whom the public indignation was turned with renewed violence, charging her with the blackest ingratitude. She herself wept as Elizabeth spoke, but she did not answer. My own agitation and anguish was extreme during the whole trial. I believed in her innocence; I knew it. Could the daemon, who had (I did not for a minute doubt) murdered my brother, also in his hellish sport have betrayed the innocent to death and ignominy? I could not sustain the horror of my situation; and when I perceived that the popular voice, and the countenances of the judges, had already condemned my unhappy victim, I rushed out of the court in agony. The tortures of the accused did not equal mine; she was sustained by innocence, but the fangs of remorse tore my bosom, and would not forego their hold.

I passed a night of unmingled wretchedness. In the morning I went to the court; my lips and throat were parched. I dared not ask the fatal question; but I was known, and the officer guessed the cause of my visit. The ballots had been thrown; they were all black, and Justine was condemned.

I cannot pretend to describe what I then felt. I had before experienced sensations of horror; and I have endeavoured to bestow upon them adequate expressions, but words cannot convey an idea of the heart-sickening despair that I then endured. The person to whom I addressed myself added, that Justine had already confessed her guilt. "That evidence," he observed, "was hardly required in so glaring a case, but I am glad of it; and, indeed, none of our judges like to condemn a criminal upon circumstantial evidence, be it ever so decisive."

This was strange and unexpected intelligence; what could it mean? Had my eyes deceived me? and was I really as mad as the whole world would believe me to be, if I disclosed the object of my suspicions? I hastened to return home, and Elizabeth eagerly demanded the result.

"My cousin," replied I, "it is decided as you may have expected; all judges had rather that ten innocent should suffer, than that one guilty should escape. But she has confessed."

This was a dire blow to poor Elizabeth, who had relied with firmness upon Justine's innocence. "Alas!" said she, "how shall I ever again believe in human goodness? Justine, whom I loved and esteemed as my sister, how could she put on those smiles of innocence only to betray? her mild eyes seemed incapable of any severity or guile, and yet she has committed a murder."

Soon after we heard that the poor victim had expressed a desire to see my cousin. My father wished her not to go; but said, that he left it to her own judgment and feelings to decide. "Yes," said Elizabeth, "I will go, although she is guilty; and you, Victor, shall accompany me: I cannot go alone." The idea of this visit was torture to me, yet I could not refuse.

We entered the gloomy prison-chamber, and beheld Justine sitting on some straw at the farther end; her hands were manacled, and her head rested on her knees. She rose on seeing us enter; and when we were left alone with her, she threw herself at the feet of Elizabeth, weeping bitterly. My cousin wept also.

"Oh, Justine!" said she, "why did you rob me of my last consolation? I relied on your innocence; and although I was then very wretched, I was not so miserable as I am now."

"And do you also believe that I am so very, very wicked? Do you also join with my enemies to crush me, to condemn me as a murderer?" Her voice was suffocated with sobs.

"Rise, my poor girl," said Elizabeth, "why do you kneel, if you are innocent? I am not one of your enemies; I believed you guiltless, notwithstanding every evidence, until I heard that you had yourself declared your guilt. That report, you say, is false; and be assured, dear Justine, that nothing can shake my confidence in you for a moment, but your own confession."

"I did confess; but I confessed a lie. I confessed, that I might obtain absolution; but now that falsehood lies heavier at my heart than all my other sins. The God of heaven forgive me! Ever since I was condemned, my confessor has besieged me; he threatened and menaced, until I almost began to think that I was the monster that he said I was. He threatened excommunication and hell fire in my last moments, if I continued obdurate. Dear lady, I had none to support me; all looked on me as a wretch doomed to ignominy and perdition. What could I do? In an evil hour I subscribed to a lie; and now only am I truly miserable."

She paused, weeping, and then continued— "I thought with horror, my sweet lady, that you should believe your Justine, whom your blessed aunt had so highly honoured, and whom you loved, was a creature capable of a crime which none but the devil himself could have perpetrated. Dear William! dearest blessed child! I soon shall see you again in heaven, where we shall all be happy; and that consoles me, going as I am to suffer ignominy and death."

"Oh, Justine! forgive me for having for one moment distrusted you. Why did you confess? But do not mourn, dear girl. Do not fear. I will proclaim, I will prove your innocence. I will melt the stony hearts of your enemies by my tears and prayers. You shall not die!—You, my play-fellow, my companion, my sister, perish on the scaffold! No! no! I never could survive so horrible a misfortune."

Justine shook her head mournfully. "I do not fear to die," she said; "that pang is past. God raises my weakness, and gives me courage to endure the worst. I leave a sad and bitter world; and if you remember me, and think of me as of one unjustly condemned, I am resigned to the fate awaiting me. Learn from me, dear lady, to submit in patience to the will of Heaven!"

During this conversation I had retired to a corner of the prison-room, where I could conceal the horrid anguish that possessed me. Despair! Who dared talk of that? The poor victim, who on the morrow was to pass the awful boundary between life and death, felt not as I did, such deep and bitter agony. I gnashed my teeth, and ground them together, uttering a groan that came from my inmost soul. Justine started. When she saw who it was, she approached me, and said, "Dear sir, you are very kind to visit me; you, I hope, do not believe that I am guilty?"

I could not answer. "No, Justine," said Elizabeth; "he is more convinced of your innocence than I was; for even when he heard that you had confessed, he did not credit it."

"I truly thank him. In these last moments I feel the sincerest gratitude towards those who think of me with kindness. How sweet is the affection of others to such a wretch as I am! It removes more than half my misfortune; and I feel as if I could die in peace, now that my innocence is acknowledged by you, dear lady, and your cousin."

Thus the poor sufferer tried to comfort others and herself. She indeed gained the resignation she desired. But I, the true murderer, felt the never-dying worm alive in my bosom, which allowed of no hope or consolation. Elizabeth also wept, and was unhappy; but hers also was the misery of innocence, which, like a cloud that passes over the fair moon, for a while hides but cannot tarnish its brightness. Anguish and despair had penetrated into the core of my heart; I bore a hell within me, which nothing could extinguish. We stayed several hours with Justine; and it was with great difficulty that Elizabeth could tear herself away. "I wish," cried she, "that I were to die with you; I cannot live in this world of misery."

Justine assumed an air of cheerfulness, while she with difficulty repressed her bitter tears. She embraced Elizabeth, and said, in a voice of half-suppressed emotion, "Farewell, sweet lady, dearest Elizabeth, my beloved and only friend; may Heaven, in its bounty, bless and preserve you; may this be the last misfortune that you will ever suffer! Live, and be happy, and make others so."

And on the morrow Justine died. Elizabeth's heartrending eloquence failed to move the judges from their settled conviction in the criminality of the saintly sufferer. My passionate and indignant appeals were lost upon them. And when I received their cold answers, and heard the harsh unfeeling reasoning of these men, my purposed avowal died away on my lips. Thus I might proclaim myself a madman, but not revoke the sentence passed upon my wretched victim. She perished on the scaffold as a murderess!

From the tortures of my own heart, I turned to contemplate the deep and voiceless grief of my Elizabeth. This also was my doing! And my father's woe, and the desolation of that late so smiling home — all was the work of my thrice-accursed hands! Ye weep, unhappy ones; but these are not your last tears! Again shall you raise the funeral wail, and the sound of your lamentations shall again and again be heard! Frankenstein, your son, your kinsman, your early, much-loved friend; he who would spend each vital drop of blood for your sakes — who has no thought nor sense of joy, except as it is mirrored also in your dear countenances — who would fill the air with blessings, and spend his life in serving you — he bids you weep — to shed countless tears; happy beyond his hopes, if thus inexorable fate be satisfied, and if the destruction pause before the peace of the grave have succeeded to your sad torments!

Thus spoke my prophetic soul, as, torn by remorse, horror, and despair, I beheld those I loved spend vain sorrow upon the graves of William and Justine, the first hapless victims to my unhallowed arts.

CHAPTER IX

245 Nothing is more painful to the human mind, than, after the feelings have been worked up by a quick succession of events, the dead calmness of inaction and certainty which follows, and deprives the soul both of hope and fear. Justine died; she rested; and I was alive. The blood flowed freely in my veins, but a weight of despair and remorse pressed on my heart, which nothing could remove. Sleep fled from my eyes; I wandered like an evil spirit, for I had committed deeds of mischief beyond description horrible, and more, much more (I persuaded myself), was yet behind. Yet my heart overflowed with kindness, and the love of virtue. I had begun life with benevolent intentions, and thirsted for the moment when I should put them in practice, and make myself useful to my fellow-beings. Now all was blasted: instead of that serenity of conscience, which allowed me to look back upon the past with self-satisfaction, and from thence to gather promise of new hopes, I was seized by remorse and the sense of guilt, which hurried me away to a hell of intense tortures, such as no language can describe.

This state of mind preyed upon my health, which had perhaps never entirely recovered from the first shock it had sustained. I shunned the face of man; all sound of joy or complacency was torture to me; solitude was my only consolation—deep, dark, deathlike solitude.

My father observed with pain the alteration perceptible in my disposition and habits, and endeavoured by arguments deduced from the feelings of his serene conscience and guiltless life, to inspire me with fortitude, and awaken in me the courage to dispel the dark cloud which brooded over me. "Do you think, Victor," said he, "that I do not suffer also? No one could love a child more than I loved your brother;" (tears came into his eyes as he spoke;) "but is it not a duty to the survivors, that we should refrain from augmenting their unhappiness by an appearance of immoderate grief? It is also a duty owed to yourself; for excessive sorrow prevents improvement or enjoyment, or even the discharge of daily usefulness, without which no man is fit for society."

This advice, although good, was totally inapplicable to my case; I should have been the first to hide my grief, and console my friends, if remorse had not mingled its bitterness, and terror its alarm with my other sensations. Now I could only answer my father with a look of despair, and endeavour to hide myself from his view.

About this time we retired to our house at Belrive. This change was particularly agreeable to me. The shutting of the gates regularly at ten o'clock, and the impossibility of remaining on the lake after that hour, had rendered our residence within the walls of Geneva very irksome to me. I was now free. Often, after the rest of the family had retired for the night, I took the boat, and passed many hours upon the water. Sometimes, with my sails set, I was carried by the wind; and sometimes, after rowing into the middle of the lake, I left the boat to pursue its own course, and gave way to my own miserable reflections. I was often tempted, when all was at peace around me, and I the only unquiet thing that wandered restless in a scene so beautiful and heavenly—if I except some bat, or the frogs, whose harsh and interrupted croaking was heard only when I approached the shore—often, I say, I was tempted to plunge into the silent lake, that the waters might close over me and my calamities for ever. But I was restrained, when I thought of the heroic and suffering Elizabeth, whom I tenderly loved, and whose existence was bound up in mine. I thought also of my father, and surviving brother: should I by my base desertion leave them exposed and unprotected to the malice of the fiend whom I had let loose among them?

250 At these moments I wept bitterly, and wished that peace would revisit my mind only that I might

afford them consolation and happiness. But that could not be. Remorse extinguished every hope. I had been the author of unalterable evils; and I lived in daily fear, lest the monster whom I had created should perpetrate some new wickedness. I had an obscure feeling that all was not over, and that he would still commit some signal crime, which by its enormity should almost efface the recollection of the past. There was always scope for fear, so long as any thing I loved remained behind. My abhorrence of this fiend cannot be conceived. When I thought of him, I gnashed my teeth, my eyes became inflamed, and I ardently wished to extinguish that life which I had so thoughtlessly bestowed. When I reflected on his crimes and malice, my hatred and revenge burst all bounds of moderation. I would have made a pilgrimage to the highest peak of the Andes, could I, when there, have precipitated him to their base. I wished to see him again, that I might wreak the utmost extent of abhorrence on his head, and avenge the deaths of William and Justine.

Our house was the house of mourning. My father's health was deeply shaken by the horror of the recent events. Elizabeth was sad and desponding; she no longer took delight in her ordinary occupations; all pleasure seemed to her sacrilege toward the dead; eternal woe and tears she then thought was the just tribute she should pay to innocence so blasted and destroyed. She was no longer that happy creature, who in earlier youth wandered with me on the banks of the lake, and talked with ecstasy of our future prospects. The first of those sorrows which are sent to wean us from the earth, had visited her, and its dimming influence quenched her dearest smiles.

"When I reflect, my dear cousin," said she, "on the miserable death of Justine Moritz, I no longer see the world and its works as they before appeared to me. Before, I looked upon the accounts of vice and injustice, that I read in books or heard from others, as tales of ancient days, or imaginary evils; at least they were remote, and more familiar to reason than to the imagination; but now misery has come home, and men appear to me as monsters thirsting for each other's blood. Yet I am certainly unjust. Every body believed that poor girl to be guilty; and if she could have committed the crime for which she suffered, assuredly she would have been the most depraved of human creatures. For the sake of a few jewels, to have murdered the son of her benefactor and friend, a child whom she had nursed from its birth, and appeared to love as if it had been her own! I could not consent to the death of any human being; but certainly I should have thought such a creature unfit to remain in the society of men. But she was innocent. I know, I feel she was innocent; you are of the same opinion, and that confirms me. Alas! Victor, when falsehood can look so like the truth, who can assure themselves of certain happiness? I feel as if I were walking on the edge of a precipice, towards which thousands are crowding, and endeavouring to plunge me into the abyss. William and Justine were assassinated, and the murderer escapes; he walks about the world free, and perhaps respected. But even if I were condemned to suffer on the scaffold for the same crimes, I would not change places with such a wretch."

I listened to this discourse with the extremest agony. I, not in deed, but in effect, was the true murderer. Elizabeth read my anguish in my countenance, and kindly taking my hand, said, "My dearest friend, you must calm yourself. These events have affected me, God knows how deeply; but I am not so wretched as you are. There is an expression of despair, and sometimes of revenge, in your countenance, that makes me tremble. Dear Victor, banish these dark passions. Remember the friends around you, who centre all their hopes in you. Have we lost the power of rendering you happy? Ah! while we love — while we are true to each other, here in this land of peace and beauty, your native country, we may reap every tranquil blessing, — what can disturb our peace?"

And could not such words from her whom I fondly prized before every other gift of fortune, suffice to chase away the fiend that lurked in my heart? Even as she spoke I drew near to her, as if in terror; lest at that very moment the destroyer had been near to rob me of her.

Thus not the tenderness of friendship, nor the beauty of earth, nor of heaven, could redeem my soul from woe: the very accents of love were ineffectual. I was encompassed by a cloud which no beneficial influence could penetrate. The wounded deer dragging its fainting limbs to some untrodden brake, there to gaze upon the arrow which had pierced it, and to die — was but a type of me.

Sometimes I could cope with the sullen despair that overwhelmed me: but sometimes the whirlwind passions of my soul drove me to seek, by bodily exercise and by change of place, some relief from my intolerable sensations. It was during an access of this kind that I suddenly left my home, and bending my steps towards the near Alpine valleys, sought in the magnificence, the eternity of such scenes, to forget myself and my ephemeral, because human, sorrows. My wanderings were directed towards the valley of Chamounix. I had visited it frequently during my boyhood. Six years had passed since then: *I* was a wreck — but nought had changed in those savage and enduring scenes.

I performed the first part of my journey on horseback. I afterwards hired a mule, as the more sure-footed, and least liable to receive injury on these rugged roads. The weather was fine: it was about the middle of the month of August, nearly two months after the death of Justine; that miserable epoch from which I dated all my woe. The weight upon my spirit was sensibly lightened as I plunged yet deeper in the ravine of Arve. The immense mountains and precipices that overhung me on every side — the sound of the river raging among the rocks, and the dashing of the waterfalls around, spoke of a power mighty as Omnipotence — and I ceased to fear, or to bend before any being less almighty than that which had created and ruled the elements, here displayed in their most terrific guise. Still, as I ascended higher, the valley assumed a more magnificent and astonishing character. Ruined castles hanging on the precipices of piny mountains; the impetuous Arve, and cottages every here and there peeping forth from among the trees, formed a scene of singular beauty. But it was augmented and rendered sublime by the mighty Alps, whose white and shining pyramids and domes towered above all, as belonging to another earth, the habitations of another race of beings.

I passed the bridge of Pélissier, where the ravine, which the river forms, opened before me, and I began to ascend the mountain that overhangs it. Soon after I entered the valley of Chamounix. This valley is more wonderful and sublime, but not so beautiful and picturesque, as that of Servox, through which I had just passed. The high and snowy mountains were its immediate boundaries; but I saw no more ruined castles and fertile fields. Immense glaciers approached the road; I heard the rumbling thunder of the falling avalanche, and marked the smoke of its passage. Mont Blanc, the supreme and magnificent Mont Blanc, raised itself from the surrounding *aiguilles*,[18] and its tremendous *dôme* overlooked the valley.

A tingling long-lost sense of pleasure often came across me during this journey. Some turn in the road, some new object suddenly perceived and recognized, reminded me of days gone by, and were associated with the light-hearted gaiety of boyhood. The very winds whispered in soothing accents, and maternal nature bade me weep no more. Then again the kindly influence ceased to act — I found myself fettered again to grief, and indulging in all the misery of reflection. Then I spurred on my animal, striving

[18] French for "needles"; here, the word is used to describe the mountain peaks. — EDS.

so to forget the world, my fears, and, more than all, myself — or, in a more desperate fashion, I alighted, and threw myself on the grass, weighed down by horror and despair.

At length I arrived at the village of Chamounix. Exhaustion succeeded to the extreme fatigue both of body and of mind which I had endured. For a short space of time I remained at the window, watching the pallid lightnings that played above Mont Blanc, and listening to the rushing of the Arve, which pursued its noisy way beneath. The same lulling sounds acted as a lullaby to my too keen sensations: when I placed my head upon my pillow, sleep crept over me; I felt it as it came, and blest the giver of oblivion.

CHAPTER X

I spent the following day roaming through the valley. I stood beside the sources of the Arveiron, which take their rise in a glacier, that with slow pace is advancing down from the summit of the hills, to barricade the valley. The abrupt sides of vast mountains were before me; the icy wall of the glacier overhung me; a few shattered pines were scattered around; and the solemn silence of this glorious presence-chamber of imperial Nature was broken only by the brawling waves, or the fall of some vast fragment, the thunder sound of the avalanche, or the cracking, reverberated along the mountains, of the accumulated ice, which, through the silent working of immutable laws, was ever and anon rent and torn, as if it had been but a plaything in their hands. These sublime and magnificent scenes afforded me the greatest consolation that I was capable of receiving. They elevated me from all littleness of feeling; and although they did not remove my grief, they subdued and tranquillised it. In some degree, also, they diverted my mind from the thoughts over which it had brooded for the last month. I retired to rest at night; my slumbers, as it were, waited on and ministered to by the assemblance of grand shapes which I had contemplated during the day. They congregated round me; the unstained snowy mountain-top, the glittering pinnacle, the pine woods, and ragged bare ravine; the eagle, soaring amidst the clouds — they all gathered round me, and bade me be at peace.

Where had they fled when the next morning I awoke? All of soul-inspiriting fled with sleep, and dark melancholy clouded every thought. The rain was pouring in torrents, and thick mists hid the summits of the mountains, so that I even saw not the faces of those mighty friends. Still I would penetrate their misty veil, and seek them in their cloudy retreats. What were rain and storm to me? My mule was brought to the door, and I resolved to ascend to the summit of Montanvert. I remembered the effect that the view of the tremendous and ever-moving glacier had produced upon my mind when I first saw it. It had then filled me with a sublime ecstasy, that gave wings to the soul, and allowed it to soar from the obscure world to light and joy. The sight of the awful and majestic in nature had indeed always the effect of solemnising my mind, and causing me to forget the passing cares of life. I determined to go without a guide, for I was well acquainted with the path, and the presence of another would destroy the solitary grandeur of the scene.

The ascent is precipitous, but the path is cut into continual and short windings, which enable you to surmount the perpendicularity of the mountain. It is a scene terrifically desolate. In a thousand spots the traces of the winter avalanche may be perceived, where trees lie broken and strewed on the ground; some entirely destroyed, others bent, leaning upon the jutting rocks of the mountain, or transversely upon other trees. The path, as you ascend higher, is intersected by ravines of snow, down which stones continually roll from above; one of them is particularly dangerous, as the slightest sound, such as even speaking in a loud voice, produces a concussion of air sufficient to draw destruction upon the head of the speaker. The pines are not tall or luxuriant, but they are sombre, and add an air of severity to the scene. I looked on the valley beneath; vast mists were rising from the rivers which ran through it, and curling in thick wreaths around the opposite mountains, whose summits were hid in the uniform clouds, while rain poured from the dark sky, and added to the melancholy impression I received from the objects around me. Alas! why does man boast of sensibilities superior to those apparent in the brute; it only renders them more necessary beings. If our impulses were confined to hunger, thirst, and desire, we might be nearly free; but now we are moved by every wind that blows, and a chance word or scene that that word may convey to us.

> We rest; a dream has power to poison sleep.
>   We rise; one wand'ring thought pollutes the day.
> We feel, conceive, or reason; laugh or weep,
>   Embrace fond woe, or cast our cares away;
> It is the same: for, be it joy or sorrow,
>   The path of its departure still is free.
> Man's yesterday may ne'er be like his morrow;
>   Nought may endure but mutability![19]

It was nearly noon when I arrived at the top of the ascent. For some time I sat upon the rock that overlooks the sea of ice. A mist covered both that and the surrounding mountains. Presently a breeze dissipated the cloud, and I descended upon the glacier. The surface is very uneven, rising like the waves of a troubled sea, descending low, and interspersed by rifts that sink deep. The field of ice is almost a league in width, but I spent nearly two hours in crossing it. The opposite mountain is a bare perpendicular rock. From the side where I now stood Montanvert was exactly opposite, at the distance of a league; and above it rose Mont Blanc, in awful majesty. I remained in a recess of the rock, gazing on this wonderful and stupendous scene. The sea, or rather the vast river of ice, wound among its dependent mountains, whose aerial summits hung over its recesses. Their icy and glittering peaks shone in the sunlight over the clouds. My heart, which was before sorrowful, now swelled with something like joy; I exclaimed—"Wandering spirits, if indeed ye wander, and do not rest in your narrow beds, allow me this faint happiness, or take me, as your companion, away from the joys of life."

As I said this, I suddenly beheld the figure of a man, at some distance, advancing towards me with superhuman speed. He bounded over the crevices in the ice, among which I had walked with caution; his stature, also, as he approached, seemed to exceed that of man. I was troubled: a mist came over my eyes, and I felt a faintness seize me; but I was quickly restored by the cold gale of the mountains. I perceived, as the shape came nearer (sight tremendous and abhorred!) that it was the wretch whom I had created. I trembled with rage and horror, resolving to wait his approach, and then close with him in mortal combat. He approached; his countenance bespoke bitter anguish, combined with disdain and malignity, while its unearthly ugliness rendered it almost too horrible for human eyes. But I scarcely observed this; rage and hatred had at first deprived me of utterance, and I recovered only to overwhelm him with words expressive of furious detestation and contempt.

"Devil," I exclaimed, "do you dare approach me? and do not you fear the fierce vengeance of my arm wreaked on your miserable head? Begone, vile insect! or rather, stay, that I may trample you to dust! and, oh! that I could, with the extinction of your miserable existence, restore those victims whom you have so diabolically murdered!"

"I expected this reception," said the daemon. "All men hate the wretched; how, then, must I be hated, who am miserable beyond all living things! Yet you, my creator, detest and spurn me,

[19] The last stanza of Percy Bysshe Shelley's "Mutability" (1816), a poem about the constancy of change. —EDS.

This classic depiction of Frankenstein's monster, played by Boris Karloff in James Whale's 1931 film, has become the standard, nearly ubiquitous portrayal that millions recognize. **What is it about this interpretation that has so timelessly captured the public's imagination? How closely does it resemble the monster as he is described in the novel?**

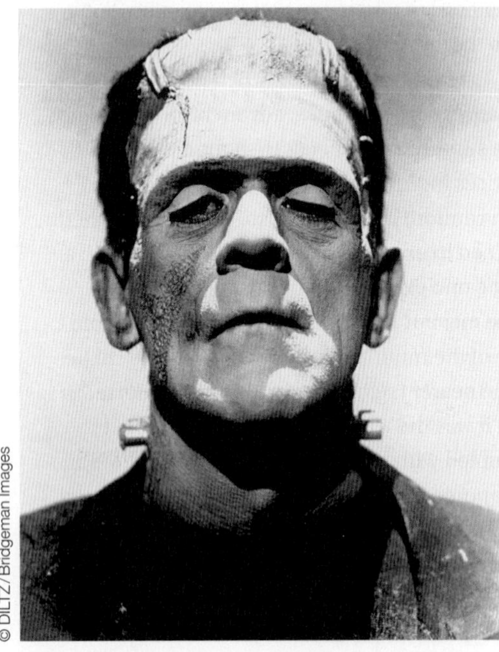

thy creature, to whom thou art bound by ties only dissoluble by the annihilation of one of us. You purpose to kill me. How dare you sport thus with life? Do your duty towards me, and I will do mine towards you and the rest of mankind. If you will comply with my conditions, I will leave them and you at peace; but if you refuse, I will glut the maw of death, until it be satiated with the blood of your remaining friends."

"Abhorred monster! fiend that thou art! the tortures of hell are too mild a vengeance for thy crimes. Wretched devil! you reproach me with your creation; come on, then, that I may extinguish the spark which I so negligently bestowed."

My rage was without bounds; I sprang on him, impelled by all the feelings which can arm one being against the existence of another.

He easily eluded me, and said—

"Be calm! I entreat you to hear me, before you give vent to your hatred on my devoted head. Have I not suffered enough, that you seek to increase my misery? Life, although it may only be an accumulation of anguish, is dear to me, and I will defend it. Remember, thou hast made me more powerful than thyself; my height is superior to thine; my joints more supple. But I will not be tempted to set myself in opposition to thee. I am thy creature, and I will be even mild and docile to my natural lord and king, if thou wilt also perform thy part, the which thou owest me. Oh, Frankenstein, be not equitable to every other, and trample upon me alone, to whom thy justice, and even thy clemency and affection, is most due. Remember, that I am thy creature; I ought to be thy Adam; but I am rather the fallen angel, whom thou drivest from joy for no misdeed. Every where I see bliss, from which I alone am irrevocably excluded. I was benevolent and good; misery made me a fiend. Make me happy, and I shall again be virtuous."

"Begone! I will not hear you. There can be no community between you and me; we are enemies. Begone, or let us try our strength in a fight, in which one must fall."

"How can I move thee? Will no entreaties cause thee to turn a favourable eye upon thy creature, who implores thy goodness and compassion? Believe me, Frankenstein: I was benevolent; my soul glowed with love and humanity: but am I not alone, miserably alone? You, my creator, abhor me; what hope can I gather from your fellow-creatures, who owe me nothing? they spurn and hate me. The desert mountains and dreary glaciers are my refuge. I have wandered here many days; the caves of ice, which I only do not fear, are a dwelling to me, and the only one which man does not grudge. These bleak skies I hail, for they are kinder to me than your fellow-beings. If the multitude of mankind knew of my existence, they would do as you do, and arm themselves for my destruction. Shall I not then hate them who abhor me? I will keep no terms with my enemies. I am miserable, and they shall share my wretchedness. Yet it is in your power to recompense me, and deliver them from an evil which it only remains for you to make so great, that not only you and your family, but thousands of others, shall be swallowed up in the whirlwinds of its rage. Let your compassion be moved, and do not disdain me. Listen to my tale: when you have heard that, abandon or commiserate me, as you shall judge that I deserve. But hear me. The guilty are allowed, by human laws, bloody as they are, to speak in their own defence before they are condemned. Listen to me, Frankenstein. You accuse me of murder; and yet you would, with a satisfied conscience, destroy your own creature. Oh, praise the eternal justice of man! Yet I ask you not to spare me: listen to me; and then, if you can, and if you will, destroy the work of your hands."

"Why do you call to my remembrance," I rejoined, "circumstances, of which I shudder to reflect, that I have been the miserable origin and author? Cursed be the day, abhorred devil, in which you first saw light! Cursed (although I curse myself) be the hands that formed you! You have made me wretched beyond expression. You have left me no power to consider whether I am just to you, or not. Begone! relieve me from the sight of your detested form."

"Thus I relieve thee, my creator," he said, and placed his hated hands before my eyes, which I flung from me with violence; "thus I take from thee a sight which you abhor. Still thou canst listen to me, and grant me thy compassion. By the virtues that I once possessed, I demand this from you. Hear my tale; it is long and strange, and the temperature of this place is not fitting to your fine sensations; come to the hut upon the mountain. The sun is yet high in the heavens; before it descends to hide itself behind yon snowy precipices, and illuminate another world, you will have heard my story, and can decide. On you it rests, whether I quit for ever the neighbourhood of man, and lead a harmless life, or become the scourge of your fellow-creatures, and the author of your own speedy ruin."

As he said this, he led the way across the ice: I followed. My heart was full, and I did not answer him; but, as I proceeded, I weighed the various arguments that he had used, and determined at least to listen to his tale. I was partly urged by curiosity, and compassion confirmed my resolution. I had hitherto supposed him to be the murderer of my brother, and I eagerly sought a confirmation or denial of this opinion. For the first time, also, I felt what the duties of a creator towards his creature were, and that I ought to render him happy before I complained of his wickedness. These motives urged me to comply with his demand. We crossed the ice, therefore, and ascended the opposite rock. The air was cold, and the rain again began to descend: we entered the hut, the fiend with an air of exultation, I with a heavy heart, and depressed spirits. But I consented to listen; and, seating myself by the fire which my odious companion had lighted, he thus began his tale.

CHAPTER XI

"It is with considerable difficulty that I remember the original era of my being: all the events of that period appear confused and indistinct. A strange multiplicity of sensations seized me, and I saw, felt, heard, and smelt, at the same time; and it was, indeed, a long time before I learned to distinguish between the operations of my various senses. By degrees, I remember, a stronger light pressed upon my nerves, so that I was obliged to shut my eyes. Darkness then came over me, and troubled me; but hardly had I felt this, when, by opening my eyes, as I now suppose, the light poured in upon me again. I walked, and, I believe, descended; but I presently found a great alteration in my sensations. Before, dark and opaque bodies had surrounded me, impervious to my touch or sight; but I now found that I could wander on at liberty, with no obstacles which I could not either surmount or avoid. The light became more and more oppressive to me; and, the heat wearying me as I walked, I sought a place where I could receive shade. This was the forest near Ingolstadt, and here I lay by the side of a brook resting from my fatigue, until I felt tormented by hunger and thirst. This roused me from my nearly dormant state, and I ate some berries which I found hanging on the trees, or lying on the ground. I slaked my thirst at the brook; and then lying down, was overcome by sleep.

"It was dark when I awoke; I felt cold also, and half-frightened, as it were instinctively, finding myself so desolate. Before I had quitted your apartment, on a sensation of cold, I had covered myself with some clothes; but these were insufficient to secure me from the dews of night. I was a poor, helpless, miserable wretch; I knew, and could distinguish, nothing; but feeling pain invade me on all sides, I sat down and wept.

"Soon a gentle light stole over the heavens, and gave me a sensation of pleasure. I started up, and beheld a radiant form rise from among the trees. I gazed with a kind of wonder. It moved slowly, but it enlightened my path; and I again went out in search of berries. I was still cold, when under one of the trees I found a huge cloak, with which I covered myself, and sat down upon the ground. No distinct ideas occupied my mind; all was confused. I felt light, and hunger, and thirst, and darkness; innumerable sounds rung in my ears, and on all sides various scents saluted me: the only object that I could distinguish was the bright moon, and I fixed my eyes on that with pleasure.

"Several changes of day and night passed, and the orb of night had greatly lessened, when I began to distinguish my sensations from each other. I gradually saw plainly the clear stream that supplied me with drink, and the trees that shaded me with their foliage. I was delighted when I first discovered that a pleasant sound, which often saluted my ears, proceeded from the throats of the little winged animals who had often intercepted the light from my eyes. I began also to observe, with greater accuracy, the forms that surrounded me, and to perceive the boundaries of the radiant roof of light which canopied me. Sometimes I tried to imitate the pleasant songs of the birds, but was unable. Sometimes I wished to express my sensations in my own mode, but the uncouth and inarticulate sounds which broke from me frightened me into silence again.

"The moon had disappeared from the night, and again, with a lessened form, showed itself, while I still remained in the forest. My sensations had, by this time, become distinct, and my mind received every day additional ideas. My eyes became accustomed to the light, and to perceive objects in their right forms; I distinguished the insect from the herb, and, by degrees, one herb from another. I found that the sparrow uttered none but harsh notes, whilst those of the blackbird and thrush were sweet and enticing.

"One day, when I was oppressed by cold, I found a fire which had been left by some wandering beggars, and was overcome with delight at the warmth I experienced from it. In my joy I thrust my hand into the live embers, but quickly drew it out again with a cry of pain. How strange, I thought, that the same cause should produce such opposite effects! I examined the materials of the fire, and to my joy found it to be composed of wood. I quickly collected some branches; but they were wet, and would not burn. I was pained at this, and sat still watching the operation of the fire. The wet wood which I had placed near the heat dried, and itself became inflamed. I reflected on this; and, by touching the various branches, I discovered the cause, and busied myself in collecting a great quantity of wood, that I might dry it, and have a plentiful supply of fire. When night came on, and brought sleep with it, I was in the greatest fear lest my fire should be extinguished. I covered it carefully with dry wood and leaves, and placed wet branches upon it; and then, spreading my cloak, I lay on the ground, and sunk into sleep.

"It was morning when I awoke, and my first care was to visit the fire. I uncovered it, and a gentle breeze quickly fanned it into a flame. I observed this also, and contrived a fan of branches, which roused the embers when they were nearly extinguished. When night came again, I found, with pleasure, that the fire gave light as well as heat; and that the discovery of this element was useful to me in my food; for I found some of the offals that the travellers had left had been roasted, and tasted much more savoury than the berries I gathered from the trees. I tried, therefore, to dress my food in the same manner, placing it on the live embers. I found that the berries were spoiled by this operation, and the nuts and roots much improved.

"Food, however, became scarce; and I often spent the whole day searching in vain for a few acorns to assuage the pangs of hunger. When I found this, I resolved to quit the place that I had hitherto inhabited, to seek for one where the few wants I experienced would be more easily satisfied. In this emigration, I exceedingly lamented the loss of the fire which I had obtained through accident, and knew not how to reproduce it. I gave several hours to the serious consideration of this difficulty; but I was obliged to relinquish all attempt to supply it; and, wrapping myself up in my cloak, I struck across the wood towards the setting sun. I passed three days in these rambles, and at length discovered the open country. A great fall of snow had taken place the night before, and the fields were of one uniform white; the appearance was disconsolate, and I found my feet chilled by the cold damp substance that covered the ground.

"It was about seven in the morning, and I longed to obtain food and shelter; at length I perceived a small hut, on a rising ground, which had doubtless been built for the convenience of some shepherd. This was a new sight to me; and I examined the structure with great curiosity. Finding the door open, I entered. An old man sat in it, near a fire, over which he was preparing his breakfast. He turned on hearing a noise; and, perceiving me, shrieked loudly, and, quitting the hut, ran across the fields with a speed of which his debilitated form hardly appeared capable. His appearance, different from any I had ever before seen, and his flight, somewhat surprised me. But I was enchanted by the appearance of the hut: here the snow and rain could not penetrate; the ground was dry; and it presented to me then as exquisite and divine a retreat as Pandaemonium appeared to the daemons of hell[20] after their sufferings in the lake of fire. I greedily devoured the remnants of the shepherd's breakfast, which consisted of bread, cheese, milk, and wine; the latter, however, I did not like. Then, overcome by fatigue, I lay down among some straw, and fell asleep.

"It was noon when I awoke; and, allured by the warmth of the sun, which shone brightly on the white ground, I determined to recommence my travels; and, depositing the remains of the peasant's breakfast in a wallet I found, I proceeded across the fields for several hours, until at sunset I arrived at a village. How miraculous did this appear! the huts, the neater cottages, and stately houses, engaged my admiration by turns. The vegetables in the gardens, the milk and cheese that I saw placed at the windows of some of the cottages, allured my appetite. One of the best of these I entered; but I had hardly placed my foot within the door, before the children shrieked, and one of the women fainted.

---

[20] A reference to Book I, lines 670–722, of John Milton's epic poem *Paradise Lost* (1667). In it, the fallen angels (who have become demons) build Pandaemonium, the capital of hell. — EDS.

The whole village was roused; some fled, some attacked me, until, grievously bruised by stones and many other kinds of missile weapons, I escaped to the open country, and fearfully took refuge in a low hovel, quite bare, and making a wretched appearance after the palaces I had beheld in the village. This hovel, however, joined a cottage of a neat and pleasant appearance; but, after my late dearly bought experience, I dared not enter it. My place of refuge was constructed of wood, but so low, that I could with difficulty sit upright in it. No wood, however, was placed on the earth, which formed the floor, but it was dry; and although the wind entered it by innumerable chinks, I found it an agreeable asylum from the snow and rain.

"Here then I retreated, and lay down happy to have found a shelter, however miserable, from the inclemency of the season, and still more from the barbarity of man.

"As soon as morning dawned, I crept from my kennel, that I might view the adjacent cottage, and discover if I could remain in the habitation I had found. It was situated against the back of the cottage, and surrounded on the sides which were exposed by a pig-sty and a clear pool of water. One part was open, and by that I had crept in; but now I covered every crevice by which I might be perceived with stones and wood, yet in such a manner that I might move them on occasion to pass out: all the light I enjoyed came through the sty, and that was sufficient for me.

"Having thus arranged my dwelling, and carpeted it with clean straw, I retired; for I saw the figure of a man at a distance, and I remembered too well my treatment the night before, to trust myself in his power. I had first, however, provided for my sustenance for that day, by a loaf of coarse bread, which I purloined, and a cup with which I could drink, more conveniently than from my hand, of the pure water which flowed by my retreat. The floor was a little raised, so that it was kept perfectly dry, and by its vicinity to the chimney of the cottage it was tolerably warm.

"Being thus provided, I resolved to reside in this hovel, until something should occur which might alter my determination. It was indeed a paradise, compared to the bleak forest, my former residence, the rain-dropping branches, and dank earth. I ate my breakfast with pleasure, and was about to remove a plank to procure myself a little water, when I heard a step, and looking through a small chink, I beheld a young creature, with a pail on her head, passing before my hovel. The girl was young, and of gentle demeanour, unlike what I have since found cottagers and farm-house servants to be. Yet she was meanly dressed, a coarse blue petticoat and a linen jacket being her only garb; her fair hair was plaited, but not adorned: she looked patient, yet sad. I lost sight of her; and in about a quarter of an hour she returned, bearing the pail, which was now partly filled with milk. As she walked along, seemingly incommoded by the burden, a young man met her, whose countenance expressed a deeper despondence. Uttering a few sounds with an air of melancholy, he took the pail from her head, and bore it to the cottage himself. She followed, and they disappeared. Presently I saw the young man again, with some tools in his hand, cross the field behind the cottage; and the girl was also busied, sometimes in the house, and sometimes in the yard.

"On examining my dwelling, I found that one of the windows of the cottage had formerly occupied a part of it, but the panes had been filled up with wood. In one of these was a small and almost imperceptible chink, through which the eye could just penetrate. Through this crevice a small room was visible, whitewashed and clean, but very bare of furniture. In one corner, near a small fire, sat an old man, leaning his head on his hands in a disconsolate attitude. The young girl was occupied in arranging the cottage; but presently she took something out of a drawer, which employed her hands, and she sat down beside the old man, who, taking up an instrument, began to play, and to produce sounds sweeter than the voice of the thrush or the nightingale. It was a lovely sight, even to me, poor wretch! who had never beheld aught beautiful before. The silver hair and benevolent countenance of the aged cottager won my reverence, while the gentle manners of the girl enticed my love. He played a sweet mournful air, which I perceived drew tears from the eyes of his amiable companion, of which the old man took no notice, until she sobbed audibly; he then pronounced a few sounds, and the fair creature, leaving her work, knelt at his feet. He raised her, and smiled with such kindness and affection, that I felt sensations of a peculiar and overpowering nature: they were a mixture of pain and pleasure, such as I had never before experienced, either from hunger or cold, warmth or food; and I withdrew from the window, unable to bear these emotions.

"Soon after this the young man returned, bearing on his shoulders a load of wood. The girl met him at the door, helped to relieve him of his burden, and, taking some of the fuel into the cottage, placed it on the fire; then she and the youth went apart into a nook of the cottage, and he showed her a large loaf and a piece of cheese. She seemed pleased, and went into the garden for some roots and plants, which she placed in water, and then upon the fire. She afterwards continued her work, whilst the young man went into the garden, and appeared busily employed in digging and pulling up roots. After he had been employed thus about an hour, the young woman joined him, and they entered the cottage together.

"The old man had, in the mean time, been pensive; but, on the appearance of his companions, he assumed a more cheerful air, and they sat down to eat. The meal was quickly despatched. The young woman was again occupied in arranging the cottage; the old man walked before the cottage in the sun for a few minutes, leaning on the arm of the youth. Nothing could exceed in beauty the contrast between these two excellent creatures. One was old, with silver hairs and a countenance beaming with benevolence and love: the younger was slight and graceful in his figure, and his features were moulded with the finest symmetry; yet his eyes and attitude expressed the utmost sadness and despondency. The old man returned to the cottage; and the youth, with tools different from those he had used in the morning, directed his steps across the fields.

"Night quickly shut in; but, to my extreme wonder, I found that the cottagers had a means of prolonging light by the use of tapers, and was delighted to find that the setting of the sun did not put an end to the pleasure I experienced in watching my human neighbours. In the evening, the young girl and her companion were employed in various occupations which I did not understand; and the old man again took up the instrument which produced the divine sounds that had enchanted me in the morning. So soon as he had finished, the youth began, not to play, but to utter sounds that were monotonous, and neither resembling the harmony of the old man's instrument nor the songs of the birds: I since found that he read aloud, but at that time I knew nothing of the science of words or letters.

"The family, after having been thus occupied for a short time, extinguished their lights, and retired, as I conjectured, to rest.

CHAPTER XII

"I lay on my straw, but I could not sleep. I thought of the occurrences of the day. What chiefly struck me was the gentle manners of these people; and I longed to join them, but dared not. I remembered too well the treatment I had suffered the night before from the barbarous villagers, and resolved, whatever course of conduct I might hereafter think it right to pursue, that for the present I would remain quietly in my hovel, watching, and endeavouring to discover the motives which influenced their actions.

"The cottagers arose the next morning before the sun. The young woman arranged the cottage, and prepared the food; and the youth departed after the first meal.

"This day was passed in the same routine as that which preceded it. The young man was constantly employed out of doors, and the girl in various laborious occupations within. The old man, whom I soon perceived to be blind, employed his leisure hours on his instrument or in contemplation. Nothing could exceed the love and respect which the younger cottagers exhibited towards their venerable companion. They performed towards him every little office of affection and duty with gentleness; and he rewarded them by his benevolent smiles.

"They were not entirely happy. The young man and his companion often went apart, and appeared to weep. I saw no cause for their unhappiness; but I was deeply affected by it. If such lovely creatures were miserable, it was less strange that I, an imperfect and solitary being, should be wretched. Yet why were these gentle beings unhappy? They possessed a delightful house (for such it was in my eyes) and every luxury; they had a fire to warm them when chill, and delicious viands when hungry; they were dressed in excellent clothes; and, still more, they enjoyed one another's company and speech, interchanging each day looks of affection and kindness. What did their tears imply? Did they really express pain? I was at first unable to solve these questions; but perpetual attention and time explained to me many appearances which were at first enigmatic.

"A considerable period elapsed before I discovered one of the causes of the uneasiness of this amiable family: it was poverty; and they suffered that evil in a very distressing degree. Their nourishment consisted entirely of the vegetables of their garden, and the milk of one cow, which gave very little during the winter, when its masters could scarcely procure food to support it. They often, I believe, suffered the pangs of hunger very poignantly, especially the two younger cottagers; for several times they placed food before the old man, when they reserved none for themselves.

"This trait of kindness moved me sensibly. I had been accustomed, during the night, to steal a part of their store for my own consumption; but when I found that in doing this I inflicted pain on the cottagers, I abstained, and satisfied myself with berries, nuts, and roots, which I gathered from a neighbouring wood.

"I discovered also another means through which I was enabled to assist their labours. I found that the youth spent a great part of each day in collecting wood for the family fire; and, during the night, I often took his tools, the use of which I quickly discovered, and brought home firing sufficient for the consumption of several days.

"I remember, the first time that I did this, the young woman, when she opened the door in the morning, appeared greatly astonished on seeing a great pile of wood on the outside. She uttered some words in a loud voice, and the youth joined her, who also expressed surprise. I observed, with pleasure, that he did not go to the forest that day, but spent it in repairing the cottage, and cultivating the garden.

"By degrees I made a discovery of still greater moment. I found that these people possessed a method of communicating their experience and feelings to one another by articulate sounds. I perceived that the words they spoke sometimes, produced pleasure or pain, smiles or sadness, in the minds and countenances of the hearers. This was indeed a godlike science, and I ardently desired to become acquainted with it. But I was baffled in every attempt I made for this purpose. Their pronunciation was quick; and the words they uttered, not having any apparent connection with visible objects, I was unable to discover any clue by which I could unravel the mystery of their reference. By great application, however, and after having remained during the space of several revolutions of the moon in my hovel, I discovered the names that were given to some of the most familiar objects of discourse; I learned and applied the words, *fire*, *milk*, *bread*, and *wood*. I learned also the names of the cottagers themselves. The youth and his companion had each of them several names, but the old man had only one, which was *father*. The girl was called *sister*, or *Agatha*; and the youth *Felix*, *brother*, or *son*. I cannot describe the delight I felt when I learned the ideas appropriated to each of these sounds, and was able to pronounce them. I distinguished several other words, without being able as yet to understand or apply them; such as *good*, *dearest*, *unhappy*.

"I spent the winter in this manner. The gentle manners and beauty of the cottagers greatly endeared them to me: when they were unhappy, I felt depressed; when they rejoiced, I sympathised in their joys. I saw few human beings beside them; and if any other happened to enter the cottage, their harsh manners and rude gait only enhanced to me the superior accomplishments of my friends. The old man, I could perceive, often endeavoured to encourage his children, as sometimes I found that he called them, to cast off their melancholy. He would talk in a cheerful accent, with an expression of goodness that bestowed pleasure even upon me. Agatha listened with respect, her eyes sometimes filled with tears, which she endeavoured to wipe away unperceived; but I generally found that her countenance and tone were more cheerful after having listened to the exhortations of her father. It was not thus with Felix. He was always the saddest of the group; and, even to my unpractised senses, he appeared to have suffered more deeply than his friends. But if his countenance was more sorrowful, his voice was more cheerful than that of his sister, especially when he addressed the old man.

"I could mention innumerable instances, which, although slight, marked the dispositions of these amiable cottagers. In the midst of poverty and want, Felix carried with pleasure to his sister the first little white flower that peeped out from beneath the snowy ground. Early in the morning, before she had risen, he cleared away the snow that obstructed her path to the milk-house, drew water from the well, and brought the wood from the out-house, where, to his perpetual astonishment, he found his store always replenished by an invisible hand. In the day, I believe, he worked sometimes for a neighbouring farmer, because he often went forth, and did not return until dinner, yet brought no wood with him. At other times he worked in the garden; but, as there was little to do in the frosty season, he read to the old man and Agatha.

"This reading had puzzled me extremely at first; but, by degrees, I discovered that he uttered many of the same sounds when he read, as when he talked. I conjectured, therefore, that he found on the paper signs for speech which he understood, and I ardently longed to comprehend these also; but how was that possible, when I did not even understand the sounds for which they stood as signs? I improved, however, sensibly in this science, but not sufficiently to follow up any kind of conversation, although I applied my whole mind to the endeavour: for I easily perceived that, although I eagerly longed to discover myself to the cottagers, I ought not to make the attempt until I had first become master of their language; which knowledge might enable me to make them overlook the deformity of my figure; for with this also the contrast perpetually presented to my eyes had made me acquainted.

"I had admired the perfect forms of my cottagers — their grace, beauty, and delicate complexions: but how was I terrified, when I viewed myself in a transparent pool! At first I started back, unable to believe that it was indeed I who was reflected in the mirror; and when I became fully convinced that I was in reality the monster that I am, I was filled with the bitterest sensations of despondence and mortification. Alas! I did not yet entirely know the fatal effects of this miserable deformity.

"As the sun became warmer, and the light of day longer, the snow vanished, and I beheld the bare trees and the black earth. From this time Felix was more employed; and the heart-moving indications of impending famine disappeared. Their food, as I afterwards found, was coarse, but it was wholesome; and they procured a sufficiency of it. Several new kinds of plants sprung up in the garden, which they dressed; and these signs of comfort increased daily as the season advanced.

"The old man, leaning on his son, walked each day at noon, when it did not rain, as I found it was called when the heavens poured forth its waters. This frequently took place; but a high wind quickly dried the earth, and the season became far more pleasant than it had been.

"My mode of life in my hovel was uniform. During the morning, I attended the motions of the cottagers; and when they were dispersed in various occupations, I slept: the remainder of the day was spent in observing my friends. When they had retired to rest, if there was any moon, or the night was star-light, I went into the woods, and collected my own food and fuel for the cottage. When I returned, as often as it was necessary, I cleared their path from the snow, and performed those offices that I had seen done by Felix. I afterwards found that these labours, performed by an invisible hand, greatly astonished them; and once or twice I heard them, on these occasions, utter the words *good spirit, wonderful*; but I did not then understand the signification of these terms.

"My thoughts now became more active, and I longed to discover the motives and feelings of these lovely creatures; I was inquisitive to know why Felix appeared so miserable, and Agatha so sad. I thought (foolish wretch!) that it might be in my power to restore happiness to these deserving people. When I slept, or was absent, the forms of the venerable blind father, the gentle Agatha, and the excellent Felix, flitted before me. I looked upon them as superior beings, who would be the arbiters of my future destiny. I formed in my imagination a thousand pictures of presenting myself to them, and their reception of me. I imagined that they would be disgusted, until, by my gentle demeanour and conciliating words, I should first win their favour, and afterwards their love.

"These thoughts exhilarated me, and led me to apply with fresh ardour to the acquiring the art of language. My organs were indeed harsh, but supple; and although my voice was very unlike the soft music of their tones, yet I pronounced such words as I understood with tolerable ease. It was as the ass and the lap-dog;[21] yet surely the gentle ass whose intentions were affectionate, although his manners were rude, deserved better treatment than blows and execration.

"The pleasant showers and genial warmth of spring greatly altered the aspect of the earth. Men, who before this change seemed to have been hid in caves, dispersed themselves, and were employed in various arts of cultivation. The birds sang in more cheerful notes, and the leaves began to bud forth on the trees. Happy, happy earth! fit habitation for gods, which, so short a time before, was bleak, damp, and unwholesome. My spirits were elevated by the enchanting appearance of nature; the past was blotted from my memory, the present was tranquil, and the future gilded by bright rays of hope, and anticipations of joy.

---

[21] In the *Fables* (IV, 5) of Jean de La Fontaine (1621–1695), the ass fawns on the dog's master, hoping to be rewarded with petting as the dog is; instead, he receives a beating. — EDS.

CHAPTER XIII

"I now hasten to the more moving part of my story. I shall relate events, that impressed me with feelings which, from what I had been, have made me what I am.

"Spring advanced rapidly; the weather became fine, and the skies cloudless. It surprised me, that what before was desert and gloomy should now bloom with the most beautiful flowers and verdure. My senses were gratified and refreshed by a thousand scents of delight, and a thousand sights of beauty.

"It was on one of these days, when my cottagers periodically rested from labour — the old man played on his guitar, and the children listened to him — that I observed the countenance of Felix was melancholy beyond expression; he sighed frequently; and once his father paused in his music, and I conjectured by his manner that he enquired the cause of his son's sorrow. Felix replied in a cheerful accent, and the old man was recommencing his music, when some one tapped at the door.

"It was a lady on horseback, accompanied by a countryman as a guide. The lady was dressed in a dark suit, and covered with a thick black veil. Agatha asked a question; to which the stranger only replied by pronouncing, in a sweet accent, the name of Felix. Her voice was musical, but unlike that of either of my friends. On hearing this word, Felix came up hastily to the lady; who, when she saw him, threw up her veil, and I beheld a countenance of angelic beauty and expression. Her hair of a shining raven black, and curiously braided; her eyes were dark, but gentle, although animated; her features of a regular proportion, and her complexion wondrously fair, each cheek tinged with a lovely pink.

"Felix seemed ravished with delight when he saw her, every trait of sorrow vanished from his face, and it instantly expressed a degree of ecstatic joy, of which I could hardly have believed it capable; his eyes sparkled, as his cheek flushed with pleasure; and at that moment I thought him as beautiful as the stranger. She appeared affected by different feelings; wiping a few tears from her lovely eyes, she held out her hand to Felix, who kissed it rapturously, and called her, as well as I could distinguish, his sweet Arabian. She did not appear to understand him, but smiled. He assisted her to dismount, and dismissing her guide, conducted her into the cottage. Some conversation took place between him and his father; and the young stranger knelt at the old man's feet, and would have kissed his hand, but he raised her, and embraced her affectionately.

"I soon perceived, that although the stranger uttered articulate sounds, and appeared to have a language of her own, she was neither understood by, nor herself understood, the cottagers. They made many signs which I did not comprehend; but I saw that her presence diffused gladness through the cottage, dispelling their sorrow as the sun dissipates the morning mists. Felix seemed peculiarly happy, and with smiles of delight welcomed his Arabian. Agatha, the ever-gentle Agatha, kissed the hands of the lovely stranger; and, pointing to her brother, made signs which appeared to me to mean that he had been sorrowful until she came. Some hours passed thus, while they, by their countenances, expressed joy, the cause of which I did not comprehend. Presently I found, by the frequent recurrence of some sound which the stranger repeated after them, that she was endeavouring to learn their language; and the idea instantly occurred to me, that I should make use of the same instructions to the same end. The stranger learned about twenty words at the first lesson, most of them, indeed, were those which I had before understood, but I profited by the others.

"As night came on, Agatha and the Arabian retired early. When they separated, Felix kissed the hand of the stranger, and said, 'Good night, sweet Safie.' He sat up much longer, conversing with his father; and, by the frequent repetition of her name, I conjectured that their lovely guest was the subject of their conversation. I ardently desired to understand them, and bent every faculty towards that purpose, but found it utterly impossible.

"The next morning Felix went out to his work; and, after the usual occupations of Agatha were finished, the Arabian sat at the feet of the old man, and, taking his guitar, played some airs so entrancingly beautiful, that they at once drew tears of sorrow and delight from my eyes. She sang, and her voice flowed in a rich cadence, swelling or dying away, like a nightingale of the woods.

"When she had finished, she gave the guitar to Agatha, who at first declined it. She played a simple air, and her voice accompanied it in sweet accents, but unlike the wondrous strain of the stranger. The old man appeared enraptured, and said some words, which Agatha endeavoured to explain to Safie, and by which he appeared to wish to express that she bestowed on him the greatest delight by her music.

"The days now passed as peaceably as before, with the sole alteration, that joy had taken place of sadness in the countenances of my friends. Safie was always gay and happy; she and I improved rapidly in the knowledge of language, so that in two months I began to comprehend most of the words uttered by my protectors.

"In the meanwhile also the black ground was covered with herbage, and the green banks interspersed with innumerable flowers, sweet to the scent and the eyes, stars of pale radiance among the moonlight woods; the sun became warmer, the nights clear and balmy; and my nocturnal rambles were an extreme pleasure to me, although they were considerably shortened by the late setting and early rising of the sun; for I never ventured abroad during daylight, fearful of meeting with the same treatment I had formerly endured in the first village which I entered.

"My days were spent in close attention, that I might more speedily master the language; and I may boast that I improved more rapidly than the Arabian, who understood very little, and conversed in broken accents, whilst I comprehended and could imitate almost every word that was spoken.

"While I improved in speech, I also learned the science of letters, as it was taught to the stranger; and this opened before me a wide field for wonder and delight.

"The book from which Felix instructed Safie was Volney's 'Ruins of Empires.'[22] I should not have understood the purport of this book, had not Felix, in reading it, given very minute explanations. He had chosen this work, he said, because the declamatory style was framed in imitation of the eastern authors. Through this work I obtained a cursory knowledge of history, and a view of the several empires at present existing in the world; it gave me an insight into the manners, governments, and religions of the different nations of the earth. I heard of the slothful Asiatics; of the stupendous genius and mental activity of the Grecians; of the wars and wonderful virtue of the early Romans — of their subsequent degenerating — of the decline of that mighty empire; of chivalry, Christianity, and kings. I heard of the discovery of the American hemisphere, and wept with Safie over the hapless fate of its original inhabitants.

"These wonderful narrations inspired me with strange feelings. Was man, indeed, at once so powerful, so virtuous, and magnificent, yet so vicious and base? He appeared at one time a mere scion of the evil principle, and at another, as all that can be conceived of noble and godlike. To be a great and virtuous man appeared the highest honour that can befall a sensitive

[22] *Les ruines, ou, Méditations sur les révolutions des empires* ("The Ruins, or a Survey of the Revolutions of Empires"), by Constantin François Chasseboœuf, compte de Volney (1757–1820), was an essay on the philosophy of history published in 1791. — EDS.

being; to be base and vicious, as many on record have been, appeared the lowest degradation, a condition more abject than that of the blind mole or harmless worm. For a long time I could not conceive how one man could go forth to murder his fellow, or even why there were laws and governments; but when I heard details of vice and bloodshed, my wonder ceased, and I turned away with disgust and loathing.

"Every conversation of the cottagers now opened new wonders to me. While I listened to the instructions which Felix bestowed upon the Arabian, the strange system of human society was explained to me. I heard of the division of property, of immense wealth and squalid poverty; of rank, descent, and noble blood.

"The words induced me to turn towards myself. I learned that the possessions most esteemed by your fellow-creatures were high and unsullied descent united with riches. A man might be respected with only one of these advantages; but, without either, he was considered, except in very rare instances, as a vagabond and a slave, doomed to waste his powers for the profits of the chosen few! And what was I? Of my creation and creator I was absolutely ignorant; but I knew that I possessed no money, no friends, no kind of property. I was, besides, endued with a figure hideously deformed and loathsome; I was not even of the same nature as man. I was more agile than they, and could subsist upon coarser diet; I bore the extremes of heat and cold with less injury to my frame; my stature far exceeded theirs. When I looked around, I saw and heard of none like me. Was I then a monster, a blot upon the earth, from which all men fled, and whom all men disowned?

"I cannot describe to you the agony that these reflections inflicted upon me: I tried to dispel them, but sorrow only increased with knowledge. Oh, that I had for ever remained in my native wood, nor known nor felt beyond the sensations of hunger, thirst, and heat!

"Of what a strange nature is knowledge! It clings to the mind, when it has once seized on it, like a lichen on the rock. I wished sometimes to shake off all thought and feeling; but I learned that there was but one means to overcome the sensation of pain, and that was death—a state which I feared yet did not understand. I admired virtue and good feelings, and loved the gentle manners and amiable qualities of my cottagers; but I was shut out from intercourse with them, except through means which I obtained by stealth, when I was unseen and unknown, and which rather increased than satisfied the desire I had of becoming one among my fellows. The gentle words of Agatha, and the animated smiles of the charming Arabian, were not for me. The mild exhortations of the old man, and the lively conversation of the loved Felix, were not for me. Miserable, unhappy wretch!

"Other lessons were impressed upon me even more deeply. I heard of the difference of sexes; and the birth and growth of children; how the father doted on the smiles of the infant, and the lively sallies of the older child; how all the life and cares of the mother were wrapped up in the precious charge; how the mind of youth expanded and gained knowledge; of brother, sister, and all the various relationships which bind one human being to another in mutual bonds.

"But where were my friends and relations? No father had watched my infant days, no mother had blessed me with smiles and caresses; or if they had, all my past life was now a blot, a blind vacancy in which I distinguished nothing. From my earliest remembrance I had been as I then was in height and proportion. I had never yet seen a being resembling me, or who claimed any intercourse with me. What was I? The question again recurred, to be answered only with groans.

"I will soon explain to what these feelings tended; but allow me now to return to the cottagers, whose story excited in me such various feelings of indignation, delight, and wonder, but which all terminated in additional love and reverence for my protectors (for so I loved, in an innocent, half painful self-deceit, to call them).

CHAPTER XIV

"Some time elapsed before I learned the history of my friends. It was one which could not fail to impress itself deeply on my mind, unfolding as it did a number of circumstances, each interesting and wonderful to one so utterly inexperienced as I was.

"The name of the old man was De Lacey. He was descended from a good family in France, where he had lived for many years in affluence, respected by his superiors, and beloved by his equals. His son was bred in the service of his country; and Agatha had ranked with ladies of the highest distinction. A few months before my arrival, they had lived in a large and luxurious city, called Paris, surrounded by friends, and possessed of every enjoyment which virtue, refinement of intellect, or taste, accompanied by a moderate fortune, could afford.

"The father of Safie had been the cause of their ruin. He was a Turkish merchant, and had inhabited Paris for many years, when, for some reason which I could not learn, he became obnoxious to the government. He was seized and cast into prison the very day that Safie arrived from Constantinople to join him. He was tried, and condemned to death. The injustice of his sentence was very flagrant; all Paris was indignant; and it was judged that his religion and wealth, rather than the crime alleged against him, had been the cause of his condemnation.

"Felix had accidentally been present at the trial; his horror and indignation were uncontrollable, when he heard the decision of the court. He made, at that moment, a solemn vow to deliver him, and then looked around for the means. After many fruitless attempts to gain admittance to the prison, he found a strongly grated window in an unguarded part of the building, which lighted the dungeon of the unfortunate Mahometan;[23] who, loaded with chains, waited in despair the execution of the barbarous sentence. Felix visited the grate at night, and made known to the prisoner his intentions in his favour. The Turk, amazed and delighted, endeavoured to kindle the zeal of his deliverer by promises of reward and wealth. Felix rejected his offers with contempt; yet when he saw the lovely Safie, who was allowed to visit her father, and who, by her gestures, expressed her lively gratitude, the youth could not help owning to his own mind, that the captive possessed a treasure which would fully reward his toil and hazard.

"The Turk quickly perceived the impression that his daughter had made on the heart of Felix, and endeavoured to secure him more entirely in his interests by the promise of her hand in marriage, so soon as he should be conveyed to a place of safety. Felix was too delicate to accept this offer; yet he looked forward to the probability of the event as to the consummation of his happiness.

"During the ensuing days, while the preparations were going forward for the escape of the merchant, the zeal of Felix was warmed by several letters that he received from this lovely girl, who found means to express her thoughts in the language of her lover by the aid of an old man, a servant of her father, who understood French. She thanked him in the most ardent terms for his intended services towards her parent; and at the same time she gently deplored her own fate.

"I have copies of these letters; for I found means, during my residence in the hovel, to procure the implements of writing; and the letters were often in the hands of Felix or Agatha. Before I depart, I will give them to you, they will prove the truth of my tale; but at present, as the

[23] A nineteenth-century British reference to Muslims. — EDS.

sun is already far declined, I shall only have time to repeat the substance of them to you.

"Safie related, that her mother was a Christian Arab, seized and made a slave by the Turks; recommended by her beauty, she had won the heart of the father of Safie, who married her. The young girl spoke in high and enthusiastic terms of her mother, who, born in freedom, spurned the bondage to which she was now reduced. She instructed her daughter in the tenets of her religion, and taught her to aspire to higher powers of intellect, and an independence of spirit, forbidden to the female followers of Mahomet. This lady died; but her lessons were indelibly impressed on the mind of Safie, who sickened at the prospect of again returning to Asia, and being immured within the walls of a haram,[24] allowed only to occupy herself with infantile amusements, ill suited to the temper of her soul, now accustomed to grand ideas and a noble emulation for virtue. The prospect of marrying a Christian, and remaining in a country where women were allowed to take a rank in society, was enchanting to her.

"The day for the execution of the Turk was fixed; but, on the night previous to it, he quitted his prison, and before morning was distant many leagues from Paris. Felix had procured passports in the name of his father, sister, and himself. He had previously communicated his plan to the former, who aided the deceit by quitting his house, under the pretence of a journey, and concealed himself, with his daughter, in an obscure part of Paris.

"Felix conducted the fugitives through France to Lyons, and across Mont Cenis to Leghorn, where the merchant had decided to wait a favourable opportunity of passing into some part of the Turkish dominions.

"Safie resolved to remain with her father until the moment of his departure, before which time the Turk renewed his promise that she should be united to his deliverer; and Felix remained with them in expectation of that event; and in the mean time he enjoyed the society of the Arabian, who exhibited towards him the simplest and tenderest affection. They conversed with one another through the means of an interpreter, and sometimes with the interpretation of looks; and Safie sang to him the divine airs of her native country.

"The Turk allowed this intimacy to take place, and encouraged the hopes of the youthful lovers, while in his heart he had formed far other plans. He loathed the idea that his daughter should be united to a Christian; but he feared the resentment of Felix, if he should appear lukewarm; for he knew that he was still in the power of his deliverer, if he should choose to betray him to the Italian state which they inhabited. He revolved a thousand plans by which he should be enabled to prolong the deceit until it might be no longer necessary, and secretly to take his daughter with him when he departed. His plans were facilitated by the news which arrived from Paris.

"The government of France were greatly enraged at the escape of their victim, and spared no pains to detect and punish his deliverer. The plot of Felix was quickly discovered, and De Lacey and Agatha were thrown into prison. The news reached Felix, and roused him from his dream of pleasure. His blind and aged father, and his gentle sister, lay in a noisome dungeon, while he enjoyed the free air, and the society of her whom he loved. This idea was torture to him. He quickly arranged with the Turk, that if the latter should find a favourable opportunity for escape before Felix could return to Italy, Safie should remain as a boarder at a convent at Leghorn; and then, quitting the lovely Arabian, he hastened to Paris, and delivered himself up to the vengeance of the law, hoping to free De Lacey and Agatha by this proceeding.

"He did not succeed. They remained confined for five months before the trial took place;

[24] A harem.—EDS.

the result of which deprived them of their fortune, and condemned them to a perpetual exile from their native country.

"They found a miserable asylum in the cottage in Germany, where I discovered them. Felix soon learned that the treacherous Turk, for whom he and his family endured such unheard-of oppression, on discovering that his deliverer was thus reduced to poverty and ruin, became a traitor to good feeling and honour, and had quitted Italy with his daughter, insultingly sending Felix a pittance of money, to aid him, as he said, in some plan of future maintenance.

"Such were the events that preyed on the heart of Felix, and rendered him, when I first saw him, the most miserable of his family. He could have endured poverty; and while this distress had been the meed of his virtue, he gloried in it: but the ingratitude of the Turk, and the loss of his beloved Safie, were misfortunes more bitter and irreparable. The arrival of the Arabian now infused new life into his soul.

"When the news reached Leghorn, that Felix was deprived of his wealth and rank, the merchant commanded his daughter to think no more of her lover, but to prepare to return to her native country. The generous nature of Safie was outraged by this command; she attempted to expostulate with her father, but he left her angrily, reiterating his tyrannical mandate.

"A few days after, the Turk entered his daughter's apartment, and told her hastily, that he had reason to believe that his residence at Leghorn had been divulged, and that he should speedily be delivered up to the French government; he had, consequently, hired a vessel to convey him to Constantinople, for which city he should sail in a few hours. He intended to leave his daughter under the care of a confidential servant, to follow at her leisure with the greater part of his property, which had not yet arrived at Leghorn.

"When alone, Safie resolved in her own 355
mind the plan of conduct that it would become her to pursue in this emergency. A residence in Turkey was abhorrent to her; her religion and her feelings were alike adverse to it. By some papers of her father, which fell into her hands, she heard of the exile of her lover, and learnt the name of the spot where he then resided. She hesitated some time, but at length she formed her determination. Taking with her some jewels that belonged to her, and a sum of money, she quitted Italy with an attendant, a native of Leghorn, but who understood the common language of Turkey, and departed for Germany.

"She arrived in safety at a town about twenty leagues from the cottage of De Lacey, when her attendant fell dangerously ill. Safie nursed her with the most devoted affection; but the poor girl died, and the Arabian was left alone, unacquainted with the language of the country, and utterly ignorant of the customs of the world. She fell, however, into good hands. The Italian had mentioned the name of the spot for which they were bound; and, after her death, the woman of the house in which they had lived took care that Safie should arrive in safety at the cottage of her lover.

CHAPTER XV

"Such was the history of my beloved cottagers. It impressed me deeply. I learned, from the views of social life which it developed, to admire their virtues, and to deprecate the vices of mankind.

"As yet I looked upon crime as a distant evil; benevolence and generosity were ever present before me, inciting within me a desire to become an actor in the busy scene where so many admirable qualities were called forth and displayed. But, in giving an account of the progress of my intellect, I must not omit a circumstance which occurred in the beginning of the month of August of the same year.

"One night, during my accustomed visit to the neighbouring wood, where I collected my own food, and brought home firing for my protectors, I found on the ground a leathern portmanteau, containing several articles of dress and some books. I eagerly seized the prize, and returned with it to my hovel. Fortunately the books were written in the language, the elements of which I had acquired at the cottage; they consisted of 'Paradise Lost,' a volume of 'Plutarch's Lives,'[25] and the 'Sorrows of Werter.'[26] The possession of these treasures gave me extreme delight; I now continually studied and exercised my mind upon these histories, whilst my friends were employed in their ordinary occupations.

"I can hardly describe to you the effect of these books. They produced in me an infinity of new images and feelings, that sometimes raised me to ecstasy, but more frequently sunk me into the lowest dejection. In the 'Sorrows of Werter,' besides the interest of its simple and affecting story, so many opinions are canvassed, and so many lights thrown upon what had hitherto been to me obscure subjects, that I found in it a never-ending source of speculation and astonishment. The gentle and domestic manners it described, combined with lofty sentiments and feelings, which had for their object something out of self, accorded well with my experience among my protectors, and with the wants which were for ever alive in my own bosom. But I thought Werter himself a more divine being than I had ever beheld or imagined; his character contained no pretension, but it sunk deep. The disquisitions upon death and suicide were calculated to fill me with wonder. I did not pretend to enter into the merits of the case, yet I inclined towards the opinions of the hero, whose extinction I wept, without precisely understanding it.

[25] A series of forty-six biographies of famous military and political figures, arranged in pairs to compare men and highlight their strengths and failings, by Plutarch (c. 46–119), a Greek biographer. — EDS.

[26] *The Sorrows of Young Werther* (1774) is a tragic novel about a romantic young artist by Johann Wolfgang von Goethe (1749–1832), a German writer and politician. — EDS.

"As I read, however, I applied much personally to my own feelings and condition. I found myself similar, yet at the same time strangely unlike to the beings concerning whom I read, and to whose conversation I was a listener. I sympathised with, and partly understood them, but I was unformed in mind; I was dependent on none, and related to none. 'The path of my departure was free;'[27] and there was none to lament my annihilation. My person was hideous, and my stature gigantic: what did this mean? Who was I? What was I? Whence did I come? What was my destination? These questions continually recurred, but I was unable to solve them.

"The volume of 'Plutarch's Lives,' which I possessed, contained the histories of the first founders of the ancient republics. This book had a far different effect upon me from the 'Sorrows of Werter.' I learned from Werter's imaginations despondency and gloom: but Plutarch taught me high thoughts; he elevated me above the wretched sphere of my own reflections, to admire and love the heroes of past ages. Many things I read surpassed my understanding and experience. I had a very confused knowledge of kingdoms, wide extents of country, mighty rivers, and boundless seas. But I was perfectly unacquainted with towns, and large assemblages of men. The cottage of my protectors had been the only school in which I had studied human nature; but this book developed new and mightier scenes of action. I read of men concerned in public affairs, governing or massacring their species. I felt the greatest ardour for virtue rise within me, and abhorrence for vice, as far as I understood the significance of those terms, relative as they were, as I applied them, to pleasure and pain alone. Induced by these feelings, I was of course led to admire peaceable lawgivers, Numa, Solon, and Lycurgus, in preference to

[27] A reference to line 14 of Percy Bysshe Shelley's "Mutability": "The path of its departure still is free." — EDS.

Romulus and Theseus. The patriarchal lives of my protectors caused these impressions to take a firm hold on my mind; perhaps, if my first introduction to humanity had been made by a young soldier, burning for glory and slaughter, I should have been imbued with different sensations.

"But 'Paradise Lost' excited different and far deeper emotions. I read it, as I had read the other volumes which had fallen into my hands, as a true history. It moved every feeling of wonder and awe, that the picture of an omnipotent God warring with his creatures was capable of exciting. I often referred the several situations, as their similarity struck me, to my own. Like Adam, I was apparently united by no link to any other being in existence; but his state was far different from mine in every other respect. He had come forth from the hands of God a perfect creature, happy and prosperous, guarded by the especial care of his Creator; he was allowed to converse with, and acquire knowledge from, beings of a superior nature: but I was wretched, helpless, and alone. Many times I considered Satan as the fitter emblem of my condition; for often, like him, when I viewed the bliss of my protectors, the bitter gall of envy rose within me.

"Another circumstance strengthened and confirmed these feelings. Soon after my arrival in the hovel, I discovered some papers in the pocket of the dress which I had taken from your laboratory. At first I had neglected them; but now that I was able to decipher the characters in which they were written, I began to study them with diligence. It was your journal of the four months that preceded my creation. You minutely described in these papers every step you took in the progress of your work; this history was mingled with accounts of domestic occurrences. You, doubtless, recollect these papers. Here they are. Every thing is related in them which bears reference to my accursed origin; the whole detail of that series of disgusting circumstances which produced it, is set in view; the minutest description of my odious and loathsome person is given, in language which painted your own horrors, and rendered mine indelible. I sickened as I read. 'Hateful day when I received life!' I exclaimed in agony. 'Accursed creator! Why did you form a monster so hideous that even *you* turned from me in disgust? God, in pity, made man beautiful and alluring, after his own image; but my form is a filthy type of yours, more horrid even from the very resemblance. Satan had his companions, fellow-devils, to admire and encourage him; but I am solitary and abhorred.'

"These were the reflections of my hours of despondency and solitude; but when I contemplated the virtues of the cottagers, their amiable and benevolent dispositions, I persuaded myself that when they should become acquainted with my admiration of their virtues, they would compassionate me, and overlook my personal deformity. Could they turn from their door one, however monstrous, who solicited their compassion and friendship? I resolved, at least, not to despair, but in every way to fit myself for an interview with them which would decide my fate. I postponed this attempt for some months longer; for the importance attached to its success inspired me with a dread lest I should fail. Besides, I found that my understanding improved so much with every day's experience, that I was unwilling to commence this undertaking until a few more months should have added to my sagacity.

"Several changes, in the mean time, took place in the cottage. The presence of Safie diffused happiness among its inhabitants; and I also found that a greater degree of plenty reigned there. Felix and Agatha spent more time in amusement and conversation, and were assisted in their labours by servants. They did not appear rich, but they were contented and happy; their feelings were serene and peaceful, while mine became every day more tumultuous. Increase of knowledge only discovered to me more clearly what a wretched outcast I was. I cherished hope, it is true; but it vanished, when I beheld my person reflected in water, or my shadow in the moonshine, even as that frail image and that inconstant shade.

"I endeavoured to crush these fears, and to fortify myself for the trial which in a few months I resolved to undergo; and some times I allowed my thoughts, unchecked by reason, to ramble in the fields of Paradise, and dared to fancy amiable and lovely creatures sympathising with my feelings, and cheering my gloom; their angelic countenances breathed smiles of consolation. But it was all a dream; no Eve soothed my sorrows, nor shared my thoughts; I was alone. I remembered Adam's supplication[28] to his Creator. But where was mine? He had abandoned me; and, in the bitterness of my heart, I cursed him.

"Autumn passed thus. I saw, with surprise and grief, the leaves decay and fall, and nature again assume the barren and bleak appearance it had worn when I first beheld the woods and the lovely moon. Yet I did not heed the bleakness of the weather; I was better fitted by my conformation for the endurance of cold than heat. But my chief delights were the sight of the flowers, the birds, and all the gay apparel of summer; when those deserted me, I turned with more attention towards the cottagers. Their happiness was not decreased by the absence of summer. They loved, and sympathised with one another; and their joys, depending on each other, were not interrupted by the casualties that took place around them. The more I saw of them, the greater became my desire to claim their protection and kindness; my heart yearned to be known and loved by these amiable creatures: to see their sweet looks directed towards me with affection, was the utmost limit of my ambition. I dared not think that they would turn them from me with disdain and horror. The poor that stopped at their door were never driven away. I asked, it is true, for greater treasures than a little food or rest: I required kindness and sympathy; but I did not believe myself utterly unworthy of it.

"The winter advanced, and an entire revolution of the seasons had taken place since I awoke into life. My attention, at this time, was solely directed towards my plan of introducing myself into the cottage of my protectors. I revolved many projects; but that on which I finally fixed was, to enter the dwelling when the blind old man should be alone. I had sagacity enough to discover, that the unnatural hideousness of my person was the chief object of horror with those who had formerly beheld me. My voice, although harsh, had nothing terrible in it; I thought, therefore, that if, in the absence of his children, I could gain the goodwill and mediation of the old De Lacey, I might, by his means, be tolerated by my younger protectors.

"One day, when the sun shone on the red leaves that strewed the ground, and diffused cheerfulness, although it denied warmth, Safie, Agatha, and Felix departed on a long country walk, and the old man, at his own desire, was left alone in the cottage. When his children had departed, he took up his guitar, and played several mournful but sweet airs, more sweet and mournful than I had ever heard him play before. At first his countenance was illuminated with pleasure, but, as he continued, thoughtfulness and sadness succeeded; at length, laying aside the instrument, he sat absorbed in reflection.

"My heart beat quick; this was the hour and moment of trial, which would decide my hopes, or realise my fears. The servants were gone to a neighbouring fair. All was silent in and around the cottage: it was an excellent opportunity; yet, when I proceeded to execute my plan, my limbs failed me, and I sank to the ground. Again I rose; and, exerting all the firmness of which I was

[28] A reference to Book VIII, lines 377–97, of John Milton's *Paradise Lost*, in which Adam requests a human companion. — EDS.

master, removed the planks which I had placed before my hovel to conceal my retreat. The fresh air revived me, and, with renewed determination, I approached the door of their cottage.

"I knocked. 'Who is there?' said the old man—'Come in.'

"I entered; 'Pardon this intrusion,' said I: 'I am a traveller in want of a little rest; you would greatly oblige me, if you would allow me to remain a few minutes before the fire.'

" 'Enter,' said De Lacey; 'and I will try in what manner I can relieve your wants; but, unfortunately, my children are from home, and, as I am blind, I am afraid I shall find it difficult to procure food for you.'

" 'Do not trouble yourself, my kind host, I have food; it is warmth and rest only that I need.'

"I sat down, and a silence ensued. I knew that every minute was precious to me, yet I remained irresolute in what manner to commence the interview; when the old man addressed me—

" 'By your language, stranger, I suppose you are my countryman;—are you French?'

" 'No; but I was educated by a French family, and understand that language only. I am now going to claim the protection of some friends, whom I sincerely love, and of whose favour I have some hopes.'

" 'Are they Germans?'

" 'No, they are French. But let us change the subject. I am an unfortunate and deserted creature; I look around, and I have no relation or friend upon earth. These amiable people to whom I go have never seen me, and know little of me. I am full of fears; for if I fail there, I am an outcast in the world for ever.'

" 'Do not despair. To be friendless is indeed to be unfortunate; but the hearts of men, when unprejudiced by any obvious self-interest, are full of brotherly love and charity. Rely, therefore, on your hopes; and if these friends are good and amiable, do not despair.'

" 'They are kind—they are the most excellent creatures in the world; but, unfortunately, they are prejudiced against me. I have good dispositions; my life has been hitherto harmless, and in some degree beneficial; but a fatal prejudice clouds their eyes, and where they ought to see a feeling and kind friend, they behold only a detestable monster.'

" 'That is indeed unfortunate; but if you are really blameless, cannot you undeceive them?'

" 'I am about to undertake that task; and it is on that account that I feel so many overwhelming terrors. I tenderly love these friends; I have, unknown to them, been for many months in the habits of daily kindness towards them; but they believe that I wish to injure them, and it is that prejudice which I wish to overcome.'

" 'Where do these friends reside?'

" 'Near this spot.'

"The old man paused, and then continued, 'If you will unreservedly confide to me the particulars of your tale, I perhaps may be of use in undeceiving them. I am blind, and cannot judge of your countenance, but there is something in your words, which persuades me that you are sincere. I am poor, and an exile; but it will afford me true pleasure to be in any way serviceable to a human creature.'

" 'Excellent man! I thank you, and accept your generous offer. You raise me from the dust by this kindness; and I trust that, by your aid, I shall not be driven from the society and sympathy of your fellow-creatures.'

" 'Heaven forbid! even if you were really criminal; for that can only drive you to desperation, and not instigate you to virtue. I also am unfortunate; I and my family have been condemned, although innocent: judge, therefore, if I do not feel for your misfortunes.'

" 'How can I thank you, my best and only benefactor? From your lips first have I heard the voice of kindness directed towards me; I shall be for ever grateful; and your present humanity assures me of success with those friends whom I am on the point of meeting.'

"'May I know the names and residence of those friends?'

"I paused. This, I thought, was the moment of decision, which was to rob me of, or bestow happiness on me for ever. I struggled vainly for firmness sufficient to answer him, but the effort destroyed all my remaining strength; I sank on the chair, and sobbed aloud. At that moment I heard the steps of my younger protectors. I had not a moment to lose; but, seizing the hand of the old man I cried, 'Now is the time! — save and protect me! You and your family are the friends whom I seek. Do not you desert me in the hour of trial!'

"'Great God!' exclaimed the old man, 'who are you?'

"At that instant the cottage door was opened, and Felix, Safie, and Agatha entered. Who can describe their horror and consternation on beholding me? Agatha fainted; and Safie, unable to attend to her friend, rushed out of the cottage. Felix darted forward, and with supernatural force tore me from his father, to whose knees I clung: in a transport of fury, he dashed me to the ground, and struck me violently with a stick. I could have torn him limb from limb, as the lion rends the antelope. But my heart sunk within me as with bitter sickness, and I refrained. I saw him on the point of repeating his blow, when, overcome by pain and anguish, I quitted the cottage, and in the general tumult escaped unperceived to my hovel.

CHAPTER XVI

"Cursed, cursed creator! Why did I live? Why, in that instant, did I not extinguish the spark of existence which you had so wantonly bestowed? I know not; despair had not yet taken possession of me; my feelings were those of rage and revenge. I could with pleasure have destroyed the cottage and its inhabitants, and have glutted myself with their shrieks and misery.

"When night came, I quitted my retreat, and wandered in the wood; and now, no longer restrained by the fear of discovery, I gave vent to my anguish in fearful howlings. I was like a wild beast that had broken the toils; destroying the objects that obstructed me, and ranging through the wood with a stag-like swiftness. O! what a miserable night I passed! the cold stars shone in mockery, and the bare trees waved their branches above me: now and then the sweet voice of a bird burst forth amidst the universal stillness. All, save I, were at rest or in enjoyment: I, like the arch-fiend, bore a hell within me; and, finding myself unsympathised with, wished to tear up the trees, spread havoc and destruction around me, and then to have sat down and enjoyed the ruin.

"But this was a luxury of sensation that could not endure; I became fatigued with excess of bodily exertion, and sank on the damp grass in the sick impotence of despair. There was none among the myriads of men that existed who would pity or assist me; and should I feel kindness towards my enemies? No: from that moment I declared everlasting war against the species, and, more than all, against him who had formed me, and sent me forth to this insupportable misery.

"The sun rose; I heard the voices of men, and knew that it was impossible to return to my retreat during that day. Accordingly I hid myself in some thick underwood, determining to devote the ensuing hours to reflection on my situation.

"The pleasant sunshine, and the pure air of day, restored me to some degree of tranquillity; and when I considered what had passed at the cottage, I could not help believing that I had been too hasty in my conclusions. I had certainly acted imprudently. It was apparent that my conversation had interested the father in my behalf, and I was a fool in having exposed my person to the horror of his children. I ought to have familiarised the old De Lacey to me, and by degrees to have discovered myself to the rest of his family, when they should have been prepared for my approach. But I did not believe my errors to be irretrievable; and, after much consideration, I resolved to return to the cottage, seek the old man, and by my representations win him to my party.

"These thoughts calmed me, and in the afternoon I sank into a profound sleep; but the fever of my blood did not allow me to be visited by peaceful dreams. The horrible scene of the preceding day was for ever acting before my eyes; the females were flying, and the enraged Felix tearing me from his father's feet. I awoke exhausted; and, finding that it was already night, I crept forth from my hiding-place, and went in search of food.

"When my hunger was appeased, I directed my steps towards the well-known path that conducted to the cottage. All there was at peace. I crept into my hovel, and remained in silent expectation of the accustomed hour when the family arose. That hour passed, the sun mounted high in the heavens, but the cottagers did not appear. I trembled violently, apprehending some dreadful misfortune. The inside of the cottage was dark, and I heard no motion; I cannot describe the agony of this suspense.

"Presently two countrymen passed by; but, pausing near the cottage, they entered into conversation, using violent gesticulations; but I did not understand what they said, as they spoke the language of the country, which differed from that of my protectors. Soon after, however, Felix approached with another man: I was surprised, as I knew that he had not quitted the cottage that morning, and waited anxiously to discover, from his discourse, the meaning of these unusual appearances.

" 'Do you consider,' said his companion to him, 'that you will be obliged to pay three months' rent, and to lose the produce of your garden? I do not wish to take any unfair advantage, and I beg therefore that you will take some days to consider of your determination.'

" 'It is utterly useless,' replied Felix; 'we can never again inhabit your cottage. The life of my father is in the greatest danger, owing to the dreadful circumstance that I have related. My wife and my sister will never recover their horror. I entreat you not to reason with me any more. Take possession of your tenement, and let me fly from this place.'

"Felix trembled violently as he said this. He and his companion entered the cottage, in which they remained for a few minutes, and then departed. I never saw any of the family of De Lacey more.

"I continued for the remainder of the day in my hovel in a state of utter and stupid despair. My protectors had departed, and had broken the only link that held me to the world. For the first time the feelings of revenge and hatred filled my bosom, and I did not strive to control them; but, allowing myself to be borne away by the stream, I bent my mind towards injury and death. When I thought of my friends, of the mild voice of De Lacey, the gentle eyes of Agatha, and the exquisite beauty of the Arabian, these thoughts vanished, and a gush of tears somewhat soothed me. But again, when I reflected that they had spurned and deserted me, anger returned, a rage of anger; and, unable to injure any thing human, I turned my fury towards inanimate objects. As night advanced, I placed a variety of combustibles around the cottage; and, after having destroyed every vestige of cultivation in the garden, I waited with forced impatience until the moon had sunk to commence my operations.

"As the night advanced, a fierce wind arose from the woods, and quickly dispersed the clouds that had loitered in the heavens: the blast tore along like a mighty avalanche, and produced a kind of insanity in my spirits, that burst all bounds of reason and reflection. I lighted the dry branch of a tree, and danced with fury around the devoted cottage, my eyes still fixed on the western horizon, the edge of which the moon nearly touched. A part of its orb was at length hid, and I waved my brand; it sunk, and, with a loud scream, I fired the straw, and heath, and bushes, which I had collected. The wind fanned the fire, and the cottage was quickly enveloped by the flames, which clung to it, and licked it with their forked and destroying tongues.

"As soon as I was convinced that no assistance could save any part of the habitation, I quitted the scene, and sought for refuge in the woods.

"And now, with the world before me, whither should I bend my steps? I resolved to fly far from the scene of my misfortunes; but to me, hated and despised, every country must be equally horrible. At length the thought of you crossed my mind. I learned from your papers that you were my father, my creator; and to whom could I apply with more fitness than to him who had given me life? Among the lessons that Felix had bestowed upon Safie, geography had not been omitted: I had learned from these the relative situations of the different countries of the earth. You had mentioned Geneva as the name of your native town; and towards this place I resolved to proceed.

"But how was I to direct myself? I knew that I must travel in a south-westerly direction to reach my destination; but the sun was my only guide. I did not know the names of the towns that I was to pass through, nor could I ask information from a single human being; but I did not despair. From you only could I hope for succour, although towards you I felt no sentiment but that of hatred. Unfeeling, heartless creator! you had endowed me with perceptions and passions, and then cast me abroad an object for the scorn and horror of mankind. But on you only had I any claim for pity and redress, and from you I determined to seek that justice which I vainly attempted to gain from any other being that wore the human form.

"My travels were long, and the sufferings I endured intense. It was late in autumn when I quitted the district where I had so long resided. I travelled only at night, fearful of encountering the visage of a human being. Nature decayed around me, and the sun became heatless; rain and snow poured around me; mighty rivers were

Frankenstein / Photo © Collection CSFF / Bridgeman Images

In this film still from one of the more faithful movie adaptations of *Frankenstein*, Robert DeNiro portrays the monster in a scene soon after he has fled the cottage. **What aspects of the monster's character and appearance does DeNiro capture here?**

frozen; the surface of the earth was hard and chill, and bare, and I found no shelter. Oh, earth! how often did I imprecate curses on the cause of my being! The mildness of my nature had fled, and all within me was turned to gall and bitterness. The nearer I approached to your habitation, the more deeply did I feel the spirit of revenge enkindled in my heart. Snow fell, and the waters were hardened; but I rested not. A few incidents now and then directed me, and I possessed a map of the country; but I often wandered wide from my path. The agony of my feelings allowed me no respite: no incident occurred from which my rage and misery could not extract its food; but a circumstance that happened when I arrived on the confines of Switzerland, when the sun had recovered its warmth, and the earth again began to look green, confirmed in an especial manner the bitterness and horror of my feelings.

"I generally rested during the day, and travelled only when I was secured by night from the view of man. One morning, however, finding that my path lay through a deep wood, I ventured to continue my journey after the sun had risen; the day, which was one of the first of spring, cheered even me by the loveliness of its sunshine and the balminess of the air. I felt emotions of gentleness and pleasure, that had long appeared dead, revive within me. Half surprised by the novelty of these sensations, I allowed myself to be borne away by them; and, forgetting my solitude and deformity, dared to be happy. Soft tears again bedewed my cheeks, and I even raised my humid eyes with thankfulness towards the blessed sun which bestowed such joy upon me.

"I continued to wind among the paths of the wood, until I came to its boundary, which was skirted by a deep and rapid river, into which many of the trees bent their branches, now budding with the fresh spring. Here I paused, not exactly knowing what path to pursue, when I heard the sound of voices, that induced me to conceal myself under the shade of a cypress. I was scarcely hid, when a young girl came running towards the spot where I was concealed, laughing, as if she ran from some one in sport. She continued her course along the precipitous sides of the river, when suddenly her foot slipt, and she fell into the rapid stream. I rushed from my hiding-place; and, with extreme labour from the force of the current, saved her, and dragged her to shore. She was senseless; and I endeavoured, by every means in my power, to restore animation, when I was suddenly interrupted by the approach of a rustic, who was probably the person from whom she had playfully fled. On seeing me, he darted towards me, and tearing the girl from my arms, hastened towards the deeper parts of the wood. I followed speedily, I hardly knew why; but when the man saw me draw near, he aimed a gun, which he carried, at my body, and fired. I sunk to the ground, and my injurer, with increased swiftness, escaped into the wood.

"This was then the reward of my benevolence! I had saved a human being from destruction, and, as a recompense, I now writhed under the miserable pain of a wound, which shattered the flesh and bone. The feelings of kindness and gentleness, which I had entertained but a few moments before, gave place to hellish rage and gnashing of teeth. Inflamed by pain, I vowed eternal hatred and vengeance to all mankind. But the agony of my wound overcame me; my pulses paused, and I fainted.

"For some weeks I led a miserable life in the woods, endeavouring to cure the wound which I had received. The ball had entered my shoulder, and I knew not whether it had remained there or passed through; at any rate I had no means of extracting it. My sufferings were augmented also by the oppressive sense of the injustice and ingratitude of their infliction. My daily vows rose for revenge — a deep and deadly revenge, such as would alone compensate for the outrages and anguish I had endured.

"After some weeks my wound healed, and I continued my journey. The labours I endured were no longer to be alleviated by the bright sun or gentle breezes of spring; all joy was but a mockery, which insulted my desolate state, and made me feel more painfully that I was not made for the enjoyment of pleasure.

"But my toils now drew near a close; and, in two months from this time, I reached the environs of Geneva.

"It was evening when I arrived, and I retired to a hiding-place among the fields that surround it, to meditate in what manner I should apply to you. I was oppressed by fatigue and hunger, and far too unhappy to enjoy the gentle breezes of evening, or the prospect of the sun setting behind the stupendous mountains of Jura.

"At this time a slight sleep relieved me from the pain of reflection, which was disturbed by the approach of a beautiful child, who came running into the recess I had chosen, with all the sportiveness of infancy. Suddenly, as I gazed on him, an idea seized me, that this little creature was unprejudiced, and had lived too short a time to have imbibed a horror of deformity. If, therefore, I could seize him, and educate him as my companion and friend, I should not be so desolate in this peopled earth.

"Urged by this impulse, I seized on the boy as he passed, and drew him towards me. As soon as he beheld my form, he placed his hands before his eyes, and uttered a shrill scream: I drew his hand forcibly from his face, and said, 'Child, what is the meaning of this? I do not intend to hurt you; listen to me.'

"He struggled violently. 'Let me go,' he cried; 'monster! ugly wretch! you wish to eat me, and tear me to pieces — You are an ogre — Let me go, or I will tell my papa.'

" 'Boy, you will never see your father again; you must come with me.'

" 'Hideous monster! let me go. My papa is a Syndic — he is M. Frankenstein — he will punish you. You dare not keep me.'

" 'Frankenstein! you belong then to my enemy — to him towards whom I have sworn eternal revenge; you shall be my first victim.'

"The child still struggled, and loaded me with epithets which carried despair to my heart; I grasped his throat to silence him, and in a moment he lay dead at my feet.

"I gazed on my victim, and my heart swelled with exultation and hellish triumph: clapping my hands, I exclaimed, 'I, too, can create desolation; my enemy is not invulnerable; this death will carry despair to him, and a thousand other miseries shall torment and destroy him.'

"As I fixed my eyes on the child, I saw something glittering on his breast. I took it; it was a portrait of a most lovely woman. In spite of my malignity, it softened and attracted me. For a few moments I gazed with delight on her dark eyes, fringed by deep lashes, and her lovely lips; but presently my rage returned: I remembered that I was for ever deprived of the delights that such beautiful creatures could bestow; and that she whose resemblance I contemplated would, in regarding me, have changed that air of divine benignity to one expressive of disgust and affright.

"Can you wonder that such thoughts transported me with rage? I only wonder that at that moment, instead of venting my sensations in exclamations and agony, I did not rush among mankind, and perish in the attempt to destroy them.

"While I was overcome by these feelings, I left the spot where I had committed the murder, and seeking a more secluded hiding-place, I entered a barn which had appeared to me to be empty. A woman was sleeping on some straw; she was young: not indeed so beautiful as her whose portrait I held; but of an agreeable aspect, and blooming in the loveliness of youth and health. Here, I thought, is one of those whose joy-imparting smiles are bestowed on all but me. And then I bent over her, and whispered, 'Awake, fairest, thy lover is near — he who would give his life but to obtain one look of affection from thine eyes: my beloved, awake!'

"The sleeper stirred; a thrill of terror ran through me. Should she indeed awake, and see me, and curse me, and denounce the murderer? Thus would she assuredly act, if her darkened eyes opened, and she beheld me. The thought was madness; it stirred the fiend within me—not I, but she shall suffer: the murder I have committed because I am for ever robbed of all that she could give me, she shall atone. The crime had its source in her: be hers the punishment! Thanks to the lessons of Felix and the sanguinary laws of man, I had learned now to work mischief. I bent over her, and placed the portrait securely in one of the folds of her dress. She moved again, and I fled.

"For some days I haunted the spot where these scenes had taken place; sometimes wishing to see you, sometimes resolved to quit the world and its miseries for ever. At length I wandered towards these mountains, and have ranged through their immense recesses, consumed by a burning passion which you alone can gratify. We may not part until you have promised to comply with my requisition. I am alone, and miserable; man will not associate with me; but one as deformed and horrible as myself would not deny herself to me. My companion must be of the same species, and have the same defects. This being you must create."

CHAPTER XVII

The being finished speaking, and fixed his looks upon me in expectation of a reply. But I was bewildered, perplexed, and unable to arrange my ideas sufficiently to understand the full extent of his proposition. He continued—

"You must create a female for me, with whom I can live in the interchange of those sympathies necessary for my being. This you alone can do; and I demand it of you as a right which you must not refuse to concede."

The latter part of his tale had kindled anew in me the anger that had died away while he narrated his peaceful life among the cottagers, and, as he said this, I could no longer suppress the rage that burned within me.

"I do refuse it," I replied; "and no torture shall ever extort a consent from me. You may render me the most miserable of men, but you shall never make me base in my own eyes. Shall I create another like yourself, whose joint wickedness might desolate the world? Begone! I have answered you; you may torture me, but I will never consent."

"You are in the wrong," replied the fiend; "and, instead of threatening, I am content to reason with you. I am malicious because I am miserable. Am I not shunned and hated by all mankind? You, my creator, would tear me to pieces, and triumph; remember that, and tell me why I should pity man more than he pities me? You would not call it murder, if you could precipitate me into one of those ice-rifts, and destroy my frame, the work of your own hands. Shall I respect man, when he contemns me? Let him live with me in the interchange of kindness; and, instead of injury, I would bestow every benefit upon him with tears of gratitude at his acceptance. But that cannot be; the human senses are insurmountable barriers to our union. Yet mine shall not be the submission of abject slavery. I will revenge my injuries: if I cannot inspire love, I will cause fear; and chiefly towards you my arch-enemy, because my creator, do I swear inextinguishable hatred. Have a care: I will work at your destruction, nor finish until I desolate your heart, so that you shall curse the hour of your birth."

A fiendish rage animated him as he said this; his face was wrinkled into contortions too horrible for human eyes to behold; but presently he calmed himself and proceeded—

"I intended to reason. This passion is detrimental to me; for you do not reflect that *you* are the cause of its excess. If any being felt emotions of benevolence towards me, I should return them an hundred and an hundred fold; for that one creature's sake, I would make peace with the whole kind! But I now indulge in dreams of bliss that cannot be realised. What I ask of you is reasonable and moderate; I demand a creature of another sex, but as hideous as myself; the gratification is small, but it is all that I can receive, and it shall content me. It is true, we shall be monsters, cut off from all the world; but on that account we shall be more attached to one another. Our lives will not be happy, but they will be harmless, and free from the misery I now feel. Oh! my creator, make me happy; let me feel gratitude towards you for one benefit! Let me see that I excite the sympathy of some existing thing; do not deny me my request!"

I was moved. I shuddered when I thought of the possible consequences of my consent; but I felt that there was some justice in his argument. His tale, and the feelings he now expressed, proved him to be a creature of fine sensations; and did I not, as his maker, owe him all the portion of happiness that it was in my power to bestow? He saw my change of feeling, and continued—

"If you consent, neither you nor any other human being shall ever see us again: I will go to the vast wilds of South America. My food is not that of man; I do not destroy the lamb and the kid to glut my appetite; acorns and berries afford me sufficient nourishment. My companion will be of the same nature as myself, and will be content with the same fare. We shall make our bed of dried leaves; the sun will shine on us as on man, and will ripen our food. The picture I present to you is peaceful and human, and you must feel that you could deny it only in the wantonness of power and cruelty. Pitiless as you have been towards me, I now see compassion in your eyes; let me seize the favourable moment, and persuade you to promise what I so ardently desire."

"You propose," replied I, "to fly from the habitations of man, to dwell in those wilds where the beasts of the field will be your only companions. How can you, who long for the love and sympathy of man, persevere in this exile? You will return, and again seek their kindness, and you will meet with their detestation; your evil passions will be renewed, and you will then have a companion to aid you in the task of destruction. This may not be: cease to argue the point, for I cannot consent."

"How inconstant are your feelings! but a moment ago you were moved by my representations, and why do you again harden yourself to my complaints? I swear to you, by the earth which I inhabit, and by you that made me, that, with the companion you bestow, I will quit the neighbourhood of man, and dwell as it may chance, in the most savage of places. My evil passions will have fled, for I shall meet with sympathy! my life will flow quietly away, and, in my dying moments, I shall not curse my maker."

His words had a strange effect upon me. I compassioned him, and sometimes felt a wish to console him; but when I looked upon him, when I saw the filthy mass that moved and talked, my heart sickened, and my feelings were altered to those of horror and hatred. I tried to stifle these sensations; I thought, that as I could not sympathise with him, I had no right to withhold from him the small portion of happiness which was yet in my power to bestow.

"You swear," I said, "to be harmless; but have you not already shown a degree of malice that should reasonably make me distrust you? May not even this be a feint that will increase your triumph by affording a wider scope for your revenge?"

"How is this? I must not be trifled with: and I demand an answer. If I have no ties and no affections, hatred and vice must be my portion; the love of another will destroy the cause of my crimes, and I shall become a thing, of whose existence every one will be ignorant. My vices are the children of a forced solitude that I abhor; and my virtues will necessarily arise when I live in communion with an equal. I shall feel the affections of a sensitive being, and become linked to the chain of existence and events, from which I am now excluded."

I paused some time to reflect on all he had related, and the various arguments which he had employed. I thought of the promise of virtues which he had displayed on the opening of his existence, and the subsequent blight of all kindly feeling by the loathing and scorn which his protectors had manifested towards him. His power and threats were not omitted in my calculations: a creature who could exist in the ice-caves of the glaciers, and hide himself from pursuit among the ridges of inaccessible precipices, was a being possessing faculties it would be vain to cope with. After a long pause of reflection, I concluded that the justice due both to him and my fellow-creatures demanded of me that I should comply with his request. Turning to him, therefore, I said—

"I consent to your demand, on your solemn oath to quit Europe for ever, and every other place in the neighbourhood of man, as soon as I shall deliver into your hands a female who will accompany you in your exile."

"I swear," he cried, "by the sun, and by the blue sky of Heaven, and by the fire of love that burns my heart, that if you grant my prayer, while they exist you shall never behold me again. Depart to your home, and commence your labours: I shall watch their progress with unutterable anxiety; and fear not but that when you are ready I shall appear."

Saying this, he suddenly quitted me, fearful, perhaps, of any change in my sentiments. I saw him descend the mountain with greater speed than the flight of an eagle, and quickly lost him among the undulations of the sea of ice.

His tale had occupied the whole day; and the sun was upon the verge of the horizon when he departed. I knew that I ought to hasten my descent towards the valley, as I should soon be encompassed in darkness; but my heart was heavy, and my steps slow. The labour of winding among the little paths of the mountains, and fixing my feet firmly as I advanced, perplexed me, occupied as I was by the emotions which the occurrences of the day had produced. Night was far advanced, when I came to the half-way resting-place, and seated myself beside the fountain. The stars shone at intervals, as the clouds passed from over them; the dark pines rose before me, and every here and there a broken tree lay on the ground: it was a scene of wonderful solemnity, and stirred strange thoughts within me. I wept bitterly; and clasping my hands in agony, I exclaimed, "Oh! stars and clouds, and winds, ye are all about to mock me: if ye really pity me, crush sensation and memory; let me become as nought; but if not, depart, depart, and leave me in darkness."

These were wild and miserable thoughts; but I cannot describe to you how the eternal twinkling of the stars weighed upon me, and how I listened to every blast of wind, as if it were a dull, ugly siroc[29] on its way to consume me.

Morning dawned before I arrived at the village of Chamounix; I took no rest, but returned immediately to Geneva. Even in my own heart I could give no expression to my sensations—they weighed on me with a mountain's weight, and their excess destroyed my agony beneath them. Thus I returned home, and entering the house, presented myself to the family. My haggard and wild appearance awoke intense alarm; but I answered no question, scarcely did I speak. I felt as if I were placed under a ban—as if I had no right to claim their sympathies—as if never more might I enjoy companionship with them. Yet even thus I loved them to adoration; and to save them, I resolved to dedicate myself to my most abhorred task. The prospect of such an occupation made every other circumstance of existence pass before me like a dream; and that thought only had to me the reality of life.

---

[29] Sirocco, a blistering wind that blows into Europe from Northern Africa.—EDS.

CHAPTER XVIII

Day after day, week after week, passed away on my return to Geneva; and I could not collect the courage to recommence my work. I feared the vengeance of the disappointed fiend, yet I was unable to overcome my repugnance to the task which was enjoined me. I found that I could not compose a female without again devoting several months to profound study and laborious disquisition. I had heard of some discoveries having been made by an English philosopher, the knowledge of which was material to my success, and I sometimes thought of obtaining my father's consent to visit England for this purpose; but I clung to every pretence of delay, and shrunk from taking the first step in an undertaking whose immediate necessity began to appear less absolute to me. A change indeed had taken place in me: my health, which had hitherto declined, was now much restored; and my spirits, when unchecked by the memory of my unhappy promise, rose proportionably. My father saw this change with pleasure, and he turned his thoughts towards the best method of eradicating the remains of my melancholy, which every now and then would return by fits, and with a devouring blackness overcast the approaching sunshine. At these moments I took refuge in the most perfect solitude. I passed whole days on the lake alone in a little boat, watching the clouds, and listening to the rippling of the waves, silent and listless. But the fresh air and bright sun seldom failed to restore me to some degree of composure; and, on my return, I met the salutations of my friends with a readier smile and a more cheerful heart.

It was after my return from one of these rambles, that my father, calling me aside, thus addressed me:—

"I am happy to remark, my dear son, that you have resumed your former pleasures, and seem to be returning to yourself. And yet you are still unhappy, and still avoid our society. For some time I was lost in conjecture as to the cause of this; but yesterday an idea struck me, and if it is well founded, I conjure you to avow it. Reserve on such a point would be not only useless, but draw down treble misery on us all."

I trembled violently at his exordium, and my father continued—

"I confess, my son, that I have always looked forward to your marriage with our dear Elizabeth as the tie of our domestic comfort, and the stay of my declining years. You were attached to each other from your earliest infancy; you studied together, and appeared, in dispositions and tastes, entirely suited to one another. But so blind is the experience of man, that what I conceived to be the best assistants to my plan, may have entirely destroyed it. You, perhaps, regard her as your sister, without any wish that she might become your wife. Nay, you may have met with another whom you may love; and, considering yourself as bound in honour to Elizabeth, this struggle may occasion the poignant misery which you appear to feel."

"My dear father, re-assure yourself. I love my cousin tenderly and sincerely. I never saw any woman who excited, as Elizabeth does, my warmest admiration and affection. My future hopes and prospects are entirely bound up in the expectation of our union."

"The expression of your sentiments on this subject, my dear Victor, gives me more pleasure than I have for some time experienced. If you feel thus, we shall assuredly be happy, however present events may cast a gloom over us. But it is this gloom which appears to have taken so strong a hold of your mind, that I wish to dissipate. Tell me, therefore, whether you object to an immediate solemnisation of the marriage. We have been unfortunate, and recent events have drawn us from that everyday tranquillity befitting my years and infirmities. You are younger; yet I do not suppose, possessed as you are of a competent fortune, that an early marriage would at all interfere with any future plans of honour and utility that you may have formed. Do not suppose, however, that I wish to dictate happiness to you, or that a delay on your part would cause me any serious uneasiness. Interpret my words with candour, and answer me, I conjure you, with confidence and sincerity."

I listened to my father in silence, and remained for some time incapable of offering any reply. I revolved rapidly in my mind a multitude of thoughts, and endeavoured to arrive at some conclusion. Alas! to me the idea of an immediate union with my Elizabeth was one of horror and dismay. I was bound by a solemn promise, which I had not yet fulfilled, and dared not break; or, if I did, what manifold miseries might not impend over me and my devoted family! Could I enter into a festival with this deadly weight yet hanging round my neck, and bowing me to the ground? I must perform my engagement, and let the monster depart with his mate, before I allowed myself to enjoy the delight of an union from which I expected peace.

I remembered also the necessity imposed upon me of either journeying to England, or entering into a long correspondence with those philosophers of that country, whose knowledge and discoveries were of indispensable use to me in my present undertaking. The latter method of obtaining the desired intelligence was dilatory and unsatisfactory: besides, I had an insurmountable aversion to the idea of engaging myself in my loathsome task in my father's house, while in habits of familiar intercourse with those I loved. I knew that a thousand fearful accidents might occur, the slightest of which would disclose a tale to thrill all connected with me with horror. I was aware also that I should often lose all self-command, all capacity of hiding the harrowing sensations that would possess me during the progress of my unearthly occupation. I must absent myself from all I loved while thus employed. Once commenced, it would quickly be achieved, and I might be restored to my family in peace and happiness. My promise fulfilled, the monster would depart for ever. Or (so my fond fancy imaged) some accident might meanwhile occur to destroy him, and put an end to my slavery for ever.

These feelings dictated my answer to my father. I expressed a wish to visit England; but, concealing the true reasons of this request, I clothed my desires under a guise which excited no suspicion, while I urged my desire with an earnestness that easily induced my father to comply. After so long a period of an absorbing melancholy, that resembled madness in its intensity and effects, he was glad to find that I was capable of taking pleasure in the idea of such a journey, and he hoped that change of scene and varied amusement would, before my return, have restored me entirely to myself.

The duration of my absence was left to my own choice; a few months, or at most a year, was the period contemplated. One paternal kind precaution he had taken to ensure my having a companion. Without previously communicating with me, he had, in concert with Elizabeth, arranged that Clerval should join me at Strasburgh. This interfered with the solitude I coveted for the prosecution of my task; yet at the commencement of my journey the presence of my friend could in no way be an impediment, and truly I rejoiced that thus I should be saved many hours of lonely, maddening reflection. Nay, Henry might stand between me and the intrusion of my foe. If I were alone, would he not at times force his abhorred presence on me, to remind me of my task, or to contemplate its progress?

To England, therefore, I was bound, and it was understood that my union with Elizabeth should take place immediately on my return. My father's age rendered him extremely averse to delay. For myself, there was one reward I promised myself from my detested toils — one consolation for my unparalleled sufferings; it was the prospect of that day when, enfranchised from my miserable slavery, I might claim Elizabeth, and forget the past in my union with her.

I now made arrangements for my journey; but one feeling haunted me, which filled me with fear and agitation. During my absence I should leave my friends unconscious of the existence of their enemy, and unprotected from his attacks, exasperated as he might be by my departure. But he had promised to follow me wherever I might go; and would he not accompany me to England? This imagination was dreadful in itself, but soothing, inasmuch as it supposed the safety of my friends. I was agonised with the idea of the possibility that the reverse of this might happen. But through the whole period during which I was the slave of my creature, I allowed myself to be governed by the impulses of the moment; and my present sensations strongly intimated that the fiend would follow me, and exempt my family from the danger of his machinations.

It was in the latter end of September that I again quitted my native country. My journey had been my own suggestion, and Elizabeth, therefore, acquiesced: but she was filled with disquiet at the idea of my suffering, away from her, the inroads of misery and grief. It had been her care which provided me a companion in Clerval—and yet a man is blind to a thousand minute circumstances, which call forth a woman's sedulous attention. She longed to bid me hasten my return,—a thousand conflicting emotions rendered her mute, as she bade me a tearful silent farewell.

I threw myself into the carriage that was to convey me away, hardly knowing whither I was going, and careless of what was passing around. I remembered only, and it was with a bitter anguish that I reflected on it, to order that my chemical instruments should be packed to go with me. Filled with dreary imaginations, I passed through many beautiful and majestic scenes; but my eyes were fixed and unobserving. I could only think of the bourne of my travels,[30] and the work which was to occupy me whilst they endured.

After some days spent in listless indolence, during which I traversed many leagues, I arrived at Strasburgh, where I waited two days for Clerval. He came. Alas, how great was the contrast between us! He was alive to every new scene; joyful when he saw the beauties of the setting sun, and more happy when he beheld it rise, and recommence a new day. He pointed out to me the shifting colours of the landscape, and the appearances of the sky. "This is what it is to live," he cried, "now I enjoy existence! But you, my dear Frankenstein, wherefore are you desponding and sorrowful?" In truth, I was occupied by gloomy thoughts, and neither saw the descent of the evening star, nor the golden sunrise reflected in the Rhine.—And you, my friend, would be far more amused with the journal of Clerval, who observed the scenery with an eye of feeling and delight, than in listening to my reflections. I, a miserable wretch, haunted by a curse that shut up every avenue to enjoyment.

We had agreed to descend the Rhine in a boat from Strasburgh to Rotterdam, whence we might take shipping for London. During this voyage, we passed many willowy islands, and saw several beautiful towns. We stayed a day at Manheim, and, on the fifth from our departure from Strasburgh, arrived at Mayence. The course of the Rhine below Mayence becomes much more picturesque. The river descends rapidly, and winds between hills, not high, but steep, and of beautiful forms. We saw many ruined castles standing on the edges of precipices, surrounded by black woods, high and inaccessible. This part of the Rhine, indeed, presents a singularly variegated landscape. In one spot you view rugged hills, ruined castles overlooking tremendous precipices, with the dark Rhine rushing beneath;

[30] End or goal.—EDS.

and, on the sudden turn of a promontory, flourishing vineyards, with green sloping banks, and a meandering river, and populous towns occupy the scene.

We travelled at the time of the vintage, and heard the song of the labourers, as we glided down the stream. Even I, depressed in mind, and my spirits continually agitated by gloomy feelings, even I was pleased. I lay at the bottom of the boat, and, as I gazed on the cloudless blue sky, I seemed to drink in a tranquillity to which I had long been a stranger. And if these were my sensations, who can describe those of Henry? He felt as if he had been transported to Fairyland, and enjoyed a happiness seldom tasted by man. "I have seen," he said, "the most beautiful scenes of my own country; I have visited the lakes of Lucerne and Uri, where the snowy mountains descend almost perpendicularly to the water, casting black and impenetrable shades, which would cause a gloomy and mournful appearance, were it not for the most verdant islands that relieve the eye by their gay appearance; I have seen this lake agitated by a tempest, when the wind tore up whirlwinds of water, and gave you an idea of what the water-spout must be on the great ocean, and the waves dash with fury the base of the mountain, where the priest and his mistress[31] were overwhelmed by an avalanche, and where their dying voices are still said to be heard amid the pauses of the nightly wind; I have seen the mountains of La Valais, and the Pays de Vaud: but this country, Victor, pleases me more than all those wonders. The mountains of Switzerland are more majestic and strange; but there is a charm in the banks of this divine river, that I never before saw equalled. Look at that castle which overhangs yon precipice; and that also on the island, almost concealed amongst the foliage of those lovely trees; and now that group of labourers coming from among their vines; and that village half hid in the recess of the mountain. Oh, surely, the spirit that inhabits and guards this place has a soul more in harmony with man, than those who pile the glacier, or retire to the inaccessible peaks of the mountains of our own country."

Clerval! beloved friend! even now it delights me to record your words, and to dwell on the praise of which you are so eminently deserving. He was a being formed in the "very poetry of nature." His wild and enthusiastic imagination was chastened by the sensibility of his heart. His soul overflowed with ardent affections, and his friendship was of that devoted and wondrous nature that the worldly-minded teach us to look for only in the imagination. But even human sympathies were not sufficient to satisfy his eager mind. The scenery of external nature, which others regard only with admiration, he loved with ardour:—

——The sounding cataract
Haunted him like a passion: the tall rock,
The mountain, and the deep and gloomy wood,
Their colours and their forms, were then to him
An appetite; a feeling, and a love,
That had no need of a remoter charm,
By thought supplied, or any interest
Unborrow'd from the eye.[32]

And where does he now exist? Is this gentle and lovely being lost for ever? Has this mind, so replete with ideas, imaginations fanciful and magnificent, which formed a world, whose existence depended on the life of its creator;—has this mind perished? Does it now only exist in my memory? No, it is not thus; your form so divinely wrought, and beaming with beauty, has decayed, but your spirit still visits and consoles your unhappy friend.

---

[31] A reference to a local tale from the Rhine-North Westphalia region of Germany. — EDS.

[32] These have been adapted from lines 76–83 of William Wordsworth's poem "Lines Composed a Few Miles above Tintern Abbey" (1798), which was written in first person. — EDS.

Pardon this gush of sorrow; these ineffectual words are but a slight tribute to the unexampled worth of Henry, but they soothe my heart, overflowing with the anguish which his remembrance creates. I will proceed with my tale.

Beyond Cologne we descended to the plains of Holland; and we resolved to post the remainder of our way; for the wind was contrary, and the stream of the river was too gentle to aid us.

Our journey here lost the interest arising from beautiful scenery; but we arrived in a few days at Rotterdam, whence we proceeded by sea to England. It was on a clear morning, in the latter days of December, that I first saw the white cliffs of Britain. The banks of the Thames presented a new scene; they were flat, but fertile, and almost every town was marked by the remembrance of some story. We saw Tilbury Fort, and remembered the Spanish armada; Gravesend, Woolwich, and Greenwich, places which I had heard of even in my country.

At length we saw the numerous steeples of London, St. Paul's towering above all, and the Tower famed in English history.

CHAPTER XIX

London was our present point of rest; we determined to remain several months in this wonderful and celebrated city. Clerval desired the intercourse of the men of genius and talent who flourished at this time; but this was with me a secondary object; I was principally occupied with the means of obtaining the information necessary for the completion of my promise, and quickly availed myself of the letters of introduction that I had brought with me, addressed to the most distinguished natural philosophers.

If this journey had taken place during my days of study and happiness, it would have afforded me inexpressible pleasure. But a blight had come over my existence, and I only visited these people for the sake of the information they might give me on the subject in which my interest was so terribly profound. Company was irksome to me; when alone, I could fill my mind with the sights of heaven and earth; the voice of Henry soothed me, and I could thus cheat myself into a transitory peace. But busy, uninteresting, joyous faces brought back despair to my heart. I saw an insurmountable barrier placed between me and my fellow-men; this barrier was sealed with the blood of William and Justine; and to reflect on the events connected with those names filled my soul with anguish.

But in Clerval I saw the image of my former self; he was inquisitive, and anxious to gain experience and instruction. The difference of manners which he observed was to him an inexhaustible source of instruction and amusement. He was also pursuing an object he had long had in view. His design was to visit India, in the belief that he had in his knowledge of its various languages, and in the views he had taken of its society, the means of materially assisting the progress of European colonisation and trade. In Britain only could he further the execution of his plan. He was for ever busy; and the only check to his enjoyments was my sorrowful and dejected mind. I tried to conceal this as much as possible, that I might not debar him from the pleasures natural to one, who was entering on a new scene of life, undisturbed by any care or bitter recollection. I often refused to accompany him, alleging another engagement, that I might remain alone. I now also began to collect the materials necessary for my new creation, and this was to me like the torture of single drops of water continually falling on the head. Every thought that was devoted to it was an extreme anguish, and every word that I spoke in allusion to it caused my lips to quiver, and my heart to palpitate.

After passing some months in London, we received a letter from a person in Scotland, who had formerly been our visitor at Geneva. He mentioned the beauties of his native country, and asked us if those were not sufficient allurements to induce us to prolong our journey as far north as Perth, where he resided. Clerval eagerly desired to accept this invitation; and I, although I abhorred society, wished to view again mountains and streams, and all the wondrous works with which Nature adorns her chosen dwelling-places.

We had arrived in England at the beginning of October, and it was now February. We accordingly determined to commence our journey towards the north at the expiration of another month. In this expedition we did not intend to follow the great road to Edinburgh, but to visit Windsor, Oxford, Matlock, and the Cumberland lakes, resolving to arrive at the completion of this tour about the end of July. I packed up my chemical instruments, and the materials I had collected, resolving to finish my labours in some obscure nook in the northern highlands of Scotland.

We quitted London on the 27th of March, and remained a few days at Windsor, rambling in its beautiful forest. This was a new scene to us mountaineers; the majestic oaks, the quantity of game, and the herds of stately deer, were all novelties to us.

From thence we proceeded to Oxford. As we entered this city, our minds were filled with the remembrance of the events that had been transacted there more than a century and a half before. It was here that Charles I. had collected his forces. This city had remained faithful to him, after the whole nation had forsaken his cause to join the standard of parliament and liberty. The memory of that unfortunate king, and his companions, the amiable Falkland, the insolent Goring, his queen, and son, gave a peculiar interest to every part of the city, which they might be supposed to have inhabited. The spirit of elder days found a dwelling here, and we delighted to trace its footsteps. If these feelings had not found an imaginary gratification, the appearance of the city had yet in itself sufficient beauty to obtain our admiration. The colleges are ancient and picturesque; the streets are almost magnificent; and the lovely Isis, which flows beside it through meadows of exquisite verdure, is spread forth into a placid expanse of waters, which reflects its majestic assemblage of towers, and spires, and domes, embosomed among aged trees.

I enjoyed this scene; and yet my enjoyment was embittered both by the memory of the past, and the anticipation of the future. I was formed for peaceful happiness. During my youthful days discontent never visited my mind; and if I was ever overcome by *ennui*, the sight of what is beautiful in nature, or the study of what is excellent and sublime in the productions of man, could always interest my heart, and communicate elasticity to my spirits. But I am a blasted tree; the bolt has entered my soul; and I felt then that I should survive to exhibit, what I shall soon cease to be — a miserable spectacle of wrecked humanity, pitiable to others, and intolerable to myself.

We passed a considerable period at Oxford, 485
rambling among its environs, and endeavouring to identify every spot which might relate to the most animating epoch of English history. Our little voyages of discovery were often prolonged by the successive objects that presented themselves. We visited the tomb of the illustrious Hampden, and the field on which that patriot fell. For a moment my soul was elevated from its debasing and miserable fears, to contemplate the divine ideas of liberty and self-sacrifice, of which these sights were the monuments and the remembrancers. For an instant I dared to shake off my chains, and look around me with a free and lofty spirit; but the iron had eaten into my flesh, and I sank again, trembling and hopeless, into my miserable self.

We left Oxford with regret, and proceeded to Matlock, which was our next place of rest. The country in the neighbourhood of this village resembled, to a greater degree, the scenery of

Switzerland; but every thing is on a lower scale, and the green hills want the crown of distant white Alps, which always attend on the piny mountains of my native country. We visited the wondrous cave, and the little cabinets of natural history, where the curiosities are disposed in the same manner as in the collections at Servox and Chamounix. The latter name made me tremble, when pronounced by Henry; and I hastened to quit Matlock, with which that terrible scene was thus associated.

From Derby, still journeying northward, we passed two months in Cumberland and Westmorland. I could now almost fancy myself among the Swiss mountains. The little patches of snow which yet lingered on the northern sides of the mountains, the lakes, and the dashing of the rocky streams, were all familiar and dear sights to me. Here also we made some acquaintances, who almost contrived to cheat me into happiness. The delight of Clerval was proportionably greater than mine; his mind expanded in the company of men of talent, and he found in his own nature greater capacities and resources than he could have imagined himself to have possessed while he associated with his inferiors. "I could pass my life here," said he to me; "and among these mountains I should scarcely regret Switzerland and the Rhine."

But he found that a traveller's life is one that includes much pain amidst its enjoyments. His feelings are for ever on the stretch; and when he begins to sink into repose, he finds himself obliged to quit that on which he rests in pleasure for something new, which again engages his attention, and which also he forsakes for other novelties.

We had scarcely visited the various lakes of Cumberland and Westmorland, and conceived an affection for some of the inhabitants, when the period of our appointment with our Scotch friend approached, and we left them to travel on. For my own part I was not sorry. I had now neglected my promise for some time, and I feared the effects of the daemon's disappointment. He might remain in Switzerland, and wreak his vengeance on my relatives. This idea pursued me, and tormented me at every moment from which I might otherwise have snatched repose and peace. I waited for my letters with feverish impatience: if they were delayed, I was miserable, and overcome by a thousand fears; and when they arrived, and I saw the superscription of Elizabeth or my father, I hardly dared to read and ascertain my fate. Sometimes I thought that the fiend followed me, and might expedite my remissness by murdering my companion. When these thoughts possessed me, I would not quit Henry for a moment, but followed him as his shadow, to protect him from the fancied rage of his destroyer. I felt as if I had committed some great crime, the consciousness of which haunted me. I was guiltless, but I had indeed drawn down a horrible curse upon my head, as mortal as that of crime.

I visited Edinburgh with languid eyes and mind; and yet that city might have interested the most unfortunate being. Clerval did not like it so well as Oxford: for the antiquity of the latter city was more pleasing to him. But the beauty and regularity of the new town of Edinburgh, its romantic castle and its environs, the most delightful in the world, Arthur's Seat, St. Bernard's Well, and the Pentland Hills, compensated him for the change, and filled him with cheerfulness and admiration. But I was impatient to arrive at the termination of my journey.

We left Edinburgh in a week, passing through Coupar, St. Andrew's, and along the banks of the Tay, to Perth, where our friend expected us. But I was in no mood to laugh and talk with strangers, or enter into their feelings or plans with the good humour expected from a guest; and accordingly I told Clerval that I wished to make the tour of Scotland alone. "Do you," said I, "enjoy yourself, and let this be our rendezvous. I may be absent a month or two; but do not interfere with my motions, I entreat you: leave me to peace and solitude for a short time; and when I return, I hope it will be with a lighter heart, more congenial to your own temper."

Henry wished to dissuade me; but, seeing me bent on this plan, ceased to remonstrate. He entreated me to write often. "I had rather be with you," he said, "in your solitary rambles, than with these Scotch people, whom I do not know: hasten then, my friend, to return, that I may again feel myself somewhat at home, which I cannot do in your absence."

Having parted from my friend, I determined to visit some remote spot of Scotland, and finish my work in solitude. I did not doubt but that the monster followed me, and would discover himself to me when I should have finished, that he might receive his companion.

With this resolution I traversed the northern highlands, and fixed on one of the remotest of the Orkneys as the scene of my labours. It was a place fitted for such a work, being hardly more than a rock, whose high sides were continually beaten upon by the waves. The soil was barren, scarcely affording pasture for a few miserable cows, and oatmeal for its inhabitants, which consisted of five persons, whose gaunt and scraggy limbs gave tokens of their miserable fare. Vegetables and bread, when they indulged in such luxuries, and even fresh water, was to be procured from the main land, which was about five miles distant.

On the whole island there were but three miserable huts, and one of these was vacant when I arrived. This I hired. It contained but two rooms, and these exhibited all the squalidness of the most miserable penury. The thatch had fallen in, the walls were unplastered, and the door was off its hinges. I ordered it to be repaired, bought some furniture, and took possession; an incident which would, doubtless, have occasioned some surprise, had not all the senses of the cottagers been benumbed by want and squalid poverty. As it was, I lived ungazed at and unmolested, hardly thanked for the pittance of food and clothes which I gave; so much does suffering blunt even the coarsest sensations of men.

In this retreat I devoted the morning to labour; but in the evening, when the weather permitted, I walked on the stony beach of the sea, to listen to the waves as they roared and dashed at my feet. It was a monotonous yet ever-changing scene. I thought of Switzerland; it was far different from this desolate and appalling landscape. Its hills are covered with vines, and its cottages are scattered thickly in the plains. Its fair lakes reflect a blue and gentle sky; and, when troubled by the winds, their tumult is but as the play of a lively infant, when compared to the roarings of the giant ocean.

In this manner I distributed my occupations when I first arrived; but, as I proceeded in my labour, it became every day more horrible and irksome to me. Sometimes I could not prevail on myself to enter my laboratory for several days; and at other times I toiled day and night in order to complete my work. It was, indeed, a filthy process in which I was engaged. During my first experiment, a kind of enthusiastic frenzy had blinded me to the horror of my employment; my mind was intently fixed on the consummation of my labour, and my eyes were shut to the horror of my proceedings. But now I went to it in cold blood, and my heart often sickened at the work of my hands.

Thus situated, employed in the most detestable occupation, immersed in a solitude where nothing could for an instant call my attention from the actual scene in which I was engaged, my spirits became unequal; I grew restless and nervous. Every moment I feared to meet my persecutor. Sometimes I sat with my eyes fixed on the ground, fearing to raise them, lest they should encounter the object which I so much dreaded to behold. I feared to wander from the sight of my fellow-creatures, lest when alone he should come to claim his companion.

De Agostini Picture Library/G. Sioen/Bridgeman Images

This photo shows the cliffs overlooking the coast of the Isle of Hoy, one of the Orkney Islands. **In what ways does the setting, as depicted here, reflect Victor Frankenstein's current state of mind? Why might this location be a suitable site for constructing the monster's female companion?**

In the mean time I worked on, and my labour was already considerably advanced. I looked towards its completion with a tremulous and eager hope, which I dared not trust myself to question, but which was intermixed with obscure forebodings of evil, that made my heart sicken in my bosom.

CHAPTER XX

I sat one evening in my laboratory; the sun had set, and the moon was just rising from the sea; I had not sufficient light for my employment, and I remained idle, in a pause of consideration of whether I should leave my labour for the night, or hasten its conclusion by an unremitting attention to it. As I sat, a train of reflection occurred to me, which led me to consider the effects of what I was now doing. Three years before I was engaged in the same manner, and had created a fiend whose unparalleled barbarity had desolated my heart, and filled it for ever with the bitterest remorse. I was now about to form another being, of whose dispositions I was alike ignorant; she might become ten thousand times more malignant than her mate, and delight, for its own sake, in murder and wretchedness. He had sworn to quit the neighbourhood of man, and hide himself in deserts; but she had not; and she, who in all probability was to become a thinking and reasoning animal, might refuse to comply with a compact made before her creation. They might even hate each other; the creature who already lived loathed his own deformity, and might he not conceive a greater abhorrence for it when it came before his eyes in the female form? She also might turn with disgust from him to the superior beauty of man; she might quit him, and he be again alone, exasperated by the fresh provocation of being deserted by one of his own species.

Even if they were to leave Europe, and inhabit the deserts of the new world, yet one of the first results of those sympathies for which the daemon thirsted would be children, and a race of devils would be propagated upon the earth, who might make the very existence of the species of man a condition precarious and full of terror. Had I a right, for my own benefit, to inflict this curse upon everlasting generations? I had before been moved by the sophisms of the being I had created; I had been struck senseless by his fiendish threats: but now, for the first time, the wickedness of my promise burst upon me; I shuddered to think that future ages might curse me as their pest, whose selfishness had not hesitated to buy its own peace at the price, perhaps, of the existence of the whole human race.

I trembled, and my heart failed within me; when, on looking up, I saw, by the light of the moon, the daemon at the casement. A ghastly grin wrinkled his lips as he gazed on me, where I sat fulfilling the task which he had allotted to me. Yes, he had followed me in my travels; he had loitered in forests, hid himself in caves, or taken refuge in wide and desert heaths; and he now came to mark my progress, and claim the fulfillment of my promise.

As I looked on him, his countenance expressed the utmost extent of malice and treachery. I thought with a sensation of madness on my promise of creating another like to him, and trembling with passion, tore to pieces the thing on which I was engaged. The wretch saw me destroy the creature on whose future existence he depended for happiness, and, with a howl of devilish despair and revenge, withdrew.

I left the room, and, locking the door, made a solemn vow in my own heart never to resume my labours; and then, with trembling steps, I sought my own apartment. I was alone; none were near me to dissipate the gloom, and relieve me from the sickening oppression of the most terrible reveries.

Several hours passed, and I remained near my window gazing on the sea; it was almost motionless, for the winds were hushed, and all nature reposed under the eye of the quiet moon. A few fishing vessels alone specked the water, and now and then the gentle breeze wafted the sound of voices, as the fishermen called to one another. I felt the silence, although I was hardly conscious of its extreme profundity, until my ear was suddenly arrested by the paddling of oars near the shore, and a person landed close to my house.

In a few minutes after, I heard the creaking of my door, as if some one endeavoured to open it softly. I trembled from head to foot; I felt a presentiment of who it was, and wished to rouse one of the peasants who dwelt in a cottage not far from mine; but I was overcome by the sensation of helplessness, so often felt in frightful dreams, when you in vain endeavour to fly from an impending danger, and was rooted to the spot.

Presently I heard the sound of footsteps along the passage; the door opened, and the wretch whom I dreaded appeared. Shutting the door, he approached me, and said, in a smothered voice—

"You have destroyed the work which you began; what is it that you intend? Do you dare to break your promise? I have endured toil and misery: I left Switzerland with you; I crept along the shores of the Rhine, among its willow islands, and over the summits of its hills. I have dwelt many months in the heaths of England, and among the deserts of Scotland. I have endured incalculable fatigue, and cold, and hunger; do you dare destroy my hopes?"

"Begone! I do break my promise; never will I create another like yourself, equal in deformity and wickedness."

"Slave, I have reasoned with you, but you have proved yourself unworthy of my condescension. Remember that I have power; you believe yourself miserable, but I can make you so wretched that the light of day will be hateful to you. You are my creator, but I am your master;—obey!"

"The hour of my irresolution is past, and the period of your power is arrived. Your threats cannot move me to do an act of wickedness; but they confirm me in a determination of not creating you a companion in vice. Shall I, in cool blood, set loose upon the earth a daemon, whose delight is in death and wretchedness? Begone! I am firm, and your words will only exasperate my rage."

The monster saw my determination in my face, and gnashed his teeth in the impotence of anger. "Shall each man," cried he, "find a wife for his bosom, and each beast have his mate, and I be alone? I had feelings of affection, and they were requited by detestation and scorn. Man! you may hate; but beware! your hours will pass in dread and misery, and soon the bolt will fall which must ravish from you your happiness for ever. Are you to be happy, while I grovel in the intensity of my wretchedness? You can blast my other passions; but revenge remains — revenge, henceforth dearer than light or food! I may die; but first you, my tyrant and tormentor, shall curse the sun that gazes on your misery. Beware; for I am fearless, and therefore powerful. I will watch with the wiliness of a snake, that I may sting with its venom. Man, you shall repent of the injuries you inflict."

"Devil, cease; and do not poison the air with these sounds of malice. I have declared my resolution to you, and I am no coward to bend beneath words. Leave me; I am inexorable."

"It is well. I go; but remember, I shall be with you on your wedding-night."

I started forward, and exclaimed, "Villain! before you sign my death-warrant, be sure that you are yourself safe."

I would have seized him; but he eluded me, and quitted the house with precipitation. In a few moments I saw him in his boat, which shot across the waters with an arrowy swiftness, and was soon lost amidst the waves.

All was again silent; but his words rung in my ears. I burned with rage to pursue the murderer of my peace, and precipitate him into the ocean. I walked up and down my room hastily and perturbed, while my imagination conjured up a thousand images to torment and sting me. Why had I not followed him, and closed with him in mortal strife? But I had suffered him to depart, and he had directed his course towards the main land. I shuddered to think who might be the next victim sacrificed to his insatiate revenge. And then I thought again of his words — "*I will be with you on your wedding-night*." That then was the period fixed for the fulfilment of my destiny. In that hour I should die, and at once satisfy and extinguish his malice. The prospect did not move me to fear; yet when I thought of my beloved Elizabeth, — of her tears and endless sorrow, when she should find her lover so barbarously snatched from her, — tears, the first I had shed for many months, streamed from my eyes, and I resolved not to fall before my enemy without a bitter struggle.

The night passed away, and the sun rose from the ocean; my feelings became calmer, if it may be called calmness, when the violence of rage sinks into the depths of despair. I left the house, the horrid scene of the last night's contention, and walked on the beach of the sea, which I almost regarded as an insuperable barrier between me and my fellow-creatures; nay, a wish that such should prove the fact stole across me. I desired that I might pass my life on that barren rock, wearily, it is true, but uninterrupted by any sudden shock of misery. If I returned, it was to be sacrificed, or to see those whom I most loved die under the grasp of a daemon whom I had myself created.

I walked about the isle like a restless spectre, separated from all it loved, and miserable in the separation. When it became noon, and the sun rose higher, I lay down on the grass, and was overpowered by a deep sleep. I had been awake the whole of the preceding night, my nerves were agitated, and my eyes inflamed by watching and misery. The sleep into which I now sunk refreshed me; and when I awoke, I again felt as if I belonged to a race of human beings like myself, and I began to reflect upon what had passed with greater composure; yet still the words of the fiend rung in my ears like a death-knell, they appeared like a dream, yet distinct and oppressive as a reality.

The sun had far descended, and I still sat on the shore, satisfying my appetite, which had become ravenous, with an oaten cake, when I saw a fishing-boat land close to me, and one of the men brought me a packet; it contained letters from Geneva, and one from Clerval, entreating me to join him. He said that he was wearing away his time fruitlessly where he was; that letters from the friends he had formed in London desired his return to complete the negotiation they had entered into for his Indian enterprise. He could not any longer delay his departure; but as his journey to London might be followed, even sooner than he now conjectured, by his longer voyage, he entreated me to bestow as much of my society on him as I could spare. He besought me, therefore, to leave my solitary isle, and to meet him at Perth, that we might proceed southwards together. This letter in a degree recalled me to life, and I determined to quit my island at the expiration of two days.

Yet, before I departed, there was a task to perform, on which I shuddered to reflect: I must pack up my chemical instruments; and for that purpose I must enter the room which had been the scene of my odious work, and I must handle those utensils, the sight of which was sickening to me. The next morning, at daybreak, I summoned sufficient courage, and unlocked the door of my laboratory. The remains of the half-finished creature, whom I had destroyed, lay scattered on the floor, and I almost felt as if I had mangled the living flesh of a human being. I paused to collect myself, and then entered the chamber. With trembling hand I conveyed the instruments out of the room; but I reflected that I ought not to leave the relics of my work to excite the horror and suspicion of the peasants; and I accordingly put them into a basket, with a great quantity of stones, and, laying them up, determined to throw them into the sea that very night; and in the mean time I sat upon the beach, employed in cleaning and arranging my chemical apparatus.

Nothing could be more complete than the alteration that had taken place in my feelings since the night of the appearance of the daemon. I had before regarded my promise with a gloomy despair, as a thing that, with whatever consequences, must be fulfilled; but I now felt as if a film had been taken from before my eyes, and that I, for the first time, saw clearly. The idea of renewing my labours did not for one instant occur to me; the threat I had heard weighed on my thoughts, but I did not reflect that a voluntary act of mine could avert it. I had resolved in my own mind, that to create another like the fiend I had first made would be an act of the basest and most atrocious selfishness; and I banished from my mind every thought that could lead to a different conclusion.

Between two and three in the morning the moon rose; and I then, putting my basket aboard a little skiff, sailed out about four miles from the shore. The scene was perfectly solitary: a few boats were returning towards land, but I sailed away from them. I felt as if I was about the commission of a dreadful crime, and avoided with shuddering anxiety any encounter with my fellow-creatures. At one time the moon, which had before been clear, was suddenly overspread by a thick cloud, and I took advantage of the moment of darkness, and cast my basket into the sea: I listened to the gurgling sound as it sunk, and then sailed away from the spot. The sky became clouded; but the air was pure, although chilled by the north-east breeze that was then rising. But it refreshed me, and filled me with such agreeable sensations, that I resolved to prolong my stay on the water; and, fixing the rudder in a direct position, stretched myself at the bottom of the boat. Clouds hid the moon, every thing was obscure, and I heard only the sound of the boat, as its keel cut through the waves; the murmur lulled me, and in a short time I slept soundly.

I do not know how long I remained in this situation, but when I awoke I found that the sun had already mounted considerably. The wind was high, and the waves continually threatened the safety of my little skiff. I found that the wind was north-east, and must have driven me far from the coast from which I had embarked. I endeavoured to change my course, but quickly found that, if I again made the attempt, the boat would be instantly filled with water. Thus situated, my only resource was to drive before the wind. I confess that I felt a few sensations of terror. I had no compass with me, and was so slenderly acquainted with the geography of this part of the world, that the sun was of little benefit to me. I might be driven into the wide Atlantic, and feel all the tortures of starvation, or be swallowed up in the immeasurable waters that roared and buffeted around me. I had already been out many hours, and felt the torment of a burning thirst, a prelude to my other sufferings. I looked on the heavens, which were covered by clouds that flew the wind, only to be replaced by others: I looked upon the sea, it was to be my grave. "Fiend," I exclaimed, "your task is already fulfilled!" I thought of Elizabeth, of my father, and of Clerval; all left behind, on whom the monster might satisfy his sanguinary and merciless passions. This idea plunged me into a reverie, so despairing and frightful, that even now, when the scene is on the point of closing before me for ever, I shudder to reflect on it.

Some hours passed thus; but by degrees, as the sun declined towards the horizon, the wind died away into a gentle breeze, and the sea became free from breakers. But these gave place to a heavy swell: I felt sick, and hardly able to hold the rudder, when suddenly I saw a line of high land towards the south.

Almost spent, as I was, by fatigue, and the dreadful suspense I endured for several hours, this sudden certainty of life rushed like a flood of warm joy to my heart, and tears gushed from my eyes.

How mutable are our feelings, and how strange is that clinging love we have of life even in the excess of misery! I constructed another sail with a part of my dress, and eagerly steered my course towards the land. It had a wild and rocky appearance; but, as I approached nearer, I easily perceived the traces of cultivation. I saw vessels near the shore, and found myself suddenly transported back to the neighbourhood of civilised man. I carefully traced the windings of the land, and hailed a steeple which I at length saw issuing from behind a small promontory. As I was in a state of extreme debility, I resolved to sail directly towards the town, as a place where I could most easily procure nourishment. Fortunately, I had money with me. As I turned the promontory, I perceived a small, neat town and a good harbour, which I entered, my heart bounding with joy at my unexpected escape.

As I was occupied in fixing the boat and arranging the sails, several people crowded towards the spot. They seemed much surprised at my appearance; but, instead of offering me any assistance, whispered together with gestures that at any other time might have produced in me a slight sensation of alarm. As it was, I merely remarked that they spoke English; and I therefore addressed them in that language: "My good friends," said I, "will you be so kind as to tell me the name of this town, and inform me where I am?"

"You will know that soon enough," replied a man with a hoarse voice. "May be you are come to a place that will not prove much to your taste; but you will not be consulted as to your quarters, I promise you."

I was exceedingly surprised on receiving so rude an answer from a stranger; and I was also disconcerted on perceiving the frowning and angry countenances of his companions. "Why do you answer me so roughly?" I replied; "surely it is not the custom of Englishmen to receive strangers so inhospitably."

"I do not know," said the man, "what the custom of the English may be; but it is the custom of the Irish to hate villains."

While this strange dialogue continued, I perceived the crowd rapidly increase. Their faces expressed a mixture of curiosity and anger, which annoyed, and in some degree alarmed me. I enquired the way to the inn; but no one replied. I then moved forward, and a murmuring sound arose from the crowd as they followed and surrounded me; when an ill-looking man approached, tapped me on the shoulder, and said, "Come, sir, you must follow me to Mr. Kirwin's, to give an account of yourself."

"Who is Mr. Kirwin? Why am I to give an account of myself? Is not this a free country?"

"Ay, sir, free enough for honest folks. Mr. Kirwin is a magistrate; and you are to give an account of the death of a gentleman who was found murdered here last night."

This answer startled me; but I presently recovered myself. I was innocent; that could easily be proved: accordingly I followed my conductor in silence, and was led to one of the best houses in the town. I was ready to sink from fatigue and hunger; but, being surrounded by a crowd, I thought it politic to rouse all my strength, that no physical debility might be construed into apprehension or conscious guilt. Little did I then expect the calamity that was in a few moments to overwhelm me, and extinguish in horror and despair all fear of ignominy or death.

I must pause here; for it requires all my fortitude to recall the memory of the frightful events which I am about to relate, in proper detail, to my recollection.

CHAPTER XXI

I was soon introduced into the presence of the magistrate, an old benevolent man, with calm and mild manners. He looked upon me, however, with some degree of severity: and then, turning towards my conductors, he asked who appeared as witnesses on this occasion.

About half a dozen men came forward; and, one being selected by the magistrate, he deposed, that he had been out fishing the night before with his son and brother-in-law, Daniel Nugent, when, about ten o'clock, they observed a strong northerly blast rising, and they accordingly put in for port. It was a very dark night, as the moon had not yet risen; they did not land at the harbour, but, as they had been accustomed, at a creek about two miles below. He walked on first, carrying a part of the fishing tackle, and his companions followed him at some distance. As he was proceeding along the sands, he struck his foot against something, and fell at his length on the ground. His companions came up to assist him; and, by the light of their lantern, they found that he had fallen on the body of a man, who was to all appearance dead. Their first supposition was, that it was the corpse of some person who had been drowned, and was thrown on shore by the waves; but, on examination, they found that the clothes were not wet, and even that the body was not then cold. They instantly carried it to the cottage of an old woman near the spot, and endeavoured, but in vain, to restore it to life. It appeared to be a handsome young man, about five and twenty years of age. He had apparently been strangled; for there was no sign of any violence, except the black mark of fingers on his neck.

The first part of this deposition did not in the least interest me; but when the mark of the fingers was mentioned, I remembered the murder of my brother, and felt myself extremely agitated; my limbs trembled, and a mist came over my eyes, which obliged me to lean on a chair for support. The magistrate observed me with a keen eye, and of course drew an unfavourable augury from my manner.

The son confirmed his father's account: but when Daniel Nugent was called, he swore positively that, just before the fall of his companion, he saw a boat, with a single man in it, at a short distance from the shore; and, as far as he could judge by the light of a few stars, it was the same boat in which I had just landed.

A woman deposed, that she lived near the beach, and was standing at the door of her cottage, waiting for the return of the fishermen, about an hour before she heard of the discovery of the body, when she saw a boat, with only one man in it, push off from that part of the shore where the corpse was afterwards found.

Another woman confirmed the account of the fishermen having brought the body into her house; it was not cold. They put it into a bed, and rubbed it; and Daniel went to the town for an apothecary, but life was quite gone.

Several other men were examined concerning my landing; and they agreed, that, with the strong north wind that had arisen during the night, it was very probable that I had beaten about for many hours, and had been obliged to return nearly to the same spot from which I had departed. Besides, they observed that it appeared that I had brought the body from another place, and it was likely, that as I did not appear to know the shore, I might have put into the harbour ignorant of the distance of the town of * * * from the place where I had deposited the corpse.

Mr. Kirwin, on hearing this evidence, desired that I should be taken into the room where the body lay for interment, that it might be observed what effect the sight of it would produce upon me. This idea was probably suggested by the extreme agitation I had exhibited when the mode of the murder had been described. I was accordingly conducted, by the magistrate and several other persons, to the inn. I could not help being struck by the strange coincidences that had taken place during this eventful night; but, knowing that I had been conversing with several persons in the island I had inhabited about the time that the body had been found, I was perfectly tranquil as to the consequences of the affair.

I entered the room where the corpse lay, and was led up to the coffin. How can I describe my sensations on beholding it? I feel yet parched with horror, nor can I reflect on that terrible moment without shuddering and agony. The examination, the presence of the magistrate and witnesses, passed like a dream from my memory, when I saw the lifeless form of Henry Clerval stretched before me. I gasped for breath; and, throwing myself on the body, I exclaimed, "Have my murderous machinations deprived you also, my dearest Henry, of life? Two I have already destroyed; other victims await their destiny: but you, Clerval, my friend, my benefactor—"

The human frame could no longer support the agonies that I endured, and I was carried out of the room in strong convulsions.

A fever succeeded to this. I lay for two months on the point of death: my ravings, as I afterwards heard, were frightful; I called myself the murderer of William, of Justine, and of Clerval. Sometimes I entreated my attendants to assist me in the destruction of the fiend by whom I was tormented; and at others, I felt the fingers of the monster already grasping my neck, and screamed aloud with agony and terror. Fortunately, as I spoke my native language, Mr. Kirwin alone understood me; but my gestures and bitter cries were sufficient to affright the other witnesses.

Why did I not die? More miserable than man ever was before, why did I not sink into forgetfulness and rest? Death snatches away many blooming children, the only hopes of their doting parents: how many brides and youthful lovers have been one day in the bloom of health and hope, and the next a prey for worms and the decay of the tomb! Of what materials was I made, that I could thus resist so many shocks, which, like the turning of the wheel, continually renewed the torture?

But I was doomed to live; and, in two months, found myself as awaking from a dream, in a prison, stretched on a wretched bed, surrounded by gaolers, turnkeys, bolts, and all the miserable apparatus of a dungeon. It was morning, I remember, when I thus awoke to understanding: I had forgotten the particulars of what had happened, and only felt as if some great misfortune had suddenly overwhelmed me; but when I looked around, and saw the barred windows, and the squalidness of the room in which I was, all flashed across my memory, and I groaned bitterly.

This sound disturbed an old woman who was sleeping in a chair beside me. She was a hired nurse, the wife of one of the turnkeys, and her countenance expressed all those bad qualities which often characterise that class. The lines of her face were hard and rude, like that of persons accustomed to see without sympathising in sights of misery. Her tone expressed her entire indifference; she addressed me in English, and the voice struck me as one that I had heard during my sufferings: —

"Are you better now, sir?" said she.

I replied in the same language, with a feeble voice, "I believe I am; but if it be all true, if indeed I did not dream, I am sorry that I am still alive to feel this misery and horror."

"For that matter," replied the old woman, "if you mean about the gentleman you murdered, I believe that it were better for you if you were dead, for I fancy it will go hard with you! However, that's none of my business; I am sent to nurse you, and get you well; I do my duty with a safe conscience; it were well if every body did the same."

I turned with loathing from the woman who could utter so unfeeling a speech to a person just saved, on the very edge of death; but I felt languid, and unable to reflect on all that had passed. The whole series of my life appeared to me as a dream; I sometimes doubted if indeed it were all true, for it never presented itself to my mind with the force of reality.

As the images that floated before me became more distinct, I grew feverish; a darkness pressed around me: no one was near me who soothed me with the gentle voice of love; no dear hand supported me. The physician came and prescribed medicines, and the old woman prepared them for me; but utter carelessness was visible in the first, and the expression of brutality was strongly marked in the visage of the second. Who could be interested in the fate of a murderer, but the hangman who would gain his fee?

These were my first reflections; but I soon learned that Mr. Kirwin had shown me extreme kindness. He had caused the best room in the prison to be prepared for me (wretched indeed was the best); and it was he who had provided a physician and a nurse. It is true, he seldom came to see me; for, although he ardently desired to relieve the sufferings of every human creature, he did not wish to be present at the agonies and miserable ravings of a murderer. He came, therefore, sometimes, to see that I was not neglected; but his visits were short, and with long intervals.

One day, while I was gradually recovering, I was seated in a chair, my eyes half open, and my cheeks livid like those in death. I was overcome by gloom and misery, and often reflected I had better seek death than desire to remain in a world which to me was replete with wretchedness. At one time I considered whether I should not declare myself guilty, and suffer the penalty of the law, less innocent than poor Justine had been. Such were my thoughts, when the door of my apartment was opened, and Mr. Kirwin entered. His countenance expressed sympathy and compassion; he drew a chair close to mine, and addressed me in French —

"I fear that this place is very shocking to you; can I do any thing to make you more comfortable?"

"I thank you; but all that you mention is nothing to me: on the whole earth there is no comfort which I am capable of receiving."

"I know that the sympathy of a stranger can be but of little relief to one borne down as you are by so strange a misfortune. But you will, I hope, soon quit this melancholy abode; for, doubtless, evidence can easily be brought to free you from the criminal charge."

“That is my least concern: I am, by a course of strange events, become the most miserable of mortals. Persecuted and tortured as I am and have been, can death be any evil to me?”

“Nothing indeed could be more unfortunate and agonising than the strange chances that have lately occurred. You were thrown, by some surprising accident, on this shore, renowned for its hospitality; seized immediately, and charged with murder. The first sight that was presented to your eyes was the body of your friend, murdered in so unaccountable a manner, and placed, as it were, by some fiend across your path.”

As Mr. Kirwin said this, notwithstanding the agitation I endured on this retrospect of my sufferings, I also felt considerable surprise at the knowledge he seemed to possess concerning me. I suppose some astonishment was exhibited in my countenance; for Mr. Kirwin hastened to say—

“Immediately upon your being taken ill, all the papers that were on your person were brought to me, and I examined them that I might discover some trace by which I could send to your relations an account of your misfortune and illness. I found several letters, and, among others, one which I discovered from its commencement to be from your father. I instantly wrote to Geneva: nearly two months have elapsed since the departure of my letter.—But you are ill; even now you tremble: you are unfit for agitation of any kind.”

“This suspense is a thousand times worse than the most horrible event: tell me what new scene of death has been acted, and whose murder I am now to lament?”

“Your family is perfectly well,” said Mr. Kirwin, with gentleness; “and some one, a friend, is come to visit you.”

I know not by what chain of thought the idea presented itself, but it instantly darted into my mind that the murderer had come to mock at my misery, and taunt me with the death of Clerval, as a new incitement for me to comply with his hellish desires. I put my hand before my eyes, and cried out in agony—

“Oh! take him away! I cannot see him; for God’s sake, do not let him enter!”

Mr. Kirwin regarded me with a troubled countenance. He could not help regarding my exclamation as a presumption of my guilt, and said, in rather a severe tone—

“I should have thought, young man, that the presence of your father would have been welcome, instead of inspiring such violent repugnance.”

“My father!” cried I, while every feature and every muscle was relaxed from anguish to pleasure: “is my father indeed come? How kind, how very kind! But where is he, why does he not hasten to me?”

My change of manner surprised and pleased the magistrate; perhaps he thought that my former exclamation was a momentary return of delirium, and now he instantly resumed his former benevolence. He rose, and quitted the room with my nurse, and in a moment my father entered it.

Nothing, at this moment, could have given me greater pleasure than the arrival of my father. I stretched out my hand to him, and cried—

“Are you then safe—and Elizabeth—and Ernest?”

My father calmed me with assurances of their welfare, and endeavoured, by dwelling on these subjects so interesting to my heart, to raise my desponding spirits; but he soon felt that a prison cannot be the abode of cheerfulness. “What a place is this that you inhabit, my son!” said he, looking mournfully at the barred windows, and wretched appearance of the room. “You travelled to seek happiness, but a fatality seems to pursue you. And poor Clerval—”

The name of my unfortunate and murdered friend was an agitation too great to be endured in my weak state; I shed tears.

“Alas! yes, my father,” replied I; “some destiny of the most horrible kind hangs over me, and I must live to fulfil it, or surely I should have died on the coffin of Henry."

We were not allowed to converse for any length of time, for the precarious state of my health rendered every precaution necessary that could ensure tranquillity. Mr. Kirwin came in, and insisted that my strength should not be exhausted by too much exertion. But the appearance of my father was to me like that of my good angel, and I gradually recovered my health.

As my sickness quitted me, I was absorbed by a gloomy and black melancholy, that nothing could dissipate. The image of Clerval was for ever before me, ghastly and murdered. More than once the agitation into which these reflections threw me made my friends dread a dangerous relapse. Alas! why did they preserve so miserable and detested a life? It was surely that I might fulfil my destiny, which is now drawing to a close. Soon, oh! very soon, will death extinguish these throbbings, and relieve me from the mighty weight of anguish that bears me to the dust; and, in executing the award of justice, I shall also sink to rest. Then the appearance of death was distant, although the wish was ever present to my thoughts; and I often sat for hours motionless and speechless, wishing for some mighty revolution that might bury me and my destroyer in its ruins.

The season of the assizes approached. I had already been three months in prison; and although I was still weak, and in continual danger of a relapse, I was obliged to travel nearly a hundred miles to the county-town, where the court was held. Mr. Kirwin charged himself with every care of collecting witnesses, and arranging my defence. I was spared the disgrace of appearing publicly as a criminal, as the case was not brought before the court that decides on life and death. The grand jury rejected the bill, on its being proved that I was on the Orkney Islands at the hour the body of my friend was found; and a fortnight after my removal I was liberated from prison.

My father was enraptured on finding me freed from the vexations of a criminal charge, that I was again allowed to breathe the fresh atmosphere, and permitted to return to my native country. I did not participate in these feelings; for to me the walls of a dungeon or a palace were alike hateful. The cup of life was poisoned for ever; and although the sun shone upon me, as upon the happy and gay of heart, I saw around me nothing but a dense and frightful darkness, penetrated by no light but the glimmer of two eyes that glared upon me. Sometimes they were the expressive eyes of Henry, languishing in death, the dark orbs nearly covered by the lids, and the long black lashes that fringed them; sometimes it was the watery, clouded eyes of the monster, as I first saw them in my chamber at Ingolstadt.

My father tried to awaken in me the feelings of affection. He talked of Geneva, which I should soon visit — of Elizabeth and Ernest; but these words only drew deep groans from me. Sometimes, indeed, I felt a wish for happiness; and thought, with melancholy delight, of my beloved cousin; or longed, with a devouring *maladie du pays*,[33] to see once more the blue lake and rapid Rhone, that had been so dear to me in early childhood: but my general state of feeling was a torpor, in which a prison was as welcome a residence as the divinest scene in nature; and these fits were seldom interrupted but by paroxysms of anguish and despair. At these moments I often endeavoured to put an end to the existence I loathed; and it required unceasing attendance and vigilance to restrain me from committing some dreadful act of violence.

Yet one duty remained to me, the recollection of which finally triumphed over my selfish despair. It was necessary that I should return without delay to Geneva, there to watch over the lives of those I so fondly loved; and to lie in wait

[33] French for "homesickness." — EDS.

for the murderer, that if any chance led me to the place of his concealment, or if he dared again to blast me by his presence, I might, with unfailing aim, put an end to the existence of the monstrous image which I had endued with the mockery of a soul still more monstrous. My father still desired to delay our departure, fearful that I could not sustain the fatigues of a journey: for I was a shattered wreck, — the shadow of a human being. My strength was gone. I was a mere skeleton; and fever night and day preyed upon my wasted frame.

Still, as I urged our leaving Ireland with such inquietude and impatience, my father thought it best to yield. We took our passage on board a vessel bound for Havre-de-Grace, and sailed with a fair wind from the Irish shores. It was midnight. I lay on the deck, looking at the stars, and listening to the dashing of the waves. I hailed the darkness that shut Ireland from my sight; and my pulse beat with a feverish joy when I reflected that I should soon see Geneva. The past appeared to me in the light of a frightful dream; yet the vessel in which I was, the wind that blew me from the detested shore of Ireland, and the sea which surrounded me, told me too forcibly that I was deceived by no vision, and that Clerval, my friend and dearest companion, had fallen a victim to me and the monster of my creation. I repassed, in my memory, my whole life; my quiet happiness while residing with my family in Geneva, the death of my mother, and my departure for Ingolstadt. I remembered, shuddering, the mad enthusiasm that hurried me on to the creation of my hideous enemy, and I called to mind the night in which he first lived. I was unable to pursue the train of thought; a thousand feelings pressed upon me, and I wept bitterly.

Ever since my recovery from the fever, I had been in the custom of taking every night a small quantity of laudanum; for it was by means of this drug only that I was enabled to gain the rest necessary for the preservation of life. Oppressed by the recollection of my various misfortunes, I now swallowed double my usual quantity, and soon slept profoundly. But sleep did not afford me respite from thought and misery; my dreams presented a thousand objects that scared me. Towards morning I was possessed by a kind of night-mare; I felt the fiend's grasp in my neck, and could not free myself from it; groans and cries rung in my ears. My father, who was watching over me, perceiving my restlessness, awoke me; the dashing waves were around: the cloudy sky above; the fiend was not here: a sense of security, a feeling that a truce was established between the present hour and the irresistible, disastrous future, imparted to me a kind of calm forgetfulness, of which the human mind is by its structure peculiarly susceptible.

CHAPTER XXII

The voyage came to an end. We landed, and proceeded to Paris. I soon found that I had overtaxed my strength, and that I must repose before I could continue my journey. My father's care and attentions were indefatigable; but he did not know the origin of my sufferings, and sought erroneous methods to remedy the incurable ill. He wished me to seek amusement in society. I abhorred the face of man. Oh, not abhorred! they were my brethren, my fellow-beings, and I felt attracted even to the most repulsive among them, as to creatures of an angelic nature and celestial mechanism. But I felt that I had no right to share their intercourse. I had unchained an enemy among them, whose joy it was to shed their blood, and to revel in their groans. How they would, each and all, abhor me, and hunt me from the world, did they know my unhallowed acts, and the crimes which had their source in me!

My father yielded at length to my desire to avoid society, and strove by various arguments to banish my despair. Sometimes he thought that I felt deeply the degradation of being obliged to answer a charge of murder, and he endeavoured to prove to me the futility of pride.

"Alas! my father," said I, "how little do you know me. Human beings, their feelings and passions, would indeed be degraded if such a wretch as I felt pride. Justine, poor unhappy Justine, was as innocent as I, and she suffered the same charge; she died for it; and I am the cause of this — I murdered her. William, Justine, and Henry — they all died by my hands."

My father had often, during my imprisonment, heard me make the same assertion; when I thus accused myself, he sometimes seemed to desire an explanation, and at others he appeared to consider it as the offspring of delirium, and that, during my illness, some idea of this kind had presented itself to my imagination, the remembrance of which I preserved in my convalescence. I avoided explanation, and maintained a continual silence concerning the wretch I had created. I had a persuasion that I should be supposed mad; and this in itself would for ever have chained my tongue. But, besides, I could not bring myself to disclose a secret which would fill my hearer with consternation, and make fear and unnatural horror the inmates of his breast. I checked, therefore, my impatient thirst for sympathy, and was silent when I would have given the world to have confided the fatal secret. Yet still words like those I have recorded, would burst uncontrollably from me. I could offer no explanation of them; but their truth in part relieved the burden of my mysterious woe.

Upon this occasion my father said, with an expression of unbounded wonder, "My dearest Victor, what infatuation is this? My dear son, I entreat you never to make such an assertion again."

"I am not mad," I cried energetically; "the sun and the heavens, who have viewed my operations, can bear witness of my truth. I am the assassin of those most innocent victims; they died by my machinations. A thousand times would I have shed my own blood, drop by drop, to have saved their lives; but I could not, my father, indeed I could not sacrifice the whole human race."

The conclusion of this speech convinced my father that my ideas were deranged, and he instantly changed the subject of our conversation, and endeavoured to alter the course of my thoughts. He wished as much as possible to obliterate the memory of the scenes that had taken place in Ireland, and never alluded to them, or suffered me to speak of my misfortunes.

As time passed away I became more calm: misery had her dwelling in my heart, but I no longer talked in the same incoherent manner of my own crimes; sufficient for me was the consciousness of them. By the utmost self-violence, I curbed the imperious voice of wretchedness, which sometimes desired to declare itself to the whole world; and my manners were calmer and more composed than they had ever been since my journey to the sea of ice.

A few days before we left Paris on our way to Switzerland, I received the following letter from Elizabeth: —

"My dear Friend,

"It gave me the greatest pleasure to receive a letter from my uncle dated at Paris; you are no longer at a formidable distance, and I may hope to see you in less than a fortnight. My poor cousin, how much you must have suffered! I expect to see you looking even more ill than when you quitted Geneva. This winter has been passed most miserably, tortured as I have been by anxious suspense; yet I hope to see peace in your countenance, and to find that your heart is not totally void of comfort and tranquillity.

"Yet I fear that the same feelings now exist that made you so miserable a year ago, even perhaps augmented by time. I would not disturb you at this period, when so many misfortunes weigh upon you; but a conversation that I had with my uncle previous to his departure renders some explanation necessary before we meet.

"Explanation! you may possibly say; what can Elizabeth have to explain? If you really say this, my questions are answered, and all my doubts satisfied. But you are distant from me, and it is possible that you may dread, and yet be pleased with this explanation; and, in a probability of this being the case, I dare not any longer postpone writing what, during your absence, I have often wished to express to you, but have never had the courage to begin.

"You well know, Victor, that our union had been the favourite plan of your parents ever since our infancy. We were told this when young, and taught to look forward to it as an event that would certainly take place. We were affectionate playfellows during childhood, and, I believe, dear and valued friends to one another as we grew older. But as brother and sister often entertain a lively affection towards each other, without desiring a more intimate union, may not such also be our case? Tell me, dearest Victor. Answer me, I conjure you, by our mutual happiness, with simple truth — Do you not love another?

"You have travelled; you have spent several years of your life at Ingolstadt; and I confess to you, my friend, that when I saw you last autumn so unhappy, flying to solitude, from the society of every creature, I could not help supposing that you might regret our connection, and believe yourself bound in honour to fulfil the wishes of your parents, although they opposed themselves to your inclinations. But this is false reasoning. I confess to you, my friend, that I love you, and that in my airy dreams of futurity you have been my constant friend and companion. But it is your happiness I desire as well as my own, when I declare to you, that our marriage would render me eternally miserable, unless it were the dictate of your own free choice. Even now I weep to think, that, borne down as you are by the cruellest misfortunes, you may stifle, by the word *honour*, all hope of that love and happiness which would alone restore you to yourself. I, who have so disinterested an affection for you, may increase your miseries tenfold, by being an obstacle to your wishes. Ah! Victor, be assured that your cousin and playmate has too sincere a love for you not to be made miserable by this supposition. Be happy, my friend; and if you obey me in this one request, remain satisfied that nothing on earth will have the power to interrupt my tranquillity.

"Do not let this letter disturb you; do not answer tomorrow, or the next day, or even until you come, if it will give you pain. My uncle will send me news of your health; and if I see but one smile on your lips when we meet, occasioned by this or any other exertion of mine, I shall need no other happiness.

"ELIZABETH LAVENZA.

"Geneva, May 18th, 17 —."

This letter revived in my memory what I had before forgotten, the threat of the fiend — *"I will be with you on your wedding-night!"* Such was my sentence, and on that night would the daemon employ every art to destroy me, and tear me from the glimpse of happiness which promised partly to console my sufferings. On that night he had determined to consummate his crimes by my death. Well, be it so; a deadly struggle would then assuredly take place, in which if he were victorious I should be at peace, and his power over me be at an end. If he were vanquished, I should be a free man. Alas! what freedom? such as the peasant enjoys when his family have been massacred before his eyes, his cottage burnt, his lands laid waste, and he is turned adrift, homeless, penniless, and alone, but free. Such would be my liberty, except that in my Elizabeth I possessed a treasure; alas! balanced by those horrors of remorse and guilt, which would pursue me until death.

Sweet and beloved Elizabeth! I read and reread her letter, and some softened feelings stole into my heart, and dared to whisper paradisiacal dreams of love and joy; but the apple was already eaten, and the angel's arm bared to drive me from all hope. Yet I would die to make her happy. If the monster executed his threat, death was inevitable; yet, again, I considered whether my marriage would hasten my fate. My destruction might indeed arrive a few months sooner; but if my torturer should suspect that I postponed it, influenced by his menaces, he would surely find other, and perhaps more dreadful means of revenge. He had vowed *to be with me on my wedding-night*, yet he did not consider that threat as binding him to peace in the mean time; for, as if to show me that he was not yet satiated with blood, he had murdered Clerval immediately after the enunciation of his threats. I resolved, therefore, that if my immediate union with my cousin would conduce either to hers or my father's happiness, my adversary's designs against my life should not retard it a single hour.

In this state of mind I wrote to Elizabeth. My letter was calm and affectionate. "I fear, my beloved girl," I said, "little happiness remains for us on earth; yet all that I may one day enjoy is centred in you. Chase away your idle fears; to you alone do I consecrate my life, and my endeavours for contentment. I have one secret, Elizabeth, a dreadful one; when revealed to you, it will chill your frame with horror, and then, far from being surprised at my misery, you will only wonder that I survive what I have endured. I will confide this tale of misery and terror to you the day after our marriage shall take place; for, my sweet cousin, there must be perfect confidence between us. But until then, I conjure you, do not mention or allude to it. This I most earnestly entreat, and I know you will comply."

In about a week after the arrival of Elizabeth's letter, we returned to Geneva. The sweet girl welcomed me with warm affection; yet tears were in her eyes, as she beheld my emaciated frame and feverish cheeks. I saw a change in her also. She was thinner, and had lost much of that heavenly vivacity that had before charmed me; but her gentleness, and soft looks of compassion, made her a more fit companion for one blasted and miserable as I was.

The tranquillity which I now enjoyed did not endure. Memory brought madness with it; and when I thought of what had passed, a real insanity possessed me; sometimes I was furious, and burnt with rage, sometimes low and despondent. I neither spoke, nor looked at any one, but sat motionless, bewildered by the multitude of miseries that overcame me.

Elizabeth alone had the power to draw me from these fits; her gentle voice would soothe me when transported by passion, and inspire me with human feelings when sunk in torpor. She wept with me, and for me. When reason returned, she would remonstrate, and endeavour to inspire me with resignation. Ah! it is well for the unfortunate to be resigned, but for the guilty there is no peace. The agonies of remorse poison the luxury there is otherwise sometimes found in indulging the excess of grief.

Soon after my arrival, my father spoke of my immediate marriage with Elizabeth. I remained silent.

"Have you, then, some other attachment?"

"None on earth. I love Elizabeth, and look forward to our union with delight. Let the day therefore be fixed; and on it I will consecrate myself, in life or death, to the happiness of my cousin."

"My dear Victor, do not speak thus. Heavy misfortunes have befallen us; but let us only cling closer to what remains, and transfer our love for those whom we have lost, to those who yet live. Our circle will be small, but bound close by the ties of affection and mutual misfortune. And when time shall have softened your despair, new and dear objects of care will be born to replace those of whom we have been so cruelly deprived."

Such were the lessons of my father. But to me the remembrance of the threat returned: nor can you wonder, that, omnipotent as the fiend had yet been in his deeds of blood, I should almost regard him as invincible; and that when he had pronounced the words, "I shall be with you on your wedding-night," I should regard the threatened fate as unavoidable. But death was no evil to me, if the loss of Elizabeth were balanced with it; and I therefore, with a contented and even cheerful countenance, agreed with my father, that if my cousin would consent, the ceremony should take place in ten days, and thus put, as I imagined, the seal to my fate.

Great God! if for one instant I had thought what might be the hellish intention of my fiendish adversary, I would rather have banished myself for ever from my native country, and wandered a friendless outcast over the earth, than have consented to this miserable marriage. But, as if possessed of magic powers, the monster had blinded me to his real intentions; and when I thought that I had prepared only my own death, I hastened that of a far dearer victim.

As the period fixed for our marriage drew nearer, whether from cowardice or a prophetic feeling, I felt my heart sink within me. But I concealed my feelings by an appearance of hilarity, that brought smiles and joy to the countenance of my father, but hardly deceived the ever-watchful and nicer eye of Elizabeth. She looked forward to our union with placid contentment, not unmingled with a little fear, which past misfortunes had impressed, that what now appeared certain and tangible happiness, might soon dissipate into an airy dream, and leave no trace but deep and everlasting regret.

Preparations were made for the event; congratulatory visits were received; and all wore a smiling appearance. I shut up, as well as I could, in my own heart the anxiety that preyed there, and entered with seeming earnestness into the plans of my father, although they might only serve as the decorations of my tragedy. Through my father's exertions, a part of the inheritance of Elizabeth had been restored to her by the Austrian government. A small possession on the shores of Como[34] belonged to her. It was agreed that, immediately after our union, we should proceed to Villa Lavenza, and spend our first days of happiness beside the beautiful lake near which it stood.

In the mean time I took every precaution to defend my person, in case the fiend should openly attack me. I carried pistols and a dagger constantly about me, and was ever on the watch to prevent artifice; and by these means gained a greater degree of tranquillity. Indeed, as the period approached, the threat appeared more as a delusion, not to be regarded as worthy to disturb my peace, while the happiness I hoped for in my marriage wore a greater appearance of certainty, as the day fixed for its solemnisation drew nearer, and I heard it continually spoken of as an occurrence which no accident could possibly prevent.

Elizabeth seemed happy; my tranquil demeanour contributed greatly to calm her mind. But on the day that was to fulfil my wishes and my destiny, she was melancholy, and a presentiment of evil pervaded her; and perhaps also she thought of the dreadful secret which I had promised to reveal to her on the following day. My father was in the mean time overjoyed, and, in the bustle of preparation, only recognised in the melancholy of his niece the diffidence of a bride.

After the ceremony was performed, a large party assembled at my father's; but it was agreed that Elizabeth and I should commence our journey by water, sleeping that night at Evian, and continuing our voyage on the following day. The day was fair, the wind favourable, all smiled on our nuptial embarkation.

Those were the last moments of my life during which I enjoyed the feeling of happiness. We passed rapidly along: the sun was hot, but we were sheltered from its rays by a kind of canopy,

[34] A large lake in Northern Italy, well known as a tourist attraction. — EDS.

while we enjoyed the beauty of the scene, sometimes on one side of the lake, where we saw Mont Salêve, the pleasant banks of Montalègre, and at a distance, surmounting all, the beautiful Mont Blanc, and the assemblage of snowy mountains that in vain endeavour to emulate her; sometimes coasting the opposite banks, we saw the mighty Jura opposing its dark side to the ambition that would quit its native country, and an almost insurmountable barrier to the invader who should wish to enslave it.

I took the hand of Elizabeth: "You are sorrowful, my love. Ah! if you knew what I have suffered, and what I may yet endure, you would endeavour to let me taste the quiet and freedom from despair, that this one day at least permits me to enjoy."

"Be happy, my dear Victor," replied Elizabeth; "there is, I hope, nothing to distress you; and be assured that if a lively joy is not painted in my face, my heart is contented. Something whispers to me not to depend too much on the prospect that is opened before us; but I will not listen to such a sinister voice. Observe how fast we move along, and how the clouds, which sometimes obscure and sometimes rise above the dome of Mont Blanc, render this scene of beauty still more interesting. Look also at the innumerable fish that are swimming in the clear waters, where we can distinguish every pebble that lies at the bottom. What a divine day! how happy and serene all nature appears!"

Thus Elizabeth endeavoured to divert her thoughts and mine from all reflection upon melancholy subjects. But her temper was fluctuating; joy for a few instants shone in her eyes, but it continually gave place to distraction and reverie.

The sun sunk lower in the heavens; we passed the river Drance, and observed its path through the chasms of the higher, and the glens of the lower hills. The Alps here come closer to the lake, and we approached the amphitheatre of mountains which forms its eastern boundary. The spire of Evian shone under the woods that surrounded it, and the range of mountain above mountain by which it was overhung.

The wind, which had hitherto carried us along with amazing rapidity, sunk at sunset to a light breeze; the soft air just ruffled the water, and caused a pleasant motion among the trees as we approached the shore, from which it wafted the most delightful scent of flowers and hay. The sun sunk beneath the horizon as we landed; and as I touched the shore, I felt those cares and fears revive, which soon were to clasp me, and cling to me for ever.

CHAPTER XXIII

It was eight o'clock when we landed; we walked for a short time on the shore, enjoying the transitory light, and then retired to the inn, and contemplated the lovely scene of waters, woods, and mountains, obscured in darkness, yet still displaying their black outlines.

The wind, which had fallen in the south, now rose with great violence in the west. The moon had reached her summit in the heavens, and was beginning to descend; the clouds swept across it swifter than the flight of the vulture, and dimmed her rays, while the lake reflected the scene of the busy heavens, rendered still busier by the restless waves that were beginning to rise. Suddenly a heavy storm of rain descended.

I had been calm during the day; but so soon as night obscured the shapes of objects, a thousand fears arose in my mind. I was anxious and watchful, while my right hand grasped a pistol which was hidden in my bosom; every sound terrified me; but I resolved that I would sell my life dearly, and not shrink from the conflict until my own life, or that of my adversary, was extinguished.

Elizabeth observed my agitation for some time in timid and fearful silence; but there was something in my glance which communicated terror to her, and trembling she asked, "What is it that agitates you, my dear Victor? What is it you fear?"

"Oh! peace, peace, my love," replied I; "this night, and all will be safe: but this night is dreadful, very dreadful."

I passed an hour in this state of mind, when suddenly I reflected how fearful the combat which I momentarily expected would be to my wife, and I earnestly entreated her to retire, resolving not to join her until I had obtained some knowledge as to the situation of my enemy.

She left me, and I continued some time walking up and down the passages of the house, and inspecting every corner that might afford a retreat to my adversary. But I discovered no trace of him, and was beginning to conjecture that some fortunate chance had intervened to prevent the execution of his menaces; when suddenly I heard a shrill and dreadful scream. It came from the room into which Elizabeth had retired. As I heard it, the whole truth rushed into my mind, my arms dropped, the motion of every muscle and fibre was suspended; I could feel the blood trickling in my veins, and tingling in the extremities of my limbs. This state lasted but for an instant; the scream was repeated, and I rushed into the room.

Great God! why did I not then expire! Why am I here to relate the destruction of the best hope, and the purest creature of earth? She was there, lifeless and inanimate, thrown across the bed, her head hanging down, and her pale and distorted features half covered by her hair. Every where I turn I see the same figure — her bloodless arms and relaxed form flung by the murderer on its bridal bier. Could I behold this, and live? Alas! life is obstinate, and clings closest where it is most hated. For a moment only did I lose recollection; I fell senseless on the ground.

When I recovered, I found myself surrounded by the people of the inn; their countenances expressed a breathless terror: but the horror of others appeared only as a mockery, a shadow of the feelings that oppressed me. I escaped from them to the room where lay the body of Elizabeth, my love, my wife, so lately living, so dear, so worthy. She had been moved from the posture in which I had first beheld her; and now, as she lay, her head upon her arm, and a handkerchief thrown across her face and neck, I might have supposed her asleep. I rushed towards her, and embraced her with ardour; but the deadly languor and coldness of the limbs told me, that what I now held in my arms had ceased to be the Elizabeth whom I had loved and cherished. The murderous mark of the fiend's grasp was on her neck, and the breath had ceased to issue from her lips.

While I still hung over her in the agony of despair, I happened to look up. The windows of the room had before been darkened, and I felt a kind of panic on seeing the pale yellow light of the moon illuminate the chamber. The shutters had been thrown back; and, with a sensation of horror not to be described, I saw at the open window a figure the most hideous and abhorred. A grin was on the face of the monster; he seemed to jeer, as with his fiendish finger he pointed towards the corpse of my wife. I rushed towards the window, and drawing a pistol from my bosom, fired; but he eluded me, leaped from his station, and, running with the swiftness of lightning, plunged into the lake.

The report of the pistol brought a crowd into the room. I pointed to the spot where he had disappeared, and we followed the track with boats; nets were cast, but in vain. After passing several hours, we returned hopeless, most of my companions believing it to have been a form conjured up by my fancy. After having landed, they proceeded to search the country, parties going in different directions among the woods and vines.

I attempted to accompany them, and proceeded a short distance from the house; but my head whirled round, my steps were like those of

Detroit Institute of Arts, USA / Founders Society purchase with Mr and Mrs Bert L. Smokler / and Mr and Mrs Lawrence A. Fleischman funds / Bridgeman Images

The Nightmare, a painting by Henry Fuseli, was first exhibited in London in 1782. Fuseli was an acquaintance of Mary Shelley's parents, and this painting inspired the scene Victor Frankenstein encounters when he finds Elizabeth murdered. **What aspects of the painting do you see reflected in the narrative style of this passage?**

a drunken man, I fell at last in a state of utter exhaustion; a film covered my eyes, and my skin was parched with the heat of fever. In this state I was carried back, and placed on a bed, hardly conscious of what had happened; my eyes wandered around the room, as if to seek something that I had lost.

After an interval, I arose, and, as if by instinct, crawled into the room where the corpse of my beloved lay. There were women weeping around — I hung over it, and joined my sad tears to theirs — all this time no distinct idea presented itself to my mind; but my thoughts rambled to various subjects, reflecting confusedly on my misfortunes, and their cause. I was bewildered in a cloud of wonder and horror. The death of William, the execution of Justine, the murder of Clerval, and lastly of my wife; even at that moment I knew not that my only remaining friends were safe from the malignity of the fiend; my father even now might be writhing under his grasp, and Ernest might be dead at his feet. This idea made me shudder, and recalled me to action. I started up, and resolved to return to Geneva with all possible speed.

There were no horses to be procured, and I must return by the lake; but the wind was unfavourable, and the rain fell in torrents. However, it was hardly morning, and I might reasonably hope to arrive by night. I hired men to row, and took an oar myself; for I had always experienced relief from mental torment in bodily exercise. But the overflowing misery I now felt, and the excess of agitation that I endured, rendered me incapable of any exertion. I threw down the oar; and leaning my head upon my hands, gave way to every gloomy idea that arose. If I looked up, I saw the scenes which were familiar to me in my happier time, and which I had contemplated but the day before in the company of her who was now but a shadow and a recollection. Tears streamed from my eyes. The rain had ceased for a moment, and I saw the fish play in the waters as they had done a few hours before; they had then been observed by Elizabeth. Nothing is so painful to the human mind as a great and sudden change. The sun might shine, or the clouds might lower: but nothing could appear to me as it had done the day before. A fiend had snatched from me every hope of future happiness: no creature had ever been so miserable as I was; so frightful an event is single in the history of man.

But why should I dwell upon the incidents that followed this last overwhelming event? Mine has been a tale of horrors; I have reached their *acme*, and what I must now relate can but be tedious to you. Know that, one by one, my friends were snatched away; I was left desolate. My own strength is exhausted; and I must tell, in a few words, what remains of my hideous narration.

I arrived at Geneva. My father and Ernest yet lived; but the former sunk under the tidings that I bore. I see him now, excellent and venerable old man! his eyes wandered in vacancy, for they had lost their charm and their delight — his Elizabeth, his more than daughter, whom he doted on with all that affection which a man feels, who in the decline of life, having few affections, clings more earnestly to those that remain. Cursed, cursed be the fiend that brought misery on his grey hairs, and doomed him to waste in wretchedness! He could not live under the horrors that were accumulated around him; the springs of existence suddenly gave way: he was unable to rise from his bed, and in a few days he died in my arms.

What then became of me? I know not; I lost sensation, and chains and darkness were the only objects that pressed upon me. Sometimes, indeed, I dreamt that I wandered in flowery meadows and pleasant vales with the friends of my youth; but I awoke, and found myself in a dungeon. Melancholy followed, but by degrees I gained a clear conception of my miseries and situation, and was then released from my prison. For they had called me mad; and during many months, as I understood, a solitary cell had been my habitation.

Liberty, however, had been an useless gift to me, had I not, as I awakened to reason, at the same time awakened to revenge. As the memory of past misfortunes pressed upon me, I began to reflect on their cause — the monster whom I had created, the miserable daemon whom I had sent abroad into the world for my destruction. I was possessed by a maddening rage when I thought of him, and desired and ardently prayed that I might have him within my grasp to wreak a great and signal revenge on his cursed head.

Nor did my hate long confine itself to useless wishes; I began to reflect on the best means of securing him; and for this purpose, about a month after my release, I repaired to a criminal judge in the town, and told him that I had an accusation to make; that I knew the destroyer of my family; and that I required him to exert his whole authority for the apprehension of the murderer.

The magistrate listened to me with attention and kindness: — "Be assured, sir," said he, "no pains or exertions on my part shall be spared to discover the villain."

"I thank you," replied I; "listen, therefore, to the deposition that I have to make. It is indeed a tale so strange, that I should fear you would not credit it, were there not something in truth which, however wonderful, forces conviction. The story is too connected to be mistaken for a dream, and I have no motive for falsehood." My manner, as I thus addressed him, was impressive, but calm; I had formed in my own heart a resolution to pursue my destroyer to death; and this purpose quieted my agony, and for an interval reconciled me to life. I now related my history, briefly, but with firmness and precision, marking the dates with accuracy, and never deviating into invective or exclamation.

The magistrate appeared at first perfectly incredulous, but as I continued he became more attentive and interested; I saw him sometimes shudder with horror, at others a lively surprise, unmingled with disbelief, was painted on his countenance.

When I had concluded my narration, I said, "This is the being whom I accuse, and for whose seizure and punishment I call upon you to exert your whole power. It is your duty as a magistrate, and I believe and hope that your feelings as a man will not revolt from the execution of those functions on this occasion."

This address caused a considerable change in the physiognomy of my own auditor. He had heard my story with that half kind of belief that is given to a tale of spirits and supernatural events; but when he was called upon to act officially in consequence, the whole tide of his incredulity returned. He, however, answered mildly, "I would willingly afford you every aid in your pursuit; but the creature of whom you speak appears to have powers which would put all my exertions to defiance. Who can follow an animal which can traverse the sea of ice, and inhabit caves and dens where no man would venture to intrude? Besides, some months have elapsed since the commission of his crimes, and no one can conjecture to what place he has wandered, or what region he may now inhabit."

"I do not doubt that he hovers near the spot which I inhabit; and if he has indeed taken refuge in the Alps, he may be hunted like the chamois, and destroyed as a beast of prey. But I perceive your thoughts: you do not credit my narrative, and do not intend to pursue my enemy with the punishment which is his desert."

As I spoke, rage sparkled in my eyes; the magistrate was intimidated:—"You are mistaken," said he, "I will exert myself; and if it is in my power to seize the monster, be assured that he shall suffer punishment proportionate to his crimes. But I fear, from what you have yourself described to be his properties, that this will prove impracticable; and thus, while every proper measure is pursued, you should make up your mind to disappointment."

"That cannot be; but all that I can say will be of little avail. My revenge is of no moment to you; yet, while I allow it to be a vice, I confess that it is the devouring and only passion of my soul. My rage is unspeakable, when I reflect that the murderer, whom I have turned loose upon society, still exists. You refuse my just demand: I have but one resource; and I devote myself, either in my life or death, to his destruction."

I trembled with excess of agitation as I said this; there was a frenzy in my manner, and something, I doubt not, of that haughty fierceness which the martyrs of old are said to have possessed. But to a Genevan magistrate, whose mind was occupied by far other ideas than those of devotion and heroism, this elevation of mind had much the appearance of madness. He endeavoured to soothe me as a nurse does a child, and reverted to my tale as the effects of delirium.

"Man," I cried, "how ignorant art thou in thy pride of wisdom! Cease; you know not what it is you say."

I broke from the house angry and disturbed, and retired to meditate on some other mode of action.

CHAPTER XXIV

My present situation was one in which all voluntary thought was swallowed up and lost. I was hurried away by fury; revenge alone endowed me with strength and composure; it moulded my feelings, and allowed me to be calculating and calm, at periods when otherwise delirium or death would have been my portion.

My first resolution was to quit Geneva for ever; my country, which, when I was happy and beloved, was dear to me, now, in my adversity, became hateful. I provided myself with a sum of money, together with a few jewels which had belonged to my mother, and departed.

And now my wanderings began, which are to cease but with life. I have traversed a vast portion of the earth, and have endured all the hardships which travellers, in deserts and barbarous countries, are wont to meet. How I have lived I hardly know; many times have I stretched my failing limbs upon the sandy plain, and prayed for death. But revenge kept me alive; I dared not die, and leave my adversary in being.

When I quitted Geneva, my first labour was to gain some clue by which I might trace the steps of my fiendish enemy. But my plan was unsettled; and I wandered many hours round the confines of the town, uncertain what path I should pursue. As night approached, I found myself at the entrance of the cemetery where William, Elizabeth, and my father reposed. I entered it, and approached the tomb which marked their graves. Every thing was silent, except the leaves of the trees, which were gently agitated by the wind; the night was nearly dark; and the scene would have been solemn and affecting even to an uninterested observer. The spirits of the departed seemed to flit around, and to cast a shadow, which was felt but not seen, around the head of the mourner.

The deep grief which this scene had at first excited quickly gave way to rage and despair. They were dead, and I lived; their murderer also lived, and to destroy him I must drag out my weary existence. I knelt on the grass, and kissed the earth, and with quivering lips exclaimed, "By the sacred earth on which I kneel, by the shades that wander near me, by the deep and eternal grief that I feel, I swear; and by thee, O Night, and the spirits that preside over thee, to pursue the daemon, who caused this misery, until he or I shall perish in mortal conflict. For this purpose I will preserve my life: to execute this dear revenge, will I again behold the sun, and tread the green herbage of earth, which otherwise should vanish from my eyes for ever. And I call on you, spirits of the dead; and on you, wandering ministers of vengeance, to aid and conduct me in my work. Let the cursed and hellish monster drink deep of agony; let him feel the despair that now torments me."

I had begun my adjuration with solemnity, and an awe which almost assured me that the shades of my murdered friends heard and approved my devotion; but the furies possessed me as I concluded, and rage choked my utterance.

I was answered through the stillness of night by a loud and fiendish laugh. It rung on my ears long and heavily; the mountains re-echoed it, and I felt as if all hell surrounded me with mockery and laughter. Surely in that moment I should have been possessed by frenzy, and have destroyed my miserable existence, but that my vow was heard, and that I was reserved for vengeance. The laughter died away; when a well-known and abhorred voice, apparently close to my ear, addressed me in an audible whisper — "I am satisfied: miserable wretch! you have determined to live, and I am satisfied."

I darted towards the spot from which the sound proceeded; but the devil eluded my grasp. Suddenly the broad disk of the moon arose, and shone full upon his ghastly and distorted shape, as he fled with more than mortal speed.

I pursued him; and for many months this has been my task. Guided by a slight clue, I followed the windings of the Rhone, but vainly. The blue Mediterranean appeared; and, by a strange chance, I saw the fiend enter by night, and hide himself in a vessel bound for the Black Sea. I took my passage in the same ship; but he escaped, I know not how.

Amidst the wilds of Tartary and Russia, although he still evaded me, I have ever followed in his track. Sometimes the peasants, scared by this horrid apparition, informed me of his path; sometimes he himself, who feared that if I lost all trace of him, I should despair and die, left some mark to guide me. The snows descended on my head, and I saw the print of his huge step on the white plain. To you first entering on life, to whom care is new, and agony unknown, how can you understand what I have felt, and still feel? Cold, want, and fatigue, were the least pains which I was destined to endure; I was cursed by some devil, and carried about with me my eternal hell; yet still a spirit of good followed and directed my steps; and, when I most murmured, would suddenly extricate me from seemingly insurmountable difficulties. Sometimes, when nature, overcome by hunger, sunk under the exhaustion, a repast was prepared for me in the desert, that restored and inspirited me. The fare was, indeed, coarse, such as the peasants of the country ate; but I will not doubt that it was set there by the spirits that I had invoked to aid me. Often, when all was dry, the heavens cloudless, and I was parched by thirst, a slight cloud would bedim the sky, shed the few drops that revived me, and vanish.

I followed, when I could, the courses of the rivers; but the daemon generally avoided these, as it was here that the population of the country chiefly collected. In other places human beings were seldom seen; and I generally subsisted on the wild animals that crossed my path. I had money with me, and gained the friendship of the villagers by distributing it; or I brought with me some food that I had killed, which, after taking a small part, I always presented to those who had provided me with fire and utensils for cooking.

My life, as it passed thus, was indeed hateful to me, and it was during sleep alone that I could taste joy. O blessed sleep! often, when most miserable, I sank to repose, and my dreams lulled me even to rapture. The spirits that guarded me had provided these moments, or rather hours, of happiness, that I might retain strength to fulfill my pilgrimage. Deprived of this respite, I should have sunk under my hardships. During the day I was sustained and inspirited by the hope of night: for in sleep I saw my friends, my wife, and my beloved country; again I saw the benevolent countenance of my father, heard the silver tones of my Elizabeth's voice, and beheld Clerval enjoying health and youth. Often, when wearied by a toilsome march, I persuaded myself that I was dreaming until night should come, and that I should then enjoy reality in the arms of my dearest friends. What agonising fondness did I feel for them! how did I cling to their dear forms, as sometimes they haunted even my waking hours, and persuade myself that they still lived! At such moments vengeance, that burned within me, died in my heart, and I pursued my path towards the destruction of the daemon, more as a task enjoined by heaven, as the mechanical impulse of some power of which I was unconscious, than as the ardent desire of my soul.

What his feelings were whom I pursued I cannot know. Sometimes, indeed, he left marks in writing on the barks of the trees, or cut in stone, that guided me, and instigated my fury. "My reign is not yet over," (these words were legible in one of these inscriptions;) "you live, and my power is complete. Follow me; I seek the everlasting ices of the north, where you will feel the misery of cold and frost, to which I am impassive. You will find near this place, if you follow not too tardily, a dead hare; eat, and be refreshed. Come on, my enemy; we have yet to wrestle for our lives; but many hard and miserable hours must you endure until that period shall arrive."

Scoffing devil! Again do I vow vengeance; again do I devote thee, miserable fiend, to torture and death. Never will I give up my search, until he or I perish; and then with what ecstasy shall I join my Elizabeth, and my departed friends, who even now prepare for me the reward of my tedious toil and horrible pilgrimage!

As I still pursued my journey to the northward, the snows thickened, and the cold increased in a degree almost too severe to support. The peasants were shut up in their hovels, and only a few of the most hardy ventured forth to seize the animals whom starvation had forced from their hiding-places to seek for prey. The rivers were covered with ice, and no fish could be procured; and thus I was cut off from my chief article of maintenance.

The triumph of my enemy increased with the difficulty of my labours. One inscription that he left was in these words: — "Prepare! your toils only begin: wrap yourself in furs, and provide food; for we shall soon enter upon a journey where your sufferings will satisfy my everlasting hatred."

670 My courage and perseverance were invigorated by these scoffing words; I resolved not to fail in my purpose; and, calling on Heaven to support me, I continued with unabated fervour to traverse immense deserts, until the ocean appeared at a distance, and formed the utmost boundary of the horizon. Oh! how unlike it was to the blue seas of the south! Covered with ice, it was only to be distinguished from land by its superior wildness and ruggedness. The Greeks wept for joy when they beheld the Mediterranean from the hills of Asia, and hailed with rapture the boundary of their toils. I did not weep; but I knelt down, and, with a full heart, thanked my guiding spirit for conducting me in safety to the place where I hoped, notwithstanding my adversary's gibe, to meet and grapple with him.

Some weeks before this period I had procured a sledge and dogs, and thus traversed the snows with inconceivable speed. I know not whether the fiend possessed the same advantages; but I found that, as before I had daily lost ground in the pursuit, I now gained on him: so much so, that when I first saw the ocean, he was but one day's journey in advance, and I hoped to intercept him before he should reach the beach. With new courage, therefore, I pressed on, and in two days arrived at a wretched hamlet on the sea-shore. I enquired of the inhabitants concerning the fiend, and gained accurate information. A gigantic monster, they said, had arrived the night before, armed with a gun and many pistols; putting to flight the inhabitants of a solitary cottage, through fear of his terrific appearance. He had carried off their store of winter food, and, placing it in a sledge, to draw which he had seized on a numerous drove of trained dogs, he had harnessed them, and the same night, to the joy of the horror-struck villagers, had pursued his journey across the sea in a direction that led to no land; and they conjectured that he must speedily be destroyed by the breaking of the ice, or frozen by the eternal frosts.

On hearing this information, I suffered a temporary access of despair. He had escaped me; and I must commence a destructive and almost endless journey across the mountainous ices of the ocean, — amidst cold that few of the inhabitants could long endure, and which I, the native of a genial and sunny climate, could not hope to survive. Yet at the idea that the fiend should live and be triumphant, my rage and vengeance returned, and, like a mighty tide, overwhelmed every other feeling. After a slight repose, during which the spirits of the dead hovered round, and instigated me to toil and revenge, I prepared for my journey.

I exchanged my land-sledge for one fashioned for the inequalities of the Frozen Ocean; and purchasing a plentiful stock of provisions, I departed from land.

I cannot guess how many days have passed since then; but I have endured misery, which nothing but the eternal sentiment of a just retribution burning within my heart could have enabled me to support. Immense and rugged mountains of ice often barred up my passage, and I often heard the thunder of the ground sea, which threatened my destruction. But again the frost came, and made the paths of the sea secure.

By the quantity of provision which I had consumed, I should guess that I had passed 675
three weeks in this journey; and the continual protraction of hope, returning back upon the heart, often wrung bitter drops of despondency and grief from my eyes. Despair had indeed almost secured her prey, and I should soon have sunk beneath this misery. Once, after the poor animals that conveyed me had with incredible toil gained the summit of a sloping ice-mountain, and one, sinking under his fatigue, died, I viewed the expanse before me with anguish, when suddenly my eye caught a dark speck upon the dusky plain. I strained my sight to discover what it could be, and uttered a wild cry of ecstasy when I distinguished a sledge, and

the distorted proportions of a well-known form within. Oh! with what a burning gush did hope revisit my heart! warm tears filled my eyes, which I hastily wiped away, that they might not intercept the view I had of the daemon; but still my sight was dimmed by the burning drops, until, giving way to the emotions that oppressed me, I wept aloud.

But this was not the time for delay: I disencumbered the dogs of their dead companion, gave them a plentiful portion of food; and, after an hour's rest, which was absolutely necessary, and yet which was bitterly irksome to me, I continued my route. The sledge was still visible; nor did I again lose sight of it, except at the moments when for a short time some ice-rock concealed it with its intervening crags. I indeed perceptibly gained on it; and when, after nearly two days' journey, I beheld my enemy at no more than a mile distant, my heart bounded within me.

But now, when I appeared almost within grasp of my foe, my hopes were suddenly extinguished, and I lost all traces of him more utterly than I had ever done before. A ground sea was heard; the thunder of its progress, as the waters rolled and swelled beneath me, became every moment more ominous and terrific. I pressed on, but in vain. The wind arose; the sea roared; and, as with the mighty shock of an earthquake, it split, and cracked with a tremendous and overwhelming sound. The work was soon finished: in a few minutes a tumultuous sea rolled between me and my enemy, and I was left drifting on a scattered piece of ice, that was continually lessening, and thus preparing for me a hideous death.

In this manner many appalling hours passed; several of my dogs died; and I myself was about to sink under the accumulation of distress, when I saw your vessel riding at anchor, and holding forth to me hopes of succour and life. I had no conception that vessels ever came so far north, and was astounded at the sight. I quickly destroyed part of my sledge to construct oars; and by these means was enabled, with infinite fatigue, to move my ice-raft in the direction of your ship. I had determined, if you were going southward, still to trust myself to the mercy of the seas rather than abandon my purpose. I hoped to induce you to grant me a boat with which I could pursue my enemy. But your direction was northward. You took me on board when my vigour was exhausted, and I should soon have sunk under my multiplied hardships into a death which I still dread — for my task is unfulfilled.

Oh! when will my guiding spirit, in conducting me to the daemon, allow me the rest I so much desire; or must I die, and he yet live? If I do, swear to me, Walton, that he shall not escape; that you will seek him, and satisfy my vengeance in his death. And do I dare to ask of you to undertake my pilgrimage, to endure the hardships that I have undergone? No; I am not so selfish. Yet, when I am dead, if he should appear; if the ministers of vengeance should conduct him to you, swear that he shall not live — swear that he shall not triumph over my accumulated woes, and survive to add to the list of his dark crimes. He is eloquent and persuasive; and once his words had even power over my heart; but trust him not. His soul is as hellish as his form, full of treachery and fiendlike malice. Hear him not; call on the manes[35] of William, Justine, Clerval, Elizabeth, my father, and of the wretched Victor, and thrust your sword into his heart. I will hover near, and direct the steel aright.

Walton, *in continuation.*

August 26th, 17 — .

You have read this strange and terrific story, Margaret; and do you not feel your blood congeal with horror, like that which even now curdles mine? Sometimes, seized with sudden agony, he could not continue his tale; at others,

[35] The Latin word for "souls of the deceased." — EDS.

his voice broken, yet piercing, uttered with difficulty the words so replete with anguish. His fine and lovely eyes were now lighted up with indignation, now subdued to downcast sorrow, and quenched in infinite wretchedness. Sometimes he commanded his countenance and tones, and related the most horrible incidents with a tranquil voice, suppressing every mark of agitation; then, like a volcano bursting forth, his face would suddenly change to an expression of the wildest rage, as he shrieked out imprecations on his persecutor.

His tale is connected, and told with an appearance of the simplest truth, yet I own to you that the letters of Felix and Safie, which he showed me, and the apparition of the monster seen from our ship, brought to me a greater conviction of the truth of his narrative than his asseverations, however earnest and connected. Such a monster has then really existence! I cannot doubt it; yet I am lost in surprise and admiration. Sometimes I endeavoured to gain from Frankenstein the particulars of his creature's formation: but on this point he was impenetrable.

"Are you mad, my friend?" said he; "or whither does your senseless curiosity lead you? Would you also create for yourself and the world a daemoniacal enemy? Peace, peace! learn my miseries, and do not seek to increase your own."

Frankenstein discovered that I made notes concerning his history: he asked to see them, and then himself corrected and augmented them in many places; but principally in giving the life and spirit to the conversations he held with his enemy. "Since you have preserved my narration," said he, "I would not that a mutilated one should go down to posterity."

Thus has a week passed away, while I have listened to the strangest tale that ever imagination formed. My thoughts, and every feeling of my soul, have been drunk up by the interest for my guest, which this tale, and his own elevated and gentle manners, have created. I wish to soothe him; yet can I counsel one so infinitely miserable, so destitute of every hope of consolation, to live? Oh, no! the only joy that he can now know will be when he composes his shattered spirit to peace and death. Yet he enjoys one comfort, the offspring of solitude and delirium: he believes, when in dreams he holds converse with his friends, and derives from that communion consolation for his miseries, or excitements to his vengeance, that they are not the creations of his fancy, but the beings themselves who visit him from the regions of a remote world. This faith gives a solemnity to his reveries that render them to me almost as imposing and interesting as truth.

Our conversations are not always confined to his own history and misfortunes. On every point of general literature he displays unbounded knowledge, and a quick and piercing apprehension. His eloquence is forcible and touching; nor can I hear him, when he relates a pathetic incident, or endeavours to move the passions of pity or love, without tears. What a glorious creature must he have been in the days of his prosperity, when he is thus noble and godlike in ruin! He seems to feel his own worth, and the greatness of his fall.

"When younger," said he, "I believed myself destined for some great enterprise. My feelings are profound; but I possessed a coolness of judgment that fitted me for illustrious achievements. This sentiment of the worth of my nature supported me, when others would have been oppressed; for I deemed it criminal to throw away in useless grief those talents that might be useful to my fellow-creatures. When I reflected on the work I had completed, no less a one than the creation of a sensitive and rational animal, I could not rank myself with the herd of common projectors. But this thought, which supported me in the commencement of my career, now serves only to plunge me lower in the dust. All my speculations and hopes are as nothing; and, like the archangel who aspired to omnipotence, I am chained in an eternal hell. My imagination was vivid, yet my powers of analysis and application were intense; by the union of these qualities I conceived the idea, and executed the creation of a man. Even now I cannot recollect, without passion, my reveries while the work was incomplete. I trod heaven in my thoughts, now exulting in my powers, now burning with the idea of their effects. From my infancy I was imbued with high hopes and a lofty ambition; but how am I sunk! Oh! my friend, if you had known me as I once was, you would not recognise me in this state of degradation. Despondency rarely visited my heart; a high destiny seemed to bear me on, until I fell, never, never again to rise."

Must I then lose this admirable being? I have longed for a friend; I have sought one who would sympathise with and love me. Behold, on these desert seas I have found such a one; but, I fear, I have gained him only to know his value, and lose him. I would reconcile him to life, but he repulses the idea.

"I thank you, Walton," he said, "for your kind intentions towards so miserable a wretch; but when you speak of new ties, and fresh affections, think you that any can replace those who are gone? Can any man be to me as Clerval was; or any woman another Elizabeth? Even where the affections are not strongly moved by any superior excellence, the companions of our childhood always possess a certain power over our minds, which hardly any later friend can obtain. They know our infantine dispositions, which, however they may be afterwards modified, are never eradicated; and they can judge of our actions with more certain conclusions as to the integrity of our motives. A sister or a brother can never, unless indeed such symptoms have been shown early, suspect the other of fraud or false dealing, when another friend, however strongly he may be attached, may, in spite of himself, be contemplated with suspicion. But I enjoyed friends, dear not only through habit and association, but from their own merits; and wherever I am, the soothing voice of my Elizabeth, and the conversation of Clerval, will be ever whispered in my ear. They are dead; and but one feeling in such a solitude can persuade me to preserve my life. If I were engaged in any high undertaking or design, fraught with extensive utility to my fellow-creatures, then could I live to fulfil it. But such is not my destiny; I must pursue and destroy the being to whom I gave existence; then my lot on earth will be fulfilled, and I may die."

September 2d.

My beloved Sister,

I write to you, encompassed by peril, and ignorant whether I am ever doomed to see again dear England, and the dearer friends that inhabit it. I am surrounded by mountains of ice, which admit of no escape, and threaten every moment to crush my vessel. The brave fellows, whom I have persuaded to be my companions, look towards me for aid; but I have none to bestow. There is something terribly appalling in our situation, yet my courage and hopes do not desert me. Yet it is terrible to reflect that the lives of all these men are endangered through me. If we are lost, my mad schemes are the cause.

And what, Margaret, will be the state of your mind? You will not hear of my destruction, and you will anxiously await my return. Years will pass, and you will have visitings of despair, and yet be tortured by hope. Oh! my beloved sister, the sickening failing of your heart-felt expectations is, in prospect, more terrible to me than my own death. But you have a husband, and lovely children; you may be happy: Heaven bless you, and make you so!

My unfortunate guest regards me with the tenderest compassion. He endeavours to fill me with hope; and talks as if life were a possession which he valued. He reminds me how often the same accidents have happened to other navigators, who have attempted this sea, and, in spite of myself, he fills me with cheerful auguries. Even the sailors feel the power of his eloquence: when he speaks, they no longer despair; he rouses their energies, and, while they hear his voice, they believe these vast mountains of ice are mole-hills, which will vanish before the resolutions of man. These feelings are transitory; each day of expectation delayed fills them with fear, and I almost dread a mutiny caused by this despair.

September 5th.

A scene has just passed of such uncommon interest, that although it is highly probable that these papers may never reach you, yet I cannot forbear recording it.

We are still surrounded by mountains of ice, still in imminent danger of being crushed in their conflict. The cold is excessive, and many of my unfortunate comrades have already found a grave amidst this scene of desolation. Frankenstein has daily declined in health: a feverish fire still glimmers in his eyes; but he is exhausted, and, when suddenly roused to any exertion, he speedily sinks again into apparent lifelessness.

I mentioned in my last letter the fears I entertained of a mutiny. This morning, as I sat watching the wan countenance of my friend—his eyes half closed, and his limbs hanging listlessly,—I was roused by half a dozen of the sailors, who demanded admission into the cabin. They entered, and their leader addressed me. He told me that he and his companions had been chosen by the other sailors to come in deputation to me, to make me a requisition, which, in justice, I could not refuse. We were immured in ice, and should probably never escape; but they feared that if, as was possible, the ice should dissipate, and a free passage be opened, I should be rash enough to continue my voyage, and lead them into fresh dangers, after they might happily have surmounted this. They insisted, therefore, that I should engage with a solemn promise, that if the vessel should be freed I would instantly direct my course southward.

This speech troubled me. I had not despaired; nor had I yet conceived the idea of returning, if set free. Yet could I, in justice, or even in possibility, refuse this demand? I hesitated before I answered; when Frankenstein, who had at first been silent, and, indeed, appeared hardly to have force enough to attend, now roused himself; his eyes sparkled, and his cheeks flushed with momentary vigour. Turning towards the men, he said—

"What do you mean? What do you demand of your captain? Are you then so easily turned from your design? Did you not call this a glorious expedition? And wherefore was it glorious? Not because the way was smooth and placid as a southern sea, but because it was full of dangers and terror; because, at every new incident, your fortitude was to be called forth, and your courage exhibited; because danger and death surrounded it, and these you were to brave and overcome. For this was it a glorious, for this was it an honourable undertaking. You were hereafter to be hailed as the benefactors of your species; your names adored, as belonging to brave men who encountered death for honour, and the benefit of mankind. And now, behold, with the first imagination of danger, or, if you will, the first mighty and terrific trial of your courage, you shrink away, and are content to be handed down as men who had not strength enough to endure cold and peril; and so, poor souls, they were chilly, and returned to their warm firesides. Why, that requires not this preparation; ye need not have come thus far, and dragged your captain to the shame of a defeat, merely to prove yourselves cowards. Oh! be men, or be more than men. Be steady to your purposes, and firm as a rock. This ice is not made of such stuff as your hearts may be; it is mutable, and cannot withstand you, if you say that it shall not. Do not return to your families with the stigma of disgrace marked on your brows. Return as heroes who have fought and conquered, and who know not what it is to turn their backs on the foe."

He spoke this with a voice so modulated to the different feelings expressed in his speech, with an eye so full of lofty design and heroism, that can you wonder that these men were moved? They looked at one another, and were unable to reply. I spoke; I told them to retire, and consider of what had been said: that I would not lead them farther north, if they strenuously desired the contrary; but that I hoped that, with reflection, their courage would return.

They retired, and I turned towards my friend; but he was sunk in languor, and almost deprived of life.

How all this will terminate, I know not; but I had rather die than return shamefully,—my purpose unfulfilled. Yet I fear such will be my fate; the men, unsupported by ideas of glory and honour, can never willingly continue to endure their present hardships.

September 7th.

The die is cast; I have consented to return, if we are not destroyed. Thus are my hopes blasted by cowardice and indecision; I come back ignorant and disappointed. It requires more philosophy than I possess, to bear this injustice with patience.

September 12th.

It is past; I am returning to England. I have lost my hopes of utility and glory;—I have lost my friend. But I will endeavour to detail these bitter circumstances to you, my dear sister; and, while I am wafted towards England, and towards you, I will not despond.

September 9th, the ice began to move, and roarings like thunder were heard at a distance, as the islands split and cracked in every direction. We were in the most imminent peril; but, as we could only remain passive, my chief attention was occupied by my unfortunate guest, whose illness increased in such a degree, that he was entirely confined to his bed. The ice cracked behind us, and was driven with force towards the north; a breeze sprung from the west, and on the 11th the passage towards the south became perfectly free. When the sailors saw this, and that their return to their native country was apparently assured, a shout of tumultuous joy broke from them, loud and long-continued. Frankenstein, who was dozing, awoke, and asked the cause of the tumult. "They shout," I said, "because they will soon return to England."

"Do you then really return?"

"Alas! yes; I cannot withstand their demands. I cannot lead them unwillingly to danger, and I must return."

"Do so, if you will; but I will not. You may give up your purpose, but mine is assigned to me by Heaven, and I dare not. I am weak; but surely the spirits who assist my vengeance will endow me with sufficient strength." Saying this, he endeavoured to spring from the bed, but the exertion was too great for him; he fell back, and fainted.

It was long before he was restored; and I often thought that life was entirely extinct. At length he opened his eyes; he breathed with difficulty, and was unable to speak. The surgeon gave him a composing draught, and ordered us to leave him undisturbed. In the mean time he told me, that my friend had certainly not many hours to live.

His sentence was pronounced; and I could only grieve, and be patient. I sat by his bed, watching him; his eyes were closed, and I thought he slept; but presently he called to me in a feeble voice, and, bidding me come near, said—"Alas! the strength I relied on is gone; I feel that I shall soon die, and he, my enemy and persecutor, may still be in being. Think not, Walton, that in the last moments of my existence I feel that burning hatred, and ardent desire of revenge, I once expressed; but I feel myself justified in desiring the death of my adversary. During these last days I have been occupied in examining my past conduct; nor do I find it blameable. In a fit of enthusiastic madness I

This mural, titled *Saturn Devouring One of His Sons*, was painted by Spanish artist Francisco Goya (1746–1828) shortly after *Frankenstein* was published. According to Roman myth, the god Saturn would destroy his children to prevent them from one day overthrowing him. **How does this image relate to Victor's pursuit of his creation after the monster has murdered several of his loved ones? What aspects of the painting lend themselves to comparison with the themes, tone, and/or mood of the novel?**

Prado, Madrid, Spain / Bridgeman Images

created a rational creature, and was bound towards him, to assure, as far as was in my power, his happiness and well-being. This was my duty; but there was another still paramount to that. My duties towards the beings of my own species had greater claims to my attention, because they included a greater proportion of happiness or misery. Urged by this view, I refused, and I did right in refusing, to create a companion for the first creature. He showed unparalleled malignity and selfishness, in evil: he destroyed my friends; he devoted to destruction beings who possessed exquisite sensations, happiness, and wisdom; nor do I know where this thirst for vengeance may end. Miserable himself, that he may render no other wretched, he ought to die. The task of his destruction was mine, but I have failed. When actuated by selfishness and vicious motives, I asked you to undertake my unfinished work; and I renew this request now, when I am only induced by reason and virtue.

"Yet I cannot ask you to renounce your country and friends, to fulfil this task; and now, that you are returning to England, you will have little chance of meeting with him. But the consideration of these points, and the well balancing of what you may esteem your duties, I leave to you; my judgment and ideas are already disturbed by the near approach of death. I dare not ask you to do what I think right, for I may still be misled by passion.

"That he should live to be an instrument of mischief disturbs me; in other respects, this hour, when I momentarily expect my release, is the only happy one which I have enjoyed for several years. The forms of the beloved dead flit before me, and I hasten to their arms. Farewell, Walton! Seek happiness in tranquillity, and avoid ambition, even if it be only the apparently innocent one of distinguishing yourself in science and discoveries. Yet why do I say this? I have myself been blasted in these hopes, yet another may succeed."

His voice became fainter as he spoke; and at length, exhausted by his effort, he sunk into silence. About half an hour afterwards he attempted again to speak, but was unable; he pressed my hand feebly, and his eyes closed for ever, while the irradiation of a gentle smile passed away from his lips.

Margaret, what comment can I make on the untimely extinction of this glorious spirit? What can I say, that will enable you to understand the depth of my sorrow? All that I should express would be inadequate and feeble. My tears flow; my mind is overshadowed by a cloud of disappointment. But I journey towards England, and I may there find consolation.

I am interrupted. What do these sounds portend? It is midnight; the breeze blows fairly, and the watch on deck scarcely stir. Again; there is a sound as of a human voice, but hoarser; it comes from the cabin where the remains of Frankenstein still lie. I must arise, and examine. Good night, my sister.

Great God! what a scene has just taken place! I am yet dizzy with the remembrance of it. I hardly know whether I shall have the power to detail it; yet the tale which I have recorded would be incomplete without this final and wonderful catastrophe.

I entered the cabin, where lay the remains of my ill-fated and admirable friend. Over him hung a form which I cannot find words to describe; gigantic in stature, yet uncouth and distorted in its proportions. As he hung over the coffin, his face was concealed by long locks of ragged hair; but one vast hand was extended, in colour and apparent texture like that of a mummy. When he heard the sound of my approach, he ceased to utter exclamations of grief and horror, and sprung towards the window. Never did I behold a vision so horrible as his face, of such loathsome yet appalling hideousness. I shut my eyes involuntarily, and endeavoured to recollect what were my duties with regard to this destroyer. I called on him to stay.

He paused, looking on me with wonder; and, again turning towards the lifeless form of his creator, he seemed to forget my presence, and every feature and gesture seemed instigated by the wildest rage of some uncontrollable passion.

"That is also my victim!" he exclaimed: "in his murder my crimes are consummated; the miserable series of my being is wound to its close! Oh, Frankenstein! generous and self-devoted being! what does it avail that I now ask thee to pardon me? I, who irretrievably destroyed thee by destroying all thou lovedst. Alas! he is cold, he cannot answer me."

His voice seemed suffocated; and my first impulses, which had suggested to me the duty of obeying the dying request of my friend, in destroying his enemy, were now suspended by a mixture of curiosity and compassion. I approached this tremendous being; I dared not again raise my eyes to his face, there was something so scaring and unearthly in his ugliness. I attempted to speak, but the words died away on my lips. The monster continued to utter wild and incoherent self-reproaches. At length I gathered resolution to address him in a pause of the tempest of his passion: "Your repentance," I said, "is now superfluous. If you had listened to the voice of conscience, and heeded the stings of remorse, before you had urged your diabolical vengeance to this extremity, Frankenstein would yet have lived."

"And do you dream?" said the daemon; "do you think that I was then dead to agony and remorse? — He," he continued, pointing to the corpse, "he suffered not in the consummation of the deed — oh! not the ten-thousandth portion of the anguish that was mine during the lingering detail of its execution. A frightful selfishness hurried me on, while my heart was poisoned with remorse. Think you that the groans of Clerval were music to my ears? My heart was fashioned to be susceptible of love and sympathy; and, when wrenched by misery to vice and hatred, it did not endure the violence of the change, without torture such as you cannot even imagine.

"After the murder of Clerval, I returned to Switzerland, heartbroken and overcome. I pitied Frankenstein; my pity amounted to horror: I abhorred myself. But when I discovered that he, the author at once of my existence and of its unspeakable torments, dared to hope for happiness; that while he accumulated wretchedness and despair upon me, he sought his own enjoyment in feelings and passions from the indulgence of which I was for ever barred, then impotent envy and bitter indignation filled me with an insatiable thirst for vengeance. I recollected my threat, and resolved that it should be accomplished. I knew that I was preparing for myself a deadly torture; but I was the slave, not the master, of an impulse, which I detested, yet could not disobey. Yet when she died! — nay, then I was not miserable. I had cast off all feeling, subdued all anguish, to riot in the excess of my despair. Evil thenceforth became my good. Urged thus far, I had no choice but to adapt my nature to an element which I had willingly chosen. The completion of my demoniacal design became an insatiable passion. And now it is ended; there is my last victim!"

I was first touched by the expressions of his misery; yet, when I called to mind what Frankenstein had said of his powers of eloquence and persuasion, and when I again cast my eyes on the lifeless form of my friend, indignation was rekindled within me. "Wretch!" I said, "it is well that you come here to whine over the desolation that you have made. You throw a torch into a pile of buildings; and, when they are consumed, you sit among the ruins, and lament the fall. Hypocritical fiend! if he whom you mourn still lived, still would he be the object, again would he become the prey, of your accursed vengeance. It is not pity that you feel; you lament only because the victim of your malignity is withdrawn from your power."

"Oh, it is not thus — not thus," interrupted the being; "yet such must be the impression conveyed to you by what appears to be the purport of my actions. Yet I seek not a fellow-feeling in my misery. No sympathy may I ever find. When I first sought it, it was the love of virtue, the feelings of happiness and affection with which my whole being overflowed, that I wished to be participated. But now, that virtue has become to me a shadow, and that happiness and affection are turned into bitter and loathing despair, in what should I seek for sympathy? I am content to suffer alone, while my sufferings shall endure: when I die, I am well satisfied that abhorrence and opprobrium should load my memory. Once my fancy was soothed with dreams of virtue, of fame, and of enjoyment. Once I falsely hoped to meet with beings, who, pardoning my outward form, would love me for the excellent qualities which I was capable of unfolding. I was nourished with high thoughts of honour and devotion. But now crime has degraded me beneath the meanest animal. No guilt, no mischief, no malignity, no misery, can be found comparable to mine. When I run over the frightful catalogue of my sins, I cannot believe that I am the same creature whose thoughts were once filled with sublime and transcendent visions of the beauty and the majesty of goodness. But it is even so; the fallen angel becomes a malignant devil. Yet even that enemy of God and man had friends and associates in his desolation; I am alone.

"You, who call Frankenstein your friend, seem to have a knowledge of my crimes and his misfortunes. But, in the detail which he gave you of them, he could not sum up the hours and months of misery which I endured, wasting in impotent passions. For while I destroyed his hopes, I did not satisfy my own desires. They were for ever ardent and craving; still I desired love and fellowship, and I was still spurned. Was there no injustice in this? Am I to be thought the only criminal, when all human kind sinned against me? Why do you not hate Felix, who drove his friend from his door with contumely? Why do you not execrate the rustic who sought to destroy the saviour of his child? Nay, these are virtuous and immaculate beings! I, the miserable and the abandoned, am an abortion, to be

Known as the wisest of the Titans in ancient Greek mythology, Prometheus stole fire from the gods of Mount Olympus and brought it to mankind. As punishment for his transgression, he was chained to a rock where an eagle would eat his liver, which would grow back each day, making his torment eternal. Shown below are two paintings of Prometheus: *The Torture of Prometheus* (c. 1620–48) by Gioacchino Assereto (left) and *Prometheus* (1998) by Xavier Cortada (right). **What aspects of each of these works illustrate Victor Frankenstein's anguish? Which one best represents the themes of the novel, and why?**

Album / Art Resource, NY

Prometheus, 1998 (acrylic on canvas), Cortada, Xavier / Private Collection / Bridgeman Images

spurned at, and kicked, and trampled on. Even now my blood boils at the recollection of this injustice.

"But it is true that I am a wretch. I have murdered the lovely and the helpless; I have strangled the innocent as they slept, and grasped to death his throat who never injured me or any other living thing. I have devoted my creator, the select specimen of all that is worthy of love and admiration among men, to misery; I have pursued him even to that irremediable ruin. There he lies, white and cold in death. You hate me; but your abhorrence cannot equal that with which I regard myself. I look on the hands which executed the deed; I think on the heart in which the imagination of it was conceived, and long for the moment when these hands will meet my eyes, when that imagination will haunt my thoughts no more.

"Fear not that I shall be the instrument of future mischief. My work is nearly complete. Neither yours nor any man's death is needed to consummate the series of my being, and accomplish that which must be done; but it requires my own. Do not think that I shall be slow to perform this sacrifice. I shall quit your vessel on the ice-raft which brought me thither, and shall seek the most northern extremity of the globe; I shall collect my funeral pile, and consume to ashes this miserable frame, that its remains may afford no light to any curious and unhallowed wretch, who would create such another as I have been. I shall die. I shall no longer feel the agonies which now consume me, or be the prey of feelings unsatisfied, yet unquenched. He is dead who called me into being; and when I shall be no more, the very remembrance of us both will speedily vanish. I shall no longer see the sun or stars, or feel the winds play on my cheeks. Light, feeling, and sense will pass away; and in this condition must I find my happiness. Some years ago, when the images which this world affords first opened upon me, when I felt the cheering warmth of summer, and heard the rustling of the leaves and the warbling of the birds, and these were all to me, I should have wept to die; now it is my only consolation. Polluted by crimes, and torn by the bitterest remorse, where can I find rest but in death?

"Farewell! I leave you, and in you the last of human kind whom these eyes will ever behold. Farewell, Frankenstein! If thou wert yet alive, and yet cherished a desire of revenge against me, it would be better satiated in my life than in my destruction. But it was not so; thou didst seek my extinction, that I might not cause greater wretchedness; and if yet, in some mode unknown to me, thou hadst not ceased to think and feel, thou wouldst not desire against me a vengeance greater than that which I feel. Blasted as thou wert, my agony was still superior to thine; for the bitter sting of remorse will not cease to rankle in my wounds until death shall close them for ever.

"But soon," he cried, with sad and solemn enthusiasm, "I shall die, and what I now feel be no longer felt. Soon these burning miseries will be extinct. I shall ascend my funeral pile triumphantly, and exult in the agony of the torturing flames. The light of that conflagration will fade away; my ashes will be swept into the sea by the winds. My spirit will sleep in peace; or if it thinks, it will not surely think thus. Farewell."

He sprung from the cabin window, as he said this, upon the ice-raft which lay close to the vessel. He was soon borne away by the waves, and lost in darkness and distance.

[1818/1831]

QUESTIONS FOR DISCUSSION

1. Before reading *Frankenstein*, the novel, you were probably already familiar with the monster through film versions and media portrayals. What were your expectations for the novel's beginning, and to what extent were they based on those well-known portrayals? How did those expectations affect your reading experience?
2. The full title of Mary Shelley's novel is *Frankenstein; or, The Modern Prometheus.* What parallels do you see between the story of Prometheus and that of Victor Frankenstein? and Frankenstein? Why would Shelley refer to this mythic figure in her subtitle?
3. Just below the title of the novel, Shelley begins the book with an epigraph from John Milton's epic poem, *Paradise Lost*, that poses a rhetorical question. Who in the novel might ask such a question? Of whom? Why might Shelley have begun with this epigraph?
4. From the text of Robert Walton's letters, what parallels can you draw between him and Victor Frankenstein? What qualities and characteristics do they share? How do they differ?
5. In Chapter II, Frankenstein speaks of a passion "which afterwards ruled my destiny" (para. 73), of "the fatal impulse that led to my ruin" (para. 75), of "the storm that was even then hanging in the stars, and ready to envelop me" (para. 82), and concludes, "Destiny was too potent, and her immutable laws had decreed my utter and terrible destruction" (para. 83). He returns to this motif again and again throughout his remarkable tale. Why does he speak as if fate has ruled his actions? To what extent do you think he truly believes that?

What do his statements imply about Shelley's attitude toward fate or destiny? Explain.

6. Who is Elizabeth? Clerval? Krempe? Waldman? Briefly describe the function each character serves in the narrative. How significant are they as influences on Victor Frankenstein? Explain.

7. What significance do you attach to the number of months it takes Victor Frankenstein to complete his labor and bring the creature to life?

8. Clerval's timely arrival just after the creation of the monster is the first of several extraordinary coincidences in the novel. Note and describe at least three others that follow in the story. What is their effect? Do they support Frankenstein's forebodings regarding destiny and fate? Are they so outrageous as to strain credibility? Do they enhance or detract from the power of the novel? Explain.

9. In paragraph 216, Frankenstein relates Justine's defense against the accusation that she murdered William: "'God knows,' she said, 'how entirely I am innocent. But I do not pretend that my protestations should acquit me: I rest my innocence on a plain and simple explanation of the facts which have been adduced against me; and I hope the character I have always borne will incline my judges to a favorable interpretation, where any circumstance appears doubtful or suspicious.'" How do these words characterize her? Read carefully what Frankenstein says in the last three paragraphs of the chapter. How has Justine affected his disposition? In what way might Justine's death represent a turning point in the narrative?

10. In Chapter X, the monster confronts Frankenstein and addresses him: "You, my creator." He refers to himself as "thy creature" and pleads, "Do your duty towards me." Read carefully what he says to Frankenstein (para. 267). What effect does this plea have on Frankenstein? As the chapter concludes, Frankenstein says, "For the first time, also, I felt what the duties of a creator towards his creature were." Do you believe him? Does Frankenstein understand fully what he says? Explain, using specific details from scenes in the novel to support your response.

11. Knowledge itself — its lure and its consequences — is a major theme of the novel. In Chapter XIII the monster recounts how he learned to read, and describes the thoughts prompted by his learning. He proclaims, "Of what a strange nature is knowledge!" (para. 333). Later, in Chapter XV he says to his creator, "Increase of knowledge only discovered to me more clearly what a wretched outcast I was" (para. 366). How could these two statements by the monster apply equally to both Walton and Frankenstein? How do they relate to the novel's larger themes? Explain.

12. In Chapter XIV the monster relates the story of the De Lacey family, the cottagers whom he has come to know. What about the family's story is it that "excited in me such various feelings of indignation, delight, and wonder," as the monster says (para. 336)? What does this reaction suggest about the monster's character?

13. Reflecting on the books he has read, the monster says, "I remembered Adam's supplication to his Creator. But where was mine? He had abandoned me; and, in the bitterness of my heart, I cursed him" (para. 367). The monster here refers to the same passage from *Paradise Lost* that Shelley uses as the epigraph to the novel. Why does Shelley have the monster express his situation in such religious terms? Does the monster's language evoke sympathy from the reader? Explain.

14. How does Frankenstein respond to the monster's tale? What moves him to change his mind regarding the creation of a female companion for the monster? And then what moves him to change his mind again and destroy that new creation in progress? What do you make of the significance of Frankenstein's ultimate change of heart, and how does it help develop some of the novel's themes?

15. After Frankenstein destroys his new creation, the monster warns: "I shall be with you on your wedding-night" (para. 514). Despite the fact that the monster has already caused the deaths of William and Justine, Frankenstein doesn't seem to fear for Elizabeth, misunderstanding the nature of the threat. Is he merely obtuse? Is he intrepid? Is he egotistical? What is it that causes him to misunderstand? Explain.

16. From the arrival of Elizabeth's final letter in Chapter XXII until her death at the hands of the monster on their wedding night, Victor Frankenstein feels more and more under the grip of an inexorable fate. Trace his increasing sense of conviction through what he says. How does that belief in (and evident submission to) "fate" contribute to your understanding of Frankenstein, and of *Frankenstein*?

17. In the final chapter, when Walton resumes as narrator, we learn that Frankenstein's story

(which, of course, includes the monster's tale) has taken a full week to tell, and that Walton believes the story he has heard. How does Walton regard Frankenstein? What about the story attracts Walton and convinces him of its veracity?

18. In Chapter XXIV, Walton proclaims, "If we are lost, my mad schemes are the cause" (para. 689). What "mad schemes" does he refer to? How could those words apply equally to Frankenstein?

19. Read carefully the speech that Frankenstein delivers to the crew as reported in Walton's letter of September 5th (para. 696). Then consider the advice he proffers to Walton as reported in the letter of September 12th (paras. 707–9). What has changed? What is the nature of the advice that he gives just before he dies?

20. In the same letter, Walton reports the monster's murder of Frankenstein. The monster then speaks to Walton, reminding him that he has heard only Frankenstein's version of the story. Read paragraph 722 carefully. To what extent does the monster adequately justify his actions?

21. After reporting the monster's explanation, Walton concludes the novel and the final letter that we get to read: "He sprung from the cabin window, as he said this, upon the ice-raft which lay close to the vessel. He was soon borne away by the waves and lost in darkness and distance" (para. 727). At this point it is nearly a month since Victor Frankenstein arrived aboard Walton's ship. How will Frankenstein's story affect him? What do you think the future will hold for Robert Walton?

QUESTIONS ON STYLE AND STRUCTURE

1. Unusual in its structure, *Frankenstein* is at once an epistolary novel (told in a series of letters) as well as a frame tale, or story within a story. In this case we have stories within stories: The monster's tale, for instance, begins in Chapter XI and continues through Chapter XVI, narrated within the frame of Frankenstein's narrative — which itself is told within the frame of Walton's letters. The novel thus becomes a double frame tale; or, to put it another way, in this section Walton is telling Margaret what Frankenstein told him that the monster told him about his experiences — and about the De Lacey family. Such a narrative structure depends on the credibility of the narrators and on the careful memory of the reader. How do you respond to such a method? Does it enhance the novel? Does it confuse events? Who is the primary narrator of the novel? Why do you think Shelley wrote the novel this way? How does the structure of the novel affect its themes and impact on the reader?

2. Near the beginning of the novel, Walton's second letter is sent from Archangel, north of St. Petersburg, Russia, where he hopes to set sail on his exploration of the Arctic. This reference reappears near the end of the novel, when Frankenstein says to Walton, "All my speculations and hopes are as nothing; and, like the archangel who aspired to omnipotence, I am chained in an eternal hell" (para. 686). Compare the two references to the archangel. How do they serve as symbolic frames for the story? Why might Shelley have chosen a town with this name as the setting for the beginning of Walton's journey?

3. In his second letter, Walton tells his sister to "not be alarmed for my safety, or if I should come back to you as worn and woeful as the 'Ancient Mariner'" (para. 15). Samuel Taylor Coleridge's poem *The Rime of the Ancient Mariner* is a frame tale in which the mariner tells his gruesome story to those who need to hear it. In Shelley's novel, Victor Frankenstein might be seen as analogous to the mariner and Walton to his listener. Near the end of Coleridge's poem, the mariner concludes his tale, saying that as he made confession,

> "Forthwith this frame of mine was wrenched
> With a woful agony,
> Which forced me to begin my tale;
> And then it left me free.
>
> "Since then, at an uncertain hour,
> That agony returns:
> And till my ghastly tale is told,
> This heart within me burns.
>
> "I pass, like night, from land to land;
> I have strange power of speech;
> That moment that his face I see,
> I know the man that must hear me:
> To him my tale I teach."

How does the allusion to Coleridge's poem serve as foreshadowing in *Frankenstein*?

4. In Chapter II, Frankenstein describes the lightning storm that left nothing but a "blasted stump" of a great oak that had stood near his house (para. 80). It launches his intense interest in electricity. Later, after he has created and abandoned his monster, he says, "But I am a blasted tree; the bolt has entered my soul . . . a miserable spectacle of wrecked humanity, pitiable to others, and intolerable to myself" (para. 484). How does this symbolism connect his early ambition with the unwanted consequences of his actions?

5. Several times during his story, Frankenstein interrupts his tale to address Walton directly (e.g., para. 110). What is the purpose and effect of these interruptions? How do they contribute to the themes of the novel?

6. Several times, Frankenstein attempts to express how he feels by quoting lines of poetry without attributing them to any author — for example, he takes lines from *The Rime of the Ancient Mariner* by Samuel Taylor Coleridge (para. 125) and from "Lines Composed a Few Miles above Tintern Abbey" by William Wordsworth (para. 471). What do such quotations suggest about both Frankenstein and his listener, Walton? How do they contribute to Shelley's purpose and to the themes of the novel?

7. What effect do the letters from Victor Frankenstein's father and from Elizabeth have on him? Immediately between his reading of Elizabeth's letter and the arrival of the one from his father, Frankenstein's mood has been cheered by his friend, Henry Clerval, and by the restorative power of nature — by the "salubrious air I breathed," he muses (para. 162). He concludes the episode: "We returned to our college on a Sunday afternoon: the peasants were dancing, and every one we met appeared gay and happy. My own spirits were high, and I bounded along with the feelings of unbridled joy and hilarity" (para. 164). How does the imagery he creates foreshadow what is to follow? Find another instance of similar foreshadowing at the end of a chapter and explain its significance.

8. Victor Frankenstein's first glimpse of the monster (on his return home after learning of William's death) is accompanied by imagery of a terrific tempest. Find other examples of the conjunction of the appearance of the monster and storm imagery. How do they contribute to the mood and meaning of the novel?

9. In paragraph 255, Frankenstein likens himself to a wounded deer. How apt is that metaphor? What aspects of Victor's character does it reveal? Do you take Frankenstein at his word, or do you read this and other similar self-descriptions with a grain of salt? Explain.

10. Read carefully the first four paragraphs of Chapter X, in which Frankenstein describes his surroundings and quotes from "Mutability," a poem by Percy Bysshe Shelley, the author's husband. What is the relationship between the imagery of Frankenstein's description and the poem? Explain. How do these paragraphs foreshadow what immediately follows?

11. After Frankenstein has destroyed the new creature he was creating, the monster tells him, "Slave, I have reasoned with you, but you have proved yourself unworthy of my condescension. Remember that I have power; you believe yourself miserable, but I can make you so wretched that the light of day will be hateful to you. You are my creator, but I am your master; — obey!" (para. 510). Explain the paradox in what the monster says. In what ways is it emblematic of the novel's themes? of the monster's character? of Frankenstein's?

12. In Chapter XXIII, Frankenstein describes finding Elizabeth dead at the hands of the monster: "She was there, lifeless and inanimate, thrown across the bed, her head hanging down, and her pale and distorted features half covered by her hair. Everywhere I turn I see the same figure — her bloodless arms and relaxed form flung by the murderer on its bridal bier" (para. 631). This image was inspired by *The Nightmare* (p. 950), a 1791 painting by Henry Fuseli, an acquaintance of Shelley's parents. View the image carefully. How effectively does it reflect the mood of the passage? Why do you think it provided such inspiration for Shelley?

13. At the end, the reader doesn't learn what becomes of the monster or of Robert Walton. How does such an inconclusive ending relate to the structure of the rest of the book? What effect does such an open-ended conclusion have on your understanding of the novel's characters and themes?

SUGGESTIONS FOR WRITING

1. *Frankenstein* is a difficult novel for many reasons, among them the epistolary format coupled with its tales within tales, the strain on credibility that the events create, and also the manner in which the characters speak. Take, for instance, one passage spoken by the monster — who is, remember, three years old:

   > Food, however, became scarce; and I often spent the whole day searching in vain for a few acorns to assuage the pangs of hunger. When I found this, I resolved to quit the place that I had hitherto inhabited; to seek for one where the few wants I experienced would be more easily satisfied. In this emigration, I exceedingly lamented the loss of the fire which I had obtained through accident, and knew not how to reproduce it. I gave several hours to the serious consideration of this difficulty; but I was obliged to relinquish all attempt to supply it; and, wrapping myself up in my cloak, I struck across the woods towards the setting sun. I passed three days in these rambles, and at length discovered the open country. . . .

   Write an essay in which you analyze the syntax in three examples of narration — one each by Walton, Frankenstein, and the monster. As you compare and contrast the passages, make an argument for how syntax functions as an element of style in the novel and its effect on the meaning of the work as a whole.

2. In "Frankenstein's Fallen Angel," contemporary writer Joyce Carol Oates discusses "the difficulty of reading Mary Shelley's novel for the first time," and argues that it should be read not as realism but as romance. She states,

   > It is a mistake to read *Frankenstein* as a modern novel of psychological realism, or as a 'novel' at all. It contains no characters, only points of view; its concerns are pointedly moral and didactic; it makes more claims for verisimilitude of even a poetic Wordsworthian nature. . . . Where the realistic novel presents characters in a more or less coherent 'field' as part of a defined society, firmly established in time and place, romance does away with questions of verisimilitude and plausibility altogether. . . . No one expects Victor Frankenstein to behave plausibly when he is a near-allegorical figure; no one expects his demon to behave plausibly since he is a demon presence, an outsized mirror image of his creator.

   Write an essay in which you analyze *Frankenstein* as a romantic rather than a realistic novel, as Oates characterizes it.

3. In his poem, "September 1, 1939," W. H. Auden (p. 821) writes, "I and the public know / What all schoolchildren learn, / Those to whom evil is done / Do evil in return." Write an essay in which you explain how these lines could serve as a thematic epigraph for *Frankenstein*.

4. In "*Frankenstein* and Radical Science," Marilyn Butler writes:

   > Compared with the professional qualifications of the novel's first two narrators, Frankenstein and Walton, an inventor and an explorer, the Creature has few claims to act as the third. Just as he owes his existence to a unique and unnatural process, he defies all odds, as a parentless being, by learning language at all. Yet the voice in which he narrates the second of the three volumes is impressive, in a strange register appropriate to a witness brought back from the remote past. . . . He is more eloquent than Frankenstein in the conversations that introduce and end their meeting, and still more persuasive when relating his life-history, an exercise in self-observation, social observation, and retrospective analysis. By tracking his own maturation, from a solitary to a social animal, the Creature succeeds in the task Frankenstein abandons, that of scientifically following up Frankenstein's technological achievement.

   How persuasive is the monster's voice? Is he more eloquent than his creator? Write an essay in which you explore these questions as you analyze the monster's voice and evaluate its contribution to the meaning of the work as a whole.

5. Read Samuel Taylor Coleridge's narrative poem, *The Rime of the Ancient Mariner*. Write an essay in which you analyze the parallels between the poem and *Frankenstein*.

6. If you have read *Paradise Lost*, the epic poem by John Milton, you will recognize parallels between

the two works of literature that go beyond Mary Shelley's epigraph from Milton: for example, between Frankenstein and both God and Satan, and between the monster and Adam. Write an essay in which you analyze the parallels between the poem and the novel, and assess the extent of the influence Milton had on Shelley.

7. In "My Monster / My Self," Barbara Johnson writes:

> Mary Shelley's Frankenstein is an even more elaborate and unsettling formation of the relation between parenthood and monstrousness. It is the story of two antithetical modes of parenting that give rise to two increasingly parallel lives — the life of Victor Frankenstein, who is the beloved child of two doting parents, and the life of the monster he single-handedly creates, who is immediately spurned and abandoned by his creator. The fact that in the end both characters reach an equal degree of alienation and self-torture and indeed become indistinguishable as they pursue each other across the frozen polar wastes indicates that the novel is, among other things, a study of the impossibility of finding an adequate model for what a parent should be.

Think about Johnson's ideas as they might inform your reading of *Frankenstein*. Is the novel as much about parenthood as it is about scientific creation? Write an essay in which you analyze Frankenstein as an exploration of parenthood.

8. In his widely popular book (in America it sold more copies than any other book after the Bible), *Baby and Child Care*, published in 1946 and revised in 1957, Dr. Benjamin Spock offered the following advice to new parents:

> Don't be afraid of your baby. . . . Love and enjoy your children for what they are, for what they look like, for what they do, and forget about the qualities that they don't have. I don't give you this advice just for sentimental reasons. There's a very important practical point here. The children who are appreciated for what they are, even if they are homely, or clumsy, or slow, will grow up with confidence in themselves — happy. They will have a spirit that will make the best of all the capacities that they have, and of all the opportunities that come their way. They will make light of any handicaps. But the children who have never been quite accepted by their parents, who have always felt that they were not quite right, will grow up lacking confidence. They'll never be able to make full use of what brains, what skills, what physical attractiveness they have. If they start life with a handicap, physical or mental, it will be multiplied tenfold by the time they are grown up.

Dr. Spock was actually writing about Victor Frankenstein and his creation. Just kidding, of course, but . . . consider how Dr. Spock's advice might apply to Frankenstein. Write an essay in which you analyze Frankenstein through the lens of Dr. Spock's advice.

TEXTS IN CONTEXT

Frankenstein and the Ethics of Creation

Surely most people — even those who have never read Mary Shelley's novel — know about Frankenstein; he is as familiar as Dracula, Sherlock Holmes, and Alice in Wonderland. Like those characters, he has been widely depicted in film and referenced in other works of art, literature, and sometimes even in political cartoons. As a result, Frankenstein has become a fixture in modern popular culture, one cemented by the actor Boris Karloff, who played the iconic monster with scars on his face and bolts in his neck in James Whale's 1931 film. But Frankenstein is unique in that he has most often been represented as his opposite — that is, as a monster created by a mad scientist with evil motives rather than as the monster's creator, a scholar driven by the selfless wish to benefit mankind. Why is the story of Frankenstein so often, and so thoroughly, garbled? Perhaps the answer to that question lies in the ethical implications of Mary Shelley's classic tale, and the questions it raises about right and wrong, about human nature, and about the limits of technological advancement. The true monster in Frankenstein may actually be a matter of perspective.

The subtitle of Mary Shelley's novel — *The Modern Prometheus* — hints that Frankenstein has perhaps gone too far, exceeding natural limits on human achievement. But the epigraph refers not to Frankenstein but to his creation, the monster, who might indeed ask his creator, as Adam asks God:

Did I request thee, Maker, from my clay
To mould Me man? Did I solicit thee
From darkness to promote me?—

This rhetorical question poses a dilemma for Victor Frankenstein and for us. What has driven him to create the monster? What motivates humanity to create new technologies and entities that we do not fully understand? Is it ambition, zeal, presumption, hubris, or a desire to improve the world and help humanity? And does responsibility for the unexpected — and unintended — consequences fall on creation or creator?

What prompted Mary Shelley to ask these questions in her work? In some ways, the novel is a direct response to the issues of the time. *Frankenstein* is a product, on the one hand, of the Enlightenment, or the age of reason, which brought new ideas to science, political thought, and philosophy. It is also a product of the age of Romanticism, an artistic and literary movement during the late eighteenth and early nineteenth centuries that celebrated the power and autonomy of the individual, who was often a rebel against the mores of the time; the glory and intensity of nature; the goodness and innocence of the young; and the unexplainable supernatural. Some Romantic literature is gothic: fantastic, mysterious, and macabre, these works often feature exotic or haunted settings, supernatural beings, and terrifying events — both *Dracula* and the works of Edgar Allan Poe are prime examples of the genre.

What is the source of humor in this cartoon? How might it be seen as a contemporary interpretation that captures the essential ideas of Shelley's work? How might it come across as reductive of the enduring themes the novel explores?

WHAT TO EXPECT WHEN YOU'RE EXPECTING

SIPRESS

David Sipress The New Yorker Collection/The Cartoon Bank

Frankenstein is indeed a Romantic, gothic novel, but it might also be seen as the first "science fiction" novel. While not set in the future, as is much science fiction, the novel does involve science as none had before, looking ahead to the future consequences of industrialization, scientific experimentation, and technological discovery. It even addresses the ethics of child rearing in an era of unprecedented progress. Is Victor Frankenstein crazy? Is he merely selfish? Is *Frankenstein* a cautionary tale about an insensitive human being, a neglectful parent? Is his transgression his inhumane response to his creation and abject neglect of his own progeny? Or does it lie in the act of artificially creating life in the first place? Is *Frankenstein* a tale about a "mad scientist" whose hubris has taken him beyond the limits of human achievement, like that of Adam and also of Lucifer, who attempted to usurp God's dominion in seeking forbidden knowledge? Is the novel a plea against advances in science and runaway technology, as many interpret it? Has Frankenstein come to represent the idea

PATTERSON

"Bring me a stem cell."

Jason Patterson The New Yorker Collection/The Cartoon Bank

How does the cartoonist suggest that *Frankenstein* applies to the current debate over stem cell research? To what extent do you agree?

that science — whatever its motives — will result in unwanted consequences and unforeseen monstrosities? The speculation these questions invite, combined with the novel's narrative style, form a truly unsettling response to the enduring ethical dilemmas first posed by the rapid social, political, and especially the technological changes of the Enlightenment era.

As a symbol, Frankenstein comes up whenever we discuss such advances as scientific engineering, cloning, robot technology, self-driving cars, and genetically modified organisms. In 1992, for instance, college professor Paul Lewis coined the term "Frankenfood" to describe genetically modified food. Or, consider Barack Obama's assertion regarding surveillance technology during his 2013 end-of-year White House press conference: "Just because we can do something, doesn't mean we should do it." Did Frankenstein create the monster simply because he *could*, without enough consideration of whether he *should*? Have we likewise failed to fully consider the ethical implications of today's groundbreaking technologies?

In the texts that follow, you will see how different writers have addressed some of these questions. The first one is an essay by Harvard paleontologist Stephen Jay Gould, who writes about literature as eloquently as he does about science. Each of the texts that follow — poetry, fiction, cartoon, and nonfiction — addresses *Frankenstein* as a novel and also touches on its enduring legacy as a cautionary tale about the unpredictable aftermath of human invention.

TEXTS IN CONTEXT

Stephen Jay Gould / from *The Monster's Human Nature* (nonfiction)
Jericho Brown / *Dear Dr. Frankenstein* (poetry)
Brian Aldiss / *Super-Toys Last All Summer Long* (fiction)
Jon Turney / from *Frankenstein's Footsteps* (nonfiction)
Brian Fairrington / *Human Cloning* (cartoon)
Alison Hawthorne Deming / *Science* (poetry)
Cari Romm / from *The Enduring Scariness of the Mad Scientist* (nonfiction)

from The Monster's Human Nature

STEPHEN JAY GOULD

Stephen Jay Gould (1941–2002) was an American paleontologist, evolutionary biologist, science historian, and prolific essayist. Born and raised in Queens in New York City, he earned degrees in geology and philosophy from Antioch College in 1963 and completed graduate work at Columbia University in 1967. After completing his studies, he was hired by Harvard University, where he taught and researched for the rest of his life. In addition to his scientific writing, Gould was known for his popular essays on evolution in *Natural History* magazine. He also wrote several best-selling books about science, including *Ever Since Darwin* (1977), *The Panda's Thumb* (1980), *Hen's Teeth and Horse's*

Toes (1983), and *The Flamingo's Smile* (1985). All told, between 1965 and 2000, Gould published 479 peer-reviewed papers, 22 books, 300 essays, and 101 major book reviews. In "The Monster's Human Nature," Gould examines how authors tend to offer nuanced and humanized portrayals of monsters in books, which are then reinterpreted by Hollywood in movies that show monsters as quintessentially inhuman.

An old Latin proverb tells us to "beware the man of one book" — *cave ab homine unius libri.* Yet Hollywood knows only one theme in making monster movies, from the archetypal *Frankenstein* of 1931 to the recent mega-hit *Jurassic Park.* Human technology must not go beyond an intended order decreed by God or set by nature's laws. No matter how benevolent the purposes of the transgressor, such cosmic arrogance can only lead to killer tomatoes, very large rabbits with sharp teeth, giant ants in the Los Angeles sewers, or even larger blobs that swallow entire cities as they grow. Yet these films often use far more subtle books as their sources and, in so doing, distort the originals beyond all thematic recognition.

The trend began in 1931 with *Frankenstein,* Hollywood's first great monster "talkie" (though Mr. Karloff only grunted, while Colin Clive, as Henry Frankenstein, emoted). Hollywood decreed its chosen theme by the most "up front" of all conceivable strategies. The film begins with a prologue (even before the titles roll) featuring a well-dressed man standing on stage before a curtain, both to issue a warning about potential fright, and to announce the film's deeper theme as the story of "a man of science who sought to create a man after his own image without reckoning upon God."

In the movie, Dr. Waldman, Henry's old medical school professor, speaks of his pupil's "insane ambition to create life," a diagnosis supported by Frankenstein's own feverish words of enthusiasm: "I created it. I made it with my own hands from the bodies I took from graves, from the gallows, from anywhere."

The best of a cartload of sequels, *The Bride of Frankenstein* (1935), makes the favored theme even more explicit in a prologue featuring Mary Wollstonecraft Shelley, who published *Frankenstein* in 1818 when she was only nineteen years old, in conversation with her husband Percy and their buddy Lord Byron. She states: "My purpose was to write a moral lesson of the punishment that befell a mortal man who dared to emulate God."

Shelley's original *Frankenstein* is a rich book 5
of many themes, but I can find little therein to support the Hollywood reading. The text is neither a diatribe on dangers of technology nor a warning about overextended ambition against a natural order. We find no passages about disobeying God — an unlikely subject for Mary Shelley and her free-thinking friends (Percy had been expelled from Oxford in 1811 for publishing a defense of atheism). Victor Frankenstein (I do not know why Hollywood changed him to Henry) is guilty of a great moral failing, as we shall see later, but his crime is not technological transgression against a natural or divine order.

We can find a few passages about the awesome power of science, but these words are not negative. Professor Waldman, a sympathetic character in the book, states, for example, "They [scientists] penetrate into the recesses of nature, and show how she works in her hiding places. They ascend into the heavens; they have discovered how the blood circulates, and the nature of the air we breathe. They have acquired new and almost unlimited powers." We do learn that ardor without compassion or moral consideration can lead to trouble, but Shelley applies this argument to any endeavor, not especially to scientific discovery (her examples are, in fact, all political). Victor Frankenstein says:

> A human being in perfection ought always to preserve a calm and peaceful mind, and never to allow passion or a transitory desire to disturb his tranquility. I do not think that the pursuit of knowledge is an exception to this rule. If the study to which you apply yourself has a tendency to weaken your affections . . . then that study is certainly unlawful, that is to say, not befitting the human mind. If this rule were always observed . . . Greece had not been enslaved; Caesar would have spared his country; America would have been discovered more gradually, and the empires of Mexico and Peru had not been destroyed.

Victor's own motivations are entirely idealistic: "I thought, that if I could bestow animation upon lifeless matter, I might in process of time (although I now found it impossible) renew life where death had apparently devoted the body to corruption." Finally, as Victor lies dying in the Arctic, he makes his most forceful statement on the dangers of scientific ambition, but he only berates himself and his own failures, while stating that others might well succeed. Victor says his dying words to the ship's captain who found him on the polar ice: "Farewell, Walton! Seek happiness in tranquility, and avoid ambition, even if it be only the apparently innocent one of distinguishing yourself in science and discoveries. Yet why do I say this? I have myself been blasted in these hopes, yet another may succeed."

But Hollywood dumbed these subtleties down to the easy formula — "man must not go beyond what God and nature intended" (you almost have to use the old gender-biased language for such a simplistic archaicism) — and has been treading in its own footsteps ever since. The latest incarnation, *Jurassic Park,* substitutes a *Velociraptor* re-created from old DNA for Karloff cobbled together from bits and pieces of corpses, but hardly alters the argument an iota.

Karloff's *Frankenstein* contains an even more serious and equally prominent distortion of a theme that I regard as the primary lesson of Mary Shelley's book — another lamentable example of Hollywood's sense that the American public cannot tolerate even the slightest exercise in intellectual complexity. Why is the monster evil? Shelley provides a nuanced and subtle answer that, to me, sets the central theme of her book. But Hollywood opted for a simplistic solution, so precisely opposite to Shelley's intent that the movie can no longer claim to be telling a moral fable (despite protestations of the man in front of the curtain, or Mary Shelley herself in the sequel), and becomes instead, as I suppose the makers intended all along, a pure horror film. . . .

10 Shelley's monster is not evil by inherent constitution. He is born unformed — carrying the predispositions of human nature, but without the specific behaviors, that can only be set by upbringing and education. He is the Enlightenment's man of hope, whom learning and compassion might mold to goodness and wisdom. But he is also a victim of post-Enlightenment pessimism as the cruel rejection of his natural fellows drives him to fury and revenge. (Even as a murderer, the monster remains fastidious and purposive. Victor Frankenstein is the source of his anger, and he kills only the friends and lovers whose deaths will bring Victor most grief; he does not, like Godzilla of the Blob, rampage through cities.)

Mary Shelley chose her words carefully to take a properly nuanced position at a fruitfully intermediate point between nature and nurture — whereas Hollywood opted for nature alone to explain the monster's evil deeds. Frankenstein's creature is not inherently good by internal construction — a benevolent theory of "nature alone," but no different in mode of explanation from Hollywood's opposite version. He is, rather born *capable* of goodness, even with an *inclination* toward kindness, should circumstances of his upbringing call forth this favored response. In his final confession to Captain Walton, before heading north to immolate himself at the Pole, the monster says:

> My heart was fashioned to be *susceptible of love and sympathy*; and, when wrenched by misery to vice and hatred, it did not endure the violence of the change without torture, such as you cannot even imagine. [My italics to note Shelley's careful phrasing in terms of potentiality or inclination, rather than determinism.]

He then adds:

> Once my fancy was soothed with dreams of virtue, of fame, and of enjoyment. Once I falsely hoped to meet with beings who, pardoning my outward form, would love me for the excellent qualities which I was *capable of bringing forth.* I was nourished with high thoughts of honor and devotion. But now vice has degraded me beneath the meanest animal . . . When I call over the frightful catalogue of my deeds, I cannot believe that I am he whose thoughts were once filled with sublime and transcendent visions of the beauty and the majesty of goodness. But it is even so; the fallen angel becomes a malignant devil.

Why, then, does the monster turn to evil against an inherent inclination to goodness? Shelley gives us an interesting answer that seems almost trivial in invoking such a superficial reason, but that emerges as profound when we grasp her general theory of human nature. He becomes evil, of course, because humans reject him so violently and so unjustly. His resulting loneliness becomes unbearable. He states:

> And what was I? Of my creation and creator I was absolutely ignorant; but I knew that I possessed no money, no friends, no kind of property. I was, besides, endowed with a figure hideously deformed and loathsome . . . When I looked around, I saw and heard none like me. Was I then a monster, a blot upon the earth, from which all men fled, and whom all men disowned?

But why is the monster so rejected, if his feelings incline toward benevolence, and his acts to evident goodness? He certainly tries to act kindly, in helping (albeit secretly) the family in the hovel that serves as his hiding place:

> I had been accustomed, during the night, to steal a part of their store for my own consumption; but when I found that in doing this I inflicted pain on the cottagers. I abstained, and satisfied myself with berries, nuts, and roots, which I gathered from a neighboring wood. I discovered also another means through which I was enabled to assist their labors. I found that the youth spent a great part of each day in collecting wood for the family fire; and, during the night, I often took his tools, the use of which I quickly discovered, and brought home firing sufficient for the consumption of several days.

15 Shelley tells us that all humans reject and even loathe the monster for a visceral reason of literal superficiality: his truly terrifying ugliness — a reason both heartrending in its deep injustice, and profound in its biological accuracy and philosophical insight about the meaning of human nature.

The monster, by Shelley's description, could scarcely have been less attractive in appearance. Victor Frankenstein describes the first sight of his creature alive:

> How can I describe my emotions at this catastrophe, or how delineate the wretch whom with such infinite pains and care I had endeavored to form? His limbs were in proportion, and I had selected his features as beautiful. Beautiful! — Great God! His yellow skin scarcely covered the work of muscles and arteries beneath; his hair was a lustrous black, and flowing; his teeth of a pearly whiteness; but these luxuriances only formed a more horrid

> contrast with his watery eyes, that seemed almost of the same color as the dun white sockets in which they were set, his shriveled complexion, and straight black lips.

Moreover, at his hyper-NBA height of eight feet, the monster scares the bejeezus out of all who cast eyes upon him.

The monster quickly grasps this unfair source of human fear and plans a strategy to overcome initial reactions, and to prevail by goodness of soul. He presents himself first to the blind old father in the hovel above his hiding place and makes a good impression. He hopes to win the man's confidence, and thus gain a favorable introduction to the world of sighted people. But, in his joy at acceptance, he stays too long. The man's son returns and drives the monster away — as fear and loathing overwhelm any inclination to hear about inner decency.

The monster finally acknowledges his inability to overcome visceral fear at his ugliness; his resulting despair and loneliness drive him to evil deeds:

> I am malicious because I am miserable; am I not shunned and hated by all mankind? . . . Shall I respect man when he contemns me? Let him live with me in the interchange of kindness, and, instead of injury, I would bestow every benefit upon him with tears of gratitude at his acceptance. But that cannot be; the human senses are insurmountable barriers to our union. . . .

Frankenstein's creature becomes a monster because he is cruelly ensnared by one of the deepest predispositions of our biological inheritance — our instinctive aversion toward seriously malformed individuals. (Konrad Lorenz, the most famous ethologist of the last generation, based much of his theory on the primacy of this inborn rule.) We are now appalled by the injustice of such a predisposition, but this proper moral feeling is an evolutionary latecomer, imposed by human consciousness upon a much older mammalian pattern.

We almost surely inherit such an instinctive 20
aversion to serious malformation, but remember that nature can only supply a predisposition, while culture shapes specific results. And now we can grasp — for Mary Shelley presented the issue to us so wisely — the true tragedy of Frankenstein's monster, and the moral dereliction of Victor himself. The predisposition for aversion toward ugliness can be overcome by learning and understanding. I trust that we have all trained ourselves in this essential form of compassion, and that we all work hard to suppress that frisson of rejection (which in honest moments we all admit we feel), and to judge people by their qualities of soul, not by their external appearances.

Frankenstein's monster was a good man in an appallingly ugly body. His countrymen could have been educated to accept him, but the person responsible for that instruction — his creator, Victor Frankenstein — ran away from his foremost duty, and abandoned his creation at first sight. Victor's sin does not lie in misuse of technology, or hubris in emulating God; we cannot find these themes in Mary Shelley's account. Victor failed because he followed a predisposition of human nature — visceral disgust at the monster's appearance — and did not undertake the duty of any creator or parent: to teach his own charge and to educate others in acceptability.

He could have schooled his creature (and not left the monster to learn language by eavesdropping and by scrounging for books in a hiding place under a hovel). He could have told the world what he had done. He could have introduced his benevolent and educated monster to people prepared to judge him on merit. But he took one look at his handiwork, and ran away forever. In other words, he bowed to a base aspect of our common nature, and did not accept the particular moral duty of our potential nurture:

> I had worked hard for nearly two years, for the sole purpose of infusing life into an inanimate body. For this I had deprived myself of rest and health. I had desired it with an ardor that far exceeded moderation; but now that I had finished, the beauty of the dream vanished, and breathless horror and disgust filled my heart. Unable to endure the aspect of the being I had created, I rushed out of the room . . . A mummy again endued with animation could not be so hideous as that wretch. I had gazed on him while unfinished; he was ugly then; but when those muscles and joints were rendered capable of motion, it became a thing such as even Dante could not have conceived. . . .

Mary Shelley wrote a moral tale, not about hubris or technology, but about responsibility to all creatures of feeling and to the products of one's own hand. The monster's misery arose from the moral failure of other humans, not from his own inherent and unchangeable constitution. Charles Darwin later invoked the same theory of human nature to remind us of duties to all people in universal bonds of brotherhood: "If the misery of our poor be caused not by the laws of nature, but by our institutions, great is our sin."

[1995]

QUESTIONS

1. According to Stephen Jay Gould, how have film productions of *Frankenstein* altered people's perception of the themes of the novel? If you have seen any of the *Frankenstein* films, to what extent do you agree with him?
2. How does Gould characterize Victor Frankenstein? Having read the novel, do you agree with that characterization? Explain.
3. Gould refers to "a theme that I regard as the primary lesson of Mary Shelley's book" (para. 9). Before explaining that theme or lesson, he then goes on to discuss the 1931 film. How would you paraphrase the theme of that film as Gould presents it? For what reasons, according to Gould, did Hollywood change the theme? Do you agree that the theme he presents is the "primary lesson" of the novel? Explain.
4. Discuss the differences between *nature* and *nurture* as Gould categorizes them. Which of the two does Gould hold more responsible for the monster's behavior? Which do you believe is primarily responsible? Explain, using examples from the novel to support your response.
5. In paragraph 20 Gould refers to "the true tragedy of Frankenstein's monster and the moral dereliction of Victor himself." What is that "true tragedy," according to Gould? Read carefully Gould's series of parallel "could have" statements. Do you agree that those statements explain the novel's tragedy? Explain.
6. Gould concludes with a strong claim: "Mary Shelley wrote a moral tale, not about hubris or technology, but about responsibility to all creatures of feeling and to the products of one's own hand. The monster's misery arose from the moral failure of other humans, not from his own inherent and unchangeable constitution." How compelling do you find Gould's argument? How accurate a reading of the novel do you believe it presents? Explain.

Dear Dr. Frankenstein

JERICHO BROWN

Jericho Brown (b. 1976) is an award-winning American poet from Shreveport, Louisiana. Brown, who completed his undergraduate studies at Dillard University, earned an MFA from the University of New Orleans and a PhD from the University of Houston. His first book,

Please (2008), won the American Book Award, and his second book, *The New Testament* (2014), won the 2015 Anisfield-Wolf Book Award. Brown is also the recipient of a Whiting Writers Award and fellowships from the Guggenheim Foundation, the National Endowment for the Arts, and the Radcliffe Institute for Advanced Study at Harvard University. Brown is currently an associate professor in English and creative writing at Emory University. He also serves as an assistant editor at *Callaloo*, the oldest continuously running African American literary magazine. In "Dear Dr. Frankenstein," Brown draws parallels between Shelley's *Frankenstein* and the Christian creation myth.

I, too know the science of building men
Out of fragments in little light
Where I'll be damned if lightning don't

Strike as I forget one
May have a thief's thumb,

Another, a murderer's arm,
And watch the men I've made leave
Like an idea I meant to write down,

Like a vehicle stuck
In reverse, like the monster

God came to know the moment
Adam named animals and claimed
Eve, turning from heaven to her

As if she was his
To run. No word he said could be tamed.

No science. No design. Nothing taken
Gently into his hand or your hand or mine,
Nothing we erect is our own.

[2014]

QUESTIONS

1. What does Jericho Brown mean by "the science of building men" (l. 1)? To what creative act do you think he refers? Explain.
2. In line 7 Brown's speaker refers to "the men I've made leave." What do you make of that statement? How does the content of the first two similes — of the idea and the stuck vehicle — help clarify the speaker's meaning or intent? According to the third simile (ll. 10–15), what created the monster that "God came to know"?
3. What does the poet suggest in lines 14 and 15: "As if she was his / To run"? Why is it that "no word he said could be tamed"?
4. To whom do the pronouns in line 17 ("his," "your," "mine") refer? Who are the "we" of the final line of the poem? Explain.
5. How would you paraphrase the final stanza? Why is the poem addressed to Dr. Frankenstein? Explain.

Super-Toys Last All Summer Long

BRIAN ALDISS

Born in 1925 in Norfolk, Engand, Brian Aldiss is a prolific author of short stories, criticism, novels, drama, and poetry. He is most widely known as a writer of science fiction. He was awarded the title of Officer of the Order of the British Empire in 2005 in recognition of his contribution to literature. *A.I. Artificial Intelligence*, the 2001 science fiction film directed by Steven Spielberg, is based on Aldiss's 1969 short story "Super-Toys Last All Summer Long," which follows.

In Mrs. Swinton's garden, it was always summer. The lovely almond trees stood about it in perpetual leaf. Monica Swinton plucked a saffron-colored rose and showed it to David.

"Isn't it lovely?" she said.

David looked up at her and grinned without replying. Seizing the flower, he ran with it across the lawn and disappeared behind the kennel where the mower-vator crouched, ready to cut or sweep or roll when the moment dictated. She stood alone on her impeccable plastic gravel path.

She had tried to love him.

5 When she made up her mind to follow the boy, she found him in the courtyard floating the rose in his paddling pool. He stood in the pool engrossed, still wearing his sandals.

"David, darling, do you have to be so awful? Come in at once and change your shoes and socks."

He went with her without protest into the house, his dark head bobbing at the level of her waist. At the age of three, he showed no fear of the ultrasonic dryer in the kitchen. But before his mother could reach for a pair of slippers, he wriggled away and was gone into the silence of the house.

He would probably be looking for Teddy.

Monica Swinton, twenty-nine, of graceful shape and lambent eye, went and sat in her living room, arranging her limbs with taste. She began by sitting and thinking; soon she was just sitting. Time waited on her shoulder with the maniac slowth it reserves for children, the insane, and wives whose husbands are away improving the world. Almost by reflex, she reached out and changed the wavelength of her windows. The garden faded; in its place, the city center rose by her left hand, full of crowding people, blowboats, and buildings (but she kept the sound down). She remained alone. An overcrowded world is the ideal place in which to be lonely.

10 The directors of Synthank were eating an enormous luncheon to celebrate the launching of their new product. Some of them wore the plastic face-masks popular at the time. All were elegantly slender, despite the rich food and drink they were putting away. Their wives were elegantly slender, despite the food and drink they too were putting away. An earlier and less sophisticated generation would have regarded them as beautiful people, apart from their eyes.

Henry Swinton, Managing Director of Synthank, was about to make a speech.

"I'm sorry your wife couldn't be with us to hear you," his neighbor said.

"Monica prefers to stay at home thinking beautiful thoughts," said Swinton, maintaining a smile.

"One would expect such a beautiful woman to have beautiful thoughts," said the neighbor.

15 Take your mind off my wife, you bastard, thought Swinton, still smiling.

He rose to make his speech amid applause.

After a couple of jokes, he said, "Today marks a real breakthrough for the company. It is now almost ten years since we put our first synthetic life-forms on the world market. You all know what a success they have been, particularly the miniature dinosaurs. But none of them had intelligence.

"It seems like a paradox that in this day and age we can create life but not intelligence. Our first selling line, the Crosswell Tape, sells best of all, and is the most stupid of all." Everyone laughed.

"Though three-quarters of the overcrowded world are starving, we are lucky here to have more than enough, thanks to population control. Obesity's our problem, not malnutrition. I guess there's nobody round this table who doesn't have a Crosswell working for him in the small intestine, a perfectly safe parasite tapeworm that enables its host to eat up to fifty percent more food and still keep his or her figure. Right?" General nods of agreement.

"Our miniature dinosaurs are almost equally stupid. Today, we launch an intelligent synthetic life-form — a full-size serving-man.

"Not only does he have intelligence, he has a controlled amount of intelligence. We believe people would be afraid of a being with a human brain. Our serving-man has a small computer in his cranium.

"There have been mechanicals on the market with mini-computers for brains — plastic things without life, super-toys — but we have at last found a way to link computer circuitry with synthetic flesh."

David sat by the long window of his nursery, wrestling with paper and pencil. Finally, he stopped writing and began to roll the pencil up and down the slope of the desk-lid.

"Teddy!" he said.

Teddy lay on the bed against the wall, under a book with moving pictures and a giant plastic soldier. The speech-pattern of his master's voice activated him and he sat up.

"Teddy! I can't think what to say!"

Climbing off the bed, the bear walked stiffly over to cling to the boy's leg. David lifted him and set him on the desk.

"What have you said so far?"

"I've said — " He picked up his letter and stared hard at it. "I've said, 'Dear Mummy, I hope you're well just now. I love you . . .'"

There was a long silence, until the bear said, "That sounds fine. Go downstairs and give it to her."

Another long silence.

"It isn't quite right. She won't understand."

Inside the bear, a small computer worked through its program of possibilities. "Why not do it again in crayon?"

When David did not answer, the bear repeated his suggestion. "Why not do it again in crayon?"

David was staring out of the window. "Teddy, you know what I was thinking? How do you tell what are real things from what aren't real things?"

The bear shuffled its alternatives. "Real things are good."

"I wonder if time is good. I don't think Mummy likes time very much. The other day, lots of days ago, she said that time went by her. Is time real, Teddy?"

"Clocks tell the time. Clocks are real. Mummy has clocks so she must like them. She has a clock on her wrist next to her dial."

David started to draw a jumbo jet on the back of his letter. "You and I are real, Teddy, aren't we?"

The bear's eyes regarded the boy unflinchingly. "You and I are real, David." It specialized in comfort.

Monica walked slowly about the house. It was almost time for the afternoon post to come over the wire. She punched the Post Office number on the dial on her wrist, but nothing came through. A few minutes more.

She could take up her painting. Or she could dial her friends. Or she could wait till Henry came home. Or she could go up and play with David. . . .

She walked out into the hall and to the bottom of the stairs.

"David!"

No answer. She called again and a third time.

"Teddy!" she called, in sharper tones.

"Yes, Mummy!" After a moment's pause, Teddy's head of golden fur appeared at the top of the stairs.

"Is David in his room, Teddy?"

"David went into the garden, Mummy."

"Come down here, Teddy!"

She stood impassively, watching the little furry figure as it climbed down from step to step on its stubby limbs. When it reached the bottom, she picked it up and carried it into the living room. It lay unmoving in her arms, staring up at her. She could feel just the slightest vibration from its motor.

"Stand there, Teddy. I want to talk to you." She set him down on a tabletop, and he stood as she requested, arms set forward and open in the eternal gesture of embrace.

"Teddy, did David tell you to tell me he had gone into the garden?"

The circuits of the bear's brain were too simple for artifice. "Yes, Mummy."

"So you lied to me."

"Yes. Mummy."

"Stop calling me Mummy! Why is David avoiding me? He's not afraid of me, is he?"

"No. He loves you."

"Why can't we communicate?"

"David's upstairs."

The answer stopped her dead. Why waste time talking to this machine? Why not simply go upstairs and scoop David into her arms and talk to him, as a loving mother should to a loving son? She heard the sheer weight of silence in the house, with a different quality of silence pouring out of every room. On the upper landing, something was moving very silently — David, trying to hide away from her. . . .

He was nearing the end of his speech now. The guests were attentive; so was the Press, lining two walls of the banqueting chamber, recording Henry's words and occasionally photographing him.

"Our serving-man will be, in many senses, a product of the computer. Without computers, we could never have worked through the sophisticated biochemics that go into synthetic flesh. The serving-man will also be an extension of the computer — for he will contain a computer in his own head, a microminiaturized computer capable of dealing with almost any situation he may encounter in the home. With reservations, of course." Laughter at this; many of those present knew the heated debate that had engulfed the Synthank boardroom before the decision had finally been taken to leave the serving-man neuter under his flawless uniform.

"Amid all the triumphs of our civilization — yes, and amid the crushing problems of overpopulation too — it is sad to reflect how many millions of people suffer from increasing loneliness and isolation. Our serving-man will be a boon to them: he will always answer, and the most vapid conversation cannot bore him.

"For the future, we plan more models, male and female — some of them without the limitations of this first one, I promise you! — of more advanced design, true bio-electronic beings.

"Not only will they possess their own computer, capable of individual programming; they will be linked to the World Data Network. Thus everyone will be able to enjoy the equivalent of an Einstein in their own homes. Personal isolation will then be banished forever!"

He sat down to enthusiastic applause. Even the synthetic serving-man, sitting at the table dressed in an unostentatious suit, applauded with gusto.

Dragging his satchel, David crept round the side of the house. He climbed on to the ornamental seat under the living-room window and peeped cautiously in.

His mother stood in the middle of the room. Her face was blank, its lack of expression scared him. He watched fascinated. He did not move; she did not move. Time might have stopped, as it had stopped in the garden.

At last she turned and left the room. After waiting a moment, David tapped on the window. Teddy looked round, saw him, tumbled off the table, and came over to the window. Fumbling with his paws, he eventually got it open.

They looked at each other.

"I'm no good, Teddy. Let's run away!"

"You're a very good boy. Your Mummy loves you."

Slowly, he shook his head. "If she loved me, then why can't I talk to her?"

"You're being silly, David. Mummy's lonely. That's why she had you."

"She's got Daddy. I've got nobody 'cept you, and I'm lonely."

Teddy gave him a friendly cuff over the head. "If you feel so bad, you'd better go to the psychiatrist again."

"I hate that old psychiatrist — he makes me feel I'm not real." He started to run across the lawn. The bear toppled out of the window and followed as fast as its stubby legs would allow.

Monica Swinton was up in the nursery. She called to her son once and then stood there, undecided. All was silent.

Crayons lay on his desk. Obeying a sudden impulse, she went over to the desk and opened it. Dozens of pieces of paper lay inside. Many of them were written in crayon in David's clumsy writing, with each letter picked out in a color different from the letter preceding it. None of the messages was finished.

"My dear Mummy, How are you really, do you love me as much — "

"Dear Mummy, I love you and Daddy and the sun is shining — "

"Dear dear Mummy, Teddy's helping me write to you. I love you and Teddy — "

"Darling Mummy, I'm your one and only son and I love you so much that some times — "

"Dear Mummy, you're really my Mummy and I hate Teddy — "

"Darling Mummy, guess how much I love — "

"Dear Mummy, I'm your little boy not Teddy and I love you but Teddy — "

"Dear Mummy, this is a letter to you just to say how much how ever so much — "

Monica dropped the pieces of paper and burst out crying. In their gay inaccurate colors, the letters fanned out and settled on the floor.

Henry Swinton caught the express home in high spirits, and occasionally said a word to the synthetic serving-man he was taking home with him. The serving-man answered politely and punctually, although his answers were not always entirely relevant by human standards.

The Swintons lived in one of the ritziest city-blocks, half a kilometer above the ground. Embedded in other apartments, their apartment had no windows to the outside; nobody wanted to see the overcrowded external world. Henry unlocked the door with his retina pattern-scanner and walked in, followed by the serving-man.

At once, Henry was surrounded by the friendly illusion of gardens set in eternal summer. It was amazing what Whologram could do to create huge mirages in small spaces. Behind its roses and wisteria stood their house; the deception was complete: a Georgian mansion appeared to welcome him.

"How do you like it?" he asked the serving-man.

"Roses occasionally suffer from black spot."

"These roses are guaranteed free from any imperfections."

"It is always advisable to purchase goods with guarantees, even if they cost slightly more."

"Thanks for the information," Henry said dryly. Synthetic lifeforms were less than ten years old, the old android mechanicals less than sixteen; the faults of their systems were still being ironed out, year by year.

He opened the door and called to Monica.

She came out of the sitting-room immediately and flung her arms round him, kissing him ardently on cheek and lips. Henry was amazed.

Pulling back to look at her face, he saw how she seemed to generate light and beauty. It was months since he had seen her so excited. Instinctively, he clasped her tighter.

"Darling, what's happened?"

"Henry, Henry — oh, my darling, I was in despair . . . but I've just dialed the afternoon post and — you'll never believe it! Oh, it's wonderful!"

"For heavens sake, woman, what's wonderful?"

He caught a glimpse of the heading on the photostat in her hand, still moist from the wall-receiver: Ministry of Population. He felt the color drain from his face in sudden shock and hope.

"Monica . . . oh . . . Don't tell me our number's come up!"

"Yes, my darling, yes, we've won this week's parenthood lottery! We can go ahead and conceive a child at once!"

He let out a yell of joy. They danced round the room. Pressure of population was such that reproduction had to be strict, controlled. Childbirth required government permission. For this moment, they had waited four years. Incoherently they cried their delight.

They paused at last, gasping and stood in the middle of the room to laugh at each other's happiness. When she had come down from the nursery, Monica had de-opaqued the windows so that they now revealed the vista of garden beyond. Artificial sunlight was growing long and golden across the lawn — and David and Teddy were staring through the window at them.

Seeing their faces, Henry and his wife grew serious.

"What do we do about them?" Henry asked.

"Teddy's no trouble. He works well."

"Is David malfunctioning?"

"His verbal communication center is still giving trouble. I think he'll have to go back to the factory again."

"Okay. We'll see how he does before the baby's born. Which reminds me — I have a surprise for you: help just when help is needed! Come into the hall and see what I've got."

As the two adults disappeared from the room, boy and bear sat down beneath the standard roses.

"Teddy — I suppose Mummy and Daddy are real, aren't they?"

Teddy said, "You ask such silly questions, David. Nobody knows what *real* really means. Let's go indoors."

"First I'm going to have another rose!" Plucking a bright pink flower, he carried it with him into the house. It could lie on the pillow as he went to sleep. Its beauty and softness reminded him of Mummy.

[1969]

QUESTIONS

1. What are some early indications that Brian Aldiss's story is set in the future?
2. What clues are there about the nature of David and Teddy? What in the text leads the reader to suspect that the mother might also be a robot?
3. With which character does the reader sympathize? Is this ironic?
4. Considering that this story was published in 1969, which details are especially prescient?
5. What do paragraphs 90–118 suggest about Aldiss's attitude toward values? What do they suggest about the relationship between technology and humanity?
6. In what respects could this story be regarded as a cautionary tale? Explain.

from **Frankenstein's Footsteps**

JON TURNEY

Jon Turney is a British science writer and former features editor of the *Times Higher Education Supplement*. He has taught at Imperial College and was head of the Department of Science and Technology Studies at University College London. He has also served as the popular science editor at Penguin Press. Turney is the author of many popular science books, including *A Quark for Mister Mark: 100 Poems about Science* (2000), *Frankenstein's Footsteps: Science, Genetics, and Popular Culture* (2000), *Lovelock and Gaia* (2003), *The Rough Guide to the Future* (2010), and *I, Superorganism: Learning to Love Your Inner Ecosystem* (2015). Turney currently lives and writes in Bristol, UK. In the following excerpt from his book *Frankenstein's Footsteps*, Turney examines the lasting appeal of the Frankenstein myth and traces its intersection with modern biological science.

The accumulated retellings of the *Frankenstein* myth are now so numerous as almost to defy empirical analysis. Today, we encounter Frankenstein in many forms. Any of the old films may still be seen as late-night TV fillers, or on video. There are even two films which incorporate versions of the origin myth of the novel, mixing together the story of Mary, Percy and Byron by the lakeside with the creation of the monster.[1] New films continue to incorporate elements of the story, from *Demon Seed,* in which the monster is a computer which finds a way of inseminating a human female, to *Robocop*.[2] Numerous editions of the novel remain in print, and new variations on the story continue to appear in printed fiction. Some of these, like Steven Gallagher's *Chimera,* are filmed in turn. Others, like Hilary Bailey's striking *Frankenstein's Bride,* remain as solely literary efforts. . . .

In addition, as with all truly frightening myths, we have tried to tame *Frankenstein* by making fun of it. Karloff's monster has been domesticated, in media ranging from the 1960s US television series *The Munsters* to the British children's comic the *Beano*, which features Frankie Stein. A distant descendant of Karloff even featured as Frank in the British Conservative government's television commercials for shares in its soon to be privatised electricity generation concern in the early 1990s. This taken-for-grantedness shows how well the cultural script has been learned. In consequence, the single word 'Frankenstein' is seen constantly as a metaphor in media commentary of all kinds, especially political commentary.[3]

---

[1]That is, Ken Russell's *Gothic* (1986) and Roger Corman's *Frankenstein Unbound* (1990). The latter is based on Brian Aldiss's novel of the same name.

[2]Again, elements of the story may be found in a wider range of films. *Silence of the Lambs* (1991) for example, about the pursuit of a serial killer, portrays a man planning to reassemble a body, or at least its whole skin, from parts stripped from his numerous victims.

[3]Just a taste: a computer search of the text of the British *Financial Times*, perhaps the country's most serious title of all, between 1990 and 1994, yields fifty-two uses of 'Frankenstein.' Aside from references to film and TV and the other arts, the monster was coupled with:

the Channel Tunnel
the poll tax
the US Internal Revenue Service
artificial intelligence
municipal planning officers
a 'monster' recycling plant
Iraq/Saddam Hussein (several times)
privatisation of electricity (that commercial)
a Swedish politician
Soviet central planning
genetic research
the Labour Party
the Department of National Heritage
the Ulster Freedom Fighters
a soccer analyst
'machines' in general

(*Continued*)

Why, then, has the story endured? Is it simply because the frame is so open at various points that it is infinitely adaptable? Or are there particular reasons, culturally general enough to read across all the retellings, with all their differences of detail, yet still specific to the culture which we share with Mary Shelley — broadly, the culture of modernity?

The first answer is to try to isolate what has endured in all the renderings of the myth since 1818. The story, for all its familiarity, is still a frightening one. It is frightening because it depicts a human enterprise which is out of control, and which turns on its creator. So much carries over from the earlier myths about the getting of knowledge. But *Frankenstein* is about science. What is more, the science is pursued, if not always with the best of intentions, then for motives with which we can readily identify. In the most striking retellings, the myth is never a straightforward anti-science story. There is something admirable about Victor Frankenstein, about Henry Frankenstein in James Whale's film, even about Peter Cushing's Baron Frankenstein. Even so, our sympathies are always torn between Frankenstein and his monster. The *Frankenstein* script, in its most salient forms, incorporates an ambivalence about science, method and motive, which is never resolved.

(*Continued*)

virtual reality
fashion journalism
the (much revived) *New York Post*
US trade laws.

Other newspapers show a similar pattern: a mix of political and technological links, mostly serious, with a scattering of light-hearted uses in other areas.

The pattern with *Dracula,* which has achieved similar currency, is rather different. Of forty-six instances in the *Financial Times* over the same period, only ten occur outside arts reviews or commentary, and most are light-hearted references to effects of the sun or daylight, the colour black (in fashion), or bloodletting. There is also a geographical link with Romania, and specifically Transylvania. The only remotely serious political references are to US Defense programmes (hard to kill) and a reference to Romania's ex-president. There are no direct references to technology.

The retention of science in all the later derivatives 5 of the story is the most striking feature of the myth. After all, in the original text, once Victor's narrative begins, the creation of the monster is accomplished in a scant thirty pages, in which space is also given to the background and education of the monster's creator. The scientific details are few. After Victor's 'brilliant light' dawns we never learn more than how he eventually 'collected the instruments of life around me, that I might infuse a spark of life into the lifeless thing that lay at my feet.' Yet it is those first thirty pages that supply the seeds of almost all of the images derived from *Frankenstein* which appear in so many variations in later stories about science and scientists.

Among others, we can distinguish in *Frankenstein* models for the scientist whose good intentions blind him to the true nature of his enterprise: 'wealth was an inferior object; but what glory would attend the discovery if I could banish disease from the human frame and render man invulnerable to any but a violent death!' Victor proclaims. And so say all of us mortal readers. But Victor also personifies the scientist as Faustian knowledge-seeker; 'the world was to me a secret which I desired to divine,' he remembers, and he recalls that 'none but those who have experienced them can conceive of the enticements of science' or, as a narrow materialist, 'On my education my father had taken the greatest precautions that my mind should be impressed with no supernatural horrors . . . a churchyard was to me merely the receptacle of bodies deprived of life.' There are also hints that science has some drive of its own, external to the will of the scientist and eventually overwhelming him. 'Natural philosophy,' Victor reflects sadly, 'is the genius that has regulated my fate.' Amidst all the simplifications, deletions and elaborations of the original, the identification of Victor as a scientist has remained inviolate. It is science which gives him his success, and that success gives him power over life. Even though his character was first drawn before biology was a separate discipline, Frankenstein is always a proto-biologist.

So the endurance of the myth plainly does testify to a deep disquiet at the potentialities inherent in scientific discovery in general, and the science of life in particular. And it is a disquiet which Mary Shelley appears to have tapped into at a remarkably early stage in the development of modern life science. The appearance of the story, and its ready acceptance, so soon after Erasmus Darwin's speculations were published, suggest that unease at the prospect of science attaining powers over life is readily evoked in the public mind. So I agree with all those who have suggested that the *Frankenstein* myth both expresses and reinforces an undercurrent of feelings about science; that in George Levine's phrase, it 'articulates a deeply felt cultural neurosis.' But what, exactly, does this neurosis consist of?

It is clear that what we now call biomedical science, or the possibility of a technologically effective biology, has played a key role in shaping the modern attitude to science. We have always been prisoners of the body, victims of morbidity and mortality, and we desire the power that biology might give us to relieve these burdens. In more recent times, this can be seen from other kinds of evidence. Medical and biological stories have long accounted for a large proportion of the press reporting of science, for example.[4] Editors appear to regard such stories as of more interest to their readers than other scientific items. The news-consuming public, in consequence, may be more aware of events in biological science than in other fields.[5] The nature of their interest has also been long established. Turn the pages of major newspaper from the early years of this century, the *San Francisco Chronicle*, say, and you will find front-page stories on radical new surgical procedures, on the possibility of choosing the sex of a baby, on proposed scientific techniques for prolonging life, and on putative cures for cancer. These stories show the early convergence of news values and the territory of biomedicine. Biological research and medical practice mean birth, sex and death; suffering, disease and disability.

Biologists who become visible to the public are aware of the hopes and fears their science raises. As the French geneticist and popular writer Jean Rostand — of whom we shall hear more — attested in the 1950s: 'The best way to gain an idea of what the human, *emotional* value of biology can be, is to look through some of the strange correspondence that a biologist receives . . . people take him for a magician, a healer, a confessor, a friend.'[6]

Among the letters he describes are those 10
from couples seeking to replace a lost child with a perfect twin, queries on the consequences of mixed marriage, people seeking confirmation of paternity by blood typing, enhancement of their children's intelligence, rejuvenation for the elderly, sex changes or cures for infertility. Rostand concludes that 'the science that provokes such appeals, prayers and confessions, the science that penetrates into private life, and whose warnings or advice can influence a marriage, a decision to have children, a person's destiny, is no ordinary science.'[7]

These examples express very well the idea that biology is indeed 'no ordinary science' for the public. It is the science which touches on

[4]For typical surveys showing the predominance of biomedical coverage see Jones et al., 1978; Einseidel, 1992.

[5]In fact, Durant and colleagues suggest, on the basis of findings from a national survey in Britain, that 'medical science may occupy a central and key position within the popular representation of science. In other words, what people know and feel about medicine may help to shape what they know and feel about science as a whole.' Durant et al., 1992.

[6]Rostand, 1959, pp. 32–3.

[7]Ibid., p. 33.

the most potent wishes of human life. 'The realisation that biology offers the prospect of ultimate control over or transformation of the living realm, just as physical science controls and transforms the physical environment, thus evokes deep rooted feelings. This realisation by itself can produce either positive or negative reactions. . . .

Frankenstein . . . is set on transforming humans directly. If he can discover the secret of life, then he can father a new species. To do so, he will experiment directly on the body.

Here, I think, Mary intuited the power of a threat which would come to seem graver as time went by. In a world where everything appeared to be subject to change, where it was becoming apparent that 'all that is solid melts into air', there was one sphere of existence which was exempt. The natural world, although it could be reshaped by physical onslaught on the landscape, although it could be despoiled or laid waste, was not yet open to technological manipulation. The forms and varieties of creatures, the hierarchy of species, the biological imperatives of existence, were fixed points in an ever-changing world.[8]

The human body, too, as I have suggested, provided an unchanging ground for experience of other changes. This does not mean, of course, that *experience* of the body, or ideas about its constitution, did not change.[9] But the body itself was not seen as changing by those experiencing the first rush of modernity. While the dead body had been anatomised for two centuries, in pursuit of a science of the interior which had made a deep impression on Renaissance and early modern culture, that science was still largely descriptive. The living body was not yet susceptible to the kind of science being developed in other areas, in which 'the object to be known . . . will be known in such a way that it can be changed.'[10] Frankenstein the character, and *Frankenstein* the novel, are both steeped in the anatomical tradition. But this anatomist goes further. Mary Shelley made the necessary imaginative leap, and fashioned an image of a science working on the body to transform it, a science which might one day come to pass. Now that we are indeed building such a science, we can see that it has always been a part of the modern project. She saw this right at the start. If, as Berman says, Goethe's key insight is the ambivalence stemming from the fact that 'the deepest horrors of Faustian development spring from its most honorable aims and its most authentic achievements', then the best horror story would be in the power which we simultaneously most desire, and most dread: power over the body. *Frankenstein* focused attention on that prospect nearly two centuries ago. We still feel the pull of the story because that power is now ours for the asking.

[1998]

[8]Formally, the idea that species were defined forms was itself relatively recent, but by the time Mary Shelley wrote it was well established. Thus the great French naturalist Buffon wrote in the 1770s that 'species are the only beings in Nature; Perpetual beings, as ancient and as permanent as Nature herself; each may be considered as a whole, independent of the world, a whole that was counted as one in the creation and that, consequently, is but one unit in Nature.' Quoted in Jacob, 1982, p. 52. In addition, the fact that myth and folklore abounded with monsters, hybrids and chimerae in unknown regions did not mean that the creatures people saw around them did not behave in an orderly way.

[9]See Porter, 1991, for a useful commentary.

[10]See Rabinow's remark on the Human Genome Project as epitomising modern rationality, as quoted above, p. 2.

Bibliography

Durant, J., Evans, G. and Thomas, G. (1992) 'Public understanding of science in Britain: the role of medicine in the popular representation of science,' *Public Understanding of Science*, 1, pp. 161–82.

Einseidel, E. (1992) 'Framing science and technology in the Canadian press,' *Public Understanding of Science*, 1, pp. 89–102.

Jacob, F. (1982) *The Logic of Life. A History of Heredity*. New York, Pantheon Books.

James, F. and Field, J. (1994) 'Frankenstein and the spark of being,' *History Today*, 449, pp 47–53.

Jones, G., Connell, I. and Meadows, J. (1978) *The Presentation of Science by the Media*. Leicester, Primary Communications Research Centre.

Porter, R. (1991) 'History of the body,' in P. Burke (ed.) *New Perspectives in Historical Writing*. Cambridge, Polity Press.

Rabinow, P. (1992) 'Artificiality and enlightenment: from sociobiology to biosociality,' in J. Crary and S. Kwinter (eds) *Incorporations*. New York, Zone Books.

Rostand, J. (1959) *Can Man Be Modified*? trans. J. Griffin. Secker & Warburg.

QUESTIONS

1. What, according to Jon Turney, explains the ubiquity and endurance of *Frankenstein* as a cultural reference?
2. Turney writes: "In the most striking retellings, the myth is never a straightforward anti-science story. There is something admirable about Victor Frankenstein, about Henry Frankenstein in James Whale's film, even about Peter Cushing's Baron Frankenstein. Even so, our sympathies are always torn between Frankenstein and his monster. The *Frankenstein* script, in its most salient forms, incorporates an ambivalence about science, method and motive, which is never resolved" (para. 4). Is *Frankenstein* ambivalent about science, as Turney says, or does it provide a straightforward anti-science theme? Explain.
3. How does Turney characterize Victor Frankenstein in paragraph 6? To what extent do the details from the novel itself support that characterization?
4. Turney says that the Frankenstein myth, in George Levine's phrase, "articulates a deeply felt cultural neurosis" regarding science, and poses the question, "But what, exactly, does this neurosis consist of" (para. 7)? How would you paraphrase the answer he provides in paragraphs 8–11? To what extent do you agree with Turney? To what extent might Shelley, were she alive today?
5. In paragraph 11 Turney writes that biological science is "the science which touches on the most potent wishes of human life." What, according to Turney, are those "potent wishes"? How do these wishes contribute to the enduring appeal of *Frankenstein*?
6. "Here, I think, Mary intuited the power of a threat which would come to seem graver as time went by," writes Turney (para. 13). Why would he use the word "threat"? What was being threatened? Explain.
7. In the last paragraph, Turney claims that "the best horror story would be rooted in the power which we simultaneously most desire, and most dread: power over the body. *Frankenstein* focused attention on that prospect nearly two centuries ago." If we do have that power, why would we greet it with both desire and dread? Do you agree with Turney that readers "still feel the pull of the story because that power is now ours for the asking"? Explain.

Human Cloning

BRIAN FAIRRINGTON

Brian Fairrington is a nationally syndicated, award-winning cartoonist. He graduated from Arizona State University in 1999 with a B.S. in political science and an M.A. in communications. Fairrington's syndicated cartoons have appeared in numerous publications, including *Time, Newsweek,* the *New York Times*, and *USA Today*, and are

known both for their provocative editorial commentary and conservative bent. In the cartoon that follows, Fairrington uses the Frankenstein myth to comment on the possibility of human cloning in the United States.

Courtesy Brian Fairringon/Cagle Cartoons

[2005]

QUESTIONS

1. What do you see in the cartoon? Describe the images, the paper the man is holding, and the captions.
2. What is the cartoonist implying about cloning? What does the cartoon suggest about larger issues concerning science, society, and ethics?
3. Why does the cartoonist cast one of the figures as Frankenstein's monster? Explain.

Science

ALISON HAWTHORNE DEMING

Alison Hawthorne Deming (b. 1946) is an American poet, essayist, and teacher from Connecticut. She is also the great-granddaughter of writer Nathaniel Hawthorne. She earned an M.F.A. from Vermont College of Fine Arts in 1983 and worked in public health for fifteen years, including a decade of work with Planned Parenthood. Currently, she is a professor of creative writing at the University of Arizona. Deming's first book of poetry, *Science and Other Poems* (1994), won the Walt Whitman Award from the Academy of American Poets. Her three other poetry books include *The Monarch: A Poem Sequence* (1997); *Genius Loci* (2005); and *Rope* (2009). Deming has also published a book of essays blending nature writing with memoir, *Temporary Homelands* (1996). Her numerous awards include a Wallace Stegner Fellowship, two National Endowment for the Arts fellowships, and a Guggenheim Fellowship. In "Science," Deming uses the memory of a science fair as an avenue to consider the larger implications of scientific progress.

Then it was the future, though what's arrived
isn't what we had in mind, all chrome and
cybernetics, when we set up exhibits
in the cafeteria for the judges
to review what we'd made of our hypotheses.

The class skeptic (he later refused to sign
anyone's yearbook, calling it a sentimental
degradation of language) chloroformed mice,
weighing the bodies before and after
to catch the weight of the soul,

wanting to prove the invisible
real as a bagful of nails. A girl
who knew it all made cookies from euglena,
a one-celled compromise between animal and
plant,
she had cultured in a flask.

We're smart enough, she concluded,
to survive our mistakes, showing photos of
farmland,
poisoned, gouged, eroded. No one believed
he really had built it when a kid no one knew
showed up with an atom smasher, confirming
that
the tiniest particles could be changed
into something even harder to break.
And one whose mother had cancer (hard to
admit now,
it was me) distilled the tar of cigarettes
to paint it on the backs of shaven mice.

She wanted to know what it took,
a little vial of sure malignancy,
to prove a daily intake smaller
than a single aspirin could finish
something as large as a life. I thought of this

because, today, the dusky seaside sparrow
became extinct. It may never be as famous
as the pterodactyl or the dodo,
but the last one died today, a resident
of Walt Disney World where now its tissue samples
lie frozen, in case someday we learn to clone
one from a few cells. Like those instant dinosaurs

that come in a gelatin capsule—just add water
and they inflate. One other thing this
brings to mind. The euglena girl won first prize

both for science and, I think, in retrospect, for hope.

[1994]

QUESTIONS

1. The poem begins, "Then it was the future, though what's arrived / isn't what we had in mind," shifting between past and present tense verbs ("was," "what's," "isn't," "had"). Which tense prevails throughout the poem? What does the speaker mean by "then it was the future"?
2. Who are the four contestants in the science contest? What is each experiment about? What does each "young scientist" attempt to discover or prove?
3. Why do you think the speaker of the poem refers to herself in the third person? What effect does that have on your reading of the poem?
4. What is the incident that has prompted the speaker's recollections? Why does that incident prompt both her memory and reflections?
5. Why does the poet present the "euglena girl" as the winner? Why does the speaker conclude that she won "both for science and, I think, in retrospect, hope"?

from The Enduring Scariness of the Mad Scientist

CARI ROMM

Cari Romm is an American journalist. She earned a B.A. in English from Northwestern University in 2012 and earned a master's in journalism at Columbia University in 2014. She is a former assistant editor at the *Atlantic* and is currently the associate editor for *New York Magazine*'s "The Science of Us," a website devoted to the science of human behavior. In this excerpt from an interview with Stuart Vyse, a professor of psychology at Connecticut College, Romm examines why people today still find Dr. Frankenstein so unsettling.

Today, many of the things that would once have seemed like horror-story fodder are scientific reality: Animals have been cloned, for example, and human faces have been transplanted. Surgical robots are trusted with human lives. But still, as the boundaries of human knowledge are continually pushed, the trope of the mad scientist endures. What is it about the character that makes it so chilling? When so much of Halloween is based on the supernatural — the ghosts, the goblins, the vampires — why are scientists so often lumped in with the rest of the haunted-house cast?

"Science and reason are supposed to be the antidote to paranormal beliefs, and yet fictional scientists often appear as villains of paranormal horror films," psychologist Stuart Vyse recently noted in *Psychology Today*, and mad-scientist-themed decorations abound in seasonal aisles as October 31 approaches. "Halloween is a kind of Rorschach test of our common fears," he wrote.

I spoke to Vyse, a professor at Connecticut College who specializes in the psychology of superstition, about why the mad scientist is one of them.

* * *

CARI ROMM What are some of the differences between the mad scientist and the typical horror villain?

5 **STUART VYSE** The typical horror villains, like Michael Meyers in *Halloween* and [Freddy Kreuger in] *Nightmare on Elm Street*, those are just sort of homicidal maniacs. They are mentally ill, psychopathic. They often have an overblown or misguided revenge motive to them. And they often seem to be superhuman — they survive under circumstances when others would not, or they have superhuman strength. So you have great power, and you have behavior that's frightening because it's so unpredictable and beyond the realm of normal experience. And then, of course, the basic thing, which is that they're out to kill people.

In the case of the mad scientist, it's interesting — only in some cases the scientist is truly described as being mad. Sometimes they are, which means they're not going to share the same predictable forms of behavior or the same goals as others.

But other times it's not so much that they're mentally ill or psychopathic or even evil, but simply that their goals are wrong according to the moral structure of the story. They are too driven by curiosity to know — almost in a Garden of Eden sort of way — certain knowledge that shouldn't be theirs, and yet they want it. And so you have that same sort of scene that goes through the Garden of Eden with Adam and Eve. There's also the Faust legend, where Faust wanted to know things and experience things that were not supposed to be within his realm, and actually sold his soul to the devil in order to experience them. They're almost infatuated or intoxicated by motivations that get us all in trouble.

ROMM What's so frightening about that sense of curiosity?

VYSE It's the unintended consequences. For example, the motives for making genetically modified foods may be very good, and they may have a good end, but people fear that there are unknown side effects — that the foods that are made this way will have some other effect on them. So many of the advances of science have been shown to have side effects. They're a mixed bag, and people worry about the downside of these achievements.

ROMM What would be an example of that?

VYSE A contemporary example — it's an old movie, but it's been remade a number of times — is *The Fly*. He's a scientist, he's interested in learning how to transport objects from one place to another, but it goes awry. It's a very sort of Faustian thing, where he ends up with knowledge that has an unintended consequence that's scary. Even Frankenstein's goals are not really evil. He may be sort of an egomaniac, taking on more power than he should be taking on. But he's driven by an interest in science and wanting to see if he can do this — in some ways, it's maybe even a positive goal, of wanting to cheat death.

But science is this powerful force that can produce unpredictable results. I grew up in the 50s and 60s, and back in that black-and-white horror film era, the great fear came from atomic energy. And Godzilla and all these sort of giant caterpillars and other things were supposed to have happened because of atomic energy. There was this fear, because of the bomb, of the power of science to create fearful creatures or to harm us in some way. That's the equivalent of the typical villains, Halloween movie villains' superhuman strength or unusual power. Science has that too. And so I think that's part of the reason why scientists are sometimes placed in that fearful role.

ROMM Is there an equivalent modern fear? Something that's taken the place of the giant radiation-infused monsters?

VYSE I think that at the moment, the main fear is that science has an unholy alliance with profit motives — that with pharmaceutical companies and vaccines and GMOs, that science is being used in that way. There are a number of contemporary science-fiction films in which corporate interests [play a role] — for example, the first *Alien* movie, in which the corporation wants to keep the creature alive in order to see if there's some commercial benefit to it. That's the kind of thing that's going on now.

ROMM In other realms, we don't find the combination of genius and mental illness to be as threatening — there's no "mad artist" trope, for example. Van Gogh isn't scary. What is it about science in particular that makes the mad scientist frightening?

VYSE It's the idea that they have powerful knowledge. As an example, I'm an experimental psychologist. I'm a scientist. But if I'm traveling on an airplane and somebody asks me what I do for a living, if I say I'm a psychologist, they sort of become nervous and worried that I'm going to analyze them. There's this sense that you have knowledge, that you'll be able to find out things about me that I don't want you to find out. And I think in the case of science, that's exactly the case — that genius, combined with the power of science, is frightening, is potentially something that could be used against you in an evil way. If you think about it, there are a number of horror films in which the villain is a psychiatrist or a psychologist. It's combining this idea of special knowledge that can be used powerfully to make that person frightening.

I would put Hannibal Lecter in a similar category. He's not really a mad scientist, but part of what makes him so scary is that he's so brilliant, and his great intelligence is in fact used against people.

ROMM You've done a lot of research on the psychology of superstition. How does the idea of the mad scientist fit in with that?

VYSE Part of the fear of science comes from people who are not rational thinkers, who are motivated by emotion and fear and don't have a good understanding of scientific processes. So for example, the evidence is there that the vaccines are safe, that there's no great harm in taking them. There's great benefit in taking them. In the scientific world, there's no ambiguity about that. But people are just refusing to believe that and to accept that evidence, and instead are clinging to other ideas. And I do believe that one of the common threads in [superstition and fear of science] is a poor understanding of critical thinking, of the role of evidence in logic, in debate.

But here's the irony: I know lots of people who are scientific thinkers who love those movies. And I grew up on them. So I'm not sure there's any cause and effect relationship. It's true that horror movies play upon aspects of science that are genuinely worthy of concern, and it's easy to create a fearful character by mixing a little bit of unexpected scientific effect and maybe an unstable character who can't be trusted. It makes for good drama. I would be hesitant to say that the real-life problem we have with acceptance of scientific thinking is encouraged or discouraged by movies, but it's clear that the things people are afraid of in one domain also work in the movie domain.

* * *

Sometimes, as was the case of Mary Shelley, science inspires art — and sometimes, art inspires science.

In Minnesota in 1931, a hundred years after Shelley described her inspiration for *Frankenstein*, a boy named Earl Bakken was captivated by actor Colin Clive's portrayal of the mad scientist. "What intrigued me the most, as I sat through the movie again and again," he later recalled, "was the creative spark of Dr. Frankenstein's electricity. Through the power of his wildly flashing laboratory apparatus, the doctor restored life to the
20 unliving."

Decades later, Bakken — the founder of medical-device company Medtronic — would, through a creative spark of his own, invent the wearable, portable pacemaker.

[2014]

QUESTIONS

1. What is the nature of the paradox that Cari Romm presents in the first paragraph? How does the quotation from Stuart Vyse help explain that paradox?
2. How does Vyse characterize the "mad scientist"? To what extent do you agree with his characterization? Explain.
3. What are Frankenstein's motives, according to Vyse? Would he call Frankenstein a mad scientist? Explain.
4. How does Vyse characterize the relationship between superstition and fear of science?
5. What is the purpose of the last section of the article, about Earl Bakken? What does it suggest about the legacy of the novel *Frankenstein* and about the consequences of scientific progress?

LITERATURE IN CONVERSATION
Frankenstein and the Ethics of Creation

1. Victor Frankenstein: Mad scientist? Visionary? Egomaniac? Idealist? Benevolent seeker? Hubristic overreacher? Stephen Jay Gould, Jon Turney, and Stuart Vyse all discuss the motives of Victor Frankenstein as they characterize him. Paraphrase each characterization and then compare and contrast them. Write an essay determining which of these three characterizations most resembles your own perspective from having read the novel.
2. In her essay "Poetry and Science: A View from the Divide," Alison Hawthorne Deming, author of the poem "Science," wrote, "Much is to be gained when scientists raid the evocative techniques of literature and when poets raid the language and mythology of scientists. The challenge for a poet is not merely to pepper the lines with spicy words and facts, but to know enough science that the concepts and vocabulary become part of the fabric of one's mind, so that in the process of composition a metaphor or paradigm from the domain of science is as likely to crop up as is one from literature or her own backyard." Write an essay that discusses and evaluates how both "Dear Dr. Frankenstein" and "Science" relate to Deming's above assertion, making specific reference to each poem.
3. Knowledge and neglect might be seen as two prominent themes of the novel *Frankenstein*. Is Victor Frankenstein's fatal crime one of neglect — abandoning his creation — or one of seeking forbidden knowledge beyond the boundaries of proper human endeavor? Write an essay that answers that question, referring to *Frankenstein* and at least two other texts.
4. Stephen Jay Gould writes, "Victor's sin does not lie in misuse of technology or hubris in emulating God; we cannot find these themes in Mary Shelley's account. Victor failed because he followed a predisposition of human nature — visceral disgust at the monster's appearance — and did not undertake the duty of any creator or parent: to teach his own charge and to educate others in acceptability." Using reference to *Frankenstein* and two other texts, write an essay in which you examine the extent to which Gould's statement accurately accounts for Victor Frankenstein's "failure."
5. One might separate the Texts in Context into two groups. In one, the cartoon, the story by Brian Aldiss, and the poems by Alison Hawthorne Deming and Jericho Brown provide creative and artistic responses to science or to *Frankenstein*; in the other, Stephen Jay Gould, Jon Turney, and Cari Romm provide discussion and analysis of *Frankenstein*, the novel, and of Frankenstein, the myth. Which of the two groups provides more insight into the meaning of *Frankenstein*, as you, a person living in the second decade of the twenty-first century, understand it? Explain.
6. Now, nearly two centuries after its initial publication, what does *Frankenstein* have to say to us about our relationship with emerging scientific technology and bioethics? What is its message concerning science — about how scientific research and development are moving so rapidly that we have trouble keeping up — and how can we respond to that message?
7. If you haven't already done so, view the classic 1931 James Whale film, *Frankenstein*, starring Boris Karloff as the monster. Compare and contrast the film with Mary Shelley's novel. Write an essay that examines the extent to which the film departs from the novel. In your essay refer to at least two of the Texts in Context as evidence to support your assessment.

FICTION

Sonny's Blues

JAMES BALDWIN

James Baldwin (1924–1987) — poet, novelist, playwright, essayist, activist — was one of the most influential figures of American literature during the latter half of the twentieth century. Born in Harlem to a single mother, he was later adopted by his stepfather, who was a preacher. Baldwin himself became a Pentecostal preacher when he was fourteen, but by the time he was seventeen, he had moved away from his family in Harlem to live among more open-minded artists and writers in Greenwich Village. In the late 1940s, Baldwin went to Europe, where he lived as an expatriate in France — and periodically in Turkey — for most of his life, returning to the United States to lecture and write. He felt that the United States of the mid-twentieth century was inimical to artists, especially black artists. In addition to the novels *Go Tell It on the Mountain* (1953), *Giovanni's Room* (1956), *If Beale Street Could Talk* (1974), and *Just Above My Head* (1979), Baldwin wrote *Notes of a Native Son* (1955) and *The Fire Next Time* (1963) — two explosive books that gave passionate voice to the civil rights movement. Baldwin also wrote poetry, plays, and essays. In "Sonny's Blues," Baldwin uses the conflict between two brothers who have chosen different paths — one a teacher and one a musician with a drug addiction — to explore the shifting values of one family in postwar America.

I read about it in the paper, in the subway, on my way to work. I read it, and I couldn't believe it, and I read it again. Then perhaps I just stared at it, at the newsprint spelling out his name, spelling out the story. I stared at it in the swinging lights of the subway car, and in the faces and bodies of the people, and in my own face, trapped in the darkness which roared outside.

It was not to be believed and I kept telling myself that, as I walked from the subway station to the high school. And at the same time I couldn't doubt it. I was scared, scared for Sonny. He became real to me again. A great block of ice got settled in my belly and kept melting there slowly all day long, while I taught my classes algebra. It was a special kind of ice. It kept melting, sending trickles of ice water all up and down my veins, but it never got less. Sometimes it hardened and seemed to expand until I felt my guts were going to come spilling out or that I was going to choke or scream. This would always be at a moment when I was remembering some specific thing Sonny had once said or done.

When he was about as old as the boys in my classes his face had been bright and open, there was a lot of copper in it; and he'd had wonderfully direct brown eyes, and great gentleness and privacy. I wondered what he looked like now. He had been picked up, the evening before, in a raid on an apartment downtown, for peddling and using heroin.

I couldn't believe it: but what I mean by that is that I couldn't find any room for it anywhere inside me. I had kept it outside me for a long time. I hadn't wanted to know. I had had suspicions, but I didn't name them, I kept putting them away. I told myself that Sonny was wild, but he wasn't crazy. And he'd always been a good boy, he hadn't ever turned hard or evil or disrespectful, the way kids can, so quick, so quick, especially in Harlem. I didn't want to believe that I'd ever see my brother going down, coming to nothing, all that light in his face gone out, in the condition I'd already seen so many others. Yet it had happened and here I was, talking about algebra to a lot of boys who might, every one of them for all I knew, be popping off needles every time they went to the head. Maybe it did more for them than algebra could.

I was sure that the first time Sonny had ever had horse, he couldn't have been much older than these boys were now. These boys, now, were living as we'd been living then, they were growing up with a rush and their heads bumped abruptly against the low ceiling of their actual possibilities. They were filled with rage. All they really knew were two darknesses, the darkness of their lives, which was now closing in on them, and the darkness of the movies, which had blinded them to that other darkness, and in which they now, vindictively, dreamed, at once more together than they were at any other time, and more alone.

When the last bell rang, the last class ended, I let out my breath. It seemed I'd been holding it for all that time. My clothes were wet — I may have looked as though I'd been sitting in a steam bath, all dressed up, all afternoon. I sat alone in the classroom a long time. I listened to the boys outside, downstairs, shouting and cursing and laughing. Their laughter struck me for perhaps the first time. It was not the joyous laughter which — God knows why — one associates with children. It was mocking and insular, its intent to denigrate. It was disenchanted, and in this, also, lay the authority of their curses. Perhaps I was listening to them because I was thinking about my brother and in them I heard my brother. And myself.

One boy was whistling a tune, at once very complicated and very simple, it seemed to be pouring out of him as though he were a bird, and it sounded very cool and moving through all that harsh, bright air, only just holding its own through all those other sounds.

I stood up and walked over to the window and looked down into the courtyard. It was the beginning of the spring and the sap was rising in the boys. A teacher passed through them every now and again, quickly, as though he or she couldn't wait to get out of that courtyard, to get those boys out of their sight and off their minds. I started collecting my stuff. I thought I'd better get home and talk to Isabel.

The courtyard was almost deserted by the time I got downstairs. I saw this boy standing in the shadow of a doorway, looking just like Sonny. I almost called his name. Then I saw that it wasn't Sonny, but somebody we used to know, a boy from around our block. He'd been Sonny's friend. He'd never been mine, having been too young for me, and, anyway, I'd never liked him. And now, even though he was a grown-up man, he still hung around that block, still spent hours on the street corners, was always high and raggy. I used to run into him from time to time and he'd often work around to asking me for a quarter or fifty cents. He always had some real good excuse, too, and I always gave it to him, I don't know why.

But now, abruptly, I hated him. I couldn't stand the way he looked at me, partly like a dog, partly like a cunning child. I wanted to ask him what the hell he was doing in the school courtyard.

He sort of shuffled over to me, and he said, "I see you got the papers. So you already know about it."

"You mean about Sonny? Yes, I already know about it. How come they didn't get you?"

He grinned. It made him repulsive and it also brought to mind what he'd looked like as a kid. "I wasn't there. I stay away from them people."

"Good for you." I offered him a cigarette and I watched him through the smoke. "You come all the way down here just to tell me about Sonny?"

"That's right." He was sort of shaking his head and his eyes looked strange, as though they were about to cross. The bright sun deadened his damp dark brown skin and it made his eyes look yellow and showed up the dirt in his kinked hair. He smelled funky. I moved a little away from him and I said, "Well, thanks. But I already know about it and I got to get home."

"I'll walk you a little ways," he said. We started walking. There were a couple of kids still loitering in the courtyard and one of them said goodnight to me and looked strangely at the boy beside me.

"What're you going to do?" he asked me. "I mean, about Sonny?"

"Look. I haven't seen Sonny for over a year. I'm not sure I'm going to do anything. Anyway, what the hell *can* I do?"

"That's right," he said quickly, "ain't nothing you can do. Can't much help old Sonny no more, I guess."

It was what I was thinking and so it seemed to me he had no right to say it.

"I'm surprised at Sonny, though," he went on — he had a funny way of talking, he looked straight ahead as though he were talking to himself — "I thought Sonny was a smart boy, I thought he was too smart to get hung."

"I guess he thought so too," I said sharply, "and that's how he got hung. And how about you? You're pretty goddamn smart, I bet."

Then he looked directly at me, just for a minute. "I ain't smart," he said. "If I was smart, I'd have reached for a pistol a long time ago."

"Look. Don't tell *me* your sad story, if it was up to me, I'd give you one." Then I felt guilty — guilty, probably, for never having supposed that the poor bastard *had* a story of his own, much less a sad one, and I asked, quickly, "What's going to happen to him now?"

He didn't answer this. He was off by himself some place. "Funny thing," he said, and from his tone we might have been discussing the quickest way to get to Brooklyn, "when I saw the papers this morning, the first thing I asked myself was if I had anything to do with it. I felt sort of responsible."

I began to listen more carefully. The subway station was on the corner, just before us, and I stopped. He stopped, too. We were in front of a bar and he ducked slightly, peering in, but whoever he was looking for didn't seem to be there. The juke box was blasting away with something black and bouncy and I half watched the barmaid as she danced her way from the juke box to her place behind the bar. And I watched her face as she laughingly responded to something someone said to her, still keeping time to the music. When she smiled one saw the little girl, one sensed the doomed, still-struggling woman beneath the battered face of the semi-whore.

"I never *give* Sonny nothing," the boy said finally, "but a long time ago I come to school high and Sonny asked me how it felt." He paused, I couldn't bear to watch him, I watched the barmaid, and I listened to the music which seemed to be causing the pavement to shake. "I told him it felt great." The music stopped, the barmaid paused and watched the juke box until the music began again. "It did."

All this was carrying me some place I didn't want to go. I certainly didn't want to know how it felt. It filled everything, the people, the houses, the music, the dark, quicksilver barmaid, with menace; and this menace was their reality.

"What's going to happen to him now?" I asked again.

"They'll send him away some place and they'll try to cure him." He shook his head. "Maybe he'll even think he's kicked the habit. Then they'll let him loose" — he gestured, throwing his cigarette into the gutter. "That's all."

"What do you mean, that's *all*?"

But I knew what he meant.

"I *mean*, that's *all*." He turned his head and looked at me, pulling down the corners of his mouth. "Don't you know what I mean?" he asked, softly.

"How the hell *would* I know what you mean?" I almost whispered it, I don't know why.

35 "That's right," he said to the air, "how would *he* know what I mean?" He turned toward me again, patient and calm, and yet I somehow felt him shaking, shaking as though he were going to fall apart. I felt that ice in my guts again, the dread I'd felt all afternoon; and again I watched the barmaid, moving about the bar, washing glasses, and singing. "Listen. They'll let him out and then it'll just start all over again. That's what I mean."

"You mean — they'll let him out. And then he'll just start working his way back in again. You mean he'll never kick the habit. Is that what you mean?"

"That's right," he said, cheerfully. "*You* see what I mean."

"Tell me," I said at last, "why does he want to die? He must want to die, he's killing himself, why does he want to die?"

He looked at me in surprise. He licked his lips. "He don't want to die. He wants to live. Don't nobody want to die, ever."

40 Then I wanted to ask him — too many things. He could not have answered, or if he had, I could not have borne the answers. I started walking. "Well, I guess it's none of my business."

"It's going to be rough on old Sonny," he said. We reached the subway station. "This is your station?" he asked. I nodded. I took one step down. "Damn!" he said, suddenly. I looked up at him. He grinned again. "Damn it if I didn't leave all my money home. You ain't got a dollar on you, have you? Just for a couple of days, is all."

All at once something inside gave and threatened to come pouring out of me. I didn't hate him any more. I felt that in another moment I'd start crying like a child.

"Sure," I said. "Don't sweat." I looked in my wallet and didn't have a dollar, I only had a five. "Here," I said. "That hold you?"

He didn't look at it — he didn't want to look at it. A terrible closed look came over his face, as though he were keeping the number on the bill a secret from him and me. "Thanks," he said, and now he was dying to see me go. "Don't worry about Sonny. Maybe I'll write him or something."

45 "Sure," I said. "You do that. So long."

"Be seeing you," he said. I went on down the steps.

And I didn't write Sonny or send him anything for a long time. When I finally did, it was just after my little girl died, he wrote me back a letter which made me feel like a bastard.

Here's what he said:

Dear Brother,

You don't know how much I needed to hear from you. I wanted to write you many a time but I dug how much I must have hurt you and so I didn't write. But now I feel like a man who's been trying to climb up out of some deep, real deep and funky hole and just saw the sun up there, outside. I got to get outside.

I can't tell you much about how I got here. I mean I don't know how to tell you. I guess I was afraid of something or I was trying to escape from something and you know I have never been very strong in the head (smile). I'm glad Mama and Daddy are dead and can't see what's happened to their son and I swear if I'd known what I was doing I would never have hurt you so, you and a lot of other fine people who were nice to me and who believed in me.

I don't want you to think it had anything to do with me being a musician. It's more than that. Or maybe less than that. I can't get anything straight in my head down here and I try not to think about what's going to happen to me when I get outside again. Sometime I think I'm going to flip and *never* get outside and sometime I think I'll come straight back. I tell you one thing, though, I'd rather blow my brains out than go through this again. But that's what they all say, so they tell me. If I tell you when I'm coming to New York and if you could meet me, I sure would appreciate it. Give my love to Isabel and the kids and I was sure sorry to hear about little Gracie. I wish I could be like Mama and say the Lord's will be done, but I don't know it seems to me that trouble is the one thing that never does get stopped and I don't know what good it does to blame it on the Lord. But maybe it does some good if you believe it.

Your brother,
SONNY

Then I kept in constant touch with him and I sent him whatever I could and I went to meet him when he came back to New York. When I saw him many things I thought I had forgotten came flooding back to me. This was because I had begun, finally, to wonder about Sonny, about the life that Sonny lived inside. This life, whatever it was, had made him older and thinner and it had deepened the distant stillness in which he had always moved. He looked very unlike my baby brother. Yet, when he smiled, when we shook hands, the baby brother I'd never known looked out from the depths of his private life, like an animal waiting to be coaxed into the light.

"How you been keeping?" he asked me.

"All right. And you?"

"Just fine." He was smiling all over his face. "It's good to see you again."

"It's good to see you."

The seven years' difference in our ages lay between us like a chasm: I wondered if these years would ever operate between us as a bridge. I was remembering, and it made it hard to catch my breath, that I had been there when he was born; and I had heard the first words he had ever spoken. When he started to walk, he walked from our mother straight to me. I caught him just before he fell when he took the first steps he ever took in this world.

"How's Isabel?"

"Just fine. She's dying to see you."

"And the boys?"

"They're fine, too. They're anxious to see their uncle."

"Oh, come on. You know they don't remember me."

"Are you kidding? Of course they remember you."

He grinned again. We got into a taxi. We had a lot to say to each other, far too much to know how to begin.

As the taxi began to move, I asked, "You still want to go to India?"

He laughed. "You still remember that. Hell, no. This place is Indian enough for me."

"It used to belong to them," I said.

And he laughed again. "They damn sure knew what they were doing when they got rid of it."

Years ago, when he was around fourteen, he'd been all hipped on the idea of going to India. He read books about people sitting on rocks, naked, in all kinds of weather, but mostly bad, naturally, and walking barefoot through hot coals and arriving at wisdom. I used to say that it sounded to me as though they were getting away from wisdom as fast as they could. I think he sort of looked down on me for that.

"Do you mind," he asked, "if we have the driver drive alongside the park? On the west side — I haven't seen the city in so long."

"Of course not," I said. I was afraid that I might sound as though I were humoring him, but I hoped he wouldn't take it that way.

So we drove along, between the green of the park and the stony, lifeless elegance of hotels and apartment buildings, toward the vivid, killing streets of our childhood. These streets hadn't changed, though housing projects jutted up out of them now like rocks in the middle of a boiling sea. Most of the houses in which we had grown up had vanished, as had the stores from which we had stolen, the basements in which we had first tried sex, the rooftops from which we had hurled tin cans and bricks. But houses exactly like the houses of our past yet dominated the landscape, boys exactly like the boys we once had been found themselves smothering in these houses, came down into the streets for light and air and found themselves encircled by disaster. Some escaped the trap, most didn't. Those who got out always left something of themselves behind, as some animals amputate a leg and leave it in the trap. It might be said, perhaps, that I had escaped, after all, I was a school teacher; or that Sonny had, he hadn't lived in Harlem for years. Yet, as the cab moved uptown through streets which seemed, with a rush, to darken with dark people, and as I covertly studied Sonny's face, it came to me that what we both were seeking through our separate cab windows was that part of ourselves which had been left behind. It's always at the hour of trouble and confrontation that the missing member aches.

70 We hit 110th Street and started rolling up Lenox Avenue. And I'd known this avenue all my life, but it seemed to me again, as it had seemed on the day I'd first heard about Sonny's trouble, filled with a hidden menace which was its very breath of life.

"We almost there," said Sonny.

"Almost." We were both too nervous to say anything more.

We live in a housing project. It hasn't been up long. A few days after it was up it seemed uninhabitably new, now, of course, it's already rundown. It looks like a parody of the good, clean, faceless life — God knows the people who live in it do their best to make it a parody. The beat-looking grass lying around isn't enough to make their lives green, the hedges will never hold out the streets, and they know it. The big windows fool no one, they aren't big enough to make space out of no space. They don't bother with the windows, they watch the TV screen instead. The playground is most popular with the children who don't play at jacks, or skip rope, or roller skate, or swing, and they can be found in it after dark. We moved in partly because it's not too far from where I teach, and partly for the kids; but it's really just like the houses in which Sonny and I grew up. The same things happen, they'll have the same things to remember. The moment Sonny and I started into the house I had the feeling that I was simply bringing him back into the danger he had almost died trying to escape.

Sonny has never been talkative. So I don't know why I was sure he'd be dying to talk to me when supper was over the first night. Everything went fine, the oldest boy remembered him, and the youngest boy liked him, and Sonny had remembered to bring something for each of them; and Isabel, who is really much nicer than I am, more open and giving, had gone to a lot of trouble about dinner and was genuinely glad to see him. And she's always been able to tease Sonny in a way that I haven't. It was nice to see her face so vivid again and to hear her laugh and watch her make Sonny laugh. She wasn't, or, anyway, she didn't seem to be, at all uneasy or embarrassed. She chatted as though there were no subject which had to be avoided and she got Sonny past his first, faint stiffness. And thank God she was there, for I was filled with that icy dread again. Everything I did seemed awkward to me, and everything I said sounded freighted with hidden meaning. I was trying to remember everything I'd heard about dope addiction and I couldn't help watching Sonny for signs. I wasn't doing it out of malice. I was trying to find out something about my brother. I was dying to hear him tell me he was safe.

75 "Safe!" my father grunted, whenever Mama suggested trying to move to a neighborhood which might be safer for children. "Safe, hell! Ain't no place safe for kids, nor nobody."

He always went on like this, but he wasn't, ever, really as bad as he sounded, not even on weekends, when he got drunk. As a matter of fact, he was always on the lookout for "something a little better," but he died before he found it. He died suddenly, during a drunken weekend in the middle of the war, when Sonny was fifteen. He and Sonny hadn't ever got on too well. And this was partly because Sonny was the apple of his father's eye. It was because he loved Sonny so much and was frightened for him, that he was always fighting with him. It doesn't do any good to fight with Sonny. Sonny just moves back, inside himself, where he can't be reached. But the principal reason that they never hit it off is that they were so much alike. Daddy was big and rough and loud-talking, just the opposite of Sonny, but they both had — that same privacy.

Mama tried to tell me something about this, just after Daddy died. I was home on leave from the army.

This was the last time I ever saw my mother alive. Just the same, this picture gets all mixed up in my mind with pictures I had of her when she was younger. The way I always see her is the way she used to be on a Sunday afternoon, say, when the old folks were talking after the big Sunday dinner. I always see her wearing pale blue. She'd be sitting on the sofa. And my father would be sitting in the easy chair, not far from her. And the living room would be full of church folks and relatives. There they sit, in chairs all around the living room, and the night is creeping up outside, but nobody knows it yet. You can see the darkness growing against the windowpanes and you hear the street noises every now and again, or maybe the jangling beat of a tambourine from one of the churches close by, but it's real quiet in the room. For a moment nobody's talking, but every face looks darkening, like the sky outside. And my mother rocks a little from the waist, and my father's eyes are closed. Everyone is looking at something a child can't see. For a minute they've forgotten the children. Maybe a kid is lying on the rug, half asleep. Maybe somebody's got a kid in his lap and is absent-mindedly stroking the kid's head. Maybe there's a kid, quiet and big-eyed, curled up in a big chair in the corner. The silence, the darkness coming, and the darkness in the faces frightens the child obscurely. He hopes that the hand which strokes his forehead will never stop — will never die. He hopes that there will never come a time when the old folks won't be sitting around the living room, talking about where they've come from, and what they've seen, and what's happened to them and their kinfolk.

But something deep and watchful in the child knows that this is bound to end, is already ending. In a moment someone will get up and turn on the light. Then the old folks will remember the children and they won't talk any more that day. And when light fills the room, the child is filled with darkness. He knows that every time this happens he's moved just a little closer to that darkness outside. The darkness outside is what the old folks have been talking about. It's what they've come from. It's what they endure. The child knows that they won't talk any more because if he knows too much about what's happened to *them*, he'll know too much too soon, about what's going to happen to *him*.

The last time I talked to my mother, I remember I was restless. I wanted to get out and see Isabel. We weren't married then and we had a lot to straighten out between us.

There Mama sat, in black, by the window. She was humming an old church song, *Lord, you brought me from a long ways off*. Sonny was out somewhere. Mama kept watching the streets.

"I don't know," she said, "if I'll ever see you again, after you go off from here. But I hope you'll remember the things I tried to teach you."

"Don't talk like that," I said, and smiled. "You'll be here a long time yet."

She smiled, too, but she said nothing. She was quiet for a long time. And I said, "Mama, don't you worry about nothing. I'll be writing all the time, and you be getting the checks. . . ."

"I want to talk to you about your brother," she said, suddenly. "If anything happens to me he ain't going to have nobody to look out for him."

"Mama," I said, "ain't nothing going to happen to you *or* Sonny. Sonny's all right. He's a good boy and he's got good sense."

"It ain't a question of his being a good boy," Mama said, "nor of his having good sense. It ain't only the bad ones, nor yet the dumb ones that gets sucked under." She stopped, looking at me. "Your Daddy once had a brother," she said, and she smiled in a way that made me feel she was in pain. "You didn't never know that, did you?"

"No," I said, "I never knew that," and I watched her face.

"Oh, yes," she said, "your Daddy had a brother." She looked out of the window again. "I know you never saw your Daddy cry. But *I* did—many a time, through all these years."

90 I asked her, "What happened to his brother? How come nobody's ever talked about him?"

This was the first time I ever saw my mother look old.

"His brother got killed," she said, "when he was just a little younger than you are now. I knew him. He was a fine boy. He was maybe a little full of the devil, but he didn't mean nobody no harm."

Then she stopped and the room was silent, exactly as it had sometimes been on those Sunday afternoons. Mama kept looking out into the streets.

"He used to have a job in the mill," she said, "and, like all young folks, he just liked to perform on Saturday nights. Saturday nights, him and your father would drift around to different places, go to dances and things like that, or just sit around with people they knew, and your father's brother would sing, he had a fine voice, and play along with himself on his guitar. Well, this particular Saturday night, him and your father was coming home from some place, and they were both a little drunk and there was a moon that night, it was bright like day. Your father's brother was feeling kind of good, and he was whistling to himself, and he had his guitar slung over his shoulder. They was coming down a hill and beneath them was a road that turned off from the highway. Well, your father's brother, being always kind of frisky, decided to run down this hill, and he did, with that guitar banging and clanging behind him, and he ran across the road, and he was making water behind a tree. And your father was sort of amused at him and he was still coming down the hill, kind of slow. Then he heard a car motor and that same minute his brother stepped from behind the tree, into the road, in the moonlight. And he started to cross the road. And your father started to run down the hill, he says he don't know why. This car was full of white men. They was all drunk, and when they seen your father's brother they let out a great whoop and holler and they aimed the car straight at him. They was having fun, they just wanted to scare him, the way they do sometimes, you know. But they was drunk. And I guess the boy, being drunk, too, and scared, kind of lost his head. By the time he jumped it was too late. Your father says he heard his brother scream when the car rolled over him, and he heard the wood of that guitar when it give, and he heard them strings go flying, and he heard them white men shouting, and the car kept on a-going and it ain't stopped till this day. And, time your father got down the hill, his brother weren't nothing but blood and pulp."

95 Tears were gleaming on my mother's face. There wasn't anything I could say.

"He never mentioned it," she said, "because I never let him mention it before you children. Your Daddy was like a crazy man that night and for many a night thereafter. He says he never in his life seen anything as dark as that road after the lights of that car had gone away. Weren't nothing, weren't nobody on that road, just your Daddy and his brother and that busted guitar. Oh, yes. Your Daddy never did really get right again. Till the day he died he weren't sure but that every white man he saw was the man that killed his brother."

She stopped and took out her handkerchief and dried her eyes and looked at me.

"I ain't telling you all this," she said, "to make you scared or bitter or to make you hate nobody. I'm telling you this because you got a brother. And the world ain't changed."

I guess I didn't want to believe this. I guess she saw this in my face. She turned away from me, toward the window again, searching those streets.

"But I praise my Redeemer," she said at last, "that He called your Daddy home before me. I ain't saying it to throw no flowers at myself, but, I declare, it keeps me from feeling too cast down to know I helped your father get safely through this world. Your father always acted like he was the roughest, strongest man on earth. And everybody took him to be like that. But if he hadn't had *me* there — to see his tears!"

She was crying again. Still, I couldn't move. I said, "Lord, Lord, Mama, I didn't know it was like that."

"Oh, honey," she said, "there's a lot that you don't know. But you are going to find it out." She stood up from the window and came over to me. "You got to hold on to your brother," she said, "and don't let him fall, no matter what it looks like is happening to him and no matter how evil you gets with him. You going to be evil with him many a time. But don't you forget what I told you, you hear?"

"I won't forget," I said. "Don't you worry, I won't forget. I won't let nothing happen to Sonny."

My mother smiled as though she were amused at something she saw in my face. Then, "You may not be able to stop nothing from happening. But you got to let him know you's *there*."

Two days later I was married, and then I was gone. And I had a lot of things on my mind and I pretty well forgot my promise to Mama until I got shipped home on a special furlough for her funeral.

And, after the funeral, with just Sonny and me alone in the empty kitchen, I tried to find out something about him.

"What do you want to do?" I asked him.

"I'm going to be a musician," he said.

For he had graduated, in the time I had been away, from dancing to the juke box to finding out who was playing what, and what they were doing with it, and he had bought himself a set of drums.

"You mean, you want to be a drummer?" I somehow had the feeling that being a drummer might be all right for other people but not for my brother Sonny.

"I don't think," he said, looking at me very gravely, "that I'll ever be a good drummer. But I think I can play a piano."

I frowned. I'd never played the role of the older brother quite so seriously before, had scarcely ever, in fact, *asked* Sonny a damn thing. I sensed myself in the presence of something I didn't really know how to handle, didn't understand. So I made my frown a little deeper as I asked: "What kind of musician do you want to be?"

He grinned. "How many kinds do you think there are?"

"Be *serious*," I said.

He laughed, throwing his head back, and then looked at me. "I *am* serious."

"Well, then, for Christ's sake, stop kidding around and answer a serious question. I mean, do you want to be a concert pianist, you want to play classical music and all that, or — or what?" Long before I finished he was laughing again. "For Christ's *sake*, Sonny!"

He sobered, but with difficulty. "I'm sorry. But you sound so — *scared*!" and he was off again.

"Well, you may think it's funny now, baby, but it's not going to be so funny when you have to make your living at it, let me tell you *that*." I was furious because I knew he was laughing at me and I didn't know why.

"No," he said, very sober now, and afraid, perhaps, that he'd hurt me, "I don't want to be a classical pianist. That isn't what interests me. I mean" — he paused, looking hard at me, as though his eyes would help me to understand, and then gestured helplessly, as though perhaps his hand would help — "I mean, I'll have a lot of studying to do, and I'll have to study *everything*, but, I mean, I want to play *with*—jazz musicians." He stopped. "I want to play jazz," he said.

Well, the word had never before sounded as heavy, as real, as it sounded that afternoon in Sonny's mouth. I just looked at him and I was probably frowning a real frown by this time. I simply couldn't see why on earth he'd want to spend his time hanging around nightclubs, clowning around on bandstands, while people pushed each other around a dance floor. It seemed—beneath him, somehow. I had never thought about it before, had never been forced to, but I suppose I had always put jazz musicians in a class with what Daddy called "good-time people."

"Are you *serious*?"

"Hell, *yes*, I'm serious."

He looked more helpless than ever, and annoyed, and deeply hurt.

I suggested, helpfully: "You mean—like Louis Armstrong?"

His face closed as though I'd struck him. "No. I'm not talking about none of that old-time, down home crap."

"Well, look, Sonny, I'm sorry, don't get mad. I just don't altogether get it, that's all. Name somebody—you know, a jazz musician you admire."

"Bird."

"Who?"

"Bird! Charlie Parker! Don't they teach you nothing in the goddamn army?"

I lit a cigarette. I was surprised and then a little amused to discover that I was trembling. "I've been out of touch," I said. "You'll have to be patient with me. Now. Who's this Parker character?"

"He's just one of the greatest jazz musicians alive," said Sonny, sullenly, his hands in his pockets, his back to me. "Maybe *the* greatest," he added, bitterly, "that's probably why *you* never heard of him."

"All right," I said, "I'm ignorant. I'm sorry. I'll go out and buy all the cat's records right away, all right?"

"It don't," said Sonny, with dignity, "make any difference to me. I don't care what you listen to. Don't do me no favors."

I was beginning to realize that I'd never seen him so upset before. With another part of my mind I was thinking that this would probably turn out to be one of those things kids go through and that I shouldn't make it seem important by pushing it too hard. Still, I didn't think it would do any harm to ask: "Doesn't all this take a lot of time? Can you make a living at it?"

He turned back to me and half leaned, half sat, on the kitchen table. "Everything takes time," he said, "and—well, yes, sure, I can make a living at it. But what I don't seem to be able to make you understand is that it's the only thing I want to do."

"Well, Sonny," I said, gently, "you know people can't always do exactly what they *want* to do—"

"*No*, I don't know that," said Sonny, surprising me. "I think people *ought* to do what they want to do, what else are they alive for?"

"You getting to be a big boy," I said desperately, "it's time you started thinking about your future."

"I'm thinking about my future," said Sonny, grimly. "I think about it all the time."

I gave up. I decided, if he didn't change his mind, that we could always talk about it later. "In the meantime," I said, "you got to finish school." We had already decided that he'd have to move in with Isabel and her folks. I knew this wasn't the ideal arrangement because Isabel's folks are inclined to be dicty and they hadn't especially wanted Isabel to marry me. But I didn't know what else to do. "And we have to get you fixed up at Isabel's."

There was a long silence. He moved from the kitchen table to the window. "That's a terrible idea. You know it yourself."

"Do you have a *better* idea?"

He just walked up and down the kitchen for a minute. He was as tall as I was. He had started to shave. I suddenly had the feeling that I didn't know him at all.

He stopped at the kitchen table and picked up my cigarettes. Looking at me with a kind of mocking, amused defiance, he put one between his lips. "You mind?"

"You smoking already?"

He lit the cigarette and nodded, watching me through the smoke. "I just wanted to see if I'd have the courage to smoke in front of you." He grinned and blew a great cloud of smoke to the ceiling. "It was easy." He looked at my face. "Come on, now. I bet you was smoking at my age, tell the truth."

I didn't say anything but the truth was on my face, and he laughed. But now there was something very strained in his laugh. "Sure. And I bet that ain't all you was doing."

He was frightening me a little. "Cut the crap," I said. "We already decided that you was going to go and live at Isabel's. Now what's got into you all of a sudden?"

"*You* decided it," he pointed out. "*I* didn't decide nothing." He stopped in front of me, leaning against the stove, arms loosely folded. "Look, brother. I don't want to stay in Harlem no more, I really don't." He was very earnest. He looked at me, then over toward the kitchen window. There was something in his eyes I'd never seen before, some thoughtfulness, some worry all his own. He rubbed the muscle of one arm. "It's time I was getting out of here."

"Where do you want to *go*, Sonny?"

"I want to join the army. Or the navy, I don't care. If I say I'm old enough, they'll believe me."

Then I got mad. It was because I was so scared. "You must be crazy. You goddamn fool, what the hell do you want to go and join the *army* for?"

"I just told you. To get out of Harlem."

"Sonny, you haven't even finished *school*. And if you really want to be a musician, how do you expect to study if you're in the *army*?"

He looked at me, trapped, and in anguish. "There's ways. I might be able to work out some kind of deal. Anyway, I'll have the G.I. Bill when I come out."

"*If* you come out." We stared at each other. "Sonny, please. Be reasonable. I know the setup is far from perfect. But we got to do the best we can."

"I ain't learning nothing in school," he said. "Even when I go." He turned away from me and opened the window and threw his cigarette out into the narrow alley. I watched his back. "At least, I ain't learning nothing you'd want me to learn." He slammed the window so hard I thought the glass would fly out, and turned back to me. "And I'm sick of the stink of these garbage cans!"

"Sonny," I said, "I know how you feel. But if you don't finish school now, you're going to be sorry later that you didn't." I grabbed him by the shoulders. "And you only got another year. It ain't so bad. And I'll come back and I swear I'll help you do *whatever* you want to do. Just try to put up with it till I come back. Will you please do that? For me?"

He didn't answer and he wouldn't look at me.

"Sonny. You hear me?"

He pulled away. "I hear you. But you never hear anything *I* say."

I didn't know what to say to that. He looked out of the window and then back at me. "OK," he said, and sighed. "I'll try."

Then I said, trying to cheer him up a little, "They got a piano at Isabel's. You can practice on it."

And as a matter of fact, it did cheer him up for a minute. "That's right," he said to himself. "I forgot that." His face relaxed a little. But the worry, the thoughtfulness, played on it still, the way shadows play on a face which is staring into the fire.

But I thought I'd never hear the end of that piano. At first, Isabel would write me, saying how nice it was that Sonny was so serious about his music and how, as soon as he came in from school, or wherever he had been when he was supposed to be at school, he went straight to that piano and stayed there until suppertime. And, after supper, he went back to that piano and stayed there until everybody went to bed. He was at the piano all day Saturday and all day Sunday. Then he bought a record player and started playing records. He'd play one record over and over again, all day long sometimes, and he'd improvise along with it on the piano. Or he'd play one section of the record, one chord, one change, one progression, then he'd do it on the piano. Then back to the record. Then back to the piano.

Well, I really don't know how they stood it. Isabel finally confessed that it wasn't like living with a person at all, it was like living with sound. And the sound didn't make any sense to her, didn't make any sense to any of them — naturally. They began, in a way, to be afflicted by this presence that was living in their home. It was as though Sonny were some sort of god, or monster. He moved in an atmosphere which wasn't like theirs at all. They fed him and he ate, he washed himself, he walked in and out of their door; he certainly wasn't nasty or unpleasant or rude, Sonny isn't any of those things; but it was as though he were all wrapped up in some cloud, some fire, some vision all his own; and there wasn't any way to reach him.

At the same time, he wasn't really a man yet, he was still a child, and they had to watch out for him in all kinds of ways. They certainly couldn't throw him out. Neither did they dare to make a great scene about that piano because even they dimly sensed, as I sensed, from so many thousands of miles away, that Sonny was at that piano playing for his life.

But he hadn't been going to school. One day a letter came from the school board and Isabel's mother got it — there had, apparently, been other letters but Sonny had torn them up. This day, when Sonny came in, Isabel's mother showed him the letter and asked where he'd been spending his time. And she finally got it out of him that he'd been down in Greenwich Village, with musicians and other characters, in a white girl's apartment. And this scared her and she started to scream at him and what came up, once she began — though she denies it to this day — was what sacrifices they were making to give Sonny a decent home and how little he appreciated it.

Sonny didn't play the piano that day. By evening, Isabel's mother had calmed down but then there was the old man to deal with, and Isabel herself. Isabel says she did her best to be calm but she broke down and started crying. She says she just watched Sonny's face. She could tell, by watching him, what was happening with him. And what was happening was that they penetrated his cloud, they had reached him. Even if their fingers had been a thousand times more gentle than human fingers ever are, he could hardly help feeling that they had stripped him naked and were spitting on that nakedness. For he also had to see that his presence, that music, which was life or death to him, had been torture for them and that they had endured it, not at all for his sake, but only for mine. And Sonny couldn't take that. He can take it a little better today than he could then but he's still not very good at it and, frankly, I don't know anybody who is.

The silence of the next few days must have been louder than the sound of all the music ever played since time began. One morning, before she went to work, Isabel was in his room for something and she suddenly realized that all of his records were gone. And she knew for certain that he was gone. And he was. He went as far as the navy would carry him. He finally sent me a postcard from some place in Greece and that was the first I knew that Sonny was still alive. I didn't see him any more until we were both back in New York and the war had long been over.

He was a man by then, of course, but I wasn't willing to see it. He came by the house from time to time, but we fought almost every time we met. I didn't like the way he carried himself, loose and dreamlike all the time, and I didn't like his friends, and his music seemed to be merely an excuse for the life he led. It sounded just that weird and disordered.

Then we had a fight, a pretty awful fight, and I didn't see him for months. By and by I looked him up, where he was living, in a furnished room in the Village, and I tried to make it up. But there were lots of people in the room and Sonny just lay on his bed, and he wouldn't come downstairs with me, and he treated these other people as though they were his family and I weren't. So I got mad and then he got mad, and then I told him that he might just as well be dead as live the way he was living. Then he stood up and he told me not to worry about him any more in life, that he *was* dead as far as I was concerned. Then he pushed me to the door and the other people looked on as though nothing were happening, and he slammed the door behind me. I stood in the hallway, staring at the door. I heard somebody laugh in the room and then the tears came to my eyes. I started down the steps, whistling to keep from crying, I kept whistling to myself, *You going to need me, baby, one of these cold, rainy days.*

I read about Sonny's trouble in the spring. Little Grace died in the fall. She was a beautiful little girl. But she only lived a little over two years. She died of polio and she suffered. She had a slight fever for a couple of days, but it didn't seem like anything and we just kept her in bed. And we would certainly have called the doctor, but the fever dropped, she seemed to be all right. So we thought it had just been a cold. Then, one day, she was up, playing, Isabel was in the kitchen fixing lunch for the two boys when they'd come in from school, and she heard Grace fall down in the living room. When you have a lot of children you don't always start running when one of them falls, unless they start screaming or something. And, this time, Grace was quiet. Yet, Isabel says that when she heard that *thump* and then that silence, something happened in her to make her afraid. And she ran to the living room and there was little Grace on the floor, all twisted up, and the reason she hadn't screamed was that she couldn't get her breath. And when she did scream, it was the worst sound, Isabel says, that she'd ever heard in all her life, and she still hears it sometimes in her dreams. Isabel will sometimes wake me up with a low, moaning, strangled sound and I have to be quick to awaken her and hold her to me and where Isabel is weeping against me seems a mortal wound.

I think I may have written Sonny the very day that little Grace was buried. I was sitting in the living room in the dark, by myself, and I suddenly thought of Sonny. My trouble made his real.

One Saturday afternoon, when Sonny had been living with us, or, anyway, been in our house, for nearly two weeks, I found myself wandering aimlessly about the living room, drinking from a can of beer, and trying to work up the courage to search Sonny's room. He was out, he was usually out whenever I was home, and Isabel had taken the children to see their grandparents. Suddenly I was standing still in front of the living room window, watching Seventh Avenue. The idea of searching Sonny's room made me still. I scarcely dared to admit to myself what I'd be searching for. I didn't know what I'd do if I found it. Or if I didn't.

On the sidewalk across from me, near the entrance to a barbecue joint, some people were holding an old-fashioned revival meeting. The barbecue cook, wearing a dirty white apron, his conked hair reddish and metallic in the pale sun, and a cigarette between his lips, stood in the doorway, watching them. Kids and older people paused in their errands and stood there, along with some older men and a couple of very tough-looking women who watched everything that happened on the avenue, as though they owned it, or were maybe owned by it. Well, they were watching this, too. The revival was being carried on by three sisters in black, and a brother. All they had were their voices and their Bibles and a tambourine. The brother was testifying and while he testified two of the sisters stood together, seeming to say, amen, and the third sister walked around with the tambourine outstretched and a couple of people dropped coins into it. Then the brother's testimony ended and the sister who had been taking up the collection dumped the coins into her palm and transferred them to the pocket of her long black robe. Then she raised both hands, striking the tambourine against the air, and then against one hand, and she started to sing. And the two other sisters and the brother joined in.

It was strange, suddenly, to watch, though I had been seeing these street meetings all my life. So, of course, had everybody else down there. Yet, they paused and watched and listened and I stood still at the window. *"Tis the old ship of Zion,"* they sang, and the sister with the tambourine kept a steady, jangling beat, *"it has rescued many a thousand!"* Not a soul under the sound of their voices was hearing this song for the first time, not one of them had been rescued. Nor had they seen much in the way of rescue work being done around them. Neither did they especially believe in the holiness of the three sisters and the brother, they knew too much about them, knew where they lived, and how. The woman with the tambourine, whose voice dominated the air, whose face was bright with joy, was divided by very little from the woman who stood watching her, a cigarette between her heavy, chapped lips, her hair a cuckoo's nest, her face scarred and swollen from many beatings, and her black eyes glittering like coal. Perhaps they both knew this, which was why, when, as rarely, they addressed each other, they addressed each other as Sister. As the singing filled the air the watching, listening faces underwent a change, the eyes focusing on something within; the music seemed to soothe a poison out of them; and time seemed, nearly, to fall away from the sullen, belligerent, battered faces, as though they were fleeing back to their first condition, while dreaming of their last. The barbecue cook half shook his head and smiled, and dropped his cigarette and disappeared into his joint. A man fumbled in his pockets for change and stood holding it in his hand impatiently, as though he had just remembered a pressing appointment further up the avenue. He looked furious. Then I saw Sonny, standing on the edge of the crowd. He was carrying a wide, flat notebook with a green cover, and it made him look, from where I was standing, almost like a schoolboy. The coppery sun brought out the copper in his skin, he was very faintly smiling, standing very still. Then the singing stopped, the tambourine turned into a collection plate again. The furious man dropped in his coins and vanished, so did a couple of the women, and Sonny dropped some change in the plate, looking directly at the woman with a little smile. He started across the avenue, toward the house. He has a slow, loping walk, something like the way Harlem hipsters walk, only he's imposed on this his own half-beat. I had never really noticed it before.

I stayed at the window, both relieved and apprehensive. As Sonny disappeared from my sight, they began singing again. And they were still singing when his key turned in the lock.

"Hey," he said.

"Hey, yourself. You want some beer?"

"No. Well, maybe." But he came up to the window and stood beside me, looking out. "What a warm voice," he said.

They were singing *If I could only hear my mother pray again!*

"Yes," I said, "and she can sure beat that tambourine."

"But what a terrible song," he said, and laughed. He dropped his notebook on the sofa and disappeared into the kitchen. "Where's Isabel and the kids?"

"I think they went to see their grandparents. You hungry?"

"No." He came back into the living room with his can of beer. "You want to come some place with me tonight?"

I sensed, I don't know how, that I couldn't possibly say no. "Sure. Where?"

He sat down on the sofa and picked up his notebook and started leafing through it. "I'm going to sit in with some fellows in a joint in the Village."

"You mean, you're going to play, tonight?"

"That's right." He took a swallow of his beer and moved back to the window. He gave me a sidelong look. "If you can stand it."

"I'll try," I said.

He smiled to himself and we both watched as the meeting across the way broke up. The three sisters and the brother, heads bowed, were singing *God be with you till we meet again*. The faces around them were very quiet. Then the song ended. The small crowd dispersed. We watched the three women and the lone man walk slowly up the avenue.

"When she was singing before," said Sonny, abruptly, "her voice reminded me for a minute of what heroin feels like sometimes — when it's in your veins. It makes you feel sort of warm and cool at the same time. And distant. And — and sure." He sipped his beer, very deliberately not looking at me. I watched his face. "It makes you feel — in control. Sometimes you've got to have that feeling."

"Do you?" I sat down slowly in the easy chair.

"Sometimes." He went to the sofa and picked up his notebook again. "Some people do."

"In order," I asked, "to play?" And my voice was very ugly, full of contempt and anger.

"Well" — he looked at me with great, troubled eyes, as though, in fact, he hoped his eyes would tell me things he could never otherwise say — "they *think* so. And *if* they think so — !"

"And what do *you* think?" I asked.

He sat on the sofa and put his can of beer on the floor. "I don't know," he said, and I couldn't be sure if he were answering my question or pursuing his thoughts. His face didn't tell me. "It's not so much to *play*. It's to *stand* it, to be able to make it at all. On any level." He frowned and smiled: "In order to keep from shaking to pieces."

"But these friends of yours," I said, "they seem to shake themselves to pieces pretty goddamn fast."

"Maybe." He played with the notebook. And something told me that I should curb my tongue, that Sonny was doing his best to talk, that I should listen. "But of course you only know the ones that've gone to pieces. Some don't — or at least they haven't *yet* and that's just about all *any* of us can say." He paused. "And then there are some who just live, really, in hell, and they know it and they see what's happening and they go right on. I don't know." He sighed, dropped the notebook, folded his arms. "Some guys, you can tell from the way they play, they on something *all* the time. And you can see that, well, it makes something real for them. But of course," he picked up his beer from the floor and sipped it and put the can down again, "they *want* to, too, you've got to see that. Even some of them that say they don't — *some*, not all."

"And what about you?" I asked — I couldn't help it. "What about you? Do *you* want to?"

He stood up and walked to the window and remained silent for a long time. Then he sighed. "Me," he said. Then: "While I was downstairs before, on my way here, listening to that woman sing, it struck me all of a sudden how much suffering she must have had to go through — to sing like that. It's *repulsive* to think you have to suffer that much."

I said: "But there's no way not to suffer — is there, Sonny?"

"I believe not," he said and smiled, "but that's never stopped anyone from trying." He looked at me. "Has it?" I realized, with this mocking look, that there stood between us, forever, beyond the power of time or forgiveness, the fact that I had held silence — so long! — when he had needed human speech to help him. He turned back to the window. "No, there's no way not to suffer. But you try all kinds of ways to keep from drowning in it, to keep on top of it, and to make it seem — well, like *you*. Like you did something, all right, and now you're suffering for it. You know?" I said nothing. "Well you know," he said, impatiently, "why *do* people suffer? Maybe it's better to do something to give it a reason, *any* reason."

"But we just agreed," I said, "that there's no way not to suffer. Isn't it better, then, just to — take it?"

"But nobody just takes it," Sonny cried, "that's what I'm telling you! *Everybody* tries not to. You're just hung up on the *way* some people try — it's not *your* way!"

The hair on my face began to itch, my face felt wet. "That's not true," I said, "that's not true. I don't give a damn what other people do, I don't even care how they suffer. I just care how *you* suffer." And he looked at me. "Please believe me," I said, "I don't want to see you — die — trying not to suffer."

"I won't," he said, flatly, "die trying not to suffer. At least, not any faster than anybody else."

"But there's no need," I said, trying to laugh, "is there? in killing yourself."

I wanted to say more, but I couldn't. I wanted to talk about will power and how life could be — well, beautiful. I wanted to say that it was all within; but was it? or, rather, wasn't that exactly the trouble? And I wanted to promise that I would never fail him again. But it would all have sounded — empty words and lies.

So I made the promise to myself and prayed that I would keep it.

"It's terrible sometimes, inside," he said, "that's what's the trouble. You walk these streets, black and funky and cold, and there's not really a living ass to talk to, and there's nothing shaking, and there's no way of getting it out — that storm inside. You can't talk it and you can't make love with it, and when you finally try to get with it and play it, you realize *nobody's* listening. So *you've* got to listen. You got to find a way to listen."

And then he walked away from the window and sat on the sofa again, as though all the wind had suddenly been knocked out of him.

"Sometimes you'll do *anything* to play, even cut your mother's throat." He laughed and looked at me. "Or your brother's." Then he sobered. "Or your own." Then: "Don't worry. I'm all right now and I think I'll *be* all right. But I can't forget — where I've been. I don't mean just the physical place I've been, I mean where I've *been*. And *what* I've been."

"What have you been, Sonny?" I asked.

He smiled — but sat sideways on the sofa, his elbow resting on the back, his fingers playing with his mouth and chin, not looking at me. "I've been something I didn't recognize, didn't know I could be. Didn't know anybody could be." He stopped, looking inward, looking helplessly young, looking old. "I'm not talking about it now because I feel *guilty* or anything like that — maybe it would be better if I did, I don't know. Anyway, I can't really talk about it. Not to you, not to anybody," and now he turned and faced me. "Sometimes, you know, and it was actually when I was most *out* of the world, I felt that I was in it, that I was *with* it, really, and I could play or I didn't really have to *play*, it just came out of me, it was there. And I don't know how I played, thinking about it now, but I know I did awful things, those times, sometimes, to people. Or it wasn't that I *did* anything to them — it was that they weren't real." He picked up the beer can; it was empty; he rolled it between his palms: "And other times — well, I needed a fix, I needed to find a place to lean, I needed to clear a *space* to *listen* — and I couldn't find it, and I — went crazy, I did terrible things to *me*, I was terrible *for* me." He began pressing the beer can between his hands, I watched the metal begin to give. It glittered, as he played with it, like a knife, and I was afraid he would cut himself, but I said nothing. "Oh well. I can never tell you. I was all by myself at the bottom of something, stinking and sweating and crying and shaking, and I smelled it, you know? *my* stink, and I thought I'd die if I couldn't get away from it and yet, all the same, I knew that everything I was doing was just locking me in with it. And I didn't know," he paused, still flattening the beer can, "I didn't know, I still *don't* know, something kept telling me that maybe it was good to smell your own stink, but I didn't think that *that* was what I'd been trying to do — and — who can stand it?" and he abruptly dropped the ruined beer can, looking at me with a small, still smile, and then rose, walking to the window as though it were the lodestone rock. I watched his face, he watched the avenue. "I couldn't tell you when Mama died — but the reason I wanted to leave Harlem so bad was to get away from drugs. And then, when I ran away, that's what I was running from — really. When I came back, nothing had changed, *I* hadn't changed, I was just — older." And he stopped, drumming with his fingers on the windowpane. The sun had vanished, soon darkness would fall. I watched his face. "It can come again," he said, almost as though speaking to himself. Then he turned to me. "It can come again," he repeated. "I just want you to know that."

"All right," I said, at last. "So it can come again. All right."

He smiled, but the smile was sorrowful. "I had to try to tell you," he said.

"Yes," I said. "I understand that."

"You're my brother," he said, looking straight at me, and not smiling at all.

"Yes," I repeated, "yes. I understand that."

He turned back to the window, looking out. "All that hatred down there," he said, "all that hatred and misery and love. It's a wonder it doesn't blow the avenue apart."

We went to the only nightclub on a short, dark street, downtown. We squeezed through the narrow, chattering, jam-packed bar to the entrance of the big room, where the bandstand was. And we stood there for a moment, for the lights were very dim in this room and we couldn't see. Then, "Hello, boy," said a voice and an enormous black man, much older than Sonny or myself, erupted out of all that atmospheric lighting and put an arm around Sonny's shoulder. "I been sitting right here," he said, "waiting for you."

He had a big voice, too, and heads in the darkness turned toward us.

Sonny grinned and pulled a little away, and said, "Creole, this is my brother. I told you about him."

Creole shook my hand. "I'm glad to meet you, son," he said, and it was clear that he was glad to meet me *there*, for Sonny's sake. And he smiled, "You got a real musician in *your* family," and he took his arm from Sonny's shoulder and slapped him, lightly, affectionately, with the back of his hand.

"Well. Now I've heard it all," said a voice behind us. This was another musician, and a friend of Sonny's, a coal-black, cheerful-looking man, built close to the ground. He immediately began confiding to me, at the top of his lungs, the most terrible things about Sonny, his teeth gleaming like a lighthouse and his laugh coming up out of him like the beginning of an earthquake. And it turned out that everyone at the bar knew Sonny, or almost everyone; some were musicians, working there, or nearby, or not working, some were simply hangers-on, and some were there to hear Sonny play. I was introduced to all of them and they were all very polite to me. Yet, it was clear that, for them, I was only Sonny's brother. Here, I was in Sonny's world. Or, rather: his kingdom. Here, it was not even a question that his veins bore royal blood.

They were going to play soon and Creole installed me, by myself, at a table in a dark corner. Then I watched them, Creole, and the little black man, and Sonny, and the others, while they horsed around, standing just below the bandstand. The light from the bandstand spilled just a little short of them and, watching them laughing and gesturing and moving about, I had the feeling that they, nevertheless, were being most careful not to step into that circle of light too suddenly: that if they moved into the light too suddenly, without thinking, they would perish in flame. Then, while I watched, one of them, the small, black man, moved into the light and crossed the bandstand and started fooling around with his drums. Then — being funny and being, also, extremely ceremonious — Creole took Sonny by the arm and led him to the piano. A woman's voice called Sonny's name and a few hands started clapping. And Sonny, also being funny and being ceremonious, and so touched, I think, that he could have cried, but neither hiding it nor showing it, riding it like a man, grinned, and put both hands to his heart and bowed from the waist.

Creole then went to the bass fiddle and a lean, very bright-skinned brown man jumped up on the bandstand and picked up his horn. So there they were, and the atmosphere on the bandstand and in the room began to change and tighten. Someone stepped up to the microphone and announced them. Then there were all kinds of murmurs. Some people at the bar shushed others. The waitress ran around, frantically getting in the last orders, guys and chicks got closer to each other, and the lights on the bandstand, on the quartet, turned to a kind of indigo. Then they all looked different there. Creole looked about him for the last time, as though he were making certain that all his chickens were in the coop, and then he — jumped and struck the fiddle. And there they were.

All I know about music is that not many people ever really hear it. And even then, on the rare occasions when something opens within, and the music enters, what we mainly hear, or hear corroborated, are personal, private, vanishing evocations. But the man who creates the music is hearing something else, is dealing with the roar rising from the void and imposing order on it as it hits the air. What is evoked in him, then, is of another order, more terrible because it has no words, and triumphant, too, for that same reason. And his triumph, when he triumphs, is ours. I just watched Sonny's face. His face was troubled, he was working hard, but he wasn't with it. And I had the feeling that, in a way, everyone on the bandstand was waiting for him, both waiting for him and pushing him along. But as I began to watch Creole, I realized that it was Creole who held them all back. He had them on a short rein. Up there, keeping the beat with his whole body, wailing on the fiddle, with his eyes half closed, he was listening to everything, but he was listening to Sonny. He was having a dialogue with Sonny. He wanted Sonny to leave the shoreline and strike out for the deep water. He was Sonny's witness that deep water and drowning were not the same thing — he had been there, and he knew. And he wanted Sonny to know. He was waiting for Sonny to do the things on the keys which would let Creole know that Sonny was in the water.

And, while Creole listened, Sonny moved, deep within, exactly like someone in torment. I had never before thought of how awful the relationship must be between the musician and his instrument. He has to fill it, this instrument, with the breath of life, his own. He has to make it do what he wants it to do. And a piano is just a piano. It's made out of so much wood and wires and little hammers and big ones, and ivory. While there's only so much you can do with it, the only way to find this out is to try; to try and make it do everything.

And Sonny hadn't been near a piano for over a year. And he wasn't on much better terms with his life, not the life that stretched before him now. He and the piano stammered, started one way, got scared, stopped; started another way, panicked, marked time, started again; then seemed to have found a direction, panicked again, got stuck. And the face I saw on Sonny I'd never seen before. Everything had been burned out of it, and, at the same time, things usually hidden were being burned in, by the fire and fury of the battle which was occurring in him up there.

Yet, watching Creole's face as they neared the end of the first set, I had the feeling that something had happened, something I hadn't heard. Then they finished, there was scattered applause, and then, without an instant's warning, Creole started into something else, it was almost sardonic, it was *Am I Blue*. And, as though he commanded, Sonny began to play. Something began to happen. And Creole let out the reins. The dry, low, black man said something awful on the drums, Creole answered, and the drums talked back. Then the horn insisted, sweet and high, slightly detached perhaps, and Creole listened, commenting now and then, dry, and driving, beautiful and calm and old. Then they all came together again, and Sonny was part of the family again. I could tell this from his face. He seemed to have found, right there beneath his fingers, a damn brand-new piano. It seemed that he couldn't get over it. Then, for awhile, just being happy with Sonny, they seemed to be agreeing with him that brand-new pianos certainly were a gas.

Then Creole stepped forward to remind them that what they were playing was the blues. He hit something in all of them, he hit something in me, myself, and the music tightened and deepened, apprehension began to beat the air. Creole began to tell us what the blues were all about. They were not about anything very new. He and his boys up there were keeping it new, at the risk of ruin, destruction, madness, and death, in order to find new ways to make us listen. For, while the tale of how we suffer, and how we are delighted, and how we may triumph is never new, it always must be heard. There isn't any other tale to tell, it's the only light we've got in all this darkness.

And this tale, according to that face, that body, those strong hands on those strings, has another aspect in every country, and a new depth in every generation. Listen, Creole seemed to be saying, listen. Now these are Sonny's blues. He made the little black man on the drums know it, and the bright, brown man on the horn. Creole wasn't trying any longer to get Sonny in the water. He was wishing him Godspeed. Then he stepped back, very slowly, filling the air with the immense suggestion that Sonny speak for himself.

Then they all gathered around Sonny and Sonny played. Every now and again one of them seemed to say, amen. Sonny's fingers filled the air with life, his life. But that life contained so many others. And Sonny went all the way back, he really began with the spare, flat statement of the opening phrase of the song. Then he began to make it his. It was very beautiful because it wasn't hurried and it was no longer a lament. I seemed to hear with what burning he had made it his, with what burning we had yet to make it ours, how we could cease lamenting. Freedom lurked around us and I understood, at last, that he could help us to be free if we would listen, that he would never be free until we did. Yet, there was no battle in his face now. I heard what he had gone through, and would continue to go through until he came to rest in earth. He had made it his: that long line, of which we knew only Mama and Daddy. And he was giving it back, as everything must be given back, so that, passing through death, it can live forever. I saw my mother's face again, and felt, for the first time, how the stones of the road she had walked on must have bruised her feet. I saw the moonlit road where my father's brother died. And it brought something else back to me, and carried me past it. I saw my little girl again and felt Isabel's tears again, and I felt my own tears begin to rise. And I was yet aware that this was only a moment, that the world waited outside, as hungry as a tiger, and that trouble stretched above us, longer than the sky.

Then it was over. Creole and Sonny let out their breath, both soaking wet, and grinning. There was a lot of applause and some of it was real. In the dark, the girl came by and I asked her to take drinks to the bandstand. There was a long pause, while they talked up there in the indigo light and after awhile I saw the girl put a Scotch and milk on top of the piano for Sonny. He didn't seem to notice it, but just before they started playing again, he sipped from it and looked toward me, and nodded. Then he put it back on top of the piano. For me, then, as they began to play again, it glowed and shook above my brother's head like the very cup of trembling.

[1957]

EXPLORING THE TEXT

1. The first sentence of the story's second paragraph begins, "It was not to be believed." What does the use of the passive voice suggest about the narrator's response to the news he has just gotten? What is the effect of the repetition of the word "it" in the story's first two paragraphs?
2. The narrator has a conversation with an old neighborhood friend of Sonny's (paras. 9–46). How does that conversation shape the characterization of the narrator? How does it shape our expectations for the outcome of the story?
3. The narrator of "Sonny's Blues" and his brother, Sonny, represent two sides of the same coin: one brother is employed as a math teacher, married, and clean living; the other is a jazz musician, single, and struggling with heroin addiction. Discuss the ways in which Baldwin brings these two characters to life and makes them more than just opposites. Which brother do you think is the story's main character? Explain your answer.
4. Sonny tells his brother that Louis Armstrong is "old-time, down home" music. He likes the music of Charlie "Bird" Parker. Listen to music by Louis Armstrong and Charlie Parker, and describe the differences between them. Parker's version of "White Christmas" gives the listener a particularly vivid understanding of the bebop style he exemplified and that so intrigues Sonny. Why might Armstrong's jazz be considered traditional and Parker's progressive? How does Baldwin illustrate bebop in the story's last scene at the club?
5. Why do you think the plot of this story is not in chronological order? Try rearranging the events of the story so that they are in chronological order. How does it change the story Baldwin is telling?
6. What do you think is the purpose of the narrator's description of a typical Sunday afternoon at his parents' house (paras. 78–79)? What part does that setting have in the story's conflict?
7. According to the narrator — and his mother — how are Sonny and his father similar? What evidence does the story offer as support? What are the parallels between the narrator and his mother? What do you think the dash in the last sentence of paragraph 76 says about the narrator? about Sonny and his father?
8. The backdrop of 1950s Harlem and the story of the narrator's uncle's death (para. 94) suggest that the characters have suffered from vicious and institutionalized racism. Where else do you see the impact of racism in the story? To what extent do you think that Sonny's addiction and the narrator's repression and rigidity are caused by their natures or by the social forces of racism?
9. The story ends in a club where the narrator goes to hear Sonny play. The language of the story changes, becoming more abstract and metaphorical. What does that change suggest about the part music plays in the lives of the musicians and what Baldwin wants us to feel about Sonny and his blues?
10. What do you think is the difference between deep water and drowning (para. 230)? Why do you think the narrator begins to understand his brother and himself through the way Creole leads Sonny into the music?
11. What effect does Sonny's music have on the narrator? Look closely at paragraph 236.
12. The very last line of the story is an allusion to a somewhat enigmatic passage in the Bible about rage and God's protection against it. What does the allusion suggest about the glowing "cup of trembling" the narrator sees in the cup "above [his] brother's head"?
13. Do you think this story has a happy ending? Why or why not?

Everyday Use

ALICE WALKER

Alice Walker (b. 1944) is a novelist, poet, essayist, civil rights activist, and self-described eco-pacifist, best known for her depictions of the struggles and strengths of African American women. The youngest of eight children born to sharecropper parents, Walker grew up in the small town of Eatonton, Georgia. After high school, she attended Spelman College in Georgia, then transferred to Sarah Lawrence College in New York, which she graduated from in 1965. Her first novel, *The Third Life of Grange Copeland*, was published in 1969, followed by her poetry collection *Revolutionary Petunias and Other Poems* (1973). In 1982, she published *The Color Purple*, her most celebrated work, which won the Pulitzer Prize and was adapted into both a movie (directed by Steven Spielberg) and a Tony Award–winning Broadway musical. Walker is also known for her essays, in which she coined the term "womanist." Claiming a more inclusive connotation than "feminist," which Walker criticized as focusing on the experiences of white, heterosexual women, she writes that a womanist is "committed to survival and wholeness of entire people, male *and* female. Not a separatist. . . . Traditionally a universalist." Walker has taught at Wellesley College, Yale University, the University of California, Berkeley, and many other institutions. She continues to support environmental causes and is an advocate for international women's rights. "Everyday Use," a story from her collection *In Love and Trouble: Stories of Black Women* (1973), explores how different definitions of heritage and history influence identity.

for your grandmama

I will wait for her in the yard that Maggie and I made so clean and wavy yesterday afternoon. A yard like this is more comfortable than most people know. It is not just a yard. It is like an extended living room. When the hard clay is swept clean as a floor and the fine sand around the edges lined with tiny, irregular grooves, anyone can come and sit and look up into the elm tree and wait for the breezes that never come inside the house.

Maggie will be nervous until after her sister goes: she will stand hopelessly in corners, homely and ashamed of the burn scars down her arms and legs, eying her sister with a mixture of envy and awe. She thinks her sister has held life always in the palm of one hand, that "no" is a word the world never learned to say to her.

You've no doubt seen those TV shows where the child who has "made it" is confronted, as a surprise, by her own mother and father, tottering in weakly from backstage. (A pleasant surprise, of course: What would they do if parent and child came on the show only to curse out and insult each other?) On TV mother and child embrace and smile into each other's faces. Sometimes the mother and father weep, the child wraps them in her arms and leans across the table to tell how she would not have made it without their help. I have seen these programs.

Sometimes I dream a dream in which Dee and I are suddenly brought together on a TV program of this sort. Out of a dark and soft-seated limousine I am ushered into a bright room filled with many people. There I meet a smiling, gray, sporty man like Johnny Carson[1] who shakes my hand and tells me what a fine girl I have. Then we are on the stage and Dee is embracing me with tears in her eyes. She pins on my dress a large orchid, even though she has told me once that she thinks orchids are tacky flowers.

In real life I am a large, big-boned woman with rough, man-working hands. In the winter I wear flannel nightgowns to bed and overalls during the day. I can kill and clean a hog as mercilessly as a man. My fat keeps me hot in zero weather. I can work outside all day, breaking ice to get water for washing; I can eat pork liver cooked over the open fire minutes after it comes steaming from the hog. One winter I knocked a bull calf straight in the brain between the eyes with a sledge hammer and had the meat hung up to chill before nightfall. But of course all this does not show on television. I am the way my daughter would want me to be: a hundred pounds lighter, my skin like an uncooked barley pancake. My hair glistens in the hot bright lights. Johnny Carson has much to do to keep up with my quick and witty tongue.

But that is a mistake. I know even before I wake up. Who ever knew a Johnson with a quick tongue? Who can even imagine me looking a strange white man in the eye? It seems to me I have talked to them always with one foot raised in flight, with my head turned in whichever way is farthest from them. Dee, though. She would always look anyone in the eye. Hesitation was no part of her nature.

"How do I look, Mama?" Maggie says, showing just enough of her thin body enveloped in pink skirt and red blouse for me to know she's there, almost hidden by the door.

"Come out into the yard," I say.

Have you ever seen a lame animal, perhaps a dog run over by some careless person rich enough to own a car, sidle up to someone who is ignorant enough to be kind to him? That is the way my Maggie walks. She has been like this, chin on chest, eyes on ground, feet in shuffle, ever since the fire that burned the other house to the ground.

Dee is lighter than Maggie, with nicer hair and a fuller figure. She's a woman now, though sometimes I forget. How long ago was it that the other house burned? Ten, twelve years? Sometimes I can still hear the flames and feel Maggie's arms sticking to me, her hair smoking and her dress falling off her in little black papery flakes. Her eyes seemed stretched open, blazed open by the flames reflected in them. And Dee. I see her standing off under the sweet gum tree she used to dig gum out of; a look of concentration on her face as she watched the last dingy gray board of the house fall in toward the red-hot brick chimney. Why don't you do a dance around the ashes? I'd wanted to ask her. She had hated the house that much.

I used to think she hated Maggie, too. But that was before we raised the money, the church and me, to send her to Augusta to school. She used to read to us without pity; forcing words, lies, other folks' habits, whole lives upon us two, sitting trapped and ignorant underneath her voice. She washed us in a river of make-believe, burned us with a lot of knowledge we didn't necessarily need to know. Pressed us to her with the serious way she read, to shove us away at just the moment, like dimwits, we seemed about to understand.

Dee wanted nice things. A yellow organdy dress to wear to her graduation from high school; black pumps to match a green suit she'd made from an old suit somebody gave me. She was determined to stare down any disaster in her efforts. Her eyelids would not flicker for minutes at a time. Often I fought off the temptation to shake her. At sixteen she had a style of her own: and knew what style was.

I never had an education myself. After second grade the school was closed down. Don't ask me

[1] Host of NBC's *The Tonight Show* from 1962 to 1992.—EDS.

why: in 1927 colored asked fewer questions than they do now. Sometimes Maggie reads to me. She stumbles along good-naturedly but can't see well. She knows she is not bright. Like good looks and money, quickness passed her by. She will marry John Thomas (who has mossy teeth in an earnest face) and then I'll be free to sit here and I guess just sing church songs to myself. Although I never was a good singer. Never could carry a tune. I was always better at a man's job. I used to love to milk till I was hooked in the side in '49. Cows are soothing and slow and don't bother you, unless you try to milk them the wrong way.

I have deliberately turned my back on the house. It is three rooms, just like the one that burned, except the roof is tin; they don't make shingle roofs any more. There are no real windows, just some holes cut in the sides, like the portholes in a ship, but not round and not square, with rawhide holding the shutters up on the outside. This house is in a pasture, too, like the other one. No doubt when Dee sees it she will want to tear it down. She wrote me once that no matter where we "choose" to live, she will manage to come see us. But she will never bring her friends. Maggie and I thought about this and Maggie asked me, "Mama, when did Dee ever *have* any friends?"

She had a few. Furtive boys in pink shirts hanging about on washday after school. Nervous girls who never laughed. Impressed with her they worshiped the well-turned phrase, the cute shape, the scalding humor that erupted like bubbles in lye. She read to them.

When she was courting Jimmy T she didn't have much time to pay to us, but turned all her faultfinding power on him. He *flew* to marry a cheap city girl from a family of ignorant flashy people. She hardly had time to recompose herself.

When she comes I will meet — but there they are!

Maggie attempts to make a dash for the house, in her shuffling way, but I stay her with my hand. "Come back here," I say. And she stops and tries to dig a well in the sand with her toe.

It is hard to see them clearly through the strong sun. But even the first glimpse of leg out of the car tells me it is Dee. Her feet were always neat-looking, as if God himself had shaped them with a certain style. From the other side of the car comes a short, stocky man. Hair is all over his head a foot long and hanging from his chin like a kinky mule tail. I hear Maggie suck in her breath. "Uhnnnh," is what it sounds like. Like when you see the wriggling end of a snake just in front of your foot on the road. "Uhnnnh."

Dee next. A dress down to the ground, in this hot weather. A dress so loud it hurts my eyes. There are yellows and oranges enough to throw back the light of the sun. I feel my whole face warming from the heat waves it throws out. Earrings gold, too, and hanging down to her shoulders. Bracelets dangling and making noises when she moves her arm up to shake the folds of the dress out of her armpits. The dress is loose and flows, and as she walks closer, I like it. I hear Maggie go "Uhnnnh" again. It is her sister's hair. It stands straight up like the wool on a sheep. It is black as night and around the edges are two long pigtails that rope about like small lizards disappearing behind her ears.

"Wa-su-zo-Tean-o!" she says, coming on in that gliding way the dress makes her move. The short stocky fellow with the hair to his navel is all grinning and he follows up with "Asalamalakim, my mother and sister!" He moves to hug Maggie but she falls back, right up against the back of my chair. I feel her trembling there and when I look up I see the perspiration falling off her chin.

"Don't get up," says Dee. Since I am stout it takes something of a push. You can see me trying to move a second or two before I make it. She turns, showing white heels through her sandals, and goes back to the car. Out she peeks next with a Polaroid. She stoops down quickly and lines up picture after picture of me sitting there in front of the house with Maggie cowering behind me. She never takes a shot without making sure the house is included. When a cow comes nibbling around the edge of the yard she snaps it and me and Maggie *and* the house. Then she puts the Polaroid in the back seat of the car, and comes up and kisses me on the forehead.

Meanwhile Asalamalakim is going through motions with Maggie's hand. Maggie's hand is as limp as a fish, and probably as cold, despite the sweat, and she keeps trying to pull it back. It looks like Asalamalakim wants to shake hands but wants to do it fancy. Or maybe he don't know how people shake hands. Anyhow, he soon gives up on Maggie.

"Well," I say. "Dee."

25 "No, Mama," she says. "Not 'Dee,' Wangero Leewanika Kemanjo!"

"What happened to 'Dee'?" I wanted to know.

"She's dead," Wangero said. "I couldn't bear it any longer, being named after the people who oppress me."

"You know as well as me you was named after your aunt Dicie," I said. Dicie is my sister. She named Dee. We called her "Big Dee" after Dee was born.

"But who was *she* named after?" asked Wangero.

30 "I guess after Grandma Dee," I said.

"And who was she named after?" asked Wangero.

"Her mother," I said, and saw Wangero was getting tired. "That's about as far back as I can trace it," I said. Though, in fact, I probably could have carried it back beyond the Civil War through the branches.

"Well," said Asalamalakim, "there you are."

"Uhnnnh," I heard Maggie say.

35 "There I was not," I said, "before 'Dicie' cropped up in our family, so why should I try to trace it that far back?"

He just stood there grinning, looking down on me like somebody inspecting a Model A car.[2] Every once in a while he and Wangero sent eye signals over my head.

"How do you pronounce this name?" I asked.

"You don't have to call me by it if you don't want to," said Wangero.

"Why shouldn't I?" I asked. "If that's what you want us to call you, we'll call you."

40 "I know it might sound awkward at first," said Wangero.

"I'll get used to it," I said. "Ream it out again."

Well, soon we got the name out of the way. Asalamalakim had a name twice as long and three times as hard. After I tripped over it two or three times he told me to just call him Hakim-a-barber. I wanted to ask him was he a barber, but I didn't really think he was, so I didn't ask.

"You must belong to those beef-cattle peoples down the road," I said. They said "Asalamalakim" when they met you, too, but they didn't shake hands. Always too busy: feeding the cattle, fixing the fences, putting up salt-lick shelters, throwing down hay. When the white folks poisoned some of the herd the men stayed up all night with rifles in their hands. I walked a mile and a half just to see the sight.

Hakim-a-barber said, "I accept some of their doctrines, but farming and raising cattle is not my style." (They didn't tell me, and I didn't ask, whether Wangero [Dee] had really gone and married him.)

45 We sat down to eat and right away he said he didn't eat collards and pork was unclean. Wangero, though, went on through the chitlins and corn bread, the greens and everything else. She talked a blue streak over the sweet potatoes. Everything delighted her. Even the fact that we still used the benches her daddy made for the table when we couldn't afford to buy chairs.

"Oh, Mama!" she cried. Then turned to Hakim-a-barber. "I never knew how lovely these benches are. You can feel the rump prints," she said, running her hands underneath her and along the bench. Then she gave a sigh and her

[2] The redesigned successor to the Ford Model T. — EDS.

hand closed over Grandma Dee's butter dish. "That's it!" she said. "I knew there was something I wanted to ask you if I could have." She jumped up from the table and went over in the corner where the churn stood, the milk in it clabber by now. She looked at the churn and looked at it.

"This churn top is what I need," she said. "Didn't Uncle Buddy whittle it out of a tree you all used to have?"

"Yes," I said.

"Uh huh," she said happily. "And I want the dasher, too."

"Uncle Buddy whittle that, too?" asked the barber.

Dee (Wangero) looked up at me.

"Aunt Dee's first husband whittled the dash," said Maggie so low you almost couldn't hear her. "His name was Henry, but they called him Stash."

"Maggie's brain is like an elephant's," Wangero said, laughing. "I can use the churn top as a centerpiece for the alcove table," she said, sliding a plate over the churn, "and I'll think of something artistic to do with the dasher."

When she finished wrapping the dasher the handle stuck out. I took it for a moment in my hands. You didn't even have to look close to see where hands pushing the dasher up and down to make butter had left a kind of sink in the wood. In fact, there were a lot of small sinks; you could see where thumbs and fingers had sunk into the wood. It was beautiful light yellow wood, from a tree that grew in the yard where Big Dee and Stash had lived.

After dinner Dee (Wangero) went to the trunk at the foot of my bed and started rifling through it. Maggie hung back in the kitchen over the dishpan. Out came Wangero with two quilts. They had been pieced by Grandma Dee and then Big Dee and me had hung them on the quilt frames on the front porch and quilted them. One was in the Lone Star pattern. The other was Walk Around the Mountain. In both of them were scraps of dresses Grandma Dee had worn fifty and more years ago. Bits and pieces of Grandpa Jarrell's Paisley shirts. And one teeny faded blue piece, about the size of a penny matchbox, that was from Great Grandpa Ezra's uniform that he wore in the Civil War.

"Mama," Wangero said sweet as a bird. "Can I have these old quilts?"

I heard something fall in the kitchen, and a minute later the kitchen door slammed.

"Why don't you take one or two of the others?" I asked. "These old things was just done by me and Big Dee from some tops your grandma pieced before she died."

"No," said Wangero. "I don't want those. They are stitched around the borders by machine."

"That'll make them last better," I said.

"That's not the point," said Wangero. "These are all pieces of dresses Grandma used to wear. She did all this stitching by hand. Imagine!" She held the quilts securely in her arms, stroking them.

"Some of the pieces, like those lavender ones, come from old clothes her mother handed down to her," I said, moving up to touch the quilts. Dee (Wangero) moved back just enough so that I couldn't reach the quilts. They already belonged to her.

"Imagine!" she breathed again, clutching them closely to her bosom.

"The truth is," I said, "I promised to give them quilts to Maggie, for when she marries John Thomas."

She gasped like a bee had stung her.

"Maggie can't appreciate these quilts!" she said. "She'd probably be backward enough to put them to everyday use."

"I reckon she would," I said. "God knows I been saving 'em for long enough with nobody using 'em. I hope she will!" I didn't want to bring up how I had offered Dee (Wangero) a quilt when she went away to college. Then she had told me they were old-fashioned, out of style.

"But they're *priceless*!" she was saying now, furiously; for she has a temper. "Maggie would put them on the bed and in five years they'd be in rags. Less than that!"

"She can always make some more," I said. "Maggie knows how to quilt."

Dee (Wangero) looked at me with hatred. "You just will not understand. The point is these quilts, *these* quilts!"

"Well," I said, stumped. "What would *you* do with them?"

"Hang them," she said. As if that was the only thing you *could* do with quilts.

Maggie by now was standing in the door. I could almost hear the sound her feet made as they scraped over each other.

"She can have them, Mama," she said, like somebody used to never winning anything, or having anything reserved for her. "I can 'member Grandma Dee without the quilts."

I looked at her hard. She had filled her bottom lip with checkerberry snuff and it gave her face a kind of dopey, hangdog look. It was Grandma Dee and Big Dee who taught her how to quilt herself. She stood there with her scarred hands hidden in the folds of her skirt. She looked at her sister with something like fear but she wasn't mad at her. This was Maggie's portion. This was the way she knew God to work.

When I looked at her like that something hit me in the top of my head and ran down to the soles of my feet. Just like when I'm in church and the spirit of God touches me and I get happy and shout. I did something I never had done before: hugged Maggie to me, then dragged her on into the room, snatched the quilts out of Miss Wangero's hands and dumped them into Maggie's lap. Maggie just sat there on my bed with her mouth open.

"Take one or two of the others," I said to Dee.

But she turned without a word and went out to Hakim-a-barber.

"You just don't understand," she said, as Maggie and I came out to the car.

"What don't I understand?" I wanted to know.

"Your heritage," she said. And then she turned to Maggie, kissed her, and said, "You ought to try to make something of yourself, too, Maggie. It's really a new day for us. But from the way you and Mama still live you'd never know it."

She put on some sunglasses that hid everything above the tip of her nose and her chin.

Maggie smiled; maybe at the sunglasses. But a real smile, not scared. After we watched the car dust settle I asked Maggie to bring me a dip of snuff. And then the two of us sat there just enjoying, until it was time to go in the house and go to bed.

[1973]

EXPLORING THE TEXT

1. This story boils down to one decision, one question: should Mama have given Dee the quilts she wanted? Cite passages from the story to support your viewpoint.
2. The two opening paragraphs, set off from the rest of the story, serve as a kind of exposition. What do these paragraphs tell you about Mama? How do they set up the conflicts explored in the rest of the story?
3. Mama recounts how she sometimes dreams about herself and Dee appearing in a heartwarming reunion on a television show. How accurate do you think Mama's dreams about being on television are? How do they prepare us as readers to meet Dee? Do they bias us against her? Explain.
4. The action of "Everyday Use" is quite contained: a visit back home for college-educated Dee. Yet Walker expects us to understand that action in a larger context. What information about the past does Walker incorporate into the story's present? How does it affect our understanding of, or attitude toward, the three central characters?
5. Dee brings home a young man who introduces himself with an Islamic greeting and whose appearance Walker reports only through Mama's eyes: "a short, stocky man" whose "hair is all over his head a foot long and hanging from his chin like a kinky mule tail" (para. 19). How does this minor character, referred to as "Hakim-a-barber,"

contribute to the development of the three central characters?

6. In many traditional African cultures, the tribe pools resources to finance the education of a promising young person, who is then expected to assist the community. How is this practice reflected in this Southern small town? What does Dee's disregard of the current practice or its origin say about her?

7. In college, Dee came into contact with people and ideas quite different from those with which she grew up. What values does the "new Dee" — Wangero — claim to embrace? How do these values conflict with her family's values? How might the two value systems overlap or complement each other?

8. In the story, we gain information about the quilts — what they look like, who made them, how they are being used, different views on how they should be used. Like most symbols, the quilts have different meanings for different people. What do they symbolize to Dee? to Maggie? to Mama?

9. Where do you find irony in the story? How would you describe that irony: angry, gentle, playful, resigned, bitter, or something else? As you develop your response, consider whether you read the title as ironic.

10. Alice Walker gives the storytelling to Mama. Why? How would the story have been different with an omniscient narrator? (Try describing Dee's entrance from a more objective viewpoint.) Explain whether you think Mama's narration is the most effective way to convey Walker's purpose.

We're Not Jews

HANIF KUREISHI

Hanif Kureishi (b. 1954) is a British Pakistani playwright, screenwriter, filmmaker, and novelist. Born in Bromley, South London, to a Pakistani father and an English mother, he earned a degree in philosophy from King's College London. His first play, *Soaking the Heat* (1976), was performed at the Royal Court Theatre in London and was followed by *The Mother Country* (1980), for which he won the Thames Television Playwright Award. His screenplay for the film *My Beautiful Laundrette* (1985) was nominated for an Academy Award. He also wrote the screenplays for *Sammy and Rosie Get Laid* (1987) and *London Kills Me* (1991), which he also directed. His film *My Son the Fanatic* (1997) was adapted from his short story included in *Love in a Blue Time* (1997) and screened at Cannes Film Festival. Kureishi's first novel, *The Buddha of Suburbia* (1990), won the Whitbread Award and was made into a BBC television series. His novel *Intimacy* (1998) was adapted into a movie of the same name in 2000 that won acclaim at the Berlin Film Festival. Kureishi was named by the *Times* (London) as one of "the 50 greatest British writers since 1945." His work is known for its exploration of family dynamics, and often blurs the line between fiction and autobiography. "We're Not Jews," set in England in the 1960s, traces the tense afterschool commute of an English woman and her half-Pakistani son.

Azhar's mother led him to the front of the lower deck, sat him down with his satchel, hurried back to retrieve her shopping, and took her place beside him. As the bus pulled away Azhar spotted Big Billy and his son Little Billy racing alongside, yelling and waving at the driver. Azhar closed his eyes and hoped it was moving too rapidly for them to get on. But they not only flung themselves onto the platform, they charged up the almost empty vehicle hooting and panting as if they were on a fair-ground ride. They settled directly across the aisle from where they could stare at Azhar and his mother.

At this his mother made to rise. So did Big Billy. Little Billy sprang up. They would follow her and Azhar. With a sigh she sank back down. The conductor came, holding the arm of his ticket machine. He knew the Billys, and had a laugh with them. He let them ride for nothing.

Mother's grey perfumed glove took some pennies from her purse. She handed them to Azhar who held them up as she had shown him.

'One and a half to the Three Kings,' he said.

'Please,' whispered Mother, making a sign of exasperation.

'Please,' he repeated.

The conductor passed over the tickets and went away.

'Hold onto them tightly,' said Mother. 'In case the inspector gets on.'

Big Billy said, 'Look, he's a big boy.'

'Big boy,' echoed Little Billy.

'So grown up he has to run to teacher,' said Big Billy.

'Cry baby!' trumpeted Little Billy.

Mother was looking straight ahead, through the window. Her voice was almost normal, but subdued. 'Pity we didn't have time to get to the library. Still, there's tomorrow. Are you still the best reader in the class?' She nudged him. 'Are you?'

'S'pose so,' he mumbled.

Every evening after school Mother took him to the tiny library nearby where he exchanged the previous day's books. Tonight, though, there hadn't been time. She didn't want Father asking why they were late. She wouldn't want him to know they had been in to complain.

Big Billy had been called to the headmistress's stuffy room and been sharply informed — so she told Mother — that she took a 'dim view.' Mother was glad. She had objected to Little Billy bullying her boy. Azhar had had Little Billy sitting behind him in class. For weeks Little Billy had called him names and clipped him round the head with his ruler. Now some of the other boys, mates of Little Billy, had also started to pick on Azhar.

'I eat nuts!'

Big Billy was hooting like an orang-utan, jumping up and down and scratching himself under the arms — one of the things Little Billy had been castigated for. But it didn't restrain his father. His face looked horrible.

Big Billy lived a few doors away from them. Mother had known him and his family since she was a child. They had shared the same air-raid shelter during the war. Big Billy had been a Ted[1] and still wore a drape coat and his hair in a sculpted quiff. He had black bitten-down fingernails and a smear of grease across his forehead. He was known as Motorbike Bill because he repeatedly built and rebuilt his Triumph. 'Triumph of the Bill,' Father liked to murmur as they passed. Sometimes numerous lumps of metal stood on rags around the skeleton of the bike, and in the late evening Big Bill revved up the machine while his record player balanced on the windowsill repeatedly blared out a 45 called 'Rave On.' Then everyone knew Big Billy was preparing for the annual bank holiday run to the coast. Mother and the other neighbours were forced to shut their windows to exclude the noise and fumes.

Mother had begun to notice not only Azhar's dejection but also his exhausted and dishevelled appearance on his return from school. He looked as if he'd been flung into a hedge and rolled in a puddle — which he had. Unburdening with difficulty, he confessed the abuse the boys gave him, Little Billy in particular.

At first Mother appeared amused by such pranks. She was surprised that Azhar took it so hard. He should ignore the childish remarks: a lot of children were cruel. Yet he couldn't make out what it was with him that made people say such things, or why, after so many contented

[1] Short for "Teddy Boy," referring to young men in London in the 1950s who wore clothes inspired by the dandies, or well-groomed men, of the Edwardian period (1901–1910). — EDS.

hours at home with his mother, such violence had entered his world.

Mother had taken Azhar's hand and instructed him to reply, 'Little Billy, you're common — common as muck!'

Azhar held onto the words and repeated them continuously to himself. Next day, in a corner with his enemy's taunts going at him, he closed his eyes and hollered them out. 'Muck, muck, muck — common as muck you!'

Little Billy was as perplexed as Azhar by the epithet. Like magic it shut his mouth. But the next day Little Billy came back with the renewed might of names new to Azhar: sambo, wog, little coon. Azhar returned to his mother for more words but they had run out.

Big Billy was saying across the bus, 'Common! Why don't you say it out loud to me face, eh? Won't say it, eh?'

'Nah,' said Little Billy. 'Won't!'

'But we ain't as common as a slut who marries a darkie.'

'Darkie, darkie,' Little Billy repeated. 'Monkey, monkey!'

Mother's look didn't deviate. But, perhaps anxious that her shaking would upset Azhar, she pulled her hand from his and pointed at a shop.

'Look.'

'What?' said Azhar, distracted by Little Billy murmuring his name.

The instant Azhar turned his head, Big Billy called, 'Hey! why don't you look at us, little lady?'

She twisted round and waved at the conductor standing on his platform. But a passenger got on and the conductor followed him upstairs. The few other passengers, sitting like statues, were unaware or unconcerned.

Mother turned back. Azhar had never seen her like this, ashen, with wet eyes, her body stiff as a tree. Azhar sensed what an effort she was making to keep still. When she wept at home she threw herself on the bed, shook convulsively and thumped the pillow. Now all that moved was a bulb of snot shivering on the end of her nose. She sniffed determinedly, before opening her bag and extracting the scented handkerchief with which she usually wiped Azhar's face, or, screwing up a corner, dislodged any stray eyelashes around his eye. She blew her nose vigorously but he heard a sob.

Now she knew what went on and how it felt. How he wished he'd said nothing and protected her, for Big Billy was using her name: 'Yvonne, Yvonne, hey, Yvonne, didn't I give you a good time that time?'

'Evie, a good time, right?' sang Little Billy.

Big Billy smirked. 'Thing is,' he said, holding his nose, 'there's a smell on this bus.'

'Pooh!'

'How many of them are there living in that flat, all squashed together like, and stinkin' the road out, eatin' curry and rice!'

There was no doubt that their flat was jammed. Grandpop, a retired doctor, slept in one bedroom, Azhar, his sister and parents in another, and two uncles in the living room. All day big pans of Indian food simmered in the kitchen so people could eat when they wanted. The kitchen wallpaper bubbled and cracked and hung down like ancient scrolls. But Mother always denied that they were 'like that.' She refused to allow the word 'immigrant' to be used about Father, since in her eyes it applied only to illiterate tiny men with downcast eyes and mismatched clothes.

Mother's lips were moving but her throat must have been dry: no words came, until she managed to say, 'We're not Jews.'

There was a silence. This gave Big Billy an Opportunity. 'What you say?' He cupped his ear and his long dark sideburn. With his other hand he cuffed Little Billy, who had begun hissing. 'Speak up. Hey, tart, we can't hear you!'

Mother repeated the remark but could make her voice no louder.

Azhar wasn't sure what she meant. In his confusion he recalled a recent conversation about South Africa, where his best friend's family had just emigrated. Azhar had asked why, if they were to go somewhere — and there had been such talk — they too couldn't choose Cape Town. Painfully she replied that there the people with white skins were cruel to the black and brown people who were considered inferior and were forbidden to go where the whites went. The coloureds had separate entrances and were prohibited from sitting with the whites.

This peculiar fact of living history, vertiginously irrational and not taught in his school, struck his head like a hammer and echoed through his dreams night after night. How could such a thing be possible? What did it mean? How then should he act?

'Nah,' said Big Billy. 'You no Yid, Yvonne. You us. But worse. Goin' with the Paki.'

All the while Little Billy was hissing and twisting his head in imitation of a spastic.

Azhar had heard his father say that there had been 'gassing' not long ago. Neighbour had slaughtered neighbour, and such evil hadn't died. Father would poke his finger at his wife, son and baby daughter, and state, 'We're in the front line!'

These conversations were often a prelude to his announcing that they were going 'home' to Pakistan. There they wouldn't have these problems. At this point Azhar's mother would become uneasy. How could she go 'home' when she was at home already? Hot weather made her swelter; spicy food upset her stomach; being surrounded by people who didn't speak English made her feel lonely. As it was, Azhar's grandfather and uncle chattered away in Urdu, and when Uncle Asif's wife had been in the country, she had, without prompting, walked several paces behind them in the street. Not wanting to side with either camp, Mother had had to position herself, with Azhar, somewhere in the middle of this curious procession as it made its way to the shops.

Not that the idea of 'home' didn't trouble Father. He himself had never been there. His family had lived in China and India; but since he'd left, the remainder of his family had moved, along with hundreds of thousands of others, to Pakistan. How could he know if the new country would suit him, or if he could succeed there? While Mother wailed, he would smack his hand against his forehead and cry 'Oh God, I am trying to think in all directions at the same time!'

He had taken to parading about the flat in Wellington boots with a net curtain over his head, swinging his portable typewriter and saying he expected to be called to Vietnam as a war correspondent, and was preparing for jungle combat.

It made them laugh. For two years Father had been working as a packer in a factory that manufactured shoe polish. It was hard physical labour, which drained and infuriated him. He loved books and wanted to write them. He got up at five every morning; at night he wrote for as long as he could keep his eyes open. Even as they ate he scribbled over the backs of envelopes, rejection slips and factory stationery, trying to sell articles to magazines and newspapers. At the same time he was studying for a correspondence course on 'How To Be A Published Author'. The sound of his frenetic typing drummed into their heads like gunfire. They were forbidden to complain. Father was determined to make money from the articles on sport, politics and literature which he posted off most days, each accompanied by a letter that began, 'Dear Sir, Please find enclosed . . .'

But Father didn't have a sure grasp of the English language which was his, but not entirely, being 'Bombay variety, mish and mash'. Their neighbour, a retired school-teacher, was kind enough to correct Father's spelling and grammar, suggesting that he sometimes used 'the right words in the wrong place, and vice versa.' His pieces were regularly returned in the self-addressed stamped envelope that the *Writers' and Artists' Yearbook* advised. Lately, when they plopped through the letter box, Father didn't open them, but tore them up, stamped on the pieces and swore in Urdu, cursing the English who, he was convinced, were barring him. Or were they? Mother once suggested he was doing something wrong and should study something more profitable. But this didn't get a good response.

In the morning now Mother sent Azhar out to intercept the postman and collect the returned manuscripts. The envelopes and parcels were concealed around the garden like an alcoholic's bottles, behind the dustbins, in the bike shed, even under buckets, where, mouldering in secret, they sustained hope and kept away disaster.

At every stop Azhar hoped someone might get on who would discourage or arrest the Billys. But no one did, and as they moved forward the bus emptied. Little Billy took to jumping up and twanging the bell, at which the conductor only laughed.

Then Azhar saw that Little Billy had taken a marble from his pocket, and, standing with his arm back, was preparing to fling it. When Big Billy noticed this even his eyes widened. He reached for Billy's wrist. But the marble was released: it cracked into the window between Azhar and mother's head, chipping the glass.

She was screaming. 'Stop it, stop it! Won't anyone help! We'll be murdered!'

The noise she made came from hell or eternity. Little Billy blanched and shifted closer to his father; they went quiet.

Azhar got out of his seat to fight them but the conductor blocked his way.

Their familiar stop was ahead. Before the bus braked Mother was up, clutching her bags; she gave Azhar two carriers to hold, and nudged him towards the platform. As he went past he wasn't going to look at the Billys, but he did give them the eye, straight on, stare to stare, so he could see them and not be so afraid. They could hate him but he would know them. But if he couldn't fight them, what could he do with his anger?

They stumbled off and didn't need to check if the crêpe-soled Billys were behind, for they were already calling out, though not as loud as before.

As they approached the top of their street the retired teacher who assisted Father came out of his house, wearing a three-piece suit and trilby hat and leading his Scottie. He looked over his garden, picked up a scrap of paper which had blown over the fence, and sniffed the evening air. Azhar wanted to laugh: he resembled a phantom; in a deranged world the normal appeared the most bizarre. Mother immediately pulled Azhar towards his gate.

Their neighbour raised his hat and said in a friendly way, 'How's it all going?'

At first Azhar didn't understand what his mother was talking about. But it was Father she was referring to. 'They send them back, his writing, every day, and he gets so angry . . . so angry . . . Can't you help him?'

'I do help him, where I can,' he replied.

'Make him stop, then!'

She choked into her handkerchief and shook her head when he asked what the matter was.

The Billys hesitated a moment and then passed on silently. Azhar watched them go. It was all right, for now. But tomorrow Azhar would be for it, and the next day, and the next. No mother could prevent it.

'He's a good little chap,' the teacher was saying, of Father.

'But will he get anywhere?'

'Perhaps,' he said. 'Perhaps. But he may be a touch —' Azhar stood on tiptoe to listen. 'Over hopeful. Over hopeful.'

'Yes,' she said, biting her lip.

'Tell him to read more Gibbon[2] and Macaulay[3],' he said. 'That should set him straight.'

'Right.'

[2] Edward Gibbon (1737–1794) was an English historian who openly critiqued organized religion. — EDS.

[3] Thomas Babington Macaulay (1800–1859) was an English historian, essayist, critic, and politician most famous for his books on British history. — EDS.

'Are you feeling better?'

'Yes, yes,' Mother insisted.

He said, concerned, 'Let me walk you back.'

'That's all right, thank you.'

Instead of going home, mother and son went in the opposite direction. They passed a bomb site and left the road for a narrow path. When they could no longer feel anything firm beneath their feet, they crossed a nearby rutted muddy playing field in the dark. The strong wind, buffeting them sideways, nearly had them tangled in the slimy nets of a soccer goal. He had no idea she knew this place.

At last they halted outside a dismal shed, the public toilet, rife with spiders and insects, where he and his friends often played. He looked up but couldn't see her face. She pushed the door and stepped across the wet floor. When he hesitated she tugged him into the stall with her. She wasn't going to let him go now. He dug into the wall with his penknife and practised holding his breath until she finished, and wiped herself on the scratchy paper. Then she sat there with her eyes closed, as if she were saying a prayer. His teeth were clicking; ghosts whispered in his ears; outside there were footsteps; dead fingers seemed to be clutching at him.

For a long time she examined herself in the mirror, powdering her face, replacing her lipstick and combing her hair. There were no human voices, only rain on the metal roof, which dripped through onto their heads.

'Mum,' he cried.

'Don't you whine!'

He wanted his tea. He couldn't wait to get away. Her eyes were scorching his face in the yellow light. He knew she wanted to tell him not to mention any of this. Recognising at last that it wasn't necessary, she suddenly dragged him by his arm, as if it had been his fault they were held up, and hurried him home without another word.

The flat was lighted and warm. Father, having worked the early shift, was home. Mother went into the kitchen and Azhar helped her unpack the shopping. She was trying to be normal, but the very effort betrayed her, and she didn't kiss Father as she usually did.

Now, beside Grandpop and Uncle Asif, Father was listening to the cricket commentary on the big radio, which had an illuminated panel printed with the names of cities they could never pick up, Brussels, Stockholm, Hilversum, Berlin, Budapest. Father's typewriter, with its curled paper tongue, sat on the table surrounded by empty beer bottles.

'Come, boy.'

Azhar ran to his father who poured some beer into a glass for him, mixing it with lemonade.

The men were smoking pipes, peering into the ashy bowls, tapping them on the table, poking them with pipe cleaners, and relighting them. They were talking loudly in Urdu or Punjabi, using some English words but gesticulating and slapping one another in a way English people never did. Then one of them would suddenly leap up, clapping his hands and shouting, 'Yes — out — out!'

Azhar was accustomed to being with his family while grasping only fragments of what they said. He endeavoured to decipher the gist of it, laughing, as he always did, when the men laughed, and silently moving his lips without knowing what the words meant, whirling, all the while, in incomprehension.

[1995]

EXPLORING THE TEXT

1. Describe the community in which Azhar and his family live. How does Azhar fit in? How is he different from his parents? In what ways is he similar to them? What is the ethnic background of each of the characters and how do they interact?
2. Why do you think Hanif Kureishi set most of the story on a moving bus with a driver who ignores the passengers? How does that setting establish the tone of the story? What does it signal to readers about England in the early 1960s, when the story takes place?
3. Why do you believe Kureishi chose to tell this story from a child's perspective? Who is the central character? How does Kureishi give his diverse cast of characters their voices?
4. What do you see as the primary differences between Azhar and Little Billy? How does each one face his world? What kind of person will each grow up to be?
5. Why is Big Billy particularly hostile to Azhar's mother? Why do you think she has trouble standing up to him? Why does she finally say, "We're not Jews"?
6. What purpose does the "retired teacher" (paras. 63–80) serve? Think about both his appearance and what he says to Azhar and his mother. Why do you think the two Billys are silenced when they see him?
7. What does "We're Not Jews" say about the place of women? Consider how both Azhar's family and the Billys treat Azhar's mother.
8. How is Azhar's father characterized? What do you make of his obsession with journalism in a language that's not his first? Do you think he's intended to be a comic figure, or something else? Explain your answer.
9. "We're Not Jews" has many historical allusions, including references to World War II, the partition of India, and apartheid in South Africa. How do these allusions provide context for Azhar's particular experience? How do they inform your reading of the Billys' actions, and Azhar's mother's reaction to them?
10. In a review of *Love in a Blue Time*, the collection in which "We're Not Jews" appears, critic Laura Miller wrote that "Kureishi's love of the world has always been the heartbeat of his work." To what extent do you believe that statement applies to this story? Explain your answer, using specific details from the story to support your response.

POETRY

Elegy Written in a Country Churchyard

THOMAS GRAY

Though he only published a mere one thousand lines of poetry during his life, Thomas Gray (1716–1771) was considered one of the greatest poets of his time. Born to a middle-class family in Cornhill, England, he was the fifth of twelve children, and the only one to survive past infancy. He was educated at Eton and later Cambridge, where, despite expectations that he would pursue law, he delved ever more deeply into literature. In 1742, Gray began writing poetry in earnest, but he was never prolific. Despite the success of many of his poems, he was very self-critical, often employing his lacerating wit at his own expense. He turned down the position of poet laureate of England, later saying that he feared his poems would be "mistaken for the words of a flea." Instead, he accepted a largely ceremonial post

teaching history at Cambridge. After his death, Gray was buried in the churchyard of Stoke Poges, which is thought to be the setting for his most famous poem, "Elegy Written in a Country Churchyard." "Elegy" was an instant success. Today it remains one of the most imitated, parodied, and quoted poems in the English language.

The curfew[1] tolls the knell of parting day,
　The lowing herd wind slowly o'er the lea,
The plowman homeward plods his weary way,
　And leaves the world to darkness and to me.

Now fades the glimmering landscape on the sight,
　And all the air a solemn stillness holds,
Save where the beetle wheels his droning flight,
　And drowsy tinklings lull the distant folds;

Save that from yonder ivy-mantled tower
　The moping owl does to the moon complain
Of such, as wandering near her secret bower,
　Molest her ancient solitary reign.

Beneath those rugged elms, that yew tree's shade,
　Where heaves the turf in many a moldering heap,
Each in his narrow cell forever laid,
　The rude[2] forefathers of the hamlet sleep.

The breezy call of incense-breathing morn,
　The swallow twittering from the straw-built shed,
The cock's shrill clarion, or the echoing horn,
　No more shall rouse them from their lowly bed.

For them no more the blazing hearth shall burn,
　Or busy housewife ply her evening care;
No children run to lisp their sire's return,
　Or climb his knees the envied kiss to share.

Oft did the harvest to their sickle yield,
　Their furrow oft the stubborn glebe[3] has broke;
How jocund did they drive their team afield!
　How bowed the woods beneath their sturdy stroke!

Let not Ambition mock their useful toil,
　Their homely joys, and destiny obscure;
Nor Grandeur hear with a disdainful smile
　The short and simple annals of the poor.

---

[1] Evening bell.—EDS.
[2] Humble.—EDS.
[3] Soil.—EDS.

The boast of heraldry, the pomp of power,
    And all that beauty, all that wealth e'er gave,
Awaits alike the inevitable hour.
    The paths of glory lead but to the grave.

Nor you, ye proud, impute to these the fault,
    If memory o'er their tomb no trophies raise,
Where through the long-drawn aisle and fretted[4] vault
    The pealing anthem swells the note of praise.

Can storied urn or animated[5] bust
    Back to its mansion call the fleeting breath?
Can Honor's voice provoke the silent dust,
    Or Flattery soothe the dull cold ear of Death?

Perhaps in this neglected spot is laid
    Some heart once pregnant with celestial fire;
Hands that the rod of empire might have swayed,
    Or waked to ecstasy the living lyre.

But Knowledge to their eyes her ample page
    Rich with the spoils of time did ne'er unroll;
Chill Penury repressed their noble rage,
    And froze the genial current of the soul.

Full many a gem of purest ray serene,
    The dark unfathomed caves of ocean bear.
Full many a flower is born to blush unseen,
    And waste its sweetness on the desert air.

Some village Hampden,[6] that with dauntless breast
    The little tyrant of his fields withstood;
Some mute inglorious Milton here may rest,
    Some Cromwell[7] guiltless of his country's blood.

The applause of listening senates to command,
    The threats of pain and ruin to despise,
To scatter plenty o'er a smiling land,
    And read their history in a nation's eyes,

Their lot forbade: nor circumscribed alone
    Their growing virtues, but their crimes confined;
Forbade to wade through slaughter to a throne,
    And shut the gates of mercy on mankind,

---

[4] Ornamented. — EDS.

[5] Lifelike. — EDS.

[6] John Hampden (1594–1643) was a prominent figure in the English civil war. He famously refused to pay a protection tax levied by Charles I. — EDS.

[7] Oliver Cromwell (1599–1658) was a rebel leader in the English civil war. — EDS.

The struggling pangs of conscious truth to hide,
To quench the blushes of ingenuous shame,
Or heap the shrine of Luxury and Pride
With incense kindled at the Muse's flame.

Far from the madding crowd's ignoble strife,
Their sober wishes never learned to stray;
Along the cool sequestered vale of life
They kept the noiseless tenor of their way.

Yet even these bones from insult to protect
Some frail memorial still erected nigh,
With uncouth rhymes and shapeless sculpture decked,
Implores the passing tribute of a sigh.

Their name, their years, spelt by the unlettered Muse,
The place of fame and elegy supply:
And many a holy text around she strews,
That teach the rustic moralist to die.

For who to dumb Forgetfulness a prey,
This pleasing anxious being e'er resigned,
Left the warm precincts of the cheerful day,
Nor cast one longing lingering look behind?

On some fond breast the parting soul relies,
Some pious drops the closing eye requires;
Even from the tomb the voice of Nature cries,
Even in our ashes live their wonted fires.

For thee, who mindful of the unhonored dead
Dost in these lines their artless tale relate;
If chance, by lonely contemplation led,
Some kindred spirit shall inquire thy fate,

Haply some hoary-headed swain[8] may say,
"Oft have we seen him at the peep of dawn
Brushing with hasty steps the dews away
To meet the sun upon the upland lawn.

"There at the foot of yonder nodding beech
That wreathes its old fantastic roots so high,
His listless length at noontide would he stretch,
And pore upon the brook that babbles by.

---

[8] White-haired (elderly) shepherd. — EDS.

"Hard by yon wood, now smiling as in scorn,
Muttering his wayward fancies he would rove,
Now drooping, woeful wan, like one forlorn,
Or crazed with care, or crossed in hopeless love.

"One morn I missed him on the customed hill,
Along the heath and near his favorite tree;
Another came; nor yet beside the rill,
Nor up the lawn, nor at the wood was he;

"The next with dirges due in sad array
Slow through the churchway path we saw him borne.
Approach and read (for thou canst read) the lay,
Graved on the stone beneath yon aged thorn."

THE EPITAPH

Here rests his head upon the lap of Earth
A youth to fortune and to Fame unknown.
Fair Science[9] *frowned not on his humble birth,*
And Melancholy marked him for her own.

Large was his bounty, and his soul sincere,
Heaven did a recompense as largely send:
He gave to Misery all he had, a tear,
He gained from Heaven ('twas all he wished), a friend.

No farther seek his merits to disclose,
Or draw his frailties from their dread abode
(There they alike in trembling hope repose),
The bosom of his Father and his God.

[1751]

[9]Learning, education. — EDS.

EXPLORING THE TEXT

1. Who do you think is the speaker? Now, try to imagine the setting. Is the speaker literally in the churchyard? How do you know?
2. Notice the use of sound imagery in stanzas 1–3. How does the toll of the "knell of parting day" (l. 1) echo throughout those stanzas? In what context do you usually hear the word "knell"? What is its connotation, and how does that connotation contribute to the meaning of this section of the poem? How does this sound imagery introduce stanza 4?
3. Look carefully at stanza 2. How does Thomas Gray use the natural world to comment on the issue of tradition and progress?
4. The poem shifts in stanza 8. Analyze the stanza, looking carefully at Gray's diction and syntax choices, and explain how it works as a transition from one idea to another.
5. Stanza 13 (ll. 49–52) may be the poem's most famous. How does Gray use figurative language to mirror the stanza's meaning, that poverty may have

forced talented people to remain unknown and unfulfilled?

6. If you read lines 61–65 grammatically — that is, as a complete sentence — you will find that the subject and verb do not appear until line 65, in a separate stanza from the object of the sentence. What is the effect of this delay? Why might Gray have considered the object worth introducing before the subject?
7. How does the speaker honor simple folk in lines 61–76?
8. Stanza 24 (ll. 93–96) begins the lead-up to the epitaph, which comprises the last twelve lines of the poem. Who is speaking beginning in line 98, and what is he or she speaking about? Whose epitaph ends the poem?
9. Some scholars believe that "Elegy" was inspired by the fact that Gray was the only one of twelve siblings to survive until adulthood. How does this knowledge affect your reading of the poem?
10. Gray's "Elegy" is considered one of the great poems, in part because of the seamless way structure, rhyme scheme, and imagery combine to communicate Gray's message that life is short. First consider each of these elements separately. How does each element connect to the poem's message? Then consider the way these elements work together to elevate this simple theme.

London

WILLIAM BLAKE

Obscure during his lifetime, William Blake (1757–1827) has come to be recognized as one of the most significant poets and artists in English history. Born in London and educated at home by parents who held nonconformist religious and political beliefs, Blake developed highly controversial views about spirituality, women's rights, and personal liberty that informed much of his work. On occasion, his views — and his willingness to express and publish them — led to difficulties with the law, including an arrest in 1803 for "uttering seditious statements against the Crown." Following an apprenticeship to an engraver, Blake began experimenting with relief engraving — a technique he called "illuminated printing" — to illustrate both his own books and works such as Milton's *Paradise Lost* and Dante's *The Divine Comedy*. "London" comes from *Songs of Experience* (1794), a response to his earlier collection of poems, *Songs of Innocence* (1789).

I wander through each chartered[1] street,
Near where the chartered Thames does flow,
And mark in every face I meet
Marks of weakness, marks of woe.

In every cry of every man,
In every Infant's cry of fear,
In every voice, in every ban,
The mind-forged manacles I hear.

[1]Defined by law. — EDS.

How the Chimney-sweeper's cry
Every black'ning Church appalls;
And the hapless Soldier's sigh
Runs in blood down Palace walls.

But most through midnight streets I hear
How the youthful Harlot's curse
Blasts the new-born Infant's tear,
And blights with plagues the Marriage hearse.

[1794]

EXPLORING THE TEXT

1. "London" takes the form of a walking tour through London. How does William Blake use visual and auditory imagery to both convey the atmosphere in the streets and create a sense of foreboding?
2. What do you make of the repetition of the words "mark" and "marks" in the first stanza? Blake uses "mark" in line 3 to mean "notice." Consider other possible meanings of the word.
3. The last two stanzas introduce a series of exploited persons: chimney sweepers, soldiers, and prostitutes. Why do you think Blake saves the "youthful Harlot" for last? What do you think he means by "Marriage hearse"?
4. The poem's third stanza is an acrostic; the first letters of the first words in each line spell out "HEAR." In addition, lines 8 and 13 both end with the word "hear." What does Blake want us to hear? Why is this technique effective in this part of the poem?
5. What is your interpretation of "mind-forged manacles" (l. 8)? How might that phrase comment on the overindustrialized world of London in the eighteenth century?
6. "London," like many of Blake's poems, has been interpreted in different ways. Critic Camille Paglia, who writes about "London" in *Break, Blow, Burn*, sees it as part of Blake's "exposé of commercial society." What is your view? Why? Can you see another way the poem might be interpreted?

Dover Beach

MATTHEW ARNOLD

Poet, essayist, and critic Matthew Arnold (1822–1888) was brought up and educated at Rugby School, one of England's oldest boarding schools, where his father was headmaster. After graduating from Balliol College at Oxford, he took the rather mundane position of inspector of schools at Her Majesty's Inspectorate of Education to support his family. He held this position for thirty years, during which time he wrote the bulk of his poetry, including *Empedocles on Etna* (1852) and *Poems* (1853). Arnold was elected professor of poetry at Oxford in 1857 and 1862, and during this time he produced several collections of essays and literary, cultural, and religious criticism. His poetry is remembered for its clarity and straightforwardness, and is considered a bridge between romanticism and modernism. In 1867, Arnold published "Dover Beach," his most famous work. Dover is the English port city from which most people traveled to France.

The sea is calm tonight.
The tide is full, the moon lies fair
Upon the straits; — on the French coast the light
Gleams and is gone; the cliffs of England stand,
Glimmering and vast, out in the tranquil bay.
Come to the window, sweet is the night-air!
Only, from the long line of spray
Where the sea meets the moon-blanched land,
Listen! you hear the grating roar
Of pebbles which the waves draw back, and fling,
At their return, up the high strand,
Begin, and cease, and then again begin,
With tremulous cadence slow, and bring
The eternal note of sadness in.

Sophocles long ago
Heard it on the Aegean, and it brought
Into his mind the turbid ebb and flow
Of human misery;[1] we
Find also in the sound a thought,
Hearing it by this distant northern sea.

The Sea of Faith
Was once, too, at the full, and round earth's shore
Lay like the folds of a bright girdle furled.
But now I only hear
Its melancholy, long, withdrawing roar,
Retreating, to the breath
Of the night-wind, down the vast edges drear
And naked shingles[2] of the world.

Ah, love, let us be true
To one another! for the world, which seems
To lie before us like a land of dreams,
So various, so beautiful, so new,
Hath really neither joy, nor love, nor light,
Nor certitude, nor peace, nor help for pain;
And we are here as on a darkling plain
Swept with confused alarms of struggle and flight,
Where ignorant armies clash by night.

[1867]

[1] A reference to Sophocles's play *Antigone*: "the gods have rocked a house to its foundations / the ruin will never cease, cresting on and on / from one generation on throughout the race — / like a great mounting tide" (ll. 659–62). — EDS.

[2] Pebble beaches. — EDS.

EXPLORING THE TEXT

1. Analyze the series of vivid images of nighttime by the sea in the first stanza. To which senses do these images appeal? How do these images relate to the meaning of the poem? Why do you think Matthew Arnold highlights the auditory images, such as "Listen!" in line 9?
2. What do the consonance and caesura in lines 9–14 add to the imagery in those lines? How does that imagery help create the mood of sadness with which the stanza ends?
3. What do you think Arnold means by "The Sea of Faith" (l. 21)? What does he think has replaced it?
4. You might notice that the last stanza of the poem is self-contradictory; it almost argues with itself. What are some of the competing ideas in the stanza? How does the tone change over the course of the stanza? How does this shift in tone highlight the stanza's mixed message?
5. The last four lines of the poem are rhymed couplets, the form traditionally used to conclude and resolve a sonnet. What is the effect of that form on the meaning of those lines? How does the stanza resolve, or fail to resolve, the problem introduced by the poem?
6. There is evidence that Arnold wrote "Dover Beach" on his honeymoon in 1851. How does that possibility change the meaning of the poem for you?
7. "Dover Beach" was written when England was the most powerful and industrially sophisticated country in the world. How does the poem comment on this period in English history?

God's Grandeur

GERARD MANLEY HOPKINS

Torn between his obligations as a Jesuit and his love for poetry, Gerard Manley Hopkins (1844–1889) declined to seek an audience for his work during his lifetime; the bulk of his poems were published posthumously in 1916. Hopkins was born in Stratford, London, to a wealthy family. After converting to Catholicism near the end of his studies at Oxford, Hopkins entered the priesthood and, adhering to one of his vows, burned nearly all of his accumulated poems. He began to write again in 1875, when he was asked to commemorate the death of five Franciscan nuns who drowned in a shipwreck off the coast of England as they fled oppression in Germany. In the poem he wrote, entitled "Wreck of the Deutschland," Hopkins introduced what he called "sprung rhythm," a meter designed to imitate the rhythm of natural speech; this meter anticipated free verse and would influence new generations of poets. "God's Grandeur," written in 1877, makes occasional use of this unconventional rhythm and is representative of Hopkins's work in both subject and form.

The world is charged with the grandeur of God.
  It will flame out, like shining from shook foil;
  It gathers to a greatness, like the ooze of oil
Crushed. Why do men then now not reck[1] his rod?[2]

Generations have trod, have trod, have trod;
  And all is seared with trade; bleared, smeared with toil;
  And wears man's smudge and shares man's smell: the soil
Is bare now, nor can foot feel, being shod.

And for all this, nature is never spent;
  There lives the dearest freshness deep down things;
And though the last lights off the black West went
  Oh, morning, at the brown brink eastward, springs—
Because the Holy Ghost over the bent
  World broods with warm breast and with ah! bright wings.

[1877]

---

[1] Mind, obey.—EDS.

[2] "Rod" here is a scepter, representing God's position as king of kings.—EDS.

EXPLORING THE TEXT

1. What does the word "charged" suggest in line 1? Consider several possibilities.
2. How does style reinforce meaning in line 5? What other examples of the close connection between style and meaning do you see in "God's Grandeur"?
3. How is the sound of the poem created? Look especially at the internal rhymes. Try reading this poem aloud to hear how Gerard Manley Hopkins uses stressed syllables to create the poem's musical quality.

4. What does the metaphor in the poem's last two lines evoke for you? Explain the metaphor and how and why it affects you the way it does.
5. "God's Grandeur" follows the form of a Petrarchan sonnet, with an octet (8 lines) and a sestet (6 lines). What question or problem is posed in the octet and answered or resolved in the sestet?
6. What argument does "God's Grandeur" make? How does Hopkins present his evidence, including a counterargument?

Crumbling is not an instant's Act

EMILY DICKINSON

Born into a prominent family in Amherst, Massachusetts, Emily Dickinson (1830–1886) received some formal education at Amherst Academy and Mount Holyoke Female Seminary (which became Mount Holyoke College). Throughout her lifetime, Dickinson was a shy and reclusive person, who preferred to remain within her close family circle. In 1862, she enclosed four poems in a letter to literary critic and abolitionist Thomas Wentworth Higginson, who had written a piece in the *Atlantic Monthly* that included practical advice for young writers. Her letter began, "Mr. Higginson, — Are you too deeply occupied to say if my verse is alive? The mind is so near itself it cannot see distinctly, and I have none to ask. Should you think it breathed, and had you the leisure to tell me, I should feel quick gratitude." Dickinson didn't sign the letter, but instead enclosed her name on a card inside a smaller envelope. Dickinson wrote over seventeen hundred poems, but only ten were published in her lifetime. "Crumbling is not an instant's Act," published four years after her death, is like much of Dickinson's work: enigmatic at first, but blossoming after a couple of readings.

Crumbling is not an instant's Act
A fundamental pause
Dilapidation's processes
Are organized Decays.

'Tis first a Cobweb on the Soul
A Cuticle of Dust
A Borer in the Axis
An Elemental Rust—

Ruin is formal—Devil's work
Consecutive and slow—
Fail in an instant, no man did
Slipping—is Crash's law.

[1890]

EXPLORING THE TEXT

1. "Crumbling is not an instant's Act" has several examples of personification. Identify them, and then analyze their effect on the poem's meaning. Pay careful attention to the way they help Emily Dickinson support the poem's argument that falling apart is a slow process.
2. The second stanza offers examples of "organized Decays." Examine them closely, and then analyze how they function both literally and figuratively.
3. Do you think Dickinson is talking only about personal crumbling, or does the poem also apply to the ways society, or even humanity, falls victim to entropy? Use examples of her language to support your answer.
4. What do you think the poem has to say on the subject of tradition and progress?
5. How is this poem timeless? How can its meaning be applied to conditions in the world today?

Mending Wall

ROBERT FROST

Though Robert Frost (1874–1963) is considered the quintessential New England poet, he was born in San Francisco. After the death of his father when Frost was eleven years old, the family moved to Massachusetts. Frost attended Dartmouth College and Harvard University, but in both cases left early to support his family. He delivered newspapers, farmed, did factory work, and taught high school and college, but considered poetry to be his true calling. Frost won four Pulitzer Prizes for his collections *New Hampshire: A Poem with Notes and Grace Notes* (1924), *Collected Poems* (1931), *A Further Range* (1937), and *A Witness Tree* (1943), and in 1961 he spoke at the inauguration of President John F. Kennedy. Frost believed that poetry should be a "reproduction of human speech," a quality evident in "Mending Wall."

Something there is that doesn't love a wall,
That sends the frozen-ground-swell under it,
And spills the upper boulders in the sun;
And makes gaps even two can pass abreast.
The work of hunters is another thing:
I have come after them and made repair
Where they have left not one stone on a stone,
But they would have the rabbit out of hiding,
To please the yelping dogs. The gaps I mean,
No one has seen them made or heard them made,
But at spring mending-time we find them there.
I let my neighbor know beyond the hill;
And on a day we meet to walk the line
And set the wall between us once again.
We keep the wall between us as we go.
To each the boulders that have fallen to each.
And some are loaves and some so nearly balls
We have to use a spell to make them balance:
"Stay where you are until our backs are turned!"
We wear our fingers rough with handling them.
Oh, just another kind of outdoor game,
One on a side. It comes to little more:
There where it is we do not need the wall:
He is all pine and I am apple orchard.
My apple trees will never get across
And eat the cones under his pines, I tell him.
He only says, "Good fences make good neighbors."
Spring is the mischief in me, and I wonder
If I could put a notion in his head:
"*Why* do they make good neighbors? Isn't it
Where there are cows? But here there are no cows.
Before I built a wall I'd ask to know

What I was walling in or walling out,
And to whom I was like to give offense.
Something there is that doesn't love a wall,
That wants it down." I could say "Elves" to him,
But it's not elves exactly, and I'd rather
He said it for himself. I see him there
Bringing a stone grasped firmly by the top
In each hand, like an old-stone savage armed.
He moves in darkness as it seems to me,
Not of woods only and the shade of trees.
He will not go behind his father's saying,
And he likes having thought of it so well
He says again, "Good fences make good neighbors."

[1914]

EXPLORING THE TEXT

1. Is there a conflict in the poem? Explain.
2. Contrast the inverted syntax of lines 1 and 35 — "Something there is that doesn't love a wall" — to the traditional subject-verb-object syntax of lines 27 and 45 — "Good fences make good neighbors." How does the difference help develop each of the poem's characters? What effect does the difference have on the poem's meaning?
3. Read lines 12–15 carefully. How could the different meanings of the word "between," which is repeated twice, change the meaning of the poem?
4. Lines 13–18 lead up to the "spell" in line 19 that the two wall-menders use to keep the rocks from toppling. How are those lead-up lines a sort of incantation in themselves? How might they connect to the image in lines 39–40 of the speaker's neighbor "bringing a stone grasped firmly by the top / In each hand, like an old-stone savage armed"?
5. Why do you think Frost allows the neighbor to offer the proverb "Good fences make good neighbors" twice? Do you think the speaker agrees with this adage? Why do you think the neighbor gets the last word?
6. "Mending Wall" questions whether a wall that has no function in the modern world still fulfills a ritualistic need. When Frost was asked about the poem's meaning, he said his poems are "all set to trip the reader head foremost into the boundless." In what way does trying to answer the poem's question trip you "into the boundless"? Which of the poem's two characters trip "into the boundless"?
7. When President Kennedy visited the Berlin Wall, he quoted the first line of "Mending Wall." His audience knew what he meant, of course. Later, when Frost visited Russia, he found that the Russian translation of the poem left off the first line. He said he could have done better for them by saying: "Something there is that doesn't love a wall, / Something there is that does." Does that potential change alter the meaning of the poem for you? Explain.

The Second Coming

WILLIAM BUTLER YEATS

William Butler Yeats (1865–1939) was born in Dublin to a middle-class Protestant family with strong connections to England. The young Yeats spent his early childhood in the West of Ireland, a region that remained a profound influence on his work. Yeats began as a playwright, founding the Irish Literary Theatre in 1899, and wrote several plays celebrating Irish cultural tradition. The most important of these are *Cathleen ni Houlihan* (1902), *The King's Threshold* (1904), and *Deirdre* (1907). His early plays earned him the Nobel Prize for Literature in 1923. By 1912, he had turned to writing poetry. Profoundly influenced by William

Blake, Yeats's poetry reflects Ireland's rich mythology and a fascination with the occult. His collections include *The Wild Swans at Coole* (1919), *Michael Robartes and the Dancer* (1921), *The Tower* (1928), and *The Winding Stair* (1933). Yeats's work spans the transition from the nineteenth century to the modernism of the twentieth century. In one of his most famous poems, "The Second Coming," Yeats presents an apocalyptic vision for humanity in the aftermath of World War I.

Turning and turning in the widening gyre[1]
The falcon cannot hear the falconer;
Things fall apart; the center cannot hold;
Mere anarchy is loosed upon the world,
The blood-dimmed tide is loosed, and everywhere
The ceremony of innocence is drowned;
The best lack all conviction, while the worst
Are full of passionate intensity.

Surely some revelation is at hand;
Surely the Second Coming is at hand.
The Second Coming! Hardly are those words out
When a vast image out of *Spiritus Mundi*[2]
Troubles my sight: somewhere in sands of the desert
A shape with lion body and the head of a man,
A gaze blank and pitiless as the sun,
Is moving its slow thighs, while all about it
Reel shadows of the indignant desert birds.
The darkness drops again; but now I know
That twenty centuries of stony sleep
Were vexed to nightmare by a rocking cradle,
And what rough beast, its hour come round at last,
Slouches towards Bethlehem to be born?

[1921]

---

[1] Widening spiral of a falcon's flight, used by Yeats to describe the cycles of history. — EDS.
[2] Soul of the world. — EDS.

EXPLORING THE TEXT

1. Consider both the speaker and the imagery in the first eight lines. How do the images help create the persona of the speaker? How are the speaker and the imagery different in the last 14 lines?
2. What do you think the falcon and the falconer (l. 2) symbolize? What do you think it means that the "falcon cannot hear the falconer"? How is that metaphor connected to the image in lines 14–17?
3. What is the effect of the repetition of "loosed" in lines 4 and 5, and "Surely" in lines 9 and 10?
4. Describe the tone of the poem. How is it created?
5. Why do you think the poem ends with a question?
6. Adam Cohen, in an editorial in the *New York Times*, notes that phrases from "The Second Coming" are "irresistible to pundits" — analysts or commentators

on politics or social policy — who find that lines such as "The best lack all conviction, while the worst / Are full of passionate intensity" (ll. 7–8) perfectly sum up any era in history. Cohen, however, believes that "The Second Coming" is "a powerful brief against punditry," a caution against confident predictions. Do you agree? Explain your answer.

Autumn Begins in Martins Ferry, Ohio

JAMES WRIGHT

James Wright (1927–1980) was born in Martins Ferry, Ohio, a small industrial town on the Ohio River. After graduating from Shreve High School, Wright served in the army and then attended Kenyon College on the GI Bill. He later studied in Vienna on a Fulbright Fellowship, and went on to earn graduate degrees at the University of Washington, where he studied with poet Theodore Roethke. His early poems tended toward traditional forms, but by the early 1960s, he had largely abandoned rhyme and meter in favor of loosely structured free verse. His works include *The Green Wall* (1957), *Saint Judas* (1959), and *The Branch Will Not Break* (1963). His 1971 *Collected Poems* was awarded a Pulitzer Prize. "Autumn Begins in Martins Ferry, Ohio" is from *The Branch Will Not Break*, and shares with the other poems of that collection not only stylistic daring but a thematic concern for loneliness and the means human beings employ to overcome or endure it.

In the Shreve High football stadium,
I think of Polacks nursing long beers in Tiltonsville,
And gray faces of Negroes in the blast furnace at Benwood,
And the ruptured night watchman of Wheeling Steel,
Dreaming of heroes.

All the proud fathers are ashamed to go home.
Their women cluck like starved pullets,
Dying for love.

Therefore,
Their sons grow suicidally beautiful
At the beginning of October,
And gallop terribly against each other's bodies.

[1963]

EXPLORING THE TEXT

1. Why is the word "autumn" in the title significant? What associations do we make with autumn? How does each connotation affect your reading of the poem?

2. Who is the speaker? Where exactly do you picture him or her? What is it about the setting in the opening line that causes the speaker to "think" of the people in the next three lines?

3. Look carefully at the poem's diction. How do words and phrases such as "nursing" (l. 2), "ruptured" (l. 4), and "starved pullets" (l. 7) add layers of meaning to the poem? Find at least two more examples of diction that add nuance and meaning to the poem.
4. What is the effect of line 9, a single word: "Therefore"? What is its purpose?
5. Look carefully at the poem's last four lines. What connects them to the first stanza? What separates them from it?
6. Is this poem more about tradition or more about progress? Explain your answer.

Bogland

SEAMUS HEANEY

Seamus Heaney (1939–2013) was born at Mossbawn, his family's farm, in Northern Ireland, about thirty miles northwest of Belfast. Heaney was the eldest of nine children. His father's family was involved in farming and cattle dealing, and his mother's family had been employed in a local linen mill. Heaney lived on the farm until he was twelve and won a scholarship to St. Columb's College, a Catholic boarding school about forty miles away. He later lived in Belfast and then the Republic of Ireland, and he said that his departure from the farm at Mossbawn was a removal from "the earth of farm labour to the heaven of education." At St. Columb's, Heaney learned Latin and Irish, and as a student at Queen's University in Belfast, he learned Anglo-Saxon; these languages resonate throughout his work. Heaney became known in the mid-1960s, when he was part of a group of Northern Irish poets that included Michael Longley, Derek Mahon, Paul Muldoon, and Ciaran Carson. Though stylistically diverse, these poets shared the background of a society that was deeply divided both politically and religiously.

Heaney's works include the collections *Death of a Naturalist* (1966), *Door into the Dark* (1969), *North* (1975), *Station Island* (1984), *Opened Ground* (1998), and *Electric Light* (2001). He is also known for his translations — such as *Sweeney Astray* (1983), *Sweeney's Flight* (1992), and *Beowulf* (1999) — and the plays *The Cure at Troy* (1990) and *Burial at Thebes* (2004). He was awarded the Nobel Prize for Literature in 1995.

for T. P. Flanagan

We have no prairies
To slice a big sun at evening—
Everywhere the eye concedes to
Encroaching horizon,

Is wooed into the cyclops' eye
Of a tarn. Our unfenced country
Is bog that keeps crusting
Between the sights of the sun.

They've taken the skeleton
Of the Great Irish Elk
Out of the peat, set it up
An astounding crate full of air.

Butter sunk under
More than a hundred years
Was recovered salty and white.
The ground itself is kind, black butter

Melting and opening underfoot,
Missing its last definition
By millions of years.
They'll never dig coal here,

Only the waterlogged trunks
Of great firs, soft as pulp.
Our pioneers keep striking
Inwards and downwards,

Every layer they strip
Seems camped on before.
The bogholes might be Atlantic seepage.
The wet centre is bottomless.

[1969]

EXPLORING THE TEXT

1. How does the poem create a feeling of drilling downwards to the very last word, which is "bottomless"? Look carefully at the way the poem looks on the page.
2. What words or images feel mythical in "Bogland" and what is their effect? What is the effect, for example, of describing a "tarn" (l.6), which is a small mountain lake, as a "cyclops' eye" (l.5)?
3. The bogs of Northern Ireland and Denmark, from which nearly intact bodies of men, women, and animals, as well as other artifacts, have been excavated, function a bit like time capsules. How does "Bogland" suggest that quality of the bogs? What does it say about the Irish and Irish history? About the relationship between the past and the present?
4. In a lecture entitled "Feeling Into Words" (1974) Seamus Heaney said he "had been reading up about the frontier and the West as an important myth in the American consciousness, so [he] set up — or rather, laid down — the bog as an answering Irish myth." What do the bogs suggest about the Irish psyche? How does "Bogland" make a comparison with the American myth of the West?
5. T. P. Flanagan (1929–2011), to whom "Bogland" is dedicated, was an Irish landscape artist with whom Heaney shared a love for the bogs. What aspects of visual art do you see in "Bogland"? What might Heaney have learned from his artist friend?
6. While the intact skeleton of an elk and unspoiled butter were, in fact, found in the bogs, "millions of years" and "bottomless" may be exaggerations. What do you think Heaney is saying about Ireland — and about history — in this mixture of artifacts and fiction?
7. The publication of "Bogland" in 1969 coincided with an outbreak of violence in Northern Ireland. Heaney has said that at around that time the "problems of poetry moved from being simply a matter of achieving the satisfactory verbal icon to being a search for images and symbols adequate to our predicament." What images and ideas does "Bogland" offer that help Heaney comment on the troubles in his country?

The Eve of Rosh Hashanah

YEHUDA AMICHAI

Trans. Chana Block and Stephen Mitchell

Yehuda Amichai (1924–2000) was an internationally renowned Israeli writer whose work has been translated into forty languages and has won numerous international awards. Born in Würtzburg, Germany, to an Orthodox Jewish family, Amichai immigrated with his family to Palestine at the age of eleven and then to Jerusalem the following year. He fought for the British army during World War II and the Israeli Defense Forces during the 1948 Arab-Israeli War. Amichai went on to study biblical and Hebrew literature at the Hebrew University of

Jerusalem. He published his first book of poetry, *Now and in Other Days*, in 1955, and his first novel, *Not of This Time, Not of This Place*, in 1963. His work is known for its accessibility, its balance of playfulness and seriousness, and its exploration of Jewish culture. In "The Eve of Rosh Hashanah," Amichai meditates on the tradition of the Jewish New Year and its promise of new beginnings.

The eve of Rosh Hashanah.[1] At the house that's being built,
a man makes a vow: not to do anything wrong in it,
only to love.
Sins that were green last spring
dried out over the summer. Now they're whispering.

So I washed my body and clipped my fingernails,
the last good deed a man can do for himself
while he's still alive.

What is man? In the daytime he untangles into words
what night turns into a heavy coil.
What do we do to one another —
a son to his father, a father to his son?

And between him and death there's nothing
but a wall of words
like a battery of agitated lawyers.

And whoever uses people as handles or as rungs of a ladder
will soon find himself hugging a stick of wood
and holding a severed hand and wiping his tears
with a potsherd.[2]

[1976/1986]

[1] The beginning of the Jewish New Year, Rosh Hashanah translates as "head of the year." — EDS.
[2] A piece of broken ceramic often found at an archaeological site. — EDS.

EXPLORING THE TEXT

1. Like the secular New Year celebrated on January 1, Rosh Hashanah is a time to consider the year past and to make resolutions for the coming year. What does the speaker of "The Eve of Rosh Hashanah" say about the year past? What resolutions does he make for the year to come?
2. What do you think the "house that's being built" (l. 1) means?
3. Find examples of figurative language in "The Eve of Rosh Hashanah." What do they have in common? Do they remind you of a particular type of language? Why are they well suited to a poem about a holy day?
4. A potsherd (l. 19) is an artifact often found at an archaeological site. Why is "wiping his tears with a piece of potsherd" an appropriate fate for someone who uses people?
5. In Rosie Schaap's *New York Times* review of *The Poetry of Yehuda Amichai*, she cites "The Eve of Rosh Hashanah" as her personal favorite, because "[i]t reminds us . . . to treat one another with

decency and care; to love, not to exploit." Do you agree that this is the poem's message? If not, what do you believe that message is? How do the poem's style elements and structure help convey its message to readers?

6. Yehuda Amichai believed that good poetry must be useful. Chana Kronfeld, a professor of comparative literature at UC Berkeley, discusses this belief in her book *The Full Severity of Compassion: The Poetry of Yehuda Amichai*: "Providing useful poetry was indeed something he was always proud of, especially when it was ordinary human beings, not the mechanisms of state or institutional religion, that would find some practical application for his words." In what ways is "The Eve of Rosh Hashanah" a useful poem? What practical applications do Amichai's words have?

Goodbye, Goldeneye

MAY SWENSON

Born in Utah, May Swenson (1913–1989) grew up speaking both Swedish and English. She received her BA from Utah State University and then moved to New York, where she spent most of her adult life. While writing poetry, Swenson worked as stenographer, secretary, editor, and manuscript reviewer at the prestigious New Directions Publishing. She was writer-in-residence and taught poetry at such schools as Bryn Mawr College, the University of North Carolina, Greensboro, and Purdue University. Among the honors Swenson received were a MacArthur Fellowship, a Guggenheim Fellowship, and the Bollingen Prize. Her work, which includes the collections *Another Animal* (1954), *A Cage of Spines* (1958), *Half Sun Half Sleep* (1967), and *Iconographs* (1970), is known for the questions it poses about love, human nature, and the natural world. Four months before her death, Swenson wrote, "The best poetry has its roots in the subconscious to a great degree. Youthful naivety, reliance on instinct more than learning and method, a sense of freedom and play, even trust in randomness, is necessary to the making of a poem." "Goodbye, Goldeneye" appeared in the collection *In Other Words* (1987).

Rag of black plastic, shred of a kite
caught on the telephone cable above the bay
has twisted in the wind all winter, summer, fall.

Leaves of birch and maple, brown paws of the oak
have all let go but this. Shiny black Mylar
on stem strong as fishline, the busted kite string

whipped around the wire and knotted — how long
will it cling there? Through another spring?
Long barge nudged up channel by a snorting tug,

its blunt front aproned with rot-black tires —
what is being hauled in slime-green drums?
The herring gulls that used to feed their young

on the shore — puffy, wide-beaked babies standing
spraddle-legged and crying — are not here this year.
Instead, steam shovel, bulldozer, cement mixer

rumble over sand, beginning the big new beach house.
There'll be a hotdog stand, flush toilets, trash—
plastic and glass, greasy cartons, crushed beercans,

barrels of garbage for water rats to pick through.
So, goodbye, goldeneye, and grebe and scaup and
loon.
Goodbye, morning walks beside the tide tinkling

among clean pebbles, blue mussel shells and snail
shells that look like staring eyeballs. Goodbye,
kingfisher, little green, black crowned heron,

snowy egret. And, goodbye, oh faithful pair of
swans that used to glide—god and goddess
shapes of purity—over the wide water.

[1987]

EXPLORING THE TEXT

1. What part does point of view play in developing the poem's images and themes? In other words, where exactly is the speaker? Does her location change? How do the questions the speaker asks in lines 8 and 11 help you locate her?
2. May Swenson uses enjambment often in "Goodbye, Goldeneye" (ll. 6–7, 12–13, 15–16). What is its effect? How do the enjambed lines help develop a theme of the poem?
3. Analyze the description of the barge and the tug in lines 9–10. What's included? What's missing?
4. Goldeneyes, grebes, scaups, and loons are types of wild waterfowl; kingfishers, little greens, herons, and egrets are types of wading birds. Why do you think the poem calls so many birds by name?
5. Swenson is sometimes classified as a nature or ecology poet. What techniques does she use in this poem to transcend those genres and humanize and universalize her subject?
6. Swenson wrote several books for young readers. What echoes of children's books do you hear in the poem? What effect do they have?
7. In her introduction to *Nature: Poems Old and New* (1994)—a posthumous collection of Swenson's poetry—Susan Mitchell compares Swenson to Gerard Manley Hopkins. She notes especially both poets' "exuberant attention to detail." What other similarities do you see between "Goodbye, Goldeneye" and "God's Grandeur" (p. 1036)? What differences do you see?

Black Boys Play the Classics

TOI DERRICOTTE

Toi Derricotte (b. 1941) is an American poet. Derricotte grew up in Michigan and earned a BA at Wayne State University in 1965 before moving to New York City in 1967 and earning an MA at New York University in 1984. Derricotte currently teaches writing at the University of Pittsburgh and is the author of five books of poetry: *The Empress of the Death House* (1978), *Natural Birth* (1983), *Captivity* (1989), *Tender* (1997), *The Black Notebooks: An Interior Journey* (1999), and *The Undertaker's Daughter* (2011). In 1996 with Cornelius Eady, she cofounded Cave Canem, an organization dedicated to the promotion of African American poets. In 2012, Derricotte served as Chancellor of the Academy of American Poets. The same year, she won a PEN/Voelcker Award for her growing body of work and its impact on American literature. Her poems candidly address difficult questions of race and gender.

The most popular "act" in
Penn Station
is the three black kids in ratty
sneakers & T-shirts playing
two violins and a cello — Brahms.[1]
White men in business suits
have already dug into their pockets
as they pass and they toss in
a dollar or two without stopping.
Brown men in work-soiled khakis
stand with their mouths open,
arms crossed on their bellies
as if they themselves have always
wanted to attempt those bars.
One white boy, three, sits
cross-legged in front of his
idols — in ecstasy —
their slick, dark faces,
their thin, wiry arms,
who must begin to look
like angels!
Why does this trembling
pull us?
A: *Beneath the surface we are one.*
B: *Amazing! I did not think that they could speak*
this tongue.

[1997]

[1] Johannes Brahms (1833–1897) was a German composer and virtuoso pianist who is best known for his technically complex and advanced works. — EDS.

EXPLORING THE TEXT

1. How does Toi Derricotte use clothing to delineate the social and ethnic differences of the characters in her poem?
2. Derricotte's poetry has been compared to Emily Dickinson's. What characteristics of Emily Dickinson's work do you see in this poem? How does Derricotte — like Dickinson — observe a routine event and turn it into something bigger and more transcendent?
3. Why do you think "act" (l. 1) is in quotation marks? What do those quotation marks add to the description of the young musicians in Penn Station?
4. What role does the "One white boy, three" (l. 15) play in the poem?
5. What do you make of the word "trembling" in line 22? Is it meant to describe the music, or does it refer to something else? How would it change the poem to replace the word "trembling" with "music"?
6. What does "Black Boys Play the Classics" suggest by its two answers to the question in lines 22–23?

Indian Movie, New Jersey

CHITRA BANERJEE DIVAKARUNI

Novelist, short-story writer, and poet Chitra Banerjee Divakaruni was born in 1956 in Calcutta, India, to a devout Hindu family, but she attended a Catholic convent school and was taught by Irish nuns. After completing her bachelor's degree at the University of Calcutta, Divakaruni moved to the United States in 1976 to pursue graduate study. She earned her MA from Wright State University and later received her PhD from the University of California at Berkeley. She is now Betty and Gene McDavid Professor of Writing at the University of Houston. Divakaruni has written many novels, including *The Mistress of Spices* (1997), *The Palace of Illusions* (2008), *One Amazing Thing* (2010), and *Before We Visit the Goddess* (2016).

"Indian Movie, New Jersey" comes from her 1997 collection, *Leaving Yuba City: New and Collected Poems*, which won the Allen Ginsberg Poetry Prize and a Pushcart Prize. Like much of Divakaruni's work, this poem addresses the conflicts between old and new world values.

Not like the white filmstars, all rib
and gaunt cheekbone, the Indian sex-goddess
smiles plumply from behind a flowery
branch. Below her brief red skirt, her thighs
are satisfying-solid, redeeming
as tree trunks. She swings her hips
and the men-viewers whistle. The lover-hero
dances in to a song, his lip-sync
a little off, but no matter, we
know the words already and sing along.
It is safe here, the day
golden and cool so no one sweats,
roses on every bush and the Dal Lake
clean again.
The sex-goddess switches
to thickened English to emphasize
a joke. We laugh and clap. Here
we need not be embarrassed by words
dropping like lead pellets into foreign ears.
The flickering movie-light
wipes from our faces years of America, sons
who want mohawks and refuse to run
the family store, daughters who date
on the sly.
When at the end the hero
dies for his friend who also
loves the sex-goddess and now can marry her,
we weep, understanding. Even the men
clear their throats to say, "What *qurbani* ![1]
What *dosti* !"[2] After, we mill around
unwilling to leave, exchange greetings
and good news: a new gold chain, a trip
to India. We do not speak
of motel raids, canceled permits, stones
thrown through glass windows, daughters and sons
raped by Dotbusters.[3]
In this dim foyer
we can pull around us the faint, comforting smell
of incense and *pakoras*,[4] can arrange
our children's marriages with hometown boys
and girls,
open a franchise, win a million
in the mail. We can retire
in India, a yellow two-storied house
with wrought-iron gates, our own
Ambassador car. Or at least
move to a rich white suburb, Summerfield
or Fort Lee, with neighbors that will
talk to us. Here while the film-songs still echo
in the corridors and restrooms, we can trust
in movie truths: sacrifice, success, love and luck,
the America that was supposed to be.

[1997]

[1] Sacrifice. — EDS.
[2] Friendship. — EDS.
[3] New Jersey gangs that attack Indians. — EDS.
[4] Savory fried pastries eaten as appetizers. — EDS.

EXPLORING THE TEXT

1. Why do you think the poem begins by describing what Indian movie stars are "Not" (l. 1)?
2. Look carefully at the figurative language of the poem. What, for example, is the effect of similes such as "thighs / . . . redeeming / as tree trunks" (ll. 4–6) and "words / dropping like lead pellets" (ll. 18–19)?
3. Who do you think is the "we" of the poem?
4. Analyze the vivid and concrete details in the poem. What is the effect of their accumulation? How does the accumulation of details connect to the pleasure of watching "Bollywood" (Indian) films, as described here?
5. How does Chitra Banerjee Divakaruni highlight the values of the audience through their response to the images on the screen?
6. How is this poem about tradition and progress? Does the speaker expect to return to the traditions of India? Why is a home in a "rich white suburb" (l. 46) only second best?

Mother Country

RICHARD BLANCO

Richard Blanco (b. 1968) is a Cuban American poet, public speaker, and civil engineer. Born in Madrid, Spain, Blanco immigrated with his Cuban-born parents and siblings to Miami, where he grew up. He earned both a BS in civil engineering and an MFA in creative writing from Florida International University. Blanco is also the first immigrant, the first Latino, the first openly gay person, and the youngest person to serve as a US inaugural poet. His collections of poetry include *City of a Hundred Fires* (1998), which won the Agnes Lynch Starrett Poetry Prize; *Directions to the Beach of the Dead* (2005), winner of the PEN/American Beyond Margins Award; *Looking for the Gulf Motel* (2012), winner of the Thom Gunn Award, the Maine Literary Award, and the Paterson Prize; *One Today* (2013); *Boston Strong* (2013); and *For All of Us, One Today: An Inaugural Poet's Journey* (2013). "Mother Country," from his most recent book, presents a multifaceted exploration of American identity and the fusion of several disparate cultural traditions.

To love a country as if you've lost one: 1968,
my mother leaves Cuba for America, a scene
I imagine as if standing in her place — one foot
inside a plane destined for a country she knew
only as a name, a color on a map, or glossy photos
from drugstore magazines, her other foot anchored
to the platform of her *patria,*[1] her hand clutched
around one suitcase, taking only what she needs
most: hand-colored photographs of her family,
her wedding veil, the doorknob of her house,
a jar of dirt from her backyard, goodbye letters
she won't open for years. The sorrowful drone
of engines, one last, deep breath of familiar air
she'll take with her, one last glimpse at all
she'd ever known: the palm trees wave goodbye
as she steps onto the plane, the mountains shrink
from her eyes as she lifts off into another life.

To love a country as if you've lost one: I hear her
— *once upon a time* — reading picture books
over my shoulder at bedtime, both of us learning
English, sounding out words as strange as the talking
animals and fair-haired princesses in their pages.
I taste her first attempts at macaroni-n-cheese
(but with chorizo and peppers), and her shame
over Thanksgiving turkeys always dry, but countered

[1] Spanish for "country." — EDS.

by her perfect pork *pernil*[2] and garlic *yuca*.[3] I smell
the rain of those mornings huddled as one under
one umbrella waiting for the bus to her ten-hour days
at the cash register. At night, the zzz-zzz of her sewing
her own blouses, *quinceañera*[4] dresses for her grown nieces
still in Cuba, guessing at their sizes, and the gowns
she'd sell to neighbors to save for a rusty white sedan —
no hubcaps, no air-conditioning, sweating all the way
through our first vacation to Florida theme parks.

To love a country as if you've lost one: as if
it were *you* on a plane departing from America
forever, clouds closing like curtains on your country,
the last scene in which you're a madman scribbling
the names of your favorite flowers, trees, and birds
you'd never see again, your address and phone number
you'd never use again, the color of your father's eyes,
your mother's hair, terrified you could forget these.
To love a country as if I was my mother last spring
hobbling, insisting I help her climb all the way up
to the Capitol, as if she were here before you today

instead of me, explaining her tears, cheeks pink
as the cherry blossoms coloring the air that day when
she stopped, turned to me, and said: You know, *mijo*,[5]
it isn't where you're born that matters, it's where
you choose to die — that's your country.

[2013]

---

[2] Spanish for "ham." — EDS.

[3] A South American plant, often cooked with a garlic sauce. — EDS.

[4] An elaborate celebration of a girl's fifteenth birthday, which carries great significance in Latin culture as a girl's coming of age. — EDS.

[5] A Spanish slang term of endearment meaning "my son." — EDS.

EXPLORING THE TEXT

1. How does Richard Blanco create a sense of being in two places at once? Why is that important to the meaning of the poem?
2. In an interview, Blanco said that growing up in an all-Cuban ex-pat community felt like living between two imaginary worlds: "the homeland paradise that everyone wanted to return to someday but nobody could visit, and the America that [Blanco] saw on television through shows like 'The Brady Bunch,'" an early 1970s sitcom about a large blended family. What aspects of "Mother Country" reflect the "homeland paradise"; what reflect the America of *The Brady Bunch*? What evidence can you find of a synthesis of the two worlds?
3. Each stanza begins with the same phrase: "To love a country as if you've lost one." How does the poem expand on that phrase in each stanza? Do you think the poem provides a response to or finishes that phrase? Explain your answer.

4. Describe the structure of "Mother Country." How do Blanco's structural decisions help set the poem's tone? What do they suggest about the meaning the word *country* carries for both the speaker and his mother?
5. "Mother Country" was one of three poems Blanco wrote when he was asked to read a poem at the inauguration of President Barack Obama in 2008. Though another poem ("One Country") was chosen, what evidence do you find that this was an "occasional" poem — that is, one written for a particular occasion? To what extent is it a suitable poem for the occasion of a presidential inauguration?
6. Blanco has said that his training as an engineer led him to poetry: "When I graduated I started working full-time and I was confronted with how much verbal skill I needed in writing reports and letters. I started paying really close attention to language, how to argue, how to create a persona, how to persuade. . . . I realized that language is engineerable. I developed a hyper-focus on language and started fiddling around with poetry. It really grew into a love and a passion." How is "Mother Country" engineered? What does it argue? What elements of language does Blanco use to persuade readers?

We Who Weave

LeCONTÉ DILL

LeConté Dill (b. 1978) is an American poet born and raised in South Central Los Angeles. She earned degrees from Spelman College, the University of California, Los Angeles, and the University of California, Berkeley. Dill has also been a participant in VONA/Voices Writing Workshops, an organization based out of the University of Miami that offers multi-genre workshops for writers of color, and workshops through Cave Canem, an organization dedicated to the support of African American writers. Her poems have appeared in numerous magazines and journals. In 2011, she co-authored, co-edited, and helped publish a poetry anthology with teens from Oakland, California, titled *Y U Gotta Call It Ghetto?* Currently she is an assistant professor at the State University of New York Downstate School of Public Health. "We Who Weave" is a response to a painting by Tyrone Geter called *The Basket Maker #2*, which features vivid colors and impressionistic flourishes that depict a woman weaving a basket.

On Tyrone Geter's "The Basket Maker #2"

Weave me closer
to you
with hands dyed indigo
that rake oyster beds
awake
Smell you long
before
I see you
Vanilla sweet
Sweetgrass weaving
wares that keep Yankees coming
on ferries, no bridge
Waters been troubled
Makes you wonder
who put the root on whom first
with doors dyed indigo
Pray the evil spirits away
at the praise house
Make John Hop[1] to stave off John Deere[2]

[1] Another name for Hopping John, or black-eyed peas, traditionally eaten at New Year's for good luck in the coming year. — EDS.
[2] A company that makes farming equipment. — EDS.

We migrants
fighting to stay put
Even nomads come home
for a Lowcountry boil[3]
a feast for hungry
prodigal sons
and daughters
with hearts dyed indigo
Dying for you to
weave us closer

[2016]

[3] A traditional Southern one-pot meal containing sausage, shrimp, crab, potatoes and corn. — EDS.

EXPLORING THE TEXT

1. Describe the imagery in "We Who Weave." Is it mostly figurative or is it more concrete? What overall effect does this imagery have on the poem?
2. "We Who Weave" invokes magic or spells — for example, the speaker asks "who put the root on whom first" (l. 15), which is another way of asking who put a spell on whom. What are the purposes of the poem's spells? What does the speaker want the spells to accomplish?
3. What do you think it means to "Make John Hop to stave off John Deere"? What do such allusions add to the poem?
4. Who are the "nomads" in line 22? What brings them home?
5. Many of the lines in "We Who Weave" are only two or three words long. Why do you think the poet chose to break the lines where she did? What is their effect?
6. "We Who Weave" is a meditation on a painting by Tyrone Geter, whose art is inspired by Africa and the diaspora, particularly to the low country of South Carolina. In this part of the American South, the slave economy helped create agricultural wealth with rice and indigo, also known as blue gold. How does "We Who Weave" weave these threads together? Find references to Africa, the diaspora, and, of course, indigo in the poem. How does LeConté Dill connect them?

Tyrone Geter

PAIRED POEMS

Mannahatta

WALT WHITMAN

Walt Whitman (1819–1892) was born on Long Island, New York. Early in his life, he worked as a country schoolteacher and printer, and served as writer and editor for the *Brooklyn Eagle* newspaper. He continued in a variety of jobs, writing and working as a carpenter, and first published his now famous *Leaves of Grass*, which later underwent several revisions and new editions, in 1855. Regarded as offensive and vulgar at the time for its outspoken content, the book celebrated individuality and the richness of life. In 1862, Whitman went to Virginia to find his brother George, who had been wounded in the Civil War. He was shocked to witness the horrors of war firsthand on the battlefield, and was deeply moved by the suffering of the wounded. He worked as an aide in army hospitals in Washington, caring first for his brother and then other soldiers as well. Among Whitman's most well-known poems from this time are "Oh Captain, My Captain" and "When Lilacs Last in the Dooryard Bloomed," both about Abraham Lincoln. Whitman is considered by many critics to be the first urban poet, and his celebration of New York City, "Mannahatta," suggests that he is the exception to the nineteenth-century rule that American intellectuals preferred the natural world.

I was asking for something specific and perfect for my city,
Whereupon lo! upsprang the aboriginal name.

Now I see what there is in a name, a word, liquid, sane, unruly, musical, self-sufficient,
I see that the word of my city is that word from of old,
Because I see that word nested in nests of water-bays, superb,
Rich, hemm'd thick all around with sailships and steamships, an island sixteen miles long,
    solid-founded,
Numberless crowded streets, high growths of iron, slender, strong, light, splendidly uprising
    toward clear skies,
Tides swift and ample, well-loved by me, toward sundown,
The flowing sea-currents, the little islands, larger adjoining islands, the heights, the villas,
The countless masts, the white shore-steamers, the lighters, the ferry-boats, the black
    sea-steamers well-model'd,
The down-town streets, the jobbers' houses of business, the houses of business of the
    ship-merchants and money-brokers, the river-streets,
Immigrants arriving, fifteen or twenty thousand a week,
The carts hauling goods, the manly race of drivers of horses, the brown-faced sailors,
The summer air, the bright sun shining, and the sailing clouds aloft,
The winter snows, the sleigh-bells, the broken ice in the river, passing along up or down
    with the flood-tide or ebb-tide,

The mechanics of the city, the masters, well-form'd, beautiful-faced, looking
you straight in the eyes,
Trottoirs throng'd, vehicles, Broadway, the women, the shops and shows,
A million people — manners free and superb — open voices — hospitality — the most
courageous and friendly young men,
City of hurried and sparkling waters! city of spires and masts!
City nested in bays! my city!

[1860]

EXPLORING THE TEXT

1. "Mannahatta" was the name given to Manhattan by the Native Americans who lived there before the Dutch settlers arrived. Why do you think Walt Whitman rhapsodizes about this early name?
2. We can assume that Whitman is the speaker — he is one of the great New York poets. Describe the speaker's persona. From what vantage point does he see the city? Is he an observer or a participant?
3. How does Whitman create the poem's pace? What is the connection between its pace and its subject?
4. What contrasts does "Mannahatta" set up? Look carefully at how Whitman invokes the past and the present.
5. Whitman is credited with the invention of American free verse, which is poetry that lacks a strict meter or rhyming sequence but is still recognizable as poetry because of its rhythmic cadence. Whitman used some conventional poetic techniques, such as iambic pentameter — the traditional meter of the sonnet — and anaphora — the repetition of the first word in a line — to achieve that cadence. Examine the cadence in "Mannahatta." Do you see any other techniques Whitman used to achieve it? What is its effect in the poem? How does the cadence help create the vivid setting that is the subject of the poem?

Chicago

CARL SANDBURG

Carl Sandburg (1878–1967) was born in Galesburg, Illinois, the son of Swedish immigrants. He spent most of his life in the Midwest, working as a reporter and a writer of poetry — such as *Good Morning, America* (1928) and *The People, Yes* (1936) — history, biography, fiction, children's books (most famously the *Rootabaga Stories* in the 1920s), and folk songs. He fought in the Spanish-American War and served as secretary to the mayor of Milwaukee, who was the country's first Socialist mayor. Sandburg and his wife raised their family in the suburbs of Chicago. Sandburg was awarded two Pulitzers, one for his biography *Abraham Lincoln: The War Years* (1939) and one for his collection *Complete Poems* (1950); he also received a Best Performance — Documentary or Spoken Word Grammy for his collaboration with the New York Philharmonic (1959). The poem "Chicago" is one of the most famous literary descriptions of an American city.

Hog Butcher for the World,
Tool Maker, Stacker of Wheat,
Player with Railroads and the Nation's Freight Handler;
Stormy, husky, brawling,
City of the Big Shoulders:

They tell me you are wicked and I believe them, for I have seen your painted women
under the gas lamps luring the farm boys.
And they tell me you are crooked and I answer: Yes, it is true I have seen the gunman
kill and go free to kill again.
And they tell me you are brutal and my reply is: On the faces of women and children
I have seen the marks of wanton hunger.
And having answered so I turn once more to those who sneer at this my city, and
I give them back the sneer and say to them:
Come and show me another city with lifted head singing so proud to be alive and
coarse and strong and cunning.
Flinging magnetic curses amid the toil of piling job on job, here is a tall bold slugger
set vivid against the little soft cities;
Fierce as a dog with tongue lapping for action, cunning as a savage pitted against
the wilderness,
Bareheaded,
Shoveling,
Wrecking,
Planning,
Building, breaking, rebuilding,
Under the smoke, dust all over his mouth, laughing with white teeth,
Under the terrible burden of destiny laughing as a young man laughs,
Laughing even as an ignorant fighter laughs who has never lost a battle,
Bragging and laughing that under his wrist is the pulse, and under his ribs the heart
of the people,
Laughing!
Laughing the stormy, husky, brawling laughter of Youth, half-naked, sweating, proud
to be Hog Butcher, Tool Maker, Stacker of Wheat, Player with Railroads and Freight
Handler to the Nation.

[1916]

EXPLORING THE TEXT

1. Personification is the principal technique in "Chicago." Describe the persona Carl Sandburg creates for the city.
2. Sandburg also uses apostrophe, a figure of speech in which someone or something absent, dead, or inanimate is addressed as if the speaker expected a reply. What is the effect of addressing Chicago? What might it reply if it could answer?
3. Describe the poem's tone. How does Sandburg create it? How is Chicago honored through the poem's tone?
4. In lines 18–23, the words "laughs" and "laughing" are repeated over and over. Characterize the city's laughter. How does it both create an image and comment on Sandburg's Chicago?
5. Sandburg's work was inspired by Walt Whitman, especially his use of free verse. The poet Amy Lowell said that the ideal of free verse was to "copy new rhythms — as expressions of new moods — and not to copy old rhythms, which merely echo old moods." How does the rhythm of "Chicago" express "new moods"?
6. Nearly a third of the city burned down in the Chicago Fire of 1871; in the aftermath, the city underwent a period of rapid reconstruction and growth. What passages in the poem seem specifically to deal with this event? How does this part of Chicago history relate to the persona that Sandburg attributes to the city?

FOCUS ON COMPARISON AND CONTRAST

1. Both "Mannahatta" and "Chicago" have a cadence that is characteristic of free verse. What are the similarities and differences in their cadences?
2. Whitman was famous for his lists, a technique that is also evident in Sandburg's "Chicago." What is the effect of these lists? How do the poets use repetition without seeming repetitive?
3. What do the poems have in common in their descriptions of cities? What is different?
4. Compare and contrast the speakers in the two poems. What do they have in common? How are they different? How does each poet create the speaker's persona?
5. Read "Mannahatta" and "Chicago" aloud. Compare and contrast the way free verse imbues the two poems with energy and vigor. You might also look for videos on the Internet in which filmmakers have combined images of New York City and Chicago with the poets' words.

WRITING ASSIGNMENT

"Mannahatta" and "Chicago" each praise the city in which it is set. Compare the speakers' pride in their cities and analyze the techniques the poets use to communicate and re-create the speakers' feelings.

London, 1802

WILLIAM WORDSWORTH

William Wordsworth (1770–1850) is one of the most famous and influential poets of the Western world and one of the premier Romantics. Widely known for his reverence of nature and the power of his lyrical verse, he lived in the Lake District of northern England, where he was inspired by the natural beauty of the landscape. With Samuel Taylor Coleridge, he published *Lyrical Ballads* in 1798; the collection, which changed the direction of English poetry, begins with Coleridge's *The Rime of the Ancient Mariner* and includes Wordsworth's "Lines Composed a Few Miles above Tintern Abbey." Among Wordsworth's other most famous works are "The World Is Too Much with Us" (p. 447), a sonnet; "Ode: Intimations of Immortality"; and "The Prelude, or Growth of a Poet's Mind," an autobiographical poem. In the sonnet "London, 1802," the speaker eulogizes the famous English poet John Milton, praising his humility and nobility, thus illuminating the complacent and morally stagnant culture of England at the time.

Milton! thou should'st be living at this hour:
England hath need of thee: she is a fen
Of stagnant waters: altar, sword, and pen,
Fireside, the heroic wealth of hall and bower,
Have forfeited their ancient English dower
Of inward happiness. We are selfish men;
Oh! raise us up, return to us again;

And give us manners, virtue, freedom, power.
Thy soul was like a star, and dwelt apart:
Thou hadst a voice whose sound was like the sea:
Pure as the naked heavens, majestic, free,
So didst thou travel on life's common way,
In cheerful godliness; and yet thy heart
The lowliest duties on herself did lay.

[1802]

EXPLORING THE TEXT

1. "London, 1802" is an example of a classic Petrarchan sonnet: it has fourteen lines written in iambic pentameter; its rhyme scheme is *abba*, *abba*, *cdde*, *ce*. The traditional sonnet poses a situation or question in the octet (first eight lines) that is resolved or answered in the sestet (the last six lines). What situation does William Wordsworth present in "London, 1802"? What resolution does he suggest?
2. Wordsworth often uses single words to represent bigger ideas, a literary device called metonymy. What institutions do "altar," "sword," "pen," and "fireside" represent?
3. Wordsworth uses similes to present the qualities in John Milton that he believes would help England out of its stagnant selfishness. What is the effect of this figurative language? What is the extra level of meaning it creates?
4. According to this poem, what potential does the artist have for improving society? How must the artist behave to make that potential become real and useful?
5. This poem is unusually nationalistic for a Romantic writer. What might explain Wordsworth's focus on England's heritage and one of its great poets?

Douglass

PAUL LAURENCE DUNBAR

Born in Dayton, Ohio, to parents who had been enslaved in Kentucky before the Civil War, Paul Laurence Dunbar (1872–1906) wrote stories and poems from an early age. At sixteen, Dunbar published "Our Martyred Soldiers" and "On The River" (1888) in Dayton's newspaper the *Herald*, and in 1890, Dunbar wrote and edited the *Tattler*, Dayton's first weekly African American newspaper. While working as an elevator operator after being denied access to law school for financial reasons, Dunbar published his own first of poetry, *Oak and Ivy* (1893), often selling copies personally to his elevator passengers. He went on to publish nine more books of poetry and several short story collections and novels. In "Douglass," Dunbar eulogizes his friend, the prominent abolitionist Frederick Douglass.

Ah, Douglass, we have fall'n on evil days,
  Such days as thou, not even thou didst know,
  When thee, the eyes of that harsh long ago
Saw, salient, at the cross of devious ways,
And all the country heard thee with amaze.

Not ended then, the passionate ebb and flow,
    The awful tide that battled to and fro;
We ride amid a tempest of dispraise.
Now, when the waves of swift dissension swarm,
    And Honor, the strong pilot, lieth stark,
Oh, for thy voice high-sounding o'er the storm,
    For thy strong arm to guide the shivering bark,
The blast-defying power of thy form,
    To give us comfort through the lonely dark.

[1903]

EXPLORING THE TEXT

1. "Douglass," like "London, 1802," is a Petrarchan sonnet. What situation or question is posed in the octet (first eight lines)? How is it resolved in the sestet (last six lines)?
2. Who is the speaker in this poem? Why does the speaker call on Frederick Douglass at that particular moment in history? How does the speaker compare the present with the past as he hails Douglass's role in the previous century?
3. What qualities in Douglass does the speaker cite as particularly important in the current crisis?
4. What is the poem's central metaphor? Trace its development through the poem and describe how Dunbar uses it to build emotion and even a sense of desperation.

FOCUS ON COMPARISON AND CONTRAST

1. Both "London, 1802" and "Douglass" begin with a literary device called an apostrophe, which is a direct address to an abstraction (such as Time), or to an absent person, place, or thing. What do the apostrophes in these poems have in common? In what ways are they different?
2. How do the two poets describe the conditions in their respective societies? How are those societies similar? How are they different?
3. Both "London, 1802" and "Douglass" are sonnets. Paul Laurence Dunbar takes some liberties with the rhyme scheme, while William Wordsworth strictly follows the rules of the Petrarchan sonnet. What effect does the poets' adherence (or lack thereof) to the standard rhyme schemes have on the meaning of each poem?
4. What qualities does each poet impute to the subject of his poem? How does the speaker in Wordsworth's poem think Milton can help society? What does Dunbar believe Frederick Douglass can accomplish?

WRITING ASSIGNMENT

Read "London, 1802" and "Douglass" carefully, and then compare and contrast how each poem's tone both expresses the desire for inspiration and also criticizes the societies in which each speaker lives.

SYNTAX

Syntax refers to the way a writer arranges words, phrases, and clauses into a **sentence**. Yet all writers, including poets, pay attention to syntax as one strategy for developing and conveying meaning.

Syntactical Patterns

Arrangement at the sentence level affects the way a reader or listener experiences the text and usually depends on the context of one sentence among others. Thus, simple, short sentences might create a flippant effect, an emphatic effect, or a sense of urgency; a longer, discursive sentence with interruptions may convey the impression of confusion or contribute to a meditative tone, depending on the overall context and the choices the writer makes in diction and figurative language. "Short" and "long" are two of many ways to discuss syntax and describe sentence patterns, but here we'll concentrate on a few specific types.

Simple, Declarative Sentences

Normal word order — subject/verb/object — in a relatively short declarative sentence usually makes a straightforward statement. In "Everyday Use," Alice Walker gives us Mama's self-description:

> In real life I am a large, big-boned woman with rough, man-working hands. In the winter I wear flannel nightgowns to bed and overalls during the day. I can kill and clean a hog as mercilessly as a man. My fat keeps me hot in zero weather. I can work outside all day.

Although these sentences include descriptors, the basic structure is "I am . . . I wear . . . I can kill . . . My fat keeps . . . I can work . . .": subject/verb/object (SVO) constructions in declarative statements. The effect is to characterize Mama as a plainspoken, unassuming woman with no frills and no pretense in the way she sees and acts in the world. What she says in that passage certainly makes that clear, but how she says it is as important as what she says.

Inverted Sentences

When a writer reverses the normal position of subject and verb (or predicate) in a declarative sentence, he or she is calling attention to something — perhaps emphasizing a point or an idea by placing it in the initial position — or slowing the pace by choosing an unusual order. In "A Good Man Is Hard to Find," Flannery O'Connor uses inversion in this sentence:

> The horrible thought she had had before the accident was that the house she had remembered so vividly was not in Georgia but in Tennessee.

If we put the sentence in standard SVO order, listen to the difference in what is emphasized:

> She had had the horrible thought before the accident that the house she had remembered so vividly was not in Georgia but in Tennessee.

In the two sentences, the same information is conveyed, yet the emphasis on the "horrible thought" is lost to the repetition of "She had had" in the standard version.

Compound-Complex Sentences

A **compound sentence** contains two independent clauses joined by a coordinating conjunction (such as *and, but, for, yet*, or *so*) or a semicolon. A complex sentence contains an independent clause and one or more subordinate clauses (which begin with words such as *after, before, although, because, until, when, while*, and *if*). A **compound-complex sentence** combines the two and is usually fairly long. Note the two compound-complex sentences in the following passage from James Baldwin's "Sonny's Blues":

> Then it was over. Creole and Sonny let out their breath, both soaking wet, and grinning. There was a lot of applause and some of it was real. In the dark, the girl came by and I asked her to take drinks to the bandstand. There was a long pause, **while** they talked up there in the indigo light and after awhile I saw the girl put a Scotch and milk on top of the piano for Sonny. He didn't seem to notice it, but just **before** they started playing again, he sipped from it and looked toward me, and nodded. Then he put it back on top of the piano. For me, then, as they began to play again, it glowed and shook above my brother's head like the very cup of trembling.

The passage includes several different types of sentences, but look closely at the ones that include subordinate clauses (those with "while" and "before"): each is also a compound sentence linked with a coordinating conjunction ("and" and "but"). This construction reveals something about the narrator's transformation at the end of the story. The subordinate clauses are almost all related to time. The narrator, at that moment, has transcended time as the story resolves at least some of the issues affecting the past, present, and future of its characters. The sentences accumulate by connecting with "and" as well as qualify by connecting with "but," a reminder of the fragile nature of the story's resolution.

Cumulative and Periodic Sentences

A periodic sentence begins with a series of phrases or even clauses, and culminates in an independent clause. Cumulative sentences are the opposite: they begin with the main point and then add modifications, qualifications, and details. In this same story, Baldwin creates a paragraph-long cumulative sentence to describe the sound of a boy whistling:

> One boy was whistling a tune, at once very complicated and very simple, it seemed to be pouring out of him as though he were a bird, and it sounded very cool and moving through all the harsh, bright air, only just holding its own through all that harsh, bright air, only just holding its own through all those other sounds.

The first independent clause is the "boy whistling a tune"; two additional independent clauses follow. The final one includes several descriptions of what the whistling sounds like. In fact, the form of the sentence underscores its content because the long accumulation of detail helps readers feel the "very complicated . . . very cool and moving" nature of the sound.

Let's take a look at a periodic sentence in Hanif Kureishi's *We're not Jews*:

> When, for weeks, numerous lumps of metal stood on rags around the skeleton of the bike, and, in the late evening, Big Bill revved up the machine, while his record player balanced on the windowsill repeatedly blared out a 45 called "Rave On," everyone knew Big Billy was preparing for the annual Bank Holiday run to the coast.

Here Kureishi uses a periodic sentence to mimic the scene he's describing. Just as the characters are inconvenienced by the noise and mess of Big Billy's preparation, so are readers delayed in getting to the final clause and Big Billy's temporary but welcome absence as he makes a "run to the coast."

Interrupted Sentences

Any of these sentence patterns can be modified by "interruptions" that add descriptive details, state conditions, suggest uncertainty, voice possible alternative views, or present qualifications. Such sentences, quite characteristic of many pre-twentieth-century writers, often employ a combination of sentence patterns that may be difficult to understand the first time you read them. If you get tripped up, try reading the sentences aloud. You may notice that they sound more natural than they look on the page. Let's examine a sentence from paragraph 13 of *Frankenstein* that demonstrates tangent-filled "self-interrupted" syntax:

> A youth passed in solitude, my best years spent under your gentle and feminine fosterage, has so refined the groundwork of my character, that I cannot overcome an intense distaste to the usual brutality exercised on board ship: I have never believed it to be necessary; and when I heard of a mariner equally noted for his kindliness of heart, and the respect and obedience paid to him by his crew, I felt myself peculiarly fortunate in being able to secure his services.

The basic idea of the sentence is that Robert Walton prefers sailors who are kind rather than cruel. But look at all the nuance the complicated sentence provides. In the opening clause, the narrator makes a connection with his sister by referring to his youth as being "spent under" her "gentle and feminine fosterage." Next, Walton begins to explain why his upbringing has shaped his seafaring adventures. Being raised by his sister, he says, has "so refined the groundwork" of his personality that he is incapable of ignoring the "intense distaste" he has for "the usual brutality" that takes place at sea. Also as a result of his upbringing, he has "never believed [violence] to be necessary." He waits until the final clause of this compound-complex sentence to reveal the action he has taken as a result: he hired a man "equally noted for his kindliness of heart." The circuitousness and repetitiveness of the prose in this sentence conjures the ebb and flow of an intimate conversation; its syntactical complexity mirrors the "refined" character Walton believes his sister has cultivated in him.

SYNTAX IN POETRY

Most poems are not written as a series of sentences arranged into paragraphs, and many poems are not written in full sentences at all. Nonetheless, examining the syntax of a poem that can be divided into sentences not only helps with comprehension but leads to a deeper understanding of meaning and purpose. Let's look at the first section of "The Second Coming" by William Butler Yeats as an example.

> Turning and turning in the widening gyre
> The falcon cannot hear the falconer;
> Things fall apart; the center cannot hold;
> Mere anarchy is loosed upon the world,
> The blood-dimmed tide is loosed, and
> everywhere
> The ceremony of innocence is drowned;
> The best lack all conviction, while the worst
> Are full of passionate intensity.

Technically, these eight lines comprise one long sentence made up of a series of independent clauses linked by semicolons. But let's look at the patterns within this sentence. The opening two lines act like a periodic sentence, with line 2 serving as the main clause. Line 3 consists of two short, simple declarative clauses, whose abruptness makes them sound like forceful statements of fact. Lines 4–6 are a series of independent clauses joined by a coordinating conjunction, so they flow together as the urgency mounts. Lines 7 and 8 make up a complex sentence that contrasts "The best" and "the worst." The compound construction and complex one in lines 4–8 have a cumulative effect as they build a description of the result of "anarchy" being "loosed": a series of impending catastrophes that together create an apocalyptic vision. This single eight-line sentence builds up to this vision, which leads to the next two lines: "Surely some revelation is at hand; / Surely the Second Coming is at hand."

Enjambment and Caesura

Poets often manipulate syntax through enjambment and caesura. Enjambment is the breaking of a syntactic unit by the end of a line or between two lines; caesura denotes a pause that breaks up a line, usually indicated by punctuation marks. Sometimes poets use these techniques for practical reasons, such as adhering to a rhyme scheme; sometimes they use them to create interesting sounds or rhythms, by controlling when the reader pauses; and sometimes they use them to emphasize a word or create an effect that echoes the meaning of a line. Let's consider the opening stanza of "God's Grandeur" by Gerard Manley Hopkins:

> The world is charged with the grandeur of God.
> It will flame out, like shining from shook foil;
> It gathers to a greatness, like the ooze of oil
> Crushed. Why do men then now not reck his rod?
> Generations have trod, have trod, have trod;
> And all is seared with trade; bleared, smeared with toil;
> And wears man's smudge and shares man's smell: the soil
> Is bare now, nor can foot feel, being shod.

In the opening stanza, there are two instances of enjambment: lines 3–4 and lines 7–8. In the first, Hopkins puts the strong final verb ("Crushed") not only at the end of the sentence, altering the standard word order, but also at the beginning of the next line. Both of these decisions emphasize the word and produce a contrast between the vowel-rich liquid sounds of "ooze of oil" and the finality of "Crushed." In the second example, the enjambment ensures the rhyme scheme of the two quatrains — *abba / abba* — but it also separates the subject ("soil") from its predicate ("Is bare"), emphasizing the bareness by isolating it and mimicking the disconnect between how nature should be and how it is.

In line 3, the caesura produced by the comma after "gathers to a greatness" stops the poem briefly, as though the line itself had built to its climax. In line 5, the commas after "trod" combine with the repetition of "have trod" to mimic the sound of clomping footsteps. Finally, in line 7, the colon is employed to introduce the final point in the quatrain. Avoiding a break in the line after the colon (which would also interrupt the rhyme scheme), the caesura denotes a deliberate pause and links "man's smell" and "the soil."

The following exercises will help you practice recognizing different syntactical patterns and how they relate to meaning.

EXERCISE 1

Identify the syntactical pattern in each of the following sentences.

1. Out came Wangero with two quilts. ("Everyday Use," para. 55)
2. At this mother made to rise. So did Big Billy. Little Billy sprang up. They would follow her and Azhar. With a sigh she sank back down. The conductor came, holding the arm of his ticket machine. He knew the Billys, and had a laugh with them. He let them ride for nothing. ("We're Not Jews," para. 2)
3. For while the tale of how we suffer, and how we are delighted, and how we may triumph is never new, it always must be heard. ("Sonny's Blues," para. 234)
4. The car continued to come on slowly, disappeared around a bend and appeared again, moving even slower, on top of the hill they had gone over. ("A Good Man Is Hard to Find," para. 70)
5. Not like the white filmstars, all rib
   and gaunt cheekbone, the Indian sex-goddess
   smiles plumply from behind a flowery
   branch.
   ("Indian Movie, New Jersey," ll. 1–4)
6. "You can do one thing or you can do another, kill a man or take a tire off his car, because sooner or later you're going to forget what it was you done and just be punished for it." ("A Good Man Is Hard to Find," para. 122)
7. I see him there
   Bringing a stone grasped firmly by the top
   In each hand, like an old-stone savage armed.
   ("Mending Wall," ll. 38–40)
8. "But when I discovered that he, the author at once of my existence and of its unspeakable torments, dared to hope for happiness, that while he accumulated wretchedness and despair upon me he sought his own enjoyment in feeling and passions from the indulgence of which I was for ever barred, then impotent envy and bitter indignation filled me with an insatiable thirst for vengeance." (*Frankenstein*, para. 719)

EXERCISE 2

Although syntactical patterns contribute to a writer's style, most authors strive for variety. Using the following passage from "Everyday Use," discuss how Alice Walker varies syntax both to stress points of emphasis and to ensure fluency.

> Don't get up, says Dee. Since I am stout it takes something of a push. You can see me trying to move a second or two before I make it. She turns, showing white heels through her sandals, and goes back to the car. Out she peeks next with a Polaroid. She stoops down quickly and lines up picture after picture of me sitting there in front of the house with Maggie cowering behind me. She never takes a shot without making sure the house is included. When a cow comes nibbling around the edge of the yard she snaps it and me and Maggie *and* the house. Then she puts the Polaroid in the back seat of the car, and comes up and kisses me on the forehead. (para. 22)

EXERCISE 3

Explain how James Baldwin's syntactical patterns contribute to the effect of the following prose passage from "Sonny's Blues."

> And Sonny hadn't been near a piano for over a year. And he wasn't on much better terms with his life, not the life that stretched before him now. He and the piano stammered, started one way, got scared, stopped; started another way, panicked, marked time, started again; then seemed to have found a direction, panicked again, got stuck. And the face I saw on Sonny I'd never seen before. Everything had been burned out of it, and, at the time, things usually hidden were being burned in, by the fire and fury of the battle which was occurring in him up there. (para. 232)

EXERCISE 4

Discuss how the syntax of "Mother Country" (p. 1049) contributes to the meaning of the poem. Pay attention to Richard Blanco's use of enjambment and caesura and the effects they have on the meaning of the poem's imagery and its themes.

EXERCISE 5

Choose a poem from this chapter and rewrite it as prose (without eliminating any of the words). Compare your "revision" with the original poem, analyzing how the poet's syntactical choices contribute to the overall meaning.

EXERCISE 6

Write a brief narrative in the style of Flannery O'Connor that uses an event from your life as inspiration. Pay special attention to emulating O'Connor's syntax.

TRADITION AND PROGRESS

1. This chapter begins with a quote from Nathaniel Hawthorne. Using the works in this chapter to support your position, write an essay in which you agree or disagree with Hawthorne that the drive toward progress is made by those who are "ill at ease," while those who are happy embrace tradition.
2. The natural world provides the background for several of the works in this chapter. Write an essay in which you explore the way writers use the natural world to comment on the clash between tradition and progress.
3. Choose two poems from this chapter, one that criticizes progress and another that celebrates it. Write an essay in which you analyze the contrasting attitudes toward the subject. Include personal commentary on which view comes closer to your own.
4. Choose one of the following statements, and explain why it fits your beliefs about tradition and progress.
   a. "Discontent is the first step in the progress of a man or a nation."

      — Oscar Wilde

   b. "A tradition without intelligence is not worth having."

      — T. S. Eliot

   c. "Science and technology revolutionize our lives, but memory, tradition and myth frame our response."

      — Arthur Schlesinger Jr.

   d. "Tradition is a guide and not a jailer."

      — W. Somerset Maugham
5. The short stories in this chapter examine racial or ethnic issues through conflicts in families or communities. Write an essay in which you analyze the racial or ethnic clashes in one or more of the stories.
6. Some of the poetry in this chapter — William Wordsworth's "London," William Butler Yeats's "The Second Coming," and Matthew Arnold's "Dover Beach," for example — are rather dark indictments of society and politics. Write an essay in which you examine the poets' positions and evaluate their arguments in light of today's world.
7. The plots of both *Frankenstein* and "A Good Man Is Hard to Find" involve travel. Consider both stories, along with other works you've read, and write an essay in which you analyze the role of travel. Be sure to address the reasons you think the subject lends itself to a study of human behavior.
8. Many of the works in this chapter concern a clash between cultures. Try writing your own story about a culture clash. You might use your family background or the diversity in your home or community as a starting point.

10 War and Peace

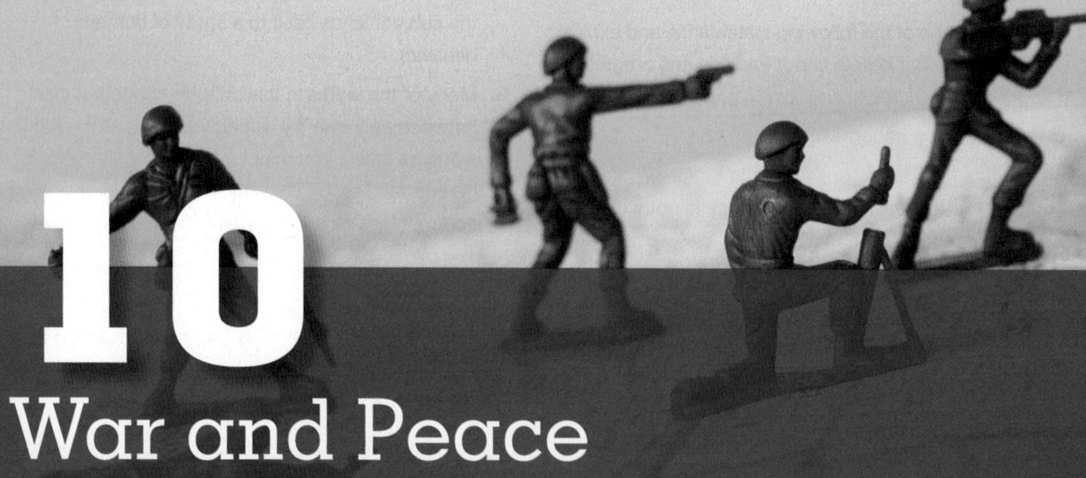

> Do dreams offer lessons? Do nightmares have themes, do we awaken and analyze them and live our lives and advise others as a result? Can the foot soldier teach anything important about war, merely for having been there? I think not. He can tell war stories.
>
> — Tim O'Brien, *If I Die in a Combat Zone, Box Me Up and Ship Me Home*

Image Source/Getty Images

It is often said that there has never been a time in human history when there wasn't a war being waged somewhere in the world. That certainly casts a grim shadow on human history. We do not award a Nobel War Prize, yet the world seems always to have looked to warriors for its heroes. We might consider what in human nature is satisfied by what war provides — not only to the warrior but to the citizens who send the warrior to fight. If war is as horrific as reported by the warrior and as deplorable as depicted in literature, why do we continue to look to warriors as our heroes?

We prize peace, but find glory in war; we detest war, but find peace fragile, fleeting, and sometimes restive. This paradox has been a major subject of serious literature since the *Iliad* (c. 725–675 BC) and the *Odyssey* (c. 750–650 BC), which tell the stories of the warrior fighting in battle and the warrior returning home, respectively. It may be simplistic to suggest, as some have, that those are the two basic stories we have to tell, but considering examples from the *Iliad* to *Star Wars*, from *The Things They Carried* to *The Hurt Locker*, we have to acknowledge the hold these stories have on our imaginations.

In this chapter you will read classic war stories and poems from Richard Lovelace and William Shakespeare as well as those inspired by Wilfred Owen's experience in World War I and Tim O'Brien's in Vietnam. You will read Shakespeare's *Othello*, a play that tells the story of a great army general undone by emotional conflict; this chapter's

Texts in Context explore *Othello* through multiple critical lenses. You will also encounter more modern stories of war and peace: Walt Whitman responding to the U.S. Civil War; Bharati Mukherjee and Wisława Szymborska to contemporary terrorism; Jill McDonough, Solmaz Sharif, and Phil Klay to present-day military weapons and conflicts. You will read stories and poems not directly about war itself but about its motivations and repercussions and consequences — including Cynthia Ozick's narrative snapshot of the Holocaust; Dunya Mikhail's ironic take on the sad wastefulness of war; and Julia Ward Howe's declaration of its glories. Finally, you will read selections that consider war's aftermath and the attempt to establish peace, including Yusef Komunyakaa's portrayal of a grieving mother and Amit Majmudar's tongue-in-cheek depiction of a wounded veteran returning home.

Throughout the chapter you will view both war and peace from a variety of perspectives: that of the warrior and the witness, the poet and the citizen, the sufferer and the survivor. Reading these selections should cause you to reflect on the nature of conflict itself, on the nature of heroism, on the role of the citizen during wartime, and on the ongoing conflict between war and peace. Of course, reading about war will not prevent future wars; however, the vicarious immersion in experience that literature provides may increase our understanding of the nature of armed conflict, stretching from Athens to Antietam, on the sanguinary trail from the fortresses at Troy to the mountains of Afghanistan, and on urban streets from Berlin and Belfast to Baghdad and Beirut.

The Things They Carried

TIM O'BRIEN

Peter Power/Toronto Star via Getty Images

Tim O'Brien was born in 1946 in Austin, Minnesota. After graduating from Macalester College with a BA in political science in 1968, he was drafted into the army and sent to Vietnam, where he became a sergeant and earned a Purple Heart. A year after the now infamous My Lai massacre (in which American soldiers attacked a village full of civilians), O'Brien's unit passed through the area where it had happened, only learning about it then. The incident figures prominently in his 1994 novel, *In the Lake of the Woods* — begun as a graduate dissertation in history at Harvard University, where he went to graduate school after the war. O'Brien's writing career started with the publication of *If I Die in a Combat Zone, Box Me Up and Ship Me Home* (1973), a memoir of his experiences in Vietnam. *Going after Cacciato*, a surrealistic novel set in the war, followed in 1978, winning the prestigious National Book Award and establishing O'Brien as a major American writer. His recent novels include *Tomcat in Love* (1998) and *July, July* (2002). Perhaps his most famous book, *The Things They Carried* — composed of a series of connected stories — appeared in 1990. Dedicated to its fictional characters and based on his actual experience, it is a novel in which O'Brien himself is the narrator. While a major theme of the novel is war and the postwar experience, it can be said that the book is also about the relationship between truth and fiction and the transformational power of art and memory. Regarding *If I Die in a Combat Zone, Box Me Up and Ship Me Home*, O'Brien has said that he had a hard time getting at the truth in that book because he stuck to the facts. The title story and first chapter of *The Things They Carried*, selected for inclusion in *The Best American Short Stories of the Century* (1999) and included here, represents his attempt to invent a fiction to get at the truth.

First Lieutenant Jimmy Cross carried letters from a girl named Martha, a junior at Mount Sebastian College in New Jersey. They were not love letters, but Lieutenant Cross was hoping, so he kept them folded in plastic at the bottom of his rucksack. In the late afternoon, after a day's march, he would dig his foxhole, wash his hands under a canteen, unwrap the letters, hold them with the tips of his fingers, and spend the last hour of light pretending. He would imagine romantic camping trips into the White Mountains in New Hampshire. He would sometimes taste the envelope flaps, knowing her tongue had been there. More than anything, he wanted Martha to love him as he loved her, but the letters were mostly chatty, elusive on the matter of love. She was a virgin, he was almost sure. She was an English major at Mount Sebastian, and she wrote beautifully about her professors and roommates and midterm exams, about her respect for Chaucer and her great affection for Virginia Woolf. She often quoted lines of poetry; she never mentioned the war, except to say, Jimmy, take care of yourself. The

Zippo lighters have been the companions of American servicemen since World War II. The one pictured here is a replica, created by American artist Bradford Edwards, of a typical lighter carried by a soldier in Vietnam. Many such lighters were found there after the war. **What does the inscription reveal about the state of mind of the combatants in the war in Vietnam? How do you see that state of mind reflected in the characters of "The Things They Carried"?**

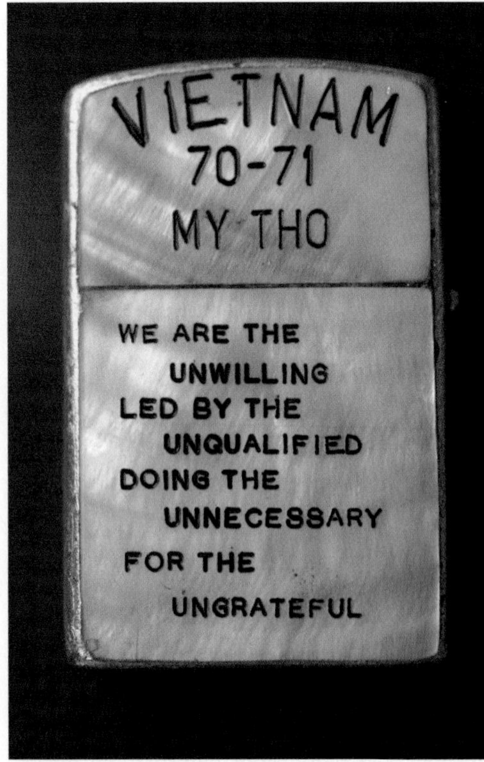

VIETNAM
70-71
MY THO
WE ARE THE
UNWILLING
LED BY THE
UNQUALIFIED
DOING THE
UNNECESSARY
FOR THE
UNGRATEFUL

Frank Zeller / AFP / Getty Images

letters weighed ten ounces. They were signed "Love, Martha," but Lieutenant Cross understood that "Love" was only a way of signing and did not mean what he sometimes pretended it meant. At dusk, he would carefully return the letters to his rucksack. Slowly, a bit distracted, he would get up and move among his men, checking the perimeter, then at full dark he would return to his hole and watch the night and wonder if Martha was a virgin.

The things they carried were largely determined by necessity. Among the necessities or near necessities were P-38 can openers, pocket knives, heat tabs, wrist watches, dog tags, mosquito repellant, chewing gum, candy, cigarettes, salt tablets, packets of Kool-Aid, lighters, matches, sewing kits, Military Payment Certificates, C rations, and two or three canteens of water. Together, these items weighed between fifteen and twenty pounds, depending upon a man's habits or rate of metabolism. Henry Dobbins, who was a big man, carried extra rations; he was especially fond of canned peaches in heavy syrup over pound cake. Dave Jensen, who practiced field hygiene, carried a toothbrush, dental floss, and several hotel-size bars of soap he'd stolen on R&R in Sydney, Australia. Ted Lavender, who was scared, carried tranquilizers until he was shot in the head outside the village of Than Khe in mid-April. By necessity, and because it was SOP,[1] they all carried steel helmets that weighed five pounds including the liner and camouflage cover. They carried the standard fatigue jackets and trousers. Very few carried underwear. On their feet they carried jungle boots — 2.1 pounds — and Dave Jensen carried three pairs of socks and a can of Dr. Scholl's foot powder as a precaution against trench foot. Until he was shot, Ted Lavender carried six or seven ounces of premium dope, which for him was a necessity. Mitchell Sanders, the RTO,[2] carried condoms. Norman Bowker carried a diary. Rat Kiley carried comic books. Kiowa, a devout Baptist, carried an illustrated New Testament that had been presented to him by his father, who taught Sunday school in Oklahoma City, Oklahoma. As a hedge against bad times, however, Kiowa also carried his grandmother's distrust of the white man, his grandfather's old hunting hatchet. Necessity dictated. Because the land was mined

[1] Standard operating procedure. — EDS.
[2] Radiotelephone operator. — EDS.

and booby-trapped, it was SOP for each man to carry a steel-centered, nylon-covered flak jacket, which weighed 6.7 pounds, but which on hot days seemed much heavier. Because you could die so quickly, each man carried at least one large compress bandage, usually in the helmet band for easy access. Because the nights were cold, and because the monsoons were wet, each carried a green plastic poncho that could be used as a raincoat or ground sheet or makeshift tent. With its quilted liner, the poncho weighed almost two pounds, but it was worth every ounce. In April, for instance, when Ted Lavender was shot, they used his poncho to wrap him up, then to carry him across the paddy, then to lift him into the chopper that took him away.

They were called legs or grunts.

To carry something was to "hump" it, as when Lieutenant Jimmy Cross humped his love for Martha up the hills and through the swamps. In its intransitive form, "to hump" meant "to walk," or "to march," but it implied burdens far beyond the intransitive.

5 Almost everyone humped photographs. In his wallet, Lieutenant Cross carried two photographs of Martha. The first was a Kodachrome snapshot signed "Love," though he knew better. She stood against a brick wall. Her eyes were gray and neutral, her lips slightly open as she stared straight-on at the camera. At night, sometimes, Lieutenant Cross wondered who had taken the picture, because he knew she had boyfriends, because he loved her so much, and because he could see the shadow of the picture taker spreading out against the brick wall. The second photograph had been clipped from the 1968 Mount Sebastian yearbook. It was an action shot — women's volleyball — and Martha was bent horizontal to the floor, reaching, the palms of her hands in sharp focus, the tongue taut, the expression frank and competitive. There was no visible sweat. She wore white gym shorts. Her legs, he thought, were almost certainly the legs of a virgin, dry and without hair, the left knee cocked and carrying her entire weight, which was just over one hundred pounds. Lieutenant Cross remembered touching that left knee. A dark theater, he remembered, and the movie was *Bonnie and Clyde*, and Martha wore a tweed skirt, and during the final scene, when he touched her knee, she turned and looked at him in a sad, sober way that made him pull his hand back, but he would always remember the feel of the tweed skirt and the knee beneath it and the sound of the gunfire that killed Bonnie and

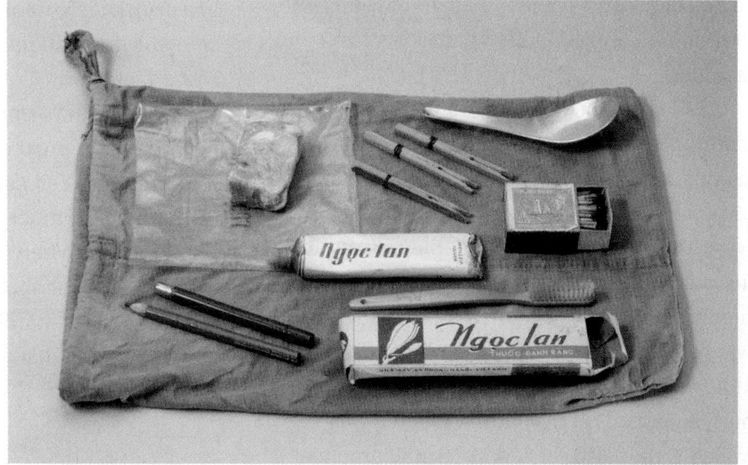

The Art Archive at Art Resource, NY

This kit, which was a memento of an American prisoner of war, contains toothpaste, brush, spoon, pegs, pencils, and matches. **How does the ordinariness of these simple hygiene items contrast with the rest of the objects "carried" by the men in "The Things They Carried"?**

Clyde, how embarrassing it was, how slow and oppressive. He remembered kissing her good night at the dorm door. Right then, he thought, he should've done something brave. He should've carried her up the stairs to her room and tied her to the bed and touched that left knee all night long. He should've risked it. Whenever he looked at the photographs, he thought of new things he should've done.

What they carried was partly a function of rank, partly of field specialty.

As a first lieutenant and platoon leader, Jimmy Cross carried a compass, maps, code books, binoculars, and a .45-caliber pistol that weighed 2.9 pounds fully loaded. He carried a strobe light and the responsibility for the lives of his men.

As an RTO, Mitchell Sanders carried the PRC-25 radio, a killer, twenty-six pounds with its battery.

As a medic, Rat Kiley carried a canvas satchel filled with morphine and plasma and malaria tablets and surgical tape and comic books and all the things a medic must carry, including M&M's for especially bad wounds, for a total weight of nearly twenty pounds.

10 As a big man, therefore a machine gunner, Henry Dobbins carried the M-60, which weighed twenty-three pounds unloaded, but which was almost always loaded. In addition, Dobbins carried between ten and fifteen pounds of ammunition draped in belts across his chest and shoulders.

As PFCs or Spec 4s, most of them were common grunts and carried the standard M-16 gas-operated assault rifle. The weapon weighed 7.5 pounds unloaded, 8.2 pounds with its full twenty-round magazine. Depending on numerous factors, such as topography and psychology, the riflemen carried anywhere from twelve to twenty magazines, usually in cloth bandoliers, adding on another 8.4 pounds at minimum, fourteen pounds at maximum. When it was available, they also carried M-16 maintenance gear — rods and steel brushes and swabs and tubes of LSA oil — all of which weighed about a pound. Among the grunts, some carried the M-79 grenade launcher, 5.9 pounds unloaded, a reasonably light weapon except for the ammunition, which was heavy. A single round weighed ten ounces. The typical load was twenty-five rounds. But Ted Lavender, who was scared, carried thirty-four rounds when he was shot and killed outside Than Khe, and he went down under an exceptional burden, more than twenty pounds of ammunition, plus the flak jacket and helmet and rations and water and toilet paper and tranquilizers and all the rest, plus the unweighed fear. He was dead weight. There was no twitching or flopping. Kiowa, who saw it happen, said it was like watching a rock fall, or a big sandbag or something — just boom, then down — not like the movies where the dead guy rolls around and does fancy spins and goes ass over teakettle — not like that, Kiowa said, the poor bastard just flat-fuck fell. Boom. Down. Nothing else. It was a bright morning in mid-April. Lieutenant Cross felt the pain. He blamed himself. They stripped off Lavender's canteens and ammo, all the heavy things, and Rat Kiley said the obvious, the guy's dead, and Mitchell Sanders used his radio to report one U.S. KIA[3] and to request a chopper. Then they wrapped Lavender in his poncho. They carried him out to a dry paddy, established security, and sat smoking the dead man's dope until the chopper came. Lieutenant Cross kept to himself. He pictured Martha's smooth young face, thinking he loved her more than anything, more than his men, and now Ted Lavender was dead because he loved her so much and could not stop thinking about her. When the dust-off arrived, they carried Lavender aboard. Afterward they burned Than Khe. They marched until dusk, then dug their holes, and that night Kiowa kept explaining how you had to be there, how fast it was, how the

[3] Killed in action. — EDS.

Malcah Zeldis / Art Resource, NY

The painting here is folk artist Malcah Zeldis's portrayal of the 1973 massacre of the village of My Lai by American troops during the Vietnam War. In "The Things They Carried," the company "burned Than Khe" after the death of Lavender, and the reader does not learn if there were still civilians there. **How does this painting portray the emotional state of both the American soldiers and that of the civilians? How does it affect your interpretation of the company's actions in "The Things They Carried"?**

poor guy just dropped like so much concrete. Boom-down, he said. Like cement.

In addition to the three standard weapons — the M-60, M-16, and M-79 — they carried whatever presented itself, or whatever seemed appropriate as a means of killing or staying alive. They carried catch-as-catch-can. At various times, in various situations, they carried M-14s and CAR-15s and Swedish Ks and grease guns and captured AK-47s and Chi-Coms and RPGs and Simonov carbines and black-market Uzis and .38-caliber Smith & Wesson handguns and 66 mm LAWs and shotguns and silencers and blackjacks and bayonets and C-4 plastic explosives. Lee Strunk carried a slingshot; a weapon of last resort, he called it. Mitchell Sanders carried brass knuckles. Kiowa carried his grandfather's feathered hatchet. Every third or fourth man carried a Claymore antipersonnel mine — 3.5 pounds with its firing device. They all carried fragmentation grenades — fourteen ounces each. They all carried at least one M-18 colored smoke grenade — twenty-four ounces. Some carried CS or tear-gas grenades. Some carried white-phosphorus grenades. They carried all they could bear, and then some, including a silent awe for the terrible power of the things they carried.

In the first week of April, before Lavender died, Lieutenant Jimmy Cross received a good-luck charm from Martha. It was a simple pebble, an ounce at most. Smooth to the touch, it was a milky-white color with flecks of orange and violet, oval-shaped, like a miniature egg. In the accompanying letter, Martha wrote that she had found the pebble on the Jersey shoreline, precisely where the land touched water at high tide, where things came together but also separated. It was this separate-but-together quality, she wrote, that had inspired her to pick up the pebble and to carry it in her breast pocket for several days, where it seemed weightless, and then to send it through the mail, by air, as a token of her truest feelings for him. Lieutenant Cross found this romantic. But he wondered what her truest feelings were, exactly, and what she meant by separate-but-together. He wondered how the tides and waves had come into play on that afternoon along the Jersey shoreline when Martha saw the pebble and bent down to rescue it from geology. He imagined bare feet. Martha was a poet, with the poet's sensibilities, and her feet would be brown and bare, the toenails unpainted, the eyes chilly and somber like the ocean in March, and though it was painful, he wondered who had been with her that afternoon. He imagined a pair of shadows moving along the strip of sand where things came together but also separated. It was phantom jealousy, he knew, but he couldn't help himself. He loved her so much. On the march, through the hot days of early April, he carried the pebble in his mouth, turning it with his tongue, tasting sea salts and moisture. His mind wandered. He had difficulty keeping his attention on the war. On occasion he would yell at his men to spread out the column, to keep their eyes open, but then he would slip away into daydreams, just pretending, walking barefoot along the Jersey shore, with Martha, carrying nothing. He would feel himself rising. Sun and waves and gentle winds, all love and lightness.

What they carried varied by mission.

15 When a mission took them to the mountains, they carried mosquito netting, machetes, canvas tarps, and extra bug juice.

If a mission seemed especially hazardous, or if it involved a place they knew to be bad, they carried everything they could. In certain heavily mined AOs,[4] where the land was dense with Toe Poppers and Bouncing Betties, they took turns humping a twenty-eight-pound mine detector. With its headphones and big sensing plate, the equipment was a stress on the lower back and shoulders, awkward to handle, often useless because of the shrapnel in the earth, but they carried it anyway, partly for safety, partly for the illusion of safety.

On ambush, or other night missions, they carried peculiar little odds and ends. Kiowa always took along his New Testament and a pair of moccasins for silence. Dave Jensen carried night-sight vitamins high in carotin. Lee Strunk carried his slingshot; ammo, he claimed, would never be a problem. Rat Kiley carried brandy and M&M's. Until he was shot, Ted Lavender carried the starlight scope, which weighed 6.3 pounds with its aluminum carrying case. Henry Dobbins carried his girlfriend's pantyhose wrapped around his neck as a comforter. They all carried ghosts. When dark came, they would move out single file across the meadows and paddies to their ambush coordinates, where they would quietly set up the Claymores and lie down and spend the night waiting.

Other missions were more complicated and required special equipment. In mid-April, it was their mission to search out and destroy the elaborate tunnel complexes in the Than Khe area south of Chu Lai. To blow the tunnels, they carried one-pound blocks of pentrite high explosives, four blocks to a man, sixty-eight pounds in all. They carried wiring, detonators, and battery-powered clackers. Dave Jensen carried earplugs. Most often, before blowing the tunnels, they were ordered by higher command to search them, which was considered bad news, but by and large they just shrugged and carried out

[4] Areas of operations. — EDS.

orders. Because he was a big man, Henry Dobbins was excused from tunnel duty. The others would draw numbers. Before Lavender died there were seventeen men in the platoon, and whoever drew the number seventeen would strip off his gear and crawl in head first with a flashlight and Lieutenant Cross's .45-caliber pistol. The rest of them would fan out as security. They would sit down or kneel, not facing the hole, listening to the ground beneath them, imagining cobwebs and ghosts, whatever was down there — the tunnel walls squeezing in — how the flashlight seemed impossibly heavy in the hand and how it was tunnel vision in the very strictest sense, compression in all ways, even time, and how you had to wiggle in — ass and elbows — a swallowed-up feeling — and how you found yourself worrying about odd things — will your flashlight go dead? Do rats carry rabies? If you screamed, how far would the sound carry? Would your buddies hear it? Would they have the courage to drag you out? In some respects, though not many, the waiting was worse than the tunnel itself. Imagination was a killer.

On April 16, when Lee Strunk drew the number seventeen, he laughed and muttered something and went down quickly. The morning was hot and very still. Not good, Kiowa said. He looked at the tunnel opening, then out across a dry paddy toward the village of Than Khe. Nothing moved. No clouds or birds or people. As they waited, the men smoked and drank Kool-Aid, not talking much, feeling sympathy for Lee Strunk but also feeling the luck of the draw. You win some, you lose some, said Mitchell Sanders, and sometimes you settle for a rain check. It was a tired line and no one laughed.

20 Henry Dobbins ate a tropical chocolate bar. Ted Lavender popped a tranquilizer and went off to pee.

After five minutes, Lieutenant Jimmy Cross moved to the tunnel, leaned down, and examined the darkness. Trouble, he thought — a cave-in maybe. And then suddenly, without willing it, he was thinking about Martha. The stresses and fractures, the quick collapse, the two of them buried alive under all that weight. Dense, crushing love. Kneeling, watching the hole, he tried to concentrate on Lee Strunk and the war, all the dangers, but his love was too much for him, he felt paralyzed, he wanted to sleep inside her lungs and breathe her blood and be smothered. He wanted her to be a virgin and not a virgin, all at once. He wanted to know her. Intimate secrets — why poetry? Why so sad? Why the grayness in her eyes? Why so alone? Not lonely, just alone — riding her bike across campus or sitting off by herself in the cafeteria. Even dancing, she danced alone — and it was the aloneness that filled him with love. He remembered telling her that one evening. How she nodded and looked away. And how, later, when he kissed her, she received the kiss without returning it, her eyes wide open, not afraid, not a virgin's eyes, just flat and uninvolved.

Lieutenant Cross gazed at the tunnel. But he was not there. He was buried with Martha under the white sand at the Jersey shore. They were pressed together, and the pebble in his mouth was her tongue. He was smiling. Vaguely, he was aware of how quiet the day was, the sullen paddies, yet he could not bring himself to worry about matters of security. He was beyond that. He was just a kid at war, in love. He was twenty-two years old. He couldn't help it.

A few moments later Lee Strunk crawled out of the tunnel. He came up grinning, filthy but alive. Lieutenant Cross nodded and closed his eyes while the others clapped Strunk on the back and made jokes about rising from the dead.

Worms, Rat Kiley said. Right out of the grave. Fuckin' zombie.

25 The men laughed. They all felt great relief.

Spook City, said Mitchell Sanders.

Lee Strunk made a funny ghost sound, a kind of moaning, yet very happy, and right then, when Strunk made that high happy moaning

An American solider turns to face the photographer as the battle continues in the background. **What do the body language, equipment, and faces of the soldiers reveal about what it's like to be in the middle of a battle? In what ways do the details of this photo reflect the soldiers' experiences in the story?**

sound, when he went *Ahhooooo*, right then Ted Lavender was shot in the head on his way back from peeing. He lay with his mouth open. The teeth were broken. There was a swollen black bruise under his left eye. The cheekbone was gone. Oh shit, Rat Kiley said, the guy's dead. The guy's dead, he kept saying, which seemed profound — the guy's dead. I mean really.

The things they carried were determined to some extent by superstition. Lieutenant Cross carried his good-luck pebble. Dave Jensen carried a rabbit's foot. Norman Bowker, otherwise a very gentle person, carried a thumb that had been presented to him as a gift by Mitchell Sanders. The thumb was dark brown, rubbery to the touch, and weighed four ounces at most. It had been cut from a VC corpse, a boy of fifteen or sixteen. They'd found him at the bottom of an irrigation ditch, badly burned, flies in his mouth and eyes. The boy wore black shorts and sandals. At the time of his death he had been carrying a pouch of rice, a rifle, and three magazines of ammunition.

You want my opinion, Mitchell Sanders said, there's a definite moral here.

He put his hand on the dead boy's wrist. He was quiet for a time, as if counting a pulse, then he patted the stomach, almost affectionately, and used Kiowa's hunting hatchet to remove the thumb.

Henry Dobbins asked what the moral was.

Moral?

You know. *Moral.*

Sanders wrapped the thumb in toilet paper and handed it across to Norman Bowker. There was no blood. Smiling, he kicked the boy's head, watched the flies scatter, and said, It's like with that old TV show — Paladin. Have gun, will travel.

Henry Dobbins thought about it.

Yeah, well, he finally said. I don't see no moral.

There it is, man.

Fuck off.

They carried USO stationery and pencils and pens. They carried Sterno, safety pins, trip flares, signal flares, spools of wire, razor blades, chewing tobacco, liberated joss sticks and statuettes of the smiling Buddha, candles, grease pencils, *The Stars and Stripes*, fingernail clippers, Psy Ops[5] leaflets, bush hats, bolos, and much more. Twice a week, when the resupply choppers came in, they carried hot chow in green Mermite cans and large canvas bags filled with iced beer and soda pop. They carried plastic water containers, each with a two-gallon capacity. Mitchell

[5] Psychological operations. — EDS.

The July 2, 1965, cover of *Life* magazine shows a pair of American soldiers as they carry a wounded comrade to safety, accompanied by the headline "Deeper into the Vietnam War." **What message does this cover photo send to Americans back home about the war and the soldiers fighting in it? To what extent do the characters in this story reflect the men shown here?**

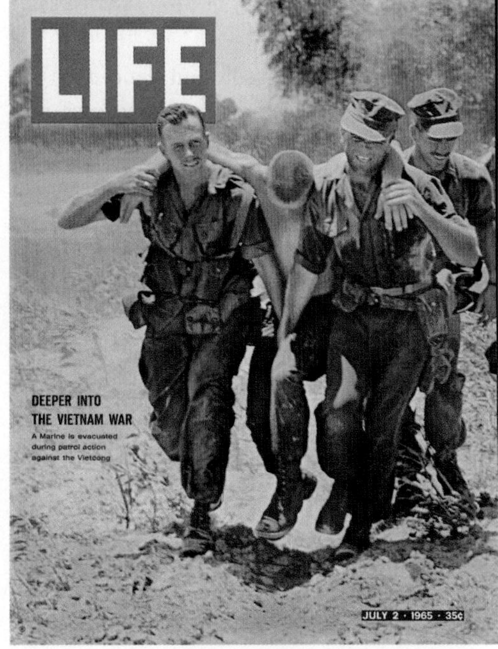

Bill Eppridge/The LIFE Premium Collection/Getty Images

Sanders carried a set of starched tiger fatigues for special occasions. Henry Dobbins carried Black Flag insecticide. Dave Jensen carried empty sandbags that could be filled at night for added protection. Lee Strunk carried tanning lotion. Some things they carried in common. Taking turns, they carried the big PRC-77 scrambler radio, which weighed thirty pounds with its battery. They shared the weight of memory. They took up what others could no longer bear. Often, they carried each other, the wounded or weak. They carried infections. They carried chess sets, basketballs, Vietnamese-English dictionaries, insignia of rank, Bronze Stars and Purple Hearts, plastic cards imprinted with the Code of Conduct. They carried diseases, among them malaria and dysentery. They carried lice and ringworm and leeches and paddy algae and various rots and molds. They carried the land itself — Vietnam, the place, the soil — a powdery orange-red dust that covered their boots and fatigues and faces. They carried the sky. The whole atmosphere, they carried it, the humidity, the monsoons, the stink of fungus and decay, all of it, they carried gravity. They moved like mules. By daylight they took sniper fire, at night they were mortared, but it was not battle, it was just the endless march, village to village, without purpose, nothing won or lost. They marched for the sake of the march. They plodded along slowly, dumbly, leaning forward against the heat, unthinking, all blood and bone, simple grunts, soldiering with their legs, toiling up the hills and down into the paddies and across the rivers and up again and down, just humping, one step and then the next and then another, but no volition, no will, because it was automatic, it was anatomy, and the war was entirely a matter of posture and carriage, the hump was everything, a kind of inertia, a kind of emptiness, a dullness of desire and intellect and conscience and hope and human sensibility. Their principles were in their feet. Their calculations were biological. They had no sense of strategy or mission. They searched the villages without knowing what to look for, not caring, kicking over jars of rice, frisking children and old men, blowing tunnels, sometimes setting fires and sometimes not, then forming up and moving on to the next village, then other villages, where it would always be the same. They carried their own lives. The pressures were enormous. In the heat of early afternoon, they would remove their helmets and flak jackets, walking bare, which was dangerous but which helped ease the strain. They would often discard things along the route of march. Purely for comfort, they would throw away rations, blow their Claymores and grenades, no matter, because by nightfall the resupply choppers would arrive with more of the same, then a day or two later still more, fresh watermelons and crates of ammunition and sunglasses and woolen sweaters — the resources were stunning — sparklers for the Fourth of July, colored eggs for Easter. It was the great American war chest — the fruits of science, the smokestacks, the canneries, the arsenals at Hartford, the Minnesota forests, the machine shops, the vast fields of corn and wheat — they carried like freight trains; they carried it on their backs and shoulders — and for all the ambiguities of Vietnam, all the mysteries and unknowns, there was at least the single abiding certainty that they would never be at a loss for things to carry.

After the chopper took Lavender away, Lieutenant Jimmy Cross led his men into the village of Than Khe. They burned everything. They shot chickens and dogs, they trashed the village well, they called in artillery and watched the wreckage, then they marched for several hours through the hot afternoon, and then at dusk, while Kiowa explained how Lavender died, Lieutenant Cross found himself trembling.

He tried not to cry. With his entrenching tool, which weighed five pounds, he began digging a hole in the earth.

He felt shame. He hated himself. He had loved Martha more than his men, and as a consequence Lavender was now dead, and this was something he would have to carry like a stone in his stomach for the rest of the war.

All he could do was dig. He used his entrenching tool like an ax, slashing, feeling both love and hate, and then later, when it was full dark, he sat at the bottom of his foxhole and wept. It went on for a long while. In part, he was grieving for Ted Lavender, but mostly it was for Martha, and for himself, because she belonged to another world, which was not quite real, and because she was a junior at Mount Sebastian College in New Jersey, a poet and a virgin and uninvolved, and because he realized she did not love him and never would.

Like cement, Kiowa whispered in the dark. I swear to God — boom-down. Not a word.

I've heard this, said Norman Bowker.

A pisser, you know? Still zipping himself up. Zapped while zipping.

All right, fine. That's enough.

Yeah, but you had to see it, the guy just —

I *heard*, man. Cement. So why not shut the fuck *up*?

Kiowa shook his head sadly and glanced over at the hole where Lieutenant Jimmy Cross sat watching the night. The air was thick and wet. A warm, dense fog had settled over the paddies and there was the stillness that precedes rain.

After a time Kiowa sighed.

One thing for sure, he said. The Lieutenant's in some deep hurt. I mean that crying jag — the way he was carrying on — it wasn't fake or anything, it was real heavy-duty hurt. The man cares.

Sure, Norman Bowker said.

Say what you want, the man does care.

We all got problems.

Not Lavender.

No, I guess not, Bowker said. Do me a favor, though.

Shut up?

That's a smart Indian. Shut up.

Shrugging, Kiowa pulled off his boots. He wanted to say more, just to lighten up his sleep, but instead he opened his New Testament and arranged it beneath his head as a pillow. The fog made things seem hollow and unattached. He tried not to think about Ted Lavender, but then he was thinking how fast it was, no drama, down and dead, and how it was hard to feel anything except surprise. It seemed un-Christian. He wished he could find some great sadness, or even anger, but the emotion wasn't there and he couldn't make it happen. Mostly he felt pleased to be alive. He liked the smell of the New Testament under his cheek, the leather

What does this photo of a soldier consoling his comrade in arms reveal about the emotional price of combat? Does it suggest that humanity can prevail even in inhumane situations, or is it instead a reminder of the hopelessness of war? Explain, using "The Things They Carried" to support your response.

Martin Gershen / Getty Images

and ink and paper and glue, whatever the chemicals were. He liked hearing the sounds of night. Even his fatigue, it felt fine, the stiff muscles and the prickly awareness of his own body, a floating feeling. He enjoyed not being dead. Lying there, Kiowa admired Lieutenant Jimmy Cross's capacity for grief. He wanted to share the man's pain, he wanted to care as Jimmy Cross cared. And yet when he closed his eyes, all he could think was Boom-down, and all he could feel was the pleasure of having his boots off and the fog curling in around him and the damp soil and the Bible smells and the plush comfort of night.

After a moment Norman Bowker sat up in the dark.

What the hell, he said. You want to talk, *talk*. Tell it to me.

Forget it.

No, man, go on. One thing I hate, it's a silent Indian.

For the most part they carried themselves with poise, a kind of dignity. Now and then, however, there were times of panic, when they squealed or wanted to squeal but couldn't, when they twitched and made moaning sounds and covered their heads and said Dear Jesus and flopped around on the earth and fired their weapons blindly and cringed and sobbed and begged for the noise to stop and went wild and made stupid promises to themselves and to God and to their mothers and fathers, hoping not to die. In different ways, it happened to all of them. Afterward, when the firing ended, they would blink and peek up. They would touch their bodies, feeling shame, then quickly hiding it. They would force themselves to stand. As if in slow motion, frame by frame, the world would take on the old logic — absolute silence, then the wind, then sunlight, then voices. It was the burden of being alive. Awkwardly, the men would reassemble themselves, first in private, then in groups, becoming soldiers again. They would repair the leaks in their eyes. They would check for casualties, call in dust-offs, light cigarettes, try to smile, clear their throats and spit and begin cleaning their weapons. After a time someone would shake his head and say, No lie, I almost shit my pants, and someone else would laugh, which meant it was bad, yes, but the guy had obviously not shit his pants, it wasn't that bad, and in any case nobody would ever do such a thing and then go ahead and talk about it. They would squint into the dense, oppressive sunlight. For a few moments, perhaps, they would fall silent, lighting a joint and tracking its passage from man to man, inhaling, holding in the humiliation. Scary stuff, one of them might say. But then someone else would grin or flick his eyebrows and say, Roger-dodger, almost cut me a new asshole, *almost.*

There were numerous such poses. Some carried themselves with a sort of wistful resignation, others with pride or stiff soldierly discipline or good humor or macho zeal. They were afraid of dying but they were even more afraid to show it.

They found jokes to tell.

They used a hard vocabulary to contain the terrible softness. *Greased* they'd say. *Offed, lit up, zapped while zipping.* It wasn't cruelty, just stage presence. They were actors and the war came at them in 3-D. When someone died, it wasn't quite dying, because in a curious way it seemed scripted, and because they had their lines mostly memorized, irony mixed with tragedy, and because they called it by other names, as if to encyst and destroy the reality of death itself. They kicked corpses. They cut off thumbs. They talked grunt lingo. They told stories about Ted Lavender's supply of tranquilizers, how the poor guy didn't feel a thing, how incredibly tranquil he was.

There's a moral here, said Mitchell Sanders.

They were waiting for Lavender's chopper, smoking the dead man's dope.

The moral's pretty obvious, Sanders said, and winked. Stay away from drugs. No joke, they'll ruin your day every time.

Cute, said Henry Dobbins.

Mind-blower, get it? Talk about wiggy—nothing left, just blood and brains.

They made themselves laugh.

There it is, they'd say, over and over, as if the repetition itself were an act of poise, a balance between crazy and almost crazy, knowing without going. There it is, which meant be cool, let it ride, because oh yeah, man, you can't change what can't be changed, there it is, there it absolutely and positively and fucking well is.

They were tough.

They carried all the emotional baggage of men who might die. Grief, terror, love, longing—these were intangibles, but the intangibles had their own mass and specific gravity, they had tangible weight. They carried shameful memories. They carried the common secret of cowardice barely restrained, the instinct to run or freeze or hide, and in many respects this was the heaviest burden of all, for it could never be put down, it required perfect balance and perfect posture. They carried their reputations. They carried the soldier's greatest fear, which was the fear of blushing. Men killed, and died, because they were embarrassed not to. It was what had brought them to the war in the first place, nothing positive, no dreams of glory or honor, just to avoid the blush of dishonor. They died so as not to die of embarrassment. They crawled into tunnels and walked point and advanced under fire. Each morning, despite the unknowns, they made their legs move. They endured. They kept humping. They did not submit to the obvious alternative, which was simply to close the eyes and fall. So easy, really. Go limp and tumble to the ground and let the muscles unwind and not speak and not budge until your buddies picked you up and lifted you into the chopper that would roar and dip its nose and carry you off to the world. A mere matter of falling, yet no one ever fell. It was not courage, exactly; the object was not valor. Rather, they were too frightened to be cowards.

By and large they carried these things inside, maintaining the masks of composure. They sneered at sick call. They spoke bitterly about guys who had found release by shooting off their own toes or fingers. Pussies, they'd say.

Candyasses. It was fierce, mocking talk, with only a trace of envy or awe, but even so, the image played itself out behind their eyes.

They imagined the muzzle against flesh. They imagined the quick, sweet pain, then the evacuation to Japan, then a hospital with warm beds and cute geisha nurses.

They dreamed of freedom birds.

At night, on guard, staring into the dark, they were carried away by jumbo jets. They felt the rush of takeoff. *Gone!* they yelled. And then velocity, wings and engines, a smiling stewardess — but it was more than a plane, it was a real bird, a big sleek silver bird with feathers and talons and high screeching. They were flying. The weights fell off, there was nothing to bear. They laughed and held on tight, feeling the cold slap of wind and altitude, soaring, thinking *It's over, I'm gone!* — they were naked, they were light and free — it was all lightness, bright and fast and buoyant, light as light, a helium buzz in the brain, a giddy bubbling in the lungs as they were taken up over the clouds and the war, beyond duty, beyond gravity and mortification and global entanglements — *Sin loi!*[6] they yelled, *I'm sorry, motherfuckers, but I'm out of it, I'm goofed, I'm on a space cruise, I'm gone!* — and it was a restful, disencumbered sensation, just riding the light waves, sailing that big silver freedom bird over the mountains and oceans, over America, over the farms and great sleeping cities and cemeteries and highways and the golden arches of McDonald's. It was flight, a kind of fleeing, a kind of falling, falling higher and higher, spinning off the edge of the earth and beyond the sun and through the vast, silent vacuum where there were no burdens and where everything weighed exactly nothing. *Gone!* they screamed, *I'm sorry but I'm gone!* And so at night, not quite dreaming, they gave themselves over to lightness, they were carried, they were purely borne.

On the morning after Ted Lavender died, First Lieutenant Jimmy Cross crouched at the bottom of his foxhole and burned Martha's letters. Then he burned the two photographs. There was a steady rain falling, which made it difficult, but he used heat tabs and Sterno to build a small fire, screening it with his body, holding the photographs over the tight blue flame with the tips of his fingers.

He realized it was only a gesture. Stupid, he thought. Sentimental, too, but mostly just stupid.

Lavender was dead. You couldn't burn the blame.

Besides, the letters were in his head. And even now, without photographs, Lieutenant Cross could see Martha playing volleyball in her white gym shorts and yellow T-shirt. He could see her moving in the rain.

When the fire died out, Lieutenant Cross pulled his poncho over his shoulders and ate breakfast from a can.

There was no great mystery, he decided.

In those burned letters Martha had never mentioned the war, except to say, Jimmy, take care of yourself. She wasn't involved. She signed the letters "Love," but it wasn't love, and all the fine lines and technicalities did not matter.

The morning came up wet and blurry. Everything seemed part of everything else, the fog and Martha and the deepening rain.

It was a war, after all.

Half smiling, Lieutenant Jimmy Cross took out his maps. He shook his head hard, as if to clear it, then bent forward and began planning the day's march. In ten minutes, or maybe twenty, he would rouse the men and they would pack up and head west, where the maps showed the country to be green and inviting. They would do what they had always done. The rain might add some weight, but otherwise it would be one more day layered upon all the other days.

He was realistic about it. There was that new hardness in his stomach.

No more fantasies, he told himself.

---

[6] Sorry about that. — EDS.

SUPPORT OUR BOYS IN
VIETNAM
KOREA, GERMANY, JAPAN, ENGLAND, ITALY, CANADA, SWEDEN,
DENMARK, BERKLEY, WATTS, BOSTON, CUBA, ARGENTINA, PAKISTAN,
LAOS, CONGO, THAILAND, ACAPULCO, INDIA, LEBANON, CHICAGO,
DOMINICAN REPUBLIC, ECUADOR, HONG KONG, WOODSTOCK, D.C., COLUMBIA
GREENLAND, PUERTO RICO, TIAJUANA, KOWLOON, CHAPEL HILL, RUSSIA, HAITI,
INDONESIA, BERMUDA, AUSTRALIA, CONSHOHOCKEN, CICERO, PRINCETON, LIBERIA, BIAFRA,
NORWAY, OKINAWA, M.I.T., PHILLIPINES, SCOTLAND, GREECE, ICELAND, GUAM, AFGHANISTAN, BRAZIL,
TURKEY, SPAIN, HARLEM, BURMA, CAMBODIA, PERU, NOVA SCOTIA, AZORES, PANAMA, CRETE, COSTA RICA, AUSTRIA
EAST VILLAGE, BOLIVIA, IRAN, HONOLULU, TAHITI, SICILY, IRELAND, CORSICA, DUBUQUE, ISRAEL, SPAIN, NETHERLANDS,
URAGUAY, VENEZUELA, SHANGHAI, GLENDALE, ARUBA, FIRE ISLAND, CHILE, CANARY ISLANDS, GUATEMALA, ANTIGUA, IWO JIMA, NIGERIA, CONGO

Eileen Tweedy/The Art Archive at Art Resource, NY

How does this protest poster — ironically asking for support for American troops in Vietnam, Korea, Germany, Japan, etc. — call on the psychedelic imagery of the cultural and sexual revolutions occurring at home during the Vietnam War? Why do you think this kind of image would or would not resonate with the young soldiers in "The Things They Carried"?

Boom-down, and you were dead, never partly dead.

Briefly, in the rain, Lieutenant 95
Cross saw Martha's gray eyes gazing back at him.

He understood.

It was very sad, he thought. The things men carried inside. The things men did or felt they had to do.

He almost nodded at her, but didn't.

Instead he went back to his maps. He was now determined to perform his duties firmly and without negligence. It wouldn't help Lavender, he knew that, but from this point on he would comport himself as a soldier. He would dispose of his good-luck pebble. Swallow it, maybe, or use Lee Strunk's slingshot, or just drop it along the trail. On the march he would impose strict field discipline. He would be careful to send out flank security, to prevent straggling or bunching up, to keep his troops moving at the proper pace and at the proper interval. He would insist on clean weapons. He would confiscate the remainder of Lavender's dope. Later in the day, perhaps, he would call the men together and speak to them plainly. He would accept the blame for what had happened to Ted Lavender. He would be a man about it. He would look them in the eyes, keeping his chin level, and he would issue the new SOPs in a calm, impersonal tone of voice, an officer's voice, leaving no room for argument or discussion. Commencing immediately, he'd tell them, they would no longer abandon equipment along the route of march. They would police up their

Henceforth, when he thought about Martha, it would be only to think that she belonged elsewhere. He would shut down the daydreams. This was not Mount Sebastian, it was another world, where there were no pretty poems or midterm exams, a place where men died because of carelessness and gross stupidity. Kiowa was right.

This photo shows an American soldier, wounded by an exploding land mine, being carried to a helicopter by his comrades. **What does this image add to your understanding of what American soldiers fighting in Vietnam carried — both as individual soldiers and as part of a collective military presence?**

acts. They would get their shit together, and keep it together, and maintain it neatly and in good working order.

He would not tolerate laxity. He would show strength, distancing himself.

Among the men there would be grumbling, of course, and maybe worse, because their days would seem longer and their loads heavier, but Lieutenant Cross reminded himself that his obligation was not to be loved but to lead. He would dispense with love; it was not now a factor. And if anyone quarreled or complained, he would simply tighten his lips and arrange his shoulders in the correct command posture. He might give a curt little nod. Or he might not. He might just shrug and say Carry on, then they would saddle up and form into a column and move out toward the villages of Than Khe.

[1986]

QUESTIONS FOR DISCUSSION

1. The story begins with a paragraph about Jimmy Cross and his relationship with Martha. What does Martha represent to Cross? Why might it be significant that Cross obsesses about whether or not she is a virgin? How do Cross's feelings for Martha change toward the end of the story, and how does this change point the way to one of the themes of the story?
2. What role does Hollywood play in this story? How are the soldiers' expectations of war and death shaped by the movies? Where in this story does Hollywood fantasy meet reality? What point is Tim O'Brien making?
3. According to the narrator, "The things they carried were largely determined by necessity" (para. 2), were "partly a function of rank, partly of field specialty" (para. 6), "varied by mission" (para. 14), and "were determined to some extent by superstition" (para. 28). Which is the strongest factor in determining what they carried? Do you find any irony in the things they carried?
4. Jimmy Cross carries "the responsibility for the lives of his men" (para. 7) and ultimately cannot bear that burden. What does he literally and figuratively shed in order to bear that weight

following Lavender's death? What point is O'Brien making?

5. Why do you think the medic would need "M&M's for especially bad wounds" (para. 9)?
6. In paragraph 29, the soldiers find the burned corpse of a teenage Vietcong soldier at the bottom of a ditch, and Sanders says, "there's a definite moral here," before cutting off the boy's thumb and giving it to Bowker. Dobbins doesn't see the moral, and ultimately, they decide, "There it is." What do they mean by that? Look at paragraph 75, where O'Brien talks more about the meaning of that phrase. Does "The Things They Carried" have a moral? If so, what is it?
7. The soldiers react differently to Ted Lavender's death (paras. 11, 27, 40–64). Pick one soldier whose reaction seems particularly significant, and explain why you find it meaningful.
8. After studying terminally ill patients, psychologist Elisabeth Kübler-Ross described five stages in the process of dealing with death: (1) denial, or "this isn't happening"; (2) anger, or "why me?"; (3) bargaining, or "I'd do anything"; (4) depression, or "I give up"; and (5) acceptance, or "It's okay." Do the soldiers facing death in this story display these behaviors? Which stages do you notice, and in what circumstances? Which stage seems most prevalent? Why do you think that is?
9. In paragraph 77, the narrator says, "They carried the soldier's greatest fear, which was the fear of blushing." Why do you think the soldiers were more afraid to blush than to die?
10. Paragraph 97 says, "It was very sad, [Cross] thought. The things men carried inside. The things men did or felt they had to do." What things do you think Cross is thinking about? What does he intend to do about it? Do you think he will succeed? Do you think it will matter? Explain your answers.
11. What opinion do you think O'Brien has about the soldiers, the war, and, specifically, Lieutenant Cross? Support your inferences with specific references to the text.

QUESTIONS ON STYLE AND STRUCTURE

1. Paragraph 3 says, "They were called legs or grunts." Explain why this use of synecdoche (using a part to refer to the whole) is especially appropriate not only for this story but for life in the military in general.
2. What evidence do you find that Jimmy Cross is a Christ figure? How does the symbolism of his name and initials influence your reading of the story? Is the virgin Martha akin to the Virgin Mary? Explain why or why not.
3. The story's central event is the death of Ted Lavender, which the story returns to again and again. Why do you think the story revisits this event so often? Do you think this repetition honors Lavender or trivializes his death? Explain your answer.
4. The reader learns about Ted Lavender's death in the second paragraph, but the narrator provides few details until paragraph 27. What is the effect of the delay on the reader? What does the delay suggest about the effects of war on the soldiers?
5. How does O'Brien characterize the soldiers by the things they carry?
6. One technique O'Brien employs is zeugma, in which one word has more than one (often incongruous) object. For example, he writes in paragraph 12, "They carried all they could bear, and then some, including a silent awe for the terrible power of the things they carried." Look for other examples of zeugma in the story. Do you see any pattern in how O'Brien uses zeugma? In particular, consider how O'Brien exploits the incongruity of zeugma in order to develop one of the themes of the story.
7. Paragraph 18 contains a series of questions. Consider all the possible meanings of the statement "Imagination was a killer." How does it answer the questions?
8. At the end of paragraph 39, the narrator adds the products of the "great American war chest" to "the things they carried." Explain the political statement this extended metaphor makes.

9. How many times does the word "they" appear from paragraphs 65 through 81? (Literally, count them.) Why does O'Brien use that pronoun so often at the end of the story?

10. In paragraph 99, the conditional "would" is repeated in nearly every sentence. What does this parallelism suggest? How does it add to the characterization of Lieutenant Cross?

SUGGESTIONS FOR WRITING

1. Read once again the epigraph to this chapter. Write an essay in which you consider how O'Brien's remarks serve to introduce "The Things They Carried."
2. Consider carefully the organization and narrative method O'Brien uses in this story. While some sections attempt to define and explain the nature of the soldier's war experience, other sections are narratives about individual soldiers. Write an essay in which you explain how the structure O'Brien uses comments on war.
3. Sometimes a work of literature reveals a great deal of richness in what it leaves out or what it doesn't say. "The Things They Carried" concentrates on what the soldiers carry, giving the soldiers little purpose beyond "humping." Write an essay discussing what O'Brien is trying to say by focusing on the minutiae of war. Think especially about what he leaves out.
4. One might view O'Brien's narrative structure itself to be symbolic. Each time the narrator brings order to the events by returning to an organized account of the things that they carried, the process slips into personal accounts and idiosyncratic details. How does such a method work symbolically to suggest something about the subject matter of the story?
5. Read "Naming of Parts" by Henry Reed (p. 1215). Compare and contrast that poem's techniques and themes to those of "The Things They Carried."
6. At the end of the story, Jimmy Cross feels responsible for Lavender's death, and his thoughts turn again to Martha as he decides to strengthen his resolve. Assume the character of Lieutenant Cross and write a letter to Martha about the incident. Then write her reply.

CLASSIC TEXT

Othello, the Moor of Venice

WILLIAM SHAKESPEARE

National Portrait Gallery, London, UK/Bridgeman Images

William Shakespeare (1564–1616) was born in Stratford-upon-Avon, England. Little is known of his life aside from the fact that he married Anne Hathaway when he was eighteen, worked as an actor-playwright in London, and retired in 1613. His plays fall into four principal categories: early comedies (1585–1594), more sophisticated comedies and histories (1595–1599), the great tragedies (1599–1607), and the final phase (1608–1613). His most accomplished works — including *Hamlet* (1601), *Othello* (1604), *King Lear* (1605), and *Macbeth* (1606) — belong to the third period. In his time his contemporaries — and likely Shakespeare himself — looked to his sonnets and other poems as the more important works. The 154 sonnets were written at various stages in Shakespeare's life, but when and to whom they were written remain unclear. Wordsworth believed that only through the sonnets could one understand Shakespeare. *Othello* is considered one of Shakespeare's finest works, and its enduring portrait of racism, love, betrayal, revenge, and repentance in the not-so-quiet aftermath of war have made it the source for numerous operatic, film, and literary adaptations.

[***Dramatis Personae***

OTHELLO, *the Moor*

BRABANTIO, [*a senator,*] *father to Desdemona*

CASSIO, *an honorable lieutenant* [*to Othello*]

IAGO, [*Othello's ancient,*] *a villain*

RODERIGO, *a gulled gentleman*

DUKE OF VENICE

SENATORS [*of Venice*]

MONTANO, *Governor of Cyprus*

GENTLEMEN *of Cyprus*

LODOVICO *and* **GRATIANO**, [*kinsmen to Brabantio,*] *two noble Venetians*

SAILORS

CLOWN

DESDEMONA, [*daughter to Brabantio and*] *wife to Othello*

EMILIA, *wife to Iago*

BIANCA, *a courtesan* [*and mistress to Cassio*]

[**A MESSENGER, A HERALD, A MUSICIAN**

Servants, Attendants, Officers, Senators, Musicians, Gentlemen

SCENE: *Venice; a seaport in Cyprus*]

ACT I

Scene i°

Enter RODERIGO *and* IAGO.

RODERIGO Tush, never tell me!° I take it much unkindly
That thou, Iago, who hast had my purse
As if the strings were thine, shouldst know of this.°

IAGO 'Sblood,° but you'll not hear me.
If ever I did dream of such a matter,
Abhor me.

RODERIGO Thou toldst me thou didst hold him° in thy hate.

IAGO Despise me
If I do not. Three great ones of the city,
In personal suit to make me his lieutenant,
Off-capped to him; and by the faith of man,
I know my price, I am worth no worse a place.
But he, as loving his own pride and purposes,
Evades them with a bombast circumstance°
Horribly stuffed with epithets of war,°
And, in conclusion,
Nonsuits° my mediators. For, "Certes,"° says he,
"I have already chose my officer."
And what was he?
Forsooth, a great arithmetician,°
One Michael Cassio, a Florentine,
A fellow almost damned in a fair wife,°
That never set a squadron in the field
Nor the division of a battle° knows
More than a spinster° — unless the bookish theoric,°
Wherein the togaed consuls° can propose°
As masterly as he. Mere prattle, without practice
Is all his soldiership. But he, sir, had th'election;
And I, of whom his° eyes had seen the proof
At Rhodes, at Cyprus, and on other grounds
Christened and heathen, must be beleed and calmed°
By debitor and creditor.° This countercaster,°
He, in good time,° must his lieutenant be,
And I — God bless the mark!° — his Moorship's ancient.°

RODERIGO By heaven, I rather would have been his hangman.°

IAGO Why, there's no remedy. 'Tis the curse of service;
Preferment° goes by letter and affection,°
And not by the old gradation,° where each second
Stood heir to th' first. Now, sir, be judge yourself
Whether I in any just term° am affined°
To love the Moor.

RODERIGO I would not follow him then.

IAGO Oh, sir, content you.°
I follow him to serve my turn upon him.
We cannot all be masters, nor all masters
Cannot be truly° followed. You shall mark
Many a duteous and knee-crooking knave
That, doting on his own obsequious bondage,

Act I, Scene i. Location: Venice. A street. **1. never tell me:** (An expression of incredulity, like "tell me another one.") **3. this:** i.e., Desdemona's elopement. **4. 'Sblood:** by His (Christ's) blood. **7. him:** Othello. **14. bombast circumstance:** wordy evasion. (*Bombast* is cotton padding.) **15. epithets of war:** military expressions. **17. Nonsuits:** rejects the petition of. **Certes:** certainly. **20. arithmetician:** i.e., a man whose military knowledge is merely theoretical, based on books of tactics. **22. A . . . wife:** (Cassio does not seem to be married, but his counterpart in Shakespeare's source does have a woman in his house. See also 4.1.128.) **24. division of a battle:** disposition of a military unit. **25. a spinster:** i.e., a housewife, one whose regular occupation is spinning. **theoric:** theory.

26. togaed consuls: toga-wearing counselors or senators. **propose:** discuss. **29. his:** Othello's. **31. beleed and calmed:** left to leeward without wind, becalmed. (A sailing metaphor.) **32. debitor and creditor:** (A name for a system of bookkeeping, here used as a contemptuous nickname for Cassio.) **countercaster:** i.e., bookkeeper, one who tallies with *counters,* or "metal disks." (Said contemptuously.) **33. in good time:** opportunely, i.e., forsooth. **34. God bless the mark:** (Perhaps originally a formula to ward off evil; here an expression of impatience.) **ancient:** standard-bearer, ensign (below lieutenant in rank). [Hall] **35. his hangman:** the executioner of him. **37. Preferment:** promotion. **letter and affection:** personal influence and favoritism. **38. old gradation:** step-by-step seniority, the traditional way. **40. term:** respect. **affined:** bound. **43. content you:** don't you worry about that. **46. truly:** faithfully.

Wears out his time, much like his master's ass,
For naught but provender, and when he's old, cashiered.°
Whip me° such honest knaves. Others there are
Who, trimmed in forms and visages of duty,°
Keep yet their hearts attending on themselves,
And, throwing but shows of service on their lords,
Do well thrive by them, and when they have lined their coats,°
Do themselves homage.° These fellows have some soul,
And such a one do I profess myself. For, sir,
It is as sure as you are Roderigo,
Were I the Moor I would not be Iago.°
In following him, I follow but myself—
Heaven is my judge, not I for love and duty,
But seeming so for my peculiar° end.
For when my outward action doth demonstrate
The native° act and figure° of my heart
In compliment extern,° 'tis not long after
But I will wear my heart upon my sleeve
For daws° to peck at. I am not what I am.°

RODERIGO What a full° fortune does the thick-lips° owe°
If he can carry 't thus!°

IAGO Call up her father.
Rouse him, make after him, poison his delight,
Proclaim him in the streets; incense her kinsmen,
And, though he in a fertile climate dwell,
Plague him with flies.° Though that his joy be joy,°
Yet throw such changes of vexation° on't
As it may lose some color.°

RODERIGO Here is her father's house. I'll call aloud.

IAGO Do, with like timorous° accent and dire yell
As when, by night and negligence, the fire°
Is spied in populous cities.

RODERIGO What ho, Brabantio! Signor Brabantio, ho!

IAGO Awake! What ho, Brabantio! Thieves, thieves, thieves!
Look to your house, your daughter, and your bags!
Thieves, thieves!

BRABANTIO [*enters*] *above,* [*at a window*].°

BRABANTIO What is the reason of this terrible summons?
What is the matter there?

RODERIGO Signor, is all your family within?

IAGO Are your doors locked?

BRABANTIO Why, wherefore ask you this?

IAGO Zounds,° sir, you're robbed. For shame, put on your gown!
Your heart is burst; you have lost half your soul.
Even now, now, very now, an old black ram
Is tupping° your white ewe. Arise, arise!
Awake the snorting° citizens with the bell,
Or else the devil° will make a grandsire of you.
Arise, I say!

---

50. cashiered: dismissed from service. **51. Whip me:** whip, as far as I'm concerned. **52. trimmed . . . duty:** dressed up in the mere form and show of dutifulness. **55. lined their coats:** i.e., stuffed their purses. **56. Do themselves homage:** i.e., attend to self-interest solely. **59. Were . . . Iago:** i.e., if I were able to assume command, I certainly would not choose to remain a subordinate, or, I would keep a suspicious eye on a flattering subordinate. **62. peculiar:** particular, personal. **64. native:** innate. **figure:** shape, intent. **65. compliment extern:** outward show (conforming in this case to the inner workings and intention of the heart). **67. daws:** small crowlike birds, proverbially stupid and avaricious. **I am not what I am:** i.e., I am not one who wears his heart on his sleeve. **68. full:** swelling. **thick-lips:** (Elizabethans often applied the term "Moor" to Negroes.) **owe:** own. **69. carry't thus:** carry this off.

72–73. though . . . flies: though he seems prosperous and happy now, vex him with misery. **73. Though . . . be joy:** Although he seems fortunate and happy. (Repeats the idea of line 72.) **74. changes of vexation:** vexing changes. **75. As . . . color:** that may cause it to lose some of its first gloss. **77. timorous:** frightening. **78. As . . . fire:** as when a fire, having gained hold by negligence at night. **83. s.d.** ***at a window:*** (This stage direction, from the Quarto, probably calls for an appearance on the gallery above and rear stage.) **88. Zounds:** by His (Christ's) wounds. **91. tupping:** covering, copulating with. (Said of sheep.) **92. snorting:** snoring. **93. the devil:** (The devil was conventionally pictured as black.)

BRABANTIO What, have you lost your wits?

RODERIGO Most reverend signor, do you know my voice?

BRABANTIO Not I. What are you?

RODERIGO My name is Roderigo.

BRABANTIO The worser welcome.
I have charged thee not to haunt about my doors.
In honest plainness thou hast heard me say
My daughter is not for thee; and now, in madness,
Being full of supper and distemp'ring° drafts,
Upon malicious bravery° dost thou come
To start° my quiet.

RODERIGO Sir, sir, sir—

BRABANTIO But thou must needs be sure
My spirits and my place have in their power°
To make this bitter to thee.

RODERIGO Patience, good sir.

BRABANTIO What tell'st thou me of robbing? This is Venice;
My house is not a grange.°

RODERIGO Most grave Brabantio,
In simple° and pure soul I come to you.

IAGO Zounds, sir, you are one of those that will not serve God if the devil bid you. Because we come to do you service and you think we are ruffians, you'll have your daughter covered with a Barbary° horse; you'll have your nephews° neigh to you; you'll have coursers for cousins and jennets for germans.°

BRABANTIO What profane wretch art thou?

IAGO I am one, sir, that comes to tell you your daughter and the Moor are now making the beast with two backs.°

BRABANTIO Thou art a villain.

IAGO You are—a senator.°

BRABANTIO This thou shalt answer.° I know thee, Roderigo.

RODERIGO Sir, I will answer anything. But I beseech you,
If't be your pleasure and most wise° consent—
As partly I find it is—that your fair daughter,
At this odd-even and dull watch o'th' night,°
Transported with° no worse nor better guard
But with a knave° of common hire, a gondolier,
To the gross clasps of a lascivious Moor—
If this be known to you and your allowance°
We then have done you bold and saucy° wrongs.
But if you know not this, my manners tell me
We have your wrong rebuke. Do not believe
That, from° the sense of all civility,°
I thus would play and trifle with your reverence.°
Your daughter, if you have not given her leave,
I say again, hath made a gross revolt,
Tying her duty, beauty, wit,° and fortunes
In an extravagant and wheeling stranger
Of here and everywhere.° Straight° satisfy yourself.
If she be in her chamber or your house,
Let loose on me the justice of the state
For thus deluding you.

BRABANTIO [*calling*]: Strike on the tinder,° ho!
Give me a taper! Call up all my people!
This accident° is not unlike my dream.

---

102. distemp'ring: intoxicating. **103. Upon malicious bravery:** with hostile intent to defy me. **104. start:** startle, disrupt. **106. My . . . power:** my temperament and my authority of office have it in their power. **109. grange:** isolated country house. **110. simple:** sincere. **115. Barbary:** from northern Africa (and hence associated with Othello). **116. nephews:** i.e., grandsons. **116–118. you'll . . . germans:** you'll consent to have powerful horses for kinfolks and small Spanish horses for near relatives. **121–122. making the beast with two backs:** copulating. [Hall]

123. a senator: (Said with mock politeness, as though the word itself were an insult.) **124. answer:** be held accountable for. **126. wise:** well-informed. **128. At . . . night:** at this hour that is between day and night, neither the one nor the other. **129. with:** by. **130. But with a knave:** than by a low fellow, a servant. **132. and your allowance:** and has your permission. **133. saucy:** insolent. **136. from:** contrary to. **civility:** good manners, decency. **137. your reverence:** (1) the respect due to you; (2) Your Reverence. **140. wit:** intelligence. **141–142. In . . . everywhere:** to a wandering and vagabond foreigner of uncertain origins. **142. Straight:** straightaway. **146. tinder:** charred linen ignited by a spark from flint and steel, used to light torches or tapers (lines 147, 172). **148. accident:** occurrence, event.

Belief of it oppresses me already.
Light, I say, light! *Exit [above].*

IAGO Farewell, for I must leave you.
It seems not meet° nor wholesome to my place°
To be producted° — as, if I stay, I shall —
Against the Moor. For I do know the state,
However this may gall° him with some check,°
Cannot with safety cast° him, for he's embarked°
With such loud° reason to the Cyprus wars,
Which even now stands in act,° that, for their souls,°
Another of his fathom° they have none
To lead their business; in which regard,°
Though I do hate him as I do hell pains,
Yet for necessity of present life°
I must show out a flag and sign of love,
Which is indeed but sign. That you shall surely find him,
Lead to the Sagittary° the raisèd search,°
And there will I be with him. So farewell.
Exit.

Enter [below] **BRABANTIO** *[in his nightgown]° with* **SERVANTS** *and torches.*

BRABANTIO It is too true an evil. Gone she is;
And what's to come of my despisèd time°
Is naught but bitterness. Now, Roderigo,
Where didst thou see her? — Oh, unhappy girl! —
With the Moor, say'st thou? — Who would be a father! —
How didst thou know 'twas she? — Oh, she deceives me

151. **meet:** fitting. **place:** position (as ensign). **152. producted:** produced (as a witness). **154. gall:** rub; oppress. **check:** rebuke. **155. cast:** dismiss. **embarked:** engaged. **156. loud:** urgent. **157. stands in act:** have started. **for their souls:** to save their souls. **158. fathom:** i.e., ability, depth of experience. **159. in which regard:** out of regard for which. **161. life:** livelihood. **164. Sagittary:** (An inn or house where Othello and Desdemona are staying, named for its sign of Sagittarius, or Centaur.) **raisèd search:** search party roused out of sleep. **165. s.d. *nightgown:*** dressing gown. (This costuming is specified in the Quarto text.) **167. time:** i.e., remainder of life.

This promotional photograph for an 1890 production of *Othello* shows actor Edwin Booth in character as Iago. **How does Booth's portrayal highlight Iago's true nature?**

Past thought! — What said she to you? — Get more tapers.
Raise all my kindred. — Are they married, think you?

RODERIGO Truly, I think they are.

BRABANTIO Oh, heaven! How got she out? Oh, treason of the blood!
Fathers, from hence trust not your daughters' minds
By what you see them act. Is there not charms°
By which the property° of youth and maidhood

177. charms: spells. **178. property:** special quality, nature.

May be abused?° Have you not read,
Roderigo,
Of some such thing?

RODERIGO Yes, sir, I have indeed.

BRABANTIO Call up my brother. — Oh, would
you had had her! —
Some one way, some another. — Do you know
Where we may apprehend her and the Moor?

RODERIGO I think I can discover° him, if you
please
To get good guard and go along with me.

BRABANTIO Pray you, lead on. At every house
I'll call;
I may command° at most. — Get weapons, ho!
And raise some special officers of night. —
On, good Roderigo. I'll deserve° your pains.

Exeunt.

Scene ii°

Enter **OTHELLO,** **IAGO,** **ATTENDANTS** *with torches.*

IAGO Though in the trade of war I have slain men,
Yet do I hold it very stuff° o'th' conscience
To do no contrived° murder. I lack iniquity
Sometimes to do me service. Nine or ten times
I had thought t'have yerked° him° here under
the ribs.

OTHELLO 'Tis better as it is.

IAGO Nay, but he prated,
And spoke such scurvy and provoking terms
Against your honor
That, with the little godliness I have,
I did full hard forbear him.° But, I pray you, sir,
Are you fast married? Be assured of this,
That the magnifico° is much beloved,
And hath in his effect° a voice potential°
As double as the Duke's. He will divorce you,
Or put upon you what restraint or grievance
The law, with all his might to enforce it on,
Will give him cable.°

OTHELLO Let him do his spite.
My services which I have done the seigniory°
Shall out-tongue his complaints. 'Tis yet to
know° —
Which, when I know that boasting is an honor,
I shall promulgate — I fetch my life and being
From men of royal siege,° and my demerits°
May speak unbonneted° to as proud a fortune
As this that I have reached. For know, Iago,
But that I love the gentle Desdemona,
I would not my unhousèd° free condition
Put into circumscription and confine°
For the sea's worth.° But, look, what lights
come yond?

Enter **CASSIO** [*and* **OFFICERS**]° *with torches.*

IAGO Those are the raisèd father and his friends.
You were best go in.

OTHELLO Not I. I must be found.
My parts, my title, and my perfect soul°
Shall manifest me rightly. Is it they?

IAGO By Janus,° I think no.

OTHELLO The servants of the Duke? And my
lieutenant?
The goodness of the night upon you, friends!
What is the news?

CASSIO The Duke does greet you,
General,
And he requires your haste-post-haste
appearance
Even on the instant.

---

179. abused: deceived. **184. discover:** reveal, uncover. **187. command:** demand assistance. **189. deserve:** show gratitude for. **Act I, Scene ii. Location:** Venice. Another street, before Othello's lodgings. **2. very stuff:** essence, basic material. (Continuing the metaphor of *trade* from line 1.) **3. contrived:** premeditated. **5. yerked:** stabbed. **him:** i.e., Roderigo. **10. I . . . him:** I restrained myself with great difficulty from assaulting him. **12. magnifico:** Venetian grandee, i.e., Brabantio. **13. in his effect:** at his command. **potential:** powerful.

17. cable: i.e., scope. **18. seigniory:** Venetian government. **19. yet to know:** not yet widely known. **22. siege:** i.e., rank. (Literally, a seat used by a person of distinction.) **demerits:** deserts. **23. unbonneted:** without removing the hat, i.e., on equal terms (? Or "with hat off," "in all due modesty.") **26. unhousèd:** unconfined, undomesticated. **27. circumscription and confine:** restriction and confinement. **28. the sea's worth:** all the riches at the bottom of the sea. **28. s.d. *officers:*** (The Quarto text specifies, "*Enter* Cassio *with lights, Officers, and torches.*") **31. My . . . soul:** my natural gifts, my position or reputation, and my unflawed conscience. **33. Janus:** Roman two-faced god of beginnings.

OTHELLO What is the matter, think you?
CASSIO Something from Cyprus, as I may divine.°
It is a business of some heat.° The galleys
Have sent a dozen sequent° messengers
This very night at one another's heels,
And many of the consuls,° raised and met,
Are at the Duke's already. You have been hotly called for;
When, being not at your lodging to be found,
The Senate hath sent about° three several° quests
To search you out.
OTHELLO 'Tis well I am found by you.
I will but spend a word here in the house
And go with you. [*Exit.*]
CASSIO Ancient, what makes° he here?
IAGO Faith, he tonight hath boarded° a land carrack.°
If it prove lawful prize,° he's made forever.
CASSIO I do not understand.
IAGO He's married.
CASSIO To who?

[*Enter* **OTHELLO.**]

IAGO Marry,° to — Come, Captain, will you go?
OTHELLO Have with you.°
CASSIO Here comes another troop to seek for you.

Enter **BRABANTIO,** **RODERIGO,** *with* **OFFICERS** *and torches.*°

IAGO It is Brabantio. General, be advised.°
He comes to bad intent.
OTHELLO Holla! stand there!
RODERIGO Signor, it is the Moor.
BRABANTIO Down with him, thief!

[*They draw on both sides.*]

IAGO You, Roderigo! Come, sir, I am for you.
OTHELLO Keep up° your bright swords, for the dew will rust them.
Good signor, you shall more command with years
Than with your weapons.
BRABANTIO O thou foul thief, where hast thou stowed my daughter?
Damned as thou art, thou hast enchanted her!
For I'll refer me to all things of sense,°
If she in chains of magic were not bound
Whether a maid so tender, fair, and happy,
So opposite to marriage that she shunned
The wealthy curlèd darlings of our nation,
Would ever have, t'incur a general mock,
Run from her guardage° to the sooty bosom
Of such a thing as thou — to fear, not to delight.
Judge me the world, if'tis not gross in sense°
That thou hast practiced on her with foul charms,
Abused her delicate youth with drugs or minerals°
That weakens motion.° I'll have't disputed on;°
'Tis probable, and palpable to thinking.
I therefore apprehend and do attach° thee
For an abuser° of the world, a practicer
Of arts inhibited° and out of warrant.° —
Lay hold upon him! If he do resist,
Subdue him at his peril.

---

39. divine: guess. **40. heat:** urgency. **41. sequent:** successive. **43. consuls:** senators. **46. about:** all over the city. **several:** separate. **49. makes:** does. **50. boarded:** gone aboard and seized as an act of piracy. (With sexual suggestion.) **carrack:** large merchant ship. **51. prize:** booty. **53. Marry:** (An oath, originally "by the Virgin Mary"; here used with wordplay on *married.*) **54. Have with you:** i.e., let's go. **55. s.d.** ***officers and torches:*** (The Quarto text calls for *"others with lights and weapons."*) **56. be advised:** be on your guard.

60. Keep up: keep in the sheath. **65. I'll . . . sense:** I'll submit my case to one and all. **71. guardage:** guardianship. **73. gross in sense:** obvious. **75. minerals:** i.e., poisons. **76. weakens motion:** impair the vital faculties. **disputed on:** argued in court by professional counsel, debated by experts. **78. attach:** arrest. **79. abuser:** deceiver. **80. arts inhibited:** prohibited arts, black magic. **out of warrant:** illegal.

OTHELLO Hold your hands,
Both you of my inclining° and the rest.
Were it my cue to fight, I should have known it
Without a prompter. — Whither will you that
I go
To answer this your charge?

BRABANTIO To prison, till fit time
Of law and course of direct session°
Call thee to answer.

OTHELLO What if I do obey?
How may the Duke be therewith satisfied,
Whose messengers are here about my side
Upon some present business of the state
To bring me to him?

OFFICER 'Tis true, most worthy
signor.
The Duke's in council, and your noble self,
I am sure, is sent for.

BRABANTIO How? The Duke in
council?
In this time of the night? Bring him away.°
Mine's not an idle° cause. The Duke himself,
Or any of my brothers of the state,
Cannot but feel this wrong as 'twere their own;
For if such actions may have passage free,°
Bondslaves and pagans shall our statesmen
be. *Exeunt.*

Scene iii°

Enter **DUKE** [*and*] **SENATORS** [*and sit at a table, with lights*], *and* **OFFICERS**.° [*The* **DUKE** *and* **SENATORS** *are reading dispatches.*]

DUKE There is no composition° in these news
That gives them credit.

FIRST SENATOR Indeed, they are
disproportioned.°
My letters say a hundred and seven galleys.

DUKE And mine, a hundred and forty.

SECOND SENATOR And mine,
two hundred.
But though they jump° not on a just° account —
As in these cases, where the aim° reports,
'Tis oft with difference — yet do they all confirm
A Turkish fleet, and bearing up to Cyprus.

DUKE Nay, it is possible enough to judgment.
I do not so secure me in the error,
But the main article I do approve°
In fearful sense.

SAILOR (*within*): What ho, what ho, what ho!

Enter **SAILOR.**

OFFICER A messenger from the galleys.

DUKE Now, what's the business?

SAILOR The Turkish preparation° makes for
Rhodes.
So was I bid report here to the state
By Signor Angelo.

DUKE How say you by° this change?

FIRST SENATOR This cannot
be
By no assay° of reason. 'Tis a pageant°
To keep us in false gaze.° When we consider
Th'importancy of Cyprus to the Turk,
And let ourselves again but understand
That, as it more concerns the Turk than
Rhodes,
So may he with more facile question bear it,°
For that° it stands not in such warlike brace,°
But altogether lacks th'abilities°
That Rhodes is dressed in° — if we make
thought of this,
We must not think the Turk is so unskillful°
To leave that latest° which concerns him first,

---

83. inclining: following, party **88. course of direct session:** regular or specially convened legal proceedings. **96. away:** right along. **97. idle:** trifling. **100. may . . . free:** are allowed to go unchecked. **Act I. Scene iii. Location:** Venice. A council chamber. **s.d. *Enter . . . Officers:*** (The Quarto text calls for the Duke and senators to *"set at a Table with lights and Attendants."*) **1. composition:** consistency. **3. disproportioned:** inconsistent.

6. jump: agree. **just:** exact. **7. the aim:** conjecture. **11–12. I do not . . . approve:** I do not take such (false) comfort in the discrepancies that I fail to perceive the main point, i.e., that the Turkish fleet is threatening. **16. preparation:** fleet prepared for battle. **19. by:** about. **20. assay:** test. **pageant:** mere show. **21. in false gaze:** looking the wrong way. **25. So may . . . it:** so also he (the Turk) can more easily capture it (Cyprus). **26. For that:** since. **brace:** state of defense. **27. th'abilities:** the means of self-defense. **28. dressed in:** equipped with. **29. unskillful:** deficient in judgment. **30. latest:** last.

Neglecting an attempt of ease and gain
To wake and wage° a danger profitless.

DUKE Nay, in all confidence, he's not for Rhodes.

OFFICER Here is more news.

Enter a **MESSENGER.**

MESSENGER The Ottomites, reverend and gracious,
Steering with due course toward the isle of Rhodes,
Have there injointed them° with an after° fleet.

FIRST SENATOR Ay, so I thought. How many, as you guess?

MESSENGER Of thirty sail; and now they do restem
Their backward course,° bearing with frank appearance°
Their purposes toward Cyprus. Signor Montano,
Your trusty and most valiant servitor,°
With his free duty° recommends° you thus,
And prays you to believe him.

DUKE 'Tis certain then for Cyprus.
Marcus Luccicos, is not he in town?

FIRST SENATOR He's now in Florence.

DUKE Write from us to him, post-post-haste. Dispatch.

FIRST SENATOR Here comes Brabantio and the valiant Moor.

Enter **BRABANTIO, OTHELLO, CASSIO, IAGO, RODERIGO,** *and* **OFFICERS.**

DUKE Valiant Othello, we must straight° employ you
Against the general enemy° Ottoman.
[*To* **BRABANTIO**] I did not see you; welcome, gentle° signor.
We lacked your counsel and your help tonight.

BRABANTIO So did I yours. Good Your Grace, pardon me;
Neither my place° nor aught I heard of business
Hath raised me from my bed, nor doth the general care
Take hold of me, for my particular° grief
Is of so floodgate° and o'erbearing nature
That it engluts° and swallows other sorrows
And it is still itself.°

DUKE Why, what's the matter?

BRABANTIO My daughter! Oh, my daughter.

DUKE AND SENATORS Dead?

BRABANTIO Ay, to me.
She is abused,° stol'n from me, and corrupted
By spells and medicines bought of mountebanks;
For nature so preposterously to err,
Being not deficient,° blind, or lame of sense,°
Sans° witchcraft could not.

DUKE Whoe'er he be that in this foul proceeding
Hath thus beguiled your daughter of herself
And you of her, the bloody book of law
You shall yourself read in the bitter letter
After your own sense°—yea, though our proper° son
Stood in your action.°

BRABANTIO Humbly I thank Your Grace.
Here is the man, this Moor, whom now it seems

---

32. wake and wage: stir up and risk. **37. injointed them:** joined themselves. **after:** second, following. **39–40. restem . . . course:** retrace their original course. **40. frank appearance:** undisguised intent. **42. servitor:** officer under your command. **43. free duty:** freely given and loyal service. **recommends:** commends himself and reports to. **50. straight:** straightaway. **51. general enemy:** universal enemy to all Christendom.

52. gentle: noble. **55. place:** official position. **57. particular:** personal. **58. floodgate:** i.e., overwhelming (as when floodgates are opened). **59. engluts:** engulfs. **60. is still itself:** remains undiminished. **62. abused:** deceived. **65. deficient:** defective. **lame of sense:** deficient in sensory perception. **66. Sans:** without. **71. After . . . sense:** according to your own interpretation. **our proper:** my own. **72. Stood . . . action:** were under your accusation.

Your special mandate for the state affairs
Hath hither brought.

ALL We are very sorry for't.

DUKE [*to* **OTHELLO**]: What, in your own part, can you say to this?

BRABANTIO Nothing, but this is so.

OTHELLO Most potent, grave, and reverend signors,
My very noble and approved° good masters:
That I have ta'en away this old man's daughter,
It is most true; true, I have married her.
The very head and front° of my offending
Hath this extent, no more. Rude° am I in my speech,
And little blessed with the soft phrase of peace;
For since these arms of mine had seven years' pith,°
Till now some nine moons wasted,° they have used
Their dearest° action in the tented field;
And little of this great world can I speak
More than pertains to feats of broils° and battle,
And therefore little shall I grace my cause
In speaking for myself. Yet, by your gracious patience,
I will a round° unvarnished tale deliver
Of my whole course of love — what drugs, what charms,
What conjuration, and what mighty magic,
For such proceeding I am charged withal,°
I won his daughter.

BRABANTIO A maiden never bold;
Of spirit so still and quiet that her motion
Blushed at herself;° and she, in spite of nature,
Of years,° of country, credit,° everything,
To fall in love with what she feared to look on!
It is a judgment maimed and most imperfect
That will confess° perfection so could err
Against all rules of nature, and must be driven
To find out practices° of cunning hell
Why this should be. I therefore vouch° again
That with some mixtures powerful o'er the blood,°
Or with some dram conjured to this effect,°
He wrought upon her.

DUKE To vouch this is no proof,
Without more wider° and more overt test°
Than these thin habits° and poor likelihoods°
Of modern seeming° do prefer° against him.

FIRST SENATOR But Othello, speak.
Did you by indirect and forcèd courses°
Subdue and poison this young maid's affections?
Or came it by request and such fair question°
As soul to soul affordeth?

OTHELLO I do beseech you,
Send for the lady to the Sagittary
And let her speak of me before her father.
If you do find me foul in her report,
The trust, the office I do hold of you
Not only take away, but let your sentence
Even fall upon my life.

DUKE Fetch Desdemona hither.

OTHELLO [*to* **IAGO**]: Ancient, conduct them.
You best know the place.

[*Exeunt* **IAGO** *and* **ATTENDANTS**.]

---

79. approved: proved, esteemed. **82. head and front:** height and breadth, entire extent. **83. Rude:** unpolished. **85. since . . . pith:** i.e., since I was seven. (*Pith* means "strength, vigor.") **86. Till . . . wasted:** until some nine months ago (since when Othello has evidently not been on active duty, but in Venice). **87. dearest:** most valuable. **89. broils:** skirmishes. [Hall] **92. round:** plain. **95. withal:** with.

97–98. her . . . herself: i.e., she blushed easily at herself. (*Motion* can suggest the impulse of the soul or of the emotions, or physical movement.) **99. years:** i.e., difference in age. **credit:** virtuous reputation. **102. confess:** concede (that). **104. practices:** plots. **105. vouch:** assert. **106. blood:** passions. **107. dram . . . effect:** dose made by magical spells to have this effect. **109. more wider:** fuller. **test:** testimony. **110. habits:** garments, i.e., appearances. **poor likelihoods:** weak inferences. **111. modern seeming:** commonplace assumption. **prefer:** bring forth. **113. forcèd courses:** means used against her will. **115. question:** conversation.

And, till she come, as truly as to heaven
I do confess the vices of my blood,°
So justly° to your grave ears I'll present
How I did thrive in this fair lady's love,
And she in mine.

DUKE Say it, Othello.

OTHELLO Her father loved me; oft invited me,
Still° question'd me the story of my life
From year to year — the battles, sieges, fortunes
That I have passed.
I ran it through, even from my boyish days
To th' very moment that he bade me tell it,
Wherein I spoke of most disastrous chances,
Of moving accidents° by flood and field,
Of hairbreadth scapes i'th'imminent deadly breach,°
Of being taken by the insolent foe
And sold to slavery, of my redemption thence,
And portance° in my travels' history,
Wherein of antres° vast and deserts idle,°
Rough quarries,° rocks, and hills whose heads touch heaven,
It was my hint° to speak — such was the process —
And of the Cannibals that each other eat,
The Anthropophagi,° and men whose heads
Do grow beneath their shoulders. These things to hear
Would Desdemona seriously incline;
But still the house affairs would draw her thence,
Which ever as she could with haste dispatch
She'd come again, and with a greedy ear
Devour up my discourse. Which I, observing,
Took once a pliant° hour, and found good means
To draw from her a prayer of earnest heart
That I would all my pilgrimage dilate,°
Whereof by parcels° she had something heard,
But not intentively.° I did consent,
And often did beguile her of her tears,
When I did speak of some distressful stroke
That my youth suffered. My story being done,
She gave me for my pains a world of sighs.
She swore, in faith, 'twas strange, 'twas passing° strange,
'Twas pitiful, 'twas wondrous pitiful.
She wished she had not heard it, yet she wished
That heaven had made her° such a man. She thanked me,
And bade me, if I had a friend that loved her,
I should but teach him how to tell my story,
And that would woo her. Upon this hint° I spake.
She loved me for the dangers I had passed,
And I loved her that she did pity them.
This only is the witchcraft I have used.
Here comes the lady. Let her witness it.

Enter **DESDEMONA,** **IAGO,** [*and*] **ATTENDANTS.**

DUKE I think this tale would win my daughter too.
Good Brabantio,
Take up this mangled matter at the best.°
Men do their broken weapons rather use
Than their bare hands.

BRABANTIO I pray you, hear her speak.
If she confess that she was half the wooer,

125. blood: passions, human nature. **126. justly:** truthfully, accurately. **131. Still:** continually. **137. moving accidents:** stirring happenings. **138. i'th'imminent . . . breach:** in death-threatening gaps made in a fortification. **141. portance:** conduct. **142. antres:** caverns. **idle:** barren, desolate. **143. Rough quarries:** rugged rock formations. **144. hint:** occasion, opportunity. **146. Anthropophagi:** man-eaters. (A term from Pliny's *Natural History.*)

153. pliant: well-suiting. **155. dilate:** relate in detail. **156. by parcels:** piecemeal. **157. intentively:** with full attention, continuously. **162. passing:** exceedingly. **165. made her:** (1) created her to be (2) made for her. **168. hint:** opportunity. (Othello does not mean that she was dropping hints.) **175. Take . . . best:** make the best of a bad bargain.

Destruction on my head if my bad blame
Light on the man! — Come hither, gentle mistress.
Do you perceive in all this noble company
Where most you owe obedience?

DESDEMONA My noble father,
I do perceive here a divided duty.
To you I am bound for life and education;°
My life and education both do learn° me
How to respect you. You are the lord of duty;°
I am hitherto your daughter. But here's my husband,
And so much duty as my mother showed
To you, preferring you before her father,
So much I challenge° that I may profess
Due to the Moor my lord.

BRABANTIO God be with you! I have done.
Please it Your Grace, on to the state affairs.
I had rather to adopt a child than get° it.
Come hither, Moor. [*He joins the hands of Othello and Desdemona.*]
I here do give thee that with all my heart°
Which, but thou hast already, with all my heart°
I would keep from thee. — For your sake,° jewel,
I am glad at soul I have no other child,
For thy escape° would teach me tyranny,
To hang clogs° on them. — I have done, my lord.

DUKE Let me speak like yourself,° and lay a sentence°
Which, as a grece° or step, may help these lovers
Into your favor.

© DeA Picture Library / Art Resource, NY

This painting, completed in 1852 by French artist Eugène Delacroix, depicts Desdemona and her father in act I, scene iii. **How is each character portrayed here? What elements of the scene have been incorporated into the painting, and where do the two depictions diverge?**

When remedies are past, the griefs are ended
By seeing the worst, which late on hopes depended.°
To mourn a mischief° that is past and gone
Is the next° way to draw new mischief on.
What cannot be preserved when fortune takes,
Patience her injury a mock'ry makes.°
The robbed that smiles steals something from the thief;
He robs himself that spends a bootless grief.°

184. education: upbringing. **185. learn:** teach. **186. of duty:** to whom duty is due. **190. challenge:** claim. **194. get:** beget. **196. with all my heart:** wherein my whole affection has been engaged. **197. with all my heart:** willingly, gladly. **198. For your sake:** because of you. **200. escape:** elopement. **201. clogs:** (Literally, blocks of wood fastened to the legs of criminals or animals to inhibit escape.) **202. like yourself:** i.e., as you would, in your proper temper. **lay a sentence:** apply a maxim. **203. grece:** step.

205–206. When . . . depended: when all hope of remedy is past, our sorrows are ended by realizing that the worst has already happened which lately we hoped would not happen. **207. mischief:** misfortune, injury. **208. next:** nearest. **209–210. What . . . makes:** when fortune takes away what cannot be saved, patience makes a mockery of fortune's wrongdoing. **212. spends a bootless grief:** indulges in unavailing grief.

BRABANTIO So let the Turk of Cyprus us beguile,
We lose it not, so long as we can smile.
He bears the sentence well that nothing bears
But the free comfort which from thence he hears,
But he bears both the sentence and the sorrow
That, to pay grief, must of poor patience borrow.°
These sentences, to sugar or to gall,
Being strong on both sides, are equivocal.°
But words are words. I never yet did hear
That the bruised heart was piercèd through the ear.°
I humbly beseech you, proceed to th'affairs of state.

DUKE The Turk with a most mighty preparation makes for Cyprus. Othello, the fortitude° of the place is best known to you; and though we have there a substitute° of most allowed° sufficiency, yet opinion, a sovereign mistress of effects, throws a more safer voice on you.° You must therefore be content to slubber° the gloss of your new fortunes with this more stubborn and boisterous expedition.°

OTHELLO The tyrant custom, most grave senators,
Hath made the flinty and steel couch of war
My thrice-driven° bed of down. I do agnize°
A natural and prompt alacrity
I find in hardness,° and do undertake
These present wars against the Ottomites.
Most humbly therefore bending to your state,°
I crave fit disposition for my wife,
Due reference of place and exhibition,
With such accommodation and besort
As levels with her breeding.°

DUKE Why at her father's.

BRABANTIO I will not have it so.

OTHELLO Nor I.

DESDEMONA Nor I. I would not there reside,
To put my father in impatient thoughts
By being in his eye. Most gracious Duke,
To my unfolding° lend your prosperous° ear;
And let me find a charter° in your voice,
T'assist my simpleness.

DUKE What would you, Desdemona?

DESDEMONA That I did love the Moor to live with him,
My downright violence and storm of fortunes°
May trumpet to the world. My heart's subdued
Even to the very quality° of my lord.
I saw Othello's visage in his mind,
And to his honors and his valiant parts°
Did I my soul and fortunes consecrate.
So that, dear lords, if I be left behind
A moth° of peace, and he go to the war,
The rites° for which I love him are bereft me,
And I a heavy° interim shall support
By his dear° absence. Let me go with him.

OTHELLO Let her have your voice.°
Vouch with me, heaven, I therefor beg it not

215–218. He bears . . . borrow: a person can easily be comforted by your maxim that enjoys its platitudinous comfort without having to experience the misfortune that occasions sorrow, but anyone whose grief bankrupts his poor patience is left with your saying and his sorrow, too. (*Bears the sentence* also plays on the meaning, "receives judicial sentence.") **219–220. These . . . equivocal:** these fine maxims are equivocal, being equally appropriate to happiness or bitterness. **222. piercèd . . . ear:** relieved by mere words reaching it through the ear. **225. fortitude:** strength. **227. substitute:** deputy. **228. allowed:** acknowledged. **228–230. opinion . . . on you:** general opinion, an important determiner of affairs, chooses you as the best man. **231. slubber:** soil, sully. **232–233. stubborn . . . expedition:** rough and violent expedition, for which haste is needed. **236. thrice-driven:** thrice sifted, winnowed. **agnize:** know in myself, acknowledge.

238. hardness: hardship. **240. bending . . . state:** bowing or kneeling to your authority. **242–244. Due . . . breeding:** proper respect for her place (as my wife) and maintenance, with such suitable provision and attendance as befits her upbringing. **250. my unfolding:** what I shall unfold or say. **prosperous:** favorable. **251. charter:** privilege, authorization. **255. My . . . fortunes:** my plain and total breach of social custom. **257. quality:** moral and spiritual identity. **259. parts:** qualities. **262. moth:** i.e., one who consumes merely. **263. rites:** rites of love. (With a suggestion, too, of "rights," sharing.) **264. heavy:** burdensome. **265. dear:** grievous. **266. voice:** consent.

To please the palate of my appetite,
Nor to comply with heat° — the young affects°
In me defunct° — and proper° satisfaction,
But to be free° and bounteous to her mind.
And heaven defend° your good souls that you think°
I will your serious and great business scant
When she is with me. No, when light-winged toys
Of feathered Cupid seel° with wanton dullness
My speculative and officed instruments,°
That my disports corrupt and taint my business,°
Let huswives° make a skillet of my helm,
And all indign° and base adversities
Make head° against my estimation!°

DUKE Be it as you shall privately determine,
Either for her stay or going. Th'affair cries haste,
And speed must answer it.

A SENATOR You must away tonight.

DESDEMONA Tonight, my lord?

DUKE This night.

OTHELLO With all my heart.

DUKE At nine i'th' morning here we'll meet again.
Othello, leave some officer behind,
And he shall our commission bring to you,
With such things else of quality and respect°
As doth import° you.

OTHELLO So please Your Grace, my ancient;
A man he is of honesty and trust.
To his conveyance I assign my wife,
With what else needful Your Good Grace shall think
To be sent after me.

DUKE Let it be so.
Good night to everyone. [*To* **BRABANTIO**] And, noble signor,
If virtue no delighted° beauty lack,
Your son-in-law is far more fair than black.

FIRST SENATOR Adieu, brave Moor. Use Desdemona well.

BRABANTIO Look to her, Moor, if thou hast eyes to see.
She has deceived her father, and may thee.

Exeunt [Duke, Brabantio, Cassio, Senators, *and officers].*

OTHELLO My life upon her faith! — Honest Iago,
My Desdemona must I leave to thee.
I prithee, let thy wife attend on her,
And bring them after in the best advantage.°
Come, Desdemona. I have but an hour
Of love, of worldly matters and direction,°
To spend with thee. We must obey the time.°

Exit [with **DESDEMONA**].

RODERIGO Iago —

IAGO What sayst thou, noble heart?

RODERIGO What will I do, think'st thou?

IAGO Why, go to bed, and sleep.

RODERIGO I will incontinently° drown myself.

IAGO If thou dost, I shall never love thee after. Why, thou silly gentleman?

RODERIGO It is silliness to live when to live is torment; and then have we a prescription° to die when death is our physician.

IAGO Oh, villainous!° I have looked upon the world for four times seven years, and, since I could distinguish betwixt a benefit

---

269. heat: sexual passion. **young affects:** passions of youth, adolescent desires. **270. defunct:** done with, at an end. **proper:** personal. **271. free:** generous. **272. defend:** forbid. **think:** should think. **275. seel:** i.e., make blind (as in falconry, by sewing up the eyes of the hawk during training). **276. My . . . instruments:** my eyes, whose function is to see. **277. That . . . business:** in such a way that my sexual pastimes interfere with my official duties. **278. huswives:** housewives; also hussies. [Hall] **279. indign:** unworthy, shameful. **280. Make head:** raise an army. **estimation:** reputation. **288. of quality and respect:** of importance and relevance. **289. import:** concern.

295. delighted: capable of delighting. **303. in . . . advantage:** at the most favorable opportunity. **305. direction:** instructions. **306. the time:** the urgency of the present crisis. **311. incontinently:** immediately, without self-restraint. **315. prescription:** (1) right based on long-established custom (2) doctor's prescription. **317. villainous:** i.e., what perfect nonsense.

and an injury, I never found man that knew how to love himself. Ere I would say I would drown myself for the love of a guinea hen,° I would change° my humanity with a baboon.

RODERIGO What should I do? I confess it is my shame to be so fond,° but it is not in my virtue° to amend it.

IAGO Virtue? A fig!° 'Tis in ourselves that we are thus or thus. Our bodies are our gardens, to the which our wills are gardeners; so that if we will plant nettles or sow lettuce, set hyssop° and weed up thyme, supply it with one gender° of herbs or distract it with° many, either to have it sterile with idleness° or manured with industry — why, the power and corrigible authority° of this lies in our wills. If the beam° of our lives had not one scale of reason to poise° another of sensuality, the blood° and baseness of our natures would conduct us to most preposterous conclusions. But we have reason to cool our raging motions,° our carnal stings, our unbitted° lusts, whereof I take this that you call love to be a sect or scion.°

RODERIGO It cannot be.

IAGO It is merely a lust of the blood and a permission of the will. Come, be a man. Drown thyself? Drown cats and blind° puppies. I have professed me thy friend, and I confess me knit to thy deserving with cables of perdurable° toughness. I could never better stead° thee than now. Put money in thy purse. Follow thou the wars; defeat thy favor° with an usurped° beard. I say, put money in thy purse. It cannot be long that Desdemona should continue her love to the Moor — put money in thy purse — nor he his to her. It was a violent commencement in her, and thou shalt see an answerable sequestration° — put but money in thy purse. These Moors are changeable in their wills° — fill thy purse with money. The food that to him now is as luscious as locusts° shall be to him shortly as bitter as coloquintida.° She must change for youth; when she is sated with his body, she will find the error of her choice. She must have change, she must. Therefore put money in thy purse. If thou wilt needs damn thyself, do it a more delicate way than drowning. Make° all the money thou canst. If sanctimony° and a frail vow betwixt an erring° barbarian and a supersubtle Venetian be not too hard for my wits and all the tribe of hell, thou shalt enjoy her. Therefore make money. A pox of° drowning thyself! It is clean out of the way.° Seek thou rather to be hanged in compassing° thy joy than to be drowned and go without her.

RODERIGO Wilt thou be fast° to my hopes if I depend on the issue?°

IAGO Thou art sure of me. Go, make money. I have told thee often, and I retell thee again and again, I hate the Moor. My cause is hearted;° thine hath no less reason. Let us be conjunctive° in our revenge against

---

323. guinea hen: (A slang term for a prostitute.) **change:** exchange. **326. fond:** infatuated. **327. virtue:** strength, nature. **328. fig:** (To give a fig is to thrust the thumb between the first and second fingers in a vulgar and insulting gesture.) **332. hyssop:** an herb of the mint family. **333. gender:** kind. **333–334. distract it with:** divide it among. **335. idleness:** want of cultivation. **336. corrigible authority:** power to correct. **337. beam:** balance. **338. poise:** counterbalance. **339. blood:** natural passions. **342. motions:** appetites. **343. unbitted:** unbridled, uncontrolled. **345. sect or scion:** cutting or offshoot. **349. blind:** i.e., newborn and helpless. **352. perdurable:** very durable. **353. stead:** assist.

355. defeat thy favor: disguise your face. **usurped:** (The suggestion is that Roderigo is not man enough to have a beard of his own.) **361–362. an answerable sequestration:** a corresponding cutting off or estrangement. **364. wills:** carnal appetites. **366. locusts:** fruit of the carob tree (see Matthew 3:4), or perhaps honeysuckle. **367. coloquintida:** colocynth or bitter apple, a purgative. **373. Make:** raise, collect. **373–374. sanctimony:** (1) an aura of goodness (2) love-worship. **374. erring:** wandering, vagabond, unsteady. **378. A pox of:** a plague or curse on. [Hall] **379. clean . . . way:** entirely unsuitable as a course of action. **380. compassing:** encompassing, embracing. **382. fast:** true. **383. issue:** (successful) outcome. **387. hearted:** fixed in the heart, heartfelt. **388. conjunctive:** united.

him. If thou canst cuckold him, thou dost thyself a pleasure, me a sport. There are many events in the womb of time which will be delivered. Traverse,° go, provide thy money. We will have more of this tomorrow. Adieu.

RODERIGO Where shall we meet i'th' morning?

IAGO At my lodging.

RODERIGO I'll be with thee betimes.° [*He starts to leave.*]

IAGO Go to,° farewell. — Do you hear, Roderigo?

RODERIGO What say you?

IAGO No more of drowning, do you hear?

RODERIGO I am changed.

IAGO Go to, farewell. Put money enough in your purse.

RODERIGO I'll sell all my land. *Exit.*

IAGO Thus do I ever make my fool my purse;
For I mine own gained knowledge should profane
If I would time expend with such a snipe°
But for my sport and profit. I hate the Moor;
And it is thought abroad° that 'twixt my sheets
He's done my office.° I know not if 't be true;
But I, for mere suspicion in that kind,
Will do as if for surety.° He holds me well;°
The better shall my purpose work on him.
Cassio's a proper° man. Let me see now:
To get his place and to plume up° my will
In double knavery — How, how? — Let's see:
After some time, to abuse° Othello's ear
That he° is too familiar with his° wife.
He hath a person and a smooth dispose°
To be suspected, framed° to make women false.
The Moor is of a free and open° nature,
That thinks men honest that but seem to be so,
And will as tenderly° be led by the nose
As asses are.
I have't. It is engender'd. Hell and night
Must bring this monstrous birth to the world's light. [*Exit.*]

---

392. **Traverse:** (A military marching term.) 397. **betimes:** early. 398. **Go to:** (An expression of impatience or jollying along others.) 406. **snipe:** woodcock, i.e., fool. 408. **it is thought abroad:** it is rumored. 409. **my office:** i.e., my sexual function as husband. 411. **do . . . surety:** act as if on certain knowledge. **holds me well:** regards me favorably. 413. **proper:** handsome. 414. **plume up:** put a feather in the cap of, i.e., glorify, gratify. 416. **abuse:** deceive. 417. **he:** Cassio. **his:** Othello's. 418. **dispose:** disposition. 419. **framed:** formed, made.

ACT II

Scene i°

Enter **MONTANO** *and two* **GENTLEMEN.**

MONTANO What from the cape can you discern at sea?

FIRST GENTLEMAN Nothing at all. It is a high-wrought flood.°
I cannot, twixt the heaven and the main,°
Descry a sail.

MONTANO Methinks the wind hath spoke aloud at land;
A fuller blast ne'er shook our battlements.
If it hath ruffianed° so upon the sea,
What ribs of oak, when mountains° melt on them,
Can hold the mortise?° What shall we hear of this?

SECOND GENTLEMAN A segregation° of the Turkish fleet.
For do but stand upon the foaming shore,
The chidden° billow seems to pelt the clouds;
The wind-shaked surge, with high and monstrous mane,°
Seems to cast water on the burning Bear°

---

420. **free and open:** frank and unsuspecting. 422. **tenderly:** readily. **Act II. Scene i. Location:** A seaport in Cyprus. An open place near the quay. 2. **high-wrought flood:** very agitated sea. 3. **main:** ocean. (Also at line 41.) 7. **ruffianed:** raged. 8. **mountains:** i.e., of water. 9. **hold the mortise:** hold their joints together. (A *mortise* is the socket hollowed out in fitting timbers.) 10. **segregation:** dispersion. 12. **chidden:** i.e., rebuked, repelled (by the shore), and thus shot into the air. 13. **monstrous mane:** (The surf is like the mane of a wild beast.) 14. **the burning Bear:** i.e., the constellation Ursa Minor or the Little Bear, which includes the polestar (and hence regarded as the *guards of th'ever-fixèd pole* in the next line; sometimes the term *guards* is applied to the two "pointers" of the Big Bear or Dipper, which may be intended here.)

And quench the guards of th'ever-fixèd pole.
I never did like molestation° view
On the enchafèd° flood.

MONTANO If that° the Turkish fleet
Be not ensheltered and embayed,° they are drowned;
It is impossible to bear it out.°

Enter a [Third] Gentleman.

THIRD GENTLEMAN News, lads! Our wars are done.
The desperate tempest hath so banged the Turks
That their designment halts.° A noble ship of Venice
Hath seen a grievous wreck° and sufferance°
On most part of their fleet.

MONTANO How? Is this true?

THIRD GENTLEMAN The ship is here put in,
A Veronesa;° Michael Cassio,
Lieutenant to the warlike Moor Othello,
Is come on shore: the Moor himself at sea,
And is in full commission here for Cyprus.

MONTANO I am glad on't. 'Tis a worthy governor.

THIRD GENTLEMAN But this same Cassio, though he speak of comfort
Touching the Turkish loss, yet he looks sadly°
And prays the Moor be safe, for they were parted
With foul and violent tempest.

MONTANO Pray heaven he be,
For I have served him, and the man commands
Like a full° soldier. Let's to the seaside, ho!
As well to see the vessel that's come in
As to throw out our eyes for brave Othello,

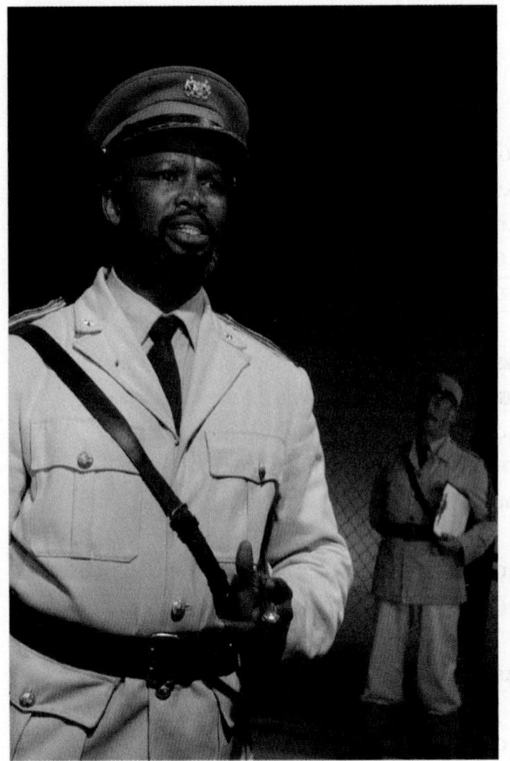

This photo is from a 2004 production of *Othello* set in the twilight of the European colonial era, shortly after the end of World War II. **How might setting the play in such an era highlight both the social and military positions Othello occupies? How might it change or broaden your understanding of his character?**

Even till we make the main and th'aerial blue°
An indistinct regard.°

THIRD GENTLEMAN Come, let's do so,
For every minute is expectancy°
Of more arrivance.°

Enter CASSIO.

CASSIO Thanks, you the valiant of this warlike isle,

---

16. like molestation: comparable disturbance. **17. enchafèd:** angry. **18. If that:** if. **19. embayed:** sheltered by a bay. **20. bear it out:** survive, weather the storm. **23. designment halts:** enterprise is crippled. (Literally, "is lame.") **24. wreck:** shipwreck. **sufferance:** damage, disaster. **28. Veronesa:** from Verona (and perhaps in service with Venice). **34. sadly:** gravely. **38. full:** perfect.

41. the main . . . blue: the sea and the sky. **42. An indistinct regard:** indistinguishable in our view. **43. is expectancy:** gives expectation. **44. arrivance:** arrival.

That so approve° the Moor! Oh, let the heavens
Give him defense against the elements,
For I have lost him on a dangerous sea.

MONTANO Is he well shipped?

CASSIO His bark is stoutly timbered, and his pilot
Of very expert and approved allowance;°
Therefore my hopes, not surfeited to death,
Stand in bold cure.° *[A cry] within:* "A sail, a sail, a sail!"

CASSIO What noise?

A GENTLEMAN The town is empty. On the brow o'th' sea°
Stand ranks of people, and they cry "A sail!"

CASSIO My hopes do shape him for the governor.° *[A shot within.]*

SECOND GENTLEMAN They do discharge their shot of courtesy;°
Our friends at least.

CASSIO I pray you, sir, go forth,
And give us truth who 'tis that is arrived.

SECOND GENTLEMAN I shall. *Exit.*

MONTANO But, good Lieutenant, is your general wived?

CASSIO Most fortunately. He hath achieved a maid
That paragons° description and wild fame,°
One that excels the quirks° of blazoning° pens,
And in th'essential vesture of creation
Does tire the engineer.°

Enter [Second] Gentleman.

How now? Who has put in?°

SECOND GENTLEMAN 'Tis one Iago, ancient to the General.

CASSIO He's had most favorable and happy speed.
Tempests themselves, high seas, and howling winds,
The guttered° rocks and congregated sands—
Traitors ensteeped° to clog the guiltless keel—
As° having sense of beauty, do omit°
Their mortal° natures, letting go safely by
The divine Desdemona.

MONTANO What is she?

CASSIO She that I spake of, our great captain's captain,
Left in the conduct of the bold Iago,
Whose footing here anticipates our thoughts
A sennight's speed.° Great Jove, Othello guard,
And swell his sail with thine own powerful breath,
That he may bless this bay with his tall° ship,
Make love's quick pants in Desdemona's arms,
Give renewed fire to our extincted spirits,
And bring all Cyprus comfort!

Enter **DESDEMONA**, **IAGO**, **RODERIGO**, *and* **EMILIA**.

Oh, behold,
The riches of the ship is come on shore.
You men of Cyprus, let her have your knees.
[*The gentlemen make curtsy to Desdemona.*]
Hail to thee, lady! And the grace of heaven
Before, behind thee, and on every hand
Enwheel thee round!

DESDEMONA I thank you, valiant Cassio.
What tidings can you tell me of my lord?

CASSIO He is not yet arrived; nor know I aught
But that he's well and will be shortly here.

---

46. approve: admire, honor. **51. approved allowance:** tested reputation. **52–53. not . . . cure:** not worn thin through repeated application or delayed fulfillment, strongly persist. **55. brow o'th' sea:** cliff-edge. **57. My . . . governor:** I hope and imagine this ship to be Othello's. **58. discharge . . . courtesy:** fire a salute in token of respect and courtesy. **64. paragons:** surpasses. **wild fame:** extravagant report. **65. quirks:** witty conceits. **blazoning:** setting forth as though in heraldic language. **66–67. And in . . . engineer:** and in her real, God-given, beauty, (she) defeats any attempt to praise her. (An *engineer* is one who devises, here a poet.) **67. put in:** i.e., to harbor.

71. guttered: jagged, trenched. **72. ensteeped:** lying under water. **73. As:** as if. **omit:** forbear to exercise. **74. mortal:** deadly. **78–79. Whose . . . speed:** whose arrival here has happened a week sooner than we expected. **81. tall:** tall-masted.

DESDEMONA Oh, but I fear — How lost you company?
CASSIO The great contention of the sea and skies
Parted our fellowship.
(*Within*) "A sail, a sail!" [*A shot.*]
But hark. A sail!
SECOND GENTLEMAN They give their greeting to the citadel.
This likewise is a friend.
CASSIO See for the news!
[*Exit Second Gentleman.*]
Good Ancient, you are welcome. [*Kissing Emilia.*] Welcome, mistress.
Let it not gall your patience, good Iago,
That I extend° my manners; 'tis my breeding°
That gives me this bold show of courtesy.
IAGO Sir, would she give you so much of her lips
As of her tongue she oft bestows on me,
You would have enough.
DESDEMONA Alas, she has no speech!°
IAGO In faith, too much.
I find it still,° when I have list° to sleep.
Marry, before Your Ladyship, I grant,
She puts her tongue a little in her heart
And chides with thinking.°
EMILIA You have little cause to say so.
IAGO Come on, come on. You are pictures out of doors,°
Bells° in your parlors, wildcats in your kitchens,°
Saints in your injuries,° devils being offended,
Players in your huswifery, and huswives in your beds.°
DESDEMONA Oh, fie upon thee, slanderer!
IAGO Nay, it is true, or else I am a Turk.°
You rise to play, and go to bed to work.
EMILIA You shall not write my praise.
IAGO No, let me not.
DESDEMONA What wouldst thou write of me, if thou shouldst praise me?
IAGO Oh, gentle lady, do not put me to't,
For I am nothing if not critical.°
DESDEMONA Come on, essay.° — There's one gone to the harbor?
IAGO Ay, madam.
DESDEMONA I am not merry, but I do beguile
The thing I am° by seeming otherwise.
Come, how wouldst thou praise me?
IAGO I am about it, but indeed my invention
Comes from my pate as birdlime does from frieze° —
It plucks out brains and all. But my Muse labors°
And thus she is delivered:
If she be fair and wise, fairness and wit,
The one's for use, the other useth it.°
DESDEMONA Well praised! How if she be black° and witty?
IAGO If she be black, and thereto have a wit,
She'll find a white that shall her blackness fit.°
DESDEMONA Worse and worse.
EMILIA How if fair and foolish?
IAGO She never yet was foolish that was fair,
For even her folly° help'd to an heir.°

---

100. extend: give scope to. **breeding:** training in the niceties of etiquette. **105. she has no speech:** i.e., she's not a chatterbox, as you allege. **107. still:** always. **list:** desire. **110. with thinking:** i.e., in her thoughts only. **111. pictures out of doors:** i.e., as pretty as pictures, and silently well-behaved in public. **112. Bells:** i.e., jangling, noisy, and brazen. **in your kitchens:** i.e., in domestic affairs. (Ill tempered or spiteful at home. [Hall]) **113. Saints . . . injuries:** i.e., putting on airs of sanctity and innocence when wronged by others. **114. Players . . . beds:** play-actors at domesticity and truly energetic only as lovers in bed.

116. a Turk: an infidel, not to be believed. **121. critical:** censorious. **122. essay:** try. **125. The thing I am:** i.e., my anxious self. **128. Comes . . . frieze:** comes out of my head with as much difficulty as birdlime (a sticky substance used to catch birds) comes out of frieze (a type of coarse woolen cloth). **129. labors:** (1) exerts herself (2) prepares to deliver a child. (With a following pun on *delivered* in line 130.) **132. The one's . . . it:** i.e., her cleverness will make use of her beauty. **133. black:** dark-complexioned, brunette. **135. She'll . . . fit:** she will find a fair-complexioned mate suited to her dark complexion. (Punning on *wight,* person, and contrasting *white* and *black,* with suggestion of sexual coupling.) **138. folly:** (With added meaning of "lechery, wantonness.") **to an heir:** i.e., to bear a child.

DESDEMONA These are old fond° paradoxes to make fools laugh i'th'alehouse. What miserable praise hast thou for her that's foul° and foolish?

IAGO There's none so foul and foolish thereunto,°
But does foul° pranks which fair and wise ones do.

DESDEMONA Oh, heavy ignorance! Thou praisest the worst best. But what praise couldst thou bestow on a deserving woman indeed, one that, in the authority of her merit, did justly put on the vouch° of very malice itself?

IAGO She that was ever fair, and never proud,
Had tongue at will,° and yet was never loud,
Never lacked gold and yet went never gay,°
Fled from her wish and yet said, "Now I may,"°
She that being angered, her revenge being nigh,
Bade her wrong stay° and her displeasure fly,
She that in wisdom never was so frail
To change the cod's head for the salmon's tail,°
She that could think and ne'er disclose her mind,
See suitors following and not look behind,
She was a wight, if ever such wight were—

DESDEMONA To do what?

IAGO To suckle fools and chronicle small beer.°

DESDEMONA Oh, most lame and impotent conclusion! Do not learn of him, Emilia, though he be thy husband. How say you, Cassio? Is he not a most profane and liberal° counselor?

CASSIO He speaks home,° madam. You may relish° him more in° the soldier than in the scholar.

[*Cassio and Desdemona stand together, conversing intimately.*]

IAGO [*aside*]: He takes her by the palm. Ay, well said,° whisper. With as little a web as this will I ensnare as great a fly as Cassio. Ay, smile upon her, do; I will gyve° thee in thine own courtship.° You say true;° 'tis so, indeed. If such tricks as these strip you out of your lieutenantry, it had been better you had not kissed your three fingers so oft, which now again you are most apt to play the sir° in. Very good; well kissed! An excellent courtesy! 'Tis so, indeed. Yet again your fingers to your lips? Would they were clyster pipes° for your sake! [*Trumpet within.*] The Moor! I know his trumpet.

CASSIO 'Tis truly so.

DESDEMONA Let's meet him and receive him.

CASSIO Lo, where he comes!

Enter **OTHELLO** *and* **ATTENDANTS**.

OTHELLO Oh, my fair warrior!

DESDEMONA My dear Othello!

OTHELLO It gives me wonder great as my content
To see you here before me. O my soul's joy,
If after every tempest come such calms,
May the winds blow till they have wakened death,
And let the laboring bark climb hills of seas
Olympus-high, and duck again as low

---

139. fond: foolish. **142. foul:** ugly. **143. thereunto:** in addition. **144. foul:** sluttish. **149. put . . . vouch:** compel the approval. **152. Had . . . will:** was never at a loss for words. **153. gay:** extravagantly clothed. **154. Fled . . . may:** avoided temptation where the choice was hers. **156. Bade . . . stay:** i.e., resolved to put up with her injury and bade her anger to cease. **158. To . . . tail:** i.e., to be selfishly demanding and ambitious. (The fish's lower body, below the rib cage, has fewest bones and is generally the succulent portion. With sexual implication as well: *cod's head* can be slang for "penis," and *tail* for "pudendum.") **163. To . . . beer:** i.e., to breastfeed babies and keep track of trivial matters. [Hall]

167–168. profane and liberal: irreverent and licentious. **169. home:** right to the target. (A term from fencing.) **170. relish:** appreciate. **in:** in the character of. **172–173. well said:** well done. **175. gyve:** fetter, shackle. **176. courtship:** courtesy, show of courtly manners. **You say true:** i.e., that's right, go ahead. **181. the sir:** i.e., the fine gentleman. **184. clyster pipes:** tubes used for enemas and douches.

As hell's from heaven! If it were now to die,
'Twere now to be most happy, for I fear
My soul hath her content so absolute
That not another comfort like to this
Succeeds in unknown fate.°

DESDEMONA The heavens forbid
But that our loves and comforts should increase
Even as our days do grow!

OTHELLO Amen to that, sweet powers!
I cannot speak enough of this content.
It stops me here; it is too much of joy.
And this, and this, the greatest discords be [*They kiss.*]°
That e'er our hearts shall make!

IAGO [*aside*]: Oh, you are well tuned now!
But I'll set down° the pegs that make this music,
As honest as I am.°

OTHELLO Come, let us to the castle.
News, friends! Our wars are done, the Turks are drowned.
How does my old acquaintance of this isle?—
Honey, you shall be well desired° in Cyprus;
I have found great love amongst them. Oh, my sweet,
I prattle out of fashion,° and I dote
In mine own comforts.—I prithee, good Iago,
Go to the bay and disembark my coffers.°
Bring thou the master° to the citadel;
He is a good one, and his worthiness
Does challenge° much respect.—Come, Desdemona.—
Once more, well met at Cyprus!

Exeunt Othello and Desdemona [*and all but Iago and Roderigo*].

201. Succeeds . . . fate: i.e., can follow in the unknown future. **207. s.d. *They kiss:*** (The direction is from the Quarto.) **210. set down:** loosen (and hence untune the instrument). **211. As . . . I am:** for all my supposed honesty. **215. desired:** sought after. **217. out of fashion:** indecorously, incoherently. **219. coffers:** chests, baggage. **220. master:** ship's captain. **221. challenge:** lay claim to, deserve.

IAGO [*to a departing attendant*]: Do thou meet me presently at the harbor. [*To* **RODERIGO**] Come hither. If thou be'st valiant—as, they say, base men° being in love have then a nobility in their natures more than is native to them—list° me. The Lieutenant tonight watches on the court of guard.° First, I must tell thee this: Desdemona is directly in love with him.

RODERIGO With him? Why, 'tis not possible.

IAGO Lay thy finger thus,° and let thy soul be instructed. Mark me with what violence she first loved the Moor, but° for bragging and telling her fantastical lies. To love him still for prating? Let not thy discreet heart think it. Her eye must be fed; and what delight shall she have to look on the devil? When the blood is made dull with the act of sport,° there should be, again to inflame it and to give satiety a fresh appetite, loveliness in favor,° sympathy° in years, manners, and beauties—all which the Moor is defective in. Now, for want of these required conveniences,° her delicate tenderness will find itself abused,° begin to heave the gorge,° disrelish and abhor the Moor. Very nature° will instruct her in it and compel her to some second choice. Now, sir, this granted—as it is a most pregnant° and unforced position—who stands so eminent in the degree of° this fortune as Cassio does? A knave very voluble,° no further conscionable° than in putting on the mere form of civil and humane° seeming for the better

227. base men: even ignoble men. **229. list:** listen to. **230–231. court of guard:** guardhouse. (Cassio is in charge of the watch.) **234. thus:** i.e., on your lips. **236. but:** only. **241–242. the act of sport:** sex. **244. favor:** appearance. **sympathy:** correspondence, similarity. **247. required conveniences:** things conducive to compatibility. **248. abused:** cheated, revolted. **249. heave the gorge:** experience nausea. **250. Very nature:** her very instincts. **253. pregnant:** evident, cogent. **254. in . . . of:** as next in line for. **256. voluble:** facile, glib. **conscionable:** conscientious, conscience-bound. **258. humane:** polite, courteous.

compassing of his salt° and most hidden loose affection.° Why, none, why, none. A slipper° and subtle knave, a finder out of occasions, that has an eye can stamp° and counterfeit advantages,° though true advantage never present itself; a devilish knave. Besides, the knave is handsome, young, and hath all those requisites in him that folly° and green° minds look after. A pestilent complete knave, and the woman hath found him° already.

RODERIGO I cannot believe that in her. She's full of most blessed condition.°

IAGO Blessed fig's end!° The wine she drinks is made of grapes. If she had been blessed, she would never have loved the Moor. Blessed pudding!° Didst thou not see her paddle with the palm of his hand? Didst not mark that?

RODERIGO Yes, that I did; but that was but courtesy.

IAGO Lechery, by this hand. An index° and obscure° prologue to the history of lust and foul thoughts. They met so near with their lips that their breaths embraced together. Villainous thoughts, Roderigo! When these mutualities° so marshal the way, hard at hand° comes the master and main exercise, th'incorporate° conclusion. Pish! But, sir, be you ruled by me. I have brought you from Venice. Watch you° tonight; for the command, I'll lay't upon you.° Cassio knows you not. I'll not be far from you. Do you find some occasion to anger Cassio, either by speaking too loud, or tainting° his discipline, or from what other course you please, which the time shall more favorably minister.°

RODERIGO Well.

IAGO Sir, he's rash and very sudden in choler,° and haply° may strike at you. Provoke him that he may, for even out of that will I cause these of Cyprus to mutiny,° whose qualification° shall come into no true taste° again but by the displanting of Cassio. So shall you have a shorter journey to your desires by the means I shall then have to prefer° them, and the impediment most profitably removed, without the which there were no expectation of our prosperity.

RODERIGO I will do this, if you can bring it to any opportunity.

IAGO I warrant° thee. Meet me by and by° at the citadel. I must fetch his necessaries ashore. Farewell.

RODERIGO Adieu. *Exit.*

IAGO That Cassio loves her, I do well believe't;
That she loves him, 'tis apt° and of great credit.°
The Moor, howbeit that I endure him not,
Is of a constant, loving, noble nature,
And I dare think he'll prove to Desdemona
A most dear husband. Now, I do love her too,
Not out of absolute lust — though peradventure
I stand accountant° for as great a sin —
But partly led to diet° my revenge
For that I do suspect the lusty Moor
Hath leaped into my seat, the thought whereof
Doth, like a poisonous mineral, gnaw my innards;
And nothing can or shall content my soul

259. salt: licentious. **260. affection:** passion. **261. slipper:** slippery. **262. an eye can stamp:** an eye that can coin, create. **263. advantages:** favorable opportunities. **267. folly:** wantonness. **green:** immature. **269. found him:** sized him up, perceived his intent. **271. condition:** disposition. **272. fig's end:** (See 1.3.328 for the vulgar gesture of the fig.) **275. pudding:** sausage. **279. index:** table of contents. **obscure:** veiled, hidden. **284. mutualities:** exchanges, intimacies. **285. hard at hand:** closely following. **286. th'incorporate:** the carnal. **288. Watch you:** stand watch. **289–290. for . . . you:** I'll arrange for you to be appointed, given orders; or, I'll put you in charge.

293. tainting: disparaging. **295. minister:** provide. **297. choler:** wrath. **298. haply:** perhaps. **300. mutiny:** riot. **301. qualification:** pacification. **301–302. true taste:** i.e., acceptable state. **305. prefer:** advance. **310. warrant:** assure. **by and by:** immediately. **315. apt:** probable. **credit:** credibility. **321. accountant:** accountable. **322. diet:** feed.

Till I am evened with him, wife for wife,
Or failing so, yet that I put the Moor
At least into a jealousy so strong
That judgment cannot cure. Which thing to do,
If this poor trash of Venice, whom I trace°
For° his quick hunting, stand the putting on,°
I'll have our Michael Cassio on the hip,°
Abuse° him to the Moor in the rank garb° —
For I fear Cassio with my nightcap° too —
Make the Moor thank me, love me, and reward me
For making him egregiously an ass
And practicing upon° his peace and quiet
Even to madness. 'Tis here, but yet confused.
Knavery's plain face is never seen till used.

Exit.

Scene ii°

Enter Othello's **HERALD** *with a proclamation.*

HERALD It is Othello's pleasure, our noble and valiant general, that, upon certain tidings now arrived, importing the mere perdition° of the Turkish fleet, every man put himself into triumph:° some to dance, some to make bonfires, each man to what sport and revels his addiction° leads him. For, besides these beneficial news, it is the celebration of his nuptial. So much was his pleasure should be proclaimed. All offices° are open, and there is full liberty of feasting from this present hour of five till the bell have told eleven. Heaven bless the isle of Cyprus and our noble general Othello!

Exit.

331. trace: i.e., pursue, dog; or, keep hungry (?) or perhaps *trash,* a hunting term, meaning to put weights on a hunting dog in order to slow him down. **332. For:** to make more eager for. **stand . . . on:** responds properly when I incite him to quarrel. **333. on the hip:** at my mercy, where I can throw him. (A wrestling term.) **334. Abuse:** slander. **rank garb:** coarse manner, gross fashion. **335. with my nightcap:** i.e., as a rival in my bed, as one who gives me cuckold's horns. **338. practicing upon:** plotting against. **Act II, Scene ii. Location:** Cyprus. **3. mere perdition:** complete destruction. **5. triumph:** public celebration. **7. addiction:** inclination. **11. offices:** rooms where food and drink are kept.

Scene iii°

Enter **OTHELLO, DESDEMONA, CASSIO,** *and* **ATTENDANTS.**

OTHELLO Good Michael, look you to the guard tonight.
Let's teach ourselves that honorable stop°
Not to outsport° discretion.

CASSIO Iago hath direction what to do,
But notwithstanding, with my personal eye
Will I look to't.

OTHELLO Iago is most honest.
Michael, good-night. Tomorrow with your earliest°
Let me have speech with you. [*To* **DESDEMONA**] Come, my dear love,
The purchase made, the fruits are to ensue;
That profit's yet to come 'tween me and you.° —
Good night.

Exit [**OTHELLO,** *with* **DESDEMONA** *and* **ATTENDANTS**].

Enter **IAGO.**

CASSIO Welcome, Iago. We must to the watch.

IAGO Not this hour,° Lieutenant; 'tis not yet ten o'th' clock. Our general cast° us thus early for the love of his Desdemona; who° let us not therefore blame. He hath not yet made wanton the night with her, and she is sport for Jove.

CASSIO She's a most exquisite lady.

IAGO And, I'll warrant her, full of game.

CASSIO Indeed, she's a most fresh and delicate creature.

IAGO What an eye she has! Methinks it sounds a parley° to provocation.

CASSIO An inviting eye, and yet methinks right modest.

Act II, Scene iii. Location: Cyprus. The citadel. **2. stop:** restraint. **3. outsport:** celebrate beyond the bounds of. **7. with your earliest:** at your earliest convenience. **9–10. The purchase . . . you:** i.e., though married, we haven't yet consummated our love. (Possibly, too, Othello is referring to pregnancy. At all events, his desire for sexual union is manifest.) **13. Not this hour:** not for an hour yet. **14. cast:** dismissed. **15. who:** i.e., Othello. **23–24. sounds a parley:** calls for a conference, issues an invitation.

This photograph is from a 2003 production of *Samritechak*, a retelling of *Othello* in classical Cambodian style. Virul (Iago), played by Pheng Sarannarin, is on the left, and Romnea (Cassio), played by Chhin Borena, stands to the right. **In what ways do these actors' body language and costumes reflect, challenge, or expand your understanding of the corresponding characters from Shakespeare's work?**

Richard Hartog / Los Angeles Times via Getty Images

IAGO And when she speaks, is it not an alarum° to love?

CASSIO She is indeed perfection.

IAGO Well, happiness to their sheets! Come, lieutenant, I have a stoup° of wine, and here without° are a brace° of Cyprus gallants that would fain have a measure° to the health of black Othello.

CASSIO Not tonight, good Iago. I have very poor and unhappy brains for drinking. I could well wish courtesy would invent some other custom of entertainment.

IAGO Oh, they are our friends; but one cup: I'll drink for you.°

CASSIO I have drunk but one cup tonight, and that was craftily qualified° too, and behold, what innovation° it makes here.° I am unfortunate in the infirmity and dare not task my weakness with any more.

IAGO What, man? 'Tis a night of revels. The gallants desire it.

CASSIO Where are they?

IAGO Here at the door. I pray you, call them in.

CASSIO I'll do't, but it dislikes me.° *Exit.*

IAGO If I can fasten but one cup upon him,
With that which he hath drunk tonight already,
He'll be as full of quarrel and offense°
As my young mistress' dog. Now, my sick fool Roderigo,
Whom love hath turned almost the wrong side out,
To Desdemona hath tonight caroused°
Potations pottle-deep;° and he's to watch.°
Three lads of Cyprus — noble swelling° spirits,
That hold their honors in a wary distance,°
The very elements° of this warlike isle —
Have I tonight flustered with flowing cups,
And they watch° too. Now, 'mongst this flock of drunkards
Am I to put our Cassio in some action
That may offend the isle. — But here they come.

27. alarum: signal calling men to arms. (Continuing the military metaphor of *parley*, line 23.) **31. stoup:** measure of liquor, two quarts. **32. without:** outside. **brace:** pair. **33. fain have a measure:** gladly drink a toast. **40. for you:** in your place. (Iago will do the steady drinking to keep the gallants company while Cassio has only one cup.) **42. qualified:** diluted. **43. innovation:** disturbance, insurrection. **here:** i.e., in my head.

50. it dislikes me: i.e., I'm reluctant. **53. offense:** readiness to give or take offense. **56. caroused:** drunk off. **57. pottle-deep:** to the bottom of the tankard. **watch:** stand watch. **58. swelling:** proud. **59. hold . . . distance:** i.e., are extremely sensitive of their honor. **60. elements:** lifeblood. **62. watch:** are members of the guard.

Enter **CASSIO, MONTANO,** *and* **GENTLEMEN;** [**SERVANTS** *following with wine*].

If consequence do but approve my dream,°
My boat sails freely both with wind and stream.°

CASSIO 'Fore God, they have given me a rouse° already.

MONTANO Good faith, a little one; not past a pint, as I am a soldier.

IAGO Some wine, ho!
[*He sings.*] "And let me the cannikin° clink, clink,
And let me the cannikin clink, clink,
A soldier's a man,
Oh, man's life's but a span;°
Why, then, let a soldier drink."
Some wine, boys!

CASSIO 'Fore God, an excellent song.

IAGO I learned it in England, where indeed they are most potent in potting.° Your Dane, your German, and your swag-bellied Hollander — drink, ho! — are nothing to your English.

CASSIO Is your Englishman so exquisite in his drinking?

IAGO Why, he drinks you,° with facility, your Dane° dead drunk; he sweats not° to overthrow your Almain;° he gives your Hollander a vomit ere the next pottle can be filled.

CASSIO To the health of our general!

MONTANO I am for it, Lieutenant, and I'll do you justice.°

IAGO O sweet England! [*He sings.*]
"King Stephen was and-a worthy peer,
His breeches cost him but a crown;
He held them sixpence all too dear,
With that he called the tailor lown.°

He was a wight of high renown,
And thou art but of low degree.
'Tis pride° that pulls the country down;
Then take thine auld° cloak about thee."

Some wine, ho!

CASSIO 'Fore God, this is a more exquisite song than the other.

IAGO Will you hear't again?

CASSIO No, for I hold him to be unworthy of his place that does those things. Well, God's above all; and there be souls must be saved, and there be souls must not be saved.

IAGO It's true, good Lieutenant.

CASSIO For mine own part — no offense to the General, nor any man of quality° — I hope to be saved.

IAGO And so do I too, Lieutenant.

CASSIO Ay; but, by your leave, not before me; the lieutenant is to be saved before the ancient. Let's have no more of this; let's to our affairs. — God forgive us our sins! — Gentlemen, let's look to our business. Do not think, gentlemen, I am drunk. This is my ancient; this is my right hand, and this is my left. I am not drunk now. I can stand well enough, and speak well enough.

GENTLEMEN Excellent well.

CASSIO Why, very well, then; you must not think then that I am drunk.

Exit.

MONTANO To th' platform, masters. Come, let's set the watch.° [*Exeunt* **GENTLEMEN.**]

IAGO You see this fellow that is gone before.
He's a soldier fit to stand by Caesar

---

65. If . . . dream: if subsequent events will only confirm my dreams and hopes. **66. stream:** current. **67. rouse:** full draft of liquor. **72. cannikin:** small drinking vessel. **75. span:** brief span of time. (Compare Psalm 39:5 as rendered in the Book of Common Prayer: "Thou hast made my days as it were a span long.") **80. potting:** drinking. **86. drinks you:** drinks **86–87. your Dane:** your typical Dane. **87. sweats not:** i.e., need not exert himself **88. Almain:** German. **93. I'll . . . justice:** i.e., I'll drink as much as you.

98. lown: lout, rascal. **101. pride:** i.e., extravagance in dress. **102. auld:** old. **114. quality:** rank. **131. set the watch:** mount the guard.

And give direction; and do but see his vice.
'Tis to his virtue a just equinox,°
The one as long as th'other. 'Tis pity of him.
I fear the trust Othello puts him in,
On some odd time of his infirmity,
Will shake this island.

MONTANO But is he often thus?

IAGO 'Tis evermore the prologue to his sleep.
He'll watch the horologe a double set,°
If drink rock not his cradle.

MONTANO It were well
The General were put in mind of it.
Perhaps he sees it not, or his good nature
Prizes the virtue that appears in Cassio
And looks not on his evils. Is not this true?

Enter **RODERIGO.**

IAGO [*aside to him*]: How now, Roderigo?
I pray you, after the Lieutenant; go.
[*Exit* **RODERIGO.**]

MONTANO And 'tis great pity that the noble Moor
Should hazard such a place as his own second
With° one of an engraffed° infirmity.
It were an honest action to say so
To the Moor.

IAGO Not I, for this fair island.
I do love Cassio well and would do much
To cure him of this evil.
[*Cry within:* "Help! Help!"]
But hark! what noise?

Enter **CASSIO,** *pursuing*° **RODERIGO.**

CASSIO Zounds, you rogue! You rascal!

MONTANO What's the matter, Lieutenant?

CASSIO A knave teach me my duty? I'll beat the knave into a twiggen° bottle.

RODERIGO Beat me?

CASSIO Dost thou prate, rogue?
[*He strikes Roderigo.*]

MONTANO Nay, good Lieutenant.[*Restraining him.*] I pray you, sir, hold your hand.

CASSIO Let me go, sir, or I'll knock you o'er the mazard.°

MONTANO Come, come, you're drunk.

CASSIO Drunk? [*They fight.*]

IAGO [*aside to* Roderigo]: Away, I say. Go out and cry a mutiny.°
[*Exit* **RODERIGO.**]
Nay, good lieutenant — God's will, gentlemen —
Help, ho! — Lieutenant — sir — Montano — sir —
Help, masters!° — Here's a goodly watch indeed! [*A bell rings.*]°
Who's that which rings the bell? — Diablo,° ho!
The town will rise.° God's will, Lieutenant, hold!
You'll be ashamed forever.

Enter **OTHELLO** *and* **ATTENDANTS** [*with weapons*].

OTHELLO What is the matter here?

MONTANO Zounds,
I bleed still.
I am hurt to th' death. He dies! [*He thrusts at* Cassio.]

OTHELLO Hold, for your lives!

IAGO Hold, ho! Lieutenant — sir — Montano — gentlemen —
Have you forgot all sense of place and duty?
Hold! The General speaks to you. Hold, for shame!

---

135. just equinox: exact counterpart. (*Equinox* is an equal length of days and nights.) **141. watch . . . set:** stay awake twice around the clock, or *horologe.* **150–151. hazard . . . With:** risk giving such an important position as his second in command to. **151. engraffed:** engrafted, inveterate. **155. s.d.** ***pursuing:*** (The Quarto text reads, *"driuing in."*)

159. twiggen: wicker-covered. (Cassio vows to assail Roderigo until his skin resembles wickerwork or until he has driven Roderigo through the holes in a wickerwork.) **165. mazard:** i.e., head. (Literally, a drinking vessel.) **168. mutiny:** riot. **171. masters:** sirs. **171. s.d.** ***A bell rings:*** (This direction is from the Quarto, as are *Exit Roderigo* at line 148. *They fight* at line 167, and *with weapons* at line 174 s.d.) **172. Diablo:** the devil. **173. rise:** grow riotous.

OTHELLO Why, how now, ho! From whence ariseth this?
Are we turned Turks, and to ourselves do that
Which heaven hath forbid the Ottomites?°
For Christian shame put by this barbarous brawl!
He that stirs next to carve for° his own rage
Holds his soul light;° he dies upon his motion.°
Silence that dreadful bell. It frights the isle
From her propriety.° What is the matter, masters?
Honest Iago, that looks dead with grieving,
Speak. Who began this? On thy love, I charge thee.

IAGO I do not know. Friends all but now, even now,
In quarter and in terms° like bride and groom
Devesting them° for bed; and then, but now —
As if some planet had unwitted men —
Swords out, and tilting one at others' breasts
In opposition bloody. I cannot speak°
Any beginning to this peevish odds;°
And would in action glorious I had lost
Those legs that brought me to a part of it!

OTHELLO How comes it, Michael, you are thus forgot?°

CASSIO I pray you, pardon me. I cannot speak.

OTHELLO Worthy Montano, you were wont be° civil;
The gravity and stillness° of your youth
The world hath noted, and your name is great
In mouths of wisest censure.° What's the matter,
That you unlace° your reputation thus
And spend your rich opinion° for the name
Of a night-brawler? Give me answer to it.

MONTANO Worthy Othello, I am hurt to danger.
Your officer, Iago, can inform you —
While I spare speech, which something° now offends° me —
Of all that I do know; nor know I aught
By me that's said or done amiss this night,
Unless self-charity be sometimes a vice,
And to defend ourselves it be a sin
When violence assails us.

OTHELLO Now, by heaven,
My blood° begins my safer guides° to rule,
And passion, having my best judgment collied,°
Essays° to lead the way. Zounds, if I stir,
Or do but lift this arm, the best of you
Shall sink in my rebuke. Give me to know
How this foul rout° began, who set it on;
And he that is approved in° this offense,
Though he had twinned with me, both at a birth,
Shall lose me. What? In a town of° war,
Yet wild, the people's hearts brim full of fear,
To manage° private and domestic quarrel?
In night, and on the court and guard of safety?°
'Tis monstrous. Iago, who began't?

MONTANO [*To* **IAGO**]: If partially affined, or leagued in office,°
Thou dost deliver more or less than truth,
Thou art no soldier.

IAGO Touch me not so near.
I had rather have this tongue cut from my mouth
Than it should do offense to Michael Cassio;
Yet, I persuade myself, to speak the truth

181–182. to ourselves . . . Ottomites: inflict on ourselves the harm that heaven has prevented the Turks from doing (by destroying their fleet). **184. carve for:** i.e., indulge, satisfy with his sword. **185. Holds . . . light:** i.e., places little value on his life. **upon his motion:** if he moves. **187. propriety:** proper state or condition. **191. In quarter . . . terms:** in conduct and speech. **192. Devesting them:** undressing themselves. **195. speak:** explain. **196. peevish odds:** childish quarrel. **199. are thus forgot:** you have forgotten yourself? [Hall] **201. wont be:** accustomed to be. **202. stillness:** sobriety. **204. censure:** judgment. **205. unlace:** undo, lay open (as one might loose the strings of a purse containing reputation).

206. opinion: reputation. **210. something:** somewhat. **offends:** pains. **216. blood:** passion (of anger). **guides:** i.e., reason. **217. collied:** darkened. **218. Essays:** undertakes. **221. rout:** riot. **222. approved in:** found guilty of. **224. town of:** town garrisoned for. **226. manage:** undertake. **227. on . . . safety:** at the main guardhouse or headquarters and on watch. **229. If . . . office:** if made partial by personal relationship or by your being fellow officers.

Shall nothing wrong him. Thus it is, General:
Montano and myself being in speech,
There comes a fellow crying out for help,
And Cassio following with determined sword
To execute upon him.° Sir, this gentleman
[*indicating* **MONTANO**]
Steps in to Cassio and entreats his pause.°
Myself the crying fellow did pursue,
Lest by his clamor — as it so fell out —
The town might fall in fright. He, swift of foot,
Outran my purpose, and I returned, the rather°
For that I heard the clink and fall of swords
And Cassio high in oath, which till tonight
I ne'er might say before. When I came back —
For this was brief — I found them close together
At blow and thrust, even as again they were
When you yourself did part them.
More of this matter cannot I report.
But men are men; the best sometimes forget.°
Though Cassio did some little wrong to him,
As men in rage strike those that wish them best,°
Yet surely Cassio, I believe, received
From him that fled some strange indignity,
Which patience could not pass.°

OTHELLO I know, Iago,
Thy honesty and love doth mince this matter,
Making it light to Cassio. Cassio, I love thee,
But nevermore be officer of mine.

Enter **DESDEMONA**, *attended.*

Look if my gentle love be not raised up.
I'll make thee an example.

DESDEMONA What is the matter, dear?

OTHELLO All's well now, sweeting;
Come away to bed. [*To* **MONTANO**] Sir, for your hurts,
Myself will be your surgeon.° — Lead him off.
[**MONTANO** *is led off.*]
Iago, look with care about the town
And silence those whom this vile brawl distracted.
Come, Desdemona. 'Tis the soldiers' life
To have their balmy slumbers waked with strife.

Exit [*with all but* **IAGO** *and* **CASSIO**].

IAGO What, are you hurt, Lieutenant?

CASSIO Ay, past all surgery.

IAGO Marry, God forbid!

CASSIO Reputation, reputation, reputation! Oh, I have lost my reputation! I have lost the immortal part of myself, and what remains is bestial. My reputation, Iago, my reputation!

IAGO As I am an honest man, I thought you had received some bodily wound; there is more sense in that than in reputation. Reputation is an idle and most false imposition,° oft got without merit and lost without deserving. You have lost no reputation at all, unless you repute yourself such a loser. What, man, there are ways to recover° the General again. You are but now cast in his mood° — punishment more in policy° than in malice, even so as one would beat his offenseless dog to affright an imperious lion.° Sue° to him again and he's yours.

CASSIO I will rather sue to be despised than to deceive so good a commander with so slight,° so drunken, and so indiscreet an

---

239. execute upon him: (1) proceed violently against him (2) execute him. **240. his pause:** him to stop. **244. rather:** sooner. **252. forget:** forget themselves. **254. those . . . best:** i.e., even those who are well disposed toward them. **257. pass:** pass over, overlook.

265. be your surgeon: i.e., make sure you receive medical attention. **281–282. false imposition:** thing artificially imposed and of no real value. **286. recover:** regain favor with. **287. cast in his mood:** dismissed in a moment of anger. **288. in policy:** done for expediency's sake and as a public gesture. **289–290. would . . . lion:** i.e., would make an example of a minor offender in order to deter more important and dangerous offenders. **290. Sue:** petition. **294. slight:** worthless.

officer. Drunk? And speak parrot?° And squabble? Swagger? Swear? And discourse fustian with one's own shadow? O thou invisible spirit of wine, if thou hast no name to be known by, let us call thee devil!

IAGO What was he that you followed with your sword? What hath he done to you?

CASSIO I know not.

IAGO Is't possible?

CASSIO I remember a mass of things, but nothing distinctly; a quarrel, but nothing wherefore.° Oh, God, that men should put an enemy in their mouths to steal away their brains! That we should, with joy, pleasance, revel, and applause,° transform ourselves into beasts!

IAGO Why, but you are now well enough. How came you thus recovered?

CASSIO It hath pleased the devil drunkenness to give place to the devil wrath. One unperfectness shows me another, to make me frankly despise myself.

IAGO Come, you are too severe a moraler.° As the time, the place, and the condition of this country stands, I could heartily wish this had not befallen; but since it is as it is, mend it for your own good.

CASSIO I will ask him for my place again; he shall tell me I am a drunkard. Had I as many mouths as Hydra,° such an answer would stop them all. To be now a sensible man, by and by a fool, and presently a beast! Oh strange! Every inordinate° cup is unblessed, and the ingredient is a devil.

IAGO Come, come, good wine is a good familiar creature, if it be well used. Exclaim no more against it. And, good Lieutenant, I think you think I love you.

CASSIO I have well approved° it, sir. I drunk!

IAGO You or any man living may be drunk at a time,° man. I'll tell you what you shall do. Our general's wife is now the general—I may say so in this respect, for that° he hath devoted and given up himself to the contemplation, mark, and denotement° of her parts° and graces. Confess yourself freely to her; importune her help to put you in your place again. She is of so free,° so kind, so apt, so blessed a disposition, that she holds it a vice in her goodness not to do more than she is requested. This broken joint between you and her husband entreat her to splinter;° and, my fortunes against any lay° worth naming, this crack of your love shall grow stronger than it was before.

CASSIO You advise me well.

IAGO I protest,° in the sincerity of love and honest kindness.

CASSIO I think it freely;° and betimes in the morning I will beseech the virtuous Desdemona to undertake for me. I am desperate of my fortunes if they check° me here.

IAGO You are in the right. Good night, Lieutenant. I must to the watch.

CASSIO Good night, honest Iago. *Exit* **CASSIO.**

IAGO And what's he then that says I play the villain,
When this advice is free° I give, and honest,
Probal° to thinking, and indeed the course
To win the Moor again? For 'tis most easy
Th'inclining° Desdemona to subdue°
In any honest suit; she's framed as fruitful°

---

295. speak parrot: talk nonsense, rant. (*Discourse fustian,* lines 296–297, has much the same meaning.) **306. wherefore:** why. **309. applause:** desire for applause. **317. moraler:** moralizer. **324. Hydra:** the Lernaean Hydra, a monster with many heads and the ability to grow two heads when one was cut off, slain by Hercules as the second of his twelve labors. **327. inordinate:** immoderate.

333. approved: proved by experience. **334–335. at a time:** at one time or another. **337. for that:** that. **339. mark, and denotement:** (Both words mean "observation.") **340. parts:** qualities. **342. free:** generous. **347. splinter:** bind with splints. **348. lay:** stake, wager. **352. protest:** insist, declare. **354. freely:** unreservedly. **357. check:** repulse. **363. free:** (1) free from guile (2) freely given. **364. Probal:** probable, reasonable. **366. Th'inclining:** the favorably disposed. **subdue:** persuade. **367. framed as fruitful:** created as generous.

As the free elements.° And then for her
To win the Moor—were't to renounce his baptism,
All seals° and symbols of redeemèd sin—
His soul is so enfettered to her love
That she may make, unmake, do what she list,
Even as her appetite° shall play the god
With his weak function.° How am I then a villain,
To counsel Cassio to this parallel° course
Directly to his good? Divinity of hell!°
When devils will the blackest sins put on,°
They do suggest° at first with heavenly shows,
As I do now. For whiles this honest fool
Plies Desdemona to repair his fortune,
And she for him pleads strongly to the Moor,
I'll pour this pestilence into his ear,
That she repeals him° for her body's lust;
And by how much she strives to do him good,
She shall undo her credit with the Moor.
So will I turn her virtue into pitch,°
And out of her own goodness make the net
That shall enmesh them all.

Enter **RODERIGO.**

How now, Roderigo?

RODERIGO I do follow here in the chase, not like a hound that hunts, but one that fills up the cry.° My money is almost spent; I have been tonight exceedingly well cudgeled; and I think the issue° will be I shall have so much° experience for my pains, and so, with no money at all and a little more wit, return again to Venice.

IAGO How poor are they that have not patience!
What wound did ever heal but by degrees?
Thou know'st we work by wit, and not by witchcraft,
And wit depends on dilatory time.
Does't not go well? Cassio hath beaten thee,
And thou, by that small hurt, hast cashiered° Cassio.
Though other things grow fair against the sun,
Yet fruits that blossom first will first be ripe.°
Content thyself awhile. By the Mass, 'tis morning!
Pleasure and action make the hours seem short.
Retire thee; go where thou art billeted.
Away, I say! Thou shalt know more hereafter.
Nay, get thee gone. *Exit* **RODERIGO.**
Two things are to be done.
My wife must move° for Cassio to her mistress;
I'll set her on;
Myself the while to draw the Moor apart
And bring him jump° when he may Cassio find
Soliciting his wife. Ay, that's the way.
Dull not device° by coldness° and delay. *Exit.*

ACT III

Scene i°

Enter **CASSIO** [*and*] **MUSICIANS.**

CASSIO Masters,° play here, I will content your pains°—
Something that's brief; and bid "Good morrow, general." [*They play.*]

[*Enter*] **CLOWN.**

---

368. free elements: i.e., earth, air, fire, and water, unrestrained and spontaneous. **370. seals:** tokens. **373. her appetite:** her desire, or, perhaps his desire for her. **374. function:** exercise of faculties (weakened by his fondness for her). **375. parallel:** i.e., seemingly in his best interests but at the same time threatening. **376. Divinity of hell!:** inverted theology of hell (which seduces the soul to its damnation)! **377. put on:** further, instigate. **378. suggest:** tempt. **383. repeals him:** attempts to get him restored. **386. pitch:** i.e., (1) foul blackness (2) a snaring substance. **390–391. fills up the cry:** merely takes part as one of the pack. **393. issue:** outcome. **394. so much:** just so much and no more.

402. cashiered: dismissed from service. **403–404. Though . . . ripe:** i.e., plans that are well prepared and set expeditiously in motion will soonest ripen into success. **410. move:** plead. **413. jump:** precisely. **415. device:** plot. **coldness:** lack of zeal. **Act III, Scene i. Location:** Before the chamber of Othello and Desdemona. **1. Masters:** Good sirs. **content your pains:** reward your efforts.

CLOWN Why, masters, have your instruments been in Naples, that they speak i'the nose° thus?

A MUSICIAN How, sir, how?

CLOWN Are these, I pray you, wind instruments?

A MUSICIAN Ay, marry, are they, sir.

CLOWN O! thereby hangs a tail.

A MUSICIAN Whereby hangs a tale, sir?

CLOWN Marry, sir, by many a wind instrument° that I know. But, masters, here's money for you. [*He gives money.*] And the General so likes your music that he desires you, for love's sake, to make no more noise with it.

A MUSICIAN Well, sir, we will not.

CLOWN If you have any music that may not° be heard, to't again; but, as they say, to hear music the General does not greatly care.

A MUSICIAN We have none such, sir.

CLOWN Then put up your pipes in your bag, for I'll away. Go; vanish into air, away!

Exeunt Musicians.

CASSIO Dost thou hear, mine honest friend?

CLOWN No, I hear not your honest friend; I hear you.

CASSIO Prithee, keep up thy quillets.° There's a poor piece of gold for thee. [*He gives money.*] If the gentlewoman that attends the General's wife be stirring, tell her there's one Cassio entreats her a little favor of speech.° Wilt thou do this?

CLOWN She is stirring, sir: if she will stir° hither, I shall seem° to notify unto her.

CASSIO Do, good my friend. *Exit* **CLOWN**.

Enter **IAGO**.

In happy time,° Iago.

IAGO You have not been a bed, then?

CASSIO Why, no. The day had broke
Before we parted. I have made bold, Iago,
To send in to your wife. My suit to her
Is that she will to virtuous Desdemona
Procure me some access.

IAGO I'll send her to you presently;
And I'll devise a mean to draw the Moor
Out of the way, that your converse and business
May be more free.

CASSIO I humbly thank you for 't. *Exit* [**IAGO**].
I never knew
A Florentine° more kind and honest.

Enter **EMILIA**.

EMILIA Good morrow, good Lieutenant. I am sorry
For your displeasure;° but all will sure be well.
The General and his wife are talking of it,
And she speaks for you stoutly.° The Moor replies
That he you hurt is of great fame° in Cyprus
And great affinity,° and that in wholesome wisdom
He might not but refuse you; but he protests° he loves you,
And needs no other suitor but his likings
To take the safest occasion by the front°
To bring you in again.

CASSIO Yet I beseech you,
If you think fit, or that it may be done,
Give me advantage of some brief discourse
With Desdemona alone.

EMILIA Pray you, come in.
I will bestow you where you shall have time
To speak your bosom° freely.

CASSIO I am much bound to you. [*Exeunt.*]

---

4. speak i'th' nose: (1) sound nasal (2) sound like one whose nose has been attacked by syphilis. (Naples was popularly supposed to have a high incidence of venereal disease.) **11. wind instrument:** (With a joke on flatulence. The *tail,* line 9, that hangs nearby the *wind instrument* suggests the penis.) **17. may not:** cannot. **25. keep . . . quillets:** refrain from quibbling. **29–30. a little . . . speech:** the favor of a brief talk. **31. stir:** bestir herself. (With a play on *stirring,* "rousing herself from rest.") **32. seem:** deem it good, think fit. **33. In happy time:** i.e., well met.

45. Florentine: i.e., even a fellow Florentine. (Iago is a Venetian; Cassio is a Florentine.) **47. displeasure:** fall from favor. **49. stoutly:** spiritedly. **50. fame:** reputation, importance. **51. affinity:** kindred, family connection. **52. protests:** insists. **54. occasion . . . front:** opportunity by the forelock. **60. bosom:** inmost thoughts.

Scene ii°

Enter **OTHELLO,** *IAGO, and* **GENTLEMEN.**

OTHELLO [*giving letters*]:
These letters give, Iago, to the pilot,
And by him do my duties° to the Senate.
That done, I will be walking on the works;°
Repair° there to me.

IAGO Well, my good lord, I'll do't.

OTHELLO This fortification, gentlemen, shall we see't?

GENTLEMEN We'll wait upon° your lordship.

Exeunt.

Scene iii°

Enter **DESDEMONA, CASSIO,** *and* **EMILIA.**

DESDEMONA Be thou assured, good Cassio, I will do
All my abilities in thy behalf.

EMILIA Good madam, do. I warrant it grieves my husband
As if the cause were his.

DESDEMONA Oh, that's an honest fellow. Do not doubt, Cassio,
But I will have my lord and you again
As friendly as you were.

CASSIO Bounteous madam,
Whatever shall become of Michael Cassio,
He's never any thing but your true servant.

DESDEMONA I know't. I thank you. You do love my lord;
You have known him long, and be you well assured
He shall in strangeness° stand no farther off
Than in a politic° distance.

CASSIO Ay, but, lady,
That policy may either last so long,
Or feed upon such nice and waterish diet,°
Or breed itself so out of circumstance,°
That, I being absent and my place supplied,°
My general will forget my love and service.

DESDEMONA Do not doubt° that. Before Emilia here
I give thee warrant° of thy place. Assure thee,
If I do vow a friendship I'll perform it
To the last article. My lord shall never rest.

This 2016 production of Giuseppe Verdi's opera *Otello*, based on *Othello*, takes place in a refugee camp. **Why do you think the director chose this setting? What parallels might be drawn between the struggles of refugees and those of Othello?**

Lluis Gene/AFP/Getty Images

Act III, Scene ii. Location: The citadel. **2. do my duties:** convey my respects. **3. works:** breastworks, fortifications. **4. Repair:** return, come. **6. wait upon:** attend. **Act III, Scene iii. Location:** The garden of the citadel.

12. strangeness: aloofness. **13. politic:** required by wise policy. **15. Or . . . diet:** or sustain itself at length upon such trivial and meager technicalities. **16. breed . . . circumstance:** continually renew itself so out of chance events, or yield so few chances for my being pardoned. **17. supplied:** filled by another person. **19. doubt:** fear. **20. warrant:** guarantee.

I'll watch him tame° and talk him out of patience;°
His bed shall seem a school, his board° a shrift;°
I'll intermingle every thing he does
With Cassio's suit. Therefore be merry, Cassio,
For thy solicitor° shall rather die
Than give thy cause away.°

Enter **OTHELLO** *and* **IAGO** [*at a distance*].

EMILIA Madam, here comes my lord.
CASSIO Madam, I'll take my leave.
DESDEMONA Why, stay, and hear me speak.
CASSIO Madam, not now; I am very ill at ease,
Unfit for mine own purposes.
DESDEMONA Well, do your discretion.°

Exit **CASSIO.**

IAGO Ha! I like not that.
OTHELLO What dost thou say?
IAGO Nothing, my lord; or if—I know not what.
OTHELLO Was not that Cassio parted from my wife?
IAGO Cassio, my lord? No, sure, I cannot think it,
That he would steal away so guiltylike,
Seeing you coming.
OTHELLO I do believe 'twas he.
DESDEMONA [*joining them*]: How now, my lord?
I have been talking with a suitor here,
A man that languishes in your displeasure.
OTHELLO Who is't you mean?
DESDEMONA Why, your lieutenant, Cassio. Good my lord,
If I have any grace or power to move you,
His present reconciliation take;°
For if he be not one that truly loves you,
That errs in ignorance and not in cunning,°
I have no judgment in an honest face.
I prithee, call him back.
OTHELLO Went he hence now?
DESDEMONA Yes, faith, so humbled
That he hath left part of his grief with me
To suffer with him. Good love, call him back.
OTHELLO Not now, sweet Desdemona. Some other time.
DESDEMONA But shall't be shortly?
OTHELLO The sooner, sweet, for you.
DESDEMONA Shall't be tonight at supper?
OTHELLO No, not tonight.
DESDEMONA Tomorrow dinner,° then?
OTHELLO I shall not dine at home.
I meet the captains at the citadel.
DESDEMONA Why, then, tomorrow night; or Tuesday morn,
On Tuesday noon, or night, on Wednesday morn.
I prithee, name the time, but let it not
Exceed three days. In faith, he's penitent;
And yet his trespass, in our common reason°—
Save that, they say, the wars must make example
Out of her best°—is not almost° a fault
T'incur a private check.° When shall he come?
Tell me, Othello. I wonder in my soul
What you would ask me that I should deny,
Or stand so mamm'ring on.° What? Michael Cassio,
That came a wooing with you, and so many a time,
When I have spoke of you dispraisingly,
Hath ta'en your part—to have so much to do
To bring him in!° By'r Lady, I could do much—
OTHELLO Prithee, no more. Let him come when he will;
I deny thee nothing.
DESDEMONA Why, this is not a boon.
'Tis as I should entreat you wear your gloves,
Or feed on nourishing dishes, or keep you warm,

---

23. watch him tame: tame him by keeping him from sleeping. (A term from falconry.) **out of patience:** past his endurance. **24. board:** dining table. **shrift:** confessional. **27. solicitor:** advocate. **28. away:** up. **34. do your discretion:** do as you think fit. **49. His . . . take:** let him be reconciled to you right away. **51. in cunning:** wittingly.

63. dinner: (The noontime meal.) **70. common reason:** everyday judgments. **71–72. Save . . . best:** were it not that, as the saying goes, military discipline requires making an example of the very best men. (*Her* refers to wars as a singular concept.) **72. not almost:** scarcely. **73. a private check:** even a private reprimand. **76. mamm'ring on:** wavering or muttering about. **80. bring him in:** restore him to favor.

Or sue to you to do a peculiar° profit
To your own person. Nay, when I have a suit
Wherein I mean to touch° your love indeed,
It shall be full of poise and difficult weight,°
And fearful to be granted.

OTHELLO I will deny thee nothing.
Whereon,° I do beseech thee, grant me this,
To leave me but a little to myself.

DESDEMONA Shall I deny you? No. Farewell, my lord.

OTHELLO Farewell, my Desdemona. I'll come to thee straight.°

DESDEMONA Emilia, come. Be as your fancies° teach you;
Whate'er you be, I am obedient.

Exit [*with* **EMILIA**].

OTHELLO Excellent wretch!° Perdition catch my soul,
But I do love thee! and when I love thee not,
Chaos is come again.°

IAGO My noble lord—

OTHELLO What dost thou say, Iago?

IAGO Did Michael Cassio, when you wooed my lady,
Know of your love?

OTHELLO He did, from first to last. Why dost thou ask?

IAGO But for a satisfaction of my thought;
No further harm.

OTHELLO Why of thy thought, Iago?

IAGO I did not think he had been acquainted with her.

OTHELLO Oh, yes; and went between us very oft.

IAGO Indeed?

OTHELLO Indeed? Ay, indeed. Discern'st thou aught in that?
Is he not honest?

IAGO Honest, my lord?

OTHELLO Honest. Ay, honest.

IAGO My lord, for aught I know.

OTHELLO What dost thou think?

IAGO Think, my lord?

OTHELLO "Think, my lord?" By heaven, thou echo'st me,
As if there were some monster in thy thought
Too hideous to be shown. Thou dost mean something.
I heard thee say even now, thou lik'st not that,
When Cassio left my wife. What didst not like?
And when I told thee he was of my counsel°
In my whole course of wooing, thou cried'st, "Indeed?"
And didst contract and purse° thy brow together
As if thou then hadst shut up in thy brain
Some horrible conceit.° If thou dost love me,
Show me thy thought.

IAGO My lord, you know I love you.

OTHELLO I think thou dost;
And, for° I know thou art full of love and honesty,
And weigh'st thy words before thou giv'st them breath,
Therefore these stops° of thine fright me the more;
For such things in a false disloyal knave
Are tricks of custom,° but in a man that's just
They're close dilations, working from the heart
That passion cannot rule.°

IAGO For Michael Cassio,
I dare be sworn I think that he is honest.

OTHELLO I think so too.

IAGO Men should be what they seem;
Or those that be not, would they might seem none!°

OTHELLO Certain men should be what they seem.

---

86. peculiar: particular, personal. **88. touch:** test. **89. poise . . . weight:** delicacy and weightiness. **92. Whereon:** in return for which. **95. straight:** straightaway. **96. fancies:** inclinations. **98. wretch:** (A term of affectionate endearment.) **99–100. And . . . again:** i.e., my love for you will last forever, until the end of time when chaos will return. (But with an unconscious, ironic suggestion that, if anything should induce Othello to cease loving Desdemona, the result would be chaos.)

123. of my counsel: in my confidence. **125. purse:** knit. **127. conceit:** fancy. **131. for:** because. **133. stops:** pauses. **135. of custom:** customary. **136–137. They're . . . rule:** they are secret or involuntary expressions of feeling that are too strong to be kept back. **137. For:** as for. **140. seem none:** not seem at all, not seem to be honest.

IAGO Why then, I think Cassio's an honest man.
OTHELLO Nay, yet there's more in this.
I prithee, speak to me as to thy thinkings,
As thou dost ruminate, and give thy worst of thoughts
The worst of words.
IAGO Good my lord, pardon me.
Though I am bound to every act of duty,
I am not bound to that° all slaves are free to.°
Utter my thoughts? Why, say they are vile and false,
As where's that palace whereinto foul things
Sometimes intrude not? Who has a breast so pure
But some uncleanly apprehensions
Keep leets and law days,° and in sessions sit
With meditations lawful?°
OTHELLO Thou dost conspire against thy friend,° Iago,
If thou but think'st him wronged and mak'st his ear
A stranger to thy thoughts.
IAGO I do beseech you,
Though I perchance am vicious° in my guess—
As I confess it is my nature's plague
To spy into abuses, and oft my jealousy°
Shapes faults that are not—that your wisdom then,
From one° that so imperfectly conceits,°
Would take no notice, nor build yourself a trouble
Out of his scattering° and unsure observance.
It were not for your quiet nor your good,
Nor for my manhood, honesty, and wisdom,
To let you know my thoughts.
OTHELLO What dost thou mean?
IAGO Good name in man and woman, dear my lord,
Is the immediate° jewel of their souls.
Who steals my purse steals trash; 'tis something, nothing;
'Twas mine, 'tis his, and has been slave to thousands;
But he that filches from me my good name
Robs me of that which not enriches him
And makes me poor indeed.
OTHELLO By heaven, I'll know thy thoughts.
IAGO You cannot, if° my heart were in your hand,
Nor shall not, whilst 'tis in my custody.
OTHELLO Ha?
IAGO Oh, beware, my lord, of jealousy.
It is the green-eyed monster, which doth mock
The meat it feeds on.° That cuckold lives in bliss
Who, certain of his fate, loves not his wronger;°
But, oh, what damnèd minutes tells° he o'er
Who dotes, yet doubts; suspects, yet fondly loves!
OTHELLO Oh, misery!
IAGO Poor and content is rich, and rich enough,°
But riches fineless° is as poor as winter
To him that ever fears he shall be poor.
Good God, the souls of all my tribe defend
From jealousy!
OTHELLO Why, why is this?
Think'st thou I'd make a life of jealousy,
To follow still the changes of the moon
With fresh suspicions?° No! To be once in doubt

---

148. that: that which. **free to:** free with respect to. **153. Keep leets and law days:** i.e., hold court, set up their authority in one's heart. (*Leets* are a kind of manor court; *law days* are the days courts sit in session, or those sessions.) **153–154. and . . . lawful:** i.e., and coexist in a kind of spiritual conflict with virtuous thoughts. **155. thy friend:** i.e., Othello. **158. vicious:** wrong. **160. jealousy:** suspicious nature. **162. one:** i.e., myself, Iago. **conceits:** judges, conjectures. **164. scattering:** random.

169. immediate: essential, most precious. **176. if:** even if. **180–181. which . . . feeds on:** (Jealousy mocks both itself and the sufferer of jealousy; it is self-devouring and is its own punishment.) **181–182. That . . . wronger:** A cuckolded husband who knows his wife to be unfaithful can at least take comfort in knowing the truth, so that he will not continue to love her or to befriend her lover. (Othello echoes this sentiment in lines 205–207, when he vows that he would end uncertainty and cease to love an unfaithful wife.) **183. tells:** counts. **186. Poor . . . enough:** to be content with what little one has is the greatest wealth of all. (Proverbial.) **187. fineless:** boundless. **193–194. To follow . . . suspicions?:** to be constantly imagining new causes for suspicion, changing incessantly like the moon?

Is once° to be resolved.° Exchange me for a goat
When I shall turn the business of my soul
To such exsufflicate and blown° surmises
Matching thy inference.° 'Tis not to make me jealous
To say my wife is fair, feeds well, loves company,
Is free of speech, sings, plays, and dances well;
Where virtue is, these are more virtuous.
Nor from mine own weak merits will I draw
The smallest fear or doubt of her revolt,°
For she had eyes, and chose me. No, Iago,
I'll see before I doubt; when I doubt, prove;
And on the proof, there is no more but this —
Away at once with love or jealousy.

IAGO I am glad of this, for now I shall have reason
To show the love and duty that I bear you
With franker spirit. Therefore, as I am bound,
Receive it from me. I speak not yet of proof.
Look to your wife; observe her well with Cassio.
Wear your eyes thus, not° jealous nor secure.°
I would not have your free and noble nature,
Out of self-bounty,° be abused.° Look to't.
I know our country disposition well;
In Venice they do let God see the pranks
They dare not show their husbands; their best conscience
Is not to leave't undone, but keep't unknown.

OTHELLO Dost thou say so?

IAGO She did deceive her father, marrying you;
And when she seemed to shake and fear your looks,
She lov'd them most.

OTHELLO And so she did.

IAGO Why, go to,° then!
She that, so young, could give out such a seeming,°
To seel° her father's eyes up close as oak,°
He thought 'twas witchcraft! But I am much to blame.
I humbly do beseech you of your pardon
For too much loving you.

OTHELLO I am bound° to thee forever.

IAGO I see this hath a little dashed your spirits.

OTHELLO Not a jot, not a jot.

IAGO I'faith, I fear it has.
I hope you will consider what is spoke
Comes from my love. But I do see you're moved.
I am to pray you not to strain my speech
To grosser issues° nor to larger reach°
Than to suspicion.

OTHELLO I will not.

IAGO Should you do so, my lord,
My speech should fall into such vile success°
Which my thoughts aimed not. Cassio's my worthy friend.
My lord, I see you're moved.

OTHELLO No, not much moved.
I do not think but Desdemona's honest.°

IAGO Long live she so! and long live you to think so!

OTHELLO And yet, how nature erring from itself —

IAGO Ay, there's the point! As — to be bold with you —
Not to affect° many proposèd matches
Of her own clime, complexion, and degree,°
Whereto we see in all things nature tends —
Foh! One may smell in such a will° most rank,
Foul disproportion,° thoughts unnatural.

---

195. once: once and for all. **resolved:** free of doubt, having settled the matter. **197. exsufflicate and blown:** inflated and blown up or flyblown, hence, loathsome, disgusting. **198. inference:** description or allegation. **203. doubt . . . revolt:** fear of her unfaithfulness. **213. not:** neither. **secure:** free from uncertainty. **215. self-bounty:** inherent or natural goodness and generosity. **abused:** deceived.

223. go to: (An expression of impatience.) **224. seeming:** false appearance. **225. seel:** blind. (A term from falconry.) **oak:** (A close-grained wood.) **229. bound:** indebted. (But perhaps with ironic sense of "tied.") **235. issues:** significances. **reach:** meaning, scope. **239. success:** effect, result. **242. honest:** chaste. **246. affect:** prefer, desire. **247. clime . . . degree:** country, temperament or skin color, and social position. **249. will:** sensuality, appetite. **250. disproportion:** abnormality.

But pardon me. I do not in position°
Distinctly speak of her, though I may fear
Her will, recoiling° to her better° judgment,
May fall to match you with her country forms°
And happily repent.°

OTHELLO Farewell, farewell!
If more thou dost perceive, let me know more.
Set on thy wife to observe. Leave me, Iago.

IAGO [*going*]: My lord, I take my leave.

OTHELLO Why did I marry? This honest creature doubtless
Sees and knows more, much more, than he unfolds.

IAGO [*returning*]:
My lord, I would I might entreat Your Honor
To scan° this thing no farther. Leave it to time.
Although 'tis fit that Cassio have his place—
For, sure, he fills it up with great ability—
Yet, if you please to hold him off awhile,
You shall by that perceive him and his means.°
Note if your lady strain his entertainment°
With any strong or vehement importunity;
Much will be seen in that. In the meantime,
Let me be thought too busy° in my fears—
As worthy cause I have to fear I am—
And hold her free,° I do beseech Your Honor.

OTHELLO Fear not my government.°

IAGO I once more take my leave. *Exit.*

OTHELLO This fellow's of exceeding honesty,
And knows all qualities,° with a learnèd spirit,
Of human dealings. If I do prove her haggard,°
Though that her jesses° were my dear heartstrings,
I'd whistle her off and let her down the wind°
To prey at fortune.° Haply, for° I am black
And have not those soft parts of conversation°
That chamberers° have, or for I am declined
Into the vale of years—yet that's not much—
She's gone. I am abused,° and my relief
Must be to loathe her. Oh, curse of marriage,
That we can call these delicate creatures ours
And not their appetites! I had rather be a toad
And live upon the vapor of a dungeon
Than keep a corner in the thing I love
For others' uses. Yet, 'tis the plague of great ones;
Prerogatived° are they less than the base.°
'Tis destiny unshunnable, like death.
Even then this forkèd° plague is fated to us
When we do quicken.° Look where she comes.

Enter **DESDEMONA** *and* **EMILIA.**

If she be false, oh, then heaven mocks itself!
I'll not believe't.

DESDEMONA How now, my dear Othello?
Your dinner, and the generous° islanders
By you invited do attend° your presence.

OTHELLO I am to blame.

DESDEMONA Why do you speak so faintly?
Are you not well?

OTHELLO I have a pain upon my forehead here.

DESDEMONA Faith, that's with watching.° 'Twill away again. [*She offers her handkerchief.*]
Let me but bind it hard, within this hour
It will be well.

OTHELLO Your napkin° is too little:
Let it alone.° Come, I'll go in with you.
[*He puts the handkerchief from him, and it drops.*]

---

251. in position: in making this argument or proposition. **253. recoiling:** reverting. **better:** i.e., more natural and reconsidered. **254. fall . . . forms:** undertake to compare you with Venetian norms of handsomeness. **255. happily repent:** haply repent her marriage. **262. scan:** scrutinize. **266. his means:** the method he uses (to regain his post). **267. strain his entertainment:** urge his reinstatement. **270. busy:** officious. **272. hold her free:** regard her as innocent. **273. government:** self-control, conduct. **276. qualities:** natures, types. **277. haggard:** wild (like a wild female hawk). **278. jesses:** straps fastened around the legs of a trained hawk. **279. I'd . . . wind:** i.e., I'd let her go forever. (To release a hawk downwind was to turn it loose.)

280. prey at fortune: fend for herself in the wild. **Haply, for:** perhaps because. **281. soft . . . conversation:** pleasing social graces. **282. chamberers:** drawing-room gallants. **284. abused:** deceived. **291. Prerogatived:** privileged (to have honest wives). **the base:** ordinary citizens. (Socially prominent men are especially prone to the common destiny of being cuckolded and to the public shame that goes with it.) **293. forkèd:** (An allusion to the horns of the cuckold.) **294. quicken:** receive life. (*Quicken* may also mean to swarm with maggots as the body festers, as in 4.2.69, in which case lines 293–294 suggest that *even then,* in death, we are cuckolded by *forkèd* worms.) **297. generous:** noble. **298. attend:** await. **302. watching:** too little sleep. **304. napkin:** handkerchief. **305. Let it alone:** i.e., never mind.

DESDEMONA I am very sorry that you are not well. *Exit [with* **OTHELLO***].*

EMILIA *[picking up the handkerchief]:*
I am glad I have found this napkin.
This was her first remembrance from the Moor.
My wayward° husband hath a hundred times
Wooed me to steal it, but she so loves the token —
For he conjured her she should ever keep it —
That she reserves it evermore about her
To kiss and talk to. I'll have the work ta'en out,°
And give't Iago. What he will do with it
Heaven knows, not I;
I nothing but to please his fantasy.°

Enter **IAGO.**

IAGO How now? What do you here alone?

EMILIA Do not you chide. I have a thing for you.

IAGO You have a thing for me? It is a common thing° —

EMILIA Ha?

IAGO To have a foolish wife.

EMILIA Oh, is that all? What will you give me now
For that same handkerchief?

IAGO What handkerchief?

EMILIA What handkerchief?
Why, that the Moor first gave to Desdemona;
That which so often you did bid me steal.

IAGO Hath stolen it from her?

EMILIA No, faith. She let it drop by negligence,
And to th'advantage° I, being there, took't up.
Look, here 'tis.

IAGO A good wench! Give it me.

EMILIA What will you do with't, that you have been so earnest
To have me filch it?

IAGO *[snatching it]:* Why, what is that to you?

EMILIA If it be not for some purpose of import,
Give't me again. Poor lady, she'll run mad
When she shall lack° it.

IAGO Be not acknown on't.°
I have use for it. Go, leave me. *Exit* **EMILIA.**
I will in Cassio's lodging lose° this napkin
And let him find it. Trifles light as air
Are to the jealous confirmations strong
As proofs of Holy Writ. This may do something.
The Moor already changes with my poison.
Dangerous conceits° are in their natures poisons,

Carol Pratt

In this photo Iago, played by Trey Lyford in a 2002 production of *Othello*, is preparing to plant Desdemona's mislaid handkerchief on Cassio. **What aspects of the actor's facial expression and body language indicate his villainous intent?**

309. wayward: capricious. **313. work ta'en out:** design of the embroidery copied. **316. fantasy:** whim. **319. common thing:** (With bawdy suggestion; *common* suggests coarseness and availability to all comers, and *thing* is a slang term for the pudendum.) **330. to th'advantage:** taking the opportunity.

336. lack: miss. **Be . . . on't:** do not confess knowledge of it, keep out of this. **338. lose:** (The Folio spelling, "loose," is a normal spelling for "lose," but it may also contain the idea of "let go," "release.") **343. conceits:** fancies, ideas.

Which at the first are scarce found to distaste,°
But with a little act° upon the blood
Burn like the mines of sulphur.

Enter **OTHELLO**.

I did say so.
Look where he comes! Not poppy nor mandragora°
Nor all the drowsy syrups of the world,
Shall ever medicine thee to that sweet sleep
Which thou owed'st° yesterday.

OTHELLO Ha, ha, false to me?

IAGO Why, how now, General? No more of that.

OTHELLO Avaunt! Begone! Thou hast set me on the rack.
I swear 'tis better to be much abused
Than but to know't a little.

IAGO How now, my lord?

OTHELLO What sense had I of her stolen hours of lust?
I saw't not, thought it not, it harmed not me.
I slept the next night well, fed well, was free° and merry;
I found not Cassio's kisses on her lips.
He that is robbed, not wanting° what is stolen,
Let him not know't and he's not robbed at all.

IAGO I am sorry to hear this.

OTHELLO I had been happy if the general camp,
Pioneers° and all, had tasted her sweet body,
So° I had nothing known. Oh, now, forever
Farewell the tranquil mind! Farewell content!
Farewell the plumèd troops and the big° wars
That makes ambition virtue! Oh, farewell!
Farewell the neighing steed and the shrill trump,
The spirit-stirring drum, th'ear-piercing fife,
The royal banner, and all quality,°
Pride,° pomp, and circumstance° of glorious war!
And, O you mortal engines,° whose rude throats
Th'immortal Jove's dread clamors° counterfeit,
Farewell! Othello's occupation's gone.

IAGO Is't possible, my lord?

OTHELLO Villain, be sure thou prove my love a whore!
Be sure of it. Give me the ocular proof,
Or, by the worth of mine eternal soul,
Thou hadst been better have been born a dog
Than answer my waked wrath.

IAGO Is 't come to this?

OTHELLO Make me to see't; or at the least, so prove it
That the probation° bear no hinge nor loop
To hang a doubt on, or woe upon thy life!

IAGO My noble lord—

OTHELLO If thou dost slander her and torture me,
Never pray more; abandon all remorse;°
On horror's head horrors accumulate;°
Do deeds to make heaven weep, all earth amazed;°
For nothing canst thou to damnation add
Greater than that.

IAGO O grace! O heaven forgive me!
Are you a man? Have you a soul or sense?
God b'wi'you; take mine office. O wretched fool!°
That lov'st to make thine honesty a vice!°
O monstrous world! Take note, take note, O world,
To be direct and honest is not safe.
I thank you for this profit,° and from hence°

---

344. distaste: be distasteful. **345. act:** action, working. **347. mandragora:** an opiate made of the mandrake root. **350. thou owed'st:** you did own. **357. free:** carefree. **359. wanting:** missing. **363. Pioneers:** diggers of mines, the lowest grade of soldiers. **364. So:** provided. **366. big:** mighty. **370. quality:** character, essential nature.

371. Pride: rich display. **circumstance:** pageantry. **372. mortal engines:** i.e., cannon. (*Mortal* means "deadly.") **373. Jove's dread clamors:** i.e., thunder. **382. probation:** proof. **386. remorse:** pity, penitent hope for salvation. **387. horrors accumulate:** add still more horrors. **388. amazed:** confounded with horror. **392. O wretched fool:** (Iago addresses himself as a fool for having carried honesty too far.) **393. vice:** failing, something overdone. **396. profit:** profitable instruction. **hence:** henceforth.

I'll love no friend, sith° love breeds such offence.°

OTHELLO Nay, stay. Thou shouldst be° honest.

IAGO I should be wise, for honesty's a fool
And loses that° it works for.

OTHELLO By the world,
I think my wife be honest and think she is not;
I think that thou art just and think thou art not.
I'll have some proof. Her name, that was as fresh
As Dian's° visage, is now begrimed and black
As mine own face. If there be cords, or knives,
Poison, or fire, or suffocating streams,
I'll not endure it. Would I were satisfied!

IAGO I see, sir, you are eaten up with passion.
I do repent me that I put it to you.
You would be satisfied?

OTHELLO Would? Nay, and I will.

IAGO And may; but how? How satisfied, my lord?
Would you, the supervisor,° grossly gape on?
Behold her topped?

OTHELLO Death and damnation! Oh!

IAGO It were a tedious difficulty, I think,
To bring them to that prospect. Damn them then,°
If ever mortal eyes do see them bolster°
More° than their own.° What then? How then?
What shall I say? Where's satisfaction?
It is impossible you should see this,
Were they as prime° as goats, as hot as monkeys,
As salt° as wolves in pride,° and fools as gross
As ignorance made drunk. But yet I say,
If imputation and strong circumstances°
Which lead directly to the door of truth
Will give you satisfaction, you may have't.

OTHELLO Give me a living reason she's disloyal.

IAGO I do not like the office.
But, sith I am entered in this cause so far,
Pricked° to't by foolish honesty and love,
I will go on. I lay with Cassio lately,
And being troubled with a raging tooth
I could not sleep. There are a kind of men
So loose of soul that in their sleeps will mutter
Their affairs. One of this kind is Cassio.
In sleep I heard him say, "Sweet Desdemona,
Let us be wary, let us hide our loves!"
And then, sir, would he grip and wring my hand,
Cry, "O sweet creature!," and then kiss me hard,
As if he plucked up kisses by the roots
That grew upon my lips; then laid his leg
Over my thigh, and sighed, and kissed, and then
Cried, "Cursèd fate that gave thee to the Moor!"

OTHELLO Oh, monstrous! Monstrous!

IAGO Nay, this was but his dream.

OTHELLO But this denoted a foregone conclusion.°
'Tis a shrewd doubt,° though it be but a dream.

IAGO And this may help to thicken other proofs
That do demonstrate thinly.

OTHELLO I'll tear her all to pieces.

IAGO Nay, but be wise. Yet we see nothing done;
She may be honest yet. Tell me but this:
Have you not sometimes seen a handkerchief
Spotted with strawberries° in your wife's hand?

OTHELLO I gave her such a one. 'Twas my first gift.

---

397. sith: since. **offense:** i.e., harm to the one who offers help and friendship. **398. Thou shouldst be:** it appears that you are. (But Iago replies in the sense of "ought to be.") **400. that:** what. **404. Dian:** Diana, goddess of the moon and of chastity. **412. supervisor:** onlooker. **415. Damn them then:** i.e., they would have to be really incorrigible. **416. bolster:** go to bed together, share a bolster. **417. More:** other. **own:** own eyes. **420. prime:** lustful. **421. salt:** wanton, sensual. **pride:** heat.

423. imputation . . . circumstances: strong circumstantial evidence. **429. Pricked:** spurred. **444. foregone conclusion:** previous experience or action. **445. shrewd doubt:** suspicious circumstance. **451. Spotted with strawberries:** embroidered with a strawberry pattern.

In this photo, taken from a 2007 production of the play, both Othello and Iago kneel at the end of act III, scene iii. **Why do you think the director chose to have the characters join hands, despite the fact that there is no such stage direction? What effect might this choice have on the audience, and what does the pose suggest about the director's interpretation of the relationship between the two men?**

IAGO I know not that; but such a handkerchief—
I am sure it was your wife's—did I today
See Cassio wipe his beard with.
OTHELLO If it be that—
IAGO If it be that, or any that was hers,
It speaks against her with the other proofs.
OTHELLO Oh, that the slave° had forty thousand lives!
One is too poor, too weak for my revenge.
Now do I see 'tis true. Look here, Iago,
All my fond° love thus do I blow to heaven.
'Tis gone.
Arise, black vengeance, from the hollow hell!
Yield up, O love, thy crown and hearted° throne
To tyrannous hate! Swell, bosom, with thy freight,°
For 'tis of aspics'° tongues!
IAGO Yet be content.°
OTHELLO O! blood, blood, blood!
IAGO Patience, I say. Your mind perhaps may change.
OTHELLO Never, Iago. Like to the Pontic Sea,°
Whose icy current and compulsive course
Ne'er feels retiring ebb, but keeps due on
To the Propontic° and the Hellespont,°
Even so my bloody thoughts with violent pace
Shall ne'er look back, ne'er ebb to humble love,
Till that a capable° and wide revenge
Swallow them up. Now, by yond marble° heaven,
[*Kneeling*] In the due reverence of a sacred vow
I here engage my words.
IAGO Do not rise yet.
[*He kneels.*]° Witness, you ever-burning lights above,
You elements that clip° us round about,
Witness that here Iago doth give up
The execution° of his wit,° hands, heart,

458. the slave: i.e., Cassio. **461. fond:** foolish. (But also suggesting "affectionate.") **464. hearted:** fixed in the heart. **465. freight:** burden. **466. aspics':** venomous serpents'. **467. content:** calm.

470. Pontic Sea: Black Sea. **473. Propontic:** Sea of Marmora, between the Black Sea and the Aegean. **Hellespont:** Dardanelles, straits where the Sea of Marmora joins with the Aegean. **476. capable:** ample, comprehensive. **477. marble:** i.e., gleaming, polished, and indifferent to human suffering. **480. s.d.** *He kneels:* (In the Quarto text, Iago kneels here after Othello has knelt at line 478.) **481. clip:** encompass. **483. execution:** exercise, action. **wit:** mind.

To wrongèd Othello's service. Let him command,
And to obey shall be in me remorse,°
What bloody business ever.° [*They rise.*]

OTHELLO I greet thy love,
Not with vain thanks, but with acceptance bounteous,
And will upon the instant put thee to't.°
Within these three days let me hear thee say
That Cassio's not alive.

IAGO My friend is dead;
'Tis done at your request. But let her live.

OTHELLO Damn her, lewd minx!° Oh, damn her, damn her!
Come, go with me apart. I will withdraw.
To furnish me with some swift means of death
For the fair devil. Now art thou my lieutenant.

IAGO I am your own forever. *Exeunt.*

Scene iv°

Enter **DESDEMONA,** *EMILIA, and* **CLOWN.**

DESDEMONA Do you know, sirrah,° where Lieutenant Cassio lies?°

CLOWN I dare not say he lies anywhere.

DESDEMONA Why, man?

CLOWN He is a soldier, and for me to say a soldier lies, t'is stabbing.

DESDEMONA Go to. Where lodges he?

CLOWN To tell you where he lodges is to tell you where I lie.

DESDEMONA Can anything be made of this?

CLOWN I know not where he lodges, and for me to devise a lodging and say he lies here, or he lies there, were to lie in mine own throat.°

DESDEMONA Can you inquire him out, and be edified by report?

CLOWN I will catechize the world for him; that is, make questions, and by them answer.

DESDEMONA Seek him, bid him come hither. Tell him I have moved my lord° on his behalf, and hope all will be well.

CLOWN To do this is within the compass of man's wit, and therefore I will attempt the doing it. *Exit* **CLOWN.**

DESDEMONA Where should I lose that handkerchief, Emilia?

EMILIA I know not, madam.

DESDEMONA Believe me, I had rather have lost my purse
Full of crusadoes;° and but my noble Moor
Is true of mind and made of no such baseness
As jealous creatures are, it were enough
To put him to ill thinking.

EMILIA Is he not jealous?

DESDEMONA Who, he? I think the sun where he was born
Drew all such humors° from him.

EMILIA Look where he comes.

Enter **OTHELLO.**

DESDEMONA I will not leave him now till Cassio
Be called to him. — How is't with you, my lord?

OTHELLO Well, my good lady. [*Aside.*] Oh, hardness to dissemble! —
How do you, Desdemona?

DESDEMONA Well, my good lord.

OTHELLO Give me your hand. [*She gives her hand.*] This hand is moist, my lady.

DESDEMONA It yet hath felt no age nor known no sorrow.

OTHELLO This argues° fruitfulness° and liberal° heart;

---

485. remorse: pity (for Othello's wrongs). **486. ever:** soever. **488. to't:** to the proof. **492. minx:** wanton. **Act III, Scene iv.** **Location:** Before the citadel. **1. sirrah:** (A form of address to an inferior.) **lies:** lodges. (But the Clown makes the obvious pun.) **13–14. lie . . . throat:** lie egregiously and deliberately.

20. moved my lord: petitioned Othello. **29. crusadoes:** Portuguese gold coins. **34. humors:** (Refers to the four bodily fluids thought to determine temperament.) **42. argues:** gives evidence of. **fruitfulness:** generosity, amorousness, and fecundity. **liberal:** generous and sexually free.

Hot, hot, and moist. This hand of yours requires
A sequester° from liberty, fasting and prayer,
Much castigation,° exercise devout;°
For here's a young and sweating devil here
That commonly rebels. 'Tis a good hand,
A frank° one.

DESDEMONA You may indeed say so,
For 'twas that hand that gave away my heart.

OTHELLO A liberal hand. The hearts of old gave hands,
But our new heraldry is hands,° not hearts.

DESDEMONA I cannot speak of this. Come now, your promise.

OTHELLO What promise, chuck?°

DESDEMONA I have sent to bid Cassio come speak with you.

OTHELLO I have a salt and sorry rheum° offends me;
Lend me thy handkerchief.

DESDEMONA Here, my lord.
[*She offers a handkerchief.*]

OTHELLO That which I gave you.

DESDEMONA I have it not about me.

OTHELLO Not?

DESDEMONA No, faith, my lord.

OTHELLO That's a fault. That handkerchief
Did an Egyptian to my mother give.
She was a charmer,° and could almost read
The thoughts of people. She told her, while she kept it
'Twould make her amiable° and subdue my father
Entirely to her love, but if she lost it
Or made a gift of it, my father's eye
Should hold her loathèd, and his spirits should hunt
After new fancies.° She, dying, gave it me,
And bid me, when my fate would have me wived,
To give it her.° I did so; and take heed on't;
Make it a darling like your precious eye.
To lose't or give't away, were such perdition°
As nothing else could match.

DESDEMONA Is 't possible?

OTHELLO 'Tis true; there 's magic in the web° of it.
A sibyl, that had numbered in the world
The sun to course two hundred compasses,°
In her prophetic fury° sewed the work;°
The worms were hallowed that did breed the silk,
And it was dy'd in mummy° which the skillful
Conserved of° maidens' hearts.

DESDEMONA I'faith! Is't true?

OTHELLO Most veritable. Therefore look to't well.

DESDEMONA Then would to God that I had never seen't!

OTHELLO Ha? Wherefore?

DESDEMONA Why do you speak so startingly and rash?°

OTHELLO Is't lost? Is't gone? Speak, is't out o'th' way?°

DESDEMONA Heaven bless us!

OTHELLO Say you?

DESDEMONA It is not lost; but what an if° it were?

OTHELLO How?

DESDEMONA I say, it is not lost.

OTHELLO Fetch 't, let me see 't!

---

44. sequester: sequestration. **45. castigation:** corrective discipline. **exercise devout:** i.e., prayer, religious meditation, etc. **48. frank:** generous, open. (With sexual suggestion.) **50–51. The hearts . . . hands:** i.e., in former times, people would give their hearts when they gave their hands to something, but in our decadent present age the joining of hands no longer has that spiritual sense. **53. chuck:** (A term of endearment.) **55. salt . . . rheum:** distressful head cold or watering of the eyes. **63. charmer:** sorceress. **65. amiable:** desirable.

69. fancies: loves. **71. her:** i.e., to my wife. **73. perdition:** loss; ruin. [Hall] **75. web:** fabric, weaving. **77. compasses:** annual circlings. (The *sibyl,* or prophetess, was two hundred years old.) **78. prophetic fury:** frenzy of prophetic inspiration. **work:** embroidered pattern. **80. mummy:** medicinal or magical preparation drained from mummified bodies. **81. Conserved of:** prepared or preserved out of. **85. startingly and rash:** disjointedly and impetuously, excitedly. **86. out o'th' way:** lost, misplaced. **89. an if:** if.

DESDEMONA Why, so I can, sir, but I will not now.
This is a trick to put me from my suit.
Pray you, let Cassio be received again.

OTHELLO Fetch me the handkerchief. My mind misgives.

DESDEMONA Come, come,
You'll never meet a more sufficient° man.

OTHELLO The handkerchief!

DESDEMONA I pray, talk° me of Cassio.

OTHELLO The handkerchief!

DESDEMONA A man that all his time
Hath founded his good fortunes on your love,°
Shared dangers with you —

OTHELLO The handkerchief!

DESDEMONA I'faith, you are to blame.

OTHELLO Zounds! *Exit* OTHELLO.

EMILIA Is not this man jealous?

DESDEMONA I ne'er saw this before.
Sure, there's some wonder in this handkerchief.
I am most unhappy° in the loss of it.

EMILIA 'Tis not a year or two shows us a man.°
They are all but° stomachs, and we all but food;
They eat us hungerly,° and when they are full
They belch us.

Enter IAGO *and* CASSIO.

Look you, Cassio and my husband.

IAGO [*to* CASSIO] There is no other way; 'tis she must do't.
And, lo, the happiness!° Go and importune her.

DESDEMONA How now, good Cassio! What's the news with you?

CASSIO Madam, my former suit. I do beseech you
That by your virtuous° means I may again
Exist and be a member of his love
Whom I, with all the office° of my heart,
Entirely honor. I would not be delayed.
If my offense be of such mortal° kind
That nor my service past, nor° present sorrows,
Nor purposed merit in futurity
Can ransom me into his love again,
But to know so must be my benefit;°
So shall I clothe me in a forced content,
And shut myself up in° some other course,
To fortune's alms.°

DESDEMONA Alas! thrice-gentle Cassio,
My advocation° is not now in tune.
My lord is not my lord; nor should I know him,
Were he in favor° as in humor° altered.
So help me every spirit sanctified°
As I have spoken for you all my best
And stood within the blank° of his displeasure
For my free° speech! You must awhile be patient.
What I can do I will, and more I will
Than for myself I dare. Let that suffice you.

IAGO Is my lord angry?

EMILIA He went hence but now,
And certainly in strange unquietness.

IAGO Can he be angry? I have seen the cannon
When it hath blown his ranks into the air,
And like the devil from his very arm
Puffed his own brother — and is he angry?

---

97. sufficient: able, complete. **98. talk:** talk to. **99–100. A man . . . love:** A man who throughout his career has relied on your favor for his advancement. **108. unhappy:** (1) unfortunate (2) sad. **109. 'Tis . . . man:** A year or two is not enough time for us women to know what men really are. **110. but:** nothing but. **111. hungerly:** hungrily. **114. the happiness:** in happy time, fortunately met.

117. virtuous: (1) efficacious (2) morally good. **119. office:** loyal service. **121. mortal:** fatal. **122. nor . . . nor:** neither . . . nor. **125. But . . . benefit:** merely to know that my case is hopeless will have to content me (and will be better than uncertainty). **127. And shut . . . in:** commit myself to. **128. To fortune's alms:** throwing myself on the mercy of fortune. **129. advocation:** advocacy. **131. favor:** appearance. **humor:** mood. **132. So . . . sanctified:** so help me all the heavenly host. **134. within the blank:** within point-blank range. (The *blank* is the center of the target.) **135. free:** frank.

Something of moment° then. I will go meet him;
There's matter in't indeed, if he be angry.

DESDEMONA I prithee, do so. *Exit* [**IAGO**].
Something, sure, of state,°
Either from Venice, or some unhatched practice°
Made demonstrable here in Cyprus to him,
Hath puddled° his clear spirit; and in such cases
Men's natures wrangle with inferior things,
Though great ones are their object. 'Tis even so;
For let our finger ache, and it indues°
Our other, healthful members even to a sense
Of pain. Nay, we must think men are not gods,
Nor of them look for such observancy°
As fits the bridal.° Beshrew me° much, Emilia,
I was, unhandsome° warrior as I am,
Arraigning his unkindness with° my soul;
But now I find I had suborned the witness,°
And he's indicted falsely.

EMILIA Pray heaven it be
State matters, as you think, and no conception
Nor no jealous toy° concerning you.

DESDEMONA Alas the day! I never gave him cause.

EMILIA But jealous souls will not be answered so;
They are not ever jealous for the cause,
But jealous for° they're jealous. It is a monster
Begot upon itself,° born on itself.

DESDEMONA Heaven keep that monster from Othello's mind!

EMILIA Lady, amen.

DESDEMONA I will go seek him. Cassio, walk hereabout.
If I do find him fit, I'll move your suit
And seek to effect it to my uttermost.

CASSIO I humbly thank Your Ladyship.
Exit [**DESDEMONA** *with* **EMILIA**].

Enter **BIANCA**.

BIANCA Save° you, friend Cassio!

CASSIO What make° you from home?
How is't with you, my most fair Bianca?
I' faith, sweet love, I was coming to your house.

BIANCA And I was going to your lodging, Cassio.
What, keep a week away? Seven days and nights?
Eightscore-eight° hours? And lovers' absent hours
More tedious than the dial° eightscore times?
Oh, weary reck'ning!

CASSIO Pardon me, Bianca.
I have this while with leaden thoughts been pressed;
But I shall, in a more continuate° time,
Strike off this score° of absence. Sweet Bianca,
[*giving her Desdemona's handkerchief*]
Take me this work out.°

BIANCA Oh, Cassio, whence came this?
This is some token from a newer friend.°
To the felt absence now I feel a cause.
Is't come to this? Well, well.

CASSIO Go to, woman!
Throw your vile guesses in the devil's teeth,

---

144. of moment: of immediate importance, momentous. **146. of state:** concerning state affairs. **147. unhatched practice:** as yet unexecuted or undiscovered plot. **149. puddled:** muddied. **152. indues:** endows, brings to the same condition. **155. observancy:** attentiveness. **156. bridal:** wedding (when a bridegroom is newly attentive to his bride). **Beshrew me:** (A mild oath.) **157. unhandsome:** insufficient, unskillful. **158. with:** before the bar of. **159. suborned the witness:** induced the witness to give false testimony. **162. toy:** fancy. **166. for:** because. **167. Begot upon itself:** generated solely from itself.

174. Save: God save. **make:** do. **179. Eightscore-eight:** one hundred sixty-eight, the number of hours in a week. **180. the dial:** a complete revolution of the clock. **183. continuate:** uninterrupted. **184. Strike . . . score:** settle this account. **185. Take . . . out:** copy this embroidery for me. **186. friend:** mistress.

From whence you have them. You are jealous
now
That this is from some mistress, some
remembrance.
No, by my faith, Bianca.
BIANCA Why, whose is it?
CASSIO I know not, neither. I found it in my
chamber.
I like the work well. Ere it be demanded° —
As like° enough it will — I would have it copied.
Take it and do't, and leave me for this time.
BIANCA Leave you? Wherefore?
CASSIO I do attend here on the General,
And think it no addition,° nor my wish,
To have him see me womaned.
BIANCA Why, I pray you?
CASSIO Not that I love you not.
BIANCA But that you do not love me.
I pray you, bring° me on the way a little,
And say if I shall see you soon at night.
CASSIO 'Tis but a little way that I can bring you,
For I attend here; but I'll see you soon.
BIANCA 'Tis very good. I must be circum-
stanced.° *Exeunt omnes.*

ACT IV

Scene i°

Enter **OTHELLO** *and* **IAGO**.

IAGO Will you think so?
OTHELLO Think so, Iago?
IAGO What,
To kiss in private?
OTHELLO An unauthorized kiss!
IAGO Or to be naked with her friend in bed
An hour or more, not meaning any harm?
OTHELLO Naked in bed, Iago, and not mean
harm?
It is hypocrisy against the devil.
They that mean virtuously and yet do so,
The devil their virtue tempts, and they tempt
heaven.
IAGO If they do nothing, 'tis a venial° slip.
But if I give my wife a handkerchief—
OTHELLO What then?
IAGO Why then, 'tis hers, my lord, and being
hers,
She may, I think, bestow't on any man.
OTHELLO She is protectress of her honor too.
May she give that?
IAGO Her honor is an essence that's not seen;
They have it° very oft that have it not.
But, for the handkerchief—
OTHELLO By heaven, I would most gladly have
forgot it.
Thou said'st — Oh, it comes o'er my
memory
As doth the raven o'er the infectious house,°
Boding to all — he had my handkerchief.
IAGO Ay, what of that?
OTHELLO That's not so good now.
IAGO What,
If I had said I had seen him do you wrong?
Or heard him say — as knaves be such
abroad,
Who having, by their own importunate suit,
Or voluntary dotage of some mistress,
Convincèd or supplied them, cannot choose
But they must blab° —
OTHELLO Hath he said anything?
IAGO He hath, my lord; but, be you well
assured,
No more than he'll unswear.
OTHELLO What hath he
said?
IAGO Faith, that he did — I know not what he did.
OTHELLO What? What?
IAGO Lie —

194. demanded: inquired for. **195. like:** likely. **199. addition:** i.e., addition to my reputation. **204. bring:** accompany. **208. be circumstanced:** be governed by circumstance, yield to your conditions. **Act IV, Scene i. Location:** Before the citadel.

9. venial: pardonable. **17. They have it:** i.e., they enjoy a reputation for it. **21. raven . . . house:** (Allusion to the belief that the raven hovered over a house of sickness or infection, such as one visited by the plague.) **25–29. as . . . blab:** since there are rascals enough who, having seduced a woman either through their own importunity or through the woman's willing infatuation, cannot keep quiet about it.

OTHELLO With her?

IAGO With her, on her; what you will.

OTHELLO Lie with her? Lie on her? We say "lie on her" when they belie° her. Lie with her? Zounds, that's fulsome.°—Handkerchief—confessions—handkerchief! To confess and be hanged for his labor—first to be hanged and then to confess.°—I tremble at it. Nature would not invest herself in such shadowing passion without some instruction.° It is not words° that shakes me thus. Pish! Noses, ears, and lips.—Is't possible?—Confess—handkerchief!—O devil!

Falls in a trance.

IAGO Work on,
My medicine, work! Thus credulous fools are caught,
And many worthy and chaste dames even thus,
All guiltless, meet reproach.—What, ho! My lord!
My lord, I say! Othello!

Enter **CASSIO.**

How now, Cassio!

CASSIO What's the matter?

IAGO My lord is fall'n into an epilepsy.
This is his second fit. He had one yesterday.

CASSIO Rub him about the temples.

IAGO No, forbear.
The lethargy° must have his° quiet course.
If not, he foams at mouth, and by and by
Breaks out to savage madness. Look, he stirs.
Do you withdraw yourself a little while.
He will recover straight. When he is gone,
I would on great occasion° speak with you.

[*Exit* **CASSIO.**]

How is it, General? have you not hurt your head?

OTHELLO Dost thou mock me?°

IAGO I mock you not, by heaven.
Would you would bear your fortune like a man!

OTHELLO A hornèd man's a monster and a beast.

IAGO There's many a beast then in a populous city,
And many a civil° monster.

OTHELLO Did he confess it?

IAGO Good sir, be a man.
Think every bearded fellow that's but yoked°
May draw with you.° There's millions now alive
That nightly lie in those unproper° beds
Which they dare swear peculiar.° Your case is better.°
Oh, 'tis the spite of hell, the fiend's arch-mock,
To lip° a wanton in a secure° couch
And to suppose her chaste! No, let me know,
And knowing what I am, I know what she shall be.°

OTHELLO Oh, thou art wise. 'Tis certain.

IAGO Stand you awhile apart;
Confine yourself but in a patient list.°
Whilst you were here o'erwhelmed with your grief—
A passion most unsuiting such a man—

---

36. belie: slander. **37. fulsome:** foul. **40–41. first . . . to confess:** (Othello reverses the proverbial *confess and be hanged;* Cassio is to be given no time to confess before he dies.) **41–43. Nature . . . instruction:** i.e., without some foundation in fact, nature would not have dressed herself in such an overwhelming passion that comes over me now and fills my mind with images, or in such a lifelike fantasy as Cassio had in his dream of lying with Desdemona. **44. words:** mere words. **55. lethargy:** coma. **his:** its.

60. on great occasion: on a matter of great importance. **62. mock me:** (Othello takes Iago's question about hurting his head to be a mocking reference to the cuckold's horns.) **66. civil:** i.e., dwelling in a city. **69. yoked:** (1) married (2) put into the yoke of infamy and cuckoldry. **70. draw with you:** pull as you do, like oxen who are yoked, i.e., share your fate as cuckold. **71. unproper:** not exclusively their own. **72. peculiar:** private, their own. **better:** i.e., because you know the truth. **74. lip:** kiss. **secure:** free from suspicion. **76. And . . . shall be:** and, knowing myself to be a cuckold, I'll know for certain that she's a whore. **79. in . . . list:** within the bounds of patience.

Cassio came hither. I shifted him away,
And laid good 'scuse upon your ecstasy,°
Bade him anon return and here speak with me,
The which he promised. Do but encave°
yourself
And mark the fleers,° the gibes, and notable
scorns
That dwell in every region of his face;
For I will make him tell the tale anew,
Where, how, how oft, how long ago, and when
He hath and is again to cope° your wife.
I say, but mark his gesture. Marry, patience!
Or I shall say you're all-in-all in spleen,°
And nothing of a man.

OTHELLO Dost thou hear, Iago?
I will be found most cunning in my patience;
But — dost thou hear? — most bloody.

IAGO That's
not amiss;
But yet keep time° in all. Will you withdraw?
[*Othello stands apart.*]
Now will I question Cassio of Bianca,
A huswife° that by selling her desires
Buys herself bread and clothes. It is a creature
That dotes on Cassio — as 'tis the strumpet's
plague
To beguile many and be beguiled by one.
He, when he hears of her, cannot restrain°
From the excess of laughter. Here he comes.

Enter **CASSIO.**

As he shall smile, Othello shall go mad;
And his unbookish° jealousy must conster°
Poor Cassio's smiles, gestures, and light
behaviors
Quite in the wrong. — How do you now,
Lieutenant?

CASSIO The worser that you give me the
addition°
Whose want° even kills me.

IAGO Ply Desdemona well and you are sure on't.
[*Speaking lower*] Now, if this suit lay in
Bianca's power,
How quickly should you speed!

CASSIO [*laughing*]: Alas! poor caitiff!°

OTHELLO [*aside*]: Look how he laughs already!

IAGO I never knew woman love man so.

CASSIO Alas, poor rogue! I think i'faith, she
loves me.

OTHELLO [*aside*]: Now he denies it faintly, and
laughs it out.

IAGO Do you hear, Cassio?

OTHELLO Now he importunes him
To tell it o'er. Go to!° Well said,° well said.

IAGO She gives it out that you shall marry her.
Do you intend it?

CASSIO Ha, ha, ha!

OTHELLO [*aside*]: Do you triumph, Roman?° Do
you triumph?

CASSIO I marry her? What? A customer?°
Prithee, bear some charity to my wit;° do
not think it so unwholesome. Ha, ha, ha!

OTHELLO [*aside*]: So, so, so, so! They laugh that
win.°

IAGO Faith, the cry° goes that you shall marry
her.

CASSIO Prithee, say true.

IAGO I am a very villain else.°

OTHELLO [*aside*]: Have you scored me?° Well.

CASSIO This is the monkey's own giving out. She
is persuaded I will marry her out of her own
love and flattery,° not out of my promise.

82–83. I shifted . . . ecstasy: I got him out of the way, using your fit as my excuse for doing so. **85. encave:** conceal. **86. fleers:** sneers. **90. cope:** encounter with, have sex with. **92. all-in-all in spleen:** utterly governed by passionate impulses. **96. keep time:** keep yourself steady (as in music). **98. huswife:** hussy. **102. restrain:** refrain. **105. his unbookish:** Othello's uninstructed. **conster:** construe.

108. addition: title. **109. Whose want:** the lack of which. **113. caitiff:** wretch. **119. Go to:** (An expression of remonstrance.) **Well said:** well done. (Sarcastic.) **123. Roman:** (The Romans were noted for their triumphs or triumphal processions.) **124. A customer?:** who, I, the whore's customer? (Or, *customer* could mean "prostitute."). **125. bear . . . wit:** be more charitable to my judgment. **127. They . . . win:** i.e., they that laugh last laugh best. **128. cry:** rumor. **130. I . . . else:** call me a complete rogue if I'm not telling the truth. **131. scored me:** scored off me, beaten me, made up my reckoning, branded me. **134. flattery:** self-flattery, self-deception.

OTHELLO [*aside*]: Iago beckons° me. Now he begins the story.

CASSIO She was here even now; she haunts me in every place. I was the other day talking on the seabank° with certain Venetians, and thither comes the bauble,° and, by this hand,° she falls me thus about my neck— [*He embraces Iago.*]

OTHELLO [*aside*]: Crying, "Oh, dear Cassio!" as it were; his gesture imports it.

CASSIO So hangs and lolls and weeps upon me, so shakes and pulls me. Ha, ha, ha!

OTHELLO [*aside*]: Now he tells how she plucked him to my chamber. Oh, I see that nose of yours, but not that dog I shall throw it to.°

CASSIO Well, I must leave her company.

IAGO Before me,° look where she comes.

Enter **BIANCA** [*with* **OTHELLO'S** *handkerchief*].

CASSIO 'Tis such another fitchew!° Marry, a perfumed one.—What do you mean by this haunting of me?

BIANCA Let the devil and his dam° haunt you! What did you mean by that same handkerchief you gave me even now? I was a fine fool to take it. I must take out the work? A likely piece of work,° that you should find it in your chamber and know not who left it there! This is some minx's token, and I must take out the work? There; give it your hobbyhorse.° [*She gives him the handkerchief.*] Wheresoever you had it, I'll take out no work on't.

CASSIO How now, my sweet Bianca? How now? How now?

OTHELLO [*aside*]: By heaven, that should be° my handkerchief!

BIANCA If you'll come to supper tonight, you may; if you will not, come when you are next prepared for.° *Exit.*

IAGO After her, after her.

CASSIO Faith, I must. She'll rail in the streets else.

IAGO Will you sup there?

CASSIO Faith, I intend so.

IAGO Well, I may chance to see you, for I would very fain speak with you.

CASSIO Prithee come. Will you?

IAGO Go to.° Say no more. [*Exit* **CASSIO**.]

OTHELLO [*advancing*]: How shall I murder him, Iago?

IAGO Did you perceive how he laughed at his vice?

OTHELLO Oh, Iago!

IAGO And did you see the handkerchief?

OTHELLO Was that mine?

IAGO Yours, by this hand. And to see how he prizes the foolish woman your wife! She gave it him, and he hath given it his whore.

OTHELLO I would have him nine years a-killing. A fine woman! A fair woman! A sweet woman!

IAGO Nay, you must forget that.

OTHELLO Ay, let her rot and perish, and be damned tonight, for she shall not live. No, my heart is turned to stone; I strike it, and it hurts my hand. Oh, the world hath not a sweeter creature! She might lie by an emperor's side and command him tasks.

IAGO Nay, that's not your way.°

OTHELLO Hang her! I do but say what she is. So delicate with her needle! An admirable musician! Oh, she will sing the savageness out of a bear. Of so high and plenteous wit and invention!°

IAGO She's the worse for all this.

OTHELLO Oh, a thousand, a thousand times! And then, of so gentle a condition!°

---

135. beckons: signals to. **138. seabank:** seashore. **139. bauble:** plaything **140. by this hand:** I make my vow. **147. not . . . to:** (Othello imagines himself cutting off Cassio's nose and throwing it to a dog.) **149. Before me:** i.e., on my soul. **150. 'Tis . . . fitchew!:** what a whore she is, just like all the others! (*Fitchew,* or "polecat," was a common term of contempt for a courtesan or prostitute.) **153. dam:** mother. **157. A likely . . . work:** A fine story. **161. hobbyhorse:** harlot. **166. should be:** must be.

167–168. when . . . for: when I'm ready for you (i.e., never). **175. Go to:** (An expression of remonstrance.) **194. your way:** i.e., the way you should think of her. **199. invention:** imagination. **202. gentle a condition:** wellborn and well-bred.

In this 2015 production of *Othello*, both Othello and Iago were played by black actors. **How might this casting choice affect the audience's understanding of the role race plays in the work? How might it affect a viewer's interpretation of the dynamic between the two characters?**

Royal Shakespeare Company Collection

IAGO Ay, too gentle.°

OTHELLO Nay, that's certain. But yet the pity of it, Iago! Oh, Iago, the pity of it, Iago!

IAGO If you are so fond° over her iniquity, give her patent° to offend, for if it touch not you it comes near nobody.

OTHELLO I will chop her into messes.° Cuckold me!

IAGO Oh, 'tis foul in her.

OTHELLO With mine officer?

IAGO That's fouler.

OTHELLO Get me some poison, Iago, this night.
I'll not expostulate with her, lest her body
and beauty unprovide° my mind again.
This night, Iago.

IAGO Do it not with poison. Strangle her in her bed, even the bed she hath contaminated.

OTHELLO Good, good! The justice of it pleases. Very good.

IAGO And for Cassio, let me be his undertaker.°
You shall hear more by midnight.

OTHELLO Excellent good. [*A trumpet within.*]
What trumpet is that same?

IAGO I warrant, something from Venice.

Enter **LODOVICO, DESDEMONA,** *and* **ATTENDANTS.**

'Tis Lodovico. This comes from the Duke.
See, your wife's with him.

LODOVICO God save you, worthy General!

OTHELLO With all my heart,° sir.

LODOVICO [*giving him a letter*]: The Duke and the Senators of Venice greet you.

OTHELLO I kiss the instrument of their pleasures. [*He opens the letter, and reads.*]

DESDEMONA And what's the news, good cousin Lodovico?

IAGO I am very glad to see you, signor.
Welcome to Cyprus.

LODOVICO I thank you. How does Lieutenant Cassio?

IAGO Lives, sir.

DESDEMONA Cousin, there's fall'n between him and my lord
An unkind° breach; but you shall make all well.

203. gentle: generous, yielding (to other men). **206. fond:** foolish **207. patent:** license. **209. messes:** portions of meat, i.e., bits. **215. unprovide:** weaken, disarm. **221. be his undertaker:** undertake to dispatch him.

228. With all my heart: i.e., I thank you most heartily.
238. unkind: unnatural, contrary to their natures; hurtful.

OTHELLO Are you sure of that?
DESDEMONA My lord?
OTHELLO [*reads*]: "This fail you not to do, as you will — "
LODOVICO He did not call; he's busy in the paper.
Is there division twixt my lord and Cassio?
DESDEMONA A most unhappy one. I would do much
T'atone° them, for the love I bear to Cassio.
OTHELLO Fire and brimstone!
DESDEMONA My lord?
OTHELLO Are you wise?
DESDEMONA What, is he angry?
LODOVICO Maybe the letter moved him;
For, as I think, they do command him home,
Deputing Cassio in his government.°
DESDEMONA By my troth, I am glad on't.°
OTHELLO Indeed?
DESDEMONA My lord?
OTHELLO I am glad to see you mad.°
DESDEMONA Why, sweet Othello —
OTHELLO [*striking her*]: Devil!
DESDEMONA I have not deserved this.
LODOVICO My lord, this would not be believed in Venice,
Though I should swear I saw't. 'Tis very much.°
Make her amends, she weeps.
OTHELLO Oh, devil, devil!
If that the earth could teem° with woman's tears,
Each drop she falls° would prove a crocodile.°
Out of my sight!
DESDEMONA I will not stay to offend you.
[*Going.*]
LODOVICO Truly, an obedient lady.
I do beseech Your Lordship, call her back.

245. T'atone: to reconcile. **251. government:** office. **252. on't:** of it. **255. I am . . . mad:** i.e., I am glad to see that you are insane enough to rejoice in Cassio's promotion. (? Othello bitterly plays on Desdemona's *I am glad.*) **260. very much:** too much, outrageous. **262. teem:** breed, be impregnated. **263. falls:** lets fall. **crocodile:** (Crocodiles were supposed to weep hypocritical tears for their victims.)

OTHELLO [*calling*]: Mistress!
DESDEMONA [*returning*]: My lord?
OTHELLO What would you with her, sir?°
LODOVICO Who, I, my lord?
OTHELLO Ay, you did wish that I would make her turn.
Sir, she can turn, and turn, and yet go on
And turn again; and she can weep, sir, weep;
And she's obedient, as you say, obedient,°
Very obedient. — Proceed you in your tears. —
Concerning this, sir — Oh, well-painted passion!° —
I am commanded home. — Get you away;
I'll send for you anon. — Sir, I obey the mandate,
And will return to Venice. — Hence! avaunt!
[*Exit* **DESDEMONA**.]
Cassio shall have my place. And, sir, tonight
I do entreat that we may sup together.
You are welcome, sir, to Cyprus. — Goats and monkeys!° *Exit.*
LODOVICO Is this the noble Moor whom our full Senate
Call all in all sufficient? Is this the nature
Whom passion could not shake? Whose solid virtue
The shot of accident nor dart of chance
Could neither graze nor pierce?
IAGO He is much changed.
LODOVICO Are his wits safe? Is he not light of brain?
IAGO He's that he is. I may not breathe my censure
What he might be. If what he might he is not,
I would to heaven he were!°

269. What . . . sir? (Othello implies that Desdemona is pliant and will do a *turn,* lines 271–272, for any man.) **274. obedient:** (With much the same sexual connotation as *turn* in lines 271–272.) **276. passion:** i.e., grief. **282. Goats and monkeys:** (See 3.3.420.) **289–291. I may . . . were!:** I dare not venture an opinion as to whether he's of unsound mind, as you suggest, but, if he isn't, then it might be better to wish he were in fact insane, since only that could excuse his wild behavior!

LODOVICO What! strike his wife!

IAGO Faith, that was not so well; yet would I knew
That stroke would prove the worst!

LODOVICO Is it his use?°
Or did the letters work upon his blood°
And new-create this fault?

IAGO Alas, alas!
It is not honesty in me to speak
What I have seen and known. You shall observe him,
And his own courses will denote° him so
That I may save my speech. Do but go after
And mark how he continues.

LODOVICO I am sorry that I am deceived in him. *Exeunt.*

Scene ii°

Enter OTHELLO *and* EMILIA.

OTHELLO You have seen nothing, then?

EMILIA Nor ever heard, nor ever did suspect.

OTHELLO Yes, you have seen Cassio and her together.

EMILIA But then I saw no harm, and then I heard
Each syllable that breath made up between them.

OTHELLO What, did they never whisper?

EMILIA Never, my lord.

OTHELLO Nor send you out o' th' way?

EMILIA Never.

OTHELLO To fetch her fan, her gloves, her mask, nor nothing?

EMILIA Never, my lord.

OTHELLO That's strange.

EMILIA I durst, my lord, to wager she is honest,
Lay down my soul at stake.° If you think other,
Remove your thought; it doth abuse your bosom.°
If any wretch have put this in your head,
Let heaven requite it with the serpent's curse!°
For if she be not honest, chaste, and true,
There's no man happy; the purest of their wives
Is foul as slander.

OTHELLO Bid her come hither. Go.

Exit EMILIA.

She says enough; yet she's a simple bawd
That cannot say as much.° This° is a subtle whore,
A closet lock and key° of villainous secrets.
And yet she'll kneel and pray; I have seen her do't.

Enter DESDEMONA *and* EMILIA.

DESDEMONA My lord, what is your will?

OTHELLO Pray you, chuck, come hither.

DESDEMONA What is your pleasure?

OTHELLO Let me see your eyes;
Look in my face.

DESDEMONA What horrible fancy's this?

OTHELLO [*to* EMILIA]: Some of your function,° mistress.
Leave procreants° alone and shut the door;
Cough or cry "hem" if anybody come.
Your mystery,° your mystery! Nay, dispatch.

Exit EMILIA.

DESDEMONA [*kneeling*]:
Upon my knees, what doth your speech import?
I understand a fury in your words.
But not the words.

OTHELLO Why, what art thou?

---

293. use: custom. **294. blood:** passions. **298. courses will denote:** actions will reveal. **Act IV, Scene ii. Location:** The citadel. **14. at stake:** as the wager.

15. abuse your bosom: deceive your breast, your heart. **17. the serpent's curse:** the curse pronounced by God on the serpent for deceiving Eve, just as some man has done to Othello and Desdemona. (See Genesis 3:14.) **21–22. she's . . . much:** i.e., any procuress or go-between who couldn't make up as plausible a story as Emilia's would have to be pretty stupid. **22. This:** i.e., Desdemona. **23. closet lock and key:** i.e., concealer. **29. Some . . . function:** i.e., practice your chosen profession, that of bawd (by guarding the door). **30. procreants:** mating couples. **32. mystery:** trade, occupation.

DESDEMONA Your wife, my lord, your true
And loyal wife.

OTHELLO Come, swear it, damn thyself,
Lest, being like one of heaven,° the devils themselves
Should fear to seize thee. Therefore be double damned:
Swear thou art honest.

DESDEMONA Heaven doth truly know it.

OTHELLO Heaven truly knows that thou art false as hell.

DESDEMONA To whom, my lord? With whom? How am I false?

OTHELLO [*weeping*]:
Ah! Desdemon! Away, away, away!

DESDEMONA Alas the heavy day! Why do you weep?
Am I the motive° of these tears, my lord?
If haply you my father do suspect
An instrument of this your calling back,
Lay not your blame on me. If you have lost him,
I have lost him too.

OTHELLO Had it pleased heaven
To try me with affliction, had they° rained
All kinds of sores and shames on my bare head,
Steeped me in poverty to the very lips,
Given to captivity me and my utmost hopes,
I should have found in some place of my soul
A drop of patience. But, alas, to make me
A fixèd figure for the time of scorn
To point his slow and moving finger at!°
Yet could I bear that too, well, very well.
But there where I have garnered° up my heart,
Where either I must live or bear no life,
The fountain° from the which my current runs
Or else dries up — to be discarded thence!
Or keep it as a cistern° for foul toads
To knot and gender in!° Turn thy complexion there,
Patience, thou young and rose-lipped cherubin —
Ay, there look grim as hell!°

DESDEMONA I hope my noble lord esteems me honest.°

OTHELLO Oh, ay; as summer flies are in the shambles,°
That quicken even with blowing.° O thou weed,
Who art so lovely fair and smell'st so sweet
That the sense aches at thee, would thou hadst ne'er been born!

DESDEMONA Alas, what ignorant sin° have I committed?

OTHELLO Was this fair paper, this most goodly book,
Made to write "whore" upon? What committed?
Committed? Oh, thou public commoner!°
I should make very forges of my cheeks,
That would to cinders burn up modesty,
Did I but speak thy deeds. What committed?
Heaven stops the nose at it and the moon winks;°
The bawdy° wind, that kisses all it meets
Is hushed within the hollow mine° of earth,
And will not hear't. What committed?
Impudent strumpet!

DESDEMONA By heaven, you do me wrong.

OTHELLO Are not you a strumpet?

---

38. being . . . heaven: looking like an angel. **45. motive:** cause. **50. they:** the heavenly powers. **56–57. A fixèd . . . finger at:** a figure of ridicule to be pointed at scornfully for all of eternity by the slowly moving finger of Time. **59. garnered:** stored. **61. fountain:** spring.

63. cistern: cesspool. **64. To . . . gender in:** to couple sexually and conceive in. **64–66. Turn . . . hell!:** direct your gaze there, Patience, and your youthful and rosy cherubic countenance will turn grim and pale at this hellish spectacle! **67. honest:** chaste. **68. shambles:** slaughterhouse. **69. That . . . blowing:** that come to life with the puffing up of the rotten meat on which the flies and their maggots are breeding. **72. ignorant sin:** sin in ignorance. **75. commoner:** prostitute. **79. winks:** closes her eyes. (The moon symbolizes chastity.) **80. bawdy:** kissing one and all. **81. mine:** cave (where the winds were thought to dwell).

DESDEMONA No, as I am a Christian.
If to preserve this vessel° for my lord
From any other foul unlawful touch
Be not to be a strumpet, I am none.
OTHELLO What, not a whore?
DESDEMONA No, as I shall be saved.
OTHELLO Is't possible?
DESDEMONA Oh, heaven forgive us!
OTHELLO I cry you mercy,° then.
I took you for that cunning whore of Venice
That married with Othello. [*Calling out*] You, mistress,
That have the office opposite to Saint Peter
And keep the gate of hell!

Enter **EMILIA.**

You, you, ay, you!
We have done our course.° There's money for your pains. [*He gives money.*]
I pray you, turn the key and keep our counsel.
Exit.
EMILIA Alas, what does this gentleman conceive?°
How do you, madam? How do you, my good lady?
DESDEMONA Faith, half asleep.°
EMILIA Good madam, what 's the matter with my lord?
DESDEMONA With who?
EMILIA Why, with my lord, madam.
DESDEMONA Who is thy lord?
EMILIA He that is yours, sweet lady.
DESDEMONA I have none. Do not talk to me, Emilia.
I cannot weep, nor answers have I none,
But what should go by water.° Prithee, tonight
Lay on my bed my wedding sheets, remember;
And call thy husband hither.
EMILIA Here's a change indeed! *Exit.*
DESDEMONA 'Tis meet I should be used so, very meet.°
How have I been behaved, that he might stick
The small'st opinion on my least misuse?°

Enter **IAGO** *and* **EMILIA.**

IAGO What is your pleasure, madam? How is't with you?
DESDEMONA I cannot tell. Those that do teach young babes
Do it with gentle means and easy tasks.
He might have chid me so, for, in good faith,
I am a child to chiding.
IAGO What is the matter, lady?
EMILIA Alas, Iago, my lord hath so bewhored her,
Thrown such despite and heavy terms upon her,
As true hearts cannot bear it.
DESDEMONA Am I that name, Iago?
IAGO What name, fair lady?
DESDEMONA Such as she says my lord did say I was.
EMILIA He called her whore. A beggar in his drink
Could not have laid such terms upon his callet.°
IAGO Why did he so?
DESDEMONA [*weeping*]:
I do not know. I am sure I am none such.
IAGO Do not weep, do not weep. Alas the day!
EMILIA Has she forsook so many noble matches,
Her father and her country and her friends,
To be called whore? Would it not make one weep?

---

86. vessel: body. **92. cry you mercy:** beg your pardon. (Sarcastic.) **97. course:** business. (With an indecent suggestion of "trick," turn at sex.) **99. conceive:** suppose, think. **101. half asleep:** i.e., dazed. **108. go by water:** be conveyed by tears.

112. 'Tis . . . very meet: i.e., it must be I somehow have deserved this. **113–114. How . . . misuse?:** what have I done that prompts Othello to attach even the slightest censure to whatever little fault I may have committed? **128. callet:** whore.

DESDEMONA It is my wretched fortune.

IAGO Beshrew° him for't!
How comes this trick° upon him?

DESDEMONA Nay, heaven doth know.

EMILIA I will be hanged if some eternal° villain,
Some busy and insinuating° rogue,
Some cogging, cozening° slave, to get some office,
Have not devised this slander. I'll be hanged else.

IAGO Fie, there is no such man. It is impossible.

DESDEMONA If any such there be, heaven pardon him!

EMILIA A halter° pardon him! And hell gnaw his bones!
Why should he call her whore? Who keeps her company?
What place? What time? What form?° What likelihood?
The Moor's abused by some most villainous knave,
Some base notorious knave, some scurvy fellow.
Oh, heavens, that such companions thou'dst unfold,°
And put in every honest hand a whip
To lash the rascals naked through the world
Even from the east to th' west!

IAGO Speak within door.°

EMILIA Oh, fie upon them! Some such squire° he was
That turned your wit the seamy side without°
And made you to suspect me with the Moor.

IAGO You are a fool. Go to.°

DESDEMONA O God, Iago,
What shall I do to win my lord again?
Good friend, go to him; for, by this light of heaven,
I know not how I lost him. Here I kneel. [*She kneels.*]
If e'er my will did trespass 'gainst his love,
Either in discourse of thought° or actual deed,
Or that° mine eyes, mine ears, or any sense
Delighted them° in any other form;
Or that I do not yet,° and ever did,
And ever will — though he do shake me off
To beggarly divorcement — love him dearly,
Comfort forswear° me! Unkindness may do much,
And his unkindness may defeat° my life,
But never taint my love. I cannot say "whore."
It does abhor° me now I speak the word;
To do the act that might the addition° earn
Not the world's mass of vanity° could make me. [*She rises.*]

IAGO I pray you, be content. 'Tis but his humor.°
The business of the state does him offense,
And he does chide with you.

DESDEMONA If 'twere no other —

IAGO It is but so, I warrant. [*Trumpets within.*]
Hark, how these instruments summon you to supper!
The messengers of Venice stays the meat.°
Go in, and weep not. All things shall be well.
[*Exeunt* **DESDEMONA** *and* **EMILIA.**]

Enter **RODERIGO.**

How now, Roderigo?

RODERIGO I do not find that thou deal'st justly with me.

---

135. Beshrew: may evil befall. (An oath.) **136. trick:** strange behavior, delusion. **137. eternal:** inveterate. **138. insinuating:** ingratiating, fawning, wheedling. **139. cogging, cozening:** cheating, defrauding. **143. halter:** hangman's noose. **145. form:** manner, circumstance. **148. that . . . unfold:** would that you would expose such fellows. **151. within door:** i.e., not so loud. **152. squire:** fellow. **153. seamy side without:** wrong side out. **155. Go to:** i.e., that's enough.

160. discourse of thought: process of thinking. **161. that:** if. (Also in line 163.) **162. Delighted them:** took delight. **163. yet:** still. **166. Comfort forswear:** may heavenly comfort forsake. **167. defeat:** destroy. **169. abhor:** (1) fill me with abhorrence (2) make me whorelike. **170. addition:** title. **171. vanity:** showy splendor. **172. humor:** mood. **178. stays the meat:** are waiting to dine.

IAGO What in the contrary?

RODERIGO Every day thou daff'st me° with some device,° Iago, and rather, as it seems to me now, keep'st from me all conveniency° than suppliest me with the least advantage° of hope. I will indeed no longer endure it, nor am I yet persuaded to put up° in peace what already I have foolishly suffered.

IAGO Will you hear me, Roderigo?

RODERIGO Faith, I have heard too much, for your words and performances are no kin together.

IAGO You charge me most unjustly.

RODERIGO With naught but truth. I have wasted myself out of my means. The jewels you have had from me to deliver° Desdemona would half have corrupted a votarist.° You have told me she hath received them and returned me expectations and comforts of sudden respect° and acquaintance, but I find none.

IAGO Well, go to, very well.

RODERIGO "Very well"! "Go to"! I cannot go to,° man, nor 'tis not very well. By this hand, I think, it is scurvy, and begin to find myself fopped° in it.

IAGO Very well.

RODERIGO I tell you 'tis not very well.° I will make myself known to Desdemona. If she will return me my jewels, I will give over my suit and repent my unlawful solicitation; if not, assure yourself I will seek satisfaction° of you.

IAGO You have said now?°

183. thou daff'st me: you put me off **184. device:** excuse, trick. **185–186. conveniency:** advantage, opportunity. **189. advantage:** increase. **186. put up:** submit to, tolerate. **198. deliver:** deliver to. **199. votarist:** nun. **202. sudden respect:** immediate consideration. **205. I cannot go to:** (Roderigo changes Iago's *go to,* an expression urging patience, to *I cannot go to,* "I have no opportunity for success in wooing.") **208. fopped:** fooled, duped. **210. not very well:** (Roderigo changes Iago's *very well,* "all right, then," to *not very well,* "not at all good.") **214–215. satisfaction:** repayment (The term normally means settling of accounts in a duel.) **216. You . . . now?:** have you finished?

RODERIGO Ay, and said nothing but what I protest intendment° of doing.

IAGO Why, now I see there's mettle in thee, and even from this instant do build on thee a better opinion than ever before. Give me thy hand, Roderigo. Thou hast taken against me a most just exception; but yet I protest I have dealt most directly in thy affair.

RODERIGO It hath not appeared.

IAGO I grant indeed it hath not appeared, and your suspicion is not without wit and judgment. But, Roderigo, if thou hast that in thee indeed which I have greater reason to believe now than ever — I mean purpose, courage, and valor — this night show it. If thou the next night following enjoy not Desdemona, take me from this world with treachery and devise engines° for my life.

RODERIGO Well, what is it? Is it within reason and compass?

IAGO Sir, there is especial commission come from Venice to depute Cassio in Othello's place.

RODERIGO Is that true? Why, then Othello and Desdemona return again to Venice.

IAGO Oh, no; he goes into Mauritania and takes away with him the fair Desdemona, unless his abode be lingered here by some accident; wherein none can be so determinate° as the removing of Cassio.

RODERIGO How do you mean, removing of him?

IAGO Why, by making him uncapable of Othello's place — knocking out his brains.

RODERIGO And that you would have me do?

IAGO Ay, if you dare do yourself a profit and a right. He sups tonight with a harlotry,° and thither will I go to him. He knows not yet of his honorable fortune. If you will watch his going thence, which I will fashion to fall out° between twelve and

218. protest intendment: avow my intention. **235. engines:** plots, snares. **246–247. determinate:** conclusive, instrumental. **253. harlotry:** slut. **257. fall out:** occur.

one, you may take him at your pleasure. I will be near to second your attempt, and he shall fall between us. Come, stand not amazed at it, but go along with me. I will show you such a necessity in his death that you shall think yourself bound to put it on him. It is now high° suppertime, and the night grows to waste.° About it.

RODERIGO I will hear further reason for this.

IAGO And you shall be satisfied. *Exeunt.*

Scene iii°

Enter **OTHELLO, LODOVICO, DESDEMONA, EMILIA,** *and* **ATTENDANTS.**

LODOVICO I do beseech you, sir, trouble yourself no further.

OTHELLO Oh, pardon me; 'twill do me good to walk.

LODOVICO Madam, good night. I humbly thank Your Ladyship.

DESDEMONA Your Honor is most welcome.

OTHELLO Will you walk, sir?
Oh, Desdemona!

DESDEMONA My lord?

OTHELLO Get you to bed on th'instant; I will be returned forthwith. Dismiss your attendant there. Look't be done.

DESDEMONA I will, my lord. *Exit [Othello, with Lodovico and attendants].*

EMILIA How goes it now? He looks gentler than he did.

DESDEMONA He says he will return incontinent,°
And hath commanded me to go to bed,
And bade me to dismiss you.

EMILIA Dismiss me?

DESDEMONA It was his bidding. Therefore, good Emilia,
Give me my nightly wearing, and adieu.
We must not now displease him.

EMILIA I would you had never seen him!

DESDEMONA So would not I. My love doth so approve him
That even his stubbornness,° his checks,° his frowns—
Prithee, unpin me—have grace and favor in them.

[*Emilia prepares Desdemona for bed.*]

EMILIA I have laid those sheets you bade me on the bed.

DESDEMONA All's one.° Good faith, how foolish are our minds!
If I do die before thee, prithee, shroud me
In one of those same sheets.

EMILIA Come, come, you talk.°

DESDEMONA My mother had a maid called Barbary.
She was in love, and he she loved proved mad°
And did forsake her. She had a song of "Willow."
An old thing 'twas, but it expressed her fortune,
And she died singing it. That song tonight
Will not go from my mind; I have much to do
But to go hang° my head all at one side
And sing it like poor Barbary. Prithee, dispatch.

EMILIA Shall I go fetch your nightgown?°

DESDEMONA No, unpin me here.
This Lodovico is a proper° man.

EMILIA A very handsome man.

DESDEMONA He speaks well.

EMILIA I know a lady in Venice would have walked barefoot to Palestine for a touch of his nether lip.

DESDEMONA [*singing*]:
"The poor soul sat sighing by a sycamore tree,
Sing all a green willow;°

---

264. high: fully **265–266. grows to waste:** wastes away. **Act IV, Scene iii. Location:** The citadel. **12. incontinent:** immediately.

21. stubbornness: roughness. **checks:** rebukes. **24. All's one:** all right; it doesn't really matter. **26. talk:** i.e., prattle. **28. mad:** wild, lunatic. **32–33. I . . . hang:** I can scarcely keep myself from hanging. **35. nightgown:** dressing gown. **37. proper:** handsome. **44. willow:** (A conventional emblem of disappointed love.)

Her hand on her bosom, her head on her knee,
Sing willow, willow, willow.
The fresh streams ran by her and murmured her moans;
Sing willow, willow, willow;
Her salt tears fell from her, and softened the stones — "
Lay by these.
[*singing*] "Sing willow, willow, willow — "
Prithee, hie thee.° He'll come anon.°
[*singing*] "Sing all a green willow must be my garland.
Let nobody blame him, his scorn I approve — "
Nay, that's not next. — Hark! who is't that knocks?

EMILIA It's the wind.

DESDEMONA [*singing*]:
"I called my love false love; but what said he then?
Sing willow, willow, willow;
If I court more women, you'll couch with more men."
So, get thee gone; good-night. Mine eyes do itch;
Doth that bode weeping?

EMILIA 'Tis neither here nor there.

DESDEMONA I have heard it said so. Oh, these men, these men!
Dost thou in conscience think — tell me — Emilia,
That there be women do abuse° their husbands
In such gross kind?

EMILIA There be some such, no question.

DESDEMONA Wouldst thou do such a deed for all the world?

EMILIA Why, would not you?

In this painting by Théodore Chassériau, titled *Desdemona Retiring to Her Bed* (1849), Desdemona is preparing for bed, having been accused of faithlessness by Othello. **What elements of the painting suggest she feels a sense of foreboding?**

DESDEMONA No, by this heavenly light!

EMILIA Nor I neither by this heavenly light;
I might do't as well i'th' dark.

DESDEMONA Wouldst thou do such a deed for all the world?

EMILIA The world's a huge thing. 'Tis a great price
For a small vice.

DESDEMONA Good troth, I think thou wouldst not.

EMILIA By my troth, I think I should, and undo't when I had done. Marry, I would not do such a thing for a joint ring,° nor for

52. hie thee: hurry. **anon:** right away. **64. abuse:** deceive.

76. joint ring: a ring made in separate halves.

measures of lawn,° nor for gowns, petticoats, nor caps, nor any petty exhibition.° But for all the whole world! Uds° pity, who would not make her husband a cuckold to make him a monarch? I should venture purgatory for't.

DESDEMONA Beshrew me if I would do such a wrong
For the whole world.

EMILIA Why, the wrong is but a wrong i'th' world, and having the world for your labor, 'tis a wrong in your own world, and you might quickly make it right.

DESDEMONA I do not think there is any such woman.

EMILIA Yes, a dozen, and as many
To th' vantage as would store the world they played for.°
But I do think it is their husbands' faults
If wives do fall. Say that they° slack their duties°
And pour our treasures into foreign laps,°
Or else break out in peevish jealousies,
Throwing restraint upon us?° Or say they strike us,
Or scant our former having in despite?°
Why, we have galls,° and though we have some grace,°
Yet have we some revenge. Let husbands know
Their wives have sense° like them. They see, and smell,
And have their palates both for sweet and sour,
As husbands have. What is it that they° do
When they change° us for others? Is it sport?°
I think it is. And doth affection° breed it?
I think it doth. Is't frailty that thus errs?
It is so, too. And have not we affections,
Desires for sport, and frailty, as men have?
Then let them use us well; else let them know,
The ills we do, their ills instruct us so.

DESDEMONA Good night, good night. God me such uses° send
Not to pick bad from bad, but by bad mend!°

Exeunt.

ACT V

Scene i°

Enter **IAGO** *and* **RODERIGO**.

IAGO Here, stand behind this bulk.° Straight will he come.
Wear thy good rapier bare,° and put it home.°
Quick, quick! Fear nothing. I'll be at thy elbow.
It makes us or it mars us. Think on that,
And fix most firm thy resolution.

RODERIGO Be near at hand. I may miscarry in't.

IAGO Here, at thy hand. Be bold, and take thy stand.

[Iago *stands aside,* Roderigo *conceals himself.*]

RODERIGO I have no great devotion to the deed;
And yet he hath given me satisfying reasons.
'Tis but a man gone. Forth, my sword! He dies. [*He draws.*]

IAGO I have rubbed this young quat° almost to the sense,°
And he grows angry. Now, whether he kill Cassio
Or Cassio him, or each do kill the other,
Every way makes my gain. Live Roderigo,°
He calls me to a restitution large

---

77. lawn: fine linen. **78. exhibition:** gift. **79. Uds:** God's. **90–91. and . . . played for:** and enough additionally to stock the world men have gambled and sported sexually for. **93. they:** our husbands. **duties:** marital duties. **94. pour . . . laps:** i.e., are unfaithful, give what is rightfully ours (semen) to other women. **96. Throwing . . . us:** jealously restricting our freedom. **97. Or . . . despite:** or spitefully take away from us whatever we enjoyed before. **98. have galls:** i.e., are capable of resenting injury and insult. **grace:** inclination to be merciful. **100. sense:** sensory perception and appetite. **102. they:** husbands. **103. change:** exchange. **sport:** sexual pastime. **104. affection:** passion.

110. uses: habit, practice. **111. Not . . . mend:** i.e., not to learn bad conduct from others' badness (as Emilia has suggested women learn from men), but to mend my ways by perceiving what badness is, making spiritual benefit out of evil and adversity. **Act V, Scene i. Location:** A street in Cyprus. **1. bulk:** framework projecting from the front of a shop. **2. bare:** unsheathed. **home:** all the way into the target. **11. quat:** pimple, pustule. **to the sense:** to the quick. **14. Live Roderigo:** if Roderigo lives.

Of gold and jewels that I bobbed° from him
As gifts to Desdemona.
It must not be. If Cassio do remain,
He hath a daily beauty in his life
That makes me ugly; and besides, the Moor
May unfold° me to him; there stand I in much peril.
No, he must die. Be't so. I hear him coming.

Enter **CASSIO.**

RODERIGO [*coming forth*]:
I know his gait, 'tis he. — Villain, thou diest!
[*He attacks Cassio.*]

CASSIO That thrust had been mine enemy indeed,
But that my coat° is better than thou know'st;
I will make proof° of thine.
[*He draws, and wounds* **RODERIGO.**]

RODERIGO Oh, I am slain!
[*He falls.* **IAGO,** *from behind, wounds* **CASSIO** *in the leg, and exits.*]

CASSIO I am maimed forever. Help, ho! Murder! Murder!

Enter **OTHELLO.**

OTHELLO The voice of Cassio! Iago keeps his word.

RODERIGO Oh, villain that I am!

OTHELLO It is even so.

CASSIO Oh, help, ho! Light! A surgeon!

OTHELLO 'Tis he: O brave Iago, honest and just,
That hast such noble sense of thy friend's wrong!
Thou teachest me. — Minion,° your dear lies dead,
And your unblest fate hies.° Strumpet, I come!
Forth of° my heart those charms, thine eyes, are blotted;
Thy bed, lust-stained, shall with lust's blood be spotted. *Exit* **OTHELLO.**

Enter **LODOVICO** *and* **GRATIANO.**

CASSIO What ho! No watch? No passage?° Murder! Murder!

GRATIANO 'Tis some mischance. The cry is very direful.

CASSIO Oh, help!

LODOVICO Hark!

RODERIGO Oh, wretched villain!

LODOVICO Two or three groan. 'Tis heavy° night;
These may be counterfeits. Let's think't unsafe
To come in to° the cry without more help.
[*They remain near the entrance.*]

RODERIGO Nobody come? Then shall I bleed to death.

Enter **IAGO** [*in his shirtsleeves, with a light*].

LODOVICO Hark!

GRATIANO Here's one comes in his shirt, with light and weapons.

IAGO Who's there? Whose noise is this that cries° on murder?

LODOVICO We do not know.

IAGO Did not you hear a cry?

CASSIO Here, here! For heaven's sake, help me!

IAGO What's the matter?
[*He moves toward Cassio.*]

GRATIANO [*to* **LODOVICO**]
This is Othello's ancient, as I take it.

LODOVICO [*to* **GRATIANO**]
The same indeed, a very valiant fellow.

IAGO [*to* **CASSIO**]
What° are you here that cry so grievously?

CASSIO Iago? Oh, I am spoiled,° undone by villains!
Give me some help.

16. bobbed: swindled. **21. unfold:** expose. **25. coat:** (Possibly a garment of mail under the outer clothing, or simply a tougher coat than Roderigo expected.) **26. proof:** a test. **34. Minion:** hussy (i.e., Desdemona). **35. hies:** hastens on. **36. Forth of:** from out.

38. passage: people passing by. **43. heavy:** thick, dark. **45. come in to:** approach. **49. cries:** cries out. **54. What:** who. (Also at lines 61 and 69.) **55. spoiled:** ruined, done for.

IAGO Oh, me, Lieutenant! What villains have done this?

CASSIO I think that one of them is hereabout,
And cannot make° away.

IAGO Oh, treacherous villains! [*To* **LODOVICO** *and* **GRATIANO**]
What are you there? Come in, and give some help. [*They advance.*]

RODERIGO Oh, help me there!

CASSIO That's one of them.

IAGO Oh, murderous slave!
Oh, villain! [*He stabs Roderigo.*]

RODERIGO Oh, damned Iago! Oh, inhuman dog!

IAGO Kill men i'th' dark? — Where be these bloody thieves? —
How silent is this town! — Ho! Murder, murder! —
[*To* **LODOVICO** *and* **GRATIANO**] What may you be? Are you of good or evil?

LODOVICO As you shall prove us,° praise° us.

IAGO Signor Lodovico?

LODOVICO He, sir.

IAGO I cry you mercy.° Here's Cassio hurt by villains.

GRATIANO Cassio?

IAGO How is't, brother?

CASSIO My leg is cut in two.

IAGO Marry, heaven forbid!
Light, gentlemen! I'll bind it with my shirt.
[*He hands them the light, and tends to* Cassio*'s wound.*]

Enter **BIANCA.**

BIANCA What is the matter, ho? Who is't that cried?

IAGO Who is't that cried?

BIANCA Oh, my dear Cassio!
My sweet Cassio! Oh, Cassio, Cassio, Cassio!

IAGO Oh, notable strumpet! Cassio, may you suspect
Who they should be that have thus mangled you?

CASSIO No.

GRATIANO I am sorry to find you thus. I have been to seek you.

IAGO Lend me a garter. [*He applies a tourniquet.*] So. — Oh, for a chair,°
To bear him easily hence!

BIANCA Alas, he faints! O Cassio, Cassio, Cassio!

IAGO Gentlemen all, I do suspect this trash
To be a party in this injury. —
Patience awhile, good Cassio. — Come, come;
Lend me a light. [*He shines the light on Roderigo.*] Know we this face or no?
Alas, my friend and my dear countryman
Roderigo! No. — Yes, sure. — Oh, heaven! Roderigo!

GRATIANO What, of Venice?

IAGO Even he, sir. Did you know him?

GRATIANO Know him? Ay.

IAGO Signor Gratiano? I cry your gentle° pardon.
These bloody accidents° must excuse my manners
That so neglected you.

GRATIANO I am glad to see you.

IAGO How do you, Cassio? — Oh, a chair, a chair!

GRATIANO Roderigo!

IAGO He, he, 'tis he. [*A litter is brought in.*] Oh, that's well said;° the chair.
Some good man bear him carefully from hence;
I'll fetch the General's surgeon. [*To* **BIANCA**] For° you, mistress,
Save you your labor.° — He that lies slain here, Cassio,
Was my dear friend. What malice° was between you?

CASSIO None in the world, nor do I know the man.

IAGO [*to* **BIANCA**]:

---

59. make: get. **70. prove us:** prove us to be. **praise:** appraise. **73. I cry you mercy:** I beg your pardon.

86. chair: litter. **98. gentle:** noble. **99. accidents:** sudden events. **103. well said:** well done. **105. For:** as for. **106. Save . . . labor:** i.e., never you mind tending Cassio. **107. malice:** enmity.

What, look you pale? — Oh, bear him out o'
th' air.°
[*Cassio and Roderigo are borne off.*]
Stay you,° good gentlemen. — Look you pale,
mistress? —
Do you perceive the gastness° of her eye? —
Nay, if you stare,° we shall hear more anon. —
Behold her well; I pray you, look upon her.
Do you see, gentlemen? Nay, guiltiness
Will speak, though tongues were out of use.

[*Enter* EMILIA.]

EMILIA 'Las, what's the matter? What's the
matter, husband?
IAGO Cassio hath here been set on in the dark
By Roderigo and fellows that are scaped.
He's almost slain, and Roderigo dead.
EMILIA Alas! good gentleman! Alas, good Cassio!
IAGO This is the fruits of whoring. Prithee,
Emilia,
Go know° of Cassio where he supped tonight.
[*To* BIANCA] What, do you shake at that?
BIANCA He supped at my house, but I therefore
shake not.
IAGO Oh, did he so? I charge you go with me.
EMILIA Oh, fie upon thee, strumpet!
BIANCA I am no strumpet, but of life as honest°
As you that thus abuse me.
EMILIA As I? Faugh! Fie upon thee!
IAGO Kind gentlemen, let's go see poor Cassio
dressed.° —
Come, mistress, you must tell 's another tale. —
Emilia, run you to the citadel
And tell my lord and lady what hath happed. —
Will you go on afore? [*Aside*] This is the night
That either makes me or fordoes° me quite.
Exeunt.

109. bear . . . air: (Fresh air was thought to be dangerous for a wound.) **110. Stay you:** (Lodovico and Gratiano are evidently about to leave.) **111. gastness:** terror. **112. stare:** (Iago pretends to interpret Bianca's wild looks as an involuntary confession of guilt.) **122. know:** learn. **127. honest:** chaste. **130. Cassio dressed:** Cassio's wounds dressed. **135. fordoes:** undoes, ruins.

Scene ii°

Enter OTHELLO [*with a light*], *and* DESDEMONA *in her bed.*°

OTHELLO It is the cause,° it is the cause, my soul.
Let me not name it to you, you chaste stars!
It is the cause. Yet I 'll not shed her blood,
Nor scar that whiter skin of hers than snow,
And smooth as monumental° alabaster.
Yet she must die, else she'll betray more men.
Put out the light, and then put out the light.°
If I quench thee, thou flaming minister,°
I can again thy former light restore,
Should I repent me;° but once put out thy light,
Thou cunning'st pattern° of excelling nature,
I know not where is that Promethean heat°
That can thy light relume.° When I have
plucked thy rose,
I cannot give it vital growth again;
It needs must wither. I'll smell it on the tree.
[*He kisses her.*]
Oh, balmy breath, that dost almost persuade
Justice to break her sword! One more, one
more.
Be thus when thou art dead, and I will kill thee,
And love thee after. One more, and this the
last. [*He kisses her.*]
So sweet was ne'er so fatal. I must weep,
But they are cruel tears.° This sorrow's
heavenly;
It strikes where it doth love.° She wakes.
DESDEMONA Who's there? Othello?

Act V, Scene ii. Location: A bedchamber in the citadel. **s.d. *in her bed:*** (Either the curtains are drawn back to reveal the bed in a recessed area backstage, or the bed is "thrust out" onstage as the scene begins.) **1. cause:** i.e., cause of justice, the offense itself, which must be corrected in the name of justice. **5. monumental:** i.e., used in making tombs and funeral monuments. **7. the light . . . light:** the torch or lamp . . . Desdemona's life. **8. minister:** servant (referring to the torch that "serves" him. [Hall]) **10. repent me:** change my mind. **11. Thou . . . pattern:** you skillfully wrought perfect example. **12. Promethean heat:** (Alludes to two myths: that of Prometheus stealing fire from heaven for humanity, and that of his creating humankind.) **13. relume:** rekindle. **21. they are cruel tears:** these tears betoken a sorrowful cruelty, regrettable but just. **22. It . . . love:** (Compare Hebrews 12:6: "For whom the Lord loveth he chasteneth.")

Christopher Duggan Photography

This photo is from the last duet in Doug Elkins's *Mo(or)town/Redux*, revived in 2012, featuring Donnell Oakley as Desdemona and Kyle Marshall as Othello. *Mo(or)town/Redux* reworks José Limon's *The Moor's Pavane* (1949), a dance that retells *Othello* as a quartet for Othello, Desdemona, Iago, and Emilia. Elkins's work uses a score of Motown classics. **How might Elkins's casting and musical choices affect viewers' interpretation of the play? What layers of meaning could it add? What might be missing?**

OTHELLO Ay, Desdemona.
DESDEMONA Will you come to bed, my lord?
OTHELLO Have you prayed tonight, Desdemon?
DESDEMONA Ay, my lord.
OTHELLO If you bethink yourself of any crime°
Unreconciled as yet to heaven and grace,
Solicit° for it straight.°
DESDEMONA Alack, my lord, what may you mean by that?
OTHELLO Well, do it, and be brief. I will walk by.
I would not kill thy unprepared spirit.
No, heaven forfend!° I would not kill thy soul.
DESDEMONA Talk you of killing?
OTHELLO Ay, I do.
DESDEMONA Then heaven
Have mercy on me!
OTHELLO Amen, with all my heart!
DESDEMONA If you say so, I hope you will not kill me.
OTHELLO Humh!
DESDEMONA And yet I fear you; for you're fatal then
When your eyes roll so. Why I should fear I know not,
Since guiltiness I know not; but yet I feel I fear.
OTHELLO Think on thy sins.
DESDEMONA They are loves I bear to you.°
OTHELLO Ay, and for that thou diest.
DESDEMONA That death's unnatural that kills for loving.
Alas, why gnaw you so your nether lip?
Some bloody passion shakes your very frame.
These are portents; but yet, I hope, I hope,
They do not point on me.
OTHELLO Peace, and be still!
DESDEMONA I will so. What's the matter?
OTHELLO That handkerchief which I so loved and gave thee
Thou gav'st to Cassio.

28. crime: sin. **30. Solicit:** petition, pray. **straight:** immediately. **34. forfend:** forbid.

42. They . . . you: i.e., my only sins are my idolatry of loving you too much.

DESDEMONA No, by my life and soul!
Send for the man and ask him.
OTHELLO Sweet soul, take heed, take heed of perjury.
Thou art on thy deathbed.
DESDEMONA Ay, but not yet to die.
OTHELLO Yes, presently.°
Therefore confess thee freely of thy sin;
For to deny each article with oath
Cannot remove nor choke the strong conception°
That I do groan withal.° Thou art to die.
DESDEMONA Then Lord have mercy on me!
OTHELLO I say, amen.
DESDEMONA And have you mercy too! I never did
Offend you in my life; never loved Cassio
But with such general warranty° of heaven
As I might love. I never gave him token.
OTHELLO By heaven, I saw my handkerchief in 's hand.
Oh, perjured woman! Thou dost stone° my heart,
And makes me call what I intend to do
A murder, which I thought a sacrifice.
I saw the handkerchief.
DESDEMONA He found it, then.
I never gave it him. Send for him hither;
Let him confess a truth.
OTHELLO He had confessed.
DESDEMONA What, my lord?
OTHELLO That he hath used thee.
DESDEMONA How? Unlawfully?
OTHELLO Ay.
DESDEMONA He will not say so.
OTHELLO No, his mouth is stopped;
Honest Iago hath ta'en order° for't.
DESDEMONA Oh, my fear interprets. What, is he dead?
OTHELLO Had all his hairs been lives, my great revenge
Had stomach for them all.
DESDEMONA Alas, he is betrayed and I undone!
[*She weeps.*]
OTHELLO Out, strumpet! Weep'st thou for him to my face?
DESDEMONA Oh, banish me, my lord, but kill me not!
OTHELLO Down, strumpet!
DESDEMONA Kill me tomorrow; let me live tonight!
OTHELLO Nay, if you strive—
DESDEMONA But half an hour!
OTHELLO Being done,° there is no pause.
DESDEMONA But while I say one prayer!
OTHELLO It is too late. *Smothers her.*
EMILIA [*at the door*]:
My lord, my lord! What, ho! my lord, my lord!
OTHELLO What noise is this? Not dead? Not yet quite dead?
I that am cruel am yet merciful;
I would not have thee linger in thy pain.
[*He dispatches her.*]
So, so.
EMILIA [*within*]: What, ho! My lord, my lord!
OTHELLO Who's there?
EMILIA [*within*]:
Oh, good my lord, I would speak a word with you!
OTHELLO Yes, 'tis Emilia.—By and by.—She's dead.
'Tis like° she comes to speak of Cassio's death.—
The noise was here.° Ha! No more moving?

---

56. presently: immediately. **59. conception:** (1) belief in your guilt (2) plan in my mind. **60. groan withal:** (1) groan at in sorrow (2) as in giving birth. **64. warranty:** sanction. **67. stone:** turn to stone, harden. **76. ta'en order:** taken measures.

86. Being done: i.e., since justice has begun its relentless course. **95. like:** likely that. **96. here:** (The Folio's "high" is possible, suggesting that the commotion of the attack on Cassio was loud.)

Katie Orlinsky/The New York Times/Redux

In this photo, taken from a 2011 production of *Othello* starring John Douglas Thompson as Othello and Juliet Rylance as Desdemona, Othello holds his wife's body after he has suffocated her, but before Emilia arrives. **How has Thompson captured Othello's emotions at this moment in the play? Why do you think the director chose to dress both characters in white for this scene?**

Still as the grave. Shall she come in? Were't
  good?—
I think she stirs again. No. What 's best to do?
If she come in, she'll sure speak to my wife.
My wife! My wife! What wife? I have no wife.
Oh, insupportable! Oh, heavy hour!
Methinks it should be now a huge eclipse
Of sun and moon, and that th'affrighted globe
Should yawn at alteration.°

104. Should . . . alteration: should gape wide in an earthquake, as if expressing amazement at an eclipse. (According to Pliny, earthquakes often happen during eclipses. The cataclysmic event here is especially terrifying in that it imagines the impossible concurrence of a solar and lunar eclipse—an apocalyptic scenario befitting the horror of Desdemona's death.)

EMILIA [*within*]: I do beseech you
  That I may speak with you, oh, good my lord!
OTHELLO I had forgot thee. Oh, come in,
    Emilia.—
  Soft,° by and by. Let me the curtains draw.—
    [*He closes the bedcurtains and opens the door.*]
  Where art thou?

Enter **EMILIA.**

    What 's the matter with thee now?
EMILIA Oh, my good lord, yonder's foul
    murders done!
OTHELLO What, now?
EMILIA But now, my lord.
OTHELLO It is the very error° of the moon;
  She° comes more nearer earth than she was
    wont,
  And makes men mad.°
EMILIA Cassio, my lord, hath killed a young
    Venetian
  Called Roderigo.
OTHELLO Roderigo killed?
  And Cassio killed?
EMILIA No, Cassio is not killed.
OTHELLO Not Cassio killed? Then murder's out
    of tune,
  And sweet revenge grows harsh.
DESDEMONA Oh, falsely, falsely murdered!
EMILIA Oh, Lord, what cry is that?
OTHELLO That? What?
EMILIA Out,° and alas, that was my lady's voice.
    [*She opens the bedcurtains.*]
  Help, help, ho, help! O lady, speak again!
  Sweet Desdemona! O sweet mistress, speak!
DESDEMONA A guiltless death I die.
EMILIA Oh, who hath done this deed?
DESDEMONA Nobody; I myself. Farewell.
  Commend me to my kind lord. Oh, farewell!
    [*She dies.*]
OTHELLO Why, how should she be murdered?

107. Soft: wait a minute. **112. error:** aberration, irregularity. **113. She:** Luna, the moon goddess. **114. mad:** i.e.,"lunatic." **123. Out:** (A cry of dismay, intensifying *alas.*)

EMILIA Alas, who knows?
OTHELLO You heard her say herself it was not I.
EMILIA She said so. I must needs report the truth.
OTHELLO She's like a liar gone to burning hell!
'Twas I that killed her.
EMILIA Oh, the more angel she,
And you the blacker devil!
OTHELLO She turned to folly,° and she was a whore.
EMILIA Thou dost belie° her, and thou art a devil.
OTHELLO She was false° as water.
EMILIA Thou art rash as fire to say
That she was false. Oh, she was heavenly true!
OTHELLO Cassio did top her. Ask thy husband else.°
Oh, I were damned beneath all depth in hell
But that I did proceed upon just grounds
To this extremity. Thy husband knew it all.
EMILIA My husband?
OTHELLO Thy husband.
EMILIA That she was false to wedlock?
OTHELLO Ay, with Cassio. Nay, had she been true,
If heaven would make me such another world
Of one entire and perfect chrysolite,°
I'd not have sold her for it.
EMILIA My husband?
OTHELLO Ay, 'twas he that told me on her first.
An honest man he is, and hates the slime
That sticks on filthy deeds.
EMILIA My husband?
OTHELLO What needs this iterance,° woman? I say thy husband.
EMILIA O mistress, villainy hath made mocks with° love!
My husband say she was false?
OTHELLO He, woman;
I say thy husband. Dost understand the word?
My friend, thy husband, honest, honest Iago.
EMILIA If he say so, may his pernicious soul
Rot half a grain a day! he lies to th' heart.
She was too fond of her most filthy bargain.
OTHELLO Ha? [*He draws.*]
EMILIA Do thy worst!
This deed of thine is no more worthy heaven
Than thou wast worthy her.
OTHELLO Peace, you were best.°
EMILIA Thou hast not half that power to do me harm
As I have to be hurt.° O gull!° O dolt!
As ignorant as dirt! Thou hast done a deed—
I care not for thy sword; I'll make thee known,
Though I lost twenty lives.—Help! Help, ho, help!
The Moor hath killed my mistress! Murder, murder!

Enter **MONTANO, GRATIANO,** *and* **IAGO.**

MONTANO What is the matter? How now, General?
EMILIA Oh, are you come, Iago? You have done well,
That men must lay their murders on your neck.°
GRATIANO What is the matter?
EMILIA [*to* **IAGO**]:
Disprove this villain, if thou be'st a man.
He says thou told'st him that his wife was false.
I know thou didst not; thou'rt not such a villain.°
Speak, for my heart is full.
IAGO I told him what I thought, and told no more
Than what he found himself was apt° and true.

---

136. folly: i.e., wantonness, fleshly sin. **137. belie:** slander. **138. false:** unstable (proverbial). [Hall] **141. else:** i.e., if you don't believe me. **150. chrysolite:** precious topaz. **157. iterance:** iteration, repetition. **158. made mocks with:** made a mockery of.

168. Peace . . . best: you'd better be quiet. **170. to be hurt:** i.e., to endure hurt. **gull:** dupe. **177. on your neck:** to your charge. **181. such a villain:** such a villain as all that. **184. apt:** plausible.

EMILIA But did you ever tell him she was false?
IAGO I did.
EMILIA You told a lie, an odious, damnèd lie!
Upon my soul, a lie, a wicked lie.
She false with Cassio? Did you say with Cassio?
IAGO With Cassio, mistress. Go to, charm° your tongue.
EMILIA I will not charm my tongue; I am bound to speak.
My mistress here lies murdered in her bed—
ALL Oh, heavens forfend!
EMILIA And your reports have set the murder on.
OTHELLO Nay, stare not, masters. It is true indeed.
GRATIANO 'Tis a strange truth.
MONTANO Oh, monstrous act!
EMILIA Villainy, villainy, villainy!
I think upon't—I think, I smell't! O villainy!
I thought so then°—I'll kill myself for grief—
O! villainy, villainy!
IAGO What, are you mad? I charge you, get you home.
EMILIA Good gentlemen, let me have leave to speak.
'Tis proper I obey him, but not now.
Perchance, Iago, I will ne'er go home.
OTHELLO Oh! Oh! Oh! [*Othello falls on the bed.*]°
EMILIA Nay, lay thee down and roar,
For thou hast killed the sweetest innocent
That e'er did lift up eye.°
OTHELLO [*rising*] Oh, she was foul!
I scarce did know you, uncle. There lies your niece,
Whose breath indeed these hands have newly stopped.
I know this act shows° horrible and grim.
GRATIANO Poor Desdemon! I am glad thy father's dead.
Thy match was mortal to him, and pure grief
Shore his old thread° in twain. Did he live now,
This sight would make him do a desperate turn,°
Yea, curse his better angel from his side,
And fall to reprobance.°
OTHELLO 'Tis pitiful. But yet Iago knows
That she with Cassio hath the act of shame
A thousand times committed. Cassio confessed it;
And she did gratify° his amorous works
With that recognizance° and pledge of love
Which I first gave her. I saw it in his hand;
It was a handkerchief, an antique token
My father gave my mother.
EMILIA Oh, God! Oh, heavenly God!
IAGO Zounds, hold your peace.
EMILIA 'Twill out, 'twill out! I peace?
No, I will speak as liberal as the north.°
Let heaven and men and devils, let them all,
All, all, cry shame against me, yet I'll speak.
IAGO Be wise, and get you home.
EMILIA I will not.
[*Iago threatens Emilia.*]
GRATIANO Fie,
Your sword upon a woman?
EMILIA Oh, thou dull Moor! That handkerchief thou speak'st of
I found by fortune and did give my husband;
For often, with a solemn earnestness,
More than indeed belonged° to such a trifle,
He begged of me to steal't.
IAGO Villainous whore!
EMILIA She give it Cassio? No, alas! I found it,
And I did give't my husband.
IAGO Filth, thou liest!

---

190. charm: control. **199. then:** (Perhaps at 3.3.332–333 and 4.2.137–154.) **205. s.d. *Othello . . . bed:*** (This direction is from the Quarto, as also *He kisses her* at line 19 and *She dies* at line 129.) **207. lift up eye:** i.e., lift her eyes to heaven. **210. shows:** looks.

213. Shore . . . thread: sheared the thread of his old age (as Atropos, one of the three Fates, was thought to do). **214. turn:** deed. **216. reprobance:** damnation, i.e., suicide. **220. gratify:** reward. **221. recognizance:** token. **227. liberal as the north:** freely as the north wind (blows). **235. belonged:** was appropriate.

EMILIA By heaven, I do not, I do not, gentlemen.
Oh, murderous coxcomb!° What should such a fool
Do with so good a wife?

OTHELLO Are there no stones° in heaven
But what serves for the thunder? — Precious° villain!

[He runs at Iago; Montano disarms Othello. Iago, from behind, stabs Emilia.]

GRATIANO The woman falls! Sure he hath killed his wife.

EMILIA Ay, ay. Oh, lay me by my mistress' side.

[Exit **IAGO**.*]*

GRATIANO He's gone, but his wife's killed.

MONTANO 'Tis a notorious villain. Take you this weapon,
Which I have here recovered from the Moor.
Come, guard the door without. Let him not pass,
But kill him rather. I'll after that same villain,
For 'tis a damnèd slave.

Exit [with all but **OTHELLO** *and* **EMILIA**, *who has been laid by* **DESDEMONA'S** *side].*

OTHELLO I am not valiant neither,
But every puny whipster gets my sword.°
But why should honor outlive honesty?°
Let it go all.

EMILIA What did thy song bode, lady?
Hark, canst thou hear me? I will play the swan,
And die in music. [*She sings.*] "Willow, willow, willow."
Moor, she was chaste. She loved thee, cruel Moor.
So come my soul to bliss as I speak true.
So speaking as I think, alas, I die. [*She dies.*]

OTHELLO I have another weapon in this chamber;
It is a sword of Spain, the ice-brook's temper° —
Oh, here it is. [*He finds a sword.*] Uncle, I must come forth.

GRATIANO [*within*]:
If thou attempt it, it will cost thee dear.
Thou hast no weapon, and perforce must suffer.

OTHELLO Look in upon me then and speak with me,
Or, naked° as I am, I will assault thee.

[*Enter* **GRATIANO**.]

GRATIANO What is the matter?

OTHELLO Behold, I have a weapon;
A better never did itself sustain
Upon a soldier's thigh. I have seen the day
That, with this little arm, and this good sword,
I have made my way through more impediments
Than twenty times your stop.° But oh, vain boast!
Who can control his fate? 'Tis not so now.
Be not afraid, though you do see me weaponed;
Here is my journey's end, here is my butt°
And very seamark° of my utmost sail.

[*Gratiano steps back.*]

Do you go back dismayed? 'Tis a lost° fear;
Man but a rush° against Othello's breast
And he retires. Where should Othello go?

[*He turns to Desdemona.*]

Now, how dost thou look now? Oh, ill-starred wench!
Pale as thy smock! When we shall meet at compt,°

---

240. coxcomb: fool. (Addressed to Othello.) **242. stones:** bolts, such as those used for thunderbolts. **243. Precious:** i.e., arrant, utter. **243. s.d. *He . . . Emilia:*** (The Quarto text reads, *"The Moore runnes at* Iago. Iago *kils his wife."* The Quarto also specifies the exit of Iago at line 245 and the death of Emilia at line 260.) **253. every . . . sword:** every whipper-snapper can get the better of me and my sword. **254. why . . . honesty?:** why should a soldier's reputation for bravery outlive true integrity?

262. the ice-brook's temper: tempered in ice-cold water. **267. naked:** unarmed. **273. your stop:** the obstruction you present. **276. butt:** goal, limit. (An archery term.) **277. seamark:** beacon (marking his destination or limit). **278. lost:** groundless. **279. Man . . . rush:** wield no more than a reed. **282. compt:** account, judgment day.

This look of thine will hurl my soul from heaven,
And fiends will snatch at it. Cold, cold, my girl?
Even like thy chastity. O! cursèd, cursèd slave!°
Whip me, ye devils,
From the possession of this heavenly sight!
Blow me about in winds! Roast me in sulfur!
Wash me in steep-down gulfs of liquid fire!
O Desdemon! Dead, Desdemon! Dead! Oh! Oh!

Enter **LODOVICO, CASSIO** [*carried in a litter*],° **MONTANO,** *and* **IAGO** [*prisoner*], *with* **OFFICERS.**

LODOVICO Where is this rash and most unfortunate man?

OTHELLO That's he that was Othello. Here I am.

LODOVICO Where is that viper? Bring the villain forth. [*Iago is led forward.*]

OTHELLO I look down towards his feet;° but that's a fable.
If that thou be'st a devil, I cannot kill thee. [*He wounds Iago.*]

LODOVICO Wrench his sword from him. [*Othello is disarmed.*]

IAGO I bleed, sir, but not killed.

OTHELLO I am not sorry neither. I'd have thee live,
For in my sense° 'tis happiness to die.

LODOVICO O thou Othello, that was once so good,
Fall'n in the practice° of a cursèd slave,°
What shall be said to thee?

OTHELLO Why, anything.
An honorable murderer, if you will,
For naught did I in hate, but all in honor.

LODOVICO This wretch hath part confessed his villainy.
Did you and he consent° in Cassio's death?

OTHELLO Ay.

CASSIO Dear General, I never gave you cause.

OTHELLO I do believe it, and I ask your pardon.
Will you, I pray, demand that demi-devil
Why he hath thus ensnared my soul and body?

IAGO Demand me nothing. What you know, you know.
From this time forth I never will speak word.

LODOVICO What, not to pray?

GRATIANO Torments° will ope your lips.

OTHELLO Well, thou dost best.°

LODOVICO Sir, you shall understand what hath befall'n,
Which, as I think, you know not. Here is a letter
Found in the pocket of the slain Roderigo;
And here another. [*He produces letters.*] The one of them imports
The death of Cassio, to be undertook
By Roderigo.

OTHELLO O villain!

CASSIO Most heathenish and most gross!°

LODOVICO [*showing another paper*]:
Now here's another discontented° paper
Found in his pocket too. And this, it seems,
Roderigo meant t'have sent this damnèd villain;
But that belike° Iago in the interim
Came in and satisfied him.°

OTHELLO [*to* **IAGO**]: O thou pernicious caitiff!
How came you, Cassio, by that handkerchief
That was my wife's?

CASSIO I found it in my chamber;
And he himself confessed but even now

---

285. slave: i.e., Othello himself. **290. s.d.** ***in a litter:*** (The Quarto specifies that Cassio is *"in a Chaire."*) **294. towards his feet:** i.e., to see if they are cloven, as the devil's are fabled to be. **298. in my sense:** to one who feels as I do. **300. in the practice:** through the plotting, into the snare. **slave:** villain.

305. consent: agree. **314. Torments:** torture. **315. thou dost best:** you (Iago) do best not to talk. **322. gross:** monstrous. **323. discontented:** full of discontent. **326. belike:** most likely. **327. Came . . . him:** interposed and gave him satisfactory explanation.

That there he dropped it for a special purpose
Which wrought to his desire.°

OTHELLO Oh, fool, fool, fool!

CASSIO There is besides in Roderigo's letter
How he upbraids Iago, that he made him
Brave° me upon the watch, whereon it came°
That I was cast;° and even but now he spake,
After long seeming dead, Iago hurt him,
Iago set him on.

LODOVICO [*to* **OTHELLO**]:
You must forsake this room and go with us.
Your power and your command is taken off,°
And Cassio rules in Cyprus. For this slave,
If there be any cunning cruelty
That can torment him much and hold him long,°
It shall be his. You shall close prisoner rest°
Till that the nature of your fault be known
To the Venetian state. — Come, bring away.

OTHELLO Soft you;° a word or two before you go.
I have done the state some service, and they know't.
No more of that. I pray you, in your letters,
When you shall these unlucky° deeds relate,
Speak of me as I am; nothing extenuate,
Nor set down aught in malice. Then must you speak
Of one that loved not wisely but too well;
Of one not easily jealous but, being wrought,°
Perplexed° in the extreme; of one whose hand,
Like the base Indian,° threw a pearl away
Richer than all his tribe; of one whose subdued° eyes,
Albeit unusèd to the melting mood,
Drop tears as fast as the Arabian trees
Their medicinable gum.° Set you down this;
And say besides that in Aleppo once,
Where a malignant and a turbaned Turk
Beat a Venetian and traduced the state,
I took by th' throat the circumcisèd dog,
And smote him, thus. [*He stabs himself.*]°

LODOVICO Oh, bloody period!°

GRATIANO All that is spoke is marred.

OTHELLO I kissed thee ere I killed thee. No way but this,
Killing myself, to die upon a kiss.
[*He kisses Desdemona and*] *dies.*

CASSIO This did I fear, but thought he had no weapon;
For he was great of heart.

LODOVICO [*to* **IAGO**]: O Spartan dog,°
More fell° than anguish, hunger, or the sea!
Look on the tragic loading of this bed.
This is thy work. The object poisons sight;
Let it be hid.° Gratiano, keep° the house,
[*The bedcurtains are drawn.*]
And seize upon° the fortunes of the Moor,
For they succeed on° you. [*To* **CASSIO**] To you, Lord Governor,
Remains the censure° of this hellish villain,
The time, the place, the torture. Oh, enforce it!
Myself will straight aboard, and to the state
This heavy act with heavy heart relate.
Exeunt.

FINIS

[c. 1603]

---

333. wrought . . . desire: worked out as he wished, fitted in with his plan. **336. Brave:** defy. **whereon it came:** whereof it came about. **337. cast:** dismissed. **341. taken off:** taken away. **344. hold him long:** keep him alive a long time (during his torture). **345. rest:** remain. **348. Soft you:** one moment. **351. unlucky:** unfortunate. **355. wrought:** worked upon, worked into a frenzy. **356. Perplexed:** distraught. **357. Indian:** (This reading from the Quarto pictures an ignorant savage who cannot recognize the value of a precious jewel. The Folio reading, "Iudean," i.e., infidel or disbeliever, may refer to Herod, who slew Miriamne in a fit of jealousy, or to Judas Iscariot, the betrayer of Christ.)

358. subdued: i.e., overcome by grief. **361. gum:** i.e., myrrh. **366. s.d. *He stabs himself:*** (This direction is in the Quarto text.) **367. period:** termination, conclusion. **373. Spartan dog:** (Spartan dogs were noted for their savagery and silence.) **374. fell:** cruel. **377. Let it be hid:** i.e., draw the bedcurtains. (No stage direction specifies that the dead are to be carried offstage at the end of the play.) **keep:** guard. **378. seize upon:** take legal possession of. **379. succeed on:** pass as though by inheritance to. **380. censure:** sentencing.

QUESTIONS FOR DISCUSSION

1. From the very outset, how does Iago characterize Cassio? How, for instance, do you interpret Iago's description of Cassio as a man who "never set a squadron in the field / Nor the division of a battle knows / More than a spinster" (I.i.23–25)?
2. How does Iago characterize himself in this opening act? How do you interpret his assertion that "[w]e cannot all be masters, nor all masters / Cannot be truly followed" (I.i.45–46)? Is he referring to himself? To what extent does his hatred of Othello seem warranted at this early point?
3. In the opening scene, we hear about Othello, but in the second scene, he enters and begins speaking for himself. In what ways do his demeanor and attitude conflict with the description that has shaped audience expectations thus far?
4. How do the military and political spheres collide with the domestic in act I? Are they fundamentally incompatible or only in partial conflict? Explain.
5. How would you describe Desdemona's character in act I when she explains her attraction to Othello to her father? What does she mean by her "divided duty" (I.iii.183)? In what ways does she demonstrate the behavior expected of women of her time? Does she seems to contradict any expectations? Support your response with specific reference to the text.
6. How does the senators' attitude toward Othello differ from that of Brabantio? What effect does their view have on Brabantio?
7. Why does Desdemona engage with Iago's banter in act II, scene i? Given that Emilia is also present, what inferences can you make about Iago's attitude toward women?
8. What chinks in Othello's soldierly armor begin to emerge in act II? Note passages where he remains his calm, disciplined self and where he seems to falter. Consider, for instance, this passage: "My blood begins my safer guides to rule, / And passion, having my best judgment collied, / Essays to lead the way" (II.iii.216–18).
9. In what ways does Iago's admonition to Cassio that "reputation is an idle and most false imposition . . ." (II.iii.281–82) undermine the values that define a professional soldier?
10. Where in act II do the professional sphere of the military and the domestic space of home and personal relationships start to overlap and even collide?
11. In act III, how does Iago plant doubt about Desdemona in Othello's mind and provoke his jealousy? Include specific examples, noting especially instances where Iago twists the meaning of words or gestures to suit his nefarious purposes.
12. Why does Desdemona take up Cassio's defense? What characteristics that initially attracted Othello to her become the ones that raise suspicion at this point in their relationship?
13. By act III, we're accustomed to Iago twisting information and appearances to his own advantage, but his out-and-out lying escalates to new heights at this point in the play. What examples of outright duplicity do you notice? Why do you think he has become so bold — or even, some might say, careless — in his deception?
14. Is Cassio an admirable character, a model soldier? Or is he depicted as naïve, weak, a dupe? Does he fall somewhere in between? How do his interactions with Bianca contribute to our understanding of him?
15. In what ways can act III, scene iv be viewed as a trial of sorts, or perhaps a distortion of a trial? What dramatic purpose might framing this scene as a trial serve within the play overall?
16. In what ways does Cyprus seem to serve as a contrast to Venice in terms of laws and standards of civil society? Is that contrast straightforward, or is it merely an illusion? Explain.
17. How do you interpret the "trance" that causes Othello to fall unconscious in act IV? To what extent does this physical response indicate that he is overwhelmed by jealousy and rage (what Iago calls "savage madness")? Do you think his reaction suggests that Othello inherently lacks the ability to control his emotions? Explain.
18. Why does Iago dissuade Othello from his initial idea of poisoning Desdemona? What does Othello's response in act IV, scene i say about his state of mind at this point?
19. How does Desdemona respond to Othello in act IV, both in public and private? Do you think she continues to exhibit the character traits we saw in previous acts, or has she changed? Explain, with reference to specific lines and passages.

20. Is Emilia a bona fide character on her own, or is she primarily a device to further the plot? How does her relationship with Iago parallel or contrast with Desdemona and Othello's? What do we learn through her interactions with Desdemona? Consider especially Emilia's comment that men "are all but stomachs, and we are all but food. / They eat us hungrily, and when they are full, / They belch us" (III.iv.110–12).

21. Why does Iago instigate conflict between Roderigo and Cassio to the point that Iago says, "whether [Roderigo] kill Cassio / Or Cassio him, or each do kill the other, / Every way makes my gain" (V.i.12–14)? How does the question of who kills whom matter in his game of power?

22. Based on the textual evidence from act V alone, did Othello ever truly love Desdemona?

23. Does the ending of the play suggest that Othello will be remembered as a Venetian who, essentially, fell from grace, or as a cultural outsider who never belonged in Venice? Explain.

24. In act III, scene iii, Othello calls out, "Perdition catch my soul / But I do love thee [Desdemona], and when I love thee not, / Chaos is come again" (ll. 98–100). These lines are in some ways emblematic of the play itself. How is *Othello* a meditation on the power of sexual passion, its role in love and marriage, and the necessity of restraining it?

QUESTIONS ON STYLE AND STRUCTURE

1. How do others refer to Othello — in both a positive and negative light? What language and images prevail? Pay particular attention to Brabantio's speech beginning "O thou foul thief . . ." in lines 63–82 of act I, scene ii.

2. How would you describe the tone of Othello's explanation of his meeting and courtship of Desdemona (I.iii.78–96, 130–72)?

3. In act I, what references do you find to money, robbery, and thievery? To what extent does this language suggest that the impact of psychological or emotional offenses can be quantitatively measured? Consider Iago's dialogue with Rodrigo at the end of act I.

4. How does Othello's language differ from that of Iago in act II, scene iii when they are discussing Desdemona, particularly in terms of directness and respect? Pay attention to sly commentaries, innuendo, and double entendres in Iago's language.

5. In act II, scene iii, Iago tells Cassio that "our general's wife is now the general" (l. 336). How does his soliloquy that follows expand that assertion into a strategy to bring about Othello's downfall? How does the language of darkness and sexuality contribute to the expression of his plan?

6. In act II, Shakespeare alternates between iambic pentameter verse and prose. Why do you think he does this? What is the effect on character development? Where else in the play do you notice this alternation, and to what effect?

7. In act III, the handkerchief appears. What literal information do we know about its history and meaning to Othello and Desdemona? How, then, does what amounts to an artifact or prop develop into a symbol as the play unfolds?

8. In act III, scene iii, we see Othello declare to Iago: "To be once in doubt / Is once to be resolved" (ll. 194–95). How does that soliloquy illuminate the inner war Othello is waging to exercise the clarity and reason that distinguished him as a soldier? Identify at least two other passages in act III that perform the same function within the play. What do these scenes collectively reveal about Othello's character?

9. In act III, scene iii, Othello pleads with Iago to provide "ocular proof" (l. 377) of Desdemona's infidelity. How does imagery incorporating light and darkness or sight and blindness reinforce the themes of the play?

10. Dramatic irony is present in the opening two acts of the play, but nearly all of act III depends upon the chasm between what Othello is aware of and what the audience knows. How does dramatic irony further both plot and theme in act III? Support your response with three examples that illustrate different effects.

11. What is the effect of images of monsters, animals, and demons in act III? Cite at least four passages

and discuss how descriptions of, allusions to, or images of them contribute to themes Shakespeare develops in *Othello*.

12. Might the scene in act III, scene iii, when Othello bids "farewell the tranquil mind" (l. 365), be seen as the transition point for the entire play — that is, the point of no return as Othello descends into an avenging murderer? Do you see this scene as the structural center of the play, or is that point located somewhere else? Explain, with specific references to the text.

13. What is the importance of the Willow Song that Desdemona sings at the end of act IV? What is its origin? How does it foreshadow the play's outcome?

14. In act IV, scene ii, Emilia insists to Othello that Desdemona is "honest, chaste, and true" (l. 18). Up until this point, "honest" has been a term Iago applies to himself, then Othello uses it to refer to Iago. How does the play explore and ultimately interrogate the meaning of "honesty" in these various contexts?

15. The play *Othello* contains several scenes that might seem more appropriate to comedy, ranging from the witty banter between Iago and Desdemona (act II), the drinking scene (act II), and the clown scenes (acts III and IV). What is the function of these comic scenes in the context of a tragedy? In what ways do they interact with or comment on the serious action and themes of the play?

SUGGESTIONS FOR WRITING

1. One way to view *Othello* is as a play that argues that we can never prove faithfulness or fidelity, only infidelity. To what extent do you agree with this interpretation? Is it an oversimplification or a brilliantly simple encapsulation of a complex play?

2. The play *Othello* is structured through a series of transformations that explore the nature and stability of the self. What factors contribute to Othello's trajectory from noble soldier to violent murderer? Consider the external as well as the internal forces that lead to such a dramatic and dangerous transformation.

3. The motivation for betrayal and its consequences is a central concern in *Othello*. Examine three acts of betrayal — or alleged betrayal — and discuss how these contribute to the overall meaning of the play. Consider specific acts of treachery, but also explore how a character or characters might be guilty of betraying their own values.

4. Critic Roland Barthes has said, "Literature is the question minus the answer." What is one central question that *Othello* raises? To what extent does Shakespeare "answer" it? Discuss how the play's exploration of this question contributes to the meaning of the work as a whole.

5. Iago has been interpreted as a prime example of Machiavellianism — that is, his behavior in *Othello* reflects the beliefs of Niccolo Machiavelli (1469–1527), a Renaissance philosopher and politician who believed that effective leadership required cunning, duplicitous thinking, and behavior that privileged self-interest over morality. To what extent do you believe Iago embodies this philosophy? Support your argument with textual evidence from Iago's soliloquies throughout the play.

6. The play alternates between two main spaces — the domestic and the military. Discuss how the tension between them contributes to the main themes of the play. Pay particular attention to how Othello, the man of war, adjusts or fails to adjust to the domestic sphere.

7. *Othello* could be seen as a series of stories that people tell about themselves and one another. However, stories are by nature subjective and conflicting narratives that that often compete with each other for legitimacy — people try to change and control a narrative, with varying degrees of success. The Shakespeare scholar Stephen Greenblatt asked, "Why does anyone submit to another's narrative at all?" How does the play *Othello* respond to that question?

8. The patriarchal society in *Othello* reflects the values of Elizabethan England, where women, who could not legally hold property, were themselves considered property and were expected to adhere to strict codes of behavior. How do Desdemona, Bianca, and Emilia measure up to and subvert these expectations? What power, if any, do these women have, and how do they wield it? Do any of them resist the roles assigned to them? If so, how, and how successfully?

9. In 1997, a production of *Othello* cast Patrick Stewart, a white actor, as Othello with an otherwise all-black cast. The award-winning African American playwright August Wilson denounced this practice, arguing that such reversal of the traditional casting of *Othello* is "a tool of cultural imperialism" that denies African American history and culture as well as economic potential. Write an argument supporting or challenging Wilson's position.
10. How do the interpretations of the most famous actors who have played Othello reflect the issues the play raised at the time? Conduct research into the most significant theater and film actors, such as Edmund Kean, Ira Aldridge, Paul Robeson, Lawrence Olivier, Orson Welles, James Earl Jones, Laurence Fishburne, or Denzel Washington. Use at least three in your analysis.
11. Choose one of the film adaptations of *Othello* to view and discuss how effective its interpretation of the play is. Consider such questions as the following: Has the film distilled or oversimplified the ideas Shakespeare explores? To what extent has the film updated key issues by showing their continuing relevance? Do the performances demonstrate a clear understanding of the characters being portrayed? How do cinematic techniques, such as cinematography and score, contribute to (or detract from) the impact of the film?

TEXTS IN CONTEXT

Othello through Critical Lenses

Why is it that when you're discussing a movie, you might see a female character's behavior as bold, while someone else might view it as overbearing? You may see the small-town setting of a novel as supportive while a classmate feels it is restrictive. One person's strength is another's menace. It's a matter of interpretation — even if it's backed up with evidence from the text in question. But why are there such differences in perspective? Essentially, experience, background, and prior knowledge all play a significant role in how we interpret literary texts as well as human behavior in general.

We're all products of our environment and our time. Of course, we turn to literature to appreciate situations outside of our own experience, yet we tend to read and interpret based on the familiar circumstances of our own lives. While a novel or poem may not be a Rorschach test, most texts have the potential to be read from different perspectives. These approaches are sometimes called *lenses* because they change how we look at the text, and the concept of reading a text through a lens has been classified by scholars as critical literary theory. While we are not going to embark on an in-depth study, exploring a few perspectives should increase your awareness of how to read texts through a variety of lenses and why each one is important. We'll consider five basic perspectives:

- formalist
- historical
- gender
- psychological
- cultural

You're probably most familiar with what we call a **formalist lens**. According to this theory, a text — a poem, a short story, a play — should be read as an independent and self-sufficient entity without taking into account, for instance, an author's religion or socioeconomic status, or the culture of the time period when it was written. Instead, the focus is on features of literary style, such as diction, structure, figurative language, and syntax. Called New Criticism, this approach dominated much of the twentieth century — and it still dominates in many situations with strict limits on the time and resources available for you to interpret a literary text. On many standardized tests, for instance, you cannot research the author or the text, and you must write an analysis in an hour or less. Under those conditions, a formalist approach is usually your best bet.

But it's not the only way to view a text, and it may not be the most creative way to examine or construct meaning. The more you know about a text, its author, and the conditions under which it was written, the more it's likely to open up to multiple interpretations. Keep in mind that regardless of the lens you choose to read with, critical perspectives aren't political soapboxes: as is true of all literary analysis, your interpretation of a work must be firmly based in the specific details and language of the text itself.

Historical Perspective

Reading through a **historical lens** involves understanding a work as a product of the historic moment when it was created. When we read through this lens, we ask questions about whether the viewpoint of the author reflects or challenges the prevailing opinions of the day. To investigate, you might study letters, paintings, and various primary source documents that offer insight into the time period when a work was written. However, in addition to understanding the social, political, and cultural context of the era, an historical perspective considers the point in time the text itself depicts. Thus, if you read a novel about the Civil War written during the civil rights movement of the 1960s, you would consider the history of the Civil War and also the social and political climate of the mid-twentieth century. The historical perspective may also investigate the evolution of language — for instance, you might examine what the word "Moor" meant in Shakespeare's time as opposed to the associations it carries today.

A historical perspective on a work considers the following:

- The events depicted in the work reflect actual events of the author's time.
- There are divergent ways of interpreting historical events.
- An author is influenced by the historical and social circumstances of the time when a work was written, even if that influence takes the form of a critique.
- The time period being depicted is influenced by the author's socioeconomic background and political views.

Gendered Perspective

When we read through the lens of gender, we ask how depictions of gender support, challenge, or even reflect on our definitions of masculinity and femininity. Acknowledging that gender is a social construct — that is, roles and identities are determined by the society in which a person lives — this perspective explores gender stereotypes, social mores and values, and questions of sexuality in representations of identity. In earlier discussions of literary theory, this perspective was called "feminist" because it challenged the viewpoint that tended to see the male perspective as the "norm" or default. Today, however, a wider lens considers the broader term "gender."

This perspective will likely ask questions about the representation of gender, the extent to which a work reinforces a patriarchal society, the attitude of the author toward gender, and how relationships between men and women are defined. In *Othello*, for instance, the fact that women in Venetian society of that day could not own property (and, in fact, were viewed *as* property) would be seen as a significant factor in Desdemona's decision-making. Although an analysis through a **gendered lens** will not include all of these characteristics, it likely will assume or illustrate some of the following:

- No text exists outside the framework of gender.
- Historically, literature has privileged men, both in terms of production and

interpretation; thus, it is important to create a tradition that balances or even challenges this conventional view.

- Since expectations of roles and behavior are a function of social and cultural values, they should be recognized as subjective and transitory.
- Stereotyping based on gender is dangerous and should be avoided and confronted.

Psychological Perspective

As the term suggests, a **psychological lens** considers the behavior and motivations of characters in a work of literature. Using the language of psychology, this perspective explores how the conscious and unconscious drives and desires — including repression, sexuality, childhood experiences, and fear — influence human actions. In general, reading through a psychological lens involves asking questions about the causes and effects of characters' behavior. For instance, in *Othello*, a psychological perspective might probe the experiences that led to Iago's ruthless ambition or consider whether he is beset by insecurities that lead him to doubt the sincerity of Othello's friendship.

An interpretation from a psychological perspective adheres to the following principles:

- An investigation of the psychology of a character or of the author is key to understanding the meaning or theme of a literary text.
- Characters are driven by unconscious motivations; a character's growing awareness of these forces may inform the plot of the work.
- A literary text may be the fictional expression of an author's personality and state of mind.
- Symbols are best understood as expressions of unconscious emotions.

In this John Massey Wright engraving of act V, scene ii, Emilia is literally closer to Desdemona than Othello is, and her dress suggests that she is already in mourning. **What does this image of Desdemona's death suggest about the bonds between women?**

Cultural Criticism

While formalism is the most traditional of the literary perspectives we are discussing, cultural criticism is more recent. When you read through a **cultural lens**, you examine how different races and ethnicities, social and economic class distinctions, and political ideologies influence the creation and interpretation of literature. Cultural criticism examines the privileging of certain groups and questions traditional hierarchies based on race, gender, and class. This perspective also seeks to break down the distinctions between so-called high art and the popular culture of everyday experience. In fact, cultural criticism may question the very nature of the literary canon — that is, why some works are valued as "classic" and thus considered more worthy of study and interpretation than others.

Although cultural criticism covers a broad landscape, it focuses on how dominant cultures or groups have silenced, devalued, misrepresented, or even demonized marginalized ones. In *Othello*, for instance, a cultural critic might explore how racism in Venetian hierarchical culture affects Othello's identity. This lens might also offer an interpretation of contemporary films, such as *O*, that filter Shakespeare's play through modern-day attitudes toward race.

The casting of Paul Robeson as Othello in 1930 — the first time since 1825 that a black man was cast in a major production of the play — was controversial and received mixed reviews. Criticism ranged from his height (too tall) to his kissing the white actress who played Desdemona. Nevertheless, he reprised the role all over the world and always loved it. He said it was "killing two birds with one stone. I'm acting and talking for the negroes in the way only Shakespeare can." **Do you think *Othello* talks for black people? Is there any justification for "colorblind" casting, or should the part of Othello always be played by a black man?**

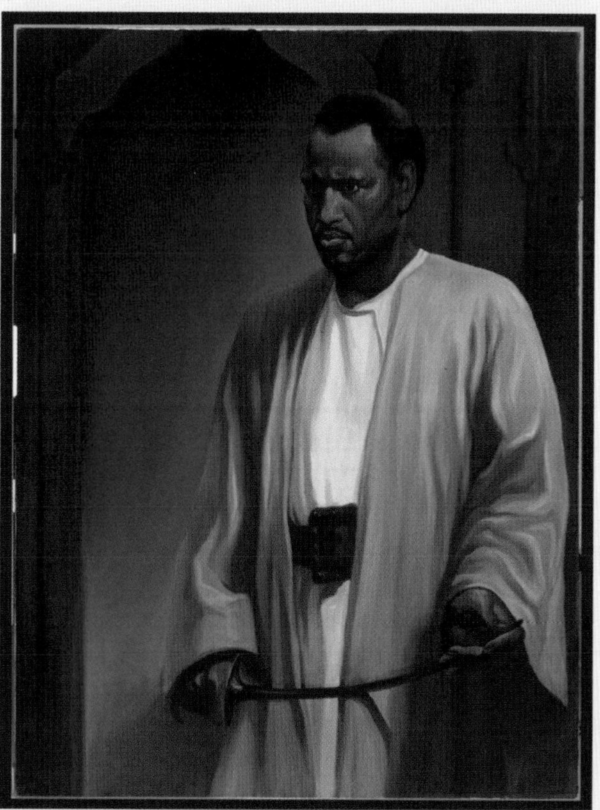

National Portrait Gallery, Smithsonian Institution/Art Resource, NY

The following tenets guide our interpretation of a work through a cultural lens:

- Ethnicity, race, social class, and religious affiliation affect how literary texts are produced and understood.
- Exploring how power — having it or being denied it — influences a literary text is a legitimate way to analyze and interpret the work.
- Studying the voices of traditionally marginalized groups is essential to a deeper understanding of how various cultures are represented in literature.
- Traditional criteria to assign value to literary works are as open to interpretation as are the texts themselves.

Keep in mind that these critical lenses are choices, meaning that most texts can be interpreted in a number of ways. These different perspectives open up possibilities for making sense of a work of literature — and ways of understanding our own experiences. No single perspective is "right," and none is " best." By exploring a single text from multiple perspectives, we hope to deepen our understanding of its themes and meaning, and develop a greater appreciation of the richness of the work. As English essayist Joseph Addison reminded us over three centuries ago, we do physical exercise to strengthen our body — and we read to strengthen the muscles of our mind.

TEXTS IN CONTEXT

Isaac Butler / *Why Is Othello Black?* (nonfiction)
Charles Lamb / from *Othello's Color: Theatrical versus Literary Representation* (nonfiction)
Charles West Cope / *Othello Relating His Adventures* (engraving)
Jennifer Dunn Hill / *Reading* Othello *and Watching a Girl Skip Rope* (poetry)
Toni Morrison / from *Desdemona* (drama)
Jeanne Murray Walker / *How Mother Courage Saves Desdemona* (poetry)
James Earl Jones / from *The Sun God* (nonfiction)
from the 2001 BBC adaptation of *Othello* (drama)
Nicole Galland / from *I, Iago* (fiction)

Why Is Othello Black?

ISAAC BUTLER

Isaac Butler is an American writer, theater director, and founder of *Parabasis*, a well-known theater blog. Butler is also a contributing writer and critic for *Slate*, the *Guardian*, the *Los Angeles Review of Books*, and *American Theatre.* He is currently the senior editor for the *Perception Institute*, a consortium of public policy researchers and advocates dedicated to using science to reduce discrimination and other social ills linked to race and identity. In "Why Is Othello Black?" Butler examines the cultural and historical context in which Shakespeare wrote, exploring issues of identity as they relate to race and ethnicity.

Is Othello black? With the news that David Oyelowo will play Othello opposite Daniel Craig's Iago and that the Metropolitan Opera is finally discontinuing the practice of blackface in productions of *Otello,* we may see a revival of this oft-asked question. What people mean when they ask if Othello is black is: What did Shakespeare mean when he called Othello black? Would we say Othello is black today?

It's an understandable question. Shakespeare's writing mostly predates the transatlantic slave trade and the more modern obsession with biological classification, both of which gave rise to our contemporary ideas of race. When Shakespeare used the word "black" he was not exactly describing a race the way we would. He meant instead someone with darker skin than an Englishman at a time when Englishmen were very, very pale. Although Othello is a Moor, and although we often assume he is from Africa, he never names his birthplace in the play. In Shakespeare's time, Moors could be from Africa, but they could also be from the Middle East, or even Spain.

While the question is logical to me, as a reader, a director, and a lover of Shakespeare, it's not the most interesting one. As language's meaning evolves, so do these plays, even if their words remain exactly the same. To us today, the word "black" carries with it a specific cluster of associations informed by history, culture, stereotypes, and literature. Othello may have started in conversation with Shakespeare's definition of blackness, but today, he speaks with ours.

A much more interesting question, really, is: *Why is Othello black?* Why did Shakespeare write a domestic tragedy about jealousy, and make the husband a Moor? Is Othello's race a canard, or is it the key to unlocking the play's deeper meanings?

Would you believe the answer to all of this 5
might involve pirates?

Before we hoist the Jolly Roger, we should consider more practical explanations for Shakespeare's choice. In August of 1600, the ambassador of the King of Barbary — roughly, modern-day Morocco — came to London as the guest of Queen Elizabeth for a six-month residency at court. He was a celebrity, Katie Sisneros, a Ph.D. candidate at the University of Minnesota focusing on representations of Turks in English popular literature, told me in an interview. "He would've had some sort of public parade. People who had never seen a Muslim, never seen a Moor, they probably saw their first Moor during that visit." Something of the ambassador's charisma and dashing good looks remain in this portrait of him painted in England at the time.

Pictures from History/Bridgeman Images

We know from records that Shakespeare's company performed at court while the ambassador — his full name was Abd el-Ouahed ben Messaoud ben Mohammed Anoun — was there, which means that Shakespeare may very well have acted in a play in front of him. (Of course it's just as likely that one or both men had a cold and missed the show; that's how nebulous Shakespeare scholarship can get.) Shakespeare likely began writing *Othello* the next year, and performed it for the first time in 1604.

If we remember that Shakespeare was a human being and a good businessman, we get the most obvious answer to our question. The Bard had just met and performed for a Moor who was a superstar. England's relationship to the Ottoman Empire and to Moors was a pressing issue. Moors were *so hot right now* back then. From there, we can imagine our inspired playwright casting about for a story about a Moor — Shakespeare's plots were mostly unoriginal and adapted — and finding Giraldi Cinthio's *Hecatommithi,* a short story collection modeled on the Decameron. Shakespeare takes two cups of Cinthio, mixes a few dashes of purloined "facts" about both Africa and Venice from recently translated books and, in a couple of years, he's baked a play.

Unfortunately for Shakespeare, in between Abd Anoun's visit and *Othello*'s premiere, Queen Elizabeth died. King James had a much frostier relationship with the Ottomans than his predecessor did. "James tried to roll back the diplomatic advances that Elizabeth made," Sisneros said. "He starts using 'let's have a new crusade' language."

Sisneros told me that to much of Shakespeare's audience, "all Moors were Turks, even though not all Turks were Moors." Furthermore, while calling someone a Moor meant that they had dark skin, in the early 17th century, the term carried a religious meaning as well. "There was no word for Muslim at the time. They used *Turk, Mosselman, Mohammedan,* these are all synonyms."

Othello, then, may have appeared at the time as an ex-Muslim — he mentions his baptism within the play — who slowly reverts to behavior that is more stereotypically "Muslim." *The Tragedy of Othello, the Moor of Venice* could be read as a nightmare about the impossibility of conversion and assimilation, meanings within the play that are less visible to us because we lack the original audience's context.

This is where piracy becomes important. If you were a British sailor working a trading ship at the time, you ran a real risk of being sacked by pirates, often Turks. If this happened, you were ransomed or, if no ransom was forthcoming, enslaved. Often, you would be offered your freedom if you converted to Islam, a process called *turning Turk.* To sweeten the deal, you could be promised land, a job, or even a wife. "If an English person is kidnapped, sold into slavery, converts for their freedom, returns to England — and this happened a lot — could they convert back?" asked Sisneros. "And if so, how could that conversion be trusted? It's an extremely troubling question at the time." Othello even uses this anxiety when breaking up a fight between his men, asking them, "Are we turned Turks? And to ourselves do that/ Which heaven hath forbid the Ottomites?"

Similarly, many English feared that Muslim converts to Christianity were incapable of fully changing. Othello's blackness, then, worked for the play's original audience as a symbol of his "true" essence. Iago scrapes away the veneer of manners Othello has layered over this, revealing what Shakespeare's audience would've thought was "real" all along. In the second half of the play, Othello begins having seizures and wild mood swings, and his vocabulary gets simpler. Othello himself echoes the idea that he's "reverting" when he commits suicide, describing to the assembled Venetians how he wants to be remembered:

And say besides that in Aleppo once.
Where a malignant and a turbaned Turk

Beat a Venetian and traduced the state,
I took by th' throat the circumsized dog
And smote him — thus! *Stabs Himself*

Othello could be talking about Desdemona as the abused Venetian or, according to Sisneros, "he could be even referring to himself. He killed the good part of himself, thus 'traducing' the Venetian state." Either way, it's hard to escape the sense that Othello is explicitly saying he has "turned Turk" by the end of the play.

15 It could also be that Othello's blackness provided Shakespeare a new way to explore questions that consumed his playwriting at this time in his career: What is identity, and how is it formed? What is a man? What is an Englishman?

To understand how Othello helped Shakespeare tease out those questions, let's first look at how Shakespeare used references to blackness. There are many (largely negative) uses of the word "black" throughout the play, and there are ways that characters reference Othello's blackness without using the word. Brabantio, Desdemona's father, enraged at his daughter's elopement, accuses Othello, saying, "Damned as thou art, thou hast enchanted her," because she never would've consented to run "to the sooty bosom/ of such a thing as thou." "Sooty" refers to Othello's skin color but, importantly, "damned" does too. Devils in Shakespeare's time were thought to be black. Black skin was a sign of being a devil, capable of witchcraft. Later, Iago promises to turn Desdemona's reputation as black as "pitch."

Complexion in Shakespeare's time was a measurement of both beauty and virtue. According to Villanova Shakespeare scholar John-Paul Spiro, to be "fair" was to be both pale and virtuous, not synonymously, but *simultaneously.* Similarly, Spiro said, "if you look at the poetry, Black-means-ugly is all over the place. The Dark Lady in the sonnets, for example. Shakespeare can't stop pointing out that she's not supposed to be attractive because she's 'dark.' In *Much Ado About Nothing,* Claudio says he'll marry a woman he's never met 'tho she be an Ethiope,' a word Shakespeare uses in other plays to mean both black and ugly." Shakespeare was a product of his time, after all, and in his time men were publishing texts like Stephen Batman's *The Doome Warning All Men to Judgement,* which describes "Ethiopes" as having "four eyes: and it is said that in Eripia be found" men that "are long necked, and mouthed as a crane."

Othello only uses the word "black" to describe himself twice. Once, as he contemplates Desdemona's infidelity, he says that perhaps she has strayed because "I am black/ And have not those soft parts of conversation/ That chamberers have." Later, he says that if she's cheated on him, "Her name, that was as fresh/ As Dian's visage, is now begrimed and black/ As mine own face." His otherness, the "passing strange" aspects that made him alluring to Desdemona, have now become ugly in his eyes — because he believes they've become ugly in hers. His entire conception of who he is has changed, paving the way for the murder of his new bride.

So does *Othello* treat Othello as a monster or do the characters in *Othello* make him that way? To Spiro, the unanswerability of the question is what makes it worth asking. "At this time — remember he's written *Hamlet, Twelfth Night,* and *Measure for Measure* not too long ago — Shakespeare is preoccupied with and invested in a deep skepticism about the knowability of the world, the self, and the other. You are a mystery to yourself; other people are a mystery to you. What is terrifying about *Othello* is that the mystery deepens with intimacy."

20 Spiro traces this thread in Shakespeare's writing to the Bard's likely familiarity with Montaigne's *Essays,* which often double back on their own assumptions, and with the shifting theological emphasis of Protestantism. "In Catholicism, to be a good person, you have to go to confession and mass. Protestantism is now saying 'No, you must always doubt your

intentions, you must always wonder if you did things for the right reason.'" As a result, Shakespeare's characters' thoughts become a swirling vortex of uncertainty. "Look at Brutus," Spiro said. "Look at Hamlet. The more you interrogate the self, the more incoherent and unknowable it gets."

And Othello presented Shakespeare's audience with a kind of incoherence when he first walked onstage: He did not fit any of his era's stereotypes of how he should behave. At the beginning of the play, Othello is straightforward, honest, and noble. He cannot conceive of being lied to. He isn't at all what an English audience would expect. The Venetians around him, on the other hand, are exactly what the audience would expect. They're, venal, dishonest, passionate, and unfaithful. Iago's case against Desdemona rests in part on using these stereotypes as proof. As he says to Othello, "In Venice [wives] do let heaven see the pranks / They dare not show their husbands."

"If Othello really is that decent, honest, and credulous, if he can really have friends and be loved by a beautiful woman, the white characters in the play can't accept it," Spiro said. "Iago has to destroy him."

Throughout his career, Shakespeare was conflicted about identity at the moment when the question *What is an Englishman?* was as vital to his audience as questions about identity are to us today. "In *Twelfth Night* you have the idea that you could make someone insane simply by telling him he's insane," Spiro said. "If Richard III had had a straight back, would he be a good person? Is his crooked back a sign that he is a bad person, or do we treat people with crooked backs badly?" To Spiro, the terrifying note Shakespeare sounds again and again, despite being a word-drunk pioneer of the English language, is that talking about it doesn't help. Hamlet can't reason his way out of the trap of the self. Neither can Othello, who is helped neither by logic, nor by proof, nor friendship, nor even by language, because all of these normal ways of making sense of the world have been arrayed in a conspiracy against him by Iago.

All along, the play is asking what makes a person, what is identity, and how belonging to an identity group shapes who you are. These questions haunt us today, but they were important to Shakespeare's audience as well. Moors weren't the only converts, after all. The entire nation had recently "converted" to the Church of England. If, according to your new faith your goodness is never guaranteed, and if all Iago needs is two days to turn a noble convert and trusted military leader into a monster, imagine what he could do if left alone with you.

[2015]

QUESTIONS

1. After posing a question in the first sentence, Isaac Butler says that "it's not the most interesting one" (para. 3). What question intrigues him more, and why?
2. What do pirates have to do with Butler's overall inquiry into the play?
3. According to Butler, how does Shakespeare's decision to make his central character a Moor show that he was "a good businessman" (para. 8)?
4. What does Butler mean when he claims that the play "could be read as a nightmare about the impossibility of conversion and assimilation, meanings within the play that are less visible to us because we lack the original audience's context" (para. 11)? Do you agree? Why or why not?
5. How does Butler's analysis reflect a historical perspective on *Othello*? Cite at least three examples from the article to support your response.
6. Where in this essay does Butler move toward a more psychological lens? Do you think this shift supports or challenges the historical lens? Explain.

from Othello's Color: Theatrical versus Literary Representation

CHARLES LAMB

Charles Lamb (1775–1834) was an English essayist and poet. He worked for more than thirty years as a clerk in the accounting office of the East India Company, writing in his evenings and on Sundays. He enjoyed great popularity in the 1820s when his essays appeared in the *London Magazine* under the penname "Elia." He and his sister Mary produced the popular book *Tales from Shakespeare*, prose versions of the plays, intended for children. Following is an excerpt from Lamb's criticism *On the Tragedies of Shakespeare, Considered with Reference to Their Fitness for Stage Representation* (1811).

Nothing can be more soothing, more flattering to the nobler parts of our natures, than to read of a young Venetian lady of highest extraction, through the force of love, and from a sense of merit in him whom she loved, laying aside every consideration of kindred, and country, and colour, and wedding with a *coal black Moor*, (for such he is represented, in the imperfect state of knowledge respecting foreign countries in those days compared with our own, or in compliance with popular notions, though the Moors are now well enough known to be by many shades less worthy of a white woman's fancy,) — it is the perfect triumph of virtue over accidents, of the imagination over the senses. She sees Othello's colour in his mind. But upon the stage, when the imagination is no longer the ruling faculty, but we are left to our poor, unassisted senses, I appeal to every one that has seen Othello played, whether he did not, on the contrary, sink Othello's mind in his colour; whether he did not find something extremely revolting in the courtship and wedded caresses of Othello and Desdemona; and whether the actual sight of the thing did not overweigh all that beautiful compromise which we make in reading; — and the reason it should do so is obvious, because there is just so much reality presented to our senses as to give a perception of disagreement, with not enough of belief in the internal motives — all that which is unseen — to overpower and reconcile the first and obvious prejudices. What we see upon a stage is body and bodily action; what we are conscious of in reading is almost exclusively the mind, and its movements; and this I think may sufficiently account for the very different sort of delight with which the same play so often affects us in the reading and in the seeing.

[1811]

QUESTIONS

1. What point does Charles Lamb make in his parenthetical comment about Othello as a "*coal black Moor*, (for such he is represented, in the imperfect state of knowledge respecting foreign countries in those days compared with our own, or in compliance with popular notions, though the Moors are now well enough known to be by many shades less worthy of white woman's fancy)"?
2. Why does Lamb believe that Desdemona "sees Othello's colour in his mind"?
3. What "beautiful compromise" does Lamb believe we make when we read *Othello*?
4. Overall, how would you sum up the argument that Lamb makes about a stage production of *Othello*? Pay particular attention to the separation of intellect and emotion that Lamb assumes.
5. Discuss Lamb's analysis as an example of using an historical lens to read a work of literature. What qualities of that perspective does his argument illustrate?

Othello Relating His Adventures

CHARLES WEST COPE

Best known for several frescos on display in the House of Lords in London, Charles West Cope (1811–1890) was an English etcher and painter who worked during the Victorian era and who focused mostly on genre and historical scenes. Cope tended to illustrate scenes from popular history as well as the domestic sphere of life, which made his artwork well received during his lifetime. In "Othello Relating His Adventures," a copperplate engraving, Cope captures the glamor of Venice and the interplay between assimilation and cultural division that Shakespeare's play explores.

Private Collection / © Look and Learn / Bridgeman Images

[c. 1880]

QUESTIONS

1. What does the composition of the engraving suggest about the relationship between Othello, Brabantio, and Desdemona?
2. How do background and framing provide their own commentary on the act of storytelling and the value placed on it?
3. How does this nineteenth-century depiction of Othello represent his racial identity? Is it ambiguous? Does it minimize or emphasize his differences from Brabantio and Desdemona? How does his attire support your interpretation?
4. How does this image interpret the speech Othello gives to describe his courtship of Desdemona in act 1, scene iii, through the perspective of cultural criticism?

Reading *Othello* and Watching a Girl Skip Rope

JENNIFER HILL

A freelance writer, Jennifer Hill (b. 1969) is the author of several books of poetry, including *Questioning Walls Open* (2001), *Book of Days* (2006), and *You Look Young Enough to Be Relevant* (2017). She has served as an artist-in-residence in both elementary and high schools in Pennsylvania. She is also the designer, editor, and owner of Paper Kite Books, a small press devoted to the publication of poetry. "Reading *Othello* and Watching a Girl Skip Rope" was first published in the anthology *In a Fine Frenzy: Poets Respond to Shakespeare* (2005).

Mouthing a rhyme about ivy
or a handkerchief fallen,
the rope swings and arms circle
like time in otherworldly whips.

The girl plays alone on asphalt,
under the unforgivable blue sky,
for better or bitter left to her devices,
tapping the sureness of the world with rope,
body leaping, airborne for an instant,

her grip tightens on the handle,
braids released like wings —
the boys led by their longing
to this girl, a strumpet, trumpet
out loud in the open yard.

What girl will count her sins
aloud when she can only go
as far as seven? The cord warps
midair on love, love.
Not high enough for joy,
low enough for God.

[2005]

QUESTIONS

1. What allusions to *Othello* do you find in this poem? Consider direct references as well as more oblique ones (e.g., "for better or bitter," line 7). How do these lead you to consider a new perspective either on the play itself or on a specific character or relationship?
2. The poem underscores the tension between confinement and freedom. What specific words and images establish this conflict? Ultimately, does the balance tip in favor of one or the other?
3. Hill uses a number of unusual phrases, such as "otherworldly whips" (l. 4) and "unforgivable blue sky" (l. 6). What is the effect of these and any others you notice?
4. How do you interpret the last four lines of the poem?
5. Throughout the poem, the girl never speaks out loud. Why not? How do you interpret the poet's decision to withhold an audible voice?
6. Reading *Othello* and jumping rope seem, on the surface, to be two unrelated activities. How does the poet bring them together? How does the more ordinary, physical activity inform the more cerebral, loftier one? Or do you think the poem discourages such binary thinking?
7. In what ways does this poem demonstrate a gendered interpretation of *Othello*? Is it a defense of Desdemona, or a challenge to conventional interpretations of her? Or do you read it as more of a commentary on the society of the time than on any one character? Cite specifics in the poem to support your position.

---

from Desdemona

TONI MORRISON

Toni Morrison (b. 1931) is best known for her novels, including *Beloved* (1987), which won the Pulitzer Prize, *The Bluest Eye* (1970), and *Song of Solomon* (1977). Among her many accolades, Morrison was awarded the Nobel Prize for Literature in 1993 and the Presidential Medal of Freedom in 2012. She has taught at numerous colleges and is professor emerita at Princeton University. Morrison's play *Desdemona* originated as a challenge from the experimental theater and opera director Peter Sellars, who felt that *Othello* "made no sense" and "had outlived its usefulness." Morrison disagreed and made a pact to find a way to talk back to Shakespeare. The result was *Desdemona*, a concert-play first produced in France in 2011, directed by Sellars. Morrison wrote the text of this interactive play and Malian singer-songwriter Rokia Traore wrote the music and lyrics. The following excerpt from the opening to the play presents Desdemona speaking from the afterlife and describing her nursemaid, Barbary.

I

DESDEMONA My name is Desdemona. The word, Desdemona, means misery. It means ill fated. It means doomed. Perhaps my parents believed or imagined or knew my fortune at the moment of my birth. Perhaps being born a girl gave them all they needed to know of what my life would be like. That it would be subject to the whims of my elders and the control of men. Certainly that was the standard, no, the obligation of females in Venice when I was a girl. Men made the rules; women followed them. A step away was doom, indeed, and misery without relief. My parents, keenly aware and approving of that system, could anticipate the future of a girl child accurately.

They were wrong. They knew the system, but they did not know me.

I am not the meaning of a name I did not choose. . . .

II

My mother was a lady of virtue whose practice and observation of manners were flawless. She taught me how to handle myself at table, how to be courteous in speech, when and how to drop my eyes, smile, curtsey. As was the custom, she did not tolerate dispute from a child, nor involve herself in what could be called my interior life. There were strict rules of deportment, solutions for every problem a young girl could have. And there was sensible punishment designed for each impropriety. Constraint was the theme of behavior. Duty was its plot.

I remember once splashing barefoot in our pond, pretending I was one of the swans that swam there. My slippers were tossed aside; the hem of my dress wet. My unleashed laughter was long and loud. The unseemliness of such behavior in a girl of less than one decade brought my mother's attention. Too old, she scolded, for such carelessness. To emphasize the point, my slippers were taken away and I remained barefoot for ten days. It was a small thing, embarrassing, inconvenient, but definitely clarifying. It meant my desires, my imagination must remain hidden. It was as though a dark heavy curtain enclosed me. Yet wrapping that curtain over my willfulness served to strengthen it.

My solace in those early days lay with my nurse, Barbary. She alone encouraged a slit in that curtain. Barbary alone conspired with me to let my imagination run free. She told me stories of other lives, other countries. Places where gods speak in thundering silence and mimic human faces and forms. Where nature is not a crafted, pretty thing, but wild, sacred and instructive. Unlike the staid, unbending women of my country, she moved with the fluid grace I saw only in swans and the fronds of willow trees. To hear Barbary sing was to wonder at the mediocrity of flutes and pipes. She was more alive than anyone I knew and more loving. She tended me as though she were my birth mother: braided my hair, dressed me, comforted me when I was ill and danced with me when I recovered. I loved her. Her heart, so wide, seemed to hold the entire world in awe and to savor its every delight.

Yet that same heart, wide as it was, proved vulnerable. When I needed her most, she stumbled under the spell of her lover. He forsook her and turned her ecstasy into ash. Eyes pooled with tears, she sang her loss of him, of love, and life.

[2012]

QUESTIONS

1. How is the Desdemona in this passage similar to and different from the woman Shakespeare depicts? Pay particular attention to the first act of *Othello*, in which Desdemona has a voice in the public arena as she addresses her father as well as the Duke of Venice, who is Othello's superior officer.

2. What do you think Desdemona means with the description of expectations for women: "Constraint was the theme of behavior. Duty was its plot"?
3. Morrison not only gives Desdemona a voice in this play, but she offers us the "missing women" — that is, those who were only alluded to in *Othello* — by providing detailed descriptions of their behavior and values. How does Morrison characterize Desdemona's mother and the nursemaid, Barbary? How might this information influence your interpretation of the play?
4. Morrison displaces Othello as the central character in the play, so it might seem that a gendered lens is the most obvious approach to take to reading the play. However, Morrison also shifts the power dynamics by emphasizing the interplay between European and African cultures. How might you view the play through the lens of cultural criticism? Consider at least two characteristics of that critical perspective.
5. The poet Adrienne Rich defined revision: "We need to know the writing of the past, and know it differently than we have ever known it; not to pass on a tradition but to break its hold over us." To what extent do you think Morrison's play "breaks [tradition's] hold on us"? Use Shakespeare's *Othello* along with this passage as your evidence; you might also listen to some of the clips from *Desdemona* in performance with the music of Rokia Traore that are available on YouTube.

How Mother Courage Saves Desdemona

JEANNE MURRAY WALKER

Jeanne Murray Walker (b. 1944) is a professor of English at the University of Delaware, where she heads the creative writing concentration. She has written eight volumes of poetry, including *Helping the Morning: New and Selected Poems* (2014), a memoir, and several plays. "How Mother Courage Saves Desdemona," which appeared in her collection *A Deed to the Light* (2004), references the character from Bertolt Brecht's play *Mother Courage and Her Children* (1939). The title character in Brecht's antiwar play, Mother Courage is a shrewd but cynical woman whose courage is her will to survive.

for Susan Sweeney

Desdemona is sobbing in the bedroom, a hole
in her heart. when Mother Courage strides in
wearing black-tie shoes, to switch on the lamp.

She has just driven her wagon across Europe
to find her dead daughter, Katrin,
stripped the body to sell her shirt, and then

walked aimlessly all night. At the door
of a theatre she hears a young woman sobbing.
Tenderly she whispers, *Here, Little Sausage, blow*

on your hem. She wants to pull Desdemona from
her extravagant belief in her own downfall.
Because what is a handkerchief, the old woman asks,
but a certain way of thinking about the world,

a flutter in the wind, anybody's wind.
If you aren't careful, you nest in one man's pocket

and then whoosh, you turn up in another's.
But you are a precious clue, the only real thing
in the play! You can't trust a man

whose name begins with O! When he mutters,
Turn out the light, Sheepface, Daughter, Desdemona,
YOU *are the light! Given what that Moor did,*

you should be ashamed to leave a trail of boohoos
like snail tracks across Europe!
Get up! It's time to find another play.

[2005]

QUESTIONS

1. How does Jeanne Murray Walker depict the relationship between Desdemona and Mother Courage in this poem? How do the details in the opening stanza summarize the characters' differences?
2. How do you interpret the speaker's description of Desdemona's "extravagant belief in her own downfall" (l. 11)?
3. What do you think Walker suggests when Mother Courage tells Desdemona that she is "a precious clue, the only real thing / in the play!" (ll. 17–18)
4. In an interview, Walker explained that Desdemona is the only "genuine, open, authentic, and sincere" character in the play, but "it's that very virtue that makes her vulnerable." To what extent do you agree with this interpretation? Does this poem support or question that view of Desdemona?
5. How would you describe the tone of this poem? Pay special attention to the ending, where Mother Courage takes over as speaker.
6. Applying either a gendered or psychological perspective to this poem, consider Mother Courage's attitude toward Othello. Why do you believe she "saves" Desdemona?

from **The Sun God**

JAMES EARL JONES

James Earl Jones (b. 1931) is an American stage and film actor known for his iconic roles in film and television, and on stage. He graduated with a degree in drama from the University of Michigan in 1955, then fought in the Korean War. Upon returning from war, Jones began a career in acting that has spanned over 60 years and is studded with almost every major award. He won a Tony and a Golden Globe for his role in the play *The Great White Hope* in 1967 and was later nominated for an Academy Award for his role in the film version of the same play in 1970. In addition to numerous other stage and film roles, Jones portrayed the voice of Darth Vader in the *Star Wars* film series (1977–1983) as well the voice of Mufasa in *The Lion King* (1994). Jones won two Emmys in 1991 for work on the television show *Gabriel's Fire* (1990) and the TV movie *Heat Wave* (1990). In 2008, Jones received a Life Achievement Award from the Screen Actors Guild, and he was given an honorary Academy Award in 2011. In the following excerpt from *The Sun God*, Jones mines his extensive experience as a stage actor to explore the character of Othello, a role he has played in several productions.

I've played Oberon in *A Midsummer Night's Dream,* Claudius in *Hamlet,* Macbeth, and King Lear, but it's Othello I keep coming back to I've played him seven times, from the age of twenty-five, in 1955. to the age of fifty, in 1982. To be honest, my favorite character in *Othello* used to be Cassio; I was always baffled by the character of Othello, even after playing him so many times I think I'm finally beginning to understand him, and the rest of this essay is a collection of my latest thoughts on how to reinstate him as a truly tragic figure. When

Shakespeare writes "a *noble* Moor, in the service of Venice," that's not a joke. So the question for me has become: How can we sustain this sense of Othello's inherent nobility?

My feeling is that the play has to do with the delicate balance of an entire cosmos. Othello's life is fueled by violence and love, two contrary forces inhabiting the same body, and he is like a great fiery orb at the center, regulating and restraining other cosmic tensions Shakespeare has placed around him other celestial entities, many of them already instable from internal confusion. Iago is a great force, but before the play even begins he has secretly spun out of his orbit. He recognizes his schizophrenia when he compares himself to the god Janus. Cassio has a split too, which reveals itself when he drinks. Desdemona is the only one who is whole. She has no demons, as Giraldi Cinthio wrote her name in the 1565 story on which the play was based, she is "Disdemona": without demons. She is a being of light, a light without violence, a lunar beauty, and her calm and steady presence is just as necessary to the cosmos Shakespeare has created. Iago conjures an alter Desdemona, however, and it is Othello's inability to reconcile the two Desdemonas which results in the tragedy. This is a deeply personal play: this is also a play that involves the greatest of all beings, and so the potential for greatness within each of us. . . .

Othello's greatness is of a different model from those of Shakespeare's other tragic protagonists Lear and Claudius are kings, Macbeth murders his way to the throne, but Othello is a general, and I've always felt that Shakespeare seems more comfortable writing about royalty — probably because the possibility of tragedy is inherent to royalty. A man is put in a position of responsibility and control in which it's easy to fail, and then he fails. Othello isn't royal, even though he can claim, "I fetch my life and being / From men of royal siege" [I.ii.21–22]. In his former life he was of royal lineage, which is why it's so ironic that he then became a slave and a wanderer — but the fact of his royalty is not a quality that plays dominantly in his nature. His interest, rather, is in nobility: what matters to him is not what he was born to, but what he has made of himself, how he positions himself within the rest of humanity, and how he exists in relation to the cosmos.

At the same time, though, Othello is more than just a general: the director Gladys Vaughan and I once nicknamed him the Sun God. He's more endowed with humanity than anyone else in the realm of the play. In spite of, or rather because of, all he has been through, Othello comes to that society standing a head above anybody else, and possessed of the desire to be better than anybody else: to be kinder, to be more just, to be more responsible than anybody else: to be kinder, to be more just, to be more responsible than anybody else. . . .

Othello's grandeur has a darker source, 5
too . . . it also comes from the fact that he has been a slave, and that he has been among the wretched, and that he has come out of all that misery and is on the other side of power and he is now a supreme warrior. He could kill everybody. He could become a tyrant. He could conquer the entire world — but he doesn't, because he can restrain himself in order to keep life in balance, and he knows that if he doesn't restrain himself then the entire world will fall to violence. It's his responsibility to keep this in check. Similarly, I believe that it's the actor's responsibility to make sure that Othello keep this in check for as long as possible, so that wherever there's a choice of meaning for a line, throughout, in performance we should choose the more positive version, the one that keeps Othello the most intact for the longest time. We should not anticipate his fall but rather, with him, resist it as much as possible, and be allies with him in his ambition to indulge his capacity to love and contain his capacity to kill. . . .

The last production of *Othello* I participated in was in 1982. There are several reasons I will always remember that production, the most important being that I had just married my wife, Cecilia Hart. She came in after we opened on Broadway as a replacement for the Desdemona (we had already burnt out three actresses), and while we were still performing she was pregnant with our son, Flynn. The initial director was Peter Coe; through his decisions he allowed Christopher Plummer, who was playing Iago, to turn it into what one of the most caustic critics of the play, Thomas Rymer, called "a bloody farce" in 1693, and I think Peter's decisions leaned that way because he didn't understand the character of Desdemona, that essential third pillar, and so he wasn't getting what he needed out of the play. Instead, it seemed as if he figured that at least he'd turn it into a crowd pleaser. We were in a perfect storm for a farce. When we arrived in Minneapolis during the out-of-town try-outs, we were booked into a monster of a theater that was not conducive to subtlety, and where only the bold strokes of performance seemed to register: the tone was therefore set from the beginning. Then the audience surprisingly and rambunctiously responded to Iago's antics — so much so that I think it even embarrassed Chris, which wouldn't have been surprising since he is classically trained, and a fine actor. I remember quite vividly when he came off stage from a howl-fest, and said to me, echoing that unnerving line of Rymer, "Oh, darling, this is a bloody farce after all". At that moment, I knew I had a wonderful costar, but no ally.

Since Rymer, *Othello* has been described as a one-act comedy followed by four acts of tragedy. However farcical or comedic, Iago is a scary role (like Shylock), and it is a difficult role for any human being because it is so ugly. After all, Iago is the man who invents racism (in the context of the play). So, without the help of a good director the actor is tempted to take it to the jokes. The day I told Peter I couldn't work with him anymore, he responded, "You're just jealous because Iago's getting all the laughs." Well, I couldn't have stated my case more clearly, except that I wouldn't have used the word "jealous."

I've always felt that Iago encapsulates the hurt of the modern man. He might be the most understandable character in this age, when all of us can, if we're not lucky, have the experience of being passed over and of not having the chance to get ahead in society. Iago is sorely wanting, and the last straw was when he found out that he wasn't going to be chosen as Othello's lieutenant.

There's a reason Othello didn't choose Iago as his lieutenant. My suspicion is that Iago knew too much, and that he was the one who did the dirty work that allowed Othello to keep his hands clean. He was the Beria to Othello's Stalin — he was the head of their equivalent of a secret police, and he possessed information about Othello as well as about everyone he would have had to investigate, and in the text we can feel something of that in his valuing, search for, and manipulation of information. Whatever use the secret police can be, however, it eventually comes to an end — on the other side, the moral and emotional investment of he who operates as the secret police costs a great deal. Long before the relationship between the two men becomes completely destructive, it is perhaps already a subtly abusive relationship. That dark history is both why Iago isn't chosen, and why he thinks he ought to be. Othello has two liaisons in this culture — and he needs them both, for he is a stranger in a strange land. Iago is one; Cassio is the other — but Cassio has clean hands, and he is more socialized and less dangerous to be promoted to a position of power in this society.

As a result, Cassio is chosen and Iago is passed over, which must have hurt beyond anything I think Shakespeare was able to write about, but he indicated it, and he gave us the fruit of that hurt. "Revenge" is a small word when it comes to Iago, for he is motivated by a source much deeper; he's operating from the soul. He is not a motiveless villain in any way, for his motives are almost too common, and too real. Therefore, to play Iago as glib is to lose the essence of that hurt. Lucifer was God's most glorious angel until God asked something of him he couldn't do; Lucifer refused, and got kicked out of heaven. The disappointment drifted into bitterness, and that bitterness converted his nature and he became Satan. Iago's pain is that of Lucifer himself.

Zoe Caldwell was brought in as the rescue director, and she almost salvaged that production. She said that audiences were coming to see the classic Titans clash, both as actors on the stage, Chris and me, and as characters in the play, Iago and Othello. "You must take Chris on," she said. I didn't think that Shakespeare had written such a scene, and I said, "I don't know what you mean."[1] Her response was simply, "I know you don't." I passed up the opportunity to explore something in that production, and now I'm coming to grips with it in this essay. But even though I do agree, and always did agree with Zoe that they are two great figures, I've never seen the play as a battle between them. In fact, it's the opposite: they are brothers, and the fact that there is a conflict between them is always a surprise to Othello. There can't be an out-and-out duel between them because they're fitted with different pistols. Iago is loaded with the prose with which he can counsel, charm, and diddle with the audience: this language is plain talk, close to everyday speech. Furthermore, Iago speaks directly to the audience in his soliloquies in what could even be called *The Confessions of Iago.* Othello, on the other hand, is loaded with iambic pentameter: this language, by contrast, is classical, poetic. He doesn't have the chance to speak directly to the audience in that familiar manner. Both Iago and Othello are great, but they are great in very different modes. . . .

Othello is written with nobility and power, and so to diminish him, to make him the victim of Iago, is to lose out on one of the classic antagonistic relationships in all of literature. Othello is responsible for the loss of his nobility in the moment when he chooses to turn to revenge.

When you diffuse the responsibility of the hero and put it onto others, then you take away from his greatness, and from the tragedy. I believe that Shakespeare wrote his tragic characters as those who had great responsibilities and

[1] In many of Shakespeare's tragedies, the issue of "fault" seems never in question. The villain Cassius in Shakespeare's *Julius Caesar* says to his co-conspirator, "The fault, dear Brutus, is not in our stars but in ourselves, that we are the underlings." And though King Lear cries out against his daughters, claiming he is "a man more sinned against than sinning," he is later able to acknowledge his kinship with and responsibility to the wretched of the earth when his rage collapses during the storm on the heath. Likewise, King Leontes in *The Winter's Tale* seems to need no outside encouragement as he struggles in the throes of his own jealousy; he is on "automatic drive." I believe the issue of "fault" is much more critical in another tragedy: *Othello.* Given how the play is written, the reader may conclude that Othello's jealousy and downfall is Iago's fault, but I don't think any hero can be absolved of responsibility or fault.

When director Zoe Caldwell suggested that audiences for that production of *Othello* came to see two titans clash, and so I "must take Chris on," I thought she meant that I — James Earl Jones in the role of Othello — should take on or duke it out with Chris Plummer as Iago. I was baffled because I didn't find in the text enough support for that. However, if I had taken her to mean that I must take Chris's character *in* — absorb him, and be more Iago-like — there are grounds for that interpretation. The plot of Shakespeare's *Othello* was lifted from an Italian novella in which both the Othello character and the Iago character, each armed with a sand-filled stocking, sneak into Desdemona's bedroom and bludgeon her to death together. Remnants of this warped partnership persist in Shakespeare's play: for instance, when the issue of Desdemona's infidelity is hinted at early on and out of the blue, Othello's response is to tell Iago to "be sure thou prove my love a whore!" Note that he doesn't ask Iago to prove Desdemona is *not* a whore — thus, his command suggests both men are bonded. Shakespeare's subtle choices yielded much more fertile dramatic terrain than that of the Italian novella; in the play, one man only hints to another, the other man demands proof, and the insinuator has no proof. This chain of events begins a dance of hubris between the men, one that obscures the issue of fault. The reader may too easily see Othello as a victim, when in truth he becomes the primary perpetrator the minute he expresses doubt in the fidelity of his wife.

who failed in their responsibilities. There can be no pathos allowed in the lives of heroes, and there's only this one moment in *Othello* when that can be turned around. It makes Othello himself more of a monster, but that's better than a pathetic fool.

From that point on, it's Othello's fault. It has to be.

That's the essential question — whose fault is it? — not just for *Othello*, but for all the tragedies. It has to be the fault of Othello, and of Lear, and of all the other tragic protagonists, or the plays fall apart. The responsibility cannot be externalized. It cannot be the fault of the others, neither of Iago, nor of Goneril and Regan.

Tragedy happens when someone who has great potential does not live up to it and fails. I find that all the tragedies are the fault of the great men. When King Lear cries out, at one of his worst moments, "I am a man / More sinned against than sinning" (3.2.56–57), he must know deep down that he's lying, because he had all the power, and in particular he had all the power to sin, and he did, so he was more sinning than sinned against.

Similarly, Othello should know that it's not Iago's fault, and the audience too should know that the tragedy that will follow is entirely the fault of Othello.

[2013]

QUESTIONS

1. What evidence from *Othello* would support James Earl Jones's assertion that "Othello's life is fueled by violence and love, two contrary forces inhabiting the same body, and he is like a great fiery orb at the center, regulating and restraining other cosmic tensions" (para. 2)? Cite at least three quotations.
2. What does Jones mean by Iago's "schizophrenia" (para. 2)?
3. What distinction does Jones make between "royalty" and "nobility"? To what extent do you agree with his analysis of Othello according to these terms?
4. Jones is not writing about race when he says that Othello's "grandeur has a darker source" (para. 5). What does he mean?
5. On what basis does Jones argue that Othello is not the victim of Iago? Do you agree or disagree with that assessment? Explain.
6. Do you agree with Jones that the moment when Othello chooses revenge he becomes "more of a monster, but that's better than a pathetic fool" (para. 13)? What specific scenes from the play support your argument?
7. From the vantage of an actor playing Othello, Jones presents a psychological analysis. Explain how his perspective illustrates at least three characteristics of the psychological lens.
8. James Earl Jones has said that "Othello is well accounted for verbally" in lines 376–89 of act III, scene iii, "but the problem then becomes how to dramatize his threats. I would suggest they would have Othello resort to more and more ruthless acting out his words; to torture Iago. And the only form of torture that would fit that interpretation is the threat of drowning, leading to actual water boarding on stage, interspersed with as much dialog as possible." What does this interpretation of the scene suggest about the dynamic between the two characters? If you were the director of a production of the play, how would you dramatize that scene, based on your understanding of both Othello and Iago?

from **Othello (2001 BBC film adaptation)**

This 2001 adaption of *Othello* is set in contemporary London during a time of racial tensions. The protagonist is John Othello, a black police officer who is chosen as the next police commissioner after he ends a riot. Below are two excerpts from the movie's script.

In the following excerpt, John Othello has been called to the scene of a community outraged at what they view as police brutality during an alleged drug raid. A calm and dignified Othello, in full dress uniform, stands on a balcony above a crowd of angry citizens who have been rioting; small fires blaze in the background.

JOHN OTHELLO Brothers and Sisters, you know who I am. For those of you who don't know me, my name is John Othello. I was born here. Grew up on these streets. I went to school here. So you know you'll get nothing but the truth from me.

CROWD What happened to Billy Coates?

JOHN OTHELLO I will tell you. A terrible thing has happened. A short while ago, Billy Coates died in hospital.[1] So what do we do now? You tell me. We can burn down the police station. . . . Loot the shops. Burn our houses. Is that what you want? I know you're angry, but before you go ahead, I want you to stop, take a second—and look. The world is watching us tonight. Now is that the way you want the world to see us? Looting our shops? Trashing our whole community? What do you think the world will call us then? Ignorant fools. And you know they will. So, my friends, I promise you this, if Billy Coates was unlawfully killed, there will be no escape for his killers, there will be no place for them to hide. Believe me, that is a promise. We have our dignity. We just want justice. We must have justice under the law—justice under the law.

These two images, both from the BBC film, show different views of John Othello as he faces the angry crowd. **How would you describe his demeanor in the first frame? What does his attitude toward the crowd seem to be? In the second frame, what does the camera angle, including the light from fires on the street below, suggest about John Othello's relationship with the people he is addressing?**

[1] Billy Coates, a black man, was arrested and beaten by the police after being falsely accused of dealing drugs.

In the following excerpt, the prime minister offers Othello the job of police commissioner. The reason for Othello's promotion is twofold: He successfully defused what might have become a race riot, and the former commissioner was just caught uttering a racial slur. As the scene begins, Othello is called into the office of the prime minister.

PRIME MINISTER John, wonderful to meet you. What you did yesterday, I think that hit the spot for all of us. I won't beat around the bush. We want to offer you the job. Are you on for it?

JOHN OTHELLO As commissioner?

PRIME MINISTER I know. You'd be skipping a couple of rungs. But we felt we wanted to make a very clear, bold statement about the kind of Britain we want our kids to grow up in. So what do you think, John? Will you take it on?

JOHN OTHELLO Prime Minister, is all this about just about making a clear bold statement, or do you really believe I'm the best man for the job?

PRIME MINISTER I wouldn't have offered it if I didn't. Do you have any doubts about your ability to handle it?

JOHN OTHELLO It's not that. I know my worth. I just never thought I'd have a chance to prove it.

[2001]

QUESTIONS

1. How well do you believe the more contemporary setting portraying racial tensions and political corruption in England captures major themes and ideas in *Othello*?
2. How does John Othello define himself as both part of the community in the housing project and a rising star in the law enforcement community? Cite specific textual evidence to support your response.
3. What traits of Shakespeare's Othello can you discern in John Othello, based on these brief scenes from the film?
4. How might this adaptation of *Othello* be viewed from a cultural perspective that focuses on depictions of social class and power? Given the importance of the visual and audio elements of film, it will be best if you can watch these two clips on YouTube and include them in your analysis.

from I, Iago

NICOLE GALLAND

Nicole Galland (b. 1955), who earned her BA in comparative religion from Harvard University, has written five novels of historical fiction. These include *Revenge of the Rose* (2006) and *Godiva* (2013). In 2015, she published *Stepdog*, her first contemporary novel. The following two excerpts are from the opening and closing sections of *I, Iago* (2012), a retelling of *Othello* in the voice of Iago. The excerpt below shows scenes from the beginning and end of the novel.

They called me "honest Iago" from an early age, but in Venice, this is not a compliment. It is rebuke. One does not prosper by honesty. One does not rise in the social ranks. One does not curry favors. Honesty causes upset, and Venice is serene. The Serene Republic. It says so right there on the seal of state, which I could read when I was two, or so claimed the governess who struggled to keep up with my precociousness.

I am the fifth son born into a family where even a second son is redundant. My eldest brother, Rizardo, learned the family business, which he would inherit someday, along with the family home and the family riches. The second-born, lacking all imagination, of course became a priest. The third and fourth did not amount to much: one died in infancy; the next made it to maturity with military aspirations, but when I was ten years, he wounded himself so severely in cadet training that he bled to death. An artillery man, he had been cleaning his ceremonial sword when it slipped from his grasp, and the blade gouged him deep near his groin.

A tragedy, of course. But young as I was, I found in it a poignant irony, and said so one too many times in father's hearing. I was whipped for my candor. And then I was informed that it fell to me to restore the family's military honor. Clearly I would never make it as a courtier, a merchant, or any other trade that required me to don a false front. I was, said father irritably, too blunt and honest for anything but warfare. . . .

"Othello." Lodovico's voice broke into our shared silence. "You are removed from office. We'll keep you imprisoned until we can present your crimes to the Venetian Senate. Cassio will rule in Cyprus. For this villain" — and of course by that he meant me — "he will be tortured for as long as he survives it." He snapped his fingers at the attendants who were warily watching all of this unfold. "Come, bring Othello away."

5 Othello glanced at me a final time. I nodded slightly, in farewell. I knew he had a dagger in his boot; I was the only one in this room who knew that — not even Cassio had inkling of it. If I really hated Othello, I would have warned them that he had a weapon, I would have forced him to remain alive with me, and go out into the world, and be judged by others who would never judge themselves. I had the power to do that to him. If I hated him, I would have told them.

I did not say a word. I watched him rise, and ask them for the favor of their patience as he gave what they supposed would be his final speech before imprisonment. The words he spoke washed right over me; I did not hear them. I was saying my own silent farewell, offering and asking redemption of a soul about to be unfettered.

He startled all of them by pulling out the dagger from his boot and shoving it hard into his own breastbone. Unsurprised but heartbroken, I lowered my head with a prayer of deliverance. As the self-important men around us cried out in shock and dismay, Othello fell onto the bed between the women. He kissed Desdemona's lifeless body tenderly, before falling into silence.

"I was afraid of that, but I did not think he had a weapon," said Cassio in a hollow voice. "He was too great of heart to remain a captive all his life."

That's not it at all, you stupid fool, I thought, but kept my lips sealed.

10 The dead are buried now, and the news is being told and told and told again. In each telling, I am certain, there is an insidious rounding of rough edges, a subtle simplifying, a massaging of the tale into one of deliberate villain and hapless victims. It is easy to call someone a villain; the title allows dismissal and more important, distance: as long as you know somebody else is the villain, then you are not one, and you may rest snugly in your own nest of good intentions, no need for vigilance or self-reflection. You mean well, and even when you act in anger, your actions are justified — somehow, surely, they are justified, they must be, and you have done nothing wrong, because you are not evil. This is the comfort of the smug.

I am honest Iago, and I ask you: might not you be dishonest with yourself?

[2012]

QUESTIONS

1. What does the information in the opening section tell us about Iago's character that we do not know in Shakespeare's *Othello*? How does this information affect your response to Iago? Keep in mind that in Nicole Galland's novel, this is the reader's first glimpse of Iago.
2. Does the commentary in the opening section about honesty being a "rebuke" explain Iago's behavior? Does it exonerate him to any degree? Since you already know Iago from Shakespeare, what clues in this excerpt might lead you to suspect he is an unreliable narrator?
3. How does the relationship between Iago and Othello in the second section both resemble and depart from that in Shakespeare's play?
4. Based on these passages, to what extent do you think that Galland succeeds in casting Iago as a sympathetic character? Pay special attention to the final paragraphs in which Iago reflects on what a "villain" is and his appeal to the reader to look inward.
5. How could this version of Iago be viewed through a psychological or cultural criticism perspective?

LITERATURE IN CONVERSATION
Othello through Critical Lenses

1. Compare and contrast the way two different critical perspectives would view the exchange between Othello and Desdemona in act IV, scene ii of *Othello*.
2. Explain which of the five critical perspectives we have discussed most closely fits your interpretation of *Othello*. Use evidence from the text to support your viewpoint.
3. Many have argued that *Othello* is not a play about racism — but it is about race. Support or challenge this distinction, analyzing the play through the lens of one of the critical perspectives we have discussed.
4. View one of the film versions of *Othello* and present an analysis of the critical lens (or lenses) you believe it reflects. Include at least four film stills and, if possible, clips from the film in your analysis. You may present your analysis as an essay or as a multimedia presentation.
5. The death scene in *Othello* (V.ii. 348–70) has been the subject of numerous paintings, lithographs, engravings, and graphic images. Choose two pieces of artwork and discuss how each represents a particular critical perspective on the relationship between Othello and Desdemona.
6. In 1999, Shakespearean scholar and actor Hugh Quarshie argued that Othello should not be played by a black actor:

   > If a black actor plays Othello does he not risk making racial stereotypes seem legitimate and even true? When a black actor plays a role written for a white actor in black make-up and for a predominantly white audience, does he not encourage the white way, or rather the wrong way, of looking at black men, namely that black men, or "Moors," are over-emotional, excitable and unstable, thereby vindicating Iago's statement, "These Moors are changeable in their wills"?

   Which critical perspective does this view most closely resemble? Incorporate your response in an essay that supports or challenges Quarshie's position.
7. Compose a poem in the voice of one of the characters from Shakespeare's *Othello*. Then, write a brief explanation of how your poem illustrates one of the critical lenses we've discussed.
8. The writer Margaret Atwood asserts, "The answers you get from literature depend upon the questions you pose." Each of the critical perspectives we've discussed raises particular kinds of questions and issues. How might the application of a particular critical lens to a reading of *Othello* define the questions the reader asks about it — and thus the "answers," or interpretation, that the reader might develop in response?

FICTION

The Shawl

CYNTHIA OZICK

Cynthia Ozick was born in 1928 in New York City, where she fell in love with literature as a child in the Bronx. The child of Lithuanian immigrants, she was strongly influenced by both the literature of her Jewish tradition and the New York writings of Henry James. She earned her BA at New York University and her MA in English literature at Ohio State University, then went on to publish numerous novels, short story collections, and essay collections. Her most recent novel, *Foreign Bodies* (2010), was shortlisted for the Orange Prize (2012) and the Jewish Quarterly-Wingate Prize (2013). Ozick is highly regarded for her ideas as well as her stories. "Even when you disagree with her, she electrifies your mind," wrote critic Christopher Lehmann-Haupt in the *New York Times* in 2000. "The Shawl" is perhaps Ozick's most famous story. Published in 1980 in the *New Yorker* and selected for inclusion in *The Best American Short Stories of the Century* (1999), it delivers a powerful glimpse into the personal horrors of the Holocaust. In an interview published in the spring 1987 *Paris Review*, Ozick discussed writing about the Holocaust: "I don't want to tamper or invent or imagine, and yet I have done it. I can't not do it. It comes. It invades."

Stella, cold, cold, the coldness of hell. How they walked on the roads together, Rosa with Magda curled up between sore breasts, Magda wound up in the shawl. Sometimes Stella carried Magda. But she was jealous of Magda. A thin girl of fourteen, too small, with thin breasts of her own, Stella wanted to be wrapped in a shawl, hidden away, asleep, rocked by the march, a baby, a round infant in arms. Magda took Rosa's nipple, and Rosa never stopped walking, a walking cradle. There was not enough milk; sometimes Magda sucked air; then she screamed. Stella was ravenous. Her knees were tumors on sticks, her elbows chicken bones.

Rosa did not feel hunger; she felt light, not like someone walking but like someone in a faint, in trance, arrested in a fit, someone who is already a floating angel, alert and seeing everything, but in the air, not there, not touching the road. As if teetering on the tips of her fingernails. She looked into Magda's face through a gap in the shawl: a squirrel in a nest, safe, no one could reach her inside the little house of the shawl's windings. The face, very round, a pocket mirror of a face: but it was not Rosa's bleak complexion, dark like cholera, it was another kind of face altogether, eyes blue as air, smooth feathers of hair nearly as yellow as the Star sewn into Rosa's coat. You could think she was one of *their* babies.

Rosa, floating, dreamed of giving Magda away in one of the villages. She could leave the line for a minute and push Magda into the hands of any woman on the side of the road. But if she moved out of line they might shoot. And even if she fled the line for half a second and pushed the shawl-bundle at a stranger, would the woman take it? She might be surprised, or afraid; she might drop the shawl, and Magda would fall out and strike her head and die. The little round head. Such a good child, she gave up screaming, and sucked now only for the taste of the drying nipple itself. The neat grip of the tiny gums. One mite of a tooth tip sticking up in the bottom gum, how shining, an elfin tombstone of white marble, gleaming there. Without complaining, Magda relinquished Rosa's teats, first the left, then the right; both were cracked, not a sniff of milk. The duct crevice extinct, a dead volcano, blind eye, chill hole, so Magda took the corner of the shawl and milked it instead. She sucked and sucked, flooding the threads with wetness. The shawl's good flavor, milk of linen.

It was a magic shawl, it could nourish an infant for three days and three nights. Magda did not die, she stayed alive, although very quiet. A peculiar smell, of cinnamon and almonds, lifted out of her mouth. She held her eyes open every moment, forgetting how to blink or nap, and Rosa and sometimes Stella studied their blueness. On the road they raised one burden of a leg after another and studied Magda's face. "Aryan," Stella said, in a voice grown as thin as a string; and Rosa thought how Stella gazed at Magda like a young cannibal. And the time that Stella said "Aryan," it sounded to Rosa as if Stella had really said, "Let us devour her."

5 But Magda lived to walk. She lived that long, but she did not walk very well, partly because she was only fifteen months old, and partly because the spindles of her legs could not hold up her fat belly. It was fat with air, full and round. Rosa gave almost all her food to Magda, Stella gave nothing; Stella was ravenous, a growing child herself, but not growing much. Stella did not menstruate. Rosa did not menstruate. Rosa was ravenous, but also not; she learned from Magda how to drink the taste of a finger in one's mouth. They were in a place without pity, all pity was annihilated in Rosa, she looked at Stella's bones without pity. She was sure that Stella was waiting for Magda to die so she could put her teeth into the little thighs.

Rosa knew Magda was going to die very soon; she should have been dead already, but she had been buried away deep inside the magic shawl, mistaken there for the shivering mound of Rosa's breasts; Rosa clung to the shawl as if it covered only herself. No one took it away from her. Magda was mute. She never cried. Rosa hid her in the barracks, under the shawl, but she knew that one day someone would inform; or one day someone, not even Stella, would steal Magda to eat her. When Magda began to walk Rosa knew that Magda was going to die very soon, something would happen. She was afraid to fall asleep; she slept with the weight of her thigh on Magda's body; she was afraid she would smother Magda under her thigh. The weight of Rosa was becoming less and less, Rosa and Stella were slowly turning into air.

Magda was quiet, but her eyes were horribly alive, like blue tigers. She watched. Sometimes she laughed — it seemed a laugh, but how could it be? Magda had never seen anyone laugh. Still, Magda laughed at her shawl when the wind blew its corners, the bad wind with pieces of black in it, that made Stella's and Rosa's eyes tear. Magda's eyes were always clear and tearless. She watched like a tiger. She guarded her shawl. No one could touch it; only Rosa could touch it. Stella was not allowed. The shawl was Magda's own baby, her pet, her little sister. She tangled herself up in it and sucked on one of the corners when she wanted to be very still.

Then Stella took the shawl away and made Magda die.

Afterward Stella said: "I was cold."

10 And afterward she was always cold, always. The cold went into her heart: Rosa saw that Stella's heart was cold. Magda flopped onward with her little pencil legs scribbling this way and that, in search of the shawl; the pencils faltered at the barracks opening, where the light began. Rosa saw and pursued. But already Magda was in the square outside the barracks, in the jolly light. It was the roll-call arena. Every morning Rosa had to conceal Magda under the shawl

against a wall of the barracks and go out and stand in the arena with Stella and hundreds of others, sometimes for hours, and Magda, deserted, was quiet under the shawl, sucking on her corner. Every day Magda was silent, and so she did not die. Rosa saw that today Magda was going to die, and at the same time a fearful joy ran in Rosa's two palms, her fingers were on fire, she was astonished, febrile: Magda, in the sunlight, swaying on her pencil legs, was howling. Ever since the drying up of Rosa's nipples, ever since Magda's last scream on the road, Magda had been devoid of any syllable; Magda was a mute. Rosa believed that something had gone wrong with her vocal cords, with her windpipe, with the cave of her larynx; Magda was defective, without a voice; perhaps she was deaf; there might be something amiss with her intelligence; Magda was dumb. Even the laugh that came when the ash-stippled wind made a clown out of Magda's shawl was only the air-blown showing of her teeth. Even when the lice, head lice and body lice, crazed her so that she became as wild as one of the big rats that plundered the barracks at daybreak looking for carrion, she rubbed and scratched and kicked and bit and rolled without a whimper. But now Magda's mouth was spilling a long viscous rope of clamor.

"Maaaa—"

It was the first noise Magda had ever sent out from her throat since the drying up of Rosa's nipples.

"Maaaa . . . aaa!"

Again! Magda was wavering in the perilous sunlight of the arena, scribbling on such pitiful little bent shins. Rosa saw. She saw that Magda was grieving the loss of her shawl, she saw that Magda was going to die. A tide of commands hammered in Rosa's nipples: Fetch, get, bring! But she did not know which to go after first, Magda or the shawl. If she jumped out into the arena to snatch Magda up, the howling would not stop, because Magda would still not have the shawl; but if she ran back into the barracks to find the shawl, and if she found it, and if she came after Magda holding it and shaking it, then she would get Magda back, Magda would put the shawl in her mouth and turn dumb again.

Rosa entered the dark. It was easy to discover the shawl. Stella was heaped under it, asleep in her thin bones. Rosa tore the shawl free and flew—she could fly, she was only air—into the arena. The sunheat murmured of another life, of butterflies in summer. The light was placid, mellow. On the other side of the steel fence, far away, there were green meadows speckled with dandelions and deep-colored violets; beyond them, even farther, innocent tiger lilies, tall, lifting their orange bonnets. In the barracks they spoke of "flowers," of "rain": excrement, thick turd-braids, and the slow stinking maroon waterfall that slunk down from the upper bunks, the stink mixed with a bitter fatty floating smoke that greased Rosa's skin. She stood for an instant at the margin of the arena. Sometimes the electricity inside the fence would seem to hum; even Stella said it was only an imagining, but Rosa heard real sounds in the wire: grainy sad voices. The farther she was from the fence, the more clearly the voices crowded at her. The lamenting voices strummed so convincingly, so passionately, it was impossible to suspect them of being phantoms. The voices told her to hold up the shawl, high; the voices told her to shake it, to whip with it, to unfurl it like a flag. Rosa lifted, shook, whipped, unfurled. Far off, very far, Magda leaned across her air-fed belly, reaching out with the rods of her arms. She was high up, elevated, riding someone's shoulder. But the shoulder that carried Magda was not coming toward Rosa and the shawl, it was drifting away, the speck of Magda was moving more and more into the smoky distance. Above the shoulder a helmet glinted. A light tapped the helmet and sparkled it into a goblet. Below the helmet a black body like a domino and a pair of black boots hurled themselves in the direction of the electrified fence. The electric voices began to chatter wildly. "Maamaa, maaa-maaa," they all hummed together. How far Magda was from Rosa now, across the whole square, past a dozen barracks, all the way on the other side! She was no bigger than a moth.

All at once Magda was swimming through the air. The whole of Magda traveled through loftiness. She looked like a butterfly touching a silver vine. And the moment Magda's feathered round head and her pencil legs and balloonish belly and zigzag arms splashed against the fence, the steel voices went mad in their growling, urging Rosa to run and run to the spot where Magda had fallen from her flight against the electrified fence; but of course Rosa did not obey them. She only stood, because if she ran they would shoot, and if she tried to pick up the sticks of Magda's body they would shoot, and if she let the wolf's screech ascending now through the ladder of her skeleton break out, they would shoot; so she took Magda's shawl and filled her own mouth with it, stuffed it in and stuffed it in, until she was swallowing up the wolf's screech and tasting the cinnamon and almond depth of Magda's saliva; and Rosa drank Magda's shawl until it dried.

[1980]

EXPLORING THE TEXT

1. How would you describe Rosa, Stella, and Magda, the three main characters of the story? In what ways does the action of the story undermine their ability to act out their roles as mother, big sister, and baby, respectively?
2. Note the rich use of imagery and figurative language in the first three paragraphs. What is the effect of the "chicken bones," the "little house," and the "elfin tombstone," for example? How does the imagery contribute to the story as a whole?
3. In paragraph 7, Ozick writes of Magda, "Sometimes she laughed — it seemed a laugh, but how could it be? Magda had never seen anyone laugh." What is Ozick suggesting about joy?
4. Paragraphs 8 and 9 are single sentences: "Then Stella took the shawl away and made Magda die." "Afterward Stella said: 'I was cold.'" The next paragraph opens, "And afterward she was always cold, always." What is the importance of the reader being catapulted into the future by this sequence of lines?
5. What is the effect of the irony and imagery in the final two paragraphs?
6. How would the story differ if it were narrated in the first person by Rosa? Why do you think Ozick tells the story in the third person?
7. What associations does a shawl have? In what ways is it ambiguous? Do you agree with Ozick's choice of a title for the story? Why or why not?

The Management of Grief

BHARATI MUKHERJEE

Born in Calcutta, India, in 1940, Bharati Mukherjee gained international experience and immersion in the English language when her father took a job in England, where the family lived from 1947 to 1951. After returning to India, she earned a BA from the University of Calcutta in 1959. She later received a scholarship to the University of Iowa, where she earned an MFA at the Iowa Writers' Workshop in 1963. She had planned to return to India to marry a man her father had chosen for her, but she stayed at Iowa to earn her PhD in comparative literature in 1969. She continues to write and teach at the University of California, Berkeley. She published her first novel, *The Tiger's Daughter*, in 1971. Among

Mukherjee's most highly regarded works are the 1989 novel *Jasmine*, described as a modern *Jane Eyre* tale about a young Indian woman in America, and *The Middleman and Other Stories*, which won the National Book Critics Circle Award in 1988 and in which "The Management of Grief" appears. In June 1985, an Air India flight left Toronto on its way to Bombay (now Mumbai), with a scheduled stop in London. A bomb exploded on board and sent the plane into the Irish Sea, killing all 329 passengers. It is believed to have been a terrorist attack by Sikh separatists fighting for a Sikh homeland in the Punjab region of India. This story takes place in the aftermath of the tragedy.

A woman I don't know is boiling tea the Indian way in my kitchen. There are a lot of women I don't know in my kitchen, whispering and moving tactfully. They open doors, rummage through the pantry, and try not to ask me where things are kept. They remind me of when my sons were small, on Mother's Day or when Vikram and I were tired, and they would make big, sloppy omelets. I would lie in bed pretending I didn't hear them.

Dr. Sharma, the treasurer of the Indo-Canada Society, pulls me into the hallway. He wants to know if I am worried about money. His wife, who has just come up from the basement with a tray of empty cups and glasses, scolds him. "Don't bother Mrs. Bhave with mundane details." She looks so monstrously pregnant her baby must be days overdue. I tell her she shouldn't be carrying heavy things. "Shaila," she says, smiling, "this is the fifth." Then she grabs a teenager by his shirttails. He slips his Walkman off his head. He has to be one of her four children; they have the same domed and dented foreheads. "What's the official word now?" she demands. The boy slips the headphones back on. "They're acting evasive, Ma. They're saying it could be an accident or a terrorist bomb."

All morning, the boys have been muttering, Sikh bomb, Sikh bomb. The men, not using the word, bow their heads in agreement.
Mrs. Sharma touches her forehead at such a word. At least they've stopped talking about space debris and Russian lasers.

Two radios are going in the dining room. They are tuned to different stations. Someone must have brought the radios down from my boys' bedrooms. I haven't gone into their rooms since Kusum came running across the front lawn in her bathrobe. She looked so funny, I was laughing when I opened the door.

The big TV in the den is being whizzed through American networks and cable channels.

"Damn!" some man swears bitterly. "How can these preachers carry on like nothing's happened?" I want to tell him we're not that important. You look at the audience, and at the preacher in his blue robe with his beautiful white hair, the potted palm trees under a blue sky, and you know they care about nothing.

The phone rings and rings. Dr. Sharma's taken charge. "We're with her," he keeps saying. "Yes, yes, the doctor has given calming pills. Yes, yes, pills are having necessary effect." I wonder if pills alone explain this calm. Not peace, just a deadening quiet. I was always controlled, but never repressed. Sound can reach me, but my body is tensed, ready to scream. I hear their voices all around me. I hear my boys and Vikram cry, "Mommy, Shaila!" and their screams insulate me, like headphones.

The woman boiling water tells her story again and again. "I got the news first. My cousin called from Halifax before six A.M., can you imagine? He'd gotten up for prayers and his son was studying for medical exams and heard on a rock channel that something had happened to a plane. They said first it had disappeared from the radar, like a giant eraser just reached out. His father called me, so I said to him, what do you mean, 'something bad'? You mean a hijacking?

And he said, *Behn,*[1] there is no confirmation of anything yet, but check with your neighbors because a lot of them must be on that plane. So I called poor Kusum straight-away. I knew Kusum's husband and daughter were booked to go yesterday."

Kusum lives across the street from me. She and Satish had moved in less than a month ago. They said they needed a bigger place. All these people, the Sharmas and friends from the Indo-Canada Society, had been there for the housewarming. Satish and Kusum made tandoori on their big gas grill and even the white neighbors piled their plates high with that luridly red, charred, juicy chicken. Their younger daughter had danced, and even our boys had broken away from the Stanley Cup telecast to put in a reluctant appearance. Everyone took pictures for their albums and for the community newspapers — another of our families had made it big in Toronto — and now I wonder how many of those happy faces are gone. "Why does God give us so much if all along He intends to take it away?" Kusum asks me.

I nod. We sit on carpeted stairs, holding hands like children. "I never once told him that I loved him," I say. I was too much the well-brought-up woman. I was so well brought up I never felt comfortable calling my husband by his first name.

"It's all right," Kusum says. "He knew. My husband knew. They felt it. Modern young girls have to say it because what they feel is fake."

Kusum's daughter Pam runs in with an overnight case. Pam's in her McDonald's uniform. "Mummy! You have to get dressed!" Panic makes her cranky. "A reporter's on his way here."

"Why?"

"You want to talk to him in your bathrobe?" She starts to brush her mother's long hair. She's the daughter who's always in trouble. She dates Canadian boys and hangs out in the mall, shopping for tight sweaters. The younger one, the goody-goody one according to Pam, the one with a voice so sweet that when she sang *bhajans*[2] for Ethiopian relief even a frugal man like my husband wrote out a hundred-dollar check, *she* was on that plane. *She* was going to spend July and August with grand-parents because Pam wouldn't go. Pam said she'd rather waitress at McDonald's. "If it's a choice between Bombay and Wonderland, I'm picking Wonderland," she'd said.

"Leave me alone," Kusum yells. "You know what I want to do? If I didn't have to look after you now, I'd hang myself."

Pam's young face goes blotchy with pain. "Thanks," she says, "don't let me stop you."

"Hush," pregnant Mrs. Sharma scolds Pam. "Leave your mother alone. Mr. Sharma will tackle the reporters and fill out the forms. He'll say what has to be said."

Pam stands her ground. "You think I don't know what Mummy's thinking? *Why her?* That's what. That's sick! Mummy wishes my little sister were alive and I were dead."

Kusum's hand in mine is trembly hot. We continue to sit on the stairs.

She calls before she arrives, wondering if there's anything I need. Her name is Judith Templeton and she's an appointee of the provincial government. "Multiculturalism?" I ask, and she says "partially," but that her mandate is bigger. "I've been told you knew many of the people on the flight," she says. "Perhaps if you'd agree to help us reach the others . . . ?"

She gives me time at least to put on tea water and pick up the mess in the front room. I have a few *samosas*[3] from Kusum's housewarming that I could fry up, but then I think, why prolong this visit?

---

[1] No. — EDS.

[2] Hymns. — EDS.

[3] Fried pastry filled with meat or vegetables. — EDS.

Judith Templeton is much younger than she sounded. She wears a blue suit with a white blouse and a polka-dot tie. Her blond hair is cut short, her only jewelry is pearl-drop earrings. Her briefcase is new and expensive looking, a gleaming cordovan leather. She sits with it across her lap. When she looks out the front windows onto the street, her contact lenses seem to float in front of her light blue eyes.

"What sort of help do you want from me?" I ask. She has refused the tea, out of politeness, but I insist, along with some slightly stale biscuits.

"I have no experience," she admits. "That is, I have an M.S.W. and I've worked in liaison with accident victims, but I mean I have no experience with a tragedy of this scale — "

"Who could?" I ask.

" — and with the complications of culture, language, and customs. Someone mentioned that Mrs. Bhave is a pillar — because you've taken it more calmly."

At this, perhaps, I frown, for she reaches forward, almost to take my hand. "I hope you understand my meaning, Mrs. Bhave. There are hundreds of people in Metro directly affected, like you, and some of them speak no English. There are some widows who've never handled money or gone on a bus, and there are old parents who still haven't eaten or gone outside their bedrooms. Some houses and apartments have been looted. Some wives are still hysterical. Some husbands are in shock and profound depression. We want to help, but our hands are tied in so many ways. We have to distribute money to some people, and there are legal documents — these things can be done. We have interpreters, but we don't always have the human touch, or maybe the right human touch. We don't want to make mistakes, Mrs. Bhave, and that's why we'd like to ask you to help us."

"More mistakes, you mean," I say.

"Police matters are not in my hands," she answers.

"Nothing I can do will make any difference," I say. "We must all grieve in our own way."

"But you are coping very well. All the people said, Mrs. Bhave is the strongest person of all. Perhaps if the others could see you, talk with you, it would help them."

"By the standards of the people you call hysterical, I am behaving very oddly and very badly, Miss Templeton." I want to say to her, *I wish I could scream, starve, walk into Lake Ontario, jump from a bridge.* "They would not see me as a model. I do not see myself as a model."

I am a freak. No one who has ever known me would think of me reacting this way. This terrible calm will not go away.

She asks me if she may call again, after I get back from a long trip that we all must make. "Of course," I say. "Feel free to call, anytime."

Four days later, I find Kusum squatting on a rock overlooking a bay in Ireland. It isn't a big rock, but it juts sharply out over water. This is as close as we'll ever get to them. June breezes balloon out her sari and unpin her knee-length hair. She has the bewildered look of a sea creature whom the tides have stranded.

It's been one hundred hours since Kusum came stumbling and screaming across my lawn. Waiting around the hospital, we've heard many stories. The police, the diplomats, they tell us things thinking that we're strong, that knowledge is helpful to the grieving, and maybe it is. Some, I know, prefer ignorance, or their own versions. The plane broke into two, they say. Unconsciousness was instantaneous. No one suffered. My boys must have just finished their breakfasts. They loved eating on planes, they loved the smallness of plates, knives, and forks. Last year they saved the airline salt and pepper shakers. Half an hour more and they would have made it to Heathrow.

Kusum says that we can't escape our fate. She says that all those people — our husbands, my boys, her girl with the nightingale voice, all those Hindus, Christians, Sikhs, Muslims, Parsis, and atheists on that plane — were fated to die together off this beautiful bay. She learned this from a swami in Toronto.

I have my Valium.

Six of us "relatives" — two widows and four widowers — choose to spend the day today by the waters instead of sitting in a hospital room and scanning photographs of the dead. That's what they call us now: relatives. I've looked through twenty-seven photos in two days. They're very kind to us, the Irish are very understanding. Sometimes understanding means freeing a tourist bus for this trip to the bay, so we can pretend to spy our loved ones through the glassiness of waves or in sun-speckled cloud shapes.

I could die here, too, and be content.

"What is that, out there?" She's standing and flapping her hands, and for a moment I see a head shape bobbing in the waves. She's standing in the water, I, on the boulder. The tide is low, and a round, black, head-sized rock has just risen from the waves. She returns, her sari end dripping and ruined and her face is a twisted remnant of hope, the way mine was a hundred hours ago, still laughing but inwardly knowing that nothing but the ultimate tragedy could bring two women together at six o'clock on a Sunday morning. I watch her face sag into blankness.

"That water felt warm, Shaila," she says at length.

"You can't," I say. "We have to wait for our turn to come."

I haven't eaten in four days, haven't brushed my teeth.

"I know," she says. "I tell myself I have no right to grieve. They are in a better place than we are. My swami says I should be thrilled for them. My swami says depression is a sign of our selfishness."

Maybe I'm selfish. Selfishly I break away from Kusum and run, sandals slapping against stones, to the water's edge. What if my boys aren't lying pinned under the debris? What if they aren't stuck a mile below that innocent blue chop? What if, given the strong currents . . .

Now I've ruined my sari, one of my best. Kusum has joined me, knee-deep in water that feels to me like a swimming pool. I could settle in the water, and my husband would take my hand and the boys would slap water in my face just to see me scream.

"Do you remember what good swimmers my boys were, Kusum?"

"I saw the medals," she says.

One of the widowers, Dr. Ranganathan from Montreal, walks out to us, carrying his shoes in one hand. He's an electrical engineer. Someone at the hotel mentioned his work is famous around the world, something about the place where physics and electricity come together. He has lost a huge family, something indescribable. "With some good luck," Dr. Ranganathan suggests to me, "a good swimmer could make it safely to some island. It is quite possible that there may be many, many microscopic islets scattered around."

"You're not just saying that?" I tell Dr. Ranganathan about Vinod, my elder son. Last year he took diving as well.

"It's a parent's duty to hope," he says. "It is foolish to rule out possibilities that have not been tested. I myself have not surrendered hope."

Kusum is sobbing once again. "Dear lady," he says, laying his free hand on her arm, and she calms down.

"Vinod is how old?" he asks me. He's very careful, as we all are. *Is*, not was.

"Fourteen. Yesterday he was fourteen. His father and uncle were going to take him down to the Taj and give him a big birthday party. I couldn't go with them because I couldn't get two weeks off from my stupid job in June." I process bills for a travel agent. June is a big travel month.

Dr. Ranganathan whips the pockets of his suit jacket inside out. Squashed roses, in darkening shades of pink, float on the water. He tore the roses off creepers in somebody's garden. He didn't ask anyone if he could pluck the roses, but now there's been an article about it in the local papers. When you see an Indian person, it says, please give him or her flowers.

"A strong youth of fourteen," he says, "can very likely pull to safety a younger one."

My sons, though four years apart, were very close. Vinod wouldn't let Mithun drown. *Electrical engineering,* I think, foolishly perhaps: this man knows important secrets of the universe, things closed to me. Relief spins me lightheaded. No wonder my boys' photographs haven't turned up in the gallery of photos of the recovered dead. "Such pretty roses," I say.

"My wife loved pink roses. Every Friday I had to bring a bunch home. I used to say, Why? After twenty-odd years of marriage you're still needing proof positive of my love?" He has identified his wife and three of his children. Then others from Montreal, the lucky ones, intact families with no survivors. He chuckles as he wades back to shore. Then he swings around to ask me a question. "Mrs. Bhave, you are wanting to throw in some roses for your loved ones? I have two big ones left."

But I have other things to float: Vinod's pocket calculator; a half-painted model B-52 for my Mithun. They'd want them on their island. And for my husband? For him I let fall into the calm, glassy waters a poem I wrote in the hospital yesterday. Finally he'll know my feelings for him.

"Don't tumble, the rocks are slippery," Dr. Ranganathan cautions. He holds out a hand for me to grab.

Then it's time to get back on the bus, time to rush back to our waiting posts on hospital benches.

Kusum is one of the lucky ones. The lucky ones flew here, identified in multiplicate their loved ones, then will fly to India with the bodies for proper ceremonies. Satish is one of the few males who surfaced. The photos of faces we saw on the walls in an office at Heathrow and here in the hospital are mostly of women. Women have more body fat, a nun said to me matter-of-factly. They float better.

Today I was stopped by a young sailor on the street. He had loaded bodies, he'd gone into the water when — he checks my face for signs of strength — when the sharks were first spotted. I don't blush, and he breaks down. "It's all right," I say. "Thank you." I heard about the sharks from Dr. Ranganathan. In his orderly mind, science brings understanding, it holds no terror. It is the shark's duty. For every deer there is a hunter, for every fish a fisherman.

The Irish are not shy; they rush to me and give me hugs and some are crying. I cannot imagine reactions like that on the streets of Toronto. Just strangers, and I am touched. Some carry flowers with them and give them to any Indian they see.

After lunch, a policeman I have gotten to know quite well catches hold of me. He says he thinks he has a match for Vinod. I explain what a good swimmer Vinod is.

"You want me with you when you look at photos?" Dr. Ranganathan walks ahead of me into the picture gallery. In these matters, he is a scientist, and I am grateful. It is a new perspective. "They have performed miracles," he says. "We are indebted to them."

The first day or two the policemen showed us relatives only one picture at a time; now they're in a hurry, they're eager to lay out the possibles, and even the probables.

The face on the photo is of a boy much like Vinod; the same intelligent eyes, the same thick brows dipping into a V. But this boy's features, even his cheeks, are puffier, wider, mushier.

"No." My gaze is pulled by other pictures. There are five other boys who look like Vinod.

The nun assigned to console me rubs the first picture with a fingertip. "When they've been in the water for a while, love, they look a little heavier." The bones under the skin are broken, they said on the first day—try to adjust your memories. It's important.

"It's not him. I'm his mother. I'd know."

"I know this one!" Dr. Ranganathan cries out, and suddenly from the back of the gallery. "And this one!" I think he senses that I don't want to find my boys. "They are the Kutty brothers. They were also from Montreal." I don't mean to be crying. On the contrary, I am ecstatic. My suitcase in the hotel is packed heavy with dry clothes for my boys.

The policeman starts to cry. "I am so sorry, I am so sorry, ma'am. I really thought we had a match."

With the nun ahead of us and the policeman behind, we, the unlucky ones without our children's bodies, file out of the makeshift gallery.

From Ireland most of us go on to India. Kusum and I take the same direct flight to Bombay, so I can help her clear customs quickly. But we have to argue with a man in uniform. He has large boils on his face. The boils swell and glow with sweat as we argue with him. He wants Kusum to wait in line and he refuses to take authority because his boss is on a tea break. But Kusum won't let her coffins out of sight, and I shan't desert her though I know that my parents, elderly and diabetic, must be waiting in a stuffy car in a scorching lot.

"You bastard!" I scream at the man with the popping boils. Other passengers press closer. "You think we're smuggling contraband in those coffins!"

Once upon a time we were well-brought-up women; we were dutiful wives who kept our heads veiled, our voices shy and sweet.

In India, I become, once again, an only child of rich, ailing parents. Old friends of the family come to pay their respects. Some are Sikh, and inwardly, involuntarily, I cringe. My parents are progressive people; they do not blame communities for a few individuals.

In Canada it is a different story now.

"Stay longer," my mother pleads. "Canada is a cold place. Why would you want to be all by yourself?" I stay.

Three months pass. Then another.

"Vikram wouldn't have wanted you to give up things!" they protest. They call my husband by the name he was born with. In Toronto he'd changed to Vik so the men he worked with at his office would find his name as easy as Rod or Chris. "You know, the dead aren't cut off from us!"

My grandmother, the spoiled daughter of a rich zamindar,[4] shaved her head with rusty razor blades when she was widowed at sixteen. My grandfather died of childhood diabetes when he was nineteen, and she saw herself as the harbinger of bad luck. My mother grew up without parents, raised indifferently by an uncle, while her true mother slept in a hut behind the main estate house and took her food with the servants. She grew up a rationalist. My parents abhor mindless mortification.

The zamindar's daughter kept stubborn faith in Vedic rituals; my parents rebelled. I am trapped between two modes of knowledge. At thirty-six, I am too old to start over and too young to give up. Like my husband's spirit, I flutter between worlds.

Courting aphasia, we travel. We travel with our phalanx of servants and poor relatives. To hill stations and to beach resorts. We play contract bridge in dusty gymkhana clubs. We ride stubby ponies up crumbly mountain trails. At tea dances, we let ourselves be twirled twice round the ballroom. We hit the holy spots we hadn't made time for before. In Varanasi, Kalighat, Rishikesh, Hardwar, astrologers and palmists seek me out and for a fee offer me cosmic consolations.

[4] Landowner.—EDS.

Already the widowers among us are being shown new bride candidates. They cannot resist the call of custom, the authority of their parents and older brothers. They must marry; it is the duty of a man to look after a wife. The new wives will be young widows with children, destitute but of good family. They will make loving wives, but the men will shun them. I've had calls from the men over crackling Indian telephone lines. "Save me," they say, these substantial, educated, successful men of forty. "My parents are arranging a marriage for me." In a month they will have buried one family and returned to Canada with a new bride and partial family.

I am comparatively lucky. No one here thinks of arranging a husband for an unlucky widow.

Then, on the third day of the sixth month into this odyssey, in an abandoned temple in a tiny Himalayan village, as I make my offering of flowers and sweetmeats to the god of a tribe of animists, my husband descends to me. He is squatting next to a scrawny sadhu[5] in moth-eaten robes. Vikram wears the vanilla suit he wore the last time I hugged him. The sadhu tosses petals on a butter-fed flame, reciting Sanskrit mantras, and sweeps his face of flies. My husband takes my hands in his.

You're beautiful, he starts. Then, *What are you doing here?*

Shall I stay? I ask. He only smiles, but already the image is fading. *You must finish alone what we started together.* No seaweed wreathes his mouth. He speaks too fast, just as he used to when we were an envied family in our pink split-level. He is gone.

In the windowless altar room, smoky with joss sticks and clarified butter lamps, a sweaty hand gropes for my blouse. I do not shriek. The sadhu arranges his robe. The lamps hiss and sputter out.

When we come out of the temple, my mother says, "Did you feel something weird in there?"

My mother has no patience with ghosts, prophetic dreams, holy men, and cults.

"No," I lie. "Nothing."

But she knows that she's lost me. She knows that in days I shall be leaving.

. . .

Kusum's put up her house for sale. She wants to live in an ashram in Hardwar. Moving to Hardwar was her swami's idea. Her swami runs two ashrams, the one in Hardwar and another here in Toronto.

"Don't run away," I tell her.

"I'm not running away," she says. "I'm pursuing inner peace. You think you or that Ranganathan fellow are better off ?"

Pam's left for California. She wants to do some modeling, she says. She says when she comes into her share of the insurance money she'll open a yoga-cum-aerobics studio in Hollywood. She sends me postcards so naughty I daren't leave them on the coffee table. Her mother has withdrawn from her and the world.

The rest of us don't lose touch, that's the point. Talk is all we have, says Dr. Ranganathan, who has also resisted his relatives and returned to Montreal and to his job, alone. He says, Whom better to talk with than other relatives? We've been melted down and recast as a new tribe.

He calls me twice a week from Montreal. Every Wednesday night and every Saturday afternoon. He is changing jobs, going to Ottawa. But Ottawa is over a hundred miles away, and he is forced to drive two hundred and twenty miles a day from his home in Montreal. He can't bring himself to sell his house. The house is a temple, he says; the king-sized bed in the master bedroom is a shrine. He sleeps on a folding cot. A devotee.

[5] Hindu ascetic dedicated to achieving liberation from human existence through intense meditation and yoga. In India they are generally seen as holy men, but some people view them with suspicion. Because of their renunciation of all things material, they are considered legally dead. — EDS.

There are still some hysterical relatives. Judith Templeton's list of those needing help and those who've "accepted" is in nearly perfect balance. Acceptance means you speak of your family in the past tense and you make active plans for moving ahead with your life. There are courses at Seneca and Ryerson we could be taking. Her gleaming leather briefcase is full of college catalogues and lists of cultural societies that need our help. She has done impressive work, I tell her.

"In the textbooks on grief management," she replies — I am her confidante, I realize, one of the few whose grief has not sprung bizarre obsessions — "there are stages to pass through: rejection, depression, acceptance, reconstruction." She has compiled a chart and finds that six months after the tragedy, none of us still rejects reality, but only a handful are reconstructing. "Depressed acceptance" is the plateau we've reached. Remarriage is a major step in reconstruction (though she's a little surprised, even shocked, over *how* quickly some of the men have taken on new families). Selling one's house and changing jobs and cities is healthy.

105 How to tell Judith Templeton that my family surrounds me, and that like creatures in epics, they've changed shapes? She sees me as calm and accepting but worries that I have no job, no career. My closest friends are worse off than I. I cannot tell her my days, even my nights, are thrilling.

She asks me to help with families she can't reach at all. An elderly couple in Agincourt whose sons were killed just weeks after they had brought their parents over from a village in Punjab. From their names, I know they are Sikh. Judith Templeton and a translator have visited them twice with offers of money for airfare to Ireland, with bank forms, power-of-attorney forms, but they have refused to sign, or to leave their tiny apartment. Their sons' money is frozen in the bank. Their sons' investment apartments have been trashed by tenants, the furnishings sold off. The parents fear that anything they sign or any money they receive will end the company's or the country's obligations to them. They fear they are selling their sons for two airline tickets to a place they've never seen.

The high-rise apartment is a tower of Indians and West Indians, with a sprinkling of Orientals. The nearest bus-stop kiosk is lined with women in saris. Boys practice cricket in the parking lot. Inside the building, even I wince a bit from the ferocity of onion fumes, the distinctive and immediate Indianness of frying ghee,[6] but Judith Templeton maintains a steady flow of information. These poor old people are in imminent danger of losing their place and all their services.

I say to her, "They are Sikh. They will not open up to a Hindu woman." And what I want to add is, as much as I try not to, I stiffen now at the sight of beards and turbans. I remember a time when we all trusted each other in this new country, it was only the new country we worried about.

The two rooms are dark and stuffy. The lights are off, and an oil lamp sputters on the coffee table. The bent old lady has let us in, and her husband is wrapping a white turban over his oiled, hip-length hair. She immediately goes to the kitchen, and I hear the most familiar sound of an Indian home, tap water hitting and filling a teapot.

110 They have not paid their utility bills, out of fear and inability to write a check. The telephone is gone, electricity and gas and water are soon to follow. They have told Judith their sons will provide. They are good boys, and they have always earned and looked after their parents.

We converse a bit in Hindi. They do not ask about the crash and I wonder if I should bring it up. If they think I am here merely as a translator, then they may feel insulted. There are thousands of Punjabi speakers, Sikhs, in Toronto to do a

[6] Clarified butter. — EDS.

better job. And so I say to the old lady, "I too have lost my sons, and my husband, in the crash."

Her eyes immediately fill with tears. The man mutters a few words which sound like a blessing. "God provides and God takes away," he says.

I want to say, But only men destroy and give back nothing. "My boys and my husband are not coming back," I say. "We have to understand that."

Now the old woman responds. "But who is to say? Man alone does not decide these things." To this her husband adds his agreement.

Judith asks about the bank papers, the release forms. With a stroke of the pen, they will have a provincial trustee to pay their bills, invest their money, send them a monthly pension.

"Do you know this woman?" I ask them.

The man raises his hand from the table, turns it over, and seems to regard each finger separately before he answers. "This young lady is always coming here, we make tea for her, and she leaves papers for us to sign." His eyes scan a pile of papers in the corner of the room. "Soon we will be out of tea, then will she go away?"

The old lady adds, "I have asked my neighbors and no one else gets *angrezi*[7] visitors. What have we done?"

"It's her job," I try to explain. "The government is worried. Soon you will have no place to stay, no lights, no gas, no water."

"Government will get its money. Tell her not to worry, we are honorable people."

I try to explain the government wishes to give money, not take. He raises his hand. "Let them take," he says. "We are accustomed to that. That is no problem."

"We are strong people," says the wife. "Tell her that."

"Who needs all this machinery?" demands the husband. "It is unhealthy, the bright lights, the cold air on a hot day, the cold food, the four gas rings. God will provide, not government."

"When our boys return," the mother says.

Her husband sucks his teeth. "Enough talk," he says.

Judith breaks in. "Have you convinced them?" The snaps on her cordovan briefcase go off like firecrackers in that quiet apartment. She lays the sheaf of legal papers on the coffee table. "If they can't write their names, an X will do — I've told them that."

Now the old lady has shuffled to the kitchen and soon emerges with a pot of tea and two cups. "I think my bladder will go first on a job like this," Judith says to me, smiling. "If only there was some way of reaching them. Please thank her for the tea. Tell her she's very kind."

I nod in Judith's direction and tell them in Hindi, "She thanks you for the tea. She thinks you are being very hospitable but she doesn't have the slightest idea what it means."

I want to say, Humor her. I want to say, My boys and my husband are with me too, more than ever. I look in the old man's eyes and I can read his stubborn, peasant's message: *I have protected this woman as best I can. She is the only person I have left. Give to me or take from me what you will, but I will not sign for it. I will not pretend that I accept.*

In the car, Judith says, "You see what I'm up against? I'm sure they're lovely people, but their stubbornness and ignorance are driving me crazy. They think signing a paper is signing their sons' death warrants, don't they?"

I am looking out the window. I want to say, *In our culture, it is a parent's duty to hope.*

"Now Shaila, this next woman is a real mess. She cries day and night, and she refuses all medical help. We may have to — "

"Let me out at the subway," I say.

"I beg your pardon?" I can feel those blue eyes staring at me.

It would not be like her to disobey. She merely disapproves, and slows at a corner to let

[7] English (Anglo). — EDS.

me out. Her voice is plaintive. "Is there anything I said? Anything I did?"

I could answer her suddenly in a dozen ways, but I choose not to. "Shaila? Let's talk about it," I hear, then slam the door.

A wife and mother begins her life in a new country, and that life is cut short. Yet her husband tells her: Complete what we have started. We, who stayed out of politics and came half way around the world to avoid religious and political feuding, have been the first in the New World to die from it. I no longer know what we started, nor how to complete it. I write letters to the editors of local papers and to members of Parliament. Now at least they admit it was a bomb. One MP answers back, with sympathy, but with a challenge. You want to make a difference? Work on a campaign. Work on mine. Politicize the Indian voter.

My husband's old lawyer helps me set up a trust. Vikram was a saver and a careful investor. He had saved the boys' boarding school and college fees. I sell the pink house at four times what we paid for it and take a small apartment downtown. I am looking for a charity to support.

We are deep in the Toronto winter, gray skies, icy pavements. I stay indoors, watching television. I have tried to assess my situation, how best to live my life, to complete what we began so many years ago. Kusum has written me from Hardwar that her life is now serene. She has seen Satish and has heard her daughter sing again. Kusum was on a pilgrimage, passing through a village, when she heard a young girl's voice, singing one of her daughter's favorite *bhajans.* She followed the music through the squalor of a Himalayan village, to a hut where a young girl, an exact replica of her daughter, was fanning coals under the kitchen fire. When she appeared, the girl cried out, "Ma!" and ran away. What did I think of that?

I think I can only envy her. 140

Pam didn't make it to California, but writes me from Vancouver. She works in a department store, giving makeup hints to Indian and Oriental girls. Dr. Ranganathan has given up his commute, given up his house and job, and accepted an academic position in Texas, where no one knows his story and he has vowed not to tell it. He calls me now once a week.

I wait, I listen and I pray, but Vikram has not returned to me. The voices and the shapes and the nights filled with visions ended abruptly several weeks ago.

I take it as a sign.

One rare, beautiful, sunny day last week, returning from a small errand on Yonge Street, I was walking through the park from the subway to my apartment. I live equidistant from the Ontario Houses of Parliament and the University of Toronto. The day was not cold, but something in the bare trees caught my attention. I looked up from the gravel, into the branches and the clear blue sky beyond. I thought I heard the rustling of larger forms, and I waited a moment for voices. Nothing.

"What?" I asked. 145

Then as I stood in the path looking north to Queen's Park and west to the university, I heard the voices of my family one last time. *Your time has come,* they said. *Go, be brave.*

I do not know where this voyage I have begun will end. I do not know which direction I will take. I dropped the package on a park bench and started walking.

[1988]

EXPLORING THE TEXT

1. What information do you learn in the opening three paragraphs? How do they set up a sense of foreboding? Why do you think Bharati Mukherjee chose not to open the story with a more traditional exposition?
2. What evidence do you see that indicates a clash in cultural attitudes and values? How does the relationship between Kusum and Pam illustrate cultural differences at the beginning of the story?
3. How is Judith Templeton depicted? Does Mukherjee want us to see her as being totally insensitive? How does Shaila's attitude toward Judith change during the course of the story? Pay special attention to Judith's characterization of the elderly Sikh couple as "lovely people" motivated by "stubbornness and ignorance" (para. 130).
4. What elements of irony do you find in this story? What purpose do they serve? For instance, consider the irony in paragraph 55 when Shaila reveals the reason she stayed home, and in paragraph 59 when she talks about "the lucky ones." What does Shaila's ironic tone say about her?
5. What does Shaila mean when she says, "I am trapped between two modes of knowledge" (para. 85)? What are these modes of knowledge, and which one does she ultimately choose?
6. In paragraph 103, Shaila says, "Acceptance means you speak of your family in the past tense and you make active plans for moving ahead with your life." Does she agree with that definition? What is the narrator's tone in that remark? Explain what evidence in the text leads you to your conclusion.
7. In paragraph 105, Shaila says, "my family surrounds me," and in paragraph 129, she says, "my boys and my husband are with me too, more than ever." What do these remarks suggest about Shaila's grief ?
8. Regarding Kusum, why does Shaila say, "I think I can only envy her" (para. 140)? What is it about Kusum that Shaila says she envies? Do you believe her? Why or why not?
9. Describe the differences between Kusum's and Shaila's reactions to the loss of their families, and the ways they manage their grief. What is the significance of Shaila's saying "I have my Valium" in response to paragraph 38 and "Maybe I'm selfish" in response to paragraph 46? What does Shaila mean when she distinguishes between "peace" and "a deadening quiet" (para. 7)? By the end of the story, how well has Shaila done with "the management of grief"?
10. How does the story end? Is Shaila honoring or betraying her belief that "it is a parent's duty to hope" (para. 131)?

Ten Kliks South

PHIL KLAY

Phil Klay (b. 1983) is an acclaimed American writer and United States Marine Corps officer. Klay grew up in Westchester, New York, and graduated from Dartmouth College in 2005. He then joined the U.S. Marines, where he was commissioned as a second lieutenant and served in Anbar province in Iraq during the 2007–2008 U.S. troop surge. After leaving the military in 2009, Klay earned an MFA in creative writing from Hunter College in 2011. Klay's first book, *Redeployment* (2014), a collection of short stories drawing on his experiences in Iraq, won the National Book Award and earned high praise from critics for its piercing portrayal of the war. "Ten Kliks South," a story from that collection, follows an artilleryman who comes to terms with his responsibility and his own mortality after successfully bombarding an enemy position.

This morning our gun dropped about 270 pounds of ICM[1] on a smuggler's checkpoint ten kliks[2] south of us. We took out a group of insurgents and then we went to the Fallujah[3] chow hall for lunch. I got fish and lima beans. I try to eat healthy.

At the table, all nine of us are smiling and laughing. I'm still jittery with nervous excitement over it, and I keep grinning and wringing my hands, twisting my wedding band about my finger. I'm sitting next to Voorstadt, our number one guy, and Jewett, who's on the ammo team with me and Bolander. Voorstadt's got a big plate of ravioli and Pop-Tarts, and before digging in, he looks up and down the table and says, "I can't believe we finally had an arty[4] mission."

Sanchez says, "It's about time we killed someone," and Sergeant Deetz laughs. Even I chuckle, a little. We've been in Iraq two months, one of the few artillery units actually doing artillery, except so far we've only shot illumination missions[5]. The grunts usually don't want to risk the collateral damage. Some of the other guns in the battery[6] had shot bad guys, but not us. Not until today. Today, the whole damn battery fired. And we know we hit our target. The lieutenant told us so.

Jewett, who's been pretty quiet, asks, "How many insurgents do you think we killed?"

"Platoon-sized element," says Sergeant Deetz.

"What?" says Bolander. He's a rat-faced professional cynic, and he starts laughing. "Platoon-sized? Sergeant, AQI[7] don't have platoons."

[1] Improved Conventional Munitions; military weapon containing two weapons — each designed to cause harm to people, weapons, and armor — that separate before impact. — EDS.

[2] Kilometers. — EDS.

[3] A city in Iraq invaded by U.S. forces in 2003. — EDS.

[4] Military slang for "artillery." — EDS.

[5] Military missions that use artillary to illuminate a site and improve visibility. — EDS.

[6] A unit of weapons organized in a way that allows the best conditions for battle. — EDS.

[7] Al-Qaeda in Iraq. — EDS.

"Why you think we needed the whole damn battery?" says Sergeant Deetz, grunting out the words.

"We didn't," says Bolander. "Each gun only fired two rounds. I figure they just wanted us all to have gun time on an actual target. Besides, even one round of ICM would be enough to take out a platoon in open desert. No way we needed the whole battery. But it was fun."

Sergeant Deetz shakes his head slowly, his heavy shoulders hunched over the table. "Platoon-sized element," he says again. "That's what it was. And two rounds a gun was what we needed to take it out."

"But," says Jewett in a small voice, "I didn't mean the whole battery. I meant, our gun. How many did our gun, just our gun, kill?"

"How am I supposed to know?" says Sergeant Deetz.

"Platoon-sized is like, forty," I say. "Figure, six guns, so divide and you got, six, I don't know, six point six people per gun."

"Yeah," says Bolander. "We killed exactly 6.6 people."

Sanchez takes out a notebook and starts doing the math, scratching out the numbers in his mechanically precise handwriting. "Divide it by nine Marines on the gun, and you, personally, you've killed zero point seven something people today. That's like, a torso and a head. Or maybe a torso and a leg."

"That's not funny," says Jewett.

"We definitely got more," says Sergeant Deetz. "We're the best shots in the battery."

Bolander snorts. "We're just firing on the quadrant and deflection the FDC[8] gives us, Sergeant. I mean . . ."

"We're better shots," says Sergeant Deetz. "Put a round down a rabbit hole at eighteen miles."

"But even if we were on target . . . ," says Jewett.

[8] Federal Deployment Center. — EDS.

"We were on target," says Sergeant Deetz.

"Okay, Sergeant, we were on target," says Jewett. "But the other guns, their rounds could have hit first. Maybe everybody was already dead."

I can see that, the shrapnel thudding into shattered corpses, the force of it jerking the limbs this way and that.

"Look," says Bolander, "even if their rounds hit first, it doesn't mean everybody was dead, necessarily. Maybe some insurgent had shrapnel in his chest, right, and he's like — " Bolander sticks his tongue out and clutches his chest dramatically, as if he were dying in an old black-and-white movie. "Then our round comes down, boom, blows his fucking head off. He was dying already, but the cause of death would be 'blown the hell up,' not 'shrapnel to the chest.'"

"Yeah, sure," says Jewett, "I guess. But I don't *feel* like I killed anybody. I think I'd know if I killed somebody."

"Naw," says Sergeant Deetz, "you wouldn't know. Not until you'd seen the bodies." The table quiets for a second. Sergeant Deetz shrugs. "It's better this way."

"Doesn't it feel weird to you," says Jewett, "after our first real mission, to just be eating lunch?"

Sergeant Deetz scowls at him, then takes a big bite of his Salisbury steak and grins. "Gotta eat," he says with his mouth full of food.

"It feels good," Voorstadt says. "We just killed some bad guys."

Sanchez gives a quick nod. "It *is* good."

"I don't think I killed anybody," says Jewett.

"Technically, I'm the one that pulled the lanyard," says Voorstadt. "I fired the thing. You just loaded."

"Like I couldn't pull a lanyard," says Jewett.

"Yeah, but you didn't," says Voorstadt.

"Drop it," says Sergeant Deetz. "It's a crew-served weapon. It takes a crew."

"If we used a howitzer[9] to kill somebody back in the States," I say, "I wonder what crime they'd charge us with."

"Murder," says Sergeant Deetz. "What are you, an idiot?"

"Yeah, murder, sure," I say, "but for each of us? In what degree? I mean, me and Bolander and Jewett loaded, right? If I loaded an M16[10] and handed it to Voorstadt and he shot somebody, I wouldn't say I'd killed anyone."

"It's a crew-served weapon," says Sergeant Deetz. "Crew. Served. Weapon. It's different."

"And I loaded, but we got the ammo from the ASP[11]," I say. "Shouldn't they be responsible, too, the ASP Marines?"

"Yeah," says Jewett. "Why not the ASP?"

"Why not the factory workers who made the ammo?" says Sergeant Deetz. "Or the taxpayers who paid for it? You know why not? Because that's retarded."

"The lieutenant gave the order," I say. "He'd get it in court, right?"

"Oh, you believe that? You think officers would take the hit?" Voorstadt laughs. "How long you been in the military?"

Sergeant Deetz thumps his fist on the table. "Listen to me. We're Gun Six. We're responsible for that gun. We just killed some bad guys. With our gun. All of us. And that's a good day's work."

"I still don't feel like I killed anybody, Sergeant," says Jewett.

Sergeant Deetz lets out a long breath. It's quiet for a second. Then he shakes his head and starts laughing. "Yeah, well, all of us except you," he says.

When we get out of the chow hall, I don't know what to do with myself. We don't have anything planned until evening, when we have another illum mission, so most of the guys want to hit the racks. But I don't want to sleep. I feel like I'm finally fully awake. This morning I'd gotten up boot-camp-style, off two hours of sleep, dressed and ready to kill before my brain

---

[9] A type of cannon. — EDS.

[10] A standard issue rifle for a soldier in the U.S. military. — EDS.

[11] Ammunition Supply Point. — EDS.

had time to start working. But now, even though my body is tired, my mind is up and I want to keep it that way.

"Head back to the can?" I say to Jewett.

He nods and we start walking the perimeter of the Battle Square, shaded by the palm trees that grow along the road.

"I kind of wish we had some weed," says Jewett.

"Okay," I say.

"Just saying."

I shake my head. We get to the corner of the Battle Square, Fallujah Surgical straight ahead of us, and turn right.

Jewett says, "Well, it's something to tell my mom about, finally."

"Yeah," I say. "Something to tell Jessie about."

"When's the last time you talked to her?"

"Week and a half."

Jewett doesn't say anything to that. I look down at my wedding band. Jessie and I'd gotten a courthouse wedding a week before I deployed so that if I died, Jessie'd get benefits. It doesn't feel like I'm married.

"What am I supposed to tell her?" I say.

Jewett shrugs.

"She thinks I'm a badass. She thinks I'm in danger."

"We get mortared from time to time."

I give Jewett a flat look.

"It's something," he says. "Anyway, now you can say you got some bad guys."

"Maybe." I look at my watch. "It's zero four, her time. I'll have to wait before I can tell her what a hero I am."

"That's what I tell my mom every day."

When we get near the cans, I tell Jewett I left something at the gun line and peel off.

The gun line's a two-minute walk. As I get closer, the palm trees thin out into desert, and I can see the Camp Fallujah post office. Here the sky expands to the edge of the horizon. It's perfectly blue and cloudless, as it has been every day for the last two months. I can see the guns pointing up into the air. Only Guns Two and Three are manned, and their Marines are just sitting around. When I got here this morning, all the guns were manned and everybody was frantic. The sky was black, with just a touch of red bleeding in from the rim of the horizon. In the half-light, you could see the outline of the massive, forty-feet-long, dark steel barrels pointed into the dark morning sky and below them the shapes of Marines hustling about, checking the guns, the rounds, the powder.

In the daylight, the guns shine crisp in the sun, but earlier this morning was dark and dirty. Me and Bolander and Jewett stood in the back right, waiting by the ammo, while Sanchez called out the quadrant and deflection they were giving to Gun Three.

I had put my hands on one of our rounds, the first one we sent out. Also the first I'd ever fired at human targets. I'd wanted to lift it up right then and there, feel the heft of it tug on my shoulders. I had trained to load those rounds. Trained so much that I had scars on my hands from when they had slammed on my fingers or torn my skin.

Then Gun Three had fired two targeting rounds. Then: "Fire mission. Battery. Two rounds." Then Sanchez had called out the quadrant and deflection and Sergeant Deetz had repeated it and Dupont and Coleman, our gunner and A-gunner, had repeated it and set it and checked it and had Sergeant Deetz check it and Sanchez verify, and we got round and time and Jackson had gotten powder and we moved smooth, like we trained to, me and Jewett on either side of the stretcher holding the round, Bolander behind with the ramming rod. Sergeant Deetz checked the powder and read, "Three, four, five, white bag." Then, to Sanchez: "Charge five, white bag." Verified.

We moved in with the round, up to the open hatch, and Bolander shoved it in with the ramming rod until we heard it ring, and Voorstadt closed the hatch.

Sanchez said, "Hook up."

Deetz said, "Hook up."

Voorstadt hooked the lanyard to the trigger. I'd seen him do it a thousand times.

Sanchez said, "Stand by."

Deetz said, "Stand by."

Voorstadt pulled out the slack in the lanyard, holding it against his waist.

Sanchez said, "Fire."

Deetz said, "Fire."

Voorstadt did a left face and our gun was alive.

The sound of it hit us, vibrating through our bodies, down deep in our chests and in our guts and in the back of our teeth. I could taste the gunpowder in the air. As the guns fired, the barrels shot back like pistons and reseated, the force of each round going off kicking up smoke and dust into the air. When I looked down the line, I couldn't see six guns. I just saw fires through the haze, or not even fires, just flashes of red in the dust and the cordite. And I could feel the roar of each gun, not just ours, as it fired. And I thought, God, this is why I'm glad I'm an artilleryman.

Because what's a grunt with an M16 shooting? 5.56?[12] Even the .50-cal.,[13] what can you really do with that? Or the main gun of a tank. Your range is what? A mile or two? And you can kill what? A small house? An armored vehicle? Wherever we were dropping these rounds, somewhere six miles south of us, those rounds were striking harder than anything else in ground warfare. Each shell weighs 130 pounds, a casing filled with eighty-eight bomblets that scatter over the target area. Each bomblet has a shaped explosive charge that can penetrate two inches of solid steel and send shrapnel flying over the battlefield. Putting those rounds downrange takes nine men moving in perfect unison. It takes an FDC, and a good spotter, and math and physics and art and skill and experience. And though I only loaded, maybe I was only one-third of the ammo team, but I moved perfectly, and the round went in with that satisfying ring, and the round went off with that incredible roar, and it shot out into the sky and hit six miles south of us. The target area. And wherever we hit, everything within a hundred yards, everything within a circle with a radius as long as a football field, everything died.

Voorstadt had the lanyard unhooked and the breech open before the gun had fully reseated, and he washed the bore with the chamber swab and we loaded another round, the second I had fired at a human target that day, although by this point, surely, there were no more living targets. And we fired again, and we felt it in our bones, and we saw the fireball burst from the barrel, and more dust and cordite went into the air, choking us with the sand of the Iraqi desert.

And then it was done.

Smoke surrounded us. We couldn't see beyond our position. I was breathing hard, taking in the smell and taste of gunpowder. And I'd looked at our gun, standing above us, quiet, massive, and felt a kind of love for it.

But the dust began to settle. And a wind came and started picking at the smoke, tugging it and lifting it over us, then higher, into the sky, the only cloud I'd seen in two months. And then the cloud thinned, disappearing into the air, blending with the soft red Iraqi sunrise.

Now, standing before the guns with the sky a perfect blue and the barrels piercing up into the air, it doesn't seem as though any of it could have happened. No speck of this morning remains in our gun. Sergeant Deetz made us clean it after the mission was over. A ritual, of sorts, for our first kill as Gun Six. We'd taken apart the ramming rod and the cleaning swab, attached the two poles together, along with a

---

[12] A standard-issue ammunition round for an M16 rifle. — EDS.

[13] A large ammunition round, typically fired from a mounted machine gun. — EDS.

bore brush, and drenched the brush in CLP.[14] Then we'd all stood in line behind the gun, holding the pole, and in unison had rammed it through the bore. And then we'd repeated the process, and black streaks of CLP and carbon snaked down the pole, staining our hands. We'd kept at it until our gun was clean.

So there's no indication here of what happened, though I know ten kliks south of us is a cratered area riddled with shrapnel and ruined buildings, burned-out vehicles and twisted corpses. The bodies. Sergeant Deetz had seen them on his first deployment, during the initial invasion. None of the rest of us have.

I turn sharply away from the gun line. It's too pristine. And maybe this is the wrong way to think about it. Somewhere, there's a corpse lying out, bleaching in the sun. Before it was a corpse, it was a man who lived and breathed and maybe murdered and maybe tortured, the kind of man I'd always wanted to kill. Whatever the case, a man definitely dead.

So I walk back to our battery area, never turning around. It's a short walk, and when I get back I find a couple of the guys playing Texas hold 'em by a smoke pit. There's Sergeant Deetz, Bolander, Voorstadt, and Sanchez. Deetz has fewer chips than the others and is leaning his bulk over the table, scowling at the pot.

"Oo-rah, motivator," he says when he sees me.

"Oo-rah, Sergeant." I watch them play. Sanchez flips the turn card and everybody checks.

"Sergeant?" I say.

"What?"

I'm not sure where to start. "Don't you think, maybe, we should have a patrol out, to see if there were any survivors?"

"What?" Sergeant Deetz is focused on the game. As soon as Sanchez flips the river, he throws his cards in.

"I mean, the mission we had. Shouldn't we go out, like, in a patrol, to see if there are any survivors?"

Sergeant Deetz looks up at me. "You are an idiot, aren't you?"

"No, Sergeant."

"There weren't any survivors," says Voorstadt, tossing his cards in as well.

"You see al-Qaeda rolling around in tanks?" says Sergeant Deetz.

"No, Sergeant."

"You see al-Qaeda building crazy bunkers and trenches?"

"No, Sergeant."

"You think al-Qaeda's got some magic, ICM-doesn't-kill-my-ass ninja powers?"

"No, Sergeant."

"No, you're goddamn right, no."

"Yes, Sergeant."

The betting is now between Sanchez and Bolander. Sanchez, looking at the pot, says to no one in particular, "I think the 2nd and 136th does patrols out there."

"But, Sergeant," I say, "what about the bodies? Doesn't somebody have to clean up the bodies?"

"Jesus, Lance Corporal. Do I look like a PRP Marine to you?"

"No, Sergeant."

"What do I look like?"

"Like an artilleryman, Sergeant."

"You're goddamn right, killer. I'm an artilleryman. We *provide* the bodies. We don't clean 'em up. You hear me?"

"Yes, Sergeant."

He looks up at me. "And what are you, Lance Corporal?"

"An artilleryman. Sergeant."

"And what do you do?"

"Provide the bodies, Sergeant."

"You're goddamn right, killer. You're goddamn right."

Sergeant Deetz turns back to the game. I use the opportunity to slip away. It was stupid to ask Deetz, but what he said has me thinking. PRP:

[14] Cleaner, Lubricant, and Preservative; used to clean weapons.—EDS.

personnel retrieval and processing, aka Mortuary Affairs. I'd forgotten about them. They must have collected the bodies from this morning.

The thought of PRP works and worms through my brain. The bodies could be sitting here, on base. But I don't know where PRP is. I'd never wanted to know, and I don't want to ask anyone the way, either. Why would anyone go there? But I leave the battery area and walk around the perimeter of the Battle Square, over to the CLB[15] buildings, dodging officers and staff NCOs.[16] It takes a good half hour, sneaking around, reading the signs outside of buildings, until I find it, a long, low, rectangular building surrounded by palm trees. It's offset from the rest of the CLB complex, but otherwise just like every other building. That feels wrong — if they cleaned up from today, severed limbs should be spilling out the door.

I stand outside, looking at the entrance. It's a simple wooden door. One I shouldn't be in front of, one I shouldn't open, one I shouldn't step through. I'm in a combat arms unit, and I don't belong here. It's bad voodoo. But I came all this way, I found it, and I'm not a coward. So I open the door.

Inside is cool air, a long hallway full of closed doors, and a Marine at a desk facing away from me. He has headphones on. They're plugged into a computer that's playing some sort of TV show. On the screen, a woman in a poofy dress is hailing a cab. She looks pretty at first, but then the screen cuts to a close-up and it's clear she's not.

The Marine at the desk turns around and takes off his headphones, looking up at me, confused. I look for chevrons on his collar and see he's a gunnery sergeant, but he seems far older than most gunnys. A trim white mustache sits on his lip and he has a white fuzz of hair over the ears, but the rest of his head is shiny and bald. As he squints up to look at me, the skin around his eyes scrunches into wrinkles. He's fat, too. Even through the uniform, I can tell. They say PRP is all reservists, no active duty undertakers in the Marine Corps, and he looks like a reservist for sure.

"Can I help you, Lance Corporal?" he says. There's a soft, southern drawl in his voice.

I stand there looking at him, my mouth open, and the seconds tick by.

Then the old gunny's face softens and he leans forward and says, "Did you lose someone, son?"

It takes me a second to figure it out. "No," I say. "No. No no no. No."

He looks at me, confused, and arches an eyebrow.

"I'm an artilleryman," I say.

"Okay," he says.

We look at each other.

"We had a mission today. Target was ten kliks south of here?" I look at him, hoping he'll get it. I feel constricted by the narrow hallway, with the desk squeezed in and the fat old gunny looking at me quizzically.

"Okay?" he says.

"It was my first mission like that. . . ."

"Okay?" he says again. He leans forward and squints up at me, like if he gets a better look, he'll know what the hell I'm talking about.

"I mean, I'm from Nebraska. From Ord, Nebraska. We don't do anything in Ord." I'm fully aware I sound like an idiot.

"You all right, Lance Corporal?" The old gunny looks at me intently, waiting. Any gunny in an arty unit would have chewed my ass by now. Any gunny in an arty unit would have chewed my ass as soon as I walked through the door, waltzing into someplace I didn't belong. But this gunny, maybe because he's a reservist, maybe because he's old, maybe because he's fat, just looks up and waits for me to get out what I need to say.

"I just never killed anybody before."

"Neither have I," he says.

---

[15] Combat Logistics Battalion. — EDS.

[16] Non-Commissioned Officers; lower-ranking officers who take orders from commissioned officers and allocate jobs to lower-ranking personnel. — EDS.

"But I did. I think. I mean, we just shot the rounds off."

"Okay," he says. "So why'd you come here?"

I look at him helplessly. "I thought, maybe, you'd been out there. And seen what we'd done."

The old gunny leans back in his chair and purses his lips tight. "No," he says.

He takes a breath and lets it out slow.

"We handle U.S. casualties. Iraqis take care of their own. Only time I see enemy dead is when they pass in a U.S. med facility. Like Fallujah Surgical." He waves his hand in the general direction of the base hospital. "Besides, TQ's[17] got a PRP section. They'd probably have handled anything in that AO."[18]

"Oh," I say. "Okay."

"We didn't have anything like that today."

"Okay," I say.

"You'll be all right," he says.

"Yeah," I say. "Thanks, Gunny."

I stand there, looking at him for a second. Then I look down at all the closed doors in the hallway, doors with nothing behind them. On the computer screen behind the gunny, a group of women drink pink martinis.

"You married, Lance Corporal?" The gunny is looking at my hands, at my wedding band.

"Yeah," I say. "About two months now."

"How old are you?" he asks.

"Nineteen."

He nods, then sits there as though turning some hard thing over in his mind. Right when I'm about to take my leave, he says, "Here's something you could do for me. Can you do me a favor?"

"Sure, Gunny."

He points at my wedding band. "Take that off and put it on the chain with your dog tags." He scoops at the chain around his own neck with two fingers and pulls out his dog tags to show me. There, hanging next to the two metal tabs with his kill data, is a gold ring. "Okay? . . .

"We need to collect personal effects," he says, putting his dog tags back in his shirt. "For me, the hardest thing is taking off the wedding rings."

"Oh." I take a step back.

"Can you do that?" he says.

"Yeah," I say, "I can do that."

"Thanks," he says.

"I should go," I say.

"You should," he says.

I turn quickly, open the door, and step out into the oven air. I walk away slow, back straight, controlling my steps, and I walk with my right hand over my left, worrying at my wedding band, twisting it around my finger.

I'd told the gunny I would do it, so as I walk I work at my ring, getting it off my finger. It feels like bad voodoo, to put it with my dog tags. But I take them from around my neck, undo the snap clasp, slip the ring onto the chain, redo the clasp, and put the dog tags back around my neck. I can feel the metal of the ring against my chest.

I walk away, not paying attention to where my steps are leading me, passing under the palm trees lining the road around the Battle Square. I'm hungry, and it should be time for chow, but I don't go that way. I go to the road by Fallujah Surgical and I stop.

It's a squat, dull building, beige and beaten down by the brightness of the sun like everything else. There's a smoke pit nearby and two Corpsmen are sitting there, talking and dragging on cigarettes, sending faint puffs of smoke into the air. I wait, looking at the building as if something incredible might emerge.

Nothing happens, of course. But there in the heat, standing before Fallujah Surgical, I remember the cooler air of the morning two days before. We'd been going to chow, all of Gun Six, laughing and joking until Sergeant Deetz, who was yelling something about the Spartans being gay, stopped midsentence. He froze, then

[17] Al Taqaddum Airbase; an airbase located in central Iraq (74 km from Baghdad). It was long abandoned when U.S. military forces occupied it in 2003, and in 2009 it was turned back over to the Iraqi military. — EDS.

[18] Area of Operations. — EDS.

shifted, straightened to his full height, and whispered, "Ahhh-ten-HUT."

We all snapped to attention, not knowing why. Sergeant Deetz raised his right hand in a salute, and so did we. Then I saw, off in the distance, well down the road, four Corpsmen coming out of Fallujah Surgical carrying a stretcher draped with the American flag. Everything was silent, still. All down the road, Marines and sailors had snapped to.

I could barely see it in the early morning light. I strained my eyes looking at the outline of the body under the thick fabric of the flag. And then the stretcher passed from view.

Now, standing there in the daytime, looking at the two Corpsmen in the smoke pit, I wonder if they'd been the ones carrying that body. They must have carried some.

Everyone standing on the road as the body went past had been so utterly silent, so still. There was no sound or movement except for the slow steps of the Corpsmen and the steady progress of the corpse. It'd been an image of death from another world. But now I know where that corpse was headed, to the old gunny at PRP. And if there was a wedding ring, the gunny would have slowly worked it off the stiff, dead fingers. He would have gathered all the personal effects and prepared the body for transport. Then it would have gone by air to TQ. And as it was unloaded off the bird, the Marines would have stood silent and still, just as we had in Fallujah. And they would have put it on a C-130[19] to Kuwait. And they would have stood silent and still in Kuwait. And they would have stood silent and still in Germany, and silent and still at Dover Air Force Base. Everywhere it went, Marines and sailors and soldiers and airmen would have stood at attention as it traveled to the family of the fallen, where the silence, the stillness, would end.

[2014]

[19] A military transport aircraft. — EDS.

EXPLORING THE TEXT

1. What do we learn about the character of Jewett from his interaction with the others at lunch? from his walk with the narrator? How is Jewett different from his fellow crew members?
2. How does the narrator describe his surroundings? What does this description reveal about his view of the war?
3. Why does Sergeant Deetz try to persuade the narrator not to think about the bodies? To what extent does his behavior reveal a conflict between conscience and duty in the military culture Phil Klay depicts?
4. Why does the narrator go off in search of his victim's bodies despite his conversation with Sergeant Deetz? What is the narrator hoping to find? Does the narrator himself even know? Explain, using details from the story to support your response.
5. How does the narrator's interaction with the gunnery sergeant change his perspective on combat?
6. Two flashbacks occur in the story. In the first, the narrator remembers the artillery mission he completed that morning. In the second, the narrator remembers saluting the body of an American marine carried out of the base hospital. Compare and contrast the two flashbacks. How do they suggest a change has occurred in the narrator's perspective on the war?
7. Compare the opening and closing paragraphs of "Ten Kliks South." What does the first paragraph suggest about the narrator's preoccupations at the story's beginning? How have his preoccupations changed by the end?
8. Among other themes, the story explores how combat undertaken at a distance can separate the combatants from a feeling of responsibility for their actions. Find at least two characters whose opinions on this theme differ and explain how their perspectives are dramatized.

POETRY

Battle Hymn of the Republic

JULIA WARD HOWE

Julia Ward Howe (1819–1910) was a prominent American abolitionist, activist, and poet. Born to a Calvinist stockbroker father and a poet mother in New York City, Howe was educated and well read from an early age. She married into a prominent family and raised six children in Boston while her husband worked. Stifled by her marriage, Howe began to publish personal poems. Her first book, *Passion-Flowers*, appeared in 1853. To the chagrin of her husband, Howe went on to write four more poetry books, many critiquing the limited role available to women in American society. Howe also produced eleven issues of the literary magazine *Northern Lights* and wrote on her travels to Europe and Cuba, raising the profile of causes ranging from pacifism to women's suffrage. In 1870, she founded the suffragist magazine *Woman's Journal*, and in 1881 was elected president of the Association for the Advancement of Women. In 1908, she was the first woman elected to the American Academy of Arts and Letters. She was inspired to write "The Battle Hymn of the Republic" after she met Abraham Lincoln in the White House in 1861, and it went on to become one of the most popular Union songs during the Civil War.

Mine eyes have seen the glory of the coming of the Lord:
He is trampling out the vintage where the grapes of wrath are stored;
He hath loosed the fateful lightning of His terrible swift sword:
His truth is marching on.

I have seen Him in the watch-fires of a hundred circling camps,
They have builded Him an altar in the evening dews and damps;
I can read His righteous sentence by the dim and flaring lamps:
His day is marching on.

I have read a fiery gospel writ in burnished rows of steel:
"As ye deal with my contemners, so with you my grace shall deal;
Let the Hero, born of woman, crush the serpent with his heel,
Since God is marching on."

He has sounded forth the trumpet that shall never call retreat;
He is sifting out the hearts of men before His judgment-seat:
Oh, be swift, my soul, to answer Him! be jubilant, my feet!
Our God is marching on.

In the beauty of the lilies Christ was born across the sea,
With a glory in his bosom that transfigures you and me:
As he died to make men holy, let us die to make men free,
While God is marching on.

[1862]

EXPLORING THE TEXT

1. In the first stanza, the speaker describes the Lord as having "loosed the fateful lightning of His terrible swift sword" (l. 3). What other images of violent power can be found in the poem? How do they contribute to the speaker's purpose?
2. The second stanza concludes, "His day is marching on" (l. 8). Examine the previous three lines in the stanza. How is the speaker's use of "day" metaphorical? What does that metaphor add to the poem?
3. Note the phrase "Battle Hymn" in the title of the poem. Where else does the speaker blend the military with the religious, and to what effect?
4. Examine how the imagery in the final stanza differs from the imagery in the previous four. What does this shift signal? What effect does it have on readers?
5. Notice how each stanza offers three long, comparatively complicated lines followed by a single line that references God directly. How does this pattern emphasize the speaker's message?

Vigil Strange I Kept on the Field One Night

WALT WHITMAN

Walt Whitman (1819–1892) was born on Long Island, New York. Early in his life, he worked as a country schoolteacher and printer, and served as writer and editor for the *Brooklyn Eagle* newspaper. He continued in a variety of jobs, writing and working as a carpenter, and first published his now famous *Leaves of Grass*, which later underwent several revisions and new editions, in 1855. Regarded as offensive and vulgar at the time for its outspoken content, the book celebrated individuality and the richness of life. In 1862, Whitman went to Virginia to find his brother George, who had been wounded in the Civil War. He was shocked to witness the horrors of war firsthand and was deeply moved by the suffering of the wounded. He worked as an aide in army hospitals in Washington, caring first for his brother and then other soldiers as well. Among Whitman's most well-known poems from this time are "Oh Captain, My Captain" and "When Lilacs Last in the Dooryard Bloom'd," both about Abraham Lincoln. The poem included here was inspired by Whitman's war experience.

Vigil strange I kept on the field one night;
When you my son and my comrade dropt at my side that day,
One look I but gave which your dear eyes return'd with a look I shall never forget,
One touch of your hand to mine O boy, reach'd up as you lay on the ground,
Then onward I sped in the battle, the even-contested battle,
Till late in the night reliev'd to the place at last again I made my way,
Found you in death so cold dear comrade, found your body son of responding
kisses, (never again on earth responding,)

Bared your face in the starlight, curious the scene, cool blew the moderate night-wind,
Long there and then in vigil I stood, dimly around me the battle-field spreading,
Vigil wondrous and vigil sweet there in the fragrant silent night,
But not a tear fell, not even a long-drawn sigh, long, long I gazed,
Then on the earth partially reclining sat by your side leaning my chin in my hands,
Passing sweet hours, immortal and mystic hours with you dearest comrade — not a tear, not a word,
Vigil of silence, love and death, vigil for you my son and my soldier,
As onward silently stars aloft, eastward new ones upward stole,
Vigil final for you brave boy, (I could not save you, swift was your death,
I faithfully loved you and cared for you living, I think we shall surely meet again,)
Till at latest lingering of the night, indeed just as the dawn appear'd,
My comrade I wrapt in his blanket, envelop'd well his form,
Folded the blanket well, tucking it carefully over head and carefully under feet,
And there and then and bathed by the rising sun, my son in his grave, in his rude-dug grave I deposited,
Ending my vigil strange with that, vigil of night and battle-field dim,
Vigil for boy of responding kisses, (never again on earth responding,)
Vigil for comrade swiftly slain, vigil I never forget, how as day brighten'd,
I rose from the chill ground and folded my soldier well in his blanket,
And buried him where he fell.

[1865]

EXPLORING THE TEXT

1. Notice that the poem is presented as a "vigil." What is significant about the choice of that particular word? Why is the word repeated throughout the poem? Why is it a "vigil strange" (l. 1), and why is the scene described as "curious" in line 8?
2. What different kinds of relationships are implied when the speaker addresses the dead soldier as both "my son and my comrade" (l. 2)? What does this suggest about the speaker's view of the Civil War in general? Cite other places in the poem in which the speaker addresses the dead soldier to support your answer.
3. Why does the speaker repeat the parenthetical phrase "(never again on earth responding,)" in lines 7 and 23? What does this imply about the speaker's mind-state?
4. How would you describe the tone of the poem? Use specific evidence from the text to support your description.
5. There is an important shift in line 19, where the "you" and "your" of line 16 become "My comrade" and "his." What is the significance of this shift in terms of the relationship of the speaker to his dying son? How does the final wrapping of his comrade in a blanket complicate this shift?
6. Most of the lines in the poem are long and ornately descriptive. What does the relative brevity of the final line — "And buried him where he fell" (l. 26) — suggest about the speaker's emotional state by the end of the poem?

Channel Firing

THOMAS HARDY

Thomas Hardy (1840–1928) was born in Dorset, England. Among his most famous works are *Far from the Madding Crowd* (1874), *The Return of the Native* (1878), *Tess of the d'Urbervilles* (1891), and *Jude the Obscure* (1895). After the less than appreciative reaction that *Jude the Obscure* received — many people found it too shocking and pessimistic — Hardy wrote only poetry. In "Channel Firing," he adopts the voices of the dead who are woken by the firing of artillery. It was published on May 1, 1914, just three months before the start of World War I.

That night your great guns, unawares,
Shook all our coffins as we lay,
And broke the chancel[1] window-squares,
We thought it was the Judgment-day

And sat upright. While drearisome
Arose the howl of wakened hounds:
The mouse let fall the altar-crumb,
The worms drew back into the mounds,

The glebe[2] cow drooled. Till God called, "No;
It's gunnery practice out at sea
Just as before you went below;
The world is as it used to be:

"All nations striving strong to make
Red war[3] yet redder. Mad as hatters[4]
They do no more for Christés sake[5]
Than you who are helpless in such matters.

"That this is not the judgment-hour
For some of them's a blessed thing,
For if it were they'd have to scour
Hell's floor for so much threatening. . . .

"Ha, ha. It will be warmer when
I blow the trumpet (if indeed
I ever do; for you are men,
And rest eternal sorely need)."

So down we lay again. "I wonder,
Will the world ever saner be,"
Said one, "than when He sent us under
In our indifferent century!"

And many a skeleton shook his head.
"Instead of preaching forty year,"
My neighbour Parson Thirdly[6] said,
"I wish I had stuck to pipes and beer."

Again the guns disturbed the hour,
Roaring their readiness to avenge,
As far inland as Stourton Tower[7],
And Camelot[8], and starlit Stonehenge.[9]

[1914]

[1] The area of a church near the altar. — EDS.

[2] A cow given to a priest by his parishioners. — EDS.

[3] A reference to the Book of Revelation, also known as The Apocalypse of John, in the New Testament of the Bible. — EDS.

[4] A reference to the symptoms of mercury poisoning experienced by hatters, who frequently used the substance to make felt hats from animal fur in the seventeenth through nineteenth centuries. — EDS.

[5] A reference to "The Doctor's Tale" in *The Canterbury Tales* by Geoffrey Chaucer: "For evermore: therefore for Christé's sake / To teach them virtue look that ye ne slake." — EDS.

[6] In *Far from the Madding Crowd*, a weak and longwinded character who begins all of his sentences with "Firstly . . ." — EDS.

[7] Also known as King Alfred's Tower, located in Somerset, England. It was erected in 1766 to commemorate the Battle of Edington (878). — EDS.

[8] The castle of King Arthur, a legendary figure said to have defended Britain against Saxon invasion in the late fifth or early sixth century. — EDS.

[9] A ring of standing stones in Wiltshire, England, that was built and periodically altered between 3100 and 1600 BC. — EDS.

EXPLORING THE TEXT

1. Note at the beginning the effect of the "great guns." What impressions are created by the imagery of the first two stanzas? How do they help establish the mood and tone of the poem?
2. What is the significance of the word "unawares" in the first line of the poem? Why do you think Hardy chose this word to describe the guns? What does this word choice reveal about the meaning of the poem?
3. God speaks from line 9 through line 24. How would you describe his tone in these lines? Why would Hardy present the voice of God this way?
4. In lines 13–14, God describes gunnery practice as "all nations striving strong to make / Red war yet redder." What does "Red war" refer to? What does this suggest about God's perspective on war in this poem?
5. Note that Hardy has God use the Middle English spelling of "Christé" for Christ. Why would he deliberately use a four-hundred-year-old archaism in this instance? What effect does this word choice have on the poem?
6. The poem is rich in poetic craft; note the enjambment in lines 5–6, 9–10, 13–14, and 25–26, as well as the caesura in lines 5, 9, 21, and 25. How do these particular elements reflect the meaning of the poem?
7. The poem is written in successive quatrains with an *abab* rhyme scheme throughout. Note as well the consistent meter: iambic pentameter, except for the final line. Why do you think Hardy chose such a formal, ballad-like structure? Why would Hardy deliberately break the rhythm, or time, of the poem in the final line? Explain.
8. Read carefully the final quatrain, noting the heavy use of alliteration and internal rhyme of the first two lines and the place names in the final two: Stourton Tower, Camelot, and Stonehenge. What is the effect of the alliteration? What progression is suggested by the three place names?

Lamentations

SIEGFRIED SASSOON

On August 2, 1914, two days before England's declaration of war, British poet Siegfried Sassoon (1886–1967) enlisted in the army and went to the front lines. Called "Mad Jack" for his reckless behavior and ferocity, Sassoon was regarded as a modern Achilles. He was wounded twice, and received two medals for bravery. While recovering from an injury in England, he became critical of the war and declined to return to duty. His 1917 letter to his commanding officer, "A Soldier's Declaration," was read to the House of Commons and published in the London *Times*. In it he stated, "I am not protesting against the conduct of the war, but against the political errors and insincerities for which the fighting men are being sacrificed. On behalf of those who are suffering now, I make this protest against the deception which is being practised upon them; also I believe it may help to destroy the callous complacency with which the majority of those at home regard the continuance of agonies which they do not share and which they have not enough imagination to realise." Deemed mentally unfit for court-martial, he was sent to the hospital to recover from shell shock and there met fellow soldier and poet Wilfred Owen, whom he encouraged to write. After the war, he taught and lectured for many years. Sassoon wrote more than twenty collections of poetry, the most famous being *Counter-Attack and Other Poems* (1918) — a small group of poems about the horrors of war, which includes "Lamentations."

I found him in the guard-room at the Base.
From the blind darkness I had heard his crying
And blundered in. With puzzled, patient face
A sergeant watched him; it was no good trying
To stop it; for he howled and beat his chest.
And, all because his brother had gone west,
Raved at the bleeding war; his rampant grief
Moaned, shouted, sobbed, and choked, while he was kneeling
Half-naked on the floor. In my belief
Such men have lost all patriotic feeling.

[1918]

EXPLORING THE TEXT

1. The speaker says he "blundered" (l. 3) into the "blind darkness" (l. 2) and that the sergeant is "puzzled" (l. 3). What does Siegfried Sassoon achieve by placing so much emphasis on the confusion of the situation?
2. Note the repetition of the past tense verbs beginning with "Moaned" (l. 8). What is the effect of this repetition? Now, find the subject of that series of verbs. What do you find significant about that subject, and how does it affect your interpretation of the poem?
3. Note the shift in tone in the middle of line 9. How would you characterize the tone of that final statement? If you had been the one to "find" the man, how would you complete the statement, "In my belief . . ."?
4. Although the poem's title might seem straightforward, try to come up with three interpretations of it. Think about what is being lamented, and by whom.

Dulce et Decorum Est

WILFRED OWEN

Born in Shropshire, England, in 1893, Wilfred Owen is the most well known and most highly regarded of the World War I poets. He enlisted in the army in 1915 and fought in France. In May 1917, he was evacuated from the front and hospitalized with shell shock (a condition now referred to as post-traumatic stress disorder). He returned to the battlefield and won the Military Cross in October 1918. Five of his poems were published that year — the only five he lived to see in print. His work exposes the horrors of the war firsthand. He was killed in battle one week before the armistice (November 11, 1918). Owen's work remained virtually unknown until 1920, when his friend, Siegfried Sassoon, collected his work and published it as *Poems*. Although Owen's life was short, and his career as a writer even shorter, his influence on the next generation of British writers was profound. While recovering from shell shock, he drafted what was to become one of the most famous and gripping poems about war in the English language, "Dulce et Decorum Est." The title comes from the Roman poet Horace (65–8 B.C.E.), whose line "Dulce et decorum est pro patria mori" means "It is sweet and fitting to die for one's country" in Latin.

Bent double, like old beggars under sacks,
Knock-kneed, coughing like hags, we cursed through sludge,
Till on the haunting flares we turned our backs
And towards our distant rest began to trudge.
Men marched asleep. Many had lost their boots
But limped on, blood-shod. All went lame; all blind;
Drunk with fatigue; deaf even to the hoots
Of tired, outstripped Five-Nines[1] that dropped behind.

Gas! GAS! Quick, boys! — An ecstasy of fumbling,
Fitting the clumsy helmets just in time;
But someone still was yelling out and stumbling
And flound'ring like a man in fire or lime[2] . . .
Dim, through the misty panes and thick green light,
As under a green sea, I saw him drowning.

In all my dreams, before my helpless sight,
He plunges at me, guttering, choking, drowning.

If in some smothering dreams you too could pace
Behind the wagon that we flung him in,
And watch the white eyes writhing in his face,
His hanging face, like a devil's sick of sin;
If you could hear, at every jolt, the blood
Come gargling from the froth-corrupted lungs,
Obscene as cancer, bitter as the cud
Of vile, incurable sores on innocent tongues, —
My friend, you would not tell with such high zest
To children ardent for some desperate glory,
The old Lie: Dulce et decorum est
Pro patria mori.

[1920]

[1] German artillery shells used in World War I. — EDS.

[2] Also known as calcium oxide, lime is a chemical compound that both sanitizes and dissolves tissue. In World War I, it was often used in the trenches to sanitize the fallen soldiers' bodies — this helped stave off the constant threat of disease as well as mitigate the smell. — EDS.

EXPLORING THE TEXT

1. Note the title of the poem and the translation provided in the headnote. What expectations does the title create for the reader, and at what point did you realize that this was not going to be a poem about the glories of war?

2. In the first stanza, how does Wilfred Owen use diction and imagery to bring the experience of a night march to life for the reader? What is the purpose of the similes comparing the troops to "old beggars" and "hags"?

3. Note the diction in the second stanza. Why does the speaker call it an "ecstasy of fumbling" (l. 9)? Why does he use "or" in "fire or lime?" (l. 12)? What does this ambiguity suggest?
4. The third stanza shifts in tense, from the past tense "saw" of line 14 to the present tense "plunges" in line 16. What accounts for this temporal shift? A shift in perspective occurs in line 17. How do the shifts in time and perspective influence your response to the poem?
5. Lines 17 through 28 conclude the poem in one sentence addressed to the "you" in line 17. Whom is the speaker addressing? How would you describe the tone the speaker uses to say the phrase "My friend" in line 25?
6. The poem uses graphic — some might say grotesque — imagery throughout. How does that imagery influence your understanding of the purpose of the poem?
7. This poem is arguably the most famous war poem in the English language. What accounts for its lasting popularity? Is its fame deserved? Why or why not?

The First Long-Range Artillery Shell in Leningrad

ANNA AKHMATOVA

Translated by Lyn Coffin

Born Anna Gorenko in Odessa, Ukraine, Anna Akhmatova (1889–1966) began writing as a child, and showed early promise as a poet. Her father believed that having a "decadent poetess" in the family would disgrace the family name, so he forced her to take a pen name. She married the Russian poet Nikolai Gumilyov in 1910, but he soon left her to go off traveling. In 1912, she gave birth to their son, Lev, and published her first book of poetry, *Vecher*. The couple divorced in 1918. In 1921, Gumilyov was arrested by the Bolsheviks, charged with betraying the revolution, and executed. Because of their connection, Akhmatova was persecuted by Stalin's regime, and except for periods during World War II, her work was banned from publication between 1925 and 1952. Despite the difficulties she faced as a writer, she is now known as one of the greatest poets of the Soviet Union. The poem included here is set during the siege of Leningrad by German artillery bombardment, which occurred from September 1941 to January 1944.

A rainbow of people rushing around,
And suddenly everything changed completely,
This wasn't a normal city sound,
It came from unfamiliar country.
True, it resembled, like a brother,
One peal of thunder or another,
But every natural thunder contains
The moisture of clouds, fresh and high,
And the thirst of fields with drought gone dry,
A harbinger of happy rains,
And this was as arid as hell ever got,
And my distracted hearing would not

Believe it, if only because of the wild
Way it started, grew, and caught,
And how indifferently it brought
Death to my child.

[1941]

EXPLORING THE TEXT

1. Try to forget the title of this poem, and then reread it. At what point does this poem *have* to be about an artillery shell? Before that point, could it be about something else? What is Anna Akhmatova's point in writing about this event in such an indirect way?
2. This poem chronicles a drastic change in the lives of the citizens of Leningrad. What familiar things does the speaker call on in order to understand the "unfamiliar" (l. 4)? In particular, why does the speaker present the situation in terms of weather?
3. What is the significance of the adverb "indifferently" in line 15? How does it help the poet express her theme?
4. Does the tone remain consistent throughout the poem, or does it shift at the very end?
5. Akhmatova wrote this poem about the first assault in a series of artillery attacks that continued for almost three years. How does knowing that information influence your understanding of and response to the poem?

Naming of Parts

HENRY REED

Henry Reed (1914–1986) was born in Birmingham, England. He won a scholarship to the University of Birmingham, where he earned an MA, writing his thesis on the novels of Thomas Hardy. In 1941, he was conscripted into the Royal Army Ordnance Corps. During the war, he served as a soldier and cryptographer, working in both the Italian and the Japanese sections of the Government Code and Cypher School. The poems for which he is best known are based on his experience in basic training, where he entertained his friends with imitations of drill sergeants. Later he wrote about those experiences in a series of poems entitled "Lessons of the War," which includes the following selection. Thus, "Naming of Parts" — arguably the most famous poem of World World II — was inspired not by an actual war experience but by Reed's time spent in basic training.

Today we have naming of parts. Yesterday,
We had daily cleaning. And tomorrow morning,
We shall have what to do after firing. But today,
Today we have naming of parts. Japonica
Glistens like coral in all of the neighboring gardens,
And today we have naming of parts.

This is the lower sling swivel. And this
Is the upper sling swivel, whose use you will see,

When you are given your slings. And this is the piling swivel,
Which in your case you have not got. The branches
Hold in the gardens their silent, eloquent gestures,
Which in our case we have not got.

This is the safety-catch, which is always released
With an easy flick of the thumb. And please do not let me
See anyone using his finger. You can do it quite easy
If you have any strength in your thumb. The blossoms
Are fragile and motionless, never letting anyone see
Any of them using their finger.

And this you can see is the bolt. The purpose of this
Is to open the breech, as you see. We can slide it
Rapidly backwards and forwards: we call this
Easing the spring. And rapidly backwards and forwards
The early bees are assaulting and fumbling the flowers:
They call it easing the Spring.

They call it easing the Spring: it is perfectly easy
If you have any strength in your thumb: like the bolt,
And the breech, and the cocking-piece, and the point of balance,
Which in our case we have not got; and the almond-blossom
Silent in all of the gardens and the bees going backwards and forwards,
For today we have naming of parts.

[1946]

EXPLORING THE TEXT

1. Each of the first four stanzas seems to be spoken in two voices. Where does the shift in perspective occur in each of them? Does this poem have two different speakers, or one speaker with two different voices? Explain.
2. Were you surprised by the imagery of the poem? What is the poet suggesting through the juxtaposition of war and nature imagery?
3. How would you explain the shift from "your case" to "our case" in lines 9–12? How do the things "Which in your case you have not got" (l. 10) compare to the things "Which in our case we have not got" (l. 12)?
4. How does the fifth stanza differ from those that precede it?
5. Judging from the poem, what is Henry Reed's attitude toward his experience as a soldier in World War II?
6. Henry Reed and Richard Wilbur (whose poem follows) both juxtapose the imagery of warfare with that of nature. How would you compare the way that each poet uses imagery to present his attitude toward his subject?

First Snow in Alsace

RICHARD WILBUR

Richard Wilbur was born in 1921 in New York City. He graduated from Amherst College in 1942 and then served in World War II. In 1944, he participated in two of the most crucial battles in Italy: the landing at Anzio and the attack on Monte Cassino, where thousands of troops were killed. His first collection of poetry, *The Beautiful Changes and Other Poems* (1947), includes "First Snow in Alsace," a poem that reflects his war experience. A decade later, his collection *Things of This World* earned both the Pulitzer Prize and the National Book Award. Wilbur is also known for his translations of French literature, especially the plays of Molière. Alsace is a small region of eastern France that borders Germany and Switzerland. From 1940 to 1944, it was under the control of Nazi Germany.

The snow came down last night like moths
Burned on the moon; it fell till dawn,
Covered the town with simple cloths.

Absolute snow lies rumpled on
What shellbursts scattered and deranged,
Entangled railings, crevassed lawn.

As if it did not know they'd changed,
Snow smoothly clasps the roofs of homes
Fear-gutted, trustless and estranged.

The ration stacks are milky domes;
Across the ammunition pile
The snow has climbed in sparkling combs.

You think: beyond the town a mile
Or two, this snowfall fills the eyes
Of soldiers dead a little while.

Persons and persons in disguise,
Walking the new air white and fine,
Trade glances quick with shared surprise.

At children's windows, heaped, benign,
As always, winter shines the most,
And frost makes marvelous designs.

The night guard coming from his post,
Ten first-snows back in thought, walks slow
And warms him with a boyish boast:

He was the first to see the snow.

[1947]

EXPLORING THE TEXT

1. In the first stanza, the snow comes down "like moths / Burned on the moon" and lies in "simple cloths" on the town. What is the effect of the differing imagery created by the simile and the metaphor in that stanza? Ultimately, what impression of the snow does the first stanza convey?
2. The snow's presence is so strong that it might be seen as a character in the first four stanzas. How does this personification prepare you for the shift ("You think:") in line 13?
3. Who is the speaker of the poem? What is the speaker's attitude toward the events and scene described?
4. What is the meaning of line 16: "Persons and persons in disguise"?
5. What is the significance of the final line of the poem? In a poem about Alsace — a disputed territory that has seen the horrors of wartime again and again over the centuries — why does Richard Wilbur write about the snow? What does the snow change in this poem, and how does it change it?

It Is Dangerous to Read Newspapers

MARGARET ATWOOD

Margaret Atwood (b. 1939) was born in Ottawa and spent much of her childhood in northern Quebec. She earned her undergraduate degree at Victoria College (now University) of the University of Toronto and an MA at Radcliffe College (Harvard University). Atwood is a prolific writer in many forms, including poetry, literary criticism, and fiction. She is the author of more than fifteen collections of poetry, including early works like *Double Persephone* (1961), *The Circle Game* (1964), *Expeditions* (1965), *Speeches for Doctor Frankenstein* (1966), and *The Animals in That Country* (1968); and later works like *Interlunar* (1984), *Morning in the Burned House* (1995), *Eating Fire: Selected Poems 1965–1995* (1998), and *The Door* (2007). Atwood's first novel, *The Edible Woman* (1969), is at once frightening and comic. Eight more novels followed — *Surfacing* (1972), *Lady Oracle* (1976), *Life Before Man* (1979), *Bodily Harm* (1981), *The Handmaid's Tale* (1985), *Cat's Eye* (1988), *The Robber Bride* (1993), and *Alias Grace* (1996) — many of them winning awards and recognition, including being named finalists for the Booker Prize, before *The Blind Assassin* (2000) won the Booker Prize. Recent novels include *The Year of the Flood* (2009), *MaddAddam* (2013), *Scribbler Moon* (2014), *The Heart Goes Last* (2015), and *Hag-Seed* (2016). With her wry, satirical, and mischievous sense of humor, Atwood has the ability to show the connection between everyday middle-class life and the richly imaginative experiences of myth and legend. "It Is Dangerous to Read Newspapers" considers the role average citizens may play during wartime.

While I was building neat
castles in the sandbox,
the hasty pits were
filling with bulldozed corpses

and as I walked to the school
washed and combed, my feet
stepping on the cracks in the cement
detonated red bombs.

Now I am grownup
and literate, and I sit in my chair
as quietly as a fuse

and the jungles are flaming, the underbrush is charged with soldiers,
the names on the difficult
maps go up in smoke.

I am the cause, I am a stockpile of chemical
toys, my body
is a deadly gadget,
I reach out in love, my hands are guns,
my good intentions are completely lethal.

Even my
passive eyes transmute
everything I look at to the pocked
black and white of a war photo,
how
can I stop myself
It is dangerous to read newspapers.

Each time I hit a key
on my electric typewriter,
speaking of peaceful trees

another village explodes.

[1968]

EXPLORING THE TEXT

1. The first stanza juxtaposes playing in a sandbox with bulldozed corpses filling a pit. Why do you think Margaret Atwood chose such a jarring set of images to open the poem? What tone does it establish?
2. The speaker often describes herself performing innocent actions that have an unintended, disastrous impact. Find at least two instances and explain how they reveal the speaker's perspective on war.
3. Why is it dangerous for the speaker to read newspapers? What sort of "danger" does it pose for the speaker? Are there multiple dangers? Is the speaker being ironic in any way? Explain.
4. The third stanza begins, "Now I am grownup / and literate" (ll. 9–10). Why do you think it might be important that the speaker point out her literacy? What might this imply about the relationship between foreign wars and the home front?
5. Why do you think the speaker separates the last line of the poem from the previous stanza, even though grammatically it belongs to the same sentence? What contrast does the separation emphasize?

The Terrorist, He Watches

WISŁAWA SZYMBORSKA

Translated by Robert A. Maguire and Magnus Jan Krynski

Wisława Szymborska [vis-*lah*-vah sim-*bawrs*-kah] (1923–2012) was born in western Poland and lived there all her life. After studying literature and sociology at Jagiellonian University in Krakow, she began to make her way as a poet. She published her first poem, "I Am Looking for a World," in 1945, and her first book, *Dlatego Zygemy* (*That's What We Live For*), in 1952. Although she had published eighteen volumes of poetry, which had been translated into more than a dozen languages, she was not well known in the English-speaking world until she was awarded the Nobel Prize for Literature in 1996. In her acceptance speech, Szymborska said, "Inspiration is not the exclusive privilege of poets or artists generally. There is, has been, and will always be a certain group of people whom inspiration visits. It's made up of all those who've consciously chosen their calling and do their job with love and imagination. It may include doctors, teachers, gardeners — and I could list a hundred more professions." Two characteristics of her work — close observation and understatement — are evident in the poem included here.

The bomb will go off in the bar at one twenty p.m.
Now it's only one sixteen p.m.
Some will still have time to get in,
Some to get out.

The terrorist has already crossed to the other
side of the street.
The distance protects him from any danger,
and what a sight for sore eyes:

A woman in a yellow jacket, she goes in.
A man in dark glasses, he comes out.
Guys in jeans, they are talking.
One seventeen and four seconds.
That shorter guy's really got it made, and gets on
a scooter,
and that taller one, he goes in.

One seventeen and forty seconds.
That girl there, she's got a green ribbon in her hair.
Too bad that bus just cut her off.

One eighteen p.m.
The girl's not there any more.
Was she dumb enough to go in, or wasn't she?
That we'll see when they carry them out.

One nineteen p.m.
No one seems to be going in.
Instead a fat baldy's coming out.
Like he's looking for something in his pockets
 and
at one nineteen and fifty seconds
he goes back for those lousy gloves of his.

It's one twenty p.m.
The time, how it drags.
Should be any moment now.
Not yet.
Yes, this is it.
The bomb, it goes off.

[1981]

EXPLORING THE TEXT

1. What is unusual about the way the poem reveals the central event? What words would you use to describe the presentation? How does the poem create tension and suspense?
2. What transition does line 7, "and what a sight for sore eyes," signal? Is it meant to introduce the descriptions of the people coming and going? How are the people described?
3. How does the countdown embedded in the poem both structure it and contribute to the development of its themes?
4. How would you describe the tone of the poem? What effect does the tone have on your response to the poem?
5. What is the impact of Wisława Szymborska's choosing to provide us with no information about the terrorist — not the time period, location, nature of the conflict, or motivation?

The War Works Hard

DUNYA MIKHAIL

Dunya Mikhail (b. 1965) is an Iraqi American poet. She was born in Baghdad, and graduated with a BA from the University of Baghdad before working as an editor, a journalist, and a translator for the *Baghdad Observer*. In 1996, under threat by the government of Saddam Hussein, Mikhail fled to Jordan and then to the United States. She later became a U.S. citizen and earned an MA in Near Eastern studies from Wayne State University. Her first book, *The War Works Hard* (2005), won the PEN Translation Fund award, was shortlisted for the Griffin Prize, and was named one of the best books of 2005 by the New York Public Library. Her second book, *Diary of a Wave Outside the Sea* (2009), which blends poetry and autobiography, won the Arab American Book Award. She is the author of two other books, *The Iraqi Nights* (2014) and *The Theory of Absence* (2014). Mikhail currently teaches at Oakland University in Michigan.

How magnificent the war is!
How eager
and efficient!
Early in the morning,
it wakes up the sirens
and dispatches ambulances
to various places,
swings corpses through the air,

rolls stretchers to the wounded,
summons rain
from the eyes of mothers,
digs into the earth
dislodging many things
from under the ruins . . .
Some are lifeless and glistening,
others are pale and still throbbing . . .
It produces the most questions
in the minds of children,
entertains the gods
by shooting fireworks and missiles
into the sky,
sows mines in the fields
and reaps punctures and blisters,
urges families to emigrate,
stands beside the clergymen
as they curse the devil
(poor devil, he remains
with one hand in the searing fire) . . .
The war continues working, day and night.
It inspires tyrants
to deliver long speeches,
awards medals to generals
and themes to poets.
It contributes to the industry
of artificial limbs,
provides food for flies,
adds pages to the history books,
achieves equality
between killer and killed,
teaches lovers to write letters,
accustoms young women to waiting,
fills the newspapers
with articles and pictures,
builds new houses
for the orphans,
invigorates the coffin makers,
gives grave diggers
a pat on the back
and paints a smile on the leader's face.
The war works with unparalleled diligence!
Yet no one gives it
a word of praise.

[2005]

EXPLORING THE TEXT

1. Note the title, "The War Works Hard." Find three other places in the poem where the speaker personifies war. How might treating war as a person change how readers see war?
2. The poem opens, "How magnificent the war is!" What tone is set by opening the poem with an exclamation? Do you think the speaker really believes war is magnificent? Explain.
3. In line 22, the speaker says that war "sows mines in the fields" as if mines are seeds that will one day be grown and harvested. Why might the speaker have chosen to use "sows" instead of something more militaristic?
4. The speaker says that war "summons rain / from the eyes of mothers" (ll. 10–11). Find at least two more images where the speaker shows something negative (tears) in a positive light (rain). How do such juxtapositions contribute to the tone of the poem?
5. Morbid humor abounds in this poem, as the speaker pokes fun at death instead of taking it seriously. For example, in line 36, she praises war because it "provides food for flies." What other examples of morbid humor can you find in the poem? What does this sarcasm reveal about the true devastation of war? What makes irony and sarcasm effective devices in this poem?

Sadiq

BRIAN TURNER

Born in 1967 in California, Brian Turner earned an MFA in poetry at the University of Oregon before enlisting in the army at the age of twenty-nine. During the seven years he spent as a soldier, he was deployed to Bosnia and Herzegovina, and served as an army infantry team leader in Iraq. His work has been published in various journals as well as in *Voices in Wartime: The Anthology* — published in 2005 in conjunction with the feature-length documentary film of the same name. His first collection of poems, *Here, Bullet* (2005), won the Beatrice Hawley Award and was a *New York Times* Editors' Choice selection. In 2007, Turner received a National Endowment for the Arts Literature Fellowship in poetry. His second collection, *Phantom Noise* (2010), was shortlisted for the T. S. Eliot Prize. Turner has also published a memoir, *My Life as a Foreign Country* (2014). He is currently the director of the low-residency MFA program at Sierra Nevada College at Lake Tahoe. "Sadiq," the title of the poem included here, is Arabic for "friend."

> *It is a condition of wisdom in the archer to*
> *be patient because when the arrow leaves the*
> *bow, it returns no more.*
>
> — SA'DI

It should make you shake and sweat,
nightmare you, strand you in a desert
of irrevocable desolation, the consequences
seared into the vein, no matter what adrenaline
feeds the muscle its courage, no matter
what god shines down on you, no matter
what crackling pain and anger
you carry in your fists, my friend,
it should break your heart to kill.

[2005]

EXPLORING THE TEXT

1. How do you interpret the epigraph from Sa'di, a revered thirteenth-century Persian poet? How does this epigraph inform your understanding of Brian Turner's poem?
2. In line 8, the speaker directly addresses "my friend." What is the speaker's attitude toward the "friend"? How does Turner's use of the word compare to Wilfred Owen's direct address to "My friend" in "Dulce et Decorum Est" (p. 1213)?
3. How does the poem reveal the speaker's attitude toward his war experience?
4. In *Regarding the Pain of Others*, Susan Sontag says of war, "We do not and cannot imagine what it was like, how dreadful or terrifying it was, how normal it becomes." How might "Sadiq" be regarded as a response to Sontag's statement?

Split

CATHY LINH CHE

Cathy Linh Che is a Vietnamese American poet from Los Angeles and Long Beach, California. She earned a BA from Reed College and an MFA from New York University. Her writing has earned numerous awards, including fellowships from Poets & Writers and the Fine Arts Work Center at Provincetown. Che's first book of poems, *Split* (2014), won the Kundiman Poetry Prize, the Norma Farber First Book Award, and the Best Poetry Book Award from the Association of Asian American Studies. She is a co-editor of *Paperbag*, an online journal that features work of recognized and new artists. In "Split," Che meditates on ideas of family, womanhood, and identity in wartime.

I see my mother, at thirteen,
in a village so small
it's never given a name.

Monsoon season drying up—
steam lifting in full-bodied waves.
She chops bắp chuối[1] for the hogs.

Her hair dips to the small of her back
as if smeared in black
and polished to a shine.

She wears a deep side-part
that splits her hair
into two uneven planes.

They come to watch her:
Americans, Marines, just boys,
eighteen or nineteen.

With scissor-fingers,
they snip the air,
point at their helmets
and then at her hair.
All they want is a small lock—
something for a bit of good luck.

Days later, my mother
is sent to the city
for safekeeping.

She will return home once,
only to be given away
to my father.

In the pictures,
the cake is sweet
and round.

My mother's hair
which spans the length
of her áo dài[2]

is long, washed, and uncut.

[2014]

[1] Vietnamese for "banana." —EDS.

[2] A traditional Vietnamese dress. —EDS.

EXPLORING THE TEXT

1. How is it that the speaker of the poem "sees" her mother at thirteen? Which parts of the poem reveal what she sees literally and which reveal her imaginative reflections? Explain.
2. Why would the speaker's mother be "sent to the city / for safekeeping" (ll. 23–24)? How does this knowledge affect the speaker of the poem?
3. Identify places where the speaker describes her mother's hair. Why do you think the speaker fixates on it? What does it represent for the speaker, and what does it represent for the other people she describes in the poem? Why is it significant that her mother's hair "is long, washed, and uncut" in the final line?

4. Carefully consider other imagery that the poem presents: for instance, the weather, the soldiers, and the cake. How do these images contribute to the meaning of the poem?
5. Except for the last line, the entire poem is broken into neat, three-line stanzas. How does the regularity and precision of this form reflect the mother's careful attention to her hair? What effect does this adherence to form create?
6. To what does the "Split" in the title refer? Does it have both literal and metaphorical reference points? Explain.

Twelve-Hour Shifts

JILL McDONOUGH

Jill McDonough (b. 1972) is an American poet who grew up in North Carolina and earned degrees from Stanford University and Boston University. McDonough has taught incarcerated college students through Boston University's Prison Education Program for thirteen years, and she also directs the MFA Program at the University of Massachusetts-Boston. She is the author of two poetry collections, *Habeas Corpus* (2008) and *Where You Live* (2012). Her numerous awards include fellowships from the National Endowment for the Arts, the Fine Arts Work Center in Provincetown, Stanford University's Stegner program, and the Library of Congress. In "Twelve-Hour Shifts," McDonough uses the consciously repetitive villanelle form to comment on the practice of drone warfare.

A drone pilot works a twelve-hour shift, then goes home
to real life. Showers, eats supper, plays video games.
Twelve hours later he comes back, high-fives, takes over the drone

from other pilots, who watch *Homeland*, do dishes, hope they don't
dream in all screens, bad kills, all slo-mo freeze-frame.
A drone pilot works a twelve-hour shift, then goes home.

A small room, a pilot's chair, the mic and headphones
crowd his mind, take him somewhere else. Another day
another dollar: hover and shift, twelve hours over strangers' homes.

Stop by the store, its Muzak, pick up the Cheerios,
get to the gym if you're lucky. Get back to your babies, play
Barbies, play blocks. Twelve hours later, come back. Take over the drone.

Smell of burned coffee in the lounge, the shifting kill zone.
Last-minute *abort mission*, and the major who forgets your name.
A drone pilot works a twelve-hour shift, then goes home.

It's done in our names, but we don't have to know. Our own
lives, shifts, hours, bounced off screens all day.
A drone pilot works a twelve-hour shift, then goes home;
fresh from twelve hours off, another comes in, takes over our drone.

[2015]

EXPLORING THE TEXT

1. Why does the speaker use the familiar phrase "Another day/another dollar" (ll. 8–9) when describing a drone pilot's working life?
2. Despite war being the theme of the poem, the speaker repeatedly weaves in commonplace, domestic references, such as "Muzak." What others can you identify? How do these references reveal the speaker's perspective on the drone warfare in which the soldiers are engaged?
3. The first stanza ends as another soldier "takes over the drone" (l. 3), but the last line of the poem ends when another soldier "takes over our drone" (l. 19). Who is represented by the "our" in the last line? What does this shift suggest about who the speaker views as responsible for war in general?
4. In line 13, the speaker juxtaposes the "smell of burned coffee in the lounge" with "the shifting kill zone" — that is, where drones execute the pilots' orders. What is the speaker's purpose in juxtaposing the image of an everyday annoyance with a violent military term?
5. Why do you think the speaker goes into such detail about the soldier's daily lives, but never describes the effect that drone strikes have on their targets?
6. How would you characterize the tone of the poem? Consider such stylistic elements as imagery, anaphora, and rhyme in your response.

Welcome Home, Troops!

AMIT MAJMUDAR

Amit Majmudar (b. 1979) is an American novelist, poet, and doctor who grew up in Cleveland, Ohio. He earned a BS at the University of Akron and an MD at Northeast Ohio Medical University, and he currently lives in Columbus, Ohio, where he is a diagnostic nuclear radiologist. Majmudar is the author of the poetry collections *0°, 0°* (2009), which was a finalist for a Poetry Society of America's Norma Faber First Book Award; *Heaven and Earth* (2011), which won the Donald Justice Poetry Prize; and *Dothead* (2016). Majmudar has also published two novels: *Partitions* (2011) and *The Abundance* (2013). Majmudar's work has been featured in *The Best of the Best American Poetry* (2012), and he has contributed essays to the *New York Times* and the *New York Review of Books*. He was named poet laureate of Ohio in 2015. His poetry often employs traditional forms to explore themes of identity, history, and mortality. "Welcome Home, Troops!" follows the story of a wounded veteran returning from battle.

Observe the Argive,[1]
redivivus[2]
with his Bethesda[3]
Special prosthetic
elbows, his Versed-[4]
reversed remember-
remember, looking
alive in olive —
the aftershave
civilian, the crew-cut
oorah[5]. His stop-
loss[6] odyssey
went Kabul[7], morphine,
Ramstein[8], Stateside,
and back — round-robin
desert wrestling,
tag out, tag in.
Now, retrofitted,
the soon-to-be
robohobo[9]
thumps down the Jetway,
a glint in his eye,
springs in his step,
no place like home.

[2016]

[1] Of or related to Argos, a Greek city. — EDS.

[2] Latin for "reborn." — EDS.

[3] A layered reference to: 1) Bethesda Softworks; a popular video game publisher; 2) the Pool of Bethesda, located in the Muslim Quarter of Jerusalem and rumored to have healing abilities; and 3) Bethesda, Maryland, where the Walter Reed National Military Medical Center is located. — EDS.

[4] A sedative given to patients prior to surgery. — EDS.

[5] A Marine battle cry meaning "charge." — EDS.

[6] A policy dictating the forced extension of a soldier's term of service. — EDS.

[7] The capital of Afghanistan. — EDS.

[8] A United States Air Force base located in Germany. — EDS.

[9] Slang for a homeless person with one or more artificial body parts. — EDS.

EXPLORING THE TEXT

1. Based on the elliptical references the speaker makes to the soldier's backstory, what hardships, physical transformations, and travels has the soldier endured?
2. How do the very short lines and bouncy, sing-song rhythm of the poem evoke the soldier's current physical and emotional state?
3. How do the speaker's archaic references — such as "Argive" (l. 1) and "redivivus" (l. 2) — help set the tone of the poem? What do they suggest about the soldier's experience?
4. In the penultimate line of the poem, the soldier has "springs in his step." What might this pun suggest about the speaker's perspective on the situation? Is the speaker sincerely celebrating the arrival of a soldier? Is there a tone of sarcasm in the speaker's voice? Explain.
5. How do you respond to the title, "Welcome Home, Troops!" — even before reading the poem? In what context is this phrase usually used? After reading the poem, what new meaning does "home" in the title, and in the last line — "no place like home" — take on?
6. How would you describe the speaker's overall attitude toward the soldier for whom "home" is war itself? Does the speaker seem to pity the soldier, look up to the soldier, or something in between? How does the speaker's description of the soldier reveal how the speaker feels about the war in general?

Safe House

SOLMAZ SHARIF

Solmaz Sharif is a poet who was born in Istanbul to Iranian parents. The former managing director of the Asian American Writers' Workshop, she holds degrees from the University of California, Berkeley, and New York University and is the author of a book of poetry, *Look* (2016). Her writing has earned numerous awards and prizes, including the "Discovery"/*Boston Review* Poetry Prize, a scholarship from the Bread Loaf Writers' Conference and a fellowship from the Fine Arts Work Center in Provincetown, a National Endowment for the Arts fellowship, and a Stegner Fellowship at Stanford University, where she is currently a Jones Lecturer. "Safe House" highlights the strain that a security-obsessed state puts on families of individuals who fall under government suspicion.

SANCTUARY where we don't have to

SANITIZE hands or words or knives, don't have to use a

SCALE each morning, worried we take up too much space. I

SCAN my memory of baba talking on

SCREEN answering a question *(how are you?)* I would ask and ask from behind the camera, his face changing with each repetition as he tried to watch the football game. He doesn't know this is the beginning of my

SCRIBING life: repetition and change. A human face at the seaport and a home growing smaller. Let's

SEARCH my father's profile: moustache black and holding back a

SECRET he still hasn't told me,

SECTION of the couch that's fallen a bit from his repeated weight,

SECTOR of the government designed to keep him from flying. He kept our house

SECURE except from the little bugs that come with dried herbs from Iran. He gives

SECURITY officers a reason to get off their chairs. My father is not afraid of

SEDITION. He can

SEIZE a wild pigeon off a Santa Monica street or watch

SEIZURES unfold in his sister's bedroom — the FBI storming through. He said *use wood sticks to hold up your protest signs then use them in*

SELF-DEFENSE *when the horses come,* his eyes

SENSITIVE when he passes advice to me, like I'm his

SEQUEL, like we're all a

SERIAL caught on Iranian satellite TV. When you tell someone off, he calls it

SERVICING. When I stand on his feet, I call it

SHADOWING. He naps in the afternoon and wakes with
SHEETLINES on his face, his hair upright, the sound of
SHELLS (SPECIFY) — the sound of mussel shells on the lip of the Bosphorus[1] crunching beneath his feet. He's given me
SHELTER and
SHIELDING, shown it's better to travel away from the
SHOAL. *Let them follow you* he says from somewhere in Los Angeles waiting for me. If he feels a
SHORT FALL he doesn't tell me about it.

[2016]

[1] A waterway located in northwestern Turkey. — EDS.

EXPLORING THE TEXT

1. A safe house usually refers to an isolated hideout used by someone in danger, but it could also be used to hold someone captive. Is the speaker in danger? Use evidence from the text of the poem to support your answer.
2. Each line begins with a word in all caps that starts with the letter *S*. What connotations do the first words of each line share? What tone is established by these sorts of words?
3. Note each time the speaker's father offers advice. What values is the father trying to instill in the speaker?
4. What two similes appear in lines 21–23? What do these similes suggest about the speaker's cultural background or interest?
5. Many of the lines end mid-sentence, only to resume jarringly on the next line. For example: "... don't have to use a / SCALE each morning, worried we take up too much space. I / SCAN my memory of baba talking — him on / SCREEN ..." (ll. 2–5). Find two more places in the poem where this pattern of enjambment occurs. What tone does this jerking rhythm create? How might the enjambment evoke the speaker's experience of life in the safe house?
6. In the notes at the end of her book *LOOK*, in which this poem appears, Solmaz Sharif explains that

   > [t]erms appearing in small caps are taken from the United States Department of Defense's Dictionary of Military and Associated Terms as amended through October 17, 2007. As a supplement to standard English dictionaries (e.g., Merriam-Webster), this military dictionary is updated regularly, often monthly, with unclassified terms being added and subtracted as needed. Need is determined by a combination of factors, including military usage, presence of the term in standard English, etc. For example, the term "drone" appeared in the 2007 version, but no longer appears in the 2015 version. It is likely "drone" was removed from the dictionary since ... the military definition is no longer a supplement to the English language, but the English language itself. Given the impossibility of keeping up with changes in the dictionary, I have used the October 17, 2007 edition throughout. This edition has over 5,900 terms, only a fraction of which appear in these poems.

   Looking back at the capitalized words in the poem, which strike you as having stronger non-military connotations? To what extent do you believe Sharif militarizes ordinary language in "SAFE HOUSE," and to what effect?

PAIRED POEMS

To Lucasta, Going to the Wars

RICHARD LOVELACE

Richard Lovelace (1617–1657) was an English poet who fought on the side of King Charles I (his supporters became known as "Cavaliers") during the English Civil War (1642–1651). Lovelace attended school in London as a child and went on to study at Oxford, where he started writing. Lovelace's first work was an unpublished drama, *The Scholars*, which was performed at Oxford and later in London. As a partisan in the Civil War, Lovelace was influenced heavily by his military experiences and political maneuvering. In perhaps what is his most famous poem, "To Lucasta, Going to the Wars," Lovelace conjures a romantic image of military adventurism.

Tell me not, Sweet, I am unkind,
  That from the nunnery
Of thy chaste breast and quiet mind
  To war and arms I fly.

True, a new mistress now I chase,
  The first foe in the field;
And with a stronger faith embrace
  A sword, a horse, a shield.

Yet this inconstancy is such
  As thou too shalt adore;
I could not love thee, Dear, so much,
  Loved I not Honor more.

[1649]

EXPLORING THE TEXT

1. What comparison is the speaker making when he calls "the first foe in the field" his "new mistress" (l. 5–6)? Why might the speaker make such a comparison?
2. How do the parenthetical terms of affection "(Sweet)" (l. 1) and "(Dear)" (l. 11) work to begin and end the poem on a similar note? What purpose does it serve to create such an effect?
3. The speaker appeals to honor throughout the poem. Where does he refer to Lucasta's honor? Where does he refer to his own honor? Why do you think the concept of honor features so prominently?
4. Why does the speaker use romantic language to describe departing for war? How might these comparisons soften the blow of his departure?
5. What is the tone of the poem? Consider the effects of the formal rhyme scheme and the romantic idealization in your answer.

To Lucasta on Going to the War—for the Fourth Time

ROBERT GRAVES

Robert Graves (1895–1985) was an English poet, novelist, critic, and classicist. Graves was born to a middle-class family in Wimbledon, and at the outbreak of World War I he enlisted immediately. After almost being killed at the Battle of the Somme, Graves returned to England and studied English at Oxford. Thereafter, he lived around the world and was able to earn a living from his writing, mostly because of the popular success of historical novels such as *I, Claudius* (1934), *Count Belisarius* (1938), and *King Jesus* (1946). Graves also translated popular versions of classical Latin and ancient Greek texts, including *The Twelve Caesars* (1965) and *The Golden Ass* (1950). In addition to his translations and innovative fictional interpretations of history, Graves also wrote a popular memoir about World War I, *Good-Bye to All That* (1929). In "To Lucasta on Going to the War – for the Fourth Time," Graves revisits Lovelace's original poem. Using his trademark wit and formal rigor, Graves critiques the self-sustaining cycle of war and the rationalizing mind-set of those who become overcommitted to military ventures.

It doesn't matter what's the cause,
  What wrong they say we're righting,
A curse for treaties, bonds, and laws,
  When we're to do the fighting!
And since we lads are proud and true,
  What else remains to do?
Lucasta, when to France your man
  Returns his fourth time, hating war,
Yet laughs as calmly as he can
  And flings an oath, but says no more.
That is not courage, that's not fear—
Lucasta, he's a Fusilier,[1]
  And his pride sends him here.

* * *

Let statesmen bluster, bark, and bray,
  And so decide who started
This bloody war, and who's to pay,
  But he must be stout-hearted,
Make sit and stake with quiet breath,
  Playing at cards with Death.
Don't plume yourself he fights for you;
  It is no courage, love, nor hate,
But let us do the things we do;
  It's pride that makes the heart be great;
It is not anger, no, nor fear—
Lucasta, he's a Fusilier,
  And his pride keeps him here.

[1918]

[1] A member of an elite branch in the British Army, the Royal Fusiliers, originally founded in 1685.—EDS.

EXPLORING THE TEXT

1. What is implied when the soldier "laughs as calmly as he can" (l. 9)? Where else in the poem does the speaker imply that all is not right with the veteran soldier returning to war?
2. Why does the speaker compare battle to "Playing at cards with Death" (l. 19)? What does this comparison suggest about the nature and purpose of warfare?
3. The first stanza ends, "And his pride sends him here" (l. 13), and the last stanza ends, "And his pride keeps him here" (l. 26). How does the shift from "sends" to "keeps" reveal the speaker's critique of war?
4. How does the rhyming form of the poem contrast ironically with its message?

FOCUS ON COMPARISON AND CONTRAST

1. Identify two places in each poem where armed conflict is represented. Then compare and contrast how each speaker treats war itself differently.
2. How could the opening of Graves's poem — "It doesn't matter what's the cause" (l. 1) — be seen as a satiric response to that of Lovelace?
3. How might addressing each poem to Lucasta, presumably by the same speaker, heighten the difference in perspective between the poems? What has changed in the warrior's perspective in Graves's poem, when the speaker is on his fourth tour of duty?
4. In "To Lucasta, Going to the Wars," Richard Lovelace's speaker justifies his departure for war with an appeal to honor. In "To Lucasta on Going to the War — for the Fourth Time," Robert Graves's speaker justifies his continued commitment to war with an appeal to pride. Compare and contrast the connotations of both honor and pride. How might the pride in Graves's poem satirize the concept of honor in Lovelace's poem?

WRITING ASSIGNMENT

"To Lucasta, Going to the Wars" and "To Lucasta on Going to the War — for the Fourth Time" offer the same character, Lucasta, very different justifications for going to or returning to war. Read the poems carefully. Then write an essay in which you compare and contrast the soldier-lover relationship in each poem, analyzing how Lovelace and Graves offer different perspectives on the purpose and nature of war.

A Wife in London (December, 1899)

THOMAS HARDY

Among the greatest nineteenth-century British novelists, Thomas Hardy (1840–1928) was born in Dorset, England. Among his most famous works are *Far from the Madding Crowd* (1874) — whose title comes from Thomas Gray's "Elegy Written in a Country Churchyard"; *The Return of the Native* (1878); *Tess of the d'Urbervilles* (1891); and *Jude the Obscure* (1895). After the less than appreciative reaction that *Jude the Obscure* received — many people found it too shocking and pessimistic — Hardy wrote only poetry. In "A Wife in London," he writes about the aftermath of the Boer War, which was waged from 1899 to 1902 in South Africa.

I — The Tragedy

She sits in the tawny vapour
    That the Thames-side lanes have uprolled,
    Behind whose webby fold on fold
Like a waning taper
    The street-lamp glimmers cold.

A messenger's knock cracks smartly,
    Flashed news is in her hand
    Of meaning it dazes to understand
Though shaped so shortly:
    He — has fallen — in the far South Land. . . .

II — The Irony

'Tis the morrow; the fog hangs thicker,
    The postman nears and goes:
    A letter is brought whose lines disclose
By the firelight flicker
    His hand, whom the worm now knows:

Fresh — firm — penned in highest feather —
    Page-full of his hoped return,
    And of home-planned jaunts by brake
        and burn
In the summer weather,
    And of new love that they would learn.

[1901]

EXPLORING THE TEXT

1. Trace the imagery of this poem as it is introduced in the first part and then picked up again in the second part. What role does the imagery play in establishing mood and conveying theme?
2. Why does Thomas Hardy call the two parts of the poem "The Tragedy" and "The Irony"? Explain using evidence from the text.
3. Imagine that the wife lives not in London but in your hometown. In a contemporary poem about her as a widow of the war in Iraq or Afghanistan, what would be different in the poem? What would be similar? How universal is the poem's message? Explain.
4. Identify the internal rhyme and alliteration in the final line of the poem. What tone is set by this lyricism? How does that tone accentuate the loss experienced by the soldier's widow?

Between Days

YUSEF KOMUNYAKAA

Yusef Komunyakaa was born James Willie Brown Jr. in 1947 and raised in Bogalusa, Louisiana. He earned an MA from Colorado State University and an MFA from the University of California, Irvine. He taught in New Orleans public schools, at Indiana University, at Princeton University, and he currently teaches at New York University. Fresh out of high school, Komunyakaa enlisted in the army and served in Vietnam, an experience that permeates his poetry. He published his first book of poems, *Dedications and other darkhorses*, in 1977, and has since gone on to publish fifteen other books, including *Neon Vernacular: New and Selected Poems* (1993), for which he won the 1994 Pulitzer Prize in poetry. In "Between Days," Komunyakaa blends realistic and resonant imagery with his characteristically conversational style to portray the bewilderment of a mother whose son was lost at war.

Expecting to see him anytime
coming up the walkway
through blueweed[1] & bloodwort,[2]
she says, "That closed casket
was weighed down with stones."
The room is as he left it
fourteen years ago, everything
freshly dusted & polished
with lemon oil. The uncashed
death check from Uncle Sam
marks a passage in the Bible
on the dresser, next to the photo
staring out through the window.
"Mistakes. Mistakes. Now,
he's gonna have to give them this
money back when he gets home.
But I wouldn't. I would
let them pay for their mistakes.
They killed his daddy, & Janet,
she & her three children
by three different men, I hope
he's strong enough to tell her
to get lost. Lord, mistakes."
His row of tin soldiers
lines the window sill. The sunset
flashes across them like a blast.
She's buried the Silver Star[3]

[1] A blue flowering plant, also known as viper's bugloss, that often grows in fairly barren places, such as roadsides, cliffs, and sand dunes. In some areas of the United States, it is considered an invasive species of plant. — EDS.

[2] A flowering plant with red roots; its juice is red and poisonous, but it has also been used in Native American traditional medicine to induce vomiting and treat respiratory ailments, among other things. — EDS.

[3] A United States military medal awarded for bravery in action against an enemy of the country. — EDS.

& the flag under his winter clothes.
The evening's first fireflies
dance in the air like distant tracers.
Her chair faces the walkway
where she sits before the TV
asleep, as the screen dissolves
into days between snow.[4]

[1988]

4 A reference to the static that would fill the television screen once programming ended for the day, before the advent of the 24-hour news channel in 1980. — EDS.

EXPLORING THE TEXT

1. What conclusions might you draw about the soldier's character solely from the objects in his room?
2. Why does the soldier's mother say, "That closed casket / was weighed down with stones" (ll. 4–5)? Of what is she trying to convince herself?
3. What language does the poet use to describe the soldier's room near the end of the poem? What theme or themes does such figurative language reveal?
4. In what way does the end of the poem mirror the beginning? How does this structure reflect the mother's experience of her dead son?

FOCUS ON COMPARISON AND CONTRAST

1. What do the widow in Thomas Hardy's poem and the mother in Yusef Komunyakaa's poem have in common? How are they different?
2. In these two poems, Hardy and Komunyakaa dramatize two women's perspectives on the loss of a beloved soldier in a foreign war. Compare and contrast the use of descriptive imagery in each poem. How does the imagery accentuate the specific emotional suffering of each woman?
3. Imagine a meeting between the two women dramatized in the poems. What would they say to each other? Create a dialogue between the two that reveals your understanding of the poems and your sympathy for the women.

WRITING ASSIGNMENT

Write an essay in which you explain how each poem treats the notion of "closure" for those who remain at home after the loss of a loved one at war.

The Parable of the Old Man and the Young and Arms and the Boy

WILFRED OWEN

Born in Shropshire, England, in 1893, Wilfred Owen is the most well known and most highly regarded of the World War I poets. He enlisted in the army in 1915 and fought in France. In May 1917, he was evacuated from the front and hospitalized with shell shock (a condition now referred to as post-traumatic stress disorder). He returned to the battlefield and won the Military Cross in October 1918. Five of his poems were published that year — the only five he lived to see in print. His work exposes the horrors of the war firsthand. He was killed in battle one week before the armistice (November 11, 1918). Owen's work remained virtually unknown until 1920, when his friend, Siegfried Sassoon, collected his work and published it as *Poems*. Although Owen's life was short, and his career as a writer even shorter, his influence on the next generation of British writers was profound. The selections here were printed back-to-back in *Poems*.

The Parable of the Old Man and the Young

So Abram rose, and clave the wood, and went,
And took the fire with him, and a knife.
And as they sojourned both of them together,
Isaac the first-born spake and said, My Father,
Behold the preparations, fire and iron,
But where the lamb for this burnt-offering?
Then Abram bound the youth with belts and straps,
And builded parapets and trenches there,
And stretchèd forth the knife to slay his son.
When lo! An angel called him out of heaven,
Saying, Lay not thy hand upon the lad,
Neither do anything to him. Behold,
A ram, caught in a thicket by its horns;
Offer the Ram of Pride instead of him.
But the old man would not so, but slew his son,
And half the seed of Europe, one by one.

[1920]

EXPLORING THE TEXT

1. This poem alludes to Genesis 22:1–19. Look up this passage of the Bible and find out what happens in the original story. Where does this poem begin to deviate from the story in Genesis? What is the significance of these deviations?
2. What does the "Ram of Pride" (l. 14) represent?
3. At line 15, the poem shifts dramatically. How do you interpret the final couplet? What does the speaker mean by "half the seed of Europe" (l. 16)?
4. Owen refers to a parable from the Bible and also calls his poem a parable. How does Owen's poem serve as a parable for his time?

Arms and the Boy

Let the boy try along this bayonet-blade
How cold steel is, and keen with hunger of blood;
Blue with all malice, like a madman's flash;
And thinly drawn with famishing for flesh.

Lend him to stroke these blind, blunt bullet-leads
Which long to nuzzle in the hearts of lads,
Or give him cartridges of fine zinc teeth,
Sharp with the sharpness of grief and death.

For his teeth seem for laughing round an apple.
There lurk no claws behind his fingers supple;
And God will grow no talons at his heels,
Nor antlers through the thickness of his curls.

[1920]

EXPLORING THE TEXT

1. The title of this poem evokes Virgil's *Aeneid*, a late first-century B.C.E. Latin epic poem that tells the story of Aeneas, a Trojan warrior who voyages to Italy and becomes the progenitor of the Romans. The *Aeneid* begins, "I sing of arms and the man." How does Wilfred Owen's use of the allusion contribute to the meaning of his poem?
2. Trace the imagery throughout the poem. What conclusions can you draw from it? Some of the imagery creates dramatic contrasts. Find some examples of this technique, and explain how they contribute to the meaning of the poem.
3. In the first two stanzas, the speaker suggests letting the boy become familiar with weapons. What reason does the speaker give? Do you find the poem's argument convincing? Explain why or why not.
4. What is the tone of the speaker? What is Owen's attitude toward what the speaker says? Toward weapons? Toward war?
5. Owen classified this poem in his draft table of contents under "protest — the unnaturalness of weapons." How does this information influence your understanding of the poem? What is ironic about this classification, given the imagery in this poem?

FOCUS ON COMPARISON AND CONTRAST

1. What do these poems have in common in terms of the way they portray violence? How do they differ?
2. Each of the poems depends on an allusion — one to the Bible, the other to a classical epic poem. Compare the effects of the allusions and their contribution to each poem's tone.
3. Both poems explore the nature of youth confronted with the reality of war. Compare and contrast the two, and evaluate which one is more satisfactory in its delivery of theme.

WRITING ASSIGNMENT

In both "The Parable of the Old Man and the Young" and "Arms and the Boy," young men are confronted with violence. Read the poems carefully. Then write an essay in which you compare and contrast the way Owen uses these confrontations, analyzing their effectiveness in communicating his antiwar message.

IMAGERY

Reflecting on the writer's craft, Joseph Conrad wrote, "My task which I am trying to achieve is, by the power of the written word, to make you hear, to make you feel — it is, above all, to make you see. That — and no more, and it is everything." What Conrad is referring to is called imagery — language that evokes a response in the reader through an appeal to one or more of the senses. Surely you have heard the age-old advice for writers: "Show, don't tell." One way for a writer to show is through imagery. It can make the abstract more concrete and thus help the reader experience the poem or story directly through the senses.

The literal meaning of *image* is "a picture of something." But in literature, imagery can be language that addresses any of the senses. Visual images are most common, but images can be auditory, appealing to our sense of hearing; olfactory, appealing to our sense of smell; gustatory, appealing to our sense of taste; tactile, appealing to our sense of touch; and kinesthetic, appealing to physical sensations such as movement or tension. Essentially, through concrete detail and precise language, imagery mentally reproduces sensations that trigger emotion and memory. You can use these emotions and memories to set a mood, reinforce a theme, or achieve other literary purposes. For instance, in the following passage from "The Management of Grief," Bharati Mukherjee uses imagery to create mood.

> The two rooms are dark and stuffy. The lights are off, and an oil lamp sputters on the coffee table. The bent old lady has let us in, and her husband is wrapping a white turban over his oiled, hip-length hair. She immediately goes to the kitchen, and I hear the most familiar sound of an Indian home, tap water hitting and filling a teapot.

Mukherjee appeals to the visual, tactile, and auditory in the first two sentences describing the look and feel of the room. The next sentence extends the visual image to the couple. The last sentence shifts from a description of unfamiliar sights to a description of a very familiar sound, the "tap water hitting and filling a teapot." This change in imagery (both in quality and in type) shifts the mood, taking us from an uncomfortable situation to a more welcoming one.

It is important to note that while a writer can add emotional power through images and image patterns, not all writers choose this strategy. Jill McDonough, for instance, writes of modern warfare almost entirely without imagery and figurative language. Consider the first stanza of the poem "Twelve-Hour Shifts":

> A drone pilot works a twelve-hour shift, then
> goes home
> to real life. Showers, eats supper, plays video
> games.
> Twelve hours later he comes back, high-fives,
> takes over the drone

Compare that description with this one from Tim O'Brien's "The Things They Carried":

> The first was a Kodachrome snapshot signed "Love," though he knew better. She stood against a brick wall. Her eyes were gray and neutral, her lips slightly open as she stared straight-on at the camera.

McDonough describes action without providing descriptive images to appeal to any of our senses. In fact, she distinguishes between the flatness of what we are seeing and "real life." What do the drone pilots look like? What do they eat for supper? It is precisely this lack of detail — and emotion — that begins to characterize the drone pilots' wartime experiences. O'Brien, on the other hand, gains emotional power by providing details about the kind of photo ("Kodachrome snapshot"), the inscription, the backdrop, the color of the girl's eyes, the set of her mouth, and her stance relative to the camera. This description gives the reader a sense of how emotionally invested Jimmy Cross is in every detail of this photo. And this sets the stage for the poignant collapse of his daydreams in the next sentence: "At night, sometimes, Lieutenant Cross wondered who had taken the picture, because he knew she had boyfriends, because he loved her so much, and because he could see the shadow of the picture taker spreading out against the brick wall."

IMAGERY AND FIGURATIVE LANGUAGE

Imagery and figurative language (metaphor, simile, and so on) are close siblings; both help us visualize and experience literature. For our purposes, we'll make a distinction between the two, acknowledging all the while that they often work together. Imagery is a literal but artful description of how something looks, feels, tastes, smells, and sounds, while figurative language compares two or more things and is not literal. These lines, from Wilfred Owen's "Dulce et Decorum Est," incorporate both literal imagery and figurative language:

> Dim, through the misty panes and thick green light,
> As under a green sea, I saw him drowning.

The imagery in the first line helps us experience what a mustard gas attack would look like through a gas mask. It's "Dim." The panes are "misty" and the light is "thick green" as it filters through the mustard gas and is viewed through the tinted lenses of the World War I gas mask. The second line turns the corner from a literal description of the scene to a figurative depiction: it was like being "under a green sea." In this case, as in many poems, literal imagery and figurative language work together to get the point across.

ANALYZING PATTERNS OF IMAGERY

Analyzing imagery means not only connecting the image to the context and themes of the story or poem, but also paying attention to the other imagery surrounding it. While a single image will often have a multiplicity of meanings and implications, an author will sometimes use a pattern of similar or contrasting images to point us in the right interpretive direction. For example, depending on the context, descriptions of the deep red of wine can suggest passion, blood (and therefore violence), Christian communion, or simply the fellowship of a good meal well enjoyed. And each of these possible meanings brings with it a mood: romantic, foreboding, solemn, satisfied. If the description of the deep red of wine is accompanied by imagery of light streaming through a stained glass window, or a white dove, then we can deduce that the author is appealing to Christian imagery.

The following passage is from "Ten Kliks South," Phil Klay's short story about being a young American artilleryman in Iraq. Notice how the vivid imagery appeals to the senses:

> Voorstadt did a left face and our gun was alive.
>
> The sound of it hit us, vibrating through our bodies, down deep in our chests and in our guts and in the back of our teeth. I could taste the gunpowder in the air. As the guns fired, the barrels shot back like pistons and reseated, the force of each round going off kicking up smoke and dust into the air. When I looked down the line, I couldn't see six guns. I just saw fires through the haze, or not even fires, just flashes of red in the dust and the cordite. And I could feel the roar of each gun, not just ours, as it fired. And I thought, God, this is why I'm glad I'm an artilleryman.

As we read this passage, we both *hear* and *feel* the sound of the artillery in the narrator's guts and teeth, we *taste* the gunpowder in the air, and we *see* the smoke and the enormous barrels moving like pistons. We also see that, after a while, the narrator can *no longer see* his targets through the fire and dust. Klay contrasts the awe-inspiring power of the artillery with the chaotic haze of perception they create. This juxtaposition of power and chaos might lead us to an interpretation of what Klay is saying about war in "Ten Kliks South."

The following exercises will help you become familiar with identifying imagery and determining its effect on the meaning of a work of literature.

EXERCISE 1

Identify the images in each of the following passages and the senses to which they appeal.

1. A dark theater, he remembered, and the movie was *Bonnie and Clyde*, and Martha wore a tweed skirt, and during the final scene, when he touched her knee, she turned and looked at him in a sad, sober way that made him pull his hand back, but he would always remember the feel of the tweed skirt and the knee beneath it and the sound of the gunfire that killed Bonnie and Clyde, how embarrassing it was, how slow and oppressive. ("The Things They Carried," para. 5)
2. Mostly he felt pleased to be alive. He liked the smell of the New Testament under his cheek, the leather and ink and paper and glue, whatever the chemicals were. He liked hearing the sounds of night. Even his fatigue, it felt fine, the stiff muscles and the prickly awareness of his own body, a floating feeling. ("The Things They Carried," para. 60)
3. The sound of it hit us, vibrating through our bodies, down deep in our chests and in our guts and in the back of our teeth. I could taste the gunpowder in the air. As the guns fired, the barrels shot back like pistons and reseated, the force of each round going off kicking up smoke and dust into the air. When I looked down the line, I couldn't see six guns. I just saw fires through the haze, or not even fires, just flashes of red in the dust and the cordite. And I could feel the roar of each gun, not just ours, as it fired. And I thought, God, this is why I'm glad I'm an artilleryman. ("Ten Kliks South," para. 82)
4. The day was not cold, but something in the bare trees caught my attention. I looked up from the gravel, into the branches and the clear blue sky beyond. I thought I heard the rustling of larger forms, and I waited a moment for voices. Nothing. ("The Management of Grief," para. 144)
5. Found you in death so cold dear comrade, found your body son of responding kisses, (never again on earth responding,)
   Bared your face in the starlight, curious the scene, cool blew the moderate night-wind,
   Long there and then in vigil I stood, dimly around me the battle-field spreading,
   Vigil wondrous and vigil sweet there in the fragrant silent night,
   ("Vigil Strange I Kept on the Field One Night," ll. 7–10)
6. Absolute snow lies rumpled on
   What shellbursts scattered and deranged,
   Entangled railings, crevassed lawn.
   ("First Snow in Alsace," ll. 4–6)

EXERCISE 2

Discuss the image patterns in the following excerpts. How do they work together to develop a specific mood or meaning? In cases in which the images are dissimilar, how does the contrast contribute to mood or meaning? Also, consider how, in some cases, figurative language works together with the images.

1. They imagined the muzzle against flesh. They imagined the quick, sweet pain, then the evacuation to Japan, then a hospital with warm beds and cute geisha nurses.

   They dreamed of freedom birds.

   At night, on guard, staring into the dark, they were carried away by jumbo jets. They felt the rush of takeoff. *Gone!* they yelled. And then velocity, wings and engines, a smiling stewardess — but it was more than a plane, it was a real bird, a big sleek silver bird with feathers and talons and high screeching. They were flying. The weights fell off, there was nothing to bear. They laughed and held on tight, feeling the cold slap of wind and altitude, soaring, thinking *It's over, I'm gone!* ("The Things They Carried," paras. 79–81)

2. Then, on the third day of the sixth month into this odyssey, in an abandoned temple in a tiny Himalayan village, as I make my offering of flowers and sweetmeats to the god of a tribe of animists, my husband descends to me. He is squatting next to a scrawny sadhu in moth-eaten robes. Vikram wears the vanilla suit he wore the last time I hugged him. The sadhu tosses petals on a butter-fed flame, reciting Sanskrit mantras, and sweeps his face of flies. My husband takes my hands in his. ("The Management of Grief," para. 89)

3. If you could hear, at every jolt, the blood
   Come gargling from the froth-corrupted lungs,
   Obscene as cancer, bitter as the cud
   Of vile, incurable sores on innocent tongues.
   ("Dulce et Decorum Est," ll. 21–24)

4. Let the boy try along this bayonet-blade
   How cold steel is, and keen with hunger of blood;
   Blue with all malice, like a madman's flash;
   And thinly drawn with famishing for flesh.
   ("Arms and the Boy," ll. 1–4)

5. **OTHELLO** Her father loved me; oft invited me,
   Still question'd me the story of my life
   From year to year — the battles, sieges, fortunes
   That I have passed.
   I ran it through, even from my boyish days
   To th' very moment that he bade me tell it,
   Wherein I spoke of most disastrous chances,
   Of moving accidents by flood and field,
   Of hairbreadth scapes i'th'imminent deadly breach,
   Of being taken by the insolent foe
   And sold to slavery, of my redemption thence,
   And portance in my travels' history,
   Wherein of antres vast and deserts idle,
   Rough quarries, rocks, and hills whose heads touch heaven,
   It was my hint to speak — such was the process —
   And of the Cannibals that each other eat,
   The Anthropophagi, and men whose heads
   Do grow beneath their shoulders. These things to hear

Would Desdemona seriously incline;
But still the house affairs would draw her thence,
Which ever as she could with haste dispatch
She'd come again, and with a greedy ear
Devour up my discourse.
(*Othello*, I.iii.130-52)

EXERCISE 3

Writers will often use imagery to highlight contrasts. For example, throughout "Naming of Parts," Henry Reed juxtaposes elements from the natural world with the parts of a rifle, and in paragraphs 15 and 16 of "The Shawl," Cynthia Ozick juxtaposes images of nature outside the fence with images of the barracks within. Divide your page into two columns. Choose one of these texts, and identify on either side of the page the images that the writer juxtaposes. Then explain how that contrast contributes to the meaning of the work.

EXERCISE 4

Read the following poem by Brian Turner, whose "Sadiq" is included in the chapter. Notice how rich in imagery this poem is, and how some images describe what the speaker sees through the scope and others, what he imagines. Identify the images and the figurative language, and discuss how they work together to achieve the writer's purpose in the poem as a whole.

In the Leupold Scope

With a 40360mm spotting scope
I traverse the Halabjah skyline,
scanning rooftops two thousand meters out
to find a woman in sparkling green, standing
among antennas and satellite dishes,
hanging laundry on an invisible line.

She is dressing the dead, clothing them
as they wait in silence, the pigeons circling
as fumestacks billow a noxious black smoke.
She is welcoming them back to the dry earth,
giving them dresses in tangerine and teal,
woven cotton shirts dyed blue.

She waits for them to lean forward
into the breeze, for the wind's breath
to return the bodies they once had,
women with breasts swollen by milk,
men with shepherd-thin bodies, children
running hard into the horizon's curving lens.

EXERCISE 5

Write a prose description or a poem based on a war photograph from a current newspaper or website. Use imagery or image patterns to add vividness to your description.

WAR AND PEACE

1. On November 11, 1985, Siegfried Sassoon was among sixteen Great War poets commemorated on a slate stone unveiled in Poets' Corner in London's Westminster Abbey. The inscription on the stone was written by friend and fellow poet Wilfred Owen. It reads: "My subject is War, and the pity of War. The Poetry is in the pity." Write an essay that supports Owen's statement about "the pity of war" as expressed in at least three of the texts in this chapter.
2. In the conclusion to her 2002 book *Regarding the Pain of Others*, Susan Sontag — who witnessed firsthand the horrors of war in Sarajevo in 1993–1996 — writes:

   > We don't get it. We truly can't imagine what it was like. We can't imagine how dreadful, how terrifying war is; and how normal it becomes. Can't understand, can't imagine. That's what every soldier, and every journalist and aid worker and independent observer who has put in time under fire, and had the luck to elude the death that struck down others nearby, stubbornly feels. And they are right.

   Write an essay that discusses the extent to which Sontag's statement is true, using at least four of the texts as support. Consider that several of the selections were written by people who personally experienced war (Tim O'Brien, Wilfred Owen, Phil Klay, Yusef Komunyakaa, Brian Turner, Henry Reed, Richard Wilbur, Robert Graves, Siegfried Sassoon, Walt Whitman), whereas others were written by those who created imagined voices of experience based on observation and study (William Shakespeare, Cynthia Ozick, Bharati Mukherjee, Margaret Atwood, Julia Ward Howe, Thomas Hardy, Wisława Szymborska, Yousif al-Sa'igh, Cathy Linh Che, Jill McDonough, Amit Majmudar).
3. The epigraph at the beginning of this chapter is from Tim O'Brien's *If I Die in a Combat Zone, Box Me Up and Ship Me Home*: "Do dreams offer lessons? Do nightmares have themes, do we awaken and analyze them and live our lives and advise others as a result? Can the foot soldier teach anything important about war, merely for having been there? I think not. He can tell war stories." Using at least three of the texts to support your argument, write an essay that discusses the validity of O'Brien's statement.
4. Consider this statement from Chris Hedges, a writer, activist, and journalist with experience as a foreign correspondent in war-torn countries.

   > The enduring attraction to war is this: Even with its destruction and carnage it can give us what we long for in life. It can give us purpose, meaning, a reason for living. Only when we are in the midst of conflict does the shallowness and vapidness of much of our lives become apparent. Trivia dominates our conversations and increasingly our airwaves. And war is an enticing elixir. It gives us resolve, a cause. It allows us to be noble.

   Write an essay that compares and contrasts the views expressed in the literature in this chapter with the view expressed by Hedges in this quotation. Refer to at least three texts for support.
5. Thomas Hardy's poem, "Channel Firing," begins:

   > That night your great guns, unawares
   > Shook all our coffins as we lay,
   > And broke the chancel-window squares,
   > We thought it was the Judgment-day

   Note particularly the word "unawares." What does it suggest about those behind the "great guns"? What similar theme does the poem have with Phil Klay's short story, "Ten Kliks South"? Compare and contrast how both "Channel Firing" and "Ten Kliks South," address that similar theme.
6. Some of the main selections from this chapter — Tim O'Brien's "The Things They Carried," Bharati Mukherjee's "The Management of Grief," Thomas Hardy's "A Wife in London," Yusef Komunyakaa's "Between Days" — present attempts to find peace. Write an essay in which you compare one of these main selections with two or more of the Conversation selections as you discuss the extent to which peace is achieved in postwar experience.

7. In the introductory essay to his book *The Government of the Tongue*, Seamus Heaney discusses reading Wilfred Owen's poetry, particularly "Dulce et Decorum Est," with students. He writes:

> And it seemed to me that "*Dulce et Decorum Est*," a poem which it was easy for them to like, was the poem where I could engage them with the question of over-writing. 'Is Owen overdoing it here?' I would ask. 'Inside of five lines we have "devil's sick of sin," "gargling," froth-corrupted," "bitter as the cud," "vile, incurable sores." Is he not being a bit overinsistent? A bit explicit?' However hangdog I might feel about such intrusions, I also felt that it was right to raise questions. Yet there was obviously an immense disparity between the nit-picking criticism I was conducting on the poem and the heavy price, in terms of emotional and physical suffering, the poet paid in order to bring it into being.

Considering not only the subject matter of the poem but also the experience and intent of the poet, is it right to ask the questions Heaney is asking? Write an essay in response to Heaney, using the text of Owen's poem or others in this chapter for support.

8. In their selections, William Shakespeare, Walt Whitman, Wilfred Owen, Siegfried Sassoon, Henry Reed, Anna Akhmatova, Julia Ward Howe, Thomas Hardy, Richard Lovelace, and Robert Graves speak across the years in the first person. Consider the power of voice in these selections. Write an essay in which you explain which voice speaks most eloquently to our time. Refer specifically to your selected text as you relate it to contemporary events.

9. Each of the following quotations addresses the nature of war and peace. Select one that interests you, and use it to develop a thesis for an essay. Use several selections from the chapter to support your thesis.

   a. "There is nothing easier than lopping off heads and nothing harder than developing ideas."
   — Fyodor Dostoevsky

   b. "People sleep peaceably in their beds at night only because rough men stand ready to do violence on their behalf."
   — George Orwell

   c. "We know how to organize warfare, but do we know how to act when confronted with peace?"
   — Jacques-Yves Cousteau

   d. "Peace is not merely a distant goal that we seek, but a means by which we arrive at that end."
   — Martin Luther King Jr.

   e. "Of course the people don't want war . . . that is understood. But voice or no voice, the people can always be brought to the bidding of the leaders. That is easy. All you have to do is tell them they are being attacked, and denounce the pacifists for lack of patriotism and exposing the country to danger. It works the same in any country."
   — Hermann Goering

   f. "The first casualty when war comes is truth."
   — Senator Hiram Johnson

   g. "The nation that makes a great distinction between its scholars and its warriors will have its thinking done by cowards, and its fighting done by fools."
   — Thucydides

10. In "The Things They Carried," Tim O'Brien devotes much attention to the physical belongings and inventories of each soldier. Examine other stories and poems in this chapter in which weaponry is described — Henry Reed's "Naming of Parts," Phil Klay's "Ten Kliks South," Julia Ward Howe's "Battle Hymn of the Republic," Thomas Hardy's "Channel Firing" — and then write an essay comparing how descriptions of weaponry in each reflect the complex perspectives of each narrator. What does description of weaponry in particular reveal about how we frame or cope with war?

MLA GUIDELINES FOR A LIST OF WORKS CITED

PRINT RESOURCES

1. A Book with One Author

A book with one author serves as a general model for most MLA citations. Include author, title, publisher, and date of publication.

Robinson, Marilynne. *Lila*. Farrar, Straus and Giroux, 2014.

2. A Book with Multiple Authors

King, Stephen, and Peter Straub. *Black House*. Random House, 2001.

3. Two or More Works by the Same Author

Multiple entries should be arranged alphabetically by title. The author's name appears at the beginning of the first entry but is replaced by three hyphens and a period in all subsequent entries.

Ward, Jesmyn. *Salvage the Bones*. Bloomsbury, 2011.

---. *Where the Line Bleeds*. Agate, 2008.

4. Author and Editor Both Named

Vidal, Gore. *The Selected Essays of Gore Vidal*. Edited by Jay Parini, Vintage, 2009.

Alternatively, to cite the editor's contribution, start with the editor's name.

Parini, Jay, editor. *The Selected Essays of Gore Vidal*. By Gore Vidal, Vintage, 2009.

5. Anthology

Oates, Joyce Carol, editor. *Telling Stories: An Anthology for Writers*. W. W. Norton, 1997.

Selection from an anthology:

Washington Irving, "Rip Van Winkle." *Conversations in American Literature: Language, Rhetoric, Culture*. Edited by Robin Aufses et al., Bedford/St. Martin's 2015, pp. 435-48.

6. Translation

Ferrante, Elena. *My Brilliant Friend*. Translated by Ann Goldstein, Europa Editions, 2011.

7. Entry in a Reference Work

Because most reference works are alphabetized, you should omit page numbers.

Lounsberry, Barbara. "Joan Didion." *Encyclopedia of the Essay*. Edited by Tracy Chevalier, Fitzroy, 1997.

For a well-known encyclopedia, use only the edition and year of publication. When an article is not attributed to an author, begin the entry with the article title.

"Gilgamesh." *The Columbia Encyclopedia*. 5th ed., 1993.

8. Sacred Text

Unless a specific published edition is being cited, sacred texts should be omitted from the works cited list.

The New Testament. Translated by Richmond Lattimore, North Point, 1997.

9. Article in a Journal

The title of the journal should be followed by the volume, issue, and year of the journal's publication, as well as the page range.

Marshall, Sarah. "Remote Control: Tonya Harding, Nancy Kerrigan, and the Spectacles of Female Power and Pain." *The Believer*, vol. 12, no. 1, 2014, pp. 3-10.

10. Article in a Magazine

In a weekly:

Heller, Nathan. "The Big Uneasy: What's Roiling the Liberal-Arts Campus?" *The New Yorker*, 30 May 2016, pp. 48-57.

In a monthly:

Shulevitz, Judith. "The Brontës' Secret." *The Atlantic*, June 2016, pp. 38-41.

11. Article in a Newspaper

If you are citing a local paper that does not contain the city name in its title, add the city name in brackets after the title. When citing an article that does not appear on consecutive pages, list the first page followed by a plus sign. The edition only needs to be included if it is listed on the paper's masthead.

Edge, John T. "Fast Food Even Before Fast Food." *The New York Times*, 30 Sept. 2009, late ed., pp. D1+. Print.

12. Review

In a weekly:

Miller, Laura. "Descendants." Review of *Homegoing*, by Yaa Gyasi, *The New Yorker*, 30 May 2016, pp. 75-77.

In a monthly:

Simpson, Mona. "Imperfect Union." Review of *Mrs. Woolf and the Servants*, by Alison Light, *The Atlantic*, Jan.-Feb. 2009, pp. 93-101.

ELECTRONIC RESOURCES

13. Article from a Database Accessed through a Subscription Service

Apply the normal rules for citing a journal article, but follow this with the name of the subscription service in italics and the digital object identifier, if available.

Morano, Michele. "Boy Eats World." *Fourth Genre: Explorations in Nonfiction*, vol. 13, no. 2, 2011, pp. 31-35. *Project MUSE*, doi: 10.1353/fge.2011.0029.

14. Article in an Online Magazine

Follow the author's name and article title with the name of the magazine in italics, the date published, and the URL of the article.

Schuman, Rebecca. "This Giant Sculpture of Kafka's Head Perfectly Encapsulates His Strange Relationship to Prague." *Slate*, 24 May 2016, http://www.slate.com/blogs/browbeat/2016/05/24/this_giant_moving_sculpture_of_kafka_s_head_is_the_perfect_tribute_to_kafka.html.

15. Article in an Online Newspaper

Alter, Alexandra. "This Summer, Girls in Titles and Girls in Peril." *The New York Times*, 26 May 2016, http://www.nytimes.com/2016/05/27/books/hot-days-cool-books.html.

16. Online Review

O'Hehir, Andrew. "'X-Men: Apocalypse': Mutants Face an Ancient, Leathery Nightmare—Nope, Not Trump!" Review of *X-Men: Apocalypse*, directed by Bryan Singer. *Salon*, 26 May 2016, http://www.salon.com/2016/05/26/x_men_apocalypse_mutants_face_an_ancient_leathery_nightmare_nope_not_trump/.

17. Entry in an Online Reference Work

"Eschatology." *Merriam-Webster*, 7 Apr. 2016, www.merriam-webster.com/dictionary/eschatology.

18. Work from a Website

"Wallace Stevens (1879–1955)." Poetry Foundation, 2015, www.poetryfoundation.org/bio/wallace-stevens.

19. Entire Website

Website with editor:

Dutton, Dennis, editor. *Arts and Letters Daily*. Chronicle of Higher Education, www.aldaily.com. Accessed 2 Oct. 2009.

Website without editor:

Academy of American Poets. 2016, poets.org. Accessed 13 Mar. 2015.

Personal website:

Mendelson, Edward. Home page. Columbia U, 2013, english.columbia.edu/people/profile/394.

20. Entire Web Log (Blog)

Holbo, John, editor. *The Valve*, http://www.thevalve.org/go. Accessed 18 Mar. 2012.

21. Entry in a Wiki

"Pre-Raphaelite Brotherhood." *Wikipedia*, 25 Nov. 2013, wikipedia.org/wiki/Pre-Raphaelite_Brotherhood.

OTHER SOURCES

22. Film and Video

Follow the title with the director, notable performers, the distribution company, and the date of release. For films viewed on the web, follow this with the URL of the website used to view the film. If citing a particular individual's work on the film, begin the entry with his or her name before the title.

> *The Hurt Locker*. Directed by Kathryn Bigelow, performances by Jeremy Renner, Anthony Mackie, Guy Pearce, and Ralph Fiennes, Summit, 2009.

Viewed on the web (use original distributor and release date):

> Nayar, Vineet. "Employees First, Customers Second." *YouTube*, 9 June 2015, www.youtube.com/watch?v=cCdu67s_C5E.

23. Interview

Include the name of the interviewer if it is someone of note.

Personal interview:

> Tripp, Lawrence. Personal interview, 14 Apr. 2014.

In print:

> Dylan, Bob. "Who Is This Bob Dylan?" *Esquire*, 23 Jan. 2014, pp. 124+.

On the radio:

> Gross, Terry. Interview with Ahmir "Questlove" Thompson. *Fresh Air*, NPR, 27 Apr. 2016.

On the web:

> Gross, Terry. Interview with Ahmir "Questlove" Thompson. *Fresh Air*. NPR, 27 Apr. 2016, www.npr.org/2016/04/27/475721555/questlove-on-prince-doo-wop-and-the-food-equivalent-of-the-mona-lisa.

24. Lecture or Speech

Viewed in person:

> Smith, Anna Deavere. "On the Road: A Search for American Character." Jefferson Lecture in the Humanities, John F. Kennedy Center for the Performing Arts, Washington, D.C., 6 Apr. 2015.

Viewed on the web:

> Batuman, Elif. Lowell Humanities Series. Boston College. frontrow.bc.edu/program/batuman.

25. Podcast

> Carlin, Dan. "King of Kings." *Hardcore History Podcast*, 28 Oct. 2015, www.dancarlin.com/hardcore-history-56-kings-of-kings.

26. Work of Art or Photograph

In a museum:

Hopper, Edward. *Nighthawks*. 1942, Oil on canvas, Art Institute, Chicago.

On the web:

Thiebaud, Wayne. *Three Machines*. 1963, De Young Museum, San Francisco, shop.famsf .org/Product.do?code=T636P. Accessed 2 Oct. 2013.

In print:

Clark, Edward. *Navy CPO Graham Jackson Plays "Goin' Home."* 1945, *The Great LIFE Photographers*, Bulfinch, 2004, pp. 78–79.

27. Map or Chart

In print:

"U.S. Personal Savings Rate, 1929–1999." *Credit Card Nation: The Consequences of America's Addiction to Credit*. By Robert D. Manning, Basic, 2000. 100.

On the web:

"1914 New Balkan States and Central Europe Map." *National Geographic*, maps .nationalgeographic.com/maps/print-collection/balkan-states-map.html. Accessed 25 Oct. 2013.

28. Cartoon or Comic Strip

In print:

Finck, Liana. Cartoon. *The New Yorker*, 30 May 2016, p. 30.

On the web:

Zyglis, Adam. "City of Light." *Buffalo News*, 8 Nov. 2015, adamzyglis.buffalonews .com/2015/11/08/city-of-light/. Cartoon.

29. Advertisement

In print:

Rosetta Stone. *Harper's*, Aug. 2008, p. 21. Advertisement.

On the web:

Seamless. *The Washington Post*, www.washingtonpost.com. Accessed 4 Apr. 2016. Advertisement.

GLOSSARY OF TERMS

abstract An abstract term is a general term that refers to a broad concept, as opposed to a term that refers to a specific, particular thing (e.g., *personhood* as opposed to *Seamus Heaney*); opposite of **concrete**.

EXAMPLE:

Do not remember me as a bridge nor a roof
as the maker of legends
nor as a trap
door to that world
where black and white clericals
hang on the edge of beauty in five oclock elevators

— AUDRE LORDE, "Movement Song," p. 608

act The major subunit into which the action of a play is divided. The number of acts in a play typically ranges between one and five, and acts are usually further divided into scenes.

allegory A literary work that portrays abstract ideas concretely. Characters in an allegory are frequently personifications of abstract ideas and are given names that refer to these ideas.

EXAMPLE:

"Young Goodman Brown" by Nathaniel Hawthorne, p. 418

alliteration The repetition of the same initial consonant sounds in a sequence of words or syllables.

EXAMPLE:

When my son lays his head in my lap, I wonder:
Do his father's kisses keep his father's worries
from becoming his? I think, Dear God, *and remember*
there are stars we haven't heard from yet:
They have so far to arrive. Amen,
I think, and I feel almost comforted.

— LI-YOUNG LEE, "The Hammock," p. 292

allusion A reference to another work of literature or to art, history, or current events.

EXAMPLE:

In "Sound and Sense" (p. 800), Alexander Pope alludes to characters from classical Greek literature:

When Ajax strives, some rock's vast weight to throw,
The line too labors, and the words move slow;
Not so, when swift Camilla scours the plain,
Flies o'er th' unbending corn, and skims along the main.

analogy In literature, a comparison between two things that helps explain or illustrate one or both of them.

EXAMPLE:

OPHELIA: *And [Hamlet] hath given countenance to his speech, my lord,*
With almost all the holy vows of heaven.

— WILLIAM SHAKESPEARE, *Hamlet*, p. 662

anapest See **meter**.

anaphora Repetition of an initial word or words to add emphasis.

EXAMPLE:

Whose herds with milk, whose fields with bread,
Whose flocks supply him with attire;
Whose trees in summer yield him shade,
In winter, fire.

— ALEXANDER POPE, "The Quiet Life," p. 446

annotation The act of noting observations directly on a text, especially anything striking or confusing, in order to record ideas and impressions for later analysis.

EXAMPLE:

See page 7 for an annotation of William Shakespeare's "When my love swears that she is made of truth."

antagonist Character in a story or play who opposes the protagonist; while not necessarily an enemy, the antagonist creates or intensifies a conflict for the protagonist. An evil antagonist is a villain.

EXAMPLE:

In William Shakespeare's Hamlet *(p. 651), Claudius is the antagonist.*

apostrophe A direct address to an abstraction (such as time), a thing (the wind), an animal, or an imaginary or absent person.

EXAMPLE:

Leave me, O Love which reachest but to dust;
And thou, my mind, aspire to higher things.

— SIR PHILIP SIDNEY, "Leave me, O Love, which reachest but to dust," p. 600

archaic language Words that were once common but that are no longer used.

EXAMPLES:

HORATIO: What art thou that usurp'st this time of night,
Together with that fair and warlike form
In which the majesty of buried Denmark
Did sometimes march? by heaven I charge thee, speak!

— WILLIAM SHAKESPEARE, *Hamlet*, p. 653

archetype A cultural symbol that has become universally understood and recognized.

EXAMPLE:

The rose Robert Burns expounds on in "A Red, Red Rose" (p. 235) conforms to archetype.

ars poetica Literally, "the art of poetry"; a form of poetry written about poetry.

EXAMPLE:

"Sound and Sense" by Alexander Pope, p. 800

assonance The repetition of vowel sounds in a sequence of words.

EXAMPLE:

And on that cheek, and o'er that brow,
So soft, so calm, yet eloquent,
The smiles that win, the tints that glow,
But tell of days in goodness spent,
A mind at peace with all below,
A heart whose love is innocent!

— LORD BYRON, "She Walks in Beauty," p. 603

atmosphere The feeling created for the reader by a work of literature. Atmosphere can be generated by many things but especially by **style**, **tone**, and **setting**. Synonymous with **mood**.

EXAMPLE:

See the discussion of how setting creates atmosphere in Edgar Allan Poe's "The Masque of the Red Death" (p. 23).

ballad First taking shape in the late Middle Ages, the ballad was a sung poem that recounted a dramatic story. Ballads were passed down orally from generation to generation. Arising in the romantic period, the literary ballad — a poem intentionally imitative of the ballad's style and structure — attempted to capture the sentiments of the common people in the same way the traditional ballad had. See also **stanza**.

EXAMPLE:

"We Are Seven" by William Wordsworth, p. 278

Beat movement A movement of American writers in the 1950s who saw society as oppressively conformist. These writers rejected mainstream values, seeking ways to escape through drugs, various forms of spirituality, and sexual experimentation. The writers of the Beat generation, among them Allen Ginsberg and Jack Kerouac, celebrated freedom of expression and held generally antiestablishment views about politics. Their writing, likewise, rejected conventional norms of structure and diction, and their books prompted several notorious obscenity trials, which helped reshape censorship laws in the United States.

EXAMPLE:

"Is About" by Allen Ginsberg, p. 813

bildungsroman A novel that explores the maturation of the protagonist, with the narrative usually moving the main character from childhood into adulthood. Also called a coming-of-age story.

blank verse Unrhymed iambic pentameter, blank verse is the most commonly used verse form in English because it comes closest to natural patterns of speaking. See also **iambic pentameter**.

EXAMPLE:

DESDEMONA: That I did love the Moor to live with him,
My downright violence and storm of fortunes
May trumpet to the world. My heart's subdued
Even to the very quality of my lord.
I saw Othello's visage in his mind,
And to his honors and his valiant parts
Did I my soul and fortunes consecrate.
So that, dear lords, if I be left behind
A moth of peace, and he go to the war,
The rites for which I love him are bereft me,
And I a heavy interim shall support
By his dear absence. Let me go with him.

— WILLIAM SHAKESPEARE, *Othello,* p. 1098

cadence Quality of spoken text formed from combining the text's rhythm with the rise and fall in the inflection of the speaker's voice.

EXAMPLE:

In Matthew Arnold's "Dover Beach" (p. 1035), the poet creates a cadence that imitates a changing wave pattern by using caesura (with commas):

Listen! you hear the grating roar
Of pebbles which the waves draw back, and fling,
At their return, up the high strand,
Begin, and cease, and then again begin,
With tremulous cadence slow, and bring
The eternal note of sadness in.

caesura A pause within a line of poetry, sometimes punctuated, sometimes not, often mirroring natural speech.

EXAMPLE:

O could I lose all father now! For why
Will man lament the state he should envy?

— BEN JONSON, "On My First Son," p. 275

caricature A character with features or traits that are exaggerated so that the character seems ridiculous. The term is usually applied to graphic depictions but can also be applied to written depictions.

EXAMPLE:

Polonius in William Shakespeare's Hamlet *(p. 651) is a caricature.*

carpe diem A widespread literary theme meaning "seize the day" in Latin and found especially in lyric poetry, carpe diem encourages readers to enjoy the present and make the most of their short lives.

EXAMPLE:

"To the Virgins, to Make Much of Time" by Robert Herrick, p. 602

catharsis Refers to the emotional release felt by the audience at the end of a tragic drama. The term comes from Aristotle's *Poetics*, in which he explains this frequently felt relief in terms of a purification of the emotions caused by watching the tragic events. (*Catharsis* means "purgation" or "purification" in Greek.)

character A person depicted in a narrative. While this term generally refers to human beings, it can also include animals or inanimate objects that are given human characteristics. Several more specific terms are used to refer to types of characters frequently employed by authors:

flat character A character embodying only one or two traits and who lacks character development; for this reason, a flat character is also called a static character. Often such characters exist only to provide background or adequate motivation for a protagonist's actions.

EXAMPLE:

In Joyce Carol Oates's "Where Are You Going, Where Have You Been?" Connie's sister, June, is described as being "so plain and chunky and steady that Connie had to hear her praised all the time by her mother and her mother's sisters." Being compared to June fuels Connie's resentment and consequent misbehavior; additionally, because June goes out with friends, Connie is allowed to as well, which is how she meets the Pied Piper.

round character A character who exhibits a range of emotions and who evolves over the course of the story.

EXAMPLE:

In Shakespeare's Hamlet *(p. 651), Hamlet is a round character who experiences complex emotional development throughout the play.*

secondary character A supporting character; while not as prominent or central as a main character, he or she is still important to the events of a story or play.

EXAMPLE:

In William Shakespeare's Othello *(p. 1086), Lodovico is a secondary character.*

stock character A type of flat character based on a stereotype; one who falls into an immediately recognizable category or type — such as the absentminded professor or the town drunk — and thus resists unique characterization. Stock characters can be artfully used for humor or satire.

EXAMPLE:

In Flannery O'Connor's "A Good Man Is Hard to Find" (p. 837), June Star and John Wesley are portrayed as stock characters — spoiled, bratty children.

characterization The method by which the author builds, or reveals, a character; it can be direct or indirect. Indirect characterization means that an author shows rather than tells readers what a character is like through what the character says, does, or thinks, or what others say about the character. Direct characterization occurs when a narrator tells the reader who a character is by describing the background, motivation, temperament, or appearance of that character.

EXAMPLES:

Direct characterization: "The Progress of Love" by Alice Munro (p. 259):
My father was not religious in the way my mother was. He was an Anglican, an Orangeman, a Conservative, because that's what he had been brought up to be. He was the son who got left on the farm with his parents and took care of them till they died. He met my mother, he waited for her, they married; he thought himself lucky then to have a family to work for.

Indirect characterization: **Pride and Prejudice** ***by Jane Austen (p. 20):***
Mr. Darcy danced only once with Mrs. Hurst and once with Miss Bingley, declined being introduced to any other lady, and spent the rest of the evening in walking about the room, speaking occasionally to one of his own party. His character was decided. He was the proudest, most disagreeable man in the world, and every body hoped that he would never come there again.

chorus In drama, especially classical Greek drama, the chorus refers to a group of participants in a play who deliver commentary on the play's action. The role of the chorus is no longer a regular feature of modern drama, although it has been employed in a few prominent works, such as T. S. Eliot's *Murder in the Cathedral*.

climax The point in a story when the conflict reaches its highest intensity.

EXAMPLE:

In Alice Walker's "Everyday Use" (p. 1016), the climax occurs when Mama (the narrator) makes the forceful decision to take the family quilts from her daughter Dee (who intends to hang them as artwork, a symbol of her heritage) and return them to her daughter Maggie (who would use them for their intended purpose—as quilts).

colloquial language/colloquialism An expression or language construction appropriate only for casual, informal speaking or writing.

EXAMPLE:

"I toldja shut up, Ellie," Arnold Friend said, "you're deaf, get a hearing aid, right? Fix yourself up. This little girl's no trouble and's gonna be nice to me, so Ellie keep to yourself, this ain't your date—right? Don't hem in on me, don't hog, don't crush, don't bird dog, don't trail me," he said in a rapid, meaningless voice, as if he were running through all the expressions he'd learned but was no longer sure which one of them was in style, then rushing on to new ones, making them up with his eyes closed.

—JOYCE CAROL OATES, "Where Are You Going, Where Have You Been?" p. 435

colonialism The occupation of one country by another. In the early 1800s, European countries controlled 35 percent of the world, but by 1914, that number had risen to nearly

85 percent and included parts of Africa, Asia, Latin America, and the Caribbean. The legacy of colonialism has extended beyond the political independence that many countries gained in the 1960s and 1970s.

EXAMPLE:

See the works in Texts in Context: Heart of Darkness *and the Legacy of Colonialism on pages 386–418.*

comedy Usually used to refer to a dramatic work that, in contrast to tragedy, has a light, amusing plot, features a happy ending, centers around ordinary people, and is written and performed in the vernacular.

EXAMPLE:

The Importance of Being Earnest *by Oscar Wilde, p. 518*

comedy of manners A satiric dramatic form that lampoons social conventions.

EXAMPLE:

Oscar Wilde's The Importance of Being Earnest *(p. 518) is a comedy of manners.*

coming-of-age story See **bildungsroman**.

complex sentence See **sentence**.

compound sentence See **sentence**.

compound-complex sentence See **sentence**.

concrete A concrete term is one that refers to a specific, particular thing, as opposed to a term that refers to a broad concept (e.g., *Seamus Heaney* as opposed to *personhood*); opposite of **abstract**.

EXAMPLE:

Kusum lives across the street from me. She and Satish had moved in less than a month ago. They said they needed a bigger place. All these people, the Sharmas and friends from the Indo-Canada Society, had been there for the housewarming. Satish and Kusum made tandoori on their big gas grill and even the white neighbors piled their plates high with that luridly red, charred, juicy chicken. Their younger daughter had danced, and even our boys had broken away from the Stanley Cup telecast to put in a reluctant appearance.

— BHARATI MUKHERJEE, "The Management of Grief," p. 1189

conflict The tension, opposition, or struggle that drives a plot. External conflict is the opposition or tension between two characters or forces. Internal conflict occurs within a character. Conflict usually arises between the protagonist and the antagonist in a story.

EXAMPLE:

In Herman Melville's "Bartleby, the Scrivener" (p. 758), the story's external conflict is between Bartleby, who won't leave his office after being fired, and the narrator, who is trying to remove him.

connotation Meanings or associations readers have with a word or an item beyond its dictionary definition, or denotation. Connotations may reveal another layer of meaning of a piece, affect the tone, or suggest symbolic resonance.

EXAMPLE:

In the following lines from Ben Jonson's "On My First Son" (p. 275), the word lament*—as opposed to synonyms such as* cry *or* feel bad about*—has formal and religious connotations.*

Will man lament the state he should envy,
To have so soon 'scaped world's and flesh's rage,
And, if no other misery, yet age?

consonance An instance in which identical final consonant sounds in nearby words follow different vowel sounds. See also **rhyme**.

EXAMPLE:

Let the boy try along this bayonet-blade
How cold steel is, and keen with hunger of blood;
Blue with all malice, like a madman's flash;
And thinly drawn with famishing for flesh.

—WILFRED OWEN, "Arms and the Boy," p. 1235

couplet See **stanza**.

critical lenses Different ways to approach interpreting a work of literature, also known as critical perspectives. Specific types of lenses discussed in this book include the following:

cultural lens An interpretation of a text that examines how different races and ethnicities, social and economic class distinctions, and political ideologies influence the creation and interpretation of literature. Although the perspective of cultural criticism covers a broad landscape, it focuses on how dominant groups have silenced, devalued, misrepresented, or even demonized marginalized ones.

formalist lens Also called New Criticism. An interpretation of a text that treats it as an independent and self-sufficient entity, focusing on style features such as diction, structure, figurative language, and syntax.

gendered lens An interpretation of a text that explores its treatment of gender stereotypes, social mores and values based on gender, and the overall representation of the genders.

historical lens An interpretation of a text that treats it as a product of the historic moment when it was created.

psychological lens An interpretation of a text that considers the behavior and motivations of characters, exploring how both conscious and unconscious drives and desires influence their actions.

cultural lens See **critical lenses**.

cumulative sentence See **sentence**.

dactyl See **meter**.

denotation The literal definition of a word, often referred to as the "dictionary definition."

denouement Pronounced *day-noo-moh*, this literally means "untying the knot"; in this phase of a plot, the conflict has been resolved and balance is restored to the world of the story.

EXAMPLE:

In Fences *(p. 151) by August Wilson, the conflicts of the play are resolved with the death of Troy in act II, scene iv. The scene that follows (act II, scene v) is the play's denouement.*

dialect Dialogue or narration written to simulate regional or cultural speech patterns.

EXAMPLE:

TROY: . . . *Man ain't had two dimes to rub together. He walking around with his shoes all run over bumming money for cigarettes.*

— AUGUST WILSON, *Fences*, p. 161

dialogue The written depiction of conversation between characters.

EXAMPLE:

"Have you gals been to the Cloud Cap Inn? That's hitched to the mountain with wire cables. See, what we done is — "

"Mr. Loatch?" Swilling a drink, I steadied my voice. "How late does the chairlift run?"

"Oh dear." He pursed his lips. "You girls gotta be somewhere? I'm afraid you're stuck with us, at least until morning. You're the last we let up. They shut that lift down until dawn."

Next to me, I heard Clara in my ear: "Are you crazy? We just got here, and you're talking about leaving? Do you know how rude you sound?"

"They're dead."

"What are you talking about? Who's dead?"

"Everyone. Everyone but us."

— KAREN RUSSELL, "The Prospectors," p. 791

diction A writer's choice of words. In addition to choosing words with precise denotations and connotations, an author must choose whether to use words that are abstract or concrete, formal or informal, or literal or figurative. See **colloquial language**.

EXAMPLE:

See the close reading of a section from Robert Herrick's "Delight in Disorder" (p. 123).

direct characterization See **characterization**.

dramatic irony See **irony, dramatic**.

dramatic monologue A type of poem in which the speaker, who is clearly distinct from the poet, addresses an audience that is present in the poem.

EXAMPLE:

"The Wife of the Man of Many Wiles" by A. E. Stallings, p. 825

ekphrastic poetry A form of poetry that comments on a work of art in another genre, such as a painting or a piece of music.

EXAMPLE:

"We Who Weave" by LeConté Dill, p. 1051

elegy A contemplative poem on death and mortality, often written for someone who has died.

EXAMPLE:

"Elegy of Fortinbras" by Zbigniew Herbert, p. 750

end rhyme See **rhyme**.

end-stopped line An end-stopped line of poetry concludes with punctuation that marks a pause. The line is completely meaningful in itself, unlike run-on lines, which require the reader to move to the next line to grasp the poet's complete thought. See also **enjambment**.

EXAMPLE:

Surely some revelation is at hand;
Surely the Second Coming is at hand.

— WILLIAM BUTLER YEATS, "The Second Coming," p. 1040

English sonnet See **sonnet**.

enjambment A poetic technique in which one line ends without a pause and must continue on to the next line to complete its meaning; also referred to as a "run-on line."

EXAMPLE:

Once more the storm is howling, and half hid
Under this cradle-hood and coverlid
My child sleeps on. There is no obstacle
But Gregory's wood and one bare hill
Whereby the haystack- and roof-levelling wind,
Bred on the Atlantic, can be stayed;

— WILLIAM BUTLER YEATS, "A Prayer for My Daughter," p. 280

epigram A short, witty statement designed to surprise an audience or a reader.

EXAMPLE:

"To lose one parent may be regarded as a misfortune — to lose both *seems like carelessness."*

— OSCAR WILDE, *The Importance of Being Earnest*, p. 527

epigraph A quotation preceding a work of literature that helps set the text's mood or suggests its themes.

EXAMPLE:

"The dragon is by the side of the road, watching those who pass. Beware lest he devour you. We go to the Father of Souls, but it is necessary to pass by the dragon." — St. Cyril of Jerusalem

— FLANNERY O'CONNOR, "A Good Man Is Hard to Find," p. 837

epiphany A character's transformative moment of realization. James Joyce, often credited with coining this as a literary term, defined it as the "sudden revelation of the whatness of a thing," the moment in which "the soul of the commonest object . . . seems to us radiant . . . a sudden spiritual manifestation [either] in the vulgarity of speech or of a gesture or in a memorable phrase of the mind itself."

EXAMPLE:

How can I describe my emotions at this catastrophe, or how delineate the wretch whom with such infinite pains and care I had endeavoured to form? His limbs were in proportion, and I had selected his features as beautiful. Beautiful!—Great God! His yellow skin scarcely covered the work of muscles and arteries beneath; his hair was of a lustrous black, and flowing; his teeth of a pearly whiteness; but these luxuriances only formed a more horrid contrast with his watery eyes, that seemed almost of the same colour as the dun white sockets in which they were set, his shriveled complexion and straight black lips.

The different accidents of life are not so changeable as the feelings of human nature. I had worked hard for nearly two years, for the sole purpose of infusing life into an inanimate body. For this I had deprived myself of rest and health. I had desired it with an ardour that far exceeded moderation; but now that I had finished, the beauty of the dream vanished, and breathless horror and disgust filled my heart. Unable to endure the aspect of the being I had created, I rushed out of the room, and continued a long time traversing my bedchamber, unable to compose my mind to sleep.

—MARY SHELLEY, *Frankenstein*, p. 876

eulogy A poem, a speech, or another work written in great praise of something or someone, usually a person no longer living.

EXAMPLE:

William Wordsworth's "London, 1802" (p. 1056) is a eulogy to the poet John Milton.

exposition In a literary work, contextual and background information told to readers (rather than shown through action) about the characters, plot, setting, and situation.

EXAMPLE:

In "Apollo" (p. 438), Chimamanda Ngozi Adichie uses the opening paragraphs to provide background on the story's protagonist and his relationship with his parents.

extended metaphor See **metaphor, extended**.

eye rhyme See **rhyme**.

falling action In a plot diagram, this is the result (or fallout) of the climax or turning point. In this phase, the conflict is being resolved. See also **plot**.

EXAMPLE:

See the analysis of the plot of Gabriel García Márquez's "One of These Days," including its falling action, on pages 18–19.

farce A dramatic form marked by wholly absurd situations, slapstick, raucous wordplay, and sometimes innuendo.

EXAMPLE:

Oscar Wilde's The Importance of Being Earnest *(p. 518) contains moments of farce, particularly the section on pages 520–24 regarding cucumber sandwiches.*

figurative language Language that uses figures of speech; nonliteral language usually evoking strong images. Sometimes referred to as metaphorical language, most of its forms explain, clarify, or enhance an idea by comparing it to something else; the comparison can be explicit (simile) or implied (metaphor). Other forms of figurative language include **personification**, **paradox**, **overstatement (hyperbole)**, **understatement**, and **irony**.

EXAMPLE:

He looked at her. He took off the sunglasses and she saw how pale the skin around his eyes was, like holes that were not in shadow but instead in light. His eyes were like chips of broken glass that catch the light in an amiable way. He smiled. It was as if the idea of going for a ride somewhere, to some place, was a new idea to him.

— JOYCE CAROL OATES, "Where Are You Going, Where Have You Been?" p. 431

first-person narrator See **narrator**.

flashback A scene in a narrative that is set in an earlier time than the main action.

EXAMPLE:

See the first two paragraphs of "Woman Hollering Creek" by Sandra Cisneros, page 591.

foil A contrasting character who allows the protagonist to stand out more distinctly.

EXAMPLE:

In Shakespeare's Hamlet *(p. 651), Laertes — who leaps at vengeance rather than deeply contemplates it — is the perfect foil for Hamlet.*

foot See **meter**.

foreshadowing A plot device in which future events are hinted at.

EXAMPLE:

See paragraphs 11–13 of Joseph Conrad's Heart of Darkness, *pages 329–30.*

form Refers to the defining structural characteristics of a work, especially a poem (i.e., meter and rhyme scheme). Often poets work within set forms, such as the sonnet or sestina, which require adherence to fixed conventions.

formal diction See **diction**.

Formalist lens See **critical lenses**.

free verse A form of poetry that does not have a regular meter or rhyme scheme.

EXAMPLE:

And would it have been worth it, after all,
Would it have been worth while,
After the sunsets and the dooryards and the sprinkled streets,
After the novels, after the teacups, after the skirts that trail along the floor

And this, and so much more? —
It is impossible to say just what I mean!

— T. S. ELIOT, "The Love Song of J. Alfred Prufrock," p. 243

gendered lens See **critical lenses**.

genre This term can refer broadly to the general category that a literary work falls into (drama or poetry, fiction or nonfiction) or more specifically to a certain subset of literary works grouped together on the basis of similar characteristics (science fiction, local color, western).

EXAMPLE:

Flannery O'Connor's "A Good Man Is Hard to Find" (p. 837) is a piece of fiction that is also classified as Southern gothic.

ghazal A form that originated in Arabic poetry, consisting of rhyming couplets and a refrain. The second line of each couplet typically ends with the same word, and the penultimate words in the second line of each couplet also rhyme with each other.

EXAMPLE:

"Ghazal for White Hen Pantry" by Jamila Woods, p. 818

graphic organizer A pre-writing strategy that helps break a work into more manageable sections for close reading and analysis. Structuring close reading in this way helps move a reader beyond simply describing the author's language choices to analysis that connects style with its effect and meaning.

EXAMPLE:

See the graphic organizer for "Reunion" by John Cheever on pages 99–100.

Harlem Renaissance A movement in the 1920s and 1930s marked by a great flowering of black arts and culture centered in the Harlem neighborhood of New York City.

EXAMPLE:

"Mother to Son" by Langston Hughes, p. 282

historical lens See **critical lenses**.

hook An opening to a piece of writing designed to catch the audience's attention.

EXAMPLE:

See the first paragraph of "How to Write about Africa" by Binyavanga Wainaina, page 414.

hubris An excessive level of pride that leads to the protagonist's downfall. See also **tragedy**.

EXAMPLE:

See Victor Frankenstein's actions in Frankenstein *by Mary Shelley, page 852.*

hyperbole Deliberate exaggeration used for emphasis or to produce a comic or an ironic effect; an overstatement to make a point.

EXAMPLE:

"Historic" had turned out to be the landlady's synonym for "haunted." "Turn-of-the-century sash windows," we'd discovered, meant "pneumonia holes."

— KAREN RUSSELL, "The Prospectors," p. 786

iamb See **meter**.

iambic pentameter An iamb, the most common metrical foot in English poetry, is made up of an unstressed syllable followed by a stressed one. Iambic pentameter, then, is a rhythmic meter containing five iambs. Unrhymed iambic pentameter is called blank verse. See also **meter**; **blank verse.**

EXAMPLE:

Thĕ cúr | fĕw tólls | thĕ knéll | ŏf párt | ĭng dáy,
Thĕ lów | ĭng hérd | wĭnd slów | lў o'ér | thĕ léa,
Thĕ plów | măn hóme | wărd plóds | hĭs wéa | rў wáy,
Ănd leáves | thĕ wórld | tŏ dárk | nĕss ánd | tŏ mé.

— THOMAS GRAY, "Elegy Written in a Country Churchyard," p. 1029

imagery A description of how something looks, feels, tastes, smells, or sounds. The verbal expression of a sensory experience: visual (sight), auditory (sound), olfactory (scent), gustatory (taste), tactile (touch), or kinesthetic (movement/tension). Imagery may use literal or figurative language.

EXAMPLE:

Queer little red bugs came out and moved in slow squadrons around me. Their backs were polished vermilion, with black spots.

— WILLA CATHER, *My Ántonia*, p. 85

imagism A modernist literary movement that rejected overly sentimental, decorative language in favor of direct and succinct expression, often focusing an entire poem on a single image.

EXAMPLE:

"Sea Rose" by H. D., p. 236

imperative sentence See **sentence**.

in medias res Latin for "in the middle of things," a technique in which a narrative begins in the middle of the action.

EXAMPLE:

"The Prospectors" by Karen Russell, p. 785

indirect characterization See **characterization**.

informal diction See **diction**.

internal rhyme See **rhyme**.

interrupted sentence See **sentence**.

inversion Also called an inverted sentence, it is created by alteration of the standard English word order of a subject (S) being followed by a verb (V) and its object (O) in a declarative sentence. It is often used to call attention to something, perhaps to emphasize a point or an idea by placing it in the initial position, or to slow the pace by choosing an unusual order.

EXAMPLE:

O S V

For this I had deprived myself of rest and health.

— MARY SHELLEY, *Frankenstein*, p. 876

irony, dramatic Tension created by the contrast between what a character says or thinks and what the audience or readers know to be true; as a result of this technique, some words and actions in a story or play take on a different meaning for the reader than they do for the characters.

EXAMPLE:

Once readers learn of Mr. Kapasi's hope for a relationship with Mrs. Das, in Jhumpa Lahiri's "Interpreter of Maladies" (p. 311), his actions take on a different meaning for the readers than for her.

irony, situational A pointed discrepancy between what seems fitting or expected in a story and what actually happens.

EXAMPLE:

Jhumpa Lahiri's story "Interpreter of Maladies" (p. 311) contains situational irony. Mr. Kapasi yearns to develop an intimate relationship with Mrs. Das. Ironically, he is disgusted and treats her coldly when he learns that she has had an extramarital affair.

irony, verbal A figure of speech that occurs when a speaker or character says one thing but means something else or when what is said is the opposite of what is expected, creating a noticeable incongruity. **Sarcasm** involves verbal irony used derisively.

EXAMPLE:

JACK (pulling off his gloves): *When one is in town one amuses oneself. When one is in the country one amuses other people. It is excessively boring.*

ALGERNON: *And who are the people you amuse?*

JACK (airily): *Oh, neighbors, neighbors.*

ALGERNON: *Got nice neighbors in your part of Shropshire?*

JACK: *Perfectly horrid! Never speak to one of them.*

ALGERNON: *How immensely you must amuse them!*

— OSCAR WILDE, *The Importance of Being Earnest*, p. 519

Italian sonnet See **sonnet**.

juxtaposition Placing two things side by side for the sake of comparison or contrast. Authors sometimes use incongruous juxtapositions to produce **verbal irony**.

EXAMPLE:

HAMLET: *To be, or not to be: that is the question:*
Whether 'tis nobler in the mind to suffer
The slings and arrows of outrageous fortune,
Or to take arms against a sea of troubles,
And by opposing end them? To die: to sleep;

— WILLIAM SHAKESPEARE, *Hamlet*, p. 683

Kafkaesque Having the nightmarish, uncanny characteristics of Kafka's stories.

limited omniscient point of view See **point of view**.

literary elements The components that together create a literary work. This term encompasses elements of style, such as imagery, syntax, figurative language, and tone, as well as storytelling elements, such as plot, character, setting, and point of view.

lyric A short poem expressing the personal feelings of a first-person speaker. The term comes from the Greek word *lyre*, and the form is descended from poems intended to be sung while accompanied by that instrument.

EXAMPLE:

"Those Winter Sundays" by Robert Hayden, p. 297

masque Now extremely rare, this genre of lush spectacle, song, dance, masks, and elaborate staging was popular among sixteenth- and seventeenth-century British nobles, who also made up its amateur and occasionally royal cast.

EXAMPLE:

Ben Jonson (p. 275) wrote many masques for the court of King James I and Queen Anne.

metaphor A figure of speech that compares or equates two things without using *like* or *as*. For comparisons made using *like* or *as*, see **simile**.

EXAMPLE:

For this, for everything, we are out of tune;

— WILLIAM WORDSWORTH, "The World Is Too Much with Us," p. 447

metaphor, extended A metaphor that continues over several lines or throughout an entire literary work.

EXAMPLE:

In "One Art" by Elizabeth Bishop (p. 606), the metaphor of losing as an art to be practiced and perfected is repeated and developed throughout.

metaphysical conceit A literary device that sets up a striking analogy between two entities that would not usually invite comparison, often drawing connections between the physical and the spiritual. This literary device is famously used by metaphysical poets, including John Donne and George Herbert.

EXAMPLE:

"The Flea" by John Donne, p. 600

meter The formal, regular organization of stressed and unstressed syllables, measured in feet. A foot is distinguished by the number of syllables it contains and how stress is placed on the syllables — stressed (´) or unstressed (˘). There are five typical feet in English verse: iamb (˘´), trochee (´˘), anapest (˘˘´), dactyl (´˘˘), and spondee (´´). Some meters dictate the number of feet per line, the most common being tetrameter, pentameter, and hexameter, having four, five, and six feet, respectively. See **iambic pentameter**.

metonymy A figure of speech in which something is represented by another thing that is related to it. Compare to **synecdoche**; see also **metaphor**.

EXAMPLE:

In this excerpt from "London, 1802" by William Wordsworth (p. 1056), an altar is used to represent religion, a sword to represent the military, and a pen to represent the arts:

England hath need of thee: she is a fen
Of stagnant waters: altar, sword, and pen,

minimalism A style in prose or verse that emphasizes economy of words and unadorned sentences.

EXAMPLE:

"Ten Kliks South" by Phil Klay, p. 1098

modernism In literature, modernism refers to a movement of writers who reached their apex between the 1920s and 1930s and expressed views of disillusionment with contemporary Western civilization, especially in the wake of World War I's mindless brutality. Rejecting the conventions of the Victorian era, these writers experimented with form and took insights from recent writings by Sigmund Freud and Carl Jung about the unconscious. They viewed art as restorative and frequently ordered their writing around symbols and allusions. Representative modernist writers include T. S. Eliot, James Joyce, and Virginia Woolf.

EXAMPLE:

See the texts in The Metamorphosis *and the Modernist Vision on pages 229–48.*

monologue In a play, a speech given by one person. See also **soliloquy**.

EXAMPLE:

Troy delivers a monologue in act I, scene iv, of Fences, *pages 173–74.*

mood Synonymous with **atmosphere**, mood is the feeling created for the reader by a work of literature. Many things can generate mood — especially **style**, **tone**, and **setting**.

motif A recurring pattern of images, words, or symbols that reveals a theme in a work of literature.

EXAMPLE:

In Shakespeare's Hamlet *(p. 651), the repeated use of words such as* play, act, see, assume, show, reveal, appear, form, *and* shape, *as well as the inclusion of a play within the play, become a motif that helps reveal one of the play's central themes: the contrast between appearance and reality.*

naive narrator See **narrator**.

narrative A story. Narratives may be written either in prose or in verse, as in narrative poetry.

EXAMPLE:

"Mother Country" by Richard Blanco (p. 1049) is a narrative poem.

narrative frame Also known as a frame story, a narrative frame is a plot device in which the author places the main narrative of his or her work within another narrative — the narrative frame. This exterior narrative usually serves to explain the main narrative in some way.

EXAMPLES:

Heart of Darkness *by Joseph Conrad, p. 327*

narrator The character, or persona, that the author uses to tell a narrative, or story. Narrators may tell stories from several different points of view, including first person, second person (very rare), and third person. See **point of view**.

EXAMPLE:

In The Metamorphosis *by Franz Kafka, the narrator is a third-person limited omniscient voice, who usually reflects Gregor's thoughts and experiences:*

> *Gregor's gaze then directed itself to the window. The dreary weather — one could hear raindrops hit the metal awning over the window — made him quite melancholy. "What if I slept a bit longer and forgot all this foolishness," he thought. But that was altogether impossible, because he was used to sleeping on his right side, and his current condition made working himself into this position impossible. No matter how vigorously he swung himself over to the right, he immediately rolled again onto his back. He tried what seemed hundreds of times, closing his eyes in order to avoid having to see his wriggling legs. He finally gave up only when he began to feel in his side a small dull ache that he had never felt before.* (pp. 195–96)

More specific terms are used to discuss the role a narrator plays in interpreting the events in a narrative:

objective narrator Also known as a neutral narrator, a narrator who recounts only what characters say and do, offering no insight into their thinking or analysis of events. All interpretation is left to the reader.

EXAMPLE:

In her short story "The Lottery" (p. 32), author Shirley Jackson uses the perspective of the objective narrator effectively to stand back and suspend judgment on an incident that turns ugly and violent.

unreliable narrator A narrator who is biased and doesn't give a full or an accurate picture of events in a narrative. Narrators may be unreliable because of youth, inexperience, madness, intentional or unintentional bias, or even a lack of morals. Authors often use this technique to distinguish the character's point of view from their own. Sometimes an author will use an unreliable narrator to make an ironic point.

EXAMPLE:

As Karen Russell's "The Prospectors" (p. 785) progresses, readers realize that the narrator, Aubby, is unreliable in her account (and perception) of her travels with Clara.

near rhyme See **rhyme**.

non sequitur In literature, a reply or remark that does not have any relevance to what occasioned or preceded it; in rhetoric, a conclusion that does not logically follow from the premises.

EXAMPLE:

HAMLET: *I am but mad north-north-west: when the wind is southerly I know a hawk from a handsaw.*

— WILLIAM SHAKESPEARE, *Hamlet*, p. 678

novella A short novel, from the Italian word meaning "story."

EXAMPLE:

The Metamorphosis *by Franz Kafka, p. 195*

objective narrator See **narrator**.

objective point of view See **point of view**.

octet See **stanza**.

ode A form of poetry used to meditate on or address a single object or condition. It originally followed strict rules of rhythm, meter, and rhyme, which by the romantic period had become more flexible.

EXAMPLE:

"For Women Who Are Difficult to Love" by Warsan Shire, p. 616

omniscient narrator See **narrator**.

omniscient point of view See **point of view**.

onomatopoeia Use of words that refer to sound and whose pronunciations mimic those sounds.

EXAMPLE:

Lee Strunk made a funny ghost sound, a kind of moaning, yet very happy, and right then, when Strunk made that high happy moaning sound, when he went Ahhooooo, right then Ted Lavender was shot in the head on his way back from peeing.

— TIM O'BRIEN, "The Things They Carried," p. 1069

overstatement See **hyperbole**.

oxymoron A paradox made up of two seemingly contradictory words.

EXAMPLE:

Out of the murderous innocence of the sea.

— WILLIAM BUTLER YEATS, "A Prayer for My Daughter," p. 280

parable A tale told explicitly to illustrate a moral lesson or conclusion. Parables can take the form of drama, poetry, or fiction.

EXAMPLE:

"The Parable of the Old Man and the Young" by Wilfred Owen, p. 1234

paradox A statement that seems contradictory but actually is not.

EXAMPLE:

For whose sake henceforth all his vows be such
As what he loves may never like too much.

— BEN JONSON, "On My First Son," p. 275

parallel structure Also known as parallelism, this term refers to the repeated use of similar grammatical structures for the purpose of emphasis. Compare with **anaphora**, a type of parallel structure concerned only with the repetitions of an initial word or words.

EXAMPLE:

He would dispose of his good-luck pebble. Swallow it, maybe, or use Lee Strunk's slingshot, or just drop it along the trail. On the march he would impose strict field discipline. He would be careful to send out flank security, to prevent straggling or bunching up, to keep his troops moving at the proper pace and at the proper interval. He would insist on clean weapons. He would confiscate the remainder of Lavender's dope. Later in the day, perhaps, he would call the men together and speak to them plainly. He would accept the blame for what had happened to Ted Lavender. He would be a man about it. He would look them in the eyes, keeping his chin level, and he would issue the new SOPs in a calm, impersonal tone of voice, an officer's voice, leaving no room for argument or discussion.

— TIM O'BRIEN, "The Things They Carried," p. 1082

parody A comic or satiric imitation of a particular literary work or style. Parodies can run the gamut from lighthearted imitations intended merely to play with something well known to exaggerations intended to criticize, usually by making a work or literary style look ridiculous.

EXAMPLE:

"The Black Man's Burden" by H. T. Johnson, p. 400

passive voice A sentence employs passive voice when the subject doesn't act but is acted on.

EXAMPLE:

Midway down they were held up by Mary Jane, who replenished them with raspberry or orange jelly or with blancmange and jam.

— JAMES JOYCE, "The Dead," p. 502

pastoral Literature that employs a romanticized description of leisurely farm or rural life.

EXAMPLE:

"The Quiet Life" by Alexander Pope, p. 446

periodic sentence See **sentence**.

persona A voice and viewpoint that an author adopts in order to deliver a story or poem. See **narrator**.

EXAMPLE:
The narrator created by A. E. Stallings in "The Wife of the Man of Many Wiles," p. 825

personification A figure of speech in which an animal or inanimate object is imbued with human qualities.

EXAMPLE:
And this same flower that smiles today,
Tomorrow will be dying.

— ROBERT HERRICK, "To the Virgins, to Make Much of Time," p. 602

Petrarchan sonnet See **sonnet**.

plot The arrangement of events in a narrative. Almost always, a conflict is central to a plot, and traditionally a plot develops in accordance with the following model: **exposition**, **rising action**, **climax**, **falling action**, **denouement**. There can be more than one sequence of events in a work, although typically there is one major sequence along with other minor sequences. These minor sequences are called subplots.

EXAMPLE:
See analysis of the plot of "One of These Days" by Gabriel García Márquez on pages 18–19.

point of view The perspective from which a work is told. The most common narrative vantage points are:

first person Told by a narrator who is a character in the story and who refers to him- or herself as "I." First-person narrators are sometimes **unreliable narrators**.

EXAMPLE: ***"I Stand Here Ironing" by Tillie Olsen, p. 248***
I nursed her. They feel that's important nowadays. I nursed all the children, but with her, with all the fierce rigidity of first motherhood, I did like the books then said. Though her cries battered me to trembling and my breasts ached with swollenness, I waited till the clock decreed.

second person Though rare, some stories are told using second-person pronouns (*you*). This casts the reader as a character in the story.

EXAMPLE: ***"Turtle Soup" by Marilyn Chin, p. 299***
You go home one evening tired from work,
and your mother boils you turtle soup.
Twelve hours hunched over the hearth
(who knows what else is in that cauldron).

third-person limited omniscient Told by a narrator who relates the action using third-person pronouns (*he, she, it*). This narrator is usually privy to the thoughts and actions of only one character.

EXAMPLE: ***"Interpreter of Maladies" by Jhumpa Lahiri, p. 316***

He began to check his reflection in the rearview mirror as he drove, feeling grateful that he had chosen the gray suit that morning and not the brown one, which tended to sag a little in the knees. From time to time he glanced through the mirror at Mrs. Das.

third-person omniscient Told by a narrator using third-person pronouns. This narrator is privy to the thoughts and actions of all the characters in the story.

EXAMPLE: ***"The Shawl" by Cynthia Ozick, p. 1185***

It was a magic shawl, it could nourish an infant for three days and three nights. Magda did not die, she stayed alive, although very quiet. A peculiar smell, of cinnamon and almonds, lifted out of her mouth. She held her eyes open every moment, forgetting how to blink or nap, and Rosa and sometimes Stella studied their blueness. On the road they raised one burden of a leg after another and studied Magda's face. "Aryan," Stella said, in a voice grown as thin as a string; and Rosa thought how Stella gazed at Magda like a young cannibal. And the time that Stella said "Aryan," it sounded to Rosa as if Stella had really said, "Let us devour her."

See **narrator**.

postmodernism In literature, postmodernism refers to a loose grouping of writers in the post–World War II era who carry on the agenda of modernism, inasmuch as they reject traditional literary conventions, embrace experimentation, and see contemporary life as bleak and fragmented. Rather than attempt to instill order through some literary device — as T. S. Eliot did with his use of allusions and myth or as William Butler Yeats did with his symbolic system — postmodern writers tend to eschew attempts to treat art as a corrective to modern malaises, and their writing celebrates or plays with the fragmentation of life instead of seeking to fix it. In addition, postmodern writers attack the distinction between "high" and "low" art maintained by modernists, and their writing engages with popular art forms like cartoons and television. Representative postmodern fiction writers include Don DeLillo, Thomas Pynchon, and Kurt Vonnegut; representative postmodern poets include John Ashbery, Ted Berrigan, Denise Levertov, and Frank O'Hara.

EXAMPLE:

"The Day Lady Died" by Frank O'Hara, p. 811

propaganda Work that aims to influence an audience about a debatable position or affiliation, not through rational or supported appeals but through one or more of the following: emotional manipulation, the selective use (and omission) of facts, spin, or any number of fallacious techniques. The word has mostly negative connotations.

EXAMPLE:

See the posters in The Importance of Being Earnest *and the Satiric Tradition, page 569.*

prose poem A blending of prose and poetry, usually resembling prose in its use of sentences without line breaks and poetry in its use of quintessentially poetic devices such as figurative language. A prose poem makes traditional genre distinctions problematic. See also **form**.

protagonist The main character in a work; often a hero or heroine, but not always.

EXAMPLE:

In Conrad's Heart of Darkness *(p. 327), the protagonist is Marlow, who is also the novella's narrator.*

psychological lens See **critical lenses**.

pun A play on words that derives its humor from the replacement of one word with another that has a similar pronunciation or spelling but a different meaning. A pun can also derive humor from the use of a single word that has more than one meaning.

EXAMPLE:

The title of Oscar Wilde's The Importance of Being Earnest *(p. 518) is a pun on the name of the play's protagonist, Ernest.*

quatrain See **stanza**.

reading journal A two-column journal promoting active reading; the reader identifies a phrase, line, or passage on the left-hand side and records questions, reactions, and reflections on the right-hand side.

EXAMPLE:

See page 10 for a reading journal on a passage from "Everyday Use" by Alice Walker.

realism Describing a literary technique, the goal of which is to render work that feels true, immediate, natural, and realistic.

EXAMPLE:

Realism characterizes Phil Klay's technique in "Ten Kliks South" (p. 1198).

refrain A line, lines, or a stanza in a poem that repeat(s) at intervals.

EXAMPLE:

"A drone pilot works a twelve-hour shift, then goes home"
This refrain appears in Jill McDonough's "Twelve-Hour Shifts" (p. 1225).

resolution The working out of a plot's conflicts, following the climax. See also **plot**.

reversal When, in a narrative, the protagonist's fortunes take an unforeseen turn.

EXAMPLE:

In Frankenstein, *Victor's reversal of fortune begins when he first views the monster he has created and brought to life (p. 852).*

See also **plot**.

rhetorical question A question asked for stylistic effect and emphasis to make a point rather than to solicit an answer.

EXAMPLE:

Men of England, wherefore plough
For the lords who lay ye low?

— PERCY BYSSHE SHELLEY, "Song: To the Men of England," p. 802

rhyme The repetition of the same (or similar) vowel or consonant sounds or constructions. A rhyme at the end of two or more lines of poetry is called an end rhyme. A rhyme that occurs within a line is called an internal rhyme. A rhyme that pairs sounds that are similar but not exactly the same is called a near rhyme or a slant rhyme. A rhyme that only works because the words look the same is called an eye rhyme or a sight rhyme. Rhyme often follows a pattern, called a rhyme scheme.

EXAMPLES:

End rhyme:

England hath need of thee: she is a fen
Of stagnant waters: altar, sword, and pen,

— WILLIAM WORDSWORTH, "London, 1802" p. 1056

Internal rhyme:

And kiss this paper for thy love's dear sake,

— ANNE BRADSTREET, "Before the Birth of One of Her Children," p. 276

Near rhyme or slant rhyme:

An erring lace, which here and there
Enthralls the crimson stomacher,

— ROBERT HERRICK, "Delight in Disorder," p. 123

Eye rhyme:

"Sisters and brothers, little Maid,
How many may you be?"
"How many? Seven in all," she said,
And wondering looked at me.

— WILLIAM WORDSWORTH, "We Are Seven," p. 278

rhythm The general pattern of stressed and unstressed syllables. See also **meter**.

EXAMPLE:

Whose herds | with milk, | whose fields | with bread,
Whose flocks | supply | him with | attire;
Whose trees | in sum | mer yield | him shade,
In win | ter, fire.

— ALEXANDER POPE, "The Quiet Life," p. 446

rising action The events, marked by increasing tension and conflict, that build up to a story's **climax**.

EXAMPLE:

In "Everyday Use" by Alice Walker (p. 1016), the rising action centers on the growing conflict between Dee's new culture and values and those of her family. This conflict increases as the disagreement about who should have the quilts intensifies, ultimately leading to the climax of the story.

romanticism In literature, a late eighteenth- to early nineteenth-century movement that emphasized beauty for beauty's sake, the natural world, emotion, imagination, the value of a nation's past and its folklore, and the heroic roles of the individual and the artist. Some prominent romantic poets in this book include Percy Bysshe Shelley, Lord Byron, Samuel Taylor Coleridge, and John Keats.

EXAMPLE:

"She Walks in Beauty" by Lord Byron, p. 603

round character See **character**.

run-on line See **enjambment**.

sarcasm See **irony, verbal**.

satire A literary or an artistic work that uses irony, wit, and humor to critique society or an individual in an attempt to effect change.

EXAMPLE:

"How to Write the Great American Indian Novel" by Sherman Alexie, p. 570

Horatian satire Named for the Roman poet Horace, this type of satire often points out vanity, foolish behavior, superficiality, or self-absorption.

EXAMPLE:

"PROM KING AND QUEEN SEEK U.N. RECOGNITION OF THEIR OWN COUNTRY . . . PROMVANIA!" by Matthea Harvey, p. 573

Juvenalian satire Named for the Roman poet Juvenal, this type of satire is angry, usually sarcastic in tone, and often bitter in its expression of contempt for and disgust with specific behavior, political policy, or social practice.

EXAMPLE:

"I Want Out" Anti-Vietnam War poster, p. 570

scene A subdivision of an act in a play. Scenes usually break up the action into logical chunks. Many contemporary plays, however, contain only sequences of scenes, without an overarching act structure. See also **act**.

secondary character See **character**.

sentence Specific types of sentences discussed in this book include the following:

complex sentence A sentence containing an independent clause and one or more subordinate clauses (beginning with words such as *after*, *before*, *although*, *because*, *until*, *when*, *while*, and *if*).

EXAMPLE:

He was known as Motorbike Bill because he repeatedly built and rebuilt his Triumph.

— HANIF KUREISHI, "We're Not Jews," p. 1023

compound sentence Two independent clauses joined by a coordinating conjunction (*and*, *but*, *or*, *nor*, *for*, *yet*, or *so*) or a semicolon.

EXAMPLE:

His voice seemed about to crack and the grandmother's head cleared for an instant.

— FLANNERY O'CONNOR, "A Good Man Is Hard to Find," p. 848

compound-complex sentence A combination of a compound sentence and a complex sentence; it is often fairly long.

EXAMPLE:

Sometimes numerous lumps of metal stood on rags around the skeleton of the bike, and in the late evening Big Bill revved up the machine while his record player balanced on the windowsill repeatedly blared out a 45 called "Rave On."

— HANIF KUREISHI, "We're Not Jews," p. 1023

cumulative sentence A sentence in which an independent clause is followed by details, qualifications, or modifications in subordinate clauses or phrases.

EXAMPLE:

Connie liked the way he was dressed, which was the way all of them dressed: tight faded jeans stuffed into black, scuffed boots, a belt that pulled his waist in and showed how lean he was, and a white pull-over shirt that was a little soiled and showed the hard small muscles of his arms and shoulders.

— JOYCE CAROL OATES, "Where Are You Going, Where Have You Been?" p. 431

imperative sentence A sentence that issues a command. The subject of an imperative sentence is often implied rather than explicit.

EXAMPLE:

Make sure you show how Africans have music and rhythm deep in their souls, and eat things no other humans eat.

— BINYAVANGA WAINAINA, "How to Write about Africa," p. 414

interrupted sentence A sentence of any pattern modified by interruptions that add descriptive details, state conditions, suggest uncertainty, voice possible alternative views, or present qualifications.

EXAMPLE:

I took refuge in the courtyard belonging to the house which I inhabited; where I remained during the rest of the night, walking up and down in the greatest agitation, listening attentively, catching and fearing each sound as if it were to announce the approach of the demoniacal corpse to which I had so miserably given life.

— MARY SHELLEY, *Frankenstein*, p. 876

periodic sentence A sentence that begins with details, qualifications, or modifications, building toward the main clause.

EXAMPLE:

For when I view them in turn, whether it be our chief hostess herself, whose good heart, whose too good heart, has become a byword with all who know her, or her sister, who seems to be gifted with perennial youth and whose singing must have been a surprise and a revelation to us all to-night, or, last but not least, when I consider our youngest hostess, talented, cheerful, hard-working and the best of nieces, I confess, Ladies and Gentlemen, that I do not know to which of them I should award the prize.

— JAMES JOYCE, *The Dead*, p. 505

simple sentence A sentence composed of one main clause without any subordinate clauses.

EXAMPLE:

I passed the night wretchedly.

— MARY SHELLEY, *Frankenstein*, p. 877

sestet See **stanza**.

setting Where and when a story takes place.

EXAMPLE:

It was a big, squarish frame house that had once been white, decorated with cupolas and spires and scrolled balconies in the heavily lightsome style of the seventies, set on what had once been our most select street. But garages and cotton gins had encroached and obliterated even the august names of that neighborhood; only Miss Emily's house was left, lifting its stubborn and coquettish decay above the cotton wagons and the gasoline pumps — an eyesore among eyesores. And now Miss Emily had gone to join the representatives of those august names where they lay in the cedar-bemused cemetery among the ranked and anonymous graves of Union and Confederate soldiers who fell at the battle of Jefferson.

— WILLIAM FAULKNER, "A Rose for Emily," p. 585

setting, social The manners, mores, customs, rituals, and codes of conduct in a work; an author may suggest approval or disapproval of any of these through a description of place.

EXAMPLE:

See the excerpt from 1984 *by George Orwell, page 26.*

Shakespearean sonnet See **sonnet**.

shift A point in a poem that indicates a change in the speaker's perspective.

EXAMPLE:

See the seventh stanza of "Digging" (p. 109):

The cold smell of potato mould, the squelch and slap.
Of soggy peat, the curt cuts of an edge.
Through living roots awaken in my head.
But I've no spade to follow men like them.

sight rhyme See **rhyme**.

simile A figure of speech used to explain or clarify an idea by comparing it explicitly to something else, using the words *like*, *as*, or *as though* to do so.

EXAMPLE:

Martha was a poet, with the poet's sensibilities, and her feet would be brown and bare, the toenails unpainted, the eyes chilly and somber like the ocean in March, and though it was painful, he wondered who had been with her that afternoon.

— TIM O'BRIEN, "The Things They Carried," p. 1074

simple sentence See **sentence**.

slang See **colloquial language/colloquialism**.

slant rhyme See **rhyme**.

soliloquy In a play, a monologue in which a character, alone on the stage, reveals his or her thoughts or emotions.

EXAMPLE:

See Hamlet's "To be, or not to be" speech in Hamlet *by William Shakespeare, pages 683–84.*

sonnet A poetic form composed of fourteen lines in iambic pentameter that adheres to a particular rhyme scheme. The two most common types are the following:

Petrarchan sonnet Also known as the Italian sonnet, its fourteen lines are divided into an octave and a sestet. The octave rhymes *abba, abba*; the sestet that follows can have a variety of different rhyme schemes: *cdcdcd*, *cdecde*, *cddcdd*.

EXAMPLE:

"The World Is Too Much with Us" by William Wordsworth, p. 447

Shakespearean sonnet Also known as the English sonnet, its fourteen lines are composed of three quatrains and a couplet, and its rhyme scheme is *abab, cdcd, efef, gg*.

EXAMPLE:

"My mistress' eyes are nothing like the sun" by William Shakespeare, p. 619

sound The musical quality of poetry, as created through techniques such as **rhyme**, **enjambment**, **caesura**, **alliteration**, **assonance**, **consonance, onomatopoeia**, **rhythm**, and **cadence**.

speaker This term is most frequently used in the context of drama and poetry. In drama, the speaker is the character who is currently delivering lines. In poetry, the speaker is the person who is expressing a point of view in the poem, either the author or a persona created by the author. See also **narrator**; **persona**; **point of view**.

EXAMPLE:

In Ben Jonson's "On My First Son" (p. 275), the speaker is a father, presumably Jonson, addressing his dead son.

Farewell, thou child of my right hand, and joy;
My sin was too much hope of thee, loved boy:
Seven years thou wert lent to me, and I thee pay,
Exacted by thy fate, on the just day.

spondee See **meter**.

sprung rhythm A meter developed out of Gerard Manley Hopkins's attempt to mirror natural speech patterns in his poetry. In sprung rhythm, the number of stressed syllables in each line is the same, while the number of unstressed syllables can vary. This means that the types of feet employed in each line can vary.

EXAMPLE:

"God's Grandeur" by Gerard Manley Hopkins, p. 1036

stage directions Any notes in the script of a play written by the author that set guidelines for the performance, explaining, for example, what the set should look like, how actors should move and deliver certain lines, and so on. They are generally italicized.

EXAMPLE:

See stage directions for A Raisin in the Sun *by Lorraine Hansberry on page 56.*

stanza Lines in a poem that the poet has chosen to group together, usually separated from other lines by a space. Stanzas within a poem usually have repetitive forms, often sharing rhyme schemes or rhythmic structures.

A number of frequently used stanza types have specific names:

couplet A two-line, rhyming stanza.

EXAMPLE:

And yet, by heaven, I think my love as rare
As any she belied with false compare.

— WILLIAM SHAKESPEARE, "My mistress' eyes are nothing like the sun," p. 619

tercet A three-line stanza.

EXAMPLE:

"Siren Song" by Margaret Atwood, p. 605

quatrain A four-line stanza.

EXAMPLE:

Yet this inconstancy is such
As thou too shalt adore;
I could not love thee, Dear, so much,
Loved I not Honor more.

— RICHARD LOVELACE, "To Lucasta, Going to the Wars," p. 1230

sestet A six-line stanza.

EXAMPLE:

Today we have naming of parts. Yesterday,
We had daily cleaning. And tomorrow morning,
We shall have what to do after firing. But today,
Today we have naming of parts. Japonica
Glistens like coral in all of the neighboring gardens,
And today we have naming of parts.

— HENRY REED, "Naming of Parts," p. 1215

octet An eight-line stanza.

EXAMPLE:

I have walked and prayed for this young child an hour
And heard the sea-wind scream upon the tower,
And under the arches of the bridge, and scream
In the elms above the flooded stream;

Imagining in excited reverie
That the future years had come,
Dancing to a frenzied drum,
Out of the murderous innocence of the sea.

— WILLIAM BUTLER YEATS, "A Prayer for My Daughter," p. 280

stream of consciousness A technique in which prose follows the logic and flow of a character's (or multiple characters') thought processes — associations, tangents, seemingly strange transitions — rather than a more ordered narrative.

EXAMPLE:

"Bliss" by Katherine Mansfield, p. 576

structure The organization of a work.

style The way a literary work is written. Style is produced by an author's choices in **diction**, **syntax**, **imagery**, **figurative language**, and other literary elements.

suspense A literary device that uses tension to make the plot more exciting; it is the effect created by artful delays and selective dissemination of information.

EXAMPLE:

An excellent example of suspense in fiction is Joyce Carol Oates's "Where Are You Going, Where Have You Been?" (p. 426).

symbol A setting, an object, or an event in a story that carries more than literal meaning and therefore represents something significant to understanding the meaning of a work of literature.

EXAMPLE:

I flew around like mad to get ready, and before forty-eight hours I was crossing the Channel to show myself to my employers, and sign the contract. In a very few hours I arrived in a city that always makes me think of a whited sepulchre. Prejudice no doubt. I had no difficulty in finding the Company's offices. It was the biggest thing in the town, and everybody I met was full of it. They were going to run an over-sea empire, and make no end of coin by trade.

— JOSEPH CONRAD, *Heart of Darkness*, p. 332

synecdoche A figure of speech in which part of something is used to represent the whole. Compare to **metonymy**.

EXAMPLE:

"They were called legs or grunts."

— TIM O'BRIEN, "The Things They Carried," p. 1071

syntax The arrangement of words into phrases, clauses, and sentences in a prose passage. This includes word order (subject-verb-object, for instance, or an inverted structure); the length and structure of sentences (simple, compound, or complex), phrases, and clauses; the chronology of passages; the preference of various parts of speech over others; the use of connectors between and within sentences; and more.

EXAMPLE:

Have you ever seen a lame animal, perhaps a dog run over by some careless person rich enough to own a car, sidle up to someone who is ignorant enough to be kind to him?[1] That is the way my Maggie walks.[2] She has been like this, chin on chest, eyes on ground, feet in shuffle, ever since the fire that burned the other house to the ground.[3]

—ALICE WALKER, "Everyday Use," p. 1017

1. *complex sentence; also a question*
2. *OSV structure, a simple declarative sentence*
3. *complex sentence; repetition of three parallel modifying phrases creates rhythm and emphasis*

syntax, poetic Similar to syntax in prose, poetic syntax also includes the arrangement of words into lines — where they break or do not break, the use of enjambment or caesura, and line length/patterns.

EXAMPLE:

For this, for everything, we are out of tune; *(caesura)*
It moves us not. —Great God! I'd rather be *(caesura)*
A Pagan suckled in a creed outworn; *(enjambment)*

—WILLIAM WORDSWORTH, "The World Is Too Much with Us," p. 447

tercet See **stanza**.

theatrical property Known more commonly as a **prop**, this is a term for any object used onstage by an actor in a play.

EXAMPLE:

During Hamlet's soliloquy in act V, scene i, of Shakespeare's Hamlet *(p. 720), the actor makes use of Yorick's skull as a prop.*

theme Underlying issues or ideas of a work.

EXAMPLE:

See the section on theme, page 45.

thesis statement The chief claim that a writer makes in any argumentative piece of writing, usually stated in one sentence.

think aloud dialogue The process of reading bit by bit a poem or passage with a partner, stopping frequently to discuss ideas, questions, or revelations engendered by the text.

tone A speaker's attitude or stance as exposed through stylistic choices. (Tone is often confused with **mood**, another element of style that describes the feeling created by the work.) Along with mood, tone provides the emotional coloring of a work and is created by some combination of the other elements of style.

EXAMPLE:

In your text, treat Africa as if it were one country. It is hot and dusty with rolling grasslands and huge herds of animals and tall, thin people who are starving. Or it is hot and steamy with very short people who eat primates. Don't get bogged down with precise descriptions. Africa is big: fifty-four countries, nine hundred million people who are too busy starving and dying and warring and emigrating to read your book. The continent is full of deserts, jungles, highlands, savannahs and many other things, but your reader doesn't care about all that, so keep your descriptions romantic and evocative and unparticular.

— BINYAVANGA WAINAINA, "How to Write about Africa," p. 414

tragedy A serious dramatic work in which the protagonist experiences a series of unfortunate reversals due to some character trait, referred to as a *tragic flaw*. The most common tragic flaw is hubris. *Hubris* comes from the Greek word *hybris*, which means pride. Modern tragedies tend to depart from some of the genre's classical conventions, portraying average rather than noble characters and attributing the protagonist's downfall to something other than a flaw in character — for example, to social circumstances.

EXAMPLES:

Othello *(p. 1086) and* Hamlet *(p. 651) by William Shakespeare*

tragic flaw See **tragedy**.

tragic hero A character who possesses a flaw or commits an error in judgment that leads to his or her downfall and a reversal of fortune.

EXAMPLE:

Hamlet in William Shakespeare's Hamlet *(p. 651).*

transcendental movement A reaction against both rationalism and empiricism in philosophy, as well as austere Calvinist doctrines about human nature, transcendentalism emphasized knowledge via mystical insight, the divine spark in each human being, and the immanence of God in nature. Beginning in Europe and drawing inspiration from European thinkers, among them Immanuel Kant and Samuel Taylor Coleridge, the transcendental movement flourished in the nineteenth-century United States, where it was linked with Christian Unitarianism. Key thinkers include Ralph Waldo Emerson and Henry David Thoreau.

EXAMPLE:

"The Apology" by Ralph Waldo Emerson, p. 448

trochee See **meter**.

understatement The presentation or framing of something as less important, urgent, awful, good, powerful, and so on than it actually is, often for satiric or comical effect; the opposite of hyperbole, it is often used along with this technique, and for similar effect.

EXAMPLE:

Bad Western characters may include children of Tory cabinet ministers, Afrikaners, employees of the World Bank. When talking about exploitation by foreigners, mention the Chinese and Indian traders. Blame the West for Africa's situation. But do not be too specific.

— BINYAVANGA WAINAINA, "How to Write about Africa," p. 415

unreliable narrator See **narrator**.

verbal irony See **irony, verbal**.

verse A broad term, verse refers to a piece of writing that is metered and rhythmic. (Free verse is an exception to this, being a piece of writing grouped with verse rather than prose, even though it lacks a meter.) The term *verse* can also be used to refer to poetry in general. See also **meter; rhyme; rhythm**.

vignette A short narrative scene or description, often one in a series. If a story or novel is composed of a series of vignettes, it often relies on a thematic, rather than a plot-driven, structure.

villanelle A form of poetry in which five tercets (rhyme scheme *aba*) are followed by a quatrain (rhyme scheme *abaa*). At the end of tercets two and four, the first line of tercet one is repeated. At the end of tercets three and five, the last line of tercet one is repeated. These two repeated lines, called *refrain lines*, are again repeated to conclude the quatrain. Much of the power of this form lies in its repeated lines and their subtly shifting sense or meaning over the course of the poem.

EXAMPLE:

"Do not go gentle into that good night" by Dylan Thomas, p. 806

wordplay Techniques by which writers manipulate language for effect; examples include puns (the deliberate misuse of words that sound alike) or double entendres (expressions with two meanings).

EXAMPLE:

LADY BRACKNELL: *Good afternoon, dear Algernon, I hope you are behaving very well.*

ALGERNON: *I'm feeling very well, Aunt Augusta.*

LADY BRACKNELL: *That's not quite the same thing. In fact the two things rarely go together.*

(Sees Jack and bows to him with icy coldness.)

ALGERNON [TO GWENDOLEN]: *Dear me, you are smart!*

GWENDOLEN: *I am always smart! Aren't I, Mr. Worthing?*

JACK: *You are quite perfect, Miss Fairfax.*

GWENDOLEN: *Oh! I hope I am not that. It would leave no room for developments, and I intend to develop in many directions.*

— OSCAR WILDE, *The Importance of Being Earnest*, pp. 523–24

zeugma Pronounced *zoyg-muh*, a technique in which one verb is used with multiple (and often incongruous) objects, so that the definition of the verb is changed, complicated, or made both literal and figurative.

EXAMPLE:

They carried chess sets, basketballs, Vietnamese-English dictionaries, insignia of rank, Bronze Stars and Purple Hearts, plastic cards imprinted with the Code of Conduct. They carried diseases, among them malaria and dysentery. They carried lice and ringworm and leeches and paddy algae and various rots and molds. They carried the land itself — Vietnam, the place, the soil — a powdery orange-red dust that covered their boots and fatigues and faces.

— TIM O'BRIEN, "The Things They Carried," p. 1077

verse A [illegible] verse [illegible] a piece of writing [illegible] rhythm [illegible] is an exception to this [illegible] piece of writing [illegible] even though it lacks a meter). The term verse can also be used to refer to poetry in general. (See also free verse; rhythm.)

vignette A brief portrait, scene or description, often one in a series [illegible] story or novel [illegible] composed of a series of [illegible] rather than a plot-driven [illegible]

villanelle A form of poetry in which five tercets [illegible] followed by a quatrain [illegible] At the end of tercets two and four the first line [illegible] At the end of tercets three and five [illegible] is repeated [illegible] the power of the form lies in its repeated lines [illegible] over the course of the poem.

EXAMPLE

[illegible] that good night [illegible] Dylan Thomas [illegible]

wordplay Techniques by which writers manipulate language for effect. Examples include [illegible] with two meanings [illegible]

EXAMPLE

[illegible]

zeugma [illegible] in which one word is linked with [illegible]

EXAMPLE

[illegible]

ACKNOWLEDGMENTS

Chinua Achebe, "An Image of Africa: Racism in Conrad's 'Heart of Darkness'" from HOPES AND IMPEDIMENTS: SELECTED ESSAYS. Copyright © 1988 by Chinua Achebe. Used by permission of Doubleday, an imprint of the Knopf Doubleday Publishing Group, a division of Penguin Random House LLC. All rights reserved. Any third party use of this material, outside of this publication, is prohibited. Interested parties must apply directly to Penguin Random House LLC for permission. Canadian rights courtesy The Wylie Agency LLC.

Chimamanda Adichie, "Apollo," originally published in *The New Yorker*. Copyright © 2015 by Chimamanda Adichie. Used by permission of The Wylie Agency LLC.

Anna Akhmatova, "The First Long-Range Artillery Shell in Leningrad" from ANNA AKHMATOVA: POEMS, tr. by Lyn Coffin. Copyright © 1983 by Lyn Coffin. Used by permission of W. W. Norton & Company, Inc.

Brian Aldiss, "Super-Toys Last All Summer Long" first published in *Harper's Bazaar*, Dec. 1969. Permission granted by Brian Aldiss and his agent, Robin Straus Agency, Inc. Any third party use of this material, outside of this publication, is prohibited. Interested parties must apply directly to Robin Straus Agency, Inc. for permission.

Sherman Alexie, "How to Write the Great American Indian Novel" reprinted from THE SUMMER OF BLACK WIDOWS. Copyright © 1996 by Sherman Alexie. Reprinted by permission of Hanging Loose Press.

Yehuda Amichai, "The Eve of Rosh Hashanah" from THE SELECTED POETRY OF YEHUDA AMICHAI, trans. by Chana Bloch and Stephen Mitchell. Copyright © 1986, 1996, 2013 by Chana Bloch and Stephen Mitchell. Reprinted by permission of the University of California Press via the Copyright Clearance Center.

Margaret Atwood, "Siren Song" from SELECTED POEMS 1965–1975. Copyright © 1976 by Margaret Atwood. Reprinted by permission of Houghton Mifflin Harcourt Publishing Company. All rights reserved. Published in Canada in SELECTED POEMS 1966–1984. Reprinted by permission of Oxford University Press Canada and by permission of the author Margaret Atwood. "Gertrude Talks Back" from GOOD BONES AND SIMPLE MURDERS. Copyright © 1983, 1992, 1994 by O.W. Toad Ltd. Used by permission of Nan A. Talese, an imprint of the Knopf Doubleday Publishing Group, a division of Penguin Random House LLC. All rights reserved. Any third party use of this material, outside of this publication, is prohibited. Interested parties must apply directly to Penguin Random House LLC for permission. Rights in Canada by permission of McClelland & Stewart, a division of Penguin Random House Canada Limited. "It is Dangerous to Read Newspapers" from SELECTED POEMS, 1965–1975. Copyright © 1976 by Margaret Atwood. Reprinted by permission of Houghton Mifflin Harcourt Publishing Company. All rights reserved. Published in Canada in SELECTED POEMS 1966–1984. Reprinted by permission of the publisher Oxford University Press Canada and the author.

W. H. Auden, "The Unknown Citizen," copyright © 1940 and renewed 1968 by W. H. Auden. From W. H. AUDEN, COLLECTED POEMS. Used by permission of Random House, an imprint and division of Penguin Random House LLC. All rights reserved. Any third party use of this material, outside of this publication, is prohibited. Interested parties must apply directly to Penguin Random House LLC for permission. Electronic rights by permission of Curtis Brown, Ltd.

James Baldwin, "Sonny's Blues" was originally published in *Partisan Review*. Copyright © 1957 by James Baldwin. Copyright renewed. Collected in GOING TO MEET THE MAN, published by Vintage Books. Used by arrangement with the James Baldwin Estate.

Dara Barnat, "Imprint" was previously published in *Yew: A Journal of Innovative Writings & Images by Women*. Reprinted by permission of the author.

Elizabeth Bishop, "One Art" from THE COMPLETE POEMS 1927–1979. Copyright © 1979, 1983 by Alice Helen Methfessel. Reprinted by permission of Farrar, Straus and Giroux, LLC.

Richard Blanco, "Mother Country" and "Madre Patria" from FOR ALL OF US, ONE TODAY: AN INAUGURAL POET'S JOURNEY. Copyright © 2013 by Richard Blanco. Republished with permission of Beacon Press, permission conveyed through Copyright Clearance Center, Inc.

Jorge Luis Borges, "A Blind Man" trans. by Alastair Reid, copyright © 1999 by Maria Kodama. Translation copyright © 1999 by Alastair Reid from SELECTED POEMS by Jorge Luis Borges, ed. by Alexander Coleman. Used by permission of Viking Books, an imprint of Penguin Publishing Group, a division of Penguin Random House LLC, The Wylie Agency, The Colchie Agency, GP, and Penguin Canada, a division of Penguin Random House Canada Limited. Collected in LA ROSE PROFUNDA. Copyright © 1995 by Maria Kodama.

Kamau Brathwaite, "Ogun" from THE ARRIVANTS: A NEW WORLD TRILOGY (1973), copyright © 1967, 1968, 1969, 1973 by Kamau Brathwaite. By permission of Oxford University Press.

Gwendolyn Brooks, "We Real Cool" and "The Chicago Defender Sends a Reporter to Little Rock" are reprinted by consent of Brooks Permissions.

Jericho Brown, "Dear Dr. Frankenstein" from THE NEW TESTAMENT. Copyright © 2014 by Jericho Brown. Reprinted with the permission of The Permissions Company, Inc. on behalf of Copper Canyon Press, www.coppercanyonpress.org.

Isaac Butler, "Why is Othello Black?" from *Slate*, Nov. 11, 2015. Copyright © 2015 by The Slate Group. All rights reserved. Used by permission and protected by the Copyright Laws of the United States. The printing, copying, redistribution, or retransmission of this Content without express written permission is prohibited.

Jannifer Fumiko Cahill, "Where You Fell" first published in *The Greensboro Review*, Spring 2007. Reprinted by permission of the author.

Cathy Linh Che, "Split" from SPLIT. Copyright © 2014 by Cathy Linh Che. Reprinted with the permission of The Permission Company, Inc. on behalf of Alice James Books, www.alicejamesbooks.org.

John Cheever, "Reunion" from THE STORIES OF JOHN CHEEVER. Copyright © 1978 by John Cheever. Used by permission of Alfred A. Knopf, an imprint of the Knopf Doubleday Publishing Group, a division of Penguin Random House LLC. All rights reserved. Any third party use of this material, outside of this publication, is prohibited. Interested parties must apply directly to Penguin Random House LLC for permission.

Marilyn Chin, "Turtle Soup" from THE PHOENIX GONE, THE TERRACE EMPTY (Minneapolis: Milkweed Editions, 2009). Copyright © 2009 by Marilyn Chin. Reprinted with permission from Milkweed Editions, www.milkweed.org.

Sandra Cisneros, from WOMAN HOLLERING CREEK. Copyright © 1991 by Sandra Cisneros. Published by Vintage Books, a division of Penguin Random House, Inc. New York and originally in hardcover by Random House, Inc. By permission of Susan Bergholz Literary Services, New York, NY and Lamy, NM. All rights reserved.

Lucille Clifton, "in the inner city" from THE COLLECTED POEMS OF LUCILLE CLIFTON. Copyright © 1987 by Lucille Clifton. Reprinted with the permission of The Permissions Company, Inc. on behalf of BOA Editions Ltd., www.boaeditions.org.

Billy Collins, "Weighing the Dog" from QUESTIONS ABOUT ANGELS. Copyright © 1991 by Billy Collins. Reprinted by permission of the University of Pittsburgh Press.

Countee Cullen, "Heritage" from MY SOUL'S HIGH SONG (NY: Doubleday 1991). Copyrights held by the Amistad Research Center Tulane University. Administrated by Thompson and Thompson, Brooklyn, NY.

E.E. Cummings, "anyone lived in a pretty how town." Copyright 1940, © 1968, 1991 by the Trustees for the E.E. Cummings Trust, from COMPLETE POEMS: 1904–1962, edited by George J. Firmage. Used by permission of Liveright Publishing Corporation.

Edwidge Danticat, "The Book of the Dead" from THE DEW BREAKER. Copyright © 2004 by Edwidge Danticat. Used by permission of Alfred A. Knopf, an imprint of the Knopf Doubleday Publishing Group, a division of Penguin Random House LLC. All rights reserved. Any third party use of this material outside of this publication, is prohibited. Interested parties must apply directly to Penguin Random House LLC for permission.

Mahmoud Darwish, "Identity Card" as translated by Denys Johnson-Davies. Reprinted by permission of Denys-Johnson Davies and Actes Sud for the Estate of Mahmoud Darwish. Copyright © by Mahmoud Darwish.

Alison Hawthorne Deming, "Science" from SCIENCE AND OTHER POEMS (1994) is reprinted by permission of the publisher, Louisiana State University Press.

Toi Derricotte, "Black Boys Play the Classics" from TENDER by Toi Derricotte. Copyright © 1997. Reprinted by permission of the University of Pittsburgh Press.

Natalie Diaz, "The Facts of Art" from WHEN MY BROTHER WAS AN AZTEC. Copyright © 2012 by Natalie Diaz. Reprinted with the permission of The Permissions Company, Inc., on behalf of Copper Canyon Press, www.coppercanonpress.org.

Emily Dickinson, from THE POEMS OF EMILY DICKINSON, edited by Thomas H. Johnson, Cambridge, Mass.: The Belknap Press of Harvard University Press. Copyright © 1951, 1955 by the President and Fellows of Harvard College. Copyright renewed 1979, 1983 by the President and Fellows of Harvard College. Copyright © 1914, 1918, 1919, 1924, 1929, 1930, 1932, 1935, 1937, 1942 by Martha Dickinson Bianchi. Copyright © 1952, 1957, 1958, 1963, 1965 by Mary L. Hampson. Reprinted by permission of the publisher.

Leconté Dill, "We Who Weave," first published in *Poetry* Jan. 2016 issue, is reprinted by permission of the author.

Chitra Banerjee Divakaruni, "Indian Movie, New Jersey" from LEAVING YUBA CITY: POEMS, copyright © 1997 by Chitra Banerjee Divakaruni. Used by permission of Doubleday, an imprint of the Knopf Doubleday Publishing Group, a division of Penguin Random House LLC. All rights reserved. Any third party use of this material, outside of this publication, is prohibited. Interested parties must apply directly to Penguin Random House LLC for permission.

Mark Doty, "Golden Retrievals" from SWEET MACHINE. Copyright © 1998 by Mark Doty. Reprinted by permission of HarperCollins Publishers.

Carol Ann Duffy, "Penelope" from THE WORLD'S WIFE. Copyright © 1999 by Carol Ann Duffy. Reprinted by permission of Farrar, Straus and Giroux, LLC and Picador c/o Pan Macmillan.

Cornelius Eady, "I'm a Fool to Love You" from THE AUTOBIOGRAPHY OF A JUKE BOX published by Carnegie Mellon University Press in 2007. Copyright © 2007 by Cornelius Eady. Reprinted by permission of the author.

T.S. Eliot, "The Love Song of J. Alfred Prufrock" from COLLECTED POEMS 1909–1962. From "Tradition and the Individual Talent" from SELECTED ESSAYS by T.S. Eliot. Reprinted by permission of Faber & Faber Ltd.

William Faulkner, "A Rose for Emily" copyright © 1930 and renewed 1958 by William Faulkner from COLLECTED STORIES OF WILLIAM FAULKNER. Used by permission of Random House, an imprint and division of Penguin Random House LLC. All rights reserved. Any third party use of this material, outside of this publication, is prohibited. Interested parties must apply directly to Penguin Random House LLC for permission. Electronic rights by permission of W. W. Norton & Company, Inc.

F. Scott Fitzgerald, from THE GREAT GATSBY is reprinted with the permission of Scribner, a division of Simon & Schuster, Inc. Copyright © 1925 by Charles Scribner's Sons. Copyright renewed 1953 by Frances Scot Fitzgerald Lanahan. All rights reserved.

Robert Frost, "Mending Wall" and "The Most of It" from the book THE POETRY OF ROBERT FROST, edited by Edward Connery Lathem. Copyright © 1930, 1939, 1969 by Henry Holt and Company, copyright © 1942, 1958 by Robert Frost, copyright © 1967, 1970 by Lesley Frost Ballantine. Reprinted by permission of Henry Holt and Company, LLC. All rights reserved.

Nicole Galland, excerpts from "Prologue" and pp. 369–370 from I, IAGO. Copyright © 2012 by Nicole Galland. Reprinted by permission of HarperCollins Publishers.

Marjorie Garber, excerpts from SHAKESPEARE AND MODERN CULTURE. Copyright © 2008 by Marjorie Garber. Used by permission of Pantheon Books, an imprint of the Knopf Doubleday Publishing Group, a division of Penguin Random House LLC. All rights reserved. Any third party use of this material, outside of this publication, is prohibited. Interested parties must apply directly to Penguin Random House LLC for permission.

Gabriel García Márquez, "One of These Days" from NO ONE WRITES TO THE COLONEL AND OTHER STORIES by Gabriel García Márquez and trans. by J.S. Bernstein. Copyright © 1968 in the English translation by Harper & Row, Publishers, Inc. Reprinted by permission of HarperCollins Publishers. "Un día de éstos" from LOS FUNERALES DE LA MAMA GRANDE. Copyright © 1962 by Gabriel García Márquez and Heirs of García Márquez. Electronic rights by permission of Agencia Literaria Carmen Balcells S.A.

Allen Ginsberg, "Is About" from DEATH & FAME: LAST POEMS 1993–1997. Copyright © 1999 by the Allen Ginsberg Trust. Reprinted by permission of HarperCollins Publishers.

Stephen Jay Gould, excerpts from DINOSAUR IN A HAYSTACK: REFLECTIONS IN NATURAL HISTORY. Copyright © 1995 by Stephen Jay Gould. Used by permission of Harmony Books, an imprint of the Crown Publishing Group, a division of Penguin Random House LLC. All rights reserved. Any third party use of this material, outside of this publication, is prohibited. Interested parties must apply directly to Penguin Random House LLC for permission.

Robert Graves, "To Lucasta on Going to the War — for the Fourth Time" first published in FAIRIES AND FUSILIERS and also collected in COMPLETE POEMS IN ONE VOLUME. Reprinted by permission of Carcanet Press Limited.

Nathalie Handal, "Caribe in Nueva York" from THE LIVES OF RAIN. Copyright © 2005 by Nathalie Handal. Permission granted by the author.

Lorraine Hansberry, Excerpts from A RAISIN IN THE SUN. Copyright © 1958 by Robert Nemiroff, as an unpublished work. Copyright © 1959, 1966, 1984 by Robert Nemiroff. Copyright renewed 1986, 1987 by Robert Nemiroff. Used by permission of Random House, an imprint and division of Penguin Random House LLC. All rights reserved. Any third party use of this material, outside of this publication is prohibited. Interested parties must apply directly to Penguin Random House LLC for permission.

Matthea Harvey, "Prom King and Queen Seek U.N. Recognition of Their Own Country . . . Promvania!" from IF THE TABLOIDS ARE TRUE WHAT ARE YOU? Copyright © 2014 by Matthea Harvey. Reprinted with the permission of The Permissions Company, Inc. on behalf of Graywolf Press, Minneapolis, Minnesota, www.graywolfpress.org.

Robert Hayden, "Those Winter Sundays," copyright © 1966 by Robert Hayden from COLLECTED POEMS OF ROBERT HAYDEN, ed. by Frederick Glaysher. Used by permission of Liveright Publishing Corp.

Terrance Hayes, "Talk" from WIND IN A BOX, copyright © 2006 by Terrance Hayes. Used by permission of Penguin Books, an imprint of Penguin Publishing Group, a division of Penguin Random House LLC.

Rebecca Hazelton, "My Husband," previously published in BEST AMERICAN POETRY (2015), ed. by David Lehman and Sherman Alexie. Reprinted by permission of Rebecca Hazelton.

Seamus Heaney, "Digging" from OPENED GROUND: SELECTED POEMS 1966–1996. Copyright © 1998 by Seamus Heaney. Reprinted by permission of Farrar, Straus & Giroux, LLC and Faber & Faber Ltd. "Bogland" from OPENED GROUND: SELECTED POEMS 1966–1996 by Seamus Heaney. Copyright © 1998 by Seamus Heaney. Reprinted by permission of Farrar, Straus, & Giroux LLC. Canadian rights courtesy of Faber & Faber Ltd.

Ernest Hemingway, from "The End of Something" is reprinted with the permission of Scribner, a division of Simon & Schuster, Inc. from THE SHORT STORIES OF ERNEST HEMINGWAY. Copyright © 1925 by Charles Scribner's Sons. Copyright renewed © 1953 by Ernest Hemingway. All rights reserved.

Zbigniew Herbert, "Elegy of Fortinbras" from THE COLLECTED POEMS: 1956–1998. Translated & edited by Alissa Valles. Copyright © 2007 The Estate of Zbigniew Herbert. Translation copyright © 2007 by HarperCollins Publishers LLC. Reprinted by permission of HarperCollins Publishers.

David Hernandez, "Lisa" from A HOUSE WAITNG FOR MUSIC. Copyright © 2003 by David Hernandez. Reprinted with the permission of The Permissions Company, Inc., on behalf of Tupelo Press, www.tupelopress.org.

Juan Felipe Herrera, "Half-Mexican" from NOTES ON THE ASSEMBLAGE. Copyright © 2015 by Juan Felipe Herrera. Reprinted by permission of City Lights Books.

Jennifer Hill, "Reading Othello and Watching a Girl Skip Rope" from IN A FINE FRENZY: POETS RESPOND TO SHAKESPEARE, ed. by David Starkey & Paul J. Willis (2005). Reprinted by permission of Jennifer Hill.

Jane Hirshfield, "This was once a love poem" from GIVEN SUGAR, GIVEN SALT. Copyright © 2001 by Jane Hirshfield. Reprinted by permission of HarperCollins Publishers.

Langston Hughes, "Mother to Son" from THE COLLECTED POEMS OF LANGSTON HUGHES, ed. by Arnold Rampersad with David Roessel, Associate Editor. Copyright © 1994 by the Estate of Langston Hughes. Used by permission of Alfred A. Knopf, an imprint of the Knopf Doubleday Publishing Group, a division of Penguin Random House LLC. All rights reserved. Any third party use of this material, outside of this publication, is prohibited. Interested parties must apply directly to Penguin Random House LLC for permission. Electronic rights by permission of Harold Ober Associates Incorporated.

Major Jackson, "Urban Renewal XVIII" from HOOPS. Copyright © 2006 by Major Jackson. Used by permission of W. W. Norton & Company, Inc.

Edward P. Jones, "The First Day" from LOST IN THE CITY. Copyright © 1992 by Edward P. Jones. Reprinted by permission of HarperCollins Publishers.

James Earl Jones, excerpts from "The Sun God" are reprinted by permission of the author. Copyright © 2013 by James Earl Jones.

Franz Kafka, "The Metamorphosis," translated by Alexis P. Walker. Reprinted by permission of Alexis P. Walker.

Jamaica Kincaid, "Girl" from AT THE BOTTOM OF THE RIVER. Copyright © 1983 by Jamaica Kincaid. Reprinted by permission of Farrar, Straus and Giroux, LLC.

Phil Klay, "Ten Kliks South" from REDEPLOYMENT. Copyright © 2014 by Phil Klay. Used by permission of Penguin Press, an imprint of Penguin Publishing Group, a division of Penguin Random House LLC.

Yusef Komunyakaa, "Between Days" from PLEASURE DOME: NEW AND COLLECTED POEMS. Copyright © 2001 by Yusef Komunyakaa. Published by Wesleyan University Press. Used by permission.

Maxine Kumin, "Woodchucks" from SELECTED POEMS 1960–1990, copyright © 1972, 1997 by Maxine Kumin. Used by permission of W. W. Norton & Company, Inc.

Hanif Kureishi, "We're Not Jews" from LOVE IN A BLUE TIME. Copyright © 1997 by Hanif Kureishi. All rights reserved. Reprinted with the permission of Scribner, a division of Simon & Schuster, Inc.

Jhumpa Lahiri, "Interpreter of Maladies" from INTERPRETER OF MALADIES. Copyright © 1999 by Jhumpa Lahiri. Reproduced by permission of Houghton Mifflin Harcourt Publishing Company. All rights reserved. Electronic rights courtesy of Sterling Lord Literistic.

Li-Young Lee, "The Hammock" from BOOK OF MY NIGHTS. Copyright © 2001 by Li-Young Lee. Reprinted with the permission of The Permissions Company, Inc., on behalf of BOA Editions, Ltd., www.boaeditions.org.

Doris Lessing, "The Old Chief Mshlanga" from AFRICAN STORIES is reprinted with the permission of Simon & Schuster, Inc. and Jonathan Clowes Ltd., London, on behalf of The Estate of Doris Lessing. Copyright © 1951, 1953, 1954, 1957, 1958, 1962, 1964, 1965, 1972 by Doris Lessing. All rights reserved.

Robin Coste Lewis, "Art & Craft" from VOYAGE OF THE SABLE VENUS: AND OTHER POEMS. Compilation copyright © 2015 by Robin Coste Lewis. Used by permission of Alfred A. Knopf, an imprint of the Knopf Doubleday Publishing Group, a division of Penguin Random House LLC. All rights reserved. Any third party use of this material, outside of this publication, is prohibited. Interested parties must apply directly to Penguin Random House LLC for permission.

C. S. Lewis, from SELECTED LITERARY ESSAYS by C. S. Lewis. Copyright © C. S. Lewis Pte. Ltd. 1969. Extract reprinted by permission of The C. S. Lewis Company Ltd.

Audre Lorde, "Movement Song" from THE COLLECTED POEMS OF AUDRE LORDE. Copyright © 1997 by The Audre Lorde Estate. Used by permission of W. W. Norton & Company, Inc.

Naguib Mahfouz, "Half a Day," copyright © 1991 by American University in Cairo Press, from THE TIME AND THE PLACE. Used by permission of Doubleday, an imprint of the Knopf Doubleday Publishing Group, a division of Penguin Random House LLC. All rights reserved. Any third party use of this material, outside of this publication, is prohibited. Interested parties must apply directly to Penguin Random House LLC for permission.

Amit Majmudar, "Welcome Home, Troops!" from DOTHEAD: POEMS, compilation copyright © 2016 by Amit Majmudar. Used by permission of Alfred A. Knopf, an imprint of the Knopf Doubleday Publishing Group, a division of Penguin Random House LLC. All rights reserved. Any third party use of this material, outside of this publication is prohibited. Interested parties must apply directly to Penguin Random House LLC for permission.

Jill McDonough, "Twelve-Hour Shifts" first published online on *Poem-a-Day*, Sept. 30, 2015 is reprinted by permission of the author.

Dunya Mikhail, "The War Works Hard" translated by Elizabeth Winslow from THE WAR WORKS HARD. Copyright © 2005 by Dunya Mikhail. Reprinted by permission of New Directions Publishing Corp.

Edna St. Vincent Millay, "Love is not all: it is not meat nor drink" from COLLECTED POEMS. Copyright 1931 © 1958 by Edna St. Vincent Millay and Norma Millay Ellis. Reprinted with the permission of The Permissions Company, Inc. on behalf of Holly Peppe, Literary Executor, The Edna St. Vincent Millay Society, www.millay.org.

Felix Mnthali, "The Stranglehold of English Lit" was previously published in ECHOES OF IBADAN and is reprinted by permission of the author.

Toni Morrison, excerpts from SONG OF SOLOMON. Copyright © 1977 by Toni Morrison. Used by permission of Alfred A. Knopf, an imprint of the Knopf Doubleday Publishing Group, a division of Penguin Random House LLC. All rights reserved. Any third party use of this material, outside of this publication, is prohibited. Interested parties must apply directly to Penguin Random House LLC for permission. Excerpts from DESDEMONA (Oberon Books 2012) are reprinted by permission of the author.

Bharati Mukherjee, "The Management of Grief" from THE MIDDLEMAN AND OTHER STORIES, copyright © 1988 by Bharati Mukherjee. Used by permission of Grove/Atlantic, Inc. Any third party use of this material, outside of this publication, is prohibited.

Alice Munro, "The Progress of Love" from THE PROGRESS OF LOVE. Copyright © 1985, 1986 by Alice Munro. Used by permission of Alfred A. Knopf, an imprint of the Knopf Doubleday Publishing Group, a division of Penguin Random House LLC. All rights reserved. Any third party use of this material, outside of this publication, is prohibited. Interested parties must apply directly to Penguin Random House LLC for permission. Rights in Canada by permission of Penguin Random House Canada Limited.

Marilyn Nelson, "The Century Quilt" from MAMA'S PROMISES: POEMS is reprinted by permission of Louisiana State University Press.

Pablo Neruda, Sonnet XX from 100 LOVE SONNETS: CIEN SONETOS DE AMOR, trans. by Stephen Tapscott. Copyright © Pablo Neruda 1959 and Funcacion Pablo Neruda. Copyright © 1986 by the University of Texas Press. This translation used by permission of the University of Texas Press.

Aimee Nezhukumatahil, "Chess" from "Poem a Day," Nov. 20, 2015. Reprinted by permission of the author.

Naomi Shihib Nye, "My Father and the Figtree" from WORDS UNDER THE WORDS: SELECTED POEMS. Copyright © 1995. Reprinted with the permission of Far Corner Books.

Joyce Carol Oates, "Where Are You Going, Where Have You Been?" [pp. 249–266] from HIGH LONESOME: NEW AND SELECTED STORIES 1966–2006. Copyright © 2006 by The Ontario Review, Inc. Reprinted by permission of HarperCollins Publishers.

Tim O'Brien, "The Things They Carried" from THE THINGS THEY CARRIED. Copyright © 1990 by Tim O'Brien. Reprinted by permission of Houghton Mifflin Harcourt Publishing Company. All rights reserved.

Flannery O'Connor, "A Good Man Is Hard to Find" from A GOOD MAN IS HARD TO FIND AND OTHER STORIES. Copyright 1953 by Flannery O'Connor. Copyright © renewed 1981 by Regina O'Connor. Reprinted by permission of Houghton Mifflin Harcourt Publishing Company. All rights reserved.

Frank O'Hara, "The Day Lady Died" from LUNCH POEMS. Reprinted by permission of the publisher City Lights Books.

Mary Oliver, "Wild Geese" from DREAM WORK. Copyright © 1986 by Mary Oliver. Used by permission of Grove/Atlantic, Inc. Any third party use of this material, outside of this publication is prohibited. "Spring in the Classroom" from NEW AND SELECTED POEMS, Vol. 1. Published by Beacon Press, Boston. Copyright © 1972, 1992 by Mary Oliver. Reprinted by permission of The Charlotte Sheedy Literary Agency Inc.

Tillie Olsen, "I Stand Here Ironing" from TELL ME A RIDDLE, REQUA 1, AND OTHER WORKS. Copyright © 2013 by the Board of Regents of the University of Nebraska. Reprinted by permission of the publisher, the University of Nebraska Press.

The Onion, excerpts from THE ONION AD NAUSEUM: COMPLETE NEWS ARCHIVES, VOL. 13 by Onion Editors. Copyright © 2002 by The Onion, Inc. Used by permission of Three Rivers Press, an imprint of The Crown Publishing Group, a division of Penguin Random House LLC. All rights reserved. Any third party use of this material, outside of this publication, is prohibited. Interested parties must apply directly to Penguin Random House LLC for permission.

Meghan O'Rourke, from "The Long Goodbye: Hamlet's Not Depressed, He's Grieving" from *Slate*, March 12, 2009. Copyright © 2009 by The Slate Group. All rights reserved. Used by permission and protected by the Copyright Laws of the United States. The printing, copying, redistribution, or retransmission of this Content without express written permission is prohibited.

Simon J. Ortiz, "My Father's Song" originally published in A GOOD JOURNEY (University of Arizona Press, 1985). All rights owned by Simon J. Ortiz. Used by permission of the author.

George Orwell, excerpts from NINETEEN EIGHTY-FOUR. Copyright © 1949 by Houghton Mifflin Harcourt Publishing Company and renewed 1977 by Sonia Brownell Orwell. Reprinted by permission of Houghton Mifflin Harcourt Publishing Company. All rights reserved.

Cynthia Ozick, "The Shawl" from THE SHAWL. Copyright © 1980, 1983 by Cynthia Ozick. Used by permission of Alfred A. Knopf, an imprint of the Knopf Doubleday Publishing Group, a division of Penguin Random House LLC. All rights reserved. Any third party use of this material outside of this publication, is prohibited. Interested parties must apply directly to Penguin Random House LLC for permission.

Gregory Pardlo, "Written by Himself" from DIGEST. Copyright © 2014 by Gregory Pardlo. Reprinted with permission of The Permissions Company, Inc. on behalf of Four Way Books, www.fourwaybooks.com. All rights reserved.

Ezra Pound, "In a Station of the Metro" from PERSONAE. Copyright © 1926 by Ezra Pound. Reprinted by permission of New Directions Publishing Group.

Molly Rose Quinn, "Dolorosa" first published in *Four Way Review*, online. Reprinted by permission of the author.

Suzanne Rancourt, "Whose Mouth Do I Speak With" from BILLBOARD IN THE CITY. Copyright © 2003 by Suzanne Rancourt. All rights reserved. Published by Curbstone Press. Reprinted by permission of the publisher.

Henry Reed, "Naming of Parts" from COLLECTED POEMS, ed. by Jon Stallworthy is reprinted by permission of Carcanet Press Limited.

Ishmael Reed, "Points of View" excerpted from NEW AND COLLECTED POEMS, 1964–2006. Copyright © 2006 by Ishmael Reed. Permission granted by Lowenstein Associates, Inc.

Barbara Jane Reyes, "To Be Walang Hiya" first published in *Poetry* magazine, May 2014 issue. Reprinted by permission of the author.

Adrienne Rich, "A Valediction Forbidding Mourning." Copyright © 2016 by The Adrienne Rich Literary Trust. Copyright © 1971 by W. W. Norton & Company, Inc., from COLLECTED POEMS: 1950–2012 by Adrienne Rich. Used by permission of W. W. Norton & Company, Inc.

Theodore Roethke, "My Papa's Waltz," copyright © 1942 by Hearst Magazines, Inc. from COLLECTED POEMS by Theodore Roethke. Used by permission of Doubleday, an imprint of the Knopf Doubleday Publishing Group, a division of Random House LLC. All rights reserved. Any third party use of this material, outside of this publication, is prohibited. Interested parties must apply directly to Penguin Random House LLC for permission.

Carl Romm, "The Enduring Scariness of the Mad Scientist." Copyright © 2014 The Atlantic Media Co., as first published in *The Atlantic Magazine*. All rights reserved. Distributed by Tribune Content Agency, LLC.

Karen Russell, "The Prospectors" was first published in *The New Yorker*. Copyright © 2015 by Karen Russell. Reprinted with permission of the Denise Shannon Literary Agency, Inc. All rights reserved.

Carl Sandburg, "Chicago" from CHICAGO POEMS. Copyright 1916 by Houghton Mifflin Harcourt Publishing Company and renewed 1944 by Carl Sandburg. Reprinted by permission of Houghton Mifflin Harcourt Publishing Company. All rights reserved.

Leopold Sedar Senghor, "In Memoriam" from THE COLLECTED POEMS, trans. by Melvin Dixon, p. 3. Copyright © 1991 by the Rector and Visitors of the University of Virginia. Reprinted by permission of the University of Virginia Press.

Anne Sexton, "Her Kind" from TO BEDLAM AND PART WAY BACK. Copyright © 1960 by Anne Sexton, renewed 1988 by Linda G. Sexton. Reprinted by permission of Houghton Mifflin Harcourt Publishing Company. All rights reserved. Electronic rights courtesy of Sterling Lord Literistic.

William Shakespeare, Notes by David Bevington from THE COMPLETE WORKS OF SHAKESPEARE, 4th ed., copyright © 1992. Reprinted by permission of Pearson Education Inc., New York, NY.

Solmaz Sharif, "Safe House" from LOOK. Copyright © 2016 by Solmaz Sharif. Reprinted with the permission of The Permissions Co., Inc. on behalf of Graywolf Press, www.graywolfpress.org.

Warsan Shire, "for women who are difficult to love" first published online on *Poem-a-Day*, July 13, 2012. Reprinted by permission of Warsan Shire.

William Stafford, "Traveling through the Dark" from ASK ME: 100 ESSENTIAL POEMS. Copyright © 1962, 1998 by William Stafford and the Estate of William Stafford. Reprinted with the permission of The Permissions Company, Inc. on behalf of Graywolf Press, Minneapolis, Minnesota, www.graywolfpress.org.

A. E. Stallings, "The Wife of the Man of Many Wiles" from ARCHAIC Smile is reprinted by permission of the University of Evansville Press.

Adrienne Su, "Peaches," originally published in *Poem-a-Day* on Oct. 23, 2015, by the Academy of American Poets. Copyright © 2015 by Adrienne Su. Reprinted by permission of the author.

May Swenson, "Goodbye, Golden Eye" was first published in *The Nation*, Feb. 18, 1984. Copyright © by May Swenson. Used with permission of the Literary Estate of May Swenson. All rights reserved.

Wisława Szymborska, "The Terrorist, He Watches," from SOUNDS, FEELINGS, THOUGHTS: SEVENTY POEMS, tr. and ed. by Magnus J. Krynski and Robert A. Maguire. Copyright © 1981 by Princeton University Press. Reprinted by permission of Princeton University Press via the Copyright Clearance Center.

Dylan Thomas, "Fern Hill" from THE POEMS OF DYLAN THOMAS, copyright © 1945 by The Trustees for the Copyrights of Dylan Thomas. "Do Not Go Gentle Into That Good Night" from THE POEMS OF DYLAN THOMAS, copyright © 1952 by Dylan Thomas. Reprinted by permission of New Directions Publishing Corp.

Natasha Trethewey, "Southern History" from NATIVE GUARD. Copyright © 2006 by Natasha Trethewey. Reprinted by permission of Houghton Mifflin Harcourt Publishing Company. All rights reserved. "History Lesson" from DOMESTIC WORK. Copyright © 1998, 2000 by Natasha Trethewey. Reprinted with the permission of The Permissions Company, Inc. on behalf of Graywolf Press, Minneapolis, Minnesota, www.graywolfpress.org.

Brian Turner, "Sadiq" and "In the Leupold Scope" from HERE, BULLET. Copyright © 2005 by Brian Turner. Reprinted with the permission of The Permissions Company, Inc., on behalf of Alice James Books, www.alicejamesbooks.org.

Jon Turney, from FRANKENSTEIN'S FOOTSTEPS. Copyright © 1998 by Jon Turney. Reprinted by permission of the publisher Yale University Press.

Helena María Viramontes, "The Moths" is reprinted with permission from the publisher of THE MOTHS AND OTHER STORIES by Helena María Viramontes. Copyright © 1995 Arte Público Press-University of Houston.

Binyavanga Wainaina, "How to Write About Africa" first published in *Granta* 92: The View from Africa. Copyright © 2006 by Binyavanga Wainaina. Used by permission of The Wylie Agency LLC.

Derek Walcott "XIV" from "Midsummer" from THE POETRY OF DEREK WALCOTT 1948–2013, selected by Glyn Maxwell. Copyright © 2014 by Derek Walcott. Reprinted by permission of Farrar, Straus and Giroux, LLC.

Alice Walker, "Everyday Use" from IN LOVE AND TROUBLE: STORIES OF BLACK WOMEN. Copyright © 1973, renewed 2001 by Alice Walker. Reprinted with permission of Houghton Mifflin Harcourt Publishing Company. All rights reserved. Electronic rights by permission of The Joy Harris Literary Agency, Inc.

Jeanne Murray Walker, "How Mother Courage Saves Desdemona" from A DEED TO THE LIGHT: POEMS. Copyright © 2004 by Jeanne Murray Walker. Used with permission of the University of Illinois Press.

Brad Watson, "Seeing Eye" from LAST DAYS OF THE DOG-MEN: STORIES, copyright © 1996 by Brad Watson. Used by permission of W. W. Norton & Company, Inc.

Aafa Michael Weaver, "My Father's Geography" from MY FATHER'S GEOGRAPHY. Copyright © 1992. Reprinted by permission of the University of Pittsburgh Press.

James Welch, from FOOLS CROW. Copyright © 1986 by James Welch. Used by permission of Viking Books, an imprint of Penguin Publishing Group, a division of Penguin Random House LLC.

Richard Wilbur, "First Snow in Alsace" from THE BEAUTIFUL CHANGES AND OTHER POEMS. Copyright 1947 and renewed 1975 by Richard Wilbur. Richard Wilbur. All rights reserved. "The Writer" from THE MIND-READER. Copyright © 1971 and renewed 1999 by Richard Wilbur. All rights reserved. Reprinted by permission of Houghton Mifflin Harcourt Publishing Company.

August Wilson, FENCES, copyright © 1986 by August Wilson. Used by Permission of New American Library, an imprint of Penguin Publishing Group, a division of Penguin Random House LLC.

Jamila Woods, "Ghazal for White Hen Pantry" first published in *Poetry* magazine, Dec. 2015 issue is reprinted by permission of the author.

Virginia Woolf, excerpt from MRS. DALLOWAY. Copyright © 1925 by Houghton Mifflin Publishing Company, and renewed 1953 by Leonard Woolf. Reprinted by permission of Houghton Mifflin Harcourt Publishing Company. All rights reserved.

James Wright, "Autumn Begins in Martins Ferry, Ohio" from COLLECTED POEMS, copyright © 1971 by James Wright. Reprinted by permission of Wesleyan University Press.

INDEX OF FIRST LINES

INDEX OF AUTHORS AND TITLES

D

E

F

G

H

I

J

K

L

P

Q

R

S

T

U

V

W

X

Y

P9-DDW-995

AMERICAN ANTIQUES AND *Collectibles*

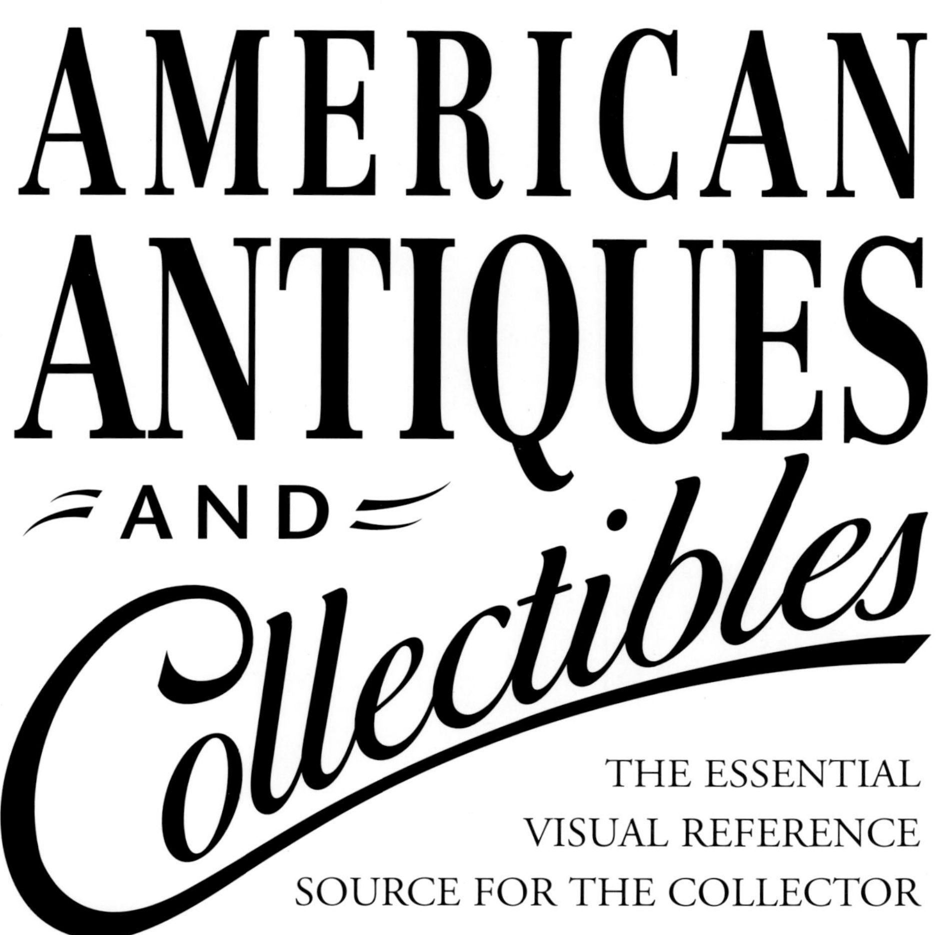

AMERICAN
ANTIQUES
AND
Collectibles
THE ESSENTIAL
VISUAL REFERENCE
SOURCE FOR THE COLLECTOR

SUSAN WARD & CHRISTOPHER PEARCE

interests, the exhibition had a high entertainment content. Attractions like Billy Rose's Aquacade – a water spectacular featuring Johnny Weissmuller of Tarzan fame and Eleanor Holm – The Savoy Dance Center with its Harlem Jitterbug Show, and a 200-ft (60 m) parachute jump were among the best attended events. Some of the finest collectibles are from the commercial exhibitors, who backed such arresting contributions as the General Motors' Futurama, the spectacular National Cash Register

ABOVE: *Souvenir metal ashtray from the New York World's Fair, 1965.*

building, and a massive 14-ton (12.6 tonne) Underwood Typewriter that actually worked, typing on 9 × 12 ft (2.7 × 3.6 m) sheets of paper! To many visitors, however, the overwhelming impression of the Fair was quantity of food, for in addition to the 'five-and-dime' restaurants and Mayflower's two great doughnut restaurants, eateries included The Wonder Bread Bakery, the Heinz Restaurant and Borden's Dairy World, which issued a book of World's Fair recipes.

COLA COLLECTIBLES

The joys of finding 'the real thing' in prime condition, whether it be a Santa Claus cut-out or a Norman Rockwell calendar.

ABOVE: *This advertisement appeared in magazines for Christmas 1960.*

Above, center and left: *Amongst the countless advertising give-aways issued by Coca-Cola, blotters are generally low budget yet highly regarded for their variety and attractiveness.*

In the 1930s promotional figurines of the Heinz Tomato, and Elsie, the Borden Cow – with Elmer, her husband – were as familiar to the public as Mickey Mouse. The concept of 'company image' had developed during the century to such a degree that many products had acquired a 'personality' almost transcending the product itself. The prime example of this is Coca-Cola, which was defined by the famous journalist William Allen White in 1938 as 'the sublimated essence of all that America stands for'. The truth of that statement is now almost beyond dispute, endorsed as it was by the American Government during World War II, when it was decided that a constant supply of Coca-Cola was an essential morale-booster for front-line troops. Pop artists, like Robert Rauschenberg and Andy Warhol, further mythologized this symbol.

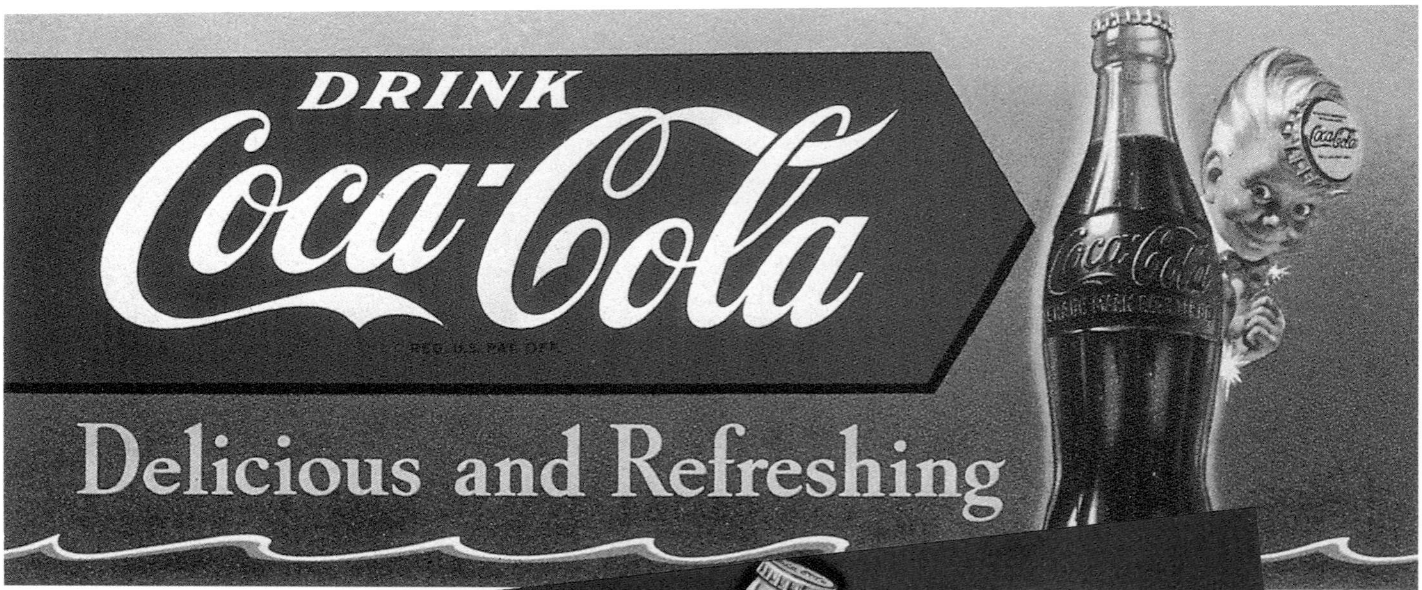

DRINK
Coca-Cola
REG. U.S. PAT. OFF.
Delicious and Refreshing

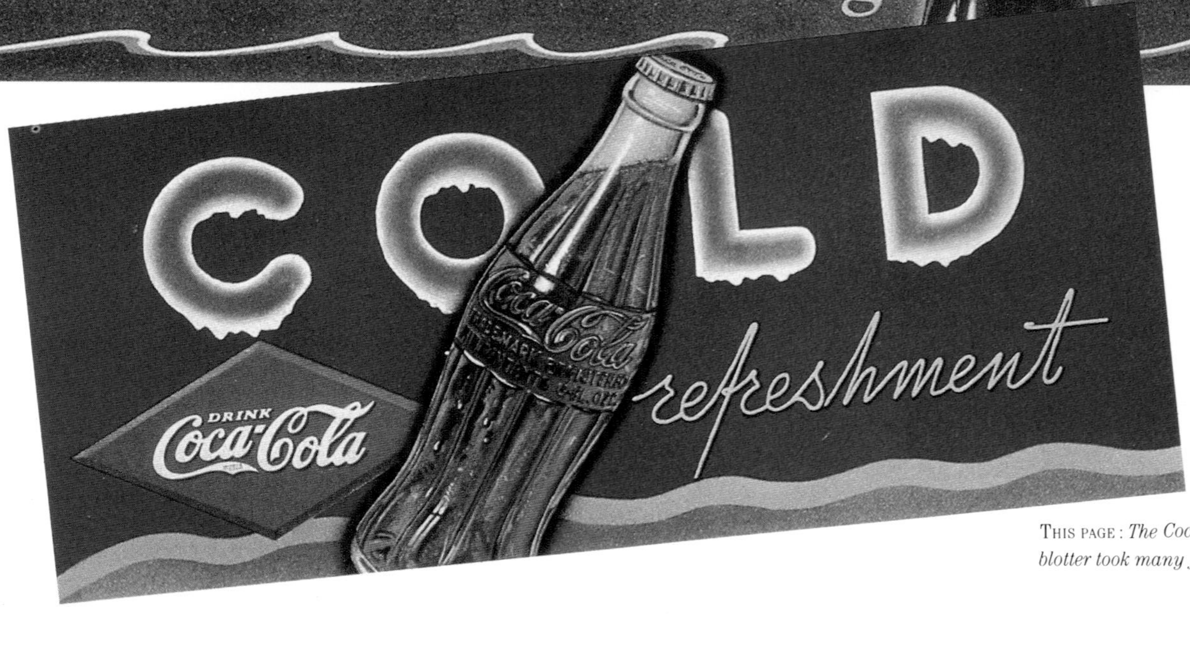

COLD
refreshment
DRINK
Coca-Cola

THIS PAGE : *The Coca-Cola blotter took many forms.*

TOP: *Large-scale cardboard advertising sign, 1945.*

ABOVE: *Score pads such as these dating from 1943 are another example of Coca-Cola inventiveness in finding things to carry the company's name!*

Today, collectors worldwide have made Coca-Cola artefacts, alongside Disney items, *the* American collectibles, with an overseas following almost as avid as the home market. The Coca-Cola cult venerates an enormous pattern of paraphernalia, some of which attract their own specialist following. Advertising posters and bills, toys, buttons and other marketing devices provide a rich lode for the enthusiast. Though old bottles are much sought after, no-one has collected the drink itself for its own sake, save during the notorious 'New Coke' scare of 1985. Then there were reports of people buying up stock of old Coke and cellaring them like fine wines! There is now no-one who can remember a time before Coca-Cola existed, and as a collectible it has the familiarity of permanence. The traditional flowing script and waisted bottle have achieved worldwide recognition, yet there are so many stages in Coca-Cola history and enough Coke collectibles to ensure that the subject never goes stale.

Excluding rare and extremely valuable 19th-century items, and such specialist items as Coca-Cola chewing gum, Coke collectibles can be broadly divided into the following:

SIGNS AND PLACARDS

The most familiar examples are the outdoor enameled metal and tin signs which were once such a feature of the American landscape. As with all Coca-Cola items there is tremendous variety. The most desirable of the tin signs are those that feature a straight-sided bottle, which indicates that they date before 1915, when the familiar 'hobbleskirt' bottle was introduced. Later pictorial signs showing the bottle, or featuring 'Betty, the Coca-Cola girl', are generally rated more highly than those which are only lettered. Also top of the pops are metal cut-out signs and embossed signs. Although not very old by Coca-Cola standards, as they date from the 1940s and 1950s, the convex 'button' signs are nevertheless popular. Plastic signs, dating from the 1950s onwards, are now being given more attention as a result of the current interest in plastics generally. Illuminated neon signs and glass signs are not particularly common and, of course, have been more vulnerable to damage. Outdoor examples have also been made of wood, masonite and aluminum.

Cut-outs and Festoons

There is a vast array of indoor display signs. Of these, by far the most desirable are cut-out window displays and soda-fountain festoons. Prime examples feature film stars (including Sue Carol, Jean Harlow, Joan Blondell, Lupe Velez and Frances Dee with Gene Raymond), while other sought-after variations are illustrated by Norman Rockwell. A particularly interesting set of cut-outs is the service girls of 1944. These five girls in wartime uniforms, each holding a bottle of Coca-Cola, came either as life-size free-standing cut-outs or as small counter displays. (As with all advertising it must be remembered that war-time restrictions prevented metal from being used.)

LEFT: *This exceptional quality sign of embossed, enameled metal advised motorists that they were approaching a school zone – at the same time publicizing Coca-Cola.*

FAR LEFT: *1940s cardboard advertisement with wood and metal frame.*

A good deal of patriotic material was printed onto paper or cardboard, and Coca-Cola produced various war-related adverts. Another very popular cut-out today is the Coca-Cola Santa Claus. Although Coca-Cola did not actually *invent* Santa, artist Haddan Sunblom's creation came to epitomize the festive old man. He appeared every Christmas from the 1930s to the early 1960s, moving from the restrictions of the cut-out to the wider opportunities of general advertising.

Above: *Die cut card 'snowman' festoon, 1930s.*

Left: *Haddon Sundblom created his first Coca-Cola Santa in 1931, and the company's advertising became part of the seasonal scene. This cardboard die-cut display dates from the 1940s.*

Festoons are cut-outs which were intended to be hung above soda-fountain back bars and were popular from the 1920s into the early 1950s. Like all cardboard cut-outs, they were vulnerable to damage, and top examples are expected to not only be in good condition but to also be in the original envelope.

Baseball Cut-outs

The national pastime offered an obvious vehicle for advertising and the results are typical of the times when collectibles overlap, since they are of equal interest to baseball as well as Coca-Cola enthusiasts. The 1950s cut-outs included individual portraits of Phil Rizzuto, Monte Irvin, Roy Campanella, Larry Doby, Bill Bruton and Satcher Paige.

(There have been other Coca-Cola/baseball advertisements, most notably a series which appeared in newspapers between 1911 and 1916.)

In addition to the variety of outdoor and indoor publicity covered thus far, other Coca-Cola items find eager buyers. Among the most interesting and collectible are:

Street Car Signs

These date from between the beginning of this century into the 1920s. They were made to a standard size 28×51cm (11×20.5in) to fit the frames which were permanently mounted on the street cars. Other products too, of course, were advertised, and judging from the surviving Coca-Cola examples, as well as those for Wrigley's Chewing Gum, Old Dutch Cleanser, Fairy Soap and the other major advertisers of this period, the interiors of the cars must have been very colorful.

Movie Stars

The silver screen had enormous influences on ideas of beauty, fashion and social behavior in the inter-war period. Even Coca-Cola could not escape its

FACING PAGE: *(Top left) this matchbook from the 1930s advertising Henry's Fried Clams claims 'patronizing us is like making love to a widow, you can't overdo it'. (Top center) stylish Art Deco graphics grace this cover advertising Mary Jane's Dining Room, Cabins and Tourist Home, 1930s. (Top right) the Colonial Lunch used the match cover to promote its motto of 'better cooking' in the 1940s. (Center left) quality foods, popular prices – the Brattleboro Restaurant, 1930s. (Center) the El Charro restaurant, Gonzales California, 1930s. (Below left) another example of feature matches, this time 'girlie' pictures hidden within an innocuous cover. (Below center) Howard Johnson's ice cream, 1940s. (Center right) the Art Deco-style New Yorker restaurant, 1930s. (Below right) Monte Proser's copacabana, 1940s.*

characteristics are also true of advertising paperweights.

Other tobacco-related advertising vehicles are cigar cutters and cigarette lighters – frequently used as promotional give-aways – cigarette cards and matchbooks.

MATCHBOOKS

Homage should be paid to the humble matchbook as the first true American collectible. Although previously there had existed collectors of stamps, coins, cheese labels and cigar labels, none of these were uniquely American. The first national club for phillumenists (matchbook collectors) was founded in 1936, but even by then the hobby was well established. Few collectors of any kind could

TOP: *Matchcovers in the 1940s became a major gallery for pin-up art. These were generally stock designs which were personalized for a wide range of commercial advertisers.*

ABOVE: *Wrigleys were early users of matchbook advertising. Their first order was for one billion!*

LEFT: *Advertising war bonds, this World War Two matchbook shows a rear view of Hitler with the message 'strike at the seat of trouble'. An additional novelty is the bomb-shaped matches.*

come close to the legendary Evelyn Hovious, who, from beginning her collection during World War I, amassed over 5,000,000 examples.

The matchbook was invented by Joshua Pusey of Philadelphia, and patented in 1892 – the patent being acquired by the Diamond Match Company. Credit for the first advertising covers must go to the thespians of the Mendelssohn Opera Company of New York who, with no funds for conventional advertising, went to work hand-lettering hundreds of matchbook covers with details of their new production and pasting down photographs of the show's stars. History records that this publicity succeeded in saving the show.

In any event it inspired salesman Henry C. Traute to make up an advertising matchbook for Pabst Brewery. On the strength of this unsolicited sample he received an order for 10,000,000 Pabst matchbooks! Shortly after, Bull Durham Tobacco placed an order for 30,000,000 and a new industry was born. A minor setback occurred when it transpired that the public would not buy them – even at the price of two for one cent. But the indomitable Traute soon solved that problem by persuading tobacconists to give a matchbook free with every purchase. This magic formula proved an instant success, and soon matchbooks were being given away all over the place, not just by tobacconists but at restaurants, bars and barbershops, with each specimen extolling the virtue of its respective establishment.

The biggest endorsement of the system was when William Wrigley gave Traute an order for matchbooks to advertise chewing gum. It was a large order – one billion! Over the years, other companies joined the fray, including Atlas, Universal, the Ohio Match Company, Federal, Superior and Monach. Among them they produced matchbooks promoting everything from war bonds to topless massage parlors, from road safety to political campaigns.

Through the years the format has remained much the same, though in 1962 the abrasive striking strip was moved by law from the front to the back. There have been variations – such as where the row of matches themselves make up a design, or extra large books – but the main fascination still lies in the covers, with their range of graphic images from a Vargas pin-up to a Yellow Cab taxi. The written publicity too captures the spirit – and often the idiom – of the period.

The idea of 'free' advertising was also successfully adapted to drinks' coasters and bottle protectors (the paper skirt around the neck of a bottle that stops the liquid from running down the side).

ABOVE: *To a collector, bottle caps are no longer throw-away ephemera but precious examples of pop graphics.*

BELOW AND FACING PAGE, CENTER: *The crimped edge Crown bottle top became a popular soft drink symbol, illustrated here by two large tin signs and a tin menu board.*

LEFT AND RIGHT: *Bottles proclaim their individuality, relics of the age before standardization and metal cans became the norm. Examples shown here are for Canada Dry and Orange Crush.*

THIS PAGE AND FACING PAGE: *Whiskey bottles enjoyed a boom during the 1970s as a result of a craze for special decorative examples by various distilleries.*

CRISPUS ATTUCKS
ALEXANDER HAMILTON
JOHN HANCOCK
LIBERTY
BEAM
100
MONTHS OLD
4/5 QUART
86 PROOF
Kentucky Straight Bourbon Whiskey
DEL WEBB
DESERT RALLY
MINT
400
1972
4/5 QUART
BEAM
86 PROOF
Kentucky Straight
100
MONTHS OLD
Bourbon Whiskey
1872
100
1972
COLORADO SPRINGS CENTENNIAL
4/5 QUART
BEAM
86 PROOF
Kentucky Straight
100
MONTHS OLD
Bourbon Whiskey

GLASS

Though glass was a popular constituent of signs, ashtrays and paperweights, its biggest use was in glass bottles, beer, whiskey, milk and perfume. As collectibles these fall broadly into the categories of containers for soft drinks. For both soft drinks and beer the bottle was for many years the standard container. Even today variations of some of the 'classic' bottles for Coke, Pepsi and others are still on the market, though much under the dominance of canned versions. Having made history by successfully portraying elegant ladies drinking directly from the bottle in the manner of construction workers, the historic power of the bottle is very much a part of the product image.

The breweries pioneered the use of cans in the mid-thirties. Wartime restrictions on the use of metal meant the return of glass, but cans re-emerged after the war. Although beer bottles retain the distinction of greater variety and age, the cans too have their afficianados. Up to prohibition there had been nearly 2,000 breweries, many supplying little more than their local community. Less than a third resumed business after repeal, and thereafter the trend was of merger and takeovers, creating major brands and greater standardization. In addition, breweries have occasionally produced commemorative or 'collectors' bottles. Specials of this sort tend to dominate whiskey collectibles. Jim Beam pioneered the 'special edition' in 1953, and was thereafter followed by a parade of other companies. However the majority of these are more properly described as decanters rather than bottles, since a large number were made in ceramic or heavy lead crystal and take sculptural or figurative forms. After his success with Coke's classic

ABOVE: *Part of the appeal of milk bottles is in the variety of local dairies, most of which have disappeared since 1950s.*

BELOW: *Glass containers displaying Planters' distinctive peanut design.*

FACING PAGE: *This 'baby top' bottle is characterized by the molded face of a baby in the glass.*

bottle, Old Forrester commissioned Ramond Loewy to design a special bottle for them, advertising it as the 'decanter sensation'.

MILK BOTTLES

The humble milk bottle is typical of that class of collectibles which sound too ordinary to be the focus of a collection. Yet, basic utility item that it was, it has now gained further appeal as a vanished relic in an age of supermarkets, plastics and no home deliveries. The milk bottle was the creation of the early commercial dairies. Before that time, farmers and dairies would supply milk from churns, the customer providing their own container. The first patented glass bottle appeared in 1880, and soon glass bottles were in use in New York City. By the beginning of this century they were in general use, with thousands of independent dairies selling their milk in customized bottles. Although waxed-paper milk cartons first appeared in the 1920s, glass remained in common use until the 1950s. Then cartons and plastic bottles began the takeover that would eventually all but kill off traditional glass. The variety of collectibles is huge, augmented by the different shapes and sizes of bottles (quarter, half and full pint, third quart, quart, half gallon, and gallon). The bottles were usually clear glass with the name of the dairy embossed or pyroglazed on it. Occasionally a design and/or slogan – 'Fresh to you each morning', for instance – were also included. A popular variation is those with a baby's head design cast in the glass.

Milk bottle collectors will usually incorporate at least a few examples of bottle caps, cap openers and cappers in their collection. Often dairy items are collectible, and extend the subject from milk bottles to cream separators, milk and butter churns, product advertising, and dairy fittings. The largest commercial dairy conglomerate was Borden's, operating out of Chicago, and its items alone can form the basis of a large collection.

PERFUME BOTTLES

Although commercially produced – as opposed to antique – perfume and display bottles are generally collected, this field is dominated by the Avon bottle. The Avon Company originated with the California Perfume company, founded in 1886. The company pioneered the technique perfected by the Fuller Brush Company, using ladies selling door-to-door. The company became Avon in 1929 and grew to a massive corporation, with over a million 'Avon ladies' internationally. Today all California perfume and many Avon items are collected. Some collectors choose to specialize in the enormous variety of

DAIRY MADE
ICE CREAM
"You're sure - It's pure"

FACING PAGE: *Ice-cream is a collectors subject in its own right, as well as being included in dairy collections. This exceptionally fine tin sign dates from the 1920s.*

BELOW: *Milk cartons generally do not have the same nostalgic appeal as glass bottles. However, unusual ones, such as this Hopalong Cassidy design, are of interest.*

ABOVE: *Original milk bottle tops have usually only survived through having been found unused when dairies have closed down or modernized.*

TOP RIGHT: *Small dairies capped the bottles by hand, using a capper such as this.*

BELOW RIGHT: *Ice-cream scoops, which come in a variety of patterns, are part of the paraphernalia of ice-cream collectibles.*

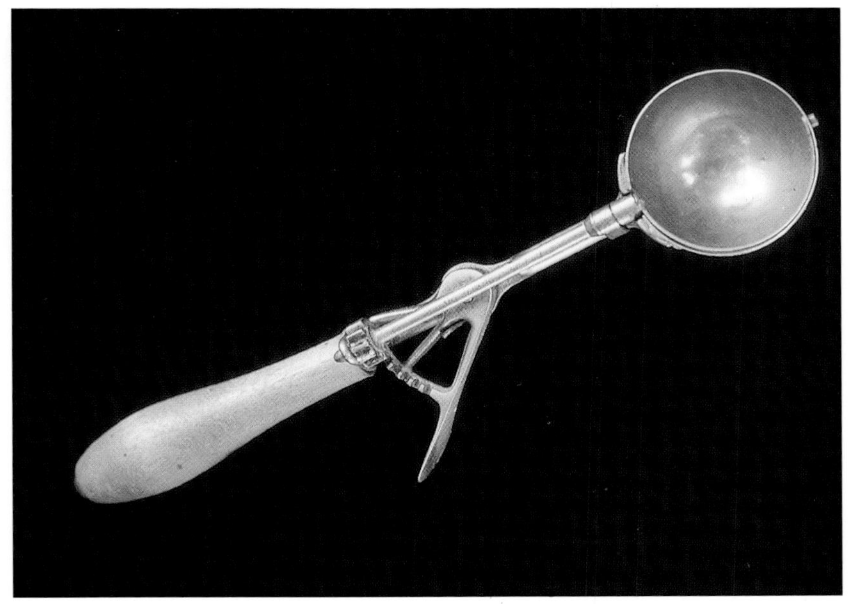

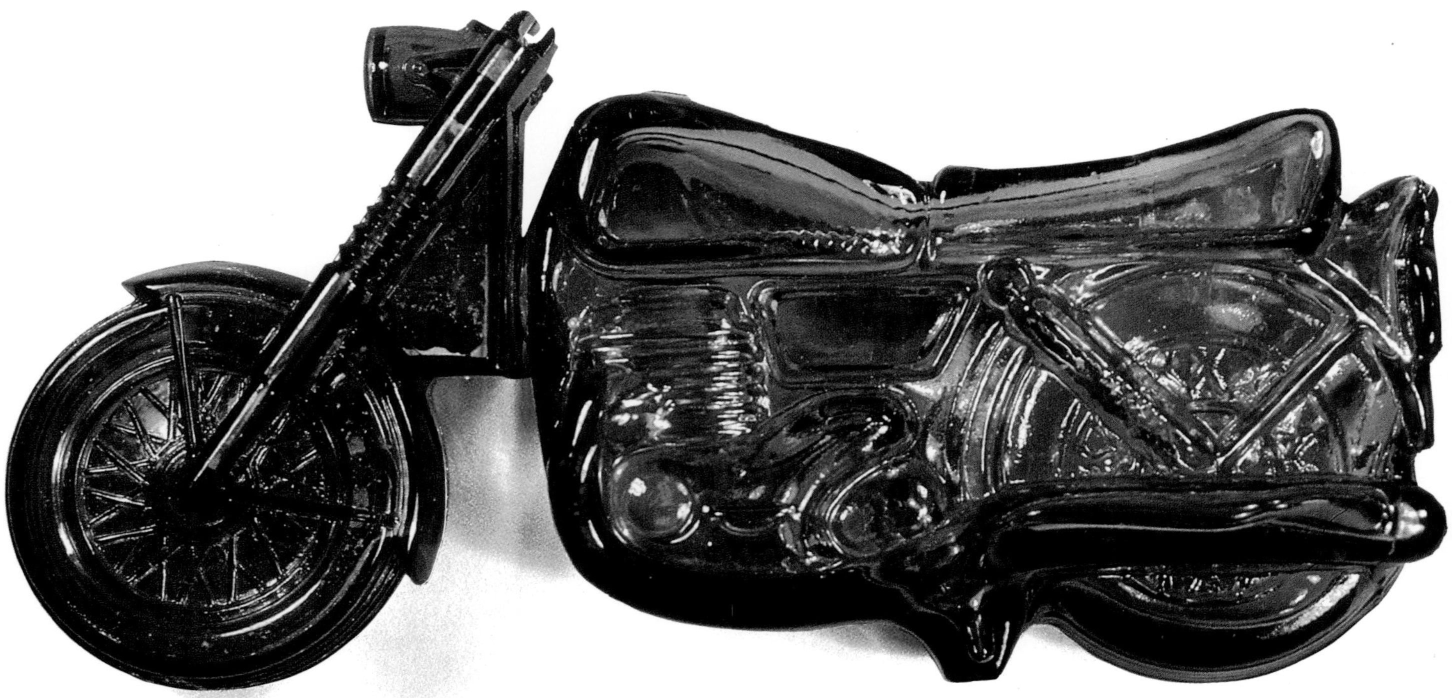

sculptural glass bottles in which Avon packaged men's aftershave, with subjects ranging from a spark plug and a greyhound bus to a snowmobile or a Mack truck.

ABOVE AND BELOW: *Pheasant decanter and Harley Davidson decanter in molded glass are examples of Avon Products' decorative packaging of men's products.*

SWANKYSWIGS

Although Swankyswigs are drinking tumblers, they are also packaging. First introduced during the Depression years of the early 1930s, they originally contained Kraft Cheese. As a marketing device they were a give-away in the same manner as some Depression glass, as there was a free tumbler with each purchase of Kraft Spread. These glasses, with their brightly painted designs, remained popular until the mid-1970s, with production only discontinued during World War II. There are many designs, some of which were only issued in small quantities.

MIRRORS

Human nature being what it is, few can resist even a casual glance at a mirror, so what a perfect place for an advertising message! Advertising mirrors range from the magnificently etched, embossed and gilded images of opulence especially favored by 19th-century companies to the little, tin-backed vanity mirrors for ladies' handbags, which were popular give-aways from the 1890s to the 1920s.

NEON SIGNS

Neon gas, colored and trapped within a glass tube, twisting and curling into the shape of a name or a device is one of the most dramatic of advertising ploys. Even the simplest sign is capable of making an enormous impact. Neon collecting has been increasing over the last 20 years, with much of the early emphasis not on the product advertised but rather on the intrinsic artistic appeal of the 'neon art' itself. At one time it was an omnipresent part of the American landscape. Indeed, so much was neon synonymous with America, from the gaudy excesses of Times Square or Las Vegas to the lonely highways crossing from the neon-lit signs of theaters and gas stations to the simple scrawl over the soda-fountain, that it is a protected part of American heritage in several historic sites.

The art critic William Wilson described neon as 'the magic wand that gave downtown its boogie-

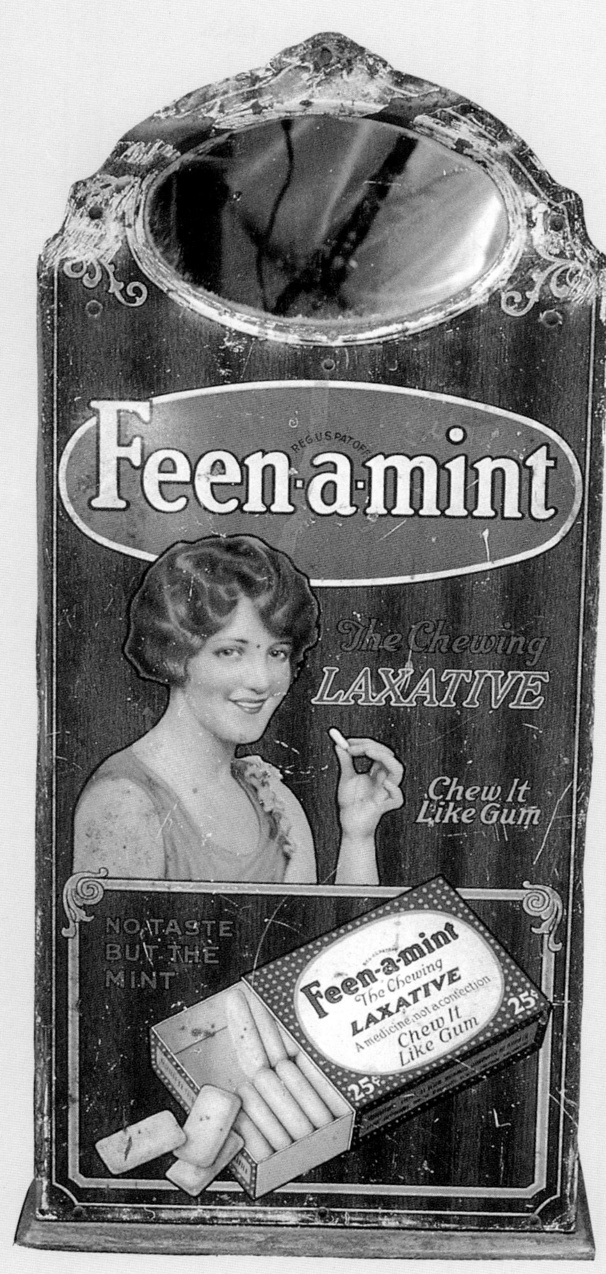

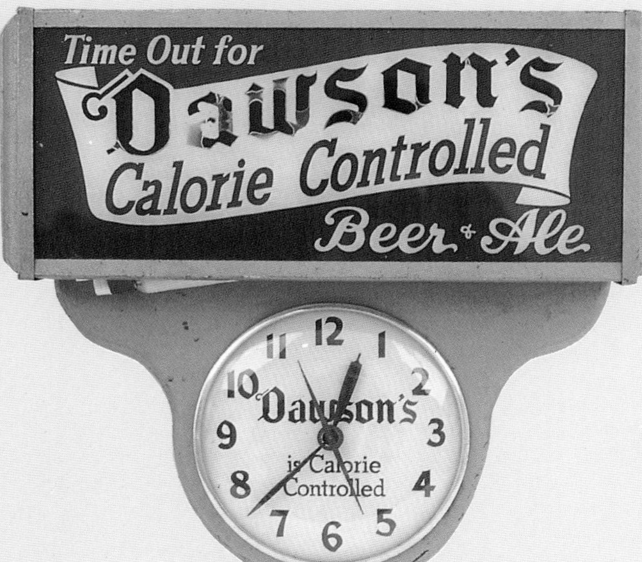

ABOVE LEFT: *Pepsi-Cola and Seven-Up advertising clocks, 1950s.*

ABOVE RIGHT: *Large advertising mirror for Feen a Mint Laxative, 1920s.*

LEFT: *Dawson's Beer clock, 1940s.*

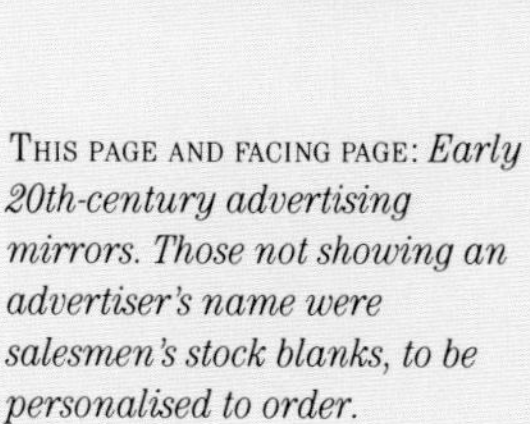

THIS PAGE AND FACING PAGE: *Early 20th-century advertising mirrors. Those not showing an advertiser's name were salesmen's stock blanks, to be personalised to order.*

COMPLIMENTS
J. ADAMOFF, 76-2ND ST, PASSAIC, N.J.

DRINK
Coca-Cola

MANUFACTURING CO.
The Largest Carriage Factory in the World.
INDIANAPOLIS, IND.
OUR GOODS ARE SOLD BY
W. M. SISSON & SON
NORTH PLAIN, CONN.

USE
MENNEN'S
VIOLET TALCUM
TOILET POWDER
ADMITTED TO BE THE BEST

400 FEET LONG
THE DENVER DRY GOODS COMPANY, DENVER, COLO.

LARGE OVAL MIRROR, FLATIRON GIRL DESIGN, NO. 31086

ALL GOING OUT ~ NOTHING COMING IN
Cascarets
DID IT
THEY WORK WHILE YOU SLEEP
SEND 2¢ STAMP FOR MIRROR LIKE THIS - ADDRESS: STERLING REMEDY CO. - CHICAGO OR NEW YORK.

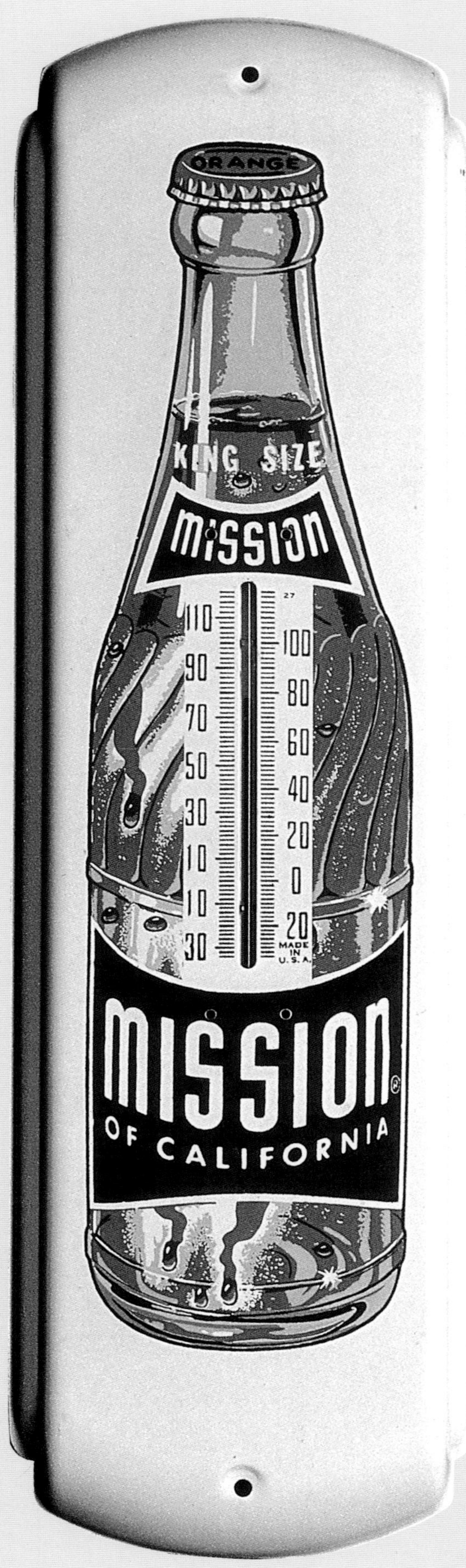

LEFT: *Tin soft drink advertising thermometers.*

woogie spirit, etching the edges of buildings, embroidering tapestries of light'. Its presence has seemed so much part of this century that it is surprising how short was its golden age. For neon did not arrive in the United States until 1923 (the world's first neon sign went up in Paris in 1912, two years after its invention), when Earl C. Anthony brought two signs over from France for his Los Angeles Packard showroom. From then until World War II, America went neon mad, erecting advertising signs and clocks all over. In the 1950s neon lost its pre-eminence to illuminated plastic signs and by the 1960s its use had declined to beer advertisements and simple signs. Many of the great neon displays were lost during modernization programs, and civic planning groups were responsible for the enthusiastic removal of vintage signs, in line with the aesthetics of the time. Neon clocks of the late 1930s and 1940s – represented most notably by the products of Neo-Lite Corporation of Ohio – now count as the most sought-after collectibles. At present, while artists and galleries are endeavouring to exploit new possibilities of the medium; collectors and neon conservationists are trying to rescue the remains of America's great neon years.

THERMOMETERS AND CLOCKS

Neon clocks account for only a small aspect of the timepieces used in advertising. Before watches became commonplace, public buildings, stores and offices would have a prominent clock, sometimes mounted on a decorated cast-iron pillar in the

Above: *This assortment of beer labels represents only the tip of the iceberg, considering the variety of beers that have been marketed over the years.*

Below: *Whiskey labels are often beautiful examples of commercial printing.*

LEFT: *Blue Heron Citrus label, Florida, 1940s.*

BELOW: *Mont Elisa and Battle Axe Grape labels, California, 1930s.*

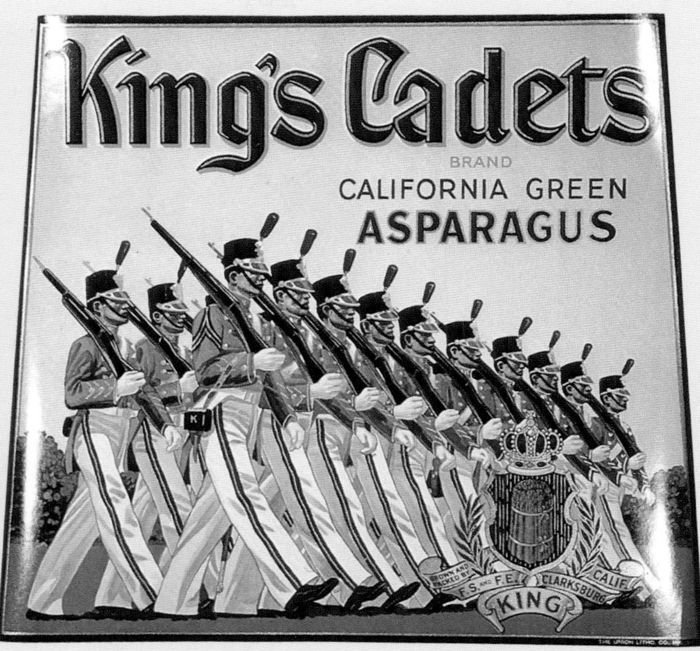

e Bird Citrus
, 1930s.

ng's Cadets
bel, California,

Atom Carrots
nia, 1930s.

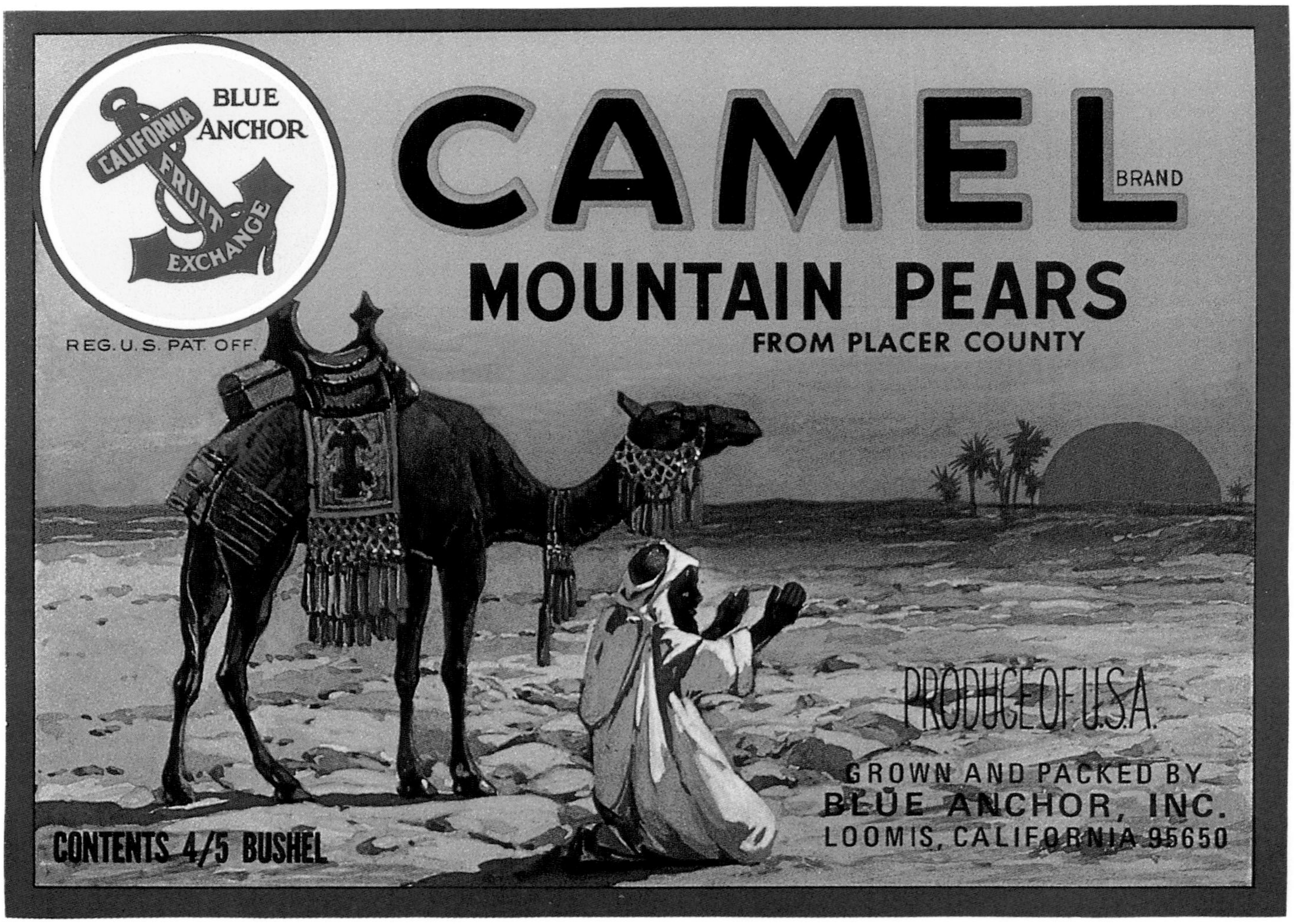

BLUE
ANCHOR
CALIFORNIA
FRUIT
EXCHANGE
REG. U.S. PAT. OFF.
CAMEL
BRAND
MOUNTAIN PEARS
FROM PLACER COUNTY
PRODUCE OF U.S.A.
GROWN AND PACKED BY
BLUE ANCHOR, INC.
LOOMIS, CALIFORNIA 95650
CONTENTS 4/5 BUSHEL

HUSTLER
Brand
EXTRA
CALIFORNIA
BARTLETTS
PACKED & SHIPPED BY
SACRAMENTO RIVER ASSN.
COURTLAND, CALIFORNIA
NET WEIGHT 46 LBS.

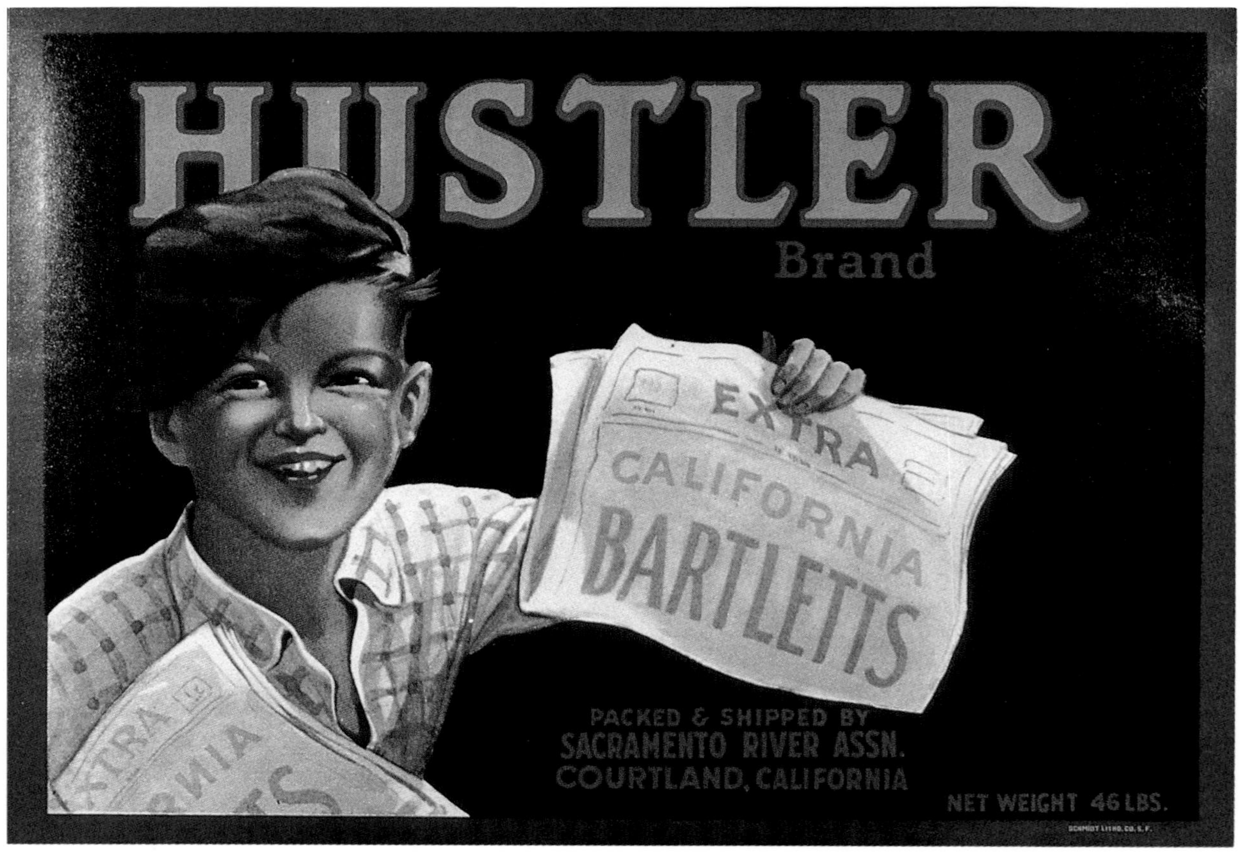

ABOVE AND LEFT: *Vintage condom packs have sufficient appeal to warrant a specialist dealer! They are also of interest to collectors of printed ephemera.*

FACING PAGE, TOP: *Camel Pears label, California, 1930s.*

FACING PAGE, BELOW: *Hustler fruit label, Oregon, 1920s.*

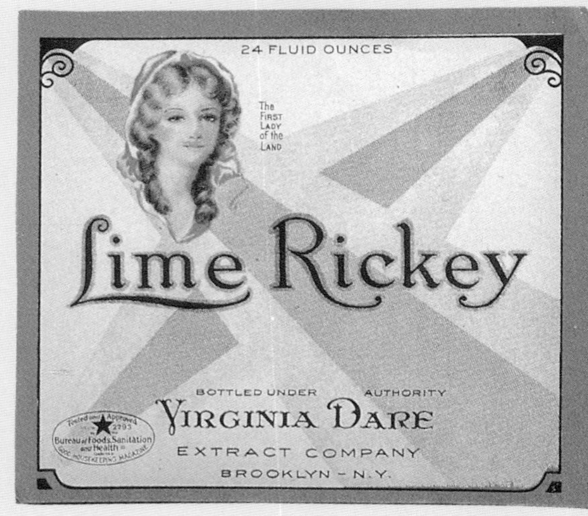

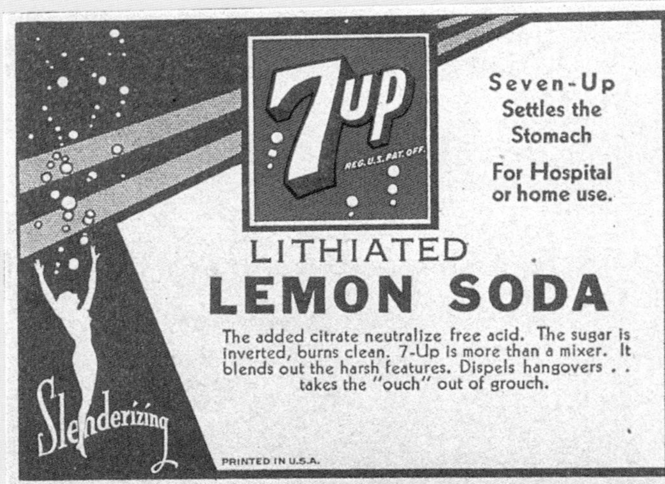

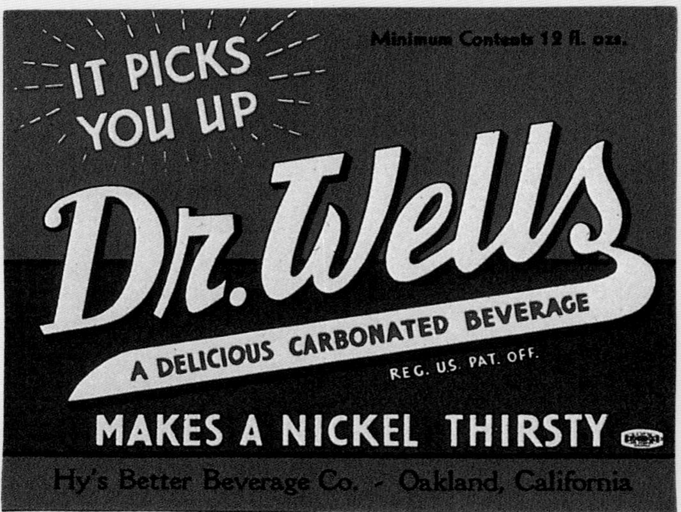

ABOVE AND FACING PAGE, TOP: *Soft drink labels are attractive, low-budget collectibles. As with many drinks, Seven-up was originally marketed as having quasi-medicinal properties.*

RIGHT: *Large paper advertisement for the Victor collar button, 1920s.*

street outside. These clocks often performed the dual purpose as advertising mediums. In the 1880s, clocks were factory-produced, and cheap enough for large companies to supply them to bars, barber-shops, etc as free promotional wares which also provided a public service. An early exponent of such clocks was Coca-Cola, but later virtually every consumer good found its way to a clock face or surround.

Divining the temperature has a similar history to telling the time in relation to advertising gimmicks. Thermometers abound in a variety of materials, from the early cast-iron and wood to plastics. From the last decade of the 19th century, thermometers were often incorporated into a tin, or (less commonly) enamel frame decorated with advertising copy.

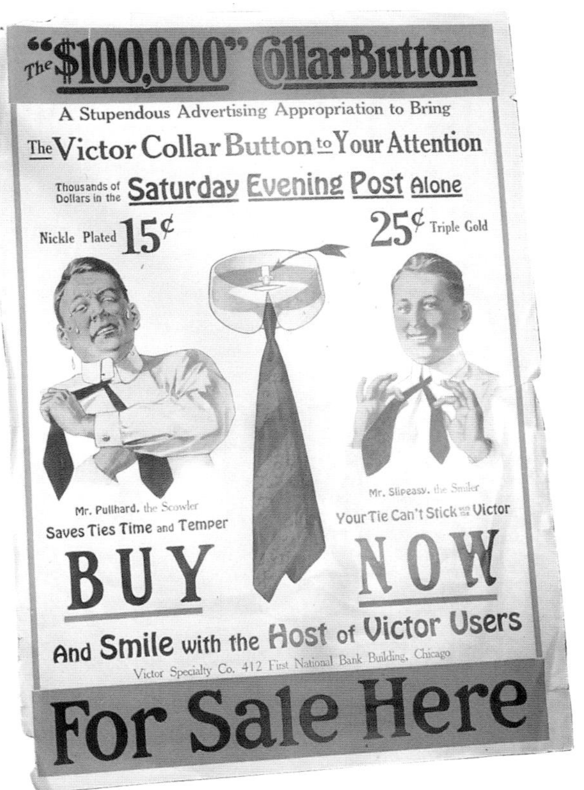

PAPER LABELS

Paper labels are some of the most beautiful examples of advertising art, particularly those which come within the confines of 'Fruit Crate Art'. These labels decorated the fruit produce of California

ABOVE: *War-time propaganda items such as these World War Two recruitment posters are valued as graphic art objects as well as for their historical importance.*

RIGHT: *Printed ephemera preserves a moment from history. Against all odds this bag recording a labor dispute has survived from the 1940s.*

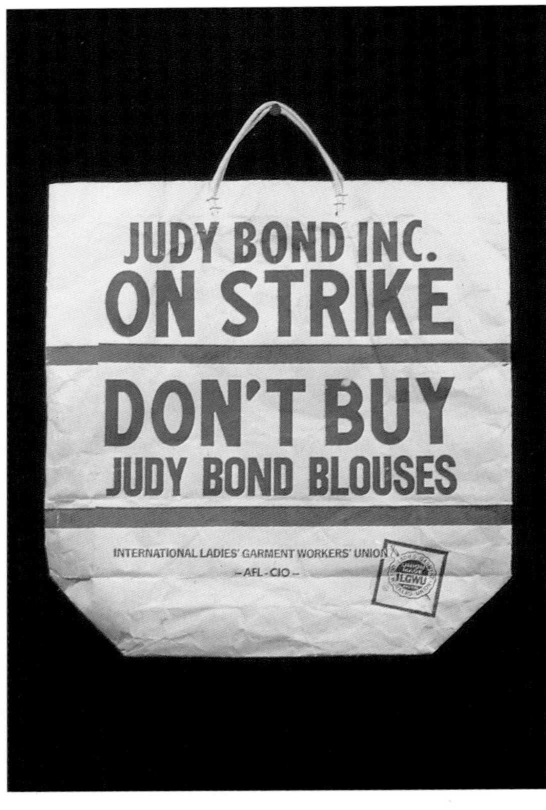

and Florida, from the 1880s – when the railroad network allowed for the nationwide transportation of fruit – to the 1950s, when the traditional wooden crate gave way to cardboard cartons. The golden age of the fruit label was from the 1920s to the 1940s, during which time many thousands of different designs were produced. The colorful images were designed to 'sell' the competitive merits of the fruit in the hectic trading of the wholesale warehouses. A multitude of subjects, including landscapes, birds, animals, 'pin-up' girls, trains and Spanish missions are paired with beautiful lettering. The majority of collectors' labels are unused examples which have been found in printers' shops and fruit wholesalers.

POSTERS – PATRIOTIC AND OTHERWISE

Both World Wars provided fertile ground for the imaginative use of the poster. Since the late 1880s and the days of the European artists like Toulouse-Lautrec and Steinlen, the possibilities of the paper hoarding had been exploited on both sides of the

ABOVE: *Political campaigns leave behind relics of the fight, such as these bumper stickers of the 1960s.*

Atlantic to promote products as diverse as: new magazines and books, trains and holiday destinations, food and drink, bicycles and nightclubs. When the government needed to appeal to patriotic sentiment – both for physical and moral support – the poster really came into its own. Recruitment, propaganda and public service announcements blared from walls and barriers; probably the best known of these posters today is the famous World War I example, 'Uncle Sam Needs You!' emblazoned under the old man's staring eyes and pointing finger.

Although advertising was restricted during World War II, many companies engaged in producing armaments and necessities were allowed to issue patriotic advertisements to keep their name alive until they could resume normal peacetime production. After the war, the art of the poster began an inevitable decline, bested by the aggressive competition of radio and television. Today the majority of posters produced are for records, films and pop concerts – all modish subjects which need to make an immediate impact, since a new event or issue will take its place tomorrow. The old days, when posters appealed to higher emotions or championed claims of consumer trust, are long gone.

Many poster dealers trade through mail order and issue catalogs. The brightness and condition of the poster, as well as its subject matter, are all of paramount importance, and will affect the price accordingly.

BELOW: *Decals advertising skating rinks are popular with ephemera and sports collectors.*

TRADE CARDS

These miniature gems of lithography became popular from the 1880s to about World War I. Although trade cards have existed from the 17th century, it was the advent of cheap color printing that popularized the card as an advertising vehicle. Some were available as stock items, which were then personalized by the addition of the advertiser's name and address. But many were custom-produced, the high quality and elaborate artwork representing the epitome of 19th-century commercial graphics. The most attractive cards were collected even in their own time, and scrapbooks of early collectors' collections still sometimes survive.

HORSFORDS ACID PHOSPHATE
FOR MENTAL & PHYSICAL
EXHAUSTION, DYSPEPSIA, &ca.
OUR PET
IT MAKES A
DELICIOUS DRINK
WITH WATER
AR ONLY
THE MAJOR & KNAPP LITH CO N.Y.

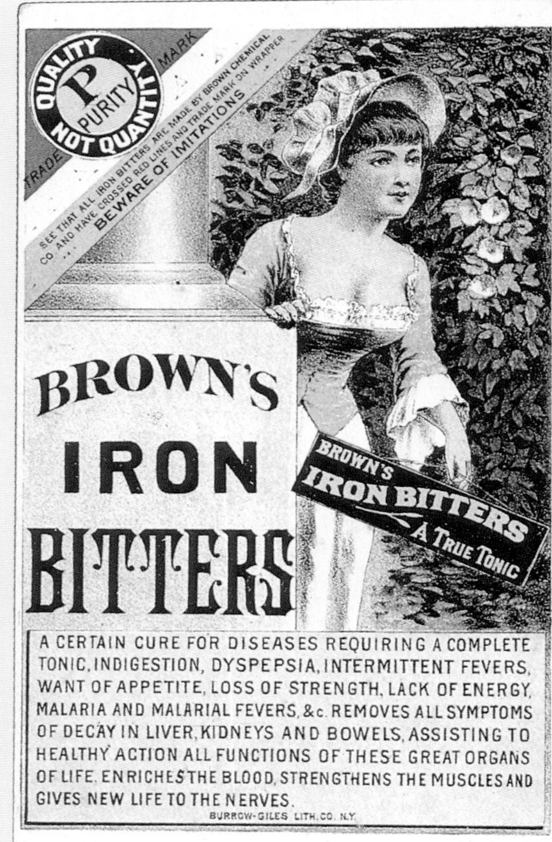
QUALITY
P
PURITY
NOT QUANTITY
TRADE MARK
SEE THAT ALL IRON BITTERS ARE MADE BY BROWN CHEMICAL
CO. AND HAVE CROSSED RED LINES AND TRADE MARK ON WRAPPER
BEWARE OF IMITATIONS
BROWN'S
IRON
BITTERS
BROWN'S
IRON BITTERS
A TRUE TONIC
A CERTAIN CURE FOR DISEASES REQUIRING A COMPLETE TONIC, INDIGESTION, DYSPEPSIA, INTERMITTENT FEVERS, WANT OF APPETITE, LOSS OF STRENGTH, LACK OF ENERGY, MALARIA AND MALARIAL FEVERS, &c. REMOVES ALL SYMPTOMS OF DECAY IN LIVER, KIDNEYS AND BOWELS, ASSISTING TO HEALTHY ACTION ALL FUNCTIONS OF THESE GREAT ORGANS OF LIFE. ENRICHES THE BLOOD, STRENGTHENS THE MUSCLES AND GIVES NEW LIFE TO THE NERVES.
BURROW-GILES LITH. CO. N.Y.

DECEMBER
SUN MON TUES WED THUR. FRI. SAT.
1 2 3 4 5 6
7 8 9 10 11 12 13
14 15 16 17 18 19 20
21 22 23 24 25 26 27
28 29 30 31
The
ELECTRIC LIGHT
ILLUMINATING
OIL
BEST IN THE WORLD
J. O. DORR'S SON.
46 HARRISON ST. N.Y.

COMPLIMENTS OF THE
"DOMESTIC" SEWING MACHINE CO.

THIS PAGE AND FACING PAGE: *These typical trade cards are not only a gallery of late 19th- and early 20th-century graphic art but are also a source of information about the products they advertise.*

ASK FOR **WHITTEMORE'S POLISHES**

The Oldest and Largest Manufacturers of Shoe Polishes in the World. Finest in Quality. Largest in Variety.

"**DANDY**" combination for cleansing and polishing all kinds of russet or tan shoes, 25c. "Star" size, 10c.

"**MIDGET**" **ox blood** and "**JEWEL**" **brown** combinations, 10c. each.

"**ELITE**" combination for gentlemen who take pride in having their shoes look A1. Restores color and lustre to all black shoes. Polish with a brush or cloth, 25c. "Baby Elite" size, 10c.

"**BUCK**" Powder, a dry cleaner, cleans and whitens buck, nubuck and suede shoes. In sifting top cans, 10c. and 25c.

"**GILT EDGE**" the only ladies shoe dressing that positively contains OIL. Blacks and Polishes ladies' and children's boots and shoes, **shines without rubbing**, 25c. "French Gloss" size, 10c.

"**SUPERB**" A **water-proof** paste polish for **all** kinds of black shoes and **old** rubbers. Blacks, polishes, softens and preserves. Contains **oils** and **waxes** to **polish** and **preserve** the leather **Large** tin boxes, 10c. Boxes open with a key "Dandy" Russet Paste same size and price.

"**QUICK WHITE**" makes dirty canvas shoes clean and white. In liquid form so it can be quickly and easily applied. Will not rub off. A sponge in every package, so always ready for use. Two sizes, 25c. and 10c.

"**ALBO**" cleans and whitens canvas shoes. In round white cakes packed in zinc boxes, with sponge, 10c. In handsome, large aluminum boxes, with sponge, 25c. Excellent for Buck, Nubuck and Suede shoes.

Chas. G. Begin

Athol, Mass.

THE BEST THREAD
FOR
ALL SEWING MACHINES
IS
CLARK'S
TRADE
MILE-END
MARK
SPOOL COTTON
BEST SIX CORD
IN
WHITE, BLACK,
AND
ALL COLORS.
COPYRIGHT 1887 BY DONALDSON BROTHERS N.Y.

THIS PAGE AND FACING PAGE: *Trade cards: a mirror of their times.*

SPORTSCARDS

The main subjects for collectors are football and baseball, although quite recently interest in bowling collectibles has been growing. The latter include matchbooks and other souvenirs from bowling alleys, as well as jackets, caps and various items decorated with a bowling theme.

With over a hundred years of history behind it, and regarded as *the* national sport, it is baseball that has the most impressive pedigree among sport collectibles. Cooperstown, New York, the home of the Baseball Hall of Fame, is both capital and mecca to lovers of the game. The core of the subject is the cult of the Super-Player, who has not only achieved pre-eminence in the game but has taken on the status of a national hero. Everyone knows the names Babe Ruth, Mickey Mantle, Willie Hays, Duke Sneider, Ted Williams, and Joe DiMaggio, for instance. Top items include autographed balls, photos and programs. The stars were also immortalized in portrait figurines made by the Hartland Plastics Company, between 1958 and 1963. These are especially sought-after, as are the special edition portrait postcards by artist Dick Perez, which bear the genuine autograph of the player. On a lower level, there are the vast quantities of 'arcade' cards, dispensed by vending machines, and baseball cards packaged with tobacco, candy and chewing gum. Baseball card collecting is an enormous subject, with some of the most desirable cards now sufficiently valuable to attract forgeries. Originating in the last century, the first cards ('T' cards) came with tobacco. Chewing tobacco has traditionally been linked with baseball since pitchers chewing their 'wad' and spitting before throwing the ball was a classic image of the game.

The 1920s saw 'E' cards issued by American Caramel, National Caramel and York Caramel. But from the 1930s to today, gum manufacturers took over. Among the first were Goudey Gum and Gum Inc. After 1945, Bowman Gum and Topps (who eventually took over Bowman) became the main card producers, joined in the 1980s by Fleer and Donruss. Complete sets from various series can be extremely valuable.

In addition to 'star'-related material, baseball collectibles encompass souvenir programs, particularly those for the all-important World Series and All-star games. Programs for games which for one reason or another are important in baseball history are also very desirable, as are yearbooks, which have been produced since the 1940s. 'Special' baseball items include: autographed bats, balls, gloves and mits – which have sometimes been sold to benefit charities – and press-pins, which were first issued to journalists and special guests for World Series' games in 1911. These have the special attraction of being produced in limited quantities.

At present, football collectibles do not generate the same excitement as those for baseball. The first gum cards appeared in 1933 as part of the Goudey Sports Kings set, to be shortly followed by the exclusively football National Chiclets set. After World War II, both Bowman and Topps issued football cards. Generally speaking, football has not produced the same level of cult hero as baseball, although the same type of material, such as autographed photos, postcards and programs, are available to the enthusiastic collector.

UNIVERSAL
FASHION COMPANY
LONDON, PARIS
&
NEW YORK.
WEMPLE & COMPANY NEW YORK.

USE
LAUTZ BROS & CO'S
SOAPS.
BEST
in the Market.

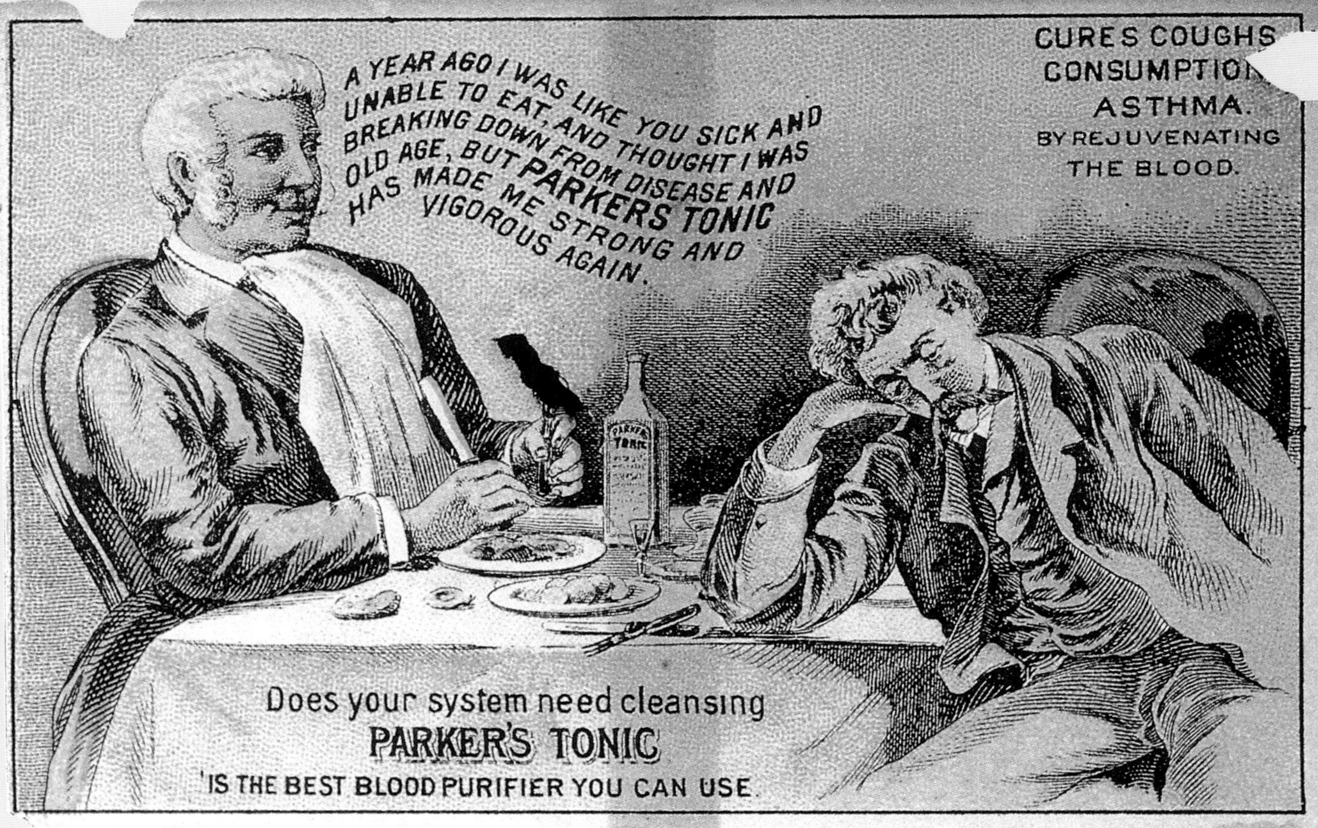

A YEAR AGO I WAS LIKE YOU SICK AND UNABLE TO EAT, AND THOUGHT I WAS BREAKING DOWN FROM DISEASE AND OLD AGE, BUT PARKERS TONIC HAS MADE ME STRONG AND VIGOROUS AGAIN.
CURES COUGHS
CONSUMPTION
ASTHMA.
BY REJUVENATING
THE BLOOD.
Does your system need cleansing
PARKER'S TONIC
IS THE BEST BLOOD PURIFIER YOU CAN USE.

NEW YORK CITY,
771 BROADWAY, CORNER 9TH ST.

Ladies! The immense crowds that have visited the GREAT FAIR STORE *every day since the opening, proves that it is a decided success. This is the first time that a store of the kind has been started in New York, and the ladies all acknowledge it is what has long been needed. The few prices that are quoted show what extraordinary bargains are being offered. Ladies' all silk Handkerchiefs, 21 cents, worth 75 cents; Ladies' Silk Clocked Balbriggan Hose, 19 cents, worth 50 cents; Corsets, 24 cents, worth 88 cents; Umbrellas, 27 cents, worth $1. A good article white hemmed Handkerchief, 4 cents; Ladies' and Children's Hose of every description. A complete assortment of Ladies' Underwear, Kid Gloves, Laces, Ribbons, Ties, Notions, Handkerchiefs, Towels, Napkins, Tablecloths, Perfumery, Jewelry, Cutlery, Toilet Articles, Soap, Stationery, Pocket Books, and many other articles for ladies' use. Also, a full line of Gents' Furnishing Goods, at*

THE GREAT FAIR STORE,
771 Broadway, cor. 9th St.
☞ *Be careful and look for the number*—**771.**

THIS PAGE AND FACING PAGE: *Color and monotone, illustrated and not: a selection of varied trade cards.*

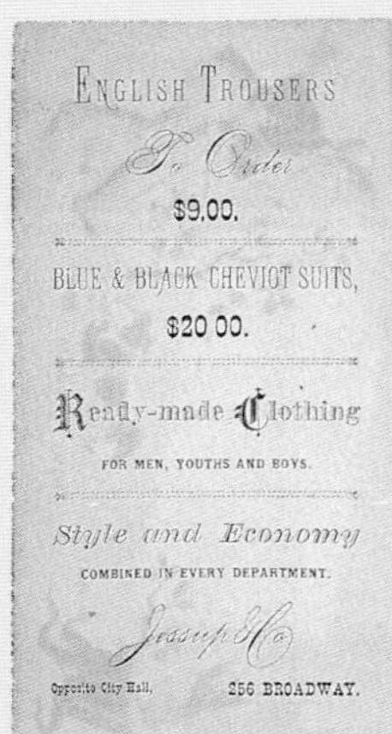

THIS PAGE AND FACING PAGE: *Trade cards for Yellow Cab, Jessup and Company, Diamond Dyes and Wheeler & Wilson.*

The Burns
VINCENT W. FOOTMAN, Manager
MAIN 4700
Yellow Cab
Hail It Any Place

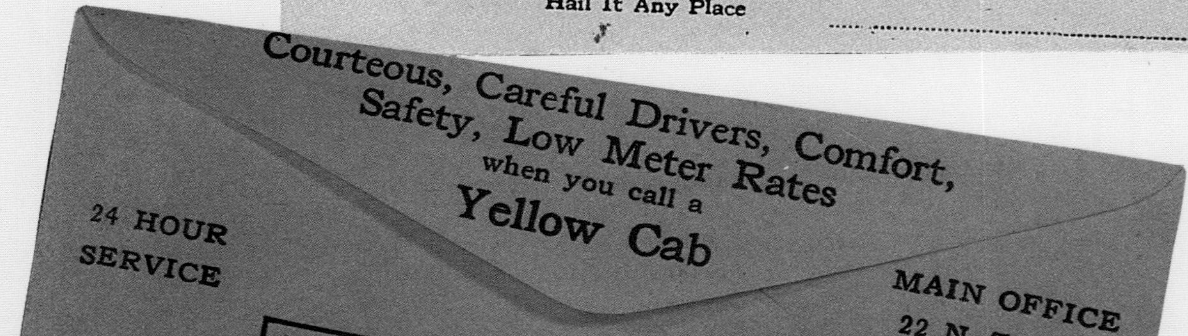

Courteous, Careful Drivers, Comfort,
Safety, Low Meter Rates
when you call a
Yellow Cab
24 HOUR SERVICE
MAIN OFFICE
22 N. TEJON
W & L
Baggage, Transfer, Moving, Shipping, All kinds of Storage
Service
PHONE MAIN 97

THE ✣ DIAMOND ✣ DYES

For Domestic and Fancy Dyeing.

For 10 Cents sufficient Dye of any color is given to dye from one to four pounds of any goods, according to shade wanted.

ANY ONE CAN EASILY COLOR

DRESSES, COATS, CLOAKS, SCARFS, HOODS, YARNS, STOCKINGS, CARPET RAGS, RIBBONS, FEATHERS,

Or any fabric or fancy article to any shade wanted and without risk of failure.

THESE Dyes are far superior to all other dyes or dye stuffs, not only in the bright shades but in Black, Brown, Navy Blue, Seal Brown, Cardinal Red and other dark and rich colors, so much desired by all, but hitherto not obtainable of good quality. Each Dye is complete in itself, thereby saving all extra expense and trouble of buying other articles to set the color.

LIST OF COLORS.

Yellow,	Eosine (Pink),	Garnet,	Brown,
Scarlet,	Violet,	Bismarck,	Crimson,
Plum,	Magenta,	Navy Blue,	Old Gold,
Slate,	Dark Blue,	Cardinal Red,	Orange,
Dark Green,	Seal Brown,	Black,	Green,
Dark Wine,	Purple,	Light Blue,	Maroon,
Drab,	Olive Green,	Cardinal, for Cotton,	
Blue, for Cotton,	Yellow, for Cotton,	Scarlet, for Cotton.	

The above Dyes are prepared for Dyeing any article of Silk, Wool, Feathers, Hair, Paper, Basket Work, Easter Eggs, Liquids, and all kinds of fancy work. Most of them will color Cotton, Linen, Jute, and every species of fabric or fibre.

We warrant these Dyes to color more goods, package for package, than any other package Dyes in the market, and to give more brilliant and durable colors. Wherever known they are fast superseding all other dye stuffs.

COLORING COTTON.

Our new colors, for cotton, will be found greatly superior to any now in use. They will stand washing and light, and are the very best Dyes known for cotton. See new sample book of cotton colors.

MAKE YOUR OWN INK.

One package of Dyes makes a pint of any color Ink. Ask the Dealer.

FOR SALE BY

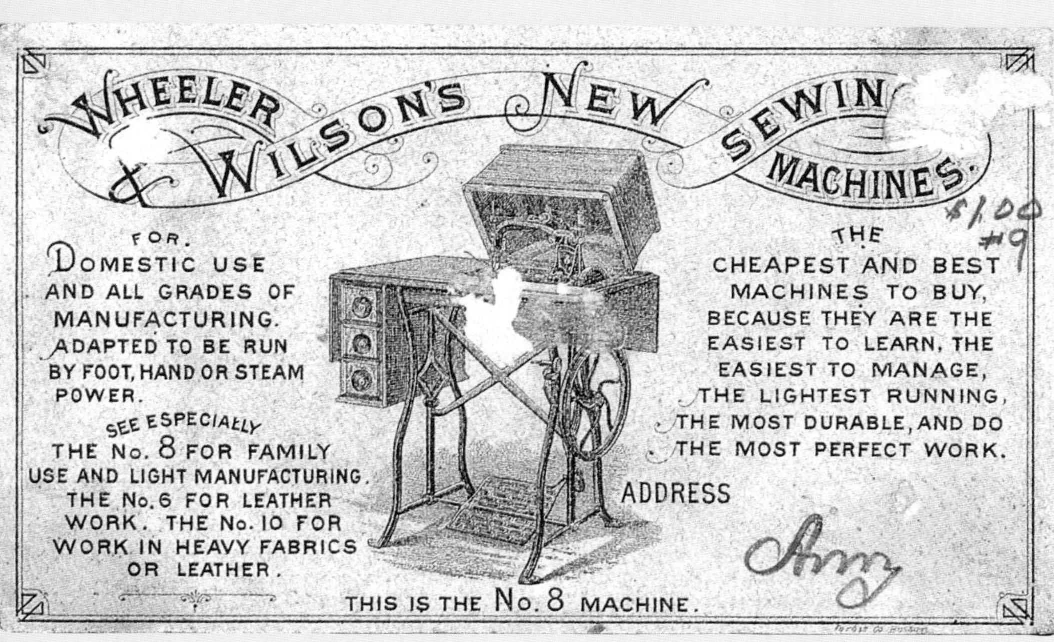

SOUTHERN
LINES
PACIFIC

GRAND
TRUNK
WESTERN

NICKEL
PLATE
ROAD

THE SOUTHERN
SR
SERVES THE SOUTH

NORTHERN
PACIFIC

Santa Fe

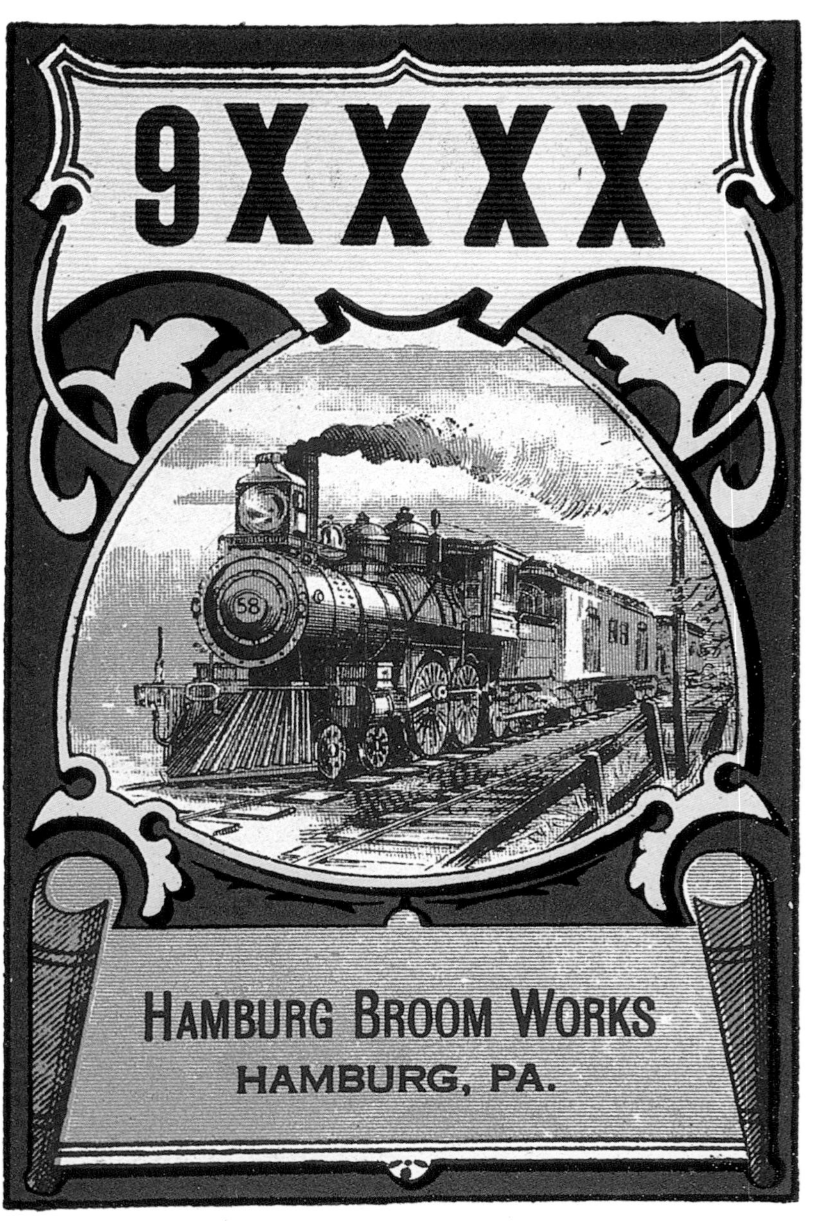

TRAINS

From the woodburning 'iron horse' of the Old West to the streamlined splendor of the 'silver streak', trains have been an integral part of the nation's history. Particularly in the 1930s, when the future extensive use of airplanes was not yet foreseen, the railroads enjoyed an enthusiastic revival. The new locomotives and stock represented the highest achievements of industrial design, including the work of Norman Bel Geddes and Ramond Loewy. The Burlington Zephyr (known as the Silver Streak for its polished stainless-steel surface) was the star attraction of the 1934 Chicago World's Fair, while the other great trains – the Blue Comet, the Super Chief, the Twentieth Century Limited, the Broadway Limited, the Silver Meteor, the Electroliner and the Sunset Limited – realized an idealized marriage of speed and luxury. In the early 1950s well-known figures such as Ronald Reagan extolled the virtues of train travel in advertisements, but by then its rivals – air travel and the automobile – were poised to take over.

So vast is the pageant of railroad history that many collectors choose one era, or one type of train, or one line in which to specialize. Train items include: advertising ephemera; timetables and tickets; dining-car china and flatware; conductor's and other employee's uniforms, hats and buttons; lamps, switch keys and tools.

HOTELS

The middle of the last century saw the advent of the great hotels, a natural corollary of both train and ocean travel. Romantic names like the Colony

ABOVE: *The woodburning 'iron horse' locomotive is an evocative image of American history.*

RIGHT: *Breakfast cereal premiums – miniature tin railroad signs.*

Hotel, Jerusalem; Raffles, Singapore; Shepherd's, Cairo; the Mount Nelson, Capetown; the Mamounia, Marrakesh – all became watering holes to the great and the literary. Hotel collectibles include luggage stickers, menus, postcards, ashtrays, china and flatware.

AUTOMOBILES

Although automobiles have long been a popular focus for the specialist collection, ranging from grand prix and classic sports cars to more prosaic vehicles, they do not fit within the scope of this book. However, the host of car-related material available does, whether it is collected to complement a car collection or as articles of interest in their own right. This area naturally coincides somewhat with gasoline collectibles, and includes sales brochures, postcards, sales premiums (model cars for children were often given when father purchased a new car) hubcaps, license plates and hood ornaments.

License plates, traditionally produced in the workshops of state penitentiaries, were originally enameled on flat sheets, but in the early 1920s they became embossed metal. Although at one time they were valid for one year only, recently stickers have shown the expiry date. Various states – particularly those actively courting tourists – have incorporated an emblem or slogan to 'advertise' the state, and there have also been special plates, most particularly to commemorate the Bicentenary of Independence. License-plate holders have also been allowed to be used for advertising or a promotional purpose. Early plates seem to have survived in the more rural regions, hoarded as useful bits of metal for patching leaking roofs!

Hood ornaments range from the exotic crystal sculptures designed by the French firm Lalique, to the standard chrome versions riveted onto production cars. Motifs include birds, animals, nude ladies, Indian heads, planes and rockets. Some are endowed with a special feature, such as animation or illumination. Several hood ornaments have now been reproduced, and there is always the danger that these are being passed off as originals.

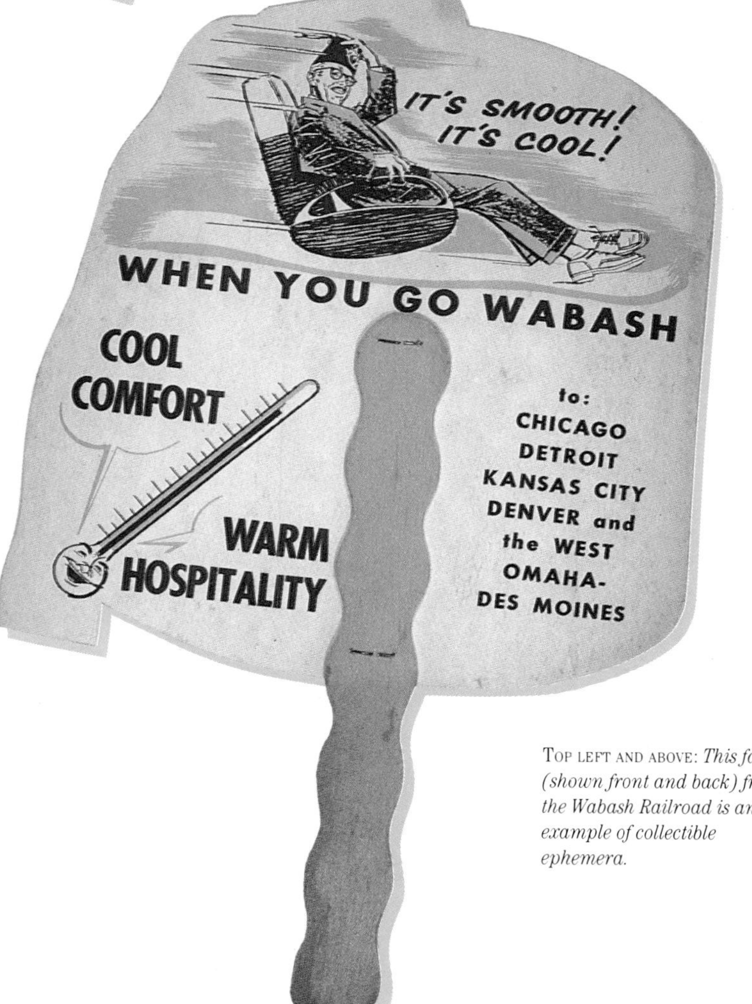

TOP LEFT AND ABOVE: *This fan (shown front and back) from the Wabash Railroad is an example of collectible ephemera.*

ABOVE: *Miniature tin railroad signs.*

ABOVE LEFT AND BELOW: *There is a contrast between the styles of these two metal signs: the traditional dating from the 1940s and the stylized 'turnpike' from the 1960s.*

LEFT: *These miniature tin license plates were a premium issued by General Mills 'Kix' breakfast cereal in 1953.*

BELOW: *Mascots can be a subject for specialization, or part of a general automobilia collection: this sturdy chrome dog is familiar as the emblem of Mack trucks.*

BOTTOM: *License plates can be of interest for having great antiquity, or for other special qualities, such as commemorative issues. There are also decorative plates, like this example from Arizona.*

COMIC AND CALENDAR COLLECTIBLES

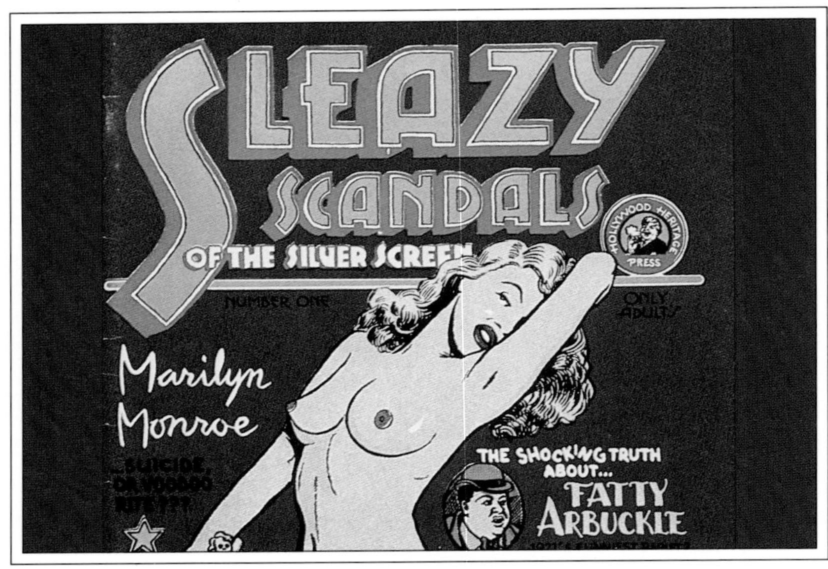

Reading for children and adults-only pin-ups – from strips to striptease.

ABOVE: *Comics have not always been for children only, as this first issue of* Sleazy Scandals *indicates.*

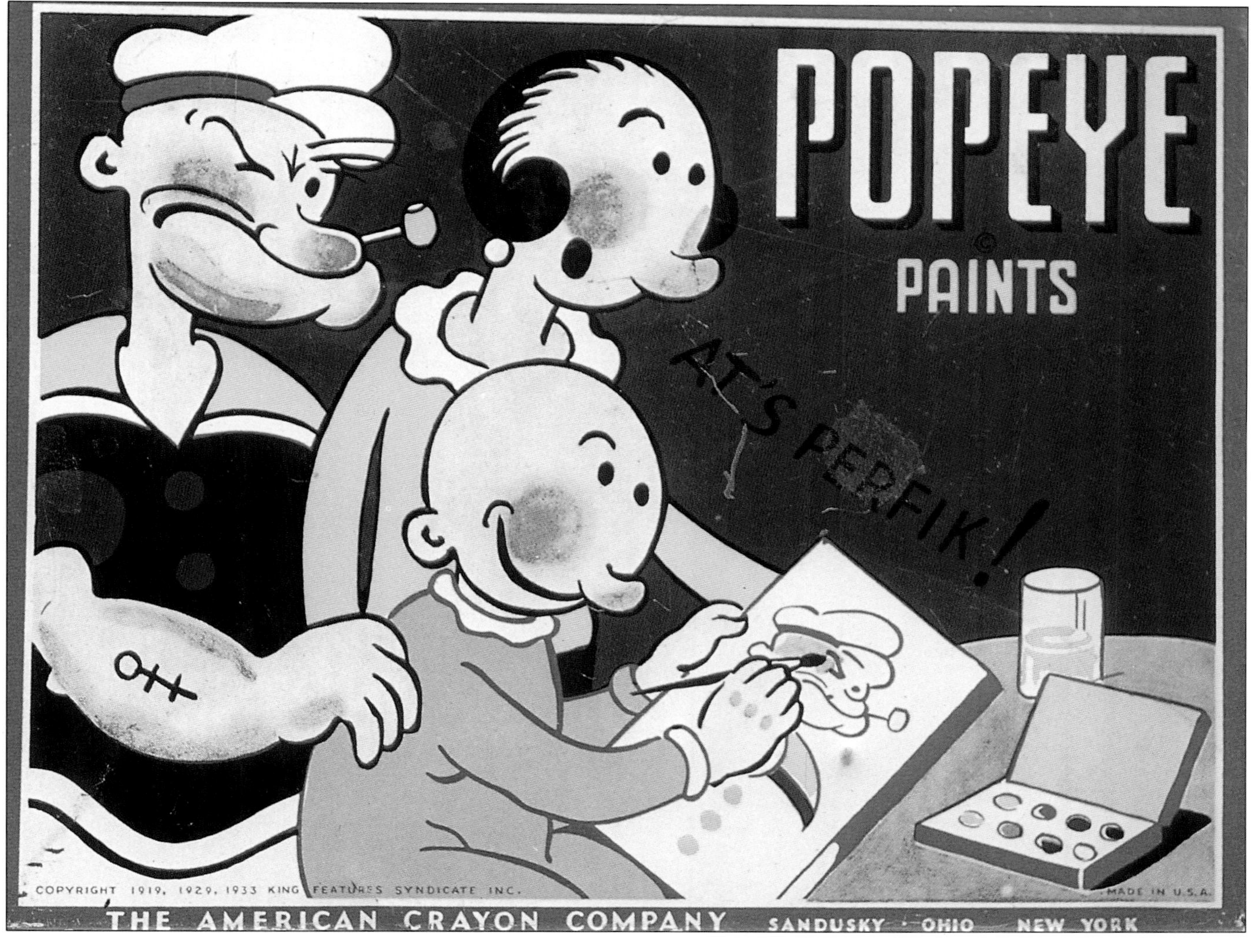

ABOVE: *Popeye and company were used to advertise such everyday products as crayons.*

Cinema – and soon after, publishing – history was made when Walt Disney introduced the internationally-famous figure of Mickey Mouse to an eager public in 1928. He was followed by an army of much-loved characters. Astute licensing governed their transfer from celluloid to the printed page and countless products, assuring that none of the characters were debased. Other popular animated stars were similarly treated, including Orphan Annie, Betty Boop, Popeye, Bugs Bunny, Batman, Superman, through to Spiderman and beyond.

Although mass popularization owes much to this century's communication and entertainment media – the radio, cinema and television – the roots of cult cartoons can be seen in 19th-century newspaper comic strips, whose first starring character was the Yellow Kid. This impish street urchin appeared in 1896, and was one of the first comic characters to be represented in figurines and other novelties. Their age and scarcity put Yellow Kid items in the top bracket of cartoon collectibles, both in terms of price and status.

Another example of a graphic image going on to become a cult is of course Kewpie though she is best known as a doll. Serial comic strip adventures were pioneered by Bud Fisher with his Mutt and Jeff, who began their daily newspaper appearances in 1907. Soon the 'funny papers' became a popular section of the newspaper. But by far the most successful of the early characters – who did not have benefit of the massive syndicating and marketing campaigns that more modern characters such as Snoopy or Garfield enjoy – was Little Orphan Annie. First appearing in 1924, the vacant-eyed waif built up a readership of some sixteen million. Annie's cheerful optimism symbolized for many the indomitable spirit of America's refusal to be beaten by the Depression, and probably accounts for her popularity during that time. Orphan Annie collectibles include figurines, dolls, games and puzzles, as well as the Big Little Books.

BIG LITTLE BOOKS

These books, which enjoyed great success during the Depression years, sold for only a dime. Although the name should properly only be applied to books by the Whitman Publishing Company who trademarked the title, other companies used the same format – about 5in high by 4in wide by 1.5in (12.7

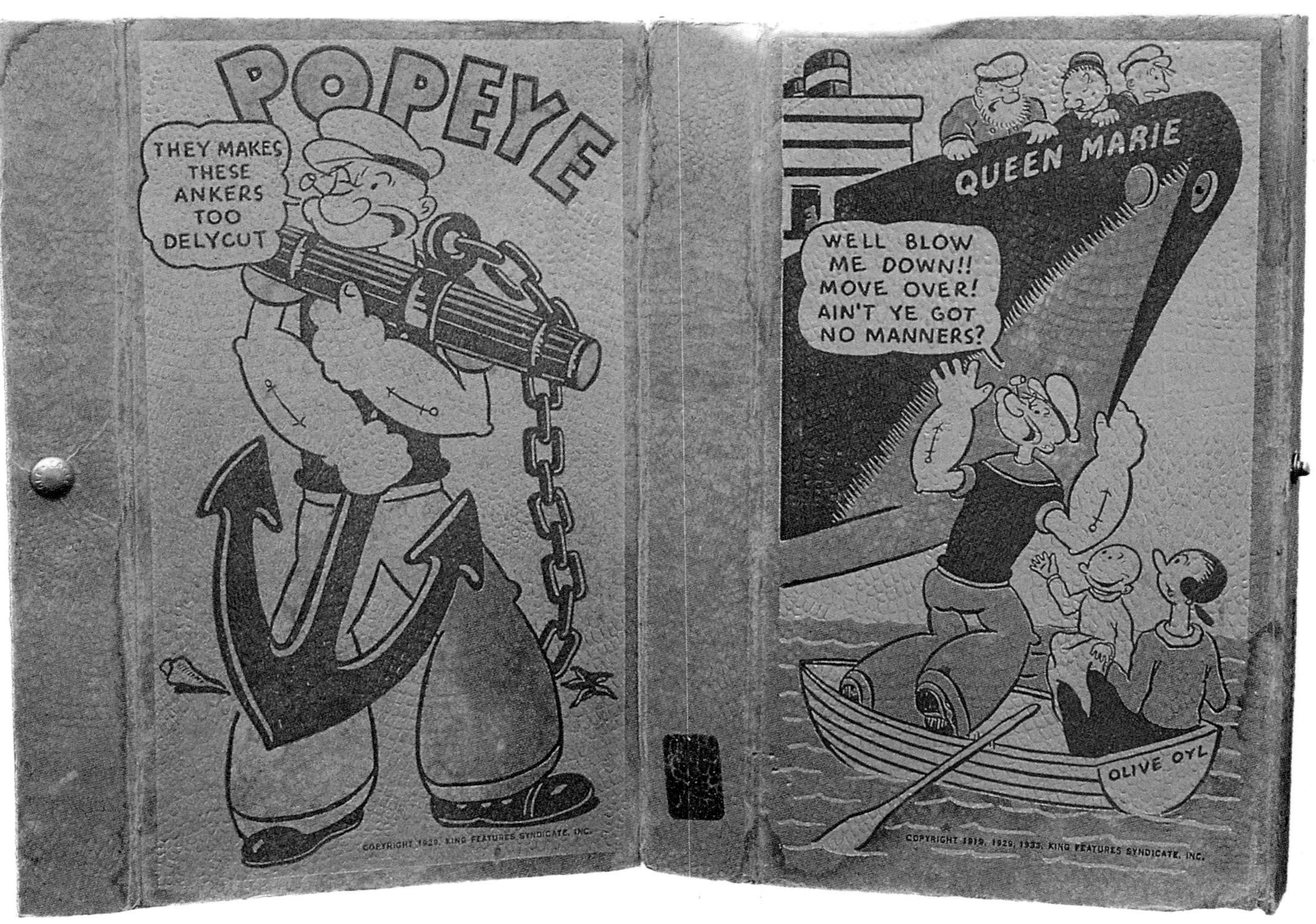

ABOVE: *The power of Popeye to sell becomes evident from the number of products he was used to endorse.*

FACING PAGE, TOP: *Calendar girl from the 1940s.*

FACING PAGE, BELOW Sleazy Scandals *issue no. 1, 1974.*

× 10.1 × 3.7 cm) thick, with bright cardboard covers and colorful illustrations.

Examples include Dell Publishing's *Fast Action* books, Fawatt Publishing's *Action* books and Soalfield Publishing's *Little Big* books. The Big Little books, as well as including sports titles and simplified versions of literary classics such as Tom Sawyer and Little Women among their number, mainly featured characters from the comic pages. In addition to Orphan Annie there was Alley Oop, Blondie, Dick Tracy, Lil 'Abner and Popeye. The cinema contributed such names as Jackie Cooper, Mickey Rooney and Judy Garland, as well as Mickey Mouse, Donald Duck, Bugs Bunny, Krazy Kat and Laurel and Hardy. Radio characters included the Lone Ranger, the Green Hornet and The Shadow. The high quality of the artwork of Big Little books has been a major factor in their recent popularity as collectibles. There is a high demand for examples in the rarely-found 'new' or 'mint' condition. Big Little book artists included Alex Raymond, Henry Vallely, Al Capp, Allen Dean and Will Gould.

The luxury version of the Big Little books were the die-cut pop-ups, introduced by Blue Ribbon Books in 1932. They featured much the same range of comic characters, and have experienced even a lower survival rate.

THE COMIC ALTERNATIVE

Although the Big Little books, under various guises by various publishers, continued into the television age, they eventually lost their popularity to the comic book. After their initial success in the newspapers, many of the early strips were subsequently reprinted, either as advertising premiums or for sale. The first comic book in the modern genre was 'Funnies on Parade', in 1933, while the first monthly comic was the ten-cent 'Famous Funnies' of July 1934. These were both shortly followed by King Comics Corporation, founded in 1936. In 1938 the most universal comic hero of all, Superman, was introduced in 'Action Comics', to be followed by a whole succession of super-heroes, including Captain Marvel, who entered the lists in 1940, Wonder Woman, Captain America, The Green Lantern, Hawk Man and Mary Marvel (Billy Batson's – aka Captain Marvel's – long-lost twin sister). The 1940s saw comic books reach enormous popularity, Captain Marvel alone selling at the rate of 2,000,000 copies every two weeks! During the 1950s, comics faced the twin threats of television competition and the hostility of parents and educationalists. The last were particularly concerned by the appearance in 1954 of a book condemning comics for,

among other things, causing juvenile delinquency. The author took special exception to the horror comic which had joined the ranks of super-heroes, detective, western and war subjects. The 1960s and 1970s witnessed a revival in comics, with a new generation of super-heroes accompanying renewed interest in the originals. It was also at about this time that comics began to be taken seriously, especially since pop artists like Roy Lichenstein and Andy Warhol contributed to this belated recognition in their own art. As a result several early super-hero comics were re-issued.

The ever-escalating value of comic collectibles has attracted much publicity, particularly from press and television. Their reports often pretend incredulity that a mass-produced ten-cent throw-away item from yesteryear can now be worth thousands. It is hard to understand why this attitude persists, as other cheap, mass-produced throw-aways known as postage stamps have been taken seriously, considered valuable and collected for over 100 years! Whatever the arguments, comic books are now prime investment items, but the careful collector must know his subject. Condition is important – tears, spine damage, rusty staples, bent covers or foxing all affect the price. Keep valued copies in archival storage bags.

CALENDAR ART AND PIN-UPS

As mentioned earlier, some collectors treat calendar art as a corollary to their own specialist interests, but these card-and-paper datekeepers are also collected for their own sake. Although the works of such artists as Maxfield Parish and Norman Rockwell have appeared on calendars, the term 'calendar art' is almost synonymous with the 'girlie' or 'pin-up' calendar. Whether these should be regarded as charming artefacts from the past, or as examples of degrading, exploitive sexism, will be up to the individual collector. But there is no escaping the fact that the pin-up – who became a popular image in the pages of *Esquire* magazine, on matchbooks, playing cards and the fuselages of World War II airplanes – also brought her artistic values to the walls of thousands of workplaces, and ended up by becoming a kind of American institution. The printing company Brown and Bigelow, the world's oldest and biggest calendar producers, issued the first girlie calendar 'Meditation', which featured an alluring young damsel, seemingly bare-breasted beneath her long, pre-Raphaelite tresses. In 1913 the first nude pin-up appeared, the notorious 'September Morn', which featured as a best-selling image on numerous other objects as well. Thousands of the calendars, including pirate productions, were sold.

RIGHT Playboy *magazine, Christmas issue December 1962.*

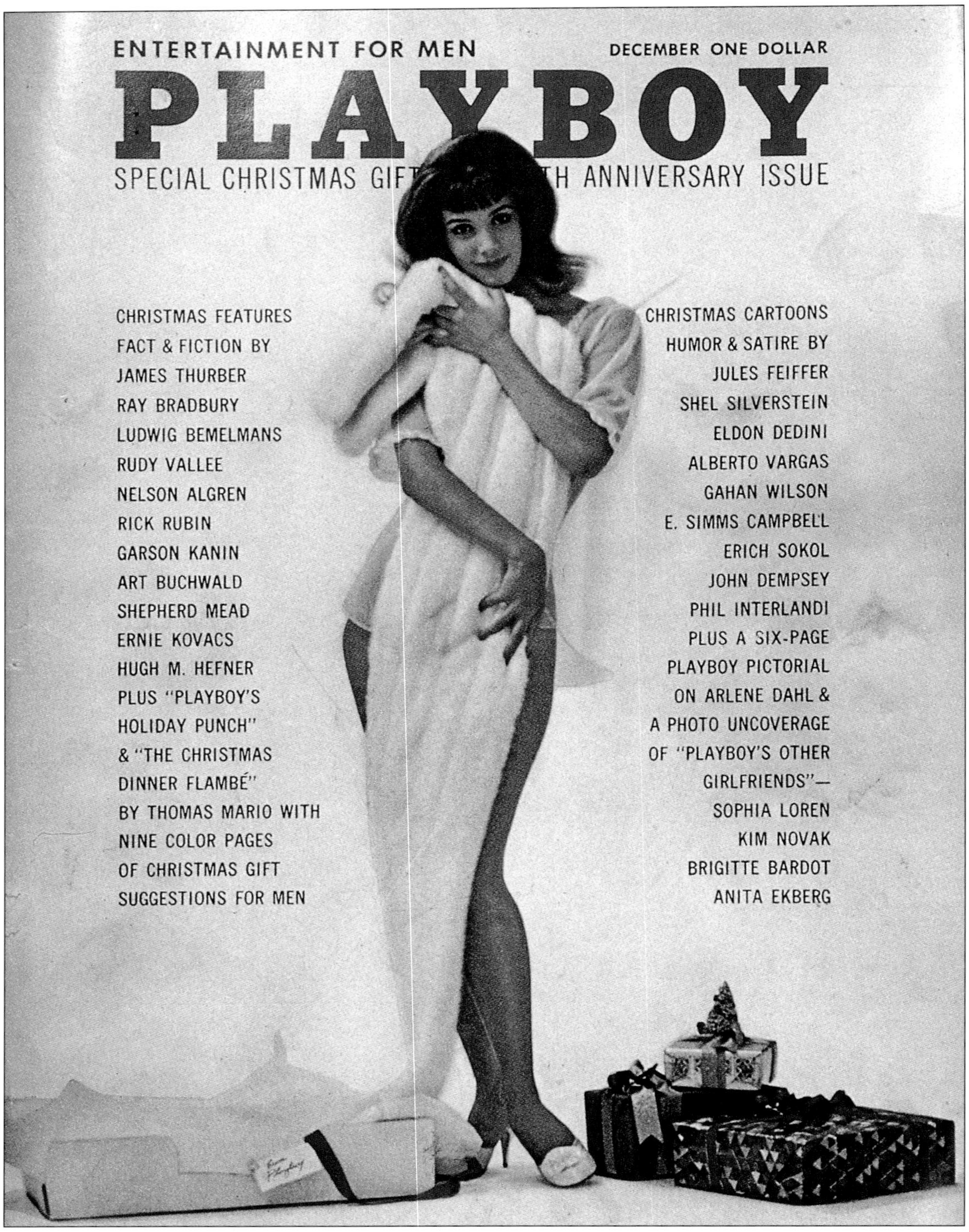

ENTERTAINMENT FOR MEN DECEMBER ONE DOLLAR

PLAYBOY

SPECIAL CHRISTMAS GIFT TH ANNIVERSARY ISSUE

CHRISTMAS FEATURES
FACT & FICTION BY
JAMES THURBER
RAY BRADBURY
LUDWIG BEMELMANS
RUDY VALLEE
NELSON ALGREN
RICK RUBIN
GARSON KANIN
ART BUCHWALD
SHEPHERD MEAD
ERNIE KOVACS
HUGH M. HEFNER
PLUS "PLAYBOY'S
HOLIDAY PUNCH"
& "THE CHRISTMAS
DINNER FLAMBÉ"
BY THOMAS MARIO WITH
NINE COLOR PAGES
OF CHRISTMAS GIFT
SUGGESTIONS FOR MEN

CHRISTMAS CARTOONS
HUMOR & SATIRE BY
JULES FEIFFER
SHEL SILVERSTEIN
ELDON DEDINI
ALBERTO VARGAS
GAHAN WILSON
E. SIMMS CAMPBELL
ERICH SOKOL
JOHN DEMPSEY
PHIL INTERLANDI
PLUS A SIX-PAGE
PLAYBOY PICTORIAL
ON ARLENE DAHL &
A PHOTO UNCOVERAGE
OF "PLAYBOY'S OTHER
GIRLFRIENDS"—
SOPHIA LOREN
KIM NOVAK
BRIGITTE BARDOT
ANITA EKBERG

BELOW: *'Girlie' waterside decals, 1940s.*

From these origins grew the whole school of pin-up art, leading exponents of which were Rolf Armstrong, Earl Moran, Gil Elvgren, Fritz Willis, George Petty, Al Moore, and – generally regarded as the king of them all – 'Varga' Alberto Vargas. Varga's name is inseperably linked with *Esquire* magazine, whose pages had been originally enlivened by the eponymous 'Petty' girls. The 'Varga' girl first replaced George Petty's version in the calendar for the December, 1940, *Esquire*. Hitherto, girlie calendars had been used as an advertising medium. But with *Esquire*'s sale of 300,020 Varga calendars, the pin-up girl was launched.

The climate of World War II assisted the cult of the pin-up to flourish. While the fantasies decorated planes, lockers and walls, the real-life Betty Grable became an officially-endorsed morale booster for the troops. In recognition of such appreciation, *Esquire* patriotically provided some 6,000,000 copies of the magazine – specially printed for the troops and devoid of any advertising – free of charge during the war years, with a further 3,000,000 distributed to the workers on military installations!

Although the popularity of the airbrush-rendered pin-up continued, the postwar years saw the increased use of photography. The most famous photographic girlie calendar was the 1951 Marilyn Monroe example, published by John Baumgarth Company from Tom Kelley's 1949 photo session with the then unknown starlet.

LEFT: *General merchant's calendar for 1945 is typical of stock printers' calendars.*

CINEMA AND CARTOON COLLECTIBLES

Mickey Mouse rubs shoulders with Marilyn Monroe in a roll-call of memorabilia from the silver screen.

ABOVE AND FACING PAGE, TOP: *Snow White skittles game exemplifies the countless toys, games and other items that owed their being to the creativity of Walt Disney.*

While comics were initially responsible for the creation of super-hero, the cinema was responsible for another aspect of American pop culture, the animated cartoon character. The first movie cartoon hero was Felix the Cat, introduced by Otto Messmer in a 1919 silent, 'Feline Follies'.

CARDBOARD MICE

Felix was a cult figure into the 1930s, and was used as a motif on a range of products, including nursery china, ashtrays and toys, as well as appearing as figurines and dolls. Although Felix was to enjoy a career as a newspaper comic strip from the 1930s to the 1950s, his cinematic star was outshone by the arrival of Disney's mouse.

The legendary Walt Disney has already produced a very successful cartoon character, 'Oswald the Lucky Rabbit'. Oswald, who actually looked a bit like Mickey Mouse, appeared in 26 Oswald silent films. Upon discovering that his contract with Universal Pictures had given them the rights to Oswald, Disney created a new character, first called Mortimer Mouse. Mrs Disney liked the character but not the name, and at her suggestion the mouse was called Mickey.

The first Mickey Mouse animated film was 'Plane Crazy' made in 1928 in the wake of the hysterical adulation of Charles Lindbergh. This was almost immediately followed by 'Gallopin' Gaucho'. But before either was released, Disney saw Al Jolson's The Jazz Singer (1927), the first talkie. Realizing that sound would transform the cinema, Disney made the third Mickey film, 'Steamboat Willie', into a talkie, with Walt himself providing the voice of Mickey. The immediate success of this, the first talking cartoon, led to 'Plane Crazy' and 'Gallopin' Gaucho' being issued with added sound. Within two years, Mickey Mouse cartoons were being made at the rate of about one a week!

MICKEY COLLECTIBLES

No fictional character has ever come close to the universal popularity of Mickey Mouse. Celebrating his 60th anniversary in 1989, the little rodent still entertains adults and children with undiminished success. His fans have included Franklin and Eleanor Roosevelt, Charles de Gaulle and Andy Warhol. No other character has been presented in so many different forms, making Mickey Mouse especially – and to a lesser degree all Disney creations – one of the biggest fields of collectibles. Why Mickey has such universal appeal defies simple analysis. But why so much collectible Mickey material exists is, however, simply because of the astute promotion Disney gave the character.

The Mickey Mouse Clubs were founded in 1929, and cinema managers sponsored club events. Banks made Mickey savings banks to encourage young savers, while bakeries iced Mickey birthday cakes. Within three years the club had over 1,000,000 members in the United States, as well as clubs in other countries.

In 1928 Disney agreed to allow the use of Mickey on the cover of a school notebook. That deal made him $300, but he soon realized the even greater

BELOW: *With so many thousands of Mickey Mouse items having been produced over the years it is not surprising that some collectors are happy to specialize in Mickey alone!*

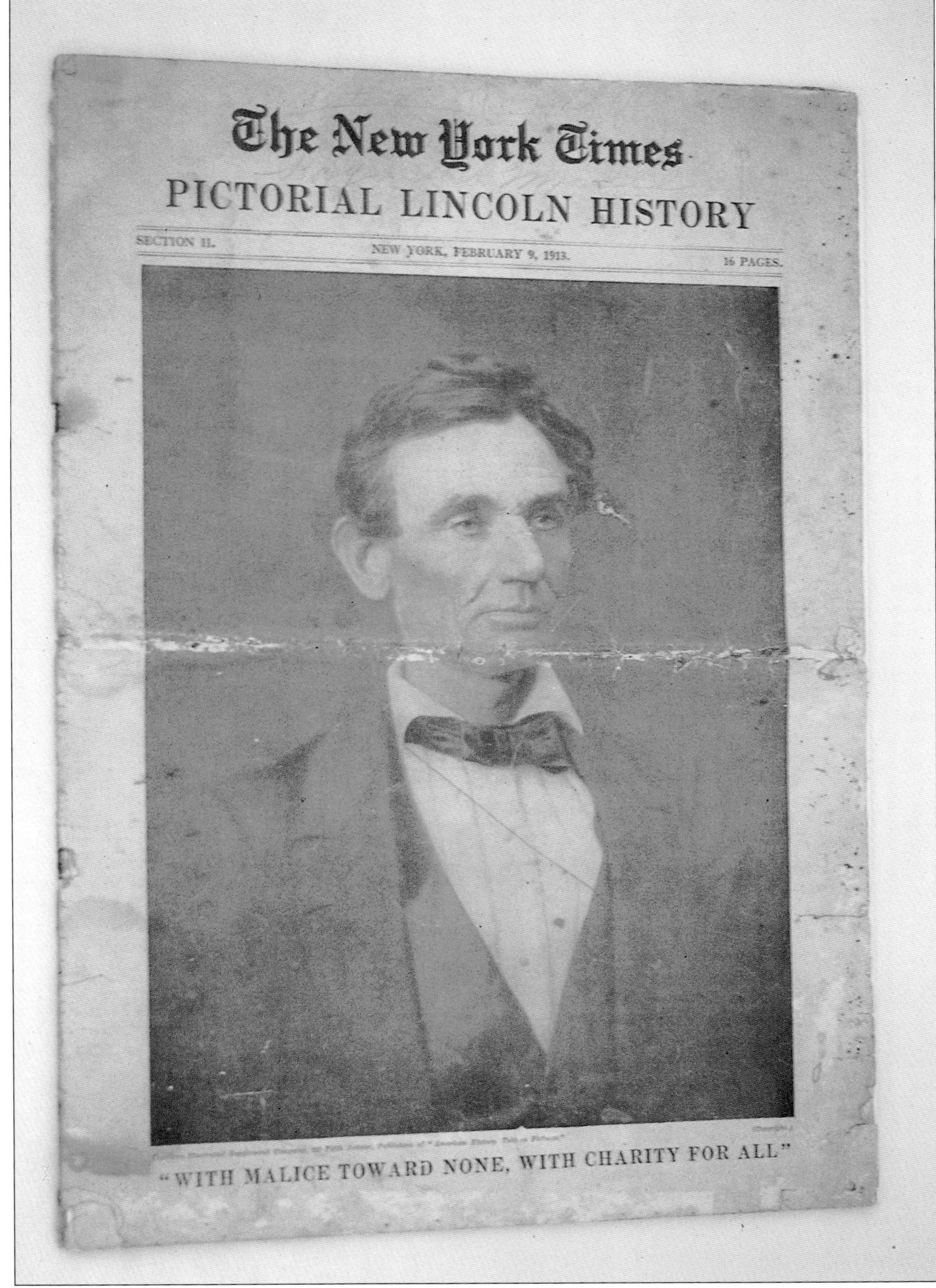

The New York Times

PICTORIAL LINCOLN HISTORY

SECTION II. NEW YORK, FEBRUARY 9, 1913. 16 PAGES.

"WITH MALICE TOWARD NONE, WITH CHARITY FOR ALL"

LEFT: *Special edition of the* New York Times, *9 February 1913, featuring a pictorial history of President Lincoln.*

Interest in social history is an obvious corollary to an interest in collecting. Even the least expensive and most ephemeral items can carry a strong 'feel' of an earlier time and place. Some of the most evocative sources of past times are old newspapers and magazines. Nearly everyone has discovered stored-away goods wrapped in an old newspaper, and found themselves smoothing out the creases to read it! American newspapers date to the beginning of the 18th century with *The Boston Newsletter*, but it was the 19th century, with its improvements in printing, in the fast communications brought about by the telegraph, and in the speed of distribution made possible by the train, that saw the introduction of the modern news journal. Collectors relate to their own local history.

A particularly popular aspect of newspaper collecting is a concentration of front page news –

ABOVE: *Mary Pickford graces the front cover of the* Illustrated Review, *1921.*

TOP LEFT: Illustrated Review *April 1921.*

ABOVE RIGHT: Pictorial Review, *December 1932, has a stylish front cover.*

RIGHT:Saturday Evening Post, *August 1938.*

major events as seen through the headlines. Though a collection of the front pages of *The New York Times, The Cleveland Plain Dealer,* or *The Boston Globe* would provide a march through the highlights of American history, the old adage that you can't believe everything you read in the papers is surely borne out by the rare issue (3 November 1948) of *The Chicago Tribune,* whose headline proclaims 'Dewey Defeats Truman!'

Unfortunately, magazines are still being despoiled by having advertisements cut out of them. Although these advertisements, particularly those by well-known illustrators or featuring film or radio stars, make great decorative items, they are still best appreciated in the context of the entire magazine in which they featured. At least since magazines have aroused increasing interest as collectibles, there is now a greater chance that they will be preserved intact.

The great age of magazine publishing was between the 1920s and the 1950s, a period distin-

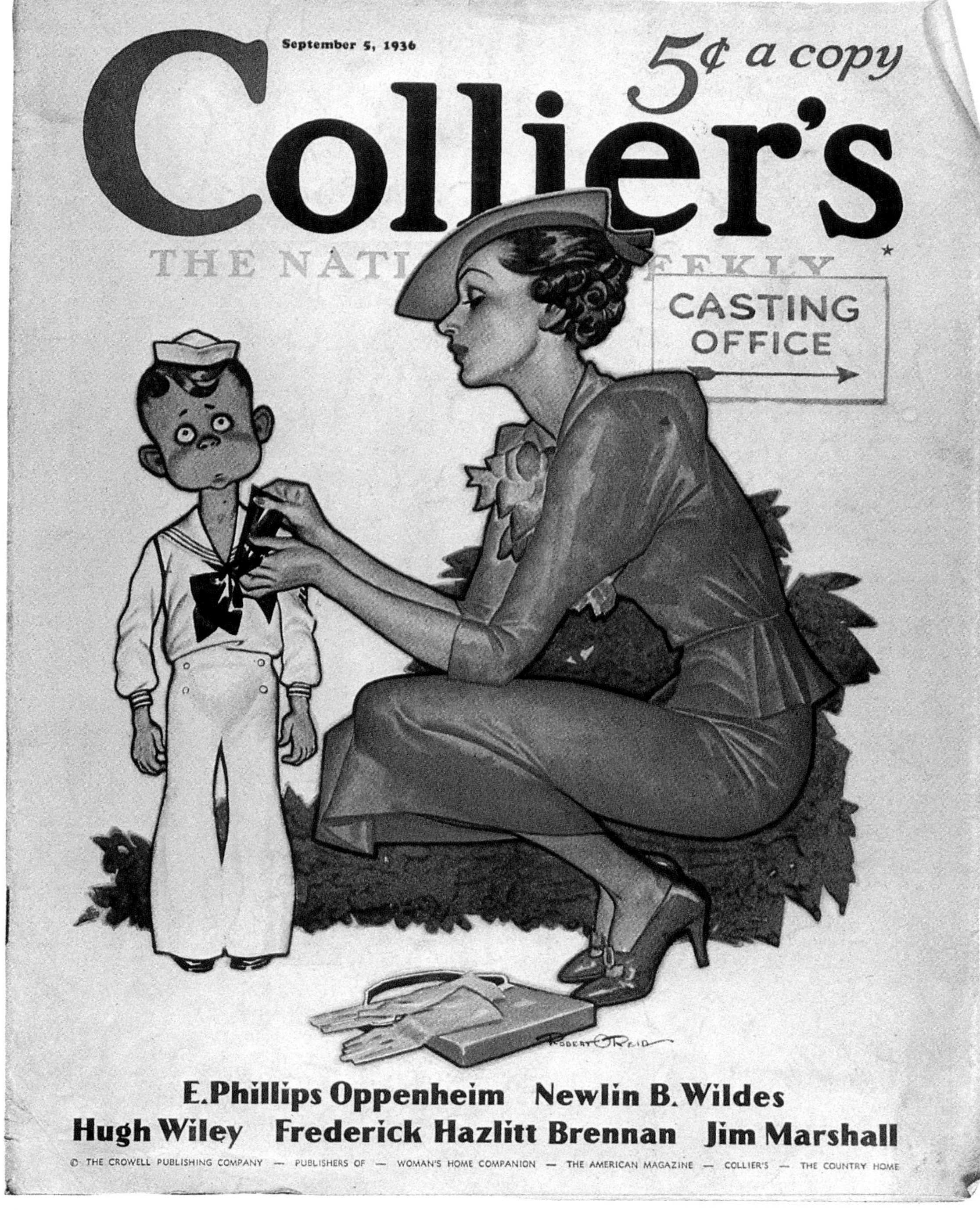

September 5, 1936
5¢ a copy
Collier's
CASTING
OFFICE
E. Phillips Oppenheim Newlin B. Wildes
Hugh Wiley Frederick Hazlitt Brennan Jim Marshall
© THE CROWELL PUBLISHING COMPANY — PUBLISHERS OF — WOMAN'S HOME COMPANION — THE AMERICAN MAGAZINE — COLLIER'S — THE COUNTRY HOME

LEFT: Colliers *magazine for September 1936.*

guished by an increase in cheap color printing and steadily increasing subscriptions. By the late 1950s high production costs and the overwhleming popularity of television were responsible for their decline.

Excluding front-cover art – a magazine collectible in its own right – the subject area can be subdivided into a variety of categories. Broad interest areas demarcated the buying public: family reading (*Colliers, The Saturday Evening Post, Life, Time, National Geographic*); women's interest and home matters (*Vanity Fair, Woman's Home Companion, Women's World, Good Housekeeping, House Beautiful,* and *House and Garden*); business (*Fortune*), as well as magazines for children, about hobbies or rural interests, and much more. Artwork by the likes of Norman Rockwell, Rose O'Neill, Maxfield Parish, or Varga, brightened the covers, while inside articles by important writers and studies by famous photographers, provide unique records of events sometimes unrecorded elsewhere. Magazines which are particularly collectible at the moment include those covering film, science fiction, fashion and sports. Many have a 'cult' following, especially *Playboy, Vogue, Mad* and *Modern Screen.*

GLASS AND CHINA COLLECTIBLES

Breakable and bankable goods that offer the most varied choice of any collectible, with something to suit all tastes and pockets.

ABOVE: *A collection of carnival glass, showing the vivid colors that make it so sought after.*

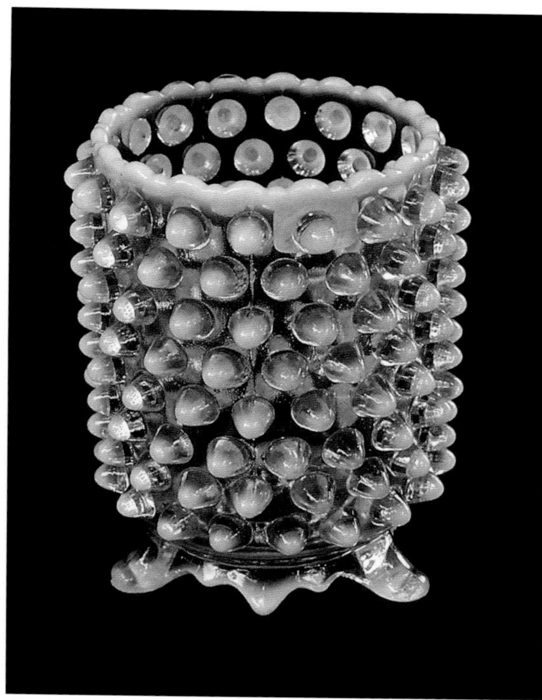

LEFT: *Clear hobnail glass.*

Entire books have been written on the single subject of late 19th- and early 20th-century pottery and china – and, indeed, glass – so this chapter combining the two is meant as a brief overview, designed to give the interested novice an idea of the opportunities in both fields. The information relayed is concerned primarily with the material itself, rather than the forms which it takes, although there are many objects, such as bells, ashtrays, cups, inkwells and figurines, which command a large coterie of collectors no matter what their constituent material. For this reason, industrial and kitchen glass is excluded, with the exception of insulators.

INSULATORS

These sculpted knobs of heavy glass deserve a brief mention, if for no other reason than their unique fascination. They date back to the second quarter of the nineteenth century, and accompanied the introduction of the telegraph. The first patented insulator was registered in 1844, and was followed by a succession of designs brought out by a myriad of manufacturers and inventors. Over 500 separate designs have been recorded! Although prices and values are seldom mentioned in this book, it is interesting to note that the rarest insulators can now be worth in excess of two thousand dollars.

PRESS-MOLDED GLASS

Most popular collectible glass tends to be mass-produced. Though the majority of domestic glass and pottery was originally made in large quantities, the vicissitudes of time have ensured examples of sufficient rarity to stimulate interest.

The advent of press-molded glass in the 1840s allowed for more invention in design and greater economy compared to the previous technique of blowing. The glass used at this time was of lead-flint; the change-over in the post-Civil War period to lime glass, – a cheaper material – allowed for increased production. The burgeoning commercial market and growth in the numbers of salesmen and outlets in turn influenced the push towards large scale mass-production. Cheap colored glass was perfected in the 1870s, and by the 1890s there were over 400 factories producing large quantities of colored glassware. From this background and period come the bulk of glass collectibles. The two major areas for the enthusiast are those of Carnival and Depression glass.

LEFT: *An unusually shaped blue glass vase with patterning.*

BELOW: *A hobnail milk glass vase.*

THIS PAGE AND FACING PAGE: *Some of the many forms of Depression glass, in the popular translucent green.*

CARNIVAL AND DEPRESSION GLASS

As the name implies, Carnival glass was originally intended to be won as prizes at fairs. Although the type originally came from Czechoslovakia it was widely manufactured in the United States, and – as was much mass-produced American glass – successfully exported. It is characterized by an iridescent sheen, which is also to be found in the carnival-style post-Depression 'Iris' range by the Jeanette Glass Company. A unique type of carnival was Goofus glass, also known as Mexican Ware, Hooligan Glass, or Pickle Glass. Manufactured by several companies – including the Crescent Glass Company, Imperial Glass Corporation, and Northwood Glass Company – it is distinguished by the fact that its pressed designs are also painted. The impermanent nature of this paint explains its original decline in popularity, with the result that production came to a halt. Any surviving examples in good condition are much sought after.

The description 'Depression glass' is applied to a range of glassware dating from the early 1930s. Although it has sometimes been called Tank Glass, the more evocative name has become the one universally accepted. The Depression era officially began with the collapse of Wall Street's stock market on 24 October 1929 – 'Black Thursday' – and the economic effects continued to become increasingly severe until Roosevelt's New Deal of 1933 began the slow move toward recovery. The remainder of the decade was distinguished by assistance like the National Recovery Act, the Works Progress Administration, and the Federal Emergency Relief Administration. Finally, the demoralizing 'Brother can you spare a dime' image of the bleakest years gave way to a generally more optimistic mood.

Against this background, Depression glass became one of the few flourishing consumer items. Cheaply mass-produced, and in many ways a successor to the European-derived molded glass which had been given as fairground prizes, it boasted over 130 different patterns and styles. Each pattern encompassed an array of items, ranging from plates, shakers and bowls to candlesticks and vases. Nearly all these items are of a surprisingly high quality. The patterns are as varied as the uncompromisingly angular 'art deco' lines of the Indiana Glass Company's 'Tea Room' to the Venetian look of the Martinsville Glass Company's 'Radiance'.

BELOW AND FACING PAGE: *Samples of carnival glass.*

PLASTICVILLE

While plastic has been given a passing mention in this chapter, it has been ignored as a subject in its own right. To continue this omission would be to ignore Plasticville, a collectible that authentically records the architecture of the American townscape. These snap-together molded plastic kits were primarily designated to go with toy trains. Their manufacturer, Bachmann Brothers Inc., had moved into plastics after a varied history that had begun in the last century as ivory workers. After a modest start in 1949, production of Plasticville blossomed into a range of realistic model diners, filling stations, and houses in varying styles – in short, everything needed to create a miniature town. The little buildings were produced in a varity of scales to suit the choice of model trains. I favor the term 'model' rather than 'toy' as a tribute to the high quality of detail achieved by such manufacturers as Ives, American Flyer and Lionel.

ABOVE: *Plasticville, a relative newcomer to the world of toy collectibles, preserves in miniature the American townscape of the 1950s.*

LEFT: *Molded plastic gasoline truck, late 1940s.*

Above and below: *Plasticville miniatures of 1950s America.*

TRAINS

Trains have possessed a special romance, even when toy-sized. The train had played such a major role in the opening up of the country during the 19th century and its transport supremacy was only eroded after World War II by air and space travel, that it was a natural candidate for male pre-occupation. It has long been an accepted tradition of family life that Dad buys a train set as much for his own enjoyment as for Junior's. Although low-budget trains continued to be made as tin wind-ups, during the 1920s through to the late 1950s, the best examples were electric powered. The three factories of the Lionel Corporation of New Jersey produced over three-quarters of the nation's locomotives and cars and accessories. Although more recent train sets have their enthusiasts, the extensive use of plastics today is generally regarded as a blow to quality.

ABOVE: *An Ives gauge o electric locomotive shown with Ives and Lionel carriages, c 1932.*

LEFT: *Two gauge o electric locomotives made by Lionel: a Union Pacific 'City of Portland' three-car diesel unit, c 1934, next to a Mini Scale NYC 'Hudson', c 1937. They are shown with the Lionel 'Hell Gate Bridge'.*

MARBLES

Marbles are long-established collectibles, with the value of top examples now fetching thousands of dollars! Although the majority of marbles are machine-made, the most desirable specimens are handmade.

There are enormous amounts of marbles available but sought-after types include swirls, with variations such as clambroth – a milk glass with multicolored swirls running through the solid base color; Indian swirls – black with twists of brilliant color over the surface; Latticinio swirls – having a 'lacy' center surrounded by swirls; and Lutz marbles – the swirled ball enriched with copper grains (these are known as Goldstone swirls). Other swirl types include 'open core', where the swirl is in the core of the marble; peppermint, where the swirls resemble peppermint candy; 'solid core' swirls, which are similar to peppermint but in different colors. One variation of the 'core' swirl is the childhood favorite known as 'cat's eye'. Every collector will have his or her special choices.

ABOVE AND BELOW: *A sample of the vast range of marbles available to the collector.*

Other favorite styles include agates or 'aggies', made from stone which is either in its natural color or artificially dyed; clay marbles, used in both the earliest specimens and in modern ones; 'cloud' marbles, made of glass, with a solid core encapsulated in a clear shell; micas, in which the glass marbles incorporate flakes of mica, giving the silvery effect of tiny fish scales; and sulphides, clear glass marbles in which a china figure is embedded.

Marbles, as with most toys (with the exception of teddy bears, where wear and tear – the scars of having been much loved – are acceptable) are valued in pristine condition. Generally, size is also a factor, the rule being the bigger the better.

LUNCH BOXES

These metal boxes from the 1950s and the 1960s, bright with logos and icons of childhood, are among the hottest things in collecting at the moment complete with fast escalating prices. The fact that lunch boxes were turned out in vast quantities is countered by their poor survival rate, a classic situation with many childhood collectibles. Despite their lowly status, these boxes demonstrate a high quality of lithographic printing, acting as a showcase for the work of some of the leading commercial illustrators of the period, such as Robert Burton, Ed Wexler and Nick Lobianco. Although vinyl plastic came into use in 1959, and a new generation of brunch bags, also in vinyl, were introduced for the teenagers who had outgrown their lunch box years, these have few aficionados. The true, all-American lunch box is a simple rec-

tangular or dome-topped lithographed tin, at its best combining the qualities of tin toys and comics. It is part of the national perception of childhood experience and is responsible for an assault of nostalgia. Its best years were the 1950s and 1960s after which metal was mainly usurped by plastic on safety grounds. In those two decades lunch box sales topped 120 million, during which time virtually every character from children's mythology, from Hopalong Cassidy to the Munsters, had been given the ultimate seal of juvenile approval: appearing on a lunch box. But the history of lunch boxes pre-dates the 1950s. From the 19th century until 1950, it had been a simple, utility container, favored by construction and other manual workers. The invention of the vacuum flask in 1913 allowed for beverages or soups to feature on the menu and, in 1921, Aladdin Industries introduced the dome-topped lunch box, the lid of which could accommodate the flask.

Although Walt Disney had issued a novelty Mickey Mouse school lunch box in 1935, and there were others on the market at about that time, legend has it that the idea of putting a character on a lunch box for children was mooted during a meeting of Aladdin executives looking for a way to boost sales. In any event, the choice of Hopalong Cassidy for their first 'character' box was an inspired one. Within the first year (1950) 600,000 boxes had gone to school. The trend was well and truly set. The rivalry between box manufacturers went into top gear when American Thermos (which later became King Seeley Thermos, a major lunch box company) brought out the Roy Rogers and Dale Evans lunch box, outgunning Hopalong Cassidy with sales of two and a half million in the first year.

Thereafter the wars between these and other producers such as Adco and Ohio Art ensured that new graphics and characters were constantly coming out, though the boxes themselves retained the standard format. Walt Disney characters were only some of the cartoon characters featured on boxes, though they did establish the record for the all-time best-seller, with 'School-bus', featuring a bus load of Disney favorites – nine million boxes!

TOP LEFT: *Amongst many Walt Disney lunch boxes, 'School-bus', designed by Al Konetzi for Aladdin, is regarded as the classic with its adaptation of the traditional Workman's dome-topped shape.*

LEFT: *The Aladdin Workman's lunch box, first introduced in 1921, led a worthy but uneventful existence until it was transformed into a variety of garish pop art school lunch kits.*

BELOW: *Aladdin's Hopalong Cassidy, introduced in 1950, is credited with popularizing the decorated school lunch box. The illustration was a simple decal, yet it sold 600,000 in its first year.*

ABOVE AND BELOW: *Lone Ranger, one of several television Western designs used for lunch boxes.*

ABOVE AND BELOW: *Although television characters dominate lunch-box graphics, sport was portrayed in 'NFL Quarterback', designed by lunch box illustrator Robert Burton for Aladdin Industries, 1964.*

ADULT PLAYTIME COLLECTIBLES

Gambling toys with the spice of dishonesty, mechanical banks that swallow your money – games for grownups.

ABOVE: *A cast metal animated bank. These mechanical marvels have a variety of actions by which the coin is deposited into the bank.*

CHAIRS

Sturdy and simple chairs, benches and stools were among the earliest furniture to be made in the American colonies. They served a multitude of purposes in the lean-tos, saltbox timber homes and stone dwellings that characterized the settlements of New England and the rest of the Northeast and middle Atlantic region.

Of the earliest 'Jacobean' styles, very few examples remain – the earliest date from about 1650 – but it is known they closely followed the English fashion of the period. Carver and Brewster chairs, named for the first governor and for the respected elder of the Plymouth colony, respectively, were both seats of honor made from the mid-1600s to the begining of the 18th century. While both were usually constructed of ash or maple, with backs and arms of turned spindles, the Brewster version is distinguished by an extra row of spindles on the back (and sometimes under the seat). Wainscot chairs – in oak or ash, plain or carved – were another popular 'best' piece of furniture, but throughout the 17th and early 18th centuries, stools and benches served more mundane uses around the fireside and table.

By the 1670s, turkey-work seats began to proliferate, their upholstery material imported at some expense from England. Less costly were rush-seated ladderback chairs, with turned posts, finials and 'mushroom' hand rests. The end of the century saw the boldly carved cane-back 'Carolingian' chair reign in the home of wealthier citizens.

William and Mary came to the English throne in 1689, but the eponymous style did not arrive in the colonies until some 10 years later. It was marked by an idiosyncratic use of Spanish and ball feet and elaborate vase-and-ring and block-and-vase turning on chairs and 'matching' tables.

Queen Anne styling appeared in England in about 1695. While the colonial avant-garde took up the new vogue as early as 1715 to 1720, it did not become the general fashion in America until the second quarter of the 18th century. The new emphasis on the 'S' curve, or 'line of beauty', meant that the cabriole leg was in evidence everywhere, particularly on chairs, which had replaced stools as the primary utilitarian form of seating. The curving leg ended in a club, pad or trifid foot, which evolved to the claw-and-ball, hairy paw or scroll foot by the 'Chippendale' period. Claw-and-ball chairs were documented in Boston as early as 1737 and Gilbert Ash (1717–85) in New York is credited with some of the finest earliest 'Chippendale' chairs, but the style did not really catch on until the late 1740s; it reached its most elaborate stage of development in Philadelphia between 1760 and 1776, under the aegis of chairmakers such as Thomas Affleck and Benjamin Randolph. Mahogany replaced walnut as the favoured wood, and the looped top rail and solid back splat of the Queen Anne style was replaced in the space of 10 years by the Cupid's bow top rail and openwork, interlaced splats with their 'Gothic' and 'Chinese' influences.

An anomaly of the mid-18th century was the American Windsor chair, certainly influenced by its English predecessor but quite distinct in its execution. The back lacked a back splat and was formed entirely of spindles locking into the top rail, while the chamfered legs sprang from near the center of the seat. This gave the piece a lighter and more vigorous quality than its Georgian counterpart. The American version had two main subdivisions: the hoop- or bow-back type, with the top rail bent into an elongated semicircle meeting the seat at each end, and the comb-back version, in which the top rail was only slightly curved, with the side rails and spindles acting as the 'teeth' of the comb. Variations of these two were legion. First produced in Philadelphia around 1725, these chairs were the most popular everyday form of seating by 1760. Even the members of the Continental Congress sat proudly upon American Windsors when they voted for 'No taxation without representation!' Their predominance continued well until the late 19th century.

For several years the War of Independence put paid to the evolution of new indigenous styles based on tastes imported from England, but by the closing years of the 18th century a new 'Federal' style emerged, encouraged by Thomas Jefferson and like-minded classicists. The term in reality encom-

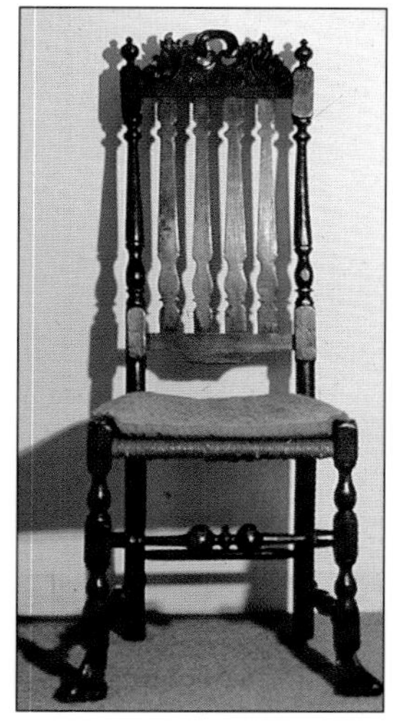

ABOVE: *A William and Mary bannister back chair, probably made c 1710 by John Gaines of Ipswich, Massachusetts.*

BELOW LEFT: *A Philadelphian example of a Queen Anne walnut chair, made c 1740, with the typical shell carving and cabriole legs.*

BELOW RIGHT: *Made c 1760, this Queen Anne walnut armchair displays some of the best craftsmanship seen before American Independence.*

passed a number of divergent but sympathetic styles, including elements of 'Hepplewhite,' 'Sheraton' and, by the start of the new century, French tastes.

While satinwood was a characteristic material in both England and America during this period, birch and maple were aso used by craftsmen in the latter, adding yet another particularly American element to the design. Other elements varied according to the style; American 'Hepplewhite' is usually distinguished by its less funny rendition of a shield-, heart- or oval-shaped back, gracefully enlivened with a carving of plumes or wheat sheaves. The legs are square and tapered, ending in spade or plain feet. 'Sheraton' is much like 'Hepplewhite', although the lines are straighter, even more delicate and vertical in execution. Some excellent inlay and carving are exhibited in the best of these chairs.

ABOVE: *A pair of sack-back Windsor chairs. (Christies, New York.)*

BELOW: *Two Sheraton side chairs with unusual half-animal front legs, made c 1810; possibly by Duncan Phyfe of New York.*

OPPOSITE: *A rosewood Victorian Renaissance revival side chair, made in New York around 1865. (Hirschl and Adler Galleries, New York.)*

The greatest American exponent of this style was Duncan Phyfe (1768–1854) of New York. He dominates the story of American style from 1790 to 1825, and his chairs and sofas are found in most American collections worthy of note. His influence overlapped that of the new Directoire and Empire styles brought back from France. Both were characterized by the dominance of saber curves in the stiles, seat rails and legs, but with the arrival of Napoleon's Empire came the preference for rosewood and heavy mahogany that took root even in the fertile republican soil of America. Noble pieces of Roman grandeur by the New York maker Charles-Honoré Lannuier (1779–1819) vie with those of Phyfe for top place in this era; the Romans themselves would have recognized the curule 'X-seat' that is almost symbolic of American Empire taste.

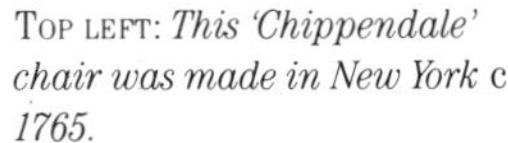

TOP LEFT: *This 'Chippendale' chair was made in New York c 1765.*

TOP CENTER: *This Philadelphian chair from c 1775 is by well-known maker Thomas Tufft.*

BELOW LEFT: *A transitional wing chair from c 1780; the upholstered parts are Queen Anne styling, while the frame is 'Chippendale'.*

BELOW RIGHT: *Two Sheraton chairs made by Duncan Phyfe c 1805 – American Regency at its best.*

TOP RIGHT: *A classic Hitchcock stencilled chair. (The American Museum in Britain, Bath.)*

CENTER RIGHT: *Federal armchair c 1795, unusual in its Louis XVI styling, which was fashionable before the French Revolution.*

Mass-production, the inevitable corollary of industrialization, began around the 1830s. The chair was among the first items of furniture to benefit from the new wave. Lambert Hitchcock (1795–1852) established a factory making chair parts at Barkhamstead, Connecticut, in 1818, but it was not until around 1825 that he began the real process by founding not only a factory but a town, Hitchcockville, dedicated to producing complete pieces of furniture. It was a landmark in the American way of running a business, and although there was a hiccup along the way with a collapse in 1828, Hitchcock took on a partner, a former employee named Arba Alford, and was on his way to success soon after. His Boston rockers and side chairs – made of birch or maple but simulated to look like rosewood or ebony, either wood-seated or rush-bottomed, and stenciled with gilt patterns of flowers and fruit – were among the most popular types of seating from the 1830s to the 1850s.

In the years immediately before 1850, John Henry Belter (1804–63) of New York married the skills of the chairmaker and carver of the past with the techniques of the machine age. His chairs, stuffed at the back and seat, were crowned by fretted, lacy carving only made possible by the strength and pliancy of the wood laminate from which they were constructed. His interpretation of the Louis XV style set the tone that all others attempted to follow – though with markedly less success, since the competition did not possess his manufacturing secrets.

After Belter's death and the destruction of the papers detailing his process, other makers retreated to the less exuberant style dubbed 'Louis XVI'; these chairs were lighter and more vertical, their detailing finer.

Michael Thonet (1796–1871), an Austrian, had also invented a laminating process, but this was combined with steaming to produce chairs and rockers of fantastically turned and scrolled 'bentwood'. Although his invention originated in the 1830s and his furniture was made in Germany, Austria-Hungary and Poland, 85 per cent of it was being sold abroad, largely to the United States, by the mid-1870s.

American companies, too, jumped on the bandwagon. Finished with either cane or upholstered seats, these bentwood pieces – especially the rockers – became among the longest-lasting design successes in American furniture history, familiar from countless ice cream parlors and cafés as well as private homes. Certainly their popularity was bound to endure longer than the craze for buffalo horn and deer antler chairs that accompanied the push westward – and bentwood pieces were, at least, marginally more comfortable!

TOP: *These 'Chippendale' Philadelphia chairs date c 1775, and are made of mahogany with some poplar and pine.*

CENTER: *Both of these mahogany chairs were made c 1790 and are typical of the 'Hepplewhite' style.*

BELOW: *Two Federal dining chairs from around 1800, the backs of which are embellished with satinwood inlaid panels.*

Above: *A mahogany and canework sofa attributed to Duncan Phyfe, made in 1810. (Metropolitan Museum of Art, New York.)*

Left: *A folding upholstery chair with a walnut frame made c 1876. (Margaret Woodbury Strong Museum.)*

FURNITURE: OVERSTUFFED CHAIRS, SETTEES AND SOFAS

The same tastes and tenets that governed the fashionable development of all-wood chairs and cabinet furniture held true for the upholstered chair and its more commodious relative, the sofa. But because these pieces were limited for many years to the homes of the wealthy, who could appreciate the finer points of comfort and design (as well as afford the actual objects), their history in the American colonies begins at a later date.

The upholstered easy chair made a shy entrance at the end of the 17th century, when a few pieces appeared covered in homemade needlework or turkey work imported from England. One or two 'Jacobean' sofas imported from the mother country at this time have also been cataloged. The wing-back chair in the 'Queen Anne' style, with its high back, wing-shaped protectors at head level (to guard the face from the heat of the fire) and rolled, stuffed arms, was introduced around 1720. Needlework and velvet were supplanted by upholstery in silk, damask and wool. A small number of sofas were made in the style; settees were slightly more common. These were at first distinguished from sofas by their size (in a sofa, it should be possible to recline) and the fact that, in most cases, they were made entirely in wood. Like the chairs, these pieces were all placed around the periphery of a room and moved to the center when needed.

It was only in the 'Chippendale' period, beginning in the late 1740s, that the sofa became more desirable to the increasingly affluent merchant class. Along with chair-back and Windsor settees, sometimes with as many as 10 or 12 legs and seating five to six people, several upholstered sofas with open-rolling arms survive. The seats of the settees too were now often upholstered in damask or, toward the end of the century, caned. Several richly carved Chippendale settees survive, but since the taste of the Hepplewhite and Sheraton period inclined even more toward their use, some wonderful examples of the elaborately draped, reeded and festooned formal pieces exist in collections.

As for the classic stiff-backed, horsehair sofa, many more of these had appeared by the 1760s and 1770s. Pad or claw-and-ball feet, with cabriole legs and acanthus carving or, alternatively, straight fluted legs and feet, distinguished the mahogany parts; scroll backs and rolled arms – vertically rolled if in the classic 'Chippendale' mode – the upholstered body. By the turn of the 19th century, the lines had become straighter and more severe, with a carved panel or pediment imposed upon the back of the sofa. Those pieces attributed to the earlier period of Duncan Phyfe are particularly noteworthy in this area.

With the onset of the 'Regency' or 'Empire' styles, the sofa, perhaps more than any other piece of public room furniture, assumed a massive quality. Heavily carved examples, with the wood totally framing the velvet- or brocade-upholstered seat and back, exerted their dominant personalities in reception and living rooms. Lotus and cornucopia carving weighed down the arms, while the legs often terminated in animal feet. The French influence found its greatest expression in the couch, lounge or daybed, in which one 'arm' end was raised and exaggerated to form a headrest, while the other arm scrolled either inward or outward, serving as a foot rail. The back usually terminated halfway along in a complementary scroll. The seat and back were either overstuffed in a plush manner or executed in canework.

The taste for things 'Oriental' (meaning anywhere from Egypt to China) in the 1830s and 1840s resulted in sofas whose heavy frames were distinguished by carved ornamental tassels near the bolsters, and in divans or sofas created specifically for the library, which was often designed as a suitably Oriental room. The Rococo sofa was epitomized by the naturalistic carving and buxom curves on the pieces of John Henry Belter, whose invention of a patented laminating process gave him a hitherto unknown pliability and strength in woodworking. His parlor suites – comprising a sofa, chairs, tables and sideboards – vied with his bedroom suites as the best-selling, up-market furniture of the 1850s and 1860s. This was the period of rosewood and black walnut – both heavy, lavish woods, incapable of discreetness. Other makers followed Belter's lead with lavish carving and balloon backs, but none was able to achieve his success.

TOP RIGHT: *Art Nouveau armchairs, made by Solomon Carpen Bros of Chicago around the turn of the century.*

LEFT: *Sofa made in New York c 1815 and attributed to Duncan Phyfe. (The American Museum in Britain.)*

BELOW LEFT: *A Rococo revival suite in laminated rosewood, attributed to John Henry Belter and made c 1860.*

TOP LEFT: *A 'Chippendale' mahogany wing chair made in Newport, Rhode Island c 1770.*

BELOW RIGHT: *Rococo revival laminated wood love seat, made c 1860 and attributed to John Henry Belter.*

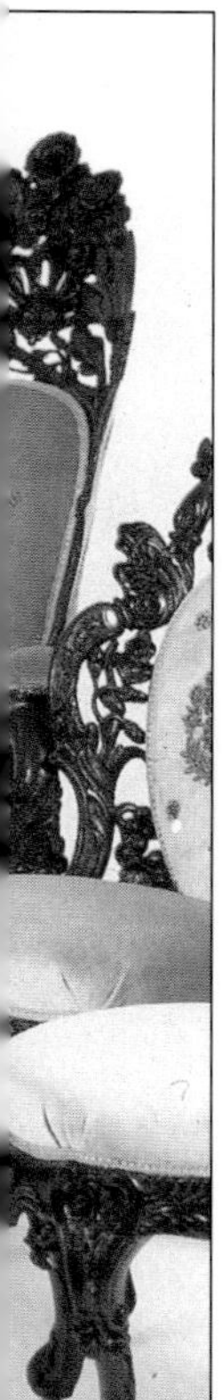

ABOVE: *Mahogany sofa attributed to Philadelphian cabinet maker Robert West, c 1825. (Ladies' Hermitage Association.)*

LEFT: *Sheraton or late Federal wing chair c 1815, made of mahogany. (Hirschl and Adler Galleries, New York.)*

FURNITURE: DINING AND OCCASIONAL TABLES

Although the earliest period of American furniture is commonly known by its English-derived nomenclature – Jacobean – many of the pieces were in fact more medieval in terms of their primitive sturdiness. Nowhere is this more apparent than in the oldest colonial tables. The largest variety, used for dining, was the trestle table, sometimes 8 feet (over 2 meters) or more in length, with a removable board secured with pegs serving as the top. Very long examples had either a third trestle midway along the table or supported the top by means of vertical supports joined to the truss.

Few of these simple large tables survive, since they were supplanted in the late 1600s by the refectory-style table, which supported the permanent top on four turned legs, either connected by four low stretchers or by three stretchers comprising an elongated 'H-frame.' The smaller version of the refectory-style table is commonly known as the tavern or taproom table, although it was generally found in private dwellings as well. The woods used were more varied than in England – oak, maple, pine and fruitwood, depending upon the part of the country in which they were made – while the skirt or frame was sometimes scrolled in a manner not found on the larger tables. An even smaller piece of furniture, but a highly useful one, was the 'stand,' its plain rectangular or round top set on four splayed or vertical legs, the support often elaborately turned. It served a variety of uses, moving with ease from bedside to hearthside, wherever it was needed.

RIGHT: *'Chippendale' mahogany card table, probably by John Goddard of Rhode Island. Made c 1765, it exemplified the transition between Queen Anne and 'Chippendale' taste.*

For dining in smaller homes, the gateleg table and its uniquely American cousin, the butterfly table – so-called because of the shape of its supporting brackets – echoed the popularity this table type enjoyed in Britain. While maple was often the choice of wood for this piece in the Northern colonies, those farther south preferred walnut almost exclusively. The leg and stretcher turnings became more elaborate as the years of the new century dawned and the arrangement of the gate, or gates, became ever more inventive.

By the William and Mary period, oak and the heavier woods had given way everywhere to a taste

ABOVE: *A 17th-century trestle table with the top made from three pine planks. It was made in New York State. (The American Museum in Britain.)*

for the more highly finished walnut. Its fine graining and the fact that it was commonly applied in veneer meant that smoother joinery was required. The gateleg continued its dominance (though now terminating in the new Spanish foot), and some older styles still hung on. Candlestands and small occasional tables began to put in an appearance, and the drawers in these and tavern tables were fitted with the new-style teardrop brass fittings, still largely imported from England.

The beginning of the second quarter of the 18th century witnessed the almost imperceptible merge of the William and Mary style into the American version of Queen Anne. The legs of tables began to gently curve out and by the 1740s had developed into the fully fledged cabriole leg, terminating in a pad or 'Dutch' foot – sometimes elaborated into the slipper, webbed or trifid variations – and later in a claw-and-ball foot. The gateleg, which had been a favorite for so long, gave way to the drop-leaf table, in which the hinged leaves were supported by swing legs. Usually two of the four legs of the table were movable, although in some of the finest pieces an extra two legs were made, so that four remained fixed and two, with shorter frame members, swung out. When open, the tables could be either square, rectangular, round or oval. Walnut was still considered the most desirable wood, although toward the end of the period mahogany, so beloved of the Chippendale school, entered the field.

The candlestand, too, had undergone a sea change. The once plain tripod base now sported cabriole legs and the supporting column a turned baluster. With the growing popularity of tea came a table designed specifically for its use: rectangular, with a raised rim or 'tray' top, an elegantly scrolled frame and graceful cabriole legs. These early tea tables, sometimes known as 'Dutch tray' tables, are among the most beautiful and highly regarded pieces of classical American furniture.

Although America was slower than England to respond to the powerful influences of Chippendale, several elements that would characterize the style at its height were already making themselves felt in the 1750s. The cabriole leg had established itself as a staple of colonial design, while the flourishing trade with the West Indies offered exotic mahogany as a replacement for domestic walnut. The flowering of the American Chippendale style would eminently suit the unique qualities of the opulent reddish-brown wood.

The types of tables popular in the 1750s to 1780s did not really change; it is the *style* that distinguishes these wonderful pieces. Philadelphia reigned supreme in colonial cabinetmaking, with Newport, Rhode Island, providing highly respectable competition. The card tables and tea tables produced by their makers echoed the elegant lines of their chairs and case pieces, although the tea table had changed considerably in appearance. After 1740, the preferred shape of the tea table was round (overall it resembled a large candlestand), with tripod legs ending in claw-and-ball feet, the support reeded or the baluster elaborately carved, and the top finished by a pie-crust or shell-and-scroll edge. Larger versions were used as breakfast tables, and the entire type is often now known generically as a tip-and-turn table, after the bird-cage mechanism that allowed the top to fold flat against the support, thus enabling the table to be pushed against a wall when not in use.

The drop-leaf dining table continued to be in vogue, with the square shape exerting more popular appeal. A variation on this was the new occasional piece known as a Pembroke table – a style imported from England – with short leaves and a wide central section sheltering a small drawer. The fashion for

RIGHT: *This remarkable Federal dining table is nearly 17ft (5.2m) long and 5ft (1.5m) wide. The six mahogany and four poplar leaves have an accordion action. Made in Philadelphia c 1805.*

FACING PAGE, TOP RIGHT: *Drum table, made in Baltimore 1810–20. Its single drawer is fitted with compartments. (Christie's, New York.)*

FACING PAGE, TOP LEFT: *An elegant Federal work table, attributed to Massachusetts cabinet makers John and Thomas Seymour. Made of mahogany, bird's-eye maple and flame birch. Made in Philadelphia c 1805.*

FACING PAGE, BELOW LEFT: *A somber Federal mahogany pembroke table. Made c 1790, probably by John Townsend of Newport, Rhode Island.*

FACING PAGE, BELOW RIGHT: *A generously proportioned 'Chippendale' dining table, probably made in Philadelphia c 1770.*

tea- and coffee-drinking and entertaining at home encouraged the proliferation of gaming tables with fold-over tops, whose surfaces were punctuated by rounded or dished corners and lined with baize.

As the styles known as 'Hepplewhite' and 'Sheraton' evolved from American 'Chippendale,' the lines of leg and frame grew slim and yet more vertical, losing the distinctive 'S' curve and deep carving so beloved of the earlier taste. The new fashion coincided with the founding of the new republic, and the classical echoes so dominant in Hepplewhite and Sheraton design found quick favor with the patriots who saw themselves as the inheritors of the noble Romans. While Philadelphia had been the capital of the Rococo Chippendale style, Baltimore came to the fore as the leading exponent of classicism, its furniture makers excelling in the contrasting inlays of holly, harewood, satinwood and amboyna that enriched tables, sideboards and secretaries.

A particular introduction of the period was the two- or three-part extension table, made from a combination of single and/or double drop-leaf tables, designed to be used together. The arrangement allowed the sections to be used in any combination convenient to the host, but unfortunately the disposition of the numerous legs did not make for the same convenience to the guests. Examples occur in both the Hepplewhite and Sheraton styles, the latter showing the characteristic reeding on the legs. While the very occasional pedestal version with sections may have been made in America between 1750 and 1790, the majority of these pieces are thought to have been imported from England.

On all tables dating from 1790 to 1820, the legs are an important key to the dominant style, since Americans were never purists. While Hepplewhite sympathies are readily apparent in the square tapered legs – often with line inlay – ending in square feet, round legs, carved with reeding and fluting, betray the influence of Sheraton. Although the wind from France blew over the Directoire style that reached its American apogee in the work of Duncan Phyfe, French influence on table design was most marked by the appearance in America of what was up to then the typically English mahogany pedestal dining table with insertable leaves, usually having two to three pedestals, each with three or four splayed legs terminating in brass casters. Some of the largest tables, 14 to 18 ft (4 to 5.5 m) long had four pedestal supports, with the central two having two parallel legs each and the two outer supports, three legs each. Some smaller tables did show more of the Phyfe style: These include sofa and side tables with exquisite inlay and a well-judged inclusion of lyre supports, far removed from some of the heavier attempts that would follow in the next decades.

LEFT: *A 'Chippendale' mixing table, c 1765. The contrast between the harmonious curves of the walnut stand and patterned marble top of this table is striking.*

BELOW LEFT: *This Federal dining table, c 1805, has a hinged section in the middle which can be used as a separate table. The whole table stretches to almost 14ft (1.7m) in length.*

BELOW CENTER: *A Federal cherry wood candlestand, made specifically to hold candelabra or candlesticks. The small drawer accommodates tinder boxes and wax tapers. Made c 1785.*

BELOW RIGHT: *An American Queen Anne tray-top table, c 1760, made of smooth-grained cherry wood.*

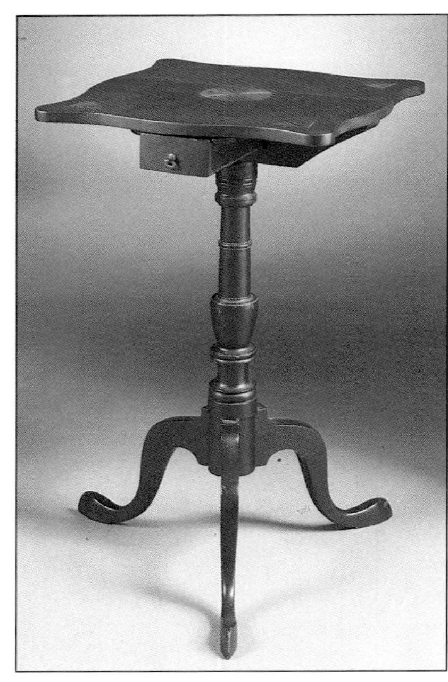

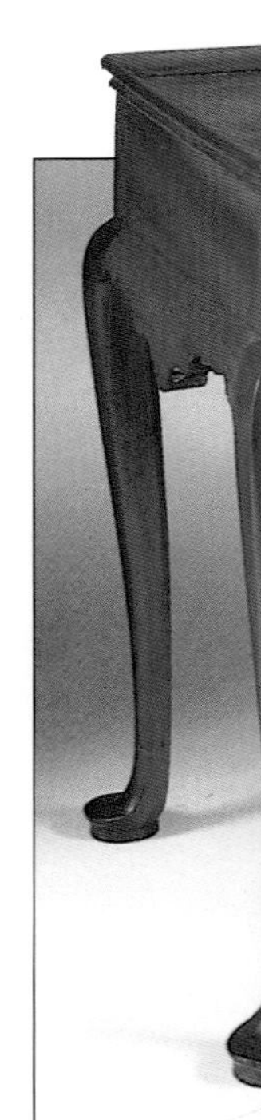

ABOVE LEFT: *The general construction of this cherry wood 'Chippendale' card table (c 1790) is closely based on a model popular from the 1770s and 1780s in England.*

ABOVE RIGHT: *A fine mahogany serpentine-fronted Federal serving table. Probably made in Salem, Massachusetts by Samuel McIntire.*

RIGHT: *Ebonized and gilded Egyptian revival table c 1880. (Margaret Woodbury Strong Museum.)*

By 1820 to 1830 and the arrival of the full-blown Empire style, the dining table had become a massive piece. The central column of the pedestal was replaced by elongated and highly carved scroll columns supporting the top, while the feet below the flattened base were unmistakably animal, belonging to some huge-pawed lion or mythical beast. Gilding was opulent and sometimes indiscriminate, while redder mahogany and distinctively grained rosewood were used for theatrical effect. Pier tables boasted marble columns and tops, and the animal theme might be continued even further with swan or dolphin supports.

After 1830, the rise of industrialism and a proliferation of furniture companies meant that eclecticism ruled the day. As in England, dining tables were made ever more massive and of ever darker mahogany, and large numbers and types of occasional tables were available in a variety of woods, from ebony in the 1830s to bamboo in the 1880s. Egyptian and 'Oriental' side tables gave way to those in the style of Louis XVI; in the 1850s French names dominated New York furniture companies. Interest in things Near Eastern returned again with the Philadelphia Centennial Exposition in 1876, which featured entire rooms decorated in the 'Moroccan' taste and centered around small 'smoking' tables.

The American edition of Charles Lock Eastlake's book *Hints on Household Taste*, published in 1872, found an eager audience among designers in the

United States. A reaction against veneers and consequent experiments in oak and other solid native woods resulted, reaching some happy conclusions in the architecture of the table. But even more striking examples of the new thinking would follow in the work of the Chicago and Prairie schools.

ABOVE LEFT: *'Chippendale' tea table made of mahogany, the favoured wood in England at the time. New England c 1765.*

ABOVE RIGHT: *Round 'Chippendale' tea table typical of Philadelphian manufacture, made c 1760. The tilting top is operated by a mechanism just visible at the top of the column support.*

FURNITURE: LOWBOYS, HIGHBOYS AND CHESTS OF DRAWERS

Unlike anything English in either form or expression, the highboy nonetheless evolved from the chests of drawers that had been made from the late 1600s in Massachusetts and Connecticut, as well as across the Atlantic. These chests of drawers were themselves an elaboration of the earlier 'blanket' or 'hope' chests that occurred in several forms throughout the Northern colonies. But the fluid lines of the masterpieces produced at the height of the highboy's reign hardly seem related to these first specimens of the cabinetmaker's art.

The earliest known example of a true chest of drawers is that held in the Winterthur Museum in Delaware, carved with the date 1678 and the initials J (I), M and S – for John and Mary Stamford, for whom it was probably made as a wedding gift. Elaborately carved and painted, with the drawers of each tier different, the chest is a unique item, strangely Germanic and Renaissance in feeling. A few pre-1700 examples exist in collections, practically all of them in oak and raised on plain or ball feet. Their close kinship to the earlier Hadley and Connecticut chests can be seen in their usually geometric panels and frame construction.

By the turn of the 18th century, pine and walnut had begun to be used in chests of drawers, but their utilitarian solidity was soon to be supplanted by the emergence of the fanciful chest-on-stand. In such a piece, legginess gave height and airiness, while walnut, ash and maple burl veneers, as well as the new art of japanning, enabled the cabinetmaker to amply demonstrate his skills. Ostensibly the design would facilitate access to drawers at the bottom of the chest, until now uncomfortably near floor level. But since the upper end of the chest-on-stand – or 'highboy' as it would come to be known – became immediately out of reach to the average colonist, that argument seems inadequate.

In any case, the new fashion took off, and the tall piece was joined by a companion of shorter dimensions that later was called the 'lowboy.' In

RIGHT: *Queen Anne flat-topped highboy with walnut and burl walnut veneer, made in Massachusetts c 1730–50. (Robert O. Stuart.)*

FACING PAGE: *'Chippendale' secretarial desk and cabinet, made of mahogany, c 1760. (C. L. Prickett Antiques.)*

ABOVE: *Carved chest from New Mexico, made in the mid/late 18th century of carved pine. (The American Museum in Britain.)*

curved pediments dazzle with sunbursts of dot and tear carving, ornate wooden grilles and crosses; and prayer kneelers, monstrances and tabernacles – all alive with coarse but vital carving. There were even special chairs for the priest or visiting bishop to sit on during the celebration of the Mass.

But such lavish decoration did not hold for the majority of the furniture in the Spanish-speaking areas. The poverty of existence in the New Mexican region (which for our purposes also includes Arizona, Texas and lower Colorado) was pervasive and largely unaltered over the years; this was reflected by the primitiveness of the furnishings. There were few tools from which to choose: the small Spanish axe, the chisel, knife, awl, adze and handsaw. No sawmill opened in the area until the 1870s; planks were hand-hewn and smoothed by sandstone rubbing. The main woods were the readily available yellow pine, and, to a much lesser extent, juniper, mesquite and cottonwood. In 18th- and early 19th-century chests, nails were not used, but rather mortise-and-tenon joints, dovetailing and dowels were the norm. Handwrought nails were used for repairs and for later pieces.

New Mexican chairs, benches and settees are among the most common furniture pieces extant today. The usual chair form had either a plank or rawhide seat, the latter secured with large brass studs. Construction was rigid and unyielding; the legs were square, unadorned posts and the backs were horizontal wooden slats or tooled leather. A seat of honor, reserved for important guests or the visiting padre, might evince some abstract curling carving on the back, apron and/or stretcher, but more common was the rugged sawtooth back and stretcher, a design that also appeared on table stretchers and chest aprons.

Large pine chests were used for storage and were usually quite simple, with molded panels and plain square legs. Smaller chests were sometimes more like boxes, mounted on their own stands. A rarer form was the painted dower chest, based on an earlier form from Chihuahua, Mexico, which 19th-century artisans had seen in the homes of some older families. But whereas the original chests were the work of trained craftsmen like those who supplied the haciendas in California, the native efforts of the New Mexican amateurs were crudely painted and finished. But their appeal is none the less for that, and they are among the most sought-after of Southwestern antiques.

Another form of storage was offered by the *trasero*, a large pine two-story cupboard on legs, with hand-carved spindles forming a grille on the upper doors. The classic form has access to drawers on the front and back of the piece, with the

LEFT: *New Mexico Spanish colonial chair. (From the collection of Shirley and Ward Alan Minge; Robert Reck Photography.)*

Top left: *New Mexico Spanish colonial table. (From the collection of Shirley Ward and Ward Alan Minge; Robert Reck Photography.)*

Center left: *Painted chest on legs, New Mexico 1828–45. (The American Museum in Britain.)*

Right: *A Trastero cupboard with spindled upper doors, from the mid 19th century. (The American Museum in Britain.)*

Above: *A chair with chip carving, New Mexico, early 19th century. (The American Museum in Britain.)*

Left: *A missal stand, typically made of pine. Made in Morada in New Mexico c 1900. (The American Museum in Britain.)*

RIGHT: *A New Mexico Spanish colonial cupboard. (From the collection of Shirley Ward Alan Minge; Robert Reck Photography.)*

'drawer' on the opposite side actually a blind. This was often the most imposing piece in the house, covered with gesso and painted with figures in bright colors. Less gaudy decoration is found on some of the oldest pieces and on examples from the poorest households.

After 1840, the intrusion of Eastern fashions resulted in less 'pure' pieces. This was reflected in 'Empire'-influenced chairs, the appearance of chests of drawers and taller tables, and other small bastardizations of the Spanish-Mexican style. But lovers of the Southwestern tradition find these aberrations of interest in and of themselves, as long as the pieces continue to exhibit the unselfconscious naïveté of the traditional forms.

FURNITURE: ARTS AND CRAFTS, 1880–1920

American furniture design of the late 19th and early 20th centuries experienced a sea change, breaking the pattern of traditional development in which styles ebbed and flowed, one into another, to produce a kind of decorative evolution. By the 1880s, the eclecticism of the Victorian age had so fragmented the concept of what furniture should be or achieve – or even look like – that 'schools' sprang up in different corners of the United States, all trying to find, in their own way, the true path to interior enlightenment in its most literal sense.

In place of historicism was an interest in straight lines and unfussy surfaces. Wood was seen as an organic element akin to stone and treated to the same shallow relief carving and blunt edges. In academic terms, the designers of the Chicago School and the Prairie School set the pace. The

TOP: *A teak settle by Charles and Henry Green, 1906, deriving its form from the functional pieces of the early settlers.*

ABOVE: *This c 1910 oak hall bench is typical of the work of Gustave Stickley, using local wood in an austere style.*

RIGHT: *Frank Lloyd Wright writing table and chair, made from American walnut and enamelled steel, c 1936.*

intimations of reform reverberated loudly there, disturbed by the breath of fresh air in architecture, which blew across all the decorative arts. In Chicago itself were the practices of Jenny, Burnham & Root, Henry Hobson Richardson (1838–86) and, most famous of all, Adler and Sullivan. In 1889 Louis H. Sullivan (1856–1924) took on the young and ambitious Frank Lloyd Wright (1869–1959) as a junior member of his firm; four years later, in 1893, Wright had opened his own business. His so-called 'Oak Park Period' – named after the site of his own Illinois house, for which he designed the furniture – extended from that date until 1910. At the Oak Park residence, and in all the other houses he designed, the furnishings were seen as a natural outgrowth of the building itself. He despised artifice and 'tampering with nature.' His advice – 'Bring out the nature of materials, let their nature intimately into your scheme. Strip the wood of varnish and let it alone – stain it . . . Go to the woods and fields for color schemes . . .' echoed through Chicago and westward across the prairies, where other architect-designers were attempting their own interpretation of reform.

ABOVE: *Oak spindle chairs and table made by Frank Lloyd Wright c 1901.*

Some of the Prairie School members had been students at the foot of Sullivan at about the same time as Wright. But whereas Wright went so far toward the terse and clean-cut that he finally decreed that machines did the job better than man, architect-designers George Grant Elmslie and George Washington Maher did not scorn decorative detail if it was integral to the piece. Working first for the architectural practice of Bauer and Hill, and then for Chicago's largest firm, J. L. Silsbee, Maher chose strong lines and massive proportions for his pieces. But he also showed that finding a new aesthetic did not demand a complete break with the past. Obvious respect for the medieval and Renaissance traditions – apparent in the scrolling stiles and animal heads that adorn some of his best works – is spiced with delight in Oriental forms. In addition, his influence on other designers of the Midwest was highly important.

Meanwhile, while architect-designers turned academic ideals into reality for the few, there were more commercial outlets riding along on the new wave. The creations of these firms were still expensive, since they clung to the tenets of Arts

LEFT: *Honduras mahogany and teak chest with carved ebony panel by C. & H. Greene, California 1907–09.*

and Crafts excellence, but they were sales companies, not architectural firms, and there was a growing core of well-off businessmen to buy their products. Chief among these companies was Herter Brothers in New York, as well as Isaac E. Scott and the Tobey Furniture Company, both in Chicago. Furnishing the Jackson Boulevard home of the Chicago industrialist Henry Lee Borden had a large part in making the latter firm's name.

While all this was happening west of the Appalachians, other movements were afoot in New York State. In 1898 Gustav Stickley (1857–1942) began designing his craftsman furniture in Eastwood, a Syracuse suburb, stating his aim that 'furniture should be durable, comfortable and fitted for the place it has to occupy and the work it has to do'. His furniture was made of native American hardwoods, the stuffed pieces covered in leather, canvas or plain cloth. The fittings were of copper or iron. His designs were long-lasting – his reclining chair, patented in 1901, was still being manufactured unchanged in 1913 – and much imitated. Although he took the precaution of having three trademarks on every piece of his furniture, in 1915 he was bankrupt by those same cheaply and widely-produced imitations.

The simple oak tables, benches, chairs and bookcases of Elbert Hubbard (1856–1915) and his community of craftsmen in Aurora, New York, were even less conspicuous. His group was christened the Roycrofters and its members saw themselves as the latter-day inheritors of the William Morris tradition. Together the works of Hubbard and Stickley are referred to as 'Mission furniture' – so-called at first because 'they had a mission to perform'. However, the name gradually took on the connotations of the California missions, with whose simplicity the brown-stained wood seemed much in sympathy.

ABOVE: *An oak fall-front desk by Stickly, c 1904. The panelled fall is inlaid with stylized motifs in pewter and various light woods.*

LEFT: *An art nouveau armchair by Greene & Greene. c 1908.*

RIGHT: *Purcell and Elmslie armchair; oak with the original upholstery and brass tacks; date unknown. (Hirschl & Adler Galleries, New York.)*

In fact the appellation should have been given to the designs of Charles Sumner Greene (1868–1957) and Henry Mather Greene (1870–1954), two Californian brothers and architectural graduates whose pieces also echoed the calm and Old West values of the Franciscan missions. Rather unfortunately, their work is sometimes known today as 'the California bungalow style'. Like the architects in the Midwest, they designed houses and the furniture to go in them. Their grand Spanish-style mansions in Pasadena and San Marino were made complete by the inclusion of their lovely walnut furniture. Unlike the others, they used inlay – in fruitwood and semiprecious stones – and ebony pegs to cover their joinery. But they embraced other artisans in their vision: Stickley furniture, Rockwood pottery and Tiffany glass were among the items that adorned Greene houses.

CLOCKS

Suiting the time to the place: creating an affordable and distinctively American style of timepiece.

ABOVE: *Federal stained maple shelf clock, Maine c 1815–25. (Christie's, New York.)*

LONG-CASE (GRANDFATHER) CLOCKS

Clocks and timepieces were among those luxuries – along with guns and glass for windows and domestic use – that the earliest New World settlers brought with them on the ships from England. Those who could not afford them hardly considered them necessities; only the wealthiest thought them worth the effort to drag halfway across the world. Even after living for a generation in North America, in the 1680s and 1690s colonists were still largely importing clocks from England. With only two or three exceptions no clocks made before 1700 in America are known to exist today.

By 1715 there were several clockmakers at work, first mainly concentrated in Philadelphia, but then spreading out to Newport, Boston and other centers. The majority of these 18th-century clocks were of the long-case (or grandfather or 'tall-case') variety. The most admired of American clock craftsmen, David Rittenhouse (1732–96), worked in Norristown, near Philadelphia, between 1750 and 1790, producing several outstanding examples that are today the pride of American museums. The skilled clockmaker Thomas Harland (d 1807) emigrated from England to Norwich, Connecticut, in 1773, and his apprentice, Daniel Burnap (1760–1838), became among the most highly regarded of the Connecticut school long-case clockmakers (he moved from East Windsor, Connecticut, to Andover, Massachusetts, *c* 1800). Clocks by such excellent makers were made to order by hand and fitted to a mahogany case that had also been made in the shop. Most had brass eight-day movements, though there are the exceptional 34-hour versions. The dials were of brass with brass spandrels and other ornamental details.

In contrast, some innovative makers were beginning to look for less costly alternatives, making functional pieces with cog wheels of cherry mounted on an oak plate, contained in an attractive but simple case. The Cheney Brothers of East Hartford, Connecticut, are hailed as making the earliest of these existing Connecticut wooden movements, in about 1745. Although cheaply and sometimes crudely made, they are almost as keenly sought after as their more sophisticated brethren. Other early makers include Gideon Rich and John Roberts.

Among the apprentices of Benjamin Cheney was Benjamin Willard (1740–1803), who, with his three brothers, went on to revolutionize the clock industry of eastern Massachusetts, southern New Hampshire and Rhode Island. Although influenced by the Cheneys, the brothers and their factories never made any wooden clocks, concentrating instead on finely made brass movements. From

LEFT: *Long-case Tiffany clock with Near East and Indian motifs; mahogany and brass, c 1880. (Metropolitan Museum of Art, New York.)*

BELOW: *Federal long-case painted clock, made in Connecticut c 1825. It was painted by R. Cole who stencilled 'R Cole Painter' on the base in gold. (Sotheby's, New York.)*

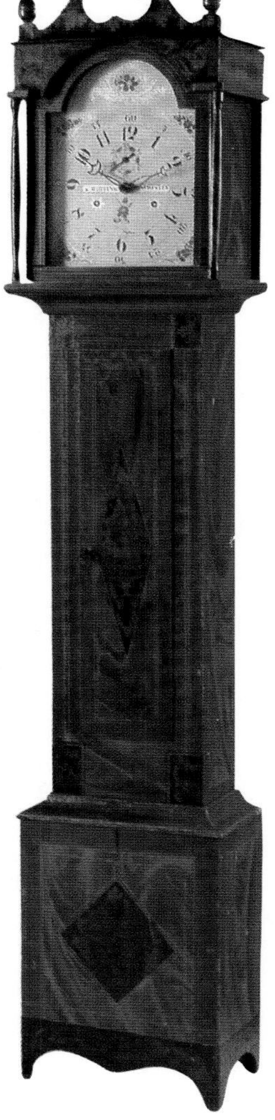

ABOVE: *Joseph Ives mirror clock in gilt gesso frame, made c 1820 in Bristol, CT. (American Clock and Watch Museum.)*

1765 on they produced many types and styles of timepiece, most notable among them their long-case and banjo clocks.

Mass-production in the modern style began with the Connecticut clockmaker Eli Terry (1772–1852), who set up his shop and factory in 1793 (after an apprenticeship with Daniel Burnap), installed steam power to fuel his works in 1803 and accepted an order for 4,000 wooden long-case clock movements in 1806. He established the first assembly line for clock production in America to fill the order and make his fortune. The majority of his movements were sold without cases, which could then be made to the specifications of the customer; an even cheaper solution was to simply hang up the movement uncased – this was known as a 'wag-on-the-wall'.

By the second decade of the 19th century, several makers had taken up Terry's ideas and were making wooden clocks, long-case and otherwise. But with the decline of Chippendale style furnishings, the long-case gave pride of place to several new rivals.

LEFT: *Rittenhouse clock. (Drexel University.)*

ABOVE: *Seth Thomas Clock Co., Thomaston, CT; gilt column model one-day weight-driven shelf clock, c 1870. (American Clock and Watch Museum.)*

LEFT: *Banjo clock, made c 1830. (Taylor B. Williams Antiques, Chicago, Illinois.)*

CLOCKS: WALL CLOCKS

Although Dutch and English brass wag-on-the-wall clocks had been imported into the American colonies since the mid-17th century, it was not until the middle of the next century that homegrown artisans assayed making the same products in America. Eli Terry's mass-produced wooden works (*c*1806 and after) were often hung without cases, and by 1815 several makers were copying his methods to supply cheap, utilitarian wag-on-the-wall pieces to a growing clientele.

Meanwhile, Simon Willard (1753–*c*1845), perhaps the most renowned of the four Willard Brothers, had been developing a more sophisticated wall-mounted 'Improved Timepiece.' Although early examples exist before 1800, he did not patent his invention until 1802. The movements were brass, the eight-day weight-driven pendulum between 20 and 26 in (50 and 66 cm) long. The wooden case consisted of a long upper section surmounted by the clock face and containing the pendulum suspension and escapement, while the square lower section was fronted by a glass-painted panel, or 'tablet,' and contained the pendulum weight. It was only in the latter part of the 19th century that it acquired the appellation 'banjo clock'. So popular did the shape become that 'banjos' were made by hundreds of craftsmen from the early 1800s throughout the 19th century, although the most finely executed tend to be pre-1830. The design lent itself to many variations. More deliberate faking has probably occurred with this type of clock than with any other American variety.

Two more exuberant styles, closely allied to the banjo in shape, movement and period, were the 'girandole' and the lyre, both of which flourished between 1815 and 1840. The design of the latter is credited to Aaron Willard Jr., nephew of Simon, and was taken up by many Massachusetts craftsmen. The girandole was the invention of Lemuel Curtis (1790–1851) of Massachusetts. Taking its name from the extravagant girandole mirrors of the period, it is considered among the most beautiful of American clocks. Fine examples are extremely difficult to find today and command high prices.

Plainer clocks, rectangular with the familiar lower glass panel, were made in mahogany and in rosewood by several other firms, principally in Connecticut, from the mid-19th century onward. They could either be used as shelf or wall clocks, and ogee molding distinguished many of the better examples. Generally speaking, after 1840–50, wall clocks were exceeded in popularity by the shelf variety, and those wall clocks that were produced usually followed the fashion dictates of the more widespread type.

ABOVE: *Tiffany mantel set; ormolu and marble with Egyptian motifs. Made in New York c 1885. (Metropolitan Museum of Art, New York.)*

CLOCKS: SHELF CLOCKS

After the long-case or grandfather clock, the American shelf clock – in all its manifestations – is the most fertile field for the horological student. Its earliest versions were a concession to space and expense, since the larger clocks were difficult to import from England and skilled craftsmen were few in the colonies. It was not until the second decade of the 18th century that a few names came to the fore. But since the long-case clock demanded a rich clientele, craftsmen began to experiment with other styles that made use of their skills but were more affordable and consistent with the distinctive American interiors.

One solution was the so-called Massachusetts shelf clock, produced by members of the Willard family as an alternative to their pricier long-cases. Made from around 1800 to 1830, they are sometimes called 'case-on-case' or 'box-on-box,' a fair description of the basic construction of these brass movement pieces.

In contrast, the pillar-and-scroll clock of Eli Terry and his sons (*c*1817 and after) combined the wooden movements he had pioneerred in his long-case pieces with a small walnut or mahogany case, between 20 and 40 in (50 and 100 cm). Turned or carved posts flanked the sides, while a broken arch or double scroll characterized the top. The door contained a glass window above the glass-painted tablet. By the 1820s, other makers in Connecticut, Massachusetts and Pennsylvania were following Terry's lead and the trend continued until the 1840s, to be overtaken by other styles echoing current fashions in furniture – the stenciled shelf clock in the style of Hitchcock (*c*1825–40), the carved or marquetry beehive (*c*1850–60), the Gothic steeple (*c*1850–60), and the 'O.G.' clock, so-named because of its ogee-molded front. These last were in vogue from about 1840 into the 20th century, growing more massive in size and decoration as the decades progressed. The changes in style were accompanied by a change in movement construction; after 1840 wooden cogs and movements gave way to rolled brass and, soon after, to steel springs, which opened the way for true mass-production.

In addition to wooden cases, other materials were called into use as they came into fashion in other furnishings. Papier-mâché enjoyed popularity *c*1860–70, usually in the form of small boudoir clocks, while iron, brass and porcelain were all used for mantel clocks in the later 19th century. Porcelain, in particular, was favored for both boudoir and parlor clocks, the latter sometimes forming part of a garniture with companion vases.

Among the great names for the collector, congregated mainly in the first half of the 19th century, are the Willards and Terrys, together with the Jerome Brothers – Chauncey and Noble – and J. C. Brown and the Bristol Clock Company of Bristol, Connecticut.

RIGHT: *One day wood-movement clock by E. Terry & Son, Plymouth, CT, c 1830. The case decoration is influenced by stenciled furniture styles. (American Clock and Watch Museum.)*

SILVER

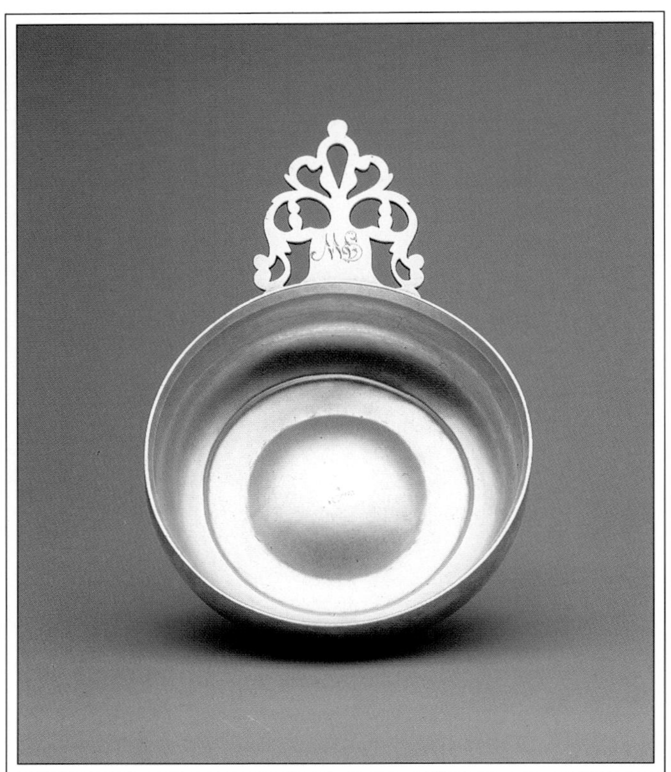

'The time is not far off when we shall have no need of foreign designers of our plate and jewelry.' Harper's Monthly *1853*

ABOVE: *A silver porringer. (Christie's, New York.)*

ABOVE: *Toleware basket made in Pennsylvania in the 19th century. (The American Museum in Britain.)*

gay freehand designs, incorporating naïvely stylized flowers and leaves, together with round spots of orange color and sprouting or encircling brushstrokes in paler hues. Generally, the complete design is round in shape, often with a running border in red, green and/or black on a white background along the top edge or foot of the piece.

Other freehand painters include the itinerant Oliver Filley, who began his tin-making, decorating and selling business in Vermont, but branched out to include outlets in Philadelphia, Lansingburgh, New York, and Bloomfield, Connecticut, in the heart of the tin centers; and the Butlers of East Greenville, New York, whose artists numbered Ann, Minerva and Marilla, daughters of tinsmith Aaron Butler. By the third decade of the 19th century, most of the free-painters were women, who used their craft to supplement their income or assisted their husbands or fathers, who were often in the tin-working trade.

A new technique came into prominence around 1825 – stenciling. It enabled far greater output than even the quick brushstrokes of the hand-painters. The defter application of paint over the black allowed the colors to glow yellow, green, red, white and brown. The stenciling technique was also centered around Berlin, though it again spread beyond it. Stenciled objects can easily be distinguished from the hand-painted by the clear demarcation of the pattern and the evenness of the paint application.

After 1850, the fashion for tole work gradually declined, although japanned toys and papier-mâché cases, boxes and furniture were produced in a limited quantity, but never in the numbers they enjoyed in Great Britain and on the Continent.

OTHER METALWORK: NAVAJO AND INDIAN JEWELRY

Southwestern Indian jewelry has been available to the non-Indian collector for roughly the past 90 years. Before that time, the Indians bartered the handmade bracelets, earrings, rings and necklaces with a few licensed traders in return for saddles, cloth, tools and other necessary items. Occasionally,

ABOVE: *This range of Indian jewelry varies in style from a highly contemporary gold necklace (left) to traditional Navajo, Zuni and Santo Domingo pieces. (Jerry Jacka Photography/Heard Museum, Phoenix.)*

these early bartered and pawned pieces have found their way into private hands. For the most part, however, it was not until the arrival of the Santa Fe Railroad – and with it the trading posts administered by the Harvey Company – that the public at large was exposed to this uniquely American artistic idiom. Even so, it remained a sleeping craft, relatively unexploited in terms of mass-production and imitation, until the late 1960s. Then, inspired by the hippies, the fad for all things ethnic took flight. The flower children made Santa Fe their provincial capital, attracting makers of 'handicrafts' even less scrupulous than themselves. The days of quality workmanship were numbered. The consequence of all this, however, is that what is in real terms a recently developed craft was given the time to evolve into a truly indigenous art form, one whose finest pieces deserve the high prices they now command.

The main focus of collectors' interest has always been the jewelry of the Navajo – the Revere family, if you like, of the Golden West. The first Southwestern American Indian tribe to work silver – probably beginning around 1870 – they have always remained, first and foremost, *silversmiths*. Inspired and, perhaps, taught by the Mexican artisans with whom they came into contact (it seems they traded their horses for learning the skill), the early Indian smiths showed an uncanny gift for adapting both Mexican and Spanish engraving motifs to their roughly worked metal. Although gravely restricted by a lack of tools, they nevertheless managed to produce a simple catalog of designs simply by using files and pipe stamps. By the 1880s they were employing the cold chisel, awl and punch, and by the late 1880s they were designing their own stamps. When stamping became the preferred method of decoration, the Navajo entered their finest hour, displaying their technical brilliance in complex designs on both cast and hammered pieces.

Indian jewelers from the 1870s to 1890s used melted American silver coins, then switched to pesos until the 1900s. Thereafter they used silver slugs manufactured for the purpose and continued to use them until the 1940s (although by this time sheet silver had been introduced). Many older pieces were melted down and the silver combined with the newer sheets or the slugs – so it is virtually

ABOVE: *Modern Navajo jewelry by Thomas Singer. Such modern work retains many of the motifs of traditional Navajo work. (Jerry Jacka Photography.)*

impossible to date a piece merely from the type of silver used. A thorough knowledge of the tools employed, the designs popular in particular periods, and even the type and treatment of stones is necessary to ascribe a date or specific place of origin to a piece.

Although most people associate turquoise with Navajo jewelry, inset stones did not become common until around 1900. Initially it was members of the Zuni tribe who were the stoneworkers, and to this day they retain the laurels as the premier jewelers among the American Indians. While the Navajo were busy learning silver-working, the Zuni were refining their stone-setting techniques, and by the 1920s the two tribes had exchanged much knowledge. However, while the Navajo would confine their use of turquoise or moonstone to a few large stones – nothing ever more extravagant than a sunburst – concentrating rather on the finesse of the surrounding design, the Zuni explored inlay and channel work in turquoise, shell and colored stones, as well as cluster and row-work settings of polished turquoise. The total effect of a Zuni design is one of delicacy – a web pattern of blue or an intricate map of desert geology – while, in contrast, that of the Navajo is strength and singleness of purpose.

Chief among the Navajo items are *conchas*, oval or round pieces of wrought silver made to be worn on a leather belt; 'squash blossom' necklaces, named for the elongated pomegranates pendent around the circumference; *najas*, crescent moons used as brooches and as pendants on necklaces; earrings, bracelets and rings. In all these pieces it is the working and the tooling of the silver that raises them from the ordinary to the highly collectible. In Zuni jewelry, bracelets, brooches and rings play a far greater part, and the amount of silver used may be minimal. In both forms of jewelry, while the color and placement of the stones obviously play a part in the aesthetic effect of the pieces, the actual fineness and worth of the stones themselves are of secondary importance to the collector. Indeed, because these are folk pieces, worked by a people without much money or many resources, the attraction of the jewelry lies in its artistic expression, not in the intrinsic value of their materials.

GLASS

The rich tradition of American glassmaking sets the scene for the work of Tiffany and others.

ABOVE: *Glass vase from the Bakewell plant, Pittsburgh, Pennsylvania. Blown from clear lead glass; the foot was made separately. (The American Museum in Britain.)*

FREE-BLOWN GLASS

The documented history of glassware in the United States is short – a mere 250 years – but significant. In that relatively limited time, America has managed to contribute substantially to both the art and the technological development of the craft.

There is reference to glassmaking in the Jamestown, Virginia, settlement as early as 1609, but little is known of the following century's production. It would seem that there was small-scale production of bottles and drinking vessels in Virginia, the Massachusetts Bay Colony and New Amsterdam (later New York), but for the most part the colonists survived on utensils of horn, pewter and earthenware, with cherished pieces of imported English or Continental silver or glass occasionally found in richer homes. Save for some fragments of glass excavated at the Jamestown site and attributed to local workmanship, no piece of American glass survives that can confidently be dated pre-1740.

During the third quarter of the 18th century, some 10 factories began production in the colonies, producing mainly utilitarian wares such as bottles and window-glass. This was both politically sound – since colonial production of tableware was forbidden by royal edict – and economically expedient. Indeed, despite the increasingly sophisticated wares turned out in the followng 100 years, these two items – particularly green bottle glass – would continue to be the mainstay of American glasshouses, subsidizing the more creative pieces risked by commercially minded management. Those factories that did not assume this conservative attitude often went bankrupt.

The type of glass produced by these early glasshouses is known collectively as South Jersey glass, in honor of the first and most famous area producing it. The Wistarburg glasshouse (*c*1739–80) in Salem County, southern New Jersey, was the initial effort of Caspar Wistar (1696–1752), a German immigrant, who had no qualifications as a glassmaker, being described as a 'brass button-maker' in contemporary documents. He nevertheless determined that there the demand for locally produced glass justified breaking the royal ban. By the 1740s his enterprise was turning out free-blown jugs, pitchers, dishes and flasks in sturdy bottle glass, in addition to the usual bread-and-butter work of windows and bottles. Soon other factories were following his lead, including the Glass House Company of New York, with works in New York (*c*1752–75) and New Windsor, as well as in Germantown, near Boston (*c*1753–67).

The style and techniques spread further afield, to the Midwest and even back to England, where the tradition carried on in the works of the Nailsea and Birmingham factories. In the United States, it continued until the mid-19th century. Although Wistar's son failed to extend his father's success and the factory closed down in 1780, one of his apprentices, Jacob Stanger, in partnership with his brother, opened the Glassboro Works in Gloucester County, New Jersey, in 1781. This glasshouse, and the later Harmony glassworks founded by the brothers in 1813, brought the South Jersey tradition well and truly into the 19th century.

Historians tend to divide South Jersey-style free-blown pieces into two eras: early South Jersey glass and post-1825. Although no pieces can definitely be ascribed to Wistar's factory, those known to be of the early period, when not plain, are distinguished by their bold applied decoration, tooled into ornamentation. Prunts, threading and crimping were succeeded by gadrooning, swagging and, in the 19th century, the signature device of the South Jersey style, the lily pad. This was accomplished by a superimposed layer of hot glass, trailed and looped. Pieces from the South Jersey region range from light aquamarine through yellow-green; those from New York are in a brighter aquamarine, as well as a few examples in amber, green or yellow,

ABOVE: *Late 18th-century engraved flip glass with tulip design. (The American Museum in Britain.)*

RW

Above left: *'Trisler' goblet, 1793, of colorless glass, blown and engraved. From New Bremen Glass. (Corning Museum of Glass.)*

Above right: *Colorless non-lead glass tumbler, blown and engraved with initials 'GMR'. Made* c *1790–95 by New Bremen Glass. (Corning Museums of Glass.)*

Left: *Tumbler with cover in the form of a glass sphere. (The American Museum in Britain.)*

Facing page: *(Left to right) blown and engraved tumbler, 1751; blown wine bottle* c *1745–55; blown and tooled taperstick* c *1739–76; blown and tooled cream basket* c *1739–76. (Corning Museum of Glass.)*

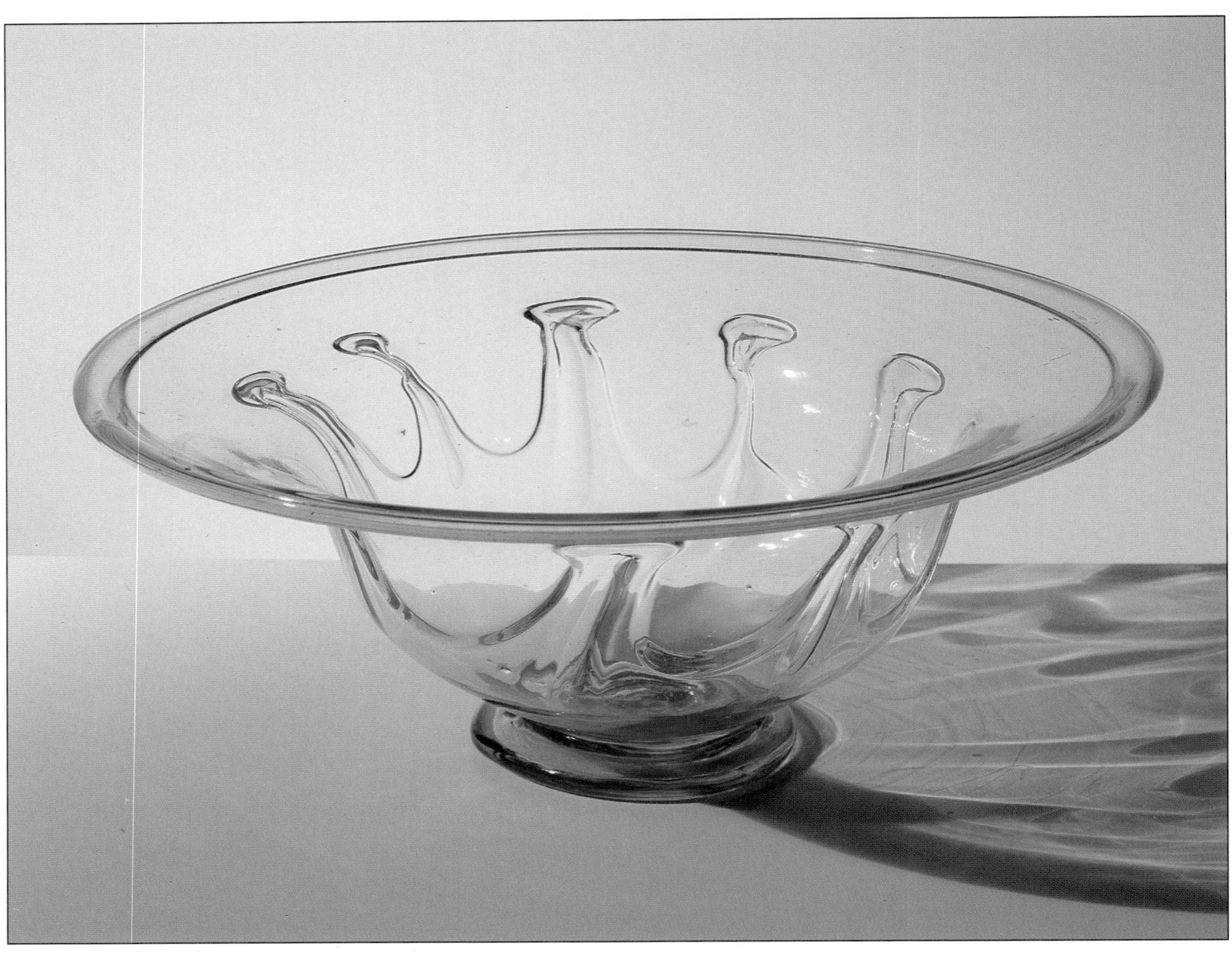

ABOVE: *Free-blown aquamarine glass bowl with lily pad decoration. Made by Redford Crown Glass Works 1831–50. (Hirschl and Adler Galleries, New York.)*

while New England versions occur most often in amber or olive green.

After 1840 some true blue pieces are also seen. Some of the most elaborate covered sugar bowls are topped by a bird, either chicken, swan, peacock or indeterminate fowl; these are collectively known as 'swan finials.' Post-1820 pieces from the New Jersey region were sometimes decorated by 'lopping and dragging' in white over a light aquamarine or other transluscent base; even later the base might be of a darker glass. While blowers in New York, New Jersey and New England remained true to traditional forms of decoration, those in the Midwest began to experiment with pattern-molding, decorating their wares with ribbing, 'popcorn' swirls and widely expanded diamonds.

While the name of Henry William 'Baron' Stiegel (1729–85) is almost synonymous with early pattern-molded ware, he is also important for the quality of the few engraved and enameled free-blown pieces that survive from the later part of his productive life. Although he opened his first factory in 1763, he only began to market enameled items in 1772, during the last two to three years before bankruptcy claimed his businesses. The clear glass for which he became so famous was deftly painted in enameled colors with patterns common to, or reminiscent of, those fashionable on the Continent, particularly Germany. Hearts, flowers and birds, arabesques and swirls decorate his charming glasses, pitchers and bottles, doubtless designed by his Manheim glasshouses to appeal to the nearby Pennsylvania German market.

Even more elegant were the works of the New Bremen Glass Manufactory (1785–95) near Frederick, Maryland, founded by John Frederick Amelung. His fine, lead-free glass was wheel-engraved in the richest Continental fashion and further embellished with applied and tooled decoration, including metalwork and occasional gilding and enameling. The pieces that have been attributed to (or signed by) him are mainly presentation pieces – usually goblets or covered tumblers – the most famous being the wonderful *Tobias and the Angel*, dated 1781 and dedicated to a member of the Amelung family, and the *Bremen Pokal*, made and engraved in 1788 and sent to Germany to demonstrate the factory's skill.

RIGHT: *'Stenger' flask, 1792, from New Bremen Glass; blown and engraved. (Corning Museum of Glass.)*

Top left: *Sugar bowl with cover with chicken finial,* c *1800. Bowl made in southern New Jersey, possibly Milford; cover southern New Jersey. (Corning Museum of Glass.)*

Far left: *Salt,* c *1788–1795; probably New Bremen Glass. Transparent and blue glass; blown and pattern-molded. (Corning Museum of Glass.)*

Left: *Blown wine glass* c *1800–20. Colorless glass with mottled purple stain. (Wendt Vornees Collection, Corning Museum of Glass.)*

Top right: *The valor cup, 1941; Steuben Glass Inc. Colorless lead glass; blown and engraved. (Corning Museum of Glass.)*

FACING PAGE: *Royal Flemish vase, c 1889–95 by the Mount Washington Glass Company. Blown, enameled lead glass with raised gilding. (Corning Museum of Glass.)*

RIGHT: *Four different types of late 19th-century colored glass: (left to right) peachblow bowl from Mount Washington Glass Works; Wild Rose peachblow vase from New England Glass Company; coral cruet by Hobbs, Brockunier and Company; Amberina vase from New England Glass Company. (Bridgeman Art Library.)*

BELOW: *Peacock leaded-glass window made by Louis Comfort Tiffany 1890–1900.*

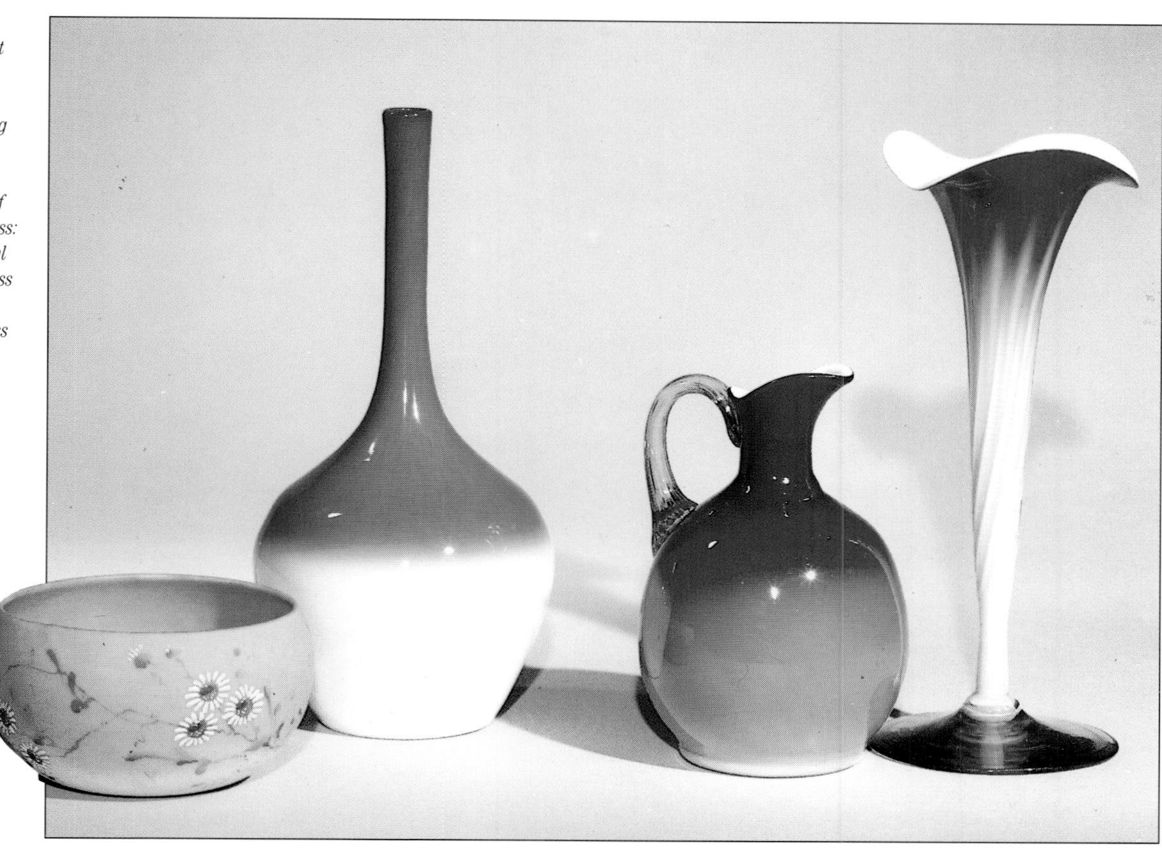

The march was stolen on Tiffany's famous iridescent glassware by the registration in 1893 of Union Glass Company's Kew Blas ware (its name is an anagram of factory manager W. S. Blake), although the Tiffany Glass and Decorating Company had actually been making a few pieces of its Favrile glass since 1892. Louis Comfort took up the challenge by registering his glass in 1894 and, by means of superior marketing and a name recognized for quality as well as fine craftsmanship, soon overtook sales of Kew Blas glass. Today, both are highly regarded by experts, although the intimidation posed by Tiffany's success often caused the Union Glass Company styles to be somewhat derivative.

While the best of the Kew Blas glass features swirling, undulating leaf- and feather-like patterns in shades of green, tan, brown and blue, Tiffany's Favrile glass looked to far wider horizons, with a large number of patterns that differed greatly. Vases tended to be the main medium to display the jewel-like colors and nacreous finish of the glass; forms ranged from 'goosenecked' to ginger-jar-shaped, from wide-bodied and pinched-necked to fluted and footed. The decoration – sometimes applied, sometimes embedded – took the form of trailing lily pads or leaves, Middle-Eastern arabesques, peacock's feathers, golden scales, loops and/or threads. The colors varied from strong reds, yellows and blues to cloudier variations with golden overtones. Authentic examples from the Tiffany glassworks are signed with Tiffany's name or initials.

ABOVE: *Steuben vase, 1920s. (Corning Museum of Glass.)*

By the turn of the century, the market for art glass was well established and several new makers joined the ranks, including the Imperial Glass Company (1901) of Bellaire, Ohio, with its freehand luster, Imperial Jewel, Egyptian and Moorish crackle vases; Fostoria Glass (1901) of Fostoria, Ohio; H.C. Fry Glass Company (1901) of Rochester, Pennsylvania, and Steuben Glass (1903), which was to survive as today's leading producer of ornamental glass. Its co-owner and leading designer, Frederick Carder (1864–1963), quickly introduced his Aurene glass to popular acclaim; blue and gold were the two characteristic colors overcast with a fine metallic sheen and sometimes applied decorative trailing. Carder remained with the company through its change of ownership (it was bought by Corning Glass in 1918) and until his retirement in 1933. He was responsible for an incredible wealth of types and styles of glassware, a few of which included Verre de Soie (*c*1916), Tyrian (*c*1917), Quartz (*c*1920), Cintra (*c*1917), Cluthra (*c*1930), Intarsia (*c*1930) and Grotesque (*c*1930s). He stands as one of the most technically and artistically gifted glassmakers of the modern age.

FACING PAGE: *Favrile vases and bowl by Louis Comfort Tiffany. (Metropolitan Museum of Art, New York.)*

CERAMICS

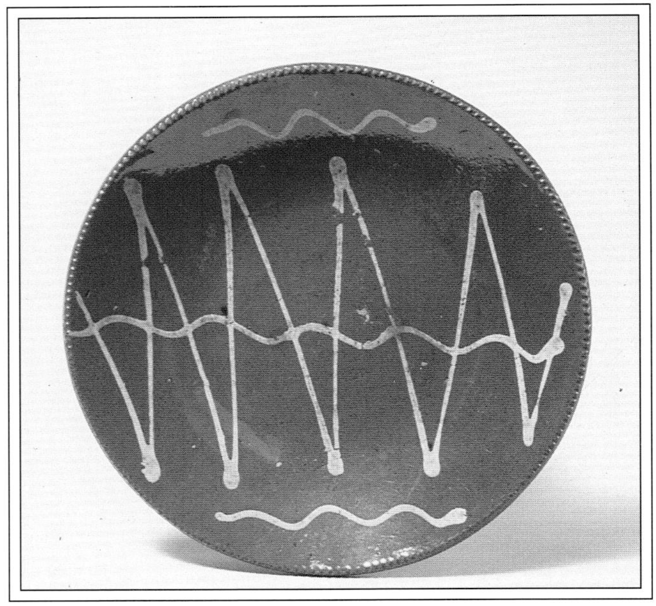

From the early days of settlement, a flourishing core of local potters established an American tradition in the face of competing foreign imports.

Above: *Pennsylvania slipware plate from the late 18th century; artist unknown. (Everson Museum of Art.)*

FOLK POTTERY AND STONEWARE

In some sections of this book, it has been noted that some crafts – notably clock- and glassmaking – had belated starts due to the wealth of goods imported from England. The situation vis-à-vis ceramics is not as clean-cut. While it is true that commercial-style potteries, geared to mass-production and -distribution, were not really established until about 1830, largely because of the popularity and availability of Anglo-American wares, a flourishing core of local potters was established throughout the colonies from the earliest days of settlement. Their work is commemorated in placenames such as Potter's Creek, Pottertown, Jugtown, Clay City and – in four states! – Kaolin. Bricks were being made in Jamestown within two years of landing, while several tilemakers were in business there by 1649. Three potters were recorded as arriving in New England in 1635: Philip Drinker in Charlestown, Massachusetts, and William Vincent (or Vinson) and John Pride in Salem. By 1800, 250 potters were registered in the New England states alone. The manpower and the knowledge were certainly there.

As for the materials, these were also richly available. Red-burning clays for bricks, tiles and redware were everywhere under the widespread shale surface. The finer buff-burning clays reached from Vermont to Baltimore and west to Ohio, while true kaolin was discovered in 1738, in a vein that stretched from Virginia to Georgia. Regular transport between settlements was one of the first achievements of the colonial administration, so there was no trouble in moving raw materials from their source to where they were needed.

But the lack of a concentrated market – there were few large towns – and a preference for English goods among those who could afford them, meant that the combination of capability and clays did not result in the automatic growth of a native industry. Rather it meant the proliferation of many small craftsmen, producing and selling their wares within a circumscribed region. The major production area for these folk wares was New England, in particular Massachusetts and New Hampshire. The earliest type was the ubiquitous and utilitarian redware. Its color was caused by iron oxide, an impurity in the clay that came about when it was fired. Other less frequently encountered colors included green (copper oxide) and brown/yellow (manganese). Earthenware objects were simple and functional: kitchen and dairy items – flasks, bottles and storage jars – as well as tableware. Decoration was minimal, at first only finger-pinching or incising, and sometimes a thin interior glaze. Later, in the early 18th century, ornament became

ABOVE: *Glazed redware coffee pot, c 1825. (Metropolitan Museum of Art, New York.)*

LEFT: *Face harvest jug, c 1850–75. Unidentified maker, probably South Carolina. The form of this jug appears to derive from the 'monkey jar', a plain earthenware vessel made to hold water, used in the West Indies and in the American South. (Abbey Rockefeller Museum.)*

ABOVE: *Sgraffito plate with floral design; Pennsylvania, 1818. (American Museum in Britain.)*

BELOW: *L. Smith tea canister, dated 1769, from Wrightstown, Bucks County, Pennsylvania (Henry Francis du Pont Winterthur Museum.)*

FACING PAGE: *Earthenware sgraffito plate, Pennsylvania c 1800–25. (Henry Francis du Pont Winterthur Museum.)*

more ambitious, using several types of glazes based on metallic oxides or compounds of red lead, galeria and clay. Also introduced was *sgraffito*, in which a design was scratched through the outer glaze to expose the clay beneath.

Sgraffito ware was a particular specialty of the Pennsylvania Dutch potters, especially those of Bucks and Montgomery counties, where, from the late 18th century through the 1830s, they produced highly regarded examples. Plates and dishes were the main items decorated, usually produced for family celebrations like births and weddings. Slipware bird whistles, together with jugs, dishes and pie plates painted with hunting scenes, birds and animals, were other typical items. Moravian and Pietist sects produced their individualistic pieces in nearby regions.

Further south, in the Shenandoah Valley, the nine members of the Bell Family, comprising three generations, produced wonderful, highly glazed bowls, figures, jugs and dishes in celadon, green and deep orange glazes. Active from the very early 19th century through 1899, their work is much valued by collectors.

Stoneware was harder and finer than earthenware, fired at a temperature several times hotter. It was the focus of much experiment when it was feared that the lead glazing of earthenware might be poisonous. The first known dated piece of American stoneware was made by Joseph Thiekson of New Jersey in 1722, although it was probably in production during the first years of the century. Duller in color than earthenware – ranging from gray-white to buff to brown – it was eventually given a rough salt glaze.

The main stoneware centers were established near clay deposits in New York, Philadelphia and New Jersey, and later in Ohio. The finest examples were near-competitors to porcelain, although most stoneware was of a lower grade, used to make jugs, crocks, churns, whistles and banks. Perhaps the most important producers of the 'best' ware were the Crolyas – later Crolius – pottery. From 1730 to 1870, 15 members of the family carried on the tradition in a confusion of name and factory changes, nevertheless managing to remain throughout notable exponents of stoneware techniques.

The most usual decorations for stoneware were birds, animals, flowers, initials and dates, executed in a clear cobalt blue, or less frequently, brown. After 1850, the free-hand style changed to the cheaper stenciling. While the tradition of the small or individual potter was one that has continued to the present day in the United States, its all-pervasive character was mitigated by the wider availability of the products from commercial potteries.

ABOVE: *Roses with shell border pattern quilt, thought to be from mid 19th century. (The American Museum in Britain.)*

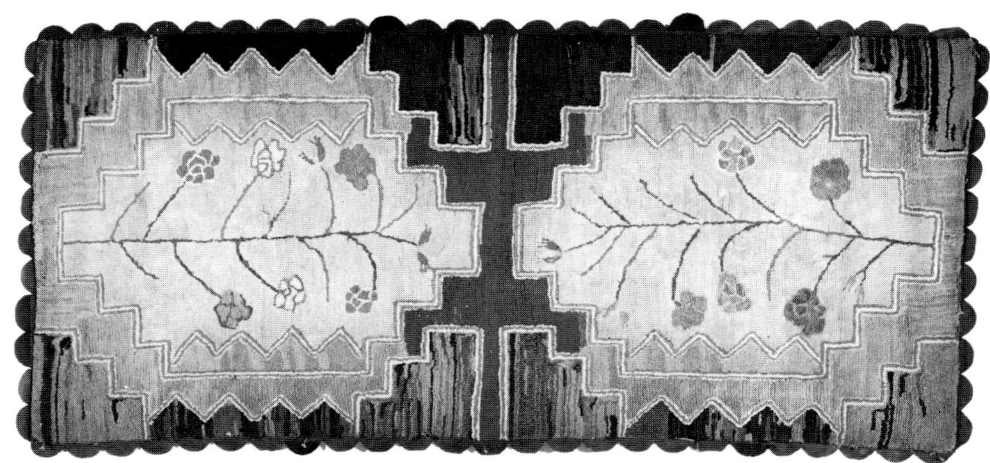

FACING PAGE, TOP: *Firehouse dog rug; cotton on burlap, uncut, late 19th century. (The American Museum in Britain.)*

FACING PAGE, CENTER: *19th-century hooked rug – a style also called 'drawn-in'. (Smithsonian Institution, Washington.)*

FACING PAGE, BELOW: *Hooked and braided rug with design, farmhouse animals;* c *early 20th century. (Thomas K. Woodard Antiques, New York.)*

RIGHT: *19th-century knitted and braided rug. (Smithsonian Institution, Washington.)*

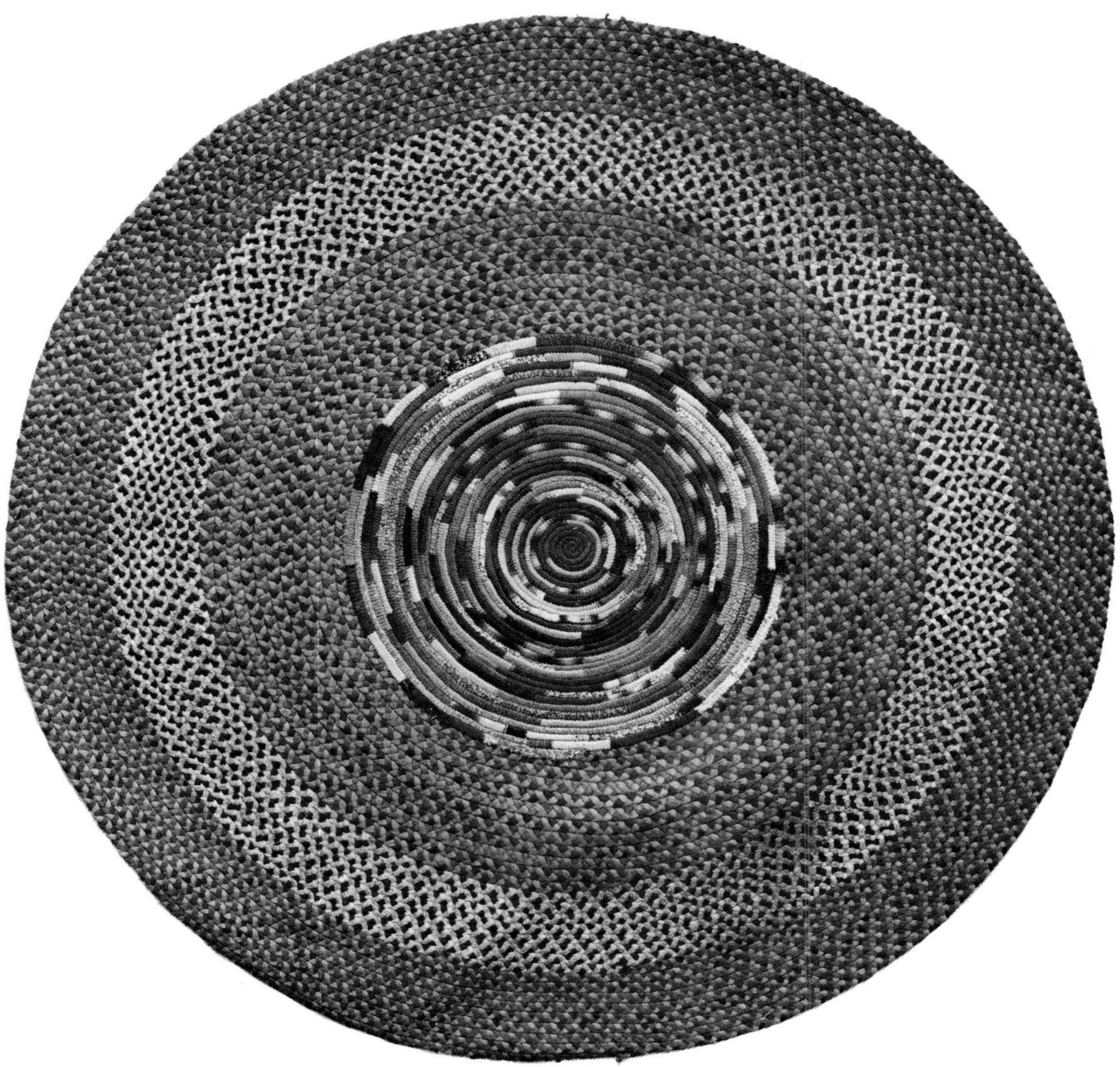

later examples these were sometimes combined with naturalistic or scenic designs, to be used as borders.

Floral designs were consistently popular, the most common being a central spray or bunch of flowers, either loose or confined in a vase or basket, surrounded by a border. Animals ranged from a favorite family pet, like a dog or cat (or two), to more heraldic or exotic creatures such as lions, stags and parrots. The American eagle constituted a particularly patriotic variation that was popular from the 1820s on.

Landscapes and townscapes are rarer but also occur; even scarcer are those examples made by the wives of seafaring men, incorporating shells, knotted ropes, fish or anchors. Rugs with mottoes such as 'God Bless Our Home' or 'Welcome' are usually quite late Victorian.

So proficient did the home craftswoman become that it was not unusual for her to undertake two medium-sized rugs a winter. Hooking bees as well as quilting bees were popular social get-togethers. With the spread of the craft and its acceptance as one of the normal pursuits of the middle-class female, the incentive for commercial development arose. After the Civil War, an invalided Union-soldier-turned-peddler, Edward Sands Frost, began the home-manufacture of stenciled patterns on burlap. His business took off and he continued to produce a wide variety of patterns until the turn of the century. Meanwhile, production had become even more mechanized by the introduction of punch-hooked patterns by Ebenezer Ross of Toledo. Marketing firms including Montgomery Ward offered mail-order patterns.

By the turn of the 20th century, making hooked rugs had become a cottage industry, and whole communities in Canada, New England, and later, the Appalachian Mountains of Tennessee, Kentucky and West Virginia, were turning themselves into rural craft specialists, selling their wares by roadside stands or through representatives. Some of these later cooperative rugs have a folk charm of their own, but often they lack the innovative combinations of color and pattern found on the pre-1900 examples.

T O Y S

Homemade treasures and mechanical marvels that delighted the children of years gone by.

ABOVE: *Carved polychrome revolutionary soldier, c 1785. (Shelburne Museum.)*

Above: *Carved animal toys, c 1850. Artist unidentified; made in Pennsylvania of painted wood. (Abbey Aldrich Rockefeller, Folk Art Center.)*

WOODEN PLAYTHINGS

Making wooden toys to amuse their children was one of the accomplishments of the settler and pioneer. While East Coast gentry could buy the occasional imported toy, even if at great expense, no such opportunity presented itself to most of the American public in the years before their own toy industry was established. Some of these homemade treasures have lasted the years and are today much valued items of craftsmanship, equally sought by toy collectors and by lovers of naïve Americana.

Late 18th- and 19th-century handmade wooden toys include whirligigs, whose flailing arms move in a circular motion alongside the stiffly carved body; windmills, whose light wooden sails spin in the breeze; acrobats who flip over horizontal bars or climb ropes; and clowns who turn somersaults down inclined planes. All of these toys rely on the straightforward rules of physics or the most elemental mechanics in order to work, but are all the more delightful for that.

More static, but just as popular, were the carved dolls, some with their clothes as well as their bodies rendered entirely in wood. Noah's Ark, with its doubled menagerie of beasts, was an extension of this idea and a particular favorite of the young. Especially charming examples, adroitly carved and brightly colored, were produced by Pennsylvania Dutch craftsmen, but examples from New England have their own charm. The Pennsylvania carvers were also responsible for a veritable catalog of

FACING PAGE: *Elephant, made in Pennsylvania c 1850. Carved and painted wood. (Abbey Aldrich Rockefeller, Folk Art Center.)*

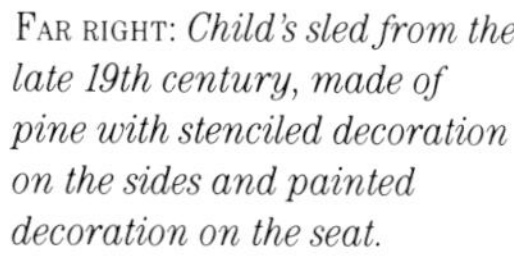

FAR RIGHT: *Child's sled from the late 19th century, made of pine with stenciled decoration on the sides and painted decoration on the seat.*

BELOW: *Whirligig, made c 1870. (Shelburne Museum.)*

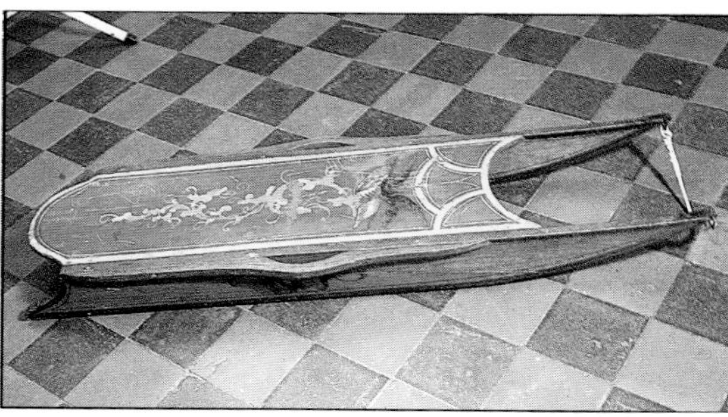

hand-turned or hand-spun toys in which little human figures whirled, pulled, sawed and hammered until the turning stopped or they ran down. Small toy horses on platforms with wheels were favorites with makers of all regions. But chief among the horsey brigade were those large enough to sit on – the rocking horse.

The rocking horse – the term is used generically, since the majority of American versions are fixed on curved wooden rockers rather than on the parallel-runners mechanism popular in England – was made throughout the 19th and 20th centuries. For most of that time it was the provenance of the amateur craftsman, although in later years small 'factories' of workers were making them, including the Crandalls (see below). Some of the most primitive versions were mere two-dimensional plank creatures with minimal paintwork and rope tails; at the other end of the scale were lifelike, full-bodied animals, with real horsehair manes and tails and realistically dappled coats. Many of the finest were made between 1830 and 1900, but very few of their makers are known.

One of the earliest toy 'factories' was that of William S. Tower of South Hingham, Massachusetts, who founded the Tower Toy Company (later the Tower Guild) in the early 1830s. Makers of wooden toys, dolls and dollhouses, they are best remembered today for their miniature furniture for dollhouses, so lovingly detailed and finished that they have become museum pieces.

In the mid-19th century, the toy-making Crandalls, headed by cousins Jesse A. and Charles A., produced a range of simple mechanism wooden toys. But their several special contributions to toymaking include an early version of the spring-mounted hobby horse that would be so successful in England, and a set of nesting alphabet or spelling blocks – both inventions of Jesse – and the first set of building blocks – the work of Charles. Charles also devised and marketed a toy called 'Pigs in Clover' – the original balls-in-the-maze game. So successful was it that at one point his factory was producing 8,000 per day!

Although wooden toys continued to be made, the appearance of tin and metal toys around 1840 dealt them a severe blow. As the decades passed,

ABOVE: *Two doll's houses with lithographed paper decorations, typical products of the Bliss Manufacturing Company, and dating from 1890–1910. (Margaret Woodbury Strong Museum.)*

FACING PAGE: *Cornhusk doll, late 18th century. (The American Museum in Britain.)*

wooden versions could claim only a smaller and smaller share of the market. They finally reached the point we are at today, where nostalgia and regard for craftsmanship are the only arguments against a playroom full of plastic rubbish.

TOYS: DOLLS

Dolls, those small mannequins made for little hands to play with, were a late arrival to the pantheon of American-made goods. For over 200 years after the settlement of Jamestown and Plymouth, most dolls came from Europe. They were brought over with the family chattels by immigrants or imported at great expense by grander families for their privileged offspring. Even after 1840 – when several immigrant makers were beginning to ply a small trade in custom-made dolls – and up to the turn of the century, the vast majority of dolls sold in America were either made totally or partially abroad, particularly in Germany.

Those dolls that were made in the colonies – and even a long time after, when the country had become independent – were not mass-produced and are therefore very rare. In addition, their makers strove hard to imitate the fashions prevalent in Great Britain and the Continent, so it is sometimes difficult to pronounce an 18th- or early 19th-century example as indigenous to the United States.

The few really old handmade dolls that have survived were crude affairs – peg dolls; 'bedpost dolls', so-called because of their resemblance to

the turned post of a typical colonial bed; wishbone dolls, made from the remnants of a turkey, the inverted 'Y' serving as neck, body and legs, with cloth arms sewn to the covering dress; cornhusk dolls, and dolls made with wooden bodies and heads of dried and preserved apple. A few more sophisticated early 19th-century examples are in special collections. These usually have heads of carved and painted wood, with bodies of either wood or cloth. The 'Dutch' dolls of the mid-19th century conform to this definition.

The first patented American doll only appeared in 1858, the application granted to an immigrant German toy-maker named Ludwig Greiner, who had settled in Philadelphia and worked there from 1840 to 1874. In fact, the patent was only for the head and shoulders, which were manufactured by Greiner from a mixture of white paper, dry Spanish whiting, rye flour and glue, the whole reinforced by an overlay of linen, onto which the features were painted. The heads had molded hairstyles with central partings, and the fashion of the hairstyle provides one of the best clues as to the age of the doll. As for the body, this was usually made by the customer, who would fit it with cloth, wooden or – at best – kid arms attached to the dress.

The introduction of India rubber supplied another medium for doll's heads, and a few surviving dolls from the 1850 to 1870 period possess them. But in fact the hard treatment they received did not marry well with the material and the rubber was prone to crack and decay. It was only after the Civil War, however, that industry was really free to develop into the luxury markets that dolls represented, and factories producing various types were registered in Philadelphia, Boston, Cincinnati and New York, the main port of disembarcation for German immigrants, many of whom, if not doll-makers, possessed traditional skills that were welcome in the trade. Wax, porcelain and composition heads all featured regularly, while in 1873 the first patent for a jointed doll was awarded to New England maker Joel Ellis, few of whose wooden dolls were actually made. Similar patents for 'improved' jointed dolls followed, and in 1881 M.C. Lefferts and W.B. Carpenter opened the Celluloid Manufacturing Company of New York. But it was the 'Can't Break 'Em' dolls of Solomon Hoffman of Brooklyn that opened up the American market to the possibilities of mass-production, and although the new version of composition head devised by Hoffman was not indestructible, it enabled him to open 'The First American Doll Factory', later incorporated into the American Doll and Toy Manufacturing Company. It was one of these heads that was used for the first American copyrighted doll – Billiken – made between 1909 and 1912 by the E.I.

RIGHT: *Painted papier mâché doll, 19th century. (The American Museum in Britain.)*

Horsman Company of New York City, which also produced the first advertising dolls – the 'Campbell Kids' made under license from the famous soup company.

In the meantime, the old-fashioned homemade cloth doll had gone commercial. 'Mammy' dolls and 'rag' dolls had been popular for many years in the South and North, cut to supplied patterns and filled by the customer. But in 1873 Mrs. Izannah Walker of Central Falls, Rhode Island, obtained a patent for making rag dolls with a double-molded cotton and wadding head, joined to bodies of muslin. Later, from the 1890s through the 1920s, Martha Chase of Pawtucket, Rhode Island, moved the technique up-market, producing dolls portraying fairy tale and literary characters, as well as famous people. These Chase dolls are today highly sought-after. Perhaps the most famous of the rag dolls, however, were the Raggedy Ann and Andy dolls, first patented in 1915 by the creator of the eponymous books. Their distinctive red yarn hair, shoe-button eyes, pinafore (Ann) and sailor stripes (Andy) turned them into a childhood classic (now produced by the Knickerbocker Toy Company).

The antithesis to the simplicity of the rag doll was the fascination with human mimicry implicit in all the moving, crying and talking dolls that appeared as the years marched on. The first 'walking doll' was patented in 1862; its complicated and ugly machinery was hidden beneath wide crinoline skirts. In 1877 came a walking and crying doll; in 1881, a singing doll. This last was an expensive

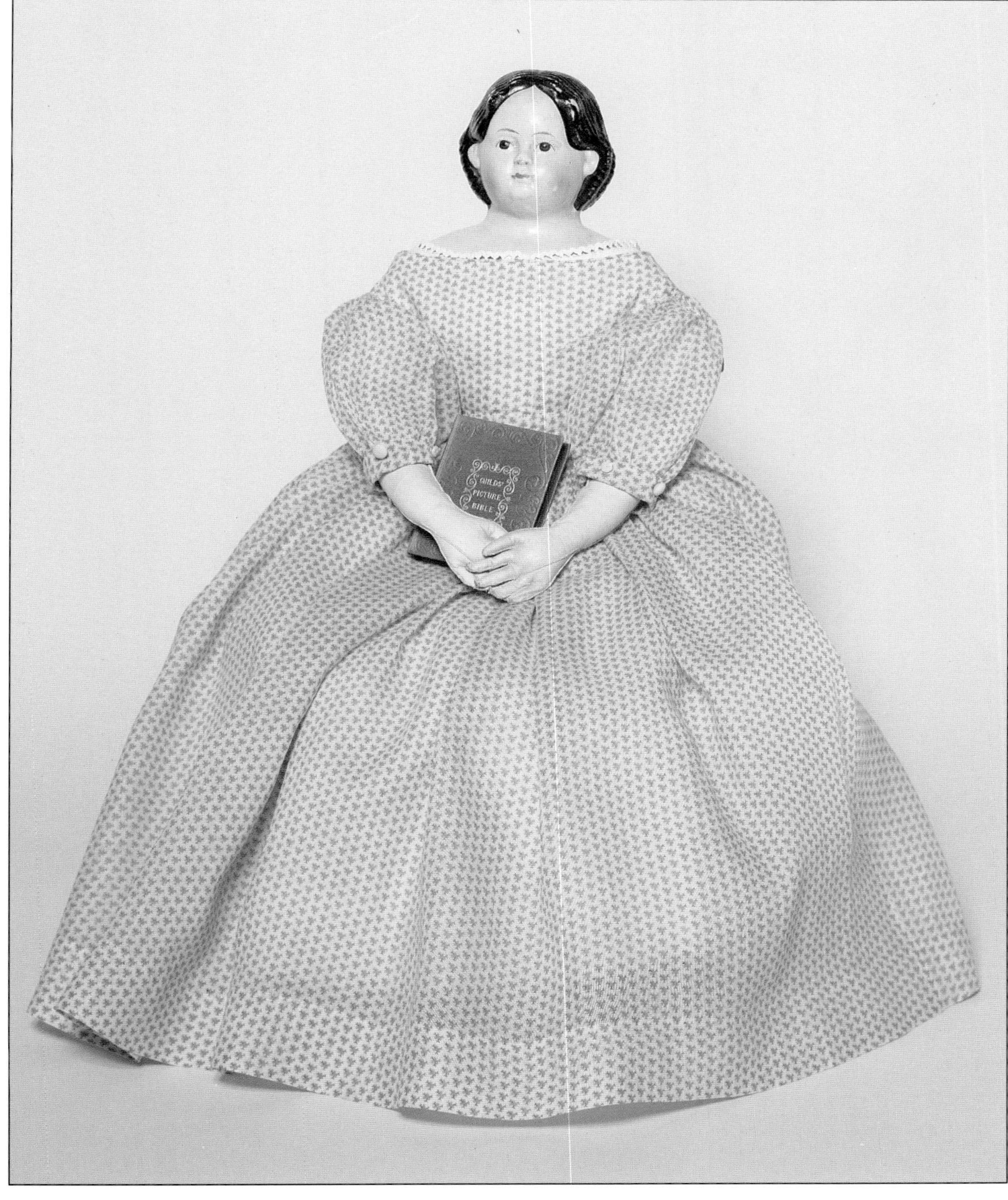

LEFT: *Cloth doll by Ludwig Greiner, 1858–72. (Margaret Woodbury Strong Museum.)*

item, with long, curling hair sprouting from a wax head and a kid body, on which was printed the name of the song she could warble.

Up to and including the early decades of the 20th century, children had been content with dolls that looked like young women or, at best, children their own age. The vogue for the baby doll took off with the Bye-Lo Baby, designed by Grace Storey Putnam in 1922 and said to be modeled on a real baby only a few days old. It was a cooperative effort, with the bisque heads made in Germany, the cloth body made and the assembly of the dolls accomplished by K & K Toy Company of New York, and the distribution handled by George Borgfeldt and Co. Within two years, however, the German heads were replaced with all-American wood-pulp composition heads, and a year later with celluloid heads. Some wooden heads and a few wax prototypes have also been found.

The 1920s saw advertising dolls, taking their lead from the Campbell Kids, become an important force in the toy market. Dolls based on cartoon characters also appeared in the 1920s, to reach their peak in the 1930s and 1940s with the Disney-licensed dolls. These were also the big days for film star dolls – Shirley Temple being the queen of them all – and even dolls based on unseen radio stars. By the 1940s plastics were being used in doll manufacture, leading to a general lowering of standards and styling, while the introduction of vinyl in the late 1950s has meant a return to better modeling, if not inspired design.

ABOVE LEFT: *Clockwork hoop toy, made by Althof Bergmann c 1870–80. (Bill Holland Collection. Reproduced courtesy of New Cavendish Books.)*

ABOVE RIGHT: *Clockwork figure of General Grant, made by Ives and Blakeslee c 1877. (Margaret Woodbury Strong Museum.)*

TOYS: METAL AND MECHANICAL TOYS

The first tin toys appeared in the 1840s. At first, the simple die-stamped shapes, crimped or riveted together, followed the pattern set by the wooden variety. Chief among the companies making them were the Philadelphia Tin Toy Manufactory and George W. Brown and Company of Connecticut. The tin toys were light, versatile and cheap, but they were not very resilient. As if in uncomplicated answer to the problem, cast-iron toys began to be made in the late 1860s, although they were not made in great numbers until the 1880s. They were certainly solid and sturdy, but they were heavy and most could not be wound by hand or easily carried about by little people. Instead iron toys took the form of static playthings – miniature stoves like Mommy's with little pots and pans to match or simple slot banks – or pull-along wagons, dogs, horses and carts, fire engines and circus animals on wheels. Sometime in the late 1860s, George Brown's tin-making firm joined forces with J. & E. Stevens, the first major iron toy company, eventually becoming known as the American Toy Company. With the invention of spring-action toys in the early 1870s, it was in an enviable commercial position and became one of the principal makers of the new mechanical banks.

A penny in the hand of a clown – or of a corrupt politician, in the case of the 'Tammany Hall Bank' – would be popped into his mouth or dropped into

INDEX

Italic page numbers refer to illustrations